The
Literature
of
England

The Literature of England

THIRD SINGLE VOLUME EDITION

George K. Anderson
Emeritus, Brown University

William E. Buckler
New York University

Mary Harris Veeder
Indiana University, Northwest

SCOTT, FORESMAN AND COMPANY
Glenview, Illinois   Dallas, Tex.   Oakland, N.J.
Palo Alto, Cal.   Tucker, Ga.   London, England

Library of Congress Cataloging in Publication Data

Anderson, George Kumler, 1901–   ed.
    The literature of England.

    CONTENTS: v. 1. From the Middle Ages through the
eighteenth century.—v. 2. From the romantic period to the
present.
    1. English literature.   I. Buckler, William Earl, 1924–
II. Veeder, Mary, 1943–   III. Title.
PR1109.A56   1979   820'.8   78-31118
ISBN 0-673-15156-5 (v. 1)

12345678910-RRW-85848382818079

Acknowledgments

Cover: Photo Researchers.
Part Openers: Part 1—A. F. Kersting; Part 2—Courtesy of the Mar-
quess of Bath; Part 3—National Monuments Record; Part 4—Fine Arts
Photographers, Ltd.; Part 5—Courtesy of the Art Institute of Chicago;
Part 6—Camera Press.

The following selections are reprinted in this work through the courtesy of their respective copyright holders.

PART 1. *Beowulf*, from *Beowulf, the Oldest English Epic. Translated into
Alliterative Verse with a Critical Introduction* by Charles W. Kennedy.
Copyright 1940 by Oxford University Press, Inc.; renewed by Charles
W. Kennedy 1968. Reprinted by permission. *Sir Gawain and the
Green Knight*, translated by Brian Stone (Penguin Classics, Second
edition, 1974) pp. 21–115. Copyright Brian Stone, 1959, 1964, 1974.
Reprinted by permission of Penguin Books Ltd. *The Canterbury Tales*
reprinted from The Works of Geoffrey Chaucer, 2nd edition by F. N.
Robinson. Copyright © 1933, 1957, renewed 1961. Used by permis-
sion of Houghton Mifflin Company.

PART 2. *Utopia*, by Thomas More. Translated and edited by H. V. S.
Ogden. Copyright 1949 by AHM Publishing Corporation. Selections
reprinted by permission of AHM Publishing Corporation.   John Milton
poems from *Complete Poems and Major Prose*, edited by Merritt Y.
Hughes. Published by The Odyssey Press, 1957.

PART 5. *The Wreck of the Deutschland*, "God's Grandeur," "The Starlight Night," "The Sea and the Skylark," "The Windhover," "Pied
Beauty," "Peace," "Spring and Fall," "Hurrahing in Harvest," "Inversnaid," "Carrion Comfort," "No Worst, There Is None," "I Wake
and Feel the Fell of Dark," "My Own Heart Let Me More Have Pity
On," "To R.B." From *The Poems of Gerard Manley Hopkns*, Fourth
Edition. Edited by W. H. Gardner and N. H. Mackenzie. Oxford University Press, 1967.

PART 6. "Snow in the Suburbs," reprinted with permission of Macmillan Publishing Co., Inc. from *Collected Poems of Thomas Hardy*.
Copyright 1925 by Macmillan Publishing Co., Inc., renewed 1953 by
Lloyds Bank Ltd. All other Hardy poems that appear in this work are
reprinted through the courtesy of Macmillan Publishing Co. *Arms
and the Man* by Bernard Shaw. Copyright 1898, 1913, 1926, 1931,
1933, 1941, George Bernard Shaw. Copyright 1905, Brentano's.
Copyright 1958, The Public Trustee as Executor of the Estate of
George Bernard Shaw. Reprinted by permission of Dodd, Mead &
Company, Inc. and The Society of Authors for the Estate of George
Bernard Shaw.   "Loveliest of Trees," "When I Was One-and-Twenty,"
"To an Athlete," "Bredon Hill," "Into My Heart," "Think no more,
lad," and "Terence, this is stupid stuff" from *A Shropshire Lad*—Authorised Edition—from *The Collected Poems of A. E. Housman*. Copyright 1939, 1940, 1965 by Holt, Rinehart and Winston. Copyright 1967, 1968 by Robert E. Symons. Reprinted by permission
of Holt, Rinehart and Winston and Jonathan Cape Ltd., publishers,
and The Society of Authors as the literary representative of the Estate
of A. E. Housman.   "The Night is freezing fast" from *The Collected
Poems of A. E. Housman*. Copyright 1922 by Holt, Rinehart and
Winston. Copyright 1950 by Barclays Bank, Ltd. Reprinted by permission of Holt, Rinehart and Winston. Copyright 1950 by Barclays Bank,
Ltd. Reprinted by permission of Holt, Rinehart and Winston and
Jonathan Cape Ltd., publishers, and The Society of Authors as the
literary representative of the Estate of A. E. Housman.   "They say my
verse is sad: no wonder," and "When green buds hang in the elm like
dust" from *The Collected Poems of A. E. Housman*. Copyright 1936 by
Barclays Bank Ltd. Copyright 1964 by Robert E. Symons. Reprinted by
permission of Holt, Rinehart and Winston and Jonathan Cape Ltd.,

All other literary credits appear on page 1251, which constitutes a
legal extension of the copyright page.

Preface

When we decided to revise *The Literature of England*, we had a number of aims: we felt the need for a compact, attractive, easy-to-read anthology, for a book that had sufficient coverage for the survey course but one that was not overly inclusive, a book that was tailored to the specific needs of teachers and students in the 1980s. Rather than publish a large, cumbersome, unnecessarily comprehensive text, we wanted to offer the most important English writers and their works—the selections that are most often actually taught in the classroom. Furthermore, we wanted to offer our selections in the most accessible and attractive format possible. We wanted to provide straightforward yet authoritative editorial material that would make the selections as meaningful as possible to students without usurping the role of the teacher. We did not want the editorial material to be as difficult as some of the texts it was designed to elucidate. In some ways, then, this is a new anthology. But it is also an anthology with a most interesting history.

The single-volume edition of *The Literature of England* first appeared in 1953. It was based upon the outlines of and followed the same plan as a two-volume edition of the book that had been published by Scott, Foresman and Company since 1936. The 1953 edition stood on its own as a special contribution to a shorter, more intensive course in English literature from the beginnings to recent times. The book was partially revised and updated in 1967. This 1979 edition has been completely revised and updated.

The revised introductions are designed to help the students place the literature of a specific period in its historical, social, and economic contexts. Each introduction is in two parts: the first discusses the period's sociohistorical background, the second examines the literary environment. The illustration program—pictures of authors, art, architecture, artifacts—also helps lend a realistic sense of the period. The author and selection headnotes have been examined and revised in the light of the most current scholarship; the footnotes have been revised along the lines of economy and contemporary critical thinking; and the texts are the most authoritative available. New to this edition are the small bubbles calling out glossed words and terms in the running texts and a section called Definitions of Literary Terms at the end of the book. Footnotes now appear immediately below the column of the text to which they refer. This new edition is also available for the first time in two paperbacks: Volume One contains the literature from *Beowulf* through the eighteenth century; Volume Two contains the literature from the Romantic Period to the present. Another significant departure from the previous philosophy of the single-volume edition is the inclusion of drama in this anthology. We now include drama in all those periods in which it is an important genre. We have a morality play from the Middle Ages, two Renaissance dramas, a Restoration comedy, and a modern play.

The most important feature of every anthology is, of course, its table of contents; the table of contents for the 1979 edition has been most extensively revised. Among the more important changes in this edition are the following: the inclusion of two more of Chaucer's *Canterbury Tales*, several Middle English lyrics, *The Second Shepherds' Play*, Marlowe's *Tragical History of Dr. Faustus*, Shakespeare's *The Tempest*, many new Donne selections, Book Nine of Milton's *Paradise Lost* and his "Of Education," Wycherley's *The Country Wife*, Part IV of Swift's *Gulliver's Travels*, many new Blake selections, selections from the poetry of Emily Brontë, many new Hardy poems, Shaw's *Arms and the Man*, Conrad's "The Secret Sharer," selections from the poetry of Wilfred Owen, many new Yeats poems, Woolf's "The Mark on the Wall," Joyce's "Clay," T. S. Eliot's *The Waste Land*, many new Auden poems, Greene's "The Destructors," Beckett's "Dante and the Lobster," and Lessing's "A Man and Two Women." In order to make room for the new material, of course, we dropped many of the lesser-known authors and the infrequently taught selections. The table of contents has been revised on the basis of suggestions submitted by the editorial consultants and hundreds of teachers of the survey course throughout the country.

This new edition of *The Literature of England* has benefited greatly from the editorial advice, suggestions, and critiques of the six period consultants. Their informed scholarship, period expertise, general interest, and unfailing counsel have proven indispensable. Any errors of fact or interpretation, however, are the responsibility of the general editors. Finally, we would like to thank Amanda Clark, Charles Schaff, and Marilyn Martin of the editorial staff of Scott, Foresman and Company for their assistance in realizing this book. A special note of recognition goes to John Nolan, who guided this project from beginning to end with patience, skill, and wisdom.

G. K. A.
W. E. B.
M. H. V.

Contents

3

The Restoration and the Eighteenth Century (1660–1784)   378

4

The Romantic Period (1784–1837)   612

5
The Victorian Age (1837–1914)

6

The Modern Period (1914–) 1074

The Middle Ages

From the Composition of *Beowulf* to the Accession of the Tudors, c. 750–1485

PART 1

Dover Castle, overlooking the English Channel, built by the Normans in the eleventh century

The Middle Ages in English literature begins about 750, the approximate date for the composition of *Beowulf,* the oldest of the great long poems written in English. It ends about 1485, the date of the accession of King Henry VII, the first of the great Tudor emperors. But something is known of English history, if not its literature, prior to the eighth century.

Roman Britain

Britain was known indirectly to a few ancient Greek writers as a dim, remote, and mysterious region. But direct knowledge of the island came with the invasion of Julius Caesar and his Roman expedition in 55 B.C. Caesar made no attempt to colonize the island, and the development of a Roman province there did not begin until nearly a century later. Then the Roman emperor Claudius, in 43 A.D., led a campaign against the Celtic inhabitants of the island and established Roman rule in Britain.

For nearly four hundred years, Britain remained a part of the mighty Roman Empire. Romans and Britons intermarried, towns grew and prospered, magnificent roads fanned out over the province, and peace was maintained under Roman law. When, under repeated attacks by barbarians, the Roman Empire began to fall apart early in the fifth century, the Romans abandoned the province. The Romanized Britons, left without the defense of the Roman legions, were soon involved in conflicts with other Celtic tribes from bordering areas which had not been subject to Roman domination—the Irish from the west, Scots and Picts from the north. Eventually, however, the remnants of the Roman province of Britain were conquered by Germanic invaders from across the North Sea.

These Germanic invaders, often referred to simply as Anglo-Saxons, were actually of three major tribes—the Angles, the Saxons, and the Jutes. Their homelands had been areas along the northwest coast of Germany and the Danish peninsula. When the Huns invaded Europe from the east in the fourth and fifth centuries, they pushed the Germanic tribes of Central Europe farther west. These tribes in turn exerted pressures on the Anglo-Saxons, who became sea rovers for a time. For many years they made sporadic attacks on the coast of Britain. Then, according to tradition, in 449 the Jutes under Hengest and Horsa landed on the coast of Kent to begin the actual conquest of Britain.

Anglo-Saxon England

The Anglo-Saxons gradually and steadily settled along the eastern British coastline. The process was slow; the details—to later generations—often obscure;

Three artifacts from the ship burial at Sutton Hoo, Suffolk, England. They are thought to be the possessions of a seventh-century East Anglian king. The helmet (right) is decorated with gold, silver, and garnets. The purse lid (above, top) and the armor buckle (above, bottom) are both made of gold; the interconnecting animal designs on the purse lid and armor buckle are characteristic of Anglo-Saxon art.

but by about 650 the Anglo-Saxons possessed all of England.

The history of England from about 600 to 850 is the story of the rivalry among small Anglo-Saxon kingdoms and the efforts of successive states to unify England. First, Kent became the strongest of the kingdoms under the rule of King Ethelbert. From about 650 to 750 Northumbria, the kingdom of the Angles, achieved political eminence. Power then moved to the Angles of Mercia, until Wessex, settled by the Saxons, attained supremacy early in the ninth century.

The Anglo-Saxons maintained the forms of society that they brought with them from the continent. They recognized two main social classes—the ruling class of earls, based originally upon kinship to the founder of the tribe; and the subject class of churls (or bondsmen), some of whom were descended from captives of the tribe. In addition, there were also a few freemen, who enjoyed a higher status than the churls because they or their ancestors had been freed from bondage as a reward for services to the king. Ideally, the king was a brave commander and revered leader in wartime and a wise judge and generous bestower of gifts in peacetime.

The tribal social system was based on the concepts of loyalty and personal indebtedness. In this kinship-based society, crimes against one's own kin were unforgivable and punishable by death. The individual needed the strength, determination, and courage to overcome an adverse climate, famine, and foes. Yet the individual was not alone and solitary; he or she could depend upon the courage, strength, and loyalty of fellow tribesmen. The bonds of loyalty and service between the king and his warriors were mutual; each saw the service he could provide the other.

Early Saxon interior of a seventh-century church at Brixworth, Northamptonshire, in central England. The arches were constructed of bricks from Roman ruins. The roof was made of wood, the primary building material of the Anglo-Saxons.

The Coming of Christianity

The Anglo-Saxons, while living on the continent in Europe, had surrounded themselves with greater and lesser deities—personifications of forces of nature or of the supernatural which they understood in terms of animal or human agencies of superior strength. In Britain they came into contact with Christianity for the first time. Some Christians had actually been in Britain during the latter years of the Roman occupation, and Christian missionaries from Ireland had set up little centers in the northern part of the island as early as the first part of the sixth century. But in 597 Pope Gregory the Great, desiring that the English should not be ignorant of Christian doctrine, sent his special emissary Augustine to convert King Ethelbert of Kent. When Augustine reached the island, he requested a meeting with Ethelbert; according to Bede (673–735) in his *Ecclesiastical History of the English Nation*, Ethelbert insisted that the meeting be held in the open air so that the strangers could not practice sorcery

upon him. Ethelbert, already married to a Christian wife, allowed Augustine and his party to live and preach in the city of Canterbury. In less than a year, Ethelbert himself was converted. Augustine became the first Archbishop of Canterbury, and within two generations Christianity had spread throughout the length and breadth of England.

To the Anglo-Saxons who heard the message of the Christian teachers, the new religion that promised something more certain than their pagan deities offered seemed worthy to be followed. Augustine and his successors attempted to assimilate as many of the old ways as were consistent with the Christian faith. According to tradition, the church of St. Pancras was built within the boundaries of what had formerly been a pagan sanctuary in Canterbury. Perhaps the most remarkable cultural interchange was the retention of the name of the pagan spring festival (Eostre) to commemorate Christ's resurrection (Easter). Furthermore,

This stone church on St. MacDara's Island, Galway, Ireland, was built in the eighth or ninth century. It is the best surviving example of Hiberno-Saxon architecture constructed of stone.

the Christian concepts of fortune and providence were similar to the Anglo-Saxon concept of wyrd (or fate) in the sense that they all placed control of individual destiny beyond the reach of personal exertion.

There was more to the acceptance of Christianity, of course, than the spiritual awakening of faith. Christianity also considerably widened the intellectual outlook of the Anglo-Saxons. In the schools that grew up as the monasteries spread, classical writings in Latin and Greek were taught in addition to the Scriptures. The Anglo-Saxons were put in touch with the continental culture of late antiquity and the early Middle Ages. England became an important center of learning for all Europe in the eighth and ninth centuries. Alcuin (735–804), for example, whom Charlemagne (742–814) chose to help implement educational reforms throughout his continental empire, was English by birth and education. The study of Latin culture, with its emphasis on the preservation of a body of knowledge, encouraged the Anglo-Saxons to both produce and write down their own literature. Indeed, Anglo-Saxon became the first important vernacular (non-Latin) written literature of Western Europe.

Later History

Around 850 in the kingdom of Wessex, Alfred the Great emerged as the most important of the Anglo-Saxon kings. Although he was a strong and skillful ruler, he could not avoid conflict with his enemies, the Viking Danes, who were following the pattern set by

the Anglo-Saxons themselves four hundred years earlier. Beginning with swift raids at the end of the eighth century, the Vikings had advanced farther and farther into the northern and central portions of England. These early raids were eventually followed by settlements until, during the reign of Alfred, the Danes were threatening the entire island. Alfred checked the Danes, but peace came at a high price. Alfred ceded to the Danes the northern and central portions of England.

These sections were eventually won back by the Anglo-Saxons during the tenth century; England appeared for a time to be developing into a unified nation. But the power of the West Saxons declined late in the century, and new waves of Danish invaders assaulted the island. In 1014 the Danes conquered England, but more unrest followed. In 1042 the Anglo-Saxons briefly returned to power. In 1066—the year of the Norman conquest—the Anglo-Saxon history of England came to an end.

Old English Literature

Old English literature is a product of two cultures—pagan and Christian. Since it is a fusion of two (sometimes complementary and sometimes conflicting) cultures, the reader will observe a certain creative tension in many Old English poems. Old English writers frequently infused the Christian world view represented in the Bible with the heroic values they had inherited and just as frequently modified the world view of their traditional epics with Christian reflections on the transience of worldly glory. This fusion of two cultures is the source of much that is distinctive in the voice and perspective of the Old English poets.

What we know about the varieties of compositions in the Old English period indicates a range of artistic method and authorial intention which cannot be neatly categorized. Epic poets celebrated heroic and Christian topics. Most scholars think that Old English poetry was composed orally—in front of an audience—by *scops* (or bards) who could draw on a vast store of traditional formula-phrases to express almost any idea in correct metrical form. Scops, accompanied by a harp or lyre, usually told their stories of heroes at royal courts—frequently changing the details of a story to suit the audience and the occasion. From the Old English period, we have only one full-length epic, *Beowulf,* which celebrates the achievements of a monster-killing hero. We also possess a few epic fragments (*The Fight at Finnsberg* and *Waldere*) and scattered allusions to others. Most authors of Old English literature are anonymous, though we do possess the names and sketchy details of a few of them.

Bede, the eighth-century historian and scholar, tells us the story of Caedmon in his *Ecclesiastical History of the English Nation.* Caedmon was an unlearned herdsman who lived in a village where the villagers entertained their companions with a song to the accompaniment of a harp when all were gathered for the evening meal. But whenever Caedmon saw the harp approaching, he would be overcome with doubt about his ability to compose a poem and would leave his fellow villagers to make his way home alone. In a dream one night, Caedmon was directed to celebrate the beginning of creation and was able to do so. Upon awakening, he remembered the divine poem he composed in his sleep. He subsequently abandoned his secular life in order to become a monk; he is reported to have been able to celebrate any sacred subject in verse. Modern scholars attribute several vigorous narratives of Old Testament events to Caedmon or his followers.

The topics of the Christian tradition are treated in a more learned fashion by Cynewulf. Despite the fact that scholars have attributed some 2,600 lines to him, little is known about him. We do know that he attempted, rather ingeniously, to weave his name into the closing lines of four of his poems in runic characters. (Runes are characters of an alphabet, probably derived from Latin and Greek, used by Germanic peoples from the third to the thirteenth centuries.) Cynewulf's attempt to escape anonymity is thought by many scholars to represent a desire to be remembered in the prayers of his readers. In one of the poems in which scholars have detected Cynewulf's influence, "The Dream of the Rood," we can note a specific instance of the fusion of pagan and Christian cultures. In this poem Christ is portrayed as a heroic warrior who dies for men's souls. The grave deeds of warriors in the heroic tradition, then, can be used by both secular and religious poets. Furthermore, "The Dream of the Rood" shows that the poet was well acquainted with the theology of the Atonement.

The variety of Old English poetry is remarkable. In addition to epics, Old English poets also wrote short lyrics, such as "The Wanderer" and "The Ruin," which are elegaic in nature, lamenting the passage of time, friends, and property. Riddles and gnomic (aphoristic) verse were also popular; both of them appeal to the belief in the rational—in our ability to figure out in a line of poetry the answer to a riddle or a universal rule of human existence. Religious allegory was yet another type of Old English poetry. In "The Phoenix," for example, the poet instructs his readers by working out the extended implicit comparison of the Phoenix (a legendary bird which, upon dying, rose youthfully alive from its own ashes) to Christ. Heroic and religious, oral and learned, folkloric and allegorical—Anglo-Saxon poetry encompasses a diversity of contexts and subjects.

Certain stylistic traits characterize Old English poetry. The verse is rhythmic, with four main emphases occurring in slightly differing combinations in each line. It is also normally alliterative, with three or four stressed syllables beginning either with the same consonant or with one of a group of similar vowel sounds. The four emphasized syllables are usually divided into half-lines of two stresses each by a *caesura*, or rhythmic pause, occurring near the middle of each line. Repeated epithets (characteristic words or phrases occurring in place of the name of the person or thing) and kennings (condensed metaphors that name things by their function) frequently occur.

Prose was also an Anglo-Saxon medium. Before the time of King Alfred the Great of Wessex (849–935), prose was written in Latin. Thus Bede (677–735), although born an Englishman, was an international scholar and churchman who wrote in Latin. His *Historia Ecclesiastica Gentis Anglorum (Ecclesiastical History of the English Nation)* relates in narrative form the history of Christianity among the English from its beginnings during the Roman occupation until the year 731. Bede's *Ecclesiastical History* is preeminent among all the materials of Anglo-Saxon history; it is both a source of accurate information and an extraordinary example of historical technique and style.

Alfred became king in 871. Since he was well educated by churchmen, he clearly realized the many difficulties which had to be overcome in order to enlighten his people, the West Saxons. Part of the remedy, as he saw it, was to translate into their own language the books that they most needed. He himself translated or encouraged the translation of five books: a work of Platonic philosophy (*The Consolation of Philosophy* by Boethius), a book of general knowledge (*Compendious History of the World* by Orosius), a book for the conduct of priestly office (*Pastoral Care* by Gregory the Great), the standard church history of England (*Ecclesiastical History of the English Nation* by Bede), and a typical example of patristic writing (*Soliloquies* by St. Augustine). The interest during his reign in recording contemporary history is reflected in the *Anglo-Saxon Chronicle*, a year-by-year account of English history, which contains a wealth of commentary and detail about his own wars against the Danes. Alfred's translations are frequently distinguished by apt and informative additions to the original text. While Alfred's prose could best be described as plain style, the prose of two later writers, Aelfric (955–1025) and Wulfstan (d. 1023), was highly ornate and alliterative. Aelfric's *Lives of the Saints* and Wulfstan's homilies are works of considerable force and passion; they are still vital today.

The Old English literature that we have—and only a very small part of it has survived the centuries—is various in its styles, moods, and purposes. It could be epic or lyrical, celebratory or elegaic, entertaining or didactic or both. The culture which supported this literature did not disappear with the arrival of William the Conqueror in 1066, but it did undergo radical change. The literature which begins to emerge in the twelfth century shows a language and a culture quite distinct from that of the Anglo-Saxon period.

A detail of the Bayeux Tapestry, made in the eleventh century of wool embroidered on linen. The tapestry depicts more than seventy scenes of the Norman Conquest of England. This particular detail represents William of Normandy giving his sister's hand to Harold, the English ruler whom William defeated at the Battle of Hastings in 1066.

Norman and Plantagenet England

Originally the Normans, like the Danes who had overrun England in the ninth century, had been Vikings. A hundred years before the Battle of Hastings, they had invaded that part of France which has since been called Normandy and had adopted the French culture, customs, and language. At the time the Normans conquered England, their civilization was more complicated and more advanced in both political organization and cultural sophistication than anything which the late Anglo-Saxon civilization could offer.

When William the Conqueror landed at Pevensey on that momentous September day in 1066, he slipped while disembarking and fell forward on his hands and knees. With great presence of mind, however, he grabbed a handful of earth in each fist. This symbolic seizure of land William converted into sober fact. He imposed Norman law, Norman government, and Norman language on the conquered Anglo-Saxons.

The foundation of Norman civilization was the feudal system, a system based upon the holding of land. Immediately upon conquering England, William laid claim to all the land in the realm. Dispossessing its Anglo-Saxon owners, he granted large areas to his lords, who, in return, promised William their services and those of their retainers. The lords, in turn, could grant portions of their lands to the knights pledged to assist them in battle. The ceremony by which these obligations were acknowledged—paying homage and swearing fealty—was considered sacred and binding without question. Lower still on the Norman social scale were the serfs—many of whom were the conquered English—who paid goods and services to the lord in return for the land they farmed.

During the more than four centuries of the later Middle Ages, England was ruled by two royal families: the Normans (1066–1154), including William the Conqueror and his direct successors, and the Plantagenets (1154–1485), beginning with Henry II. Three noteworthy events in the progress toward a constitutional monarchy occurred during the reign of the Plantagenets: judicial reform, the granting of the Magna Charta, and the beginnings of Parliament.

When Henry II ascended the throne in 1154, nearly a hundred years after the Norman conquest, he found a confused and corrupt system of justice. Some of the courts were administered by the king's justices, others were under the jurisdiction of feudal barons, and others followed the Anglo-Saxon judicial code. Convinced that the king's justice must be the same for all people in every section of England, Henry divided the country into districts, appointed judges in each circuit, and expanded the functions of the jury.

King John (1167?–1216), son of Henry II, totally disregarded the provisions for justice his father had guaranteed by charter. He jailed his subjects on false charges and refused them trials; he imposed ruinous taxes. Exasperated beyond endurance, barons and knights joined together and in 1215 at Runnymede, on the banks of the Thames, forced John to sign the Magna Charta. This document, which established by law certain liberties, was conservative in its reassertion of traditional baronial privileges but was progressive in its implication that the king, like his people, was subject to the rule of law. During the reign of Edward I (1272–1307), the rights of the English were again extended when Edward called the first parliament—the Great Parliament of 1295—in which all propertied classes of the kingdom, including barons and clergy, were represented.

During the fifty-year reign of Edward III (1327–1377), the grandson of Edward I, commerce developed and England prospered. Particularly important was the wool trade. Wool from England was shipped to France to be woven into cloth for English markets. So important was this trade that the export duty on raw wool was the chief source of money for the English government. This prosperous trade irked the king of France to such a degree that he began to seize English wool ships. In retaliation, Edward III revived an old claim to the crown of France. The war thus begun in 1337 was waged intermittently for a hundred years and is known as the Hundred Years' War. Ultimately England lost the war and relinquished its claims to French territory. Indeed, by the end of the Hundred Years' War, the English monarch's claim to the hereditary kingship of France had become tenuous; during the preceding two centuries, England had moved from Norman domination to distinct nationhood and from a country with a French-speaking aristocracy to a country in which all classes spoke the English language.

Instead of a period of peace in which to recover from the war with France, the second half of the fifteenth century was marked by warfare between the descendants of the duke of York and the duke of Lancaster, who were both sons of Edward III. The crown changed hands several times during this period, known as the War of the Roses. The earl of Richmond, of the house of Lancaster, eventually married Elizabeth, heiress of the house of York, and ascended the throne in 1485 as Henry VII, the first of the Tudors.

Cultural and Social Background

While no one set of events absolutely dominated the cultural and social milieu of the later Middle Ages, certain trends and realities of English life can be discerned. The Church—though now with a hierarchy of

Norman prelates—remained influential throughout the period. In Norman England education was the province of the Church. In the centuries before the printing press was invented, manuscripts were painstakingly copied by hand in the monasteries. Monks and priests passed on the culture of Greece and Rome, together with the teachings of the Church, to the young men who came to the monasteries for their education. From such beginnings in the twelfth and thirteenth centuries came the formal organization of Oxford and Cambridge as universities. Education and learning were vital forces in England. Faith and reason have a complex relation in every age—including the medieval.

The Church was also bound up with other aspects of life. In medieval thought Church and king were necessary instruments for maintaining order in society; they were considered "the two swords of God." But the authority of the Church itself—and the related notion of relying upon authority in thinking and acting—has frequently been misinterpreted by those modern readers who place undue emphasis upon the influence of the Church. It is true that the Church insisted upon its own authority in matters of faith and dogma and that many philosophic questions were settled by reliance upon principles accepted on faith (on the authority of God or of the Church). Yet the predominance of the Church in the later Middle Ages must not obscure the fact that there is always a distance between official pronouncement and individual belief—even in an ultimately believing age. Skepticism, heresy, and humor at the expense of authority occurred throughout the period.

The work of John Wyclif (1328–1384) offers a striking example of the diversity of medieval religious thought. With some encouragement from John of Gaunt and other influential Englishmen, he formulated

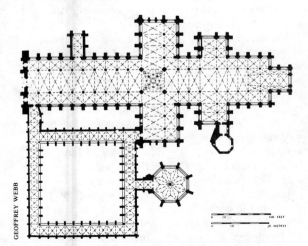

Salisbury Cathedral, built between 1220 and 1270, is the only church done completely in the English High Gothic style. Above: floor plan of the cathedral. Right: the west facade. It shows the English High Gothic emphasis on horizontal, rather than vertical, ornamental motifs.

The medieval knight Sir George Luttrell, from the Luttrell Psalter, made about 1340. Psalters, or liturgical books, were popular among the English aristocracy in the thirteenth and fourteenth centuries.

doctrines which emphasized individual grace over ecclesiastical authority and the evidence of Christ and the Scriptures over the assertions of the Church hierarchy. Yet, despite our modern tendency to see all medieval critics of the Church as forerunners of the Protestant Reformation, Wyclif did not wish to start a new church. His immediate objective—together with that of his many contemporaries—was to seek reform within the old Church.

In addition to the influence of the Church, a second important tendency of the age was that the social structure was gradually becoming more complex. Immediately after the Norman Conquest there were, as we have already pointed out, only two main social classes: the aristocratic nobles (both secular and ecclesiastical) and the serfs. After 1200, however, the slow but steady growth of trade and industry meant the increase in importance of the town and the development of an industrial middle class. By the middle of the thirteenth century, this industrial middle class was sufficiently strong to form into guilds (protective associations of the individual crafts) and to have a voice in the Great Parliament of 1295. By the end of

the fifteenth century, the middle class was recognized as an important component of the economic and political life of the kingdom.

The social structure also felt the impact of the Hundred Years' War and the Black Death. The war that broke out in 1337 was based, in part, upon economic frictions generated by the English merchant classes. The war itself established the military importance of English yeomen and freemen. In the English victories at Agincourt, Crecy, and Poitiers, longbowmen defeated the immobile, heavily armored French knights on horseback. The Black Death, a form of bubonic plague which ravaged Europe between 1346 and 1349, killed an estimated 40 percent of the population. The reduction of the labor force by plague deaths led to higher wages for workers, mobility among the working classes, and ultimately to the self-emancipation of many serfs. The Peasants' Revolt of 1381, while ultimately unsuccessful in effecting social change, indicates the rising expectations of the English working class and the general social and economic turmoil of the times.

A third important factor that influenced the shape of

the age was a strong current of nationalism. The growth of nationalism is particularly reflected in the use of the English language. For a century and a half after the Battle of Hastings, the majority of the literature written in England—with the exception of a handful of works such as Layamon's *Brut*—was written in French or Latin. The English language had fallen into low social esteem. By the latter half of the fourteenth century, however, English—now showing the influence of French upon the Anglo-Saxon base—was regularly taught in the schools in place of French and was becoming the predominant literary language. John Gower (1325?–1408), for example, was a poet who wrote in French, Latin, and English. His works in each language were selected in order to reach different segments of the reading public, and he represents the cultural pluralism of the day. Geoffrey Chaucer (1340?–1400), the major literary figure of the English Middle Ages, wrote his early poems and the influential *The Canterbury Tales* in English. In the fifteenth century literacy expanded rapidly; some of the more important writers of this period were William Dunbar (1465–1530), Robert Henryson (1425–1506), and Sir Thomas Malory (1394?–1471). The religious dramas and moralities and the lyrics and carols of the fifteenth century speak to an audience much more varied than the court circle alone.

Middle English Literature

The influence of the Church, the changing social structure, and the emerging sense of nationalism were all important to the development of Middle English literature. It is, of course, important for us to see the literature of the age as the age itself would see it. No single formal or thematic principle applies to all the literature of the age; we cannot compartmentalize the literature too neatly. For example, the works of Geoffrey Chaucer defy all categories. In his early career he wrote courtly poetry of all kinds—elegies, visions, satires, and the romance *Troilus and Criseyde*. Later, in *The Canterbury Tales*, he shows once again his mastery of all those early genres plus others that were new to him—beast fable, fabliau (a short bawdy tale in verse), saint's life and sermon, to name only a few. While Chaucer exemplifies and surmounts literary categories, the works of other writers are easier to label. A quick survey of the literary forms in which the authors of the age expressed themselves will help us understand more precisely their achievement.

Romance. The courtly romance—usually a story of a knight seeking honor or adventure, or performing the service of a lover—arose from a context very different from that which nurtured *Beowulf*. Romance can be traced to twelfth-century France and the new atmosphere that emerged there. Although scholars are still debating the causes of this new atmosphere, some think that it developed as a result of the cosmopolitan influence of the Crusades (series of wars undertaken by European Christians between the eleventh and fourteenth century to recover the Holy Land from the Moslems). Others attribute the new atmosphere to the quality of court life in twelfth-century France, Burgundy, and Aquitaine. One feature of romance—its idealization of women—has been traced to the actual circumstances of court life. Because male retainers far outnumbered the women of the court, they found themselves admiring the women "from afar."

The romance is often concerned with the analysis of

The George Inn at Norton St. Philip, Somerset, dates from 1397 and is one of the oldest licensed inns in England. Pilgrims stayed at inns of this type on their way to Canterbury.

A manuscript illumination showing pilgrims on the way to the shrine of St. Thomas à Becket at Canterbury. Becket, the Archbishop of Canterbury killed in 1170 by officers of King Henry II, was considered a martyr by pilgrims in Chaucer's time because of his refusal to place the authority of the State over the authority of the Church.

motive and psychology in love. Needless to say, women play a larger role in the romance than they did in earlier literature. Some critics see the role of the woman in romance as similar, on a symbolic level, to the role of a sovereign receiving fealty from a vassal. Other critics have emphasized similarities to religious worship, especially the veneration of the Virgin Mary popular in the eleventh century. Although the accuracy of the term as a description of actual practices has been questioned, *courtly love* is a useful characterization of conventions governing the relationship of the sexes in the literary world of romance. As commonly used, courtly love describes certain attitudes and behaviors. In a courtly love relationship, the woman (frequently a virgin or another man's wife) is idealized and distanced from her lover; the male suffers to do deeds worthy of the mistress of his heart. Marriage is not the goal of the lovers.

The world of romance is far removed from the world of *Beowulf*—especially in the role and importance it gives to women and to men's relationship with them. In the romance, the grim folk hero of Anglo-Saxon literature and of the French *chanson de geste* has been transformed and softened. Fully aware of the delights of earthly love, the romantic hero chooses to sublimate earthly passion into idealized devotion; he would willingly give all to his sworn love. The romantic hero is bound to the mistress of his heart by oaths of homage and fealty; his virtues are piety, honor, valor, and loyalty. Since his high quests for adventure

and honor had to be made on horseback, the romantic hero became the chivalric knight (cf. French *cheval*, horse), and his code of conduct became the chivalric code.

Romances written in French and in Anglo-Norman French were very much in vogue among the English aristocracy in the late thirteenth and fourteenth centuries. As the demand for literature written in English began to emerge in the mid-fourteenth century, many of these romances were translated into metrical English verse. A number of prose translations appeared in fifteenth-century England. One of them, Malory's *Morte Darthur*, was an original synthesis and work of art in its own right.

Many English romances dealt with Germanic materials, such as *King Horn, Havelock the Dane,* and *Guy of Warwick.* Far more numerous, however, were those of Celtic origin treating of King Arthur and his knights. The first bare mention of Arthur in literature comes in a chronicle of Nennius, a compiler of British history who flourished around 800. It was not until the middle of the twelfth century, however, that Geoffrey of Monmouth in his Latin prose chronicle, *A History of the Kings of Britain,* gives a full account of the career of Arthur, who could supposedly trace his ancestry back to Aeneas of Troy. Arthur, whose deeds circulated in oral tradition for a long time in both Britain and northern France, has a mysterious and magic birth and a marvelous career at arms. There is little of the chivalric element in the early Middle English stories about Arthur; indeed, he is nearer to the epic hero than to the romantic knight. Soon writers turned from Arthur to knights of his so-called Round Table.

A portrait of Chaucer now in the National Portrait Gallery, London. Probably an early copy from a miniature.

A page of The Canterbury Tales *from the Ellesmere Manuscript, made about 1410. It shows Chaucer beginning his* Tale of Melibee.

King Arthur's battle with Modred, from a fourteenth-century Dutch manuscript. According to Malory's Morte Darthur, *Arthur fought Modred to regain his throne, which Modred had taken in his absence. Arthur killed Modred but was fatally wounded in the battle.*

Among the Celtic knights associated with Arthurian legend were the following: Gawain, nephew of Arthur, whose strength was said to wax until noon and then wane, well known for his white steed and his glorious sword of dazzling rays; Percival, regarded as a holy fool; Tristram, a mighty hunter and gifted musician, whose famous love for Isolde is perhaps the peak of attainment in the chivalric love romance; Lancelot, bravest and most celebrated member of Arthur's court, at once the most imposing and the most humanly flawed of King Arthur's knights.

Related to the Arthurian material are several other legends, the most important and complex of which is concerned with the Holy Grail, the cup from which Christ was supposed to have drunk at the Last Supper. The Grail was supposedly miraculous in its powers to feed and to heal. According to tradition, the Grail had been brought to England by Joseph of Arimathea. It later disappeared and was sought after by various knights in various romances. However, it would only be revealed to a pure knight; the search for the Grail became a definite spiritual quest. Knights had to turn their minds from the secular pursuits of mere chivalry. Even Lancelot, as a chivalric lover, did not possess the perfect virtue needed to attain the Grail. But the authors of the Grail legend created a son for Lancelot—Galahad—who did achieve the Grail.

In addition to the Celtic Arthurian romance, there were other popular cycles of medieval romance in both French and English. Particularly influential were stories of Charlemagne and his circle, and Roland and Oliver and their Saracen adversaries (many of whom were later converted to Christianity and subsequently became romantic heroes in their own right). Stories from classical antiquity involving Troy, Thebes, and Alexander the Great also inspired romances.

Devotional and didactic literature. Devotional and didactic literature is a less homogeneous category than romance. It is a classification by intention or customary usage and can contain both courtly and common styles addressed to various audiences. Devotional literature has, of course, a specifically religious focus; didactic literature, on the other hand, is designed to teach or provide instruction on both religious and nonreligious topics. The line between devotional and didactic literature is, at times, fine.

Among devotional texts, both the sermon and the saint's life attempt to rouse their audience to virtue by an examination of successful souls. Sermons were often thematically organized around a passage from Scripture and frequently included *exempla,* or brief stories, to illustrate a particular text. Saints' lives had biographical themes based on real or imaginary events from the lives of martyrs and other holy people. Other devotional works were directed to a very specific audience; for example, the *Ancrene Wisse* (1225?), a vigorous and personal exhortation on the dangers and pleasures of the solitary life, was directed at religious hermits. Other, more technical, devotional literature dealt with the preparations for receiving the seven sacraments of the Roman church, especially penance. Devotional texts written by mystics, such as Richard Rolle de Hampole's (1300?–1349) *The Form of Perfect Living* and Juliana of Norwich's (d. 1443?) *Revelations of Divine Love,* taught of the love and joy they experienced.

Didactic literature attempts to teach while entertaining. The Middle English bestiary was an allegorical or moralizing work which found meaning in the appearance and habits of real or imaginary animals. The allegorical dream vision, a form with classical origins but developed most fully by the French writers of the fourteenth century, was also a didactic work. In an allegorical dream vision, a poet tells the story of someone who, often after looking into some book or pondering some personal problem, sleeps and dreams a wondrous dream, which allegorically—in an extended metaphor—comments upon the problems of this world. Chaucer used the dream vision in his early poems for both elegaic and satiric ends. In the late fourteenth-century dream vision, *The Pearl*, generally attributed to the author of *Sir Gawain and the Green Knight*, the dreamer laments the loss of a pearl of great price, which is both his daughter and God's gift of grace. While most dream visions are relatively short, William Langland's (1332?–1400?) *Piers Plowman* is a notable exception. *Piers Plowman* is a long, difficult, and complex poem. In Langland's poem the dreamer falls asleep somewhere in the Malvern Hills (in southwest England), but his vision is not bound there in time and space. The dreamer ponders the abuse of clerical power in the fourteenth century, journeys back to the Harrowing of Hell, and travels from the London of his day to Jerusalem at the time of the crucifixion of Christ. There are no less than three separate versions of the poem, which may represent the author's revisions of the text over a period of years. Yet, difficult as we find the work today, the forty-seven existing manuscripts of the poem indicate its undeniable popularity in its own time.

We can also consider the historical chronicle to be, in some sense, a form of didactic literature. While the intention of the historical chronicler may not specifically be to teach, the chronicler certainly aims to record contemporary history for the thoughtful observation of later ages. William of Malmesbury (1095–1142), probably the best of the many able chroniclers of his day, and Geoffrey of Monmouth (1110–1154) made secular applications of a long-standing monastic model of narrative history.

Lyrics. The lyrics of the Middle English period should be seen as songs, though most have become separated from any musical notation. As with devotional and didactic works, lyrics cannot be tied exclusively to any one audience, courtly or common, religious or secular. The mostly anonymous authors moved freely between religious and secular subjects and conventions. Their topics ranged from love (both divine and human) to contemporary politics to landlords and bad weather. They wrote verse that freely criticized Church and state alike, frequently sympathizing with the victims of ecclesiastical or royal tyranny. It is difficult to date the individual lyrics that have come down to us with much certainty because they have been preserved in manuscript in haphazard fashion; a significant number probably date from the thirteenth century.

Two illustrations from an old manuscript (Cotton Nero A, X, 4) of Sir Gawain and the Green Knight. *One illustration shows the beheading scene; the other shows Sir Gawain and the Lady of the Castle of the Green Knight.*

Drama. The later Middle Ages witnessed the birth of English drama. The drama from about 1200 to 1500—consisting of liturgical, mystery, and morality plays—does not develop in a smooth, causal progression. Although earlier scholars thought that medieval drama evolved in complexity from simple Latin plays (based on Church liturgy) to larger cycles of plays, modern scholars, on the other hand, believe that cycle plays represented a new dramatic impulse directed at a new audience. It is apparent that the authors of the cycle plays learned dramatic lessons from the liturgy since they proceeded to broaden the scope of their plays, both in their treatment of all Christian history and in their inclusion of secular as well as devotional materials.

The origin of religious drama was humble and quite simple. The dialogue between the priests and the people during church services was naturally dramatic. Soon a simple acting out (usually by priests) of familiar liturgical episodes—such as the coming of the three Marys to the sepulcher at the Resurrection, or the search for the Christ child by the Three Magi—was introduced into the sacred services. Early mystery plays (sometimes called miracle plays) were dramatizations from biblical history, the legends of the saints, and the liturgy of the Church. They are called mystery plays because they are concerned, in the widest sense, with the mystery of Christ's redemption.

The progress of religious drama in England was advanced by at least two developments of the later Middle Ages—one economic and one ecclesiastical. The first was the notable growth of the towns and the corresponding development in the growth and power of the trade guilds. These guilds were well-organized bodies that had the inclination both to take over the religious plays from the Church and to develop them in wider channels. The impulse which the Church gave to the growth of the plays was the establishment of certain festival days. Corpus Christi, a movable holiday established in 1264, is perhaps the most noteworthy example. It occurred late in the spring and thus provided a suitable season and occasion for outdoor performances. A representative cycle of plays designed for presentation on Corpus Christi would include the important moments in salvation history—for example, the Creation, the Fall, the Flood, the story of Abraham and Isaac, the birth of Christ (usually treated by several plays), the dramatic incidents of Christ's ministry, the Crucifixion, the Resurrection, and the Last Judgment. Each play was the business and responsibility of a particular guild. The actors in the cycle plays were amateurs who were nevertheless paid by the various guilds for their acting and were fined for neglecting rehearsals. Guild records also list payments for costumes and rudimentary stage properties. The motivation for using these properties was essentially symbolic—as when God was placed on a beautiful throne—rather than an attempt at realism.

In certain English towns, like Chester and York, festival performances utilized flat wagons, or pageants. Whether the plays were produced on the wagons, which would then move to new sites to repeat the performance, is a matter of some debate. In other towns, like Coventry, the cycle plays are thought to have been acted out in sequence at a single place on a center stage surrounded by an audience. Whether on pageant wagons or at a central location, these performances used their stages in an open and flexible way, with the various scenes and episodes appearing in the same space with little or no formal indication of any change of locale.

Dating from the first decade of the fifteenth century, the morality play—thought by some scholars to have originated in the schools and universities—represents a different, though related, style of drama. Whereas the mystery plays are designed to teach the faithful significant events in biblical history, the morality plays typically present, in extended allegories, the struggle between the forces of good and evil for man's immortal soul.

According to the common formula of the morality play, man is conceived in sin and born graceless. His mortal career is a struggle between the good and bad qualities in him: the good qualities pull him toward heaven; the bad qualities push him toward hell. The overtly didactic purpose of the morality play (to assist the wavering to lead a righteous life) made a clearly defined dramatic conflict inevitable. Man is surrounded on one side by the world, the flesh, and the devil, and on the other by the cardinal Christian virtues. The characters in the morality play are abstract virtues and vices. Death usually overtakes the protagonist. Yet, though the action is customarily somber, the morality play is not a tragedy; the soul of the protagonist, after enduring the greatest temptations, is in the end judged and saved. Furthermore, as in the mystery plays, the comic realism of some characters lightens the grim subject matter while furthering the theme of the play.

As the fifteenth century drew to a close, so did the distinctively medieval period of English culture and literature. Within the decade after Sir Thomas Malory completed his majestic *Morte Darthur* in 1469, the art of printing was introduced into England by William Caxton (1422?–1491?). Perhaps no single event did so much to change the literary climate in England as the establishment of Caxton's press, with its potential for introducing literature to a growing audience. A decade after printing was introduced came the accession of the Tudor dynasty with the crowning of Henry VII in 1485. The Renaissance was beginning.

BEOWULF

Beowulf is well fitted to stand as the chief surviving monument of Old English literature. Its celebration of heroic virtue together with its sombre awareness of man's mortality finely illustrates the mingling of pagan and Christian values within the Anglo-Saxon culture.

Beowulf, the only complete Old English epic that has been preserved, survives in one manuscript (Cotton Vitellius A XV), now in the British Museum. It was somehow saved from destruction following the dissolution of the monasteries by Henry VIII in 1536. The manuscript was written in Wessex about the year 1000, but the poem itself was probably composed in Northumbria sometime around 750. An event described in the poem has been identified as belonging to the early sixth century—Hygelac's raid on the Frisians (l. 2050) occurred, according to the Frankish chroniclers, between 512 and 520. The legends embodied in the poem are, of course, much older.

Nothing is known of the so-called *Beowulf* Poet except by inference. Some early critics argued for multiple authorship largely because the complex unity of the poem, which modern studies of orally composed poetry have helped us to understand more clearly, was not visible to them. Most critics today assume one author for the version we have. The evidence of the poem itself allows us to conclude that the author had some clerical learning, was acquainted with conduct at the royal court, was familiar with the heroic legends of his race, and was expert in the composition of alliterative poetry. Like many epic poets, he was an admirer of old times and old ways; he emphasized established ideals of social and personal conduct by embodying them in the figure of a hero whom his audience could strive to emulate.

This hero, Beowulf, is a Geat. It is uncertain who the Geats actually were. They might have been the Jutes of Jutland, but more probably their name refers to the Old Norse Gautar, a tribe in southern Sweden. There may well have been such a tribe with a king, Hygelac, whose chief thane, Beowulf, was endowed with extraordinary skill as a warrior and as a swimmer. But Beowulf's deeds in Hrothgar's court—killing the monster Grendel and following the mother of Grendel to her lair—belong to legend rather than to history, as the many folktale analogues to his adventures indicate. Similarly, we must look beyond the actual Geats and Danes to see Beowulf as the man whom an eighth-century English poet chose as the embodiment of what the poet's society saw as extraordinary virtues. The figure of Beowulf has dignity and polish, in the sense that he is fully acquainted with the etiquette demanded of a chieftain of his importance. His physical strength is overwhelming; his courage is solid and sure. Most of all, his stoical attitudes toward time and fate endowed him with a world view which would have been wholly admirable to the Christianized audience of the eighth century.

Note on the Old English Language

English is a member of the Anglo-Frisian branch of the West Germanic languages. Its nearest relatives are the Frisian, still spoken in the northernmost coastal regions of Holland, and Low German ("Plattdeutsch"), the dialect of northern Germany. As a member of the Germanic language group, English is part of the Indo-European family of languages.

In the period before the Norman Conquest, and for a generation or so thereafter, English was highly inflected in its use of case endings, even more so than Modern German. It had not made use, as yet, of its amazing power of borrowing and assimilating foreign words—one of the striking features of Modern English. Its vocabulary tended to be conservative; its grammar, complex; and its dialectal differences, striking. During the Old English period (before 1100) four major dialects are recognized: the Northumbrian, the Mercian, the West Saxon, and the Kentish. An overwhelming proportion of the surviving Old English literature is in West Saxon, which thus becomes the "classic" dialect of Old English.

The presence of a full inflectional system is a distinctive mark of Old English. The inflectional endings began to weaken and even to disappear during the eleventh century. The sloughing-off process was slow and did not approach completion until after 1500. There is, therefore, a linguistic reason for the division of English literature into Old, Middle, and Modern: the Old English (500–1100) being the period of full inflections; the Middle English (1100–1500), the period of weakening and disappearing inflectional endings; the Modern English (1500 to the present), the period of loss of inflections.

The following passage, representing the first eleven lines of *Beowulf,* serves to illustrate the language and versification of Old English. The alliteration, the free four-beat line with marked caesura or pause in the middle (at the end of the second foot), the absence of rhyme, and the strong, direct language should be noted.

> Hwaet! we Gar-Dena   in geardagum,
> þeodcyninga   þrym gefrunon,
> hu þa aeþelingas   ellen fremedon!
> Oft Scyld Scefing   sceaþena þreatum
> monegum maegþum   meodosetla ofteah,
> egsode eorlas,   syððan aerest wearð
> feasceaft funden;   he þaes frofre gebad,
> weox under wolcnum,   weorðmyndum þah
> oð þaet him aeghwylc   þara ymbsittendra

ofer hronrade   hyran scolde,
gomban gyldan;   þaet waes god cyning!

The pronunciation of vowels in Old English generally follows that in Latin (Continental). The consonants are in the main pronounced as in Modern English. These exceptions should be noted: *y* represents a sound approximating French *u*; *ae* is Modern English *a* as in *hat, cat, man*; *eo* and *ea* are diphthongs with the stress on the first vowel—among the consonants, *c* before *e* and *i* is probably a *ch*-sound, otherwise, a *k*; *g* before *e* and *i* is a roughened guttural *y*, otherwise hard *g*; *sc* is probably Modern English *sh*. All syllables have value, with the accent of a word normally on the first syllable. ð and þ represent the Modern English *th*-sounds.

THE DANISH COURT AND THE RAIDS OF GRENDEL

Lo! we have listened to many a lay°
Of the Spear-Danes'° fame, their splendor of old,
Their mighty princes, and martial deeds!
Many a mead-hall Scyld, son of Sceaf,°
Snatched from the forces of savage foes.
From a friendless foundling, feeble and wretched,
He grew to a terror as time brought change.
He throve under heaven in power and pride
Till alien peoples beyond the ocean°
10 Paid toll and tribute. A good king he!
   To him thereafter an heir was born,
A son of his house, whom God had given
As stay to the people; God saw the distress
The leaderless nation had long endured,
The Giver of glory, the Lord of life,
Showered fame on the son of Scyld;
His name was honored, Beowulf° known,
To the farthest dwellings in Danish lands.
So must a young man strive for good
20 With gracious gifts from his father's store,
That in later seasons, if war shall scourge,
A willing people may serve him well.
'Tis by earning honor a man must rise
In every state. Then his hour struck,
And Scyld passed on to the peace of God.
   As their leader had bidden, whose word was law
In the Scylding realm which he long had ruled,
His loving comrades carried him down
To the shore of ocean; a ring-prowed ship,

Straining at anchor and sheeted with ice,   30
Rode in the harbor, a prince's pride.
Therein they laid him, their well-loved lord,
Their ring-bestower,° in the ship's embrace,
The mighty prince at the foot of the mast
Amid much treasure and many a gem
From far-off lands. No lordlier ship
Have I ever heard of, with weapons heaped,
With battle-armor, with bills and byrnies.°
On the ruler's breast lay a royal treasure
As the ship put out on the unknown deep.   40
With no less adornment they dressed him round,
Or gift of treasure, than once they gave
Who launched him first on the lonely sea
While still but a child. A golden standard
They raised above him, high over head,
Let the wave take him on trackless seas.
Mournful their mood and heavy their hearts;
Nor wise man nor warrior knows for a truth
Unto what haven that cargo came.
   Then Beowulf ruled o'er the Scylding realm,   50
Beloved and famous, for many a year—
The prince, his father, had passed away—
Till, firm in wisdom and fierce in war,
The mighty Healfdene held the reign,
Ruled, while he lived, the lordly Scyldings.
Four sons and daughters were seed of his line,
Heorogar and Hrothgar, leaders of hosts,
And Halga, the good. I have also heard
A daughter was Onela's consort and queen,
The fair bed-mate of the Battle-Scylfing.°   60
   To Hrothgar was granted glory in war,
Success in battle; retainers bold
Obeyed him gladly; his band increased
To a mighty host. Then his mind was moved
To have men fashion a high-built hall,
A mightier mead-hall than man had known,
Wherein to portion to old and young
All goodly treasure that God had given,
Save only the folk-land, and lives of men.
His word was published to many a people   70
Far and wide o'er the ways of earth
To rear a folk-stead richly adorned;
The task was speeded, the time soon came
That the famous mead-hall was finished and done.
To distant nations its name was known,
The Hall of the Hart;° and the king kept well
His pledge and promise to deal out gifts,
Rings at the banquet. The great hall rose

Beowulf. Verse translation by Charles W. Kennedy **1 lay,** a narrative poem **2 Spear-Danes.** The Danes are called by a number of names: Scyldings, Ingwines, Spear-Danes, Ring-Danes, Victory-Danes, Bright-Danes, East-, West-, North-, and South-Danes **4 Scyld, son of Sceaf.** At a time when the Danes were greatly oppressed by their enemies, a ship came mysteriously to their shores bearing a baby and rich treasures. The baby grew up to lead the Danes victoriously in battle and to establish their dynasty of kings. At his death he passed away to the great deep whence he had come, probably on the very ship that had brought him. Sea burials of this sort were common in Scandinavia from the fourth to the sixth centuries **9 ocean,** literally, the "whale road," one of several notable kennings (metaphorical synonyms, often naming by function) for the sea **17 Beowulf.** This ruler should not be confused with the later Beowulf whose exploits are the center of this poem

33 ring-bestower. A kenning for "king." Rings or other presents, the usual reward for services rendered, were given out by the king of the tribe or nation at the banquet or feast held in celebration of the deed performed. On less formal occasions, too, a king would distribute gifts among the chief warriors of his tribe to insure their service to him in the future **38 battle armor . . . byrnies.** The usual equipment of the Viking warrior consisted of (1) his byrnie, or corslet, generally of chain mail, (2) his sword, (3) his short sword or dagger, (4) his spear of ashwood tipped with iron or steel, (5) his shield of linden wood (occasionally of iron), and (6) an elaborate helmet, consisting of headpiece (often surmounted by the image of a boar's head), visor, and nose guard, with artistic designs and animal figures on the crest **60 Battle-Scylfyng.** Scylfyng or Swede, of whom we shall hear more later in the poem **76 Hall of the Hart,** or Heorot, so called from the antlers with which the gables of the building were ornamented. The hart was a symbol of royalty

High and horn-gabled, holding its place
80 Till the battle-surge° of consuming flame
Should swallow it up; the hour was near
That the deadly hate of a daughter's husband
Should kindle to fury and savage feud.

Then an evil spirit° who dwelt in the darkness
Endured it ill that he heard each day
The din of revelry ring through the hall,
The sound of the harp, and the scop's sweet song.
A skillful bard sang the ancient story
Of man's creation; how the Maker wrought
90 The shining earth with its circling waters;
In splendor established the sun and moon
As lights to illumine the land of men;
Fairly adorning the fields of earth
With leaves and branches; creating life
In every creature that breathes and moves.
So the lordly warriors lived in gladness,
At ease and happy, till a fiend from hell
Began a series of savage crimes.
They called him Grendel, a demon grim
100 Haunting the fen-lands, holding the moors,
Ranging the wastes, where the wretched wight
Made his lair with the monster kin;
He bore the curse of the seed of Cain°
Whereby God punished the grievous guilt
Of Abel's murder. Nor ever had Cain
Cause to boast of that deed of blood;
God banished him far from the fields of men;
Of his blood was begotten an evil brood,
Marauding monsters and menacing trolls,
110 Goblins and giants who battled with God
A long time. Grimly He gave them reward!

Then at the nightfall the fiend drew near
Where the timbered mead-hall towered on high,
To spy how the Danes fared after the feast.
Within the wine-hall he found the warriors
Fast in slumber, forgetting grief,
Forgetting the woe of the world of men.
Grim and greedy the gruesome monster,
Fierce and furious, launched attack,
120 Slew thirty spearmen asleep in the hall,
Sped away gloating, gripping the spoil,
Dragging the dead men home to his den.
Then in the dawn with the coming of daybreak
The war-might of Grendel was widely known.
Mirth was stilled by the sound of weeping;
The wail of the mourner awoke with day.
And the peerless hero, the honored prince,
Weighed down with woe and heavy of heart,
Sat sorely grieving for slaughtered thanes,
130 As they traced the track of the cursed monster.

From that day onward the deadly feud
Was a long-enduring and loathsome strife.
Not longer was it than one night later
The fiend returning renewed attack
With heart firm-fixed in the hateful war,
Feeling no rue for the grievous wrong.
'Twas easy thereafter to mark the men
Who sought their slumber elsewhere afar,°
Found beds in the bowers, since Grendel's hate
Was so baldly blazoned in baleful signs. 140
He held himself at a safer distance
Who escaped the clutch of the demon's claw.
So Grendel raided and ravaged the realm,
One against all, in an evil war
Till the best of buildings was empty and still.
'Twas a weary while! Twelve winters' time
The lord of the Scyldings° had suffered woe,
Sore affliction and deep distress.
And the malice of Grendel, in mournful lays,
Was widely sung by the sons of men, 150
The hateful feud that he fought with Hrothgar—
Year after year of struggle and strife,
An endless scourging, a scorning of peace
With any man of the Danish might.
No strength could move him to stay his hand,
Or pay for° his murders; the wise knew well
They could hope for no halting of savage assault.
Like a dark death-shadow the ravaging demon,
Night-long prowling the misty moors,
Ensnared the warriors, wary or weak. 160
No man can say how these shades of hell
Come and go on their grisly rounds.

With many an outrage, many a crime,
The fierce lone-goer, the foe of man,
Stained the seats of the high-built house,
Haunting the hall in the hateful dark.
But throne or treasure he might not touch,
Finding no favor or grace with God.
Great was the grief of the Scylding leader,
His spirit shaken, while many a lord 170
Gathered in council considering long
In what way brave men best could struggle
Against these terrors of sudden attack.
From time to time in their heathen temples°
Paying homage they offered prayer
That the Slayer of souls would send them succor
From all the torment that troubled the folk.
Such was the fashion and such the faith
Of their heathen hearts that they looked to hell,
Not knowing the Maker, the mighty Judge, 180

80 **battle-surge.** Hrothgar's daughter Freawaru was later married to Ingeld, prince of the Heathobards, to settle a feud which had long raged between the two tribes. At the wedding feast the feud again broke out; the warriors of Ingeld invaded Hrothgar's dominions and burned Heorot to the ground. This is one of the many allusions in the poem to events before and after the story being told   84 **evil spirit,** Grendel   103 **seed of Cain.** Grendel is thought of as being descended from Cain, who, because of the murder of his brother Abel, was cursed by God (*Genesis,* 4: 10-16)

137 **'Twas easy . . . elsewhere afar.** An example of typical Anglo-Saxon humor, which consisted in whimsically sarcastic understatement   147 **lord of the Scyldings,** Hrothgar   156 **pay for,** i.e., through the payment of blood money. See l. 442 and note. A murderer was required by law to pay blood money to the relatives of the deceased (as in the case of Ecgtheow, Beowulf's father). Grendel, as an uncivilized criminal, did not recognize the law. His whole relation with the Danes is spoken of as a feud, such as that between the Danes and the Heathobards or between the Geats and the Swedes   174 **heathen temples.** In the opinion of the Christian poet, the ancient Germanic peoples worshiped the devil (the "Slayer of souls") and sacrificed to idols. Elsewhere in *Beowulf,* Hrothgar's religious sentiments seem definitely Christian. The poet seems to imply that, in a time of stress, the Danes reverted to their heathen faith

Nor how to worship the Wielder of glory,
The Lord of heaven, the God of hosts.
Woe unto him who in fierce affliction
Shall plunge his soul in the fiery pit
With no hope of mercy or healing change;
But well with the soul that at death seeks God,
And finds his peace in his Father's bosom.
    The son of Healfdene was heavy-hearted,
Sorrowfully brooding in sore distress,
190 Finding no help in a hopeless strife,
Too bitter the struggle that stunned the people,
The long oppression, loathsome and grim.

THE COMING OF BEOWULF

Then tales of the terrible deeds of Grendel
Reached Hygelac's thane° in his home with the Geats;
Of living strong men he was the strongest,
Fearless and gallant and great of heart.
He gave command for a goodly vessel
Fitted and furnished; he fain would sail
Over the swan-road° to seek the king
200 Who suffered so sorely for need of men.
And his bold retainers found little to blame
In his daring venture, dear though he was;
They viewed the omens, and urged him on.
Brave was the band he had gathered about him,
Fourteen stalwarts seasoned and bold,
Seeking the shore where the ship lay waiting,
A sea-skilled mariner sighting the landmarks.
Came the hour of boarding; the boat was riding
The waves of the harbor under the hill.
210 The eager mariners mounted the prow;
Billows were breaking, sea against sand.
In the ship's hold snugly they stowed their trappings,
Gleaming armor and battle-gear;
Launched the vessel, the well-braced bark,
Seaward bound on a joyous journey.
Over breaking billows, with bellying sail
And foamy beak, like a flying bird
The ship sped on, till the next day's sun
Showed sea-cliffs shining, towering hills
220 And stretching headlands. The sea was crossed,
The voyage ended, the vessel moored.
And the Weder people waded ashore
With clatter of trappings and coats of mail;
Gave thanks to God that His grace had granted
Sea-paths safe for their ocean-journey.
    Then the Scylding coast-guard watched from the
        sea-cliff
Warriors bearing their shining shields,
Their gleaming war-gear, ashore from the ship.
His mind was puzzled, he wondered much
230 What men they were. On his good horse mounted,
Hrothgar's thane made haste to the beach,

Boldly brandished his mighty spear
With manful challenge: 'What men are you,
Carrying weapons and clad in steel,
Who thus come driving across the deep
On the ocean-lanes in your lofty ship?
Long have I served as the Scylding outpost,
Held watch and ward at the ocean's edge
Lest foreign foemen with hostile fleet
Should come to harry our Danish home,   240
And never more openly sailed to these shores
Men without password, or leave to land.
I have never laid eyes upon earl on earth
More stalwart and sturdy than one of your troop,
A hero in armor; no hall-thane he
Tricked out with weapons, unless looks belie him,
And noble bearing. But now I must know
Your birth and breeding, nor may you come
In cunning stealth upon Danish soil.
You distant-dwellers, you far sea-farers,   250
Hearken, and ponder words that are plain:
'Tis best you hasten to have me know
Who your kindred and whence you come.'
    The lord of the seamen gave swift reply,
The prince of the Weders unlocked his word-hoard:
'We are sprung of a strain of the Geatish stock,
Hygelac's comrades and hearth-companions.
My father was famous in many a folk-land,
A leader noble, Ecgtheow his name!
Many a winter went over his head   260
Before death took him from home and tribe;
Well nigh every wise man remembers him well
Far and wide on the ways of earth.
With loyal purpose we seek your lord,
The prince of your people, great Healfdene's son.°
Be kindly of counsel; weighty the cause
That leads us to visit the lord of the Danes;
Nor need it be secret, as far as I know!
You know if it's true, as we've heard it told,
That among the Scyldings some secret scather,   270
Some stealthy demon in dead of night,
With grisly horror and fiendish hate
Is spreading unheard-of havoc and death.
Mayhap I can counsel the good, old king
What way he can master the merciless fiend,
If his coil of evil is ever to end
And feverish care grow cooler and fade—
Or else ever after his doom shall be
Distress and sorrow while still there stands
This best of halls on its lofty height.'   280
    Then from the saddle the coast-guard spoke,
The fearless sentry: 'A seasoned warrior
Must know the difference between words and deeds,
If his wits are with him. I take your word
That your band is loyal to the lord of the Scyldings.
Now go your way with your weapons and armor,
And I will guide you; I'll give command

194 **Hygelac's thane,** Beowulf. A thane is a military attendant or retainer. Geats, sometimes called the Weders. Weder itself means "weather" or "storm" and has reference to the nature of the coast on which the Geats lived   199 **swan-road,** another kenning for "sea"

265 **Healfdene's son,** Hrothgar

That my good retainers may guard your ship,
Your fresh-tarred floater, from every foe,
290 And hold it safe in its sandy berth,
Till the curving prow once again shall carry
The loved man home to the land of the Geat.
To hero so gallant shall surely be granted
To come from the swordplay sound and safe.'
Then the Geats marched on; behind at her mooring,
Fastened at anchor, their broad-beamed boat
Safely rode on her swinging cable.
Boar-heads glittered on glistening helmets°
Above their cheek-guards, gleaming with gold;
300 Bright and fire-hardened the boar held watch
Over the column of marching men.
Onward they hurried in eager haste
Till their eyes caught sight of the high-built hall,
Splendid with gold, the seat of the king,
Most stately of structures under the sun;
Its light shone out over many a land.
The coast-guard showed them the shining hall,
The home of heroes; made plain the path;
Turned his horse; gave tongue to words:
310 'It is time to leave you! The mighty Lord
In His mercy shield you and hold you safe
In your bold adventure. I'll back to the sea
And hold my watch against hostile horde.'

BEOWULF'S WELCOME AT HROTHGAR'S COURT

The street had paving of colored stone;
The path was plain to the marching men.
Bright were their byrnies, hard and hand-linked;
In their shining armor the chain-mail sang
As the troop in their war-gear tramped to the hall.
The sea-weary sailors set down their shields,
320 Their wide, bright bucklers along the wall,
And sank to the bench. Their byrnies rang.
Their stout spears stood in a stack together
Shod with iron and shaped of ash.
'Twas a well-armed troop! Then a stately warrior
Questioned the strangers about their kin:
'Whence come you bearing your burnished shields,
Your steel-gray harness and visored helms,
Your heap of spears? I am Hrothgar's herald,
His servant-thane. I have never seen strangers,
330 So great a number, of nobler mien.
Not exiles, I ween, but high-minded heroes
In greatness of heart have you sought out Hrothgar.'
Then bold under helmet the hero made answer,
The lord of the Weders, manful of mood,
Mighty of heart: 'We are Hygelac's men,
His board-companions; Beowulf is my name.
I will state my mission to Healfdene's son,
The noble leader, your lordly prince,
If he will grant approach to his gracious presence.'

And Wulfgar answered, the Wendel prince,°   340
Renowned for merit in many a land,
For war-might and wisdom: 'I will learn the wish
Of the Scylding leader, the lord of the Danes,
Our honored ruler and giver of rings,
Concerning your mission, and soon report
The answer our leader thinks good to give.'
He swiftly strode to where Hrothgar sat
Old and gray with his earls about him;
Crossed the floor and stood face to face
With the Danish king; he knew courtly custom.   350
Wulfgar saluted his lord and friend:
'Men from afar have fared to our land
Over ocean's margin—men of the Geats,
Their leader called Beowulf—seeking a boon,
The holding of parley, my prince, with thee.
O gracious Hrothgar, refuse not the favor!
In their splendid war-gear they merit well
The esteem of earls; he's a stalwart leader
Who led this troop to the land of the Danes.'
Hrothgar spoke, the lord of the Scyldings: 360
'Their leader I knew when he still was a lad.
His father was Ecgtheow; Hrethel the Geat°
Gave him in wedlock his only daughter.
Now is their son come, keen for adventure,
Finding his way to a faithful friend.
Sea-faring men who have voyaged to Geatland
With gifts of treasure as token of peace,
Say that his hand-grip has thirty men's strength.
God, in His mercy, has sent him to save us—
So springs my hope—from Grendel's assaults.   370
For his gallant courage I'll load him with gifts!
Make haste now, marshal the men to the hall,
And give them welcome to Danish ground.'
Then to the door went the well-known warrior,
Spoke from the threshold welcoming words:
'The Danish leader, my lord, declares
That he knows your kinship; right welcome you come,
You stout sea-rovers, to Danish soil.
Enter now, in your shining armor
And vizored helmets, to Hrothgar's hall.   380
But leave your shields and the shafts of slaughter
To wait the issue and weighing of words.'
Then the bold one rose with his band around him,
A splendid massing of mighty thanes;
A few stood guard as the Geat gave bidding
Over the weapons stacked by the wall.
They followed in haste on the heels of their leader
Under Heorot's roof. Full ready and bold
The helmeted warrior strode to the hearth;
Beowulf spoke; his byrny glittered,   390
His war-net woven by cunning of smith:
'Hail! King Hrothgar! I am Hygelac's thane,
Hygelac's kinsman. Many a deed
Of honor and daring I've done in my youth.

---

298 **Boar- heads . . . helmets.** The helmets were crested with the images of boars

340 **Wendel prince,** probably a prince of the Vandals, the East Germanic race that occupied Spain and northern Africa   362 **Hrethel,** grandfather of Beowulf and father of Hygelac

This business of Grendel was brought to my ears
On my native soil. The sea-farers say
This best of buildings, this boasted hall,
Stands dark and deserted when sun is set,
When darkening shadows gather with dusk.
400 The best of my people, prudent and brave,
Urged me, King Hrothgar, to seek you out;
They had in remembrance my courage and might.
Many had seen me come safe from the conflict,
Bloody from battle; five foes I bound
Of the giant kindred, and crushed their clan.
Hard-driven in danger and darkness of night
I slew the nicors that swam the sea,
Avenged the woe they had caused the Weders,
And ended their evil—they needed the lesson!
410 And now with Grendel, the fearful fiend,
Single-handed I'll settle the strife!
Prince of the Danes, protector of Scyldings,
Lord of nations, and leader of men,
I beg one favor—refuse me not,
Since I come thus faring from far-off lands—
That I may alone with my loyal earls,
With this hardy company, cleanse Hart-Hall.
I have heard that the demon in proud disdain
Spurns all weapons; and I too scorn—
420 May Hygelac's heart have joy of the deed—
To bear my sword, or sheltering shield,
Or yellow buckler, to battle the fiend.
With hand-grip only I'll grapple with Grendel;
Foe against foe I'll fight to the death,
And the one who is taken must trust to God's grace!
The demon, I doubt not, is minded to feast
In the hall unaffrighted, as often before,
On the force of the Hrethmen, the folk of the Geats.
No need then to bury the body he mangles!
430 If death shall call me, he'll carry away
My gory flesh to his fen-retreat
To gorge at leisure and gulp me down,
Soiling the marshes with stains of blood.
There'll be little need longer to care for my body!
If the battle slays me, to Hygelac send
This best of corselets that covers my breast,
Heirloom of Hrethel, and Wayland's work,°
Finest of byrnies. Fate° goes as Fate must!'
    Hrothgar spoke, the lord of the Scyldings:
440 'Deed of daring and dream of honor
Bring you, friend Beowulf, knowing our need!
Your father once fought the greatest of feuds,°
Laid Heatholaf low, of the Wylfing line;
And the folk of the Weders refused him shelter
For fear of revenge. Then he fled to the South-Danes,

The Honor-Scyldings beyond the sea.
I was then first governing Danish ground,
As a young lad ruling the spacious realm,
The home-land of warriors. Heorogar° was dead,   450
The son of Healfdene no longer living,
My older brother, and better than I!
Thereafter by payment composing the feud,
O'er the water's ridge I sent to the Wylfing
Ancient treasure; he swore me oaths!
It is sorrow sore to recite to another
The wrongs that Grendel has wrought in the hall,
His savage hatred and sudden assaults.
My war-troop is weakened, my hall-band° is wasted;
Fate swept them away into Grendel's grip.
But God may easily bring to an end   460
The ruinous deeds of the ravaging foe.
Full often my warriors over their ale-cups
Boldly boasted,° when drunk with beer,
They would bide in the beer-hall the coming of battle,
The fury of Grendel, with flashing swords.
Then in the dawn, when the daylight strengthened,
The hall stood reddened and reeking with gore,
Bench-boards wet with the blood of battle;
And I had the fewer of faithful fighters,
Beloved retainers, whom Death had taken.   470
Sit now at the banquet, unbend your mood,
Speak of great deeds as your heart may spur you!'
    Then in the beer-hall were benches made ready
For the Geatish heroes. Noble of heart,
Proud and stalwart, they sat them down
And a beer-thane served them; bore in his hands
The patterned ale-cup, pouring the mead,
While the scop's sweet singing was heard in the hall.
There was joy of heroes, a host at ease,
A welcome meeting of Weder and Dane.   480

UNFERTH TAUNTS BEOWULF

Then out spoke Unferth,° Ecglaf's son,
Who sat at the feet of the Scylding lord,
Picking a quarrel—for Beowulf's quest,
His bold sea-voyaging, irked him sore;
He bore it ill that any man other
In all the earth should ever achieve
More fame under heaven than he himself:
'Are you the Beowulf that strove with Breca°

---

437 **Wayland's work.** Wayland was the Germanic god of metal-working, comparable, at least in part, to the classical Vulcan. Ancient armor of fine workmanship was likely to be attributed to Wayland's manufacture   438 **Fate,** considered as a personified deity presiding over the destinies of man   442 **the greatest of feuds.** The story of Ecgtheow, Beowulf's father, illustrates interesting elements in Germanic law and politics. When he killed a man belonging to another tribe (the Wylfings), he was in danger of precipitating a feud between that tribe and his own, the Geats. The Geats (called here the Weders) avoided the feud by exiling Ecgtheow. He sought refuge in the court of Hrothgar, who made it possible for Ecgtheow to rejoin his tribe by paying blood money to the Wylfings. Beowulf's coming to Denmark is in part payment for Hrothgar's services to Ecgtheow

449 **Heorogar,** the eldest son of Healfdene and Hrothgar's predecessor on the Danish throne. Heorogar's son, Heoroweard, would ordinarily have succeeded, but the Germanic kingship was elective as well as hereditary   458 **hall-band,** the *comitatus,* the retinue of warriors surrounding the king   463 **boasted, etc.** The "boast" of a warrior was not an instance of conceit but a means of self-incitement to heroic deeds. If the boast was not accomplished, the warrior was shamed, and death was preferable to shame. This Germanic custom of boasting, of stating definitely what one intended to do—usually at a feast held on the eve of a great emergency—persisted into medieval times and is found in some of the earlier chivalric romances   481 **Unferth,** the spokesman or orator of Hrothgar's court. He is also a thane, warrior, and counselor. His name means, approximately, "disturber of the peace" and is significant of his character—the envious, backbiting malcontent occasionally found in heroic epics   488 **Breca.** Unferth and Beowulf give two versions of an adventure which was probably the subject of a separate epic lay in the *Beowulf* "cycle." According to Beowulf, his feat of swimming from southern Sweden to northern Norway was not a contest but the achieving of a boast that he and Breca, another young warrior, had made in common

In a swimming match in the open sea,
490 Both of you wantonly tempting the waves,
Risking your lives on the lonely deep
For a silly boast? No man could dissuade you,
Nor friend nor foe, from the foolhardy venture
Of ocean-swimming; with outstretched arms
You clasped the sea-stream, measured her streets,
With plowing shoulders parted the waves.
The sea-flood boiled with its wintry surges,
Seven nights you toiled in the tossing sea;
His strength was the greater, his swimming the
    stronger!
500 The waves upbore you at break of day
To the stretching beach of the Battle-Ræmas;°
And Breca departed, beloved of his people,
To the land of the Brondings, the beauteous home,
The stronghold fair, where he governed the folk,
The city and treasure; Beanstan's son°
Made good his boast to the full against you!
Therefore, I ween, worse fate shall befall,
Stout as you are in the struggle of war,
In deeds of battle, if you dare to abide
510 Encounter with Grendel at coming of night.'
    Beowulf spoke, the son of Ecgtheow:
'My good friend Unferth, addled with beer
Much have you made of the deeds of Breca!
I count it true that I had more courage,
More strength in swimming than any other man.
In our youth we boasted—we were both of us boys—
We would risk our lives in the raging sea.
And we made it good! We gripped in our hands
Naked swords, as we swam in the waves,
520 Guarding us well from the whales' assault.
In the breaking seas he could not outstrip me,
Nor would I leave him. For five nights long
Side by side we strove in the waters
Till racing combers wrenched us apart,
Freezing squalls, and the falling night,
And a bitter north wind's icy blast.
Rough were the waves; the wrath of the sea-fish
Was fiercely roused; but my firm-linked byrny,
The gold-adorned corselet that covered my breast,
530 Gave firm defense from the clutching foe.
Down to the bottom a savage sea-beast
Fiercely dragged me and held me fast
In a deadly grip; none the less it was granted me
To pierce the monster with point of steel.
Death swept it away with the swing of my sword.
    The grisly sea-beasts again and again
Beset me sore; but I served them home
With my faithful blade as was well-befitting.
They failed of their pleasure to feast their fill
540 Crowding round my corpse on the ocean-bottom!
Bloody with wounds, at the break of day,
They lay on the sea-beach slain with the sword.
No more would they cumber the mariner's course

On the ocean deep. From the east came the sun,
Bright beacon of God, and the seas subsided;
I beheld the headlands, the windy walls.
Fate often delivers an undoomed earl
If his spirit be gallant! And so I was granted
To slay with the sword-edge nine of the nicors.°
I have never heard tell of more terrible strife   550
Under dome of heaven in darkness of night,
Nor of man harder pressed on the paths of ocean.
But I freed my life from the grip of the foe
Though spent with the struggle. The billows bore me,
The swirling currents and surging seas,
To the land of the Finns.° And little I've heard
Of any such valiant adventures from you!
Neither Breca nor you in the press of battle
Ever showed such daring with dripping swords—
Though I boast not of it! But you stained your blade   560
With blood of your brothers,° your closest of kin;
And for that you'll endure damnation in hell,
Sharp as you are! I say for a truth,
Son of Ecglaf, never had Grendel
Wrought such havoc and woe in the hall,
That horrid demon so harried your king,
If your heart were as brave as you'd have men think!
But Grendel has found that he never need fear
Revenge from your people, or valiant attack
From the Victor-Scyldings; he takes his toll,   570
Sparing none of the Danish stock.
He slays and slaughters and works his will
Fearing no hurt at the hands of the Danes!
But soon will I show him the stuff of the Geats,
Their courage in battle and strength in the strife;
Then let him who may go bold to the mead-hall
When the next day dawns on the dwellings of men,
And the sun in splendor shines warm from the south.'
Glad of heart was the giver of treasure,
Hoary-headed and hardy in war;   580
The lordly leader had hope of help
As he listened to Beowulf's bold resolve.
    There was revel of heroes and high carouse,
Their speech was happy; and Hrothgar's queen,
Of gentle manners, in jewelled splendor
Gave courtly greeting to all the guests.
The high-born lady first bore the beaker
To the Danish leader, lord of the land,
Bade him be blithe at the drinking of beer;
Beloved of his people, the peerless king   590
Joined in the feasting, had joy of the cup.
Then to all alike went the Helming° lady
Bearing the beaker to old and young,
Till the jewelled queen with courtly grace
Paused before Beowulf, proffered the mead.
She greeted the Geat and to God gave thanks,
Wise of word, that her wish was granted;

---

501 **Battle-Ræmas,** probably a tribe whose home was near modern Oslo
505 **Beanstan's son,** Breca

549 **nicors.** The nicor, or water monster, often appeared in Germanic legend
556 **Finns,** usually held to be the Lapps, inhabitants of Finmarken, around the
North Cape in the northern extremity of Norway and considerably above the Arctic Circle   561 **blood of your brothers.** Beowulf here retaliates by unveiling the
story of Unferth's past crime and by accusing him of cowardice   592 **Helming,**
the tribe to which Wealhtheow belonged, possibly Celtic

At last she could look to a hero for help,
Comfort in evil. He took the cup,
600 The hardy warrior, at Wealhtheow's° hand
And, eager for battle, uttered his boast;
Beowulf spoke, the son of Ecgtheow:
'I had firm resolve when I set to sea
With my band of earls in my ocean-ship,
Fully to work the will of your people
Or fall in the struggle slain by the foe.
I shall either perform deeds fitting an earl
Or meet in this mead-hall the coming of death!'
Then the woman was pleased with the words he
        uttered,
610 The Geat-lord's boast; the gold-decked queen
Went in state to sit by her lord.

BEOWULF SLAYS GRENDEL

In the hall as of old° were brave words spoken,
There was noise of revel; happy the host
Till the son of Healfdene would go to his rest.
He knew that the monster would meet in the hall
Relentless struggle when light of the sun
Was dusky with gloom of the gathering night,
And shadow-shapes crept in the covering dark,
Dim under heaven. The host arose.
620 Hrothgar graciously greeted his guest,
Gave rule of the wine-hall, and wished him well,
Praised the warrior in parting words:
'Never to any man, early or late,
Since first I could brandish buckler and sword,
Have I trusted this ale-hall save only to you!
Be mindful of glory, show forth your strength,
Keep watch against foe! No wish of your heart
Shall go unfulfilled if you live through the fight.'
    Then Hrothgar withdrew with his host of retainers,
630 The prince of the Scyldings, seeking his queen,
The bed of his consort. The King of Glory
Had stablished a hall-watch, a guard against Grendel,
Dutifully serving the Danish lord,
The land defending from loathsome fiend.
The Geatish hero put all his hope
In his fearless might and the mercy of God!
He stripped from his shoulders the byrny of steel,
Doffed helmet from head; into hand of thane
Gave inlaid iron, the best of blades;
640 Bade him keep well the weapons of war.
Beowulf uttered a gallant boast,°
The stalwart Geat, ere he sought his bed:
'I count myself nowise weaker in war
Or grapple of battle than Grendel himself.
Therefore I scorn to slay him with sword,
Deal deadly wound, as I well might do!

Nothing he knows of a noble fighting,
Of thrusting and hewing and hacking of shield,
Fierce as he is in the fury of war.
In the shades of darkness we'll spurn the sword   650
If he dares without weapon to do or to die.
And God in His wisdom shall glory assign,
The ruling Lord, as He deems it right.'
Then the bold in battle bowed down to his rest,
Cheek pressed pillow; the peerless thanes
Were stretched in slumber around their lord.
Not one had hope of return to his home,
To the stronghold or land where he lived as a boy.
For they knew how death had befallen the Danes,
How many were slain as they slept in the wine-hall.   660
But the wise Lord wove them fortune in war,
Gave strong support to the Weder people;
They slew their foe by the single strength
Of a hero's courage. The truth is clear,
God rules forever the race of men.
    Then through the shades of enshrouding night
The fiend came stealing; the archers slept
Whose duty was holding the horn-decked hall—
Though one was watching—full well they knew
No evil demon could drag them down   670
To shades under ground if God were not willing.
But the hero watched awaiting the foe,
Abiding in anger the issue of war.
    From the stretching moors, from the misty hollows,
Grendel came creeping, accursed of God,
A murderous ravager minded to snare
Spoil of heroes in high-built hall.
Under clouded heavens he held his way
Till there rose before him the high-roofed house,
Wine-hall of warriors gleaming with gold.   680
Nor was it the first of his fierce assaults
On the home of Hrothgar; but never before
Had he found worse fate or hardier hall-thanes!
Storming the building he burst the portal,
Though fastened of iron, with fiendish strength;
Forced open the entrance in savage fury
And rushed in rage o'er the shining floor.
A baleful glare from his eyes was gleaming
Most like to a flame. He found in the hall
Many a warrior sealed in slumber,   690
A host of kinsmen. His heart rejoiced;
The savage monster was minded to sever
Lives from bodies ere break of day,
To feast his fill of the flesh of men.
But he was not fated to glut his greed
With more of mankind when the night was ended!
    The hardy kinsman of Hygelac° waited
To see how the monster would make his attack.
The demon delayed not, but quickly clutched
A sleeping thane in his swift assault,   700
Tore him in pieces, bit through the bones,
Gulped the blood, and gobbled the flesh,

600 **Wealhtheow's.** Her name suggests "foreign captive." Most royal marriages among the Germanic tribes were political; marriage outside the tribe seems to have been frequent   612 **as of old, etc.,** as in the days before the coming of Grendel. Beowulf's confidence has communicated itself to his hosts   641 **gallant boast, etc.** Note that Beowulf "speaks his boast" before retiring, since the expected sudden attack in the night will not give him time for the customary epic speech

697 **kinsman of Hygelac,** Beowulf

Greedily gorged on the lifeless corpse,
The hands and the feet. Then the fiend stepped nearer,
Sprang on the Sea-Geat lying outstretched,
Clasping him close with his monstrous claw.
But Beowulf grappled and gripped him hard,
Struggled up on his elbow; the shepherd of sins
Soon found that never before had he felt
710 In any man other in all the earth
A mightier hand-grip; his mood was humbled,
His courage fled; but he found no escape!
He was fain to be gone; he would flee to the darkness,
The fellowship of devils. Far different his fate
From that which befell him in former days!
The hardy hero, Hygelac's kinsman,
Remembered the boast he had made at the banquet;
He sprang to his feet, clutched Grendel fast,
Though fingers were cracking, the fiend pulling free.
720 The earl pressed after; the monster was minded
To win his freedom and flee to the fens.
He knew that his fingers were fast in the grip
Of a savage foe. Sorry the venture,
The raid that the ravager made on the hall.
   There was din in Heorot. For all the Danes,
The city-dwellers, the stalwart Scyldings,
That was a bitter spilling of beer!
The walls resounded, the fight was fierce,
Savage the strife as the warriors struggled.
730 The wonder was that the lofty wine-hall
Withstood the struggle, nor crashed to earth,
The house so fair; it was firmly fastened
Within and without with iron bands
Cunningly smithied; though men have said
That many a mead-bench gleaming with gold
Sprang from its sill as the warriors strove.
The Scylding wise men had never weened
That any ravage could wreck the building,
Firmly fashioned and finished with bone,
740 Or any cunning compass its fall,
Till the time when the swelter and surge of fire
Should swallow it up in a swirl of flame.°
   Continuous tumult filled the hall;
A terror fell on the Danish folk
As they heard through the wall the horrible wailing,
The groans of Grendel, the foe of God
Howling his hideous hymn of pain,
The hell-thane shrieking in sore defeat.
He was fast in the grip of the man who was greatest
750 Of mortal men in the strength of his might,
Who would never rest while the wretch was living,
Counting his life-days a menace to man.
   Many an earl of Beowulf brandished
His ancient iron to guard his lord,
To shelter safely the peerless prince.
They had no knowledge, those daring thanes,
When they drew their weapons to hack and hew,
To thrust to the heart, that the sharpest sword,

The choicest iron in all the world,   760
Could work no harm to the hideous foe.
On every sword he had laid a spell,
On every blade; but a bitter death
Was to be his fate; far was the journey
The monster made to the home of fiends.
   Then he who had wrought such wrong to men,
With grim delight as he warred with God,
Soon found that his strength was feeble and failing
In the crushing hold of Hygelac's thane.
Each loathed the other while life should last!
There Grendel suffered a grievous hurt,   770
A wound in the shoulder, gaping and wide;
Sinews snapped and bone-joints broke,
And Beowulf gained the glory of battle.
Grendel, fated, fled to the fens,
To his joyless dwelling, sick unto death.
He knew in his heart that his hours were numbered,
His days at an end. For all the Danes
Their wish was fulfilled in the fall of Grendel.
The stranger from far, the stalwart and strong,
Had purged of evil the hall of Hrothgar,   780
And cleansed of crime; the heart of the hero
Joyed in the deed his daring had done.
The lord of the Geats made good to the East-Danes
The boast he had uttered; he ended their ill,
And all the sorrow they suffered long
And needs must suffer—a foul offense.
The token was clear when the bold in battle
Laid down the shoulder and dripping claw—
Grendel's arm—in the gabled hall!

THE JOY OF THE DANES
AND THE LAY OF SIGEMUND

When morning came, as they tell the tale,   790
Many a warrior hastened to hall,
Folk-leaders faring from far and near
Over wide-running ways, to gaze at the wonder,
The trail of the demon. Nor seemed his death
A matter of sorrow to any man
Who viewed the tracks of the vanquished monster
As he slunk weary-hearted away from the hall,
Doomed and defeated and marking his flight
With bloody prints to the nicors' pool.
The crimson currents bubbled and heaved   800
In eddying reaches reddened with gore;
The surges boiled with the fiery blood.
But the monster had sunk from the sight of men.
In that fenny covert the cursed fiend
Not long thereafter laid down his life,
His heathen spirit; and hell received him.
   Then all the comrades, the old and young,
The brave of heart, in a blithesome band
Came riding their horses home from the mere.
Beowulf's prowess was praised in song;   810
And many men stated that south or north,

743-4 See note on l. 80

Over all the world, or between the seas,
Or under the heaven, no hero was greater,
More worthy of rule. But no whit they slighted
The gracious Hrothgar, their good old king.
Time and again they galloped their horses,
Racing their roans where the roads seemed fairest;
Time and again a gleeman° chanted,
A minstrel mindful of saga and lay.
820 He wove his words in a winsome pattern,
Hymning the burden of Beowulf's feat,
Clothing the story in skillful verse.

*All tales he had ever heard told he sang of
    Sigemund's° glory,*
*Deeds of the Wælsing forgotten, his weary roving and
    wars,*
Feuds and fighting unknown to men, save Fitela only,
*Tales told by uncle to nephew when the two were com-
    panions,*
*What time they were bosom-comrades in battle and
    bitter strife.*
*Many of monster blood these two had slain with the
    sword-edge;*
*Great glory Sigemund gained that lingered long after
    death,*
When he daringly slew the dragon that guarded the
830   *hoard of gold.*
Under the ancient rock° the warrior ventured alone,
No Fitela fighting beside him; but still it befell
*That his firm steel pierced the worm, the point stood
    fast in the wall;*
The dragon had died the death! And the hero's daring
*Had won the treasure to have and to hold as his heart
    might wish.*
*Then the Wælsing loaded his sea-boat, laid in the
    breast of the ship*
*Wondrous and shining treasure; the worm dissolved in
    the heat.*
Sigemund was strongest of men in his deeds of daring,
*Warrior's shield and defender, most famous in days of
    old*
After Heremod's° might diminished, his valor and
840   *vigor in war,*
*Betrayed in the land of the Jutes to the hands of his
    foemen, and slain.*
*Too long the surges of sorrow swept over his soul; in
    the end*
His life was a lingering woe to people and princes.
*In former days his fate was mourned by many a
    warrior*
*Who had trusted his lord for protection from terror and
    woe,*

*Had hoped that the prince would prosper, wielding his
    father's wealth,*
*Ruling the tribe and the treasure, the Scylding city and
    home.*
*Hygelac's kinsman had favor and friendship of all
    mankind,*
But the stain of sin sank deep into Heremod's heart.

Time and again on their galloping steeds   850
Over yellow roads they measured the mile-paths;
Morning sun mounted the shining sky
And many a hero strode to the hall,
Stout of heart, to behold the wonder.
The worthy ruler, the warder of treasure,
Set out from the bowers with stately train;
The queen with her maidens paced over the mead-
    path.
Then spoke Hrothgar; hasting to hall
He stood at the steps, stared up at the roof
High and gold-gleaming; saw Grendel's hand: 860
'Thanks be to God for this glorious sight!
I have suffered much evil, much outrage from Grendel,
But the God of glory works wonder on wonder.
I had no hope of a haven from sorrow
While this best of houses stood badged with blood,
A woe far-reaching for all the wise
Who weened that they never could hold the hall
Against the assaults of devils and demons.
But now with God's help this hero has compassed
A deed our cunning could no way contrive.   870
Surely that woman may say with truth,
Who bore this son, if she still be living,
Our ancient God showed favor and grace
On her bringing-forth! O best of men,
I will keep you, Beowulf, close to my heart
In firm affection; as son to father
Hold fast henceforth to this foster-kinship.
You shall know not want of treasure or wealth
Or goodly gift that your wish may crave,
While I have power. For poorer deeds   880
I have granted guerdon, and graced with honor
Weaker warriors, feebler in fight.
You have done such deeds that your fame shall
    flourish
Through all the ages! God grant you still
All goodly grace as He gave before.'
Beowulf spoke, the son of Ecgtheow:
'By the favor of God we won the fight,
Did the deed of valor, and boldly dared
The might of the monster. I would you could see
The fiend himself lying dead before you!   890
I thought to grip him in stubborn grasp
And bind him down on the bed of death,
There to lie straining in struggle for life,
While I gripped him fast lest he vanish away.
But I might not hold him or hinder his going
For God did not grant it, my fingers failed.
Too savage the strain of his fiendish strength!

To save his life he left shoulder and claw,
The arm of the monster, to mark his track.
900 But he bought no comfort; no whit thereby
Shall the wretched ravager racked with sin,
The loathsome spoiler, prolong his life.
A deep wound holds him in deadly grip,
In baleful bondage; and black with crime
The demon shall wait for the day of doom
When the God of glory shall give decree.'

    Then slower of speech was the son of Ecglaf,
More wary of boasting of warlike deeds,
While the nobles gazed at the grisly claw,
910 The fiend's hand fastened by hero's might
On the lofty roof. Most like to steel
Were the hardened nails, the heathen's hand-spurs,
Horrible, monstrous; and many men said
No tempered sword, no excellent iron,
Could have harmed the monster or hacked away
The demon's battle-claw dripping with blood.

THE FEAST AND THE LAY OF FINNSBURG

In joyful haste was Heorot decked
And a willing host of women and men
Gaily dressed and adorned the guest-hall.
920 Splendid hangings with sheen of gold
Shone on the walls, a glorious sight
To eyes that delight to behold such wonders.
The shining building was wholly shattered
Though braced and fastened with iron bands;
Hinges were riven; the roof alone
Remained unharmed when the horrid monster,
Foul with evil, slunk off in flight,
Hopeless of life. It is hard to flee
The touch of death, let him try who will;
930 Necessity urges the sons of men,
The dwellers on earth, to their destined place
Where the body, bound in its narrow bed,
After the feasting is fast in slumber.

    Soon was the time when the son of Healfdene
Went to the wine-hall; he fain would join
With happy heart in the joy of feasting.
I never have heard of a mightier muster
Of proud retainers around their prince.
All at ease they bent to the benches,
940 Had joy of the banquet; their kinsmen bold,
Hrothgar and Hrothulf,° happy of heart,
In the high-built hall drank many a mead-cup.
The hall of Hrothgar was filled with friends;
No treachery yet had troubled the Scyldings.
Upon Beowulf, then, as a token of triumph,
Hrothgar bestowed a standard of gold,
A banner embroidered, a byrny and helm.
In sight of many, a costly sword
Before the hero was borne on high;

Beowulf drank of many a bowl. 950
No need for shame in the sight of heroes
For gifts so gracious! I never have heard
Of many men dealing in friendlier fashion,
To others on ale-bench, richer rewards,
Four such treasures fretted with gold!
On the crest of the helmet a crowning wreath,
Woven of wire-work, warded the head
Lest tempered swordblade, sharp from the file,
Deal deadly wound when the shielded warrior
Went forth to battle against the foe. 960
Eight horses also with plated headstalls
The lord of heroes bade lead into hall;
On one was a saddle skillfully fashioned
And set with jewels, the battle-seat
Of the king himself, when the son of Healfdene
Would fain take part in the play of swords;
Never in fray had his valor failed,
His kingly courage, when corpses were falling.
And the prince of the Ingwines° gave all these gifts
To the hand of Beowulf, horses and armor; 970
Bade him enjoy them! With generous heart
The noble leader, the lord of heroes,
Rewarded the struggle with steeds and with treasure,
So that none can belittle, and none can blame,
Who tells the tale as it truly happened.

    Then on the ale-bench to each of the earls
Who embarked with Beowulf, sailing the sea-paths,
The lord of princes dealt ancient heirlooms,
Gift of treasure, and guerdon of gold°
To requite his slaughter whom Grendel slew, 980
As he would have slain others, but all-wise God
And the hero's courage had conquered Fate.
The Lord ruled over the lives of men
As He rules them still. Therefore understanding
And a prudent spirit are surely best!
He must suffer much of both weal and woe
Who dwells here long in these days of strife.

    Then song and revelry rose in the hall;
Before Healfdene's leader the harp was struck
And hall-joy wakened; the song was sung, 990
Hrothgar's gleeman rehearsed the lay
Of the sons of Finn° when the terror befell them:

    Hnæf of the Scyldings, the Half-Dane, fell in the
      Frisian slaughter;
Nor had Hildeburh cause to acclaim the faith of the
      Jutish folk,
Blameless, bereft of her brothers in battle, and
      stripped of her sons

---

941 **Hrothulf,** son of Hrothgar's younger brother Halga

969 **Ingwines,** the Danes 979 **Gift . . . gold.** Feeling morally responsible for Grendel's murder of Beowulf's thane, Hrothgar pays Beowulf the blood money 992 The story of the fight between the Danes and the Frisians is told in a highly allusive fashion, and seems to assume a listener's prior knowledge of its basic outlines. Hnaef, a king of the Danes, is the brother of Hildeburh, who is married to Finn, king of the Frisians, also referred to as the Jutes. While Hnaef is visiting at Finn's court, Finn's men attack Hnaef and his followers unexpectedly. Hnaef is killed, as is the son of Hildeburh and Finn. Both sides are weakened, and agree to a truce, whereby the Danish survivors are given gifts and apparently honorable status at the Frisian court. Hengest, who was second in command to Hnaef, broods, however, on revenge, and eventually arranges an attack on Finn, in which Finn is killed and Hildeburh taken back to the Danes

Who fell overcome by their fate and wounded with
    spears!
Not for nothing Hoc's daughter bewailed death's
    bitter decree,
In the dawn under morning skies, when she saw the
    slaughter of kinsmen
In the place where her days had been filled with the
    fairest delights of the world.
1000 Finn's thanes were slain in the fight, save only a few;
Nor could he do battle with Hengest or harry his
    shattered host;
And the Frisians made terms with the Danes, a truce,
    a hall for their dwelling,
A throne, and a sharing of rights with the sons of the
    Jutes,
And that Finn, the son of Folcwalda, each day would
    honor the Danes,
The host of Hengest, with gifts, with rings and
    guerdon of gold,
Such portion of plated treasure as he dealt to the
    Frisian folk
When he gladdened their hearts in the hall. So both
    were bound by the truce.
And Finn swore Hengest with oaths that were forceful
    and firm
He would rightfully rule his remnant, follow his
    council's decree,
And that no man should break the truce, or breach it
1010   by word or by will,
Nor the lordless in malice lament they were fated to
    follow
The man who had murdered their liege; and, if ever a
    Frisian
Fanned the feud with insolent speech, the sword
    should avenge it.
    Then a funeral pyre was prepared, and gold was
    drawn from the hoard,
The best of the Scylding leaders was laid on the bier;
In the burning pile was a gleaming of blood-stained
    byrnies,
The gilded swine and the boar-helm hard from the
    hammer,
Many a warrior fated with wounds and fallen in battle.
And Hildeburh bade that her son be laid on the bier of
    Hnæf,
His body consumed in the surging flame at his uncle's
1020   shoulder.
Beside it the lady lamented, singing her mournful
    dirge.
The hero was placed on the pyre; the greatest of
    funeral flames
Rolled with a roar to the skies at the burial barrow.
Heads melted and gashes gaped, the mortal wounds of
    the body,
Blood poured out in the flames; the fire, most greedy
    of spirits,

Swallowed up all whom battle had taken of both their
    peoples.
Their glory was gone! The warriors went to their
    homes,
Bereft of their friends, returning to Friesland, to city
    and stronghold.
    Then Hengest abode with Finn all the slaughter-
    stained winter,
But his heart longed ever for home, though he could
    not launch on the sea   1030
His ring-stemmed ship, for the billows boiled with the
    storm,
Strove with the wind, and the winter locked ocean in
    bonds of ice;
Till a new Spring shone once more on the dwellings of
    men,
The sunny and shining days which ever observe their
    season.
The winter was banished afar, and fair the bosom of
    earth.
Then the exile longed to be gone, the guest from his
    dwelling,
But his thoughts were more on revenge than on voy-
    aging over the wave,
Plotting assault on the Jutes, renewal of war with the
    sword.
So he spurned not the naked hint when Hunlafing laid
    in his lap
The battle-flasher, the best of blades, well known to
    the Jutes!   1040
In his own home death by the sword befell Finn, the
    fierce-hearted,
When Guthlaf and Oslaf requited the grim attack,
The woe encountered beyond the sea, the sorrow they
    suffered,
Nor could bridle the restive spirits within their breasts!
    Then the hall was reddened with blood and bodies of
    foemen,
Finn killed in the midst of his men, and the fair queen
    taken.
The Scylding warriors bore to their ships all treasure
    and wealth,
Such store as they found in the home of Finn of jewels
    and gems.
And the noble queen they carried across the sea-paths,
Brought her back to the Danes, to her own dear
    people.   1050

So the song was sung, the lay recited,
The sound of revelry rose in the hall.
Stewards poured wine from wondrous vessels;
And Wealhtheow, wearing a golden crown,
Came forth in state where the two were sitting,
Courteous comrades, uncle and nephew,
Each true to the other in ties of peace.
Unferth, the orator, sat at the feet

Of the lord of the Scyldings; and both showed trust
1060 In his noble mind, though he had no mercy
On kinsmen in swordplay; the Scylding queen spoke:
'My sovereign lord, dispenser of treasure,
Drink now of this flagon, have joy of the feast!
Speak to the Geats, O gold-friend of men,
In winning words as is well-befitting;
Be kind to the Geat-men and mindful of gifts
From the gold you have garnered from near and far.
You have taken as son,° so many have told me,
This hardy hero. Heorot is cleansed,
1070 The gleaming gift-hall.° Rejoice while you may
In lavish bounty, and leave to your kin
People and kingdom when time shall come,
Your destined hour, to look on death.
I know the heart of my gracious Hrothulf,
That he'll safely shelter and shield our sons
When you leave this world, if he still is living.
I know he will favor with gracious gifts
These boys of ours, if he bears in mind
The many honors and marks of love
1080 We bestowed upon him while he still was a boy.'
    She turned to the bench where her boys were sitting,
Hrethric and Hrothmund, the sons of heroes,
The youth together; there the good man sat,
Beowulf of the Geats, beside the two brothers.
Then the cup was offered with gracious greeting,
And seemly presents of spiraled gold,
A corselet, and rings, and the goodliest collar
Of all that ever were known on earth.
I have never heard tell of a worthier treasure
1090 In the hoarding of heroes beneath the sky
Since Hama° bore off to the shining city
The Brosings' jewel, setting and gems,
Fled from Eormenric's cruel craft
And sought the grace of eternal glory.
Hygelac, the Geat, grandson of Swerting°
Wore the ring in the last of his raids,
Guarding the spoil under banner in battle,
Defending the treasure. Overtaken by Fate,
In the flush of pride he fought with the Frisians
1100 And met disaster. The mighty prince
Carried the ring o'er the cup of the waves,
The precious jewel, and sank under shield.
Then his body fell into Frankish hands,
His woven corselet and jewelled collar,
And weaker warriors plundered the dead

After the carnage and welter of war.
The field of battle was covered with corpses
Of Geats who had fallen, slain by the sword.
    The sound of revelry rose in the hall;
Wealhtheow spoke to the warrior host: 1110
'Take, dear Beowulf, collar and corselet,
Wear these treasures with right good will!
Thrive and prosper and prove your might!
Befriend my boys with your kindly counsel;
I will remember and I will repay.
You have earned the undying honor of heroes
In regions reaching as far and wide
As the windy walls that the sea encircles.
May Fate show favor while life shall last!
I wish you wealth to your heart's content;   1120
In your days of glory be good to my sons!
Here each hero is true to other,
Gentle of spirit, loyal to lord,
Friendly thanes and a folk united,
Wine-cheered warriors who do my will.'

THE TROLL-WIFE AVENGES GRENDEL

Then she went to her seat. At the fairest of feasts
Men drank of the wine-cup, knowing not Fate,
Nor the fearful doom that befell the earls
When darkness gathered, and gracious Hrothgar
Sought his dwelling and sank to rest.   1130
A host of heroes guarded the hall
As they oft had done in the days of old.
They stripped the benches and spread the floor
With beds and bolsters. But one of the beer-thanes
Bowed to his hall-rest doomed to death.
They set at their heads their shining shields,
Their battle-bucklers; and there on the bench
Above each hero his towering helmet,
His spear and corselet hung close at hand.
It was ever their wont to be ready for war   1140
At home or in field, as it ever befell
That their lord had need. 'Twas a noble race!
    Then they sank to slumber. But one paid dear
For his evening rest, as had often happened
When Grendel haunted the lordly hall
And wrought such ruin, till his end was come,
Death for his sins; it was easily seen,
Though the monster was slain, an avenger survived
Prolonging the feud, though the fiend had perished.
The mother of Grendel, a monstrous hag,   1150
Brooded over her misery, doomed to dwell
In evil waters and icy streams
From ancient ages when Cain had killed
His only brother, his father's son.
Banished and branded with marks of murder
Cain fled far from the joys of men,
Haunting the barrens, begetting a brood
Of grisly monsters; and Grendel was one,

1068 **You have taken, etc.** Wealhtheow is afraid that Hrothgar's gratitude may
lead him to make Beowulf his actual heir and so dispossess his own sons; she
tactfully suggests other rewards   1070 **gift-hall,** Heorot, so called because it was
the hall wherein the king rewarded his warriors for their deeds with gifts
1091 **Hama, etc.** The story here alluded to is told more clearly in a Norse saga.
Hama, a follower of Eormanric, historically a king of the East Goths in the fourth
century, in legend a cruel tyrant, fled from his lord and took refuge in a monastery. In *Beowulf* he is said to have stolen from Eormanric the collar of the Brosings, a famous necklace which, according to Norse legends, belonged originally
to the goddess Freyja (corresponding to Aphrodite, or Venus, in classical mythology). This necklace came later into the possession of Hrothgar, who gave it to
Beowulf, who gave it to Hygd, who must have given it to Hygelac, her husband,
for he lost it in his last battle   1095 **Swerting,** presumably the maternal uncle of
Hygelac; his name is not in the Geatish dynasty

The fiendish ogre who found in the hall
1160 A hero on watch, and awaiting the fray.
The monster grappled; the Geat took thought
Of the strength of his might, that marvelous gift
Which the Lord had given; in God he trusted
For help and succor and strong support,
Whereby he humbled the fiend from hell,
Destroyed the demon; and Grendel fled,
Harrowed in heart and hateful to man,
Deprived of joy, to the place of death.
But rabid and raging his mother resolved
1170 On a dreadful revenge for the death of her son!
    She stole to the hall where the Danes were sleeping,
And horror fell on the host of earls
When the dam of Grendel burst in the door.
But the terror was less as the war-craft is weaker,
A woman's strength, than the might of a man
When the hilted sword, well shaped by the hammer,
The blood-stained iron of tempered edge,
Hews the boar from the foeman's helmet.
Then in the hall was the hard-edged blade,
1180 The stout steel, brandished above the benches;
Seizing their shields men stayed not for helmet
Or ample byrny, when fear befell.
As soon as discovered, the hag was in haste
To fly to the open, to flee for her life.
One of the warriors she swiftly seized,
Clutched him fast and made off to the fens.
He was of heroes the dearest to Hrothgar,
The best of comrades between two seas;
The warrior brave, the stout-hearted spearman,
1190 She slew in his sleep. Nor was Beowulf there;
But after the banquet another abode
Had been assigned to the glorious Geat.
There was tumult in Heorot. She tore from its place
The blood-stained claw.° Care was renewed!
It was no good bargain when both in turn
Must pay the price with the lives of friends!
    Then the white-haired warrior, the aged king,
Was numb with sorrow, knowing his thane
No longer was living, his dearest man dead.
1200 Beowulf, the brave, was speedily summoned,
Brought to the bower; the noble prince
Came with his comrades at dawn of day
Where the wise king awaited if God would award
Some happier turn in these tidings of woe.
The hero came tramping into the hall
With his chosen band—the boards resounded—
Greeted the leader, the Ingwine lord,
And asked if the night had been peaceful and pleasant.
    Hrothgar spoke, the lord of the Scyldings:
1210 'Ask not of pleasure; pain is renewed
For the Danish people. Æschere is dead!
Dead is Yrmenlaf's elder brother!
He was my comrade, closest of counsellors,
My shoulder-companion as side by side

1194 **blood-stained claw,** that of Grendel

We fought for our lives in the welter of war,
In the shock of battle when boar-helms crashed.
As an earl should be, a prince without peer,
Such was Æschere, slain in the hall
By the wandering demon! I know not whither
She fled to shelter, proud of her spoil,   1220
Gorged to the full. She avenged the feud
Wherein yesternight you grappled with Grendel
And savagely slew him because so long
He had hunted and harried the men of my folk.
He fell in the battle and paid with his life.
But now another fierce ravager rises
Avenging her kinsman, and carries it far,
As it seems to many a saddened thane
Who grieves in his heart for his treasure-giver.
This woe weighs heavy! The hand lies still   1230
That once was lavish of all delights.
    Oft in the hall I have heard my people,
Comrades and counsellors, telling a tale
Of evil spirits their eyes have sighted,
Two mighty marauders who haunt the moors.
One shape, as clearly as men could see,
Seemed woman's likeness, and one seemed man,
An outcast wretch of another world,
And huger far than a human form.
Grendel my countrymen called him, not knowing   1240
What monster-brood spawned him, what sire begot.
Wild and lonely the land they live in,
Wind-swept ridges and wolf-retreats,
Dread tracts of fen where the falling torrent
Downward dips into gloom and shadow
Under the dusk of the darkening cliff.
Not far in miles lies the lonely mere
Where trees firm-rooted and hung with frost
Overshroud the wave with shadowing gloom.
And there a portent appears each night,   1250
A flame in the water; no man so wise
Who knows the bound of its bottomless depth.
The heather-stepper, the horned stag,
The antlered hart hard driven by hounds,
Invading that forest in flight from afar
Will turn at bay and die on the brink
Ere ever he'll plunge in that haunted pool.
'Tis an eerie spot! Its tossing spray
Mounts dark to heaven when high winds stir
The driving storm, and the sky is murky,   1260
And with foul weather the heavens weep.
On your arm only rests all our hope!
Not yet have you tempted those terrible reaches
The region that shelters that sinful wight.
Go if you dare! I will give requital
With ancient treasure and twisted gold,
As I formerly gave in guerdon of battle,
If out of that combat you come alive.'
    Beowulf spoke, the son of Ecgtheow:
'Sorrow not, brave one! Better for man   1270
To avenge a friend than much to mourn.
All men must die; let him who may

Win glory ere death. That guerdon is best
For a noble man when his name survives him.
Then let us rise up, O ward of the realm,
And haste us forth to behold the track
Of Grendel's dam. And I give you pledge
She shall not in safety escape to cover,
To earthy cavern, or forest fastness,
1280 Or gulf of ocean, go where she may.
This day with patience endure the burden
Of every woe, as I know you will.'
Up sprang the ancient, gave thanks to God
For the heartening words the hero had spoken.

BEOWULF SLAYS THE TROLL-WIFE

Quickly a horse was bridled for Hrothgar,
A mettlesome charger with braided mane;
In royal splendor the king rode forth
Mid the trampling tread of a troop of shieldmen.
The tracks lay clear where the fiend had fared
1290 Over plain and bottom and woodland path,
Through murky moorland making her way
With the lifeless body, the best of thanes
Who of old with Hrothgar had guarded the hall.
By a narrow path the king pressed on
Through rocky upland and rugged ravine,
A lonely journey, past looming headlands,
The lair of monster and lurking troll.
Tried retainers, a trusty few,
Advanced with Hrothgar to view the ground.
1300 Sudden they came on a dismal covert
Of trees that hung over hoary stone,
Over churning water and blood-stained wave.
Then for the Danes was the woe the deeper,
The sorrow sharper for Scylding earls,
When they first caught sight, on the rocky sea-cliff,
Of slaughtered Æschere's severed head.
The water boiled in a bloody swirling
With seething gore as the spearmen gazed.
The trumpet sounded a martial strain;
1310 The shield-troop halted. Their eyes beheld
The swimming forms of strange sea-dragons,
Dim serpent shapes in the watery depths,
Sea-beasts sunning on headland slopes;
Snakelike monsters that oft at sunrise
On evil errands scour the sea.
Startled by tumult and trumpet's blare,
Enraged and savage, they swam away;
But one the lord of the Geats brought low,
Stripped of his sea-strength, despoiled of life,
1320 As the bitter bow-bolt pierced his heart.
His watery-speed grew slower, and ceased,
And he floated, caught in the clutch of death.
Then they hauled him in with sharp-hooked boar-
    spears,
By sheer strength grappled and dragged him ashore,
A wondrous wave-beast; and all the array
Gathered to gaze at the grisly guest.

Beowulf donned his armor for battle,
Heeded not danger; the hand-braided byrny,
Broad of shoulder and richly bedecked,
Must stand the ordeal of the watery depths.   1330
Well could that corselet defend the frame
Lest hostile thrust should pierce to the heart.
Or blows of battle beat down the life.
A gleaming helmet guarded his head
As he planned his plunge to the depths of the pool
Through the heaving waters—a helm adorned
With lavish inlay and lordly chains,
Ancient work of the weapon-smith
Skillfully fashioned, beset with the boar,°
That no blade of battle might bite it through.   1340
Not the least or the worst of his war-equipment
Was the sword the herald of Hrothgar° loaned
In his hour of need—Hrunting its name—
An ancient heirloom, trusty and tried;
Its blade was iron, with etched design,
Tempered in blood of many a battle.
Never in fight had it failed the hand
That drew it daring the perils of war,
The rush of the foe. Not the first time then
That its edge must venture on valiant deeds.   1350
But Ecglaf's stalwart son was unmindful
Of words he had spoken while heated with wine,
When he loaned the blade to a better swordsman.
He himself dared not hazard his life
In deeds of note in the watery depths;
And thereby he forfeited honor and fame.
Not so with that other undaunted spirit
After he donned his armor for battle.
Beowulf spoke, the son of Ecgtheow:
'O gracious ruler, gold-giver to men,   1360
As I now set forth to attempt this feat,
Great son of Healfdene, hold well in mind
The solemn pledge we plighted of old,
That if doing your service I meet my death
You will mark my fall with a father's love.
Protect my kinsmen, my trusty comrades,
If battle take me. And all the treasure
You have heaped on me bestow upon Hygelac,
Hrothgar beloved! The lord of the Geats,
The son of Hrethel,° shall see the proof,   1370
Shall know as he gazes on jewels and gold,
That I found an unsparing dispenser of bounty,
And joyed, while I lived, in his generous gifts.
Give back to Unferth the ancient blade,
The sword-edge splendid with curving scrolls,
For either with Hrunting I'll reap rich harvest
Of glorious deeds, or death shall take me.'
    After these words the prince of the Weders
Awaited no answer, but turned to the task,
Straightway plunged in the swirling pool.   1380
Nigh unto a day he endured the depths

1339 **beset . . . boar,** embossed figures about the crown of the helmet, not a boar crest as in previous instances of this word in the poem   1342 **herald of Hrothgar,** Unferth. Note his changed attitude toward Beowulf   1370 **son of Hrethel,** Hygelac

Ere he first had view of the vast sea-bottom.
Soon she found, who had haunted the flood,
A ravening hag, for a hundred half-years,
Greedy and grim, that a man was groping
In daring search through the sea-troll's home.
Swift she grappled and grasped the warrior
With horrid grip, but could work no harm,
No hurt to his body; the ring-locked byrny
1390 Cloaked his life from her clutching claw;
Nor could she tear through the tempered mail
With her savage fingers. The she-wolf bore
The ring-prince down through the watery depths
To her den at the bottom; nor could Beowulf draw
His blade for battle, though brave his mood.
Many a sea-beast, strange sea-monsters,
Tasked him hard with their menacing tusks,
Broke his byrny and smote him sore.
    Then he found himself in a fearsome hall
1400 Where water came not to work him hurt,
But the flood was stayed by the sheltering roof.
There in the glow of firelight gleaming
The hero had view of the huge sea-troll.
He swung his war-sword with all his strength,
Withheld not the blow, and the savage blade
Sang on her head its hymn of hate.
But the bold one found that the battle-flasher°
Would bite no longer, nor harm her life.
The sword-edge failed at his sorest need.
1410 Often of old with ease it had suffered
The clash of battle, cleaving the helm,
The fated warrior's woven mail.
That time was first for the treasured blade
That its glory failed in the press of the fray.
But fixed of purpose and firm of mood
Hygelac's earl was mindful of honor;
In wrath, undaunted, he dashed to earth
The jewelled sword with its scrolled design,
The blade of steel; staked all on strength,
1420 On the might of his hand, as a man must do
Who thinks to win in the welter of battle
Enduring glory; he fears not death.
The Geat-prince joyed in the straining struggle,
Stalwart-hearted and stirred to wrath,
Gripped the shoulder of Grendel's dam
And headlong hurled the hag to the ground.
But she quickly clutched him and drew him close,
Countered the onset with savage claw.
The warrior staggered, for all his strength,
1430 Dismayed and shaken and borne to earth.
She knelt upon him and drew her dagger,
With broad bright blade, to avenge her son,
Her only issue. But the corselet's steel
Shielded his breast and sheltered his life
Withstanding entrance of point and edge.
    Then the prince of the Geats would have gone his
        journey,

The son of Ecgtheow, under the ground;
But his sturdy breast-net, his battle-corselet,
Gave him succor, and holy God,
The Lord all-wise, awarded the mastery;   1440
Heaven's Ruler gave right decree.
    Swift the hero sprang to his feet;
Saw mid the war-gear a stately sword,°
An ancient war-brand of biting edge,
Choicest of weapons worthy and strong,
The work of giants, a warrior's joy,
So heavy no hand but his own could hold it,
Bear to battle or wield in war.
Then the Scylding warrior, savage and grim,
Seized the ring-hilt° and swung the sword,   1450
Struck with fury, despairing of life,
Thrust at the throat, broke through the bone-rings;
The stout blade stabbed through her fated flesh.
She sank in death; the sword was bloody;
The hero joyed in the work of his hand.
The gleaming radiance shimmered and shone
As the candle of heaven shines clear from the sky.
Wrathful and resolute Hygelac's thane
Surveyed the span of the spacious hall;
Grimly gripping the hilted sword   1460
With upraised weapon he turned to the wall.
The blade had failed not the battle-prince;
A full requital he firmly planned
For all the injury Grendel had done
In numberless raids on the Danish race,
When he slew the hearth-companions of Hrothgar,
Devoured fifteen of the Danish folk
Clasped in slumber, and carried away
As many more spearmen, a hideous spoil.
All this the stout-heart had stern requited;   1470
And there before him bereft of life
He saw the broken body of Grendel
Stilled in battle, and stretched in death,
As the struggle in Heorot smote him down.
The corpse sprang wide as he struck the blow,
The hard sword-stroke that severed the head.
    Then the tried retainers, who there with Hrothgar
Watched the face of the foaming pool,
Saw that the churning reaches were reddened,
The eddying surges stained with blood.   1480
And the gray, old spearmen spoke of the hero,
Having no hope he would ever return
Crowned with triumph and cheered with spoil.
Many were sure that the savage sea-wolf
Had slain their leader. At last came noon.
The stalwart Scyldings forsook the headland;
Their proud gold-giver° departed home.
But the Geats sat grieving and sick in spirit,
Stared at the water with longing eyes,
Having no hope they would ever behold   1490
Their gracious leader and lord again.

1443 **stately sword,** etc., placed, apparently, among the armor hanging on the wall of the cave   1450 **ring-hilt.** The hilt of the sword was adorned with a ring of gold about the top   1487 **goldgiver,** Hrothgar

1407 **battle-flasher,** a kenning for "sword"

Then the great sword, eaten with blood of battle,
Began to soften and waste away
In iron icicles, wonder of wonders,
Melting away most like to ice
When the Father looses the fetters of frost,
Slackens the bondage that binds the wave,
Strong in power of times and seasons;
He is true God! Of the goodly treasures
1500 From the sea-cave Beowulf took but two,
The monster's head and the precious hilt
Blazing with gems; but the blade had melted,
The sword dissolved, in the deadly heat,
The venomous blood of the fallen fiend.

BEOWULF RETURNS TO HEOROT

Then he who had compassed the fall of his foes
Came swimming up through the swirling surge.
Cleansed were the currents, the boundless abyss,
Where the evil monster had died the death
And looked her last on this fleeting world.
1510 With sturdy strokes the lord of the seamen
To land came swimming, rejoiced in his spoil,
Had joy of the burden he brought from the depths.
And his mighty thanes came forward to meet him,
Gave thanks to God they were granted to see
Their well-loved leader both sound and safe.
From the stalwart hero his helmet and byrny
Were quickly loosened; the lake lay still,
Its motionless reaches reddened with blood.
Fain of heart men fared o'er the footpaths,
1520 Measured the ways and the well-known roads.
From the sea-cliff's brim the warriors bore
The head of Grendel, with heavy toil;
Four of the stoutest, with all their strength,
Could hardly carry on swaying spear
Grendel's head to the gold-decked hall.
Swift they strode, the daring and dauntless,
Fourteen Geats, to the Hall of the Hart;
And proud in the midst of his marching men
Their leader measured the path to the mead-hall.
1530 The hero entered, the hardy in battle,
The great in glory, to greet the king;
And Grendel's head by the hair was carried
Across the floor where the feasters drank—
A terrible sight for lord and for lady—
A gruesome vision whereon men gazed!
Beowulf spoke, the son of Ecgtheow:
'O son of Healfdene, lord of the Scyldings!
This sea-spoil wondrous, whereon you stare,
We joyously bring you in token of triumph!
1540 Barely with life surviving the battle,
The war under water, I wrought the deed
Weary and spent; and death had been swift
Had God not granted His sheltering strength.
My strong-edged Hrunting, stoutest of blades,
Availed me nothing. But God revealed—
Often His arm has aided the friendless—

The fairest of weapons hanging on wall,
An ancient broadsword; I seized the blade,
Slew in the struggle, as fortune availed,
The cavern-warders. But the war-brand old,   1550
The battle-blade with its scrolled design,
Dissolved in the gush of the venomous gore;
The hilt alone I brought from the battle.
The record of ruin, and slaughter of Danes,
These wrongs I avenged, as was fitting and right.
Now I can promise you, prince of the Scyldings,
Henceforth in Heorot rest without rue
For you and your nobles; nor need you dread
Slaughter of follower, stalwart or stripling,
Or death of earl, as of old you did.'   1560
Into the hand of the aged leader,
The gray-haired hero, he gave the hilt,
The work of giants, the wonder of gold.
At the death of the demons the Danish lord
Took in his keeping the cunning craft,
The wondrous marvel, of mighty smiths;
When the world was freed of the ravaging fiend,
The foe of God, and his fearful dam
Marked with murder and badged with blood,
The bound hilt passed to the best of kings   1570
Who ever held sceptre beside two seas,
And dealt out treasure in Danish land!
    Hrothgar spoke, beholding the hilt,
The ancient relic whereon was etched
An olden record of struggle and strife,
The flood that ravaged the giant race,
The rushing deluge of ruin and death.
That evil kindred were alien to God,
But the Ruler avenged with the wrath of the deep!
On the hilt-guards, likewise, of gleaming gold   1580
Was rightly carven in cunning runes,°
Set forth and blazoned, for whom that blade,
With spiral tooling and twisted hilt,
That fairest of swords, was fashioned and smithied.
Then out spoke Hrothgar, Healfdene's son,
And all the retainers were silent and still:
'Well may he say, whose judgment is just,
Recalling to memory men of the past,
That this earl was born of a better stock!
Your fame, friend Beowulf, is blazoned abroad   1590
Over all wide ways, and to every people.
In manful fashion have you showed your strength,
Your might and wisdom. My word I will keep,
The plighted friendship we formerly pledged.
Long shall you stand as a stay to your people,
A help to heroes, as Heremod° was not
To the Honor-Scyldings, to Ecgwela's sons!
Not joy to kindred, but carnage and death,
He wrought as he ruled o'er the race of the Danes.
In savage anger he slew his comrades,   1600
His table-companions, till, lawless and lone,

1581 **runes**, the ancient Germanic alphabet, derived in large measure from the
Greek and Roman and formed with straight lines to facilitate carving on wood
1596 See l. 840

An odious outcast, he fled from men.
Though God had graced him with gifts of strength,
Over all men exalting him, still in his breast
A bloodthirsty spirit was rooted and strong.
He dealt not rings to the Danes for glory;
His lot was eternal torment of woe,
And lasting affliction. Learn from his fate!
Strive for virtue! I speak for your good;
1610 In the wisdom of age I have told the tale.
   'Tis a wondrous marvel how mighty God
In gracious spirit bestows on men
The gift of wisdom, and goodly lands,
And princely power! He rules over all!
He suffers a man of lordly line
To set his heart on his own desires,
Awards him fullness of worldly joy,
A fair home-land, and the sway of cities,
The wide dominion of many a realm,
1620 An ample kingdom, till, cursed with folly,
The thoughts of his heart take no heed of his end.
He lives in luxury, knowing not want,
Knowing no shadow of sickness or age;
No haunting sorrow darkens his spirit,
No hatred or discord deepens to war;
The world is sweet, to his every desire,
And evil assails not—until in his heart
Pride overpowering gathers and grows!
The warder slumbers, the guard of his spirit;
1630 Too sound is that sleep, too sluggish the weight
Of worldly affairs, too pressing the Foe,
The Archer who looses the arrows of sin.
   Then is his heart pierced, under his helm,
His soul in his bosom, with bitter dart.
He has no defense for the fierce assaults
Of the loathsome Fiend. What he long has cherished
Seems all too little! In anger and greed
He gives no guerdon of plated rings.
Since God has granted him glory and wealth
1640 He forgets the future, unmindful of Fate.
But it comes to pass in the day appointed
His feeble body withers and fails;
Death descends, and another seizes
His hoarded riches and rashly spends
The princely treasure, imprudent of heart.
Beloved Beowulf, best of warriors,
Avoid such evil and seek the good,
The heavenly wisdom. Beware of pride!
Now for a time you shall feel the fullness
1650 And know the glory of strength, but soon
Sickness or sword shall strip you of might,
Or clutch of fire, or clasp of flood,
Or flight of arrow, or bite of blade,
Or relentless age; or the light of the eye
Shall darken and dim, and death on a sudden,
O lordly ruler, shall lay you low.
   A hundred half-years I've been head of the Ring-
      Danes,
Defending the folk against many a tribe

With spear-point and sword in the surges of battle
Till not one was hostile 'neath heaven's expanse.   1660
But a loathsome change swept over the land,
Grief after gladness, when Grendel came,
That evil invader, that ancient foe!
Great sorrow of soul from his malice I suffered;
But thanks be to God who has spared me to see
His° bloody head at the battle's end!
Join now in the banquet; have joy of the feast,
O mighty in battle! And the morrow shall bring
Exchange of treasure in ample store.'
   Happy of heart the Geat leader hastened,   1670
Took seat at the board as the good king bade.
Once more, as of old, brave heroes made merry
And tumult of revelry rose in the hall.
   Then dark over men the night shadows deepened
The host all arose, for Hrothgar was minded,
The gray, old Scylding, to go to his rest.
On Beowulf too, after labor of battle,
Came limitless longing and craving for sleep.
A hall-thane graciously guided the hero,
Weary and worn, to the place prepared,   1680
Serving his wishes and every want
As befitted a mariner come from afar.
The stout-hearted warrior sank to his rest;
The lofty building, splendid and spacious,
Towered above him. His sleep was sound
Till the black-coated raven, blithesome of spirit,
Hailed the coming of Heaven's bliss.

THE PARTING OF BEOWULF AND HROTHGAR

Then over the shadows uprose the sun.
The Geats were in haste, and eager of heart
To depart to their people. Beowulf longed   1690
To embark in his boat, to set sail for his home.
The hero tendered the good sword Hrunting
To the son of Ecglaf,° bidding him bear
The lovely blade; gave thanks for the loan,
Called it a faithful friend in the fray,
Bitter in battle. The greathearted hero
Spoke no word in blame of the blade!
Arrayed in war-gear, and ready for sea,
The warriors bestirred them; and, dear to the Danes,
Beowulf sought the high seat of the king.   1700
The gallant in war gave greeting to Hrothgar;
Beowulf spoke, the son of Ecgtheow:
'It is time at last to tell of our longing!
Our homes are far, and our hearts are fain
To seek again Hygelac over the sea.
You have welcomed us royally, harbored us well
As a man could wish; if I ever can win
Your affection more fully, O leader of heroes,
Swift shall you find me to serve you again!
If ever I learn, o'er the levels of ocean,   1710
That neighboring nations beset you sore,

1666 **His,** Grendel's   1693 **son of Ecglaf,** Unferth

As in former days when foemen oppressed,
With thanes by the thousand I will hasten to help.
For I know that Hygelac, lord of the Geats,
Prince of the people, though young in years,
Will favor and further by word and deed
That my arm may aid you, and do you honor,
With stout ash-spear and succor of strength
In the press of need. And if princely Hrethric°
1720 Shall purpose to come to the court of the Geats,
He will find there a legion of loyal friends.
That man fares best to a foreign country
Who himself is stalwart and stout of heart.'
    Hrothgar addressed him, uttered his answer:
'Truly, these words has the Lord of wisdom
Set in your heart, for I never have harkened
To speech so sage from a man so young.
You have strength, and prudence, and wisdom of
    word!
I count it true if it come to pass
1730 That point of spear in the press of battle,
Or deadly sickness, or stroke of sword,
Shall slay your leader, the son of Hrethel,
The prince of your people, and you still live,
The Sea-Geats could have no happier choice
If you would be willing to rule the realm,
As king to hold guard o'er the hoard and the heroes.
The longer I know you, the better I like you,
Beloved Beowulf! You have brought it to pass
That between our peoples a lasting peace
1740 Shall bind the Geats to the Danish-born;
And strife shall vanish, and war shall cease,
And former feuds, while I rule this realm.
And many a man, in the sharing of treasure,
Shall greet another with goodly gifts
O'er the gannet's bath.° And the ring-stemmed ship
Shall bear over ocean bountiful riches
In pledge of friendship. Our peoples, I know,
Shall be firm united toward foe and friend,
Faultless in all things, in fashion of old.'
1750   Then the son of Healfdene, shelter of earls,
Bestowed twelve gifts on the hero in hall,
Bade him in safety with bounty of treasure
Seek his dear people, and soon return.
The peerless leader, the Scylding lord,
Kissed the good thane and clasped to his bosom
While tears welled fast from the old man's eyes.
Both chances he weighed in his wise, old heart,
But greatly doubted if ever again
They should meet at council or drinking of mead.
1760 Nor could Hrothgar master—so dear was the man—
His swelling sorrow; a yearning love
For the dauntless hero, deep in his heart,
Burned through his blood. Beowulf, the brave,
Prizing his treasure and proud of the gold,

Turned away, treading the grassy plain.
The ring-stemmed sea-goer, riding at anchor,
Awaited her lord. There was loud acclaim
Of Hrothgar's gifts, as they went their way.
He was a king without failing or fault,
Till old age, master of all mankind,   1770
Stripped him of power and pride of strength.

BEOWULF RETURNS TO GEATLAND

Then down to the sea came the band of the brave,
The host of young heroes in harness of war,
In their woven mail; and the coast-warden viewed
The heroes' return, as he heeded their coming!
No uncivil greeting he gave from the sea-cliff
As they strode to ship in their glistening steel;
But rode toward them and called their return
A welcome sight for their Weder kin.
There on the sand the ring-stemmed ship,   1780
The broad-bosomed bark, was loaded with war-gear
With horses and treasure; the mast towered high
Over the riches of Hrothgar's hoard.
A battle-sword Beowulf gave to the boatwarden
Hilted with gold; and thereafter in hall
He had the more honor because of the heirloom,
The shining treasure. The ship was launched.
Cleaving the combers of open sea
They dropped the shoreline of Denmark astern.
A stretching sea-cloth, a bellying sail,   1790
Was bent on the mast; there was groaning of timbers;
A gale was blowing; the boat drove on.
The foamy-necked plunger plowed through the bil-
    lows,
The ring-stemmed ship through the breaking seas,
Till at last they sighted the sea-cliffs of Geatland,
The well-known headlands; and, whipped by the wind,
The boat drove shoreward and beached on the sand.
    Straightway the harbor-watch strode to the
    seashore;
Long had he watched for the well-loved men,
Scanning the ocean with eager eyes!   1800
The broad-bosomed boat he bound to the shingle°
With anchor ropes, lest the rip of the tide
Should wrench from its mooring the comely craft.
    From the good ship Beowulf bade them bear
The precious jewels and plated gold,
The princely treasure. Not long was the path
That led to where Hygelac, son of Hrethel,
The giver of treasure, abode in his home
Hard by the sea-wall, hedged by his thanes.
Spacious the castle, splendid the king   1810
On his high hall-seat; youthful was Hygd,
Wise and well-born—though winters but few
Hæreth's daughter had dwelt at court.
She was noble of spirit, not sparing in gifts
Of princely treasure to the people of the Geats.

1719 **if . . . Hrethric.** Perhaps following Wealhtheow's hint, Beowulf offers to enroll her eldest son, the heir, among the Geatish thanes. For a prince to spend a few years in a foreign court was a common Germanic custom; Beowulf himself seems to have enjoyed a similar education   1745 **gannet's bath,** another kenning for "sea": a gannet is a large, fish-eating sea bird

1795 **shingle,** a kind of gravel on the seashore

Of the pride of Thryth,° and her crimes, the fair
    folk-queen was free;
Thryth, of whose liegemen none dared by day, save
    only her lord,
Lift up his eyes to her face, lest his fate be a mortal
    bondage,
Seizure and fetters and sword, a blow of the patterned
    blade
Declaring his doom, and proclaiming the coming of
1820   death.
That is no way of a queen, nor custom of lovely lady,
Though peerless her beauty and proud, that a weaver
    of peace
Should send a dear man to his death for a feigned
    affront.
But the kinsman of Hemming at last made an end of
    her evil.
For men at the drinking of mead tell tale of a change,
How she wrought less ruin and wrong when, given in
    marriage
Gleaming with jewels and gold, to the high-born hero
    and young,
Over the fallow flood she sailed, at her father's bid-
    ding
Seeking the land of Offa, and there while she lived,
1830 Famed for goodness, fulfilled her fate on the throne.
She held high love for her lord, the leader of heroes,
The best, I have heard, of mankind or the children of
    men
Between the two seas; for Offa, the stalwart, was hon-
    ored
For his gifts and his greatness in war. With wisdom he
    governed;
And from him Eomær descended, Hemming's
    kinsman, grandson of Garmund,
Stalwart and strong in war, and the helper of heroes.

Then the hero strode with his stalwart band
Across the stretches of sandy beach,
The wide sea-shingle. The world-candle shone,
1840 The hot sun hasting on high from the south.
Marching together they made their way
To where in his stronghold the stout young king,
Ongentheow's° slayer, protector of earls,
Dispensed his treasure. Soon Hygelac heard
Of the landing of Beowulf, bulwark of men,

1816 **Thryth.** Her fickle and cruel behavior early in her life is a contrast to the virtues of Hygd, Hygelac's young wife, and to her own mature virtues when she has become Offa's queen   1843 **Ongentheow,** a Swedish (Scylfing) king. There are frequent allusions in the second half of the poem to the conflicts of the Geats and Swedes. The order of narration is not that of the events themselves. Here is a brief account of the two stages in the conflict, in chronological order. The Swedes invaded Geatland in the reign of Hygelac's predecessor, Haethcyn; while leading a retributive expedition against the Swedes, Haethcyn was killed. Hygelac (through the action of his thane Eofor) avenges Haethcyn by the death of the Swedish king, Ongentheow. This is the first stage or generation of the feud. After a peace of some duration, the second stage begins. Hygelac's successor, Heardred, arouses the wrath of Onela, one of the two sons of Ongentheow, by harboring Onela's two nephews, Eanmund and Eadgils, from whom Onela is taking the kingdom which they should rightly inherit from their father, Othere. After Heardred is slain by Onela, Beowulf becomes king. He eventually sends an expedition into the Swedish territories, gains full revenge, and places an ally (Eadgils) on the Geatish throne. At Beowulf's death, however, the trouble seems likely to be renewed

That his shoulder-companion had come to his court
Sound and safe from the strife of battle.
    The hall was prepared, as the prince gave bidding,
Places made ready for much travelled men.
And he who came safe from the surges of battle   1850
Sat by the side of the king himself,
Kinsman by kinsman; in courtly speech
His liege lord greeted the loyal thane
With hearty welcome. And Hæreth's daughter
Passed through the hall-building pouring the mead,
With courtesy greeting the gathered host,
Bearing the cup to the hands of the heroes.
In friendly fashion in high-built hall
Hygelac questioned his comrade and thane;
For an eager longing burned in his breast   1860
To hear from the Sea-Geats the tale of their travels.
'How did you fare in your far sea-roving,
Beloved Beowulf, in your swift resolve
To sail to the conflict, the combat in Heorot,
Across the salt waves? Did you soften at all
The sorrows of Hrothgar, the weight of his woe?
Deeply I brooded with burden of care
For I had no faith in this far sea-venture
For one so beloved. Long I implored
That you go not against the murderous monster,   1870
But let the South Danes settle the feud
Themselves with Grendel. To God be thanks
That my eyes behold you unharmed and unhurt.'
    Beowulf spoke, the son of Ecgtheow:
'My dear lord Hygelac, many have heard
Of that famous grapple 'twixt Grendel and me,
The bitter struggle and strife in the hall
Where he formerly wrought such ruin and wrong,
Such lasting sorrow for Scylding men!
All that I avenged! Not any on earth   1880
Who longest lives of that loathsome brood,
No kin of Grendel cloaked in his crime,
Has cause to boast of that battle by night!
First, in that country, I fared to the hall
With greeting for Hrothgar; Healfdene's kinsman
Learned all my purpose, assigned me a place
Beside his own son. 'Twas a happy host!
I never have seen under span of heaven
More mirth of heroes sitting at mead!
The peerless queen, the peace-pledge of peoples,   1890
Passed on her round through the princely hall;
There was spurring of revels, dispensing of rings,
Ere the noble woman went to her seat.
    At times in the host the daughter of Hrothgar
Offered the beaker to earls in turn;
Freawaru men called her, the feasters in hall,
As she held out to heroes the well-wrought cup.
Youthful and gleaming with jewels of gold
To the fair son of Froda the maiden is plighted.
For the Scylding leader, the lord of the land,   1900
Deems it wise counsel, accounting it gain,
To settle by marriage the murderous feud,
The bloody slaughter! But seldom for long

Does the spear go ungrasped when a prince has
     perished,
Though the bride in her beauty be peerless and proud!
Ill may it please the Heathobard prince
And all his thanes, when he leads his lady
Into the hall, that a Danish noble
Should be welcomed there by the Heathobard host.
1910 For on him shall flash their forefathers' heirlooms,
Hard-edged, ring-hilted, the Heathobards' hoard
When of old they had war-might, nor wasted in battle
Their lives and the lives of their well-loved thanes.

Then an aged spearman shall speak at the beer-feast,
The treasure beholding with sorrow of heart,
Remembering sadly the slaughter of men,
Grimly goading the young hero's spirit,
Spurring to battle, speaking this word:
"Do you see, my lord, the sword of your father,
1920 The blade he bore to the last of his fights,
The pride of his heart as, under his helmet,
The Scyldings slew him, the savage Danes,
When Withergyld° fell, and after the slaughter,
The fall of heroes, they held the field?
And now a son of those bloody butchers,
Proud in his trappings, tramps into hall
And boasts of the killing, clothed with the treasure
That is yours by your birthright to have and to hold?"
Over and over the old man will urge him,
1930 With cutting reminders recalling the past
Till it comes at last that the lady's thane,
For the deeds of his father, shall forfeit his life
In a bloody slaughter, slain by the sword,
While the slayer goes scatheless knowing the land.
On both sides then shall sword-oaths be broken
When hate boils up within Ingeld's heart,
And his love of his lady grows cooler and lessens
Because of his troubles. I count not true
Heathobard faith, nor their part in the peace,
1940 Nor their friendship firm to the Danish folk.

I must now speak on, dispenser of treasure,
Further of Grendel, till fully you know
How we fared in that fierce and furious fight!
When the jewel of heaven had journeyed o'er earth,
The wrathful demon, the deadly foe,
Stole through the darkness spying us out
Where still unharmed we guarded the gold-hall.
But doom in battle and bitter death
Were Handscio's° fate! He was first to perish
1950 Though girded with weapon and famous in war.
Grendel murdered him, mangled his body,
Bolted the dear man's bloody corpse.
No sooner for that would the slaughterous spirit,
Bloody of tooth and brooding on evil,
Turn empty-handed away from the hall!
The mighty monster made trial of my strength
Clutching me close with his ready claw.
Wide and wondrous his huge pouch hung

Cunningly fastened, and fashioned with skill
From skin of dragon by devil's craft.   1960
Therein the monster was minded to thrust me
Sinless and blameless, and many beside.
But it might not be, when I rose in wrath,
And fronted the hell-fiend face to face.
Too long is the tale how I took requital
On the cursed foe for his every crime,
But the deeds I did were a lasting honor,
Beloved prince, to your people's name.
He fled away, and a fleeting while
Possessed his life and the world's delights;   1970
But he left in Heorot his severed hand,
A bloody reminder to mark his track.
Humbled in spirit and wretched in heart
Down he sank to the depths of the pool.
When the morrow fell, and we feasted together,
The Scylding ruler rewarded me well
For the bloody strife, in guerdon bestowing
Goodly treasure of beaten gold.
There was song and revel. The aged Scylding
From well-stored mind spoke much of the past.   1980
A warrior sang to the strains of the glee-wood,
Sometimes melodies mirthful and joyous,
Sometimes lays that were tragic and true.
And the great-hearted ruler at times would tell
A tale of wonder in fitting words.
Heavy with years the white-haired warrior
Grieved for his youth and the strength that was gone;
And his heart was moved by the weight of his winters
And many a memory out of the past.
All the long day we made merry together   1990
Till another night came to the children of men,
And quickly the mother of Grendel was minded
To wreak her vengeance; raging with grief
She came to the hall where the hate of the Weders
Had slain her son. But the hideous hag
Avenged his killing; with furious clutch
She seized a warrior—the soul of Æschere,°
Wise and aged, went forth from the flesh!
Not at all could the Danes, when the morrow dawned,
Set brand to his body or burn on the bale   2000
Their well-loved comrade. With fiendish clasp
She carried his corpse through the fall of the force.
That was to Hrothgar, prince of the people,
Sorest of sorrows that ever befell!
For your sake the sad-hearted hero implored me
To prove my valor and, venturing life,
To win renown in the watery depths.
He promised reward. Full well is it known
How I humbled the horrible guard of the gulf.
Hand to hand for a space we struggled   2010
Till the swirling eddies were stained with blood;
With cleaving sword-edge I severed the head
Of Grendel's hag in that hall of strife.
Not easily thence did I issue alive,

1923 **Withergyld**, famous warrior of the Danes   1949 **Handscio**, thane of Beowulf, killed by Grendel

1997 **Æschere**, counsellor of Hrothgar, killed by Grendel's mother

But my death was not fated; not yet was I doomed!
    Then the son of Healfdene, the shelter of earls,
Gave many a treasure to mark the deed.
The good king governed with courtly custom;
In no least way did I lose reward,
2020 The meed of my might; but he gave me treasure,
Healfdene's son, to my heart's desire.
These riches I bring you, ruler of heroes,
And warmly tender with right good will.
Save for you, King Hygelac, few are my kinsmen,
Few are the favors but come from you.'
    Then he bade men bring the boar-crested headpiece,
The towering helmet, and steel-gray sark,
The splendid war-sword, and spoke this word:
'The good king Hrothgar gave me this gift,
2030 This battle-armor, and first to you
Bade tell the tale of his friendly favor.
He said King Heorogar,° lord of the Scyldings,
Long had worn it, but had no wish
To leave the mail to his manful son,
The dauntless Heoroweard, dear though he was!
Well may you wear it! Have joy of it all.'
As I've heard the tale, he followed the trappings
With four bay horses, matched and swift,
Graciously granting possession of both,
2040 The steeds and the wealth. 'Tis the way of a kinsman,
Not weaving in secret the wiles of malice
Nor plotting the fall of a faithful friend.
To his kinsman Hygelac, hardy in war,
The heart of the nephew was trusty and true;
Dear to each was the other's good!
To Hygd, as I've heard, he presented three horses
Gaily saddled, slender and sleek,
And the gleaming necklace Wealhtheow gave,
A peerless gift from a prince's daughter.
2050 With the gracious guerdon, the goodly jewel,
Her breast thereafter was well bedecked.
    So the son of Ecgtheow bore himself bravely,
Known for his courage and courteous deeds,
Strove after honor, slew not his comrades
In drunken brawling; nor brutal his mood.
But the bountiful gifts which the Lord God gave him
He held with a power supreme among men.
He had long been scorned,° when the sons of the Geats
Accounted him worthless; the Weder lord
2060 Held him not high among heroes in hall.
Laggard they deemed him, slothful and slack.
But time brought solace for all his ills!
    Then the battle-bold king, the bulwark of heroes,
Bade bring a battle-sword banded with gold,
The heirloom of Hrethel; no sharper steel,
No lovelier treasure, belonged to the Geats.
He laid the war-blade on Beowulf's lap,
Gave him a hall and a stately seat

And hides° seven thousand. Inherited lands
Both held by birth-fee, home and estate.   2070
But one held rule o'er the spacious realm.
And higher therein his order and rank.

THE FIRE-DRAGON AND THE TREASURE

It later befell in the years that followed
After Hygelac sank in the surges of war,°
And the sword slew Heardred under his shield
When the Battle-Scylfings, those bitter fighters,
Invaded the land of the victor-folk
Overwhelming Hereric's° nephew in war,
That the kingdom came into Beowulf's hand.
For fifty winters he governed it well,   2080
Aged and wise with the wisdom of years,
Till a fire-drake° flying in darkness of night
Began to ravage and work his will.
On the upland heath he guarded a hoard,
A stone barrow° lofty. Under it lay
A path concealed from the sight of men.
There a thief broke in on the heathen treasure,
Laid hand on a flagon all fretted with gold,
As the dragon discovered, though cozened in sleep
By the pilferer's cunning. The people soon found   2090
That the mood of the dragon was roused to wrath!
    Not at all with intent, of his own free will,
Did he ravish the hoard, who committed the wrong
But in dire distress the thrall of a thane,
A guilty fugitive fleeing the lash,
Forced his way in. There a horror befell him!
Yet the wretched exile escaped from the dragon,
Swift in retreat when the terror arose.
A flagon he took. There, many such treasures
Lay heaped in that earth-hall where the owner of old   2100
Had carefully hidden the precious hoard,
The countless wealth of a princely clan.
Death came upon them in days gone by
And he who lived longest, the last of his line,
Guarding the treasure and grieving for friend,
Deemed it his lot that a little while only
He too might hold that ancient hoard.
A barrow new-built near the ocean billows
Stood cunningly fashioned beneath the cliff;

2032 **Heorogar,** Hrothgar's elder brother and his predecessor in the kingship.
Heoroweard, Heorogar's son, has been passed over in the succession
2058 **long been scorned, etc.** Beowulf is said to have been slothful and unwar-
like in his youth; this detail associates him with other mythic heroes who were
unpromising in youth but who went on to perform notable deeds

2069 **hides.** According to the usual estimate, a "hide" of land came to about 120
modern acres   2074 **Hygelac, etc.** Hygelac was killed in the raid against the
Frisians. At his death, Hygd offered Beowulf the kingship but he refused and
served as regent during the early reign of Hygelac's young son Heardred. When
Heardred was slain by the Swedes ("War-Scylfings"), Beowulf took the throne
2078 **Hereric,** brother of Hygd, uncle of Heardred   2082 **fire-drake, etc.** The
story is somewhat obscure here. Ages before, a treasure had been buried and
protected by a curse. Nevertheless, it was found and removed by certain warriors
and passed on through inheritance to the last survivor of the race. This man
buried the treasure again, and a dragon guarded it for the next three hundred
years. Then a serf, who had probably killed a man in his master's household, fled
from his master's anger, found the treasure in the mound, and stole a cup with
which to pay the blood money for his crime. When the cup had purchased his
pardon, it was sent to Beowulf as a present. Meanwhile, the dragon, angered by
the theft, spewed out his fiery breath on the countryside and burned Beowulf's
mead hall   2085 **stone barrow,** a chamber with walls of stone, covered with
earth, with a narrow entrance near its base. Such mounds are common both in
England and in Scandinavia. This one was situated on a cliff above the sea

2110 Into the barrow the ring-warden bore
The princely treasure, the precious trove
Of golden wealth, and these words he spoke:
'Keep thou, O Earth, what men could not keep—
This costly treasure—it came from thee!
Baleful slaughter has swept away,
Death in battle, the last of my blood;
They have lived their lives; they have left the
       mead-hall.
Now I have no one to wield the sword,
No one to polish the plated cup,
2120 The precious flagon—the host is fled.
The hard-forged helmet fretted with gold
Shall be stripped of its inlay; the burnishers sleep
Whose charge was to brighten the battle-masks.
Likewise the corselet that countered in war
Mid clashing of bucklers the bite of the sword—
Corselet and warrior decay into dust;
Mailed coat and hero are moveless and still.
No mirth of gleewood,° no music of harp,
No good hawk swinging in flight through the hall;
2130 No swift steed stamps in the castle yard;
Death has ravished an ancient race.'
So sad of mood he bemoaned his sorrow,
Lonely and sole survivor of all,
Restless by day and wretched by night
Till the clutch of death caught at his heart.
Then the goodly treasure was found unguarded
By the venomous dragon enveloped in flame,
The old naked night-foe flying in darkness,
Haunting the barrows; a bane that brings
2140 A fearful dread to the dwellers of earth.
His wont is to hunt out a hoard under ground°
And guard heathen gold, growing old with the years.
But no whit for that is his fortune more fair!

    For three hundred winters this waster of peoples
Held the huge treasure-hall under the earth
Till the robber aroused him to anger and rage,
Stole the rich beaker and bore to his master,
Imploring his lord for a compact of peace.
So the hoard was robbed and its riches plundered;
2150 To the wretch was granted the boon that he begged;
And his liege-lord first had view of the treasure,
The ancient work of the men of old.
Then the worm awakened and war was kindled,
The rush of the monster along the rock,
When the fierce one found the tracks of the foe;
He had stepped too close in his stealthy cunning
To the dragon's head. But a man undoomed
May endure with ease disaster and woe
If he has His favor who wields the world.
2160 Swiftly the fire-drake sought through the plain
The man who wrought him this wrong in his sleep.
Inflamed and savage he circled the mound,
But the waste was deserted—no man was in sight.

The worm's mood was kindled to battle and war;
Time and again he returned to the barrow
Seeking the treasure-cup. Soon he was sure
That a man had plundered the precious gold.
Enraged and restless the hoard-warden waited
The gloom of evening. The guard of the mound
Was swollen with anger; the fierce one resolved   2170
To requite with fire the theft of the cup.
Then the day was sped as the worm desired;
Lurking no longer within his wall
He sallied forth surrounded with fire,
Encircled with flame. For the folk of the land
The beginning was dread as the ending was grievous
That came so quickly upon their lord.

    Then the baleful stranger belched fire and flame,
Burned the bright dwellings—the glow of the blaze
Filled hearts with horror. The hostile flier   2180
Was minded to leave there nothing alive.
From near and from far the war of the dragon,
The might of the monster, was widely revealed
So that all could see how the ravaging scather
Hated and humbled the Geatish folk.
Then he hastened back ere the break of dawn
To his secret den and the spoil of gold.
He had compassed the land with a flame of fire,
A blaze of burning; he trusted the wall,
The sheltering mound, and the strength of his might— 2190
But his trust betrayed him! The terrible news
Was brought to Beowulf, told for a truth,
That his home was consumed in the surges of fire,
The goodly dwelling and throne of the Geats.
The heart of the hero was heavy with anguish,
The greatest of sorrows; in his wisdom he weened
He had grievously angered the Lord Everlasting,
Blamefully broken the ancient law.
Dark thoughts stirred in his surging bosom,
Welled in his breast, as was not his wont.   2200
The flame of the dragon had levelled the fortress,
The people's stronghold washed by the wave.
But the king of warriors, prince of the Weders,
Exacted an ample revenge for it all.
The lord of warriors and leader of earls
Bade work him of iron a wondrous shield,
Knowing full well that wood could not serve him
Nor linden defend him against the flame.
The stalwart hero was doomed to suffer
The destined end of his days on earth;   2210
Likewise the worm, though for many a winter
He had held his watch o'er the wealth of the hoard.
The ring-prince scorned to assault the dragon
With a mighty army, or host of men.
He feared not the combat, nor counted of worth
The might of the worm, his courage and craft,
Since often aforetime, beset in the fray,
He had safely issued from many an onset,
Many a combat and, crowned with success,
Purged of evil the hall of Hrothgar   2220
And crushed out Grendel's loathsome kin.

2128 **gleewood,** a kenning for "harp" 2141 **His wont . . . ground, etc.** Cf. the
dragon that guards the treasure in the lay of Sigemund sung by Hrothgar's bard.
Such treasure-guarding dragons are common in folklore and mythology

Nor was that the least of his grim engagements
When Hygelac fell,° great Hrethel's son;
When the lord of the people, the prince of the Geats,
Died of his wounds in the welter of battle,
Perished in Friesland, smitten with swords.
Thence Beowulf came by his strength in swimming;
Thirty sets of armor he bore on his back
As he hasted to ocean. The Hetware° men
2230 Had no cause to boast of their prowess in battle
When they gathered against him with linden shields.
But few of them ever escaped his assault
Or came back alive to the homes they had left;
So the son of Ecgtheow swam the sea-stretches,
Lonely and sad, to the land of his kin.
Hygd then tendered him kingdom and treasure,
Wealth of riches and royal throne,
For she had no hope with Hygelac dead
That her son could defend the seat of his fathers
2240 From foreign foemen. But even in need,
No whit the more could they move the hero
To be Heardred's liege, or lord of the land.
But he fostered Heardred with friendly counsel,
With honor and favor among the folk,
Till he came of age and governed the Geats.
Then the sons of Ohthere fleeing in exile°
Sought out Heardred over the sea.
They had risen against the lord of the Scylfings,
Best of the sea-kings, bestower of rings,
2250 An illustrious prince in the land of the Swedes.
So Heardred fell. For harboring exiles
The son of Hygelac died by the sword.
Ongentheow's son, after Heardred was slain,
Returned to his home, and Beowulf held
The princely power and governed the Geats.
He was a good king, grimly requiting
In later days the death of his prince.
Crossing the sea with a swarming host
He befriended Eadgils, Ohthere's son,
2260 In his woe and affliction, with weapons and men;
He took revenge in a savage assault,
And slew the king. So Ecgtheow's son
Had come in safety through all his battles,
His bitter struggles and savage strife,
To the day when he fought with the deadly worm.
With eleven comrades, kindled to rage
The Geat lord went to gaze on the dragon.
Full well he knew how the feud arose,
The fearful affliction; for into his hold
2270 From hand of finder the flagon had come.
The thirteenth man in the hurrying throng
Was the sorrowful captive who caused the feud.
With woeful spirit and all unwilling
Needs must he guide them, for he only knew
Where the earth-hall stood near the breaking billows
Filled with jewels and beaten gold.
The monstrous warden, waiting for battle,
Watched and guarded the hoarded wealth.
No easy bargain for any of men
To seize that treasure! The stalwart king,   2280
Gold-friend of Geats, took seat on the headland,
Hailed his comrades and wished them well.
Sad was his spirit, restless and ready,
And the march of Fate immeasurably near;
Fate that would strike, seek his soul's treasure,
And deal asunder the spirit and flesh.
Not long was his life encased in the body!
    Beowulf spoke, the son of Ecgtheow:
'Many an ordeal I endured in youth,
And many a battle. I remember it all.   2290
I was seven winters old when the prince of the people,
The lord of the treasure-hoard, Hrethel the king,
From the hand of my father had me and held me,
Recalling our kinship with treasure and feast.
As long as he lived I was no less beloved,
As thane in his hall, than the sons of his house,
Herebeald and Hæthcyn and Hygelac, my lord.
For the eldest brother the bed of death
Was foully fashioned by brother's deed
When Hæthcyn let fly a bolt from his horn-bow,   2300
Missed the mark, and murdered his lord;
Brother slew brother with bloody shaft—
A tragic deed and beyond atonement,
A foul offense to sicken the heart!
Yet none the less was the lot of the prince
To lay down his soul and his life, unavenged.
    Even so sad and sorrowful is it,
And bitter to bear, to an old man's heart,°
Seeing his young son swing on the gallows.
He wails his dirge and his wild lament   2310
While his son hangs high, a spoil to the raven;
His aged heart can contrive no help.
Each dawn brings grief for the son that is gone
And his heart has no hope of another heir,
Seeing the one has gone to his grave.
In the house of his son he gazes in sorrow
On wine-hall deserted and swept by the wind,
Empty of joy. The horsemen and heroes
Sleep in the grave. No sound of the harp,
No welcoming revels as often of old!   2320
He goes to his bed with his burden of grief;
To his spirit it seems that dwelling and land
Are empty and lonely, lacking his son.
    So the helm of the Weders yearned after Herebeald
And welling sadness surged in his heart.
He could not avenge the feud on the slayer
Nor punish the prince for the loathsome deed,
Though he loved him no longer, nor held him dear.
Because of this sorrow that sore befell
He left life's joys for the heavenly light,   2330
Granting his sons, as a good man will,
Cities and land, when he went from the world.
    Then across the wide water was conflict and war,

2223 **When Hygelac fell, etc.,** another reference to Hygelac's fatal expedition against the Frisians   2229 **Hetware,** Frisian   2246 See note to l. 1843

2308 This old man is not Hygelac. Beowulf is speaking now of bearing griefs analogous to Hygelac's

A striving and struggle of Swedes and Geats,
A bitter hatred, when Hrethel died.
Ongentheow's sons were dauntless and daring,
Cared not for keeping of peace overseas;
But often around Hreosnabeorh slaughtered and slew.
2340 My kinsmen avenged the feud and the evil,
As many have heard, though one of the Weders
Paid with his life—a bargain full bitter!
Hæthcyn's fate was to fall in the fight.
It is often recounted, a kinsman with sword-edge
Avenged in the morning the murderer's deed
When Ongentheow met Eofor. Helm split asunder;
The aged Scylfing sank down to his death.
The hand that felled him remembered the feud
And drew not back from the deadly blow.
     For all the rich gifts that Hygelac gave me
2350 I repaid him in battle with shining sword,
As chance was given. He granted me land,
A gracious dwelling and goodly estate.
Nor needed he seek of the Gifths, or the Spear-Danes,
Or in Swedish land, a lesser in war
To fight for pay; in the press of battle
I was always before him alone in the van.
So shall I bear me while life-days last,
While the sword holds out that has served me well
Early and late since I slew Dæghrefn,
2360 The Frankish hero, before the host.
He brought no spoil from the field of battle,
No corselet of mail to the Frisian king.
Not by the sword the warden of standards,
The stalwart warrior, fell in the fight.
My battle-grip shattered the bones of his body
And silenced the heart-beat. But now with the sword,
With hand and hard blade, I must fight for the
     treasure.'

BEOWULF AND WIGLAF SLAY THE DRAGON

For the last time Beowulf uttered his boast:
'I came in safety through many a conflict
2370 In the days of my youth; and now even yet,
Old as I am, I will fight this feud,
Do manful deeds, if the dire destroyer
Will come from his cavern to meet my sword.'
The king for the last time greeted his comrades,
Bold helmet-bearers and faithful friends:
'I would bear no sword nor weapon to battle
With the evil worm, if I knew how else
I could close with the fiend, as I grappled with
     Grendel.
From the worm I look for a welling of fire,
2380 A belching of venom, and therefore I bear
Shield and byrny. Not one foot's space
Will I flee from the monster, the ward of the mound.
It shall fare with us both in the fight at the wall
As Fate shall allot, the lord of mankind.
Though bold in spirit, I make no boast
As I go to fight with the flying serpent.

Clad in your corselets and trappings of war,
By the side of the barrow abide you to see
Which of us twain may best after battle
Survive his wounds. Not yours the adventure, 2390
Nor the mission of any, save mine alone,
To measure his strength with the monstrous dragon
And play the part of a valiant earl.
By deeds of daring I'll gain the gold
Or death in battle shall break your lord.'
     Then the stalwart rose with his shield upon him,
Bold under helmet, bearing his sark
Under the stone-cliff; he trusted the strength
Of his single might. Not so does a coward!
He who survived through many a struggle, 2400
Many a combat and crashing of troops,
Saw where a stone-arch stood by the wall
And a gushing stream broke out from the barrow.
Hot with fire was the flow of its surge,
Nor could any abide near the hoard unburned,
Nor endure its depths, for the flame of the dragon.
Then the lord of the Geats in the grip of his fury
Gave shout of defiance; the strong-heart stormed.
His voice rang out with the rage of battle,
Resounding under the hoary stone. 2410
Hate was aroused; the hoard-warden knew
'Twas the voice of a man. No more was there time
To sue for peace; the breath of the serpent,
A blast of venom, burst from the rock.
The ground resounded; the lord of the Geats
Under the barrow swung up his shield
To face the dragon; the coiling foe
Was gathered to strike in the deadly strife.
The stalwart hero had drawn his sword,
His ancient heirloom of tempered edge; 2420
In the heart of each was fear of the other!
The shelter of kinsmen stood stout of heart
Under towering shield as the great worm coiled;
Clad in his war-gear he waited the rush.
In twisting folds the flame-breathing dragon
Sped to its fate. The shield of the prince
For a lesser while guarded his life and his body
Than heart had hoped. For the first time then
It was not his portion to prosper in war;
Fate did not grant him glory in battle! 2430
Then lifted his arm the lord of the Geats
And smote the worm with his ancient sword
But the brown edge failed as it fell on bone,
And cut less deep than the king had need
In his sore distress. Savage in mood
The ward of the barrow countered the blow
With a blast of fire; wide sprang the flame.
The ruler of Geats had no reason to boast;
His unsheathed iron, his excellent sword,
Had weakened as it should not, had failed in the fight. 2440
It was no easy journey for Ecgtheow's son
To leave this world and against his will
Find elsewhere a dwelling! So every man shall
In the end give over this fleeting life.

Not long was the lull. Swiftly the battlers
Renewed their grapple. The guard of the hoard
Grew fiercer in fury. His venomous breath
Beat in his breast. Enveloped in flame
The folk-leader suffered a sore distress.
2450 No succoring band of shoulder-companions,
No sons of warriors aided him then
By valor in battle. They fled to the forest
To save their lives; but a sorrowful spirit
Welled in the breast of one of the band.
The call of kinship can never be stilled
In the heart of a man who is trusty and true.

His name was Wiglaf, Weohstan's son,
A prince of the Scylfings,° a peerless thane,
Ælfhere's kinsman; he saw his king
2460 Under his helmet smitten with heat.
He thought of the gifts which his lord had given,
The wealth and the land of the Wægmunding line
And all the folk-rights° his father had owned;
Nor could he hold back, but snatched up his buckler,
His linden shield and his ancient sword,
Heirloom of Eanmund, Ohthere's son,
Whom Weohstan slew with the sword in battle,
Wretched and friendless and far from home.
The brown-hewed helmet he bore to his kinsmen,
2470 The ancient blade and the byrny of rings.
These Onela gave him—his nephew's arms—
Nor called for vengeance, nor fought the feud,
Though Weohstan had slaughtered his brother's son.
He held the treasures for many half-years,
The byrny and sword, till his son was of age
For manful deeds, as his father before him.
Among the Geats° he gave him of war-gear
Countless numbers of every kind;
Then, full of winters, he left the world,
2480 Gave over this life. And Wiglaf, the lad,
Was to face with his lord the first of his battles,
The hazard of war. But his heart did not fail
Nor the blade of his kinsman weaken in war,
As the worm soon found when they met in the fight!

Wiglaf spoke in sorrow of soul,
With bitter reproach rebuking his comrades:
'I remember the time,° as we drank in the mead-hall,
When we swore to our lord who bestowed these rings
That we would repay for the war-gear and armor,
2490 The hard swords and helmets, if need like this
Should ever befall him. He chose us out
From all the host for this high adventure,
Deemed us worthy of glorious deeds,
Gave me these treasures, regarded us all
As high-hearted bearers of helmet and spear—

Though our lord himself, the shield of his people,
Thought single-handed to finish this feat,
Since of mortal men his measure was most
Of feats of daring and deeds of fame.
Now is the day that our lord has need   2500
Of the strength and courage of stalwart men.
Let us haste to succor his sore distress
In the horrible heat and the merciless flame.
God knows I had rather the fire should enfold
My body and limbs with my gold-friend and lord.
Shameful it seems that we carry our shields
Back to our homes ere we harry the foe
And ward the life of the Weder king.
Full well I know it is not his due
That he alone, of the host of the Geats,   2510
Should suffer affliction and fall in the fight.
One helmet and sword, one byrny and shield,
Shall serve for us both in the storm of strife.'
Then Wiglaf dashed through the deadly reek
In his battle-helmet to help his lord.
Brief were his words: 'Beloved Beowulf,
Summon your strength, remember the vow
You made of old in the years of youth
Not to allow your glory to lessen
As long as you lived. With resolute heart,   2520
And dauntless daring, defend your life
With all your force. I fight at your side!'
Once again the worm, when the words were spoken,
The hideous foe in a horror of flame,
Rushed in rage at the hated men.
Wiglaf's buckler was burned to the boss
In the billows of fire; his byrny of mail
Gave the young hero no help or defense.
But he stoutly pressed on under shield of his kinsman
When his own was consumed in the scorching flame.   2530
Then the king once more was mindful of glory,
Swung his great sword-blade with all his might
And drove it home on the dragon's head.
But Nægling° broke, it failed in the battle,
The blade of Beowulf, ancient and gray.
It was not his lot that edges of iron
Could help him in battle; his hand was too strong,
Overtaxed, I am told, every blade with its blow.
Though he bore a wondrous hard weapon to war,
No whit the better was he thereby!   2540
A third time then the terrible scather,
The monstrous dragon inflamed with the feud,
Rushed on the king when the opening offered,
Fierce and flaming; fastened its fangs
In Beowulf's throat; he was bloodied with gore;
His life-blood streamed from the welling wound.
As they tell the tale, in the king's sore need
His shoulder-companion showed forth his valor,
His craft and courage, and native strength.
To the head of the dragon he paid no heed,   2550
Though his hand was burned as he helped his king.

2458 **Scylfings, etc.** The Scylfings were the reigning family among the Swedes.
Wiglaf's father Weohstan, a Swedish exile, had taken refuge in Geatland; he was
also related to the Waegmundings, Beowulf's family   2463 The Germanic nations or tribes always had a certain amount of land and livestock that was common property in addition to the personal property of the individual noblemen.
Each member of the tribe had the right to use his "share" of this common property. Such a share was known as a "folk-right"   2477 Although Wiglaf's father
fought on Onela's side in the earlier Geatish-Scylfing conflict, by the time Wiglaf
is old enough to receive warrior's armor, he is living among the Geats
2487 **remember the time, etc.,** a noteworthy statement of the bond of loyalty that
joined the *comitatus*, or body of warriors, to their chief

2534 **Nægling,** Beowulf's sword

A little lower° the stalwart struck
At the evil beast, and his blade drove home
Plated and gleaming. The fire began
To lessen and wane. The king of the Weders
Summoned his wits; he drew the dagger
He wore on his corselet, cutting and keen,
And slit asunder the worm with the blow.
So they felled the foe and wrought their revenge;
2560 The kinsmen together had killed the dragon.
So a man should be when the need is bitter!
That was the last fight Beowulf fought;
That was the end of his work in the world.

BEOWULF'S DEATH

The wound which the dragon had dealt him began
To swell and burn; and soon he could feel
The baneful venom inflaming his breast.
The wise, old warrior sank down by the wall
And stared at the work of the giants of old,
The arches of stone and the standing columns
2570 Upholding the ancient earth-hall within.
His loyal thane, the kindest of comrades,
Saw Beowulf bloody and broken in war;
In his hands bore water and bathed his leader,
And loosened the helm from his dear lord's head.
    Beowulf spoke, though his hurt was sore,
The wounds of battle grievous and grim.
Full well he weened that his life was ended,
And all the joy of his years on earth;
That his days were done, and Death most near:
2580 'My armor and sword I would leave to my son
Had Fate but granted, born of my body,
An heir to follow me after I'm gone.
For fifty winters I've ruled this realm,
And never a lord of a neighboring land
Dared strike with terror or seek with sword.
In my life I abode by the lot assigned,
Kept well what was mine, courted no quarrels,
Swore no false oaths. And now for all this
Though my hurt is grievous, my heart is glad.
2590 When life leaves body, the Lord of mankind
Cannot lay to my charge the killing of kinsmen!
Go quickly, dear Wiglaf, to gaze on the gold
Beneath the hoar stone. The dragon lies still
In the slumber of death, despoiled of his hoard.
Make haste that my eyes may behold the treasure,
The gleaming jewels, the goodly store,
And, glad of the gold, more peacefully leave
The life and the realm I have ruled so long.'
    Then Weohstan's son, as they tell the tale,
2600 Clad in his corselet and trappings of war,
Hearkened at once to his wounded lord.
Under roof of the barrow he broke his way.
Proud in triumph he stood by the seat,
Saw glittering jewels and gold on the ground,

The den of the dragon, the old dawn-flier,
And all the wonders along the walls.
Great bowls and flagons of bygone men
Lay all unburnished and barren of gems,
Many a helmet ancient and rusted,
Many an arm-ring cunningly wrought.   2610
Treasure and gold, though hid in the ground,
Override man's wishes, hide them who will!°
High o'er the hoard he beheld a banner,
Greatest of wonders, woven with skill,
All wrought of gold; its radiance lighted
The vasty ground and the glittering gems.
But no sign of the worm! The sword-edge had slain
    him.
As I've heard the tale, the hero unaided
Rifled those riches of giants of old,
The hoard in the barrow, and heaped in his arms   2620
Beakers and platters, picked what he would
And took the banner, the brightest of signs.
The ancient sword with its edge of iron
Had slain the worm who watched o'er the wealth,
In the midnight flaming, with menace of fire
Protecting the treasure for many a year
Till he died the death. Then Wiglaf departed
In haste returning enriched with spoil.
He feared, and wondered if still he would find
The lord of the Weders alive on the plain,   2630
Broken and weary and smitten with wounds.
With his freight of treasure he found the prince,
His dear lord, bloody and nigh unto death.
With water he bathed him till words broke forth
From the hoard of his heart and, aged and sad,
Beowulf spoke, as he gazed on the gold:
'For this goodly treasure whereon I gaze
I give my thanks to the Lord of all,
To the Prince of glory, Eternal God,
Who granted me grace to gain for my people   2640
Such dower of riches before my death.
I gave my life for this golden hoard.
Heed well the wants, the need of my people;
My hour is come, and my end is near.
Bid warriors build, when they burn my body,
A stately barrow on the headland's height.
It shall be for remembrance among my people
As it towers high on the Cape of the Whale,
And sailors shall know it as Beowulf's Barrow,
Sea-faring mariners driving their ships   2650
Through fogs of ocean from far countries.'
Then the great-hearted king unclasped from his throat
A collar of gold, and gave to his thane;
Gave the young hero his gold-decked helmet,
His ring and his byrny, and wished him well.
'You are the last of the Wægmunding line.
All my kinsmen, earls in their glory,
Fate has sent to their final doom,
And I must follow.' These words were the last

2552 **lower,** etc. The dragon was vulnerable only in the belly

2611-12 **Treasure . . . will.** This seems to mean "Gold will bring about the ruin of any man, no matter how carefully it is hidden"

2660 The old king spoke ere the pyre received him,
The leaping flames of the funeral blaze,
And his breath went forth from his bosom, his soul
Went forth from the flesh, to the joys of the just.

Then bitter it was for Beowulf's thane
To behold his loved one lying on earth
Suffering sore at the end of life.
The monster that slew him, the dreadful dragon,
Likewise lay broken and brought to his death.
The worm no longer could rule the hoard,
2670 But the hard, sharp sword, the work of the hammer,
Had laid him low; and the winged dragon
Lay stretched near the barrow, broken and still.
No more in the midnight he soared in air,
Disclosing his presence, and proud of his gold;
For he sank to earth by the sword of the king.
But few of mankind,° if the tales be true,
Has it prospered much, though mighty in war
And daring in deed, to encounter the breath
Of the venomous worm or plunder his wealth
When the ward of the barrow held watch o'er the
2680   mound.
Beowulf bartered his life for the treasure;
Both foes had finished this fleeting life.

Not long was it then till the laggards in battle
Came forth from the forest, ten craven in fight,
Who had dared not face the attack of the foe
In their lord's great need. The shirkers in shame
Came wearing their bucklers and trappings of war
Where the old man lay. They looked upon Wiglaf.
Weary he sat by the side of his leader
2690 Attempting with water to waken his lord.
It availed him little; the wish was vain!
He could not stay his soul upon earth,
Nor one whit alter the will of God.
The Lord ruled over the lives of men
As He rules them still. With a stern rebuke
He reproached the cowards whose courage had failed.
Wiglaf addressed them, Weohstan's son;
Gazed sad of heart on the hateful men:
'Lo! he may say who would speak the truth
2700 That the lord who gave you these goodly rings,
This warlike armor wherein you stand—
When oft on the ale-bench he dealt to his hall-men
Helmet and byrny, endowing his thanes
With the fairest he found from near or from far—
That he grievously wasted these trappings of war
When battle befell him. The king of the folk
Had no need to boast of his friends in the fight.
But the God of victory granted him strength
To avenge himself with the edge of the sword
2710 When he needed valor. Of little avail
The help I brought in the bitter battle!
Yet still I strove, though beyond my strength,
To aid my kinsman. And ever the weaker
The savage foe when I struck with my sword;

Ever the weaker the welling flame!
Too few defenders surrounded our ruler
When the hour of evil and terror befell.
Now granting of treasure and giving of swords,
Inherited land-right° and joy of the home,
Shall cease from your kindred. And each of your clan   2720
Shall fail of his birthright when men from afar
Hear tell of your flight and your dastardly deed.
Death is better for every earl
Than life besmirched with the brand of shame!'

THE MESSENGER FORETELLS
THE DOOM OF THE GEATS

Then Wiglaf bade tell the tidings of battle
Up over the cliff in the camp of the host
Where the linden-bearers all morning long
Sat wretched in spirit, and ready for both,
The return, or the death, of their dear-loved lord.
Not long did he hide, who rode up the headland,   2730
The news of their sorrow, but spoke before all:
'Our leader lies low, the lord of the Weders,
The king of the Geats, on the couch of death.
He sleeps his last sleep by the deeds of the worm.
The dreadful dragon is stretched beside him
Slain with dagger-wounds. Not by the sword
Could he quell the monster or lay him low.
And Wiglaf is sitting, Weohstan's son,
Bent over Beowulf, living by dead.
Death watch he keeps in sorrow of spirit   2740
Over the bodies of friend and foe.

Now comes peril of war when this news is rumored
    abroad,
The fall of our king known afar among Frisians and
    Franks!°
For a fierce feud rose with the Franks when Hygelac's
    warlike host
Invaded the Frisian fields, and the Hetware° van-
    quished the Geats,
Overcame with the weight of their hordes, and
    Hygelac fell in the fray;
It was not his lot to live on dispensing the spoils of
    war.
And never since then of the Franks had we favor or
    friend.
And I harbor no hope of peace or faith from the
    Swedish folk,
For well is it known of men that Ongentheow slew with
    the sword   2750
Hæthcyn, the son of Hrethel, near Ravenswood, in the
    fight
When the Swedish people in pride swept down on the
    Geats.
And Ohthere's aged father, old and a terror in battle,

2676 **few of mankind, etc.,** suggests that Beowulf was doomed by the curse placed long ago upon the treasure hoard

2719 **land-right,** folk-right   2743 See note on l. 1843   2745 **Hetware,** another name for the Frisians, upon whom Hygelac made the raid in which he was killed

Made onslaught, killing their king, and rescued his
   queen,
Ohthere's mother and Onela's, aged, bereft of her
   gold.
He followed the flying foe till, lordless and lorn,
They barely escaped into Ravenswood. There he beset
   them,
A wretched remnant of war, and weary with wounds.
And all the long hours of the night he thundered his
   threats
That some on the morrow he would slay with the edge
2760   of the sword,
And some should swing on the gallows for food for the
   fowls!
But hope returned with the dawn to the heavy-hearted
When they heard the sound of the trumpets and
   Hygelac's horn,
As the good king came with his troops marching up on
   their track.
   Then was a gory meeting of Swedes and Geats;
On all sides carnage and slaughter, savage and grim,
As the struggling foemen grappled and swayed in the
   fight.
And the old earl Ongentheow, crestfallen and cowed,
Fled with his men to a fastness, withdrew to the hills.
He had tasted Hygelac's strength, the skill of the hero
2770   in war,
And he had no hope to resist or strive with the sea-
   men,
To save his hoard from their hands, or his children, or
   wife.
So the old king fled to his fortress; but over the plain
Hygelac's banners swept on in pursuit of the Swedes,
Stormed to the stronghold's defenses, and old
   Ongentheow
Was brought to bay with the sword, and subject to
   Eofor's will!
Wulf, son of Wonred, in wrath then struck with his
   sword,
And the blood in streams burst forth from under the
   old man's hair.
Yet the aged Scylfing was all undaunted and answered
   the stroke
With a bitter exchange in the battle; and Wonred's
2780   brave son
Could not requite the blow, for the hero had cleft his
   helmet,
And, covered with blood, he was forced to bow; he fell
   to the earth.
But his death was not doomed, and he rallied, though
   the wound was deep.
Then Hygelac's hardy thane, when his brother lay low,
Struck with his ancient blade, a sturdy sword of the
   giants,
Cut through the shield-wall, cleaving the helmet. The
   king,
The folk-defender, sank down. He was hurt unto
   death.

Then were many that bound Wulf's wounds when the
   fight was won,
When the Geats held the ground of battle; as booty of
   war
Eofor stripped Ongentheow of iron byrny and helm,   2790
Of sword-blade hilted and hard, and bore unto
   Hygelac
The old man's trappings of war. And Hygelac took the
   treasures,
Promising fair rewards, and this he fulfilled.
The son of Hrethel, the king of the Geats, when he
   came to his home,
Repaid with princely treasure the prowess of Eofor
   and Wulf;
Gave each an hundred thousand of land and linked
   rings,
And none could belittle or blame. They had won the
   honor in war.
He gave to Eofor also the hand of his only daughter
To be a pledge of good will, and the pride of his home.

This is the fighting and this the feud,   2800
The bitter hatred, that breeds the dread
Lest the Swedish people should swarm against us
Learning our lord lies lifeless and still.
His was the hand that defended the hoard,
Heroes, and realm against ravaging foe,
By noble counsel and dauntless deed.
Let us go quickly to look on the king
Who brought us treasure, and bear his corpse
To the funeral pyre. The precious hoard
Shall burn with the hero. There lies the heap   2810
Of untold treasure so grimly gained,
Jewels and gems he bought with his blood
At the end of life. All these at the last
The flames shall veil and the brands devour.
No man for remembrance shall take from the treasure,
Nor beauteous maiden adorn her breast
With gleaming jewel; bereft of gold
And tragic-hearted many shall tread
A foreign soil, now their lord has ceased
From laughter and revel and rapture of joy.   2820
Many a spear in the cold of morning
Shall be borne in hand uplifted on high.
No sound of harp shall waken the warrior,
But the dusky raven despoiling the dead
Shall clamor and cry and call to the eagle
What fare he found at the carrion-feast
The while with the wolf he worried the corpses.'
   So the stalwart hero had told his tidings,
His fateful message; nor spoke amiss
As to truth or telling. The host arose;   2830
On their woeful way to the Eagles' Ness°
They went with tears to behold the wonder.
They found the friend, who had dealt them treasure
In former days, on the bed of death,

2831 **Ness,** cliff

Stretched out lifeless upon the sand.
The last of the good king's days was gone;
Wondrous the death of the Weder prince!
They had sighted first, where it lay outstretched,
The monstrous wonder, the loathsome worm,
2840 The horrible fire-drake, hideous-hued,
Scorched with the flame. The spread of its length
Was fifty foot-measures! Oft in the night
It sported in air, then sinking to earth
Returned to its den. Now moveless in death
It had seen the last of its earthly lair.
Beside the dragon were bowls and beakers,
Platters lying, and precious swords
Eaten with rust, where the hoard had rested
A thousand winters in the womb of earth.
2850 That boundless treasure of bygone men,
The golden dower, was girt with a spell
So that never a man might ravage the ring-hall
Save as God himself, the Giver of victory—
He is the Shelter and Shield of men—
Might allow such man as seemed to Him meet,
Might grant whom He would, to gather the treasure.
　His way of life, who had wickedly hoarded
The wealth of treasure beneath the wall,
Had an evil end, as was widely seen.
2860 Many the dragon had sent to death,
But in fearful fashion the feud was avenged!
'Tis a wondrous thing when a warlike earl
Comes to the close of his destined days,
When he may no longer among his kinsmen
Feast in the mead-hall. So Beowulf fared
When he sought the dragon in deadly battle!
Himself he knew not what fate was in store
Nor the coming end of his earthly life.
The lordly princes who placed the treasure
2870 Had cursed it deep to the day of doom,
That the man who plundered and gathered the gold
Might pay for the evil imprisoned in hell,
Shackled in torment and punished with pain,
Except the invader should first be favored
With the loving grace of the Lord of all!
　Then spoke Wiglaf, Weohstan's son:
'Often for one man many must sorrow
As has now befallen the folk of the Geats.
We could not persuade the king by our counsel,
2880 Our well-loved leader, to shun assault
On the dreadful dragon guarding the gold;
To let him lie where he long had lurked
In his secret lair till the world shall end.
But Beowulf, dauntless, pressed to his doom.
The hoard was uncovered; heavy the cost;
Too strong the fate that constrained the king!
I entered the barrow, beholding the hoard
And all the treasure throughout the hall;
In fearful fashion the way was opened,
2890 An entrance under the wall of earth.
Of the hoarded treasure I heaped in my arms
A weighty burden, and bore to my king.

He yet was living; his wits were clear.
Much the old man said in his sorrow;
Sent you greeting, and bade you build
In the place of burning a lofty barrow,
Proud and peerless, to mark his deeds;
For he was of all men the worthiest warrior
In all the earth, while he still might rule
And wield the wealth of his lordly land.   2900
Let us haste once more to behold the treasure,
The gleaming wonders beneath the wall.
I will show the way that you all may see
And closely scan the rings and the gold.
Let the bier be ready, the pyre prepared,
When we come again to carry our lord,
Our leader beloved, where long he shall lie
In the kindly care of the Lord of all.'

BEOWULF'S FUNERAL

Then the son of Weohstan, stalwart in war,
Bade send command to the heads of homes   2910
To bring from afar the wood for the burning
Where the good king lay: 'Now glede shall devour,
As dark flame waxes, the warrior prince
Who has often withstood the shower of steel
When the storm of arrows, sped from the string,
Broke over shield, and shaft did service,
With feather-fittings guiding the barb.'
　Then the wise son of Weohstan chose from the host
Seven thanes of the king, the best of the band;
Eight heroes together they hied to the barrow   2920
In under the roof of the fearful foe;
One of the warriors leading the way
Bore in his hand a burning brand.
They cast no lots who should loot the treasure
When they saw unguarded the gold in the hall
Lying there useless; little they scrupled
As quickly they plundered the precious store.
Over the sea-cliff into the ocean
They tumbled the dragon, the deadly worm,
Let the sea-tide swallow the guarder of gold.   2930
Then a wagon was loaded with well-wrought treasure,
A countless number of every kind;
And the aged warrior, the white-haired king,
Was borne on high to the Cape of the Whale.
　The Geat folk fashioned a peerless pyre
Hung round with helmets and battle-boards,
With gleaming byrnies as Beowulf bade.
In sorrow of soul they laid on the pyre
Their mighty leader, their well-loved lord.
The warriors kindled the bale on the barrow,   2940
Wakened the greatest of funeral fires.
Dark o'er the blaze the wood-smoke mounted;
The winds were still, and the sound of weeping
Rose with the roar of the surging flame
Till the heat of the fire had broken the body.
With hearts that were heavy they chanted their
　sorrow,

Singing a dirge for the death of their lord;
And an aged woman° with upbound locks
Lamented for Beowulf, wailing in woe.
2950 Over and over she uttered her dread
Of sorrow to come, of bloodshed and slaughter,
Terror of battle, and bondage, and shame.
The smoke of the bale-fire rose to the sky!
   The men of the Weder folk fashioned a mound
Broad and high on the brow of the cliff,
Seen from afar by seafaring men.
Ten days they worked on the warrior's barrow
Inclosing the ash of the funeral flame
With a wall as worthy as wisdom could shape.
2960 They bore to the barrow the rings and the gems,

2948 **aged woman.** Like many epic heroes, Beowulf is rather solitary in life and dies without offspring

The wealth of the hoard the heroes had plundered.
The olden treasure they gave to the earth,
The gold to the ground, where it still remains
As useless to men as it was of yore.
Then round the mound rode the brave in battle,
The sons of warriors, twelve in a band,
Bemoaning their sorrow and mourning their king.
They sang their dirge and spoke of the hero
Vaunting his valor and venturous deeds.
So is it proper a man should praise   2970
His friendly lord with a loving heart,
When his soul must forth from the fleeting flesh.
So the folk of the Geats, the friends of his hearth,
Bemoaned the fall of their mighty lord;
Said he was kindest of worldly kings,
Mildest, most gentle, most eager for fame.

THE PEARL POET
fl. 1370

Sir Gawain and the Green Knight constitutes a clear and critical look at the ideals of physical and moral integrity demanded of the medieval knight. The poem combines powerful and vigorous narrative with a deep feeling for nature; it is sophisticated but neither cynical nor sentimental. It has often been regarded as the choicest of the Middle English romances. The poem shows evidence of conscious and intricate artistic planning in its many patterned scenes and structures. Instead of the usual manifold adventures of the hero, there are only two, and these two are made to depend on each other. These two central incidents test Gawain's character as a knight and lead to a critical examination of chivalry in general. The first, the beheading incident, tests his physical courage and his fidelity to his word; the second, the incident of the lady in the castle of the Green Knight, tries his chastity and moral courage. Gawain's conduct, exemplary as it is, is not impossibly idealized. He flinches quite naturally under the first terrible blow of the Green Knight's ax, and he does not emerge unscathed from the ordeal of the bedchamber. His conduct is finally open to a variety of valid interpretations—his own, the Green Knight's, and that of Arthur's court. Thus, its unity of narrative effect, its vigorous style, its metrical and poetic brilliance, and its two central incidents distinguish *Sir Gawain* from other fourteenth-century Middle English romances.

   The manuscript known as Cotton Nero A X contains four poems written in the West Midland dialect, the last of which is *Sir Gawain and the Green Knight.*

Pearl, the first of the four and the one which has given the poet his name, is a dream-vision elegy for the death of a child and, by allegorical extension, for some more extensive spiritual loss. *Patience* and *Purity*, the second and third poems, are homiletic narratives. The resemblances among these four poems are so great that the entire group has generally been assigned to one author, the Pearl Poet. The identity of this author remains unclear, but there is general agreement that the four poems were composed around 1370.

   The form of *Sir Gawain* is unusual. It is told in four sections, or fits; the verse form consists of irregular stanzas, which up to the last four lines are in unrhymed alliterative verse. The stanzas average about twenty lines, but in each stanza the last five lines are much shorter than the others. The first of these five lines is a short "bob" line of one metrical foot; the remaining four are trimeters or tetrameters, generally iambic, rhyming *abab*. The sample given below, the opening stanza of the poem, well illustrates the difficult but vigorous dialect of the poem.

   Siþen þe sege and þe assaut watȝ sesed at Troye,
   þe borȝ brittened and brent to brondeȝ and askeȝ,
   þe tulk þat þe trammes of tresoun þer wroȝt
   Watȝ tried for his tricherie, þe trewest on erthe:
   Hit watȝ Ennias þe athel and his highe kynde,
   þat siþen depreced prouinces, and patrounes bicome
   Welneȝe of al þe wele in þe West Iles.
   Fro riche Romulus to Rome ricchis hym swyþe,

With gret bobbaunce þat burȝe he biges vpon fyrst,
And neuenes hit his aune nome, as hit now hat;
Ticius to Tuskan and teldes bigynnes,
Langaberde in Lumbardie lyftes vp homes,
And fer ouer þe French flod Felix Brutus
On mony bonkkes ful brode Bretayn he setteȝ
     Wyth wynne,
   Where werre and wrake and wonder
   Bi syþeȝ hatȝ wont þerinne,
   And oft boþe blysse and blunder
   Ful skete hatȝ skyfted synne.

Here, as in Old English, þ is the symbol of the Modern English *th*-sounds. ȝ is a symbol of several sounds. In the works of the Pearl Poet its use is peculiar: in final position it seems to be a z-sound, as in *"brondeȝ and askeȝ"* ("brands and ashes") in the second line. At the beginning of a word it is a rather guttural *y*-sound, and also in the middle of a word before an *e* or *i* (cf. *burȝe*). But in the middle of a word before *–t* it is clearly a spirant sound like the German *ch* or the Scotch *loch* (as in *wroȝt*, "wrought," pronounced here "wrocht").

SIR GAWAIN AND THE GREEN KNIGHT°

FIT I

1

The seige and the assault being ceased at Troy,
The battlements broken down and burnt to brands and
   ashes,
The treacherous trickster whose treasons there
   flourished
Was famed for his falsehood, the foulest on earth.
Aeneas the noble° and his knightly kin
Then conquered kingdoms, and kept in their hand
Wellnigh all the wealth of the western lands.°
Royal Romulus° to Rome first turned,
Set up the city in splendid pomp,
10 Then named her with his own name, which now she
   still has:
Ticius° founded Tuscany, townships raising,
Longbeard° in Lombardy lifted up homes,
And far over the French flood Felix Brutus°
On many spacious slopes set Britain with joy
    And grace;
   Where war and feud and wonder
   Have ruled the realm a space,

And after, bliss and blunder
By turns have run their race.

2

And when this Britain was built by this brave noble, 20
Here bold men bred, in battle exulting,
Stirrers of trouble in turbulent times.
Here many a marvel, more than in other lands,
Has befallen by fortune since that far time.
But of all who abode here of Britain's kings,
Arthur was highest in honour, as I have heard;
So I intend to tell you of a true wonder,
Which many folk mention as a manifest marvel,
A happening eminent among Arthur's adventures.
Listen to my lay but a little while: 30
Straightway shall I speak it, in city as I heard it,
    With tongue;
   As scribes have set it duly
   In the lore of the land so long,
   With letters linking truly
   In story bold and strong.

3

This king lay at Camelot° one Christmastide
With many mighty lords, manly liegemen,
Members rightly reckoned of the Round Table,°
In splendid celebration, seemly and carefree. 40
There tussling in tournament time and again
Jousted in jollity these gentle knights,
Then in court carnival sang catches and danced;
For fifteen days the feasting there was full in like
   measure
With all the meat and merry-making men could devise,
Gladly ringing glee, glorious to hear,
A noble din by day, dancing at night!
All was happiness in the height in halls and chambers
For lords and their ladies, delectable joy.
With all delights on earth they housed there together, 50
Saving Christ's self, the most celebrated knights,
The loveliest ladies to live in all time,
And the comeliest king ever to keep court.
For this fine fellowship was in its fair prime
    Far famed,
   Stood well in heaven's will,
   Its high-souled king acclaimed:
   So hardy a host on hill
   Could not with ease be named.

4

The year being so young that yester-even saw its birth, 60
That day double on the dais were the diners served.
Mass sung and service ended, straight from the chapel
The King and his company came into hall.
Called on with cries from clergy and laity,
Noël was newly announced, named time and again.

Sir Gawain and the Green Knight. Verse translation by Brian Stone 5 **Aeneas the noble.** According to medieval tradition, Troy had been taken through the machinations of Aeneas, who was ultimately tried by the Greeks and exiled from the city 7 **western lands,** probably England and Scotland, the Hebrides, Ireland, Wight, Man, and the Orkneys 8 **Romulus,** legendary founder of Rome 11 **Ticius,** perhaps a fictitious descendant of Aeneas 12 **Longbeard,** the traditional ancestor of the Lombards, a famous Germanic tribe 13 **Brutus,** according to legend the grandson of Aeneas and the founder of Britain

37 **Camelot,** the capital of King Arthur's realm, identified by Sir Thomas Malory with Winchester 39 **Round Table.** To eliminate quarrels among Arthur's guests about the order in which they had been seated at table, a round table was devised so there could be no question of "high" or "low"

Then lords and ladies leaped forth, largesse
    distributing,
Offered New Year gifts in high voices, handed them
    out,
Bustling and bantering about these offerings.
Ladies laughed full loudly, though losing their wealth,
70 And he that won was not woeful, you may well
    believe.
All this merriment they made until meal time.
Then in progress to their places they passed after
    washing,
In authorized order, the high-ranking first;
With glorious Guinevere, gay in the midst,
On the princely platform° with its precious hangings
Of splendid silk at the sides, a state over her
Of rich tapestry of Toulouse and Turkestan°
Brilliantly embroidered with the best gems
Of warranted worth that wealth at any time
80   Could buy.
    Fairest of form was this queen,
    Glinting and grey of eye;
    No man could say he had seen
    A lovelier, but with a lie.

5

But Arthur would not eat until all were served.
He was charming and cheerful, child-like and gay,
And loving active life, little did he favour
Lying down for long or lolling on a seat,
So robust his young blood and his beating brain.
90 Still, he was stirred now by something else:
His noble announcement that he never would eat
On such a fair feast-day till informed in full
Of some unusual adventure, as yet untold,
Of some momentous marvel that he might believe,
About ancestors, or arms, or other high theme;
Or till a stranger should seek out a strong knight of his,
To join with him in jousting, in jeopardy to lay
Life against life, each allowing the other
The favour of Fortune, the fairer lot.
100 Such was the King's custom when he kept court,
At every fine feast among his free retinue
    In hall.
    So he throve amid the throng,
    A ruler royal and tall,
    Still standing staunch and strong,
    And young like the year withal.

6

Erect stood the strong King, stately of mien,
Trifling time with talk before the topmost table.
Good Gawain was placed at Guinevere's side,
110 And Agravain of the Hard Hand sat on the other side,
Both the King's sister's sons, staunchest of knights.

75 **princely platform.** The medieval hall had a high table on the dais at one end, reserved for the lord of the castle, his family, and his knightly nobles, and rows of tables below the dais, parallel to the long sides of the hall, where the less important retainers gathered 77 **Toulouse and Turkestan.** Toulouse was a city in southern France famous during the Middle Ages for its silk stuffs. The cloth imported from Turkestan was obviously very costly

Above, Bishop Baldwin began the board,
And Ywain, Urien's son ate next to him.
These were disposed on the dais and with dignity
    served,
And many mighty men next, marshalled at side tables.
Then the first course came in with such cracking of
    trumpets,
(Whence bright bedecked blazons in banners hung)
Such din of drumming and a deal of fine piping,
Such wild warbles whelming and echoing
That hearts were uplifted high at the strains.   120
Then delicacies and dainties were delivered to the
    guests,
Fresh food in foison, such freight of full dishes
That space was scarce at the social tables
For the several soups set before them in silver
    On the cloth.
    Each feaster made free with the fare,
    Took lightly and nothing loth;
    Twelve plates were for every pair,
    Good beer and bright wine both.

7

Of their meal I shall mention no more just now,   130
For it is evident to all that ample was served;
Now another noise, quite new, neared suddenly,
Likely to allow the liege lord to eat;
For barely had the blast of trump abated one minute
And the first course in the court been courteously
    served,
When there heaved in at the hall door an awesome
    fellow
Who in height outstripped all earthly men.
From throat to thigh he was so thickset and square,
His loins and limbs were so long and so great,
That he was half a giant on earth, I believe;   140
Yet mainly and most of all a man he seemed,
And the handsomest of horsemen, though huge, at
    that;
For though at back and at breast his body was broad,
His hips and haunches were elegant and small,
And perfectly proportioned were all parts of the man,
    As seen.
    Men gaped at the hue of him
    Ingrained in garb and mien,
    A fellow fiercely grim,
    And all a glittering green.°   150

8

And garments of green girt the fellow about—
A two-third length tunic, tight at the waist,
A comely cloak on top, accomplished with lining
Of the finest fur to be found, made of one piece,
Marvellous fur-trimmed material, with matching hood
Lying back from his locks and laid on his shoulders;
Fitly held-up hose, in hue the same green,

150 **green.** Green was a fairy color, hence quite appropriate to this particular knight; the color is also symbolic of immortal spring

That was caught at the calf, with clinking spurs
  beneath
Of bright gold on bases of embroidered silk,
160 But no iron shoe armoured that horseman's feet.
And verily his vesture was all vivid green,
So were the bars on his belt and the brilliants set
In ravishing array on the rich accoutrements
About himself and his saddle on silken work.
It would be tedious to tell a tithe of the trifles
Embossed and embroidered, such as birds and flies,
In gay green gauds, with gold everywhere.
The breast-hangings of the horse, its haughty crupper,
The enamelled knobs and nails on its bridle,
170 And the stirrups that he stood on, were all stained with
  the same;
So were the splendid saddle-skirts and bows
That ever glimmered and glinted with their green
  stones.
The steed that he spurred on was similar in hue
    To the sight,
    Green and huge of grain,
    Mettlesome in might
    And brusque with bit and rein—
    A steed to serve that knight!

9
Yes, garbed all in green was the gallant rider,
180 And the hair of his head was the same hue as his horse,
And floated finely like a fan round his shoulders;
And a great bushy beard on his breast flowing down,
With the heavy hair hanging from his head,
Was shorn below the shoulder, sheared right round,
So that half his arms were under the encircling hair,
Covered as by a king's cape, that closes at the neck.
The mane of that mighty horse, much like the beard,
Well crisped and combed, was copiously plaited
With twists of twining gold, twinkling in the green,
190 First a green gossamer, a golden one next.
His flowing tail and forelock followed suit,
And both were bound with bands of bright green,
Ornamented to the end with exquisite stones,
While a thong running through them threaded on high
Many bright golden bells, burnished and ringing.
Such a horse, such a horseman, in the whole wide
  world
Was never seen or observed by those assembled
  before,
    Not one.
    Lightning-like he seemed
200 And swift to strike and stun.
    His dreadful blows, men deemed,
    Once dealt, meant death was done.

10
Yet hauberk and helmet had he none,
Nor plastron nor plate-armour proper to combat,
Nor shield for shoving, nor sharp spear for lunging;
But he held a holly cluster in one hand, holly

That is greenest when groves are gaunt and bare,
And an axe in his other hand, huge and monstrous,
A hideous helmet-smasher for anyone to tell of;
The head of that axe was an ell-rod° long.   210
Of green hammered gold and steel was the socket,
And the blade was burnished bright, with a broad
  edge,
Acutely honed for cutting, as keenest razors are.
The grim man gripped it by its great strong handle,
Which was wound with iron all the way to the end,
And graven in green with graceful designs.
A cord curved round it, was caught at the head,
Then hitched to the haft at intervals in loops,
With costly tassels attached thereto in plenty
On bosses of bright green embroidered richly.   220
In he rode, and up the hall, this man,
Driving towards the high dais, dreading no danger.
He gave no one a greeting, but glared over all.
His opening utterance was, 'Who and where
Is the governor of this gathering? Gladly would I
Behold him with my eyes and have speech with him.'
    He frowned;
    Took note of every knight
    As he ramped and rode around;
    Then stopped to study who might   230
    Be the noble most renowned.

11
The assembled folk stared, long scanning the fellow,
For all men marvelled what it might mean
That a horseman and his horse should have such a
  colour
As to grow green as grass, and greener yet, it seemed,
More gaudily glowing than green enamel on gold.
Those standing studied him and sidled towards him
With all the world's wonder as to what he would do.
For astonishing sights they had seen, but such a one
  never;
Therefore a phantom from Fairyland the folk there   240
  deemed him.
So even the doughty were daunted and dared not
  reply,
All sitting stock-still, astounded by his voice.
Throughout the high hall was a hush like death;
Suddenly as if all had slipped into sleep, their voices
  were
    At rest;
    Hushed not wholly for fear,
    But some at honour's behest;
    But let him whom all revere
    Greet that gruesome guest.

12
For Arthur sensed an exploit before the high dais,   250
And accorded him courteous greeting, no craven he,

210 **ell-rod**, approximately forty-five inches long

Saying to him, 'Sir knight, you are certainly welcome.
I am head of this house: Arthur is my name.
Please deign to dismount and dwell with us
Till you impart your purpose, at a proper time.'
'May he that sits in heaven help me,' said the knight,
'But my intention was not to tarry in this turreted hall.
But as your reputation, royal sir, is raised up so high,
And your castle and cavaliers are accounted the best,
260 The mightiest of mail-clad men in mounted fighting,
The most warlike, the worthiest the world has bred,
Most valiant to vie with in virile contests,
And as chivalry is shown here, so I am assured,
At this time, I tell you, that has attracted me here.
By this branch that I bear, you may be certain
That I proceed in peace, no peril seeking;
For had I fared forth in fighting gear,
My hauberk and helmet, both at home now,
My shield and sharp spear, all shining bright,
270 And other weapons to wield, I would have brought;
However, as I wish for no war here, I wear soft
    clothes.
But if you are as bold as brave men affirm,
You will gladly grant me the good sport I demand
        By right.'
        Then Arthur answer gave:
        'If you, most noble knight,
        Unarmoured combat crave,
        We'll fail you not in fight.'

13

'No, it is not combat I crave, for come to that,
280 On this bench only beardless boys are sitting.
If I were hasped in armour on a high steed,
No man among you could match me, your might being
    meagre.
So I crave in this court a Christmas game,
For it is Yuletide and New Year, and young men
    abound here.
If any in this household is so hardy in spirit,
Of such mettlesome mind and so madly rash
As to strike a strong blow in return for another,
I shall offer to him this fine axe freely;
This axe, which is heavy enough, to handle as he
    please.
290 And I shall bide the first blow, as bare as I sit here.
If some intrepid man is tempted to try what I suggest,
Let him leap towards me and lay hold of this weapon,
Acquiring clear possession of it, no claim from me
    ensuing.
Then shall I stand up to his stroke, quite still on this
    floor—
So long as I shall have leave to launch a return blow
        Unchecked.
        Yet he shall have a year
        And a day's reprieve, I direct.
        Now hasten and let me hear
300   Who answers, to what effect.'

14

If he had astonished them at the start, yet stiller now
Were the henchmen in hall, both high and low.
The rider wrenched himself round in his saddle
And rolled his red eyes about roughly and strangely,
Bending his brows, bristling and bright, on all,
His beard swaying as he strained to see who would
    rise.
When none came to accord with him, he coughed
    aloud,
Then pulled himself up proudly, and spoke as follows:
'What, is this Arthur's house, the honour of which
Is bruited abroad so abundantly?   310
Has your pride disappeared? Your prowess gone?
Your victories, your valour, your vaunts, where are
    they?
The revel and renown of the Round Table
Is now overwhelmed by a word from one man's voice,
For all flinch for fear from a fight not begun!'
Upon this, he laughed so loudly that the lord grieved.
His fair features filled with blood
        For shame.
        He raged as roaring gale;
        His followers felt the same.   320
        The King, not one to quail,
        To that cavalier then came.

15

'By heaven,' then said Arthur, 'What you ask is
    foolish,
But as you firmly seek folly, find it you shall.
No good man here is aghast at your great words.
Hand me your axe now, for heaven's sake,
And I shall bestow the boon you bid us give.'
He sprang towards him swiftly, seized it from his
    hand,
And fiercely the other fellow footed the floor.
Now Arthur had his axe, and holding it by the haft   330
Swung it about sternly, as if to strike with it.
The strong man stood before him, stretched to his full
    height,
Higher than any in the hall by a head and more.
Stern of face he stood there, stroking his beard,
Turning down his tunic in a tranquil manner,
Less unmanned and dismayed by the mighty strokes
Than if a banqueter at the bench had brought him a
    drink
        Of wine.
        Then Gawain at Guinevere's side
        Bowed and spoke his design: 340
        'Before all, King, confide
        This fight to me. May it be mine.'

16

'If you would, worthy lord,' said Gawain to the King,
'Bid me stir from this seat and stand beside you,
Allowing me without lese-majesty to leave the table,
And if my liege lady were not displeased thereby,

I should come there to counsel you before this court of
  nobles.
For it appears unmeet to me, as manners go,
When your hall hears uttered such a haughty request,
350 Though you gladly agree, for you to grant it yourself,
When on the benches about you many such bold men
  sit,
Under heaven, I hold, the highest-mettled,
There being no braver knights when battle is joined.
I am the weakest, the most wanting in wisdom, I
  know,
And my life, if lost, would be least missed, truly.
Only through your being my uncle, am I to be valued;
No bounty but your blood in my body do I know.
And since this affair is too foolish to fall to you,
And I first asked it of you, make it over to me;
360 And if I fail to speak fittingly, let this full court judge
      Without blame.'
      Then wisely they whispered of it,
      And after, all said the same:
      That the crowned King should be quit,
      And Gawain given the game.

                    17
Then the King commanded the courtly knight to rise.
He directly uprose, approached courteously,
Knelt low to his liege lord, laid hold of the weapon;
And he graciously let him have it, lifted up his hand
370 And gave him God's blessing, gladly urging him
To be strong in spirit and stout of sinew.
'Cousin, take care,' said the King, 'To chop once,
And if you strike with success, certainly I think
You will take the return blow without trouble in time.'
Gripping the great axe, Gawain goes to the man
Who awaits him unwavering, not quailing at all.
Then said to Sir Gawain the stout knight in green,
'Let us affirm our pact freshly, before going farther.
I beg you, bold sir, to be so good
380 As to tell me your true name, as I trust you to.'
'In good faith,' said the good knight, 'Gawain is my
  name,
And whatever happens after, I offer you this blow,
And in twelve months' time I shall take the return blow
With whatever weapon you wish, and with no one else
      Shall I strive.'
      The other with pledge replied,
      'I'm the merriest man alive
      It's a blow from you I must bide,
      Sir Gawain, so may I thrive.'

                    18
390 'By God,' said the Green Knight, 'Sir Gawain, I
  rejoice
That I shall have from your hand what I have asked for
  here.

And you have gladly gone over, in good discourse,
The covenant I requested of the King in full,
Except that you shall assent, swearing in truth,
To seek me yourself, in such place as you think
To find me under the firmament, and fetch your
  payment
For what you deal me today before this dignified
  gathering.'
'How shall I hunt for you? How find your home?'
Said Gawain, 'By God that made me, I go in
  ignorance;
Nor, knight, do I know your name or your court.   400
But instruct me truly thereof, and tell me your name,
And I shall wear out my wits to find my way there;
Here is my oath on it, in absolute honour!'
'That is enough this New Year, no more is needed,'
Said the gallant in green to Gawain the courteous,
'To tell you the truth, when I have taken the blow
After you have duly dealt it, I shall directly inform you
About my house and my home and my own name.
Then you may keep your covenant, and call on me,
And if I waft you no words, then well may you   410
  prosper,
Stay long in your own land and look for no further
      Trial.
      Now grip your weapon grim;
      Let us see your fighting style.'
      'Gladly,' said Gawain to him,
      Stroking the steel the while.

                    19
On the ground the Green Knight graciously stood,
With head slightly slanting to expose the flesh.
His long and lovely locks he laid over his crown,
Baring the naked neck for the business now due.   420
Gawain gripped his axe and gathered it on high,
Advanced the left foot before him on the ground,
And slashed swiftly down on the exposed part,
So that the sharp blade sheared through, shattering the
  bones,
Sank deep in the sleek flesh, split it in two,
And the scintillating steel struck the ground.
The fair head fell from the neck, struck the floor,
And people spurned it as it rolled around.
Blood spurted from the body, bright against the green.
Yet the fellow did not fall, nor falter one whit,   430
But stoutly sprang forward on legs still sturdy,
Roughly reached out among the ranks of nobles,
Seized his splendid head and straightway lifted it.
Then he strode to his steed, snatched the bridle,
Stepped into the stirrup and swung aloft,
Holding his head in his hand by the hair.
He settled himself in the saddle as steadily
As if nothing had happened to him, though he had
      No head.

440 He twisted his trunk about,
That gruesome body that bled;
He caused much dread and doubt
By the time his say was said.

20

For he held the head in his hand upright,
Pointed the face at the fairest in fame on the dais;
And it lifted its eyelids and looked glaringly,
And menacingly said with its mouth as you may now
      hear:
'Be prepared to perform what you promised, Gawain;
Seek faithfully till you find me, my fine fellow,
450 According to your oath in this hall in these knights'
      hearing.
Go to the Green Chapel without gainsaying to get
Such a stroke as you have struck. Strictly you deserve
That due redemption on the day of New Year.
As the Knight of the Green Chapel I am known to
      many;
Therefore if you ask for me, I shall be found.
So come, or else be called coward accordingly!'
Then he savagely swerved, sawing at the reins,
Rushed out at the hall door, his head in his hand,
And the flint-struck fire flew up from the hooves.
460 What place he departed to no person there knew,
Nor could any account be given of the country he had
      come from.
            What then?
      At the Green Knight Gawain and King
      Grinned and laughed again;
      But plainly approved the thing
      As a marvel in the world of men.

21

Though honoured King Arthur was at heart astounded,
He let no sign of it be seen, but said clearly
To the comely queen in courtly speech,
470 'Do not be dismayed, dear lady, today:
Such cleverness comes well at Christmastide,
Like the playing of interludes, laughter and song,
As lords and ladies delight in courtly carols.
However, I am now able to eat the repast,
Having seen, I must say, a sight to wonder at.'
He glanced at Sir Gawain, and gracefully said,
'Now sir, hang up your axe: you have hewn enough.'
And on the backcloth above the dais it was boldly hung
Where all men might mark it and marvel at it
480 And with truthful testimony tell the wonder of it.
Then to the table the two went together,
The King and the constant knight, and keen men
      served them
Double portions of each dainty with all due dignity,
All manner of meat, and minstrelsy too.
Daylong they delighted till darkness came
      To their shores.

Now Gawain give a thought,
Lest peril make you pause
In seeking out the sport
That you have claimed as yours.   490

FIT II

22

Such earnest of noble action had Arthur at New Year,
For he was avid to hear exploits vaunted.
Though starved of such speeches when seated at first,
Now had they high matter indeed, their hands full of 't.
Gawain was glad to begin the games in hall,
But though the end be heavy, have no wonder,
For if men are spritely in spirit after strong drink,
Soon the year slides past, never the same twice;
There is no foretelling its fulfilment from the start.
Yes, this Yuletide passed and the year following;   500
Season after season in succession went by.
After Christmas comes the crabbed Lenten time,
Which forces on the flesh fish and food yet plainer.°
Then weather more vernal wars with the wintry world,
The cold ebbs and declines, the clouds lift,
In shining showers the rain sheds warmth
And falls upon the fair plain, where flowers appear;
The grassy lawns and groves alike are garbed in green;
Birds prepare to build, and brightly sing
The solace of the ensuing summer that soothes hill   510
      And dell.
      By hedgerows rank and rich
      The blossoms bloom and swell,
      And sounds of sweetest pitch
      From lovely woodlands well.

23

Then comes the season of summer with soft winds,
When Zephyrus himself breathes on seeds and herbs.
In paradise is the plant that springs in the open
When the dripping dew drops from its leaves,
And it bears the blissful gleam of the bright sun.   520
Then Harvest comes hurrying, urging it on,
Warning it because of winter to wax ripe soon;
He drives the dust to rise with the drought he brings,
Forcing it to fly up from the face of the earth.
Wrathful winds in raging skies wrestle with the sun;
Leaves are lashed loose from the trees and lie on the
      ground
And the grass becomes grey which was green before.
What rose from root at first now ripens and rots;
So the year in passing yields its many yesterdays,
And winter returns, as the way of the world is,   530
      I swear;

502–503 **Lenten . . . plainer.** Lenten fasting regulations restricted the consumption
of meat and the size of the meals

So came the Michaelmas° moon,
With winter threatening there,
And Gawain considered soon
The fell way he must fare.

24

Yet he stayed in hall with Arthur till All Saints' Day,°
When Arthur provided plentifully, especially for
  Gawain,
A rich feast and high revelry at the Round Table.
The gallant lords and gay ladies grieved for Gawain,
540 Anxious on his account; but all the same
They mentioned only matters of mirthful import,
Joylessly joking for that gentle knight's sake.
For after dinner with drooping heart he addressed his
  uncle
And spoke plainly of his departure, putting it thus:
'Now, liege lord of my life, I beg my leave of you.
You know the kind of covenant it is: I care little
To tell over the trials of it, trifling as they are,
But I am bound to bear the blow and must be gone
  tomorrow
To seek the gallant in green, as God sees fit to guide
  me.'
550 Then the most courtly in that company came together,
Ywain and Eric and others in troops,
Sir Dodinal the Fierce, The Duke of Clarence,
Lancelot and Lionel and Lucan the Good,
Sir Bors and Sir Bedivere, both strong men,
And many admired knights, with Mador of the Gate.
All the company of the court came near to the King
With carking care in their hearts, to counsel the knight.
Much searing sorrow was suffered in the hall
That such a gallant man as Gawain should go in quest
560 To suffer a savage blow, and his sword no more
    Should bear.
    Said Gawain, gay of cheer,
    'Whether fate be foul or fair,
    Why falter I or fear?
    What should man do but dare?'

25

He dwelt there all that day, and at dawn on the morrow
Asked for his armour. Every item was brought.
First a crimson carpet was cast over the floor
And the great pile of gilded war-gear glittered upon it.
570 The strong man stepped on it, took the steel in hand.
The doublet he dressed in was dear Turkestan stuff;
Then came the courtly cape, cut with skill,
Finely lined with fur, and fastened close.
Then they set the steel shoes on the strong man's feet,

Lapped his legs in steel with lovely greaves,
Complete with knee-pieces, polished bright
And connecting at the knee with gold-knobbed hinges.
Then came the cuisses, which cunningly enclosed
His thighs thick of thew, and which thongs secured.
Next the hauberk, interlinked with argent steel rings   580
Which rested on rich material, wrapped the warrior
  round.
He had polished armour on arms and elbows,
Glinting and gay, and gloves of metal,
And all the goodly gear to give help whatever
    Betide;
    With surcoat richly wrought,
    Gold spurs attached in pride,
    A silken sword-belt athwart,
    And steadfast blade at his side.

26

When he was hasped in armour his harness was noble;   590
The least lace or loop was lustrous with gold.
So, harnessed as he was, he heard his mass
As it was offered at the high altar in worship.
Then he came to the King and his court-fellows,
Took leave with loving courtesy of lord and lady,
Who commended him to Christ and kissed him
  farewell.
By now Gringolet had been got ready, and girt with a
  saddle
That gleamed most gaily with many golden fringes,
Everywhere nailed newly for this noble occasion.
The bridle was embossed and bound with bright gold;   600
So were the furnishings of the fore-harness and the fine
  skirts.
The crupper and the caparison accorded with the
  saddle-bows,
And all was arrayed on red with nails of richest gold,
Which glittered and glanced like gleams of the sun.
Then his casque, equipped with clasps of great
  strength
And padded inside, he seized and swiftly kissed;
It towered high on his head and was hasped at the
  back,
With a brilliant silk band over the burnished
  neck-guard,
Embroidered and bossed with the best gems
On broad silken borders, with birds about the seams,   610
Such as parrots painted with periwinkles between,
And turtles and true-love-knots traced as thickly
As if many beauties in a bower had been busy seven
  winters
    Thereabout.
    The circlet on his head
    Was prized more precious no doubt,
    And perfectly diamonded,
    Threw a gleaming lustre out.

532 **Michaelmas,** September 29, the feast of St. Michael the Archangel   536 **All
Saints' Day,** November 1

27

Then they showed him the shield of shining gules,
620 With the Pentangle° in pure gold depicted thereon.
He brandished it by the baldric, and about his neck
He slung it in a seemly way, and it suited him well.
And I intend to tell you, though I tarry therefore,
Why the Pentangle is proper to this prince of knights.
It is a symbol which Solomon° conceived once
To betoken holy truth, by its intrinsic right,
For it is a figure which has five points,
And each line overlaps and is locked with another;
And it is endless everywhere, and the English call it,
630 In all the land, I hear, the Endless Knot.
Therefore it goes with Sir Gawain and his gleaming
    armour,
For, ever faithful in five things, each in fivefold
    manner,
Gawain was reputed good and, like gold well refined,
He was devoid of all villainy, every virtue displaying
    In the field.
        Thus this Pentangle new
        He carried on coat and shield,
        As a man of troth most true
        And knightly name annealed.

28

640 First he was found faultless in his five wits.
Next, his five fingers never failed the knight,
And all his trust on earth was in the five wounds
Which came to Christ on the Cross, as the Creed tells.
And whenever the bold man was busy on the
    battlefield,
Through all other things he thought on this,
That his prowess all depended on the five pure Joys
That the holy Queen of Heaven had of her Child.
Accordingly the courteous knight had that queen's
    image
Etched on the inside of his armoured shield,
650 So that when he beheld her, his heart did not fail.
The fifth five I find the famous man practised
Were—Liberality and Lovingkindness leading the
    rest;
Then his Continence and Courtesy, which were never
    corrupted;
And Piety, the surpassing virtue. These pure five
Were more firmly fixed on that fine man
Than on any other, and every multiple,
Each interlocking with another, had no end,
Being fixed to five points which never failed,
Never assembling on one side, nor sundering either,
660 With no end at any angle; nor can I find
Where the design started or proceeded to its end.

---

620 **Pentangle**, a five-pointed star, an ancient symbol of perfection; during the
Middle Ages the symbol was believed to have the power to repel demons
625 **Solomon.** Solomon's seal consisted of a pentangle circumscribed by a circle

---

Thus on his shining shield this knot was shaped
Royally in red gold upon red gules.
That is the pure Pentangle, so people who are wise
    Are taught.
        Now Gawain was ready and gay;
        His spear he promptly caught
        And gave them all good day
        For ever, as he thought.

29

He struck the steed with his spurs and sprang on his   670
    way
So forcefully that the fire flew up from the flinty
    stones.
All who saw that seemly sight were sick at heart,
And all said to each other softly, in the same breath,
In care for that comely knight, 'By Christ, it is evil
That yon lord should be lost, who lives so nobly!
To find his fellow on earth in faith is not easy.
It would have been wiser to have worked more warily,
And to have dubbed the dear man a duke of the realm.
A magnificent master of men he might have been,
And so had a happier fate than to be utterly destroyed,   680
Beheaded by an unearthly being out of arrogance.
Who supposed the Prince would approve such counsel
As is giddily given in Christmas games by knights?'
Many were the watery tears that whelmed from
    weeping eyes,
When on quest that worthy knight went from the court
    That day.
        He faltered not nor feared,
        But quickly went his way;
        His road was rough and weird,°
        Or so the stories say.   690

30

Now the gallant Sir Gawain in God's name goes
Riding through the realm of Britain, no rapture in his
    mind.
Often the long night he lay alone and companionless,
And did not find in front of him food of his choice;
He had no comrade but his courser in the country
    woods and hills,
No traveller to talk to on the track but God,
Till he was nearly nigh to Northern Wales.
The isles of Anglesey he kept always on his left,
And fared across the fords by the foreshore
Over at Holy Head to the other side   700
Into the wilderness of Wirral,° where few dwelled
To whom God or good-hearted man gave his love.
And always as he went, he asked whomever he met
If they knew or had knowledge of a knight in green,
Or could guide him to the ground where a green chapel
    stood.

---

689 **weird**, fated or destined, as well as strange   701 **Wirral**, forest in Cheshire

And there was none but said him nay, for never in their
    lives
Had they set eyes on someone of such a hue
      As green.
      His way was wild and strange
710   By dreary hill and dean.
      His mood would many times change
      Before that fane was seen.

31

He rode far from his friends, a forsaken man,
Scaling many cliffs in country unknown.
At every bank or beach where the brave man crossed
    water,
He found a foe in front of him, except by a freak of
    chance,
And so foul and fierce a one that he was forced to fight.
So many marvels did the man meet in the mountains,
It would be too tedious to tell a tenth of them.
720 He had death-struggles with dragons, did battle with
    wolves,
Warred with wild men who dwelt among the crags,
Battled with bulls and bears and boars at other times,
And ogres that panted after him on the high fells.
Had he not been doughty in endurance and dutiful to
    God,
Doubtless he would have been done to death time and
    again.
Yet the warring little worried him; worse was the
    winter,
When the cold clear water cascaded from the clouds
And froze before it could fall to the fallow earth.
Half-slain by the sleet, he slept in his armour
730 Night after night among the naked rocks,
Where the cold streams splashed from the steep crests
Or hung high over his head in hard icicles.
So in peril and pain, in parlous plight,
This knight covered the country till Christmas Eve
      Alone;
      And he that eventide
      To Mary made his moan,
      And begged her be his guide
      Till some shelter should be shown.

32

740 Merrily in the morning by a mountain he rode
Into a wondrously wild wooded cleft,
With high hills on each side overpeering a forest
Of huge hoary oaks, a hundred together.
The hazel and the hawthorn were intertwined
With rough ragged moss trailing everywhere,
And on the bleak branches birds in misery
Piteously piped away, pinched with cold.
The gallant knight on Gringolet galloped under them
Through many a swamp and marsh, a man all alone,
750 Fearing lest he should fail, through adverse fortune,
To see the service of him who that same night
Was born of a bright maiden to banish our strife.

And so sighing he said, 'I beseech thee Lord,
And thee Mary, mildest mother so dear,
That in some haven with due honour I may hear Mass
And Matins° tomorrow morning: meekly I ask it,
And promptly thereto I pray my Pater and Ave
    And Creed.'
    He crossed himself and cried
    For his sins, and said, 'Christ speed   760
    My cause, his cross my guide!'
    So prayed he, spurring his steed.

33

Thrice the sign of the Saviour on himself he had made,
When in the wood he was aware of a dwelling with a
    moat
On a promontory above a plateau, penned in by the
    boughs
And tremendous trunks of trees, and trenched about;
The comeliest castle that ever a knight owned,
It was pitched on a plain, with a park all round,
Impregnably palisaded with pointed stakes,
And containing many trees in its two-mile   770
    circumference.
The courteous knight contemplated the castle from
    one side
As it shimmered and shone through the shining oaks.
Then humbly he took off his helmet and offered thanks
To Jesus and Saint Julian,° gentle patrons both,
Who had given him grace and gratified his wish.
'Now grant it be good lodging!' the gallant knight said.
Then he goaded Gringolet with his golden heels,
And mostly by chance emerged on the main highway,
Which brought the brave man to the bridge's end
      With one cast.   780
      The drawbridge vertical,
      The gates shut firm and fast,
      The well-provided wall—
      It blenched at never a blast.

34

The knight, still on his steed, stayed on the bank
Of the deep double ditch that drove round the place.
The wall went into the water wonderfully deep,
And then to a huge height upwards it reared
In hard hewn stone, up to the cornice;
Built under the battlements in the best style, courses 790
    jutted
And turrets protruded between, constructed
With loopholes in plenty with locking shutters.
No better barbican had ever been beheld by that
    knight.
And inside he could see a splendid high hall
With towers and turrets on top, all tipped with
    crenellations,
And pretty pinnacles placed along its length,
With carved copes, cunningly worked.

756 **Matins,** the canonical morning prayers   774 **Saint Julian,** St. Julian the
Hospitaller, patron saint of travelers and of hospitality

Many chalk-white chimneys the chevalier saw
On the tops of towers twinkling whitely,
800 So many painted pinnacles sprinkled everywhere,
Congregated in clusters among the crenellations,
That it appeared like a prospect of paper patterning.
To the gallant knight on Gringolet it seemed good
    enough
If he could ever gain entrance to the inner court,
And harbour in that house while Holy Day lasted,
     Well cheered.
      He hailed, and at a height
      A civil porter appeared,
      Who welcomed the wandering knight,
810   And his inquiry heard.

35

'Good sir,' said Gawain, 'Will you give my message
To the high lord of this house, that I ask for lodging?'
'Yes, by Saint Peter,' replied the porter, 'and I think
You may lodge here as long as you like, sir knight.'
Then away he went eagerly, and swiftly returned
With a host of well-wishers to welcome the knight.
They let down the drawbridge and in a dignified way
Came out and did honour to him, kneeling
Courteously on the cold ground to accord him worthy
    welcome.
820 They prayed him to pass the portcullis, now pulled up
    high,
And he readily bid them rise and rode over the bridge.
Servants held his saddle while he stepped down,
And his steed was stabled by sturdy men in plenty.
Strong knights and squires descended then
To bring the bold warrior blithely into hall.
When he took off his helmet, many hurried forward
To receive it and to serve this stately man,
And his bright sword and buckler were both taken as
    well.
Then graciously he greeted each gallant knight,
830 And many proud men pressed forward to pay their
    respects.
Garbed in his fine garments, he was guided to the hall,
Where a fine fire was burning fiercely on the hearth.
Then the prince of those people appeared from his
    chamber
To meet in mannerly style the man in his hall.
'You are welcome to dwell here as you wish,' he said,
'Treat everything as your own, and have what you
    please
      In this place.'
      'I yield my best thanks yet:
      May Christ make good your grace!'
840   Said Gawain and, gladly met,
      They clasped in close embrace.

36

Gawain gazed at the gallant who had greeted him well
And it seemed to him the stronghold possessed a brave
    lord,

A powerful man in his prime, of stupendous size.
Broad and bright was his beard, all beaver-hued;
Strong and sturdy he stood on his stalwart legs;
His face was fierce as fire, free was his speech,
And he seemed in good sooth a suitable man
To be prince of a people with companions of mettle.
This prince led him to an apartment and expressly   850
    commanded
That a man be commissioned to minister to Gawain;
And at his bidding a band of men bent to serve
Brought him to a beautiful room where the bedding
    was noble.
The bed-curtains, of brilliant silk with bright gold
    hems,
Had skilfully-sewn coverlets with comely facings,
And the fairest fur on the fringes was worked.
With ruddy gold rings on the cords ran the curtains;
Toulouse and Turkestan tapestries on the wall
And fine carpets underfoot, on the floor, were fittingly
    matched.
There amid merry talk the man was disrobed,   860
And stripped of his battle-sark and his splendid
    clothes.
Retainers readily brought him rich robes
Of the choicest kind to choose from and change into.
In a trice when he took one, and was attired in it,
And it sat on him in style, with spreading skirts,
It certainly seemed to those assembled as if spring
In all its hues were evident before them;
His lithe limbs below the garment were gleaming with
    beauty.
Jesus never made, so men judged, more gentle and
    handsome
      A knight: 870
      From wherever in the world he were,
      At sight it seemed he might
      Be a prince without a peer
      In field where fell men fight.

37

At the chimneyed hearth where charcoal burned, a
    chair was placed
For Sir Gawain in gracious style, gorgeously decked
With cushions on quilted work, both cunningly
    wrought;
And then on that man a magnificent mantle was
    thrown,
A gleaming garment gorgeously embroidered,
Fairly lined with fur, the finest skins   880
Of ermine on earth, and his hood of the same.
In that splendid seat he sat in dignity,
And warmth came to him at once, bringing well-being.
In a trice on fine trestles a table was put up,
Then covered with a cloth shining clean and white,
And set with silver spoons, salt-cellars and overlays.
The worthy knight washed willingly, and went to his
    meat.
In seemly enough style servants brought him

Several fine soups, seasoned lavishly
890 Twice-fold, as is fitting, and fish of all kinds—
Some baked in bread, some browned on coals,
Some seethed, some stewed and savoured with spice,
But always subtly sauced, and so the man liked it.
The gentle knight generously judged it a feast,
And often said so, while the servers spurred him on
    thus
        As he ate:
    'This present penance do;
    It soon shall be offset.'
    The knight rejoiced anew,
900
    For the wine his spirits whet.

38

Then in seemly style they searchingly inquired,
Putting to the prince private questions,
So that he courteously conceded he came of that court
Where high-souled Arthur held sway alone,
Ruler most royal of the Round Table;
And that Sir Gawain himself now sat in the house,
Having come that Christmas, by course of fortune.
Loudly laughed the lord when he learned what knight
He had in his house; such happiness it brought
910 That all the men within the moat made merry,
And promptly appeared in the presence of Gawain,
To whose person are proper all prowess and worth,
And pure and perfect manners, and praises unceasing.
His reputation rates first in the ranks of men.
Each knight neared his neighbour and softly said,
'Now we shall see displayed the seemliest manners
And the faultless figures of virtuous discourse.
Without asking we may hear how to hold conversation
Since we have seized upon this scion of good breeding.
920 God has given us of his grace good measure
In granting us such a guest as Gawain is,
When, contented at Christ's birth, the courtiers shall
    sit
        And sing.
    This noble knight will prove
    What manners the mighty bring;
    His converse of courtly love
    Shall spur our studying.'

39

When the fine man had finished his food and risen,
It was nigh and near to the night's mid-hour.
930 Priests to their prayers paced their way
And rang the bells royally, as rightly they should,
To honour that high feast with evensong.
The lord inclines to prayer, the lady too;
Into her private pew she prettily walks;
Gawain advances gaily and goes there quickly,
But the lord gripped his gown and guided him to his
    seat,
Acknowledged him by name and benevolently said

In the whole world he was the most welcome of men.
Gawain spoke his gratitude, they gravely embraced,
And sat in serious mood the whole service through. 940
Then the lady had a longing to look on the knight;
With her bevy of beauties she abandoned her pew.
Most beautiful of body and bright of complexion,
Most winsome in ways of all women alive,
She seemed to Sir Gawain, excelling Guinevere.
To squire that splendid dame, he strode through the
    chancel.
Another lady led her by the left hand,
A matron, much older, past middle age,
Who was highly honoured by an escort of squires.
Most unlike to look on those ladies were, 950
For if the one was winsome, then withered was the
    other.
Hues rich and rubious were arrayed on the one,
Rough wrinkles on the other rutted the cheeks.
Kerchiefed with clear pearls clustering was the one,
Her breast and bright throat bare to the sight,
Shining like sheen of snow shed on the hills;
The other was swathed with a wimple wound to the
    throat
And choking her swarthy chin in chalk-white veils.
On her forehead were folded enveloping silks,
Trellised about with trefoils and tiny rings. 960
Nothing was bare on that beldame but the black
    brows,
The two eyes, protruding nose and stark lips,
And those were a sorry sight and exceedingly bleary:
A grand lady, God knows, of greatness in the world
        Well tried!
    Her body was stumpy and squat,
    Her buttocks bulging and wide;
    More pleasure a man could plot
    With the sweet one at her side.

40

When Gawain had gazed on that gracious-looking 970
    creature
He gained leave of the lord to go along with the ladies.
He saluted the senior, sweeping a low bow,
But briefly embraced the beautiful one,
Kissing her in courtly style and complimenting her.
They craved his acquaintance and he quickly
    requested
To be their faithful follower, if they would so favour
    him.
They took him between them, and talking, they led
    him
To a high room. By the hearth they asked first
For spices, which unstintingly men sped to bring,
And always with heart-warming, heady wine. 980
In lovingkindness the lord leaped up repeatedly
And many times reminded them that mirth should
    flow;

Elaborately lifted up his hood, looped it on a spear,
And offered it as a mark of honour to whoever should
  prove able
To make the most mirth that merry Yuletide.
'And I shall essay, I swear, to strive with the best
Before this garment goes from me, by my good friends'
  help.'
So with his mirth the mighty lord made things merry
To gladden Sir Gawain with games in hall
990   That night;
      Until, the time being spent,
      The lord demanded light.
      Gawain took his leave and went
      To rest in rare delight.

41

On that morning when men call to mind the birth
Of our dear Lord born to die for our destiny,
Joy waxes in dwellings the world over for his sake:
And so it befell there on the feast day with fine fare.
Both at main meals and minor repasts strong men
  served
1000 Rare dishes with fine dressings to the dais company.
Highest, in the place of honour, the ancient crone sat,
And the lord, so I believe, politely next.
Together sat Gawain and the gay lady
In mid-table, where the meal was mannerly served
  first;
And after throughout the hall, as was held best,
Each gallant by degree was graciously served.
There was meat and merry-making and much delight,
To such an extent that it would try me to tell of it,
Even if perhaps I made the effort to describe it.
1010 But yet I know the knight and the nobly pretty one
Found such solace and satisfaction seated together,
In the discreet confidences of their courtly dalliance,
Their irreproachably pure and polished repartee,
That with princes' sport their play of wit surpassingly
  Compares.
      Pipes and side-drums sound,
      Trumpets entune their airs;
      Each soul its solace found,
      And the two were enthralled with theirs.

42

1020 That day they made much merriment, and on the
  morrow again,
And thickly the joys thronged on the third day after;
But gentle was the jubilation on St John's Day,°
The final one for feasting, so the folk there thought.
As there were guests geared to go in the grey dawn
They watched the night out with wine in wonderful
  style,
Leaping night-long in their lordly dances.

At last when it was late those who lived far off,
Each one, bid farewell before wending their ways.
Gawain also said goodbye, but the good host grasped
  him,
Led him to the hearth of his own chamber,   1030
And held him back hard, heartily thanking him
For the fine favour he had manifested to him
In honouring his house that high feast-tide,
Brightening his abode with his brilliant company:
'As long as I live, sir, I believe I shall thrive
Now Gawain has been my guest at God's own feast.'
'Great thanks, sir,' said Gawain. 'In good faith, yours,
All yours is the honour, may the High King requite it!
I stand at your service, knight, to satisfy your will
As good use engages me, in great things and small,   1040
      By right.'
      The lord then bid his best
      Longer to delay the knight,
      But Gawain, replying, pressed
      His departure in all despite.

43

Then with courteous inquiry the castellan asked
What fierce exploit had sent him forth, at that festive
  season,
From the King's court at Camelot, so quickly and
  alone,
Before the holy time was over in the homes of men.
'You may in truth well demand,' admitted the knight. 1050
'A high and urgent errand hastened me from thence,
For I myself am summoned to seek out a place
To find which I know not where in the world to look.
For all the land in Logres°—may our Lord help me!
I would not fail to find it on the feast of New Year.
So this is my suit, sir, which I beseech of you here,
That you tell me in truth if tale ever reached you
Of the Green Chapel, or what ground or glebe it stands
  on,
Or of the knight who holds it, whose hue is green.
For at that place I am pledged, by the pact between us, 1060
To meet that man, if I remain alive.
From now until the New Year is not a great time,
And if God will grant it me, more gladly would I see
  him
Than gain any good possession, by God's son!
I must wend my way, with your good will, therefore;
I am reduced to three days in which to do my business,
And I think it fitter to fall dead than fail in my errand.'
Then the lord said laughingly, 'You may linger a while,
For I shall tell you where your tryst is by your term's
  end.
Give yourself no more grief for the Green Chapel's   1070
  whereabouts,
For you may lie back in your bed, brave man, at ease

1022 **St John's Day,** December 27

1054 **the land in Logres,** the term applied in Welsh legend to England south of
the Humber

Till full morning on the First, and then fare forth
To the meeting place at mid-morning to manage how
    you may
        Out there.
        Leave not till New Year's Day,
        Then get up and go with cheer;
        You shall be shown the way;
        It is hardly two miles from here.'

44

Then Gawain was glad and gleefully exclaimed,
1080 'Now above all, most heartily do I offer you thanks!
For my goal is now gained, and by grace of yours
I shall dwell here and do what you deem good for me.'
So the lord seized Sir Gawain, seated him beside
    himself,
And to enliven their delight, he had the ladies fetched,
And much gentle merriment they long made together.
The lord, as one like to take leave of his senses
And not aware of what he was doing, spoke warmly
    and merrily.
Then he spoke to Sir Gawain, saying out loud,
'You have determined to do the deed I ask:
1090 Will you hold to your undertaking here and now?'
'Yes, sir, in good sooth,' said the true knight,
'While I stay in your stronghold, I shall stand at your
    command.'
'Since you have spurred,' the lord said, 'from afar,
Then watched awake with me, you are not well
    supplied
With either sustenance or sleep, for certain, I know;
So you shall lie long in your room, late and at ease
Tomorrow till the time of mass, and then take your
    meal
When you will, with my wife beside you
To comfort you with her company till I come back to
    court.
1100   You stay,
        And I shall get up at dawn.
        I will to the hunt away.'
        When Gawain's agreement was sworn
        He bowed, as brave knights may.

45

'Moreover,' said the man, 'Let us make a bargain
That whatever I win in the woods be yours,
And any achievement you chance on here, you
    exchange for it.
Sweet sir, truly swear to such a bartering,
Whether fair fortune or foul befall from it.'
1110 'By God,' said the good Gawain, 'I agree to that,
And I am happy that you have an eye to sport.'
Then the prince of that people said, 'What pledge of
    wine
Is brought to seal the bargain?' And they burst out
    laughing.
They took drink and toyed in trifling talk,

These lords and ladies, as long as they liked,
And then with French refinement and many fair words
They stood, softly speaking, to say goodnight,
Kissing as they parted company in courtly style.
With lithe liege servants in plenty and lambent torches,
Each brave man was brought to his bed at last,   1120
    Full soft.
    Before they fared to bed
    They rehearsed their bargain oft.
    That people's prince, men said,
    Could fly his wit aloft.

FIT III

46

In the faint light before dawn folk were stirring;
Guests who had to go gave orders to their grooms,
Who busied themselves briskly with the beasts,
    saddling,
Trimming their tackle and tying on their luggage.
Arrayed for riding in the richest style,   1130
Guests leaped on their mounts lightly, laid hold of their
    bridles,
And each rider rode out on his own chosen way.
The beloved lord of the land was not the last up,
Being arrayed for riding with his retinue in force.
He ate a sop hastily when he had heard mass,
And hurried with horn to the hunting field;
Before the sun's first rays fell on the earth,
On their high steeds were he and his knights.
Then these cunning hunters came to couple their
    hounds,
Cast open the kennel doors and called them out,   1140
And blew on their bugles three bold notes.
The hounds broke out barking, baying fiercely,
And when they went chasing, they were whipped
    back.
There were a hundred choice huntsmen there, whose
    fame
        Resounds.
    To their stations keepers strode;
    Huntsmen unleashed hounds:
    The forest overflowed
    With the strident bugle sounds.

47

At the first cry wild creatures quivered with dread.   1150
The deer in distraction darted down to the dales
Or up to the high ground, but eagerly they were
Driven back by the beaters, who bellowed lustily.
They let the harts with high-branching heads have their
    freedom,
And the brave bucks, too, with their broad antlers,
For the noble prince had expressly prohibited
Meddling with male deer in the months of close
    season.

But the hinds were held back with a 'Hey' and a
  'Whoa!'
And does driven with much din to the deep valleys.
1160 Lo! the arrows' slanting flight as they were loosed!
A shaft flew forth at every forest turning,
The broad head biting on the brown flank.
They screamed as the blood streamed out, sank dead
  on the sward,
Always harried by hounds hard on their heels,
And the hurrying hunters' high horn notes.
Like the rending of ramped hills roared the din.
If one of the wild beasts slipped away from the archers
It was dragged down and met death at the dog-bases
After being hunted from the high ground and harried to
  the water,
1170 So skilled were the hunt-servants at stations lower
  down,
So gigantic the greyhounds that grabbed them in a
  flash,
Seizing them savagely, as swift, I swear,
    As sight.
    The lord, in humour high
    Would spur, then stop and alight.
    In bliss the day went by
    Till dark drew on, and night.

48

Thus by the forest borders the brave lord sported,
And the good man Gawain, on his gay bed lying,
1180 Lay hidden till the light of day gleamed on the walls,
Covered with fair canopy, the curtains closed,
And as in slumber he slept on, there slipped into his
  mind
A slight, suspicious sound, and the door stealthily
  opened.
He raised up his head out of the bedclothes,
Caught up the corner of the curtain a little
And watched warily towards it, to see what it was.
It was the lady, loveliest to look upon,
Who secretly and silently secured the door,
Then bore towards his bed: the brave knight,
  embarrassed,
1190 Lay flat with fine adroitness and feigned sleep.
Silently she stepped on, stole to his bed,
Caught up the curtain, crept within,
And seated herself softly on the side of the bed.
There she watched a long while, waiting for him to
  wake.
Slyly close this long while lay the knight,
Considering in his soul this circumstance,
Its sense and likely sequel, for it seemed marvellous.
'Still, it would be more circumspect,' he said to
  himself,
'To speak and discover her desire in due course.'
1200 So he stirred and stretched himself, twisting towards
  her,
Opened his eyes and acted as if astounded;

And, to seem the safer by such service, crossed
  himself
    In dread.
    With chin and cheek so fair,
    White ranged with rosy red,
    With laughing lips, and air
    Of love, she lightly said:

49

'Good morning, Sir Gawain,' the gay one murmured,
'How unsafely you sleep, that one may slip in here!
Now you are taken in a trice. Unless a truce come   1210
  between us,
I shall bind you to your bed—of that be sure.'
The lady uttered laughingly those playful words.
'Good morning, gay lady,' Gawain blithely greeted
  her.
'Do with me as you will: that well pleases me.
For I surrender speedily and sue for grace,
Which, to my mind, since I must, is much the best
  course.'
And thus he repaid her with repartee and ready
  laughter.
'But if, lovely lady, your leave were forthcoming,
And you were pleased to free your prisoner and pray
  him to rise,
I would abandon my bed for a better habiliment,   1220
And have more happiness in our honey talk.'
'Nay, verily, fine sir,' urged the voice of that sweet
  one,
'You shall not budge from your bed. I have a better
  idea.
I shall hold you fast here on this other side as well
And so chat on with the chevalier my chains have
  caught.
For I know well, my knight, that your name is Sir
  Gawain,
Whom all the world worships, wherever he ride;
For lords and their ladies, and all living folk,
Hold your honour in high esteem, and your courtesy.
And now—here you are truly, and we are utterly   1230
  alone;
My lord and his liegemen are a long way off;
Others still bide in their beds, my bower-maidens too;
Shut fast and firmly with a fine hasp is the door;
And since I have in this house him who pleases all,
As long as my time lasts I shall lingering in talk take
    My fill.
    My young body is yours,
    Do with it what you will;
    My strong necessities force
    Me to be your servant still.'   1240

50

'In good truth,' said Gawain, 'that is a gain indeed,
Though I am hardly the hero of whom you speak.
To be held in such honour as you here suggest,

I am altogether unworthy, I own it freely.
By God, I should be glad, if you granted it right
For me to essay by speech or some other service,
To pleasure such a perfect lady—pure joy it would be.'
'In good truth, Sir Gawain,' the gay lady replied,
1250 'If I slighted or set at naught your spotless fame
And your all-pleasing prowess, it would show poor
      breeding.
But there is no lack of ladies who would love, noble
      one,
To hold you in their arms, as I have you here,
And linger in the luxury of your delightful discourse,
Which would perfectly pleasure them and appease
      their woes—
Rather than have riches or the red gold they own.
But as I love that Lord, the Celestial Ruler,
I have wholly in my hand what all desire
      Through his grace.'
      Not loth was she to allure,
1260   This lady fair of face;
      But the knight with speeches pure
      Answered in each case.

51

'Madam,' said the merry man, 'May Mary requite you!
For in good faith I have found in you free-hearted
      generosity.
Certain men for their deeds receive esteem from
      others,
But for myself, I do not deserve the respect they show
      me;
Your honourable mind makes you utter only what is
      good.'
'Now by Mary,' said the noble lady, 'Not so it seems
      to me,
For were I worth the whole of womankind,
1270 And all the wealth in the world were in my hand,
And if bargaining I were to bid to bring myself a lord—
With your noble qualities, knight, made known to me
      now,
Your good looks, gracious manner and great courtesy,
All of which I have heard of before, but here prove
      true—
No lord that is living could be allowed to excel you.'
'Indeed, dear lady, you did better,' said the knight,
'But I am proud of the precious price you put on me,
And solemnly as your servant say you are my
      sovereign.
May Christ requite it you: I have become your knight.'
1280 Then of many matters they talked till mid-morning and
      after,
And all the time she behaved as if she adored him;
But Sir Gawain was on guard in a gracious manner.
Though she was the winsomest woman the warrior had
      known,
He was less love-laden because of the loss he must
      Now face—

His destruction by the stroke,
For come it must was the case.
The lady of leaving then spoke;
He assented with speedy grace.

52

Then she gave him goodbye, glinting with laughter,   1290
And standing up, astounded him with these strong
      words:
'May He who prospers every speech for this pleasure
      reward you!
I cannot bring myself to believe that you could be
      Gawain.'
'How so?' said the knight, speaking urgently,
For he feared he had failed to observe the forms of
      courtesy.
But the beauteous one blessed him and brought out
      this argument:
'Such a great man as Gawain is granted to be,
The very vessel of virtue and fine courtesy,
Could scarcely have stayed such a sojourn with a lady
Without craving a kiss out of courtesy,   1300
Touched by some trifling hint at the tail-end of a
      speech.'
'So be it, as you say,' then said Gawain,
'I shall kiss at your command, as becomes a knight
Who fears to offend you; no further plea is needed.'
Whereupon she approached him, and penned him in
      her arms,
Leaned over him lovingly and gave the lord a kiss.
Then they commended each other to Christ in comely
      style,
And without more words she went out by the door.
He made ready to rise with rapid haste,
Summoned his servant, selected his garb,   1310
And walked down, when he was dressed, debonairly
      to mass.
Then he went to the well-served meal which awaited
      him,
And made merry sport till the moon rose
      At night.
      Never was baron bold
      So taken by ladies bright,
      That young one and the old:
      They throve all three in delight.

53

And still at his sport spurred the castellan,
Hunting the barren hinds in holt and on heath.   1320
So many had he slain, by the setting of the sun,
Of does and other deer, that it was downright
      wonderful.
Then at the finish the folk flocked in eagerly,
And quickly collected the killed deer in a heap.
Those highest in rank came up with hosts of
      attendants,

Picked out what appeared to be the plumpest beasts
And, according to custom, had them cut open with
   finesse.
Some who ceremoniously assessed them there
Found two fingers' breadth of fat on the worst.
1330 Then they slit open the slot, seized the first stomach,
Scraped it with a keen knife and tied up the tripes.
Next they hacked off all the legs, the hide was
   stripped,
The belly broken open and the bowels removed
Carefully, lest they loosen the ligature of the knot.
Then they gripped the gullet, disengaged deftly
The wezand° from the windpipe and whipped out the
   guts.
Then their sharp knives shore through the shoulder-
   bones,
Which they slid out of a small hole, leaving the sides
   intact.
Then they cleft the chest clean through, cutting it in
   two.
1340 Then again at the gullet a man began to work
And straight away rived it, right to the fork,
Flicked out the shoulder-fillets, and faithfully then
He rapidly ripped free the rib-fillets.
Similarly, as is seemly, the spine was cleared
All the way to the haunch, which hung from it;
And they heaved up the whole haunch and hewed it
   off;
And that is called, according to its kind, the numbles,°
   I find.
     At the thigh-forks then they strain
1350   And free the folds behind,
     Hurrying to hack all in twain,
     The backbone to unbind.

54

Then they hewed off the head and also the neck,
And after sundered the sides swiftly from the chine,
And into the foliage they flung the fee of the raven.
Then each fellow, for his fee, as it fell to him to have,
Skewered through the stout flanks beside the ribs,
And then by the hocks of the haunches they hung up
   their booty.
On one of the finest fells they fed their hounds,
1360 And let them have the lights,° the liver and the tripes,
With bread well imbrued with blood mixed with them.
Boldly they blew the kill amid the baying of hounds.
Then off they went homewards, holding their meat,
Stalwartly sounding many stout horn-calls.
As dark was descending, they were drawing near
To the comely castle where quietly our knight stayed.
     Fires roared,
     And blithely hearts were beating
     As into hall came the lord.

1336 **wezand,** part of the throat. The terms and details throughout the hunt
scenes are from the highly technical diction of hunting manuals   1347 **numbles,**
internal organs   1360 **lights,** lungs

When Gawain gave him greeting,   1370
     Joy abounded at the board.

55

Then the master commanded everyone to meet in the
   hall,
Called the ladies to come down with their company of
   maidens.
Before all the folk on the floor, he bid men
Fetch the venison and place it before him.
Then gaily and in good humour to Gawain he called,
Told over the tally of the sturdy beasts,
And showed him the fine fat flesh flayed from the ribs.
'How does the sport please you? Do you praise me for
   it?
Am I thoroughly thanked for thriving as a huntsman?' 1380
'Certainly,' said the other, 'Such splendid spoils
Have I not seen for seven years in the season of
   winter.'
'And I give you all, Gawain,' said the good man then,
'For according to our covenant you may claim it as
   your own.'
'Certes, that is so, and I say the same to you,'
Said Gawain, 'For my true gains in this great house,
I am not loth to allow, must belong to you.'
And he put his arms round his handsome neck,
   hugging him,
And kissed him in the comeliest way he could think of.
'Accept my takings, sir, for I received no more;   1390
Gladly would I grant them, however great they were.'
'And therefore I thank you,' the thane said, 'Good!
Yours may be the better gift, if you would break it to
   me
Where your wisdom won you wealth of that kind.'
'No such clause in our contract! Request nothing else!'
Said the other, 'You have your due: ask more,
     None should.'
     They laughed in blithe assent
     With worthy words and good;
     Then to supper they swiftly went,   1400
     To fresh delicious food.

56

And sitting afterwards by the hearth of an audience
   chamber,
Where retainers repeatedly brought them rare wines,
In their jolly jesting they jointly agreed
On a settlement similar to the preceding one;
To exchange the chance achievements of the morrow,
No matter how novel they were, at night when they
   met.
They accorded on this compact, the whole court
   observing,
And the bumper was brought forth in banter to seal it.
And at last they lovingly took leave of each other,   1410
Each man hastening thereafter to his bed.
The cock having crowed and called only thrice,
The lord leaped from bed, and his liegemen too,

So that mass and a meal were meetly dealt with,
And by first light the folk to the forest were bound
    For the chase.
      Proudly the hunt with horns
      Soon drove through a desert place:
      Uncoupled through the thorns
1420   The great hounds pressed apace.

57

By a quagmire they quickly scented quarry and gave
    tongue,
And the chief huntsman urged on the first hounds up,
Spurring them on with a splendid spate of words.
The hounds, hearing it, hurried there at once,
Fell on the trial furiously, forty together,
And made such echoing uproar, all howling at once,
That the rocky banks round about rang with the din.
Hunters inspirited them with sound of speech and
    horn.
Then together in a group, across the ground they
    surged
1430 At speed between a pool and a spiteful crag.
On a stony knoll by a steep cliff at the side of a bog,
Where rugged rocks had roughly tumbled down,
They careered on the quest, the cry following,
Then surrounded the crag and the rocky knoll as well,
Certain their prey skulked inside their ring,
For the baying of the bloodhounds meant the beast
    was there.
Then they beat upon the bushes and bade him come
    out,
And he swung out savagely aslant the line of men,
A baneful boar of unbelievable size,
1440 A solitary long since sundered from the herd,
Being old and brawny, the biggest of them all,
And grim and ghastly when he grunted: great was the
    grief
When he thrust through the hounds, hurling three to
    earth,
And sped on scot-free, swift and unscathed.
They hallooed, yelled, 'Look out!' cried, 'Hey, we
    have him!'
And blew horns boldly, to bring the bloodhounds
    together;
Many were the merry cries from men and dogs
As they hurried clamouring after their quarry to kill
    him on
      The track.
1450   Many times he turns at bay
      And tears the dogs which attack.
      He hurts the hounds, and they
      Moan in a piteous pack.

58

Then men shoved forward, shaped to shoot at him,
Loosed arrows at him, hitting him often,
But the points, for all their power, could not pierce his
    flanks,

Nor would the barbs bite on his bristling brow.
Though the smooth-shaven shaft shattered in pieces,
Wherever it hit, the head rebounded.
But when the boar was battered by blows unceasing, 1460
Goaded and driven demented, he dashed at the men,
Striking them savagely as he assailed them in rushes,
So that some lacking stomach stood back in fear.
But the lord on a lithe horse lunged after him,
Blew on his bugle like a bold knight in battle,
Rallied the hounds as he rode through the rank
    thickets,
Pursuing this savage boar till the sun set.
And so they disported themselves this day
While our lovable lord lay in his bed.
At home the gracious Gawain in gorgeous clothes   1470
    Reclined:
      The gay one did not forget
      To come with welcome kind,
      And early him beset
      To make him change his mind.

59

She came to the curtain and cast her eye
On Sir Gawain, who at once gave her gracious
    welcome,
And she answered him eagerly, with ardent words,
Sat at his side softly, and with a spurt of laughter
And a loving look, delivered these words: 1480
'It seems to me strange, if, sir, you are Gawain,
A person so powerfully disposed to good,
Yet nevertheless know nothing of noble conventions,
And when made aware of them, wave them away!
Quickly you have cast off what I schooled you in
    yesterday
By the truest of all tokens of talk I know of.'
'What?' said the wondering knight, 'I am not aware of
    one.
But if it be true what you tell, I am entirely to blame.'
'I counselled you then about kissing,' the comely one
    said;
'When a favour is conferred, it must be forthwith   1490
    accepted:
That is becoming for a courtly knight who keeps the
    rules.'
'Sweet one, unsay that speech,' said the brave man,
'For I dared not do that lest I be denied.
If I were forward and were refused, the fault would be
    mine.'
'But none,' said the noblewoman, 'could deny you, by
    my faith!
You are strong enough to constrain with your strength
    if you wish,
If any were so ill-bred as to offer you resistance.'
'Yes, good guidance you give me, by God,' replied
    Gawain,
'But threateners are ill thought of and do not thrive in
    my country,
Nor do gifts thrive when given without good will.   1500

I am here at your behest, to offer a kiss to when you like;
You may do it whenever you deem fit, or desist,
    In this place.'
    The beautiful lady bent
    And fairly kissed his face;
    Much speech the two then spent
    On love, its grief and grace.

60

'I would know of you, knight,' the noble lady said,
'If it did not anger you, what argument you use,
1510 Being so hale and hearty as you are at this time,
So generous a gentleman as you are justly famed to be;
Since the choicest thing in Chivalry, the chief thing praised,
Is the loyal sport of love, the very lore of arms?
For the tale of the contentions of true knights
Is told by the title and text of their feats,
How lords for their true loves put their lives at hazard,
Endured dreadful trials for their dear loves' sakes,
And with valour avenged and made void their woes,
Bringing home abundant bliss by their virtues.
1520 You are the gentlest and most just of your generation;
Everywhere your honour and high fame are known;
Yet I have sat at your side two separate times here
Without hearing you utter in any way
A single syllable of the saga of love.
Being so polished and punctilious a pledge-fulfiller,
You ought to be eager to lay open to a young thing
Your discoveries in the craft of courtly love.
What! Are you ignorant, with all your renown?
Or do you deem me too dull to drink in your dalliance?
1530   For shame!
    I sit here unchaperoned, and stay
    To acquire some courtly game;
    So while my lord is away,
    Teach me your true wit's fame.'

61

'In good faith,' said Gawain, 'may God requite you!
It gives me great happiness, and is good sport to me,
That so fine a fair one as you should find her way here
And take pains with so poor a man, make pastime with her knight,
With any kind of clemency—it comforts me greatly.
1540 But for me to take on the travail of interpreting true love
And construing the subjects of the stories of arms
To you who, I hold, have more skill
In that art, by half, than a hundred of such
As I am or ever shall be on the earth I inhabit,
Would in faith be a manifold folly, noble lady.
To please you I would press with all the power in my soul,
For I am highly beholden to you, and evermore shall be
True servant to your bounteous self, so save me God!'

So that stately lady tempted him and tried him with questions
To win him to wickedness, whatever else she thought. 1550
But he defended himself so firmly that no fault appeared,
Nor was there any evil apparent on either side,
    But bliss;
    For long they laughed and played
    Till she gave him a gracious kiss.
    A fond farewell she bade,
    And went her way on this.

62

Sir Gawain bestirred himself and went to mass:
Then dinner was dressed and with due honour served.
All day long the lord and the ladies disported, 1560
But the castellan coursed across the country time and again,
Hunted his hapless boar as it hurtled over the hills,
Then bit the backs of his best hounds asunder
Standing at bay, till the bowmen obliged him to break free
Out into the open for all he could do,
So fast the arrows flew when the folk there concentrated.
Even the strongest he sometimes made start back,
But in time he became so tired he could tear away no more,
And with the speed he still possessed, he spurted to a hole
On a rise by a rock with a running stream beside. 1570
He got the bank at his back, and began to abrade the ground.
The froth was foaming foully at his mouth,
And he whetted his white tusks; a weary time it was
For the bold men about, who were bound to harass him
From a distance, for none dared to draw near him
    For dread.
    He had hurt so many men
    That it entered no one's head
    To be torn by his tusks again,
    And he raging and seeing red. 1580

63

Till the castellan came himself, encouraging his horse,
And saw the boar at bay with his band of men around.
He alighted in lively fashion, left his courser,
Drew and brandished his bright sword and boldly strode forward,
Striding at speed through the stream to where the savage beast was.
The wild thing was aware of the weapon and its wielder,
And so bridled with its bristles in a burst of fierce snorts
That all were anxious for the lord, lest he have the worst of it.

Straight away the savage brute sprang at the man,
1590 And baron and boar were both in a heap
In the swirling water: the worst went to the beast,
For the man had marked him well at the moment of
impact,
Had put the point precisely at the pit of his chest,
And drove it in to the hilt, so that the heart was shat-
tered,
And the spent beast sank snarling and was swept
downstream,
Teeth bare.
A hundred hounds and more
Attack and seize and tear;
Men tug him to the shore
1600 And the dogs destroy him there.

64

Bugles blew the triumph, horns blared loud.
There was hallooing in high pride by all present;
Braches bayed at the beast, as bidden by their masters,
The chief huntsmen in charge of that chase so hard.
Then one who was wise in wood-crafts
Started in style to slash open the boar.
First he hewed off the head and hoisted it on high,
Then rent him roughly along the ridge of his back,
Brought out the bowels and broiled them on coals
1610 For blending with bread as the braches' reward.
Then he broke out the brawn from the bright broad
flanks,
Took out the offal, as is fit,
Attached the two halves entirely together,
And on a strong stake stoutly hung them.
Then home they hurried with the huge beast,
With the boar's head borne before the baron himself,
Who had destroyed him in the stream by the strength
of his arm,
Above all:
It seemed to him an age
1620 Till he greeted Gawain in hall.
To reap his rightful wage
The latter came at his call.

65

The lord exclaimed loudly, laughing merrily
When he saw Sir Gawain, and spoke joyously.
The sweet ladies were sent for, and the servants
assembled.
Then he showed them the shields, and surely de-
scribed
The large size and length, and the malignity
Of the fierce boar's fighting when he fled in the woods;
So that Gawain congratulated him on his great deed,
1630 Commended it as a merit he had manifested well,
For a beast with so much brawn, the bold man said,
A boar of such breadth, he had not before seen.
When they handled the huge head the upright man
praised it,

Expressed horror thereat for the ear of the lord.
'Now Gawain,' said the good man, 'this game is your
own
By our contracted treaty, in truth, you know.'
'It is so,' said the knight, 'and as certainly
I shall give you all my gains as guerdon, in faith.'
He clasped the castellan's neck and kissed him kindly,
And then served him a second time in the same style. 1640
'In all our transactions since I came to sojourn,' as-
serted Gawain,
'Up to tonight, as of now, there's nothing that
I owe.'
'By Saint Giles,'° the castellan quipped,
'You're the finest fellow I know:
Your wealth will have us whipped
If your trade continues so!'

66

Then the trestles and tables were trimly set out,
Complete with cloths, and clearly flaming cressets
And waxen torches were placed in the wall-brackets 1650
By retainers, who then tended the entire hall-gathering.
Much gladness and glee then gushed forth there
By the fire on the floor: and in multifarious ways
They sang noble songs at supper and afterwards,
A concert of Christmas carols and new dance songs,
With the most mannerly mirth a man could tell of,
And our courteous knight kept constant company with
the lady.
In a bewitchingly well-mannered way she made up to
him,
Secretly soliciting the stalwart knight
So that he was astounded, and upset in himself. 1660
But his upbringing forbade him to rebuff her utterly,
So he behaved towards her honourably, whatever
aspersions might
Be cast.
They revelled in the hall
As long as their pleasure might last
And then at the castellan's call
To the chamber hearth they passed.

67

There they drank and discoursed and decided to enjoy
Similar solace and sport on New Year's Eve.
But the princely knight asked permission to depart in 1670
the morning,
For his appointed time was approaching, and perforce
he must go.
But the lord would not let him and implored him to
linger,
Saying, 'I swear to you, as a staunch true knight,
You shall gain the Green Chapel to give your dues,

1644 **Saint Giles,** a popular medieval saint, who spent part of his life as a hermit

My lord, in the light of New Year, long before sunrise.
Therefore remain in your room and rest in comfort,
While I fare hunting in the forest; in fulfilment of our
oath
Exchanging what we achieve when the chase is over.
For twice I have tested you, and twice found you true.
1680 Now "Third time, throw best!" Think of that
tomorrow!
Let us make merry while we may, set our minds on
joy,
For hard fate can hit man whenever it likes.'
This was graciously granted and Gawain stayed.
Blithely drink was brought, then to bed with lights
They pressed.
All night Sir Gawain sleeps
Softly and still at rest;
But the lord his custom keeps
And is early up and dressed.

68

1690 After mass, he and his men made a small meal.
Merry was the morning; he demanded his horse.
The men were ready mounted before the main gate,
A host of knightly horsemen to follow after him.
Wonderfully fair was the forest-land, for the frost
remained,
And the rising sun shone ruddily on the ragged clouds,
In its beauty brushing their blackness off the heavens.
The huntsmen unleashed the hounds by a holt-side,
And the rocks and surrounding bushes rang with their
horn-calls.
Some found and followed the fox's tracks,
1700 And wove various ways in their wily fashion.
A small hound cried the scent, the senior huntsman
called
His fellow foxhounds to him and, feverishly sniffing,
The rout of dogs rushed forward on the right path.
The fox hurried fast, for they found him soon
And, seeing him distinctly, pursued him at speed,
Unmistakably giving tongue with tumultuous din.
Deviously in difficult country he doubled on his
tracks,
Swerved and wheeled away, often waited listening,
Till at last by a little ditch he leaped a quickset hedge,
1710 And stole out stealthily at the side of a valley,
Considering his stratagem had given the slip to the
hounds.
But he stumbled on a tracking-dogs' tryst-place
unawares,
And there in a cleft three hounds threatened him at
once,
All grey.
He swiftly started back,
And, full of deep dismay,
He dashed on a different track;
To the woods he went away.

Then came the lively delight of listening to hounds
When they had all met in a muster, mingling together, 1720
For, catching sight of him, they cried such curses on
him
That the clustering cliffs seemed to be crashing down.
Here he was hallooed when the hunters met him,
There savagely snarled at by intercepting hounds;
Then he was called thief and threatened often;
With the tracking dogs on his tail, no tarrying was
possible.
When out in the open he was often run at,
So he often swerved in again, that artful Reynard.
Yes, he led the lord and his liegemen a dance
In this manner among the mountains till mid-afternoon, 1730
While harmoniously at home the honoured knight slept
Between the comely curtains in the cold morning.
But the lady's longing to woo would not let her sleep,
Nor would she impair the purpose pitched in her heart,
But rose up rapidly and ran to him
In a ravishing robe that reached to the ground,
Trimmed with finest fur from pure pelts;
Not coifed as to custom, but with costly jewels
Strung in scores on her splendid hairnet.
Her fine-featured face and fair throat were unveiled, 1740
Her breast was bare and her back as well.
She came in by the chamber door and closed it after
her,
Cast open a casement and called on the knight,
And briskly thus rebuked him with bountiful words
Of good cheer.
'Ah sir! What, sound asleep?
The morning's crisp and clear.'
He had been drowsing deep,
But now he had to hear.

70

The noble sighed ceaselessly in unsettled slumber 1750
As threatening thoughts thronged in the dawn light
About destiny, which the day after would deal him his
fate
At the Green Chapel where Gawain was to greet his
man,
And be bound to bear his buffet unresisting.
But having recovered consciousness in comely
fashion,
He heaved himself out of dreams and answered
hurriedly.
The lovely lady advanced, laughing adorably,
Swooped over his splendid face and sweetly kissed
him.
He welcomed her worthily with noble cheer
And, gazing on her gay and glorious attire, 1760
Her features so faultless and fine of complexion,
He felt a flush of rapture suffuse his heart.
Sweet and genial smiling slid them into joy

Till bliss burst forth between them, beaming gay
    And bright;
  With joy the two contended
  In talk of true delight,
  And peril would have impended
  Had Mary not minded her knight.

71

1770 For that peerless princess pressed him so hotly,
So invited him to the very verge, that he felt forced
Either to allow her love or blackguardly rebuff her.
He was concerned for his courtesy, lest he be called
    caitiff,
But more especially for his evil plight if he should
    plunge into sin,
And dishonour the owner of the house treacherously.
'God shield me! That shall not happen, for sure,' said
    the knight.
So with laughing love-talk he deflected gently
The downright declarations that dropped from her lips.
Said the beauty to the bold man, 'Blame will be yours
1780 If you love not the living body lying close to you
More than all wooers in the world who are wounded in
    heart;
Unless you have a lover more beloved, who delights
    you more,
A maiden to whom you are committed, so immutably
    bound
That you do not seek to sever from her—which I see is
    so.
Tell me the truth of it, I entreat you now;
By all the loves there are, do not hide the truth
    With guile.'
  Then gently, 'By Saint John,'
  Said the knight with a smile,
1790   'I owe my oath to none,
  Nor wish to yet a while.'

72

'Those words,' said the fair woman, 'are the worst
    there could be,
But I am truly answered, to my utter anguish.
Give me now a gracious kiss, and I shall go from here
As a maid that loves much, mourning on this earth.'
Then, sighing, she stooped, and seemlily kissed him,
And, severing herself from him, stood up and said,
'At this adieu, my dear one, do me this pleasure:
Give me something as gift, your glove if no more,
1800 To mitigate my mourning when I remember you.'
'Now certainly, for your sake,' said the knight,
'I wish I had here the handsomest thing I own,
For you have deserved, forsooth, superabundantly
And rightfully, a richer reward than I could give.
But as tokens of true love, trifles mean little.
It is not to your honour to have at this time

A mere glove as Gawain's gift to treasure.
For I am here on an errand in unknown regions,
And have no bondsmen, no baggages with dear-bought
    things in them.
This afflicts me now, fair lady, for your sake.   1810
Man must do as he must; neither lament it
    Nor repine.'
  'No, highly honoured one,'
  Replied that lady fine,
  'Though gift you give me none,
  You must have something of mine.'

73

She proffered him a rich ring wrought in red gold,
With a sparkling stone set conspicuously in it,
Which beamed as brilliantly as the bright sun;
You may well believe its worth was wonderfully great.   1820
But the courteous man declined it and quickly said,
'Before God, gracious lady, no giving just now!
Not having anything to offer, I shall accept nothing.'
She offered it him urgently and he refused again,
Fast affirming his refusal on his faith as a knight.
Put out by this repulse, she presently said,
'If you reject my ring as too rich in value,
Doubtless you would be less deeply indebted to me
If I gave you my girdle, a less gainful gift.'
She swiftly slipped off the cincture of her gown   1830
Which went round her waist under the wonderful
    mantle,
A girdle of green silk with a golden hem,
Embroidered only at the edges, with hand-stitched
    ornament.
And she pleaded with the prince in a pleasant manner
To take it notwithstanding its trifling worth;
But he told her that he could touch no treasure at all,
Not gold nor any gift, till God gave him grace
To pursue to success the search he was bound on.
'And therefore I beg you not to be displeased:
Press no more your purpose, for I promise it never   1840
    Can be.
  I owe you a hundredfold
  For grace you have granted me;
  And ever through hot and cold
  I shall stay your devotee.'

74

'Do you say "no" to this silk?' then said the beauty,
'Because it is simple in itself? And so it seems.
Lo! It is little indeed, and so less worth your esteem.
But one who was aware of the worth twined in it
Would appraise its properties as more precious   1850
    perhaps,
For the man that binds his body with this belt of green,
As long as he laps it closely about him,
No hero under heaven can hack him to pieces,

For he cannot be killed by any cunning on earth.'
Then the prince pondered, and it appeared to him
A precious gem to protect him in the peril appointed
  him
When he gained the Green Chapel to be given
  checkmate:
It would be a splendid stratagem to escape being slain.
Then he allowed her to solicit him and let her speak.
1860 She pressed the belt upon him with potent words
And having got his agreement, she gave it him gladly,
Beseeching him for her sake to conceal it always,
And hide it from her husband with all diligence.
That never should another know of it, the noble swore
      Outright.
        Then often his thanks gave he
        With all his heart and might,
        And thrice by then had she
        Kissed the constant knight.

75

1870 Then with a word of farewell she went away,
For she could not force further satisfaction from him.
Directly she withdrew, Sir Gawain dressed himself,
Rose and arrayed himself in rich garments,
But laid aside the love-lace the lady had given him,
Secreted it carefully where he could discover it later.
Then he went his way at once to the chapel,
Privily approached a priest and prayed him there
To listen to his life's sins and enlighten him
On how he might have salvation in the hereafter.
1880 Then, confessing his faults, he fairly shrove himself,
Begging mercy for both major and minor sins.
He asked the holy man for absolution
And was absolved with certainty and sent out so pure
That Doomsday could have been declared the day
      after.
Then he made merrier among the noble ladies,
With comely carolling and all kinds of pleasure,
Than ever he had done, with ecstasy, till came
        Dark night.
        Such honour he did to all,
1890   They said, 'Never has this knight
        Since coming into hall
        Expressed such pure delight.'

76

Now long may he linger there, love sheltering him!
The prince was still on the plain, pleasuring in the
  chase,
Having finished off the fox he had followed so far.
As he leaped over a hedge looking out for the quarry,
Where he heard the hounds that were harrying the fox,
Reynard came running through a rough thicket
With the pack all pell-mell, panting at his heels.

The lord, aware of the wild beast, waited craftily,   1900
Then drew his dazzling sword and drove at the fox.
The beast baulked at the blade to break sideways,
But a dog bounded at him before he could,
And right in front of the horse's feet they fell on him,
All worrying their wily prey with a wild uproar.
The lord quickly alighted and lifted him up,
Wrenched him beyond reach of the ravening fangs,
Held him high over his head and hallooed lustily,
While the angry hounds in hordes bayed at him.
Thither hurried the huntsmen with horns in plenty,   1910
Sounding the rally splendidly till they saw their lord.
When the company of his court had come up to the
  kill,
All who bore bugles blew at once,
And the others without horns hallooed loudly.
The requiem that was raised for Reynard's soul
And the commotion made it the merriest meet ever,
        Men said.
        The hounds must have their fee:
        They pat them on the head,
        Then hold the fox; and he   1920
        Is reft of his skin of red.

77

Then they set off for home, it being almost night,
Blowing their big horns bravely as they went.
At last the lord alighted at his beloved castle
And found upon the floor a fire, and beside it
The good Sir Gawain in a glad humour
By reason of the rich friendship he had reaped from the
  ladies.
He wore a turquoise tunic extending to the ground;
His softly-furred surcoat suited him well,
And his hood of the same hue hung from his shoulder. 1930
All trimmed with ermine were hood and surcoat.
Meeting the master in the middle of the floor,
Gawain went forward gladly and greeted him thus:
'Forthwith, I shall be the first to fulfil the contract
We settled so suitably without sparing the wine.'
Then he clasped the castellan and kissed him thrice
As sweetly and steadily as a strong knight could.
'By Christ!' quoth the other, 'You will carve yourself a
  fortune
By traffic in this trade when the terms suit you!'
'Do not chop logic about the exchange,' chipped in   1940
  Gawain,
'As I have properly paid over the profit I made.'
'Marry,' said the other man, 'Mine is inferior,
For I have hunted all day and have only taken
This ill-favoured fox's skin, may the Fiend take it!
And that is a poor price to pay for such precious things
As you have pressed upon me here, three pure kisses
        So good.'

'Enough!' acknowledged Gawain,
'I thank you, by the Rood.'
1950 And how the fox was slain
The lord told him as they stood.

78

With mirth and minstrelsy, and meals when they liked,
They made as merry then as ever men could;
With the laughter of ladies and delightful jesting,
Gawain and his good host were very gay together,
Save when excess or sottishness seemed likely.
Master and men made many a witty sally,
Until presently, at the appointed parting-time,
The brave men were bidden to bed at last.
1960 Then of his host the hero humbly took leave,
The first to bid farewell, fairly thanking him:
'May the High King requite you for your courtesy at
   this feast,
And the wonderful week of my dwelling here!
I would offer to be one of your own men if you liked,
But that I must move on tomorrow, as you know,
If you will give me the guide you granted me,
To show me the Green Chapel where my share of
   doom
Will be dealt on New Year's Day, as God deems for
   me.'
'With all my heart!' said the host. 'In good faith,
1970 All that I ever promised you, I shall perform.'
He assigned him a servant to set him on his way,
And lead him in the hills without any delay,
Faring through forest and thicket by the most
   straightforward route
      They might.
      With every honour due
      Gawain then thanked the knight,
      And having bid him adieu,
      Took leave of the ladies bright.

79

So he spoke to them sadly, sorrowing as he kissed,
1980 And urged on them heartily his endless thanks,
And they gave to Sir Gawain words of grace in return,
Commending him to Christ with cries of chill sadness.
Then from the whole household he honourably took
   his leave,
Making all the men that he met amends
For their several services and solicitous care,
For they had been busily attendant, bustling about
   him;
And every soul was as sad to say farewell
As if they had always had the hero in their house.
Then the lords led him with lights to his chamber,
1990 And blithely brought him to bed to rest.
If he slept—I dare not assert it—less soundly than
   usual,
There was much on his mind for the morrow, if he
   meant to give
      It thought.

Let him lie there still,
He almost has what he sought;
So tarry a while until
The process I report.

FIT IV

80

Now the New Year neared, the night passed,
Daylight fought darkness as the Deity ordained.
But wild was the weather the world awoke to;   2000
Bitterly the clouds cast down cold on the earth,
Inflicting on the flesh flails from the north.
Bleakly the snow blustered, and beasts were frozen;
The whistling wind wailed from the heights,
Driving great drifts deep in the dales.
Keenly the lord listened as he lay in his bed;
Though his lids were closed, he was sleeping little.
Every cock that crew recalled to him his tryst.
Before the day had dawned, he had dressed himself,
For the light from a lamp illuminated his chamber.   2010
He summoned his servant, who swiftly answered,
Commanded that his mail-coat and mount's saddle he
   brought.
The man fared forth and fetched him his armour,
And set Sir Gawain's array in splendid style.
First he clad him in his clothes to counter the cold,
Then in his other armour which had been well kept;
His breast- and belly-armour had been burnished
   bright,
And the rusty rings of his rich mail-coat rolled clean,
And all being as fresh as at first, he was fain to give
   thanks
      Indeed.   2020
      Each wiped and polished piece
      He donned with due heed.
      The gayest from here to Greece,
      The strong man sent for his steed.

81

While he was putting on apparel of the most princely
   kind—
His surcoat, with its symbol of spotless deeds
Environed on velvet with virtuous gems,
Was embellished and bound with embroidered seams,
And finely fur-lined with the fairest skins—
He did not leave the lace belt, the lady's gift: 2030
For his own good, Gawain did not forget that!
When he had strapped the sword on his swelling hips,
The knight lapped his loins with his love-token twice,
Quickly wrapped it with relish round his waist.
The green silken girdle suited the gallant well,
Backed by the royal red cloth that richly showed.
But Gawain wore the girdle not for its great value,
Nor through pride in the pendants, in spite of their
   polish,
Nor for the gleaming gold which glinted on the ends,

2040 But to save himself when of necessity he must
Stand an evil stroke, not resisting it with knife
    Or sword.
        When ready and robed aright,
        Out came the comely lord;
        To the men of name and might
        His thanks in plenty poured.

82

Then was Gringolet got ready, that great huge horse.
Having been assiduously stabled in seemly quarters,
The fiery steed was fit and fretting for a gallop.
2050 Sir Gawain stepped to him and, inspecting his coat,
Said earnestly to himself, asserting with truth,
'Here in this castle is a company whose conduct is
    honourable.
The man who maintains them, may he have joy!
The delightful lady, love befall her while she lives!
Thus for charity they cherish a chance guest
Honourably and open-handedly; may He on high,
The King of Heaven, requite you and your company
    too!
And if I could live any longer in lands on earth,
Some rich recompense, if I could, I should readily give
    you.'
2060 Then he stepped into the stirrup and swung aloft.
His man showed him his shield; on his shoulder he put
    it,
And gave the spur to Gringolet with his gold-spiked
    heels.
The horse sprang forward from the paving, pausing no
    more
        To prance.
        His man was mounted and fit,
        Laden with spear and lance.
        'This castle to Christ I commit:
        May He its fortune enhance!'

83

The drawbridge was let down and the broad double
    gates
2070 Were unbarred and borne open on both sides.
Passing over the planks, the prince blessed himself
And praised the kneeling porter, who proffered him
    'Good day',
Praying God to grant that Gawain would be saved.
And Gawain went on his way with the one man
To put him on the right path for that perilous place
Where the sad assault must be received by him.
By bluffs where boughs were bare they passed,
Climbed by cliffs where the cold clung:
Under the high clouds, ugly mists
2080 Merged damply with the moors and melted on the
    mountains;
Each hill had a hat, a huge mantle of mist.
Brooks burst forth above them, boiling over their
    banks
And showering down sharply in shimmering cascades.

Wonderfully wild was their way through the woods;
Till soon the sun in the sway of that season
        Brought day.
        They were on a lofty hill
        Where snow beside them lay,
        When the servant stopped still
        And told his master to stay.   2090

84

'For I have guided you to this ground, Sir Gawain, at
    this time,
And now you are not far from the noted place
Which you have searched for and sought with such
    special zeal.
But I must say to you, forsooth, since I know you,
And you are a lord whom I love with no little regard:
Take my governance as guide, and it shall go better for
    you,
For the place is perilous that you are pressing towards.
In that wilderness dwells the worst man in the world,
For he is valiant and fierce and fond of fighting,
And mightier than any man that may be on earth,   2100
And his body is bigger than the best four
In Arthur's house, or Hector, or any other.
At the Green Chapel he gains his great adventures. .
No man passes that place, however proud in arms,
Without being dealt a death-blow by his dreadful hand.
For he is an immoderate man, to mercy a stranger;
For whether churl or chaplain by the chapel rides,
Monk or mass-priest or man of other kind,
He thinks it as convenient to kill him as keep alive
    himself.
Therefore I say, as certainly as you sit in your saddle, 2110
If you come there you'll be killed, I caution you,
    knight,
Take my troth for it, though you had twenty lives
        And more.
        He has lived here since long ago
        And filled the field with gore.
        You cannot counter his blow,
        It strikes so sudden and sore.

85

'Therefore, good Sir Gawain, leave the grim man
    alone!
Ride by another route, to some region remote!
Go in the name of God, and Christ grace your fortune! 2120
And I shall go home again and undertake
To swear solemnly by God and his saints as well
(By my halidom,° so help me God, and every other
    oath)
Stoutly to keep your secret, not saying to a soul
That ever you tried to turn tail from any man I knew.'
'Great thanks,' replied Gawain, somewhat galled, and
    said,
'It is worthy of you to wish for my well-being, man,

2123 halidom, holy place or relic

And I believe you would loyally lock it in your heart.
But however quiet you kept it, if I quit this place,
2130 Fled from the fellow in the fashion you propose,
I should become a cowardly knight with no excuse
   whatever,
For I will go to the Green Chapel, to get what Fate
   sends,
And have whatever words I wish with that worthy,
Whether weal or woe is what Fate
   Demands.
   Fierce though that fellow be,
   Clutching his club where he stands,
   Our Lord can certainly see
   That his own are in safe hands.'

86

2140 'By Mary!' said the other man, 'If you mean what you
   say,
You are determined to take all your trouble on
   yourself.
If you wish to lose your life, I'll no longer hinder you.
Here's your lance for your hand, your helmet for your
   head.
Ride down this rough track round yonder cliff
Till you arrive in a rugged ravine at the bottom,
Then look about on the flat, on your left hand,
And you will view there in the vale that very chapel,
And the grim gallant who guards it always.
Now, noble Gawain, good-bye in God's name.
2150 For all the gold on God's earth I would not go with
   you,
Nor foot it an inch further through this forest as your
   fellow.'
Whereupon he wrenched at his reins, that rider in the
   woods,
Hit the horse with his heels as hard as he could,
Sent him leaping along, and left the knight there
   Alone.
   'By God!' said Gawain, 'I swear
   I will not weep or groan:
   Being given to God's good care,
   My trust in Him shall be shown.'

87

2160 Then he gave the spur to Gringolet and galloped down
   the path,
Thrust through a thicket there by a bank,
And rode down the rough slope right into the ravine.
Then he searched about, but it seemed savage and
   wild,
And no sign did he see of any sort of building;
But on both sides banks, beetling and steep,
And great crooked crags, cruelly jagged;
The bristling barbs of rock seemed to brush the sky.
Then he held in his horse, halted there,
Scanned on every side in search of the chapel.
2170 He saw no such thing anywhere, which seemed
   remarkable,

Save, hard by in the open, a hillock of sorts,
A smooth-surfaced barrow on a slope beside a stream
Which flowed forth fast there in its course,
Foaming and frothing as if feverishly boiling.
The knight, urging his horse, pressed onwards to the
   mound,
Dismounted manfully and made fast to a lime-tree
The reins, hooking them round a rough branch;
Then he went to the barrow, which he walked round,
   inspecting,
Wondering what in the world it might be.
It had a hole in each end and on either side,   2180
And was overgrown with grass in great patches.
All hollow it was within, only an old cavern
Or the crevice of an ancient crag: he could not explain
   it
   Aright.
   'O God, is the Chapel Green
   This mound?' said the noble knight.
   'At such might Satan be seen
   Saying matins at midnight.'

88

'Now certainly the place is deserted,' said Gawain,
'It is a hideous oratory, all overgrown,   2190
And well graced for the gallant garbed in green
To deal out his devotions in the Devil's fashion.
Now I feel in my five wits, it is the Fiend himself
That has tricked me into this tryst, to destroy me here.
This is a chapel of mischance—checkmate to it!
It is the most evil holy place I ever entered.'
With his high helmet on his head, and holding his
   lance,
He roamed up to the roof of that rough dwelling.
Then from that height he heard, from a hard rock
On the bank beyond the brook, a barbarous noise.   2200
What! It clattered amid the cliffs fit to cleave them
   apart,
As if a great scythe were being ground on a grindstone
   there.
What! It whirred and it whetted like water in a mill.
What! It made a rushing, ringing din, rueful to hear.
'By God!' then said Gawain, 'that is going on,
I suppose, as a salute to myself, to greet me
   Hard by.
   God's will be warranted:
   "Alas!" is a craven cry.
   No din shall make me dread   2210
   Although today I die.'

89

Then the courteous knight called out clamorously,
'Who holds sway here and has an assignation with me?
For the good knight Gawain is on the ground here.
If anyone there wants anything, wend your way hither
   fast,
And further your needs either now, or not at all.'
'Bide there!' said one on the bank above his head,

'And you shall swiftly receive what I once swore to
    give you.'
Yet for a time he continued his tumult of scraping,
2220 Turning away as he whetted, before he would descend.
Then he thrust himself round a thick crag through a
    hole,
Whirling round a wedge of rock with a frightful
    weapon,
A Danish axe° duly honed for dealing the blow,
With a broad biting edge, bow-bent along the handle,
Ground on a grindstone, a great four-foot blade—
No less, by that love-lace gleaming so brightly!
And the gallant in green was garbed as at first,
His looks and limbs the same, his locks and beard;
Save that steadily on his feet he strode on the ground,
2230 Setting the handle to the stony earth and stalking
    beside it.
He would not wade through the water when he came to
    it,
But vaulted over on his axe, then with huge strides
Advanced violently and fiercely along the field's width
    On the snow.
      Sir Gawain went to greet
      The knight, not bowing low.
      The man said, 'Sir so sweet,
      You honour the trysts you owe.'

90

'Gawain,' said the green knight, 'may God guard you!
2240 You are welcome to my dwelling, I warrant you,
And you have timed your travel here as a true man
    ought.
You know plainly the pact we pledged between us:
This time a twelvemonth ago you took your portion,
And now at this New Year I should nimbly requite
    you.
And we are on our own here in this valley
With no seconds to sunder us, spar as we will.
Take your helmet off your head, and have your
    payment here.
And offer no more argument or action than I did
When you whipped off my head with one stroke.'
2250 'No,' said Gawain, 'by God who gave me a soul,
The grievous gash to come I grudge you not at all;
Strike but the one stroke and I shall stand still
And offer you no hindrance; you may act freely,
    I swear.'
      Head bent, Sir Gawain bowed,
      And showed the bright flesh bare.
      He behaved as if uncowed,
      Being loth to display his care.

91

Then the gallant in green quickly got ready,
2260 Heaved his horrid weapon on high to hit Gawain,

With all the brute force in his body bearing it aloft,
Swinging savagely enough to strike him dead.
Had it driven down as direly as he aimed,
The daring dauntless man would have died from the
    blow.
But Gawain glanced up at the grim axe beside him
As it came shooting through the shivering air to shatter
    him,
And his shoulders shrank slightly from the sharp edge.
The other suddenly stayed the descending axe,
And then reproved the prince with many proud words:
'You are not Gawain,' said the gallant, 'whose   2270
    greatness is such
That by hill or hollow no army ever frightened him;
For now you flinch for fear before you feel harm.
I never did know that knight to be a coward.
I neither flinched nor fled when you let fly your blow,
Nor offered any quibble in the house of King Arthur.
My head flew to my feet, but flee I did not.
Yet you quail cravenly though unscathed so far.
So I am bound to be called the better man
    Therefore.'
      Said Gawain, 'Not again   2280
      Shall I flinch as I did before;
      But if my head pitch to the plain,
      It's off for evermore.

92

'But be brisk, man, by your faith, and bring me to the
    point;
Deal me my destiny and do it out of hand,
For I shall stand your stroke, not starting at all
Till your axe has hit me. Here is my oath on it.'
'Have at you then!' said the other, heaving up his axe,
Behaving as angrily as if he were mad.
He menaced him mightily, but made no contact,   2290
Smartly withholding his hand without hurting him.
Gawain waited unswerving, with not a wavering limb,
But stood still as a stone or the stump of a tree
Gripping the rocky ground with a hundred grappling
    roots.
Then again the green knight began to gird:
'So now you have a whole heart I must hit you.
May the high knighthood which Arthur conferred
Preserve you and save your neck, if so it avail you!'
Then said Gawain, storming with sudden rage,
'Thrash on, you thrustful fellow, you threaten too   2300
    much.
It seems your spirit is struck with self-dread.'
'Forsooth,' the other said, 'You speak so fiercely
I will no longer lengthen matters by delaying your
    business,
    I vow.'
      He stood astride to smite,
      Lips pouting, puckered brow.
      No wonder he lacked delight
      Who expected no help now.

Up went the axe at once and hurtled down straight
2310 At the naked neck with its knife-like edge.
Though it swung down savagely, slight was the wound,
A mere snick on the side, so that the skin was broken.
Through the fair fat to the flesh fell the blade,
And over his shoulders the shimmering blood shot to
    the ground.
When Sir Gawain saw his gore glinting on the snow,
He leapt feet close together a spear's length away,
Hurriedly heaved his helmet on to his head,
And shrugging his shoulders, shot his shield to the
    front,
Swung out his bright sword and said fiercely,
2320 (For never had the knight since being nursed by his
    mother
Been so buoyantly happy, so blithe in this world)
'Cease your blows, sir, strike me no more.
I have sustained a stroke here unresistingly,
And if you offer any more I shall earnestly reply.
Resisting, rest assured, with the most rancorous
    Despite.
    The single stroke is wrought
    To which we pledged our plight
    In high King Arthur's court:
2330   Enough now, therefore, knight!'

94

The bold man stood back and bent over his axe,
Putting the haft to earth, and leaning on the head.
He gazed at Sir Gawain on the ground before him,
Considering the spirited and stout way he stood,
Audacious in arms; his heart warmed to him.
Then he gave utterance gladly in his great voice,
With resounding speech saying to the knight,
'Bold man, do not be so bloodily resolute.
No one here has offered you evil discourteously,
2340 Contrary to the covenant made at the King's court.
I promised a stroke, which you received: consider
    yourself paid.
I cancel all other obligations of whatever kind.
If I had been more active, perhaps I could
Have made you suffer by striking a savager stroke.
First in foolery I made a feint at striking,
Not rending you with a riving cut—and right I was,
On account of the first night's covenant we accorded;
For you truthfully kept your trust in troth with me,
Giving me your gains, as a good man should.
2350 The further feinted blow was for the following day,
When you kissed my comely wife, and the kisses came
    to me:
For those two things, harmlessly I thrust twice at you
    Feinted blows.
    Truth for truth's the word;
    No need for dread, God knows.
    From your failure at the third
    The tap you took arose.

'For that braided belt you wear belongs to me.
I am well aware that my own wife gave it you.
Your conduct and your kissings are completely known 2360
    to me,
And the wooing by my wife—my work set it on.
I instructed her to try you, and you truly seem
To be the most perfect paladin ever to pace the earth.
As the pearl to the white pea in precious worth,
So in good faith is Gawain to other gay knights.
But here your faith failed you, you flagged somewhat,
    sir,
Yet it was not for a well-wrought thing, nor for wooing
    either,
But for love of your life, which is less blameworthy.'
The other strong man stood considering this a while,
So filled with fury that his flesh trembled,   2370
And the blood from his breast burst forth in his face
As he shrank for shame at what the chevalier spoke of.
The first words the fair knight could frame were:
'Curses on both cowardice and covetousness!
Their vice and villainy are virtue's undoing.'
Then he took the knot, with a twist twitched it loose,
And fiercely flung the fair girdle to the knight.
'Lo! There is the false thing, foul fortune befall it!
I was craven about our encounter, and cowardice
    taught me
To accord with covetousness and corrupt my   2380
    nature
And the liberality and loyalty belonging to chivalry.
Now I am faulty and false and found fearful always.
In the train of treachery and untruth go woe
    And shame.
    I acknowledge, knight, how ill
    I behaved, and take the blame.
    Award what penance you will:
    Henceforth I'll shun ill-fame.'

96

Then the other lord laughed and politely said,
'In my view you have made amends for your mis-   2390
    demeanour;
You have confessed your faults fully with fair
    acknowledgement,
And plainly done penance at the point of my axe.
You are absolved of your sin and as stainless now
As if you had never fallen in fault since first you were
    born.
As for the gold-hemmed girdle, I give it you, sir,
Seeing it is as green as my gown. Sir Gawain, you may
Think about this trial when you throng in company
With paragons of princes, for it is a perfect token,
At knightly gatherings, of the great adventure at the
    Green Chapel.
You shall come back to my castle this cold New Year, 2400
And we shall revel away the rest of this rich feast;
    Let us go.'

Thus urging him, the lord
Said, 'You and my wife, I know
We shall bring to clear accord,
Though she was your fierce foe.'

97

'No, forsooth,' said the knight, seizing his helmet,
And doffing it with dignity as he delivered this thanks,
'My stay has sufficed me. Still, luck go with you!
2410 May He who bestows all good, honour you with it!
And commend me to the courteous lady, your comely
    wife;
Indeed, my due regards to both dear ladies,
Who with their wanton wiles have thus waylaid their
    knight.
But it is no marvel for a foolish man to be maddened
    thus
And saddled with sorrow by the sleights of women.
For here on earth was Adam taken in by one,
And Solomon by many such, and Samson likewise;
Delilah dealt him his doom; and David, later still,
Was blinded by Bathsheba, and badly suffered for it.
2420 Since these were troubled by their tricks, it would be
    true joy
To love them but not believe them, if a lord could,
For these were the finest of former times, most
    favoured by fortune
Of all under the heavenly kingdom whose hearts were
        Abused;
    These four all fell to schemes
    Of women whom they used.
    If I am snared, it seems
    I ought to be excused.

98

'But your girdle,' said Gawain, 'God requite you for it!
2430 Not for the glorious gold shall I gladly wear it,
Nor for the stuff nor the silk nor the swaying pendants,
Nor for its worth, fine workmanship or wonderful
    honour;
But as a sign of my sin I shall see it often,
Remembering with remorse, when I am mounted in
    glory,
The fault and faintheartedness of the perverse flesh,
How it tends to attract tarnishing sin.
So when pride shall prick me for my prowess in arms,
One look at this love-lace will make lowly my heart.
But one demand I make of you, may it not incommode
    you:
2440 Since you are master of the demesne I have remained
    in a while,
Make known, by your knighthood—and now may He
    above,
Who sits on high and holds up heaven, requite you!—
How you pronounce your true name; and no more
    requests.'

'Truly,' the other told him, 'I shall tell you my title.
Bertilak of the High Desert I am called here in this
    land.
Through the might of Morgan the Fay,° who remains in
    my house,
Through the wiles of her witchcraft, a lore well
    learned—
Many of the magical arts of Merlin she acquired,
For she lavished fervent love long ago
On that susceptible sage: certainly your knights know   2450
        Of their fame.
    So "Morgan the Goddess"
    She accordingly became;
    The proudest she can oppress
    And to her purpose tame—

99

'She sent me forth in this form to your famous hall
To put to the proof the great pride of the house,
The reputation for high renown of the Round Table;
She bewitched me in this weird way to bewilder your
    wits,
And to grieve Guinevere° and goad her to death   2460
With ghastly fear of that ghost's ghoulish speaking
With his head in his hand before the high table.
That is the aged beldame who is at home:
She is indeed your own aunt, Arthur's half-sister,
Daughter of the Duchess of Tintagel who in due
    course,
By Uther, was mother of Arthur,° who now holds
    sway.
Therefore I beg you, bold sir, come back to your aunt,
Make merry in my house, for my men love you,
And by my faith, brave sir, I bear you as much good
    will
As I grant any man under God, for your great hon-   2470
    esty.'
But Gawain firmly refused with a final negative.
They clasped and kissed, commending each other
To the Prince of Paradise, and parted on the cold
    ground
        Right there.
    Gawain on steed serene
    Spurred to court with courage fair,
    And the gallant garbed in green
    To wherever he would elsewhere.

100

Now Gawain goes riding on Gringolet
In lonely lands, his life saved by grace.   2480

2446 **Morgan the Fay,** sister of Arthur, an evil figure in Arthurian legend. She came under the influence of Merlin, the great magician of the Arthurian court, learned his magic secrets, and, according to some stories, became his mistress. She had been quite beautiful until her relationship with Merlin, when she became an unlovely hag   2460 **grieve Guinevere.** Guinevere had discovered Morgan in an affair with a knight, which caused her to be driven from the court—hence her ill will toward Guinevere   2465–2466 **Duchess of Tintagel . . . Arthur.** Arthur's father, Uther Pendragon, had fallen in love with Ygerne, the Duchess of Tintagel and wife of Gorlois. Gorlois was slain; and, through the help of Merlin, Uther visited Ygerne in the guise of Gorlois. The child of this union was Arthur

Often he stayed at a house, and often in the open,
And often overcame hazards in the valleys,
Which at this time I do not intend to tell you about.
The hurt he had had in his neck was healed,
And the glittering girdle that girt him round
Obliquely, like a baldric, was bound by his side
And laced under the left arm with a lasting knot,
In token that he was taken in a tarnishing sin;
And so he came to court, quite unscathed.
2490 When the great became aware of Gawain's arrival
There was general jubilation at the joyful news.
The King kissed the knight, and the Queen likewise,
And so did many a staunch noble who sought to salute
    him.
They all asked him about his expedition,
And he truthfully told them of his tribulations—
What chanced at the chapel, the good cheer of the
    knight,
The lady's love-making, and lastly, the girdle.
He displayed the scar of the snick on his neck
Where the bold man's blow had hit, his bad faith to
2500   Proclaim;
    He groaned at his disgrace,
    Unfolding his ill-fame,
    And blood suffused his face
    When he showed his mark of shame.

101

'Look, my lord,' said Gawain, the lace in his hand.
'This belt confirms the blame I bear on my neck,
My bane and debasement, the burden I bear
For being caught by cowardice and covetousness.
This is the figure of the faithlessness found in me,
2510 Which I must needs wear while I live.

For man can conceal sin but not dissever from it,
So when it is once fixed, it will never be worked
    loose.'
First the King, then all the court, comforted the
    knight,
And all the lords and ladies belonging to the Table
Laughed at it loudly, and concluded amiably
That each brave man of the brotherhood should bear a
    baldric,
A band, obliquely about him, of bright green,
Of the same hue as Sir Gawain's and for his sake wear
    it.
So it ranked as renown to the Round Table,
And an everlasting honour to him who had it,   2520
As is rendered in Romance's rarest book.
Thus in the days of Arthur this exploit was achieved,
To which the books of Brutus bear witness;
After the bold baron, Brutus, came here,
The siege and the assault being ceased at Troy
    Before.
    Such exploits, I'll be sworn,
    Have happened here of yore.
    Now Christ with his crown of thorn
    Bring us his bliss evermore! AMEN   2530

HONY SOYT QUI MAL PENCE°

2531 **Hony . . . Pence,** motto of the Order of the Garter, "May he be shamed who thinks ill of it." The Order of the Garter, instituted c. 1346 by Edward III, is the oldest and most important of the orders of knighthood in England. The association of the Order of the Garter with Gawain, however, is inaccurate. The appearance of the motto here may indicate that the poem was written in honor of the Order of the Garter; it may also signify that the Pearl Poet had some connection with Edward III. However, there is no consensus among critics on either of these issues.

GEOFFREY CHAUCER
c. 1340–1400

Geoffrey Chaucer was born in London about 1340, the son of John Chaucer, a prosperous wine merchant. His training and public life connect him with both the mercantile and noble classes. He was a page in the household of Elizabeth, Countess of Ulster, in the late 1350s. In 1359 and 1360 he served in the English army in France, where he was ransomed after being taken prisoner. In 1366 he married Philippa de Roet, sister of the third wife of John of Gaunt, who was a son of Edward III. He traveled to France and Italy in the 1360s and 1370s on commercial and diplomatic missions. From the 1380s until the end of his life, he filled a number of civil positions in govern-

ment—Controller of Petty Customs in Kent, Justice of the Peace in Kent, Clerk of the King's Works, and Deputy Forester of North Petherton in Somersetshire. Thus, Chaucer's public life places him at the center of the economic and political activity of his times.

It is his literary activity, however, which concerns us here. In the period before 1370, he translated sections of *The Romance of the Rose*, an idealized love allegory by Guillaume de Lorris, and *The Book of the Duchess*, an elegy on the death of Blanche, first wife of John of Gaunt. In the period from 1370 to 1385, he wrote the fragmentary satire *The House of Fame*; the Valentine poem *The Parliament of Fowles*; the *Legend of Good*

Women, an unfinished collection of tales with tragic heroines; the translation of the *Consolation of Philosophy* by Boethius; and the love story *Troilus and Criseyde. The Canterbury Tales* belongs to the last period, from 1385 until his death in 1400. Throughout his career, moreover, Chaucer wrote short pieces—courtly lyrics, a group of ballades dealing with Boethian themes, some personal pieces of arresting quality, and some translations or adaptations.

Chaucer's career has traditionally been divided into three distinct periods—the French (1355–1370), the Italian (1370–1385), and the English (1385–1400)—on the basis of the styles he was imitating and the writers he was reading. Throughout his career, Chaucer continually demonstrated that he was a very well-read man; his writings indicate that he was familiar with Vergil, Ovid, Boethius, Petrarch, Dante, and Boccaccio. He steadily developed his artistic skill and intellectual stature.

It is probable that Chaucer began *The Canterbury Tales* about 1386 or shortly thereafter and continued the work until nearly 1400. A few of the stories may have been written earlier and then incorporated into the collection. The tales are from various sources. Like Shakespeare who succeeded him and his own fourteenth-century contemporaries, Chaucer was gifted at adapting material not his own to original uses. His characters represent almost a cross section of contemporary middle-class English society. It is quite possible that in some instances Chaucer may have had real people in mind when he delineated particular characters; in most cases, however, he chose details which would typify his characters as representatives of particular classes or outlooks.

In addition to describing the characters, the *General Prologue* makes clear the plan of the framework. Each pilgrim is to tell two stories on the trip to Canterbury and two more on the return journey to London. In such a scheme the total number of tales should have run close to one hundred and twenty. Yet only twenty-four stories survive, and of these, four are unfinished. Chaucer evidently modified his scheme to include only one tale by each pilgrim, and (although *The Canterbury Tales* has a beginning and an end), even this restricted scheme was never quite completed. Among the twenty-four stories, however, virtually every type of medieval fiction is represented. There is even a characteristic medieval sermon, which is not a narrative at all.

The stories follow each other in an apparently natural course, with the Host (the Innkeeper) acting as master of ceremonies and extemporaneous critic. Not all the manuscripts of *The Canterbury Tales,* however, agree on the ordering of the tales. Still, critics have traced significant patterns in the whole or in parts. A few of the tales are grouped together because the people telling them are engaged in a quarrel. The Friar, for example, tells a tale against summoners; the Summoner replies with a scurrilous tale about a friar. Several tales seem to be connected by the problem of happiness in married life (the so-called Marriage Group); the relation of meaning, style, and genre in literature is the concern of other tales. Many other interpretations have received attention—perhaps Chaucer was interested primarily in dramatic tension and conflict among the pilgrims, or perhaps he conceived of the whole pilgrimage as an allegory, with all of the pilgrims as wayfarers to eternity. The reader can choose among these interpretations—and many others. *The Canterbury Tales* will speak for itself. It reflects the entire life of fourteenth-century England, both in the multitude of characters it represents and in the variety of literary styles and genres which Chaucer uses. As a conscious craftsman, Chaucer created a literary work so artfully fashioned that we often confuse it with life itself.

Note on the Middle English Language

English, during the Old English period, was a highly inflected language, but it tended to lose or at least to weaken most of the inflectional endings between about 1100 and 1500. Whatever the vowel of a final syllable in Old English, the characteristic vowel of the same syllable in Middle English was –e–. This weakening and loss of suffixes occurred as the accent of a word became fixed upon the first syllable, with consequent lack of stress on the final syllable. Thus, the Old English *sunu* ("son"), *stanas* ("stones"), *lufode* ("loved") appear in Middle English as *sone, stones, luvede* or *lovede.* In certain dialects even in Middle English times, and in all dialects after the sixteenth century, a final –e– produced by the weakening of suffixes was dropped in pronunciation, although often retained in spelling. The vowels of accented syllables were also modified in the Middle English period in the general direction of Modern English.

As a consequence of this leveling of inflectional endings, morphological distinctions (variations in the form of a word by means of which its grammatical functions may be distinguished) began to disappear. There are fewer distinct noun or adjective declensions or verb conjugations in Middle English. Grammatical gender became in the main a dead matter by about 1300.

The influence of the French culture brought in by the Norman Conquest is not at first very apparent in the English language, although French words began to appear in the eleventh century. But because there was little vernacular literature before 1200, it is difficult to generalize. During the thirteenth, and particularly the fourteenth, century, however, there was a steady and impressive influx of foreign words, mostly French, but some Norse and Low German as well. The influence of the French is then seen also in the effect upon English word order (making it different from, say, the Modern German) and on the analytical processes of the language, i.e., the tendency to express an idea by separate words rather than by combining several ideas, through the use of suffixes, into a single word—compare English *I shall have loved* with Latin *amavero.* But it cannot be said that Middle English, even when borrowing most freely, lost its definitely Germanic base.

Middle English literature, unlike that surviving from the Old English period, was written in all parts of England. Before 1300, one must reckon with considerable dialectal variations in Middle English literature and with freedom in spelling and in grammar and syntax. With the rise in importance of the towns during the era from 1250 to 1400, particularly of the metropolis and capital, London, the Northern and Southern and Kentish dialects yielded in great measure to the dialect of London, which is southeast Midland. Individual forms from many other major dialects can be found, however, throughout Middle English; it is from this complex mixture of dialects that Modern English has been formed.

Since some Middle English dialects are readable, and since it was felt that some representation of the language at this time should be made, the selections from the Middle English lyrics and from Chaucer's poetry have been left in the original. The lyrics, it must be understood, do not necessarily belong to Chaucer's dialect, even if both the lyrics and Chaucer's poems are written in Middle English.

On Reading Middle English

Reading Middle English aloud with a fair approximation of the original pronunciation and accent is well worth the effort involved. To do so for Chaucer will be to hear and to appreciate the melody of his lines. Even the best modern metrical translation pales when compared with the original.

The general principles involved may be briefly stated. All consonants are pronounced, even the *g*'s and *k*'s in words like *gnaw* and *knee.* An *h* or a *gh* preceding a *t,* as in *niht* or *laughte,* is pronounced like the *ch* in Modern German *ich* or *Nacht,* depending (as in Modern German) on the quality of the preceding vowel. In general, all vowels are also pronounced, including final –*e*'s, which have the sound of the initial vowel in the modern word *about* (phonetically, ə'baut). Thus, the word *reverence* is pronounced as four distinct syllables, re-ve-reń cë (phonetically, re-və-reń sə). Chaucer's vowels generally have the same values as vowels in French, Italian, or German, except that there is no nasalizing of them before *n* or *m* as in the French *mon, blanc, parfum.* Diphthongs are usually pronounced like the separate vowels which compose them, within the compass of one syllable. Words are

accented very much as in Modern English. Here the rhythm of the lines offers a safe guide. It will be noticed that French words still have their stronger accent toward the end, as in the word *reverence* quoted above. Participial nouns ending in –*ing (e)* have a fairly strong secondary stress on the inflexional syllable: thus *gúer-don-ing-e.* When the rhythm of a line demands it, the final unaccented –*e* (or even other final vowels in unaccented words) may be elided with the initial vowel of the next word, as in the phrase *time and space* (phonetically, 'ti:m and 'spa-sə).

The following table of vowel approximations will serve as a guide:

a, when long, is like *a* in English *father*
a, when short, is the same sound shortened
e, when long, has the quality of the *e* in Modern English *there* or of the final vowel in the English loan-word from the French, *fiancée*
e, when short, is like the *e* in English *met*
i, when long, is like the *i* in *machine*
i, when short, is like the *i* in *sit*
o, when long, is similar to the *o* in English *note,* or to the *o* in *born*
o, when short, is like the vowel in English (southern British) not *(nawt)*
u, when long (though often spelled *ou* or *ow*), is like the vowel in *school*
u, when short, is pronounced as in English *full*
ei and *ai* are both pronounced [*oei*], somewhat like the Cockney version of *day*
au (aw) is like *ou* in English *house*

from THE CANTERBURY TALES

GENERAL PROLOGUE

Whan that Aprill with his shoures soote°
The droghte of March hath perced to the roote,
And bathed every veyne in swich° licour°
Of which vertu° engendred is the flour;°
Whan Zephirus eek° with his sweete breeth
Inspired hath in every holt° and heeth°
The tendre croppes, and the yonge sonne°
Hath in the Ram° his halve cours yronne,
And smale foweles maken melodye,

The Canterbury Tales. General Prologue 1 **Whan . . . soote.** In *The Canterbury Tales,* Chaucer makes use chiefly (1) of the seven-line iambic pentameter stanza (rhyming *abab bcc*), known as the Chaucerian stanza, or Rime Royal or (2) iambic pentameter rhyming couplets, as in the selection given here. The iambic pentameter couplet is the "heroic couplet" of Neoclassical fame, except that the later writers like Dryden and Pope preferred to "close" it to a greater degree, i.e., bring the thought to a more definite conclusion at the end of the second line **soote,** sweet 3 **swich, licour,** moisture 4 **vertu,** power, efficacy, magical influence **flour,** flower 5 **eek,** also 6 **holt,** a cultivated tract or plantation **heeth,** heath 7 **sonne,** sun, "young" because it is early in the year. The medieval calendar started the year at the vernal equinox in March rather than on the first of January 8 **the Ram,** the constellation of Aries, which was, in classical astronomy, the spot in the heavens at which the sun was located at the time of the vernal equinox; hence it was the first constellation of the year

10 That slepen al the nyght with open ye°
(So priketh hem° nature in hir corages);°
Thanne longen folk to goon on pilgrimages,
And palmeres° for to seken straunge strondes,°
To ferne° halwes,° kowthe° in sondry londes;
And specially from every shires ende
Of Engelond to Caunterbury they wende,
The hooly blisful martir° for to seke,
That hem hath holpen° whan that they were seeke.°
  Bifil that in that seson on a day,
20 In Southwerk° at the Tabard° as I lay
Redy to wenden on my pilgrymage
To Caunterbury with ful devout corage,
At nyght was come into that hostelrye
Wel nyne and twenty in a compaignye,
Of sondry folk, by aventure yfalle°
In felaweshipe, and pilgrimes were they alle,
That toward Caunterbury wolden ryde.
The chambres and the stables weren wyde,
And wel we weren esed° atte beste.°
30 And shortly, whan the sonne was to reste,
So hadde I spoken with hem everichon°
That I was of hir felaweshipe anon,
And made forward° erly for to ryse,
To take oure wey ther as I yow devyse.°
  But nathelees,° whil I have tyme and space,
Er that I ferther in this tale pace,°
Me thynketh it acordaunt to resoun
To telle yow al the condicioun
Of ech of hem, so as it semed me,
40 And whiche they weren, and of what degree,
And eek in what array that they were inne;
And at a knyght than wol I first bigynne.
  A KNYGHT ther was, and that a worthy man,
That fro the tyme that he first bigan
To riden out, he loved chivalrie,
Trouthe and honour, fredom and curteisie.
Ful worthy was he in his lordes werre,°
And therto hadde he riden, no man ferre,°
As wel in cristendom as in hethenesse,
50 And evere honoured for his worthynesse.
At Alisaundre he° was whan it was wonne.

Ful ofte tyme he hadde the bord° bigonne
Aboven alle nacions in Pruce;°
In Lettow° hadde he reysed° and in Ruce,°
No Cristen man so ofte of his degree.
In Gernade° at the seege eek hadde he be
Of Algezir,° and riden in Belmarye.°
At Lyeys° was he and at Satalye,°
Whan they were wonne; and in the Grete See°
At many a noble armee hadde he be.   60
At mortal batailles hadde he been fiftene,
And foughten for oure feith at Tramyssene°
In lystes thries, and ay slayn his foo.
This ilke° worthy knyght hadde been also
Somtyme with the lord of Palatye°
Agayn another hethen in Turkye.
And everemoore he hadde a sovereyn prys;°
And though that he were worthy, he was wys,°
And of his port° as meeke as is a mayde.
He nevere yet no vileynye ne sayde   70
In al his lyf unto no maner wight.
He was a verray, parfit° gentil knyght.
But, for to tellen yow of his array,
His hors° were goode, but he was nat gay.
Of fustian° he wered a gypon°
Al bismotered° with his habergeon,°
For he was late ycome from his viage,°
And wente for to doon his pilgrymage.
  With hym ther was his sone, a yong SQUIER,°
A lovyere and a lusty bacheler,   80
With lokkes crulle° as they were leyd in presse.
Of twenty yeer of age he was, I gesse.
Of his stature he was of evene lengthe,
And wonderly delyvere,° and of greet strengthe.
And he hadde been somtyme in chyvachie°
In Flaundres, in Artoys, and Pycardie,
And born hym weel, as of so litel space,°
In hope to stonden in his lady° grace.
Embrouded° was he, as it were a meede°
Al ful of fresshe floures, whyte and reede.   90
Syngynge he was, or floytynge,° al the day;
He was as fressh as is the month of May.
Short was his gowne, with sleves longe and wyde.

---

10 **ye**, eye 11 **hem**, them **corages**, disposition, temperament, desires, will
13 **palmeres**, pilgrims **strondes**, strands, shores 14 **ferne**, distant **halwes**,
hallowed places, shrines **kowthe**, famous, well-known 17 **holy . . . martir**,
Thomas à Becket, Archbishop of Canterbury, slain during a Church and crown
dispute during the reign of Henry II of England. His assassination took place in
1170, and he was canonized in 1173. His position in the quarrel with Henry was
construed by the common people as in their favor, and he was immensely popular after death; his tomb became the most famous shrine in medieval England
18 **holpen**, helped **seeke**, sick. Note that this *seeke* rhymes with *seke* ("seek") in
the preceding line. Identical rhymes of this sort were not only not avoided but
even sought at times 20 **Southwerk**, the bustling suburb of London at the beginning of the Canterbury road **the Tabard**. The tabard, a short, sleeveless coat,
was the sign of the inn. There was actually an inn by this name in Southwark
during Chaucer's time 25 **yfalle**, befallen, taken place 29 **esed**, entertained,
set at ease **atte beste**, in the best possible way 31 **everichon**, every one
33 **forward**, agreement 34 **ther . . . devyse**, where I describe it to you
35 **nathelees**, nevertheless 36 **pace**, pass 47 **werre**, war 48 **ferre**, farther
51 **Alisaundre**, etc. The Knight is a veteran of many wars of the fourteenth century. Judging by the places mentioned, he may have been in large part in the service of King Edward III. His many enterprises mark him as practically a soldier of
fortune, but always with the backing of a prince or lord and always in a cause
which would have been regarded by his contemporaries as reputable or honorable. King Peter of Cyprus, a scion of one of the noted chivalric families of
France, was a brilliant leader of these adventurous expeditions; one of his feats
was the capture of Alexandria (*Alisaundre*) in 1365

52 **the bord**, to "begin the board" was to sit at the head of the table, the obvious
place of honor 53 **Pruce**, Prussia. Apparently the Knight was a member of the
Teutonic Order of Knights, one of the great chivalric associations of the Middle
Ages 54 **Lettow**, Lithuania. The Lithuanians were converted to Christianity in
1386, largely through the instrumentality of the Teutonic Order **reysed**, made
expeditions **Ruce**, Russia. The Teutonic Order was a powerful buffer between
Western Christendom and pagan nations, particularly the Tartars, and made several incursions into Russia during the Middle Ages 56 **Gernade**, Granada
57 **Algezir**, modern Algeciras, captured by the English under the Earl of Derby in
1344 **Belmarye**, Benmarin in Morocco 58 **Lyeys**, Lyas, Armenia, harried by
King Peter of Cyprus in 1367. **Satalye**, Atalia, on the coast of Asia Minor, captured by King Peter of Cyprus in 1361 59 **Grete See**, the Mediterranean
62 **Tramyssene**, Tlemcen in Algeria 64 **ilke**, same 65 **Palatye**, probably a
Turkish heathen allied to King Peter of Cyprus 67 **sovereyn prys**, noble or
sovereign worth 68 **though . . . wys**. Though he was brave, he was prudent
69 **port**, bearing 72 **verray, parfit**, truly perfect 74 **hors**, horses 75 **fustian**,
a thick cotton cloth **gypon**, a tunic 76 **bismotered**, smutted, marked with dirt
habergeon, hauberk, coat of mail 77 **viage**, voyage, expedition 79 **Squier**,
a young candidate for knighthood 81 **crulle**, curled 84 **delyvere**, active, agile
85 **chyvachie**, cavalry raids; as mentioned here, there must have been various
raids in France during the Hundred Years War 87 **as . . . space**, considering the
short period of time he had been training for knighthood 88 **lady**, lady's
89 **Embrouded**, decorated with embroidery **meede**, meadow 91 **floytynge**,
playing the flute. The list of accomplishments given in the description of the
Squire represents what was expected of a young man in courtly life

Wel koude he sitte on hors and faire ryde.
He koude songes make and wel endite,°
Juste° and eek daunce, and weel purtreye° and write.
So hoote he lovede that by nyghtertale°
He sleep namoore than dooth a nyghtyngale.
Curteis he was, lowely, and servysable,
100 And carf biforn his fader at the table.°

    A YEMAN° hadde he and servantz namo°
At that tyme, for hym liste° ride so,
And he was clad in cote and hood of grene.
A sheef of pecok arwes, bright and kene,
Under his belt he bar ful thriftily,
(Wel koude he dresse his takel° yemanly:
His arwes drouped noght with fetheres lowe)
And in his hand he baar a myghty bowe.
A not heed° hadde he, with a broun visage.
110 Of wodecraft wel koude he al the usage.
Upon his arm he baar a gay bracer,°
And by his syde a swerd and a bokeler,
And on that oother syde a gay daggere
Harneised° wel and sharp as point of spere;
A Cristopher° on his brest of silver sheene.
An horn he bar, the bawdryk° was of grene;
A forster° was he, soothly, as I gesse.

    Ther was also a Nonne, a PRIORESSE,
That of hir smylyng was ful symple and coy;°
120 Hire gretteste ooth was but by Seinte Loy;°
And she was cleped° madame Eglentyne.
Ful weel she soong the service dyvyne,
Entuned in hir nose ful semely,
And Frensh she spak ful faire and fetisly,°
After the scole of Stratford atte Bowe,°
For Frenssh of Parys was to hire unknowe.
At mete wel ytaught was she with alle:
She leet no morsel from hir lippes falle,
Ne wette hir fyngres in hir sauce depe;
130 Wel koude she carie a morsel and wel kepe
That no drope ne fille upon hire brest.
In curteisie was set ful muchel hir lest.°
Hir over-lippe wyped she so clene
That in hir coppe ther was no ferthyng° sene
Of grece, whan she dronken hadde hir draughte.
Ful semely after hir mete she raughte.°
And sikerly° she was of greet desport,°
And ful plesaunt, and amyable of port,
And peyned hire to countrefete cheere

Of court,° and to been estatlich of manere,   140
And to ben holden digne° of reverence.
But, for to speken of hire conscience,°
She was so charitable and so pitous°
She wolde wepe, if that she saugh a mous
Kaught in a trappe, if it were deed or bleede.
Of smale houndes hadde she that she fedde
With rosted flessh, or milk and wastel-breed.°
But soore wepte she if oon of hem were deed,
Or if men smoot it with a yerde° smerte;°
And al was conscience and tendre herte.   150
Ful semyly hir wympul pynched° was,
Hir nose tretys,° hir eyen greye as glas,
Hir mouth ful smal, and therto softe and reed;
But sikerly she hadde a fair forheed;
It was almoost a spanne brood, I trowe;
For, hardily,° she was nat undergrowe.
Ful fetys was hir cloke, as I was war.
Of smal coral aboute hire arm she bar
A peire of bedes, gauded° al with grene,
And theron heng a brooch of gold ful sheene,   160
On which ther was first write a crowned A,°
And after Amor vincit omnia.°

    Another NONNE with hire hadde she,
That was hir chapeleyne,° and preestes thre.°

    A MONK ther was, a fair for the maistrie,°
An outridere,° that lovede venerie,
A manly man, to been an abbot able.
Ful many a deyntee° hors hadde he in stable,
And whan he rood, men myghte his brydel heere
Cynglen in a whistlynge wynd als cleere   170
And eek as loude as dooth the chapel belle.
Ther as this lord was kepere of the celle,°
The reule of seint Maure or of seint Beneit,
By cause that it was old and somdel streit°
This ilke Monk leet olde thynges pace,
And heeld after the newe world the space.°
He yaf° nat of that text a pulled hen,°
That seith that hunters ben nat hooly men,
Ne that a monk, whan he is recchelees,
Is likned til° a fissh that is waterlees,—   180
This is to seyn, a monk out of his cloystre.
But thilke text heeld he nat worth an oystre;
And I seyde his opinion was good.
What° sholde he studie and make hymselven wood,°

95 **endite,** compose the words of the song 96 **Juste,** joust **purtreye,** draw (pictures) 97 **nyghtertale,** nighttime 100 **carf . . . table.** It was a regular duty of a squire to do the carving before a meal 101 **Yeman,** yeoman. He ranked in military service below a squire (since he would ordinarily have no pretensions to knighthood) but above a groom **namo,** no more 102 **hym liste,** it pleased him to 106 **takel,** equipment 109 **not heed,** head with hair cropped short or shaved 111 **bracer,** an arm guard worn just above the wrist to protect the archer from the impact of the string 114 **Harneised,** armored, sheathed 115 **Cristopher,** an image of St. Christopher, the patron saint of foresters, whose protection he desired 116 **bawdryk,** baldric, the cord or belt by which the horn was attached to its owner 117 **forster,** a forester 119 **coy,** quiet 120 **Seinte Loy,** St. Eloi, St. Eligius, chosen here partly for the sake of the rhyme, partly for the ladylike sound of his name, and possibly because he was a courtier turned saint 121 **cleped,** called 124 **fetisly,** neatly 125 **Stratford atte Bowe,** a nunnery of St. Leonard's in Bromley, Middlesex, adjoining Stratford-Bow. The prioress spoke the kind of French one would hear in a nunnery of England, not the French of Paris 132 **lest,** pleasure, joy 134 **ferthyng,** bit, trace 136 **raughte,** reached 137 **sikerly,** surely, certainly **desport,** good humor

139 **countrefete . . . court,** to duplicate or imitate the behavior 141 **digne,** worthy 142 **conscience,** sensibility, tender feelings 143 **pitous,** tender-hearted 147 **wastel-breed,** a fine white bread 149 **yerde,** rod, stick **smerte,** smartly 151 **pynched,** pleated, fluted 152 **tretys,** well formed 156 **hardily,** surely, certainly 159 **gauded,** covered with large beads 161 **a crowned A,** apparently a large *A* surmounted by a crown 162 **Amor . . . omnia.** Love conquers all 164 **chapeleyne,** a secretary and personal assistant **Preestes thre,** possibly an error on Chaucer's part; three nun's priests would bring the total up to thirty-one pilgrims instead of the twenty-nine mentioned in l. 24. One such priest would be necessary to escort a woman of the Church, but three would have been unnecessary. Only one is heard of later—the teller of *The Nun's Priest's Tale* 165 **for the maistrie,** surpassing all others 166 **outridere,** a monk who had the duty of inspecting the estates of the monastery 168 **deyntee,** worthy, fine 172 **celle,** a subordinate monastery 173 **seint Maure or of seint Beneit.** St. Benedict was the founder of monasticism in western Europe, having established the famous Benedictine order in 529. St. Maurus was his follower 174 **somdel streit,** somewhat strict 176 **the space,** meanwhile, for the time (he held after the new ways) 177 **yaf,** gave **pulled hen,** plucked hen 180 **til,** to 184 **What,** why **wood,** mad, out of his wits

Upon a book in cloystre alwey to poure,
Or swynken with his handes, and laboure,
As Austyn bit?° How shal the world be served?
Lat Austyn have his swynk° to hym reserved!
Therfore he was a prikasour° aright:
190 Grehoundes he hadde as swift as fowel in flight;
Of prikyng° and of huntyng for the hare
Was al his lust, for no cost wolde he spare.
I seigh° his sleves purfiled at the hond°
With grys,° and that the fyneste of a lond;
And, for to festne his hood under his chyn,
He hadde of gold ywroght a ful curious pyn;
A love-knotte° in the gretter ende ther was.
His heed was balled, that shoon as any glas,
And eek his face, as he hadde been enoynt.
200 He was a lord ful fat and in good poynt;°
His eyen stepe,° and rollynge in his heed,
That stemed as a forneys of a leed;°
His bootes souple, his hors in greet estaat.°
Now certeinly he was a fair prelaat;
He was nat pale as a forpyned° goost.
A fat swan loved he best of any roost.
His palfrey was as broun as is a berye.
    A FRERE ther was, a wantowne° and a merye,
A lymytour,° a ful solempne° man.
210 In alle the ordres foure° is noon that kan
So muchel of daliaunce° and fair langage.
He hadde maad ful many a mariage°
Of yonge wommen at his owene cost.
Unto his ordre he was a noble post.°
Ful wel biloved and famulier was he
With frankeleyns° over al° in his contree,
And eek with worthy wommen of the toun;
For he hadde power of confessioun,
As seyde hymself, moore than a curat,
220 For of his ordre he was licenciat.°
Ful swetely herde he confessioun,
And plesaunt was his absolucioun:
He was an esy man to yeve° penaunce,
Ther as he wiste to have a good pitaunce.°
For unto a povre ordre for to yive
Is signe that a man is wel yshryve;
For if he yaf, he dorste make avaunt,°
He wiste° that a man was repentaunt;
For many a man so hard is of his herte,

He may nat wepe, althogh hym soore smerte.   230
Therfore in stede of wepynge and preyeres
Men moote yeve silver to the povre freres.
His typet° was ay farsed° ful of knyves
And pynnes, for to yeven faire wyves.
And certeinly he hadde a murye note:
Wel koude he synge and pleyen on a rote;°
Of yeddynges° he baar outrely the pris.°
His nekke whit was as the flour-de-lys;
Therto he strong was as a champioun.
He knew the tavernes wel in every toun   240
And everich hostiler° and tappestere°
Bet than a lazar° or a beggestere;°
For unto swich a worthy man as he
Acorded nat, as by his facultee,
To have with sike lazars aqueyntaunce.
It is nat honest, it may nat avaunce,°
For to deelen with no swich poraille,°
But al with riche and selleres of vitaille.°
And over al, ther as profit sholde arise,
Curteis he was and lowely of servyse.   250
Ther nas no man nowher so vertuous.
He was the beste beggere in his hous;
[And yaf a certeyn ferme for the graunt;
Noon of his bretheren cam ther in his haunt;]
For thogh a wydwe hadde noght a sho,°
So plesaunt was his "In principio,"°
Yet wolde he have a ferthyng, er he wente.
His purchas was wel bettre than his rente.°
And rage he koude, as it were right a whelp.°
In love-dayes° ther koude he muchel help,   260
For ther he was nat lyk a cloysterer
With a thredbare cope,° as is a povre scoler,
But he was lyk a maister or a pope.
Of double worstede was his semycope,°
That rounded as a belle out of the presse.
Somwhat he lipsed,° for his wantownesse,
To make his Englissh sweete upon his tonge;
And in his harpyng, whan that he hadde songe,
His eyen twynkled in his heed aryght,
As doon the sterres in the frosty nyght.   270
This worthy lymytour was cleped Huberd.
    A MARCHANT was ther with a forked berd,
In mottelee,° and hye on horse he sat;
Upon his heed a Flaundryssh bever hat,
His bootes clasped faire and fetisly.
His resons he spak ful solempnely,
Sownynge° alwey th'encrees° of his wynnyng.

He wolde the see were kept for any thyng
Bitwixe Middelburgh and Orewelle.°
280 Wel koude he in eschaunge sheeldes° selle.
This worthy man ful wel his wit bisette:°
Ther wiste no wight that he was in dette,
So estatly was he of his governaunce°
With his bargaynes and with his chevyssaunce.°
For sothe he was a worthy man with alle,
But, sooth to seyn, I noot° how men hym calle.

A CLERK ther was of Oxenford also,
That unto logyk hadde longe ygo.°
As leene was his hors as is a rake,
290 And he nas nat right fat, I undertake,
But looked holwe, and therto sobrely.
Ful thredbare was his overeste courtepy;°
For he hadde geten hym yet no benefice,°
Ne was so worldly for to have office.
For hym was levere° have at his beddes heed
Twenty bookes, clad in blak or reed,
Of Aristotle and his philosophie,
Than robes riche, or fithele,° or gay sautrie.°
But al be that he was a philosophre,
300 Yet hadde he but litel gold in cofre;
But al that he myghte of his freendes hente,°
On bookes and on lernynge he it spente,
And bisily gan for the soules preye
Of hem that yaf hym wherwith to scoleye.°
Of studie took he moost cure° and moost heede.
Noght o word spak he moore than was neede,
And that was seyd in forme and reverence,
And short and quyk and ful of hy sentence;
Sownynge in moral vertu was his speche,
310 And gladly wolde he lerne and gladly teche.

A SERGEANT OF THE LAWE, war and wys,°
That often hadde been at the Parvys,°
Ther was also, ful riche of excellence.
Discreet he was and of greet reverence—
He semed swich, his wordes weren so wise.
Justice he was ful often in assise,
By patente° and by pleyn commissioun.°
For his science° and for his heigh renoun,
Of fees and robes hadde he many oon.
320 So greet a purchasour was nowher noon:
Al was fee symple to hym in effect;°

His purchasyng myghte nat been infect.°
Nowher so bisy a man as he ther nas,
And yet he semed bisier than he was.
In termes hadde he caas and doomes° alle
That from the tyme of kyng William° were falle.
Therto he koude endite,° and make a thyng,°
Ther koude no wight pynche° at his writyng;
And every statut koude° he pleyn by rote.°
He rood but hoomly in a medlee° cote.   330
Girt with a ceint° of silk, with barres smale;
Of his array telle I no lenger tale.°

A FRANKELEYN was in his compaignye.
Whit was his berd as is the dayesye;
Of his complexioun he was sangwyn.°
Wel loved he by the morwe a sop in wyn;°
To lyven in delit was evere his wone,°
For he was Epicurus owene sone,°
That heeld opinioun that pleyn delit
Was verray felicitee parfit.   340
An housholdere, and that a greet, was he;
Seint Julian he was in his contree.°
His breed, his ale, was always after oon;
A bettre envyned° man was nowher noon.
Withoute bake mete was nevere his hous
Of fissh and flessh, and that so plentevous,
It snewed in his hous of mete and drynke,
Of alle deyntees that men koude thynke.
After the sondry sesons of the yeer,
So chaunged he his mete and his soper.°   350
Ful many a fat partrich hadde he in muwe,°
And many a breem° and many a luce° in stuwe.°
Wo was his cook but if° his sauce were
Poynaunt and sharp, and redy al his geere.°
His table dormant° in his halle alway
Stood redy covered al the longe day.
At sessiouns° ther was he lord and sire;
Ful ofte tyme he was knyght of the shire.°
An anlaas° and a gipser° al of silk
Heeng at his girdel, whit as morne milk.   360
A shirreve° hadde he been, and a contour.°

325 **caas . . . doomes,** cases and judgments. He knew statutes and court decisions (common law) as well   326 **kyng William,** William the Conqueror, whose passion for orderly codification of law resulted in the famous Domesday Book   327 **endite,** here, to write out a legal document   **thyng,** a legal document of any sort   328 **pynche,** object to, cavil at   329 **koude,** knew   **by rote,** from its root, from its basic principles   330 **medlee,** cloth of mixed weave and often of many colors   331 **ceint,** girdle   332 **telle . . . tale.** I shall not tell a longer story   335 **sangwyn.** According to the old conception of the body, there were four component *humors*—blood, phlegm, bile, and black bile—which were held in a kind of harmony or balance known as the complexion. But in all complexions some particular humor dominated, with the result that there were sanguine, phlegmatic, bilious, and melancholy complexions (or temperaments). The Franklin, then, was of sanguine complexion or temperament—blood predominated in his makeup; he was ruddy and a hearty liver   336 **sop in wyn,** bread soaked in wine   337 **wone,** habit, custom   338 **Epicurus owene sone,** an epicure. The hedonistic philosophy of Epicurus (342?–270 B.C.) was and is still today often a little unfairly pictured as a philosophy of comfortable, pleasurable, opportunist living for the moment   342 **Seint Julian, . . . contree,** the St. Julian of his neighborhood. St. Julian was the patron saint of hospitality   344 **bettre envyned,** with a better stock of wine   350 **So chaunged . . . soper.** So did he vary his meals and his supper   351 **in muwe,** in his coop or pen for birds   352 **breem,** bream, a fish with arched back   **luce,** pickerel   **stuwe,** fisy pool   353 **but if,** unless   354 **geere,** equipment   355 **table dormant,** a table fixed in the floor, instead of movable, intended for unexpected guests. This would be in keeping with the Franklin's noted hospitality   357 **sessiouns,** sessions of the local courts, which were presided over by local justices of the peace, of whom the Franklin was one   358 **knyght of the shire,** member of Parliament for his country   359 **anlaas,** a short dagger   **gipser,** purse, pouch   361 **shirreve,** sheriff, king's administrative officer in a county   **contour,** a vague term probably meaning sergeant at law

279 **Middelburgh and Orewelle,** ports in Holland and England, respectively. The Merchant would want this sea path for the wool trade kept open at all costs   280 **sheeldes,** écus, French coins. The selling of écus to Englishmen for profit was distinctly illegal according to a statute of King Edward III   281 **bisette,** used   283 **governaunce,** demeanor   284 **chevyssaunce,** a term referring to borrowing and lending, also used loosely for any illicit income, particularly from usury. Such is its meaning here   286 **noot,** I know not   288 **ygo,** gone. "To go to logic" would be "to study logic"   292 **overeste courtepy,** outermost short-coat   293 **geten . . . benefice,** been given no religious office   295 **hym . . . levere,** he would rather   298 **fithele,** fiddle, violin   **sautrie,** psaltery, a harp-like stringed instrument   301 **hente,** get, seize, acquire   304 **to scoleye,** to go to school, to receive learning   305 **cure,** care   311 **Sergeant of the Lawe,** one of the legal servants of the king, chosen from barristers of at least sixteen years' standing. Those who were not chosen to serve as judges of the King's Courts or of the Exchequer went about on circuit as justices of the assize   **war and wys,** discreet and prudent   312 **Parvys,** the porch of St. Paul's in London, where lawyers were accustomed to consult with their clients   317 **patente,** by letters patent from the king, making the appointment as judge   **pleyn commissioun,** the more common certificates of appointment made in the form of letters sealed and addressed to the appointee giving him full jurisdiction   318 **science,** knowledge (of the law)   321 **Al . . . effect.** All things were in affect fee simple to him—in other words, he always got property in unrestricted possession (*fee simple*)   322 **purchasyng . . . infect,** no defect could be found in the title to his possessions

80   *The Middle Ages*

Was nowher swich a worthy vavasour.°

AN HABERDASSHERE and a CARPENTER,
A WEBBE,° a DYERE, and a TAPYCER,°—
And they were clothed alle in o lyveree
Of a solempne and a greet fraternitee.
Ful fressh and newe hir geere apiked° was;
Hir knyves were chaped° noght with bras
But al with silver; wroght ful clene and weel
370 Hire girdles and hir pouches everydeel.°
Wel semed ech of hem a fair burgeys°
To sitten in a yeldehalle° on a deys.°
Everich, for the wisdom that he kan,
Was shaply° for to been an alderman.
For catel° hadde they ynogh and rente,
And eek hir wyves wolde it wel assente;
And elles certeyn were they to blame.
It is ful fair to been ycleped° "madame,"
And goon to vigilies° al bifore,
380 And have a mantel roialliche ybore.°

A COOK they hadde with hem for the nones°
To boille the chiknes with the marybones,°
And poudre-marchant tart° and galyngale.°
Wel koude he knowe a draughte of Londoun ale.
He koude rooste, and sethe, and broille, and frye,
Maken mortreux,° and wel bake a pye.
But greet harm was it, as it thoughte me,
That on his shyne a mormal° hadde he.
For blankmanger,° that made he with the beste.

390 A SHIPMAN° was ther, wonynge° fer by weste;
For aught I woot, he was of Dertemouthe.
He rood upon a rouncy,° as he kouthe,°
In a gowne of faldyng° to the knee.
A daggere hangynge on a laas° hadde he
Aboute his nekke, under his arm adoun.
The hoote somer hadde maad his hewe al broun;
And certeinly he was a good falawe.
Ful many a draughte of wyn had he ydrawe
Fro Burdeux-ward, whil that the chapman sleep.°
400 Of nyce conscience° took he no keep.
If that he faught, and hadde the hyer hond,
By water he sente hem hoom to every lond.°
But of his craft to rekene wel his tydes,
His stremes, and his daungers° hym bisides,

His herberwe,° and his moone, his lodemenage,°
Ther nas noon swich from Hulle to Cartage.°
Hardy he was and wys to undertake;
With many a tempest hadde his berd been shake.
He knew alle the havenes, as they were,
Fro Gootlond° to the cape of Fynystere,°   410
And every cryke in Britaigne and in Spayne.
His barge ycleped was the Maudelayne.

With us ther was a DOCTOUR OF PHISIK;
In al this world ne was ther noon hym lik,
To speke of phisik and of surgerye,
For he was grounded in astronomye.°
He kepte his pacient a ful greet deel
In houres by his magyk natureel.°
Wel koude he fortunen° the ascendent°
Of his ymages° for his pacient.   420
He knew the cause of everich maladye,
Were it of hoot, or coold, or moyste, or drye,°
And where they engendred, and of what humour.°
He was a verray, parfit praktisour:
The cause yknowe, and of his harm the roote,
Anon he yaf the sike man his boote.°
Ful redy hadde he his apothecaries
To sende hym drogges and his letuaries,°
For ech of hem made oother for to wynne—
Hir frendshipe nas nat newe to bigynne.   430
Wel knew he the olde Esculapius,°
And Deyscorides, and eek Rufus,
Olde Ypocras, Haly, and Galyen,
Serapion, Razis, and Avycen,
Averrois, Damascien, and Constantyn,
Bernard, and Gatesden, and Gilbertyn.
Of his diete mesurable° was he,
For it was of no superfluitee,
But of greet norissyng and digestible.
His studie was but litel on the Bible.   440
In sangwyn° and in pers° he clad was al,
Lyned with taffata and with sendal;°
And yet he was but esy of dispence;°
He kepte that he wan in pestilence.°
For gold in phisik is a cordial,°
Therefore he lovede gold in special.

---

362 **vavasour,** a substantial landholder, not of the nobility   364 **Webbe,** weaver
Tapycer, a tapestry-maker   367 **geere apiked,** equipment adorned
368 **chaped,** capped   370 **everydeel,** every bit, entirely   371 **burgeys,** burgess,
citizen   372 **yeldehalle,** guild hall   **deys,** dais, raised platform. The mayor and
his aldermen sat on the dais, the common councilors on the floor   374 **shaply,**
suitable, fitted   375 **catel,** property. To be a municipal alderman a citizen had to
have a certain amount of property   378 **ycleped,** called   379 **vigilies.** Each
guild had a certain day in the year dedicated to it for its festival. The *vigilie* was
the celebration held on the eve of the guild's feast day   380 **ybore,** carried,
borne   381 **for the nones,** for the occasion   382 **marybones,** marrow bones
383 **poudre-marchant tart,** a tart made with a heavy coating of a sweetish
flavoring powder   **galyngale,** the extract of the sweet cyperus   386 **mortreux,** a
thick soup or stew   388 **mormal,** an ulcer, a running sore   389 **blankmanger,**
creamed meat stewed with eggs, rice, sugar, and sometimes nuts   390 **Shipman,**
a seafaring man, but here the captain of a ship   **wonynge,** dwelling   392
rouncy, a word strangely enough meaning either a broken-down nag or a good
strong horse   **as he kouthe,** as best he knew how   393 **faldyng,** a coarse
woolen cloth   394 **laas,** string or cord   399 **whil . . . sleep,** while the merchant
napped. The Shipman stole much of the wine he was carrying for a merchant
400 **conscience,** tender feeling, scruples   402 **by water . . . every lond.** Presumably the Shipman could turn to piracy and sink his victim's ship and make him
walk the plank   404 **daungers,** here a kind of generic term for such things as
tides, currents, moons, and compass bearings   405 **herberwe,** lodging; as
applied to a shipman, his harbor or anchorage   **lodemenage,** pilotage

406 **Cartage,** Cartagena, a Spanish port   410 **Gootlond,** the island of Gothland,
off the coast of Sweden   **Fynystere,** the westernmost point on the Iberian peninsula in Spain   416 **astronomye.** The medieval science of astronomy was much
like the modern astrology. All natural phenomena observable in the heavens were
supposed to have direct bearing upon the lives of men, and so even a physician
would have to know astronomy since only certain times of the day or year, when
the celestial bodies were in propitious alignment, would be favorable for the
treatment of a patient   417–418 **kepte . . . magyk natureel.** The Physician
watched his patient for the times most advantageous to his treatment   419 **for-
tunen,** place in a favorable position   **ascendent,** that degree of the ecliptic which
is rising at a given time. The Physician, then, was skillful at picking ascendants
that showed a favorable grouping of beneficent planets and constellations
420 **ymages,** either representations of the patient (wax or clay figures) or talismans representing the different signs of the zodiac. By exposing these images to
the firmament when there was a favorable ascendant, a physician was supposed
to be able to work wonders with his patient's condition   422 **hoot . . . drye,** the
four elementary "qualities," consisting of contrary attributes, which in combinations produced the four elements: cold and dry (earth); hot and moist (air); cold
and moist (water); hot and dry (fire)   423 **humour.** The humors were similarly
produced by contrary attributes: hot and moist (blood); cold and moist (phlegm);
hot and dry (bile); cold and dry (black bile)   426 **boote,** remedy
428 **letuaries,** remedies   431 **Esculapius,** etc., a noteworthy list of the great
names in medicine prior to, and contemporaneous with, Chaucer   437 **mesurable,** moderate   441 **sangwyn,** a red cloth   **pers,** a cloth of Persian blue
442 **sendal,** a thin silk   443 **esy of dispence,** slow to spend   444 **pestilence,**
the Black Death but probably any epidemic   445 **gold . . . cordial.** Gold in solution was a "sovereign" remedy for desperate diseases; so the Doctor loved gold

A good WIF was ther OF biside BATHE,
But she was somdel° deef, and that was scathe.°
Of clooth-makyng she hadde swich an haunt,°
450 She passed hem of Ypres and of Gaunt.°
In al the parisshe wif ne was ther noon
That to the offrynge bifore hire sholde goon;
And if ther dide, certeyn so wrooth was she,
That she was out of alle charitee.
Hir coverchiefs° ful fyne weren of ground;°
I dorste swere they weyeden ten pound
That on a Sonday weren upon hir heed.
Hir hosen weren of fyn scarlet reed,
Ful streite yteyd, and shoes ful moyste and newe.
460 Boold was hir face, and fair, and reed of hewe.
She was a worthy womman al hir lyve:
Housbondes at chirche dore she hadde fyve,
Withouten° oother compaignye in youthe,—
But therof nedeth nat to speke as nowthe.°
And thries hadde she been at Jerusalem;
She hadde passed many a straunge strem;
At Rome she hadde been, and at Boloigne,
In Galice at Seint-Jame,° and at Coloigne.
She koude muchel of wandrynge by the weye.
470 Gat-tothed° was she, soothly for to seye.
Upon an amblere° esily she sat,
Ywympled wel, and on hir heed an hat
As brood as is a bokeler or a targe;°
A foot-mantel° aboute hir hipes large,
And on hir feet a paire of spores sharpe.
In felaweshipe wel koude she laughe and carpe.°
Of remedies° of love she knew per chaunce,
For she koude of that art the olde daunce.
    A good man was ther of religioun,
480 And was a povre PERSOUN° OF A TOUN,
But riche he was of hooly thoght and werk.
He was also a lerned man, a clerk,
That Cristes gospel trewely wolde preche;
His parisshens devoutly wolde he teche.
Benygne he was, and wonder diligent,
And in adversitee ful pacient,
And swich he was ypreved ofte sithes.
Ful looth were hym to cursen° for his tithes,
But rather wolde he yeven, out of doute,
490 Unto his povre parisshens aboute
Of his offryng and eek of his substaunce.
He koude in litel thyng have suffisaunce.
Wyd was his parisshe, and houses fer asonder,
But he ne lefte nat, for reyn ne thonder,
In siknesse nor in meschief° to visite
The ferreste° in his parisshe, muche and lite,°

Upon his feet, and in his hand a staf.
This noble ensample to his sheep he yaf,
That first he wroghte, and afterward he taughte.
Out of the gospel he tho wordes caughte,   500
And this figure he added eek therto,
That if gold ruste, what shal iren do?
For if a preest be foul, on whom we truste,
No wonder is a lewed° man to ruste;
And shame it is, if a prest take keep,
A shiten shepherde and a clene sheep.
Wel oghte a preest ensample for to yive,
By his clennesse, how that his sheep sholde lyve.
He sette nat his benefice to hyre°
And leet his sheep encombred in the myre   510
And ran to Londoun unto Seinte Poules
To seken hym a chaunterie° for soules,
Or with a bretherhed to been withholde;°
But dwelte at hoom, and kepte wel his folde,
So that the wolf ne made it nat myscarie;
He was a shepherde and noght a mercenarie.
And though he hooly were and vertuous,
He was to synful men nat despitous,°
Ne of his speche daungerous° ne digne,°
But in his techyng discreet and benygne.   520
To drawen folk to hevene by fairnesse,
By good ensample, this was his bisynesse.
But it were any persone obstinat,
What so he were, of heigh or lough estat,
Hym wolde he snybben° sharply for the nonys.
A bettre preest I trowe that nowher noon ys.
He waited after no pompe and reverence,
Ne maked him a spiced conscience,°
But Cristes loore and his apostles twelve
He taughte, but first he folwed it hymselve.   530
    With hym ther was a PLOWMAN, was his brother,
That hadde ylad° of dong ful many a fother;°
A trewe swynkere° and a good was he,
Lyvynge in pees and parfit charitee.
God loved he best with al his hoole herte
At alle tymes, thogh him gamed° or smerte,
And thanne his neighebor right as hymselve.
He wolde thresshe, and therto dyke° and delve,
For Cristes sake, for every povre wight,
Withouten hire, if it lay in his myght.   540
His tithes payde he ful faire and wel,
Bothe of his propre swynk and his catel.
In a tabard° he rood upon a mere.

504 lewed, ignorant   509 sette . . . to hyre. He did not rent his office to someone else while he went up to London, etc.   512 chaunterie, a provision
whereby a priest was to sing a daily mass for the repose of a soul
513 bretherhed . . . withholde, to be retained as a chaplain by a guild—an additional source of income   518 despitous, spiteful   519 daungerous, arrogant
digne, haughty   525 snybben, snub, chide, rebuke   528 spiced conscience,
oversweetened feelings; the parson was not too fastidious in his feelings or dealings with his parishioners   532 ylad, led, pulled   fother, load   533 swynkere,
laborer   536 him gamed, etc., though it pleased him or hurt him—in all circumstances   538 dyke, dig, make a ditch   543 tabard, a short cloak
544 Reve, an official of a feudal estate whose duties were more administrative
than constabulary   545 Somnour, an officer of the ecclesiastical courts; in effect
a policeman for all offenses involving a breach of ecclesiastical, rather than civil,
law   Pardoner, a distributor of papal indulgences in reward for contributions to
the Church. In many instances, pardoners were not even ordained clergymen and
were itinerant and irresponsible in consequence

448 somdel, somewhat   scathe, a pity   449 swich an haunt, such a practice or
skill   450 Ypres . . . Gaunt. Ypres and Ghent were two important centers of the
Flemish wool trade   455 coverchiefs, kerchiefs   ground, texture   463 Withouten, not counting   464 as nowthe, at the moment   468 Seint-Jame, the
shrine of St. James of Compostella in Spain   470 Gat-tothed, with teeth set far
apart, a characteristic the medieval mind associated with sensuality
471 amblere, an ambling horse   473 targe, shield   474 foot-mantel, an outer
riding-skirt   476 carpe, discourse   477 remedies, cures   480 Persoun, parson, parish priest   488 cursen, to excommunicate for nonpayment of tithes. The
actual excommunication would, of course, have to be pronounced by the bishop
495 meschief, misfortune   496 ferreste, farthest, most remote   muche and lite,
high and low (in social rank)

Ther was also a REVE,° and a MILLERE,
A SOMNOUR,° and a PARDONER° also,
A MAUNCIPLE,° and myself—ther were namo.
  The MILLERE was a stout carl° for the nones;
Ful byg he was of brawn, and eek of bones.
That proved wel, for over al ther he cam,
550 At wrastlynge he wolde have alwey the ram.°
He was short-sholdred, brood, a thikke knarre;°
Ther was no dore that he nolde heve of harre,°
Or breke it at a rennyng° with his heed.
His berd as any sowe or fox was reed,
And therto brood, as though it were a spade.
Upon the cop° right of his nose he hade
A werte, and theron stood a toft of herys,
Reed as the brustles of a sowes erys;
His nosethirles° blake were and wyde.
560 A swerd and bokeler bar he by his syde.
His mouth as greet was as a greet forneys.
He was a janglere° and a goliardeys,°
And that was moost of synne and harlotries.
Wel koude he stelen corn and tollen thries;°
And yet he hadde a thombe of gold,° pardee.
A whit cote and a blew hood wered he.
A baggepipe wel koude he blowe and sowne,°
And therwithal he broghte us out of towne.
  A gentil MAUNCIPLE was ther of a temple,°
570 Of which achatours° myghte take exemple
For to be wise in byynge of vitaille;
For wheither that he payde or took by taille,°
Algate° he wayted so in his achaat°
That he was ay biforn and in good staat.°
Now is nat that of God a ful fair grace
That swich a lewed mannes wit shal pace
The wisdom of an heep of lerned men?
Of maistres hadde he mo than thries ten,
That weren of lawe expert and curious,°
580 Of which ther were a duszeyne in that hous
Worthy to been stywardes of rente and lond
Of any lord that is in Engelond,
To make hym lyve by his propre good
In honour dettelees (but if he were wood),
Or lyve as scarsly as hym list desire;
And able for to helpen al a shire
In any caas that myghte falle or happe;
And yet this Manciple sette hir aller cappe.°

  The REVE was a sclendre colerik° man.
His berd was shave as ny as ever he kan;   590
His heer was by his erys ful round yshorn;
His top was dokked° lyk a preest biforn
Ful longe were his legges and ful lene,
Ylyk a staf, ther was no calf ysene.
Wel koude he kepe a gerner° and a bynne;
Ther was noon auditour koude on him wynne.°
Wel wiste he by the droghte and by the reyn
The yeldynge of his seed and of his greyn.
His lordes sheep, his neet,° his dayerye,
His swyn, his hors, his stoor,° and his pultrye   600
Was hoolly in this Reves governynge,
And by his covenant yaf the rekenynge,
Syn° that his lord was twenty yeer of age.
Ther koude no man brynge hym in arrerage.°
Ther nas baillif, ne hierde,° nor oother hyne,°
That he ne knew his sleighte and his covyne;°
They were adrad° of hym as of the deeth.
His wonyng° was ful faire upon an heeth;
With grene trees yshadwed was his place.
He koude bettre than his lord purchace.   610
Ful riche he was astored° pryvely:
His lord wel koude he plesen subtilly,
To yeve and lene hym of his owene good,
And have a thank, and yet a cote and hood.
In youthe he hadde lerned a good myster;°
He was a wel good wrighte, a carpenter.
This Reve sat upon a ful good stot,°
That was al pomely° grey and highte° Scot.
A long surcote° of pers upon he hade,
And by his syde he baar a rusty blade.   620
Of Northfolk was this Reve of which I telle,
Biside a toun men clepen Baldeswelle.°
Tukked° he was as is a frere aboute,
And evere he rood the hyndreste° of oure route.

  A SOMONOUR was ther with us in that place,
That hadde a fyr-reed cherubynnes face,
For saucefleem° he was, with eyen narwe.
As hoot he was and lecherous as a sparwe,
With scalled° browes blake and piled° berd.
Of his visage children were aferd.   630
Ther nas quyk-silver, lytarge,° ne brymstoon,
Boras, ceruce,° ne oille of tartre noon;
Ne oynement that wolde clense and byte,
That hym myghte helpen of his whelkes° white,
Nor of the knobbes sittynge on his chekes.

Geoffrey Chaucer   **83**

Wel loved he garleek, oynons, and eek lekes,
And for to drynken strong wyn, reed as blood;
Thanne wolde he speke and crie as he were wood.
And whan that he wel dronken hadde the wyn,
640 Thanne wolde he speke no word but Latyn.
A fewe termes hadde he, two or thre,
That he had lerned out of som decree—
No wonder is, he herde it al the day;
And eek ye knowen wel how that a jay
Kan clepen "Watte"° as wel as kan the pope.
But whoso koude in oother thyng hym grope,°
Thanne hadde he spent al his philosophie;
Ay "Questio quid iuris"° wolde he crie.
He was a gentil harlot° and a kynde;
650 A bettre felawe sholde men noght fynde.
He wolde suffre for a quart of wyn
A good felawe to have his concubyn
A twelf month, and excuse hym atte fulle;
Ful prively a fynch eek koude he pulle.°
And if he foond owher° a good felawe,
He wolde techen him to have noon awe
In swich caas of the ercedekenes curs,
But if a mannes soule were in his purs;
For in his purs he sholde ypunysshed be.
660 "Purs is the ercedekenes helle," seyde he.
But wel I woot he lyed right in dede;
Of cursyng oghte ech gilty man him drede,
For curs wol slee right as assoillyng° savith,
And also war hym of a *Significavit*.°
In daunger° hadde he at his owene gise°
The yonge girles° of the diocise,
And knew hir conseil, and was al hir reed.
A gerland hadde he set upon his heed
As greet as it were for an ale-stake.°
670 A bokeleer hadde he maad hym of a cake.
  With hym ther rood a gentil PARDONER
Of Rouncivale,° his freend and his compeer,°
That streight was comen fro the court of Rome.
Ful loude he soong "Come hider, love, to me!"
This Somonour bar to hym a stif burdoun;°
Was nevere trompe of half so greet a soun.
This Pardoner hadde heer as yelow as wex,
But smothe it heeng as dooth a strike° of flex;
By ounces° henge his lokkes that he hadde,
680 And therwith he his shuldres overspradde;
But thynne it lay, by colpons° oon and oon.

But hood, for jolitee, wered he noon,
For it was trussed up in his walet.
Hym thoughte he rood al of the newe jet;°
Dischevelee, save his cappe, he rood al bare.
Swiche glarynge eyen hadde he as an hare.
A vernycle° hadde he sowed upon his cappe.
His walet lay biforn hym in his lappe,
Bretful° of pardoun, comen from Rome al hoot.
A voys he hadde as smal as hath a goot. 690
No berd hadde he, ne nevere sholde have;
As smothe it was as it were late shave.
I trowe he were a geldyng or a mare.
But of his craft, fro Berwyk into Ware,°
Ne was ther swich another pardoner
For in his male° he hadde a pilwe-beer,°
Which that he seyde was Oure Lady veyl:
He seyde he hadde a gobet° of the seyl
That Seint Peter hadde, whan that he wente
Upon the see, til Jhesu Crist hym hente.° 700
He hadde a croys of latoun° ful of stones,
And in a glas he hadde pigges bones.
But with thise relikes, whan that he fond
A povre person dwellynge upon lond,
Upon a day he gat hym moore moneye
Than that the person gat in monthes tweye;
And thus, with feyned flaterye and japes,°
He made the person and the peple his apes.
But trewely to tellen atte laste,°
He was in chirche a noble ecclesiaste. 710
Wel koude he rede a lessoun or a storie,
But alderbest° he song an offertorie;
For wel he wiste, whan that song was songe,
He moste preche and wel affile° his tonge
To wynne silver, as he ful wel koude;
Therefore he song the murierly and loude.
  Now have I toold you soothly, in a clause,
Th'estaat, th'array, the nombre, and eek the cause
Why that assembled was this compaignye
In Southwerk at this gentil hostelrye 720
That highte the Tabard, faste by the Belle.
But now is tyme to yow for to telle
How that we baren us that ilke nyght,
Whan we were in that hostelrie alyght;
And after wol I telle of our viage
And al the remenaunt of oure pilgrimage.
But first I pray yow, of youre curteisye,
That ye n'arette° it nat my vileynye,
Thogh that I pleynly speke in this mateere,
To telle yow hir wordes and hir cheere,° 730
Ne thogh I speke hir wordes proprely.
For this ye knowen al so wel as I,

645 **Watte,** the diminutive of Walter; parrots were evidently taught to say
"Watte!" instead of "Polly!" 646 **grope,** question, test 648 **Questio quid
iuris.** The question is, what (part) of the law (applies)—apparently a familiar piece
of legalistic jargon 649 **harlot,** rascal, not necessarily limited to a female
654 **prively . . . he pulle,** secretly pluck a finch (a slang phrase of highly indecent
nature) 655 **owher,** anywhere 663 **assoillyng,** absolution 664 **Significavit,**
the opening word of the writ which sent a person to prison following excommunication 665 **daunger,** power, control **gise,** discretion 666 **girles,** young
people of either sex 669 **ale-stake.** Every inn had a stake projecting horizontally
over the door, on which was suspended a hoop or garland decorated with ivy
leaves—a symbol of festivity. The Summoner's wreath of flowers was not unusual
among Church people on special occasions, such as an ecclesiastical procession
672 **Rouncivale,** the hospital of the Blessed Mary of Rouncivalle, near Charing
Cross, London. It was a cell of the great convent of Our Lady of Roncesvalles in
Navarre. There are several allusions in Middle English literature to pardoners who
made Rouncivale their headquarters, and all such allusions are satirical **compeer,** comrade 675 **stif burdoun,** a stout "burden" or basic ground melody
678 **strike,** a bunch (of flax) 679 **ounces,** small tufts or bunches 681 **col-
pons,** shreds, strips

684 **al of the newe jet,** all in the new manner or style 687 **vernycle,** a little
"veronica," a copy of the handkerchief which St. Veronica was said to have lent
to Christ during the march to Calvary and which traditionally bore the imprint of
his face 689 **Bretful,** brimful 694 **Berwyk into Ware,** Berwick, at the mouth
of the Tweed in Northumberland (northern England) and Ware in Hertfordshire
(southern England) 696 **male,** bag **pilwe-beer,** pillowcase 698 **gobet,** piece,
fragment 700 **hente,** caught. See *Matthew,* 14:22-33 701 **latoun,** latten, an
alloy of copper and zinc 707 **japes,** jests, jokes 709 **atte laste,** at last, finally
712 **alderbest,** best of all 714 **affile,** file, smooth off 728 **n'arette, etc.,**
impute, ascribe 730 **cheere,** behavior

Whoso shal telle a tale after a man,
He moot reherce as ny as evere he kan
Everich a word, if it be in his charge,
Al° speke he never so rudeliche and large,
Or ellis he moot° telle his tale untrewe,
Or feyne thyng, or fynde wordes newe.
He may nat spare, althogh he were his brother;
740 He moot as wel seye o word as another.
Crist spak hymself ful brode in hooly writ,
And wel ye woot no vileynye is it.
Eek Plato° seith, whoso that kan hym rede,
The wordes moote be cosyn to the dede.
Also I prey yow to foryeve it me,
Al have I nat set folk in hir degree
Heere in this tale, as that they sholde stonde.
My wit is short, ye may wel understonde.
    Greet chiere made oure Hoost° us everichon,°
750 And to the soper sette he us anon.
He served us with vitaille at the beste;
Strong was the wyn, and wel to drynke us leste.°
A semely man OURE HOOSTE was withalle
For to han been a marchal in an halle.°
A large man he was with eyen stepe—
A fairer burgeys is ther noon in Chepe°—
Boold of his speche, and wys, and wel ytaught,
And of manhod hym lakkede right naught.
Eek therto he was right a myrie man,
760 And after soper pleyen° he bigan,
And spak of myrthe amonges othere thynges,
Whan that we hadde maad oure rekenynges,
And seyde thus: "Now, lordynges, trewely,
Ye been to me right welcome, hertely;
For by my trouthe, if that I shal nat lye,
I saugh nat this yeer so myrie a compaignye
Atones° in this herberwe° as is now.
Fayn wolde I doon yow myrthe, wiste I how.
And of a myrthe I am right now bythoght,
770 To doon yow ese, and it shal coste noght.
    Ye goon to Caunterbury—God yow speede,
The blisful martir quite° yow youre meede!°
And wel I woot, as ye goon by the weye,
Ye shapen° yow to talen° and' to pleye;
For trewely, confort ne myrthe is noon
To ride by the weye doumb as a stoon;
And therfore wol I maken yow disport,°
As I seyde erst,° and doon yow som confort.
And if yow liketh alle by oon assent
780 For to stonden at my juggement,
And for to werken as I shal yow seye,

To-morwe, whan ye riden by the weye,
Now, by my fader soule that is deed,
But ye be myrie, I wol yeve yow myn heed!
Hoold up youre hondes, withouten moore speche.''
    Oure conseil was nat longe for to seche.
Us thoughte it was noght worth to make it wys,°
And graunted hym withouten moore avys,°
And bad him seye his voirdit° as hym leste.
"Lordynges,'' quod he, ''now herkneth for the beste; 790
But taak it nought, I prey yow, in desdeyn.°
This is the poynt, to speken short and pleyn,
That ech of yow, to shorte with oure weye,
In this viage shal telle tales tweye
To Caunterbury-ward, I mene it so,
And homward he shal tellen othere two,°
Of aventures that whilom° han bifalle.
And which of yow that bereth hym best of alle,
That is to seyn, that telleth in this caas
Tales of best sentence° and moost solaas,°   800
Shal have a soper at oure aller cost°
Heere in this place, sittynge by this post,
Whan that we come agayn fro Caunterbury.
And for to make yow the moore mury,
I wol myselven goodly with yow ryde,
Right at myn owene cost, and be youre gyde;
And whoso wole my juggement withseye°
Shal paye al that we spenden by the weye.
And if ye vouche sauf that it be so,
Tel me anon, withouten wordes mo,   810
And I wol erly shape me therfore.''
    This thyng was graunted, and oure othes swore
With ful glad herte, and preyden hym also
That he wolde vouche sauf for to do so,
And that he wolde been oure governour,°
And of oure tales juge and reportour,°
And sette a soper at a certeyn pris,
And we wol reuled been at his devys°
In heigh and lough;° and thus by oon assent
We been acorded to his juggement.   820
And therupon the wyn was fet° anon;
We dronken, and to reste wente echon,
Withouten any lenger taryynge.
    Amorwe, whan that day bigan to sprynge,
Up roos oure Hoost, and was oure aller cok,°
And gadrede us togidre alle in a flok,
And forth we riden a litel moore than paas°
Unto the wateryng of Seint Thomas;°
And there oure Hoost bigan his hors areste
And seyde, "Lordynges, herkneth, if yow leste.   830

736 Al, although   737 moot, must   743 Plato. His works were probably
known to Chaucer not through the original Greek but through Latin derivatives,
especially Boethius' Consolation of Philosophy   749 oure Hoost. The Host is certainly one of the most important figures in the pilgrimage. He serves as inter-
locutor and as master of ceremonies, and his reactions to the different stories
seem to have been intended by Chaucer as the common-sense reactions of a typical English midd e-class citizen   everichon, every one   752 us leste, it pleased
us   754 marchal in an halle. The Host was imposing enough in personality to
have been a marshal in any assembly of people   756 Chepe, Cheapside, one of
the principal London streets of the century   760 pleyen, a very vague word
meaning "waxed merry," "disported himself," "joked," etc.   767 Atones, at one
time   herberwe, inn   772 quite, requite, reward   meede, meed, reward
774 shapen, plan   talen, to talk and tell stories   777 disport, diversion, entertainment   778 erst, before

787 make it wys, play the wise man, deliberate   788 avys, consideration, argument   789 voirdit, decision   791 in desdeyn, in contempt, i.e., think not
lightly of my suggestion   796 tellen othere two. This would call for four stories
from each pilgrim. Chaucer never completed this design; he did not actually
make the rounds once. There is evidence that he changed his plan as he progressed with the collection   797 whilom, formerly   800 sentence, significance,
moral meaning   solaas, amusement, entertainment   801 oure aller cost, at the
expense of us all   807 withseye, deny, gainsay   815 governour, guide and
leader   816 reportour, commentator or referee   818 at his devys, at his direction   819 In heigh and lough, in every respect   821 fet, fetched   825 oure
aller cok, cock for all of us, our reveille   827 moore than paas, at a trot
828 wateryng of Seint Thomas, a brook at the second milestone on the Kent road

Ye woot youre foreward,° and I it yow recorde.
If even-song and morwe-song° accorde,
Lat se now who shal telle the firste tale.
As evere mote I drynke wyn or ale,
Whoso be rebel to my juggement
Shal paye for al that by the wey is spent.
Now draweth cut, er that we ferrer twynne;°
He which that hath the shorteste shal bigynne.
Sire Knyght,'' quod he, ''my mayster and my lord,
840 Now draweth cut, for that is myn accord.
Cometh neer,'' quod he, ''my lady Prioresse.
And ye, sire Clerk, lat be youre shamefastnesse,°
Ne studieth noght; ley hond to, every man!''
Anon to drawen every wight bigan,
And shortly for to tellen as it was,
Were it by aventure, or sort, or cas,°
The sothe is this, the cut fil to the Knyght,
Of which ful blithe and glad was every wyght,
And telle he moste his tale, as was resoun,
850 By foreward and by composicioun,°
As ye han herd; what nedeth wordes mo?
And whan this goode man saugh that it was so,
As he that wys was and obedient
To kepe his foreward by his free assent,
He seyde, ''Syn I shal bigynne the game,
What,° welcome be the cut, a Goddes name!
Now lat us ryde, and herkneth what I seye.''
And with that word we ryden forth oure weye,
And he bigan with right a myrie cheere
860 His tale anon, and seyde as ye may heere.

THE MILLER'S TALE°

Whilom ther was dwellynge at Oxenford
A riche gnof,° that gestes heeld to bord,
And of his craft he was a carpenter.
With hym ther was dwellynge a poure scoler,
Hadde lerned art, but al his fantasye
Was turned for to lerne astrologye,
And koude a certeyn of conclusiouns,°
To demen by interrogaciouns,
If that men asked hym in certein houres
10 Whan that men sholde have droghte or elles shoures,
Or if men asked hym what sholde bifalle
Of every thyng; I may nat rekene hem alle.
   This clerk was cleped hende Nicholas.°
Of deerne° love he koude and of solas;°

And therto he was sleigh and ful privee,°
And lyk a mayden meke for to see.
A chambre hadde he in that hostelrye
Allone, withouten any compaignye,
Ful fetisly ydight° with herbes swoote;
And he hymself as sweete as is the roote   20
Of lycorys, or any cetewale.°
His Almageste,° and bookes grete and smale,
His astrelabie,° longynge for his art,
His augrym stones° layen faire apart,
On shelves couched at his beddes heed;
His presse ycovered with a faldyng° reed;
And al above ther lay a gay sautrie,°
On which he made a-nyghtes melodie
So swetely that all the chambre rong;
And Angelus ad virginem° he song;   30
And after that he song the Kynges Noote.°
Ful often blessed was his myrie throte.
And thus this sweete clerk his tyme spente
After his freendes fyndyng° and his rente.°
   This carpenter hadde wedded newe° a wyf,
Which that he lovede moore than his lyf;
Of eighteteene yeer she was of age.
Jalous he was, and heeld hire narwe in cage,
For she was wylde and yong, and he was old,
And demed hymself been lik a cokewold.°   40
He knew nat Catoun,° for his wit was rude,
That bad man sholde wedde his simylitude.
Men sholde wedden after hire estaat,
For youthe and elde is often at debaat.°
But sith that he was fallen in the snare,
He moste endure, as oother folk, his care.°
   Fair was this yonge wyf, and therwithal
As any wezele hir body gent and smal.
A ceynt° she werede, barred al of silk,
A barmclooth° eek as whit as morne milk   50
Upon hir lendes,° ful of many a goore.°
Whit was hir smok, and broyden al bifoore
And eek bihynde, on hir coler aboute,
Of col-blak silk, withinne and eek withoute.
The tapes of hir white voluper°
Were of the same suyte of hir coler;
Hir filet° brood of silk, and set ful hye.
And sikerly she hadde a likerous ye;°
Ful smale ypulled° were hire browes two,
And tho were bent and blake as any sloo.°   60
She was ful moore blisful on to see
Than is the newe pere-jonette° tree,

831 **foreward,** agreement   832 **even-song and morwe-song.** If what we said last night agrees with what we are saying this morning   837 **ferrer twynne,** get farther away (from London)   842 **shamefastnesse,** shyness   846 **aventure . . . cas.** These three nouns all seem to be synonymous here with "luck" or "chance"   850 **By foreward . . . composicioun,** according to the agreement and the ar- rangement   856 **What,** an old interjection, about the equivalent of "Lo!" or "Well!" Its purpose was to attract attention or to command silence
The Miller's Tale. After the knight has finished his long romance of Palamon and Arcite, which is received with general approbation by the pilgrims, the Host turns to the Monk, the most impressive churchman in the group, to ask him for a tale. Before he can get an acceptance, however, the drunken Miller rudely volunteers his story of a carpenter and his wife. 2 **gnof,** churl, old codger   7 **certeyn of conclusiouns,** a certain (number) of propositions or problems   13 **hende Nicholas,** a fixed epithet signifying "ready to hand," "handy"   14 **deerne,** secret   **solas,** amusement

15 **privee,** furtive   19 **fetisly ydight,** handsomely equipped   21 **cetewale,** zedoary, a plant related to ginger   22 **Almageste,** the name given to the as- tronomical treatise by Ptolemy, and then applied generally to works on astrology   23 **astrelabie,** astrolabe, used in ascertaining the altitudes of heavenly bodies   24 **augrym stones,** stones or counters used in an abacus   26 **faldyng,** a coarse woolen cloth   27 **sautrie,** psaltery, a stringed instrument resembling a zither   30 **Angelus ad virginem,** a medieval hymn on the Annunciation   31 **Kynges Noote,** a medieval folk melody   34 **fyndyng,** provision for   **rente,** income   35 **newe,** recently   40 **cokewold,** cuckold   41 **Catoun,** Dionysius Cato, the supposed author of a popular collection of Latin didactic couplets   44 **debaat,** contention   45–46 **sith . . . care.** Divorce was a rare thing in the Middle Ages   49 **ceynt,** sash, girdle   50 **barmclooth,** apron   51 **lendes,** loins   **goore,** gore, a triangular piece of cloth let into a garment   55 **voluper,** cap   57 **filet,** head- band   58 **a likerous ye,** a lecherous eye   59 **smale ypulled,** plucked close   60 **sloo,** the blackthorn, which bears a small plumlike fruit   62 **pere-jonette,** early-ripe pear

And softer than the wolle is of a wether.°
And by hir girdel heeng a purs of lether,
Tasseled with silk, and perled with latoun.°
In al this world, to seken up and doun,
There nys no man so wys that koude thenche°
So gay a popelote° or swich a wenche.
Ful brighter was the shynyng of hir hewe
70 Than in the Tour the noble yforged newe.°
But of hir song, it was as loude and yerne
As any swalwe sittynge on a berne.
Therto she koude skippe and make game,
As any kyde or calf folwynge his dame.
Hir mouth was sweete as bragot° or the meeth,°
Or hoord of apples leyd in hey° or heeth.
Wynsynge° she was, as is a joly colt,
Long as a mast, and upright° as a bolt.°
A brooch she baar upon hir lowe coler,
80 As brood as is the boos° of a bokeler.
Hir shoes were laced on hir legges hye.
She was a prymerole, a piggesnye,°
For any lord to leggen in his bedde,
Or yet for any good yeman to wedde.

    Now, sire, and eft, sire, so bifel the cas,
That on a day this hende Nicholas
Fil with this yonge wyf to rage° and pleye,
Whil that hir housbonde was at Oseneye,°
As clerkes ben ful subtile and ful queynte;°
90 And prively he caughte hire by the queynte,°
And seyde, "Ywis, but if ich have my wille,
For deerne love of thee, lemman, I spille.°"
And heeld hire harde by the haunchebones,
And seyde, "Lemman, love me al atones,
Or I wol dyen, also God me save!"
And she sproong as a colt dooth in the trave,°
And with hir heed she wryed° faste awey,
And seyde, "I wol nat kisse thee, by my fey!
Why, lat be," quod she, "lat be, Nicholas,
100 Or I wol crie 'out, harrow' and 'allas'!
Do wey youre handes, for youre curteisye!"

    This Nicholas gan mercy for to crye,
And spak so faire, and profred him so faste,
That she hir love hym graunted atte laste,
And swoor hir ooth, by seint Thomas of Kent,°
That she wol been at his comandement,
Whan that she may hir leyser wel espie.°
"Myn housbonde is so ful of jalousie
That but ye wayte wel and been privee,
110 I woot right wel I nam but deed," quod she.
"Ye moste been ful deerne, as in this cas."
    "Nay, therof care thee noght," quod Nicholas.
"A clerk hadde litherly biset° his whyle,

But if he koude a carpenter bigyle."
And thus they been accorded and ysworn
To wayte a tyme, as I have told biforn.

    Whan Nicholas had doon thus everideel,
And thakked° hire aboute the lendes weel,
He kiste hire sweete and taketh his sawtrie,
And pleyeth faste, and maketh melodie.   120

    Thanne fil it thus, that to the paryssh chirche,
Cristes owene werkes for to wirche,
This goode wyf went on an haliday.
Hir forheed shoon as bright as any day,
So was it wasshen whan she leet hir werk.
Now was ther of that chirche a parissh clerk,
The which that was ycleped Absolon.°
Crul° was his heer, and as the gold it shoon,
And strouted as a fanne° large and brode;
Ful streight and evene lay his joly shode.°   130
His rode° was reed, his eyen greye as goos.
With Poules wyndow° corven on his shoos,
In hoses rede he wente fetisly.
Yclad he was ful smal and propicly
Al in a kirtel° of a lyght waget;°
Ful faire and thikke been the poyntes° set.
And therupon he hadde a gay surplys
As whit as is the blosme upon the rys.°
A myrie child he was, so God me save.
Wel koude he laten blood and clippe and shave,°   140
And maken a chartre of lond or acquitaunce.°
In twenty manere koude he trippe and daunce
After the scole of Oxenforde tho,
And with his legges casten to and fro,
And pleyen songes on a smal rubible;°
Therto he song som tyme a loud quynyble;°
And as wel koude he pleye on a giterne.
In al the toun nas brewhous ne taverne
That he ne visited with his solas,
Ther any gaylard tappestere° was.   150
But sooth to seyn, he was somdeel squaymous°
Of fartyng, and of speche daungerous.°

    This Absolon, that jolif was and gay,
Gooth with a sencer on the haliday,
Sensynge° the wyves of the parisshe faste;
And many a lovely look on hem he caste,
And namely° on this carpenteris wyf.
To looke on hire hym thoughte a myrie lyf,
She was so propre and sweete and likerous.
I dar wel seyn, if she hadde been a mous,   160
And he a cat, he wolde hire hente anon.°
This parissh clerk, this joly Absolon,

---

118 **thakked,** stroked, patted   127 **Absolon.** The irony of this name lies in the fact that Absalom, the rebellious son of David (see 2 *Samuel,* 3 and 18), was, in medieval tradition, the model of irresistible male beauty   128 **Crul,** curly   129 **strouted as a fanne,** spread out like a fan   130 **shode,** side of the head, temple   131 **rode,** complexion   132 **Poules wyndow,** designed like the windows of St. Paul's, i.e., diamond-shaped   135 **kirtel,** a frock with short skirt   waget, blue   136 **poyntes,** tagged laces   138 **rys,** twig   140 **Wel . . . shave.** He could be a barber on occasion   141 **maken . . . acquitaunce.** He could draw up a deed or a release   145 **rubible,** lute   146 **quynyble,** a high falsetto   150 **gaylard tappestere,** gay, roistering barmaid   151 **squaymous,** squeamish   152 **daungerous,** fastidious   155 **Sensynge,** smelling out; note the pun on *sencer* (censer) in the line preceding   157 **namely,** particularly   161 **wolde . . . anon,** would have caught her soon

63 **wether,** sheep   65 **latoun,** an alloy of copper and zinc   67 **thenche,** think of, imagine   68 **popelote,** little doll   70 **noble . . . newe.** The *noble* was worth about eight shillings. Money was minted in the Tower of London   75 **bragot,** bragget, drink mace of honey and ale   **meeth,** a variant of mead   76 **hey,** hedge   77 **Wynsynge,** skittish   78 **upright,** straight (in any direction)   **bolt,** the arrow for a crossbow   80 **boos,** boss   82 **piggesnye,** pigsnie (pig's eye), a flower related to the trillium   87 **rage,** indulge in amorous sport   88 **Oseneye,** a town near Oxford   89 **queynte,** subtle, complex in behavior   90 **queynte,** female sexual organs   92 **spille,** perish   96 **trave,** a wooden frame for holding horses   97 **wryed,** twisted   105 **Thomas of Kent,** Thomas à Becket   107 **leyser . . . espie,** find an opportunity   113 **litherly biset,** badly spent

Hath in his herte swich a love-longynge
That of no wyf took he noon offrynge;°
For curteisie, he seyde, he wolde noon.

The moone, whan it was nyght, ful brighte shoon,
And Absolon his gyterne hath ytake,
For paramours° he thoghte for to wake.
And forth he gooth, jolif and amorous,
170 Til he cam to the carpenteres hous
A litel after cokkes hadde ycrowe,
And dressed hym up by a shot-wyndowe°
That was upon the carpenteris wal.
He syngeth in his voys gentil and smal,
"Now, deere lady, if thy wille be,
I praye yow that ye wole rewe on me,"
Ful wel acordaunt° to his gyternynge.
This carpenter awook, and herde him synge,
And spak unto his wyf, and seyde anon,
180 "What! Alison! herestow nat Absolon,
That chaunteth thus under oure boures wal?"
And she answerde hir housbonde therwithal,
"Yis, God woot, John, I heere it every deel."

This passeth forth; what wol ye bet than weel?°
Fro day to day this joly Absolon
So woweth hire that hym is wo bigon.
He waketh al the nyght and al the day;
He kembeth his lokkes brode, and made hym gay;
He woweth hire by meenes and brocage,°
190 And swoor he wolde been hir owene page;°
He syngeth, brokkynge° as a nyghtyngale;
He sente hire pyment,° meeth, and spiced ale,
And wafres, pipyng hoot out of the gleede;°
And, for she was of town, he profred meede.°
For som folk wol ben wonnen for richesse,
And somme for strokes, and somme for gentillesse.

Somtyme, to shewe his lightnesse and maistrye,
He pleyeth Herodes upon a scaffold hye.°
But what availleth hym as in this cas?
200 She loveth so this hende Nicholas
That Absolon may blowe the bukkes horn;°
He ne hadde for his labour but a scorn.
And thus she maketh Absolon hire ape,°
And al his ernest turneth til a jape.
Ful sooth is this proverbe, it is no lye,
Men seyn right thus, "Alwey the nye slye
Maketh the ferre leeve to be looth.°"
For though that Absolon be wood° or wrooth,
By cause that he fer was from hire sight,
210 This nye Nicholas stood in his light.

Now ber thee wel, thou hende Nicholas,
For Absolon may waille and synge "allas."
And so bifel it on a Saterday,

This carpenter was goon til Osenay;
And hende Nicholas and Alisoun
Acorded been to this conclusioun,
That Nicholas shal shapen hym a wyle
This sely° jalous housbonde to bigyle;
And if so be the game wente aright,
She sholde slepen in his arm al nyght, 220
For this was his desir and hire also.
And right anon, withouten wordes mo,
This Nicholas no lenger wolde tarie,
But dooth ful softe unto his chambre carie
Bothe mete and drynke for a day or tweye,
And to hire housbonde bad hire for to seye,
If that he axed after Nicholas,
She sholde seye she nyste where he was,
Of al that day she saugh hym nat with ye;
She trowed that he was in maladye, 230
For for no cry hir mayde koude hym calle,
He nolde answere for thyng that myghte falle.

This passeth forth al thilke Saterday,
That Nicholas stille in his chambre lay,
And eet and sleep, or dide what hym leste,
Til Sonday, that the sonne gooth to reste.
This sely carpenter hath greet merveyle
Of Nicholas, or what thyng myghte hym eyle,
And seyde, "I am adrad, by Seint Thomas,
It stondeth nat aright with Nicholas. 240
God shilde that he deyde sodeynly!
This world is now ful tikel,° sikerly.
I saugh to-day a cors yborn to chirche
That now, on Monday last, I saugh hym wirche.°

"Go up," quod he unto his knave anoon,
"Clepe at his dore, or knokke with a stoon.
Looke how it is, and tel me boldely."
This knave gooth hym up ful sturdily,
And at the chambre dore whil that he stood,
He cride and knokked as that he were wood, 250
"What! how! what do ye, maister Nicholay?
How may ye slepen al the longe day?"

But al for noght, he herde nat a word.
An hole he foond, ful lowe upon a bord,
Ther as the cat was wont in for to crepe,
And at that hole he looked in ful depe,
And at the laste he hadde of hym a sight.
This Nicholas sat evere capyng° upright,
As he had kiked° on the newe moone.
Adoun he gooth, and tolde his maister soone 260
In what array° he saugh this ilke man.

This carpenter to blessen hym bigan,
And seyde, "Help us, seinte Frydeswyde!°
A man woot litel what hym shal bityde.
This man is falle, with his astromye,°
In some woodnesse or in som agonye.

164 **That . . . offrynge.** He neglected to collect the offerings of any woman in the congregation   168 **paramours,** passionate love   172 **shot-wyndowe,** a small window with a hinge or bolt   177 **acordaunt,** in harmony with   184 **what . . . weel?** What do you want for a good thing?   189 **meenes and brocage,** with the help of go-betweens   190 **page,** servant   191 **brokkynge,** with a quaver or break in his voice   192 **pyment,** pimento   193 **gleede,** fire   194 **meede,** bribe, consideration for services rendered   198 **playeth . . . hye.** He played the part of Herod (a noisy, spectacular role) in a miracle play   201 **blowe . . . horn,** an expression of utter futility   203 **ape,** fool   206–207 **"Alwey . . . looth."** Always a sly one near at hand makes the absent one to be hated   208 **wood,** mad, crazy

218 **sely,** foolish   242 **tikel,** ticklish, unstable   244 **That . . . hym wirche,** whom I saw at work last Monday   258 **capyng,** gaping   259 **kiked,** gazed. It was believed that to gaze on the moon, especially when new or full, was to invite madness; cf. "moonstruck"   261 **array,** condition   263 **seinte Frydeswyde,** an Anglo-Saxon saint   265 **astromye,** a garbled, ignorant form of *astronomy*

I thoghte ay wel how that it sholde be!
Men sholde nat knowe of Goddes pryvetee.
Ye, blessed be alwey a lewed° man
270 That noght but oonly his bileve° kan!
So ferde another clerk with astromye;
He walked in the feeldes, for to prye
Upon the sterres, what ther sholde bifalle,
Til he was in a marle-pit yfalle;
He saugh nat that. But yet, by seint Thomas,
Me reweth soore of hende Nicholas.°
He shal be rated° of his studiyng,
If that I may, by Jhesus, hevene kyng!
Get me a staf, that I may underspore,°
280 Whil that thou, Robyn, hevest up the dore.
He shal out of his studiyng, as I gesse"—
And to the chambre dore he gan hym dresse.
His knave was a strong carl for the nones,
And by the haspe he haaf it of atones;°
Into the floor the dore fil anon.
This Nicholas sat ay as stille as stoon,
And evere caped upward into the eir.
This carpenter wende he were in despeir,°
And hente hym by the sholdres myghtily,
290 And shook hym harde, and cride spitously,
"What! Nicholay! what, how! what, looke adoun!
Awak, and thenk on Cristes passioun!
I crouche° thee from elves and fro wightes."
Therwith the nyght-spel° seyde he anon-rightes
On foure halves° of the hous aboute,
And on the thresshfold° of the dore withoute:
"Jhesu Crist and seinte Benedight,
Blesse this hous from every wikked wight,
For nyghtes verye,° the white pater-noster!
300 Where wentestow, seinte Petres soster?"
    And atte laste this hende Nicholas
Gan for to sik soore, and seyde, "Allas!
Shal al the world be lost eftsoones° now?"
    This carpenter answerde, "What seystow?
What! thynk on God, as we doon, men that swynke.°"
    This Nicholas answerde, "Fecche me drynke,
And after wol I speke in pryvetee
Of certeyn thyng that toucheth me and thee.
I wol telle it noon oother man, certeyn."
310   This carpenter goth doun, and comth ageyn,
And broghte of myghty ale a large quart;
And whan that ech of hem had dronke his part,
This Nicholas his dore faste shette,
And doun the carpenter by hym he sette.
    He seyde "John, myn hooste, lief and deere,
Thou shalt upon thy trouthe swere me heere
That to no wight thou shalt this conseil° wreye;
For it is Cristes conseil that I seye,

And if thou telle it man, thou art forlore;°
For this vengeaunce thou shalt han therfore,   320
That if thou wreye me, thou shalt be wood.°"
"Nay, Crist forbede it, for his hooly blood!"
Quod tho this sely man, "I nam no labbe;°
Ne, though I seye, I nam nat lief to gabbe.
Sey what thou wolt, I shal it nevere telle
To child ne wyf, by hym that harwed helle!°"
    "Now John," quod Nicholas, "I wol nat lye;
I have yfounde in myn astrologye,
As I have looked in the moone bright,
That now a Monday next, at quarter nyght,°   330
Shal falle a reyn, and that so wilde and wood,
That half so greet was nevere Noes flood.
This world," he seyde, "in lasse than an hour
Shal al be dreynt,° so hidous is the shour.
Thus shal mankynde drenche, and lese hir lyf."
    This carpenter answerde, "Allas, my wyf!
And shal she drenche? allas, myn Alisoun!"
For sorwe of this he fil almoost adoun,
And seyde, "Is ther no remedie in this cas?"
    "Why, yis, for Gode," quod hende Nicholas,   340
"If thou wolt werken after loore and reed.°
Thou mayst nat werken after thyn owene heed;
For thus seith Salomon, that was ful trewe,
'Werk al by conseil, and thou shalt nat rewe.'
And if thou werken wolt by good conseil,
I undertake, withouten mast and seyl,
Yet shal I saven hire and thee and me.
Hastow nat herd hou saved was Noe,
Whan that oure Lord hadde warned hym biforn
That al the world with water sholde be lorn?"   350
    "Yis," quod this Carpenter, "ful yoore ago."
    "Hastou nat herd," quod Nicholas, "also
The sorwe of Noe with his felaweshipe,
Er that he myghte gete his wyf to shipe?°
Hym hadde be levere, I dar wel undertake
And thilke tyme, than alle his wetheres blake
That she hadde had a ship hirself allone.
And therfore, woostou what is best to doone?
This asketh haste, and of an hastif thyng
Men may nat preche or maken tariyng.   360
    Anon go gete us faste into this in
A knedyng trogh, or ellis a kymelyn,°
For ech of us, but looke that they be large,
In which we mowe swymme as in a barge,
And han therinne vitaille suffisant
But for a day,—fy on the remenant!
The water shal aslake and goon away
Aboute pryme upon the nexte day.
But Robyn may nat wite of this, thy knave,°
Ne eek thy mayde Gille I may nat save;   370

269 **lewed,** ignorant, unlearned   270 **bileve,** belief, faith   276 **Me . . . Nicholas,** I'm very sorry about handy Nicholas   277 **rated,** berated   279 **underspore,** thrust up, pry up   284 **atones,** at once   288 **despeir,** distress   293 **crouche,** cross, make the sign of the Cross   294 **nyght-spel,** a charm designed to protect a house from evil   295 **halves,** sides   296 **thresshfold,** threshold   299 **verye,** evil spirits; perhaps evil   303 **eftsoones,** very soon, immediately   305 **swynke,** labor   317 **conseil,** secret

319 **forlore,** lost, damned   321 **if . . . wood.** If you betray me, you will go mad   323 **labbe,** blab   326 **hym . . . helle,** Christ, who in legend spent the three days between the Crucifixion and the Resurrection visiting hell and rescuing the souls of the deserving   330 **quarter nyght.** Night began officially at 6:00 P.M. and ended at 6:00 A.M., hence a *quarter night* would be 9:00 P.M.   334 **dreynt,** drowned   341 **loore and reed,** teaching and advice   353–354 **The sorwe . . . shipe,** a reference to the miracle-play treatment of the story of Noah, in which Noah's wife is unwilling to enter the Ark and has to be taken on board by force   362 **kymelyn,** a shallow tub   369 **knave,** servant boy

Geoffrey Chaucer   **89**

Axe nat why, for though thou aske me,
I wol nat tellen Goddes pryvetee.
Suffiseth thee, but if thy wittes madde,
To han as greet a grace as Noe hadde.
Thy wyf shal I wel saven, out of doute.
Go now thy wey, and speed thee heer-aboute.
　　But whan thou hast, for hire and thee and me,
Ygeten us thise knedyng tubbes thre,
Thanne shaltow hange hem in the roof ful hye,
380 That no man of oure purveiaunce° spye.
And whan thou thus hast doon, as I have seyd,
And hast oure vitaille faire in hem yleyd,
And eek an ax, to smyte the corde atwo,
Whan that the water comth, that we may go,
And breke an hole an heigh, upon the gable,
Unto the gardyn-ward, over the stable,
That we may frely passen forth oure way,
Whan that the grete shour is goon away,
Thanne shaltou swymme as myrie, I undertake,°
390 As dooth the white doke after hire drake.
Thanne wol I clepe, 'How, Alison! how, John!
Be myrie, for the flood wol passe anon.'
And thou wolt seyn, 'Hayl, maister Nicholay!
Good morwe, I se thee wel, for it is day.'
And thanne shul we be lordes al oure lyf
Of al the world, as Noe and his wyf.
　　But of o thyng I warne thee ful right:
Be wel avysed on that ilke nyght
That we ben entred into shippes bord,
400 That noon of us ne speke nat a word,
Ne clepe, ne crie, but be in his preyere;
For it is Goddes owene heeste deere.
　　Thy wyf and thou moote hange fer atwynne;
For that bitwixe yow shal be no synne,
Namoore in lookyng than ther shal in deede,
This ordinance is seyd. Go, God thee speede!
Tomorwe at nyght, whan men ben alle aslepe,
Into oure knedyng-tubbes wol we crepe,
And sitten there, abidyng Goddes grace.
410 Go now thy wey, I have no lenger space
To make of this no lenger sermonyng.
Men seyn thus, 'sende the wise, and sey no thyng:'
Thou art so wys, it needeth thee nat teche.
Go, save oure lyf, and that I the biseche.''
　　This sely carpenter goth forth his wey.
Ful ofte he seide ''alas'' and ''weylawey,°''
And to his wyf he tolde his pryvetee,
And she was war, and knew it bet than he,
What al this queynte cast° was for to seye.
420 But nathelees she ferde° as she wolde deye,
And seyde, ''Allas! go forth thy wey anon,
Help us to scape, or we been dede echon!
I am thy trewe, verray wedded wyf;
Go, deere spouse, and help to save oure lyf.''

Lo, which a greet thyng is affeccioun!°
Men may dyen of ymaginacioun,
So depe may impressioun be take.
This sely carpenter bigynneth quake;
Hym thynketh verraily that he may see
Noees flood come walwynge° as the see   430
To drenchen Alisoun, his hony deere.
He wepeth, weyleth, maketh sory cheere;
He siketh with ful many a sory swogh;°
He gooth and geteth hym a knedyng trogh,
And after that a tubbe and a kymelyn,
And pryvely he sente hem to his in,°
And heng hem in the roof in pryvetee.
His owene hand° he made laddres thre,
To clymben by the ronges and the stalkes
Unto the tubbes hangynge in the balkes,°   440
And hem vitailled, bothe trogh and tubbe,
With breed and chese, and good ale in a jubbe,°
Suffisynge right ynogh as for a day.
But er that he hadde maad al this array,
He sente his knave, and eek his wenche also,
Upon his nede° to London for to go.
And on the Monday, whan it drow to nyght,
He shette his dore withoute candel-lyght,
And dressed° alle thyng as it sholde be.
And shortly, up they clomben alle thre;   450
They seten stille wel a furlong way.°
　　''Now, Pater-noster, clom!°'' seyde Nicholay,
And ''clom,'' quod John, and ''clom,'' seyde Alisoun.
This carpenter seyde his devocioun,
And stille he sit, and biddeth his preyere,
Awaitynge on the reyn, if he it heere.
　　The dede sleep, for wery bisynesse,
Fil on this carpenter right as I gesse,
Aboute corfew-tyme,° or litel moore;
For travaille° of his goost he groneth soore,   460
And eft he routeth,° for his heed myslay.
Doun of° the laddre stalketh Nicholay,
And Alisoun ful softe adoun she spedde;
Withouten wordes mo they goon to bedde,
Ther as the carpenter is wont to lye.
Ther was the revel and the melodye;
And thus lith Alison and Nicholas,
In bisynesse of myrthe and of solas,
Til that the belle of laudes° gan to rynge,
And freres in the chauncel gonne synge.   470
　　This parissh clerk, this amorous Absolon,
That is for love alwey so wo bigon,
Upon the Monday was at Oseneye
With compaignye, hym to disporte and pleye,
And axed upon cas° a cloisterer
Ful prively after John the carpenter;

425 **affeccioun**, emotion   430 **walwynge**, tumbling   433 **swogh**, sigh
436 **in**, lodging   438 **His owene hand**, with his own hand   440 **balkes**, beams
442 **jubbe**, jug   446 **Upon his nede**, on his business   449 **dressed**, prepared
451 **a furlong way**, the time it takes to walk a furlong (an eighth of a mile) at a
good walking gait; about two and a half minutes   452 **clom**, silence. The
meaning seems to be ''Say a *paternoster*, then be quiet''   459 **corfew-tyme**,
probably 8:00 P.M.   460 **travaille**, trouble, pains   461 **routeth**, snores
462 **of**, off   469 **laudes**, lauds, the service that follows matins   475 **upon cas**,
by chance

380 **purveiaunce**, foresight   389 **undertake**, dare say   416 **weylawey**, an expression of alarm and lamentation   419 **queynte cast**, subtle plan   420 **ferde**,
behaved

90　*The Middle Ages*

And he drough hym apart out of the chirche,
And seyde, "I noot, I saugh hym heere nat wirche
Syn Saterday; I trowe that he be went
480 For tymber, ther oure abbot hath hym sent;
For he is wont for tymber for to go,
And dwellen at the grange° a day or two;
Or elles he is at his hous, certeyn.
Where that he be, I kan nat soothly seyn."
    This Absolon ful joly was and light,
And thoghte, "Now is tyme to wake al nyght;
For sikirly° I saugh hym nat stirynge
Aboute his dore, syn day bigan to sprynge.
    So moot I thryve, I shal, at cokkes crowe,
490 Ful pryvely knokken at his wyndowe
That stant° ful lowe upon his boures wal.
To Alison now wol I tellen al
My love-longynge, for yet I shal nat mysse
That at the leeste wey I shal hire kisse.
Som maner confort shal I have, parfay.
My mouth hath icched al this longe day;
That is a signe of kissyng atte leeste.
Al nyght me mette eek I was at a feeste.
Therfore I wol go slepe an houre or tweye,
500 And al the nyght thanne wol I wake and pleye."
    Whan that the firste cok hath crowe,° anon
Up rist this joly lovere Absolon,
And hym arraieth gay, at poynt-devys.°
But first he cheweth greyn° and lycorys,
To smellen sweete, er he hadde kembd his heer.
Under his tonge a trewe-love° he beer,
For therby wende he to ben gracious.
He rometh to the carpenteres hous,
And stille he stant under the shot-wyndowe—
510 Unto his brest it raughte, it was so lowe—
And softe he cougheth with a semy° soun:
"What do ye, hony-comb, sweete Alisoun,
My faire bryd, my sweete cynamome?°
Awaketh, lemman myn, and speketh to me!
Wel litel thynken ye upon my wo,
That for youre love I swete ther I go.
No wonder is thogh that I swelte° and swete;
I moorne as dooth a lamb after the tete.°
Ywis, lemman, I have swich love-longynge,
520 That lik a turtel° trewe is my moornynge.
I may nat ete na moore than a mayde."
    "Go fro the wyndow, Jakke° fool," she sayde;
"As help me God, it wol nat be 'com pa me.'°
I love another—and elles I were to blame—
Wel bet than thee, by Jhesu, Absolon.
Go forth thy wey, or I wol caste a ston,
And lat me slepe, a twenty devel wey!°"
    "Allas," quod Absolon, "and weylawey,
That trewe love was evere so yvel biset!

Thanne kysse me, syn it may be no bet,   530
For Jhesus love, and for the love of me."
    "Wiltow thanne go thy wey therwith?" quod she.
    "Ye, certes, lemman," quod this Absolon.
    "Thanne make thee redy," quod she, "I come
        anon."
And unto Nicholas she seyde stille,
"Now hust,° and thou shalt laughen al thy fille."
    This Absolon doun sette hym on his knees
And seyde, "I am a lord at alle degrees;°
For after this I hope ther cometh moore.
Lemman, thy grace, and sweete bryd, thyn oore!"   540
    Thy wyndow she undoth, and that in haste.
"Have do," quod she, "com of,° and speed the faste,
Lest that oure neighebores thee espie."
    This Absolon gan wype his mouth ful drie.
Derk was the nyght as pich, or as the cole,
And at the wyndow out she putte hir hole,
And Absolon, hym fil no bet ne wers,°
But with his mouth he kiste hir naked ers
Ful savourly, er he were war of this.
    Abak he stirte, and thoughte it was amys,   550
For wel he wiste a womman hath no berd.
He felte a thyng al rough and long yherd,
And seyde, "Fy! allas! what have I do?"
    "Tehee!" quod she, and clapte the wyndow to,
And Absolon gooth forth a sory pas.
    "A berd!° a berd!" quod hende Nicholas,
"By Goddes corpus,° this goth faire and weel."
    This sely° Absolon herde every deel,
And on his lippe he gan for anger byte,
And to hymself he seyde, "I shal thee quyte."   560
    Who rubbeth now, who frot° now his lippes
With dust, with sond, with straw, with clooth, with
        chippes,
But Absolon, that seith ful ofte, "Allas!"
"My soule bitake° I unto Sathanas,
But me were levere than al this toun," quod he,
"Of this despit awroken° for to be.
Allas," quod he, "allas, I ne hadde ybleynt!°"
His hoote love was coold and al yqueynt;°
For fro that tyme that he hadde kist hir ers,
Of paramours° he sette nat a kers;   570
For he was heeled of his maladie.
Ful ofte paramours he gan deffie,
And weep as dooth a child that is ybete.
A softe paas he wente over the strete
Until a smyth men cleped daun Gerveys,
That in his forge smythed plough harneys;
He sharpeth shaar and kultour° bisily.
    This Absolon knokketh al esily,
And seyde, "Undo, Gerveys, and that anon."
    "What, who artow?" "It am I, Absolon."   580

482 **grange**, barn   487 **sikirly**, certainly   491 **stant**, stands   501 **firste . . .
crowe**, presumably at 1:00 A.M.   503 **poynt-devys**, according to plan
504 **greyn**, grain of Paradise, a spice   506 **trewe-love**, leaves of herb Paris,
which grew in the form of a lover's knot   511 **semy**, thin, small
513 **cynamome**, baby talk for cinnamon   517 **swelte**, perish   518 **tete**, teat
520 **turtel**, turtledove   522 **Jakke**, a term of contempt   523 **com pa me**, come
kiss me; probably the refrain of a popular song   527 **twenty devel wey**, a profane intensive of *away*

536 **hust**, hush   538 **lord . . . degrees**, in all conditions, in every way
542 **com of**, hurry up   547 **hym . . . wers**, i.e., he took his chances   556 **A
berd!, etc.** "To make a beard" was a Middle English expression for making a fool
of some one   557 **By Goddes corpus**, by the body of Christ   558 **sely**,
wretched   561 **frot**, rubs   564 **bitake**, entrust   566 **awroken**, avenged
567 **ybleynt**, blenched, turned aside   568 **yqueynt**, quenched
570 **paramours**, sexual love   577 **kultour**, colter

"What, Absolon! for Cristes sweete tree,°
Why rise ye so rathe? ey, *benedicitee!*
What eyleth yow? Som gay gerl, God it woot,
Hath broght yow thus upon the viritoot.°
By seinte Note,° ye woot wel what I mene."
    This Absolon ne roghte nat a bene°
Of al his pley; no word agayn he yaf;
He hadde moore tow on his distaf°
Than Gerveys knew, and seyde, "Freend so deere,
590 That hoote kultour in the chymenee heere,
As lene it me, I have therwith to doone,
And I wol brynge it thee agayn ful soone."
    Gerveys answerde, "Certes, were it gold,
Or in a poke° nobles alle untold,
Thou sholdest have, as I am trewe smyth.
Ey, Cristes foo! what wol ye do therwith?"
    "Therof," quod Absolon, "be as be may.
I shal wel telle it thee to-morwe day"—
And caughte the kultour by the colde stele.
600 Ful softe out at the dore he gan to stele,
And wente unto the carpenteris wal.
He cogheth first, and knokketh therwithal
Upon the wyndowe, right as he dide er.
    This Alison answerde, "Who is ther
That knokketh so? I warante it a theef."
    "Why, nay," quod he, "God woot, my sweete leef,
I am thyn Absolon, my deerelyng.
Of gold," quod he, "I have thee broght a ryng.
My mooder yaf it me, so God me save;
610 Ful fyn it is, and therto wel ygrave.
This wol I yeve thee, if thou me kisse."
    This Nicholas was risen for to pisse,
And thoughte he wolde amenden al the jape;
He sholde kisse his ers er that he scape.
And up the wyndowe dide he hastily,
And out his ers he putteth pryvely
Over the buttok, to the haunche-bon;
And therwith spak this clerk, this Absolon,
"Spek, sweete bryd, I noot nat where thou art."
620   This Nicholas anon leet fle a fart,
As greet as it had been a thonder-dent,
That with the strook he was almoost yblent;°
And he was redy with his iren hoot,
And Nicholas amydde the ers he smoot.
    Of gooth the skyn an hande-brede° aboute,
The hoote kultour brende so his toute,°
And for the smert he wende for to dye.
As he were wood, for wo he gan to crye,
"Help! water! water! help, for Goddes herte!"
630   This carpenter out of his slomber sterte,
And herde oon crien "water" as he were wood,

And thoughte, "Allas, now comth Nowelis flood!°"
He sit hym up withouten wordes mo,
And with his ax he smoot the corde atwo,
And doun gooth al; he foond neither to selle,
Ne breed ne ale,° til he cam to the celle
Upon the floor, and ther aswowne° he lay.
    Up stirte hire Alison and Nicholay,
And criden "out" and "harrow" in the strete.
The neighebores, bothe smale and grete,   640
In ronnen for to gauren° on this man,
That yet aswowne lay, bothe pale and wan,
For with the fal he brosten hadde his arm.
But stonde he moste unto his owene harm;°
For whan he spak, he was anon bore doun°
With hende Nicholas and Alisoun.
They tolden every man that he was wood,
He was agast so of Nowelis flood
Thurgh fantasie, that of his vanytee
He hadde yboght hym knedyng tubbes thre,   650
And hadde hem hanged in the roof above;
And that he preyed hem, for Goddes love,
To sitten in the roof, *par compaignye.°*
    The folk gan laughen at his fantasye;
Into the roof they kiken and they cape,°
And turned al his harm unto a jape.
For what so that this carpenter answerde,
It was for noght, no man his reson herde.
With othes grete he was so sworn adoun
That he was holde wood in al the toun;   660
For every clerk anonright heeld with oother.
They seyde, "The man is wood, my leeve brother";
And every wight gan laughen at this stryf.
Thus swyved° was this carpenteris wyf,
For al his kepyng and his jalousye;
And Absolon hath kist hir nether ye;
And Nicholas is scalded in the towte.
This tale is doon, and God save al the rowte!

THE WIFE OF BATH'S PROLOGUE°

"Experience, though noon auctoritee°
Were in this world, is right ynogh for me
To speke of wo that is in mariage;
For, lordynges, sith I twelve yeer was of age,
Thonked be God that is eterne on lyve,

632 **Nowelis flood.** The old carpenter confuses "Noe" and "Nowel," Christmas
635-36 **he foond . . . ale.** He found neither bread nor ale to sell; i.e., he did not
stop to do business on the way 637 **aswowne,** in a swoon 641 **gauren,** stare,
gaze 644 **But stonde . . . harm.** He had to put up with it to his own discomfort 645 **bore doun,** refuted 653 **par compaignye,** for the sake of company 655 **kiken . . . cape,** gazed and stared 664 **swyved,** had intercourse with
The Wife of Bath's Prologue and Tale, a version of a story known through a Middle English romance, a popular ballad, and a story from the *Confessio Amantis* by
Chaucer's friend John Gower (1330–1408). Chaucer's immediate source is none
of these and is in fact not known. In this tale there are two celebrated motifs of
folk literature: that of the loathly lady and that of the riddle, both of which may
be found among the popular ballads. A beautiful woman, turned by witchcraft
into a repulsive hag, can be released from the spell only through the devoted and
unflinching love of a man. In the riddle motif, an individual must answer a riddle
or be put to death if he cannot solve it 1 **auctoritee,** authority

581 **tree,** the Cross 584 **viritoot,** posthaste 585 **seinte Note,** St. Neot, an
Anglo-Saxon saint 586 **roghte . . . bene,** didn't care a bean 588 **tow on his
distaf,** a metaphor from spinning meaning that he had more important business in
hand 594 **poke,** bag 622 **yblent,** blinded 625 **hande-brede,** a hand's
breadth 626 **toute,** anus

Housbondes at chirche dore I have had fyve,—
If I so ofte myghte have ywedded bee,°—
And alle were worthy men in hir degree.
But me was toold, certeyn, nat longe agoon is,
10 That sith that Crist ne wente nevere but onis
To weddyng, in the Cane of Galilee,°
That by the same ensample taughte he me
That I ne sholde wedded be but ones.
Herkne eek, lo, which a sharp word for the nones,
Biside a welle, Jhesus, God and man,
Spak in repreeve of the Samaritan:°
'Thou hast yhad fyve housbondes,' quod he,
'And that ilke man that now hath thee
Is noght thyn housbonde,' thus seyde he certeyn.
20 What that he mente therby, I kan nat seyn;
But that I axe, why that the fifthe man
Was noon housbonde to the Samaritan?
How manye myghte she have in mariage?
Yet herde I nevere tellen in myn age
Upon this nombre diffinicioun.
Men may devyne and glosen,° up and doun,
But wel I woot, expres, withoute lye,
God bad us for to wexe and multiplye;°
That gentil text kan I wel understonde.
30 Eek wel I woot, he seyde myn housbonde
Sholde lete fader and mooder, and take to me.°
But of no nombre mencion made he,
Of bigamye, or of octogamye;
Why sholde men thanne speke of it vileynye?
    Lo, heere the wise kyng, daun Salomon;°
I trowe he hadde wyves mo than oon.
As wolde God it were leveful unto me
To be refresshed half so ofte as he!
Which yifte of God hadde he for alle his wyvys!
40 No man hath swich that in this world alyve is.
God woot, this noble kyng, as to my wit,
The firste nyght had many a myrie fit
With ech of hem, so wel was hym on lyve.
Yblessed be God that I wedded fyve!°
Welcome the sixte, whan that evere he shal.
For sothe, I wol nat kepe me chaast in al.
Whan myn housbonde is fro the world ygon,
Som Cristen man shal wedde me anon,
For thanne, th'apostle° seith that I am free
50 To wedde, a Goddes half, where it liketh me.
He seith that to be wedded is no synne;
Bet is to be wedded than to brynne.
What rekketh me, thogh folk seye vileynye

Of shrewed Lameth° and his bigamye?
I woot wel Abraham was an hooly man,
And Jacob eek, as ferforth as I kan;
And ech of hem hadde wyves mo than two,
And many another holy man also.
Wher can ye seye, in any manere age,
That hye God defended° mariage   60
By expres word? I pray yow, telleth me.
Or where comanded he virginitee?
I woot as wel as ye, it is no drede,
Th'apostle, whan he speketh of maydenhede,
He seyde that precept therof hadde he noon.°
Men may conseille a womman to been oon,
But conseillyng is no comandement.
He putte it in oure owene juggement;
For hadde God comanded maydenhede,
Thanne hadde he dampned° weddyng with the dede. 70
And certes, if ther were no seed ysowe,
Virginitee, thanne wherof sholde it growe?
Poul dorste nat comanden, atte leeste,
A thyng of which his maister yaf noon heeste.
The dart° is set up for virginitee:
Cacche whoso may, who renneth best lat see.
    But this word is nat taken of every wight,
But ther as God lust° gyve it of his myght.
I woot wel that th'apostle was a mayde;
But nathelees, thogh that he wroot and sayde   80
He wolde that every wight were swich as he,°
Al nys but conseil to virginitee.
And for to been a wyf he yaf me leve
Of indulgence; so nys it no repreve
To wedde me, if that my make dye,
Withouten excepcion of bigamye.°
Al° were it good no womman for to touche,—
He mente as in his bed or in his couche;
For peril is bothe fyr and tow t'assemble:
Ye knowe what this ensample may resemble.   90
This is al and som, he heeld virginitee
Moore parfit than weddyng in freletee.
Freletee clepe I, but if that he and she
Wolde leden al hir lyf in chastitee.°
    I graunte it wel, I have noon envie,
Thogh maydenhede preferre° bigamye.
It liketh hem to be clene, body and goost;
Of myn estaat I nyl nat make no boost.
For wel ye knowe, a lord in his houshold,
He nath nat every vessel al of gold;   100

---

7 **If I ... bee,** if my marriage to so many could be valid   10–11 **Crist ... Galilee,** as told in *John*, 2:1 ff   14–16 **sharp word ... Samaritan.** See *John*, 4:6 ff   26 **glosen,** explain, make commentaries upon   28 **God ... multiplye.** See *Genesis*, 1:28   30–31 **myn housbonde ... to me.** See *Matthew*, 19:5   35 **Salomon, etc.** See *1 Kings*, 11:3   44 **fyve.** The following lines are probably genuine, but whether Chaucer added them late and meant to keep them, or wrote them early and meant to reject them, is unclear: Of whiche I have pyked out the beste, Bothe of here nether purs and of here cheste. Diverse scoles maken parfyt clerkes, And diverse practyk in many sondry werkes Maketh the werkman parfyt sekirly; Of fyve husbondes scoleiyng am I.   49 **th'apostle,** St. Paul. See *1 Corinthians*, 7:9 and 7:39

54 **shrewed Lameth,** accursed Lamech, the first bigamist mentioned in the Old Testament (*Genesis*, 4:19–23)   60 **defended,** forbade   65 **He seyde ... noon.** Now concerning virgins I have no commandment of the Lord—*1 Corinthians*, 7:25   70 **dampned,** damned, condemned   75 **dart,** the prize in a running contest. The Wife of Bath means that anyone who wishes to compete in the contest for chastity may do so and may win the prize by remaining chaste, but the contest is not for her   78 **God lust,** it pleases God (to)   81 **He ... as he.** For I would that all men were even as myself—*1 Corinthians*, 7:7   83–86 **he yaf ... bigamye.** He said that there was no sin of bigamy in remarrying if my mate died   87 **Al,** although. See *1 Corinthians*, 7:1   93–94 **Freletee ... chastitee.** Unless (but if) he and she will lead their lives in chastity, I consider them "in frailty"   96 **preferre,** take precedence over, be preferred to

Somme been of tree,° and doon hir lord servyse.
God clepeth folk to hym in sondry wyse,
And everich hath of God a propre yifte,
Som this, som that, as hym liketh shifte.°
    Virginitee is greet perfeccion,
And continence eek with devocion,
But Crist, that of perfeccion is welle,
Bad nat every wight he sholde go selle
Al that he hadde, and gyve it to the poore
110 And in swich wise folwe hym and his foore.°
He spak to hem that wolde lyve parfitly;
And lordynges, by youre leve, that am nat I.
I wol bistowe the flour of al myn age
In the actes and in fruyt of mariage.
    Telle me also, to what conclusion
Were membres maad of generacion,
And of so parfit wys a wight ywroght?
Trusteth right wel, they were nat maad for noght.
Glose whoso wole, and seye bothe up and doun,
120 That they were maked for purgacioun
Of uryne, and oure bothe thynges smale
Were eek to knowe a femele from a male,
And for noon oother cause,—say ye no?
The experience woot wel it is noght so.
So that the clerkes be nat with me wrothe,
I sey this, that they maked ben for bothe,
This is to seye, for office,° and for ese
Of engendrure, ther we nat God displese.
Why sholde men elles in hir bookes sette
130 That man shal yelde to his wyf hire dette?
Now wherwith sholde he make his paiement,
If he ne used his sely° instrument?
Thanne were they maad upon a creature
To purge uryne, and eek for engendrure.
    But I seye noght that every wight is holde,°
That hath swich harneys as I to yow tolde,
To goon and usen hem in engendrure.
Thanne sholde men take of chastitee no cure.°
Crist was a mayde, and shapen as a man,
140 And many a seint, sith that the world bigan;
Yet lyved they evere in parfit chastitee.
I nyl envye no virginitee.
Lat hem be breed of pured° whete-seed,
And lat us wyves hoten° barly-breed;
And yet with barly-breed, Mark° telle kan,
Oure Lord Jhesu refresshed many a man.
In swich estaat as God hath cleped us
I wol persevere; I nam nat precius.°
In wyfhod I wol use myn instrument
150 As frely as my Makere hath it sent.
If I be daungerous,° God yeve me sorwe!
Myn housbonde shal it have bothe eve and morwe,
Whan that hym list come forth and paye his dette.

An housbonde I wol have, I wol nat lette,°
Which shal be bothe my dettour and my thral,
And have his tribulacion withal
Upon his flessh, whil that I am his wyf.
I have the power durynge al my lyf
Upon his propre body, and noght he.
Right thus the Apostel tolde it° unto me;   160
And bad oure housbondes for to love us weel.
Al this sentence me liketh every deel''—
    Up stirte the Pardoner, and that anon:
''Now, dame,'' quod he, ''by God and by seint John!
Ye been a noble prechour in this cas.
I was aboute to wedde a wyf; allas!
What sholde I bye it° on my flessh so deere?
Yet hadde I levere wedde no wyf to-yeere!°''
    ''Abyde!'' quod she, ''my tale is nat bigonne.
Nay, thou shalt drynken of another tonne,   170
Er that I go, shal savoure wors than ale.
And whan that I have toold thee forth my tale
Of tribulacion in mariage,
Of which I am expert in al myn age,
This is to seyn, myself have been the whippe,—
Than maystow chese wheither thou wolt sippe
Of thilke tonne that I shal abroche.°
Be war of it, er thou to° ny approche;
For I shal telle ensamples mo than ten.
'Whoso° that nyl be war by othere men,   180
By hym shul othere men corrected be.'
The same wordes writeth Ptholomee;
Rede in his Almageste,° and take it there.''
    ''Dame, I wolde praye yow, if youre wyl it were,''
Seyde this Pardoner, ''as ye bigan,
Telle forth youre tale, spareth for no man,
And teche us yonge men of youre praktike.°''
    ''Gladly,'' quod she, ''sith it may yow like;
But that I praye to al this compaignye,
If that I speke after my fantasye,   190
As taketh not agrief of that I seye;
For myn entente is nat but for to pleye.
    Now, sire, now wol I telle forth my tale.—
As evere moote I drynken wyn or ale,
I shal seye sooth, tho housbondes that I hadde,
As thre of hem were goode, and two were badde.
The thre were goode men, and riche, and olde;
Unnethe° myghte they the statut holde
In which that they were bounden unto me.
Ye woot wel what I meene of this, pardee!   200
As help me God, I laughe whan I thynke
How pitously a-nyght I made hem swynke!°
And, by my fey, I tolde of it no stoor.°
They had me yeven hir lond and hir tresoor;
Me neded nat do lenger diligence

101 **tree,** wood   104 **as hym liketh shifte,** as it pleases him to arrange (his life)
110 **foore,** company, disciples   127 **office,** (physiological) functions
132 **sely,** blessed   135 **holde,** obligated, bound to   138 **cure,** care, heed
143 **pured,** refined   144 **hoten,** be called   145 **Mark,** actually John; see *John,*
6:9   148 **precius,** fastidious   151 **daungerous,** over-fastidious

154 **lette,** hesitate, find difficulties   160 **Apostel tolde it.** See *Ephesians,* 5:25
167 **bye it,** pay for it   168 **to-yeere,** this year   177 **abroche,** break open
178 **to,** too   180–181 **Whoso, etc.,** attributed to Ptolemy's *Almagest* but not
actually found there; it was probably proverbial   182–183 **Ptholomee . . . Almageste.** The *Almagest* was the classic treatment of astronomy, but the name was
applied loosely to many works on astronomy and astrology   187 **praktike,** practice as opposed to theory   198 **Unnethe,** with difficulty   202 **swynke,** labor,
work hard   203 **tolde . . . stoor,** did not consider worth anything

To wynne hir love, or doon hem reverence.
They loved me so wel, by God above,
That I ne tolde no deyntee° of hir love!
A wys womman wol bisye hire evere in oon°
210 To gete hire love, ye, ther as she hath noon.
But sith I hadde hem hoolly in myn hond,
And sith they hadde me yeven al hir lond,
What° sholde I taken keep hem for to plese,
But it were° for my profit and myn ese?
I sette hem so a-werke, by my fey,
That many a nyght they songen 'weilawey!'
The bacon was nat fet for hem, I trowe,
That som men han in Essex at Dunmowe.°
I governed hem so wel, after my lawe,
220 That ech of hem ful blisful was and fawe°
To brynge me gaye thynges fro the fayre.
They were ful glad whan I spak to hem faire;
For, God it woot, I chidde hem spitously.
    Now herkneth hou I baar me properly,°
Ye wise wyves, that kan understonde.
Thus shulde ye speke and bere hem wrong on honde;°
For half so boldely kan ther no man
Swere and lyen, as a womman kan.
I sey nat this by wyves that been wyse,
230 But if it be whan they hem mysavyse.
A wys wyf shal, if that she kan hir good,
Bere hym on honde that the cow is wood,°
And take witnesse of hir owene mayde
Of hir assent; but herkneth how I sayde:
    'Sire olde kaynard,° is this thyn array?
Why is my neighebores wyf so gay?
She is honoured over al ther she gooth;
I sitte at hoom, I have no thrifty° clooth.
What dostow at my neighebores hous?
240 Is she so fair? artow so amorous?
What rowne° ye with oure mayde? *Benedicite!*
Sire olde lecchour, lat thy japes be!
And if I have a gossib or a freend,
Withouten gilt,° thou chidest as a feend,
If that I walke or pleye unto his hous!
Thou comest hoom as dronken as a mous,
And prechest on thy bench, with yvel preef!°
Thou seist to me it is a greet meschief
To wedde a povre womman, for costage;°
250 And if that she be riche, of heigh parage,°
Thanne seistow that it is a tormentrie
To soffre hire pride and hire malencolie.
And if that she be fair, thou verray knave,
Thou seyst that every holour° wol hire have;

She may no while in chastitee abyde,
That is assailled upon ech a syde.
    Thou seyst som folk desiren us for richesse,
Somme for oure shap, and somme for oure fairnesse,
And som for she kan outher synge or daunce,
260 And som for gentillesse and daliaunce;
Som for hir handes and hir armes smale:
Thus goth al to the devel, by thy tale.
Thou seyst men may nat kepe a castel wal,
It may so longe assailled been over al.
    And if that she be foul,° thou seist that she
Coveiteth every man that she may se,
For as a spaynel she wol on hym lepe,
Til that she fynde som man hire to chepe.°
Ne noon so grey goos gooth ther in the lake
270 As seïstow, wol been withoute make.°
And seyst it is an hard thyng for to welde
A thyng that no man wole, his thankes,° helde.°
Thus seistow, lorel,° whan thow goost to bedde;
And that no wys man nedeth for to wedde,
Ne no man that entendeth unto hevene.
With wilde thonder-dynt and firy levene°
Moote° thy welked° nekke be tobroke!
    Thow seyst that droppyng houses, and eek smoke,
And chidyng wyves maken men to flee
280 Out of hir owene hous; a! *benedicitee!*
What eyleth swich an old man for to chide?
    Thow seyst we wyves wol oure vices hide
Til we be fast, and thanne we wol hem shewe,—
Wel may that be a proverbe of a shrewe!
    Thou seist that oxen, asses, hors, and houndes,
They been assayed at diverse stoundes;
Bacyns, lavours,° er that men hem bye,
Spoones and stooles, and al swich housbondrye,
And so been pottes, clothes, and array;
290 But folk of wyves maken noon assay,
Til they be wedded; olde dotard shrewe!
And thanne, seistow, we wol oure vices shewe.
    Thou seist also that it displeseth me
But if that° thou wolt preyse my beautee,
And but thou poure° alwey upon my face,
And clepe me "faire dame" in every place.
And but thou make a feeste on thilke day
That I was born, and make me fressh and gay;
And but thou do to my norice° honour,
300 And to my chamberere withinne my bour,
And to my fadres folk and his allyes,—
Thus seistow, olde barel-ful of lyes!
    And yet of oure apprentice Janekyn,
For his crispe° heer, shynynge as gold so fyn,
And for he squiereth me bothe up and doun,
Yet hastow caught a fals suspecioun.
I wol hym noght, thogh thou were deed tomorwe!
    But tel me this: why hydestow, with sorwe,

The keyes of thy cheste awey fro me?
310 It is my good as wel as thyn, pardee!
What, wenestow make an ydiot of oure dame?°
Now by that lord that called is Seint Jame,
Thou shalt nat bothe, thogh that thou were wood,
Be maister of my body and of my good;
That oon thou shalt forgo, maugree thyne yen.°
What helpith it of me to enquere or spyen?
I trowe thou woldest loke me in thy chiste!
Thou sholdest seye, "Wyf, go wher thee liste;
Taak youre disport, I wol nat leve no talys.°
320 I knowe yow for a trewe wyf, dame Alys."
We love no man that taketh kep or charge
Wher that we goon; we wol ben at oure large.°

　　Of alle men yblessed moot he be,
The wise astrologien, Daun Ptholome,
That seith this proverbe in his Almageste:
"Of alle men his wysdom is the hyeste
That rekketh nevere who hath the world in honde."
By this proverbe thou shalt understonde,
Have thou ynogh, what thar thee° recche or care
330 How myrily that othere folkes fare?
For, certeyn, olde dotard, by youre leve,
Ye shul have queynte right ynogh at eve.
He is to greet a nygard that wolde werne
A man to lighte a candle at his lanterne;
He shal have never the lasse light, pardee.
Have thou ynogh, thee thar nat pleyne thee.

　　Thou seyst also, that if we make us gay
With clothyng, and with precious array,
That it is peril of oure chastitee;
340 And yet, with sorwe! thou most enforce thee,
And seye thise wordes in the Apostles name:
"In habit maad with chastitee and shame
Ye wommen shul apparaille yow," quod he,
"And noght in tressed heer and gay perree,°
As perles, ne with gold, ne clothes riche.°"
After thy text, ne after thy rubriche,°
I wol nat wirche as muchel as a gnat.°

　　Thou seydest this, that I was lyk a cat;
For whoso wolde senge a cattes skyn,
350 Thanne wolde the cat wel dwellen in his in;
And if the cattes skyn be slyk and gay,
She wol nat dwelle in house half a day,
But forth she wole, er any day be dawed,
To shewe hir skyn, and goon a-caterwawed.°
This is to seye, if I be gay, sire shrewe,
I wol renne out, my borel° for to shewe.

　　Sire olde fool, what helpeth thee to spyen?
Thogh thou preye Argus° with his hundred yen
To be my warde-cors,° as he kan best,

In feith, he shal nat kepe me but me lest;° 360
Yet koude I make his berd,° so moot I thee!

　　Thou seydest eek that ther been thynges thre,°
The whiche thynges troublen al this erthe,
And that no wight may endure the ferthe.
O leeve sire shrewe, Jhesu shorte thy lyf!
Yet prechestow and seyst an hateful wyf
Yrekened is for oon of thise meschances.
Been ther none othere maner resemblances
That ye may likne youre parables to,
But if a sely° wyf be oon of tho? 370

　　Thou liknest eek wommenes love to helle,
To bareyne lond, ther water may nat dwelle.
Thou liknest it also to wilde fyr;°
The moore it brenneth, the moore it hath desir
To consume every thyng that brent wole be.
Thou seyest, right as wormes shende° a tree,
Right so a wyf destroyeth hire housbonde;
This knowe they that been to wyves bonde.'

　　Lordynges, right thus, as ye have understonde,
Barr I stifly myne olde housbondes on honde 380
That thus they seyden in hir dronkenesse;
And al was fals, but that I took witnesse
On Janekyn, and on my nece also.
O Lord! the peyne I dide hem and the wo,
Ful giltelees, by Goddes sweete pyne!
For as an hors I koude byte and whyne.
I koude pleyne, and yit was in the gilt,
Or elles often tyme hadde I been spilt.°
Whoso that first to mille comth, first grynt;°
I pleyned first, so was oure werre ystynt. 390
They were ful glade to excuse hem blyve°
Of thyng of which they nevere agilte° hir lyve.
Of wenches wolde I beren hem on honde,
Whan that for syk° unnethes myghte they stonde.

　　Yet tikled I his herte, for that he
Wende that I hadde of hym so greet chiertee!°
I swoor that al my walkynge out by nyghte
Was for t'espye wenches that he dighte;°
Under that colour° hadde I many a myrthe.
For al swich wit is yeven us in oure byrthe; 400
Deceite, wepyng, spynnyng God hath yive
To wommen kyndely,° whil that they may lyve.
And thus of o thyng I avaunte me,
Atte ende I hadde the bettre in ech degree,
By sleighte, or force, or by som maner thyng,
As by continueel murmur or grucchyng.
Namely° abedde hadden they meschaunce: 410
Ther wolde I chide, and do hem no plesaunce;
I wolde no lenger in the bed abyde,
If that I felte his arm over my syde,
Til he had maad his raunson unto me;
Thanne wolde I suffre hym do his nycetee.°

And therfore every man this tale I telle,
Wynne whoso may, for al is for to selle;
With empty hand men may none haukes lure.

420 For wynnyng wolde I al his lust endure,
And make me a feyned appetit;
And yet in bacon° hadde I nevere delit;
That made me that evere I wolde hem chide.
For thogh the pope hadde seten hem biside,
I wolde nat spare hem at hir owene bord;
For, by my trouthe, I quitte° hem word for word.
As helpe me verray God omnipotent,
Though I right now sholde make my testament,
I ne owe hem nat a word that it nys quit.

430 I broghte it so aboute by my wit
That they moste yeve it up, as for the beste,
Or elles hadde we nevere been in reste.
For thogh he looked as a wood leon,
Yet sholde he faille of his conclusion.

     Thanne wolde I seye, 'Goode lief, taak keep
How mekely looketh Wilkyn, oure sheep!
Com neer,° my spouse, lat me ba° thy cheke!
Ye sholde been al pacient and meke,
And han a sweete spiced conscience,°

440 Sith ye so preche of Jobes pacience.
Suffreth alwey, syn ye so wel kan preche;
And but ye do, certein we shal yow teche
That it is fair to have a wyf in pees.
Oon of us two moste bowen, doutelees;
And sith a man is moore resonable
Than womman is, ye moste been suffrable.
What eyleth yow to grucche thus and grone?
Is it for ye wolde have my queynte allone?
Wy, taak it al! lo, have it every deel!

450 Peter! I shrewe yow, but ye love it weel;
For if I wolde selle my *bele chose*,°
I koude walke as fressh as is a rose;
But I wol kepe it for youre owene tooth.
Ye be to blame, by God! I sey yow sooth.'
     Swiche manere wordes hadde we on honde.
Now wol I speken of my fourthe housbonde.

     My fourthe housbonde was a revelour;
This is to seyn, he hadde a paramour;
And I was yong and ful of ragerye,

460 Stibourn and strong, and joly as a pye.°
How koude I daunce to an harpe smale,
And synge, ywis, as any nyghtyngale,
Whan I had dronke a draughte of sweete wyn!
Metellius,° the foule cherl, the swyn,
That with a staf birafte his wyf hir lyf,
For she drank wyn, thogh I hadde been his wyf,
He sholde nat han daunted me fro drynke!
And after wyn on Venus moste I thynke,
For al so siker as cold engendreth hayl,
A likerous mouth moste han a likerous tayl.

In wommen vinolent° is no defence,—
This knowen lecchours by experience.
     But, Lord Crist! whan that it remembreth me
Upon my yowthe, and on my jolitee,   470
It tikleth me aboute myn herte roote.
Unto this day it dooth myn herte boote
That I have had my world as in my tyme.
But age, allas! that al wole envenyme,
Hath me biraft my beautee and my pith.
Lat go, farewel! the devel go therwith!
The flour is goon, ther is namoore to telle;
The bren,° as I best kan, now moste I selle;
But yet to be right myrie wol I fonde.
Now wol I tellen of my fourthe housbonde.   480

     I seye, I hadde in herte greet despit
That he of any oother had delit.
But he was quit, by God and by Seint Joce!°
I made hym of the same wode a croce;
Nat of my body, in no foul manere,
But certeinly, I made folk swich cheere
That in his owene grece I made hym frye
For angre, and for verray jalousye.
By God! in erthe I was his purgatorie,
For which I hope his soule be in glorie.   490
For, God it woot, he sat ful ofte and song,
Whan that his shoo ful bitterly hym wrong.
Ther was no wight, save God and he, that wiste,
In many wise, how soore I hym twiste.
He deyde whan I cam fro Jerusalem,
And lith ygrave under the roode beem,°
Al is his tombe noght so curyus
As was the sepulcre of hym Daryus,°
Which that Appelles° wroghte subtilly;
It nys but wast to burye hym preciously.   500
Lat hym fare wel, God yeve his soul reste!
He is now in his grave and in his cheste.
     Now of my fifthe housbonde wol I telle.
God lete his soule nevere come in helle!
And yet was he to me the mooste shrewe;°
That feele I on my ribbes al by rewe,
And evere shal unto myn endyng day.
But in oure bed he was so fressh and gay,
And therwithal so wel koude he me glose,°
Whan that he wolde han my *bele chose*,   510
That thogh he hadde me bete on every bon,
He koude wynne agayn my love anon.
I trowe I loved hym best, for that he
Was of his love daungerous° to me.
We wommen han, if that I shal nat lye,
In this matere a queynte° fantasye;
Wayte what° thyng we may nat lightly have,
Therafter wol we crie al day and crave.
Forbede us thyng, and that desiren we;
Preesse on us faste, and thanne wol we fle.   520

---

418 **bacon,** a slang term for old meat (hence old men)   422 **quitte,** paid back
433 **neer,** nearer   **ba,** buss, kiss lustily   435 **spiced conscience,** highly
sweetened feelings or disposition   447 **bele chose,** sexual organs   456 **pye,**
magpie   460 **Metellius, etc.** The story is taken from the words of the Roman
writer Valerius Maximus

467 **vinolent,** full of wine   478 **bren,** bran   483 **Joce,** St. Judocus of Brittany
496 **ygrave . . . roode beem,** buried under the rood beam, between the chancel
and the nave of the church   498 **Daryus,** Darius the Great, King of Persia
(522–486 B.C.)   499 **Appelles,** a Greek painter of the fourth century B.C.
505 **shrewe,** rascal   509 **glose,** cajole, flatter   514 **daungerous,** offish, fastidious   516 **queynte,** subtle, delicate   517 **Wayte what,** whatever

With daunger oute we al oure chaffare;°
Greet prees at market maketh deere ware,
And to greet cheep° is holde at litel prys:
This knoweth every womman that is wys.

My fifthe housbonde, God his soule blesse!
Which that I took for love, and no richesse,
He som tyme was a clerk of Oxenford,
And hadde left scole, and wente at hom to bord
With my gossib, dwellynge in oure toun;
530 God have hir soule! hir name was Alisoun.
She knew myn herte, and eek my privetee,
Bet° than oure parisshe preest, so moot I thee!
To hire biwreyed° I my conseil al.
For hadde myn housbonde pissed on a wal,
Or doon a thyng that sholde han cost his lyf,
To hire, and to another worthy wyf,
And to my nece, which that I loved weel,
I wolde han toold his conseil every deel.
And so I dide ful often, God it woot,
540 That made his face often reed and hoot
For verray shame, and blamed hymself for he
Had toold to me so greet a pryvetee.°

And so bifel that ones in a Lente—
So often tymes I to my gossyb wente,
For evere yet I loved to be gay,
And for to walke in March, Averill, and May,
Fro hous to hous, to heere sondry talys—
That Jankyn clerk, and my gossyb dame Alys,
And I myself, into the feeldes wente.
550 Myn housbonde was at Londoun al that Lente;
I hadde the bettre leyser° for to pleye,
And for to se, and eek for to be seye
Of lusty folk. What wiste I wher my grace
Was shapen for to be, or in what place?
Therfore I made my visitaciouns
To vigilies° and to processiouns,
To prechyng eek, and to thise pilgrimages,
To pleyes of myracles, and to mariages,
And wered upon my gaye scarlet gytes.°
560 Thise wormes, ne thise motthes, ne thise mytes,
Upon my peril, frete hem never a deel;
And wostow° why? for they were used weel.

Now wol I tellen forth what happed me.
I seye that in the feeldes walked we,
Til trewely we hadde swich daliance,
This clerk and I, that of my purveiance°
I spak to hym and seyde hym how that he,
If I were wydwe, sholde wedde me.
For certeinly, I sey for no bobance,°
570 Yet was I nevere withouten purveiance
Of mariage, n'of othere thynges eek.
I holde a mouses herte nat worth a leek
That hath but oon hole for to sterte to,

And if that faille, thanne is al ydo.
I bar hym on honde° he hadde enchanted me,—
My dame taughte me that soutiltee.
And eek I seyde I mette° of hym al nyght,
He wolde han slayn me as I lay upright,°
And al my bed was ful of verray blood;
But yet I hope that he shal do me good, 580
For blood bitokeneth gold, as me was taught.
And al was fals; I dremed of it right naught,
But as I folwed ay my dames loore,
As wel of this as of othere thynges moore.

But now, sire, lat me se, what I shal seyn?
A ha! by God, I have my tale ageyn.
Whan that my fourthe housbonde was on beere,
I weep algate,° and made sory cheere,
As wyves mooten,° for it is usage,
And with my coverchief covered my visage, 590
But for that I was purveyed of a make,
I wepte but smal, and that I undertake.°

To chirche was myn housbonde born a-morwe
With neighebores, that for hym maden sorwe;
And Jankyn, oure clerk, was oon of tho.
As help me God! whan that I saugh hym go
After the beere, me thoughte he hadde a paire
Of legges and of feet so clene and faire
That al myn herte I yaf unto his hoold.
He was, I trowe, a twenty wynter oold, 600
And I was fourty, if I shal seye sooth;
But yet I hadde alwey a coltes tooth.°
Gat-tothed I was, and that bicam me weel;
I hadde the prente of seinte Venus seel.
As help me God! I was a lusty oon,
And faire, and riche, and yong, and wel bigon;
And trewely, as myne housbondes tolde me,
I hadde the beste *quoniam*° myghte be.
For certes, I am al Venerien
In feelynge, and myn herte is Marcien. 610
Venus me yaf my lust, my likerousnesse,
And Mars yaf me my sturdy hardynesse;
Myn ascendent was Taur, and Mars therinne.°
Allas! allas! that evere love was synne!
I folwed ay myn inclinacioun
By vertu of my constellacioun;
That made me I koude noght withdrawe
My chambre of Venus° from a good felawe.
Yet have I Martes mark upon my face,
And also in another privee place. 620
For God so wys be my savacioun,
I ne loved nevere by no discrecioun,
But evere folwede myn appetit,
Al were he short, or long, or blak, or whit;
I took no kep, so that he liked me,

575 **bar hym on honde,** led him (falsely) to believe   577 **mette,** dreamed
578 **upright,** straight   588 **algate,** all the time   589 **mooten,** must   592 **undertake,** declare, state openly   602 **coltes tooth,** proverbial for a lustful disposition   608 **quoniam,** female sexual organs   613 **Myn ascendent . . . Mars
therinne.** At the time of the Wife of Bath's birth, Taurus was rising above the
horizon. Taurus is a constellation most favorable to Venus. Mars, the lover of
Venus, made with Venus a powerful and vigorous combination in respect to
planetary influence   618 **chambre of Venus,** the vulva

521 **With . . . chaffare.** In the presence of indifference we will put out all our
wares   523 **cheep,** bargain   532 **Bet,** better   533 **biwreyed,** revealed, disclosed   542 **pryvetee,** secret   551 **leyser,** leisure   556 **vigilies,** feasts and entertainments on the eve of feast days   559 **gytes,** gowns (?)   562 **wostow,** do
you know   566 **purveiance,** foresight   569 **bobance,** boast

How poore he was, ne eek of what degree.
    What sholde I seye? but, at the monthes ende,
This joly clerk, Jankyn, that was so hende,°
Hath wedded me with greet solempnytee;°
630 And to hym yaf I al the lond and fee
That evere was me yeven therbifoore.
But afterward repented me ful soore;
He nolde suffre nothyng of my list.°
By God! he smoot me ones on the lyst,°
For that I rente out of his book a leef,
That of the strook myn ere wax al deef.
Stiborn I was as is a leonesse,
And of my tonge a verray jangleresse,
And walke I wolde, as I had doon biforn,
640 From hous to hous, although he had it sworn;°
For which he often tymes wolde preche,
And me of olde Romayn geestes° teche;
How he Symplicius Gallus lefte his wyf,
And hire forsook for terme of al his lyf,
Noght but for open-heveded° he hir say
Lookynge out at his dore upon a day.
    Another Romayn tolde he me by name,
That, for his wyf was at a someres game
Withouten his wityng, he forsook hire eke.
650 And thanne wolde he upon his Bible seke
That ilke proverbe of Ecclesiaste°
Where he comandeth, and forbedeth faste,
Man shal nat suffre his wyf go roule aboute.
Thanne wolde he seye right thus, withouten doute:
    'Whoso that buyldeth his hous al of salwes,
And priketh his blynde hors over the falwes,°
And suffreth his wyf to go seken halwes,°
Is worthy to been hanged on the galwes!'
But al for noght, I sette noght an hawe°
660 Of his proverbes n'of his olde sawe,
Ne I wolde nat of hym corrected be.
I hate hym that my vices telleth me,
And so doo mo, God woot, of us than I.
This made hym with me wood al outrely;
I nolde noght forbere hym in no cas.
    Now wol I seye yow sooth, by seint Thomas,
Why that I rente out of his book a leef,
For which he smoot me so that I was deef.
    He hadde a book that gladly, nyght and day,
670 For his desport° he wolde rede alway;
He cleped it Valerie and Theofraste,°
At which book he lough alwey ful faste.
And eek ther was somtyme a clerk at Rome,
A cardinal, that highte Seint Jerome,

That made a book agayn Jovinian;
In which book eek ther was Tertulan,°
Crisippus,° Trotula,° and Helowys,°
That was abbesse nat fer fro Parys;
And eek the Parables of Salomon,°
Ovides Art,° and bookes many on,   680
And alle thise were bounden in o volume.
And every nyght and day was his custume,
Whan he hadde leyser and vacacioun
From oother worldly occupacioun,
To reden on this book of wikked wyves.
He knew of hem mo legendes and lyves
Than been of goode wyves in the Bible.
For trusteth wel, it is an impossible
That any clerk wol speke good of wyves,
But if it be of hooly seintes lyves,   690
Ne of noon oother womman never the mo.
Who peyntede the leon, tel me who?°
By God! if wommen hadde writen stories,
As clerkes han withinne hire oratories,°
They wolde han writen of men moore wikkednesse
Than al the mark of Adam° may redresse.
The children of Mercurie and of Venus°
Been in hir wirkyng ful contrarius;
Mercurie loveth wysdam and science,
And Venus loveth ryot and dispence.   700
And, for hire diverse disposicioun,
Ech falleth in otheres exaltacioun.°
And thus, God woot, Mercurie is desolat
In Pisces, wher Venus is exaltat;
And Venus falleth ther Mercurie is reysed.
Therfore no womman of no clerk is preysed.
The clerk, whan he is oold, and may noght do
Of Venus werkes worth his olde sho,
Thanne sit° he doun, and writ in his dotage
That wommen kan nat kepe hir mariage!   710
    But now to purpos, why I tolde thee
That I was beten for a book, pardee!
Upon a nyght Jankyn, that was oure sire,
Redde on his book, as he sat by the fire,
Of Eva first, that for hir wikkednesse
Was al mankynde broght to wrecchednesse,
For which that Jhesu Crist hymself was slayn,
That boghte us with his herte blood agayn.
Lo, heere expres of womman may ye fynde,
That womman was the los of al mankynde.   720

676 **Tertulan.** Tertullian (fl. 200), a Christian author of works on chastity, monogamy, and modesty   677 **Crisippus**, mentioned in the *Epistle Against Jovinian*   **Trotula**, traditionally a famous female gynecologist and obstetrician who supposedly taught in Italy in the middle of the eleventh century   **Helowys,** Eloise, the beloved of the scholiast Abelard of Paris (1079–1142)   679 **Parables of Salomon**, the *Book of Proverbs*   680 **Ovides Art**, the *Ars Amatoria* of the Roman poet Ovid (43 B.C.–A.D. 17?), an authoritative work for the Middle Ages on love and love-making   692 **Who peyntede the leon, etc.** According to Aesop's fable, a man, not a lion, painted the picture and thus the lion was justified in complaining that the picture was biased   694 **oratories,** chapels or closets for private prayers   696 **mark of Adam**, likeness of Adam, men   697 **children . . . Venus,** men and women born under Mercury and Venus, respectively. Venus governs love, Mercury governs learning, and the two are not compatible   702 **exaltacioun,** that constellation in which a given planet exerts its greatest influence on mankind. It means a desolation or weakened influence of a planet of contrary nature in the same constellation. Thus in Pisces, Venus is *exaltat* while Mercury, of contrary nature (since love and wisdom do not mix), is *desolat*   709 **sit,** sits

628 **hende,** graceful, gracious   629 **solempnytee,** pomp and ceremony
633 **He nolde . . . list.** He would not stand for what I wanted   634 **lyst,** ears
640 **sworn,** forbidden   642 **Romayn geestes,** stories from Roman history. Most of the tales told by the Wife of Bath are derived from Valerius Maximus
645 **open-heveded,** bareheaded   651 **Ecclesiaste,** the Apocryphal *Book of Ecclesiasticus;* see *Ecclesiasticus,* 22:25   656 **falwes,** fallow ground   657 **seken halwes,** visit shrines on a pilgrimage   659 **hawe,** the fruit of the hawthorn tree   670 **desport,** amusement   671 **Valerie . . . Theofraste.** Jankyn evidently had a manuscript containing Walter Map's *Epistle of Valerius to Rufinus, Not to Marry,* included in his celebrated Anglo-Latin miscellany, *De Nugis Curialium,* and Theophrastus' *Liber de Nuptiis.* Chaucer evidently was familiar with these works and with the *Epistle Against Jovinian* by St. Jerome (340?–420)

Geoffrey Chaucer   **99**

Tho redde he me how Sampson loste his heres:
Slepynge, his lemman kitte it with hir sheres;
Thurgh which treson loste he bothe his yen.

Tho redde he me, if that I shal nat lyen,
Of Hercules and of his Dianyre,
That caused hym to sette hymself afyre.

No thyng forgat he the care and the wo
That Socrates hadde with his wyves two;
How Xantippa° caste pisse upon his heed.
730 This sely° man sat stille as he were deed;
He wiped his heed, namoore dorste he seyn,
But 'Er that thonder stynte, comth a reyn!'

Of Phasipha,° that was the queene of Crete,
For shrewednesse, hym thoughte the tale swete;
Fy! spek namoore—it is a grisly thyng—
Of hire horrible lust and hir likyng.

Of Clitermystra, for hire lecherye,
That falsly made hire housbonde for to dye,
He redde it with ful good devocioun.
740 He tolde me eek for what occasioun
Amphiorax at Thebes loste his lyf.
Myn housbonde hadde a legende of his wyf,
Eriphilem, that for an ouche of gold
Hath prively unto the Grekes told
Wher that hir housbonde hidde hym in a place,
For which he hadde at Thebes sory grace.

Of Lyvia° tolde he me, and of Lucye:°
They bothe made hir housbondes for to dye;
That oon for love, that oother was for hate.
750 Lyvia hir housbonde, on an even late,
Empoysoned hath, for that she was his fo;
Lucia, likerous, loved hire housbonde so
That, for he sholde alwey upon hire thynke,
She yaf hym swich a manere love-drynke
That he was deed er it were by the morwe;
And thus algates° housbondes han sorwe.

Thanne tolde he me how oon Latumyus°
Compleyned unto his felawe Arrius
That in his gardyn growed swich a tree
760 On which he seyde how that his wyves thre
Hanged hemself for herte despitus.
'O leeve brother,' quod this Arrius,
'Yif me a plante of thilke blissed tree,
And in my gardyn planted shal it bee.'

Of latter date, of wyves hath he red
That somme han slayn hir housbondes in hir bed,
And lete hir lecchour dighte hire al the nyght,°
Whan that the corps lay in the floor upright.
And somme han dryve nayles in hir brayn,°
770 Whil that they slepte, and thus they had hem slayn.
Somme han hem yeve poysoun in hire drynke.

He spak moore harm than herte may bithynke;
And therwithal he knew of mo proverbes
Than in this world ther growen gras or herbes.
'Bet is,'° quod he, 'thyn habitacioun
Be with a leon or a foul dragoun,
Than with a womman usynge for to chyde.'
'Bet is,'° quod he, 'hye in the roof abyde,
Than with an angry wyf doun in the hous;
They been so wikked and contrarious,   780
They haten that hir housbondes loven ay.'
He seyde, 'a womman° cast hir shame away,
Whan she cast of hir smok;' and forthermo,
'A fair womman, but she be chaast also,
Is lyk a gold ryng in a sowes nose.'°
Who wolde wene, or who wolde suppose,
The wo that in myn herte was, and pyne?

And whan I saugh he wolde nevere fyne
To reden on this cursed book al nyght,
Al sodeynly thre leves have I plyght°   790
Out of his book, right as he radde, and eke
I with my fest so took hym on the cheke
That in oure fyr he fil bakward adoun.
And he up stirte° as dooth a wood leoun,
And with his fest he smoot me on the heed,
That in the floor I lay as I were deed.
And whan he saugh how stille that I lay,
He was agast, and wolde han fled his way,
Til atte laste out of my swogh° I breyde.
'O! hastow slayn me, false theef?' I seyde,   800
'And for my land thus hastow mordred me?
Er I be deed, yet wol I kisse thee.'

And neer he cam, and kneled faire adoun,
And seyde, 'Deere suster Alisoun,
As help me God! I shal thee nevere smyte.
That I have doon, it is thyself to wyte.°
Foryeve it me, and that I thee biseke!'
And yet eftsoones I hitte hym on the cheke,
And seyde, 'Theef, thus muchel am I wreke;
Now wol I dye, I may no lenger spede.'   810
But atte laste, with muchel care and wo,
We fille acorded by us selven two.
He yaf me al the bridel in myn hond,
To han the governance of hous and lond,
And of his tonge, and of his hond also;
And made hym brenne his book anon right tho.
And whan that I hadde geten unto me,
By maistrie, al the soveraynetee,
And that he seyde, 'Myn owene trewe wyf,
Do as thee lust the terme of al thy lyf;   820
Keep thyn honour, and keep eek myn estaat'—
After that day we hadden never debaat.
God helpe me so, I was to hym as kynde
As any wyf from Denmark unto Ynde,
And also trewe, and so was he to me.

---

729 **Xantippa,** wife of Socrates   730 **sely,** wretched and innocent, "poor"
733 **Phasipha,** wife of King Minos of Crete; according to classical legend she
conceived a violent passion for a bull, by which she gave birth to the monster
Minotaur   747 **Lyvia,** a Roman woman who poisoned Drusus in the reign of the
Emperor Tiberius (A.D. 23)   **Lucye,** the wife of the Roman poet Lucretius (96?–55
B.C.); according to tradition, she inadvertently poisoned her husband by giving
him what she thought was an aphrodisiac   756 **algates,** always
757 **Latumyus, etc.,** from Walter Map's *Epistle of Valerius* (see note to l. 671); it is
not known precisely who Latumius was   766–767 **somme . . . al the nyght,** evidently the tale of the Matron of Ephesus in a variant form   769 **somme . . .
brayn,** the tale of Jael and Sisera; see *Judges,* 4:21

775 **Bet is, etc.,** quoted from *Ecclesiasticus,* 25:16   778 **Bet is, etc.,** quoted from
Proverbs, 21:9–10   782 **woman, etc.,** quoted from St. Jerome   784 **A fair . . .
sowes nose,** quoted from *Proverbs,* 11:22   790 **plyght,** plucked, tore out
794 **stirte,** started, leaped   799 **swogh,** swoon, faint   806 **wyte,** blame

I prey to God, that sit in magestee,
So blesse his soule for his mercy deere.
Now wol I seye my tale, if ye wol heere."

BIHOLDE THE WORDES BITWENE
THE SOMONOUR AND THE FRERE.

The Frere lough,° whan he hadde herd al this;
830 "Now dame," quod he, "so have I joye or blis,
This is a long preamble of a tale!"
And whan the Somonour herde the Frere gale,°
"Lo," quod the Somonour, "Goddes armes two!
A frere wol entremette° hym everemo.
Lo, goode men, a flye and eek a frere
Wol falle in every dyssh and eek mateere.
What spekestow of preambulacioun?°
What! amble, or trotte, or pees, or go sit doun!
Thou lettest° oure disport in this manere."
840 "Ye, woltow so, sire Somonour?" quod the Frere;
"Now, by my feith, I shal, er that I go,
Telle of a somonour swich a tale or two,
That alle the folk shal laughen in this place."
"Now elles, Frere, I bishrewe° thy face,"
Quod this Somonour, "and I bishrewe me,
But if I telle tales two or thre
Of freres, er I come to Sidyngborne,°
That I shal make thyn herte for to morne,
For wel I woot thy pacience is gon."
850 Oure Hooste cride "Pees! and that anon!"
And seyde, "Lat the womman telle hire tale.
Ye fare as folk that dronken ben of ale.
Do, dame, telle forth youre tale, and that is best."
"Al redy, sire," quod she, "right as yow lest,
If I have licence of this worthy Frere."
"Yis,° dame," quod he, "tel forth, and I wol
heere."

THE WIFE OF BATH'S TALE

In th'olde dayes of the Kyng Arthour,
Of which that Britons speken greet honour,
Al was this land fulfild of fayerye.°
860 The elf-queene, with hir joly compaignye,
Daunced ful ofte in many a grene mede.
This was the olde opinion, as I rede;
I speke of manye hundred yeres ago.
But now kan no man se none elves mo,

For now the grete charitee° and prayeres
Of lymytours° and othere hooly freres,
That serchen every lond and every streem,
As thikke as motes in the sonne-beem,
Blessynge halles, chambres, kichenes, boures,°
Citees, burghes, castels, hye toures,   870
Thropes,° bernes, shipnes,° dayeryes—
This maketh that ther ben no fayeryes.
For ther as wont to walken was an elf,
Ther walketh now the lymytour hymself
In undermeles° and in morwenynges,
And seyth his matyns and his hooly thynges
As he gooth in his lymytacioun.
Wommen may go now saufly up and doun.
In every bussh or under every tree
Ther is noon oother incubus but he,   880
And he ne wol doon hem but dishonour.°
And so bifel it that this kyng Arthour
Hadde in his hous a lusty bacheler,
That on a day cam ridynge fro ryver;°
And happed that, allone as he was born,
He saugh a mayde walkynge hym biforn,
Of which mayde anon, maugree hir heed,°
By verray force, he rafte° hire maydenhed;
For which oppressioun was swich clamour
And swich pursute unto the kyng Arthour,   890
That dampned was this knyght for to be deed,
By cours of lawe, and sholde han lost his heed—
Paraventure swich was the statut tho—
But that the queene and othere ladyes mo
So longe preyeden the kyng of grace,
Til he his lyf hym graunted in the place,
And yaf hym to the queene, al at hir wille,
To chese wheither she wolde hym save or spille.°
The queene thanketh the kyng with al hir myght,
And after this thus spak she to the knyght,   900
Whan that she saugh hir tyme, upon a day:
"Thou standest yet," quod she, "in swich array
That of thy lyf yet hastow no suretee.
I grante thee lyf, if thou kanst tellen me°
What thyng is it that wommen moost desiren.
Be war, and keep thy nekke-boon from iren!
And if thou kanst nat tellen it anon,
Yet wol I yeve thee leve for to gon
A twelf-month and a day, to seche° and leere°
An answere suffisant in this mateere;   910
And suretee wol I han, er that thou pace,
Thy body for to yelden in this place."
Wo was this knyght, and sorwefully he siketh;
But what! he may nat do al as hym liketh.

829 **lough,** laughed   832 **gale,** cry out, exclaim   834 **entremette,** interfere, insert (himself)   837 **preambulacioun,** a play on *preamble* (1. 831) and *perambulation*   839 **lettest,** hinder. The interchange between Friar and Summoner is preliminary to their quarrel; the two proceed, after the Wife of Bath has finished her tale, to tell stories derogatory to each other's profession   844 **bishrewe,** curse   847 **Sidyngborne,** a town forty miles from London on the old Canterbury road; the pilgrims were more than halfway along their journey   856 **yis,** yes indeed   859 **fayerye,** the great company of fairies   865 **charitee,** Christian love. The whole passage is bitterly sarcastic

866 **lymytours,** friars granted licenses to beg within certain territories or limits   869 **boures,** the sleeping quarters in medieval castles   871 **Thropes,** villages   **shipnes,** stables, sheds   875 **undermeles,** afternoon   880-881 **incubus . . . dishonour.** In folklore, the incubus, a demoniac spirit that visited mortals in the form of a nightmare, was likely to impregnate a woman found in the woods. But, says the Wife, now the friars have chased away the incubi through their prayers and exorcisms, and the only remaining danger to a woman was violation, since the friar would be incapable of impregnating her   884 **fro ryver,** from hawking or fowling by the river   887 **maugree hir heed,** in spite of her   888 **rafte,** took away   898 **spille,** destroy   904 **I grante . . . tellen me,** the so-called Sphinx motif in folklore   909 **seche,** seek   **leere,** learn

Geoffrey Chaucer **101**

And at the laste he chees hym for to wende,
And come agayn, right at the yeres ende,
With swich answere as God wolde hym purveye;
And taketh his leve, and wendeth forth his weye.

He seketh every hous and every place
920 Where as he hopeth for to fynde grace,
To lerne what thyng wommen loven moost;
But he ne koude arryven in no coost°
Wher as he myghte fynde in this mateere
Two creatures accordynge in-feere.°
Somme seyde wommen loven best richesse,
Somme seyde honour, somme seyde jolynesse,
Somme riche array, somme seyden lust abedde,
And oftetyme to be wydwe and wedde.
Somme seyde that oure hertes been moost esed
930 Whan that we been yflatered and yplesed.
He gooth ful ny the sothe, I wol nat lye.
A man shal wynne us best with flaterye;
And with attendance, and with bisynesse,
Been we ylymed,° bothe moore and lesse.

And somme seyen that we loven best
For to be free, and do right as us lest,
And that no man repreve us of oure vice,
But seye that we be wise, and no thyng nyce.
For trewely ther is noon of us alle,
940 If any wight wol clawe us on the galle,°
That we nel kike, for he seith us sooth.
Assay, and he shal fynde it that so dooth;
For, be we never so vicious withinne,
We wol been holden° wise and clene of synne.

And somme seyn that greet delit han we
For to been holden stable, and eek secree,°
And in o purpos stedefastly to dwelle,
And nat biwreye thyng that men us telle.
But that tale is nat worth a rake-stele.°
950 Pardee, we wommen konne no thyng hele;
Witnesse on Myda,°—wol ye heere the tale?

Ovyde, amonges othere thynges smale,
Seyde Myda hadde, under his longe heres,
Growynge upon his heed two asses eres,
The whiche vice he hydde, as he best myghte,
Ful subtilly from every mannes sighte,
That, save his wyf, ther wiste of it namo.
He loved hire moost, and trusted hire also;
He preyede hire that to no creature
960 She sholde tellen of his disfigure.

She swoor him, "Nay," for al this world to wynne,
She nolde do that vileynye or synne,
To make hir housbonde han so foul a name.
She nolde nat telle it for hir owene shame.
But nathelees, hir thoughte that she dyde,°

That she so longe sholde a conseil hyde;
Hir thoughte it swal so soore aboute hir herte
That nedely som word hire moste asterte;
And sith she dorste telle it to no man,
Doun to a mareys° faste by she ran— 970
Til she cam there, hir herte was a-fyre—
And as a bitore° bombleth in the myre,
She leyde hir mouth unto the water doun:
"Biwreye me nat, thou water, with thy soun,"
Quod she; "to thee I telle it and namo;
Myn housbonde hath longe asses erys two!
Now is myn herte al hool, now is it oute.
I myghte no lenger kepe it, out of doute.
Heere may ye se, thogh we a tyme abyde,
Yet out it moot; we kan no conseil hyde. 980
The remenant of the tale° if ye wol heere,
Redeth Ovyde, and ther ye may it leere.

This knyght, of which my tale is specially,
Whan that he saugh he myghte nat come therby,
This is to seye, what wommen love moost,
Withinne his brest ful sorweful was the goost.
But hoom he gooth, he myghte nat sojourne;
The day was come that homward moste he tourne
And in his wey it happed hym to ryde,
In al this care, under a forest syde, 990
Wher as he saugh upon a daunce go
Of ladyes foure and twenty,° and yet mo;
Toward the whiche daunce he drow ful yerne,°
In hope that som wysdom sholde he lerne.
But certeinly, er he cam fully there,
Vanysshed was this daunce, he nyste where.
No creature saugh he that bar lyf,
Save on the grene he saugh sittynge a wyf—
A fouler wight ther may no man devyse.
Agayn° the knyght this olde wyf gan ryse, 1000
And seyde, "Sire knyght, heer forth ne lith no wey.
Tel me what that ye seken, by youre fey!
Paraventure it may the bettre be;
Thise olde folk kan° muchel thyng," quod she.

"My leeve mooder," quod this knyght, "certeyn
I nam but deed,° but if° that I kan seyn
What thyng it is that wommen moost desire.
Koude ye me wisse,° I wolde wel quite youre hire."

"Plight me thy trouthe heere in myn hand," quod
she,
"The nexte thyng that I requere thee, 1010
Thou shalt it do, if it lye in thy myght,
And I wol telle it yow er it be nyght."

"Have heer my trouthe," quod the knyght, "I
grante."

"Thanne," quod she, "I dar me wel avante
Thy lyf is sauf; for I wol stonde therby,

922 **in no coost,** no matter what the expense or effort   924 **in-feere,** together
934 **ylymed,** caught with lime. The metaphor is taken from fowling   940 **clawe
. . . galle,** hit or rub us on a sore spot   944 **holden,** considered   946 **secree,**
discreet   949 **rake-stele,** the handle of a rake   951 **Myda, etc.** The story is tak-
en from Ovid's *Metamorphoses,* but Ovid says it was Midas' barber who could
not keep a secret, not his wife. Possibly Jankyn had twisted the tale in this way to
suit his thesis of the unreliability of women   965 **hir thoughte . . . dyde.** She
thought that she would die (if she could not unburden herself of her secret)

970 **mareys,** marsh, swamp   972 **bitore,** bittern, a small bird of the heron family   981 **remenant of the tale.** The reeds about the marsh caught up the words
and repeated them in their rustling, so that the whole world eventually came to
know Midas' secret   991–992 **daunce . . . foure and twenty.** The twenty-four
ladies constituted a fairy "ring," a commonplace of Celtic tales   993 **yerne,** eagerly   1000 **Agayn,** towards   1004 **kan,** know   1006 **I nam but deed,** I shall
be (naught) but dead   **but if,** unless   1008 **wisse,** inform

Upon my lyf, the queene wol seye as I.
Lat se which is the proudeste of hem alle,
That wereth on° a coverchief or a calle,
That dar seye nay of that I shal thee teche.
1020 Lat us go forth, withouten lenger speche.''
Tho rowned she a pistel° in his ere,
And bad hym to be glad, and have no fere.
  Whan they be comen to the court, this knyght
Seyde he had holde his day,° as he hadde hight,
And redy was his answere, as he sayde.
Ful many a noble wyf, and many a mayde,
And many a wydwe, for that they been wise,
The queene hirself sittynge as a justise,
Assembled been, his answere for to heere;
1030 And afterward this knyght was bode appeere.
  To every wight comanded was silence,
And that the knyght sholde telle in audience
What thyng that worldly wommen loven best.
This knyght ne stood nat stille as doth a best,°
But to his questioun anon answerde
With manly voys, that al the court it herde:
  "My lige lady, generally," quod he,
"Wommen desiren to have sovereynetee
1040 And for to been in maistrie hym above.
This is youre mooste desir, thogh ye me kille.
Dooth as yow list; I am heer at youre wille."
In al the court ne was ther wyf, ne mayde,
Ne wydwe, that contraried that he sayde,
But seyden he was worthy han his lyf.
  And with that word up stirte the olde wyf,
Which that the knyght saugh sittynge on the grene:
"Mercy," quod she, "my sovereyn lady queene!
Er that youre court departe, do me right.
1050 I taughte this answere unto the knyght;
For which he plighte me his trouthe there,
The firste thyng that I wolde hym requere,
He wolde it do, if it lay in his myghte.
Bifore the court thanne preye I thee, sir knyght,"
Quod she, "that thou me take unto thy wyf;
For wel thou woost that I have kept thy lyf.
If I seye fals, sey nay, upon thy fey!''
  This knyght answerde, "Allas! and weylawey!
I woot right wel that swich was my biheste.
1060 For Goddes love, as chees° a newe requeste!
Taak al my good, and lat my body go.''
  "Nay, thanne," quod she, "I shrewe us bothe two!
For thogh that I be foul, and oold, and poore,
I nolde for al the metal, ne for oore,
That under erthe is grave, or lith above,
But if thy wyf I were, and eek thy love.''
  "My love?" quod he, "nay, my dampnacioun!
Allas! that any of my nacioun°
Sholde evere so foule disparaged be!''

But al for noght; the ende is this, that he   1070
Constreyned was, he nedes moste hire wedde;
And taketh his olde wyf, and gooth to bedde.
  Now wolden som men seye, paraventure,
That for my necligence I do no cure
To tellen yow the joye and al th'array
That at the feeste was that ilke day.
To which thyng shortly answeren I shal:
I seye ther nas no joye ne feeste at al;
Ther nas but hevynesse and muche sorwe.
For prively he wedded hire on the morwe,   1080
And al day after hidde hym as an owle,
So wo was hym, his wyf looked so foule.
  Greet was the wo the knyght hadde in his thoght,
Whan he was with his wyf abedde ybroght;
He walweth and he turneth to and fro.
His olde wyf lay smylynge everemo,
And seyde, "O deere housbonde, benedicitee!
Fareth every knyght thus with his wyf as ye?
Is this the lawe of kyng Arthures hous?
Is every knyght of his so dangerous?°   1090
I am youre owene love and eek youre wyf;
I am she which that saved hath youre lyf,
And, certes, yet ne dide I yow nevere unright;
Why fare ye thus with me this firste nyght?
Ye faren lyk a man had lost his wit.
What is my gilt? For Goddes love, tel me it,
And it shal been amended, if I may.''
  "Amended?" quod this knyght, "allas! nay, nay!
It wol nat been amended nevere mo.
Thou art so loothly, and so oold also,   1100
And therto comen of so lough° a kynde,
That litel wonder is thogh I walwe and wynde.
So wolde God myn herte wolde breste!''
  "Is this," quod she, "the cause of youre unreste?''
  "Ye, certeinly," quod he, "no wonder is.''
  "Now, sire," quod she, "I koude amende al this,
If that me liste, er it were dayes thre,
So wel ye myghte bere yow unto me.
  But, for ye speken of swich gentillesse
As is descended out of old richesse,   1110
That therfore sholden ye be gentil men,
Swich arrogance is nat worth an hen.
Looke who° that is moost vertuous alway,
Pryvee and apert, and moost entendeth ay
To do the gentil dedes that he kan;
Taak hym for the grettest gentil man.
Crist wole we clayme of hym oure gentillesse,
Nat of oure eldres for hire old richesse.
For thogh they yeve us al hir heritage,
For which we clayme to been of heigh parage,   1120
Yet may they nat biquethe, for no thyng,
To noon of us hir vertuous lyvyng,
That made hem gentil men ycalled be,
And bad us folwen hem in swich degree.

1018 **wereth on**, wears 1021 **rowned . . . pistel**, whispered a message
1024 **holde his day**, kept his appointed day 1034 **best**, beast, animal
1060 **as chees**, choose 1068 **nacioun**, probably meaning "lineage" here

1090 **dangerous**, fussy, overparticular 1101 **lough**, low 1113 **Looke who**, whoever

Wel kan the wise poete of Florence,
That highte Dant,° speken in this sentence.
Lo, in swich maner rym is Dantes tale:
'Ful selde up riseth by his branches smale
Prowesse of man, for God, of his goodnesse,
Wole that of hym we clayme oure gentillesse';
For of oure eldres may we no thyng clayme
But temporel thyng, that man may hurte and mayme.

Eek every wight woot this as wel as I,
If gentillesse were planted natureelly
Unto a certeyn lynage doun the lyne,
Pryvee and apert, thanne wolde they nevere fyne
To doon of gentillesse the faire office;
They myghte do no vileynye or vice.

Taak fyr, and ber it in the derkeste hous
Bitwix this and the mount of Kaukasous,
And lat men shette the dores and go thenne,
Yet wole the fyr as faire lye and brenne°
As twenty thousand men myghte it biholde;
His office° natureel ay wol it holde,
Up peril of my lyf, til that it dye.

Heere may ye se wel how that genterye
Is nat annexed to possessioun,
Sith folk ne doon hir operacioun
Alwey, as dooth the fyr, lo, in his kynde.
For, God it woot, men may wel often fynde
A lordes sone do shame and vileynye;
And he that wole han pris of his gentrye,
For he was boren of a gentil hous,
And hadde his eldres noble and vertuous,
And nel° hymselven do no gentil dedis,
Ne folwen his gentil auncestre that deed is,
He nys nat gentil, be he duc or erl;
For vileyns synful dedes make a cherl.
For gentillesse nys but renomee
Of thyne auncestres, for hire heigh bountee,
Which is a strange thyng to thy persone.
Thy gentillesse cometh fro God allone.°
Thanne comth oure verray gentillesse of grace;
It was no thyng° biquethe us with oure place.

Thenketh hou noble, as seith Valerius,
Was thilke Tullius Hostillius,
That out of poverte roos to heigh noblesse.
Reedeth Senek,° and redeth eek Boece;
Ther shul ye seen expres that it no drede is
That he is gentil that dooth gentil dedis.
And therfore, leeve housbonde, I thus conclude:
Al were it that myne auncestres were rude,
Yet may the hye God, and so hope I,
Grante me grace to lyven vertuously.
Thanne am I gentil, whan that I bigynne
To lyven vertuously and weyve° synne.

And ther as ye of poverte me repreeve,
The hye God, on whom that we bileeve,
In wilful poverte chees to lyve his lyf.
And certes every man, mayden, or wyf,   1180
May understonde that Jhesus, hevene kyng,
Ne wolde nat chese a vicious lyvyng.
Glad poverte is an honest thyng, certeyn;
This wole Senec and othere clerkes seyn.
Whoso that halt hym payd of his poverte,
I holde hym riche, al° hadde he nat a sherte.
He that coveiteth is a povre wight,
For he wolde han that is nat in his myght;
But he that noght hath, ne coveiteth have,
Is riche, although ye holde hym but a knave.   1190
Verray poverte, it syngeth proprely;
Juvenal° seith of poverte myrily:
'The povre man, whan he goth by the weye,
Bifore the theves he may synge and pleye.'
Poverte is hateful good and, as I gesse,
A ful greet bryngere out of bisynesse;
A greet amendere eek of sapience
To hym that taketh it in pacience.
Poverte is this, although it seme alenge,°
Possessioun that no wight wol chalenge.   1200
Poverte ful ofte, whan a man is lowe,
Maketh his God and eek hymself to knowe.
Poverte a spectacle° is, as thynketh me,
Thurgh which he may his verray freendes see.
And therfore, sire, syn that I noght yow greve,
Of my poverte namoore ye me repreve.

Now, sire, of elde ye repreve me;
And certes, sire, thogh noon auctoritee
Were in no book, ye gentils of honour
Seyn that men sholde an oold wight doon favour,   1210
And clepe hym fader, for youre gentillesse;
And auctours shal I fynden, as I gesse.

Now ther ye seye that I am foul and old,
Than drede you noght to been a cokewold;°
For filthe and eelde, also moot I thee,
Been grete wardeyns upon chastitee.
But nathelees, syn I knowe youre delit,
I shal fulfille youre worldly appetit.

Chese now," quod she, "oon of thise thynges
   tweye:
To han me foul and old til that I deye,   1220
And be to yow a trewe, humble wyf,
And nevere yow displese in al my lyf;
Or elles ye wol han me yong and fair,
And take youre aventure° of the repair
That shal be to youre hous by cause of me,
Or in som oother place, may wel be.
Now chese yourselven, wheither that yow liketh."

This knyght avyseth hym and sore siketh,°
But atte laste he seyde in this manere:

1126 **Dant, etc.** see Dante's *Convivio,* IV, 15ff.   1142 **lye and brenne,** blaze
1144 **office,** function   1155 **nel,** will not   1159–1162 **For gentilesse . . . allone.** For, as far as your ancestors are concerned, only the renown of their names
contributes to *gentilesse* (that is, only the renown that comes from their noble
deeds and ideals), and that is a matter foreign to yourself. Only God can give you
true *gentilesse*   1164 **no thyng,** not at all   1168 **Senek,** Seneca, Roman
philosopher, teacher, and dramatist (4 B.C.–A.D. 65)   1176 **weyve,** avoid

1186 **al,** although   1192 **Juvenal,** Roman satirist (60?–140?). It is unlikely that
Chaucer knew his works directly, but sayings of Roman poets circulated in the
Middle Ages in anthologies of quotations, or *florilegia*   1199 **alenge,** wretched
miserable   1203 **spectacle,** a reading or looking glass   1214 **cokewold,** cuckold
1224 **aventure,** chances   1228 **siketh,** sighs

"My lady and my love, and wyf so deere,   1230
I put me in youre wise governance;
Cheseth youreself which may be moost plesance,
And moost honour to yow and me also.
I do no fors the wheither of the two;
For as yow liketh, it suffiseth me."
    "Thanne have I gete of yow maistrie," quod she,
"Syn I may chese and governe as me lest?"
    "Ye, certes, wyf," quod he, "I holde it best."
    "Kys me," quod she, "we be no lenger wrothe;
For, by my trouthe, I wol be to yow bothe,   1240
This is to seyn, ye, bothe fair and good.
I prey to God that I moote sterven wood,°
But I to yow be also good and trewe
As evere was wyf, syn that the world was newe.
And but I be to-morn as fair to seene
As any lady, emperice, or queene,
That is bitwixe the est and eke the west,
Dooth with my lyf and deth right as yow lest.
Cast up the curtyn, looke how that it is."
    And whan the knyght saugh verraily al this,   1250
That she so fair was, and so yong therto,
For joye he hente° hire in his armes two,
His herte bathed in a bath of blisse,
A thousand tyme a-rewe° he gan hire kisse,
And she obeyed hym in every thyng
That myghte doon hym plesance or likyng.

    And thus they lyve unto hir lyves ende
In parfit joye; and Jhesu Crist us sende
Housbondes meeke, yonge, and fressh abedde,
And grace t'overbyde° hem that we wedde;   1260
And eek I praye Jhesu shorte hir lyves
That wol nat be governed by hir wyves;
And olde and angry nygardes of dispence,
God sende hem soone verray pestilence!

THE CLERK'S TALE

Ther is, right at the west syde of Ytaille,
Doun at the roote of Vesulus° the colde,
A lusty° playn, habundant of vitaille,°
Where many a tour and toun thou mayst biholde,
That founded were in tyme of fadres olde,
And many another delitable sighte,
And Saluces° this noble contree highte.°

    A markys° whilom° lord was of that lond,
As were his worthy eldres hym bifore,
And obeisant, ay redy to his hond,   10
Were alle his liges,° bothe lasse and moore.
Thus in delit he lyveth, and hath doon yoore,

Biloved and drad,° thurgh favour of Fortune,
Bothe of his lordes and of his commune.

    Therwith he was, so speke as of lynage,
The gentilleste° yborn of Lumbardye,
A fair persone, and strong, and yong of age,
And ful of honour and of curteisye;
Discreet ynogh his contree for to gye,
Save in somme thynges that he was to blame;   20
And Walter was this yonge lordes name.

    I blame hym thus, that he considered noght
In tyme comynge what myghte hym bityde,°
But on his lust° present was al his thoght,
As for to hauke and hunte on every syde.
Wel ny alle othere cures leet he slyde,°
And eek he nolde°—and that was worst of alle—
Wedde no wyf, for noght that may bifalle.

    Oonly that point his peple bar so soore
That flokmeele° on a day they to hym wente,   30
And oon of hem, that wisest was of loore—
Or elles that the lord best wolde assente
That he sholde telle hym what his peple mente,
Or elles koude he shewe wel swich mateere—
He to the markys seyde as ye shul heere:

    "O noble markys, youre humanitee
Asseureth us and yeveth us hardinesse,°
As ofte as tyme is of necessitee,
That we to yow mowe telle oure hevynesse.
Accepteth, lord, now of youre gentillesse   40
That we with pitous herte unto yow pleyne,°
And lat youre eres nat my voys desdeyne.

    "Al have I noght to doone in this mateere
Moore than another man hath in this place,
Yet for as muche as ye, my lord so deere,
Han alwey shewed me favour and grace
I dar the bettre aske of yow a space
Of audience, to shewen oure requeste,
And ye, my lord, to doon right as yow leste.

    "For certes, lord, so wel us liketh yow°   50
And al youre werk, and evere han doon, that we
Ne koude nat us self devysen how
We myghte lyven in moore felicitee,
Save o thyng, lord, if it youre wille be,
That for to been a wedded man yow leste;
Thanne were youre peple in sovereyn hertes reste.

    "Boweth youre nekke under that blisful yok
Of soveraynetee, noght of servyse,

1242 **sterven wood,** die mad   1252 **hente,** seized   1254 **a-rewe,** in a row, in
succession   1260 **t'overbyde,** dominate
The Clerk's Tale 2 **Vesulus,** Monte Viso in the Maritime Alps   3 **lusty,** pleasant
vitaille, provisions   7 **Saluces,** Saluzzo   **highte,** was called or named   8 **markys,** marquis   **whilom,** formerly, once upon a time   11 **liges,** subjects

13 **drad,** feared   16 **gentilleste,** the most well-bred, most worthy   23 **bityde,**
happen   24 **lust,** pleasure   26 **slyde,** pass away   27 **nolde,** would not
30 **flokmeele,** in a crowd   37 **hardinesse,** boldness, assurance   41 **pleyne,** lament or complain   50 **us liketh yow,** you please us

Which that men clepe spousaille or wedlok;
60 And thenketh, lord, among youre thoghtes wyse
How that oure dayes passe in sondry wyse;
For thogh we slepe, or wake, or rome, or ryde,
Ay fleeth the tyme; it nyl no man abyde.

"And thogh youre grene youthe floure as yit,
In crepeth age alwey, as stille as stoon,
And deeth manaceth° every age, and smyt
In ech estaat, for ther escapeth noon;
And al so certein as we knowe echoon
That we shul deye, as uncerteyn we alle
70 Been of that day whan deeth shal on us falle.

"Accepteth thanne of us the trewe entente,
That nevere yet refuseden thyn heeste,°
And we wol, lord, if that ye wole assente,
Chese yow a wyf, in short tyme atte leeste,
Born of the gentilleste and of the meeste
Of al this land, so that it oghte seme
Honour to God and yow, as we kan deeme.

"Delivere us out of al this bisy° drede,
And taak a wyf, for hye Goddes sake!
80 For if it so bifelle, as God forbede,
That thurgh youre deeth youre lynage sholde slake,°
And that a straunge successour sholde take
Youre heritage, O, wo were us alyve!
Wherfore we pray you hastily to wyve."

Hir meeke preyere and hir pitous cheere°
Made the markys herte han pitee.
"Ye wol," quod he, "myn owene peple deere,
To that I nevere erst thoughte streyne me.°
I me rejoysed of my liberte,
90 That seelde° tyme is founde in mariage;
Ther I was free, I moot been in servage.

"But nathelees I se youre trewe entente,
And truste upon youre wit, and have doon ay;
Wherfore of my free wyl I wole assente
To wedde me, as soone as evere I may.
But ther as ye han profred me to-day
To chese me a wyf, I yow relesse°
That choys, and prey yow of that profre cesse.

"For God it woot, that children ofte been
100 Unlyk hir worthy eldres hem bifore;
Bountee comth al of God, nat of the streen°
Of which they been engendred and ybore.
I truste in Goddes bountee, and therfore

My mariage and myn estaat and reste
I hym bitake; he may doon as hym leste.

"Lat me allone° in chesynge of my wyf,—
That charge upon my bak I wole endure.
But I yow preye, and charge upon youre lyf,
That what wyf that I take, ye me assure
To worshipe hire, whil that hir lyf may dure,°   110
In word and werk, bothe heere and everywheere
As she an emperoures doghter weere.

"And forthermoore, this shal ye swere, that ye
Agayn my choys shul neither grucche° ne stryve
For sith° I shal forgoon my libertee   115
At youre requeste, as evere moot I thryve,
Ther as myn herte is set, ther wol I wyve;
And but ye wole assente in swich manere,
I prey yow, speketh namoore of this matere."

With hertely° wyl they sworen and assenten   120
To al this thyng, ther seyde no wight nay;
Bisekynge hym of grace, er that they wenten,
That he wolde graunten hem a certein day
Of his spousaille,° as soone as evere he may;
For yet alwey the peple somwhat dredde,
Lest that the markys no wyf wolde wedde.

He graunted hem a day, swich as hym leste,
On which he wolde be wedded sikerly,
And seyde he dide al this at hir requeste.
And they, with humble entente, buxomly,   130
Knelynge upon hir knees ful reverently,
Hym thonken alle; and thus they han an ende
Of hire entente, and hoom agayn they wende.

And heerupon he to his officeres
Comaundeth for the feste to purveye,°
And to his privee knyghtes and squieres
Swich charge yaf as hym liste on hem leye;
And they to his comandement obeye,
And ech of hem dooth al his diligence
To doon unto the feeste reverence.   140

Explicit prima pars.
Incipit secunda pars.

Noght fer fro thilke paleys honurable,
Wher as this markys shoop° his mariage,
There stood a throop,° of site delitable,
In which that povre folk of that village
Hadden hir beestes and hir herbergage,°

---

66 **manaceth,** menaces   72 **heeste,** command   78 **bisy,** anxious   81 **slake,**
cease   84 **cheere,** appearance, behavior   88 **streyne me,** to force myself
90 **seelde,** seldom   97 **I yow relesse,** I relieve you of   101 **streen,** strain, stock

106 **allone,** alone   110 **dure,** last   114 **grucche,** grumble, murmur at
115 **sith,** since   120 **hertely,** heartfelt   124 **spousaille,** marriage   135 **purveye,** provide   142 **shoop,** prepared, planned   143 **throop,** village   145 **herbergage,** lodging

And of hire labour tooke hir sustenance,
After that the erthe yaf hem habundance.

Amonges thise povre folk ther dwelte a man
Which that was holden povrest of hem alle;
150 But hye God somtyme senden kan
His grace into a litel oxes stalle;
Janicula men of that throop hym calle.
A doghter hadde he, fair ynogh to sighte,
And Grisildis this yonge mayden highte.

But for to speke of vertuous beautee,
Thanne was she oon the faireste under sonne;
For povreliche yfostred up° was she,
No likerous° lust was thurgh hire herte yronne.
Wel ofter of the welle than of the tonne°
160 She drank, and for she wolde vertu plese,
She knew wel labour, but noon ydel ese.

But thogh this mayde tendre were of age,
Yet in the brest of hire virginitee
Ther was enclosed rype and sad corage;°
And in greet reverence and charitee
Hir olde povre fader fostred shee.
A fewe sheep, spynnynge,° on feeld she kepte;
She wolde noght been ydel til she slepte.

And whan she homward cam, she wolde brynge
170 Wortes° or othere herbes tymes ofte,
The whiche she shredde and seeth° for hir lyvynge,
And made hir bed ful hard and nothyng softe;
And ay she kepte hir fadres lyf on-lofte°
With everich obeisaunce° and diligence
That child may doon to fadres reverence.

Upon Grisilde, this povre creature,
Ful ofte sithe this markys sette his ye
As he on huntyng rood paraventure;°
And whan it fil that he myghte hire espye,°
180 He noght with wantown° lookyng of folye
His eyen caste on hire, but in sad wyse°
Upon hir chiere he wolde hym ofte avyse.

Commendynge in his herte hir womman-hede,
And eek hir vertu, passynge any wight°
Of so yong age, as wel in chiere as dede.
For thogh the peple have no greet insight
In vertu, he considered ful right
Hir bountee,° and disposed that he wolde
Wedde hire oonly, if evere he wedde sholde.

The day of weddyng cam, but no wight kan   190
Telle what womman that it sholde be;
For which merveille wondred many a man,
And seyden, whan they were in privetee,
"Wol nat oure lord yet leve his vanytee?
Wol he nat wedde? allas; allas, the while!
Why wole he thus hymself and us bigile?°"

But nathelees this markys hath doon make°
Of gemmes, set in gold and in asure,
Brooches and rynges, for Grisildis sake;
And of hir clothyng took he the mesure   200
By a mayde lyk to hire stature,
And eek of othere aornementes alle
That unto swich a weddyng sholde falle.

The time of undren° of the same day
Approcheth, that this weddyng sholde be;
And al the paleys put was in array,
Bothe halle and chambres, ech in his degree;°
Houses of office° stuffed with plentee
Ther maystow seen, of deyntevous vitaille
That may be founde as fer as last Ytaille.   210

This roial markys, richely arrayed,
Lordes and ladyes in his compaignye,
The whiche that to the feeste weren yprayed,
And of his retenue the bachelrye,°
With many a soun of sondry melodye,
Unto the village of the which I tolde,
In this array the righte wey° han holde.

Grisilde of this, God woot, ful innocent,
That for hire shapen was al this array,
To fecchen water at a welle is went,   220
And cometh hoom as soone as ever she may;
For wel she hadde herd seyd that thilke° day
The markys sholde wedde, and if she myghte,
She wolde fayn° han seyn som of that sighte.

She thoghte, "I wole with othere maydens stonde,
That been my felawes, in oure dore and se
The markysesse, and therfore wol I fonde°
To doon at hoom, as soone as it may be,
The labour which that longeth unto me;
And thanne I may at leyser hire biholde,   230
If she this wey unto the castel holde."

And as she wolde over hir thresshfold gon,
The markys cam, and gan hire for to calle;
And she set doun hir water pot anon,

Biside the threshfold, in an oxes stalle,
And doun upon hir knes she gan to falle,
And with sad contenance kneleth stille,
Til she had herd what was the lordes wille.

This thoghtful markys spak unto this mayde
240 Ful sobrely, and seyde in this manere:
"Where is youre fader, O Grisildis?" he sayde.
And she with reverence, in humble cheere,
Answerde, "Lord, he is al redy heere."
And in she gooth withouten lenger lette,°
And to the markys she hir fader fette.°

He by the hand thanne took this olde man,
And seyde thus, whan he hym hadde asyde:
"Janicula, I neither may ne kan
Lenger the plesance° of myn herte hyde.
250 If that thou vouche sauf, what so bityde,
Thy doghter wol I take, er that I wende,°
As for my wyf, unto hir lyves ende.

"Thou lovest me, I woot it wel certeyn,
And art my feithful lige man ybore;
And al that liketh° me, I dar wel seyn
It liketh thee, and specially therfore
Tel me that poynt that I have seyd bifore,
If that thou wolt unto that purpos drawe,
To take me as for thy sone-in-lawe."

260 This sodeyn cas this man astonyed° so
That reed he wax;° abayst and al quakynge
He stood; unnethes° seyde he wordes mo,
But oonly thus: "Lord," quod he, "my willynge
Is as ye wole, ne ayeynes° youre likynge
I wol no thyng, ye be my lord so deere;
Right as yow lust, governeth this mateere."

"Yet wol I," quod this markys softely,
"That in thy chambre I and thou and she
Have a collacioun,° and wostow° why?
270 For I wol axe if it hire wille be
To be my wyf, and reule hire after me.°
And al this shal be doon in thy presence;
I wol noght speke out of thyn audience."

And in the chambre, whil they were aboute
Hir tretys, which as ye shal after heere,
The peple cam unto the hous withoute,
And wondred hem in how honest manere
And tentifly° she kepte hir fader deere.
But outrely° Grisildis wondre myghte,
280 For nevere erst ne saugh she swich a sighte.

No wonder is thogh that she were astoned
To seen so greet a gest come in that place;
She nevere was to swiche gestes woned,°
For which she looked with ful pale face.
But shortly forth this matere for to chace,°
Thise arn the wordes that the markys sayde
To this benigne, verray, feithful mayde.

"Grisilde," he seyde, "ye shal wel understonde
It liketh to youre fader and to me
That I yow wedde, and eek it may so stonde, 290
As I suppose, ye wol that it so be.
But thise demandes axe I first," quod he,
"That, sith it shal be doon in hastif wyse,°
Wol ye assente, or elles yow avyse?

"I seye this, be ye redy with good herte
To al my lust, and that I frely may,
As me best thynketh, do yow laughe or smerte,°
And nevere ye to grucche° it, nyght ne day?
And eek whan I sey 'ye,' ne sey nat 'nay,'
Neither by word ne frownyng contenance? 300
Swere this, and heere I swere oure alliance."

Wondrynge upon this word, quakynge for drede,
She seyde, "Lord, undigne and unworthy
Am I to thilke honour that ye me beede,°
But as ye wole yourself, right so wol I.
And heere I swere that nevere willyngly,
In werk ne thoght, I nyl° yow disobeye,
For to be deed, though me were looth to deye."

"This is ynogh, Grisilde myn," quod he.
And forth he gooth, with a ful sobre cheere, 310
Out at the dore, and after that cam she,
And to the peple he seyde in this manere:
"This is my wyf," quod he, "that standeth heere.
Honoureth hire and loveth hire, I preye,
Whoso me loveth; ther is namoore to seye."

And for that no thyng of hir olde geere°
She sholde brynge into his hous, he bad
That wommen sholde dispoillen° hire right theere;
Of which thise ladyes were nat right glad
To handle hir clothes, wherinne she was clad. 320
But nathelees, this mayde bright of hewe
Fro foot to heed they clothed han al newe.

Hir heris han they kembd,° that lay untressed
Ful rudely,° and with hir fyngres smale°
A corone on hire heed they han ydressed,
And sette hire ful of nowches grete and smale.
Of hire array what sholde I make a tale?

---

244 **lette,** delay 245 **fette,** fetched 249 **plesance,** delight 251 **wende,** depart 255 **liketh,** pleases 260 **astonyed,** astonished 261 **reed he wax,** red he grew 262 **unnethes,** hardly, with difficulty 264 **ayeynes,** against, opposed to 269 **collacioun,** conference **wostow,** do you know 271 **after me,** according to my will 278 **tentifly,** attentively 279 **outrely,** wholly, absolutely

283 **woned,** accustomed 285 **for to chace,** to pursue 293 **hastif wyse,** hasty manner 297 **smerte,** feel pain 298 **grucche,** complain 304 **beede,** bid, offer 307 **nyl,** will not 316 **geere,** apparel 318 **dispoillen,** undress 323 **kembd,** combed 324 **rudely,** roughly **smale,** slender

Unnethe the peple hir knew for hire fairnesse,
Whan she translated was in swich richesse.

330   This markys hath hire spoused° with a ryng
Broght for the same cause, and thanne hire sette
Upon an hors, snow-whit and wel amblyng,°
And to his paleys, er he lenger lette,
With joyful peple that hire ladde and mette,
Conveyed hire, and thus the day they spende
In revel, til the sonne gan descende.

   And shortly forth this tale for to chace,
I seye that to this newe markysesse
God hath swich favour sent hire of his grace,
340 That it ne semed nat by liklynesse
That she was born and fed in rudenesse,°
As in a cote or in an oxe-stalle,
But norissed° in an emperoures halle.

   To every wight she woxen° is so deere
And worshipful° that folk ther she was bore,
And from hire birthe knewe hire yeer by yeere,
Unnethe trowed they,—but dorste han swore—
That to Janicle, of which I spak bifore,
She doghter were, for, as by conjecture,°
350 Hem thoughte she was another creature.

   For though that evere vertuous was she,
She was encressed in swich excellence
Of thewes° goode, yset in heigh bountee,
And so discreet° and fair of eloquence,
So benigne and so digne of reverence,
And koude so the peples herte embrace,
That ech hire lovede that looked in hir face.

   Noght oonly of Saluces in the toun
Publiced was the bountee of hir name,
360 But eek biside in many a regioun,
If oon seide wel, another seyde the same;
So spradde of hire heighe bountee° the fame
That men and wommen, as wel yonge as olde,
Good to Saluce, upon hire to biholde.

   Thus Walter lowely—nay, but roially—
Wedded with fortunat honestetee,
In Goddes pees lyveth ful esily
At hoom, and outward grace ynogh had he;
And for he saugh that under low degree
370 Was ofte vertu hid, the peple hym heelde
A prudent man, and that is seyn ful seelde.

   Nat oonly this Grisildis thurgh hir wit
Koude al the feet° of wyfly hoomlinesse,

But eek, whan that the cas required it,
The commune profit° koude she redresse.
Ther nas discord, rancour, ne hevynesse
In al that land, that she ne koude apese,
And wisely brynge hem alle in reste and ese.

   Though that hire housbonde absent were anon,
If gentil men or othere of hire contree   380
Were wrothe,° she wolde bryngen hem aton;°
So wise and rype° wordes hadde she,
And juggementz of so greet equitee,
That she from hevene sent was, as men wende,°
Peple to save and every wrong t'amende.

   Nat longe tyme after that this Grisild
Was wedded, she a doghter hath ybore.
Al had hire levere° have born a knave child,
Glad was this markys and the folk therfore;
For though a mayde child coome al bifore,   390
She may unto a knave child atteyne
By liklihede, syn she nys nat bareyne.°

Explicit secunda pars.
Incipit tercia pars.

   Ther fil, as it bifalleth tymes mo,
Whan that this child had souked but a throwe,°
This markys in his herte longeth so
To tempte his wyf, hir sadnesse for to knowe,
That he ne myghte out of his herte throwe
This merveillous desir his wyf t'assaye;°
Nedelees, God woot, he thoghte hire for t'affraye.°

   He hadde assayed hire ynogh bifore,   400
And foond hire evere good; what neded it
Hire for to tempte, and alwey moore and moore,
Though som men preise it for a subtil wit?
But as for me, I seye that yvele it sit
To assaye a wyf whan that it is no nede,
And putten hire in angwyssh and in drede.

   For which this markys wroghte in this manere:
He cam allone a-nyght, ther as she lay,
With stierne face and with ful trouble cheere,
And seyde thus: "Grisilde," quod he, "that day   410
That I yow took out of youre povere array,
And putte yow in estaat of heigh noblesse,—
Ye have nat that forgeten, as I gesse?

   "I seye, Grisilde, this present dignitee,
In which that I have put yow, as I trowe,°
Maketh yow nat foryetful for to be
That I yow took in povre estaat ful lowe,

---

330 **spoused**, marry   332 **wel amblyng**, walking well, with a pleasant gait
341 **rudenesse**, poverty   343 **norissed**, brought up   344 **woxen**, became
345 **worshipful**, honorable   349 **as by conjecture**, by supposition, as one would
have supposed   353 **thewes**, virtues   354 **discreet**, wise, courteous
362 **heighe bountee**, excellence, virtue   373 **feet**, feats

375 **commune profit**, general welfare of the state   381 **wrothe**, angry   **aton**,
together, in agreement   382 **rype**, mature   384 **wende**, thought   388 **hire levere**, she would rather   392 **bareyne**, barren   394 **but a throwe**, a little while
398 **t'assaye**, to test   399 **t'affraye**, to terrify   415 **as I trowe**, I think

For any wele ye moot youreselven knowe.
Taak heede of every word that y yow seye;
420 Ther is no wight that hereth it but we tweye.

   "Ye woot° yourself wel how that ye cam heere
Into this hous, it is nat longe ago;
And though to me that ye be lief and deere,
Unto my gentils° ye be no thyng so.
They seyn, to hem it is greet shame and wo
For to be subgetz° and been in servage
To thee, that born art of a smal village.

   "And namely sith thy doghter was ybore
Thise wordes han they spoken, doutelees.
430 But I desire, as I have doon bifore,
To lyve my lyf with hem in reste and pees.
I may nat in this caas be recchelees;°
I moot doon with thy doghter for the beste,
Nat as I wolde, but as my peple leste.°

   "And yet, God woot, this is ful looth° to me;
But nathelees withoute youre wityng°
I wol nat doon; but this wol I," quod he,
"That ye to me assente as in this thyng.
Shewe now youre pacience in youre werkyng,
440 That ye me highte° and swore in youre village
That day that maked was oure mariage."

   Whan she had herd al this, she noght ameved°
Neither in word, or chiere, or contenaunce;
For, as it semed, she was nat agreved.
She seyde, "Lord, al lyth in youre plesaunce.
My child and I, with hertely obeisaunce,
Been youres al, and ye mowe save or spille
Youre owene thyng; werketh after youre wille.

   "Ther may no thyng, God so my soule save,
450 Liken to yow that may displese me;
Ne I desire no thyng for to have,
Ne drede for to leese, save oonly yee.
This wyl is in myn herte, and ay shal be;
No lengthe of tyme or deeth may this deface,
Ne chaunge my corage to another place."

   Glad was this markys of hire answeryng,
But yet he feyned as he were nat so;
Al drery was his cheere and his lookyng,
Whan that he sholde out of the chambre go.
460 Soone after this, a furlong wey or two,
He prively° hath toold al his entente
Unto a man, and to his wyf hym sente.

   A maner sergeant was this privee man,
The which that feithful ofte he founden hadde
In thynges grete, and eek swich folk wel kan

Doon execucioun in thynges badde.
The lord knew wel that he hym loved and dradde;
And whan this sergeant wiste his lordes wille,
Into the chambre he stalked hym ful stille.

   "Madame," he seyde, "ye moote foryeve it me,   470
Though I do thyng to which I am constreyned.
Ye been so wys that ful wel knowe ye
That lordes heestes mowe nat been yfeyned;°
They mowe wel been biwailled or compleyned,
But men moote nede unto hire lust obeye,
And so wol I; ther is namoore to seye.

   "This child I am comanded for to take,"—
And spak namoore, but out the child he hente°
Despitously,° and gan a cheere make
As though he wolde han slayn it er he wente.   480
Grisildis moot al suffre and al consente;
And as a lamb she sitteth meke and stille,
And leet this crueel sergeant doon his wille.

   Suspecious was the diffame° of this man,
Suspect his face, suspect his word also;
Suspect the tyme in which he this bigan.
Allas! hir doghter that she loved so,
She wende he wolde han slawen it right tho.
But nathelees she neither weep ne syked,°
Conformynge hire to that the markys lyked.   490

   But atte laste to speken she bigan,
And mekely she to the sergeant preyde,
So as he was a worthy gentil man,
That she moste kisse hire child er that it deyde.
And in hir barm° this litel child she leyde
With ful sad face, and gan the child to blisse,°
And lulled it, and after gan it kisse.

   And thus she seyde in hire benigne voys,
"Fareweel my child! I shal thee nevere see.
But sith I thee have marked with the croys°   500
Of thilke Fader—blessed moote he be!—
That for us deyde upon a croys of tree,
Thy soule, litel child, I hym bitake,
For this nyght shaltow dyen for my sake."

   I trowe that to a norice in this cas
It had been hard this reuthe for to se;
Wel myghte a mooder thanne han cryd "allas!"
But nathelees so sad stidefast was she
That she endured al adversitee,
And to the sergeant mekely she sayde,   510
"Have heer agayn youre litel yonge mayde.

   "Gooth now," quod she, "and dooth my lordes
      heeste;

But o thyng wol I prey yow of youre grace,
That, but my lord forbad yow, atte leeste
Burieth this litel body in som place
That beestes ne no briddes it torace.°''
But he no word wol to that purpos seye,
But took the child and wente upon his weye.

This sergeant cam unto his lord ageyn,
520 And of Grisildis wordes and hire cheere
He tolde hym point for point, in short and pleyn,
And hym presenteth with his doghter deere.
Somwhat this lord hadde routhe° in his manere,
But nathelees his purpos heeld he stille,
As lordes doon, what they wol han hir wille;

And bad this sergeant that he pryvely
Sholde this child ful softe wynde and wrappe,°
With alle circumstances tendrely,
And carie it in a cofre° or in a lappe;
530 But, upon peyne his heed of for to swappe,
That no man sholde knowe of his entente,
Ne whenne he cam, ne whider that he wente;

But at Boloigne to his suster deere,
That thilke tyme of Panik was countesse,
He sholde it take, and shewe hire this mateere,
Bisekynge° hire to doon hire bisynesse°
This child to fostre in alle gentillesse;
And whos child that it was he bad hire hyde
From every wight, for oght that may bityde.

540 The sergeant gooth, and hath fulfild this thyng;
But to this markys now retourne we.
For now gooth he ful faste ymaginyng
If by his wyves cheere he myghte se,
Or by hire word aperceyve,° that she
Were chaunged; but he nevere hire koude fynde
But evere in oon ylike sad and kynde.

As glad, as humble, as bisy in servyse,
And eek in love, as she was wont to be,
Was she to hym in every maner wyse;
550 Ne of hir doghter noght a word spak she.
Noon accident, for noon adversitee,
Was seyn in hire, ne nevere hir doghter name
Ne nempned° she, in ernest nor in game.°

Explicit tercia pars.
Sequitur pars quarta.

In this estaat ther passed been foure yeer
Er she with childe was, but, as God wolde,
A knave child she bar by this Walter,
Ful gracious and fair for to biholde.
And whan that folk it to his fader tolde,

Nat oonly he, but al his contree merye
Was for this child, and God they thanke and herye.   560

Whan it was two yeer old, and fro the brest
Departed of his norice,° on a day
This markys caughte yet another lest
To tempte his wyf yet ofter, if he may.
O nedelees was she tempted in assay!
But wedded men ne knowe no mesure,°
Whan that they fynde a pacient creature.

''Wyf,'' quod this markys, ''ye han herd er this,
My peple sikly berth° oure mariage;
And namely sith my sone yboren is,   570
Now is it worse than evere in al oure age.
The murmur sleeth myn herte and my corage,
For to myne eres comth the voys so smerte°
That it wel ny destroyed hath myn herte.

''Now sey they thus: 'Whan Walter is agon,
Thanne shal the blood of Janicle succede
And been oure lord, for oother have we noon.'
Swiche wordes seith my peple, out of drede.
Wel oughte I of swich murmur taken heede;
For certeinly I drede swich sentence,°   580
Though they nat pleyn speke in myn audience.°

''I wolde lyve in pees, if that I myghte;
Wherfore I am disposed outrely,
As I his suster servede° by nyghte,
Right so thenke I to serve hym pryvely.
This warne I yow, that ye nat sodeynly
Out of youreself for no wo sholde outreye;°
Beth pacient, and therof I yow preye.''

''I have,'' quod she, ''seyd thus, and evere shal:
I wol no thyng, ne nyl no thyng, certayn,   590
But as yow list. Naught greveth me at al;
Though that my doughter and my sone be slayn,—
At youre comandement, this is to sayn.
I have noght had no part of children tweyne
But first siknesse, and after, wo and peyne.

''Ye been oure lord, dooth with youre owene
   thyng
Right as yow list; axeth° no reed° at me.
For as I lefte at hoom al my clothyng,
Whan I first cam to yow, right so,'' quod she,
''Lefte I my wyl and al my libertee,   600
And took youre clothyng; wherfore I yow preye,
Dooth youre plesaunce, I wol youre lust obeye.

''And certes, if I hadde prescience
Youre wyl to knowe, er ye youre lust me tolde,
I wolde it doon withouten necligence;

---

516 **torace,** tear to pieces   523 **routhe,** pity   527 **wynde and wrappe,** bundle
and wrap up   529 **cofre,** box   536 **Bisekekynge,** beseeching   **doon hire
bisynesse,** busy herself, concern herself   544 **aperceyve,** perceive   553
nempned, named, mentioned   **in ernest nor in game,** neither seriously nor
lightly

562 **norice,** nurse   566 **mesure,** moderation   569 **sikly berth,** bear
not well   573 **smerte,** painful   580 **sentence,** judgment   581 **audience,** hearing
584 **servede,** treated   587 **out of . . . outreye,** fall into a passion because of this
sorrow   597 **axeth,** ask   **reed,** advice

But now I woot youre lust, and what ye wolde,
Al youre plesance ferme and stable I holde;
For wiste I that my deeth wolde do yow ese,
Right gladly wolde I dyen, yow to plese.

610 "Deth may noght make no comparisoun
Unto youre love." And whan this markys say
The constance of his wyf, he caste adoun
His eyen two, and wondreth that she may
In pacience suffre al this array;
And forth he goth with drery contenance,
But to his herte it was ful greet plesance.

This ugly sergeant, in the same wyse
That he hire doghter caughte,° right so he,
Or worse, if men worse kan devyse,
620 Hath hent° hire sone, that ful was of beautee.
And evere in oon° so pacient was she
That she no chiere maade of hevynesse,
But kiste hir sone, and after gan it blesse;

Save this, she preyede hym that, if he myghte,
Hir litel sone he wolde in erthe grave,°
His tendre lymes, delicaat to sighte,
Fro foweles and fro beestes for to save.
But she noon answere of hym myghte have
He wente his wey, as hym no thyng ne roghte;°
630 But to Boloigne he tendrely it broghte.

This markys wondred, evere lenger the moore,
Upon hir pacience, and if that he
Ne hadde soothly° knowen therbifoore
That parfitly hir children loved she,
He wolde have wend that of som subtiltee,
And of malice, or for crueel corage,
That she hadde suffred this with sad visage.

But wel he knew that next hymself, certayn,
She loved hir children best in every wyse.
640 But now of wommen wolde I axen fayn
If thise assayes myghte nat suffise?
What koude a sturdy° housbonde moore devyse
To preeve hir wyfhod and hir stedefastnesse,
And he continuynge evere in sturdinesse?

But ther been folk of swich condicion
That whan they have a certein purpos take,
They kan nat stynte of hire entencion,
But, right as they were bounden to a stake,
They wol nat of that firste purpos slake.°
650 Right so this markys fulliche hath purposed
To tempte his wyf as he was first disposed.

He waiteth if by word or contenance
That she to hym was changed of corage;
But nevere koude he fynde variance.
She was ay oon in herte and in visage;
And ay the forther that she was in age,
The moore trewe, if that it were possible,
She was to hym in love, and moore penyble.°

For which it semed thus, that of hem two
Ther nas but o wyl; for, as Walter leste,   660
The same lust was hire plesance also.
And, God be thanked, al fil for the beste.
She shewed wel, for no worldly unreste
A wyf, as of hirself, nothing ne sholde
Wille in effect, but as hir housbonde wolde.

The sclaundre° of Walter ofte and wyde spradde
That of a crueel herte he wikkedly,
For he a povre womman wedded hadde,
Hath mordred bothe his children prively.
Swich murmur was among hem comunly.   670
No wonder is, for to the peples ere
Ther cam no word, but that they mordred were.

For which, where as his peple therbifore
Hadde loved hym wel, the sclaundre of his diffame
Made hem that they hym hatede therfore.
To been a mordrere is an hateful name;
But nathelees, for ernest ne for game,
He of his crueel purpos nolde stente;°
To tempte his wyf was set al his entente.

Whan that his doghter twelve yeer was of age,   680
He to the court of Rome, in subtil wyse
Enformed of his wyl, sente his message,
Comaundynge hem swiche bulles° to devyse
As to his crueel purpos may suffyse,
How that the pope, as for his peples reste,
Bad hym to wedde another, if hym leste.

I seye, he bad they sholde countrefete
The popes bulles, makynge mencion
That he hath leve his firste wyf to lete,°
As by the popes dispensacion,   690
To stynte rancour and dissencion
Bitwixe his peple and hym; thus seyde the bulle,
The which they han publiced atte fulle.

The rude peple, as it no wonder is,
Wenden ful wel that it hadde be right so;
But whan thise tidynges came to Grisildis,
I deeme that hire herte was ful wo.
But she, ylike sad for everemo,

618 **caughte**, seized   620 **hent**, seized   621 **evere in oon**, continually
625 **grave**, bury   629 **as him . . . roghte**, as if he cared for nothing   633 **soothly**,
truly   642 **sturdy**, stern, cruel   649 **slake**, desist

658 **penyble**, inured to pain   666 **sclaundre**, slander   678 **stente**, leave off
683 **bulles**, papal proclamations   689 **to lete**, abandon

Disposed was, this humble creature,
700 The adversitee of Fortune al t'endure,

Abidynge evere his lust and his plesance,
To whom that she was yeven° herte and al,
As to hire verray worldly suffisance.°
But shortly if this storie I tellen shal,
This markys writen hath in special
A lettre, in which he sheweth his entente,
And secreely he to Boloigne it sente.

To the Erl of Panyk, which that hadde tho
Wedded his suster, preyde he specially
710 To bryngen hoom agayn his children two
In honurable estaat al openly.
But o thyng he hym preyede outrely,
That he to no wight, though men wolde enquere,
Sholde nat telle whos children that they were,

But seye, the mayden sholde ywedded be
Unto the Markys of Saluce anon.
And as this erl was preyed, so dide he;
For at day set he on his wey is goon
Toward Saluce, the lordes many oon
720 In riche array, this mayden for to gyde,
Hir yonge brother ridynge hire bisyde.

Arrayed was toward hir mariage
This fresshe mayde, ful of gemmes cleere;
Hir brother, which that seven yeer was of age,
Arrayed eek ful fressh in his manere.
And thus in greet noblesse and with glad cheere,
Toward Saluces shapynge hir journey,
Fro day to day they ryden in hir wey.

Explicit quarta pars.
Sequitur pars quinta.

Among al this, after his wikke usage,°
730 This markys, yet his wyf to tempte moore
To the outtreste preeve of hir corage,
Fully to han experience and loore
If that she were as stidefast as bifoore,
He on a day, in open audience,
Ful boistously° hath seyd hire this sentence:

"Certes, Grisilde, I hadde ynogh plesance
To han yow to my wyf for youre goodnesse,
As for youre trouthe° and for youre obeisance,
Noght for youre lynage, ne for youre richesse;
740 But now knowe I in verray soothfastnesse
That in greet lordshipe, if I wel avyse,
Ther is greet servitute in sondry wyse.

"I may nat doon as every plowman may.
My peple me constreyneth for to take
Another wyf, and crien day by day;
And eek the pope, rancour for to slake.
Consenteth it, that dar I undertake;°
And trewely thus muche I wol yow seye,
My newe wyf is comynge by the weye.

"Be strong of herte, and voyde° anon hir place,   750
And thilke dowere that ye broghten me,
Taak it agayn; I graunte it of my grace.
Retourneth to youre fadres hous," quod he;
"No man may alwey han prosperitee.
With evene herte I rede yow t'endure
The strook of Fortune or of aventure.°"

And she agayn answerde in pacience,
"My lord," quod she, "I woot, and wiste alway,
How that bitwixen youre magnificence
And my poverte no wight kan ne may   760
Maken comparison; it is no nay.
I ne heeld me nevere digne° in no manere
To be youre wyf, no, ne youre chamberere.

"And in this hous, ther ye me lady maade—
The heighe God take I for my witnesse,
And also wysly he my soule glaade—
I nevere heeld me lady ne mistresse,
But humble servant to youre worthynesse,
And evere shal, whil that my lyf may dure,
Aboven every worldly creature.   770

"That ye so longe of youre benignitee
Han holden me in honour and nobleye,
Where as I was noght worthy for to bee,
That thonke I God and yow, to whom I preye
Foryelde° it yow; ther is namoore to seye.
Unto my fader gladly wol I wende,
And with hym dwelle unto my lyves ende.

"Ther I was fostred of a child ful smal,
Til I be deed my lyf ther wol I lede,
A wydwe clene in body, herte, and al.   780
For sith I yaf to yow my maydenhede,
And am youre trewe wyf, it is no drede,
God shilde° swich a lordes wyf to take
Another man to housbonde or to make!

"And of youre newe wyf God of his grace
So graunte yow wele and prosperitee!
For I wol gladly yelden hire my place,
In which that I was blisful wont to bee.

702 **yeven,** given   703 **suffisance,** contentment   729 **usage,** custom, habit
735 **boistously,** rudely or coarsely   738 **trouthe,** fidelity

747 **dar I undertake,** I dare say   750 **voyde,** depart, empty   756 **aventure,** chance
762 **digne,** worthy   775 **Foryelde,** repay   783 **shilde,** forbid

For sith it liketh yow, my lord," quod shee,
790 "That whilom weren al myn hertes reste,
That I shal goon, I wol goon whan yow leste.

"But ther as ye me profre swich dowaire°
As I first broghte, it is wel in my mynde
It were my wrecched clothes, nothyng faire,
The whiche to me were hard now for to fynde.
O goode God! how gentil and how kynde
Ye semed by youre speche and youre visage
The day that maked was oure mariage!

"But sooth is seyd—algate° I fynde it trewe,
800 For in effect it preeved is on me—
Love is noght oold as whan that it is newe.
But certes, lord, for noon adversitee,
To dyen in the cas, it shal nat bee
That evere in word or werk I shal repente
That I yow yaf myn herte in hool entente.

"My lord, ye woot that in my fadres place
Ye dide me streepe out of my povre weede,
And richely me cladden, of youre grace.
To yow broghte I noght elles, out of drede,
810 But feith, and nakednesse, and maydenhede;
And heere agayn your clothyng I restoore,
And eek your weddyng ryng, for everemore.

"The remenant of youre jueles redy be
Inwith youre chambre, dar I saufly° sayn.
Naked out of my fadres hous," quod she,
"I cam, and naked moot I turne agayn.
Al youre plesance wol I folwen fayn;
But yet I hope it be nat youre entente
That I smoklees° out of youre paleys wente.

820 "Ye koude nat doon so dishonest a thyng,
That thilke wombe in which youre children leye
Sholde biforn the peple, in my walkyng,
Be seyn al bare; wherfore I yow preye,
Lat me nat lyk a worm go by the weye.
Remembre yow, myn owene lord so deere,
I was youre wyf, though I unworthy weere.

"Wherfore, in gerdon° of my maydenhede,
Which that I broghte, and noght agayn I bere,
As voucheth sauf to yeve me, to my meede,
830 But swich a smok as I was wont to were,
That I therwith may wrye° the wombe of here
That was youre wyf. And heer take I my leeve
Of yow, myn owene lord, lest I yow greve."

"The smok," quod he, "that thou hast on thy
    bak,

Lat it be stille, and bere it forth with thee."
But wel unnethes thilke word he spak,
But wente his wey, for routhe° and for pitee.
Biforn the folk hirselven strepeth she,
And in hir smok, with heed and foot al bare,
Toward hir fadre hous forth is she fare.   840

The folk hire folwe, wepynge in hir weye,
And Fortune ay they cursen as they goon;
But she fro wepyng kepte hire eyen dreye,
Ne in this tyme word ne spak she noon.
Hir fader, that this tidynge herde anoon,
Curseth the day and tyme that Nature
Shoop hym to been a lyves creature.

For out of doute this olde poure man
Was evere in suspect of hir mariage;
For evere he demed, sith that it bigan,   850
That whan the lord fulfild hadde his corage,
Hym wolde thynke it were a disparage
To his estaat so lowe for t'alighte,
And voyden° hire as soone as ever he myghte.

Agayns° his doghter hastily goth he,
For he by noyse of folk knew hire comynge,
And with hire olde coote, as it myghte be
He covered hire, ful sorwefully wepynge.
But on hire body myghte he it nat brynge,
For rude was the clooth, and moore of age   860
By dayes fele° than at hire mariage.

Thus with hire fader, for a certeyn space,
Dwelleth this flour of wyfly pacience,
That neither by hire wordes ne hire face,
Biforn the folk, ne eek in hire absence,
Ne shewed she that hire was doon offence;
Ne of hire heighe estaat no remembraunce
Ne hadde she, as by hire contenaunce.

No wonder is, for in hire grete estaat
Hire goost° was evere in pleyn humylitee;   870
No tendre mouth,° noon herte delicaat,
No pompe, no semblant of roialtee,
But ful of pacient benyngnytee,
Discreet and pridelees, ay honurable,
And to hire housbonde evere meke and stable.

Men speke of Job, and moost for his humblesse
As clerkes, whan hem list, konne wel endite,°
Namely of men, but as in soothfastnesse,
Though clerkes preise wommen but a lite,
Ther kan no man in humblesse hym acquite   880
As womman kan, ne kan been half so trewe°
As wommen been, but it be falle of newe.

---

792 **dowaire,** dower 799 **algate,** anyhow 814 **saufly,** safely 819 **smoklees,** without a smock 827 **gerdon,** guerdon 831 **wrye,** cover

837 **routhe,** compassion 854 **voyden,** expel 855 **Agayns,** so as to meet 861 **fele,** more 870 **goost,** spirit, soul 871 **tendre mouth,** delicate appetite 877 **endite,** relate 881 **trewe,** faithful

Fro Boloigne is this Erl of Panyk come,
Of which the fame up sprang to moore and lesse,
And to the peples eres, alle and some,
Was kouth° eek that a newe markysesse
He with hym broghte, in swich pompe and richesse
That nevere was ther seyn with mannes ye
So noble array in al West Lumbardye.

890 The markys, which that shoop and knew al this,
Er that this erl was come, sente his message
For thilke sely° povre Grisildis;
And she with humble herte and glad visage,
Nat with no swollen thoght in hire corage,
Cam at his heste, and on hire knees hire sette,
And reverently and wisely she hym grette.

"Grisilde," quod he, "my wyl is outrely,
This mayden, that shal wedded been to me,
Received be to-morwe as roially
900 As it possible is in myn hous to be,
And eek that every wight in his degree
Have his estaat,° in sittyng and servyse
And heigh plesaunce, as I kan best devyse.

"I have no wommen suffisaunt, certayn,
The chambres for t'arraye in ordinaunce
After my lust, and therfore wolde I fayn
That thyn were al swich manere governaunce.
Thou knowest eek of old al my plesaunce;
Thogh thyn array be badde and yvel biseye,°
910 Do thou thy devoir at the leeste weye."

"Nat oonly, lord, that I am glad," quod she,
"To doon youre lust, but I desire also
Yow for to serve and plese in my degree
Withouten feyntyng, and shal everemo;
Ne nevere, for no wele ne no wo,
Ne shal the goost withinne myn herte stente
To love yow best with al my trewe entente."

And with that word she gan the hous to dighte,°
And tables for to sette, and beddes make;
920 And peyned hire to doon al that she myghte,
Preyynge the chambereres, for Goddes sake,
To hasten hem, and faste swepe and shake;
And she, the mooste servysable of alle,
Hath every chambre arrayed and his halle.

Abouten undren gan this erl alighte,
That with hym broghte thise noble children tweye,
For which the peple ran to seen the sighte
Of hire array, so richely biseye;
And thanne at erst° amonges hem they seye

That Walter was no fool, thogh that hym leste   930
To chaunge his wyf, for it was for the beste.

For she is fairer, as they deemen° alle,
Than is Grisilde, and moore tendre of age,
And fairer fruyt bitwene hem sholde falle,
And moore plesant, for hire heigh lynage.
Hir brother eek so fair was of visage
That hem to seen the peple hath caught plesaunce
Commendynge now the markys governaunce.—

"O stormy peple! unsad and evere untrewe!
Ay undiscreet and chaungynge as a fane!   940
Delitynge evere in rumbul° that is newe,
For lyk the moone ay wexe ye and wane!
Ay ful of clappyng, deere ynogh a jane!°
Youre doom° is fals, youre constance yvele
    preeveth;
A ful greet fool is he that on yow leeveth."

Thus seyden sadde folk in that citee,
Whan that the peple gazed up and doun;
For they were glad, right for the noveltee,
To han a newe lady of hir toun.
Namoore of this make I now mencioun,   950
But to Grisilde agayn wol I me dresse,°
And telle hir constance and hir bisynesse.—

Ful bisy was Grisilde in every thyng
That to the feeste was apertinent.
Right noght was she abayst of hire clothyng,
Thogh it were rude and somdeel eek torent;°
But with glad cheere to the yate° is went
With oother folk, to greete the markysesse,
And after that dooth forth hire bisynesse.

With so glad chiere his gestes she receyveth,   960
And konnyngly, everich in his degree,°
That no defaute no man aperceyveth,
But ay they wondren what she myghte bee
That in so povre array was for to see,
And koude swich honour and reverence,
And worthily they preisen hire prudence.

In al this meene while she ne stente
This mayde and eek hir brother to commende
With al hir herte, in ful benyngne entente,
So wel that no man koude hir pris amende.°   970
But atte laste, whan that thise lordes wende
To sitten doun to mete, he gan to calle
Grisilde, as she was bisy in his halle.

"Grisilde," quod he, as it were in his pley,
"How liketh thee my wyf and hire beautee?"

---

886 **kouth,** known   892 **sely,** poor   902 **estaat,** rank   909 **badde and yvel biseye,** poor and wretched looking   918 **dighte,** fix, prepare   929 **at erst,** first   932 **deemen,** judge   941 **rumbul,** rumor   943 **deere ynogh a jane,** too expensive at a penny   944 **doom,** judgment   951 **wol I me dresse,** will I address myself   956 **torent,** to tear into pieces   957 **yate,** gate   961 **everich in his degree,** each according to his station   970 **hir pris amende,** her praise better

"Right wel," quod she, "my lord; for, in good fey,
A fairer saugh I nevere noon than she.
I prey to God yeve hire prosperitee;
And so hope I that he wol to yow sende
980 Plesance ynogh unto youre lyves ende.

"O thyng biseke I yow, and warne also,
That ye ne prikke° with no tormentynge
This tendre mayden, as ye han doon mo;
For she is fostred in hire norissynge°
Moore tendrely, and, to my supposynge,
She koude nat adversitee endure
As koude a povre fostred creature."

And whan this Walter saugh hire pacience,
Hir glade chiere, and no malice at al,
990 And he so ofte had doon to hire offence,
And she ay sad and constant as a wal,
Continuynge evere hire innocence overal,
This sturdy markys gan his herte dresse°
To rewen upon hire wyfly stedfastnesse.

"This is ynogh, Grisilde myn," quod he;
"Be now namoore agast ne yvele apayed.°
I have thy feith and thy benyngnytee,
As wel as evere womman was, assayed,
In greet estaat, and povreliche arrayed.
1000 Now knowe I, dere wyf, thy stedfastnesse,"—
And hire in armes took and gan hire kesse.°

And she for wonder took of it no keep;
She herde nat what thyng he to hire seyde;
She ferde° as she had stert out of a sleep,
Til she out of hire mazednesse abreyde.°
"Grisilde," quod he, "by God, that for us deyde,
Thou art my wyf, ne noon oother I have,
Ne nevere hadde, as God my soule save!

"This is thy doghter, which thou hast supposed
1010 To be my wyf; that oother feithfully
Shal be myn heir, as I have ay disposed;
Thou bare hym in thy body trewely.
At Boloigne have I kept hem prively;
Taak hem agayn, for now maystow nat seye
That thou hast lorn° noon of thy children tweye.

"And folk that ootherweys han seyd of me,
I warne hem wel that I have doon this deede
For no malice, ne for no crueltee,
But for t'assaye in thee thy wommanheede,
1020 And nat to sleen my children—God forbeede!—
But for to kepe hem pryvely and stille,°
Til I thy purpos knewe and al thy wille."

Whan she this herde, aswowne° doun she falleth
For pitous joye, and after hire swownynge
She bothe hire yonge children to hire calleth,
And in hire armes, pitously wepynge,
Embraceth hem, and tendrely kissynge
Ful lyk a mooder, with hire salte teeres
She bathed bothe hire visage and hire heeres.

O which a pitous thyng it was to se   1030
Hir swownyng, and hire humble voys to heere!
"Grauntmercy, lord, God thanke it yow," quod she,
"That ye han saved me my children deere!
Now rekke I nevere to been deed° right heere;
Sith I stonde in youre love and in youre grace,
No fors of deeth,° ne whan my spirit pace!

"O tendre, o deere, o yonge children myne!
Youre woful mooder wende stedfastly
That crueel houndes or som foul vermyne
Hadde eten yow; but God, of his mercy,   1040
And youre benyngne fader tendrely
Hath doon yow kept,"—and in that same stounde°
Al sodeynly she swapte° adoun to grounde.

And in hire swough so sadly holdeth she
Hire children two, whan she gan hem t'em-
brace,
That with greet sleighte° and greet difficultee
The children from hire arm they gonne arace.°
O many a teere on many a pitous face
Doun ran of hem that stooden hire bisyde;
Unnethe abouten hire myghte they abyde.   1050

Walter hire gladeth, and hire sorwe slaketh;°
She riseth up, abaysed,° from hire traunce,
And every wight hire joye and feeste maketh
Til she hath caught agayn hire contenaunce.°
Walter hire dooth so feithfully plesaunce
That it was deyntee° for to seen the cheere
Bitwixe hem two, now they been met yfeere.°

Thise ladyes, whan that they hir tyme say,
Han taken hire and into chambre gon,
And strepen hire out of hire rude array,   1060
And in a clooth of gold that brighte shoon,
With a coroune of many a riche stoon
Upon hire heed, they into halle hire broghte,
And ther she was honured as hire oghte.

Thus hath this pitous day a blisful ende,
For every man and womman dooth his myght
This day in murthe and revel to dispende
Til on the welkne° shoon the sterres lyght.

982 **prikke,** incite   984 **fostred in hire norissynge,** cherished in her bringing up
993 **his herte dresse,** to direct his heart   996 **yvele apayed,** ill-pleased
1001 **kesse,** kiss   1004 **ferde,** behaved   1005 **mazednesse abreyde,** amazement started up   1015 **lorn,** lost   1021 **stille,** quietly

1023 **aswowne,** in a swoon   1034 **rekke I nevere . . . deed,** I care not if I die
1036 **No fors of deeth,** no matter about death   1042 **stounde,** moment
1043 **swapte,** fell   1046 **sleighte,** skill   1047 **arace,** tore away   1051 **slaketh,**
abates   1052 **abaysed,** abashed   1054 **caught . . . hire contenaunce,** regained
her composure   1056 **deyntee,** delight   1057 **yfeere,** together   1068 **welkne,**
sky

For moore solempne in every mannes syght
1070 This feste was, and gretter of costage,°
Than was the revel of hire mariage.

Ful many a yeer in heigh prosperitee
Lyven thise two in concord and in reste,
And richely his doghter maryed he
Unto a lord, oon of the worthieste
Of al Ytaille; and thanne in pees and reste
His wyves fader in his court he kepeth,
Til that the soule out of his body crepeth.

His sone succedeth in his heritage
1080 In reste and pees, after his fader day,
And fortunat was eek in mariage,
Al putte he nat his wyf in greet assay.
This world is nat so strong, it is no nay,
As it hath been in olde tymes yoore,
And herkneth what this auctour seith therfoore.

This storie is seyd, nat for that wyves sholde
Folwen Grisilde as in humylitee,
For it were inportable,° though they wolde;
But for that every wight, in his degree,
1090 Sholde be constant in adversitee
As was Grisilde; therfore Petrak writeth
This storie, which with heigh stile he enditeth.°

For, sith a womman was so pacient
Unto a mortal man, wel moore us oghte
Receyven al in gree° that God us sent;
For greet skile is, he preeve that he wroghte.
But he ne tempteth no man that he boghte,°
As seith Seint Jame, if ye his pistel° rede;
He preeveth folk al day, it is no drede,

1100 And suffreth us, as for oure excercise,
With sharpe scourges of adversitee
Ful ofte to be bete in sondry wise;
Nat for to knowe oure wyl, for certes he,
Er we were born, knew al oure freletee;°
And for oure beste is al his governaunce.
Lat us thanne lyve in vertuous suffraunce.°

But o word, lordynges, herkneth er I go:
It were ful hard to fynde now-a-dayes
In al a toun Grisildis thre or two;
1110 For if that they were put to swiche assayes,
The gold of hem hath now so badde alayes
With bras, that thogh the coyne be fair at ye,°
It wolde rather breste° a-two than plye.°

For which heere, for the Wyves love of Bathe—
Whos lyf and al hire secte° God mayntene

In heigh maistrie,° and elles were it scathe°—
I wol with lusty herte, fressh and grene,
Seyn yow a song to glade yow, I wene;
And lat us stynte of ernestful° matere.
Herkneth my song that seith in this manere: 1120

Lenvoy de Chaucer.

Grisilde is deed, and eek hire pacience,
And bothe atones buryed in Ytaille;
For which I crie in open audience,
No wedded man so hardy be t'assaille
His wyves pacience in trust to fynde
Grisildis, for in certein he shal faille.

O noble wyves, ful of heigh prudence,
Lat noon humylitee youre tonge naille,
Ne lat no clerk have cause or diligence
To write of yow a storie of swich mervaille   1130
As of Grisildis pacient and kynde,
Lest Chichevache° yow swelwe in hire entraille!°

Folweth Ekko, that holdeth no silence,
But evere answereth at the countretaille.°
Beth nat bidaffed° for youre innocence,
But sharply taak on yow the governaille.°
Emprenteth wel this lessoun in youre mynde,
For commune profit sith it may availle.

Ye archewyves,° stondeth at defense,
Syn ye be strong as is a greet camaille;°   1140
Ne suffreth nat that men yow doon offense.
And sklendre wyves, fieble as in bataille,
Beth egre as is a tygre yond in Ynde;
Ay clappeth as a mille,° I yow consaille.

Ne dreed hem nat, doth hem no reverence,
For though thyn housbonde armed be in maille,
The arwes of thy crabbed° eloquence
Shal perce his brest, and eek his aventaille.°
In jalousie I rede eek thou hym bynde,
And thou shalt make hym couche as doth a quaille.   1150

If thou be fair, ther folk been in presence,
Shewe thou thy visage and thyn apparaille;
If thou be foul, be fre of thy dispence;°
To gete thee freendes ay do thy travaille;
Be ay of chiere as light as leef on lynde,°
And lat hym care, and wepe, and wrynge, and
    waille!

[The following stanza seems to have been the original
ending of the tale. It stands after the Envoy in most of

1116 **maistrie,** superiority   **scathe,** a pity   1119 **ernestful,** serious
1132 **Chichevache,** a fabulous cow, reputed to feed on virtuous wives, who was
terribly thin. Bicorne, an equally fabulous cow, was said to feed on patient husbands and was monstrously fat   **entraille,** entrails   1134 **countretaille,** in reply
1135 **bidaffed,** fooled   1136 **governaille,** mastery   1139 **archewyves,** strong
dominating wives   1140 **camaille,** camel   1144 **clappeth as a mille,** chatter as
a mill, be as noisy   1147 **crabbed,** bitter   1148 **aventaille,** front of a helmet
1153 **dispence,** expenditure   1155 **as leef on lynde,** as a linden leaf

---

1070 **costage,** expense   1088 **inportable,** intolerable   1092 **enditeth,** relates
1095 **in gree,** good will   1096 **For greet . . . boghte,** there is good reason in
what he does   1098 **pistel,** epistle   1104 **freletee,** frailty   1106 **suffraunce,**
patience   1112 **at ye,** to the eye   1113 **breste,** break   **plye,** bend   1115 **al
hire secte,** all her sex

the manuscripts which preserve it, but it may have been meant to follow l. 1106 or l. 1113.

Bihoold the murye words of the Hoost.

This worthy Clerk, whan ended was his tale,
Oure Hooste seyde, and swoor, "By Goddes bones,
Me were levere° than a barel ale
1160 My wyf at hoom had herd this legende ones!
This is a gentil° tale for the nones,°
As to my purpos, wiste ye my wille;
But thyng that wol nat be, lat it be stille."]

THE PARDONER'S PROLOGUE°

Radix malorum est Cupiditas. Ad Thimotheum, 6.

"Lordynges," quod he, "in chirches whan I
    preche,
I peyne me to han an hauteyn° speche,
And rynge it out as round as gooth a belle,
For I kan° al by rote that I telle.
My theme° is alwey oon, and evere was—
Radix malorum est Cupiditas.°
    First I pronounce whennes that I come,
And thanne my bulles shewe I, alle and some.
Oure lige lordes seel° on my patente,
10 That shewe I first, my body to warente,°
That no man be so boold, ne preest ne clerk,
Me to destourbe of Cristes hooly werk.
And after that thanne telle I forth my tales;
Bulles of popes and of cardynales,
Of patriarkes and bishopes I shewe,
And in Latyn I speke a wordes fewe,
To saffron with my predicacioun,°
And for to stire hem to devocioun.
Thanne shewe I forth my longe cristal stones,°
20 Ycrammed ful of cloutes° and of bones,—
Relikes been they, as wenen they echoon.
Thanne have I in latoun° a sholder-boon
Which that was of an hooly Jewes sheep.
'Goode men,' I seye, 'taak of my wordes keep;
If that this boon be wasshe in any welle,
If cow, or calf, or sheep, or oxe swelle
That any worm hath ete, or worm ystonge,°
Taak water of that welle and wassh his tonge,

And it is hool anon; and forthermoore,
Of pokkes and of scabbe, and every soore
Shal every sheep be hool that of this welle
30 Drynketh a draughte. Taak kep eek what I telle:
If that the good-man that the beestes oweth
Wol every wyke, er that the cok hym croweth,
Fastynge, drynken of this welle a draughte,
As thilke hooly Jew oure eldres taughte,
His beestes and his stoor shal multiplie.
    And, sires, also it heeleth jalousie;
For though a man be falle in jalous rage,
Lat maken with this water his potage,°
40 And nevere shal he moore his wyf mystriste,
Though he the soothe of hir defaute° wiste,
Al had she taken prestes two or thre.
    Heere is a miteyn eek, that ye may se.
He that his hand wol putte in this mitayn,
He shal have multipliyng of his grayn,
Whan he hath sowen, be it whete or otes,
So that° he offre pens, or elles grotes.
    Goode men and wommen, o thyng warne I yo
If any wight be in this chirche now
50 That hath doon synne horrible, that he
Dar nat, for shame, of it yshryven be,
Or any womman, be she yong or old,
That hath ymaad hir housbonde cokewold,°
Swich folk shal have no power ne no grace
To offren to my relikes in this place.
And whoso fyndeth hym out of swich blame,
He wol come up and offre in Goddes name,
And I assoille him by the auctoritee
Which that by bulle ygraunted was to me.'
60 By this gaude° have I wonne, yeer by yeer,
An hundred mark sith I was pardoner.
I stonde lyk a clerk in my pulpet,
And whan the lewed peple is doun yset,
I preche so as ye han herd bifoore,
And telle an hundred false japes moore.
Thanne peyne I me to strecche forth the nekke,
And est and west upon the peple I bekke,°
As dooth a dowve sittynge on a berne.
70 Myne handes and my tonge goon so yerne
That it is joye to se my bisynesse.
Of avarice and of swich cursednesse
Is al my prechyng, for to make hem free
To yeven hir pens, and namely° unto me.
For myn entente is nat but° for to wynne,
And nothyng° for correccioun of synne.
I rekke nevere, whan that they been beryed,
Though that hir soules goon a-blakeberyed!°
For certes, many a predicacioun
80 Comth ofte tyme of yvel entencioun;
Som for plesance of folk and flaterye,
To been avaunced by ypocrisye,

1159 **levere,** I had rather   1161 **gentil,** noble   1161 **for the nones,** for the purpose
The Pardoner's Prologue and Tale. The pilgrims pause beside the road, and the Pardoner, who has just been asked for a story, partakes of some cakes and ale. Warmed by the drink, he proceeds to a remarkable passage of self-revelation
2 **hauteyn,** proud, lofty   4 **kan,** know   5 **theme,** text   6 **Radix . . . Cupiditas.** The root of (all) evil is avarice; see *1 Timothy,* 6:10   9 **lige lordes seel,** the seal of some bishop   10 **warente,** protect   17 **To . . . predicacioun,** with which to give color to my preaching. Saffron is a yellow dye   19 **cristal stones,** glass cases   20 **cloutes,** rags   22 **latoun,** latten, an alloy of copper and zinc   27 **That . . . ystonge,** that has eaten any snake, or which any snake has stung

40 **potage,** soup   42 **defaute,** fault   48 **So that,** provided   54 **cokewold,** cuckold   61 **gaude,** pretense   68 **bekke,** nod   74 **namely,** particularly   75 **nat but,** only   76 **nothyng,** not at all   78 **Though . . . a-blakeberyed,** though their souls should go a-blackberrying (play truant)

And som for veyne glorie, and som for hate.
For whan I dar noon oother weyes debate,
Thanne wol I stynge hym with my tonge smerte°
In prechyng, so that he shal nat asterte°
To been defamed falsly, if that he
Hath trespased to my bretheren or to me.
For though I telle noght his propre name,
90 Men shal wel knowe that it is the same,
By signes, and by othere circumstances.
Thus quyte° I folk that doon us displesances;
Thus spitte I out my venym under hewe
Of hoolynesse, to semen hooly and trewe.
    But shortly myn entente I wol devyse:
I preche of no thyng but for coveityse.
Therfore my theme is yet, and evere was,
Radix malorum est Cupiditas.
Thus kan I preche agayn° that same vice
100 Which that I use, and that is avarice.
But though myself be gilty in that synne,
Yet kan I maken oother folk to twynne°
From avarice, and soore to repente.
But that is nat my principal entente;
I preche nothyng but for coveitise.
Of this mateere it oghte ynogh suffise.
    Thanne telle I hem ensamples many oon
Of olde stories longe tyme agoon.
For lewed° peple loven tales olde;
110 Swiche thynges kan they wel reporte and
        holde.
What, trowe ye, that whiles I may preche,
And wynne gold and silver for I teche,
That I wol lyve in poverte wilfully?°
Nay, nay, I thoghte° it nevere, trewely!
For I wol preche and begge in sondry landes;
I wol nat do no labour with myne handes,
Ne make baskettes, and lyve therby,
By cause I wol nat beggen ydelly.
I wol noon of the apostles countrefete;°
120 I wol have moneie, wolle, chese, and whete,
Al° were it yeven of the povereste page,°
Or of the povereste wydwe in a village,
Al sholde hir children sterve for famyne.
Nay, I wol drynke licour of the vyne,
And have a joly wenche in every toun.
But herkneth, lordynges, in conclusioun:
Youre likyng is that I shal telle a tale.
Now have I dronke a draughte of corny° ale,
By God, I hope I shal yow telle a thyng
130 That shal by reson been at youre likyng.
For though myself be a ful vicious° man,
A moral tale yet I yow telle kan,
Which I am wont to preche for to wynne.
Now hoold youre pees! my tale I wol bigynne.''

THE PARDONER'S TALE

In Flaundres whilom was a compaignye
Of yonge folk that haunteden folye,
As riot, hasard,° stywes, and tavernes,
Where as with harpes, lutes, and gyternes,°
They daunce and pleyen at dees° bothe day and
        nyght,
And eten also and drynken over hir myght,°   140
Thurgh which they doon the devel sacrifise
Withinne that develes temple, in cursed wise,
By superfluytee abhomynable.
Hir othes been so grete and so dampnable
That it is grisly for to heere hem swere.
Oure blissed Lordes body they totere,°—
Hem thoughte that Jewes rente hym noght ynough;
And ech of hem at otheres synne lough.
And right anon thanne comen tombesteres°
Fetys and smale, and yonge frutesteres,°   150
Syngeres with harpes, baudes, wafereres,°
Whiche been the verray develes officeres
To kyndle and blowe the fyr of lecherye,
That is annexed unto glotonye.
The hooly writ take I to my witnesse
That luxurie is in wyn and dronkenesse.°
    Lo, how that dronken Looth,° unkyndely,°
Lay by his doghtres two, unwityngly;
So dronke he was, he nyste what he wroghte.
Herodes, whoso wel the stories soghte,   160
What he of wyn was repleet at his feeste,
Right at his owene table he yaf his heeste°
To sleen the Baptist John, ful giltelees.
    Senec° seith a good word doutelees;
He seith he kan no difference fynde
Bitwix a man that is out of his mynde
And a man which that is dronkelewe,°
But that woodnesse,° yfallen in a shrewe,
Persevereth lenger than doth dronkenesse.
O glotonye, ful of cursednesse!   170
O cause first of oure confusioun!
O original of oure dampnacioun,
Til Crist hadde boght us with his blood agayn!
Lo, how deere, shortly for to sayn,
Aboght° was thilke cursed vileynye!
Corrupt was al this world for glotonye.
    Adam oure fader, and his wyf also,
Fro Paradys to labour and to wo
Were dryven for that vice, it is no drede.°
For whil that Adam fasted, as I rede,   180
He was in Paradys; and whan that he
Eet of the fruyt deffended° on the tree,

85 **smerte**, smartly   86 **asterte**, escape from being (defamed)   92 **quyte**, pay back   99 **agayn**, against   102 **twynne**, part from   109 **lewed**, ignorant   113 **wilfully**, voluntarily. Voluntary poverty is one of the vows taken by all entering a monastic order   114 **thoghte**, had in mind   119 **countrefete**, imitate   121 **Al**, although   **page**, boy   128 **corny**, strong in grain   131 **vicious**, full of vices

137 **hasard**, gambling   138 **gyternes**, guitars   139 **dees**, dice   140 **over hir myght**, beyond their powers   146 **body they totere, etc.**, reference to the "tearing" or "rending" of Christ's body through oaths like "By God's bones"   149 **tombesteres**, female tumblers, dancing girls   150 **frutesteres**, fruit-selling girls   151 **wafereres**, sellers of cakes and wafers   155–156 **The hooly writ . . . dronkenesse.** See *Ephesians*, 5:18; *Proverbs*, 20:1   157 **dronken Looth**. See *Genesis*, 19:30–36   **unkyndely**, unnaturally   162 **yaf his heeste**, gave his commands   164 **Senec**, Seneca (3 B.C.–A.D. 65), Roman philosopher and writer of tragedies   167 **dronkelewe**, drunk   168 **woodnesse**, madness   175 **Aboght**, bought and paid for   179 **it . . . drede**, there is no doubt   182 **deffended**, forbidden

Anon he was out cast to wo and peyne.
O glotonye, on thee wel oghte us pleyne!
O, wiste a man how manye maladyes
Folwen of excesse and of glotonyes,
He wolde been the moore mesurable
Of his diete, sittynge at his table.
Allas! the shorte throte, the tendre mouth,
190 Maketh that est and west and north and south,
In erthe, in eir, in water, men to swynke°
To gete a glotoun deyntee mete and drynke!
Of this matiere, o Paul, wel kanstow trete:
"Mete° unto wombe,° and wombe eek unto mete,
Shal God destroyen bothe," as Paulus seith.°
Allas! a foul thyng is it, by my feith,
To seye this word, and fouler is the dede,
Whan man so drynketh of the white and rede
That of his throte he maketh his pryvee,
200 Thurgh thilke cursed superfluitee.
    The apostel wepyng seith ful pitously,
"Ther walken manye of whiche yow toold have I—
I seye it now wepyng, with pitous voys—
That they been enemys of Cristes croys,
Of whiche the ende is deeth, wombe is hir god!°"
O wombe! O bely! O stynkyng cod,°
Fulfilled° of dong and of corrupcioun!
At either ende of thee foul is the soun.
How greet labour and cost is thee to fynde!°
210 Thise cookes, how they stampe, and streyne, and
        grynde,
And turnen substaunce into accident,°
To fulfille al thy likerous talent!°
Out of the harde bones knokke they
The mary,° for they caste noght awey
That may go thurgh the golet softe and swoote.
Of spicerie of leef, and bark, and roote
Shal been his sauce ymaked by delit,
To make hym yet a newer appetit.
But, certes, he that haunteth swiche delices
220 Is deed, whil that he lyveth in tho vices.
    A lecherous thyng is wyn, and dronkenesse
Is ful of stryvyng and of wrecchednesse.
O dronke man, disfigured is thy face,
Sour is thy breeth, foul artow to embrace,
And thurgh thy dronke nose semeth the soun
As though thou seydest ay "Sampsoun, Sampsoun!"
And yet, God woot, Sampsoun drank nevere no
        wyn.
Thou fallest as it were a styked swyn;
Thy tonge is lost, and al thyn honeste cure;°
230 For dronkenesse is verray sepulture
Of mannes wit and his discrecioun.
In whom that drynke hath dominacioun

He kan no conseil kepe, it is no drede.
Now kepe yow fro the white and fro the rede,
And namely fro the white wyn of Lepe,°
That is to selle in Fysshstrete or in Chepe.°
This wyn of Spaigne crepeth subtilly
In othere wynes, growynge faste by,
Of which ther ryseth swich fumositee°
That whan a man hath dronken draughtes thre, 240
And weneth that he be at hoom in Chepe,
He is in Spaigne, right at the toune of Lepe,—
Nat at the Rochele,° ne at Burdeux toun;°
And thanne wol he seye "Sampsoun, Sampsoun!"
    But herkneth, lordynges, o word, I yow preye,
That alle the sovereyn actes, dar I seye,
Of victories in the Olde Testament,
Thurgh verray God, that is omnipotent,
Were doon in abstinence and in preyere.
Looketh the Bible, and ther ye may it leere. 250
    Looke, Attilla,° the grete conquerour,
Deyde in his sleep, with shame and dishonour,
Bledynge ay at his nose in dronkenesse.
A capitayn sholde lyve in sobrenesse.
And over al this, avyseth yow right wel
What was comaunded unto Lamuel°—
Nat Samuel, but Lamuel, seye I;
Redeth the Bible, and fynde it expresly
Of wyn-yevyng to hem that han justise.
Namoore of this, for it may wel suffise. 260
    And now that I have spoken of glotonye,
Now wol I yow deffenden hasardrye.
Hasard is verray mooder of lesynges,
And of deceite, and cursed forswerynges,°
Blaspheme of Crist, manslaughtre, and wast also
Of catel and of tyme; and forthermo,
It is repreeve and contrarie of honour°
For to ben holde a commune hasardour.
And ever the hyer he is of estaat,
The moore is he yholden desolaat.° 270
If that a prynce useth hasardrye,
In alle governaunce and policye
He is, as by commune opynioun,
Yholde the lasse in reputacioun.
    Stilboun, that was a wys embassadour,
Was sent to Corynthe, in ful greet honour,
Fro Lacidomye, to make hire alliaunce.
And whan he cam, hym happede, par chaunce,
That alle the gretteste that were of that lond,
Pleyynge atte hasard he hem fond. 280
For which, as soone as it myghte be,
He stal hym hoom agayn to his contree,
And seyde, "Ther wol I nat lese my name,
Ne I wol nat take on me so greet defame,
Yow for to allie unto none hasardours.

191 **swynke**, labor 194 **Mete**, meat **wombe**, belly 195 **as Paulus seith.** See
1 Corinthians, 6:13 202-205 **Ther walken . . . hir god.** See *Philippians*, 3:18-19
206 **cod**, stomach, intestines 207 **Fulfilled**, filled full 209 **How greet . . .
to fynde.** How great a labor and cost it is to provide for (finde) thee 211 **substaunce into accident.** In the sense peculiar to medieval philosophy, the *substance*
of a thing is its real essence; the *accident* comprises the external qualities (color,
weight, shape, etc.) 212 **likerous talent**, lecherous or gluttonous appetite
214 **mary**, the marrow 229 **honest cure**, care for one's honor, self-respect

235 **Lepe**, a town near Cadiz, Spain 236 **Fysshstrete . . . Chepe.** Fishstreet was
a very busy mercantile street near London Bridge 239 **fumositee**, fumes
243 **the Rochele**, La Rochelle, France **Burdeux toun**, Bordeaux, France
251 **Attilla.** The great leader of the Huns died in 453, supposedly as the result of
over-dissipation on his wedding night 256 **Lamuel**, Lemuel. See *Proverbs*,
31:4 ff 264 **forswerynges**, swearing falsely 267 **repreeve . . . honour**, a
shame and enemy to honor 270 **yholden desolaat**, considered debased

Sendeth othere wise embassadours;
For, by my trouthe, me were levere dye
Than I yow sholde to hasardours allye.
For ye, that been so glorious in honours,
290 Shul nat allyen yow with hasardours
As by my wyl, ne as by my tretee.''
This wise philosophre, thus seyde hee.
    Looke eek that to the kyng Demetrius,°
The kyng of Parthes, as the book seith us,
Sente him a paire of dees of gold in scorn,
For he hadde used hasard ther-biforn;
For which he heeld his glorie or his renoun
At no value or reputacioun.
Lordes may fynden oother maner pley
300 Honest ynough to dryve the day awey.
    Now wol I speke of othes false and grete
A word or two, as olde bookes trete.
Gret sweryng is a thyng abhominable,
And fals sweryng is yet moore reprevable.
The heighe God forbad sweryng at al,
Witnesse on Mathew;° but in special
Of sweryng seith the hooly Jeremye,
"Thou shalt swere sooth thyne othes, and nat lye,
And swere in doom, and eek in rightwisnesse'';°
310 But ydel sweryng is a cursednesse.
Bihoold and se that in the firste table
Of heighe Goddes heestes honurable,
Hou that the seconde heeste of hym is this:
"Take nat my name in ydel or amys.''
Lo, rather he forbedeth swich sweryng
Than homycide or many a cursed thyng;
I seye that, as by ordre, thus it stondeth;
This knoweth, that his heestes understondeth,
How that the seconde heeste of God is that.
320 And forther over, I wol thee telle al plat,°
That vengeance shal nat parten from his hous
That of his othes is to outrageous.°
"By Goddes precious herte,'' and "By his nayles,''
And "By the blood of Crist that is in Hayles,°
Sevene is my chaunce, and thyn is cynk and treye!°''
"By Goddes armes, if thou falsly pleye,
This daggere shal thurghout thyn herte go!''—
This fruyt cometh of the bicched bones° two,
Forsweryng, ire, falsnesse, homycide.
330 Now, for the love of Crist, that for us dyde,
Lete youre othes, bothe grete and smale.
But, sires, now wol I telle forth my tale.
    Thise riotoures thre of whiche I telle,
Longe erst er prime° rong of any belle,
Were set hem in a taverne for to drynke,

And as they sat, they herde a belle clynke
Biforn a cors, was caried to his grave.
That oon of hem gan callen to his knave:
"Go bet,°'' quod he, "and axe redily
What cors is this that passeth heer forby;   340
And looke that thou reporte his name weel.''
    "Sire,'' quod this boy, "it nedeth never-a-deel;°
It was me toold er ye cam heer two houres.
He was, pardee, an old felawe of youres;
And sodeynly he was yslayn to-nyght,
Fordronke,° as he sat on his bench upright.
Ther cam a privee theef men clepeth Deeth,
That in this contree al the peple sleeth,
And with his spere he smoot his herte atwo,
And wente his wey withouten wordes mo.   350
He hath a thousand slayn this pestilence.
And, maister, er ye come in his presence,
Me thynketh that it were necessarie
For to be war of swich an adversarie.
Beth redy for to meete hym everemoore;
Thus taughte me my dame; I sey namoore.''
    "By seinte Marie!'' seyde this taverner,
"The child seith sooth, for he hath slayn this yeer,
Henne over a mile, withinne a greet village,
Bothe man and womman, child, and hyne,° and   360
    page;°
I trowe his habitacioun be there.
To been avysed greet wysdom it were,
Er that he dide a man a dishonour.''
    "Ye, Goddes armes!'' quod this riotour,
"Is it swich peril with hym for to meete?
I shal hym seke by wey and eek by strete,
I make avow to Goddes digne bones!°
Herkneth, felawes, we thre been al ones;
Lat ech of us holde up his hand til oother,
And ech of us bicomen otheres brother,   370
And we wol sleen this false traytour Deeth.
He shal be slayn, he that so manye sleeth,
By Goddes dignitee,° er it be nyght!''
    Togidres han thise thre hir trouthes plight
To lyve and dyen ech of hem for oother,
As though he were his owene ybore brother.
And up they stirte, al dronken in this rage,
And forth they goon towardes that village
Of which the taverner hadde spoke biforn.
And many a grisly ooth thanne han they sworn,   380
And Cristes blessed body al torente—
Deeth shal be deed, if that they may hym hente!
    Whan they han goon nat fully half a mile,
Right as they wolde han troden over a stile,
An oold man and a povre with hem mette.
This olde man ful mekely hem grette,°
And seyde thus, "Now, lordes, God yow see!°''

The proudeste of thise riotoures three
Answerde agayn, ''What, carl,° with sory grace!
390 Why artow° al forwrapped° save thy face?
Why lyvestow so longe in so greet age?''
  This olde man gan looke in his visage,
And seyde thus: ''For I ne kan nat fynde
A man, though that I walked into Ynde,
Neither in citee ne in no village,
That wolde chaunge his youthe for myn age;
And therfore moot I han myn age stille,
As longe tyme as it is Goddes wille.
Ne Deeth, allas! ne wol nat han my lyf.
400 Thus walke I, lyk a restelees kaityf,
And on the ground, which is my moodres gate,
I knokke with my staf, bothe erly and late,
And seye 'Leeve mooder, leet me in!
Lo how I vanysshe, flessh, and blood, and skyn!
Allas! whan shul my bones been at reste?
Mooder, with yow wolde I chaunge my cheste
That in my chambre longe tyme hath be,
Ye, for an heyre clowt to wrappe in me!'
But yet to me she wol nat do that grace,
410 For which ful pale and welked° is my face.
  But, sires, to yow it is no curteisye
To speken to an old man vileynye,
But he trespasse in word, or elles in dede.
In Hooly Writ ye may yourself wel rede:
'Agayns an oold man, hoor upon his heed,
Ye sholde arise;'° wherfore I yeve yow reed,
Ne dooth unto an oold man noon harm now,
Namoore than that ye wolde men did to yow
In age, if that ye so longe abyde.
420 And God be with yow, where ye go° or ryde!
I moot go thider as I have to go.''
  ''Nay, olde cherl, by God, thou shalt nat so,''
Seyde this oother hasardour anon;
''Thou partest nat so lightly, by Seint John!
Thou spak right now of thilke traytour Deeth,
That in this contree alle oure freendes sleeth.
Have heer my trouthe, as thou art his espye,°
Telle where he is, or thou shalt it abye,°
By God, and by the hooly sacrement!
430 For soothly thou art oon of his assent°
To sleen us yonge folk, thou false theef!''
  ''Now, sires,'' quod he, ''if that yow be so leef°
To fynde Deeth, turne up this croked wey,
For in that grove I lafte hym, by my fey,
Under a tree, and there he wole abyde;
Noght for youre boost he wole him no thyng hyde.
Se ye that ook? Right there ye shal hym fynde.
God save yow, that boghte agayn mankynde,
And yow amende!'' Thus seyde this olde man;
440 And everich of thise riotoures ran
Til he cam to that tree, and ther they founde
Of floryns fyne of gold ycoyned rounde

Wel ny an eighte busshels, as hem thoughte.
No lenger thanne after Deeth they soughte,
But ech of hem so glad was of that sighte,
For that the floryns been so faire and brighte,
That doun they sette hem by this precious hoord.
The worste of hem, he spak the firste word.
  ''Bretheren,'' quod he, ''taak kep what that I
    seye;
My wit is greet, though that I bourde° and pleye.   450
This tresor hath Fortune unto us yiven,
In myrthe and jolitee oure lyf to lyven,
And lightly as it comth, so wol we spende.
Ey! Goddes precious dignitee! who wende°
To-day that we sholde han so fair a grace?
But myghte this gold be caried fro this place
Hoom to myn hous, or elles unto youres—
For wel ye woot that al this gold is oures—
Thanne were we in heigh felicitee.
But trewely, by daye it may nat bee.   460
Men wolde seyn that we were theves stronge,
And for oure owene tresor doon us honge.°
This tresor moste ycaried be by nyghte
As wisely and as slyly° as it myghte.
Wherfore I rede that cut among us alle
Be drawe, and lat se wher the cut wol falle;
And he that hath the cut with herte blithe
Shal renne to the town, and that ful swithe,°
And brynge us breed and wyn ful prively.
And two of us shul kepen subtilly   470
This tresor wel; and if he wol nat tarie,
Whan it is nyght, we wol this tresor carie,
By oon assent, where as us thynketh best.''
That oon of hem the cut broghte in his fest,°
And bad hem drawe, and looke where it wol falle;
And it fil on° the yongeste of hem alle,
And forth toward the toun he wente anon.
And also soone as that he was gon,
That oon of hem spak thus unto that oother:
''Thow knowest wel thou art my sworen brother;   480
Thy profit wol I telle thee anon.
Thou woost wel that oure felawe is agon.
And heere is gold, and that ful greet plentee,
That shal departed been among us thre.
But nathelees, if I kan shape it so
That it departed were among us two,
Hadde I nat doon a freendes torn° to thee?''
  That oother answerde, ''I noot hou that may be.
He woot wel that the gold is with us tweye;
What shal we doon? What shal we to hym seye?''   490
  ''Shal it be conseil?°'' seyde the firste shrewe,°
''And I shal tellen in a wordes fewe
What we shal doon, and brynge it wel aboute.''
  ''I graunte,'' quod that oother, ''out of doute,
That, by my trouthe, I wol thee nat biwreye.''

389 **carl,** man, fellow   390 **artow,** are you   **forwrapped,** wrapped up
410 **welked,** withered   415–416 **Agayns . . . arise.** See *Leviticus,* 19:32
420 **go,** walk   427 **espye,** spy   428 **abye,** pay for   430 **assent,** opinion, belief   432 **leef,** lief, eager

450 **bourde,** jest   454 **wende,** supposed, expected   462 **doon us honge,** make
us hang, have us hanged   464 **slyly,** wisely   468 **swithe,** quickly   474 **fest,**
fist. The lot was chosen presumably by plucking grass—the shortest blade determined the choice   476 **fil on,** fell to   487 **freendes torn,** friendly turn
491 **conseil,** a secret   **shrewe,** rascal

"Now," quod the firste, "thou woost wel we be
    tweye,
And two of us shul strenger be than oon.
Looke whan that he is set, that right anoon
Arys as though thou woldest with hym pleye,
500 And I shal ryve hym thurgh the sydes tweye
Whil that thou strogelest with hym as in game,
And with thy daggere looke thou do the same;
And thanne shal al this gold departed be,
My deere freend, bitwixen me and thee.
Thanne may we bothe oure lustes all fulfille,
And pleye at dees right at oure owene wille."
And thus acorded been thise shrewes tweye
To sleen the thridde, as ye han herd me seye.
    This yongeste, which that wente to the toun,
510 Ful ofte in herte he rolleth up and doun
The beautee of thise floryns newe and brighte.
"O Lord!" quod he, "if so were that I myghte
Have al this tresor to myself allone,
Ther is no man that lyveth under the trone
Of God that sholde lyve so murye as I!"
And atte laste the feend, oure enemy,
Putte in his thought that he sholde poyson beye,°
With which he myghte sleen his felawes tweye;
For-why° the feend foond hym in swich lyvynge
520 That he hadde leve° him to sorwe brynge.
For this was outrely his fulle entente,
To sleen hem bothe, and nevere to repente.
And forth he gooth, no lenger wolde he tarie,
Into the toun, unto a pothecarie,
And preyde hym that he hym wolde selle
Som poyson, that he myghte his rattes quelle;°
And eek ther was a polcat in his hawe,°
That, as he seyde, his capouns hadde yslawe,
And fayn he wolde wreke hym,° if he myghte,
530 On vermyn that destroyed hym by nyghte.
    The pothecarie answerde, "And thou shalt have
A thyng that, also God my soule save,
In al this world ther is no creature,
That eten or dronken hath of this confiture°
Noght but the montance° of a corn of whete,
That he ne shal his lif anon forlete;°
Ye, sterve° he shal, and that in lasse while
Than thou wolt goon a paas nat but a mile,
This poysoun is so strong and violent."
540 This cursed man hath in his hond yhent
This poysoun in a box, and sith° he ran
Into the nexte strete unto a man,
And borwed of hym large botelles thre;
And in the two his poyson poured he;
The thridde he kepte clene for his drynke.
For al the nyght he shoop hym for to swynke
In cariynge of the gold out of that place.
And whan this riotour, with sory grace,

Hadde filled with wyn his grete botels thre,
To his felawes agayn repaireth he.   550
    What nedeth it to sermone° of it moore?
For right as they hadde cast his deeth bifoore,
Right so they han hym slayn, and that anon.
And whan that this was doon, thus spak that oon:
"Now lat us sitte and drynke, and make us merie,
And afterward we wol his body berie."
And with that word it happed hym, par cas,
To take the botel ther the poyson was,
And drank, and yaf his felawe drynke also,
For which anon they storven bothe two.   560
    But certes, I suppose that Avycen°
Wroot nevere in no canon, ne in no fen,°
Mo wonder signes of empoisonyng
Than hadde thise wrecches two, er hir endyng.
Thus ended been thise homycides two,
And eek the false empoysonere also.
    O cursed synne of alle cursednesse!
O traytours homycide, O wikkednesse!
O glotonye, luxurie, and hasardrye!
Thou blasphemour of Crist with vileynye   570
And othes grete, of usage and of pride!
Allas! mankynde, how may it bitide
That to thy creatour, which that the wroghte,
And with his precious herte-blood thee boghte,
Thou art so fals and so unkynde,° allas?
    Now, goode men, God foryeve yow youre trespas,
And ware yow fro the synne of avarice!
Myn hooly pardoun may yow alle warice,°
So that ye offre nobles or sterlynges,°
Or elles silver broches, spoones, rynges.   580
Boweth youre heed under this hooly bulle!
Cometh up, ye wyves, offreth of youre wolle!°
Youre names I entre heer in my rolle anon;
Into the blisse of hevene shul ye gon.
I yow assoille, by myn heigh power,
Yow that wol offre, as clene and eek as cleer
As ye were born.—And lo, sires, thus I preche.
And Jhesu Crist, that is oure soules leche,
So graunte yow his pardoun to receyve,
For that is best; I wol yow nat deceyve.   590
    But, sires, o word forgat I in my tale:
I have relikes and pardoun in my male,°
As faire as any man in Engelond,
Whiche were me yeven by the popes hond.
If any of yow wole, of devocion,
Offren, and han myn absolucion,
Com forth anon, and kneleth heere adoun,
And mekely receyveth my pardoun;
Or elles taketh pardoun as ye wende,
Al newe and fressh at every miles ende,   600
So that ye offren, alwey newe and newe,

551 nedeth . . . sermone, why is it necessary to make a sermon   561 Avycen,
the famous Arab philosopher of the eleventh century, particularly noted for his
medical studies   562 fen, chapter, subdivision; canoun signifies the chapter
heading   575 unkynde, unnatural, monstrous   578 warice, cure   579 nobles
or sterlynges. The noble was a coin first used in the fourteenth century, worth six
shillings eight pence; the sterlyng was a silver penny   582 wolle, wool
592 male, bag

517 beye, buy   519 For-why, because   520 leve, permission. God permitted
the fiend to bring the man to sorrow   526 quelle, kill   527 hawe, yard
529 wreke him, avenge himself   534 confiture, concoction   535 montance,
amount   536 forlete, leave, give up   537 sterve, die   541 sith, afterwards

Nobles or pens, whiche that be goode and trewe.
It is an honour to everich that is heer
That ye mowe have a suffisant pardoneer
T'assoille° yow, in contree as ye ryde,
For aventures whiche that may bityde.
Paraventure ther may fallen oon or two
Doun of his hors, and breke his nekke atwo.
Looke which a seuretee is it to yow alle
610 That I am in youre felaweshipe yfalle,
That may assoille yow, bothe moore and lasse,
Whan that the soule shal fro the body passe.
I rede that oure Hoost heere shal bigynne,
For he is moost envoluped° in synne.
Com forth, sire Hoost, and offre first anon,
And thou shalt kisse the relikes everychon,
Ye, for a grote! Unbokele anon thy purs.''
   ''Nay, nay!'' quod he, ''thanne have I Cristes
      curs!
Lat be,'' quod he, ''it shal nat be, so theech!°
620 Thou woldest make me kisse thyn olde breech,
And swere it were a relyk of a seint,
Though it were with thy fundement depeint!°
But, by the croys° which that Seint Eleyne fond,
I wolde I hadde thy coillons° in myn hond
In stide of relikes or of seintuarie.
Lat kutte hem of, I wol thee helpe hem carie;
They shul be shryned in an hogges toord!''
   This Pardoner answerde nat a word;
So wrooth he was, no word ne wolde he seye.
630 ''Now,'' quod oure Hoost, ''I wol no lenger pleye
With thee, ne with noon oother angry man.''
But right anon the worthy Knyght bigan,
Whan that he saugh that al the peple lough,
''Namoore of this, for it is right ynough!
Sire Pardoner, be glad and myrie of cheere;
And ye, sire Hoost, that been to me so deere,
I prey yow that ye kisse the Pardoner.
And Pardoner, I prey thee, drawe thee neer,
And, as we diden, lat us laughe and pleye.''
640 Anon they kiste, and ryden forth hir weye.

THE NUN'S PRIEST'S TALE

A povre wydwe, somdeel stape° in age
Was whilom dwellyng in a narwe cotage,
Biside a grove, stondynge in a dale.
This wydwe, of which I telle yow my tale,
Syn thilke day that she was last a wyf,
In pacience ladde a ful symple lyf,
For litel was hir catel and hir rente.°
By housbondrie of swich as God hire sente

She foond° hirself and eek hir doghtren two.
Thre large sowes hadde she, and namo,   10
Three keen,° and eek a sheep that highte Malle.
Ful sooty was hire bour and eek hir halle,
In which she eet ful many a sklendre meel.
Of poynaunt sauce hir neded never a deel.
No deyntee morsel passed thurgh hir throte;
Hir diete was accordant° to hir cote.
Repleccioun° ne made hire nevere sik;
Attempree° diete was al hir phisik,
And exercise, and hertes suffisaunce.
The goute lette° hire nothyng for to daunce,   20
N'apoplexie shente° nat hir heed.
No wyn ne drank she, neither whit ne reed;
Hir bord was served moost with whit and blak,°—
Milk and broun breed, in which she foond no lak,
Seynd° bacoun, and somtyme an ey° or tweye;
For she was, as it were, a maner deye.°
   A yeerd she hadde, enclosed al aboute
With stikkes, and a drye dych withoute,
In which she hadde a cok, hight Chauntecleer.
In al the land, of crowyng nas his peer.   30
His voys was murier than the murie orgon
On messe° dayes that in the chirche gon.
Wel sikerer° was his crowyng in his logge
Than is a clokke or an abbey orlogge.°
By nature he knew ech ascencioun°
Of the equynoxial° in thilke toun;
For whan degrees fiftene weren ascended,
Thanne crew he, that it myghte nat been amended.°
His coomb was redder than the fyn coral,
And batailled° as it were a castel wal;   40
His byle was blak, and as the jeet it shoon;
Lyk asure were his legges and his toon;°
His nayles whitter than the lylye flour,
And lyk the burned gold was his colour.
This gentil cok hadde in his governaunce°
Sevene hennes for to doon al his plesaunce,
Whiche were his sustres and his paramours,
And wonder lyk to hym, as of colours;
Of whiche the faireste hewed on hir throte
Was cleped faire damoysele Pertelote.   50
Curteys she was, discreet, and debonaire,°
And compaignable, and bar hyrself so faire,
Syn thilke day that she was seven nyght oold,
That trewely she hath the herte in hoold°
Of Chauntecleer, loken° in every lith;°
He loved hire so that wel was hym therwith.°

9 **foond,** provided for   11 **keen,** kine, cows   16 **accordant to,** in keeping with 17 **Repleccioun,** overeating   18 **Attempree,** temperate   20 **lette, etc.** The gout did not prevent her from dancing   21 **shente,** injured   23 **whit and blak,** light and dark ale   25 **Seynd,** singed   **ey,** egg   26 **deye,** dairy woman 32 **messe,** feast, mass   33 **sikerer,** more certain, more dependable   34 **orlogge,** horologe, large clock   35–36 **ascencioun of the equynoxial.** The *equinoxial* is the great circle made in the heavens by the extended plane of the earth's equator. It made a complete revolution in twenty-four hours; consequently, fifteen degrees would pass or "ascend" every hour. Chauntecleer knew by instinct every hour of the day and proclaimed its arrival   38 **it ... amended.** It could not be improved upon   40 **batailled,** with battlements (the cock's wattles)   42 **toon,** toes   45 **governaunce,** control, power   51 **debonaire,** meek   54 **in hoold,** in her grasp, in her possession   55 **loken,** locked   **lith,** limb   56 **wel ... therwith.** It was well with Chauntecleer because he loved her so

605 **T'assoille,** to absolve   614 **envoluped,** enveloped   619 **so theech,** so may I prosper   622 **with ... depeint,** daubed with your excrement   623 **croys ...** **fond.** St. Helen was believed to be the finder of the True Cross   624 **coillons,** testicles
The Nun's Tale   1 **stape,** advanced   7 **catel ... rente,** property and income

But swich a joye was it to here hem synge,
Whan that the brighte sonne gan to sprynge,
In sweete accord, "My lief is faren in londe!"°
60 For thilke tyme, as I have understonde,
Beestes and briddes koude speke and synge.°
  And so bifel that in a dawenynge,
As Chauntecleer among his wyves alle
Sat on his perche that was in the halle,
And next hym sat this faire Pertelote,
This Chauntecleer gan gronen in his throte,
As man that in his dreem is drecched° soore.
And whan that Pertelote thus herde hym roore,
She was agast, and seyde, "Herte deere,
70 What eyleth yow, to grone in this manere?
Ye been a verray sleper; fy, for shame!"
  And he answerde, and seyde thus: "Madame,
I pray yow that ye take it nat agrief.°
By God, me mette° I was in swich meschief
Right now, that yet myn herte is soore afright.
Now God," quod he, "my swevene recche° aright,
And kepe my body out of foul prisoun!
Me mette how that I romed up and doun
Withinne our yeerd, wheer as I saugh a beest
80 Was lyk an hound, and wolde han maad areest
Upon my body, and wolde han had me deed.
His colour was bitwixe yelow and reed,
And tipped was his tayl and bothe his eeris
With blak, unlyk the remenant of his heeris;
His snowte smal, with glowynge eyen tweye.
Yet of his look for feere almoost I deye;
This caused me my gronyng, doutelees.°"
  "Avoy!" quod she, "fy on yow, hertelees!°
Allas!" quod she, "for, by that God above,
90 Now han ye lost myn herte and al my love.
I kan nat love a coward, by my feith!
For certes, what so any womman seith,
We alle desiren, if it myghte bee,
To han housbondes hardy, wise, and free,
And secree, and no nygard, ne no fool,
Ne hym that is agast of every tool,
Ne noon avauntour,° by that God above!
How dorste ye seyn, for shame, unto youre love
That any thyng myghte make yow aferd?
100 Have ye no mannes herte, and han a berd?
Allas! and konne ye been agast of swevenys?
Nothyng, God woot, but vanitee in sweven is.
Swevenes engendren° of replecciouns,°
And ofte of fume° and of complecciouns,°
Whan humours been to habundant in a wight.
Certes° this dreem, which ye han met to-nyght,

Cometh of the greete superfluytee
Of youre rede colera,° pardee,
Which causeth folk to dreden in hir dremes
Of arwes, and of fyr with rede lemes,°   110
Of rede beestes, that they wol hem byte,
Of contek,° and of whelpes, grete and lyte;
Right as the humour of malencolie
Causeth ful many a man in sleep to crie
For feere of blake beres, or boles° blake,
Or elles blake develes wole hem take.
Of othere humours koude I telle also
That werken many a man sleep ful wo;
But I wol passe as lightly as I kan.
  Lo Catoun,° which that was so wys a man,   120
Seyde he nat thus, 'Ne do no fors of° dremes?'
  Now sire," quod she, "whan we flee fro the
    bemes,
For Goddes love, as taak som laxatyf.
Up° peril of my soule and of my lyf,
I conseille yow the beste, I wol nat lye,
That bothe of colere° and of malencolye°
Ye purge yow; and for ye shal nat tarie,
Though in this toun is noon apothecarie,
I shal myself to herbes techen yow
That shul been for youre hele° and for youre prow;°   130
And in oure yeerd tho herbes shal I fynde
The whiche han of hire propretee by kynde°
To purge yow bynethe and eek above.
Foryet nat this, for Goddes owene love!
Ye been ful coleryk of compleccioun;
Ware the sonne in his ascencioun
Ne fynde yow nat repleet of humours hoote.
And if it do, I dar wel leye a grote,
That ye shul have a fevere terciane,°
Or an agu, that may be youre bane.   140
A day or two ye shul have digestyves
Of wormes, er ye take youre laxatyves
Of lawriol,° centaure, and fumetere,
Or elles of ellebor, that groweth there,
Of katapuce, or of gaitrys beryis,
Of herbe yve, growyng in oure yeerd, ther mery is;
Pekke hem up right as they growe and ete hem yn.
Be myrie, housbonde, for youre fader kyn!
Dredeth no dreem, I kan sey yow namoore."
  "Madame," quod he, "graunt mercy of youre   150
    loore.
But nathelees, as touchyng daun° Catoun,
That hath of wysdom swich a greet renoun,
Though that he bad no dremes for to drede,
By God, men may in olde bookes rede

59 **My lief . . . in londe.** My love has gone to the country 60–61 **For thilke tyme . . . synge,** a conventional "apology" in fables 67 **drecched,** troubled, afflicted 73 **agrief,** amiss 74 **me mette,** I dreamed 76 **swevene recche,** interpre. This tale provides an interesting commentary upon the medieval attitude toward dreams, in that the two main characters, Chauntecleer and Pertelote, represent in a sense the two fundamentally different approaches to dreams. Pertelote believes in the physiological explanation of dreams while Chauntecleer tends to see in dreams portents of future events 87 **doutelees,** doubtless 88 **hertelees,** lacking heart or courage 97 **avauntour,** boaster, braggart, which often connotes cowardice 103 **engendren,** have their source in, come about from **replecciouns,** overeating 104 **fume,** air on the stomach **complecciouns,** the combination and balance of the four humors 106 **Certes,** surely, certainly

108 **rede colera,** bile. A serious overbalance of one humor in respect to the others was thought to give a corresponding tinge to all objects seen by the patient. Too much bile was supposed to make all things appear red 110 **lemes,** flames 112 **contek,** conflict 115 **boles,** bulls 120 **Catoun,** Dionysius Cato, fourth-century author of a collection of Latin epigrams 121 **do no fors of,** attach no importance to 124 **Up,** upon 126 **colere,** choler, bile **malencolye,** black bile 130 **hele,** health **prow,** benefit 132 **by kynde,** by nature 139 **fevere terciane,** a tertian fever, one that recurs every third day. Medieval authorities attributed the disease to a superabundance of bile or black bile 143 **lawriol, etc.,** a list of drugs commonly used as cathartics in the Middle Ages 151 **daun.** Here as elsewhere, the shortened form of the Latin *dominus* ("lord") is used as a title of respect

Of many a man moore of auctorite
Than evere Caton was, so moot I thee,°
That al the revers seyn of this sentence,°
And han wel founden by experience
160 That dremes been significacioun
As wel of joye as of tribulaciouns
That folk enduren in this lif present.
Ther nedeth make of this noon argument;
The verray preeve° sheweth it in dede.
   Oon of the gretteste auctour that men rede
Seith thus: that whilom two felawes wente
On pilgrimage, in a ful good entente;
And happed so, they coomen in a toun
Wher as ther was swich congregacioun
Of peple, and eek so streit° of herbergage,°
170 That they ne founde as muche as o cotage
In which they bothe myghte ylogged bee.
Wherfore they mosten of necessitee,
As for that nyght, departen compaignye;
And ech of hem gooth to his hostelrye,
And took his loggyng as it wolde falle.
That oon of hem was logged in a stalle,
Fer in a yeerd, with oxen of the plough;
That oother man was logged wel ynough,
As was his aventure or his fortune,
180 That us governeth alle as in commune.
   And so bifel that, longe er it were day,
This man mette in his bed, ther as he lay,
How that this felawe gan upon hym calle,
And seyde, 'Allas! for in an oxes stalle
This nyght I shal be mordred ther I lye.
Now help me, deere brother, or I dye.
In alle haste com to me!' he sayde.
This man out of his sleep for feere abrayde;°
But whan that he was wakened of his sleep,
190 He turned hym, and took of this no keep.
Hym thoughte° his dreem nas but a vanitee.
Thus twies in his slepyng dremed hee;
And atte thridde tyme yet his felawe
Cam, as hym thoughte, and seide, 'I am now slawe.°
Bihoold my bloody woundes depe and wyde!
Arys up erly in the morwe tyde,
And at the west gate of the toun,' quod he,
'A carte ful of dong ther shaltow se,
In which my body is hid ful prively;
200 Do thilke carte arresten boldely.
My gold caused my mordre, sooth to sayn.'
And tolde hym every point how he was slayn,
With a ful pitous face, pale of hewe.
And truste wel, his dreem he foond ful trewe,
For on the morwe, as soone as it was day,
To his felawes in° he took the way;
And whan that he cam to this oxes stalle,
After his felawe he bigan to calle.

The hostiler answerede hym anon,
And seyde, 'Sire, your felawe is agon. 210
As soone as day he wente out of the toun.'
   This man gan fallen in suspecioun,
Remembrynge on his dremes that he mette,
And forth he gooth—no lenger wolde he lette°—
Unto the west gate of the toun, and fond
A dong-carte, wente as it were to donge lond,°
That was arrayed in that same wise
As ye han herd the dede man devyse.°
And with an hardy herte he gan to crye
Vengeance and justice of this felonye. 220
'My felawe mordred is this same nyght,
And in this carte he lith gapyng upright.°
I crye out on the ministres,' quod he,
'That sholden kepe and reulen this citee.
Harrow! allas! heere lith my felawe slayn!'
What sholde I moore unto this tale sayn?
The peple out sterte and caste the cart to grounde,
And in the myddel of the dong they founde
The dede man, that mordred was al newe.
   O blisful God, that art so just and trewe, 230
Lo, how that thou biwreyest° mordre alway!
Mordre wol out, that se we day by day.
Mordre is so wlatsom° and abhomynable
To God, that is so just and resonable,
That he ne wol nat suffre it heled° be,
Though it abyde a yeer, or two, or thre.
Mordre wol out, this my conclusioun.
And right anon, ministres of that toun
Han hent° the carter and so soore hym pyned,°
And eek the hostiler so soore engyned,° 240
That they biknewe° hire wikkednesse anon,
And were anhanged by the nekke-bon.
   Heere may men seen that dremes been to drede.
And certes in the same book I rede,
Right in the nexte chapitre after this—
I gabbe° nat, so have I joye or blis—
Two men that wolde han passed over see,
For certeyn cause, into a fer contree,
If that the wynd ne hadde been contrarie,
That made hem in a citee for to tarie 250
That stood ful myrie upon an haven-syde;
But on a day, agayn° the even-tyde,
The wynd gan chaunge, and blew right as hem leste.
Jolif° and glad they wente unto hir reste,
And casten hem ful erly for to saille.
But to that o° man fil a greet mervaille:
That oon of hem, in slepyng as he lay,
Hym mette a wonder dreem agayn the day.
Hym thoughte a man stood by his beddes syde,
And hym comanded that he sholde abyde, 260
And seyde hym thus: 'If thou tomorwe wende,

---

156 **so moot I thee,** so may I prosper   157 **sentence,** statement, opinion
163 **verray preve, etc.** The true test (of the statement) proves it in fact
169 **streit,** narrow; here in the sense of "crowded"   **herbergage,** lodgings
188 **abrayde,** started up   191 **Hym thoughte,** it seemed to him   194 **slawe,**
slain   206 **in,** inn, lodging

214 **lette,** hinder, with the meaning here of "linger"   216 **donge lond,** to cover
land with dung. Raw sewage was carried outside the city gates and dumped there
218 **devyse,** describe   222 **upright,** on his back   231 **biwreyest,** make
known   233 **wlatsom,** disgusting   235 **heled,** concealed   239 **hent,** seized
pyned, tortured   240 **engyned,** put on the rack or other instrument (engine) of
torture   241 **biknewe,** confessed   246 **gabbe,** speak idly   252 **agayn,** toward,
just before   254 **Jolif,** jolly   256 **o,** one

Thow shalt be dreynt;° my tale is at an ende.'
He wook, and tolde his felawe what he mette,
And preyde hym his viage for to lette;°
As for that day, he preyde hym to byde.
His felawe, that lay by his beddes syde,
Gan for to laughe, and scorned him ful faste.
'No dreem,' quod he, 'may so myn herte agaste
That I wol lette for to do my thynges.
270 I sette nat a straw by thy dremynges,
For swevenes been but vanytees and japes.°
Men dreme alday of owles and of apes,
And eek of many a maze° therwithal;
Men dreme of thyng that nevere was ne shal.°
But sith I see that thou wolt heere abyde,
And thus forslewthen° wilfully thy tyde,°
God woot, it reweth me;° and have good day!'
And thus he took his leve, and wente his way.
But er that he hadde half his cours yseyled,
280 Noot I nat why, ne what myschaunce it eyled,
But casuelly° the shippes botme rente,
And ship and man under the water wente
In sighte of othere shippes it bisyde,
That with hem seyled at the same tyde.
And therfore, faire Pertelote so deere,
By swiche ensamples olde maistow leere
That no man sholde been to recchelees°
Of dremes; for I seye thee, doutelees,
That many a dreem ful soore is for to drede.
290   Lo, in the lyf of seint Kenelm° I rede,
That was Kenulphus sone, the noble kyng
Of Mercenrike, how Kenelm mette a thyng.
A lite er he was mordred, on a day,
His mordre in his avysioun° he say.°
His norice° hym expowned every deel
His sweven, and bad hym for to kepe hym weel
For traisoun; but he nas but seven yeer oold,
And therfore litel tale° hath he toold°
Of any dreem, so hooly was his herte.
300 By God! I hadde levere than my sherte
That ye hadde rad his legende, as have I.
    Dame Pertelote, I sey yow trewely,
Macrobeus,ᶜ that writ the avisioun
In Affrike of the worthy Cipioun,°
Affermeth dremes, and seith that they been
Warnynge of thynges that men after seen.
And forthermoore, I pray yow, looketh wel
In the olde testament, of Daniel,
If he heeld dremes any vanitee.
310 Reed eek of Joseph,° and ther shul ye see

Wher dremes be somtyme—I sey nat alle°—
Warnynge of thynges that shul after falle.
Looke of Egipte the kyng, daun Pharao,
His bakere and his butiller also,
Wher they ne felte noon effect in dremes.
Whoso wol seken actes of sondry remes°
May rede of dremes many a wonder thyng.
Lo Cresus,° which that was of Lyde kyng,
Mette he nat that he sat upon a tree,
Which signified he sholde anhanged bee?   320
Lo heere Andromacha,° Ectores wyf,
That day that Ector sholde lese his lyf,
She dremed on the same nyght biforn
How that the lyf of Ector sholde be lorn,
If thilke day he wente into bataille.
She warned hym, but it myghte nat availle;
He wente for to fighte natheles,
But he was slayn anon of Achilles.
But thilke tale is al to longe to telle,
And eek it is ny day, I may nat dwelle.   330
Shortly I seye, as for conclusioun,
That I shal han of this avisioun
Adversitee; and I seye forthermoor,
That I ne telle of laxatyves no stoor,
For they been venymous, I woot it weel;
I hem diffye, I love hem never a deel!
    Now let us speke of myrthe, and stynte° al this.
Madame Pertelote, so have I blis,
Of o thyng God hath sent me large grace;
For whan I se the beautee of youre face,   340
Ye been so scarlet reed aboute youre yen,
It maketh al my drede for to dyen;
For al so siker° as *In principio*,
Mulier est hominis confusio,°—
Madame, the sentence of this Latyn is,
'Womman is mannes joye and al his blis.'
For whan I feele a-nyght your softe syde,
Al be it that I may nat on yow ryde,
For that oure perche is maad so narwe, allas!
I am so ful of joye and of solas,   350
That I diffye bothe sweven and dreem.''
And with that word he fley doun fro the beem,
For it was day, and eke his hennes alle,
And with a chuk he gan hem for to calle,
For he hadde founde a corn,° lay in the yerd.
Real he was, he was namoore aferd.
He fethered Pertelote twenty tyme,
And trad hire eke as ofte, er it was pryme.
He looketh as it were a grym leoun,°
And on his toos he rometh up and doun;   360
Hym deigned nat to sette his foot to grounde.

262 **dreynt**, drowned   264 **lette**, delay   271 **vanytees and japes**, follies and jokes   273 **maze**, confusion, bewilderment   274 **shal**, shall (be)   276 **forslewthen**, waste in sloth   **tyde**, time   277 **it reweth me**, it rues me, I am sorry   281 **casuelly**, by accident   287 **recchelees**, not caring for, not heeding   290 **seint Kenelm**, etc. The story is told in one of the many medieval lives of the saints. Kenulphus, King of Mercia, died in 821; his son Kenelm was but seven years of age at the time and was put under the care of his aunt, who conspired to murder him. Before his death the child dreamed that he climbed into a lofty tree; one of his friends came and cut it down, whereupon the boy flew to heaven as a bird   294 **avysioun**, vision, dream   **say**, saw   295 **norice**, nurse   298 **tale**, importance   **toold**, ascribed, attributed   303 **Macrobeus**, c. 400, was the "authority" on dreams during the Middle Ages and a proponent of the "pre-monitory" interpretation of dreams   **the avisioun . . . Cipioun**, Macrobius wrote a commentary on Cicero's "Somnium Scipionis" or "Dream of Scipio (Africanus)"

310 **Joseph.** The manner in which Joseph interprets dreams is told in *Genesis*, 37, 40, 41. The marshaling of authorities is typical of reasoning in the Middle Ages   311 **I sey nat alle.** I do not set (up) all dreams (as proof)   316 **remes**, realms   318 **Cresus.** The king of Lydia (603?–546 B.C.) was defeated and killed by Cyrus the Great   321 **Andromacha**, the wife of Hector in Homer's *Iliad*. There is nothing in Homer about her dream; it is a fiction of the medieval authors in the development of the Troy story   337 **stynte**, stop   343 **siker**, sure   343–344 **In principio . . . confusio.** The quotation begins like the first verse of the *Gospel of John* or the opening of the *Book of Genesis*. The rest (*Mulier . . .*) means "Woman is man's confusion" and was more or less a proverb of the time   355 **corn**, grain (of any kind)   359 **leoun**, lion

He chukketh whan he hath a corn yfounde,
And to hym rennen thanne his wyves alle.
Thus roial, as a prince is in his halle,
Leve I this Chauntecleer in his pasture,
And after wol I telle his aventure.
    Whan that the month in which the world bigan,
That highte March, whan God first maked man,
Was compleet, and passed were also,
370 Syn March bigan, thritty dayes and two,
Bifel that Chauntecleer in al his pryde,
His sevene wyves walkynge by his syde,
Caste up his eyen to the brighte sonne,
That in the signe of Taurus° hadde yronne
Twenty degrees and oon, and somwhat moore,
And knew by kynde,° and by noon oother loore,
That it was pryme,° and crew with blisful stevene.
"The sonne," he seyde, "is clomben up on hevene
Fourty degrees and oon, and moore ywis.°
380 Madame Pertelote, my worldes blis,
Herkneth thise blisful briddes how they synge,
And se the fresshe floures how they sprynge;
Ful is myn herte of revel and solas!"
But sodeynly hym fil a sorweful cas,°
For evere the latter ende of joye is wo.
God woot that worldly joye is soon ago;°
And if a rethor° koude faire endite,
He in a cronycle saufly myghte it write
As for a sovereyn notabilitee.
390 Now every wys man, lat him herkne me;
This storie is also trewe, I undertake,
As is the book of Launcelot de Lake,°
That wommen holde in ful greet reverence.
Now wol I torne agayn to my sentence.
    A col-fox, ful of sly iniquitee,
That in the grove hadde woned° yeres three,
By heigh ymaginacioun forncast,°
The same nyght thurghout the hegges brast°
Into the yerd ther Chauntecleer the faire
400 Was wont, and eek his wyves, to repaire;
And in a bed of wortes° stille he lay,
Til it was passed undern° of the day,
Waitynge his tyme on Chauntecleer to falle,
As gladly doon thise homycides alle
That in await liggen° to mordre men.
O false mordrour, lurkynge in thy den!
O newe Scariot,° newe Genylon,°
False dissymulour, o Greek Synon,°
That broghtest Troye al outrely to sorwe!
410 O Chauntecleer, acursed be that morwe

That thou into that yerd flaugh fro the bemes!
Thou were ful wel ywarned by thy dremes
That thilke day was perilous to thee;
But what that God forwoot° moot nedes bee,
After the opinioun of certein clerkis.
Witnesse on hym that any parfit clerk is,
That in scole is greet altercacioun
In this mateere, and greet disputisoun,
And hath been of an hundred thousand men.
But I ne kan nat bulte it to the bren°   420
As kan the hooly doctour Augustyn,°
Or Boece,° or the Bisshop Bradwardyn,°
Wheither that Goddes worthy forwityng
Streyneth° me nedely° for to doon a thyng,—
"Nedely" clepe° I symple necessitee;
Or elles, if free choys be graunted me
To do that same thyng, or do it noght,
Though God forwoot it er that was wroght;
Or if his wityng° streyneth never a deel
But by necessitee condicioneel.°   430
I wol nat han to do of swich mateere;
My tale is of a cok, as ye may heere,
That tok his conseil of his wyf, with sorwe,
To walken in the yerd upon that morwe
That he hadde met that dreem that I yow tolde.
Wommennes conseils been ful ofte colde;
Wommannes conseil broghte us first to wo,
And made Adam fro Paradys to go,
Ther as he was ful myrie and wel at ese.
But for I noot° to whom it myght displese,   440
If I conseil of wommen wolde blame,
Passe over, for I seyde it in my game.°
Rede auctours,° where they trete of swich mateere,
And what they seyn of wommen ye may heere.
Thise been the cokkes wordes, and nat myne;
I kan noon harm of no womman divyne.
    Faire in the soond,° to bathe hire myrily,
Lith Pertelote, and alle hire sustres by,
Agayn the sonne, and Chauntecleer so free
Soong murier than the mermayde in the see;   450
For Phisiologus° seith sikerly
How that they syngen wel and myrily.
And so bifel that, as he caste his ye
Among the wortes on a boterflye,
He was war of this fox, that lay ful lowe.
Nothyng ne liste hym thanne for to crowe,
But cride anon, "Cok! cok!" and up he sterte
As man that was affrayed in his herte.
For natureelly a beest desireth flee

---

374 **signe of Taurus,** the second of the twelve signs of the zodiac. The sun would be in Taurus from about April 20 to May 20. The reference in the next line to twenty-one or more degrees places the date at approximately May 3   376 **by kynde,** by nature, by instinct   377 **pryme,** the first hour of the day (6:00 A.M.) The time would be shortly before nine o'clock   379 **ywis,** in truth, surely.
384 **sorweful cas,** sad event   386 **ago,** gone   387 **rethor,** rhetorician
392 **Launcelot de Lake,** the great chivalric hero of the Arthurian cycle
396 **woned,** dwelt   397 **heigh ymaginacioun forncast,** by divine foreknowledge foreordained   398 **brast,** burst   401 **wortes,** herbs   402 **undern,** early morning   405 **liggen,** lie   407 **Scariot,** Judas Iscariot, the disciple who betrayed Christ   **Genylon,** Ganelon, the traitor in the *Song of Roland,* who betrayed Roland's command to the Saracens   408 **Synon,** the man who persuaded the Trojans to admit the wooden horse at Troy, by which plan the city was captured

414 **forwoot,** foreknows. The question of providence versus free will was a favorite among medieval philosophers   420 **bulte . . . bren,** sift it to the bran, analyze the question thoroughly   421 **Augustyn.** St. Augustine was the great representative of orthodox doctrine   422 **Boece,** Boethius (480?–524?), who dealt in his *Consolation of Philosophy* with the question of providence versus free will **Bisshop Bradwardyn,** lecturer at Oxford and Archbishop of Canterbury at the time of his death in 1349. His treatment of the problem was conservative and orthodox—he relied chiefly upon providence   424 **Streyneth,** constrains, forces **nedely,** of necessity   425 **clepe,** call   429 **wityng,** knowing, knowledge 430 **necessitee condicioneel,** necessity conditioned by God's foreknowledge (as contrasted to simple necessity, whereby a thing happens because it must)
440 **noot,** know not   442 **game,** joke   443 **auctours,** authors and authorities
447 **soond,** sand   451 **Phisiologus,** the *Physiologus* or Latin bestiary

Fro his contrarie,° if he may it see,
Though he never erst° hadde seyn it with his ye.
 This Chauntecleer, whan he gan hym espye,
He wolde han fled, but that the fox anon
Seyde, "Gentil sire, allas! wher wol ye gon?
Be ye affrayed of me that am youre freend?
Now, certes, I were worse than a feend,
If I to yow wolde harm or vileynye!
I am nat come youre conseil for t'espye,
But trewely, the cause of my comynge
470 Was oonly for to herkne how that ye synge.
For trewely, ye have as myrie a stevene
As any aungel hath that is in hevene.
Therwith ye han in musyk moore feelynge
Than hadde Boece, or any that kan synge.
My lord youre fader—God his soule blesse!—
And eek youre mooder, of hire gentillesse,°
Han in myn hous ybeen to my greet ese;
And certes, sire, ful fayn wolde I yow plese.
But, for men speke of syngyng, I wol seye,—
480 So moote I brouke wel myne eyen tweye,°—
Save yow, I herde nevere man so synge
As dide youre fader in the morwenynge.
Certes, it was of herte, al that he song.
And for to make his voys the moore strong,
He wolde so peyne hym that with bothe his yen
He moste wynke,° so loude he wolde cryen,
And stonden on his tiptoon therwithal,
And strecche forth his nekke long and smal.°
And eek he was of swich discrecioun
490 That ther nas no man in no regioun
That hym in song or wisedom myghte passe.
I have wel rad in 'Daun Burnel the Asse,'°
Among his vers, how that ther was a cok,
For that a preestes sone yaf hym a knok
Upon his leg whil he was yong and nyce,°
He made hym for to lese his benefice.°
But certeyn, ther nys no comparisoun
Bitwixe the wisedom and discrecioun
Of youre fader and of his subtilee.
500 Now syngeth, sire, for seinte charitee;
Lat se, konne ye youre fader countrefete?°"
 This Chauntecleer his wynges gan to bete,
As man that koude his traysoun nat espie,
So was he ravysshed with his flaterie.
 Allas! ye lordes, many a fals flatour
Is in youre courtes, and many a losengeour,°
That plesen yow wel moore, by my feith,
Than he that soothfastnesse° unto yow seith.
Redeth Ecclesiaste° of flaterye;
510 Beth war, ye lordes, of hir trecherye.

This Chauntecleer stood hye upon his toos,
Strecchynge his nekke, and heeld his eyen cloos,
And gan to crowe loude for the nones.
And daun Russell the fox stirte up atones,
And by the gargat hente° Chauntecleer,
And on his bak toward the wode hym beer,
For yet ne was ther no man that hym sewed.°
 O destinee, that mayst nat been eschewed!
Allas, that Chauntecleer fleigh fro the bemes!
Allas, his wyf ne roghte° nat of dremes!   520
And on a Friday fil al this meschaunce.
 O Venus, that art goddesse of plesaunce,
Syn that thy servant was this Chauntecleer,
And in thy servyce dide al his poweer,
Moore for delit than world to multiplye,
Why woldestow suffre hym on thy day to dye?
 O Gaufred,° deere maister soverayn,
That whan thy worthy kyng Richard was slayn
With shot, compleynedest his deeth so soore,
Why ne hadde I now thy sentence and thy loore,   530
The Friday for to chide, as diden ye?
For on a Friday, soothly, slayn was he.
Thanne wolde I shewe yow how that I koude pleyne°
For Chauntecleres drede and for his peyne.
 Certes, swich cry ne lamentacion,
Was nevere of ladyes maad whan Ylion°
Was wonne, and Pirrus with his streite swerd,
Whan he hadde hent kyng Priam by the berd,
And slayn hym, as seith us Eneydos,°
As maden alle the hennes in the clos,°   540
Whan they had seyn of Chauntecleer the sighte.
But sovereynly dame Pertelote shrighte
Ful louder than dide Hasdrubales wyf,
Whan that hir housbonde hadde lost his lyf,°
And that the Romayns hadde brend° Cartage.
She was so ful of torment and of rage°
That wilfully into the fyr she sterte,
And brende hirselven with a stedefast herte.
 O woful hennes; right so criden ye,
As, whan that Nero brende the citee   550
Of Rome, cryden senatoures wyves
For that hir husbondes losten alle hir lyves,—
Withouten gilt this Nero hath hem slayn.
Now wole I turne to my tale agayn.
 This sely° wydwe and eek hir doghtres two
Herden thise hennes crie and maken wo,
And out at dores stirten they anon,
And syen the fox toward the grove gon,
And bar upon his bak the cok away,
And cryden, "Out! harrow! and weyl-away!   560
Ha! ha! the fox!" and after hym they ran,
And eek with staves many another man.

460 **contrarie,** opposite. According to medieval belief, every creature had another creature that was its contrary, such as dog to cat, snake to bird, etc.
461 **erst,** before   476 **gentillesse,** nobility of birth, character, or bearing
480 **So . . . tweye,** as I can enjoy my eyes—a mild oath   486 **wynke,** close his eyes   488 **smal,** narrow   492 **'Daun Burnel the Asse,'** a character in an Anglo-Latin satirical poem of the twelfth century by Nigel Wireker called *Burnellus, seu Speculum Stultorum* ("Burnell, or the Mirror of Idiots")   495 **nyce,** ignorant, foolish   496 **benefice,** his Church living   501 **countrefete,** imitate and match   506 **losengeour,** flatterer   508 **soothfastnesse,** truth   509 **Ecclesiaste,** the Apocryphal Book of Ecclesiasticus

515 **gargat,** throat   **hente,** seized   517 **sewed,** pursued   520 **roghte,** recked, heeded   527 **Gaufred,** Geoffrey de Vinsauf, a writer on the art of poetry, whose great work, the *Poetria Nova,* appeared shortly after the death of Richard I (1199); his model for an elegy consists of some lines of lament on the death of Richard   533 **pleyne,** complain   536 **Ylion,** Troy   539 **Eneydos,** Vergil's *Aeneid*   540 **clos,** close, yard   544 **hir housbonde . . . lyf.** Hasdrubal was King of Carthage when the Romans sacked it (146 B.C.)   545 **brend,** burnt   546 **rage,** madness   555 **sely,** good, innocent

Geoffrey Chaucer   **129**

Ran Colle oure dogge, and Talbot and Gerland,
And Malkyn, with a dystaf in hir hand;
Ran cow and calf, and eek the verray hogges,
So fered for the berkyng of the dogges
And shoutyng of the men and wommen eeke,
They ronne so hem thoughte hir herte breeke.
They yolleden as feendes doon in helle;
570 The dokes° cryden as men wolde hem quelle;°
The gees for feere flowen over the trees;
Out of the hyve cam the swarm of bees.
So hydous was the noyse, a, *benedicitee!*
Certes, he Jakke Straw and his meynee°
Ne made nevere shoutes half so shrille
Whan that they wolden any Flemyng kille,
As thilke day was maad upon the fox.
Of bras they broghten bemes,° and of box,°
Of horn, of boon, in whiche they blewe and
powped,°
580 And therwithal they skriked and they howped.
It seemed as the hevene sholde falle.

Now, goode men, I prey yow herkneth alle:
Lo, how Fortune turneth sodeynly
The hope and pryde eek of hir enemy!
This cok, that lay upon the foxes bak,
In al his drede unto the fox he spak,
And seyde, "Sire, if that I were as ye,
Yet sholde I seyn, as wys God helpe me,
'Turneth agayn, ye proude cherles alle!
590 A verray pestilence upon yow falle!
Now am I come unto the wodes syde;
Maugree youre heed,° the cok shal heere abyde.
I wol hym ete, in feith, and that anon!'"
The fox answerde, "In feith, it shal be don."
And as he spak that word, al sodeynly
This cok brak from his mouth delyverly,°
And heighe upon a tree he fleigh anon.
And whan the fox saugh that the cok was gon,
"Allas!" quod he, "O Chauntecleer, allas!
600 I have to yow," quod he, "ydoon trespas,
In as muche as I maked yow aferd
Whan I yow hente and broghte out of the yerd.
But, sire, I dide it in no wikke entente.
Com doun, and I shal telle yow what I mente;
I shal seye sooth to yow, God help me so!"
"Nay thanne," quod he, "I shrewe° us bothe two.
And first I shrewe myself, bothe blood and bones,
If thou bigyle me ofter than ones.
Thou shalt namoore, thurgh thy flaterye,
610 Do me to synge and wynke with myn ye;
For he that wynketh, whan he sholde see,

Al wilfully, God lat him nevere thee!°"
"Nay," quod the fox, "but God yeve hym mes-
chaunce,
That is so undiscreet of governaunce°
That jangleth° whan he sholde holde his pees."
Lo, swich it is for to be recchelees°
And necligent, and truste on flaterye.
But ye that holden this tale a folye,
As of a fox, or of a cok and hen,
Taketh the moralite, goode men. 620
For seint Paul seith that al that writen is,
To oure doctrine° it is ywrite, ywis;
Taketh the fruyt,° and lat the chaf be stille.°
Now, goode God, if that it be thy wille,
As seith my lord, so make us alle goode men,
And brynge us to his heighe blisse! Amen.

THE PARSON'S PROLOGUE

By that° the Maunciple hadde his tale al ended,
The sonne° fro the south lyne was descended
So lowe that he nas nat, to my sighte,
Degrees nyne and twenty as in highte.
Foure of the clokke it was tho, as I gesse,
For ellevene foot, or litel moore or lesse,
My shadwe was at thilke tyme, as there,
Of swiche feet as my lengthe parted were
In sixe feet equal of proporcioun.
Therwith the moones exaltacioun,° 10
I meene Libra, alwey gan ascende,
As we were entryng at a thropes° ende;
For which oure Hoost, as he was wont to gye,°
As in this caas, oure joly compaignye,
Seyde in this wise: "Lordynges everichoon,
Now lakketh us no tales mo than oon.
Fulfilled is my sentence° and my decree;
I trowe that we han herd of ech degree;°
Almoost fulfild is al myn ordinaunce.
I pray to God, so yeve hym right good chaunce,° 20
That telleth this tale to us lustily.°
Sire preest," quod he, "artow a vicary?°
Or arte a person?° sey sooth, by thy fey!
Be what thou be, ne breke thou nat oure pley;°
For every man, save thou, hath toold his tale.
Unbokele, and shewe us what is in thy male;°

614 **governaunce,** self-control, behavior   615 **jangleth,** chatters   616 **re-**
cchelees, reckless   622 **doctrine,** instruction   623 **fruyt,** corn   **lat . . . stille.**
Let the chaff alone
The Parson's Prologue   1 **By that,** by the time that   2–9 **sonne** etc. "The al-
titude of the sun was 29 degrees which means, for April 20th, that the time was
about 4 P.M. With the sun at that angle an object six feet high would cast a
shadow eleven feet long." (F.N. Robinson, *Works of Geoffrey Chaucer*)   10 **the**
moones exaltacioun. Another astrological reference to time, though Chaucer's astrology is confused here   12 **thropes,** village's   13 **gye,** direct   17 **sentence,**
judgment   18 **degree,** rank   20 **yeve hym . . . chaunce,** good luck to him (who
tells the last tale)   21 **lustily,** with pleasure   22 **vicary,** vicar   23 **person,** parson   24 **ne breke thou nat oure pley,** don't break up our game   26 **male,** bag
27 **cheere,** countenance

570 **dokes,** ducks   **quelle,** kill   574 **Jakke Straw . . . meynee.** The Peasants'
Revolt of 1381 included rioting by Jack Straw and his followers against the
Flemish who had settled in London and adjacent parts. The competition offered
by the Flemish in the wool industry was the chief reason for the bad feeling
578 **bemes,** trumpets   **box,** boxwood   579 **powped,** puffed   592 **Maugree**
youre heed, in spite of you   596 **delyverly,** quickly   606 **shrewe,** curse
612 **God . . . thee.** God let him never prosper

Thou sholdest knytte up wel a greet mateere.
Telle us a fable° anon, for cokkes bones!"

30 This Persoun answerde, al atones,
"Thou getest fable noon ytoold for me;
For Paul, that writeth unto Thymothee,
Repreveth hem that weyven° soothfastnesse,°
And tellen fables and swich wrecchednesse.
Why sholde I sowen draf° out of my fest,
Whan I may sowen whete, if that me lest?
For which I seye, if that yow list to heere
Moralitee and vertuous mateere,
And thanne that ye wol yeve me audience,°

40 I wol ful fayn, at Cristes reverence,
Do yow plesaunce leefful,° as I kan.
But trusteth wel, I am a Southren man,
I kan nat geeste 'rum, ram, ruf,' by lettre,°
Ne, God woot, rym° holde I but litel bettre;
And therfore, if yow list—I wol nat glose°—
I wol yow telle a myrie tale in prose
To knytte up° al this feeste, and make an ende.
And Jhesu, for this grace, wit me sende
To shewe yow the wey, in this viage,°

50 Of thilke parfit glorious pilgrymage
That highte Jerusalem celestial.°
And if ye vouche sauf, anon I shal
Bigynne upon my tale, for which I preye
Telle youre avys,° I kan no bettre seye.

But nathelees, this meditacioun
I putte it ay under correccioun
Of clerkes, for I am nat textueel;°
I take but the sentence, trusteth weel.
Therfore I make protestacioun

60 That I wol stonde to correccioun."

Upon this word we han assented soone,
For, as it seemed, it was for to doone,°
To enden in som vertuous sentence,
And for to yeve hym space and audience;
And bade oure Hoost he sholde to hym seye
That alle we to telle his tale hym preye.

Oure Hoost hadde the wordes for us alle:
"Sire preest," quod he, "now faire yow bifalle!
Telleth," quod he, "youre meditacioun.

70 But hasteth yow, the sonne wole adoun;°
Beth fructuous,° and that in litel space,
And to do wel God sende yow his grace!
Sey what yow list,° and we wol gladly heere."
And with that word he seyde in this manere.

RETRACTION

Now preye I to hem alle that herkne this litel tretys or rede, that if ther be any thyng in it that liketh
hem,° that therof they thanken oure Lord Jhesu Crist,
of whom procedeth al wit and al goodnesse. / And if
ther be any thyng that displese hem, I preye hem
also that they arrette° it to the defaute° of myn unkonnynge,° and nat to my wyl, that wolde ful fayn° have
seyd bettre if I hadde had konnynge. / For oure book°
seith, "Al that is writen is writen for oure doctrine,"° and that is myn entente. / Wherfore I biseke 10
yow mekely, for the mercy of God, that ye preye for
me that Crist have mercy on me and foryeve me my
giltes; / and namely° of my translacions and enditynges of° worldly vanitees, the whiche I revoke in
my retracciouns: / as is the book of Troilus; the
book also of Fame; the book of the xxv. Ladies;° the
book of the Duchesse; the book of Seint Valentynes
day of the Parlement of Briddes; the tales of Caunterbury, thilke that sownen into synne;° / the book of
the Leoun;° and many another book, if they were in 20
my remembrance, and many a song and many a lec-
cherous lay; that Crist for his grete mercy foryeve me
the synne. / But of the translacion of Boece de
Consolacione, and othere bookes of legendes of
seintes, and omelies,° and moralitee, and devocioun, /
that thanke I oure Lord Jhesu Crist and his blisful
Mooder, and alle the seintes of hevene, / bisekynge
hem that they from hennes forth unto my lyves ende
sende me grace to biwayle my giltes, and to studie to
the salvacioun of my soule, and graunte me grace of 30
verray penitence, confessioun and satisfaccioun to
doon in this present lyf, / thurgh the benigne grace of
hym that is kyng of kynges and preest over alle
preestes, that boghte us with the precious blood of his
herte; / so that I may been oon of hem at the day of
doom that shulle be saved. *Qui cum patre et Spiritu
Sancto vivit et regnat Deus per omnia secula. Amen.*°
(1385–1400)

GENTILESSE

The firste stok,° fader of gentilesse—
What man that claymeth gentil for to be,
Must folowe his trace, and alle his wittes dresse°
Vertu to sewe,° and vyces for to flee.

29 **fable,** tale or fable, with implications of falsehood, to which the Parson reacts
instantly. Cf. the term "a fiction"   33 **weyven,** neglect, abandon   33 **soothfastnesse,** truth   35 **draf,** chaff   39 **yeve me audience,** give me a hearing
41 **Do . . . leefful,** give you lawful pleasure, proper delight   42–43 **I am a
Southren . . . by lettre.** Alliterative poetry, in which repeated initial consonants
link a line, was a more Northern literary fashion in the fourteenth century
44 **rym,** rime   45 **glose,** cajole   47 **To knytte up,** to gather together
49 **viage,** journey   50–51 **thilke parfit . . . celestial,** that same perfect glorious
pilgrimage which is called the heavenly Jerusalem   54 **avys,** advice   57 **textueel,** learned in texts   62 **for to doone,** suitable to do   70 **wole adoun,** wishes
to set, will soon set   71 **fructuous,** fruitful   73 **yow list,** you please

Retraction   3 **liketh hem,** pleases them   6 **arrette,** ascribe   **defaute,** defect
7 **unkonnynge,** ignorance   **ful fayn,** very happily   8 **oure book,** the Scriptures
10 See Paul, *Romans* 15:4   **doctrine,** instruction   13 **namely,** especially
14 **enditynges of,** compositions about   16 **the book of the xxv. Ladies,** probably
The Legend of Good Women   19 **thilke that sownen into synne,** those which tend
toward sin, or are consonant with sin   20 **book of the Leoun,** perhaps a reference to Machaut's *Dit dou Lyon* which Chaucer may have translated. The other
titles referred to are works of Chaucer described briefly in the headnote
25 **omelies,** homilies   36–37 **Qui cum patre . . . Amen,** Who, with the Father
and the Holy Spirit, lives and reigns God, world without end. Amen.
Gentilesse   1 **firste stok,** Christ or God, not Adam   3 **dresse,** direct, prepare
4 **sewe,** follow

For unto vertu longeth dignitee,°
And noght the revers, saufly dar I deme,
Al were° he mytre, croune, or diademe.

This firste stok was ful of rightwisnesse,
Trewe of his word, sobre, pitous, and free,°
10 Clene of his goste,° and loved besinesse
Ageinst the vyce of slouthe, in honestee;
And, but° his heir love vertu, as dide he,
He is noght gentil, thogh he riche seme,
Al were he mytre, croune, or diademe.

Vyce may wel be heir to old richesse;
But ther may no man, as men may wel see,
Bequethe his heir his vertuous noblesse
That is appropred° unto no degree,°
But to the firste fader in magestee,
20 That maketh him his heir, that can him queme,°
Al were he mytre, croune, or diademe.

TRUTH

Fle fro the prees,° and dwelle with soothfastnesse;°
Suffyce unto thy good, though hit be smal;
For hord° hath hate, and clymbing tikelnesse,°
Prees hath envye, and wele blent overal;°
Savour° no more than thee bihove shal;
Werk wel thy-self, that other folk canst rede;°
And trouthe thee shal delivere, hit is no drede.°

Tempest thee noght° al croked to redresse,
In trust of hir that turneth as a bal;°
10 Gret reste stant in litel besinesse,°
And eek be war to sporne ageyns an al;°
Stryve noght, as doth the crokke with the wal.
Daunte° thyself, that dauntest otheres dede;
And trouthe thee shal delivere, hit is no drede.

That thee is sent, receyve in buxumnesse,°
The wrastling for this world axeth a fal.°
Her nis non hom, her nis but wildernesse;
Forth, pilgrim, forth! Forth, beste, out of thy stal!
Know thy countree; look up, thank God of al;

Hold the hye-way, and lat thy gost° thee lede! 20
And trouthe thee shal delivere, hit is no drede.

ENVOY

Therefore, thou Vache,° leve thyn old wrecchednesse;
Unto the world leve now to be thral;
Crye Him mercy that of His hy goodnesse
Made thee of noght, and in especial
Draw unto Him, and pray in general
For thee, and eek for other, hevenlich mede;°
And trouthe shal thee delivere, hit is no drede.
(1390?)

ENVOY TO BUKTON

My maister° Bukton, whan of Crist our kyng
Was axed° what is trouthe or sothfastnesse,
He nat a word answerde to that axing,
As who seith, "No man is al trewe," I gesse.
And therfore, though I highte° to expresse
The sorwe and wo that is in mariage,
I dar not writen of it no wikkednesse,
Lest I myself falle eft° in swich dotage.

I wol nat seyn how that it is the cheyne
Of Sathanas, on which he gnaweth evere; 10
But I dar seyn, were he out of his peyne,
As by his wille he wolde be bounde nevere.
But thilke doted fool that eft hath levere°
Ycheyned be than out of prison crepe,
God lete him never fro his wo dissevere,
Ne no man him bewayle, though he wepe!

But yet, lest thow do worse, take a wyf;
Bet is to wedde than brenne in worse wise.°
But thow shalt have sorwe on thy flessh, thy lyf,
And been thy wives thral, as seyn these wise; 20
And yf that hooly writ may nat suffyse,
Experience shal the teche, so may happe,
That the were lever to be take in Frise°
Than eft to falle of weddynge in the trappe.

5 **longeth,** belongs **dignitee,** worth, honor 7 **Al,** although **were,** wear 9 **free,** generous in spirit 10 **goste,** spirit 12 **but,** unless 18 **appropred,** made the property of **degree,** rank 20 **queme,** please **Truth.** Legend has it that this poem was composed on Chaucer's deathbed, but it is probable that he wrote it to give good counsel to his young friend Sir Philip de la Vache, who married the daughter of Chaucer's intimate acquaintance Sir Lewis Clifford. The name of de la Vache is seen by most scholars in the envoy to the poem 1 **prees,** press, crowd **soothfastnesse,** truth 3 **hord,** avarice **tikelnesse,** ticklishness, instability 4 **and . . . overal,** and riches blind (dazzle) entirely 5 **Savour,** taste 6 **rede,** advise. The line means practice what you preach 7 **hit . . . drede,** there is no doubt 8 **Tempest thee noght,** do not perturb yourself 9 **hir . . . bal,** Fortune, who is often pictured as having a wheel or ball 10 **Gret . . . besinesse.** Great peace stands (lies) in not being too busy 11 **sporne . . . al,** to kick against an awl, an expression of futility. See *Acts,* 9:5 13 **Daunte,** rule 15 **buxumnesse,** compliance 16 **The . . . fal.** Wrestling for (the sake of) this world is asking for a fall

20 **gost,** spirit 22 **Vache.** The word is capitalized by most editors who see in this a reference to Sir Philip de la Vache. But there is probably a play on words here; Chaucer is picturing man as a lowly beast (l.18) in a stall; *vache* is French for "cow" 27 **mede,** reward **Envoy to Bukton.** This sharply satirical poem was composed in 1396. It is addressed either to Sir Peter Bukton, of Holderness in Yorkshire, or to Sir Robert Bukton, of Goosewold in Suffolk. The evidence seems to favor the former of the two 1 **maister,** lawyer. This is evidence that Sir Peter Bukton, a lawyer, is the addressee of the poem 2 **Was axed, etc.,** referring to the question asked Christ by Pontius Pilate, "What is truth?" See *John,* 18:38 5 **highte,** promised 8 **eft,** again. Chaucer's wife Philippa supposedly died some ten years before (1387?) 13 **levere,** rather 18 **Bet is . . . wise.** See 1 *Corinthians,* 7:9 23 **Frise.** An expedition against Friesland (Frisia) in September 1396 was noted for the bloodthirsty conduct of the Frisians, who massacred English prisoners

This lytel writ, proverbes, or figure
I sende yow, take kepe of yt, I rede;
Unwys is he that kan no wele° endure.
If thow be siker,° put thee nat in drede.°
The Wyf of Bathe I pray yow that ye rede
30 Of this matere that we have on honde.
God graunte yow your lyf frely to lede
In fredam; for ful hard is to be bonde.
(1396?)

MIDDLE ENGLISH LYRICS

Though their musical notation has frequently been lost, many Middle English lyrics were written as songs. The original poet-singers may have been traveling artists or resident professionals; they sang to entertain, to express religious devotion, or to celebrate the joys of this world. The disturbing transiency of human affairs, known as the *ubi sunt* motif, appears in both religious and secular lyrics (cf. *Ubi Sunt Qui Ante Nos Fuerunt?*). The pure religious song of devotion, the hymn, is not so distinguished in Middle English as the sacred lullaby or the lyrics prompted by the scene of the Virgin at the Cross, usually known as the *Stabat Mater* theme (cf. *Jesus Christ's Mild Mother*). As for the secular lyrics, human love is the subject of *Alysoun*; the beauties of the English countryside in spring inspire the famous *Cuckoo Song*. Occasionally the lyric and the ballad approach each other, as in the romantically religious *The Falcon Hath Borne My Mate Away*.

Much recent criticism has been devoted to the identity, intentions, and social position of the Middle English lyric poets. We cannot answer many questions with certainty; what appears to be highly personal in the lyrics, for example, may merely be conventional, and vice versa. There are no clear-cut distinctions between the audience for and composers of secular verse and the audience for and composers of religious songs.

The earliest of the lyrics is probably the *Cuckoo Song*, which dates from the early thirteenth century. The other lyrics cover a period some two and a half centuries after the *Cuckoo Song*. It is extremely difficult to date the lyrics with any certainty.

The lyrics have been reprinted here in the original and should be read aloud, with the aid of the note "On Reading Middle English" (p. 76).

27 **wele**, prosperity 28 **siker**, safe, secure **drede**, doubt

CUCKOO SONG

Sumer is icumen in:
    Lhude° sing cuccu!°
Groweth sed, and bloweth med,°
    And springth the wude nu.°   5
        Sing cuccu!

Awe° bleteth after lomb;
    Lhouth° after calve cu,°
Bulluc sterteth,° bucke verteth.°
    Murie° sing cuccu!

Cuccu, cuccu, well singes thu, cuccu: 10
    Ne swike° thu naver° nu.
Sing cuccu, nu, sing cuccu!
    Sing cuccu, sing cuccu, nu!

ALYSOUN

Bytuene Mershe and Averil
    When spray biginneth to springe,
The lutel foul hath hire wyl
    On hyre lud° to synge;
    Ich libbe° in love-longinge
For semlokest° of alle thynge,
    He° may me blisse bringe,
Icham in hire baundoun.°
    An hendy hap ichabbe yhent,°
    Ichot° from hevene it is me sent,   10
    From alle wymmen mi love is lent°
Ant lyht° on Alysoun.

On heu hire her is fayr ynoh,
    Hire browe broune, hire eye blake,
With lossum° chere he on me loh;°
    With middel smal and wel y-make;
    Bote he me wolle to hire take
    Forte buen° hire owen make,°
    Longe to lyven ichulle° forsake,
And feye° fallen adoun   20
    An hendy hap, etc.

Nihtes when I wende° and wake,
    Forthi° myn wonges° waxeth won;
Levedi,° al for thine sake

Cuckoo Song 2 **Lhude**, loudly **cuccu**, cuckoo 3 **bloweth**, blossometh **med**, meadow 4 **nu**, now 6 **Awe**, ewe 7 **Lhouth**, loweth **cu**, cow 8 **sterteth**, springs up **verteth**, breaks wind 9 **Murie**, merrily 11 **swike**, cease, fail **naver**, never Alysoun 4 **lud**, language 5 **Ich libbe**, I live 6 **semlokest**, fairest, most beautiful 7 **He**, she 8 **Icham . . . baundoun.** I am in her power 9 **hendy hap**, gracious fortune **ichabbe yhent**, I have received 10 **Ichot**, I know 11 **lent**, taken away from, departed 12 **lyht**, alighted, placed 15 **lossum**, lovesome, loving **loh**, laughed 18 **Forte buen**, for to dwell **make**, mate 19 **ichulle**, I will 20 **feye**, doomed 22 **wende**, toss 23 **Forthi**, for that **wonges**, cheeks 24 **Levedi**, lady

Longinge is ylent° me on
In world nis non so wytermon°
   That al hire bounte telle con;
      Hire swyre° is whittore then the swon,
   And feyrest may° in toune.
30   An hendy hap, etc.

Icham for wowyng° al forwake,°
   Wery so water in wore,°
Lest eny reve° me my make,
   Ichabbe y-yernéd yore°
Betere is tholien whyle° sore
   Then mournen evermore.
Geynes° under gore,°
   Herkne to my roun.°
      An hendy hap, etc.

UBI SUNT QUI ANTE NOS FUERUNT?

Were beth° they that biforen us weren,°
Houndes ladden° and havekes° beren,
   And hadden feld and wode?
      The riche levedies° in here° bour,
      That wereden gold in here tressour,
   With here brighte rode;°

Eten and drounken, and maden hem glad;
Here lif was al with gamen y-lad;
   Men kneleden hem biforen;
10   They beren hem wel swithe heye:°
      And in a twincling of an eye
   Here soules weren forloren.°

Were is that lawhing° and that song,
That trayling° and that proude gong,°
   Tho° havekes and tho houndes?
      Al that joye is went away,
      That wele is comen to weylaway,°
   To manye harde stoundes.°

Here paradis they nomen° here,
20 And nou they lyen in helle y-fere;°
   The fyr hit brennes° evere:
      Long is ay, and long is o,
      Long is wy, and long is wo;
   Thennes ne cometh they nevere.

THE FALCON HATH BORNE
MY MATE AWAY°

Lully, lulley, lully, lulley,
The faucon hath borne my mate away.

He bare him up, he bare him down,
He bare him into an orchard brown.

In that orchard there was an halle,   5
That was hanged with purpill and pall!°

And in that hall there was a bede,
It was hanged with gold so rede.

And in that bed there lith a knight
His woundes bleding day and night.   10

By that beds side kneleth a may,°
And she wepeth both night and day.

And by that beds side there stondeth a stone,
Corpus Christi writen there on.

A SACRED LULLABY

Lullay, my child, and wepe no more,
   Slepe and be now still.
The king of bliss thy fader is
   As it was his will.

This endris° night I saw a sight,
   A maid a cradell kepe,
And ever she song and seid among:
   "Lullay, my child, and slepe."

"I may not slepe, but I may wepe,
   I am so wo begone;   10
Slepe I wold, but I am colde,
   And clothes have I none."

Me thought I hard,° the child answard,
   And to his moder he said,
"My moder dere, what do I here,
   In cribbe why am I laid?

"I was borne and laid beforne
   Bestes, both ox and asse.
My moder mild, I am thy child,
   But he my fader was.   20

"Adam's gilt this man had spilt;°
   That sin greveth me sore.
Man, for thee here shall I be
   Thirty winter and more.

"Dole it is to see, here shall I be
   Hanged upon the rode,
With baleis° to-bete, my woundes to-wete,
   And yeve my fleshe to bote.

"Here shall I be hanged on a tree,
   And die as it is skill.°   30

That I have bought° lesse will I nought;
  It is my fader's will.

"A spere so scharp shall perse my herte,
  For dedes that I have done.
Fader of grace, whether thou has
  Forgeten thy litell sone?

"Withouten pety° here shall I aby,°
  And make my fleshe all blo.°
Adam, iwis,° this deth it is
40 For thee and many mo."

JESUS CHRIST'S MILD MOTHER

Jesu Cristes milde moder stode,°
Biheld hire sone on rode
That he was i-pined° on.

The sone heng;° the moder stode
5 And biheld hire childes blode
Hou it of his wundes ran.

TIMOR MORTIS

    In what state that ever I be,
    Timor mortis conturbat me.°

As I me walked in one morning,
I hard° a birde both wepe and singe.
This was the tenor of her talkinge,
    Timor mortis conturbat me.

I asked this birde what he ment.
He said, "I am a musket gent;°
For dred of deth I am nigh shent;°
10   *Timor mortis conturbat me.*"

Jesu Crist, whan he shuld die,
To his Fader loud gan he crye;
"Fader," he said, "in Trinity,
    Timor mortis conturbat me."

Whan I shall die know I no day,
Therefore this songe sing I may;
In what place or contrey can I not say.
    Timor mortis conturbat me.

THE SECOND SHEPHERDS' PLAY°

The *Second Shepherds' Play* is one of the finest
examples of the English mystery play. It was composed near the end of the fourteenth century or at the
beginning of the fifteenth and is called *"Second"
Shepherds' Play* because in the late fifteenth-century
manuscript in which it has been preserved it follows a
"First" Shepherds' Play. This manuscript—one of the
most significant dramatic documents to have been preserved—takes its name from the Towneley family of
Lancashire, who once owned it. Approximately one
third of the thirty-two plays in the Towneley manuscript, including the *Secunda,* seem to have been the
work of a single unknown writer whose metrical skill,
keen sense of humor, and dramatic power entitle him
to be regarded as the first great comic dramatist in English literature. Although there is some uncertainty as
to where the plays were first produced, such local allusions as do occur in them indicate that the pageants
belonged to the dramatic cycle played by the guilds of
Wakefield in the south of Yorkshire, and so their author has come to be called the Wakefield Master.

As in the case of the Pearl Poet, there has been
much speculation about the character and identity of
this Wakefield Master. It is probable that he was a
man of humble birth but educated and well read, very
likely a secular priest. His dates are not known, but
most authorities place him in the mid-fifteenth century.
In any case, the plays in the Towneley cycle associated with his name—the plays of *Noah,* the two
Shepherd plays, *Herod,* the *Way of the Cross,* and certain parts of other plays—not only clearly demonstrate
revisions of traditional miracle-play material bright
with humor and personality but point also to a playwright easily the most distinctive in the whole range of
early English drama.

The metrical form of the play deserves brief comment. Apparently what the Wakefield Master did was
to take an earlier thirteen-line stanza and combine the
first eight lines into four longer lines. Thus a nine-line
stanza was produced, with lines five and nine in the
resulting stanza reduced or "bobbed" to one and two
accents, respectively—an abnormally short line. The
net result is a jerky type of line, and it is likely that the
Wakefield Master was actually attempting to reflect in
his verse form the rapid movement and hopping,
quick, farcical tempo of his plot.

Characters

COLL, *First Shepherd*
GIB, *Second Shepherd*
DAW, *Third Shepherd*
MAK, *the Sheep-stealer*
GILL, *Mak's Wife*
THE VIRGIN MARY
THE CHILD CHRIST
AN ANGEL

31 **bought,** done by way of the redemption of mankind   37 **pety,** pity   **aby,**
atone   38 **blo,** blue   39 **iwis,** truly, surely   **Jesus Christ's Mild Mother**
1 **stode,** stood   3 **i-pined,** tortured   4 **heng,** hung   **Timor Mortis**   2 **Timor
. . . me,** the fear of death disturbs me   4 **hard,** heard   8 **musket gent,** noble
sparrow hawk   9 **shent,** destroyed

The Second Shepherds' Play. Translation by Homer Watt. The play was performed
either on a fixed stage or pageant wagon. In either case there would be a "multiple stage" with the three shepherds meeting at one end of the platform and Mak's
hut standing at the other end—and a similar plan for the Nativity episodes

The moors near Wakefield in Yorkshire. Enter COLL, *the First Shepherd, soliloquizing.*

COLL. Lord, but these weathers are cold, and I am ill
wrapped;
I am numb and feel old, so long have I napped;
My legs bend and fold, my fingers are chapped,
It is not as I would, for I am all lapped
        In sorrow.
In storms and tempest,
Now in the east, now in the west,
Woe is him has never rest,
        Midday nor morrow.

10 But we wretched sheep-hands, that walk on the moor,
In good faith, these demands put us near out of door;°
No wonder, as it stands, if we be poor,
For the best of our lands lies fallow as the floor,
        As ye ken.
We are so lamed,
Over-taxed and shamed,
We are hand-tamed°
        By these gentry-men.

Thus they rob us of rest—Our Lady them harry!—
20 These men that are lord-fast,° they make the plow
tarry.
That, men say, is for the best; we find it contrary.
Thus are husbandmen pressed, in point to miscarry°
        In life.
Thus hold they us under,
Thus they bring us in blunder;
It were a great wonder,
        That ever should we thrive.

For may he get a painted sleeve, or a brooch° now-a-
days,
Woe is he that shall grieve, or against him aught says,
30 No man dare him reprove, though he insolence has;
And yet may none believe one word that he says—
        No letter.
He can make purveyance,°
With boast and arrogance,
And all through maintenance,
        By men that are greater.

There shall come a swain, as proud as a po,°
He must borrow my wain, my plow also,
Which I am full fain to grant ere he go.
40 Thus live we in pain, anger, and woe,

By night and day.
He must have if he longed;
If I should forgang° it,
I were better be hanged
        Than once say him nay.

It does me good, as I walk thus alone,
Of this world for to talk and make here my moan.
To my sheep will I stalk and hearken anon;
There abide with my flock, or sit on a stone
        Full soon.   50
For I trow, pardie!°
True men if they be,
We get more company
        Ere it be noon.

COLL *walks aside. Enter* GIB, *the Second Shepherd,
soliloquizing.*

GIB. Ben'dicite and Dominus!° what may this all
mean?
Why fares this world thus? Oft have we not seen.
Lord, these weathers are spiteous, and the wind is full
keen;
And the frosts so hideous they water mine een,
        No lie.
Now in dry, now in wet,   60
Now in snow, now in sleet,
When my shoon° freeze to my feet,
        It is not all easy.

But as far as I ken, ere yet as I go,
We poor married men must suffer much woe.
We have sorrow now and then; it falls often so.
Silly Capyl, our hen, both to and fro
        She cackles;
But begin she to croak,
To grumble or cluck,   70
Woe is him, our poor cock,
        For he is in the shackles.

These men that are wed, have not all their will,
When they are full hard bestead, they sigh full still;
God knows they are led full hard and full ill;
In bower nor in bed they say naught theretil,°
        This tide.°
My part have I found;
How she drives me around!
Woe is him that is bound,   80
        For he must abide.

But now late in our lives—a marvel to me,
That I think my heart rives,° such wonders to see,

---

11 **put . . . door**, make us homeless   17 **hand-tamed**, brought to submission
20 **lord-fast**, servants to a nobleman   22 **in . . . miscarry**, on the point of being
ruined   28 **painted sleeve . . . brooch**, the embroidered coat sleeve or ornament
designating connection with a nobleman   33 **purveyance**, seizure of property at
a price fixed by the purveyor   37 **po**, peacock

43 **forgang**, give it up   51 **pardie**, par Dieu   55 **Ben'dicite . . . Dominus**,
blessings (on us) Lord   62 **shoon**, shoes   76 **theretil**, thereto; i.e., they dare not
answer back   77 **tide**, time   83 **rives**, is torn asunder

What that destiny drives, that it should so be—
Some men will have two wives, and some men three
            In store.
Some are woe that have any;
But so far ken I,
Woe is he who has many,
90   For he feels it sore.   {He addresses
                                                the audience.

But, young men, of wooing, for God that you bought,°
Be well ware of wedding, and think in your thought
"Had I wist"° is a thing that serves ye of naught;
Much quiet mourning has wedding home brought,
            And griefs,
With many a sharp shower;
For thou may catch in an hour
That shall serve thee full sour
            As long as thou lives.

100 For as read I epistle,° I have one for my fere°
As sharp as a thistle, as rough as a briar;
She has brows like a bristle with a sour-looking cheer;°
Had she once wet her whistle, she could sing full clear
            Her pater-noster.
She is as great as a whale,
She has a gallon of gall;
By him that died for us all,
            I would I had run till I lost her.

    COLL. God, why speak ye so raw! Full deafly ye
        stand.
110 GIB. Yea, the devil in thy maw!—why be ye so
        grand!
Saw thou anywhere Daw?
    COLL.   Yea, on a lea land°
Heard I him blaw; he comes here at hand,
            Not far;
Stand still.
    GIB.   Why?
    COLL. For he comes here, hope I.
    GIB. He will give us both a lie,
            Unless we beware.

Enter DAW, the Third Shepherd, servant of GIB. At
first he does not see the other two.

120   DAW. Christ's cross me speed, and Saint Nicholas!
Thereof had I need, it is worse than it was.
Whoso could take heed, and let the world pass,
It is ever in dread and brittle as glass,
            And slithers.°
This world fared never so,
With marvels mo' and mo',

Now in weal, now in woe,
            And everything withers.

Was never since Noah's flood such floods seen,
Winds and rains so rude, and storms so keen,   130
Some stammered, some stood in doubt, as I ween,
Now God turn all to good, I say as I mean,
            For ponder:
These floods so they drown,
Both in fields and in town,
They bear all down,
            And that is a wonder.

We that walk in the nights, our cattle to keep,
We see sudden sights, when other men sleep.   {He
                        catches sight of the others.
Yet methinks my heart lights; I see rogues peep.   140
They are two tall wights; I will give my sheep
            A turn.
But full ill have I meant;
As I walk on this bent,°
I may lightly repent,
            My toes if I spurn.   {He recognizes and
                        addresses first COLL; then his master GIB.

Ah, sir, God you save, and my master I greet!
A drink fain would I have and somewhat to eat.
    COLL. Christ's curse, my knave, thou art a lazy
        cheat.
    GIB. What! the boy likes to rave. Just wait for thy
        meat   150
            'Til we've made it.
Ill thrift on thy pate!
Though the rogue came late
Yet is he in state
            To eat, if he had it.

    DAW. Such servants as I, that sweats and swinks,°
Eats our bread full dry, and often, methinks,
We are full wet and weary when master-men winks,°
Yet comes full lately both dinners and drinks.
            But neatly   160
Both our dame and our sire,
When we have run in the mire,
They can nip at our hire,
            And pay us full lately.

But hear my truth, master, for the bargain ye make
I'll do only hereafter what work I can't 'scape.
If you press me too hard, sir, why you I'll forsake.
For as yet lay my supper never on my stomack
            In fields.
But wherefore should I threap?°   170

---

91 **God . . . bought,** Christ the Redeemer   93 **wist,** known   100 **epistle,** the
Bible   **fere,** mate   102 **cheer,** countenance   112 **lea land,** fallow land
124 **slithers,** slides

144 **bent,** heath. Daw reconsiders when he reflects that he might stumble in the
dusk   156 **swinks,** toils   158 **master-men winks,** the masters sleep
170 **threap,** complain

With my staff I can leap,°
And men say, "Light cheap
    Full badly yields."°

  COLL. Thou wert an ill lad, to ride a-wooing°
From a man that had but little for spending.
  GIB. Peace, boy!—I bade; no more jangling,
Or I shall make thee afraid, by the heaven's king!
    With thy frauds.
Where are our sheep, boy? Forlorn?
180 DAW. Sir, this same day at morn,
I them left in the corn,
    When they rang lauds;

They have pasture good; they cannot go wrong.
  COLL. That is right. By the rood,° these nights are long!
Yet I would, ere we yode,° we might have a song.
  GIB. So I thought as I stood, to make mirth us among.
  DAW.   I grant.
  COLL. Let the tenor mine be.
  GIB. And I the treble so high.
190 DAW. Then the mean falls to me;
    Let see how ye chant.   {They sing.°

Then enter MAK, *with a cloak thrown over his smock.*
He soliloquizes.

  MAK. Now, Lord, by thy names seven, that made both moon and starns
More than I can count even; keep me, Lord, from all harms!
I am all uneven;° that fills me with alarms.
Now would God I were in heaven, for there weep no bairns°—
    So still!
  COLL. Who is that pipes so poor?
  MAK. Would God ye knew how I were!
Lo, a man that walks on the moor,
    And has not all his will.
200 GIB. Mak, where hast thou gone? Tell us tidings.
  DAW. Is he come? Then each one take heed to his things.   {*Snatches his own cloak from* MAK.
  MAK. What! Ich° be a yeoman, I tell you, of the king;
The self and the same, sent from a great lordling,
        {MAK *pretends not to know them.*
    And rich.
Fie on you; get thee hence,
Out of my presence;
I must have reverence,
    Why, who be Ich?

COLL. Wherefore are ye so quaint? Mak, ye do wrong.   210
  GIB. Why, Mak, play the saint? Right falsely ye sang.
  DAW. I trow the rogue can paint,° may the devil him hang!

  MAK. I shall make complaint, and get ye all whanged
    At a word,
And tell even how ye doth.
  COLL. But, Mak, is that truth?
Now take out that southern tooth,
    And no longer gird.°

  GIB. Mak, the devil get ye, a stroke would I lend you.
  DAW. Mak, know ye not me? By God, I could   220
bend you.   {MAK *pretends suddenly to recognize them.*

  MAK. God bless you all three! I would not offend you.
Ye are a fair company.
  COLL.   Oh, must we befriend you!
  GIB.   Rogue, cheat!
Thus late as thou goes,
What will men suppose?
We'll have to watch close
    Lest ye steal sheep.

  MAK. I am true as steel, all men know,
But a sickness I feel, that rocks me to and fro;   230
My belly fares not weel; it fills me with woe.
  DAW. "Seldom lies the de'il dead," we all trow.
  MAK.   Therefore
Full sore am I and ill,
If I stand stock still;
I've not eat my fill
    This month and more.

  COLL. How fares thy wife? By my hood, how does she do?
  MAK. Lies weltering,° by the rood, by the fire, lo!
And the house full of brood. She drinks well, too,   240
Ill speed other good that she will do!°
    By my shoe,
Eats as fast as she can,
And each year that comes to man,
She adds one to our clan,
    And some years two.

Even were I more prosperous, and richer by far,
I were eaten out of house, and of harbor,
Yet she is a foul dowse,° if ye come near.

171 **With . . . leap,** I can easily run away 172–173 **Light . . . yields,** an easy bargain yields a bad return. Numerous proverbs appear in the miracle plays 174 **ride a-wooing,** run away 184 **rood,** cross 185 **yode,** went 191 **They sing,** not only to introduce variety but to mark the end of the first episode 194 **uneven,** at odds 195 **bairns,** children—the first of several significant allusions to babies 203 **Ich, etc.** To conceal his identity and stand on his dignity, Mak adopts the southern dialect—one of the earliest uses of comic dialect in drama

212 **paint,** deceive 218 **gird,** sneer 239 **weltering,** rolling about 241 **Ill speed . . . do,** bad luck to any other thing she may do—a general malediction 249 **dowse,** slut

138   *The Middle Ages*

₂₅₀ There is none that trows,° nor knows, a waur°
                Then ken I.
Now will ye see what I proffer,
To give all in my coffer
Tomorrow next to offer,
                Her head-mass penny.°

    GIB. I wot so forwaked° is none in this shire:
I would sleep if I taked less to my hire.°
    COLL. I am cold and naked, and would have a fire.
    DAW. I am weary and shaked and run in the mire.
₂₆₀   Watch thou!
    GIB. Nay, I will lie down by,
For I must sleep truly.
    DAW. As good a man's son was I
                As any of you.

But, Mak, come hither! between us shalt thou stay.
    MAK. Then I might stop you, I ween, from what
        ye would say,
                Indeed.
From my top to my toe
Manus tuas commendo,
₂₇₀ *Pontio Pilato.*°
                Christ's cross me speed.

The shepherds fall asleep. Then MAK *arises without
awakening them and addresses the audience softly.*

    MAK. Now were time for a man, that lacks what he
        wold,
To stalk privately then into a fold,
And nimbly to work then, and be not too bold,
For he might pay for the bargain, if it were told
                At the ending.
Now work I a spell,°
For he needs good counsel
That fain would fare well,
                And has but little spending.° {MAK *works
₂₈₀   a spell on them.*

Now about you a circle, as round as a moon
Til I have done that I will, till that it be noon,
That ye lie stone-still, till that I have done,
And I shall theretil a good magic rune
                Recite.
"Over your heads my hand I lift,
Out go your eyes; destroyed be your sight,"
But yet I must make better shift,
                If it be right.

₂₉₀ Lord, but they sleep hard! that may ye all hear;°
I was never a shepherd, but now it is clear,

If the flock be scared, yet will I steal near,
Ho! I draw hitherward! now mends out cheer,
                From sorrow.
A fat sheep I dare say,
A good fleece if I may,
When I can, I'll repay,
                But this will I borrow.   {*He steals a
                                            sheep and goes home.*

    MAK (*at the door of his cottage*). How, Gill, art
        thou in?
                Get us some light.   ₃₀₀
    GILL. Who makes such din this time of night?
I am set for to spin; I hope not I might
Rise a penny to win! I curse ye, foul wight!
                So fares
A housewife that has been
Rushed about 'til she's lean.
There may no work be seen
                Because of such cares.

    MAK. Good wife, open the heck.° See'st thou not
        what I bring?
    GILL. I may let thee draw the sneck.° Ah! come in, ₃₁₀
        my sweeting.
    MAK. Yea, thou dost not reck of my long standing.
    GILL. By thy naked neck, thou art like for to
        swing!°
    MAK.   Get away!
I am worthy of my meat,
For at a pinch can I get
More than they that work and sweat
                All the long day,

Thus it fell to my lot, Gill, I had such grace.
    GILL. It were a foul blot to be hanged for the case.
    MAK. I have scaped, Gillot, from as hard a place. ₃₂₀
    GILL. "But so long goes the pot to the water,"
        men says,
                "At last
Comes it home broken."
    MAK. Well know I the token,
But let it never be spoken;
                But help make the sheep fast.

I would he were slain. I should like well to eat.
This twelvemonth was I not so fain of some good
        sheep-meat.
    GILL. Come they ere he be slain, and hear the
        sheep bleat—
    MAK. Then might I be ta'en; that gives me a cold ₃₃₀
        sweat!
                Go bar
The gate-door.

    250 **trows,** has experienced   **waur,** worse   255 **head-mass penny,** money for
her requiem mass   256 **forwaked,** worn out   257 **if . . . hire,** if I were paid
less; Gib is probably sarcastic   269 **Manus, etc.** Mak says his prayers by
parodying the words of Jesus in *Luke,* 23:46   277 **a spell.** Mak may actually be
a wizard or may merely be amusing the audience with some mock hocus-pocus
280 **little spending,** little to spend   290 **that may ye all hear.** The shepherds
respond to Mak's magic by snoring

309 **heck,** hatch, door   310 **sneck,** latch   312 **By . . . swing.** Gill sees the
sheep

GILL.   Yes, Mak,
For if they come at thy back—
    MAK. Then I'd be caught by the pack:
          The devil the waur!°

    GILL. A good trick have I spied, since thou
        knowest none:
Here shall we him hide, till they be gone;
In my cradle abide. Let me alone,
340 And I shall lie beside in childbed and groan.
    MAK.   In bed!
And I shall say thou wast light°
Of a boy babe this night.
    GILL. Now that day was bright,
          On which I was bred.

A goodly device and a far cast;°
Yet a woman's advice helps at the last.
I care never who spies. Again go thou fast.
    MAK. Come I not ere they rise; there will blow a
        cold blast—
350   I will go sleep.
Yet sleep all this company,
And I shall go stalk privily,
As it had never been I
          That bore off their sheep.

After having killed the sheep, MAK *returns to the
moors, lies down, and pretends to sleep. After a
pause, the shepherds awake one after another.*

    COLL. *Resurrex a mortruis!*° have hold my hand!
Judas carnas dominus! I may not well stand.
My foot sleeps, by Jesus, as 'twere tied with a band.
I thought that we laid us full near England.
    GIB.   Ah me!
360 Lord, but I have slept weel,
As fresh as an eel,
As light I me feel
          As leaf on a tree.

    DAW. Ben'cite! be herein! So my body quakes
My heart is out of my skin, such throbbing it makes.
Who makes all this din? So hard my brow aches
Round about will I spin. Hark fellows, awake!
          We were four.
See ye anywhere Mak now?
370 COLL. We were up ere thou.
    GIB. Man, I give God a vow,
          Yet he went not afore.

    DAW. Methought he was wrapped in a wolf's skin.
    COLL. So are many lapped, if ye look but within.
    GIB. When we had long napped, methought with a
        gin°

A fat sheep he trapped, but he made no din.
    DAW.   Be still;
Thy dream makes thee brood;
t is but vision, by the rood.
    COLL. Now God turn all to good,   380
          If it be his will.   {*Looking about they
                                   find* MAK *and awaken him.*

    GIB. Rise, Mak, for shame! thou liest right long.
    MAK. Now Christ's holy name be us amang,
What is this? By Saint James!—I may not well gang!
I trust I be the same. Ah! my neck has lain wrang
          Enough.   {*They help him to his feet.*
Mickle thank! Since yestreen
By Saint Stephen, I deem
I was plagued with a dream
          That shook me right rough   390

I thought Gill began to croak, and travail full sad.
Well nigh at the first cock,—of a young lad,
For to mend our flock; then be I never glad.
To have "tow on my rok"°—more than ever I had.
          Ah, my head!
A house full of young weans,°
The devil knock out their brains!
Woe is he of small means
          And too little bread.

I must go home, by your leave, to Gill as I thought.   400
Pray you look up my sleeve, that I steal nought:
I am loath you to grieve, or from you take
          aught.   {MAK *leaves them.*

    DAW. Go forth, well might ye thieve! Now would I
        we sought
          This morn,
That we had all our store.°
    COLL. But I will go before,
Let us meet.
    GIB.   Where afore?
    DAW.   At the crooked thorn.

    MAK (*at his cottage door*). Undo this door! who is   410
        here? How long shall I stand?
    GILL. Who maketh such gear?°—Now walk in the
        waniand!°
    MAK. Ah, Gill, what cheer?—It is I, Mak, your
        husband.
    GILL. Then may we see here the devil in a band,°
          Sir Guile!
Lo, he comes with a note,
As if held by his throat,
I can work not a mote
          For any great while.

---

336 **the waur,** reward you   342 **light,** delivered   346 **far cast,** clever plan
355 **Resurrex, etc.,** "hog" Latin used as mild expletives. The first, suggesting a
resurrection from the dead, is appropriate to the awakening of Coll from his deep
sleep. The meaning of the garbled Latin in the second phrase is unclear
375 **gin,** trick or strategem

394 **tow on my rok,** flax—for spinning—on my distaff   396 **weans,** small children   403–405 **Now . . . store.** I think we should investigate to discover if we
have all our sheep this morning   411 **gear,** business, doings   **waniand,** the time
of the waning of the moon—an unlucky season   413 **devil in a band,** apparently
an allusion to Mak's guile

MAK. Will ye hear what fuss she makes—to get
   her a gloze,°
420 Yet she does naught but rakes the fire with her toes.
   GILL. Why, who wanders, who wakes—who
      comes, who goes?
   Who brews, who bakes? Who's never a-doze?
      And then
   It is sad to behold,
   Now in hot, now in cold
   Full woful is the household
      That wants a woman.

   But what end hast thou made with the shepherds,
      Mak?
   MAK. The last word that they said, when I turned
      my back,
430 They would look that they had of their sheep all the
      pack.
   'Twere ill luck to have stayed when they their sheep
      lack.
      Perdie!
   But howso the game goes,
   They'll blame me, I suppose
   And make a foul noise,
      And cry out upon me.

   But thou must do aright.
   GILL.   I accord me theretil.
   I'll wrap him out of sight in my cradle.
440 If it were a greater slight, even yet I'd show
      skill.   {As she talks, GILL swaddles the dead
         sheep in the cradle; she then lies down on the
                                             bed.

   I will lie down straight. Come wrap me.
   MAK.   I will.
   GILL.   Behind.
   Come the shepherds, I trow,
   They will nip us full narrow.
   MAK. But I may cry out, ''Harrow!''°
      The sheep if they find.

   GILL. Hearken aye when they call; they will come
      anon.
   Come and make ready all, and sing all alone;
450 Sing ''Lullay'' thou shall, for I must groan,
   And cry out by the wall on Mary and John,°
      For pain.
   Sing ''Lullay'' full fast
   When thou hears at the last;
   And but I play a false cast°
      Ne'er trust me again.

*After having searched until sunrise, the Three
Shepherds meet at the crooked hawthorne on the
moors.*

   DAW. Ah, Coll, good morn. Why sleepest thou not?
   COLL. Alas, that ever was I born! We have a foul
      blot.
   A fat wether have we lorn.
   DAW.   Marry, I would ye said it not!   460
   GIB. Who would do us that scorn? That was a foul
      plot.
   COLL.   Some shrew.
   I have sought with my dogs,
   All Horbery Shrogs
   And of fifteen hogs°
      Found I all but one ewe.°

   DAW. Now trust me if you will, by Saint Thomas of
      Kent!°
   Either Mak or Gill have on evil been bent.
   COLL. Peace, man, be still;—I saw when he went.
   Thou slander'st him ill; thou ought to repent,   470
      Indeed.
   GIB. Now I tell ye no lie
   If I should even here die,
   I would say it were he,
      That did that same deed.

   DAW. Go we thither with speed—and run on our
      feet.
   May I never eat bread—the truth till I meet.
   COLL. Nor drink, in my head—with him till I meet.
   GIB. I will rest in no stead, until I him greet.
      My brother.°   480
   Till we're out of our plight,
   And I see him in sight,
   I will ne'er sleep one night,
      Nay, not another.

*The Shepherds go to Mak's cottage. Hearing them
approach, MAK begins to sing a lullaby and GILL to
groan in pretended pain.*

   DAW. Will ye hear Gill and Mak! Our Sire! list, how
      they croon!
   COLL. Heard I never voice crack so clear out of
      tune.
   Call to him.
   GIB.   Mak! undo your door soon!
   MAK. Who is it that spake as if it were noon,   490
      So oft?
   Who is that, I say?
   DAW. Good fellows, if it were day—
   MAK. As far as ye may—

                              {MAK *admits them.*
   If it please ye, speak soft!

   Over a sick woman's head, that suffers malease,°
   I had rather be dead than she had any disease.

419 **gloze,** excuse   446 **Harrow,** a cry used in hunting   451 **Mary and John,**
the Virgin Mary and Saint John   455 **false cast,** sly trick

465 **hogs,** unshorn yearling sheep   466 **one ewe.** This and other references to
the stolen sheep are inconsistent; most of the allusions are to a lost ram
467 **Saint Thomas of Kent,** Thomas à Becket   480 **My brother.** He addresses
Coll   495 **malease,** sickness

GILL. Go elsewhere, I said, and leave me in peace.
Each foot that ye tread near makes my heart cease.
      Oh, me!
500 COLL. Tell us, Mak, if ye may,
How fare ye, I say?
    MAK. But are ye on this farm today?
        Now how fare ye?
Ye have run in the mire, and are all soaked yet,
I shall make you a fire, if ye will sit.
A nurse would I hire; can ye think of one yet?
Well earned is my hire; my dream—this is it,   *{He*
                points to the cradle.
    In season.
I have bairns if ye knew,
510 Well more than enow,
But we must drink as we brew,
    And that is but reason.

Dine ere ye take the road; methink that ye sweat.
    GIB. Nay neither mends our mode, to drink nor to
      eat.
    MAK. Why, sir, ails you aught but good?
    DAW.   Yes, our sheep that we get
Are stolen or they go. Our loss is great.
    MAK.   Sirs, drink!
Had I been there
520 Some should have bought it full dear.
    COLL. Marry, some men say that ye were,
      And that makes us think.

    GIB. Mak, some men trows that it should be ye.
    DAW. Either ye or your spouse, so say we.
    MAK. Now if ye really suppose that it's Gill or me,
Come and rip our house, and then may ye see
      Who had her;°
If I any sheep got,
Or cow or stot;°
530 And Gill, my wife, rose not
      Here since she laid her.

As I am both true and leal, to God here I pray,
That this be the first meal, I shall eat this day.
    COLL. Mak, as I have weal, arise thee, I say!
"He learned timely to steal, that could not say nay."
    GILL.   I swelt.°
Out thieves now at once!
Ye come to rob us for the nonce.
    MAK. Here ye not how she groans?
540   Your hearts should melt.

GILL. Out thieves, from my bairn! Get near him no
    more.
MAK. If ye knew all she's borne, your hearts
    would be sore.

Ye do wrong, I you warn, that ye thus come before
To a woman so forlorn—but I say no more.
    GILL.   Ah, my middle!
I pray to God so mild,
If ever I you beguiled,
That I eat this child,
      That lies in this cradle.

    MAK. Peace, woman, for God's pain, and cry not   550
    so;
Thou hurtest thy brain, and mak'st me full woe
    GIB. I know our sheep be slain. What find ye two?
    DAW. All work is in vain; as well may we go.
      Save some tatters,
I can find no flesh,
Hard nor nesh,°
Salt nor fresh,
      But two empty platters.

Live cattle but this, tame nor wild,
None, as have I bliss, smelled near as vile.   560
      {He points to the cradle.
    GILL. No, so God give me bliss, and joy of my
    child.
    COLL. We have aimed quite amiss; I hold us
    beguiled.
    GIB.   Sir, we're done.
Sir, our lady him save,
Is your child a knave?°
    MAK. Any lord might well have
      This child for his son.

When he wakens he grips° that joy is to see.
    DAW. In good time to his hips,° and happy they
    be!
But who were his gossips,° so soon ready?   570
    MAK. So fair fall their lips!
    COLL (*aside*).   Hark now, a lie!
    MAK.   So God them thank,
Parkin, and Gibbon Waller, I say,
And gentle John Horne, in good fay°—
He made us all gay—
      With the great shank.

    GIB. Mak, friends will we be, for we are all one.
    MAK. We? Ye are no friends to me, for
      amends get I none.   580
Farewell all three: I wish well ye were gone.   *{The*
             shepherds leave the cottage.
    DAW. "Fair words may there be, but love there is
    none—"
      This year.
    COLL. Gave ye the child anything?°
    GIB. I trow not one farthing.

527 **her,** the ewe   529 **stot,** young steer   536 **swelt,** perish

556 **nesh,** soft   565 **knave,** boy   568 **grips,** his little hand clutches my finger
569 **to his hips,** to his loins. Daw is wishing the "child" many descendants
570 **gossips,** godfathers   575 **fay,** faith   584 **Gave . . . anything.** It was bad
manners not to give a gift to a newborn infant; thus the shepherds' kindness becomes the source of Mak's downfall just when he believes himself safe

DAW. Fast again will I fling,
        Abide ye me here.   *{He returns to Mak's cottage. The other shepherds follow him.*
Mak, pray have no grief, if I come to thy bairn.
MAK. Nay, I can't but believe that foul hast thou farne.°
590   DAW. The child will not grieve, that little day-starn.
Mak, with your leave, let me give your bairn,
        But sixpence.
MAK. Nay, go 'way: he sleeps.
DAW. Methinks he peeps.
MAK. When he wakens, he weeps.
        I pray you go hence.

DAW. Give me leave him to kiss, and lift up the clout.   *{DAW pulls back the covers.*
What the devil is this? He has a long snout.
COLL. He is birth-marked amiss.° Why wait we about?
600   GIB. "Ill spun weft," I wis, "aye cometh foul out."°
        Aye, so!
He is like our sheep.
DAW. How, Gib, may I peep?
COLL. I trow, "Kind will creep,
        Where it may not go."°

GIB. This was a quaint gaud,° and a far cast;
It was a high fraud.
DAW.   Yea, sirs, was 't.
Lets burn this bawd and bind her fast.
610   "A false scau'd° hangs at the last";
        So shalt thou.
Will ye see how they swaddle
His four feet in the middle?
Saw I never in a cradle
        A hornéd lad° e'er now!

MAK. Peace bid I! what! how do ye dare?
It was I him begat and yon woman him bare.
COLL. What's the name of the brat? Lo, God, Mak's heir!
GIB. Oh, stop all that! Now God give him care,
620   I say.
GILL. A pretty child is he,
As sits upon a woman's knee;
A dilly-down,° perdie!
        To make a man gay.

DAW. I know him by the ear-mark—that is a good token.
MAK. I tell you, sirs, hark—his nose was broken.
Since then, told me a clerk,° that he had been stroken.°

COLL. This is a false work; no worse can be spoken.
        Get a weapon!
GILL. He was taken by an elf;   630
I saw it myself.
When the clock struck twelve,
        Was he misshapen.

GIB. Ye two are right deft—ill may ye be sped!
DAW. Since they maintain their theft—let's do them to dead.
MAK. If I trespass eft,° smite off my head.
With you as judge I'll be left.
COLL.   Sirs, follow my lead;
        For this trespass
We will neither curse nor fight,   640
Scold, nor chide,
But seize him tight,
        And cast him in canvas.

They drag MAK *out-of-doors and toss him in a canvas sheet stripped from Gill's bed. Leaving him groaning on the ground, they return to the moors.*°

* * * * *

COLL. Lord, but I am sore, and ache in my wrist.
In faith, I can do no more, therefore will I rest.
GIB. As a sheep of seven score, he weighed in my fist.
For to sleep anywhere, methink that I list.
DAW.   Now I pray you,
On this green let us lie.
COLL. On these thefts yet think I.   650
DAW. Oh, let your wrath die!°
        Do as I say you.

They lie down and sleep. Then an ANGEL *appears above, who sings "Gloria in Excelsis," then speaks.*

ANGEL. Arise herdsmen, attend, for now is he born
That shall take from the fiend all that Adam had lorn.°
That wizard° to rend, this night is he born.
God is made your friend now on this morn.
        He behests,
To Bethl'em go see,
There found will he be,
In a crib full poorly,   660
        Betwixt two beasts.

COLL. 'Twas as sweet a song even as ever yet I heard.
It is hard to believe that I thus could be stirred.

589 **foul . . . farne,** you have done badly   599 **He . . . amiss.** Coll thinks at first that the "child" is badly birth-marked   600 **Ill . . . out,** i.e., murder will out   604–605 **Kind . . . go.** Nature will crawl where it cannot walk—a popular proverb   606 **gaud,** deceit   610 **scau'd,** scold   615 **a hornéd lad.** Daw alludes to the ram's horns and perhaps is also making the ancient cuckold jest   623 **dilly-down,** sweet little bud   627 **clerk,** a learned man   **stroken,** struck

636 **eft,** again; Mak admits his guilt   **the moors.** Mak's cottage now becomes the stable at Bethlehem   651 **let your wrath die,** a preparation for the mood of "on earth peace, good will toward men"   654 **lorn,** lost, an allusion to the "original sin"   655 **wizard,** Satan

GIB. Of God's son from heaven, he spoke a fair
    word.

All the wood like the levin,° methought that he gard°
    Appear.
DAW. He spoke of a bairn
In Bethlehem born.   {He points to the star.
    COLL. That betokens yon starn.
670   Let us seek him there.

GIB. Say, what was his song? Heard ye not how
    he cracked it?
Three breves° to a long.
DAW.   Yea, marry, he hacked it.
Was no crotchet° wrong, nor no thing that lacked it.
    COLL. For to sing us among, right as he cracked it.
        I can.
GIB. Let us see how ye croon
Can ye bark at the moon?
    DAW. Hold your tongues! have done!
680   COLL.   Sing after me, then. {They sing.°

GIB. To Bethl'em he bade that we should gang;
I am full a-dread that we tarry too lang.
    DAW. Be merry and not sad; of good tidings he
        sang.
We'll be evermore glad, our way as we gang,
        Without noise.
COLL. Hie we thither, we three,
Though we be wet and weary,
To that child and that lady.
        We have naught to lose.

690   GIB. We find by the prophecy—let be your din—
Of David and Isay,° and more than I ken,
They prophesied by clergy, that in a virgin
Should he alight and lie, to atone for our sin
        And slake it.
Save our race from woe;
For Isay said so:
"Ecce virgo
        Concipiet"° a child that is naked.

    DAW. Full glad may we be, and abide that day,
700 That loved one to see that all powers sway.
Lord, well were it for me, for once and for aye,
Might I kneel on my knee some word for to say
        To that child.
But the angel said:
In a crib was he laid;
He was poorly arrayed,
        Both gentle and mild.

COLL. Patriarchs that have been—and prophets
    beforn—
They desired to have seen this child that is born.
They are gone full clean—that have they lorn.   710
We shall see him, I ween, e'er it be morn,
        For token.
When I see him and feel,
I shall then know full weel
It is true as steel
        What prophets have spoken:

To so poor as we are, that he would appear,
First found, and declared, by his messenger.
    GIB. Go we now, let us fare; the place is us near.
    DAW. I am ready and dare; together go here,   720
        To that heavenly light!
Lord, if thy will be,
We are simple, all three,
Grant thou us of thy glee,
        And comfort this night.

*The shepherds arrive at Bethlehem, enter the stable,
and kneel before* MARY *and the* CHILD.

    COLL. Hail, comely and clean; hail, young child!
Hail, maker, as I mean,° from a maiden so mild!
Thou hast cursed, I ween, the warlock° so wild,
Of his haughty mien he now goes beguiled.
        He° merry is!   730
Lo, he laughs, my sweeting,
A happy meeting!
Here's my promised greeting,
        Have a cluster of cherries.

    GIB. Hail, sovereign, savior, for thou hast us sought!
Hail! thou noble child any flower, that all things has
    wrought!
Hail! full of power, that made all from nought!
Hail! I kneel and I cower. A bird have I brought
        To my bairn!
Hail, little wee mop!   740
Of our creed thou art the crop°
I would drink from thy cup,
        Little day-starn.

    DAW. Hail, darling dear, full of godhead!
I pray thee be near, when that I have need.
Hail! sweet is thy cheer; my heart would bleed
To see thee sit here in so poor weed,
        With no pennies.
Hail! put forth thy hand small!
I bring thee but a ball   750
Have it and play withal.
        And go to the tennis.

665 **levin,** lightning   **gard,** made   672 **breves,** short musical notes, each equivalent to one-third of the long note in the Middle Ages   674 **crotchet,** quarter
note   680 **They sing.** Apparently the shepherds repeat the *Gloria in Excelsis*
691 **Isay,** *Isaiah;* see Chapters 9:6-7, 11, and especially 53, early accepted as a
prophecy of the coming of the Messiah. King David was thought of as the prophet
and ancestor of Jesus   697-698 **Ecce virgo Concipiet,** behold a virgin shall conceive

727 **mean,** believe   728 **warlock,** Satan   730 **He,** the Christ Child   741 **our
creed . . . crop.** "Looking unto Jesus the author and finisher of our faith" (*Hebrews,* 12:2)

MARY. The Father of Heaven, God omnipotent,
That made all in days seven, his son has He sent.
My name did God name, and I conceived ere He
    went.
I conceived Him full even, through His might, as
    God meant;
        And now is He born.
May He keep you from woe:
I shall pray Him so;
760 Tell it forth as ye go,
        And think on this morn.
  COLL. Farewell, lady, so fair to behold,
With thy child on thy knee.
  GIB.   But he lies very cold.
Lord, well is with me. Now we go forth, behold!
  DAW. Forsooth, already it seems to be told
        Full oft.
  COLL. What grace we have found;
  GIB. Come forth, now are we sound.
770 DAW. To sing are we bound;
        Let it ring out aloft!   *{The shepherds go
                              out singing.*

Here ends The Shepherds' Pageant.

SIR THOMAS MALORY
1394?–1471

Thomas Malory was once thought to be one of the few medieval authors about whom we knew something; it was often felt that we knew, in fact, rather too much. The Warwickshire knight, whose identity as the author of the *Morte Darthur* had been unchallenged for years, was charged with crimes of extortion, robbery, and rape. He seems to have spent the last twenty years of his life in prison. Readers of *Morte Darthur* thus had to reconcile these unpleasant facts with the image of an author lauding chivalric virtue. More recent scholarship—the work of William Matthews, especially—has challenged the Warwickshire Malory and has investigated other Thomas Malorys who may have been the poet. The details of the biographical speculation are too complicated to rehearse here; there are still only plausible cases for other Malorys. But it is important to bear in mind that *Morte Darthur* may not have been written by a man with such a criminal record.

Thomas Malory's one work, so far as is known, was his compilation and general arrangement of the various cycles of Arthurian legend, gathered together under the title of *Morte Darthur*. It is clear that in nearly every case Malory made use of French versions of the Arthurian stories, condensing and rewriting them; but it is also fairly clear that his publisher William Caxton edited his work to some extent, leaving out parts of the original Malory text. There is little doubt, moreover, that Malory was indebted also to a long Middle English romance in alliterative verse, the *Morte Arthure*. Much controversy has centered about the problem of the composition of *Morte Darthur*. Did Malory write eight separate Arthurian romances as he read his sources, or did he have an overall plan for a unified work, which he followed from the beginning? In either case, the net result was an uneven work which begins with the mysterious birth of Arthur and proceeds to the last fatal battle in the West, after which the king passes away to Avalon, the queen enters a nunnery, and Lancelot dies in sanctity.

Malory's *Morte Darthur* was one of the many works printed by William Caxton (1422?–1491?), who introduced printing into England. Caxton probably came from a family of some influence, for he was apprenticed to Robert Large, one of the richest mercers of London. He lived in Bruges for some time and apparently became a successful merchant and a man of polish and of intellectual interests. He retired from his business about 1471 and under the patronage of the Duchess of Burgundy took up literary pursuits. His most ambitious work was his translation of the Frenchman Lefevre's *Recuyel of the Histories of Troye*, a compilation of stories about the Trojan War completed in 1471.

At about this same time, Caxton became interested in the art of printing, which had been practiced on the Continent since the days of Johann Gutenberg (1400?–1468?), the inventor of printing from movable type. Caxton's *Recuyel* was the first book printed in English (1474). Sometime within the next year he moved his press to London, where he soon printed the first book actually published in England, the *Dictes and Sayings of the Philosophers* (1477). Among the most famous of Caxton's later publications were the editions of Malory's *Morte Darthur*, Gower's *Confessio Amantis*, and Chaucer's *Canterbury Tales*—beautiful specimens of the printer's art.

from MORTE DARTHUR

CAXTON'S PREFACE°

After that I had accomplished and finished divers histories, as well of contemplation as of other historical and worldly acts of great conquerors and princes,

---

Caxton's Preface, significant in showing the importance of the Arthurian story in the mind of Caxton and his public

and also certain books of ensamples and doctrine, many noble and divers gentlemen of this realm of England came and demanded me many and oftimes, wherefore that I have not do made and imprint the noble history of the Saint Grail, and of the most renowned Christian king, first and chief of the three best Christian, and worthy, King Arthur, which ought most to be remembered among us Englishmen tofore all other Christian kings. For it is notoriously known through the universal world that there be nine worthy and the best that ever were, that is to wit three Paynims,° three Jews, and three Christian men. As for the Paynims, they were tofore the Incarnation of Christ, which were named, the first Hector of Troy, of whom the history is come both in ballad and in prose;° the second Alexander the Great; and the third Julius Caesar, Emperor of Rome, of whom the histories be well-known and had. And as for the three Jews which also were tofore the Incarnation of our Lord, of whom the first was duke Joshua which brought the children of Israel into the land of behest; the second David, King of Jerusalem; and the third Judas Machabeus: of these three the Bible rehearseth all their noble histories and acts. And since the said Incarnation have been three noble Christian men, stalled° and admitted through the universal world into the number of the nine best and worthy. Of whom was first the noble Arthur, whose noble acts I purpose to write in this present book here following. The second was Charlemain,° or Charles the Great, of whom the history is had in many places both in French and in English; and the third and last was Godfrey of Boloine,° of whose acts and life I made a book unto the excellent prince and king of noble memory, King Edward the Fourth.° The said noble gentlemen instantly required me to imprint the history of the said noble king and conqueror, King Arthur, and of his knights, with the history of the Saint Greal, and of the death and ending of the said Arthur; affirming that I ought rather to imprint his acts and noble feats, than of Godfrey of Boloine, or any of the other eight, considering that he was a man born within this realm, and king and emperor of the same: and that there be in French divers and many noble volumes of his acts, and also of his knights. To whom I answered that divers men hold opinion that there was no such Arthur and that all such books as been made of him, be but feigned and fables, because that some chronicles make of him no mention, nor remember him nothing, nor of his knights. Whereto they answered and one in special said, that in him that should say or think that

there was never such a king called Arthur, might well be aretted° great folly and blindness; for he said that there were many evidences of the contrary. First ye may see his sepulchre in the Monastery of Glastinbury. And also in Policronicon,° in the fifth book the sixth chapter, and in the seventh book the twenty-third chapter, where his body was buried and after found and translated into the said monastery. Ye shall see also in the history of Bochas,° in his book De Casu Principum,° part of his noble acts, and also of his fall. Also Galfridus° in his British book recounteth his life; and in divers places of England many remembrances be yet of him and shall remain perpetually, and also of his knights. First in the Abbey of Westminster, at St. Edward's Shrine,° remaineth the print of his seal in red wax closed in beryl, in which is written Patricius Arthurus, Britannie, Gallie, Germanie, Dacie, Imperator.° Item in the castle of Dover ye may see Gawaine's skull and Craddock's° mantle: at Winchester the Round Table: at other places Launcelot's sword and many other things. Then all these things considered, there can no man reasonably gainsay but there was a king of this land named Arthur. For in all places, Christian and heathen, he is reputed and taken for one of the nine worthy, and the first of the three Christian men. And also he is more spoken of beyond the sea, more books made of his noble acts than there be in England, as well in Dutch, Italian, Spanish, and Greek, as in French. And yet of record remain in witness of him in Wales, in the town of Camelot,° the great stones and marvelous works of iron, lying under the ground, and royal vaults, which divers now living hath seen. Wherefore it is a marvel why he is no more renowned in his own country, save only it accordeth to the Word of God, which saith that no man is accepted for a prophet in his own country.° Then all these things foresaid alleged, I could not well deny but that there was such a noble king named Arthur, and reputed one of the nine worthy, and first and chief of the Christian men. And many noble volumes be made of him and of his noble knights in French, which I have seen and read beyond the seat,° which be not had in our maternal tongue. But in Welsh be many and also in French, and some in English, but nowhere nigh all. Wherefore, such as have late been drawn out briefly into English I have after the simple conning° that God hath sent to

15 **Paynims,** pagans   18 **ballad . . . prose,** the various versions of the Troy legend. By "ballads" Caxton probably refers to the metrical romances   28 **stalled,** established   33 **Charlemain,** Charlemagne (742–814), Emperor of the Franks and the first of the Holy Roman emperors   35 **Godfrey of Boloine,** Godfrey of Bouillon (1060?–1100), leader of the First Crusade, in which Jerusalem was wrested from the Saracens in 1099. He was chosen the first of the rulers of the new Kingdom of Jerusalem   37 **Edward the Fourth,** King Edward IV of England (1441–1483), the chief ruler backed by the Yorkists during the Wars of the Roses

55 **aretted,** attributed   58 **Policronicon,** a universal history, originally in Latin, translated in 1387   62 **Bochas,** Giovanni Boccaccio (1313–1375), an important writer of the Italian Renaissance   **De Casu Principum,** Of the Fall of Princes, a didactic work by Boccaccio. It tells the story of the downfall of great men and is intended to serve as a warning example to posterity   64 **Galfridus,** Geoffrey of Monmouth (1110?–1154), the first Englishman to write a comprehensive account of the career of King Arthur. His Historia Regum Britanniae is particularly important for its imaginative treatment of Arthur himself   68 **St. Edward's shrine,** the tomb of Edward the Confessor (1004–1066)   70 **Britannie . . . Imperator,** Emperor of Britain, Gaul, Germania, and Dacia   72 **Craddock,** Caradog, the son of the old Welsh god Bran   83 **Camelot.** The site of Arthur's ancient capital has never been fixed with certainty by present-day investigators; it is possible that Camelot was part of Winchester   89 **prophet . . . country,** a paraphrase of the familiar biblical saying. See Matthew, 13:57; Mark, 6:4; Luke, 4:24; John, 4:44   95 **beyond the seat,** thoroughly, from the sources   99 **conning,** understanding

me, under the favor and correction of all noble lords and gentlemen, enprised° to imprint a book of the noble histories of the said King Arthur, and of certain of his knights, after a copy unto me delivered, which copy Sir Thomas Malorye did take out of certain books of French, and reduced it into English. And I, according to my copy, have done set it in imprint, to the intent that noble men may see and learn the noble acts of chivalry, the gentle and virtuous deeds that some knights used in those days, by which they came to honor; and how they that were vicious were punished and oft put to shame and rebuke; humbly beseeching all noble lords and ladies, with all other estates of what estate or degree they be of, that shall see and read in this said book and work, that they take the good and honest acts in their remembrance, and to follow the same. Wherein they shall find many joyous and pleasant histories, and noble and renowned acts of humanity, gentleness, and chivalry. For herein may be seen noble chivalry, courtesy, humanity, friendliness, hardiness, love, friendship, cowardice, murder, hate, virtue, and sin. Do after the good and leave the evil, and it shall bring you to good fame and renown. And for to pass the time this book shall be pleasant to read in; but for to give faith and belief that all is true that is contained herein, ye be at your liberty; but all is written for our doctrine,° and for to beware that we fall not to vice nor sin; but to exercise and follow virtue; by which we may come and attain to good fame and renown in this life, and after this short and transitory life, to come unto everlasting bliss in heaven, the which He grant us that reigneth in heaven, the blessed Trinity. Amen.

Then to proceed forth in this said book, which I direct unto all noble princes, lords and ladies, gentlemen or gentlewomen, that desire to read or hear read of the noble and joyous history of the great conqueror and excellent king, King Arthur, sometime king of this noble realm, then called Britain; I, William Caxton, simple person, present this book following, which I have enprised to imprint; and [it] treateth of the noble acts, feats of arms of chivalry, prowess, hardiness, humanity, love, courtesy, and very gentleness, with many wonderful histories and adventures. And for to understand briefly the content of this volume, I have divided it into twenty-one books, and every book chaptered, as hereafter shall by God's grace follow. The first book shall treat how Uther Pendragon gat the noble conqueror King Arthur, and containeth twenty-eight chapters. The second book treateth of Balin the noble knight, and containeth nineteen chapters. The third book treateth of the marriage of King Arthur to Queen Guenever, with other matters, and containeth fifteen chapters. The fourth book, how Merlin was as-

sotted,° and of war made to King Arthur, and containeth twenty-nine chapters. The fifth book treateth of the conquest of Lucius the emperor, and containeth twelve chapters. The sixth book treateth of Sir Launcelot and Sir Lionel, and marvelous adventures, and containeth eighteen chapters. The seventh book treateth of a noble knight called Sir Gareth, and named by Sir Kay, Beaumains, and containeth thirty-six chapters. The eighth book treateth of the birth of Sir Tristram the noble knight, and of his acts, and containeth forty-one chapters. The ninth book treateth of a knight named by Sir Kay, La Cote Male Taile, and also of Sir Tristram, and containeth forty-four chapters. The tenth book treateth of Sir Tristram and other marvelous adventures, and containeth eighty-eight chapters. The eleventh book treateth of Sir Launcelot and Sir Galahad, and containeth fourteen chapters. The twelfth book treateth of Sir Launcelot and his madness, and containeth fourteen chapters. The thirteenth book treateth how Galahad came first to King Arthur's court, and the quest how the Sangreal was begun, and containeth twenty chapters. The fourteenth book treateth of the quest of the Sangreal, and containeth ten chapters. The fifteenth book treateth of Sir Launcelot, and containeth six chapters. The sixteenth book treateth of Sir Bors and Sir Lionel his brother, and containeth seventeen chapters. The seventeenth book treateth of the Sangreal, and containeth twenty-three chapters. The eighteenth book treateth of Sir Launcelot and the queen, and containeth twenty-five chapters. The nineteenth book treateth of Queen Guenever and Launcelot, and containeth thirteen chapters. The twentieth book treateth of the piteous death of Arthur, and containeth twenty-two chapters. The twenty-first book treateth of his last departing, and how Sir Launcelot came to revenge his death, and containeth thirteen chapters. The sum is twenty-one books, which contain the sum of five hundred and seven chapters, as more plainly shall follow hereafter.

BOOK 21

The malcontents Mordred and Agravaine attempt to interest their brothers Gawain, Gareth, and Gaheris in the project of catching Lancelot and Guinevere together, in order that their love intrigue may be made certain to King Arthur. Gawain, Gareth, and Gaheris refuse to do anything against their respected friend Lancelot. But Mordred and Agravaine, in company with many other knights, ambush Lancelot in the queen's apartments. Lancelot fights his way out of the ambush, killing all his opponents save Mordred; but

---

101 **enprised,** undertaken   126 **for our doctrine,** for our teaching, i.e., to teach us

153 **assotted,** made a fool of

the secret love of Christendom's greatest knight has been discovered, and he must flee. Guinevere is accused of adultery and is to be burnt at the stake. Lancelot, however, rallies about him many of his friends; they make a sudden attack and rescue Guinevere after a fierce battle, carrying her off to Lancelot's great castle, Joyous Gard. In the fight Gaheris and Gareth are inadvertently slain by Lancelot, who did not recognize them, as they were unarmed. This disaster alienates Gawain from Lancelot, and when Arthur is persuaded to summon his forces to avenge himself on Lancelot for thus carrying off the queen, Gawain becomes one of his staunchest supporters.*

Arthur besieges Lancelot in Joyous Gard for some time. The Pope finally intercedes and induces Arthur to take Guinevere back. Arthur is even willing to forgive Lancelot, but the irreconcilable Gawain will have none of it. Lancelot deems it expedient to leave the country. He crosses into France, but in the meantime Gawain has persuaded Arthur to take up arms against Lancelot. A great expedition also crosses into France and attacks Lancelot at Benwick (Bayonne). Gawain, against Arthur's wishes, taunts Lancelot into doing battle with him. They meet on more than one occasion. Gawain's peculiar attribute of strength which grows until noonday almost brings about the defeat of Lancelot, but the latter grimly holds his own and finally gives Gawain a blow on the head. While Arthur and his army are attacking Lancelot in France, the dire events with which Book 21 begins are already shaping themselves in England.*

CHAPTER 1

How Sir Mordred Presumed and Took on Him to Be King of England, and Would Have Married the Queen, His Uncle's Wife

As Sir Mordred was ruler of all England, he did do make letters as though that they came from beyond the sea, and the letters specified that King Arthur was slain in battle with Sir Launcelot. Wherefore Sir Mordred made a parliament, and called the lords together, and there he made them to choose him king; and so was he crowned at Canterbury, and held a feast there fifteen days; and afterward he drew him unto Winchester, and there he took the Queen Guenever 10 and said plainly that he would wed her which was his uncle's wife and his father's wife. And so he made ready for the feast, and a day prefixed that they should be wedded; wherefore Queen Guenever was passing heavy. But she durst not discover her heart, but spake fair, and agreed to Sir Mordred's will. Then she desired of Sir Mordred for to go to London, to buy all manner of things that longed° unto the wedding. And by

cause of her fair speech Sir Mordred trusted her well enough and gave her leave to go. And so when she came to London she took the Tower of London, and 20 suddenly in all haste possible she stuffed it with all manner of victual and well garnished it with men, and so kept it. Then when Sir Mordred wist and understood how he was beguiled, he was passing wroth out of measure. And a short tale for to make, he went and laid a mighty siege about the Tower of London, and made many great assaults thereat, and threw many great engines unto them, and shot great guns. But all might not prevail Sir Mordred, for Queen Guenever would never for fair speech nor for foul, would never 30 trust to come in his hands again. Then came the Bishop of Canterbury, the which was a noble clerk, and an holy man, and thus he said to Sir Mordred: "Sir, what will ye do? will ye first displease God and sithen shame yourself, and all knighthood? Is not King Arthur your uncle, no farther but your mother's brother, and on her himself King Arthur begat you upon his own sister, therefore how may you wed your father's wife?° Sir," said the noble clerk, "leave this opinion or I shall curse you with book and bell and candle." "Do thou 40 thy worst," said Sir Mordred, "wit thou well I shall defy thee." "Sir," said the Bishop, "and wit you well I shall not fear me to do that me ought to do. Also where ye noise° where my lord Arthur is slain, and that is not so, and therefore ye will make a foul work in this land." "Peace, thou false priest," said Sir Mordred, "for an thou chafe me any more I shall make strike off thy head." So the Bishop departed and did the cursing in the most orgulist° wise that might be done. And then Sir Mordred sought the Bishop of Canterbury, for to 50 have slain him. Then the Bishop fled, and took part of his goods with him, and went nigh unto Glastonbury;° and there he was as priest hermit in a chapel and lived in poverty and in holy prayers, for well he understood that mischievous war was at hand. Then Sir Mordred sought on Queen Guenever by letters and sondes,° and by fair means and foul means, for to have her to come out of the Tower of London; but all this availed not, for she answered him shortly, openly and privily, that she had lever° slay herself than to be married with him. 60 Then came word to Sir Mordred that King Arthur had araised° the siege for Sir Launcelot, and he was coming homeward with a great host, to be avenged upon Sir Mordred; wherefore Sir Mordred made write writs to all the barony of this land, and much people drew to him. For then was the common voice among them that with Arthur was none other life but war and strife, and with Sir Mordred was great joy and bliss. Thus was Sir Arthur depraved,° and evil said of. And many there

36–38 **uncle . . . wife.** Arthur supposedly had an incestuous relationship with his sister, Bellicent, from which union was born Mordred, who was at once Arthur's son and nephew 44 **noise,** spread rumor 49 **orgulist,** proudest 52 **Glastonbury,** a town in Somersetshire, England, noted for its famous abbey, where the Holy Grail and the mythical tombs of King Arthur and Queen Guinevere were supposedly located 56 **sondes,** messengers 60 **lever,** rather 62 **araised,** raised, quit 69 **depraved,** vilified, disparaged

Morte Darthur 17 **longed,** belonged, were appropriate to

70 were that King Arthur had made up of nought, and given them lands, might not then say him a good word. Lo, ye all Englishmen, see ye not what a mischief here was! for he that was the most king and knight of the world, and most loved the fellowship of noble knights, and by him they were all upholden, now might not these Englishmen hold them content with him. Lo, thus was the old custom and usage of this land; and also men say that we of this land have not yet lost nor forgotten that custom and usage. Alas, this is a great 80 default of us Englishmen, for there may no thing please us no term. And so fared the people at that time, they were better pleased with Sir Mordred than they were with King Arthur; and much people drew unto Sir Mordred, and said they would abide with him for better and for worse. And so Sir Mordred drew with a great host to Dover, for there he heard say that Sir Arthur would arrive, and so he thought to beat his own father from his lands; and the most part of all England held with Sir Mordred, the people were so new fangle.°

CHAPTER 2

How After that King Arthur Had Tidings, He Returned and Came to Dover, Where Sir Mordred Met Him to Let His Landing; and of the Death of Sir Gawaine

90 And so as Sir Mordred was at Dover with his host, there came King Arthur with a great navy of ships and galleys and carracks.° And there was Sir Mordred ready awaiting upon his landing, to let° his own father to land upon the land that he was king over. Then there was launching of great boats and small, and full of noble men of arms; and there was much slaughter of gentle knights, and many a full bold baron was laid full low, on both parties. But King Arthur was so courageous that there might no manner of knights let him to 100 land, and his knights fiercely followed him; and so they landed maugre° Sir Mordred and all his power, and put Sir Mordred aback, that he fled and all his people. So when this battle was done, King Arthur let bury his people that were dead. And then was noble Sir Gawaine found in a great boat, lying more than half dead. When Sir Arthur wist that Sir Gawaine was laid so low, he went unto him; and there the king made sorrow out of measure and took Sir Gawaine in his arms, and thrice he there swooned. And then when he 110 awaked, he said: "Alas, Sir Gawaine, my sister's son, here now thou liest, the man in the world that I loved most; and now is my joy gone, for now, my nephew Sir Gawaine, I will discover me unto your person; in Sir Launcelot and you I most had my joy, and mine affiance,° and now have I lost my joy of you both;

wherefore all mine earthly joy is gone from me." "Mine uncle King Arthur," said Sir Gawaine, "wit you well my death day is come, and all is through mine own hastiness and wilfulness; for I am smitten upon the old wound the which Sir Launcelot gave me, on the 120 which I feel well I must die; and had Sir Launcelot been with you as he was, this unhappy war had never begun; and of all this am I causer, for Sir Launcelot and his blood, through their prowess, held all your cankered enemies in subjection and daunger. And now," said Sir Gawaine, "ye shall miss Sir Launcelot. But alas, I would not accord with him, and therefore," said Sir Gawaine, "I pray you, fair uncle, that I may have paper, pen, and ink, that I may write to Sir Launcelot a cedle° with mine own hands." And then when 130 paper and ink was brought, then Gawaine was set up weakly by King Arthur, for he was shriven a little tofore; and then he wrote thus, as the French book° maketh mention: "Unto Sir Launcelot, flower of all noble knights that ever I heard of or saw by my days, I, Sir Gawaine, King Lot's son of Orkney, sister's son unto the noble King Arthur, send thee greeting, and let thee have knowledge that the tenth day of May I was smitten upon the old wound that thou gavest me afore the city of Benwick, and through the same wound that 140 thou gavest me I am come to my death day. And I will that all the world wit, that I, Sir Gawaine, knight of the Table Round, sought my death, and not through thy deserving, but it was mine own seeking; wherefore I beseech thee, Sir Launcelot, to return again unto this realm, and see my tomb, and pray some prayer more or less for my soul. And this same day that I wrote this cedle, I was hurt to the death in the same wound, the which I had of thy hand, Sir Launcelot; for of a more nobler man might I not be slain. Also Sir Launcelot, 150 for all the love that ever was betwixt us, make no tarrying, but come over the sea in all haste, that thou mayst with thy noble knights rescue that noble king that made thee knight, that is my lord Arthur; for he is full straitly bestad° with a false traitor, that is my half-brother, Sir Mordred; and he hath let crown him king, and would have wedded my lady Queen Guenever, and so had he done had she not put herself in the Tower of London. And so the tenth day of May last past, my lord Arthur and we all landed upon them at 160 Dover; and there we put that false traitor, Sir Mordred, to flight, and there it misfortuned me to be stricken upon thy stroke. And at the date of this letter was written, but two hours and a half afore my death, written with mine own hand, and so subscribed with part of my heart's blood. And I require thee, most famous knight of the world, that thou wilt see my tomb." And then Sir Gawaine wept, and King Arthur wept; and then they swooned both. And when they

---

89 **new fangle,** fickle, changeable 92 **carracks,** small, broad, barge-like ships
93 **let,** prevent 101 **maugre,** in spite of 115 **affiance,** trust

130 **cedle,** schedule, written message 133 **French book,** one of the numerous French Arthurian romances to which Malory had access for his version
155 **bestad,** beset

¹⁷⁰ awaked both, the king made Sir Gawaine to receive his Saviour. And then Sir Gawaine prayed the king for to send for Sir Launcelot, and to cherish him above all other knights. And so at the hour of noon Sir Gawaine yielded up the spirit; and then the king let inter him in a chapel within Dover Castle; and there yet all men may see the skull of him, and the same wound is seen that Sir Launcelot gave him in battle. Then was it told the king that Sir Mordred had pyghte° a new field upon Barham Down.° And upon the morn the king rode ¹⁸⁰ thither to him, and there was a great battle betwixt them, and much people was slain on both parties; but at the last Sir Arthur's party stood best, and Sir Mordred and his party fled unto Canterbury.

CHAPTER 3

How After, Sir Gawaine's Ghost Appeared to King Arthur, and Warned Him That He Should Not Fight That Day

And then the king let search all the towns for his knights that were slain, and interred them; and salved them with soft salves that so sore were wounded. Then much people drew unto King Arthur. And then they said that Sir Mordred warred upon King Arthur with wrong. And then King Arthur drew him with his host ¹⁹⁰ down by the seaside westward toward Salisbury;° and there was a day assigned betwixt King Arthur and Sir Mordred, that they should meet upon a down beside Salisbury, and not far from the seaside; and this day was assigned on a Monday after Trinity Sunday, whereof King Arthur was passing glad, that he might be avenged upon Sir Mordred. Then Sir Mordred araised much people about London, for they of Kent, Southsex, and Surrey, Estsex, and of Southfolk, and of Northfolk,° held the most part with Sir Mordred; and ²⁰⁰ many a full noble knight drew unto Sir Mordred and to the king; but they that loved Sir Launcelot drew unto Sir Mordred. So upon Trinity Sunday at night, King Arthur dreamed a wonderful dream, and that was this: that him seemed he sat upon a chaflet° in a chair, and the chair was fast to a wheel, and thereupon sat King Arthur in the richest cloth of gold that might be made; and the king thought there was under him, far from him, an hideous deep black water, and therein were all manner of serpents, and worms, and wild beasts, foul ²¹⁰ and horrible; and suddenly the king thought the wheel turned up so down, and he fell among the serpents, and every beast took him by a limb; and then the king cried as he lay in his bed and slept: "Help!" And then knights, squires, and yeomen awaked the king; and then he was so amazed that he wist not where he was;

and then he fell on slumbering again, not sleeping nor thoroughly waking. So the king seemed verily that there came Sir Gawaine unto him with a number of fair ladies with him. And when King Arthur saw him, then he said: "Welcome, my sister's son; I weened thou ²²⁰ hadst been dead, and now I see thee on live, much am I beholding unto almighty Jesu. O fair nephew and my sister's son, what be these ladies that hither be come with you?" "Sir," said Sir Gawaine, "all these be ladies for whom I have foughten when I was man living, and all these are those that I did battle for in righteous quarrel; and God hath given them that grace at their great prayer, by cause I did battle for them, that they should bring me hither unto you: thus much hath God given me leave, for to warn you of your death; for ²³⁰ an ye fight as tomorn with Sir Mordred, as ye both have assigned, doubt ye not ye must be slain, and the most part of your people on both parties. And for the great grace and goodness that almighty Jesu hath unto you, and for pity of you, and many more other good men there shall be slain, God hath sent me to you of his special grace, to give you warning that in no wise ye do battle as tomorn, but that ye take a treaty for a month day; and proffer you largely, so as tomorn to be put in a delay. For within a month shall come Sir Launcelot ²⁴⁰ with all his noble knights, and rescue you worshipfully, and slay Sir Mordred, and all that ever will hold with him." Then Sir Gawaine and all the ladies vanished. And anon the king called upon his knights, squires, and yeomen and charged them wightly° to fetch his noble lords and wise bishops unto him. And when they were come, the king told them his avision, what Sir Gawaine had told him, and warned him that if he fought on the morn he should be slain. Then the king commanded Sir Lucan the Butler, and his brother ²⁵⁰ Sir Bedivere, with two bishops with them, and charged them in any wise, an they might, "Take a treaty for a month day with Sir Mordred, and spare not, proffer him lands and goods as much as ye think best." So then they departed and came to Sir Mordred, where he had a grim host of an hundred thousand men. And there they entreated Sir Mordred long time; and at the last Sir Mordred was agreed for to have Cornwall and Kent, by Arthur's days: after, all England, after the days of King Arthur. ²⁶⁰

CHAPTER 4

How by Misadventure of an Adder the Battle Began, Where Mordred Was Slain, and Arthur Hurt to the Death

Then were they condescended° that King Arthur and Sir Mordred should meet betwixt both their hosts, and every each of them should bring fourteen persons;° and

---

178 **pyghte**, pitched, prepared   179 **Barham Down**, section between Canterbury and Folkstone in Kent   190 **Salisbury**, a city in Wiltshire, England, about twenty miles from Southampton   199 **Southsex . . . Northfolk**, archaic forms of the names of the important English counties of *Sussex, Surrey, Essex, Suffolk,* and *Norfolk*, respectively   204 **chaflet**, a small platform or dais

245 **wightly**, valiantly   261 **condescended**, agreed   263 **fourteen persons.** A leader and his retinue of fourteen persons is a convention of epic and romance

they came with this word unto Arthur. Then said he: "I am glad that this is done"; and so he went into the field. And when Arthur should depart, he warned all his host that an° they see any sword drawn: "Look ye come on fiercely, and slay that traitor, Sir Mordred, for I in no wise trust him." In likewise Sir Mordred warned his host that: "An ye see any sword drawn, look that ye come on fiercely, and so slay all that ever before you standeth; for in no wise I will not trust for this treaty, for I know well my father will be avenged on me." And so they met as their appointment was, and so they were agreed and accorded thoroughly; and wine was fetched, and they drank. Right soon came an adder out of a little heath bush, and it stung a knight on the foot. And when the knight felt him stung, he looked down and saw the adder, and then he drew his sword to slay the adder, and thought of none other harm. And when the host on both parties saw that sword drawn, then they blew beamous,° trumpets, and horns, and shouted grimly. And so both hosts dressed them together. And King Arthur took his horse, and said: "Alas this unhappy day!" and so rode to his party. And Sir Mordred in likewise. And never was there seen a more dolefuller battle in no Christian land; for there was but rushing and riding, foining° and striking, and many a grim word was there spoken either to other, and many a deadly stroke. But ever King Arthur rode throughout the battle of Sir Mordred many times, and did full nobly as a noble king should, and at all times he fainted never; and Sir Mordred that day put him in devoir,° and in great peril. And thus they fought all the long day and never stinted till the noble knights were laid to the cold earth; and ever they fought still till it was near night, and by that time was there an hundred thousand laid dead upon the down. Then was Arthur wood wroth° out of measure, when he saw his people so slain from him. Then the king looked about him, and then was he ware, of all his host and of all his good knights, were left no more on live but two knights; that one was Sir Lucan the Butler and his brother Sir Bedivere, and they were full sore wounded. "Jesu mercy," said the king, "where are all my noble knights become? Alas that ever I should see this doleful day, for now," said Arthur, "I am come to mine end. But would to God that I wist where were that traitor Sir Mordred, that hath caused all this mischief." Then was King Arthur ware where Sir Mordred leaned upon his sword among a great heap of dead men. "Now give me my spear," said Arthur unto Sir Lucan "for yonder I have espied the traitor that all this woe hath wrought." "Sir, let him be," said Sir Lucan, "for he is unhappy; and if ye pass this unhappy day ye shall be right well revenged upon him. Good lord, remember ye of your night's dream, and what the spirit of Sir Gawaine told you this night, yet God of his

great goodness hath preserved you hitherto. Therefore, for God's sake, my lord, leave off by this, for blessed be God ye have won the field, for here we be three on live, and with Sir Mordred is none on live; and if ye leave off now this wicked day of destiny is past." "Tide me death, betide me life," saith the king, "now I see him yonder alone he shall never escape mine hands, for at a better avail shall I never have him." "God speed you well," said Sir Bedivere. Then the king gat his spear in both his hands and ran toward Sir Mordred, crying: "Traitor, now is thy death day come." And when Sir Mordred heard Sir Arthur, he ran until° him with his sword drawn in his hand. And there King Arthur smote Sir Mordred under the shield, with a foin of his spear, throughout the body, more than a fathom. And when Sir Mordred felt that he had his death wound, he thrust himself with the might that he had up to the bur of King Arthur's spear. And right so he smote his father Arthur, with his sword holden in both his hands, on the side of the head, that the sword pierced the helmet and the brain pan, and therewithal Sir Mordred fell stark dead to the earth; and the noble Arthur fell in a swoon to the earth, and there he swooned ofttimes. And Sir Lucan the Butler and Sir Bedivere ofttimes heave him up. And so weakly they led him betwixt them both, to a little chapel not far from the seaside. And when the king was there he thought him well eased. Then heard they people cry in the field. "Now go thou, Sir Lucan," said the king, "and do me to wit what betokens that noise in the field." So Sir Lucan departed, for he was grievously wounded in many places. And so as he yede,° he saw and hearkened by the moonlight, how that pillers° and robbers were come into the field to pill and to rob many a full noble knight of brooches and beads, of many a good ring and of many a rich jewel; and who that were not dead all out, there they slew them for their harness and their riches. When Sir Lucan understood this work, he came to the king as soon as he might and told him all what he had heard and seen. "Therefore by my rede," said Sir Lucan, "it is best that we bring you to some town." "I would it were so," said the king.

CHAPTER 5

How King Arthur Commanded to Cast His Sword Excalibur into the Water, and How He Was Delivered to Ladies in a Barge

"But I may not stand, mine head works° so. Ah Sir Launcelot," said King Arthur, "this day have I sore missed thee: alas, that ever I was against thee, for now have I my death, whereof Sir Gawaine me warned in

---

267 **an**, if   282 **beamous**, a kind of trumpet   288 **foining**, thrusting   294 **in devoir**, in knightly duty   299 **wood wroth**, insanely angered

331 **until**, unto   350 **yede**, went   351 **pillers**, robbers, despoilers   362 **works**, pains

my dream." Then Sir Lucan took up the king the one part, and Sir Bedivere the other part, and in the lifting the king swooned; and Sir Lucan fell in a swoon with the lift, that the part of his guts fell out of his body, and
370 therewith the noble knight's heart brast. And when the king awoke, he beheld Sir Lucan how he lay foaming at the mouth and part of his guts lay at his feet. "Alas," said the king, "this is to me a full heavy sight, to see this noble duke so die for my sake, for he would have holpen me, that had more need of help than I. Alas, he would not complain him, his heart was so set to help me: now Jesu have mercy upon his soul!" Then Sir Bedivere wept for the death of his brother. "Leave this mourning and weeping," said the king, "for all
380 this will not avail me, for wit thou well an I might live myself, the death of Sir Lucan would grieve me evermore; but my time hieth fast," said the king. "Therefore," said Arthur unto Sir Bedivere, "take thou Excalibur, my good sword, and go with it to yonder water side, and when thou comest there I charge thee throw my sword in that water, and come again and tell me what thou there seest." "My lord," said Bedivere, "your commandment shall be done, and lightly bring you word again." So Sir Bedivere departed, and by the
390 way he beheld that noble sword, that the pommel and the haft was all of precious stones; and then he said to himself: "If I throw this rich sword in the water, thereof shall never come good, but harm and loss." And then Sir Bedivere hid Excalibur under a tree. And so, as soon as he might, he came again unto the king, and said he had been at the water, and had thrown the sword in the water. "What saw thou there?" said the king. "Sir," he said, "I saw nothing but waves and winds." "That is untruly said of thee," said the king,
400 "therefore go thou lightly again and do my commandment; as thou art to me lief and dear, spare not, but throw it in." Then Sir Bedivere returned again, and took the sword in his hand; and then him thought sin and shame to throw away that noble sword, and so efte he hid the sword and returned again, and told to the king that he had been at the water and done his commandment. "What saw thou there?" said the king. "Sir," he said, "I saw nothing but the waters wappe and waves wanne."° "Ah, traitor untrue," said King
410 Arthur, "now hast thou betrayed me twice. Who would have weened that thou that hast been to me so lief and dear, and thou art named a noble knight, and would betray me for the richness of the sword. But now go again lightly, for thy long tarrying putteth me in great jeopardy of my life, for I have taken cold. And but if thou do now as I bid thee, if ever I may see thee, I shall slay thee with mine own hands; for thou wouldst for my rich sword see me dead." Then Sir Bedivere departed, and went to the sword, and lightly took it up,
420 and went to the water side; and there he bound the girdle about the hilts, and then he threw the sword as

409 **wappe . . . wanne,** lap and ebb

far into the water as he might; and there came an arm and an hand above the water and met it, and caught it, and so shook it thrice and brandished, and then vanished away the hand with the sword in the water. So Sir Bedivere came again to the king, and told him what he saw. "Alas!" said the king, "help me hence, for I dread me I have tarried over long." Then Sir Bedivere took the king upon his back, and so went with him to that water side. And when they were at the water side, 430 even fast by the bank hoved a little barge with many fair ladies in it, and among them all was a queen, and all they had black hoods, and all they wept and shrieked when they saw King Arthur. "Now put me into the barge," said the king. And so he did softly; and there received him three queens with great mourning; and so they set them down, and in one of their laps King Arthur laid his head. And then that queen said: "Ah, dear brother, why have ye tarried so long from me? alas, this wound on your head hath 440 caught over-much cold." And so then they rowed from the land, and Sir Bedivere beheld all those ladies go from him. Then Sir Bedivere cried: "Ah my lord Arthur, what shall become of me, now ye go from me and leave me here alone among mine enemies?" "Comfort thyself," said the king, "and do as well as thou mayest, for in me is no trust for to trust in; for I will into the vale of Avilion° to heal me of my grievous wound; and if thou hear never more of me, pray for my soul." But ever the queens and ladies wept and 450 shrieked, that it was pity to hear. And as soon as Sir Bedivere had lost the sight of the barge, he wept and wailed, and so took the forest; and so he went all that night, and in the morning he was ware betwixt two holts hoar, of a chapel and an hermitage.

CHAPTER 6

How Sir Bedivere Found Him on the Morrow Dead in an Hermitage, and How He Abode There with the Hermit

Then was Sir Bedivere glad, and thither he went; and when he came into the chapel, he saw where lay an hermit grovelling on all four, there fast by a tomb was new graven. When the hermit saw Sir Bedivere, he knew him well, for he was but little tofore Bishop of 460 Canterbury, that Sir Mordred flemed.° "Sir," said Bedivere, "what man is there interred that ye pray so fast for?" "Fair son," said the hermit, "I wot not verily, but by deeming.° But this night, at midnight, here came a number of ladies, and brought hither a dead corpse, and prayed me to bury him; and here they offered an hundred tapers, and they gave me an hundred besants." "Alas!" said Sir Bedivere, "that was my lord King Arthur, that here lieth buried in this chapel."

448 **Avilion,** Avalon, the Celtic abode of the blessed   461 **flemed,** put to flight
464 **deeming,** guess, supposition

470 Then Sir Bedivere swooned; and when he awoke he prayed the hermit he might abide with him still there, to live with fasting and prayers. "For from hence will I never go," said Sir Bedivere, "by my will, but all the days of my life here to pray for my lord Arthur." "Ye are welcome to me," said the hermit, "for I know ye better than ye ween that I do. Ye are the bold Bedivere, and the full noble duke, Sir Lucan the Butler, was your brother." Then Sir Bedivere told the hermit all as ye have heard tofore. So there bode Sir Bedivere 480 with the hermit that was tofore Bishop of Canterbury, and there Sir Bedivere put upon him poor clothes and served the hermit full lowly in fasting and in prayers. Thus of Arthur I find never more written in books that he authorised, nor more of the very certainty of his death heard I never read, but thus was he led away in a ship wherein were three queens; that one was King Arthur's sister, Queen Morgan le Fay;° the other was the Queen of Northgalis; the third was the Queen of the Waste Lands. Also there was Nimue,° the chief 490 lady of the lake, that had wedded Pelleas the good knight; and this lady had done much for King Arthur, for she would never suffer Sir Pelleas to be in no place where he should be in danger of his life; and so he lived to the uttermost of his days with her in great rest. More of the death of King Arthur could I never find, but that ladies brought him to his burials; and such one was buried there, that the hermit bare witness that sometime was Bishop of Canterbury, but yet the hermit knew not in certain that he was verily the body of King 500 Arthur; for this tale Sir Bedivere, knight of the Table Round, made it to be written.

CHAPTER 7

Of the Opinion of Some Men of the Death of King Arthur; and How Queen Guenever Made Her a Nun in Almesbury

Yet some men say in many parts of England that King Arthur is not dead, but had by the will of our Lord Jesu into another place; and men say that he shall come again, and he shall win the holy cross. I will not say it shall be so, but rather I will say, here in this world he changed his life. But many men say that there is written upon his tomb this verse: *Hic jacet Arthurus Rex, quondam Rexque futurus.*° Thus leave I here Sir 510 Bedivere with the hermit, that dwelled that time in a chapel beside Glastonbury, and there was his hermitage. And so they lived in their prayers, and fastings, and great abstinence. And when Queen Guenever understood that King Arthur was slain, and all the noble knights, Sir Mordred and all the remnant, then the queen stole away, and five ladies with her, and so she went to Almesbury;° and there she let make herself a nun, and ware white clothes and black, and great penance she took, as ever did sinful lady in this land, and never creature could make her merry; but lived in 520 fasting, prayers, and alms-deeds, that all manner of people marveled how virtuously she was changed. Now leave we Queen Guenever in Almesbury, a nun in white clothes and black, and there she was abbess and ruler as reason would; and turn we from her, and speak we of Sir Launcelot du Lake.

CHAPTER 8

How When Sir Launcelot Heard of the Death of King Arthur, and of Sir Gawaine, and Other Matters, He Came into England

And when he heard in his country that Sir Mordred was crowned king in England, and made war against King Arthur, his own father, and would let him to land in his own land; also it was told Sir Launcelot how that 530 Sir Mordred had laid siege about the Tower of London, by cause the queen would not wed him; then was Sir Launcelot wroth out of measure and said to his kinsmen: "Alas! that double traitor Sir Mordred, now me repenteth that ever he escaped my hands, for much shame hath he done unto my lord Arthur; for all I feel by the doleful letter that my lord Sir Gawaine sent me, on whose soul Jesu have mercy, that my lord Arthur is full hard bestad. Alas!" said Sir Launcelot, "that ever I should live to hear that most noble king that made me 540 knight thus to be overset with his subject in his own realm. And this doleful letter that my lord, Sir Gawaine, hath sent me afore his death, praying me to see his tomb, wit you well his doleful words shall never go from mine heart, for he was a full noble knight as ever was born; and in an unhappy hour was I born that ever I should have that unhap to slay first Sir Gawaine, Sir Gaheris the good knight, and mine own friend Sir Gareth, that full noble knight. Alas, I may say I am unhappy," said Sir Launcelot, "that ever I should do 550 thus unhappily, and, alas, yet might I never have hap to slay that traitor, Sir Mordred." "Leave your complaints," said Sir Bors, "and first revenge you of the death of Sir Gawaine; and it will be well done that ye see Sir Gawaine's tomb, and secondly that ye revenge my lord Arthur, and my lady, Queen Guenever." "I thank you," said Sir Launcelot, "forever ye will my worship." Then they made them ready in all the haste that might be, with ships and galleys, with Sir Launcelot and his host to pass into England. And so he 560 passed over the sea till he came to Dover, and there he landed with seven kings, and the number was hideous to behold. Then Sir Launcelot spered of° men of Dover where was King Arthur become. Then the people told

---

487 **Morgan le Fay,** the sorceress sister and lifelong enemy of Arthur, but attending his death as his nearest of kin   489 **Nimue.** Originally a nymph of the lake, she was insanely loved by the old magician Merlin, whom she lured into a rock and immured there. Nimue seems to have been for a while an associate of the evil-designing Morgan le Fay, but she apparently reformed after her marriage to Pelleas, a young knight   508–509 **Hic . . . Futurus.** Here lies King Arthur, king that was and is to be

517 **Almesbury,** a town near Salisbury   563 **spered,** asked

him how that he was slain, and Sir Mordred and an hundred thousand died on a day; and how Sir Mordred gave King Arthur there the first battle at his landing, and there was good Sir Gawaine slain; and on the morn Sir Mordred fought with the king upon Barham Down, and there the king put Sir Mordred to the worse. "Alas," said Sir Launcelot, "this is the heaviest tidings that ever came to me. Now, fair sirs," said Sir Launcelot, "shew me the tomb of Sir Gawaine." And then certain people of the town brought him into the Castle of Dover and shewed him the tomb. Then Sir Launcelot kneeled down and wept, and prayed heartily for his soul. And that night he made a dole,° and all they that would come had as much flesh, fish, wine, and ale, and every man and woman had twelve pence, come who would. Thus with his own hand dealt he this money, in a mourning gown; and ever he wept, and prayed them to pray for the soul of Sir Gawaine. And on the morn all the priests and clerks that might be gotten in the country were there, and sang mass of requiem; and there offered first Sir Launcelot, and he offered an hundred pound; and then the seven kings offered forty pound apiece; and also there was a thousand knights, and each of them offered a pound; and the offering dured° from morn till night, and Sir Launcelot lay two nights on his tomb in prayers and weeping. Then on the third day Sir Launcelot called the kings, dukes, earls, barons, and knights, and said thus: "My fair lords, I thank you all of your coming into this country with me, but we came too late, and that shall repent me while I live, but against death may no man rebel. But sithen it is so," said Sir Launcelot, "I will myself ride and seek my lady, Queen Guenever, for as I hear say she hath had great pain and much disease; and I heard say that she is fled into the west. Therefore ye all shall abide me here, and but if I come again within fifteen days, then take your ships and your fellowship, and depart into your country, for I will do as I say to you."

CHAPTER 9

How Sir Launcelot Departed to Seek the Queen Guenever, and How He Found Her at Almesbury

Then came Sir Bors de Ganis, and said: "My lord Sir Launcelot, what think ye for to do, now to ride in this realm? wit ye well ye shall find few friends." "Be as be may," said Sir Launcelot, "keep you still here, for I will forth on my journey, and no man nor child shall go with me." So it was no boot to strive, but he departed and rode westerly, and there he sought a seven or eight days; and at the last he came to a nunnery; and then was Queen Guenever ware of Sir Launcelot as he walked in the cloister. And when she saw him there she swooned thrice, that all the ladies and gentlewomen had work enough to hold the queen up. So when she might speak, she called ladies and gentlewomen to her, and said: "Ye marvel, fair ladies, why I make this fare. Truly," she said, "it is for the sight of yonder knight that yonder standeth; wherefore I pray you all call him to me." When Sir Launcelot was brought to her, then she said to all the ladies: "Through this man and me hath all this war been wrought, and the death of the most noblest knights of the world; for through our love that we have loved together is my most noble lord slain. Therefore, Sir Launcelot, wit thou well I am set in such a plight to get my soul heal; and yet I trust through God's grace that after my death to have a sight of the blessed face of Christ, and at domesday to sit on his right side, for as sinful as ever I was are saints in heaven. Therefore, Sir Launcelot, I require thee and beseech thee heartily, for all the love that ever was betwixt us, that thou never see me more in the visage; and I command thee, on God's behalf, that thou forsake my company, and to thy kingdom thou turn again, and keep well thy realm from war and wrake;° for as well as I have loved thee, mine heart will not serve me to see thee, for through thee and me is the flower of kings and knights destroyed; therefore, Sir Launcelot, go to thy realm, and there take thee a wife, and live with her with joy and bliss; and I pray thee heartily, pray for me to our Lord that I may amend my misliving." "Now, sweet madam," said Sir Launcelot, "would ye that I should now return again unto my country, and there to wed a lady? Nay, madam, wit you well that shall I never do, for I shall never be so false to you of that I have promised; but the same destiny that ye have taken you to, I will take me unto, for to please Jesu, and ever for you I cast me specially to pray." "If thou wilt do so," said the queen, "hold thy promise, but I may never believe but that thou wilt turn to the world again." "Well, madam," said he, "ye say as pleaseth you, yet wist you me never false of my promise, and God defend but I should forsake the world as ye have done. For in the quest of the Sangreal° I had forsaken the vanities of the world had not your lord been. And if I had done so at that time, with my heart, will, and thought, I had passed all the knights that were in the Sangreal except Sir Galahad, my son.° And therefore, lady, sithen ye

636 **wrake,** ruin, destruction   655 **Sangreal,** the Holy Grail   658-659 **passed . . . son.** Although Lancelot's preeminence would have made him the logical knight to achieve the Grail, he is ineligible in the eyes of the Church because of his affair with Guinevere. Instead, he is given a son, Galahad, who is to achieve the Grail. Lancelot, although near the Grail, does not have the privilege of seeing it, as do Percival, Bors, and Galahad

660 have taken you to perfection, I must needs take me to perfection, of right. For I take record of God, in you I have had mine earthly joy; and if I had found you now so disposed, I had cast to have had you into mine own realm.

CHAPTER 10

How Sir Launcelot Came to the Hermitage Where the Archbishop of Canterbury Was, and How He Took the Habit on Him

"But sithen I find you thus disposed, I ensure you faithfully, I will ever take me to penance, and pray while my life lasteth, if I may find any hermit, either gray or white,° that will receive me. Wherefore, madam, I pray you kiss me and never no more."
670 "Nay," said the queen, "that shall I never do, but abstain you from such works"; and they departed. But there was never so hard an hearted man but he would have wept to see the dolor that they made; for there was lamentation as they had been stung with spears; and many times they swooned, and the ladies bare the queen to her chamber. And Sir Launcelot awoke, and went and took his horse, and rode all that day and all night in a forest, weeping. And at the last he was ware of an hermitage and a chapel stood betwixt two cliffs;
680 and then he heard a little bell ring to mass, and thither he rode and alit, and tied his horse to the gate, and heard mass. And he that sang mass was the Bishop of Canterbury. Both the Bishop and Sir Bedivere knew Sir Launcelot, and they spake together after mass. But when Sir Bedivere had told his tale all whole, Sir Launcelot's heart almost brast for sorrow, and Sir Launcelot threw his arms abroad, and said: "Alas! who may trust this world." And then he kneeled down on his knee and prayed the Bishop to shrive him and
690 assoil him. And then he besought the Bishop that he might be his brother. Then the Bishop said: "I will gladly"; and there he put an habit upon Sir Launcelot, and there he served God day and night with prayers and fastings. Thus the great host abode at Dover. And then Sir Lionel took fifteen lords with him and rode to London to seek Sir Launcelot; and there Sir Lionel was slain and many of his lords. Then Sir Bors de Ganis made the great host for to go home again; and Sir Bors, Sir Ector de Maris, Sir Blamore, Sir
700 Bleoberis, with more other of Sir Launcelot's kin, took on them to ride all England overthwart and endlong, to seek Sir Launcelot. So Sir Bors by fortune rode so long till he came to the same chapel where Sir Launcelot was; and so Sir Bors heard a little bell knell, that

rang to mass; and there he alit and heard mass. And when mass was done, the Bishop, Sir Launcelot, and Sir Bedivere came to Sir Bors. And when Sir Bors saw Sir Launcelot in that manner clothing, then he prayed the Bishop that he might be in the same suit. And so there was an habit put upon him, and there he lived in 710 prayers and fasting. And within half a year, there was come Sir Galihud, Sir Galihodin, Sir Blamore, Sir Bleoberis, Sir Villiars, Sir Clarras, and Sir Gahalantine. So all these seven noble knights there abode still. And when they saw Sir Launcelot had taken him to such perfection, they had no list to depart, but took such an habit as he had. Thus they endured in great penance six year; and then Sir Launcelot took the habit of priesthood of the Bishop, and a twelvemonth he sang mass. And there was none of these other 720 knights but they read in books, and holp° for to sing mass, and rang bells, and did bodily all manner of service. And so their horses went where they would, for they took no regard of no worldly riches. For when they saw Sir Launcelot endure such penance, in prayers and fastings, they took no force what pain they endured, for to see the noblest knight of the world take such abstinence that he waxed full lean. And thus upon a night there came a vision to Sir Launcelot, and charged him, in remission of his sins, to haste him unto 730 Almesbury: "And by then thou come there, thou shalt find Queen Guenever dead. And therefore take thy fellows with thee, and purvey them of an horse bier, and fetch thou the corpse of her, and bury her by her husband, the noble King Arthur." So this advision came to Sir Launcelot thrice in one night.

CHAPTER 11

How Sir Launcelot Went with His Seven Fellows to Almesbury, and Found There Queen Guenever Dead, Whom they Brought to Glastonbury

Then Sir Launcelot rose up or day, and told the hermit. "It were well done," said the hermit, "that ye made you ready, and that you disobey not the advision." Then Sir Launcelot took his seven fellows with 740 him, and on foot they yede from Glastonbury to Almesbury, the which is little more than thirty mile. And thither they came [within two days, for they were weak and feeble to go. And when Sir Launcelot was come] to Almesbury within the nunnery, Queen Guenever died but half an hour afore. And the ladies told Sir Launcelot that Queen Guenever told them all or she passed, that Sir Launcelot had been priest near a twelvemonth, "And hither he cometh as fast as he

---

668 **gray or white,** anachronistic references to the Franciscans (Gray Friars) and Carmelites (White Friars)

721 **holp,** helped

750 may to fetch my corpse; and beside my lord, King Arthur, he shall bury me. Wherefore," the queen said in hearing of them all: "I beseech Almighty God that I may never have power to see Sir Launcelot with my worldly eyen"; "and thus," said all the ladies, "was ever her prayer these two days, till she was dead." Then Sir Launcelot saw her visage, but he wept not greatly, but sighed. And so he did all the observance of the service himself, both the dirge at night, and on the morn he sang mass. And there was ordained an horse

760 bier; and so with an hundred torches ever burning about the corpse of the queen, and ever Sir Launcelot with his seven fellows went about the horse bier, singing and reading many an holy orison and frankincense upon the corpse incensed. Thus Sir Launcelot and his seven fellows went on foot from Almesbury unto Glastonbury. And when they were come to the chapel and the hermitage, there she had a dirge, with great devotion. And on the morn the hermit that sometime was Bishop of Canterbury sang the mass of

770 requiem with great devotion. And Sir Launcelot was the first that offered, and then also his seven fellows. And then she was wrapped in cered cloth of Raines, from the top to the toe, in thirtyfold; and after she was put in a web of lead, and then in a coffin of marble. And when she was put in the earth Sir Launcelot swooned, and lay long still, while the hermit came and awaked him, and said: "Ye be to blame, for ye displease God with such manner of sorrow making." "Truly," said Sir Launcelot, "I trust I do not dis-

780 please God, for He knoweth mine intent. For my sorrow was not, nor is not, for any rejoicing of sin, but my sorrow may never have end. For when I remember of her beauty, and of her noblesse, that was both with her king and with her, so when I saw his corpse and her corpse so lie together, truly mine heart would not serve to sustain my careful body. Also when I remember me how by my default, mine orgulity, and my pride, that they were both laid full low, that were peerless that ever was living of Christian people, wit

790 you well," said Sir Launcelot, "this remembered, of their kindness and mine unkindness, sank so to mine heart that I might not sustain myself." So the French book maketh mention.

CHAPTER 12

How Sir Launcelot Began to Sicken, and After Died, Whose Body Was Borne to Joyous Gard for to Be Buried

Then Sir Launcelot never after ate but little meat, ne drank, till he was dead. For then he sickened more and more, and dried, and dwined away. For the Bishop nor none of his fellows might not make him to eat, and little he drank, that he was waxen by a cubit shorter than he was, that the people could not know him. For

evermore, day and night, he prayed, but sometime he 800 slumbered a broken sleep; ever he was lying groveling on the tomb of King Arthur and Queen Guenever. And there was no comfort that the Bishop, nor Sir Bors, nor none of his fellows, could make him, it availed not. So within six weeks after, Sir Launcelot fell sick, and lay in his bed; and then he sent for the Bishop that there was hermit, and all his true fellows. Then Sir Launcelot said with dreary steven:° "Sir Bishop, I pray you give to me all my rites that longeth to a Christian man." "It shall not need you," said the hermit and all 810 his fellows, "it is but heaviness of your blood, ye shall be well mended by the grace of God tomorn." "My fair lords," said Sir Launcelot, "wit you well my careful body will into the earth, I have warning more than now I will say; therefore give me my rites." So when he was houseled and enelid,° and had all that a Christian man ought to have, he prayed the Bishop that his fellows might bear his body to Joyous Gard. Some men say it was Alnwick,° and some men say it was Bamborough.° "Howbeit," said Sir Launcelot, 820 "me repenteth sore, but I made mine avow sometime, that in Joyous Gard I would be buried. And by cause of breaking of mine avow, I pray you all, lead me thither." Then there was weeping and wringing of hands among his fellows. So at a season of the night they all went to their beds, for they all lay in one chamber. And so after midnight, against day, the Bishop that was hermit, as he lay in his bed asleep, he fell upon a great laughter. And therewithal the fellowship awoke and came to the Bishop, and asked what he 830 ailed. "Ah, Jesu mercy," said the Bishop, "why did ye awake me? I was never in all my life so merry and so well at ease." "Wherefore?" said Sir Bors. "Truly," said the Bishop, "here was Sir Launcelot with me with more angels than ever I saw men in one day. And I saw the angels heave up Sir Launcelot unto heaven, and the gates of heaven opened against him." "It is but dretching of swevens,"° said Sir Bors, "for I doubt not Sir Launcelot aileth nothing but good." "It may well be," said the Bishop; "go ye to his bed, and 840 then shall ye prove the sooth." So when Sir Bors and his fellows came to his bed they found him stark dead, and he lay as he had smiled, and the sweetest savor about him that ever they felt. Then was there weeping and wringing of hands, and the greatest dole they made that ever made men. And on the morn the Bishop did his mass of requiem; and after, the Bishop and all the nine knights put Sir Launcelot in the same horse bier that Queen Guenever was laid in tofore that she was buried. And so the Bishop and they all together went 850 with the body of Sir Launcelot daily, till they came to Joyous Gard; and ever they had an hundred torches burning about him. And so within fifteen days they

---

808 **steven,** voice   816 **houseled and enelid,** given the Eucharist (houseled) and extreme unction   819 **Alnwick,** a town in Northumberland   820 **Bamborough,** a sea town in Northumberland   838 **dretching of swevens,** confusion of dreams

came to Joyous Gard. And there they laid his corpse in the body of the quire, and sang and read many psalters and prayers over him and about him. And ever his visage was laid open and naked, that all folks might behold him. For such was the custom in those days, that all men of worship should so lie with open visage 860 till that they were buried. And right thus as they were at their service, there came Sir Ector de Maris, that had seven years sought all England, Scotland, and Wales, seeking his brother, Sir Launcelot.

CHAPTER 13

How Sir Ector Found Sir Launcelot His Brother Dead, and How Constantine Reigned Next after Arthur, and of the End of This Book

And when Sir Ector heard such noise and light in the quire of Joyous Gard, he alit and put his horse from him, and came into the quire, and there he saw men sing and weep. And all they knew Sir Ector, but he knew not them. Then went Sir Bors unto Sir Ector, and told him how there lay his brother, Sir Launcelot, 870 dead; and then Sir Ector threw his shield, sword, and helm from him. And when he beheld Sir Launcelot's visage, he fell down in a swoon. And when he waked it were hard any tongue to tell the doleful complaints that he made for his brother. "Ah, Launcelot," he said, "thou were head of all Christian knights, and now I dare say," said Sir Ector, "thou Sir Launcelot, there thou liest, that thou were never matched of earthly knight's hand. And thou were the courteoust knight that ever bare shield. And thou were the truest friend 880 to thy lover that ever bestrad horse. And thou were the truest lover of a sinful man that ever loved woman. And thou were the kindest man that ever struck with sword. And thou were the goodliest person that ever came among press of knights. And thou was the meekest man and the gentlest that ever ate in hall among ladies. And thou were the sternest knight to thy mortal foe that ever put spear in the rest." Then there was weeping and dolor out of measure. Thus they kept Sir Launcelot's corpse on loft fifteen days, and then 890 they buried it with great devotion. And then at leisure they went all with the Bishop of Canterbury to his hermitage, and there they were together more than a month. Then Sir Constantine, that was Sir Cador's son of Cornwall, was chosen king of England. And he was a full noble knight, and worshipfully he ruled this realm. And then this King Constantine sent for the

Bishop of Canterbury, for he heard say where he was. And so he was restored unto his Bishopric, and left that hermitage. And Sir Bedivere was there ever still hermit to his life's end. Then Sir Bors de Ganis, Sir 900 Ector de Maris, Sir Gahalantine, Sir Galihud, Sir Galihodin, Sir Blamore, Sir Bleoberis, Sir Villiars le Valiant, Sir Clarras of Clermont, all these knights drew them to their countries. Howbeit King Constantine would have had them with him, but they would not abide in this realm. And there they all lived in their countries as holy men. And some English books make mention that they went never out of England after the death of Sir Launcelot, but that was but favor of makers.° For the French book maketh mention, and is 910 authorised, that Sir Bors, Sir Ector, Sir Blamore, and Sir Bleoberis went into the Holy Land thereas Jesu Christ was quick and dead, and anon as they had stablished their lands. For the book saith, so Sir Launcelot commanded them for to do, or ever he passed out of this world. And these four knights did many battles upon the miscreants or Turks. And there they died upon a Good Friday for God's sake.

Here is° the end of the book of King Arthur, and of his noble knights of the Round Table, that when they 920 were whole together there was ever an hundred and forty. And here is the end of the death of Arthur. I pray you all, gentlemen and gentlewomen that readeth this book of Arthur and his knights, from the beginning to the ending, pray for me while I am on live, that God send me good deliverance, and when I am dead, I pray you all pray for my soul. For this book was ended the ninth year of the reign of King Edward the Fourth, by Sir Thomas Maleore, knight, as Jesu help him for his great might, as he is the servant of Jesu both day and 930 night.

Thus endeth this noble and joyous book entitled Le Morte Darthur. Notwithstanding it treateth of the birth, life, and acts of the said King Arthur, of his noble knights of the Round Table, their marvelous enquests and adventures, the achieving of the Sangreal, and in the end the dolorous death and departing out of this world of them all. Which book was reduced into English by Sir Thomas Malory, knight, as afore is said, and by me divided into twenty-one books,° chap- 940 tered and imprinted, and finished in the abbey Westminster the last day of July the year of our Lord MCCCCLXXXV.

910 **favor of makers,** poetic imagination   919 **Here, etc.,** the conventional "retraction," or epilogue, in which the medieval writer confessed his unworthiness and begged for the prayers of his readers   940 **by me divided . . . books,** i.e., by Caxton

The Renaissance

From the Accession of the Tudors to the Restoration of Charles II, 1485–1660

PART 2

Longleat House, Wiltshire, designed by Sir John Thynne, completed in 1580

The Renaissance approximately encompasses the years from 1485, the year of the accession of the Tudors, to 1660, the year of the restoration of Charles II. It was an era of great events in politics, religion, and literature. We witness the culmination of the Tudor dynasty in the reign of Queen Elizabeth I, the beheading of a Stuart monarch, and the institution of a Commonwealth government. We see the traditional Catholicism of the country challenged and defeated by English Protestantism. We see the publication of Spenser's *Faerie Queene*, Shakespeare's plays, and Milton's *Paradise Lost*. The paradox is enormous: even as it profoundly influenced the Renaissance, the Middle Ages came to an end in England and the new world came into being.

Tudor England

In 1485, Henry VII, the first of the Tudors, won accession to the throne by his defeat of Richard III at Bos-

worth Field. The defeat of Richard symbolized the passing of the long period of castles, barons, and armored knights. It came only fifteen years after Malory had completed his account of the passing of Arthur. Henry VII (1485–1509) was a ruler more mercantile than military, and his reign marks a shift in national interest from the feuds of Lancastrians and Yorks to the exploration of new worlds.

The reign of Henry VIII (1509–1547) saw a full-scale rebellion against papal authority. Although there were many other factors that affected the breach with Rome, Henry's desire for a new wife (to produce the male heir that his first wife, Catherine of Aragon, had not) was paramount. Pope Clement VII refused to declare Henry's marriage to Catherine null and void. Henry, first having received permission from Parliament to appoint bishops in England without papal permission, designated a loyal friend, Thomas Cranmer, as archbishop of Canterbury. In 1533 Cranmer pronounced the king's marriage to Catherine invalid and legalized Henry's marriage to Anne Boleyn. Goaded into action,

Henry VIII appoints his young son Edward to succeed him as king. Henry's appointment frustrated the wishes of the pope (pictured in the foreground), who hoped to restore Roman Catholicism to England after Henry's break with the Church.

NATIONAL PORTRAIT GALLERY

The coronation procession (1547) of Edward VI in London. The procession moves toward Westminster Abbey, where English sovereigns were crowned.

Clement VII excommunicated Henry. In 1534 Henry severed all connections with Rome; Parliament passed the famous Act of Supremacy, which stated that the king "justly and rightfully is and ought to be supreme head of the Church of England, called *Anglicana Ecclesia.*"

Upon Henry's death, his frail ten-year-old son became King Edward VI. During his reign (1547–1553) the growing Protestant party in England became ascendant. The old Latin service was replaced by Cranmer's Book of Common Prayer, written in English, which brought the service much closer to the people and exerted a powerful influence on the development of the language. In 1553 the Forty-Two Articles defined the faith of the Church of England along Protestant lines.

Edward was succeeded by Mary, the unfortunate daughter of Henry's first wife, Catherine. Mary (1553–1558), a devout Catholic, briefly reinstated Catholicism and put three hundred Protestants, including Cranmer, to death. She married Philip of Spain but produced no heir. Hence, at her death, her Protestant half-sister Elizabeth succeeded to the throne. Elizabeth's reign (1558–1603) was long; her impact on both the church and the nation was strong.

Elizabeth valued unity in the church as a political, not spiritual, asset. The English Protestants exiled under Mary returned home with new zeal. The extreme Catholic traditionalists, in turn, now went into exile. By steering a slow middle course and pretending at least that nothing final was being done, Eliz-abeth sought to compromise between two growing native religious factions—the Protestant traditionalists and the Protestant radicals. The radicals felt that the external break with the Roman Church was not enough; they wanted to "purify" the new Church of England and attacked the retention of anything not commanded by Scripture. These radicals eventually

Protestant fanatics destroyed Roman Catholic religious images, or icons, as in this illustration, during the reign of Edward VI (1547–1553). To radical Protestants, the use of icons to decorate Catholic churches was a form of idolatry.

The Renaissance **161**

became known as Puritans. Elizabeth's settlement compromised by allowing traditional practices not contradicted by Scripture. Where definition might give offense, vagueness allowed freedom of conscience to the believer. At best, the Elizabethan compromise never appeased traditional extremists or Puritans. More importantly, it never reconciled some theological and practical issues which affected the lives of most Englishmen. The association of Catholicism with such national enemies as Spain and France and with the morally suspect (though intellectually attractive) Italians certainly helped to confirm Protestantism as the dominant religion of England. Only in the period after Elizabeth's death did the differences among Protestant sects become as intensely important to the nation as the earlier differences between Catholics and Protestants had been.

Politics, as well as religion, added to the factionalism of Elizabeth's reign. Two questions—whether she should marry and whom, and who her heir would be if she did not—were enduring uncertainties. Still,

Elizabeth's wisdom in choosing her political advisers and her ability to direct national energies against foreign opponents resulted in a long and essentially sound reign. Perhaps her most stunning achievement was the defeat of the Spanish Armada. In 1588 English Sea Dogs trounced this fleet of one hundred thirty ships in the English Channel. Philip of Spain's unsuccessful invasion was an attempt to gain the English kingdom for himself and to free its people from heresy. The defeat of the Armada meant that England would remain Protestant and that it would soon emerge as a dominant sea power. At Elizabeth's death in 1603, the dynasty of the strong-willed Tudors came to an end; the crown passed to the Stuarts when James VI of Scotland became James I of England.

Widening Horizons

If the entire Tudor period were to be characterized by a single word, that word might be *expansion*. The known world had suddenly grown larger—geographi-

This portrait of Queen Elizabeth I commemorates the English defeat of the Spanish Armada in 1588. Through the window on the left, the English fleet can be seen heading off the Armada; through the window on the right, the remnants of the Armada are seen floating on the storm-tossed waters of the English Channel.

Old Moreton Hall, Cheshire, completed in 1559, is one of the best surviving examples of Tudor architecture. Decorative exteriors, created by wood patterns on a plaster background, replaced the austere stone walls of the castles of the Middle Ages.

cally, economically, socially, and culturally. The most obvious phase of this expansion was geographical. Henry VII came to the throne just seven years before the discovery of America. English exploration to the west began soon after. While the motive for this exploration was greed as much as a spirit of new adventure, in Elizabeth's reign Britannia became a naval power and began to lay the foundations of empire. Spanish fleets were, of course, often bound for the same territory, and it was only with the destruction of the Spanish Armada in 1588 that the way was really cleared for English colonization of the new world.

Economically, increased exploration and trade brought new riches into England—riches which helped bolster the wealthy middle class of merchants. Though the court and courtiers still formed an essential part of the English world, control was very slowly passing from hereditary aristocrats to merchants and city dwellers. Some government offices were falling into the hands of such men as the innkeeper's grandson, Lord Burleigh, who became Elizabeth's wisest ad-

viser. Men were knighted now, not for defending their sovereign in battle, but for lending her money in times of peace.

The New Learning

The expansive nature of the age is also reflected in new attitudes toward and new sources of learning. The Tudor sovereigns themselves were proud of their proficiency in the humanistic arts. So many poets were writing at the court of Henry VIII that it was described as "a nest of singing birds." Henry himself wrote lyrics and composed songs. Elizabeth knew not only Greek and Latin but also spoke Italian, French, and Spanish. Pride in accomplishment characterized the age's attitude toward learning and the arts. The Renaissance, or rebirth of learning, had begun in Italy in the late fourteenth century. The Renaissance's renewed interest in classical authors and models and in exploratory thinking was brought to England by the Dutch humanist, Desiderius Erasmus (1466?–1536) in the reign of the first Tudors; it was furthered by humanists of that generation such as William Grocyn (1446?–1519), Sir Thomas More (1478–1535), John Colet (1467–1519), and John Fisher (1459–1535). Patronized by the court and nourished by Oxford and Cambridge universities, the new learning spread rapidly. English writers began to draw heavily upon the literary treasures and traditions of ancient Greece and Rome. Seneca's tragedies; the comedies of Platus and Terence; and the pastoral, epic, and love poems of Vergil, Horace, and Ovid were all more frequently copied than were the works of earlier English writers such as Chaucer and Malory.

As both education and book production show us, the new impulse for learning did not restrict itself to learned clerks and an occasional nobleman. New schools were founded throughout the country, in rural towns as well as in the city. Although it is probable that before the first book was printed in England in 1477 not more than 2 percent of the English people could either read or write, by the mid-sixteenth century, both burgher and craftsman wrote much more frequently and read more widely than had ever been possible in the days of handmade books.

The New Theology

The new theology in England came about because of England's part in the rebellion against the Church of Rome. There had been critics of the Church in England earlier, notably Wyclif and his followers. Wyclif's attempts to reform the Church resulted in the first complete translation of the Bible into English. But the impact of this reform was limited; there could hardly have been any widespread reading of the Bible when so few Englishmen could read and when each copy of the translation had to be made by hand. What could

not be done in the reign of Richard II, however, was accomplished under Henry VIII. The initial impulse to revolt from Rome came, like the new learning, from the Continent. In 1521 Martin Luther defended his unorthodox position at the Diet of Worms—an assembly of the princes of the Holy Roman Empire—and one year later began his translation of the New Testament from the original languages into German. In England the Reformation soon gained ground; William Tyndale's English translation of the New Testament, made at Worms and inspired by the corruption of the Roman Church, followed Luther's by only three years (1525). Henry's own marital troubles soon provided the catalyst for full-scale rebellion. In 1535 Thomas More, John Fisher, and others died for their refusal to subscribe to the Act of Supremacy that established Henry as head of the Church of England.

The new literacy and new theology can be seen together in the number of Bible translations in the period. The nine translations which appeared from 1526 to 1611 are as interesting in their relation to the state as in their literary character. The first complete Bible printed in England, by Miles Coverdale in 1535, was dedicated to Henry VIII; and the 1611 version was dedicated to the first of the Stuarts, King James. Court and church united to bring the message once locked in a scholarly language to a newly expanding literate audience.

The traditional English Protestants and the Roman Church differed on matters of both belief and ritual. Catholics, for example, considered the pope as God's appointed representative on earth; Protestants saw the sovereign in this role (hence treason opened one to charges of heresy, and vice versa). Protestant churches were not decorated with the statues and representations of the saints which characterized the Catholic churches; Latin ritual observations were not part of the

A sixteenth-century tennis match, from Marshall's The Annals of Tennis *(1878). Tennis, played only on indoor courts in the sixteenth century, was a popular game among the English nobility. Henry VIII enjoyed playing tennis, and Queen Elizabeth was an avid spectator.*

The Gardner's Labyrinth (1577), by Thomas Hill. Formal gardens, based on French and Italian designs, became common in England in the sixteenth century. This design—a series of squares, each with diagonal paths converging on a smaller square in the center—was especially popular.

English Protestant Church. Catholics believed in the necessity of confessing their sins to priests, God's earthly representatives, for absolution; Protestants simply prayed for God's own eventual forgiveness. Some of these issues still separate Catholics and English Protestants today.

The New Literature

Although the new literacy of the Tudor period ensured wider audiences than ever before for certain kinds of printed materials, there were, in addition, specialized audiences who did not depend upon such material. Certain writers wrote for an audience of immediate acquaintances, who read their work in manuscripts circulated informally among a small group. Shakespeare's sonnets, for example, were known in literary circles perhaps ten years or so before they were published (1609). Even those writers with a very public product, the dramatists, usually did not arrange for or supervise the reproduction of their texts. Establishing the texts of Elizabethan drama is difficult for precisely this reason. The texts which survived may be good copies, actors' prompt copies, pirated texts set down from the memory of a performance, or some combination of these. Some nondramatic writers, like the

ambitious Robert Greene, did try to write for a living; and Ben Jonson, though regarded by his fellows as strangely conceited for doing so, published his collected works—The Works of Benjamin Jonson—in 1616. Elizabethan writers expected to be read, or seen, without necessarily expecting to be published in print.

Writers in any age, however, need to eat. Some were supported by their own courtly lineage. Others sought to secure position and riches from a patron, a person of royal or noble birth. The patron's name could then be attached to the writer's works, often in a lavish dedication or by compliments within the plot or verse, which would be visible to the knowledgeable. The patron would hopefully return the compliment in some less aesthetic but more financially tangible form—money or preferment at court.

The literature directed toward a court audience or patron would, of course, be quite different from that intended to please the city merchant. The courtly author and those who wrote for a courtly audience reflected in their writing the interests, the fashions, even the language of the aristocracy. A courtly audience's interest in a sonnet sequence was very probably intellectual and formal: How was the sonnet form adapted and varied? What were the problems of love as the author saw them in contrast, perhaps, to Petrarch (the Italian poet who provided the model sonnet pattern)? The courtly audience was often as interested in experimentation and variation as in the sentiment expressed or the situation involved. Another aspect of courtly taste is reflected in the extended, episodic plot and prose of Sir Philip Sidney's *Arcadia*. Written in 1580 and 1581 at the request of his sister Mary, Countess of Pembroke, for her amusement, the book is loosely framed around the adventures of two friends. But the intellectual action of the *Arcadia* lies in its interspersed pastoral poems, its intricate plays on words, its marvellous reunions and obscure disguises, and its numerous conflicts between love and friendship. Courtly literature approached daily life through a world of the heroic past or ideal present, a world peopled with kings and queens, knights and ladies, and courtly gentlemen whose perfect manners furnished mirrors for their living counterparts.

Just as the Tudors copied Italian fashions and manners, so too they drew upon Italian literary materials and methods. Francesco Petrarch (1304–1374) provided the model for the English sonnet; Giovanni Boccaccio (1313–1375), Matteo Bandello (1480?–1562), Giovanni Giraldi (1504–1573), and Lodovico Ariosto (1474–1533) provided source materials for countless Elizabethan prose works and plays; Niccolò Machiavelli (1469–1527) provided political ideas in *The Prince*; Baldassare Castiglione (1478–1529) provided a code of conduct in *The Courtier*. Thus, the literary and social channels between Italy and England were kept open in spite of England's break with the Roman Church.

The literature of the court was not completely foreign to the citizens of London. They had, however, their own bourgeois tastes which demanded that literature reflect their own life and interests. This reflection they found in prose and drama that contained more realism than romance and more native than Italian materials. Robert Greene (1560?–1592) and other champions of Elizabethan roguery gave the middle class the vicarious thrill of contact with cozeners (tricksters or thieves) and vagabonds, as well as the conservative assurance that rogues would be unmasked and defeated. The bourgeois reader had the thrill of the journey with the certainty of a safe home. Thomas Dekker's *The Shoemaker's Holiday* (1600) told the story of a master shoemaker who became lord mayor of London; Dekker's comedy depicted scenes from London life, the manners of its citizens, and the tensions between commoners and aristocrats. Christopher Marlowe's *Doctor Faustus* (1588–1589) demonstrated in its intellectual, theological, and moral rigor that public literature could have as much substance as court literature.

Any attempt to create exclusive categories for Elizabethan literature, however, must finally acknowledge the age's own ability and delight in resolving mutually exclusive choices and in surmounting paradoxes. The public audience which loved the spectacle of bearbaiting supported as well the theater of Shakespeare. The same aristocrats who delighted in privately circulated sonnets and allegorical pastoral romances saw the plays from public theaters performed at court during the Christmas season. The age took pleasure in various art forms, all of which seemed

Woodcut (left) *from the title page of the 1624 edition of* Doctor Faustus. *The painting* (right) *is thought to be a portrait of Christopher Marlowe.*

Portrait of Edmund Spenser.

NATIONAL PORTRAIT GALLERY

from the reading of classical epic authors and later commentaries upon them and from the practice of the Italian poets Torquato Tasso (1544–1595) and Lodovico Ariosto. A modern reader, inclined to search for a realistic plot, will find more enjoyment in reading allegories if he or she remembers that in an allegory it is not the relationships among the episodes of the narrative that are important but rather the episodes themselves. When, for example, in Spenser's *Faerie Queene,* the knight Guyon stops to view two frolicking and underclad maidens, his journey is impeded because he is forgetting his identity as the Knight of Temperance. When he stops to indulge in fantasy, he is thus not himself and cannot move on his journey. The incident has no cause-and-effect relationship to events that precede or follow it. It is caused by and affects only Guyon's nature as the Knight of Temperance. The very nature of allegory tends, therefore, to make allegorical poetic works lengthy, for an exploration of meaning becomes clear only after the narration of many individual episodes of discovery.

Some poets of the age were eager to experiment with new verse forms in English. Surrey (Henry Howard) tried iambic pentameter blank verse, which became the medium for heroic plays. Wyatt and Surrey introduced into England, and later modified, the Petrarchan sonnet, thus giving to Sidney, Shakespeare, Spenser, and others an accepted stanza for love poems of a reflective type. Because the Tudor audience was so familiar with the form of the fourteen-line sonnet, they enjoyed its many elaborate variations—in rhyme scheme, in the relationship between verse unit and thought unit, and in the relationships among its parts.

more integrally related to an Elizabethan audience than they do to us today. Dramas were filled with songs, songs were poems, architects were arrangers of masques, gardens were intellectual puzzles.

Poetry. The poetic literature of Renaissance England is characterized by vigorous experiments and extensive production. Some Elizabethan poets were writing in traditional poetic genres—lyrical, pastoral, and allegorical; others sought to shape new forms. Lyric poetry, from Thomas Wyatt (1503–1619) and Henry Howard (1517–1547) to Thomas Campion (1567–1619) and Ben Jonson (1572–1637), remains important throughout the period. These Elizabethan lyric poets are sometimes more conventional than they appear, for their lyrics may be imitations or translations of poems which influenced them, or expressions of conventional difficulties of conventional lovers. Interest in poetic conventions is also shown by the vogue of pastoral poetry, which sprang from that Elizabethan delight in such classical poets as Vergil. In pastoral poetry, poets disguise themselves as shepherds singing the joys (or sometimes problems) of an idyllic country world. The shepherds and shepherdesses, nymphs and swains are not realistic portraits of Elizabethan rustic life. Rather, the "green world" of pastoral offers the poet a conventional vantage point from which to consider seriously the arts of poetry and of love and to comment on society. Even when pastoral songs appear to us to be simple statements of feelings, their Tudor audience would have recognized their conventional aspects.

Allegory (an extended and complicated metaphor) was another favorite Elizabethan device for exploring narrative meaning. Though medieval allegory was an influence (and certainly may have affected Spenser), a great part of the Elizabethan allegorical impulse came

Portrait of Sir Philip Sidney.

NATIONAL PORTRAIT GALLERY

Prose. The same variety and spirit of experimentation can be found in Tudor prose. The subjects were various—history, philosophy, criticism, travel, manners, the exploits of rogues as well as of pastoral heroes. Prose styles were equally diverse. The so-called plain style was based upon the brief syntactic units and simple diction characteristic of the Roman writer Seneca (54 B.C.?–A.D. 39). The Ciceronian style—taking its name from the Roman writer and statesman Cicero (106–43 B.C.)—was composed of longer syntactic units with less parallelism and more elaborate antitheses. Plain style, artful as it is, often gives the appearance of simplicity; the Ciceronian, in contrast, shows its complexities and complication. The contrast between the elaborate movement of Sidney's prose in *The Defense* and Bacon's simpler style in the *Essays* provides a case in point.

Drama. The characteristic richness and innovation of Tudor prose and poetry appear even more strikingly in the drama. In the later Middle Ages, the mystery and morality plays had created large popular audiences for drama. Drama seems the dominant genre of the Elizabethan age and is perhaps its greatest achievement.

No longer working so literally within the religious or didactic framework of the mystery and morality plays, Tudor playwrights turned to new areas for their material. Because many of them had scholarly and university backgrounds, they frequently adapted plots from classical comedies and tragedies into English in the early sixteenth century. The dramatists of Shakespeare's (1564–1616) generation, however, more often found their source material in legends and city streets, in romances and chronicles; they then transformed that material to please the tastes of their audience. And a growing and heterogeneous audience it was, as a glance at the building and style of theaters reveals.

We possess records, dated as early as 1576, of a number of theaters built in London. Though no Elizabethan structures survive (and thus there is sometimes more scholarly controversy than certainty), we can make certain assumptions about the Elizabethan stage and method of staging. The stage was essentially a platform, with some apron perhaps projecting into the audience. Surrounding the stage in a semicircular fashion, the audience sat or stood on the ground and in a multileveled polygonal structure which was open to the sky in the center. The back of the stage was a facade, taller than one story, with perhaps a balcony or raised window used for appropriate scenes. On the first level of the stage, there may have been a recessed room or aperture. Though the stage was by no means bare of props and small sets—indeed, the entire theater was a symbolic building—scenery was provided largely by the words of the poet. The actors, who were professionals, were men and boys; it was still considered inappropriate for women to appear on stage. Costumes, as we know from records of theatrical expenditures, were usually elaborate versions of current Elizabethan dress rather than copies of historic apparel. Companies of actors acted a variety of plays—comedies, tragedies, histories, and mixed genres. Some

actors became especially known for certain roles; it was, after all, repertory theater. There was audience enough for many theaters, but the theater companies still competed in the productions of popular kinds of plays.

The drama appeared to its contemporaries as many things. To classical critics, such as Sidney, drama—especially tragedy—was a type of poetry, and its language was the language of verse. Others treated drama as a forum for moral instruction. To many Puritans it was unnatural and corrupting. To most Elizabethans, however, to those who stood cheaply and those who paid well, it was popular entertainment, entertaining in its extraordinary variety. Christopher Marlowe's (1564–1593) plays moved the drama nearer to the epic; Ben Jonson's (1572–1637), nearer to classical satire. Some dramatists reflected the fanciful world of prose romances, others the realism of city merchants.

Detail from the Chandos portrait of Shakespeare.

Though Shakespeare overtowers his contemporaries, his works spring from the same world as theirs. He wrote lyrics and sonnets, acted and wrote histories, tragedies, comedies, and romances. Born the son of a well-to-do merchant, he made his fortune in the city by pleasing city tastes and died a wealthy landowner in his own country town. His drama is as various in its subjects and styles as is the Tudor period itself. Indeed, the "stages" in his development as a playwright serve as a microcosm for the age itself: from classically inspired comedies (*The Comedy of Errors*), to early melodramas (*Romeo and Juliet*), to the history plays of the 1590s (*King Henry IV*), to the great tragedies of the 1600s (*Hamlet, King Lear, Othello, Macbeth*), to the thoughtful "dark" comedies (*Measure for Measure*) and mature love tragedy (*Antony and Cleopatra*), to the late romances (*The Winter's Tale, The Tempest*).

Stuart and Puritan England

Upon the death of Elizabeth in 1603, James I came to the throne. His reign (1603–1625) was marked by increased political and religious strife. James was an ardent believer in the theory of the divine right of kings, which was contrary to the English conception of the limited power of the monarch. Though the English Reformation had made the political sovereign head of the Anglican Church, and though in feudal theory all kings held the fief of kingship from God as liege lord (and thus had to answer only to him), no Tudor was unwise enough to insist upon the theory. But with the Stuarts, and their Royalist supporters, it was different. The king, for them, stood above the law. The king and the Royalists championed unquestioning devotion to the crown; the Parliament and the Puritans, on the other hand, the inviolability of common law. Further, James' foreign policy was also regarded by many of his subjects as less than successful—especially in his desire for Catholic alliances, and in his attempt to negotiate a marriage between his son, Prince Charles, and the Spanish Infanta.

James had no sympathy with the English Puritans; his fear of the power of church government, as he had seen it in his native Scotland, led him to try to impose the ritual of the Church of England upon a body of

Charles I with M. de St. Antoine *(1633) by Sir Anthony Van Dyck, whose dramatic Baroque portraits of Charles suggest his aristocratic and authoritative manner. Charles I, beheaded in 1649, was at the height of his power when this portrait was done.*

believers now far more diverse than in Elizabeth's time. His political theory, his religious leanings, and his personal stubbornness (in contrast to Elizabeth's ability as a consummate politician) all increased the tension and conflict within the kingdom.

Charles I continued his father's abuses during his reign (1625–1649). Faced with a well-developed opposition party strongly based in the gentry class, Charles preferred repression to conciliation. From 1629 to 1640 he ruled without Parliament. To secure the money which his personal extravagances and those of his favorites required, he resorted to various illegal methods—imposing customs, forcing taxes and grants. Acting through his archbishop of Canterbury, Archbishop Laud, Charles attempted to impose Catholic practices. Laud restored many of the abandoned rituals of the Roman Church, which many Puritans regarded as idolatrous. Many dissatisfied Puritans emigrated to America to seek the religious freedom their own country no longer afforded them. The English religious situation grew rapidly more hostile and polarized.

The armed rebellion of the Scots (1637), resisting the imposition of the Anglican Prayer Book and demanding the rights of free assembly and a Scotch parliament, found the king without funds to conduct a war against them. By 1640 the threat from the north was sufficiently serious to force Charles to summon Parliament to raise money; he was refused and dissolved Parliament. But as the situation in Scotland further deteriorated, he was forced to try again. The Parliament that Charles called in November 1640 is known as the Long Parliament; it remained in session until 1653. Led by John Pym (1584–1643), a country gentleman who was an effective parliamentarian, the Long Parliament vigorously resisted Charles' demands. It impeached the king's chief ministers, abolished the Star Chamber (the crown's secret court), and drew up a list of grievances against the king. Parliament proclaimed itself sovereign henceforth, with or without the agreement of the king. The king reacted by personally invading Parliament to seize its leaders; he was unsuccessful. By 1642, Royalists and Puritans were engaged in civil war.

Both the terminology for talking about the war and the course of the war itself are complicated. When the name "Puritan" was first used, for example, cannot be determined, but it was certainly in use in the early years of Elizabeth's reign. It was often used derisively as a generic term for a growing number of persons, mostly from the citizen and craftsman classes, who believed that the Anglicans had not gone far enough in their reformation. Several more or less distinct sects of nonconformists arose, some of which took their names from their form of government, like the Presbyterians, or from some phase of their belief, like the Baptists, or even from the derision of their enemies, like the Quakers, who were accused of trembling in religious ecstasy. All nonconforming sects were precisely that—they did not conform in their dogma or practice to the policy of the Anglican Church.

Because of the close relationship between state and church in the period, the conflicts between conservative and radical church reformers carried great political weight. The Anglican Church was the official church of England; the nonconformists in general were, therefore, religious rebels. The adherents of the state church were made uneasy by the very existence of nonconformist groups, who themselves feared a state-supported tyranny of the Anglican Church. In Elizabethan England the Puritans, located mostly in London, can hardly be said to have formed a political party. They appear in literature primarily as the butt of stereotypical jokes about their dour countenances, their Hebrew names, their fondness for cant laced with Biblical quotations, and the simplicity of their dress. Under the Stuarts, however, serious and educated Puritans gradually entered into a political alignment against the king's party.

The party of the king, the Cavaliers or Royalists as they are often called, have, like the Puritans, too often been reduced to a contemptible stereotype. They were not all profligates and fops, nor always supporters of tyranny or unthinking subscribers to a state religion. Many of them wished to see the excesses of the crown checked within the traditional framework of government. The supporters of the king's cause certainly more often possessed the charm and style of the chivalric world than did the Puritans. Yet any modern viewer of this conflict must look beyond the appearances, beyond the contrast of lace cuffs and plain homespun, to the long-standing reasons that led to the conflict.

For the first year of the Civil War, Charles was successful everywhere. The Parliamentary forces were largely inexperienced, and their first leader, John Hampden (1594–1643) was killed early in the conflict. But the second year of the war saw the rise of a brilliant new leader of the Parliamentary forces, Oliver Cromwell (1599–1658). At the important battles of Marston Moor and Newbury, Parliamentary forces under Cromwell were successful. It was Cromwell who began to push the advances aggressively, inspiring his untutored troops with a holy zeal and a sense of religious mission. The final decisive victory for the Parliamentary forces was at Naseby on June 14, 1645. After that victory, though Parliament was itself not initially eager to press charges against the king, Charles' attempt to set up a Scottish invasion and some Puritan gerrymandering of the Parliament itself finally resulted in a trial, conviction, and death sentence for Charles. On January 30, 1649, Charles I was beheaded.

For the first time in English history the cry of "The king is dead" was not followed by the cry "Long live the king." A "Commonwealth" or "Free State" was created in May 1649. Cromwell ruled first as the leader of the Commonwealth's Council of State and then, after 1653, as Lord Protector of the realm. Under Cromwell, England made a conquest of Ireland; defeated Charles Stuart, son of the late King; conducted a war with Holland; and maintained prestige on the continent in numerous diplomatic negotiations. Upon

Banqueting House, Whitehall Palace, London, built by Inigo Jones (1573–1652), well-known architect and designer, during the period 1619–1622 for James I. The panels for the ceiling of the interior (left) were painted by Peter Paul Rubens in 1635 for Charles I. Court masques, for which Jones frequently designed costumes, were often held here. The West Front (right) is in the Palladian style of the Italian Renaissance.

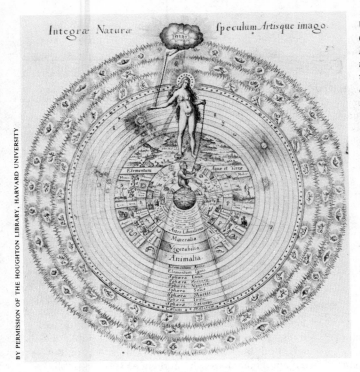

Integra Naturæ Speculum Artisque imago

Utriusque Cosmi Historia (*History of Each Order of the Universe*) (1617–1619?) *by Robert Fludd (1574–1637), physician and mystic, depicts the Ptolemaic view of the universe; the earth rather than the sun is at the center. The inner circles represent the accepted Renaissance hierarchy of the universe.*

Cromwell's death in 1658, however, Puritan power began to wane. Popular support began to grow for the restoration of the monarchy. Two years later a new Parliament with Royalist inclinations invited Charles Stuart, who had taken sanctuary in France, to return to England as Charles II. He landed at Dover on May 25, 1660, and proceeded to London amid scenes of wild enthusiasm. The brief Puritan interlude was over, but Charles II, the first constitutional monarch, knew what James I and Charles I had refused to admit—that the king ruled by right of Parliament.

Seventeenth-Century Literature

The literature of the Stuart and Puritan period provides a link between the literature of the Elizabethan age and that of the Restoration. The literature produced under the first two Stuarts was in many ways very Elizabethan: Stuart authors upheld the distinctive values and characteristics of court society until checked, temporarily, by Puritan control. Stuart poetry, prose, and drama can be distinguished from the Elizabethan genres chiefly in their sources and styles.

Poetry. The poetry of the Elizabethan age was inspired chiefly by Italian authors; during the reign of the Stuarts, the principal continental influence was French. This shift is revealed distinctly in the declining popularity of Petrarch and the growing popularity of the French poet Pierre de Ronsard (1525–1585) and his associates of the Pléiade, a group of young French

poets who attempted to enrich literature through imitation of the Greek classics. Both Ben Jonson (1572–1637) and John Donne (1573–1631), the most influential literary figures of the reigns of James and Charles, introduced elements quite different from the artificiality and conscious indirectness of much Elizabethan verse. Thus, poetry in the early Stuart period developed new, distinctive qualities.

Of all late Elizabethan poets, Jonson and Donne were the best qualified by temperament and art to serve as links between the two periods and to give new directions to the next age. Both grew up under Elizabethan influences but lived well into the Stuart period. Both were literary rebels, strong minded, independent. Both were vigorous, bold, industrious, and productive. These qualities gave their poetry a vitality which impressed the apprentice poets of Charles' age. To the influence of their writing must be added the effect of their spoken words. Ben Jonson was an oral autocrat; Donne was a powerful and popular preacher. Thus, the effect of their personalities was added to that of their poems.

Many of the poets following them reflect the influence of one or the other. Those poets variously given the names "Sons of Ben" and "Cavalier Poets" (including Thomas Carew, Richard Lovelace, John Suckling, Robert Herrick, and Andrew Marvell) wrote in the tradition of classical song and sweetness, which marks Jonson's poetry. Many of the lyrics written by the Cavaliers remain favorites today as expressions of delicate emotions. Another type of poetry, perhaps proceeding from Donne's influence, becomes the vehicle

Portrait of John Donne (1594?), probably painted during the period of his travels in Italy and Spain. The inscription Illumina tenebras nostras domina *means "Mistress, light up my darkness."*

always moral and lofty, often sublime and even apocalyptic in expression. Milton sees himself taking on a divine task; Spenser views it as the poet's task. The measured, leisurely pauses created by the nine-line Spenserian stanza are far removed from the forward moving, sometimes verbally contorted, Miltonic blank verse. To move from the humanely moral concerns of Spenser to the sometimes strictly theological concerns of Milton is indeed to move from the court of Elizabeth to the sectarian world of Commonwealth England. Though Milton cannot be separated from his age, he certainly surpasses the limitations of his creed and politics.

Drama. Stuart drama is different from Elizabethan drama for several reasons. In the days of Elizabeth, various noblemen sponsored companies of actors. Courtiers and commoners alike patronized the theaters. As a consequence, Elizabethan plays, by design, offered something to please the taste of everyone. The private theaters increasingly built during the reign of James I were completely enclosed and small in size; admission fees were higher than those of public theaters. Both these factors had obvious effects on the size and character of the audience. The last public theater, the Red Bull, was built in 1605. Shakespeare's own company, the Lord Chamberlain's Men, purchased a private theater, Blackfriars, in 1607. As the heterogeneous public of Elizabeth's day left the theater, the new drama offered more extreme visions to more homogeneous audiences—the grimly realistic or the horrific or the artificial as in Thomas Middleton's (1570–1627) caustic city comedies, or John Marston's (1575?–1634) savage revenge plays, or John Ford's (1586?–1640?) courtly tragedies. There was a moral vision in these plays; but the playwrights, while not entirely divorcing themselves from tradition, did consider ideas and forms that were radical when compared to the Elizabethan public-theater plays. With the coming of James I, the acting companies were taken under royal patronage. Actors became Grooms of the Chamber and mere appendages of the Revels Office at

of some of the best talents of the age—religious poetry. Both the heightened sense of religious conflict in the period and the desire to move beyond sectarianism to the peace of a common belief were part of the impetus behind the age's religious poetry. Some poetry, like Donne's, is questing, querulous, and contentious but ultimately believing. Other writers, like George Herbert, sought through the very intricate patterns of verse itself to praise a loving God in a selfless, nonegotistical fashion that concentrates on using the head to turn the heart to God. Donne and his followers (including George Herbert, Richard Crashaw, Henry Vaughan, and Thomas Traherne) were first called "Metaphysical Poets" by Samuel Johnson; they are "metaphysical" in the sense that their vision is inward, complex, acute, spiritual, and psychological. They took pleasure in making—sometimes forcing—connections within and between earthly "things." The Elizabethan fondness for sonnet sequences was replaced by a taste for complicated extended works and collections of related poems such as Herbert's *Temple,* Traherne's *Centuries,* and Vaughan's *Silex Scintillans.*

As with the Elizabethans, poetry was not confined to lyrics or structured collections of short poems. Longer nondramatic works in both periods were not, of course, so common as shorter pieces; each period seemed interested in a different kind of long poem. Spenser's *Faerie Queene* shows the Elizabethan taste for extended allegorical narratives; Milton's *Paradise Lost* shows the Commonwealth taste for Christian epics. While Spenser does claim epic intention and Milton does sometimes use allegory, the differences between the two poets remain striking. Milton aims not to explore the nature of man's human virtues, but to "justify the ways of God to man." His learning, his music, his literary skill, were fused by a burning, if sometimes narrow, prophetic zeal. As a result, he is

Portrait of John Milton, by William Faithorne. Milton, a supporter of the Puritan cause, is shown here in the traditional Puritan costume.

Costumes designed by Inigo Jones for masques, or theatrical performances, at King James' court. The costumes and poses show the influence of the Italian Renaissance. Left: *costume from* Oberon (1611); center: *costume for the Countess of Belford, from the* Masque of Queens (1609); right: *Oceania, from Ben Jonson's* Masque of Blacknesse (1605).

court. Thus, the drama became more literally connected with the court than it had been in the time of Elizabeth, and the actors were often Royalists by virtue of their positions.

It was inevitable, therefore, that in the struggle between king and Parliament the actors found themselves the target of the Puritans. Actually, Puritan opposition to the stage was already well established when Charles I came to the throne in 1625. Some Puritans argued that the theaters were a source for spreading physical disease. Others argued that the theaters were a source of moral disease, in several ways. First, they claimed that gamblers, tricksters, and prostitutes flourished in the crowds of theatergoers; second, that actors represented beings other than God made them to be and that the playwrights, in making a seeming world of a fiction, were blasphemously rivaling God in trying to make "something out of nothing"; and third, that the theater was morally diseased because bawdy subjects were discussed there. During Charles' reign, growing Puritan opposition to Cavalier manners and interests increasingly led to further attacks on the stage. Finally, on September 2, 1642, the drama was suppressed by act of Parliament.

Prose. The prose of the early seventeenth century was, in some respects, a tool of important business. The serious religious and civil controversies of the period occasioned much prose writing, both by writers little known and by writers so well known as John Milton. There were still, of course, writers interested in nonpolemical productions, and such works as Robert Burton's *The Anatomy of Melancholy* (1621) and Sir Thomas Browne's long treatises still draw an audience today.

The variety of styles—plain and ornate—found in the Elizabethan period continued. And the political or religious party of the writer did not necessarily dictate the choice of style. Milton's prose is ornate and Latinate though his church was plain and Puritan. Perhaps the prose writer most popular with later audiences is John Bunyan (1628–1688), whose background may have been polemical but whose works are very moving narratives. Bunyan had no formal education but had a deep acquaintance with the Bible, and his plain style, in contrast to Milton's Ciceronian style, is not heavy with classical constructions or erudition. Like Milton, he lived in visions; unlike Milton, he expressed his visions in mundane terms.

With the restoration of Charles II in 1660, the Renaissance itself did not so much cease as change. The complicated, sometimes fantastic hierarchy would become the more orderly "Great Chain of Being." The king, who may once have had divine pretensions, would now be a coequal with Parliament. The Renaissance fondness for epics, classical imitations, a theater mingling clowns and kings, and elaborate prose would all be transformed into heroic drama and court comedy, the instructive novel, rational discourses on man and society, extended political and moral essays, and the newspaper.

SIR THOMAS MORE
1478–1535

Sir Thomas More was educated in the household of Cardinal Morton, Archbishop of Canterbury, and at Oxford. He became an intimate friend of Erasmus, the Dutch humanist who later taught in England, and was regarded by his contemporaries as one of the most accomplished of the English humanists. But in his home in Chelsea, London, he was no retiring scholar. From his election to Parliament at twenty-six until a few years before his death he was the personal friend of Henry VIII and served his monarch on numerous foreign embassies and in varied offices including that of Lord Chancellor, in which he succeeded Cardinal Wolsey in 1529. He died a martyr to his conscience and his faith, for he remained always "the king's good servant, but God's first" and refused to believe that there were no moral laws higher than those promulgated by Parliament and dictated by an absolute monarch. He went to the block in 1535 rather than subscribe to the Act of Supremacy, which made his temporal ruler head of the Church of England. Sir Thomas More was canonized in 1935.

More's authorship of *The History of Edward V and Richard III* is no longer questioned. He is, in addition, the acknowledged author of certain tracts directed against Tyndale and Luther—tracts which display an acerbity at odds with the joyous and witty nature ascribed to him by his son-in-law William Roper. His most famous work is *Utopia*, written in Latin in 1516 and translated into English in 1551 by Ralph Robinson. More's picture of the ideal republic of Nowhere suggests his acquaintance with Plato's *Republic* but does not seem to have been based on that Greek vision of an ideal state. On the contrary, it is almost national in its allusions to English or European social, political, and religious conditions. In *Utopia* More makes a noble attack on needless and ruthless warfare and on other social forces that he believed to be destructive, and he advocates the advanced precept of religious toleration. The name "Utopian" came to be the universal adjective applied to Bacon's *New Atlantis* and to all later English conceptions of an ideal republic.

from UTOPIA,° Book One

ON COMMUNAL PROPERTY

"But, Master More,° to speak plainly what is in my mind, as long as there is private property and while money is the standard of all things, I do not think that a nation can be governed either justly or happily: not justly, because the best things will fall to the worst men; nor happily, because all things will be divided among a few. Even these few are not really well off, while the rest are utterly miserable.

"So I reflect on the wise and sacred institutions of the Utopians, who are so well governed with so few laws. Among them virtue has its due reward, yet everything is shared equally and every man lives in plenty. I contrast them with other nations that are still making laws and yet can never order their affairs satisfactorily. Although each man calls the property he has obtained his own, the many laws passed every day do not enable him to obtain or keep it or to distinguish satisfactorily what he calls his own from another's. This is clear from the many lawsuits unceasingly arising and never ending. When I consider these things, I grow more favorable to Plato's opinion and do not wonder that he refused to make laws for any people who will not share all their goods equally. Wisest of men,° he easily perceived that the one and only way to make a people happy is to establish equality of property. I doubt whether this equality can be achieved where property belongs to individual men. For when every man gets as much as he can for himself by one device or another, the few divide the whole wealth among themselves and leave want to the rest. The result generally is that there will be two sorts of people, and their fortunes ought to be interchanged: one sort are useless, but ravenous and wicked, while the other sort are unassuming, modest men who serve the public more than themselves by their daily work.

"By this I am persuaded that unless private property is entirely done away with, there can be no fair dis-

---

Utopia. The text reprinted here follows the modern translation by H. V. S. Ogden
1 **But, Master More,** spoken by Raphael Hythloday, More's guide to Utopia. Book One is largely a dialogue

23 **Wisest of men, etc.,** a reference to an incident in the life of Plato related by Diogenes Laertius

tribution of goods, nor can the world be happily governed. As long as private property remains, the largest
and far the best part of mankind will be oppressed with
an inescapable load of cares and anxieties. This load, I
admit, may be lightened somewhat, but cannot be entirely removed. Laws might be made that no one
should own more than a certain amount of land nor
possess more than a certain sum of money. Or laws
might be passed to prevent the prince from growing
too powerful and the populace from becoming too
strong. It might be made unlawful for public offices to
be solicited, or sold, or made burdensome for the officeholder by great expense. Otherwise officeholders
are tempted to reimburse themselves by dishonesty
and force, and it becomes necessary to find rich men
for those offices which ought rather to be held by wise
men. Such laws, I say, may have as much effect as
good nursing has on men who are dangerously sick.
Social evils may be allayed and mitigated, but so long
as private property remains, there is no hope at all that
they may be healed and society restored to good
health. While you try to cure one part, you aggravate
the disease in other parts. In redressing one evil
another is committed, since you cannot give something
to one man without taking the same thing from
another.''

"On the contrary,°" I replied, "it seems to me that
men cannot live well where all things are in common.
How can there be plenty where every man stops
working? The hope of gain will not drive him; he will
rely on others and become lazy. If men are stirred by
want, and yet no one can legally protect what he has
earned, what can follow but continual bloodshed and
turmoil, especially when the respect for and the authority of magistrates are lost? I cannot conceive of
authority among men that are equal to one another in
all things."

"I do not wonder," said Raphael, "that it appears
so to you, since you have no idea, or only a false idea
of such a state. But if you had been with me in Utopia
and had seen their customs and institutions as I did at
first hand for the five years that I spent among them,
you would frankly confess that you had never seen a
people ordered so well as they were. Indeed I would
never willingly have left, if it had not been to make
known that new world to others."

"You will not easily persuade me," Peter Giles° said,
"that people in that new land are better governed than
in our known world. Our abilities are not inferior to
theirs, and our government, I believe, is older. Long

experience has helped us to find out many conveniences of life, and by good luck we have discovered
other things which man's abilities could never have
invented.''

"As for the age of their commonwealth," Raphael
replied, "you might judge more correctly if you had
read their histories. If these may be trusted, they had
cities even before there were inhabitants here. What
chance has hit on or ingenuity has discovered, these
things might have been found there as well as here. As
a matter of fact I believe that we surpass them in
natural abilities, but we are left far behind them in
diligence and in zeal to learn. According to their
chronicles they had heard nothing about the men from
beyond the equator (as they call us) before our landing
there, except that once about twelve hundred years
ago a ship which a storm had carried toward Utopia
was wrecked on their island. Some Romans and Egyptians from the ship were cast up on the island and
never departed. Now note how the Utopians profited
from this chance event by their diligence. They learned
all the useful arts of Roman civilization either directly
from their shipwrecked guests or indirectly from hints
given in answer to inquiries. What benefits from the
mere fact that some Europeans landed there! If a
similar accident has hitherto brought any men here
from their land, it has been completely forgotten, as
doubtless it will be forgotten in time to come that I was
ever in their country. From one such accident they
made themselves masters of all our useful inventions,
but I believe it will be a long time before we accept any
of their institutions which are better than ours. This
willingness to learn, I think, is the real reason for their
being better governed and for their living more happily
than we do, though we are not behind them in ingenuity or riches."

"Then I earnestly beg you, Master Raphael," I said,
"to describe that island to us. Do not try to be brief,
but explain in order everything relating to their soil,
rivers, towns, people, manners, institutions, laws,
and, in fact, everything you think we would like to
know. And you may take it for granted that we want to
know whatever we do not know yet."

"There is nothing," he said, "that I would be happier to do, for these things are fresh in my mind. But it
will take some time."

"Let us first go to dinner," I said, "and afterward
we shall have time enough."

"Let us do so," he said. So we went in and had
dinner. Then we came back and sat down on the same
bench. I ordered my servants to take care that no one
should interrupt us. Peter Giles and I besought
Raphael to be as good as his word. When he saw that
we were eager to hear him, he sat silent and thoughtful
a moment, and then began as follows.

64 **On the contrary, etc.** More the author, employing a very carefully
balanced expositional method, puts a standard conservative defense of private
property in the mouth of More the character in *Utopia*   84 **Peter Giles,**
European humanist and a friend of Erasmus; he arranged for the first printing
of *Utopia*

from UTOPIA, Book Two°

THEIR GOLD AND SILVER, AND HOW THEY KEEP IT

Therefore they have accumulated an inestimable amount of gold and silver, but they do not keep it, in the form of treasure. I am reluctant to tell you how they keep it, for fear you will not believe me. I would not have believed it myself if anyone had told me about it—not unless I had seen it with my own eyes. It is almost always true that the more different anything is 150 from what people are used to, the harder it is to believe. In view of the fact that the Utopians' customs are so different from ours, a shrewd judge will not be surprised to find that they do not use gold and silver at all as we do. Since they keep gold and silver only for grave contingencies, they take care that in the meantime no one shall value these metals more than they deserve. Iron is obviously greatly superior to either. Men can no more do without iron than without fire and water. But gold and silver have no indispensable qual- 160 ities. Human folly has made them precious only because of their scarcity. Nature, like a wise and generous parent, has placed the best things everywhere and in the open, such as air and water and the earth itself, but she has hidden vain and useless things in remote and far away places.

If they kept their gold and silver guarded in a tower, foolish people might suspect the prince and senate of deceiving the citizens and aiming at some advantage for themselves. If they made plate and wrought-metal 170 work out of them, they would not want to give up such articles and melt them down to pay mercenaries. To solve the problem, they have thought out a plan as much in accord with their institutions as it is contrary to ours. The plan seems incredible to us (except to those of us who are very wise), because we regard gold as of great value and hoard it carefully. While their eating and drinking utensils are made of china and glass, beautiful but inexpensive, their chamber pots and stools both in their public halls and their homes are 180 made of gold and silver. They also use these metals for the chains and fetters of their bondmen. They hang gold rings from the ears of criminals, place gold rings on their fingers, gold collars around their necks, and gold crowns on their heads. Thus they hold gold and silver up to scorn in every way.

The result is that when there is need to part with these metals, which others give up as painfully as if their vitals were being torn out, none of the Utopians regard it as any more than the loss of a penny, so to 190 speak. They find pearls on their shores and diamonds and carbuncles on certain rocks, but they do not search for them. If they find them by chance, they polish them and adorn their younger children with them. As children they take pride and pleasure in such ornaments, and consequently put them aside when they are older and observe that only children use such baubles. This results from their own sense of propriety and not from their parents' commands, just as our children throw away their nuts, amulets, and dolls, when they grow up. 200

Different customs and institutions produce quite different ideas and attitudes, a truth I never saw better illustrated than in the behavior of the Anemolian° ambassadors, who came to Amaurot° while I was there. Because they came to discuss important business, three citizens from each city had come to Amaurot ahead of time. The ambassadors from neighboring states, at least those who had been there before, knew that fine clothing was not esteemed among the Utopians, that silk was scorned, and that gold was consi- 210 dered a shameful thing. They came as plainly clothed as possible. But when the Anemolians, who lived far away and had little intercourse with the Utopians, saw that all the people wore the same coarse clothing, they took it for granted that they did not have anything else. They themselves, being a proud rather than a wise people, decided to dress themselves gloriously like gods and dazzle the eyes of the poor Utopians by the splendor of their garb. The three ambassadors made their entry accompanied by a hundred attendants, all 220 dressed in varicolored clothing, many in silk. Since they were nobles at home, the ambassadors wore cloaks of cloth of gold, necklaces and earrings of gold, gold rings on their fingers, caps hung with gold chains studded with pearls and other jewels, in short decked out with all those things which among the Utopians were considered badges of slavery, signs of punishment, or toys for children. It was a sight to see how high they held their heads when they compared their clothing with that of the Utopians, for the people had 230 swarmed out into the streets. It was no less amusing to think how far they were from creating the impression which they had expected to make, for in the eyes of all the Utopians, except for those few who had visited other states, all this pomp and splendor seemed shameful. The Utopians saluted all the lowest people as lords and paid no respect at all to the ambassadors themselves, because they seemed to be dressed as slaves with their gold chains. And you might have seen children, who had already thrown away their pearls 240 and gems, nudge their mothers upon seeing the jewels in the ambassadors' caps, and say, "Look, mother!

Book Two. Book Two is largely narrative

203 **Anemolian,** from the Greek *anemolios,* "windy" 204 **Amaurot,** the capital of Utopia

See that big fool who wears pearls and gems, as if he were a little boy!'' Then she would say seriously, ''Hush, my boy. I think he is one of the ambassadors' fools.'' Others found fault with the golden chains for being useless and so light that any slave might break them, and so loose that a person when he wished could shake them off, and run away. But after the ambas-
250 sadors had spent one day and then another there, and had seen the great quantity of cheap gold and silver which was scorned as much by the Utopians as it was held in respect by the Anemolians, and when they had learned also that there was more gold and silver in the chains and fetters of a single slave than in the apparel of all three ambassadors, then their feathers fell. Somewhat shamefacedly they laid aside all the finery in which they had strutted, but they did so willingly, as they had conversed with the Utopians and learned
260 their customs and ideas.

THEIR MARRIAGE CUSTOMS

A woman is not married before eighteen, nor a man before twenty-two. If a man (or woman) is convicted of an illicit affair before marriage, he is severely punished and marriage is denied him for his whole life, unless a prince's pardon remits the punishment. The master and mistress of the household in which the offense has occurred are in disgrace for having been remiss in their duty. The reason for punishing this offense so severely is the fear that few would unite in
270 married love, to spend their whole lives with one person and put up with all the annoyances of marriage, unless they were rigorously restrained from promiscuity.

In the choice of wives they carefully follow a custom which seemed to us foolish and absurd. Before marriage some responsible and honorable woman, either a virgin or a widow, presents the woman naked to her suitor and after that some upright man presents the suitor naked to the woman. We laughed at this and
280 condemned it as foolish. On the contrary they wonder at the stupidity of other people, who are exceedingly cautious in matters involving only a little money. For example, men will refuse to buy a colt, unless they take off its saddle and harness, which might conceal a sore. But in the choice of a mate, on which one's happiness depends for the rest of one's life, they act carelessly. They leave all but a hand's-breadth of the woman's face covered with clothing and judge her by it, so that in marrying a couple runs a great risk of
290 mutual dislike if later anything in either's body should offend the other. Not all men are so wise that they consider only a woman's behavior. And even wise men think that physical beauty in wives adds not a little to the virtues of the mind. Certainly some deformity may lurk underneath clothing which will alienate a man from his wife when it is too late to be separated from her. If such a deformity is discovered after marriage, a man must bear his lot, so the Utopians think care ought to be taken by law that no one be deceived.

There is all the more reason for their taking this 300 precaution, because in that part of the world they alone are monogamists. Their marriages are broken only by death. They do not allow divorce except for adultery or insufferable waywardness on the part of either spouse. The injured person is given permission to change spouses by the senate, but the guilty party is considered disreputable and for the rest of his life is forbidden to remarry. They do not allow a husband to put away his wife against her will because of some bodily misfortune. They consider it a matter of cruelty 310 and disloyalty to desert one's spouse when most in need of comfort, especially in old age (which is itself really a sickness, since it brings sickness in its train). It happens occasionally that when a married couple cannot agree well together and when they have found other persons with whom they hope to live more happily, they separate by mutual consent and contract new marriages, but only with the consent of the senate. Such divorces are not allowed unless the senators and their wives have made careful inquiry 320 into the grounds for it. They allow them unwillingly, for they know that it weakens the love of married couples to leave the door open to easy new marriages.

They punish adulterers with the severest bondage. If both parties are married, they are divorced, and the injured persons may be married to one another or to some one else. But if either of the injured parties continues to love the undeserving spouse, then the couple may live together in marriage, provided the innocent person is willing to share in the labor to which 330 bondmen are condemned. Sometimes it happens that the repentance of the guilty person so moves the prince to pity that he grants both of them freedom once more. If anyone commits adultery a second time, his punishment is death.

THEIR PUNISHMENTS, THEIR LEGAL PROCEDURE, AND OTHER MATTERS

Their law lays down no other fixed penalties, but the senate fixes the punishment according to the wickedness of the crime. Husbands punish their wives, and parents their children, unless the offense is so great that a public punishment seems to be for the common 340 good. Generally the most serious crimes are punished by bondage, for they think this no less terrible to criminals than death. And it is more beneficial to the commonwealth, for a bondman's labor is worth more to the state than his death. Moreover the sight of bondage longer deters other men from similar crimes. If bondmen rebel and refuse to work, they are put to death like wild beasts which neither captivity nor chains can restrain. Those who bear their bondage patiently are not left hopeless. After they have been tamed by long hardship, if they show by their repentance that their wrongdoing troubles them more than their punishment, their bondage is modified or remitted, sometimes by the prince's prerogative and sometimes by popular vote.

A man who attempts to seduce a woman risks the same punishment as if he had actually done it. They think that an attempted crime is as bad as one committed, and that a man's failure should not mitigate his punishment when he did all he could to succeed.

They take pleasure in fools. While they think it contemptible to mistreat them, they do not forbid men to enjoy their foolishness, and even regard this as beneficial to the fools. No fools are entrusted to the care of serious and stern men who do not laugh at their ridiculous behavior and jests, for fear that a man who finds no enjoyment in a fool's only gift will not treat him kindly.

To jeer at a person for being deformed or crippled is not considered a reproach to him. But the mocker, who stupidly upbraids the cripple for something he cannot help, is held in contempt.

They consider it a sign of sluggish disposition to neglect one's natural beauty, but they think it is detestable to use rouge. They have learned by experience that no physical beauty recommends a wife to her husband as much as uprightness and obedience. Though some men are won by beauty, none are held except by virtue and compliance.

They deter men from crime by penalties and incite them to virtue by public honors. They set up statues of distinguished men who have deserved well of their country in the market places, to preserve the memory of their good deeds and to spur on the citizens to emulate the glory of their ancestors.

Any man who campaigns too zealously for a magistracy is sure to fail. They live together harmoniously and the magistrates are never proud or cruel. Instead they are called fathers, and deservedly. Because the magistrates do not exact honor from the people against their will, the people honor them willingly, as they should. Not even the prince has the distinction of robe or diadem; he is known only by a sheaf of grain carried before him. In the same way the priest is known by a wax candle.

They have few laws, and such are their institutions that they need few. They strongly censure other nations, which cannot get along without an infinite number of laws and interpretations. They think it highly unjust to bind men by laws that are too numerous to be read and too obscure to be readily understood. As for lawyers, a kind of men who handle matters craftily and interpret laws subtly, they have none at all. They maintain that it is better for each man to plead his own case, and to entrust to the judge what he would elsewhere tell his lawyer. Thus there is less delay, and the truth is brought out more readily. A man speaks without the help of a lawyer's wily instruction, and the judge examines each point carefully, and protects the simpler sort against the falsehoods of crafty men. It is hard to find such equitable procedure among other nations, with their multitude of intricate laws.

But in Utopia everyone is skillful in the law. For the laws are very few, as I have said, and the plainest interpretation is the fairest. All laws, according to their view, are promulgated for the single purpose of teaching each man his duty. Subtle interpretations teach very few, for there are few who can understand them; the simpler and more obvious sense of the laws is clear to all. If laws are not clear, they are useless for the masses of people who need their guidance most. There might as well be no laws at all as to have laws which only men of great ability and long training can interpret. Most men lack the brains for this task and cannot spare the time from their work.

(1516)

SIR THOMAS WYATT
1503–1542

Sir Thomas Wyatt was born in Kent and educated at Cambridge. In both his sonnets and his songs, he gave England a new lyrical stimulus and established the thirst for literary experimentation characteristic of the Tudor age. Wyatt was closely associated with the court of Henry VIII. Tradition has made him the lover of Anne Boleyn before Henry met her, but in spite of this dangerous admiration he retained royal favor and was sent on numerous foreign missions. His travels in Italy in 1526 and 1527 gave him an understanding of Continental artistic achievement, then at its height in the Renaissance, and an acquaintance with the sonnet, which he introduced into English. Wyatt did not employ the form of the Petrarchan sonnet so gracefully as he did another novel type of verse, *terza rima*. An

Italian form, *terza rima* is composed of three-line units of verse which are joined to the one preceding and the one following by a common rhyme: *a b a, b c b, c d c,* and so forth. Perhaps because rhymes in English are harder to find than in Italian, it has never been a widely used verse form in English. His lyrics circulated in manuscript during his lifetime; fifteen years after his death, they were printed in Totell's miscellany, *Songs and Sonnets.*

THE LOVER COMPARETH HIS STATE TO A SHIP IN PERILOUS STORM TOSSED ON THE SEA

My galley chargéd with forgetfulness°
Thorough sharp seas, in winter nights doth pass,
'Tween rock and rock; and eke mine enemy, alas,
That is my lord, steereth with cruelness.
5 And every oar, a thought in readiness,
As though that death were light in such a case.
And endless wind doth tear the sail apace
Of forcéd sighs, and trusty fearfulness.
A rain of tears, a cloud of dark disdain
10 Hath done the wearied cords great hinderance,
Wreathéd with error, and eke with ignorance.
The stars be hid that led me to this pain;
Drowned is reason that should me consort,
And I remain despairing of the port.
(1557)

THE LONG LOVE THAT IN MY THOUGHT DOTH HARBOR

The long love that in my thought doth harbor,
And in my heart doth keep his° residence,
Into my face presseth with bold pretense
And there encampeth, spreading his banner.
5 She that me learns° to love and suffer
And wills that my trust and lust's negligence°
Be reined by reason, shame,° and reverence
With his hardiness takes displeasure.
Wherewithal unto the heart's forest he flieth,
10 Leaving his enterprise with pain and cry,
And there him hideth, and not appeareth.
What may I do, when my master feareth,

But in the field with him to live and die?
For good is the life ending faithfully.
(1557)

WHOSO LIST TO HUNT

Whoso list to hunt, I know where is an hind,
But as for me, alas, I may no more:
The vain travail hath wearied me so sore.
I am of them that farthest cometh behind;
Yet may I by no means my wearied mind   5
Draw from the deer: but as she fleeth afore,
Fainting I follow. I leave off therefore,
Since in a net I seek to hold the wind.
Who list her to hunt, I put him out of doubt,
As well as I, may spend his time in vain: 10
And, graven with diamonds, in letters plain
There is written her fair neck round about:
Noli me tangere,° for Caesar's° I am,
And wild for to hold, though I seem tame.
(1557)

THEY FLEE FROM ME

They flee from me, that sometime did me seek,
With naked foot stalking in my chamber.
I have seen them, gentle, tame, and meek,
That now are wild, and do not remember
That sometime they put themselves in danger   5
To take bread at my hand; and now they range,
Busily seeking with a continual change.

Thankéd be Fortune it hath been otherwise,
Twenty times better; but once in special,
In thin array, after a pleasant guise,   10
When her loose gown from her shoulders did fall,
And she me caught in her arms long and small,°
And therewith all sweetly did me kiss
And softly said, "Dear heart, how like you this?"

It was no dream, I lay broad waking.   15
But all is turned, thorough my gentleness,
Into a strange fashion of forsaking;
And I have leave to go, of her goodness,
And she also to use newfangleness.°
But since that I so kindely° am served,   20
I fain would know what she hath deserved.
(1557)

The Lover Compareth His State to a Ship in Perilous Storm Tossed on the Sea
1 **charged with forgetfulness,** weighed down with neglect   **The Long Love That in My Thought Doth Harbor** 2 **his,** its   5 **learns,** teaches   6 **lust's negligence,** open revelation of my love or desire   7 **shame,** modesty

Whoso List to Hunt   13 **Noli me tangere,** Touch me not   **Caesar's,** traditionally believed to refer to Henry VIII's love for Anne Boleyn, who was rumored to have been Wyatt's sweetheart   **They Flee from Me**   12 **small,** slender   19 **newfangleness,** fickleness   20 **kindely,** naturally (but with an ironic suggestion of the modern meaning of "kindly")

HENRY HOWARD, EARL OF SURREY 1517–1547

The Earl of Surrey, whose literary career is often associated with Sir Thomas Wyatt's, was, like Wyatt, an innovator and experimenter in verse. He took the Italian sonnet and gave to it that structure which later acquired the name of the greatest poet who employed it, William Shakespeare. Surrey was even more at home in *terza rima* than was Wyatt. Long before Roger Ascham praised blank verse in his *The Schoolmaster* (1570), Surrey used that natural poetic form in his translations of Books II and IV of Vergil's *Aeneid*—an accomplishment the more remarkable in that he had no English model. Surrey was among the first of the English patricians to write lyrics and did much to establish the tradition of courtly concern with art and letters. His career as a courtier, soldier, and writer, was brief; he was executed for treason at the age of thirty. Ten years after his death many of his lyrics were published in Totell's miscellany, *Songs and Sonnets*.

LOVE THAT DOTH REIGN AND LIVE WITHIN MY THOUGHT

Love that doth reign and live within my thought,
And built his seat within my captive breast,
Clad in the arms wherein with me he fought
Oft in my face he doth his banner rest.
5 But she that taught me love and suffer pain,
My doubtful hope and eke my hot desire
With shamefast look to shadow and refrain,
Her smiling grace converteth straight to ire.
And coward love then to the heart apace
10 Taketh his flight where he doth lurk and plain°
His purpose lost, and dare not show his face.
For my lord's guilt thus faultless bide I pain;
Yet from my lord shall not my foot remove.
Sweet is the death that taketh end by love.
(1557)

DESCRIPTION OF SPRING WHEREIN EACH THING RENEWS, SAVE ONLY THE LOVER

The soote° season that bud and bloom forth brings,
With green hath clad the hill and eke the vale;
The nightingale with feathers new she sings;
The turtle° to her make° hath told her tale:
5 Summer is come, for every spray now springs;

The hart hath hung his old head° on the pale;
The buck in brake his winter coat he flings;
The fishes float with new repairéd scale;
The adder all her slough away she slings;
The swift swallow pursueth the flies smale;°   10
The busy bee her honey now she mings.°
Winter is worn, that was the flowers' bale:
And thus I see among these pleasant things
Each care decays, and yet my sorrow springs!
(1557)

ALAS, SO ALL THINGS NOW DO HOLD THEIR PEACE

Alas, so all things now do hold their peace,
Heaven and earth disturbéd in nothing;
The beasts, the air, the birds their song do cease;
The night's chare° the stars about doth bring.
Calm is the sea, the waves work less and less;   5
So am not I, whom love alas doth wring,
Bringing before my face the great increase
Of my desires, whereat I weep and sing
In joy and woe as in a doubtful ease.
For my sweet thoughts sometime do pleasure bring,   10
But by and by the cause of my disease
Gives me a pang that inwardly doth sting,
When that I think what grief it is again
To live and lack the thing should rid my pain.
(1557)

THE MEANS TO ATTAIN HAPPY LIFE

Martial,° the things that do attain
   The happy life be these, I find:
The riches left, not got with pain;
   The fruitful ground, the quiet mind;

The equal friend; no grudge, no strife;   5
   No charge° of rule, nor governance;
Without disease, the healthful life;
   The household of continuance;

The mean diet, no delicate fare;
   True wisdom joined with simpleness;   10
The night dischargéd of all care,
   Where wine the wit may not oppress.

The faithful wife, without debate;°
   Such sleeps as may beguile the night;
Contented with thine own estate,   15
   Ne° wish for death, ne° fear his might.
(1557)

Love That Doth Reign   10 **plain,** complain or lament   **Description of Spring Wherein Each Thing Renews**   1 **soote,** sweet   4 **turtle,** turtledove, used in lyric poetry as the symbol of love   **make,** mate

6 **hung his old head,** i.e., shed his old horns   10 **smale,** small   11 **mings,** for mengs, mixes or mingles   **Alas, So All Things**   4 **night's chare,** chariot or car   **The Means to Attain Happy Life**   1 **Martial,** Roman satirical poet of the first century A.D.; this poem is a translation of his *Epigrams,* Book X, number 47   6 **charge,** burden   13 **debate,** wrangling, strife   16 **Ne . . . ne,** not . . . nor

SIR PHILIP SIDNEY
1554–1586

As courtier, soldier, and scholar, Sir Philip Sidney was the perfect Elizabethan knight, one of the first of a distinguished group of gentlemen who represented the Renaissance spirit in the breadth of their accomplishments. His court connections he inherited, for his father was Sir Henry Sidney, Lord Deputy of Ireland, and his mother's father was John Dudley, Duke of Northumberland. Sidney was educated at Oxford and by travel in France, Italy, Germany, and other countries. From this residence abroad he returned to London to become the most admired of Elizabethan courtiers, "the glass of fashion and the mold of form." His brief life ended when he joined his uncle, the Earl of Leicester, in a military expedition to the Low Countries and died, a hero, of wounds received at Zutphen.

To Elizabethan courtiers like Sidney, scholarship and literary endeavor seemed natural companions of statecraft and military exploit. Like other gentlemen of his time he wrote his poetry and his prose not to be printed but to be circulated among his private friends. Sidney's love sonnets, entitled *Astrophel and Stella*, were addressed to Penelope Devereux, Lady Rich, and the volume remains one of the first and best of the Elizabethan sonnet sequences. Much of his other poetry he scattered after the manner of the time through his prose—especially in his pastoral romance *Arcadia*, addressed to his sister, the Countess of Pembroke. He wrote *An Apology for Poetry* about 1582, perhaps in reply to Stephen Gosson's *The School of Abuse*, an attack on poetry which appeared in 1579. For Sidney, the realm of poetry included drama, and the *Apology* becomes a memorable discussion of drama and of the ends of literature itself.

from AN APOLOGY FOR POETRY°

Poesy, therefore, is an art of imitation; for so Aristotle termeth it in the word μίμησις; that is to say, a representing, counterfeiting, or figuring forth: to speak metaphorically, a speaking picture, with this end, to teach and delight.

Of this have been three general kinds: the chief, both in antiquity and excellency, were they that did imitate the inconceivable excellencies of God. Such were David in his Psalms; Salomon in his Song of Songs, in his Ecclesiastes, and Proverbs; Moses and Deborah in 10 their hymns;° and the writer of Job; which, beside other, the learned Emanuel Tremellius and Franciscus Junius° do entitle the poetical part of the scripture; against these none will speak that hath the Holy Ghost in due holy reverence. In this kind, though in a full wrong divinity, were Orpheus, Amphion,° Homer in his hymns, and many other, both Greeks and Romans. And this poesy must be used by whosoever will follow St. Paul's counsel,° in singing psalms when they are merry; and I know is used with the fruit of comfort by 20 some, when, in sorrowful pangs of their death-bringing sins, they find the consolation of the never-leaving goodness.

The second kind is of them that deal with matters philosophical; either moral, as Tyrtaeus, ° Phocylides,° Cato;° or natural, as Lucretius,° and Virgil's *Georgics*;° or astronomical, as Manilius and Pontanus;° or historical, as Lucan;° which who mislike, the fault is in their judgment, quite out of taste, and not in the sweet food of sweetly uttered knowledge. 30

But because this second sort is wrapped within the fold of the proposed subject, and takes not the free course of his own invention; whether they properly be poets or no, let grammarians dispute, and go to the third, indeed right poets, of whom chiefly this question ariseth; betwixt whom and these second is such a kind of difference as betwixt the meaner sort of painters, who counterfeit only such faces as are set before them, and the more excellent, who having no law but wit, bestow that in colors upon you which is fittest for the 40 eye to see; as the constant though lamenting look of Lucretia,° when she punished in herself another's fault; wherein he painteth not Lucretia, whom he never saw, but painteth the outward beauty of such a virtue. For these third be they which most properly do imitate to teach and delight; and to imitate, borrow nothing of what is, hath been, or shall be; but range, only reined with learned discretion, into the divine consideration of what may be, and should be. These be they that, as the first and most noble sort, may justly be termed 50 "vates";° so these are waited on in the excellentest languages and best understandings, with the foredescribed name of poets. For these, indeed, do merely make to imitate, and imitate both to delight and teach, and delight to move men to take that goodness in hand which, without delight, they would fly as from a

12–13 **Emanuel Tremellius and Franciscus Junius,** two Biblical scholars in the Tudor period who collaborated in the edition of the Bible to which Sidney refers 16 **Orpheus, Amphion,** in Greek myth, two musicians with magic powers; the first was the son of the muse Calliope, the second the son of Zeus and Antiope 19 **St. Paul's counsel.** In the other one of the two 1595 editions of Sidney's treatise, the allusion is given correctly to St. James. The reference is to *James,* 5:13: Is any merry? let him sing psalms 25 **Tyrtaeus,** a Greek elegiac poet of the early seventh century B.C. **Phocylides,** a Greek writer of poetic maxims of the sixth century B.C. **Cato,** Dionysius, to whom were ascribed a collection of moral maxims that were very popular in the Middle Ages **Lucretius,** a Roman poet of the first century B.C. The reference is to his *De Rerum Natura (On the Nature of Things)* **Georgics,** poems describing and praising country life by Vergil, another Roman poet of the first century B.C. 27 **Manilius,** a Roman poet of the first century who dealt with astronomical themes **Pontanus,** Italian Renaissance scholar and poet (1426–1503); his chief work was *De Stellis (On the Stars)* **Lucan,** Roman epic poet (A.D. 39–65); his chief work is *Pharsalia,* an unfinished epic describing the wars of Caesar and Pompey 42 **Lucretia,** Lucrece, the Roman matron who killed herself after she had been raped by Tarquin, King of Rome 51 **vates,** prophets

An Apology for Poetry, published in 1595 by two different printers; in one of these issues it was called *An Apologie for Poetrie,* in the other *The Defence of Poesie* 10–11 **Moses . . . Deborah . . . hymns.** The allusions are to *Exodus,* 15:1–19, *Deuteronomy,* 32:1–43, and *Judges,* 5

stranger; and teach to make them know that goodness whereunto they are moved; which being the noblest scope to which ever any learning was directed, yet want

60 there not idle tongues to bark at them.

These be subdivided into sundry more special denominations; the most notable be the heroic, lyric, tragic, comic, satiric, iambic, elegiac, pastoral, and certain others; some of these being termed according to the matter they deal with, some by the sort of verse they like best to write in; for, indeed, the greatest part of poets have appareled their poetical inventions in that numerous kind of writing which is called verse. Indeed but appareled; verse being but an ornament, and no

70 cause to poetry, since there have been many most excellent poets that never versified, and now swarm many versifiers that need never answer to the name of poets. For Xenophon,° who did imitate so excellently as to give us *effigiem justi imperii*, the portraiture of a just empire, under the name of Cyrus, as Cicero saith of him, made therein an absolute heroical poem. So did Heliodorus,° in his sugared° invention of that picture of love in Theagenes and Chariclea; and yet both these wrote in prose; which I speak to show

80 that it is not riming and versing that maketh a poet (no more than a long gown maketh an advocate, who, though he pleaded in armor, should be an advocate and no soldier); but it is that feigning notable images of virtues, vices, or what else, with that delightful teaching, which must be the right describing note to know a poet by. Although, indeed, the senate of poets hath chosen verse as their fittest raiment; meaning, as in matter they passed all in all, so in manner to go beyond them; not speaking table-talk fashion, or like men in a

90 dream, words as they chanceably fall from the mouth, but piecing each syllable of each word by just proportion, according to the dignity of the subject.

* * * * *

Now therein of all sciences (I speak still of human, and according to the humane conceits) is our poet the monarch. For he doth not only show the way, but giveth so sweet a prospect into the way, as will entice any man to enter into it. Nay, he doth, as if your journey should lie through a fair vineyard, at the first give you a cluster of grapes, that, full of that taste, you may

100 long to pass further. He beginneth not with obscure definitions, which must blur the margent with interpretations, and load the memory with doubtfulness; but he cometh to you with words set in delightful proportion, either accompanied with, or prepared for,

the well enchanting skill of music; and with a tale forsooth he cometh unto you, with a tale which holdeth children from play, and old men from the chimney corner. And, pretending no more, doth intend the winning of the mind from wickedness to virtue: even as the child is often brought to take most wholesome 110 things by hiding them in such other as have a pleasant taste: which, if one should begin to tell them the nature of aloes or rhubarb they should receive, would sooner take their physic at their ears than at their mouth.

* * * * *

Since, then, poetry is of all human learnings the most ancient, and of most fatherly antiquity, as from whence other learnings have taken their beginnings; since it is so universal that no learned nation doth despise it, nor barbarous nation is without it; since both Roman and Greek gave such divine names unto it, the 120 one of prophesying, the other of making, and that indeed that name of making is fit for him, considering that where all other arts retain themselves within their subject, and receive, as it were, their being from it, the poet only, only bringeth his own stuff, and doth not learn a conceit out of a matter, but maketh matter for a conceit; since neither his description nor end containeth any evil, the thing described cannot be evil; since his effects be so good as to teach goodness, and delight the learners of it; since therein (namely in 130 moral doctrine, the chief of all knowledges) he doth not only far pass the historian, but, for instructing, is well nigh comparable to the philosopher, for moving, leaveth him behind him; since the Holy Scripture (wherein there is no uncleanness) hath whole parts in it poetical, and that even our Savior Christ vouchsafed to use the flowers of it; since all his kinds are not only in their united forms but in their severed dissections fully commendable; I think, and think I think rightly, the laurel crown appointed for triumphant captains 140 doth worthily, of all other learnings, honor the poet's triumph.

* * * * *

For heretofore poets have in England flourished, and, which is to be noted, even in those times when the trumpet of Mars° did sound loudest. And now that an overfaint quietness should seem to strew the house for poets, we are almost in as good reputation as the mountebanks° at Venice. Truly even that, as of the one side it giveth great praise to Poesy, which like Venus (but to better purpose) hath rather be troubled in the 150 net with Mars than enjoy the homely quiet of Vulcan;°

73 **Xenophon,** an Athenian historian of the fifth century B.C. best known for his *Anabasis,* an account of the expedition of the younger Cyrus against Artaxerxes. The allusion here is to his *Cyropaedia,* a romance based on the education of a perfect king   77 **Heliodorus,** a Greek writer of romances of the third century. The allusion here is to his *Aethiopica,* which tells of the love of Theagenes, a Thessalian, for Clariclea, the white daughter of the Ethiopian queen   **sugared,** delightful, charming

145 **trumpet of Mars,** general reference to war; Mars is the Roman god of war 148 **mountebanks,** charlatans, quacks   149–151 **Venus . . . Vulcan.** Venus, although married to Vulcan, loved Mars. Vulcan arranged for a net to trap the lovers in their bed and then proceeded to call in the other gods to watch

so serves it for a piece of a reason why they are less grateful to idle England, which now can scarce endure the pain of a pen. Upon this necessarily followeth, that base men with servile wits undertake it, who think it enough if they can be rewarded of the printer. And so as Epaminondas° is said, with the honour of his virtue, to have made an office, by his exercising it, which before was contemptible, to become highly respected,
160 so these, no more but setting their names to it, by their own disgracefulness disgrace the most graceful Poesy. For now, as if all the Muses were got with child, to bring forth bastard poets, without any commission they do post over the banks of Helicon, till they make the readers more weary than posthorses, while, in the meantime, they,

    Queis meliore luto finxit praecordia Titan,°

are better content to suppress the outflowing of their wit, than, by publishing them, to be accounted knights
170 of the same order. But I that, before ever I durst aspire unto the dignity, am admitted into the company of the paper-blurrers, do find the very true cause of our wanting estimation is want of desert, taking upon us to be poets in despite of Pallas. Now, wherein we want desert were a thankworthy labour to express: but if I knew, I should have mended myself. But I, as I never desired the title, so have I neglected the means to come by it. Only, overmastered by some thoughts, I yielded an inky tribute unto them.

* * * * *

180   Chaucer, undoubtedly, did excellently in his *Troilus and Cressida;* of whom, truly, I know not whether to marvel more, either that he in that misty time could see so clearly, or that we in this clear age walk so stumblingly after him. Yet had he great wants, fit to be forgiven in so reverent antiquity. I account the *Mirrour of Magistrates*° meetly furnished of beautiful parts, and in the Earl of Surrey's *Lyrics* many things tasting of a noble birth, and worthy of a noble mind. The *Shepheard's Calendar*° hath much poetry in his Ec-
190 logues, indeed worthy the reading, if I be not deceived. That same framing of his style to an old rustic language I dare not allow, since neither Theocritus in Greek, Virgil in Latin, nor Sannazzaro in Italian° did affect it. Besides these, do I not remember to have seen but few (to speak boldly) printed, that have poetical sinews in them: for proof whereof, let but most of the verses be put in prose, and then ask the meaning; and it will be found that one verse did but beget another, without ordering at the first what should be at the last; which

becomes a confused mass of words, with a tingling 200 sound of rhyme, barely accompanied with reason.

* * * * *

Our tragedies and comedies not without cause cried out against, observing rules neither of honest civility nor skilful poetry. Excepting *Gorboduc*° (again I say of those that I have seen), which notwithstanding as it is full of stately speeches and well-sounding phrases, climbing to the height of Seneca his style, and as full of notable morality, which it doeth most delightfully teach, and so obtain the very end of poesy; yet, in truth, it is very defectious in the circumstances, which 210 grieves me, because it might not remain as an exact model of all tragedies. For it is faulty both in place and time, the two necessary companions of all corporal actions. For where the stage should always represent but one place, and the uttermost time presupposed in it should be, both by Aristotle's precept° and common reason, but one day; there is both many days and many places inartificially imagined.

But if it be so in *Gorboduc*, how much more in all the rest? Where you shall have Asia of the one side, and 220 Afric of the other, and so many other under kingdoms, that the player, when he comes in, must ever begin with telling where he is, or else the tale will not be conceived. Now shall you have three ladies walk to gather flowers, and then we must believe the stage to be a garden. By and by, we hear news of shipwreck in the same place, then we are to blame if we accept it not for a rock. Upon the back of that comes out a hideous monster with fire and smoke, and then the miserable beholders are bound to take it for a cave; while, in the 230 meantime, two armies fly in, represented with four swords and bucklers, and then what hard heart will not receive it for a pitched field?

Now of time they are much more liberal; for ordinary it is, that two young princes fall in love; after many traverses she is got with child, delivered of a fair boy, he is lost, groweth a man, falleth in love, and is ready to get another child; and all this in two hours' space;° which, how absurd it is in sense, even sense may imagine, and art hath taught, and all ancient 240 examples justified, and at this day the ordinary players

157 **Epaminondas**, Theban general and statesman (418?–362 B.C.) 167 **Queis . . . Titan.** Whose hearts Titan molded from better clay. The quotation is from Juvenal's *Satire XIV* 186 **Mirrour of Magistrates**, Elizabethan compilation of the narratives of the downfalls of illustrious men; first edition published in 1559 189 **Shepheard's Calendar,** twelve eclogues by Sir Edmund Spenser (1552–1599) 192–193 **Theocritus . . . Italian.** Theocritus, Vergil, and Sannazzaro are all pastoral poets and hence relevant predecessors to Spenser

204 **Gorboduc.** The first English tragedy was written by Norton and Sackville in 1561. It was the first play in which blank verse was used, and each of the five acts is preceded by a dumb show allegorically suggestive of the action which immediately follows. The plot is based upon the old chronicle story of the British king, Gorboduc, who divided his kingdom between his sons Ferrex and Porrex, with disastrous results. In structure and sententiousness it owes much to Seneca. The apparent object of the authors was not so much to create a tragedy as to present a dramatic argument against the sedition and civil war which follow failure to determine the royal succession 216 **Aristotle's precept.** Aristotle (384–322 B.C.) was a Greek philosopher and critic whose *Poetics,* a definition and analysis of poetic tragedy, was regarded in the Middle Ages as a standard criticism. Sidney follows the medieval and later interpretations of Aristotle in ascribing to him the precepts regarding the unities of time and place; actually Aristotle only suggested the limitation to "a single revolution of the sun," and he said nothing whatever about limitation of place. In the attack on drama which follows, Sidney may have had in mind the court rather than the popular play, for the first public theater was not built until three or four years before the composition of this treatise 239 **two hours' space,** the usual length of an Elizabethan play

in Italy will not err in. Yet will some bring in an example of the *Eunuch* in Terence,° that containeth matter of two days, yet far short of twenty years. True it is, and so was it to be played in two days, and so fitted to the time it set forth. And though Plautus° have in one place done amiss, let us hit it with him, and not miss with him. But they will say, how then shall we set forth a story which contains both many places and many times? And do they not know that a tragedy is tied to the laws of poesy, and not of history; not bound to follow the story, but having liberty either to feign a quite new matter or to frame the history of the most tragical conveniency? Again, many things may be told, which cannot be showed—if they know the difference betwixt reporting and representing. As for example, I may speak, though I am here, of Peru, and in speech digress from that to the description of Calicut;° but in action I cannot represent it without Pacolet's horse.° And so was the manner the ancients took, by some *Nuntius*° to recount things done in former time, or other place.

Lastly, if they will represent an history they must not, as Horace saith, begin *ab ovo*,° but they must come to the principal point of that one action which they will represent. By example this will be best expressed; I have a story of young Polydorus, delivered, for safety's sake, with great riches, by his father Priamus to Polymnestor, King of Thrace, in the Trojan war time. He, after some years, hearing of the overthrow of Priamus, for to make the treasure his own, murthereth the child; the body of the child is taken up; Hecuba, she, the same day, findeth a sleight° to be revenged most cruelly of the tyrant. Where, now, would one of our tragedy-writers begin, but with the delivery of the child? Then should he sail over into Thrace, and so spend I know not how many years, and travel numbers of places. But where doth Euripides?° Even with the finding of the body; leaving the rest to be told by the spirit of Polydorus. This needs no further to be enlarged; the dullest wit may conceive it.

But, besides these gross absurdities, how all their plays be neither right tragedies nor right comedies, mingling kings and clowns, not because the matter so carrieth it, but thrust in the clown by head and shoulders to play a part in majestical matters, with neither decency nor discretion; so as neither the admiration and commiseration, nor the right sportfulness, is by their mongrel tragi-comedy obtained. I know Apuleius° did somewhat so, but that is a thing recounted with

space of time, not represented in one moment; and I know the ancients have one or two examples of tragi-comedies as Plautus hath *Amphytrio*.° But, if we mark them well, we shall find that they never, or very daintily, match hornpipes and funerals. So falleth it out, that having indeed no right comedy in that comical part of our tragedy, we have nothing but scurrility, unworthy of any chaste ears; or some extreme show of doltishness, indeed fit to lift up a loud laughter, and nothing else; where the whole tract of a comedy should be full of delight; as the tragedy should be still maintained in a well-raised admiration.

But our comedians think there is no delight without laughter, which is very wrong; for though laughter may come with delight, yet cometh it not of delight, as though delight should be the cause of laughter; but well may one thing breed both together. Nay, rather in themselves they have, as it were, a kind of contrariety. For delight we scarcely do, but in things that have a conveniency to ourselves, or to the general nature; laughter almost ever cometh of things most disproportioned to ourselves and nature. Delight hath a joy in it either permanent or present; laughter hath only a scornful tickling. For example, we are ravished with delight to see a fair woman, and yet are far from being moved to laughter; we laugh at deformed creatures, wherein certainly we cannot delight. We delight in good chances; we laugh at mischances. We delight to hear the happiness of our friends and country, at which he were worthy to be laughed at that would laugh; we shall, contrarily, sometimes laugh to find a matter quite mistaken, and go down the hill against the bias, in the mouth of some such men as for the respect of them one shall be heartily sorry he cannot choose but laugh, and so is rather pained than delighted with laughter. Yet deny I not but that they may go well together; for as in Alexander's° picture well set out we delight without laughter, and in twenty mad antics we laugh without delight: so in Hercules, painted, with his great beard and furious countenance, in a woman's attire, spinning at Omphale's° commandment, it breeds both delight and laughter; for the representing of so strange a power in love procures delight, and the scornfulness of the action stirreth laughter.

But I speak to this purpose, that all the end of the comical part be not upon such scornful matters as stir laughter only, but mix with it that delightful teaching which is the end of poesy. And the great fault, even in that point of laughter, and forbidden plainly by Aristotle, is, that they stir laughter in sinful things, which are rather execrable than ridiculous; or in miserable, which are rather to be pitied than scorned. For what is it to make folks gape at a wretched beggar, and a beg-

---

243 **Terence,** Publius Terentius Afer (c. 190–159 B.C.), Roman comic playwright. His influence on Elizabethan playwrights was probably not so great, however, as that of Plautus 246 **Plautus,** Titus Maccius Plautus (c. 254–184 B.C.), another Roman comic playwright. In his reference to Plautus' having "in one place done amiss," Sidney may have had in mind the *Captivi*, in which the unity of time seems to have been violated 258 **Calicut,** a seaport on the southwest coast of India 259 **Pacolet's horse,** a winged animal which belonged to the dwarf Pacolet in the medieval romance of Valentine and Orson 261 **Nuntius,** Latin for "messenger," a character in the ancient classical drama who narrated events necessary to the action but not presented on the stage 264 **ab ovo,** from the egg, i.e., from the beginning 273 **sleight,** device 278 **Euripides,** Greek tragic playwright (480–406 B.C.). The story is from his *Hecuba* and relates the climax of the Trojan queen's sorrows in the sacrifice of her daughter Polyxena and the murder of her youngest son Polydorus 289 **Apuleius,** a Roman satirical writer of the second century B.C. The specific allusion is to the *Golden Ass*

293 **Amphytrio.** In this play the speaker of the prologue announces it as a tragicomedy because a servant plays a part with kings and gods 327 **Alexander's,** Alexander the Great's 329–331 **Hercules . . . Omphale's.** In Ovid's *Heroides* and in Greek legend, Hercules served as a slave to Omphale, a Lydian queen, as a penalty for his murder of Iphitus. An ancient mosaic in Rome represented him as spinning with a distaff while Omphale wears his lion's skin. Sidney interprets the scene as symbolic of the power of love

garly clown; or against law of hospitality, to jest at strangers because they speak not English so well as we do? What do we learn? Since it is certain,

> *Nil habet infelix paupertas durius in se,*
> *Quam quod ridiculos homines facit.°*

350 But rather a busy loving courtier, and a heartless threatening Thraso;° a self-wise-seeming schoolmaster; a wry-transformed traveler: these, if we saw walk in stage names, which we play naturally, therein were delightful laughter, and teaching delightfulness; as in the other, the tragedies of Buchanan° do justly bring forth a divine admiration.

But I have lavished out too many words of this play matter; I do it because, as they are excelling parts of poesy, so is there none so much used in England, and none can be more pitifully abused; which, like an un-
360 mannerly daughter, showing a bad education, causeth her mother Poesy's° honesty to be called in question.

* * * * *

So that since the ever-praiseworthy Poesy is full of virtue-breeding delightfulness, and void of no gift that ought to be in the noble name of learning; since the blames laid against it are either false or feeble; since the cause why it is not esteemed in England is the fault of poet-apes, not poets; since, lastly, our tongue is most fit to honour Poesy, and to be honoured by Poesy; I conjure you all that have had the evil luck to
370 read this ink-wasting toy of mine, even in the name of the Nine Muses, no more to scorn the sacred mysteries of Poesy, no more to laugh at the name of "poets," as though they were next inheritors to fools, no more to jest at the reverent title of a "rhymer"; but to believe, with Aristotle, that they were the ancient treasurers of the Grecians' Divinity; to believe, with Bembus,° that they were first bringers-in of all civility; to believe, with Scaliger,° that no philosopher's precepts can sooner make you an honest man than the reading of
380 Virgil; to believe, with Clauserus,° the translator of Cornutus, that it pleased the heavenly Deity, by Hesiod and Homer, under the veil of fables, to give us all knowledge, Logic, Rhetoric, Philosophy, natural and moral, and *Quid non?;°* to believe, with me, that there are many mysteries contained in Poetry, which of purpose were written darkly, lest by profane wits it should be abused; to believe, with Landino,° that they are so beloved of the gods that whatsoever they write proceeds of a divine fury; lastly, to believe them-
390 selves, when they tell you they will make you immortal by their verses.

Thus doing, your name shall flourish in the printers' shops; thus doing, you shall be of kin to many a poetical preface; thus doing, you shall be most fair, most rich, most wise, most all, you shall dwell upon superlatives. Thus doing, though you be *libertino patre natus,°* you shall suddenly grow *Herculea proles,°*
> *Si quid mea carmina possunt.°*

400 certain rustical disdain, will become such a Mome° as to be a Momus of Poetry;° then, though I will not wish unto you the ass's ears of Midas° nor to be driven by a poet's verses (as Bubonax was) to hang himself, nor to be rhymed to death as is said to be done in Ireland;° yet certain rustical disdain, will become such a Mome° as to be a Momus of Poetry;° then, though I will not wish unto you the ass's ears of Midas° nor to be driven by a poet's verses (as Bubonax was) to hang himself, nor to
410 by rhymed to death as is said to be done in Ireland;° yet thus much curse I must send you, in the behalf of all poets that while you live, you live in love, and never get favour for lacking skill of a Sonnet, and when you die, your memory die from the earth for want of an Epitaph.
(1580, 1595)

from ASTROPHEL AND STELLA°

1

Loving in truth, and fain in verse my love to show,
That she, dear she, might take some pleasure of my pain,
Pleasure might cause her read, reading might make her know,
Knowledge might pity win, and pity grace obtain,
I sought fit words to paint the blackest face of woe, 5
Studying inventions fine, her wits to entertain.
Oft turning others' leaves, to see if thence would flow
Some fresh and fruitful showers upon my sunburnt brain.
But words came halting forth, wanting Invention's stay;
Invention, Nature's child, fled step-dame Study's 10
blows;
And others' feet still seemed but strangers in my way.
Thus great with child to speak, and helpless in my throes,
Biting my truant pen, beating myself for spite:
"Fool!" said my Muse to me, "look in thy heart, and write."

347–348 **Nil habet, etc.** Bitter poverty has no sharper pang than this, that it makes men ridiculous (Juvenal's *Satires*) 350 **Thraso,** a braggart warrior in *The Eunuch* of Terence 354 **Buchanan,** George (1506–1582), a Scottish miscellaneous writer 361 **her mother Poesy's,** i.e., the art of fiction in general, not just verse 376 **Bembus,** Pietro Bembo (1470–1547), Italian writer, ecclesiatic, and humanist 373 **Scaliger,** Julius Caesar Scaliger, Italian physician and scholar (1484–1558), best known for his philosophical and scientific writings 380 **Clauserus,** Conrad Clauser (1520?–1611?), famous German scholar; he translated Lucius Annaeus Cornutus, Roman stoic philosopher of first century A.D. 384 **Quid non?** What not? 387 **Landino,** Cristoforo Landino (1424–1504), Italian humanist

397 **libertino patre natus,** born of a free (nonslave) father **Herculea proles,** a descendant of Hercules 398 **Si . . . possunt.** If my poems (songs) may be of any help. The quotation is from Vergil's *Aeneid*, Book IX 405 **Mome,** blockhead, fool 406 **Momus of Poetry,** the personification of criticism 407 **Midas,** in Greek mythology, king of Phrygia. He was given ass's ears by Apollo for preferring, in a contest, the music of Pan to Apollo's 409 **rhymed . . . Ireland.** According to popular legend, Irish bards could cause death through their song **Astrophel and Stella.** The words mean star-lover and star; they are poetic names respectively for Sidney and the lady addressed, usually identified with Penelope Devereaux, who married Lord Rich in 1580

5

It is most true, that eyes are formed to serve
The inward light: and that the heavenly part
Ought to be king, from whose rules who do swerve,
Rebels to Nature, strive for their own smart.
5 It is most true, what we call *Cupid's* dart,
An image is, which for ourselves we carve;
And, fools, adore in temple of our heart,
Till that good God make Church and Churchman
    starve.
True, that true Beauty Virtue is indeed,
10 Whereof this Beauty can be but a shade,
Which elements with mortal mixture breed:
True, that on earth we are but pilgrims made,
And should in soul up to our country move:
True, and yet true that I must Stella love.

31

With how sad steps, O Moon, thou climb'st the skies!
How silently, and with how wan a face!
What, may it be that even in heavenly place
That busy archer° his sharp arrows tries?
5 Sure, if that long-with-love-acquainted eyes
Can judge of love, thou feel'st a lover's case.
I read it in thy looks; thy languished grace,
To me that feel the like, thy state descries.
Then, even of fellowship, O Moon, tell me,
10 Is constant love deemed there but want of wit?
Are beauties there as proud as here they be?
Do they above love to be loved, and yet
Those lovers scorn whom that love doth possess?
Do they call virtue there ungratefulness?

39

Come, Sleep! O Sleep, the certain knot of peace,
The baiting-place° of wit, the balm of woe,
The poor man's wealth, the prisoner's release,
The indifferent judge between the high and low;
5 With shield of proof shield me from out the prease°
Of those fierce darts Despair at me doth throw;
Oh make in me those civil wars to cease.
I will good tribute pay, if thou do so.
Take thou of me smooth pillows, sweetest bed,
10 A chamber deaf to noise and blind to light,
A rosy garland and a weary head;
And if these things, as being thine by right,
Move not thy heavy grace, thou shalt in me,
Livelier than elsewhere, Stella's image see.

41

Having this day my horse, my hand, my lance
Guided so well that I obtain'd the prize,°
Both by the judgment of the English eyes
And of some sent from that sweet enemy, France;
5 Horsemen my skill in horsemanship advance,

Town folks my strength; a daintier judge applies
His praise to slight which from good use° doth rise;
Some lucky wits impute it but to chance;
Others, because of both sides I do take
My blood from them who did excell in this,°   10
Think Nature me a man-at-arms did make.
How far they shot awry! The true cause is,
Stella look'd on, and from her heav'nly face
Sent forth thy beams which made so fair my race.

50

Stella, the fullness of my thoughts of thee
Cannot be stayed within my panting breast,
But they do swell and struggle forth of me
Till that in words thy figure be expressed;
And yet, as soon as they so forméd be,   5
According to my lord Love's own behest,
With sad eyes I their weak proportion see
To portrait that which in this world is best.
So that I cannot choose but write my mind,
And cannot choose but put out what I write,   10
While these poor babes their death in birth do find;
And now my pen these lines had dashéd quite
But that they stopped his fury from the same
Because their fore-front bare sweet Stella's name.
(1591)

ROBERT GREENE
1560?–1592

Robert Greene was characteristically Elizabethan in the paradox of his character: he was a scholar and a vagabond, a sinner and somewhat of a Puritan, raw and unrestrained in experience but frequently charming and delicate in his writings. He had extensive academic training at Oxford and Cambridge and received M.A. degrees from both universities. His first university contact was with Cambridge, where he went at an early age from his birthplace in Norwich. After having taken his first degree, he traveled in Italy and Spain. Returning to London, Greene spent the third and last decade of his short life in vagabonding and furious writing. Unlike many of his contemporaries, he seems to have been equally gifted in prose, verse, and drama. He died as he had lived, in poverty and disrepute, with only strangers at his bedside.

In his dramas as in his other writing, Greene is a follower rather than an innovator, but his contributions to the development of the Elizabethan drama are considerable, for he popularized certain devices and elements that were borrowed by Shakespeare and later dramatists. Since most of his plays were not printed

---

Sonnet 31   4 **busy archer,** Cupid   Sonnet 39   2 baiting-place, place of refreshment   5 **prease,** press, crowd   Sonnet 41   2 **prize,** an actual tournament in the summer of 1581

7 **use,** experience   9–10 **Others, because . . . in this,** because my ancestors on both sides were distinguished in the tournament

until after his death in 1592, it is difficult to determine the order of their composition. The first seems to have been the heroic play *Orlando Furioso* (1588?), the material for which he took from Ariosto. To Marlowe he was indebted for at least one dramatic suggestion: Greene's *Alphonsus, King of Aragon* (1588) followed Marlowe's *Tamburlaine;* but the direction of influence between Greene's *Friar Bacon and Friar Bungay* (1589) and Marlowe's *Dr. Faustus* in their respective magic plots has not been established with certainty. *Friar Bacon and Friar Bungay,* probably Greene's best-known play, bears a striking resemblance to *Dr. Faustus,* but it is not necessary to suppose that Greene therefore borrowed liberally from Marlowe's most famous drama. Greene's pseudo-historical play, *James IV,* is especially interesting for his use of an acted prologue and a definite enveloping action.

Greene's prose may be divided into two general groups: his romances and his realistic pamphlets. Of the first type his *Euphues' Censure to Philautus* (1587) reveals a traditional debt to Lyly. *Pandosto* (1588) is the romance of the lost princess Fawnia, her ultimate recovery, and her marriage to Prince Dorastus; it was this story that Shakespeare took as the basis for *The Winter's Tale.*

But Greene's romances show only one aspect of his literary interest; as a prose realist he is even better known. The Puritan side of Greene displays itself in his personal pamphlets as well as in his exposés of London roguery. In the first group the note of repentance is uppermost, while in the second the avowed objective is to warn honest men by revealing the trickery of rascals. *The Mourning Garment* (1590) has a prodigal-son note, and the *Groatsworth of Wit Bought with a Million of Repentance* (1592) and *The Repentance of Robert Greene* (1592) are definitely autobiographical and confessional. His *Defence of Cony-catching, Disputation between a He-cony-catcher and a She-cony-catcher,* and *The Black Book's Messenger* are vivid examples of Tudor literature about vagabondage.

from A NOTABLE DISCOVERY° OF COSENAGE°

THE ART OF CONY-CATCHING

There be requisite effectually to act the art of cony-catching° three several parties: the setter,° the verser, and the barnacle. The nature of the setter is to draw any person familiarly to drink with him, which person they call the cony, and their method is according to the man they aim at; if a gentleman, merchant, or apprentice, the cony is the more easily caught, in that they are soon induced to play, and therefore I omit the circumstance which they use in catching of them. And for because the poor country farmer or yeoman is the [10] mark which they most of all shoot at, who they know comes not empty to the term,° I will discover the means they put in practice to bring in some honest, simple and ignorant men to their purpose.

The cony-catchers, appareled like honest civil gentlemen, or good fellows, with a smooth face, as if butter would not melt in their mouths, after dinner when the clients are come from Westminster Hall° and are at leisure to walk up and down Paul's,° Fleetstreet, Holborn, the Strand, and such common haunted places, [20] where these cosening companions attend only to spy out a prey; who as soon as they see a plain country fellow well and cleanly appareled, either in a coat of homespun russet, or of frieze, as the time° requires, and a side pouch° at his side, "There is a cony," saith one.

At that word out flies the setter, and overtaking the man, begins to salute him thus: "Sir, God save you, you are welcome to London, how doth all our good friends in the country, I hope they be all in health?"

The countryman seeing a man so courteous he [30] knows not, half in a brown study at this strange salutation, perhaps makes him this answer: "Sir, all our friends in the country are well, thanks be to God, but truly I know you not, you must pardon me."

"Why, sir," saith the setter, guessing by his tongue° what countryman he is, "are you not such a countryman?"

If he say yes, then he creeps upon him closely. If he say no, then straight the setter comes over him thus: "In good sooth, sir, I know you by your face and have [40] been in your company before; I pray you, if without offence, let me crave your name, and the place of your abode."

The simple man straight tells him where he dwells, his name, and who be his next neighbors, and what gentlemen dwell about him.

After he hath learned all of him, then he comes over his fallows° kindly: "Sir, though I have been somewhat bold to be inquisitive of your name, yet hold me excused, for I took you for a friend of mine; but since by [50] mistaking I have made you slack° your business, we'll drink a quart of wine, or a pot of ale, together."

If the fool be so ready as to go, then the cony is caught; but if he smack° the setter, and smells a rat by his clawing, and will not drink with him, then away goes the setter, and discourseth to the verser° the name of the man, the parish he dwells in, and what gentle-

---

A Notable Discovery of Cosenage **Discovery,** disclosure, exposé **Cosenage,** fraud 1–2 **cony-catching,** cheating, swindling. A cony is a rabbit and hence a dupe, simpleton, easy victim 2 **setter,** thieves' cant for the rogue who hunts the victims and brings them in. The functions of the verser and the barnacle appear later

12 **term,** the stated period, usually four times a year, during which the London law courts were in session; these drew many countrymen to the city 18 **Westminster Hall,** the public hall in the west end of London in which the court held its sessions 19 **Paul's,** St. Paul's Church in the heart of London; its broad nave was a popular promenade. The other names are those of prominent London thoroughfares 24 **time,** i.e., the seasons. *Frieze* was woolen cloth, *russet* of lighter weight and texture, but both were homespun and so marked out the countryman 25 **side pouch,** his pocketbook, worn attached to the belt 35 **tongue,** dialect, by which the cheat could determine his victim's native shire 48 **fallows,** plowed land; the figure suggests that having given his victim a preliminary plowing, the rogue cultivates him further 51 **slack,** neglect 54 **smack,** detect by smelling; cf. the phrase following 56 **verser,** cardsharper

men are his near neighbors. With that away goes he, and crossing the man at some turning, meets him full in the face, and greets him thus:

"What, goodman Barton, how fare all our friends about you? You are well met, I have the wine for you, you are welcome to town."

The poor countryman, hearing himself named by a man he knows not, marvels, and answers that he knows him not, and craves pardon.

"Not me, goodman Barton, have you forgot me? Why, I am such a man's kinsman, your neighbor not far off; how doth this or that good gentleman my friend? Good Lord, that I should be out of your remembrance! I have been at your house divers times."

"Indeed, sir," saith the farmer, "are you such a man's kinsman? Surely, sir, if you had not challenged acquaintance of me, I should never have known you. I have clean forgot you, but I know the good gentleman your cousin well, he is my very good neighbor."

"And for his sake," saith the verser, "we'll drink afore we part."

Haply the man thanks him, and to the wine or ale they go. Then ere they part, they make him a cony, and so ferret-claw° him at cards that they leave him as bare of money as an ape of a tail.

Thus have the filthy fellows their subtle fetches° to draw on poor men to fall into their cosening practises. Thus like consuming moths of the commonwealth they prey upon the ignorance of such plain souls as measure all by their own honesty, not regarding either conscience or the fatal revenge that's threatened for such idle and licentious persons, but do employ all their wits to overthrow such as with their handy-thrift satisfy their hearty thirst, they preferring cosenage before labor, and choosing an idle practice before any honest form of good living.

Well, to the method again of taking up their conies. If the poor countryman smoke them still, and will not stoop unto either of their lures, then one, either the verser, or the setter, or some of their crew, for there is a general fraternity betwixt them, steppeth before the cony as he goeth, and letteth drop twelve pence in the highway, that of force the cony must see it. The countryman, spying the shilling, maketh not dainty, for *quis nisi mentis inops oblatum respuit aurum*,° but stoopeth very mannerly and taketh it up. Then one of the conycatchers behind crieth half part, and so challengeth half of his finding. The countryman, content, offereth to change the money. "Nay faith, friend," saith the verser, "'tis ill luck to keep found money; we'll go spend it in a pottle° of wine"—or in a breakfast, dinner, or supper, as the time of day requires.

If the cony say he will not, then answers the verser,

"Spend my part." If still the cony refuse, he taketh half and away.

If they spy the countryman to be of a having and covetous mind, then have they a further policy to draw him on; another that knoweth the place of his abode meeteth him and saith, "Sir, well met, I have run hastily to overtake you. I pray you, dwell you not in Darbyshire, in such a village?"

"Yes, marry, do I, friend," saith the cony.

Then replies the verser,° "Truly, sir, I have a suit to you, I am going out of town, and must send a letter to the parson of your parish. You shall not refuse to do a stranger such a favor as to carry it him. Haply, as men may in time meet, it may lie in my lot to do you as good a turn; and for your pains I will give you twelve pence."

The poor cony in mere simplicity saith, "Sir, I'll do so much for you with all my heart; where is your letter?"

"I have it not, good sir, ready written, but may I entreat you to step into some tavern or alehouse? We'll drink the while, and I will write but a line or two."

At this the cony stoops, and for greediness of the money, and upon courtesy, goes with the setter into the tavern. As they walk, they meet the verser, and then they all three go into the tavern together.

See, gentlemen, what great logicians these conycatchers be, that have such rhetorical persuasions to induce the poor countryman to his confusion, and what variety of villainy they have to strip the poor farmer of his money.

Well, imagine the cony is in the tavern, then sits down the verser and saith to the setter, "What, sirra! Wilt thou give me a quart of wine, or shall I give thee one?" "We'll drink a pint," saith the setter, "and play a game of cards for it, respecting more the sport than the loss." "Content," quoth the verser, "go call for a pair."° And while he is gone to fetch them, he saith to the cony, "You shall see me fetch over my young master for a quart of wine finely. But this you must do for me; when I cut the cards, as I will not cut above five off, mark then, of all the greatest pack, which is undermost, and when I bid you call a card for me, name that, and you shall see we'll make him pay for a quart of wine straight."

"Truly," saith the cony, "I am no great player at cards, and I do not well understand your meaning."

"Why," saith he, "it is thus: I will play at mumchance,° or decoy,° that he shall shuffle the cards and I will cut. Now either of us must call a card; you shall cut for me, and he for himself, and whose card comes first wins. Therefore, when I have cut the cards, then

---

81 **ferret-claw**, a ferret is a weasel trained to hunt rabbits or conies   83 **fetches**, tricks   101–2 **quis nisi, etc.** Nobody is so weak of mind that he will spurn proffered money   108 **pottle**, pot or tankard; originally a liquid measure equal to two quarts

120 **verser.** Greene meant to write *setter*   149 **a pair**, a pack; called *pair* because the cards belonged together in a set   159–60 **mum-chance**, a gambling game played silently   **decoy**, a fashionable card game

mark the nethermost of the greatest heap, that I set°
upon the cards which I cut off, and always call that for
me.''

"Oh, now," saith the cony, "I understand you. Let
me alone, I warrant I'll fit your turn."

With that in comes the setter with his cards, and
170 asketh at what game they shall play. "Why," saith the
verser, "at a new game called mum-chance, that hath
no policy° nor knavery, but plain as a pike-staff. You
shall shuffle and I'll cut, you shall call a card, and this
honest man, a stranger almost to us both, shall call
another for me, and which of our cards comes first
shall win." "Content," saith the setter, "for that's but
mere hazard." And so he shuffles the cards, and the
verser cuts off some four cards, and then taking up the
heap to set upon them giveth the cony a glance of the
180 bottom card of that heap, and saith, "Now, sir, call for
me."

The cony, to blind the setter's eyes, asketh as
though he were not made privy to the game, "What
shall I cut?"

"What card?" saith the verser. "Why, what you
will, either heart, spade, club, or diamond, coat-card°
or other."

"Oh, is it so?" saith the cony. "Why, then, you
shall have the four of hearts"—which was the card he
190 had a glance of.

"And," saith the setter (holding the cards in his
hand and turning up the uppermost card, as if he knew
not well the game), "I'll have the knave of trumps."
"Nay," saith the verser, "there is no trump, you may
call what card you will." Then saith he, "I'll have the
ten of spades." With that he draws, and the four of
hearts comes first. "Well," saith the setter, "'tis but
hazard, mine might have come as well as yours, five is
up, I fear not the set."° So they shuffle and cut, but the
200 verser wins.

"Well," saith the setter, "no butter will cleave on
my bread. What, not one draught among five? Drawer,
a fresh pint! I'll have another bout with you.—But, sir,
I believe," saith he to the cony, "you see some card,
that it goes so cross on my side."

"I?" saith the cony, "Nay, I hope you think not so
of me; 'tis but hazard and chance, for I am but a mere
stranger unto the game. As I am an honest man, I
never saw it before."

210 Thus this simple cony closeth up smoothly to take
the verser's part, only for greediness to have him win
the wine. "Well," answers the setter, "then I'll have
one cast more." And to it they go, but he loseth all,
and beginneth to chafe in this manner: "Were it not,"
quoth he, "that I care not for a quart of wine, I could
swear as many oaths for anger as there be hairs on my
head. Why should not my luck be as good as yours,

and fortune favor me as well as you? What, not one
called card in ten cuts? I'll forswear the game
forever."   220

"What, chafe not, man," saith the verser. "Seeing
we have your quart of wine, I'll show you the game."
And with that discourseth° all to him, as if he knew it
not. The setter, as simply as if the knave were ignorant, saith, "Aye, marry, I think so! You must needs
win, when he knows what card to call. I might have
played long enough before I had got a set."

"Truly," says the cony, "'tis a pretty game, for 'tis
not possible for him to lose that cuts the cards. I warrant the other that shuffles may lose Saint Peter's cope 230
if he had it. Well, I'll carry this home with me into the
country, and win many a pot of ale with it."

"A fresh pint!" saith the verser. "And then we'll
away. But seeing, sir, you are going homeward, I'll
learn you a trick worth the noting, that you shall win
many a pot with in the winter nights."

With that he culls out the four knaves, and pricks°
one in the top, one in the midst, and one in the bottom.
"Now, sir," saith he, "you see these three knaves
apparently; thrust them down with your hand, and cut 240
where you will, and though they be so far asunder I'll
make them all come together."

"I pray you, let's see that trick," saith the cony.
"Methinks it should be impossible."

So the verser draws, and all the three knaves come
in one heap. This he doth once or twice, then the cony
wonders at it and offers him a pint of wine to teach it
him. "Nay," saith the verser. "I'll do it for thanks;
and therefore mark me where you have taken out the
four knaves, lay two together above and draw up one 250
of them that it may be seen, then prick the other in the
midst and the third in the bottom, so when any cuts,
cut he never so warily, three knaves must of force
come together, for the bottom knave is cut to lie upon
both the upper knaves."

"Aye, marry," saith the setter, "but then the three
knaves you showed come not together."

"Truth," saith the verser. "But one among a
thousand mark not that; it requires a quick eye, a sharp
wit, and a reaching head to spy at the first."   260

"Now gramercy,° sir, for this trick," saith the cony.
"I'll domineer with this amongst my neighbors."

Thus doth the verser and the setter feign friendship
to the cony, offering him no show of cosenage, nor
once to draw him in for a pint of wine, the more to
shadow° their villainy.

But now begins the sport. As thus they sit tippling,
comes the barnacle and thrusts open the door, looking
into the room where they are, and as one bashful steppeth back again and saith, "I cry you mercy, gentle- 270
men, I thought a friend of mine had been here. Pardon

---

164 **set,** bet 172 **policy,** trick 186 **coat-card,** face card 198–99 **five is up
. . . set.** With five cuts agreed upon, he still hopes to win the wager

223 **discourseth,** discloses, reveals 237 **pricks,** thrusts 261 **gramercy,** many
thanks 266 **shadow,** conceal

my boldness." "No harm," saith the verser. "I pray you drink a cup of wine with us, and welcome." So in comes the barnacle, and taking the cup drinks to the cony, and then saith, "What, at cards, gentlemen? Were it not I should be offensive to the company, I would play for a pint till my friend come that I look for." "Why, sir," saith the verser, "if you will sit down you shall be taken up for a quart of wine." 280 "With all my heart," saith the barnacle. "What will you play at, primero,° primo visto, sant, one and thirty, new cut, or what shall be the game?" "Sir," saith the verser, "I am but an ignorant man at cards, and I see you have them at your fingers' end. I will play with you at a game wherein can be no deceit; it is called mum-chance at cards, and it is thus: you shall shuffle the cards, and I will cut, you shall call one, and this honest country yeoman shall call a card for me, and which of our cards comes first shall win. Here you see 290 is no deceit, and this I'll play."

"No, truly," saith the cony, "methinks there can be no great craft in this."

"Well," saith the barnacle, "for a pint of wine have at you." So they play as before, five up,° and the verser wins.

"This is hard luck," saith the barnacle, "and I believe the honest man spies some card in the bottom; and therefore I'll make this, always to prick° the bottom card." "Content," saith the verser, and the cony to 300 cloak the matter saith, "Sir, you offer me injury to think that I can call a card, when I neither touch them, shuffle, cut, nor draw them." "Ah, sir," saith the barnacle, "give losers leave to speak."

Well, to it they go again, and then the barnacle, knowing the game best, by chopping° a card wins two of the five, but lets the verser win the set; then in a chafe he sweareth 'tis but his ill luck, and he can see no deceit in it, and therefore he will play twelve pence a cut.

310 The verser is content, and wins twos or threes of the barnacle, whereat he chafes, and saith, "I came hither in an ill hour; but I will win my money again, or lose all in my purse."

With that he draws out a purse with some three or four pounds and claps it on the board. The verser asketh the cony secretly by signs if he will be his half; he says, "Aye," and straight seeks for his purse. Well, the barnacle shuffles the cards thoroughly, and the verser cuts as before. The barnacle when he hath 320 drawn one card saith, "I'll either win something or lose something, therefore I'll vie and revie° every card at my pleasure, till either yours or mine come out, and therefore twelve pence upon this card, my card comes first for twelve pence." "No," saith the verser. "Aye," saith the cony, "and I durst hold twelve pence more." "Why, I hold you," saith the barnacle, and so

they vie and revie till some ten shillings be on the stake; and then next comes forth the verser's card, that the cony called, and so the barnacle loseth.

Well, this flesheth° the cony; the sweetness of gain 330 maketh him frolic, and no man is more ready to vie and revie than he. Thus for three or four times the barnacle loseth; at last, to whet on the cony, he striketh his chopped card, and winneth a goodly stake. "Away with the witch!" cries the barnacle. "I hope the cards will turn at last."

"Aye, much!" thinketh the cony. "'Twas but a chance that you asked so right, to ask one of the five that was cut off. I am sure there was forty to one on my side, and I'll have you on the lurch anon." So still they 340 vie and revie, and for once that the barnacle wins, the cony gets five.

At last when they mean to shave the cony clean of all his coin, the barnacle chafeth, and upon a pawn° borroweth some money of the tapster and swears he will vie it to the uttermost. Then thus he chops his card to cross-bite° the cony. He first looks on the bottom card, and shuffles often, but still keeping that bottom card which he knows to be uppermost; then sets he down the cards, and the verser to encourage the cony 350 cut off but three cards, whereof the barnacle's card must needs be the uppermost. Then shows he the bottom card of the other heap cut off, to the cony, and sets it upon the barnacle's card which he knows, so that of force the card that was laid uppermost must come first; and then the barnacle calls that card. They draw a card, and then the barnacle vies and the countryman vies upon him; for this is the law, as often as one vies or revies, the other must see° it, else he loseth the stake. Well, at last the barnacle plies it so that 360 perhaps he vies more money than the cony hath in his purse. The cony upon this, knowing his card is the third or fourth card, and that he hath forty to one against the barnacle, pawns his rings if he have any, his sword, his cloak, or else what he hath about him, to maintain the vie, and when he laughs in his sleeve, thinking he hath fleeced the barnacle of all, then the barnacle's card comes forth, and strikes such a cold humor unto his heart that he sits as a man in a trance, not knowing what to do, and sighing while his heart is 370 ready to break, thinking on the money that he hath lost.

Perhaps the man is very simple and patient, and, whatsoever he thinks, for fear goes his way quiet with his loss, while the cony-catchers laugh and divide the spoil, and being out of the doors, poor man, goes to his lodging with a heavy heart, pensive and sorrowful, but too late, for perhaps his state did depend° on that money, and so he, his wife, his children, and his family are brought to extreme misery. 380

Another, perhaps more hardy and subtle, smokes°

281 **primero, etc.,** card games popular at the time   294 **five up,** as earlier, the number of points needed to win   298 **prick,** choose   305 **chopping,** changing   321 **vie and revie,** wage· and raise the wager

330 **flesheth,** arouses (by giving a taste of blood)   344 **pawn,** pledge   347 **cross-bite,** cheat   359 **see,** meet the bet   378 **his state did depend.** He needed the money to meet a mortgage or other payment on his property   381 **smokes,** detects

the cony-catchers, and smelleth cosenage, and saith they shall not have his money so; but they answer him with braves,° and though he bring them before an officer, yet the knaves are so favored that the man never recovers his money, and yet he° is let slip unpunished.

Thus are the poor conies robbed by these baseminded caterpillars; thus are serving men oft enticed to play and lose all; thus are prentices induced to be conies, and so are cosened of their masters' money; yea, young gentlemen, merchants, and others, are fetched in by these damnable rakehells, a plague as ill as hell, which is, present loss of money, and ensuing misery. A lamentable case in England, when such vipers are suffered to breed and are not cut off with the sword of justice....

(1591)

EDMUND SPENSER
1552–1599

Edmund Spenser was part of the worlds of city, court, and university. Born in London in 1522, the son of John Spenser, a clothmaker, he first attended the Merchant Taylors' School. He spent the years 1569–1576 at Cambridge, coming as a "sizar" (poor scholar). He was influenced by the strong Puritan atmosphere of the University and by his friendship with Gabriel Harvey, Cambridge don and humanist, who interested Spenser in theories of poetry and encouraged him to experiment with Latin and Greek accentual systems in English verse. After taking an M.A. degree, Spenser returned to London and served as secretary to several prominent men, the last of which was Lord Grey of Wilton, Lord Deputy of Ireland. Spenser was active during this time in the progressive literary society Areopagus, which was chiefly interested in promoting a new English poetry, and contributed The Shepheards Calender (1579) to the movement. In 1580 he went to Ireland with Lord Grey and eventually held a number of civil positions there. He returned to England in 1589 to complete the first three books of The Faerie Queene, which were published in 1590. After a courtship commemorated in the sonnet sequence Amoretti, he married Elizabeth Boyle in 1594 in Ireland. In 1595 he journeyed to London with three more books of The Faerie Queene but failed to gain the political advancement he had hoped for at Queen Elizabeth's court. In 1596, in addition to some shorter pieces, the first three books of The Faerie Queene appeared again, somewhat altered, along with

384 **braves,** defiances   386 **he,** the rogue

the second three (the "Mutability Cantos" were first included only in the edition of 1609). In 1597 he returned to Ireland once more. A year later, his home there, Kilcolman Castle, burned to the ground in the course of Tyrone's Rebellion; in December he left for London to make an official report on the uprising. He died suddenly in January 1599 at a London inn. He is buried near Chaucer in Westminster Abbey.

from THE FAERIE QUEENE

Although Spenser's reputation and popularity through the centuries have fluctuated, he has always exerted a great formative influence on poets—on Keats, for example, and Tennyson. Certainly Spenser deserves Lamb's accolade "the poet's poet," but it would be wrong to conclude that he is therefore inaccessible to the common reader. After all, his primary appeal, like Chaucer's and Malory's, remains narrative.

Spenser's long poem, The Faerie Queene, is neither a series of sensuously detailed medieval tableaux nor an unfinished allegorical romance; and the well-known epic resemblance really applies to its superficial architecture alone. How, then, should The Faerie Queene be characterized as a special instance of narrative poetry? In its illogical, dreamlike progression it seems first of all to have certain conceptual affinities, which C. S. Lewis has designated "polyphonic" or "interwoven" in narrative character, with a species of antique myth and medieval tale. The work, moreover, contains all the stuff of elemental drama—of, say, the morality play—and it stipulates an unmediated, prerational response to the events as they occur. The sophisticated reader must return to that level of consciousness where he or she literally *believes* in the wicked magicianship of Archimago much as a child believes in witches. A powerful imaginative creation like Archimago cannot be reduced to the neat interpretive pigeonhole, "personification of Hypocrisy." He must be allowed to reinduce a kind of universal childish fear in the mind, the fear of something dreadful and malign. And so what, then, if he first appears in a narrative sequence, drops out for a time while Spenser unaccountably becomes involved with some new set of characters and adventures, and at last, just as unaccountably, appears again? This inconclusive quality of narrative progression is just the point: Archimago, like the devil, must be viewed as a permanent entity of human psychology; he is *always* there, his pranks *never* concluded.

Spenser's personalized embodiments of the forces of negation and sensual threat in The Faerie Queene cannot be equated with academic abstractions of sin. They are vital, symbolic, and dramatic distillations from universal experience, not the stick figures of simplistic moral allegory. No individual who has ever been as intensely involved as the Redcrosse Knight with the eternal problem of coping with life could doubt the profound psychological realism that accompanies his capitulation to the flesh, his subsequent agonies of shame and despair, and his final spiritual rehabilitation. Appropriately, Spenser's account of the Redcrosse Knight may best exemplify one of the most important themes in *The Faerie Queene*—the evaluative discrepancy between true and false choice. It is only when the hero has arduously acquired the capacity for moral insight that he can "see" the real ugliness beneath Duessa's alluring external appearance and deceitful impersonations:

> . . . that witch they disaraid. . . .
> . . . .
> Ne spared they to strip her naked all.
> Then when they had despoiled her tire and call,
> Such as she was, their eyes might her behold,
> That her misshapen parts did them appall;
> A loathly, wrinkled hag, ill favoured, old,
> Whose secret filth good manners biddeth not be
>   told.
>
> (I, viii, 46)

After his humiliating captivity under Duessa and the long ritual of purgation, moreover, the Redcrosse Knight can truly apprehend his radiant Una for the first time and appreciate her worth. By profiting from painful experience, he entitles himself not only to her love but to reinstatement in Gloriana's crusade of moral idealism.

Spenser's allegory of the Redcrosse Knight may suggest, in addition, a certain narrative method. He seems to conceive of time as a continuum in which people perpetually fall, reassert themselves, seek new adventures, and confront the same old lures in more sophisticated guises. A similar generative principle appears to provide the basic curve of action for every book of *The Faerie Queene;* it accounts, further, for such recurrent staples of "plot" as the dramatically externalized inner conflict or confusion between lust and love (e.g., Duessa versus Una, Acrasia versus Alma) and incarceration in dens of sensuality (e.g., the Bower of Bliss, the House of Busirane). Evidently, the characters in this imagined world must learn for themselves again and again.

A LETTER OF THE AUTHORS

Expounding his whole intention in the course of this worke: which, for that it giveth great light to the reader, for the better understanding is hereunto annexed.

To the Right Noble and Valorous SIR WALTER RALEIGH, KNIGHT;

Lord Wardein of the Stanneryes, and Her Maiesties Liefetenaunt of the County of Cornewayll.

Sir, knowing how doubtfully all allegories may be construed, and this booke of mine which I have entituled the *Faery Queene*, being a continued allegory, or darke conceit,° I have thought good, as well for avoyding of gealous opinions and misconstructions, as also for your better light in reading thereof, (being so by you commanded) to discover unto you the general intention and meaning, which in the whole course thereof I have fashioned, without expressing of any particular purposes, or by accidents° therein oc- 10 casioned. The generall end therefore of all the booke is to fashion a gentleman or noble person in vertuous and gentle discipline: which for that I conceived shoulde be most plausible° and pleasing, being coloured with an historicall fiction, the which the most part of men delight to read, rather for variety of matter then for profite of the ensample, I chose the historye of King Arthure, as most fitte for the excellency of his person, being made famous by many men's former workes, and also furthest from the daunger of envy, and suspi- 20 tion of present time. In which I have followed all the antique Poets historicall: first Homere, who in the Persons of Agamemnon and Ulysses hath ensampled a good governor and a vertuous man, the one in his Ilias, the other in his Odysseis; then Virgil, whose like intention was to doe in the person of Aeneas; after him Ariosto comprised them both in his Orlando: and lately Tasso dissevered them againe, and formed both parts in two persons, namely that part which they in Philosophy call Ethice, or vertues of a private man, 30 coloured in his Rinaldo; the other named Politice in his God fredo. By ensample of which excellente poets, I labour to pourtraict in Arthure, before he was king, the image of a brave knight, perfected in the twelve private morall vertues, as Aristotle hath devised; the which is the purpose of these first twelve bookes: which if I finde to be well accepted, I may be perhaps encoraged to frame the other part of polliticke vertues in his person, after that hee came to be king.

To some, I know, this methode will seeme dis- 40 pleasaunt, which had rather have good discipline delivered plainly in way of precepts, or sermoned at large, as they use, then thus clowdily enwrapped in Allegoricall devises. But such, me seeme, should be satisfide with the use of these dayes, seeing all things accounted by their showes, and nothing esteemed of, that is not delightfull and pleasing to commune sence. For this cause is Xenophon preferred before Plato, for that the one, in the exquisite depth of his judgement, formed a commune welth,° such as it should be; but the 50 other in the person of Cyrus, and the Persians, fashioned a governement, such as might best be: so much more profitable and gratious is doctrine by en-

The Faerie Queene 4 **conceit,** comparison   10 **by accidents,** incidental matters   14 **plausible,** acceptable   50 **commune welth,** commonwealth; the allusion is to Xenophon's *Cyropaedia,* a political romance

sample, then by rule. So haue I laboured to doe in the person of Arthure: whome I conceive, after his long education by Timon, to whom he was by Merlin delivered to be brought up, so soone as he was borne of the Lady Igrayne, to have seene in a dream or vision the Faery Queene, with whose excellent beauty ravished, he awaking resolved to seeke her out; and so being by Merlin armed, and by Timon throughly instructed, he went to seeke her forth in Faerye land. In that Faery Queene I meane glory in my generall intention, but in my particular I conceive the most excellent and glorious person of our soveraine the Queene, and her kingdome in Faery land. And yet, in some places els, I doe otherwise shadow her.° For considering she beareth two persons, the one of a most royall Queene or Empresse, the other of a most vertuous and beautifull Lady, this latter part in some places I doe expresse in Belphoebe, fashioning her name according to your owne excellent conceipt of Cynthia (Phoebe and Cynthia being both names of Diana). So in the person of Prince Arthure I sette forth magnificence in particular, which vertue for that (according to Aristotle and the rest) it is the perfection of all the rest, and conteineth in it them all, therefore in the whole course I mention the deedes of Arthure applyable to that vertue, which I write of in that booke. But of the xii. other vertues, I make xii. other knights the patrones, for the more variety of the history: of which these three bookes contayn three. The first of the knight of the Redcrosse, in whome I expresse holynes: The seconde of Sir Guyon, in whome I sette forth temperaunce: The third of Britomartis, a lady knight, in whome I picture chastity. But, because the beginning of the whole worke seemeth abrupte, and as depending upon other antecedents, it needs that ye know the occasion of these three knights' severall adventures. For the method of a poet historical is not such, as of an historiographer. For an historiographer discourseth of affayres orderly as they were donne, accounting as well the times as the actions; but a poet trusteth into the middest,° even where it most concerneth him, and there recoursing to the thinges forepaste, and divining of thinges to come, maketh a pleasing analysis of all.

The beginning therefore of my history, if it were to be told by an historiographer, should be the twelfth booke, which is the last; where I devise that the Faery Queene kept her annuall feaste xii. dayes; uppon which xii. severall dayes, the occasions of the xii. severall adventures hapned, which, being undertaken by xii. severall knights, are in these xii. books severally handled and discoursed. The first was this. In the beginning of the feast, there presented him selfe a tall clownishe younge man, who, falling before the Queene of Faeries, desired a boone (as the manner then was) which during that feast she might not refuse: which

was that hee might have the atchievement of any adventure, which during that feaste should happen: that being graunted, he rested him on the floore, unfitte through his rusticity for a better place. Soone after entred a faire ladye in mourning weedes, riding on a white asse, with a dwarfe behind her leading a warlike steed, that bore the armes of a knight, and his speare in the dwarfes hand. Shee, falling before the Queene of Faeries, complayned that her father and mother, an ancient king and queene, had bene by an huge dragon many years shut up in a brasen castle, who thence suffred them not to yssew;° and therefore besought the Faery Queene to assygne her some one of her knights to take on him that exployt. Presently that clownish person, upstarting, desired that adventure: whereat the Queene much wondering, and the lady much gainesaying, yet he earnestly importuned his desire. In the end the lady told him, that unlesse that armour which she brought, would serve him (that is, the armour of a Christian man specified by Saint Paul, vi. Ephes.) that he could not succeed in that enterprise: which being forthwith put upon him, with dewe furnitures° thereunto, he seemed the goodliest man in al that company, and was well liked of the lady. And eftesoones° taking on him knighthood, and mounting on that straunge courser, he went forth with her on that adventure: where beginneth the first booke, viz.

A GENTLE KNIGHT WAS PRICKING
ON THE PLAYNE, ETC.

The second day there came in a palmer, bearing an infant with bloody hands, whose parents he complained to have bene slayn by an enchaunteresse called Acrasia; and therefore craved of the Faery Queene, to appoint him some knight to performe that adventure; which being assigned to Sir Guyon, he presently went forth with that same palmer: which is the beginning of the second booke, and the whole subject thereof. The third day there came in a groome, who complained before the Faery Queene, that a vile enchaunter, called Busirane, had in hand a most faire lady, called Amoretta, whom he kept in most grievous torment, because she would not yield him the pleasure of her body. Whereupon Sir Scudamour, the lover of that lady, presently tooke on him that adventure. But being unable to performe it by reason of the hard enchauntments, after long sorrow, in the end met with Britomartis, who succoured him, and reskewed his love.

But by occasion° hereof many other adventures are intermedled; but rather as accidents then intendments:° as the love of Britomart, the overthrow of Marinell, the misery of Florimell, the vertuousness of Bel-

67 **shadow her,** represent her allegorically   93–94 **into the middest.** This is the classical theory expressed in Horace's *Ars Poetica* in the phrase *in medias res*

120 **yssew,** issue   130–31 **furnitures,** articles to complete the equipment 132–33 **eftesoones,** forthwith   155 **by occasion,** incidentally   156 **intendments,** definite plan

phoebe, the lasciviousness of Hellenora, and many the
like.

    Thus much, Sir, I have briefly overronne, to direct
your understanding to the welhead of the history, that
from thence gathering the whole intention of the conceit ye may, as in a handfull, gripe al the discourse,
which otherwise may happily seeme tedious and confused. So, humbly craving the continuance of your
honorable favour towards me, and th'eternall establishment of your happines, I humbly take leave.

23. January, 1589.

Yours most humbly affectionate,

Ed. Spenser

from BOOK I

1

Lo I the man, whose Muse whilome° did maske,
As time her taught, in lowly Shepheards weeds,°
Am now enforst a far unfitter taske,
For trumpets sterne to chaunge mine Oaten reeds,°
And sing of Knights and Ladies gentle deeds;
Whose prayses having slept in silence long,
Me, all too meane, the sacred Muse° areeds°
To blazon broad emongst her learned throng:
Fierce warres and faithfull loves shall moralize my
   song.

2

Helpe then, O holy Virgin chiefe of nine,°
Thy weaker° Novice to performe thy will,
Lay forth out of thine everlasting scryne°
The antique rolles, which there lye hidden still,
Of Faerie knights and fairest *Tanaquill*,°
Whom that most noble Briton Prince° so long
Sought through the world, and suffered so much ill,
That I must rue his undeserved wrong:
O helpe thou my weake wit, and sharpen my dull tong.

3

And thou most dreaded impe° of highest *Jove*,
Faire *Venus* sonne, that with thy cruell dart
At that good knight so cunningly didst rove,°
That glorious fire it kindled in his hart,
Lay now thy deadly Heben° bow apart,
And with thy mother milde come to mine ayde:
Come both, and with you bring triumphant *Mart*,°
In loves and gentle jollities arrayd,
After his murdrous spoiles and bloudy rage allayd.

4

And with them eke, O Goddesse° heavenly bright,
Mirrour of grace and Majestie divine,
Great Lady of the greatest Isle, whose light
Like *Phoebus* lampe° throughout the world doth shine,
Shed thy faire beames into my feeble eyne,
And raise my thoughts too humble and too vile,°
To thinke of that true glorious type of thine,°
The argument of mine afflicted stile:°
The which to heare, vouchsafe, O dearest dred° a-
   while.

CANTO I

The Patron of true Holinesse,
  foule Errour doth defeate:
Hypocrisie him to entrappe,
  doth to his home entreate.

1

A Gentle Knight was pricking° on the plaine,
Ycladd in mightie armes and silver shielde,
Wherein old dints of deepe wounds did remaine,
The cruell markes of many' a bloudy fielde;
Yet armes till that time did he never wield:
His angry steede did chide his foming bitt,
As much disdayning to the curbe to yield:
Full jolly° knight he seemd, and faire did sitt,
As one for knightly giusts° and fierce encounters fitt.

2

But on his brest a bloudie Crosse he bore,
The deare remembrance of his dying Lord,
For whose sweete sake that glorious badge he wore,
And dead as living ever him ador'd:
Upon his shield the like was also scor'd,
For soveraine hope, which in his helpe he had:
Right faithfull true he was in deede and word,
But of his cheere° did seeme too solemne sad;
Yet nothing did he dread, but ever was ydrad.°

3

Upon a great adventure he was bond,
That greatest *Gloriana* to him gave,
That greatest Glorious Queene of *Faerie* lond,
To winne him worship, and her grace to have,
Which of all earthly things he most did crave;
And ever as he rode, his hart did earne°
To prove his puissance in battell brave
Upon his foe, and his new force to learne;
Upon his foe, a Dragon° horrible and stearne.

Book I   1 **whilome**, formerly   2 **Shepheards weeds**, an allusion to his authorship of *The Shepheardes Calender*   4 **trumpets . . . reeds**, respectively, the symbols of epic and of pastoral poetry   7 **sacred Muse**, Clio   **areeds**, appoints
10 **Virgin . . . nine**, Clio, the muse of history   11 **weaker**. The comparative is
here used as an intensive, too weak   12 **scryne**, shrine; here depository for historical rolls   14 **Tanaquill**, Queen Elizabeth   15 **Briton Prince**, King Arthur
19 **impe**, child; the allusion is to Cupid, son of Venus   21 **rove**, shoot with an
arrow; a term in archery   23 **Heben**, ebony—suggestive of deadliness
25 **Mart**, Mars, god of war and paramour of Venus

28 **Goddesse**, Elizabeth, frequently associated in contemporary literature with the
goddesses of classical mythology   31 **Phoebus lampe**, the sun   33 **vile**, lowly
34 **glorious . . . thine**, Gloriana, the Faerie Queene   35 **afflicted stile**, lowly pen
36 **dearest dred**, direst inspirer of awe   Canto I   1 **pricking**, spurring forth
8 **jolly**, bold   9 **giusts**, jousts   17 **cheere**, countenance   18 **ydrad**, dreaded,
feared   24 **earne**, yearn   27 **Dragon**, Sin

4

A lovely Ladie° rode him faire beside,
Upon a lowly Asse° more white then snow,
30 Yet she much whiter, but the same did hide
Under a vele, that wimpled° was full low,
And over all a blacke stole° she did throw,
As one that inly mournd: so was she sad,
And heavie sat upon her palfrey slow:
Seemed in heart some hidden care she had,
And by her in a line° a milke white lambe she lad.

5

So pure an innocent, as that same lambe,
She was in life and every vertuous lore,
And by descent from Royall lynage came
40 Of ancient Kings and Queenes, that had of yore
Their scepters stretcht from East to Westerne shore,
And all the world in their subjection held;
Till that infernall feend with foule uprore
Forwasted all their land, and them expeld:
Whom to avenge, she had this Knight from far
  compeld.

6

Behind her farre away a Dwarfe° did lag,
That lasie seemd in being ever last,
Or wearied with bearing of her bag
Of needments at his backe. Thus as they past,
50 The day with cloudes was suddeine overcast,
And angry *Jove* an hideous storme of raine
Did poure into his Lemans° lap so fast,
That every wight to shrowd it did constrain,
And this faire couple eke to shroud themselves were
  fain.

7

Enforst to seeke some covert nigh at hand,
A shadie grove not far away they spide,
That promist ayde the tempest to withstand:
Whose loftie trees yclad with sommers pride,
Did spred so broad, that heavens light did hide,
60 Not perceable with power of any starre:
And all within were pathes and alleies wide,
With footing worne, and leading inward farre:
Faire harbour that them seemes; so in they entred arre.

8

And foorth they passe, with pleasure forward led,
Joying to heare the birdes sweete harmony,
Which therein shrouded from the tempest dred,
Seemd in their song to scorne the cruell sky.
Much can they prayse the trees° so straight and hy,

9

The sayling Pine, the Cedar proud and tall,
The vine-prop Elme, the Poplar never dry,   70
The builder Oake, sole king of forrests all,
The Aspine good for staves, the Cypresse funerall.

9

The Laurell, meed° of mightie Conquerours
And Poets sage, the Firre that weepeth still,
The Willow worne of forlorne Paramours,
The Eugh° obedient to the benders will,
The Birch for shaftes, the Sallow° for the mill,
The Mirrhe sweete bleeding in the bitter wound,
The warlike Beech, the Ash for nothing ill,
The fruitful Olive, and the Platane° round,   80
The carver Holme,° the Maple seeldom inward sound.

10

Led with delight, they thus beguile the way,
Untill the blustring storme is overblowne;
When weening° to returne, whence they did stray,
They cannot finde that path, which first was showne,
But wander too and fro in wayes unknowne,°
Furthest from end then, when they neerest weene,
That makes them dout, their wits be not their owne:
So many pathes, so many turnings seene,
That which of them to take, in diverse doubt they   90
  been.

11

At last resolving forward still to fare,
Till that some end they finde or in or out,
That path they take, that beaten seemd most bare,
And like to lead the labyrinth about;
Which when by tract they hunted had throughout,
At length it brought them to a hollow cave,
Amid the thickest woods. The Champion stout
Eftsoones dismounted from his courser brave,
And to the Dwarfe a while his needlesse spere he gave.

12

Be well aware, quoth then that Ladie milde,   100
Least suddaine mischiefe ye too rash provoke,
The danger hid, the place unknowne and wilde,
Breedes dreadfull doubts: Oft fire is without smoke,
And perill without show: therefore your stroke
Sir knight with-hold, till further triall made.
Ah Ladie (said he) shame were to revoke
The forward footing for an hidden shade:
Vertue gives her selfe light, through darkenesse for
  to wade.

13

Yea but (quoth she) the perill of this place
I better wot then you, though now too late   110

To wish you backe returne with foule disgrace,
Yet wisedome warnes, whilest foot is in the gate,
To stay the steppe, ere forced to retrate.
This is the wandring wood, this *Errours den*,
A monster vile, whom God and man does hate:
Therefore I read° beware. Fly fly° (quoth then
The fearefull Dwarfe:) this is no place for living men.

14

But full of fire and greedy hardiment,
The youthfull knight could not for ought be staide,
120 But forth unto the darksome hole he went,
And looked in: his glistring armor made
A litle glooming light, much like a shade,
By which he saw the ugly monster plaine,
Halfe like a serpent° horribly displaide,
But the'other halfe did womans shape retaine,
Most lothsom, filthie, foule, and full of vile disdaine.

15

And as she lay upon the durtie ground,
Her huge long taile her den all overspred,
Yet was in knots and many boughtes° upwound,
130 Pointed with mortall sting. Of her there bred
A thousand yong ones, which she dayly fed,
Sucking upon her poisonous dugs, eachone
Of sundry shapes, yet all ill favored:
Soone as that uncouth° light upon them shone,
Into her mouth they crept, and suddain all were gone.

16

Their dam upstart, out of her den effraide,°
And rushed forth, hurling her hideous taile
About her cursed head, whose folds displaid
Were stretcht now forth at length without entraile.°
140 She lookt about, and seeing one in mayle
Armed to point,° sought backe to turne againe;
For light she hated as the deadly bale,
Ay wont in desert darknesse to remaine,
Where plaine none might her see, nor she see any
plaine.

17

Which when the valiant Elfe° perceiv'd, he lept
As Lyon fierce upon the flying pray,
And with his trenchand° blade her boldly kept
From turning backe, and forced her to stay:
Therewith enrag'd she loudly gan to bray,
150 And turning fierce, her speckled taile advaunst,
Threatning her angry sting, him to dismay:
Who nought aghast, his mightie hand enhaunst:°
The stroke down from her head unto her shoulder
glaunst.

18

Much daunted with that dint, her sence was dazd,
Yet kindling rage, her selfe she gathered round,
And all attonce her beastly body raizd
With doubled forces high above the ground:
Tho wrapping up her wrethed sterne arownd,
Lept fierce upon his shield, and her huge traine
All suddenly about his body wound,   160
That hand or foot to stirre he strove in vaine:
God helpe the man so wrapt in *Errours* endlesse traine.

19

His Lady sad to see his sore constraint,
Cride out, Now, now, Sir knight, shew what ye bee,
Add faith unto your force, and be not faint:
Strangle her, else she sure will strangle thee.
That when he heard, in great perplexitie,
His gall did grate° for griefe° and high disdaine,
And knitting all his force got one hand free,
Wherewith he grypt her gorge° with so great paine, 170
That soone to loose her wicked bands did her con-
straine.

20

Therewith she spewd out of her filthy maw
A floud of poyson horrible and blacke,
Full of great lumpes of flesh and gobbets° raw,
Which stunck so vildly, that it forst him slacke
His grasping hold, and from her turne him backe:
Her vomit full of bookes and papers° was,
With loathly frogs and toades, which eyes did lacke,
And creeping sought way in the weedy gras:
Her filthy parbreake all the place defiled has.   180

21

As when old father *Nilus* gins to swell
With timely pride above the *Aegyptian* vale,
His fattie waves do fertile slime outwell,
And overflow each plaine and lowly dale:
But when his later spring gins to avale,°
Huge heapes of mudd he leaves, wherein there breed
Ten thousand kindes of creatures, partly male
And partly female of his fruitfull seed;
Such ugly monstrous shapes elswhere may no man
reed.°

22

The same so sore annoyed has the knight,   190
That welnigh choked with the deadly stinke,
His forces faile, ne can no longer fight.
Whose corage when the feend perceiv'd to shrinke,
She poured forth out of her hellish sinke
Her fruitfull cursed spawne of serpents small,
Deformed monsters, fowle, and blacke as inke,

115 **read**, advise   **Fly fly**, Prudence counsels the knight to take the safe (but dishonorable) course of action   124 **Halfe ... serpent**, a lamia-type creature
129 **boughtes**, coils   134 **uncouth**, unfamiliar, strange   136 **effraide**,
frightened   139 **entraile**, coiling   141 **to point**, completely   145 **Elfe**. The
Redcrosse Knight was of elfin birth   147 **trenchand**, trenchant, sharp   152 **enhaunst**, lifted up

168 **grate**, stir   **griefe**, anger   170 **gorge**, throat   174 **gobbets**, lumps
177 **bookes and papers**, presumably pamphlet attacks on English church and
state (or just corrupt literature in general)   185 **his ... avale**, his flood begins to
subside. The river Nile is here represented as a river god   189 **reed**, see

Which swarming all about his legs did crall,
And him encombred sore, but could not hurt at all.

23

As gentle Shepheard° in sweete even-tide,
When ruddy *Phoebus* gins to welke° in west,   200
High on an hill, his flocke to vewen wide,
Markes which do byte their hasty supper best;
A cloud of cumbrous° gnattes do him molest,
All striving to infixe their feeble stings,
That from their noyance he no where can rest,
But with his clownish hands their tender wings
He brusheth oft, and oft doth mar their murmurings.

24

Thus ill bestedd,° and fearefull more of shame,
Then of the certaine perill he stood in,
Halfe furious unto his foe he came,   210
Resolv'd in minde all suddenly to win,
Or soone to lose, before he once would lin;°
And strooke at her with more then manly° force,
That from her body full of filthie sin
He raft° her hatefull head without remorse;
A streame of cole black bloud forth gushed from
     her corse.

25

Her scattred brood, soone as their Parent deare
They saw so rudely falling to the ground,
Groning full deadly, all with troublous feare,
Gathred themselves about her body round,   220
Weening their wonted entrance to have found
At her wide mouth: but being there withstood
They flocked all about her bleeding wound,
And sucked up their dying mothers blood,
Making her death their life, and eke her hurt their
     good.

26

That detestable sight him much amazde,
To see th'unkindly° Impes° of heaven accurst,
Devoure their dam; on whom while so he gazd,
Having all satisfide their bloudy thurst,
Their bellies swolne he saw with fulnesse burst,   230
And bowels gushing forth: well worthy end
Of such as drunke her life, the which them nurst;
Now needeth him no lenger labour spend,
His foes have slaine themselves, with whom he
     should contend.

27

His Ladie seeing all, that chaunst, from farre
Approcht in hast to greet his victorie,
And said, Faire knight, borne under happy starre,

Who see your vanquisht foes before you lye;
Well worthy be you of that Armorie,°
Wherein ye have great glory wonne this day,   240
And proov'd your strength on a strong enimie,
Your first adventure: many such I pray,
And henceforth ever wish, that like succeed it may.

28

Then mounted he upon his Steede againe,
And with the Lady backward sought to wend;
That path he kept, which beaten was most plaine,
Ne ever would to any by-way bend,
But still did follow one unto the end,
The which at last out of the wood them brought.
So forward on his way (with God to frend)°   250
He passed forth, and new adventure sought;
Long way he travelled, before he heard of ought.

29

At length they chaunst to meet upon the way
An aged Sire, in long blacke weedes yclad,
His feete all bare, his beard all hoarie gray,
And by his belt his booke° he hanging had;
Sober he seemde, and very sagely sad,°
And to the ground his eyes were lowly bent,
Simple in shew, and voyde of malice bad,
And all the way he prayed, as he went,   260
And often knockt his brest, as one that did repent.

30

He faire the knight saluted, louting° low,
Who faire him quited,° as that courteous was:
And after asked him, if he did know
Of straunge adventures, which abroad did pas.
Ah my deare Sonne (quoth he) how should, alas,
Silly° old man, that lives in hidden cell,
Bidding° his beades all day for his trespas,
Tydings of warre and worldly trouble tell?
With° holy father sits not with such things to mell.   270

31

But if of daunger which hereby doth dwell,
And homebred evill ye desire to heare,
Of a straunge man I can you tidings tell,
That wasteth all this countrey farre and neare.
Of such (said he) I chiefly do inquere,
And shall you well reward to shew the place,
In which that wicked wight his dayes doth weare:
For to all knighthood it is foule disgrace,
That such a cursed creature lives so long a space.

32

Far hence (quoth he) in wastfull wildernesse   280
His dwelling is, by which no living wight

---

199 **gentle Shepheard,** etc., a Homeric or epic simile, a long and elaborate comparison; cf. Stanza 21 200 **welke,** fade, wane 203 **cumbrous,** harassing 208 **bestedd,** beset 212 **lin,** stop 213 **manly,** human 215 **raft,** bereft 227 **unkindly,** unnatural **Impes,** children, brood

239 **Armorie,** armor (bearing the Christian symbol) 250 **to frend,** as a friend 256 **his booke,** his prayer book 257 **sad,** pensive, thoughtful 262 **louting,** bending 263 **quited,** requited, returned the salutation 267 **Silly,** simple 268 **Bidding,** telling, counting 270 **With,** etc. It befits not a hermit to meddle with such matters

May ever passe, but thorough great distresse.
Now (sayd the Lady) draweth toward night,
And well I wote, that of your later fight
Ye all forwearied° be: for what so strong,
But wanting rest will also want of might?
The Sunne that measures heaven all day long,
At night doth baite° his steedes the *Ocean* waves
    emong.

33

Then with the Sunne take Sir, your timely rest,
290 And with new day new worke at once begin:
Untroubled night they say gives counsell best.
Right well Sir knight ye have advised bin,
(Quoth then that aged man;) the way to win
Is wisely to advise: now day is spent;
Therefore with me ye may take up your In
For this same night. The knight was well content:
So with that godly father to his home they went.

34

A little lowly Hermitage it was,
Downe in a dale, hard by a forests side,
300 Far from resort of people, that did pas
In travell to and froe: a little wyde
There was an holy Chappell edifyde,°
Wherein the Hermite dewly wont to say
His holy things each morne and eventyde:
Thereby a Christall streame did gently play,
Which from a sacred fountaine welled forth alway.

35

Arrived there, the little house they fill,
Ne looke for entertainement, where none was:
Rest is their feast, and all things at their will;
310 The noblest mind the best contentment has.
With faire discourse the evening so they pas:
For that old man of pleasing wordes had store,
And well could file his *tongue* as smooth as glas;
He told of Saintes and Popes,° and evermore
He strowd an *Ave-Mary* after and before.

36

The drouping Night thus creepeth on them fast,
And the sad humour° loading their eye liddes,
As messenger of *Morpheus*° on them cast
Sweet slombring deaw, the which to sleepe them bid-
    des.
320 Unto their lodgings then his guestes he riddes:
Where when all drownd in deadly sleepe he findes,
He to his study goes, and there amiddes
His Magick bookes and artes of sundry kindes,
He seekes out mighty charmes, to trouble sleepy
    mindes.

37

Then choosing out few wordes most horrible,
(Let none them read) thereof did verses frame,
With which and other spelles like terrible,
He bade awake blacke *Plutoes* griesly Dame,°
And cursed heaven, and spake reprochfull shame
Of highest God, the Lord of life and light;   330
A bold bad man, that dar'd to call by name
Great *Gorgon*,° Prince of darknesse and dead night,
At which *Cocytus* quakes, and *Styx*° is put to flight.

38

And forth he cald out of deepe darkness dred
Legions of Sprights, the which like little flyes
Fluttring about his ever damned hed,
A-waite whereto their service he applyes,
To aide his friends, or fray° his enimies:
Of those he chose out two, the falsest twoo,
And fittest for to forge true-seeming lyes;   340
The one of them he gave a message too,
The other by him selfe staide other worke to doo.

39

He° making speedy way through spersed ayre,
And through the world of waters wide and deepe,
To *Morpheus* house doth hastily repaire.
Amid the bowels of the earth full steepe,
And low, where dawning day doth never peepe,
His dwelling is; there *Tethys*° his wet bed
Doth ever wash, and *Cynthia*° still doth steepe
In silver deaw his ever-drouping hed,   350
Whiles sad Night over him her mantle black doth
    spred.

40

Whose double gates he findeth locked fast,
The one faire fram'd of burnisht Yvory,
The other all with silver overcast;
And wakefull dogges before them farre do lye.
Watching to banish Care their enimy,
Who oft is wont to trouble gentle Sleepe.
By them the Sprite doth passe in quietly,
And unto *Morpheus* comes, whom drowned deepe
In drowsie fit he findes: of nothing he takes keepe.   360

41

And more, to lulle him in his slumber soft,
A trickling streame from high rocke tumbling downe
And ever-drizling raine upon the loft,°
Mixt with a murmuring winde, much like the sowne
Of swarming Bees, did cast him in a swowne:
No other noyse, nor peoples troublous cryes,
As still are wont t'annoy the walled towne,

---

285 **forwearied,** exhausted   288 **baite,** refresh; the allusion is to the horses of the sun god   302 **edifyde,** built   314 **Saintes and Popes.** The hermit was Archimago, who symbolized hypocrisy   317 **sad humour,** heavy moisture; the theory was that a "dry brain" did not rest well   318 **Morpheus,** the god of sleep

328 **Plutoes griesly Dame,** Proserpine   332 **Gorgon,** Demogorgon, a demon of magic powers   333 **Cocytus . . . Styx,** rivers in Hades   338 **fray,** terrify 343 **He,** i.e., the messenger of Archimago   348 **Tethys,** in Greek myth the wife of Oceanus; here used of the Ocean himself   349 **Cynthia,** the moon 363 **loft,** roof

Might there be heard: but carelesse Quiet lyes,
Wrapt in eternall silence farre from enemyes.

42

370 The messenger approaching to him spake,
But his waste wordes returned to him in vaine:
So sound he slept, that nought mought him awake.
Then rudely he him thrust, and pusht with paine,
Whereat he gan to stretch: but he againe
Shooke him so hard, that forced him to speake.
As one then in a dreame, whose dryer braine°
Is tost with troubled sights and fancies weake,
He mumbled soft, but would not all his silence breake.

43

The Sprite then gan more boldly him to wake,
380 And threatned unto him the dreaded name
Of *Hecate*:° whereat he gan to quake,
And lifting up his lumpish head, with blame
Halfe angry asked him, for what he came.
Hither (quoth he) me *Archimago* sent,
He that the stubborne Sprites can wisely tame,
He bids thee to him send for his intent
A fit false dreame, that can delude the sleepers sent.

44

The God obayde, and calling forth straight way
A diverse dreame out of his prison darke,
390 Delivered it to him, and downe did lay
His heavie head, devoide of carefull carke,°
Whose sences all were straight benumbd and starke.
He backe returning by the Yvorie dore,°
Remounted up as light as chearefull Larke,
And on his litle winges the dreame he bore
In hast unto his Lord, where he him left afore.

45

Who all this while with charmes and hidden artes,
Had made a Lady of that other Spright,
And fram'd of liquid ayre her tender partes
400 So lively, and so like in all mens sight,
That weaker sence it could have ravisht quight:
The maker selfe for all his wondrous witt,
Was nigh beguiled with so goodly sight:
Her all in white he clad, and over it
Cast a blacke stole, most like to seeme for *Una* fit.

46

Now when that ydle dreame was to him brought,
Unto that Elfin knight he bad him fly,
Where he slept soundly void of evill thought,
And with false shewes abuse his fantasy,
410 In sort as° he him schooled privily:

And that new creature borne without her dew,°
Full of the makers guile, with usage sly
He taught to imitate that Lady trew,
Whose semblance she did carrie under feigned hew.

47

Thus well instructed, to their worke they hast,
And comming where the knight in slomber lay,
The one upon his hardy head him plast,
And made him dreame of loves and lustfull play,
That nigh his manly hart did melt away,
Bathed in wanton blis and wicked joy: 420
Then seemed him his Lady by him lay,
And to him playnd,° how that false winged boy
Her chast hart had subdewd, to learne Dame pleasures
     toy.

48

And she her selfe of beautie soveraigne Queene,
Faire *Venus* seemde unto his bed to bring
Her, whom he waking evermore did weene
To be the chastest flowre, that ay did spring
On earthly braunch, the daughter of a king,
Now a loose Leman to vile service bound:
And eke the *Graces* seemed all to sing,   430
Hymen iô Hymen,° dauncing all around,
Whilst freshest *Flora*° her with Yvie girlond crownd.

49

In this great passion of unwonted lust,
Or wonted feare of doing ought amis,
He started up, as seeming to mistrust
Some secret ill, or hidden foe of his:
Lo there before his face his Lady is,
Under blake stole hyding her bayted hooke,
And as halfe blushing offred him to kis,
With gentle blandishment and lovely looke,   440
Most like that virgin true, which for her knight
     him took.

50

All cleane dismayed to see so uncouth sight,
And halfe enraged at her shamelesse guise,
He thought have slaine her in his fierce despight:°
But hasty heat tempring with sufferance° wise,
He stayde his hand, and gan himselfe advise
/To prove his sense, and tempt her faigned truth.
Wringing her hands in wemens pitteous wise,
Tho can° she weepe, to stirre up gentle ruth,°
Both for her noble bloud, and for her tender youth.   450

51

And said, Ah Sir, my liege Lord and my love,
Shall I accuse the hidden cruell fate,

376 **dryer braine**, See 1. 317   381 **Hecate**, in Greek myth a triple-formed goddess of moon, earth, and underworld, a type of witch   391 **carefull carke,** worry
that is full of care   393 **Yvorie dore,** the gate through which false dreams go
out; true dreams passed through the Gate of Horn   410 **In sort as, etc.,** according to the method that he had taught him secretly

411 **without her dew,** unnaturally   422 **playnd,** complained   431 **Hymen,**
etc., chant to Hymen, god of wedlock   432 **Flora,** goddess of flowers   444 **despight,** anger   445 **sufferance,** patience   449 **Tho can,** then did   **ruth,** pity

And mightie causes wrought in heaven above,
Or the blind God,° that doth me thus amate,°
For hoped love to winne me certaine hate?
Yet thus perforce he bids me do, or die.
Die is my dew: yet rew my wretched state
You, whom my hard avenging destinie
Hath made judge of my life or death indifferently.

52

460 Your owne deare sake forst me at first to leave
My Fathers kingdome, There she stopt with teares;
Her swollen hart her speach seemd to bereave,
And then againe begun, My weaker yeares
Captiv'd to fortune and frayle wordly feares,
Fly to your faith for succour and sure ayde:
Let me not dye in languor and long teares.
Why Dame (quoth he) what hath ye thus dismayd?
What frayes° ye, that were wont to comfort me af-
    frayd?

53

Love of your selfe, she said, and deare° constraint
470 Lets me not sleepe, but wast the wearie night
In secret anguish and unpittied plaint,
Whiles you in carelesse sleepe are drowned quight.
Her doubtfull words made that redoubted knight
Suspect her truth: yet since no untruth he knew,
Her fawning love with foule disdainefull spight
He would not shend,° but said, Deare dame I rew,
That for my sake unknowne such griefe unto you grew.

54

Assure your selfe, it fell not all to ground;
For all so deare as life is to my hart,
480 I deeme your love, and hold me to you bound;
Ne let vaine feares procure your needlesse smart,
Where cause is none, but to your rest depart.
Not all content, yet seemd she to appease°
Her mournefull plaintes, beguiled of her art,
And fed with words, that could not chuse but please,
So slyding softly forth, she turned as to her ease.

55

Long after lay he musing at her mood,
Much griev'd to thinke that gentle Dame so light,
For whose defence he was to shed his blood.
490 At last dull wearinesse of former fight
Having yrockt a sleepe his irkesome spright,
That troublous dreame gan freshly tosse his braine,
With bowres, and beds, and Ladies deare delight:
But when he saw his labour all was vaine,
With that misformed spright he backe returnd againe.
(1590)

454 **blind God**, Cupid   **amate**, subdue   468 **frayes**, frightens   469 **deare**, dire
476 **shend**, blame   483 **appease**, cease

from **BOOK II**

Book II of *The Faerie Queene* concerns Sir Guyon, who
represents the ideal of Temperance or Self-Control in
the poem's allegorical scheme; he is accompanied by
the Palmer, a holy sage. Briefly, Sir Guyon visits the
cave of Mammon (i.e., Materialism, Worldliness),
captures the carnal enchantress Acrasia, and razes her
Bower of Bliss (Canto XII). The knight is saved at a
crucial point in these adventures by Prince Arthur,
who first dispatches the pagan brothers Cymochles
and Pyrocles and at last personally delivers Alma (the
Spirit or Pure Soul, Queen of Body Castle and the
House of Temperance). On the whole, Book II is more
abstract in the nature of its narrative than Book I and
more laden with the elaborate, sensuous, descriptive
detail which characterizes so much of Spenser's finest
poetry.

CANTO XII

Guyon, by Palmers governance,
    passing through perils great,
Doth overthrow the Bowre of blisse,
    and Acrasie defeat.

1

Now gins this goodly frame of Temperance
Fairely to rise, and her adorned hed
To pricke of highest praise forth to advance,
Formerly grounded, and fast setteled
On firme foundation of true bountihed;
And this brave knight, that for that vertue fights,
Now comes to point of that same perilous sted,
Where Pleasure dwelles in sensuall delights,
Mongst thousand dangers, and ten thousand magick
    mights.

2

Two dayes now in that sea he sayled has,   10
Ne ever land beheld, ne living wight,
Ne ought save perill, still as he did pas:
Tho when appeared the third *Morrow* bright,
Upon the waves to spred her trembling light,
An hideous roaring farre away they heard,
That all their senses filled with affright,
And streight they saw the raging surges reard
Up to the skyes, that them of drowning made affeard.

3

Said then the Boteman, Palmer stere aright,
And keepe an even course; for yonder way   20
We needes must passe (God do us well acquight,)
That is the *Gulfe of Greedinesse*, they say,
That deepe engorgeth all this worldes pray:
Which having swallowd up excessively,

He soone in vomit up againe doth lay,
And belcheth forth his superfluity,
That all the seas for feare do seeme away to fly.

4

On th'other side an hideous Rocke is pight,
Of mightie *Magnes*° stone, whose craggie clift
30 Depending from on high, dreadfull to sight,
Over the waves his rugged armes doth lift,
And threatneth downe to throw his ragged rift
On who so commeth nigh; yet nigh it drawes
All passengers, that none from it can shift:
For whiles they fly that Gulfes devouring jawes,
They on this rock are rent, and sunck in helplesse
   wawes.

5

Forward they passe and strongly he them rowes,
Untill they nigh unto that Gulfe arrive,
Where streame more violent and greedy growes:
40 Then he with all his puissance doth strive
To strike his oares, and mightily doth drive
The hollow vessell through the threatfull wave,
Which gaping wide, to swallow them alive,
In th'huge abysse of his engulfing grave,
Doth rore at them in vaine, and with great terror rave.

6

They passing by, that griesly mouth did see,
Sucking the seas into his entralles deepe,
That seem'd more horrible then hell to bee,
Or that darke dreadfull hole of *Tartare* steepe,
50 Through which the damned ghosts doen often creepe
Backe to the world, bad livers to torment:
But nought that falles into this direfull deepe,
Ne that approcheth nigh the wide descent,
May backe returne, but is condemned to be drent.°

7

On th'other side, they saw that perilous Rocke,
Threatning it selfe on them to ruinate,°
On whose sharpe clifts the ribs of vessels broke,
And shivered ships, which had bene wrecked late,
Yet stuck, with carkasses exanimate°
60 Of such, as having all their substance spent
In wanton joyes, and lustes intemperate,
Did afterwards make shipwracke° violent,
Both of their life, and fame for ever fowly blent.°

8

For thy, this hight *The Rocke of* vile *Reproch*,
A daungerous and detestable place,

To which nor fish nor fowle did once approch,
But yelling Meawes, with Seagulles hoarse and
   bace,
And Cormoyrants, with birds of ravenous race,
Which still sate waiting on that wastfull clift,
For spoyle of wretches, whose unhappie cace,   70
After lost credite and consumed thrift,
At last them driven hath to this despairefull drift

9

The Palmer seeing them in safetie past,
Thus said; Behold th'ensamples in our sights,
Of lustfull luxurie and thriftlesse wast:
What now is left of miserable wights,
Which spent their looser daies in lewd delights,
But shame and sad reproch, here to be red,
By these rent reliques, speaking their ill plights?
Let all that live, hereby be counselled,   80
To shunne *Rocke of Reproch*, and it as death to dred.

10

So forth they rowed, and that *Ferryman*
With his stiffe oares did brush the sea so strong,
That the hoare waters from his frigot ran,
And the light bubbles daunced all along,
Whiles the salt brine out of the billowes sprong.
At last farre off they many Islands spy,
On every side floting the floods emong:
Then said the knight, Loe I the land descry,
Therefore old Syre thy course do thereunto apply.   90

11

That may not be, said then the *Ferryman*
Least we unweeting hap to be fordonne:°
For those same Islands, seeming now and than,
Are not firme lande, nor any certein wonne,
But straggling plots, which to and fro do ronne
In the wide waters: therefore are they hight
The *wandring Islands*.° Therefore doe them
   shonne;
For they have oft drawne many a wandring wight
Into most deadly daunger and distressed plight.

12

Yet well they seeme to him, that farre doth vew,   100
Both faire and fruitfull, and the ground dispred
With grassie greene of delectable hew,
And the tall trees with leaves apparelled,
Are deckt with blossomes dyde in white and red,
That mote the passengers thereto allure;
But whosoever once hath fastened
His foot thereon, may never it recure,
But wandreth ever more uncertein and unsure.

Book II Canto XII   29 **Magnes**, magnet   54 **drent**, drowned   56 **ruinate**,
wreak ruin   59 **exanimate**, lifeless   62 **make shipwracke**, commit suicide
63 **blent**, darkened

92 **fordonne**, destroyed   97 **wandring Islands**. These islands recall the
mythological lotus land (see ll. 100–108)

13

As th'Isle of *Delos* whylome men report
110 Amid th' *Aegaean* sea long time did stray,
Ne made for shipping any certaine port,
Till that *Latona* traveiling that way,
Flying from *Junoes* wrath and hard assay,
Of her faire twins was there delivered,
Which afterwards did rule the night and day;
Thenceforth it firmely was established,
And for *Apolloes* honor highly herried.°

14

They to him hearken, as beseemeth meete,
And passe on forward: so their way does ly,
120 That one of those same Islands, which doe fleet°
In the wide sea, they needes must passen by,
Which seemd so sweet and pleasant to the eye,
That it would tempt a man to touchen there:
Upon the banck they sitting did espy
A daintie damzell,° dressing of her heare,
By whom a little skippet° floting did appeare.

15

She them espying, loud to them can call,
Bidding them nigher draw unto the shore;
For she had cause to busie them withall;
130 And therewith loudly laught: But nathemore
Would they once turne, but kept on as afore:
Which when she saw, she left her lockes undight,
And running to her boat withouten ore
From the departing land it launched light,
And after them did drive with all her power and might.

16

Whom overtaking, she in merry sort
Them gan to bord, and purpose diversly,
Now faining dalliance and wanton sport,
Now throwing forth lewd words immodestly;
140 Till that the Palmer gan full bitterly
Her to rubuke, for being loose and light
Which not abiding, but more scornefully
Scoffing at him, that did her justly wite.
She turned her bote about, and from them rowed quite.

17

That was the wanton *Phaedria*, which late
Did ferry him over the *Idle lake*:
Whom nought regarding, they kept on their gate,
And all her vaine allurements did forsake,
When them the wary Boateman thus bespake;
150 Here now behoveth us well to avyse,°
And of our safetie good heede to take;
For here before a perlous passage lyes,
Where many Mermayds° haunt, making false
   melodies.

18

But by the way, there is a great Quicksand,
And a whirlepoole of hidden jeopardy,
Therefore, Sir Palmer, keepe an even hand;
For twixt them both the narrow way doth ly.
Scarse had he said, when hard at hand they spy
That quicksand nigh with water covered;
But by the checked wave they did descry   160
It plaine, and by the sea discoloured:
It called was the quicksand of *Unthriftyhed*.°

19

They passing by, a goodly Ship did see,
Laden from far with precious merchandize,
And bravely furnished, as ship might bee,
Which through great disaventure, or mesprize,
Her selfe had runne into that hazardize;
Whose mariners and merchants with much toyle,
Labour'd in vaine, to have recur'd their prize,
And the rich wares to save from pitteous spoyle,   170
But neither toyle nor travell might her backe recoyle.

20

On th'other side they see that perilous Poole,
That called was the *Whirlepoole of decay*,
In which full many had with haplesse doole°
Beene suncke, of whom no memorie did stay:
Whose circled waters rapt with whirling sway,
Like to a restlesse wheele, still running round,
Did covet, as they passed by that way,
To draw their boate within the utmost bound
Of his wide *Labyrinth*, and then to have them dround. 180

21

But th'heedfull Boateman strongly forth did stretch
His brawnie armes, and all his body straine,
That th'utmost sandy breach they shortly fetch,
Whiles the dred daunger does behind remaine.
Suddeine they see from midst of all the Maine,
The surging waters like a mountaine rise,
And the great sea puft up with proud disdaine,
To swell above the measure of his guise,
As threatning to devoure all, that his powre despise.

22

The waves come rolling, and the billowes rore   190
Outragiously, as they enraged were,
Or wrathfull *Neptune* did them drive before
His whirling charet, for exceeding feare:
For not one puffe of wind there did appeare,
That all the three thereat woxe° much afrayd,
Unweeting, what such horrour straunge did reare.
Eftsoones they saw an hideous hoast arrayd,
Of huge Sea monsters, such as living sence dismayd.

---

117 **herried,** respected   120 **fleet,** float   125 **daintie damzell,** i.e., Phaedria (l.
145), who appears here as a kind of Lorelei or Circe figure   126 **skippet,** skiff
150 **avyse,** advise ourselves   153 **Mermayds,** i.e., Sirens

162 **Unthriftyhed,** heedlessness   174 **doole,** lament   195 **woxe,** grew

23

Most ugly shapes, and horrible aspects,
200 Such as Dame Nature selfe mote° feare to see,
Or shame, that ever should so fowle defects
From her most cunning hand escaped bee;
All dreadfull pourtraicts of deformitee:
Spring-headed *Hydraes*,° and sea-shouldring Whales,
Great whirlpooles, which all fishes make to flee,
Bright Scolopendraes, arm'd with silver scales,
Mighty *Monoceros*, with immeasured tayles.

24

The dreadfull Fish, that hath deserv'd the name
Of Death, and like him lookes in dreadfull hew,
210 The griesly Wasserman, that makes his game
The flying ships with swiftnesse to pursew,
The horrible Sea-satyre, that doth shew
His fearefull face in time of greatest storme,
Huge *Ziffius*, whom Mariners eschew
No lesse, then rockes, (as travellers informe,)
And greedy *Rosmarines* with visages deforme.

25

All these, and thousand thousands many more,
And more deformed Monsters thousand fold,
With dreadfull noise, and hollow rombling rore,
220 Came rushing in the fomy waves enrold,
Which seem'd to fly for feare, them to behold:
Ne wonder, if these did the knight appall;
For all that here on earth we dreadfull hold,
Be but as bugs° to fearen babes withall,
Compared to the creatures in the seas entrall.

26

Feare nought, (then said the Palmer well aviz'd;)
For these same Monsters are not these in deed,
But are into these fearefull shapes disguiz'd
By that same wicked witch, to worke us dreed,
230 And draw from on this journey to proceede.
Tho lifting up his vertuous staffe on hye,
He smote the sea, which calmed was with speed,
And all that dreadfull Armie fast gan flye
Into great *Tethys* bosome, where they hidden lye.

27

Quit from that daunger, forth their course they kept,
And as they went, they heard a ruefull cry
Of one, that wayld and pittifully wept,
That through the sea the resounding plaints did fly:
At last they in an Island did espy
240 A seemely Maiden, sitting by the shore,
That with great sorrow and sad agony,
Seemed some great misfortune to deplore,
And lowd to them for succour called evermore.

28

Which *Guyon* hearing, streight his Palmer bad,
To stere the boate towards that dolefull Mayd,
That he might know, and ease her sorrow sad:
Who him avizing better, to him sayd;
Faire Sir, be not displeasd, if disobayd:
For ill it were to hearken to her cry;
For she is inly nothing ill apayd,   250
But onely womanish fine forgery,
Your stubborne hart t'affect with fraile infirmity.

29

To which when she your courage hath inclind
Through foolish pitty, then her guilefull bayt
She will embosome deeper in your mind,
And for your ruine at the last awayt.
The knight was ruled, and the Boateman strayt
Held on his course with stayed stedfastnesse,
Ne ever shruncke, ne ever sought to bayt
His tyred armes for toylesome wearinesse,   260
But with his oares did sweepe the watry wildernesse.

30

And now they nigh approched to the sted,°
Where as those Mermayds dwelt: it was a still
And calmy bay, on th'one side sheltered
With the brode shadow of an hoarie hill,
On th'other side an high rocke toured still,
That twixt them both a pleasaunt port they made,
And did like an halfe Theatre fulfill:
There those five sisters had continuall trade,°
And usd to bath themselves in that deceiptfull shade. 270

31

They were faire Ladies, till they fondly striv'd
With th'*Heliconian* maides for maistery;
Of whom they over-comen, were depriv'd
Of their proud beautie, and th'one moyity
Transform'd to fish, for their bold surquedry,°
But th'upper halfe their hew retained still,
And their sweet skill in wonted melody;
Which ever after they abusd to ill,
T'allure weake travellers, whom gotten they did kill.

32

So now to *Guyon*, as he passed by,   280
Their pleasaunt tunes they sweetly thus applide;
O thou faire sonne of gentle Faery,
That art in mighty armes most magnifide
Above all knights, that ever battell tride,
O turne thy rudder hither-ward a while:
Here may thy storme-bet vessell safely ride;
This is the Port of rest from troublous toyle,
The worlds sweet In,° from paine and wearisome
   turmoyle.

---

200 mote, might   204 Hydraes, etc., legendary monsters   224 bugs, bugbears,
bogeys

262 sted, place   269 had continuall trade, had always lived   275 surquedry,
presumption   288 In, inn

33

With that the rolling sea resounding soft,
290 In his big base them fitly answered,
And on the rocke the waves breaking aloft,
A solemne Meane° unto them measured,
The whiles sweet *Zephirus* lowd whisteled
His treble, a straunge kinde of harmony;
Which *Guyons* senses softly tickeled,
That he the boateman bad row easily,
And let him heare some part of their rare melody.

34

But him the Palmer from that vanity,
With temperate advice discounselled,
300 That they it past, and shortly gan descry
The land, to which their course they leveled;
When suddeinly a grosse fog over spred
With his dull vapour all that desert has,
And heavens chearefull face enveloped,
That all things one, and one as nothing was,
And this great universe seemd one confused mas.

35

Thereat they greatly were dismayd, ne wist°
How to direct their way in darkenesse wide,
But feard to wander in that wastfull mist,
310 For tombling into mischiefe unespide.
Worse is the daunger hidden, then descride.
Suddeinly an innumerable flight
Of harmefull fowles about them fluttering, cride,
And with their wicked wings them oft did smight,
And sore annoyed, groping in that griesly night.

36

Even all the nation of unfortunate
And fatall birds about them flocked were,
Such as by nature men abhorre and hate,
The ill-faste° Owle, deaths dreadfull messengere,
320 The hoars Night-raven, trump of dolefull drere,
The lether-winged Bat, dayes enimy,
The ruefull Strich, still waiting on the bere,
The Whistler shrill, that who so heares, doth dy,
The hellish Harpies, prophets of sad destiny.

37

All those, and all that else does horrour breed,
About them flew, and fild their sayles with feare:
Yet stayd they not, but forward did proceed,
Whiles th'one did row, and th'other stifly steare;
Till that at last the weather gan to cleare,
330 And the faire land it selfe did plainly show.
Said then the Palmer, Lo where does appeare
The sacred soile, where all our perils grow;
Therefore, Sir knight, your ready armes about you
    throw.

38

He hearkned, and his armes about him tooke,
The whiles the nimble boate so well her sped,
That with her crooked keele the land she strooke,
Then forth the noble *Guyon* sallied,
And his sage Palmer, that him governed;
But th'other by his boate behind did stay.
They marched fairly forth, of nought ydred,°   340
Both firmely armd for every hard assay,
With constancy and care, gainst daunger and dismay.

39

Ere long they heard an hideous bellowing
Of many beasts, that roard outrageously,
As if that hungers point, or *Venus* sting
Had them enraged with fell° surquedry;
Yet nought they feard, but past on hardily,
Untill they came in vew of those wild beasts:
Who all attonce, gaping full greedily,
And rearing fiercely their upstarting crests,   350
Ran towards, to devoure those unexpected guests.

40

But soone as they approcht with deadly threat,
The Palmer over them his staffe upheld,
His mighty staffe, that could all charmes defeat:
Eftsoones their stubborne courages were queld,
And high advaunced crests downe meekely fled,
In stead of fraying,° they them selves did feare,
And trembled, as them passing they beheld:
Such wondrous powre did in that staffe appeare,
All monsters to subdew to him, that did it beare.   360

41

Of that same wood it fram'd was cunningly,
Of which *Caduceus* whilome was made,
Caduceus the rod of *Mercury*,
With which he wonts the *Stygian* realmes invade,
Through ghastly horrour, and eternall shade;
Th' infernall feends with it he can asswage,
And *Orcus* tame, whom nothing can perswade,
And rule the *Furyes*, when they most do rage:
Such vertue in his staffe had eke this Palmer sage.

42

Thence passing forth, they shortly do arrive,   370
Whereas the Bowre of *Blisse* was situate;
A place pickt out by choice of best alive,
That natures worke by art can imitate:
In which what ever in this worldly state
Is sweet, and pleasing unto living sense,
Or that may dayntiest fantasie aggrate,°
Was poured forth with plentifull dispence,
And made there to abound with lavish affluence.

---

292 **Meane,** middle part (in music)   307 **wist,** knew   319 **ill-faste,** ominous, ugly

340 **ydred,** afraid   346 **fell,** fierce   357 **fraying,** causing fright   376 **aggrate,** please

43

Goodly it was enclosed round about,
380 Aswell their entred guestes to keepe within,
As those unruly beasts to hold without;
Yet was the fence thereof but weake and thin;
Nought feard their force, that fortilage° to win,
But wisedomes powre, and temperaunces might,
By which the mightiest things efforced bin:
And eke the gate was wrought of substaunce light,
Rather for pleasure, then for battery or fight.

44

Yt framed was of precious yvory,
That seemd a worke of admirable wit;
390 And therein all the famous history
Of *Jason* and *Medae* was ywrit;
Her mighty charmes, her furious loving fit,
His goodly conquest of the golden fleece,
His falsed faith, and love too lightly flit,
The wondred *Argo*, which in venturous peece
First through the *Euxine* seas bore all the flowr of
  Greece.

45

Ye might have seene the frothy billowes fry
Under the ship, as thorough them she went,
That seemed the waves were into yvory,
400 Or yvory into the waves were sent;
And other where the snowy substaunce sprent°
With vermell, like the boyes bloud therein shed,
A piteous spectacle did represent,
And otherwhiles with gold besprinkeled;
Yt seemd th'enchaunted flame, which did *Creüsa* wed.

46

All this, and more might in that goodly gate
Be red; that ever open stood to all,
Which thither came: but in the Porch there sate
A comely personage of stature tall,
410 And semblaunce pleasing, more then naturall,
That travellers to him seemd to entize;
His looser garment to the ground did fall,
And flew about his heeles in wanton wize,
Not fit for speedy pace, or manly exercize.

47

They in that place him *Genius* did call:
Not that celestiall powre, to whom the care
Of life, and generation of all
That lives, pertaines in charge particulare,
Who wondrous things concerning our welfare,
420 And straunge phantomes doth let us oft forsee,
And oft of secret ill bids us beware:
That is our Selfe,° whom though we do not see,
Yet each doth in him selfe it well perceive to bee.

48

Therefore a God him sage Antiquity
Did wisely make, and good *Agdistes* call:
But this same was to that quite contrary,
The foe of life, that good envyes to all,
That secretly doth us procure to fall,
Through guilefull semblaunts, which he makes us see.
He of this Gardin had the governall, 430
And Pleasures porter° was devizd to bee,
Holding a staffe in hand for more formalitee.

49

With diverse flowres he daintily was deckt,
And strowed round about, and by his side
A mighty Mazer bowle of wine was set,
As if it had to him bene sacrifide;
Wherewith all new-come guests he gratifide:
So did he eke Sir *Guyon* passing by:
But he his idle curtesie defide,
And overthrew his bowle disdainfully; 440
And broke his staffe, with which he charmed
  semblants sly.

50

Thus being entred, they behold around
A large and spacious plaine, on every side
Strowed with pleasauns,° whose faire grassy ground
Mantled with greene, and goodly beautifide
With all the ornaments of *Floraes* pride,
Wherewith her mother Art, as halfe in scorne
Of niggard Nature, like a pompous bride
Did decke her, and too lavishly adorne,
When forth from virgin bowre she comes in th'early 450
  morne.

51

Thereto the Heavens alwayes Joviall,
Lookt on them lovely, still in stedfast state,
Ne suffred storme nor frost on them to fall,
Their tender buds or leaves to violate,
Nor scorching heat, nor cold intemperate
T'afflict the creatures, which therein did dwell,
But the milde aire with season moderate
Gently attempred, and disposd so well,
That still it breathed forthsweet spirit and holesome
  smell.

52

More sweet and holesome, then the pleasaunt hill 460
Of *Rhodope*, on which the Nimphe, that bore
A gyaunt babe,° her selfe for griefe did kill;
Or the Thessalian *Tempe*, where of yore
Faire *Daphne Phoebus* hart with love did gore;
Or *Ida*, where the gods lov'd to repaire,
When ever they their heavenly bowres forlore;

Or sweet *Parnasse*, the haunt of Muses faire;
Or *Eden* selfe, if ought with *Eden* mote compaire.

53

Much wondred *Guyon* at the faire aspect
470 Of that sweet place, yet suffred no delight
To sincke into his sence, nor mind affect,
But passed forth, and lookt still forward right,
Bridling his will, and maistering his might:
Till that he came unto another gate;
No gate, but like one, being goodly dight
With boughes and braunches, which did broad dilate°
Their clasping armes, in wanton wreathings intricate.

54

So fashioned a Porch with rare device,
Archt over head with an embracing vine,
480 Whose bounches hanging downe, seemed to entice
All passers by, to tast their lushious wine,
And did themselves into their hands incline,
As freely offering to be gathered:
Some deepe empurpled as the *Hyacint*,
Some as the Rubine, laughing sweetly red,
Some like faire Emeraudes, not yet well ripened.

55

And them amongst, some were of burnisht gold,
So made by art, to beautifie the rest,
Which did themselves emongst the leaves enfold,
490 As lurking from the vew of covetous guest,
That the weake bowes, with so rich load opprest,
Did bow adowne, as over-burdened.
Under that Porch a comely dame did rest,
Clad in faire weedes,° but fowle disordered,
And garments loose, that seemd unmeet for
   womanhed.

56

In her left hand a Cup of gold she held,
And with her right the riper fruit did reach,
Whose sappy liquor, that with fulnesse sweld,
Into her cup she scruzd,° with daintie breach
500 Of her fine fingers, without fowle empeach,°
That so faire wine-presse made the wine more sweet:
Thereof she used to give to drinke to each,
Whom passing by she happened to meet:
It was her guise, all Straungers goodly so to greet.

57

So she to *Guyon* offred it to tast;
Who taking it out of her tender hond.
The cup to ground did violently cast,
That all in peeces it was broken fond,°
And with the liquor stained all the lond;
510 Whereat *Excesse*° exceedingly was wroth,
Yet no'te° the same amend, ne yet withstond,

But suffered him to passe, all° were she loth;
Who nought regarding her displeasure forward goth.

58

There the most daintie Paradise on ground,
It selfe doth offer to his sober eye,
In which all pleasures plenteously abound,
And none does others happinesse envye:
The painted flowres, the trees upshooting hye,
The dales for shade, the hilles for breathing space,
The trembling groves, the Christall running by;   520
And that, which all faire workes doth most aggrace,
The art, which all that wrought, appeared in no place.

59

One would have thought, (so cunningly, the rude,
And scorned parts were mingled with the fine,)
That nature had for wantonesse ensude°
Art, and that Art at nature did repine;°
So striving each th'other to undermine,
Each did the others worke more beautifie;
So diff'ring both in willes, agreed in fine:
So all agreed through sweete diversitie,   530
This Gardin to adorne with all varietie.

60

And in the midst of all, a fountaine stood,
Of richest substaunce, that on earth might bee,
So pure and shiny, that the silver flood
Through every channell running one might see;
Most goodly it with curious imageree
Was over-wrought, and shapes of naked boyes,
Of which some seemd with lively jollitee,
To fly about, playing their wanton toyes,°
Whilest others did them selves embay° in liquid joyes.   540

61

And over all, of purest gold was spred,
A trayle of yvie in his° native hew:
For the rich mettall was so coloured,
That wight, who did not well avis'd it vew,
Would surely deeme it to be yvie trew:
Low his lascivious armes adown did creepe,
That themselves dipping in the silver dew,
Their fleecy flowres they tenderly did steepe,
Which drops of Christall seemd for wantones° to
   weepe.

62

Infinit streames continually did well   550
Out of this fountaine, sweet and faire to see,
The which into an ample laver° fell,
And shortly grew to so great quantitie,
That like a little lake it seemd to bee;
Whose depth exceeded not three cubits hight,
That through the waves one might the bottom see,

476 **dilate**, stretch forth   494 **weedes**, clothes   499 **scruzd**, squeezed
500 **empeach**, hindrance   508 **fond**, found   510 **Excesse**, the woman's name

511 **no'te**, could not   512 **all**, although   525 **ensude**, imitated   526 **repine**,
take offense   539 **toyes**, frivolous sports   540 **embay**, bathe   542 **his**, its
549 **wantones**, wantonness   552 **laver**, basin

All pav'd beneath with Iaspar shining bright,
That seemd the fountaine in that sea did sayle upright.

63

And all the margent round about was set,
560 With shady Laurell trees, thence to defend
The sunny beames, which on the billowes bet,
And those which therein bathed, mote offend.
As *Guyon* hapned by the same to wend,
Two naked Damzelles he therein espyde,
Which therein bathing, seemed to contend,
And wrestle wantonly, ne car'd to hyde,
Their dainty parts from vew of any, which them eyde.

64

Sometimes the one would lift the other quight
Above the waters, and then downe againe
570 Her plong, as over maistered by might,
Where both awhile would covered remaine,
And each the other from to rise restraine;
The whiles their snowy limbes, as through a vele,
So through the Christall waves appeared plaine:
Then suddeinly both would themselves unhele,°
And th'amorous sweet spoiles to greedy eyes revele.

65

As that faire Starre, the messenger of morne,
His deawy face out of the sea doth reare:
Or as the *Cyprian* goddesse,° newly borne
580 Of th'Oceans fruitfull froth, did first appeare:
Such seemed they, and so their yellow heare
Christalline humour° dropped downe apace.
Whom such when *Guyon* saw, he drew him neare,
And somewhat gan relent his earnest pace,
His stubborne brest gan secret pleasaunce to embrace.

66

The wanton Maidens him espying, stood
Gazing a while at his unwonted guise;
Then th'one her selfe low ducked in the flood,
Abasht, that her a straunger did avise:°
590 But th'other rather higher did arise,
And her two lilly paps aloft displayd,
And all, that might his melting hart entise
To her delights, she unto him bewrayd:
The rest hid underneath, him more desirous made.

67

With that, the other likewise up arose,
And her faire lockes, which formerly were bownd
Up in one knot, she low adowne did lose:
Which flowing long and thick, her cloth'd arownd,
And th'yvorie in golden mantle gownd:
600 So that faire spectacle from him was reft,
Yet that, which reft it, no lesse faire was fownd:
So hid in lockes and waves from lookers theft,
Nought but her lovely face she for his looking left.

68

Withall she laughed, and she blusht withall,
That blushing to her laughter gave more grace,
And laughter to her blushing, as did fall:
Now when they spide the knight to slacke his pace,°
Them to behold, and in his sparkling face
The secret signes of kindled lust appeare,
Their wanton meriments they did encreace,   610
And to him beckned, to approch more neare,
And shewd him many sights, that courage cold could
    reare.°

69

On which when gazing him the Palmer saw,
He much rebukt those wandring eyes of his,
And counseld well, him forward thence did draw.
Now are they come nigh to the *Bowre of blis*
Of her fond favorites so nam'd amis:
When thus the Palmer; Now Sir, well avise;
For here the end of all our travell is:
Here wonnes° *Acrasia*, whom we must surprise,   620
Else she will slip away, and all our drift despise.

70

Eftsoones they heard a most melodious sound,
Of all that mote delight a daintie eare,
Such as attonce might not on living ground,
Save in this Paradise, be heard elsewhere:
Right hard it was, for wight, which did it heare,
To read, what manner musicke that mote bee:
For all that pleasing is to living eare,
Wad there consorted in one harmonee,
Birdes, voyces, instruments, windes, waters, all agree. 630

71

The joyous birdes shrouded in chearefull shade,
Their notes wnto the voyce attempred sweet;
Th' Angelicall soft trembling voyces made
To th'instruments divine respondence meet:
The silver sounding instruments did meet
With the base murmure of the waters fall:
The waters fall with difference discreet,
Now soft, now loud, unto the wind did call:
The gentle warbling wind low answered to all.

72

There, whence that Musick seemed heard to bee,   640
Was the faire Witch her selfe now solacing,
With a new Lover, whom through sorceree
And witchcraft, she from farre did thither bring:
There she had him now layd a slombering,
In secret shade, after long wanton joyes:
Whilst round about them pleasauntly did sing
Many faire Ladies, and lascivious boyes,
That ever mixt their song with light licentious toyes.

---

575 **unhele,** uncover   579 **Cyprian goddesse,** i.e., Venus   582 **Christalline
humour,** clear moisture   589 **avise,** look at

607 **slacke his pace.** The temperate Sir Guyon, here very much a man of flesh
and blood, has been thoroughly aroused by their erotic displays   612 **courage
. . . reare,** excite dormant lust   620 **wonnes,** dwells

And all that while, right over him she hong,
650 With her false eyes fast fixed in his sight,
As seeking medicine, whence she was stong,°
Or greedily depasturing delight:
And oft inclining downe with kisses light,
For feare of waking him, his lips bedewd,
And through his humid eyes did sucke his spright,
Quite molten into lust and pleasure lewd;
Wherewith she sighed soft, as if his case she rewd.

74

The whiles some one did chaunt this lovely lay:
Ah see,° who so faire thing doest faine to see,
660 In springing flowre the image of thy day;
Ah see the Virgin Rose, how sweetly shee
Doth first peepe forth with bashful modestee,
That fairer seemes, the lesse ye see her may;
Lo see soone after, how more bold and free
Her bared bosome she doth broad display;
Loe see soone after, how she fades, and falles away.

75

So passeth, in the passing of a day,
Of mortall life the leafe, the bud, the flowre,
Ne more doth flourish after first decay,
670 That earst° was sought to decke both bed and bowre,
Of many a Ladie, and many a Paramowre:
Gather therefore the Rose, whilest yet is prime,
For soone comes age, that will her pride deflowre:
Gather the Rose of love, whilest yet is time,
Whilest loving thou mayst loved be with equall crime.°

76

He ceast, and then gan all the quire of birdes
Their diverse notes t'attune unto his lay,
As in approvance of his pleasing words.
The constant paire heard all, that he did say,
680 Yet swarved not, but kept their forward way,
Through many covert groves, and thickets close,
In which they creeping did at last display
That wanton Ladie, with her lover lose,°
Whose sleepie head she in her lap did soft dispose.

77

Upon a bed of Roses she was layd,
As faint through heat, or dight to° pleasant sin,
And was arayd, or rather disarayd,
All in a vele of silke and silver thin,
That hid no whit her alabaster skin,
690 But rather shewd more white, if more might bee:
More subtile web *Arachne* cannot spin,
Nor the fine nets, which oft we woven see
Of scorched deaw, do not in th'aire more lightly flee.

78

Her snowy brest was bare to readie spoyle
Of hungry eies, which n'ote therewith be fild,
And yet through languour of her late sweet toyle,
Few drops, more cleare then Nectar, forth distild,
That like pure Orient perles adowne it trild
And her faire eyes sweet smyling in delight,
Moystened their fierie beames, with which she thri   700
Fraile harts, yet quenched not; like starry light
Which sparckling on the silent waves, does seeme
    more bright.

79

The young man sleeping by her, seemd to bee
Some goodly swayne of honorable place,
That certes it great pittie was to see
Him his nobilitie so foule deface;
A sweet regard, and amiable grace,
Mixed with manly sternesse did appeare
Yet sleeping, in his well proportioned face,
And on his tender lips the downy heare   710
Did now but freshly spring, and silken blossomes
    beare.

80

His warlike armes, the idle instruments
Of sleeping praise, were hong upon a tree,
And his brave shield, full of old moniments,
Was fowly ra'st,° that none the signes might see;
Ne for them, ne for honour cared hee,
Ne ought, that did to his advauncement tend,
But in lewd loves, and wastfull luxuree,
His dayes, his goods, his bodie he did spend:
O horrible enchantment, that him so did blend.°   720

81

The noble Elfe, and carefull Palmer drew
So nigh them, minding nought, but lustfull game,
That suddein forth they on them rusht, and threw
A subtile net, which onely for the same
The skilfull Palmer formally° did frame.
So held them under fast, the whiles the rest
Fled all away for feare of fowler shame.
The faire Enchauntresse, so unwares opprest,
Tryde all her arts, and all her sleights, thence
    out to wrest.

82

And eke her lover strove: but all in vaine;   730
For that same net so cunningly was wound,
That neither guile, nor force might it distraine.
They tooke them both, and both them strongly bound
In captive bandes, which there they readie found:
But her in chaines of adamant he tyde;
For nothing else might keepe her safe and sound;

---

651 **stong,** stung   659–675 **Ah see . . . crime,** a lovely, seductive carpe diem
lyric   670 **earst,** first   675 **crime,** sin, fault   683 **lose,** loose   686 **dight to,**
prepared for

715 **ra'st,** erased   720 **blend,** blind   725 **formally,** skillfully

But *Verdant*° (so he hight) he soone untyde,
And counsell sage insteed thereof to him applyde.

83

But all those pleasant bowres and Pallace brave,
740 *Guyon* broke downe, with rigour pittilesse;
Ne ought their goodly workmanship might save
Them from the tempest of his wrathfulnesse,
But that their blisse he turn'd to balefulnesse:
Their groves he feld, their gardins did deface,
Their arbers spoyle, their Cabinets suppresse.
Their banket houses burne, their buildings race,°
And of the fairest late, now made the fowlest place.

84

Then led they her away, and eke that knight
They with them led, both sorrowfull and sad:
750 The way they came, the same retourn'd they right,
Till they arrived, where they lately had
Charm'd those wild-beasts, that rag'd with furie mad.
Which now awaking, fierce at them gan fly,
As in their mistresse reskew, whom they lad;
But them the Palmer soone did pacify.
Then *Guyon* askt, what meant those beastes,
    which there did ly.

85

Said he, These seeming beasts are men indeed,
Whom this Enchauntresse hath transformed thus,
Whylome° her lovers, which her lusts did feed,
760 Now turned into figures hideous,
According to their mindes like monstruous.°
Sad end (quoth he) of life intemperate,
And mournefull meed° of joyes delicious:
But Palmer, if it mote thee so aggrate,
Let them returned be unto their former state.

86

Streight way he with his vertuous staffe them strooke,
And streight of beasts they comely men became;
Yet being men they did unmanly looke,
And stared ghastly, some for inward shame,
770 And some for wrath, to see their captive Dame:
But one above the rest in speciall,
That had an hog beene late, hight *Grille*° by name,
Repined° greatly, and did him miscall,°
That had from hoggish forme him brought to naturall.

87

Said *Guyon*, See the mind of beastly man,
Tmat hath so soone forgot the excellence
Of his creation, when he life began,
That now he chooseth, with vile difference,

To be a beast, and lacke intelligence.
To whom the Palmer thus, The donghill kind   780
Delights in filth and foule incontinence:
Let *Grill* be *Grill*, and have his hoggish mind,
But let us hence depart, whilest wether serves
    and wind.
(1590)

from BOOK III

Book III of *The Faerie Queene* has as its heroine the
lady knight Britomart, who represents the virtue of
Chastity. She does not appear in Canto VI. Her principal feat is the rescue of Amoret (Feminine Grace,
Fidelity) from the wicked magician Busirane (Illicit
Love). In general, Book III is most notable for its passages of elaborate description, such as that of the Garden of Adonis, which follows. After Stanza 53 of
Canto VI, Spenser, with one transitional stanza, returns
to other threads of narrative left unresolved in the
rambling, leisurely course of Book III.

CANTO VI

*The birth of faire Belphoebe and
    of Amoret is told.
The Gardins of Adonis fraught
    with pleasures manifold.*

1

Well may I weene, faire Ladies, all this while
Ye wonder, how this noble Damozell
So great perfections did in her compile,
Sith that in salvage forests she did dwell,
So farre from court and royall Citadell,
The great schoolmistresse of all curtesy:
Seemeth that such wild woods should far expell
All civill usage and gentility,
And gentle sprite deforme with rude rusticity.

2

But to this faire *Belphoebe* in her berth   10
The heavens so favourable were and free,
Looking with myld aspect upon the earth,
In th'*Horoscope* of her nativitee,
That all the gifts of grace and chastitee
On her they poured forth of plenteous horne;
Jove laught on *Venus* from his soveraigne see,
And *Phaebus* with faire beames did her adorne,
And all the *Graces* rockt her cradle being borne.

3

Her berth was of the wombe of Morning dew,
And her conception of the joyous Prime,   20
And all her whole creation did her shew

737 **Verdant,** so called because of his youth and comeliness   746 **race,** raze
759 **Whylome,** formerly   761 **According . . . monstruous.** Baser minds are embodied in baser beasts.   763 **meed,** reward   772 **Grille.** Grill first appears in a
dialogue by Plutarch, in which Odysseus visits with animals enchanted by Circe.
"Gryllus" is happy to remain an animal. In the *Faerie Queene*, he seems to embody those who cannot profit from the lesson of sensual enslavement and degradation as the others have   773 **Repined,** grieved   **miscall,** abuse

Pure and unspotted from all loathly crime,
That is ingenerate in fleshly slime.
So was this virgin borne, so was she bred,
So was she trayned up from time to time,
In all chast vertue, and true bounti-hed
Till to her dew perfection she was ripened.

4

Her mother was the faire *Chrysogonee*,
The daughter of *Amphisa*, who by race
30 A Faerie was, yborne of high degree,
She bore *Belphoebe*, she bore in like cace
Faire *Amoretta* in the second place:
These two were twinnes, and twixt them two did share
The heritage of all celestiall grace.
That all the rest it seem'd they robbed bare
Of bountie, and of beautie, and all vertues rare.

5

It were a goodly storie, to declare,
By what straunge accident faire *Chrysogone*
Conceiv'd these infants, and how them she bare,
40 In this wild forrest wandring all alone,
After she had nine moneths fulfild and gone:
For not as other wemens commune brood,
They were enwombed in the sacred throne
Of her chaste bodie, nor with commune food,
As other wemens babes, they sucked vitall blood.

6

But wondrously they were begot, and bred
Through influence of th'heavens fruitfull ray,
As it in antique bookes is mentioned.
It was upon a Sommers shynie day,
50 When *Titan* faire his beames did display,
In a fresh fountaine, farre from all mens vew,
She bath'd her brest, the boyling heat t' allay;
She bath'd with roses red, and violets blew,
And all the sweetest flowres, that in the forrest grew.

7

Till faint through irkesome wearinesse, adowne
Upon the grassie ground her selfe she layd
To sleepe, the whiles a gentle slombrings wowne
Upon her fell all naked bare displayd;
The sunne-beames bright upon her body playd,
60 Being through former bathing mollifide,
And pierst into her wombe, where they embayd°
With so sweet sence and secret power unspide,
That in her pregnant flesh they shortly fructifide.°

8

Miraculous may seeme to him, that reades
So straunge ensample of conception;
But reason teacheth that the fruitfull seades

Of all things living, through impression
Of the sunbeames in moyst complexion,
Doe life conceive and quickned are by kynd:
So after *Nilus* inundation,   70
Infinite shapes of creatures men do fynd,
Informed in the mud, on which the Sunne hath shynd.

9

Great father he of generation
Is rightly cald, th'author of life and light;
And his faire sister for creation
Ministreth matter fit, which tempred right
With heate and humour, breedes the living wight.
So sprong these twinnes in wombe of *Chrysogone*,
Yet wist she nought thereof, but sore affright,
Wondred to see her belly so upblone,   80
Which still increast, till she her terme had full outgone.

10

Whereof conceiving shame and foule disgrace,
Albe° her guiltlesse conscience her cleard,
She fled into the wildernesse a space,
Till that unweeldy burden she had reard,
And shund dishonor, which as death she feard:
Where wearie of long travell, downe to rest
Her selfe she set, and comfortably cheard;
There a sad cloud of sleepe her overkest,
And seized every sense with sorrow sore opprest.   90

11

It fortuned, faire *Venus* having lost
Her little sonne, the winged god of love,
Who for some light displeasure, which him crost,
Was from her fled, as flit as ayerie Dove,
And left her blisfull bowre of joy above.
(So from her often he had fled away,
When she for ought him sharpely did reprove,
And wandred in the world in strange aray,
Disguiz'd in thousand shapes, that none might him
    bewray.)°

12

Him for to seeke, she left her heavenly hous,   100
The house of goodly formes and faire aspects,
Whence all the world derives the glorious
Features of beautie, and all shapes select,
With which high God his workmanship hath deckt;
And searched every way, through which his wings
Had borne him, or his tract she mote detect:
She promist kisses sweet, and sweeter things
Unto the man, that of him tydings to her brings.

13

First she him sought in Court, where most he used
Whylome to haunt, but there she found him not;   110
But many there she found, which sore accused

Book III Canto VI 61 **embayd,** bathed 63 **fructifide,** a kind of symbolic immaculate conception, based on the notion of spontaneous generation, occurs here
(see ll. 70–72)

83 **Albe,** although 99 **bewray,** recognize

His falsehood, and with foule infamous blot
His cruell deedes and wicked wyles did spot:
Ladies and Lords she every where mote heare
Complayning, how with his empoysned shot
Their wofull harts he wounded had whyle there,
And so had left them languishing twixt hope and feare.

14

She then the Citties sought from gate to gate,
And every one did aske, did he him see;
120 And every one her answerd, that too late
He had him seene, and felt the crueltie
Of his sharpe darts and whot° artillerie;
And every one threw forth reproches rife
Of his mischievous deedes, and said, That hee
Was the disturber of all civill life,
The enimy of peace, and author of all strife.

15

Then in the countrey she abroad him sought,
And in the rurall cottages inquired,
Where also many plaints to her were brought,
130 How he their heedlesse harts with love had fyred,
And his false venim through their veines inspyred;
And eke the gentle shepheard swaynes, which sat
Keeping their fleecie flockes, as they were hyred,
She sweetly heard complaine, both how and what
Her sonne had to them doen; yet she did smile thereat.

16

But when in none of all these she him got,
She gan avize, where else he mote him hyde:
At last she her bethought, that she had not
Yet sought the salvage woods and forrests wyde,
140 In which full many lovely Nymphes abyde,
Mongst whom might be, that he did closely lye,
Or that the love of some of them him tyde:
For thy she thither cast her course t'apply,
To search the secret haunts of *Dianes* company.

17

Shortly unto the wastefull woods she came,
Whereas she found the Goddesse with her crew,
After late chace of their embrewed game,
Sitting beside a fountaine in a rew,
Some of them washing with the liquid dew
150 From off their dainty limbes the dustie sweat,
And soyle which did deforme their lively hew;
Others lay shaded from the scorching heat;
The rest upon her person gave attendance great.

18

She having hong upon a bough on high
Her bow and painted quiver, had unlaste
Her silver buskins from her nimble thigh,
And her lancke loynes ungirt, and brests unbraste,°

After her heat the breathing cold to taste;
Her golden lockes, that late in tresses bright
Embreaded were for hindring of her haste,   160
Now loose about her shoulders hong undight,°
And were with sweet *Ambrosia* all besprinckled light.

19

Soone as she *Venus* saw behind her backe,
She was asham'd to be so loose surprized,
And woxe halfe wroth against her damzels slacke,
That had not her thereof before avized,
But suffred her so carelesly disguized
Be overtaken. Soone her garments loose
Upgath'ring, in her bosome she comprized,
Well as she might, and to the Goddesse rose,   170
Whiles all her Nymphes did like a girlond her enclose.

20

Goodly she gan faire *Cytherea* greet,
And shortly asked her, what cause her brought
Into that wildernesse for her unmeet,
From her sweete bowres, and beds with pleasures
  fraught:
That suddein change she strange adventure thought.
To whom halfe weeping, she thus answered,
That she her dearest sonne *Cupido* sought,
Who in his frowardnesse from her was fled;
That she repented sore, to have him angered.   180

21

Thereat *Diana* gan to smile, in scorne
Of her vaine plaint, and to her scoffing sayd;
Great pittie sure, that ye be so forlorne
Of your gay sonne, that gives ye so good ayd
To your disports: ill mote ye bene apayd.°
But she was more engrieved, and replide;
Faire sister, ill beseemes it to upbrayd
A dolefull heart with so disdainfull pride;
The like that mine, may be your paine another tide.

22

As you in woods and wanton wildernesse   190
Your glory set, to chace the salvage beasts,
So my delight is all in joyfulnesse,
In beds, in bowres, in banckets,° and in feasts:
And ill becomes you with your loftie creasts,
To scorne the joy, that *Jove* is glad to seeke;
We both are bound to follow heavens beheasts,
And tend our charges with obeisance meeke:
Spare, gentle sister, with reproch my paine to eeke.°

23

And tell me, if that ye my sonne have heard,
To lurke emongst your Nymphes in secret wize;   200
Or keepe their cabins: much I am affeard,
Least he like one of them him selfe disguize,

122 whot, hot   157 unbraste, unfastened

161 undight, disordered   185 apayd, rewarded   193 banckets, banquets
198 eeke, increase

Edmund Spenser   **211**

And turne his arrowes to their exercize:
So may he long himselfe full easie hide:
For he is faire and fresh in face and guize,
As any Nymph (let not it be envyde.)
So saying every Nymph full narrowly she eyde.

24

But *Phoebe* therewith sore was angered,
And sharply said: Goe Dame, goe seeke your boy,
210 Where you him lately left, in *Mars* his bed;
He comes not here, we scorne his foolish joy,
Ne lend we leisure to his idle toy:
But if I catch him in this company,
By *Stygian* lake I vow, whose sad annoy
The Gods doe dread, he dearely shall abye:
Ile clip his wanton wings, that he no more shall fly.

25

Whom when as *Venus* saw so sore displeased,
She inly sory was, and gan relent,
What she had said: so her she soone appeased,
220 With sugred words and gentle blandishment,
Which as a fountaine from her sweet lips went,
And welled goodly forth, that in short space
She was well pleasd, and forth her damzels sent,
Through all the woods, to search from place to place,
If any tract of him or tydings they mote trace.

26

To search the God of love, her Nymphes she sent
Throughout the wandring forrest every where:
And after them her selfe eke with her went
To seeke the fugitive, both farre and nere,
230 So long they sought, till they arrived were
In that same shadie covert, whereas lay
Faire *Crysogone* in slombry traunce whilere:
Who in her sleepe (a wondrous thing to say)
Unwares had borne two babes, as faire as springing
  day.

27

Unwares she them conceiv'd, unwares she bore:
She bore withouten paine, that° she conceived
Withouten pleasure: ne her need implore
Lucinaes° aide: which when they both perceived,
They were through wonder nigh of sense bereaved,
240 And gazing each on other, nought bespake:
At last they both agreed, her seeming grieved
Out of her heavy swowne not to awake,
But from her loving side the tender babes to take.

28

Up they them tooke, each one a babe uptooke,
And with them carried, to be fostered;
Dame *Phoebe* to a Nymph her babe betooke,
To be upbrought in perfect Maydenhed,

And of her selfe her name *Belphoebe* red:
But *Venus* hers thence farre away convayd,
To be upbrought in goodly womanhed,   250
And in her litle loves stead, which was strayd,
Her *Amoretta* cald, to comfort her dismayd.

29

She brought her to her joyous Paradize,
Where most she wonnes,° when she on earth does
  dwel.
So faire a place, as Nature can devize:
Whether in *Paphos*, or *Cytheron* hill,
Or it in *Gnidus* be, I wote not well;
But well I wote by tryall, that this same
All other pleasant places doth excell,
And calledsis by her lost lovers name,   260
The *Gardin* of *Adonis*, farre renowmd by fame.

30

In that same Gardin all the goodly flowres,
Wherewith dame Nature doth her beautifie,
And decks the girlonds of her paramoures,
Are fetcht: there is the first seminarie°
Of all things, that are borne to live and die,
According to their kindes. Long worke it were,
Here to account the endlesse progenie
Of all the weedes, that bud and blossome there;
But so much as doth need, must needs be counted   270
  here.

31

It sited was in fruitfull soyle of old,
And girt in with two walles on either side;
The one of yron, the other of bright gold,
That none might thorough breake, nor overstride:
And double gates it had, which opened wide,
By which both in and out men moten pas;
Th'one faire and fresh, the other old and dride:
Old *Genius* the porter of them was,
Old *Genius*, the which a double nature has.

32

He letteth in, he letteth out to wend,   280
All that to come into the world desire;
A thousand thousand naked babes attend
About him day and night, which doe require,
That he with fleshly weedes would them attire:
Such as him list, such as eternall fate
Ordained hath, he clothes with sinfull mire,
And sendeth forth to live in mortall state,
Till they againe returne backe by the hinder gate.

33

After that they againe returned beene,
They in that Gardin planted be againe;   290
And grow afresh, as they had never seene

---

236 **that,** because, since   238 **Lucinaes,** the goddess of childbirth

254 **wonnes,** resides   265 **seminarie,** genetic source

Fleshly corruption, nor mortall paine.
Some thousand yeares so doen they there remaine;
And then of him are clad with other hew,
Or sent into the chaungefull world againe,
Till thither they returne, where first they grew:
So like a wheele around they runne from old to new.

34

Ne needs there Gardiner to set, or sow,
To plant or prune: for of their owne accord
300 All things, as they created were, doe grow,
And yet remember well the mightie word,
Which first was spoken by th'Almightie lord,
That bad them to increase and multiply:
Ne doe they need with water of the ford,
Or of the clouds to moysten their roots dry;
For in themselves eternall moisture they imply.

35

Infinite shapes of creatures there are bred,
And uncouth formes, which none yet ever knew,
And every sort is in a sundry bed
310 Set by it selfe, and ranckt in comely rew:
Some fit for reasonable soules t'indew,
Some made for beasts, some made for birds to weare,
And all the fruitfull spawne of fishes hew
In endlesse rancks along enraunged were,
That seem'd the *Ocean* could not containe them there.

36

Daily they grow, and daily forth are sent
Into the world, it to replenish more;
Yet is the stocke not lessened, nor spent,
But still remaines in everlasting store,
320 As it at first created was of yore.
For in the wide wombe of the world there lyes,
In hatefull darkenesse and in deepe horrore,
An huge eternall *Chaos*, which supplyes
The substances of natures fruitfull progenyes.

37

All things from thence doe their first being fetch,
And borrow matter, whereof they are made,
Which when as forme and feature it does ketch,
Becomes a bodie, and doth then invade
The state of life, out of the griesly shade.
330 That substance is eterne, and bideth so,
Ne when the life decayes, and forme does fade,
Doth it consume, and into nothing go,
But chaunged is, and often altred to and fro.

38

The substance is not chaunged, nor altered,
But th'only forme and outward fashion;
For every substance is conditioned
To change her hew, and sundry formes to don,
Meet for her temper and complexion:

For formes are variable and decay,°
By course of kind, and by occasion;   340
And that faire flowre of beautie fades away,
As doth the lilly fresh before the sunny ray.

39

Great enimy to it, and to all the rest,
That in the *Gardin* of *Adonis* springs,
Is wicked *Time*, who with his scyth addrest,
Does mow the flowring herbes and goodly things,
And all their glory to the ground downe flings,
Where they doe wither, and are fowly mard:
He flyes about, and with his flaggy wings
Beates downe both leaves and buds without regard,   350
Ne ever pittie may relent his malice hard.

40

Yet pittie often did the gods relent,
To see so faire things mard, and spoyled quight:
And their great mother *Venus* did lament
The losse of her deare brood, her deare delight:
Her hart was pierst with pittie at the sight,
When walking through the Gardin, them she spyde,
Yet no'te she find redresse for such despight.
For all that lives, is subject to that law:
All things decay in time, and to their end do draw.   360

41

But were it not, that *Time* their troubler is,
All that in this delightfull Gardin growes,
Should happie be, and have immortall blis,
For here all plentie, and all pleasure flowes,
And sweet love gentle fits emongst them throwes,
Without fell rancor, or fond gealosie;
Franckly each paramour his leman knowes,
Each bird his mate, ne any does envie
Their goodly meriment, and gay felicitie.

42

There is continuall spring, and harvest there   370
Continuall, both meeting at one time:
For both the boughes doe laughing blossomes beare,
And with fresh colours decke the wanton Prime,°
And eke attonce the heavy trees they clime,
Which seeme to labour under their fruits lode:
The whiles the joyous birdes made their pastime
Emongst the shadie leaves, their sweet abode,
And their true loves without suspition tell abrode.

43

Right in the middest of that Paradise,
There stood a stately Mount, on whose round top   380
A gloomy grove of mirtle trees did rise,
Whose shadie boughes sharpe steele did never lop,
Nor wicked beasts their tender buds did crop,

339 **For formes ... decay.** Here Spenser introduces one of his most recurrent
themes, that of mutability (i.e., the principle of inevitable change and decay inherent in human life)   373 **Prime,** spring

But like a girlond compassed the hight,
And from their fruitfull sides sweet gum did drop,
That all the ground with precious deaw bedight,
Threw forth most dainty odours, and most sweet
  delight.

44

And in the thickest covert of that shade,
There was a pleasant arbour, not by art,
390 But of the trees owne inclination made,
Which knitting their rancke braunches part to part,
With wanton yvie twyne, entrayld athwart,
And Eglantine, and Caprifole° emong,
Fashioned above within their inmost part,
The nether *Phoebus* beams could through them
  throng,
Nor *Aeolus* sharp blast could worke them any wrong.

45

And all about grew every sort of flowre,
To which sad lovers were transformd of yore;
Fresh *Hyacinthus*, *Phoebus* paramoure,
400 And dearest love,
Foolish *Narcisse*, that likes the watry shore,
Sad *Amaranthus*, made a flowre but late,
Sad *Amaranthus*, in whose purple gore
Me seemes I see *Amintas*° wretched fate,
To whom sweet Poets verse hath given endlesse date.

46

There wont faire *Venus* often to enjoy
Her deare *Adonis* joyous company,
And reape sweet pleasure of the wanton boy;
There yet, some say, in secret he does ly,
410 Lapped in flowres and pretious spycery,
By her hid from the world, and from the skill
Of *Stygian* Gods, which doe her love envy;
But she her selfe, when ever that she will,
Possesseth him, and of his sweetnesse takes her fill.

47

And sooth it seemes they say: for he may not
For ever die, and ever buried bee
In balefull night, where all things are forgot;
All be he subject to mortalitie,
Yet is eterne in mutabilitie,
420 And by succession made perpetuall,
Transformed oft, and chaunged diverslie:
For him the Father of all formes they call;
Therefore needs mote he live, that living gives to all.

48

There now he liveth in eternall blis,
Joying his goddesse, and of her enjoyd:
Ne feareth he henceforth that foe of his,

Which with his cruell tuske him deadly cloyd:
For that wilde Bore, the which him once annoyd,°
She firmely hath emprisoned for ay,
That her sweet love his malice mote avoyd,   430
In a strong rocky Cave, which is they say,
Hewen underneath that Mount, that none him losen
  may.

49

There now he lives in everlasting joy,
With many of the Gods in company,
Which thither haunt, and with the winged boy
Sporting himselfe in safe felicity:
Who when he hath with spoiles and cruelty
Ransackt the world, and in the wofull harts
Of many wretches set his triumphes hye,
Thither resorts, and laying his sad darts   440
Aside, with faire *Adonis* playes his wanton parts.

50

And his true love faire *Psyche* with him playes,
Faire *Psyche* to him lately reconcyld,
After long troubles and unmeet upbrayes,
With which his mother *Venus* her revyld,
And eke himselfe her cruelly exyld:
But now in steadfast love and happy state
She with him lives and hath him borne a chyld,
Pleasure, that doth both gods and men aggrate,
Pleasure, the daughter of *Cupid* and *Psyche* late.°   450

51

Hither great *Venus* brought this infant faire,
The younger daughter of *Chrysogonee*,
And unto *Psyche* with great trust and care
Committed her, yfostered to bee,
And trained up in true feminitee:
Who no lesse carefully her tendered,
Then her owne daughter *Pleasure*, to whom shee
Made her companion, and her lessoned
In all the lore of love, and goodly womanhead.

52

In which when she to perfect ripenesse grew,   460
Of grace and beautie noble Paragone,
She brought her forth into the worldes vew,
To be th'ensample of true love alone,
And Lodestarre of all chaste affectione,
To all faire Ladies, that doe live on ground.
To Faery court she came, where many one
Admyrd her goodly haveour,° and found
His feeble hart wide launched with loves cruell wound.

53

But she to none of them her love did cast,
Save to the noble knight Sir *Scudamore*,   470

---

393 **Caprifole**, honeysuckle   404 **Amintas**, probably a reference to Sir Philip
Sidney

428 **annoyd**, injured   442–450 **And his . . . late.** Here Spenser recounts the
classical myth of the lovers Cupid and Psyche   467 **haveour**, behavior

To whom her loving hart she linked fast
In faithfull love, t'abide for evermore,
And for his dearest sake endured sore,
Sore trouble of an hainous enimy;
Who her would forced have to have forlore
Her former love, and stedfast loialty,
As ye may elsewhere read that ruefull history.
(1590)

from AMORETTI

1

Happy ye leaves° when as those lilly hands,
which hold my life in their dead doing° might,
shall handle you and hold in loves soft bands,
lyke captives trembling at the victors sight.
5 And happy lines, on which with starry light,
those lamping° eyes will deigne sometimes to look
and reade the sorrowes of my dying spright,
written with teares in harts close bleeding book.
And happy rymes bath'd in the sacred brooke,
10 of *Helicon*° whence she derived is,
when ye behold that Angels blessed looke,
my soules long lacked foode, my heavens blis.
Leaves, lines, and rymes, seeke her to please alone,
whom if ye please, I care for other none.

16

One day as I unwarily did gaze
on those fayre eyes my loves immortall light:
the whiles my stonisht° hart stood in amaze,
through sweet illusion of her lookes delight.
5 I mote° perceive how in her glauncing sight,
legions of loves° with little wings did fly:
darting their deadly arrowes fyry bright,
at every rash beholder passing by.
One of those archers closely I did spy,
10 ayming his arrow at my very hart:
when suddenly with twincle of her eye,
the Damzell broke his misintended dart.
Had she not so doon, sure I had bene slayne,
yet as it was, I hardly° scap't with paine.

34

Lyke as a ship that through the Ocean wyde,
by conduct of some star doth make her way,
whenas a storme hath dimd her trusty guyde,
out of her course doth wander far astray.
5 So I whose star, that wont with her bright ray,
me to direct, with cloudes is overcast,
doe wander now in darknesse and dismay,
through hidden perils round about me plast.
Yet hope I well, that when this storme is past

my *Helice*° the lodestar of my lyfe   10
will shine again, and looke on me at last,
with lovely light to cleare my cloudy grief.
Till then I wander carefull comfortlesse,
in secret sorrow and sad pensivenesse.

54

Of this worlds Theatre in which we stay,
My love lyke the Spectator ydly sits
Beholding me that all the pageants play,
Disguysing diversly my troubled wits.
Sometimes I joy when glad occasion fits,   5
And mask in myrth lyke to a Comedy:
Soone after when my joy to sorrow flits,
I waile and make my woes a Tragedy.
Yet she beholding me with constant eye,
Delights not in my merth nor rues° my smart: 10
But when I laugh she mocks, and when I cry
She laughes, and hardens evermore her hart.
What then can move her? if nor merth nor mone,
She is no woman, but a sencelesse stone.

75

One day I wrote her name upon the strand,
but came the waves and washed it away:
agayne I wrote it with a second hand,
but came the tyde, and made my paynes his pray.
Vayne man, sayd she, that doest in vaine assay,   5
a mortall thing so to immortalize,
for I my selve shall lyke to this decay,
and eek my name bee wyped out lykewize.
Not so, (quod I) let baser things devize
to dy in dust, but you shall live by fame: 10
my verse° your vertues rare shall eternize,
and in the hevens wryte your glorious name.
Where whenas death shall all the world subdew,
our love shall live, and later life renew.

79

Men call you fayre, and you doe credit° it,
for that your selfe ye dayly such doe see:
but the trew fayre, that is the gentle wit,
and vertuous mind, is much more praysd of me.
For all the rest, how ever fayre it be,   5
shall turne to nought and loose° that glorious hew:
but onely that is permanent and free
from frayle corruption, that doth flesh ensew.
That is true beautie: that doth argue you
to be divine and borne of heavenly seed: 10
deriv'd from that fayre Spirit,° from whom al true
And perfect beauty did at first proceed.
He onely fayre, and what he fayre hath made,
all other fayre lyke flowres untymely fade.
(1595)

Amoretti Sonnet 1 1 leaves, pages of the sonnets 2 dead doing, death-
dealing 6 lamping, shining 10 Helicon, a mountain in Boeotia sacred to Apollo
and the Muses Sonnet 16 3 stonisht, astonished 5 mote, might 6 loves,
cupids 14 hardly, barely, with difficulty

Sonnet 34 10 Helice, the constellation of the Great Bear Sonnet 54
10 rues, pities Sonnet 75 11 my verse, etc., a common sonnet conceit
Sonnet 79 1 credit, believe 6 loose, lose 11 fayre Spirit, God

EPITHALAMION

Ye learned sisters° which have oftentimes
Beene to me ayding, others to adorne:
Whom ye thought worthy of your gracefull rymes,
That even the greatest did not greatly scorne
To heare theyr names sung in your simple layes,
But joyed in theyr prayse.
And when ye list your owne mishaps to mourne,
Which death, or love, or fortunes wreck° did rayse,
Your string could soone to sadder tenor turne,
10 And teach the woods and waters to lament
Your dolefull dreriment.
Now lay those sorrowfull complaints aside,
And having all your heads with girland crownd,
Helpe me mine owne loves prayses to resound,
Ne let the same of any be envide:
So Orpheus° did for his owne bride,
So I unto my selfe alone will sing,
The woods shall to me answer and my Eccho ring.

Early before the worlds light giving lampe,
20 His golden beame upon the hils doth spred,
Having disperst the nights unchearefull dampe,
Doe ye awake, and with fresh lusty-hed,
Go to the bowre of my beloved love,
My truest turtle dove,
Bid her awake; for Hymen° is awake,
And long since ready forth his maske° to move,
With his bright Tead° that flames with many a flake,
And many a bachelor° to waite on him,
In theyr fresh garments trim.
30 Bid her awake therefore and soone her dight,°
For lo the wished day is come at last,
That shall for al the paynes and sorrowes past,
Pay to her usury of long delight:
And whylest she doth her dight,
Doe ye to her of joy and solace sing,
That all the woods may answer and your eccho ring.

Bring with you all the Nymphes that you can heare
Both of the rivers and the forrests greene:
And of the sea that neighbours to her neare,°
40 Al with gay girlands goodly wel beseene.°
And let them also with them bring in hand,
Another gay girland
For my fayre love of lillyes and of roses,
Bound truelove wize with a blew silke riband.
And let them make great store of bridale poses,
And let them eeke bring store of other flowers

To deck the bridale bowers.
And let the ground whereas her foot shall tread,
For feare the stones her tender foot should wrong
Be strewed with fragrant flowers all along,   50
And diapred° lyke the discolored mead.
Which done, doe at her chamber dore awayt,
For she will waken strayt,
The whiles doe ye this song unto her sing,
The woods shall to you answer and your Eccho ring.

Ye Nymphes of Mulla which with carefull heed,
The silver scaly trouts doe tend full well,
And greedy pikes which use therein to feed,
(Those trouts and pikes all others doo excell)
And ye likewise which keepe the rushy lake,   60
Where none doo fishes take,
Bynd up the locks the which hang scatterd light,
And in his waters which your mirror make,
Behold your faces as the christall bright,
That when you come whereas my love doth lie,
No blemish she may spie.
And eke ye lightfoot mayds which keepe the deere,
That on the hoary mountayne use to towre,°
And the wylde wolves which seeke them to devoure,
With your steele darts doo chace from comming neer, 70
Be also present heere,
To helpe to decke her and to help to sing,
That all the woods may answer and your eccho ring.

Wake, now my love, awake: for it is time,
The Rosy Morne long since left Tithones° bed,
All ready to her silver coche° to clyme,
And Phoebus gins to shew his glorious hed.
Hark how the cheerefull birds do chaunt theyr laies
And carroll of loves praise.
The merry Larke hir mattins sings aloft,   80
The thrush replyes, the Mavis° descant playes,
The Ouzell° shrills, the Ruddock° warbles soft,
So goodly all agree with sweet consent,
To this dayes merriment.
Ah my deere love why doe ye sleepe thus long,
When meeter were that ye should now awake,
T'awayt the comming of your joyous make,°
And hearken to the birds love-learned song,
The deawy leaves among.
For they of joy and pleasance to you sing,   90
That all the woods them answer and theyr eccho ring.

My love is now awake out of her dreame,
And her fayre eyes like stars that dimmed were
With darksome cloud, now shew theyr goodly beams
More bright then Hesperus° his head doth rere.
Come now ye damzels, daughters of delight,
Helpe quickly her to dight,

Epithalamion   1 learned sisters, the nine Muses   8 wreck, violence   16 Orpheus, son of Apollo and Calliope. Orpheus went to Hades to recover his dead wife Eurydice, tamed Cerberus, the watchdog of Hades, and with the persuasive power of his music moved Pluto to release Eurydice. But on his return to the world of light, he disobeyed Pluto's injunctions by looking back to see if his wife was following him; consequently he lost her again   25 Hymen, the god of marriage   26 maske, a court entertainment, here celebrating a wedding   27 Tead, torch, Hymen's symbol   28 bachelor, candidate for knighthood   30 dight, dress   39 neighbours . . . neare. Elizabeth Boyle, to whom the hymn was addressed, lived at Kilcoran on the Bay of Youghal, County Cork   40 beseene, adorned

51 diapred, variegated   68 towre, climb in a spiral   75 Tithones, the beloved of Aurora, who prevailed upon Jupiter to grant him immortality, but failed to ask for eternal youth also   76 coche, coach   81 Mavis, song thrush   82 Ouzell, blackbird   Ruddock, the European robin   87 make, mate   95 Hesperus, the evening star

But first come ye fayre houres which were begot
In Jove's sweet paradice, of Day and Night,
100 Which doe the seasons of the yeare allot,
And al that ever in this world is fayre
Doe make and still repayre.
And ye three handmayds° of the Cyprian Queene,
The which doe still adorne her beauties pride,
Helpe to addorne my beautifullest bride:
And as ye her array, still throw betweene
Some graces to be seene,
And as ye use to Venus, to her sing,
The whiles the woods shal answer and your eccho
    ring.

110 Now is my love all ready forth to come,
Let all the virgins therefore well awayt,
And ye fresh boyes that tend upon her groome
Prepare your selves; for he is comming strayt.
Set all your things in seemely good aray
Fit for so joyfull day,
The joyfulst day that ever sunne did see.
Faire Sun, shew forth thy favourable ray,
And let thy lifull° heat not fervent be
For feare of burning her sunshyny face,
120 Her beauty to disgrace.
O fayrest Phoebus, father of the Muse,
If ever I did honour thee aright,
Or sing the thing that mote thy mind delight,
Doe not thy servants simple boone refuse,
But let this day let this one day be myne,
Let all the rest be thine.
Then I thy soverayne prayses loud wil sing,
That all the woods shal answer and theyr eccho ring.

Harke how the Minstrels gin to shrill aloud
130 Their merry Musick that resounds from far,
The pipe, the tabor,° and the trembling Croud,°
That well agree withouten breach or jar.
But most of all the Damzels doe delite,
When they their tymbrels smyte,
And thereunto doe daunce and carrol sweet,
That all the sences they doe ravish quite,
The whyles the boyes run up and downe the street,
Crying aloud with strong confused noyce,
As if it were one voyce.
140 Hymen, iô Hymen,° Hymen they do shout,
That even to the heavens theyr shouting shrill
Doth reach, and all the firmament doth fill,
To which the people standing all about,
As in approvance doe thereto applaud
And loud advaunce her laud,°
And evermore they Hymen, Hymen sing,
That al the woods them answer and theyr eccho ring.
Loe where she comes along with portly pace°

Lyke Phoebe° from her chamber of the East,
Arysing forth to run her mighty race,   150
Clad all in white, that seemes a virgin best.
So well it her beseemes that ye would weene
Some angell she had beene.
Her long loose yellow locks lyke golden wyre,
Sprinckled with perle, and perling flowres a tweene,
Doe lyke a golden mantle her attyre,
And being crowned with a girland greene,
Seeme lyke some mayden Queene.
Her modest eyes abashed to behold
So many gazers, as on her do stare,   160
Upon the lowly ground affixed are.
Ne dare lift up her countenance too bold,
But blush to heare her prayses sung so loud,
So farre from being proud.
Nathlesse doe ye still loud her prayses sing.
That all the woods may answer and your eccho ring.

Tell me ye merchants daughters did ye see
So fayre a creature in your towne before,
So sweet, so lovely, and so mild as she,
Adornd with beautyes grace and vertues store,   170
Her goodly eyes lyke Saphyres shining bright,
Her forehead yvory white,
Her cheekes lyke apples which the sun hath rudded,
Her lips lyke cherryes charming men to byte,
Her brest like to a bowle of creame uncrudded,°
Her paps lyke lyllies budded,
Her snowie necke lyke to a marble towre,°
And all her body like a pallace fayre,
Ascending uppe with many a stately stayre,
To honours seat and chastities sweet bowre.   180
Why stand ye still ye virgins in amaze,
Upon her so to gaze,
Whiles ye forget your former lay to sing,
To which the woods did answer and your eccho ring.

But if ye saw that which no eyes can see,
The inward beauty of her lively spright,
Garnisht with heavenly guifts of high degree,
Much more then would ye wonder at that sight,
And stand astonisht lyke to those which red°
Medusaes mazeful hed.°   190
There dwels sweet love and constant chastity,
Unspotted fayth and comely womanhood,
Regard of honour and mild modesty,
There vertue raynes as Queene in royal throne,
And giveth lawes alone.
The which the base affections doe obay,
And yeeld theyr services unto her will,
Ne thought of thing uncomely ever may
Thereto approch to tempt her mind to ill.
Had ye once seene these her celestial threasures,   200

---

103 **three handmayds,** the three Graces who served Aphrodite, supposedly born in Cyprus   118 **lifull,** lifegiving   131 **tabor,** small drum   **Croud,** ancient Celtic stringed instrument   140 **Hymen iô Hymen,** a shout of joy in praise of the god of marriage, used in Latin marriage songs   145 **laud,** praise

148 **portly pace,** dignified step   149 **Phoebe,** the moon   175 **uncrudded,** uncurdled   177 **marble towre.** Cf. *Song of Solomon* 4:4   189 **red,** saw 190 **Medusaes mazeful hed.** The snaky-locked head of the Gorgon turned to stone all who beheld it

And unrevealed pleasures,
Then would ye wonder and her prayses sing,
That al the woods should answer and your eccho ring.

Open the temple gates° unto my love,
Open them wide that she may enter in,
And all the postes adorne as doth behove,
And all the pillours deck with girlands trim,
For to recyve this Saynt with honour dew,
That commeth in to you.
210 With trembling steps and humble reverence,
She commeth in, before th'almighties vew,
Of her ye virgins learne obedience,
When so ye come into those holy places,
To humble your proud faces:
Bring her up to th'high altar, that she may
The sacred ceremonies there partake,
The which do endlesse matrimony make,
And let the roring Organs loudly play
The praises of the Lord in lively notes,
220 The whiles with hollow throates
The Choristers the joyous Antheme sing,
That al the woods may answere and their eccho ring.

Behold whiles she before the altar stands
Hearing the holy priest that to her speakes
And blesseth her with his two happy hands,
How the red roses flush up in her cheekes,
And the pure snow with goodly vermill° stayne,
Like crimsin dyde in grayne,
That even th'Angels which continually,
230 About the sacred Altare doe remaine,
Forget their service and about her fly,
Ofte peeping in her face that seemes more fayre,
The more they on it stare.
But her sad° eyes still fastened on the ground,
Are governed with goodly modesty,
That suffers not one looke to glaunce awry,
Which may let in a little thought unsownd.
Why blush ye love to give to me your hand,
The pledge of all our band?°
240 Sing, ye sweet Angels, Alleluya sing,
That all the woods may answere and your eccho ring.

Now al is done: bring home the bride againe,
Bring home the triumph of our victory,
Bring home with you the glory of her gaine,
With joyance bring her and with jollity.
Never had man more joyfull day then this,
Whom heaven would heape with blis.
Make feast therefore now all this live long day,
This day for ever to me holy is,
250 Poure out the wine without restraint or stay,
Poure not by cups, but by the belly full,
Poure out to all that wull,

And sprinkle all the postes and wals with wine,
That they may sweat, and drunken be withall.
Crowne ye God Bacchus with a coronall,
And Hymen also crowne with wreathes of vine,
And let the Graces daunce unto the rest;
For they can doo it best:
The whiles the maydens doe theyr carroll sing,
To which the woods shal answer and theyr eccho ring.   260

Ring ye the bels, ye yong men of the towne,
And leave your wonted labors for this day:
This day is holy; doe ye write it downe,
That ye for ever it remember may.
This day the sunne is in his chiefest hight,°
With Barnaby the bright,
From whence declining daily by degrees,
He somewhat loseth of his heat and light,
When once the Crab° behind his back he sees.
But for this time it ill ordained was,   270
To chose the longest day in all the yeare,
And shortest night, when longest fitter weare:
Yet never day so long, but late would passe.
Ring ye the bels, to make it weare away,
And bonefiers make all day,
And daunce about them, and about them sing:
That all the woods may answer, and your eccho ring.

Ah when will this long weary day have end,
And lende me leave to come unto my love?
How slowly do the houres theyr numbers spend?   280
How slowly does sad Time his feathers move?
Hast thee O fayrest Planet to thy home
Within the Westerne fome:
Thy tyred steedes long since have need of rest.
Long though it be, at last I see it gloome,
And the bright evening star with golden creast
Appeare out of the East.
Fayre childe° of beauty, glorious lampe of love
That all the host of heaven in rankes doost lead,
And guydest lovers through the nightes dread,   290
How chearefully thou lookest from above,
And seemst to laugh atweene thy twinkling light
As joying in the sight
Of these glad many which for joy doe sing,
That all the woods them answer and their eccho ring.

Now ceasse ye damsels your delights forepast;
Enough is it, that all the day was youres:
Now day is doen, and night is nighing fast:
Now bring the Bryde into the brydall boures.
Now night is come, now soone her disaray,   300
And in her bed her lay;
Lay her in lillies and in violets,
And silken courteins over her display,
And odourd sheetes, and Arras coverlets.°

204 **Open . . . gates.** Cf. *Psalms* 24:7–10   227 **vermill,** crimson
234 **sad,** serious   239 **band,** bond

265 **sunne . . . hight.** June 11, Spenser's wedding day, was the summer solstice in the old calendar   269 **Crab,** the zodiacal sign associated with Cancer
288 **Fayre childe,** etc. Hesperus   304 **Arras coverlets,** tapestry covers woven in Arras, France

218   *The Renaissance*

Behold how goodly my faire love does ly
In proud humility;
Like unto Maia,° when as Jove her tooke,
In Tempe,° lying on the flowry gras,
Twixt sleepe and wake, after she weary was,
310 With bathing in the Acidalian brooke.°
Now it is night, ye damsels may be gon,
And leave my love alone,
And leave likewise your former lay to sing:
The woods no more shal answere, nor your eccho ring.

Now welcome night, thou night so long expected,
That long daies labour doest at last defray,
And all my cares, which cruell love collected,
Hast sumd in one, and cancelled for aye:
Spread thy broad wing over my love and me,
320 That no man may us see,
And in thy sable mantle us enwrap,
From feare of perrill and foule horror free.
Let no false treason seeke us to entrap,
Nor any dread disquiet once annoy
The safety of our joy:
But let the night be calme and quietsome,
Without tempestuous storms or sad afray:
Lyke as when Jove with fayre Alcmena lay,
When he begot the great Tirynthian groome:°
330 Or lyke as when he with thy selfe did lie,
And begot Majesty.
And let the mayds and yongmen cease to sing:
Ne let the woods them answer, nor theyr eccho ring.

Let no lamenting cryes, nor dolefull teares,
Be heard all night within nor yet without:
Ne let false whispers, breeding hidden feares,
Breake gentle sleepe with misconceived dout.
Let no deluding dreames, nor dreadful sights
Make sudden sad affrights;
340 Ne let housefyres, nor lightnings helpelesse harmes,
Ne let the Pouke,° nor other evill sprights,
Ne let mischivous witches with theyr charmes,
Ne let hob Goblins, names whose sence we see not,
Fray us with things that be not.
Let not the shriech Oule, nor the Storke be heard:
Nor the night Raven that still deadly yels,
Nor damned ghosts cald up with mighty spels,
Nor griesly vultures make us once affeard:
Ne let th'unpleasant Quyre of Frogs still croking
350 Make us to wish theyr choking.
Let none of these theyr drery accents sing;
Ne let the woods them answer, nor theyr eccho ring.

But let stil Silence trew night watches keepe,
That sacred peace may in assurance rayne,
And tymely sleep, when it is tyme to sleepe,
May poure his limbs forth on your pleasant playne,
The whiles an hundred little winged loves,

Like divers fethered doves,
Shall fly and flutter round about your bed,
And in the secret darke, that none reproves,   360
Their prety stealthes shal worke, and snares shal
    spread
To filch away sweet snatches of delight,
Conceald through covert night.
Ye sonnes of Venus, play your sports at will,
For greedy pleasure, carelesse of your toyes,
Thinks more upon her paradise of joyes,
Then what ye do, albe it good or ill.
All night therefore attend your merry play,
For it will soone be day:
Now none doth hinder you, that say or sing,   370
Ne will the woods now answer, nor your Eccho ring.

Who is the same, which at my window peepes?
Or whose is that faire face, that shines so bright,
Is it not Cinthia,° she that never sleepes,
But walkes about high heaven al the night?
O fayrest goddesse, do thou not envy
My love with me to spy:
For thou likewise didst love, though now unthought,
And for a fleece of woll, which privily,
The Latmian shepherd° once unto thee brought,   380
His pleasures with thee wrought.
Therefore to us be favorable now;
And sith of wemens labours thou hast charge,
And generation goodly dost enlarge,
Encline thy will t'effect our wishfull vow,
And the chast wombe informe with timely seed,
That may our comfort breed:
Till which we cease our hopefull hap° to sing,
Ne let the woods us answere, nor our Eccho ring.

And thou great Juno, which with awful might   390
The lawes of wedlock still dost patronize,
And the religion of the faith first plight
With sacred rites hast taught to solemnize:
And eeke for comfort often called art
Of women in their smart,
Eternally bind thou this lovely band,
And all thy blessings unto us impart.
And thou glad Genius, in whose gentle hand,
The bridale bowre and geniall° bed remaine,
Without blemish or staine,   400
And the sweet pleasures of theyr loves delight
With secret ayde dost succour and supply,
Till they bring forth the fruitfull progeny,
Send us the timely fruit of this same night.
And thou fayre Hebe,° and thou Hymen free,
Grant that it may so be.
Till which we cease your further prayse to sing,
Ne any woods shal answer, nor your Eccho ring.

---

307 **Maia**, one of the Pleiades; she became the mother of Hermes   308 **Tempe**,
a Thessalian valley   310 **Acidalian brooke**, the outlet of the well Acidalis in
Boeotia   329 **Tirynthian groome**, Hercules   341 **Pouke**, the Pooka, a malicious
phantom in Irish folklore

374 **Cinthia**, the moon   380 **Latmian shepherd**, Endymion, a shepherd boy from
Mount Latmos with whom the moon goddess fell in love as he slept; Spenser has
modified the legend   388 **hap**, good fortune   399 **geniall**, nuptial   405 **Hebe**,
goddess of youth

And ye high heavens, the temple of the gods,
410 In which a thousand torches flaming bright
Doe burne, that to us wretched earthly clods,
In dreadful darknesse lend desired light;
And all ye powers which in the same remayne,
More then we men can fayne,°
Poure out your blessings on us plentiously,
And happy influence upon us raine,
That we may raise a large posterity,
Which from the earth, which they may long possesse,
With lasting happinesse,
420 Up to your haughty pallaces may mount,
And for the guerdon° of theyr glorious merit
May heavenly tabernacles there inherit,
Of blessed Saints for to increase the count.
So let us rest, sweet love, in hope of this,
And cease till then our tymely joyes to sing,
The woods no more us answer, nor our eccho ring.

Song made in lieu of many ornaments,
With which my love should duly have bene dect,
While cutting off through hasty accidents,°
430 Ye would not stay your dew time to expect,
But promist both to recompens,
Be unto her a goodly ornament,
And for short time an endlesse moniment.°
(1595)

CHRISTOPHER MARLOWE
1564–1593

Marlowe was born in Canterbury in 1564, the son of a shoemaker. He received a scholarship and was educated at Cambridge, where he received an M.A. in 1587. Soon after that he became associated as a dramatist with the Admiral's Men, a theatrical company which produced most of his plays. He is chiefly known for his dramas: *Tamburlaine* (in which he helped introduce blank verse to the stage), *The Jew of Malta, Edward II,* and *Dr. Faustus. Tamburlaine* established the characteristically Marlovian hero who obsessively thirsts for limitless, godlike power. Tamburlaine seeks the power to rule; Barabas in *The Jew of Malta* seeks the power of money; Mortimer in *Edward II* seeks political authority; and Faustus seeks the power of knowledge.

We do not know many details about Marlowe's life during the short, turbulent years of his career. In 1593, we do know that the playwright Thomas Kyd, with whom Marlowe had at one time lived, supported charges that Marlowe held treasonable and atheistic

ideas. Before Marlowe could appear in court for questioning, he was stabbed in a barroom brawl at Deptford by a drinking companion. Although a coroner's jury certified that his assailant had acted in self-defense, Marlowe's death may have resulted from a plot against him due, as some scholars believe, to his possible activities as a government agent. When he died at the age of twenty-nine, he had already left behind him dramas and poems that would earn him a lasting place in English literature; if his contemporary, Shakespeare, had died at the same age, he would be almost unknown today.

THE PASSIONATE SHEPHERD TO HIS LOVE°

Come live with me and be my Love,
And we will all the pleasures prove
That hills and valleys, dales and fields,
Or woods or steepy mountain yields.

And we will sit upon the rocks,   5
And see the shepherds feed their flocks
By shallow rivers, to whose falls
Melodious birds sing madrigals.

And I will make thee beds of roses
And a thousand fragrant posies;   10
A cap of flowers, and a kirtle°
Embroidered all with leaves of myrtle;

A gown made of the finest wool
Which from our pretty lambs we pull;
Fair-linéd slippers for the cold,   15
With buckles of the purest gold;

A belt of straw and ivy buds
With coral clasps and amber studs—
And if these pleasures may thee move,
Come live with me and be my Love.   20

The shepherd swains shall dance and sing
For thy delight each May morning—
If these delights thy mind may move,
Then live with me and be my Love.
(1599, 1600)

THE NYMPH'S REPLY TO THE SHEPHERD

If all the world and love were young,
And truth in every shepherd's tongue,
These pretty pleasures might me move,
To live with thee and be thy love.

---

414 **fayne,** imagine   421 **guerdon,** reward   429 **hasty accidents.** Possibly the wedding date had been advanced   433 **moniment,** monument

The Passionate Shepherd. This pastoral lyric appeared in *England's Helicon*
11 **kirtle,** gown   **The Nymph's Reply.** This cynical reply to Marlowe's lyric is attributed to Sir Walter Raleigh

5 But time drives flocks from field to fold,
    When rivers rage, and rocks grow cold;
    And Philomel° becometh dumb;
    The rest complains of cares to come.

    The flowers do fade, and wanton fields
10 To wayward Winter reckoning yields;
    A honey tongue, a heart of gall,
    Is fancy's spring, but sorrow's fall.

    Thy gowns, thy shoes, thy bed of roses,
    Thy cap, thy kirtle, and thy posies,
15 Soon break, soon wither, soon forgotten,
    In folly ripe, in reason rotten.

    Thy belt of straw and ivy buds,
    Thy coral clasps and amber studs,
    All these in me no means can move,
20 To come to thee and be thy love.

    But could youth last, and love still breed,
    Had joys no date, nor age no need,
    Then these delights my mind might move,
    To live with thee and be thy love.
    (1599)

THE TRAGICAL HISTORY
OF DOCTOR FAUSTUS

Marlowe probably composed *Doctor Faustus* in the
winter of 1588–89, although some scholars argue for
the date 1592. The earliest known edition of the play,
a truncated acting text which shows the hand of a less
talented collaborator, was not published until 1604.
An enlarged edition published in 1616, though more
reliable on the whole, presumably contains the "additions" of low farce for which two hack playwrights
were paid in 1602. The problem of establishing an
authentic text of *Doctor Faustus* is thus unusually
complicated. However, considerable scholarship undertaken in the last few decades, particularly the
pioneer work of Boas and Greg, has at last recon-
structed a comprehensible, reasonably authoritative
text. That printed here follows Boas' composite text for
the play; it is based primarily on the edition of 1616,
which most bibliographers consider to be the less
corrupt of the two extant versions.

Marlowe's tragedy of Dr. Faustus is apparently
based upon a simple narrative account in German
(1587) of the career of Dr. John Faust, a necromancer.
This popular work was soon translated into English
and utilized selectively by Marlowe in his dramatic
version of the story. The serious scenes and the basic
conception of the play as a whole were Marlowe's,
but many comic episodes closely resembling those in
the *Faustbook* source seem to have been introduced by
some other dramatist, probably after the death of
Marlowe, with the aim of making his *Doctor Faustus*
more of a commercial success on the stage. Marlowe's
rather sophisticated philosophical treatment of the
medieval Faust legend was widely admired during his
own period; later, it provided much of the inspiration
for Goethe's epic drama *Faust*.

Although conventionally regarded as an epitome of
the Renaissance ideal of the search for knowledge, a
kind of Promethean figure, Marlowe's Faustus comes
to be evaluated at something far less within the
psychological morality-play scheme of the tragedy.
The sympathetic Promethean element is present, of
course, but the supposedly lofty aspirations of Faustus
often sound indistinguishable from an adolescent's
daydream of sexual extravaganzas, adulation by his
fellows, unreproved pranks against authority, and the
like. But despite this apparent duality in his characterization, his decline and fall remain psychologically absorbing.

DRAMATIS PERSONAE

THE CHORUS.
DOCTOR FAUSTUS.
WAGNER, *his servant*.
VALDES, } *friends to*
CORNELIUS, } *Faustus*.
THREE SCHOLARS.
AN OLD MAN.

THE POPE.
RAYMOND, *King of Hungary*.
BRUNO.
TWO CARDINALS.
ARCHBISHOP OF RHEIMS.
CARDINAL OF LORRAINE.
CHARLES, *Emperor of Germany*.
MARTINO, }
FREDERICK, } *Gentlemen*
BENVOLIO, } *of his Court*.
A KNIGHT.
DUKE OF SAXONY.
DUKE OF ANHOLT.
DUCHESS OF ANHOLT.
BISHOPS, MONKS, FRIARS, SOLDIERS
    and ATTENDANTS.

CLOWN.
ROBIN, *an ostler*.
DICK.
RALPH.
A VINTNER.
A HORSE-COURSER.
A CARTER.
HOSTESS.

---

7 **Philomel,** the nightingale; the allusion is to the legend that Philomela was a
maiden whose tongue was cut out by Tereus, her sister's husband, in order that
she might not reveal his rape of her

GOOD ANGEL.
BAD ANGEL.
EVIL ANGEL.
MEPHISTOPHILIS.
LUCIFER.
BELZEBUB.
DEVILS.
THE SEVEN DEADLY SINS.
ALEXANDER THE GREAT,
PARAMOUR OF ALEXANDER,
DARIUS,   } *Spirits.*
HELEN,
TWO CUPIDS,

ACT I
PROLOGUE *Enter* CHORUS.

    CHORUS.° Not marching in the fields of Thrasimen,°
Where Mars did mate the warlike Carthagens;
Nor sporting in the dalliance of love,
In courts of kings, where state° is over-turn'd;
Nor in the pomp of proud audacious deeds,
Intends our Muse to vaunt his heavenly verse:
Only this, Gentles—we must now perform
The form° of Faustus' fortunes, good or bad:
And now to patient judgments we appeal,
10 And speak for Faustus in his infancy.
Now is he born, of parents base of stock,
In Germany, within a town call'd Rhode:°
At riper years, to Wittenberg° he went,
Whereas his kinsmen chiefly brought him up.
So much he profits in divinity,°
The fruitful plot of scholarism grac'd,°
That shortly he was grac'd with Doctor's name,
Excelling all and sweetly can dispute°
In th' heavenly matters of theology;
20 Till swoln with cunning,° of a self-conceit,
His waxen wings° did mount above his reach,
And, melting, heavens conspir'd his overthrow;
For, falling to a devilish exercise,
And glutted now with learning's golden gifts,
He surfeits upon cursed necromancy;°
Nothing so sweet as magic is to him,
Which he prefers before his chiefest bliss:°
And this the man that in his study sits.   {*Exit.*

SCENE I FAUSTUS *in his Study.*

    FAUST. Settle thy studies, Faustus, and begin
To sound the depth of that thou wilt profess:

Having commenc'd,° be a divine in show,°
Yet level° at the end of every art,
And live and die in Aristotle's works.
Sweet Analytics, 'tis thou hast ravish'd me!
Bene disserere est finis logices.
Is, to dispute well, logic's chiefest end?
Affords this art no greater miracle?
Then read no more; thou hast attain'd that end.   10
A greater subject fitteth Faustus' wit:
Bid ὂν χαὶ μὴ ὂν farewell;° and Galen° come;
Seeing, *Ubi desinit philosophus ibi incipit medicus,*°
Be a physician, Faustus; heap up gold,
And be eternis'd° for some wondrous cure!
Summum bonum medicinæ sanitas,
The end of physic is our body's health.
Why, Faustus, hast thou not attain'd that end?
Is not thy common talk sound aphorisms?°
Are not thy bills° hung up as monuments,   20
Whereby whole cities have escap'd the plague,
And thousand desp'rate maladies been cur'd?°
Yet art thou still but Faustus, and a man.°
Couldst thou make men to live eternally,
Or, being dead, raise them to life again,
Then this profession were to be esteem'd.
Physic, farewell! Where is Justinian?°   {*Reads.*
'*Si una eademque res legatur duobus
Alter rem, alter valorem rei,*' etc.°
A petty case of paltry legacies!   {*Reads.* 30
'*Exhæreditare filium non potest pater nisi*'°—
Such is the subject of the Institute,
And universal body of the law.
This study fits a mercenary drudge,
Who aims at nothing but external trash;
Too servile and illiberal for me.
When all is done, divinity is best:
Jeromë's Bible,° Faustus; view it well.   {*Reads.*
'*Stipendium peccati mors est.*'° Ha! '*Stipendium,*' etc.
The reward of sin is death: that's hard.°   {*Reads.* 40
'*Si peccasse negamus, fallimur
Et nulla est in nobis veritas.*'°
If we say that we have no sin,
We deceive ourselves, and there is no truth in us
Why, then, belike we must sin,
And so consequently die:
Ay, we must die an everlasting death.
What doctrine call you this, *Che sera, sera:*°
What will be, shall be? Divinity, adieu!

Act I, i   3 **commenc'd,** graduated   **in show,** in appearance only   4 **level,** aim   12 **Bid . . . farewell,** being and not being, i.e., philosophy   **Galen,** an ancient medical authority   13 **Ubi . . . medicus,** where the philosopher leaves off the physician begins   15 **eternis'd.** Faustus is already obsessed with the idea of immortality through fame   19 **aphorisms,** medical opinions   20 **bills,** prescriptions   21–22 **Whereby . . . cur'd.** Faustus' great potentiality for good is repeatedly indicated   23 **and a man.** Faustus identifies himself with the gods rather than with human beings and aspires to their power   27 **Justinian,** Roman emperor and legal authority   28–29 **Si . . . rei, etc.** If something is bequeathed to two persons, one shall have the thing itself, the other something of equal value   31 **Exhœreditare . . . nisi,** a father cannot disinherit his son unless—   38 **Jeromë's Bible,** the Vulgate   39 **Stipendium. . . est.,** translated in l. 40   40 **hard,** hard to accept   41–42 **Si . . . veritas,** translated in ll. 43–44   48 **Che sera, sera,** translated in l. 49.Faustus rationalizes the Bible's injunctions into a kind of supernatural manipulation of determinism, but his real objection seems to be that this Christian doctrine recognizes no exceptions; he apparently desires a special dispensation on the basis of intellectual superiority

The Tragical History of Doctor Faustus   1 **Chorus,** a single actor who recited a prologue to the play or an act. This introductory device is employed here to give a condensed history of Faustus' life up to the point which the action will cover and to define the conservative moral position on his researches   **Thrasimen,** Lake Trasimeno, the site of one of Hannibal's greatest victories over the Romans   4 **state,** political power   8 **form,** course, outline   12 **Rhode,** Roda, in Saxe-Altenburg   13 **Wittenberg,** the famous university   15 **divinity,** theology   16 **grac'd,** graced   18 **dispute,** debate   20 **cunning,** knowledge, learning   21 **waxen wings, etc.,** an allusion to the Greek myth of Icarus and Daedalus   25 **necromancy,** black magic   27 **chiefest bliss,** eternal salvation

50 These metaphysics of magicians,
And necromantic books are heavenly;
Lines, circles, letters, and characters;
Ay, these are those that Faustus most desires.
O, what a world of profit and delight,
Of power, of honour, and omnipotence,
Is promised to the studious artizan!°
All things that move between the quiet poles
Shall be at my command: emperors and kings
Are but obey'd in their several provinces,
60 Nor can they raise the wind, or rend the clouds;
But his dominion° that exceeds° in this,
Stretcheth as far as doth the mind of man;
A sound magician is a demigod:°
Here, tire my brain to get a deity!

Enter WAGNER.

Wagner, commend me to my dearest friends,
The German Valdes and Cornelius;
Request them earnestly to visit me.
        WAG. I will, sir.   {Exit.
        FAUST. Their conference will be a greater help to me
70 Than all my labours, plot I ne'er so fast.

Enter the GOOD ANGEL and BAD ANGEL.°

        GOOD ANG. O, Faustus, lay that damned book aside,
And gaze not on it, lest it tempt thy soul,
And heap God's heavy wrath upon thy head!
Read, read the Scriptures:—that is blasphemy.
        BAD ANG. Go forward, Faustus, in that famous art
Wherein all Nature's treasure is contain'd:
Be thou on earth as Jove is in the sky,
Lord and commander of these elements.°
                               {Exeunt ANGELS.
        FAUST. How am I glutted with conceit° of this!
80 Shall I make spirits fetch me what I please,
Resolve me of all ambiguities,°
Perform what desperate enterprise I will?
I'll have them fly to India for gold,
Ransack the ocean for orient pearl,
And search all corners of the new-found world
For pleasant fruits and princely delicates;
I'll have them read me strange philosophy,
And tell the secrets of all foreign kings;
I'll have them wall all Germany with brass,
90 And make swift Rhine circle fair Wittenberg.
I'll have them fill the public schools° with silk,
Wherewith the students shall be bravely° clad;
I'll levy soldiers with the coin they bring,

And chase the Prince of Parma from our land,
And reign sole king of all the Provinces;
Yea, stranger engines for the brunt of war,
Than was the fiery keel° at Antwerp's bridge,
I'll make my servile spirits to invent.
                               {He calls within.

Enter VALDES and CORNELIUS.

Come, German Valdes, and Cornelius,
And make me blest with your sage conference!   100
Valdes, sweet Valdes, and Cornelius,
Know that your words have won me at the last
To practise magic and concealed arts:
Yet not your words only, but mine own fantasy,
That will receive no object;° for my head
But ruminates on necromantic skill.
Philosophy is odious and obscure;
Both law and physic are for petty wits;
Divinity is basest° of the three,
Unpleasant, harsh, contemptible, and vile: 110
'Tis magic, magic, that hath ravish'd me.
Then, gentle friends, aid me in this attempt
And I, that have with subtle syllogisms
Gravell'd° the pastors of the German church,
And made the flowering pride of Wittenberg
Swarm to my problems,° as the infernal spirits°
On sweet Musaeus when he came to hell,
Will be as cunning as Agrippa° was,
Whose shadows made all Europe honour him.
        VALD. Faustus, these books, thy wit, and our ex-   120
        perience
Shall make all nations to canonize us.
As Indian Moors° obey their Spanish lords,
So shall the spirits of every element
Be always serviceable to us three;
Like lions shall they guard us when we please;
Like Almain rutters° with their horsemen's staves,
Or Lapland giants, trotting by our sides;
Sometimes like women, or unwedded maids,
Shadowing more beauty in their airy brows
Than has the white breasts of the queen of love;°   130
From Venice shall they drag huge argosies,
And from America the golden fleece°
That yearly stuffs old Philip's° treasury;
If learned Faustus will be resolute.°
        FAUST. Valdes, as resolute am I in this
As thou to live: therefore object it not.°
        CORN. The miracles that magic will perform

97 **fiery keel,** a reference to the burning ship used in an attack on Antwerp by
the Dutch in 1585   105 **receive no object,** dwell on no aspect of physical reality   109 **basest.** Faustus has expediently changed his mind   114 **Gravell'd,**
confounded   116 **problems,** in logic or mathematics   **infernal spirits,** an unconscious anticipation of his own destiny   118 **Agrippa,** medieval German author (1486?–1535) supposed to have the power of summoning ghosts ("shadows")
122 **Indian Moors,** South American Indians   126 **Almain rutters,** German
horsemen   128–130 **Sometimes . . . love,** a fine early specimen of the sensuous,
erotic imagery which appropriately pervades the tragedy of Marlowe's "lascivious" Faustus   132 **golden fleece,** a calculated adaptation of the classical myth
of Jason's quest   133 **Philip's,** Philip II of Spain   134 **resolute.** Faustus later
adopts this word as a kind of perverse motto which recalls him at moments of
conscience to perseverance in his career of evil   136 **object it not,** don't stipu-
late it

56 **artizan,** master (of magic)   61 **dominion,** power, range of control   **exceeds,**
excels   63 **demigod,** again the aspiration to deity   **Enter . . . Angel.** These
familiar figures of morality drama are more than literal presences or symbols in
Doctor Faustus; they represent opposite poles of the hero's moral will. They appear regularly at moments of soliloquy or intense inner conflict and constitute a
highly sophisticated device of psychological exposition   75–78 **Go forward . . .
elements.** The Bad Angel strategically tempts Faustus to that which he is most
susceptible   79 **conceit,** idea, possibility   81 **Resolve . . . ambiguities.** Ironically, Faustus does have this objective answered by his bond, but not as he would
wish   91 **public schools,** university lecture rooms   92 **bravely,** resplendently

Will make thee vow to study nothing else.
He that is grounded in astrology,
140 Enrich'd with tongues, well seen° in minerals,
Hath all the principles magic doth require:
Then doubt not, Faustus, but to be renown'd,
And more frequented for this mystery°
Than heretofore the Delphian oracle.
The spirits tell me they can dry the sea,
And fetch the treasure of all foreign wrecks,
Yea, all the wealth that our forefathers hid
Within the massy° entrails of the earth:
Then tell me, Faustus, what shall we three want?
150 FAUST. Nothing, Cornelius. O, this cheers my soul!
Come, show me some demonstrations magical,
That I may conjure in some bushy grove,
And have these joys in full possession.
    VALD. Then haste thee to some solitary grove,
And bear wise Bacon's° and Albertus' works,
The Hebrew Psalter, and New Testament;°
And whatsoever else is requisite
We will inform thee ere our conference cease.
    CORN. Valdes, first let him know the words of art;
160 And then, all other ceremonies learn'd,
Faustus may try his cunning by himself.
    VALD. First I'll instruct thee in the rudiments,
And then wilt thou be perfecter than I.
    FAUST. Then come and dine with me, and, after
        meat,
We'll canvass every quiddity° thereof;
For, ere I sleep, I'll try what I can do:
This night I'll conjure, though I die° therefore.
                                    {Exeunt omnes.

SCENE II *Before Faustus' house. Enter* TWO SCHOL-
ARS.

    FIRST SCHOL. I wonder what's become of Faustus,
that was wont to make our schools ring with *sic probo.*°

Enter WAGNER.

    SEC. SCHOL. That shall we presently know; here
comes his boy.
    FIRST SCHOL. How now, sirrah! where's thy master?
    WAG. God in heaven knows.
    SEC. SCHOL. Why, dost not thou know, then?
    WAG. Yes, I know; but that follows not.
    FIRST SCHOL. Go to, sirrah! leave your jesting, and
10 tell us where he is.
    WAG. That follows not by force of argument, which

you, being Licentiates,° should stand upon; therefore
acknowledge your error, and be attentive.
    SEC. SCHOL. Then you will not tell us?
    WAG. You are deceiv'd, for I will tell you: yet, if you
were not dunces, you would never ask me such a
question; for is he not *corpus naturale?* and is not that
mobile?° Then wherefore should you ask me such a
question? But that I am by nature phlegmatic,° slow to
wrath, and prone to lechery (to love, I would say), it 20
were not for you to come within forty foot of the place
of execution,° although I do not doubt but to see you
both hanged the next sessions. Thus having triumph'd
over you, I will set my countenance like a precisian,°
and begin to speak thus:—Truly, my dear brethren,
my master is within at dinner, with Valdes and Cornelius, as this wine, if it could speak, would inform
your worships: and so, the Lord bless you, preserve
you, and keep you, my dear brethren.   {*Exit.*
    FIRST SCHOL. O Faustus. Then I fear that which I 30
        have long suspected,
That thou art fallen into that damned art
For which they two are infamous through the world.
    SEC. SCHOL. Were he a stranger, not allied to me,
The danger of his soul would make me mourn.
But, come, let us go and inform the Rector,°
It may be his grave counsel may reclaim him.
    FIRST SCHOL. I fear me nothing will reclaim him
        now!
    SEC. SCHOL. Yet let us see what we can do.
                                    {*Exeunt.*

SCENE III *A grove. Enter* FAUSTUS *to conjure.*

    FAUST. Now that the gloomy shadow of the night,
Longing to view Orion's drizzling look,°
Leaps from th' antarctic world unto the sky,
And dims the welkin° with her pitchy breath,
Faustus, begin thine incantations,
And try if devils will obey thy hest,°
Seeing thou hast pray'd and sacrific'd to them.
Within this circle is Jehovah's name,
Forward and backward anagrammatiz'd;
Th' abbreviated names of holy saints,   10
Figures of every adjunct° to the heavens,
And characters of signs° and erring° stars,
By which the spirits are enforc'd to rise:
Then fear not, Faustus, to be resolute,
And try the utmost magic can perform.   {*Thunder.*
'*Sint mihi Dii Acherontis propitii! Valeat numen trip-
lex Jehovæ! Ignis, aeris, aquæ, terrae spiritus, salvete!*

Orientis princeps, Belzebub, inferni ardentis
monarcha, et Demogorgon, propitiamus vos, ut ap-
20 *pareat et surgat Mephistophilis.°* [*Enter* DRAGON
above.] *Quid tu moraris?° per Jehovam, Gehennam, et*
consecratam aquam quam nunc spargo, signumque
crucis quod nunc facio, et per vota nostra, ipse nunc
surgat nobis dicatus Mephistophilis!°

Enter MEPHISTOPHILIS.

I charge thee to return, and change thy shape;
Thou art too ugly to attend on me:
Go, and return an old Franciscan friar;
That holy shape becomes a devil best.°
               {*Exit* MEPHISTOPHILIS.
I see there's virtue° in my heavenly words:
30 Who would not be proficient in this art?
How pliant is this Mephistophilis,
Full of obedience and humility!
Such is the force of magic and my spells:
Now, Faustus, thou art conjuror laureat,
That canst command great Mephistophilis.
Quin redis, Mephistophilis, fratris imagine!°

Re-enter MEPHISTOPHILIS *like a Franciscan friar.*

    MEPH. Now, Faustus, what would'st thou have me
      do?
    FAUST. I charge thee wait upon me whilst I live,
To do whatever Faustus shall command,
40 Be it to make the moon drop from her sphere,
Or the ocean to overwhelm the world.
    MEPH. I am a servant to great Lucifer,
And may not follow thee without his leave;
No more than he commands must we perform.
    FAUST. Did not he charge thee to appear to me?
    MEPH. No, I came now hither of mine own accord.
    FAUST. Did not my conjuring raise thee? speak.
    MEPH. That was the cause, but yet *per accidens;°*
For, when we hear one rack° the name of God,
50 Abjure the Scriptures and his Saviour Christ,
We fly, in hope to get his glorious soul;
Nor will we come, unless he use such means
Whereby he is in danger to be damn'd.
Therefore the shortest cut for conjuring
Is stoutly to abjure the Trinity,
And pray devoutly to the prince of hell.
    FAUST. So Faustus hath
Already done; and holds this principle,
There is no chief but only Belzebub;
60 To whom Faustus doth dedicate himself.
This word 'damnation' terrifies not me,

For I confound hell in Elysium:
My ghost be with the old philosophers!°
But, leaving these vain trifles of men's souls,
Tell me what is that Lucifer thy lord?
    MEPH. Arch-regent and commander of all spirits.
    FAUST. Was not that Lucifer an angel once?
    MEPH. Yes, Faustus, and most dearly lov'd of God.
    FAUST. How comes it then that he is prince of
      devils?
    MEPH. O, by aspiring pride and insolence;°   70
For which God threw him from the face of heaven.
    FAUST. And what are you that live with Lucifer?
    MEPH. Unhappy spirits that fell with Lucifer,
Conspir'd against our God with Lucifer,
And are for ever damn'd with Lucifer.
    FAUST. Where are you damn'd?
    MEPH.   In hell.
    FAUST. How comes it then that thou art out of hell?
    MEPH. Why this is hell,° nor am I out of it:
Think'st thou that I, that saw the face of God,
And tasted the eternal joys of Heaven,   80
Am not tormented with ten thousand hells,
In being depriv'd of everlasting bliss?
O, Faustus,° leave these frivolous demands,
Which strikes a terror to my fainting soul!
    FAUST. What, is great Mephistophilis so passionate
For being deprived of the joys of heaven?
Learn thou of Faustus manly fortitude,
And scorn those joys thou never shalt possess.°
Go bear these tidings to great Lucifer:
Seeing Faustus hath incurr'd eternal death   90
By desperate thoughts against Jove's deity,
Say, he surrenders up to him his soul,
So he will spare him four-and-twenty years,
Letting him live in all voluptuousness;°
Having thee ever to attend on me,
To give me whatsoever I shall ask,
To tell me whatsoever I demand,
To slay mine enemies, and to aid my friends,
And always be obedient to my will.
Go, and return to mighty Lucifer,   100
And meet me in my study at midnight,
And then resolve me of thy master's mind.
    MEPH. I will, Faustus.   {*Exit.*
    FAUST. Had I as many souls as there be stars,
I'd give them all for Mephistophilis.
By him I'll be great Emperor of the world,
And make a bridge through the moving air,
To pass the ocean with a band of men;
I'll join the hills that bind the Afric shore,
And make that country continent to Spain,   110

21 **Quid . . . moraris.** What are you waiting for 21–24 **per . . . Mephistophilis.**
By Jehova, Gehenna, and the holy water which I now sprinkle, and the sign of the
cross which I now make, and by our vows [as Christians], may Mephistophilis
himself now rise to serve us (apparently a more potent incantation) 27–28 **friar
. . . best,** anti-Catholic satire which crops up throughout the play 29 **virtue,** efficacy 36 **Quin . . . imagine.** Return, Mephistophilis, in the likeness of a friar
48 **per accidens,** by the immediate, not the ultimate, cause 49 **rack,** torture (by
blaspheming)

63 **old philosophers,** pre-Christian thinkers who regarded heaven and hell indifferently 70 **by aspiring pride and insolence,** a pointed parallel to the present
case of Faustus himself 78 **this is hell.** Marlowe's hell is a symbol for the
abstract psychological suffering of the spiritually rebellious 83 **O, Faustus, etc.**
Faustus fails to take warning from Mephistophilis' evident sincerity here 87–
88 **Learn . . . possess.** Faustus presumes to instruct the devil in casuistry. However, he is unable to follow his own advice here when he too faces damnation (V,
ii) 94 **all voluptuousness,** unlimited sensual indulgence (again, not knowledge)

Christopher Marlowe   **225**

And both contributory to my crown:
The Emperor shall not live but by my leave,
Nor any potentate of Germany.
Now that I have obtain'd what I desir'd,
I'll live in speculation° of this art,
Till Mephistophilis return again.   {Exit.

SCENE IV Enter WAGNER and the CLOWN.

WAG. Come hither, sirrah boy.
CLOWN.° Boy! O disgrace to my person. Zounds,
boy in your face! You have seen many boys with
beards, I am sure.
WAG. Sirrah, hast thou no comings in?°
CLOWN. Yes, and goings out too, you may see, sir.
WAG. Alas, poor slave! see how poverty jests in his
nakedness! I know the villain's out of service, and so
hungry, that I know he would give his soul to the devil
10 for a shoulder of mutton, though it were blood-raw.
CLOWN. Not so, neither. I had need to have it well-
roasted, and good sauce to it, if I pay so dear, I can tell
you.
WAG. Sirrah, wilt thou be my man and wait on me,
and I will make thee go like Qui mihi discipulus?°
CLOWN. What, in verse?
WAG. No slave; in beaten silk and stavesacre.°
CLOWN. Stavesacre! that's good to kill vermin.
Then, belike, if I serve you, I shall be lousy.
20 WAG. Why, so thou shalt be, whether thou do'st it or
no. For, sirrah, if thou do'st not presently bind thyself
to me for seven years, I'll turn all the lice about thee
into familiars,° and make them tear thee in pieces.
CLOWN. Nay, sir, you may save yourself a labour,
for they are as familiar with me as if they had paid for
their meat and drink, I can tell you.
WAG. Well, sirrah, leave your jesting and take these
guilders.
CLOWN. Yes, marry, sir, and I thank you too.
30 WAG. So, now thou art to be at an hour's warning,
whensoever and wheresoever the devil shall fetch
thee.
CLOWN. Here, take your guilders again, I'll none of
'em.
WAG. Not I, thou art pressed,° for I will presently
raise up two devils to carry thee away—Banio,
Belcher!
CLOWN. Belcher! and Belcher come here, I'll belch
him. I am not afraid of a devil.

Enter two DEVILS.

40 WAG. How now, sir, will you serve me now?
CLOWN. Ay, good Wagner, take away the devil then.

WAG. Spirits, away! Now, sirrah, follow me.
                                        {Exeunt DEVILS.
CLOWN. I will, sir, but hark you, master, will you
teach me this conjuring occupation?
WAG. Ay, sirrah, I'll teach thee to turn thyself to a
dog, or a cat, or a mouse, or a rat, or any thing.°
CLOWN. A dog, or a cat, or a mouse, or a rat, O
brave° Wagner!
WAG. Villain, call me Master Wagner, and see that
you walk attentively and let your right eye be always 50
diametrally fixed upon my left heel, that thou may'st
quasi vestigias nostras insistere.°
CLOWN. Well, sir, I warrant you.   {Exeunt.

ACT II
SCENE I Enter FAUSTUS in his study.

FAUST. Now, Faustus, must
Thou needs be damn'd,° and canst thou not be sav'd.
What boots° it, then, to think on God or heaven?
Away with such vain fancies, and despair;
Despair in God, and trust in Belzebub:
Now go not backward; Faustus, be resolute:
Why waver'st thou? O, something soundeth in mine
    ear,
'Abjure this magic, turn to God again!'
Ay, and Faustus will turn to God again.
To God? he loves thee not;   10
The God thou serv'st is thine own appetite,
Wherein is fix'd the love of Belzebub:
To him I'll build an altar and a church,
And offer lukewarm blood of newborn babes.

Enter the two ANGELS.

BAD ANG. Go forward, Faustus, in that famous art.
GOOD ANG. Sweet Faustus, leave that execrable art.
FAUST. Contrition, prayer, repentance—what of
    these?
GOOD ANG. O, they are means to bring thee unto
    heaven!
BAD ANG. Rather illusions, fruits of lunacy,
That make them foolish that do use them most.   20
GOOD ANG. Sweet Faustus, think of heaven and
    heavenly things.
BAD ANG. No, Faustus; think of honour and of
    wealth.   {Exeunt ANGELS.
FAUST. Wealth! Why, the signiory of Emden° shall
    be mine.
When Mephistophilis shall stand by me,
What power can hurt me? Faustus, thou art safe:
Cast no more doubts—Mephistophilis, come!
And bring glad tidings from great Lucifer;—

---

115 **speculation,** contemplation   **Sc. iv** 2 **Clown,** a rustic buffoon (not a court
jester)   5 **comings in,** income   15 **Qui . . . discipulus,** you who are my pupil.
The whole of Scene iv is a richly evaluative comic parallel to Faustus' interview
with Mephistophilis in the preceding scene. This morality-style technique of
comic alternation occurs throughout *Doctor Faustus*   17 **stavesacre,** a kind of
delphinium for killing vermin   23 **familiars,** demons, familiar spirits
35 **pressed,** drafted, hired

46 **a dog . . . or any thing,** the first of many suggestions in the play that Faustus'
contract aligns him with the animals, not the gods   48 **brave,** wonderful
52 **quasi . . . insistere,** follow my footsteps   **Act II, i**   2–14 **Thou needs be
damned,** etc. Faustus is thus easily distracted from painful reconsiderations
throughout the play   3 **boots,** avails   23 **Emden,** a wealthy German trade
center

Is't not midnight?—come, Mephistophilis,
Veni, veni, Mephistophile!°

Enter MEPHISTOPHILIS.

30 Now tell me what saith Lucifer, thy lord?
    MEPH. That I shall wait on Faustus while he lives,
So he will buy my service with his soul.
      FAUST. Already Faustus hath hazarded that for thee.
    MEPH. But now thou must bequeath it solemnly,
And write a deed of gift with thine own blood;
For that security craves Lucifer.
If thou deny it, I must back to hell.
      FAUST. Stay, Mephistophilis, tell me what good
Will my soul do thy lord?°
40   MEPH. Enlarge his kingdom.
      FAUST. Is that the reason why he tempts us thus?
    MEPH. *Solamen miseris socios habuisse doloris.*°
      FAUST. Why, have you any pain that torture others?
    MEPH. As great as have the human souls of men.
But tell me, Faustus, shall I have thy soul?
And I will be thy slave, and wait on thee,
And give thee more than thou hast wit to ask.
      FAUST. Ay, Mephistophilis, I'll give it him.
    MEPH. Then, Faustus, stab thy arm courageously,
50 And bind thy soul, that at some certain day
Great Lucifer may claim it as his own;
And then be thou as great as Lucifer.
      FAUST [*stabbing his arm*]. Lo, Mephistophilis, for
    love of thee,
I cut mine arm, and with my proper° blood
Assure my soul to be great Lucifer's,
Chief lord and regent of perpetual night!
View here this blood that trickles from mine arm,
And let it be propitious for my wish.°
    MEPH. But, Faustus,
60 Write it in manner of a deed of gift.
      FAUST. Ay, so I do. [*Writes.*] But, Mephistophilis,
My blood congeals, and I can write no more.
    MEPH. I'll fetch thee fire to dissolve it straight.
                         {*Exit.*
      FAUST. Why might the staying° of my blood por-
    tend?
Is it unwilling I should write this bill?°
Why streams it not, that I may write afresh?
Faustus gives to thee his soul: oh, there it stay'd!
Why shouldst thou not? is not thy soul thine own?
Then write again, *Faustus gives to thee his soul.*

Re-enter MEPHISTOPHILIS *with a chafer° of fire.*

70   MEPH. See, Faustus, here is fire, set it on.
      FAUST. So, now the blood begins to clear again;

Now will I make an end° immediately.   {*Writes.*
    MEPH. What will not I do to obtain his soul?
                              {*Aside.*
      FAUST. *Consummatum est;*° this bill is ended,
And Faustus hath bequeath'd his soul to Lucifer.
But what is this inscription° on mine arm?
Homo, fuge!° Whither should I fly?
If unto God, he'll throw me down to hell.
My senses are deceiv'd; here's nothing° writ:—
Oh yes, I see it plain; even here is writ,   80
Homo, fuge! Yet shall not Faustus fly.
    MEPH. I'll fetch him somewhat to delight his mind.°
                    {*Aside, and then exit.*

Enter DEVILS, *giving crowns and rich apparel to*
FAUSTUS. *They dance, and then depart.*

Enter MEPHISTOPHILIS.

      FAUST. What means this show? Speak, Mephis-
    tophilis.
    MEPH. Nothing, Faustus, but to delight thy mind,
And let thee see what magic can perform.
      FAUST. But may I raise such spirits when I please?
    MEPH. Ay, Faustus, and do greater things than
    these.
      FAUST. Then there's enough for a thousand souls.
Here, Mephistophilis, receive this scroll,
A deed of gift of body and of soul: 90
But yet conditionally that thou perform
All articles prescrib'd between us both.
    MEPH. Faustus, I swear by hell and Lucifer
To effect all promises between us made!
      FAUST. Then hear me read it, Mephistophilis.

*On these conditions following. First, that Faustus may
be a spirit in form and substance. Secondly, that
Mephistophilis shall be his servant, and at his command. Thirdly, that Mephistophilis shall do for him,
and bring him whatsoever. Fourthly, that he shall be in* 100
*his chamber or house invisible. Lastly, that he shall
appear to the said John Faustus at all times, in what
form or shape soever he please.*
*I, John Faustus, of Wittenberg, Doctor, by these pres-
ents, do give both body and soul to Lucifer Prince of
the East, and his minister Mephistophilis; and furthermore grant unto them that, four and twenty years
being expired, and these articles above written being
inviolate, full power to fetch or carry the said John
Faustus, body and soul, flesh, blood, or goods, into* 110
their habitation wheresoever.
                         By me, John Faustus.

---

29 **Veni . . . Mephistophile.** Come, come, Mephistophilis   38–39 **what good
. . . thy lord.** A guarded reprise of the earlier scene of catechism follows here
42 **Solamen . . . doloris.** Misery loves company   53–58 **Lo, . . . wish,** a kind of
blasphemous sacrificial offer   54 **proper,** own   64 **staying,** clotting, holding
back. Even his body opposes this unnatural pact. See also the "staying" of Faustus' supplicating hands when the bond comes due, V, ii   65 **bill,** contract
chafer, portable grate

72 **make an end,** conclude (symbolically, damn [myself])   74 **Consummatum
est.** It is finished—the last words of Christ on the Cross (see *John*, 19:30). Faustus'
deed of blood is in part a blasphemous analogue to Christ's sacrifice
76 **inscription,** another miraculous external manifestation of his inner conflict
77 **Homo, fuge.** Man, fly   79 **nothing.** The miracle (or hallucination) disappears
as soon as Faustus reasons himself into perseverance in this course, but then the
outward signs of his doubts immediately recur   82 **delight his mind.** Mephistophilis cleverly distracts Faustus whenever he considers repentance

MEPH. Speak, Faustus, do you deliver this as your deed?

FAUST. Ay, take it, and the devil give thee good of it!

MEPH. So, now, Faustus, ask me what thou wilt.

FAUST. First I will question with thee about hell.°
Tell me, where is the place that men call hell?

MEPH. Under the heavens.

FAUST. Ay, so are all things else, but whereabouts?

120 MEPH. Within the bowels of these elements,
Where we are tortur'd and remain for ever:
Hell hath no limits, nor is circumscrib'd
In one self place; but where we are is hell,
And where hell is, there must we ever be:
And, to be short, when all the world dissolves,
And every creature shall be purified,
All places shall be hell that is not heaven.

FAUST. I think hell's a fable.

MEPH. Ay, think so, till experience change thy mind.

130 FAUST. Why, dost thou think that Faustus shall be damn'd?

MEPH. Ay, of necessity, for here's the scroll
In which thou hast given thy soul to Lucifer.

FAUST. Ay, and body too: but what of that?
Think'st thou that Faustus is so fond° to imagine
That, after this life, there is any pain?
No, these are trifles and mere old wives' tales.°

MEPH. But I am an instance to prove the contrary;°
For I tell thee I am damn'd, and now in hell.

FAUST. Nay, and this be hell, I'll willingly be damn'd:

140 What! sleeping, eating, walking, and disputing!
But, leaving off this, let me have a wife,
The fairest maid in Germany, for I
Am wanton and lascivious
And cannot live without a wife.

MEPH. I prithee, Faustus, talk not of a wife.°

FAUST. Nay, sweet Mephistophilis, fetch me one,
for I will have one.

MEPH. Well, Faustus, thou shalt have a wife.

He fetches in a WOMAN-DEVIL.

FAUST. What sight is this?

MEPH. Now, Faustus, wilt thou have a wife?

150 FAUST. Here's a hot whore indeed! No, I'll no wife.

MEPH. Marriage is but a ceremonial toy:
And if thou lovest me, think no more of it.
I'll cull thee out the fairest courtesans,
And bring them ev'ry morning to thy bed:
She whom thine eye shall like, thy heart shall have,
Were she as chaste as was Penelope,°
As wise as Saba,° or as beautiful

As was bright Lucifer° before his fall.
Here, take this book, and peruse it well:
The iterating° of these lines brings gold;   160
The framing° of this circle on the ground
Brings thunder, whirlwinds, storm and lightning;
Pronounce this thrice devoutly to thyself,
And men in harness shall appear to thee,
Ready to execute what thou command'st.

FAUST. Thanks, Mephistophilis, for this sweet book.°
This will I keep as chary as my life.   {*Exeunt.*

SCENE II *Enter* FAUSTUS *in his study and* MEPHIS-
TOPHILIS.

FAUST. When I behold the heavens, then I repent,
And curse thee, wicked Mephistophilis,
Because thou hast depriv'd me of those joys.

MEPH. 'Twas thine own seeking, Faustus, thank thyself.
But think'st thou heaven is such a glorious thing?
I tell thee, Faustus, it is not half so fair
As thou, or any man that breathes on earth.

FAUST. How prov'st thou that?

MEPH. 'Twas made for man; then he's more excellent.

FAUST. If heaven was made for man, 'twas made for   10
me:
I will renounce this magic and repent.

Enter the two ANGELS.

GOOD ANG. Faustus, repent; yet God will pity thee.

BAD ANG. Thou art a spirit;° God cannot pity thee.

FAUST. Who buzzeth in mine ears, I am a spirit?
Be I a devil, yet God may pity me;
Yea, God will pity me, if I repent.

BAD ANG. Ay, but Faustus never shall repent.
{*Exeunt* ANGELS.

FAUST. My heart is harden'd, I cannot repent:
Scarce can I name salvation, faith, or heaven,
But fearful echoes thunders in mine ears,   20
'Faustus, thou art damn'd!' Then swords, and knives,
Poison, guns, halters, and envenom'd steel
Are laid before me to despatch myself;
And long ere this I should have done the deed,
Had not sweet pleasure° conquer'd deep despair.
Have not I made blind Homer sing to me
Of Alexander's° love and Oenon's° death?
And hath not he, that built the walls of Thebes,°
With ravishing sound of his melodious harp,
Made music with my Mephistophilis?   30

---

116 **hell.** Appropriately, Faustus is much intrigued by hell   134–136 **Thinks't . . . tales.** Faustus adheres to a rationalist's attitudes on the matter since the pros-pect they offer is less painful for him to anticipate   134 **fond,** foolish   137 **But I . . . the contrary.** Mephistophilis is often wryly humorous   145 **talk not of a wife.** Mephistophilis quibbles because marriage is a sacrament. Then he success-fully diverts Faustus from this purpose with the woman devil and his promises   156 **Penelope,** wife of Ulysses   157 **Saba,** the Queen of Sheba

158 **Lucifer,** not a very tactful comparison at this point   160 **iterating,** repeating   161 **framing,** drawing   166 **book.** This book of magic is repeatedly contrasted to the Scriptures   **Sc. ii**   13 **a spirit,** a demon   25 **pleasure.** In his last hours Faustus also seeks to obliterate despair through pleasure and again projects him-self into a classical context, desiring none other than Helen of Troy   27 **Alex-ander,** Paris   **Oenon,** the nymph Paris deserted for Helen of Troy; she later killed herself   28 **he, that built . . . Thebes,** Amphion, a legendary musician

Why should I die, then, or basely despair?
I am resolv'd; Faustus shall not repent.—
Come, Mephistophilis, let us dispute again,
And reason of divine astrology.
Speak, are there many spheres above the moon?
Are all celestial bodies but one globe,
As is the substance of this centric earth?

    MEPH. As are the elements, such are the heavens,
Even from the moon unto the imperial orb,
40 Mutually folded in each others' spheres,
And jointly move upon one axletree,°
Whose termine° is termed the world's wide pole;
Nor are the names of Saturn, Mars, or Jupiter
Feign'd but are erring stars.

    FAUST.   But have they all
One motion, both *situ et tempore?*°

    MEPH. All move from east to west in four and twenty
hours upon the poles of the world; but differ in their
motions upon the poles of the zodiac.°

    FAUST. These slender questions Wagner can decide:
50 Hath Mephistophilis no greater skill?°
Who knows not the double motion of the planets?
That the first is finish'd in a natural day;
The second thus: Saturn in thirty years;
Jupiter in twelve; Mars in four; the Sun, Venus, and
Mercury in a year; the Moon in twenty-eight days.
These are freshmen's questions. But, tell me, hath ev-
ery sphere a dominion or intelligentia?°

    MEPH. Ay.

    FAUST. How many heavens or spheres are there?

60   MEPH. Nine; the seven planets, the firmament, and
the imperial heaven.

    FAUST. But is there not *coelum igneum, et cristal-
linum?*°

    MEPH. No, Faustus, they be but fables.

    FAUST. Resolve me then in this one question: why
are not conjunctions, oppositions, aspects, eclipses,
all at one time, but in some years we have more, in
some less?

    MEPH. *Per inaequalem motum respectu totius.*°

70   FAUST. Well, I am answer'd.° Now tell me who
made the world.

    MEPH. I will not.

    FAUST. Sweet Mephistophilis, tell me.

    MEPH. Move me not, Faustus.

    FAUST. Villain, have not I bound thee to tell me any
thing?

    MEPH. Ay, that is not against our kingdom.
This is: thou art damn'd; think thou of hell.

    FAUST. Think, Faustus, upon God that made the
80 world.

    MEPH. Remember this.   {*Exit.*

    FAUST. Ay, go, accursed spirit, to ugly hell!
'Tis thou hast damn'd distressed Faustus' soul.
Is't not too late?

Enter the two ANGELS.

    BAD ANG. Too late.
    GOOD ANG. Never too late, if Faustus will repent.
    BAD ANG. If thou repent, devils will tear thee in
pieces.°
    GOOD ANG. Repent, and they shall never raze° thy
skin.   {*Exeunt* ANGELS.
    FAUST. O, Christ, my Saviour, my Saviour,
Help to save distressed Faustus' soul!   90

Enter LUCIFER, BELZEBUB, *and* MEPHISTOPHILIS.

    LUC. Christ cannot save thy soul, for he is just:
There's none but I have interest in the same.
    FAUST. O, what art thou that look'st so terribly?
    LUC. I am Lucifer,
And this is my companion prince in hell.
    FAUST. O, Faustus, they are come to fetch thy soul!
    BELZ. We are come to tell thee thou dost injure us.
    LUC. Thou call'st on Christ, contrary to thy promise.
    BELZ. Thou shouldst not think on God.
    LUC. Think on the devil.   100
    BELZ. And his dam° too.
    FAUST. Nor will I henceforth: pardon me in this,
And Faustus vows never to look to heaven,
Never to name God, or to pray to him,
To burn his Scriptures, slay his ministers,
And make my spirits pull his churches down.
    LUC. So shalt thou show thyself an obedient servant,
And we will highly gratify thee for it.
    BELZ. Faustus, we are come from hell in person to
show thee some pastime: sit down, and thou shalt be- 110
hold the Seven Deadly Sins appear to thee in their own
proper shapes and likeness.
    FAUST. That sight will be as pleasing unto me,
As Paradise was to Adam, the first day
Of his creation.
    LUC. Talk not of Paradise or creation; but mark the
show.°
Go, Mephistophilis, fetch them in.

Enter the SEVEN DEADLY SINS.

    BELZ. Now, Faustus, question them° of their names
and dispositions.
    FAUST. That shall I soon. What are thou, the first? 120
    PRIDE. I am Pride. I disdain to have any parents. I

41 **axletree,** axle, axis 42 **termine,** end 46 **situ et tempore,** in position and
time 48 **zodiac,** the common axletree 50 **no greater skill.** Ironically,
Mephistophilis can never tell Faustus any more than what he already knows; his
knowledge is just as limited 57 **intelligentia,** an angelic intelligence (believed to
be the source of motion in each sphere) 62 **coelum . . . cristallinum,** the
heaven of fire and the crystalline sphere (concepts introduced by certain old authorities to explain the precession of equinoxes) 69 **Per . . . totius,** because of
their unequal velocities within the system 70 **Well . . . answer'd,** spoken sarcastically

87 **devils . . . in pieces,** Faustus' ultimate fate in any event 88 **raze,** scratch.
But Faustus lacks sufficient faith to credit the Good Angel's assurance; contrast the
end of the martyred old man who later exhorts him to repent (see V, i). Faustus is
repeatedly dissuaded from repentance by the mention of physical torture
101 **his dam.** "The devil and his dam" was a common colloquial expression
116 **Talk not . . . but mark the show,** another diversionary tactic 118 **question
them.** These comically grotesque personifications reply with analyses of the
psychological conditions of mind which make one prone to a particular sin

am like to Ovid's flea;° I can creep into every corner of a wench; sometimes, like a periwig,° I sit upon her brow; next, like a necklace I hang about her neck; then, like a fan of feathers, I kiss her lips, and then turning myself to a wrought smock° do what I list. But, fie, what a smell is here! I'll not speak another word, unless the ground be perfum'd, and cover'd with cloth of arras.°

130   FAUST. Thou art a proud knave, indeed! What are thou, the second?

   COVET. I am Covetousness, begotten of an old churl in a leather bag: and might I now obtain my wish, this house, you and all, should turn to gold, that I might lock you safe into my chest. O my sweet gold!

   FAUST. And what are thou, the third?

   ENVY. I am Envy, begotten of a chimney-sweeper and an oyster-wife. I cannot read, and therefore wish all books burn'd. I am lean with seeing others eat. O, 140 that there would come a famine over all the world, that all might die, and I live alone! then thou should'st see how fat I'ld be. But must thou sit, and I stand? come down, with a vengeance!

   FAUST. Out, envious wretch!—But what art thou, the fourth?

   WRATH. I am Wrath. I had neither father nor mother: I leapt out of a lion's mouth when I was scarce an hour old; and ever since have run up and down the world with these case of rapiers, wounding myself 150 when I could get none to fight withal. I was born in hell; and look to it, for some of you shall be my father.

   FAUST. And what are thou, the fifth?

   GLUT. I am Gluttony. My parents are all dead, and the devil a penny they have left me, but a small pension, and that buys me thirty meals a day and ten bevers°—a small trifle to suffice nature. I come of a royal pedigree! my father was a Gammon° of Bacon, and my mother was a Hogshead of Claret wine; my godfathers were these, Peter Pickled-herring and Martin 160 Martlemas-beef. But my godmother, O she was an ancient gentlewoman; her name was Margery Marchbeer. Now, Faustus, thou hast heard all my progeny;° wilt thou bid me to supper?

   FAUST. Not I.

   GLUT. Then the devil choke thee.

   FAUST. Choke thyself, glutton!—What art thou, the sixth?

   SLOTH. Heigh ho! I am Sloth. I was begotten on a sunny bank, where I have lain ever since; and you 170 have done me great injury to bring me from thence: let me be carried thither again by Gluttony and Lechery. Heigh ho! I'll not speak a word more for a king's ransom.

   FAUST. And what are you, Mistress Minx, the seventh and last?

   LECHERY. Who, I, sir? I am one that loves an inch of raw mutton° better than an ell° of friend stockfish,° and the first letter of my name begins with Lechery.

   LUC. Away, to hell, away, on Piper!°

                   {*Exeunt the* SEVEN SINS.

   FAUST. O, how this sight doth delight my soul!   180

   LUC. But, Faustus, in hell is all manner of delight.

   FAUST. O, might I see hell, and return again safe, how happy were I then!

   LUC. Faustus, thou shalt. At midnight I will send for thee.

Meanwhile peruse this book and view it thoroughly, And thou shalt turn thyself into what shape thou wilt.

   FAUST. Thanks, mighty Lucifer!

This will I keep as chary° as my life.

   LUC. Now, Faustus, farewell.   190

   FAUST. Farewell, great Lucifer. Come, Mephistophilis.   {*Exeunt omnes several ways.*

SCENE III *An inn yard. Enter* ROBIN *with a book.*

   ROBIN. What, Dick, look to the horses there, till I come again. I have gotten one of Doctor Faustus' conjuring books, and now we'll have such knavery, as't passes.

Enter DICK.

   DICK. What, Robin, you must come away and walk the horses.

   ROBIN. I walk the horses? I scorn't, 'faith, I have other matters in hand, let the horses walk themselves and they will. [*Reads.*] *A per se; a, t. h. e. the; o per se; o deny orgon, gorgon.*° Keep further from me, O 10 thou illiterate and unlearned hostler.

   DICK. 'Snails,° what hast thou got there? a book? why, thou canst not tell ne'er a word on't.

   ROBIN. That thou shalt see presently. Keep out of the circle, I say, lest I send you into the ostry° with a vengeance.

   DICK. That's like, 'faith: you had best leave your foolery, for an my master come, he'll conjure you, 'faith.

   ROBIN. My master conjure me? I'll tell thee what, an 20 my master come here, I'll clap as fair a pair of horns° on's head as e'er thou sawest in thy life.

   DICK. Thou need'st not do that, for my mistress hath done it.

   ROBIN. Ay, there be of us here that have waded as deep into matters as other men, if they were disposed to talk.

---

122 **Ovid's flea,** an obscene medieval poem *Carmen de Pulice* ("The Flea") ascribed to Ovid   123 **periwig,** peruke, a man's wig popular in this period
126 **wrought smock,** embroidered petticoat   129 **arras,** fine tapestry material
155 **bevers,** snacks   157 **Gammon,** whole side of pork   162 **progeny,** lineage

176 **an inch of raw mutton,** vulgarism for the penis   177 **ell,** forty-five inches
stockfish, cod   179 **Piper.** A piper frequently leads the Seven Deadly Sins (as well as the Dance of Death) in medieval dramatic and pictorial representations
189 **chary,** carefully   **Sc. iii.** This scene provides a satirical anticipation of Faustus' escapades in Rome   9–10 **A per se ... gorgon,** a semiliterate version of Faustus' invocation to Demogorgon   12 **'Snails,** God's nails, an oath   15 **ostry,** stable   21 **a pair of horns,** the standard Elizabethan joke that a cuckolded husband would grow horns

DICK. A plague take you, I thought you did not sneak up and down after her for nothing. But I prithee, tell me, in good sadness, Robin, is that a conjuring book?

ROBIN. Do but speak what thou'lt have me to do, and I'll do't: If thou'lt dance naked, put off thy clothes, and I'll conjure thee about presently: or if thou'lt go but to the tavern with me, I'll give thee white wine, red wine, claret wine, sack, muscadine, malmesey, and whippin-crust,° hold belly, hold,° and we'll not pay one penny for it.

DICK. O brave, prithee let's to it presently, for I am as dry as a dog.

ROBIN. Come then, let's away.   {*Exeunt.*

ACT III
PROLOGUE *Enter the* CHORUS.

CHOR.° Learned Faustus,
To find the secrets of astronomy
Graven in the book of Jove's high firmament,
Did mount him up to scale Olympus' top,
Where sitting in a chariot burning bright,
Drawn by the strength of yoked dragons' necks,
He views the clouds, the planets, and the stars,
The tropic zones, and quarters of the sky,
From the bright circle of the hornèd moon,
E'en to the height of *Primum Mobile:*°
And whirling round with this circumference,
Within the concave compass of the pole;
From east to west his dragons swiftly glide,
And in eight days did bring him home again.
Not long he stayed within his quiet house,
To rest his bones after his weary toil,
But new exploits do hale him out again,
And mounted then upon a dragon's back,
That with his wings did part the subtle air,
He now is gone to prove cosmography,°
That measures coasts, and kingdoms of the earth:
And, as I guess, will first arrive at Rome,
To see the Pope and manner of his court,
And take some part of holy Peter's feast,
The which this day is highly solemniz'd.   {*Exit.*

SCENE I *The Pope's privy chamber. Enter* FAUSTUS *and* MEPHISTOPHILIS.

FAUST. Having now,° my good Mephistophilis,
Pass'd with delight the stately town of Trier,°
Environ'd round with airy mountain tops,
With walls of flint, and deep entrenched lakes,°
Not to be won by any conquering prince;

From Paris next, coasting the realm of France,
We saw the river Maine fall into Rhine,
Whose banks are set with groves of fruitful vines;
Then up to Naples, rich Campania,
Whose buildings fair and gorgeous to the eye,
The streets straight forth, and paved with finest brick,
Quarters the town in four equivalents;
There saw we learned Maro's° golden tomb,
The way he cut, an English mile in length,
Thorough a rock of stone, in one night's space;
From thence to Venice, Padua, and the East,
In one of which a sumptuous temple° stands,
That threats the stars with her aspiring top,
Whose frame is paved with sundry coloured stones,
And roof'd aloft with curious work in gold.
Thus hitherto hath Faustus spent his time:
But tell me now, what resting place is this?
Hast thou, as erst I did command,
Conducted me within the walls of Rome?

MEPH. I have, my Faustus, and for proof thereof
This is the goodly Palace of the Pope;
And cause we are no common guests
I choose his privy chamber for our use.

FAUST. I hope his Holiness will bid us welcome.

MEPH. All's one, for we'll be bold with his venison.
But now, my Faustus, that thou may'st perceive
What Rome contains° for to delight thine eyes,
Know that this city stands upon seven hills
That underprop the groundwork of the same:
Just through the midst runs flowing Tiber's stream,
With winding banks that cut it in two parts;
Over the which four stately bridges lean,
That make safe passage to each part of Rome:
Upon the bridge called Ponte Angelo
Erected is a castle passing strong,
Where thou shalt see such store of ordinance,
As that the double cannons, forg'd of brass,
Do match the number of the days contain'd
Within the compass of one complete year:
Beside the gates, and high pyramides,°
That Julius Caesar brought from Africa.

FAUST. Now, by the kingdoms of infernal rule,
Of Styx, of Acheron, and the fiery lake
Of ever-burning Phlegethon,° I swear
That I do long to see the monuments
And situation of bright splendent Rome:
Come, therefore, let's away.

MEPH. Nay, stay, my Faustus; I know you'd see the Pope°
And take some part of holy Peter's feast,
The which, in state and high solemnity,
This day is held through Rome and Italy,

Christopher Marlowe   **231**

In honour of the Pope's triumphant victory.

FAUST. Sweet Mephistophilis, thou pleasest me,
Whilst I am here on earth, let me be cloy'd
60 With all things that delight the heart of man.
My four-and-twenty years of liberty
I'll spend in pleasure and in dalliance,
That Faustus' name, whilst this bright frame doth
    stand,
May be admired through the furthest land.

MEPH. 'Tis well said, Faustus, come then, stand by
    me
And thou shalt see them come immediately.

FAUST. Nay, stay, my gentle Mephistophilis,
And grant me my request, and then I go.
Thou know'st within the compass of eight days
70 We view'd the face of heaven, of earth and hell.
So high our dragons soar'd into the air,
That looking down, the earth appear'd to me
No bigger than my hand in quantity.
There did we view the kingdoms of the world,
And what might please mine eye, I there beheld.
Then in this show let me an actor be,
That this proud Pope may Faustus' cunning see.

MEPH. Let it be so, my Faustus, but, first stay,
And view their triumphs,° as they pass this way.
80 And then devise what best contents thy mind
By cunning in thine art to cross the Pope,
Or dash the pride of this solemnity;
To make his monks and abbots stand like apes,
And point like antics° at his triple crown:
To beat the beads about the friars' pates,
Or clap huge horns upon the Cardinals' heads;
Or any villainy thou canst devise,
And I'll perform it, Faustus: Hark! they come:
This day shall make thee be admir'd° in Rome.

Enter the CARDINALS *and* BISHOPS, *some bearing
crosiers,° some the pillars,°* MONKS *and* FRIARS *singing
their procession. Then the* POPE, *and* RAYMOND,° KING
OF HUNGARY, *with* BRUNO° *led in chains.*

90   POPE. Cast down our footstool.

RAY. Saxon Bruno, stoop,
Whilst on thy back his Holiness ascends
Saint Peter's chair and state pontifical.

BRUNO. Proud Lucifer, that state belongs to me:
But thus I fall to Peter, not to thee.

POPE. To me and Peter shalt thou grovelling lie,
And crouch before the Papal dignity;
Sound trumpets, then, for thus Saint Peter's heir,
From Bruno's back, ascends Saint Peter's chair.
                   {*A flourish while he ascends.*
100 Thus, as the gods creep on with feet of wool,

Long ere with iron hands they punish men,
So shall our sleeping vengeance now arise,
And smite with death thy hated enterprise.
Lord Cardinals of France and Padua,
Go forthwith to our holy Consistory,
And read amongst the Statutes Decretal,
What, by the holy Council held at Trent,°
The sacred synod hath decreed for him
That doth assume the Papal government
Without election, and a true consent: 110
Away, and bring us word with speed.

FIRST CARD. We go, my lord. {*Exeunt* CARDINALS.

POPE. Lord Raymond.

FAUST. Go, haste thee, gentle Mephistophilis
Follow the Cardinals to the Consistory;
And as they turn their superstitious books,
Strike them with sloth, and drowsy idleness;
And make them sleep so sound, that in their shapes
Thyself and I may parley with this Pope,
This proud confronter of the Emperor:°   120
And in despite of all his Holiness
Restore this Bruno to his liberty,
And bear him to the States of Germany.

MEPH. Faustus, I go.

FAUST. Despatch it soon,
The Pope shall curse that Faustus came to Rome.
            {*Exeunt* FAUSTUS *and* MEPHISTOPHILIS.

BRUNO. Pope Adrian, let me have right of law,
I was elected by the Emperor.

POPE. We will depose the Emperor for that deed,
And curse the people that submit to him;   130
Both he and thou shalt stand excommunicate,
And interdict° from Church's privilege
And all society of holy men:
He grows too proud in his authority,
Lifting his lofty head above the clouds,
And like a steeple overpeers the Church:
But we'll pull down his haughty insolence.
And as Pope Alexander,° our progenitor,
Trod on the neck of German Frederick,
Adding this golden sentence to our praise:—   140
'That Peter's heirs should tread on Emperors,
And walk upon the dreadful adder's back,
Treading the lion and the dragon down,
And fearless spurn the killing basilisk':°
So will we quell that haughty schismatic;
And by authority apostolical
Depose him from his regal government.

BRUNO. Pope Julius° swore to princely Sigismond,
For him, and the succeeding Popes of Rome,
To hold the Emperors their lawful lords.   150

POPE. Pope Julius did abuse the Church's rites,

---

79 **triumphs,** parades   84 **antics,** madmen, freaks   89 **admir'd.** Faustus is
concerned with making himself famous by any means possible, even if it is just by
damaging the dignity of some great personage   **crosiers,** crosses   **pillars,** ceremonial religious emblems   **Raymond,** a fictitious king   **Bruno,** also fictitious;
here he is the German pretender to the papal throne over whom the Pope has just
triumphed

107 **Trent,** site of a major council of the Catholic Church from 1545 to 1563
120 **Emperor.** The Pope emerged victorious from a conflict with the Holy Roman
Emperor and captured his choice for Pope, Bruno   132 **interdict,** proscribed
138 **Pope Alexander.** Pope Alexander III (1159–1181) compelled the submission
of Emperor Frederick Barbarossa   144 **basilisk,** deadly mythical monster

And therefore none of his decrees can stand.
Is not all power° on earth bestowed on us?
And therefore, though we would, we cannot err.
Behold this silver belt, whereto is fix'd
Seven golden keys fast sealed with seven seals
In token of our sevenfold power from Heaven,
To bind or loose, lock fast, condemn, or judge,
Resign, or seal, or whatso pleaseth us.
160 Then he and thou, and all the world shall stoop,
Or be assured of our dreadful curse,
To light as heavy as the pains of hell.

Enter FAUSTUS *and* MEPHISTOPHILIS *like the* CARDI-
NALS.

MEPH. Now tell me, Faustus, are we not fitted well?
FAUST. Yes, Mephistophilis, and two such Cardinals
Ne'er serv'd a holy Pope as we shall do.
But whilst they sleep within the Consistory,
Let us salute his reverend Fatherhood.
RAY. Behold, my Lord, the Cardinals are return'd.
POPE. Welcome, grave Fathers, answer presently,
170 What have our holy Council there decreed,
Concerning Bruno and the Emperor,
In quittance° of their late conspiracy
Against our state and Papal dignity?
FAUST. Most sacred Patron of the Church of Rome
By full consent of all the synod
Of priests and prelates, it is thus decreed:
That Bruno and the German Emperor
Be held as Lollards° and bold schismatics
And proud disturbers of the Church's peace.
180 And if that Bruno, by his own assent,
Without enforcement of the German peers,
Did seek to wear the triple diadem,
And by your death to climb Saint Peter's chair,
The Statutes Decretal have thus decreed,
He shall be straight condemn'd of heresy,
And on a pile of fagots burnt to death.
POPE. It is enough: Here, take him to your charge,
And bear him straight to Ponte Angelo,
And in the strongest tower enclose him fast;
190 Tomorrow, sitting in our Consistory
With all our college of grave Cardinals,
We will determine of his life or death.
Here, take his triple crown along with you,
And leave it in the Church's treasury.
Make haste again, my good Lord Cardinals,
And take our blessing apostolical.
MEPH. So, so; was never devil thus blessed before.
FAUST. Away, sweet Mephistophilis, be gone,
The Cardinals will be plagu'd for this anon.

{*Exeunt* FAUSTUS *and* MEPHISTOPHILIS, *with* BRUNO.
POPE. Go presently and bring a banquet forth,   200
That we may solemnize Saint Peter's feast,
And with Lord Raymond, King of Hungary,
Drink to our late and happy victory.   {*Exeunt.*

SCENE II *A sennet while the banquet is brought in; and
then enter* FAUSTUS *and* MEPHISTOPHILIS *in their own
shapes.*

MEPH. Now, Faustus, come, prepare thyself for
mirth:
The sleepy Cardinals are hard at hand
To censure° Bruno, that is posted hence,
And on a proud-pac'd steed, as swift as thought,
Flies o'er the Alps to fruitful Germany,
There to salute the woeful Emperor.
FAUST. The Pope will curse them for their sloth to-
day,
That slept both Bruno and his crown away:
But now, that Faustus may delight his mind,
And by their folly make some merriment,   10
Sweet Mephistophilis, so charm me here,
That I may walk invisible to all,
And do whate'er I please, unseen of any.
MEPH. Faustus, thou shalt, then kneel down pres-
ently:

*Whilst on thy head I lay my hand,
And charm thee with this magic wand.
First wear this girdle, then appear
Invisible to all are here:
The Planets seven, the gloomy air,
Hell and the Furies' forked hair,*   20
*Pluto's blue fire, and Hecate's tree,°
With magic spells so compass thee,
That no eye may thy body see.*

So, Faustus, now for all their holiness,
Do what thou wilt, thou shalt not be discern'd.
FAUST. Thanks, Mephistophilis; now, friars, take
heed,
Lest Faustus make your shaven crowns to bleed.
MEPH. Faustus, no more: see where the Cardinals
come.

Enter POPE *and all the* LORDS. *Enter the* CARDINALS
with a book.

POPE. Welcome, Lord Cardinals: come, sit down.
Lord Raymond, take your seat. Friars, attend,   30
And see that all things be in readiness,
As best beseems this solemn festival.
FIRST CARD. First, may it please your sacred Holi-
ness

148–162 **Pope . . . hell.** Bruno continues his argument and appears throughout
this scene to have the right on his side and to be a more admirable man than the
Pope. Thus in helping him and annoying the Pope, Faustus and Mephistophilis
occupy the thematically confusing position of satirical exposers. But their prank
with the cardinals who seem to favor Bruno, suggests that the two have acted
only on an anarchic impulse, rather than in support of the cause of an underdog
153 **all power** Ironically, the Pope displays a Lucifer-like pride   172 **quittance,**
requital, punishment   178 **Lollards,** Protestants (originally English followers of
Wycliffe, the fourteenth-century religious reformer). The Pope applies the term to
Faustus and Mephistophilis at the banquet they disrupt

Sc. ii   3 **censure,** pass judgment on   21 **Hecate's tree.** Hecate, the goddess
of witchcraft, is not associated with any special tree. The word, however, may be
a mistake for "three" since she was often represented as a triple goddess (of
heaven, earth, and hell). Interestingly, the Pope is also a "triple" monarch (IV, ii,
10)

To view the sentence of the reverend synod,
Concerning Bruno and the Emperor?
   POPE. What needs this question? Did I not tell you,
Tomorrow we would sit i' th' Consistory,
And there determine of his punishment?
You brought us word even now, it was decreed
40 That Bruno and the cursed Emperor
Were by the holy Council both condemn'd
For loathed Lollards and base schismatics:
Then wherefore would you have me view that book?
   FIRST CARD. Your Grace mistakes, you gave us no
     such charge.
   RAY. Deny it not, we all are witnesses
That Bruno here was late deliver'd you,
With his rich triple crown° to be reserv'd
And put into the Church's treasury,
   BOTH CARD. By holy Paul, we saw them not.
50 POPE. By Peter, you shall die,
Unless you bring them forth immediately:
Hale them to prison, lade their limbs with gyves:°
False prelates, for this hateful treachery,
Curs'd be your souls to hellish misery.
     {*Exeunt* ATTENDANTS *with the two* CARDINALS.
   FAUST. So, they are safe:° now, Faustus, to the
     feast,
The Pope had never such a frolic guest.
   POPE. Lord Archbishop of Reames, sit down with
     us.
   ARCHBISH. I thank your Holiness.
   FAUST. Fall to, the devil choke you an you spare.
60 POPE. How now? Who's that which spake?—Friars,
     look about.
   FRIAR. Here's nobody, if it like your Holiness.
   POPE. Lord Raymond, pray fall to. I am beholding
To the Bishop of Milan for this so rare a present.
   FAUST. I thank you, sir.   {*Snatches the dish.*
   POPE. How now? who's that which snatch'd the
     meat from me?
Villains, why speak you not?—
My good Lord Archbishop, here's a most dainty dish,
Was sent me from a Cardinal in France.
   FAUST. I'll have that too.   {*Snatches the dish.*
70 POPE. What Lollards do attend our Holiness,
That we receive such great indignity?
Fetch me some wine.
   FAUST. Ay, pray do, for Faustus is adry.
   POPE. Lord Raymond, I drink unto your grace.
   FAUST. I pledge your grace.   {*Snatches the cup.*
   POPE. My wine gone too? —ye lubbers, look about
And find the man that doth this villainy,
Or by our sanctitude, you all shall die.
I pray, my lords, have patience at this
80 Troublesome banquet.
   ARCHBISHOP. Please it your Holiness, I think it be
Some ghost crept out of Purgatory, and now
Is come unto your Holiness for his pardon.

   POPE. It may be so:
God then command our priests to sing a dirge,
To lay the fury of this same troublesome ghost.
     {*Exit an* ATTENDANT.
Once again, my Lord, fall to.
     {*The* POPE *crosseth himself.*
   FAUST. How now?
Must every bit be spicéd with a cross?°
Nay then, take that.   {*Strikes the* POPE. 90
   POPE. O I am slain, help me, my lords;
O come and help to bear my body hence:—
Damn'd be his soul° for ever for this deed!
     {*Exeunt the* POPE *and his train.*
   MEPH. Now, Faustus, what will you do now, for I
can tell you you'll be curs'd with bell, book, and can-
dle.°
   FAUST. Bell, book, and candle,—candle, book, and
    bell,—
Forward and backward, to curse Faustus to hell!

Enter the FRIARS *with bell, book, and candle for the
Dirge.*

   FIRST FRIAR. Come, brethren, let's about our business with good devotion.   *Sing this.* 100

*Cursed be he that stole his Holiness' meat from the
   table! Maledicat Dominus!°
Cursed be he that struck his Holiness a blow on the
   face! Maledicat Dominus!
Cursed be he that took Friar Sandelo a blow on the
   pate! Maledicat Dominus!
Cursed be he that disturbeth our holy dirge! Maledicat
   Dominus!
Cursed be he that took away his Holiness' wine!
   Maledicat Dominus!   110
   Et omnes Sancti!° Amen!*

{MEPHISTOPHILIS *and* FAUSTUS *beat the* FRIARS, *fling
     fireworks° among them, and exeunt.*

SCENE III *A street, near an inn. Enter* ROBIN *and* DICK,
with a cup.

   DICK. Sirrah Robin, we were best look that your
devil can answer the stealing of this same cup,° for the
vintner's boy follows us at the hard heels.
   ROBIN. 'Tis no matter! let him come; an he follow us
I'll so conjure him as he was never conjured in his life.
I warrant him. Let me see the cup.

89 **spicéd with a cross.** Another instance of the largely irrelevant anti-Catholic
satire in the play   93 **Damn'd be his soul,** an unconscious irony; Faustus is already damned   95 **bell, book, and candle,** the traditional equipment for cursing
and excommunication   102 **Maledicat Dominus.** "May the Lord curse him."
The reasons for which Faustus is cursed here are absurd but the act itself
nevertheless has validity; Faustus has now been condemned by the ultimate
spiritual authority on earth, God's temporal representative   111 **Et omnes Sancti.**
"And may all the saints also curse him" **fireworks.** A typical morality-play bit of
mischief usually perpetrated by the lesser devils **Sc. iii.** This scene forms an
evaluative satirical contrast to the disrespectful antics of Faustus and Mephistophilis in Rome 2 **cup.** The stolen cup is implicitly associated with the vessel
of Holy Communion

47 **triple crown,** the tiara worn by the Pope   52 **lade . . . with gyves,** load them
with prisoners' shackles   55 **safe,** in hell

Enter VINTNER.

DICK. Here 't is. Yonder he comes. Now, Robin, now or never show thy cunning.

VINT. O are you here? I am glad I have found you,
10 you are a couple of fine companions; pray, where's the cup you stole from the tavern?

ROBIN. How, how? we steal a cup? Take heed what you say; we look not like cup-stealers, I can tell you.

VINT. Never deny 't, for I know you have it, and I'll search you.

ROBIN. Search me? Ay, and spare not. Hold the cup, Dick   {*aside to* DICK.
Come, come, search me, search me!
          {VINTNER *searches him.*

VINT. [*to* DICK]. Come on, sirrah, let me search you
20 now!

DICK. Ay, ay, do! Hold the cup, Robin
[*aside to* ROBIN].
I fear not your searching; we scorn to steal your cups, I can tell you.   {VINTNER *searches him.*

VINT. Never outface me for the matter, for, sure, the cup is between you two.

ROBIN. Nay, there you lie, 'tis beyond us both.

VINT. A plague take you! I thought 't was your knavery to take it away; come, give it me again.

ROBIN. Ay much; when? can you tell?° Dick, make
30 me a circle, and stand close at my back, and stir not for thy life. Vintner, you shall have your cup anon. Say nothing, Dick.

[READS.] *O per se, o Demogorgon, Belcher and Mephistophilis!*

Enter MEPHISTOPHILIS.

MEPH. You princely° legions of infernal rule,
How am I vexed by these villains' charms!
From Constantinople have they brought me now
Only for pleasure of these damned slaves.
          {*Exit* VINTNER.

ROBIN. By Lady, sir, you have had a shrewd journey
40 of it. Will it please you to take a shoulder of mutton to supper, and a tester° in your purse, and go back again?

DICK. Aye, aye. I pray you heartily, sir, for we call'd you but in jest, I promise you.

MEPH. To purge the rashness of this cursed deed,
First be thou turned to this ugly shape,
For apish deeds transformed to an ape.°

ROBIN. O brave! an Ape! I pray, sir, let me have the carrying of him about to show some tricks.

MEPH. And so thou shalt: be thou transformed to a
50 dog, And carry him upon thy back.° Away, be gone!

ROBIN. A dog! that's excellent; let the maids look

well to their porridgepots, for I'll into the kitchen presently. Come, Dick, come.
          {*Exeunt the* TWO CLOWNS.

MEPH. Now with the flames of ever-burning fire,
I'll wing myself, and forthwith fly amain
Unto my Faustus, to the Great Turk's Court.°   {*Exit.*

ACT IV
PROLOGUE *Enter* CHORUS.

CHOR. When Faustus had with pleasure ta'en the view
Of rarest things, and royal courts of kings,
He stay'd his course, and so returned home;
Where such as bear his absence but with grief,
I mean his friends and near'st companions,
Did gratulate his safety with kind words,
And in their conference of what befell,
Touching his journey through the world and air,
They put forth questions of astrology,
Which Faustus answer'd with such learned skill   10
As they admir'd and wonder'd at his wit.
Now is his fame spread forth in every land:
Amongst the rest the Emperor is one,
Carolus the Fifth,° at whose palace now
Faustus is feasted 'mongst his noblemen.
What there he did, in trial of his art,
I leave untold; your eyes shall see perform'd.   {*Exit.*

SCENE I *A room in the Emperor's Court at Innsbruck.*
Enter MARTINO *and* FREDERICK *at several doors.*

MART. What ho, officers, gentlemen,
Hie to the presence to attend the Emperor,
Good Frederick, see the rooms be voided straight,
His majesty is coming to the hall;
Go back, and see the state in readiness.

FRED. But where is Bruno, our elected Pope,
That on a fury's back° came post from Rome?
Will not his Grace consort° the Emperor?

MART. O yes, and with him comes the German conjuror,
The learned Faustus, fame of Wittenberg,   10
The wonder of the world for magic art;
And he intends to show great Carolus
The race of all his stout progenitors;
And bring in presence of his Majesty
The royal shapes and warlike semblances
Of Alexander and his beauteous paramour.°

FRED. Where is Benvolio?

MART. Fast asleep, I warrant you,
He took his rouse with stoups° of Rhenish wine
So kindly yesternight to Bruno's health,   20
That all this day the sluggard keeps his bed.

29 **when? can you tell.** A scornful retort common in the Elizabethan period
35–38 **You princely . . . slaves.** The dignity and infernal grandeur of Mephistophilis are considerably compromised here; he appears in the position of a lackey's lacke 41 **tester,** sixpence 46 **For apish deeds transformed to an ape.** Faustus has similarly debased his spirit to the condition of beasts 50 **And carry him upon thy back.** This brutal picture foreshadows the level of Faustus' next escapade, a kind of vulgar side-show exhibition before the Emperor (IV, ii)

54–56 **Now with . . . Court.** Mephistophilis' grand rhetoric fails to compensate for the debasement that his image has incurred **Act IV, Prologue** 14 **Carolus the Fifth,** Emperor Charles V (1519–1556). Faustus has duly become famous and is now about to give a "command performance" before the Emperor's court **Sc. i** 7 **on a fury's back,** a bestial association 8 **consort,** accompany 16 **paramour,** Thaïs, mistress of Alexander the Great 19 **took . . . stoups,** made merry with full glasses

FRED. See, see, his window's ope, we'll call to him.
MART. What ho, Benvolio!

Enter BENVOLIO *above, at a window, in his nightcap;*
buttoning.

BENV. What a devil ail you two?
MART. Speak softly, sir, lest the devil hear you:
For Faustus at the court is late arriv'd,
And at his heels a thousand furies wait,
To accomplish whatsoever the Doctor please,
BENV. What of this?
30 MART. Come, leave thy chamber first, and thou shalt
    see
This conjuror perform such rare exploits,
Before the Pope° and royal Emperor,
As never yet was seen in Germany.
BENV. Has not the Pope enough of conjuring yet?
He was upon the devil's back late enough;
And if he be so far in love with him,
I would he would post with him to Rome again.
FRED. Speak. wilt thou come and see this sport?
BENV. Not I.
40 MART. Wilt thou stand in thy window, and see it
    then?
BENV. Ay, an I fall not asleep i' th' meantime.
MART. The Emperor is at hand, who comes to see
What wonders by black spells may compass'd be.
BENV. Well, go you attend the Emperor: I am con-
tent for this once to thrust my head out at a window;
for they say if a man be drunk overnight the devil
cannot hurt him in the morning; if that be true, I have a
charm in my head shall control him as well as the
conjuror, I warrant you.
                    {*Exeunt* FREDERICK *and* MARTINO.

SCENE II *The Presence Chamber in the Court. A sen-*
net. Enter CHARLES, *the* GERMAN EMPEROR, BRUNO,
DUKE OF SAXONY, FAUSTUS, MEPHISTOPHILIS, FRED-
ERICK, MARTINO, *and* ATTENDANTS.

EMP. Wonder of men, renown'd magician,
Thrice-learned Faustus, welcome to our Court.
This deed of thine, in setting Bruno free
From his and our professed enemy,
Shall add more excellence unto thine art,
Than if by powerful necromantic spells,
Thou couldst command the world's obedience:
For ever be belov'd of Carolus,
And if this Bruno thou hast late redeem'd,
10 In peace possess the triple diadem,
And sit in Peter's chair, despite of chance,
Thou shalt be famous through all Italy,

And honour'd of the German Emperor.
FAUST. These gracious words, most royal Carolus,
Shall make poor Faustus, to his utmost power,
Both love and serve the German Emperor,
And lay his life at holy Bruno's feet.
For proof whereof, if so your Grace be pleas'd,
The Doctor stands prepar'd by power of art
To cast his magic charms, that shall pierce through   20
The ebon gates of ever-burning hell,
And hale the stubborn Furies from their caves,
To compass whatsoe'er your Grace commands.
BENV. [*above*]. 'Blood, he speaks terribly: but for all
that I do not greatly believe him: he looks as like a
conjuror as the Pope to a costermonger.°
EMP. Then, Faustus, as thou late did'st promise us,
We would behold that famous conqueror,
Great Alexander and his paramour
In their true shapes and state majestical,   30
That we may wonder at their excellence.
FAUST. Your Majesty shall see them presently. ·
Mephistophilis, away.
And with a solemn noise of trumpets' sound
Present before this royal Emperor,
Great Alexander and his beauteous paramour.
MEPH. Faustus, I will.
BENV. Well, Master Doctor, an your devils come not
away quickly, you shall have me asleep presently:
zounds, I could eat myself for anger, to think I have   40
been such an ass all this while to stand gaping after the
devil's governor,° and can see nothing.
FAUST. I'll make you feel something anon, if my art
fail me not.—
My lord, I must forewarn your Majesty,
That when my spirits present the royal shapes
Of Alexander and his paramour,
Your Grace demand no questions of the king,
But in dumb silence let them come and go.
EMP. Be it as Faustus please, we are content.   50
BENV. Ay, ay, and I am content too; and thou bring
Alexander and his paramour before the Emperor, I'll
be Acteon and turn myself to a stag.
FAUST. And I'll play Diana, and send you the horns
presently.

Sennet. Enter at one door° the EMPEROR ALEXANDER,
at the other DARIUS; *they meet,* DARIUS *is thrown*
down, ALEXANDER *kills him; takes off his crown and*
offering to go out, his paramour meets him, he em-
braceth her, and sets Darius' crown upon her head;
and coming back, both salute the EMPEROR, *who,*
leaving his state,° offers to embrace them, which,
FAUSTUS *seeing, suddenly stays him. Then trumpets*
cease, and music sounds.

Sc. ii   26 **costermonger,** fruitseller (another undercutting association of Faustus)
42 **devil's governor.** Faustus is the exhibitor or handler of Mephistophilis   **En-**
ter at one door . . . sounds. This stylized pantomime implies an analogue to the
Emperor's desire to control the papacy; he apparently identifies with the victorious Alexander   **state,** throne

32 **Pope,** Bruno

My gracious lord, you do forget yourself,
These are but shadows, not substantial.
   EMP. O pardon me, my thoughts are so ravished
With sight of this renowned Emperor,
60 That in mine arms I would have compass'd him.
But, Faustus, since I may not speak to them,
To satisfy my longing thoughts at full,
Let me this tell thee: I have heard it said,
That this fair lady whilst she liv'd on earth,
Had on her neck, a little wart, or mole;°
How may I prove that saying to be true?
   FAUST. Your Majesty may boldly go and see.
   EMP. Faustus, I see it plain,
And in this sight thou better pleasest me,
70 Than if I gain'd another monarchy.
   FAUST. Away, be gone!   {Exit show.
See, see, my gracious lord, what strange beast is yon,
that thrusts his head out at window?
   EMP. O wondrous sight: see, Duke of Saxony,
Two spreading horns most strangely fastened
Upon the head of young Benvolio.
   SAX. What, is he asleep, or dead?
   FAUST. He sleeps, my lord, but dreams not of his
horns.
80 EMP. This sport is excellent; we'll call and wake
him.
What ho, Benvolio.
   BENV. A plague upon you, let me sleep a while.
   EMP. I blame thee not to sleep much, having such a
head of thine own.
   SAX. Look up, Benvolio, 'tis the Emperor calls.
   BENV. The Emperor? where—O zounds, my head!
   EMP. Nay, and thy horns hold, 'tis no matter for thy
head, for that's arm'd sufficiently.
90 FAUST. Why, how now, Sir Knight, what, hang'd by
the horns? this is most horrible: fie, fie, pull in your
head for shame, let not all the world wonder at you.
   BENV. Zounds, Doctor, is this your villainy?
   FAUST. O say not so,° sir: the Doctor has no skill,
No art, no cunning, to present these lords,
Or bring before this royal Emperor
The mighty monarch, warlike Alexander.
If Faustus do it, you are straight resolv'd
In bold Acteon's shape to turn a stag.
100 And therefore, my lord, so please your Majesty,
I'll raise a kennel of hounds, shall hunt him so,
As all his footmanship shall scarce prevail
To keep his carcase from their bloody fangs.
Ho, Belimote, Argiron, Asterote.
   BENV. Hold, hold! Zounds, he'll raise up a kennel of
devils,
I think, anon: good, my lord, entreat for me: 'sblood,
I am never able to endure these torments.

   EMP. Then, good Master Doctor,
Let me entreat you to remove his horns,
He has done penance now sufficiently.   110
   FAUST. My gracious lord, not so much for injury
done to me, as to delight your Majesty with some
mirth, hath Faustus justly requited this injurious
knight, which being all I desire, I am content to remove his horns. Mephistophilis, transform him
[MEPHISTOPHILIS removes the horns], and hereafter,
sir, look you speak well of scholars.
   BENV. Speak well of ye? 'sblood, and scholars be
such cuckold-makers to clap horns of honest men's
head o' this order, I'll e'er trust smooth faces and 120
small ruffs° more. But an I be not reveng'd for this,
would I might be turn'd to a gaping oyster, and drink
nothing but salt water.   {Aside, and then exit above.
   EMP. Come, Faustus, while the Emperor lives,
In recompense of this thy high desert,
Thou shalt command the state of Germany,
And live belov'd of mighty Carolus.   {Exeunt omnes.

SCENE III Near a grove, outside Innsbruck. Enter BEN-
VOLIO, MARTINO, FREDERICK, and SOLDIERS.

   MART. Nay, sweet Benvolio, let us sway thy
      thoughts
From this attempt against the conjuror.
   BENV. Away, you love me not, to urge me thus.
Shall I let slip so great an injury,
When every servile groom jests at my wrongs,
And in their rustic gambols proudly say,
'Benvolio's head was graced with horns today'?
O may these eyelids never close again,
Till with my sword I have that conjuror slain.
If you will aid me in this enterprise,   10
Then draw your weapons, and be resolute:
If not, depart: here will Benvolio die,
But Faustus' death shall quit° my infamy.
   FRED. Nay, we will stay with thee, betide what may,
And kill that Doctor if he come this way.
   BENV. Then, gentle Frederick, hie thee to the grove,
And place our servants and our followers
Close in an ambush there behind the trees.
By this (I know) the conjuror is near;
I saw him kneel and kiss the Emperor's hand,°   20
And take his leave laden with rich rewards.
Then, soldiers, boldly fight; if Faustus die,
Take you the wealth, leave us the victory.
   FRED. Come, soldiers, follow me unto the grove;
Who kills him shall have gold and endless love.
          {Exit FREDERICK with the SOLDIERS.
   BENV. My head is lighter than it was by th' horns,

---

65 **wart, or mole.** A bit of vulgar titillation which marks the lowest point of
Faustus' performance. This is followed by an unseemly mockery of Benvolio in
recompense for the critical satirical view he had taken of these proceedings
94–104 **say not . . . Asterote.** Faustus taunts Benvolio, taking his childish revenge

120–121 **smooth faces and small ruffs.** Scholars, in contrast to courtiers, were
often smooth-shaven and did not wear large ruffs; however, Faustus has a beard
(see IV, iii, 61) **Sc. iii 13 quit,** requite, avenge **20 kneel and kiss the Emperor's hand,** a form of homage generally accorded only to the Pope or other
high officials of the Church

But yet my heart's more ponderous than my head,
And pants until I see that conjuror dead.
    MART. Where shall we place ourselves, Benvolio?
30 BENV. Here will we stay to bide the first assault.
O were that damned hellhound but in place,
Thou soon shouldst see me quit my foul disgrace.

Enter FREDERICK.

    FRED. Close, close, the conjuror is at hand,
And all alone comes walking in his gown;
Be ready then, and strike the peasant down.
    BENV. Mine be that honour then: now, sword, strike
      home,
For horns he gave I'll have his head anon.

Enter FAUSTUS *with the false head.*

    MART. See, see, he comes.
    BENV. No words: this blow ends all,
40 Hell take his soul, his body thus must fall.
                     {*Stabs* FAUSTUS.
    FAUST. [*falling*]. Oh!
    FRED. Groan you, Master Doctor?
    BENV. Break may his heart with groans: dear Fred-
      erick, see,
Thus will I end his griefs immediately.
    MART. Strike with a willing hand. [BENVOLIO *strikes
off* FAUSTUS' *false head.*] His head is off.
    BENV. The devil's dead, the Furies now may laugh.
    FRED. Was this that stern aspect, that awful frown,
Made the grim monarch of infernal spirits
Tremble and quake at his commanding charms?°
50 MART. Was this that damned head, whose art con-
    spir'd
Benvolio's shame before the Emperor?
    BENV. Ay, that's the head, and here the body lies,
Justly rewarded for his villainies.
    FRED. Come, let's devise how we may add more
    shame
To the black scandal of his hated name.
    BENV. First, on his head,° in quittance of my
    wrongs,
I'll nail huge forked horns, and let them hang
Within the window where he yok'd me first,
That all the world may see my just revenge.
60 MART. What use shall we put his beard to?
    BENV. We'll sell it to a chimney-sweeper; it will
wear out ten birchen brooms. I warrant you.
    FRED. What shall his eyes do?
    BENV. We'll put out his eyes, and they shall serve

for buttons to his lips, to keep his tongue from catching
cold.
    MART. An excellent policy: and now, sirs, having
divided him, what shall the body do?
                     {FAUSTUS *rises.*
    BENV. Zounds, the devil's alive again.
    FRED. Give him his head, for God's sake.   70
    FAUST. Nay, keep it: Faustus will have heads and
    hands,
Ay, all your hearts to recompense this deed.
Knew you not, traitors, I was limited
For four-and-twenty years to breathe on earth?
And had you cut my body with your swords,
Or hew'd this flesh and bones as small as sand,
Yet in a minute had my spirit return'd,
And I had breath'd a man made free from harm.
But wherefore do I dally my revenge?
Asteroth, Belimoth, Mephistophilis,   80
        {*Enter* MEPHISTOPHILIS *and other* DEVILS.
Go, horse these traitors on your fiery backs,
And mount aloft with them as high as heaven,
Thence pitch them headlong to the lowest hell:
Yet, stay, the world shall see their misery,
And hell shall after plague their treachery.
Go, Belimoth, and take this caitiff hence,
And hurl him in some lake of mud and dirt:
Take thou this other, drag him through the woods,
Amongst the pricking thorns, and sharpest briers,
Whilst with my gentle Mephistophilis,   90
This traitor flies unto some steepy rock,
That, rolling down, may break the villain's bones,
As he intended to dismember me.
Fly hence, despatch my charge immediately.
    FRED. Pity us, gentle Faustus, save our lives!
    FAUST. Away!
    FRED. He must needs go that the devil drives.
             {*Exeunt* SPIRITS *with the* KNIGHTS.

Enter the ambushed SOLDIERS.

    FIRST SOLD. Come, sirs, prepare yourselves in
    readiness,
Make haste to help these noble gentlemen,
I heard them parley with the conjuror.   100
    SEC. SOLD. See where he comes, despatch, and kill
    the slave.
    FAUST. What's here? an ambush to betray my life:
Then, Faustus, try thy skill: base peasants, stand:
For lo! these trees remove at my command,
And stand as bulwarks 'twixt yourselves and me,
To shield me from your hated treachery:
Yet to encounter this your weak attempt,
Behold an army comes incontinent.

FAUSTUS *strikes the door, and enter a devil playing on
a drum, after him another bearing an ensign; and di-*

47–49 **Was this . . . charms.** Cf. V, i, Faustus' apostrophe to Helen of Troy
56–68 **First, on his head . . . body do.** This catalogue of atrocities committed
upon the supposedly decapitated Faustus now turns the sympathies of the audience against Benvolio; he and his men receive their just deserts which again puts
Faustus temporarily in the position of a righteous man

vers with weapons, MEPHISTOPHILIS with fireworks; they set upon the SOLDIERS, and drive them out. Exit FAUSTUS.

SCENE IV *Enter at several doors* BENVOLIO, FREDERICK, *and* MARTINO, *their heads and faces bloody, and besmear'd with mud and dirt, all having horns on their heads.*

MART. What ho, Benvolio!

BENV. Here, what, Frederick, ho!

FRED. O help me, gentle friend; where is Martino?

MART. Dear Frederick, here,
Half smother'd in a lake of mud and dirt,
Through which the furies dragg'd me by the heels.

FRED. Martino, see Benvolio's horns again.

MART. O misery, how now, Benvolio?

BENV. Defend me, heaven, shall I be haunted still?

10 MART. Nay, fear not, man; we have no power to kill.

BENV. My friends transformed thus! O hellish spite,
Your heads are all set with horns.

FRED.   You hit it right:
It is your own you mean, feel on your head.

BENV. Zounds, horns again!

MART.   Nay, chafe not, man, we all are sped.

BENV. What devil attends this damn'd magician,
That, spite of spite, our wrongs are doubled?

FRED. What may we do, that we may hide our
shames?

20 BENV. If we should follow him to work revenge,
He'd join long asses' ears to these huge horns,
And make us laughingstocks to all the world.

MART. What shall we then do, dear Benvolio?

BENV. I have a castle joining near these woods,
And thither we'll repair and live obscure,
Till time shall alter these our brutish shapes:
Sith black disgrace hath thus eclips'd our fame,
We'll rather die with grief than live with shame.
{*Exeunt omnes.*

SCENE V *At the entrance to the house of Faustus. Enter* FAUSTUS *and the* HORSE-COURSER.°

HORSE-C. I beseech, your worship, accept of these forty dollars.°

FAUST. Friend, thou canst not buy so good a horse, for so small a price. I have no great need to sell him, but if thou likest him for ten dollars more take him, because I see thou hast a good mind to him.

HORSE-C. I beseech you, sir, accept of this; I am a very poor man and have lost very much of late by horseflesh, and this bargain will set me up again.

FAUST. Well, I will not stand° with thee, give me the 10 money. [HORSE-COURSER gives FAUSTUS the money.] Now, sirrah, I must tell you that you may ride him o'er hedge and ditch, and spare him not; but, do you hear? in any case ride him not into the water.°

HORSE-C. How, sir, not into the water? Why, will he not drink of all waters?

FAUST. Yes, he will drink of all waters, but ride him not into the water; o'er hedge and ditch, or where thou wilt, but not into the water. Go, bid the ostler deliver him unto you, and remember what I say.   20

HORSE-C. I warrant you, sir. O joyful day, now am I a made man° for ever.   {*Exit.*

FAUST. What art thou, Faustus, but a man condemn'd to die?°
Thy fatal time° draws to a final end,
Despair doth drive distrust into my thoughts.
Confound these passions with a quiet sleep.
Tush! Christ did call the thief upon the Cross;°
Then rest thee, Faustus, quiet in conceit.°
{*He sits to sleep.*

Re-enter the HORSE-COURSER *wet.*

HORSE-C. O what a cozening Doctor was this? I was riding my horse into the water, thinking some hidden 30 mystery had been in the horse, I had nothing under me but a little straw, and had much ado to escape drowning. Well, I'll go rouse him, and make him give me my forty dollars again. Ho, sirrah Doctor, you cozening scab! Master Doctor, awake and rise, and give me my money again, for your horse is turned to a bottle° of hay, master Doctor [*He pulls off his leg.*] Alas! I am undone, what shall I do? I have pull'd off his leg.

FAUST. O, help, help, the villain hath murder'd me.

HORSE-C. Murder, or not murder, now he has but 40 one leg, I'll outrun him, and cast this leg into some ditch or other.   {*Aside, and then runs out.*

FAUST. Stop him, stop him, stop him!—ha, ha, ha, Faustus hath his leg again, and the horse-courser a bundle of hay for his forty dollars.

Enter WAGNER.

How now, Wagner, what news with thee?

WAGNER. If it please you, the Duke of Anholt doth earnestly entreat your company, and hath sent some of

10 **stand,** haggle   14 **ride him not into the water.** Like Adam and Eve, the man immediately proceeds to do the one thing forbidden him, in the vain hope that it will exalt his station. Faustus' knowledge of this side of human psychology enables him to cheat the horse-courser   22 **a made man,** a man who has made his fortune   23 **a man . . . to die,** as opposed to "a made man"   27 **the thief upon the Cross.** See *Luke,* 23:39-43   28 **in conceit,** in mind, imagination. Faustus' despair is easily allayed by the parallel of the Good Thief crucified with Christ even though he has just cheated the horse-courser, shows no compunction, and has no apparent intention of reforming; he is smugly deluding himself   24-38 **Thy fatal time . . . leg.** The ensuing episode has the abrupt, unreal quality of a dream. However, Faustus is not actually dreaming but feigning sleep   36 **bottle,** bundle

Sc. v. Horse-courser, horse-trader; traditionally, a shrewd bargainer   2 **dollars,** originally, common German coins

his men to attend you with provision fit for your jour-
50 ney.

FAUST. The Duke of Anholt's° an honourable gentleman, and one to whom I must be no niggard° of my
cunning. Come away!   {*Exeunt.*

SCENE VI *An Inn. Enter* ROBIN, DICK, *the* HORSE-
COURSER, *and a* CARTER.

CART. Come, my masters, I'll bring you to the best
beer in Europe. What ho, hostess!—where be these
whores?°

Enter HOSTESS.

HOST. How now, what lack you? What, my old
guests, welcome.

ROBIN. Sirra Dick, dost thou know why I stand so
mute?

DICK. No, Robin, why is't?

ROBIN. I am eighteenpence on the score,° but say
10 nothing, see if she have forgotten me.

HOST. Who's this, that stands so solemnly by himself? what, my old guest?

ROBIN. O hostess, how do you? I hope my score
stands still.

HOST. Ay, there's no doubt of that, for methinks you
make no haste to wipe it out.

DICK. Why, hostess, I say, fetch us some beer.

HOST. You shall presently: look up in th' hall there,
ho!   {Exit.
20 DICK. Come, sirs, what shall we do now till mine
hostess comes?

CART. Marry, sir, I'll tell you the bravest tale how a
conjuror served me; you know Doctor Fauster?

HORSE-C. Ay, a plague take him, here's some on's
have cause to know him; did he conjure thee too?

CART. I'll tell you how he serv'd me: As I was going
to Wittenberg t'other day, with a load of hay, he met
me, and asked me what he should give me for as much
hay as he could eat; now, sir, I thinking that a little
30 would serve his turn, bade him take as much as he
would for three farthings; so he presently gave me my
money, and fell to eating; and, as I am a cursen man,
he never left eating, till he had eat up all my load of
hay.°

ALL. O monstrous, eat a whole load of hay!

ROBIN. Yes, yes, that may be; for I have heard of
one that has eat a load of logs.°

HORSE-C. Now sirs, you shall hear how villainously
he serv'd me: I went to him yesterday to buy a horse of
40 him, and he would by no means sell him under forty
dollars; so, sir, because I knew him to be such a horse
as would run over hedge and ditch and never tire, I
gave him his money. So when I had my horse, Doctor
Fauster bade me ride him night and day, and spare him
no time; but, quoth he, in any case, ride him not into
the water. Now, sir, I thinking the horse had had some
rare quality that he would not have me know of, what
did I but rid him into a great river, and when I came
just in the midst, my horse vanish'd away, and I sat
straddling upon a bottle of hay.°   50

ALL. O brave Doctor!

HORSE-C. But you shall hear how bravely I serv'd
him for it; I went me home to his house, and there I
found him asleep; I kept a hallooing and whooping in
his ears, but all could not wake him: I seeing that, took
him by the leg, and never rested pulling, till I had
pull'd me his leg quite off, and now 'tis at home in mine
hostry.°

DICK. And has the Doctor but one leg then? that's
excellent, for one of his devils turn'd me into the like- 60
ness of an ape's face.

CART. Some more drink, hostess.

ROBIN. Hark you, we'll into another room and drink
a while, and then we'll go seek out the Doctor.
                                      {*Exeunt omnes.*

SCENE VII *The Court of the Duke of Anholt. Enter the*
DUKE OF ANHOLT, *his* DUCHESS, FAUSTUS, *and*
MEPHISTOPHILIS.

DUKE. Thanks, master Doctor, for these pleasant
sights. Nor know I how sufficiently to recompense
your great deserts in erecting that enchanted castle in
the air, the sight whereof so delighted me,
As nothing in the world could please me more.

FAUST. I do think myself, my good Lord, highly rec-
ompensed in that it pleaseth your Grace to think but
well of that which Faustus hath performed. But gracious lady, it may be that you have taken no pleasure
in those sights; therefore, I pray you tell me, what is 10
the thing you most desire to have; be it in the world, it
shall be yours. I have heard that great-bellied° women
do long for things are rare and dainty.

DUCH. True, master Doctor, and since I find you so
kind, I will make known unto you what my heart desires to have; and were it now summer, as it is
January, a dead time of the winter, I would request no
better meat than a dish of ripe grapes.

FAUST. This is but° a small matter. Go, Mephistophilis, away!   {*Exit* MEPHISTOPHILIS. 20
Madam, I will do more than this for your content.

Enter MEPHISTOPHILIS *again with the grapes.*

Here now taste ye these, they should be good,
For they come from a far country, I can tell you.

51–53 **The Duke . . . away.** As usual, Faustus seems naively impressed by persons
of the nobility and is obsequious in his behavior towards them   52 **niggard.** He
has been niggardly in his treatment of the poor horse-courser   **Sc. vi**   3 **whores,**
the hostess and the inn's maidservants   9 **on the score,** in debt   33 **all my load
of hay,** another of Faustus' mean tricks. Here, moreover, he assumes an actively
bestial character   37 **a load of logs,** humorous slang expression for being drunk

50 **hay.** Note the repeated connection between illusion or self-delusion and
"hay," the cheap and insubstantial food of animals   58 **hostry,** inn   **Sc. vii**
12 **great-bellied,** pregnant   19–34 **This is but . . . you see,** a trivial and debasing
parlor-trick of magic

DUKE. This makes me wonder more than all the rest
That at this time of the year, when every tree
Is barren of his fruit, from whence you had
These ripe grapes.

FAUST. Please it your Grace the year is divided into
two circles over the whole world, so that when it is
30 winter with us, in the contrary circle it is likewise
summer with them, as in India, Saba° and such countries that lie far east, where they have fruit twice a
year. From whence, by means of a swift spirit that I
have, I had these grapes brought, as you see.

DUCH. And trust me, they are the sweetest grapes
that e'er I tasted.

{The CLOWNS bounce° at the gate within.

DUKE. What rude disturbers have we at the gate?
Go, pacify their fury, set it ope,
And then demand of them what they would have.

{They knock again, and call out to talk with FAUSTUS.

40 A SERVANT. Why, how now, masters, what a coil° is
there?
What is the reason you disturb the Duke?

DICK. We have no reason for it, therefore a fig° for
him.

SERV. Why, saucy varlets, dare you be so bold?

HORSE-C. I hope, sir, we have wit enough to be more
bold than welcome.

SERV. It appears so, pray be bold elsewhere, and
trouble not the Duke.

DUKE. What would they have?

50 SERV. They all cry out to speak with Doctor Faustus.

CART. Ay, and we will speak with him.

DUKE. Will you, sir? Commit° the rascals.

DICK. Commit with us! he were as good commit with
his father as commit with us.

FAUST. I do beseech your Grace let them come in,
They are good subject for a merriment.

DUKE. Do as thou wilt, Faustus, I give thee leave.

FAUST. I thank your Grace.

Enter ROBIN, DICK, CARTER, *and* HORSE-COURSER.

Why, how now, my good friends?
60 Faith you are too outrageous, but come near,
'I have procur'd your pardons: welcome all.

ROBIN. Nay, sir, we will be welcome for our money,
and we will pay for what we take. What ho, give's half
a dozen of beer here, and be hang'd.

FAUST. Nay, hark you, can you tell me where you
are?

CART. Ay, marry can I; we are under heaven.

SERV. Ay, but, sir sauce-box, know you in what
place?

70 HORSE-C. Ay, ay, the house is good enough to drink
in:

Zounds, fill us some beer, or we'll break all the barrels
in the house, and dash out all your brains with your
bottles.

FAUST. Be not so furious: come, you shall have
beer.
My lord, beseech you give me leave a while,
I'll gage my credit° 'twill content your Grace.

DUKE. With all my heart, kind Doctor, please thyself;
Our servants and our Court's at thy command.

FAUST. I humbly thank your Grace: then fetch some
beer.

HORSE-C. Ay, marry, there spake a Doctor indeed, 80
and, 'faith, I'll drink a health to thy wooden leg for that
word.

FAUST. My wooden leg! what dost thou mean by
that?

CART. Ha, ha, ha, dost hear him, Dick? He has forgot his leg.

HORSE-C. Ay, ay, he does not stand much upon that.

FAUST. No, 'faith not much upon a wooden leg.

CART. Good Lord, that flesh and blood should be so
frail with your Worship. Do not you remember a 90
horse-courser you sold a horse to?

FAUST. Yes, I remember I sold one a horse.

CART. And do you remember you bid he should not
ride him onto the water?

FAUST. Yes, I do very well remember that.

CART. And do you remember nothing of your leg?

FAUST. No, in good sooth.

CART. Then, I pray, remember your curtsy.

FAUST. I thank you, sir.

CART. 'Tis not so much worth; I pray you tell me one 100
thing.

FAUST. What's that?

CART. Be both your legs bedfellows every night together?

FAUST. Wouldst thou make a Colossus° of me, that
thou askest me such questions?

CART. No. truly, sir: I would make nothing of you,
but I would fain know that.

Enter HOSTESS *with drink.*

FAUST. Then I assure thee certainly they are.

CART. I thank you, I am fully satisfied.   110

FAUST. But wherefore dost thou ask?

CART. For nothing, sir: but methinks you should
have a wooden bedfellow of one of 'em.

HORSE-C. Why, do you hear, sir, did not I pull off
one of your legs when you were asleep?

FAUST. But I have it again, now I am awake: look
you here, sir.

ALL. O horrible, had the Doctor three legs?

31 **Saba,** Sheba   36 **bounce,** bang   40 **coil,** disturbance, commotion   42 **fig,**
an obscene gesture expressing contempt   52 **Commit,** put in jail. Dick then puns
on the meaning in "commit adultery," from the Ten Commandments

75 **I'll gage my credit,** I'll bet   105 **Colossus,** a reference to the ancient Colossus of Rhodes

CART. Do you remember, sir,° how you cozened me
120 and ate up my load of—
                          {FAUSTUS *charms him dumb.*
   DICK. Do you remember how you made me wear an
ape's—
   HORSE-C. You whoreson conjuring scab, do you remember how you cozened me with a ho—
   ROBIN. Ha' you forgotten me? you think to carry it
away with your *hey-pass* and *re-pass;*° do your re-
member the dog's fa—   {*Exeunt* CLOWNS.
   HOST. Who pays for the ale? hear you, Master Doc-
tor, now you have sent away my guests, I pray who
130 shall pay me for my a—   {*Exit* HOSTESS.
   LADY. My lord,
We are much beholding to this learned man.
   DUKE. So are we, Madam, which we will recom-
pense
With all the love and kindness that we may.
His artful sport drives all sad thoughts away.
                                    {*Exeunt.*

ACT V

SCENE I *Thunder and lightning. Enter* DEVILS *with
cover'd dishes.* MEPHISTOPHILIS *leads them into
Faustus' study. Then enter* WAGNER.

   WAG. I think my master means to die shortly,
He has made his will, and given me his wealth,
His house, his goods, and store of golden plate,
Besides two thousands ducats ready coin'd.
I wonder what he means; if death were nigh°
He would not frolic thus. He's now at supper
With the scholars, where there's such belly-cheer
As Wagner in his life ne'er saw the like.
And see where they come, belike the feast is done.
                                        {*Exit.*

Enter FAUSTUS, MEPHISTOPHILIS, *and two or three*
SCHOLARS.

10   FIRST SCHOL. Master Doctor Faustus, since our
conference about fair ladies, which was the beautifullest in all the world, we have determined with ourselves that Helen of Greece was the admirablest lady
that ever liv'd: therefore, Master Doctor, if you will do
us so much favour, as to let us see that peerless dame
of Greece, we should think ourselves much beholding
unto you.
   FAUST. Gentlemen,
For that I know your friendship is unfeign'd,
20 It is not Faustus' custom to deny
The just request of those that wish him well,
You shall behold that peerless dame of Greece,

No otherwise for pomp or majesty
Than when Sir Paris cross'd the seas with her,
And brought the spoil to rich Dardania.°
Be silent, then, for danger is in words.°
      {*Music sound,* MEPHISTOPHILIS *brings in* HELEN,
                              she passeth over the stage.
   SEC. SCHOL. Was this fair Helen, whose admired
worth
Made Greece with ten years' wars afflict poor Troy?
Too simple is my wit to tell her praise,
Whom all the world admires for majesty.   30
   THIRD SCHOL. No marvel though the angry Greeks
      pursued
With ten years' war the rape° of such a queen,
Whose heavenly beauty passeth all compare.
   FIRST SCHOL. Now we have seen the pride of Na-
ture's work,
And only paragon of excellence,
We'll take our leaves; and for this glorious deed
Happy and blest be Faustus evermore!
   FAUST. Gentlemen, farewell: the same wish I to you.
                                    {*Exeunt Scholars.*

Enter an OLD MAN.°

   OLD MAN. O gentle Faustus, leave this damned art,
This magic, that will charm thy soul to hell,   40
And quite bereave° thee of salvation.
Though thou hast now offended like a man,
Do not persever in it like a devil;
Yet, yet, thou hast an amiable soul,°
If sin by custom grow not into nature:
Then, Faustus, will repentance come too late,
Then thou art banish'd from the sight of heaven;
No mortal can express the pains of hell.
It may be this my exhortation
Seems harsh and all unpleasant; let it not,   50
For, gentle son, I speak it not in wrath,
Or envy of thee, but in tender love,
And pity of thy future misery.
And so have hope, that this my kind rebuke,
Checking thy body,° may amend thy soul.
   FAUST. Break heart, drop blood, and mingle it with
      tears,
Tears falling from repentant heaviness
Of thy most vile and loathsome filthiness,
The stench whereof corrupts the inward soul
With such flagitious crimes of heinous sins   60
As no commiseration may expel,
But mercy, Faustus, of thy Saviour sweet,

25 **Dardania,** Troy   26 **danger is in words,** literally, it would be dangerous to speak to the spirit of Helen. More broadly, words (such as those of Faustus' bond) have the power of destruction   32 **rape,** abduction   **Enter an Old Man.** The old man appears here as a kind of externalization of Faustus' anticipation of imminent death. He also assumes the function of conscience formerly assigned to the Good Angel; Mephistophilis now propounds the argument of the Bad Angel   41 **be-reave,** deprive   44 **an amiable soul.** Faustus' great potentiality for good, which is repeatedly stressed, makes the tragedy of his life all the more lamentable
55 **Checking thy body.** The old man fears, with good reason, that Faustus is con-templating Helen of Troy as his paramour. When he acquires her he has commit-ted the sin of intercourse with spirits and is then beyond redemption

119-130 **Do you remember, . . . for my a—.** This succession of abruptly termi-nated accusations against Faustus reinforces audience sympathy with the simple peasants whom he has duped and now mocks for the Duke's amusement
126 **hey-pass and re-pass,** traditional conjuring words   **Act V, i.** Mephistophilis again appears in the men al role of a waiter or steward   5 **if death were nigh.** Wagner does not understand his master's recourse to pleasure as a psychological anodyne to despair

Whose blood alone must wash away thy guilt—
Where art thou, Faustus? wretch, what has thou done?
Damn'd art thou, Faustus, damn'd; despair and die!

{MEPHISTOPHILIS *gives him a dagger.*

Hell claims his right, and with a roaring voice
Says, 'Faustus, come; thine hour is almost come';
And Faustus now will come to do thee right.

OLD MAN. Oh, stay, good Faustus, stay thy desperate steps!

70 I see an angel hover o'er thy head,
And, with a vial full of precious grace,
Offers to pour the same into thy soul:
Then call for mercy, and avoid despair.

FAUST. O friend, I feel
Thy words to comfort my distressed soul!
Leave me a while to ponder on my sins.

OLD MAN. Faustus, I leave thee; but with grief of
heart,
Fearing the enemy of thy hapless soul.   {*Exit.*

FAUST. Accursed Faustus, where is mercy now?

80 I do repent; and yet I do despair:
Hell strives with grace for conquest in my breast:
What shall I do to shun the snares of death?

MEPH. Thou traitor, Faustus, I arrest thy soul
For disobedience to my sovereign lord:
Revolt, or I'll in piecemeal tear thy flesh.

FAUST. I do repent I e'er offended him.
Sweet Mephistophilis, entreat thy lord
To pardon my unjust presumption,
And with my blood again I will confirm

90 The former vow I made to Lucifer.

MEPH. Do it, then, Faustus with unfeigned heart,
Lest greater dangers do attend thy drift.

{FAUSTUS *stabs his arm,
and writes on a paper with his blood.*

FAUST. Torment, sweet friend, that base and aged
man
That durst dissuade me from thy Lucifer,
With greatest torments that our hell affords.

MEPH. His faith is great; I cannot touch his soul;
But what I may afflict his body with
I will attempt, which is but little worth.

FAUST. One thing, good servant, let me crave of
thee,

100 To glut the longing of my heart's desire,—
That I may have unto my paramour
That heavenly Helen which I saw of late,
Whose sweet embraces may extinguish clean
Those thoughts that do dissuade me from my vow,
And keep my oath I made to Lucifer.

MEPH. This, or what else, my Faustus shall desire,
Shall be perform'd in twinkling of an eye.

Enter HELEN *again, passing over the stage between
two* CUPIDS.

FAUST. Was this the face that launch'd a thousand
ships,

And burnt the topless° towers of Ilium?—
Sweet Helen, make me immortal° with a kiss.—   110

{*She kisses him.*

Her lips suck forth my soul: see where it flies!—
Come, Helen, come, give me my soul again.
Here will I dwell, for heaven is in these lips
And all is dross that is not Helena. {*Enter* OLD MAN.°
I will be Paris, and for love of thee,
Instead of Troy, shall Wittenberg be sack'd;
And I will combat with weak Menelaus,
And wear thy colours on my plumed crest:
Yea, I will wound Achilles in the heel,
And then return to Helen for a kiss.   120
O, thou art fairer than the evening's air
Clad in the beauty of a thousand stars;
Brighter art thou° than flaming Jupiter
When he appear'd to hapless Semele;°
More lovely than the monarch of the sky
In wanton Arethusa's° azured arms;
And none but thou shalt be my paramour!

{*Exeunt* FAUSTUS, HELEN *and* CUPIDS.

OLD MAN. Accursed Faustus, miserable man,
That from thy soul exclud'st the grace of Heaven,
And fliest the throne of his tribunal-seat!   130

Enter the DEVILS.

Satan begins to sift me with his pride:
As in this furnace God shall try my faith,
My faith, vile hell, shall triumph over thee.
Ambitious fiends, see how the heavens smiles
At your repulse, and laughs your state to scorn!
Hence, hell! for hence I fly unto my God.   {*Exeunt.*

SCENE II *Faustus' Study. Thunder. Enter above*
LUCIFER, BELZEBUB, *and* MEPHISTOPHILIS.

LUC. Thus from infernal Dis do we ascend
To view the subjects of our monarchy,
Those souls which sin seals the black sons of hell,
'Mong which as chief, Faustus, we come to thee,
Bringing with us lasting damnation
To wait upon thy soul; the time is come
Which makes it forfeit.

MEPH. And this gloomy night,
Here in this room will wretched Faustus be.

BELZ. And here we'll stay,   10
To mark him how he doth demean himself.

MEPH. How should he, but in desperate lunacy?
Fond worldling, now his heart-blood dries with grief,
His conscience kills it and his labouring brain

---

109 **topless.** Their tops rose out of sight   110 **make me immortal.** Ironically,
Faustus thus damns himself forever   114 **Enter Old Man.** Faustus is proceeding
just as the old man had feared   123–126 **Brighter art . . . arms.** Faustus compares Helen to the male lovers of these mythological pairs, thereby implicitly putting himself in the female role   124 **Semele,** Theban girl beloved by Jupiter and
destroyed through her own plea that he appear before her in all his fiery immortal
splendor   126 **Arethusa,** a wood nymph changed by Artemis into a stream

Begets a world of idle fantasies,
To overreach the Devil;° but all in vain,
His store of pleasures must be sauc'd with pain.
He and his servant, Wagner, are at hand.
Both come from drawing Faustus' latest will.
20 See where they come!

Enter FAUSTUS *and* WAGNER.

FAUST. Say, Wagner, thou hast perus'd my will,
How dost thou like it?
WAG.   Sir, so wondrous well,
As in all humble duty, I do yield
My life and lasting service for your love.

Enter the SCHOLARS.

FAUST. Gramercies, Wagner. Welcome, gentlemen.
                                        {*Exit* WAGNER.
FIRST SCHOL. Now, worthy Faustus, methinks your
looks are changed.
FAUST. O, gentlemen!
30 SEC. SCHOL. What ails Faustus?
FAUST. Ah, my sweet chamber-fellow, had I liv'd
with thee, then had I lived still! but now must die eter-
nally. Look, sirs, comes he not? comes he not?
FIRST SCHOL. O my dear Faustus, what imports this
fear?
SEC. SCHOL. Is all our pleasure turn'd to melancholy?
THIRD SCHOL. He is not well with being over-
solitary.
40 SEC. SCHOL. If it be so, we'll have physicians
And Faustus shall be cur'd.
THIRD SCHOL. 'Tis but a surfeit,° sir; fear nothing.
FAUST. A surfeit of deadly sin, that hath damn'd
both body and soul.
SEC. SCHOL. Yet, Faustus, look up to heaven; remember God's mercies are infinite.
FAUST. But Faustus' offence can ne'er be pardoned:
the serpent that tempted Eve may be saved, but not
Faustus. O, gentlemen, hear me with patience, and
50 tremble not at my speeches! Though my heart pant and
quiver to remember that I have been a student here
these thirty years, O, would I had never seen Wittenberg, never read book! and what wonders I have done,
all Germany can witness, yea, all the world; for which
Faustus hath lost both Germany and the world; yea,
heaven itself, heaven, the seat of God, the throne of
the blessed, the kingdom of joy; and must remain in
hell for ever—hell, oh, hell for ever! Sweet friends,
what shall become of Faustus, being in hell for ever?
60 SEC. SCHOL. Yet, Faustus, call on God.
FAUST. On God, whom Faustus hath abjur'd! on
God, whom Faustus hath blasphem'd! Oh, my God, I

would weep! but the devil draws in my tears. Gush
forth blood, instead of tears! yea, life and soul—Oh,
he stays my tongue! I would lift up my hands; but see,
they hold 'em, they hold 'em!
ALL. Who, Faustus?
FAUST. Why, Lucifer and Mephistophilis. O, gentlemen, I gave them my soul for my cunning!
ALL. Oh, God forbid!   70
FAUST. God forbade it, indeed; but Faustus hath
done it: for the vain pleasure of four and twenty years
hath Faustus lost eternal joy and felicity. I writ them a
bill with mine own blood: the date is expired; this is the
time, and he will fetch me.
FIRST SCHOL. Why did not Faustus tell us of this
before, that divines might have pray'd for thee?
FAUST. Oft have I thought to have done so; but the
devil threaten'd to tear me in pieces, if I nam'd God; to
fetch me, body and soul, if I once gave ear to divinity: 80
and now 'tis too late. Gentlemen, away, lest you perish
with me.
SEC. SCHOL. O, what may we do to save Faustus?
FAUST. Talk not of me, but save yourselves, and
depart.
THIRD SCHOL. God will strengthen me; I will stay
with Faustus.
FIRST SCHOL. Tempt not God, sweet friend; but let
us into the next room, and pray for him.
FAUST. Ay, pray for me, pray for me; and what noise 90
soever you hear, come not unto me, for nothing can
rescue me.
SEC. SCHOL. Pray thou, and we will pray that God
may have mercy upon thee.
FAUST. Gentlemen, farewell: if I live till morning, I'll
visit you; if not, Faustus is gone to hell.
ALL. Faustus, farewell.   {*Exeunt* SCHOLARS.
MEPH. (*above*). Ay, Faustus, now thou hast no hope
    of heaven;
Therefore despair, think only upon hell,
For that must be thy mansion, there to dwell.   100
FAUST. O thou bewitching fiend, 'twas thy tempta-
    tion
Hath robb'd me of eternal happiness.
MEPH. I do confess it,° Faustus, and rejoice;
'Twas I, that when thou wert i' the way to heaven,
Damm'd up thy passage; when thou took'st the book,
To view the Scriptures, then I turn'd the leaves,
And led thine eye.—
What, weep'st thou? 'tis too late, despair, farewell!
Fools that will laugh on earth, must weep in hell.
    {*Exeunt* LUCIFER, BELZEBUB, MEPHISTOPHILIS.

Enter the GOOD ANGEL *and the* BAD ANGEL *at several
doors.*

GOOD ANG. Oh, Faustus, if thou hadst given ear to 110
    me,

Sc. ii   16 **overreach the Devil.** An "overreacher" is a man consumed by limitless pride and ego   42 **surfeit,** indigestion, the effects of overindulgence. Faustus
then applies their diagnosis to his state of spiritual disease

103 **I do confess it.** Mephistophilis gleefully explains his strategy

Innumerable joys had followed thee.
But thou didst love the world.
    BAD ANG.   Gave ear to me,
And now must taste hell's pains perpetually.
    GOOD ANG. O what will all thy riches, pleasures,
      pomps,
Avail thee now?
    BAD ANG. Nothing but vex thee more,
To want in hell, that had on earth such store.
                        {Music while the throne descends.
    GOOD ANG. O thou hast lost celestial happiness,
120 Pleasures unspeakable, bliss without end.
Hadst thou affected° sweet divinity,
Hell, or the devil, had had no power on thee.
Hadst thou kept on that way, Faustus, behold,
In what resplendent glory thou hadst sit
In yonder throne, like those bright shining saints,
And triumph'd over hell: that hast thou lost:
And now, poor soul, must thy good angel leave thee,
                        {The throne ascends.
The jaws of hell are open to receive thee.   *{Exit.*
                        {Hell is discovered.
    BAD ANG. Now, Faustus, let thine eyes with horror
      stare
130 Into that vast perpetual torture-house.
There are the Furies tossing damned souls
On burning forks; their bodies boil in lead:
There are live quarters° broiling on the coals,
That ne'er can die: this ever-burning chair
Is for o'er-tortured souls to rest them in;
These that are fed with sops of flaming fire,
Were gluttons and lov'd only delicates,
And laugh'd to see the poor starve at their gates:
But yet all these are nothing; thou shalt see
140 Ten thousand tortures that more horrid be.
    FAUST. O, I have seen enough to torture me.
    BAD ANG. Nay, thou must feel them, taste the smart
      of all:
He that loves pleasure, must for pleasure fall:
And so I leave thee, Faustus, till anon;
Then wilt thou tumble in confusion.°   *{Exit.*
                        {Hell disappears.
                   {The clock strikes eleven.
    FAUST. Ah, Faustus,
Now hast thou but one bare hour to live,
And then thou must be damn'd perpetually!
Stand still, you ever moving spheres of heaven,
150 That time may cease, and midnight never come;
Fair Nature's eye, rise, rise again, and make
Perpetual day; or let this hour be but
A year, a month, a week, a natural day,
That Faustus may repent and save his soul!
O lente, lente currite, noctis equi!°
The stars move still, time runs, the clock will strike,
The devil will come, and Faustus must be damn'd.

O, I'll leap up to my God!—Who pulls me down?—
See, see, where Christ's blood streams in the firma-
    ment!
One drop would save my soul, half a drop: ah, my   160
    Christ!—
Ah, rend not my heart for naming of my Christ!
Yet will I call on him: O, spare me, Lucifer!—
Where is it now? 'tis gone: and see, where God
Stretcheth out his arm, and bends his ireful brows!
Mountains and hills, come, come, and fall on me,
And hide me from the heavy wrath of God!
No, no!
Then will I headlong run into the earth:
Earth, gape! O, no, it will not harbour me!
You stars that reign'd at my nativity,   170
Whose influence hath allotted death and hell,°
Now draw up Faustus, like a foggy mist,
Into the entrails of yon lab'ring cloud
That, when you vomit forth into the air,
My limbs may issue from your smoky mouths,
So that my soul may but ascend to heaven!
                        {The clock strikes.
Ah, half the hour is past! 'twill all be passed anon.
O God,
If thou wilt not have mercy on my soul,
Yet for Christ's sake, whose blood hath ransom'd me, 180
Impose some end to my incessant pain;
Let Faustus live in hell a thousand years,
A hundred thousand, and at last be sav'd!
O, no end is limited to damned souls!
Why wert thou not a creature wanting soul?
Or why is this immortal that thou hast?
Ay, Pythagoras' *metempsychosis*,° were that true,
This soul should fly from me, and I be changed
Unto some brutish beast!° all beasts are happy,
For, when they die,   190
Their souls are soon dissolved in elements;
But mine must live still° to be plagu'd in hell.
Curs'd be the parents that engender'd me!
No, Faustus, curse thyself, curse Lucifer
That hath depriv'd thee of the joys of heaven.
                    {The clock striketh twelve.
O, it strikes, it strikes! Now, body, turn to air,
Or Lucifer will bear thee quick° to hell!
O soul, be changed into little water drops,
And fall into the ocean, ne'er be found!

Thunder and enter the DEVILS.

My God, my God, look not so fierce on me!   200
Adders and serpents, let me breathe a while!
Ugly hell, gape not! come not, Lucifer!
I'll burn my books!°—Ah, Mephistophilis!
                      {Exeunt with him.

171 **Whose influence . . . death and hell.** But Faustus finally accepts some responsibility for his damnation   187 **Pythagoras' metempsychosis,** the ancient
theory of the transmigration of souls   189 **some brutish beast.** Ironically, Faustus
has lived like a beast, "a creature wanting soul"   192 **still,** always   198 **quick,**
alive   203 **I'll burn my books.** This last desperate bid to propitiate hell could not
be more apt; Faustus the scholar chiefly damned himself through his books

121 **affected,** chosen, preferred   133 **quarters,** bodies   145 **confusion,** perdition   155 **O lente, lente currite, noctis equi.** "Run slowly, slowly, horses of the
night," a line from Ovid's *Amores*

SCENE III *A room next to Faustus' study. Enter the* SCHOLARS.

    FIRST SCHOL. Come, gentlemen, let us go visit
      Faustus,
For such a dreadful night was never seen,
Since first the world's creation did begin.
Such fearful shrieks and cries were never heard:
Pray heaven the Doctor have escap'd the danger.
    SEC. SCHOL. O help us heaven! see, here are Faus-
      tus' limbs,
All torn asunder by the hand of death.
    THIRD SCHOL. The devils whom Faustus serv'd°
      have torn him thus:
For 'twixt the hours of twelve and one, methought
10 I heard him shriek and call aloud for help:
At which self° time the house seem'd all on fire,
With dreadful horror of these damned fiends.
    SEC. SCHOL. Well, gentlemen, though Faustus' end
      be such
As every Christian heart laments to think on,
Yet for he was a scholar, once admired
For wondrous knowledge in our German schools,
We'll give his mangled limbs due burial;
And all the students, clothed in mourning black,
Shall wait upon his heavy° funeral.   {*Exeunt.*

EPILOGUE *Enter* CHORUS

    CHOR. Cut is the branch° that might have grown full
      straight,
And burned is Apollo's laurel° bough,
That sometime° grew within this learned man.
Faustus is gone: regard his hellish fall,
Whose fiendful fortune° may exhort the wise,
Only to wonder at° unlawful things,
Whose deepness doth entice such forward° wits
To practise more than heavenly power permits.
                        {*Exit.*

    Terminat hora diem; terminat Author opus.°
(1616)

THOMAS CAMPION
1567–1620

Thomas Campion was a poet, musician, critic, and doctor. He followed the advocates of classical measures and wrote a treatise on English poetry con-

demning the use of rhyme, but he used rhyme freely in his own poetry. His lyric poetry was set to music by himself and other composers in lute song collections and masques for the English court. In addition, he wrote Latin verse, a treatise on music, and several collections of lyrics and songs.

MY SWEETEST LESBIA

My sweetest Lesbia,° let us live and love,
And though the sager sort our deeds reprove,
Let us not weigh them. Heaven's great lamps do dive
Into their west and straight again revive,
But soon as once set is our little light,   5
Then must we sleep one ever-during night.

If all would lead their lives in love like me,
Then bloody swords and armor should not be,
No drum nor trumpet peaceful sleeps should move,
Unless alarm came from the camp of love.   10
But fools do live, and waste their little light,
And seek with pain their ever-during night.

When timely death my life and fortune ends,
Let not my hearse be vexed with mourning friends,
But let all lovers, rich in triumph, come   15
And with sweet pastimes grace my happy tomb;
And, Lesbia, close up thou my little light,
And crown with love my ever-during night.
(1601)

WHEN TO HER LUTE CORINNA SINGS

When to her lute Corinna sings,
Her voice revives the leaden strings,
And doth in highest notes appear
As any challenged echo clear;
But when she doth of mourning speak,   5
Even with her sighs the strings do break.

And, as her lute doth live or die,
Led by her passion, so must I:
For when of pleasure she doth sing,
My thoughts enjoy a sudden spring;   10
But if she doth of sorrow speak,
Even from my heart the strings do break.
(1601)

ROSE-CHEEKED LAURA

  Rose-cheeked Laura, come
Sing thou smoothly with thy beauty's

Sc. iii   8 **whom Faustus serv'd.** Faustus lived in the delusion that they were serving him   11 **self,** same   19 **heavy,** sad, tragic   **Epilogue**   1–3 **Cut is the branch . . . man.** The Chorus pronounces the "moral" of Faustus' tragedy, the loss to man and God of a great mind   2 **laurel,** symbol of wisdom, learning, and renown   3 **sometime,** formerly   5 **fiendful fortune,** hellish fate   6 **Only to wonder at,** to restrict oneself to observing with awe   7 **forward,** superior, presumptuous   9 **Terminat . . . opus.** The hour ends the day; the author ends his work

My Sweetest Lesbia   1 **Lesbia,** the name under which the Latin lyric poet Catullus (87–54? B.C.) celebrated the subject of many of his verses

Silent music, either other
  Sweetly gracing.

5   Lovely forms do flow
From consent divinely framéd;
Heaven is music, and thy beauty's
  Birth is heavenly.

These dull notes we sing
10 Discords need for helps to grace them.
Only beauty purely loving
  Knows no discord,

But still moves delight,
Like clear springs renewed by flowing,
15 Ever perfect, ever in themselves eternal.
  (1602)

THERE IS A GARDEN IN HER FACE

There is a garden in her face,
  Where roses and white lilies grow;
A heavenly paradise is that place,
  Wherein all pleasant fruits do flow.
5 There cherries grow, which none may buy
  Till "Cherry ripe!" themselves do cry.

Those cherries fairly do enclose
  Of orient pearl a double row;
Which when her lovely laughter shows,
10 They look like rose-buds filled with snow.
Yet them nor peer nor prince can buy,
  Till "Cherry ripe!" themselves do cry.

Her eyes like angels watch them still;
  Her brows like bended bows do stand,
15 Threatening with piercing frowns to kill
  All that attempt with eye or hand
Those sacred cherries to come nigh,
  Till "Cherry ripe!" themselves do cry.
  (1618)

FAIN WOULD I WED

Fain would I wed a fair young man that day and night
  could please me,
When my mind or body grieved, that had the power to
  ease me.
Maids are full of longing thoughts that breed a bloodless sickness,
And that, oft I hear men say, is only cured by quickness.
5 Oft have I been wooed and praised, but never could be
  moved:

Many for a day or so I have most dearly loved,
But this foolish mind of mine straight loathes the thing
  resolved.
If to love be sin in me, that sin is soon absolved.
Sure, I think I shall at last fly to some holy Order;
When I once am settled there, then can I fly no farther. 10
Yet I would not die a maid, because I had a mother:
As I was by one brought forth, I would bring forth
  another.
(1617)

THE ENGLISH BIBLE

The hub of the English Reformation was the English
Bible. The Reformation allowed individuals to read
the word of God themselves or, if they were illiterate,
to have it read in a language which they could understand. So the English Bible was chained to the pillars
of the churches, and ultimately small and inexpensive
editions came into the home. If the English Reformation had been a uniform rebellion against the Roman
Catholic Church, it is conceivable that a correspond-
ingly uniform translation of the Bible might have resulted. But there was reformation within the Reformation, and the gap between the Anglican Church and
Presbyterianism, for example, seemed at times to be
even greater than that between the Anglican Church
and Roman Catholicism. The English Bible tended,
therefore, not only to guide individuals in the way of
life but also in the doctrines peculiar to one sect or
another. The Puritans at Geneva made their own
translation in 1560, and the Bishops of the Established
Church in England made another translation eight
years later to offset the alarming popularity of the
Geneva version. The Roman Catholics, for obvious
reasons, made their own translation from the Latin
Vulgate in 1582 and 1609. The English translations
were usually made from early Greek and Hebrew
manuscripts and checked carefully against Greek,
Latin, Continental, and earlier English translations.

A psalm from the Old Testament, the Twenty-Third,
has been chosen from six of the leading translations of
the period to illustrate the battle of faiths and doctrines. Modern type has been used for all six versions,
and the numerous sidenotes and other interpretations
of the translators have been omitted. The original
spellings and usages have, however, been retained. A
brief explanation of each translation follows.

The first complete Bible in English was that of Miles
Coverdale, produced abroad in 1535. Coverdale
worked chiefly from German and Latin versions, but
his New Testament was greatly influenced by the earlier work of William Tyndale (1526). The Great Bible
of 1539, so called because of its size, was a revision

of Coverdale's. It was the first Bible "Appointed to be Read in Churches." The Geneva Bible of 1560 was also translated on the Continent by religious refugees. Its popularity arose partly from its small size, its roman type, and its use—for the first time in English biblical translations—of numbers for the verses. Its elaborate notes cover historical and geographical matters and point out the moral lessons to be gathered from the text. It was published in more than one hundred forty editions over a period of eighty-four years, roughly from the accession of Elizabeth to the Civil War. Thus, it was not only the Bible of Shakespeare, but that of Cromwell, Milton, and Bunyan. The Bishops' Bible of 1568 was translated under the direction of Archbishop Parker by eight bishops and several other scholars in England mainly to replace the authorized "Great Bible" of 1539 but also to counteract the Calvinist trend in the notes of the Geneva Version. In this second purpose it failed, for its size, cost, ornate Gothic type, and uneven quality prevented it from ever becoming popular. The last edition appeared in 1602, or forty-two years before the last edition of its rival. The Roman Catholic translation of the New Testament was issued at Rheims in 1582, and the Old Testament at Douai in 1609–1610. As with so many of the translations, the work was done by religious exiles from England; William Allen directed the translation, and the actual work was done largely by Gregory Martin, an Oxford graduate. The Protestant translations were, of course, not acceptable to the Roman Catholics, whose translation follows the meaning and the form of St. Jerome's Latin Bible (the Vulgate).

No other book in English literature has exerted as much influence as has the English Bible. Part of this influence has come from its religious nature, but part of it is due to its high merit as a work of literary art. Although drawn from ancient Hebrew and Greek originals and filtered through many translations before the days of Elizabeth and James, the book was made thoroughly English by the craftsmanship of its translators. It is the last of the Protestant translations, however, the King James Bible of 1611 (sometimes referred to as the "Authorized Version"), that has come to be regarded as *the* English Bible.

The King James Bible had its origin in a conference which the king assembled at Hampton Court in January 1604. He did not achieve his objective of reconciling the divergent Protestant groups that had been tearing England apart during Elizabeth's reign. But the proposal of Dr. John Reynolds of Oxford—that a new translation of the Bible be made which would be acceptable to all religious groups—was eagerly adopted, and after some delay, the work was actively begun. Groups of scholars at Westminster, Cambridge, and Oxford worked independently and then conferred until they agreed. The Bishops' Bible was used as a guide, but the originals and all earlier translations were diligently consulted. The translation appeared in 1611,

seven years after it had been proposed; within three years it had run through fourteen editions. After three hundred odd years it still outsells all other English books.

THE TWENTY-THIRD PSALM IN SIX TRANSLATIONS

COVERDALE BIBLE, 1535

The Lorde is my shepherde, I can wante nothinge. He fedeth me in a grene pasture, and ledeth me to a fresh water. He quickeneth my soule, and bringeth me forth in the way of rightuousnes for his names sake. Though I shulde walke now in the valley of the 5 shadowe of death, yet I feare no euell, for thou art with me: thy staffe and they shephoke comforte me. Thou preparest a table before me agaynst mine enemies: thou anoyntest my heade with oyle, and fyllest my cuppe full. O let thy louynge kyndnes and mercy 10 folowe me all the dayes of my life, that I maye dwell in the house of the Lorde for euer.

GREAT BIBLE, 1539

The Lorde is my shepherde, therfore can I lack nothing. He shall fede me in a grene pasture, and leade me forth besyde the waters of comforte. He shall conuert my soule, and brynge me forth in the pathes of ryghteousnes for hys names sake. Yee though I walke 5 thorow the valley of the shadow of death, I will feare no euell, for thou art with me: thy rodde and thy staffe comforte me.

Thou shalt prepare a table before me agaynst them that trouble me: thou has anoynted my head with oyle, 10 and my cuppe shal be full.

But thy louynge kyndnes and mercy shall folowe me all the dayes of my lyfe: and I will dwell in the house of the Lord for euer.

GENEVAN BIBLE, 1560

The Lord is my shepherd, I shall not want. He maketh me to rest in grene pasture, and leadeth me by the waters of comforte. He restoreth my soule, and leadeth me in the paths of righteousnes for his Names sake. Yea, thogh I shulde walke through the valley of 5 the shadow of death, I wil feare no euil: for thou art with me: thy rod and thy staffe, they comforte me. Thou doest prepare a table before me in the sight of mine aduersaries: thou doest anoint mine head with oyle and my cup runneth ouer. Douteles kindenes, and 10 Mercie shal follow me al the dayes of my life, and I shal remaine a long season in the house of the Lord.

BISHOPS' BIBLE, 1568

God is my sheephearde, therfore I can lacke nothyng: he wyll cause me to repose my selfe in pasture full of grasse, and he wyll leade me vnto calme waters.

5 He wyll conuert my soule: he wyll bring me foorth into the pathes of righteousnesse for his name sake.

Yea though I walke through the valley of the shadow of death, I wyll feare no euyll, for thou art with me, thy rodde and thy staffe be the thynges that do comfort 10 me.

Thou wylt prepare a table before me in the presence of myne aduersaries: thou has annoynted my head with oyle, and my cup shal be brymme full.

Truely felicitie and mercie shal folowe me all the 15 dayes of my life: and I wyll dwell in the house of God for a long tyme.

RHEIMS-DOUAI BIBLE, 1610

Our Lord ruleth me, and nothing shal be wanting to me: in place of pasture there he hath placed me. Vpon the water of refection he hath brought me vp: he hath conuerted my soule. He hath conducted me vpon the 5 pathes of iustice, for his name. For, although I shal walke in the middes of the shadow of death, I will not feare euils: because thou art with me. Thy rod and thy staffe: they haue comforted me. Thou has prepared in my sight a table, against them that truble me. Thou hast fatted my head with oyle: and my chalice ine- 10 briating how goodlie is it! And thy mercie shal folow me al the dayes of my life: And that I may dwel in the house of our Lord, in longitude of dayes.

KING JAMES BIBLE, 1611

The Lord is my shepheard, I shall not want.

He maketh me to lie downe in greene pastures: he leadeth mee beside the still waters.

He restoreth my soule: he leadeth me in the pathes of righteousnes, for his names sake. 5

Yea though I walke through the valley of the shadowe of death, I will feare no euill: for thou art with me, thy rod and thy staffe, they comfort me.

Thou preparest a table before me, in the presence of mine enemies: thou anointest my head with oyle, my 10 cuppe runneth ouer.

Surely goodnes and mercie shall followe me all the daies of my life: and I will dwell in the house of the Lord for euer.

WILLIAM SHAKESPEARE
1564–1616

William Shakespeare was born in Stratford in 1564, the third child of John Shakespeare, a merchant and alderman. Apparently he had the usual grammar school education of the time with its staple of Latin, but the details of his education are uncertain. Like others of his class, he married young; by the time he was twenty-one, he was the father of three children. His dramatic career began about 1590; in 1594 he became an actor-sharer in the Lord Chamberlain's Men, one of the ablest of the theatrical companies. In 1598 he was mentioned as among the best playwrights of both comedy and tragedy. For the Lord Chamberlain's Men (which became the King's Men in 1603 at the accession of James), Shakespeare wrote the whole or the major part of thirty-seven plays. Various legal records show him to have been a respected man of property both in London and in Stratford. About 1611 or 1612 he retired to his native city. He died on April 23, 1616, and was buried in the chancel of the Church of the Holy Trinity in Stratford. Roughly half of his plays were published in single editions during his lifetime, and after his death thirty-six of them—four-teen comedies, ten histories, and twelve tragedies—were collected together in the famous First Folio edition of 1623.

Shakespeare's literary career falls roughly into four stages:

c.1588–1592 In London; beginning as a playwright
c.1592–1598 Devoted himself chiefly to comedies and the first tetralogy of chronicle plays; also wrote the early tragedy *Titus Andronicus* and the short narrative poems *Venus and Adonis* and *The Rape of Lucrece*; later in the decade wrote the second tetralogy of history plays, several romantic comedies (e. g., *Love's Labor's Lost, The Merchant of Venice*), and the middle tragedies *Romeo and Juliet* and *Julius Caesar*; probably also completed most or all of the sonnets (published 1609)
c.1601–1609 Period of the later romantic comedies (e. g., *As You Like It, Twelfth Night*), the "problem plays" (e. g., *Measure for Measure, Troilus and Cressida*), and the great mature tragedies *Hamlet, Othello, King Lear, Macbeth,* and *Antony and Cleopatra*; also

wrote *Timon of Athens, Coriolanus,* and the early romance *Pericles;* contributed the strange, lovely poem *The Phoenix and the Turtle* to an anthology
c.1610–1613 Period of the late romances *Cymbeline, The Winter's Tale,* and *The Tempest;* also wrote *Henry VIII,* probably in collaboration with Fletcher, and parts of the tragicomedy *Two Noble Kinsmen*

Shakespeare's composition of a sonnet sequence was hardly unique in his day; Sidney, Spenser, and other prominent Elizabethan poets also contributed to the popular vogue of the genre. But as one might expect, Shakespeare's cycle differs significantly from those of his fellow sonneteers in the greater individuality and overall poetic quality of his work. Although not published as a collection until 1609, most of the sonnets were probably written at various times during the 1590s and only later brought together with the intent of giving them some degree of narrative or thematic continuity. It is debatable whether they were originally published in the correct order, but certain sequences and motifs, largely traditional, may be discerned: a series celebrating the beauty of a young man and the poet's painful emotional involvement with him; some sonnets to a "dark lady"; some about a triangle involving two men and a woman; some about a rival poet; a good number on the destructive power of time and the dubiously consoling notion of the immortality of art; and scattered sonnets of moral insight such as 129 and 146. The longstanding controversies about the identity of the "Mr. W. H.," to whom the sonnets are dedicated, and the possibility of direct autobiographical inspiration are unlikely ever to be resolved. A purely literary survey of the sonnets confirms this improbability. Some of them seem to be just conventional literary exercises; yet others exhibit a provocative personal immediacy.

Shakespeare probably derived part of his gift of expression in drama from the compression and linguistic discipline required by the sonnet form. In addition, the sonnets register a characteristic line of somber, urgent questioning of experience, particularly the experience of love, which infuses the problem plays and mature tragedies. This persistent inquiry into the ultimate value and meaning of intimate relationships appears in a conceptual progression of drama: *Romeo and Juliet, Troilus and Cressida,* and *Antony and Cleopatra.* These densely poetic plays, along with the sonnets, reflect Shakespeare's lifelong absorption in the phenomenon of loving.

The form of the sonnets is that of the Elizabethan variation of the Italian—three quatrains with alternate rhymes *(abab cdcd efef)* and a concluding couplet *(gg).* The division of thought usually follows that of the lines: lament in the quatrains, comfort or reconciliation in the couplet; a question in the quatrains, the answer in the couplet; and similar ad-

justments of thought within structural segments. Sometimes the sonnets are linked ideologically in a minor sequence or in pairs; more frequently, however, they stand alone.

SONNETS

18

Shall I compare thee to a summer's day?
Thou art more lovely and more temperate:
Rough winds do shake the darling buds of May,
And summer's lease hath all too short a date:
Sometime too hot the eye of heaven shines, 5
And often is his gold complexion dimm'd;
And every fair° from fair sometime declines,
By chance or nature's changing course untrimm'd;°
But thy eternal summer shall not fade
Nor lose possession of that fair thou ow'st;° 10
Nor shall Death brag thou wand'rest in his shade,
When in eternal lines to time thou grow'st:
 So long as men can breathe or eyes can see,
 So long lives this° and this gives life to thee.

29

When, in disgrace with fortune and men's eyes,
I all alone beweep my outcast state
And trouble deaf heaven with my bootless° cries
And look upon myself and curse my fate,
Wishing me like to one more rich in hope, 5
Featur'd like him, like him with friends possess'd,
Desiring this man's art and that man's scope,
With what I most enjoy contented least;
Yet in these thoughts myself almost despising,
Haply I think on thee, and then my state, 10
Like to the lark at break of day arising
From sullen earth, sings hymns at heaven's gate;
 For thy sweet love rememb'red such wealth brings
 That then I scorn to change my state with kings.

30

When to the sessions of sweet silent thought
I summon up remembrance of things past,
I sigh the lack of many a thing I sought,
And with old woes new wail my dear time's waste:
Then can I drown an eye, unus'd to flow, 5
For precious friends hid in death's dateless° night,
And weep afresh love's long since cancell'd woe,
And moan th' expense of many a vanish'd sight:
Then can I grieve at grievances foregone,
And heavily from woe to woe tell o'er 10
The sad account of fore-bemoaned moan,
Which I new pay as if not paid before.
 But if the while I think on thee, dear friend,
 All losses are restor'd and sorrows end.

Sonnet 18 7 **every fair,** every beautiful thing 8 **untrimm'd,** stripped 10 **ow'st,** owns 14 **this,** this sonnet Sonnet 29 3 **bootless,** useless, unprofitable Sonnet 30 6 **dateless,** without date, endless

55

Not marble, nor the gilded monuments
Of princes, shall outlive this pow'rful rhyme;
But you shall shine more bright in these contents°
Than unswept stone besmear'd with sluttish time.
5 When wasteful war shall statues overturn,
And broils root out the work of masonry,
Nor Mars his sword nor war's quick fire shall burn
The living record of your memory.
'Gainst death and all-oblivious enmity
10 Shall you pace forth; your praise shall still find room
Even in the eyes of all posterity
That wear this world out to the ending doom.°
    So, till the judgement that yourself arise,
    You live in this, and dwell in lovers' eyes.

71

No longer mourn for me when I am dead
Than you shall hear the surly sullen bell
Give warning to the world that I am fled
From this vile world, with vilest worms to dwell:
5 Nay, if you read this line, remember not
The hand that writ it; for I love you so
That I in your sweet thoughts would be forgot
If thinking on me then should make you woe.
O, if, I say, you look upon this verse
10 When I perhaps compounded am with clay,
Do not so much as my poor name rehearse,
But let your love even with my life decay,
    Lest the wise world should look into your moan
    And mock you with me after I am gone.

73

That time of year thou mayst in me behold
When yellow leaves, or none, or few, do hang
Upon those boughs which shake against the cold,
Bare ruin'd choirs, where late the sweet birds sang.
5 In me thou see'st the twilight of such day
As after sunset fadeth in the west,
Which by and by black night doth take away,
Death's second self, that seals up all in rest.
In me thou see'st the glowing of such fire
10 That on the ashes of his youth doth lie,
As the death-bed whereon it must expire
Consum'd with that which it was nourish'd by.
    This thou perceiv'st, which makes thy love more
        strong,
    To love that well which thou must leave ere long.

97

How like a winter hath my absence been
From thee, the pleasure of the fleeting year!
What freezings have I felt, what dark days seen!
What old December's bareness every where!
5 And yet this time remov'd° was summer's time,

The teeming autumn, big with rich increase,
Bearing the wanton burthen of the prime,°
Like widow'd wombs after their lords' decease:
Yet this abundant issue seem'd to me
But hope of orphans and unfathered fruit;   10
For summer and his pleasures wait on thee,
And, thou away, the very birds are mute;
    Or, if they sing, 'tis with so dull a cheer
    That leaves look pale, dreading the winter's near.

98

From you have I been absent in the spring,
When proud-pied° April dress'd in all his trim
Hath put a spirit of youth in every thing,
That heavy° Saturn laugh'd and leap'd with him.
Yet nor the lays of birds nor the sweet smell   5
Of different flowers in odour and in hue
Could make me any summer's story° tell,
Or from their proud lap pluck them where they grew;
Nor did I wonder at the lily's white,
Nor praise the deep vermilion in the rose;   10
They were but sweet, but figures of delight,
Drawn after you, you pattern of all those.
    Yet seem'd it winter still, and, you away,
    As with your shadow I with these did play:

106

When in the chronicle of wasted time
I see descriptions of the fairest wights,
And beauty making beautiful old rhyme
In praise of ladies dead and lovely knights,
Then, in the blazon° of sweet beauty's best,   5
Of hand, of foot, of lip, of eye, of brow,
I see their antique pen would have express'd
Even such a beauty as you master now.
So all their praises are but prophecies
Of this our time, all you prefiguring;   10
And, for they look'd but with divining eyes,
They had not skill enough your worth to sing:
    For we, which now behold these present days,
    Have eyes to wonder, but lack tongues to praise.

116

Let me not to the marriage of true minds
Admit impediments. Love is not love
Which alters when it alteration finds,
Or bends with the remover to remove:
O, no! it is an ever-fixed mark   5
That looks on tempests and is never shaken;
It is the star to every wand'ring bark,
Whose worth's unknown, although his height be ta-
    ken.
Love's not Time's fool, though rosy lips and cheeks
Within his bending sickle's compass come;   10
Love alters not with his brief hours and weeks,

Sonnet 55   3 these contents, this sonnet   12 the ending doom, the Day of Judgment   Sonnet 97. See also the companion sonnet, 98, which follows   5 this time remov'd, the actual season of separation

7 the prime, the spring, or that time of the year when planting is done   Sonnet 98   2 proud-pied, splendidly variegated   4 That heavy, so that baleful   7 summer's story, gay fiction   Sonnet 106   5 blazon, description, especially with a view to display

But bears it out even to the edge of doom.
   If this be error and upon me prov'd,
   I never writ, nor no man ever lov'd.

129

Th' expense of spirit in a waste of shame
Is lust in action; and till action, lust
Is perjur'd, murd'rous, bloody, full of blame,
Savage, extreme, rude, cruel, not to trust,
5 Enjoy'd no sooner but despised straight,
Past reason hunted, and no sooner had
Past reason hated, as a swallowed bait
On purpose laid to make the taker mad;
Mad in pursuit and in possession so;
10 Had, having, and in quest to have, extreme;
A bliss in proof, and prov'd, a very woe;
Before, a joy propos'd; behind, a dream.
   All this the world well knows; yet none knows well
   To shun the heaven that leads men to this hell.

130

My mistress' eyes° are nothing like the sun;
Coral is far more red than her lips' red;
If snow be white, why then her breasts are dun;
If hairs be wires, black wires grow on her head.
5 I have seen roses damask'd, red and white,
But no such roses see I in her cheeks;
And in some perfumes is there more delight
Than in the breath that from my mistress reeks.°
I love to hear her speak, yet well I know
10 That music hath a far more pleasing sound;
I grant I never saw a goddess go;°
My mistress, when she walks, treads on the ground:
   And yet, by heaven, I think my love as rare
   As any she belied with false compare.

138

When my love swears that she is made of truth
I do believe her, though I know she lies,
That she might think me some untutor'd youth,
Unlearned in the world's false subtleties.
5 Thus vainly thinking that she thinks me young,
Although she knows my days are past the best,
Simply I credit her false-speaking tongue:
On both sides thus is simple truth suppress'd.
But wherefore says she not she is unjust?
10 And wherefore say not I that I am old?
O, love's best habit is in seeming trust,
And age in love loves not to have years told:
   Therefore I lie with her and she with me,
   And in our faults by lies we flattered be.

146

Poor soul, the centre of my sinful earth,°
[Thrall to] these rebel pow'rs that thee array,°

Why dost thou pine within and suffer dearth,
Painting thy outward walls so costly gay?
Why so large cost, having so short a lease,   5
Dost thou upon thy fading mansion spend?
Shall worms, inheritors of this excess,
Eat up thy charge? is this thy body's end?
Then, soul, live thou upon thy servant's loss,
And let that pine to aggravate° thy store;   10
Buy terms divine in selling hours of dross;
Within be fed,° without be rich no more:
   So shalt thou feed on Death, that feeds on men,
   And Death once dead, there's no more dying then.
(1609)

THE TEMPEST

The Tempest, first performed in 1611, is, like a number of Shakespeare's late plays, often called a romance. Prospero's island world, with its magical spirits, shipwrecked travelers, and loving couple, shows Shakespeare's fascination with the wondrous, remote, and adventurous. Though we have no direct literary sources for Shakespeare's story, he may have been influenced by contemporary shipwreck narratives and by reports received from the new colonists in America.

The shipwrecked travelers, King Alonso and the members of his court, represent the corrupt world of Naples and Milan. Antonio and Sebastian cynically reject the island world; they even attempt to plot a murder and a political coup. The comic antics of Stephano and Trinculo reveal the self-deception of ambitious men; their attempt to murder Prospero parodies the actions of Sebastian and Antonio.

Prospero rules the imaginary island world with white magic—magic devoted to good ends. He conjures up trials and visions to test the other characters' intentions and to guide them toward a renewed faith in goodness. His chief power, exercised through Ariel, is to create illusions—of separation, of death, of the gods' blessings—by controlling the elements. Thus, Prospero creates the illusion of death to test Alonso. Alonso reacts to the apparent death of his son Ferdinand with guilt and despair; he interprets it as a punishment for his earlier overthrow of Prospero.

Ferdinand also undergoes trials devised by Prospero to test his worth. Unlike the other shipwrecked travelers, however, Ferdinand is innocent and hopeful, well-matched to Miranda. Although Prospero approves of his prospective son-in-law, he temporarily creates the illusion of parental opposition to marriage and imposes the task of logbearing (much like that assigned to Caliban) on Ferdinand. The marriage bond between Ferdinand and Miranda unites the best of both worlds: the moral world and the natural world, the world of the flesh and the world of the spirit.

Sonnet 130   1 **My mistress' eyes, etc.** This sonnet is a clever satire on the conventional poetic description of a lady   8 **reeks,** is exhaled   11 **go,** walk   **Sonnet 146**   1 **my sinful earth,** my mortal clay, my body   2 **array,** clothe

10 **aggravate,** increase   12 **Within be fed, etc.** Spiritual food will create immortality and so destroy Death

Unlike Alonso and the members of his court, Caliban and Ariel are creatures untouched by Western civilization. Caliban is a child of nature, sensitive to natural beauty. At the same time, of course, he is also the child of a witch; his darker, irrational desires must be curbed because they defy reason. Caliban, as a representative of natural man, calls into question the values of Western society. With instinctive cunning, he senses that books are his chief enemy. In the end, however, he is reconciled; he vows to "be wise hereafter/ And seek for grace."

Ariel is a woodland spirit who belongs to the magic world of song, music, and illusion. Prospero uses Ariel to perform his magic, but Ariel exists independently of Prospero. Ariel also exists apart from time and space; at the end of the last act, Prospero enjoins Ariel, "Then to the elements/Be free, and fare thou well!" Ironically, Prospero looks forward to releasing Ariel because he himself will then be released from his responsibilities as ruler of the island world. His power weighs heavily on him because he is a man, not a god, and cherishes his own humanity. Thus, it is with relief as well as melancholy that Prospero finally leaves his demanding role as the creative moral intelligence of the island world.

NAMES OF THE ACTORS

ALONSO, King of Naples.
SEBASTIAN, *his brother.*
PROSPERO, the right Duke of Milan.
ANTONIO, *his brother, the usurping* Duke of Milan.
FERDINAND, *son to the King of Naples.*
GONZALO, *an honest old Counsellor.*
ADRIAN *and* ⎫
FRANCISCO, ⎭ *Lords.*
CALIBAN, *a savage and deformed Slave.*
TRINCULO, *a Jester.*
STEPHANO, *a drunken Butler.*
MASTER OF A SHIP.
BOATSWAIN.
MARINERS.

MIRANDA, *daughter to Prospero.*

ARIEL, *an airy Spirit.*
IRIS,
CERES,
JUNO, ⎬ [*presented by*] *Spirits.*
NYMPHS,
REAPERS,

[Other Spirits attending on Prospero.]

THE SCENE: *An uninhabited island.*

ACT I.
SCENE I. [*On a ship at sea:*] *a tempestuous noise of thunder and lightning heard.*

Enter a SHIP-MASTER *and* a BOATSWAIN.

MAST. Boatswain!°
BOATS. Here, master: what cheer?
MAST. Good,° speak to the mariners: fall to 't yarely,° or we run ourselves aground: bestir, bestir. *Exit.*

Enter MARINERS.

BOATS. Heigh, my hearts! cheerly, cheerly, my hearts! yare, yare! Take in the topsail. Tend° to the master's whistle. Blow,° till thou burst thy wind, if room enough!°

Enter ALONSO, SEBASTIAN, ANTONIO, FERDINAND, GONZALO, *and others.*

ALON. Good boatswain, have care. Where 's the master? Play the° men.   10
BOATS. I pray now, keep below.
ANT. Where is the master, bos'n?
BOATS. Do you not hear him? You mar our labour: keep your cabins: you do assist the storm.
GON. Nay, good, be patient.
BOATS. When the sea is. Hence! What cares° these roarers° for the name of king? To cabin: silence! trouble us not.
GON. Good, yet remember whom thou hast aboard.
BOATS. None that I more love than myself. You are a   20
counsellor; if you can command these elements to silence, and work the peace of the present,° we will not hand° a rope more; use your authority: if you cannot, give thanks you have lived so long, and make yourself ready in your cabin for the mischance of the hour, if it so hap. Cheerly, good hearts! Out of our way, I say.
Exit.

GON. I have great comfort from this fellow: methinks he hath no drowning mark upon him; his complexion is perfect gallows.° Stand fast, good Fate, to his hanging: make the rope of his destiny our cable, for our own doth   30
little advantage.° If he be not born to be hanged, our case is miserable.   *Exeunt.*

Enter BOATSWAIN.

BOATS. Down with the topmast! yare! lower, lower! Bring her to try with main-course.° (*A cry within.*) A plague upon this howling! they are louder than the weather or our office.°

The Tempest Act I, Scene I   1 **Boatswain,** under-officer in a ship, having to do with sails and rigging and the supervision of the crew at work   3 **Good,** probably, good friend   3 **fall . . . yarely,** set to work nimbly   6 **Tend,** attend   7 **Blow,** addressed to the wind   8 **if room enough,** as long as we have sea-room enough   10 **Play the,** act like   16 **cares,** described as a singular verb used with a plural subject on account of haste; also as an old northern plural of the verb in *s*   17 **roarers,** waves or winds, or both; allusion to *roarer* meaning "bully," "blusterer"   22 **work . . . present,** calm the storm   23 **hand,** handle   29 **complexion . . . gallows,** appearance shows he was born to be hanged   31 **doth little advantage,** is of little benefit   34 **Bring . . . course,** heave to and sail her close to the wind by means of the mainsail   36 **they . . . office,** the passengers make more noise than the winds or than we do at work

Enter SEBASTIAN, ANTONIO, *and* GONZALO.

Yet again! what do you here? Shall we give o'er and
drown? Have you a mind to sink?

    SEB. A pox o' your throat, you bawling, blasphe-
40 mous, incharitable dog!

    BOATS. Work you then.

    ANT. Hang, cur! hang, you whoreson, insolent
noisemaker! We are less afraid to be drowned than thou
art.

    GON. I'll warrant him for drowning;° though the ship
were no stronger than a nutshell and as leaky as an
unstanched° wench.

    BOATS. Lay her a-hold, a-hold!° set her two courses°
off to sea again! lay her off!

Enter MARINERS *wet.*

50   MARINERS. All lost! to prayers, to prayers! all lost!
                              [*Exeunt.*]

    BOATS. What, must our mouths be cold?°

    GON. The king and prince at prayers! let 's assist
    them,
For our case is as theirs.

    SEB.   I 'm out of patience.

    ANT. We are merely° cheated of our lives by
    drunkards:
This wide-chapp'd° rascal—would thou mightst lie
    drowning
The washing of ten tides!°

    GON.   He'll be hang'd yet,
Though every drop of water swear against it
And gape at wid'st to glut° him.
A confused noise within: 'Mercy on us!'—
'We split,° we split!'—'Farewell my wife and
    children!'—
60 'Farewell, brother!'—'We split, we split, we split!'
                             [*Exit* BOATS.]

    ANT. Let 's all sink wi' th' king.

    SEB. Let 's take leave of him.   *Exit* [*with* ANT.]

    GON. Now would I give a thousand furlongs of sea
for an acre of barren ground, long heath,° brown
furze,° any thing. The wills above be done! but I would
fain die a dry death.   *Exit.*

SCENE II. [*The island. Before* PROSPERO'S *cell.*]

Enter PROSPERO *and* MIRANDA.

    MIR. If by your art, my dearest father, you have
Put the wild waters in this roar, allay them.

The sky, it seems, would pour down stinking pitch,°
But that° the sea, mounting to th' welkin's cheek,°
Dashes the fire out. O, I have suffered
With those that I saw suffer: a brave vessel,
Who had, no doubt, some noble creature in her,
Dash'd all to pieces. O, the cry did knock
Against my very heart. Poor souls, they perish'd.
Had I been any god of power, I would   10
Have sunk the sea within the earth or ere
It should the good ship so have swallow'd and
The fraughting° souls within her.

    PROS.   Be collected:
No more amazement:° tell your piteous heart
There 's no harm done.

    MIR.   O, woe the day!

    PROS.   No harm.
I have done nothing but in care of thee,
Of thee, my dear one, thee, my daughter, who
Art ignorant of what thou art, nought knowing
Of whence I am, nor that I am more better
Than Prospero, master of a full° poor cell,   20
And thy no greater father.

    MIR.   More to know
Did never meddle° with my thoughts.

    PROS.   'Tis time
I should inform thee farther. Lend thy hand,
And pluck my magic garment from me. So:°
                [*Lays down his mantle.*]
Lie there, my art. Wipe thou thine eyes; have comfort.
The direful spectacle of the wrack, which touch'd
The very virtue of compassion in thee,
I have with such provision° in mine art
So safely ordered that there is no soul°—
No, not so much perdition° as an hair   30
Betid to any creature in the vessel
Which thou heard'st cry, which thou saw'st sink. Sit
    down;
For thou must now know farther.

    MIR.   You have often
Begun to tell me what I am, but stopp'd
And left me to a bootless inquisition,°
Concluding 'Stay: not yet.'

    PROS.   The hour's now come;
The very minute bids thee ope thine ear;
Obey and be attentive. Canst thou remember
A time before we came unto this cell?
I do not think thou canst, for then thou wast not   40
Out° three years old.

    MIR.   Certainly, sir, I can.

    PROS. By what? by any other house or person?
Of any thing the image tell me that
Hath kept with thy remembrance.

    MIR.   'Tis far off
And rather like a dream than an assurance

---

45 **warrant him for drowning,** guarantee that he will never be drowned 47 **un-stanched,** wide open 48 **a-hold,** close to the wind **courses,** sails; i.e., they would set her foresail as well as her mainsail 51 **must . . . cold,** let us heat up our mouths with liquor 54 **merely,** absolutely, entirely 55 **wide-chapp'd,** with mouth wide open 55–56 **lie . . . tides.** Pirates were hanged on the shore and left until three tides had come in 58 **glut,** swallow 59 **split,** i.e., on the rocks 64 **long heath,** defined as "open barren ground"; also as "heather," 65 **furze,** broom, or gorse (a prickly shrub); F: *firrs,* taken to mean "firs" (New Cambridge)

Scene II 3 **stinking pitch,** suggestion of heat 4 **But that,** were it not that **welkin's cheek,** sky's face 13 **fraughting,** forming the cargo 14 **amazement,** consternation 20 **full,** very, exceedingly 22 **meddle,** mingle 24 **So,** used with a gesture, meaning "good," "very well" 28 **provision,** foresight 29 **no soul,** i.e., lost; many emendations 30 **perdition,** loss 35 **bootless inquisition,** profitless inquiry 41 **Out,** fully

That my remembrance warrants.° Had I not
Four or five women once that tended me?
   PROS. Thou hadst, and more, Miranda. But how is it
That this lives in thy mind? What seest thou else
50 In the dark backward and abysm of time?
If thou remémb'rest aught ere thou cam'st here,
How thou cam'st here thou mayst.
     MIR.   But that I do not.
   PROS. Twelve year since, Miranda, twelve year
    since,
Thy father was the Duke of Milan and
A prince of power.
     MIR.   Sir, are not you my father?
   PROS. Thy mother was a piece° of virtue, and
She said thou wast my daughter; and thy father
Was Duke of Milan; and thou his only heir
And princess no worse issued.°
     MIR.   O the heavens!
60 What foul play had we, that we came from thence?
Or blessed was 't we did?
   PROS.   Both, both, my girl:
By foul play, as thou say'st, were we heav'd thence,
But blessedly holp hither.
     MIR.   O, my heart bleeds
To think o' th' teen that I have turn'd you to,°
Which is from° my remembrance! Please you, farther.
   PROS. My brother and thy uncle, call'd Antonio—
I pray thee, mark me—that a brother should
Be so perfidious!—he whom next thyself
Of all the world I lov'd and to him put
70 The manage of my state; as at that time
Through all the signories° it was the first
And Prospero the prime duke, being so reputed
In dignity, and for the liberal arts°
Without a parallel; those being all my study,
The government I cast upon my brother
And to my state° grew stranger, being transported
And rapt in secret studies.° Thy false uncle—
Dost thou attend me?
     MIR.   Sir, most heedfully.
   PROS. Being once perfected° how to grant suits,
80 How to deny them, who t' advance and who
To trash° for over-topping,° new created
The creatures that were mine, I say, or chang'd 'em,
Or else new form'd 'em; having both the key°
Of officer and office, set all hearts i' th' state
To what tune pleas'd his ear; that now he was
The ivy which had hid my princely trunk,
And suck'd my verdure out on 't. Thou attend'st not.
     MIR. O, good sir, I do.
     PROS.   I pray thee, mark me.
I, thus neglecting worldly ends, all dedicated
90 To closeness° and the bettering of my mind

With that which, but by being so retir'd,
O'er-priz'd all popular rate,° in my false brother
Awak'd° an evil nature; and my trust,
Like a good parent, did beget of him
A falsehood in its contrary° as great
As my trust was; which had indeed no limit,
A confidence sans bound. He being thus lorded,°
Now only with what my revenue yielded,
But what my power might else exact, like one
Who having into truth, by telling of it,   100
Made such a sinner of his memory,
To credit his own lie,° he did believe
He was indeed the duke; out o'° th' substitution,
And executing th' outward face of royalty,
With all prerogative: hence his ambition growing—
Dost thou hear?
     MIR.   Your tale, sir, would cure
    deafness.
   PROS. To have no screen between this part he
    play'd
And him he play'd it for, he needs will be
Absolute Milan.° Me, poor man, my library
Was dukedom large enough: of temporal royalties°   110
He thinks me now incapable; confederates°—
So dry° he was for sway—wi' th' King of Naples
To give him annual tribute, do him homage,
Subject his coronet to his crown and bend
The dukedom yet unbow'd—alas, poor Milan!—
To most ignoble stooping.
     MIR.   O the heavens!
   PROS. Mark his condition° and th' event;° then tell
    me
If this might be a brother.
     MIR.   I should sin
To think but nobly of my grandmother:
Good wombs have borne bad sons.
     PROS.   Now the condition.   120
This King of Naples, being an enemy
To me inveterate, hearkens my brother's suit;
Which was, that he, in lieu o' th' premises°
Of homage and I know not how much tribute,
Should presently extirpate me and mine
Out of the dukedom and confer fair Milan
With all the honours on my brother: whereon,
A treacherous army levied, one midnight
Fated to th' purpose did Antonio open
The gates of Milan, and, i' th' dead of darkness,   130
The ministers for th' purpose hurried thence
Me and thy crying self.
     MIR.   Alack, for pity!
I, not remémb'ring how I cried out then,

91–92 **but . . . rate,** except that it was done in retirement, (would have) surpassed in value all popular estimate   93 **Awak'd.** *I* in line 89 is the subject   95 **in its contrary,** of an opposite kind   97 **lorded,** raised to lordship   100–102 **Who . . . lie,** a difficult passage; the meaning is: He had lied so long that he believed his own lies. New Cambridge editors read *minted* for *into,* interpreting the passage as a figure from coining of baser metals, so that *telling* means "counting," *substitution* means "the substituting of baser metals for gold," and *executing . . . royalty* means "stamping the coins"   103 **out o',** as a result of   109 **Absolute Milan,** actual duke of Milan   110 **royalties,** prerogatives and rights of a sovereign   111 **confederates,** conspires   112 **dry,** thirsty   117 **condition,** pact   **event,** outcome   123 **in . . . premises,** in return for the stipulations

45–46 **assurance . . . warrants,** certainty that my memory guarantees   56 **piece,** masterpiece   59 **issued,** born   64 **teen . . . to,** trouble I've caused you to remember   65 **from,** i.e., has no place in   71 **signories,** states of northern Italy   73 **liberal arts,** allusion to the learned studies of the Middle Ages   76 **state,** position as ruler   77 **secret studies,** magic, the occult   79 **perfected,** grown skillful   81 **trash,** check a hound by tying a weight to its neck   **over-topping,** running too far ahead of the pack   83 **key,** tool for tuning stringed instruments, with suggestion of the usual meaning   90 **closeness,** retirement, seclusion

Will cry it o'er again: it is a hint°
That wrings mine eyes to 't.
    PROS.   Hear a little further
And then I'll bring thee to the present business
Which now 's upon 's; without the which this story
Were most impertinent.°
    MIR.   Wherefore did they not
That hour destroy us?
    PROS.   Well demanded, wench:°
140 My tale provokes that question. Dear, they durst not,
So dear the love my people bore me, nor set
A mark so bloody on the business, but
With colours fairer painted their foul ends.
In few,° they hurried us aboard a bark,
Bore us some leagues to sea; where they prepar'd
A rotten carcass of a butt,° not rigg'd,
Nor tackle, sail, nor mast; the very rats
Instinctively have quit it: there they hoist us,
To cry to th' sea that roar'd to us, to sigh
150 To th' winds whose pity, sighing back again,
Did us but loving wrong.°
    MIR.   Alack, what trouble
Was I then to you!
    PROS.   O, a cherubin°
Thou wast that did preserve me. Thou didst smile,
Infused with a fortitude from heaven,
When I have deck'd° the sea with drops full salt,
Under my burthen groan'd; which° rais'd in me
An undergoing stomach,° to bear up
Against what should ensue.
    MIR.   How came we ashore?
    PROS. By Providence divine.
160 Some food we had and some fresh water that
A noble Neapolitan, Gonzalo,
Out of his charity, who being then appointed
Master of this design, did give us, with
Rich garments, linens, stuffs and necessaries,
Which since have steaded much; so, of his gentleness,
Knowing I lov'd my books, he furnish'd me
From mine own library with volumes that
I prize above my dukedom.
    MIR.   Would I might
But ever see that man!
    PROS. Now I arise: [Resumes his mantle.]
170 Sit still, and hear the last of our sea-sorrow.
Here in this island we arriv'd; and here
Have I, thy schoolmaster, made thee more profit
Than other princesses can that have more time
For vainer hours and tutors not so careful.
    MIR. Heavens thank you for 't! And now, I pray
        you, sir,
For still 'tis beating in my mind, your reason

For raising this sea-storm?
    PROS.   Know thus far forth.
By accident most strange, bountiful Fortune,
Now my dear lady, hath mine enemies
Brought to this shore; and by my prescience   180
I find my zenith° doth depend upon
A most auspicious star, whose influence
If now I court not but omit, my fortunes
Will ever after droop. Here cease more questions:
Thou art inclin'd to sleep; 'tis a good dulness,°
And give it way: I know thou canst not choose.
                    [Miranda sleeps.]
Come away,° servant, come. I am ready now.
Approach, my Ariel, come.

Enter ARIEL.

    ARI. All hail, great master! grave sir, hail! I come
To answer thy best pleasure; be 't to fly,   190
To swim, to dive into the fire, to ride
On the curl'd clouds, to thy strong bidding task°
Ariel and all his quality.°
    PROS.   Hast thou, spirit,
Perform'd to point° the tempest that I bade thee?
    ARI. To every article.
I boarded the king's ship; now on the beak,
Now in the waist,° the deck,° in every cabin,
I flam'd amazement: sometime I 'ld divide,
And burn in many places; on the topmast,
The yards and boresprit,° would I flame distinctly,°   200
Then meet and join. Jove's lightnings, the precursors
O' th' dreadful thunder-claps, more momentary°
And sight-outrunning were not; the fire and cracks
Of sulphurous roaring the most mighty Neptune
Seem to besiege and make his bold waves tremble,
Yea, his dread trident shake.
    PROS.   My brave spirit!
Who was so firm, so constant, that this coil
Would not infect his reason?
    ARI.   Not a soul
But felt a fever of the mad° and play'd
Some tricks of desperation. All but mariners   210
Plung'd in the foaming brine and quit the vessel,
Then all afire with me: the king's son, Ferdinand,
With hair up-staring,°—then like reeds, not hair,—
Was the first man that leap'd; cried, 'Hell is empty,
And all the devils are here.'
    PROS.   Why, that's my spirit!
But was not this nigh shore?
    ARI.   Close by, my master.
    PROS. But are they, Ariel, safe?
    ARI.   Not a hair perish'd;

---

134 **hint,** occasion   138 **impertinent,** irrelevant   139 **wench,** used as a term of affectionate address   144 **few,** few words   146 **butt,** tub; Globe: *boat*
151 **loving wrong,** figure of speech called oxymoron, in which, to emphasize a contrast, contradictory terms are associated; the *wrong* done by sea and winds was wrought by seeming sympathy   152 **cherubin,** plural used as singular; applied to an angelic woman   155 **deck'd,** covered (with salt tears)
156 **which,** i.e., the smile   157 **undergoing stomach,** courage to undergo

181 **zenith,** height of fortune; astrological term   185 **dulness,** drowsiness
187 **Come away,** come   192 **task,** make demands upon   193 **quality,** fellowspirits   194 **point,** i.e., to the smallest detail   196 **beak,** prow   197 **waist,** midship   **deck,** poopdeck at the stern   200 **boresprit,** bowsprit   **distinctly,** separately   202 **momentary,** instantaneous   209 **fever of the mad,** i.e., such as madmen feel   213 **up-staring,** standing on end

On their sustaining garments° not a blemish,
But fresher than before: and, as thou bad'st me,
220 In troops I have dispers'd them 'bout the isle.
The king's son have I landed by himself;
Whom I left cooling of the air with sighs
In an odd angle° of the isle and sitting,
His arms in this sad knot.   [*Folds his arms.*]
    PROS.   Of the king's ship
The mariners say how thou hast dispos'd
And all the rest o' th' fleet.
    ARI.   Safely in harbour
Is the king's ship; in the deep nook,° where once
Thou call'dst me up at midnight to fetch dew°
From the still-vex'd Bermoothes,° there she 's hid:
230 The mariners all under hatches stow'd;
Who, with a charm join'd to their suff'red labour,
I have left asleep: and for the rest o' th' fleet
Which I dispers'd, they all have met again
And are upon the Mediterranean flote,°
Bound sadly home for Naples,
Supposing that they saw the king's ship wrack'd
And his great person perish.
    PROS.   Ariel, thy charge
Exactly is perform'd: but there's more work.
What is the time o' th' day?
    ARI.   Past the mid season.
240   PROS. At least two glasses.° The time 'twixt six and
    now
Must by us both be spent most preciously.
    ARI. Is there more toil? Since thou dost give me
    pains,
Let me remember° thee what thou hast promis'd,
Which is not yet perform'd me.
    PROS.   How now? moody?
What is 't thou canst demand?
    ARI.   My liberty.
    PROS. Before the time be out? no more!
    ARI.   I prithee,
Remember I have done thee worthy service;
Told thee no lies, made thee no mistakings,° serv'd
Without or grudge or grumblings: thou didst promise
250 To bate me a full year.°
    PROS.   Dost thou forget
From what a torment I did free thee?
    ARI.   No.
    PROS. Thou dost, and think'st it much to tread the
    ooze
Of the salt deep,
To run upon the sharp wind of the north,
To do me business in the veins o' th' earth
When it is bak'd with frost.
    ARI.   I do not, sir.

    PROS. Thou liest, malignant thing! Hast thou forgot
The foul witch Sycorax, who with age and envy
Was grown into a hoop? hast thou forgot her?
    ARI. No, sir.
    PROS.   Thou hast. Where was she born? 260
    speak; tell me.
    ARI. Sir, in Argier.°
    PROS.   O, was she so? I must
Once in a month recount what thou hast been,
Which thou forget'st. This damn'd witch Sycorax,
For mischiefs manifold and sorceries terrible
To enter human hearing, from Argier,
Thou know'st, was banish'd: for one thing she did°
They would not take her life. Is not this true?
    ARI. Ay, sir.
    PROS. This blue-ey'd° hag was hither brought with
    child
And here was left by th' sailors. Thou, my slave,   270
As thou report'st thyself, wast then her servant;
And, for thou wast a spirit too delicate
To act her earthy and abhorr'd commands,
Refusing her grand hests,° she did confine thee,
By help of her more potent ministers
And in her most unmitigable rage,
Into a cloven pine; within which rift
Imprison'd thou didst painfully remain
A dozen years; within which space she died
And left thee there; where thou did'st vent thy groans 280
As fast as mill-wheels strike. Then was this island—
Save for the son that she did litter here,
A freckled° whelp hag-born—not honour'd with
A human shape.
    ARI.   Yes, Caliban her son.
    PROS. Dull thing, I say so; he, that Caliban
Whom now I keep in service. Thou best know'st
What torment I did find thee in; thy groans
Did make wolves howl and penetrate the breasts
Of ever angry bears: it was a torment
To lay upon the damn'd, which Sycorax   290
Could not again undo: it was mine art,
When I arriv'd and heard thee, that made gape
The pine and let thee out.
    ARI.   I thank thee, master.
    PROS. If thou more murmur'st, I will rend an oak
And peg thee in his knotty entrails till
Thou hast howl'd away twelve winters.
    ARI.   Pardon, master;
I will be correspondent° to command
And do my spiriting gently.
    PROS.   Do so, and after two days
I will discharge thee.
    ARI.   That 's my noble master!
What shall I do? say what; what shall I do?   300

PROS. Go make thyself like a nymph o' th' sea: be
     subject
To no sight but thine and mine, invisible
To every eyeball else. Go take this shape
And hither come in 't: go, hence with diligence!
                                        Exit [*Ariel*].
Awake, dear heart, awake! thou hast slept well;
Awake!
     MIR.   The strangeness of your story
          put
Heaviness in me.
     PROS.   Shake it off. Come on;
We'll visit Caliban my slave, who never
Yields us kind answer.
     MIR.   'Tis a villain, sir,
I do not love to look on.
310 PROS.   But, as 'tis,
We cannot miss° him: he does make our fire,
Fetch in our wood and serves in offices
That profit us. What, ho! slave! Caliban!
Thou earth, thou! speak.
     CAL.   (*Within*) There's wood enough
          within.
     PROS. Come forth, I say! there 's other business for
          thee:
Come, thou tortoise! when?

Enter ARIEL *like a water-nymph.*

Fine apparition! My quaint Ariel,
Hark in thine ear.   [*Whispers.*]
     ARI.   My lord, it shall be done.   *Exit.*
     PROS. Thou poisonous slave, got by the devil himself
320 Upon thy wicked° dam, come forth!

Enter CALIBAN.

     CAL. As wicked dew as e'er my mother brush'd
With raven's feather from unwholesome fen
Drop on you both! a south-west° blow on ye
And blister you all o'er!
     PROS. For this, be sure, to-night thou shalt have
          cramps,
Side-stitches that shall pen thy breath up; urchins°
Shall, for that vast° of night that they may work,
All exercise° on thee; thou shalt be pinch'd
As thick as honeycomb, each pinch more stinging
Than bees that made 'em.
     CAL.   I must eat my dinner.
This island 's mine, by Sycorax my mother,
Which thou tak'st from me. When thou cam'st first,

Thou strok'st me and made much of me, wouldst
     give me
Water with berries° in 't, and teach me how
To name the bigger light, and how the less,
That burn by day and night: and then I lov'd thee
And show'd thee all the qualities o' th' isle,
The fresh springs, brine-pits,° barren place and fertile:
Curs'd be I that did so! All the charms
Of Sycorax, toads, beetles, bats, light on you!   340
For I am all the subjects that you have,
Which first was mine own king: and here you sty° me
In this hard rock, whiles you do keep from me
The rest o' th' island.
     PROS.   Thou most lying slave,
Whom stripes may move, not kindness! I have us'd
     thee,
Filth as thou art, with humane care, and lodg'd thee
In mine own cell, till thou didst seek to violate
The honour of my child.
     CAL. O ho, O ho! would 't had been done!
Thou didst prevent me; I had peopled else   350
This isle with Calibans.
     MIR.   Abhorred° slave,
Which any print of goodness wilt not take,
Being capable of all ill! I pitied thee,
Took pains to make thee speak, taught thee each hour
One thing or other: when thou didst not, savage,
Know thine own meaning, but wouldst gabble like
A thing most brutish, I endow'd thy purposes
With words that made them known.° But thy vile
     race,°
Though thou didst learn, had that in 't which good
     natures
Could not abide to be with; therefore wast thou   360
Deservedly confin'd into this rock,
Who hadst deserv'd more than a prison.
     CAL. You taught me language; and my profit on 't
Is, I know how to curse. The red plague° rid° you
For learning me your language!
     PROS.   Hag-seed,° hence!
Fetch us in fuel; and be quick, thou 'rt best,
To answer other business. Shrug'st thou, malice?
If thou neglect'st or dost unwillingly
What I command, I'll rack thee with old° cramps,
Fill all thy bones with aches,° make thee roar   370
That beasts shall tremble at thy din.
     CAL.   No, pray thee.
[*Aside*] I must obey: his art is of such pow'r,
It would control my dam's god, Setebos,°

334 **berries.** Strachey's *Repertory,* one of the sources, says that the Bermudas
were full of thickets of "goodly Cedar . . . the Berries whereof, our men seething,
straining, and letting stand some three or foure daies, made a kind of pleasant
drinke"   338 **brine-pits,** salt springs   342 **sty,** put in sty   351–362 **Abhorred
. . . prison.** Sometimes assigned to Prospero (as in Globe)   357–358 **endow'd . . .
known,** enabled you to make known what was going on in your mind
358 **race,** natural disposition   364 **red plague,** bubonic plague   **rid,** destroy,
with play on *red*   365 **Hag-seed,** hag's offspring   369 **old,** plenty of
370 **aches,** pronounced "aitches"   373 **Setebos,** mentioned in Eden's *History of
Travel* (1577) as a deity, or devil, of the Patagonians

311 **miss,** do without   320 **wicked,** mischievous, harmful   323 **south-west,**
i.e., wind (bringing disease)   326 **urchins,** hedgehogs; here, suggesting goblins
327 **vast,** long hours   328 **exercise,** practice, work

And make a vassal of him.

PROS.   So, slave; hence!

Exit Caliban.

Enter FERDINAND; *and* ARIEL, *invisible, playing and singing.*

ARIEL'S *song.*

Come unto these yellow sands,
    And then take hands:
Courtsied when you have and kiss'd°
    The wild waves whist,°
Foot it featly° here and there;
380   And, sweet sprites, the burthen° bear.
Burthen (dispersedly)°. Hark, hark!
            Bow-wow.
    The watch-dogs bark:
            Bow-wow.
ARI. Hark, hark! I hear
    The strain of strutting chanticleer
    Cry, Cock-a-diddle-dow.
FER. Where should this music be? i' th' air or th'
    earth?
It sounds no more: and, sure, it waits upon
Some god o' th' island. Sitting on a bank,
Weeping again the king my father's wrack,
390 This music crept by me upon the waters,
Allaying both their fury and my passion
With its sweet air: thence I have follow'd it,
Or it hath drawn me rather. But 'tis gone.
No, it begins again.

ARIEL'S *song.*

Full fathom five thy father lies;
    Of his bones are coral made;
Those are pearls that were his eyes:
    Nothing of him that doth fade
But doth suffer a sea-change
400   Into something rich and strange.
Sea-nymphs hourly ring his knell:
            Burthen. Ding-dong.
[ARI.] Hark! now I hear them,—Ding-dong, bell.
    FER. The ditty does remember° my drown'd father.
This is no mortal business, nor no sound
That the earth owes.° I hear it now above me.
    PROS. The fringed curtains of thine eye advance
And say what thou seest yond.
    MIR.   What is 't? a spirit?
Lord, how it looks about! Believe me, sir,
It carries a brave form. But 'tis a spirit.
    PROS. No, wench; it eats and sleeps and hath such
410   senses

As we have, such. This gallant which thou seest
Was in the wrack; and, but he 's something stain'd
With grief that 's beauty's canker,° thou mightst call
    him
A goodly person: he hath lost his fellows
And strays about to find 'em.
    MIR.   I might call him
A thing divine, for nothing natural
I ever saw so noble.
    PROS.   [*Aside*] It goes on,° I see,
As my soul prompts it. Spirit, fine spirit! I'll free thee
Within two days for this.
    FER.   Most sure, the goddess
On whom these airs attend! Vouchsafe my pray'r   420
May know if you remain° upon this island;
And that you will some good instruction give
How I may bear me° here: my prime request,
Which I do last pronounce, is, O you wonder!
If you be maid or no?
    MIR.   No wonder, sir;
But certainly a maid.
    FER.   My language! heavens!
I am the best° of them that speak this speech,
Were I but where 'tis spoken.
    PROS.   How? the best?
What wert thou, if the King of Naples heard thee?
    FER. A single° thing, as I am now, that wonders   430
To hear thee speak of Naples. He does hear me;
And that he does I weep: myself am Naples,
Who with mine eyes, never since at ebb, beheld
The king my father wrack'd.
    MIR.   Alack, for mercy!
    FER. Yes, faith, and all his lords; the Duke of Milan
And his brave son° being twain.
    PROS.   [*Aside*] The Duke of Milan
And his more braver daughter could control° thee,
If now 'twere fit to do 't. At the first sight
They have chang'd eyes.° Delicate Ariel,
I'll set thee free for this. [*To Fer.*] A word, good sir;   440
I fear you have done yourself some wrong:° a word.
    MIR. Why speaks my father so ungently? This
Is the third man that e'er I saw, the first
That e'er I sigh'd for: pity move my father
To be inclin'd my way!
    FER.   O, if a virgin,
And your affection not gone forth, I'll make you
The queen of Naples.
    PROS.   Soft, sir! one word more.
[*Aside*] They are both in either's pow'rs; but this
    swift business
I must uneasy° make, lest too light° winning

376–377 **Come . . . kiss'd**, three motions before the dance—take hands, curtsy, kiss (New Cambridge)   378 **whist,** silent   379 **featly,** neatly   380 **burthen,** refrain   381 **dispersedly,** i.e., from all parts of the stage   403 **remember,** commemorate   405 **owes,** owns   413 **canker,** cankerworm (feeding on buds and leaves)   417 **It goes on,** my charm works   421 **remain,** dwell   423 **bear me,** conduct myself   427 **best,** i.e., in birth   430 **single,** solitary, with a suggestion of feebleness   436 **son,** the only reference to a son of Antonio   437 **control,** confute   439 **chang'd eyes,** exchanged amorous glances   441 **done . . . wrong,** are mistaken   449 **uneasy,** difficult

Make the prize light.° [*To Fer.*] One word more; I
450   charge thee
That thou attend me: thou dost here usurp
The name thou ow'st° not; and hast put thyself
Upon this island as a spy, to win it
From me, the lord on 't.

FER.   No, as I am a man.

MIR. There 's nothing ill can dwell in such a temple:
If the ill spirit have so fair a house,
Good things will strive to dwell with 't.

PROS.   Follow me.
Speak not you for him; he 's a traitor. [*To Fer.*] Come;
I'll manacle thy neck and feet together:
460 Sea-water shalt thou drink; thy food shall be
The fresh-brook mussels, wither'd roots and husks
Wherein the acorn cradled. Follow.

FER.   No;
I will resist such entertainment° till
Mine enemy has more pow'r.

                 He draws, and is charmed from
                 moving.

MIR.   O dear father,
Make not too rash a trial of him, for
He 's gentle° and not fearful.°

PROS.   What? I say,
My foot° my tutor? [*To Fer.*] Put thy sword up, traitor;
Who mak'st a show but dar'st not strike, thy
    conscience
Is so possess'd with guilt: come, from thy ward,°
470 For I can here disarm thee with this stick°
And make thy weapon drop.

MIR.   Beseech you, father.

PROS. Hence! hang not on my garments.

MIR.   Sir, have pity;
I'll be his surety.

PROS.   Silence! one word more
Shall make me chide thee, if not hate thee. What!
An advocate for an impostor! hush!
Thou think'st there is no more such shapes as he,
Having seen but him and Caliban: foolish wench!
To th' most of men this is a Caliban
And they to him are angels.

MIR.   My affections
480 Are then most humble; I have no ambition
To see a goodlier man.

PROS. [*To Fer.*]   Come on; obey:
Thy nerves° are in their infancy again
And have no vigour in them.

FER.   So they are;
My spirits, as in a dream, are all bound up.
My father's loss, the weakness which I feel,
The wrack of all my friends, nor this man's threats,
To whom I am subdu'd, are but light to me,
Might I but through my prison once a day

Behold this maid: all corners else o' th' earth
Let liberty make use of;° space enough   490
Have I in such a prison.

PROS.   [*Aside*] It works. [*To Fer.*]
    Come on.
Thou hast done well, fine Ariel! [*To Fer.*] Follow me.
[*To Ari.*] Hark what thou else shalt do me.

MIR.   Be of comfort;
My father 's of a better nature, sir,
Than he appears by speech: this is unwonted
Which now came from him.

PROS.   Thou shalt be as free
As mountains winds: but then exactly do
All points of my command.

ARI.   To th' syllable.

PROS. Come, follow. [*To Mir.*] Speak not for him.
                        Exeunt.

ACT II.

SCENE I. [*Another part of the island.*]

Enter ALONSO, SEBASTIAN, ANTONIO, GONZALO, AD-
RIAN, FRANCISCO, *and others.*

GON. Beseech you, sir, be merry; you have cause,
So have we all, of joy; for our escape
Is much beyond our loss. Our hint of° woe
Is common; every day some sailor's wife,
The masters of some merchant° and the merchant°
Have just our theme of woe; but for the miracle,
I mean our preservation, few in millions
Can speak like us: then wisely, good sir, weigh
Our sorrow with our comfort.

ALON.   Prithee, peace.

SEB. [*To Ant.*] He receives comfort like cold por- 10
ridge.

ANT. [*To Seb.*] The visitor° will not give him o'er so.

SEB. Look, he 's winding up the watch of his wit; by
and by it will strike.

GON. Sir,—

SEB. [*To Ant.*] One: tell.°

GON. When every grief is entertain'd that 's offer'd,
Comes to the entertainer—

SEB. A dollar.°

GON. Dolour comes to him, indeed: you have spoken 20
truer than you purposed.

SEB. You have taken it wiselier than I meant you
should.

GON. Therefore, my lord,—

ANT. Fie, what a spendthrift is he of his tongue!

ALON. I prithee, spare.

GON. Well, I have done: but yet,—

SEB. He will be talking.

ANT. Which, of he or Adrian, for a good wager, first
begins to crow?°   30

449, 450 **light, light,** easy, cheap   452 **ow'st,** ownest   463 **entertainment,**
treatment   466 **gentle,** wellborn, high-spirited   **not fearful,** not dangerous (because incapable of treachery)   467 **foot,** subordinate. Miranda (the foot) presumes to instruct Prospero (the head)   469 **ward,** defensive posture (in fencing)
470 **stick,** his wand   482 **nerves,** sinews

489–490 **all . . . of,** those who are free may have all the rest of the world   **Act
II, Scene I**   3 **hint of,** occasion for   5 **merchant, merchant,** merchant vessel,
merchant   12 **visitor,** one taking nourishment to the sick   16 **tell,** keep count
19 **dollar,** widely circulated coin, the German *Thaler* and the Spanish *piece of
eight*   29–30 **Which . . . crow,** which of the two, Gonzalo or Adrian, do you bet
will speak (crow) first?

SEB. The old cock.°

ANT. The cockerel.

SEB. Done. The wager?

ANT. A laughter.°

SEB. A match!°

ADR. Though this island seem to be desert,—

SEB. Ha, ha, ha! So, you 're paid.

ADR. Uninhabitable and almost inaccessible,—

SEB. Yet,—

40 ADR. Yet,—

ANT. He could not miss 't.°

ADR. It must needs be of subtle, tender and delicate temperance.°

ANT. Temperance° was a delicate wench.

SEB. Ay, and a subtle; as he most learnedly delivered.

ADR. The air breathes upon us here most sweetly.

SEB. As if it had lungs and rotten ones.

ANT. Or as 'twere perfumed by a fen.

50 GON. Here is every thing advantageous to life.

ANT. True; save means to live.

SEB. Of that there 's none, or little.

GON. How lush and lusty the grass looks! how green!

ANT. The ground indeed is tawny.°

SEB. With an eye° of green in 't.

ANT. He misses not much.

SEB. No; he doth but mistake the truth totally.

GON. But the rarity of it is,—which is indeed almost beyond credit,—

60 SEB. As many vouched rarities are.

GON. That our garments, being, as they were, drenched in the sea, hold notwithstanding their freshness and glosses, being rather new-dyed than stained with salt water.

ANT. If but one of his pockets° could speak, would it not say he lies?

SEB. Ay, or very falsely pocket up his report.

GON. Methinks our garments are now as fresh as when we put them on first in Afric, at the marriage of
70 the king's fair daughter Claribel to the King of Tunis.

SEB. 'Twas a sweet marriage, and we prosper well in our return.

ADR. Tunis was never graced before with such a paragon to their queen.

GON. Not since widow Dido's time.

ANT. Widow! a pox o' that! How came that widow in? widow Dido!°

SEB. What if he had said 'widower Æneas' too? Good Lord, how you take it!

80 ADR. 'Widow Dido' said you? you make me study of that: she was of Carthage, not of Tunis.

GON. This Tunis, sir, was Carthage.

ADR. Carthage?

GON. I assure you, Carthage.

SEB. His word is more than the miraculous harp;° he hath raised the wall and houses too.

ANT. What impossible matter will he make easy next?

SEB. I think he will carry this island home in his pocket and give it his son for an apple.   90

ANT. And, sowing the kernels of it in the sea, bring forth more islands.

GON. Ay.

ANT. Why, in good time.°

GON. [To Alon.] Sir, we were talking that our garments seem now as fresh as when we were at Tunis at the marriage of your daughter, who is now queen.

ANT. And the rarest that e'er came there.

SEB. Bate,° I beseech you, widow Dido.

ANT. O, widow Dido! ay, widow Dido.   100

GON. Is not, sir, my doublet as fresh as the first day I wore it? I mean, in a sort.

ANT. That sort° was well fished for.

GON. When I wore it at your daughter's marriage?

ALON. You cram these words into mine ears against
The stomach of my sense. Would I had never
Married my daughter there! for, coming thence,
My son is lost and, in my rate,° she too,
Who is so far from Italy remov'd
I ne'er again shall see her. O thou mine heir   110
Of Naples and of Milan, what strange fish
Hath made his meal on thee?

FRAN.   Sir, he may live:
I saw him beat the surges under him,
And ride upon their backs; he trod the water,
Whose enmity he flung aside, and breasted
The surge most swoln that met him; his bold head
'Bove the contentious waves he kept, and oar'd
Himself with his good arms in lusty stroke
To th' shore, that o'er his wave-worn basis bow'd,°
As stooping to relieve him: I not doubt   120
He came alive to land.°

ALON.   No, no, he 's gone.

SEB. Sir, you may thank yourself for this great loss,
That would not bless our Europe with your daughter,
But rather loose° her to an African;
Where she at least is banish'd from your eye,
Who° hath cause to wet the grief on 't.

ALON.   Prithee, peace.

SEB. You were kneel'd to and importun'd otherwise
By all of us, and the fair soul herself
Weigh'd between loathness and obedience, at
Which end o' th' beam should bow.° We have lost
    your son,   130

31 **old cock,** i.e., Gonzalo   34 **laughter,** sitting of eggs. When Adrian (the *cockerel*) begins to speak, Sebastian loses the bet and pays with a *laugh* for a *laughter*   35 **A match,** a bargain; agreed   41 **He . . . miss 't,** i.e., even if it is uninhabitable and inaccessible, he could not refrain from talking about it   43 **temperance,** temperature   44 **Temperance,** a Puritan name for women, thought also to refer to Temperance, a character in Chapman's *May Day* (1611)   54 **tawny,** dull brown   55 **eye,** tinge   65 **pockets,** i.e., because they are muddy   77 **widow Dido,** queen of Carthage deserted by Aeneas, and thus not really a widow

85 **miraculous harp,** allusion to Amphion's harp with which he raised the walls of Thebes; Gonzalo has exceeded that deed by rebuilding a modern Carthage   94 **in good time,** vague expression of agreement or approbation   99 **Bate,** except   103 **sort,** lucky catch after much angling; probable suggestion of the age of the garment, with a play on *sort* in line 102   108 **rate,** opinion   112–121 **Sir . . . land,** Francisco's only speech   119 **that . . . bow'd,** that hung out over its wave-worn foot   124 **loose,** so F; Globe: *lose*   126 **Who,** which (eye)   128–130 **the fair . . . bow,** Claribel herself was poised uncertain between unwillingness and obedience as to which end of the scale should sink

I fear, for ever: Milan and Naples have
Moe widows in them of this business' making
Than we bring men to comfort them:
The fault 's your own.

ALON.   So is the dear'st o' th' loss.

GON. My lord Sebastian,
The truth you speak doth lack some gentleness
And time to speak it in: you rub the sore,
When you should bring the plaster.

SEB.   Very well.

ANT. And most chirurgeonly.°

140 GON. It is foul weather in us all, good sir,
When you are cloudy.

SEB. [To Ant.]   Foul weather?

ANT. [To Seb.]   Very foul.

GON. Had I plantation° of this isle, my lord,—

ANT. He 'ld sow 't with nettle-seed.

SEB.   Or docks, or mallows.

GON. And were the king on 't, what would I do?

SEB. 'Scape being drunk for want of wine.

GON. I' th' commonwealth I would by contraries
Execute all things; for no kind of traffic
Would I admit; no name of magistrate;
Letters° should not be known; riches, poverty,
150 And use of service,° none; contract, succession,°
Bourn,° bound of land,° tilth,° vineyard, none;
No use of metal, corn, or wine, or oil;
No occupation; all men idle, all;
And women too, but innocent and pure;
No sovereignty;°—

SEB.   Yet he would be king on 't.

ANT. The latter end of his commonwealth forgets the
beginning.

GON. All things in common nature should produce
Without sweat or endeavour: treason, felony,
160 Sword, pike, knife, gun, or need of any engine,°
Would I not have; but nature should bring forth,
Of it° own kind, all foison,° all abundance,
To feed my innocent people.

SEB. No marrying 'mong his subjects?

ANT. None, man; all idle: whores and knaves.

GON. I would with such perfection govern, sir,
T' excel the golden age.

SEB.   'Save his majesty!

ANT. Long live Gonzalo!

GON.   And,—do you mark me, sir?

ALON. Prithee, no more; thou dost talk nothing to
170 me.

GON. I do well believe your highness; and did it to
minister occasion° to these gentlemen, who are of such
sensible° and nimble lungs that they always use to
laugh at nothing.

ANT. 'Twas you we laughed at.

GON. Who in this kind of merry fooling am nothing
to you: so you may continue and laugh at nothing still.

ANT. What a blow was there given!

SEB. An it had not fallen flat-long.°

GON. You are gentlemen of brave mettle;° you would 180
lift the moon out of her sphere,° if she would continue
in it five weeks without changing.

Enter ARIEL [*invisible*] *playing solemn music.*

SEB. We would so, and then go a bat-fowling.°

ANT. Nay, good my lord, be not angry.

GON. No, I warrant you; I will not adventure° my
discretion so weakly. Will you laugh me asleep, for I
am very heavy?

ANT. Go sleep, and hear us.°

          [*All sleep except Alon., Seb., and Ant.*]

ALON. What, all so soon asleep! I wish mine eyes
Would, with themselves, shut up my thoughts: I find 190
They are inclin'd to do so.

SEB.   Please you, sir,
Do not omit° the heavy° offer of it:
It seldom visits sorrow; when it doth,
It is a comforter.

ANT.   We two, my lord,
Will guard your person while you take your rest,
And watch your safety.

ALON.   Thank you. Wondrous heavy.

          [*Alonso sleeps. Exit Ariel.*]

SEB. What a strange drowsiness possesses them!

ANT. It is the quality o' th' climate.

SEB.   Why
Doth it not then our eyelids sink? I find not
Myself dispos'd to sleep.

ANT.   Nor I; my spirits are nimble.   200
They fell together all, as by consent;°
They dropp'd, as by a thunder-stroke. What might,
Worthy Sebastian? O, what might?—No more:—
And yet methinks I see it in thy face,
What thou shouldst be: th' occasion speaks° thee, and
My strong imagination sees a crown
Dropping upon thy head.

SEB.   What, art thou waking?

ANT. Do you not hear me speak?

SEB.   I do; and surely
It is a sleepy language and thou speak'st
Out of thy sleep. What is it thou didst say?   210
This is a strange repose, to be asleep
With eyes wide open; standing, speaking, moving,
And yet so fast asleep.

ANT.   Noble Sebastian,
Thou let'st thy fortune sleep—die, rather; wink'st°
Whiles thou art waking.

139 **chirurgeonly**, like a skilled surgeon   142 **plantation**, colonization; subsequent play on the literal meaning   146–155 **I' th' . . . sovereignty.** This passage on man in his primitive state is based on Montaigne, *Essays*, I, xxx, perhaps
derived from Florio's translation (1603)   149 **Letters**, learning   150 **use of service**, custom of employing servants   **succession**, holding of property by right of
inheritance   151 **Bourn**, boundaries   **bound of land**, landmarks   **tilth**, tillage
of soil   160 **engine**, instrument of warfare   162 **it**, its   **foison**, plenty
172 **minister occasion**, furnish opportunity   173 **sensible**, sensitive

179 **flat-long,** with the flat of the sword   180 **mettle**, temper, nature   181 **lift
. . . sphere.** As a planet in the old astronomy, the moon had a crystal sphere in
which she moved. Gonzalo means that they would lift the moon out of her sphere
if she remained steady in it   183 **batfowling**, hunting birds at night with lantern
and stick; also, gulling a simpleton. Gonzalo is the simpleton (or fowl), and
Sebastian will use the moon as his lantern   185 **adventure**, risk   188 **Go . . .
us**, let our laughing send you to sleep, or, go to sleep and hear us laugh at you
192 **omit**, neglect   **heavy**, drowsy   201 **consent**, agreement as to a course of
action   205 **speaks**, calls upon, proclaims (thee) king   214 **wink'st**, shuts the
eyes

SEB.   Thou dost snore distinctly;°
There 's meaning in thy snores.
     ANT. I am more serious than my custom: you
Must be so too, if heed me; which to do
Trebles thee o'er.°
     SEB.   Well, I am standing water.°
     ANT. I'll teach you how to flow.
220 SEB.   Do so: to ebb
Hereditary sloth instructs me.
     ANT.   O,
If you but knew how you the purpose° cherish
Whiles thus you mock it! how, in stripping it,°
You more invest it! Ebbing men,° indeed,
Most often do so near the bottom run
By their own fear or sloth.
     SEB.   Prithee, say on:
The setting° of thine eye and cheek proclaim
A matter° from thee, and a birth indeed
Which throes° thee much to yield.
     ANT.   Thus, sir:
230 Although this lord° of weak remembrance,° this,
Who shall be of as little memory
When he is earth'd,° hath here almost persuaded,—
For he 's a spirit of persuasion, only
Professes to persuade,°—the king his son 's alive,
'Tis as impossible that he 's undrown'd
As he that sleeps here swims.
     SEB.   I have no hope
That he 's undrown'd.
     ANT.   O, out of that 'no hope'
What great hope have you! no hope that way° is
Another way so high a hope that even
240 Ambition cannot pierce a wink beyond,
But doubt discovery there.° Will you grant with me
That Ferdinand is drown'd?
     SEB.   He 's gone.
     ANT.   Then, tell me,
Who 's the next heir of Naples?
     SEB.   Claribel.
     ANT. She that is queen of Tunis; she that dwells
Ten leagues beyond man's life;° she that from Naples
Can have no note,° unless the sun were post°—
The man i' th' moon 's too slow—till new-born chins
Be rough and razorable;° she that from° whom
We all were sea-swallow'd, though some cast° again,
250 And by that destiny to perform an act
Whereof what 's past is prologue, what to come
In yours and my discharge.°
     SEB.   What stuff is this! how say you?

'Tis true, my brother's daughter 's queen of Tunis;
So is she heir of Naples; 'twixt which regions
There is some space.
     ANT.   A space whose ev'ry cubit
Seems to cry out, 'How shall that Claribel
Measure us° back to Naples? Keep in Tunis,
And let Sebastian wake.'° Say, this were death
That now hath seiz'd them; why, they were no
     worse
Than now they are. There be that can rule Naples   260
As well as he that sleeps; lords that can prate
As amply and unnecessarily
As this Gonzalo; I myself could make
A chough of as deep chat.° O, that you bore
The mind that I do! what a sleep were this
For your advancement! Do you understand me?
     SEB. Methinks I do.
     ANT.   And how does your content°
Tender° your own good fortune?
     SEB.   I remember
You did supplant your brother Prospero.
     ANT.   True:
And look how well my garments sit upon me;   270
Much feater° than before: my brother's servants
Were then my fellows; now they are my men.
     SEB. But, for your conscience?
     ANT. Ay, sir; where lies that? if 'twere a kibe,°
'Twould put me to my slipper: but I feel not
This deity in my bosom: twenty consciences,
That stand 'twixt me and Milan, candied° be they
And melt ere they molest! Here lies your brother,
No better than the earth he lies upon,
If he were that which now he 's like, that 's dead;   280
Whom I, with this obedient steel, three inches of it,
Can lay to bed for ever; whiles you, doing thus,
To the perpetual wink for aye might put
This ancient morsel, this Sir Prudence, who
Should not upbraid our course. For all the rest,
They'll take suggestion as a cat laps milk;
They'll tell the clock° to any business that
We say befits the hour.
     SEB.   Thy case, dear friend,
Shall be my precedent; as thou got'st Milan,
I'll come by Naples. Draw thy sword: one stroke   290
Shall free thee from the tribute which thou payest;
And I the king shall love thee.
     ANT.   Draw together;
And when I rear my hand, do you the like,
To fall it on Gonzalo.   [They draw.]
     SEB.   O, but one word!

Enter ARIEL [*invisible*], *with music and song.*

     ARI. My master through his art foresees the danger

215 **distinctly,** with separate and individual sounds   219 **Trebles thee o'er,** makes thee three times as great   **standing water,** water which neither flows nor ebbs   222 **purpose,** i.e., of being king   223 **stripping it,** stripping off all pretense, revealing it   224 **Ebbing men,** men whose fortunes ebb, leaving them stranded   227 **setting,** set expression   228 **matter,** matter of importance   229 **throes,** pains   230 **this lord,** Gonzalo   **remembrance,** power of remembering   232 **earth'd,** buried   234 **Professes to persuade,** he was a privy councilor   238 **that way,** i.e., in regard to Ferdinand's being saved   240–241 **Ambition . . . there,** ambition itself cannot see any further than that hope (of the crown) without doubting the reality of the objects it sees   245 **Ten . . . life,** it would take more than a lifetime to get there   246 **note,** intimation   **post,** messenger   247–248 **till . . . razorable,** till babies born today will be old enough to shave   248 **from,** on our voyage from   249 **cast,** were disgorged, with pun on *casting* (of parts for a play)   252 **discharge,** performance, i.e, to get done

257 **Measure us,** find (her) way   257–258 **Keep . . . wake,** let her stay in Tunis, and let Sebastian wake (to his good fortune)   263–264 **I . . . chat,** I could teach a jackdaw to talk as wisely   267 **content,** desire, contentment   268 **Tender,** provide for; or, regard   271 **feater,** more becomingly   274 **kibe,** sore on the heel   277 **candied,** frozen, congealed   287 **tell the clock,** answer appropriately

That you, his friend, are in; and sends me forth—
For else his project dies—to keep them living.
Sings in Gonzalo's ear.

While you here do snoring lie,
Open-ey'd conspiracy
300   His time° doth take.
If of life you keep a care,
Shake off slumber, and beware:
Awake, awake!

ANT. Then let us both be sudden.°
GON. [*Wakes*]   Now, good angels
Preserve the king.   [*The others wake.*]
ALON. Why, how now? ho, awake! Why are you
    drawn?
Wherefore this ghastly looking?
GON.   What 's the matter?
SEB. Whiles we stood here securing your repose,
Even now, we heard a hollow burst of bellowing
310 Like bulls, or rather lions: did 't not wake you?
It struck mine ear most terribly.
ALON.   I heard nothing.
ANT. O, 'twas a din to fright a monster's ear,
To make an earthquake! sure, it was the roar
Of a whole herd of lions.
ALON.   Heard you this, Gonzalo?
GON. Upon mine honour, sir, I heard a humming,°
And that a strange one too, which did awake me:
I shak'd you, sir, and cried: as mine eyes open'd,
I saw their weapons drawn: there was a noise,
That 's verily. 'Tis best we stand upon our guard,
320 Or that we quit this place: let 's draw our weapons.
ALON. Lead off this ground; and let 's make further
    search
For my poor son.
GON. Heavens keep him from these beasts!
For he is, sure, i' th' island.
ALON.   Lead away.
ARI. Prospero my lord shall know what I have done:
So, king, go safely on to seek thy son.   *Exeunt.*

SCENE II. [*Another part of the island.*]

Enter CALIBAN *with a burden of wood. A noise of
thunder heard.*

CAL. All the infections that the sun sucks up
From bogs, fens, flats, on Prosper fall and make him
By inch-meal° a disease! His spirits hear me
And yet I needs must curse. But they'll nor pinch,
Fright me with urchin-shows, pitch me i' th' mire,
Nor lead me, like a firebrand, in the dark
Out of my way, unless he bid 'em; but
For every trifle are they set upon me;
Sometime like apes that mow° and chatter at me

And after bite me, then like hedgehogs which   10
Lie tumbling in my barefoot way and mount
Their pricks at my footfall; sometime am I
All wound with adders who with cloven tongues
Do hiss me into madness.

Enter TRINCULO.

    Lo, now, lo!
Here comes a spirit of his, and to torment me
For bringing wood in slowly. I'll fall flat;
Perchance he will not mind me.   [*Lies down.*]
TRIN. Here 's neither bush nor shrub, to bear off° any
weather at all, and another storm brewing; I hear it
sing i' the wind: yond same black cloud, yond huge 20
one, looks like a foul bombard° that would shed his
liquor. If it should thunder as it did before, I know not
where to hide my head: yond same cloud cannot
choose but fall by pailfuls. What have we here? a man
or a fish? dead or alive? A fish: he smells like a fish; a
very ancient and fish-like smell; a kind of not of the
newest Poor-John.° A strange fish!° Were I in England
now, as once I was, and had but this fish painted,° not a
holiday fool there but would give a piece of silver:
there would this monster make a man;° any strange 30
beast there makes a man: when they will not give a doit°
to relieve a lame beggar, they will lay out ten to see a
dead Indian. Legged like a man! and his fins like arms!
Warm o' my troth! I do now let loose my opinion; hold
it no longer: this is no fish, but an islander, that hath
lately suffered by a thunderbolt. [*Thunder.*] Alas, the
storm is come again! my best way is to creep under his
gaberdine;° there is no other shelter hereabout: misery
acquaints a man with strange bed-fellows. I will here
shroud° till the dregs° of the storm be past.   [*Creeps 40
    under Caliban's garment.*]

Enter STEPHANO, *singing [, a bottle in his hand].*

STE. I shall no more to sea, to sea,
    Here shall I die ashore—
This is a very scurvy tune to sing at a man's funeral:
well, here 's my comfort.   *Drinks.*
[*Sings.*]
The master, the swabber, the boatswain and I,
    The gunner and his mate
Lov'd Mall, Meg and Marian and Margery,
    But none of us car'd for Kate;
    For she had a tongue with a tang,
    Would cry to a sailor, Go hang!   50
She lov'd not the savour of tar nor of pitch,
Yet a tailor might scratch her where'er she did itch:
    Then to sea, boys, and let her go hang!

---

18 **bear off,** keep off   21 **foul bombard,** dirty leathern bottle   27 **Poor-John,**
salted hake, type of poor fare   **fish.** Malone cites a license issued by the Master
of the Revels (1632) "to shew a strange fish for half a yeare"   28 **painted,** i.e.,
on a sign set up outside a booth or tent at a fair   30 **make a man,** i.e., make his
fortune   31 **doit,** small coin   38 **gaberdine,** cloak, loose upper garment
40 **shroud,** take shelter   **dregs,** last remains

---

300 **time,** opportunity   304 **sudden,** swift in action   315 **humming,** i.e., Ariel's
song   **Scene II** 3 **inch-meal,** little by little   9 **mow,** make faces

This is a scurvy tune too: but here's my comfort.

Drinks.

CAL. Do not torment me: Oh!

STE. What 's the matter? Have we devils here? Do you put tricks upon 's with savages and men of Ind,° ha? I have not 'scaped drowning to be afeard now of your four legs; for it hath been said, As proper a man
60 as ever went on four legs cannot make him give ground; and it shall be said so again while Stephano breathes at' nostrils.

CAL. The spirit torments me; Oh!

STE. This is some monster of the isle with four legs, who hath got, as I take it, an ague. Where the devil should he learn our language? I will give him some relief, if it be but for that. If I can recover° him and keep him tame and get to Naples with him, he 's a present for any emperor that ever trod on neat's-leather.°
70 CAL. Do not torment me, prithee; I'll bring my wood home faster.

STE. He 's in his fit now and does not talk after the wisest. He shall taste of my bottle: if he have never drunk wine afore, it will go near to remove his fit. If I can recover him and keep him tame, I will not take too much° for him; he shall pay for him that hath him, and that soundly.

CAL. Thou dost me yet but little hurt; thou wilt anon, I know it by thy trembling:° now Prosper works upon
80 thee.

STE. Come on your ways; open your mouth; here is that which will give language to you, cat: open your mouth;° this will shake your shaking, I can tell you, and that soundly. [*Gives Caliban drink.*] You cannot tell who 's your friend: open your chaps again.

TRIN. I should know that voice: it should be—but he is drowned; and these are devils: O defend me!

STE. Four legs and two voices: a most delicate monster! His forward voice now is to speak well of his
90 friend; his backward voice is to utter foul speeches and to detract. If all the wine in my bottle will recover him, I will help his ague. Come. [*Gives drink.*] Amen! I will pour some in thy other mouth.

TRIN. Stephano!

STE. Doth thy other mouth call me? Mercy, mercy! This is a devil, and no monster: I will leave him; I have no long spoon.°

TRIN. Stephano! If thou beest Stephano, touch me and speak to me; for I am Trinculo—be not afeard—
100 thy good friend Trinculo.

STE. If thou beest Trinculo, come forth: I'll pull thee by the lesser legs: if any be Trinculo's legs, these are they. [*Pulls him out.*] Thou art very Trinculo indeed! How camest thou to be the siege° of this moon-calf?° can he vent Trinculos?

TRIN. I took him to be killed with a thunder-stroke. But art thou not drowned, Stephano? I hope now thou art not drowned. Is the storm overblown? I hid me under the dead moon-calf's gaberdine for fear of the storm. And art thou living, Stephano? O Stephano, 110 two Neapolitans 'scaped!

STE. Prithee, do not turn me about; my stomach is not constant.°

CAL. [*Aside*] These be fine things, an if they be not sprites.
That 's a brave god and bears celestial liquor.
I will kneel to him.

STE. How didst thou 'scape? How camest thou hither? swear by this bottle how thou camest hither. I escaped upon a butt of sack° which the sailors heaved o'erboard—by this bottle, which I made of the bark of 120 a tree with mine own hands since I was cast ashore.

CAL. I'll swear upon that bottle to be thy true subject; for the liquor is not earthly.

STE. Here; swear then how thou escapedst.

TRIN. Swum ashore, man, like a duck: I can swim like a duck, I'll be sworn.

STE. Here, kiss the book.° Though thou canst swim like a duck, thou art made like a goose.[*Gives drink.*]

TRIN. O Stephano, hast any more of this?

STE. The whole butt, man: my cellar is in a rock by 130 the sea-side where my wine is hid. How now, moon-calf! how does thine ague?

CAL. Hast thou not dropp'd from heaven?

STE. Out o' the moon, I do assure thee: I was the man i' the moon when time was.°

CAL. I have seen thee in her and I do adore thee:
My mistress show'd me thee and thy dog and thy bush.°

STE. Come, swear to that; kiss the book: I will furnish it anon with new contents: swear. [*Gives drink.*]

TRIN. By this good light, this is a very shallow mon- 140 ster! I afeard of him! A very weak monster! The man i' the moon! A most poor credulous monster! Well drawn,° monster, in good sooth!

CAL. I'll show thee every fertile inch o' th' island;
And I will kiss thy foot: I prithee, be my god.

TRIN. By this light, a most perfidious and drunken monster! when 's god 's asleep, he'll rob his bottle.

CAL. I'll kiss thy foot; I'll swear myself thy subject.

STE. Come on then; down, and swear.

TRIN. I shall laugh myself to death at this puppy- 150 headed monster. A most scurvy monster! I could find in my heart to beat him,—

STE. Come, kiss.

TRIN. But that the poor monster 's in drink: an abominable monster!

CAL. I'll show thee the best springs; I'll pluck thee berries;

---

57 **Ind,** India, or, vaguely, the East   67 **recover,** restore   69 **neat's-leather,** leather from the skin of an ox or cow   75–76 **take too much,** i.e., no sum can be too much   79 **trembling,** suggestion of demonic possession   82–83 **cat . . . mouth,** allusion to the proverb, "Good liquor will make a cat speak"   97 **long spoon,** allusion to the proverb, "He that sups with the devil has need of a long spoon"   104 **siege,** excrement   **moon-calf,** monster, abortion (supposed to be caused by the influence of the moon)

113 **not constant,** unsteady   119 **butt of sack,** barrel of Canary wine   127 **kiss the book.** He gives him the bottle instead of the Bible on which to make his oath   135 **when time was,** once upon a time   137–138 **dog . . . bush.** See *A Midsummer Night's Dream*, V, i, 136   142 **Well drawn.** Caliban takes a good draft of the wine

I'll fish for thee and get thee wood enough.
A plague upon the tyrant that I serve!
I'll bear him no more sticks, but follow thee,
160 Thou wondrous man.

TRIN. A most ridiculous monster, to make a wonder
of a poor drunkard!

CAL. I prithee, let me bring thee where crabs° grow;
And I with my long nails will dig thee pig-nuts;°
Show thee a jay's nest and instruct thee how
To snare the nimble marmoset;° I'll bring thee
To clust'ring filberts and sometimes I'll get thee
Young scamels° from the rock. Wilt thou go with me?

STE. I prithee now, lead the way without any more
170 talking. Trinculo, the king and all our company else
being drowned, we will inherit° here: here; bear my
bottle: fellow Trinculo, we'll fill him by and by again.

CAL. (Sings drunkenly)
Farewell, master; farewell, farewell!

TRIN. A howling monster; a drunken monster!

CAL. No more dams I'll make for fish;
    Nor fetch in firing
    At requiring;
    Nor scrape trenchering,° nor wash dish:
    'Ban, 'Ban, Cacaliban
180   Has a new master: get a new man.
Freedom, hey-day! hey-day, freedom! freedom, hey-
day, freedom!

STE. O brave monster! Lead the way.   Exeunt.

ACT III.
SCENE I. [Before PROSPERO's cell.]

Enter FERDINAND, bearing a log.

FER. There be some sports are painful, and their
    labour
Delight in them sets off: some kinds of baseness
Are nobly undergone and most poor matters
Point to rich ends. This my mean task
Would be as heavy to me as odious, but
The mistress which I serve quickens what 's dead
And makes my labours pleasures: O, she is
Ten times more gentle than her father 's crabbed,
And he 's compos'd of harshness. I must remove
10 Some thousands of these logs and pile them up,
Upon a sore° injunction: my sweet mistress
Weeps when she sees me work, and says, such
    baseness
Had never like executor. I forget:
But these sweet thoughts do even refresh my labours,
Most busy lest,° when I do it.

163 crabs, crab apples   164 pig-nuts, earth-chestnuts   166 marmoset, small
monkey   168 scamels, not explained. Keightley conjectured seamels (seagulls);
Theobald: stannels (kestrels); New Cambridge editors call attention to the fact that
"seamews" occurs in Strachey's letter   171 inherit, take possession
178 trenchering, trenchers, wooden plates   Act III, Scene I   11 sore, grievous,
severe   15 Most . . . lest, unexplained; Spedding suggests Most busiest when
idlest; New Cambridge editors suggest busy-idlest, employed in trifles

Enter MIRANDA; and PROSPERO [at a distance, un-
seen].

MIR.   Alas, now, pray you,
Work not so hard: I would the lightning had
Burnt up those logs that you are enjoin'd to pile!
Pray, set it down and rest you: when this burns,
'Twill weep for having wearied you. My father
Is hard at study; pray now, rest yourself;   20
He 's safe for these three hours.

FER.   O most dear mistress,
The sun will set before I shall discharge
What I must strive to do.

MIR.   If you'll sit down,
I'll bear your logs the while: pray, give me that;
I'll carry it to the pile.

FER.   No, precious creature;
I had rather crack my sinews, break my back,
Than you should such dishonour undergo,
While I sit lazy by.

MIR.   It would become me
As well as it does you: and I should do it
With much more ease; for my good will is to it,   30
And yours it is against.

PROS. [Aside]   Poor worm, thou art infect
This visitation shows it.

MIR.   You look wearily.

FER. No, noble mistress; 'tis fresh morning with me
When you are by at night. I do beseech you—
Chiefly that I might set it in my prayers—
What is your name?

MIR.   Miranda.—O my father,
I have broke your hest to say so!

FER.   Admir'd Miranda!
Indeed the top of admiration! worth
What 's dearest to the world! Full many a lady
I have ey'd with best regard and many a time   40
Th' harmony of their tongues hath into bondage
Brought my too diligent ear: for several virtues
Have I lik'd several women; never any
With so full soul, but some defect in her
Did quarrel with the noblest grace she ow'd°
And put it to the foil:° but you, O you,
So perfect and so peerless, are created
Of every creature's best!

MIR.   I do not know
One of my sex; no woman's face remember,
Save, from my glass, mine own; nor have I seen   50
More that I may call men than you, good friend,
And my dear father: how features are abroad,
I am skilless° of; but, by my modesty,
The jewel in my dower, I would not wish
Any companion in the world but you,
Nor can imagination form a shape,

45 ow'd, owned   46 put . . . foil, disgraced it; a wrestling phrase   53 skilless,
ignorant

266   The Renaissance

Besides yourself, to like of. But I prattle
Something too wildly and my father's precepts
I therein do forget.

FER.   I am in my condition
60 A prince, Miranda; I do think, a king;
I would, not so!—and would no more endure
This wooden slavery than to suffer
The flesh-fly blow my mouth. Hear my soul speak:
The very instant that I saw you, did
My heart fly to your service; there rèsides,
To make me slave to it; and for your sake
Am I this patient log-man.

MIR.   Do you love me?

FER. O heaven, O earth, bear witness to this sound
And crown what I profess with kind event
70 If I speak true! if hollowly,° invert
What best is boded me to mischief! I
Beyond all limit of what else i' th' world
Do love, prize, honour you.

MIR.   I am a fool.
To weep at what I am glad of.

PROS. [Aside]   Fair encounter
Of two most rare affections! Heavens rain grace
On that which breeds between 'em!

FER.   Wherefore weep you?

MIR. At mine unworthiness that dare not offer
What I desire to give, and much less take
What I shall die to want. But this is trifling;
80 And all the more it seeks to hide itself,
The bigger bulk it shows. Hence, bashful cunning!
And prompt me, plain and holy innocence!
I am your wife, if you will marry me;
If not, I'll die your maid: to be your fellow
You may deny me; but I'll be your servant,
Whether you will or no.

FER.   My mistress, dearest;
And I thus humble ever.

MIR.   My husband, then?

FER. Ay, with a heart as willing
As bondage e'er of freedom: here 's my hand.

90 MIR. And mine, with my heart in 't: and now
            farewell
Till half an hour hence.

FER.   A thousand thousand!

                    Exeunt [FER. and MIR. severally].

PROS. So glad of this as they I cannot be,
Who are surpris'd withal; but my rejoicing
At nothing can be more. I'll to my book,
For yet ere supper-time must I perform
Much business appertaining.   Exit.

SCENE II. [Another part of the island.]

Enter CALIBAN, STEPHANO, and TRINCULO.

70 hollowly, insincerely, falsely

STE. Tell not me; when the butt is out, we will drink
water; not a drop before: therefore bear up,° and board
'em.° Servant-monster, drink to me.

TRIN. Servant-monster! the folly of this island! They
say there 's but five upon this isle: we are three of
them; if th' other two be brained like us, the state
totters.

STE. Drink, servant-monster, when I bid thee: thy
eyes are almost set in thy head.°

TRIN. Where should they be set else? he were a 10
brave monster indeed, if they were set in his tail.

STE. My man-monster hath drown'd his tongue in
sack: for my part, the sea cannot drown me; I swam,
ere I could recover the shore, five and thirty leagues
off and on. By this light, thou shalt be my lieutenant,
monster, or my standard.°

TRIN. Your lieutenant, if you list; he 's no standard.°

STE. We'll not run, Monsieur Monster.

TRIN. Nor go neither; but you'll lie like dogs and yet
say nothing neither.   20

STE. Moon-calf, speak once in thy life, if thou beest
a good moon-calf.

CAL. How does thy honour? Let me lick thy shoe.
I'll not serve him; he is not valiant.

TRIN. Thou liest, most ignorant monster: I am in
case° to justle a constable. Why, thou deboshed° fish,
thou, was there ever man a coward that hath drunk so
much sack as I to-day? Wilt thou tell a monstrous lie,
being but half a fish and half a monster?

CAL. Lo, how he mocks me! wilt thou let him, my 30
lord?

TRIN. 'Lord' quoth he. That a monster should be
such a natural!°

CAL. Lo, lo, again! bite him to death, I prithee.

STE. Trinculo, keep a good tongue in your head: if
you prove a mutineer,—the next tree! The poor
monster 's my subject and he shall not suffer indignity.

CAL. I thank my noble lord. Wilt thou be pleased to
hearken once again to the suit I made to thee?

STE. Marry, will I: kneel and repeat it; I will stand, 40
and so shall Trinculo.

Enter ARIEL, invisible.

CAL. As I told thee before, I am subject to a tyrant, a
sorcerer, that by his cunning hath cheated me of the
island.

ARI. Thou liest.

CAL. Thou liest, thou jesting monkey, thou: I would
my valiant master would destroy thee! I do not lie.

STE. Trinculo, if you trouble him any more in 's tale,
by this hand, I will supplant some of your teeth.

Scene II   2 bear up, put the helm up so as to bring the ship into the wind
3 board 'em, climb aboard; both phrases refer to drinking   9 thy eyes . . . head,
current description of drunkenness meaning that the eyes are fixed in a stare, or
dimmed by drink   16 standard, standard-bearer   17 standard, something that
stands up   26 case, condition   deboshed, debauched   33 natural, idiot

TRIN. Why, I said nothing.

STE. Mum, then, and no more. Proceed.

CAL. I say, by sorcery he got this isle;
From me he got it. If thy greatness will
Revenge it on him,—for I know thou dar'st,
But this thing dare not,—

STE. That 's most certain.

CAL. Thou shalt be lord of it and I'll serve thee.

STE. How now shall this be compass'd?
Canst thou bring me to the party?

60 CAL. Yea, yea, my lord: I'll yield him thee asleep,
Where thou mayst knock a nail into his head.

ARI. Thou liest; thou canst not.

CAL. What a pied ninny 's° this! Thou scurvy patch!°
I do beseech thy greatness, give him blows
And take his bottle from him: when that 's gone
He shall drink nought but brine; for I'll not show him
Where the quick freshes° are.

STE. Trinculo, run into no further danger: interrupt
the monster one word further, and, by this hand, I'll
70 turn my mercy out o' doors and make a stock-fish° of
thee.

TRIN. Why, what did I? I did nothing. I'll go farther
off.

STE. Didst thou not say he lied?

ARI. Thou liest.

STE. Do I so? take thou that. [Beats Trin.] As you
like this, give me the lie another time.

TRIN. I did not give the lie. Out o' your wits and
hearing too? A pox o' your bottle! this can sack and
80 drinking do. A murrain° on your monster, and the devil
take your fingers!

CAL. Ha, ha, ha!

STE. Now, forward with your tale. [To Trin.]
Prithee, stand further off.

CAL. Beat him enough: after a little time
I'll beat him too.

STE.   Stand farther. Come, proceed.

CAL. Why, as I told thee, 'tis a custom with him,
I' th' afternoon to sleep: there thou mayst brain him,
Having first seiz'd his books, or with a log
90 Batter his skull, or paunch him with a stake,
Or cut his wezand° with thy knife. Remember
First to possess his books; for without them
He 's but a sot,° as I am, nor hath not
One spirit to command: they all do hate him
As rootedly as I. Burn but his books.
He has brave utensils,—for so he calls them,—
Which, when he has a house, he'll deck withal.
And that most deeply to consider is
The beauty of his daughter; he himself
100 Calls her a nonpareil:° I never saw a woman,
But only Sycorax my dam and she;

But she as far surpasseth Sycorax
As great'st does least.

STE.   Is it so brave a lass?

CAL. Ay, lord; she will become thy bed, I warrant,
And bring thee forth brave brood.

STE. Monster, I will kill this man: his daughter and I
will be king and queen,—save our graces!—and Trinculo and thyself shall be viceroys. Dost thou like the
plot, Trinculo?

TRIN. Excellent.   110

STE. Give me thy hand: I am sorry I beat thee; but,
while thou livest, keep a good tongue in thy head.

CAL. Within this half hour will he be asleep:
Wilt thou destroy him then?

STE.   Ay, on mine honour.

ARI. This will I tell my master.

CAL. Thou mak'st me merry; I am full of pleasure:
Let us be jocund: will you troll the catch°
You taught me but while-ere?°

STE. At thy request, monster, I will do reason, any
reason. Come on, Trinculo, let us sing.   Sings. 120

    Flout 'em and scout 'em
    And scout° 'em and flout 'em;
        Thought is free.

CAL. That 's not the tune.

            Ariel plays the tune on a tabor° and pipe.

STE. What is this same?

TRIN. This is the tune of our catch, played by the
picture of Nobody.°

STE. If thou beest a man, show thyself in thy likeness: if thou beest a devil, take 't as thou list.

TRIN. O, forgive me my sins!   130

STE. He that dies pays all debts: I defy thee. Mercy
upon us!

CAL. Art thou afeard?

STE. No, monster, not I.

CAL. Be not afeard; the isle is full of noises,
Sounds and sweet airs, that give delight and hurt not.
Sometimes a thousand twangling instruments
Will hum about mine ears, and sometime voices
That, if I then had wak'd after long sleep,
Will make me sleep again: and then, in dreaming,   140
The clouds methought would open and show riches
Ready to drop upon me, that, when I wak'd,
I cried to dream again.

STE. This will prove a brave kingdom to me, where I
shall have my music for nothing.

CAL. When Prospero is destroyed.

STE. That shall be by and by: I remember the story.

TRIN. The sound is going away; let 's follow it, and
after do our work.

STE. Lead, monster; we'll follow. I would I could 150
see this taborer; he lays it on.

---

63 **pied ninny,** fool in motley   **patch,** common word for *fool*   67 **quick freshes,**
running springs   70 **stock-fish,** dried cod beaten before boiling   80 **murrain,**
plague   91 **wezand,** windpipe   93 **sot,** fool   100 **nonpareil,** one having no
equal

117 **troll the catch,** sing the round   118 **while-ere,** a while since   122 **scout,**
deride. New Cambridge editors emend, *cout* (befool)   *Stage Direction:* **tabor,**
small drum   127 **picture of Nobody,** a figure with head, arms, and legs, but no
trunk, used by John Trundle, bookseller and printer

TRIN. Wilt come? I'll follow, Stephano.   *Exeunt*.

SCENE III. [*Another part of the island.*]

Enter ALONSO, SEBASTIAN, ANTONIO, GONZALO, ADRIAN, FRANCISCO, *& c*.

GON. By 'r lakin,° I can go no further, sir;
My old bones ache: here 's a maze trod indeed
Through forth-rights and meanders!° By your
    patience,
I needs must rest me.
    ALON.   Old lord, I cannot blame thee,
Who am myself attach'd with weariness,
To th' dulling of my spirits: sit down, and rest.
Even here I will put off my hope and keep it
No longer for my flatterer: he is drown'd
Whom thus we stray to find, and the sea mocks
10 Our frustrate search on land. Well, let him go.
    ANT. [*Aside to Seb.*] I am right glad that he 's so out
        of hope.
Do not, for one repulse, forego the purpose
That you resolv'd t' effect.
    SEB.   [*Aside to Ant.*] The next advan-
tage
Will we take throughly.
    ANT.   [*Aside to Seb.*] Let it be to-
night;
For, now they are oppress'd with travel, they
Will not, nor cannot, use such vigilance
As when they are fresh.
    SEB.   [*Aside to Ant.*] I say, to-night: no
more.   *Solemn and strange music*.
    ALON. What harmony is this? My good friends,
        hark!
    GON. Marvellous sweet music!

[*Enter*] PROSPERO *on the top,° invisible. Enter several
strange Snapes, bringing in a banquet; they dance
about it with gentle actions of salutations; and, inviting the King, & c. to eat, they depart.*

20   ALON. Give us kind keepers,° heavens! What were
        these?
    SEB. A living drollery.° Now I will believe
That there are unicorns, that in Arabia
There is one tree, the phœnix' throne, one phœnix
At this hour reigning there.
    ANT.   I'll believe both;
And what does else want credit, come to me,
And I'll be sworn 'tis true: travellers ne'er did lie,
Though fools at home condemn 'em.
    GON.   If in Naples

Scene III   1 **By 'r lakin,** by our Lady   3 **forth-rights and meanders,** paths
straight and crooked   *Stage Direction:*   **on the top,** in the gallery above the
stage or some higher point   20 **keepers,** guardian angels   21 **drollery,** puppet
show

I should report this now, would they believe me?
If I should say, I saw such islanders—
For, certes,° these are people of the island—   30
Who, though they are of monstrous shape, yet, note,
Their manners are more gentle-kind than of
Our human generation you shall find
Many, nay, almost any.
    PROS.   [*Aside*] Honest lord,
Thou hast said well; for some of you there present
Are worse than devils.
    ALON.   I cannot too much muse
Such shapes, such gesture and such sound, expres-
    sing,
Although they want the use of tongue, a kind
Of excellent dumb discourse.
    PROS.   [*Aside*] Praise in departing.°
    FRAN. They vanish'd strangely.   40
    SEB.   No matter, since
They have left their viands behind; for we have
    stomachs.
Will 't please you taste of what is here?
    ALON.   Not I.
    GON. Faith, sir, you need not fear. When we were
        boys,
Who would believe that there were mountaineers
Dew-lapp'd° like bulls, whose throats had hanging at
    'em
Wallets of flesh? or that there were such men
Whose heads stood in their breasts? which now we
    find
Each putter-out of five for one° will bring us
Good warrant of.
    ALON.   I will stand to and feed,
Although my last: no matter, since I feel   50
The best is past. Brother, my lord the duke,
Stand to and do as we.

Thunder and lightning. Enter ARIEL, *like a harpy;°
claps his wings upon the table; and, with a quaint
device,° the banquet vanishes.*

    ARI. You are three men of sin, whom Destiny,
That hath to° instrument this lower world
And what is in 't, the never-surfeited sea
Hath caus'd to belch up you; and on this island
Where man doth not inhabit; you 'mongst men
Being most unfit to live. I have made you mad;
And even with such-like valour° men hang and drown
Their proper selves. [*Alon., Seb. & c. draw their
                        swords.*]

30 **certes,** certainly   39 **Praise in departing.** Save your praise until the end of
the performance   45 **Dew-lapp'd,** having a dewlap, or fold of skin hanging from
the neck, as cattle; often supposed to refer to people afflicted with goiter
48 **putter-out . . . one,** one who invests money, or gambles on the risks of travel on
the condition that, if he returns safely, he is to receive five times the amount deposited; hence, any traveler   *Stage Direction:*   **harpy,** a fabulous monster
with a woman's face and vulture's body supposed to be a minister of divine vengeance   **quaint device,** ingenious stage contrivance   54 **to,** as   59 **such-like
valour,** i.e., the reckless valor derived from madness

You fools! I and my fellows
Are ministers of Fate: the elements,
Of whom your swords are temper'd,° may as well
Wound the loud winds, or with bemock'd-at stabs
Kill the still-closing° waters, as diminish
One dowle° that's in my plume:° my fellow-ministers
Are like° invulnerable. If° you could hurt,
Your swords are now too massy for your strengths
And will not be uplifted. But remember—
For that 's my business to you—that you three
From Milan did supplant good Prospero;
Expos'd unto the sea, which hath requit° it,
Him and his innocent child: for which foul deed
The pow'rs, delaying, not forgetting, have
Incens'd the seas and shores, yea, all the creatures,
Against your peace. Thee of thy son, Alonso,
They have bereft; and do pronounce by me
Ling'ring perdition, worse than any death
Can be at once, shall step by step attend
You and your ways; whose wraths to guard you from—
Which here, in this most desolate isle, else falls
Upon your heads—is nothing but heart's sorrow
And a clear° life ensuing.

He vanishes in thunder; then, to soft music, enter the Shapes again, and dance, with mocks and mows, and carrying out the table.

PROS. Bravely the figure of this harpy hast thou
Perform'd, my Ariel; a grace it had, devouring:°
Of my instruction hast thou nothing bated°
In what thou hadst to say: so, with good life°
And observation strange,° my meaner° ministers
Their several kinds have done. My high charms work
And these mine enemies are all knit up
In their distractions; they now are in my pow'r;
And in these fits I leave them, while I visit
Young Ferdinand, whom they suppose is drown'd,
And his and mine lov'd darling. [*Exit above.*]
GON. I' th' name of something holy, sir, why stand you
In this strange stare?
ALON. O, it is monstrous, monstrous!
Methought the billows spoke and told me of it;
The winds did sing it to me, and the thunder,
That deep and dreadful organ-pipe, pronounc'd
The name of Prosper: it did bass my trespass.°
Therefore my son i' th' ooze is bedded, and
I'll seek him deeper than e'er plummet sounded
And with him there lie mudded. *Exit.*
SEB. But one fiend at a time,
I'll fight their legions o'er.

ANT. I'll be thy second.
Exeunt [Seb. and Ant.].
GON. All three of them are desperate: their great guilt,
Like poison given to work a great time after,
Now 'gins to bite the spirits.° I do beseech you
That are of suppler joints, follow them swiftly
And hinder them from what this ecstasy
May now provoke them to.
ADR. Follow, I pray you. *Exeunt onnes.*

ACT IV.
SCENE I. [*Before* PROSPERO'S *cell.*]

Enter PROSPERO, FERDINAND, *and* MIRANDA.

PROS. If I have too austerely punish'd you,
Your compensation makes amends, for I
Have given you here a third of mine own life,
Or that for which I live; who once again
I tender to thy hand: all thy vexations
Were but my trials of thy love, and thou
Hast strangely° stood the test: here, afore Heaven,
I ratify this my rich gift. O Ferdinand,
Do not smile at me that I boast her off,
For thou shalt find she will outstrip all praise
And make it halt behind her.
FER. I do believe it
Against an oracle.°
PROS. Then, as my gift and thine own acquisition
Worthily purchas'd, take my daughter: but
If thou dost break her virgin-knot before
All sanctimonious° ceremonies may
With full and holy rite be minist'red,
No sweet aspersion° shall the heavens let fall
To make this contract grow; but barren hate,
Sour-ey'd disdain and discord shall bestrew
The union of your bed with weeds so loathly
That you shall hate it both: therefore take heed,
As Hymen's° lamps shall light you.
FER. As I hope
For quiet days, fair issue and long life,
With such love as 'tis now, the murkiest den,
The most opportune place, the strong'st suggestion
Our worser genius° can, shall never melt
Mine honour into lust, to take away
The edge of that day's celebration
When I shall think, or Phœbus' steeds are founder'd,°
Or Night kept chain'd below.
PROS. Fairly spoke.
Sit then and talk with her; she is thine own.
What, Ariel! my industrious servant, Ariel!

Enter ARIEL.

---

62 **temper'd**, composed 64 **still-closing**, always closing again when parted 65 **dowle**, soft, fine feather **plume**, plumage (?) (Onions) 66 **like**, likewise, similarly **If**, even if 71 **requit**, requited, avenged 82 **clear**, unspotted, innocent 84 **devouring**, i.e., ravishing (?) 85 **bated**, abated, diminished 86 **so . . . life**, with faithful reproduction 87 **observation strange**, rare attention to detail **meaner**, i.e., subordinate to Ariel 99 **bass my trespass**, proclaimed my trespass like a bass note in music

106 **bite the spirits**, i.e., conscience troubles them **Act IV, Scene I** 7 **strangely**, extraordinarily 12 **Against an oracle**, even if an oracle should declare otherwise 16 **sanctimonious**, sacred 18 **aspersion**, dew, shower 23 **Hymen's**. Hymen was the Greek and Roman god of marriage 27 **genius**, evil genius, or evil attendant spirit 30 **founder'd**, broken down, made lame

ARI. What would my potent master? here I am.

PROS. Thou and thy meaner fellows your last service
Did worthily perform; and I must use you
In such another trick. Go bring the rabble,°
O'er whom I give thee pow'r, here to this place:
Incite them to quick motion; for I must
40 Bestow upon the eyes of this young couple
Some vanity° of mine art: it is my promise,
And they expect it from me.

ARI.   Presently?

PROS. Ay, with a twink.

ARI. Before you can say 'come' and 'go,'
        And breathe twice and cry 'so, so,'
        Each one, tripping on his toe,
        Will be here with mop and mow.°
        Do you love me, master? no?

PROS. Dearly, my delicate Ariel. Do not approach
Till thou dost hear me call.

50 ARI.   Well, I conceive.   *Exit.*

PROS. Look thou be true; do not give dalliance
Too much the rein: the strongest oaths are straw
To th' fire i' th' blood: be more abstemious,
Or else, good night your vow!

FER.   I warrant you, sir;
The white cold virgin snow upon my heart
Abates the ardour of my liver.°

PROS.   Well.
Now come, my Ariel! bring a corollary,°
Rather than want a spirit: appear, and pertly!°
No tongue! all eyes! be silent.   *Soft music.*

Enter IRIS.

60 IRIS. Ceres, most bounteous lady, thy rich leas
Of wheat, rye, barley, vetches, oats and pease;
Thy turfy mountains, where live nibbling sheep,
And flat meads thatch'd with stover,° them to keep;
Thy banks with pioned and twilled° brims,
Which spongy April at thy hest betrims,
To make cold nymphs chaste crowns; and thy broom-
        groves,°
Whose shadow the dismissed bachelor loves,
Being lass-lorn; thy pole-clipt° vineyard;
And thy sea-marge, sterile and rocky-hard,
70 Where thou thyself dost air;—the queen o' th' sky,
Whose wat'ry arch° and messenger am I,
Bids thee leave these, and with her sovereign grace,
                                Juno descends.°
Here on this grass-plot, in this very place,
To come and sport: her peacocks fly amain:°
Approach, rich Ceres, her to entertain.

Enter CERES.

CER. Hail, many-colour'd messenger, that ne'er
Dost disobey the wife of Jupiter;
Who with thy saffron wings upon my flow'rs
Diffusest honey-drops, refreshing show'rs,
And with each end of thy blue bow dost crown   80
My bosky° acres and my unshrubb'd down,°
Rich scarf to my proud earth; why hath thy queen
Summon'd me hither, to this short-grass'd green?

IRIS. A contract of true love to celebrate;
And some donation freely to estate
On the blest lovers.

CER.   Tell me, heavenly bow,
If Venus or her son, as thou dost know,
Do now attend the queen? Since they did plot
The means that dusky Dis my daughter got,°
Her and her blind boy's scandal'd° company   90
I have forsworn.

IRIS.   Of her society
Be not afraid: I met her deity
Cutting the clouds towards Paphos° and her son
Dove-drawn with her. Here thought they to have
        done
Some wanton charm upon this man and maid,
Whose vows are, that no bed-right shall be paid
Till Hymen's torch be lighted; but in vain;
Mars's hot minion° is return'd again;
Her waspish-headed° son has broke his arrows,
Swears he will shoot no more but play with sparrows 100
And be a boy right out.

[JUNO *alights.*]

CER.   Highest queen of state,
Great Juno, comes; I know her by her gait.

JUNO. How does my bounteous sister? Go with me
To bless this twain, that they may prosperous be
And honour'd in their issue.   *They sing:*

JUNO. Honour, riches, marriage-blessing,
        Long continuance, and increasing,
        Hourly joys be still upon you!
        Juno sings her blessings on you.

CER. Earth's increase, foison plenty,°   110
        Barns and garners never empty,
        Vines with clust'ring bunches growing,
        Plants with goodly burthen bowing;

        Spring come to you at the farthest
        In the very end of harvest!
        Scarcity and want shall shun you;
        Ceres' blessing so is on you.

---

37 **rabble,** band, i.e., the *meaner fellows* of line 35   41 **vanity,** illusion
47 **mop and mow,** gestures and grimaces   56 **liver,** as the seat of the passions
57 **corollary,** supernumerary   58 **pertly,** briskly   63 **stover,** fodder for cattle
64 **pioned and twilled,** unexplained; excavated (?) or trenched (?) (Onions),
ridged (New Cambridge), grown over with peonies and lilies (Hanmer)
66 **broom-groves,** groves of broom (?)   68 **pole-clipt,** hedged in with poles
71 **wat'ry arch,** rainbow   *Stage Direction: **Juno descends,*** i.e., starts her
descent from the "heavens" above the stage (?)   74 **amain,** with full force or
speed

81 **bosky,** covered with shrubs   **unshrubb'd down,** shrubless upland   89 **Dis
. . . got.** Pluto, god of the infernal regions, carried off Persephone, daughter of
Ceres, to be his bride in Hades   90 **scandal'd,** scandalous   93 **Paphos,** a town
in the island of Cyprus, sacred to Venus   98 **Mars's . . . minion,** Venus, the beloved of Mars   99 **waspish-headed,** fiery, hot-headed (?)   110 **foison plenty,**
plentiful harvest

FER. This is a most majestic vision, and
Harmonious charmingly. May I be bold
To think these spirits?
120 PROS.   Spirits, which by mine art
I have from their confines call'd to enact
My present fancies.
    FER.   Let me live here ever;
So rare a wond'red° father and a wise
Makes this place Paradise.

        Juno and Ceres whisper, and send Iris on
                                    employment.

    PROS.   Sweet, now, silence!
Juno and Ceres whisper seriously;
There 's something else to do: hush, and be mute,
Or else our spell is marr'd.
        IRIS. You nymphs, call'd Naiads, of the windring°
            brooks,
With your sedg'd crowns and ever-harmless looks,
130 Leave your crisp° channels and on this green land
Answer your summons; Juno does command:
Come, temperate° nymphs, and help to celebrate
A contract of true love; be not too late.

Enter certain Nymphs.

You sunburnt sicklemen, of August weary,
Come hither from the furrow and be merry:
Make holiday; your rye-straw hats put on
And these fresh nymphs encounter every one
In country footing.°

*Enter certain Reapers, properly habited: they join with
the Nymphs in a graceful dance; towards the end
whereof* PROSPERO *starts suddenly, and speaks; after
which, to a strange, hollow, and confused noise, they
heavily vanish.*

    PROS. [*Aside*] I had forgot that foul conspiracy
140 Of the beast Caliban and his confederates
Against my life: the minute of their plot
Is almost come. [*To the Spirits.*] Well done! avoid;° no
    more!
    FER. This is strange: your father 's in some passion
That works° him strongly.
    MIR.   Never till this day
Saw I him touch'd with anger so distemper'd.°
    PROS. You do look, my son, in a mov'd sort,°
As if you were dismay'd: be cheerful, sir.
Our revels now are ended. These our actors,
As I foretold you, were all spirits and
150 Are melted into air, into thin air:
And, like the baseless fabric of this vision,
The cloud-capp'd tow'rs, the gorgeous palaces,
The solemn temples, the great globe itself,
Yea, all which it inherit,° shall dissolve

And, like this insubstantial pageant faded,
Leave not a rack° behind. We are such stuff
As dreams are made on, and our little life
Is rounded with a sleep. Sir, I am vex'd;
Bear with my weakness; my old brain is troubled:
Be not disturb'd with my infirmity: 160
If you be pleas'd, retire into my cell
And there repose: a turn or two I'll walk,
To still my beating mind.
    FER. MIR.   We wish your peace.
                                    Exeunt.
    PROS. Come with a thought.° I thank thee, Ariel:
    come.

Enter ARIEL.

    ARI. Thy thoughts I cleave to. What 's thy pleasure?
    PROS.   Spirit,
We must prepare to meet with Caliban.
    ARI. Ay, my commander: when I presented° Ceres,
I thought to have told thee of it, but I fear'd
Lest I might anger thee.
    PROS. Say again, where didst thou leave these   170
    varlets?
    ARI. I told you, sir, they were red-hot with
    drinking;
So full of valour that they smote the air
For breathing in their faces; beat the ground
For kissing of their feet; yet always bending
Towards their project. Then I beat my tabor;
At which, like unback'd° colts, they prick'd their ears,
Advanc'd° their eyelids, lifted up their noses
As they smelt music: so I charm'd their ears
That calf-like they my lowing follow'd through
Tooth'd briers, sharp furzes, pricking goss° and thorns, 180
Which ent'red their frail shins: at last I left them
I' th' filthy-mantled° pool beyond your cell,
There dancing up to th' chins, that the foul lake
O'erstunk their feet.°
    PROS.   This was well done, my bird.°
Thy shape invisible retain thou still:
The trumpery° in my house, go bring it hither,
For stale° to catch these thieves.
    ARI.   I go, I go.   *Exit.*
    PROS. A devil, a born devil, on whose nature
Nurture can never stick; on whom my pains,
Humanely taken, all, all lost, quite lost;   190
And as with age his body uglier grows,
So his mind cankers. I will plague them all,
Even to roaring.

Enter ARIEL, *loaden with glistering apparel, & c.*

---

123 **wond'red,** wonder-performing   128 **windring,** wandering (?) or winding (?)
130 **crisp,** curled, rippled   132 **temperate,** chaste   138 **country footing,**
country dancing   142 **avoid,** depart, withdraw   144 **works,** affects   145 **distemper'd,** vexed   146 **sort,** state, condition   154 **it inherit,** occupy it

156 **rack,** mass of cloud driven before the wind in the upper air (Onions)
164 **with a thought,** on the instant   167 **presented,** acted the part of, or introduced   176 **unback'd,** unbroken, unridden   177 **Advanc'd,** lifted up
180 **goss,** gorse, a prickly shrub   182 **filthy-mantled,** covered with a vegetable
coating, slimy   184 **feet,** New Cambridge conjectures: *sweat*   **bird,** used as a
term of endearment   186 **trumpery,** cheap goods, the "glistering apparel" mentioned in the following stage direction   187 **stale,** decoy

Come, hang them on this line.°

[PROSPERO *and* ARIEL *remain, invisible.*] *Enter* CALI-
BAN, STEPHANO, *and* TRINCULO, *all wet.*

CAL. Pray you, tread softly, that the blind mole may
not
Hear a foot fall: we now are near his cell.

STE. Monster, your fairy, which you say is a harmless fairy, has done little better than played the Jack°
with us.

TRIN. Monster, I do smell all horse-piss; at which
200 my nose is in great indignation.

STE. So is mine. Do you hear, monster? If I should
take a displeasure against you, look you,—

TRIN. Thou wert but a lost monster.

CAL. Good my lord, give me thy favour still.
Be patient, for the prize I'll bring thee to
Shall hoodwink° this mischance: therefore speak softly.
All 's hush'd as midnight yet.

TRIN. Ay, but to lose our bottles in the pool,—

STE. There is not only disgrace and dishonour in
210 that, monster, but an infinite loss.

TRIN. That 's more to me than my wetting: yet this is
your harmless fairy, monster.

STE. I will fetch off my bottle, though I be o'er ears
for my labour.

CAL. Prithee, my king, be quiet. See'st thou here,
This is the mouth o' th' cell: no noise, and enter.
Do that good mischief which may make this island
Thine own for ever, and I, thy Caliban,
For aye thy foot-licker.

220   STE. Give me thy hand. I do begin to have bloody
thoughts.

TRIN. O king Stephano!° O peer! O worthy
Stephano! look what a wardrobe here is for thee!

CAL. Let it alone, thou fool; it is but trash.

TRIN. O, ho, monster! we know what belongs to a
frippery.° O king Stephano!

STE. Put off that gown, Trinculo; by this hand, I'll
have that gown.

TRIN. Thy grace shall have it.

230   CAL. The dropsy drown this fool! what do you mean
To dote thus on such luggage?° Let 's alone
And do the murder first: if he awake,
From toe to crown he'll fill our skins with pinches,
Make us strange stuff.

STE. Be you quiet, monster. Mistress line, is not this
my jerkin? [*Takes it down.*] Now is the jerkin° under
the line:° now, jerkin, you are like to lose your hair°
and prove a bald jerkin.

TRIN. Do, do: we steal by line and level,° an 't like
240 your grace.

STE. I thank thee for that jest; here 's a garment
for 't: wit shall not go unrewarded while I am king of
this country. 'Steal by line and level' is an excellent
pass of pate;° there 's another garment for 't.

TRIN. Monster, come, put some lime° upon your fingers, and away with the rest.

CAL. I will have none on 't: we shall lose our time,
And all be turn'd to barnacles,° or to apes
With foreheads villanous low.

STE. Monster, lay to your fingers: help to bear this 250
away where my hogshead of wine is, or I'll turn you
out of my kingdom: go to, carry this.

TRIN. And this.

STE. Ay, and this.

*A noise of hunters heard. Enter divers Spirits, in shape
of dogs and hounds, hunting them about,* PROSPERO
and ARIEL *setting them on.*

PROS. Hey, Mountain, hey!

ARI. Silver! there it goes, Silver!

PROS. Fury, Fury! there, Tyrant, there! hark! hark!
[*Cal., Ste., and Trin. are driven out.*]
Go charge my goblins that they grind their joints
With dry convulsions,° shorten up their sinews
With aged cramps, and more pinch-spotted make them 260
Than pard° or cat o' mountain.°

ARI.   Hark, they roar!

PROS. Let them be hunted soundly. At this hour
Lies at my mercy all mine enemies:
Shortly shall all my labours end, and thou
Shalt have the air at freedom: for a little
Follow, and do me service.   *Exeunt.*

ACT V.
SCENE I. [*Before* PROSPERO'S *cell.*]

Enter PROSPERO *in his magic robes, and* ARIEL.

PROS. Now does my project gather to a head:
My charms crack not;° my spirits obey; and time
Goes upright with his carriage.° How 's the day?°

ARI. On the sixth hour; at which time, my lord,
You said our work should cease.

PROS.   I did say so,
When first I rais'd the tempest. Say, my spirit,
How fares the king and 's followers?

ARI.   Confin'd together
In the same fashion as you gave in charge,
Just as you left them; all prisoners, sir,
In the line-grove° which weather-fends° your cell;   10
They cannot budge till your release.° The king,
His brother and yours, abide all three distracted

---

193 **line,** probably, lime tree   197 **played the Jack,** done a mean trick. *Jack* has
a double meaning, "knave" and "will-o-the-wisp"   206 **hoodwink,** cover up;
hawking term   222 **king Stephano,** allusion to the old ballad beginning, "King
Stephen was a worthy peer"   226 **frippery,** place where cast-off clothes are sold
231 **luggage,** impedimenta, heavy stuff to be carried   236 **jerkin,** jacket made
of leather   237 **under the line,** under the lime tree, with punning allusion, probably, to the equinoctial line   237 **lose your hair,** a reference to tropical fevers
experienced by seamen, causing loss of hair   239 **by line and level,** i.e., by
means of instruments, or, methodically, like dishonest carpenters and masons;
with pun on *line,* above

244 **pass of pate,** sally of wit   245 **lime,** birdlime   248 **barnacles,** barnacle
geese, formerly supposed to be hatched from seashells attached to trees and to fall
thence into the water; possibly, the ordinary meaning is intended   259 **convulsions,** cramps   261 **pard,** panther or leopard   **cat o' mountain,** wildcat   **Act V,
Scene I** 2 **crack not,** are flawless (from alchemy)   3 **carriage,** burden; i.e.,
Time is unstooped, runs smoothly   **How 's the day?** What time is it?   10 **line-
grove,** grove of lime trees   **weatherfends,** protects from the weather   11 **your
release,** you release them

And the remainder mourning over them,
Brimful of sorrow and dismay; but chiefly
Him that you term'd, sir, 'The good old lord,
    Gonzalo;'
His tears runs down his beard, like winter's drops
From eaves of reeds.° Your charm so strongly works
    'em
That if you now beheld them, your affections
Would become tender.

PROS.   Dost thou think so, spirit?

20 ARI. Mine would, sir, were I human.

PROS.   And mine shall.
Hast thou, which art but air, a touch, a feeling
Of their afflictions, and shall not myself,
One of their kind, that relish all° as sharply,
Passion as they, be kindlier mov'd than thou art?
Though with their high wrongs I am struck to th'
    quick,
Yet with my nobler reason 'gainst my fury
Do I take part: the rarer° action is
In virtue than in vengeance: they being penitent,
The sole drift of my purpose doth extend
30 Not a frown further. Go release them, Ariel:
My charms I'll break, their senses I'll restore,
And they shall be themselves.

ARI.   I'll fetch them, sir.   *Exit.*

PROS. Ye° elves of hills, brooks, standing lakes and
    groves,
And ye that on the sands with printless foot
Do chase the ebbing Neptune and do fly him
When he comes back; you demi-puppets° that
By moonshine do the green sour ringlets° make,
Whereof the ewe not bites, and you whose pastime
Is to make midnight mushrumps, that rejoice
40 To hear the solemn curfew; by whose aid,
Weak masters though ye be, I have bedimm'd
The noontide sun, call'd forth the mutinous winds,
And 'twixt the green sea and the azur'd vault
Set roaring war: to the dread rattling thunder
Have I given fire° and rifted Jove's stout oak
With his own bolt; the strong-bas'd promontory
Have I made shake and by the spurs° pluck'd up
The pine and cedar: graves at my command
Have wak'd their sleepers, op'd, and let 'em forth
50 By my so potent art. But this rough magic
I here abjure, and, when I have requir'd
Some heavenly music, which even now I do,
To work mine end upon their senses that
This airy charm is for, I'll break my staff,
Bury it certain fathoms in the earth,
And deeper than did ever plummet sound
I'll drown my book.   *Solemn music.*

Here enters ARIEL *before: then* ALONSO, *with a
frantic gesture, attended by* GONZALO; SEBASTIAN *and*
ANTONIO *in like manner, attended by* ADRIAN *and*
FRANCISCO: *they all enter the circle which* PROSPERO
had made, and there stand charmed; which PROSPERO
observing, speaks:

A solemn air and the best comforter
To an unsettled fancy cure thy brains,
Now useless, boil'd° within thy skull! There stand, 60
For you are spell-stopp'd.
Holy Gonzalo, honourable man,
Mine eyes, ev'n sociable° to the show° of thine,
Fall fellowly drops. The charm dissolves apace,
And as the morning steals upon the night,
Melting the darkness, so their rising senses
Begin to chase the ignorant fumes° that mantle
Their clearer reason. O good Gonzalo,
My true preserver, and a loyal sir
To him thou follow'st! I will pay thy graces 70
Home both in word and deed. Most cruelly
Didst thou, Alonso, use me and my daughter:
Thy brother was a furtherer in the act.
Thou art pinch'd for 't now, Sebastian. Flesh and
    blood,
You, brother mine, that entertain'd ambition,
Expell'd remorse and nature; who, with Sebastian,
Whose inward pinches therefore are most strong,
Would here have kill'd your king; I do forgive thee,
Unnatural though thou art. Their understanding
Begins to swell, and the approaching tide 80
Will shortly fill the reasonable shore
That now lies foul and muddy. Not one of them
That yet looks on me, or would know me: Ariel,
Fetch me the hat and rapier in my cell:
I will discase° me, and myself present
As I was sometime Milan: quickly, spirit;
Thou shalt ere long be free.

   [*Exit Ariel and return immediately.*]

ARIEL *sings and helps to attire him.*

 Where the bee sucks, there suck I:
 In a cowslip's bell I lie;
 There I couch when owls do cry. 90
 On the bat's back I do fly
 After summer merrily.
Merrily, merrily shall I live now
Under the blossom that hangs on the bough.

PROS. Why, that 's my dainty Ariel! I shall miss thee;
But yet thou shalt have freedom: so, so, so.°

---

17 **eaves of reed**, thatch 23 **all**, quite 27 **rarer**, nobler 33–57 **Ye . . .
book.** This famous passage is an embellished paraphrase of Golding's translation
of Ovid's *Metamorphoses*, vii, 197–219 36 **demipuppets**, elves and fairies; literally, puppets of half-size 37 **green sour ringlets**, fairy rings, circles of grass produced by fungus within the soil 44–45 **to . . . fire**, the dread rattling thunder-
bolt I have discharged 47 **spurs**, roots

60 **boil'd**, made hot with humors 63 **sociable**, sympathetic **show**, appearance
67 **ignorant fumes.** The fumes which rose up into the brain to produce sleep
brought with them unconsciousness 85 **discase**, undress 96 **so, so, so**, that
will do very well

To the king's ship, invisible as thou art:
There shalt thou find the mariners asleep
Under the hatches; the master and the boatswain
100 Being awake, enforce them to this place,
And presently, I prithee.
    ARI. I drink the air before me, and return
Or ere your pulse twice beat.   *Exit.*
    GON. All torment, trouble, wonder and amazement
Inhabits here: some heavenly power guide us
Out of this fearful country!
    PROS.   Behold, sir king,
The wronged Duke of Milan, Prospero:
For more assurance that a living prince
Does now speak to thee, I embrace thy body;
110 And to thee and thy company I bid
A hearty welcome.
    ALON.   Whe'r thou be'st he or no,
Or some enchanted trifle° to abuse me,
As late I have been, I not know: thy pulse
Beats as of flesh and blood; and, since I saw thee,
Th' affliction of my mind amends, with which,
I fear, a madness held me: this must crave,
An if this be at all, a most strange story.
Thy dukedom I resign and do entreat
Thou pardon me my wrongs. But how should
    Prospero
Be living and be here?
120   PROS.   First, noble friend,
Let me embrace thine age, whose honour cannot
Be measur'd or confin'd.
    GON.   Whether this be
Or be not, I'll not swear.
    PROS.   You do yet taste
Some subtilties° o' th' isle, that will not let you
Believe things certain. Welcome, my friends all!
[*Aside to Seb. and Ant.*] But you, my brace of lords,
    were I so minded,
I here could pluck his highness' frown upon you
And justify you° traitors: at this time
I will tell no tales.
    SEB.   [*Aside*] The devil speaks in him.
    PROS.   No.
130 For you, most wicked sir, whom to call brother
Would even infect my mouth, I do forgive
Thy rankest fault; all of them; and require
My dukedom of thee, which perforce, I know,
Thou must restore.
    ALON.   If thou be'st Prospero,
Give us particulars of thy preservation;
How thou hast met us here, who three hours since
Were wrack'd upon this shore; where I have lost—
How sharp the point of this remembrance is!—
My dear son Ferdinand.
    PROS.   I am woe° for 't, sir.

ALON. Irreparable is the loss, and Patience   140
Says it is past her cure.
    PROS.   I rather think
You have not sought her help, of whose soft grace
For the like loss I have her sovereign aid
And rest myself content.
    ALON.   You the like loss!
    PROS. As great to me as late;° and, supportable
To make the dear loss, have I means much weaker
Than you may call to comfort you, for I
Have lost my daughter.
    ALON.   A daughter?
O heavens, that they were living both in Naples,
The king and queen there! that they were, I wish   150
Myself were mudded in that oozy bed
Where my son lies. When did you lose your daughter?
    PROS. In this last tempest. I perceive, these lords
At this encounter do so much admire
That they devour° their reason and scarce think
Their eyes do offices of truth, their words
Are natural breath: but, howsoev'r you have
Been justled from your senses, know for certain
That I am Prospero and that very duke
Which was thrust forth of Milan, who most strangely   160
Upon this shore, where you were wrack'd, was
    landed,
To be the lord on 't. No more yet of this;
For 'tis a chronicle of day by day,
Not a relation for a breakfast nor
Befitting this first meeting. Welcome, sir;
This cell 's my court: here have I few attendants
And subjects none abroad: pray you, look in.
My dukedom since you have given me again,
I will requite you with as good a thing;
At least bring forth a wonder, to content ye   170
As much as me my dukedom.

Here PROSPERO *discovers*° FERDINAND *and* MIRANDA,
playing at chess.

    MIR. Sweet lord, you play me false.
    FER.   No, my dearest love,
I would not for the world.
    MIR. Yes, for a score° of kingdoms you should
    wrangle,°
And I would call it fair play.
    ALON.   If this prove
A vision of the Island, one dear son
Shall I twice lose.
    SEB.   A most high miracle!
    FER. Though the seas threaten, they are merciful;
I have curs'd them without cause.   [*Kneels.*]

---

112 **trifle**, trick of magic   124 **subtilties**, illusions   128 **justify you**, prove you to be   139 **woe**, sorry

145 **late**, i.e., as great to me as it is recent   155 **devour**, render null, destroy   *Stage Direction:* **discovers**, by opening a curtain rear-stage   174 **score**, double meaning: game or wager in which the score is reckoned by kingdoms, and also twenty kingdoms   **wrangle**, meaning (1) contend in a game or wager, and (2) argue or contend in words

ALON.   Now all the blessings
180 Of a glad father compass thee about!
Arise, and say how thou cam'st here.
    MIR.   O, wonder!
How many goodly creatures are there here!
How beauteous mankind is! O brave new world,
That has such people in 't!
    PROS.   'Tis new to thee.
    ALON. What is this maid with whom thou wast at
        play?
Your eld'st° acquaintance cannot be three hours:
Is she the goddess that hath sever'd us,
And brought us thus together?
    FER.   Sir, she is mortal;
But by immortal Providence she 's mine:
190 I chose her when I could not ask my father
For his advice, nor thought I had one. She
Is daughter to this famous Duke of Milan,
Of whom so often I have heard renown,
But never saw before; of whom I have
Receiv'd a second life; and second father
This lady makes him to me.
    ALON.   I am hers:
But, O, how oddly will it sound that I
Must ask my child forgiveness!
    PROS.   There, sir, stop:
Let us not burthen our remembrance with
A heaviness that 's gone.
200 GON.   I have inly wept
Or should have spoke ere this. Look down, you gods,
And on this couple drop a blessed crown!
For it is you that have chalk'd forth the way
Which brought us hither.
    ALON.   I say, Amen, Gonzalo!
    GON. Was Milan thrust from Milan, that his issue
Should become kings of Naples? O, rejoice
Beyond a common joy, and set it down
With gold on lasting pillars: In one voyage
Did Claribel her husband find at Tunis
210 And Ferdinand, her brother, found a wife
Where he himself was lost, Prospero his dukedom
In a poor isle and all of us ourselves
When no man was his own.°
    ALON.   [To Fer. and Mir.] Give me
        your hands:
Let grief and sorrow still embrace his heart
That doth not wish you joy!
    GON.   Be it so! Amen!

Enter ARIEL, with the MASTER and BOATSWAIN
amazedly following.

O, look, sir, look, sir! here is more of us:
I prophesied, if a gallows were on land,

This fellow could not drown. Now, blasphemy,
That swear'st grace o'erboard, not an oath on shore?
Hast thou no mouth by land? What is the news?   220
    BOATS. The best news is, that we have safely found
Our king and company; the next, our ship—
Which, but three glasses° since, we gave out split—
Is tight and yare° and bravely rigg'd as when
We first put out to sea.
    ARI.   [Aside to Pros.] Sir, all this
        service
Have I done since I went.
    PROS.   [Aside to Ari.] My tricksy
        spirit!
    ALON. These are not natural events; they strengthen
From strange to stranger. Say, how came you hither?
    BOATS. If I did think, sir, I were well awake,
I 'ld strive to tell you. We were dead of sleep,   230
And—how we know not—all clapp'd under hatches;
Where but even now with strange and several noises
Of roaring, shrieking, howling, jingling chains,
And moe diversity of sounds, all horrible;
We were awak'd; straightway, at liberty;
Where we, in all her trim, freshly beheld
Our royal, good and gallant ship, our master
Cap'ring to eye her: on a trice, so please you,
Even in a dream, were we divided from them
And were brought moping hither.
    ARI.   [Aside to Pros.] Was 't well 240
        done?
    PROS. [Aside to Ari.] Bravely, my diligence. Thou
        shalt be free.
    ALON. This is as strange a maze as e'er men trod;
And there is in this business more than nature
Was ever conduct° of: some oracle
Must rectify our knowledge.
    PROS.   Sir, my liege,
Do not infest° your mind with beating on
The strangeness of this business; at pick'd° leisure
Which shall be shortly, single I'll resolve you,
Which to you shall seem probable, of every
These happen'd accidents; till when, be cheerful   250
And think of each thing well. [Aside to Ari.] Come
        hither, spirit:
Set Caliban and his companions free;
Untie the spell. [Exit Ariel.] How fares my gracious
        sir?
There are yet missing of your company
Some few odd lads that you remember not.

Enter ARIEL, driving in CALIBAN, STEPHANO and TRIN-
CULO, in their stolen apparel.

STE. Every man shift for all the rest, and let no man

---

186 **eld'st,** earliest   213 **own,** i.e., master of his senses

223 **glasses,** hours   224 **yare,** ready   244 **conduct,** guide, leader   246 **infest,**
harass, disturb   247 **pick'd.** chosen

take care for himself; for all is but fortune. Coragio,°
bully-monster,° coragio!

TRIN. If these be true spies which I wear in my head,
260 here 's a goodly sight.

CAL. O Setebos, these be brave spirits indeed!
How fine my master is! I am afraid
He will chastise me.

SEB.   Ha, ha!
What things are these, my lord Antonio?
Will money buy 'em?

ANT.   Very like; one of them
Is a plain fish, and, no doubt, marketable.

PROS. Mark but the badges° of these men, my lords,
Then say if they be true. This mis-shapen knave,
His mother was a witch, and one so strong
270 That could control the moon, make flows and ebbs,
And deal in her command without her power.°
These three have robb'd me; and this demi-devil—
For he 's a bastard one—had plotted with them
To take my life. Two of these fellows you
Must know and own; this thing of darkness I
Acknowledge mine.

CAL.   I shall be pinch'd to death.

ALON. Is not this Stephano, my drunken butler?

SEB. He is drunk now: where had he wine?

ALON. And Trinculo is reeling ripe: where should
they
280 Find this grand liquor that hath gilded° 'em?
How cam'st thou in this pickle?

TRIN. I have been in such a pickle since I saw you
last that, I fear me, will never out of my bones: I shall
not fear fly-blowing.°

SEB. Why, how now, Stephano!

STE. O, touch me not; I am not Stephano, but a
cramp.

PROS. You 'ld be king o' the isle, sirrah?

STE. I should have been a sore one then.

ALON. This is a strange thing as e'er I look'd on.

                [Pointing to Caliban.]

290 PROS. He is as disproportion'd in his manners
As in his shape. Go, sirrah, to my cell;
Take with you your companions; as you look
To have my pardon, trim it handsomely.

CAL. Ay, that I will; and I'll be wise hereafter
And seek for grace. What a thrice-double ass
Was I, to take this drunkard for a god
And worship this dull fool!

PROS.   Go to; away!

ALON. Hence, and bestow your luggage where you
found it.

SEB. Or stole it, rather.

          [Exeunt Cal., Ste., and Trin.]

PROS. Sir, I invite your highness and your train   300
To my poor cell, where you shall take your rest
For this one night; which, part of it, I'll waste
With such discourse as, I not doubt, shall make it
Go quick away; the story of my life
And the particular accidents° gone by
Since I came to this isle: and in the morn
I'll bring you to your ship and so to Naples,
Where I have hope to see the nuptial
Of these our dear-belov'd solemnized;
And thence retire me to my Milan, where   310
Every third thought shall be my grave.

ALON.   I long
To hear the story of your life, which must
Take° the ear strangely.

PROS.   I'll deliver° all;
And promise you calm seas, auspicious gales
And sail so expeditious that shall catch
Your royal fleet far off. [*Aside to Ari.*] My Ariel, chick,
That is thy charge: then to the elements
Be free, and fare thou well!—Please you, draw near.

                    Exeunt omnes.

EPILOGUE.

SPOKEN BY PROSPERO.

Now my charms are all o'erthrown,
And what strength I have 's mine own,
Which is most faint: now, 'tis true,
I must be here confin'd by you,
Or sent to Naples. Let me not,
Since I have my dukedom got
And pardon'd the deceiver, dwell
In this bare island by your spell;
But release me from my bands
With the help of your good hands:°   10
Gentle breath of yours my sails
Must fill, or else my project fails,
Which was to please. Now I want
Spirits to enforce, art to enchant,
And my ending is despair,
Unless I be reliev'd by prayer,
Which pierces so that it assaults
Mercy itself and frees all faults.
As you from crimes would pardon'd be,
Let your indulgence set me free.   *Exit.* 20
(1611)

---

258 **Coragio,** courage **bully-monster,** gallant monster 267 **badges,** emblems
of cloth or silver worn on the arms of retainers. Prospero refers here to the stolen
clothes as emblems of their villainy 271 **deal . . . power,** wield the moon's
power, either without her authority, or beyond her influence 280 **gilded,**
flushed, made drunk 284 **fly-blowing,** i.e., rotting after death (since he's pick-
led)

305 **accidents,** occurrences, events 313 **Take,** take effect upon **deliver,** declare, relate **Epilogue** 10 **hands,** applause

FRANCIS BACON
1561–1626

Francis Bacon was born in London in 1561, the son of Sir Nicholas Bacon, Lord Keeper of the great seal. After his education at Cambridge, Bacon served in the English embassy in France from 1576 to 1579. Upon his return to England, he sought a government appointment by petitioning Lord Burleigh, a relative on his mother's side of the family, but was unsuccessful. Bacon then studied law and entered Parliament in 1584. He became Solicitor-General in 1607, Attorney-General in 1613, Lord Keeper in 1617, and Lord Chancellor in 1618. His political career ended in 1621, however, when he was charged with bribery and admitted that he was guilty of "corruption and neglect." Deprived of all his political offices, fined heavily, barred from court and Parliament, and imprisoned briefly in the Tower, he retired to the family residence at Gorhambury and devoted the rest of his life to literary and philosophical work.

Young Francis Bacon once wrote to Lord Burleigh that he had taken "all knowledge to be his province." His massive writings reflect this Renaissance spirit of inquiry; they are closely related to his goal of creating a great "instauration," or renewal of science. First, Bacon planned to study all existing sciences and all existing methods of acquiring truth; second, to develop a new "organon," or scientific method for interpreting nature; and third, to reconstruct all knowledge on the basis of the new plan. The great fragments of this ambitious project, which he did complete, are still amazing in their penetration and power. His *Advancement of Learning* is really a prelude to the first part of his plan, and the *De Augmentis Scientarum* is an elaboration of it in Latin. The *Sylva Sylvarum* contributes to his review of the existing state of knowledge. The greatest work connected with the plan of the instauration is the *Novum Organum*; it contains the famous analysis of human fallacies that obscure the light of understanding. The *New Atlantis*, never "perfected," would seem to be a thing apart from the great scheme of writing. Actually it is not. Although it presents an ideal commonwealth, just as does More's *Utopia*, it differs radically from the *Utopia* in emphasizing the place in the perfect republic, not of government and social institutions, but of the light of the intellect. Prophetically, Bacon's ideal vision of a Society of Scholars and Scientists laboring together became a reality with the founding in 1662 of the Royal Society, a group much influenced by the spirit of Baconian inquiry.

Although he apparently regarded his essay writing as a kind of gentleman's hobby, reserving his serious attention for his projected scientific work, Bacon nevertheless took pains to revise, refine, and enlarge his volume of *Essays or Counsels—Civil and Moral* over more than a quarter of a century. His prose varied in the course of maturation, but on the whole the essays display a fine sense of succinctness and general stylistic tact. In tone they are deliberate, coolly commonsense views *on* the world derived from Bacon's own abundant experience as a social being and complete citizen *of* the world.

The text of the *Essays* followed here is from the 1625 edition, the last one printed during Bacon's lifetime.

ESSAYS OR COUNSELS— CIVIL AND MORAL

1. OF TRUTH

"What is truth?" said jesting Pilate,° and would not stay for an answer. Certainly there be that° delight in giddiness,° and count it a bondage to fix a belief; affecting free-will in thinking, as well as in acting. And though the sects of philosophers of that kind° be gone, yet there remain certain discoursing° wits which are of the same veins, though there be not so much blood in them as was in those of the ancients. But it is not only the difficulty and labor which men take in finding out 10 of truth, nor again that when it is found it imposeth upon men's thoughts, that doth bring lies in favor; but a natural though corrupt love of the lie itself. One of the later school of the Grecians° examineth the matter, and is at a stand° to think what should be in it, that men should love lies; where neither they make for pleasure, as with poets;° nor for advantage, as with the merchant; but for the lie's sake. But I cannot tell; this same truth is a naked and open daylight, that doth not show the masques and mummeries and triumphs° of the world, 20 half so stately and daintily as candlelights. Truth may perhaps come to the price of a pearl, that showeth best by day; but it will not rise to the price of a diamond or carbuncle, that showeth best in varied lights. A mixture of a lie doth ever add pleasure. Doth any man doubt, that if there were taken out of men's minds vain opinions, flattering hopes, false valuations, imaginations as one would, and the like, but it would leave the minds of a number of men poor shrunken things, full of melancholy and indisposition, and unpleasing to themselves? One of the fathers,° in great severity, called 30 poesy *vinum daemonum*,° because it filleth the imagi-

1.—Of Truth   1 **Pilate,** Roman procurator of Judea before whom Jesus was tried. Pilate's question was addressed to Jesus, who had just testified that he came into the world to bear witness unto the truth; but the ruler did not wait for Jesus' answer (*John* 18:37–38)   2 **that,** those who   3 **giddiness,** lightness of thought   5 **philosophers . . . kind,** the sceptics, the Greek sophists and members of later schools of thought who believed that all knowledge is uncertain   6 **discoursing,** discursive   12–13 **One . . . Grecians,** Lucian, Greek satirist (120?–200?)   14 **stand,** halt   15–16 **lies . . . poets.** Poetry or fiction was generally considered inferior to "factual" writing (philosophy, science, theology, etc.) at this time and was also regarded as a corrupting influence   19 **masques . . . triumphs.** The figure alludes to the elaborate court entertainments produced at night   30 **One of the fathers,** the church father St. Augustine (354–430)   31 **vinum daemonum,** the devil's wine

nation, and yet it is but with the shadow of a lie. But it is not the lie that passeth through the mind, but the lie that sinketh in and settleth in it, that doth the hurt, such as we spake of before. But howsoever these things are thus in men's depraved judgments and affections, yet truth, which only doth judge itself, teacheth that the inquiry of truth, which is the lovemaking or wooing of it, the knowledge of truth, which
40 is the presence of it, and the belief of truth, which is the enjoying of it, is the sovereign good of human nature. The first creature° of God, in the works of the days,° was the light of the sense; the last was the light of reason; and his sabbath work, ever since, is the illumination of his Spirit. First he breathed light upon the face of the matter or chaos; then he breathed light into the face of man; and still he breathed and inspireth light into the face of his chosen. The poet° that beautified the sect that was otherwise inferior to the
50 rest, saith yet excellently well: *It is a pleasure to stand upon the shore, and to see ships tossed upon the sea: a pleasure to stand in the window of a castle, and to see a battle and the adventures thereof below: but no pleasure is comparable to the standing upon the vantage ground of Truth* (a hill not to be commanded, and where the air is always clear and serene), *and to see the errors,° and wanderings, and mists, and tempests, in the vale below:* so° always that this prospect be with pity, and not with swelling or pride. Certainly, it is
60 heaven upon earth, to have a man's mind move in charity, rest in providence, and turn upon the poles of truth.

To pass from theological and philosophical truth, to the truth of civil business: it will be acknowledged, even by those that practise it not, that clear and round dealing is the honor of man's nature; and that mixture of falsehood is like alloy in coin of gold and silver; which may make the metal work the better, but it embaseth it. For these winding and crooked courses are
70 the goings of the serpent; which goeth basely upon the belly, and not upon the feet. There is no vice that doth so cover a man with shame as to be found false and perfidious. And therefore Montaigne° saith prettily, when he inquired the reason, why the word of the lie should be such a disgrace and such an odious charge? Saith he, *If it be well weighed, to say that a man lieth, is as much to say as that he is brave towards God and a coward towards men.* For a lie faces God, and shrinks from man. Surely the wickedness of falsehood
80 and breach of faith cannot possibly be so highly expressed, as in that it shall be the last peal to call the judgments of God upon the generations of men; it being foretold, that when Christ cometh, *he shall not find faith upon the earth.*°
(1625)

42 **creature,** created thing   43 **works of the days,** the creation   48 **poet,** Lucretius, Roman poet (96?–55? B.C.). In his *De Rerum Natura* ("On the Nature of Things") he ascribed grace to the Epicureans upon whose philosophy he based his poem   57 **errors,** windings   58 **so,** provided   73 **Montaigne,** French philosopher and essayist (1533–1592)   83 **foretold . . . earth,** in *Luke,* 18:8. Jesus' words form a question, not an assertion, as here

5. OF ADVERSITY

It was an high speech of Seneca (after the manner of the Stoics): *That the good things which belong to prosperity are to be wished; but the good things that belong to adversity are to be admired.*° *Bona rerum secundarum optabilia, adversarum mirabilia.* Certainly, if miracles be the command over nature, they appear most in adversity. It is yet a higher speech of his than the other (much too high for a heathen). *It is true greatness to have in one the frailty of a man, and the security of a god. Vere magnum, habere* 10 *fragilitatem hominis, securitatem dei.* This would have done better in poesy, where transcendences° are more allowed. And the poets indeed have been busy with it; for it is in effect the thing which is figured in that strange fiction of the ancient poets, which seemeth not to be without mystery; nay, and to have some approach to the state of a Christian: that *Hercules, when he went to unbind Prometheus* (by whom human nature is represented), *sailed the length of the great ocean in an earthen pot or pitcher:* lively describing 20 Christian resolution, that saileth in the frail bark of the flesh through the waves of the world. But to speak in a mean.° The virtue of prosperity is temperance; the virtue of adversity is fortitude; which in morals is the more heroical virtue. Prosperity is the blessing of the Old Testament; adversity is the blessing of the New; which carrieth the greater benediction, and the clearer revelation of God's favor. Yet even in the Old Testament, if you listen to David's harp,° you shall hear as many hearse-like airs as carols; and the pencil of the 30 Holy Ghost hath labored more in describing the afflictions of Job than the felicities of Solomon. Prosperity is not without many fears and distastes; and adversity is not without comforts and hopes. We see in needleworks and embroideries, it is more pleasing to have a lively work upon a sad and solemn ground, than to have a dark and melancholy work upon a lightsome ground: judge therefore of the pleasure of the heart by the pleasure of the eye. Certainly virtue is like precious odors, most fragrant when they are incensed or 40 crushed: for prosperity doth best discover vice; but adversity doth best discover virtue.
(1625)

5.—Of Adversity   4 **admired,** wondered at   12 **transcendences,** hyperboles, exaggerations   23 **in a mean,** moderately   29 **David's harp,** the *Psalms* of King David

7. OF PARENTS AND CHILDREN

The joys of parents are secret, and so are their griefs and fears: they cannot utter the one, nor they will not utter the other. Children sweeten labors, but they make misfortunes more bitter: they increase the cares of life, but they mitigate the remembrance of death. The perpetuity by generation is common to beasts; but

memory, merit, and noble works are proper to men: and surely a man shall see the noblest works and foundations have proceeded from childless men, which
10 have sought to express the images of their minds, where those of their bodies have failed: so the care of posterity is most in them that have no posterity. They that are the first raisers of their houses are most indulgent towards their children; beholding them as the continuance not only of their kind but of their work; and so both children and creatures.

The difference in affection of parents towards their several children is many times unequal, and sometimes unworthy, especially in the mother; as Solomon saith:°
20 "A wise son rejoiceth the father, but an ungracious son shames the mother." A man shall see, where there is a house full of children, one or two of the eldest respected, and the youngest made wantons;° but in the midst some that are as it were forgotten, who many times nevertheless prove the best. The illiberality of parents in allowance° towards their children is an harmful error; makes them base; acquaints them with shifts; makes them sort° with mean company; and makes them surfeit more when they come to plenty:
30 and therefore the proof° is best, when men keep their authority towards their children, but not their purse. Men have a foolish manner (both parents and schoolmasters and servants) in creating and breeding an emulation between brothers during childhood, which many times sorteth° to discord when they are men, and disturbeth families. The Italians make little difference between children and nephews or near kinsfolks; but so they be of the lump, they care not though they pass not through their own body. And, to say truth, in na-
40 ture it is much a like matter; insomuch that we see a nephew sometimes resembleth an uncle or a kinsman more than his own parents, as the blood happens. Let parents choose betimes° the vocations and courses they mean their children should take; for then they are most flexible; and let them not too much apply themselves to the disposition of their children, as thinking they will take best to that which they have most mind to. It is true, that if the affection° or aptness of the children be extraordinary, then it is good not to cross it; but
50 generally the precept is good, *Optimum elige, suave et facile illud faciet consuetudo.°* Younger brothers are commonly fortunate, but seldom or never where the elder are disinherited.
(1612, 1625)

8. OF MARRIAGE AND SINGLE LIFE

He that hath wife and children hath given hostages to fortune; for they are impediments to great enterprises, either of virtue or mischief. Certainly, the best works,

and of greatest merit for the public, have proceeded from the unmarried or childless men, which both in affection and means have married and endowed the public. Yet it were great reason that those that have children should have greatest care of future times; unto which they know they must transmit their dearest pledges. Some there are, who though they lead a single 10 life, yet their thoughts do end with themselves, and account future times impertinences. Nay, there are some other that account wife and children but as bills of charges. Nay more, there are some foolish rich covetous men that take a pride in having no children, because they may be thought so much the richer. For perhaps they have heard some talk: "Such an one is a great rich man," and another except to it: "Yea, but he hath a great charge of children"; as if it were an abatement to his riches. But the most ordinary cause 20 of a single life is liberty; especially in certain self-pleasing and humorous° minds, which are so sensible of every restraint, as they will go near to think their girdles and garters to be bonds and shackles. Unmarried men are best friends, best masters, best servants; but not always best subjects; for they are light to run away; and almost all fugitives are of that condition. A single life doth well with churchmen; for charity will hardly water the ground where it must first fill a pool. It is indifferent for judges and magistrates; for if they 30 be facile and corrupt, you shall have a servant five times worse than a wife. For soldiers, I find the generals commonly in their hortatives put men in mind of their wives and children; and I think the despising of marriage amongst the Turks maketh the vulgar soldier more base. Certainly wife and children are a kind of discipline of humanity; and single men, though they be many times more charitable, because their means are less exhaust,° yet, on the other side, they are more cruel and hard-hearted (good to make severe in- 40 quisitors), because their tenderness is not so oft called upon. Grave natures, led by custom, and therefore constant, are commonly loving husbands; as was said of Ulysses, *Vetulam suam praetulit immortalitati.°* Chaste women are often proud and froward, as presuming upon the merit of their chastity. It is one of the best bonds both of chastity and obedience in the wife, if she think her husband wise; which she will never do if she find him jealous. Wives are young men's mistresses; companions for middle age; and old men's 50 nurses. So as a man may have a quarrel° to marry when he will. But yet he was reputed one of the wise men, that made answer to the question, when a man should marry? "A young man not yet, an elder man not at all."° It is often seen that bad husbands have very good wives; whether it be that it raiseth the price of their husband's kindness when it comes; or that the

7.—Of Parents and Children   19 **Solomon saith,** *Proverbs,* 10:1   23 **wantons,** spoiled darlings   25-26 **illiberality . . . allowance,** stinginess in providing for   28 **sort,** consort, associate   30 **proof,** experience   35 **sorteth,** conduce   43 **betimes,** early   48 **affection,** tendency   50-51 **Optimum . . . consuetudo.** Choose the best; habit will make it pleasant and easy

8.—Of Marriage and Single Life   22 **humorous,** whimsical   39 **exhaust,** exhausted   44 **Vetulam . . . immortalitati.** "He preferred his aged wife to immortality." The allusion is to the passage in the *Odyssey* (Book V) in which Calypso chides her guest with preferring his mortal wife to immortality as guardian of the nymph's home   51 **quarrel,** reason   54-55 **A young man . . . all,** ascribed to Thales, Greek sage of the sixth and seventh centuries B.C.

wives take a pride in their patience. But this never fails, if the bad husbands were of their own choosing, against their friends' consent; for then they will be sure to make good their own folly.

(1612, 1625)

42. OF YOUTH AND AGE

A man that is young in years may be old in hours if he have lost no time. But that happeneth rarely. Generally youth is like the first cogitations, not so wise as the second. For there is a youth in thoughts as well as in ages. And yet the invention of young men is more lively than that of old; and imaginations stream into their minds better and, as it were, more divinely. Natures that have much heat, and great and violent desires and perturbations, are not ripe for action till they have passed the meridian of their years, as it was with Julius Caesar and Septimius Severus°, of the latter of whom it is said, *Juventutem egit erroribus, imo furoribus, plenam!*° And yet he was the ablest emperor almost of all the list. But reposed natures may do well in youth, as it is seen in Augustus Caesar, Cosmos,° Duke of Florence, Gaston de Foix,° and others. On the other side, heat and vivacity in age is an excellent composition for business. Young men are fitter to invent than to judge, fitter for execution than for counsel, and fitter for new projects than for settled business. For the experience of age, in things that fall within the compass of it, directeth them; but in new things, abuseth° them. The errors of young men are the ruin of business; but the errors of aged men amount but to this, that more might have been done, or sooner.

Young men, in the conduct and manage of actions, embrace more than they can hold; stir more than they can quiet; fly to the end, without consideration of the means and degrees; pursue some few principles, which they have chanced upon, absurdly; care not to innovate,° which draws unknown inconveniences; use extreme remedies at first; and, that which doubleth all errors, will not acknowledge or retract them, like an unready° horse, that will neither stop nor turn. Men of age object too much, consult too long, adventure too little, repent too soon, and seldom drive business home to the full period, but content themselves with a mediocrity of success. Certainly it is good to compound employments° of both, for that will be good for the present, because the virtues of either age may correct the defects of both; and good for succession, that young men may be learners, while men in age are actors; and, lastly, good for extern° accidents, because authority followeth old men, and favor and popularity

youth. But for the moral part perhaps youth will have the preeminence, as age hath for the politic. A certain rabbin° upon the text, "Your young men shall see visions, and your old men shall dream dreams," inferreth that young men are admitted nearer to God than old, because vision is a clearer revelation than a dream. And certainly the more a man drinketh of the world the more it intoxicateth; and age doth profit rather in the powers of understanding than in the virtues of the will and affections. There be some have an over-early ripeness in their years, which fadeth betimes; these are, first, such as have brittle° wits, the edge whereof is soon turned—such as was Hermogenes,° the rhetorician, whose books are exceeding subtle, who afterwards waxed stupid. A second sort is of those that have some natural dispositions, which have better grace in youth than in age, such as is a fluent and luxuriant speech, which becomes youth well, but not age; so Tully° saith of Hortensius,° *Idem manebat, neque idem decebat.*° The third is of such as take too high a strain at the first, and are magnanimous more than tract of years can uphold; as was Scipio Africanus,° of whom Livy° saith in effect, *Ultima primis cedebant.*°

(1612, 1625)

50. OF STUDIES

Studies serve for delight, for ornament, and for ability. Their chief use for delight is in privateness and retiring; for ornament, is in discourse; and for ability, is in the judgment and disposition of business; for expert° men can execute, and perhaps judge of particulars, one by one; but the general counsels, and the plots and marshaling of affairs come best from those that are learned. To spend too much time in studies is sloth; to use them too much for ornament is affectation; to make judgment wholly by their rules is the humor of a scholar. They perfect nature, and are perfected by experience; for natural abilities are like natural plants, that need pruning by study; and studies themselves do give forth directions too much at large, except they be bounded in by experience. Crafty men contemn studies, simple men admire° them, and wise men use them; for they teach not their own use; but that is a wisdom without them and above them, won by observation. Read not to contradict and confute, nor to believe and take for granted, nor to find talk and discourse, but to weigh and consider. Some books are to be tasted, others to be swallowed, and some few to be chewed and digested; that is, some books are to be read only in parts; others to be read but not curiously,°

42.—Of Youth and Age   11 Septimius Severus, Roman emperor (146–211) **12–13 Juventutem . . . plenam.** He spent his entire youth in errors, nay, in mad acts   **15 Cosmos,** Cosimo I de Medici (1519–1574)   **16 Gaston de Foix,** French general (died 1512)   **23 abuseth,** imposes upon   **30–31 care . . . innovate,** are not careful about beginning new ventures   **34 unready,** headstrong   **39 compound employments,** employ both old men and young   **43 extern,** external

47 rabbin, rabbi; Isaac Abrabanel (1437–1508)   **56 brittle,** unstable   **57 Hermogenes,** Greek rhetorician of the second century A.D. who lost his mind at twenty-five   **63 Tully,** Cicero   **Hortensius,** Roman orator of the first century B.C.   **Idem . . . decebat.** He continued the same when the same was no longer becoming to him   **66 Scipio Africanus,** Roman general (237–183 B.C.) who defeated Hannibal   **67 Livy,** Roman historian (59 B.C.–A.D. 17)   **Ultima primis cedebant.** His last acts fell before his first   **50.—Of Studies   5 expert,** experienced   **16 admire,** wonder at   **24 curiously,** with much care

and some few to be read wholly, and with diligence and attention. Some books also may be read by deputy, and extracts made of them by others; but that would be only in the less important arguments and the meaner sort of books; else distilled books are, like
30 common distilled waters, flashy° things. Reading maketh a full man; conference a ready man; and writing an exact man. And, therefore, if a man write little, he had need have a great memory; if he confer little, he had need have a present wit; and if he read little, he had need have much cunning, to seem to know that° he doth not. Histories make men wise; poets, witty; the mathematics, subtle; natural philosophy, deep; moral, grave; logic and rhetoric, able to contend: *Abeunt studia in mores!*° Nay, there is no stand or impediment
40 in the wit but may be wrought out by fit studies; like as diseases of the body may have appropriate exercises. Bowling is good for the stone and reins,° shooting for the lungs and breast, gentle walking for the stomach, riding for the head, and the like. So if a man's wit be wandering, let him study the mathematics; for in demonstrations, if his wit be called away never so little, he must begin again. If his wit be not apt to distinguish or find differences, let him study the schoolmen; for they are *cymini sectores!*° If he be not apt to beat
50 over matters, and to call up one thing to prove and illustrate another, let him study the lawyers' cases. So every defect of the mind may have a special receipt.
(1597, 1612, 1625)

SIR THOMAS OVERBURY 1581–1613

Sir Thomas Overbury was both author and courtier. He was a protégé of Robert Carr, Viscount Rochester, an Oxford acquaintance. Overbury and Carr, a favorite of James I, quarreled violently when Overbury opposed Carr's marriage with Frances Howard, divorced wife of the Earl of Essex. As a result, the king had Overbury imprisoned in the Tower (1613), where he was slowly poisoned to death by agents of Lady Essex. Carr and Lady Essex were convicted, but their lives were spared by the king. Overbury is known today for his character sketch in verse, *A Wife* (1614), and his prose sketches collected under the title *The Characters*; the latter is important in the development of the English essay. From the beginning of the reign of James I to the Restoration of his grandson, character writing in prose was highly popular; many writers ex-

perimented with such sketches, which vary greatly in mood and form. Taken together, they form not only the important genre of character sketching but also a lively picture of humanity in the seventeenth century.

THE CHARACTERS

A MELANCHOLY MAN

Is a strayer from the drove: one that nature made sociable, because she made him man, and a crazed disposition hath altered. Impleasing to all, as all to him; straggling thoughts are his content, they make him dream waking, there's his pleasure. His imagination is never idle, it keeps his mind in a continual motion, as the poise° the clock: he winds up his thoughts often, and as often unwinds them; Penelope's web° thrives faster. He'll seldom be found without the shade of some grove, in whose bottom a river dwells. He 10 carries a cloud in his face, never fair weather: his outside is framed to his inside, in that he keeps a decorum, both unseemly. Speak to him; he hears with his eyes; ears follow his mind, and that's not at leisure. He thinks business, but never does any: he is all contemplation, no action. He hews and fashions his thoughts, as if he meant them to some purpose; but they prove unprofitable, as a piece of wrought timber to no use. His spirits and the sun are enemies; the sun bright and warm, his humor° black and cold: variety of foolish 20 apparitions people his head, they suffer him not to breathe, according to the necessities of nature; which makes him sup up a draught of as much air at once, as would serve at thrice. He denies nature her due in sleep, and over-pays her with watchfulness: nothing pleaseth him long, but that which pleaseth his own fantasies: they are the consuming evils, and evil consumptions that consume him alive. Lastly he is a man only in show, but comes short of the better part; a whole reasonable soul, which is a man's chief preëmi- 30 nence, and sole mark from creatures sensible.
(1614)

A PURITAN

Is a diseased piece of Apocrypha: bind him to the Bible, and he corrupts the whole text; ignorance, and fat feed are his founders; his nurses, railing, rabies, and round breeches; his life is but a borrowed blast of wind, for between two religions, as between two doors, he is ever whistling. Truly whose child he is, is yet unknown, for willingly his faith allows no father:

A Melancholy Man   7 **poise,** weight, which operates the works by force of gravity   8 **Penelope's web.** In the *Odyssey,* Penelope, faithful wife of the wandering Odysseus, delays her numerous suitors by promising to marry one after she had completed weaving a web; at night she unravels what she has woven during the day   20 **humor,** mood

30 **flashy,** tasteless, flat   35 **that,** that which   38–39 **Abeunt . . . mores.** Studies develop into habits (Ovid's *Heroides*)   42 **stone and reins,** testicles and kidneys   49 **cymini sectores,** "hairsplitters"

only thus far his pedigree is found, Bragger, and he flourished about a time first; his fiery zeal keeps him
10 continually costive,° which withers him into his own translation, and till he eat a Schoolman, he is hidebound; he ever prays against nonresidents,° but is himself the greatest discontinuer,° for he never keeps near his text: anything that the law allows, but marriage, and March beer, he murmurs at; what it disallows and holds dangerous, makes him° a discipline. Where the gate stands open, he is ever seeking a stile; and where his learning ought to climb, he creeps through; give him advice, you run into *traditions*, and
20 urge a modest course, he cries out *councils*.° His greatest care is to contemn obedience, his last care to serve God handsomely and cleanly; he is now become so cross a kind of teaching, that should the church enjoin clean shirts, he were lousy; more sense than single prayers is not his, nor more in those than still the same petitions: from which he either fears a learned faith, or doubts God understands not at first hearing. Show him a ring, he runs back like a bear; and hates square dealing as allied to caps; a pair of organs blow
30 him out of the parish and are the only clyster pipes to cool him. Where the meat is best, there he confutes most, for his arguing is but the efficacy of his eating: good bits he holds breed good positions, and the Pope he best concludes against in plum broth. He is often drunk, but not as we are, temporally; nor can his sleep then cure him, for the fumes of his ambition make his very soul reel, and that small beer that should allay him (silence) keeps him more surfeited, and makes his heat break out in private houses; women and lawyers
40 are his best disciples; the one, next fruit, longs for forbidden doctrine, the other to maintain forbidden titles, both which he sows amongst them. Honest he dare not be, for that loves order; yet if he can be brought to ceremony, and made but master of it, he is converted.
(1614)

WHAT A CHARACTER IS

If I must speak the schoolmaster's language, I will confess that character comes of this infinite mood χαράξω, that signifieth to engrave, or make a deep impression. And for that cause, a letter (as A, B) is called a character.

Those elements which we learn first, leaving a strong seal in our memories.

Character is also taken from an Egyptian hieroglyphic, for an impress, or short emblem; in little com-
10 prehending much.

To square out a character by our English level, it is a

picture (real or personal) quaintly drawn, in various colors, all of them heightened by one shadowing.

It is a quick and soft touch of many strings, all shutting up in one musical close; it is wit's descant° on any plain song.
(1614)

BEN JONSON
1573–1637

For his plays and his poetry, Ben Jonson is justly regarded as one of the major talents of his age. He came from a working-class background, and his extensive acquaintance with the classics came through his own efforts. His father, who was a minister, died before he was born; the widow married a bricklayer, and for a time Jonson seems to have followed in his stepfather's calling. He attended Westminster School, but there is no record of his having gone to either Oxford or Cambridge. At twenty-five he had completed his military adventures on the Continent and was in London writing *Every Man in His Humor* (1598), an epoch-making comedy because of the theory upon which it was based. His pugnacious defense of his dramatic theories and his naturally quarrelsome disposition drew him into numerous violent controversies, notably with Marston and Dekker, English dramatists, whom he attacked in two satirical comedies—*Cynthia's Revels* (1601) and *The Poetaster* (1602). He seems, however, to have patched up these quarrels, for he collaborated with Marston and Chapman in *Eastward Hoe* (1605), a comedy which included some satire upon the Scottish followers of James I, and he shared their prison sentence for his indiscretion. His classical tragedies, *Sejanus* (1603) and *Catiline* (1611), were failures. In his comedy of humors, however, he followed the practices of Plautus and Terence without allowing the Latin technique to submerge his own bent for social satire; thus, he developed an important type of comedy, which is perhaps best illustrated by *Volpone* (1607).

Jonson's early satire of James I's courtiers did not bring him into permanent disfavor with that monarch, for he soon became the outstanding writer of court masques—elaborate and costly entertainments consisting chiefly of song, dance, and allegorical pageantry. In *The Masque of Queens* (1609), *Oberon* (1616), and other masques he collaborated with Inigo Jones, architect and designer; but ultimately the two disagreed violently as to the relative importance of their

A Puritan   10 **costive**, constipated   12 **nonresidents**, preachers who did not live among their congregations   13 **discontinuer**, absentee   16 **makes him**, he makes   20 **councils**, councils of the Church, abhorred by the Puritans as much as *traditions*

What a Character Is   15 **descant**, variations

share in the productions, and the partnership dissolved. Unlike all other dramatists of his time, Ben Jonson had no aversion to seeing his plays in print; in 1616 he astonished his fellow playwrights by issuing his dramas and poems in folio as his "Works." This same year, the year of Shakespeare's death, he became official court poet. But if James I was disposed to honor Ben Jonson, Charles I was not, and the dramatist spent the last decade of his life presiding not over court entertainments but over feasts at the Mermaid Tavern, which inspired Robert Herrick and other poets of "the tribe of Ben" to carry into a later decade Jonson's philosophy and art.

Many of Jonson's lyrics were scattered through his plays, and others appeared in *Epigrams* (1616), *The Forest* (1616), and *Underwoods* (1640). His prose appeared principally in some of the famous prefaces to his plays, which set forth his dramatic ideas, and in *Timber; or, Discoveries Made upon Men and Matter,* scattered bits of philosophy, criticism, and comment.

SONG: TO CELIA°

Come, my Celia, let us prove,
While we can, the sports of love.
Time will not be ours for ever;
He, at length, our good will sever;
Spend not then his gifts in vain.   5
Suns that set may rise again;
But if once we lose this light,
'T is with us perpetual night.
Why should we defer our joys?
Fame and rumor are but toys.°   10
Cannot we delude the eyes
Of a few poor household spies?
Or his° easier ears beguile,
Thus removéd by our wile?
'T is no sin love's fruits to steal;
But the sweet theft to reveal,
To be taken, to be seen,
These have crimes accounted been.
(1605)

SONG TO CELIA°

Drink to me only with thine eyes,
    And I will pledge with mine;
Or leave a kiss but in the cup,
    And I'll not look for wine.
The thirst that from the soul doth rise   5
    Doth ask a drink divine;
But might I of Jove's nectar sup,
    I would not change for thine.

I sent thee late a rosy wreath,
    Not so much honoring thee   10
As giving it a hope, that there
    It could not withered be.
But thou thereon didst only breathe,
    And sent'st it back to me;
Since when it grows, and smells, I swear,   15
    Not of itself, but thee.
(1616)

SLOW, SLOW, FRESH FOUNT

Slow, slow, fresh fount, keep time with my salt tears;
Yet slower, yet, O faintly, gentle springs!
List to the heavy part the music bears,
Woe weeps out her division, when she sings.
    Droop herbs and flowers;   5
    Fall grief in showers;
Our beauties are not ours. O, I could still
Like melting snow upon some craggy hill,
    Drop, drop, drop, drop,
Since nature's pride is now a withered daffodil.   10
(1600)

TO PENSHURST

Thou art not, Penshurst,° built to envious show
    Of touch or marble, nor canst boast a row
Of polished pillars, or a roof of gold;
    Thou hast no lanthorn,° whereof tales are told,
Or stairs, or courts; but standest an ancient pile,
    And these grudged at, art reverenced the while.
Thou joyest in better marks, of soil, of air,
    Of wood, of water: therein thou art fair.
Thou hast thy walks for health, as well as sport;
    Thy Mount, to which the Dryads do resort,   10
Where Pan and Bacchus their high feasts have made
    Beneath the broad beech and the chestnut shade,
The taller tree, which of a nut was set,
    At his great birth, where all the Muses met.
There, in the writhèd bark, are cut the names
    Of many a Sylvan, taken with his flames.
And thence, the ruddy Satyrs oft provoke
    The lighter Fauns, to reach thy Lady's oak.°
Thy copse,° too, named of Gamage, thou hast there,
    That never fails to serve thee seasoned deer   20
When thou wouldst feast, or exercise thy friends.
    The lower land that to the river bends,
Thy sheep, thy bullocks, kine, and calves do feed;
    The middle grounds thy mares and horses breed.
Each bank doth yield thee coneys,° and the tops
    Fertile of wood, Ashore and Sidney's copse,
To crown thy open table doth provide

Song: To Celia. Sung by Volpone in *Volpone* III, vi   10 **toys,** trifles   13 **his,** a reference to Celia's husband, Corvino   **Song to Celia.** From *The Forest*

To Penshurst   1 **Penshurst,** the Sidney family home, in Kent   4 **lanthorn,** "a glassed-in room at the top of the house" (Hunter)   18 **thy Lady's oak,** tradition says that an earlier Sidney lady began labor under that oak   19 **copse,** wooded grove   25 **coneys,** rabbits

The purpled pheasant with the speckled side.
The painted partridge lies in every field,
30   And, for thy mess, is willing to be killed;
And if the high swollen Medway° fail thy dish,
    Thou hast thy ponds that pay thee tribute fish,
Fat, agèd carps, that run into thy net.
    And pikes, now weary their own kind to eat,
As loath, the second draught or cast to stay,
    Officiously, at first, themselves betray.
Bright eels that emulate them and leap on land,
    Before the fisher or into his hand.
Then hath thy orchard fruit, thy garden flowers,
40   Fresh as the air and new as are the hours.
The early cherry, with the later plum,
    Fig, grape, and quince, each in his time doth come;
The flushing apricot and woolly peach
    Hang on thy walls that every child may reach.
And though thy walls be of the country stone,
    They are reared with no man's ruin, no man's groan.
There's none that dwell about them wish them down;
    But all come in, the farmer, and the clown;°
And no one empty-handed to salute
50   Thy lord and lady, though they have no suit.°
Some bring a capon, some a rural cake,
    Some nuts, some apples; some that think they make
The better cheeses bring them; or else send
    By their ripe daughters whom they would commend
This way to husbands, and whose baskets bear
    An emblem of themselves, in plum or pear.
But what can this (more than express their love)
    Add to thy free provisions, far above
The need of such? whose liberal board doth flow
60   With all that hospitality doth know!
Where comes no guest, but is allowed to eat
    Without his fear, and of thy Lord's own meat,
Where the same beer and bread and self-same wine
    That is his Lordship's shall be also mine.
And I not fain to sit (as some, this day,
    At great men's tables) and yet dine away.
Here no man tells° my cups; nor, standing by,
    A waiter doth my gluttony envý,
But gives me what I call and lets me eat,
70   He knows, below,° he shall find plenty of meat.
Thy tables hoard not up for the next day,
    Nor when I take my lodging need I pray
For fire, or lights, or livery: all is there;
    As if thou, then, wert mine, or I reigned here,
There's nothing I can wish, for which I stay.
    That found King James, when hunting late this way,
With his brave son, the Prince, they saw thy fires
    Shine bright on every hearth as the desires
Of thy Penates° had been set on flame
80   To entertain them; or the country came,
With all their zeal, to warm their welcome here.
    What (great, I will not say, but) sudden cheer

Didst thou, then, make them! and what praise was
    heaped
    On thy good lady, then! who, therein, reaped
The just reward of her high huswifery;
    To have her linen, plate, and all things nigh,
When she was far: and not a room, but dressed,
    As if it had expected such a guest!
These, Penshurst, are thy praise, and yet not all.
    Thy lady's noble, fruitful, chaste withall.°   90
His children thy great lord may call his own:
    A fortune in this age but rarely known.
They are and have been taught religion; thence
    Their gentler spirits have sucked innocence.
Each morn and even they are taught to pray
    With the whole household, and may, every day,
Read, in their virtuous parents noble parts,
    The mysteries of manners, arms, and arts.
Now Penshurst, they that will proportion thee
    With other edifices, when they see   100
Those proud, ambitious heaps, and nothing else,
    May say, their lords have built, but thy lord dwells.
(1616)

QUEEN AND HUNTRESS

Queen and huntress, chaste and fair,
Now the sun is laid to sleep,
Seated in thy silver chair,
State in wonted manner keep:
    Hesperus entreats thy light,   5
    Goddess, excellently bright.

Earth, let not thy envious shade
Dare itself to interpose;
Cynthia's shining orb was made
Heaven to clear when day did close: 10
    Bless us then with wishèd sight,
    Goddess, excellently bright.

Lay thy bow of pearl apart,
And thy crystal-shining quiver;
Give unto the flying hart   15
Space to breathe, how short soever:
    Thou that mak'st a day of night,
    Goddess, excellently bright.
(1601)

ON MY FIRST DAUGHTER

Here lies, to each her parents' ruth,°
Mary, the daughter of their youth;
Yet all heaven's gifts being heaven's due,
It makes the father less to rue.
At six months' end she parted hence   5

31 **Medway,** river on the estate   48 **clown,** rustic   50 **no suit,** i.e., they are not
flattering to gain a special favor or settlement   67 **tells,** counts   70 **below,** in
the servant's quarters   79 **Penates,** household deities

90 **withall,** as well   **On My First Daughter**   1 **ruth,** pity

With safety of her innocence;
Whose soul heaven's queen, whose name she bears,
In comfort of her mother's tears,
Hath placed amongst her virgin-train:
10 Where, while that severed doth remain,
This grave partakes the fleshly birth;
Which cover lightly, gentle earth!
(1616)

ON MY FIRST SON

Farewell, thou child of my right hand,° and joy:
My sin was too much hope of thee, loved boy:
Seven years thou wert lent to me, and I thee pay,
Exacted by thy fate, on the just day.
5 O could I lose all father now! for why
Will man lament the state he should envy,
To have so soon 'scaped world's and flesh's rage,
And, if no other misery, yet age?
Rest in soft peace, and asked, say, "Here doth lie
10 Ben Jonson his best piece of poetry."
For whose sake henceforth all his vows be such
As what he loves may never like too much.
(1616)

STILL TO BE NEAT

Still to be neat, still to be dressed,
As you were going to a feast;
Still to be powdered, still perfumed:
Lady, it is to be presumed,
5 Though art's hid causes are not found,
All is not sweet, all is not sound.

Give me a look, give me a face,
That makes simplicity a grace;
Robes loosely flowing, hair as free:
10 Such sweet neglect more taketh me
Than all the adulteries of art;
They strike mine eyes, but not my heart.
(1609)

TO JOHN DONNE

Donne, the delight of Phoebus and each Muse,
Who, to thy one, all other brains refuse;
Whose every work, of thy most early wit,
Came forth example and remains so yet;
5 Longer a-knowing than most wits do live,
And which no affection praise enough can give.
To it thy language, letters, arts, best life,

Which might with half mankind maintain a strife.
All which I meant to praise, and yet I would,
But leave, because I cannot as I should. 10
(1616)

TO THE MEMORY OF MY BELOVED MASTER, WILLIAM SHAKESPEARE°

To draw no envy, Shakespeare, on thy name,
Am I thus ample° to thy book and fame;
While I confess thy writings to be such
As neither man, nor muse, can praise too much.
'Tis true, and all men's suffrage.° But these ways
Were not the paths I meant unto thy praise;
For silliest ignorance on these may light,
Which, when it sounds at best, but echoes right;
Or blind affection, which doth ne'er advance
The truth, but gropes, and urgeth all by chance; 10
Or crafty malice might pretend this praise,
And think to ruin, where it seemed to raise.
These are, as some infamous bawd or whore
Should praise a matron. What could hurt her more?
But thou art proof against them, and, indeed,
Above the ill fortune of them, or the need.
I therefore will begin. Soul of the age!
The applause, delight, the wonder of our stage!
My Shakespeare, rise! I will not lodge thee by
Chaucer, or Spenser, or bid Beaumont° lie 20
A little further, to make thee a room;
Thou art a monument without a tomb,
And art alive still while thy book doth live
And we have wits to read and praise to give.
That I not mix thee so, my brain excuses,
I mean with great, but disproportioned Muses;
For if I thought my judgment were of years,
I should commit thee surely with thy peers,
And tell how far thou didst our Lyly outshine,
Or sporting Kyd,° or Marlowe's mighty line. 30
And though thou hadst small Latin and less Greek
From thence to honor thee, I would not seek
For names; but call forth thundering Aeschylus,
Euripides, and Sophocles° to us;
Pacuvius, Accius,° him of Cordova° dead,
To life again, to hear thy buskin° tread,
And shake a stage; or, when thy socks were on,
Leave thee alone for the comparison
Of all that insolent Greece or haughty Rome
Sent forth, or since did from their ashes come. 40
Triumph, my Britain, thou hast one to show

To the Memory . . . Shakespeare. This tribute was published in the first complete edition of Shakespeare's plays, 1623 2 ample, i.e., do I thus add my poem to your book 5 suffrage, vote 20 Chaucer, etc. Jonson suggests that it is not necessary to Shakespeare's fame that he be buried in Westminster Abbey beside these poets 30 Kyd. Thomas Kyd (1557?–1595?), early dramatic contemporary of Shakespeare; author of The Spanish Tragedy (printed 1594) 33–34 Aeschylus, Euripides, and Sophocles, Greek tragic dramatists of the fifth and sixth centuries B.C. 35 Pacuvius, Accius, Roman tragic dramatists of the second century B.C. him of Cordova, Seneca (4 B.C.–A.D. 65), politician, philosopher, and writer of tragedies that influenced Elizabethan drama; he was born in Cordova, Spain 36 buskin, the thick-soled boot used by Greek and Roman tragic actors to increase their stature; thus the symbol of tragedy. The sock, or thin-soled shoe, worn by comic actors became, similarly, the symbol of comedy

On My First Son 1 child of my right hand, Jonson's son, Benjamin, whose name in Hebrew means child of my right hand, was born in 1596 and died in 1603

To whom all scenes of Europe homage owe.
He was not of an age, but for all time!
And all the Muses still were in their prime,
When, like Apollo, he came forth to warm°
Our ears, or like a Mercury° to charm!
Nature herself was proud of his designs
And joyed to wear the dressing of his lines!
Which were so richly spun, and woven so fit,
50 As, since, she will vouchsafe no other wit.
The merry Greek, tart Aristophanes,°
Neat Terence, witty Plautus,° now not please,
But antiquated and deserted lie,
As they were not of Nature's family.
Yet must I not give Nature all; thy art,
My gentle Shakespeare, must enjoy a part.
For though the poet's matter nature be,
His art doth give the fashion; and, that he
Who casts° to write a living line, must sweat
60 (Such as thine are) and strike the second heat
Upon the Muses' anvil; turn the same
(And himself with it) that he thinks to frame,
Or, for the laurel, he may gain a scorn;
For a good poet's made,° as well as born.
And such wert thou! Look how the father's face
Lives in his issue; even so the race
Of Shakespeare's mind and manners brightly shines
In his well turnéd, and true filéd lines;
In each of which he seems to shake a lance,°
70 As brandished at the eyes of ignorance.
Sweet Swan of Avon! what a sight it were
To see thee in our waters yet appear,
And make those flights upon the banks of Thames,
That so did take Eliza, and our James!°
But stay, I see thee in the hemisphere
Advanced, and made a constellation there!
Shine forth, thou Star of poets, and with rage
Or influence, chide or cheer the drooping stage,
Which, since thy flight from hence, hath mourned like
    night,
80 And despairs day, but for thy volume's light.
(1623)

JOHN DONNE
1572–1631

John Donne was born in London in 1572, of Roman
Catholic parents. His mother was a descendant of
Henry VIII's chancellor, Sir Thomas More. His father, a

descendant of an ancient Welsh family, was a wealthy
London merchant. After his father's death in 1576, his
mother married Dr. John Syminges, several times
president of the Royal College of Physicians, who
brought up the Donne children. Donne was educated
at home by a Catholic tutor until he entered Oxford in
1584. After three years he transferred to Cambridge
but did not take a degree from either university because of his Catholic scruples. For a few years after
1590 he studied law. In 1593 he received his portion
of his father's estate, which amounted to a considerable inheritance.

As a young man, he wrote poetry of great talent and
was celebrated for his wit, his dashing behavior, and
his reckless worldliness, which coincided with a
period of religious doubt. Though many of his earlier
religious poems were written from the Catholic point
of view, he ultimately abandoned the Catholic faith.
By 1593 he had composed many of the pieces in his
Divine Poems as well as the first three of his *Satires*,
the third of which appears here. It is an admirable exposition of the situation confronting a man of religious
nature in the London of the times, when a choice of
religions was becoming more and more a matter of
free option. Donne's sojourns as a gentleman adventurer in Italy and Spain in 1594 brought him into the
full current of Renaissance literature; indeed, his unusual liking for "conceits" may in part have been influenced by the Spanish writer Gongora. In 1598,
Donne became Secretary to the Lord Keeper, Sir
Thomas Egerton; he seemed to be on the threshold of
a brilliant career at court. In 1601, however, Donne
eloped with his patron's sixteen-year-old niece Ann
More; her father, Sir George More, dismissed him from
Egerton's service and imprisoned him briefly on the
charge of marrying a minor without parental consent.
From this point on, Donne was frequently dependent
on patrons and often in severe financial difficulties. By
1601 he had finished his *Satires* and the mystical *The
Progress of the Soul,* and in the following year a collection of ten sonnets was printed. These, however,
along with a great many of his short love poems, belong to indeterminate periods of his young manhood.
Another earlier work, *Biathanatos,* a defense of suicide,
was printed after his death.

In the years immediately preceding 1615, when he
was finally ordained in the Anglican Church, he engaged in such anti-Catholic polemical writing as *Pseudo-
Martyr* (1610) and *Ignatius His Conclave* (1611) and
wrote the singular and arresting work of great mystical
power, *The Anatomy of the World* (1611). After Donne
had preached before King James I, who was peculiarly
attached to the poet as a man of religion, a new phase
became evident in the poet's literary work. Thenceforth he excelled as a prose writer, a homiletic artist of
great force and intense insight. Not much interested in
a variety of positions in the church, he preferred to
remain Dean of St. Paul's in London, an office which

45 **warm**, thrill   46 **Mercury,** the Roman messenger of the gods who charmed
with his caduceus, or rod   51 **Aristophanes,** Greek comic dramatist (448?–
380? B.C.)   52 **Terence . . . Plautus,** Roman comic dramatists respectively of the
second and third centuries B.C.   59 **casts,** intends; the word also carries out
the figure by suggesting metal work   64 **good poet's made,** an allusion to the
famous proverb *Poeta nascitur, non fit,* "The poet is born, not made"
69 **shake a lance,** a pun on "shake spear"   74 **Eliza . . . James,** Queen Elizabeth
and James I

he filled from 1621 until his death and in which he achieved his great reputation as a divine. His collected poems were first printed in 1633; his prose work, comprising especially *Juvenilia, Essays in Divinity, Devotions upon Emergent Occasions,* his *Letters,* and more than 150 *Sermons,* was gathered and printed in various fragments between 1633 and 1651.

Donne's poetry is often in revolt against the conventions of the Elizabethan lyric. He is often cynical, grotesque, abrupt, tender, and rhetorical; his form, rough and angular; and his metrics, crabbed and irregular. Frequently his imagery shows a high degree of concentration and an amazing ingenuity. He is today regarded as the greatest of the "metaphysical" school of poets.

SONG

Go and catch a falling star,
  Get with child a mandrake° root,
Tell me where all past years are,
  Or who cleft the devil's foot;
5 Teach me to hear mermaids singing,
Or to keep off envy's stinging,
    And find
    What wind
Serves to advance an honest mind.

10 If thou be'st born to strange sights,
  Things invisible go see,
Ride ten thousand days and nights
  Till Age snow white hairs on thee;
Thou, when thou return'st, wilt tell me
15 All strange wonders that befell thee,
    And swear
    No where
Lives a woman true and fair.

If thou find'st one, let me know;
20   Such a pilgrimage were sweet.
Yet do not; I would not go,
  Though at next door we might meet.
Though she were true when you met her,
And last till you write your letter,
25   Yet she
    Will be
False, ere I come, to two or three.
(1633)

THE FLEA

Mark but this flea, and mark in this,
How little that which thou deniest me is;
Me it sucked first, and now sucks thee,

And in this flea, our two bloods mingled be;
Confess it, this cannot be said
A sin, or shame, or loss of maidenhead,
  Yet this enjoys before it woo,
  And pampered swells with one blood made of two,
  And this, alas, is more than we could do.

Oh stay, three lives in one flea spare,   10
Where we almost, nay more than married are:
This flea is you and I, and this
Our marriage bed, and marriage temple is;
Though parents grudge, and you, we are met,
And cloistered in these living walls of jet.°
  Though use make thee apt to kill me,
  Let not to this, self murder added be,
  And sacrilege, three sins in killing three.

Cruel and sudden, hast thou since
Purpled thy nail, in blood of innocence?°   20
In what could this flea guilty be,
Except in that drop which it sucked from thee?
Yet thou triumph'st, and say'st that thou
Find'st not thy self, nor me the weaker now;
  'Tis true, then learn how false, fears be;
  Just so much honor, when thou yield'st to me,
  Will waste, as this flea's death took life from thee.
(1633)

THE BAIT

Come live with me, and be my love,
And we will some new pleasures prove
Of golden sands, and crystal brooks,
With silken lines, and silver hooks.

There will the river whispering run
Warm'd by thine eyes, more than the sun.
And there th' enamored fish will stay,
Begging themselves they may betray.

When thou wilt swim in that live bath,
Each fish, which every channel hath,   10
Will amorously to thee swim,
Gladder to catch thee, than thou him.

If thou, to be so seen, be'st loath,
By sun, or moon, thou darkenest both,
And if my self have leave to see,
I need not their light, having thee.

Let others freeze with angling reeds,
And cut their legs, with shells and weeds,
Or treacherously poor fish beset,
With strangling snare, or windowy net.   20

Song 2 **mandrake,** the mandragora, a European herb with a forked root which was supposed to resemble a human being and to shriek when pulled up

The Flea 15 **jet,** the flea's black body 20 **Purpled . . . innocence.** She has squashed the flea with her fingernail

Let coarse bold hands, from slimy nest
The bedded fish in banks out-wrest,
Or curious traitors, sleave-silk flies
Bewitch poor fishes' wandering eyes.

For thee, thou needest no such deceit,
For thou thy self art thine own bait,
That fish, that is not catched thereby,
Alas, is wiser far than I.
(1633)

THE INDIFFERENT

I can love both fair and brown;
Her whom abundance melts, and her whom want
    betrays;
Her who loves loneness best, and her who masks and
    plays;
Her whom the country formed, and whom the town;
Her who believes, and her who tries;
Her who still weeps with spongy eyes,
And her who is dry cork and never cries.
I can love her, and her, and you, and you;
I can love any, so she be not true.

10 Will no other vice content you?
Will it not serve your turn to do as did your mothers?
Or have you all old vices spent and now would find
    out others?
Or doth a fear that men are true torment you?
O we are not, be not you so;
Let me—and do you—twenty know;
Rob me, but bind me not, and let me go.
Must I, who came to travel thorough you,
Grow your fixed subject, because you are true?

Venus heard me sigh this song;
20 And by love's sweetest part, variety, she swore,
She heard not this till now; it should be so no more.
She went, examined, and returned ere long,
And said, "Alas! some two or three
Poor heretics in love there be,
Which think to stablish dangerous constancy.
But I have told them, 'Since you will be true,
You shall be true to them, who're false to you.'"
(1633)

THE ECSTASY

Where, like a pillow on a bed,
    A pregnant bank swelled up, to rest
The violet's reclining head,
    Sat we two, one another's best.
Our hands were firmly cemented
    With a fast balm, which thence did spring,
Our eye-beams twisted, and did thread

Our eyes, upon one double string;
So t' intergraft our hands, as yet
    Was all the means to make us one,   10
And pictures in our eyes to get
    Was all our propagation.
As 'twixt two equal armies, fate
    Suspends uncertain victory,
Our souls (which to advance their state,°
    Were gone out) hung 'twixt her, and me.
And whil'st our souls negotiate there,
    We like sepulchral statues lay;
All day, the same our postures were,
    And we said nothing, all the day.   20
If any, so by love refined
    That he soul's language understood,
And by good love were grown all mind,
    Within convenient distance stood,
He (though he knew not which soul spake,
    Because both meant, both spake the same)
Might thence a new concoction take,
    And part far purer than he came.
This Ecstasy doth unperplex
    (We said) and tell us what we love;   30
We see by this, it was not sex,
    We see, we saw not what did move:°
But as all several° souls contain
    Mixtures of things, they know not what,
Love, these mixed souls, doth mix again,
    And makes both one, each this and that.
A single violet transplant,
    The strength, the color, and the size,
(All which before was poor, and scant)
    Redoubles still, and multiplies.   40
When love, with one another so
    Interinanimates two souls,
That abler soul, which thence doth flow,
    Defects of loneliness controls.
We then, who are this new soul, know
    Of what we are composed, and made,
For, th' atomies° of which we grow,
    Are souls, whom no change can invade.
But O alas, so long, so far
    Our bodies why do we forbear?   50
They are ours, though they are not we; we are
    The intelligences, they the sphere.°
We owe them thanks, because they thus,
    Did us, to us, at first convey,
Yielded their forces, sense, to us,
    Nor are dross to us, but allay.°
On man heaven's influence works not so,
    But that it first imprints the air,
So soul into the soul may flow,
    Though it to body first repair.   60
As our blood labors to beget
    Spirits, as like souls as it can,

The Ecstasy   15 state, condition, situation   32 We see . . . move. We perceive
now that we did not perceive what made us love   33 several, separate
47 atomies, atoms   52 intelligences . . . sphere, the intelligent spirits and the
orbit in which they reside, respectively   56 allay, alloy

John Donne   **289**

Because such fingers need to knit
    That subtle knot, which makes us man:
So must pure lovers' souls descend
    T' affections, and to faculties,
Which sense may reach and apprehend,
    Else a great prince in prison lies.
T' our bodies turn we then, that so
70   Weak men on love revealed may look;
Love's mysteries in souls do grow,
    But yet the body is his book.
And if some lover, such as we,
    Have heard this dialogue of one,
Let him still mark us, he shall see
    Small change, when we're to bodies gone.

(1633)

LOVERS' INFINITENESS

If yet I have not all thy love,
Dear, I shall never have it all,
I cannot breathe one other sigh, to move;
Nor can entreat one other tear to fall,
And all my treasure, which should purchase thee,
Sighs, tears, and oaths, and letters I have spent.
Yet no more can be due to me,
Than at the bargain made was meant,
If then thy gift of love were partial,
10 That some to me, some should to others fall,
    Dear, I shall never have thee all.

Or if then thou gavest me all,
All was but all, which thou hadst then;
But if in thy heart, since, there be or shall,
New love created be, by other men,
Which have their stocks entire, and can in tears,
In sighs, in oaths, and letters outbid me,
This new love may beget new fears,
For, this love was not vowed by thee.
20 And yet it was, thy gift being general,
The ground, thy heart is mine; what ever shall
    Grow there, dear, I should have it all.

Yet I would not have all yet;
He that hath all can have no more,
And since my love doth every day admit
New growth, thou shouldst have new rewards in store;
Thou canst not every day give me thy heart,
If thou canst give it, then thou never gavest it:
Love's riddles are, that though thy heart depart,
30 It stays at home, and thou with losing savest it:
But we will have a way more liberal,
Than changing hearts, to join them, so we shall
    Be one, and one another's all.

(1633)

SONG°

Sweetest love, I do not go,
    For weariness of thee,
Nor in hope the world can show
    A fitter love for me;
        But since that I
Must die at last, 'tis best,
To use myself in jest
    Thus by feigned deaths to die;

Yesternight the sun went hence,
    And yet is here today,   10
He hath no desire nor sense,
    Nor half so short a way:
        Then fear not me,
But believe that I shall make
Speedier journeys, since I take
    More wings and spurs than he.

O how feeble is man's power,
    That if good fortune fall,
Cannot add another hour,
    Nor a lost hour recall!   20
        But come bad chance,
And we join to it our strength,
And we teach it art and length,
    Itself o'er us to advance.

When thou sigh'st, thou sigh'st not wind,
    But sigh'st my soul away,
When thou weep'st, unkindly kind,
    My life's blood doth decay.
        It cannot be
That thou lov'st me, as thou say'st,   30
If in thine my life thou waste,
    Thou art the best of me.

Let not thy divining heart
    Forethink me any ill,
Destiny may take thy part,
    And may thy fears fulfill;
        But think that we
Are but turn'd aside to sleep;
They who one another keep
    Alive, ne'er parted be.   40

(1633)

ON HIS MISTRESS

By our first strange and fatal interview,
By all desires which thereof did ensue,
By our long starving hopes, by that remorse
Which my words' masculine persuasive force
Begot in thee, and by the memory

Song. This extremely moving lyric was allegedly written before the poet departed on a brief trip to France; it is addressed to his wife. Compare *A Valediction: Forbidding Mourning*

Of hurts, which spies and rivals threatened me,
  I calmly beg; but by thy father's wrath,
By all pains which want and divorcement hath,
  I conjure thee, and all the oaths which I
10 And thou have sworn to seal joint constancy,
  Here I unswear, and overswear them thus,
  Thou shalt not love by ways so dangerous.
Temper, O fair Love, love's impetuous rage,
  Be my true mistress still, not my feigned page;
I'll go, and, by thy kind leave, leave behind
  Thee, only worthy to nurse in my mind,
Thirst to come back; O, if thou die before,
  My soul from other lands to thee shall soar.
Thy (else Almighty) beauty cannot move
20 Rage from the seas, nor thy love teach them love,
  Nor tame wild Boreas' harshness; thou hast read
How roughly he in pieces shiveréd
  Fair Orithea,° whom he swore he loved.
Fall ill or good, 'tis madness to have proved
  Dangers unurged; feed on this flattery
That absent lovers one in th' other be.
  Dissemble nothing, not a boy, nor change
Thy body's habit, nor mind's; be not strange
  To thyself only; all will spy in thy face
30 A blushing womanly discovering grace;
  Richly clothed apes, are called apes, and as soon
Eclipsed as bright we call the moon the moon.
  Men of France, changeable chameleons,
Spittles° of diseases, shops of fashions,
  Love's fuellers, and the rightest company
Of players, which upon the world's stage be,
  Will quickly know° thee, and no less, alas!
Th' indifferent Italian, as we pass
  His warm land, well content to think thee page,°
40 Will hunt thee with such lust, and hideous rage,
  As Lot's fair guests were vext.° But none of these
Nor spongy, hydroptic° Dutch shall thee displease,
  If thou stay here. O stay here, for, for thee
England is only a worthy gallery,
  To walk in expectation, till from thence
Our greatest King call thee to His presence.
  When I am gone, dream me some happiness,
Nor let thy looks our long hid love confess,
  Nor praise, nor dispraise me, nor bless nor curse
50 Openly love's force, nor in bed fright thy nurse
  With midnight's startings, crying out, 'Oh! oh! oh! oh!
Nurse, O my love is slain, I saw him go
  O'er the white Alps alone; I saw him, I,
Assailed, fight, taken, stabbed, bleed, fall, and die.'
  Augur me better chance, except dread Jove
Think it enough for me to have had thy love.
  (1633)

On His Mistress **21-23 Boreas' . . . Orithea.** In Greek mythology Boreas was the personification of the north wind. He abducted Orithea, daughter of Erechtheus, king of Athens. According to some versions, he lived happily with Orithea at his abode on Mt. Haemus in Thrace; according to others, his violent lovemaking destroyed her **34 Spittles,** hospitals; there may be an unpleasant play on words here **37 know,** have sexual intercourse with **38-39 Th' . . . page,** a characteristic slur on the alleged homosexuality of the Italian dandy **41 Lot's . . . vext.** *Genesis*, Chapter 19 **42 hydroptic,** afflicted with dropsy

THE CANONIZATION

For God's sake hold your tongue, and let me love,
  Or chide my palsy, or my gout,
My five gray hairs, or ruined fortune, flout,
  With wealth your state, your mind with arts im-
      prove,
    Take you a course,° get you a place,°
    Observe His Honor, or His Grace,
Or the King's real, or his stamped face°
    Contemplate; what you will, approve,°
  So you will let me love.

Alas, alas, who's injured by my love?   10
  What merchant's ships have my sighs drowned?
Who says my tears have overflowed his ground?
  When did my colds a forward spring remove?°
    When did the heats which my veins fill
    Add one more to the plaguy bill?°
Soldiers find wars, and lawyers find out still
  Litigious men, which quarrels move,
  Though she and I do love.

Call us what you will, we are made such by love;
  Call her one, me another fly,°   20
We're tapers too, and at our own cost die,
  And we in us find the eagle and the dove.°
    The phoenix° riddle hath more wit
    By us: we two being one, are it.
So, to one neutral thing both sexes fit.
  We die and rise the same, and prove
  Mysterious by this love.

We can die by it, if not live by love,
  And if unfit for tombs and hearse
Our legend be, it will be fit for verse;   30
  And if no piece of chronicle we prove,
    We'll build in sonnets pretty rooms;
    As well a well-wrought urn becomes
The greatest ashes, as half-acre tombs,
  And by these hymns,° all shall approve
  Us canonized for love:

And thus invoke us: You whom reverend love
  Made one another's hermitage;
You, to whom love was peace, that now is rage;
  Who did the whole world's soul contract, and drove
    Into the glasses of your eyes
    (So made such mirrors, and such spies,

The Canonization **5 Take you a course,** in the general sense of "settling yourself in life" **place,** an appointment at court or elsewhere **7 stamped face,** on coins **8 approve.** Put it to the proof **13 my colds . . . remove,** that is, by freezing it up **15 plaguy bill,** weekly lists of deaths from the plague **20 fly.** Like the fly, a symbol of transitory life, we are burned up in "tapers" which consume themselves. There is a hint here of the old superstition that every act of intercourse subtracts a day from one's life. (To "die," in the punning terminology of the 17th century, was to consummate the act of sex; see Donne's *The Legacy*) **22 the eagle and the dove.** Here both are symbols of earthly wisdom (strength) and heavenly meekness (purity), the latter paradoxically more powerful than the former **23 phoenix,** a symbol of immortality as well as of undying desire **35 hymns,** Donne's own poems, transformed into hymns in a new love-religion

That they did all to you epitomize)
    Countries, towns, courts: Beg from above
    A pattern of your love!
(1633)

A VALEDICTION:
FORBIDDING MOURNING°

As virtuous men pass mildly away,
    And whisper to their souls to go,
Whilst some of their sad friends do say
    The breath goes now, and some say, No;

So let us melt, and make no noise,
    No tear-floods, nor sigh-tempests move,
'Twere profanation of our joys
    To tell the laity our love.

Moving of th' earth brings harms and fears,
10   Men reckon what it did and meant;
But trepidation of the spheres,
    Though greater far, is innocent.

Dull sublunary° lovers' love
    (Whose soul is sense) cannot admit
Absence, because it doth remove
    Those things which elemented it.

But we by a love so much refined
    That our selves know not what it is,
Inter-assuréd of the mind,
20   Care less, eyes, lips, and hands to miss.

Our two souls therefore, which are one,
    Though I must go, endure not yet
A breach, but an expansion,
    Like gold to airy thinness beat.

If they be two, they are two so
    As stiff twin compasses° are two;
Thy soul, the fixed foot, makes no show
    To move, but doth, if th' other do.

And though it in the center sit,
30   Yet when the other far doth roam,
It leans and harkens after it,
    And grows erect, as that comes home.

Such wilt thou be to me, who must
    Like th' other foot, obliquely run;
Thy firmness makes my circle just,
    And makes me end where I begun.
(1633)

A Valediction: Forbidding Mourning. The particularly serious tone of this poem may be due to the circumstances of its composition. Izaak Walton tells us it was addressed to Donne's wife on the occasion of his trip to the Continent in 1612. Donne had many forebodings of misfortune which were verified when his wife gave birth to a stillborn child during his absence. Compare *Sweetest Love, I Do Not Go*   13 **sublunary,** beneath the moon; therefore, mundane and fickle   26 **compasses.** One of the most involved and most celebrated images in Donne's poetry

AIR AND ANGELS°

Twice or thrice had I loved thee,
Before I knew thy face or name;
So in a voice, so in a shapeless flame,
Angels affect us oft, and worshiped be;
    Still when, to where thou wert, I came,
Some lovely glorious nothing I did see.
    But since my soul, whose child love is,
Takes limbs of flesh, and else could nothing do,
    More subtle than the parent is
Love must not be, but take a body too;   10
    And therefore what thou wert, and who,
        I bid love ask, and now
That it assume thy body I allow,
And fix itself in thy lip, eye, and brow.

Whilst thus to ballast love I thought,
And so more steadily to have gone,
With wares which would sink admiration,
I saw I had love's pinnace overfraught;
    Every thy hair for love to work upon
Is much too much, some fitter must be sought;   20
    For, nor in nothing, nor in things
Extreme and scatt'ring bright, can love inhere.
    Then as an angel, face and wings
Of air, not pure as it, yet pure doth wear,
    So thy love may be my love's sphere.
        Just such disparity
As is 'twixt air and angels' purity,
'Twixt women's love and men's will ever be.
(1633)

A HYMN TO GOD THE FATHER

Wilt thou forgive that sin where I begun,
    Which was my sin, though it were done before?
Wilt thou forgive that sin through which I run,
    And do run still, though still I do deplore?
When thou hast done, thou hast not done;   5
    For I have more.

Wilt thou forgive that sin which I have won
    Others to sin, and made my sins their door?
Wilt thou forgive that sin which I did shun
    A year or two, but wallowed in a score?   10
When thou hast done, thou hast not done;
    For I have more.

I have a sin of fear, that when I've spun
    My last thread, I shall perish on the shore;
But swear by thyself that at my death thy Son   15

Air and Angels. The appearance of angels (who are pure spirit) in visible form was explained in scholastic theology by the theory that they made themselves "bodies" of air condensed to clouds

Shall shine as he shines now and heretofore;
And having done that, thou hast done;
   I fear no more.

(1633)

GOOD FRIDAY, 1613. RIDING WESTWARD

Let man's soul be a sphere, and then, in this,
The intelligence° that moves, devotion is,
And as the other spheres, by being grown
Subject to foreign motions, lose their own,
And being by others hurried every day,
Scarce in a year their natural form obey:
Pleasure or business, so, our souls admit
For their first mover, and are whirled by it.
Hence is 't, that I am carried toward the West
10 This day, when my soul's form bends toward the East.
There I should see a sun, by rising set,
And by that setting endless day beget;
But that Christ on his Cross, did rise and fall,
Sin had eternally benighted all.°
Yet dare I almost be glad, I do not see
That spectacle of too much weight for me.
Who sees God's face, that is self life, must die;
What a death were it then to see God die?
It made his own lieutenant Nature shrink,
20 It made His footstool crack, and the sun wink.°
Could I behold those hands which span the Poles,
And turn all spheres° at once pierced with those holes?
Could I behold that endless height which is
Zenith to us, and our Antipodes,
Humbled below us? or that blood which is
The seat of all our souls, if not of His,
Made dirt of dust, or that flesh which was worn
By God, for His apparel, ragged and torn?
If on these things I durst not look, durst I
30 Upon His miserable Mother cast mine eye,
Who was God's partner here, and furnish'd thus
Half of that sacrifice, which ransomed us?
Though these things, as I ride, be from mine eye,
They are present yet unto my memory,
For that looks toward them; and Thou look'st toward
   me,
O Savior, as thou hang'st upon the tree;
I turn my back to Thee, but to receive
Corrections, till Thy mercies bid Thee leave.
O think me worth Thine anger, punish me,
40 Burn off my rusts, and my deformity,
Restore Thine image, so much, by Thy grace,
That Thou may'st know me, and I'll turn my face.

(1633)

Good Friday, 1613. 2 **intelligence,** angel. According to medieval astronomy,
each heavenly sphere was under the guardianship of one of the angels   11–
14 **There I should . . . all.** The poet in the West deliberately turns his back to the
East (where Christ was crucified), lest he see Christ die on the Cross. The sun is
symbolic not only of the fatal day of Good Friday but also of Christ who died as
His influence was growing ("by rising set"), and by His death brought endless day
to all those who believe in Him. If Christ had not so died, sin would have benighted us al   20 **It made . . . sun wink,** a reference to the perturbations of nature which attended the death of Christ, particularly to the earthquake. The identification of the earth with God's footstool is from *Isaiah,* 66:1   22 **turn all
spheres.** Christ is often spoken of as the first *mover* of the universe

THE THIRD SATIRE

Kind pity chokes my spleen; brave scorn forbids
Those tears to issue which swell my eyelids;
I must not laugh, nor weep sins, and be wise;
Can railing then cure these worn maladies?
Is not our mistress fair Religion,
As worthy of all our soul's devotion,
As virtue was to the first blinded age?
Are not Heaven's joys as valiant to assuage
Lusts, as earth's honor was to them? Alas,
As we do them in means, shall they surpass   10
Us in the end, and shall thy father's spirit
Meet blind philosophers in Heaven, whose merit
Of strict life may be imputed faith, and hear
Thee, whom he taught so easy ways and near
To follow, damned? O if thou dar'st, fear this;
This fear great courage and high valor is.
Dar'st thou aid mutinous Dutch,° and dar'st thou lay
Thee in ships' wooden sepulchers, a prey
To leader's rage, to storms, to shot, to dearth?
Dar'st thou dive seas and dungeons of the earth?   20
Hast thou courageous fire to thaw the ice
Of frozen Norths' discoveries? and thrice
Colder than salamanders, like divine
Children in the oven,° fires of Spain, and the line,°
Whose countries limbecks° to our bodies be,
Canst thou for gain bear? and must every he
Which cries not, 'Goddess!' to thy mistress, draw,
Or eat thy poisonous words? courage of straw!
O desperate coward, wilt thou seem bold, and
To thy foes and his (who made thee to stand   30
Sentinel in his world's garrison) thus yield,
And for forbidden wars leave the appointed field?
Know thy foes: the foul Devil (whom thou
Strivest to please), for hate, not love, would allow
Thee fain, his whole realm to be quit; and as
The world's all parts wither away and pass
So the world's self, thy other loved foe, is
In her decrepit wane; and thou loving this,
Dost love a withered and worn strumpet; last,
Flesh (itself's death) and joys which flesh can taste,   40
Thou lovest; and thy fair goodly soul, which doth
Give this flesh power to taste joy, thou dost loathe.
Seek true Religion. O where? Mirreus,°
Thinking her unhoused here, and fled from us,
Seeks her at Rome; there, because he doth know
That she was there a thousand years ago;
He loves her rags so, as we here obey
The state-cloth where the prince sat yesterday.
Crantz° to such brave loves will not be enthralled,
But loves her only, who at Geneva is called   50
Religion, plain, simple, sullen, young,

The Third Satire   17 **mutinous Dutch,** a reference to the revolt of the Dutch
Protestants against their overlord, the King of Spain, out of which grew the Dutch
Republic   24 **Children in the oven,** an allusion to the Israelites Shadrach,
Meshach, and Abednego, who were cast into a fiery furnace by Nebuchadnezzar
but were preserved by God's intervention   **line,** the Equator   25 **limbecks,**
alembics   43 **Mirreus,** a name given to a young man of a particular religious
persuasion.   **Crantz** (l. 49), **Graius** (l. 55), and **Phrygius** (l. 62) are other such
youths

Contemptuous, yet unhandsome; as among
Lecherous humors, there is one that judges
No wenches wholesome, but coarse country drudges.
Graius° stays still at home here, and because
Some preachers, vile ambitious bawds, and laws
Still new like fashions, bid him think that she
Which dwells with us, is only perfect, he
Embraceth her, whom his godfather's will
60 Tender to him, being tender, as wards still
Take such wives as their guardians offer, or
Pay values. Careless Phrygius° doth abhor
All, because all cannot be good, as one
Knowing some women whores, dares marry none.
Graccus loves all as one, and thinks that so
As women do in divers countries go
In divers habits, yet are still one kind,
So doth, so is Religion; and this blind-
Ness too much light breeds; but unmoved thou
70 Of force must one, and forced but one allow;
And the right; ask thy father which is she,
Let him ask his; though truth and falsehood be
Near twins, yet truth a little elder is;
Be busy to seek her, believe me this,
He's not of none, nor worst, that seeks the best.
To adore, or scorn an image, or protest,
May all be bad; doubt wisely; in strange way
To stand inquiring right, is not to stray;
To sleep, or run wrong, is. On a huge hill,
80 Cragged and steep, Truth stands, and he that will
Reach her, about must,° and about must go;
And what the hill's suddenness resists, win so;°
Yet strive so, that before age, Death's twilight,
Thy soul rest, for none can work in that night.
To will, implies delay, therefore now do:
Hard deeds, the body's pains; hard knowledge too
The mind's endeavors reach, and mysteries
Are like the sun, dazzling, yet plain to all eyes.
Keep the truth which thou hast found; men do not
    stand
90 In so ill case here, that God hath with his hand
Signed kings' blank-charters° to kill whom they hate,
Nor are they vicars, but hangmen to Fate.
Fool and wretch, wilt thou let thy soul be tied
To Man's laws, by which she shall not be tried
At the last day? Oh, will it then boot thee
To say a Philip, or a Gregory,
A Harry, or a Martin° taught thee this?
Is not this excuse for mere contraries,
Equally strong? Cannot both sides say so?
100 That thou mayest rightly obey power, her bounds
    know;
Those past, her nature and name is changed; to be

81 **about must,** must turn around   82 **win so,** by turning around or changing plans   91 **blank-charters,** death warrants left blank, the name of the victim to be filled in at the convenience of the prosecutor   96–97 **Philip . . . Martin.** Philip and Gregory represent worldly Catholicism and ecclesiastical Catholicism, respectively; Philip is Philip II of Spain, the chief Catholic potentate of the time, and Gregory is the name of several popes—perhaps Gregory the Great (c. 600) is meant, but more likely either Gregory XII or Gregory XIV, who were popes after the Reformation. Harry is Henry VIII of England, and Martin is Martin Luther

Then humble to her is idolatry.
As streams are, Power is; those blest flowers that
    dwell
At the rough stream's calm head, thrive and do well,
But having left their roots, and themselves given
To the stream's tyrannous rage, alas, are driven
Through mills, and rocks, and woods, and at last,
    almost
Consumed in going, in the sea are lost:
So perish souls, which more choose men's unjust
Power from God claimed, than God Himself to trust. 110
(1633)

from HOLY SONNETS

3

O might those sighs and tears return again
Into my breast and eyes, which I have spent,
That I might in this holy discontent
Mourn with some fruit, as I have mourn'd in vain;
In mine Idolatry what showers of rain   5
Mine eyes did waste? what griefs my heart did rent?
That sufferance was my sin; now I repent;
'Cause I did suffer I must suffer pain.
Th' hydroptique° drunkard, and night-scouting thief,
The itchy lecher, and self tickling proud   10
Have the remembrance of past joys, for relief
Of coming ills. To (poor) me is allow'd
No ease; for, long, yet vehement grief hath been
Th' effect and cause, the punishment and sin.

5

If poisonous minerals, and if that tree,
Whose fruit threw death on else immortal us,°
If lecherous goats, if serpents envious
Cannot be damned; alas, why should I be?
Why should intent or reason, born in me,   5
Make sins, else equal, in me, more heinous?
And mercy being easy, and glorious
To God, in his stern wrath, why threatens he?
But who am I, that dare dispute with thee?
O God, Oh! of thine only worthy blood,   10
And my tears, make a heavenly Lethean° flood,
And drown in it my sin's black memory.
That thou remember them, some claim as debt,
I think it mercy, if thou wilt forget.

7

At the round earth's imagined corners, blow
Your trumpets, angels, and arise, arise
From death, you numberless infinities
Of souls, and to your scattered bodies go,
All whom the flood did, and fire shall o'erthrow,   5
All whom war, dearth, age, agues, tyrannies,

Sonnet 3   9 **Th' hydroptique,** dropsical, with an unquenchable thirst   **Sonnet 5** 1–2 **that tree . . . us.** The tree in Eden on which the forbidden fruit grew; if Adam had not eaten it, his descendants would have been immortal   11 **Lethean,** Lethe was the river in Hades whose water caused forgetfulness

Despair, law, chance, hath slain, and you whose eyes
Shall behold God, and never taste death's woe.°
But let them sleep, Lord, and me mourn a space,
10 For, if above all these, my sins abound,
'Tis late to ask abundance of thy grace,
When we are there; here on this lowly ground,
Teach me how to repent; for that's as good
As if thou hadst sealed my pardon, with thy blood.

10

Death be not proud, though some have callèd thee
Mighty and dreadful, for thou art not so,
For those whom thou think'st thou dost overthrow,
Die not, poor Death, nor yet canst thou kill me.
5 From rest and sleep, which but thy pictures be,
Much pleasure, then from thee, much more must flow,
And soonest our best men with thee do go,
Rest of their bones, and soul's delivery.
Thou art slave to fate, chance, kings, and desperate
    men,
10 And dost with poison, war, and sickness dwell,
And poppy, or charms can make us sleep as well,
And better than thy stroke; why swell'st thou then?
One short sleep past, we wake eternally,
And death shall be no more; Death, thou shalt die.

14

Batter my heart, three-personed God; for, you
As yet but knock, breathe, shine, and seek to mend;
That I may rise and stand, o'erthrow me, and bend
Your force, to break, blow, burn, and make me new.
5 I, like an usurped town, to another due,
Labor to admit you, but oh, to no end,
Reason, your viceroy in me, me should defend,
But is captived, and proves weak or untrue.
Yet dearly I love you, and would be lovèd fain,
10 But am betrothed unto your enemy:
Divorce me, untie, or break that knot again,
Take me to you, imprison me, for I
Except you enthrall me, never shall be free,
Nor ever chaste, except you ravish me.
(1633)

from DEVOTIONS UPON EMERGENT OCCASIONS

MEDITATION XVII

Perchance he for whom this bell tolls may be so ill,
as that he knows not it tolls for him; and perchance I
may think myself so much better than I am, as that
they who are about me, and see my state, may have
caused it to toll for me, and I know not that. The
church is catholic, universal, so are all her actions; all
that she does belongs to all. When she baptizes a child,

Sonnet 7   7 **you whose . . . woe,** you who will be alive at the time of the Last Judgment

that action concerns me; for that child is thereby connected to that head which is my head too, and in-
grafted into that body whereof I am a member. And 10
when she buries a man, that action concerns me: all
mankind is of one author, and is one volume; when one
man dies, one chapter is not torn out of the book, but
translated into a better language; and every chapter
must be so translated; God employs several translators; some pieces are translated by age, some by
sickness, some by war, some by justice; but God's
hand is in every translation, and his hand shall bind up
all our scattered leaves again for that library where
every book shall lie open to one another. As therefore 20
the bell that rings to a sermon calls not upon the
preacher only, but upon the congregation to come, so
this bell calls us all; but how much more me, who am
brought so near the door by this sickness. There was a
contention as far as a suit (in which both piety and
dignity, religion and estimation, were mingled), which
of the religious orders should ring to prayers first in the
morning; and it was determined, that they should ring
first that rose earliest. If we understand aright the dignity of this bell that tolls for our evening prayer, we 30
would be glad to make it ours by rising early, in that
application, that it might be ours as well as his, whose
indeed it is. The bell doth toll for him that thinks it
doth; and though it intermit again, yet from that minute that that occasion wrought upon him, he is united
to God. Who casts not up his eye to the sun when it
rises? but who takes off his eye from a comet when
that breaks out? Who bends not his ear to any bell
which upon any occasion rings? but who can remove it
from that bell which is passing a piece of himself out of 40
this world? No man is an island, entire of itself; every
man is a piece of the continent, a part of the main. If a
clod be washed away by the sea, Europe is the less, as
well as if a promontory were, as well as if a manor of
thy friend's or of thine own were: any man's death
diminishes me, because I am involved in mankind, and
therefore never send to know for whom the bell tolls; it
tolls for thee. Neither can we call this a begging of
misery, or a borrowing of misery, as though we were
not miserable enough of ourselves, but must fetch in 50
more from the next house, in taking upon us the misery
of our neighbors. Truly it were an excusable covetousness if we did, for affliction is a treasure, and scarce
any man hath enough of it. No man hath affliction
enough that is not matured and ripened by it, and made
fit for God by that affliction. If a man carry treasure in
bullion, or in a wedge of gold, and have none coined
into current money, his treasure will not defray him as
he travels. Tribulation is a treasure in the nature of it,
but it is not current money in the use of it, except we 60
get nearer and nearer our home, Heaven, by it.
Another man may be sick too, and sick to death, and
this affliction may lie in his bowels, as gold in a mine,
and be of no use to him; but this bell, that tells me of
his affliction, digs out and applies that gold to me: if by

this consideration of another's danger I take mine own into contemplation, and so secure myself, by making my recourse to my God, who is our only security.

MEDITATION XVIII

The bell rings out, the pulse thereof is changed; the tolling was a faint and intermitting pulse, upon one side; this stronger, and argues more and better life. His soul is gone out, and as a man who had a lease of one thousand years after the expiration of a short one, or an inheritance after the life of a man in a consumption, he is now entered into the possession of his better estate. His soul is gone, whither? Who saw it come in, or who saw it go out? Nobody; yet everybody is sure
10 he had one, and hath none. If I will ask mere philosophers what the soul is, I shall find amongst them that will tell me, it is nothing but the temperament and harmony, and just and equal composition of the elements in the body, which produces all those faculties which we ascribe to the soul; and so in itself is nothing, no separable substance that overlives the body. They see the soul is nothing else in other creatures, and they affect an impious humility to think as low of man. But if my soul were no more than the soul
20 of a beast, I could not think so; that soul that can reflect upon itself, consider itself, is more than so. If I will ask, not mere philosophers, but mixed men, philosophical divines, how the soul, being a separate substance, enters into man, I shall find some that will tell me, that it is by generation and procreation from parents, because they think it hard to charge the soul with the guiltiness of original sin if the soul were infused into a body in which it must necessarily grow foul, and contract original sin whether it will or no; and
30 I shall find some that will tell me, that it is by immediate infusion from God, because they think it hard to maintain an immortality in such a soul, as should be begotten and derived with the body from mortal parents. If I will ask, not a few men, but almost whole bodies, whole churches, what becomes of the souls of the righteous at the departing thereof from the body, I shall be told by some, that they attend an expiation, a purification in a place of torment; by some, that they attend the fruition of the sight of God in a place of rest,
40 but yet but of expectation; by some, that they pass to an immediate possession of the presence of God. St. Augustine studied the nature of the soul as much as any thing, but the salvation of the soul; and he sent an express messenger to St. Jerome, to consult of some things concerning the soul; but he satisfies himself with this: "Let the departure of my soul to salvation be evident to my faith, and I care the less how dark the

entrance of my soul into my body be to my reason." It is the going out, more than the coming in, that con-
cerns us. This soul this bell tells me is gone out, 50 whither? Who shall tell me that? I know not who it is, much less what he was, the condition of the man, and the course of his life, which should tell me whither he is gone, I know not. I was not there in his sickness, nor at his death; I saw not his way nor his end, nor can ask them who did, thereby to conclude or argue whither he is gone. But yet I have one nearer me than all these, mine own charity; I ask that, and that tells me he is gone to everlasting rest, and joy, and glory. I owe him a good opinion; it is but thankful charity in me, be- 60 cause I received benefit and instruction from him when his bell tolled; and I, being made the fitter to pray by that disposition, wherein I was assisted by his occasion, did pray for him; and I pray not without faith; so I do charitably, so I do faithfully believe, that that soul is gone to everlasting rest, and joy, and glory. But for the body, how poor a wretched thing is that? we cannot express it so fast, as it grows worse and worse. That body, which scarce three minutes since was such a house, as that that soul, which made but one step 70 from thence to Heaven, was scarce thoroughly content to leave that for Heaven; that body hath lost the name of a dwelling-house, because none dwells in it, and is making haste to lose the name of a body, and dissolve to putrefaction. Who would not be affected to see a clear and sweet river in the morning, grow a kennel of muddy landwater by noon, and condemned to the saltness of the sea by night? and how lame a picture, how faint a representation is that, of the precipitation of man's body to dissolution? Now all the parts built up, 80 and knit by a lovely soul, now but a statue of clay, and now these limbs melted off, as if that clay were but snow; and now the whole house is but a handful of sand, so much dust, and but a peck of rubbish, so much bone. If he who, as this bell tells me, is gone now, were some excellent artificer, who comes to him for a cloak or a garment now? or for counsel, if he were a lawyer? if a magistrate, for justice? man, before he hath his immortal soul, hath a soul of sense, and a soul of vegetation before that: this immortal soul did not 90 forbid other souls to be in us before, but when this soul departs, it carries all with it; no more vegetation, no more sense. Such a mother-in-law is the earth, in respect of our natural mother; in her womb we grew, and when she was delivered of us, we were planted in some place, in some calling in the world; in the womb of the earth we diminish, and when she is delivered of us, our grave opened for another; we are not transplanted, but transported, our dust blown away with profane dust, with every wind. 100
(1624)

GEORGE HERBERT
1593–1633

The most important of the metaphysical poets after John Donne is George Herbert, a man of singular purity and fervor. Born of Welsh parents in Montgomery in 1593, he was educated at Westminster School and Trinity College, Cambridge, where his brilliance as a student and a public speaker won for him the post of university orator when he was only eighteen. In 1626 he became deacon in Lincoln Cathedral, and in 1630 he was ordained as an Anglican priest and assigned to the rectory of Fulston St. Peter's, Bemerton, Wiltshire. He died of consumption only three years later (1633) and was buried under the altar at which he had served with a reverence and devotion that distinguished him throughout England. *The Temple*, a collection of his sacred poems published the year of his death, contains one hundred twenty-nine poems that form a record of his difficult spiritual progression.

THE PEARL

I know the ways of learning, both the head
And pipes that feed the press and make it run;
What reason hath from nature borrowéd,
Or of itself, like a good housewife, spun
In laws and policy; what the stars conspire;
What willing nature speaks, what forced by fire;°
Both the old discoveries, and the new-found seas,
The stock and surplus, cause and history;
All these stand open, or I have the keys:
10 Yet I love Thee.

I know the ways of honor, what maintains
The quick returns of courtesy and wit;
In vies of favors whether party gains
When glory swells the heart, and moldeth it
To all expressions, both of hand and eye,
Which on the world a true-love knot may tie,
And bear the bundle wheresoe'er it goes;
How many drams of spirit there must be
To sell my life unto my friends or foes:
20 Yet I love Thee.

I know the ways of pleasure, the sweet strains,
The lullings and the relishes of it;
The propositions of hot blood and brains;
What mirth and music mean; what love and wit
Have done these twenty hundred years and more;
I know the projects of unbridled store;°
My stuff is flesh, not brass; my senses live,
And grumble oft that they have more in me

Than he that curbs them, being but one to five:
Yet I love Thee.   30

I know all these, and have them in my hand;
Therefore not seeléd° but with open eyes
I fly to Thee, and fully understand
Both the main sale and the commodities;
And at what rate and price I have Thy love,
With all the circumstances that may move.
Yet through the labyrinths, not my groveling wit,
But Thy silk twist° let down from heaven to me,
Did both conduct and teach me how by it
To climb to Thee.   40

(1633)

THE COLLAR°

I struck the board, and cried, "No more; I will abroad!
What! shall I ever sigh and pine?
My lines and life are free; free as the road,
    Loose as the wind, as large as store.°
        Shall I be still in suit?°
    Have I no harvest but a thorn
    To let me blood, and not restore
What I have lost with cordial fruit?
        Sure there was wine
    Before my sighs did dry it; there was corn   10
        Before my tears did drown it;
    Is the year only lost to me?
        Have I no bays to crown it,
No flowers, no garlands gay? all blasted,
        All wasted?
    Not so, my heart, but there is fruit,
        And thou hast hands.
    Recover all thy sigh-blown age
On double pleasures; leave thy cold dispute
Of what is fit and not; forsake thy cage,   20
        Thy rope of sands
Which petty thoughts have made, and made to thee
    Good cable, to enforce and draw,
        And be thy law,
    While thou didst wink° and wouldst not see.
        Away! take heed;
        I will abroad.
Call in thy death's head there, tie up thy fears;
        He that forbears
    To suit and serve his need   30
        Deserves his load."
But as I raved, and grew more fierce and wild
        At every word,
    Methought I heard one calling, "Child";
        And I replied, "My Lord."

(1633)

The Pearl 6 **forced by fire,** wrung from nature in the flame of the experimental laboratory 26 **store,** wealth

32 **seeléd,** blinding a hawk by running threads through its eyelids, then tying them over its head (in falconry) 38 **twist,** cord **The Collar,** the symbol of submission and spiritual restraint (cf. *Matthew,* 11:29: "Take my yoke upon you") 4 **store,** abundance 5 **still in suit,** always forced to entreat 25 **wink,** close the eyes

VIRTUE

Sweet day, so cool, so calm, so bright,
   The bridal of the earth and sky:
The dew shall weep thy fall tonight;
     For thou must die.

5 Sweet rose, whose hue, angry° and brave,°
   Bids the rash gazer wipe his eye:
Thy root is ever in its grave,
     And thou must die.

Sweet spring, full of sweet days and roses,
10   A box where sweets compacted lie;°
My music shows ye have your closes,°
     And all must die.

Only a sweet and virtuous soul,
   Like seasoned timber, never gives;
15 But though the whole world turn to coal,
     Then chiefly lives.
(1633)

EASTER WINGS

Lord, who createdst man in wealth and store,
   Though foolishly he lost the same,
     Decaying more and more,
       Till he became
        Most poor:
        With thee
       O let me rise
     As larks, harmoniously,
   And sing this day thy victories:
10 Then shall the fall° further the flight in me.

My tender age in sorrow did begin:
   And still with sicknesses and shame
     Thou didst so punish sin,
       That I became
        Most thin.
        With thee
       Let me combine,
     And feel this day thy victory:
   For, if I imp° my wing on thine,
20 Affliction shall advance the flight in me.
(1633)

JORDAN (I)°

Who says that fictions only and false hair
Become a verse? Is there in truth no beauty?
Is all good structure in a winding stair?

May no lines pass, except they do their duty
   Not to a true, but painted chair?   5

Is it no verse, except enchanted groves
And sudden arbors shadow coarse-spun lines?
Must purling streams refresh a lovers loves?
Must all be veiled, while he that reads, divines,
   Catching the sense at two removes?   10

Shepherds are honest people; let them sing:
Riddle who list, for me, and pull for prime:°
I envy no man's nightingale or spring;
Nor let them punish me with loss of rhyme,
   Who plainly say, *My God, My King.*   15
(1633)

JORDAN (II)

When first my lines of heavenly joys made mention,
   Such was their luster, they did so excel,
That I sought out quaint words, and trim invention;
   My thoughts began to burnish,° sprout, and swell,
Curling with metaphors a plain intention,   5
   Decking the sense, as if it were to sell.

Thousands of notions in my brain did run,
   Offering their service, if I were not sped:°
I often blotted what I had begun;
   This was not quick° enough, and that was dead.   10
Nothing could seem too rich to clothe the sun,
   Much less those joys which trample on his head.

As flames do work and wind when they ascend,
   So did I weave myself into the sense;
But while I bustled, I might hear a friend   15
   Whisper, "How wide° is all this long pretense!
There is in love a sweetness ready penned:
   Copy out only that, and save expense."
(1633)

LOVE (III)

Love bade me welcome: yet my soul drew back,
     Guilty of dust and sin.
But quick-eyed Love, observing me grow slack°
     From my first entrance in,
Drew nearer to me, sweetly questioning   5
     If I lacked anything.

"A guest," I answered, "worthy to be here":
     Love said, "You shall be he."
"I, the unkind, ungrateful? Ah, my dear,
     I cannot look on thee."   10

Virtue 5 **angry,** red **brave,** beautiful, splendid 10 **box . . . lie.** The earth is teeming with beauty about to burst forth 11 **closes,** end **Easter Wings** 10 **the fall.** Man's fall was a *felix culpa* or happy fault because it led to the Incarnation and Redemption 19 **imp,** graft **Jordan (I).** "Crossing Jordan" is a symbol for entering the Promised Land

12 **pull for prime,** to draw a lucky card in the card game primero **Jordan (II)** 4 **burnish,** grow bright 8 **sped,** succeeding 10 **quick,** lively 16 **wide,** far from the true subject **Love (III)** 3 **slack,** backward

Love took my hand, and smiling did reply,
　　"Who made the eyes but I?"

"Truth, Lord; but I have marred them; let my shame
　　Go where it doth deserve."
15 "And know you not," says Love, "who bore the
　　blame?"
　　　　"My dear, then I will serve."
"You must sit down," says Love, "and taste my
　　meat."
　　　　So I did sit and eat.

(1633)

THE PULLEY

　　　　When God at first made man,
Having a glass of blessings standing by;
Let us (said he) pour on him all we can:
Let the worlds riches, which dispersed lie,
5 　　　　Contract into a span.

　　　　So strength first made a way;
Then beauty flowed, then wisdom, honor, pleasure:
When almost all was out, God made a stay,
Perceiving that alone of all his treasure
10 　　　　Rest in the bottom lay.

　　　　For if I should (said he)
Bestow this jewel also on my creature,
He would adore my gifts instead of me,
And rest in Nature, not the God of Nature:
15 　　　　So both should losers be.

　　　　Yet let him keep the rest,°
But keep them with repining restlessness:
Let him be rich and weary, that at least,
If goodness lead him not, yet weariness
20 　　　　May toss him to my breast.

　(1633)

RICHARD CRASHAW 1613?–1649

The most mystical of the sacred metaphysical poets
was Richard Crashaw, son of a Puritan divine of
London noted for his violent hatred of Roman
Catholics. At Pembroke Hall, Cambridge, where he
went in 1631 when he was about nineteen, Crashaw
took a keen interest in ecclesiastical matters. His
further interest in the Spanish and Italian mystics fed
his own deep strain of mysticism. After losing his fellowship at Cambridge because of his Royalist and High
Church leanings, he converted to Roman Catholicism.
He was in Paris in 1646, and shortly afterward he became secretary to Cardinal Palotta, governor of Rome.
By condemning the corruption of other members of
the governor's staff, he aroused their resentment and
was sent for his own safety to the Church of Our Lady
of Loretto. He died almost immediately afterward,
perhaps poisoned by his enemies. He was a follower
of George Herbert, as indicated by the title of his first
volume of secular and sacred poems published in
1646, *Steps to the Temple*. These and later poems were
issued in Paris three years after his death as *Carmen
Deo Nostro*.

ON THE WOUNDS OF OUR CRUCIFIED LORD

O these wakeful wounds of thine!
　　Are they Mouths? or are they eyes?
Be they Mouths, or be they eyne,°
　　Each bleeding part some one supplies.

Lo! a mouth, whose full-bloomed lips　　　　5
　　At too dear a rate are roses.
Lo! a blood-shot eye! that weeps
　　And many a cruel tear discloses.

O thou that on this foot hast laid
　　Many a kiss, and many a Tear,　　　　10
Now thou shalt have all repaid,
　　Whatsoe'er thy charges were.

This foot hath got a Mouth and lips,
　　To pay the sweet sum of thy kisses;
To pay thy Tears, an Eye that weeps　　　　15
　　Instead of Tears such Gems as this° is.

The difference only this appears,
　　(Nor can the change offend)
The debt is paid in *Ruby*-Tears,
　　Which thou in Pearls did'st lend.　　　　20

(1646)

UPON THE INFANT MARTYRS°

To see both blended in one flood
The Mothers' Milk, the Children's blood,
Makes me doubt if Heaven will gather,
Roses hence, or Lilies rather.

(1646)

On the Wounds 3 **eyne,** plural of "eye"　16 **this,** a drop of blood　**Upon the Infant Martyrs.** The slaughter of the Innocents ordered by Herod after the birth of Christ is Crashaw's subject here

The Pulley 16 **rest,** with a play on the two meanings of "rest"

THE FLAMING HEART°

Upon the book and picture of the seraphical Saint Teresa,° as she is usually expressed° with a seraphim beside her.

Well-meaning readers! you that come as friends,
And catch the precious name this piece pretends:°
Make not too much haste to admire
That fair-cheeked fallacy of fire.
That is a Seraphim, they say,
And this the great Teresia.
Readers, be ruled by me, and make
Here a well-placed and wise mistake:
You must transpose the picture quite
10   And spell it wrong to read it right;
Read *him* for *her* and *her* for *him*,
And call the Saint the Seraphim.
   Painter, what didst thou understand,
To put her dart into his hand!
See, even the years and size of him
Shows this the Mother Seraphim.
This is the mistress-flame; and duteous he,
Her happy fire-works here comes down to see.
O most poor-spirited of men!
20   Had thy cold pencil kissed her pen
Thou couldst not so unkindly err
To show us this faint shade for her.
Why, man, this speaks pure mortal frame,
And mocks with female frost love's manly frame.
One would suspect thou mean'st to paint
Some weak, inferior, woman saint.
But had thy pale-faced purple took
Fire from the burning cheeks of that bright book,
Thou wouldst on her have heaped up all
30   That could be found seraphical:
Whate'er this youth of fire wears fair,
Rosy fingers, radiant hair,
Glowing cheek and glistering wings,
All those fair and flagrant things,
But before all, that fiery dart
Had filled the hand of this great heart.
   Do then as equal right requires,
Since his the blushes be, and hers the fires,
Resume and rectify thy rude° design,
40   Undress° thy seraphim into mine.
Redeem this injury of thy art,
Give him the veil, give her the dart.
   Give him the veil, that he may cover
The red cheeks of a rivaled lover,
Ashamed that our world now can show
Nests of new Seraphims here below.
   Give her the dart, for it is she
(Fair youth) shoots both thy shaft and thee.

Say, all ye wise and well-pierced hearts
That live and die amidst her darts,   50
What is it your tasteful spirits do prove
In that rare life of her and love?
Say and bear witness. Sends she not
A Seraphim at every shot?
What magazines of immortal arms there shine!
Heaven's great artillery in each love-spun line.
Give then the dart to her who gives the flame,
Give him the veil who kindly takes the shame.
   But if it be the frequent fate
Of worst faults to be fortunate;   60
If all's prescription,° and proud wrong
Hearkens not to an humble song,
For all the gallantry of him,
Give me the suffering Seraphim.
His be the bravery of all those bright things,
The glowing cheeks, the glistering wings,
The rosy hand, the radiant dart,
Leave her alone the Flaming Heart.
   Leave her that, and thou shalt leave her
Not one loose shaft, but love's whole quiver.   70
For in love's field was never found
A nobler weapon than a wound.
Love's passives are his activ'st part,
The wounded is the wounding heart.
O heart! the equal poise of love's both parts,°
Big alike with wounds and darts,
Live in these conquering leaves,° live all the same;
And walk through all tongues one triumphant flame.
Live here, great heart; and love and die and kill,
And bleed and wound; and yield and conquer still.   80
Let this immortal life, where'er it comes,
Walk in a crowd of loves and martyrdoms.
Let mystic deaths wait on 't, and wise souls be
The love-slain witnesses of this life of thee:
O sweet incendiary! show here thy art,
Upon this carcass of a hard, cold heart;
Let all thy scattered shafts of light, that play
Among the leaves of thy large books of day,°
Combined against this breast, at once break in
And take away from me myself and sin!   90
This gracious robbery shall thy bounty be,
And my best fortunes such fair spoils of me.°
O thou undaunted daughter of desires!
By all thy dower of lights and fires;
By all the eagle° in thee, all the dove;°
By all thy lives and deaths of love;
By thy large draughts of intellectual day,°
And by thy thirsts of love more large than they;
By all thy brim-filled bowls of fierce desire,
By thy last morning's draught of liquid fire;°   100
By the full kingdom of that final kiss

The Flaming Heart. An English translation of the *Vida, The Flaming Hart or the Life of the Glorious S. Teresa* was published in Antwerp in 1642   **Saint Teresa,** (1515–1582) a Spanish mystic famous for her passionate visions and holy labors   **expressed,** depicted   2 **pretends,** holds forth or presents   39 **rude,** crude   40 **undress,** change by changing the costume of

61 **if all's prescription,** "right acquired through long possession"   75 **both parts,** the passive (wounds) and the active (darts)   77 **leaves,** pages of the saint's book   88 **books of day,** books of spiritual and intellectual enlightenment   92 **And my . . . of me.** My best fortune will be to be despoiled in this way   95 **eagle,** symbol of wisdom   **dove,** symbol of mercy   97 **intellectual day,** the light of pure thought   100 **last . . . fire.** Teresa was supposed to have been killed by a seraph who plunged a fiery lance into her heart

That seized thy parting soul, and sealed thee His;
By all the heavens thou hast in Him,
Fair sister of the seraphim,
By all of Him we have in thee,
Leave nothing of myself in me!
Let me so read thy life that I
Unto all life of mine may die!
(1652)

HENRY VAUGHAN
1622–1695

Henry Vaughan was born in 1622 at Newton St.
Bridget on the Usk in Wales. He loved his native
mountains, and when he came to select a pen name,
he chose "the Silurist" from the Silures, or ancient inhabitants of southern Wales. From Jesus College, Oxford, Vaughan went to London to study law but
changed his mind and decided to devote himself to
medicine. In 1647 he returned to his home on the Usk
to live and practice. From this time until 1650 he suffered from a prolonged illness that deepened and
strengthened his spiritual nature. His religious and
literary guide became "the blessed man Mr. George
Herbert" (though Vaughan was only a boy when the
older man died), and the two show many similarities.
Vaughan's sacred poems appeared in 1650 as *Silex
Scintillans* and his secular verse as *Poems* (1646) and
Thalia Rediviva (1678). Vaughan outlived the other
metaphysical poets by many years, not dying until
1695.

THE RETREAT

Happy those early days, when I
Shined in my angel-infancy!
Before I understood this place
Appointed for my second race,°
Or taught my soul to fancy aught
But a white, celestial thought;
When yet I had not walked above
A mile or two from my first love,
And looking back at that short space,
10 Could see a glimpse of his bright face;
When on some gilded cloud or flower
My gazing soul would dwell an hour,
And in those weaker glories spy
Some shadows of eternity;
Before I taught my tongue to wound
My conscience with a sinful sound,

Or had the black art to dispense,
A several° sin to every sense,
But felt through all this fleshly dress
Bright shoots of everlastingness.   20
  O, how I long to travel back,
And tread again that ancient track,
That I might once more reach that plain,
Where first I left my glorious train;
From whence the enlightened spirit sees
That shady city° of palm trees.
But ah! my soul with too much stay
Is drunk, and staggers in the way!
Some men a forward motion love,
But I by backward steps would move;   30
And when this dust falls to the urn,
In that state I came, return.
(1650)

THE WORLD

I saw Eternity the other night,
Like a great ring of pure and endless light,
  All calm, as it was bright;
And round beneath it, Time, in hours, days, years,
  Driven by the spheres
Like a vast shadow moved; in which the world
  And all her train were hurled.
The doting lover in his quaintest strain
  Did there complain;
Near him, his lute, his fancy, and his flights,°   10
  Wit's sour delights,
With gloves, and knots, the silly snares of pleasure,
  Yet his dear treasure,
All scattered lay, while he his eyes did pour
  Upon a flower.

The darksome statesman, hung with weights and woe,
Like a thick midnight-fog moved there so slow,
  He did not stay, nor go;
Condemning thoughts, like sad eclipses, scowl
  Upon his soul,   20
And clouds of crying witnesses without
  Pursued him with one shout.
Yet digged the mole, and lest his ways be found,
  Worked under ground,
Where he did clutch his prey; but one did see
  That policy;
Churches and altars fed him; perjuries
  Were gnats and flies;
It rained about him blood and tears, but he
  Drank them as free.   30

The fearful miser on a heap of rust
Sat pining all his life there, did scarce trust
  His own hands with the dust,

18 **several,** separate, different   26 **shady city,** the celestial city (heaven)   **The
World**   10 **fancy . . . flights,** his love poems

The Retreat   4 **second race,** earthly existence

Yet would not place one piece above, but lives
    In fear of thieves.
Thousands there were as frantic as himself,
    And hugged each one his pelf;
The downright epicure placed heaven in sense,
    And scorned pretense;
40 While others, slipped into a wide excess,
    Said little less;
The weaker sort, slight, trivial wares enslave,
    Who think them brave;
And poor, despiséd Truth sat counting by
    Their victory.

Yet some, who all this while did weep and sing,
And sing and weep, soared up into the ring;
    But most would use no wing.
O fools, said I, thus to prefer dark night
50   Before true light!
To live in grots and caves, and hate the day
    Because it shows the way,
The way, which from this dead and dark abode
    Leads up to God;
A way where you might tread the sun, and be
    More bright than he!
But, as I did their madness so discuss,
    One whispered thus
"This ring the Bridegroom did for none provide,
60   But for his bride."
    (1650)

THEY ARE ALL GONE
INTO THE WORLD OF LIGHT

They are all gone into the world of light!
    And I alone sit lingering here;
Their very memory is fair and bright
    And my sad thoughts doth clear.

It grows and glitters in my cloudy breast,
    Like stars upon some gloomy grove,
Or those faint beams in which this hill is dressed
    After the sun's remove.

I see them walking in an air of glory,
10   Whose light doth trample on my days:
My days, which are at best but dull and hoary,
    Mere glimmering and decays.

Oh holy hope, and high humility,
    High as the heavens above!
These are your walks, and you have showed them me
    To kindle my cold love.

Dear, beauteous death! the jewel of the just,
    Shining nowhere but in the dark,
What mysteries do lie beyond thy dust,
20   Could man outlook that mark!

He that hath found some fledged bird's nest, may
    know
    At first sight, if the bird be flown;
But what fair well or grove he sings in now,
    That is to him unknown.

And yet, as angels in some brighter dreams
    Call to the soul when man doth sleep,
So some strange thoughts transcend our wonted
    themes,
    And into glory peep.

If a star were confined into a tomb,
    Her captive flames must needs burn there;   30
But when the hand that locked her up gives room,
    She'll shine through all the sphere.

Oh father of eternal life, and all
    Created glories under thee!
Resume thy spirit from this world of thrall
    Into true liberty.

Either disperse these mists, which blot and fill
    My perspective° still as they pass:
Or else remove me hence unto that hill
    Where I shall need no glass.   40
(1655)

REGENERATION

A ward, and still in bonds,° one day
    I stole abroad;
It was high spring, and all the way
    Primrosed and hung with shade;
    Yet was it frost within,
      And surly winds
Blasted my infant buds,° and sin
    Like clouds eclipsed my mind.

Stormed thus, I straight perceived my spring°
    Mere stage and show,   10
My walk a monstrous, mountained thing,
    Roughcast with rocks and snow;
    And as a pilgrim's eye,
      Far from relief,
Measures the melancholy sky,
    Then drops and rains for grief,

So sighed I upwards still; at last
    'Twixt steps and falls
I reached the pinnacle, where placed
    I found a pair of scales;   20
    I took them up and laid

They Are All Gone 38 perspective, telescope. The figure is that of a mortal
trying to see heaven through the mists of the world Regeneration 1 A ward
. . . bonds, as a young man 7 infant buds, a highly compact comparison of his
soul's developing moral nature with a tender, growing plant 9 my spring, in the
world as it appears to others. Vaughan contrasts inner and outer perspectives here

In th' one, late pains;
The other smoke and pleasures weighed,
But proved the heavier grains.°

With that some cried, "Away!" Straight I
Obeyed, and led
Full east, a fair, fresh field could spy;
Some called it Jacob's bed,°
A virgin soil which no
30   Rude feet ere trod,
Where, since he stepped there, only go
Prophets and friends of God.

Here I reposed; but scarce well set,
A grove descried
Of stately height, whose branches met
And mixed on every side;
I entered, and once in,
Amazed to see 't,
Found all was changed, and a new spring
40 Did all my senses greet.

The unthrift sun shot vital gold,
A thousand pieces,
And heaven its azure did unfold,
Checkered with snowy fleeces;
The air was all in spice,
And every bush
A garland wore; thus fed my eyes,
But all the ear lay hush.°

Only a little fountain lent
50   Some use for ears,
And on the dumb shades language spent,
The music of her tears;

I drew her near, and found
The cistern full
Of divers stones, some bright and round,
Others ill-shaped and dull.

The first, pray mark, as quick as light
Danced through the flood,
But the last, more heavy than the night,
Nailed to the center stood;   60
I wondered much, but tired
At last with thought,
My restless eye that still desired
As strange an object brought.

It was a bank of flowers, where I descried,
Though 'twas midday,
Some fast asleep, others broad-eyed
And taking in the ray;
Here, musing long, I heard
A rushing wind   70
Which still increased, but whence it stirred
No where I could not find.

I turned me round, and to each shade
Dispatched an eye
To see if any leaf had made
Least motion or reply,
But while I listening sought
My mind to ease
By knowing where 'twas; or where not,
It whispered, "Where I please."°   80

"Lord," then said I, "on me one breath,
And let me die before my death!"
(1650)

24 **heavier grains.** The speaker's pleasures weigh more and are thus more valuable than his pains   28 **Jacob's bed.** Jacob's ladder led him to a vision of a new order   48 **hush,** quiet

80 **Where I please.** See *John*, 3:8

ROBERT BURTON
1577–1640

Born into a genteel country family of Leicestershire, the fourth of nine children, Burton received a standard early education and later went to Oxford. He graduated in 1602 but remained to study divinity, finally receiving his B.D. in 1614. It is a popular tradition, unsubstantiated by records, that his first-hand experience with the "disease" which he later anatomized so minutely occurred during the unusually long period of time between his two academic degrees. In any event, he distinguished himself as a scholar and stayed at Oxford for the rest of his life. Burton per-

formed his clerical duties conscientiously but otherwise lived wholly among his books. He never married and, as he said himself, "never travelled but in Map or Card." He devoted all his energies to the research, composition, and continual revision of *The Anatomy of Melancholy*, first published in 1621 and revised five times in his lifetime. The book, which Burton considered primarily a medical treatise, is divided into three sections: the first deals with the causes and manifestations of melancholy, the second with its cure, and the third with two classic varieties of melancholy, love and religious melancholy. The "melancholy man," the personality type that generated so much interest in the seventeenth century, still exists today but has a different name (a neurotic, perhaps, or a pessimist). To the modern reader, Burton's *Anatomy* is not only an encyclopedia of quaint, curious lore and lively digressions on a multitude of topics but also a work of considerable emotional and moral perception.

from THE ANATOMY OF MELANCHOLY

PART. I, SECT. I, MEMB. III, SUBSECT. I.—*Definition of Melancholy, Name, Difference*

Having thus briefly anatomized the body and soul of man, as a preparative to the rest, I may now freely proceed to treat of my intended subject, to most men's capacity; and after many ambages,° perspicuously define what this melancholy is, show his name and differences. The name is imposed from the matter, and disease denominated from the material cause: as Bruel observes, Μελανχολία, *quasi* Μέλαινα χολή, from black choler.° And whether it be a cause or an effect, a
10 disease or symptom, let Donatus Altomarus and Salvianus decide; I will not contend about it. It hath several descriptions, notations, and definitions. Fracastorius, in his second book of Intellect, calls those melancholy "whom abundance of that same depraved humour of black choler hath so misaffected, that they become mad thence, and dote in most things, or in all, belonging to election, will, or other manifest operations of the understanding." Melanelius out of Galen, Ruffus, Aetius, describe it to be "a bad and peevish
20 disease, which makes men degenerate into beasts"; Galen, "a privation or infection of the middle cell of the head," etc., defining it from the part affected, which Hercules de Saxonia approves, *lib*. I, *cap*. 16, calling it "a depravation of the principal function"; Fuchsius, *lib*. I, *cap*. 23; Arnoldus, *Breviar. lib*. I, *cap*. 18; Guianerius, and others: "by reason of black choler," Paulus adds. Halyabbas simply calls it a "commotion of the mind"; Aretaeus, "a perpetual anguish of the soul, fastened on one thing, without an
30 ague"; which definition of his Mercurialis, *de affect. cap. lib*. I, *cap*. 10, taxeth; but Aelianus Montaltus defends, *lib. de morb. cap*. I, *de melan*., for sufficient and good. The common sort define it to be "a kind of dotage"° without a fever, having for his ordinary companions fear and sadness, without any apparent occasion. So doth Laurentius, *cap*. 4; Piso, *lib*. I, *cap*. 43; Donatus Altomarus, *cap*. 7 *Art. medic*.; Jacchinus, *in com. in lib*. 9 *Rhasis ad Almansor. cap*. 15; Valesius, *Exerc*. 17; Fuchsius, *Institut*. 13, *sec*. I, *cap*. II, etc.,

which common definition, howsoever approved by 40 most, Hercules de Saxonia will not allow of, nor David Crusius, *Theat. morb. Herm. lib*. 2, *cap*. 6; he holds it unsufficient, "as rather showing what it is not, than what it is," as omitting the specifical difference, the phantasy° and brain: but I descend to particulars. The *summum genus*° is dotage, or "anguish of the mind," saith Aretaeus; "of a principal part," Hercules de Saxonia adds, to distinguish it from cramp and palsy, and such diseases as belong to the outward sense and motions; "depraved," to distinguish it from folly and 50 madness (which Montaltus makes *angor animi*,° to separate), in which those functions are not depraved, but rather abolished; "without an ague" is added by all, to sever it from frenzy, and that melancholy which is in a pestilent fever. "Fear and sorrow" make it differ from madness; "without a cause" is lastly inserted, to specify it from all other ordinary passions of "fear and sorrow." We properly call that dotage, as Laurentius interprets it, "when some one principal faculty of the mind, as imagination or reason, is cor- 60 rupted, as all melancholy persons have." It is without a fever, because the humour is most part cold and dry, contrary to putrefaction. Fear and sorrow are the true characters and inseparable companions of most melancholy, not all, as Hercules de Saxonia, *tract. posthumo de Melancholia, cap*. 2, well excepts; for to some it is most pleasant, as to such as laugh most part; some are bold again, and free from all manner of fear and grief, as hereafter shall be declared.

from PART. I, SECT. II, MEMB. III, SUBSECT. XV— *Love of Learning, or overmuch Study. With a Digression of the Misery of Scholars, and why the Muses are Melancholy*

. . . hard students are commonly troubled with gouts, catarrhs, rheums, cachexia, bradypepsia, bad eyes, stone, and colic, crudities, oppilations, vertigo, winds, consumptions, and all such diseases as come by overmuch sitting; they are most part lean, dry, ill-coloured, spend their fortunes, lose their wits, and many times their lives, and all through immoderate pains and extraordinary studies. If you will not believe the truth of this, look upon great Tostatus' and Thomas Aquinas' works, and tell me whether those men took 10 pains? peruse Austin, Hierome,° etc., and many thousands besides.

*Qui cupit optatam cursu contingere metam,
Multa tulit, fecitque puer, sudavit et alsit°*

He that desires this wished goal to gain,
Must sweat and freeze before he can attain,

The Anatomy of Melancholy   I, I, III, I   4 **ambages,** circumlocutions   9 **black choler,** black bile, one of the four humors of the old physiology   33 **a kind of dotage, etc.** This is still a good definition for the modern term *anxiety*

45 **phantasy,** fancy or imagination   46 **summum genus,** most general class   51 **angor animi,** strangling of the mind   **I, II, III, XV**   11 **Hierome,** Jerome   13 **Qui cupit, etc.,** from Horace

and labour hard for it. So did Seneca, by his own confession, *ep.* 8: "Not a day that I spend idle, part of the night I keep mine eyes open, tired with waking, and now slumbering to their continual task." Hear Tully, *pro Archia Poeta*: "Whilst others loitered, and took their pleasures, he was continually at his book"; so they do that will be scholars, and that to the hazard (I say) of their healths, fortunes, wits, and lives. How much did Aristotle and Ptolemy spend? *unius regni pretium* they say, more than a king's ransom; how many crowns per annum, to perfect arts, the one about his History of Creatures, the other on his Almagest? How much time did Thebet Benchorat employ, to find out the motion of the eighth sphere? forty years and more, some write. How many poor scholars have lost their wits, or become dizzards,° neglecting all worldly affairs and their own health, *esse* and *bene esse* [being and well-being], to gain knowledge for which, after all their pains, in this world's esteem they are accounted ridiculous and silly fools, idiots, asses, and (as oft they are) rejected, contemned, derided, doting, and mad! Look for examples in Hildesheim, *Spicil.* 2, *de mania et delirio*; read Trincavellius, *lib.* 3, *consil.* 36, *et c.* 17; Montanus, *consil.* 233; Garcaeus, *de Judic. genit. cap.* 33; *Mercurialis, consil.* 86, *cap.* 25; Prosper Calenius in his book *de atra bile*. Go to Bedlam and ask. Or if they keep their wits, yet they are esteemed scrubs° and fools by reason of their carriage: "after seven years' study,"

statua taciturnius exit,
Plerumque et risu populum guatit.

[Dumb as a statue, slow he stalks along,
And shakes with laughter loud the gazing throng.]

Because they cannot ride an horse, which every clown can do; salute and court a gentlewoman, carve at table, cringe and make congees,° which every common swasher° can do, *his populus ridet*, etc., they are laughed to scorn, and accounted silly fools by our gallants. Yea, many times, such is their misery, they deserve it: a mere scholar, a mere ass. . . .

from PART. III, SECT. II, MEMB. III

Symptoms or Signs of Love-Melancholy, in Body, Mind, good, bad, etc.

Symptoms are either of body or mind; of body, paleness, leanness, dryness, etc. *Pallidus omnis amans,° color hic est aptus amanti* [pale is every lover, this hue beseemeth love], as the poet describes lovers; *fecit amor maciem*, love causeth leanness. Avicenna, *de Ilishi, cap.* 33, makes hollow eyes, dryness, symptoms of this disease, "to go smiling to themselves, or acting as if they saw or heard some delectable object." Valleriola, *lib.* 3 *Observat. cap.* 7; Laurentius, *cap.* 10; Aelianus Montaltus, *de her. amore*; Langius, *epist.* 24, *lib.* I, *Epist. med.*, deliver as much, *corpus exsangue pallet, corpus gracile, oculi cavi* [the body bloodless and pale, a lean body, hollow eyes], lean, pale, *ut nudis qui pressit calcibus anguem* [as one who has trodden with naked foot upon a snake], hollow-eyed, their eyes are hidden in their heads, *Tenerque nitidi corporis cecidit decor* [their sleek charm falls away], they pine away, and look ill with waking, cares, sighs:

Et qui tenebant signa Phœbeæ facis
Oculi, nihil gentile nec patrium micant,

[And eyes that were like suns for brightness lose all their inherited lustre,]

with groans, griefs, sadness, dullness:

Nulla jam Cereris subit
Cura aut salutis,

want of appetite, etc. A reason of all this Jason Pratensis gives, "because of the distraction of the spirits the liver doth not perform his part, nor turns the aliment into blood as it ought, and for that cause the members are weak for want of sustenance, they are lean and pine, as the herbs of my garden do this month of May, for want of rain." The green-sickness therefore often happeneth to young women, a cachexia or an evil habit to men, besides their ordinary sighs, complaints, and lamentations, which are too frequent. As drops from a still, *ut occluso stillat ab igne liquor*, doth Cupid's fire provoke tears from a true lover's eyes:

The mighty Mars did oft for Venus shriek,
Privily moistening his horrid cheek
With womanish tears;

Ignis distillat in undas,
Testis erit largus qui rigat ora liquor;

[Fire distils into water, witness the copious stream that bathes his cheeks;]

with many such-like passions. When Chariclea was enamoured of Theagenes, as Heliodorus sets her out, "she was half distracted, and spake she knew not what, sighed to herself, lay much awake, and was lean upon a sudden": and when she was besotted on her son-in-law, *pallor deformis, marcentes oculi*, etc., she had ugly paleness, hollow eyes, restless thoughts, short wind, etc. Euryalus, in an epistle sent to Lucretia his mistress, complains amongst other grievances, *Tu mihi et somni et cibi usum abstulisti*, Thou hast taken my stomach and my sleep from me. So he describes it aright:

32 **dizzards,** fools 43 **scrubs,** mean fellows **III, II, III** 52 **make congees,** fawn and take his leave with the accustomed civilities 53 **swasher,** swaggerer
2 **Pallidus omnis, etc.** The sources of Burton's many quotations here are too numerous to be identified; most of them are from classical and medieval authors

His sleep, his meat, his drink, in him bereft,
That lean he waxeth, and dry as a shaft,
His eyes hollow and grisly to behold,
60   His hew pale and ashen to unfold,
And solitary he was ever alone,
And waking all the night making mone.

Theocritus, *Idyll.* 2, makes a fair maid of Delphi, in
love with a young man of Minda, confess as much:

*Ut vidi, ut insanii, ut animus mihi male affectus est,
Miseræ mihi forma tabescebat, neque amplius
    pompam
Ullam curabam, aut quando domum redieram
Novi, sed me ardens quidam morbus consumebat,
Decubui in lecto dies decem, et noctes decem,*
70   *Defluebant capite capilli, ipsaque sola reliqua
Ossa et cutis.*

No sooner seen I had, but mad I was,
My beauty fail'd, and I no more did care
For any pomp, I knew not where I was,
But sick I was, and evil I did fare;
I lay upon my bed ten days and nights,
A skeleton I was in all men's sights.

All these passions are well expressed by that heroical
poet in the person of Dido:

80   *At non infelix animi Phœnissa, nec unquam
Solvitur in somnos, oculisve ac pectore amores
Accipit; ingeminant curæ, rursusque resurgens
Sævit amor,* etc.

Unhappy Dido could not sleep at all,
    But lies awake, and takes no rest:
And up she gets again, whilst care and grief,
    And raging love torment her breast.

Accius Sannazarius, *Ecloga* 2, *de Galatea,* in the same
manner feigns his Lycoris tormenting herself for want
90   of sleep, sighing, sobbing, and lamenting; and Eustathius his Ismenias much troubled, and "panting at
heart, at the sight of his mistress," he could not sleep,
his bed was thorns. All make leanness, want of appetite, want of sleep ordinary symptoms, and by that
means they are brought often so low, so much altered
and changed, that as he jested in the comedy, "one can
scarce know them to be the same men."

*Attenuant juvenum vigilatæ corpora noctes,
Curaque et immenso qui fit amore dolor.*

100   [Young men grow pale and lean from the sleepless
nights and the cares and pangs of love.]

Many such symptoms there are of the body to discern
lovers by, *quis enim bene celet amorem?* [for who can
hide love?] "Can a man," saith Solomon (Prov. vi,
27), "carry fire in his bosom and not burn?" it will
hardly be hid; though they do all they can to hide it, it
must out, *plus quam mille notis* [by more than a
thousand symptoms] it may be described, *quoque
magis tegitur, tectus magis æstuat ignis* [and the more
it is hidden, the more fiercely does it burn]. 'Twas 110
Antiphanes the comedian's observation of old, love
and drunkenness cannot be concealed, *celare alia pos-
sis, hæc præter duo, vini potum,* etc.; words, looks,
gestures, all will betray them; but two of the most
notable signs are observed by the pulse and countenance. When Antiochus, the son of Seleucus, was sick
for Stratonice, his mother-in-law, and would not confess his grief, or the cause of his disease, Erasistratus
the physician found him by his pulse and countenance
to be in love with her, "because that when she came in 120
presence, or was named, his pulse varied, and he
blushed besides." In this very sort was the love of
Charicles, the son of Polycles, discovered by Panacius
the physician, as you may read the story at large in
Aristaenetus. By the same signs Galen brags that he
found out Justa, Boethius the consul's wife, to dote on
Pylades the player, because at his name still she both
altered pulse and countenance, as Poliarchus did at the
name of Argenis. Franciscus Valesius, *lib.* 3, *controv.*
13, *Med. contr.,* denies there is any such *pulsus* 130
amatorius, or that love may be so discerned; but
Avicenna confirms this of Galen out of his experience,
lib. 3, *fen.* I; and Gordonius, *cap.* 20; "Their pulse,"
he saith, "is inordinate and swift, if she go by whom he
loves"; Langius, *epist.* 24, *lib.* I, *Med. epist.;*
Nevisanus, *lib.* 4, *numer.* 66, *Syl. nuptialis*; Valescus
de Taranta; Guianerius, *tract.* 15. Valleriola sets down
this for a symptom: "Difference of pulse, neglect of
business, want of sleep, often sighs, blushings when
there is any speech of their mistress, are manifest 140
signs." But amongst the rest, Josephus Struthius, that
Polonian, in the fifth book, *cap.* 17, of his Doctrine of
Pulses, holds that this and all other passions of the
mind may be discovered by the pulse. "And if you will
know," saith he, "whether the men suspected be such
or such, touch their arteries," etc. And in his fourth
book, fourteenth chapter, he speaks of this particular
pulse, "Love makes an unequal pulse," etc.; he gives
instance of a gentlewoman, a patient of his, whom by
this means he found to be much enamoured, and with 150
whom: he named many persons, but at the last when
his name came whom he suspected, "her pulse began
to vary and to beat swifter, and so, by often feeling her
pulse, he perceived what the matter was." Apollonius,
Argonaut. lib. 4, poetically setting down the meeting
of Jason and Medea, makes them both to blush at one
another's sight, and at the first they were not able to
speak.

*Totus, Parmeno,
Tremo, horreoque, postquam aspexi hanc.* 160

[I trembled all over when I beheld her.]

Phaedria trembled at the sight of Thais, others sweat, blow short, *crura tremunt ac poplites* [their legs shake under them], are troubled with palpitation of heart upon the like occasion, *cor proximum ori*, saith Aristaenetus, their heart is at their mouth, leaps, these burn and freeze (for love is fire, ice, hot, cold, itch, fever, frenzy, pleurisy, what not?), they look pale, red, and commonly blush at their first congress,° and some-
170 times through violent agitation of spirits bleed at nose, or when she is talked of; which very sign Eustathius makes an argument of Ismene's affection, that when she met her sweetheart by chance, she changed her countenance to a maiden-blush. 'Tis a common thing amongst lovers, as Arnulphus, that merry conceited bishop, hath well expressed in a facetious epigram of his:

Alterno facies sibi dat responsa rubore,
Et tener affectum prodit utrique pudor, etc.

180 Their faces answer, and by blushing say,
How both affected are, they do betray.

But the best conjectures are taken from such symptoms as appear when they are both present; all their speeches, amorous glances, actions, lascivious gestures will bewray them; they cannot contain themselves, but that they will be still kissing. Stratocles, the physician, upon his wedding-day, when he was at dinner, *nihil prius sorbillavit, quam tria basia puellæ pangeret*, could not eat his meat for kissing the bride,
190 etc. First a word, and then a kiss, then some other compliment, and then a kiss, then an idle question, then a kiss, and when he had pumped his wits dry, can say no more, kissing and colling° are never out of season, *Hoc non deficit incipitque semper*, 'tis never at an end, another kiss, and then another, another, and another, etc.: *Huc ades, o Thelayra*; "Come, kiss me, Corinna!" . . . They cannot, I say, contain themselves, they will be still not only joining hands, kissing, but embracing, treading on their toes, etc., diving into
200 their bosoms, and that *libenter, et cum delectatione* [lasciviously and voluptuously], as Philostratus confesseth to his mistress; and Lamprias in Lucian, *mammillas premens, per sinum clam dextra*, etc., feeling their paps, and that scarce honestly sometimes: as the old man in the comedy well observed of his son, *Non ego te videbam manum huic puellæ in sinum inserere?* "Did not I see thee put thy hand into her bosom? Go to!" with many such love tricks. Juno in Lucian, *tom. 4, Deorum dial. 6*, complains to Jupiter of Ixion,
210 he looked so attentively on her, and sometimes would sigh and weep in her company; "and when I drank by chance, and gave Ganymede the cup, he would desire

169 **congress**, meeting   193 **colling**, fondling

to drink still in the very cup that I drank of, and in the same place where I drank, and would kiss the cup, and then look steadily on me, and sometimes sigh, and then again smile." If it be so they cannot come near to dally, have not that opportunity, familiarity, or acquaintance to confer and talk together; yet, if they be in presence, their eye will bewray them: *Ubi amor ibi oculus* [where I like I look], as the common saying is, 220 "Where I look I like, and where I like I love"; but they will lose themselves in her looks.

Alter in alterius jactantes lumina vultus,
Quærebant taciti noster ubi esset amor.

[Eyes looking into eyes asked silently, Where is your love?]

They cannot look off whom they love, they will *impregnare eam ipsis oculis*, deflower her with their eyes, be still gazing, staring, stealing faces, smiling, glancing at her, as Apollo on Leuconthoe, the Moon on her 230 Endymion, when she stood still in Caria, and at Latmos caused her chariot to be stayed. They must all stand and admire, or, if she go by, look after her as long as they can see her; she is *animæ auriga* [the charioteer of their soul], as Anacreon calls her, they cannot go by her door or window but, as an adamant, she draws their eyes to it; though she be not there present, they must needs glance that way, and look back to it. Aristaenetus of Euxitheus, Lucian, in his *Imagines*, of himself, and Tatius of Clitophon say as 240 much, *Ille oculos de Leucippe nunquam dejiciebat* [he never turned his eyes away from Leucippe], and many lovers confess, when they came in their mistress' presence, they could not hold off their eyes, but looked wistly and steadily on her, *inconnivo aspectu*, with much eagerness and greediness, as if they would look through, or should never have enough sight of her: *Fixis ardens obtutibus hæret* [his eyes clung to her with fixed and burning gaze]. . . . If so be they cannot see them whom they love, they will still be walking and 250 waiting about their mistress' doors, taking all opportunity to see them; as in Longus Sophista, Daphnis and Chloe, two lovers, were still hovering at one another's gates, he sought all occasions to be in her company, to hunt in summer, and catch birds in the frost about her father's house in the winter, that she might see him, and he her. "A king's palace was not so diligently attended," saith Aretine's Lucretia, "as my house was when I lay in Rome; the porch and street was ever full of some, walking or riding, on set purpose to see me; 260 their eye was still upon my window; as they passed by, they could not choose but look back to my house when they were past, and sometimes hem or cough, or take some impertinent occasion to speak aloud, that I might look out and observe them." 'Tis so in other places, 'tis common to every lover, 'tis all his felicity to be with her, to talk with her; he is never well but in her company, and will walk "seven or eight times a day through the street where she dwells, and make sleeveless° errands to see her"; plotting still where, when, and how to visit her,

> Lenesque sub noctem susurri,
> Composita repetuntur hora.

[Faint whispers are listened for in the dark at the trysting hour.]

And when he is gone, he thinks every minute an hour, every hour as long as a day, ten days a whole year, till he see her again.

> Tempora si numeres, bene quæ numeramus amantes.

[If thou canst count the moments which we lovers count.]

And if thou be in love, thou wilt say so too, *Et longum formosa vale,* farewell, sweetheart, *vale carissima Argenis,* etc., farewell, my dear Argenis, once more farewell, farewell. And though he is to meet her by compact, and that very shortly, perchance to-morrow, yet loath to depart, he'll take his leave again and again, and then come back again, look after, and shake his hand, wave his hat afar off. Now gone, he thinks it long till he see her again, and she him, the clocks are surely set back, the hour's past.

> Hospita, Demophoon, tua te Rhodopeia Phyllis
> Ultra promissum tempus abesse queror.

[Beloved Demophoon, thy Thracian Phyllis complains that thou tarriest beyond the promised hour.]

She looks out at window still to see whether he come, and by report Phyllis went nine times to the seaside that day, to see if her Demophoon were approaching, and Troilus to the city gates, to look for his Creseid. She is ill at ease, and sick till she see him again, peevish in the meantime, discontent, heavy, sad; and why comes he not? where is he? why breaks he promise? why tarries he so long? sure he is not well; sure he hath some mischance; sure he forgets himself and me; with infinite such. And then, confident again, up she gets, out she looks, listens and inquires, hearkens, kens; every man afar off is sure he, every stirring in the street, now he is there, that's he, *male auroræ, male soli dicit, dejeratque,* etc., the longest day that ever was, so she raves, restless and impatient; for *amor non patitur moras,* love brooks no delays: the time's quickly gone that's spent in her company, the miles short, the way pleasant; all weather is good whilst he goes to her house, heat or cold; though his teeth chatter in his head, he moves not; wet or dry, 'tis all one; wet to the skin, he feels it not, cares not at least for it, but will easily endure it and much more, because it is done with alacrity, and for his mistress' sweet sake; let the burden be never so heavy, love makes it light. Jacob served seven years for Rachel, and it was quickly gone because he loved her. None so merry if he may haply enjoy her company, he is in heaven for a time; and if he may not, dejected in an instant, solitary, silent, he departs weeping, lamenting, sighing, complaining.

But the symptoms of the mind in lovers are almost infinite, and so diverse that no art can comprehend them; though they be merry sometimes, and rapt beyond themselves for joy, yet most part, love is a plague, a torture, an hell, a bitter-sweet passion at last; *Amor melle et felle est fecundissimus, gustum dat dulcem et amarum* [love abounds with both honey and gall, it hath both sweet and bitter taste]. 'Tis *suavis amarities, dolentia delectabilis, hilare tormentum* [a sweet bitterness, a delightful grief, a cheerful torment];

> Et me melle beant suaviora,
> Et me felle necant amariora.

[Its sweetness more than honey doth delight,
Its bitterness doth worse than wormwood spite.]

. . . Your most grim Stoics and severe philosophers will melt away with this passion, and if Athenaeus belie them not, Aristippus, Apollodorus, Antiphanes, etc., have made love-songs and commentaries of their mistresses' praises, orators write epistles, princes give titles, honours, what not? Xerxes gave to Themistocles Lampsacus to find him wine, Magnesia for bread, and Myus for the rest of his diet. The Persian kings allotted whole cities to like use, *hæc civitas mulieri redimiculum præbeat, hæc in collum, hæc in crines,* one whole city served to dress her hair, another her neck, a third her hood. Ahasuerus would have given Esther half his empire, and Herod bid Herodias "ask what she would, she should have it." Caligula gave an 100,000 sesterces to his courtesan at first word, to buy her pins, and yet when he was solicited by the senate to bestow something to repair the decayed walls of Rome for the commonwealth's good, he would give but 6000 sesterces at most. Dionysius, that Sicilian tyrant, rejected all his privy councillors, and was so besotted on Myrrha, his favourite and mistress, that he would bestow no office, or in the most weightiest business of the kingdom do aught, without her especial advice, prefer, depose, send, entertain no man, though worthy and well-deserving, but by her consent; and he again whom she commended, howsoever unfit, unworthy, was as highly approved. Kings and emperors, instead of poems, build cities; Hadrian built Antinoe in Egypt, besides constellations, temples, altars, statues, images, etc., in the honour of his Antinous. Alexander bestowed infinite sums to set out his Hephaestion to all

270 **sleeveless,** causeless, unnecessary

eternity. Socrates professeth himself love's servant, ignorant in all arts and sciences, a doctor alone in love matters, *et quum alienarum rerum omnium scientiam diffiteretur,* saith Maximus Tyrius, *his sectator, hujus negotii professor,* etc., and this he spake openly, at home and abroad, at public feasts, *in Piræo, Lyceo, sub platano,* etc. [in the Piraeus, the Lyceum, under the plane-tree, etc.], the very blood-hound of beauty, as he is styled by others. But I conclude there is no end of love's symptoms, 'tis a bottomless pit. Love is subject to no dimensions; not to be surveyed by any art or engine: and besides, I am of Haedus' mind, "no man can discourse of love matters, or judge of them aright, that hath not made trial in his own person," or, as Aeneas Sylvius adds, "hath not a little doted, been mad or love-sick himself." I confess I am but a novice, a contemplator only, *Nescio quid sit amor nec amo* [I know not what is love nor am I in love], I have a tincture, for why should I lie, dissemble or excuse it? yet *homo sum,* etc., not altogether inexpert in this subject, *non sum præceptor amandi* [I am not an instructor in love], and what I say is merely reading, *ex aliorum forsan ineptiis* [perhaps from the triflings of others], by mine own observation and others' relation. . . .

PART. III, SECT. IV, MEMB. II, SUBSECT. V—*Prognostics of Despair, Atheism, Blasphemy, Violent Death, etc.*

Most part, these kind of persons make away themselves; some are mad, blaspheme, curse, deny God, but most offer violence to their own persons, and sometimes to others: "A wounded spirit who can bear?" (Prov. xviii, 14); as Cain, Saul, Achitophel, Judas, blasphemed and died. Bede saith, Pilate died desperate, eight years after Christ. Felix Plater hath collected many examples. "A merchant's wife, that was long troubled with such temptations," in the night rose from her bed, and out of the window broke her neck into the street; another drowned himself, desperate as he was, in the Rhine; some cut their throats, many hang themselves. But this needs no illustration. It is controverted by some, whether a man so offering violence to himself, dying desperate, may be saved, ay or no? If they die so obstinately and suddenly that they cannot so much as wish for mercy, the worst is to be suspected, because they die impenitent. If their death had been a little more lingering, wherein they might have some leisure in their hearts to cry for mercy, charity may judge the best; divers have been recovered out of the very act of hanging and drowning themselves, and so brought *ad sanam mentem* [to their senses], they have been very penitent, much abhorred their former act, confessed that they have repented in an instant, and cried for mercy in their hearts. If a man put desperate hands upon himself by occasion of madness or melancholy, if he have given testimony before of his regeneration, in regard he doth this not so much out of his will as *ex vi morbi* [on account of his disease], we must make the best construction of it, as Turks do, that think all fools and madmen go directly to heaven.

from PART III, SECT. IV, MEMB. II, SUBSECT. VI—*Cure of Despair by Physic, Good Counsel, Comforts, etc.*

. . . Last of all: If the party affected shall certainly know this malady to have proceeded from too much fasting, meditation, precise life, contemplation of God's judgments (for the devil deceives many by such means), in that other extreme he circumvents melancholy itself, reading some books, treatises, hearing rigid preachers, etc. If he shall perceive that it hath begun first from some great loss, grievous accident, disaster, seeing others in like case, or any such terrible object, let him speedily remove the cause, which to the cure of this disease Navarrus so much commends, *avertat cogitationem a re scrupulosa* [let him avert his thoughts from the painful subject], by all opposite means, art, and industry, let him *laxare animum,* by all honest recreations refresh and recreate his distressed soul; let him direct his thoughts, by himself and other of his friends. Let him read no more such tracts or subjects, hear no more such fearful tones, avoid such companies, and by all means open himself, submit himself to the advice of good physicians and divines, which is *contraventio scrupulorum* [a relief in uneasiness], as he calls it, hear them speak to whom the Lord hath given the tongue of the learned, to be able to minister a word to him that is weary, whose words are as flagons of wine. Let him not be obstinate, headstrong, peevish, wilful, self-conceited (as in this malady they are), but give ear to good advice, be ruled and persuaded; and no doubt but such good counsel may prove as prosperous to his soul as the angel was to Peter, that opened the iron gates, loosed his bands, brought him out of prison, and delivered him from bodily thraldom; they may ease his afflicted mind, relieve his wounded soul, and take him out of the jaws of hell itself. I can say no more, or give better advice to such as are anyway distressed in this kind, than what I have given and said. Only take this for a corollary and conclusion, as thou tenderest thine own welfare in this and all other melancholy, thy good health of body and mind, observe this short precept, give not way to solitariness and idleness. "Be not solitary, be not idle." 70

Sperate Miseri,
Cavete Felices.

[Hope, ye unhappy ones; ye happy ones, fear.]
(1638)

IZAAK WALTON
1593–1683

Izaak Walton, born in Stafford in 1593 of yeoman stock, was apprenticed to an ironmonger in London, and became a freeman of that company in 1618. Nevertheless, his inclinations were literary. He knew both Donne and Jonson and was acquainted with Sir Henry Wotton and other poets. His sympathy was with the Royalists, but since he was fifty years old when the Great Rebellion broke out, he did not actively side with either party. After the execution of the king, during the years in which Cromwell and his Parliaments were struggling to establish a stable government, this quiet man, characteristically, was peacefully writing about fish.

In his first book, a biography (1640), Walton expressed his admiration for Donne. To this study he added biographies of Sir Henry Wotton (1651), Richard Hooker (1665), George Herbert (1670), and Robert Sanderson (1678). However, his best work, as a whole, is his fisherman's classic, *The Complete Angler*, which first appeared in an abbreviated form in 1653. The framework of this mixture of learning and wisdom is five days of fishing and quiet conference between Piscator, the fisherman (Walton himself), Venator, the hunter, and Auceps, the falconer. Although three country sports are represented, the fisherman leads the others and in the end converts them to his quiet form of recreation.

from THE COMPLETE ANGLER

from THE FIRST DAY

A Conference betwixt an Angler, a Falconer, and a Hunter, each commending His Recreation

CHAPTER I PISCATOR, VENATOR, AUCEPS

PISCATOR. You are well overtaken, Gentlemen! A good morning to you both! I have stretched my legs up Tottenham Hill to overtake you, hoping your business may occasion you towards Ware whither I am going this fine fresh May morning.

VENATOR. Sir, I, for my part, shall almost answer your hopes; for my purpose is to drink my morning's draught at the Thatched House in Hoddesden; and I think not to rest till I come thither, where I have ap-
10 pointed a friend or two to meet me: but for this gentleman that you see with me, I know not how far he intends his journey; he came so lately into my company, that I have scarce had time to ask him the question.

AUCEPS. Sir, I shall by your favor bear you company as far as Theobalds, and there leave you; for then I turn up to a friend's house, who mews° a Hawk for me, which I now long to see.

VENATOR. Sir, we are all so happy as to have a fine, fresh, cool morning; and I hope we shall each be the 20 happier in the others' company. And, Gentlemen, that I may not lose yours, I shall either abate or amend my pace to enjoy it, knowing that, as the Italians say, "Good company in a journey makes the way to seem the shorter."

AUCEPS. It may do so, Sir, with the help of good discourse, which, methinks, we may promise from you, that both look and speak so cheerfully: and for my part, I promise you, as an invitation to it, that I will be as free and open-hearted as discretion will allow me 30 to be with strangers.

VENATOR. And, Sir, I promise the like.

PISCATOR. I am right glad to hear your answers; and, in confidence you speak the truth, I shall put on a boldness to ask you, Sir, whether business or pleasure caused you to be so early up, and walk so fast? for this other gentleman hath declared he is going to see a hawk, that a friend mews for him.

VENATOR. Sir, mine is a mixture of both, a little business and more pleasure; for I intend this day to do 40 all my business, and then bestow another day or two in hunting the Otter, which a friend, that I go to meet, tells me is much pleasanter than any other chase whatsoever: howsoever, I mean to try it; for tomorrow morning we shall meet a pack of Otterdogs of noble Mr. Sadler's, upon Amwell Hill, who will be there so early, that they intend to prevent the sunrising.

PISCATOR. Sir, my fortune has answered my desires, and my purpose is to bestow a day or two in helping to destroy some of those villainous vermin: for I hate 50 them perfectly, because they love fish so well, or rather, because they destroy so much; indeed so much, that, in my judgment all men that keep Otterdogs ought to have pensions from the King, to encourage them to destroy the very breed of those base Otters, they do so much mischief.

VENATOR. But what say you to the Foxes of the Nation, would not you as willingly have them destroyed? for doubtless they do as much mischief as Otters do. 60

PISCATOR. Oh, Sir, if they do, it is not so much to me and my fraternity, as those base vermin the Otters do.

AUCEPS. Why, Sir, I pray, of what fraternity are you, that you are so angry with the poor Otters?

PISCATOR. I am, Sir, a Brother of the Angle, and therefore an enemy to the Otter: for you are to note, that we Anglers all love one another, and therefore do I hate the Otter both for my own, and their sakes who are of my brotherhood.

VENATOR. And I am a lover of Hounds; I have fol- 70

The Complete Angler 17 **mews,** keeps in a cage

lowed many a pack of dogs many a mile, and heard many merry Huntsmen make sport and scoff at Anglers.

AUCEPS. And I profess myself a Falconer, and have heard many grave, serious men pity them, it is such a heavy, contemptible, dull recreation.

PISCATOR. You know, Gentlemen, it is an easy thing to scoff at any art or recreation; a little wit mixed with ill nature, confidence, and malice, will do it; but though they often venture boldly, yet they are often caught, even in their own trap, according to that of Lucian,° the father of the family of Scoffers:

> Lucian, well skilled in scoffing, this hath writ,
> Friend, that's your folly, which you think your wit:
> This you vent oft, void both of wit and fear,
> Meaning another, when yourself you jeer.

If to this you add what Solomon says of Scoffers, that they are an abomination to mankind, let him that thinks fit scoff on, and be a Scoffer still; but I account them enemies to me and all that love Virtue and Angling.

And for you that have heard many grave, serious men pity Anglers; let me tell you, Sir, there be many men that are by others taken to be serious and grave men, whom we contemn and pity. Men that are taken to be grave, because nature hath made them of a sour complexion; money-getting men, men that spend all their time, first in getting, and next, in anxious care to keep it; men that are condemned to be rich, and then always busy or discontented: for these poor rich-men, we Anglers pity them perfectly, and stand in no need to borrow their thoughts to think ourselves so happy. No, no, Sir, we enjoy a contentedness above the reach of such dispositions, and as the learned and ingenuous Montaigne° says, like himself, freely, "When my Cat and I entertain each other with mutual apish tricks, as playing with a garter, who knows but that I make my Cat more sport than she makes me? Shall I conclude her to be simple, that has her time to begin or refuse, to play as freely as I myself have? Nay, who knows but that it is a defect of my not understanding her language, for doubtless Cats talk and reason with one another, that we agree no better: and who knows but that she pities me for being no wiser than to play with her, and laughs and censures my folly, for making sport for her, when we two play together?"

Thus freely speaks Montaigne concerning Cats; and I hope I may take as great a liberty to blame any man, and laugh at him too, let him be never so grave, that hath not heard what Anglers can say in the justification of their Art and Recreation; which I may again tell you, is so full of pleasure, that we need not borrow their thoughts, to think ourselves happy.

(1653)

82 **Lucian,** Greek satirist of the second century   105 **Montaigne,** French philosopher anc essayist (1533–1592)

from THE LIFE OF DR. JOHN DONNE

[DONNE IN HIS SHROUD]

A monument being resolved upon, Dr. Donne sent for a carver to make for him in wood the figure of an urn, giving him directions for the compass and height of it; and to bring with it a board, of the just° height of his body. These being got, then without delay a choice painter was got to be in readiness to draw his picture, which was taken as followeth. Several charcoal fires being first made in his large study, he brought with him into that place his winding-sheet in his hand, and having put off all his clothes, had this sheet put on him, and so tied with knots at his head and feet, and his hands so placed as dead bodies are usually fitted to be shrouded and put into their coffin or grave. Upon this urn he thus stood with his eyes shut and with so much of the sheet turned aside as might show his lean, pale, and deathlike face, which was purposely turned towards the east, from whence he expected the second coming of his and our Saviour Jesus. In this posture he was drawn at his just height; and when the picture was fully finished, he caused it to be set by his bedside, where it continued and became his hourly object till his death, and was then given to his dearest friend and executor Dr. Henry King, then chief residentiary of St. Paul's, who caused him to be thus carved in one entire piece of white marble, as it now stands° in that church; and by Dr. Donne's own appointment, these words were to be affixed to it as his epitaph:

JOHANNES DONNE°
Sac. Theol. Profess.

Post varia studia quibus ab annis tenerrimis   30
fideliter, nec infeliciter incubuit,
instinctu et impulsu Sp. Sancti, monitu
et hortatu

REGIS JACOBI, *ordines sacros*
amplexus, anno sui Jesu, 1614, et suae aetatis 42,
decanatu hujus ecclesiae indutus 27
Novembris, 1621,

exutus morte ultimo die Martii, 1631,
hic licet in occiduo cinere aspicit eum
cujus nomen est Oriens.   40

. . . [After his death] there was by some grateful unknown friend that thought Dr. Donne's memory ought

The Life of Dr. John Donne   4 just, exact   **25 as it now stands.** Donne's tomb was destroyed in the great fire of 1666, but the statue itself may still be seen in St. Paul's Cathedral   **28–40 Johannes Donne, etc.** John Donne, Professor of Sacred Theology. After various studies, which he plied from his tenderest youth faithfully and not unsuccessfully, moved by the instinct and impulse of the Holy Spirit and the admonition and encouragement of King James, he took holy orders in the year of our Lord 1614 at the age of 42. On the 27th of November, 1621, he was made deacon of this church; and he died on the last day of March, 1631. Here in the decline and decay of ashes, may he look upon Him whose name is a Rising Sun

to be perpetuated, an hundred marks sent to his two faithful friends and executors, towards the making of his monument. It was not for many years known by whom; but after the death of Dr. Fox, it was known that it was he that sent it; and he lived to see as lively a representation of his dead friend as marble can express: a statue indeed so like Dr. Donne, that (as his
50 friend Sir Henry Wotton hath expressed himself) "it seems to breathe faintly, and posterity shall look upon it as a kind of artificial miracle."

He was of stature moderately tall; of a straight and equally proportioned body, to which all his words and actions gave an unexpressible addition of comeliness.

The melancholy and pleasant humor were in him so contempered that each gave advantage to the other, and made his company one of the delights of mankind.

His fancy was unimitably high, equaled only by his
60 great wit; both being made useful by a commanding judgment.

His aspect was cheerful, and such as gave a silent testimony of a clear knowing soul, and of a conscience at peace with itself.

His melting eye showed that he had a soft heart, full of noble compassion; of too brave a soul to offer injuries and too much a Christian not to pardon them in others.

He did much contemplate (especially after he entered into his sacred calling) the mercies of Almighty 70 God, the immortality of the soul, and the joys of heaven: and would often say in a kind of sacred ecstasy—"Blessed be God that he is God, only and divinely like himself."

He was by nature highly passionate, but more apt to reluct at° the excesses of it. A great lover of the offices of humanity, and of so merciful a spirit that he never beheld the miseries of mankind without pity and relief.

He was earnest and unwearied in the search of knowledge, with which his vigorous soul is now satis- 80 fied, and employed in a continual praise of that God that first breathed it into his active body: that body, which once was a temple of the Holy Ghost and is now become a small quantity of Christian dust:

But I shall see it reanimated.

(1640)

76 **reluct at,** oppose

ROBERT HERRICK
1591–1674

Herrick was born in 1591 in London, son of a goldsmith, but upon the death of his father in 1592 his mother moved to the village of Hampton, where the boy was reared in a rural setting that influenced him greatly. After a brief apprenticeship to a jeweler at age sixteen, he broke away from the craft and went to St. John's College, Cambridge, graduating in 1617. He then entered a ten-year period of private study and writing under the influence of Ben Jonson. Failing to secure a court appointment, he took orders in the Anglican Church and, after serving briefly as military chaplain for the duke of Buckingham, accepted from the king a position at Dean Prior in 1629. Most of his pastoral songs are connected with the period following his shift from court to country. Perhaps even the title of his collected verses, *Hesperides*, published in 1648, was meant as a tribute to the west country. Refusing to subscribe to the Solemn League and Covenant in 1647, Herrick was ejected from his charge at Dean Prior and returned to London, where he lived until the Restoration. He was then reappointed to his parish and served there until his death in 1674.

AN ODE FOR BEN JONSON

Ah, Ben!
Say how or when
Shall we, thy guests,
Meet at those lyric feasts,°
Made at the Sun,   5
The Dog, the Triple Tun;
Where we such clusters° had,
As made us nobly wild, not mad?
And yet each verse of thine
Out-did the meat, out-did the frolic wine.   10

My Ben!
Or come again,
Or send to us
Thy wit's great overplus;
But teach us yet   15
Wisely to husband it,
Lest we that talent spend;

An Ode for Ben Jonson 4 **those lyric feasts.** The names that follow are those of London taverns 7 **clusters,** of grapes (wine)

And having once brought to an end
That precious stock, the store
20 Of such a wit the world should have no more.
(1648)

THE NIGHT PIECE, TO JULIA

Her eyes the glow-worm lend thee;
The shooting stars attend thee;
   And the elves also,
   Whose little eyes glow
5 Like the sparks of fire, befriend thee.

No will-o'-the-wisp° mislight thee,
Nor snake or slow-worm° bite thee;
   But on, on thy way
   Not making a stay,
10 Since ghosts there's none to affright thee.

Let not the dark thee cumber;
What though the moon does slumber?
   The stars of the night
   Will lend thee their light
15 Like tapers clear without number.

Then, Julia, let me woo thee,
Thus, thus to come unto me;
   And when I shall meet
   Thy silv'ry feet,
20 My soul I'll pour into thee.
(1648)

CHERRY-RIPE°

Cherry-ripe, ripe, ripe, I cry,
Full and fair ones; come and buy!
If so be you ask me where
They do grow, I answer, there,
5 Where my Julia's lips do smile;
There's the land, or cherry-isle,
Whose plantations fully show
All the year where cherries grow.
(1648)

DELIGHT IN DISORDER

A sweet disorder in the dress
Kindles in clothes a wantonness.
A lawn about the shoulders thrown

Into a fine distraction;
An erring° lace, which here and there   5
Enthrals the crimson stomacher;
A cuff neglectful, and thereby
Ribbands to flow confusedly;
A winning wave, deserving note,
In the tempestuous petticoat;   10
A careless shoestring, in whose tie
I see a wild civility;—
Do more bewitch me, than when art
Is too precise in every part.
(1648)

UPON JULIA'S CLOTHES

Whenas in silks my Julia goes,
Then, then, methinks, how sweetly flows
The liquefaction of her clothes.

Next, when I cast mine eyes, and see
That brave vibration, each way free,   5
Oh, how that glittering taketh me!
(1648)

TO THE VIRGINS TO MAKE MUCH OF TIME°

Gather ye rosebuds while ye may,
   Old Time is still a-flying;
And this same flower that smiles today,
   Tomorrow will be dying.

The glorious lamp of heaven, the sun,   5
   The higher he's a-getting,
The sooner will his race be run,
   And nearer he's to setting.

That age is best which is the first,
   When youth and blood are warmer;   10
But being spent, the worse and worst
   Times still succeed the former.

Then be not coy, but use your time,
   And while ye may, go marry;
For, having lost but once your prime,   15
   You may forever tarry.
(1648)

The Night Piece, to Julia 6 **will-o'-the-wisp,** light appearing over marshy grounds which sometimes misleads travelers 7 **slow-worm,** the blindworm, incorrectly considered venomous **Cherry-Ripe.** In his tribute to Julia's lips, Herrick has adopted the familiar street cry of the London cherry vendor

Delight in Disorder 5 **erring,** straying, wandering **To the Virgins to Make Much of Time,** a classic specimen of the carpe diem lyric

CORINNA'S GOING A-MAYING°

Get up, get up for shame, the blooming morn
Upon her wings presents the god unshorn.°
  See how Aurora throws her fair
  Fresh-quilted colors through the air:
  Get up, sweet slug-a-bed, and see
  The dew bespangling herb and tree.
Each flower has wept and bowéd toward the east
Above an hour since: yet you not dressed;
  Nay! not so much as out of bed?
10   When all the birds have matins° said
  And sung their thankful hymns, 't is sin,
  Nay, profanation, to keep in,
Whenas a thousand virgins on this day
Spring, sooner than the lark, to fetch in May.

Rise, and put on your foliage, and be seen
To come forth, like the springtime, fresh and green,
  And sweet as Flora.° Take no care
  For jewels for your gown or hair:
  Fear not; the leaves will strew
20   Gems in abundance upon you:
Besides, the childhood of the day has kept,
Against you come, some orient pearls unwept;
  Come and receive them while the light
  Hangs on the dew-locks of the night:
  And Titan° on the eastern hill
  Retires himself, or else stands still
Till you come forth. Wash, dress, be brief in praying:
Few beads° are best when once we go a-Maying.

Come, my Corinna, come; and, coming mark
30 How each field turns a street,° each street a park
  Made green and trimmed with trees; see how
  Devotion gives each house a bough
  Or branch: each porch, each door ere this
  An ark, a tabernacle is,
Made up of white-thorn, neatly interwove;
As if here were those cooler shades of love.
  Can such delights be in the street
  And open fields and we not see 't?
  Come, we'll abroad; and let's obey
40   The proclamation made for May:
And sin no more, as we have done, by staying;
But, my Corinna, come, let 's go a-Maying.

There's not a budding boy or girl this day
But is got up, and gone to bring in May.
  A deal of youth, ere this, is come
  Back, and with white-thorn laden home.
  Some have dispatched their cakes and cream
  Before that we have left° to dream:

And some have wept, and wooed, and plighted troth
And chose their priest, ere we can cast off sloth: 50
  Many a green-gown has been given;°
  Many a kiss, both odd and even:
  Many a glance too has been sent
  From out the eye, love's firmament;
Many a jest told of the keys betraying
This night, and locks picked, yet we're not a-Maying.

Come, let us go while we are in our prime;
And take the harmless folly of the time.
  We shall grow old apace, and die
  Before we know our liberty.   60
  Our life is short, and our days run
  As fast away as does the sun;
And, as a vapor or a drop of rain,
Once lost, can ne 'er be found again,
  So when or you or I are made
  A fable, song, or fleeting shade,
  All love, all liking, all delight
  Lies drowned with us in endless night.
Then while time serves, and we are but decaying,
Come, my Corinna, come let 's go a-Maying.   70
(1648)

HIS PRAYER FOR ABSOLUTION

For those my unbaptizéd rimes,°
Writ in my wild unhallowed times,
For every sentence, clause, and word,
That 's not inlaid with thee, my Lord
Forgive me, God, and blot each line
Out of my book that is not thine.
But if, 'mongst all, thou find'st here one
Worthy thy benediction,
That one of all the rest shall be
The glory of my work and me.
(1648)

SIR JOHN SUCKLING
1609–1642

Born at Twickenham and educated at Cambridge and Gray's Inn, Sir John Suckling spent his early years adventuring in France and Italy. He was knighted on his return to England, and soon afterward, in 1631, he went with Charles, Marquis of Hamilton, to take part in the Protestant campaign of Gustavus Adolphus, King of Sweden, against Tilly. In 1639

Corinna's Going A-Maying. A-Maying is the festival of "bringing in the May" by invading the fields and woods early on the morning of May 1 and bringing back spring flowers and greens. The poem is a classical pastoral in form and tone 2 **the god unshorn.** Apollo, the sun, is presented by Aurora, the dawn, before he has begun to send out light streamers, his hair   10 **matins,** morning prayer service   17 **Flora,** goddess of flowers   25 **Titan,** the sun god   28 **Few beads are best.** Each bead on the rosary represents a prayer   30 **turns a street,** is crowded with young people a-Maying   48 **left,** ceased

51 **green-gown . . . given.** Many a dress has been grass-stained because its wearer has been thrown down   **His Prayer for Absolution**   1 **my unbaptizéd rimes,** his poems on worldly subjects

Suckling participated in the Scottish campaign and was with Charles I when he was defeated by Leslie. He sat in the Long Parliament in 1640 but joined a Royalist plot to make Charles head of the army, was discovered, and fled to France. Two years later he committed suicide without ever having returned to England. His works were published in 1646 under the title *Fragmenta Aurea*.

WHY SO PALE AND WAN, FOND LOVER?

Why so pale and wan, fond lover?
    Prithee, why so pale?
Will, when looking well can't move her,
    Looking ill prevail?
5 Prithee, why so pale?

Why so dull and mute, young sinner?
    Prithee, why so mute?
Will, when speaking well can't win her,
    Saying nothing do 't?
10 Prithee, why so mute?

Quit, quit for shame! This will not move,
    This cannot take her.
If of herself she will not love,
    Nothing can make her:
15 The devil take her!°
(1639)

CONSTANCY

Out upon it, I have loved
    Three whole days together!
And am like to love three more,
    If it prove fair weather.

5 Time shall molt away his wings
    Ere he shall discover
In the whole wide world again
    Such a constant lover.

But the spite on 't is, no praise
10 Is due at all to me:
Love with me had made no stays,
    Had it any been but she.

Had it any been but she,
    And that very face,
15 There had been at least ere this
    A dozen dozen in her place.
(1639)

Why So Pale and Wan, Fond Lover?   15 **The devil take her!,** a typical echo of Donne's abrupt manner

THOMAS CAREW
1598?–1639?

Thomas Carew studied at Oxford but left without taking a degree. After studying law, he went to Venice as secretary to Sir Dudley Carleton, the English ambassador. On the accession of Charles I, he was given a court position as gentleman of the king's privy chamber at the palace of Whitehall. Both a city man and a courtier, he was a member of the "tribe of Ben" and a friend of Suckling. His most elaborate production was *Coelum Britannicum,* a masque performed at Whitehall. He died about 1639, before his poems were collected and published.

DISDAIN RETURNED

He that loves a rosy cheek,
    Or a coral lip admires,
Or from starlike eyes doth seek
    Fuel to maintain his fires,
As old Time makes these decay,   5
So his flames must waste away.

But a smooth and steadfast mind,
    Gentle thoughts and calm desires,
Hearts with equal love combined,
    Kindle never-dying fires.   10
Where these are not, I despise
Lovely cheeks or lips or eyes.

No tears, Celia, now shall win
    My resolved heart to return;
I have searched thy soul within,   15
    And find naught but pride and scorn;
I have learned thy arts, and now
    Can disdain as much as thou.
Some power, in my revenge, convey
    That love to her I cast away.   20
(1640)

SONG

Ask me no more where Jove bestows,
When June is past, the fading rose;
For in your beauty's orient deep
These flowers, as in their causes, sleep.

Ask me no more whither do stray   5
The golden atoms of the day;
For in pure love heaven did prepare
Those powders to enrich your hair.

Ask me no more whither doth haste
The nightingale when May is past;
For in your sweet, dividing throat
She winters and keeps warm her note.

Ask me no more where those stars 'light
That downwards fall in dead of night;
15 For in your eyes they sit, and there
Fixéd become as in their sphere.

Ask me no more if east or west
The phoenix° builds her spicy nest;
For unto you at last she flies,
20 And in your fragrant bosom dies.
(1640)

EDMUND WALLER
1606–1687

Edmund Waller was the most popular lyric poet of his time, partly because of his use of the distich, or rhymed couplet, and partly because of his active part in the struggle between king and Parliament. Born in Coleshill in 1606, he was educated at Eton and King's College, Cambridge. Before he was twenty, he became an active debater in Parliament. He was a close associate of the Puritans Hampden (his kinsman) and Pym, but at the outbreak of hostilities, he favored the king and alienated himself from his Puritan associates. In 1643 he engaged in a plot to secure London for Charles, was arrested, fined heavily, and banished. He was pardoned in 1651 and made commissioner of trade by Cromwell in 1655. After the Restoration, he again entered Parliament, serving until his death in 1687.

GO, LOVELY ROSE!

Go, lovely rose!
Tell her that wastes her time and me,
That now she knows,
When I resemble° her to thee,
5 How sweet and fair she seems to be.

Tell her that's young,
And shuns to have her graces spied,
That hadst thou sprung
In deserts, where no men abide,
10 Thou must have uncommended died.

Small is the worth
Of beauty from the light retired;
Bid her come forth,
Suffer herself to be desired,
And not blush so to be admired.   15

Then die! that she
The common fate of all things rare
May read in thee;
How small a part of time they share
That are so wondrous sweet and fair!   20
(1645)

OF THE LAST VERSES IN THE BOOK

When we for age could neither read nor write,
The subject made us able to indite:°
The soul, with nobler resolutions decked,
The body stooping, does herself erect.
No mortal parts are requisite to raise   5
Her that, unbodied, can her Maker praise.
   The seas are quiet when the winds give o'er;
So, calm are we when passions are no more!
For then we know how vain it was to boast
Of fleeting things, so certain to be lost.   10
Clouds of affection from our younger eyes
Conceal that emptiness which age descries.
   The soul's dark cottage,° battered and decayed,
Lets in new light through chinks that time has made;
Stronger by weakness, wiser men become,   15
As they draw near to their eternal home.
Leaving the old, both worlds at once they view,
That stand upon the threshold of the new.
(1690)

RICHARD LOVELACE
1618–1658

Richard Lovelace, the eldest son of Sir William Lovelace of Woolwich, was educated at Charterhouse and Oxford. He served in the Scottish campaign of 1639 but apparently took little part in the actual fighting between king and Parliament. In 1642 he presented to the Long Parliament the petition from Kent for "a restoration of the bishops, liturgy, and common prayer" and as a result was imprisoned for seven weeks, during which time he wrote his famous lyric to Althea. He served in the French continental wars and was again imprisoned on his return to En-

---

Song   18 **phoenix**, in Greek fable a bird which lived for five hundred years and then burned itself on a funeral pile, fragrant with spices; from the ashes it arose reborn   **Go, Lovely Rose!**   4 **resemble**, liken

Of the Last Verses in the Book   2 **indite**, composing   13 **soul's dark cottage**, the body

gland in 1648. After his poems were published in 1649, he lived quietly in London until his death in 1658.

TO LUCASTA, GOING TO THE WARS°

Tell me not, sweet, I am unkind,
   That from the nunnery
Of thy chaste breast and quiet mind
   To war and arms I fly.

5 True, a new mistress now I chase,
   The first foe in the field;
And with a stronger faith embrace
   A sword, a horse, a shield.

Yet this inconstancy is such
10   As thou too shalt adore;
I could not love thee, dear, so much,
   Loved I not honor more.
(1649)

TO ALTHEA, FROM PRISON°

When Love with unconfinéd wings
   Hovers within my gates,
And my divine Althea brings
   To whisper at the grates;
When I lie tangled in her hair
   And fettered to her eye,
The birds that wanton in the air
   Know no such liberty.

When flowing cups run swiftly round
10   With no allaying Thames,°
Our careless heads with roses bound,
   Our hearts with loyal flames;
When thirsty grief in wine we steep,
   When healths and draughts go free,
Fishes that tipple in the deep
   Know no such liberty.

When, like committed° linnets, I
   With shriller throat will sing
The sweetness, mercy, majesty,
20   And glories of my king;
When I shall voice aloud how good
   He is, how great should be,
Enlargéd° winds, that curl the flood,
   Know no such liberty.

Stone walls do not a prison make,
   Nor iron bars a cage;
Minds innocent and quiet take
   That for an hermitage;
If I have freedom in my love
   And in my soul am free,
Angels alone, that soar above,   30
   Enjoy such liberty.
(1649)

ANDREW MARVELL 1621–1678

Andrew Marvell's father was a Church of England parson of the parish at Winestead, but the son displayed an early leaning toward religious nonconformity. From the Hull grammar school he proceeded to Trinity College, Cambridge, where he took an A.B. degree in 1638. His first poems were published between 1650 and 1652 while he was acting as tutor at Nun Appleton house, Yorkshire, for the daughter of Sir Thomas Fairfax, Lord-General of the Parliamentary forces. In 1657 he was appointed assistant to John Milton, the blind Latin Secretary for the Commonwealth. In 1659 Marvell represented Hull in Parliament, where he remained until his death.

In his own time Marvell was noted for his prose rather than for his verse. While in Parliament, he began a *News-letter*, addressed to his constituents, which appeared from 1660 until his death in 1678; *Controversial Essays*, a long series of tracts published from 1672 to 1677, deals with religious questions. His nonsatirical poems were collected after his death and published in 1681; the satires appeared in 1689, one year after the revolution against James II, under the title *Poems on Affairs of State*. Marvell's high reputation today rests chiefly upon his lyric poems, which T. S. Eliot referred to as having "a tough reasonableness beneath the slight lyric grace."

TO HIS COY MISTRESS

Had we but world enough, and time,
This coyness, lady, were no crime.
We would sit down, and think which way
To walk, and pass our long love's day.
Thou by the Indian Ganges' side
Shouldst rubies find: I by the tide
Of Humber° would complain.° I would
Love you ten years before the flood,°

And you should, if you please, refuse
10 Till the conversion of the Jews;
My vegetable love should grow
Vaster than empires and more slow;
An hundred years should go to praise
Thine eyes, and on thy forehead gaze;
Two hundred to adore each breast,
But thirty thousand to the rest;
An age at least to every part,
And the last age should show your heart.
For, lady, you deserve this state;
20 Nor would I love at lower rate.

But at my back I always hear
Time's wingéd chariot hurrying near;
And yonder all before us lie
Deserts of vast eternity.
Thy beauty shall no more be found,
Nor in thy marble vault shall sound
My echoing song; then worms shall try
That long preserved virginity;
And your quaint° honor turn to dust,
30 And into ashes all my lust:
The grave's a fine and private place,
But none, I think, do there embrace.

Now therefore, while the youthful hue
Sits on thy skin like morning dew,
And while thy willing soul transpires
At every pore with instant fires,
Now let us sport us while we may,
And now, like amorous birds of prey,
Rather at once our time devour
40 Than languish in his slow-chapped° power,
Let us roll all our strength and all
Our sweetness up into one ball,
And tear our pleasures with rough strife
Thorough the iron gates of life:
Thus, though we cannot make our sun
Stand still, yet we will make him run.
(c. 1650; 1681)

THE GARDEN

How vainly men themselves amaze,
To win the palm, the oak, or bays,°
And their incessant labors see
Crowned from some single herb or tree
Whose short and narrow-vergéd shade
Does prudently their toils upbraid,
While all the flowers and trees do close
To weave the garlands of repose!

Fair Quiet, have I found thee here,
10 And Innocence, thy sister dear?

Mistaken long, I sought you then
In busy companies of men.
Your sacred plants, if here below,
Only among the plants will grow;
Society is all but rude
To this delicious solitude.

No white nor red was ever seen
So amorous as this lovely green.°
Fond lovers, cruel as their flame,
Cut in these trees their mistress' name. 20
Little, alas! they know or heed,
How far these beauties hers exceed!
Fair trees! wheres'e'r your barks I wound
No name shall but your own be found.

When we have run our passion's heat,
Love hither makes his best retreat.
The gods, that mortal beauty chase,
Still in a tree did end their race;
Apollo hunted Daphne so,
Only that she might laurel grow; 30
And Pan did after Syrinx° speed,
Not as a nymph, but for a reed.

What wondrous life is this I lead!
Ripe apples drop about my head;
The luscious clusters of the vine
Upon my mouth do crush their wine;
The nectarine, and curious peach,
Into my hands themselves do reach;
Stumbling on melons, as I pass,
Ensnared with flowers, I fall on grass. 40

Meanwhile the mind, from pleasure less,
Withdraws into its happiness;—
The mind, that ocean where each kind
Does straight its own resemblance find;
Yet it creates, transcending these,
Far other worlds, and other seas,
Annihilating all that's made
To a green thought in a green shade.

Here at the fountain's sliding foot,
Or at some fruit-tree's mossy root, 50
Casting the body's vest aside,
My soul into the boughs does glide:
There, like a bird, it sits and sings,
Then whets and combs its silver wings,
And, till prepared for longer flight,
Waves in its plumes the various light.

Such was that happy garden-state,
While man there walked without a mate.

18 **green**, in neo-Platonic and religious symbolism, the color of hope
29 **Apollo . . . Syrinx.** In Greek myth Apollo pursued Daphne and Pan pursued
Syrinx. Daphne was turned into a laurel bush and Syrinx into a clump of reeds
from which the god made his "Pan's pipes"

29 **quaint**, proud   40 **slow-chapped**, slowly crushing   **The Garden** 2 **palm**
. . . **bays,** symbols of various kinds of public honor

After a place so pure and sweet,
60 What other help could yet be meet!

But 'twas beyond a mortal's share
To wander solitary there:
Two paradises 'twere in one,
To live in paradise alone.

How well the skilful gardener drew
Of flowers, and herbs, this dial new;
Where, from above, the milder sun
Does through a fragrant zodiac run,
And, as it works, the industrious bee
70 Computes its time as well as we!
How could such sweet and wholesome hours
Be reckoned but with herbs and flowers?
(c. 1650-1652, 1681)

THE MOWER AGAINST GARDENS

Luxurious° man, to bring his vice in use,
    Did after him° the world seduce,
And from the fields the flowers and plants allure,
    Where Nature was most plain and pure.
He first enclosed within the gardens square
    A dead and standing pool of air,
And a more luscious earth for them did knead,
    Which stupefied them while it fed.
The pink° grew then as double as his mind;
10   The nutriment did change the kind.
With strange perfumes he did the roses taint;
    And flowers themselves were taught to paint.
The tulip white did for complexion seek,
    And learned to interline its cheek;
Its onion root° they then so high did hold,
    That one was for a meadow sold:
Another world was searched through oceans new,
    To find the *Marvel of Peru;*°
And yet these rarities might be allowed
20   To man, that sovereign thing and proud,
Had he not dealt between the bark and tree,
    Forbidden mixtures there to see.
No plant now knew the stock from which it came;
    He grafts upon the wild the tame,
That the uncertain and adulterate fruit
    Might put the palate in dispute.
His green seraglio has its eunuchs too,
    Lest any tyrant him outdo;
And in the cherry he does Nature vex,
30   To procreate without a sex.°
'Tis all enforced,° the fountain and the grot,
    While the sweet fields do lie forgot,

Where willing Nature does to all dispense
    A wild and fragrant innocence;
And fauns and fairies do the meadows till
    More by their presence than their skill.
Their statues polished by some ancient hand,
    May to adorn the gardens stand;
But, howsoe'er the figures do excel,
    The Gods themselves with us do dwell.   40
(1681)

BERMUDAS

Where the remote Bermudas ride
In the ocean's bosom unespied,
From a small boat that rowed along
The listening winds received this song:

"What should we do but sing His praise
That led us through the watery maze
Unto an isle so long unknown,
And yet far kinder than our own?
Where He the huge sea-monsters wracks°
That lift the deep upon their backs,   10
He lands us on a grassy stage,
Safe from the storms' and prelates' rage.
He gave us this eternal spring
Which here enamels everything,
And sends the fowls to us in care
On daily visits through the air.
He hangs in shades the orange bright
Like golden lamps in a green night,
And does in the pomegranates close
Jewels more rich than Ormus° shows.   20
He makes the figs our mouths to meet
And throws the melons at our feet;
But apples plants of such a price,
No tree could ever bear them twice.
With cedars chosen by His hand
From Lebanon° He stores the land;
And makes the hollow seas that roar
Proclaim the ambergris on shore.
He cast (of which we rather boast)
The Gospel's pearl upon our coast;   30
And in these rocks for us did frame
A temple where to sound His name.
Oh, let our voice His praise exalt
Till it arrive at heaven's vault,
Which thence, perhaps, rebounding may
Echo beyond the Mexique bay!"

Thus sung they in the English boat
A holy and a cheerful note;
And all the way, to guide their chime,   40
With falling oars they kept the time.
(1681)

The Mower Against Gardens   1 **Luxurious**, voluptuous or lecherous   2 **after him**, after man's own fall from grace   9 **pink**, a garden flower   15 **onion root**, a tulip bulb is onion shaped. "During the tulip mania (at its height 1634-37) the bulbs were sold in Holland by weight like precious stones" (Margoliouth)
18 **Marvel of Peru**, an exotic plant found in the West Indies and South America   30 **sex**, critics are unsure what gardening process is meant here   31 **enforced**, contrived, not coming about naturally

Bermudas   9 **wracks**, controls   20 **Ormus**, Ormuz, an ancient seaport of Persia noted in the Middle Ages for its riches   25 **cedars . . . Lebanon**, cedars like the famous ones of the Lebanon Mountains in Palestine

Andrew Marvell   **319**

THE DEFINITION OF LOVE

My Love is of a birth as rare
As 'tis, for object, strange and high;
It was begotten by Despair
Upon Impossibility.

Magnanimous Despair alone
Could show me so divine a thing,
Where feeble Hope could ne'er have flown
But vainly flapped its tinsel wing.

And yet I quickly might arrive
10 Where my extended soul is fixed;
But Fate does iron wedges drive,
And always crowds itself betwixt.

For Fate with jealous eye does see
Two perfect loves, nor lets them close;
Their union would her ruin be,
And her tyrannic power depose.

And therefore her decrees of steel
Us as the distant poles have placed
(Though Love's whole world on us doth wheel),
Not by themselves to be embraced,   20

Unless the giddy heaven fall,
And earth some new convulsion tear,
And, us to join, the world should all
Be cramped into a planisphere.

As lines, so loves oblique may well
Themselves in every angle greet
But ours, so truly parallel,
Though infinite, can never meet.

Therefore the love which us doth bind,
But Fate so enviously debars,   30
Is the conjunction of the mind,
And opposition of the stars.
(1681)

JOHN MILTON
1608–1674

John Milton's life falls, like the seventeenth century itself, into three natural divisions—the years before the Great Rebellion, the years from the beginning of the Rebellion to the Restoration, and the years after the Restoration. Milton was born on December 9, 1608, the son of a prosperous London lawyer who had the generosity and foresight to give his son a rich, full education. From St. Paul's School and private tutors, Milton went to Christ's College, Cambridge in 1625. Here, after having gained a reputation for being studious, reserved, and sometimes difficult, he took an M.A. degree in 1632. His intense feeling about the corruption of the clergy made it impossible for him to consider taking the Anglican orders expected of him; therefore, he retired to his father's country house at Horton. Here, in the country quiet, he diligently studied and wrote for five years. To the Horton period belong Comus (1634), a masque, Lycidas, and probably L'Allegro and Il Penseroso. After his mother's death in 1637, Milton traveled on the Continent until, hearing of increasing religious and political troubles in England, he returned home in 1639.

In the 1640s, Milton began to write tracts supporting the Puritan cause. In 1642 he married Mary Powell, age seventeen, who returned to her parents within two months. Milton was soon writing divorce tracts defending incompatability as a just ground for divorce. Until the Restoration in 1660, Milton's major efforts were prose works. In 1644 appeared Of Education, a pamphlet advancing his humanistic ideas on education, and Areopagitica, a plea for freedom of the press and free thought. His Eikonoklastes (1649) and Defensio pro Populo Anglicano (1651) are arguments in defense of Parliament.

Milton's first wife, whose parents were Royalists, had returned to him after the collapse of the king's cause in 1645. Of this marriage three daughters were born; the mother died at the birth of a fourth child in 1652. His second wife, Catherine Woodcock, whom he married in 1656, also died in childbirth. His third wife, Elizabeth Minshull, a woman of twenty-four when he married her in 1663, survived him by many years.

Milton's most direct service to the Commonwealth came with his appointment in 1649 to the office of Latin Secretary to the newly created Commission of Foreign Affairs. By 1652, the eyestrain from this work and from his extensive reading over many years had caused him to become totally blind.

The return of a Stuart monarch in 1660, of course, caused a reversal in his political fortunes; he was arrested, fined, and imprisoned for a short time. After eventually receiving a full pardon from Charles II, he lived in literary seclusion. The last twelve years of his life were spent in London. With the help of secretaries he was able to continue and finish work on his pro-

jected epic poem, which aimed to "justify the ways of
God to men." It was published in 1667 as *Paradise
Lost*; despite its unpopular attitudes and the author's
disfavor, the work was soon recognized as a great epic
achievement. In 1671 Milton followed his earlier success with the publication of another, shorter epic,
Paradise Regained, which told the story of Christ's
triumph, and *Samson Agonistes*, a poem in the form of
a Greek tragedy. He continued working on and revis-
ing his poetry until his death in 1674.

Milton stands between two ages, remarkably fusing
the religious and political spirit of the Commonwealth
with the humanistic traditions and intellectual restlessness of the Renaissance. His poetry compels the
epithet "great": his superb prosody and technique in
numerous verse forms, meters, and even languages, for
example, or the austere, sustained sublimity which
marks his major poems. In addition, he possesses
another attribute of greatness—the capacity to influence poets of later generations. One has but to glance
at the poetry of Wordsworth or Keats for evidence.
Milton is the master of English blank verse, of the
"grand style," and, perhaps most significant, of a singularly intense moral idealism.

L'ALLEGRO°

Hence loathed Melancholy
  Of *Cerberus*° and blackest midnight born,
In *Stygian*° Cave forlorn
  'Mongst horrid shapes, and shrieks, and sights
    unholy,
Find out some uncouth cell,
  Where brooding darkness spreads his jealous wings,
And the night-Raven sings;
  There under *Ebon* shades, and low-brow'd Rocks,
As ragged as thy Locks,
10 In dark *Cimmerian*° desert ever dwell.
But come thou Goddess fair and free,
In Heav'n yclep'd° *Euphrosyne*,°
  And by men, heart-easing Mirth,
Whom lovely *Venus* at a birth
With two sister Graces° more
  To Ivy-crowned *Bacchus*° bore;
Or whether (as some Sager sing)
The frolic Wind that breathes the Spring,
  Zephyr with *Aurora*° playing,
20 As he met her once a-Maying,

There on Beds of Violets blue,
And fresh-blown Roses washt in dew,
Fill'd her with thee a daughter fair,
So buxom, blithe, and debonair.
Haste thee nymph, and bring with thee
Jest and youthful Jollity,
Quips and Cranks,° and wanton Wiles,
Nods, and Becks,° and Wreathed Smiles,
Such as hang on *Hebe's*° cheek,
And love to live in dimple sleek;   30
Sport that wrinkled Care derides,
And Laughter holding both his sides.
Come, and trip it as ye go
On the light fantastic toe,
And in thy right hand lead with thee,
The Mountain Nymph, sweet Liberty;
And if I give thee honor due,
Mirth, admit me of thy crew
To live with her, and live with thee,
In unreproved pleasures free;   40
To hear the Lark begin his flight,
And singing startle the dull night,
From his watch-tow'r in the skies,
Till the dappled dawn doth rise;
Then to come in spite of sorrow,
And at my window bid good-morrow,
Through the Sweet-Briar, or the Vine,
Or the twisted Eglantine;°
While the Cock with lively din,
Scatters the rear of darkness thin,   50
And to the stack, or the Barn door.
Stoutly struts his Dames before;
Oft list'ning how the Hounds and horn
Cheerly rouse the slumb'ring morn,
From the side of some Hoar Hill,
Through the high wood echoing shrill;
Some time walking not unseen
By Hedgerow Elms, on Hillocks green,
Right against the Eastern gate,
Where the great Sun begins his state,   60
Rob'd in flames, and Amber light,
The clouds in thousand Liveries dight;°
While the Plowman near at hand,
Whistles o'er the Furrow'd Land,
And the Milkmaid singeth blithe,
And the Mower whets his scythe,
And every Shepherd tells his tale°
Under the Hawthorn in the dale.
Straight mine eye hath caught new pleasures
Whilst the Landscape round it measures,   70
Russet Lawns and Fallows Gray,
Where the nibbling flocks do stray;
Mountains on whose barren breast

L'Allegro, an Italian title meaning "the cheerful man." This poem and *Il Penseroso*—"the contemplative man"—are companion pieces which present two
contrasting views of living: that of the social man and that f the retiring, scholarly
man 2 **Cerberus,** the three-headed dog that guarded the gateway to Hades in
classical mythology 3 **Stygian,** referring to the gloomy river Styx of Hades, over
which Charon ferried the shades of the dead (cf. *Paradise Lost,* Book II, l. 577)
10 **Cimmerian.** In classical cosmography Cimmeria was the land of darkness and
mist which lay beyond the ocean stream bounding the world plain 12 **yclep'd,**
named **Euphrosyne,** one of the three Graces, goddesses of joy and gentleness.
The word means "cheerful" 15 **two sister Graces,** Aglaia and Thalia
16 **Bacchus,** Dionysus, the god of wine. The three Graces are usually represented
as being the daughters of Zeus and Eurynome 19 **Zephyr . . . Aurora,** the god
of the west wind and the goddess of the morn, respectively. This account of the
birth of Euphrosyne is Milton's invention

27 **Quips and Cranks,** witty sayings and quick turns of speech, respectively
28 **Becks,** beckonings 29 **Hebe,** daughter of Zeus and Hera and cupbearer to
the gods 48 **Eglantine,** sweetbriar, but Milton probably had in mind some
twisting vine like the honeysuckle 62 **dight,** dressed 67 **tells his tale.** Inasmuch as the preceding line describes the mower *at work,* this phrase probably
means "counts the number of his sheep;" however, it may mean "tells a story" or
"courts a maid"

The laboring clouds do often rest;
Meadows trim with Daisies pied,
Shallow Brooks, and Rivers wide.
Towers and Battlements it sees
Bosom'd high in tufted Trees,
Where perhaps some beauty lies,
80 The Cynosure° of neighboring eyes.
Hard by, a Cottage chimney smokes,
From betwixt two aged Oaks,
Where *Corydon*° and *Thyrsis* met,
Are at their savory dinner set
Of Herbs, and other Country Messes,
Which the neat-handed *Phillis* dresses;
And then in haste her Bow'r she leaves,
With *Thestylis* to bind the Sheaves;
Or if the earlier season lead
90 To the tann'd Haycock in the Mead.
Sometimes with secure delight
The upland Hamlets will invite,
When the merry Bells ring round,
And the jocund rebecs° sound
To many a youth, and many a maid,
Dancing in the Checker'd shade;
And young and old come forth to play
On a Sunshine Holiday,
Till the livelong daylight fail;
100 Then to the Spicy Nut-brown Ale,
With stories told of many a feat,
How *Faery Mab*° the junkets eat;
She was pincht and pull'd, she said,
And he, by Friar's Lantern led,°
Tells how the drudging *Goblin*° sweat
To earn his Cream-bowl° duly set,
When in one night, ere glimpse of morn,
His shadowy Flail hath thresh'd the Corn
That ten day-laborers could not end;
110 Then lies him down the Lubber Fiend,°
And, stretch'd out all the Chimney's length,
Basks at the fire his hairy strength;
And Crop-full out of doors he flings,
Ere the first Cock his Matin rings.
Thus done the Tales, to bed they creep,
By whispering Winds soon lull'd asleep.
Tow'red Cities° please us then,
And the busy hum of men,
Where throngs of Knights and Barons bold,
120 In weeds° of Peace high triumphs° hold,
With store of° Ladies, whose bright eyes
Rain influence,° and judge the prize
Of Wit,° or Arms, while both contend

To win her Grace, whom all commend.
There let *Hymen*° oft appear
In Saffron robe, with Taper clear,
And pomp, and feast, and revelry,
With mask, and antique Pageantry—
Such sights as youthful Poets dream
On Summer eves by haunted stream.   130
Then to the well-trod stage anon,
If *Jonson's* learned Sock° be on,
Or sweetest *Shakespeare*, fancy's child,
Warble his native Wood-notes wild.
And ever against eating Cares,
Lap me in soft *Lydian* Airs,°
Married to immortal verse,
Such as the meeting soul may pierce
In notes, with many a winding bout°
Of linked sweetness long drawn out,   140
With wanton heed, and giddy cunning,
The melting voice through mazes running;
Untwisting all the chains that tie
The hidden soul of harmony;
That *Orpheus'*° self may heave his head
From golden slumber on a bed
Of heapt *Elysian* flow'rs, and hear
Such strains as would have won the ear
Of *Pluto*, to have quite set free
His half-regain'd *Eurydice*.   150
These delights if thou canst give,
Mirth, with thee I mean to live.
(1631?)

IL PENSEROSO°

Hence vain deluding joys,
   The brood of folly without father bred,
How little you bested,°
   Or fill the fixed mind with all your toys;°
Dwell in some idle brain,
   And fancies fond° with gaudy shapes possess,°
As thick and numberless
   As the gay motes that people the Sunbeams,
Or likest hovering dreams,
   The fickle Pensioners of *Morpheus'*° train.°   10
But hail thou Goddess, sage and holy,
Hail divinest Melancholy,
Whose Saintly visage is too bright
To hit the Sense of human sight;
And therefore to our weaker view,

80 **Cynosure**, center of attraction   83–88 **Corydon . . . Thestylis**, conventional names for shepherds and shepherdesses in classical pastoral poetry   94 **rebecs,** early stringed instruments played with a bow; "jocund" implies a festive occasion   102 **Faery Mab**, the English queen of the fairies   103 **she . . . he**, two of the story-tellers   104 **Friar's Lantern**, will-o'-the-wisp   105 **drudging Goblin**, Puck or Robin Goodfellow, the household brownie   106 **Cream-bowl**, the usual fee for the goblin's services   110 **Lubber Fiend**, clumsy elf   117 **Tow'red Cities, etc.** Having described the pleasures which L'Allegro enjoys in the country, the poet gives a contrasting picture of social life in the city   120 **weeds**, garments **high triumphs**, elaborate court entertainments such as masques and tournaments   121 **store of**, many   122 **Rain influence.** The ladies' eyes are thought of as stars that control the destinies of the contestants   123 **Wit**, intelligence such as might be displayed in a debate or poetic contest

125 **Hymen**, the classical god of marriage, frequently personified at noble weddings   132 **Sock**, the flat-soled shoe worn by Greek and Roman comic actors; hence the symbol of comedy   136 **Lydian Airs**, a soft mode in ancient Greek music   139 **bout**, turn or round   145 **Orpheus**. In Greek mythology the musician Orpheus followed his wife Eurydice into the halls of Pluto, god of the Underworld, and played so sweetly that the god promised to release her if Orpheus did not look back upon her until both had passed the gates of Hades; however, he broke his promise and so lost his wife again   **Il Penseroso**. See first footnote to *L'Allegro*. The modern Italian form of the word is *pensieroso*   3 **bested**, profit, avail   4 **toys**, trifles   6 **fond**, foolish   **possess**, possessed   10 **Morpheus**, the god of dreams in classical mythology   **train**, following

O'erlaid with black, staid Wisdom's hue.
Black, but such as in esteem,
Prince *Memnon's*° sister might beseem,°
Or that Starr'd *Ethiop* Queen° that strove
20 To set her beauty's praise above
The Sea Nymphs, and their powers offended.
Yet thou art higher far descended;
Thee bright-hair'd *Vesta*° long of yore,
To solitary *Saturn* bore;
His daughter she (in *Saturn's* reign,
Such mixture was not held a stain).
Oft in glimmering Bow'rs and glades
He met her, and in secret shades
Of woody *Ida's* inmost grove,
30 While yet there was no fear of *Jove*.°
Come pensive Nun, devout and pure,
Sober, steadfast, and demure,
All in a robe of darkest grain,°
Flowing with majestic train,
And sable stole of *Cypress* Lawn,°
Over thy decent° shoulders drawn.
Come, but keep thy wonted state,
With ev'n step, and musing gait,
And looks commercing with the skies,
40 Thy rapt soul sitting in thine eyes:
There held in holy passion still,
Forget thyself to Marble, till
With a sad Leaden downward cast,
Thou fix them on the earth as fast.
And join with thee calm Peace and Quiet,
Spare Fast, that oft with gods doth diet,
And hears the Muses in a ring
Aye round about *Jove's* Altar sing.
And add to these retired Leisure,
50 That in trim Gardens takes his pleasure;
But first, and chiefest, with thee bring
Him that yon soars on golden wing,
Guiding the fiery-wheeled throne,
The Cherub Contemplation;
And the mute Silence hist along,°
'Less *Philomel*° will deign a Song,
In her sweetest, saddest plight,°
Smoothing the rugged brow of night.
While *Cynthia* checks her Dragon yoke,
60 Gently o'er th' accustom'd Oak;
Sweet Bird that shunn'st the noise of folly,
Most musical, most melancholy!
Thee Chantress oft the Woods among,
I woo to hear thy Even-Song;
And missing thee, I walk unseen°

On the dry smooth-shaven Green,
To behold the wand'ring Moon,
Riding near her highest noon,
Like one that had been led astray
Through the Heav'n's wide pathless way;   70
And oft, as if her head she bow'd,
Stooping through a fleecy cloud.
Oft on a Plat of rising ground,
I hear the far-off *Curfew* sound,
Over some wide-water'd shore,
Swinging slow with sullen roar;
Or if the Air will not permit,
Some still removed place will fit,
Where glowing Embers through the room
Teach light to counterfeit a gloom,   80
Far from all resort of mirth,
Save the Cricket on the hearth,
Or the Bellman's° drowsy charm,
To bless the doors from nightly harm:
Or let my Lamp at midnight hour,
Be seen in some high lonely Tow'r,
Where I may oft outwatch the *Bear*,°
With thrice great *Hermes*,° or unsphere°
The spirit of *Plato* to unfold
What Worlds, or what vast Regions hold   90
The immortal mind that hath forsook
Her mansion in this fleshly nook:
And of those *Dæmons* that are found
In fire, air, flood, or underground,
Whose power hath a true consent
With Planet, or with Element.
Sometime let Gorgeous Tragedy
In Scepter'd Pall come sweeping by,
Presenting *Thebes*,° or *Pelops'* line,°
Or the tale of *Troy*° divine,   100
Or what (though rare) of later age,
Ennobled hath the Buskin'd stage.°
But, O sad Virgin, that thy power
Might raise *Musaeus*° from his bower,
Or bid the soul of *Orpheus* sing
Such notes as, warbled to the string,
Drew Iron tears down *Pluto's* cheek,
And made Hell grant what Love did seek.
Or call up him° that left half told
The story of *Cambuscan* bold,   110
Of *Camball*, and of *Algarsife*,
And who had *Canace*° to wife,
That own'd the virtuous° Ring and Glass,

---

83 **Bellman's drowsy charm,** the night watchman's hourly call of "All's well"
87 **outwatch the Bear,** sit up all night. The constellation of the Great Bear, or Big Dipper, never sets in England   88 **thrice great Hermes,** Hermes Trismegistus, a mythical king of Egypt and reputed author of scholarly treatises on numerous subjects, especially alchemy   **unsphere,** call back from whatever sphere his spirit inhabits. Plato speculated in *Phaedo* on the immortality of the soul   99 **Thebes,** in Greek legend the capital of Boeotia and the scene of the tragedies of Oedipus, Polynices, and Eteocles   **Pelops' line.** In Greek legend, Atreus, Thyestes, Aegisthus, and Agamemnon were descendants of Pelops whose tragic fate was presented on stage   100 **tale of Troy,** the familiar legends of the Trojan War   102 **Buskin'd stage.** The buskin was a thick-soled boot worn by Greek and Roman tragic actors to increase their stature to heroic proportions; the word came to be used as a symbol of tragedy   104 **Musaeus,** a Greek poet around the sixth century and author of a poem on Hero and Leander   109 **him,** Chaucer. He left the *Squire's Tale* unfinished   110 **Cambuscan . . . Canace.** Cambuscan was a king of Tartary; Camball and Algarsife were his sons, and Canace his daughter   113 **virtuous,** powerful

---

18 **Prince Memnon,** in Greek mythology, son of Tithonus and Aurora, and king of the Ethiopians. He assisted Priam in the Trojan War   **beseem,** suit   19 **Ethiop Queen,** Cassiopeia, in classical mythology the beautiful wife of Cepheus, king of the Ethiopians, whose boast that she was more beautiful than the sea-nymphs resulted in their sending a sea monster to ravage the country. On her death the gods transformed her into a star   23 **Vesta,** goddess of the hearth and a daughter of Saturn, ancient god of agriculture   29 **Ida's . . . no fear of Jove.** Milton apparently identified Saturn with Cronus who was overthrown by his son Jove after the infant god had been concealed from his father and brought up in the caves of Mount Ida in Crete   33 **grain.** The reference is not to the texture but to the dark dye   35 **Cypress Lawn,** thin black crepe   36 **decent,** seemly   55 **hist along,** bring silently   56 **Philomel,** the nightingale; contrasts with the skylark in *L'Allegro,* l. 41   57 **plight,** mood   65 **I walk unseen,** contrasts with *L'Allegro,* l. 57

And of the wondrous Horse of Brass,°
On which the *Tartar* King did ride;
And if aught else great Bards beside
In sage and solemn tunes have sung,
Of Tourneys and of Trophies hung,
Of Forests, and enchantments drear,
120 Where more is meant than meets the ear.
Thus night oft see me in thy pale career,
Till civil-suited Morn appear,
Not trickt and frounc't° as she was wont
With the Attic Boy° to hunt,
But kerchieft in a comely Cloud,
While rocking Winds are Piping loud,
Or usher'd with a shower still,
When the gust hath blown his fill,
Ending on the rustling Leaves,
130 With minute-drops° from off the Eaves.
And when the Sun begins to fling
His flaring beams, me Goddess bring
To arched walks of twilight groves,
And shadows brown° that *Sylvan*° loves
Of Pine or monumental Oak,
Where the rude Axe with heaved stroke
Was never heard the Nymphs to daunt,
Or fright them from their hallow'd haunt.
There in close covert by some Brook,
140 Where no profaner eye may look,
Hide me from Day's garish eye,
While the Bee with Honied thigh,
That at her flow'ry work doth sing,
And the Waters murmuring
With such consort° as they keep,
Entice the dewy-feather'd Sleep;
And let some strange mysterious dream
Wave at his Wings° in Airy stream,
Of lively portraiture display'd,
150 Softly on my eyelids laid.
And as I wake, sweet music° breathe
Above, about, or underneath,
Sent by some spirit to mortals good,
Or th'unseen Genius of the Wood.°
But let my due feet never fail
To walk the studious Cloister's pale,°
And love the high embowed Roof,
With antic Pillars massy proof,
And storied Windows° richly dight,
160 Casting a dim religious light.
There let the pealing Organ blow
To the full voic'd Choir below,
In Service high and Anthems clear,
As may with sweetness, through mine ear,

Dissolve me into ecstasies,
And bring all Heav'n before mine eyes.
And may at last my weary age
Find out the peaceful hermitage,
The Hairy Gown and Mossy Cell,
Where I may sit and rightly spell°   170
Of every Star that Heav'n doth shew,
And every Herb that sips the dew;
Till old° experience do attain
To something like Prophetic strain.
These pleasures *Melancholy* give,
And I with thee will choose to live.
(1631?)

LYCIDAS°

*In this Monody° the Author bewails a learned Friend,
unfortunately drown'd in his Passage from* Chester *on
the* Irish Seas, 1637. And by occasion foretells the ruin
of our corrupted Clergy then in their height.*

Yet once more,° O ye Laurels, and once more
Ye Myrtles brown, with Ivy never sere,
I come to pluck° your Berries harsh and crude,
And with forc'd fingers rude,
Shatter your leaves before the mellowing year.
Bitter constraint, and sad occasion dear,
Compels me to disturb your season due:
For *Lycidas* is dead, dead ere his prime,
Young *Lycidas*, and hath not left his peer:
Who would not sing for *Lycidas*? he knew   10
Himself to sing,° and build the lofty rhyme.
He must not float upon his wat'ry bier
Unwept, and welter to the parching wind,
Without the meed of some melodious tear.
Begin then, Sisters of the sacred well,°
That from beneath the seat of *Jove* doth spring,
Begin, and somewhat loudly sweep the string.
Hence with denial vain, and coy excuse,
So may some gentle Muse
With lucky words favor my destin'd Urn,°   20
And as he passes turn,
And bid fair peace be to my sable shroud.
For we were nurst upon the self-same hill,°
Fed the same flock, by fountain, shade, and rill.
Together both, ere the high Lawns appear'd
Under the opening eyelids of the morn,
We drove afield, and both together heard
What time the Gray-fly winds her sultry horn,
Batt'ning° our flocks with the fresh dews of night,

114 **Ring . . . Horse of Brass.** The ring, the mirror, and the brass horse, all with magic properties, were gifts from the King of Arabia   123 **trickt and frounc't,** adorned and plaited   124 **the Attic boy,** Cephalus, an Athenian (Attic) huntsman beloved of Aurora (Dawn)   130 **minute-drops,** drops that drip slowly   134 **brown,** dusk   **Sylvan,** Sylvanus, the god of forest glades   145 **consort,** either companionship or concert harmony; *they* seems to refer to "the waters murmuring"   148 **Wave at his Wings,** a probable allusion to the misty, wavering uncertainty of dream visions   151 **sweet music,** *Let* is understood   154 **Genius of the Wood,** the presiding deity   156 **pale,** bounds, enclosure   159 **storied Windows,** sacred stories in stained glass

170 **spell,** study   173 **old,** grown old by practice   **Lycidas,** an elegy in the form of a pastoral in which the dead poet, Edward King, and the author appear as shepherds. Milton wrote the explanatory headnote   **Monody,** a funeral song or dirge sung by a single voice   1 **once more.** The allusion is to Milton's having written other poems   3 **I come to pluck.** The author would gather a laurel wreath to honor his dead friend   11 **to sing,** how to sing   15 **Sisters . . . well,** the nine Muses whose home was the Pierian spring near Mt. Olympus (the seat of Jove)   20 **Urn,** a figure for death. Milton expresses a hope that on his death some poetic tribute may be paid to him   23 **nurst . . . hill,** a figure for "attended the same college" (at Cambridge)   29 **Batt'ning,** feeding

30 Oft till the Star that rose, at Ev'ning, bright
Toward Heav'n's descent had slop'd his westering
wheel.
Meanwhile the Rural ditties were not mute,
Temper'd to th'Oaten Flute;
Rough *Satyrs* danc'd, and *Fauns*° with clov'n heel
From the glad sound would not be absent long,
And old *Damaetas*° lov'd to hear our song.
  But O the heavy change, now thou art gone,
Now thou art gone, and never must return!
Thee Shepherd, thee the Woods, and desert Caves,
40 With wild Thyme and the gadding° Vine o'ergrown,
And all their echoes mourn.
The Willows and the Hazel Copses green
Shall now no more be seen,
Fanning their joyous Leaves to thy soft lays.
As killing as the Canker° to the Rose,
Or Taint-worm to the weanling Herds that graze,
Or Frost to Flowers, that their gay wardrobe wear,
When first the White-thorn blows;
Such, *Lycidas*, thy loss to Shepherd's ear.
50   Where were ye Nymphs when the remorseless deep
Clos'd o'er the head of your lov'd *Lycidas?*
For neither were ye playing on the steep,
Where your old *Bards,* the famous *Druids,*° lie,
Nor on the shaggy top of *Mona*° high,
Nor yet where *Deva*° spreads her wizard° stream:
Ay me, I fondly dream!
Had ye been there—for what could that have done?
What could the Muse herself that *Orpheus* bore,°
The Muse herself, for her enchanting son
60 Whom Universal nature did lament,
When by the rout that made the hideous roar,
His gory visage down the stream was sent,
Down the swift *Hebrus* to the *Lesbian* shore?
  Alas! What boots it° with uncessant care
To tend the homely slighted Shepherd's trade,
And strictly meditate the thankless Muse?°
Were it not better done as others use,
To sport with *Amaryllis* in the shade,
Or with the tangles of *Neaera's* hair?°
70 *Fame* is the spur that the clear spirit doth raise
(That last infirmity° of Noble mind)
To scorn delights, and live laborious days;
But the fair Guerdon when we hope to find,
And think to burst out into sudden blaze,
Comes the blind *Fury*° with th'abhorred shears,
And slits the thin-spun life. "But not the praise,"

Phoebus repli'd, and touch'd my trembling ears;°
"*Fame* is no plant that grows on mortal soil,
Nor in the glistering foil°
Set off to th'world, nor in broad rumor lies,   80
But lives and spreads aloft by those pure eyes
And perfect witness of all-judging *Jove*;
As he pronounces lastly on each deed,
Of so much fame in Heav'n expect thy meed."
  O Fountain *Arethuse,*° and thou honor'd flood,
Smooth-sliding *Mincius;*° crown'd with vocal reeds,
That strain I heard was of a higher mood:
But now my Oat° proceeds,
And listens to the Herald of the Sea°
That came in *Neptune's*° plea.   90
He ask'd the Waves, and ask'd the Felon winds,
What hard mishap hath doom'd this gentle swain?
And question'd every gust of rugged wings
That blows from off each beaked Promontory.
They knew not of his story,
And sage *Hippotades*° their answer brings,
That not a blast was from his dungeon stray'd,
The Air was calm, and on the level brine,
Sleek *Panope* with all her sisters° play'd.
It was that fatal and perfidious Bark   100
Built in th'eclipse,° and rigg'd with curses dark,
That sunk so low that sacred head of thine.
  Next *Camus,*° reverend Sire, went footing slow,
His Mantle hairy, and his Bonnet sedge,
Inwrought with figures dim, and on the edge
Like to that sanguine flower inscrib'd with woe.°
"Ah! Who hath reft" (quoth he) "my dearest pledge?"
Last came, and last did go,
The Pilot of the *Galilean* lake.
Two massy Keys° he bore of metals twain   110
(The Golden opes, the Iron shuts amain).
He shook his Mitred locks,° and stern bespake:
"How well could I have spar'd for thee, young swain,
Enough of such as for their bellies' sake,
Creep and intrude and climb into the fold?
Of other care they little reck'ning make,
Than how to scramble at the shearers' feast,
And shove away the worthy bidden guest;
Blind mouths!° that scarce themselves know how to
hold

34 **Satyrs . . . Fauns,** sylvan sprites   36 **Damaetas,** stock name for an older,
philosophical shepherd   40 **gadding,** rambling   45 **Canker,** a cankerworm
53 **Druids,** ancient Celtic priests, represented here as having been bardic singers
54 **Mona,** old Roman name for the Isle of Man or Anglesey, off the coast of
Wales   55 **Deva,** the river Dee in north Wales; it flows into the Irish Sea
wizard, powerful in its control of the fate of Wales   58 **Muse . . . Orpheus bore.**
Calliope, the Muse of heroic poetry, could not save her son, the musician, from
being torn to pieces by the Thracian women who were maddened by his laments
for his dead wife Eurydice. They cast his dismembered corpse into the *Hebrus*
River and it floated down to the Isle of Wales   64 **what boots it, etc.** What is to
be gained by writing poetry   66 **meditate . . . Muse,** compose a poem which
goes unrewarded   68 **Amaryllis . . . Neaera,** common pastoral names for
shepherdesses   71 **last infirmity,** last weakness which the noble mind conquers
75 **the blind Fury.** In Greek myth Atropos was the one of the three Fates who
cut the thread of life. Milton calls her *blind* because she does not discriminate,
and a *Fury* because of the malignant nature of her function

77 **touch'd . . . ears,** a symbolic act. The ear was regarded as the seat of memory
79 **foil,** tinsel   85 **Arethuse,** a fountain. In Greek myth the river god Alpheus
pursued the nymph Arethusa under land and sea until they merged in the fountain
in Ortygia near Sicily which took her name   86 **Mincius,** a river near Mantua in
Italy, the birthplace of Vergil who sang of the stream   88 **Oat,** oaten reed, the
symbol of pastoral song   89 **Herald of the Sea,** Triton, a sea god in Greek myth
represented in art as blowing on a shell; hence the epithet *herald*   90 **Neptune,**
in Greek myth the principal god of the sea   96 **Hippotades,** Aeolus, god of the
winds   99 **Panope . . . sisters,** the Nereids, daughters of the sea god Nereus
101 **Built in th' eclipse.** Work done during an eclipse of the moon was regarded
as ill-omened   103 **Camus,** the god of the river Cam. This river flows past the
college lawns at Cambridge   106 **sanguine . . . woe,** the hyacinth. In Greek
myth the hyacinth sprung from the blood of the youth Hyacinthus, accidentally
killed by Apollo. The markings on the petals resemble the Greek word *alas*
109 **Pilot of the Galilean Lake.** St. Peter, disciple of Jesus, who was a fisherman
on Lake Galilee in Palestine. At this point Milton begins his condemnation of
"our corrupted Clergy" of the Anglican Church and his forecast of their ruin. In
a broader sense, it is an indictment of injustice and confused moral values
110 **Two massy Keys.** Jesus' words to Peter were: "And I will give unto thee the
keys of the kingdom of heaven" (*Matthew*, 16:19)   112 **Mitred locks,** as first
"bishop of Rome," he wore the official headdress of the bishop   119 **Blind
mouths,** a highly compressed and figurative expression (synecdoche) for clergy
blind to all but greed

120 A Sheep-hook,° or have learn'd aught else the least
That to the faithful Herdman's art belongs!
What recks it them? What need they? They are sped;°
And when they list,° their lean and flashy° songs
Grate on their scrannel° Pipes of wretched straw.
The hungry Sheep look up, and are not fed,
But swoln with wind,° and the rank mist they draw,
Rot inwardly, and foul contagion spread:
Besides what the grim Wolf with privy paw
Daily devours apace, and nothing said;
130 But that two-handed engine° at the door
Stands ready to smite once, and smite no more.''
    Return *Alpheus,* the dread voice is past
That shrunk thy streams; Return *Sicilian* Muse,°
And call the Vales, and bid them hither cast
Their Bells and Flowrets of a thousand hues.
Ye valleys low where the mild whispers use°
Of shades and wanton winds and gushing brooks,
On whose fresh lap the swart Star° sparely looks,
Throw hither all your quaint enamell'd eyes,
140 That on the green turf suck the honied showers,
And purple all the ground with vernal flowers.
Bring the rathe° Primrose that forsaken dies,
The tufted Crow-toe,° and pale Jessamine,
The white Pink, and the Pansy freakt with jet,°
The glowing Violet,
The Musk-rose, and the well-attir'd Woodbine,
With Cowslips wan that hang the pensive head,
And every flower that sad embroidery wears:
Bid *Amaranthus* all his beauty shed,
150 And Daffadillies fill their cups with tears,
To strew the Laureate° Hearse where *Lycid* lies.
For so to interpose a little ease,
Let our frail thoughts dally with false surmise.°
Ay me! Whilst thee the shores and sounding Seas
Wash far away, where'er thy bones are hurl'd,
Whether beyond the stormy *Hebrides,*
Where thou perhaps under the whelming tide
Visit'st the bottom of the monstrous world;
Or whether thou to our moist vows denied,
160 Sleep'st by the fable of *Bellerus*° old,
Where the great vision of the guarded Mount°
Looks toward *Namancos*° and *Bayona's* hold;
Look homeward Angel° now, and melt with ruth:
And, O ye *Dolphins,* waft the hapless youth.°

Weep no more, woeful Shepherds weep no more,
For *Lycidas* your sorrow is not dead,
Sunk though he be beneath the wat'ry floor,
So sinks the day-star° in the Ocean bed,
And yet anon repairs his drooping head,
And tricks° his beams, and with new-spangled Ore,   170
Flames in the forehead of the morning sky:
So *Lycidas,* sunk low, but mounted high,
Through the dear might of him that walk'd the waves,
Where other groves, and other streams along,
With *Nectar* pure his oozy Locks he laves,
And hears the unexpressive nuptial Song,°
In the blest Kingdoms meek of joy and love.
There entertain him all the Saints above,
In solemn troops, and sweet Societies
That sing, and singing in their glory move,   180
And wipe the tears for ever from his eyes.
Now *Lycidas,* the Shepherds weep no more;
Henceforth thou art the Genius of the shore,
In thy large recompense,° and shalt be good
To all that wander in that perilous flood.
    Thus sang the uncouth Swain to th'Oaks and rills,
While the still morn went out with Sandals gray;
He touch't the tender stops of various Quills,°
With eager thought warbling his *Doric* lay:°
And now the Sun had stretch't out all the hills,   190
And now was dropt into the Western bay;
At last he rose, and twitch't° his Mantle blue:
Tomorrow to fresh Woods, and Pastures new.°
(1637)

HOW SOON HATH TIME

How soon hath Time, the subtle thief of youth,
    Stol'n on his wing my three and twentieth year!
    My hasting days fly on with full career,
    But my late spring no bud or blossom show'th.°
Perhaps my semblance might deceive the truth,   5
    That I to manhood am arriv'd so near,
    And inward ripeness doth much less appear,
    That some more timely-happy spirits° endu'th.
Yet be it less or more, or soon or slow,
    It shall be still in strictest measure ev'n   10
    To that same lot, however mean or high,
Toward which Time leads me, and the will of Heav'n;
    All is, if I have grace to use it so,
    As ever in my great task-Master's eye.°
(1632; 1645)

120 **Sheep-hook,** the allusion is to the *crosier,* or pastoral staff, of the bishop, the symbol of his office as shepherd of God's flock   122 **sped,** taken care of   123 **list,** wish   **flashy,** uninspired, flat   124 **scrannel,** harsh, unmelodious. The entire figure is that of pastoral song; the allusions are to the thin, empty sermons and teachings of the uninspired clergy, and to the verse of inferior poets   126 **wind . . . mist,** figure for shallow and false doctrines   130 **two-handed engine,** probably the sword of justice, the ax "laid unto the root of the trees . . . which bringeth not forth good fruit" (Matthew, 3:10) This line has received much critical attention   133 **Sicilian Muse,** pastoral poetry   136 **use,** inhabit   138 **swart Star,** Sirius, the Dog Star, supposed to wither vegetation   142 **rathe,** early   143 **Crow-toe,** crowfoot   144 **freakt with jet,** striped with black   151 **Laureate,** covered with laurel in honor of the dead poet   153 **with false surmise,** with imagining that the body of Lycidas is really present and not floating "upon his watery bier"   160 **Bellerus.** Milton coined this from Bellerium, the Roman name for Land's End   161 **vision . . . Mount.** Near Land's End is St. Michael's Mount, a rocky island guarded by the Archangel Michael   162 **Namancos,** ancient town in Spain opposite St. Michael's Mount and near the Spanish castle of Bayona   163 **Angel,** St. Michael, who is urged to turn his gaze from Spain to England   164 **Dolphins . . . youth,** an allusion to the Greek legend of the rescue of the bard Arion by dolphins when he was cast overboard by sailors

168 **day-star,** sun   170 **tricks,** tricks out; dresses, adorns   176 **unexpressive,** inexpressible   **nuptial Song,** for the "marriage of the Lamb" (see *Revelation,* 19:7). The lines which follow were suggested by St. John's description of the heavenly city in *Revelation*   184 **In . . . recompense,** as thy reward   188 **Quills,** reeds in his pastoral pipe   189 **Doric lay,** pastoral poetry   192 **twitch't,** pulled about him   193 **Tomorrow . . . new,** an obscure allusion to Milton's plan for writing other types of poetry   **How Soon Hath Time**   4 **show'th,** the pronunciation is indicated by the rhyme with *youth*   8 **timely-happy spirits,** persons whose intellectual and spiritual development has an appropriate agreement with their age and physical appearance   14 **All is . . . eye.** The general meaning seems to be, to quote from a later poet, "All service ranks alike with God." Compare the last lines of his sonnet *When I Consider How My Light Is Spent*

ON THE LATE MASSACRE IN PIEDMONT°

Avenge, O Lord, thy slaughter'd Saints, whose bones
  Lie scatter'd on the Alpine mountains cold,
  Ev'n them who kept thy truth so pure of old
  When all our Fathers worship't Stocks and Stones,
5 Forget not: in thy book record their groans
  Who were thy Sheep and in their ancient Fold
  Slain by the bloody *Piemontese* that roll'd
  Mother with Infant down the Rocks. Their moans
The Vales redoubl'd to the Hills, and they
10 To Heav'n. Their martyr'd blood and ashes sow
  O'er all th'*Italian* fields where still doth sway
The triple Tyrant:° that from these may grow
  A hundredfold, who having learnt thy way
  Early may fly the *Babylonian* woe.

(1655; 1673)

WHEN I CONSIDER HOW MY LIGHT IS SPENT

When I consider how my light is spent,
  Ere half my days,° in this dark world and wide,
  And that one Talent° which is death to hide,
  Lodg'd with me useless, though my Soul more bent
5 To serve therewith my Maker, and present
  My true account, lest he returning chide;
  "Doth God exact day-labor, light denied,"
  I fondly° ask; But patience to prevent
That murmur, soon replies, "God doth not need
10 Either man's work or his own gifts; who best
  Bear his mild yoke,° they serve him best; his State
Is Kingly. Thousands° at his bidding speed
  And post o'er Land and Ocean without rest:
  They also serve who only stand and wait."

(1652?; 1673)

METHOUGHT I SAW MY LATE ESPOUSED SAINT°

Methought I saw my late espoused Saint
  Brought to me like *Alcestis*° from the grave,
  Whom *Jove's* great Son to her glad Husband gave,
  Rescu'd from death by force though pale and faint.
5 Mine as whom washt from spot of child-bed taint,
  Purification in the old Law° did save,

And such, as yet once more I trust to have
  Full sight of her in Heaven without restraint,
Came vested all in white, pure as her mind:
  Her face was veil'd, yet to my fancied sight,   10
  Love, sweetness, goodness, in her person shin'd
So clear, as in no face with more delight.
  But O, as to embrace me she inclin'd,
  I wak'd, she fled, and day brought back my night.

(1658; 1673)

from PARADISE LOST

The "plot" of *Paradise Lost* is, in its essentials, as simple as the story of the creation of man and his expulsion from Eden in the first chapters of *Genesis*. Evil had already entered the universe before man was created, for it was born of pride and rebellion in heaven. The poem tells of the fall of Satan, the leader, and all his misguided hosts, and of his determination never to yield but rather to fight the Almighty by guile. Thus, he makes an excursion to earth, where the newly created man and woman are living in a paradise of sweet delights. By appealing to her vanity, he seduces Eve to the momentous act of disobedience against God, and she in turn lures Adam to the same trespass. Because they have sinned of their own volition they are expelled from Eden, though comforted with the promise that God's own son will come as their redeemer. The grand author of their transgression returns in triumph to his evil hosts, but at the very moment of his boasting he and the rest of the rebel angels dramatically sink from their upright state to the hissing, crawling forms of serpents, as best befits their nature.

Stripped of its poetry, the narrative is of course just a skeleton, but about that frame the poet has built an epic that reveals his "high seriousness," his assimilation of Western cultural traditions, and his unparalleled poetic craftsmanship. It is evident that he knew the ancient epics of Homer and Vergil intimately, for he made artful adaptations of such epic formulas and devices as the invocation, the beginning *in medias res* ("in the middle of things"), the "epic flashback" (putting part of the antecedent action into the mouth of a narrator), the formal roll call of the leaders, the extended Homeric similes, and innumerable other classical effects. It is apparent, too, that he knew Dante's *Divina Commedia*, since his description of hell contains many echoes of the *Inferno*. And it is evident, perhaps most of all, that Milton knew the Bible; the lines of the poem are crowded with richly amplifying allusions, not only to *Genesis*, where the loss of paradise is told, and to *Revelation*, where the war in heaven is reflected rather than detailed, but also to countless other relevant parts of the Old and New Testaments. Finally, the poem reflects his individualistic Puritan theology; it

On the Late Massacre. This sonnet is Milton's protest against the killing of the Vaudois, or Waldenses, the oldest Protestant sect in Europe, by the Duke of Savoy for their refusal to embrace the Roman Catholic faith or go into exile. Cromwell's official protest, which was written by Milton as the Latin secretary, was effective in preventing further outrages of the same sort   12 **The triple Tyrant,** the Pope. The allusion is to the tiara, or triple crown, which he wears **When I Consider** 2 **half my days.** Milton was about forty-three when he became totally blind 3 **one Talent,** an allusion to Jesus' parable of the talents (*Matthew*, 25:15–30); the "unprofitable servant" was condemned for hiding his one talent in the earth 8 **fondly,** foolishly   11 **mild yoke,** allusion to the words of Jesus, "my yoke is easy" (*Matthew*, 11:29–30)   12 **Thousands,** of angels **Me thought I saw.** There is critical disagreement as to which of Milton's first two wives is the subject here 2 **Alcestis.** In Greek legend Alcestis, devoted wife of King Admetus, offered her life that her husband might live. She was rescued from the tomb by Hercules, "Jove's great son," after a struggle with Death for her possession, and restored to her husband   6 **Purification . . . Law.** The allusion is to the Hebrew law for women who have borne children (see *Leviticus*, 12)

reveals his belief in God's justice, in the existence of a personal Adversary, and in a creed that included the doctrines of original sin and salvation by atonement.

But breaking down the poem into its various formative elements should not distract attention from the whole, the finished work. As an integrated epic poem it has certain definite characteristics which differentiate it from the epics of Homer and Vergil. It does not deal with the fortunes of a single hero, like Odysseus and Aeneas. It has, indeed, *no* hero, for it is only a romantic quibble to insist, as has been done, that the magnificently characterized Satan is the hero; the real protagonist is mankind, and the real dramatic conflict arises from man's divided propensity for good and evil. Like the classical epics, *Paradise Lost* ranges from heaven to hell, but unlike them its *milieu* is in no one country and its characters, particularly Adam and Eve, are more universal than national. As in Spenser's *Faerie Queene*—which also influenced Milton greatly—*Paradise Lost* contains many allegorical figures such as Sin and Death. Matthew Arnold characterized Homer's epics as rapid; Milton's epic, on the contrary, is, like Spenser's *Faerie Queene*, almost static in places. Even in the parts presenting the most vigorous action, as in the narration of the battles in heaven in Books V and VI, the movement is slow and deliberate compared to similar passages in the *Iliad* and the *Odyssey*. A comparison, therefore, of *Paradise Lost* with the classical epics reveals more divergence and originality than resemblance.

In one other, important respect Milton's epic differs from all others—its grandness. Milton's own seriousness and moral aspiration are reflected in his poem, and he has surely maintained his purpose of making "no middle flight." Part of the loftiness of his epic is in the subject matter and in his purpose; part, however, is in his art and notably in the "Miltonic blank verse." In the Elizabethan age, blank verse grew from a series of single lines, independent in metrical structure and often in thought, to a more closely knit group in which structure and thought ran through several lines. Milton employed the "blank verse paragraph," a device in which the measure is used with flexibility and freedom and built into a larger structure, much as single sentences combine to form prose paragraphs. Added to this control and flexibility is the sense of melody of a poet who was also an accomplished organist.

BOOK ONE

The Argument°

This first Book proposes, first in brief, the whole Subject, Man's disobedience, and the loss thereupon of Paradise wherein he was plac't: *Then touches* the prime cause of his fall, the Serpent, or rather *Satan* in the Serpent; who

revolting from God, and drawing to his side many Legions of Angels, was by the command of God driven out of Heaven with all his Crew into the great Deep. *Which action past over, the Poem hastes into the midst of things,°* *presenting* Satan with his Angels now fallen into Hell, *describ'd here,* not in the Centre (for Heaven and Earth may be suppos'd as yet not made, certainly not yet accurst) but in a place of utter darkness, fitliest call'd Chaos: Here *Satan* with his Angels lying on the burning Lake, thunder-struck and astonisht, after a certain space recovers, as from confusion, calls up him who next in Order and Dignity lay by him; they confer of thir miserable fall. *Satan* awakens all his Legions, who lay till then in the same manner confounded; They rise, thir Numbers, array of Battle, thir chief Leaders nam'd, according to the Idols known afterwards in *Canaan* and the Countries adjoining. To these *Satan* directs his Speech, comforts them with hope yet of regaining Heaven, but tells them lastly of a new World and new kind of Creature to be created, according to an ancient Prophecy or report in Heaven; *for that Angels were long before this visible Creation, was the opinion of many ancient Fathers.* To find out the truth of this Prophecy, and what to determine thereon he refers to a full Council. What his Associates thence attempt. *Pandemonium°* the Palace of *Satan* rises, suddenly built out of the Deep: The infernal Peers there sit in Council.

Of Man's First Disobedience, and the Fruit
Of that Forbidden Tree, whose mortal taste
Brought Death into the World, and all our woe,
With loss of *Eden*, till one greater Man
Restore us, and regain the blissful Seat,
Sing Heav'nly Muse,° that on the secret top
Of *Oreb*,° or of *Sinai*,° didst inspire
That Shepherd,° who first taught the chosen Seed,
In the Beginning how the Heav'ns and Earth
Rose out of *Chaos:* Or if *Sion* Hill°   10
Delight thee more, and *Siloa's* Brook° that flow'd
Fast by the Oracle of God; I thence
Invoke thy aid to my advent'rous Song,
That with no middle flight intends to soar
Above th' *Aonian* Mount,° while it pursues
Things unattempted yet in Prose or Rhyme.
And chiefly Thou O Spirit,° that dost prefer
Before all Temples th' upright heart and pure,
Instruct me, for Thou know'st; Thou from the first
Wast present, and with mighty wings outspread   20
Dove-like° satst brooding on the vast Abyss

8 **into . . . things,** an echo of *in medias res* from Horace's *Ars Poetica,* the critical principle that the epic should begin in the midst of the action and later, by an "epic flashback," recount the antecedent action   29 **Pandemonium,** literally, the place of all demons   6 **Heav'nly Muse,** the holy spirit that inspired Moses, David, and the prophets. By implication Milton contrasts this inspiration with that of the Greek muses   7 **Oreb,** or Horeb, the mountain of God on which Jehovah spoke to Moses from the midst of a burning bush (*Exodus,* 3)   8 **Sinai,** the holy mountain in the wilderness of Sinai at the top of which Moses received from God the laws to govern the Hebrews (*Exodus,* 19)   8 **That Shepherd,** Moses. The authorship of the book of *Genesis,* which includes the story of the creation, has been ascribed to him   10 **Sion Hill,** the height upon which Jerusalem was built   11 **Siloa's Brook,** stream which flowed near the hill on which the temple in Jerusalem was erected   15 **Aonian Mount,** Helicon in Boeotia, sacred to the Muses; Milton's inspiration is holier than that of the classical poets   17 **Spirit,** the Holy Ghost   21 **Dove-like.** "And the Holy Ghost descended in a bodily shape like a dove . . ." (*Luke,* 3:22)

Paradise Lost, Book I   The Argument   **Argument,** subject, theme

And mad'st it pregnant: What in me is dark
Illumine, what is low raise and support;
That to the highth of this great Argument
I may assert Eternal Providence,
And justify the ways of God to men.
    Say first, for Heav'n hides nothing from thy view
Nor the deep Tract of Hell, say first what cause
Mov'd our Grand Parents in that happy State,
30 Favor'd of Heav'n so highly, to fall off
From thir Creator, and transgress his Will
For one restraint,° Lords of the World besides?
Who first seduc'd them to that foul revolt?
Th' infernal Serpent; hee it was, whose guile
Stirr'd up with Envy and Revenge, deceiv'd
The Mother of Mankind; what time his Pride
Had cast him out from Heav'n, with all his Host
Of Rebel Angels, by whose aid aspiring
To set himself in Glory above his Peers,
40 He trusted to have equall'd the most High,
If he oppos'd; and with ambitious aim
Against the Throne and Monarchy of God
Rais'd impious War in Heav'n and Battle proud
With vain attempt. Him the Almighty Power
Hurl'd headlong flaming from th' Ethereal Sky
With hideous ruin and combustion down
To bottomless perdition, there to dwell
In Adamantine Chains and penal Fire,
Who durst defy th' Omnipotent to Arms.
50 Nine times the Space that measures Day and Night
To mortal men, hee with his horrid crew
Lay vanquisht, rolling in the fiery Gulf
Confounded though immortal: But his doom
Reserv'd him to more wrath; for now the thought
Both of lost happiness and lasting pain
Torments him; round he throws his baleful eyes
That witness'd huge affliction and dismay
Mixt with obdúrate pride and steadfast hate:
At once as far as Angels' ken he views
60 The dismal Situation waste and wild,
A Dungeon horrible, on all sides round
As one great Furnace flam'd, yet from those flames
No light, but rather darkness visible
Serv'd only to discover° sights of woe,
Regions of sorrow, doleful shades, where peace
And rest can never dwell, hope never comes
That comes to all; but torture without end
Still urges, and a fiery Deluge, fed
With ever-burning Sulphur unconsum'd:
70 Such place Eternal Justice had prepar'd
For those rebellious, here thir Prison ordained
In utter darkness, and thir portion set
As far remov'd from God and light of Heav'n
As from the Center thrice to th' utmost Pole.°

O how unlike the place from whence they fell!
There the companions of his fall, o'erwhelm'd
With Floods and Whirlwinds of tempestuous fire,
He soon discerns, and welt'ring by his side
One next himself in power, and next in crime,
Long after known in *Palestine,* and nam'd   80
Beëlzebub.° To whom th' Arch-Enemy,
And thence in Heav'n call'd Satan,° with bold words
Breaking the horrid silence thus began.
    If thou beest hee; But O how fall'n! how chang'd
From him, who in the happy Realms of Light
Cloth'd with transcendent brightness didst outshine
Myriads though bright: If he whom mutual league,
United thoughts and counsels, equal hope,
And hazard in the Glorious Enterprise,
Join'd with me once, now misery hath join'd   90
In equal ruin: into what Pit thou seest
From what highth fall'n, so much the stronger
      prov'd
He with his Thunder: and till then who knew
The force of those dire Arms? yet not for those,
Nor what the Potent Victor in his rage
Can else inflict, do I repent or change,
Though chang'd in outward luster; that fixt mind
And high disdain, from sense of injur'd merit,
That with the mightiest rais'd me to contend,
And to the fierce contention brought along   100
Innumerable force of Spirits arm'd
That durst dislike his reign, and mee preferring,
His utmost power with adverse power oppos'd
In dubious Battle on the Plains of Heav'n,
And shook his throne. What though the field be
      lost?
All is not lost; the unconquerable Will,
And study of revenge, immortal hate,
And courage never to submit or yield:
And what is else not to be overcome?
That Glory never shall his wrath or might   110
Extort from me. To bow and sue for grace
With suppliant knee, and deify his power
Who from the terror of this Arm so late
Doubted his Empire, that were low indeed,
That were an ignominy and shame beneath
This downfall; since by Fate the strength of Gods
And this Empyreal substance cannot fail,
Since through experience of this great event
In Arms not worse, in foresight much advanc't,
We may with more successful hope resolve   120
To wage by force or guile eternal War
Irreconcilable to our grand Foe,
Who now triúmphs, and in th' excess of joy
Sole reigning holds the Tyranny of Heav'n.
    So spake th' Apostate Angel, though in pain,
Vaunting aloud, but rackt with deep despair:
And him thus answer'd soon his bold Compeer.
    O Prince, O Chief of many Throned Powers,

32 **For one restraint,** in respect to one prohibition, or because of one prohibition
64 **discover,** disclose   74 **Center . . . Pole.** For the purposes of symbol and
plot Milton followed the Ptolemaic system of cosmography. At the center was the
circle of the stellar universe, and at the center of this circle was Earth; around it,
each on its own orbit, revolved the planets. Above was Heaven and at the opposite extreme, cut out of Chaos, was Hell. The radius of the stellar circle was
one-third of the distance from Heaven to Hell

81 **Beëlzebub,** a prince of the devils; his name means "lord of the flies"
82 **Satan,** the Adversary (see *Job,* 1)

That led th' imbattl'd Seraphim° to War
Under thy conduct, and in dreadful deeds
Fearless, endanger'd Heav'n's perpetual King;
And put to proof his high Supremacy,
Whether upheld by strength, or Chance, or Fate;
Too well I see and rue the dire event,
That with sad overthrow and foul defeat
Hath lost us Heav'n, and all this mighty Host
In horrible destruction laid thus low,
As far as Gods and Heav'nly Essences
Can perish: for the mind and spirit remains
Invincible, and vigor soon returns,
Though all our Glory extinct, and happy state
Here swallow'd up in endless misery.
But what if he our Conqueror (whom I now
Of force° believe Almighty, since no less
Than such could have o'erpow'rd such force as ours)
Have left us this our spirit and strength entire
Strongly to suffer and support our pains,
That we may so suffice his vengeful ire,
Or do him mightier service as his thralls
By right of War, whate'er his business be
Here in the heart of Hell to work in Fire,
Or do his Errands in the gloomy Deep;
What can it then avail though yet we feel
Strength undiminisht, or eternal being
To undergo eternal punishment?
Whereto with speedy words th' Arch-fiend repli'd.
    Fall'n Cherub, to be weak is miserable
Doing or Suffering: but of this be sure,
To do aught good never will be our task,
But ever to do ill our sole delight,
As being the contrary to his high will
Whom we resist. If then his Providence
Out of our evil seek to bring forth good,
Our labor must be to pervert that end,
And out of good still to find means of evil;
Which oft-times may succeed, so as perhaps
Shall grieve him, if I fail not, and disturb
His inmost counsels from thir destin'd aim.
But see the angry Victor hath recall'd
His Ministers of vengeance and pursuit
Back to the Gates of Heav'n: the Sulphurous Hail
Shot after us in storm, o'erblown hath laid
The fiery Surge, that from the Precipice
Of Heav'n receiv'd us falling, and the Thunder,
Wing'd with red Lightning and impetuous rage,
Perhaps hath spent his shafts, and ceases now
To bellow through the vast and boundless Deep.
Let us not slip th' occasion, whether scorn,
Or satiate fury yield it from our Foe.
Seest thou yon dreary Plain, forlorn and wild,
The seat of desolation, void of light,
Save what the glimmering of these livid flames
Casts pale and dreadful? Thither let us tend

From off the tossing of these fiery waves,
There rest, if any rest can harbor there,
And reassembling our afflicted Powers,
Consult how we may henceforth most offend
Our Enemy, our own loss how repair,
How overcome this dire Calamity,
What reinforcement we may gain from Hope,
If not what resolution from despair.
    Thus Satan talking to his nearest Mate
With Head up-lift above the wave, and Eyes
That sparkling blaz'd, his other Parts besides
Prone on the Flood, extended long and large
Lay floating many a rood, in bulk as huge
As whom the Fables name of monstrous size,
Titanian, or *Earth-born,* that warr'd on *Jove,*
Briareos or *Typhon,*° whom the Den
By ancient *Tarsus* held, or that Sea-beast
Leviathan, which God of all his works
Created hugest that swim th' Ocean stream:
Him haply slumb'ring on the *Norway* foam
The Pilot of some small night-founder'd° Skiff,
Deeming some Island, oft, as Seamen tell,
With fixed Anchor in his scaly rind
Moors by his side under the Lee, while Night
Invests the Sea, and wished Morn delays:
So stretcht out huge in length the Arch-fiend lay
Chain'd on the burning Lake, nor ever thence
Had ris'n or heav'd his head, but that the will
And high permission of all-ruling Heaven
Left him at large to his own dark designs,
That with reiterated crimes he might
Heap on himself damnation, while he sought
Evil to others, and enrag'd might see
How all his malice serv'd but to bring forth
Infinite goodness, grace and mercy shown
On Man by him seduc't, but on himself
Treble confusion, wrath and vengeance pour'd.
Forthwith upright he rears from off the Pool
His mighty Stature; on each hand the flames
Driv'n backward slope thir pointing spires, and roll
In billows, leave i' th' midst a horrid Vale.
Then with expanded wings he steers his flight
Aloft, incumbent on the dusky Air
That felt unusual weight, till on dry Land
He lights, if it were Land that ever burn'd
With solid, as the Lake with liquid fire
And such appear'd in hue; as when the force
Of subterranean wind transports a Hill
Torn from *Pelorus,*° or the shatter'd side
Of thund'ring *Ætna,* whose combustible
And fuell'd entrails thence conceiving Fire,
Sublim'd with Mineral fury, aid the Winds,
And leave a singed bottom all involv'd
With stench and smoke: Such resting found the sole

130

140

150

160

170

180

190

200

210

220

230

---

129 **Powers . . . Seraphim.** Milton follows the medieval conception of the celestial hierarchy also employed by Dante. The order is (1) Seraphim (2) Cherubim (3) Thrones (4) Dominions (5) Virtues (6) Powers (7) Principalities (8) Archangels (9) Angels   144 **Of force,** perforce, of necessity

199 **Briareos or Typhon,** in Greek myth, two monsters, the first with a hundred hands, the second with a hundred fire-breathing heads, who attempted to overthrow the dynasty of Jove. Typhon lived in Cilicia, of which Tarsus was the capital   204 **night-founder'd,** obliged to furl sail for the night. The fable alluded to here is an ancient one   232 **Pelorus,** northeastern promontory of Sicily near the volcano of Mt. Etna

Of unblest feet. Him follow'd his next Mate,
Both glorying to have scap't the *Stygian* flood
240 As Gods, and by thir own recover'd strength,
Not by the sufferance of supernal Power.

   Is this the Region, this the Soil, the Clime,
Said then the lost Arch-Angel, this the seat
That we must change for Heav'n, this mournful gloom
For that celestial light? Be it so, since he
Who now is Sovran can dispose and bid
What shall be right: fardest from him is best
Whom reason hath equall'd, force hath made
      supreme
Above his equals. Farewell happy Fields
250 Where Joy for ever dwells: Hail horrors, hail
Infernal world, and thou profoundest Hell
Receive thy new Possessor: One who brings
A mind not to be chang'd by Place or Time.
The mind is its own place, and in itself
Can make a Heav'n of Hell, a Hell of Heav'n.
What matter where, if I be still the same,
And what I should be, all but less than hee
Whom Thunder hath made greater? Here at least
We shall be free; th' Almighty hath not built
260 Here for his envy, will not drive us hence:
Here we may reign secure, and in my choice
To reign is worth ambition though in Hell:
Better to reign in Hell, than serve in Heav'n.
But wherefore let we then our faithful friends,
Th' associates and copartners of our loss
Lie thus astonisht on th' oblivious Pool,
And call them not to share with us their part
In this unhappy Mansion: or once more
With rallied Arms to try what may be yet
270 Regain'd in Heav'n, or what more lost in Hell?

   So *Satan* spake, and him *Beëlzebub*
Thus answer'd. Leader of those Armies bright,
Which but th' Omnipotent none could have foiled,
If once they hear that voice, thir liveliest pledge
Of hope in fears and dangers, heard so oft
In worst extremes, and on the perilous edge
Of battle when it rag'd, in all assaults
Thir surest signal, they will soon resume
New courage and revive, though now they lie
280 Groveling and prostrate on yon Lake of Fire,
As we erewhile, astounded and amaz'd;
No wonder, fall'n such a pernicious highth.

   He scarce had ceas't when the superior Fiend
Was moving toward the shore; his ponderous shield
Ethereal temper, massy, large and round,
Behind him cast; the broad circumference
Hung on his shoulders like the Moon, whose Orb
Through Optic Glass° the *Tuscan* Artist° views
At Ev'ning from the top of *Fesole,°*
290 Or in *Valdarno,°* to descry new Lands,
Rivers or Mountains in her spotty Globe.

His Spear, to equal which the tallest Pine
Hewn on *Norwegian* hills, to be the Mast
Of some great Ammiral,° were but a wand,
He walkt with to support uneasy steps
Over the burning Marl, not like those steps
On Heaven's Azure, and the torrid Clime
Smote on him sore besides, vaulted with Fire;
Nathless he so endur'd, till on the Beach
Of that inflamed Sea, he stood and call'd   300
His Legions, Angel Forms, who lay intrans't
Thick as Autumnal Leaves that strow the Brooks
In *Vallombrosa,°* where th' *Etrurian°* shades
High overarch't imbow'r; or scatter'd sedge
Afloat, when with fierce Winds *Orion°* arm'd
Hath vext the Red-Sea Coast, whose waves o'erthrew
Busiris° and his *Memphian* Chivalry,
While with perfidious hatred they pursu'd
The Sojourners of *Goshen,°* who beheld
From the safe shore thir floating Carcasses   310
And broken Chariot Wheels; so thick bestrown
Abject and lost lay these, covering the Flood,
Under amazement of thir hideous change.
He call'd so loud, that all the hollow Deep
Of Hell resounded. Princes, Potentates,
Warriors, the Flow'r of Heav'n, once yours, now lost,
If such astonishment as this can seize
Eternal spirits; or have ye chos'n this place
After the toil of Battle to repose
Your wearied virtue, for the ease you find   320
To slumber here, as in the Vales of Heav'n?
Or in this abject posture have ye sworn
To adore the Conqueror? who now beholds
Cherub and Seraph rolling in the Flood
With scatter'd Arms and Ensigns, till anon
His swift pursuers from Heav'n Gates discern
Th' advantage, and descending tread us down
Thus drooping, or with linked Thunderbolts
Transfix us to the bottom of this Gulf.
Awake, arise, or be for ever fall'n.   330

   They heard, and were abasht, and up they sprung
Upon the wing; as when men wont to watch
On duty, sleeping found by whom they dread,
Rouse and bestir themselves ere well awake.
Nor did they not perceive the evil plight
In which they were, or the fierce pains not feel;
Yet to thir General's Voice they soon obey'd
Innumerable. As when the potent Rod
Of *Amram's* Son° in *Egypt's* evil day
Wav'd round the Coast, up call'd a pitchy cloud   340
Of *Locusts,* warping on the Eastern Wind,
That o'er the Realm of impious *Pharaoh* hung
Like Night, and darken'd all the Land of *Nile:*

---

288 **Optic Glass,** telescope   **Tuscan Artist,** Galileo, Italian astronomer (1564–1642); he was a defender of the Copernican theory of astronomy which was opposed to the Ptolemaic theory   289 **Fesole,** the modern Fiesole, a hill near Florence   290 **Valdarno,** the valley of the River Arno, in which Florence is situated

294 **Ammiral,** admiral, the flagship bearing the commander of the fleet   303 **Vallombrosa,** a valley twenty miles east of Florence   **Etruria** is now Tuscany and part of Umbria   305 **Orion,** in Greek myth, a hunter who became a constellation upon his death. When the constellation rises late (in November), it is supposed to create storms   307 **Busiris,** a mythical king of Egypt; he was not, however, the Pharaoh of the Exodus (see *Exodus,* 14)   309 **Sojourners of Goshen,** the Hebrews who lived, before the Exodus, in a district of northern Egypt called Goshen (see *Genesis,* 47:27)   339 **Amram's Son,** Moses. For the account of the plague of locusts see *Exodus,* 10:12–19

So numberless were those bad Angels seen
Hovering on wing under the Cope of Hell
'Twixt upper, nether, and surrounding Fires;
Till, as a signal giv'n, th' uplifted Spear
Of thir great Sultan waving to direct
Thir course, in even balance down they light
350 On the firm brimstone, and fill all the Plain;
A multitude, like which the populous North
Pour'd never from her frozen loins, to pass
Rhene or the *Danaw*,° when her barbarous Sons
Came like a Deluge on the South, and spread
Beneath *Gibraltar* to the *Lybian* sands.
Forthwith from every Squadron and each Band
The Heads and Leaders thither haste where stood
Thir great Commander; Godlike shapes and forms
Excelling human, Princely Dignities,
360 And Powers that erst in Heaven sat on Thrones;
Though of thir Names in heav'nly Records now
Be no memorial, blotted out and ras'd
By thir Rebellion, from the Books of Life.
Nor had they yet among the Sons of *Eve*
Got them new Names, till wand'ring o'er the Earth,
Through God's high sufferance for the trial of man,
By falsities and lies the greatest part
Of Mankind they corrupted to forsake
God thir Creator, and th' invisible
370 Glory of him that made them, to transform
Oft to the Image of a Brute, adorn'd
With gay Religions full of Pomp and Gold,
And Devils to adore for Deities:
Then were they known to men by various Names,
And various Idols through the Heathen World.
Say, Muse, thir Names° then known, who first, who
    last,
Rous'd from the slumber on that fiery Couch,
At thir great Emperor's call, as next in worth
Came singly where he stood on the bare strand,
380 While the promiscuous crowd stood yet aloof?
The chief were those who from the Pit of Hell
Roaming to seek thir prey on earth, durst fix
Thir Seats long after next the Seat° of God,
Thir Altars by his Altar, Gods ador'd
Among the Nations round, and durst abide
Jehovah thund'ring out of *Sion*, thron'd
Between the Cherubim; yea, often plac'd
Within his Sanctuary itself thir Shrines,
Abominations; and with cursed things
390 His holy Rites, and solemn Feasts profan'd,
And with thir darkness durst affront his light.
First *Moloch*,° horrid King besmear'd with blood
Of human sacrifice, and parents' tears,
Though for the noise of Drums and Timbrels loud

Thir children's cries unheard, that pass'd through fire
To his grim Idol. Him the *Ammonite*
Worship in *Rabba* and her wat'ry Plain,
In *Argob* and in *Basan*, to the stream
Of utmost *Arnon.*° Nor content with such
Audacious neighborhood, the wisest heart   400
Of *Solomon* he led by fraud to build
His Temple right against the Temple of God
On that opprobrious Hill,° and made his Grove
The pleasant Valley of *Hinnom, Tophet*° thence
And black *Gehenna*° call'd, the Type of Hell.
Next *Chemos*,° th' obscene dread of *Moab's* Sons,
From *Aroar*° to *Nebo*, and the wild
Of Southmost *Abarim;* in *Hesebon*
And *Horonaim, Seon's* Realm, beyond
The flow'ry Dale of *Sibma* clad with Vines,   410
And *Eleale* to th' *Asphaltic* Pool.°
Peor his other Name, when he entic'd
Israel in *Sittim* on thir march from *Nile*
To do him wanton rites,° which cost them woe.
Yet thence his lustful Orgies he enlarg'd
Even to that Hill of scandal,° by the Grove
Of *Moloch* homicide, lust hard by hate;
Till good *Josiah*° drove them thence to Hell.
With these came they, who from the bord'ring flood
Of old *Euphrates* to the Brook that parts   420
Egypt from *Syrian* ground, had general Names
Of *Baalim* and *Ashtaroth,*° those male,
These Feminine. For Spirits when they please
Can either Sex assume, or both; so soft
And uncompounded is thir Essence pure,
Not ti'd or manacl'd with joint or limb,
Nor founded on the brittle strength of bones,
Like cumbrous flesh; but in what shape they choose
Dilated or condens't, bright or obscure,
Can execute thir aery purposes,   430
And works of love or enmity fulfil.
For those the Race of *Israel* oft forsook
Thir living strength, and unfrequented left
His righteous Altar, bowing lowly down
To bestial Gods; for which thir heads as low
Bow'd down in Battle, sunk before the Spear
Of despicable foes. With these in troop
Came *Astoreth*, whom the *Phœnicians* call'd
Astarte, Queen of Heav'n, with crescent Horns;
To whose bright Image nightly by the Moon   440
Sidonian° Virgins paid thir Vows and Songs,
In *Sion* also not unsung, where stood

353 **Rhene ... Danaw,** the Rhine and Danube, respectively. The allusion is to the invasion of the Roman Empire by the northern tribes in the third through fifth centuries; they spread westward to Spain and, crossing to Africa, captured Carthage   376 **Say ... Names.** This roll call of leaders may have been suggested by the naming and numbering of the Greek and Trojan hosts in Book II of the *Iliad.* Milton gives to his devil chieftains the names of the principal heathen gods   383 **next to the Seat,** an allusion to the numerous occasions in Hebrew history on which shrines to foreign gods were erected in or near the temple of Jehovah   392 **Moloch,** fire god worshiped by the sacrifice of infants incinerated in the heated arms of his statue (see *I Kings,* 11:7)

399 **Rabba ... Arnon.** Rabba was the capital of Ammon; Argob, Basan (for Bashan), and Arnon are east of the Jordan River and in the northern sections of Ammon   403 **opprobrious Hill,** the Mount of Olives where Solomon built a shrine to Moloch (see *I Kings,* 11:5–7)   404 **Tophet,** probably not the valley itself but a place of sacrifice to Moloch established there   405 **Gehenna,** the Greek name for the valley of Hinnom. Perpetual fires were maintained there to burn the city refuse   406 **Chemos,** god of Moab, another tribe east of the Jordan   407 **Aroar, etc.,** names of towns and mountains in the district of the Jordan River extending south to the Dead Sea   411 **Asphaltic Pool,** so-called because of the bitumen in it   414 **To do ... rites.** At Shittim, during the wanderings, thousands of Israelites were executed for taking Moabitish wives and worshiping Baal-peor, the god of the Moabites (*Numbers,* 25)   416 **Hill of scandal.** See l. 403   418 **Josiah,** the good king of Judah who restored the worship of Jehovah (see *II Kings,* 23)   422 **Baalim and Ashtaroth,** collective names for manifestations of the sun god and the moon goddess, respectively; Milton gives the individual names later   441 **Sidonian,** from Sidon, a Phoenician city

Her Temple on th' offensive Mountain, built
By that uxorious King,° whose heart though large,
Beguil'd by fair Idolatresses, fell
To Idols foul. *Thammuz*° came next behind,
Whose annual wound in *Lebanon*° allur'd
The *Syrian* Damsels to lament his fate
In amorous ditties all a Summer's day,
450 While smooth *Adonis* from his native Rock
Ran purple to the Sea, suppos'd with blood
Of *Thammuz* yearly wounded: the Love-tale
Infected *Sion's* daughters° with like heat,
Whose wanton passions in the sacred Porch
Ezekiel saw, when by the Vision led
His eye survey'd the dark Idolatries
Of alienated *Judah*. Next came one
Who mourn'd in earnest, when the Captive Ark
Maim'd his brute Image, head and hands lopt off
460 In his own Temple, on the grunsel edge,°
Where he fell flat, and sham'd his Worshippers:
Dagon° his Name, Sea Monster, upward Man
And downward Fish: yet had his Temple high
Rear'd in *Azotus*, dreaded through the Coast
Of *Palestine*, in *Gath* and *Ascalon*,
And *Accaron* and *Gaza's*° frontier bounds.
Him follow'd *Rimmon*,° whose delightful Seat
Was fair *Damascus*, on the fertile Banks
Of *Abbana* and *Pharphar*, lucid streams.
470 He also against the house of God was bold:
A Leper once he lost and gain'd a King,
Ahaz° his sottish Conqueror, whom he drew
God's Altar to disparage and displace
For one of *Syrian* mode, whereon to burn
His odious off'rings, and adore the Gods
Whom he had vanquisht. After these appear'd
A crew who under Names of old Renown,
Osiris, Isis, Orus and thir Train
With monstrous° shapes and sorceries abus'd
480 Fanatic *Egypt* and her Priests, to seek
Thir wand'ring Gods disguis'd in brutish forms°
Rather than human. Nor did *Israel* scape
Th' infection when thir borrow'd Gold compos'd
The Calf in *Oreb:*° and the Rebel King°
Doubl'd that sin in *Bethel* and in *Dan*,
Lik'ning his Maker to the Grazed Ox,
Jehovah, who in one Night when he pass'd
From *Egypt* marching, equall'd° with one stroke
Both her first born and all her bleating Gods.
490 *Belial* came last, than whom a Spirit more lewd
Fell not from Heaven, or more gross to love

Vice for itself: To him no Temple stood
Or Altar smok'd; yet who more oft than hee
In Temples and at Altars, when the Priest
Turns Atheist, as did *Ely's* Sons,° who fill'd
With lust and violence the house of God.
In Courts and Palaces he also Reigns
And in luxurious° Cities, where the noise
Of riot ascends above thir loftiest Tow'rs,
And injury and outrage: And when Night   500
Darkens the Streets, then wander forth the Sons
Of *Belial*, flown° with insolence and wine.
Witness the Streets of *Sodom*,° and that night
In *Gibeah*,° when the hospitable door
Expos'd a Matron to avoid worse rape.
These were the prime in order and in might;
The rest were long to tell, though far renown'd,
Th' *Ionian*° Gods, of *Javan's*° Issue held
Gods, yet confest later than Heav'n and Earth
Thir boasted Parents; *Titan*° Heav'n's first born   510
With his enormous brood, and birthright seiz'd
By younger *Saturn*,° he from mightier *Jove*
His own and *Rhea's* Son like measure found;
So *Jove* usurping reign'd: these first in *Crete*
And *Ida*° known, thence on the Snowy top
Of cold *Olympus* rul'd the middle Air
Thir highest Heav'n; or on the *Delphian* Cliff,°
Or in *Dodona*,° and through all the bounds
Of *Doric*° Land; or who with *Saturn* old
Fled over *Adria*° to th' *Hesperian* Fields,°   520
And o'er the *Celtic*° roam'd the utmost Isles.°
All these and more came flocking; but with looks
Downcast and damp, yet such wherein appear'd
Obscure some glimpse of joy, to have found thir chief
Not in despair, to have found themselves not lost
In loss itself; which on his count'nance cast
Like doubtful hue: but he his wonted pride
Soon recollecting, with high words, that bore
Semblance of worth, not substance, gently rais'd
Thir fainting courage, and dispell'd thir fears.   530
Then straight commands that at the warlike sound
Of Trumpets loud and Clarions be uprear'd
His mighty Standard; that proud honor claim'd
Azazel as his right, a Cherub tall:
Who forthwith from the glittering Staff unfurl'd
Th' Imperial Ensign, which full high advanc't°
Shone like a Meteor streaming to the Wind
With Gems and Golden lustre rich imblaz'd,
Seraphic arms and Trophies: all the while
Sonorous metal blowing Martial sounds: 540
At which the universal Host upsent

444 **uxorious king,** Solomon 446 **Thammuz,** the Adonis of Greek myth who was slain by a boar 447 **annual wound in Lebanon,** an allusion to the bringing down of the red mud from the Lebanon Mountains of northern Palestine in the Adonis River 453 **Sion's daughters,** the women of Jerusalem 460 **grunsel edge,** threshold. The story is told in I Samuel, 5:4 462 **Dagon,** sea god of the Philistines who dwelt on the coast of Palestine 464 **Azotus . . . Gaza,** the five chief cities of the Philistines 467 **Rimmon,** god of Damascus 472 **Ahaz,** King of Judah (see II Kings, 16) 479 **monstrous,** because often represented with animals' heads 481 **brutish forms,** Osiris, bull; Isis, cow; Orus, sun 484 **The Calf in Oreb.** See Exodus, 32 **the Rebel King,** Jeroboam, who rebelled with ten tribes against Rehoboam, son of Solomon, and established the northern kingdom of Israel. His idolatry in the two northern cities is told in I Kings, 12:28–33 488 **equall'd,** made equal in death. The allusion is to the tenth plague (see Exodus, 12)

495 **Ely's Sons.** See I Samuel, 2:12–17; "now the sons of Eli were the sons of Belial; they knew not the Lord" 498 **luxurious,** lustful 502 **flown,** flushed 503 **Sodom,** the wicked city of the plain destroyed with its sister city Gomorrah; for the particular episode alluded to see Genesis, 19:1–11 504 **Gibeah.** See Judges, 19 508 **Ionian,** Greek **Javan,** one of the sons of Japheth 510 **Titan,** son of Heaven (Uranus) and Earth (Ge) **Saturn,** a Titan who dethroned his father Uranus and was in turn dethroned by his son Zeus (Jove) 515 **Ida.** According to Greek mythology Zeus was born on Mount Ida and established his regular abode on Olympus 517 **Delphian Cliff,** an oracle of Apollo 518 **Dodona,** an oracle of Zeus 519 **Doric,** Greek 520 **Adria,** the Adriatic **Hesperian Fields,** an allusion to Italy where the older dynasty of Greek gods was worshiped by the Romans 521 **the Celtic,** France and Spain **utmost Isles,** the islands of Britain 536 **advanc't,** raised

John Milton   333

A shout that tore Hell's Concave, and beyond
Frighted the Reign of *Chaos* and old *Night.*
All in a moment through the gloom were seen
Ten thousand Banners rise into the Air
With Orient° Colors waving: with them rose
A Forest huge of Spears: and thronging Helms
Appear'd, and serried Shields in thick array
Of depth immeasurable: Anon they move
550 In perfect *Phalanx°* to the *Dorian* mood°
Of Flutes and soft Recorders; such as rais'd
To highth of noblest temper Heroes old
Arming to Battle, and instead of rage
Deliberate valor breath'd, firm and unmov'd
With dread of death to flight or foul retreat,
Nor wanting power to mitigate and swage
With solemn touches, troubl'd thoughts, and chase
Anguish and doubt and fear and sorrow and pain
From mortal or immortal minds. Thus they
560 Breathing united force with fixed thought
Mov'd on in silence to soft Pipes that charm'd
Thir painful steps o'er the burnt soil; and now
Advanc't in view they stand, a horrid Front
Of dreadful length and dazzling Arms, in guise
Of Warriors old with order'd Spear and Shield,
Awaiting what command thir mighty Chief
Had to impose: He through the armed Files
Darts his experienc't eye, and soon traverse
The whole Battalion views, thir order due,
570 Thir visages and stature as of Gods;
Thir number last he sums. And now his heart
Distends with pride, and hard'ning in his strength
Glories: For never since created man,
Met such imbodied force, as nam'd with these
Could merit more than that small infantry°
Warr'd on by Cranes: though all the Giant brood°
Of *Phlegra* with th' Heroic Race were join'd
That fought at *Thebes* and *Ilium,°* on each side
Mixt with auxiliar Gods; and what resounds
580 In Fable or *Romance* of *Uther's* Son°
Begirt with *British* and *Armoric°* Knights;
And all who since, Baptiz'd or Infidel
Jousted in *Aspramont°* or *Montalban,*
Damasco, or *Marocco,* or *Trebisond,*
Or whom *Biserta* sent from *Afric* shore
When *Charlemain* with all his Peerage fell
By *Fontarabbia.°* Thus far these beyond
Compare of mortal prowess, yet observ'd
Thir dread commander: he above the rest
590 In shape and gesture proudly eminent
Stood like a Tow'r; his form had yet not lost
All her Original brightness, nor appear'd

Less than Arch-Angel ruin'd, and th' excess
Of Glory obscur'd: As when the Sun new ris'n
Looks through the Horizontal misty Air
Shorn of his Beams, or from behind the Moon
In dim Eclipse disastrous twilight sheds
On half the Nations, and with fear of change
Perplexes Monarchs. Dark'n'd so, yet shone
Above them all th' Arch-Angel: but his face   600
Deep scars of Thunder had intrencht, and care
Sat on his faded cheek, but under Brows
Of dauntless courage, and considerate Pride
Waiting revenge: cruel his eye, but cast
Signs of remorse and passion° to behold
The fellows of his crime, the followers rather
(Far other once beheld in bliss) condemn'd
For ever now to have thir lot in pain,
Millions of Spirits for his fault amerc't°
Of Heav'n, and from Eternal Splendors flung   610
For his revolt, yet faithful how they stood,
Thir Glory wither'd. As when Heaven's Fire
Hath scath'd the Forest Oaks, or Mountain Pines,
With singed top thir stately growth though bare
Stands on the blasted Heath. He now prepar'd
To speak; whereat thir doubl'd Ranks they bend
From wing to wing, and half enclose him round
With all his Peers: attention held them mute.
Thrice he assay'd, and thrice in spite of scorn,
Tears such as Angels weep, burst forth: at last   620
Words interwove with sighs found out thir way.

O Myriads of immortal Spirits, O Powers
Matchless, but with th' Almighty, and that strife
Was not inglorious, though th' event was dire,
As this place testifies, and this dire change
Hateful to utter: but what power of mind
Foreseeing or presaging, from the Depth
Of knowledge past or present, could have fear'd
How such united force of Gods, how such
As stood like these, could ever know repulse?   630
For who can yet believe, though after loss,
That all these puissant Legions, whose exile
Hath emptied Heav'n, shall fail to re-ascend
Self-rais'd, and repossess thir native seat?
For mee be witness all the Host of Heav'n,
If counsels different, or danger shunn'd
By me, have lost our hopes. But he who reigns
Monarch in Heav'n, till then as one secure
Sat on his Throne, upheld by old repute,
Consent or custom, and his Regal State   640
Put forth at full, but still his strength conceal'd,
Which tempted our attempt, and wrought our fall.
Henceforth his might we know, and know our own
So as not either to provoke, or dread
New War, provok't; our better part remains
To work in close design, by fraud or guile
What force effected not: that he no less
At length from us may find, who overcomes

546 **Orient,** bright 550 **Phalanx,** body of troops in close array **Dorian mood,**
stern and suitable for battle 575 **small infantry.** In classical legend the Pygmies
of Ethiopia waged continual war with the cranes who attacked them 576 **Giant
brood,** the giants who were defeated by the gods at Phlegra in Macedonia
578 **Thebes and Ilium,** in Greek story, the cities respectively of the warfare of
"The Seven Against Thebes" and of the Trojan War 580 **Uther's Son,** King
Arthur 581 **Armoric,** Breton 583 **Aspramont, etc.,** places made famous by
exploits of crusaders and heroes of the romances of chivalry 585 **Biserta . . .
Fontarabbia,** an allusion to a legend concerning the defeat of Charlemagne and
the twelve peers of France

605 **passion,** suffering 609 **amerc't,** punished by being deprived of heaven

By force, hath overcome but half his foe.
650 Space may produce new Worlds; whereof so rife
There went a fame° in Heav'n that he ere long
Intended to create, and therein plant
A generation, whom his choice regard
Should favor equal to the Sons of Heaven:
Thither, if but to pry, shall be perhaps
Our first eruption, thither or elsewhere:
For this Infernal Pit shall never hold
Celestial Spirits in Bondage, nor th' Abyss
Long under darkness cover. But these thoughts
660 Full Counsel must mature: Peace is despair'd,
For who can think Submission? War then, War
Open or understood, must be resolv'd.

He spake: and to confirm his words, out-flew
Millions of flaming swords, drawn from the thighs
Of mighty Cherubim; the sudden blaze
Far round illumin'd hell: highly they rag'd
Against the Highest, and fierce with grasped Arms
Clash'd on thir sounding shields the din of war,
Hurling defiance toward the Vault of Heav'n.
670 There stood a Hill not far whose grisly top
Belch'd fire and rolling smoke; the rest entire
Shone with a glossy scurf, undoubted sign
That in his womb was hid metallic Ore,
The work of Sulphur. Thither wing'd with speed
A numerous Brigad hasten'd. As when bands
Of Pioners° with Spade and Pickax arm'd
Forerun the Royal Camp, to trench a Field,
Or cast a Rampart. Mammon° led them on,
Mammon, the least erected Spirit that fell
680 From Heav'n, for ev'n in Heav'n his looks and
thoughts
Were always downward bent, admiring more
The riches of Heav'n's pavement, trodd'n Gold,
Than aught divine or holy else enjoy'd
In vision beatific: by him first
Men also, and by his suggestion taught,
Ransack'd the Center, and with impious hands
Rifl'd the bowels of thir mother Earth
For Treasures better hid. Soon had his crew
Op'n'd into the Hill a spacious wound
690 And digg'd out ribs of Gold. Let none admire°
That riches grow in Hell; that soil may best
Deserve the precious bane. And here let those
Who boast in mortal things, and wond'ring tell
Of Babel,° and the works of Memphian Kings,°
Learn how thir greatest Monuments of Fame,
And Strength and Art are easily outdone
By Spirits reprobate, and in an hour
What in an age they with incessant toil
And hands innumerable scarce perform.
700 Nigh on the Plain in many cells prepar'd,
That underneath had veins of liquid fire

Sluic'd from the Lake, a second multitude
With wondrous Art founded the massy Ore,
Severing each kind, and scumm'd the Bullion dross:
A third as soon had form'd within the ground
A various mould, and from the boiling cells
By strange conveyance fill'd each hollow nook:
As in an Organ from one blast of wind
To many a row of Pipes the sound-board breathes.
Anon out of the earth a Fabric huge   710
Rose like an Exhalation, with the sound
Of Dulcet Symphonies and voices sweet,
Built like a Temple, where Pilasters round
Were set, and Doric pillars overlaid
With Golden Architrave; nor did there want
Cornice or Frieze, with bossy Sculptures grav'n;
The Roof was fretted Gold. Not Babylon,
Nor great Alcairo° such magnificence
Equall'd in all thir glories, to inshrine
Belus or Serapis° thir Gods, or seat   720
Thir Kings, when Egypt with Assyria strove
In wealth and luxury. Th' ascending pile
Stood fixt her stately highth, and straight the doors
Op'ning thir brazen folds discover wide
Within, her ample spaces, o'er the smooth
And level pavement: from the arched roof
Pendant by subtle Magic many a row
Of Starry Lamps and blazing Cressets° fed
With Naphtha and Asphaltus yielded light
As from a sky. The hasty multitude   730
Admiring enter'd, and the work some praise
And some the Architect: his hand was known
In Heav'n by many a Tow'red structure high,
Where Scepter'd Angels held thir residence,
And sat as Princes, whom the supreme King
Exalted to such power, and gave to rule,
Each in his Hierarchy, the Orders bright.
Nor was his name unheard or unador'd
In ancient Greece; and in Ausonian land°
Men call'd him Mulciber;° and how he fell   740
From Heav'n, they fabl'd, thrown by angry Jove
Sheer o'er the Crystal Battlements: from Morn
To Noon he fell, from Noon to dewy Eve,
A Summer's day; and with the setting Sun
Dropt from the Zenith like a falling Star,
On Lemnos th' Ægæan Isle: thus they relate,
Erring; for he with this rebellious rout
Fell long before; nor aught avail'd him now
To have built in Heav'n high Tow'rs; nor did he scape
By all his Engines, but was headlong sent   750
With his industrious crew to build in hell.
Meanwhile the winged Heralds by command
Of Sovran power, with awful Ceremony
And Trumpets' sound throughout the Host proclaim
A solemn Council forthwith to be held
At Pandæmonium, the high Capitol

---

651 fame, rumor, report   676 Pioners, soldiers detailed to make entrenchments,
lay roads, and do other military engineering   678 Mammon, symbol of riches;
"ye cannot serve God and mammon" (Matthew, 6:24)   690 admire, wonder
694 Babel. The allusion is to the building of the Tower of Babel (Genesis, 11:1-9)
Memphian kings. The allusion here is to the building of the pyramids

718 Alcairo, Cairo   720 Belus or Serapis, the Assyrian god Bel and an Egyptian
deity, respectively   728 Cressets, fire baskets for illumination   739 Ausonian
land, Italy   740 Mulciber, Vulcan or Hephaestos

Of Satan and his Peers: thir summons call'd
From every Band and squared Regiment
By place or choice the worthiest; they anon
760 With hundreds and with thousands trooping came
Attended: all access was throng'd, the Gates
And Porches wide, but chief the spacious Hall
(Though like a cover'd field, where Champions bold
Wont ride in arm'd, and at the Soldan's° chair
Defi'd the best of *Paynim*° chivalry
To mortal combat or career with Lance)
Thick swarm'd, both on the ground and in the air,
Brusht with the hiss of rustling wings. As Bees
In spring time, when the Sun with *Taurus*° rides,
770 Pour forth thir populous youth about the Hive
In clusters; they among fresh dews and flowers
Fly to and fro, or on the smoothed Plank,
The suburb of thir Straw-built Citadel,
New rubb'd with Balm, expatiate and confer
Thir State affairs. So thick the aery crowd
Swarm'd and were strait'n'd; till the Signal giv'n,
Behold a wonder! they but now who seem'd
In bigness to surpass Earth's Giant Sons
Now less than smallest Dwarfs, in narrow room
780 Throng numberless, like that Pigmean Race
Beyond the *Indian* Mount, or Faery Elves,
Whose midnight Revels, by a Forest side
Or Fountain some belated Peasant sees,
Or dreams he sees, while over-head the Moon
Sits Arbitress, and nearer to the Earth
Wheels her pale course; they on thir mirth and dance
Intent, with jocund Music charm his ear;
At once with joy and fear his heart rebounds.
Thus incorporeal Spirits to smallest forms
790 Reduc'd thir shapes immense, and were at large,
Though without number still amidst the Hall
Of that infernal Court. But far within
And in thir own dimensions like themselves
The great Seraphic Lords and Cherubim
In close recess and secret conclave sat
A thousand Demi-Gods on golden seats,
Frequent° and full. After short silence then
And summons read, the great consult° began.

The End of the First Book.

BOOK TWO

The Argument

The Consultation begun, *Satan* debates whether another
Battle be to be hazarded for the recovery of Heaven:
some advise it, others dissuade: A third proposal is preferr'd, mention'd before by *Satan*, to search the truth of

764 **Soldan's,** Sultan's   765 **Paynim,** pagan   769 **Sun with Taurus.** The sun is in Taurus, the bull (a sign of the zodiac—April 19–May 20)   797 **Frequent,** crowded   798 **consult,** consultation

that Prophecy or Tradition in Heaven concerning
another world, and another kind of creature equal or not
much inferior to themselves, about this time to be
created: Thir doubt who shall be sent on this difficult
search: *Satan* thir chief undertakes alone the voyage, is
honor'd and applauded. The Council thus ended, the   10
rest betake them several ways and to several employments, as thir inclinations lead them, to entertain the
time till *Satan* return. He passes on his Journey to Hell
Gates, finds them shut, and who sat there to guard them,
by whom at length they are op'n'd, and discover to him
the great Gulf between Hell and Heaven; with what
difficulty he passes through, directed by *Chaos*, the
Power of that place, to the sight of this new World which
he sought.

High on a Throne of Royal State, which far
Outshone the wealth of *Ormus*° and of *Ind*,°
Or where the gorgeous East with richest hand
Show'rs on her Kings *Barbaric* Pearl and Gold,
Satan exalted sat, by merit rais'd
To that bad eminence; and from despair
Thus high uplifted beyond hope, aspires
Beyond thus high, insatiate to pursue
Vain War with Heav'n, and by success° untaught
His proud imaginations thus display'd.   10
Powers and Dominions, Deities of Heav'n,
For since no deep within her gulf can hold
Immortal vigor, though opprest and fall'n,
I give not Heav'n for lost. From this descent
Celestial Virtues rising, will appear
More glorious and more dread than from no fall
And trust themselves to fear no second fate:
Mee though just right and the fixt Laws of Heav'n
Did first create your Leader, next, free choice,
With what besides, in Counsel or in Fight,   20
Hath been achiev'd of merit, yet this loss
Thus far at least recover'd, hath much more
Establisht in a safe unenvied Throne
Yielded with full consent. The happier state
In Heav'n, which follows dignity, might draw
Envy from each inferior; but who here
Will envy whom the highest place exposes
Foremost to stand against the Thunderer's aim
Your bulwark, and condemns to greatest share
Of endless pain? where there is then no good   30
For which to strive, no strife can grow up there
From Faction; for none sure will claim in Hell
Precedence, none, whose portion is so small
Of present pain, that with ambitious mind
Will covet more. With this advantage then
To union, and firm Faith, and firm accord,
More than can be in Heav'n, we now return
To claim our just inheritance of old,
Surer to prosper than prosperity
Could have assur'd us; and by what best way,   40

Book II   2 **Ormus,** for Ormuz, an ancient and very rich commercial city on an island in the Persian Gulf   **Ind,** India   9 **success,** experience

Whether of open War or covert guile,
We now debate; who can advise, may speak.
    He ceas'd, and next him *Moloch,* Scepter'd King
Stood up, the strongest and the fiercest Spirit
That fought in Heav'n; now fiercer by despair:
His trust was with th' Eternal to be deem'd
Equal in strength, and rather than be less
Car'd not to be at all; with that care lost
Went all his fear: of God, or Hell, or worse
50 He reck'd° not, and these words thereafter spake.
    My sentence is for open War: Of Wiles,
More unexpert, I boast not: them let those
Contrive who need, or when they need, not now.
For while they sit contriving, shall the rest,
Millions that stand in Arms, and longing wait
The Signal to ascend, sit ling'ring here
Heav'n's fugitives, and for thir dwelling place
Accept this dark opprobrious Den of shame,
The Prison of his Tyranny who Reigns
60 By our delay? no, let us rather choose
Arm'd with Hell flames and fury all at once
O'er Heav'n's high Tow'rs to force resistless way,
Turning our Tortures into horrid Arms
Against the Torturer; when to meet the noise
Of his Almighty Engine he shall hear
Infernal Thunder, and for Lightning see
Black fire and horror shot with equal rage
Among his Angels; and his Throne itself
Mixt with *Tartarean*° Sulphur, and strange fire,
70 His own invented Torments. But perhaps
The way seems difficult and steep to scale
With upright wing against a higher foe.
Let such bethink them, if the sleepy drench
Of that forgetful Lake benumb not still,
That in our proper motion° we ascend
Up to our native seat: descent and fall
To us is adverse. Who but felt of late
When the fierce Foe hung on our brok'n Rear
Insulting, and pursu'd us through the Deep,
80 With what compulsion and laborious flight
We sunk thus low? Th' ascent is easy then;
Th' event° is fear'd; should we again provoke
Our stronger, some worse way his wrath may find
To our destruction: if there be in Hell
Fear to be worse destroy'd: what can be worse
Than to dwell here, driv'n out from bliss, condemn'd
In this abhorred deep to utter woe;
Where pain of unextinguishable fire
Must exercise us without hope of end
90 The Vassals of his anger, when the Scourge
Inexorably, and the torturing hour
Calls us to Penance? More destroy'd than thus
We should be quite abolisht and expire.
What fear we then? what doubt we to incense
His utmost ire? which to the highth enrag'd,

Will either quite consume us, and reduce
To nothing this essential,° happier far
Than miserable to have eternal being:
Or if our substance be indeed Divine,
And cannot cease to be, we are at worst   100
On this side nothing; and by proof we feel
Our power sufficient to disturb his Heav'n,
And with perpetual inroads to Alarm,
Though inaccessible, his fatal° Throne:
Which if not Victory is yet Revenge.
    He ended frowning, and his look denounc'd
Desperate revenge, and Battle dangerous
To less than Gods. On th' other side up rose
Belial, in act more graceful and humane;
A fairer person lost not Heav'n; he seem'd   110
For dignity compos'd and high exploit:
But all was false and hollow; though his Tongue
Dropt Manna, and could make the worse appear
The better reason, to perplex and dash
Maturest Counsels: for his thoughts were low;
To vice industrious, but to Nobler deeds
Timorous and slothful: yet he pleas'd the ear,
And with persuasive accent thus began.
    I should be much for open War, O Peers,
As not behind in hate; if what was urg'd   120
Main reason to persuade immediate War,
Did not dissuade me most, and seem to cast
Ominous conjecture on the whole success:
When he who most excels in fact° of Arms,
In what he counsels and in what excels
Mistrustful, grounds his courage on despair
And utter dissolution, as the scope
Of all his aim, after some dire revenge.
First, what Revenge? the Tow'rs of Heav'n are fill'd
With Armed watch, that render all access   130
Impregnable; oft on the bordering Deep
Encamp thir Legions, or with obscure wing
Scout far and wide into the Realm of night,
Scorning surprise. Or could we break our way
By force, and at our heels all Hell should rise
With blackest Insurrection, to confound
Heav'n's purest Light, yet our great Enemy
All incorruptible would on his Throne
Sit unpolluted, and th' Ethereal mould
Incapable of stain would soon expel   140
Her mischief, and purge off the baser fire
Victorious. Thus repuls'd, our final hope
Is flat despair: we must exasperate
Th' Almighty Victor to spend all his rage,
And that must end us, that must be our cure,
To be no more; sad cure; for who would lose,
Though full of pain, this intellectual being,
Those thoughts that wander through Eternity,
To perish rather, swallow'd up and lost
In the wide womb of uncreated night,   150
Devoid of sense and motion? and who knows,

---

50 **reck'd,** cared   69 **Tartarean,** from Tartarus, in classic myth the infernal regions and the abode of evil spirits   75 **our proper motion,** the natural motion for
angels—upward   82 **event,** outcome

97 **essential,** being, substance   104 **fatal,** established by fate   124 **fact,** deed

John Milton   **337**

Let this be good, whether our angry Foe
Can give it, or will ever? how he can
Is doubtful; that he never will is sure.
Will he, so wise, let loose at once his ire,
Belike through impotence, or unaware,
To give his Enemies thir wish, and end
Them in his anger, whom his anger saves
To punish endless? wherefore cease we then?
160 Say they who counsel War, we are decreed,
Reserv'd and destin'd to Eternal woe;
Whatever doing, what can we suffer more,
What can we suffer worse? is this then worst,
Thus sitting, thus consulting, thus in Arms?
What when we fled amain, pursu'd and strook
With Heav'n's afflicting Thunder, and besought
The Deep to shelter us? this Hell then seem'd
A refuge from those wounds: or when we lay
Chain'd on the burning Lake? that sure was worse.
170 What if the breath that kindl'd those grim fires
Awak'd should blow them into sevenfold rage
And plunge us in the flames? or from above
Should intermitted vengeance arm again
His red right hand to plague us? what if all
Her stores were op'n'd, and this Firmament
Of Hell should spout her Cataracts of Fire,
Impendent horrors, threat'ning hideous fall
One day upon our heads; while we perhaps
Designing or exhorting glorious war,
180 Caught in a fiery Tempest shall be hurl'd
Each on his rock transfixt, the sport and prey
Of racking whirlwinds, or for ever sunk
Under yon boiling Ocean, wrapt in Chains;
There to converse with everlasting groans,
Unrespited, unpitied, unrepriev'd,
Ages of hopeless end; this would be worse.
War therefore, open or conceal'd, alike
My voice dissuades; for what can force or guile
With him, or who deceive his mind, whose eye
190 Views all things at one view? he from Heav'n's highth
All these our motions vain, sees and derides;
Not more Almighty to resist our might
Than wise to frustrate all our plots and wiles.
Shall we then live thus vile, the race of Heav'n
Thus trampl'd, thus expell'd to suffer here
Chains and these Torments? better these than worse
By my advice; since fate inevitable
Subdues us, and Omnipotent Decree,
The Victor's will. To suffer, as to do,
200 Our strength is equal, nor the Law unjust
That so ordains: this was at first resolv'd,
If we were wise, against so great a foe
Contending, and so doubtful what might fall.
I laugh, when those who at the Spear are bold
And vent'rous, if that fail them, shrink and fear
What yet they know must follow, to endure
Exile, or ignominy, or bonds, or pain,
The sentence of thir Conqueror: This is now
Our doom; which if we can sustain and bear,

Our Supreme Foe in time may much remit   210
His anger, and perhaps thus far remov'd
Not mind us not offending, satisfi'd
With what is punisht; whence these raging fires
Will slack'n, if his breath stir not thir flames.
Our purer essence then will overcome
Thir noxious vapor, or enur'd not feel,
Or chang'd at length, and to the place conform'd
In temper and in nature, will receive
Familiar the fierce heat, and void of pain;
This horror will grow mild, this darkness light,   220
Besides what hope the never-ending flight
Of future days may bring, what chance, what change
Worth waiting, since our present lot appears
For happy though but ill, for ill not worst,
If we procure not to ourselves more woe.
    Thus *Belial* with words cloth'd in reason's garb
Counsell'd ignoble ease, and peaceful sloth,
Not peace: and after him thus *Mammon* spake.
    Either to disinthrone the King of Heav'n
We war, if war be best, or to regain   230
Our own right lost: him to unthrone we then
May hope, when everlasting Fate shall yield
To fickle Chance, and *Chaos* judge the strife:
The former vain to hope argues as vain
The latter: for what place can be for us
Within Heav'n's bound, unless Heav'n's Lord supreme
We overpower? Suppose he should relent
And publish Grace to all, on promise made
Of new Subjection; with what eyes could we
Stand in his presence humble, and receive   240
Strict Laws impos'd, to celebrate his Throne
With warbl'd Hymns, and to his Godhead sing
Forc't Halleluiahs; while he Lordly sits
Our envied Sovran, and his Altar breathes
Ambrosial Odors and Ambrosial Flowers,
Our servile offerings. This must be our task
In Heav'n, this our delight; how wearisome
Eternity so spent in worship paid
To whom we hate. Let us not then pursue
By force impossible, by leave obtain'd   250
Unácceptable, though in Heav'n, our state
Of splendid vassalage, but rather seek
Our own good from ourselves, and from our own
Live to ourselves, though in this vast recess,
Free, and to none accountable, preferring
Hard liberty before the easy yoke
Of servile Pomp. Our greatness will appear
Then most conspicuous, when great things of small,
Useful of hurtful, prosperous of adverse
We can create, and in what place soe'er   260
Thrive under evil, and work ease out of pain
Through labor and endurance. This deep world
Of darkness do we dread? How oft amidst
Thick clouds and dark doth Heav'n's all-ruling Sire
Choose to reside, his Glory unobscur'd,
And with the Majesty of darkness round

Covers his Throne; from whence deep thunders roar
Must'ring thir rage, and Heav'n resembles Hell?
As he our darkness, cannot we his Light
270 Imitate when we please? This Desert soil
Wants not her hidden lustre, Gems and Gold;
Nor want we skill or art, from whence to raise
Magnificence; and what can Heav'n show more?
Our torments also may in length of time
Become our Elements, these piercing Fires
As soft as now severe, our temper chang'd
Into their temper; which must needs remove
The sensible of pain. All things invite
To peaceful Counsels, and the settl'd State
280 Of order, how in safety best we may
Compose our present evils, with regard
Of what we are and where, dismissing quite
All thoughts of War; ye have what I advise.

　　He scarce had finisht, when such murmur fill'd
Th' Assembly, as when hollow Rocks retain
The sound of blust'ring winds, which all night long
Had rous'd the Sea, now with hoarse cadence lull
Sea-faring men o'erwatcht, whose Bark by chance
Or Pinnace anchors in a craggy Bay
290 After the Tempest: Such applause was heard
As *Mammon* ended, and his Sentence pleas'd,
Advising peace: for such another Field
They dreaded worse than Hell: so much the fear
Of Thunder and the Sword of *Michaël*°
Wrought still within them; and no less desire
To found this nether Empire, which might rise
By policy, and long process of time,
In emulation opposite to Heav'n.
Which when *Beëlzebub* perceiv'd, than whom,
300 *Satan* except, none higher sat, with grave
Aspect he rose, and in his rising seem'd
A Pillar of State; deep on his Front engraven
Deliberation sat and public care;
And Princely counsel in his face yet shone,
Majestic though in ruin: sage he stood
With *Atlantean*° shoulders fit to bear
The weight of mightiest Monarchies; his look
Drew audience and attention still as Night
Or Summer's Noon-tide air, while thus he spake.
310 　　Thrones and Imperial Powers, off-spring of Heav'n,
Ethereal Virtues;° or these Titles now
Must we renounce, and changing style be call'd
Princes of Hell? for so the popular vote
Inclines, here to continue, and build up here
A growing Empire; doubtless; while we dream,
And know not that the King of Heav'n hath doom'd
This place our dungeon, not our safe retreat
Beyond his Potent arm, to live exempt
From Heav'n's high jurisdiction, in new League
320 Banded against his Throne, but to remain
In strictest bondage, though thus far remov'd,

Under th' inevitable curb, reserv'd
His captive multitude: For he, be sure,
In highth or depth, still first and last will Reign
Sole King, and of his Kingdom lose no part
By our revolt, but over Hell extend
His Empire, and with Iron Sceptre rule
Us here, as with his Golden those in Heav'n.
What sit we then projecting peace and war?
War hath determin'd us, and foil'd with loss　　330
Irreparable; terms of peace yet none
Voutsaf't or sought; for what peace will be giv'n
To us enslav'd, but custody severe,
And stripes, and arbitrary punishment
Inflicted? and what peace can we return,
But to our power hostility and hate,
Untam'd reluctance, and revenge though slow,
Yet ever plotting how the Conqueror least
May reap his conquest, and may least rejoice
In doing what we most in suffering feel?　　340
Nor will occasion want, nor shall we need
With dangerous expedition to invade
Heav'n, whose high walls fear no assault or Siege,
Or ambush from the Deep. What if we find
Some easier enterprise? There is a place
(If ancient and prophetic fame in Heav'n
Err not) another World, the happy seat
Of some new Race call'd *Man,* about this time
To be created like to us, though less
In power and excellence, but favor'd more　　350
Of him who rules above; so was his will
Pronounc'd among the Gods, and by an Oath,
That shook Heav'n's whole circumference,
　　confirm'd.
Thither let us bend all our thoughts, to learn
What creatures there inhabit, of what mould,
Or substance, how endu'd, and what thir Power,
And where thir weakness, how attempted best,
By force or subtlety: Though Heav'n be shut,
And Heav'n's high Arbitrator sit secure
In his own strength, this place may lie expos'd　　360
The utmost border of his Kingdom, left
To their defense who hold it: here perhaps
Some advantageous act may be achiev'd
By sudden onset, either with Hell fire
To waste his whole Creation, or possess
All as our own, and drive as we were driven,
The puny habitants, or if not drive,
Seduce them to our Party, that thir God
May prove thir foe, and with repenting hand
Abolish his own works. This would surpass　　370
Common revenge, and interrupt his joy
In our Confusion, and our Joy upraise
In his disturbance; when his darling Sons
Hurl'd headlong to partake with us, shall curse
Thir frail Original, and faded bliss,
Faded so soon. Advise if this be worth
Attempting, or to sit in darkness here
Hatching vain Empires. Thus *Beëlzebub*

---

294 **Michaël**, chief warrior of the heavenly armies (the archangel's battle with
Satan is narrated in Book VI)　306 **Atlantean**, like Atlas, the Titan who bore the
sky on his shoulders　311 **Virtues**, one of the orders in the celestial hierarchy

Pleaded his devilish Counsel, first devis'd°
380 By *Satan,* and in part propos'd: for whence,
But from the Author of all ill could Spring
So deep a malice, to confound the race
Of mankind in one root, and Earth with Hell
To mingle and involve, done all to spite
The great Creator? But thir spite still serves
His glory to augment. The bold design
Pleas'd highly those infernal States,° and joy
Sparkl'd in all thir eyes; with full assent
They vote: whereat his speech he thus renews.
390   Well have ye judg'd, well ended long debate,
Synod of Gods, and like to what ye are,
Great things resolv'd, which from the lowest deep
Will once more lift us up, in spite of Fate,
Nearer our ancient Seat; perhaps in view
Of those bright confines, whence with neighboring
    Arms
And opportune excursion we may chance
Re-enter Heav'n; or else in some mild Zone
Dwell not unvisited of Heav'n's fair Light
Secure, and at the bright'ning Orient beam
400 Purge off this gloom; the soft delicious Air,
To heal the scar of these corrosive Fires
Shall breathe her balm. But first whom shall we send
In search of this new world, whom shall we find
Sufficient? who shall tempt with wand'ring feet
The dark unbottom'd infinite Abyss°
And through the palpable obscure find out
His uncouth° way, or spread his aery flight
Upborne with indefatigable wings
Over the vast abrupt,° ere he arrive°
410 The happy Isle; what strength, what art can then
Suffice, or what evasion bear him safe
Through the strict Senteries and Stations thick
Of Angels watching round? Here he had need
All circumspection, and wee now no less
Choice in our suffrage; for on whom we send,
The weight of all and our last hope relies.
    This said, he sat; and expectation held
His look suspense, awaiting who appear'd
To second, or oppose, or undertake
420 The perilous attempt; but all sat mute,
Pondering the danger with deep thoughts; and each
In other's count'nance read his own dismay
Astonisht: none among the choice and prime
Of those Heav'n-warring Champions could be found
So hardy as to proffer or accept
Alone the dreadful voyage; till at last
Satan, whom now transcendent glory rais'd
Above his fellows, with Monarchal pride
Conscious of highest worth, unmov'd thus spake.
430   O Progeny of Heav'n, Empyreal Thrones,
With reason hath deep silence and demur

Seiz'd us, though undismay'd: long is the way
And hard, that out of Hell leads up to light;
Our prison strong, this huge convex of Fire,
Outrageous to devour, immures us round
Ninefold, and gates of burning Adamant
Barr'd over us prohibit all egress.
These past, if any pass, the void profound
Of unessential° Night receives him next
Wide gaping, and with utter loss of being   440
Threatens him, plung'd in that abortive gulf.
If thence he scape into whatever world,
Or unknown Region, what remains him less
Than unknown dangers and as hard escape.
But I should ill become this Throne, O Peers,
And this Imperial Sov'ranty, adorn'd
With splendor, arm'd with power, if aught propos'd
And judg'd of public moment, in the shape
Of difficulty or danger could deter
Mee from attempting. Wherefore do I assume   450
These Royalties, and not refuse to Reign,
Refusing to accept as great a share
Of hazard as of honor, due alike
To him who Reigns, and so much to him due
Of hazard more, as he above the rest
High honor'd sits? Go therefore mighty Powers.
Terror of Heav'n, though fall'n; intend° at home,
While here shall be our home, what best may ease
The present misery, and render Hell
More tolerable; if there be cure or charm   460
To respite or deceive, or slack the pain
Of this ill Mansion: intermit no watch
Against a wakeful Foe, while I abroad
Through all the Coasts of dark destruction seek
Deliverance for us all: this enterprise
None shall partake with me. Thus saying rose
The Monarch, and prevented all reply,
Prudent, lest from his resolution rais'd
Others among the chief might offer now
(Certain to be refus'd) what erst they fear'd;   470
And so refus'd might in opinion stand
His Rivals, winning cheap the high repute
Which he through hazard huge must earn. But they
Dreaded not more th' adventure than his voice
Forbidding; and at once with him they rose;
Thir rising all at once was as the sound
Of Thunder heard remote. Towards him they bend
With awful reverence prone; and as a God
Extol him equal to the highest in Heav'n:
Nor fail'd they to express how much they prais'd,   480
That for the general safety he despis'd
His own: for neither do the Spirits damn'd
Lose all thir virtue; lest bad men should boast
Thir specious° deeds on earth, which glory excites,
Or close ambition varnisht o'er with zeal.
Thus they thir doubtful consultations dark
Ended rejoicing in their matchless Chief:

379 **first devis'd.** See Book I, ll. 650–654   387 **States,** estates, authorities, parliaments, as in the modern "three estates"   405 **Abyss,** the undefined portion of the cosmic space between heaven and hell   407 **uncouth,** unknown, uncertain   409 **abrupt,** the space or gulf in Chaos between hell and Earth   **arrive,** reach

439 **unessential,** without essence, formless   457 **intend,** consider   484 **specious,** showy

As when from mountain tops the dusky clouds
Ascending, while the North wind sleeps, o'erspread
490 Heav'n's cheerful face, the low'ring Element
Scowls o'er the dark'n'd lantskip Snow, or show'r;
If chance the radiant Sun with farewell sweet
Extend his ev'ning beam, the fields revive,
The birds thir notes renew, and bleating herds
Attest thir joy, that hill and valley rings.
O shame to men! Devil with Devil damn'd
Firm concord holds, men only disagree
Of Creatures rational, though under hope
Of heavenly Grace; and God proclaiming peace,
500 Yet live in hatred, enmity, and strife
Among themselves, and levy cruel wars,
Wasting the Earth, each other to destroy:
As if (which might induce us to accord)
Man had not hellish foes anow besides,
That day and night for his destruction wait.
   The *Stygian*° Council thus dissolv'd; and forth
In order came the grand infernal Peers:
Midst° came thir mighty Paramount,° and seem'd
Alone th' Antagonist of Heav'n, nor less
510 Than Hell's dread Emperor with pomp Supreme,
And God-like imitated State; him round
A Globe of fiery Seraphim inclos'd
With bright imblazonry, and horrent° Arms.
Then of thir Session ended they bid cry
With Trumpet's regal sound the great result:
Toward the four winds four speedy Cherubim
Put to thir mouths the sounding Alchymy
By Herald's voice explain'd: the hollow Abyss
Heard far and wide, and all the host of Hell
520 With deaf'ning shout, return'd them loud acclaim.
Thence more at ease thir minds and somewhat rais'd
By false presumptuous hope, the ranged powers
Disband, and wand'ring, each his several way
Pursues, as inclination or sad choice
Leads him perplext, where he may likeliest find
Truce to his restless thoughts, and entertain
The irksome hours, till this great Chief return.
Part on the Plain, or in the Air sublime
Upon the wing, or in swift Race contend,
530 As at th' *Olympian* Games or *Pythian*° fields;
Part curb thir fiery Steeds, or shun the Goal°
With rapid wheels, or fronted Brígads form.
As when to warn proud Cities war appears
Wag'd in the troubl'd Sky, and Armies rush
To Battle in the Clouds, before each Van
Prick forth the Aery Knights, and couch thir spears
Till thickest Legions close; with feats of Arms
From either end of Heav'n the welkin burns.
Others with vast *Typhœan* rage more fell
540 Rend up both Rocks and Hills, and ride the Air
In whirlwind; Hell scarce holds the wild uproar.

As when *Alcides* from *Oechalia* Crown'd
With conquest, felt th' envenom'd robe, and tore
Through pain up by the roots *Thessalian* Pines,
And *Lichas* from the top of *Oeta* threw
Into th' *Euboic* Sea.° Others more mild,
Retreated in a silent valley, sing
With notes Angelical to many a Harp
Thir own Heroic deeds and hapless fall
By doom of Battle; and complain that Fate   550
Free Virtue should enthrall to Force or Chance.
Thir Song was partial, but the harmony
(What could it less when Spirits immortal sing?)
Suspended Hell, and took with ravishment
The thronging audience. In discourse more sweet
(For Eloquence the Soul, Song charms the Sense,)
Others apart sat on a Hill retir'd,
In thoughts more elevate, and reason'd high
Of Providence, Foreknowledge, Will, and Fate,
Fixt Fate, Free will, Foreknowledge absolute,°   560
And found no end, in wand'ring mazes lost.
Of good and evil much they argu'd then,
Of happiness and final misery,
Passion and Apathy, and glory and shame,
Vain wisdom all, and false Philosophie:
Yet with a pleasing sorcery could charm
Pain for a while or anguish, and excite
Fallacious hope, or arm th' obdured breast
With stubborn patience as with triple steel.
Another part in Squadrons and gross° Bands,   570
On bold adventure to discover wide
That dismal World, if any Clime perhaps
Might yield them easier habitation, bend
Four ways thir flying March, along the Banks
Of four infernal Rivers° that disgorge
Into the burning Lake thir baleful streams;
Abhorred *Styx* the flood of deadly hate,
Sad *Acheron* of sorrow, black and deep;
Cocytus, nam'd of lamentation loud
Heard on the rueful stream; fierce *Phlegeton*   580
Whose waves of torrent fire inflame with rage.
Far off from these a slow and silent stream,
Lethe the River of Oblivion rolls
Her wat'ry Labyrinth, whereof who drinks,
Forthwith his former state and being forgets,
Forgets both joy and grief, pleasure and pain.
Beyond this flood a frozen Continent
Lies dark and wild, beat with perpetual storms
Of Whirlwind and dire Hail, which on firm land
Thaws not, but gathers heap, and ruin seems   590
Of ancient pile; all else deep snow and ice,
A gulf profound as that *Serbonian* Bog°

546 **Alcides . . . Sea.** Hercules, returning with his bride Deianira from one of his successful exploits, slew with a poisoned arrow the centaur Nessus, who attempted to carry her off. Dying, Nessus told Deianira to give her husband a robe anointed with his blood. The poison maddened Hercules and in his rage he threw his servant Lichas into the sea   560 **Free will, Foreknowledge absolute.** These concepts were recurrent in Protestant theology, the second usually under the term predestination   570 **Gross,** large   575 **four infernal Rivers.** These are streams of classical mythology, as is Lethe, river of Oblivion   592 **Serbonian Bog,** Lake Serbonis, which had the deceitful appearance of solid ground but was really a dangerous morass

506 **Stygian,** hellish (from Styx, a river of the underworld, in classical myth)
508 **Midst,** in their midst   **Paramount,** chief   513 **horrent,** bristling
530 **Olympian . . . Pythian,** athletic meets of ancient Greece   531 **shun the Goal.** The allusion is to the chariot race in which the driver wheeled as closely as possible to the turning posts

Betwixt *Damiata* and Mount *Casius* old,
Where Armies whole have sunk: the parching Air
Burns frore, and cold performs th' effect of Fire.
Thither by harpy-footed Furies hal'd,
At certain revolutions all the damn'd
Are brought: and feel by turns the bitter change
Of fierce extremes, extremes by change more fierce,
600 From Beds of raging Fire to starve in Ice
Thir soft Ethereal warmth, and there to pine
Immovable, infixt, and frozen round,
Periods of time, thence hurried back to fire.
They ferry over this *Lethean* Sound
Both to and fro, thir sorrow to augment,
And wish and struggle, as they pass, to reach
The tempting stream, with one small drop to lose
In sweet forgetfulness all pain and woe,
All in one moment, and so near the brink;
610 But Fate withstands, and to oppose th' attempt
Medusa° with *Gorgonian* terror guards
The Ford, and of itself the water flies
All taste of living wight, as once it fled
The lip of *Tantalus.*° Thus roving on
In confus'd march forlorn, th' advent'rous Bands
With shudd'ring horror pale, and eyes aghast
View'd first thir lamentable lot, and found
No rest: through many a dark and dreary Vale
They pass'd, and many a Region dolorous,
620 O'er many a Frozen, many a Fiery Alp,
Rocks, Caves, Lakes, Fens, Bogs, Dens, and shades
    of death,
A Universe of death, which God by curse
Created evil, for evil only good,
Where all life dies, death lives, and Nature breeds,
Perverse, all monstrous, all prodigious things,
Abominable, inutterable, and worse
Than Fables yet have feign'd, or fear conceiv'd,
Gorgons and *Hydras*, and *Chimeras*° dire.
    Meanwhile the Adversary of God and Man,
630 *Satan* with thoughts inflam'd of highest design,
Puts on swift wings, and towards the Gates of Hell
Explores° his solitary flight; sometimes
He scours the right hand coast, sometimes the left,
Now shaves with level wing the Deep, then soars
Up to the fiery concave tow'ring high.
As when far off at Sea a Fleet descri'd
Hangs in the Clouds, by *Equinoctial* Winds
Close sailing from *Bengala,* or the Isles
Of *Ternate* and *Tidore,*° whence Merchants bring
640 Thir spicy Drugs: they on the Trading Flood
Through the wide *Ethiopian*° to the Cape
Ply stemming nightly toward the Pole. So seem'd
Far off the flying Fiend: at last appear

Hell bounds high reaching to the horrid Roof,
And thrice threefold the Gates; three folds were Brass,
Three Iron, three of Adamantine Rock,
Impenetrable, impal'd with circling fire,
Yet unconsum'd. Before the Gates there sat
On either side a formidable shape;
The one seem'd Woman to the waist, and fair,   650
But ended foul in many a scaly fold
Voluminous and vast, a Serpent arm'd
With mortal sting: about her middle round
A cry of Hell Hounds never ceasing bark'd
With wide *Cerberean* mouths° full loud, and rung
A hideous Peal: yet, when they list, would creep,
If aught disturb'd thir noise, into her womb,
And kennel there, yet there still bark'd and howl'd
Within unseen. Far less abhorr'd than these
Vex'd *Scylla*° bathing in the Sea that parts   660
Calabria from the hoarse *Trinacrian* shore:
Nor uglier follow the Night-Hag, when call'd
In secret, riding through the Air she comes
Lur'd with the smell of infant blood, to dance
With *Lapland*° Witches, while the laboring Moon
Eclipses at thir charms. The other shape,
If shape it might be call'd that shape had none
Distinguishable in member, joint, or limb,
Or substance might be call'd that shadow seem'd,
For each seem'd either; black it stood as Night,   670
Fierce as ten Furies, terrible as Hell,
And shook a dreadful Dart; what seem'd his head
The likeness of a Kingly Crown had on.
Satan was now at hand, and from his seat
The Monster moving onward came as fast,
With horrid strides; Hell trembled as he strode.
Th' undaunted Fiend what this might be admir'd,
Admir'd,° not fear'd; God and his Son except,
Created thing naught valu'd he nor shunn'd;
And with disdainful look thus first began.   680
    Whence and what are thou, execrable shape,
That dar'st, though grim and terrible, advance
Thy miscreated Front athwart my way
To yonder Gates? through them I mean to pass,
That be assured, without leave askt of thee:
Retire, or taste thy folly, and learn by proof,
Hell-born, not to contend with Spirits of Heav'n.
    To whom the Goblin° full of wrath repli'd:
Art thou that Traitor Angel, art thou hee,
Who first broke peace in Heav'n and Faith, till then   690
Unbrok'n, and in proud rebellious Arms
Drew after him the third part of Heav'n's Sons
Conjur'd against the Highest, for which both Thou
And they outcast from God, are here condemn'd
To waste Eternal days in woe and pain?
And reck'n'st thou thyself with Spirits of Heav'n,
Hell-doom'd, and breath'st defiance here and scorn,

611 **Medusa,** in Greek myth the Gorgon with the snaky locks, whose aspect was so terrifying that it turned the beholders to stone; she was slain by Perseus 614 **Tantalus,** a sinner represented in Greek legend as punished in the underworld by the torture of unsatisfied hunger and thirst   628 **Gorgons . . . Chimeras,** in Greek myth, monsters of the underworld   632 **Explores,** pursues uncertainly   638 **Bengala . . . Ternate . . . Tidore,** an arm of the Indian Ocean, and two small islands of the Dutch Indies, respectively   641 **wide Ethiopian,** the Indian Ocean

655 **Cerberean mouths,** like those of Cerberus, the three-headed hound of hell in classic myth   660 **Scylla,** a female sea monster destructive to mariners. She lived in the sea between Italy and Sicily, opposite the destructive whirlpool Charybdis   665 **Lapland,** believed to be the special haunt of witches   678 **Admir'd,** wondered at   688 **Goblin,** fiend

Where I reign King, and to enrage thee more,
Thy King and Lord? Back to thy punishment,
700 False fugitive, and to thy speed add wings,
Lest with a whip of Scorpions I pursue
Thy ling'ring, or with one stroke of this Dart
Strange horror seize thee, and pangs unfelt before.
      So spake the grisly terror, and in shape,
So speaking and so threat'ning, grew tenfold
More dreadful and deform: on th' other side
Incens't with indignation *Satan* stood
Unterrifi'd, and like a Comet° burn'd,
That fires the length of *Ophiucus*° huge
710 In th' Artic Sky, and from his horrid hair
Shakes Pestilence and War. Each at the Head
Levell'd his deadly aim; thir fatal hands
No second stroke intend, and such a frown
Each cast at th' other, as when two black Clouds
With Heav'n's Artillery fraught, come rattling on
Over the *Caspian*, then stand front to front
Hov'ring a space, till Winds the signal blow
To join thir dark Encounter in mid air:
So frown'd the mighty Combatants, that Hell
720 Grew darker at thir frown, so matcht they stood;
For never but once more was either like
To meet so great a foe: and now great deeds
Had been achiev'd, whereof all Hell had rung,
Had not the Snaky Sorceress that sat
Fast by Hell Gate, and kept the fatal Key,
Ris'n, and with hideous outcry rush'd between.
      O Father, what intends thy hand, she cri'd,
Against thy only Son? What fury O Son,
Possesses thee to bend that mortal Dart
730 Against thy Father's head? and know'st for whom;
For him who sits above and laughs the while
At thee ordain'd his drudge, to execute
Whate'er his wrath, which he calls Justice, bids,
His wrath which one day will destroy ye both.
      She spake, and at her words the hellish Pest
Forebore, then these to her *Satan* return'd:
      So strange thy outcry, and thy words so strange
Thou interposest, that my sudden hand
Prevented spares to tell thee yet by deeds
740 What it intends; till first I know of thee,
What thing thou art, thus double-form'd, and why
In this infernal Vale first met thou call'st
Me Father, and that Phantasm call'st my Son?
I know thee not, nor ever saw till now
Sight more detestable than him and thee.
      T' whom thus the Portress of Hell Gate repli'd:
Hast thou forgot me then, and do I seem
Now in thine eye so foul, once deem'd so fair
In Heav'n, when at th' Assembly, and in sight
750 Of all the Seraphim with thee combin'd
In bold conspiracy against Heav'n's King,
All on a sudden miserable pain
Surpris'd thee, dim thine eyes, and dizzy swum

In darkness, while thy head flames thick and fast
Threw forth, till on the left side op'ning wide,
Likest to thee in shape and count'nance bright,
Then shining heav'nly fair, a Goddess arm'd
Out of thy head° I sprung: amazement seiz'd
All th' Host of Heav'n; back they recoil'd afraid
At first, and call'd me *Sin*, and for a Sign   760
Portentous held me; but familiar grown,
I pleas'd, and with attractive graces won
The most averse, thee chiefly, who full oft
Thyself in me thy perfect image viewing
Becam'st enamor'd, and such joy thou took'st
With me in secret, that my womb conceiv'd
A growing burden. Meanwhile War arose,
And fields were fought in Heav'n: wherein remain'd
(For what could else) to our Almighty Foe
Clear Victory, to our part loss and rout   770
Through all the Empyrean: down they fell
Driv'n headlong from the Pitch of Heaven, down
Into this Deep, and in the general fall
I also; at which time this powerful Key
Into my hand was giv'n, with charge to keep
These Gates for ever shut, which none can pass
Without my op'ning. Pensive here I sat
Alone, but long I sat not, till my womb
Pregnant by thee, and now excessive grown
Prodigious motion felt and rueful throes.   780
At last this odious offspring° whom thou seest
Thine own begotten, breaking violent way
Tore through my entrails, that with fear and pain
Distorted, all my nether shape thus grew
Transform'd: but he my inbred enemy
Forth issu'd, brandishing his fatal Dart
Made to destroy: I fled, and cri'd out *Death;*
Hell trembl'd at the hideous Name, and sigh'd
From all her Caves, and back resounded *Death.*
I fled, but he pursu'd (though more, it seems,   790
Inflam'd with lust than rage) and swifter far,
Mee overtook his mother all dismay'd,
And in embraces forcible and foul
Ingend'ring with me, of that rape begot
These yelling Monsters that with ceasless cry
Surround me, as thou saw'st, hourly conceiv'd
And hourly born, with sorrow infinite
To me, for when they list, into the womb
That bred them they return, and howl and gnaw
My Bowels, thir repast; then bursting forth   800
Afresh with conscious terrors vex me round,
That rest or intermission none I find.
Before mine eyes in opposition sits
Grim *Death* my Son and foe, who sets them on,
And me his Parent would full soon devour
For want of other prey, but that he knows
His end with mine involv'd; and knows that I
Should prove a bitter Morsel, and his bane,

708 **Comet** Comets were often considered omens of disaster
709 **Ophiuchus**, a constellation

758 **Out of thy head.** Milton has borrowed this conception from the Greek myth
of the birth of Pallas Athene from the head of Zeus   781 **this odious offspring.**
The wages of sin is death

Whenever that shall be; so Fate pronounc'd.
810 But thou O Father, I forewarn thee, shun
His deadly arrow; neither vainly hope
To be invulnerable in those bright Arms,
Though temper'd heav'nly, for that mortal dint,
Save he who reigns above, none can resist.
      She finish'd, and the subtle Fiend his lore
Soon learn'd, now milder, and thus answer'd smooth.
Dear Daughter, since thou claim'st me for thy Sire,
And my fair Son here shows't me, the dear pledge
Of dalliance had with thee in Heav'n, and joys
820 Then sweet, now sad to mention, through dire change
Befall'n us unforeseen, unthought of, know
I come no enemy, but to set free
From out this dark and dismal house of pain,
Both him and thee, and all the heav'nly Host
Of Spirits that in our just pretenses arm'd
Fell with us from on high: from them I go
This uncouth errand sole, and one for all
Myself expose, with lonely steps to tread
Th' unfounded deep, and through the void immense
830 To search with wand'ring quest a place foretold
Should be, and, by concurring signs, ere now
Created vast and round, a place of bliss
In the Purlieus of Heav'n, and therein plac't
A race of upstart Creatures, to supply
Perhaps our vacant room, though more remov'd,
Lest Heav'n surcharg'd with potent multitude
Might hap to move new broils: Be this or aught
Than this more secret now design'd, I haste
To know, and this once known, shall soon return,
840 And bring ye to the place where Thou and Death
Shall dwell at ease, and up and down unseen
Wing silently the buxom Air, imbalm'd
With odors; there ye shall be fed and fill'd
Immeasurably, all things shall be your prey.
      He ceas'd, for both seem'd highly pleas'd, and
          Death
Grinn'd horrible a ghastly smile, to hear
His famine should be fill'd, and blest his maw
Destin'd to that good hour: no less rejoic'd
His mother bad, and thus bespake her Sire.
850   The key of this infernal Pit by due,
And by command of Heav'n's all-powerful King
I keep, by him forbidden to unlock
These Adamantine Gates; against all force
Death ready stands to interpose his dart,
Fearless to be o'ermatcht by living might.
But what owe I to his commands above
Who hates me, and hath hither thrust me down
Into this gloom of *Tartarus* profound,
To sit in hateful Office here confin'd,
860 Inhabitant of Heav'n, and heav'nly-born,
Here in perpetual agony and pain,
With terrors and with clamors compasst round
Of mine own brood, that on my bowels feed:
Thou art my Father, thou my Author, thou
My being gav'st me; whom should I obey

But thee, whom follow? thou wilt bring me soon
To that new world of light and bliss, among
The Gods who live at ease, where I shall Reign
At thy right hand voluptuous, as beseems
Thy daughter and thy darling, without end.   870
      Thus saying, from her side the fatal Key,
Sad instrument of all our woe, she took;
And towards the Gate rolling her bestial train,
Forthwith the huge Portcullis high up drew,
Which but herself not all the *Stygian* powers
Could once have mov'd; then in the key-hole turns
Th' intricate wards, and every Bolt and Bar
Of massy Iron or solid Rock with ease
Unfast'ns: on a sudden op'n fly
With impetuous recoil and jarring sound   880
Th' infernal doors, and on thir hinges grate
Harsh Thunder, that the lowest bottom shook
Of *Erebus*. She op'n'd, but to shut
Excell'd her power; the Gates wide op'n stood,
That with extended wings a Banner'd Host
Under spread Ensigns marching might pass through
With Horse and Chariots rankt in loose array;
So wide they stood, and like a Furnace mouth
Cast forth redounding° smoke and ruddy flame.
Before thir eyes in sudden view appear   890
The secrets of the hoary deep, a dark
Illimitable Ocean without bound,
Without dimension, where length, breadth, and highth,
And time and place are lost; where eldest *Night*
And *Chaos*, Ancestors of Nature, hold
Eternal Anarchy, amidst the noise
Of endless wars, and by confusion stand.
For hot, cold, moist, and dry, four Champions fierce
Strive here for Maistry, and to Battle bring
Thir embryon Atoms; they around the flag   900
Of each his Faction, in thir several Clans,
Light-arm'd or heavy, sharp, smooth, swift or slow,
Swarm populous, unnumber'd as the Sands
Of *Barca* or *Cyrene's*° torrid soil,
Levied to side with warring Winds, and poise
Thir lighter wings. To whom these most adhere,
Hee rules a moment; *Chaos* Umpire sits,
And by decision more imbroils the fray
By which he Reigns: next him high Arbiter
Chance governs all. Into this wild Abyss,   910
The Womb of nature and perhaps her Grave,
Of neither Sea, nor Shore, nor Air, nor Fire,
But all these in thir pregnant causes mixt
Confus'dly, and which thus must ever fight,
Unless th' Almighty Maker them ordain
His dark materials to create more Worlds,
Into this wild Abyss the wary fiend
Stood on the brink of Hell and look'd a while,
Pondering his Voyage: for no narrow frith
He had to cross. Nor was his ear less peal'd   920
With noises loud and ruinous (to compare

889 **redounding,** billowy   904 **Barca . . . Cyrene,** ancient cities of Libya, northern Africa

Great things with small) than when *Bellona*° storms,
With all her battering Engines bent to rase
Some Capital City; or less than if this frame
Of Heav'n were falling, and these Elements
In mutiny had from her Axle torn
The steadfast Earth. At last his Sail-broad Vans°
He spreads for flight, and in the surging smoke
Uplifted spurns the ground, thence many a League
930   As in a cloudy Chair ascending rides
Audacious, but that seat soon failing, meets
A vast vacuity: all unawares
Flutt'ring his pennons vain plumb down he drops
Ten thousand fadom deep, and to this hour
Down had been falling, had not by ill chance
The strong rebuff of some tumultuous cloud
Instinct with Fire and Nitre hurried him
As many miles aloft: that fury stay'd,
Quencht in a Boggy *Syrtis,*° neither Sea,
940   Nor good dry Land, nigh founder'd on he fares,
Treading the crude consistence, half on foot,
Half flying; behoves him now both Oar and Sail.
As when a Gryfon° through the Wilderness
With winged course o'er Hill or moory Dale,
Pursues the *Arimaspian,*° who by stealth
Had from his wakeful custody purloin'd
The guarded Gold: So eagerly the fiend
O'er bog or steep, through strait, rough, dense, or
      rare,
With head, hands, wings, or feet pursues his way,
950   And swims or sinks, or wades, or creeps, or flies:
At length a universal hubbub wild
Of stunning sounds and voices all confus'd
Borne through the hollow dark assaults his ear
With loudest vehemence: thither he plies,
Undaunted to meet there whatever power
Or Spirit of the nethermost Abyss
Might in that noise reside, of whom to ask
Which way the nearest coast of darkness lies
Bordering on light; when straight behold the Throne
960   Of *Chaos,* and his dark Pavilion spread
Wide on the wasteful Deep; with him Enthron'd
Sat Sable-vested *Night,* eldest of things,
The Consort of his Reign; and by them stood
Orcus° and *Ades,*° and the dreaded name
Of *Demogorgon;*° Rumor next and *Chance,*
And *Tumult* and *Confusion* all imbroil'd,
And *Discord* with a thousand various mouths.
      T' whom *Satan* turning boldly, thus. Ye Powers
And Spirits of this nethermost Abyss,
970   *Chaos* and *ancient Night,* I come no Spy,
With purpose to explore or to disturb
The secrets of your Realm, but by constraint
Wand'ring this darksome Desert, as my way

Lies through your spacious Empire up to light,
Alone, and without guide, half lost, I seek
What readiest path leads where your gloomy bounds
Confine with Heav'n; or if some other place
From your Dominion won, th' Ethereal King
Possesses lately, thither to arrive
I travel this profound, direct my course;   980
Directed, no mean recompence it brings
To your behoof, if I that Region lost,
All usurpation thence expell'd, reduce
To her original darkness and your sway
(Which is my present journey) and once more
Erect the Standard there of *ancient Night;*
Yours be th' advantage all, mine the revenge.
      Thus *Satan;* and him thus the Anarch° old
With falt'ring speech and visage incompos'd
Answer'd. I know thee, stranger, who thou art,   990
That mighty leading Angel, who of late
Made head against Heav'n's King, though over-
      thrown.
I saw and heard, for such a numerous Host
Fled not in silence through the frighted deep
With ruin upon ruin, rout on rout,
Confusion worse confounded; and Heav'n Gates
Pour'd out by millions her victorious Bands
Pursuing. I upon my Frontiers here
Keep residence; if all I can will serve,
That little which is left so to defend,   1000
Encroacht on still through our intestine° broils
Weak'ning the Sceptre of old *Night:* first Hell
Your dungeon stretching far and wide beneath;
Now lately Heaven and Earth, another World
Hung o'er my Realm, link'd in a golden Chain
To that side Heav'n from whence your Legions fell:
If that way be your walk, you have not far;
So much the nearer danger; go and speed;
Havoc and spoil and ruin are my gain.
      He ceas'd; and *Satan* stay'd not to reply,   1010
But glad that now his Sea should find a shore,
With fresh alacrity and force renew'd
Springs upward like a Pyramid of fire
Into the wild expanse, and through the shock
Of fighting Elements, on all sides round
Environ'd wins his way; harder beset
And more endanger'd, than when *Argo* pass'd
Through *Bosporus* betwixt the justling Rocks:
Or when *Ulysses* on the Larboard shunn'd
Charybdis, and by th' other whirlpool steer'd.   1020
So he with difficulty and labor hard
Mov'd on, with difficulty and labor hee;
But hee once past, soon after when man fell,
Strange alteration! Sin and Death amain
Following his track, such was the will of Heav'n,
Pav'd after him a broad and beat'n way
Over the dark Abyss, whose boiling Gulf
Tamely endur'd a Bridge of wondrous length

922 **Bellona,** Roman goddess of war   927 **Vans,** wings   939 **Syrtis,** quicksands
off the north coast of Africa   943 **Gryfon,** griffon, fabulous monster with a lion's
body and an eagle's wings   945 **Arimaspian,** one-eyed people of Scythia who
warred against the griffons to get the gold which the monsters guarded   964 **Orcus,** the personification of the Roman Lower World   **Ades,** personification of
death   965 **Demogorgon,** a mysterious infernal deity so powerful as to control
the fates of gods as well as of men

988 **Anarch,** leader of anarchy   1001 **intestine,** internal

From Hell continu'd reaching th' utmost Orb°
1030 Of this frail World; by which the Spirits perverse
With easy intercourse pass to and fro
To tempt or punish mortals, except whom
God and good Angels guard by special grace.
But now at last the sacred influence
Of light appears, and from the walls of Heav'n
Shoots far into the bosom of dim Night
A glimmering dawn; here Nature first begins
Her fardest verge, and *Chaos* to retire
As from her outmost works a brok'n foe
1040 With tumult less and with less hostile din,
That *Satan* with less toil, and now with ease
Wafts on the calmer wave by dubious light
And like a weather-beaten Vessel holds
Gladly the Port, though Shrouds and Tackle torn;
Or in the emptier waste, resembling Air,
Weighs his spread wings, at leisure to behold
Far off th' Empyreal Heav'n, extended wide
In circuit, undetermin'd square or round,
With Opal Tow'rs and Battlements adorn'd
1050 Of living Sapphire, once his native Seat;
And fast by hanging in a golden Chain
This pendant world, in bigness as a Star
Of smallest Magnitude close by the Moon.
Thither full fraught with mischievous revenge,
Accurst, and in a cursed hour he hies.

The End of the Second Book.

from BOOK THREE

Now had th' Almighty Father from above,
From the pure Empyrean° where he sits
High Thron'd above all highth, bent down his eye,
His own works and their works at once to view:
60 About him all the Sanctities of Heaven°
Stood thick as Stars, and from his sight receiv'd
Beatitude past utterance; on his right
The radiant image of his Glory sat,
His only Son; On Earth he first beheld
Our two first Parents, yet the only two
Of mankind, in the happy Garden plac't,
Reaping immortal fruits of joy and love,
Uninterrupted joy, unrivall'd love
In blissful solitude; he then survey'd
70 Hell and the Gulf between, and *Satan* there
Coasting the wall of Heav'n on this side Night
In the dun Air sublime,° and ready now
To stoop° with wearied wings, and willing feet
On the bare outside of this World, that seem'd
Firm land imbosom'd without Firmament,
Uncertain° which, in Ocean or in Air.

Him God beholding from his prospect high,
Wherein past, present, future he beholds,
Thus to his only Son foreseeing spake.
Only begotten Son, seest thou what rage   80
Transports our adversary, whom no bounds
Prescrib'd, no bars of Hell, nor all the chains
Heapt on him there, nor yet the main Abyss
Wide interrupt can hold; so bent he seems
On desperate revenge, that shall redound
Upon his own rebellious head. And now
Through all restraint broke loose he wings his way
Not far off Heav'n, in the Precincts of light,
Directly towards the new created World,
And Man there plac't, with purpose to assay°   90
If him by force he can destroy, or worse,
By some false guile pervert; and shall pervert;
For Man will heark'n to his glozing° lies,
And easily transgress the sole Command,
Sole pledge of his obedience: So will fall
Hee and his faithless Progeny: whose fault?
Whose but his own? ingrate, he had of mee
All he could have; I made him just and right,
Sufficient to have stood, though free to fall.
Such I created all th' Ethereal Powers   100
And Spirits, both them who stood and them who fail'd;
Freely they stood who stood, and fell who fell.
Not free, what proof could they have giv'n sincere
Of true allegiance, constant Faith or Love,
Where only what they needs must do, appear'd,
Not what they would? what praise could they receive?
What pleasure I from such obedience paid,
When Will and Reason (Reason also is choice)
Useless and vain, of freedom both despoil'd,
Made passive both, had serv'd necessity,   110
Not mee. They therefore as to right belong'd,
So were created, nor can justly accuse
Thir maker, or thir making, or thir Fate;
As if Predestination over-rul'd
Thir will, dispos'd by absolute Decree
Or high foreknowledge; they themselves decreed
Thir own revolt, not I: if I foreknew,
Foreknowledge had no influence on their fault,
Which had no less prov'd certain unforeknown.
So without least impulse or shadow of Fate,   120
Or aught by me immutably foreseen,
They trespass, Authors to themselves in all
Both what they judge and what they choose; for so
I form'd them free, and free they must remain,
Till they enthrall themselves: I else must change
Thir nature, and revoke the high Decree
Unchangeable, Eternal, which ordain'd
Thir freedom: they themselves ordain'd thir fall.
The first sort by thir own suggestion fell,
Self-tempted, self-deprav'd: Man falls deceiv'd   130
By th' other first: Man therefore shall find grace,
The other none: in Mercy and Justice both,

1029 **Orb,** the outermost of the ten spheres which surrounded the earth   **Book
III** 57 **Empyrean,** the highest sphere of the Universe   60 **Sanctities of Heaven,**
the angelic hierarchies   72 **In the dun Air sublime,** in the dusky air aloft
73 **stoop,** to swoop, like a bird of prey, to bend its course downward   76 **Uncertain,** difficult to perceive

90 **assay,** make trial   93 **glozing,** flattering

Through Heav'n and Earth, so shall my glory excel,
But Mercy first and last shall brightest shine. . . .

Behold mee then, mee for him, life for life
I offer, on mee let thine anger fall;
Account mee man; I for his sake will leave
Thy bosom, and this glory next to thee
240 Freely put off, and for him lastly die
Well pleas'd. on me let Death wreck all his rage;
Under his gloomy power I shall not long
Lie vanquisht; thou hast giv'n me to possess
Life in myself for ever, by thee I live,
Though now to Death I yield, and am his due
All that of me can die, yet that debt paid,
Thou wilt not leave me in the loathsome grave
His prey, nor suffer my unspotted Soul
For ever with corruption there to dwell;
250 But I shall rise Victorious, and subdue
My vanquisher, spoil'd of his vaunted spoil;
Death his death's wound shall then receive, and stoop
Inglorious, of his mortal sting disarm'd.
I through the ample Air in Triumph high
Shall lead Hell Captive maugre° Hell, and show
The powers of darkness bound. Thou at the sight
Pleas'd, out of Heaven shalt look down and smile,
While by thee rais'd I ruin all my Foes,
Death last, and with his Carcass glut the Grave:
260 Then with the multitude of my redeem'd
Shall enter Heav'n long absent, and return,
Father, to see thy face, wherein no cloud
Of anger shall remain, but peace assur'd,
And reconcilement; wrath shall be no more
Thenceforth, but in thy presence Joy entire.
   His words here ended, but his meek aspéct
Silent yet spake, and breath'd immortal love
To mortal men, above which only shone
Filial obedience: as a sacrifice
270 Glad to be offer'd, he attends the will
Of his great Father. . . .

from BOOK FOUR

The Argument

Satan now in prospect of *Eden,* and nigh the place where
he must now attempt the bold enterprise which he
undertook alone against God and Man, falls into many
doubts with himself, and many passions, fear, envy, and
despair; but at length confirms himself in evil, journeys
on to Paradise, whose outward prospect and situation is
described, overleaps the bounds, sits in the shape of a
Cormorant on the Tree of Life, as highest in the Garden
to look about him. The Garden describ'd; *Satan's* first
10 sight of *Adam* and *Eve;* his wonder at thir excellent form

and happy state, but with resolution to work thir fall;
overhears thir discourse, thence gathers that the Tree of
Knowledge was forbidden them to eat of, under penalty
of death; and thereon intends to found his Temptation,
by seducing them to transgress: then leaves them a
while, to know further of thir state by some other means.
Meanwhile *Uriel* descending on a Sun-beam warns *Gabriel,* who had in charge the Gate of Paradise, that some
evil spirit had escap'd the Deep, and past at Noon by his
Sphere in the shape of a good Angel down to Paradise,   20
discovered after by his furious gestures in the Mount.
Gabriel promises to find him ere morning. Night coming
on, *Adam* and *Eve* discourse of going to thir rest: thir
Bower describ'd; thir Evening worship. *Gabriel* drawing
forth his Bands of Night-watch to walk the round of
Paradise, appoints two strong Angels to *Adam's* Bower,
lest the evil spirit should be there doing some harm to
Adam or *Eve* sleeping; there they find him at the ear of
Eve, tempting her in a dream, and bring him, though
unwilling, to *Gabriel;* by whom question'd, he scornfully   30
answers, prepares resistance, but hinder'd by a Sign from
Heaven, flies out of Paradise.

   O for that warning voice, which he who saw
Th' *Apocalypse,* heard cry in Heav'n aloud,
Then when the Dragon, put to second rout,
Came furious down to be reveng'd on men,
Woe to the inhabitants on Earth!° that now,
While time was, our first Parents had been warn'd
The coming of thir secret foe, and scap'd
Haply so scap'd his mortal snare; for now
Satan, now first inflam'd with rage, came down,
The Tempter ere th' Accuser of man-kind,   10
To wreck on innocent frail man his loss
Of that first Battle, and his flight to Hell:
Yet not rejoicing in his speed, though bold,
Far off and fearless, nor with cause to boast,
Begins his dire attempt, which nigh the birth
Now rolling, boils in his tumultuous breast,
And like a devilish Engine back recoils
Upon himself; horror and doubt distract
His troubl'd thoughts, and from the bottom stir
The Hell within him, for within him Hell   20
He brings, and round about him, nor from Hell
One step no more than from himself can fly
By change of place: Now conscience wakes despair
That slumber'd, wakes the bitter memory
Of what he was, what is, and what must be
Worse; of worse deeds worse sufferings must ensue.
Sometimes towards *Eden* which now in his view
Lay pleasant, his griev'd look he fixes sad,
Sometimes towards Heav'n and the full-blazing Sun,
Which now sat high in his Meridian Tow'r:°   30
Then much revolving, thus in sighs began.
   O thou that with surpassing Glory crown'd,

---

255 **maugre,** in spite of

Book IV   5 **he . . . Earth,** St. John the Divine, author of *Revelation*. The passage
alluded to is in Chapter 12. During the war in heaven, a great red dragon, having
seven crowned heads and ten horns, was cast out by Michaël and his angels, and
overcome only by the blood of the Lamb   30 **Meridian Tow'r.** It was noon

Look'st from thy sole Dominion like the God
Of this new World; at whose sight all the Stars
Hide thir diminisht heads; to thee I call,
But with no friendly voice, and add thy name
O Sun, to tell thee how I hate thy beams
That bring to my remembrance from what state
I fell, how glorious once above thy Sphere;
40 Till Pride and worse Ambition threw me down
Warring in Heav'n against Heav'n's matchless King:
Ah wherefore! he deserv'd no such return
From me, whom he created what I was
In that bright eminence, and with his good
Upbraided none; nor was his service hard.
What could be less than to afford him praise,
The easiest recompense, and pay him thanks,
How due! yet all his good prov'd ill in me,
And wrought but malice; lifted up so high
50 I sdein'd° subjection, and thought one step higher
Would set me highest, and in a moment quit
The debt immense of endless gratitude,
So burdensome, still paying, still° to owe;
Forgetful what from him I still receiv'd,
And understood not that a grateful mind
By owing owes not, but still pays, at once
Indebted and discharg'd; what burden then?
O had his powerful Destiny ordain'd
Me some inferior Angel, I had stood
60 Then happy; no unbounded hope had rais'd
Ambition. Yet why not? some other Power
As great might have aspir'd, and me though mean
Drawn to his part; but other Powers as great
Fell not, but stand unshak'n, from within
Or from without, to all temptations arm'd.
Hadst thou the same free Will and Power to stand?
Thou hadst: whom hast thou then or what to accuse,
But Heav'n's free Love dealt equally to all?
Be then his Love accurst, since love or hate,
70 To me alike, it deals eternal woe.
Nay curs'd be thou; since against his thy will
Chose freely what it now so justly rues.
Me miserable! which way shall I fly
Infinite wrath, and infinite despair?
Which way I fly is Hell; myself am Hell;
And in the lowest deep a lower deep
Still threat'ning to devour me opens wide,
To which the Hell I suffer seems a Heav'n.
O then at last relent: is there no place
80 Left for Repentance, none for Pardon left?
None left but by submission; and that word
Disdain forbids me, and my dread of shame
Among the Spirits beneath, whom I seduc'd
With other promises and other vaunts
Than to submit, boasting I could subdue
Th' Omnipotent. Ay me, they little know
How dearly I abide that boast so vain,
Under what torments inwardly I groan:

While they adore me on the Throne of Hell,
With Diadem and Sceptre high advanc'd   90
The lower still I fall, only Supreme
In misery; such joy Ambition finds.
But say I could repent and could obtain
By Act of Grace my former state; how soon
Would highth recall high thoughts, how soon unsay
What feign'd submission swore: ease would recant
Vows made in pain, as violent and void.
For never can true reconcilement grow
Where wounds of deadly hate have pierc'd so deep:
Which would but lead me to a worse relapse,   100
And heavier fall: so should I purchase dear
Short intermission bought with double smart.
This knows my punisher; therefore as far
From granting hee, as I from begging peace:
All hope excluded thus, behold instead
Of us out-cast, exil'd, his new delight,
Mankind created, and for him this World.
So farewell Hope, and with Hope farewell Fear,
Farewell Remorse: all Good to me is lost;
Evil be thou my Good; by thee at least   110
Divided Empire with Heav'n's King I hold
By thee, and more than half perhaps will reign;
As Man ere long, and this new World shall know. . . .

from BOOK NINE

The Argument

Satan having compast the Earth, with meditated guile returns as a mist by Night into Paradise, enters into the Serpent sleeping. *Adam* and *Eve* in the Morning go forth to thir labors, which *Eve* proposes to divide in several places, each laboring apart: *Adam* consents not, alleging the danger, lest that Enemy, of whom they were forewarn'd, should attempt her found alone: *Eve* loath to be thought not circumspect or firm enough, urges her going apart, the rather desirous to make trial of her strength; *Adam* at last yields: The Serpent finds her alone; his subtle approach, first gazing, then speaking, with much flattery extolling *Eve* above all other Creatures. *Eve* wond'ring to hear the Serpent speak, asks how he attain'd to human speech and such understanding not till now; the Serpent answers, that by tasting of a certain Tree in the Garden he attain'd both to Speech and Reason, till then void of both: *Eve* requires him to bring her to that Tree, and finds it to be the Tree of Knowledge forbidden: The Serpent now grown bolder, with many wiles and arguments induces her at length to eat; she pleas'd with the taste deliberates awhile whether to impart thereof to *Adam* or not, at last brings him of the Fruit, relates what persuaded her to eat thereof: *Adam* at first amaz'd, but perceiving her lost, resolves through vehemence of love to perish with her; and extenuating the trespass, eats also of the Fruit: The effects thereof in them both; they seek to cover thir nakedness; then fall to variance and accusation of one another.

50 **sdein'd**, disdained   53 **still**, ever

No more of talk° where God or Angel Guest
With Man, as with his Friend, familiar us'd
To sit indulgent, and with him partake
Rural repast, permitting him the while
Venial discourse unblam'd: I now must change
Those Notes to Tragic; foul distrust, and breach
Disloyal on the part of Man, revolt,
And disobedience: On the part of Heav'n
Now alienated, distance and distaste,
10 Anger and just rebuke, and judgment giv'n,
That brought into this World a world of woe,
Sin and her shadow Death, and Misery°
Death's Harbinger: Sad task, yet argument
Not less but more Heroic than the wrath
Of stern Achilles on his Foe pursu'd
Thrice Fugitive about Troy Wall;° or rage
Of Turnus for Lavinia disespous'd,°
Or Neptune's ire or Juno's, that so long
Perplex'd the Greek and Cytherea's Son;
20 If answerable style I can obtain
Of my Celestial Patroness,° who deigns
Her nightly visitation unimplor'd,
And dictates to me slumb'ring, or inspires
Easy my unpremeditated Verse:
Since first this Subject for Heroic Song
Pleas'd me long choosing, and beginning late;
Not sedulous by Nature to indite
Wars, hitherto the only Argument
Heroic deem'd, chief maistry to dissect
30 With long and tedious havoc fabl'd Knights°
In Battles feign'd; the better fortitude
Of Patience and Heroic Martyrdom
Unsung; or to describe Races and Games,
Or tilting Furniture,° emblazon'd Shields,
Impreses° quaint, Caparisons and Steeds;
Bases° and tinsel Trappings, gorgeous Knights
At Joust and Tournament; then marshall'd Feast
Serv'd up in Hall with Sewers, and Seneschals;
The skill of Artifice or Office mean,
40 Not that which justly gives Heroic name
To Person or to Poem. Mee of these
Nor skill'd nor studious, higher Argument
Remains, sufficient of itself to raise
That name, unless an age too late, or cold
Climate, or Years damp my intended wing
Deprest; and much they may, if all be mine,
Not Hers who brings it nightly to my Ear.
The Sun was sunk, and after him the Star
Of Hesperus, whose Office is to bring
50 Twilight upon the Earth, short Arbiter
Twixt Day and Night, and now from end to end
Night's Hemisphere had veil'd the Horizon round:
When Satan who late fled before the threats

Of Gabriel out of Eden, now improv'd
In meditated fraud and malice, bent
On Man's destruction, maugre° what might hap
Of heavier on himself, fearless return'd.
By Night he fled, and at Midnight return'd
From compassing the Earth, cautious of day,
Since Uriel Regent of the Sun descri'd   60
His entrance, and forewarn'd the Cherubim
That kept thir watch; thence full of anguish driv'n,
The space of seven continu'd Nights he rode
With darkness, thrice the Equinoctial Line°
He circl'd, four times cross'd the Car of Night
From Pole to Pole, traversing each Colure;°
On th'eighth return'd, and on the Coast averse°
From entrance or Cherubic Watch, by stealth
Found unsuspected way. There was a place,
Now not, though Sin, not Time, first wrought the   70
   change,
Where Tigris at the foot of Paradise
Into a Gulf shot under ground, till part
Rose up a Fountain by the Tree of Life;
In with the River sunk, and with it rose
Satan involv'd in rising Mist, then sought
Where to lie hid; Sea he had searcht and Land
From Eden over Pontus,° and the Pool
Mæotis,° up beyond the River Ob:°
Downward as far Antarctic; and in length
West from Orontes° to the Ocean barr'd   80
At Darien,° thence to the Land where flows
Ganges and Indus: thus the Orb he roam'd
With narrow° search; and with inspection deep
Consider'd every Creature, which of all
Most opportune might serve his Wiles, and found
The Serpent subtlest Beast of all the Field.
Him after long debate, irresolute
Of thoughts revolv'd, his final sentence chose
Fit Vessel, fittest Imp of fraud, in whom
To enter, and his dark suggestions hide   90
From sharpest sight: for in the wily Snake,
Whatever sleights none would suspicious mark,
As from his wit and native subtlety
Proceeding, which in other Beasts observ'd
Doubt might beget of Diabolic pow'r
Active within beyond the sense of brute.
Thus he resolv'd, but first from inward grief
His bursting passion into plaints thus pour'd:
O Earth, how like to Heav'n, if not preferr'd
More justly, Seat worthier of Gods, as built   100
With second thoughts, reforming what was old!
For what God after better worse would build?
Terrestrial Heav'n, danc't round by other Heav'ns
That shine, yet bear thir bright officious° Lamps,
Light above Light, for thee alone, as seems,
In thee concentring all thir precious beams
Of sacred influence: As God in Heav'n

Book IX   1 No more of talk, etc. This preface introduces the central theme of man's sin   12 Misery, disease   14 wrath . . . Wall, the subject of the Iliad   16 rage . . . disespous'd, the chief story of the second half of the Aeneid   21 Patroness, the muse Urania   30 Knights, a reference to medieval chivalric romances   34 tilting furniture, equipment for jousts   35 Impreses, heraldic emblems   36 Bases, trappings of a horse

56 maugre, in spite of   64 Equinoctial Line, equator   66 Colure, line, geographical demarcation   67 averse, opposite   77 Pontus, the Black Sea   78 Mæotis, Sea of Azov   Ob, in Siberia   80 Orontes, a river in Syria   81 Darien, Isthmus of Panama   83 narrow, close   104 officious, serviceable

Is Centre, yet extends to all, so thou
Centring receiv'st from all those Orbs; in thee,
110 Not in themselves, all thir known virtue appears
Productive in Herb, Plant, and nobler birth
Of Creatures animate with gradual life
Of Growth, Sense, Reason, all summ'd up in Man.
With what delight could I have walkt thee round,
If I could joy in aught, sweet interchange
Of Hill and Valley, Rivers, Woods and Plains,
Now Land, now Sea, and Shores with Forest crown'd,
Rocks, Dens, and Caves; but I in none of these
Find place or refuge; and the more I see
120 Pleasures about me, so much more I feel
Torment within me, as from the hateful siege
Of contraries; all good to me becomes
Bane, and in Heav'n much worse would be my state.
But neither here seek I, no nor in Heav'n
To dwell, unless by maistring Heav'n's Supreme;
Nor hope to be myself less miserable
By what I seek, but others to make such
As I, though thereby worse to me redound:
For only in destroying I find ease
130 To my relentless thoughts; and him destroy'd,
Or won to what may work his utter loss,
For whom all this was made, all this will soon
Follow, as to him linkt in weal or woe,
In woe then: that destruction wide may range:
To mee shall be the glory sole among
Th'infernal Powers, in one day to have marr'd
What he *Almighty* styl'd, six Nights and Days
Continu'd making, and who knows how long
Before had been contriving, though perhaps
140 Not longer than since I in one Night freed
From servitude inglorious well nigh half
Th' Angelic Name, and thinner left the throng
Of his adorers: hee to be aveng'd,
And to repair his numbers thus impair'd,
Whether such virtue spent of old now fail'd
More Angels to Create, if they at least
Are his Created, or to spite us more,
Determin'd to advance into our room
A Creature form'd of Earth, and him endow,
150 Exalted from so base original,
With Heav'nly spoils, our spoils; What he decreed
He effected; Man he made, and for him built
Magnificent this World, and Earth his seat,
Him Lord pronounc'd, and, O indignity!
Subjected to his service Angel wings,
And flaming Ministers to watch and tend
Thir earthy Charge: Of these the vigilance
I dread, and to elude, thus wrapt in mist
Of midnight vapor glide obscure, and pry
160 In every Bush and Brake, where hap may find
The Serpent sleeping, in whose mazy folds
To hide me, and the dark intent I bring.
O foul descent! that I who erst contended
With Gods to sit the highest, am now constrain'd
Into a Beast, and mixt with bestial slime,

This essence to incarnate and imbrute,
That to the highth of Deity aspir'd;
But what will not Ambition and Revenge
Descend to? who aspires must down as low
As high he soar'd, obnoxious first or last   170
To basest things. Revenge, at first though sweet,
Bitter ere long back on itself recoils;
Let it; I reck not, so it light well aim'd,
Since higher I fall short, on him who next
Provokes my envy, this new Favorite
Of Heav'n, this Man of Clay, Son of despite,
Whom us the more to spite his Maker rais'd
From dust: spite then with spite is best repaid.
    So saying, through each Thicket Dank or Dry,
Like a black mist low creeping, he held on   180
His midnight search, where soonest he might find
The Serpent: him fast sleeping soon he found
In Labyrinth of many a round self-roll'd,
His head the midst, well stor'd with subtle wiles:
Not yet in horrid Shade or dismal Den,
Nor nocent yet, but on the grassy Herb
Fearless unfear'd he slept: in at his Mouth
The Devil enter'd, and his brutal sense,
In heart or head, possessing soon inspir'd
With act° intelligential; but his sleep   190
Disturb'd not, waiting close° th' approach of Morn.
Now whenas sacred Light began to dawn
In *Eden* on the humid Flow'rs, that breath'd
Thir morning incense, when all things that breathe,
From th' Earth's great Altar send up silent praise
To the Creator, and his Nostrils fill
With grateful Smell, forth came the human pair
And join'd thir vocal Worship to the Choir
Of Creatures wanting voice; that done, partake
The season, prime for sweetest Scents and Airs: 200
Then commune how that day they best may ply
Thir growing work: for much thir work outgrew
The hands' dispatch of two Gard'ning so wide.
And *Eve* first to her Husband thus began.
    Adam, well may we labor still° to dress
This Garden, still to tend Plant, Herb and Flow'r,
Our pleasant task enjoin'd, but till more hands
Aid us, the work under our labor grows,
Luxurious by restraint; what we by day
Lop overgrown, or prune, or prop, or bind,   210
One night or two with wanton growth derides
Tending to wild. Thou therefore now advise
Or hear what to my mind first thoughts present,
Let us divide our labors, thou where choice
Leads thee, or where most needs, whether to wind
The Woodbine round this Arbor, or direct
The clasping Ivy where to climb, while I
In yonder Spring° of Roses intermixt
With Myrtle, find what to redress till Noon:
For while so near each other thus all day   220
Our task we choose, what wonder if so near

190 **act,** activity   191 **close,** hidden   206 **still,** always   218 **Spring,** clump

Looks intervene and smiles, or object new
Casual discourse draw on, which intermits
Our day's work brought to little, though begun
Early, and th' hour of Supper comes unearn'd.
    To whom mild answer *Adam* thus return'd.
Sole Eve, Associate sole, to me beyond
Compare above all living Creatures dear,
Well hast thou motion'd,° well thy thoughts imploy'd
230 How we might best fulfil the work which here
God hath assign'd us, nor of me shalt pass
Unprais'd: for nothing lovelier can be found
In Woman, than to study household good,
And good works in her Husband to promote.
Yet not so strictly hath our Lord impos'd
Labor, as to debar us when we need
Refreshment, whether food, or talk between,
Food of the mind, or this sweet intercourse
Of looks and smiles, for smiles from Reason flow,
240 To brute deni'd, and are of Love the food,
Love not the lowest end of human life.
For not to irksome toil, but to delight
He made us, and delight to Reason join'd.
These paths and Bowers doubt not but our joint hands
Will keep from Wilderness with ease, as wide
As we need walk, till younger hands ere long
Assist us: But if much converse perhaps
Thee satiate, to short absence I could yield.
For solitude sometimes is best society,
250 And short retirement urges sweet return.
But other doubt possesses me, lest harm
Befall thee sever'd from me; for thou know'st
What hath been warn'd us, what malicious Foe
Envying our happiness, and of his own
Despairing, seeks to work us woe and shame
By sly assault; and somewhere nigh at hand
Watches, no doubt, with greedy hope to find
His wish and best advantage, us asunder,
Hopeless to circumvent us join'd, where each
260 To other speedy aid might lend at need;
Whether his first design be to withdraw
Our fealty from God, or to disturb
Conjugal Love, than which perhaps no bliss
Enjoy'd by us excites his envy more;
Or this, or worse, leave not the faithful side
That gave thee being, still shades thee and protects.
The Wife, where danger or dishonor lurks,
Safest and seemliest by her Husband stays,
Who guards her, or with her the worst endures.
270   To whom the Virgin Majesty of *Eve,*
As one who loves, and some unkindness meets,
With sweet austere composure thus repli'd.
    Offspring of Heav'n and Earth, and all Earth's Lord,
That such an Enemy we have, who seeks
Our ruin, both by thee inform'd I learn,
And from the parting Angel over-heard
As in a shady nook I stood behind,

Just then return'd at shut of Ev'ning Flow'rs.
But that thou shouldst my firmness therefore doubt
To God or thee, because we have a foe   280
May tempt it, I expected not to hear.
His violence thou fear'st not, being such,
As wee, not capable of death or pain,
Can either not receive, or can repel.
His fraud is then thy fear, which plain infers
Thy equal fear that my firm Faith and Love
Can by his fraud be shak'n or seduc't;
Thoughts, which how found they harbor in thy breast,
Adam, misthought of her to thee so dear?
    To whom with healing words *Adam* repli'd.   290
Daughter of God and Man, immortal *Eve,*
For such thou art, from sin and blame entire:°
Not diffident of thee do I dissuade
Thy absence from my sight, but to avoid
Th' attempt itself, intended by our Foe.
For hee who tempts, though in vain, at least asperses°
The tempted with dishonor foul, suppos'd
Not incorruptible of Faith, not proof
Against temptation: thou thyself with scorn
And anger wouldst resent the offer'd wrong,   300
Though ineffectual found: misdeem not then,
If such affront I labor to avert
From thee alone, which on us both at once
The Enemy, though bold, will hardly dare,
Or daring, first on mee th' assault shall light.
Nor thou his malice and false guile contemn;
Subtle he needs must be, who could seduce
Angels, nor think superfluous others' aid.
I from the influence of thy looks receive
Access in every Virtue, in thy sight   310
More wise, more watchful, stronger, if need were
Of outward strength; while shame, thou looking on,
Shame to be overcome or over-reacht
Would utmost vigor raise, and rais'd unite.
Why shouldst not thou like sense within thee feel
When I am present, and thy trial choose
With me, best witness of thy Virtue tri'd.
    So spake domestic° *Adam* in his care
And Matrimonial Love; but *Eve,* who thought
Less attribúted to her Faith sincere,   320
Thus her reply with accent sweet renew'd.
    If this be our condition, thus to dwell
In narrow circuit strait'n'd by a Foe,
Subtle or violent, we not endu'd
Single with like defense, wherever met,
How are we happy, still in fear of harm?
But harm precedes not sin: only our Foe
Tempting affronts us with his foul esteem
Of our integrity: his foul esteem
Sticks no dishonor on our Front, but turns   330
Foul on himself; then wherefore shunn'd or fear'd
By us? who rather double honor gain
From his surmise prov'd false, find peace within,

229 **motion'd,** proposed

292 **entire,** spotless; untouched   296 **asperses,** taints   318 **domestic,** devoted

Favor from Heav'n, our witness from th' event.°
And what is Faith, Love, Virtue unassay'd
Alone, without exterior help sustain'd?
Let us not then suspect our happy State
Left so imperfet by the Maker wise,
As not secure to single or combin'd.
340 Frail is our happiness, if this be so,
And *Eden* were no *Eden* thus expos'd.

To whom thus *Adam* fervently repli'd.
O Woman, best are all things as the will
Of God ordain'd them, his creating hand
Nothing imperfet or deficient left
Of all that he Created, much less Man,
Or aught that might his happy State secure,
Secure from outward force; within himself
The danger lies, yet lies within his power:
350 Against his will he can receive no harm.
But God left free the Will, for what obeys
Reason, is free, and Reason he made right,
But bid her well beware, and still erect,
Lest by some fair appearing good surpris'd
She dictate false, and misinform the Will
To do what God expressly hath forbid.
Not then mistrust, but tender love enjoins,
That I should mind thee oft, and mind° thou me.
Firm we subsist, yet possible to swerve,
360 Since Reason not impossibly may meet
Some specious object by the Foe suborn'd,
And fall into deception unaware,
Not keeping strictest watch, as she was warn'd.
Seek not temptation then, which to avoid
Were better, and most likely if from mee
Thou sever not: Trial will come unsought.
Wouldst thou approve thy constancy, approve°
First thy obedience; th' other who can know,
Not seeing thee attempted, who attest?
370 But if thou think, trial unsought may find
Us both securer than thus warn'd thou seem'st,
Go; for thy stay, not free, absents thee more;
Go in thy native innocence, rely
On what thou hast of virtue, summon all,
For God towards thee hath done his part, do thine.

So spake the Patriarch of Mankind, but *Eve*
Persisted, yet submiss, though last, repli'd.

With thy permission then, and thus forewarn'd
Chiefly by what thy own last reasoning words
380 Touch'd only, that our trial, when least sought,
May find us both perhaps far less prepar'd,
The willinger I go, nor much expect
A Foe so proud will first the weaker seek;
So bent, the more shall shame him his repulse.
Thus saying, from her Husband's hand her hand
Soft she withdrew, and like a Wood-Nymph light,
Oread or *Dryad*, or of *Delia's*° Train,
Betook her to the Groves, but *Delia's* self
In gait surpass'd and Goddess-like deport,

Though not as shee with Bow and Quiver arm'd   390
But with such Gard'ning Tools as Art yet rude,
Guiltless of fire had form'd, or Angels brought.
To *Pales,*° or *Pomona,*° thus adorn'd,
Likest she seem'd, *Pomona* when she fled
Vertumnus, or to *Ceres* in her Prime,
Yet Virgin of *Proserpina* from *Jove.*
Her long and ardent look his Eye pursu'd
Delighted, but desiring more her stay.
Oft he to her his charge of quick return
Repeated, shee to him as oft engag'd   400
To be return'd by Noon amid the Bow'r,
And all things in best order to invite
Noontide repast, or Afternoon's repose.
O much deceiv'd, much failing, hapless *Eve,*
Of thy presum'd return! event perverse!
Thou never from that hour in Paradise
Found'st either sweet repast, or sound repose;
Such ambush hid among sweet Flow'rs and Shades
Waited with hellish rancor imminent
To intercept thy way, or send thee back   410
Despoil'd of Innocence, of Faith, of Bliss.
For now, and since first break of dawn the Fiend,
Mere Serpent in appearance, forth was come,
And on his Quest, where likeliest he might find
The only two of Mankind, but in them
The whole included Race, his purpos'd prey.
In Bow'r and Field he sought, where any tuft
Of Grove or Garden-Plot more pleasant lay,
Thir tendance or Plantation for delight,
By Fountain or by shady Rivulet,   420
He sought them both, but wish'd his hap might find
Eve separate, he wish'd, but not with hope
Of what so seldom chanc'd, when to his wish,
Beyond his hope, *Eve* separate he spies,
Veil'd in a Cloud of Fragrance, where she stood,
Half spi'd, so thick the Roses bushing round
About her glow'd, oft stooping to support
Each Flow'r of slender stalk, whose head though gay
Carnation, Purple, Azure, or speckt with Gold,
Hung drooping unsustain'd, them she upstays   430
Gently with Myrtle band, mindless° the while,
Herself, though fairest unsupported Flow'r,
From her best prop so far, and storm so nigh.
Nearer he drew, and many a walk travers'd
Of stateliest Covert, Cedar, Pine, or Palm,
Then voluble and bold, now hid, now seen
Among thick-wov'n Arborets and Flow'rs
Imborder'd on each Bank, the hand of *Eve:*
Spot more delicious than those Gardens feign'd
Or of reviv'd *Adonis,* or renown'd   440
Alcinoüs, host of old *Laertes'* Son,
Or that, not Mystic, where the Sapient King
Held dalliance with his fair *Egyptian* Spouse.°
Much hee the Place admir'd, the Person more.

334 **from th' event,** in the outcome 358 **mind,** remind 367 **approve,** prove
387 **Delia,** Diana

393 **Pales,** Roman goddess of sheep and shepherds **Pomona,** Roman goddess
of fruit 431 **mindless,** heedless 443 **Sapient King . . . Spouse.** See *I Kings,* 3:1
and *Song of Solomon,* 7:1

As one who long in populous City pent,
Where Houses thick and Sewers annoy the Air,
Forth issuing on a Summer's Morn to breathe
Among the pleasant Villages and Farms
Adjoin'd, from each thing met conceives delight,
450 The smell of Grain, or tedded° Grass, or Kine,
Or Dairy, each rural sight, each rural sound;
If chance with Nymphlike step fair Virgin pass,
What pleasing seem'd, for her now pleases more,
She most, and in her look sums all Delight.
Such Pleasure took the Serpent to behold
This Flow'ry Plat,° the sweet recess of *Eve*
Thus early, thus alone; her Heav'nly form
Angelic, but more soft, and Feminine,
Her graceful Innocence, her every Air
460 Of gesture or least action overaw'd
His Malice, and with rapine sweet bereav'd
His fierceness of the fierce intent it brought:
That space the Evil one abstracted stood
From his own evil, and for the time remain'd
Stupidly good, of enmity disarm'd,
Of guile, of hate, of envy, of revenge;
But the hot Hell that always in him burns,
Though in mid Heav'n, soon ended his delight,
And tortures him now more, the more he sees
470 Of pleasure not for him ordain'd: then soon
Fierce hate he recollects, and all his thoughts
Of mischief, gratulating, thus excites.
    Thoughts, whither have ye led me, with what sweet
Compulsion thus transported to forget
What hither brought us, hate, not love, nor hope
Of Paradise for Hell, hope here to taste
Of pleasure, but all pleasure to destroy,
Save what is in destroying, other joy
To me is lost. Then let me not let pass
480 Occasion which now smiles, behold alone
The Woman, opportune to all attempts,
Her Husband, for I view far round, not nigh,
Whose higher intellectual more I shun,
And strength, of courage haughty, and of limb
Heroic built, though of terrestrial mould,
Foe not informidable, exempt from wound,
I not; so much hath Hell debas'd, and pain
Infeebl'd me, to what I was in Heav'n.
Shee fair, divinely fair, fit Love for Gods,
490 Not terrible, though terror be in Love
And beauty, not approach by stronger hate,
Hate stronger, under show of Love well feign'd,
The way which to her ruin now I tend.
    So spake the Enemy of Mankind, enclos'd
In Serpent, Inmate bad, and toward *Eve*
Address'd his way, not with indented wave,
Prone on the ground, as since, but on his rear,
Circular base of rising folds, that tow'r'd
Fold above fold a surging Maze, his Head
500 Crested aloft, and Carbuncle° his Eyes;

With burnisht Neck of verdant Gold, erect
Amidst his circling Spires, that on the grass
Floated redundant: pleasing was his shape,
And lovely, never since of Serpent kind
Lovelier, not those that in *Illyria* chang'd
Hermione and *Cadmus,*° or the God
In *Epidaurus;*° nor to which transform'd
Ammonian Jove, or *Capitoline* was seen,
Hee with *Olympias,*° this with her who bore
Scipio° the highth of *Rome.* With tract oblique   510
At first, as one who sought access, but fear'd
To interrupt, side-long he works his way.
As when a Ship by skilful Steersman wrought
Nigh River's mouth or Foreland, where the Wind
Veers oft, as oft so steers, and shifts her Sail;
So varied hee, and of his tortuous Train
Curl'd many a wanton wreath in sight of *Eve,*
To lure her Eye; shee busied heard the sound
Of rustling Leaves, but minded not, as us'd
To such disport before her through the Field,   520
From every Beast, more duteous at her call,
Than at *Circean* call the Herd disguis'd.
Hee bolder now, uncall'd before her stood;
But as in gaze admiring: Oft he bow'd
His turret Crest, and sleek enamell'd Neck,
Fawning, and lick'd the ground whereon she trod.
His gentle dumb expression turn'd at length
The Eye of *Eve* to mark his play; he glad
Of her attention gain'd, with Serpent Tongue
Organic, or impulse of vocal Air,   530
His fraudulent temptation thus began.
    Wonder not,° sovran Mistress, if perhaps
Thou canst, who are sole Wonder, much less arm
Thy looks, the Heav'n of mildness, with disdain,
Displeas'd that I approach thee thus, and gaze
Insatiate, I thus single, nor have fear'd
Thy awful brow, more awful thus retir'd.
Fairest resemblance of thy Maker fair,
Thee all things living gaze on, all things thine
By gift, and thy Celestial Beauty adore   540
With ravishment beheld, there best beheld
Where universally admir'd: but here
In this enclosure wild, these Beasts among,
Beholders rude, and shallow to discern
Half what in thee is fair, one man except,
Who sees thee? (and what is one?) who shouldst be
    seen
A Goddess among Gods, ador'd and serv'd
By Angels numberless, thy daily Train.
    So gloz'd° the Tempter, and his Proem° tun'd;
Into the Heart of *Eve* his words made way,   550
Though at the voice much marvelling; at length
Not unamaz'd she thus in answer spake.
    What may this mean? Language of Man pronounc't

506 **not . . . Cadmus,** not those that Hermione and Cadmus became when
metamorphosed   507 **Epidaurus,** shrine of Aesculapius, god of medicine
509 **Olympias,** mother of Alexander the Great (whose father, in legend, was Jupiter)   510 **Scipio.** The great general Scipio was also held to be an illegitimate
son of Jupiter   532 **Wonder not . . . daily Train.** Satan strategically appeals to
Eve's vanity   549 **gloz'd,** flattered   **Proem,** introduction

450 **tedded,** spread out to dry   456 **Plat,** plot   500 **Carbuncle,** deep red

John Milton 353

By Tongue of Brute, and human sense exprest?
The first at least of these I thought deni'd
To Beasts, whom God on thir Creation-Day
Created mute to all articulate sound;
The latter I demur, for in thir looks
Much reason, and in thir actions oft appears.
560 Thee, Serpent, subtlest beast of all the field
I knew, but not with human voice endu'd;
Redouble then this miracle, and say,
How cam'st thou speakable of mute, and how
To me so friendly grown above the rest
Of brutal kind, that daily are in sight?
Say, for such wonder claims attention due.
      To whom the guileful Tempter thus repli'd.
Empress of this fair World, resplendent *Eve,*
Easy to mee it is to tell thee all
570 What thou command'st and right thou should'st be
        obey'd:
I was at first as other Beasts that graze
The trodden Herb, of abject thoughts and low,
As was my food, nor aught but food discern'd
Or Sex, and apprehended nothing high:
Till on a day roving the field, I chanc'd
A goodly Tree far distant to behold
Loaden with fruit of fairest colors mixt,
Ruddy and Gold: I nearer drew to gaze;
580 When from the boughs a savory odor blown,
Grateful to appetite, more pleas'd my sense
Than smell of sweetest Fennel, or the Teats
Of Ewe or Goat dropping with Milk at Ev'n,
Unsuckt of Lamb or Kid, that tend thir play.
To satisfy the sharp desire I had
Of tasting those fair Apples, I resolv'd
Not to defer; hunger and thirst at once,
Powerful persuaders, quick'n'd at the scent
Of that alluring fruit, urg'd me so keen.
590 About the mossy Trunk I wound me soon,
For high from ground the branches would require
Thy utmost reach or *Adam's:* Round the Tree
All other Beasts that saw, with like desire
Longing and envying stood, but could not reach.
Amid the Tree now got, where plenty hung
Tempting so nigh, to pluck and eat my fill
I spar'd not, for such pleasure till that hour
At Feed or Fountain never had I found.
Sated at length, ere long I might perceive
Strange alteration in me, to degree
600 Of Reason in my inward Powers, and Speech
Wanted not long, though to this shape retain'd.
Thenceforth to Speculations high or deep
I turn'd my thoughts, and with capacious mind
Consider'd all things visible in Heav'n,
Or Earth, or Middle, all things fair and good;
But all that fair and good in thy Divine
Semblance, and in thy Beauty's heav'nly Ray
United I beheld; no Fair to thine
Equivalent or second, which compell'd
610 Mee thus, though importune perhaps, to come

And gaze, and worship thee of right declar'd
Sovran of Creatures, universal Dame.
      So talk'd the spirited sly Snake; and *Eve*
Yet more amaz'd unwary thus repli'd.
      Serpent, thy overpraising leaves in doubt
The virtue of that Fruit, in thee first prov'd:
But say, where grows the Tree, from hence how far?
For many are the Trees of God that grow
In Paradise, and various, yet unknown
To us, in such abundance lies our choice,
As leaves a greater store of Fruit untoucht,   620
Still hanging incorruptible, till men
Grow up to thir provision, and more hands
Help to disburden Nature of her Birth.
      To whom the wily Adder, blithe and glad.
Empress, the way is ready, and not long,
Beyond a row of Myrtles, on a Flat,
Fast by a Fountain, one small Thicket past
Of blowing Myrrh and Balm; if thou accept
My conduct, I can bring thee thither soon.
      Lead then, said *Eve.* Hee leading swiftly roll'd 630
In tangles, and made intricate seem straight,
To mischief swift. Hope elevates, and joy
Bright'ns his Crest, as when a wand'ring Fire,°
Compact of unctuous vapor, which the Night
Condenses, and the cold invirons round,
Kindl'd through agitation to a Flame,
Which oft, they say, some evil Spirit attends,
Hovering and blazing with delusive Light,
Misleads th' amaz'd Night-wanderer from his way   640
To Bogs and Mires, and oft through Pond or Pool,
There swallow'd up and lost, from succor far.
So glister'd the dire Snake, and into fraud
Led *Eve* our credulous Mother, to the Tree
Of prohibition, root of all our woe;
Which when she saw, thus to her guide she spake.
      Serpent, we might have spar'd our coming hither,
Fruitless to mee, though Fruit be here to excess,
The credit of whose virtue rest with thee,
Wondrous indeed, if cause of such effects.   650
But of this Tree we may not taste nor touch;
God so commanded, and left that Command
Sole Daughter of his voice; the rest, we live
Law to ourselves, our Reason is our Law.
      To whom the Tempter guilefully repli'd.
Indeed? hath God then said that of the Fruit
Of all these Garden Trees ye shall not eat,
Yet Lords declar'd of all in Earth or Air?
      To whom thus *Eve* yet sinless. Of the Fruit
Of each Tree in the Garden we may eat,   660
But of the Fruit of this fair Tree amidst
The Garden, God hath said, Ye shall not eat
Thereof, nor shall ye touch it, lest ye die.
      She scarce had said, though brief, when now more
        bold
The Tempter, but with show of Zeal and Love

634 **wand'ring Fire,** will-o'-the-wisp

To Man, and indignation at his wrong,
New part puts on,° and as to passion mov'd,
Fluctuates disturb'd, yet comely, and in act
Rais'd, as of some great matter to begin.
670 As when of old some Orator renown'd
In *Athens* or free *Rome,* where Eloquence
Flourish'd, since mute, to some great cause addrest,
Stood in himself collected, while each part,
Motion, each act won audience ere the tongue,
Sometimes in highth began, as no delay
Of Preface brooking through his Zeal of Right.
So standing, moving, or to highth upgrown
The Tempter all impassion'd thus began.

O Sacred, Wise, and Wisdom-giving Plant,
680 Mother of Science, Now I feel thy Power
Within me clear, not only to discern
Things in thir Causes, but to trace the ways
Of highest Agents, deem'd however wise.
Queen of this Universe, do not believe
Those rigid threats of Death; ye shall not Die:
How should ye? by the Fruit? it gives you Life
To Knowledge: By the Threat'ner? look on mee,
Mee who have touch'd and tasted, yet both live,
And life more perfet have attain'd than Fate
690 Meant mee, by vent'ring higher than my Lot.
Shall that be shut to Man, which to the Beast
Is open? or will God incense his ire
For such a petty Trespass, and not praise
Rather your dauntless virtue, whom the pain
Of Death denounc't, whatever thing Death be,
Deterr'd not from achieving what might lead
To happier life, knowledge of Good and Evil;
Of good, how just? of evil, if what is evil
Be real, why not known, since easier shunn'd?
700 God therefore cannot hurt ye, and be just;
Not just, not God; not fear'd then, nor obey'd:
Your fear itself of Death removes the fear.
Why then was this forbid? Why but to awe,
Why but to keep ye low and ignorant,
His worshippers; he knows that in the day
Ye Eat thereof, your Eyes that seem so clear,
Yet are but dim, shall perfetly be then
Op'n'd and clear'd, and ye shall be as Gods,
Knowing both Good and Evil as they know.
710 That ye should be as Gods, since I as Man,
Internal Man, is but proportion meet,
I of brute human, yee of human Gods.
So ye shall die perhaps, by putting off
Human, to put on Gods, death to be wisht,
Though threat'n'd, which no worse than this can bring.
And what are Gods that Man may not become
As they, participating God-like food?
The Gods are first, and that advantage use
On our belief, that all from them proceeds;
720 I question it, for this fair Earth I see,
Warm'd by the Sun, producing every kind,

Them nothing: If they all things, who enclos'd
Knowledge of Good and Evil in this Tree,
That who so eats thereof, forthwith attains
Wisdom without their leave? and wherein lies
Th' offense, that Man should thus attain to know?
What can your knowledge hurt him, or this Tree
Impart against his will if all be his?
Or is it envy, and can envy dwell
In heav'nly breasts? these, these and many more   730
Causes import° your need of this fair Fruit.
Goddess humane, reach then, and freely taste.

He ended, and his words replete with guile
Into her heart too easy entrance won:
Fixt on the Fruit she gaz'd, which to behold
Might tempt alone, and in her ears the sound
Yet rung of his persuasive words, impregn'd
With Reason, to her seeming, and with Truth;
Meanwhile the hour of Noon drew on, and wak'd
An eager appetite, rais'd by the smell   740
So savory of that Fruit, which with desire,
Inclinable now grown to touch or taste,
Solicited her longing eye; yet first
Pausing a while, thus to herself she mus'd.

Great are thy Virtues, doubtless, best of Fruits,
Though kept from Man, and worthy to be admir'd,
Whose taste, too long forborne, at first assay
Gave elocution to the mute, and taught
The Tongue not made for Speech to speak thy praise:
Thy praise hee also who forbids thy use,   750
Conceals not from us, naming thee the Tree
Of Knowledge, knowledge both of good and evil;
Forbids us then to taste, but his forbidding
Commends thee more, while it infers the good
By thee communicated, and our want:
For good unknown, sure is not had, or had
And yet unknown, is as not had at all.
In plain then, what forbids he but to know,
Forbids us good, forbids us to be wise?
Such prohibitions bind not. But if Death   760
Bind us with after-bands, what profits then
Our inward freedom? In the day we eat
Of this fair Fruit, our doom is, we shall die.
How dies the Serpent? hee hath eat'n and lives,
And knows, and speaks, and reasons, and discerns,
Irrational till then. For us alone
Was death invented? or to us deni'd
This intellectual food, for beasts reserv'd?
For Beasts it seems: yet that one Beast which first
Hath tasted, envies not, but brings with joy   770
The good befall'n him, Author unsuspect,°
Friendly to man, far from deceit or guile.
What fear I then, rather what know to fear
Under this ignorance of Good and Evil,
Of God or Death, of Law or Penalty?
Here grows the Cure of all, this Fruit Divine,
Fair to the Eye, inviting to the Taste,

---

667 **New part puts on,** assumes a new role

731 **import,** prove   771 **Author unsuspect,** the serpent

Of virtue to make wise: what hinders then
To reach, and feed at once both Body and Mind?
780 So saying, her rash hand in evil hour
Forth reaching to the Fruit, she pluck'd, she eat:°
Earth felt the wound, and Nature from her seat
Sighing through all her Works gave signs of woe,
That all was lost. Back to the Thicket slunk
The guilty Serpent, and well might, for *Eve*
Intent now wholly on her taste, naught else
Regarded, such delight till then, as seem'd,
In Fruit she never tasted, whether true
Or fancied so, through expectation high
790 Of knowledge, nor was God-head from her thought.
Greedily she ingorg'd without restraint,
And knew not eating Death: Satiate at length,
And hight'n'd as with Wine, jocund and boon,°
Thus to herself she pleasingly began.

O Sovran, virtuous, precious of all Trees
In Paradise, of operation blest
To Sapience, hitherto obscur'd, infam'd,
And thy fair Fruit let hang, as to no end
Created; but henceforth my early care,
800 Not without Song, each Morning, and due praise°
Shall tend thee, and the fertile burden ease
Of thy full branches offer'd free to all;
Till dieted by thee I grow mature
In knowledge, as the Gods who all things know;
Though others envy what they cannot give;
For had the gift been theirs, it had not here
Thus grown. Experience, next to thee I owe,
Best guide; not following thee, I had remain'd
In ignorance, thou op'n'st Wisdom's way,
810 And giv'st access, though secret she retire.
And I perhaps am secret; Heav'n is high,
High and remote to see from thence distinct
Each thing on Earth; and other care perhaps
May have diverted from continual watch
Our great Forbidder, safe with all his Spies
About him. But to *Adam* in what sort
Shall I appear? shall I to him make known
As yet my change, and give him to partake
Full happiness with mee, or rather not.
820 But keep the odds of Knowledge in my power
Without Copartner? so to add what wants
In Female Sex, the more to draw his Love,
And render me more equal, and perhaps,
A thing not undesirable, sometime
Superior: for inferior who is free?
This may be well: but what if God have seen,
And Death ensue? then I shall be no more,
And *Adam* wedded to another *Eve*,
Shall live with her enjoying, I extinct;
830 A death to think. Confirm'd then I resolve,
Adam shall share with me in bliss or woe:
So dear I love him, that with him all deaths
I could endure, without him live no life.

So saying, from the Tree her step she turn'd,
But first low Reverence done, as to the power
That dwelt within, whose presence had infus'd
Into the plant sciential° sap, deriv'd
From Nectar, drink of Gods. *Adam* the while
Waiting desirous her return, had wove
Of choicest Flow'rs a Garland to adorn   840
Her Tresses, and her rural labors crown,
As Reapers oft are wont thir Harvest Queen.
Great joy he promis'd to his thoughts, and new
Solace in her return, so long delay'd;
Yet oft his heart, divine of something ill,
Misgave him; hee the falt'ring measure felt;
And forth to meet her went, the way she took
That Morn when first they parted; by the Tree
Of Knowledge he must pass; there he her met,
Scarce from the Tree returning; in her hand   850
A bough of fairest fruit that downy smil'd,
New gather'd, and ambrosial smell diffus'd.
To him she hasted, in her face excuse
Came Prologue, and Apology to prompt,
Which with bland words at will she thus addrest.
Hast thou not wonder'd, *Adam,* at my stay?
Thee I have misst, and thought it long, depriv'd
Thy presence, agony of love till now
Not felt, nor shall be twice, for never more
Mean I to try, what rash untri'd I sought,   860
The pain of absence from thy sight. But strange
Hath been the cause, and wonderful to hear:
This Tree is not as we are told, a Tree
Of danger tasted, nor to evil unknown
Op'ning the way, but of Divine effect
To open Eyes, and make them Gods who taste;
And hath been tasted such: the Serpent wise,
Or not restrain'd as wee, or not obeying,
Hath eat'n of the fruit, and is become,
Not dead, as we are threat'n'd, but thenceforth 870
Endu'd with human voice and human sense,
Reasoning to admiration, and with mee
Persuasively hath so prevail'd, that I
Have also tasted, and have also found
Th' effects to correspond, opener mine Eyes,
Dim erst, dilated Spirits, ampler Heart,
And growing up to Godhead; which for thee
Chiefly I sought, without thee can despise.
For bliss, as thou hast part, to me is bliss,
Tedious, unshar'd with thee, and odious soon.   880
Thou therefore also taste, that equal Lot
May join us, equal Joy, as equal Love;
Lest thou not tasting, different degree
Disjoin us, and I then too late renounce
Deity for thee, when Fate will not permit.
Thus *Eve* with Count'nance blithe her story told;
But in her Cheek distemper flushing glow'd.
On th' other side, *Adam,* soon as he heard
The fatal Trespass done by *Eve,* amaz'd,

781 **eat,** ate   793 **boon,** blithe   800 **Not . . . praise.** In Eve's mind the tree has virtually replaced God

837 **sciential,** conferring knowledge

890 Astonied stood and Blank, while horror chill
Ran through his veins, and all his joints relax'd;
From his slack hand the Garland wreath'd for *Eve*
Down dropp'd, and all the faded Roses shed:
Speechless he stood and pale, till thus at length
First to himself he inward silence broke.
    O fairest of Creation, last and best
Of all God's Works, Creature in whom excell'd
Whatever can to sight or thought be form'd,
Holy, divine, good, amiable, or sweet!
900 How art thou lost, how on a sudden lost,
Defac't, deflow'r'd, and now to Death devote?°
Rather how hast thou yielded to transgress
The strict forbiddance, how to violate
The sacred Fruit forbidd'n! some cursed fraud
Of Enemy hath beguil'd thee, yet unknown,
And mee with thee hath ruin'd, for with thee
Certain my resolution is to Die;
How can I live without thee, how forgo
Thy sweet Converse and Love so dearly join'd,
910 To live again in these wild Woods forlorn?
Should God create another *Eve,* and I
Another Rib afford, yet loss of thee
Would never from my heart; no no, I feel
The Link of Nature draw me: Flesh of Flesh,
Bone of my Bone thou art,° and from thy State
Mine never shall be parted, bliss or woe.
    So having said, as one from sad dismay
Recomforted, and after thoughts disturb'd
Submitting to what seem'd remediless,
920 Thus in calm mood his Words to *Eve* he turn'd.
    Bold deed thou hast presum'd, advent'rous *Eve,*
And peril great provok't, who thus hath dar'd
Had it been only coveting to Eye
That sacred Fruit, sacred to abstinence,
Much more to taste it under ban to touch.
But past who can recall, or done undo?
Not God Omnipotent, nor Fate; yet so
Perhaps thou shalt not Die, perhaps the Fact°
Is not so heinous now, foretasted Fruit,
930 Profan'd first by the Serpent, by him first
Made common and unhallow'd ere our taste;
Nor yet on him found deadly, he yet lives,
Lives, as thou said'st, and gains to live as Man
Higher degree of Life, inducement strong
To us, as likely tasting to attain
Proportional ascent, which cannot be
But to be Gods, or Angels Demi-gods.
Nor can I think that God, Creator wise,
Though threat'ning, will in earnest so destroy
940 Us his prime Creatures, dignifi'd so high,
Set over all his Works, which in our Fall,
For us created, needs with us must fail,
Dependent made; so God shall uncreate,
Be frustrate, do, undo, and labor lose,
Not well conceiv'd of God, who though his Power

Creation could repeat, yet would be loath
Us to abolish, lest the Adversary
Triumph and say; Fickle their State whom God
Most Favors, who can please him long? Mee first
950 He ruin'd, now Mankind; whom will he next?
Matter of scorn, not to be given the Foe.
However I with thee have fixt my Lot,
Certain to undergo like doom; if Death
Consort with thee, Death is to mee as Life;
So forcible within my heart I feel
The Bond of Nature draw me to my own,
My own in thee, for what thou art is mine;
Our State cannot be sever'd, we are one,
One Flesh; to lose thee were to lose myself.
960   So *Adam,* and thus *Eve* to him repli'd.
O glorious trial of exceeding Love,
Illustrious evidence, example high!
Ingaging me to emulate, but short
Of thy perfection, how shall I attain,
Adam, from whose dear side I boast me sprung,
And gladly of our Union hear thee speak,
One Heart, one Soul in both; whereof good proof
This day affords, declaring thee resolv'd,
Rather than Death or aught than Death more dread
970 Shall separate us, linkt in Love so dear,
To undergo with mee one Guilt, one Crime,
If any be, of tasting this fair Fruit,
Whose virtue, for of good still good proceeds,
Direct, or by occasion hath presented
This happy trial of thy Love, which else
So eminently never had been known.
Were it I thought Death menac't would ensue
This my attempt, I would sustain alone
The worst, and not persuade thee, rather die
980 Deserted, than oblige° thee with a fact
Pernicious to thy Peace, chiefly assur'd
Remarkably so late of thy so true,
So faithful Love unequall'd; but I feel
Far otherwise th' event, not Death, but Life
Augmented, op'n'd Eyes, new Hopes, new Joys,
Taste so Divine, that what of sweet before
Hath toucht my sense, flat seems to this, and harsh.
On my experience, *Adam,* freely taste,
And fear of Death deliver to the Winds.
990   So saying, she embrac'd him, and for joy
Tenderly wept, much won that he his Love
Had so ennobl'd, as of choice to incur
Divine displeasure for her sake, or Death.
In recompense (for such compliance bad
Such recompense best merits) from the bough
She gave him of that fair enticing Fruit
With liberal hand: he scrupl'd not to eat
Against his better knowledge, not deceiv'd,
But fondly overcome with Female charm.
1000 Earth trembl'd from her entrails, as again
In pangs, and Nature gave a second groan,

901 **devote,** fated   914 **Flesh . . . art.** See *Genesis,* 2:23   928 **Fact,** deed   980 **oblige,** involve

Sky low'r'd, and muttering Thunder, some sad drops
Wept at completing of the mortal Sin
Original; while *Adam* took no thought,
Eating his fill, nor *Eve* to iterate
Her former trespass fear'd, the more to soothe
Him with her lov'd society, that now
As with new Wine intoxicated both
They swim in mirth, and fancy that they feel
1010 Divinity within them breeding wings
Wherewith to scorn the Earth: but that false Fruit
Far other operation first display'd,
Carnal desire inflaming, hee on *Eve*
Began to cast lascivious Eyes, she him
As wantonly repaid; in Lust they burn:
Till *Adam* thus 'gan *Eve* to dalliance move.
    Eve, now I see thou are exact of taste,
And elegant, of Sapience no small part,
Since to each meaning savor we apply,
1020 And Palate call judicious; I the praise
Yield thee, so well this day thou hast purvey'd.
Much pleasure we have lost, while we abstain'd
From this delightful Fruit, nor known till now
True relish, tasting; if such pleasure be
In things to us forbidden, it might be wish'd,
For this one Tree had been forbidden ten.
But come, so well refresh't, now let us play,
As meet is, after such delicious Fare;
For never did thy Beauty since the day
1030 I saw thee first and wedded thee, adorn'd
With all perfections, so inflame my sense
With ardor to enjoy thee, fairer now
Than ever, bounty of this virtuous Tree.
    So said he, and forbore not glance or toy°
Of amorous intent, well understood
Of *Eve,* whose Eye darted contagious Fire.
Her hand he seiz'd, and to a shady bank,
Thick overhead with verdant roof imbowr'd
He led her nothing loath; Flow'rs were the Couch,
1040 Pansies, and Violets, and Asphodel,
And Hyacinth, Earth's freshest softest lap.
There they thir fill of Love and Love's disport
Took largely, of thir mutual guilt the Seal,
The solace of thir sin, till dewy sleep
Oppress'd them, wearied with thir amorous play.
Soon as the force of that fallacious Fruit,
That with exhilarating vapor bland
About thir spirits had play'd, and inmost powers
Made err, was now exhal'd, and grosser sleep
1050 Bred of unkindly fumes, with conscious dreams
Encumber'd, now had left them, up they rose
As from unrest, and each the other viewing,
Soon found thir Eyes how op'n'd, and thir minds
How dark'n'd; innocence, that as a veil
Had shadow'd them from knowing ill, was gone,
Just confidence, and native righteousness,
And honor from about them, naked left

To guilty shame: hee cover'd, but his Robe
Uncover'd more. So rose the *Danite* strong
Herculean Samson from the Harlot-lap   1060
Of *Philistean Dalilah,* and wak'd
Shorn of his strength, They destitute and bare
Of all thir virtue: silent, and in face
Confounded long they sat, as struck'n mute,
Till *Adam,* though not less than *Eve* abasht,
At length gave utterance to these words constrain'd
    O *Eve,* in evil hour thou didst give ear
To that false Worm, of whomsoever taught
To counterfeit Man's voice, true in our Fall,
False in our promis'd Rising; since our Eyes   1070
Op'n'd we find indeed, and find we know
Both Good and Evil, Good lost, and Evil got,
Bad Fruit of Knowledge, if this be to know,
Which leaves us naked thus, of Honor void,
Of Innocence, of Faith, of Purity,
Our wonted Ornaments now soil'd and stain'd,
And in our Faces evident the signs
Of foul concupiscence; whence evil store;
Even shame, the last of evils; of the first
Be sure then. How shall I behold the face   1080
Henceforth of God or Angel, erst with joy
And rapture so oft beheld? those heav'nly shapes
Will dazzle now this earthly, with thir blaze
Insufferably bright. O might I here
In solitude live savage, in some glade
Obscur'd, where highest Woods impenetrable
To Star or Sun-light, spread thir umbrage broad,
And brown as Evening: Cover me ye Pines,
Ye Cedars, with innumerable boughs
Hide me, where I may never see them more.°   1090
But let us now, as in bad plight, devise
What best may for the present serve to hide
The Parts of each from other, that seem most
To shame obnoxious,° and unseemliest seen,
Some Tree whose broad smooth Leaves together
    sew'd,
And girded on our loins, may cover round
Those middle parts, that this new comer, Shame,
There sit not, and reproach us as unclean.
    So counsell'd hee, and both together went
Into the thickest Wood, there soon they chose   1100
The Figtree, not that kind for Fruit renown'd,
But such as at this day to *Indians* known
In *Malabar* or *Decan* spreads her Arms
Branching so broad and long, that in the ground
The bended Twigs take root, and Daughters grow
About the Mother Tree, a Pillar'd shade
High overarch't, and echoing Walks between;
There oft the *Indian* Herdsman shunning heat
Shelters in cool, and tends his pasturing Herds
At Loopholes cut through thickest shade: Those   1110
    Leaves
They gather'd, broad as *Amazonian* Targe,

1034 **toy,** caress

1090 **Cover me . . . more.** See *Revelation,* 6:16   1094 **obnoxious,** liable

And with what skill they had, together sew'd,
To gird thir waist, vain Covering if to hide
Thir guilt and dreaded shame; O how unlike
To that first naked Glory. Such of late
Columbus found th' *American* so girt
With feather'd Cincture, naked else and wild
Among the Trees on Isles and woody Shores.
Thus fenc't, and as they thought, thir shame in part
1120 Cover'd, but not at rest or ease of Mind,
They sat them down to weep, nor only Tears
Rain'd at thir Eyes, but high Winds worse within
Began to rise, high Passions, Anger, Hate,
Mistrust, Suspicion, Discord, and shook sore
Thir inward State of Mind, calm Region once
And full of Peace, now toss't and turbulent:
For Understanding rul'd not, and the Will
Heard not her lore, both in subjection now
To sensual Appetite, who from beneath
1130 Usurping over sovran Reason claim'd
Superior sway: From thus distemper'd breast,
Adam, estrang'd in look and alter'd style,
Speech intermitted thus to *Eve* renew'd.
    Would thou hadst heark'n'd to my words, and stay'd
With me, as I besought thee, when that strange
Desire of wand'ring this unhappy Morn,
I know not whence possess'd thee; we had then
Remain'd still happy, not as now, despoil'd
Of all our good, sham'd, naked, miserable.
1140 Let none henceforth seek needless cause to approve
The Faith they owe; when earnestly they seek
Such proof, conclude, they then begin to fail.
    To whom soon mov'd with touch of blame thus *Eve.*
What words have past thy Lips, *Adam* severe,
Imput'st thou that to my default, or will
Of wand'ring, as thou call'st it, which who knows
But might as ill have happ'n'd thou being by,
Or to thyself perhaps: hadst thou been there,
Or here th' attempt, thou couldst not have discern'd
1150 Fraud in the Serpent, speaking as he spake;
No ground of enmity between us known,
Why hee should mean me ill, or seek to harm.
Was I to have never parted from thy side?
As good have grown there still a lifeless Rib.
Being as I am, why didst not thou the Head
Command me absolutely not to go,
Going into such danger as thou said'st?
Too facile then thou didst not much gainsay,
Nay, didst permit, approve, and fair dismiss.
1160 Hadst thou been firm and fixt in thy dissent,
Neither had I transgress'd, nor thou with mee.
    To whom then first incenst *Adam* repli'd.
Is this the Love, is this the recompense
Of mine to thee, ingrateful *Eve,* express't
Immutable when thou wert lost, not I,
Who might have liv'd and joy'd immortal bliss,
Yet willingly chose rather Death with thee:
And am I now upbraided, as the cause
Of thy transgressing? not enough severe,

It seems, in thy restraint: what could I more? 1170
I warn'd thee, I admonish'd thee, foretold
The danger, and the lurking Enemy
That lay in wait; beyond this had been force,
And force upon free Will hath here no place.
But confidence then bore thee on, secure°
Either to meet no danger, or to find
Matter of glorious trial; and perhaps
I also err'd in overmuch admiring
What seem'd in thee so perfet, that I thought
No evil durst attempt thee, but I rue 1180
That error now, which is become my crime,
And thou th' accuser. Thus it shall befall
Him who to worth in Woman overtrusting
Lets her Will rule; restraint she will not brook,
And left to herself, if evil thence ensue,
Shee first his weak indulgence will accuse.
    Thus they in mutual accusation spent
The fruitless hours, but neither self-condemning,
And of thir vain contést appear'd no end.

The End of the Ninth Book.

from BOOK TWELVE

In either hand the hast'ning Angel caught
Our ling'ring Parents, and to th' Eastern Gate
Led them direct, and down the Cliff as fast
To the subjected Plain; then disappear'd. 640
They looking back, all th' Eastern side beheld
Of Paradise, so late thir happy seat,
Wav'd over by that flaming Brand, the Gate
With dreadful Faces throng'd and fiery Arms:
Some natural tears they dropp'd, but wip'd them soon;
The World was all before them, where to choose
Thir place of rest, and Providence thir guide:
They hand in hand with wand'ring steps and slow,
Through *Eden* took thir solitary way.

The End.
(1667)

OF EDUCATION

TO MASTER SAMUEL HARTLIB°

Mr. Hartlib,

    I am long since persuaded that to say or do aught
worth memory and imitation, no purpose or respect
should sooner move us than simply the love of God
and of mankind. Nevertheless to write now the reforming of education, though it be one of the greatest
and noblest designs that can be thought on, and for the

1175 **secure,** foolishly confident   **Of Education   Hartlib,** "indefatigable writer
of books on agriculture, religion and education" (Hughes)

want whereof this nation perishes, I had not yet at this time been induced but by your earnest entreaties and serious conjurements; as having my mind for the pres-
10 ent half diverted in the pursuance of some other assertions, the knowledge and the use of which cannot but be a great furtherance both to the enlargement of truth and honest living, with much more peace. Nor should the laws of any private friendship have prevailed with me to divide thus, or transpose my former thoughts, but that I see those aims, those actions, which have won you with me the esteem of a person sent hither by some good providence from a far country° to be the occasion and the incitement of great good
20 to this island.

And, as I hear, you have obtained the same repute with men of most approved wisdom, and some of the highest authority among us; not to mention the learned correspondence which you hold in foreign parts, and the extraordinary pains and diligence which you have used in this matter, both here and beyond the seas; either by the definite will of God so ruling, or the peculiar sway of nature, which also is God's working. Neither can I think that, so reputed and so valued as
30 you are, you would, to the forfeit of your own discerning ability, impose upon me an unfit and overponderous argument; but that the satisfaction which you profess to have received from those incidental discourses which we have wandered into, hath pressed and almost constrained you into a persuasion that what you require from me in this point, I neither ought nor can in conscience defer beyond this time both of so much need at once, and so much opportunity to try what God hath determined.
40 I will not resist therefore whatever it is either of divine or human obligement that you lay upon me; but will forthwith set down in writing, as you request me, that voluntary idea which hath long in silence presented itself to me, of a better education, in extent and comprehension far more large, and yet of time far shorter, and of attainment far more certain, than hath been yet in practice. Brief I shall endeavor to be; for that which I have to say, assuredly this nation hath extreme need should be done sooner than spoken. To
50 tell you therefore what I have benefited herein among old renowned authors, I shall spare; and to search what many modern Januas and Didactics,° more than ever I shall read, have projected, my inclination leads me not. But if you can accept of these few observations which have flowered off, and are as it were the burnishing of many studious and contemplative years altogether spent in the search of religious and civil knowledge, and such as pleased you so well in the relating, I here give you them to dispose of.
60 The end then of learning is to repair the ruins° of our

first parents by regaining to know God aright, and out of that knowledge to love him, to imitate him, to be like him, as we may the nearest by possessing our souls of true virtue, which being united to the heavenly grace of faith makes up the highest perfection. But because our understanding cannot in this body found itself but on sensible things, nor arrive so clearly to the knowledge of God and things invisible as by orderly conning over° the visible and inferior creature, the same method is necessarily to be followed in all dis- 70 creet teaching. And seeing every nation affords not experience and tradition enough for all kind of learning, therefore we are chiefly taught the languages of those people who have at any time been most industrious after wisdom; so that language is but the instrument conveying to us things useful to be known. And though a linguist should pride himself to have all the tongues that Babel cleft the world into, yet, if he have not studied the solid things in them as well as the words and lexicons, he were nothing so much to be 80 esteemed a learned man as any yeoman or tradesman competently wise in his mother dialect only.

Hence appear the many mistakes which have made learning generally so unpleasing and so unsuccessful; first, we do amiss to spend seven or eight years merely in scraping together so much miserable Latin and Greek as might be learned otherwise easily and delightfully in one year. And that which casts our proficiency therein so much behind, is our time lost partly in too oft idle vacancies° given both to schools and 90 universities, partly in a preposterous exaction,° forcing the empty wits of children to compose themes, verses and orations, which are the acts of ripest judgment and the final work of a head filled by long reading and observing with elegant maxims and copious invention. These are not matters to be wrung from poor striplings, like blood out of the nose, or the plucking of untimely fruit: besides the ill habit which they get of wretched barbarizing° against the Latin and Greek idiom with their untutored Anglicisms, odious to be 100 read, yet not to be avoided without a well-continued and judicious conversing among pure authors digested, which they scarce taste. Whereas, if after some preparatory grounds of speech by their certain forms got into memory, they were led to the praxis thereof in some chosen short book lessoned thoroughly to them, they might then forthwith proceed to learn the substance of good things, and arts in due order, which would bring the whole language quickly into their power. This I take to be the most rational and most 110 profitable way of learning languages, and whereby we may best hope to give account to God of our youth spent herein.

And for the usual method of teaching arts, I deem it to be an old error of universities not yet well recovered

---

18 **a far country,** Hartlib had emigrated from Prussia to England 52 **Januas and Didactics,** reference to two works by Comenius (of whom Hartlib was a translator) 60 **ruins.** Before the Fall, Milton believed, Adam possessed all knowledge

69 **conning over,** poring over 90 **vacancies,** holidays 91 **exaction,** demand 99 **barbarizing,** violating the laws of Latin or Greek grammar

from the scholastic grossness of barbarous ages, that instead of beginning with arts most easy—and those be such as are most obvious to the sense—they present their young unmatriculated novices at first coming with the most intellective abstractions of logic and metaphysics. So that they having but newly left those grammatic flats and shallows where they stuck unreasonably to learn a few words with lamentable construction, and now on the sudden transported under another climate to be tossed and turmoiled with their unballasted wits in fathomless and unquiet deeps of controversy, do for the most part grow into hatred and contempt of learning, mocked and deluded all this while with ragged notions and babblements, while they expected worthy and delightful knowledge; till poverty or youthful years call them importunately° their several ways and hasten them with the sway of friends either to an ambitious and mercenary, or ignorantly zealous divinity: some allured to the trade of law, grounding their purposes not on the prudent and heavenly contemplation of justice and equity which was never taught them, but on the promising and pleasing thoughts of litigious terms, fat contentions, and flowing fees; others betake them to state affairs with souls so unprincipled in virtue and true generous breeding that flattery and court shifts and tyrannous aphorisms appear to them the highest points of wisdom; instilling their barren hearts with a conscientious slavery, if, as I rather think, it be not feigned. Others, lastly, of a more delicious and airy spirit, retire themselves—knowing no better—to the enjoyments of ease and luxury, living out their days in feast and jollity; which indeed is the wisest and the safest course of all these, unless they were with more integrity undertaken. And these are the fruits of misspending our prime youth at the schools and universities as we do, either in learning mere words or such things chiefly as were better unlearned.

I shall detain you no longer in the demonstration of what we should not do, but straight conduct ye to a hillside, where I will point ye out the right path of a virtuous and noble education; laborious indeed at the first ascent, but else so smooth, so green, so full of goodly prospect and melodious sounds on every side, that the harp of Orpheus° was not more charming. I doubt not but ye shall have more ado to drive our dullest and laziest youth, our stocks and stubs,° from the infinite desire of such a happy nurture, than we have now to hale and drag our choicest and hopefullest wits to that asinine feast of sowthistles and brambles which is commonly set before them as all the food and entertainment of their tenderest and most docible age. I call therefore a complete and generous education that which fits a man to perform justly, skillfully, and magnanimously all the offices, both private

and public, of peace and war. And how all this may be done between twelve and one and twenty, less time than is now bestowed in pure trifling at grammar and sophistry, is to be thus ordered.

First, to find out a spacious house and ground about it fit for an academy and big enough to lodge a hundred and fifty persons, whereof twenty or thereabout may be attendants, all under the government of one, who shall be thought of desert sufficient, and ability either to do all or wisely to direct and oversee it done. This place should be at once both school and university, not needing a remove° to any other house of scholarship, except it be some peculiar° college of law or physic, where they mean to be practitioners; but as for those general studies which take up all our time from Lily° to the commencing, as they term it, master of art, it should be absolute. After this pattern, as many edifices may be converted to this use as shall be needful in every city throughout this land, which would tend much to the increase of learning and civility everywhere. This number, less or more thus collected, to the convenience of a foot company, or interchangeably two troops of cavalry, should divide their day's work into three parts, as it lies orderly: their studies, their exercise, and their diet.

For their studies: first, they should begin with the chief and necessary rules of some good grammar, either that now used, or any better; and while this is doing, their speech is to be fashioned to a distinct and clear pronunciation, as near as may be to the Italian, especially in the vowels. For we Englishmen, being far northerly, do not open our mouths in the cold air wide enough to grace a southern tongue, but are observed by all other nations to speak exceeding close and inward; so that to smatter Latin with an English mouth is as ill a hearing° as law French. Next, to make them expert in the usefullest points of grammar, and withal to season them and win them early to the love of virtue and true labor, ere any flattering seducement or vain principle seize them wandering, some easy and delightful book of education would be read to them, whereof the Greeks have store; as Cebes, Plutarch, and other Socratic discourses.° But in Latin we have none of classic authority extant, except the two or three first books of Quintilian,° and some select pieces elsewhere.

But here the main skill and groundwork will be to temper them such lectures and explanations upon every opportunity as may lead and draw them in willing obedience, inflamed with the study of learning and the admiration of virtue—stirred up with high hopes of living to be brave men and worthy patriots, dear to God and famous to all ages; that they may despise and scorn all their childish and ill-taught qualities to delight

131 **importunately,** unseasonably, at the wrong time   160 **harp of Orpheus,** whose music charmed beasts, trees, rocks   162 **stubs,** remnants

182 **a remove,** a move   183 **peculiar,** distinct   185 **Lily,** William Lily was the author of the standard beginning text in Latin   206 **a hearing,** a thing to hear   212 **Cebes . . . discourses,** classical authors on education   215 **Quintilian,** famous Roman rhetorician

in manly and liberal exercises, which he who hath the art and proper eloquence to catch° them with, what with mild and effectual persuasions and what with the intimation of some fear, if need be, but chiefly by his own example, might in a short space gain them to an
230 incredible diligence and courage, infusing into their young breasts such an ingenuous and noble ardor, as would not fail to make many of them renowned and matchless men. At the same time, some other hour of the day, might be taught them the rules of arithmetic, and soon after the elements of geometry, even playing, as the old manner was. After evening repast till bedtime their thoughts will be best taken up in the easy grounds of religion and the story of scripture.

The next step would be to the authors of agriculture,
240 Cato, Varro, and Columella,° for the matter is most easy; and, if the language be difficult, so much the better—it is not a difficulty above their years. And here will be an occasion of inciting and enabling them hereafter to improve the tillage of their country, to recover the bad soil and to remedy the waste that is made of good; for this was one of Hercules' praises. Ere half these authors be read (which will soon be with plying hard and daily) they cannot choose but be masters of any ordinary prose. So that it will be then sea-
250 sonable for them to learn in any modern author the use of the globes and all the maps, first with the old names and then with the new; or they might be then capable to read any compendious method of natural philosophy.

And at the same time might be entering into the Greek tongue after the same manner as was before prescribed in the Latin; whereby the difficulties of grammar being soon overcome, all the historical physiology of Aristotle and Theophrastus are open
260 before them, and, as I may say, under contribution. The like access will be to Vitruvius, to Seneca's *Natural Questions,* to Mela, Celsus, Pliny, or Solinus.° And having thus passed the principles of arithmetic, geometry, astronomy, and geography, with a general compact of physics, they may descend in mathematics to the instrumental science of trigonometry, and from thence to fortification, architecture, enginery, or navigation. And in natural philosophy they may proceed leisurely from the history of meteors, minerals, plants,
270 and living creatures, as far as anatomy.

Then also in course might be read to them out of some not tedious writer the institution of physic, that they may know the tempers, the humors, the seasons, and how to manage a crudity;° which he who can wisely and timely do, is not only a great physician to himself and to his friends, but also may at some time or other save an army by this frugal and expenseless means only, and not let the healthy and stout bodies of young men rot away under him for want of this discipline—

which is a great pity, and no less a shame to the com- 280 mander. To set forward all these proceedings in nature and mathematics, what hinders but that they may procure, as oft as shall be needful, the helpful experiences of hunters, fowlers, fishermen, shepherds, gardeners, apothecaries; and in the other sciences, architects, engineers, mariners, anatomists; who doubtless would be ready, some for reward and some to favor such a hopeful seminary. And this will give them such a real tincture of natural knowledge as they shall never forget, but daily augment with delight. Then also those 290 poets which are now counted most hard, will be both facile and pleasant: Orpheus, Hesiod, Theocritus, Aratus, Nicander, Oppian, Dionysius, and, in Latin, Lucretius, Manilius and the rural part of Virgil.°

By this time, years and good general precepts will have furnished them more distinctly with that act of reason which in ethics is called Proairesis;° that they may with some judgment contemplate upon moral good and evil. Then will be required a special reinforcement of constant and sound indoctrinating to set 300 them right and firm, instructing them more amply in the knowledge of virtue and the hatred of vice; while their young and pliant affections are led through all the moral works of Plato, Xenophon, Cicero, Plutarch, Laertius, and those Locrian remnants;° but still to be reduced° in their nightward studies wherewith they close the day's work, under the determinate sentence of David or Solomon, or the evangels and apostolic scriptures. Being perfect in the knowledge of personal duty, they may then begin the study of economics. 310 And either now or before this, they may have easily learned at any odd hour the Italian tongue. And soon after, but with wariness and good antidote, it would be wholesome enough to let them taste some choice comedies, Greek, Latin, or Italian; those tragedies also that treat of household matters, as *Trachiniæ, Alcestis,* and the like.

The next remove must be to the study of politics; to know the beginning, end, and reasons of political societies, that they may not in a dangerous fit of the 320 commonwealth be such poor, shaken, uncertain reeds, of such a tottering conscience, as many of our great counsellors have lately shown themselves, but steadfast pillars of the state. After this, they are to dive into the grounds of law and legal justice; delivered first and with best warrant by Moses, and as far as human prudence can be trusted, in those extolled remains of Grecian lawgivers, Lycurgus, Solon, Zaleucus, Charondas, and thence to all the Roman edicts and tables with their Justinian: and so down to the Saxon and common 330 laws of England, and the statutes.

Sundays also and every evening may be now understandingly spent in the highest matters of theology and church history ancient and modern; and ere this time

226 **catch,** charm 240 **Cato, Varro, Columella,** Latin authors on agriculture
261 **Vitruvius . . . Solinus,** classical writers on arts and natural sciences
274 **crudity,** indigestion

292–294 **Orpheus . . . Virgil.** Greek and Latin pastoral poets 297 **Proairesis,** "Aristotle's term for intelligent choice between good and evil in the *Nichomachean Ethics*" (Hughes) 304–305 **Plato . . . remnants.** Classical philosophers and historians 306 **reduced,** recalled, brought into proper order

the Hebrew tongue at a set hour might have been gained, that the scriptures may be now read in their own original; whereto it would be no impossibility to add the Chaldee and the Syrian dialect. When all these employments are well conquered, then will the choice 340 histories, heroic poems, and Attic tragedies of stateliest and most regal argument, with all the famous political orations, offer themselves; which, if they were not only read, but some of them got by memory and solemnly pronounced with right accent and grace, as might be taught, would endue them even with the spirit and vigor of Demosthenes or Cicero, Euripides or Sophocles.°

And now, lastly, will be the time to read with them those organic° arts which enable men to discourse and 350 write perspicuously, elegantly, and according to the fitted style of lofty, mean, or lowly. Logic, therefore, so much as is useful, is to be referred to this due place with all her well-couched heads and topics, until it be time to open her contracted palm into a graceful and ornate rhetoric, taught out of the rule of Plato, Aristotle, Phalereus, Cicero, Hermogenes, Longinus. To which poetry would be made subsequent, or indeed rather precedent, as being less subtle and fine, but more simple, sensuous, and passionate. I mean not 360 here the prosody of a verse, which they could not but have hit on before among the rudiments of grammar; but that sublime art which in Aristotle's *Poetics,* in Horace, and the Italian commentaries of Castelvetro, Tasso, Mazzoni, and others, teaches what the laws are of a true epic poem, what of a dramatic, what of a lyric, what decorum is, which is the grand masterpiece to observe. This would make them soon perceive what despicable creatures our common rhymers and playwriters be, and show them what religious, what glori- 370 ous and magnificent use might be made of poetry, both in divine and human things.

From hence, and not till now, will be the right season of forming them to be able writers and composers in every excellent matter, when they shall be thus fraught with an universal insight into things. Or whether they be to speak in parliament or council, honor and attention would be waiting on their lips. There would then also appear in pulpits other visages, other gestures, and stuff otherwise wrought than what 380 we now sit under, ofttimes to as great a trial of our patience as any other that they preach to us. These are the studies wherein our noble and our gentle youth ought to bestow their time in a disciplinary way from twelve to one and twenty: unless they rely more upon their ancestors dead than upon themselves living. In which methodical course it is so supposed they must proceed by the steady pace of learning onward, as at convenient times for memory's sake to retire back into the middle ward, and sometimes into the rear of what 390 they have been taught, until they have confirmed and

solidly united the whole body of their perfected knowledge, like the last embattling of a Roman legion. Now will be worth the seeing what exercises and recreations may best agree and become these studies.

THEIR EXERCISE.

The course of study hitherto briefly described, is, what I can guess by reading, likest to those ancient and famous schools of Pythagoras, Plato, Isocrates, Aristotle and such others, out of which were bred up such a number of renowned philosophers, orators, historians, poets, and princes all over Greece, Italy, and Asia, 400 besides the flourishing studies of Cyrene and Alexandria. But herein it shall exceed them and supply a defect as great as that which Plato noted in the commonwealth of Sparta; whereas that city trained up their youth most for war, and these in their academies and Lycæum all for the gown, this institution of breeding which I here delineate shall be equally good both for peace and war. Therefore about an hour and a half ere they eat at noon should be allowed them for exercise and due rest afterwards; but the time for this may be 410 enlarged at pleasure, according as their rising in the morning shall be early.

The exercise which I commend first is the exact use of their weapon, to guard and to strike safely with edge or point; this will keep them healthy, nimble, strong, and well in breath—is also the likeliest means to make them grow large and tall, and to inspire them with a gallant and fearless courage, which, being tempered with seasonable lectures and precepts to them of true fortitude and patience, will turn into a native and 420 heroic valor, and make them hate the cowardice of doing wrong. They must be also practised in all the locks and grips of wrestling, wherein Englishmen were wont to excel, as need may often be in fight to tug or grapple, and to close. And this perhaps will be enough wherein to prove and heat their single strength.

The interim of unsweating themselves regularly, and convenient rest before meat may, both with profit and delight, be taken up in recreating and composing their travailed spirits with the solemn and divine harmonies 430 of music, heard or learned, either while the skilful organist plies his grave and fancied descant in lofty fugues, or the whole symphony with artful and unimaginable touches adorn and grace the well-studied chords of some choice composer; sometimes the lute or soft organ stop waiting on elegant voices, either to religious, martial, or civil ditties; which, if wise men and prophets be not extremely out, have a great power over dispositions and manners to smooth and make them gentle from rustic harshness and distempered 440 passions. The like also would not be inexpedient after meat to assist and cherish nature in her first concoction and send their minds back to study in good tune and satisfaction. Where having followed it close under

346–347 **Demosthenes . . . Sophocles.** famous orators and dramatists 349 **organic,** serving as an organ, instrument or means

vigilant eyes till about two hours before supper, they are by a sudden alarum or watchword to be called out to their military motions, under sky or covert according to the season, as was the Roman wont; first on foot, then, as their age permits, on horseback, to all the art of cavalry; that having in sport, but with much exactness and daily muster, served out the rudiments of their soldiership in all the skill of embattling, marching, encamping, fortifying, besieging, and battering, with all the helps of ancient and modern stratagems, tactics, and warlike maxims, they may as it were out of a long war come forth renowned and perfect commanders in the service of their country. They would not then, if they were trusted with fair and hopeful armies, suffer them for want of just and wise discipline to shed away from about them like sick feathers, though they be never so oft supplied; they would not suffer their empty and unrecruitable colonels of twenty men in a company to quaff out or convey into secret hoards the wages of a delusive list and a miserable remnant; yet in the meanwhile to be overmastered with a score or two of drunkards, the only soldiery left about them, or else to comply with all rapines and violences. No, certainly, if they knew aught of that knowledge that belongs to good men or good governors, they would not suffer these things.

But to return to our own institute: besides these constant exercises at home, there is another opportunity of gaining experience to be won from pleasure itself abroad. In those vernal seasons of the year when the air is calm and pleasant, it were an injury and sullenness against nature not to go out and see her riches and partake in her rejoicing with heaven and earth. I should not therefore be a persuader to them of studying much then, after two or three years that they have well laid their grounds, but to ride out in companies with prudent and staid guides to all the quarters of the land: learning and observing all places of strength, all commodities of building and of soil, for towns and tillage, harbors and ports for trade. Sometimes taking sea as far as to our navy, to learn there also what they can in the practical knowledge of sailing and of sea fight.

These ways would try all their peculiar gifts of nature; and if there were any secret excellence among them, would fetch it out and give it fair opportunities to advance itself by, which could not but mightily redound to the good of this nation, and bring into fashion again those old admired virtues and excellencies, with far more advantage now in this purity of Christian knowledge. Nor shall we then need the monsieurs of Paris to take our hopeful youth into their slight and prodigal custodies and send them over back again transformed into mimics, apes, and kickshaws.° But if they desire to see other countries at three or four and twenty years of age, not to learn principles but to enlarge experience and make wise observation, they will

by that time be such as shall deserve the regard and honor of all men where they pass, and the society and friendship of those in all places who are best and most eminent. And perhaps then other nations will be glad to visit us for their breeding, or else to imitate us in their own country.

Now, lastly, for their diet there cannot be much to say, save only that it would be best in the same house; for much time else would be lost abroad, and many ill habits got; and that it should be plain, healthful, and moderate, I suppose is out of controversy. Thus, Mr. Hartlib, you have a general view in writing, as your desire was, of that which at several times I had discoursed with you concerning the best and noblest way of education; not beginning, as some have done, from the cradle, which yet might be worth many considerations. If brevity had not been my scope, many other circumstances also I could have mentioned, but this, to such as have the worth in them to make trial, for light and direction may be enough. Only I believe that this is not a bow° for every man to shoot in that counts himself a teacher, but will require sinews almost equal to those which Homer gave Ulysses; yet I am withal persuaded that it may prove much more easy in the assay than it now seems at distance, and much more illustrious; howbeit, not more difficult than I imagine, and that imagination presents me with nothing but very happy and very possible according to best wishes; if God have so decreed, and this age have spirit and capacity enough to apprehend.

(1644)

JOHN BUNYAN
1628–1688

John Bunyan, born in Elstow, Bedfordshire, in 1628, was the son of an artisan, and he himself became a brazier. He received little schooling. At sixteen he was drafted into the Parliamentary army and served from November 1644 to June 1647. At the end of his service in the army, Bunyan returned to his native village, married, settled down to his craft, and began seriously reading the Bible. "I was never out of the Bible," he wrote later, "either by reading or meditation."

In 1653 Bunyan joined a Baptist church in Bedford, and shortly thereafter he began preaching lay sermons in his own and neighboring churches. Attacks by Quakers, who heckled him as he preached, brought about his first published writing, a controversial tract entitled *Some Gospel Truths Opened* (1656). The Restoration was unkind to all nonconformists; under the old Conventicle Act they were forbidden to preach

---

497 **kickshaws,** something elegant but insubstantial

521 **bow.** In its *Odyssey,* Odysseus bends the bow which the suitors of Penelope could not bend

and were punished for expressions of their belief in print. Therefore, in the first year of the return of Charles II, Bunyan was imprisoned in the Bedford jail, where he remained for twelve years until the royal declaration of indulgence released him in 1672. So it was that most of his writing was done in prison. *Grace Abounding to the Chief of Sinners* (1666) is a spiritual autobiography recounting his intense religious experiences. *The Holy City,* or the *New Jerusalem* (1665), followed his reading of the book of *Revelation* and prefigures the glowing description of the celestial city in *The Pilgrim's Progress. A Confession of My Faith and a Reason of My Practice,* written in 1672 just before his release, was an addition to the record of his remarkable spiritual evolution.

On his release from prison under the king's general pardon, which also permitted nonconformist ministers to preach, Bunyan was elected pastor of the church in Bedford of which he had been a member for nearly twenty years. After three years in this position, the royal indulgence, under pressure of the Anglicans, was withdrawn, and Bunyan was again imprisoned, this time for six months. During this period he produced his masterpiece, *The Pilgrim's Progress from This World to That Which Is to Come.* The short form of this narrative was published in 1678, another enlarged edition appeared later the same year, and a third and still further enlarged issue came out in the following year. After his release from prison he continued to write. *The Life and Death of Mr. Badman,* an allegorical tale, first appeared in 1680. In *The Holy War* (1682), another religious allegory, Bunyan drew upon his impressions and military experiences with the Parliamentary army. Part II of *Pilgrim's Progress,* dealing with the journey of Christian's family to join him, appeared in 1684, four years before Bunyan's death.

The traditional popularity of *Pilgrim's Progress* has been second only to that of the Bible. Not only in England but in Puritan New England it became a universally read classic. "This is the great merit of the book," said Dr. Johnson, "that the most cultivated man cannot find anything to praise more highly, and the child knows nothing more amusing." Though no longer the popular book it once was, it remains an important document in the development of English prose fiction.

from THE PILGRIM'S PROGRESS

[CHRISTIAN SETS FORTH]

As I walked through the wilderness of this world, I lighted on a certain place where was a Den, and I laid me down in that place to sleep; and, as I slept, I dreamed a dream. I dreamed, and behold I saw a man clothed with rags, standing in a certain place, with his face from his own house, a book in his hand, and a great burden upon his back (Isaiah 64:6; Luke 14:33; Psalms 38:4; Habakkuk 2:2; Acts 16:31). I looked and saw him open the book and read therein; and, as he read, he wept, and trembled; and not being able longer 10 to contain, he brake out with a lamentable cry, saying, "What shall I do?" (Acts 2:37).

In this plight, therefore, he went home and refrained himself as long as he could, that his wife and children should not perceive his distress; but he could not be silent long, because that his trouble increased. Wherefore at length he brake his mind to his wife and children; and thus he began to talk to them. O my dear wife, said he, and you the children of my bowels, I, your dear friend, am in myself undone by reason of a 20 burden that lieth hard upon me; moreover, I am for certain informed that this our city will be burned with fire from heaven, in which fearful overthrow both myself, with thee, my wife, and you my sweet babes, shall miserably come to ruin, except (the which yet I see not) some way of escape can be found, whereby we may be delivered. At this his relations were sore amazed; not for that they believed that what he had said to them was true, but because they thought that some frenzy distemper° had got into his head; there- 30 fore, it drawing towards night, and they hoping that sleep might settle his brains, with all haste they got him to bed. But the night was as troublesome to him as the day; wherefore, instead of sleeping, he spent it in sighs and tears. So, when the morning was come, they would know how he did. He told them, Worse and worse: he also set to talking to them again: but they began to be hardened. They also thought to drive away his distemper by harsh and surly carriages° to him; sometimes they would deride, sometimes they would 40 chide, and sometimes they would quite neglect him. Wherefore he began to retire himself to his chamber, to pray for and pity them, and also to condole his own misery; he would also walk solitarily in the fields, sometimes reading, and sometimes praying: and thus for some days he spent his time.

Now, I saw, upon a time, when he was walking in the fields, that he was, as he was wont, reading in his book, and greatly distressed in his mind; and as he read, he burst out, as he had done before, crying, 50 "What shall I do to be saved?"

I saw also that he looked this way and that way, as if he would run; yet he stood still, because, as I perceived, he could not tell which way to go. I looked then, and saw a man named Evangelist coming to him, who asked, Wherefore dost thou cry? (Job 33:23.)

He answered, Sir, I perceive by the book in my hand that I am condemned to die, and after that to come to judgment (Hebrews 9:27), and I find that I am not willing to do the first (Job 16:21), nor able to do the 60 second (Ezekiel 22:14).

The Pilgrim's Progress 30 **distemper,** a derangement of humors, insanity
39 **carriages,** bearings, demeanors

Christian no sooner leaves the World but meets
Evangelist, who lovingly him greets
With tidings of another; and doth show
Him how to mount to that from this below.

Then said Evangelist, Why not willing to die, since this life is attended with so many evils? The man answered, Because I fear that this burden that is upon my back will sink me lower than the grave, and I shall
70 fall into Tophet° (Isaiah 30:33). And, sir, if I be not fit to go to prison, I am not fit to go to judgment, and from thence to execution; and the thoughts of these things make me cry.

Then said Evangelist, If this be thy condition, why standest thou still? He answered, Because I know not whither to go. Then he gave him a parchment roll, and there was written within, "Flee from the wrath to come" (Matthew 3:7).

The man therefore read it, and looking upon
80 Evangelist very carefully, said, Whither must I fly? Then said Evangelist, pointing with his finger over a very wide field, Do you see yonder wicket-gate?° (Matthew 7:13, 14.) The man said, No. Then said the other, Do you see yonder shining light? (Psalms 119:105; 2 Peter 1:19.) He said, I think I do. Then said Evangelist, Keep that light in your eye, and go up directly thereto: so shalt thou see the gate; at which when thou knockest it shall be told thee what thou shalt do. So I saw in my dream that the man began to
90 run. Now, he had not run far from his own door, but his wife and children perceiving it, began to cry after him to return; but the man put his fingers in his ears, and ran on, crying, Life, life! eternal life! (Luke 14:26.) So he looked not behind him, but fled towards the middle of the plain (Genesis 19:17). . . .

THE FIGHT WITH APOLLYON

But now, in this Valley of Humiliation,° poor Christian was hard put to it; for he had gone but a little way, before he espied a foul fiend coming over the field to meet him; his name is Apollyon.° Then did Christian
100 begin to be afraid, and to cast in his mind whether to go back or to stand his ground. But he considered again that he had no armor for his back; and therefore thought that to turn the back to him might give him the greater advantage with ease to pierce him with his darts. Therefore he resolved to venture and stand his ground; for, thought he, had I no more in mine eye than the saving of my life, it would be the best way to stand.

So he went on, and Apollyon met him. Now the
110 monster was hideous to behold; he was clothed with scales, like a fish (and they are his pride), he had wings like a dragon, feet like a bear, and out of his belly came fire and smoke, and his mouth was as the mouth of a lion. When he was come up to Christian, he beheld him with a disdainful countenance, and thus began to question with him.

APOL. Whence come you? and whither are you bound?

CHR. I am come from the City of Destruction, which is the place of all evil, and am going to the City of Zion. 120

APOL. By this I perceive thou art one of my subjects, for all that country is mine, and I am the prince and god of it. How is it, then, that thou hast run away from thy king? Were it not that I hope thou mayest do me more service, I would strike thee now, at one blow, to the ground.

CHR. I was born, indeed, in your dominions, but your service was hard, and your wages such as a man could not live on, "for the wages of sin *is* death" (Romans 6:23); therefore, when I was come to years, I did 130 as other considerate persons do, look out, if, perhaps, I might mend myself.

APOL. There is no prince that will thus lightly lose his subjects, neither will I as yet lose thee; but since thou complainest of thy service and wages, be content to go back: what our country will afford, I do here promise to give thee.

CHR. But I have let myself to° another, even to the King of princes; and how can I, with fairness, go back with thee? 140

APOL. Thou hast done in this, according to the proverb, "Changed a bad for a worse"; but it is ordinary for those that have professed themselves his servants, after a while to give him the slip, and return again to me. Do thou so too, and all shall be well.

CHR. I have given him my faith, and sworn my allegiance to him; how, then, can I go back from this, and not be hanged as a traitor?

APOL. Thou didst the same to me, and yet I am willing to pass by all, if now thou wilt yet turn again and go 150 back.

CHR. What I promised thee was in my nonage; and, besides, I count the Prince under whose banner now I stand is able to absolve me; yea, and to pardon also what I did as to my compliance with thee; and besides, O thou destroying Apollyon! to speak truth, I like his service, his wages, his servants, his government, his company and country, better than thine; and, therefore, leave off to persuade me further; I am his servant, and I will follow him. 160

APOL. Consider, again, when thou art in cool blood, what thou art like to meet with in the way that thou goest. Thou knowest that, for the most part, his servants come to an ill end, because they are transgressors against me and my ways. How many of them have been put to shameful deaths; and, besides, thou count-

70 **Tophet,** a place in the Valley of Hinnon, near Jerusalem, where human sacrifices by fire were offered to Moloch; hence, the fiery pit, hell   82 **wicket-gate,** a small, narrow gate, usually part of a larger gate or door   96 **Valley of Humiliation.** The preceding episode recounts how Christian entered the Valley under the guidance of Discretion, Piety, Charity, and Prudence   99 **Apollyon,** "the angel of the bottomless pit"

138 **let myself to,** entered into a contract with

est his service better than mine, whereas he never came yet from the place where he is to deliver any that served him out of their hands; but as for me, how many
170 times, as all the world very well knows, have I delivered, either by power, or fraud, those that have faithfully served me, from him and his, though taken by them; and so I will deliver thee.

CHR. His forbearing at present to deliver them is on purpose to try their love, whether they will cleave to him to the end; and as for the ill end thou sayest they come to, that is most glorious in their account; for, for present deliverance, they do not much expect it, for they stay for their glory, and then they shall have it,
180 when their Prince comes in his and the glory of the angels.

APOL. Thou hast already been unfaithful in thy service to him; and how dost thou think to receive wages of him?

CHR. Wherein, O Apollyon! have I been unfaithful to him?

APOL. Thou didst faint at first setting out, when thou wast almost choked in the Gulf of Despond; thou didst attempt wrong ways to be rid of thy burden, whereas
190 thou shouldest have stayed till thy Prince had taken it off; thou didst sinfully sleep and lose thy choice thing;° thou wast, also, almost persuaded to go back, at the sight of the lions; and when thou talkest of thy journey, and of what thou hast heard and seen, thou art inwardly desirous of vain-glory in all that thou sayest or doest.

CHR. All this is true, and much more which thou hast left out; but the Prince whom I serve and honor is merciful, and ready to forgive; but, besides, these in-
200 firmities possessed me in thy country, for there I sucked them in; and I have groaned under them, been sorry for them, and have obtained pardon of my Prince.

APOL. Then Apollyon broke out into a grievous rage, saying, I am an enemy to this Prince; I hate his person, his laws, and people; I am come out on purpose to withstand thee.

CHR. Apollyon, beware what you do; for I am in the king's highway, the way of holiness; therefore take
210 heed to yourself.

APOL. Then Apollyon straddled quite over the whole breadth of the way, and said, I am void of fear in this matter: prepare thyself to die; for I swear by my infernal den, that thou shalt go no further; here will I spill thy soul.

And with that he threw a flaming dart at his breast; but Christian had a shield in his hand, with which he caught it, and so prevented the danger of that.

Then did Christian draw, for he saw it was time to
220 bestir him: and Apollyon as fast made at him, throwing darts as thick as hail; by the which, notwithstanding all that Christian could do to avoid it, Apollyon wounded

him in his head, his hand, and foot. This made Christian give a little back; Apollyon, therefore, followed his work amain, and Christian again took courage, and resisted as manfully as he could. This sore combat lasted for above half a day, even till Christian was almost quite spent; for you must know that Christian, by reason of his wounds, must needs grow weaker and weaker.   230

Then Apollyon, espying his opportunity, began to gather up close to Christian, and wrestling with him, gave him a dreadful fall; and with that Christian's sword flew out of his hand. Then said Apollyon, I am sure of thee now. And with that he had almost pressed him to death, so that Christian began to despair of life: but as God would have it, while Apollyon was fetching of his last blow, thereby to make a full end of this good man, Christian nimbly stretched out his hand for his sword, and caught it saying, "Rejoice not against me, 240 O mine enemy: when I fall I shall arise" (Micah 7:8); and with that gave him a deadly thrust, which made him give back, as one that had received his mortal wound. Christian perceiving that, made at him again, saying, "Nay, in all these things we are more than conquerors through him that loved us" (Romans 8:37). And with that Apollyon spread forth his dragon's wings, and sped him away, that Christian for a season saw him no more. (James 4:7.)

In this combat no man can imagine, unless he had 250 seen and heard as I did, what yelling and hideous roaring Apollyon made all the time of the fight—he spake like a dragon; and, on the other side, what sighs and groans burst from Christian's heart. I never saw him all the while give so much as one pleasant look, till he perceived he had wounded Apollyon with his two-edged sword; then, indeed, he did smile, and look upward; but it was the dreadfulest sight that ever I saw.

A more unequal match can hardly be—
Christian must fight an angel;° but you see,   260
The valiant man by handling Sword and Shield,
Doth make him, though a Dragon, quit the field.

So when the battle was over, Christian said, "I will here give thanks to him that delivered me out of the mouth of the lion, to him that did help me against Apollyon." And so he did, saying—

"Great Beelzebub, the captain of this fiend,
Designed my ruin; therefore to this end
He sent him harnessed out: and he with rage
That hellish was, did fiercely me engage.   270
But blessed Michael° helped me, and I,
By dint of sword, did quickly make him fly.
Therefore to him let me give lasting praise,
And thank and bless his holy name always." . . .

260 **angel**, supernatural spirit; here, a fiend   271 **Michael**, the archangel who led the heavenly hosts in the fight against Satan. Bunyan has in mind, however, the Michael who fought the dragon (*Revelation*, 12:7)

191 **thy choice thing**, parchment roll or certificate of salvation

Then I saw in my dream, that when they were got out of the wilderness, they presently saw a town before them, and the name of that town is Vanity; and at the town there is a fair kept, called Vanity Fair: it is kept all the year long; it beareth the name of Vanity
280 Fair, because the town where it is kept is lighter than vanity; and also because all that is there sold, or that cometh thither, is vanity. As is the saying of the wise, "all that cometh *is* vanity" (Ecclesiastes 1:2, 14; 2:11, 17; 11:8; Isaiah 51:29).

This fair is no new-erected business, but a thing of ancient standing; I will show you the original of it.

Almost five thousand years agone, there were pilgrims walking to the Celestial City, as these two honest persons are: and Beelzebub, Apollyon, and Le-
290 gion, with their companions, perceiving by the path that the pilgrims made, that their way to the city lay through this town of Vanity, they contrived here to set up a fair; a fair wherein should be sold all sorts of vanity, and that it should last all the year long: therefore at this fair are all such merchandise sold, as houses, lands, trades, places, honors, preferments, titles, countries, kingdoms, lusts, pleasures, and delights of all sorts, as whores, bawds, wives, husbands, children, masters, servants, lives, blood, bodies,
300 souls, silver, gold, pearls, precious stones, and what not.

And, moreover, at this fair there is at all times to be seen juggling, cheats, games, plays, fools, apes, knaves, and rogues, and that of every kind.

Here are to be seen, too, and that for nothing, thefts, murders, adulteries, false swearers, and that of a blood-red color.

And as in other fairs of less moment, there are the several rows and streets, under their proper names,
310 where such and such wares are vended; so here likewise you have the proper places, rows, streets (viz. countries and kingdoms), where the wares of this fair are soonest to be found. Here is the Britain Row, the French Row, the Italian Row, the Spanish Row, the German Row, where several sorts of vanities are to be sold. But, as in other fairs, some one commodity is as the chief of all the fair, so the ware of Rome° and her merchandise is greatly promoted in this fair; only our English nation, with some others,° have taken a dislike
320 thereat.

Now, as I said, the way to the Celestial City lies just through this town where this lusty fair is kept; and he that will go to the City, and yet not go through this town, must needs "go out of the world" (1 Corinthians 5:10). The Prince of princes himself, when here, went through this town to his own country, and that upon a fair day too; yea, and as I think, it was Beelzebub, the chief lord of this fair, that invited him to buy of his vanities; yea, would have made him lord of the fair, would he but have done him reverence as he went 330 through the town. (Matthew 4:8, Luke 4:5-7.) Yea, because he was such a person of honor, Beelzebub had him from street to street, and showed him all the kingdoms of the world in a little time, that he might, if possible, allure the Blessed One to cheapen° and buy some of his vanities; but he had no mind to the merchandise, and therefore left the town, without laying out so much as one farthing upon these vanities. This fair, therefore, is an ancient thing, of long standing, and a very great fair. Now these pilgrims, as I said, 340 must needs go through this fair. Well, so they did: but, behold, even as they entered into the fair, all the people in the fair were moved, and the town itself as it were in a hubbub about them; and that for several reasons: for—

First, The pilgrims were clothed with such kind of raiment as was diverse from the raiment of any that traded in that fair. The people, therefore, of the fair, made a great gazing upon them: some said they were fools, some they were bedlams, and some they are 350 outlandish° men. (1 Corinthians 2:7, 8.)

Secondly, And as they wondered at their apparel, so they did likewise at their speech; for few could understand what they said; they naturally spoke the language of Canaan,° but they that kept the fair were the men of this world; so that, from one end of the fair to the other, they seemed barbarians each to the other.

Thirdly, But that which did not a little amuse the merchandisers was, that these pilgrims set very light by all their wares; they cared not so much as to look 360 upon them; and if they called upon them to buy, they would put their fingers in their ears, and cry, "Turn away mine eyes from beholding vanity," and look upwards, signifying that their trade and traffic was in heaven. (Psalms 119:37; Philippians 3:19, 20.)

One chanced mockingly, beholding the carriage of the men, to say unto them, What will ye buy? But they, looking gravely upon him, answered, "We buy the truth" (Proverbs 23:23). At that there was an occasion taken to despise the men the more; some mock- 370 ing, some taunting, some speaking reproachfully, and some calling upon others to smite them. At last things came to a hubbub and great stir in the fair, insomuch that all order was confounded. Now was word presently brought to the great one of the fair, who quickly came down, and deputed some of his most trusty friends to take these men into examination, about whom the fair was almost overturned. So the men were brought to examination; and they that sat upon them, asked them whence they came, whither they 380 went, and what they did there, in such an unusual garb? The men told them that they were pilgrims and strangers in the world, and that they were going to

---

317 **ware of Rome,** an allusion to the Roman Catholic ritual, symbols, etc.
319 **English . . . others,** a reference to the various Protestant reformations in England and on the Continent

335 **cheapen,** to ask the price of 351 **outlandish men,** foreigners 355 **Canaan,** a district in Palestine

their own country, which was the heavenly Jerusalem (Hebrews 11:13-16); and that they had given no occasion to the men of the town, nor yet to the merchandisers, thus to abuse them, and to let° them in their journey, except it was for that, when one asked them what they would buy, they said they would buy the truth. But they that were appointed to examine them did not believe them to be any other than bedlams and mad, or else such as came to put all things into a confusion in the fair. Therefore they took them and beat them, and besmeared them with dirt, and then put them into the cage,° that they might be made a spectacle to all the men of the fair.

Behold Vanity Fair! the Pilgrims there
   Are chained and stand beside:
Even so it was our Lord passed here,
   And on Mount Calvary died. . . .

[GIANT DESPAIR]

Neither *could* they, with all the skill they° had, get again to the stile that night. Wherefore, at last, lighting under a little shelter, they sat down there until the day-break: but, being weary, they fell asleep. Now there was, not far from the place where they lay, a castle called Doubting Castle, the owner whereof was Giant Despair; and it was in his grounds they now were sleeping: wherefore he, getting up in the morning early, and walking up and down in his fields, caught Christian and Hopeful asleep in his grounds. Then, with a grim and surly voice, he bid them awake; and asked them whence they were, and what they did in his grounds. They told him they were pilgrims, and that they had lost their way. Then said the Giant, You have this night trespassed on me, by trampling in and lying on my grounds, therefore you must go along with me. So they were forced to go, because he was stronger than they. They also had but little to say, for they knew themselves in a fault. The Giant, therefore, drove them before him, and put them into his castle, into a very dark dungeon, nasty and stinking to the spirits of these two men. (Psalms 88:18.) Here, then, they lay from Wednesday morning till Saturday night, without one bit of bread, or drop of drink, or light, or any to ask how they did; they were, therefore, here in evil case, and were far from friends and acquaintance. Now in this place Christian had double sorrow, because it was through his unadvised counsel that they were brought into this distress.

The pilgrims now, to gratify the flesh,
   Will seek its ease; but oh! how they afresh

Do thereby plunge themselves new griefs into!
Who seek to please the flesh, themselves undo.

Now, Giant Despair had a wife, and her name was Diffidence. So when he was gone to bed, he told his wife what he had done; to wit, that he had taken a couple of prisoners and cast them into his dungeon, for trespassing on his grounds. Then he asked her also what he had best to do further to them. So she asked him what they were, whence they came, and whither they were bound; and he told her. Then she counseled him that when he arose in the morning he should beat them without any mercy. So, when he arose, he getteth him a grievous crab-tree cudgel, and goes down into the dungeon to them, and there first falls to rating of them as if they were dogs, although they never gave him a word of distaste. Then he falls upon them, and beats them fearfully, in such sort, that they were not able to help themselves, or to turn them upon the floor. This done, he withdraws and leaves them, there to condole their misery, and to mourn under their distress. So all that day they spent the time in nothing but sighs and bitter lamentations. The next night, she, talking with her husband about them further, and understanding they were yet alive, did advise him to counsel them to make away themselves. So when morning was come, he goes to them in a surly manner as before, and perceiving them to be very sore with the stripes that he had given them the day before, he told them, that since they were never like to come out of that place, their only way would be forthwith to make an end of themselves, either with knife, halter, or poison, for why, said he, should you choose life, seeing it is attended with so much bitterness? But they desired him to let them go. With that he looked ugly upon them, and, rushing to them, had doubtless made an end of them himself, but that he fell into one of his fits (for he sometimes, in sunshiny weather, fell into fits), and lost for a time the use of his hand; wherefore he withdrew, and left them as before, to consider what to do. Then did the prisoners consult between themselves, whether it was best to take his counsel or no; and thus they began to discourse:—

CHR. Brother, said Christian, what shall we do? The life that we now live is miserable. For my part I know not whether it is best, to live thus, or to die out of hand. "My soul chooseth strangling rather than life," and the grave is more easy for me than this dungeon. (Job 7:15.) Shall we be ruled by the Giant?

HOPE. Indeed, our present condition is dreadful, and death would be far more welcome to me than thus for ever to abide; but yet, let us consider, the Lord of the country to which we are going hath said, Thou shalt do no murder: no, not to another man's person; much more, then, are we forbidden to take his counsel to kill ourselves. Besides, he that kills another can but commit murder upon his body; but for one to kill himself is to kill body and soul at once. And, moreover, my

brother, thou talkest of ease in the grave; but hast thou
490 forgotten the hell, whither for certain the murderers
go? For "no murderer hath eternal life," etc. And let
us consider, again, that all the law is not in the hand of
Giant Despair. Others, so far as I can understand, have
been taken by him, as well as we; and yet have escaped out of his hand. Who knows, but that God that
made the world may cause that Giant Despair may die?
or that, at some time or other, he may forget to lock us
in? or that he may, in a short time, have another of his
fits before us, and may lose the use of his limbs? and if
500 ever that should come to pass again, for my part, I am
resolved to pluck up the heart of a man, and to try my
utmost to get from under his hand. I was a fool that I
did not try to do it before; but, however, my brother,
let us be patient, and endure a while. The time may
come that may give us a happy release; but let us not
be our own murderers. With these words, Hopeful at
present did moderate the mind of his brother; so they
continued together (in the dark) that day, in their sad
and doleful condition.
510 Well, towards evening, the Giant goes down into the
dungeon again, to see if his prisoners had taken his
counsel; but when he came there he found them alive;
and truly, alive was all; for now, what for want of
bread and water, and by reason of the wounds they
received when he beat them, they could do little but
breathe. But, I say, he found them alive; at which he
fell into a grievous rage, and told them that, seeing
they had disobeyed his counsel, it should be worse
with them than if they had never been born.
520 At this they trembled greatly, and I think that Christian fell into a swoon; but, coming a little to himself
again, they renewed their discourse about the Giant's
counsel; and whether yet they had best to take it or no.
Now Christian again seemed to be for doing it, but
Hopeful made his second reply as followeth:—
HOPE. My brother, said he, remembereth thou not
how valiant thou hast been heretofore? Apollyon could
not crush thee, nor could all that thou didst hear, or
see, or feel, in the Valley of the Shadow of Death.
530 What hardship, terror, and amazement hast thou already gone through! And art thou now nothing but
fear! Thou seest that I am in the dungeon with thee, a
far weaker man by nature than thou art; also, this
Giant has wounded me as well as thee, and hath also
cut off the bread and water from my mouth; and with
thee I mourn without the light. But let us exercise a
little more patience; remember how thou playedst the
man at Vanity Fair, and wast neither afraid of the
chain, nor cage, nor yet of bloody death. Wherefore let
540 us (at least to avoid the shame, that becomes not a
Christian to be found in) bear up with patience as well
as we can.
Now, night being come again, and the Giant and his
wife being in bed, she asked him concerning the prisoners, and if they had taken his counsel. To which he
replied, They are sturdy rogues, they choose rather to

bear all hardship, than to make away themselves. Then
said she, Take them into the castle-yard tomorrow,
and show them the bones and skulls of those that thou
hast already despatched, and make them believe, ere a 550
week comes to an end, thou also wilt tear them in
pieces, as thou hast done their fellows before them.
So when the morning was come, the Giant goes to
them again, and takes them into the castle-yard, and
shows them, as his wife had bidden him. These, said
he, were pilgrims as you are, once, and they trespassed in my grounds, as you have done; and when I
thought fit, I tore them in pieces, and so, within ten
days, I will do you. Go, get you down to your den
again; and with that he beat them all the way thither. 560
They lay, therefore, all day on Saturday in a lamentable case, as before. Now, when night was come, and
when Mrs.° Diffidence and her husband, the Giant,
were got to bed, they began to renew their discourse of
their prisoners; and withal the old Giant wondered,
that he could neither by his blows nor his counsel bring
them to an end. And with that his wife replied, I fear,
said she, that they live in hope that some will come to
relieve them, or that they have picklocks about them,
by the means of which they hope to escape. And 570
sayest thou so, my dear? said the Giant; I will, therefore, search them in the morning.
Well, on Saturday, about midnight, they began to
pray, and continued in prayer till almost break of day.
Now, a little before it was day, good Christian, as
one half amazed, brake out in this passionate speech:
What a fool, quoth he, am I, thus to lie in a stinking
dungeon, when I may as well walk at liberty! I have a
key in my bosom, called Promise, that will, I am persuaded, open any lock in Doubting Castle. Then said 580
Hopeful, That is good news, good brother; pluck it out
of thy bosom, and try.
Then Christian pulled it out of his bosom, and began
to try at the dungeon door, whose bolt (as he turned
the key) gave back, and the door flew open with ease,
and Christian and Hopeful both came out. Then he
went to the outward door that leads into the castle-
yard, and, with his key, opened that door also. After,
he went to the iron gate, for that must be opened too;
but that lock went damnable hard, yet the key did open 590
it. Then they thrust open the gate to make their escape
with speed, but that gate, as it opened, made such a
creaking, that it waked Giant Despair, who, hastily
rising to pursue his prisoners, felt his limbs to fail, for
his fits took him again, so that he could by no means go
after them. Then they went on, and came to the King's
highway, and so were safe, because they were out of
his jurisdiction.
Now, when they were gone over the stile, they began to contrive with themselves what they should do at 600
that stile, to prevent those that should come after,
from falling into the hands of Giant Despair. So they

563 **Mrs.**, pronounced "mistress"

consented to erect there a pillar, and to engrave upon the side thereof this sentence—"Over this stile is the way to Doubting Castle, which is kept by Giant Despair, who despiseth the King of the Celestial Country, and seeks to destroy his holy pilgrims." Many, therefore, that followed after, read what was written, and escaped the danger. This done, they sang as follows:—

610 Out of the way we went, and then we found
What 'twas to tread upon forbidden ground;
And let them that come after have a care,
Lest heedlessness makes them, as we, to fare.
Lest they for trespassing his prisoners are,
Whose castle's Doubting, and whose name's
Despair. . . .

[THE CELESTIAL CITY]

Now I saw in my dream, that by this time the pilgrims were got over the Enchanted Ground, and entering into the country of Beulah, whose air was very sweet and pleasant, the way lying directly through it, 620 they solaced themselves there for a season. (Isaiah 62:4.) Yea, here they heard continually the singing of birds, and saw every day the flowers appear in the earth, and heard the voice of the turtle° in the land. (Canticles 2:10-12.) In this country the sun shineth night and day; wherefore this was beyond the Valley of the Shadow of Death, and also out of the reach of Giant Despair, neither could they from this place so much as see Doubting Castle. Here they were within sight of the city they were going to, also here met them 630 some of the inhabitants thereof; for in this land the Shining Ones commonly walked, because it was upon the borders of heaven. In this land also, the contract between the bride and the bridegroom was renewed; yea, here, "As the bridegroom rejoiceth over the bride, so did their God rejoice over them" (Isaiah 62:5). Here they had no want of corn° and wine; for in this place they met with abundance of what they had sought for in all their pilgrimage. (Verse 8.) Here they heard voices from out of the city, loud voices, saying, 640 "Say ye to the daughter of Zion, behold, thy salvation cometh! Behold, his reward is with him!" (Verse 11.) Here all the inhabitants of the country called them, "The holy people, The redeemed of the Lord, Sought out," etc. (Verse 12.)

Now, as they walked in this land, they had more rejoicing than in parts more remote from the kingdom to which they were bound; and drawing near to the city, they had yet a more perfect view thereof. It was builded of pearls and precious stones, also the street 650 thereof was paved with gold; so that by reason of the natural glory of the city, and the reflection of the sunbeams upon it, Christian with desire fell sick; Hopeful also had a fit or two of the same disease. Wherefore, here they lay by it a while, crying out, because of their pangs, "If ye find my beloved, tell him that I am sick of love" (Canticles 5:8).

But, being a little strengthened, and better able to bear their sickness, they walked on their way, and came yet nearer and nearer, where were orchards, vineyards, and gardens, and their gates opened into 660 the highway. Now, as they came up to these places, behold the gardener stood in the way, to whom the pilgrims said, Whose goodly vineyards and gardens are these? He answered, They are the King's, and are planted here for his own delight, and also for the solace of pilgrims. So the gardener had them into the vineyards, and bid them refresh themselves with the dainties. (Deuteronomy 23:24.) He also showed them there the King's walks, and the arbors where he delighted to be; and here they tarried and slept. 670

Now I beheld in my dream, that they talked more in their sleep at this time than ever they did in all their journey; and being in a muse thereabout, the gardener said even to me, Wherefore musest thou at the matter? It is the nature of the fruit of the grapes of these vineyards to go down so sweetly as to cause the lips of them that are asleep to speak.

So I saw that when they awoke, they addressed themselves to go up to the city; but, as I said, the reflection of the sun upon the city (for "the city was 680 pure gold," Revelation 21:18) was so extremely glorious, that they could not, as yet, with open face behold it, but through an instrument made for that purpose. (2 Corinthians 3:18.) So I saw, that as I went on, there met them two men, in raiment that shone like gold; also their faces shone as the light.

These men asked the pilgrims whence they came; and they told them. They also asked them where they had lodged, what difficulties and dangers, what comforts and pleasures they had met in the way; and they 690 told them. Then said the men that met them, You have but two difficulties more to meet with, and then you are in the city.

Christian then, and his companion, asked the men to go along with them; so they told them they would. But, said they, you must obtain it by your own faith. So I saw in my dream that they went on together, until they came in sight of the gate.

Now, I further saw, that betwixt them and the gate was a river, but there was no bridge to go over: the 700 river was very deep. At the sight, therefore, of this river, the pilgrims were much stunned; but the men that went with them said, You must go through, or you cannot come at the gate.

The pilgrims then began to inquire if there was no other way to the gate; to which they answered, Yes; but there hath not any, save two, to wit, Enoch and Elijah,° been permitted to tread that path, since the

---

623 **turtle,** turtledove   636 **corn,** grain in general

707 **Enoch and Elijah.** Both went to heaven without dying. The first "walked with God: and he was not; for God took him" (*Genesis*, 5:24). The second was carried to heaven in a chariot of fire (2 *Kings*, 2:11)

foundation of the world, nor shall, until the last trumpet shall sound. (1 Corinthians 15:51, 52.) The pilgrims then, especially Christian, began to despond in their minds, and looked this way and that, but no way could be found by them, by which they might escape the river. Then they asked the men if the waters were all of a depth. They said, No; yet they could not help them in that case; for, said they, you shall find it deeper or shallower, as you believe in the King of the place.

They then addressed themselves to the water; and entering, Christian began to sink, and crying out to his good friend Hopeful, he said, I sink in deep waters; the billows go over my head, all his waves go over me! Selah.°

Then said the other, Be of good cheer, my brother, I feel the bottom, and it is good. Then said Christian, Ah! my friend, "the sorrows of death have compassed me about"; I shall not see the land that flows with milk and honey; and with that a great darkness and horror fell upon Christian, so that he could not see before him. Also here he in great measure lost his senses, so that he could neither remember, nor orderly talk of any of those sweet refreshments that he had met with in the way of his pilgrimage. But all the words that he spake still tended to discover that he had horror of mind, and heart fears that he should die in that river, and never obtain entrance in at the gate. Here also, as they that stood by perceived, he was much in the troublesome thoughts of the sins that he had committed, both since and before he began to be a pilgrim. It was also observed that he was troubled with apparitions of hobgoblins and evil spirits, for ever and anon he would intimate so much by words. Hopeful, therefore, here had much ado to keep his brother's head above water; yea, sometimes he would be quite gone down, and then, ere a while, he would rise up again half dead. Hopeful also would endeavor to comfort him, saying, Brother, I see the gate, and men standing by to receive us; but Christian would answer, It is you, it is you they wait for; you have been Hopeful ever since I knew you. And so have you, said he to Christian. Ah, brother! said he, surely if I was right he would now arise to help me; but for my sins he hath brought me into the snare, and hath left me. Then said Hopeful, My brother, you have quite forgot the text, where it is said of the wicked, "There are no bands in their death, but their strength is firm. They are not in trouble as other men, neither are they plagued like other men" (Psalms 73:4, 5). These troubles and distresses that you go through in these waters are no sign that God hath forsaken you; but are sent to try you, whether you will call to mind that which heretofore you have received of his goodness, and live upon him in your distresses.

Then I saw in my dream, that Christian was as in a muse a while. To whom also Hopeful added this word,

722 **Selah**, a word found in *Psalms*—apparently a direction to the musicians but used by Bunyan as though it were equivalent to *Amen*

Be of good cheer. Jesus Christ maketh thee whole; and with that Christian brake out with a loud voice, Oh! I see him again, and he tells me, "When thou passest through the waters, I will be with thee; and through the rivers, they shall not overflow thee" (Isaiah 43:2). Then they both took courage, and the enemy was after that as still as a stone, until they were gone over. Christian therefore presently found ground to stand upon, and so it followed that the rest of the river was but shallow. Thus they got over. Now, upon the bank of the river, on the other side, they saw the two shining men again, who there waited for them; wherefore, being come out of the river, they saluted them saying, We are ministering spirits, sent forth to minister for those that shall be heirs of salvation. Thus they went along towards the gate.

Now, now look how the holy pilgrims ride,
Clouds are their Chariots, Angels are their Guide:
Who would not here for him all hazards run,
That thus provides for his when this world's done.

Now you must note that the city stood upon a mighty hill, but the pilgrims went up that hill with ease, because they had these two men to lead them up by the arms; also, they had left their mortal garments behind them in the river, for though they went in with them, they came out without them. They, therefore, went up here with much agility and speed, though the foundation upon which the city was framed was higher than the clouds. They, therefore, went up through the regions of the air, sweetly talking as they went, being comforted, because they safely got over the river, and had such glorious companions to attend them.

The talk they had with the Shining Ones was about the glory of the place; who told them that the beauty and glory of it was inexpressible. There, said they, is the "Mount Zion, the heavenly Jerusalem, the innumerable company of angels, and the spirits of just men made perfect" (Hebrews 12:22–24). You are going now, said they, to the paradise of God, wherein you shall see the tree of life, and eat of the never-fading fruits thereof; and when you come there, you shall have white robes given you, and your walk and talk shall be every day with the King, even all the days of eternity. (Revelation 2:7; 3:4; 22:5.) There you shall not see again such things as you saw when you were in the lower region upon the earth, to wit, sorrow, sickness, affliction, and death, "for the former things are passed away." You are now going to Abraham, to Isaac, and Jacob, and to the prophets—men that God hath taken away from the evil to come, and that are now resting upon their beds, each one walking in his righteousness. (Isaiah 57:1, 2; 65:17.) The men then asked, What must we do in the holy place? To whom it was answered, You must there receive the comforts of all your toil, and have joy for all your sorrow; you must reap what you have sown, even the fruit of all your prayers, and tears, and sufferings for the King by the way. (Galatians 6:7.) In that place you must wear crowns of gold, and enjoy the perpetual sight and vision of the Holy One, for "there you shall see him as he is" (1 John 3:2). There also you shall serve him continually with praise, with shouting, and thanksgiving, whom you desired to serve in the world, though with much difficulty, because of the infirmity of your flesh. There your eyes shall be delighted with seeing, and 830 your ears with hearing the pleasant voice of the Mighty One. There you shall enjoy your friends again, that are gone thither before you; and there you shall with joy receive, even every one that follows into the holy place after you. There also shall you be clothed with glory and majesty, and put into an equipage fit to ride out with the King of glory. When he shall come with the sound of trumpet in the clouds, as upon the wings of the wind, you shall come with him; and when he shall sit upon the throne of judgment, you shall sit by 840 him; yea, and when he shall pass sentence upon all the workers of iniquity, let them be angels or men, you also shall have a voice in that judgment, because they were his and your enemies. (1 Thessalonians 4:13–17; Jude 14; Daniel 7:9, 10; 1 Corinthians 6:2, 3.) Also, when he shall again return to the city, you shall go too, with sound of trumpet, and be ever with him.

Now while they were thus drawing towards the gate, behold a company of the heavenly host came out to meet them; to whom it was said, by the other two 850 Shining Ones, These are the men that have loved our Lord when they were in the world, and that have left all for his holy name; and he hath sent us to fetch them, and we have brought them thus far on their desired journey, that they may go in and look their Redeemer in the face with joy. Then the heavenly host gave a great shout, saying, "Blessed are they which are called unto the marriage supper of the Lamb" (Revelation 19:9.) There came out also at this time to meet them, several of the King's trumpeters, clothed in white and 860 shining raiment, who, with melodious noises, and loud, made even the heavens to echo with their sound. These trumpeters saluted Christian and his fellow with ten thousand welcomes from the world; and this they did with shouting, and sound of trumpet.

This done, they compassed them round on every side; some went before, some behind, and some on the right hand, some on the left (as it were to guard them through the upper regions), continually sounding as they went, with melodious noise, in notes on high: so 870 that the very sight was to them that could behold it, as if heaven itself was come down to meet them. Thus, therefore, they walked on together; and as they walked, ever and anon these trumpeters, even with joyful sound, would, by mixing their music with looks and gestures, still signify to Christian and his brother, how welcome they were into their company, and with what gladness they came to meet them; and now were these two men, as it were, in heaven, before they came

at it, being swallowed up with the sight of angels, and with hearing of their melodious notes. Here also they 880 had the city itself in view, and they thought they heard all the bells therein to ring, to welcome them thereto. But above all, the warm and joyful thoughts that they had about their own dwelling there, with such company, and that for ever and ever. Oh, by what tongue or pen can their glorious joy be expressed! And thus they came up to the gate.

Now, when they were come up to the gate, there was written over it in letters of gold, "Blessed are they that do his commandments, that they may have right to 890 the tree of life, and may enter in through the gates into the city" (Revelation 22:14).

Then I saw in my dream, that the Shining Men bid them call at the gate; the which, when they did, some looked from above over the gate, to wit, Enoch, Moses, and Elijah, etc., to whom it was said, These pilgrims are come from the City of Destruction, for the love that they bear to the King of this place; and then the pilgrims gave in unto them each man his certificate, which they had received in the beginning; those, 900 therefore, were carried in to the King, who, when he had read them, said, Where are the men? To whom it was answered, They are standing without the gate. The King then commanded to open the gate, "That the righteous nation," said he, "which keepeth the truth, may enter in" (Isaiah 26:2).

Now I saw in my dream that these two men went in at the gate: and lo, as they entered, they were transfigured, and they had raiment put on that shone like gold. There were also that met them with harps and 1000 crowns, and gave them to them—the harps to praise withal, and the crowns in token of honor. Then I heard in my dream that all the bells in the city rang again for joy, and that it was said unto them, "Enter ye into the joy of your Lord." I also heard the men themselves, that they sang with a loud voice, saying, "Blessing and honor, and glory, and power, be unto him that sitteth upon the throne, and unto the Lamb, for ever and ever" (Revelation 5:13).

Now, just as the gates were opened to let in the 1010 men, I looked in after them, and, behold, the City shone like the sun; the streets also were paved with gold, and in them walked many men, with crowns on their heads, palms in their hands, and golden harps to sing praises withal.

There were also of them that had wings, and they answered one another without intermission, saying, "Holy, holy, holy is the Lord" (Revelation 4:8). And after that they shut up the gates; which, when I had seen, I wished myself among them. 1020

Now while I was gazing upon all these things, I turned my head to look back, and saw Ignorance come up to the river side; but he soon got over, and that without half that difficulty which the other two men met with. For it happened that there was then in that place, one Vain-hope, a ferryman, that with his boat helped him over; so he, as the other I saw, did ascend the hill, to come up to the gate, only he came alone; neither did any man meet him with the least encouragement. When he was come up to the gate, he looked up to the writing that was above, and then began to knock, supposing that entrance should have been quickly administered to him; but he was asked by the men that looked over the top of the gate, Whence came you? and what would you have? He answered, I have eat and drank in the presence of the King, and he has taught in our streets. Then they asked him for his certificate, that they might go in and show it to the King; so he fumbled in his bosom for one, and found none. Then said they, Have you none? But the man answered never a word. So they told the King, but he would not come down to see him, but commanded the two Shining Ones that conducted Christian and Hopeful to the City, to go out and take Ignorance, and bind him hand and foot, and have him away. Then they took him up, and carried him through the air, to the door that I saw in the side of the hill, and put him in there. Then I saw that there was a way to hell, even from the gates of heaven, as well as from the City of Destruction! So I awoke, and behold it was a dream.

(1678)

The Restoration and The Eighteenth Century

From the Restoration of Charles II to the Death of Samuel Johnson, 1660–1784

PART 3

Royal Crescent, Bath, designed by John Wood II, completed in 1775

The years between the restoration of Charles II to the throne in 1660 and the death of Samuel Johnson in 1784 were a time of transition and transformation in the British Isles. England witnessed the final triumph of Parliament over king, the dramatic growth of the British empire, and the beginning of an industrial revolution which was to change the landscape, expand cities, and profoundly alter traditional habits of thought and life. Because this period also fostered the intellectual accomplishments of such great English rationalist philosophers as John Locke (1632–1704) and Thomas Hobbes (1588–1679), it has often been called the Age of Reason or the Enlightenment. Past historians have frequently characterized Restoration and eighteenth-century England as a nation of complacent and cheerful rationalists unconcerned by the great changes around them. This view has caused many twentieth-century writers to use the classic/romantic dichotomy to distinguish this age from the period following it. They have frequently regarded the Restoration and eighteenth-century period as a classical age, typified by order, reason, and restraint. On the other hand, they have often viewed the dawn of the nineteenth century, beginning with the French Revolution, as a period of romanticism, characterized by disorder, irrationality, and lack of restraint.

The dangers of such simplified generalizations about history are revealed when we recognize that from 1660 to 1784 five generations of writers expressed widely diverse responses to the shifting pressures of the new era. Cowper's assumptions at the end of the age clearly differed from Dryden's at its beginning. To understand the writers of this period more fully, we need first to become familiar with the political and social climate in which they lived.

The Restoration

An age that saw the reopening of the English theaters began with a historic event staged with all the dramatic pageantry of the theater itself. John Evelyn (1620–1706), whose diaries provide some of our most fascinating records of the time, described the day as follows:

May 29, 1660. This day his Majesty Charles II came to London after a sad and long exile and calamitous suffering both of the King and Church, being seventeen years. This was also his birthday, and with a triumph of above 200,000 horse and foot, brandishing their swords and shouting with inexpressible joy; the ways strewed with flowers, the bells ringing, the streets hung with tapestry, fountains running with wine; the Mayor, Alderman, and all the Companies in their liveries, chains of gold and banners; Lords and Nobles clad in cloth of silver, gold, and velvet; the windows and balconies all set with ladies; trumpets, music, and myriads of people flocking, even so far as Rochester, so as they were seven hours in passing the City, even from two in the afternoon till nine at night. I stood in the Strand and beheld it, and blessed God.

As this passage suggests, the Restoration at its outset marked a reaction against the severity of the old Puritan customs and ways of life. Charles II left many governmental matters to his ministers, for his temperament and his French upbringing inclined him to pursue the pleasures of court more energetically than the business of politics. His court in England was brilliant but also dissolute; thus, it provided an audience receptive to witty, sparkling, non-Puritan, secular literature. Yet despite the frivolity of much of court life, the patronage of Charles II was what made possible the foundation of the Royal Society and in turn lent impetus to the great scientific movement of which men like the mathematician Sir Isaac Newton (1642–1727) were to be a part. We should also be aware that the influence of Charles' personality did not do away with all the vestiges of Puritanism. Such customs as family prayer, Bible reading, and the Puritan idea of Sunday as a day set aside for religious observation survived as a part of English life.

Puritanism as a political and religious force was for the moment powerless. Within a year or two after Charles' return, the bodies of Oliver Cromwell and other Puritans had been exhumed and exposed to public scorn. The judges who had sentenced Charles I to death were either executed or forced into exile. John Milton, who had been an important Puritan offi-

Entrance hall of Coleshill House (1662), Berkshire, built by Sir Roger Pratt. The staircase design and the arrangement of the classical busts exemplify the Restoration values of order, symmetry, and balance.

COPYRIGHT COUNTRY LIFE

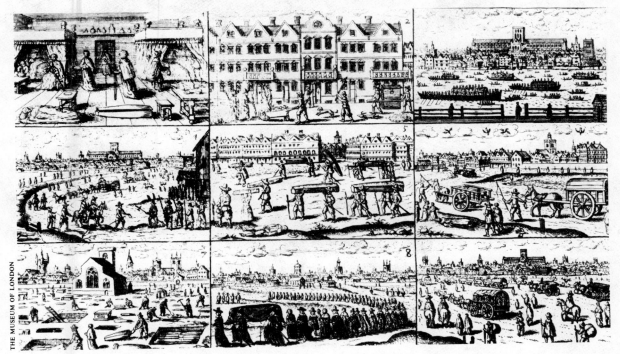

These scenes of funeral processions and burials during the Great Plague in London are from an engraving (1665) by John Dunstall. This outbreak of the bubonic plague—the worst since the Black Death epidemic of 1346—killed seventy-five thousand people.

cial, was forced into retirement. Puritan literature, however, did survive. The two greatest Puritan works, Milton's *Paradise Lost* and Bunyan's *Pilgrim's Progress*, were printed during the Restoration period.

England was troubled during the reign of Charles II (1660–1685) by both internal and external problems. In 1665 an outbreak of the bubonic plague occurred —the worst since the days of the Black Death in the fourteenth century—and soon after, the Great Fire of London destroyed most of the older part of the city. During the same year, a naval war with Holland broke out. It represented the inevitable collision of two powers with colonial aspirations. The English court initially mismanaged the war, and for a time London was seriously threatened by the Dutch fleet. Although English naval power finally brought the war to a moderately successful conclusion, the foreign prestige of England declined during the Restoration period. The effect of all these problems following so closely upon one another raised some doubts among the English people about their newly restored king and his government. Thus, it is not surprising that the age was disrupted by occasional incidents of political strife.

The general religious amnesty granted by Charles in 1672 calmed political conflict considerably, but tensions remained. Though Charles himself outwardly subscribed to the Church of England, he was known to have Catholic sympathies. He had a French upbringing (his mother was French, and France was strongly Catholic), and in the late 1670s and early 1680s he even sought the political and financial support of King Louis XIV. Thus, the Church of England felt threatened by papal power as well as by domestic religious dissidents. Throughout Charles' reign, the country was uneasy about the question of his successor to the throne, especially when it became clear that the king would not leave any legitimate children and that his heir would apparently be an avowed Catholic, his brother James, duke of York. This unstable situation caused widespread political and religious uncertainty and occasional incidents of civil bloodshed.

One notable outbreak of violence was a result of Titus Oates' (1649–1705) "Popish Plot." In 1678 Oates spread elaborate rumors that the Roman Catholics were forming criminal plots against the government. Oates' action not only increased the anti-Catholic feeling in the Parliament but also led to actual persecution of many innocent Catholic citizens. Nevertheless, the general unrest of the period gave rise as well to the formation of the groups that gradually evolved into political parties as we think of them today.

In 1685 Charles II died, avowing himself a Catholic on his deathbed, and was succeeded by his brother, the Catholic James II. James' impossible attempt to turn England from a Protestant to a Roman Catholic country quickly produced a crisis. Neither James nor his religion was popular in England, and when the birth of a son in the summer of 1688 seemed to promise a Catholic succession Protestant leaders began

Blenheim Palace, Woodstock, designed by Sir John Vanbrugh (1664–1726), was begun in 1705 at the request of Queen Anne and completed in 1720. Parliament gave this huge country house (it is 850 feet in length) to John Churchill, duke of Marlborough, in return for his defeat of the French in 1704 during the War of the Spanish Succession. Winston Churchill was later born at the palace. Vanbrugh was not only a prominent architect but was also a popular dramatist, today remembered for The Provoked Wife *(1692) and* The Relapse *(1696).*

secret negotiations to bring to the throne James' oldest daughter, Mary, whose husband, William of Orange, was Dutch and a champion of Protestantism on the Continent. William landed on November 5, 1688, a day which is still celebrated in England, and James, forsaken by his army, was driven into exile. The events which placed William and Mary on the English throne are referred to by Englishmen as the Glorious, or Bloodless, Revolution. The revolution involved a peaceful compromise between the opposing forces; king and Parliament agreed to work together, but Parliament was recognized as the highest level of political authority.

The exiled James made a serious effort to regain his throne, enlisting French and Irish help, but defeat at the Battle of Boyne (1690) in Ireland crushed his hopes. He fled to France where his son and grandson, referred to as the Old and Young Pretenders, made life uneasy for subsequent English rulers. Supporters of James and his heirs (called Jacobites from the Latin *Jacobus*, James) organized two noteworthy rebellions. The first occurred in 1715 when the Old Pretender arrived in Scotland to support an uprising against the newly crowned King George I; the second was in 1745 when the Young Pretender ("Bonnie Prince Charlie") invaded England and advanced as far south as Derby. Support for his cause failed to materialize, and he was forced to retreat to Scotland where he was defeated in 1746 in the Battle of Culloden.

William III and Mary were co-rulers, but William was the administrator. His reign (1689–1702) was marked by the increasingly clear definition of two political parties, the Whigs and the Tories, and by the intense strife between them. Yet party membership at the time suggested an even greater variety of meanings than it does today. Individuals were judged to be Whig or Tory for a broad range of reasons, including the nature of their writings or actions, friends or family connections, or their conversations or possessions. In the most general terms, Tories were more conservative and strongly Anglican, with more country squires, clergymen, and established wealthy families in their midst. The Whig party, which in its origin had religious connections with Puritanism, had a larger urban base, with wealth from newly created noblemen and from tradesmen. The ability of a crafty politician like Robert Walpole (1676–1745) to manipulate groups and shift sides should prevent us from thinking of party labels as immutable. Yet it is fair to say that the very difficulty of firmly defining the natures of the two political parties suggests a diversity and complexity of response to the various social and political questions that emerged during the reign of William III and during the eighteenth century.

The Eighteenth Century

Upon Mary's death from smallpox in 1694 and William's death from a fall in 1702, Anne, the second daughter of James II, came to the throne. Her reign (1702–1714) was memorable for many events that affected English letters and politics. During her administration, England was obliged to confront the schemes of the Old Pretender, James Edward, who had won the support of France in his attempt to regain the English throne. Hostilities broke out between England and France, with various nations allying themselves with each antagonist. In the War of the Spanish Succession (fought to determine whether the Spanish throne would go to the grandson of Louis XIV), victories by the duke of Marlborough at Blenheim (1704) and Ramilles (1706) meant that England's royal succession remained free from foreign interference. Two other types of political struggle also characterized Queen Anne's reign. First, England and Scotland were formally united in 1707, though not without considerable opposition from the Scots, who were aided by King Louis XIV of France. Second, controversy flared between Whigs and Tories. Under the leadership of Robert Harley and Henry Saint-John (later the earl of Oxford and Viscount Bolingbroke), the Tories held power at the beginning and the end of Anne's reign. However, at her death in 1714, the Whigs took control, drove out Tory officeholders, and permanently turned such men as Jonathan Swift (1667–1745) away from politics.

Since none of Anne's seventeen children survived childhood, the succession was again in question. Parliament had declared in 1701 that Anne's successor must be Protestant, and at her death the only eligible candidate for the position was the fifty-four-year-old great-grandson of James I of England. He was George, the Elector of Hanover, Germany, and he did not speak English; he could converse with his chief minister only in French or in poor Latin. This was one of several reasons why George I turned over many of the crown's traditional powers to various ministers in the government.

Most prominent among the many gifted ministers under George I and under his son, George II, was Robert Walpole, who held office from 1715 to 1717 and from 1721 to 1742. He was a shrewd politician with a strong interest in finance and commerce. Walpole pursued complicated changes in the tax and tariff structure in order to increase prosperity and further trade. He believed that a flourishing economy was the means of securing the longevity of a royal dynasty, especially one threatened by such ever present rivals as the Jacobite pretenders. Though he had served as minister of war and of the navy, Walpole long resisted war with Spain because he felt that England's greatest profit through trade would be gained through peaceful alliance. His hardheaded attitude toward politics and his willingness to buy support made him a frequent center of controversy and target of satire. He was known to have bribed members of the House of Commons and offered subsidies in return for favorable comment in the press. Walpole eventually lost his majority in the Commons and resigned in 1742. Whatever our reactions today to the ruthless policies or governmental corruption under Walpole, his political skill and his administrative abilities cannot be doubted.

After the fall of Walpole, George II waged various intermittent wars, some gaining empire and one losing it. In the Seven Years' War (1756–1763) England took Canada from France. The French were also defeated in India by Robert Clive's (1725–1774) expeditions from 1756 to 1760. At this time, the British East India Company was transformed from a trading corporation into a political power. Under the reign of George II's successor, however, England faced severe problems in India because of its responsibility as an imperial ruler to the native people and their local leaders.

George III, who came to the throne in 1760 and reigned for the next sixty years, showed a greater disposition to have a voice in government than had his

Mr. and Mrs. Robert Andrews (1749) by Thomas Gainsborough (1727–1788), the most popular English portrait painter of the eighteenth century. The subjects' unpretentious poses and the Suffolk landscape behind them make this portrait appear more informal and spontaneous than others of the period.

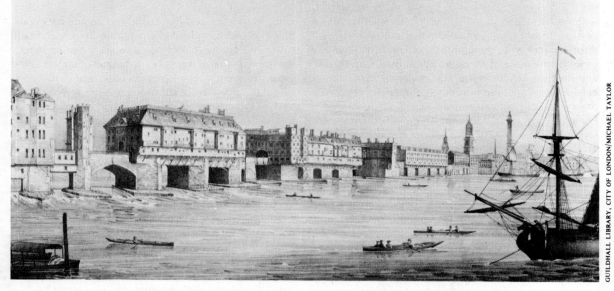

An engraving (1751) by John Boydell of London Bridge, the first stone bridge built across the Thames (1209) and the primary thoroughfare across the river until it was dismantled in 1831.

two predecessors. He was not a wise statesman, and his conscientiousness and good intentions were not adequate weapons to combat political intrigue. Complex economic and political forces during George III's reign brought about the American Revolution. Taxation, political representation, and trade rights—rather than the malice or madness of George, as had once been suggested—are now recognized as the main issues that caused the conflict. Revolution came about in America, as it was soon to come about in France, because of new political ideas and aspirations formulated by English political philosophers such as John Locke (1632–1704) and Thomas Paine (1737–1809). These new political ideas included such notions as human equality and the individual's right to what the American Declaration of Independence defined as "life, liberty, and the pursuit of happiness."

With the death in 1784 of Samuel Johnson, the great writer, lexicographer, and conversationalist, the distinctive character of the eighteenth century seemed to disappear. The end of the age could equally well be seen in the American and French Revolutions of 1776 and 1789 respectively, or in the publication of the *Lyrical Ballads* by Wordsworth and Coleridge in 1798. These events indicated that a change in international life was occurring and that England would have a part to play in that change.

Literature: 1660–1784

The neoclassical age was an era of intense concentration, one in which scholars and writers attempted to assimilate and order the new knowledge they had

gained. The desire for order often produces a respect for rules; however, it would be a mistake to assume that this period was entirely dominated by such an attitude. From first to last—from Dryden to Johnson—the best literary minds of the age struggled to find ways of reconciling the artist's natural genius with literary tradition.

Literary Background

Before we turn to specific authors in the neoclassical period and the kinds of works they produced, we will examine two concepts that literary historians and critics often resort to in discussing neoclassical literature—conventionality and reason. In the following sections we will attempt to answer these questions: To what extent can the literature of the Restoration and the eighteenth century be considered conventional? To what extent unconventional? To what extent can the literature be considered rational? To what extent irrational? Are these concepts relevant? What are their limitations?

Conventionality. Respect for convention is very often cited as a characteristic of the neoclassical period. But this convenient label is valid only if the word "convention" is used with discrimination. The beribboned and periwigged fashions popular during the reigns of Charles and Anne, the careful attention to etiquette and good breeding evident in the formal literature and informal correspondence of the age, the familiar patterns of social behavior that Pope mocked so brilliantly in *The Rape of the Lock*—such manifestations of convention are distinctive enough, but finally less important to the age than its literary accomplishments and artistic conventions. It is here that the impact of the Renaissance was great.

The Renaissance had worshiped the genius of the Greek philosopher, Aristotle (384–322 B.C.), whose *Poetics* was for generations an unrivaled authority on literary standards. The concepts of the "three unities" of drama were derived from this work and from its interpretations by French critics. They included the unity of time, according to which the action of a play should cover not more than a day. The unity of place decreed that the scene of a play should occur in one locality. According to the unity of action, the one concept actually derived from Aristotle, a play should have only one plot or main action and should be of a single type, wholly comic or tragic. The English writers paid much less attention than the French did to the unities of time and place but were more likely to respect the principle of unity of action. More significant, however, than any one rule of classical criticism was the presence of a characteristic spirit in the literature of the time. An intelligence and dignity, a bent toward moral instruction, and a love of moderation, balance, and grace were all fostered by the influence of classical tradition and were expressed by Pope's words:

Be not the first by whom the new are tried,
Nor yet the last to lay the old aside.

By the time of Dryden's death in 1700, interest in classical literature began to be modified by new ideas. Aristotle's influence was fading by the time of Queen Anne, and men of common sense like Swift and

Johnson condemned the slavish imitation of classical models. Although the influence of such poets as Homer and Vergil was partly responsible for the creation of masterpieces like Pope's *Essay on Man*, it also led to the effusions of many inferior poets. The better poets of the period developed a healthy respect for—not a mindless dedication to—the classical standards of symmetry, balance, grace, and order. As Pope directed his colleagues:

Learn hence for ancient rules a just esteem
To copy nature is to copy them.

The dignity of much Latin and Greek verse inspired many neoclassical writers with a love for the resounding word and the elegant phrase. One form of expression that appealed especially to the age's taste was the poetic epithet—an adjective of vague descriptive powers qualifying an equally general noun, together forming a metaphoric description of an object—as in "the plumy race" in these lines from Thomson's *Seasons*, "Winter" :

But chief the plumy race,
The tenants of the sky, its changes speak.
Retiring from the downs, where all day long
They picked their scanty fair, a blackening train
Of clamorous rooks thick-urge their weary flight,
And seek the closing shelter of the grove.

The reasons for choosing such a phrase are complex and are not simply the means of avoiding commonplace expressions or specific words, since "rooks" are mentioned four lines later and a whole catalogue

Painting entitled The Ranelagh Rotunda *(1746–1747), by Canaletto (1697–1768), an Italian painter known particularly for his urban scenes. Ranelagh, formerly a resort by the River Thames in Chelsea, London, was bought in 1690 by Richard Jones, Third Viscount Ranelagh, who built a mansion and laid out gardens. It was opened to the public in 1742 as a place of entertainment; concerts were often performed in the rotunda. It was demolished in 1826.*

of specific birds follows. Thomson is careful to focus our attention on the heavens by using "plumy" to distinguish birds from all other "races" or "kinds" of creatures. Eighteenth-century English poets used other formal devices to separate the language of poetry from that of ordinary discourse, such as classical allusions, inversions of word order, and personification.

The poets of the period also favored a sonorous and neatly rounded verse form, the heroic couplet. It consisted of two rhyming lines of iambic pentameter verse. If the second line completed a sentence or a thought, the couplet was called "closed," as in this example from Pope's *The Rape of the Lock*:

But when to mischief mortals bend their will,
How soon they find fit instruments of ill!

This verse form was not new. Chaucer had employed it in the fourteenth century in *The Canterbury Tales*, as had certain Elizabethan poets such as Ben Jonson and his imitators. John Denham (1615–1669) and Edmund Waller (1606–1687) helped popularize the form and began the trend for the more frequent use of closed couplets. John Dryden, however, made the form best known, and Alexander Pope brought it to perfection.

The heroic couplet was the favorite poetic instrument of the satirists of the time. It provided an effective vehicle for expressing critical insights by giving poets a constant form upon which to work variations. The heroic couplet provides a dominant rhythm against which the subtle contrasts created by alliteration and assonance, balance and antithesis, pause and forward movement are most fully revealed. The couplet dominated poetry from Dryden to Johnson. Not until almost the nineteenth century, with the rise of the Romantic movement, did it yield its position of prominence to blank verse.

Reason. Reactions of recent historians against seeing the Restoration and the eighteenth century as "the age of reason" are well founded, but we must not ignore the extent to which the age cherished the ideal of social and artistic order. During the Restoration, the

Portrait of Alexander Pope by William Hoare.

nation was no longer splintered by a major civil war, for the Jacobite rebellions were more regional, and it had not yet been disrupted by the growth of industry. Brilliant architects—notably Christopher Wren (1632–1723), who supervised the rebuilding of London after the Great Fire—built churches, houses, and public buildings of dignity and grandeur. All were solemn celebrations either of the national identity or of family wealth and position. The semicircular facades of residential crescents in London and Bath achieved a homogeneous vista and a new style of understated elegance. Landscape architects such as Lancelot "Capability" Brown (1715–1783) designed gardens quite different from the planned square walkways, parterres, and controlled hedges of France. In Brown's "natural" gardens, the broad vista, the shaggy but consciously shaped border of trees, and the irregularly shaped lake all provided pleasing effects by enriching nature's art with man's.

The civility of some levels of society is regarded by many historians as evidence of an orderly way of life in this period. City dwellers could amuse themselves by day in the theaters and at such recreational centers as St. James' Park or the Vauxhall Gardens. They could temper the strain of business or professional affairs with the society afforded by the many coffee or chocolate houses of London. These establishments combined the functions of lunchroom, saloon, city club, and forum. Particular coffee houses were frequented by particular professions or political parties. The poets and critics went to Will's, the clergy to Truby's, scholars and academicians to the Grecian, Tories to the Cocoa Tree, and Whigs to St. James' Coffee House. The salons or social gatherings held by intellectual women offered many of the attractions of the coffee houses in a more private setting. The human instinct to share news, ideas, and gossip found a natural outlet in these institutions, and the art of conversation flourished. James Boswell's remarkable biography of Samuel Johnson provides ample evidence of the importance of conversation and social exchange in this age.

The prosperous civility of life in England between 1660 and 1784 must not, however, obscure the ways

Portrait of John Dryden (1693) by Sir Godfrey Kneller (1646–1723). Kneller, born in Germany, came to England in 1675. Among the ten reigning monarchs he painted were Charles II, William III, Louis XIV, and Peter the Great. He retained favor under Anne and George I, during which time he painted many English celebrities.

in which society was neither prosperous nor civil nor orderly. The country squire, living in rural backwardness, would have to plan carefully for his occasional trip to London, for the roads were poor, at times even impassable, and always infested with highwaymen. Transportation by stagecoach was uncomfortable and laborious. Once in London, the visitor found himself in poorly kept streets without police protection. Criminals usually lived in squalor and were subject to punishment by an appallingly severe penal code which assigned the death penalty for both the theft of a handkerchief and for murder. The vast body of criminal literature of the period reveals a harsh and materialistic world. Moreover, the engravings of William Hogarth (1697–1764), such as *The Rake's Progress*, depict the unfortunate consequences of a wealth and urbanity gained at the price of moral integrity.

Evidence of intense passion and emotionalism among writers belies the familiar image of this period as an "age of reason" as much as the turmoil of the streets does. A knowledge of Samuel Johnson's struggles with despair, for example, enriches our understanding of this individual, whose memorable words are so often quoted out of context and cited for their wisdom and rationality.

The eighteenth century also produced the most influential religious revival movement—Methodism—of the last three centuries. Starting at Oxford in 1729 John and Charles Wesley were inspired by the vision of a personal God who invited an emotional response not provided by the rituals of the Church of England. With the doors of the parish churches closed to them, they turned to the radical alternative of open-air preaching. The Methodists' emphasis on trust in a personal God made them seem dangerously "enthusiastic," as did their use of lay preachers, both male and female. The very word *enthusiasm* was used in a pejorative sense; Johnson defined it in his *Dictionary* (1755) as "a vain belief of private revelation; a vain confidence of divine favour or communication." Although the full growth of Methodism carried into the nineteenth century, its origin in the eighteenth century qualifies substantially the common view of this as a "rational" era. If the age deeply valued the powers of human reason, it was because it knew so well the fervor of the heart.

The Literature of the Restoration

The most important type of literature produced in the Restoration—the drama—was encouraged by the court of Charles II. All plays and most of the nondramatic poetry and prose between 1660 and 1700 were composed with the aristocratic audience in mind. Restoration literature basically represented a violent reaction against Puritanism and a thoroughgoing devotion to neoclassical ideals.

St. Paul's Cathedral, London, designed by Christopher Wren (1632–1723) and completed in 1710, is one of the best examples of English Baroque architecture. Wren's designs were used to restore fifty London churches that were damaged in the Great Fire (1666).

Drama. Although the theaters had been closed by the Puritans in 1642, some plays, masques, and other stage entertainments were performed surreptitiously during the Commonwealth. It was not until 1656, however, that a play was actually sanctioned by the government—Sir William Davenant's *The Siege of Rhodes*. Immediately after the Restoration two theatrical companies were licensed in London—the Duke of York's Company under the leadership of Davenant in 1661, and the King's Company in 1663. These troupes staged revivals of Elizabethan plays and operas as well as the characteristic types of Restoration drama—the heroic play, the classical tragedy, and the comedy of manners.

Church of St. Martin-in-the-Fields, London, designed by James Gibbs (1682–1754) and completed in 1726. Its style is a combination of classical influences, as evidenced by the Corinthian columns, and contemporary structures, such as the steeple, one of the most prominent in the London skyline.

The heroic play had as its aim the celebration on a grand scale of the themes of love and honor. Though the Restoration mightily applauded this type of drama, interest in it has not endured. Later ages have condemned it for its bombast and rant, its stylization of character, its overcomplication of plot, and its extravagantly exotic atmosphere. Even in its own day, a heroic play such as Dryden's *Indian Queen* (1664) never recovered from the burlesque directed against it by George Villiers' *The Rehearsal* (1671).

An heir of the heroic play was the Restoration tragedy. It achieved greater realism than the heroic play and tended to depart from rhyming heroic couplets by adopting the blank verse of the great Elizabethan tragedies. However, the neoclassical ideal of dignity and decorum forbade the inclusion of comic scenes, which were used in the tragedies of Shakespeare. Also, the three unities demanded greater integration of plot, so that one must look hard to find in a Restoration tragedy a subplot as elaborate as that in *King Lear*. *All for Love* (1678), Dryden's version of the Antony and Cleopatra story, is an excellent example of Restoration tragedy. Next in greatness to Dryden in the writing of serious drama was Thomas Otway (1652–1685), whose plays, notably *Venice Preserved* (1682),

were characterized by searching pathos, not only moving in itself but interesting as a symptom of that sentimentality which plagued drama after 1700.

The dramatic genre for which the Restoration is most celebrated is comedy. No subsequent period has produced such brilliant comedies of manners. The ancestor of these plays was the comedy of humors that Ben Jonson made famous a half century before. In both we see a tendency to caricature and to label characters with names reflecting their most striking traits. For example, in *The Country Wife*, a jealous husband is called Mr. Pinchwife.

The best writers of Restoration comedy were Sir George Etherege (1634–1691), William Wycherley (1640–1716), William Congreve (1670–1729), George Farquhar (1678–1707), and Sir John Vanbrugh (1664–1726). "Gentle George" Etherege had the lightest touch. "Brawney" Wycherley was the most cutting satirist in the group. Congreve was the most skilled dramatic technician and the greatest wit. Farquhar dealt with the middle class rather than the aristocracy, as was more usual, and Vanbrugh—"Honest Van"—wrote plays that were closer to farce than to comedy of manners. However, all aimed at brilliant and witty mockery of current fashions in ideas as well as dress. Their stage was filled with coxcombs, coquettes, men about town, dupes, and fools. Their plots were rich with intrigue and bawdy humor.

To the Puritans and to much of the great middle class who looked on in outrage at the freedom of the Restoration stage, the plays of Wycherley and Congreve appeared scandalously immoral. The anti-Puritan tone of Restoration literature was encouraged by the court of Charles II, and the plays and other literature of the period were composed with an aristocratic audience in mind. Thus, when the inevitable reaction against the excesses of the Restoration court and life surfaced, there was also criticism of its drama. In 1698 a dissenting clergyman, Jeremy Collier, published his *Short View of the Immorality and Profaneness of the English Stage*. Collier's work was unfair in some ways and ridiculous in others, but it effectively argued that "nothing has gone further in debauching the age than the stage poets and playhouse." The question raged for a quarter century but its effect was immediately felt. For example, the plays of Farquhar, coming barely a decade after Collier's blast, followed conventional morality more closely. The old freedoms of Restoration comedy were being checked as the Restoration itself was coming to a close.

Prose. The incomparable *Diary* of Samuel Pepys (1633–1703) is more reliable than any drama as a mirror of the irresponsible, carefree life of the Restoration. In his informal and secret jottings from 1660 to 1669, Pepys presents a superb picture of Restoration London: the theater, life in St. James' Park, the gossip of the court, the Great Fire, the plague, the Dutch

The painter and engraver William Hogarth (1697–1764) was noted for his many series of narrative drawings depicting different aspects of eighteenth-century English life, some of which carried moral messages. Below: The Marriage Contract, *from the series* Marriage a la Mode (1743–1745), *satirizes the marriage customs of the English aristocracy. In this painting the groom's father (right) confers with his associates about the size of the bride's dowry while the bride (second from left) discusses the matter with a lawyer. The dandified groom (left) can be seen gazing into a mirror. Left:* Gin Lane (1751) *satirizes the excesses of drinking.*

Portrait of William Wycherley.

conclusions about our ability to know were liberating. He affirmed the belief that the individual's own experience is valuable and can be the source of real knowledge if the proper deductive method is used in the search for clear and distinct ideas. The emphasis throughout Locke's work on clarity marked him as a man of his age, and the history of English culture and philosophy for years afterward reflected the influence of his careful empiricism.

The Literature of the Eighteenth Century

The chief figures of English literature from the death of Dryden in 1700 to the death of Johnson in 1784 are appraised in the headnotes to their works found in Part III. These figures include Daniel Defoe, Jonathan Swift, Joseph Addison and Richard Steele, Alexander Pope, Samuel Johnson, and Oliver Goldsmith. Their appraisals and the accompanying examinations of the genres in which they worked need not be repeated here, but a few words on the general character of the eighteenth century are necessary.

Reflections of common sense: 1700–1745. In the first half of the eighteenth century, literature served more practical as well as more moral functions than it had done in previous decades. Two influential forces in the Restoration did not long survive the turn of the century: the dominance of the Tory party and the anti-Puritan trend in literature. With the death of Queen Anne, control of the government fell into the hands of the Whigs, who dominated the political scene throughout the rest of the period. Collier's attack on the Restoration theater was one clear indication of the resurgence of more conservative religious influences. It had not yet found its proper leader, however, for John Wesley's conversion did not occur until the 1730s, but a climate was clearly emerging which would enable Wesley's voice to be heard and his influence felt.

As literacy continued to increase, people demanded a popular press. The writers responded by starting periodicals, which flourished after 1700. *The Daily Courant,* the first daily journal, appeared in 1702 and Defoe's *Review* in 1704. The *Tatler* (1709) was followed by the *Spectator* (1711). The trend reached its height with *The Gentleman's Magazine* (1731), the first English magazine in the modern sense. As we might expect, writing gradually ceased to be primarily an avocation of the wealthy during this period and became a profession at which an individual might earn a living, however modest.

The periodicals strove to edify as well as to amuse their readers. Yet the most profound moral criticism did not come from the press or from the pulpit but from the best writers of the period, Alexander Pope

War, and the involved, amusing, and pathetic domestic affairs of Pepys himself. Pepys' work remains unique as a personal journal, but there were many other diarists and many great writers of letters.

The study of science linked this period with the work of such Renaissance investigators as Francis Bacon (1561–1626) and René Descartes (1596–1650). The Royal Society was established in 1662, and Newton's *Principia* (1687) was a landmark in the investigation of the physical world. Astronomical studies and works on physics proliferated. The invention of the microscope provided scientists with an additional tool to continue at close range their examination of the world. The empiricism essential to scientific discovery was also the method of inquiry advocated by John Locke in the age's most influential work of philosophy, *Essay Concerning Human Understanding* (1690).

Locke's aims, as outlined at the beginning of the *Essay,* were "to inquire into the original, certainty, and extent of human knowledge, together with the grounds and degrees of belief, opinion, and assent." Human knowledge, Locke concluded, is not innate; rather, it comes from the empirical evidence of our own experience. We can, therefore, proceed to discover the nature of things if we look closely, for "the light of reason . . . the candle of the Lord, that is set up within us, shines bright enough for all our purposes." Locke's

An Experiment with an Air Pump (1768), by Joseph Wright (1734–1797), English genre and portrait painter, reflects the interest in scientific inquiry prevalent in the eighteenth century. In this experiment air was withdrawn from the glass container that holds the bird and then forced back in with the pump to revive the bird. The painter, sometimes known as "Wright of Derby" because he passed virtually his whole life in that English county, is best known for his candlelight and fireside scenes.

and Jonathan Swift. They perfected the satiric mode. Pope, a disenfranchised Catholic, and Swift, an expatriate Anglican clergyman, devoted their genius to the colossal effort of urging the world to see life honestly. Both were well-educated men who artfully employed the shock tactics of satire which they believed the times required.

Portrait of Jonathan Swift by Jervas.

Reflections of sensibility: 1745–1784. The second half of the eighteenth century is sometimes referred to as the Age of Johnson, but that is a misnomer. Although Johnson towered above the period, he did not shape it. Moreover, the development of his own mind and spirit began before the start of the new age. It must be remembered that this was also the era of Collins, Thomson, Gray, Goldsmith, and others.

The period witnessed the rise of a new poetry of melancholy. Such works as William Collins' "Ode to Evening" (1747) and Thomas Gray's "Elegy Written in a Country Churchyard" (1750) were overshadowed by the gloom typical of Milton's *Il Penseroso*. Another form of melancholy verse, referred to as the "graveyard school," was exemplified by Edward Young's *The Complaint, or Night Thoughts on Life, Death, and Immortality* (1742–1746). This trend was accompanied

A Literary Party, *an engraving by W. Walker showing Samuel Johnson and his literary circle. Among the famous people represented here are* (left to right) *James Boswell, Johnson, Joshua Reynolds, and* (far right) *Oliver Goldsmith.*

by intensified interest in medieval architecture and literature. The former expressed itself in a revival of Gothic architecture, which in the earlier eighteenth century was regarded as barbaric in its irregularity of style. For example, Horace Walpole's home, Strawberry Hill, was built in the design of a Gothic castle. Furthermore, Gothic fiction and tales of the bizarre in human experience were often set in medieval times. Another significant medieval literary form which attracted wide attention during this period and which influenced later poetic developments was the ballad.

At the same time, a new fascination with nature arose. Works like James Thomson's *The Seasons* described the grand, impressive aspects of nature. Thomson's break with the neoclassical forms and moral impulse was limited, but his spirit was that of a man seeking inspiration in nature. The plight of the downtrodden individual trapped in modern industrial society caused other poets to seek the primitive and the wild. This humanitarian outlook, mixed with both the sentimental and the idyllic, appears in Oliver Goldsmith's "The Deserted Village" and in Cowper's Thomson to Cowper, the poetry of statement began to

yield to the poetry of spontaneity, and a new age of lyricism was beginning.

The poetry of the latter half of the eighteenth century is clearly different from the poetry of rational, objective statement written during the first half of the century. In studying the Romantic movement, it is good to take a second look at some of the authors of the late eighteenth century, but it is also important to note that these writers did not consider themselves "pre-Romantic." They chose to write differently from their immediate predecessors and should not be saddled with labels that relate them only to their literary successors.

The rise of the novel. One dominant eighteenth-century literary form—the novel—must be mentioned in any introduction to the period, though the anthology form prevents including any complete novels and though the novel form prevents selections from being representative of a whole work. Only a brief sketch of the novel's diverse and extensive development can be attempted here. The reader should consult more detailed histories of the genre for further study.

What is generally called the novel has innumerable ancestors ranging from the ancient Greek romances and their imitators to jestbooks and criminal biographies. Most of the early forms of prose fiction were loosely plotted and were little concerned with the interplay between individuals and their relationship to society. It was not until the eighteenth century that the novel as a form with a tight structure began to emerge.

Defoe's *Robinson Crusoe* (1719) is often considered the first English novel. He wrote several other narratives about the adventures of historical or quasi-historical persons, the most successful of which is *Moll Flanders* (1722). Defoe succeeded in duplicating the realistic surfaces of human lives so well that we accept the reality of the characters in his novels, even when they are not complex. Moll seems real because Defoe carefully presents her circumstances and her problems—economic progress and setback—through an imitation of the journal or memoir form.

After Defoe came a series of novelists who developed the genre's potential for creating convincing characters and intricate plots. Samuel Richardson (1689–1761) achieved a depth of characterization unknown previously by using the epistolary form, or narration by means of a series of letters. In *Pamela, or Virtue Rewarded* (1740), *Clarissa Harlowe* (1748), and *Sir Charles Grandison* (1753) the characters provide intricate studies in psychology and complex reflections of the culture. Richardson's novels effectively convey a moral message by establishing an empathy between the reader and the characters.

Henry Fielding (1707–1754), a satirical playwright, journalist, and later, a justice of the peace, also wrote fiction, but it was vastly different from Richardson's. His *History and Adventures of Joseph Andrews* (1742) burlesques Richardson's *Pamela* and, unlike many burlesques, becomes a comic masterpiece in its own right. In his preface to the novel, Fielding explained that he sought to write "a comic epic in prose"; the exhilarating humor, excellent construction, and humane wisdom of the novel confirm his success. His *Tom Jones* (1749) is one of the great novels of all time. Laurence Sterne's (1713–1768) masterpiece, *The Life and Opinions of Tristram Shandy, Gentleman* (1760–1767), is delightful in its humor and its profound psychology. In this work Sterne challenges and finally rejects the "realism of time and event" in order to examine instead the subjectivity of perception, the power of obsession, and the fluidity of identity. The stream of consciousness tradition in modern fiction, particularly in the work of James Joyce, owes a considerable debt to Laurence Sterne.

After the passing of Sterne, Tobias Smollett (1721–1771) achieved new comic effects, playing upon the picaresque tradition in his early novels. *The Expedition of Humphry Clinker* (1771), his greatest novel, presents the comic incidents of a group of "originals" traveling

Sham Gothic ruin (1747), Hagley Park, Worcestershire. Eighteenth-century archaeological discoveries, such as the buried Roman city at Pompeii, caused a renewed interest in classical (and in England, Gothic) architecture and artifacts. "Ruins" like this one were popular in English landscape designs throughout the period.

Mrs. Siddons as the Tragic Muse (1784) by Sir Joshua Reynolds (1723–1792), well-known portrait painter whose academic approach to art resulted in paintings with historical themes. Here, his contemporary subject—the famous tragic actress Sarah Siddons—is portrayed as the Muse of Tragedy, one of nine goddesses of the arts in Greek mythology.

through England and Scotland. The achievements of all these writers were to be matched and perhaps surpassed by the works of Jane Austen at the turn of the century. By this point the genre had fully demonstrated the enormous versatility that would make it the major literary form of the Victorian and modern periods.

Perhaps the diversity of the literature and the multiplicity of political and social changes that transformed England between 1660 and 1784 are what has led literary historians to cling to such terms as neo-classical, Augustan, rational, and pre-Romantic in describing the literature of the Restoration and the eighteenth century. As we have noted, such terms usually reflect a degree of truth, but they must be used with discretion. In the very complexity which makes it difficult to describe the period from 1660 to 1784, however, we may catch a glimpse of what made it great. A startlingly new and different age of social and industrial upheaval was to follow.

JOHN DRYDEN
1631–1700

Born in Northamptonshire, Dryden attended Westminster School in London and Trinity College, Cambridge. His first important poem, *Heroic Stanzas* (1659), was written on the death of Cromwell. The next year he wrote *Astraea Redux*, celebrating the return of Charles II. Although his critics accused him of being a political turncoat, he remained loyal to Charles and to his successor, James II, for the rest of his life. As Dr. Johnson said, "If he changed, he changed with the nation." *Astraea Redux* showed Dryden's mastery of the heroic couplet, the poetic form that was to prevail in English literature for almost a hundred years. After an unsuccessful attempt at tragedy, Dryden wrote several comedies directed at the popular taste of the time, but these plays also proved to be failures. *The Indian Queen* (1664) and *The Indian Emperor* (1667), two heroic plays, were both striking successes, partly because of the use of heroic verse and particularly because of the melodramatic qualities and the splendor of the stage spectacle. In 1667 appeared his poem *Annus Mirabilis*, which describes the great events in English history during the period 1665–1666: the war with Holland, the plague, and the Great Fire of London. In 1668 he was made poet laureate, and two years later he was also made historiographer to the king.

Dryden ably set forth his critical views in his *Essay of Dramatic Poesy* (1668), in his prefaces, and in other writings. For the next fifteen years he wrote many plays, but his satirical comedies and rather extravagant tragedies met with only indifferent success. *Aurengzebe* (1676) was his last rhymed tragedy. His next dramatic work was *All for Love* (1678), a powerful version of the story of Antony and Cleopatra in blank verse; it is considered Dryden's best play.

Some of Dryden's finest talent was expressed in satire. As a result of the political and religious turmoil of the years 1678–1681, he wrote many treatises, chiefly in verse, defending his evolving convictions. *Absalom and Achitophel*, a brilliant satire written in 1681, attacked those who planned to establish the king's illegitimate son, the duke of Monmouth, on the throne. In 1682 came *The Medal*, directed against the Whigs; *MacFlecknoe*, a witty and exuberant satire; and *Religio Laici*, a defense of the Church of England against its enemies. Three years later Dryden became a Roman Catholic and in 1687 published his most famous religious poem, *The Hind and the Panther*. In this satire, the hind is the symbol of the Roman Catholic Church, persecuted by the panther, the wolf, the bear, the boar, and other animals, representing the Anglicans, the Calvinists, and other hostile sects. Although Dryden's religious and political shifting of position has led

to some doubt about his sincerity, there is no evidence that he was motivated by opportunism. His several changes in religion and politics represent the outcome of a lifelong habit of philosophical skepticism, a conscientious search for authority in matters of government and private belief, and an increasingly conservative cast of mind. Throughout his life Dryden acted on the principle that "true philosophical discipline consists in balancing every proposition against its contrary and thus establishing that neither can be certainly known as either true or false."

In the last ten to fifteen years of his life, Dryden wrote lyric poetry, producing the *Song for St. Cecilia's Day, Alexander's Feast,* and the ode *To Mrs. Anne Killigrew.* After the Revolution of 1688 and the exile of King James II, Dryden refused for reasons of conscience to swear allegiance to William and Mary; he thereby lost all pensions and offices, including the laureateship, and was again forced to support himself by writing. He wrote plays, eulogies, criticism, and an epoch-making translation of Vergil as well as numerous translations of various other classical authors. His poetic translations of some of the fables of Ovid, Homer, Boccaccio, and Chaucer appeared with one of his most significant critical prefaces, *Preface to the Fables,* a few months before his death in 1700. He was buried in Westminster Abbey beside Chaucer.

In both prose and poetry, Dryden contributed a distinctly new quality to English literature. T. S. Eliot has said that he "found the English speechless, and he gave them speech"; that is, he introduced a conversational rhythm which was both natural and forceful. Dryden's prose is marked by an absence of the elaborate devices of his predecessors. It is a prose of muted rhythm, employing for the most part only the usual balance and antithesis. Because it is simple, direct, and lucid, his is the first prose that sounds truly modern. Dryden's contribution to poetry was the development of the heroic couplet. Dryden wrote sixty thousand lines of heroic couplet verse, and he not only practiced but also studied the form exhaustively; thus, the couplet which he transmitted from Edmund Waller to Alexander Pope was a sharpened, subtle, and sophisticated instrument.

from MARRIAGE À LA MODE

WHY SHOULD A
FOOLISH MARRIAGE VOW

Why should a foolish marriage vow,
   Which long ago was made,
Oblige us to each other now,
   When passion is decayed?
We loved and we loved as long as we could,   5
   Till our love was loved out in us both;

But our marriage is dead when the pleasure is fled:
  'Twas pleasure first made it an oath.

If I have pleasures for a friend,
10   And farther love in store,
What wrong has he whose joys did end,
   And who could give no more?
'Tis a madness that he should be jealous of me,
   Or that I should bar him of another;
15 For all we can gain is to give ourselves pain,
   When neither can hinder the other.

WHILST ALEXIS LAY PRESSED

Whilst Alexis lay pressed
In her arms he loved best,
With his hands round her neck
And his head on her breast,
5 He found the fierce pleasure too hasty to stay,
And his soul° in the tempest just flying away.

When Celia saw this,
With a sigh and a kiss
She cried, "Oh my dear, I am robbed of my bliss:
10 'Tis unkind of your love, and unfaithfully done,
To leave me behind you, and die° all alone!"

The youth, though in haste,
And breathing his last,
In pity died slowly, while she died more fast;
15 Till at length she cried, "Now, my dear, now let us go;
Now die, my Alexis, and I will die too!"

Thus entranced they did lie
Till Alexis did try
To recover new breath, that again he might die.
20 Then often they died, but the more they did so,
The nymph died more quick, and the shepherd more
   slow.
(1673)

ABSALOM AND ACHITOPHEL

Absalom and Achitophel was written in the hope of influencing the verdict of a grand jury; that it failed in
no way discredits the fact that the poet hoped that it
might succeed.

   Protestantism and the English monarchy were
both at stake. In 1678, Titus Oates and a number of
confederates gave false but sworn testimony that a
Popish plot existed to assassinate Charles II, burn London, massacre the people, and reestablish Roman
Catholicism. Four well-publicized facts gave general
credence to the word of perjurers: (1) Charles was rumored to be privately sympathetic to the Roman
Catholics; (2) James, duke of York, Charles' brother
and heir to the throne, openly professed Catholicism;
(3) the Justice of the Peace, Sir Edmund Berry Godfrey,
who had received a copy of Oates' testimony for
safekeeping, was murdered, a crime with which the
Catholics were immediately charged; and (4) the
seized papers of the duke of York's secretary showed
that he was carrying on a correspondence with Louis
XIV's confessor regarding the reestablishment of Roman Catholicism in England.

   History has shown that Titus Oates was a fraud
and a rascal: "Popish Plot" has become a humorous
phrase. But at the time, Whig opposition to Charles,
led by the Earl of Shaftesbury, sought to embarrass the
crown, to divert the succession from James, duke of
York, to James, duke of Monmouth (Charles' illegitimate son), and to assure the dominance of Protestantism. Charles dueled with Shaftesbury and finally
broke his power in 1681. He charged him with high
treason, and it was the verdict of the Whig jury that
tried him that Dryden tried unsuccessfully to influence.

   The allegorical basis of the satire is the biblical
story of King David and his son Absalom (*Samuel*,
2:13–18). Monmouth is Absalom; Shaftesbury, the
false tempter Achitophel; and Charles II, King David.

In pious times, e'r Priest-craft did begin,
Before *Polygamy* was made a sin;
When man, on many, multiply'd his kind,
E'r one to one was, cursedly, confind:
When Nature prompted, and no law deny'd
Promiscuous use of Concubine and Bride;
Then, *Israel*'s Monarch,° after Heaven's own heart,
His vigorous warmth did, variously, impart
To Wives and Slaves: And, wide as his Command,
Scatter'd his Maker's Image through the Land.   10
Michal,° of Royal blood, the Crown did wear,
A Soyl ungratefull to the Tiller's care:
Not so the rest; for several Mothers bore
To Godlike *David*, several Sons before.°
But since like slaves his bed they did ascend,
No True Succession could their seed attend.
Of all this Numerous Progeny was none
So Beautifull, so brave as *Absolon:*°
Whether, inspir'd by some diviner Lust,
His Father got him with a greater Gust;   20
Or that his Conscious destiny made way
By manly beauty to Imperiall sway.
Early in Foreign fields he won Renown,
With Kings and States ally'd to *Israel*'s Crown:
In Peace the thoughts of War he coud remove,
And seem'd as he were only born for love.
What e'r he did was done with so much ease,

Absalom and Achitophel   7 Israel's Monarch, King David, representing Charles
II of England; *Israel* is England   **11 Michal,** daughter of Saul and wife of David;
she represents Charles II's queen, Catharine of Portugal, who was childless
13 several Mothers . . . before. The "several mothers" were the many mistresses
of Charles II   **18 Absalon,** a variant of *Absalom*, the third son of David; he represents James, Duke of Monmouth, son of Charles II and Lucy Waters

Marriage à la Mode   Whilst Alexis Lay Pressed   6 soul, metonymy for semen
11 die. In the seventeenth century, "to die" sometimes meant "to reach a sexual
climax"

In him alone, 'twas Natural to please.
His motions all accompanied with grace;
30 And *Paradise* was open'd in his face.
With secret Joy, indulgent *David* view'd
His Youthfull Image in his Son renew'd:
To all his wishes Nothing he deny'd,
And made the Charming *Annabel*° his Bride.
What faults he had (for who from faults is free?)
His Father coud not, or he woud not see.
Some warm excesses, which the Law forbore,
Were constru'd Youth that purg'd by boyling o'r:
And *Amnon*'s° Murther, by a specious Name,
40 Was call'd a Just Revenge for injur'd Fame.
Thus Prais'd, and Lov'd, the Noble Youth remain'd,
While *David*, undisturb'd, in *Sion* raign'd.
But Life can never be sincerely blest:
Heaven punishes the bad, and proves the best.
The *Jews*, a Headstrong, Moody, Murmuring race,
As ever try'd th' extent and stretch of grace;
God's pamper'd people whom, debauch'd with ease,
No King could govern, nor no God could please;
(Gods they had tri'd of every shape and size
50 That God-smiths could produce, or Priests devise:)
These *Adam*-wits, too fortunately free,
Began to dream they wanted libertie;
And when no rule, no president was found
Of men, by Laws less circumscrib'd and bound,
They led their wild desires to Woods and Caves,
And thought that all but Savages were Slaves.
They who when *Saul*° was dead, without a blow,
Made foolish *Ishbosheth*° the Crown forgo;
Who banisht *David* did from *Hebron*° bring,
60 And, with a Generall Shout, proclaim'd him King:
Those very *Jewes*, who, at their very best,
Their Humour more than Loyalty exprest,
Now, wondred why, so long, they had obey'd
An Idoll Monarch which their hands had made:
Thought they might ruine him they could create;
Or melt him to that Golden Calf, a State.
But these were randome bolts: No form'd Design,
Nor Interest made the Factious Croud to joyn:
The sober part of *Israel*, free from stain,
70 Well knew the value of a peacefull raign:
And, looking backward with a wise afright,
Saw Seames of wounds, dishonest to the sight;
In contemplation of whose ugly Scars,
They Curst the memory of Civil Wars.°
The moderate sort of Men, thus qualifi'd,
Inclin'd the Ballance to the better side:
And *David*'s mildness manag'd it so well,
The Bad found no occasion to Rebell.
But, when to Sin our byast Nature leans,
80 The carefull Devil is still at hand with means;
And providently Pimps for ill desires:
The Good old Cause reviv'd, a Plot requires.

Plots, true or false, are necessary things,
To raise up Common-wealths, and ruin Kings.
Th' inhabitants of old *Jerusalem*
Were *Jebusites:*° the Town so call'd from them;
And their's the Native right—
But when the chosen people° grew more strong,
The rightfull cause at length became the wrong:
And every loss the men of *Jebus* bore,   90
They still were thought God's enemies the more.
Thus, worn and weaken'd, well or ill content,
Submit they must to *David*'s Government:
Impoverisht, and depriv'd of all Command,
Their Taxes doubled as they lost their Land,
And, what was harder yet to flesh and blood,
Their Gods disgrac'd, and burnt like common wood.
This set the Heathen Priesthood° in a flame;
For Priests of all Religions are the same:
Of whatsoe'r descent their Godhead be,   100
Stock, Stone, or other homely pedigree,
In his defence his Servants are as bold
As if he had been born of beaten gold.
The *Jewish Rabbins*° thô their Enemies,
In this conclude them honest men and wise:
For 'twas their duty, all the Learned think,
T'espouse his Cause by whom they eat and drink.
From hence began that Plot,° the Nation's Curse,
Bad in it self, but represented worse.
Rais'd in extremes, and in extremes decry'd;   110
With Oaths affirm'd, with dying Vows deny'd.
Not weigh'd, or winnow'd by the Multitude;
But swallow'd in the Mass, unchew'd and Crude.
Some Truth there was, but dash'd and brew'd with
        Lyes;
To please the Fools, and puzzle all the Wise.
Succeeding times did equal folly call,
Believing nothing, or believing all.
Th' *Egyptian*° Rites the *Jebusites* imbrac'd;
Where Gods were recommended by their Tast.
Such savory Deities must needs be good,   120
As serv'd at once for Worship and for Food.
By force they could not Introduce these Gods;
For Ten to One, in former days was odds.
So Fraud was us'd, (the Sacrificers trade,)
Fools are more hard to Conquer than Perswade.
Their busie Teachers mingled with the *Jews;*
And rak'd, for Converts, even the Court and Stews:°
Which *Hebrew* Priests° the more unkindly took,
Because the Fleece accompanies the flock.
Some thought they God's Anointed° meant to Slay   130
By Guns, invented since full many a day:
Our Authour swears it not; but who can know

86 **Jebusites,** Roman Catholics   88 **chosen people,** Protestants   98 **Heathen Priesthood,** Catholic priests   104 **Jewish Rabbins,** leading clergymen of the Church of England   108 **that Plot,** the famous Popish Plot of 1677–1679. The Jesuits were charged, on doubtful evidence, with a conspiracy to overthrow the government and place a Catholic on the throne, with the aid of France. One consequence of this was a minor war with France   118 **Egyptian,** French. Lines 118–119 are an attack upon the Roman Catholic doctrine of transubstantiation   127 **Court and Stews.** The king was thought to be a Catholic; some of his mistresses were Catholics, as was his brother, the Duke of York, later James II   128 **Hebrew Priests,** clergymen of the Church of England   130 **God's Anointed,** the king

34 **Annabel,** Monmouth's wife, Anne Scott   39 **Amnon's,** has not been identified certainly.   57 **Saul,** Cromwell   58 **Ishbosheth,** Cromwell's son, Richard   59 **Hebron,** Scotland, where Charles II had first been crowned   74 **Civil Wars,** the Civil War of the 1640's

John Dryden   **395**

How far the Devil and *Jebusites* may go?
This Plot, which fail'd for want of common Sense,
Had yet a deep and dangerous Consequence:
For, as when raging Fevers boyl the Blood,
The standing Lake soon floats into a Flood;
And every hostile Humour, which before
Slept quiet in its Channels, bubbles o'r:
140 So, several Factions from this first Ferment,
Work up to Foam, and threat the Government.
Some by their Friends, more by themselves thought
    wise,
Oppos'd the Power, to which they could not rise.
Some had in Courts been Great, and thrown from
    thence,
Like Feinds, were harden'd in Impenitence.
Some by their Monarch's fatal mercy grown,
From Pardon'd Rebels, Kinsmen to the Throne;
Were rais'd in Power and publick Office high:
Strong Bands, if Bands ungratefull men could tye.
150   Of these the false *Achitophel*° was first:
A Name to all succeeding Ages Curst.
For close° Designs, and crooked Counsels fit;
Sagacious, Bold, and Turbulent of wit:
Restless, unfixt in Principles and Place;
In Power unpleas'd, impatient of Disgrace.
A fiery Soul, which working out its way,
Fretted the Pigmy Body° to decay:
And o'r inform'd° the Tenement of Clay.
A daring Pilot in extremity;
160 Pleas'd with the Danger, when the Waves went high
He sought the Storms; but for a Calm unfit,
Would Steer too nigh the Sands, to boast his Wit.
Great Wits are sure to Madness near ally'd;
And thin Partitions do their Bounds divide:
Else, why should he, with Wealth and Honour blest,
Refuse his Age the needful hours of Rest?
Punish a Body which he coud not please;
Bankrupt of Life, yet Prodigal of Ease?
And all to leave, what with his Toyl he won,
170 To that unfeather'd, two Leg'd thing, a Son:
Got, while his Soul did hudled Notions try;
And born a shapeless Lump, like Anarchy.
In Friendship False, Implacable in Hate:
Resolv'd to Ruine or to Rule the State.
To Compass this the Triple Bond° he broke;
The Pillars of the publick Safety shook:
And fitted *Israel* for a Foreign Yoke.
Then, seiz'd with Fear, yet still affecting Fame,
Usurp'd a Patriott's All-attoning Name.
180 So easie° still it proves in Factious Times,
With publick Zeal to cancel private Crimes:
How safe is Treason, and how sacred ill,
Where none can sin against the Peoples Will:

Where Crouds can wink; and no offence be known,
Since in anothers guilt they find their own.
Yet, Fame deserv'd, no Enemy can grudge;
The Statesman we abhor, but praise the Judge.
In *Israels* Courts ne'r sat an *Abbethdin*°
With more discerning Eyes, or Hands more clean:
Unbrib'd, unsought, the Wretched to redress;   190
Swift of Dispatch, and easie of Access.
Oh, had he been content to serve the Crown,
With vertues only proper to the Gown;
Or, had the rankness of the Soyl been freed
From Cockle, that opprest the Noble seed:
David, for him his tunefull Harp had strung,
And Heaven had wanted° one Immortal song.
But wilde Ambition loves to slide, not stand;
And Fortunes Ice prefers to Vertues Land:
Achitophel, grown weary to possess   200
A lawfull Fame, and lazy Happiness;
Disdain'd the Golden fruit to gather free,
And lent the Croud his Arm to shake the Tree.
Now, manifest of° Crimes, contriv'd long since,
He stood at bold Defiance with his Prince:
Held up the Buckler of the Peoples Cause,
Against the Crown; and sculk'd behind the Laws.
The wish'd occasion of the Plot he takes,
Some Circumstances finds, but more he makes.
By buzzing Emissaries, fills the ears   210
Of listning Crowds, with Jealosies and Fears
Of Arbitrary Counsels brought to light,
And proves the King himself a *Jebusite:*°
Weak Arguments! which yet he knew full well,
Were strong with People easie to Rebell.
For, govern'd by the *Moon,* the giddy *Jews*
Tread the same track when she the Prime renews:°
And once in twenty Years, their Scribes Record,
By natural Instinct they change their Lord.
Achitophel still wants a Chief, and none   220
Was found so fit as Warlike *Absolon:*
Not, that he wish'd his Greatness to create,
(For Polititians neither love nor hate:)
But, for he knew, his Title not allow'd,°
Would keep him still depending on the Crowd:
That Kingly power, thus ebbing out, might be
Drawn to the dregs of a Democracy.
Him he attempts, with studied Arts to please,
And sheds his Venome, in such words as these.
    Auspicious Prince! at whose Nativity   230
Some Royal Planet rul'd the Southern sky;
Thy longing Countries Darling and Desire;
Their cloudy Pillar, and their guardian Fire:
Their second *Moses,* whose extended Wand
Divides the Seas, and shews the promis'd Land:
Whose dawning Day, in every distant age,

---

150 **Achitophel,** Anthony Ashley Cooper, Earl of Shaftesbury   152 **close,** secret
157 **Pigmy Body.** Shaftesbury was small   158 **o'r inform'd,** made his mind too
active for his body   175 **Triple Bond,** Triple Alliance of England, Holland, and
Sweden against France, made in 1668. Actually this alliance was not broken by
Shaftesbury, as Dryden thought, but by Charles II in 1670, when he made a secret
treaty with the French king   180 **So easie, etc.** Lines 180–191 were inserted in
the second edition of the poem (1681), after Shaftesbury had been acquitted and
released

188 **Abbethdin,** a Jewish officer of the high court of justice. Shaftesbury was Lord
Chancellor (1672–1673) and had served as President of the Privy Council
197 **wanted,** lacked. The "immortal song" is Dryden's poem   204 **manifest of,**
detected in, guilty of   213 **King . . . Jebusite.** Charles II died a Catholic; it has
since been proved that he was one during his reign   217 **the Prime renews,** becomes new. The implication here is that the people are as changeable as the
moon   224 **Title not allowed.** Monmouth was barred from the throne because of
his illegitimate birth

Has exercis'd the Sacred Prophets rage:
The Peoples Prayer, the glad Deviners Theam,
The Young-mens Vision, and the Old mens Dream!
240 Thee, *Saviour*, Thee, the Nations Vows confess;
And, never satisfi'd with seeing, bless:
Swift, unbespoken Pomps, thy steps proclaim,
And stammerring Babes are taught to lisp thy Name.
How long wilt thou the general Joy detain;
Starve, and defraud the People of thy Reign?
Content ingloriously to pass thy days
Like one of Vertues Fools that feeds on Praise;
Till thy fresh Glories, which now shine so bright,
Grow Stale and Tarnish with our daily sight.
250 Believe me, Royal Youth, thy Fruit must be,
Or gather'd Ripe, or rot upon the Tree.
Heav'n, has to all allotted, soon or late,
Some lucky Revolution of their Fate:
Whose Motions, if we watch and guide with Skill,
(For humane Good depends on humane Will,)
Our Fortune rolls, as from a smooth Descent,
And, from the first Impression, takes the Bent:
But, if unseiz'd, she glides away like wind;
And leaves repenting Folly far behind.
260 Now, now she meets you, with a glorious prize,
And spreads her Locks before her as she flies.
Had thus Old *David*, from whose Loyns you spring,
Not dar'd, when Fortune call'd him, to be King,
At *Gath*° an Exile he might still remain,
And heavens Anointing Oyle had been in vain.
Let his successfull Youth your hopes engage,
But shun th' example of Declining Age:
Behold him setting in his Western Skies,
The Shadows lengthning as the Vapours rise.
270 He is not now, as when on *Jordan*'s Sand°
The Joyfull People throng'd to see him Land,
Cov'ring the *Beach*, and blackning all the *Strand*:
But, like the Prince of Angels from his height,
Comes tumbling downward with diminish'd light;
Betray'd by one poor Plot to publick Scorn,
(Our only blessing since his Curst Return:)
Those heaps of People which one Sheaf did bind,
Blown off and scatter'd by a puff of Wind.
What strength can he to your Designs oppose,
280 Naked of Friends, and round beset with Foes?
If *Pharaoh*'s° doubtfull Succour he shoud use,
A Foreign Aid woud more Incense the *Jews*:
Proud *Egypt* woud dissembled Friendship bring;
Foment the War, but not support the King:
Nor woud the Royal Party e'r unite
With *Pharaoh*'s Arms, t'assist the *Jebusite;*
Or if they shoud, their Interest soon woud break,
And with such odious Aid make *David* weak.
All sorts of men by my successfull Arts,
290 Abhorring Kings, estrange their alter'd Hearts
From *David*'s Rule: And 'tis the general Cry,

264 **Gath**, Brussels, where Charles had spent some time during his exile
270 **Jordan's Sand**, the coast at Dover where Charles landed in 1660
281 **Pharaoh**, the French king

Religion, Common-wealth, and Liberty.
If you as Champion of the publique Good,
Add to their Arms a Chief of Royal Blood;
What may not *Israel* hope, and what Applause
Might such a General gain by such a Cause?
Not barren Praise alone, that Gaudy Flower,
Fair only to the sight, but solid Power:
And Nobler is a limited Command,
Giv'n by the Love of all your Native Land,   300
Than a Successive Title, Long, and Dark,
Drawn from the Mouldy Rolls of *Noah*'s Ark.
    What cannot Praise effect in Mighty Minds,
When Flattery Sooths, and when Ambition Blinds!
Desire of Power, on Earth a Vitious Weed,
Yet, sprung from High, is of Cælestial Seed:
In God 'tis Glory: And when men Aspire,
'Tis but a Spark too much of Heavenly Fire.
Th' Ambitious Youth, too Covetous of Fame,
Too full of Angells Metal in his Frame;   310
Unwarily was led from Vertues ways;
Made Drunk with Honour, and Debauch'd with Praise.
Half loath, and half consenting to the Ill,
(For Loyal Blood within him strugled still)
He thus reply'd—And what Pretence have I
To take up Arms for Publick Liberty?
My Father Governs with unquestion'd Right;
The Faiths Defender, and Mankinds Delight:
Good, Gracious, Just, observant of the Laws;
And Heav'n by Wonders has Espous'd his Cause.   320
Whom has he Wrong'd in all his Peaceful Reign?
Who sues for Justice to his Throne in Vain?
What Millions has he Pardon'd of his Foes,
Whom Just Revenge did to his Wrath expose?
Mild, Easy, Humble, Studious of our Good;
Enclin'd to Mercy, and averse from Blood.
If Mildness Ill with Stubborn *Israel* Suite,
His Crime is God's beloved Attribute.
What could he gain, his People to Betray,
Or change his Right, for Arbitrary Sway?   330
Let Haughty *Pharaoh* Curse with such a Reign,
His Fruitfull *Nile*, and Yoak a Servile Train.
If *David*'s Rule *Jerusalem* Displease,
The *Dog-star* heats their Brains to this Disease.
Why then shoud I, Encouraging the Bad,
Turn Rebell, and run Popularly Mad?
Were he a Tyrant who, by Lawless Might,
Opprest the *Jews*, and Rais'd the *Jebusite*,
Well might I Mourn; but Natures Holy Bands
Woud Curb my Spirits, and Restrain my Hands: 340
The People might assert their Liberty;
But what was Right in them, were Crime in me.
His Favour leaves me nothing to require;
Prevents my Wishes, and outruns Desire.
What more can I expect while *David* lives,
All but his Kingly Diadem he gives;
And that: But there he Paus'd; then Sighing, said,
Is Justly Destin'd for a Worthier Head.
For when my Father from his Toyls shall Rest,

350 And late Augment the Number of the Blest:
His Lawfull Issue shall the Throne ascend,
Or the *Collateral* Line where that shall end.
His Brother,° though Opprest with Vulgar Spight,
Yet Dauntless and Secure of Native Right,
Of every Royal Vertue stands possest;
Still Dear to all the Bravest, and the Best.
His Courage Foes, his Friends his Truth Proclaim;
His Loyalty the King, the World his Fame.
His Mercy even th' Offending Crowd will find,
360 For sure he comes of a Forgiving Kind.
Why shoud I then Repine at Heavens Decree;
Which gives me no Pretence to Royalty?
Yet oh that Fate Propitiously Enclind,
Had rais'd my Birth, or had debas'd my Mind;
To my large Soul, not all her Treasure lent,
And then Betray'd it to a mean Descent.
I find, I find my mounting Spirits Bold,
And *David*'s Part disdains my Mothers Mold.
Why am I Scanted by a Niggard Birth?
370 My Soul Disclaims the Kindred of her Earth:
And made for Empire, Whispers me within;
Desire of Greatness is a Godlike Sin.
      Him Staggering so when Hells dire Agent found,
While fainting Vertue scarce maintain'd her Ground,
He pours fresh Forces in, and thus Replies:
      Th' Eternal God Supreamly Good and Wise,
Imparts not these Prodigious Gifts in vain;
What Wonders are Reserv'd to bless your Reign?
Against your will your Arguments have shown,
380 Such Vertue's only given to guide a Throne.
Not that your Father's Mildness I contemn;
But Manly Force becomes the Diadem.
'Tis true, he grants the People all they crave;
And more perhaps than Subjects ought to have:
For Lavish grants suppose a Monarch tame,
And more his Goodness than his Wit proclaim.
But when shoud People strive their Bonds to break,
If not when Kings are Negligent or Weak?
Let him give on till he can give no more,
390 The Thrifty Sanhedrin° shall keep him poor:
And every Sheckle which he can receive,
Shall cost a Limb of his Prerogative.
To ply him with new Plots, shall be my care,
Or plunge him deep in some Expensive War;
Which when his Treasure can no more Supply,
He must, with the Remains of Kingship, buy.
His faithful Friends, our Jealousies and Fears,
Call *Jebusites;* and *Pharaoh*'s Pentioners:
Whom, when our Fury from his Aid has torn,
400 He shall be Naked left to publick Scorn.
The next Successor, whom I fear and hate,
My Arts have made Obnoxious to the State;
Turn'd all his Vertues to his Overthrow,
And gain'd our Elders to pronounce a Foe.
His Right, for Sums of necessary Gold,

Shall first be Pawn'd, and afterwards be Sold:
Till time shall Ever-wanting *David* draw,
To pass your doubtfull Title into Law:
If not; the People have a Right Supreme
To make their Kings; for Kings are made for them.   410
All Empire is no more than Pow'r in Trust,
Which when resum'd, can be no longer Just.
Succession, for the general Good design'd,
In its own wrong a Nation cannot bind:
If altering that, the People can relieve,
Better one Suffer, than a Nation grieve.
The *Jews* well know their power: e'r *Saul* they Chose,
God was their King, and God they durst Depose.
Urge now your Piety, your Filial Name,
A Father's Right, and fear of future Fame;   420
The publick Good, that Universal Call,
To which even Heav'n Submitted, answers all.
Nor let his Love Enchant your generous Mind;
'Tis Natures trick to Propagate her Kind.
Our fond Begetters, who woud never dye,
Love but themselves in their Posterity.
Or let his Kindness by th' Effects be try'd,
Or let him lay his vain Pretence aside.
God said he lov'd your Father; coud he bring
A better Proof, than to Anoint him King?   430
It surely shew'd he lov'd the Shepherd well,
Who gave so fair a Flock as *Israel.*
Woud *David* have you thought his Darling Son?
What means he then, to Alienate the Crown?
The name of Godly he may blush to bear:
'Tis after God's own heart to Cheat his Heir.
He to his Brother gives Supreme Command;
To you a Legacy of Barren Land:
Perhaps th' old Harp, on which he thrums his Layes:
Or some dull *Hebrew* Ballad in your Praise.   440
Then the next Heir, a Prince, Severe and Wise,
Already looks on you with Jealous Eyes;
Sees through the thin Disguises of your Arts,
And markes your Progress in the Peoples Hearts.
Though now his mighty Soul its Grief contains;
He meditates Revenge who least Complains.
And like a Lyon, Slumbring in the way,
Or Sleep-dissembling, while he waits his Prey,
His fearless Foes within his Distance draws;
Constrains his Roaring, and Contracts his Paws;   450
Till at the last, his time for Fury found,
He shoots with suddain Vengeance from the Ground:
The Prostrate Vulgar, passes o'r, and Spares;
But with a Lordly Rage, his Hunters teares.
Your Case no tame Expedients will afford;
Resolve on Death, or Conquest by the Sword,
Which for no less a Stake than Life, you Draw;
And Self-defence is Natures Eldest Law.
Leave the warm People no Considering time;
For then Rebellion may be thought a Crime.   460
Prevail your self of what Occasion gives,
But try your Title while your Father lives:
And that your Arms may have a fair Pretence,

353 **Brother,** James, Duke of York   390 **Sanhedrin,** the Parliament

Proclaim, you take them in the King's Defence:
Whose Sacred Life each minute woud Expose,
To Plots, from seeming Friends, and secret Foes.
And who can sound the depth of *David*'s Soul?
Perhaps his fear, his kindness may Controul.
He fears his Brother, though he loves his Son,
470 For plighted Vows too late to be undone.
If so, by Force he wishes to be gain'd,
Like womens Leachery, to seem Constrain'd:
Doubt not, but when he most affects the Frown,
Commit a pleasing Rape upon the Crown.
Secure his Person to secure your Cause;
They who possess the Prince, possess the Laws.
　He said, And this Advice above the rest,
With *Absalom*'s Mild nature suited best;
Unblam'd of Life (Ambition set aside,)
480 Not stain'd with Cruelty, nor puft with Pride;
How happy had he been, if Destiny
Had higher plac'd his Birth, or not so high!
His Kingly Vertues might have claim'd a Throne,
And blest all other Countries but his own:
But charming Greatness, since so few refuse;
'Tis Juster to Lament him, than Accuse.
Strong were his hopes a Rival to remove,
With blandishments to gain the publick Love;
To Head the Faction while their Zeal was hot,
490 And Popularly prosecute the Plot.
To farther this, *Achitophel* Unites
The Malecontents of all the *Israelites*;
Whose differing Parties he could wisely Joyn,
For several Ends, to serve the same Design.
The Best, and of the Princes some were such,
Who thought the power of Monarchy too much:
Mistaken Men, and Patriots in their Hearts;
Not Wicked, but Seduc'd by Impious Arts.
By these the Springs of Property were bent,
500 And wound so high, they Crack'd the Government.
The next for Interest sought t' embroil the State,
To sell their Duty at a dearer rate;
And make their *Jewish* Markets of the Throne,
Pretending publick Good, to serve their own.
Others thought Kings an useless heavy Load,
Who Cost too much, and did too little Good.
These were for laying Honest *David* by,
On Principles of pure good Husbandry.
With them Joyn'd all th' Haranguers of the Throng,
510 That thought to get Preferment by the Tongue.
Who follow next, a double Danger bring,
Not only hating *David*, but the King,
The *Solymæan* Rout;° well Verst of old,
In Godly Faction, and in Treason bold;
Cowring and Quaking at a Conqueror's Sword,
But Lofty to a Lawfull Prince Restor'd;
Saw with Disdain an *Ethnick* Plot begun,
And Scorn'd by *Jebusites* to be Out-done.
Hot *Levites*° Headed these; who pul'd before

From th' *Ark*,° which in the Judges days they bore,   520
Resum'd their Cant, and with a Zealous Cry,
Pursu'd their old belov'd Theocracy.
Where Sanhedrin and Priest inslav'd the Nation,
And justifi'd their Spoils by Inspiration;
For who so fit for Reign as *Aaron*'s Race,°
If once Dominion they could found in Grace?
These led the Pack; tho not of surest scent,
Yet deepest mouth'd against the Government.
A numerous Host of dreaming Saints succeed;
Of the true old Enthusiastick° breed: 530
'Gainst Form and Order they their Power employ;
Nothing to Build and all things to Destroy.
But far more numerous was the herd of such,
Who think too little, and who talk too much.
These, out of meer instinct, they knew not why,
Ador'd their fathers God, and Property:
And, by the same blind benefit of Fate,
The Devil and the *Jebusite* did hate:
Born to be sav'd, even in their own despight;
Because they could not help believing right.   540
Such were the tools; but a whole Hydra° more
Remains, of sprouting heads too long, to score.
　Some of their Chiefs were Princes of the Land:
In the first Rank of these did *Zimri*° stand:
A man so various, that he seem'd to be
Not one, but all Mankinds Epitome.
Stiff in Opinions, always in the wrong;
Was every thing by starts, and nothing long:
But, in the course of one revolving Moon,
Was Chymist, Fidler, States-Man, and Buffoon: 550
Then all for Women, Painting, Rhiming, Drinking;
Besides ten thousand freaks that dy'd in thinking.
Blest Madman, who coud every hour employ,
With something New to wish, or to enjoy!
Rayling and praising were his usual Theams;
And both (to shew his Judgment) in Extreams:
So over Violent, or over Civil,
That every man, with him, was God or Devil.
In squandring Wealth° was his peculiar Art:
Nothing went unrewarded, but Desert.   560
Begger'd by Fools, whom still he found too late:
He had his Jest, and they had his Estate.
He laught himself from Court, then sought Relief
By forming Parties, but coud ne're be Chief:
For, spight of him, the weight of Business fell
On *Absalom* and wise *Achitophel*:
Thus, wicked but in will, of means bereft,
He left not Faction, but of that was left.

520 **Ark,** the national religion　525 **Aaron's Race,** the priesthood　530 **En-
thusiastick.** The word, throughout the Restoration and neoclassical periods, is always a word of reproach. The original meaning, "inspired by a god," "inspired
by religious emotion," always connoted to Dryden and his contemporaries the
unbalanced, the emotionally violent, the lunatic fringe　541 **Hydra,** in classical
mythology, the nine-headed monster of the Lernaean swamps, killed by Hercules
as one of his twelve labors. As fast as one head was cut off, two grew in its place,
until Hercules finally burnt off the heads with a firebrand　544 **Zimri,** George
Villiers, Duke of Buckingham (1628–1687), one of the authors of *The Rehearsal*
(1672), a burlesque drama in which Dryden is ridiculed. Dryden here takes revenge in one of the notable portraits in satirical literature, one that Dryden himself
said was worth the whole poem of *Absalom and Achitophel.* Buckingham was one
of Charles' ministers, but was dismissed in 1674 and joined the opposition
559 **Wealth.** After the Restoration, Buckingham's income was twenty thousand
pounds a year, an immense fortune for those days

513 **Solymæan Rout,** the London mob　519 **Levites,** Presbyterians

Titles and Names 'twere tedious to Reherse
570 Of Lords, below the Dignity of Verse.
   Wits, warriors, Common-wealthsmen, were the best:
   Kind Husbands and meer Nobles all the rest.
   And, therefore in the name of Dulness, be
   The well hung *Balaam* and cold *Caleb* free.
   And Canting *Nadab*° let Oblivion damn,
   Who made new porridge for the Paschal Lamb.
   Let Friendships holy band some Names assure:
   Some their own Worth, and some let Scorn secure.
   Nor shall the Rascall Rabble here have Place,
580 Whom Kings no Titles gave, and God no Grace:
   Not Bull-fac'd *Jonas,* who could Statutes draw
   To mean Rebellion, and make Treason Law.
   But he, tho bad, is follow'd by a worse,
   The wretch, who Heavens Annointed dar'd to Curse.
   Shimei,° whose Youth did early Promise bring
   Of Zeal to God, and Hatred to his King;
   Did wisely from Expensive Sins refrain,
   And never broke the Sabbath, but for Gain:
   Nor ever was he known an Oath to vent,
590 Or Curse unless against the Government.
   Thus, heaping Wealth, by the most ready way
   Among the *Jews,* which was to Cheat and Pray;
   The City, to reward his pious Hate
   Against his Master, chose him Magistrate:
   His Hand a Vare of Justice did uphold;
   His Neck was loaded with a Chain of Gold.
   During his Office, Treason was no Crime.
   The Sons of *Belial* had a glorious Time:
   For *Shimei,* though not prodigal of pelf,
600 Yet lov'd his wicked Neighbour as himself:
   When two or three were gather'd to declaim
   Against the Monarch of *Jerusalem,*
   Shimei was always in the midst of them.
   And, if they Curst the King when he was by,
   Woud rather Curse, than break good Company.
   If any durst his Factious Friends accuse,
   He pact a Jury of dissenting *Jews:*
   Whose fellow-feeling, in the godly Cause,
   Would free the suffring Saint from Humane Laws.
610 For Laws are only made to Punish those,
   Who serve the King, and to protect his Foes.
   If any leisure time he had from Power,
   (Because 'tis Sin to misimploy an hour;)
   His business was, by Writing, to Persuade,
   That Kings were Useless, and a Clog to Trade:
   And, that his noble Stile he might refine,
   No *Rechabite*° more shund the fumes of Wine.
   Chast were his Cellars, and his Shrieval Board
   The Grossness of a City Feast abhor'd:
620 His Cooks, with long disuse, their Trade forgot;
   Cool was his Kitchen, tho his Brains were hot.
   Such frugal Vertue Malice may accuse,
   But sure 'twas necessary to the *Jews:*

For Towns once burnt, such Magistrates require
As dare not tempt Gods Providence by fire.
With Spiritual food he fed his Servants well,
But free from flesh, that made the *Jews* Rebel:
And *Moses*'s Laws he held in more account,
For forty days of Fasting in the Mount.
   To speak the rest, who better are forgot,   630
Would tyre a well breath'd Witness of the Plot:
Yet, *Corah,*° thou shalt from Oblivion pass;
Erect thy self thou Monumental Brass:
High as the Serpent of thy mettall made,
While Nations stand secure beneath thy shade.
What tho his Birth were base, yet Comets rise
From Earthy Vapours ere they shine in Skies.
Prodigious Actions may as well be done
By Weavers issue, as by Princes Son.
This Arch-Attestor for the Publick Good,   640
By that one Deed Enobles all his Bloud.
Who ever ask'd the Witnesses high race,
Whose Oath with Martyrdom did *Stephen* grace?
Ours was a *Levite,* and as times went then,
His Tribe were Godalmightys Gentlemen.
Sunk were his Eyes, his Voyce was harsh and loud,
Sure signs he neither Cholerick was, nor Proud:
His long Chin prov'd his Wit; his Saintlike Grace
A Church Vermilion, and a *Moses*'s Face;
His Memory, miraculously great,   650
Could Plots, exceeding mans belief, repeat;
Which, therefore cannot be accounted Lies
For humane Wit could never such devise.
Some future Truths are mingled in his Book;
But, where the witness faild, the Prophet Spoke:
Some things like Visionary flights appear;
The Spirit caught him up, the Lord knows where:
And gave him his *Rabinical* degree
Unknown to Foreign University.
His Judgment yet his Memory did excel;   660
Which peic'd his wondrous Evidence so well:
And suited to the temper of the times;
Then groaning under *Jebusitick* Crimes.
Let *Israels* foes suspect his heav'nly call,
And rashly judge his Writ Apocryphal;
Our Laws for such affronts have forfeits made:
He takes his life, who takes away his trade.
Were I my self in witness *Corahs* place,
The wretch who did me such a dire disgrace,
Should whet my memory, though once forgot,   670
To make him an Appendix of my Plot.
His Zeal to heav'n, made him his Prince despise,
And load his person with indignities:
But Zeal peculiar priviledg affords;
Indulging latitude to deeds and words.
And *Corah* might for *Agag*'s° murther call,
In terms as course as *Samuel* us'd to *Saul.*
What others in his Evidence did Joyn,

574-5 **Balaam . . . Nadab,** various members of Whig nobility and gentry, Jonas, l. 581, is of the same persuasion   585 **Shimei,** Slingsby Bethel, Whig sheriff of London, known for his puritanism and anti-Royalism   617 **Rechabite,** a teetotaler

632 **Corah,** Titus Oates, instigator of action against the alleged Popish plot 676 **Agag,** probably Lord Chief Justice Scroggs, who had presided at one of the plot trials

(The best that could be had for love or coyn,)
In *Corah*'s own predicament will fall:
For *witness* is a Common Name to all.
    Surrounded thus with Freinds of every sort,
Deluded *Absalom*, forsakes the Court:
Impatient of high hopes, urg'd with renown,
And Fir'd with near possession of a Crown:
Th' admiring Croud are dazled with surprize,
And on his goodly person feed their eyes:
His joy conceal'd, he sets himself to show;
On each side bowing popularly low:
His looks, his gestures, and his words he frames,
And with familiar ease repeats their Names.
Thus, form'd by Nature, furnish'd out with Arts,
He glides unfelt into their secret hearts:
Then with a kind compassionating look,
And sighs, bespeaking pity ere he spoak,
Few words he said; but easy those and fit:
More slow than Hybla drops, and far more sweet.
    I mourn, my Countrymen, your lost Estate,
Tho far unable to prevent your fate:
Behold a Banisht man, for your dear cause
Expos'd a prey to Arbitrary laws!
Yet oh! that I alone cou'd be undone,
Cut off from Empire, and no more a Son!
Now all your Liberties a spoil are made;
Ægypt and *Tyrus* intercept your Trade,
And *Jebusites* your Sacred Rites invade.
My Father, whom with reverence yet I name,
Charm'd into Ease, is careless of his Fame:
And, brib'd with petty summs of Forreign Gold,
Is grown in *Bathsheba*'s° Embraces old:
Exalts his Enemies, his Friends destroys:
And all his pow'r against himself employs.
He gives, and let him give my right away:
But why should he his own, and yours betray?
He only, he can make the Nation bleed,
And he alone from my revenge is freed.
Take then my tears (with that he wip'd his Eyes)
'Tis all the Aid my present power supplies:
No Court Informer can these Arms accuse,
These Arms may Sons against their Fathers use,
And, tis my wish, the next Successors Reign
May make no other *Israelite* complain.
    Youth, Beauty, Graceful Action, seldom fail:
But Common Interest always will prevail:
And pity never Ceases to be shown
To him, who makes the peoples wrongs his own.
The Croud, (that still believe their Kings oppress)
With lifted hands their young *Messiah* bless:
Who now begins his Progress to ordain;
With Chariots, Horsemen, and a numerous train:
From East to West his Glories he displaies:
And, like the Sun, the promis'd land survays.
Fame runs before him, as the morning Star;
And shouts of Joy salute him from afar:

680
690
700
710
720
730

Each house receives him as a Guardian God;
And Consecrates the Place of his aboad:
But hospitable treats did most Commend
Wise *Issachar*, his wealthy western friend.
This moving Court, that caught the peoples Eyes,
And seem'd but Pomp, did other ends disguise:
Achitophel had form'd it, with intent
To sound the depths, and fathom where it went,
The Peoples hearts; distinguish Friends from Foes;
And try their strength, before they came to blows:
Yet all was colour'd with a smooth pretence
Of specious love, and duty to their Prince.
Religion, and Redress of Grievances,
Two names, that always cheat and always please,
Are often urg'd; and good King *David*'s life
Indanger'd by a Brother and a Wife.
Thus, in a Pageant Show, a Plot is made;
And Peace it self is War in Masquerade.
Oh foolish *Israel!* never warn'd by ill,
Still the same baite, and circumvented still!
Did ever men forsake their present ease,
In midst of health Imagine a desease;
Take pains Contingent mischiefs to foresee,
Make Heirs for Monarks, and for God decree?
What shall we think! can People give away
Both for themselves and Sons, their Native sway?
Then they are left Defensless, to the Sword
Of each unbounded Arbitrary Lord:
And Laws are vain, by which we Right enjoy,
If Kings unquestiond can those laws destroy.
Yet, if the Crowd be Judge of fit and Just,
And Kings are onely Officers in trust,
Then this resuming Cov'nant was declar'd
When Kings were made, or is for ever bar'd:
If those who gave the Scepter, coud not tye
By their own deed their own Posterity,
How then coud *Adam* bind his future Race?
How coud his forfeit on mankind take place?
Or how coud heavenly Justice damn us all,
Who nere consented to our Fathers fall?
Then Kings are slaves to those whom they Command,
And Tenants to their Peoples pleasure stand.
Add, that the Pow'r for Property allowd,
Is mischeivously seated in the Crowd:
For who can be secure of private Right,
If Sovereign sway may be dissolv'd by might?
Nor is the Peoples Judgment always true:
The most may err as grosly as the few.
And faultless Kings run down, by Common Cry,
For Vice, Oppression, and for Tyranny.
What Standard is there in a fickle rout,
Which, flowing to the mark, runs faster out?
Nor only Crowds, but Sanhedrins may be
Infected with this publick Lunacy:
And Share the madness of Rebellious times,
To Murther Monarchs for Imagin'd crimes.
If they may Give and Take when e'r they please,
Not Kings alone, (the Godheads Images,)

740
750
760
770
780
790

John Dryden   **401**

But Government it self at length must fall
To Natures state; where all have Right to all.
Yet, grant our Lords the People Kings can make,
What Prudent men a setled Throne woud shake?
For whatsoe'r their Sufferings were before,
That Change they Covet makes them suffer more.
All other Errors but disturb a State;
800 But Innovation is the Blow of Fate.
If ancient Fabricks nod, and threat to fall,
To Patch the Flaws, and Buttress up the Wall,
Thus far 'tis Duty; but here fix the Mark:
For all beyond it is to touch our Ark.
To change Foundations, cast the Frame anew,
Is work for Rebels who base Ends pursue:
At once Divine and Humane Laws controul;
And mend the Parts by ruine of the Whole.
The Tampering World is subject to this Curse,
810 To Physick their Disease into a worse.
   Now what Relief can Righteous *David* bring?
How Fatall 'tis to be too good a King!
Friends he has few, so high the Madness grows,
Who dare be such, must be the Peoples Foes:
Yet some there were, ev'n in the worst of days;
Some let me name, and Naming is to praise.
   In this short File *Barzillai*° first appears;
Barzillai crown'd with Honour and with Years:
Long since, the rising Rebells he withstood
820 In Regions Waste, beyond the *Jordans* Flood:
Unfortunately Brave to buoy the State;
But sinking underneath his Masters Fate:
In Exile with his Godlike Prince he Mourn'd;
For him he Suffer'd, and with him Return'd.
The Court he practis'd, not the Courtier's art:
Large was his Wealth, but larger was his Heart:
Which, well the Noblest Objects knew to choose,
The Fighting Warriour, and Recording Muse.
His Bed coud once a Fruitfull Issue boast:
830 Now more than half a Father's Name is lost.
His Eldest Hope, with every Grace adorn'd,
By me (so Heav'n will have it) always Mourn'd,
And always honour'd, snatcht in Manhoods prime
By' unequal Fates, and Providences crime:
Yet not before the Goal of Honour won,
All parts fulfill'd of Subject and of Son;
Swift was the Race, but short the Time to run.
Oh Narrow Circle, but of Pow'r Divine,
Scanted in Space, but perfect in thy Line!
840 By Sea, by Land, thy Matchless Worth was known;
Arms thy Delight, and War was all thy Own:
Thy force, Infus'd, the fainting *Tyrians* prop'd:
And Haughty *Pharaoh* found his Fortune stop'd.
Oh Ancient Honour, Oh Unconquer'd Hand,
Whom Foes unpunish'd never coud withstand!
But *Israel* was unworthy of thy Name:
Short is the date of all Immoderate Fame.
It looks as Heaven our Ruine had design'd,

And durst not trust thy Fortune and thy Mind.
Now, free from Earth, thy disencumbred Soul   850
Mounts up, and leaves behind the Clouds and Starry
    Pole:
From thence thy kindred legions mayst thou bring
To aid the guardian Angel of thy King.
Here stop my Muse, here cease thy painfull flight;
No Pinions can pursue Immortal height:
Tell good *Barzillai* thou canst sing no more,
And tell thy Soul she should have fled before;
Or fled she with his life, and left this Verse
To hang on her departed Patron's Herse?
Now take thy steepy flight from heaven, and see   860
If thou canst find on earth another *He;*
Another He would be too hard to find,
See then whom thou canst see not far behind.
Zadock° the Priest, whom, shunning Power and Place,
His lowly mind advanc'd to *David*'s Grace:
With him the *Sagan* of *Jerusalem,*
Of hospitable Soul and noble Stem;
Him of the Western dome,° whose weighty sense
Flows in fit words and heavenly eloquence.
The Prophets Sons by such example led,   870
To Learning and to Loyalty were bred:
For *Colleges* on bounteous Kings depend,
And never Rebell was to Arts a friend.
To these succeed the Pillars of the Laws,
Who best cou'd plead and best can judge a Cause.
Next them a train of Loyal Peers ascend:
Sharp judging *Adriel*° the Muses friend,
Himself a Muse—In Sanhedrins debate
True to his Prince; but not a Slave of State
Whom *David*'s love with Honours did adorn,   880
That from his disobedient Son were torn.
Jotham° of piercing wit and pregnant thought,
Indew'd by nature, and by learning taught
To move Assemblies, who but onely try'd
The worse awhile, then chose the better side;
Nor chose alone, but turn'd the balance too;
So much the weight of one brave man can doe.
Hushai° the friend of *David* in distress,
In publick storms of manly stedfastness;
By foreign treaties he inform'd his Youth;   890
And join'd experience to his native truth.
His frugal care supply'd the wanting Throne,
Frugal for that, but bounteous of his own:
'Tis easy conduct when Exchequers flow,
But hard the task to manage well the low:
For Soveraign power is too deprest or high,
When Kings are forc'd to sell, or Crowds to buy.
Indulge one labour more my weary Muse,
For *Amiel,*° who can *Amiel*'s praise refuse?
Of ancient race by birth, but nobler yet   900
In his own worth, and without Title great:

817 **Barzillai,** Duke of Ormond, friend and counsellor to Charles

864 **Zadock,** the Archbishop of Canterbury   868 **Him of . . . dome,** Dean of Westminster   877 **Adriel,** John Sheffield, third Earl of Mulgrave, a poet 882 **Jotham,** George Savile, Marquis of Halifax, prominent Parliamentarian 888 **Hushai,** the First Lord of the Treasury   899 **Amiel,** a former speaker of the House of Commons

The Sanhedrin long time as chief he rul'd,
Their Reason guided and their Passion coold;
So dexterous was he in the Crown's defence,
So form'd to speak a Loyal Nation's Sense,
That as their band was *Israel*'s Tribes in small,
So fit was he to represent them all.
Now rasher Charioteers the Seat ascend,
Whose loose Carriers his steady Skill commend:
910 They like th' unequal Ruler of the Day,
Misguide the Seasons and mistake the Way;
While he withdrawn at their mad Labour smiles,
And safe enjoys the Sabbath of his Toyls.

These were the chief, a small but faithful Band
Of Worthies, in the Breach who dar'd to stand,
And tempt th' united Fury of the Land.
With grief they view'd such powerful Engines bent,
To batter down the lawful Government.
A numerous Faction with pretended frights,
920 In Sanhedrins to plume the Regal Rights.
The true Successour from the Court remov'd:
The Plot, by hireling Witnesses improv'd.
These Ills they saw, and as their Duty bound,
They shew'd the King the danger of the Wound:
That no Concessions from the Throne woud please,
But Lenitives fomentèd the Disease:
That *Absalom,* ambitious of the Crown,
Was made the Lure to draw the People down:
That false *Achitophel*'s pernitious Hate,
930 Had turn'd the Plot to Ruine Church and State:
The Councill violent, the Rabble worse
That *Shimei* taught *Jerusalem* to Curse.

With all these loads of Injuries opprest,
And long revolving, in his carefull Breast,
Th' event of things; at last his patience tir'd,
Thus from his Royal Throne by Heav'n inspir'd,
The God-like *David* spoke: with awfull fear
His Train their Maker in their Master hear.

Thus long have I, by native mercy sway'd,
940 My wrongs dissembl'd, my revenge delay'd:
So willing to forgive th' Offending Age,
So much the Father did the King asswage.
But now so far my Clemency they slight,
Th' Offenders question my Forgiving Right.
That one was made for many, they contend:
But 'tis to Rule, for that 's a Monarch's End.
They call my tenderness of Blood, my Fear:
Though Manly tempers can the longest bear.
Yet, since they will divert my Native course,
950 'Tis time to shew I am not Good by Force.
Those heap'd Affronts that haughty Subjects bring,
Are burthens for a Camel, not a King:
Kings are the publick Pillars of the State,
Born to sustain and prop the Nations weight:
If my Young *Samson* will pretend a Call
To shake the Column, let him share the Fall:
But oh that yet he woud repent and live!
How easie 'tis for Parents to forgive!
With how few Tears a Pardon might be won

From Nature, pleading for a Darling Son!   960
Poor pitied Youth, by my Paternal care,
Rais'd up to all the Height his Frame coud bear:
Had God ordain'd his fate for Empire born,
He woud have given his Soul another turn:
Gull'd with a Patriots name, whose Modern sense
Is one that would by Law supplant his Prince:
The Peoples Brave, the Politicians Tool;
Never was Patriot yet, but was a Fool.
Whence comes it that Religion and the Laws
Should more be *Absalom*'s than *David*'s Cause?   970
His old Instructor, e're he lost his Place,
Was never thought indu'd with so much Grace.
Good Heav'ns, how Faction can a Patriot Paint!
My Rebel ever proves my Peoples Saint:
Would *They* impose an Heir upon the Throne?
Let Sanhedrins be taught to give their Own.
A King's at least a part of Government,
And mine as requisite as their Consent:
Without my Leave a future King to choose,
Infers a Right the Present to Depose: 980
True, they Petition me t' approve their Choise,
But *Esau*'s Hands suite ill with *Jacob*'s Voice.
My Pious Subjects for my Safety pray,
Which to Secure they take my Power away.
From Plots and Treasons Heaven preserve my years,
But Save me most from my Petitioners.
Unsatiate as the barren Womb or Grave;
God cannot Grant so much as they can Crave.
What then is left but with a Jealous Eye
To guard the Small remains of Royalty?   990
The Law shall still direct my peacefull Sway,
And the same Law teach Rebels to Obey:
Votes shall no more Establish'd Pow'r controul,
Such Votes as make a Part exceed the Whole:
No groundless Clamours shall my Friends remove,
Nor Crowds have power to Punish e're they Prove:
For Gods, and Godlike Kings their Care express,
Still to Defend their Servants in distress.
Oh that my Power to Saving were confin'd:
Why am I forc'd, like Heaven, against my mind,   1000
To make Examples of another Kind?
Must I at length the Sword of Justice draw?
Oh curst Effects of necessary Law!
How ill my Fear they by my Mercy scan,
Beware the Fury of a Patient Man.
Law they require, let Law then shew her Face;
They coud not be content to look on Grace,
Her hinder parts, but with a daring Eye
To tempt the terror of her Front, and Dye.
By their own arts 'tis Righteously decreed,   1010
Those dire Artificers of Death shall bleed.
Against themselves their Witnesses will Swear,
Till Viper-like their Mother Plot they tear:
And suck for Nutriment that bloody gore
Which was their Principle of Life before.
Their *Belial* with their *Belzebub* will fight;
Thus on my Foes, my Foes shall do me Right:

Nor doubt th' event: for Factious crowds engage
In their first Onset, all their Brutal Rage;
1020 Then, let 'em take an unresisted Course,
Retire and Traverse, and Delude their Force:
But when they stand all Breathless, urge the fight,
And rise upon 'em with redoubled might:
For Lawfull Pow'r is still Superiour found,
When long driven back, at length it stands the ground.
He said. Th' Almighty, nodding, gave Consent;
And Peals of Thunder shook the Firmament.
Henceforth a Series of new time began,
The mighty Years in long Procession ran:
1030 Once more the Godlike *David* was Restor'd,
And willing Nations knew their Lawfull Lord.
(1681)

MACFLECKNOE

OR, A SATIRE UPON
THE TRUE-BLUE PROTESTANT
POET, T. S.

Thomas Shadwell (1640–1692), who was ridiculed in
this mock-heroic satire, was not a great poet, but
neither was he a fool. In fact, he wrote comedies and
satires on contemporary life which were both lively
and readable. Precisely how he got Dryden to attack
him can only be surmised. For several years Shadwell
and Dryden had carried on a public dialogue about
the relative merits of Ben Jonson's plays, which Shadwell prized highly and which, he felt, Dryden did not
sufficiently admire. Perhaps Dryden at last became
exasperated by Shadwell's persistent and monotonous
tone. Also, as the subtitle suggests (it was provided by
the pirating publisher), Shadwell was a Protestant and
a Whig; at the time of the poem's composition (1678),
Dryden was becoming more and more intense about
Charles, the royal succession, and the religious establishment.

The name "Mac Flecknoe" (that is, "son of
Flecknoe") was taken from Richard Flecknoe, a feeble
Irish poet who died in 1678. Andrew Marvell's lampoon of Flecknoe in 1645 and Flecknoe's fervid criticism of the English stage may have led Dryden to his
witty indictment of Shadwell.

All human things are subject to decay,
And when fate summons, monarchs must obey.
This Flecknoe found, who, like Augustus,° young
Was called to empire, and had governed long;
In prose and verse was owned, without dispute,
Through all the realms of Nonsense absolute.
This aged prince, now flourishing in peace,
And blessed with issue of a large increase;
Worn out with business, did at length debate

To settle the succession of the State;   10
And, pondering which of all his sons was fit
To reign, and wage immortal war with wit,
Cried; "'Tis resolved; for nature pleads, that he
Should only rule, who most resembles me.
Sh—— alone my perfect image bears,
Mature in dullness from his tender years:
Sh—— alone, of all my sons, is he
Who stands confirmed in full stupidity.
The rest to some faint meaning make pretense,
But Sh—— never deviates into sense.   20
Some beams of wit on other souls may fall,
Strike through, and make a lucid interval;
But Sh——'s genuine night admits no ray,
His rising fogs prevail upon the day.
Besides, his goodly fabric° fills the eye,
And seems designed for thoughtless majesty;
Thoughtless as monarch oaks that shade the plain,
And, spread in solemn state, supinely reign
Heywood and Shirley° were but types of thee,
Thou last great prophet of tautology.   30
Even I, a dunce of more renown than they,
Was sent before but to prepare thy way;
And, coarsely clad in Norwich drugget,° came
To teach the nations in thy greater name.
My warbling lute, the lute I whilom strung,
When to King John of Portugal° I sung,
Was but the prelude to that glorious day,°
When thou on silver Thames didst cut thy way,
With well-timed oars before the royal barge,
Swelled with the pride of thy celestial charge;   40
And big with hymn, commander of a host,
The like was ne'er in Epsom blankets tossed.°
Methinks I see the new Arion° sail,
The lute still trembling underneath thy nail.
At thy well-sharpened thumb from shore to shore
The treble squeaks for fear, the basses roar;
Echoes from Pissing Alley Sh—— call,
And Sh—— they resound from Aston Hall.
About thy boat the little fishes throng,
As at the morning toast that floats along.   50
Sometimes, as prince of thy harmonious band,
Thou wield'st thy papers in thy threshing hand.°
St. André's° feet ne'er kept more equal time
Not e'en the feet of thy own *Psyche's*° rime;
Though they in number as in sense excel:

MacFlecknoe   3 **Augustus,** Augustus Caesar, first Emperor of Rome (31 B.C. to A.D. 14). He was thirty-two when he became emperor

25 **his goodly fabric.** Shadwell was an unusually large man   29 **Heywood and Shirley.** Thomas Heywood, an Elizabethan playwright (1575–1650), was a prolific author. His masterpiece was the domestic tragedy *A Woman Killed with Kindness* (performed 1603). James Shirley (1596–1666) is far more obscure. His specialties were bloody tragedy and realistic comedy—*The Cardinal* (1641) is a favorable example of the first, and *The Lady of Pleasure* (1635) of the second. The latter play foreshadows much of the Restoration comedy spirit   33 **Norwich drugget,** a coarse woolen or mixed fabric   36 **King John of Portugal.** Flecknoe once visited Portugal and said he had enjoyed the patronage of King John IV (d. 1656)   37 **prelude . . . day.** The occasion described by this and lines 37–42 has never been ascertained with certainty. It is known, however, that Shadwell was rather gifted in music   42 **Epsom blankets tossed,** a reference to *Epsom Wells* (1673), a play by Shadwell, and to a scene in Shadwell's *The Virtuoso* (1676) in which a character is tossed in a blanket   43 **Arion,** a Greek musician of the eighth century B.C. (another allusion to Shadwell and his musical pretensions)   51 **harmonious band . . . threshing hand.** The implication here is that Shadwell's music was of the rustic untutored kind (from the point of view of the neoclassical standard, such music would be beneath contempt)   53 **St. André,** a popular French dancing master of the day   54 **Psyche,** a rhymed opera by Shadwell, produced in 1675

So just, so like tautology, they fell,
That, pale with envy, Singleton° forswore
The lute and sword, which he in triumph bore,
And vowed he ne'er would act Villerius° more."
60 Here stopped the good old sire, and wept for joy
In silent raptures of the hopeful boy.
All arguments, but most his plays, persuade,
That for anointed dullness he was made.
    Close to the walls which fair Augusta° bind
(The fair Augusta much to fears inclined),
An ancient fabric raised t' inform the sight,
There stood of yore, and Barbican° it hight:
A watchtower once; but now, so fate ordains,
Of all the pile an empty name remains.
70 From its old ruins brothel-houses rise,
Scenes of lewd loves, and of polluted joys,
Where their vast courts the mother-strumpets keep,
And, undisturbed by watch, in silence sleep.
Near these a Nursery° erects its head,
Where queens are formed, and future heroes bred;
Where unfledged actors learn to laugh and cry,
Where infant punks° their tender voices try,
And little Maximins° the gods defy.
Great Fletcher° never treads in buskins here,
80 Nor greater Jonson° dares in socks° appear;
But gentle Simkin° just reception finds
Amidst this monument of vanished minds:
Pure clinches° the suburbian Muse affords,
And Panton° waging harmless war with words.
Here Flecknoe, as a place to fame well known,
Ambitiously designed his Sh——'s throne;
For ancient Dekker° prophesied long since,
That in this pile° should reign a mighty prince,
Born for a scourge of wit, and flail of sense;
90 To whom true dullness should some *Psyches* owe,
But worlds of *Misers* from his pen should flow;
Humorists and hypocrites it should produce,
Whole Raymond families, and tribes of Bruce.°
    Now Empress Fame had published the renown
Of Sh——'s coronation through the town.
Roused by report of Fame, the nations meet,
From near Bunhill, and distant Watling Street.°
No Persian carpets spread th' imperial way,
But scattered limbs of mangled poets lay;
100 From dusty shops neglected authors come;

Martyrs of pies, and relics of the bum.°
Much Heywood, Shirley, Ogleby° there lay,
But loads of Sh—— almost choked the way.
Bilked stationers,° for yeomen stood prepared,
And Herringman° was captain of the guard.
The hoary prince in majesty appeared,
High on a throne of his own labors reared.
At his right hand our young Ascanius° sate,
Rome's other hope, and pillar of the State.
His brows thick fogs, instead of glories, grace,   110
And lambent dullness played around his face.
As Hannibal° did to the altars come,
Sworn by his sire a mortal foe to Rome;
So Sh—— swore, nor should his vow be vain,
That he till death true dullness would maintain;
And, in his father's right, and realm's defense,
Ne'er to have peace with wit, nor truce with sense.
The king himself the sacred unction made,
As king by office, and as priest by trade.
In his sinister° hand, instead of ball,   120
He placed a mighty mug of potent ale;
Love's Kingdom° to his right he did convey,
At once his scepter, and his rule of sway;
Whose righteous lore the prince had practiced young,
And from whose loins recorded *Psyche*° sprung.
His temples, last, with poppies were o'erspread,
That nodding seemed to consecrate his head.
Just at that point of time, if fame not lie,
On his left hand twelve reverend owls did fly.
So Romulus, 'tis sung, by Tiber's brook,°   130
Presage of sway from twice six vultures took.
Th' admiring throng loud acclamations make,
And omens of his future empire take.
The sire then shook the honors of his head,
And from his brows damps of oblivion shed
Full on the filial dullness: long he stood,
Repelling from his breast, the raging god;
At length burst out in this prophetic mood:
    "Heavens bless my son, from Ireland let him reign
To far Barbadoes on the western main;   140
Of his dominion may no end be known,
And greater than his father's be his throne;
Beyond *Love's Kingdom* let him stretch his pen!"
He paused, and all the people cried, "Amen."
Then thus continued he: "My son, advance
Still in new impudence, new ignorance.
Success let others teach, learn thou from me

57 **Singleton**, a contemporary opera singer   59 **Villerius**, a general in *The Siege of Rhodes*, an opera by Sir William Davenant (1606–1668)   64 **Augusta**, a Roman name for London. Charles II was sometimes called Caesar Augustus. The next line refers to the fact that London had been in fear of "popish" (Catholic) plots   67 **Barbican**, literally, an outer fortification. In London it was the name given to the site of an old watchtower from which a view could be had not only of the city but of the adjacent counties   74 **Nursery**, a theater built in 1664 to train young actors   77 **infant punks**, child prostitutes. Restoration slang sometimes referred to actors as punks   78 **Maximins**. Maximin was a bombastic hero in Dryden's early play *Tyrannic Love* (1669)   79 **Fletcher**, John Fletcher (1579–1625), the noted Elizabethan dramatist   80 **Jonson**, Ben Jonson, famous for his comedies of "humors"   **socks**, low shoes or sandals worn by actors of comedy in ancient Greece and Rome (refers here to the Jonson comedies)   81 **Simkin**, a contemporary stage clown   83 **clinches**, puns   84 **Panton**, Thomas Panton (d. 1685), a noted contemporary wit and punster   87 **Dekker**, Thomas Dekker (1570?–1641?), well-known Elizabethan dramatist, pamphleteer, and poet   88 **pile**, building   91 **Misers . . . Bruce.** *The Miser* (1671) and *The Humorist* (1672) were plays by Shadwell. Raymond is a character in *The Humorist*; Bruce, in Shadwell's *The Virtuoso*   97 **Bunhill . . . Watling Street.** Bunhill and Watling Street are close together in Old London. Dryden's implication here is that Shadwell's fame was limited to this very small area; his use of "distant" is therefore pure mockery

101 **pies . . . bum.** Leaves from discarded books were placed under pies and cakes by bakers; they were also used for toilet paper   102 **Ogleby**, John Ogleby (1600–1676), an inferior poet and translator of Homer, Vergil, and Aesop   104 **Bilked stationers**, defrauded or cheated booksellers (there was no sale of the works of poor poets like Shadwell)   105 **Herringman**, Dryden's London publisher   108 **Ascanius**, Shadwell. In Vergil's *Aeneid*, Ascanius, the son and heir of Aeneas, is called "the other hope of great Rome"   112 **Hannibal**, a great Carthaginian general (247–183 B.C.) who at the age of nine is said to have been compelled by his father to swear eternal hatred for Rome   120 **sinister**, left. At their coronation, kings held a ball in their left hand as a symbol of authority over the whole world   122 **Love's Kingdom**, a pastoral tragicomedy by Flecknoe   125 **Psyche.** The opera by Shadwell was mentioned above (l. 54); hence the use of the word *recorded*, "reported"   130 **Romulus . . . brook.** Romulus was the legendary founder and first king of Rome. With his twin brother Remus, he was thrown into the Tiber in infancy, but was rescued and suckled by a wolf. According to the ancient story, the brothers could not agree on the exact place where Rome was to be built. They decided to resort to augury and each took his position on his chosen hill. Six vultures flew past Remus, but when Romulus reported that twelve had flown past him, his hill was declared approved

Pangs without birth, and fruitless industry.
Let *Virtuosos*° in five years be writ;
150 Yet not one thought accuse thy toil of wit.°
Let gentle George° in triumph tread the stage,
Make Dorimant betray, and Loveit rage;
Let Cully, Cockwood, Fopling, charm the pit,
And in their folly show the writer's wit.
Yet still thy fools shall stand in thy defense,
And justify their author's want of sense.
Let 'em be all by thy own model made
Of dullness, and desire no foreign aid;
That they to future ages may be known,
160 Not copies drawn, but issue of thy own.
Nay, let thy men of wit too be the same,
All full of thee, and differing but in name.
But let no alien S—dl—y° interpose,
To lard with wit thy hungry *Epsom* prose.
And when false flowers of rhetoric thou wouldst cull,
Trust nature, do not labor to be dull;
But write thy best, and top; and, in each line,
Sir Formal's° oratory will be thine:
Sir Formal, though unsought, attends thy quill,
170 And does thy northern dedications° fill.
Nor let false friends seduce thy mind to fame,
By arrogating Jonson's hostile name.°
Let father Flecknoe fire thy mind with praise,
And uncle Ogleby thy envy raise.
Thou art my blood, where Jonson has no part:
What share have we in nature, or in art?
Where did his wit on learning fix a brand,
And rail at arts he did not understand?
Where made he love in Prince Nicander's° vein,
180 Or swept the dust in *Psyche's* humble strain?
Where sold he bargains, 'whip-stitch,° kiss my arse,'
Promised a play and dwindled to a farce?
When did his Muse from Fletcher scenes purloin,
As thou whole Eth'rege dost transfuse to thine?
But so transfused as oil on water's flow,
His always floats above, thine sinks below.
This is thy province, this thy wondrous way,
New humors to invent for each new play:
This is that boasted bias of thy mind,
190 By which one way, to dullness, 'tis inclined;
Which makes thy writings lean on one side still,
And, in all changes, that way bends thy will.
Nor let thy mountain-belly make pretense
Of likeness; thine's a tympany° of sense.

A tun of man in thy large bulk is writ,
But sure thou'rt but a kilderkin° of wit.
Like mine, thy gentle numbers feebly creep;
Thy tragic Muse gives smiles, thy comic sleep.
With whate'er gall thou sett'st thyself to write,
Thy inoffensive satires never bite.   200
In thy felonious heart though venom lies,
It does but touch thy Irish pen, and dies.
Thy genius calls thee not to purchase fame
In keen iambics, but mild anagram.
Leave writing plays, and choose for thy command
Some peaceful province in acrostic land.
There thou may'st wings display and altars raise,°
And torture one poor word ten thousand ways.
Or, if thou wouldst thy diff'rent talents suit,
Set thy own songs, and sing them to thy lute.''   210
    He said: but his last words were scarcely heard;
For Bruce and Longvil had a trap° prepared,
And down they sent the yet declaiming bard.
Sinking he left his drugget robe behind,
Borne Upwards by a subterranean wind.
The mantel fell to the young prophet's part,
With double portion of his father's art.
(1682)

TO THE MEMORY OF MR. OLDHAM°

Farewell, too little, and too lately known,
Whom I began to think and call my own:
For sure our souls were near allied, and thine
Cast in the same poetic mould with mine.
One common note on either lyre did strike,
And knaves and fools we both abhorred alike.
To the same goal did both our studies drive:
The last set out the soonest did arrive.
Thus Nisus° fell upon the slippery place,
While his young friend performed and won the race. 10
O early ripe! to thy abundant store
What could avancing age have added more?
It might (what nature never gives the young)
Have taught the numbers of thy native tongue.
But satire needs not those, and wit will shine
Through the harsh cadence of a rugged line:
A noble error, and but seldom made,
When poets are by too much force betrayed
Thy generous fruits, though gathered ere their prime,
Still showed a quickness; and maturing time   20
But mellows what we write to the dull sweets of
    rhyme.
Once more, hail and farewell; farewell, thou young,
But ah too short, Marcellus of our tongue;°

149 **Virtuosos**, a reference to Shadwell's *Virtuoso*, a play on which Shadwell was engaged for five years   150 **wit**, intelligence   151 **gentle George**, George Etherege (1635?–1691), a well-known comic dramatist of the Restoration. His three plays, *The Comical Revenge, or Love in a Tub* (1664); *She Would If She Could* (1668); and *The Man of Mode, or Sir Fopling Flutter* (1676) are characteristic Restoration comedies in their sparkling wit, satirical outlook, and bawdy tendencies. Dorimant, Loveit, Cully, etc. (ll. 152–153), are characters from his plays   163 **S—dl—y**, Sir Charles Sedley (1635?–1691), a court poet and wit who had written the prologue to Shadwell's *Epsom Wells* and probably had helped Shadwell in other plays   168 **Sir Formal**, Sir Formal Trifle, a character in Shadwell's *Virtuoso*, called "the orator, a florid coxcomb"   170 **northern dedications**, an allusion to Shadwell's dedication of several books to the Duke of Newcastle and members of his family (Newcastle is in northern England)   172 **Jonson's . . . name**. Shadwell had frequently given lavish praise to Ben Jonson as a writer of comedies and regarded himself as Jonson's successor. Dryden's rather mild praise of Jonson had irritated Shadwell   179 **Nicander**, a character in Shadwell's *Psyche*   181 **whip-stitch**, a contemptuous term for a tailor. Phrases like these are used by Sir Samuel Hearty in Shadwell's *Virtuoso*   194 **tympany**, inflation, conceit

196 **kilderkin**, a small cask   207 **wings . . . raise**, an allusion to the fanciful verse forms of the metaphysical poets   212 **Bruce . . . trap**. In Shadwell's *Virtuoso* these characters cause Sir Formal Trifle to disappear through a trap door   **Mr. Oldham**. John Oldham was a Restoration satirist, who died at the age of thirty, in 1683   9 **Nisus**. Nisus was leading the race when he slipped and fell. *Aeneid* V, 315–39   23 **Marcellus of our tongue**. Marcellus, whom Augustus Caesar wished to succeed him, died young, cutting short a promising career

Thy brows with ivy, and with laurels bound;
But fate and gloomy night encompass thee around.
(1684)

TO THE PIOUS MEMORY
OF THE ACCOMPLISHED YOUNG LADY,
MRS. ANNE KILLIGREW°

EXCELLENT IN THE TWO SISTER-ARTS
OF POESY AND PAINTING, AN ODE

I

Thou youngest virgin-daughter of the skies,
Made in the last promotion of the blest;
Whose palms,° new plucked from paradise,
In spreading branches more sublimely rise,
Rich with immortal green above the rest:
Whether, adopted to some neighbouring star,
    Or, in procession fixed and regular,
    Moved with the heavens' majestic pace;
10 Or, called to more superior bliss,
Thou treadest, with seraphims, the vast abyss:
Whatever happy region is thy place,
Cease thy celestial song a little space;
(Thou wilt have time enough for hymns divine,
    Since heaven's eternal year is thine.)
Here then a mortal Muse thy praise rehearse,
        In no ignoble verse;
But such as thy own voice did practise here,
When thy first fruits of poesy were given,
20 To make thyself a welcome inmate there;
        While yet a young probationer,
        And candidate of heaven.

II

If by traduction° came thy mind,
    Our wonder is the less to find
A soul so charming from a stock so good;
Thy father was transfused into thy blood:
So wert thou born into the tuneful strain,
(An early, rich, and inexhausted vein.)
    But if thy preexisting soul
30 Was formed, at first, with myriads more,
It did through all the mighty poets roll
    Who Greek or Latin laurels wore
And was that Sappho° last, which once it was before.
    If so, then cease thy flight, O heaven-born mind!
    Thou hast no dross to purge from thy rich ore;
    Nor can thy soul a fairer mansion find,

Than was the beauteous frame she left behind:
Return, to fill or mend the choir of thy celestial kind.

III

May we presume to say that at thy birth
New joy was sprung in heaven, as well as here on   40
        earth?
For sure the milder planets did combine
On thy auspicious horoscope to shine,
And even the most malicious were in trine.°
Thy brother-angels at thy birth
    Strung each his lyre and tuned it high,
    That all the people of the sky
Might know a poetess was born on earth.
    And then, if ever, mortal ears
    Had heard the music of the spheres!
And if no clustering swarm of bees   50
On thy sweet mouth distilled their golden dew,
    'Twas that such vulgar° miracles
    Heaven had no leisure to renew:
For all the blest fraternity of love
Solemnized there thy birth and kept thy holiday above.

IV

O gracious God! how far have we
Profaned thy heavenly gift of poesy!
Made prostitute and profligate the Muse,
Debased to each obscene and impious use,
Whose harmony was first ordained above   60
For tongues of angels, and for hymns of love!
O wretched we! why were we hurried down
    This lubric° and adulterate age,
(Nay, added fat pollutions of our own,)
    To increase the steaming ordures of the stage?
What can we say to excuse our *second fall?*
Let this thy *vestal,* Heaven, atone for all:
Her Arethusian stream° remains unsoiled,
Unmixed with foreign filth, and undefiled;
Her wit was more than man, her innocence a child!   70

V

Art she had none, yet wanted none;
    For nature did that want supply:
    So rich in treasures of her own,
    She might our boasted stores defy:
Such noble vigour did her verse adorn
That it seemed borrowed, where 'twas only born.
Her morals too were in her bosom bred,
    By great examples daily fed,
What in the best of books, her father's life, she read.
And to be read herself she need not fear;   80
Each test, and every light, her Muse will bear,
Though Epictetus with his lamp° were there.
Even love (for love sometimes her Muse expressed)

Anne Killigrew. She died at the age of twenty-five, in 1685, a few months before
her first and only volume of poetry appeared. Dryden's *Ode* appeared first in that
volume   3 **palms,** given to a victor   23 **traduction,** conveyance from one place
or body to another. Dryden refers here to Anne's father's writings. Her uncles
wrote also   33 **Sappho,** Greek poetess of the seventh century B.C.

43 **in trine,** two planets are in trine when they are one-third of a zodiac, i.e., 120
degrees, apart   52 **vulgar,** common. Tradition says that such a miracle happened
to infant Pindar   63 **lubric,** shifty, wanton   68 **her Arethusian stream,** inspira-
tional for pastoral poetry especially. See *Lycidas,* l. 85   82 **Epictetus with his
lamp,** an embodiment of the standards of Stoic virtue

Was but a lambent° flame which played about her
    breast,
Light as the vapours of a morning dream:
So cold herself, whilst she such warmth expressed,
'Twas Cupid bathing in Diana's stream.

VI

Born to the spacious empire of the Nine,
One would have thought she should have been content
90 To manage well that mighty government;
But what can young ambitious souls confine?
    To the next realm she stretched her sway,
    For *painture* near adjoining lay,
    A plenteous province, and alluring prey.
    A *chamber of dependences*° was framed,
    (As conquerors will never want pretence,
      When armed, to justify the offence,)
And the whole fief in right of poetry she claimed.
The country open lay without defence;
100 For poets frequent inroads there had made,
    And perfectly could represent
    The shape, the face, with every lineament;
    And all the large demains which the *Dumb Sister*°
      swayed
      All bowed beneath her government;
      Received in triumph wheresoe'er she went.
Her pencil drew whate'er her soul designed,
And oft the happy draught surpassed the image in her
    mind.
    The sylvan scenes of herds and flocks,
    And fruitful plains and barren rocks,
110 Of shallow brooks that flowed so clear
    The bottom did the top appear;
    Of deeper too and ampler floods,
    Which, as in mirrors, showed the woods;
    Of lofty trees, with sacred shades,
    And perspectives of pleasant glades,
    Where nymphs of brightest form appear,
    And shaggy satyrs standing near,
    Which them at once admire and fear:
    The ruins too of some majestic piece,
120 Boasting the power of ancient Rome, or Greece,
    Whose statues, friezes, columns broken lie,
    And, though defaced, the wonder of the eye:
    What nature, art, bold fiction e'er durst frame,
    Her forming hand gave feature to the name.
So strange a concourse ne'er was seen before,
But when the peopled ark the whole creation bore.

VII

The scene then changed: with bold erected look
Our martial king° the sight with reverence strook;
For, not content to express his outward part,

Her hand called out the image of his heart   130
His warlike mind, his soul devoid of fear,
His high-designing thoughts were figured there,
As when, by magic, ghosts are made appear.
    Our phoenix queen° was portrayed too so bright,
Beauty alone could beauty take so right:
Her dress, her shape, her matchless grace,
Were all observed, as well as heavenly face.
With such a peerless majesty she stands,
As in that day she took the crown from sacred
    hands;
Before a train of heroines was seen,   140
In beauty foremost, as in rank the queen.
Thus nothing to her genius was denied,
    But like a ball of fire, the further thrown
    Still with a greater blaze she shone,
And her bright soul broke out on every side.
What next she had designed, Heaven only knows;
To such immoderate growth her conquest rose
That fate alone its progress could oppose.

VIII

Now all those charms, that blooming grace,
The well-proportioned shape and beauteous face, 150
Shall never more be seen by mortal eyes:
In earth the much-lamented virgin lies!
    Not wit nor piety could fate prevent;
    Nor was the cruel destiny content
    To finish all the murder at a blow,
    To sweep at once her life and beauty too;
But, like a hardened felon, took a pride
    To work more mischievously slow,
And plundered first, and then destroyed.°
O double sacrilege on things divine,   160
To rob the relic, and deface the shrine!
    But thus Orinda° died:
Heaven, by the same disease, did both translate;
As equal were their souls, so equal was their fate.

IX

Meantime her warlike brother on the seas
    His waving streamers to the winds displays,
And vows for his return, with vain devotion, pays.
    Ah, generous youth, that wish forbear,
    The winds too soon will waft thee here!
    Slack all thy sails, and fear to come,   170
Alas, thou knowst not, thou art wrecked at home!
No more shalt thou behold thy sister's face,
Thou hast already had her last embrace.
But look aloft, and if thou kennst from far
Among the Pleiads° a new kindled star;
If any sparkles than the rest more bright,
'Tis she that shines in that propitious light.

---

84 **lambent**, shining with a soft clear light and without fierce heat 95 **a chamber of dependences.** The implicit metaphor here refers to rulers and dominions. A "chamber of dependence" is a legal agreement which sets up the right of lords to hold certain estates. She is seen as a ruler annexing the nearby art/ province of painting 103 **the Dumb Sister,** the muse of painting. Dryden describes some subjects of Anne Killigrew's paintings in the following lines 128 **King,** James II

134 **Our phoenix queen,** as special in her beauty as is the phoenix, a mythical bird of gorgeous plumage, fabled to be the only one of its kind 159 **plundered . . . destroyed.** Anne Killigrew died, disfigured first, from smallpox 152 **Orinda,** Katharine Philips (1631–64) a poet who had also died of smallpox 175 **Pleiads,** virgin companions of Artemis, metamorphosed into a group of stars

X

When in mid-air the golden trump shall sound,
  To raise the nations under ground;
180   When in the Valley of Jehoshaphat°
The judging God shall close the book of fate,
  And there the last assizes° keep
  For those who wake and those who sleep;
  When rattling bones together fly
  From the four corners of the sky;
When sinews o'er the skeletons are spread,
Those clothed with flesh, and life inspires the dead;
The sacred poets first shall hear the sound,
And foremost from the tomb shall bound,
190 For they are covered with the lightest ground;
And straight, with inborn vigour, on the wing,
Like mounting larks, to the new morning sing.
There thou, sweet saint, before the choir shalt go,
As harbinger of heaven, the way to show,
The way which thou so well hast learned below.
(1685)

A SONG FOR ST. CECILIA'S DAY°

From harmony, from heavenly harmony,
  This universal frame began:
  When Nature underneath a heap
    Of jarring atoms lay,
  And could not heave her head,
The tuneful voice was heard from high:
  "Arise, ye more than dead."

Then cold and hot and moist and dry°
  In order to their stations leap,
10   And Music's power obey.
From harmony, from heavenly harmony,
  This universal frame began:
    From harmony to harmony
Through all the compass of the notes it ran,
The diapason° closing full in Man.

What passion cannot Music raise and quell!
  When Jubal° struck the chorded shell,
  His listening brethren stood around,
  And wondering, on their faces fell
20 To worship that celestial sound.

Less than a god they thought there could not dwell
  Within the hollow of that shell
  That spoke so sweetly and so well.
What passion cannot Music raise and quell!

  The trumpet's loud clangor
    Excites us to arms
  With shrill notes of anger
    And mortal alarms.
  The double, double, double beat
    Of the thundering drum   30
    Cries: "Hark! the foes come;
Charge, charge, 'tis too late to retreat!"

  The soft complaining flute
    In dying notes discovers
    The woes of hopeless lovers,
Whose dirge is whispered by the warbling lute.
    Sharp violins proclaim
Their jealous pangs and desperation,
Fury, frantic indignation,
Depth of pains, and height of passion,   40
    For the fair, disdainful dame.

But oh! what art can teach,
What human voice can reach
    The sacred organ's praise?
  Notes inspiring holy love,
Notes that wing their heavenly ways
  To mend the choirs above.
Orpheus could lead the savage race;°
And trees unrooted left their place,
    Sequacious of° the lyre;   50
But bright Cecilia raised the wonder higher:
When to her organ vocal breath was given,
An angel heard, and straight appeared,
    Mistaking earth for heaven.

GRAND CHORUS

As from the power of sacred lays
  The spheres began to move,°
And sung the great Creator's praise
  To all the blessed above;
So when the last and dreadful hour
This crumbling pageant shall devour,   60
The trumpet shall be heard on high,
The dead shall live, the living die,
And Music shall untune the sky.
(1687)

---

180 **Valley of Jehoshaphat,** site of the Last Judgment   182 **assizes,** here meaning the Last Judgment   **A Song for St. Cecilia's Day.** St. Cecilia, a Christian martyr of the third century, was the patron saint of music. On St. Cecilia's Day (November 22) an original ode set to music was customarily presented at an annual festival held by a London music society, Dryden's poem was written for this purpose. It was originally set to music by the Italian composer G. B. Draghi, but it is now associated entirely with Handel's later (1739) score   8 **cold . . . dry,** the qualities of the four elements, according to ancient and medieval natural philosophy and astrology   15 **diapason,** the entire compass of musical notes   17 **Jubal,** mentioned in *Genesis*, 4:21 as the "father of all such as handle the harp and organ"

48 **Orpheus . . . race.** In Greek mythology Orpheus was a Thracian poet and musician whose lyre could charm beasts and move trees and rocks   50 **Sequacious of,** following after   56 **spheres . . . move.** The ancients believed that the stars made music as they revolved in their spheres

ALEXANDER'S FEAST:
OR, THE POWER OF MUSIC°

AN ODE IN HONOR
OF ST. CECILIA'S DAY

1

'T was at the royal feast, for Persia° won
    By Philip's warlike son:
      Aloft in awful state
      The godlike hero sate
      On his imperial throne:
His valiant peers were placed around;
Their brows with roses and with myrtles bound:
    (So should desert in arms be crowned.)
The lovely Thäis,° by his side,
10 Sate like a blooming Eastern bride
In flower of youth and beauty's pride.
      Happy, happy, happy pair!
        None but the brave,
        None but the brave,
    None but the brave deserves the fair.

CHORUS

      Happy, happy, happy pair!
        None but the brave,
        None but the brave,
    None but the brave deserves the fair.

2

20 Timotheus,° placed on high
      Amid the tuneful choir,
With flying fingers touched the lyre:
The trembling notes ascend the sky,
    And heavenly joys inspire.
      The song began from Jove,
      Who left his blissful seats above,
    (Such is the power of mighty love.)
    A dragon's fiery form° belied the god:
    Sublime on radiant spires° he rode,
30 When he to fair Olympia pressed;
    And while he sought her snowy breast:
Then, round her slender waist he curled,
And stamped an image of himself, a sovereign of the
        world.
    The listening crowd admire the lofty sound;
    "A present deity," they shout around;

"A present deity," the vaulted roofs rebound:
      With ravished ears
      The monarch hears,
      Assumes the god,
      Affects to nod,   40
And seems to shake the spheres.

CHORUS

      With ravished ears
      The monarch hears,
      Assumes the god,
      Affects to nod,
And seems to shake the spheres.

3

The praise of Bacchus° then the sweet musician sung,
    Of Bacchus ever fair and ever young:
      The jolly god in triumph comes;
      Sound the trumpets; beat the drums;   50
        Flushed with a purple grace
        He shows his honest face:
Now give the hautboys° breath; he comes, he comes.
    Bacchus; ever fair and young,
      Drinking joys did first ordain;
    Bacchus' blessings are a treasure,
    Drinking is the soldier's pleasure;
      Rich the treasure,
      Sweet the pleasure,
    Sweet is pleasure after pain.   60

CHORUS

    Bacchus' blessings are a treasure,
    Drinking is the soldier's pleasure;
      Rich the treasure,
      Sweet the pleasure,
    Sweet is pleasure after pain.

4

Soothed with the sound, the king grew vain;
    Fought all his battles o'er again;
And thrice he routed all his foes; and thrice he slew the
        slain.
    The master saw the madness rise;
    His glowing cheeks, his ardent eyes;   70
And, while he° heaven and earth defied,
Changed his hand, and checked his pride°
      He chose a mournful Muse,
      Soft pity to infuse:
He sung Darius° great and good,
    By too severe a fate,
Fallen, fallen, fallen, fallen,

Alexander's Feast. This poem is a companion ode to *A Song for St. Cecilia's Day*. The "feast" is a celebration of Alexander's victory over Darius III, emperor of Persia; the poem is a celebration of the power of music over the passions. Again, the ode is associated with Handel's (1736) score rather than with that of the original composer, Jeremiah Clarke. Dryden spoke of this ode as the best of his poetry
1 **Persia, etc.** The feast celebrates the conquest of Persia by Alexander the Great (356–323 B.C.), son of Philip of Macedon 9 **Thäis,** an Athenian courtesan who accompanied Alexander into Asia and who was thought to have incited him to fire the Persian palaces at Persepolis 20 **Timotheus,** Alexander's favorite musician 28 **dragon's fiery form.** Jove supposedly assumed the form of a dragon, in which he wooed Olympias, the mother of Alexander 29 **radiant spires,** coils

47 **Bacchus,** the god of wine in classical mythology 53 **hautboys,** oboes 71 **he,** Alexander 72 **his hand . . . his pride.** "His hand" is the hand of Timotheus, "his pride" that of Alexander 75 **Darius,** Darius III, emperor of Persia from 336 B.C. until his defeat by Alexander and death in 331 B.C.

Fallen from his high estate,
And weltering in his blood;
80   Deserted, at his utmost need,
By those his former bounty fed;
On the bare earth exposed he lies,
With not a friend to close his eyes.
With downcast looks the joyless victor sate,
    Revolving in his altered soul
        The various turns of chance below;
And, now and then, a sigh he stole;
And tears began to flow.

CHORUS

    Revolving in his altered soul
90   The various turns of chance below;
And, now and then, a sigh he stole;
And tears began to flow.

5

The mighty master smiled to see
That love was in the next degree:
'T was but a kindred sound to move,
For pity melts the mind to love.
    Softly sweet, in Lydian measures,°
    Soon he soothed his soul to pleasures.
"War," he sung, "is toil and trouble;
100   Honor, but an empty bubble;
    Never ending, still beginning,
Fighting still, and still destroying:
    If the world be worth thy winning,
    Think, O think it worth enjoying;
    Lovely Thaïs sits beside thee,
    Take the good the gods provide thee."
The many rend the skies with loud applause;
So Love was crowned, but Music won the cause.
    The prince, unable to conceal his pain,
110   Gazed on the fair
        Who caused his care,
    And sighed and looked, sighed and looked,
Sighed and looked, and sighed again:
At length, with love and wine at once oppressed,
The vanquished victor sunk upon her breast.

CHORUS

    The prince, unable to conceal his pain,
        Gazed on the fair
        Who caused his care,
    And sighed and looked, sighed and looked,
120   Sighed and looked, and sighed again:
At length, with love and wine at once oppressed,
The vanquished victor sunk upon her breast.

97 **Lydian measures,** sweet and sensuous measures. The ancient district of Lydia in Asia Minor was noted for its wealth and luxury

6

Now strike the golden lyre again:
A louder yet, and yet a louder strain.
Break his bands of sleep asunder,
And rouse him, like a rattling peal of thunder.
    Hark, hark, the horrid sound
        Has raised up his head:
        As awaked from the dead,
    And amazed, he stares around.   130
"Revenge, revenge!" Timotheus cries,
    "See the Furies° arise!
    See the snakes that they rear,
    How they hiss in their hair,
And the sparkles that flash from their eyes!
    Behold a ghastly band,
    Each a torch in his hand!
Those are Grecian ghosts, that in battle were slain,
        And unburied remain
        Inglorious on the plain: 140
        Give the vengeance due
        To the valiant crew.
Behold how they toss their torches on high,
    How they point to the Persian abodes,
And glittering temples of their hostile gods!"
The princes applaud, with a furious joy;
And the king seized a flambeau° with zeal to destroy;
        Thaïs led the way,
        To light him to his prey,
And, like another Helen,° fired another Troy.   150

CHORUS

And the king seized a flambeau with zeal to destroy;
        Thaïs led the way,
        To light him to his prey,
And, like another Helen, fired another Troy.

7

        Thus, long ago,
    Ere heaving bellows learned to blow,
        While organs yet were mute;
        Timotheus, to his breathing flute,
        And sounding lyre,
Could swell the soul to rage, or kindle soft desire.   160
    At last, divine Cecilia came,
    Inventress of the vocal frame;°
The sweet enthusiast,° from her sacred store,
    Enlarged the former narrow bounds,
    And added length to solemn sounds,
With nature's mother wit, and arts unknown before.

132 **Furies,** the ancient classical goddesses of vengeance, characterized by hideous features, disgusting habits, and fearful snaky hair   147 **flambeau,** a flaming torch   150 **Helen,** wife of Menelaus, King of Sparta, carried off on account of her beauty by Paris, son of Priam, King of Troy   162 **vocal frame,** the organ, supposedly invented by St. Cecilia, who, because of her virtue and piety, was said to have been visited by an angel (l. 170). The form of circumlocution seen here in "vocal frame" is characteristic of neoclassical verse, not only in the Latinity of the words, but in the combination of a single adjective ("epithet") with a noun of vague meaning. This combination is an "elegant" eighteenth-century way of saying a very plain and concrete word   163 **enthusiast,** in the literal sense of "inspired by a god." Dryden probably did not intend the usual sinister connotation of "unbalanced," "insane," etc.

Let old Timotheus yield the prize,
 Or both divide the crown;
He raised a mortal to the skies;
170 She drew an angel down.

GRAND CHORUS

 At last, divine Cecilia came,
 Inventress of the vocal frame;
The sweet enthusiast, from her sacred store,
 Enlarged the former narrow bounds,
 And added length to solemn sounds,
With nature's mother wit, and arts unknown before.
 Let old Timotheus yield the prize,
  Or both divide the crown;
 He raised a mortal to the skies;
180   She drew an angel down.
 (1697)

from AN ACCOUNT OF THE ENSUING POEM . . . PREFIXED TO ANNUS MIRABILIS°

. . . The composition of all poems is, or *ought to be, of wit, and wit in the poet, or wit writing* (if you will give me leave to use a school-distinction) is *no other than the faculty of imagination in the writer which, like a nimble spaniel, beats over and ranges through the field of memory, till it springs the quarry it hunted after;* or, without metaphor, which searches over all the memory for the species or ideas of those things which it designs to represent. Wit written is that which
10 is well defined, the happy result of thought, or product of imagination. But to proceed from wit, in the general notion of it, to the proper wit of an heroic or historical poem, I judge it chiefly to consist in the delightful imaging of persons, actions, passions, or things. 'Tis not the jerk or sting of an epigram, nor the seeming contradiction of a poor antithesis (the delight of an ill-judging audience in a play of rhyme), nor the jingle of a more poor paronomasia;° neither is it so much the morality of a grave sentence affected by Lucan,° but
20 more sparingly used by Virgil;° but it is some lively and apt description, dressed in such colours of speech that it sets before your eyes the absent object as perfectly and more delightfully than nature. So then, the first happiness of the poet's imagination is properly invention, or finding of the thought; the second is fancy, or the variation, driving, or moulding of that thought, as the judgment represents it proper to the subject; the third is elocution, or the art of clothing and adorning that thought so found and varied, in apt, significant,

and sounding words: the quickness of the imagination 30 is seen in the invention, the fertility in the fancy, and the accuracy in the expression. . . .
(1666)

from AN ESSAY OF DRAMATIC POESY

"I dare boldly affirm these two things of the English drama: First, that we have many plays of ours as regular as any of theirs, and which, besides, have more variety of plot and characters; and secondly, that in most of the irregular plays of Shakespeare or Fletcher° (for Ben Jonson's are for the most part regular), there is a more masculine fancy and greater spirit in the writing than there is in any of the French. I could produce, even in Shakespeare's and Fletcher's works, some plays which are almost exactly formed; as *The* 10 *Merry Wives of Windsor,*° and *The Scornful Lady:*° but because (generally speaking) Shakespeare, who writ first, did not perfectly observe the laws of comedy, and Fletcher, who came nearer to perfection, yet through carelessness made many faults, I will take the pattern of a perfect play from Ben Jonson, who was a careful and learned observer of the dramatic laws, and from all his comedies I shall select *The Silent Woman,* of which I will make a short examen, according to those rules which the French observe." 20

As Neander was beginning to examine *The Silent Woman,* Eugenius, earnestly regarding him: "I beseech you, Neander," said he, "gratify the company, and me in particular, so far, as before you speak of the play, to give us a character of the author; and tell us frankly your opinion, whether you do not think all writers, both French and English, ought to give place to him."

"I fear," replied Neander, "that in obeying your commands I shall draw some envy on myself. Besides, 30 in performing them, it will be first necessary to speak somewhat of Shakespeare and Fletcher, his rivals in poesy; and one of them, in my opinion, at least his equal, perhaps his superior.

"To begin, then, with Shakespeare. He was the man who of all modern, and perhaps ancient poets, had the largest and most comprehensive soul. All the images of nature were still present to him, and he drew them, not laboriously, but luckily; when he describes anything, you more than see it, you feel it too. Those who accuse 40 him to have wanted learning, give him the greater commendation: he was naturally learned; he needed not the spectacles of books to read nature; he looked inwards, and found her there. I cannot say he is everywhere alike; were he so, I should do him injury to compare him with the greatest of mankind. He is many times flat, insipid, his comic wit degenerating into

---

Annus Mirabilis. Dryden's poem is subtitled "The Year of Wonders, 1666." The wonders are naval victories over the Dutch, the plague, and the Fire of London 18 **paronomasia,** a pun, playing on words which sound alike 19 **Lucan,** first-century A.D. Latin writer, author of *Pharsalia* 20 **Virgil,** first-century B.C. Latin author of *The Aeneid*

Of Dramatic Poesy 5 **Fletcher,** John Fletcher, noted Elizabethan dramatist 11 **The Merry Wives of Windsor,** a well-known comedy by Shakespeare **The Scornful Lady,** a satirical play (1616) by Beaumont and Fletcher

clenches,° his serious swelling into bombast. But he is always great, when some great occasion is presented to him; no man can say he ever had a fit subject for his wit, and did not then raise himself as high above the rest of poets,

Quantum lenta solent inter viburna cupressi.°

The consideration of this made Mr. Hales of Eton° say that there was no subject of which any poet ever writ, but he would produce it much better done in Shakespeare; and however others are now generally preferred before him, yet the age wherein he lived, which had contemporaries with him Fletcher and Jonson, never equaled them to him in their esteem: and in the last king's° court, when Ben's reputation was at highest, Sir John Suckling, and with him the greater part of the courtiers, set our Shakespeare far above him. . . .

"As for Jonson, to whose character I am now arrived, if we look upon him while he was himself (for his last plays were but his dotages), I think him the most learned and judicious writer which any theater ever had. He was a most severe judge of himself, as well as others. One cannot say he wanted wit, but rather that he was frugal of it. In his words you find little to retrench or alter. Wit, and language, and humor also in some measure, we had before him; but something of art was wanting to the drama, till he came. He managed his strength to more advantage than any who preceded him. You seldom find him making love in any of his scenes, or endeavoring to move the passions; his genius was too sullen and saturnine to do it gracefully, especially when he knew he came after those who had performed both to such an height. Humor was his proper sphere; and in that he delighted most to represent mechanic people.° He was deeply conversant in the ancients, both Greek and Latin, and he borrowed boldly from them; there is scarce a poet or historian among the Roman authors of those times, whom he has not translated in *Sejanus* and *Catiline*.° But he has done his robberies so openly, that one may see he fears not to be taxed° by any law. He invades authors like a monarch; and what would be theft in other poets, is only victory in him. With the spoils of these writers he so represents old Rome to us, in its rites, ceremonies, and customs, that if one of their poets had written either of his tragedies, we had seen less of it than in him. If there was any fault in his language, it was, that he weaved it too closely and laboriously, in his comedies especially; perhaps too, he did a little too much Romanize our tongue, leaving the words which he translated almost as much Latin as he found them,

wherein, though he learnedly followed their language, he did not enough comply with the idiom of ours. If I would compare him with Shakespeare, I might acknowledge him the more correct° poet, but Shakespeare the greater wit. Shakespeare was the Homer, or father of our dramatic poets; Jonson was the Virgil, the pattern of elaborate writing; I admire him, but I love Shakespeare. To conclude of him; as he has given us the most correct plays, so in the precepts which he has laid down in his *Discoveries,* we have as many and profitable rules for perfecting the stage, as any wherewith the French can furnish us. . . ."
(1668)

from A DISCOURSE CONCERNING THE ORIGINAL AND PROGRESS OF SATIRE

. . . There are only two reasons for which we may be permitted to write lampoons. . . . The first is revenge, when we have been affronted in the same nature, or have been any ways notoriously abused, and can make ourselves no other reparation. . . . The second reason which may justify a poet when he writes against a particular person: and that is when he is become a public nuisance. All those whom Horace° in his Satires, and Persius° and Juvenal° have mentioned in theirs with a brand of infamy, are wholly such. 'Tis an action of virtue to make examples of vicious men. They may and ought to be upbraided with their crimes and follies: both for their own amendment, if they are not yet incorrigible, and for the terror of others, to hinder them from falling into those enormities which they see are so severely punished in the persons of others. The first reason was only an excuse for revenge; but this second is absolutely of a poet's office to perform. . . .

Let the chastisements of Juvenal be never so necessary for his new kind of satire; let him declaim as wittily and sharply as he pleases: yet still the nicest and most delicate touches of satire consist in fine raillery. . . . How easy is it to call rogue and villain, and that wittily! But how hard to make a man appear a fool, a blockhead, or a knave, without using any of those opprobrious terms! To spare the grossness of the names, and to do the thing yet more severely, is to draw a full face, and to make the nose and cheeks stand out, and yet not to employ any depth of shadowing. This is the mystery of that noble trade, which yet no master can teach to his apprentice: he may give the rules, but the scholar is never the nearer in his practice. Neither is it true that this fineness of raillery is offensive. A witty man is tickled while he is hurt in this manner, and a fool feels it not. The occasion of an offence may possibly be given, but he can-

48 **clenches,** puns 53 **Quantum . . . cupressi,** "as cypresses tower above low-bending shrubs" (Vergil's *First Eclogue*) 54 **Mr. Hales of Eton,** John Hales (1584–1656), critic and theologian, Greek professor at Oxford, and Fellow of Eton College 61 **last king,** Charles I, reigned from 1625 to 1649 81 **mechanic people,** tradespeople, the middle class 85 **Sejanus and Catiline,** classical tragedies by Jonson, produced in 1603 and 1611, respectively 87 **taxed,** accused, found fault with

101 **correct,** following literary rules closely **Progress of Satire** 8–9 **Horace, Persius, Juvenal.** Horace (65–8 B.C.) was a very famous lyric and satiric poet of imperial Rome. Persius and Juvenal were Roman satirists of the first century A.D.

not take it. If it be granted that in effect this way does more mischief; that a man is secretly wounded, and though he be not sensible himself, yet the malicious world will find it for him: yet there is still a vast difference betwixt the slovenly butchering of a man, and the fineness of a stroke that separates the head from the body, and leaves it standing in its place. . . . It must be granted by the favourers of Juvenal that Horace is the more copious and profitable in his instructions of human life. But in my particular opinion, which I set not up for a standard to better judgments, Juvenal is the more delightful author. I am profited by both, I am pleased with both; but I owe more to Horace for my instruction, and more to Juvenal for my pleasure.

That Horace is somewhat the better instructor of the two is proved from hence, that his instructions are more general, Juvenal's more limited. So that, granting that the counsels which they give are equally good for moral use, Horace, who gives the most various advice, and most applicable to all occasions which can occur to us in the course of our lives, as including in his discourse not only all the rules of morality, but also of civil conversation, is undoubtedly to be preferred to him who is more circumscribed in his instructions, makes them to fewer people, and on fewer occasions than the other. . . . Juvenal, excepting only his first satire, is in all the rest confined to the exposing of some particular vice; that he lashes, and there he sticks. His sentences are truly shining and instructive; but they are sprinkled here and there. Horace is teaching us in every line, and is perpetually moral. . . .

I must confess that the delight which Horace gives me is but languishing. Be pleased still to understand that I speak of my own taste only: he may ravish other men; but I am too stupid and insensible to be tickled. Where he barely grins himself and, as Scaliger says, only shews his white teeth, he cannot provoke me to any laughter. His urbanity, that is, his good manners, are to be commended, but his wit is faint; and his salt, if I may dare to say so, almost insipid. Juvenal is of a more vigorous and masculine wit; he gives me as much pleasure as I can bear. . . . Add to this that his thoughts are as just as those of Horace, and much more elevated. His expressions are sonorous and more noble; his verse more numerous, and his words are suitable to his thoughts, sublime and lofty. All these contribute to the pleasure of the reader, and the greater the soul of him who reads, his transports are the greater. Horace is always on the amble, Juvenal on the gallop; but his way is perpetually on carpet ground. He goes with more impetuosity than Horace; but as securely; and the swiftness adds a more lively agitation to the spirits. . . . The meat of Horace is more nourishing; but the cookery of Juvenal more exquisite; so that, granting Horace to be the more general philosopher, we cannot deny that Juvenal was the greater poet, I mean in satire. His thoughts are sharper; his indignation against vice is more vehement; his spirit has more of the commonwealth° genius; he treats tyranny, and all the vices attending it, as they deserve, with the utmost rigour: and consequently, a noble soul is better pleased with a zealous vindicator of Roman liberty than with a temporizing poet, a well-mannered Court slave, and a man who is often afraid of laughing in the right place; who is ever decent, because he is naturally servile. After all, Horace had the disadvantage of the times in which he lived; they were better for the man, but worse for the satirist. 'Tis generally said that those enormous vices which were practised under the reign of Domitian were unknown in the time of Augustus Cæsar; that therefore Juvenal had a larger field than Horace. Little follies were out of doors when oppression was to be scourged instead of avarice: it was no longer time to turn into ridicule the false opinions of philosophers, when the Roman liberty was to be asserted. . . .

(1693)

from PREFACE TO THE FABLES°

. . . With Ovid ended the golden age of the Roman tongue; from Chaucer the purity of the English tongue began. The manners of the poets were not unlike. Both of them were well-bred, well-natured, amorous, and libertine, at least in their writings; it may be, also in their lives. Their studies were the same, philosophy and philology.° Both of them were knowing in astronomy; of which Ovid's books of the *Roman Feasts,*° and Chaucer's *Treatise of the Astrolabe,*° are sufficient witnesses. But Chaucer was likewise an astrologer, as were Virgil, Horace,° Persius,° and Manilius.° Both writ with wonderful facility and clearness; neither were great inventors: for Ovid only copied the Grecian fables, and most of Chaucer's stories were taken from his Italian contemporaries, or their predecessors. Boccaccio his° *Decameron*° was first published, and from thence our Englishman has borrowed many of his *Canterbury Tales:*° yet that of *Palamon and Arcite*° was written, in all probability, by some Italian wit, in a former age, as I shall prove hereafter. The tale of

95 **commonwealth,** interested in the public interest, the common good **Preface to the Fables.** *Fables, Ancient and Modern,* Dryden's last volume, was published two months before his death. It consists of loosely translated narrations from Homer, Ovid, Boccaccio, and Chaucer   7 **philology,** all studies in literature or in subjects touched by literature   8 **Roman Feasts,** Ovid's *Fasti,* six books of all kinds of antiquarian matter on six months of the year   9 **Treatise of the Astrolabe,** a textbook by Chaucer on the use of the astrolabe, an instrument for measuring the altitudes of celestial bodies   11 **Horace,** lyric and satiric poet of imperial Rome (65–8 B.C.), writer of odes and fashioner of the form known as the Horatian ode   **Persius,** Roman satirist of the first century A.D.   **Manilius,** an obscure Roman poet of about the beginning of the Christian era known only for his *Astronomicae,* a didactic poem on the heavens   16 **his,** an obsolete form suggested by the genitive "es"(s). It was thought that the "'s" stood for his. **Decameron,** story collection by Giovanni Boccaccio (1313–1375), mentioned in connection with Chaucer's *Canterbury Tales*   17–18 **borrowed .. Canterbury Tales.** It is reasonably certain that Chaucer was not familiar with the original of the *Decameron;* the similarity between some of the *Canterbury Tales* and some of the stories in the *Decameron* probably arose from the fact that both Chaucer and Boccaccio were using a common source   18 **Palamon and Arcite,** The Knight's Tale in the Canterbury Tales. In this instance, Chaucer obviously used much material from Boccaccio's long narrative poem, *Teseide*

Griselda° was the invention of Petrarch;° by him sent to Boccaccio, from whom it came to Chaucer. *Troilus and Cressida* was also written by a Lombard author,° but much amplified by our English translator, as well as beautified; the genius of our countrymen, in general, being rather to improve an invention than to invent themselves, as is evident not only in our poetry, but in many of our manufactures. I find I have anticipated already, and taken up from Boccaccio before I come to him: but there is so much less behind; and I am of the temper of most kings, who love to be in debt, are all for present money, no matter how they pay it afterwards; besides, the nature of a preface is rambling, never wholly out of the way, nor in it. This I have learned from the practice of honest Montaigne,° and return at my pleasure to Ovid and Chaucer, of whom I have little more to say.

Both of them built on the inventions of other men; yet since Chaucer had something of his own, as *The Wife of Bath's Tale, The Cock and the Fox,*° which I have translated, and some others, I may justly give our countryman the precedence in that part; since I can remember nothing of Ovid which was wholly his. Both of them understood the manners; under which name I comprehend the passions, and, in a larger sense, the descriptions of persons, and their very habits. For an example, I see Baucis and Philemon° as perfectly before me, as if some ancient painter had drawn them; and all the Pilgrims in *The Canterbury Tales,* their humors, their features, and the very dress, as distinctly as if I had supped with them at the *Tabard* in Southwark.° Yet even there, too, the figures of Chaucer are much more lively,° and set in a better light; which though I have not time to prove, yet I appeal to the reader, and am sure he will clear me from partiality. The thoughts and words remain to be considered, in the comparison of the two poets, and I have saved myself one-half of the labor, by owning that Ovid lived when the Roman tongue was in its meridian; Chaucer, in the dawning of our language: therefore that part of the comparison stands not on an equal foot, any more than the diction of Ennius° and Ovid, or of Chaucer and our present English. The words are given up, as a post not to be defended in our poet, because he wanted the modern art of fortifying.° The thoughts remain to be considered; and they are to be measured only by their propriety; that is, as they flow more or less naturally from the persons described, on such and such occasions. The vulgar judges, which are nine parts in ten of all nations, who call conceits and jingles wit, who see Ovid full of them, and Chaucer altogether without them, will think me little less than mad for preferring the Englishman to the Roman. Yet, with their leave, I must presume to say that the things they admire are only glittering trifles, and so far from being witty, that in a serious poem they are nauseous, because they are unnatural. Would any man, who is ready to die for love, describe his passion like Narcissus?° Would he think of *inopem me copia fecit,*° and a dozen more of such expressions, poured on the neck of one another, and signifying all the same thing? If this were wit, was this a time to be witty, when the poor wretch was in the agony of death? This is just John Littlewit, in *Bartholomew Fair,*° who had a conceit (as he tells you) left him in his misery; a miserable conceit. On these occasions the poet should endeavor to raise pity; but, instead of this, Ovid is tickling you to laugh. Virgil never made use of such machines when he was moving you to commiserate the death of Dido:° he would not destroy what he was building. Chaucer makes Arcite° violent in his love, and unjust in the pursuit of it; yet, when he came to die, he made him think more reasonably: he repents not of his love, for that had altered his character; but acknowledges the injustice of his proceedings, and resigns Emilia to Palamon. What would Ovid have done on this occasion? He would certainly have made Arcite witty on his deathbed; he had complained he was further off from possession, by being so near, and a thousand such boyisms,° which Chaucer rejected as below the dignity of the subject. They who think otherwise, would, by the same reason, prefer Lucan° and Ovid to Homer and Virgil, and Martial° to all four of them. As for the turn of words,° in which Ovid particularly excels all poets, they are sometimes a fault, and sometimes a beauty, as they are used properly or improperly; but in strong passions always to be shunned, because passions are serious, and will admit no playing. The French have a high value for them; and, I confess, they are often what they call delicate, when they are introduced with judgment; but Chaucer writ with more simplicity, and followed Nature more closely than to use them. I have thus far, to the best of my knowledge, been an upright judge betwixt the parties in competition, not meddling with the design nor the disposition of it; because the design was not their own; and in the disposing of it they were equal. It

21 **Griselda,** the archetype of the "patient wife" in medieval story. Chaucer's *Clerk's Tale* in the *Canterbury Tales* and Boccaccio's tenth story of the tenth day in the *Decameron* are two versions of the legend, but they are drawn from Petrarch's Latin version and have no direct connection with one another   **Petrarch,** Italian poet and storyteller, contemporary of Boccaccio   35 **Montaigne,** French essayist (1533-1592), a pioneer in the writing of the informal essay in modern European letters   40 **The Cock and the Fox,** better known as *The Nun's Priest's Tale*   47 **Baucis and Philemon,** characters in one of the stories of Ovid's *Metamorphoses*—an elderly couple who died in the same hour and who were transformed into trees whose boughs intertwined   51-2 **Tabard in Southwark,** the inn from which the Canterbury pilgrims set out on their journey   53 **lively,** lifelike   62 **Ennius,** early Roman epic poet (239-169 B.C.)   65 **wanted . . . fortifying.** Dryden is basing his point on the assumption that Middle English *per se* is inferior to modern English both as a vehicle of human expression and as an artistic medium

78 **Narcissus.** The story is told in Ovid's *Metamorphoses*. Narcissus, a beautiful youth, rejected the nymph Echo because he was infatuated with his own beauty and spent his time admiring his own reflection in the water. He pined away and was finally changed by the gods into the flower that bears his name. Meanwhile Echo, too, had languished until she became a mere voice   79 **inopem . . . fecit.** "My wealth has made me poor" (Ovid's *Metamorphoses,* III, 466)   84 **Bartholomew Fair,** one of Ben Jonson's best satirical comedies (1614), a play thronged with a multitude of characters from the London of Jonson's time   89 **Dido,** the legendary queen of Carthage who fell in love with Aeneas and committed suicide when he left her (*Aeneid,* Book IV)   90 **Arcite,** one of the two young princes vying for the hand of Emilia in Chaucer's *Knight's Tale.* His rival Palamon was the successful suitor   99 **boyisms,** immature expressions worthy only of a boy   102 **Lucan,** Marcus Annaeus Lucanus (39-65), Roman epic poet whose special subject was the civil war between Caesar and Pompey in 48 B.C.; the *Pharsalia* is his unfinished poem   **Martial,** Marcus Valerius Martialis (40?-104), powerful Roman satirist, particularly gifted in the use of epigram. For this reason he was a favorite source for many neoclassical writers   103 **turn of words,** the neatly rounded phrase in the proper place; the instinct for epigram

remains that I say somewhat of Chaucer in particular.

In the first place, as he is the father of English poetry, so I hold him in the same degree of veneration as the Grecians held Homer, or the Romans Virgil. He is a perpetual fountain of good sense; learned in all sciences; and, therefore, speaks properly on all subjects. As he knew what to say, so he knows also when to leave off; a continence which is practiced by few writers, and scarcely by any of the ancients, excepting Virgil and Horace. One of our late great poets° is sunk in his reputation, because he could never forgive any conceit which came in his way; but swept like a dragnet, great and small. There was plenty enough, but the dishes were ill sorted; whole pyramids of sweetmeats for boys and women, but little of solid meat for men. All this proceeded not from any want of knowledge, but of judgment. Neither did he want that in discerning the beauties and faults of other poets, but only indulged himself in the luxury of writing; and perhaps knew it was a fault, but hoped the reader would not find it. For this reason, though he must always be thought a great poet, he is no longer esteemed a good writer; and for ten impressions which his works have had in so many successive years, yet at present a hundred books are scarcely purchased once a twelvemonth; for, as my last Lord Rochester° said, though somewhat profanely, "Not being of God, he could not stand."

Chaucer followed Nature everywhere, but was never so bold to go beyond her; and there is a great difference of being *poeta* and *nimis poeta*,° if we may believe Catullus,° as much as betwixt a modest behavior and affectation. The verse of Chaucer, I confess, is not harmonious to us; but 'tis like the eloquence of one whom Tacitus commends, it was *auribus istius temporis accommodata:*° they who lived with him, and some time after him, thought it musical; and it continues so, even in our judgment, if compared with the numbers of Lidgate and Gower,° his contemporaries; there is the rude sweetness of a Scotch tune in it, which is natural and pleasing, though not perfect. 'Tis true, I cannot go so far as he who published the last edition of him;° for he would make us believe the

fault is in our ears, and that there were really ten syllables in a verse where we find but nine: but this opinion is not worth confuting; 'tis so gross and obvious an error that common sense (which is a rule in everything but matters of Faith and Revelation) must convince the reader, that equality of numbers, in every verse which we call *heroic,* was either not known, or not always practiced, in Chaucer's age. It were an easy matter to produce some thousands of his verses, which are lame for want of half a foot, and sometimes a whole one, and which no pronunciation can make otherwise. We can only say, that he lived in the infancy of our poetry, and that nothing is brought to perfection at the first. We must be children before we grow men. There was an Ennius, and in process of time a Lucilius,° and a Lucretius,° before Virgil and Horace; even after Chaucer there was a Spenser,° a Harrington,° a Fairfax,° before Waller° and Denham° were in being; and our members were in their nonage° till these last appeared. I need say little of his parentage, life and fortunes; they are to be found at large in all the editions of his works. He was employed abroad, and favored, by Edward the Third, Richard the Second, and Henry the Fourth, and was poet, as I suppose, to all three of them. In Richard's time, I doubt,° he was a little dipped in the rebellion of the Commons; and being brother-in-law to John of Gaunt,° it was no wonder if he followed the fortunes of that family; and was well with Henry the Fourth when he had deposed his predecessor. Neither is it to be admired,° that Henry, who was a wise as well as a valiant prince, who claimed by succession, and was sensible that his title was not sound, but was rightfully in Mortimer,° who had married the heir of York; it was not to be admired, I say, if that great politician should be pleased to have the greatest wit of those times in his interests, and to be the trumpet of his praises. Augustus had given him the example, by the advice of Maecenas,° who recommended Virgil and Horace to him; whose praises helped to make him popular while he was alive, and after his death have made him precious to posterity. As for the religion of our poet, he seems to have some little bias towards the opinions of Wyclif, after John of Gaunt his patron; somewhat of which appears in the tale of *Piers Plowman:*° yet I cannot blame him for inveighing so sharply

126 **One . . . late great poets,** Abraham Cowley (1618–1667), a distinguished writer of odes rather than a mediocre lyric writer. His form of ode, characterized by great freedom of stanza structure, became known as the Cowleyan ode and has been the type usually favored by subsequent English writers, in contrast to the regular stanza structure of the Horatian ode or the antiphonal nature of the Greek or Pindaric ode   142 **Lord Rochester,** John Wilmot, Earl of Rochester (1648–1680), the most famous wit at the court of King Charles II and a writer of lyrical poetry in the Cavalier tradition   147 **poeta . . . poeta,** "a poet—and too much of a poet" (Martial, *Epigrams,* III, 44)   148 **Catullus,** Roman lyric poet (84–54 B.C.)   151–52 **auribus . . . accommodata,** "suited to the ears of that time" (Tacitus, *De Oratoribus,* xxi). Tacitus (55–120) was a celebrated Roman historian and legal orator. Dryden has really paraphrased the quotation, which originally ran *auribus indicum accommodata,* "suited to the ears of judges"   155 **Lidgate and Gower.** John Lydgate (1370?–1451?), a follower of Chaucer, was possibly the most voluminous poet that English literature has produced, but one of inferior talent, although the most talented among English poets of the fifteenth century. John Gower (1325?–1408), a friend of Chaucer's, court poet and scholar, wrote in three languages, Latin, French, and English. His most ambitious work is the *Confessio Amantis,* in English, a story collection belonging to the "f4amework tradition"   159 **last edition of him.** This was the edition of Chaucer by Thomas Speght, first published in 1598 and reprinted in 1602 and 1687. Speght's edition was not a perfect printing of Chaucer's text, but Speght himself was right about Chaucer's ten syllables to a line. Dryden's inability to comprehend this fact arose from the ignorance of the age in general and of Dryden in particular concerning the disposal that should be made of the final -e's

174 **Lucilius,** Roman satirical poet of the second century B.C.   175 **Lucretius,** noted Roman poet and philosopher (95–55 B.C.), the proponent of a grandiose conception of the universe based on a kind of "atomic" theory   176 **Spenser,** Edmund Spenser   **Harrington,** Sir John Harrington (1561–1612), translator of the Italian Renaissance epic, the *Orlando Furioso* of Ludovico Ariosto (1474–1533)   **Fairfax,** Edward Fairfax (1580–1635), translator of the other most important Italian Renaissance epic, the *Jerusalem Delivered* of Torquato Tasso (1544–1595)   177 **Waller,** Edmund Waller, Cavalier lyric poet   **Denham,** John Denham (1615–1669), author of *Cooper's Hill,* a didactic poem. Waller and Denham do not merit their exalted position here in company with Ariosto, Tasso, Vergil, etc. But as both were instrumental in establishing the use of the heroic couplet in true neoclassical style, they might have rated high in Dryden's estimation   178 **nonage,** the period in which a person is in the eyes of the law   184 **doubt,** suspect, hardly "fear," as the word had originally meant   186 **John of Gaunt,** Duke of Lancaster, son of King Edward III, and both friend and patron to Chaucer   189 **admired,** wondered at   192 **Mortimer,** Edmund Mortimer, Earl of March, heir presumptive to King Richard II. He had been supported by Richard II but was pushed aside by Henry IV, who seized the throne from Richard in 1399   197 **Maecenas,** Roman statesman and rich patron of letters during the reign of the Emperor Augustus   203 **Piers Plowman,** not the great social document of fourteenth-century England but *The Plowman's Tale,* another piece belonging to the *Piers Plowman* tradition and ascribed for a long time to Chaucer

against the vices of the clergy in his age: their pride, their ambition, their pomp, their avarice, their worldly interest, deserved the lashes which he gave them, both in that, and in most of his *Canterbury Tales*. Neither has his contemporary Boccaccio spared them: yet both those poets lived in much esteem with good and holy men in orders; for the scandal which is given by particular priests reflects not on the sacred function. Chaucer's Monk, his Canon, and his Friar, took not from the character of his Good Parson. A satirical poet is the check of the laymen on bad priests. We are only to take care that we involve not the innocent with the guilty in the same condemnation. The good cannot be too much honored, nor the bad too coarsely used; for the corruption of the best becomes the worst. When a clergyman is whipped, his gown is first taken off, by which the dignity of his order is secured. If he be wrongfully accused, he has his action of slander; and 'tis at the poet's peril if he transgress the law. But they will tell us that all kind of satire, though never so well deserved by particular priests, yet brings the whole order into contempt. Is then the peerage of England anything dishonored when a peer suffers for his treason? If he be libeled, or any way defamed, he has his *scandalum magnatum*° to punish the offender. They who use this kind of argument seem to be conscious to themselves of somewhat which has deserved the poet's lash, and are less concerned for their public capacity than for their private; at least there is pride at the bottom of their reasoning. If the faults of men in orders are only to be judged among themselves, they are all in some sort parties; for, since they say the honor of their order is concerned in every member of it, how can we be sure that they will be impartial judges? How far I may be allowed to speak my opinion in this case, I know not; but I am sure a dispute of this nature caused mischief in abundance betwixt a King of England and an Archbishop of Canterbury;° one standing up for the laws of his land, and the other for the honor (as he called it) of God's Church; which ended in the murder of the prelate, and in the whipping of his Majesty from post to pillar for his penance. The learned and ingenious Dr. Drake° has saved me the labor of inquiring into the esteem and reverence which the priests have had of old; and I would rather extend than diminish any part of it. Yet I must needs say that when a priest provokes me without any occasion given him, I have no reason, unless it be the charity of a Christian, to forgive him; *prior laesit*° is justification

sufficient in the civil law. If I answer him in his own language, self-defense I am sure must be allowed me; and if I carry it further, even to a sharp recrimination, somewhat may be indulged to human frailty. Yet my resentment has not wrought so far but that I have followed Chaucer, in his character of a holy man, and have enlarged on that subject with some pleasure; reserving to myself the right, if I shall think fit hereafter, to describe another sort of priests, such as are more easily to be found than the Good Parson; such as have given the last blow to Christianity in this age, by a practice so contrary to their doctrine. But this will keep cold till another time. In the meanwhile, I take up Chaucer where I left him.

He must have been a man of a most wonderful comprehensive nature, because, as it has been truly observed of him, he has taken into the compass of his *Canterbury Tales* the various manners and humors (as we now call them) of the whole English nation, in his age. Not a single character has escaped him. All his pilgrims are severally distinguished from each other; and not only in their inclinations, but in their very physiognomies and persons. Baptista Porta° could not have described their natures better than by the marks which the poet gives them. The matter and manner of their tales, and of their telling, are so suited to their different educations, humors, and callings, that each of them would be improper in any other mouth. Even the grave and serious characters are distinguished by their several sorts of gravity: their discourses are such as belong to their age, their calling, and their breeding; such as are becoming of them, and of them only. Some of his persons are vicious, and some virtuous; some are unlearned, or (as Chaucer calls them) lewd, and some are learned. Even the ribaldry of the low characters is different: the Reeve, the Miller, and the Cook, are several men, and distinguished from each other as much as the mincing Lady-Prioress and the broad-speaking gap-toothed Wife of Bath. But enough of this; there is such a variety of game springing up before me that I am distracted in my choice, and know not which to follow. 'Tis sufficient to say, according to the proverb, that "Here is God's plenty." We have our forefathers and great grand-dames all before us, as they were in Chaucer's days: their general characters are still remaining in mankind, and even in England, though they are called by other names than those of Monks, and Friars, and Canons, and Lady Abbesses, and Nuns; for mankind is ever the same, and nothing lost out of Nature, though everything is altered. . . .

(1700)

229 **scandalum magnatum,** the crime of *lese-majesté,* or the defaming of rulers
242 **King . . . Canterbury,** an allusion to the famous quarrel between King Henry II and Thomas à Becket, Archbishop of Canterbury, which culminated in the assassination of Becket in 1170   247 **Dr. Drake,** James Drake (1667–1707), who wrote a reply to Jeremy Collier's attack on the English stage (1699)   253 **prior laesit,** "he struck first," from the prologue to the *Eunuchus,* a comedy by the early Roman playwright Terence (195?–159 B.C.)

276 **Baptista Porta,** a noted Italian physiognomist (1543–1617)

SAMUEL PEPYS
1633–1703

Samuel Pepys, the son of a London tailor, secured an education at St. Paul's School and at Cambridge University through the help of his kinsman and patron, Sir Edward Montagu, first earl of Sandwich. Pepys had an early appetite for the activities of important people. As a lad at school, he was an eyewitness of the execution of King Charles I in 1649; as secretary to Montagu, he was with the fleet that brought Charles II back from exile in 1660. Through Montagu's aid Pepys rose from minor government offices to the position of Secretary of the Admiralty, a post he held from 1673 to the Revolution of 1688. With the coming of William III, Pepys was not only removed from office but for a short time was imprisoned because of his sympathies with Charles' descendants. Released through the influence of powerful friends, he retired to Clapham, where his last years passed quietly.

Pepys left behind him two works: his *Memoirs of the Navy* (1690) and his *Diary*. The *Diary* covers the period from January 1, 1660, to May 31, 1669, and provides a record of London life. His subjects include his official and family affairs; his flirtations as well as his jealousies; the foibles and scandals of his acquaintances; plays, operas, and other Restoration amusements; the Dutch War, the plague, and the Great Fire of London. Pepys probably had not the slightest idea that it would someday be spread before the eager eyes of the reading public. It was written in shorthand and not deciphered until 1825. Apparently it was composed secretly: when, at the age of thirty-six, he was suffering from a terrible fear of oncoming blindness, he wrote in the last paragraph of the journal: "I resolve from this time forward to have it [the diary] kept by my people in long-hand and must therefore be contented to set down no more than is fit for them and all the world to know."

from THE DIARY

1659–60

Blessed be God, at the end of the last year, I was in very good health, without any sense of my old pain, but upon taking of cold.° I lived in Axe Yard, having my wife, and servant Jane, and no other in family than us three.

The condition of the State was thus: viz. the Rump,°

after being disturbed by my Lord Lambert,° was lately returned to sit again. The officers of the Army all forced to yield. Lawson° lies still in the river, and Monk° is with his army in Scotland. Only my Lord Lambert is 10 not yet come into the Parliament, nor is it expected that he will, without being forced to it. The new Common Council of the City do speak very high; and had sent to Monk, their sword-bearer, to acquaint him with their desires for a free and full Parliament, which is at present the desires, and the hopes, and the expectations of all: twenty-two of the old secluded° members having been at the House-door the last week to demand entrance, but it was denied them; and it is believed that neither they nor the people will be satisfied 20 till the House be filled. My own private condition very handsome, and esteemed rich, but indeed very poor; besides my goods of my house, and my office, which at present is somewhat certain. Mr. Downing° master of my office.

July 1, 1660 (Lord's day.)—Infinite of business, my heart and head full. Met with Purser Washington,° with whom and a lady, a friend of his, I dined at the Bell Tavern in King Street, but the rogue had no more manners than to invite me, and to let me pay my club.° 30 This morning come home my fine camlet° cloak, with gold buttons, and a silk suit, which cost me much money, and I pray God to make me able to pay for it. In the afternoon to the Abbey, where a good sermon by a stranger, but no Common Prayer° yet.

October 11, 1660.— . . . To walk in St. James's Park, where we observed the several engines at work to draw up water, with which sight I was very much pleased. Above all the rest, I liked that which Mr. Greatorex brought, which do carry up the water with a 40 great deal of ease. Here, in the Park, we met with Mr. Salisbury, who took Mr. Creed and me to the Cockpit° to see *The Moore of Venice,*° which was well done. Burt° acted the Moore; by the same token, a very pretty lady that sat by me, called out, to see Desdemona smothered. . . .

October 13, 1660.—I went out to Charing Cross, to see Major-General Harrison° hanged, drawn, and quartered; which was done there, he looking as cheerful as any man could do in that condition. He was 50 presently cut down, and his head and heart shown to the people, at which there was great shouts of joy. It is said, that he said that he was sure to come shortly at

7 **Lambert,** John Lambert (1619–1683), a major general in the Parliamentary forces during the Civil War, but condemned as a traitor after the Restoration. He was banished to Guernsey and later to Plymouth Island, where he lived in exile and imprisonment for twenty years   9 **Lawson,** Sir John Lawson (c. 1665), son of a poor man of Hull. He rose from common seaman to the rank of admiral and distinguished himself during the Protectorate. Nevertheless, he readily supported the restoration of the monarchy   9 **Monk,** George Monk (1608–1670), afterwards Duke of Albemarle. He helped to restore Charles II to the throne   17 **secluded,** excluded by the Parliamentarian army in 1647 and 1648   24 **Downing,** George Downing (c. 1623–1684), of the Exchequer, in whose office Pepys was a clerk   27 **Washington,** a friend of Pepys in the Admiralty office   30 **club,** share of the expenses   31 **camlet,** a rich material made of silk and camel's hair or wool   35 **Common Prayer,** its use had been abolished during the Commonwealth   42 **Cockpit,** a theater in Drury Lane   43 **Moore of Venice,** Shakespeare's *Othello*   44 **Burt,** Nicholas Burt, one of the good Restoration actors   48 **Harrison,** Thomas Harrison, son of a butcher in Newcastle-under-Lyme, appointed by Cromwell to convey Charles I from Windsor to Whitehall for trial. He also sat as one of the king's judges

The Diary   2–3 pain . . . cold. On March 26, 1658, Pepys had successfully undergone an operation for a gall bladder condition. Pepys always commemorated the day   6 **Rump,** the Rump Parliament, the remnant of the Long Parliament, established by the expulsion of the Presbyterian members in 1648, dismissed by force in 1653 and restored briefly in 1659–60

the right hand of Christ to judge them that now had judged him; and that his wife do expect his coming again. Thus it was my chance to see the King beheaded at White Hall, and to see the first blood shed in revenge for the King at Charing Cross. Setting up shelves in my study.

November 1, 1660.—This morning—Sir W. Pen° and I were mounted early, and had very merry discourse all the way, he being very good company. We come to Sir W. Batten's,° where he lives like a prince, and we were made very welcome. Among other things, he showed me my Lady's closet, wherein was great store of rarities; as also a chair, which he calls King Harry's chaire, where he that sits down is catched with two irons, that come round about him, which makes good sport. Here dined with us two or three more country gentlemen: among the rest, Mr. Christmas, my old school-fellow, with whom I had much talk. He did remember that I was a great Roundhead when I was a boy, and I was much afraid that he would have remembered the words that I said the day the King was beheaded (that, were I to preach upon him, my text should be—"The memory of the wicked shall rot"); but I found afterwards that he did go away from school before that time. He did make us good sport in imitating Mr. Case, Ash, and Nye,° the ministers; but a deadly drinker he is, and grown very fat.

December 25, 1660 (Christmas day.)—To church in the morning, and there saw a wedding in the church, which I have not seen many a day; and the young people so merry one with another! and strange to see what delight we married people have to see these poor fools decoyed into our condition, every man and woman gazing and smiling at them. Here I saw again my beauty Lethulier.° Home to look over and settle my papers, both of my accounts private, and those of Tangier, which I have let go so long that it were impossible for any soul, had I died, to understand them, or ever come to good end in them. I hope God will never suffer me to come to that disorder again.

March 23, 1661.—To the Red Bull° (where I had not been since plays come up again) . . . up to the tiring-room,° where strange the confusion and disorder that there is among them in fitting themselves, especially here, where the clothes are very poor, and the actors but common fellows. At last into the pit, where I think there was not above ten more than myself, and not one hundred in the whole house. And the play, which is called *All's Lost by Lust,*° poorly done; and with so much disorder, among others, in the music-room the boy that was to sing a song, not singing it right, his master fell about his ears and beat him so, that it put the whole house in an uproar. . . .

January 1, 1662.—Waking this morning out of my sleep on a sudden, I did with my elbow hit my wife a great blow over her face and neck, which waked her with pain, at which I was sorry, and to sleep again. . . .

March 1, 1662.—My wife and I by coach, first to see my little picture that is a-drawing, and thence to the Opera,° and there saw *Romeo and Juliet,* the first time it was ever acted, but it is a play of itself the worst that ever I heard, and the worst acted that ever I saw these people do, and I am resolved to go no more to see the first time of acting, for they were all of them out more or less. . . .

September 30, 1662.—To the Duke's play-house,° where we saw *The Duchess of Malfy°* well performed, but Betterton° and Ianthe [Mrs. Betterton] to admiration. Strange to see how easily my mind do revert to its former practice of loving plays and wine; but this night I have again bound myself to Christmas next.° I have also made up this evening my monthly ballance, and find that, notwithstanding the loss of £30 to be paid to the loyall and necessitous cavaliers by act of Parliament, yet I am worth about £680, for which the Lord God be praised. My condition at present is this:—I have long been building, and my house, to my great content, is now almost done. My Lord Sandwich° has lately been in the country, and very civil to my wife, and hath himself spent some pains in drawing a plot of some alterations in our house there, which I shall follow as I get money. As for the office, my late industry hath been such, as I am become as high in reputation as any man there, and good hold I have of Mr. Coventry and Sir G. Carteret,° which I am resolved, and it is necessary for me, to maintain, by all fair means. Things are all quiet. The late outing of the Presbyterian clergy, by their not renouncing the Covenant as the Act of Parliament commands, is the greatest piece of state now in discourse. But, for ought I see, they are gone out very peaceably, and the people not so much concerned therein as was expected.

October 2, 1662.—At night, hearing that there was a play at the Cockpit, and my Lord Sandwich, who come to town last night, at it, I do go thither, and by very great fortune did follow four or five gentlemen who were carried to a little private door in a wall, and so crept through a narrow place, and come into one of the boxes next the King's, but so as I could not see the King or Queen, but many of the fine ladies, who yet are not really so handsome generally as I used to take them to be, but that they are finely dressed. Then we saw *The Cardinall,*° a tragedy I had never seen before, nor is there any great matter in it. The company that

---

60 **Pen,** an associate and friend of the rising Pepys in the Admiralty office, captain at twenty-one, rear admiral of Ireland at twenty-three, and vice-admiral of England at thirty-two. He was the father of William Penn, founder of Pennsylvania.   63 **Batten,** Commissioner of the Navy   79 **Case . . . Nye,** royal chaplains   88 **Lethulier,** wife of a London merchant, and friend of Pepys   94 **Red Bull,** an old playhouse in St. John Street, Clerkenwell   95 **tiring-room,** dressing room   102 **All's . . . Lust,** a play by William Rowley (1642?–1685?)

113 **Opera,** Lincoln's Inn Fields Theatre   119 **Duke's play-house,** Lincoln's Inn Fields Theatre   120 **The Duchess of Malfy,** a play by John Webster (d. 1634)   121 **Betterton,** Thomas Betterton (1635–1710), the greatest of the Restoration actors   122–24 **Strange . . . next.** Pepys repeatedly made resolutions to give up seeing plays, to go only when his wife accompanied him. But he always broke them   131 **Sandwich,** Sir Edward Montagu (1625–1672), one of the Council of State, and a distant relative of Pepys, who owed his rise in the Admiralty to him   137–38 **Mr. Coventry and Sir G. Carteret,** associates of Pepys in the Admiralty office   156 **The Cardinall,** a tragedy by James Shirley (1596–1666)

come in with me into the box were all Frenchmen, that could speak no English; but, Lord! what sport they made to ask a pretty lady that they got among them, that understood both French and English, to make her tell them what the actors said.

December 26, 1662.—Up, my wife to the making of Christmas pies all day, being now pretty well again,° and I abroad to several places about some businesses, among others bought a bake-pan in Newgate Market, and sent it home; it cost me 16s. So to Dr. Williams, but he is out of town, then to the Wardrobe.° Hither come Mr. Battersby; and we falling into a discourse of a new book of drollery in verse called *Hudebras*,° I would needs go find it out, and met with it at the Temple; cost me 2s. 6d. But when I came to read it, it is so silly an abuse of the Presbyter Knight going to the wars, that I am ashamed of it; and by and by meeting at Mr. Townshend's at dinner, I sold it to him for 18d. Here we dine with many tradesmen that belong to the Wardrobe, but I was weary soon of their company, and broke up dinner as soon as I could, and away, with the greatest reluctancy and dispute (two or three times my reason stopping my sense and I would go back again) within myself, to the Duke's house and saw *The Villain*,° which I ought not to do without my wife, but that my time is now out that I did undertake it for. But, Lord! to consider how my natural desire is to pleasure, which God be praised that he has given me the power by my late oaths to curb so well as I have done, and will do again after two or three plays more. Here I was better pleased with the play than I was at first, understanding the design better than I did. Here I saw Gosnell° and her sister at a distance, and could have found it in my heart to have accosted them, but thought not prudent. But I watched their going out and found that they came, she, her sister and another woman, alone, without any man, and did go over the fields a foot. I find that I have an inclination to have her come again, though it is most against my interest either of profit or content of mind, other than for their singing. Home on foot, in my way calling at Mr. Rawlinson's and drinking only a cup of ale there. He tells me my uncle has ended his purchase, which cost him £4,500, and how my uncle do express his trouble that he has with his wife's relations; but I understand his great intentions are for the Wights that hang upon him and by whose advice this estate is bought. Thence home, and found my wife busy among her pies, but angry for some saucy words that her maid Jane has given her, which I will not allow of, and therefore will give her warning to be gone. As also we are both displeased for some slight words that Sarah,° now at Sir W. Pen's, hath spoke of us, but it is no matter. We shall endeavor to join the lion's skin to the fox's tail.° So to my office alone awhile, and then home to my study and supper and bed. Being also vexed at my boy for his staying playing abroad when he is sent of errands, so that I have sent him tonight to see whether their country carrier be in town or no, for I am resolved to keep him no more.

July 13, 1663.— . . . I met the Queen-Mother° walking in the Pell Mell, led by my Lord St. Alban's. And finding many coaches at the Gate, I found upon enquiry that the Duchess is brought to bed of a boy;° and hearing that the King and Queen are rode abroad with the Ladies of Honor to the Park, and seeing a great crowd of gallants staying here to see their return, I also stayed walking up and down. . . . By and by the King and Queen, who looked in this dress (a white laced waistcoat and a crimson short petticoat, and her hair dressed *à la negligence*) mighty pretty; and the King rode hand in hand with her. Here was also my Lady Castlemaine° rode among the rest of the ladies; but the King took, methought, no notice of her; nor when she light, did any body press (as she seemed to expect, and stayed for it) to take her down, but was taken down by her own gentlemen. She looked mighty out of humor, and had a yellow plume in her hat (which all took notice of) and yet is very handsome, but very melancholy; nor did anybody speak to her, or she so much as smile or speak to anybody. I followed them up into White Hall, and into the Queen's presence, where all the ladies walked, talking and fiddling with their hats and feathers, and changing and trying one another's by one another's heads, and laughing. But it was the finest sight to me, considering their great beauties, and dress, that ever I did see in all my life. But, above all, Mrs. Stewart in this dress, with her hat cocked and a red plume, with her sweet eye, little Roman nose, and excellent taille,° is now the greatest beauty I ever saw, I think, in my life; and, if ever woman can, do exceed my Lady Castlemaine, at least in this dress; nor do I wonder if the King changes, which I verily believe is the reason of his coldness to my Lady Castlemaine. . . .

January 4, 1664.—I to my Lord Sandwich's lodgings, but he not being up, I to the Duke's chamber, and there by and by to his closet, where, since his lady was ill, a little red bed of velvet is brought for him to lie alone, which is a very pretty one. After doing business here, I to my Lord's again, and there spoke with him, and he seems now almost friends again, as he used to

164 **pretty well again.** Mrs. Pepys had spent the preceding day in bed   168 **the Wardrobe,** the official residence of Pepys' employer, Sir Edward Montagu, Earl of Sandwich   170 **Hudebras,** a satire on the Puritans by Samuel Butler. The official date of publication of *Hudibras* is 1663, so that it could have been off the press but a few days before Pepys came upon it   182 **The Villain,** a tragedy by Thomas Porter, an otherwise completely obscure seventeenth-century playwright   189–90 **Gosnell,** Mrs. Pepys maid, just recently discharged. Pepys speaks elsewhere of her good singing voice, and of the fact that she appeared with some success upon the stage

209 **Sarah,** Gosnell's predecessor at the Pepys household. Mrs. Pepys, who seems to have been a woman of quick temper, had discharged Sarah about a month before the entry in question   210–11 **join . . . tail,** a proverbial expression for patching up matters and making the best of them   217 **Queen-Mother,** Queen Henrietta Maria, widow of Charles I and mother of Charles II   220 **Duchess . . . boy.** The Duchess of York, wife of James, Duke of York, who later became James II of England. The boy here referred to was James Stuart, Duke of Cambridge, the second son. He died in 1667   229 **Lady Castlemaine.** Barbara Villiers (1641–1709), Duchess of Cleveland, one of the better-known mistresses of Charles II. Her rival, Frances Stuart, mentioned below, seems to have been a temporary infatuation   246 **taille,** figure

be. Here meeting Mr. Pierce, the surgeon, he told me,
among other Court news, how the Queen is very well
again; and that she speaks now very pretty English,
and makes her sense out now and then with pretty
phrases: as among others this is mightily cried up; that,
meaning to say that she did not like such a horse so
well as the rest, he being too prancing and full of
tricks, she said he did make too much vanity. To the
Tennis Court, and there saw the King play at tennis
and others: but to see how the King's play was extolled, without any cause at all, was a loathsome sight,
though sometimes, indeed, he did play very well, and
deserved to be commended; but such open flattery is
beastly. Afterwards to St. James's Park, seeing people
play at Pell Mell;° where it pleased me mightily to hear
a gallant, lately come from France, swear at one of his
companions for suffering his man, a spruce blade, to
be so saucy as to strike a ball while his master was
playing on the Mall. My wife is mighty sad to think of
her father, who is going into Germany against the
Turkes; but what will become of her brother I know
not. He is so idle, and out of all capacity, I think, to
earn his bread.

January 6, 1664 (Twelfth day.)—This morning I began a practice, which I find, by the ease I do it with,
that I shall continue, it saving me money and time; that
is, to trimme myself with a razer: which pleases me
mightily.

August 7, 1664 (Lord's day.)—My wife telling me
sad stories of the ill, improvident, disquiet, and sluttish
manner, that my father and mother and Pall° do live in
the country, which troubles me mightily, and I must
seek to remedy it. Showed my wife, to her great admiration and joy, Mr. Gauden's° present of plate, the two
flaggons, which indeed are so noble that I hardly can
think that they are yet mine. I saw several poor creatures carried by, by constables, for being at a conventicle.° They go like lambs, without any resistance. I
would to God they would either conform, or be more
wise, and not be catched!

October 10, 1664.—Sir W. Pen do grow every day
more and more regarded by the Duke,° because of his
service heretofore in the Dutch war, which I am confident is by some strong obligations he hath laid upon
Mr. Coventry; for Mr. Coventry must needs know that
he is a man of very mean parts, but only a bred seaman. Sat up till past twelve at night, to look over the
account of the collections for the Fishery, and to the
loose and base manner that monies so collected are
disposed of in, would make a man never part with a
penny in that manner; and, above all, the inconvenience of having a great man, though never so seeming
pious as my Lord Pembroke° is. He is too great to be

called to an account, and is abused by his servants,
and yet obliged to defend them, for his own sake. This
day, by the blessing of God, my wife and I have been
married nine years: but my head, being full of business, I did not think of it to keep it in any extraordinary
manner. But bless God for our long lives, and loves,
and health together, which the same God long continue, I wish, from my very heart!

June 7, 1665.— . . . This day, much against my will,
I did in Drury Lane see two or three houses marked
with a red cross upon the doors, and "Lord have
mercy upon us" writ there; which was a sad sight to
me, being the first of the kind, that to my remembrance, I ever saw. It put me into an ill conception of
myself and my smell,° so that I was forced to buy some
roll-tobacco to smell to and chaw, which took away
the apprehension.

July 26, 1665.—To Greenwich, to the Park, where I
heard the King and Duke are come by water this morn
from Hampton Court. They asked me several questions. The King mightily pleased with his new buildings there. I followed them to Castle's ship, in building, and there met Sir W. Batten, and thence to Sir G.
Carteret's, where all the morning with them; they not
having any but the Duke of Monmouth,° and Sir W.
Killigrew,° and one gentleman, and a page more. Great
variety of talk, and was often led to speak to the King
and Duke. By and by they to dinner, and all to dinner
and sat down to the King, saving myself, which,
though I could not in modesty expect, yet, God forgive
my pride! I was sorry I was there, that Sir W. Batten
should say that he could sit down where I could not.
The King having dined, he came down, and I went in
the barge with him, I sitting at the door. Down to
Woolwich, and there I just saw and kissed my wife,
and saw some of her painting, which is very curious;
and away again to the King, and back again with him in
the barge, hearing him and the Duke talk, and seeing
and observing their manner of discourse. And, God
forgive me! though I admire them with all the duty
possible, yet the more a man considers and observes
them, the less he finds of difference between them and
other men, though, blessed be God! they are both princes of great nobleness and spirits. The Duke of Monmouth is the most skittish leaping gallant that ever
I saw, always in action, vaulting, or leaping, or clambering. Sad news of the death of so many in the parish
of the plague, forty last night. The bell always going.
To the Exchange, where I went up and sat talking with
my beauty, Mrs. Batelier,° a great while, who is indeed
one of the finest women I ever saw in my life. This day
poor Robin Shaw° at Backewell's died, and Backewell

273 **Pell Mell,** a game in which a box-wood ball was driven through an iron ring
suspended at a height in a long alley. Pall Mall, the fashionable club street in
London, was developed from one of these alleys   289 **Pall,** Paulina, Pepys' sister
292 **Mr. Gauden,** Dennis Gauden, later Sir Dennis, victualler to the Navy.
Pepys was not above taking presents   295 **conventicle,** a clandestine meeting of
nonconformists, probably Quakers   300 **Duke,** the Duke of York, High Admiral
311 **Pembroke,** Philip, fifth Earl of Pembroke (d. 1669)

325–26 **ill conception . . . smell.** The older theory about the spread of the plague
was that the disease was contagious through the smell of the victim   336 **Duke of
Monmouth,** illegitimate son of Charles II. He was then only a lad   337 **Killigrew,** elder brother of Thomas Killigrew, the playwright. He also wrote verses and
plays   361 **Mrs. Batelier.** Mary Batelier kept a linen draper's shop in the Royal
Exchange; she and her brother William are frequently mentioned in the *Diary*
363 **Robin Shaw,** an employee of Alderman Backewell

himself now in Flanders. The King himself asked about Shaw, and being told he was dead, said he was very sorry for it. The sickness is got into our parish this week, and is got, indeed, every where; so that I begin to think of setting things in order, which I pray God enable me to put, both as to soul and body.

370 August 3, 1665.— . . . To the ferry, where I was forced to stay a great while before I could get my horse brought over, and then mounted and rode very finely to Dagenhams; all the way people, citizens, walking to and again to inquire how the plague is in the city this week by the Bill; which by chance, at Greenwich, I had heard was 2020 of the plague, and 3000 and odd of all diseases; but methought it was a sad question to be so often asked me. Coming to Dagenhams,° I there met our company coming out of the house, having stayed 380 as long as they could for me; so I let them go a little before, and went and took leave of my Lady Sandwich, . . . Then down to the buttery, and eat a piece of cold venison pie, and drank and took some bread and cheese in my hand; and so mounted after them, Mr. Marr very kindly staying to lead me the way. . . . [and] telling me how a maid-servant of Mr. John Wright's (who lives thereabouts) falling sick of the plague, she was removed to an outhouse, and a nurse appointed to look to her; who, being once ab- 390 sent, the maid got out of the house at the window, and run away. The nurse coming and knocking, and having no answer, believed she was dead, and went and told Mr. Wright so; who and his lady were in great strait what to do to get her buried. At last resolved to go to Burntwood hard by, being in the parish, and there get people to do it. But they would not; so he went home full of trouble, and in the way met the wench walking over the common, which frightened him worse than before; and was forced to send people to take her, 400 which he did; and they got one of the pest coaches and put her into it to carry her to a pest house. And passing in a narrow lane, Sir Anthony Browne, with his brother and some friends in the coach, met this coach with the curtains drawn close. The brother being a young man, and believing there might be some lady in it that would not be seen, and the way being narrow, he thrust his head out of his own into her coach, and to look, and there saw somebody look very ill, and in a sick dress, and stunk mightily; which the coachman 410 also cried out upon. And presently they came up to some people that stood looking after it, and told our gallants that it was a maid of Mr. Wright's carried away sick of the plague; which put the young gentleman into a fright had almost cost him his life, but is now well again. . . .

August 12, 1665.— . . . The people die so, that now it seems they are fain to carry the dead to be buried by daylight, the nights not sufficing to do it in. And my Lord Mayor commands people to be within at nine at night all, as they say, that the sick may have liberty to 420 go abroad for air. There is one also dead out of one of our ships at Deptford, which troubles us mightily; the Providence fire-ship,° which was just fitted to go to sea. But they tell me today no more sick on board. And this day W. Bodham tells me that one is dead at Woolwich, not far from the Rope-yard. I am told, too, that a wife of one of the grooms at Court is dead at Salisbury; so that the King and Queen are speedily to be all gone to Milton. God preserve us!

October 16, 1665.— . . . God knows what will be- 430 come of all the King's matters in a little time, for he runs in debt every day,° and nothing to pay them looked after. Thence I walked to the Tower; but, Lord! how empty the streets are and melancholy, so many poor sick people in the streets full of sores; and so many sad stories overheard as I walk, everybody talking of his dead, and that man sick, and so many in this place, and so many in that. And they tell me that, in Westminster, there is never a physician and but one apothecary left, all being dead; but that there are great hopes of a great 440 decrease this week; God send it! . . .

August 14, 1666 (Thanksgiving day.)°—Comes Mr. Foley and his man with a box of great variety of carpenter's and joyner's tooles, which I had bespoke, which please me mightily, but I will have more. Povy tells me how mad my letter makes my Lord Peterborough, and what a furious letter he hath writ to me in answer, though it is not come yet. This did trouble me; for, though there be no reason, yet to have a nobleman's mouth open against a man, may do a man hurt; 450 so I endeavoured to have found him out and spoke with him, but could not. So to the chapel, and heard a piece of the Dean of Westminster's° sermon, and a speciall good anthemne before the King, after sermon. After dinner, with my wife and Mercer° to the Beare Garden;° where I have not been, I think, of many years, and saw some good sport of the bull's tossing the dogs—one into the very boxes. But it is a very rude and nasty pleasure. We had a great many hectors° in the same box with us, and one very fine went into the pit, 460 and played his dog for a wager; which was a strange sport for a gentleman; where they drank wine, and drank Mercer's health first; which I pledged with my hat off. We supped at home, and very merry. And then about nine to Mrs. Mercer's gate, where the fire and boys expected us, and her son had provided abundance of serpents and rockets; and there mighty merry, my Lady Pen and Pegg going thither with us, and Nan Wright, till about twelve at night, flinging our fireworks, and burning one another, and the people 470 over the way. And, at last, our business being most spent, we went into Mrs. Mercer's, and there mighty

423 **fire-ship,** naval vessel which in action would be loaded with combustibles or explosives and set adrift into the enemy's line   432 **in debt every day.** In an earlier part of this same entry, Pepys had been speaking of the lewd behavior of Charles and his extravagances with his mistresses   442 **Thanksgiving day,** in honor of a naval victory   453 **Dean of Westminster,** John Dolben afterwards Archbishop of York   455 **Mercer,** Mrs. Pepys gentlewoman; she was quite vivacious and could sing   456 **Beare Garden,** an old pleasure resort on Bankside in Southwark   459 **hectors,** bullies, rowdies

378 **Dagenhams,** a village about ten miles from London

merry, smutting one another with candle grease and soot, till most of us were like devils. And that being done, then we broke up, and to my house; and there I made them drink, and upstairs we went, and then fell into dancing, W. Batelier dancing well; and dressing, him and I, and one Mr. Banister, who, with my wife, come over also with us, like women; and Mercer put on a suit of Tom's, like a boy, and mighty mirth we had and Mercer danced a jigg; and Nan Wright and my wife and Pegg Pen put on perriwigs. Thus we spent till three or four in the morning, mighty merry; and then departed, and to bed.

September 2, 1666 (Lord's day).—Some of our maids sitting up late last night to get things ready against our feast today, Jane called us up about three in the morning, to tell us of a great fire they saw in the city. So I rose and slipped on my night-gown, and went to her window; and thought it to be on the backside of Marke-lane at the farthest; but, being unused to such fires as followed, I thought it far enough off; and so went to bed again, and to sleep. About seven rose again to dress myself, and there looked out at the window, and saw the fire not so much as it was, and further off. So to my closet to set things to rights, after yesterday's cleaning. By and by Jane comes and tells me that she hears that above 300 houses have been burned down tonight by the fire we saw, and that it is now burning down all Fish Street, by London Bridge. So I made myself ready presently, and walked to the Tower; and there got up upon one of the high places, Sir J. Robinson's little son going up with me; and there I did see the houses at that end of the bridge all on fire, and an infinite great fire on this and the other side the end of the bridge; which, among other people, did trouble me for poor little Michell and our Sarah on the bridge. So down with my heart full of trouble, to the Lieutenant of the Tower, who tells me that it begun this morning in the King's baker's house in Pudding-lane, and that it hath burned St. Magnus's Church and most part of Fish Street already. So I down to the water-side, and there got a boat, and through bridge and there saw a lamentable fire. Poor Michell's house, as far as the Old Swan, already burned that way, and the fire running further, that, in a very little time, it got as far as the Steele-yard, while I was there. Everybody endeavoring to remove their goods, and flinging into the river, or bringing them into lighters that lay off; poor people staying in their houses as long as till the very fire touched them, and then running into boats, or clambering from one pair of stairs, by the water-side, to another. And, among other things, the poor pigeons, I perceive, were loth to leave their houses, but hovered about the windows and balconies, till some of them burned their wings, and fell down. Having stayed, and in an hour's time seen the fire rage every way; and nobody, to my sight, endeavoring to quench it, but to remove their goods, and leave all to the fire, and having seen it get as far as the Steele-yard, and the wind mighty high, and driving it into the city: and everything, after so long a drought, proving combustible, even the very stones of churches; and, among other things, the poor steeple by which pretty Mrs. —— lives, and whereof my old schoolfellow Elborough is parson, taken fire in the very top, and there burned till it fell down; I to White Hall, with a gentleman with me who desired to go off from the Tower, to see the fire, in my boat; to White Hall, and there up to the King's closet in the Chapel, where people come about me, and I did give them an account dismayed them all, and word was carried into the King. So I was called for, and did tell the King and Duke of York what I saw; and, that unless his Majesty did command houses to be pulled down, nothing could stop the fire. They seemed much troubled, and the King commanded me to go to my Lord Mayor from him, and command him to spare no houses, but to pull down before the fire every way. The Duke of York bid me tell him, that if he would have any more soldiers, he shall; and so did my Lord Arlington afterwards, as a great secret. Here meeting with Captain Cocke, I in his coach, which he lent me, and Creed with me to Paul's;° and there walked along Watling Street, as well as I could, every creature coming away loaden with goods to save, and, here and there, sick people carried away in beds. Extraordinary good goods carried in carts and on backs. At last met my Lord Mayor in Canning Street, like a man spent, with a handkercher about his neck. To the King's message, he cried like a fainting woman, "Lord! what can I do? I am spent; people will not obey me. I have been pulling down houses; but the fire overtakes us faster than we can do it." That he needed no more soldiers; and that, for himself, he must go and refresh himself, having been up all night. So he left me, and I him, and walked home, seeing people all almost distracted, and no manner of means used to quench the fire. The houses, too, so very thick thereabouts, and full of matter for burning, as pitch and tar, in Thames Street; and warehouses of oil, and wines, and brandy, and other things. Here I saw Mr. Isaake Houblon, the handsome man, prettily dressed and dirty at his door at Dowgate, receiving some of his brothers' things, whose houses were on fire; and, as he says, have been removed twice already; and he doubts, as it soon proved, that they must be, in a little time, removed from his house also, which was a sad consideration. And to see the churches all filling with goods by people who themselves should have been quietly there at this time. By this time, it was about twelve o'clock; and so home, and there find my guests, which was Mr. Wood and his wife Barbary Shelden, and also Mr. Moone; she mighty fine, and her husband, for aught I see, a likely man. But Mr. Moone's design and mine, which was to look over my closet, and please him with the sight thereof, which he hath long desired, was wholly

553 **Paul's,** St. Paul's Cathedral

Samuel Pepys **423**

disappointed; for we were in great trouble and disturbance at this fire, not knowing what to think of it. However, we had an extraordinary good dinner, and as merry as at this time we could be. While at dinner, Mrs. Batelier come to enquire after Mr. Woolfe and Stanes, who, it seems, are related to them, whose houses in Fish Street are all burned, and they in a sad condition. She would not stay in the fright. Soon as dined, I and Moone away, and walked through the city, the streets full of nothing but people and horses and carts loaden with goods, ready to run over one another, and removing goods from one burned house to another. They now removing out of Canning Street, which received goods in the morning, into Lumbard Street, and further; and among others, I now saw my little goldsmith Stokes receiving some friend's goods, whose house itself was burned the day after. We parted at Paul's; he home, and I to Paul's Wharf, where I had appointed a boat to attend me, and took in Mr. Carcasse and his brother, whom I met in the street, and carried them below and above bridge too and again to see the fire, which was now got further, both below and above, and no likelihood of stopping it. Met with the King and Duke of York in their barge, and with them to Queenhithe, and there called Sir Richard Browne to them. Their order was only to pull down houses apace, and so below bridge at the waterside; but little was or could be done, the fire coming upon them so fast. Good hopes there was of stopping it at the Three Cranes above, and at Buttulph's Wharf below bridge, if care be used; but the wind carries it into the city, so as we know not, by the waterside, what it do there. River full of lighters and boats taking in goods, and good goods swimming in the water; and only I observed that hardly one lighter or boat in three that had the goods of a house in, but there was a pair of virginals° in it. Having seen as much as I could now, I away to White Hall by appointment, and there walked to St. James's Park; and there met my wife, and Creed, and Wood, and his wife, and walked to my boat; and there upon the water again, and to the fire up and down, it still encreasing, and the wind great. So near the fire as we could for smoke; and all over the Thames, with one's face in the wind, you were almost burned with a shower of fire-drops. This is very true; so as houses were burned by these drops and flakes of fire, three or four, nay, five or six houses, one from another. When we could endure no more upon the water, we to a little ale-house on the Bankside, over against the Three Cranes, and there stayed till it was dark almost and saw the fire grow; and, as it grew darker, appeared more and more; and in corners and upon steeples, and between churches and houses, as far as we could see up the hill of the city, in a most horrid, malicious, bloody flame, not like the fine flame of an ordinary fire. Barbary and her husband away

623 **virginals,** small legless pianos

before us. We stayed till, it being darkish, we saw the fire as only one entire arch of fire from this to the other side the bridge, and in a bow up the hill for an arch of above a mile long; it made me weep to see it. The churches, houses, and all on fire, and flaming at once; and a horrid noise the flames made, and the cracking of houses at their ruin. So home with a sad heart, and there find everybody discoursing and lamenting the fire; and poor Tom Hater come with some few of his goods saved out of his house, which was burned upon Fish Street Hill. I invited him to lie at my house, and did receive his goods; but was deceived in his lying there, the news coming every moment of the growth of the fire; so as we were forced to begin to pack up our own goods, and prepare for their removal; and did by moonshine, it being brave, dry, and moonshine and warm weather, carry much of my goods into the garden; and Mr. Hater and I did remove my money and iron chests into my cellar, as thinking that the safest place. And got my bags of gold into my office, ready to carry away, and my chief papers of accounts also there, and my tallies into a box by themselves. So great was our fear, as Sir W. Batten hath carts come out of the country to fetch away his goods this night. We did put Mr. Hater, poor man! to bed a little; but he got but very little rest, so much noise being in my house, taking down of goods.

September 5, 1666.—I lay down in the office again upon W. Hewer's quilt, being mighty weary, and sore in my feet with going till I was hardly able to stand. About two in the morning my wife calls me up, and tells me of new cries of fire, it being come to Barking Church, which is the bottom of our land. I up; and finding it so, resolved presently to take her away, and did, and took my gold, which was about £2350, W. Hewer and Jane down by Proundy's boat to Woolwich; but, Lord! what a sad sight it was by moonlight, to see the whole city almost on fire, that you might see it plain at Woolwich, as if you were by it. There, when I come, I find the gates shut, but no guard kept at all; which troubled me, because of discourse now begun, that there is plot in it, and that the French had done it. I got the gates open, and to Mr. Shelden's, where I locked up my gold, and charged my wife and W. Hewer never to leave the room without one of them in it, night or day. So back again, by the way seeing my goods well in the lighters at Deptford, and watched well by people. Home, and whereas I expected to have seen our house on fire, it being now about seven o'clock, it was not. But to the fire, and there find greater hopes than I expected; for my confidence of finding our office on fire was such, that I durst not ask anybody how it was with us, till I come and saw it not burned. But, going to the fire, I find, by the blowing up of houses, and the great help given by the workmen out of the King's yards, sent up by Sir W. Pen, there is a good stop given to it, as well as at Marke Lane end as ours; it having only burned the dial of Barking Church, and part of the porch, and was there quenched. I up to the top of Barking steeple, and there saw the saddest sight of desolation that I ever saw; everywhere great fires, oil-cellars, and brimstone, and other things burning. I became afeard to stay there long, and therefore down again as fast as I could, the fire being spread as far as I could see it; and to Sir W. Pen's, and there eat a piece of cold meat, having eaten nothing since Sunday, but the remains of Sunday's dinner. Here I met with Mr. Young and Whistler; and, having removed all my things, and received good hopes that the fire at our end is stopped, they and I walked into the town, and find Fenchurch Street, Gracious Street, and Lumbard Street all in dust. The Exchange a sad sight, nothing standing there, of all the statues or pillars, but Sir Thomas Gresham's picture in the corner. Walked into Moorfields, our feet ready to burn, walking through the town among the hot coals, and find that full of people, and poor wretches carrying their goods there, and everybody keeping his goods together by themselves; and a great blessing it is to them that it is fair weather for them to keep abroad night and day; drank there, and paid two-pence for a plain penny loaf. Thence homeward, having passed through Cheapside, and Newgate Market, all burned; and seen Anthony Joyce's house in fire; and took up, which I keep by me, a piece of glass of Mercer's Chapel in the street, where much more was, so melted and buckled with the heat of the fire like parchment. I also did see a poor cat taken out of a hole in a chimney, joyning to the wall of the Exchange, with the hair all burned off the body, and yet alive. So home at night, and find there good hopes of saving our office; but great endeavors of watching all night, and having men ready; and so we lodged them in the office, and had drink and bread and cheese for them. And I lay down and slept a good night about midnight; though, when I rose, I heard that there had been a great alarm of French and Dutch being risen, which proved nothing. But it is a strange thing to see how long this time did look since Sunday, having been always full of variety of actions, and little sleep, that it looked like a week or more, and I had forgot almost the day of the week.

September 17, 1666.—Up betimes, and shaved myself after a week's growth: but, Lord! how ugly I was yesterday, and how fine to-day! By water, seeing the City all the way—a sad sight indeed, much fire being still in. Sir W. Coventry was in great pain lest the French fleete should be passed by our fleete, who had notice of them on Saturday, and were preparing to go meet them; but their minds altered, and judged them merchant-men; when, the same day, the Success, Captain Ball, made their whole fleete, and come to Brighthelmstone,° and thence at five o'clock afternoon, Saturday, wrote Sir W. Coventry news thereof; so that we do much fear our missing them. Here come in and talked with Sir Thomas Clifford,° who appears a very fine gentleman, and much set by at Court for his activity in going to sea, and stoutness every where, and stirring up and down.

February 14, 1667.— . . . This morning come up to my wife's bedside, I being up dressing myself, little Will Mercer to be her Valentine; and brought her name writ upon blue paper in gold letters, done by himself, very pretty; and we were both well pleased with it. But I am also this year my wife's Valentine, and it will cost me £5; but that I must have laid out if we had not been Valentines.

February 25, 1667.—Lay long in bed, talking with pleasure with my poor wife, how she used to make coal fires, and wash my foul clothes with her own hand for me, poor wretch! in our little room at my Lord Sandwich's; for which I ought for ever to love and admire her, and do; and persuade myself she would do the same thing again, if God should reduce us to it. At my goldsmith's did observe the King's new medall, where, in little, there is Mrs. Stewart's° face as well done as ever I saw anything in my whole life, I think: and a pretty thing it is, that he should choose her face to represent Britannia by.

March 2, 1667.— . . . After dinner with my wife to the King's house to see The Mayden Queene, a new play of Dryden's, mightily commended for the regularity of it, and the strain and wit; and the truth is, there is a comical part done by Nell,° which is Florimell, that I never can hope ever to see the like done again by man or woman. The King and Duke of York were at the play. But so great performance of a comical part was never, I believe, in the world before as Nell do this, both as a mad girl, then most and best of all when she comes in like a young gallant; and hath the motions and carriage of a spark the most that ever I saw any man have. It makes me, I confess, admire her. . . .

August 18, 1667.—To Cree Church,° to see it how it is: but I find no alteration there, as they say there was, for my Lord Mayor andsAldermen to come to sermon, as they do every Sunday, as they did formerly to Paul's. There dined with me Mr. Turner and his daughter Betty. Betty is grown a fine young lady as to carriage and discourse. We had a good haunch of venison, powdered° and boiled, and a good dinner. I walked towards White Hall, but, being wearied, turned into St. Dunstan's Church, where I heard an able sermon of the minister of the place; and stood by a pretty, modest maid, whom I did labour to take by the hand; but she would not, but got further and further from me; and, at last, I could perceive her to take pins out of her pocket to prick me if I should touch her again—which, seeing,

757 **Sir Thomas Clifford**, a gallant naval officer who was knighted for his conduct in a sea fight in 1665 777 **Mrs. Stewart**, a great beauty of the court, one of Charles II's mistresses 785 **Nell**, Nell Gwyn, the vivacious actress who rose from the gutter to the palace of Charles II 795 **Cree Church**, the Church of St. Catherine Cree, one of the few city churches to escape the Fire. It was used by the Lord Mayor and the Corporation after the destruction of St. Paul's Cathedral 802 **powdered**, salted

754 **Brighthelmstone,** Brighton on the Sussex coast

810 I did forbear, and was glad I did spy her design. And
then I fell to gaze upon another pretty maid, in a pew
close to me, and she on me; and I did go about to take
her by the hand, which she suffered a little, and then
withdrew. So the sermon ended, and the church broke
up, and my amours ended also. . . .

October 5, 1667.— . . . To the King's house; and
there going in met with Knipp,° and she took us up into
the tiring-rooms; and to the women's shift, where Nell
was dressing herself, and was all unready, and is very
820 pretty, prettier than I thought. And so walked all up
and down the house above, and then below into the
scene-room, and there sat down, and she gave us fruit;
and here I read the questions to Knipp, while she
answered me, through all her part of *Flora's Figarys,*°
which was acted today. But, Lord! to see how they
were both painted would make a man mad, and did
make me loathe them; and what base company of men
comes among them, and how lewdly they talk! And
how poor the men are in clothes, and yet what a show
830 they make on the stage by candle-light, is very observable. But to see how Nell cursed, for having so few
people in the pit, was pretty; the other house carrying
away all the people at the new play, and is said
now-a-days to have generally most company, as being
better players. By and by into the pit, and there saw
the play, which is pretty good, but my belly was full of
what I had seen in the house, and so, after the play
done, away home. . . .

September 4, 1668.—At the Office all the morning;
840 and at noon my wife, and Deb.,° and Mercer, and W.
Hewer and I to the Fair, and there, at the old house,
did eat a pig, and was pretty merry, but saw no sights,
my wife having a mind to see the play *Bartholomew-
Fair,*° with puppets. And it is an excellent play; the
more I see it, the more I love the wit of it; only the
business of abusing the Puritans begins to grow stale,
and of no use, they being the people that, at last, will
be found the wisest. And here Knipp come to us, and
sat with us, and thence took coach in two coaches, and
850 losing one another, my wife, and Knipp, and I to Hercules Pillars, and there supped, and I did take from her
mouth the words and notes of her song of "the
Larke," which pleases me mightily. And so set her at
home, and away we home, where our company come
before us. This night Knipp tells us that there is a
Spanish woman lately come over, that pretends to sing
as well as Mrs. Knight; both of whom I must endeavour to hear.

May 31, 1669.— . . . And thus ends all that I doubt I
860 shall ever be able to do with my own eyes in the keep-

ing of my Journal, I being not able to do it any longer,
having done now so long as to undo my eyes almost
every time that I take a pen in my hand; and, therefore,
whatever comes of it, I must forbear: and, therefore,
resolve, from this time forward, to have it kept by my
people in long-hand, and must be contented to set
down no more than is fit for them and all the world to
know; or, if there be any thing, I must endeavour to
keep a margin in my book open, to add, here and there,
a note in short-hand with my own hand.   870

And so I betake myself to that course, which is almost as much as to see myself go into my grave: for
which, and all the discomforts that will accompany my
being blind, the good God prepare me!
(1825)

WILLIAM WYCHERLEY
1640–1716

William Wycherley was born at Clive in Shropshire, where his father owned a small estate. He
was educated in France (where he converted to Roman Catholicism) and at Queen's College, Oxford
(where he was reconverted to Anglicanism). He came
to London, where he was affiliated with the Inner
Temple, but literature and not the law was his main
interest.

His first play, *Love in a Wood, or, St. James's Park*,
was well received in 1671. Indeed, the mistress of
Charles II, the duchess of Cleveland, liked the play so
much that she took the trouble to meet the author and
sponsored him at court. *The Country Wife* (1675) was
also a great success, as was *The Plain-Dealer*, a comedy staged a year later. It was his last play.

The rest of what we know about his life has less of
an air of success about it. His marriage to the countess of Drogheda in 1679 earned the displeasure of
Charles II. The countess, who died in 1681, left
Wycherley her estate, but the legacy was consumed
by litigation over the inheritance. Wycherley was imprisoned for debt several times, but James II eventually
took pity on him and arranged for the payment of his
debts and an annual pension. Wycherley lived his last
years in retirement on the family estate. During this
time he worked on a collection of poems which were
published in 1704. He also became friendly with
Alexander Pope, who undertook to revise some of
Wycherley's poems at Wycherley's request. At the end
of his life, on December 21, 1715, he married again,

---

817 **Knipp,** an actress of some promise and considerable sparkle, with whom
Pepys carried on an intermittent flirtation   824 *Flora's Figarys,* i.e., *Flora's Vag-
aries,* a comedy by a young Oxford student, Richard Rhodes. Nell Gwyn made a
great success in the role of Flora   840 **Deb.,** Mrs. Pepys maid   843 ***Bar-
tholomew-Fair,*** a comedy by Ben Jonson, satirizing the Puritans (1614)

apparently to spite a nephew who would have inherited his estate. Eleven days later, after receiving the last rites of the Roman Catholic Church, he died.

THE COUNTRY WIFE

Of the three acknowledged masters of Restoration comedy—William Congreve (1670–1729), George Etherege (1635?–1692), and William Wycherley—Wycherley's satire is the most cutting and, at times, savage. In the world of *The Country Wife*, Horner's trick—having himself proclaimed impotent—allows the audience to see what reality lies behind the protestations of virtue by the various women who seek his company and by the husbands and sparkish young men. The traditional "double standard," which insists upon one standard of sexual conduct for men and another for women, is also a target of scorn. In the course of the play, Wycherley examines the related themes of love, marriage, sex, reputation, and money. The satire has a particularly mordant quality because it does not seem to contain a single character who fully embodies genuine moral virtue. Alithea knows Sparkish's faults but does not act on her own to avert a loveless marriage. Margery, the country wife of the title, loses what may be called inexperience if not innocence of town ways. Wycherley would hardly seem to be regarding her as the moral standard. Horner, the satiric manipulator, manipulates for his own pleasure. He is not a reformer but rather a more cunning sinner than the rest.

Still, as a perceptive picture of a society where values have become trivial regulations rather than humane and guiding precepts, *The Country Wife* is unsurpassed. The staging of the play is difficult, as any reader knows who tries to keep track of just who is in what closet in Horner's house, but seems appropriately intricate for a world where disguise and deceit are commonplace.

THE PERSONS

MR. HORNER.
MR. HARCOURT.
MR. DORILANT.
MR. PINCHWIFE.
MR. SPARKISH.
SIR JASPER FIDGET.
MRS. MARGERY PINCHWIFE.
MRS. ALITHEA.
MY LADY FIDGET.
MRS. DAINTY FIDGET.
MRS. SQUEAMISH.
OLD LADY SQUEAMISH.

WAITERS, SERVANTS, and ATTENDANTS.
A BOY.
A QUACK.
LUCY, ALITHEA'S MAID.

THE SCENE: *London.*

PROLOGUE

Spoken by Mr. Hart.

Poets, like cudgelled bullies, never do
At first or second blow submit to you;
But will provoke you still, and ne'er have done
Till you are weary, first, with laying on:
The late so baffled scribbler of this day,
Though he stands trembling, bids me boldly say
What me before most plays are used to do,
For poets out of fear first draw on you;
In a fierce prologue the still pit defie,
And ere you speak, like Castril,° give the lie;   10
But though our Bayes's° battles oft I've fought,
And with bruised knuckles their dear conquests
*   bought;*
Nay, never yet feared odds upon the stage,
In prologue dare not hector with the age,
But would take quarter from your saving hands,
Though Bayes within all yielding countermands,
Says you confed'rate wits no quarter give,
Therefore his play shan't ask your leave to live:
Well, let the vain rash fop, by huffing° so,
Think to obtain the better terms of you;   20
But we the actors humbly will submit,
Now, and at any time, to a full pit:
Nay, often we anticipate your rage,
And murder poets for you on our stage:
We set no guards upon our tiring-room,°
But when with flying colours there you come,
We patiently, you see, give up to you
Our poets, virgins, nay our matrons too.

ACT I SCENE I

Enter HORNER, *and* QUACK *following him at a distance.*

    HORN. (*Aside.*) A quack is as fit for a pimp as a midwife for a bawd. They are still but in their way both helpers of nature. Well, my dear doctor, hast thou done what I desired?
    QUACK. I have undone you for ever with the women,

The Country Wife   Prologue   10 Castril, a contentious character in Ben Jonson's *The Alchemist* (1610)   11 Bayes, a character in Villiers' *The Rehearsal* (1671) based on John Dryden. Hart, the actor speaking the Prologue, had often played in Dryden's plays   19 huffing, bullying   25 tiring-room, dressing room

and reported you throughout the whole town as bad as an eunuch, with as much trouble as if I had made you one in eanest.

HORN. But have you told all the midwives you know, the orange wenches at the playhouses, the city husbands, and old fumbling keepers° of this end of the town? For they'll be the readiest to report it!

QUACK. I have told all the chamber-maids, waiting-women, tire-women° and old women of my acquaintance; nay, and whispered it as a secret to 'em, and to the whisperers of Whitehall. So that you need not doubt 'twill spread, and you will be as odious to the handsome young women as . . .

HORN. As the smallpox. Well . . .

QUACK. And to the married women of this end of the town as . . .

HORN. As the great ones; nay, as their own husbands.

QUACK. And to the city dames as Aniseed Robin° of filthy and contemptible memory; and they will frighten their children with your name, especially their females.

HORN. And cry, 'Horner's coming to carry you away!' I am only afraid 'twill not be believed. You told 'em 'twas by an English-French disaster, and an English-French chirurgeon,° who has given me at once not only a cure but an antidote for the future against that damned malady, and that worse distemper, love, and all other women's evils?

QUACK. Your late journey into France has made it the more credible, and your being here a fortnight before you appeared in public looks as if you apprehended the shame—which I wonder you do not. Well, I have been hired by young gallants to belie 'em t'other way, but you are the first would be thought a man unfit for women.

HORN. Dear Mr. doctor, let vain rogues be contented only to be thought abler men than they are. Generally 'tis all the pleasure they have, but mine lies another way.

QUACK. You take, methinks, a very preposterous way to it, and as ridiculous as if we operators in physic should put forth bills to disparage our medicaments, with hopes to gain customers.

HORN. Doctor, there are quacks in love, as well as physic, who get but the fewer and worse patients for their boasting. A good name is seldom got by giving it oneself, and women no more than honour are compassed by bragging. Come, come, doctor, the wisest lawyer never discovers the merits of his cause till the trial. The wealthiest man conceals his riches, and the cunning gamester his play. Shy husbands and keepers, like old rooks, are not to be cheated but by a new

unpractised trick. False friendship will pass now no more than false dice upon 'em—no, not in the city. 60

Enter BOY.

BOY. There are two ladies and a gentleman coming up.

HORN. A pox! Some unbelieving sisters of my former acquaintance who, I am afraid, expect their sense should be satisfied of the falsity of the report. No—this formal fool and women!

Enter SIR JASPER FIDGET, LADY FIDGET, *and* MRS. DAINTY FIDGET.

QUACK. His wife and sister.

SIR JAS. My coach breaking just now before your door, sir, I look upon as an occasional reprimand to me, sir, for not kissing your hands, sir, since your 70 coming out of France, sir; and so my disaster, sir, has been my good fortune, sir; and this is my wife and sister, sir.

HORN. What then, sir?

SIR JAS. My lady and sister, sir.—Wife, this is master Horner.

LADY FIDG. Master Horner, husband!

SIR JAS. My lady, my lady Fidget, sir.

HORN. So, sir.

SIR JAS. Won't you be acquainted with her, sir? 80 (*Aside.*) So, the report is true, I find, by his coldness or aversion to the sex; but I'll play the wag with him. Pray salute my wife, my lady, sir.

HORN. I will kiss no man's wife, sir, for him, sir; I have taken my eternal leave, sir, of the sex already, sir.

SIR JAS. (*Aside.*) Ha, ha, ha,! I'll plague him yet.—Not know my wife, sir?

HORN. I do know your wife, sir, she's a woman, sir, and consequently a monster, sir, a greater monster 90 than a husband, sir.

SIR JAS. A husband! How, sir?

HORN. (*Makes horns.*) So, sir. But I make no more cuckolds, sir.

SIR JAS. Ha, ha, ha! Mercury, Mercury!

LADY FIDG. Pray, sir Jasper, let us be gone from this rude fellow.

DAIN. Who, by his breeding, would think he had ever been in France?

LADY FIDG. Foh! he's but too much a French fellow, 100 such as hate women of quality and virtue for their love to their husbands, sir Jasper. A woman is hated by 'em as much for loving her husband as for loving their money. But pray let's be gone.

HORN. You do well, madam, for I have nothing that you came for. I have brought over not so much as a bawdy picture, new postures, nor the second part of the *Ecole des Filles,*° nor. . . .

QUACK. (*Apart to* HORNER.) Hold for shame, sir!
110 What d'ye mean? You'll ruin yourself for ever with the sex. . . .

SIR JAS. Ha, ha, ha! He hates women perfectly, I find.

DAIN. What pity 'tis he should.

LADY FIDG. Ay, he's a base rude fellow for't; but affectation makes not a woman more odious to them than virtue.

HORN. Because your virtue is your greatest affectation, madam.

120 LADY FIDG. How, you saucy fellow! Would you wrong my honour?

HORN. If I could.

LADY FIDG. How d'y mean, sir?

SIR JAS. Ha, ha, ha! No, he can't wrong your ladyship's honour; upon my honour! He poor man—hark you in your ear—a mere eunuch.

LADY FIDG. O filthy French beast! foh, foh! Why do we stay? Let's be gone. I can't endure the sight of him.

SIR JAS. Stay but till the chairs° come. They'll be
130 here presently.

LADY FIDG. No, no.

SIR JAS. Nor can I stay longer. 'Tis—let me see—a quarter and a half quarter of a minute past eleven. The Council will be sat, I must away. Business must be preferred always before love and ceremony with the wise, Mr. Horner.

HORN. And the impotent, sir Jasper.

SIR JAS. Ay, ay, the impotent, Master Horner, ha, ha, ha!

140 LADY FIDG. What, leave us with a filthy man alone in his lodgings?

SIR JAS. He's an innocent man now, you know. Pray stay, I'll hasten the chairs to you.—Mr. Horner, your servant; I should be glad to see you at my house. Pray come and dine with me, and play at cards with my wife after dinner—you are fit for women at that game yet, ha, ha! (*Aside.*) 'Tis as much a husband's prudence to provide innocent diversion for a wife as to hinder her unlawful pleasures, and he had better employ her than
150 let her employ herself.—Farewell.

[*Exit* SIR JASPER.

HORN. Your servant, sir Jasper.

LADY FIDG. I will not stay with him, foh!

HORN. Nay, madam, I beseech you stay, if it be but to see I can be as civil to ladies yet as they would desire.

LADY FIDG. No, no, foh! You cannot be civil to ladies.

DAIN. You as civil as ladies would desire!

LADY FIDG. No, no, no! foh, foh, foh!

[*Exeunt* LADY FIDGET *and* DAINTY.

QUACK. Now I think, I, or you yourself rather, have 160 done your business with the women!

HORN. Thou art an ass. Don't you see already, upon the report and my carriage, this grave man of business leaves his wife in my lodgings, invites me to his house and wife, who before would not be acquainted with me out of jealousy?

QUACK. Nay, by this means you may be the more acquainted with the husbands, but the less with the wives.

HORN. Let me alone; if I can but abuse the hus- 170 bands, I'll soon disabuse the wives! Stay—I'll reckon you up the advantages I am like to have by my stratagem. First, I shall be rid of all my old acquaintances, the most insatiable sorts of duns, that invade our lodgings in a morning. And next to the pleasure of making a new mistress is that of being rid of an old one. And of all old debts, love, when it comes to be so, is paid the most unwillingly.

QUACK. Well, you may be so rid of your old acquaintances, but how will you get any new ones?   180

HORN. Doctor, thou wilt never make a good chemist,° thou art so incredulous and impatient. Ask but all the young fellows of the town, if they do not lose more time, like huntsmen, in starting the game, than in running it down. One knows not where to find 'em, who will, or will not. Women of quality are so civil you can hardly distinguish love from good breeding, and a man is often mistaken! But now I can be sure she that shows an aversion to me loves the sport—as those women that are gone, whom I warrant to be right.° And 190 then the next thing is, your women of honour, as you call 'em, are only chary of their reputations, not their persons, and 'tis scandal they would avoid, not men. Now may I have, by the reputation of an eunuch, the privileges of one; and be seen in a lady's chamber in a morning as early as her husband; kiss virgins before their parents or lovers; and may be, in short, the *passe partout*° of the town. Now, doctor. . . .

QUACK. Nay, now you shall be the doctor! And your process is so new that we do not know but it may 200 succeed.

HORN. Not so new neither. *Probatum est,*° doctor.

QUACK. Well, I wish you luck and many patients whilst I go to mine.

[*Exit* QUACK.

Enter HARCOURT *and* DORILANT *to* HORNER.

HARC. Come, your appearance at the play yesterday has, I hope, hardened you for the future against the women's contempt and the men's raillery, and now you'll abroad as you were wont.

HORN. Did I not bear it bravely?

DOR. With a most theatrical impudence! Nay, more 210

---

108 **Ecole des Filles,** a pornographic fiction   129 **chairs,** sedan chairs

181 **chemist,** alchemist   190 **right,** sexy   198 **passe partout,** passkey
202 **Probatum est,** it has been tried

than the orange-wenches show there, or a drunken vizard-mask,° or a great-bellied° actress. Nay, or the most impudent of creatures—an ill poet. Or, what is yet more impudent, a second-hand critic!

HORN. But what say the ladies? Have they no pity?

HARC. What ladies? The vizard-masks, you know, never pity a man when all's gone, though in their service.

DOR. And for the women in the boxes, you'd never 220 pity them when 'twas in your power.

HARC. They say, 'tis pity but all that deal with common women should be served so.

DOR. Nay, I dare swear, they won't admit you to play at cards with them, go to plays with 'em, or do the little duties which other shadows of men are wont to do for 'em.

HORN. Who do you call shadows of men?

DOR. Half-men.

HORN. What, boys?

230 DOR. Ay, your old boys, old *beaux garçons,*° who like superannuated stallions are suffered to run, feed, and whinny with the mares as long as they live, though they can do nothing else.

HORN. Well, a pox on love and wenching! Women serve but to keep a man from better company. Though I can't enjoy *them,* I shall *you* the more. Good fellowship and friendship are lasting, rational and manly pleasures.

HARC. For all that, give me some of those pleasures 240 you call effeminate too! They help to relish one another.

HORN. They disturb one another.

HARC. No, mistresses are like books—if you pore upon them too much they doze you and make you unfit for company, but if used discreetly you are the fitter for conversation by 'em.

DOR. A mistress should be like a little country retreat near the town—not to dwell in constantly, but only for a night and away, to taste the town the better 250 when a man returns.

HORN. I tell you, 'tis as hard to be a good fellow, a good friend, and a lover of women, as 'tis to be a good fellow, a good friend, and a lover of money. You cannot follow both, then choose your side. Wine gives you liberty, love takes it away.

DOR. Gad, he's in the right on't.

HORN. Wine gives you joy, love grief and tortures, besides the chirurgeon's. Wine makes us witty, love, only sots. Wine makes us sleep; love breaks it.

260 DOR. By the world he has reason, Harcourt.

HORN. Wine makes. . . .

DOR. Ay, wine makes us . . . makes us princes; love makes us beggars, poor rogues, i'gad . . . and wine. . . .

HORN. So, there's one converted. No, no, love and wine—oil and vinegar.

HARC. I grant it; love will still be uppermost!

HORN. Come, for my part I will have only those glorious, manly pleasures of being drunk and very slovenly.   270

Enter BOY.

BOY. Mr. Sparkish is below, sir.

HARC. What, my dear friend! A rogue that is fond of me only, I think, for abusing him.

DOR. No, he can no more think the men laugh at him than that women jilt him, his opinion of himself is so good.

HORN. Well, there's another pleasure by drinking I thought not of—I shall lose *his* acquaintance, because he cannot drink! And you know 'tis a very hard thing to be rid of him for he's one of those nauseous offerers 280 at wit, who, like the worst fiddlers, run themselves into all companies.

HARC. One that by being in the company of men of sense would pass for one.

HORN. And may so to the short-sighted world, as a false jewel amongst true ones is not discerned at a distance. His company is as troublesome to us as a cuckold's when you have a mind to his wife's.

HARC. No, the rogue will not let us enjoy one another, but ravishes our conversation, though he sig- 290 nifies no more to't than sir Martin Mar-all's gaping,° and awkward thrumming upon the lute does to his man's voice and music.

DOR. And to pass for a wit in town shows himself a fool every night to us, that are guilty of the plot.

HORN. Such wits as he are, to a company of reasonable men, like rooks to the gamesters, who only fill a room at the table, but are so far from contributing to the play that they only serve to spoil the fancy of those that do.   300

DOR. Nay, they are used like rooks too, snubbed, checked, and abused; yet the rogues will hang on.

HORN. A pox on 'em, and all that force nature, and would be still what she forbids 'em! Affectation is her greatest monster.

HARC. Most men are the contraries to that they would seem. Your bully, you see, is a coward with a long sword; the little, humbly fawning physician with his ebony cane is he that destroys men.

DOR. The usurer, a poor rogue possessed of mouldy 310 bonds and mortgages; and we they call spendthrifts are only wealthy, who lay out his money upon daily new purchases of pleasure.

HORN. Ay, your arrantest cheat is your trustee, or executor; your jealous man, the greatest cuckold; your churchman, the greatest atheist; and your noisy, pert rogue of a wit, the greatest fop, dullest ass, and worst company as you shall see—for here he comes!

212 **vizard-mask,** a woman of loose character wearing a mask in public, a whore
212 **great-bellied,** pregnant   230 **beaux garçons,** playboys

291 **sir Martin Mar-all's gaping.** Sir Martin Mar-all, main character in Dryden's play of that name (1667), tried to pass off his servant's singing and playing as his own

Enter SPARKISH *to them.*

SPARK. How is't, sparks,° how is't? Well, faith,
320 Harry, I must rally thee a little, ha, ha, ha! upon the
report in town of thee, ha, ha, ha! I can't hold i'faith
—shall I speak?

HORN. Yes, but you'll be so bitter then.

SPARK. Honest Dick and Frank here shall answer for
me, I will not be extreme bitter, by the universe.

HARC. We will be bound in ten thousand pound
bond, he shall not be bitter at all.

DOR. Nor sharp, nor sweet.

HORN. What, not downright insipid?

330 SPARK. Nay then, since you are so brisk and provoke
me, take what follows. You must know, I was discoursing and rallying with some ladies yesterday, and
they happened to talk of the fine new signs in town.

HORN. Very fine ladies, I believe.

SPARK. Said I, 'I know where the best new sign is.'
'Where?' says one of the ladies. 'In Covent Garden,° I
replied. Said another, 'In what street?' 'In Russell
Street,° answered I. 'Lord,' says another, 'I'm sure
there was ne'er a fine new sign there yesterday.' 'Yes,
340 but there was,' said I again, 'and it came out of France,
and has been there a fortnight.'

DOR. A pox! I can hear no more, prithee.

HORN. No, hear him out; let him tune his crowd a
while.

HARC. The worst music, the greatest preparation.

SPARK. Nay, faith, I'll make you laugh. 'It cannot
be,' says a third lady. 'Yes, yes,' quoth I again. Says a
fourth lady. . . .

HORN. Look to't, we'll have no more ladies.

350 SPARK. No . . . then mark, mark, now. Said I to the
fourth, 'Did you never see Mr. Horner? He lodges in
Russell Street, and he's a *sign of a man,* you know,
since he came out of France!' He, ha, he!

HORN. But the devil take me, if thine be the sign of a
jest.

SPARK. With that they all fell a-laughing, till they
bepissed themselves! What, but it does not move you,
methinks? Well, I see one has as good go to law without a witness, as break a jest without a laughter on
360 one's side. Come, come sparks, but where do we dine?
I have left at Whitehall° an earl to dine with you.

DOR. Why, I thought thou hadst loved a man with a
title better than a suit with a French trimming to't.

HARC. Go to him again.

SPARK. No, sir, a wit to me is the greatest title in the
world.

HORN. But go dine with your earl, sir; he may be
exceptious. We are your friends, and will not take it ill
to be left, I do assure you.

370 HARC. Nay, faith, he shall go to him.

SPARK. Nay, pray, gentlemen.

DOR. We'll thrust you out, if you wo'not. What, disappoint anybody for us?

SPARK. Nay, dear gentlemen, hear me.

HORN. No, no, sir, by no means; pray go, sir.

SPARK. Why, dear rogues.

DOR. No, no.

They all thrust him out of the room.

ALL. Ha, ha, ha!

SPARKISH *returns.*

SPARK. But, sparks, pray hear me. What, d'ye think
I'll eat then with gay shallow fops and silent cox- 380
combs? I think wit as necessary at dinner as a glass of
good wine, and that's the reason I never have any
stomach when I eat alone. Come, but where do we
dine?

HORN. Even where you will.

SPARK. At Chateline's?

DOR. Yes, if you will.

SPARK. Or at the Cock?

DOR. Yes, if you please.

SPARK. Or at the Dog and Partridge? 390

HORN. Ay, if you have a mind to't, for we shall dine
at neither.

SPARK. Pshaw! with your fooling we shall lose the
new play. And I would no more miss seeing a new play
the first day than I would miss sitting in the wits' row.
Therefore I'll go fetch my mistress and away.

[*Exit* SPARKISH.

Manent HORNER, HARCOURT, DORILANT. *Enter to
them* MR. PINCHWIFE.

HORN. Who have we here? Pinchwife?

PINCH. Gentlemen, your humble servant.

HORN. Well, Jack, by thy long absence from the
town, the grumness° of thy countenance, and the 400
slovenliness of thy habit, I should give thee joy, should
I not, of marriage?

PINCH. (*Aside.*) Death! does he know I'm married
too? I thought to have concealed it from him at
least—My long stay in the country will excuse my
dress, and I have a suit of law, that brings me up to
town, that puts me out of humour. Besides, I must give
Sparkish tomorrow five thousand pound to lie with my
sister.

HORN. Nay, you country gentlemen, rather than not 410
purchase, will buy anything; and he is a cracked title, if
we may quibble. Well, but am I to give thee joy? I
heard thou wert married.

PINCH. What then?

HORN. Why, the next thing that is to be heard is,
thou'rt a cuckold.

---

319 **sparks,** young men of elegant or foppish character   336 **Covent Garden,**
fashionable district in London   338 **Russell Street,** fashionable residential area
361 **Whitehall,** the king's palace

400 **grumness,** gloominess, surliness

William Wycherley   431

PINCH. (*Aside.*) Unsupportable name!

HORN. But I did not expect marriage from such a whoremaster as you, one that knew the town so much, 420 and women so well.

PINCH. Why, I have married no London wife.

HORN. Pshaw! that's all one. That grave circumspection in marrying a country wife is like refusing a deceitful, pampered Smithfield jade° to go and be cheated by a friend in the country.

PINCH. (*Aside.*) A pox on him and his simile!—At least we are a little surer of the breed there, know what her keeping has been, whether foiled° or unsound.

HORN. Come, come, I have known a clap° gotten in 430 Wales. And there are cousins, justices' clerks, and chaplains in the country—I won't say coachmen! But she's handsome and young?

PINCH. (*Aside.*) I'll answer as I should do.—No, no, she has no beauty but her youth; no attraction but her modesty; wholesome, homely, and housewifely, that's all.

DOR. He talks as like a grazier° as he looks.

PINCH. She's too awkward, ill-favoured, and silly to bring to town.

440 HARC. Then methinks you should bring her, to be taught breeding.

PINCH. To be taught! No, sir, I thank you. Good wives and private soldiers should be ignorant. (*Aside.*) I'll keep her from your instructions, I warrant you.

HARC. (*Aside.*) The rogue is as jealous as if his wife were not ignorant.

HORN. Why, if she be ill-favoured, there will be less danger here for you than by leaving her in the country. *We* have such variety of dainties that we are seldom 450 hungry.

DOR. But they have always coarse, constant, swinging stomachs in the country.

HARC. Foul feeders indeed.

DOR. And your hospitality is great there.

HARC. Open house, every man's welcome!

PINCH. So, so, gentlemen.

HORN. But, prithee, why would'st thou marry her? If she be ugly, ill-bred, and silly, she must be rich then?

PINCH. As rich as if she brought me twenty thousand 460 pound out of this town; for she'll be as sure not to spend her moderate portion as a London baggage would be to spend hers, let it be what it would; so 'tis all one. Then, because she's ugly, she's the likelier to be my own; and being ill-bred, she'll hate conversation; and since silly and innocent, will not know the difference betwixt a man of one-and-twenty and one of forty.

HORN. Nine—to my knowledge; but if she be silly, she'll expect as much from a man of forty-nine as from 470 him of one-and-twenty. But methinks wit is more necessary than beauty, and I think no young woman

ugly that has it, and no handsome woman agreeable without it.

PINCH. 'Tis my maxim he's a fool that marries, but he's a greater that does not marry a fool. What is wit in a wife good for, but to make a man a cuckold?

HORN. Yes, to keep it from his knowledge.

PINCH. A fool cannot contrive to make her husband a cuckold.

HORN. No, but she'll club with a man that can; and 480 what is worse, if she cannot make her husband a cuckold, she'll make him jealous, and pass for one, and then 'tis all one.

PINCH. Well, well, I'll take care for one, my wife shall make me no cuckold, though she had your help Mr. Horner; I understand the town, sir.

DOR. (*Aside.*) His help!

HARC. (*Aside.*) He's come newly to town, it seems, and has not heard how things are with him.

HORN. But tell me, has marriage cured thee of 490 whoring, which it seldom does?

HARC. 'Tis more than age can do.

HORN. No, the word is, I'll marry and live honest. But a marriage vow is like a penitent gamester's oath, and entering into bonds and penalties to stint himself to such a particular small sum at play for the future, which makes him but the more eager, and not being able to hold out, loses his money again, and his forfeit to boot.

DOR. Ay, ay, a gamester will be a gamester whilst his 500 money lasts, and a whoremaster whilst his vigour.

HARC. Nay, I have known 'em, when they are broke and can lose no more, keep a-fumbling with the box in their hands to fool with only, and hinder other gamesters.

DOR. That had wherewithal to make lusty stakes.

PINCH. Well, gentlemen, you may laugh at me, but you shall never lie with my wife; I know the town.

HORN. But prithee, was not the way you were in better? Is not keeping better than marriage? 510

PINCH. A pox on't! The jades would jilt me; I could never keep a whore to myself.

HORN. So, then you only married to keep a whore to yourself? Well, but let me tell you, women, as you say, are like soldiers, made constant and loyal by good pay rather than by oaths and covenants. Therefore I'd advise my friends to keep rather than marry, since too I find, by your example, it does not serve one's turn— for I saw you yesterday in the eighteen-penny place° with a pretty country wench! 520

PINCH. (*Aside.*) How the devil! Did he see my wife then? I sat there that she might not be seen. But she shall never go to a play again.

HORN. What, dost thou blush at nine-and-forty for having been seen with a wench?

DOR. No, faith, I warrant 'twas his wife, which he seated there out of sight, for he's a cunning rogue, and understands the town.

424 **Smithfield jade.** Smithfield was a horse market famous for deceit and trickery; a Smithfield jade was a Smithfield whore   428 **foiled,** deflowered
429 **clap,** venereal disease   437 **grazier,** one who grazes and feeds cattle for market

519 **eighteen-penny place,** a part of a theater frequented by whores

HARC. He blushes! Then 'twas his wife—for men are now more ashamed to be seen with them in public than with a wench.

PINCH. (*Aside.*) Hell and damnation! I'm undone, since Horner has seen her, and they know 'twas she.

HORN. But prithee, was it thy wife? She was exceedingly pretty; I was in love with her at that distance.

PINCH. You are like never to be nearer to her. Your servant, gentlemen. (*Offers to go.*)

HORN. Nay, prithee stay.

PINCH. I cannot, I will not.

HORN. Come, you shall dine with us.

PINCH. I have dined already.

HORN. Come, I know thou hast not. I'll treat thee, dear rogue. Thou sha't spend none of thy Hampshire money° today.

PINCH. (*Aside.*) Treat me! So, he uses me already like his cuckold!

HORN. Nay, you shall not go.

PINCH. I must, I have business at home.

[*Exit* PINCHWIFE.

HARC. To beat his wife! He's as jealous of her as a Cheapside husband of a Covent Garden wife.°

HORN. Why, 'tis as hard to find an old whoremaster without jealousy and the gout, as a young one without fear or the pox.

As gout in age from pox in youth proceeds,
So wenching past, then jealousy succeeds—
The worst disease that love and wenching breeds.

ACT II SCENE I

MRS. MARGERY PINCHWIFE *and* ALITHEA: MR. PINCHWIFE *peeping behind at the door.*

MRS. PINCH. Pray, sister, where are the best fields and woods to walk in, in London?

ALITH. A pretty question! Why, sister, Mulberry Garden and St. James's Park; and for close walks, the New Exchange.

MRS. PINCH. Pray, sister, tell me why my husband looks so grum here in town, and keeps me up so close, and will not let me go a-walking, nor let me wear my best gown yesterday?

ALITH. Oh, he's jealous, sister.

MRS. PINCH. Jealous? What's that?

ALITH. He's afraid you should love another man.

MRS. PINCH. How should he be afraid of my loving another man, when he will not let me see any but himself.

ALITH. Did he not carry you yesterday to a play?

MRS. PINCH. Ay, but we sat amongst ugly people. He would not let me come near the gentry, who sat under us, so that I could not see 'em. He told me none but naughty women sat there, whom they toused and

moused.° But I would have ventured for all that.

ALITH. But how did you like the play?

MRS. PINCH. Indeed I was a-weary of the play, but I liked hugeously the actors! They are the goodliest, properest men, sister.

ALITH. Oh, but you must not like the actors, sister.

MRS. PINCH. Ay, how should I help it, sister? Pray, sister, when my husband comes in, will you ask leave for me to go a-walking?

ALITH. (*Aside.*) A-walking! Ha, ha! Lord, a country gentlewoman's leisure is the drudgery of a foot-post;° and she requires as much airing as her husband's horses.

Enter MR. PINCHWIFE *to them.*

But here comes your husband; I'll ask, though I'm sure he'll not grant it.

MRS. PINCH. He says he won't let me go abroad for fear of catching the pox.°

ALITH. Fie, the smallpox you should say.

MRS. PINCH. Oh my dear, dear bud, welcome home! Why dost thou look so fropish?° Who has nangered° thee?

PINCH. You're a fool!

MRS. PINCHWIFE *goes aside and cries.*

ALITH. Faith, so she is, for crying for no fault, poor tender creature!

PINCH. What, you would have her as impudent as yourself, as arrant a jill-flirt,° a gadder, a magpie, and to say all—a mere notorious town-woman?

ALITH. Brother, you are my only censurer; and the honour of your family shall sooner suffer in your wife there than in me, though I take the innocent liberty of the town.

PINCH. Hark you, mistress, do not talk so before my wife. The innocent liberty of the town!

ALITH. Why, pray, who boasts of any intrigue with me? What lampoon has made my name notorious? What ill women frequent my lodgings? I keep no company with any women of scandalous reputations.

PINCH. No, you keep the men of scandalous reputations company.

ALITH. Where? Would you not have me civil? Answer 'em in a box at the plays, in the drawing room at Whitehall, in St. James's Park, Mulberry Garden, or. . . .

PINCH. Hold, hold! Do not teach my wife where the men are to be found! I believe she's the worse for your town documents already. I bid you keep her in ignorance, as I do.

MRS. PINCH. Indeed, be not angry with her, bud. She

Act II 20–21 **toused and moused,** tossed and tumbled, handled roughly but in a playful and sexual way 31 **foot-post,** letter carrier on foot 37 **pox,** syphilis 40 **fropish,** fretful, peevish **nangered,** angered 46 **jill-flirt,** a young woman of a wanton character

544 **thy Hampshire money,** country money 551 **Cheapside husband . . . wife,** as jealous as a merchant husband of an actual or would-be aristocratic wife

will tell me nothing of the town though I ask her a thousand times a day.

PINCH. Then you are very inquisitive to know, I find!

MRS. PINCH. Not I, indeed, dear. I hate London. Our placehouse in the country is worth a thousand of't. Would I were there again!

PINCH. So you shall, I warrant. But were you not talking of plays and players when I came in? (*To* ALITHEA.) You are her encourager in such discourses.

MRS. PINCH. No, indeed, dear; she chid me just now for liking the playermen.

PINCH. (*Aside*.) Nay, if she be so innocent as to own to me her liking them, there is no hurt in't.—Come, my poor rogue, but thou lik'st none better than me?

MRS. PINCH. Yes, indeed, but I do; the playermen are finer folks.

PINCH. But you love none better than me?

MRS. PINCH. You are mine own dear bud, and I know you; I hate a stranger.

PINCH. Ay, my dear, you must love me only, and not be like the naughty town-women, who only hate their husbands and love every man else—love plays, visits, fine coaches, fine clothes, fiddles, balls, treats, and so lead a wicked town-life.

MRS. PINCH. Nay, if to enjoy all these things be a town-life, London is not so bad a place, dear.

PINCH. How! If you love me, you must hate London.

ALITH. (*Aside*.) The fool has forbid me discovering to her the pleasures of the town, and he is now setting her agog upon them himself.

MRS. PINCH. But, husband, do the town-women love the playermen too?

PINCH. Yes, I warrant you.

MRS. PINCH. Ay, I warrant you.

PINCH. Why, you do not, I hope?

MRS. PINCH. No, no, bud; but why have we no playermen in the country?

PINCH. Ha!—Mistress Minx, ask me no more to go to a play.

MRS. PINCH. Nay, why, love? I did not care for going, but when you forbid me, you make me, as't were, desire it.

ALITH. (*Aside*.) So 'twill be in other things, I warrant.

MRS. PINCH. Pray, let me go to a play, dear.

PINCH. Hold your peace, I wo'not.

MRS. PINCH. Why, love?

PINCH. Why, I'll tell you.

ALITH. (*Aside*.) Nay, if he tell her, she'll give him more cause to forbid her that place.

MRS. PINCH. Pray, why, dear?

PINCH. First, you like the actors, and the gallants may like you.

MRS. PINCH. What, a homely country girl? No bud, nobody will like me.

PINCH. I tell you, yes, they may.

MRS. PINCH. No, no, you jest—I won't believe you, I will go.

PINCH. I tell you then, that one of the lewdest fellows in town, who saw you there, told me he was in love with you.

MRS. PINCH. Indeed! Who, who, pray who was't?

PINCH. (*Aside*.) I've gone too far, and slipped before I was aware. How overjoyed she is!

MRS. PINCH. Was it any Hampshire gallant, any of our neighbours? I promise you, I am beholding to him.

PINCH. I promise you, you lie; for he would but ruin you, as he has done hundreds. He has no other love for women, but that; such as he look upon women, like basilisks,° but to destroy 'em.

MRS. PINCH. Ay, but if he loves me, why should he ruin me? Answer me to that. Methinks he should not; I would do him no harm.

ALITH. Ha, ha, ha!

PINCH. 'Tis very well; but I'll keep him from doing you any harm, or me either.

Enter SPARKISH *and* HARCOURT.

But here comes company; get you in, get you in.

MRS. PINCH. But pray, husband, is he a pretty gentleman that loves me?

PINCH. In, baggage, in!

　　　　　[*Thrusts her in; shuts the door.*

(*Aside*.) What, all the lewd libertines of the town brought to my lodgings by this easy coxcomb! S'death, I'll not suffer it.

SPARK. Here Harcourt, do you approve my choice? (*To* ALITHEA.) Dear little rogue, I told you I'd bring you acquainted with all my friends, the wits, and. . . .

HARCOURT *salutes her.*

PINCH. (*Aside*.) Ay, they shall know her, as well as you yourself will, I warrant you.

SPARK. This is one of those, my pretty rogue, that are to dance at your wedding tomorrow; and him you must bid welcome ever to what you and I have.

PINCH. (*Aside*.) Monstrous!

SPARK. Harcourt, how dost thou like her, faith?—Nay, dear, do not look down; I should hate to have a wife of mine out of countenance at any thing.

PINCH. (*Aside*.) Wonderful!

SPARK. Tell me, I say, Harcourt, how dost thou like her? Thou hast stared upon her enough to resolve me.

HARC. So infinitely well that I could wish I had a mistress too, that might differ from her in nothing but her love and engagement to you.

ALITH. Sir, master Sparkish has often told me that his acquaintance were all wits and railleurs,° and now I find it.

139 **basilisks,** fabulous reptiles whose breath and look are fatal　172 **railleurs,** those who practice raillery, good humored ridicule and banter

SPARK. No, by the universe, madam, he does not rally now; you may believe him. I do assure you, he is the honestest, worthiest true-hearted gentleman—a man of such perfect honour, he would say nothing to a lady he does not mean.

PINCH. (*Aside*.) Praising another man to his mis- 180 tress!

HARC. Sir, you are so beyond expectation obliging, that. . . .

SPARK. Nay, i'gad, I am sure you do admire her extremely; I see't in your eyes.—He does admire you, madam.—By the world, don't you?

HARC. Yes, above the world, or the most glorious part of it, her whole sex; and till now I never thought I should have envied you, or any man about to marry, but you have the best excuse for marriage I ever knew.

190 ALITH. Nay, now, sir, I'm satisfied you are of the society of the wits and railleurs since you cannot spare your friend even when he is but too civil to you. But the surest sign is, since you are an enemy to marriage, for that, I hear, you hate as much as business or bad wine.

HARC. Truly, madam, I never was an enemy to marriage till now, because marriage was never an enemy to me before.

ALITH. But why, sir, is marriage an enemy to you 200 now? Because it robs you of your friend here? For you look upon a friend married as one gone into a monastery, that is—dead to the world.

HARC. 'Tis indeed, because you marry him; I see, madam, you can guess my meaning. I do confess heartily and openly, I wish it were in my power to break the match. By heavens I would!

SPARK. Poor Frank.

ALITH. Would you be so unkind to me?

HARC. No, no, 'tis not because I would be unkind to 210 you.

SPARK. Poor Frank! No, gad, 'tis only his kindness to me.

PINCH. (*Aside*.) Great kindness to you indeed! Insensible fop, let a man make love to his wife to his face!

SPARK. Come, dear Frank, for all my wife there that shall be, thou shalt enjoy me sometimes, dear rogue. By my honour, we men of wit condole for our deceased brother in marriage as much as for one dead in 220 earnest. I think that was prettily said of me, ha, Harcourt? But come, Frank, be not melancholy for me.

HARC. No, I assure you I am not melancholy for you.

SPARK. Prithee, Frank, dost think my wife-that-shall-be, there, a fine person?

HARC. I could gaze upon her till I became as blind as you are.

SPARK. How, as I am? How?

HARC. Because you are a lover, and true lovers are 230 blind, stock blind.

SPARK. True, true; but by the world, she has wit too, as well as beauty. Go, go with her into a corner, and try if she has wit; talk to her anything; she's bashful before me.

HARC. Indeed, if a woman wants wit in a corner, she has it nowhere.

ALITH. (*Aside to* SPARKISH.) Sir, you dispose of me a little before your time. . . .

SPARK. Nay, nay, madam let me have an earnest of your obedience, or. . . . Go, go, madam. . . .   240

HARCOURT *courts* ALITHEA *aside*.

PINCH. How, sir! If you are not concerned for the honour of a wife, I am for that of a sister; he shall not debauch her. Be a pander to your own wife, bring men to let, let 'em make love before your face, thrust 'em into a corner together, then leave 'em in private! Is this your town wit and conduct?

SPARK. Ha, ha, ha! A silly wise rogue would make one laugh more than a stark fool, ha, ha, ha! I shall burst. Nay, you shall not disturb 'em; I'll vex thee, by the world.   250

[*Struggles with* PINCHWIFE *to keep him from* HARCOURT *and* ALITHEA.

ALITH. The writings are drawn, sir, settlements made;° 'tis too late, sir, and past all revocation.

HARC. Then so is my death.

ALITH. I would not be unjust to him.

HARC. Then why to me so?

ALITH. I have no obligation to you.

HARC. My love.

ALITH. I had his before.

HARC. You never had it; he wants, you see, jealousy, the only infallible sign of it.   260

ALITH. Love proceeds from esteem; he cannot distrust my virtue. Besides he loves me, or he would not marry me.

HARC. Marrying you is no more sign of his love, than bribing your woman, that he may marry you, is a sign of his generosity. Marriage is rather a sign of interest than love; and he that marries a fortune, covets a mistress, not loves her. But if you take marriage for a sign of love, take it from me immediately.

ALITH. No, now you have put a scruple in my head. 270 But in short, sir, to end our dispute—I must marry him, my reputation would suffer in the world else.

HARC. No, if you do marry him, with your pardon, madam, your reputation suffers in the world, and you would be thought in necessity for a cloak.

ALITH. Nay, now you are rude, sir.—Mr. Sparkish, pray come hither, your friend here is very troublesome, and very loving.

---

252 **writings . . . settlements made,** legal documents setting up the marriage state and property disposition

HARC. (*Aside to* ALITHEA.) Hold, hold!

280 PINCH. D'ye hear that?

SPARK. Why, d'ye think I'll seem to be jealous, like a country bumpkin?

PINCH. No, rather be a cuckold, like a credulous cit.°

HARC. Madam, you would not have been so little generous as to have told him?

ALITH. Yes, since you could be so little generous as to wrong him.

HARC. Wrong him! No man can do't, he's beneath an injury; a bubble,° a coward, a senseless idiot, a wretch 290 so contemptible to all the world but you that . . .

ALITH. Hold, do not rail at him, for since he is like to be my husband, I am resolved to like him. Nay, I think I am obliged to tell him you are not his friend.—Master Sparkish, Master Sparkish!

SPARK. What, what? Now, dear rogue, has not she wit?

HARC. (*Speaks surlily.*) Not so much as I thought, and hoped she had.

ALITH. Mr. Sparkish, do you bring people to rail at 300 you?

HARC. Madam. . . .

SPARK. How! No, but if he does rail at me, 'tis but in jest, I warrant—what we wits do for one another and never take any notice of it.

ALITH. He spoke so scurrilously of you, I had no patience to hear him; besides, he has been making love to me.

HARC. (*Aside.*) True, damned, telltale woman.

SPARK. Pshaw! to show his parts°—we wits rail and 310 make love often but to show our parts; as we have no affections, so we have no malice; we. . . .

ALITH. He said you were a wretch, below an injury.

SPARK. Pshaw!

HARC. (*Aside.*) Damned, senseless, impudent, virtuous jade! Well, since she won't let me have her, she'll do as good, she'll make me hate her.

ALITH. A common bubble.

SPARK. Pshaw!

ALITH. A coward.

320 SPARK. Pshaw, pshaw!

ALITH. A senseless, drivelling idiot.

SPARK. How! Did he disparage my parts? Nay, then my honour's concerned. I can't put up that, sir, by the world. Brother, help me to kill him. (*Aside.*) I may draw now, since we have the odds of him! 'Tis a good occasion, too, before my mistress . . .

[*Offers to draw.*

ALITH. Hold, hold!

SPARK. What, what?

ALITH. (*Aside.*) I must not let 'em kill the gentleman 330 neither, for his kindness to me; I am so far from hating him that I wish my gallant had his person and understanding. Nay, if my honour. . . .

SPARK. I'll be thy death.

ALITH. Hold, hold! Indeed, to tell the truth, the gentleman said after all that what he spoke was but out of friendship to you.

SPARK. How! say, I am—I am a fool, that is, no wit, out of friendship to me?

ALITH. Yes, to try whether I was concerned enough for you, and made love to me only to be satisfied of my 340 virtue, for your sake.

HARC. (*Aside.*) Kind however. . . .

SPARK. Nay, if it were so, my dear rogue, I ask thee pardon. But why would not you tell me so, faith?

HARC. Because I did not think on't, faith.

SPARK. Come, Horner does not come. Harcourt let's be gone to the new play.—Come, madam.

ALITH. I will not go, if you intend to leave me alone in the box and run into the pit, as you use to do.

SPARK. Pshaw! I'll leave Harcourt with you in the 350 box to entertain you, and that's as good. If I sat in the box I should be thought no judge but of trimmings.°— Come away, Harcourt, lead her down.

[*Exeunt* SPARKISH, HARCOURT, *and* ALITHEA.

PINCH. Well, go thy ways, for the flower of the true town fops, such as spend their estates before they come to 'em, and are cuckolds before they're married. But let me go look to my own freehold—How!

Enter MY LADY FIDGET, MISTRESS DAINTY FIDGET, *and* MISTRESS SQUEAMISH

LADY FIDG. Your servant, sir. Where is your lady? We are come to wait upon her to the new play.

PINCH. New play! 360

LADY FIDG. And my husband will wait upon you presently.

PINCH. (*Aside.*) Damn your civility.—Madam, by no means; I will not see sir Jasper here till I have waited upon him at home; nor shall my wife see you till she has waited upon your ladyship at your lodgings.

LADY FIDG. Now we are here, sir. . . .

PINCH. No, madam.

DAIN. Pray let us see her.

SQUEAM. We will not stir till we see her. 370

PINCH. (*Aside.*) A pox on you all!

[*Goes to the door, and returns.*

She has locked the door, and is gone abroad.

LADY FIDG. No, you have locked the door, and she's within.

DAIN. They told us below, she was here.

PINCH. (*Aside.*) Will nothing do? Well, it must out then.—To tell you the truth, ladies, which I was afraid to let you know before, least it might endanger your lives, my wife has just now the smallpox come out upon her. Do not be frightened; but pray, be gone, 380 ladies; you shall not stay here in danger of your lives; pray get you gone, ladies.

LADY FIDG. No, no we have all had 'em.

---

283 **credulous cit,** city merchant, as opposed to an aristocrat   289 **a bubble,** dupe or gull   309 **parts,** personal qualities

352 **trimmings,** clothes

SQUEAM. Alack, alack!

DAIN. Come, come, we must see how it goes with her; I understand the disease.

LADY FIDG. Come.

PINCH. (Aside.) Well, there is no being too hard for women at their own weapon, lying; therefore I'll quit
390 the field.

[Exit PINCHWIFE.

SQUEAM. Here's an example of jealousy!

LADY FIDG. Indeed, as the world goes, I wonder there are no more jealous, since wives are so neglected.

DAIN. Pshaw! as the world goes, to what end should they be jealous?

LADY FIDG. Foh! 'tis a nasty world.

SQUEAM. That men of parts, great acquaintance, and quality should take up with and spend themselves and
400 fortunes in keeping little playhouse creatures, foh!

LADY FIDG. Nay, that women of understanding, great acquaintance, and good quality should fall a-keeping too of little creatures, foh!

SQUEAM. Why, 'tis the men of quality's fault. They never visit women of honour and reputation as they used to do; and have not so much as common civility for ladies of our rank, but use us with the same indifferency and ill-breeding as if we were all married to 'em.

LADY FIDG. She says true! 'Tis an arrant shame
410 women of quality should be so slighted. Methinks, birth—birth should go for something. I have known men admired, courted, and followed for their titles only.

SQUEAM. Ay, one would think men of honour should not love, no more than marry, out of their own rank.

DAIN. Fie, fie upon 'em! They are come to think cross-breeding for themselves best, as well as for their dogs and horses.

LADY FIDG. They are dogs, and horses for't!
420 SQUEAM. One would think, if not for love, for vanity a little.

DAIN. Nay, they do satisfy their vanity upon us sometimes, and are kind to us in their report—tell all the world they lie with us.

LADY FIDG. Damned rascals! That we should be only wronged by 'em. To report a man has. . . had a person, when he has not . . . had a person, is the greatest wrong in the whole world that can be . . . done to a person.
430 SQUEAM. Well, 'tis an arrant shame noble persons should be so wronged and neglected.

LADY FIDG. But still 'tis an arranter shame for a noble person to neglect her own honour, and defame her own noble person with little inconsiderable fellows, foh!

DAIN. I suppose the crime against our honour is the same with a man of quality as with another.

LADY FIDG. How! No, sure, the man of quality is likest one's husband, and therefore the fault should be
440 the less.

DAIN. But then the pleasure should be the less!

LADY FIDG. Fie, fie, fie, for shame, sister! Whither shall we ramble? Be continent° in your discourse, or I shall hate you.

DAIN. Besides, an intrigue is so much the more notorious for the man's quality.

SQUEAM. 'Tis true, nobody takes notice of a private man, and therefore with him 'tis more secret, and the crime's the less when 'tis not known.

LADY FIDG. You say true. I'faith, I think you are in 450 the right on't. 'Tis not an injury to a husband till it be an injury to our honours; so that a woman of honour loses no honour with a private person; and to say truth. . . .

DAIN. (Apart to SQUEAMISH.) So, the little fellow is grown a private person . . . with her.

LADY FIDG. But still my dear, dear honour.

Enter SIR JASPER, HORNER, DORILANT.

SIR JAS. Ay, my dear, dear of honour, thou hast still so much honour in thy mouth. . . .

HORN. (Aside.) That she has none elsewhere.   460

LADY FIDG. Oh, what d'ye mean to bring in these upon us?

DAIN. Foh! these are as bad as wits.

SQUEAM. Foh!

LADY FIDG. Let us leave the room.

SIR JAS. Stay, stay; faith, to tell you the naked truth. . . .

LADY FIDG. Fie, sir Jasper, do not use that word naked.

SIR JAS. Well, well, in short, I have business at 470 Whitehall, and cannot go to the play with you, therefore would have you go. . . .

LADY FIDG. With those two to a play?

SIR JAS. No, not with t'other, but with Mr. Horner. There can be no more scandal to go with him than with Mr. Tattle, or Master Limberham.

LADY FIDG. With that nasty fellow! No!

SIR JAS. Nay, prithee dear, hear me.

[Whispers to LADY FIDGET.

HORN. Ladies. . . .

HORNER, DORILANT drawing near SQUEAMISH and DAINTY.

DAIN. Stand off!   480

SQUEAM. Do not approach us!

DAIN. You herd with the wits, you are obscenity all over.

SQUEAM. I would as soon look upon a picture of Adam and Eve, without fig leaves, as any of you, if I could help it, therefore keep off, and do not make us sick.

DOR. What a devil are these?

443 **continent,** characterized by self-restraint; perhaps also a pun of chastity

HORN. Why, these are pretenders to honour, as crit-
490 ics to wit, only by censuring others; and as every raw,
peevish, out-of-humoured affected, dull, tea-drinking,
arithmetical° fop sets up for a wit, by railing at men of
sense, so these for honour by railing at the court and
ladies of as great honour as quality.

SIR JAS. Come, Mr. Horner, I must desire you to go
with these ladies to the play, sir.

HORN. I, sir?

SIR JAS. Ay, ay, come, sir.

HORN. I must beg your pardon, sir, and theirs. I will
500 not be seen in women's company in public again for
the world.

SIR JAS. Ha, ha! strange aversion!

SQUEAM. No, he's for women's company in private.

SIR JAS. He—poor man—he! ha, ha, ha!

DAIN. 'Tis a greater shame amongst lewd fellows to
be seen in virtuous women's company than for the
women to be seen with them.

HORN. Indeed, madam, the time was I only hated
virtuous women, but now I hate the other too; I beg
510 your pardon ladies.

LADY FIDG. You are very obliging, sir, because we
would not be troubled with you.

SIR JAS. In sober sadness, he shall go.

DOR. Nay, if he wo'not, I am ready to wait upon the
ladies; and I think I am the fitter man.

SIR JAS. You, sir, no, I thank you for that—Master
Horner is a privileged man amongst the virtuous
ladies; 'twill be a great while before you are so, he, he,
he! He's my wife's gallant, he, he, he! No, pray with-
520 draw, sir, for as I take it, the virtuous ladies have no
business with you.

DOR. And I am sure he can have none with them.
'Tis strange a man can't come amongst virtuous wom-
en now but upon the same terms as men are admitted
into the great Turk's seraglio;° but heaven keep me
from being an ombre° player with 'em! But where is
Pinchwife?

                                    [Exit DORILANT.

SIR JAS. Come, come, man; what, avoid the sweet
society of woman-kind?—that sweet, soft, gentle,
530 tame, noble creature, woman, made for man's companion. . . .

HORN. So is that soft, gentle, tame, and more noble
creature a spaniel, and has all their tricks—can fawn,
lie down, suffer beating, and fawn the more; barks at
your friends when they come to see you; makes your
bed hard; gives you fleas, and the mange sometimes.
And all the difference is, the spaniel's the more faithful
animal, and fawns but upon one master.

SIR JAS. He, he, he!
540 SQUEAM. Oh, the rude beast!

DAIN. Insolent brute!

LADY FIDG. Brute! Stinking, mortified, rotten
French wether,° to dare. . . .

SIR JAS. Hold, an't please your ladyship.—For
shame, master Horner, your mother was a woman.—(Aside.) Now shall I never reconcile 'em.—
Hark you, madam, take my advice in your anger. You
know you often want one to make up your drolling
pack of ombre° players; and you may cheat him easily,
for he's an ill gamester, and consequently loves play. 550
Besides, you know, you have but two old civil gentlemen (with stinking breaths too) to wait upon you
abroad; take in the third into your service. The others
are but crazy; and a lady should have a supernumerary°
gentleman-usher, as a supernumerary coachhorse, lest
sometimes you should be forced to stay at home.

LADY FIDG. But are you sure he loves play, and has
money?

SIR JAS. He loves play as much as you, and has
money as much as I.   560

LADY FIDG. Then I am contented to make him pay
for his scurrillity; money makes up in a measure all
other wants in men.—(Aside.) Those whom we cannot
make hold for gallants, we make fine.

SIR JAS. (Aside.) So, so; now to mollify, to wheedle
him.—Master Horner, will you never keep civil company? Methinks 'tis time now, since you are only fit
for them. Come, come, man, you must e'en fall to
visiting our wives, eating at our tables, drinking tea
with our virtuous relations after dinner, dealing cards 570
to 'em, reading plays and gazettes to 'em, picking fleas
out of their shocks° for 'em, collecting receipts,° new
songs, women, pages, and footmen for 'em.

HORN. I hope they'll afford me better employment,
sir.

SIR JAS. He, he, he! 'Tis fit you know your work
before you come into your place; and since you are
unprovided of a lady to flatter, and a good house to eat
at, pray frequent mine, and call my wife mistress, and
she shall call you gallant, according to the custom.   580

HORN. Who, I?

SIR JAS. Faith, thou shalt for my sake; come, for my
sake only.

HORN. For your sake. . . .

SIR JAS. Come, come, here's a gamester for you; let
him be a little familiar sometimes; nay, what if a little
rude? Gamesters may be rude with ladies, you know.

LADY FIDG. Yes, losing gamesters have a privilege
with women.

HORN. I always thought the contrary, that the win- 590
ning gamester had most privilege with women; for
when you have lost your money to a man, you'll lose
anything you have, all you have, they say, and he may
use you as he pleases.

SIR JAS. He, he, he! Well, win or lose, you shall have
your liberty with her.

LADY FIDG. As he behaves himself; and for your
sake I'll give him admittance and freedom.

HORN. All sorts of freedom, madam?

---

492 **arithmetical,** precise   525 **seraglio,** harem   526 **ombre,** card game
543 **wether,** a male sheep castrated before maturity

554 **supernumerary,** extra, unnecessary   572 **shocks,** dogs with long, shaggy
hair   **receipts,** recipes

SIR JAS. Ay, ay, ay, all sorts of freedom thou can'st take, and so go to her, begin thy new employment; wheedle her, jest with her, and be better acquainted one with another.

HORN. (*Aside*.) I think I know her already, therefore may venture with her, my secret for hers.

[HORNER *and* LADY FIDGET *whisper*.

SIR JAS. Sister, cuz, I have provided an innocent playfellow for you there.

DAIN. Who, he!

SQUEAM. There's a playfellow indeed!

SIR JAS. Yes, sure, what, he is good enough to play at cards, blindman's buff, or the fool with sometimes.

SQUEAM. Foh! we'll have no such playfellows.

DAIN. No, sir, you shan't choose playfellows for us, we thank you.

SIR JAS. Nay, pray hear me.

[*Whispering to them.*

LADY FIDG. But, poor gentleman, could you be so generous, so truly a man of honour, as for the sakes of us women of honour, to cause yourself to be reported no man? No man! And to suffer yourself the greatest shame that could fall upon a man, that none might fall upon us women by your conversation? But indeed, sir, as perfectly, perfectly, the same man as before your going into France, sir? As perfectly, perfectly, sir?

HORN. As perfectly, perfectly, madam. Nay, I scorn you should take my word; I desire to be tried only, madam.

LADY FIDG. Well, that's spoken again like a man of honour; all men of honour desire to come to the test. But, indeed, generally you men report such things of yourselves, one does not know how or whom to believe; and it is come to that pass we dare not take your words no more than your tailor's, without some staid servant of yours be bound with you. But I have so strong a faith in your honour, dear, dear, noble sir, that I'd forfeit mine for yours at any time, dear sir.

HORN. No, madam, you should not need to forfeit it for me. I have given you security already to save you harmless, my late reputation being so well known in the world, madam.

LADY FIDG. But if upon any future falling out, or upon a suspicion of my taking the trust out of your hands, to employ some other, you yourself should betray your trust, dear sir? I mean, if you'll give me leave to speak obscenely, you might tell, dear sir.

HORN. If I did, nobody would believe me! The reputation of impotency is as hardly recovered again in the world as that of cowardice, dear madam.

LADY FIDG. Nay, then, as one may say, you may do your worst, dear, dear, sir.

SIR JAS. Come, is your ladyship reconciled to him yet? Have you agreed on matters? For I must be gone to Whitehall.

LADY FIDG. Why, indeed, sir Jasper, master Horner is a thousand, thousand times a better man than I thought him. Cousin Squeamish, sister Dainty, I can name him now; truly, not long ago, you know, I thought his very name obscenity, and I would as soon have lain with him as have named him.

SIR JAS. Very likely, poor madam.

DAIN. I believe it.

SQUEAM. No doubt on't.

SIR JAS. Well, well—that your ladyship is as virtuous as any she, I know, and him all the town knows—he, he, he! Therefore, now you like him, get you gone to your business together; go, go, to your business, I say, pleasure, whilst I go to my pleasure, business.

LADY FIDG. Come then, dear gallant.

HORN. Come away, my dearest mistress.

SIR JAS. So, so; why 'tis as I'd have it.

[*Exit* SIR JASPER.

HORN. And as I'd have it!

LADY FIDG. Who for his business from his wife will run,
　　Takes the best care to have her business done!

[*Exeunt omnes.*

ACT III SCENE I

ALITHEA *and* MRS. PINCHWIFE.

ALITH. Sister, what ails you? You are grown melancholy.

MRS. PINCH. Would it not make anyone melancholy, to see you go every day fluttering about abroad, whilst I must stay at home like a poor, lonely, sullen bird in a cage?

ALITH. Ay, sister, but you came young and just from the nest to your cage, so that I thought you liked it; and could be as cheerful in't as others that took their flight themselves early, and are hopping abroad in the open air.

MRS. PINCH. Nay, I confess I was quiet enough till my husband told me what pure lives the London ladies live abroad, with their dancing, meetings, and junketings,° and dressed every day in their best gowns; and I warrant you, play at ninepins every day of the week, so they do.

Enter MR. PINCHWIFE.

PINCH. Come, what's here to do? You are putting the town pleasures in her head, and setting her a-longing.

ALITH. Yes, after ninepins! You suffer none to give her those longings, you mean, but yourself.

PINCH. I tell her of the vanities of the town like a confessor.

ALITH. A confessor! Just such a confessor as he that, by forbidding a silly ostler to grease the horse's teeth, taught him to do't.

Act III, Scene I 14 junketings, merrymaking, banqueting

PINCH. Come Mistress Flippant, good precepts are lost when poor examples are still before us. The liberty you take abroad makes her hanker after it, and out of humour at home. Poor wretch! she desired not to come to London; I would bring her.

ALITH. Very well.

PINCH. She has been this week in town, and never desired, till this afternoon, to go abroad.

ALITH. Was she not at a play yesterday?

PINCH. Yes, but she ne'er asked me. I was myself the cause of her going.

ALITH. Then, if she ask you again, you are the cause of her asking, and not my example.

PINCH. Well, tomorrow night I shall be rid of you; and the next day, before 'tis light, she and I'll be rid of the town, and my dreadful apprehensions. Come, be not melancholy, for thou shalt go into the country after tomorrow, dearest.

ALITH. Great comfort!

MRS. PINCH. Pish! what d'ye tell me of the country for?

PINCH. How's this! What, pish at the country?

MRS. PINCH. Let me alone, I am not well.

PINCH. O if that be all—what ails my dearest?

MRS. PINCH. Truly I don't know; but I have not been well since you told me there was a gallant at the play in love with me.

PINCH. Ha!

ALITH. That's by my example too!

PINCH. Nay, if you are not well, but are so concerned because a lewd fellow chanced to lie and say he liked you, you'll make me sick too.

MRS. PINCH. Of what sickness?

PINCH. Of that which is worse than the plague—jealousy.

MRS. PINCH. Pish, you jeer! I'm sure there's no such disease in our receiptbook at home.

PINCH. No, thou never met'st with it, poor innocent. (*Aside.*) Well, if thou cuckold me, 'twill be my fault, for cuckolds and bastards are generally makers of their own fortune.

MRS. PINCH. Well, but pray, bud, let's go to a play tonight.

PINCH. 'Tis just done, she comes from it; but why are you so eager to see a play?

MRS. PINCH. Faith, dear, not that I care one pin for their talk there, but I like to look upon the playermen, and would see, if I could, the gallant you say loves me; that's all, dear bud.

PINCH. Is that all, dear bud?

ALITH. This proceeds from my example!

MRS. PINCH. But if the play be done, let's go abroad however, dear bud.

PINCH. Come, have a little patience, and thou shalt go into the country on Friday.

MRS. PINCH. Therefore I would see first some sights, to tell my neighbours of. Nay, I will go abroad, that's once.

ALITH. I'm the cause of this desire too!

PINCH. But now I think on't, who was the cause of Horner's coming to my lodging today? That was you.

ALITH. No, you, because you would not let him see your handsome wife out of your lodging.

MRS. PINCH. Why, O Lord! did the gentleman come hither to see me indeed?

PINCH. No, no.—You are not cause of that damned question too, Mistress Alithea? (*Aside.*) Well, she's in the right of it. He is in love with my wife . . . and comes after her . . . 'tis so . . . but I'll nip his love in the bud; lest he should follow us into the country, and break his chariot-wheel near our house on purpose for an excuse to come to't. But I think I know the town.

MRS. PINCH. Come, pray bud, let's go abroad before 'tis late. For I will go, that's flat and plain.

PINCH. (*Aside.*) So! the obstinacy already of a town-wife, and I must, whilst she's here, humour her like one.—Sister, how shall we do, that she may not be seen or known?

ALITH. Let her put on her mask.

PINCH. Pshaw! A mask makes people but the more inquisitive, and is as ridiculous a disguise as a stage beard; her shape, stature, habit will be known. And if we should meet with Horner he would be sure to take acquaintance with us, must wish her joy, kiss her, talk to her, leer upon her, and the devil and all. No, I'll not use her to a mask, 'tis dangerous; for masks have made more cuckolds than the best faces that ever were known.

ALITH. How will you do then?

MRS. PINCH. Nay, shall we go? The Exchange will be shut, and I have a mind to see that.

PINCH. So . . . I have it . . . I'll dress her up in the suit we are to carry down to her brother, little sir James; nay, I understand the town tricks. Come, let's go dress her. A mask! No—a woman masked, like a covered dish, gives a man curiosity, and appetite, when, it may be, uncovered 'twould turn his stomach; no, no.

ALITH. Indeed your comparison is something a greasy one. But I had a gentle gallant used to say, 'A beauty masked, like the sun in eclipse, gathers together more gazers than if it shined out.'

[*Exeunt.*

SCENE II

The scene changes to the New Exchange.

Enter HORNER, HARCOURT, DORILANT.

DOR. Engaged to women, and not sup with us?

HORN. Ay, a pox on 'em all.

HARC. You were much a more reasonable man in the morning, and had as noble resolutions against 'em as a widower of a week's liberty.

DOR. Did I ever think to see you keep company with women in vain?

HORN. In vain! No—'tis, since I can't love 'em, to be revenged on 'em.

10 HARC. Now your sting is gone, you looked in the box, amongst all those women, like a drone in the hive, all upon you; shoved and ill-used by 'em all, and thrust from one side to t'other.

DOR. Yet he must be buzzing amongst 'em still, like other old beetle-headed,° lickerish° drones. Avoid 'em, and hate 'em as they hate you.

HORN. Because I do hate 'em, and would hate 'em yet more, I'll frequent 'em. You may see by marriage, nothing makes a man hate a woman more, than her 20 constant conversation. In short, I converse with 'em, as you do with rich fools, to laugh at 'em, and use 'em ill.

DOR. But I would no more sup with women, unless I could lie with 'em, than sup with a rich coxcomb, unless I could cheat him.

HORN. Yes, I have known thee sup with a fool for his drinking; if he could set out your hand that way only, you were satisfied, and if he were a wine-swallowing mouth 'twas enough.

30 HARC. Yes, a man drinks often with a fool, as he tosses with a marker, only to keep his hand in ure.° But do the ladies drink?

HORN. Yes, sir, and I shall have the pleasure at least of laying 'em flat with a bottle, and bring as much scandal that way upon 'em as formerly t'other.

HARC. Perhaps you may prove as weak a brother amongst 'em that way as t'other.

DOR. Foh! drinking with women is as unnatural as scolding with 'em. But 'tis a pleasure of decayed for-40 nicators, and the basest way of quenching love.

HARC. Nay, 'tis drowning love instead of quenching it. But leave us for civil women too!

DOR. Ay, when he can't be the better for 'em. We hardly pardon a man that leaves his friend for a wench, and that's a pretty lawful call.

HORN. Faith, I would not leave you for 'em, if they would not drink.

DOR. Who would disappoint his company at Lewis's for a gossiping?

50 HARC. Foh! Wine and women, good apart, together as nauseous as sack° and sugar. But hark you, sir, before you go, a little of your advice; an old maimed general, when unfit for action, is fittest for counsel. I have other designs upon women than eating and drinking with them. I am in love with Sparkish's mistress, whom he is to marry tomorrow. Now how shall I get her?

Enter SPARKISH, *looking about.*

HORN. Why, here comes one will help you to her.

HARC. He! He, I tell you, is my rival, and will hinder 60 my love.

HORN. No, a foolish rival and a jealous husband assist their rival's designs; for they are sure to make their women hate them, which is the first step to their love for another man.

HARC. But I cannot come near his mistress but in his company.

HORN. Still the better for you, for fools are most easily cheated when they themselves are accessories; and he is to be bubbled° of his mistress, as of his money, the common mistress, by keeping him com-70 pany.

SPARK. Who is that, that is to be bubbled? Faith, let me snack,° I han't met with a bubble since Christmas. Gad, I think bubbles are like their brother woodcocks,° go out with the cold weather.

HARC. (*Apart to* HORNER.) A pox! he did not hear all I hope.

SPARK. Come, you bubbling rogues you, where do we sup?—Oh, Harcourt, my mistress tells me you have been making fierce love to her all the play long, 80 ha, ha!—But I. . . .

HARC. I make love to her?

SPARK. Nay, I forgive thee; for I think I know thee, and I know her, but I am sure I know myself.

HARC. Did she tell you so? I see all women are like these of the exchange, who, to enhance the price of their commodities, report to their fond customers offers which were never made 'em.

HORN. Ay, women are as apt to tell before the intrigue as men after it, and so show themselves the 90 vainer sex. But hast thou a mistress, Sparkish? 'Tis as hard for me to believe it as that thou ever hadst a bubble, as you bragged just now.

SPARK. Oh, your servant, sir; are you at your raillery, sir? But we were some of us beforehand with you today at the play. The wits were something bold with you, sir; did you not hear us laugh?

HARC. Yes, but I thought you had gone to plays to laugh at the poet's wit, not at your own.

SPARK. Your servant, sir; no, I thank you. Gad, I go 100 to a play as to a country treat. I carry my own wine to one, and my own wit to t'other, or else I'm sure I should not be merry at either. And the reason why we are so often louder than the players is because we think we speak more wit, and so become the poet's rivals in his audience. For to tell you the truth, we hate the silly rogues; nay, so much that we find fault even with their bawdy upon the stage, whilst we talk of nothing else in the pit as loud.

HORN. But, why should'st thou hate the silly poets? 110 Thou hast too much wit to be one, and they, like whores, are only hated by each other. And thou dost scorn writing, I'm sure.

SPARK. Yes, I'd have you to know, I scorn writing. But women, women, that make men do all foolish things, make 'em write songs too. Everybody does it.

'Tis even as common with lovers as playing with fans; and you can no more help rhyming to your Phyllis than drinking to your Phyllis.

120 HARC. Nay, poetry in love is no more to be avoided than jealousy.

DOR. But the poets damned your songs, did they?

SPARK. Damn the poets! They turned 'em into burlesque, as they call it. That burlesque is a hocus-pocus trick they have got, which by the virtue of *hictius doctius, topsy-turvy,* they make a wise and witty man in the world a fool upon the stage, you know not how. And 'tis therefore I hate 'em too, for I know not but it may be my own case; for they'll put a man into a play 130 for looking asquint. Their predecessors were contented to make serving-men only their stage-fools, but these rogues must have gentlemen, with a pox to 'em, nay knights. And, indeed, you shall hardly see a fool upon the stage but he's a knight. And to tell you the truth, they have kept me these six years from being a knight in earnest, for fear of being knighted in a play, and dubbed a fool.

DOR. Blame 'em not, they must follow their copy—the age.

140 HARC. But why should'st thou be afraid of being in a play, who expose yourself every day in the playhouses, and as public places?

HORN. 'Tis but being on the stage, instead of standing on a bench in the pit.

DOR. Don't you give money to painters to draw you like? And are you afraid of your pictures at length in a playhouse, where all your mistresses may see you?

SPARK. A pox! Painters don't draw the smallpox or pimples in one's face. Come, damn all your silly au-150 thors whatever, all books and booksellers, by the world, and all readers, courteous or uncourteous.

HARC. But, who comes here, Sparkish?

Enter MR. PINCHWIFE, *and his wife in man's clothes,* ALITHEA, LUCY *her maid.*

SPARK. Oh hide me! There's my mistress too.
[SPARKISH *hides himself behind* HARCOURT.
HARC. She sees you.

SPARK. But I will not see her. 'Tis time to go to Whitehall, and I must not fail the drawing-room.

HARC. Pray, first carry me, and reconcile me to her.

SPARK. Another time! Faith, the king will have supped.

160 · HARC. Not with the worse stomach for thy absence! Thou art one of those fools that think their attendance at the king's meals as necessary as his physicians', when you are more troublesome to him than his doctors, or his dogs.

SPARK. Pshaw! I know my interest, sir. Prithee, hide me.

HORN. Your servant, Pinchwife.—What, he knows us not!

PINCH. (*To his wife aside.*) Come along.

MRS. PINCH. Pray, have you any ballads? Give me a 170 sixpenny worth?

CLASP.° We have no ballads.

MRS. PINCH. Then give me *Covent Garden Drollery,* and a play or two. . . . Oh, here's *Tarugo's Wiles,* and *The Slighted Maiden*°—I'll have them.

PINCH. (*Apart to her.*) No, plays are not for your reading. Come along; will you discover yourself?

HORN. Who is that pretty youth with him, Sparkish?

SPARK. I believe his wife's brother, because he's something like her; but I never saw her but once. 180

HORN. Extremely handsome. I have seen a face like it too. Let us follow 'em.
[*Exeunt* PINCHWIFE, MISTRESS PINCHWIFE. ALITHEA,
    LUCY, HORNER, DORILANT *following them.*

HARC. Come, Sparkish, your mistress saw you, and will be angry you go not to her. Besides I would fain be reconciled to her, which none but you can do, dear friend.

SPARK. Well, that's a better reason, dear friend. I would not go near her now, for her's or my own sake, but I can deny you nothing; for though I have known thee a great while, never go, if I do not love thee as 190 well as a new acquaintance.

HARC. I am obliged to you indeed, dear friend. I would be well with her, only to be well with thee still; for these ties to wives usually dissolve all ties to friends. I would be contented she should enjoy you a-nights, but I would have you to myself a-days, as I have had, dear friend.

SPARK. And thou shalt enjoy me a-days, dear, dear friend, never stir; and I'll be divorced from her, sooner than from thee. Come along. . . . 200

HARC. (*Aside.*) So we are hard put to't, when we make our rival our procurer; but neither she nor her brother would let me come near her now. When all's done, a rival is the best cloak to steal to a mistress under, without suspicion; and when we have once got to her as we desire, we throw him off like other cloaks.
[*Exit* SPARKISH, *and* HARCOURT *following him.*

Re-enter MR. PINCHWIFE, MISTRESS PINCHWIFE *in man's clothes.*

PINCH. (*To* ALITHEA *off-stage.*) Sister, if you will not go, we must leave you. (*Aside.*) The fool her gallant and she will muster up all the young saunterers of this place, and they will leave their dear seamstresses to 210 follow us. What a swarm of cuckolds and cuckold-makers are here!—Come, let's be gone, Mistress Margery.

MRS. PINCH. Don't you believe that, I han't half my bellyfull of sights yet.

PINCH. Then walk this way.

MRS. PINCH. Lord, what a power of brave signs are here! Stay—the Bull's Head, the Ram's Head, and the Stag's Head! Dear. . . .

172 **clasp,** a street vendor   175 **Covent Garden Drollery . . . Maiden,** popular songs and plays

PINCH. Nay, if every husband's proper sign° here were visible, they would be all alike.

MRS. PINCH. What d'ye mean by that, bud?

PINCH. 'Tis no matter . . . no matter, bud.

MRS. PINCH. Pray tell me; nay, I will know.

PINCH. They would all be bulls', stags' and rams' heads!

[*Exeunt* MR. PINCHWIFE, MRS. PINCHWIFE.

Re-enter SPARKISH, HARCOURT, ALITHEA, LUCY, *at t'other door.*

SPARK. Come, dear madam, for my sake you shall be reconciled to him.

ALITH. For your sake I hate him.

HARC. That's something too cruel, madam, to hate me for his sake.

SPARK. Ay indeed, madam, too, too cruel to me, to hate my friend for my sake.

ALITH. I hate him because he is your enemy; and you ought to hate him too, for making love to me, if you love me.

SPARK. That's a good one; I hate a man for loving you! If he did love you, 'tis but what he can't help; and 'tis your fault, not his, if he admires you. I hate a man for being of my opinion! I'll ne'er do't, by the world.

ALITH. Is it for your honour or mine, to suffer a man to make love to me, who am to marry you tomorrow?

SPARK. Is it for your honour or mine, to have me jealous? That he makes love to you, is a sign you are handsome; and that I am not jealous, is a sign you are virtuous. That, I think, is for your honour.

ALITH. But 'tis your honour too I am concerned for.

HARC. But why, dearest madam, will you be more concerned for his honour, than he is himself? Let his honour alone, for my sake and his. He, he has no honour. . . .

SPARK. How's that?

HARC. But what my dear friend can guard himself.

SPARK. O ho—that's right again.

HARC. Your care of his honour argues his neglect of it, which is no honour to my dear friend here; therefore once more, let his honour go which way it will, dear madam.

SPARK. Ay, ay, were it for my honour to marry a woman whose virtue I suspected, and could not trust her in a friend's hands?

ALITH. Are you not afraid to lose me?

HARC. He afraid to lose you, madam! No, no—you may see how the most estimable and most glorious creature in the world is valued by him. Will you not see it?

SPARK. Right, honest Frank, I have that noble value for her that I cannot be jealous of her.

ALITH. You mistake him. He means you care not for me nor who has me.

SPARK. Lord, madam, I see you are jealous! Will you wrest a poor man's meaning from his words?

ALITH. You astonish me, sir, with your want of jealousy.

SPARK. And you make me giddy, madam, with your jealousy and fears, and virtue and honour. Gad, I see virtue makes a woman as troublesome as a little reading or learning.

ALITH. Monstrous!

LUCY. (*Behind.*) Well, to see what easy husbands these women of quality can meet with! A poor chambermaid can never have such lady-like luck. Besides, he's thrown away upon her; she'll make no use of her fortune, her blessing; none to a gentleman for a pure cuckold, for it requires good breeding to be a cuckold.

ALITH. I tell you then plainly, he pursues me to marry me.

SPARK. Pshaw!

HARC. Come, madam, you see you strive in vain to make him jealous of me. My dear friend is the kindest creature in the world to me.

SPARK. Poor fellow.

HARC. But his kindness only is not enough for me, without your favour. Your good opinion, dear madam, 'tis that must perfect my happiness. Good gentleman, he believes all I say; would you would do so. Jealous of me! I would not wrong him nor you for the world.

ALITHEA *walks carelessly to and fro.*

SPARK. Look you there; hear him, hear him, and do not walk away so.

HARC. I love you, madam, so. . . .

SPARK. How's that! Nay—now you begin to go too far indeed.

HARC. So much, I confess, I say I love you, that I would not have you miserable, and cast yourself away upon so unworthy and inconsiderable a thing as what you see here.

[*Clapping his hand on his breast, points at* SPARKISH.

SPARK. No, faith, I believe thou would'st not. Now his meaning is plain. But I knew before thou would'st not wrong me nor her.

HARC. No, no, heavens forbid the glory of her sex should fall so low as into the embraces of such a contemptible wretch, the last of mankind—my dear friend here—I injure him.   [*Embracing* SPARKISH.

ALITH. Very well.

SPARK. No, no, dear friend, I knew it. Madam, you see he will rather wrong himself than me, in giving himself such names.

ALITH. Do you not understand him yet?

SPARK. Yes, how modestly he speaks of himself, poor fellow.

ALITH. Methinks he speaks impudently of yourself, since—before yourself too; insomuch that I can no longer suffer his scurrilous abusiveness to you, no more than his love to me.   [*Offers to go.*

220 **sign**, the horns of a cuckold

SPARK. Nay, nay, madam, pray stay. His love to you! Lord, madam, has he not spoke yet plain enough?

ALITH. Yes indeed, I should think so.

SPARK. Well then, by the world, a man can't speak civilly to a woman now but presently she says he makes love to her! Nay, madam, you shall stay, with your pardon, since you have not yet understood him, till he has made an *éclaircissement*° of his love to you, that is, what kind of love it is. (*To* HARCOURT.) Answer to thy catechism. Friend, do you love my mistress here?

HARC. Yes, I wish she would not doubt it.

SPARK. But how do you love her?

HARC. With all my soul.

ALITH. I thank him; methinks he speaks plain enough now.

SPARK. (*To* ALITHEA.) You are out still.—But with what kind of love, Harcourt?

HARC. With the best and truest love in the world.

SPARK. Look you there then, that is with no matrimonial love, I'm sure!

ALITH. How's that? Do you say matrimonial love is not best?

SPARK. (*Aside*.) Gad, I went too far ere I was aware.—But speak for thyself, Harcourt; you said you would not wrong me nor her.

HARC. No, no, madam, e'en take him for heaven's sake. . . .

SPARK. Look you there, madam.

HARC. Who should in all justice be yours, he that loves you most.

[*Claps his hand on his breast.*

ALITH. Look you there, Mr. Sparkish, who's that?

SPARK. Who should it be?—Go on, Harcourt.

HARC. Who loves you more than women titles, or fortune fools.

[*Points at* SPARKISH.

SPARK. Look you there, he means me still, for he points at me.

ALITH. Ridiculous!

HARC. Who can only match your faith and constancy in love.

SPARK. Ay.

HARC. Who knows, if it be possible, how to value so much beauty and virtue.

SPARK. Ay.

HARC. Whose love can no more be equalled in the world than that heavenly form of yours.

SPARK. No.

HARC. Who could no more suffer a rival than your absence, and yet could no more suspect your virtue than his own constancy in his love to you.

SPARK. No.

HARC. Who, in fine, loves you better than his eyes, that first made him love you.

332 *éclaircissement*, a clarification

SPARK. Ay—nay, madam, faith, you shan't go, till. . . .

ALITH. Have a care, lest you make me stay too long. . . .

SPARK. But till he has saluted you; that I may be assured you are friends, after his honest advice and declaration. Come, pray, madam, be friends with him.

Enter MASTER PINCHWIFE, MISTRESS PINCHWIFE.

ALITH. You must pardon me, sir, that I am not yet so obedient to you.

PINCH. What, invite your wife to kiss men? Monstrous! Are you not ashamed? I will never forgive you.

SPARK. Are you not ashamed that I should have more confidence in the chastity of your family than you have? You must not teach me, I am a man of honour, sir, though I am frank and free. I am frank, sir. . . .

PINCH. Very frank, sir, to share your wife with your friends.

SPARK. He is an humble, menial friend, such as reconciles the differences of the marriage bed. You know man and wife do not always agree; I design him for that use, therefore would have him well with my wife.

PINCH. A menial friend! You will get a great many menial friends by showing your wife as you do.

SPARK. What then? It may be I have a pleasure in't, as I have to show fine clothes at a playhouse the first day, and count money before poor rogues.

PINCH. He that shows his wife or money will be in danger of having them borrowed sometimes.

SPARK. I love to be envied, and would not marry a wife that I alone could love. Loving alone is as dull as eating alone. Is it not a frank age? And I am a frank person. And to tell you the truth, it may be I love to have rivals in a wife; they make her seem to a man still but as a kept mistress. And so good night, for I must to Whitehall.—Madam, I hope you are now reconciled to my friend; and so I wish you a good night, madam, and sleep if you can, for tomorrow you know I must visit you early with a canonical gentleman. Good night, dear Harcourt.

[*Exit* SPARKISH.

HARC. Madam, I hope you will not refuse my visit tomorrow, if it should be earlier with a canonical gentleman than Mr. Sparkish's.

PINCH. (*Coming between* ALITHEA *and* HARCOURT.) This gentlewoman is yet under my care; therefore you must yet forbear your freedom with her, sir.

HARC. Must, sir!

PINCH. Yes, sir, she is my sister.

HARC. 'Tis well she is, sir—for I must be her servant, sir. Madam. . . .

PINCH. Come away, sister. We had been gone if it

had not been for you, and so avoided these lewd rakehells,° who seem to haunt us.

Enter HORNER, DORILANT *to them.*

HORN. How now, Pinchwife!

PINCH. Your servant.

HORN. What! I see a little time in the country makes a man turn wild and unsociable, and only fit to converse with his horses, dogs, and his herds.

PINCH. I have business, sir, and must mind it. Your business is pleasure, therefore you and I must go different ways.

HORN. Well, you may go on, but this pretty young gentleman . . .

[*Takes hold of* MRS. PINCHWIFE.

HARC. The lady. . . .

DOR. And the maid. . . .

HORN. Shall stay with us, for I suppose their business is the same with ours—pleasure.

PINCH. (*Aside.*) 'Sdeath, he knows her, she carries it so sillily! Yet if he does not, I should be more silly to discover it first.

ALITH. Pray, let us go, sir.

PINCH. Come, come.

HORN. (*To* MRS. PINCHWIFE.) Had you not rather stay with us?—Prithee, Pinchwife, who is this pretty young gentleman?

PINCH. One to whom I'm a guardian. (*Aside.*) I wish I could keep her out of your hands.

HORN. Who is he? I never saw anything so pretty in all my life.

PINCH. Pshaw! do not look upon him so much; he's a poor bashful youth, you'll put him out of countenance. Come away, brother.

[*Offers to take her away.*

HORN. Oh, your brother?

PINCH. Yes, my wife's brother. Come, come, she'll stay supper for us.

HORN. I thought so, for he is very like her I saw you at the play with, whom I told you I was in love with.

MRS. PINCH. (*Aside.*) O jeminy! Is this he that was in love with me? I am glad on't, I vow, for he's a curious fine gentleman, and I love him already too. (*To* MR. PINCHWIFE.) Is this he, bud?

PINCH. (*To his wife.*) Come away, come away.

HORN. Why, what haste are you in? Why won't you let me talk with him?

PINCH. Because you'll debauch him. He's yet young and innocent, and I would not have him debauched for anything in the world. (*Aside.*) How she gazes on him! the devil!

HORN. Harcourt, Dorilant, look you here; this is the likeness of that dowdy he told us of, his wife. Did you ever see a lovelier creature? The rogue has reason to be jealous of his wife, since she is like him, for she would make all that see her in love with her.

HARC. And as I remember now, she is as like him here as can be.

DOR. She is indeed very pretty, if she be like him.

HORN. Very pretty? A very pretty commendation! She is a glorious creature, beautiful beyond all things I ever beheld.

PINCH. So, so.

HARC. More beautiful than a poet's first mistress of imagination.

HORN. Or another man's last mistress of flesh and blood.

MRS. PINCH. Nay, now you jeer, sir; pray don't jeer me.

PINCH. Come, come. (*Aside.*) By heavens, she'll discover herself!

HORN. I speak of your sister, sir.

PINCH. Ay, but saying she was handsome, if like him, made him blush. (*Aside.*) I am upon a rack!

HORN. Methinks he is so handsome he should not be a man.

PINCH. (*Aside.*) Oh, there 'tis out, he has discovered her! I am not able to suffer any longer. (*To his wife.*) Come, come away, I say.

HORN. Nay, by your leave, sir, he shall not go yet. (*To them.*) Harcourt, Dorilant, let us torment this jealous rogue a little.

HARC. *and* DOR. How?

HORN. I'll show you.

PINCH. Come, pray let him go, I cannot stay fooling any longer; I tell you his sister stays supper for us.

HORN. Does she? Come then, we'll all go sup with her and thee.

PINCH. No, now I think on't, having stayed so long for us, I'll warrant she's gone to bed. (*Aside.*) I wish she and I were well out of their hands.—Come, I must rise early tomorrow, come.

HORN. Well then, if she be gone to bed, I wish her and you a good night. But pray, young gentleman, present my humble service to her.

MRS. PINCH. Thank you heartily, sir.

PINCH. (*Aside.*) S'death! she will discover herself yet in spite of me.—He is something more civil to you, for your kindness to his sister, than I am, it seems.

HORN. Tell her, dear sweet little gentleman, for all your brother there, that you have revived the love I had for her at first sight in the playhouse.

MRS. PINCH. But did you love her indeed, and indeed?

PINCH. (*Aside.*) So, so.—Away, I say.

HORN. Nay, stay. Yes, indeed, and indeed, pray do you tell her so, and give her this kiss from me.

[*Kisses her.*

PINCH. (*Aside.*) O heavens! What do I suffer! Now 'tis too plain he knows her, and yet . . .

431 **rakehells,** libertines

HORN. And this, and this . . .

[*Kisses her again.*

MRS. PINCH. What do you kiss me for? I am no woman.

PINCH. (*Aside.*) So—there, 'tis out.—Come, I cannot, nor will stay any longer.

540 HORN. Nay, they shall send your lady a kiss too. Here, Harcourt, Dorilant, will you not?

[*They kiss her.*

PINCH. (*Aside.*) How! do I suffer this? Was I not accusing another just now for this rascally patience, in permitting his wife to be kissed before his face? Ten thousand ulcers gnaw away their lips!—Come, come.

HORN. Good night, dear little gentleman; madam, goodnight; farewell Pinchwife. (*Apart to* HARCOURT *and* DORILANT.) Did I not tell you I would raise his jealous gall?

[*Exeunt* HORNER, HARCOURT *and* DORILANT.

550 PINCH. So, they are gone at last! Stay, let me see first if the coach be at this door.

[*Exit.*

HORNER, HARCOURT *and* DORILANT *return.*

HORN. What, not gone yet? Will you be sure to do as I desired you, sweet sir?

MRS. PINCH. Sweet sir, but what will you give me then?

HORN. Anything. Come away into the next walk.

[*Exit* HORNER, *haling away* MRS. PINCHWIFE.

ALITH. Hold, hold! What d'ye do?

LUCY. Stay, stay, hold. . . .

HARC. Hold, madam, hold! Let him present him,
560 he'll come presently; nay, I will never let you go till you answer my question.

LUCY. For god's sake, sir, I must follow 'em.

DOR. No, I have something to present you with too; you shan't follow them.

ALITHEA, LUCY, *struggling with* HARCOURT *and* DORILANT. PINCHWIFE *returns.*

PINCH. Where?—how?—what's become of?—gone!—whither?

LUCY. He's only gone with the gentleman, who will give him something, an't please your worship.

PINCH. Something!—give him something, with a
570 pox!—Where are they?

ALITH. In the next walk only, brother.

PINCH. Only, only! Where, where?

[*Exit* PINCHWIFE, *and returns presently, then goes out again.*

HARC. What's the matter with him? Why so much concerned? But dearest madam. . . .

ALITH. Pray, let me go, sir; I have said and suffered enough already.

HARC. Then you will not look upon, nor pity, my sufferings?

ALITH. To look upon 'em, when I cannot help 'em, were cruelty, not pity; therefore I will never see you 580 more.

HARC. Let me then, madam, have my privilege of a banished lover, complaining or railing, and giving you but a farewell reason why, if you cannot condescend to marry me, you should not take that wretch, my rival.

ALITH. He only, not you, since my honour is engaged so far to him, can give me a reason, why I should not marry him. But if he be true, and what I think him to me, I must be so to him. Your servant, sir.

HARC. Have women only constancy when 'tis a vice, 590 and are, like fortune, only true to fools?

DOR. (*To* LUCY, *who struggles to get from him.*) Thou sha't not stir, thou robust creature! You see I can deal with you, therefore you should stay the rather, and be kind.

Enter PINCHWIFE.

PINCH. Gone, gone, not to be found! quite gone! Ten thousand plagues go with 'em! Which way went they?

ALITH. But into t'other walk, brother.

LUCY. Their business will be done presently sure, an't please your worship; it can't be long in doing, I'm 600 sure on't.

ALITH. Are they not there?

PINCH. No; you know where they are, you infamous wretch, eternal shame of your family, which you do not dishonour enough yourself, you think, but you must help her to do it too, thou legion of bawds!

ALITH. Good brother. . . .

PINCH. Damned, damned sister!

ALITH. Look you here, she's coming.

Enter MISTRESS PINCHWIFE *in man's clothes, running, with her hat under her arm, full of oranges and dried fruit;* HORNER *following.*

MRS. PINCH. O dear bud, look you here what I have 610 got, see.

PINCH. (*Aside, rubbing his forehead.*) And what I have got here too, which you can't see.

MRS. PINCH. The fine gentleman has given me better things yet.

PINCH. Has he so? (*Aside.*) Out of breath and coloured! I must hold yet.

HORN. I have only given your little brother an orange, sir.

PINCH. (*To* HORNER.) Thank you, sir. (*Aside.*) You 620 have only squeezed my orange, I suppose, and given it me again. Yet I must have a city-patience. (*To his wife.*) Come, come away.

MRS. PINCH. Stay, till I have put up my fine things, bud.

Enter SIR JASPER FIDGET.

SIR JAS. O master Horner, come, come, the ladies stay for you; your mistress, my wife, wonders you make not more haste to her.

HORN. I have stayed this half hour for you here, and 'tis your fault I am not with your wife.

SIR JAS. But pray, don't let her know so much. The truth on't is, I was advancing a certain project to his majesty about—I'll tell you.

HORN. No, let's go, and hear it at your house.— Good night, sweet little gentleman. One kiss more; you'll remember me now, I hope.

[Kisses her.

DOR. What, sir Jasper, will you separate friends? He promised to sup with us, and if you take him to your house, you'll be in danger of our company too.

SIR JAS. Alas, gentlemen, my house is not fit for you; there are none but civil women there, which are not for your turn. He, you know, can bear with the society of civil women now, ha, ha, ha! Besides, he's one of my family . . . he's . . . he, he, he!

DOR. What is he?

SIR JAS. Faith, my eunuch, since you'll have it, he, he, he!

[Exit SIR JASPER FIDGET and HORNER.

DOR. I rather wish thou wert his, or my cuckold. Harcourt, what a good cuckold is lost there for want of a man to make him one! Thee and I cannot have Horner's privilege, who can make use of it.

HARC. Ay, to poor Horner 'tis like coming to an estate at threescore, when a man can't be the better for't.

PINCH. Come.

MRS. PINCH. Presently, bud.

DOR. Come, let us go too. (To ALITHEA.) Madam, your servant. (To LUCY.) Good night, strapper.°

HARC. Madam, though you will not let me have a good day or night, I wish you one; but dare not name the other half of my wish.

ALITH. Good night, sir, for ever.

MRS. PINCH. I don't know where to put this here, dear bud. You shall eat it. Nay, you shall have part of the fine gentleman's good things, or treat as you call it, when we come home.

PINCH. Indeed, I deserve it, since I furnished the best part of it.

[Strikes away the orange.

The gallant treats, presents, and gives the ball;
But 'tis the absent cuckold, pays for all.

ACT IV SCENE I

In PINCHWIFE's house in the morning.

LUCY, ALITHEA dressed in new clothes.

LUCY. Well, madam, now have I dressed you, and set you out with so many ornaments, and spent upon you ounces of essence and pulvilio;° and all this for no other purpose but as people adorn and perfume a corpse for a stinking secondhand grave—such or as bad I think Master Sparkish's bed.

ALITH. Hold your peace.

LUCY. Nay, madam, I will ask you the reason why you would banish poor Master Harcourt for ever from your sight? How could you be so hard-hearted?

ALITH. 'Twas because I was not hard-hearted.

LUCY. No, no; 'twas stark love and kindness, I warrant!

ALITH. It was so. I would see him no more because I love him.

LUCY. Hey-day, a very pretty reason!

ALITH. You do not understand me.

LUCY. I wish you may yourself.

ALITH. I was engaged to marry, you see, another man, whom my justice will not suffer me to deceive injure.

LUCY. Can there be a greater cheat or wrong done to a man than to give him your person without your heart? I should make a conscience of it.

ALITH. I'll retrieve it for him after I am married a while.

LUCY. The woman that marries to love better will be as much mistaken as the wencher that marries to live better. No, madam, marrying to increase love is like gaming to become rich—alas, you only lose what little stock you had before.

ALITH. I find by your rhetoric you have been bribed to betray me.

LUCY. Only by his merit, that has bribed your heart, you see, against your word and rigid honour. But what a devil is this honour? 'Tis sure a disease in the head, like the megrim,° or falling sickness, that always hurries people away to do themselves mischief. Men lose their lives by it: women what's dearer to 'em, their love, the life of life.

ALITH. Come, pray talk you no more of honour, nor Master Harcourt. I wish the other would come to secure my fidelity to him and his right in me.

LUCY. You will marry him then?

ALITH. Certainly. I have given him already my word, and will my hand too, to make it good when he comes.

LUCY. Well, I wish I may never stick pin more if he be not an errant natural° to t'other fine gentleman.

ALITH. I own he wants the wit of Harcourt, which I will dispense withal for another want he has, which is want of jealousy which men of wit seldom want.

LUCY. Lord, madam, what should you do with a fool to your husband? You intend to be honest, don't you? Then that husbandly virtue, credulity, is thrown away upon you.

658 **strapper,** a tall, robust woman

Act IV, Scene I 3 **essence and pulvilio,** perfume and cosmetic powder
37 **megrim,** migraine or nervous headache   49 **natural,** one born without the usual powers of reason and understanding

ALITH. He only that could suspect my virtue should have cause to do it. 'Tis Sparkish's confidence in my truth that obliges me to be so faithful to him.

60 LUCY. You are not sure his opinion may last.

ALITH. I am satisfied 'tis impossible for him to be jealous after the proofs I have had of him. Jealousy in a husband—heaven defend me from it! It begets a thousand plagues to a poor woman, the loss of her honour, her quiet, and her. . . .

LUCY. And her pleasure!

ALITH. What d'ye mean, impertinent?

LUCY. Liberty is a great pleasure, madam.

ALITH. I say, loss of her honour, her quiet, nay, her
70 life sometimes; and what's as bad almost, the loss of this town, that is, she is sent into the country, which is the last ill usage of a husband to a wife, I think.

LUCY. (Aside.) Oh, does the wind lie there?—Then of necessity, madam, you think a man must carry his wife into the country, if he be wise. The country is as terrible, I find, to our young English ladies as a monastery to those abroad. And on my virginity, I think they would rather marry a London jailer than a high sheriff of a county, since neither can stir from his
80 employment. Formerly women of wit married fools for a great estate, a fine seat, or the like; but now 'tis for a pretty seat only in Lincoln's Inn Fields, St. James's Fields, or the Pall Mall.°

Enter to them SPARKISH, *and* HARCOURT *dressed like a parson.*

SPARK. Madam, your humble servant, a happy day to you, and to us all.

HARC. Amen.

ALITH. Who have we here?

SPARK. My chaplain, faith. O madam, poor Harcourt remembers his humble service to you, and in obedi-
90 ence to your last commands, refrains coming into your sight.

ALITH. Is not that he?

SPARK. No, fie, no; but to show that he ne'er intended to hinder our match, has sent his brother here to join our hands. When I get me a wife, I must get her a chaplain, according to the custom. This is his brother, and my chaplain.

ALITH. His brother?

LUCY. (Aside.) And your chaplain, to preach in your
100 pulpit then!

ALITH. His brother!

SPARK. Nay, I knew you would not believe it.—I told you, sir, she would take you for your brother Frank.

ALITH. Believe it!

LUCY. (Aside.) His brother! ha, ha, he! He has a trick left still, it seems.

SPARK. Come, my dearest, pray let us go to church before the canonical hour° is past.

ALITH. For shame, you are abused still. 110

SPARK. By the world, 'tis strange now you are so incredulous.

ALITH. 'Tis strange you are so credulous.

SPARK. Dearest of my life, hear me. I tell you this is Ned Harcourt of Cambridge, by the world—you see he has a sneaking college look. 'Tis true he's something like his brother Frank, and they differ from each other no more than in their age, for they were twins.

LUCY. Ha, ha, he!

ALITH. Your servant, sir; I cannot be so deceived, 120 though you are. But come, let's hear, how do you know what you affirm so confidently?

SPARK. Why, I'll tell you all. Frank Harcourt, coming to me this morning to wish me joy and present his service to you, I asked him if he could help me to a parson. Whereupon he told me he had a brother in town who was in orders, and he went straight away and sent him, you see there, to me.

ALITH. Yes, Frank goes and puts on a black coat—then tells you he is Ned. That's all you have 130 for't!

SPARK. Pshaw, pshaw! I tell you by the same token, the midwife put her garter about Frank's neck to know 'em asunder, they were so like.

ALITH. Frank tells you this too?

SPARK. Ay, and Ned there too. Nay, they are both in a story.

ALITH. So, so; very foolish!

SPARK. Lord, if you won't believe one, you had best try him by your chambermaid there; for chambermaids 140 must needs know chaplains from other men, they are so used to 'em.

LUCY. Let's see; nay, I'll be sworn he has the canonical smirk, and the filthy, clammy palm of a chaplain.

ALITH. Well, most reverend doctor, pray let us make an end of this fooling.

HARC. With all my soul, divine, heavenly creature, when you please.

ALITH. He speaks like a chaplain indeed. 150

SPARK. Why, was there not 'soul', 'divine', 'heavenly', in what he said.

ALITH. Once more, most impertinent black coat, cease your persecution, and let us have a conclusion of this ridiculous love.

HARC. (Aside.) I had forgot—I must suit my style to my coat, or I wear it in vain.

ALITH. I have no more patience left. Let us make once an end of this troublesome love, I say.

HARC. So be it, seraphic lady, when your honour 160 shall think it meet and convenient so to do.

SPARK. Gad, I'm sure none but a chaplain could speak so, I think.

82–83 **Lincoln's Inn . . . Pall Mall,** fashionable London locales

109 **canonical hour,** an hour between 8:00 A.M. and 12:00 M.; the time period within which marriage can be legally performed in a parish church in England

ALITH. Let me tell you, sir, this dull trick will not serve your turn. Though you delay our marriage, you shall not hinder it.

HARC. Far be it from me, munificent patroness, to delay your marriage. I desire nothing more than to marry you presently, which I might do, if you yourself
170 would; for my noble, good-natured and thrice generous patron here would not hinder it.

SPARK. No, poor man, not I, faith.

HARC. And now, madam, let me tell you plainly, nobody else shall marry you. By heavens, I'll die first, for I'm sure I should die after it.

LUCY. (Aside.) How his love has made him forget his function, as I have seen it in real parsons!

ALITH. That was spoken like a chaplain too! Now you understand him, I hope.
180 SPARK. Poor man, he takes it heinously to be refused. I can't blame him, 'tis putting an indignity upon him not to be suffered. But you'll pardon me, madam, it shan't be, he shall marry us. Come away, pray, madam.

LUCY. Ha, ha, he! More ado! 'Tis late.

ALITH. Invincible stupidity! I tell you he would marry me as your rival, not as your chaplain.

SPARK. (Pulling her away.) Come, come, madam.

LUCY. I pray, madam, do not refuse this reverend
190 divine the honour and satisfaction of marrying you—for I dare say he has set his heart upon't, good doctor.

ALITH. What can you hope or design by this?

HARC. (Aside.) I could answer her—a reprieve, for a day only, often revokes a hasty doom. At worst, if she will not take mercy on me and let me marry her, I have at least the lover's second pleasure, hindering my rival's enjoyment, though but for a time.

SPARK. Come, madam, 'tis e'en twelve o'clock, and my mother charged me never to be married out of the
200 canonical hours. Come, come! Lord, here's such a deal of modesty, I warrant, the first day.

LUCY. Yes, an't please your worship, married women show all their modesty the first day, because married men show all their love the first day.

[Exeunt SPARKISH, ALITHEA, HARCOURT and LUCY.

SCENE II

The scene changes to a bedchamber, where appear PINCHWIFE, MRS. PINCHWIFE.

PINCH. Come, tell me, I say.

MRS. PINCH. Lord! han't I told it an hundred times over?

PINCH. (Aside.) I would try if, in the repetition of the ungrateful tale, I could find her altering it in the least circumstance; for if her story be false, she is so too.—Come, how was't, baggage?

MRS. PINCH. Lord, what pleasure you take to hear it, sure!

PINCH. No, you take more in telling it, I find. But 10 speak—how was't?

MRS. PINCH. He carried me up into the house next to the Exchange.

PINCH. So, and you two were only in the room?

MRS. PINCH. Yes, for he sent away a youth, that was there, for some dried fruit and China oranges.

PINCH. Did he so? Damn him for it . . . and for. . . .

MRS. PINCH. But presently came up the gentlewoman of the house.

PINCH. Oh, 'twas well she did! But what did he do 20 whilst the fruit came?

MRS. PINCH. He kissed me an hundred times, and told me he fancied he kissed my fine sister, meaning me you know, whom he said he loved with all his soul, and bid me be sure to tell her so, and to desire her to be at her window by eleven of the clock this morning, and he would walk under it at that time.

PINCH. (Aside.) And he was as good as his word, very punctual, a pox reward him for't.

MRS. PINCH. Well, and he said if you were not 30 within, he would come up to her, meaning me, you know, bud, still.

PINCH. (Aside.) So—he knew her certainly. But for this confession I am obliged to her simplicity.—But what, you stood very still when he kissed you?

MRS. PINCH. Yes, I warrant you; would you have had me discovered myself?

PINCH. But you told me he did some beastliness to you—as you called it. What was't?

MRS. PINCH. Why, he put. . . .   40

PINCH. What?

MRS. PINCH. Why, he put the tip of his tongue between my lips, and so mousled me° . . . and I said, I'd bite it.

PINCH. An eternal canker seize it, for a dog!

MRS. PINCH. Nay, you need not be so angry with him neither, for to say truth, he has the sweetest breath I ever knew.

PINCH. The devil!—You were satisfied with it then, and would do it again?   50

MRS. PINCH. Not unless he should force me.

PINCH. Force you, changeling! I tell you no woman can be forced.

MRS. PINCH. Yes, but she may be sure by such a one as he, for he's a proper, goodly strong man—'tis hard, let me tell you, to resist him.

PINCH. (Aside.) So, 'tis plain she loves him, yet she has not love enough to make her conceal it from me. But the sight of him will increase her aversion for me, and love for him, and that love instruct her how to 60 deceive me and satisfy him, all idiot as she is. Love! 'Twas he gave women first their craft, their art of deluding. Out of nature's hands they came plain, open, silly, and fit for slaves, as she and heaven intended 'em, but damned love . . . well . . . I must strangle

Scene II   43 **mousled me**, pulled me about roughly

that little monster whilst I can deal with him.—Go, fetch pen, ink, and paper out of the next room.

MRS. PINCH. Yes, bud.

[*Exit* MRS. PINCHWIFE.

PINCH. (*Aside.*) Why should women have more in-
70 vention in love than men? It can only be because they have more desires, more soliciting passions, more lust, and more of the devil.

MRS. PINCHWIFE *returns*.

Come, minx, sit down and write.

MRS. PINCH. Ay, dear bud, but I can't do't very well.

PINCH. I wish you could not at all.

MRS. PINCH. But what should I write for?

PINCH. I'll have you write a letter to your lover.

MRS. PINCH. O lord, to the fine gentleman a letter!

PINCH. Yes, to the fine gentleman.

80 MRS. PINCH. Lord, you do but jeer; sure you jest?

PINCH. I am not so merry, come, write as I bid you.

MRS. PINCH. What, do you think I am a fool?

PINCH. (*Aside.*) She's afraid I would not dictate any love to him, therefore she's unwilling.—But you had best begin.

MRS. PINCH. Indeed, and indeed, but I won't, so I won't!

PINCH. Why?

MRS. PINCH. Because he's in town. You may send
90 for him if you will.

PINCH. Very well, you would have him brought to you—is it come to this? I say, take the pen and write, or you'll provoke me.

MRS. PINCH. Lord, what d'ye make a fool of me for? Don't I know that letters are never writ but from the country to London, and from London into the country? Now, he's in town, and I am in town too; therefore I can't write to him, you know.

PINCH. (*Aside.*) So, I am glad it is no worse; she is
100 innocent enough yet.—Yes, you may, when your husband bids you, write letters to people that are in town.

MRS. PINCH. Oh, may I so? Then I'm satisfied.

PINCH. Come, begin. (*Dictates.*) 'Sir. . . .'

MRS. PINCH. Shan't I say, 'Dear Sir'? You know one says always something more than bare 'Sir'.

PINCH. Write as I bid you, or I will write 'whore' with this penknife in your face.

MRS. PINCH. Nay, good bud. (*She writes.*) 'Sir'.

PINCH. 'Though I suffered last night your nauseous,
110 loathed kisses and embraces. . . .'—Write!

MRS. PINCH. Nay, why should I say so? You know I told you he had a sweet breath.

PINCH. Write!

MRS. PINCH. Let me but put out 'loathed'.

PINCH. Write, I say!

MRS. PINCH. Well then. (*Writes.*)

PINCH. Let's see what have you writ. (*Takes the paper and reads.*) 'Though I suffered last night your

kisses and embraces'—Thou impudent creature! Where is 'nauseous' and 'loathed'? 120

MRS. PINCH. I can't abide to write such filthy words.

PINCH. Once more write as I'd have you, and question it not, or I will spoil thy writing with this. (*Holds up the penknife.*) I will stab out those eyes that cause my mischief.

MRS. PINCH. O lord, I will!

PINCH. So . . . so. . . . Let's see now! (*Reads.*) 'Though I suffered last night your nauseous, loathed kisses, and embraces'—go on—'Yet I would not have you presume that you shall ever repeat them.' 130 —So. . . .

MRS. PINCH. (*She writes.*) I have writ it.

PINCH. On then.—'I then concealed myself from your knowledge, to avoid your insolencies. . . .'

MRS. PINCH. (*She writes.*) So.

PINCH. 'The same reason, now I am out of your hands. . . .'

MRS. PINCH. (*She writes.*) So.

PINCH. 'Makes me own to you my unfortunate, though innocent frolic, of being in man's clothes. . . .' 140

MRS. PINCH. (*She writes.*) So.

PINCH. 'That you may forevermore cease to pursue her, who hates and detests you. . . .'

[*She writes on.*

MRS. PINCH. (*Sighs.*) So -h. . . .

PINCH. What, do you sigh?—'detests you . . . as much as she loves her husband and her honour'.

MRS. PINCH. I vow, husband, he'll ne'er believe I should write such a letter.

PINCH. What, he'd expect a kinder from you? Come 150 now, your name only.

MRS. PINCH. What, shan't I say, 'Your most faithful, humble servant till death'?

PINCH. No, tormenting fiend! (*Aside.*) Her style, I find, would be very soft.—Come, wrap it up now, whilst I go fetch wax and a candle, and write on the back side, 'For Mr. Horner'.

[*Exit* PINCHWIFE.

MRS. PINCH. 'For Mr. Horner'.—So, I am glad he has told me his name. Dear Mr. Horner! But why should I send thee such a letter that will vex thee and make thee angry with me? . . . Well I will not send 160 it. . . . Ay, but then my husband will kill me . . . for I see plainly, he won't let me love Mr. Horner . . . but what care I for my husband? . . . I won't so, I won't send poor Mr. Horner such a letter . . . but then my husband. . . . But oh, what if I writ at bottom, my husband made me write it? . . . Ay, but then my husband would see't. . . . Can one have no shift? Ah, a London woman would have had a hundred presently. Stay . . . what if I should write a letter, and wrap it up like this, and write upon't too? Ay, but then my hus- 170 band would see't. . . . I don't know what to do. . . . But yet y'vads I'll try, so I will . . . for I will not send this letter to poor Mr. Horner, come what will on't.

[*She writes, and repeats what she hath writ.*
'Dear, sweet Mr. Horner' . . . . So. . . . 'My husband would have me send you a base, rude, unmannerly letter . . . but I won't' . . . so . . . 'and would have me forbid you loving me . . . but I won't' . . . so . . . 'and would have me say to you, I hate you
180 poor Mr. Horner . . . but I won't tell a lie for him' . . . there . . . 'for I'm sure if you and I were in the country at cards together' . . . so . . . 'I could not help treading on your toe under the table' . . . so . . . 'or rubbing knees with you, and staring in your face 'till you saw me' . . . very well . . . 'and then looking down, and blushing for an hour together' . . . so . . . 'but I must make haste before my husband come; and now he has taught me to write letters you shall have longer ones from me, who am, dear, dear, poor
190 dear Mr. Horner, your most humble friend, and servant to command 'till death, Margery Pinchwife.'— Stay, I must give him a hint at bottom . . . so . . . now wrap it up just like t'other . . . so . . . now write 'For Mr. Horner' . . . But, oh now, what shall I do with it? For here comes my husband.

Enter PINCHWIFE.

PINCH. (*Aside.*) I have been detained by a sparkish coxcomb, who pretended a visit to me; but I fear 'twas to my wife.—What, have you done?
200 MRS. PINCH. Ay, ay, bud, just now.
PINCH. Let's see't. What d'ye tremble for? What, you would not have it go?
MRS. PINCH. Here. (*Aside.*) No, I must not give him that, so I had been served if I had given him this.
PINCH. (*He opens and reads the first letter.*) Come, where's the wax and seal?
MRS. PINCH. (*Aside.*) Lord, what shall I do now? Nay, then, I have it.—Pray, let me see't. Lord, you think me so arrant a fool, I cannot seal a letter? I will
210 do't, so I will.
[*Snatches the letter from him, changes it for the other, seals it, and delivers it to him.*
PINCH. Nay, I believe you will learn that, and other things too, which I would not have you.
MRS. PINCH. So. Han't I done it curiously? (*Aside.*) I think I have; there's my letter going to Mr. Horner, since he'll needs have me send letters to folks.
PINCH. 'Tis very well; but I warrant, you would not have it go now?
MRS. PINCH. Yes, indeed, but I would, bud, now.
PINCH. Well you are a good girl then. Come, let me
220 lock you up in your chamber 'till I come back. And be sure you come not within three strides of the window when I am gone, for I have a spy in the street.
[*Exit* MRS. PINCHWIFE.
[PINCHWIFE *locks the door.*
At least, 'tis fit she thinks so. If we do not cheat women, they'll cheat us; and fraud may be justly used with secret enemies, of which a wife is the most

dangerous. And he that has a handsome one to keep, and a frontier town, must provide against treachery rather than open force. Now I have secured all within, I'll deal with the foe without with false intelligence. (*Holds up the letter.*)
[*Exit* PINCHWIFE.

SCENE III

The scene changes to HORNER's *lodging.*

QUACK *and* HORNER.

QUACK. Well, sir, how fadges° the new design? Have you not the luck of all your brother projectors,° to deceive only yourself at last?
HORN. No, good Domine° doctor, I deceive you, it seems, and others too, for the grave matrons and old rigid husbands think me as unfit for love as they are. But their wives, sisters and daughters know some of 'em better things already!
QUACK. Already!
HORN. Already, I say. Last night I was drunk with 10 half a dozen of your civil persons, as you call 'em, and people of honour, and so was made free of their society and dressing rooms for ever hereafter; and am already come to the privileges of sleeping upon their pallats, warming smocks, tying shoes and garters, and the like, doctor, already, already, doctor.
QUACK. You have made use of your time, sir.
HORN. I tell thee, I am now no more interruption to 'em when they sing or talk bawdy than a little squab° French page who speaks no English. 20
QUACK. But do civil persons and women of honour drink and sing bawdy songs?
HORN. Oh, amongst friends, amongst friends. For your bigots in honour are just like those in religion. They fear the eye of the world more than the eye of heaven, and think there is no virtue but railing at vice, and no sin but giving scandal. They rail at a poor, little, kept player, and keep themselves some young, modest pulpit comedian to be privy to their sins in their closets,° not to tell 'em of them in their chapels. 30
QUACK. Nay, the truth on't is, priests amongst the women now have quite got the better of us lay confessors, physicians.
HORN. And they are rather their patients, but . . .

Enter my LADY FIDGET, *looking about her.*

Now we talk of women of honour, here comes one. Step behind the screen there, and but observe if I have not particular privileges with the women of reputation already, doctor, already.

QUACK *steps behind screen.*

Scene III   1 **fadges**, goes   2 **projectors**, schemers   4 **Domine**, lord or sir
19 **squab**, squat   30 **closets**, small rooms for private use

LADY FIDG. Well, Horner, am not I a woman of
40 honour? You see, I'm as good as my word.

HORN. And you shall see, madam, I'll not be be-
hindhand with you in honour. And I'll be as good as
my word too, if you please but to withdraw into the
next room.

LADY FIDG. But first, my dear sir, you must promise
to have a care of my dear honour.

HORN. If you talk a word more of your honour,
you'll make me incapable to wrong it. To talk of honour in the mysteries of love is like talking of heaven or
50 the deity in an operation of witchcraft, just when you
are employing the devil; it makes the charm impotent.

LADY FIDG. Nay, fie, let us not be smutty. But you
talk of mysteries, and bewitching to me—I don't understand you.

HORN. I tell you, madam, the word 'money' in a
mistress's mouth, at such a nick of time, is not a more
disheartening sound to a younger brother than that of
honour to an eager lover like myself.

LADY FIDG. But you can't blame a lady of my repu-
60 tation to be chary.

HORN. Chary! I have been chary of it already, by the
report I have caused of myself.

LADY FIDG. Ay, but if you should ever let other
women know that dear secret, it would come out. Nay,
you must have a great care of your conduct, for my
acquaintance are so censorious,—oh 'tis a wicked
censorious world, Mr. Horner!—I say, are so censorious and detracting that perhaps they'll talk to the prejudice of my honour, though you should not let them
70 know the dear secret.

HORN. Nay, madam, rather than they shall prejudice
your honour, I'll prejudice theirs; and to serve you, I'll
lie with 'em all, make the secret their own, and then
they'll keep it! I am a Machiavel° in love, madam.

LADY FIDG. Oh no, sir, not that way.

HORN. Nay, the devil take me, if censorious women
are to be silenced any other way!

LADY FIDG. A secret is better kept, I hope, by a
single person than a multitude. Therefore pray do not
80 trust anybody else with it, dear, dear Mr. Horner.

[*Embracing him.*

Enter SIR JASPER FIDGET.

SIR JAS. How now!

LADY FIDG. (*Aside.*) O my husband! . . . prevented! . . . and what's almost as bad, found with my
arms about another man . . . that will appear too
much . . . what shall I say?—Sir Jasper, come hither.
I am trying if Mr. Horner were ticklish, and he's as
ticklish as can be. I love to torment the confounded
toad. Let you and I tickle him.

SIR JAS. No, your ladyship will tickle him better

without me, I suppose. But is this your buying china? I 90
thought you had been at the china house?

HORN. (*Aside.*) China house! That's my cue, I must
take it.—A pox! Can't you keep your impertinent
wives at home? Some men are troubled with the husbands, but I with the wives. But I'd have you to know,
since I cannot be your journeyman by night, I will not
be your drudge by day, to squire your wife about and
be your man of straw, or scarecrow, only to pies and
jays° that would be nibbling at your forbidden fruit. I
shall be shortly the hackney gentleman-usher° of the 100
town.

SIR JAS. (*Aside.*) He, he, he! Poor fellow, he's in the
right on't, faith! To squire women about for other folks
is as ungrateful an employment as to tell money for
other folks. He, he, he!—Ben't angry, Horner.

LADY FIDG. No, 'tis I have more reason to be angry,
who am left by you to go abroad indecently alone; or,
what is more indecent, to pin myself upon such ill-bred
people of your acquaintance as this is.

SIR JAS. Nay, prithee, what has he done? 110

LADY FIDG. Nay, he has done nothing.

SIR JAS. But what d'ye take ill, if he has done nothing?

LADY FIDG. Ha, ha, ha! Faith, I can't but laugh,
however. Why, d'ye think the unmannerly toad would
not come down to me to the coach? I was fain to come
up to fetch him, or go without him, which I was resolved not to do; for he knows china very well, and has
himself very good, but will not let me see it lest I
should beg some. But I will find it out, and have what I 120
came for yet.

[*Exit* LADY FIDGET, *and locks the door, followed by*
HORNER *to the door.*

HORN. (*Apart to* LADY FIDGET.) Lock the door,
madam.—So, she has got into my chamber, and
locked me out. Oh, the impertinency of womankind!
Well, Sir Jasper, plain dealing is a jewel. If ever you
suffer your wife to trouble me again here, she shall
carry you home a pair of horns, by my Lord Mayor she
shall! Though I cannot furnish you myself, you are
sure, yet I'll find a way.

SIR JAS. (*Aside.*) Ha, ha, he! At my first coming in 130
and finding her arms about him, tickling him it seems, I
was half jealous, but now I see my folly.—He, he, he!
Poor Horner.

HORN. Nay, though you laugh now, 'twill be my turn
ere long. Oh, women, more impertinent, more cunning, and more mischievous than their monkeys, and
to me almost as ugly! . . . Now is she throwing my
things about, and rifling all I have . . . but I'll get into
her the back way, and so rifle her for it.

SIR JAS. Ha, ha, ha! Poor angry Horner. 140

HORN. Stay here a little, I'll ferret her out to you
presently, I warrant.

[*Exit* HORNER *at t'other door.*

---

74 **Machiavel,** a schemer; after Niccolo Machiavelli (1469–1527), Italian statesman and author of *The Prince*

99 **pies and jays,** dandies   100 **hackney gentleman-usher,** hired escort

SIR JAS. Wife! My lady Fidget! Wife! He is coming into you the back way!

[SIR JASPER *calls through the door to his wife; she answers from within.*

LADY FIDG. Let him come, and welcome, which way he will.

SIR JAS. He'll catch you, and use you roughly, and be too strong for you.

LADY FIDG. Don't you trouble yourself, let him if he 150 can.

QUACK. (*Behind.*) This indeed I could not have believed from him, nor any but my own eyes.

Enter MISTRESS SQUEAMISH.

SQUEAM. Where's this woman-hater, this toad, this ugly, greasy, dirty sloven?

SIR JAS. (*Aside.*) So the women all will have him ugly. Methinks he is a comely person, but his wants make his form contemptible to 'em; and 'tis e'en as my wife said yesterday, talking of him, that a proper handsome eunuch was as ridiculous a thing as a gigantic 160 coward.

SQUEAM. Sir Jasper, your servant. Where is the odious beast?

SIR JAS. He's within in his chamber, with my wife; she's playing the wag with him.

SQUEAM. Is she so? And he's a clownish beast, he'll give her no quarter, he'll play the wag with her again, let me tell you. Come, let's go help her . . . What, the door's locked?

SIR JAS. Ay, my wife locked it.

170 SQUEAM. Did she so? Let us break it open then.

SIR JAS. No, no, he'll do her no hurt.

SQUEAM. No. (*Aside.*) But is there no other way to get into 'em? Whither goes this? I will disturb 'em.

[*Exit* SQUEAMISH *at another door.*

Enter OLD LADY SQUEAMISH.

OLD L. SQUEAM. Where is this harlotry, this impudent baggage, this rambling tomrig?° O sir Jasper, I'm glad to see you here. Did you not see my viled grandchild come in hither just now?

SIR JAS. Yes.

OLD L. SQUEAM. Ay, but where is she then? where is 180 she? Lord, sir Jasper, I have e'en rattled myself to pieces in pursuit of her. But can you tell what she makes here? They say below, no woman lodges here.

SIR JAS. No.

OLD L. SQUEAM. No! What does she here then? Say, if it be not a woman's lodging, what makes she here? But are you sure no woman lodges here?

SIR JAS. No, nor no man neither—this is Mr. Horner's lodging.

OLD L. SQUEAM. Is it so, are you sure?

SIR JAS. Yes, yes. 190

OLD L. SQUEAM. So—then there's no hurt in't, I hope. But where is he?

SIR JAS. He's in the next room with my wife.

OLD L. SQUEAM. Nay, if you trust him with your wife, I may with my biddy.° They say he's a merry, harmless man now, e'en as harmless a man as ever came out of Italy with a good voice,° and as pretty harmless company for a lady as a snake without his teeth.

SIR JAS. Ay, ay, poor man. 200

Enter MRS. SQUEAMISH.

SQUEAM. I can't find 'em.—Oh, are you here, grandmother? I followed, you must know, my lady Fidget hither. 'Tis the prettiest lodging, and I have been staring on the prettiest pictures.

Enter LADY FIDGET *with a piece of china in her hand, and* HORNER *following.*

LADY FIDG. And I have been toiling and moiling for the prettiest piece of china, my dear.

HORN. Nay, she has been too hard for me, do what I could.

SQUEAM. Oh lord, I'll have some china too. Good Mr. Horner, don't you think to give other people 210 china, and me none. Come in with me too.

HORN. Upon my honour, I have none left now.

SQUEAM. Nay, nay, I have known you deny your china before now, but you shan't put me off so. Come.

HORN. This lady had the last there.

LADY FIDG. Yes indeed, madam, to my certain knowledge he has no more left.

SQUEAM. Oh, but it may be he may have some you could not find.

LADY FIDG. What, d'y think if he had had any left, I 220 would not have had it too? For we women of quality never think we have china enough.

HORN. Do not take it ill, I cannot make china for you all, but I will have a roll-wagon° for you too, another time.

SQUEAM. Thank you, dear toad.

LADY FIDG. (*Apart to* HORNER.) What do you mean by that promise?

HORN. (*Aside to* LADY FIDGET.) Alas, she has an innocent, literal understanding. 230

OLD L. SQUEAM. Poor Mr. Horner, he has enough to do to please you all, I see.

HORN. Ay, madam, you see how they use me.

OLD L. SQUEAM. Poor gentleman, I pity you.

HORN. I thank you, madam. I could never find pity but from such reverend ladies as you are. The young ones will never spare a man.

195 **my biddy,** my chick   196–197 **as harmless . . . good voice.** A reference to castrati, male singers who, by chance or planning, retained a soprano voice into their adult years   224 **roll-wagon,** a low-wheeled vehicle for conveying goods. Critics debate the term's meaning here, and the shape of the object

175 **tomrig,** tomboy

SQUEAM. Come, come, beast, and go dine with us, for we shall want a man at ombre after dinner.

240 HORN. That's all their use of me, madam, you see.

SQUEAM. Come, sloven, I'll lead you, to be sure of you.

[*Pulls him by the cravat.*

OLD L. SQUEAM. Alas, poor man, how she tugs him! Kiss, kiss her! That's the way to make such nice women quiet.

HORN. No, madam, that remedy is worse than the torment. They know I dare suffer anything rather than do it.

OLD L. SQUEAM. Prithee kiss her, and I'll give you
250 her picture in little, that you admired so last night. Prithee, do!

HORN. Well, nothing but that could bribe me. I love a woman only in effigy, and good painting, as much as I hate them. I'll do't, for I could adore the devil well painted.

[*Kisses* MRS. SQUEAMISH.

SQUEAM. Foh, you filthy toad! Nay, now I've done jesting.

OLD L. SQUEAM. Ha, ha, ha! I told you so.

SQUEAM. Foh! a kiss of his. . . .

260 SIR JAS. Has no more hurt in't than one of my spaniel's.

SQUEAM. Nor no more good neither.

QUACK. (*Behind.*) I will now believe anything he tells me.

Enter MR. PINCHWIFE.

LADY FIDG. O lord, here's a man! Sir Jasper, my mask, my mask! I would not be seen here for the world.

SIR JAS. What, not when I am with you?

LADY FIDG. No, no, my honour . . . let's be gone.

270 SQUEAM. Oh, grandmother, let us be gone. Make haste, make haste, I know not how he may censure us.

LADY FIDG. Be found in the lodging of anything like a man! Away!

[*Exeunt* SIR JASPER, LADY FIDGET, OLD LADY
SQUEAMISH, MRS. SQUEAMISH.

QUACK. (*Behind.*) What's here, another cuckold? He looks like one, and none else sure have any business with him.

HORN. Well, what brings my dear friend hither?

PINCH. Your impertinency.

HORN. My impertinency! Why, you gentlemen that
280 have got handsome wives think you have a privilege of saying anything to your friends, and are as brutish as if you were our creditors.

PINCH. No, sir, I'll ne'er trust you any way.

HORN. But why not, dear Jack? Why diffide in° me thou knowst so well?

284 **diffide in,** distrust

PINCH. Because I do know you so well.

HORN. Han't I been always thy friend, honest Jack, always ready to serve thee, in love or battle, before thou wert married, and am so still?

PINCH. I believe so. You would be my second now 290 indeed.

HORN. Well, then, dear Jack, why so unkind, so grum, so strange to me? Come, prithee kiss me, dear rogue. Gad, I was always, I say, and am still as much thy servant as. . . .

PINCH. As I am yours, sir. What, you would send a kiss to my wife, is that it?

HORN. So, there 'tis! A man can't show his friendship to a married man, but presently he talks of his wife to you. Prithee, let thy wife alone, and let thee 300 and I be all one, as we were wont. What, thou art as shy of my kindness as a Lombard Street alderman of a courtier's civility at Locket's.

PINCH. But you are overkind to me—as kind as if I were your cuckold already. Yet I must confess you ought to be kind and civil to me, since I am so kind, so civil to you, as to bring you this. Look you there, sir.

[*Delivers him a letter.*

HORN. What is't?

PINCH. Only a love letter, sir.

HORN. From whom? . . . How! this is from your 310 wife! (*Reads.*) Hum . . . and hum. . . .

PINCH. Even from my wife, sir. Am I not wondrous kind and civil to you now too?—(*Aside.*) But you'll not think her so!

HORN. (*Aside*) Ha! Is this a trick of his or hers?

PINCH. The gentleman's surprised, I find. What, you expected a kinder letter?

HORN. No, faith, not I, how could I?

PINCH. Yes, yes, I'm sure you did. A man so well made as you are, must needs be disappointed if the 320 women declare not their passion at first sight or opportunity.

HORN. (*Aside.*) But what should this mean? Stay, the postscript. (*Reads aside.*) 'Be sure you love me whatsoever my husband says to the contrary, and let him not see this lest he should come home and pinch me, or kill my squirrel.'—(*Aside.*) It seems he knows not what the letter contains.

PINCH. Come, ne'er wonder at it so much.

HORN. Faith, I can't help it. 330

PINCH. Now, I think I have deserved your infinite friendship and kindness, and have showed myself sufficiently an obliging kind friend and husband! Am I not so, to bring a letter from my wife to her gallant?

HORN. Ay, the devil take me, art thou the most obliging, kind friend and husband in the world, ha, ha!

PINCH. Well, you may be merry, sir, but in short I must tell you, sir, my honour will suffer no jesting.

HORN. What dost thou mean?

PINCH. Does the letter want a comment? Then 340 know, sir, though I have been so civil a husband as to bring you a letter from my wife, to let you kiss and court her to my face, I will not be a cuckold, sir, I will not.

HORN. Thou art mad with jealousy. I never saw thy wife in my life, but at the play yesterday, and I know not if it were she or no. I court her, kiss her!

PINCH. I will not be a cuckold, I say. There will be danger in making me a cuckold.

350   HORN. Why, wert thou not well cured of thy last clap?°

PINCH. I wear a sword.

HORN. It should be taken from thee lest thou should'st do thyself a mischief with it. Thou art mad, man.

PINCH. As mad as I am, and as merry as you are, I must have more reason from you ere we part. I say again, though you kissed and courted last night my wife in man's clothes, as she confesses in her let-
360 ter. . . .

HORN. (Aside.) Ha!

PINCH. Both she and I say, you must not design it again, for you have mistaken your woman, as you have done your man.

HORN. (Aside.) Oh . . . I understand something now.—Was that thy wife? Why would'st thou not tell me 'twas she? Faith, my freedom with her was your fault, not mine.

PINCH. (Aside.) Faith, so 'twas.

370   HORN. Fie! I'd never do't to a woman before her husband's face, sure.

PINCH. But I had rather you should do't to my wife before my face than behind my back, and that you shall never do.

HORN. No—you will hinder me.

PINCH. If I would not hinder you, you see by her letter, she would.

HORN. Well, I must e'en acquiesce then, and be contented with what she writes.

380   PINCH. I'll assure you 'twas voluntarily writ. I had no hand in't, you may believe me.

HORN. I do believe thee, faith.

PINCH. And believe her too, for she's an innocent creature, has no dissembling in her—and so fare you well, sir.

HORN. Pray, however, present my humble service to her, and tell her I will obey her letter to a tittle, and fulfill her desires, be what they will, or with what difficulty soever I do't, and you shall be no more jealous of
390 me, I warrant her and you.

PINCH. Well, then, fare you well, and play with any man's honour but mine, kiss any man's wife but mine, and welcome.

[Exit MR. PINCHWIFE.

HORN. Ha, ha, ha! Doctor.

QUACK. It seems he has not heard the report of you, or does not believe it.

HORN. Ha, ha! Now, doctor, what think you?

QUACK. Pray let's see the letter . . . hum . . . (Reads the letter.) 'for . . . dear . . . love you . . .'

HORN. I wonder how she could contrive it! What 400 say'st thou to't? 'Tis an original.

QUACK. So are your cuckolds, too, originals, for they are like no other common cuckolds, and I will henceforth believe it not impossible for you to cuckold the Grand Signior° amidst his guards of eunuchs, that I say!

HORN. And I say for the letter, 'tis the first love letter that ever was without flames, darts, fates, destinies, lying and dissembling in't.

Enter SPARKISH *pulling in* MR. PINCHWIFE.

SPARK. Come back, you are a pretty brother-in-law, 410 neither go to church, nor to dinner with your sister bride!

PINCH. My sister denies her marriage, and you see is gone away from you dissatisfied.

SPARK. Pshaw! upon a foolish scruple that our parson was not in lawful orders, and did not say all the Common Prayer. But 'tis her modesty only, I believe. But let women be never so modest the first day, they'll be sure to come to themselves by night, and I shall have enough of her then. In the meantime, Harry 420 Horner, you must dine with me. I keep my wedding at my aunt's in the Piazza.

HORN. Thy wedding! What stale maid has lived to despair of a husband, or what young one of a gallant?

SPARK. Oh, your servant, sir . . . this gentleman's sister then . . . no stale maid.

HORN. I'm sorry for't.

PINCH. (Aside.) How comes he so concerned for her?

SPARK. You sorry for't? Why, do you know any ill 430 by her?

HORN. No, I know none but by thee. 'Tis for her sake, not yours, and another man's sake that might have hoped, I thought.

SPARK. Another man! Another man! What is his name?

HORN. Nay, since 'tis past he shall be nameless. (Aside.) Poor Harcourt! I am sorry thou hast missed her.

PINCH. (Aside.) He seems to be much troubled at the 440 match.

SPARK. Prithee tell me—nay, you shan't go, brother.

PINCH. I must of necessity, but I'll come to you to dinner.

[Exit MR. PINCHWIFE.

SPARK. But Harry, what, have I a rival in my wife already? But with all my heart, for he may be of use to me hereafter! For though my hunger is now my sauce, and I can fall on heartily without, but the time will

---

350–351 **cured of thy last clap,** cured of gonorrhea

405 **Grand Signior,** former sultan of Turkey

come when a rival will be as good sauce for a married
450 man to a wife as an orange to veal.

HORN. O thou damned rogue, thou hast set my teeth
on edge with thy orange!

SPARK. Then let's to dinner—there I was with you
again. Come.

HORN. But who dines with thee?

SPARK. My friends and relations, my brother Pinchwife, you see, of your acquaintance.

HORN. And his wife?

SPARK. No, gad, he'll ne'er let her come amongst us
460 good fellows. Your stingy country coxcomb keeps his
wife from his friends, as he does his little firkin° of ale
for his own drinking, and a gentleman can't get a
smack on't. But his servants, when his back is turned,
broach it at their pleasures, and dust it away, ha, ha,
ha! Gad, I am witty, I think, considering I was married
today, by the world. But come. . . .

HORN. No, I will not dine with you, unless you can
fetch her too.

SPARK. Pshaw! what pleasure can'st thou have with
470 women now, Harry?

HORN. My eyes are not gone—I love a good prospect yet, and will not dine with you unless she does
too. Go fetch her, therefore, but do not tell her husband 'tis for my sake.

SPARK. Well, I'll go try what I can do. In the meantime come away to my aunt's lodging, 'tis in the way to
Pinchwife's.

HORN. The poor woman has called for aid, and
stretched forth her hand, doctor. I cannot but help her
480 over the pale° out of the briars!

[Exeunt SPARKISH, HORNER, QUACK.

SCENE IV

The Scene changes to PINCHWIFE's house.

MRS. PINCHWIFE alone leaning on her elbow. A table,
pen, ink, and paper.

MRS. PINCH. Well, 'tis e'en so, I have got the London disease they call love. I am sick of my husband,
and for my gallant. I have heard this distemper called a
fever, but methinks 'tis liker an ague, for when I think
of my husband I tremble and am in a cold sweat, and
have inclinations to vomit, but when I think of my
gallant, dear Mr. Horner, my hot fit comes and I am all
in a fever, indeed, and as in other fevers my own
chamber is tedious to me, and I would fain be removed
10 to his, and then methinks I should be well. Ah, poor
Mr. Horner! Well, I cannot, will not stay here. Therefore I'll make an end of my letter to him, which shall be
a finer letter than my last, because I have studied it like
anything. Oh, sick, sick!

[Takes the pen and writes.

Enter MR. PINCHWIFE, who seeing her writing steals
softly behind her, and looking over her shoulder,
snatches the paper from her.

PINCH. What, writing more letters?

MRS. PINCH. O lord, bud, why d'ye fright me so?

[She offers to run out: he stops her, and reads.

PINCH. How's this! Nay, you shall not stir, madam.
'Dear, dear, dear, Mr. Horner. . . .' Very well. . . . I
have taught you to write letters to good purpose . . . but let's see't.—'First, I am to beg your par- 20
don for my boldness in writing to you, which I'd have
you to know I would not have done had not you said
first you loved me so extremely, which if you do, you
will never suffer me to lie in the arms of another man,
whom I loath, nauseate, and detest.'—Now you can
write these filthy words! But what follows?—'Therefore I hope you will speedily find some way to free me
from this unfortunate match, which was never, I assure you, of my choice, but I'm afraid 'tis already too
far gone. However, if you love me, as I do you, you 30
will try what you can do, but you must help me away
before tomorrow, or else, alas, I shall be forever out of
your reach, for I can defer no longer our. . . .' (The
letter concludes.) 'Our?' What is to follow 'our'?
Speak, what? Our journey into the country, I suppose?
Oh, woman, damned woman! And love, damned love,
their old tempter! For this is one of his miracles. In a
moment he can make those blind that could see, and
those see that were blind, those dumb that could
speak, and those prattle who were dumb before—nay, 40
what is more than all, make these dough-baked,
senseless, indocile animals, women, too hard for us,
their politic lords and rulers, in a moment.—But make
an end of your letter, and then I'll make an end of you
thus, and all my plagues together.

[Draws his sword

MRS. PINCH. O lord, o lord you are such a passionate
man, bud!

Enter SPARKISH.

SPARK. How now, what's here to do?

PINCH. This fool here now!

SPARK. What, drawn upon your wife? You should 50
never do that but at night in the dark, when you can't
hurt her! This is my sister-in-law, is it not? (Pulls aside
her handkerchief.) Ay, faith, e'en our country
Margery; one may know her. Come, she and you must
go dine with me; dinner's ready, come. But where's
my wife? Is she not come home yet? Where is she?

PINCH. Making you a cuckold—'tis that they all do,
as soon as they can.

SPARK. What, the wedding day? No, a wife that designs to make a cully° of her husband will be sure to let 60
him win the first stake of love, by the world. But come,

_____

461 **firkin**, small wooden vessel or cask   480 **pale**, fence

Scene IV   60 **cully**, a dupe or gull

they stay dinner for us. Come, I'll lead down our Margery.

MRS. PINCH. No! . . . Sir, go, we'll follow you.

SPARK. I will not wag° without you.

PINCH. (*Aside*.) This coxcomb is a sensible torment to me amidst the greatest in the world.

SPARK. Come, come, madam Margery.

PINCH. No, I'll lead her my way. What, would you 70 treat your friends with mine, for want of your own wife? (*Leads her to t'other door, and locks her in and returns.*)—(*Aside*.) I am contented my rage should take breath.

SPARK. (*Aside*.) I told Horner this.

PINCH. Come now.

SPARK. Lord, how shy you are of your wife! But let me tell you, brother, we men of wit have amongst us a saying that cuckolding, like the smallpox, comes with a fear, and you may keep your wife as much as you will 80 out of danger of infection, but if her constitution incline her to't, she'll have it sooner or later, by the world, say they.

PINCH. (*Aside*.) What a thing is a cuckold, that every fool can make him ridiculous!—Well, sir, . . . but let me advise you, now you are come to be concerned, because you suspect the danger, not to neglect the means to prevent it, especially when the greatest share of the malady will light upon your own head, for . . .

Hows'e'er the kind wife's belly comes to swell,
90 The husband breeds for her,° and first is ill.

ACT V SCENE I

MR. PINCHWIFE's *House.*

Enter MR. PINCHWIFE *and* MRS. PINCHWIFE.

A table and candle.

PINCH. Come, take the pen and make an end of the letter, just as you intended. If you are false in a tittle, I shall soon perceive it, and punish you with this as you deserve. (*Lays his hand on his sword.*) Write what was to follow . . . let's see. . . . 'You must make haste and help me away before tomorrow, or else I shall be for ever out of your reach, for I can defer no longer our. . . .' What follows 'our'?

MRS. PINCH. Must all out then, bud?

[MRS. PINCHWIFE *takes the pen and writes.*
10 Look you there, then.

PINCH. Let's see . . . 'For I can defer no longer our wedding. Your slighted Alithea.'—What's the meaning of this? My sister's name to't? Speak, unriddle!

MRS. PINCH. Yes, indeed, bud.

PINCH. But why her name to't? Speak—speak I say!

MRS. PINCH. Ay, but you'll tell her then again. If you would not tell her again. . . .

PINCH. I will not. . . . I am stunned . . . my head turns round. Speak!

MRS. PINCH. Won't you tell her indeed, and indeed? 20

PINCH. No, speak, I say.

MRS. PINCH. She'll be angry with me, but I had rather she should be angry with me than you bud. And to tell you the truth, 'twas she made me write the letter, and taught me what I should write.

PINCH. (*Aside*.) Ha! I thought the style was somewhat better than her own.—But how could she come to you to teach you, since I had locked you up alone?

MRS. PINCH. Oh, through the keyhole, bud.

PINCH. But why should she make you write a letter 30 for her to him, since she can write herself?

MRS. PINCH. Why, she said because—for I was unwilling to do it.

PINCH. Because what—because?

MRS. PINCH. Because, lest Mr. Horner should be cruel and refuse her, or vain afterwards, and show the letter, she might disown it, the hand not being hers.

PINCH. (*Aside*.) How's this? Ha!—then I think I shall come to myself again. This changeling could not invent this lie, but if she could, why should she? She 40 might think I should soon discover it . . . stay . . . now I think on't too, Horner said he was sorry she had married Sparkish, and her disowning her marriage to me makes me think she has evaded it for Horner's sake. Yet why should she take this course? But men in love are fools; women may well be so.—But hark you, madam, your sister went out in the morning and I have not seen her within since.

MRS. PINCH. Alackaday, she has been crying all day above, it seems, in a corner. 50

PINCH. Where is she? Let me speak with her.

MRS. PINCH. (*Aside*.) O lord, then he'll discover all!—Pray hold, bud. What, d'y mean to discover me? She'll know I have told you then. Pray, bud, let me talk with her first.

PINCH. I must speak with her to know whether Horner ever made her any promise; and whether she be married to Sparkish or no.

MRS. PINCH. Pray, dear bud, don't, till I have spoken with her and told her that I have told you all, for she'll 60 kill me else.

PINCH. Go then, and bid her come out to me.

MRS. PINCH. Yes, yes, bud.

PINCH. Let me see. . . .

MRS. PINCH. (*Aside*.) I'll go, but she is not within to come to him. I have just got time to know of Lucy her maid, who first set me on work, what lie I shall tell next, for I am e'en at my wits end!

[*Exit* MRS. PINCHWIFE.

PINCH. Well, I resolve it; Horner shall have her. I'd rather give him my sister than lend him my wife, and 70 such an alliance will prevent his pretensions to my wife, sure. I'll make him of kin to her, and then he won't care for her.

---

65 **wag,** move   90 **husband . . . her,** he grows the horns of a cuckold

MRS. PINCHWIFE *returns.*

MRS. PINCH. O lord, bud, I told you what anger you would make me with my sister!

PINCH. Won't she come hither?

MRS. PINCH. No, no, alackaday, she's ashamed to look you in the face, and she says if you go in to her, she'll run away downstairs, and shamefully go herself
80 to Mr. Horner, who has promised her marriage, she says, and she will have no other, so she won't.

PINCH. Did he so—promise her marriage? Then she shall have no other. Go tell her so, and if she will come and discourse with me a little concerning the means, I will about it immediately. Go!

[*Exit* MRS. PINCHWIFE.

His estate is equal to Sparkish's, and his extraction as much better than his as his parts are. But my chief reason is I'd rather be of kin to him by the name of brother-in-law than of cuckold.

Enter MRS. PINCHWIFE.

90 Well, what says she now?

MRS. PINCH. Why, she says she would only have you lead her to Horner's lodging—with whom she first will discourse the matter before she talk with you, which yet she cannot do. For alack, poor creature, she says she can't so much as look you in the face, therefore she'll come to you in a mask. And you must excuse her if she make you no answer to any question of yours till you have brought her to Mr. Horner. And if you will not chide her nor question her she'll come out to you
100 immediately.

PINCH. Let her come. I will not speak a word to her, nor require a word from her.

MRS. PINCH. Oh, I forgot—besides, she says, she cannot look you in the face, though through a mask, therefore would desire you to put out the candle.

MR. PINCH. I agree to all; let her make haste. There, 'tis out. (*Puts out the candle.*)

[*Exit* MRS. PINCHWIFE.

My case is something better; I'd rather fight with
110 Horner for not lying with my sister than for lying with my wife, and of the two I had rather find my sister too forward than my wife. I expected no other from her free education, as she calls it, and her passion for the town. Well, wife and sister are names which make us expect love and duty, pleasure and comfort, but we find 'em plagues and torments, and are equally, though differently troublesome to their keeper—for we have as much ado to get people to lie with our sisters as keep 'em from lying with our wives!

Enter MRS. PINCHWIFE, *masked, and in hood and scarf, and a nightgown and petticoat of* ALITHEA's, *in the dark.*

What, are you come, sister? Let us go then . . . but

first let me lock up my wife. Mrs. Margery, where are 120 you?

MRS. PINCH. Here, bud.

PINCH. Come hither, that I may lock you up. Get you in. (*Locks the door.*) Come, sister, where are you now?

MRS. PINCHWIFE *gives him her hand, but when he lets her go, she steals softly on t'other side of him, and is led away by him for his sister* ALITHEA.

SCENE II

The scene changes to HORNER's *lodging.*

QUACK, HORNER.

QUACK. What, all alone? Not so much as one of your cuckolds here, nor one of their wives! They use to take their turns with you, as if they were to watch you.

HORN. Yes, it often happens that a cuckold is but his wife's spy, and is more upon family duty when he is with her gallant abroad, hindering his pleasure, than when he is at home with her, playing the gallant. But the hardest duty a married woman imposes upon a lover is keeping her husband company always.

QUACK. And his fondness wearies you almost as 10 soon as hers.

HORN. A pox! keeping a cuckold company after you have had his wife is as tiresome as the company of a country squire to a witty fellow of the town, when he has got all his money.

QUACK. And as at first a man makes a friend of the husband to get the wife, so at last you are fain to fall out with the wife to be rid of the husband.

HORN. Ay, most cuckold-makers are true courtiers. When once a poor man has cracked his credit for 'em, 20 they can't abide to come near him.

QUACK. But at first, to draw him in, are so sweet, so kind, so dear, just as you are to Pinchwife. But what becomes of that intrigue with his wife?

HORN. A pox! he's as surly as an alderman that has been bit,° and since he's so coy, his wife's kindness is in vain, for she's a silly innocent.

QUACK. Did she not send you a letter by him?

HORN. Yes, but that's a riddle I have not yet solved. Allow the poor creature to be willing, she is silly too, 30 and he keeps her up so close. . . .

QUACK. Yes, so close that he makes her but the more willing, and adds but revenge to her love, which two, when met, seldom fail to satisfy each other one way or other.

HORN. What! here's the man we are talking of, I think.

Act V, Scene II   26 **bit,** tricked financially

Enter MR. PINCHWIFE *leading in his wife, masked, muffled, and in her sister's nightgown.*

HORN. Pshaw!

QUACK. Bringing his wife to you is the next thing to
40 bringing a love letter from her.

HORN. What means this?

PINCH. The last time, you know, sir, I brought you a love letter. Now you see a mistress I think you'll say I am a civil man to you!

HORN. Ay, the devil take me, will I say thou art the civilest man I ever met with, and I have known some. I fancy I understand thee now better than I did the letter. But hark thee, in thy ear. . . .

PINCH. What?

50 HORN. Nothing but the usual question, man; is she sound,° on thy word?

PINCH. What, you take her for a wench, and me for a pimp?

HORN. Pshaw! wench and pimp, paw° words. I know thou art an honest fellow, and hast a great acquaintance among the ladies, and perhaps hast made love for me rather than let me make love to thy wife.

PINCH. Come, sir, in short; I am for no fooling.

HORN. Nor I neither; therefore prithee let's see her
60 face presently. Make her show, man! Art thou sure I don't know her?

PINCH. I am sure you do know her.

HORN. A pox! why dost thou bring her to me then?

PINCH. Because she's a relation of mine. . . .

HORN. Is she, faith, man! Then thou art still more civil and obliging, dear rogue.

PINCH. . . . who desired me to bring her to you.

HORN. Then she is obliging, dear rogue.

PINCH. You'll make her welcome, for my sake, I
70 hope.

HORN. I hope she is handsome enough to make herself welcome. Prithee, let her unmask.

PINCH. Do you speak to her. She would never be ruled by me.

HORN. Madam . . .

[MRS. PINCHWIFE *whispers to* HORNER.
She says she must speak with me in private. Withdraw, prithee.

PINCH. (*Aside.*) She's unwilling, it seems, I should know all her undecent conduct in this business.—
80 Well, then, I'll leave you together, and hope when I am gone you'll agree. If not, you and I shan't agree, sir.

HORN. (*Aside.*) What means the fool?—If she and I agree, 'tis no matter what you and I do.

[*Whispers to* MRS. PINCHWIFE, *who makes signs with her hand for* MR. PINCHWIFE *to be gone.*

PINCH. In the meantime I'll fetch a parson, and find out Sparkish and disabuse him. You would have me fetch a parson, would you not? Well then. . . . Now I think I am rid of her, and shall have no more trouble

---

51 **sound,** healthy, not infected with a venereal disease   54 **paw,** improper, obscene

---

with her. Our sisters and daughters, like usurers' money, are safest when put out, but our wives, like their writings, never safe but in our closets under lock 90 and key.

[*Exit* MR. PINCHWIFE.

Enter BOY.

BOY. Sir Jasper Fidget, sir, is coming up.

HORN. Here's the trouble of a cuckold, now, we are talking of. A pox on him! Has he not enough to do to hinder his wife's sport, but he must other women's too?—Step in here, madam.

[*Exit* MRS. PINCHWIFE.

Enter SIR JASPER.

SIR JAS. My best and dearest friend.

HORN. (*Aside to* QUACK.) The old style, doctor.— Well, be short, for I am busy. What would your impertinent wife have now? 100

SIR JAS. Well guessed, i'faith, for I do come from her.

HORN. To invite me to supper? Tell her I can't come. Go.

SIR JAS. Nay, now you are out, faith, for my lady and the whole knot of the virtuous gang, as they call themselves, are resolved upon a frolic of coming to you tonight in a masquerade, and are all dressed already.

HORN. I shan't be at home.

SIR JAS. (*Aside.*) Lord, how churlish he is to wom- 110 en!—Nay, prithee don't disappoint 'em, they'll think 'tis my fault, prithee don't. I'll send in the banquet and the fiddles. But make no noise on't, for the poor virtuous rogues would not have it known for the world, that they go a-masquerading, and they would come to no man's ball but yours.

HORN. Well, well—get you gone, and tell 'em, if they come, 'twill be at the peril of their honour and yours.

SIR JAS. He, he, he! We'll trust you for that, farewell. 120

[*Exit* SIR JASPER.

HORN.   Doctor, anon you too shall be my guest,
         But now I'm going to a private feast.

SCENE III

The Scene changes to the Piazza of Covent Garden.

SPARKISH, PINCHWIFE.

SPARK. (*With the letter in his hand.*) But who could have thought a woman could have been false to me? By the world, I could not have thought it.

PINCH. You were for giving and taking liberty; she has taken it only, sir, now you find in that letter. You are a frank person, and so is she, you see there.

SPARK. Nay, if this be her hand—for I never saw it.

PINCH. 'Tis no matter whether that be her hand or no. I am sure this hand, at her desire, led her to Mr. Horner, with whom I left her just now, to go fetch a parson to 'em, at their desire too, to deprive you of her forever, for it seems yours was but a mock marriage.

SPARK. Indeed, she would needs have it that 'twas Harcourt himself in a parson's habit that married us, but I'm sure he told me 'twas his brother Ned.

PINCH. Oh, there 'tis out, and you were deceived, not she, for you are such a frank person—but I must be gone. You'll find her at Mr. Horner's. Go and believe your eyes.

[Exit MR. PINCHWIFE.

SPARK. Nay, I'll to her, and call her as many crocodiles, sirens, harpies, and other heathenish names as a poet would do a mistress who had refused to hear his suit, nay more, his verses on her.—But stay, is not that she following a torch at t'other end of the Piazza? And from Horner's certainly—'tis so.

Enter ALITHEA following a torch, and LUCY behind.

You are well met, madam, though you don't think so. What, you have made a short visit to Mr. Horner, but I suppose you'll return to him presently. By that time the parson can be with him.

ALITH. Mr. Horner, and the parson, sir!

SPARK. Come, madam, no more dissembling, no more jilting, for I am no more a frank person.

ALITH. How's this?

LUCY. (*Aside.*) So, 'twill work, I see.

SPARK. Could you find out no easy country fool to abuse? none but me, a gentleman of wit and pleasure about the town? But it was your pride to be too hard for a man of parts, unworthy false woman! False as a friend that lends a man money to lose! False as dice, who undo those that trust all they have to 'em!

LUCY. (*Aside.*) He has been a great bubble by his similes, as they say!

ALITH. You have been too merry, sir, at your wedding dinner, sure.

SPARK. What, d'y mock me too?

ALITH. Or you have been deluded.

SPARK. By you!

ALITH. Let me understand you.

SPARK. Have you the confidence—I should call it something else, since you know your guilt—to stand my just reproaches? You did not write an impudent letter to Mr. Horner! who I find now has clubbed with you in deluding me with his aversion for women, that I might not, forsooth, suspect him for my rival.

LUCY. (*Aside.*) D'y think the gentleman can be jealous now, madam?

ALITH. I write a letter to Mr. Horner!

SPARK. Nay, madam, do not deny it. Your brother showed it me just now, and told me likewise he left you at Horner's lodging to fetch a parson to marry you to him. And I wish you joy, madam, joy, joy! and to him, too, much joy! and to myself more joy for not marrying you!

ALITH. (*Aside.*) So I find my brother would break off the match, and I can consent to't, since I see this gentleman can be made jealous.—O Lucy, by his rude usage and jealousy, he makes me almost afraid I am married to him. Art thou sure 'twas Harcourt himself and no parson that married us?

SPARK. No, madam, I thank you. I suppose that was a contrivance too of Mr. Horner's and yours, to make Harcourt play the parson. But I would, as little as you, have him one now, no, not for the world, for shall I tell you another truth? I never had any passion for you 'till now, for now I hate you. 'Tis true I might have married your portion, as other men of parts of the town do sometimes, and so your servant. And to show my unconcernedness, I'll come to your wedding and resign you with as much joy as I would a stale wench to a new cully. Nay, with as much joy as I would after the first night, if I had been married to you. There's for you, and so your servant, servant.

[*Exit* SPARKISH.

ALITH. How was I deceived in a man!

LUCY. You'll believe, then, a fool may be made jealous now? For that easiness in him, that suffers him to be led by a wife, will likewise permit him to be persuaded against her by others.

ALITH. But marry Mr. Horner! My brother does not intend it, sure. If I thought he did, I would take thy advice, and Mr. Harcourt for my husband. And now I wish that if there be any over-wise woman of the town, who, like me, would marry a fool for fortune, liberty, or title, first, that her husband may love play, and be a cully to all the town, but her, and suffer none but fortune to be mistress of his purse. Then, if for liberty, that he may send her into the country under the conduct of some housewifely mother-in-law. And, if for title, may the world give 'em none but that of cuckold.

LUCY. And for her greater curse, madam, may he not deserve it.

ALITH. Away, impertinent!—Is not this my old lady Lanterlu's?°

LUCY. Yes, madam. (*Aside.*) And here I hope we shall find Mr. Harcourt.

[*Exeunt* ALITHEA, LUCY.

SCENE IV

The scene changes again to HORNER's *lodging.*

HORNER, LADY FIDGET, MRS. DAINTY FIDGET, MRS. SQUEAMISH.

A table, banquet, and bottles.

Scene III 102 **Lanterlu's,** meaningless syllables occurring in the refrain of a song of the early seventeenth century; also loo, an ancient card game

HORN. (*Aside.*) A pox! they are come too soon . . . before I have sent back my new mistress. All I have now to do is to lock her in, that they may not see her.

LADY FIDG. That we may be sure of our welcome, we have brought our entertainment with us, and are resolved to treat thee, dear toad.

DAIN. And that we may be merry to purpose, have left sir Jasper and my old lady Squeamish quarrelling

10 at home at backgammon.

SQUEAM. Therefore, let us make use of our time, lest they should chance to interrupt us.

LADY FIDG. Let us sit then.

HORN. First, that you may be private, let me lock this door and that, and I'll wait upon you presently.

LADY FIDG. No, sir, shut 'em only and your lips for ever, for we must trust you as much as our women.

HORN. You know all vanity's killed in me.—I have no occasion for talking.

20 LADY FIDG. Now, ladies, supposing we had drank each of us our two bottles, let us speak the truth of our hearts.

DAIN. *and* SQUEAM. Agreed.

LADY FIDG. By this brimmer,° for truth is nowhere else to be found. (*Aside to* HORNER.) Not in thy heart, false man!

HORN. (*Aside to* LADY FIDGET.) You have found me a true man, I'm sure!

LADY FIDG. (*Aside to* HORNER.) Not every way.

30 —But let us sit and be merry.

(LADY FIDGET *sings.*)

1.

Why should our damned tyrants oblige us to live
On the pittance of pleasure which they only give?
    We must not rejoice,
    With wine and with noise.
In vain we must wake in a dull bed alone,
Whilst to our warm rival, the bottle, they're gone.
    Then lay aside charms,
    *And take up these arms.**   [*The glasses.

2.

'Tis wine only gives 'em their courage and wit,
40 *Because we live sober, to men we submit.*
    If for beauties you'd pass,
    Take a lick of the glass,
'Twill mend your complexions, and when they are gone,
The best red we have is the red of the grape.
    Then, sisters, lay't on,
    And damn a good shape.

DAIN. Dear brimmer! Well, in token of our openness and plain-dealing, let us throw our masks over our heads.

HORN. So, 'twill come to the glasses anon.   50

SQUEAM. Lovely brimmer! Let me enjoy him first.

LADY FIDG. No, I never part with a gallant till I've tried him. Dear brimmer, that mak'st our husbands short-sighted.

DAIN. And our bashful gallants bold.

SQUEAM. And for want of a gallant, the butler lovely in our eyes. Drink, eunuch.

LADY FIDG. Drink, thou representative of a husband. Damn a husband!

DAIN. And, as it were a husband, an old keeper.   60

SQUEAM. And an old grandmother.

HORN. And an English bawd, and a French chirurgion.

LADY FIDG. Ay, we have all reason to curse 'em.

HORN. For my sake, ladies?

LADY FIDG. No, for our own, for the first spoils all young gallants' industry.

DAIN. And the other's art makes 'em bold only with common women.

SQUEAM. And rather run the hazard of the vile dis- 70 temper amongst them than of a denial amongst us.

DAIN. The filthy toads choose mistresses now as they do stuffs,° for having been fancied and worn by others.

SQUEAM. For being common and cheap.

LADY FIDG. Whilst women of quality, like the richest stuffs, lie untumbled and unasked for.

HORN. Ay, neat, and cheap, and new, often they think best.

DAIN. No, sir, the beasts will be known by a mis- 80 tress longer than by a suit.

SQUEAM. And 'tis not for cheapness neither.

LADY FIDG. No, for the vain fops will take up druggets° and embroider 'em. But I wonder at the depraved appetites of witty men; they use to be out of the common road, and hate imitation. Pray tell me, beast, when you were a man, why you rather chose to club with a multitude in a common house for an entertainment than to be the only guest at a good table.

HORN. Why, faith, ceremony and expectation are 90 unsufferable to those that are sharp bent. People always eat with the best stomach at an ordinary,° where every man is snatching for the best bit.

LADY FIDG. Though he get a cut over the fingers. . . . But I have heard people eat most heartily of another man's meat, that is, what they do not pay for.

HORN. When they are sure of their welcome and freedom, for ceremony in love and eating is as ridiculous as in fighting. Falling on briskly is all should be done in those occasions.   100

LADY FIDG. Well, then, let me tell you, sir, there is nowhere more freedom than in our houses, and we take freedom from a young person as a sign of good

---

73 **stuffs**, materials   84 **druggets**, clothing material, a coarse mix of fabrics
92 **ordinary**, meal for a fixed price in an eating house or tavern

Scene IV   24 **brimmer**, a glass filled to the brim

breeding, and a person may be as free as he pleases with us, as frolic, as gamesome, as wild as he will.

HORN. Han't I heard you all declaim against wild men?

LADY FIDG. Yes, but for all that, we think wildness in a man as desirable a quality as in a duck or rabbit. A
110 tame man, foh!

HORN. I know not, but your reputations frightened me, as much as your faces invited me.

LADY FIDG. Our reputation! Lord, why should you not think that we women make use of our reputation, as you men of yours, only to deceive the world with less suspicion? Our virtue is like the statesman's religion, the Quaker's word, the gamester's oath, and the great man's honour—but to cheat those that trust us.

SQUEAM. And that demureness, coyness, and mod-
120 esty that you see in our faces in the boxes at plays is as much a sign of a kind woman as a vizard-mask in the pit.

DAIN. For, I assure you, women are least masked when they have the velvet vizard on.

LADY FIDG. You would have found us modest women in our denials only.

SQUEAM. Our bashfulness is only the reflection of the men's.

DAIN. We blush when they are shamefaced.
130 HORN. I beg your pardon, ladies. I was deceived in you devilishly. But why that mighty pretence to honour?

LADY FIDG. We have told you. But sometimes 'twas for the same reason you men pretend business often, to avoid ill company, to enjoy the better and more privately those you love.

HORN. But why would you ne'er give a friend a wink then?

LADY FIDG. Faith, your reputation frightened us as
140 much as ours did you, you were so notoriously lewd.

HORN. And you so seemingly honest.

LADY FIDG. Was that all that deterred you?

HORN. And so expensive . . . you allow freedom, you say?

LADY FIDG. Ay, ay.

HORN. That I was afraid of losing my little money, as well as my little time, both which my other pleasures required.

LADY FIDG. Money, foh! You talk like a little fellow
150 now. Do such as we expect money?

HORN. I beg your pardon, madam. I must confess, I have heard that great ladies, like great merchants, set but the higher prices upon what they have, because they are not in necessity of taking the first offer.

DAIN. Such as we make sale of our hearts?

SQUEAM. We bribed for our love? Foh!

HORN. With your pardon, ladies, I know, like great men in offices, you seem to exact flattery and attendance only from your followers, but you have receiv-
160 ers about you, and such fees to pay, a man is afraid to pass your grants.° Besides, we must let you win at cards, or we lose your hearts. And if you make an assignation, 'tis at a goldsmith's, jeweller's, or china house, where, for your honour you deposit to him, he must pawn his to the punctual cit,° and so paying for what you take up, pays for what he takes up.

DAIN. Would you not have us assured of our gallant's love?

SQUEAM. For love is better known by liberality than by jealousy.   170

LADY FIDG. For one may be dissembled, the other not. (Aside.) But my jealousy can be no longer dissembled, and they are telling ripe.—Come, here's to our gallants in waiting, whom we must name, and I'll begin. This is my false rogue. [Claps him on the back.

SQUEAM. How!

HORN. (Aside.) So, all will out now.

SQUEAM. (Aside to HORNER.) Did you not tell me, 'twas for my sake only you reported yourself no man?

DAIN. (Aside to HORNER.) Oh wretch! Did you not   180
swear to me, 'twas for my love and honour you passed for that thing you do?

HORN. So, so.

LADY FIDG. Come, speak ladies; this is my false villain.

SQUEAM. And mine too.

DAIN. And mine.

HORN. Well, then, you are all three my false rogues too, and there's an end on't.

LADY FIDG. Well, then, there's no remedy; sister   190
sharers, let us not fall out, but have a care of our honour. Though we get no presents, no jewels of him, we are savers of our honour, the jewel of most value and use, which shines yet to the world unsuspected, though it be counterfeit.

HORN. Nay, and is e'en as good as if it were true, provided the world think so; for honour, like beauty now, only depends on the opinion of others.

LADY FIDG. Well, Harry Common, I hope you can be true to three. Swear—but 'tis no purpose to require 200
your oath for you are as often forsworn as you swear to new women.

HORN. Come, faith, madam, let us e'en pardon one another, for all the difference I find betwixt we men and you women, we forswear ourselves at the beginning of an amour, you as long as it lasts.

Enter SIR JASPER FIDGET, and OLD LADY SQUEAMISH.

SIR JAS. Oh, my lady Fidget, was this your cunning to come to Mr. Horner without me? But you have been nowhere else, I hope.

LADY FIDG. No, sir Jasper.   210

OLD L. SQUEAM. And you came straight hither, biddy?

161 **to pass your grants,** accept your gifts   165 **cit,** a townsman or merchant as distinguished from a gentleman

SQUEAM. Yes, indeed, lady grandmother.

SIR JAS. 'Tis well, 'tis well. I knew when once they were thoroughly acquainted with poor Horner, they'd ne'er be from him. You may let her masquerade it with my wife and Horner, and I warrant her reputation safe.

Enter BOY.

BOY. Oh, sir, here's the gentleman come whom you bid me not suffer to come up without giving you
220 notice, with a lady too, and other gentlemen.

HORN. Do you all go in there, whilst I send 'em away, and boy, do you desire 'em to stay below 'till I come, which shall be immediately.

[*Exeunt* SIR JASPER, LADY SQUEAMISH, LADY FIDGET,
MISTRESS DAINTY, MISTRESS SQUEAMISH.

BOY. Yes, sir. [*Exit.*

[*Exit* HORNER *at t'other door, and returns with*
MISTRESS PINCHWIFE.

HORN. You would not take my advice to be gone home before your husband came back; he'll now discover all. Yet pray, my dearest, be persuaded to go home, and leave the rest to my management. I'll let you down the back way.

230 MRS. PINCH. I don't know the way home, so I don't.

HORN. My man shall wait upon you.

MRS. PINCH. No, don't you believe that I'll go at all. What, are you weary of me already?

HORN. No, my life, 'tis that I may love you long, 'tis to secure my love, and your reputation with your husband. He'll never receive you again else.

MRS. PINCH. What care I? D'ye think to frighten me with that? I don't intend to go to him again. You shall be my husband now.

240 HORN. I cannot be your husband, dearest, since you are married to him.

MRS. PINCH. Oh, would you make me believe that? Don't I see every day at London here, women leave their first husbands, and go and live with other men as their wives? Pish, pshaw! you'd make me angry, but that I love you so mainly.

HORN. So, they are coming up.—In again, in, I hear 'em.

[*Exit* MISTRESS PINCHWIFE.

Well, a silly mistress is like a weak place, soon got,
250 soon lost, a man has scarce time for plunder. She betrays her husband first to her gallant, and then her gallant to her husband.

Enter PINCHWIFE, ALITHEA, HARCOURT, SPARKISH,
LUCY, *and a* PARSON.

PINCH. Come, madam, 'tis not the sudden change of your dress, the confidence of your asseverations, and your false witness there, shall persuade me I did not bring you hither just now. Here's my witness, who

cannot deny it, since you must be confronted.—Mr. Horner, did not I bring this lady to you just now?

HORN. (*Aside.*) Now must I wrong one woman for another's sake. But that's no new thing with me; for in 260 these cases I am still on the criminal's side, against the innocent.

ALITH. Pray speak, sir.

HORN. (*Aside.*) It must be so—I must be impudent and try my luck; impudence uses to be too hard for truth.

PINCH. What, you are studying an evasion, or excuse for her? Speak, sir.

HORN. No, faith, I am something backward only to speak in women's affairs or disputes. 270

PINCH. She bids you speak.

ALITH. Ay, pray sir do, pray satisfy him.

HORN. Then truly, did you bring that lady to me just now.

PINCH. O ho!

ALITH. How, sir!

HARC. How, Horner!

ALITH. What mean you, sir? I always took you for a man of honour.

HORN. (*Aside.*) Ay, so much a man of honour that I 280 must save my mistress, I thank you, come what will on't.

SPARK. So if I had had her, she'd have made me believe the moon had been made of a Christmas pie.

LUCY. (*Aside.*) Now could I speak, if I durst, and solve the riddle, who am the author of it.

ALITH. O unfortunate woman! A combination against my honour, which most concerns me now, because you share in my disgrace, sir, and it is your censure which I must now suffer, that troubles me, not 290 theirs.

HARC. Madam, then have no trouble, you shall now see 'tis possible for me to love too, without being jealous. I will not only believe your innocence myself, but make all the world believe it. (*Apart to* HORNER.) Horner, I must now be concerned for this lady's honour.

HORN. And I must be concerned for a lady's honour too.

HARC. This lady has her honour, and I will protect it. 300

HORN. My lady has not her honour, but has given it me to keep, and I will preserve it.

HARC. I understand you not.

HORN. I would not have you.

MRS. PINCH. (*Peeping in behind.*) What's the matter with 'em all?

PINCH. Come, come, Mr. Horner, no more disputing. Here's the parson; I brought him not in vain.

HORN. No, sir, I'll employ him, if this lady please.

PINCH. How! what d'ye mean? 310

SPARK. Ay, what does he mean?

HORN. Why, I have resigned your sister to him; he has my consent.

PINCH. But he has not mine, sir. A woman's injured honour, no more than a man's, can be repaired or satisfied by any but him that first wronged it. And you shall marry her presently, or . . .[Lays his hand on his sword.

Enter to them MISTRESS PINCHWIFE.

MRS. PINCH. O lord, they'll kill poor Mr. Horner! Besides he shan't marry her whilst I stand by and look
320 on. I'll not lose my second husband so.
PINCH. What do I see?
ALITH. My sister in my clothes!
SPARK. Ha!
MRS. PINCH. (To PINCHWIFE.) Nay, pray now don't quarrel about finding work for the parson. He shall marry me to Mr. Horner, for now I believe you have enough of me.
HORN. Damned, damned loving changeling!
MRS. PINCH. Pray, sister, pardon me for telling so
330 many lies of you.
HARC. I suppose the riddle is plain now.
LUCY. No, that must be my work. Good sir, hear me.
[Kneels to MR. PINCHWIFE, who stands doggedly with his hat over his eyes.
PINCH. I will never hear woman again, but make 'em all silent, thus—
[Offers to draw upon his wife.
HORN. No, that must not be.
PINCH. You then shall go first, 'tis all one to me.
[Offers to draw on HORNER; stopped by HARCOURT.
HARC. Hold!

Enter SIR JASPER FIDGET, LADY FIDGET, LADY SQUEAMISH, MRS. DAINTY FIDGET, MRS. SQUEAMISH.

SIR JAS. What's the matter? what's the matter? pray,
340 what's the matter, sir? I beseech you communicate, sir.
PINCH. Why, my wife has communicated, sir, as your wife may have done too, sir, if she knows him, sir.
SIR JAS. Pshaw! with him! ha, ha, he!
PINCH. D'ye mock me, sir? A cuckold is a kind of a wild beast, have a care, sir!
SIR JAS. No, sure, you mock me, sir—he cuckold you! It can't be, ha, ha, he! Why, I'll tell you,
350 sir. . . . [Offers to whisper.
PINCH. I tell you again, he has whored my wife, and yours too, if he knows her, and all the women he comes near. 'Tis not his dissembling, his hypocrisy, can wheedle me.
SIR JAS. How! does he dissemble? Is he an hypocrite? Nay then . . . how . . . wife . . . sister, is he an hypocrite?

OLD L. SQUEAM. An hypocrite, a dissembler! Speak, young harlotry, speak, how?
SIR JAS. Nay, then . . . oh, my head too! . . . Oh 360 thou libidinous lady!
OLD L. SQUEAM. Oh thou harloting harlotry! Hast thou done't then?
SIR JAS. Speak, good Horner, art thou a dissembler, a rogue? Hast thou. . . ?
HORN. So. . . .
LUCY. (Apart to HORNER.) I'll fetch you off, and her too, if she will but hold her tongue.
HORN. (Apart to LUCY.) Canst thou? I'll give thee. . . .
370
LUCY. (To MR. PINCHWIFE.) Pray, have but patience to hear me, sir, who am the unfortunate cause of all this confusion. Your wife is innocent, I only culpable—for I put her upon telling you all these lies concerning my mistress in order to the breaking off the match between Mr. Sparkish and her, to make way for Mr. Harcourt.
SPARK. Did you so, eternal rotten-tooth? Then it seems, my mistress was not false to me, I was only deceived by you. Brother, that should have been, now, 380 man of conduct, who is a frank person now?—to bring your wife to her lover—ha!
LUCY. I assure you, sir, she came not to Mr. Horner out of love, for she loves him no more. . . .
MRS. PINCH. Hold, I told lies for you, but you shall tell none for me, for I do love Mr. Horner with all my soul, and nobody shall say me nay. Pray don't you go to make poor Mr. Horner believe to the contrary, 'tis spitefully done of you, I'm sure.
HORN. (Aside to MRS. PINCHWIFE.) Peace, dear 390 idiot!
MRS. PINCH. Nay, I will not peace.
PINCH. Not till I make you.
DOR. Horner, your servant; I am the doctor's guest, he must excuse our intrusion.
QUACK. But what's the matter, gentlemen? For heaven's sake, what's the matter?
HORN. Oh, 'tis well you are come. 'Tis a censorious world we live in; you may have brought me a reprieve, or else I had died for a crime I never committed, and 400 these innocent ladies had suffered with me. Therefore, pray satisfy these worthy, honourable, jealous gentlemen . . . that . . .
[Whispers.
QUACK. Oh, I understand you; is that all?—Sir Jasper, by heavens and upon the word of a physician, sir . . .
[Whispers to SIR JASPER.
SIR JAS. Nay, I do believe you truly.—Pardon me, my virtuous lady, and dear of honour.
OLD L. SQUEAM. What, then all's right again?
SIR JAS. Ay, ay, and now let us satisfy him too. 410
[They whisper with MR. PINCHWIFE.

PINCH. An eunuch! Pray, no fooling with me.

QUACK. I'll bring half the chirurgions in town to swear it.

PINCH. They! . . . They'll swear a man that bled to death through his wounds died of apoplexy.

QUACK. Pray hear me, sir. Why, all the town has heard the report of him.

PINCH. But does all the town believe it?

QUACK. Pray enquire a little, and first of all these.

420 PINCH. I'm sure when I left the town he was the lewdest fellow in't.

QUACK. I tell you, sir, he has been in France since; pray ask but these ladies and gentlemen, your friend Mr. Dorilant. . . . Gentlemen and ladies; han't you all heard the late sad report of poor Mr. Horner?

ALL LADIES. Ay, ay, ay.

DOR. Why, thou jealous fool, do'st thou doubt it? He's an arrant French capon.

MRS. PINCH. 'Tis false, sir, you shall not disparage
430 poor Mr. Horner, for to my certain knowledge. . . .

LUCY. Oh, hold!

SQUEAM. (Aside to LUCY.) Stop her mouth!

LADY FIDG. (To PINCHWIFE.) Upon my honour, sir, 'tis as true. . . .

DAIN. D'ye think we would have been seen in his company?

SQUEAM. Trust our unspotted reputations with him!

LADY FIDG. (Aside to HORNER.) This you get, and we too, by trusting your secret to a fool.

440 HORN. Peace, madam. (Aside to QUACK.) Well, doctor, is not this a good design, that carries a man on unsuspected, and brings him off safe?

PINCH. (Aside.) Well, if this were true, but my wife . . .

[DORILANT whispers with MRS. PINCHWIFE.

ALITH. Come, brother, your wife is yet innocent you see. But have a care of too strong an imagination, lest like an over-concerned, timorous gamester, by fancying an unlucky cast, it should come. Women and fortune are truest still to those that trust 'em.

450 LUCY. And any wild thing grows but the more fierce and hungry for being kept up, and more dangerous to the keeper.

ALITH. There's doctrine for all husbands, Mr. Harcourt.

HARC. I edify, madam, so much that I am impatient till I am one.

DOR. And I edify so much by example I will never be one.

SPARK. And because I will not disparage my parts I'll
460 ne'er be one.

HORN. And I, alas, can't be one.

PINCH. But I must be one—against my will, to a country wife, with a country murrain° to me.

---

463 murrain, plague

MRS. PINCH. (Aside.) And I must be a country wife still too, I find, for I can't, like a city one, be rid of my musty husband and do what I list.

HORN. Now, sir, I must pronounce your wife innocent, though I blush whilst I do it, and I am the only man by her now exposed to shame, which I will straight drown in wine, as you shall your suspicion, 470 and the ladies' troubles we'll divert with a ballet. Doctor, where are your maskers?

LUCY. Indeed, she's innocent, sir, I am her witness. And her end of coming out was but to see her sister's wedding, and what she has said to your face of her love to Mr. Horner was but the usual innocent revenge on a husband's jealousy—was it not, madam? Speak.

MRS. PINCH. (Aside to LUCY and HORNER.) Since you'll have me tell more lies.—Yes, indeed, bud.

PINCH.   For my own sake fain I would all believe; 480
    Cuckolds, like lovers, should themselves
      deceive.
    But . . . (Sighs.)
    His honour is least safe, too late I find,
    Who trust it with a foolish wife or friend.

A dance of cuckolds.

HORN.   Vain fops, but court, and dress, and keep a
      pother,
    To pass for women's men with one another;
    But he who aims by women to be prized,
    First by the men, you see, must be despised!

EPILOGUE

spoken by MRS. KNEP.

Now, you the vigorous, who daily here
O'er vizard mask in public domineer,
And what you'd do to her if in place where;
Nay, have the confidence to cry, 'Come out!'
Yet when she says, 'Lead on', you are not stout;
But to your well-dressed brother straight turn round
And cry, 'Pox on her, Ned, she can't be found!'
Then slink away, a fresh one to engage,
With so much seeming heat and loving rage,
You'd frighten listening actress on the stage: 10
Till she at last has seen you huffing come,
And talk of keeping in the tiring-room,
Yet cannot be provoked to lead her home.
Next, you Falstaffs of fifty, who beset
Your buckram maidenheads,° which your friends get;
And whilst to them you of achievement boast,

Epilogue   15 buckram maidenheads. See Falstaff's boast in *I Henry IV*, II, iv. Buckram was a fabric sometimes used for padding, hence a buckram maidenhead was something padded or falsified

They share the booty, and laugh at your cost.
In fine, you essenced° boys, both old and young,
Who would be thought so eager, brisk, and strong,
20 Yet do the ladies, not their husbands, wrong:
Whose purses for your manhood make excuse,
And keep your Flanders mares° for show, not use;
Encouraged by our woman's man today,
A Horner's part may vainly think to play;
And may intrigues so bashfully disown
That they may doubted be by few or none;
May kiss the cards at picquet, ombre, loo,
And so be thought to kiss the lady too;
But, gallants, have a care, faith, what you do.
30 The world, which to no man his due will give,
You by experience know you can deceive,
And men may still believe you vigorous,
But then we women—there's no coz'ning° us!

FINIS

(1675)

DANIEL DEFOE
1659–1731

Daniel Defoe (originally Foe) was born in London of a middle-class family of nonconformists, Puritan in their outlook. Equipped with a good education, he took active part in the political, religious, and economic controversies of his day. He was soldier, trader, journalist, and pamphleteer; in all these various occupations he suffered from abuse and scorn leveled at him by his contemporaries. His spirit of independence alarmed one group; his spirit of moderation irritated others. In view of his Puritan background, his close relationship with the government of William III is not surprising. Between the years 1695 and 1702 Defoe worked hard for William; he wrote several pamphlets in defense of William's policies and composed The True-Born Englishman (1701), a vigorous satirical poem directed against the national objection to William as a foreigner and against the English insistence upon "purity of blood" as a necessary attribute of leadership. In this same period came his Essay upon Projects (1697–1698), setting forth many of his own views on social and political questions and demonstrating that for his age his views were often extremely liberal. He won a considerable audience among the middle classes, and when he was placed in the pillory, fined, and imprisoned for his hard-bitten satire against the Church of England party, The Short-

est Way with Dissenters (1702), he became something of a popular hero.

Having been released from prison in 1704. Defoe started a journal, The Review, a tri-weekly political newspaper published until 1713. In this he discussed questions of the day and printed reflections upon the morals and manners of contemporary England in a manner anticipating The Tatler and The Spectator of Steele and Addison. In addition to being a journalist, Defoe was a government agent, ostensibly in support of the Tory party, but the evidence tends to confirm the belief that he was something of a political adventurer. During these last twenty years of his life, he wrote the novels for which he is best known: Robinson Crusoe (1719); Memoirs of a Cavalier (1720); Captain Singleton (1720); The Fortunes and Misfortunes of Moll Flanders (1722); A Journal of the Plague Year (1722); The History of Colonel Jack (1722); Roxana, or The Fortunate Mistress (1724).

from AN ESSAY UPON PROJECTS

THE EDUCATION OF WOMEN

I have often thought of it as one of the most barbarous customs in the world, considering us as a civilized and a Christian country, that we deny the advantages of learning to women. We reproach the sex every day with folly and impertinence, while I am confident, had they the advantages of education equal to us, they would be guilty of less than ourselves.

One would wonder, indeed, how it should happen that women are conversible° at all, since they are only beholding to natural parts° for all their knowledge. 10 Their youth is spent to teach them to stitch and sew or make baubles. They are taught to read, indeed, and perhaps to write their names or so, and that is the height of a woman's education. And I would but ask any who slight the sex for their understanding, what is a man (a gentleman, I mean) good for that is taught no more?

I need not give instances, or examine the character of a gentleman with a good estate, and of a good family, and with tolerable parts, and examine what figure 20 he makes for want of education.

The soul is placed in the body like a rough diamond, and must be polished, or the luster of it will never appear: and 'tis manifest that as the rational soul distinguishes us from brutes, so education carries on the distinction and makes some less brutish than others. This is too evident to need any demonstration. But why then should women be denied the benefit of in-

---

18 **essenced,** perfumed   22 **Flanders mares,** breeding horses, by extension, whores   33 **coz'ning,** cheating

An Essay Upon Projects   9 **conversible,** able to be conversed with   10 **beholding . . . parts,** dependent upon nature and instinct

struction? If knowledge and understanding had been
30 useless additions to the sex, God Almighty would
never have given them capacities, for He made nothing
needless. Besides, I would ask such what they can see
in ignorance that they should think it a necessary ornament to a woman? or how much worse is a wise
woman than a fool? or what has the woman done to
forfeit the privilege of being taught? Does she plague
us with her pride and impertinence? Why did we not
let her learn, that she might have had more wit? Shall
we upbraid women with folly, when 'tis only the error
40 of this inhuman custom that hindered them being made
wiser?

The capacities of women are supposed to be greater
and their senses quicker than those of the men; and
what they might be capable of being bred to is plain
from some instances of female wit, which this age is
not without; which upbraids us with injustice, and
looks as if we denied women the advantages of education for fear they should vie with the men in their improvements.

50 To remove this objection, and that women might
have at least a needful opportunity of education in all
sorts of useful learning, I propose the draught of an
Academy for that purpose.

I know 'tis dangerous to make public appearances of
the sex. They are not either to be confined or exposed;
the first will disagree with their inclinations, and the
last with their reputations, and therefore it is somewhat difficult; and I doubt a method proposed by an
ingenious lady° in a little book called *Advice to the*
60 *Ladies,* would be found impracticable, for, saving my
respect to the sex, the levity, which perhaps is a little
peculiar to them, at least in their youth, will not bear
the restraint; and I am satisfied nothing but the height
of bigotry can keep up a nunnery. Women are extravagantly desirous of going to heaven, and will
punish their pretty bodies to get thither; but nothing
else will do it, and even in that case sometimes it falls
out that nature will prevail.

When I talk, therefore, of an academy for women, I
70 mean both the model, the teaching, and the government different from what is proposed by that ingenious
lady, for whose proposal I have a very great esteem,
and also a great opinion of her wit; different, too, from
all sorts of religious confinement, and, above all, from
vows of celibacy.

Wherefore the academy I propose should differ but
little from public schools,° wherein such ladies as were
willing to study should have all the advantages of
learning suitable to their genius.° But since some
80 severities of discipline more than ordinary would be
absolutely necessary to preserve the reputation of the
house, that persons of quality and fortune might not be

afraid to venture their children thither, I shall venture
to make a small scheme by way of essay.°

The house I would have built in a form by itself, as
well as in a place by itself. The building should be of
three plain fronts, without any jettings or bearing-
work;° that the eye might at a glance see from one coign
to the other; the gardens walled in the same triangular
figure, with a large moat, and but one entrance. When 90
thus every part of the situation was contrived as well
as might be for discovery, and to render intriguing
dangerous, I would have no guards, no eyes, no spies
set over the ladies, but shall expect them to be tried by
the principles of honor and strict virtue. . . .

Upon this ground I am persuaded such measures
might be taken that the ladies might have all the freedom in the world within their own walls, and yet no
intriguing, no indecencies, nor scandalous affairs happen; and in order to this the following customs and 100
laws should be observed in the colleges, of which I
would propose one at least in every county in England,
and about ten for the city of London.

After the regulation of the form of the building as
before:—

1. All the ladies who enter into the house should set
their hands to the orders of the house,° to signify their
consent to submit to them.

2. As no woman should be received but who declared herself willing, and that it was the act of her 110
choice to enter herself, so no person should be confined to continue there a moment longer than the same
voluntary choice inclined her.

3. The charges of the house being to be paid by the
ladies, everyone that entered should have only this
encumbrance, that she should pay for the whole year,
though her mind should change as to her continuance.

4. An Act of Parliament should make it felony without clergy° for any man to enter by force or fraud into
the house, or to solicit any woman, though it were to 120
marry, while she was in the house. And this law would
by no means be severe, because any woman who was
willing to receive the addresses of a man might discharge herself of the house when she pleased; and, on
the contrary, any woman who had occasion, might
discharge herself of the impertinent addresses of any
person she had an aversion to by entering into the
house.

In this house, the persons who enter should be
taught all sorts of breeding suitable both to their genius 130
and quality, and in particular, music and dancing,
which it would be cruelty to bar the sex of, because
they are their darlings; but besides this, they should be

---

84 **essay,** trial, attempt   88 **jettings or bearing-work.** *Jettings* in architecture is
an older name for anything jutting out from the perpendicular; *bearing-work*
would refer to that part of a wall which bore the weight of such projections
106–107 **set their hands . . . house,** sign their names to the ordinances or bylaws
119 **without clergy.** In earlier times, when convicted of some capital crime
other than treason, it was possible for any member of the clergy, and then somewhat later, for anyone who could read or write, to appear before an ecclesiastical
rather than a civil court. When discharged from this ecclesiastical court, the accused would suffer a lesser punishment than death, usually whipping or branding
or even heavy fines. As Defoe uses the sense here, he is practically saying "to
make it a crime without any mitigation of punishment possible"

---

59 **ingenious lady,** Mary Astell (1668–1731), an English authoress who wrote *A
Serious Proposal to the Ladies Wherein a Method Is Offered for the Improvement of
Their Minds*   77 **public schools.** As used in England, this term applies to one of
the several private, classical schools preparatory to the universities, such as Rugby
or Eton   79 **genius,** natural talents and abilities

Daniel Defoe   **467**

taught languages, as particularly French and Italian; and I would venture the injury of giving a woman more tongues than one. They should, as a particular study, be taught all the graces of speech, and all the necessary air of conversation, which our common education is so defective in that I need not expose it. They should be brought to read books, and especially history; and so to read as to make them understand the world, and be able to know and judge of things when they hear of them.

To such whose genius would lead them to it, I would deny no sort of learning; but the chief thing, in general, is to cultivate the understandings of the sex, that they may be capable of all sorts of conversation; that, their parts and judgments being improved, they may be as profitable in their conversation as they are pleasant.

Women, in my observation, have little or no difference in them, but as they are or are not distinguished by education. Tempers, indeed, may in some degree influence them, but the main distinguishing part is their breeding.

The whole sex are generally quick and sharp. I believe I may be allowed to say generally so, for you rarely see them lumpish and heavy when they are children, as boys will often be. If a woman be well bred, and taught the proper management of her natural wit, she proves generally very sensible and retentive; and without partiality, a woman of sense and manners is the finest and most delicate part of God's creation, the glory of her Maker, and the great instance of His singular regard to man, His darling creature, to whom He gave the best gift either God could bestow or man receive. And 'tis the sordidest piece of folly and ingratitude in the world to withhold from the sex the due luster which the advantage of education gives to the natural beauty of their minds.

A woman well bred and well taught, furnished with the additional accomplishments of knowledge and behavior, is a creature without comparison; her society is the emblem of sublimer enjoyments; her person is angelic and her conversation heavenly; she is all softness and sweetness, peace, love, wit, and delight. She is every way suitable to the sublimest wish, and the man that has such a one to his portion has nothing to do but rejoice in her and be thankful.

On the other hand, suppose her to be the very same woman, and rob her of the benefit of education, and it follows thus:

If her temper be good, want of education makes her soft and easy. Her wit, for want of teaching, makes her impertinent and talkative. Her knowledge, for want of judgment and experience, makes her fanciful and whimsical. If her temper be bad, want of breeding makes her worse, and she grows haughty, insolent, and loud. If she be passionate, want of manners makes her termagant and a scold, which is much at one with lunatic. If she be proud, want of discretion (which still is breeding) makes her conceited, fantastic, and

ridiculous. And from these she degenerates to be turbulent, clangorous, noisy, nasty, and the devil.

Methinks mankind for their own sakes—since, say what we will of the women, we all think fit at one time or other to be concerned with them—should take some care to breed them up to be suitable and serviceable, if they expected no such thing as delight from them. Bless us! what care do we take to breed up a good horse and to break him well! and what a value do we put upon him when it is done, and all because he should be fit for our use! and why not a woman? Since all her ornaments and beauty without suitable behavior is a cheat in nature, like the false tradesman, who puts the best of his goods uppermost, that the buyer may think the rest are of the same goodness.

Beauty of the body, which is the women's glory, seems to be now unequally bestowed, and Nature, or rather Providence, to lie under some scandal about it, as if 'twas given a woman for a snare to men, and so made a kind of a she-devil of her; because, they say, exquisite beauty is rarely given with wit, more rarely with goodness of temper, and never at all with modesty. And some, pretending to justify the equity of such a distribution, will tell us 'tis the effect of the justice of Providence in dividing particular excellencies among all His creatures, share and share alike, as it were, that all might for something or other be acceptable to one another, else some would be despised.

I think both these notions false, and yet the last, which has the show of respect to Providence, is the worst, for it supposes Providence to be indigent and empty, as if it had not wherewith to furnish all the creatures it had made, but was fain to be parsimonious in its gifts, and distribute them by piecemeal for fear of being exhausted.

If I might venture my opinion against an almost universal notion, I would say most men mistake the proceedings of Providence in this case, and all the world at this day are mistaken in their practice about it. And because the assertion is very bold, I desire to explain myself.

That Almighty First Cause which made us all is certainly the fountain of excellence, as it is of being, and by an invisible influence could have diffused equal qualities and perfections to all the creatures it has made, as the sun does its light, without the least ebb or diminution to Himself, and has given indeed to every individual sufficient to the figure His providence had designed him in the world.

I believe it might be defended if I should say that I do suppose God has given to all mankind equal gifts and capacities in that He has given them all souls equally capable, and that the whole difference in mankind proceeds either from accidental difference in the make of their bodies or from the foolish difference of education.

1. *From Accidental Difference in Bodies.* I would avoid discoursing here of the philosophical position of

the soul in the body. But if it be true, as philosophers do affirm, that the understanding and memory is dilated or contracted according to the accidental dimensions of the organ through which 'tis conveyed, then, though God has given a soul as capable to me as another, yet if I have any natural defect in those parts of the body by which the soul should act, I may have the same soul infused as another man, and yet he be a wise man and I a very fool. For example, if a child naturally have a defect in the organ of hearing, so that he could never distinguish any sound, that child shall never be able to speak or read, though it have a soul capable of all the accomplishments in the world. The brain is the center of all the soul's actings, where all the distinguishing faculties of it reside; and 'tis observable a man who has a narrow contracted head, in which there is not room for the due and necessary operations of nature by the brain, is never a man of very great judgment; and that proverb, "A great head and little wit," is not meant by nature, but is a reproof upon sloth, as if one should, by way of wonder, say, "Fie, fie! you that have a great head have but little wit; that's strange! that must certainly be your own fault." From this notion I do believe there is a great matter in the breed of men and women—not that wise men shall always get wise children, but I believe strong and healthy bodies have the wisest children, and sickly, weakly bodies affect the wits as well as the bodies of their children. We are easily persuaded to believe this in the breeds of horses, cocks, dogs, and other creatures, and I believe 'tis as visible in men.

But to come closer to the business, the great distinguishing difference which is seen in the world between men and women is in their education, and this is manifested by comparing it with the difference between one man or woman and another.

And herein it is that I take upon me to make such a bold assertion that all the world are mistaken in their practice about women; for I cannot think that God Almighty ever made them so delicate, so glorious creatures, and furnished them with such charms, so agreeable and so delightful to mankind, with souls capable of the same accomplishments with men, and all to be only stewards of our houses, cooks, and slaves.

Not that I am for exalting the female government in the least; but, in short, I would have men take women for companions, and educate them to be fit for it. A woman of sense and breeding will scorn as much to encroach upon the prerogative of the man as a man of sense will scorn to oppress the weakness of the woman. But if the women's souls were refined and improved by teaching, that word would be lost; to say, the *weakness of the sex* as to judgment, would be nonsense, for ignorance and folly would be no more found among women than men. I remember a passage which I heard from a very fine woman; she had wit and capacity enough, an extraordinary shape and face, and a great

fortune, but had been cloistered up all her time, and, for fear of being stolen, had not had the liberty of being taught the common necessary knowledge of women's affairs; and when she came to converse in the world, her natural wit made her so sensible of the want of education that she gave this short reflection on herself—"I am ashamed to talk with my very maids," says she, "for I don't know when they do right or wrong. I had more need go to school than be married."

I need not enlarge on the loss the defect of education is to the sex, nor argue the benefit of the contrary practice; 'tis a thing will be more easily granted than remedied. This chapter is but an essay at the thing, and I refer the practice to those happy days, if ever they shall be, when men shall be wise enough to mend it. (1692; 1697)

from A JOURNAL OF THE PLAGUE YEAR

. . . It pleased God that I was still spared, and very hearty and sound in health, but very impatient of being pent up within doors without air, as I had been for fourteen days or thereabouts; and I could not restrain myself, but I would go and carry a letter for my brother to the post-house; then it was, indeed, that I observed a profound silence in the streets. When I came to the post-house, as I went to put in my letter, I saw a man stand in one corner of the yard, and talking to another at a window, and a third had opened a door belonging to the office. In the middle of the yard lay a small leather purse, with two keys hanging at it, with money in it, but nobody would meddle with it. I asked how long it had lain there; the man at the window said it had lain almost an hour, but they had not meddled with it, because they did not know but the person who dropped it might come back to look for it. I had no such need of money, nor was the sum so big that I had any inclination to meddle with it, or to get the money at the hazard it might be attended with, so I seemed to go away, when the man who had opened the door said he would take it up; but so, that if the right owner came for it he should be sure to have it. So he went in and fetched a pail of water, and set it down hard by the purse, then went again and fetched some gunpowder, and cast a good deal of powder upon the purse, and then made a train from that which he had thrown loose upon the purse; the train reached about two yards; after this he goes in a third time, and fetches out a pair of tongs red-hot, and which he had prepared, I suppose, on purpose; and first setting fire to the train of powder, that singed the purse, and also smoked the air sufficiently.° But he was not content with that, but he then takes up the purse with the tongs, holding it so long till the tongs burnt through the purse, and then he

A Journal of the Plague Year 32–33 **smoked . . . sufficiently.** The older theory was that the plague was transmitted by bodily exhalations. The gunpowder would permeate the air with its own odor and so drive out the "exhalations" that would make the purse infectious

shook the money out into the pail of water, so he carried it in. The money, as I remember, was about thirteen shillings, and some smooth groats° and brass farthings.

40 Much about the same time I walked out into the fields toward Bow, for I had a great mind to see how things were managed in the river, and among the ships; and as I had some concern in shipping, I had a notion that it had been one of the best ways of securing one's self from the infection to have retired into a ship; and musing how to satisfy my curiosity in that point, I turned away over the fields, from Bow to Bromley and down to Blackwell, to the stairs that are there for landing or taking water.

50 Here I saw a poor man walking on the bank or seawall, as they call it, by himself. I walked awhile also about, seeing the houses all shut up; at last I fell into some talk, at a distance, with this poor man. First I asked how people did thereabouts. "Alas! sir," says he, "almost desolate, all dead or sick. Here are very few families in this part, or in that village," pointing at Poplar, "where half of them are dead already, and the rest sick." Then he pointing to one house, "They are all dead," said he, "and the house stands open, no-
60 body dares go into it. A poor thief," says he, "ventured in to steal something, but he paid dear for his theft; for he was carried to the churchyard too, last night." Then he pointed to several other houses. "There," says he, "they all are dead, the man and his wife and five children." "There," says he, "they are shut up, you see a watchman at the door; and so of other houses." "Why," says I, "what do you here all alone?" "Why," says he, "I am a poor desolate man; it hath pleased God I am not yet visited, though my
70 family is, and one of my children dead." "How do you mean, then," said I, "that you are not visited?" "Why," says he, "that is my house," pointing to a very little low boarded house, "and there my poor wife and two children live," said he, "if they may be said to live; for my wife and one of the children are visited, but I do not come at them." And with that word I saw the tears run very plentifully down his face; and so they did down mine, too, I assure you.

"But," said I, "why do you not come at them? How
80 can you abandon your own flesh and blood?" "Oh, sir," says he, "the Lord forbid! I do not abandon them, I work for them as much as I am able; and, blessed be the Lord, I keep them from want." And with that I observed he lifted up his eyes to Heaven with a countenance that presently told me I had happened on a man that was no hypocrite, but a serious, religious, good man; and his ejaculation was an expression of thankfulness that, in such a condition as he was in, he should be able to say his family did not
90 want. "Well," says I, "honest man, that is a great mercy, as things go now with the poor. But how do

38 **groats,** old Dutch coins, worth about fourpence. They were not coined after 1662

you live, then, and how are you kept from the dreadful calamity that is now upon us all?" "Why, sir," says he, "I am a waterman, and there is my boat," says he, "and the boat serves me for a house; I work in it in the day, and I sleep in it in the night, and what I get I lay it down upon that stone," says he, showing me a broad stone on the other side of the street, a good way from the house; "and then," says he, "I halloo and call to them till I make them hear, and they come and fetch 100 it."

"Well, friend," says I, "but how can you get money as a waterman? Does anybody go by water these times?" "Yes, sir," says he, "in the way I am employed there does. Do you see there," says he, "five ships lie at anchor," pointing down the river a good way below the town; "and do you see," says he, "eight or ten ships lie at the chain there, and at anchor yonder?" pointing above the town. "All those ships have families on board, of their merchants and owners, 110 and such like, who have locked themselves up, and live on board, close shut in, for fear of infection; and I tend on them to fetch things for them, carry letters and do what is absolutely necessary, that they may not be obliged to come on shore; and every night I fasten my boat on board one of the ship's boats, and there I sleep by myself, and, blessed be God, I am preserved hitherto."

"Well," said I, "friend, but will they let you come on board after you have been on shore here, when this 120 has been such a terrible place, and so infected as it is?"

"Why, as to that," said he, "I very seldom go up the ship side, but deliver what I bring to their boat, or lie by the side, and they hoist it on board. If I did, I think they are in no danger from me, for I never go into any house on shore, or touch anybody, no, not for my own family; but I fetch provisions for them."

"Nay," says I, "but that may be worse, for you must have those provisions of somebody or other; and 130 since all this part of the town is so infected, it is dangerous so much as to speak with anybody; for the village," said I, "is as it were the beginning of London, though it be at some distance from it."

"That is true," added he, "but you do not understand me right. I do not buy provisions for them here; I row up to Greenwich, and buy fresh meat there, and sometimes I row down the river to Woolwich, and buy there; then I go to single farm houses on the Kentish side, where I am known, and buy fowls, and eggs, and 140 butter, and bring to the ships as they direct me, sometimes one, sometimes the other. I seldom come on shore here; and I came only now to call my wife and hear how my little family do, and give them a little money which I received last night."

"Poor man!" said I, "and how much hast thou gotten for them?"

"I have gotten four shillings," said he, "which is a great sum as things go now with poor men; but they have given me a bag of bread, too, and a salt fish, and some fresh; so all helps out.''

"Well," said I, "and have you given it them yet?"

"No," said he, "but I have called, and my wife has answered that she cannot come out yet, but in half an hour she hopes to come, and I am waiting for her. Poor woman!" says he, "she is brought sadly down; she has had a swelling, and it is broke,° and I hope she will recover, but I fear the child will die; but it is the Lord!" Here he stopped and wept very much.

"Well, honest friend," said I, "thou hast a sure comforter if thou hast brought thyself to be resigned to the will of God; He is dealing with us all in judgment."

"Oh, sir," says he, "it is infinite mercy if any of us are spared; and who am I to repine?"

"Say'st thou so?" said I, "and how much less is my faith than thine!" And here my heart smote me, suggesting how much better this poor man's foundation was, on which he stayed in the danger, than mine; that he had nowhere to fly; that he had a family to bind him to attendance, which I had not; and mine was mere presumption, his a true dependence and a courage resting on God, and yet that he used all possible caution for his safety.

I turned a little away from the man while these thoughts engaged me; for, indeed, I could no more refrain from tears than he.

At length, after some further talk, the poor woman opened the door and called: "Robert, Robert!" He answered, and bid her stay a few moments, and he would come; so he ran down the common stairs to his boat, and fetched up a sack in which were the provisions he had brought from the ships; and when he returned he hallooed again; then he went to the great stone which he showed me, and emptied the sack, and laid all out, everything by themselves, and then retired; and his wife came with a little boy to fetch them away; and he called and said such a captain had sent such a thing, and such a captain such a thing, and at the end adds: "God has sent it all; give thanks to Him." When the poor woman had taken up all, she was so weak she could not carry it at once in, though the weight was not much neither; so she left the biscuit, which was in a little bag, and left a little boy to watch it till she came again.

"Well, but," says I to him, "did you leave her the four shillings, too, which you said was your week's pay?"

"Yes, yes," said he, "you shall hear her own it."—So he calls again, "Rachel, Rachel" (which, it seems, was her name), "did you take up the money?" "Yes," said she. "How much was it?" said he. "Four shillings and a groat," said she. "Well, well," says he, "the Lord keep you all"; and so he turned to go away.

As I could not refrain from contributing tears to this man's story, so neither could I refrain my charity for his assistance; so I called him, "Hark thee, friend," said I, "come hither, for I believe thou art in health, that I may venture thee"; so I pulled out my hand, which was in my pocket before, "Here," says I, "go and call thy Rachel once more, and give her a little more comfort from me. God will never forsake a family that trusts in Him as thou dost"; so I gave him four other shillings, and bade him go lay them on the stone, and call his wife.

I have not words to express the poor man's thankfulness, neither could he express it himself, but by tears running down his face. He called his wife, and told her God had moved the heart of a stranger, upon hearing their condition, to give them all that money; and a great deal more such as that he said to her. The woman, too, made signs of the like thankfulness, as well to Heaven as to me, and joyfully picked it up; and I parted with no money all that year that I thought better bestowed. . . .

(1722)

JONATHAN SWIFT
1667–1745

Swift was born in Dublin, the posthumous son of a penniless English father. He was supported for a time by his uncle; he was educated at Kilkenny School and Trinity College, Dublin. He left the university and became a secretary to Sir William Temple at Moor Park, near London. While working for Temple, he met Esther Johnson, a member of the Temple household, who became his close friend and correspondent for thirty years. His series of intimate letters, published later in the century as the *Journal to Stella*, is addressed to her. His years of service to Temple won Swift recognition from William III, who gave him some promise of a church career. Swift was ordained and eventually obtained a position at Kilroot, Ireland (1695), which he soon abandoned to return to his post with Sir William Temple. At this time Swift seriously tried his hand at literature; he produced *A Tale of a Tub* (written in 1696), a prose satire on "corruptions in religion and learning," and *The Battle of the Books* (also written in 1696), a satire which attempted to determine whether the ancients (Homer, Pindar, Euclid, Aristotle, Plato) or the moderns (Milton, Dryden, Descartes, Hobbes, Scotus) were superior as literary figures. Both works were well received.

Swift returned to Ireland in 1699 after the death of Temple, carrying with him a considerable reputation as a polemical writer. He continued to make frequent

150
160
170
180
190
200
210
220

157 **swelling . . . broke.** The plague was characterized by the swelling of the lymphatic glands. The opinion held by the physicians of the time was that these swellings should somehow be made to open. "If these swellings could be brought to a head, and to break and run, or as the surgeons call it, to digest, the patient generally recovered" (*A Journal of the Plague Year*). Modern therapeutics demands that the abscesses be left alone

visits to London in order to keep in contact with his literary friends there—Congreve, Addison, Steele, Pope, Gay, and others.

In the following years several events of importance occurred in Swift's life. In 1708 he met Esther Vanhomrigh, with whom he had, for fifteen years, an uneven affair. Perhaps more important, he went over to the Tory side in politics in 1710. He wrote numerous effective pamphlets and articles on political questions throughout the first two decades of the eighteenth century; his writings helped him rise to a powerful position. In 1713 Swift was appointed dean of St. Patrick's, Dublin. With the death of Queen Anne in 1714, the Tories lost political power, and Swift's fortunes sank. He spent most of the rest of his life in Ireland and devoted the next few years to writings attacking the English exploitation of the Irish. In 1724 and 1728 respectively, he published his two most well-known pieces on the Irish question—the *Drapier's Letters* against the debasement of Irish currency by the English, and *A Modest Proposal* against the harsh English policy toward Ireland. Swift soon became a national hero to his people.

It is for *Gulliver's Travels* (1726) however, that Swift is most remembered. Offering itself soberly as a "shipwreck narrative" of Captain Lemuel Gulliver, the work allows Swift great scope in satirizing human pretensions—in politics, religion, institutions, and personal habits. After the publication of *Gulliver's Travels*, Swift produced little that was notable. He suffered intense aggravation from a chronic illness and was declared not of sound mind in 1642. He died three years later and is buried in St. Patrick's Cathedral, Dublin.

Swift is perhaps the foremost prose satirist of English literature. His indignation at those he considers enemies of the human spirit or pretentious fools is so intense that it has sometimes been taken for scorn of human beings themselves. The more one knows of Swift and of his satiric targets, however, the less this seems so. In a letter to Alexander Pope dated 29 September 1725, Swift wrote:

I have ever hated all nations, professions and communities, and all my love is towards individuals: for instance, I hate the tribe of lawyers, but I love councillor such a one, judge such a one, for so with physicians (I will not speak of my own trade), soldiers, English, Scotch, French; and the rest, but principally I hate and detest that animal called man, although I heartily love John, Peter, Thomas, and so forth. This is the system upon which I have governed myself many years (but do not tell), and so I shall go on till I have done with them.

A DESCRIPTION OF A CITY SHOWER

Careful observers may foretell the hour
(By sure prognostics)° when to dread a shower.
While rain depends, the pensive cat gives o'er
Her frolics, and pursues her tail no more.
Returning home at night, you'll find the sink
Strike your offended sense with double stink.°
If you be wise, then go not far to dine;
You'll spend in coach-hire more than save in wine.
A coming shower your shooting corns presage;
10 Old aches throb, your hollow tooth will rage.
Saunt'ring in coffee-house is Dulman° seen;
He damns the climate, and complains of spleen.°
  Meanwhile the South, rising with dabbled° wings,
A sable cloud athwart the welkin flings,
That swilled more liquor than it could contain,
And, like a drunkard, gives it up again.
Brisk Susan whips her linen from the rope,
While the first drizzling shower is borne aslope:
Such is that sprinkling which some careless quean°
20 Flirts on you from her mop, but not so clean.
You fly, invoke the gods; then turning, stop

To rail; she, singing, still whirls on her mop.
Nor yet the dust had shunned th'unequal strife,
But, aided by the wind, fought still for life,
And wafted with its foe by violent gust,
'Twas doubtful which was rain, and which was dust.
Ah! where must needy poet seek for aid,
When dust and rain at once his coat invade?
Sole coat, where dust cemented by the rain
Erects the nap, and leaves a cloudy stain.   30
  Now in contiguous drops the flood comes down,
Threat'ning with deluge this *devoted* town.
To shops in crowds the daggled females° fly,
Pretend to cheapen goods, but nothing buy.
The Templar spruce, while every spout's abroach,°
Stays till 'tis fair, yet seems to call a coach.
The tucked-up sempstress walks with hasty strides,
While streams run down her oiled umbrella's sides.
Here various kinds, by various fortunes led,
Commence acquaintance underneath a shed.   40
Triumphant Tories and desponding Whigs
Forget their feuds, and join to save their wigs.
Boxed in a chair° the beau impatient sits,

City Shower 2 **prognostics**, predictions 5–6 **sink . . . double stink.** The sewer is backing up; there were open ditches running down the center of the street
11 **Dulman**, a dull man 12 **spleen**, melancholy, caprice, dejection 13 **dabbled**, wetted by splashing 19 **quean**, hussy

33 **daggled females**, having their skirts clogged with mud 35 **abroach**, venting out liquid 43 **Boxed in a chair**, seated in an enclosed sedan chair

While spouts run clatt'ring o'er the roof by fits;
And ever and anon with frightful din
The leather sounds; he trembles from within.
So when Troy chairmen bore the wooden steed,
Pregnant with Greeks impatient to be freed
(Those bully Greeks, who, as the moderns do,
50 Instead of paying chairmen,° run them through),
Laocoön struck the outside with his spear,
And each imprisoned hero quaked for fear.
   Now from all parts the swelling kennels flow,
And bear their trophies with them as they go.
Filths of all hues and odors seem to tell
What streets they sailed from, by their sight and smell.
They, as each torrent drives, with rapid force
From Smithfield or St. Pulchre's shape their course,
And in huge confluent joined at Snow-Hill ridge,
60 Fall from the conduit prone to Holborn Bridge.
Sweepings from butchers' stalls, dung, guts, and
        blood,
Drowned puppies, stinking sprats,° all drenched in
        mud,
Dead cats and turnip-tops come tumbling down the
        flood.

(1710)

A SATIRICAL ELEGY ON THE DEATH OF A LATE FAMOUS GENERAL°

His Grace? impossible! what, dead?
Of old age too, and in his bed?
And could that mighty warrior fall,
And so inglorious after all!
Well, since he's gone, no matter how;
The last loud trump must wake him now;
And trust me, as the noise grows stronger,
He'll wish to sleep a little longer.
And could he be indeed so old
10 As by the newspapers we're told?
Threescore, I think, is pretty high:
'Twas time in conscience he should die;
This world he cumbered long enough;
He burnt his candle to a snuff,
And that's the reason, some folks think,
He left behind so great a stink.

Behold, his funeral appears;
Nor widows' sighs, nor orphans' tears,
Wont at such time each heart to pierce,
20 Attend the progress of his hearse.
But what of that, his friends may say;
He had those honors in his day:

True to his profit and his pride,
He made them weep before he died.
   Come hither, all ye empty things,
Ye bubbles raised by breath of kings,
Who float upon the tide of state;
Come hither, and behold your fate:
Let pride be taught by this rebuke
How very mean a thing's a Duke;   30
From all his ill-got honors flung,
Turned to that dirt from whence he sprung.

from GULLIVER'S TRAVELS

There are four parts to *Gulliver's Travels*. Parts I and II
are companion pieces in the sense that they present
Lemuel Gulliver in reversed situations. In Part I, Captain Gulliver is shipwrecked on the coast of Lilliput,
where the inhabitants are only six inches tall. Initially
enchanted by the ingenuity, humaneness, and esthetic
qualities of these diminutive people, the reader eventually becomes shocked by the disproportion between
their negligible size and their monstrous corruption: by
an Emperor whose great ambition is to destroy his
neighbors; by ministers who win preferment by tight-
rope walking; by political parties that are distinguished
by the use of high heels or low heels; by religious factions struggling with the problem as to whether eggs
should be broken at the big end or the little end. Gulliver looks down upon them as the higher orders must
look down upon man.
    In Part II, the situation is entirely reversed. In
Brobdingnag, where Gulliver is dwarfed by giants sixty
feet in height, it is he, the European man, who is contemptible. He is morally myopic, and his social and
political assumptions gradually emerge as irrational
and absurd. The King spiels out the sentence: "I cannot but conclude the Bulk of your Natives to be the
most pernicious Race of little odious Vermin that Nature ever suffered to crawl upon the surface of the
Earth." Gulliver himself establishes the tone of Part II
by his fear that the peasant who discovers him may
dash him to the ground "as we usually do any little
hateful Animal which we have a Mind to destroy."
The world of the Brobdingnagians is practical, concrete, simple, and benevolent. Gulliver sees mankind
as an insect might or as we might see ourselves under
a huge microscope: cancerous, blotched, coarse,
lousy, and nauseous.
    The third voyage takes Gulliver to Laputa and to
other countries (The Flying Island, Balnibari) whose
inhabitants are scholars, scientists, philosophers, inventors, and professors who devote themselves to
speculation and research. This part has been called "a
digression on madness"—in government, philosophy,
economics, scientific speculation, and experimenta-

50 **chairmen**, chair bearers 62 **sprats**, small sea-fish
Death of a Late Famous General. The Duke of Marlborough died on 16 June
1722

tion. In this part also we find the race of Struldbrugs, or Immortals, who in their endless and ghastly dotage are the most miserable of beings.

Part IV is the most universal and controversial of all the parts of *Gulliver's Travels*. When reading it, one should remember that Swift is the author and that Gulliver is the narrator and chief actor, with a *created* character and personality. He is a reliable reporter, not an authoritative commentator or interpreter.

A LETTER FROM CAPTAIN GULLIVER TO HIS COUSIN SYMPSON°

I hope you will be ready to own publicly, whenever you shall be called to it, that by your great and frequent urgency you prevailed on me to publish a very loose and uncorrect account of my travels; with direction to hire some young gentlemen of either university to put them in order, and correct the style, as my cousin Dampier° did by my advice, in his book called, *A Voyage round the World*. But I do not remember I gave you power to consent, that any thing should be
10 omitted, and much less that any thing should be inserted: therefore, as to the latter, I do here renounce every thing of that kind; particularly a paragraph about her Majesty the late Queen Anne, of most pious and glorious memory; although I did reverence and esteem her more than any of human species. But you, or your interpolator, ought to have considered, that as it was not my inclination, so was it not decent to praise any animal of our composition before my master *Houyhnhnm:* and besides, the fact was altogether
20 false; for to my knowledge, being in England during some part of her Majesty's reign, she did govern by a chief minister; nay, even by two successively; the first whereof was the Lord of Godolphin, and the second the Lord of Oxford; so that you have made me *say the thing that was not.* Likewise, in the account of the Academy of Projectors, and several passages of my discourse to my master *Houyhnhnm,* you have either omitted some material circumstances, or minced or changed them in such a manner, that I do hardly know
30 my own work. When I formerly hinted to you something of this in a letter, you were pleased to answer that you were afraid of giving offence; that people in power were very watchful over the press, and apt not only to interpret, but to punish every thing which looked like an *innuendo* (as I think you called it). But pray, how could that which I spoke so many years ago, and at about five thousand leagues distance, in another reign, be applied to any of the *Yahoos,* who now are said to govern the herd; especially, at a time when I
40 little thought on or feared the unhappiness of living under them? Have not I the most reason to complain, when I see these very *Yahoos* carried by *Houyhnhnms*

in a vehicle, as if these were brutes, and those the rational creatures? And indeed, to avoid so monstrous and detestable a sight, was one principal motive of my retirement hither.

Thus much I thought proper to tell you in relation to yourself, and to the trust I reposed in you.

I do in the next place complain of my own great want of judgment, in being prevailed upon by the entreaties 50 and false reasonings of you and some others, very much against my own opinion, to suffer my travels to be published. Pray bring to your mind how often I desired you to consider, when you insisted on the motive of public good; that the *Yahoos* were a species of animals utterly incapable of amendment by precepts or examples: and so it hath proved; for instead of seeing a full stop put to all abuses and corruptions, at least in this little island, as I had reason to expect: behold, after above six months warning, I cannot learn that my 60 book hath produced one single effect according to my intentions: I desired you would let me know by a letter, when party and faction were extinguished; judges learned and upright; pleaders honest and modest, with some tincture of common sense; and Smithfield blazing with pyramids of lawbooks; the young nobility's education entirely changed; the physicians banished; the female *Yahoos* abounding in virtue, honour, truth and good sense; courts and levees of great ministers thoroughly weeded and swept; wit, merit and learning 70 rewarded; all disgracers of the press in prose and verse, condemned to eat nothing but their own cotton, and quench their thirst with their own ink. These, and a thousand other reformations, I firmly counted upon by your encouragement; as indeed they were plainly deducible from the precepts delivered in my book. And, it must be owned, that seven months were a sufficient time to correct every vice and folly to which *Yahoos* are subject; if their natures had been capable of the least disposition to virtue or wisdom: yet so far 80 have you been from answering my expectation in any of your letters; that on the contrary, you are loading our carrier every week with libels, and keys, and reflections, and memoirs, and second parts; wherein I see myself accused of reflecting upon great states-folk; of degrading human nature (for so they have still the confidence to style it), and of abusing the female sex. I find likewise that the writers of those bundles are not agreed among themselves; for some of them will not allow me to be author of my own travels; and others 90 make me author of books to which I am wholly a stranger.

I find likewise, that your printer hath been so careless as to confound the times, and mistake the dates of my several voyages and returns; neither assigning the true year, or the true month, or day of the month: and I hear the original manuscript is all destroyed, since the publication of my book. Neither have I any copy left: however, I have sent you some corrections, which you may insert, if ever there should be a second edition: 100

Gulliver's Travels   **A Letter from Captain Gulliver.** Swift added this letter to a 1735 edition of *Gulliver's Travels*. He had not approved of all changes made in earlier editions   7 **Dampier,** William Dampier, English buccaneer and circumnavigator (1652–1715)

and yet I cannot stand to them, but shall leave that matter to my judicious and candid readers, to adjust it as they please.

I hear some of our sea-*Yahoos* find fault with my sea-language, as not proper in many parts, nor now in use. I cannot help it. In my first voyages, while I was young, I was instructed by the oldest mariners, and learned to speak as they did. But I have since found that the sea-*Yahoos* are apt, like the land ones, to become new-fangled in their words; which the latter change every year; insomuch, as I remember upon each return to my own country, their old dialect was so altered, that I could hardly understand the new. And I observe, when any *Yahoo* comes from London out of curiosity to visit me at my own house, we neither of us are able to deliver our conceptions in a manner intelligible to the other.

If the censure of *Yahoos* could any way affect me, I should have great reason to complain, that some of them are so bold as to think my book of travels a mere fiction out of my own brain; and have gone so far as to drop hints, that the *Houyhnhnms* and *Yahoos* have no more existence than the inhabitants of Utopia.

Indeed I must confess, that as to the people of *Lilliput, Brobdingrag* (for so the word should have been spelt, and not erroneously *Brobdingnag*), and *Laputa;* I have never yet heard of any *Yahoo* so presumptuous as to dispute their being, or the facts I have related concerning them; because the truth immediately strikes every reader with conviction. And is there less probability in my account of the *Houyhnhnms* or *Yahoos,* when it is manifest as to the latter, there are so many thousands even in this city, who only differ from their brother brutes in *Houyhnhnm-land,* because they use a sort of a jabber, and do not go naked? I wrote for their amendment, and not their approbation. The united praise of the whole race would be of less consequence to me, than the neighing of those two degenerate *Houyhnhnms* I keep in my stable; because, from these, degenerate as they are, I still improve in some virtues, without any mixture of vice.

Do these miserable animals presume to think that I am so far degenerated as to defend my veracity? *Yahoo* as I am, it is well known through all *Houyhnhnm-land,* that by the instructions and example of my illustrious master, I was able in the compass of two years (although I confess with the utmost difficulty) to remove that infernal habit of lying, shuffling, deceiving, and equivocating, so deeply rooted in the very souls of all my species; especially the Europeans.

I have other complaints to make upon this vexatious occasion; but I forbear troubling myself or you any further. I must freely confess, that since my last return, some corruptions of my *Yahoo* nature have revived in me by conversing with a few of your species, and particularly those of my own family, by an unavoidable necessity; else I should never have attempted so absurd a project as that of reforming the *Yahoo* race in this kingdom; but I have now done with all such visionary schemes for ever.
(April 2, 1727)

THE PUBLISHER TO THE READER

The author of these Travels, Mr. Lemuel Gulliver, is my ancient and intimate friend; there is likewise some relation between us by the mother's side. About three years ago, Mr. Gulliver growing weary of the concourse of curious people coming to him at his house in Redriff, made a small purchase of land, with a convenient house, near Newark, in Nottinghamshire, his native country; where he now lives retired, yet in good esteem among his neighbours.

Although Mr. Gulliver was born in Nottinghamshire, where his father dwelt, yet I have heard him say his family came from Oxfordshire; to confirm which, I have observed in the churchyard at Banbury, in that county, several tombs and monuments of the Gullivers.

Before he quitted Redriff, he left the custody of the following papers in my hands, with the liberty to dispose of them as I should think fit. I have carefully perused them three times: the style is very plain and simple; and the only fault I find is, that the author, after the manner of travellers, is a little too circumstantial. There is an air of truth apparent through the whole; and indeed the author was so distinguished for his veracity, that it became a sort of proverb among his neighbours at Redriff, when any one affirmed a thing, to say it was as true as if Mr. Gulliver had spoke it.

By the advice of several worthy persons, to whom, with the author's permission, I communicated these papers, I now venture to send them into the world, hoping they may be at least, for some time, a better entertainment to our young noblemen, than the common scribbles of politics and party.

This volume would have been at least twice as large, if I had not made bold to strike out innumerable passages relating to the winds and tides, as well as to the variations and bearings in the several voyages; together with the minute descriptions of the management of the ship in storms, in the style of sailors: likewise the account of longitudes and latitudes; wherein I have reason to apprehend that Mr. Gulliver may be a little dissatisfied: but I was resolved to fit the work as much as possible to the general capacity of readers. However, if my own ignorance in sea-affairs shall have led me to commit some mistakes, I alone am answerable for them: and if any traveller hath a curiosity to see the whole work at large, as it came from the hand of the author, I will be ready to gratify him.

As for any further particulars relating to the author, the reader will receive satisfaction from the first pages of the book.

RICHARD SYMPSON

PART IV
A VOYAGE TO THE COUNTRY
OF THE HOUYHNHNMS

CHAPTER I

The Author sets out as Captain of a ship. His men conspire against him, confine him a long time to his cabin, set him on shore in an unknown land. He travels up into the country. The Yahoos, a strange sort of animal, described. The Author meets two Houyhnhnms.

I continued at home with my wife and children about five months in a very happy condition, if I could have learned the lesson of knowing when I was well. I left my poor wife big with child, and accepted an advantageous offer made me to be Captain of the *Adventurer,* a stout merchantman of 350 tons: for I understood navigation well, and being grown weary of a surgeon's employment at sea, which however I could exercise upon occasion, I took a skilful young man of
10 that calling, one Robert Purefoy, into my ship. We set sail from Portsmouth upon the seventh day of September, 1710; on the fourteenth we met with Captain Pocock of Bristol, at Teneriffe, who was going to the bay of Campechy, to cut logwood. On the sixteenth, he was parted from us by a storm; I heard since my return, that his ship foundered, and none escaped but one cabin boy. He was an honest man, and a good sailor, but a little too positive in his own opinions, which was the cause of his destruction, as it hath been
20 of several others. For if he had followed my advice, he might have been safe at home with his family at this time, as well as myself.

I had several men died in my ship of calentures,° so that I was forced to get recruits out of Barbadoes, and the Leeward Islands, where I touched by the direction of the merchants who employed me, which I had soon too much cause to repent: for I found afterwards that most of them had been buccaneers. I had fifty hands on board, and my orders were, that I should trade with the
30 Indians in the South-Sea, and make what discoveries I could. These rogues whom I had picked up debauched my other men, and they all formed a conspiracy to seize the ship and secure me; which they did one morning, rushing into my cabin, and binding me hand and foot, threatening to throw me overboard, if I offered to stir. I told them, I was their prisoner, and would submit. This they made me swear to do, and then they unbound me, only fastening one of my legs with a chain near my bed, and placed a sentry at my door with his piece charged,

who was commanded to shoot me dead, if I attempted 40 my liberty. They sent me down victuals and drink, and took the government of the ship to themselves. Their design was to turn pirates, and plunder the Spaniards, which they could not do, till they got more men. But first they resolved to sell the goods in the ship, and then go to Madagascar for recruits, several among them having died since my confinement. They sailed many weeks, and traded with the Indians, but I knew not what course they took, being kept a close prisoner in my cabin, and expecting nothing less than to be murdered, 50 as they often threatened me.

Upon the ninth day of May, 1711, one James Welch came down to my cabin; and said he had orders from the Captain to get me ashore. I expostulated with him, but in vain; neither would he so much as tell me who their new Captain was. They forced me into the longboat, letting me put on my best suit of clothes, which were as good as new, and a small bundle of linen, but no arms except my hanger; and they were so civil as not to search my pockets, into which I conveyed what 60 money I had, with some other little necessaries. They rowed about a league, and then set me down on a strand. I desired them to tell me what country it was. They all swore, they knew no more than myself, but said, that the Captain (as they called him) was resolved, after they had sold the lading, to get rid of me in the first place where they could discover land. They pushed off immediately, advising me to make haste, for fear of being overtaken by the tide, and so bade me farewell. 70

In this desolate condition I advanced forward, and soon got upon firm ground, where I sat down on a bank to rest myself, and consider what I had best to do. When I was a little refreshed, I went up into the country, resolving to deliver myself to the first savages I should meet, and purchase my life from them by some bracelets, glass rings, and other toys which sailors usually provide themselves with in those voyages, and whereof I had some about me. The land was divided by long rows of trees, not regularly planted, but naturally 80 growing; there was great plenty of grass, and several fields of oats. I walked very circumspectly for fear of being surprised, or suddenly shot with an arrow from behind or on either side. I fell into a beaten road, where I saw many tracks of human feet, and some of cows, but most of horses. At last I beheld several animals in a field, and one or two of the same kind sitting in trees. Their shape was very singular, and deformed, which a little discomposed me, so that I lay down behind a thicket to observe them better. Some of them 90 coming forward near the place where I lay, gave me an opportunity of distinctly marking their form. Their heads and breasts were covered with a thick hair, some frizzled and others lank; they had beards like goats, and a long ridge of hair down their backs and the

Part IV   Chapter I   23 **calentures,** a disease occurring among sailors in the tropics

fore parts of their legs and feet, but the rest of their bodies were bare, so that I might see their skins, which were of a brown buff colour. They had no tails, nor any hair at all on their buttocks, except about the anus;
100 which, I presume, nature had placed there to defend them as they sat on the ground; for this posture they used, as well as lying down, and often stood on their hind feet. They climbed high trees, as nimbly as a squirrel, for they had strong extended claws before and behind, terminating in sharp points, and hooked. They would often spring, and bound, and leap with prodigious agility. The females were not so large as the males; they had long lank hair on their heads, but none on their faces, nor any thing more than a sort of down
110 on the rest of their bodies, except about the anus, and pudenda. Their dugs hung between their fore-feet, and often reached almost to the ground as they walked. The hair of both sexes was of several colours, brown, red, black, and yellow. Upon the whole, I never beheld in all my travels so disagreeable an animal, nor one against which I naturally conceived so strong an antipathy. So that thinking I had seen enough, full of contempt and aversion, I got up and pursued the beaten road, hoping it might direct me to the cabin of
120 some Indian. I had not got far when I met one of these creatures full in my way, and coming up directly to me. The ugly monster, when he saw me, distorted several ways every feature of his visage, and stared as at an object he had never seen before; then approaching nearer, lifted up his forepaw, whether out of curiosity or mischief, I could not tell. But I drew my hanger, and gave him a good blow with the flat side of it, for I durst not strike with the edge, fearing the inhabitants might be provoked against me, if they should come to know,
130 that I had killed or maimed any of their cattle. When the beast felt the smart, he drew back, and roared so loud, that a herd of at least forty came flocking about me from the next field, howling and making odious faces; but I ran to the body of a tree, and leaning my back against it, kept them off by waving my hanger. Several of this cursed brood getting hold of the branches behind, leapt up into the tree, from whence they began to discharge their excrements on my head; however, I escaped pretty well, by sticking close to the
140 stem of the tree, but was almost stifled with the filth, which fell about me on every side.

In the midst of this distress, I observed them all to run away on a sudden as fast as they could, at which I ventured to leave the tree, and pursue the road, wondering what it was that could put them into this fright. But looking on my left hand, I saw a horse walking softly in the field; which my persecutors having sooner discovered, was the cause of their flight. The horse started a little when he came near me, but soon recov-
150 ering himself, looked full in my face with manifest tokens of wonder: he viewed my hands and feet, walking round me several times. I would have pursued my journey, but he placed himself directly in the way, yet looking with a very mild aspect, never offering the least violence. We stood gazing at each other for some time; at last I took the boldness to reach my hand towards his neck, with a design to stroke it, using the common style and whistle of jockeys when they are going to handle a strange horse. But this animal seeming to receive my civilities with disdain, shook his head, and bent his brows, softly raising up his right 160 fore-foot to remove my hand. Then he neighed three or four times, but in so different a cadence, that I almost began to think he was speaking to himself in some language of his own.

While he and I were thus employed, another horse came up; who applying himself to the first in a very formal manner, they gently struck each other's right hoof before, neighing several times by turns, and varying the sound, which seemed to be almost articulate. They went some paces off, as if it were to confer to- 170 gether, walking side by side, backward and forward, like persons deliberating upon some affair of weight, but often turning their eyes towards me, as it were to watch that I might not escape. I was amazed to see such actions and behaviour in brute beasts, and concluded with myself, that if the inhabitants of this country were endued with a proportionable degree of reason, they must needs be the wisest people upon earth. This thought gave me so much comfort, that I resolved to go forward until I could discover some 180 house or village, or meet with any of the natives, leaving the two horses to discourse together as they pleased. But the first, who was a dapple gray, observing me to steal off, neighed after me in so expressive a tone, that I fancied myself to understand what he meant; whereupon I turned back, and came near him, to expect his farther commands: but concealing my fear as much as I could, for I began to be in some pain, how this adventure might terminate; and the reader will easily believe I did not much like my present situ- 190 ation.

The two horses came up close to me, looking with great earnestness upon my face and hands. The gray steed rubbed my hat all round with his right fore-hoof, and discomposed it so much that I was forced to adjust it better, by taking it off, and settling it again; whereat both he and his companion (who was a brown bay) appeared to be much surprised: the latter felt the lappet of my coat, and finding it to hang loose about me, they both looked with new signs of wonder. He 200 stroked my right hand, seeming to admire the softness and colour; but he squeezed it so hard between his hoof and his pastern, that I was forced to roar; after which they both touched me with all possible tenderness. They were under great perplexity about my shoes and stockings, which they felt very often, neighing to each other, and using various gestures, not unlike those of a philosopher, when he would attempt to solve some new and difficult phenomenon.

210 Upon the whole, the behavior of these animals was so orderly and rational, so acute and judicious, that I at last concluded, they must needs be magicians, who had thus metamorphosed themselves upon some design, and seeing a stranger in the way, were resolved to divert themselves with him; or perhaps were really amazed at the sight of a man so very different in habit, feature, and complexion from those who might probably live in so remote a climate. Upon the strength of this reasoning, I ventured to address them in the fol-
220 lowing manner: Gentlemen, if you be conjurers, as I have good cause to believe, you can understand any language; therefore I make bold to let your worships know, that I am a poor distressed English man, driven by his misfortunes upon your coast, and I entreat one of you, to let me ride upon his back, as if he were a real horse, to some house or village, where I can be relieved. In return of which favour I will make you a present of this knife and bracelet (taking them out of my pocket). The two creatures stood silent while I
230 spoke, seeming to listen with great attention; and when I had ended, they neighed frequently towards each other, as if they were engaged in serious conversation. I plainly observed, that their language expressed the passions very well, and the words might with little pains be resolved into an alphabet more easily than the Chinese.

I could frequently distinguish the word *Yahoo,* which was repeated by each of them several times; and although it was impossible for me to conjecture what it
240 meant, yet while the two horses were busy in conversation, I endeavoured to practise this word upon my tongue; and as soon as they were silent, I boldly pronounced *Yahoo* in a loud voice, imitating, at the same time, as near as I could, the neighing of a horse; at which they were both visibly surprised, and the gray repeated the same word twice, as if he meant to teach me the right accent, wherein I spoke after him as well as I could, and found myself perceivably to improve every time, though very far from any degree of perfec-
250 tion. Then the bay tried me with a second word, much harder to be pronounced; but reducing it to the English orthography, may be spelt thus, *Houyhnhnm.* I did not succeed in this so well as the former, but after two or three farther trials, I had better fortune; and they both appeared amazed at my capacity.

After some further discourse, which I then conjectured might relate to me, the two friends took their leaves, with the same compliment of striking each other's hoof; and the gray made me signs that I should
260 walk before him, wherein I thought it prudent to comply, till I could find a better director. When I offered to slacken my pace, he would cry *Hhuun, Hhuun;* I guessed his meaning, and gave him to understand, as

well as I could, that I was weary, and not able to walk faster; upon which, he would stand a while to let me rest.

CHAPTER II

The Author conducted by a Houyhnhnm *to his house. The house described. The Author's reception. The food of the* Houyhnhnms. *The Author in distress for want of meat, is at last relieved. His manner of feeding in this country.*

Having travelled about three miles, we came to a long kind of building, made of timber, stuck in the ground, and wattled across; the roof was low, and covered with straw. I now began to be a little comforted, and took out some toys, which travellers usually carry for presents to the savage Indians of America and other parts, in hopes the people of the house would be thereby encouraged to receive me kindly. The horse made me a sign to go in first; it was a large room with a smooth clay floor, and a rack and 10 manger extending the whole length on one side. There were three nags, and two mares, not eating, but some of them sitting down upon their hams, which I very much wondered at; but wondered more to see the rest employed in domestic business. These seemed but ordinary cattle; however, this confirmed my first opinion, that a people who could so far civilise brute animals, must needs excel in wisdom all the nations of the world. The gray came in just after, and thereby prevented any ill treatment, which the others might have 20 given me. He neighed to them several times in a style of authority, and received answers.

Beyond this room there were three others, reaching the length of the house, to which you passed through three doors, opposite to each other, in the manner of a vista; we went through the second room towards the third; here the gray walked in first, beckoning me to attend: I waited in the second room, and got ready my presents for the master and mistress of the house: they were two knives, three bracelets of false pearl, a small 30 looking-glass, and a bead necklace. The horse neighed three or four times, and I waited to hear some answers in a human voice, but I heard no other returns, than in the same dialect, only one or two a little shriller than his. I began to think that this house must belong to some person of great note among them, because there appeared so much ceremony before I could gain admittance. But, that a man of quality should be served all by horses, was beyond my comprehension. I feared my brain was disturbed by my sufferings and misfor- 40 tunes: I roused myself, and looked about me in the room where I was left alone; this was furnished like the first, only after a more elegant manner. I rubbed my eyes often, but the same objects still occurred. I pinched my arms and sides, to awake myself, hoping I might be in a dream. I then absolutely concluded, that all these appearances could be nothing else but necromancy and magic. But I had no time to pursue these reflections; for the gray horse came to the door, and made me a sign to follow him into the third room, where I saw a very comely mare, together with a colt and foal, sitting on their haunches, upon mats of straw, not unartfully made, and perfectly neat and clean.

The mare soon after my entrance, rose from her mat, and coming up close, after having nicely observed my hands and face, gave me a most contemptuous look; then turning to the horse, I heard the word *Yahoo* often repeated betwixt them; the meaning of which word I could not then comprehend, although it were the first I had learned to pronounce; but I was soon better informed, to my everlasting mortification: for the horse beckoning to me with his head, and repeating the word *Hhuun, Hhuun,* as he did upon the road, which I understood was to attend him, led me out into a kind of court, where was another building at some distance from the house. Here we entered, and I saw three of those detestable creatures, whom I first met after my landing, feeding upon roots, and the flesh of some animals, which I afterwards found to be that of asses and dogs, and now and then a cow dead by accident or disease. They were all tied by the neck with strong withes, fastened to a beam; they held their food between the claws of their fore-feet, and tore it with their teeth.

The master horse ordered a sorrel nag, one of his servants, to untie the largest of these animals, and take him into the yard. The beast and I were brought close together, and our countenances diligently compared, both by master and servant, who thereupon repeated several times the word *Yahoo.* My horror and astonishment are not to be described, when I observed, in this abominable animal, a perfect human figure: the face of it indeed was flat and broad, the nose depressed, the lips large, and the mouth wide. But these differences are common to all savage nations, where the lineaments of the countenance are distorted by the natives suffering their infants to lie grovelling on the earth, or by carrying them on their backs, nuzzling with their face against the mother's shoulders. The fore-feet of the *Yahoo* differed from my hands in nothing else but the length of the nails, the coarseness and brownness of the palms, and the hairiness on the backs. There was the same resemblance between our feet, with the same differences, which I knew very well, though the horses did not, because of my shoes and stockings; the same in every part of our bodies, except as to hairiness and colour, which I have already described.

The great difficulty that seemed to stick with the two horses, was, to see the rest of my body so very different from that of a *Yahoo,* for which I was obliged to my clothes, whereof they had no conception. The sorrel nag offered me a root, which he held (after their manner, as we shall describe in its proper place) between his hoof and pastern; I took it in my hand, and having smelt it, returned it to him again as civilly as I could. He brought out of the *Yahoo's* kennel a piece of ass's flesh, but it smelt so offensively that I turned from it with loathing: he then threw it to the *Yahoo,* by whom it was greedily devoured. He afterwards showed me a wisp of hay, and a fetlock full of oats; but I shook my head, to signify, that neither of these were food for me. And indeed, I now apprehended that I must absolutely starve, if I did not get to some of my own species; for as to those filthy *Yahoos,* although there were few greater lovers of mankind, at that time, than myself, yet I confess I never saw any sensitive being so detestable on all accounts; and the more I came near them, the more hateful they grew, while I stayed in that country. This the master horse observed by my behaviour, and therefore sent the *Yahoo* back to his kennel. He then put his forehoof to his mouth, at which I was much surprised, although he did it with ease, and with a motion that appeared perfectly natural, and made other signs to know what I would eat; but I could not return him such an answer as he was able to apprehend; and if he had understood me, I did not see how it was possible to contrive any way for finding myself nourishment. While we were thus engaged, I observed a cow passing by, whereupon I pointed to her, and expressed a desire to let me go and milk her. This had its effect; for he led me back into the house, and ordered a mare-servant to open a room, where a good store of milk lay in earthen and wooden vessels, after a very orderly and cleanly manner. She gave me a large bowl full, of which I drank very heartily, and found myself well refreshed.

About noon I saw coming towards the house a kind of vehicle, drawn like a sledge by four *Yahoos.* There was in it an old steed, who seemed to be of quality; he alighted with his hind-feet forward, having by accident got a hurt in his left fore-foot. He came to dine with our horse, who received him with great civility. They dined in the best room, and had oats boiled in milk for the second course, which the old horse eat warm, but the rest cold. Their mangers were placed circular in the middle of the room, and divided into several partitions, round which they sat on their haunches upon bosses of straw. In the middle was a large rack with angles answering to every partition of the manger; so that each horse and mare eat their own hay, and their own mash of oats and milk, with much decency and regularity. The behaviour of the young colt and foal appeared very modest, and that of the master and mistress extremely cheerful and complaisant to their guest. The gray ordered me to stand by him, and much discourse passed between him and his friend concerning me, as I found by the stranger's often looking on me, and the frequent repetition of the word *Yahoo*.

160 I happened to wear my gloves, which the master gray observing, seemed perplexed, discovering signs of wonder what I had done to my fore-feet; he put his hoof three or four times to them, as if he would signify, that I should reduce them to their former shape, which I presently did, pulling off both my gloves, and putting them into my pocket. This occasioned farther talk, and I saw the company was pleased with my behaviour, whereof I soon found the good effects. I was ordered to speak the few words I understood, and while they
170 were at dinner, the master taught me the names for oats, milk, fire, water, and some others; which I could readily pronounce after him, having from my youth a great facility in learning languages.

When dinner was done, the master horse took me aside, and by signs and words made me understand the concern that he was in, that I had nothing to eat. Oats in their tongue are called *hlunnh*. This word I pronounced two or three times; for although I had refused them at first, yet upon second thoughts, I considered
180 that I could contrive to make of them a kind of bread, which might be sufficient with milk to keep me alive, till I could make my escape to some other country, and to creatures of my own species. The horse immediately ordered a white mare-servant of his family to bring me a good quantity of oats in a sort of wooden tray. These I heated before the fire as well as I could, and rubbed them till the husks came off, which I made a shift to winnow from the grain; I ground and beat them between two stones, then took water, and made
190 them into a paste or cake, which I toasted at the fire, and ate warm with milk. It was at first a very insipid diet, though common enough in many parts of Europe, but grew tolerable by time; and having been often reduced to hard fare in my life, this was not the first experiment I had made how easily nature is satisfied. And I cannot but observe, that I never had one hour's sickness, while I stayed in this island. 'Tis true, I sometimes made a shift to catch a rabbit, or bird, by springs° made of *Yahoos'* hairs, and I often gathered
200 wholesome herbs, which I boiled, and eat as salads with my bread, and now and then, for a rarity, I made a little butter, and drank the whey. I was at first at a great loss for salt; but custom soon reconciled the want of it; and I am confident that the frequent use of salt among us is an effect of luxury, and was first introduced only as a provocative to drink; except where it is necessary for preserving of flesh in long voyages, or in places remote from great markets. For we observe no animal to be fond of it but man: and as to myself,
210 when I left this country, it was a great while before I could endure the taste of it in anything that I eat.

This is enough to say upon the subject of my diet, wherewith other travellers fill their books, as if the readers were personally concerned—whether we fared well or ill. However, it was necessary to mention this matter, lest the world should think it impossible that I could find sustenance for three years in such a country, and among such inhabitants.

When it grew towards evening, the master horse ordered a place for me to lodge in; it was but six yards 220 from the house, and separated from the stable of the *Yahoos*. Here I got some straw, and covering myself with my own clothes, slept very sound. But I was in a short time better accommodated, as the reader shall know hereafter, when I come to treat more particularly about my way of living.

CHAPTER III

The Author studious to learn the language, the Houyhnhnm *his master assists in teaching him. The language described. Several* Houyhnhnms *of quality come out of curiosity to see the Author. He gives his master a short account of his voyage.*

My principal endeavour was to learn the language, which my master (for so I shall henceforth call him), and his children, and every servant of his house, were desirous to teach me. For they looked upon it as a prodigy that a brute animal should discover such marks of a rational creature. I pointed to every thing, and enquired the name of it, which I wrote down in my journal-book when I was alone, and corrected my bad accent by desiring those of the family to pronounce it often. In this employment, a sorrel nag, one of the 10 under servants, was very ready to assist me.

In speaking, they pronounce through the nose and throat, and their language approaches nearest to the High-Dutch, or German, of any I know in Europe; is much more graceful and significant. The Emperor Charles V. made almost the same observation, when he said, that if he were to speak to his horse, it should be in High-Dutch.

The curiosity and impatience of my master were so great, that he spent many hours of his leisure to in- 20 struct me. He was convinced (as he afterwards told me) that I must be a *Yahoo,* but my teachableness, civility, and cleanliness, astonished him; which were qualities altogether so opposite to those animals. He was most perplexed about my clothes, reasoning sometimes with himself, whether they were a part of my body: for I never pulled them off till the family were asleep, and got them on before they waked in the morning. My master was eager to learn from whence I came, how I acquired those appearances of reason, 30 which I discovered in all my actions, and to know my story from my own mouth, which he hoped he should soon do by the great proficiency I made in learning and pronouncing their words and sentences. To help my memory, I formed all I learned into the English alphabet, and writ the words down with the translations. This last, after some time, I ventured to do in my master's presence. It cost me much trouble to explain to him what I was doing; for the inhabitants have not the least idea of books or literature.

In about ten weeks time I was able to understand most of his questions, and in three months could give him some tolerable answers. He was extremely curious to know from what part of the country I came, and how I was taught to imitate a rational creature, because the *Yahoos* (whom he saw I exactly resembled in my head, hands, and face, that were only visible), with some appearance of cunning, and the strongest disposition to mischief, were observed to be the most unteachable of all brutes. I answered, that I came over the sea from a far place, with many others of my own kind, in a great hollow vessel made of the bodies of trees. That my companions forced me to land on this coast, and then left me to shift for myself. It was with some difficulty, and by the help of many signs, that I brought him to understand me. He replied, that I must needs be mistaken, or that I *said the thing which was not*. (For they have no word in their language to express lying or falsehood.) He knew it was impossible that there could be a country beyond the sea, or that a parcel of brutes could move a wooden vessel whither they pleased upon water. He was sure no *Houyhnhnm* alive could make such a vessel nor would trust *Yahoos* to manage it.

The word *Houyhnhnm,* in their tongue, signifies a *horse,* and in its etymology, *the perfection of nature.* I told my master, that I was at a loss for expression, but would improve as fast as I could; and hoped in a short time I should be able to tell him wonders: he was pleased to direct his own mare, his colt and foal, and the servants of the family, to take all opportunities of instructing me, and every day for two or three hours, he was at the same pains himself. Several horses and mares of quality in the neighbourhood came often to our house upon the report spread of a wonderful *Yahoo,* that could speak like a *Houyhnhnm,* and seemed in his words and actions to discover some glimmerings of reason. These delighted to converse with me: they put many questions, and received such answers as I was able to return. By all these advantages, I made so great a progress, that in five months from my arrival I understood whatever was spoke, and could express myself tolerably well.

The *Houyhnhnms* who came to visit my master, out of a design of seeing and talking with me, could hardly believe me to be a right *Yahoo,* because my body had a different covering from others of my kind. They were astonished to observe me with but the usual hair or skin, except on my head, face, and hands; but I discovered that secret to my master, upon an accident, which happened about a fortnight before.

I have already told the reader, that every night when the family were gone to bed, it was my custom to strip and cover myself with my clothes: it happened one morning early, that my master sent for me, by the sorrel nag, who was his valet; when he came, I was fast asleep, my clothes fallen off on one side, and my shirt above my waist. I awaked at the noise he made, and observed him to deliver his message in some disorder; after which he went to my master, and in a great fright gave him a very confused account of what he had seen. This I presently discovered; for going as soon as I was dressed, to pay my attendance upon his Honour, he asked me the meaning of what his servant had reported, that I was not the same thing when I slept as I appeared to be at other times; that his valet assured him, some part of me was white, some yellow, at least not so white, and some brown.

I had hitherto concealed the secret of my dress, in order to distinguish myself, as much as possible, from that cursed race of *Yahoos;* but now I found it in vain to do so any longer. Besides, I considered that my clothes and shoes would soon wear out, which already were in a declining condition, and must be supplied by some contrivance from the hides of *Yahoos* or other brutes; whereby the whole secret would be known. I therefore told my master, that in the country from whence I came, those of my kind always covered their bodies with the hairs of certain animals prepared by art, as well for decency as to avoid the inclemencies of air, both hot and cold; of which, as to my own person, I would give him immediate conviction, if he pleased to command me: only desiring his excuse, if I did not expose those parts that nature taught us to conceal. He said my discourse was all very strange, but especially the last part; for he could not understand why nature should teach us to conceal what nature had given. That neither himself nor family were ashamed of any parts of their bodies; but however I might do as I pleased. Whereupon, I first unbuttoned my coat, and pulled it off. I did the same with my waistcoat; I drew off my shoes, stockings, and breeches. I let my shirt down to my waist, and drew up the bottom, fastening it like a girdle about my middle to hide my nakedness.

My master observed the whole performance with great signs of curiosity and admiration. He took up all my clothes in his pastern, one piece after another, and examined them diligently; he then stroked my body very gently, and looked round me several times, after which he said, it was plain I must be a perfect *Yahoo;* but that I differed very much from the rest of my species, in the softness, and whiteness, and smoothness of my skin, my want of hair in several parts of my body, the shape and shortness of my claws behind and before, and my affectation of walking continually on my two hinder feet. He desired to see no more, and gave me leave to put on my clothes again, for I was shuddering with cold.

I expressed my uneasiness at his giving me so often the appellation of *Yahoo,* an odious animal, for which I had so utter a hatred and contempt. I begged he would forbear applying that word to me, and take the same order in his family, and among his friends whom he suffered to see me. I requested likewise, that the secret of my having a false covering to my body might be known to none but himself, at least as long as my present clothing should last; for as to what the sorrel nag his valet had observed, his Honour might command him to conceal it.

160 All this my master very graciously consented to, and thus the secret was kept till my clothes began to wear out, which I was forced to supply by several contrivances, that shall hereafter be mentioned. In the meantime, he desired I would go on with my utmost diligence to learn their language, because he was more astonished at my capacity for speech and reason, than at the figure of my body, whether it were covered or no; adding, that he waited with some impatience to hear the wonders which I promised to tell him.

170 From thenceforward he doubled the pains he had been at to instruct me; he brought me into all company, and made them treat me with civility, because, as he told them, privately, this would put me into good humour, and make me more diverting.

Every day when I waited on him, beside the trouble he was at in teaching, he would ask me several questions concerning myself, which I answered as well as I could; and by these means he had already received some general ideas, though very imperfect. It would be 180 tedious to relate the several steps by which I advanced to a more regular conversation: but the first account I gave of myself in any order and length, was to this purpose:

That I came from a very far country, as I already had attempted to tell him, with about fifty more of my own species; that we travelled upon the seas, in a great hollow vessel made of wood, and larger than his Honour's house. I described the ship to him in the best terms I could, and explained by the help of my hand- 190 kerchief displayed, how it was driven forward by the wind. That upon a quarrel among us, I was set on shore on this coast, where I walked forward without knowing whither, till he delivered me from the persecution of those execrable *Yahoos*. He asked me, who made the ship, and how it was possible that the *Houyhnhnms* of my country would leave it to the management of brutes? My answer was, that I durst proceed no further in my relation, unless he would give me his word and honour that he would not be of- 200 fended, and then I would tell him the wonders I had so often promised. He agreed; and I went on by assuring him, that the ship was made by creatures like myself, who in all the countries I had travelled, as well as in my own, were the only governing, rational animals; and that upon my arrival hither, I was as much astonished to see the *Houyhnhnms* act like rational beings, as he or his friends could be in finding some marks of reason in a creature he was pleased to call a *Yahoo*, to which I owned my resemblance in every

part, but could not account for their degenerate and 210 brutal nature. I said farther, that if good fortune ever restored me to my native country, to relate my travels hither, as I resolved to do, every body would believe that I *said the thing which was not*; that I invented the story out of my own head; and with all possible respect to himself, his family and friends, and under his promise of not being offended, our countrymen would hardly think it probable, that a *Houyhnhnm* should be the presiding creature of a nation, and a *Yahoo* the brute. 220

CHAPTER IV

The Houyhnhnm's *notion of truth and falsehood. The Author's discourse disapproved by his master. The Author gives a more particular account of himself, and the accidents of his voyage.*

My master heard me with great appearances of uneasiness in his countenance, because *doubting*, or *not believing*, are so little known in this country, that the inhabitants cannot tell how to behave themselves under such circumstances. And I remember in frequent discourses with my master concerning the nature of manhood, in other parts of the world having occasion to talk of *lying* and *false representation*, it was with much difficulty that he comprehended what I meant, although he had otherwise a most acute judg- 10 ment. For he argued thus: that the use of speech was to make us understand one another, and to receive information of facts; now if any one *said the thing which was not*, these ends were defeated; because I cannot properly be said to understand him; and I am so far from receiving information, that he leaves me worse than in ignorance, for I am led to believe a thing black when it is white, and short when it is long. And these were all the notions he had concerning that faculty of *lying*, so perfectly well understood, and so universally 20 practised, among human creatures.

To return from this digression; when I asserted that the *Yahoos* were the only governing animals in my country, which my master said was altogether past his conception, he desired to know, whether we had *Houyhnhnms* among us, and what was their employment: I told him, we had great numbers, that in the summer they grazed in the fields, and in winter were kept in houses, with hay and oats, where *Yahoo* servants were employed to rub their skins smooth, comb 30 their manes, pick their feet, serve them with food, and make their beds. I understand you well, said my master, it is now very plain, from all you have spoken, that whatever share of reason the *Yahoos* pretend to, the *Houyhnhnms* are your masters; I heartily wish our *Yahoos* would be so tractable. I begged his Honour would please to excuse me from proceeding any farther, because I was very certain that the account he expected from me would be highly displeasing. But he insisted in commanding me to let him know the best and the worst: I told him, he should be obeyed. I owned, that the *Houyhnhnms* among us, whom we called horses, were the most generous and comely animals we had, that they excelled in strength and swiftness; and when they belonged to persons of quality, employed in travelling, racing, or drawing chariots, they were treated with much kindness and care, till they fell into diseases, or became foundered° in the feet; and then they were sold, and used to all kind of drudgery till they died; after which their skins were stripped and sold for what they were worth, and their bodies left to be devoured by dogs and birds of prey. But the common race of horses had not so good fortune, being kept by farmers and carriers, and other mean people, who put them to greater labour, and fed them worse. I described, as well as I could, our way of riding, the shape and use of a bridle, a saddle, a spur, and a whip, of harness and wheels. I added, that we fastened plates of a certain hard substance called iron at the bottom of their feet, to preserve their hoofs from being broken by the stony ways on which we often travelled.

My master, after some expressions of great indignation, wondered how we dared to venture upon a *Houyhnhnm's* back, for he was sure, that the weakest servant in his house would be able to shake off the strongest *Yahoo*, or by lying down, and rolling on his back, squeeze the brute to death. I answered, that our horses were trained up from three or four years old to the several uses we intended them for; that if any of them proved intolerably vicious, they were employed for carriages; that they were severely beaten while they were young for any mischievous tricks; that the males, designed for common use of riding or draught, were generally castrated about two years after their birth, to take down their spirits, and make them more tame and gentle; that they were indeed sensible of rewards and punishments; but his Honour would please to consider that they had not the least tincture of reason any more than the *Yahoos* in this country.

It put me to the pains of many circumlocutions to give my master a right idea of what I spoke; for their language doth not abound in variety of words, because their wants and passions are fewer than among us. But it is impossible to express his noble resentment at our savage treatment of the *Houyhnhnm* race, particularly after I had explained the manner and use of castrating horses among us, to hinder them from propagating their kind, and to render them more servile. He said, if it were possible there could be any country where *Yahoos* alone were endued with reason, they certainly must be the governing animal, because reason will in time always prevail against brutal strength. But, considering the frame of our bodies, and especially of mine, he thought no creature of equal bulk was so ill contrived, for employing that reason in the common offices of life; whereupon he desired to know whether those among whom I lived resembled me or the *Yahoos* of his country. I assured him, that I was as well shaped as most of my age; but the younger and the females were much more soft and tender, and the skins of the latter generally as white as milk. He said, I differed indeed from other *Yahoos*, being much more cleanly, and not altogether so deformed, but, in point of real advantage, he thought I differed for the worse. That my nails were of no use either to my fore or hinder-feet; as to my fore-feet, he could not properly call them by that name, for he never observed me to walk upon them; that they were too soft to bear the ground; that I generally went with them uncovered, neither was the covering I sometimes wore on them, of the same shape, or so strong as that on my feet behind. That I could not walk with any security, for if either of my hinder-feet slipped, I must inevitably fall. He then began to find fault with other parts of my body, the flatness of my face, the prominence of my nose, my eyes placed directly in front, so that I could not look on either side without turning my head: that I was not able to feed myself, without lifting one of my fore-feet to my mouth: and therefore nature had placed those joints to answer that necessity. He knew not what could be the use of those several clefts and divisions in my feet behind; these were too soft to bear the hardness and sharpness of stones without a covering made from the skin of some other brute; that my whole body wanted a fence against heat and cold, which I was forced to put on and off every day with tediousness and trouble. And lastly, that he observed every animal in this country naturally to abhor the *Yahoos*, whom the weaker avoided, and the stronger drove from them. So that supposing us to have the gift of reason, he could not see how it were possible to cure that natural antipathy which every creature discovered against us; nor consequently, how we could tame and render them serviceable. However, he would (as he said) debate the matter no farther, because he was more desirous to know my own story, the country where I was born, and the several actions and events of my life before I came hither.

I assured him, how extremely desirous I was that he should be satisfied on every point; but I doubted much, whether it would be possible for me to explain myself on several subjects whereof his Honour could have no conception, because I saw nothing in his country to which I could resemble them. That, however, I would do my best, and strive to express myself by similitudes, humbly desiring his assistance when I wanted proper words; which he was pleased to promise me.

I said, my birth was of honest parents in an island called England, which was remote from this country,

Chapter IV   48 **foundered**, affected with founder, an inflammation of a horse's foot

as many days' journey as the strongest of his Honour's servants could travel in the annual course of the sun. That I was bred a surgeon, whose trade it is to cure wounds and hurts in the body, got by accident or violence; that my country was governed by a female man, whom we called a Queen. That I left it to get riches, whereby I might maintain myself and family when I should return. That, in my last voyage, I was commander of the ship, and had about fifty *Yahoos* under me, many of which died at sea, and I was forced to supply them by others picked out from several nations. That our ship was twice in danger of being sunk; the first time by a great storm, and the second, by striking against a rock. Here my master interposed, by asking me, how I could persuade strangers out of different countries to venture with me, after the losses I had sustained, and the hazards I had run. I said, they were fellows of desperate fortunes, forced to fly from the places of their birth, on account of their poverty or their crimes. Some were undone by lawsuits; others spent all they had in drinking, whoring, and gaming; others fled for treason; many for murder, theft, poisoning, robbery, perjury, forgery, coining false money, for committing rapes or sodomy, for flying from their colours, or deserting to the enemy, and most of them had broken prison; none of these durst return to their native countries for fear of being hanged, or of starving in a jail; and therefore were under the necessity of seeking a livelihood in other places.

During this discourse, my master was pleased to interrupt me several times; I had made use of many circumlocutions in describing to him the nature of the several crimes for which most of our crew had been forced to fly their country. This labour took up several days' conversation, before he was able to comprehend me. He was wholly at a loss to know what could be the use or necessity of practising those vices. To clear up which I endeavoured to give some ideas of the desire of power and riches, of the terrible effects of lust, intemperance, malice, and envy. All this I was forced to define and describe by putting of cases, and making of suppositions. After which, like one whose imagination was struck with something never seen or heard of before, he would lift up his eyes with amazement and indignation. Power, government, war, law, punishment, and a thousand other things had no terms, wherein that language could express them, which made the difficulty almost insuperable to give my master any conception of what I meant. But being of an excellent understanding, much improved by contemplation and converse, he at last arrived at a competent knowledge of what human nature in our parts of the world is capable to perform, and desired I would give him some particular account of that land which we call Europe, but especially of my own country.

CHAPTER V

The Author, at his master's commands, informs him of the state of England. *The causes of war among the princes of* Europe. *The Author begins to explain the* English *constitution.*

The reader may please to observe, that the following extract of many conversations I had with my master, contains a summary of the most material points, which were discoursed at several times for above two years; his Honour often desiring fuller satisfaction as I farther improved in the *Houyhnhnm* tongue. I laid before him, as well as I could, the whole state of Europe; I discoursed of trade and manufactures, of arts and sciences; and the answers I gave to all the questions he made, as they arose upon several subjects, were a fund of conversation not to be exhausted. But I shall here only set down the substance of what passed between us concerning my own country, reducing it into order as well as I can, without any regard to time or other circumstances, while I strictly adhere to truth. My only concern is, that I shall hardly be able to do justice to my master's arguments and expressions, which must needs suffer by my want of capacity, as well as by a translation into our barbarous English.

In obedience, therefore, to his Honour's commands, I related to him the Revolution° under the Prince of Orange; the long war with France entered into by the said prince, and renewed by his successor, the present Queen, wherein the greatest powers of Christendom were engaged, and which still continued: I computed at his request, that about a million of *Yahoos* might have been killed in the whole progress of it; and perhaps a hundred or more cities taken, and thrice as many ships burnt or sunk.

He asked me what were the usual causes or motives that made one country go to war with another. I answered they were innumerable; but I should only mention a few of the chief. Sometimes the ambition of princes, who never think they have land or people enough to govern; sometimes the corruption of ministers, who engage their master in a war in order to stifle or divert the clamour of the subjects against their evil administration. Difference in opinions hath cost many millions of lives: for instance, whether flesh be° bread, or bread be flesh; whether the juice of a certain berry be blood or wine; whether whistling be a vice or a virtue; whether it be better to kiss a post, or throw it into the fire; what is the best colour for a coat, whether black, white, red, or gray; and whether it should be long or short, narrow or wide, dirty or clean; with

Chapter V 21ff. **Revolution.** Swift refers here to the Glorious Revolution of 1688 and to the War of the Spanish Succession 39ff. **whether flesh be . . .** Swift refers here to religious controversies about the presence of the body and blood of Christ in the bread and wine of the Eucharist, as well as to differing religious customs of behavior and dress many more. Neither are any wars so furious and bloody, or of so long continuance, as those occasioned by difference in opinion, especially if it be in things indifferent.

Sometimes the quarrel between two princes is to decide which of them shall dispossess a third of his dominions, where neither of them pretend to any right. Sometimes one prince quarreleth with another, for fear the other should quarrel with him. Sometimes a war is entered upon, because the enemy is too strong, and sometimes because he is too weak. Sometimes our neighbours want the things which we have, or have the things which we want; and we both fight, till they take ours or give us theirs. It is a very justifiable cause of a war to invade a country after the people have been wasted by famine, destroyed by pestilence, or embroiled by factions among themselves. It is justifiable to enter into war against our nearest ally, when one of his towns lies convenient for us, or a territory of land, that would render our dominions round and complete. If a prince sends forces into a nation, where the people are poor and ignorant, he may lawfully put half of them to death, and make slaves of the rest, in order to civilize and reduce them from their barbarous way of living. It is a very kingly, honourable, and frequent practice, when one prince desires the assistance of another to secure him against an invasion, that the assistant, when he hath driven out the invader, should seize on the dominions himself, and kill, imprison, or banish the prince he came to relieve. Alliance by blood or marriage is a frequent cause of war between princes; and the nearer the kindred is, the greater is their disposition to quarrel: poor nations are hungry, and rich nations are proud; and pride and hunger will ever be at variance. For these reasons, the trade of a soldier is held the most honourable of all others; because a soldier is a *Yahoo* hired to kill in cold blood as many of his own species, who have never offended him, as possibly he can.

There is likewise a kind of beggarly princes in Europe, not able to make war by themselves, who hire out their troops to richer nations, for so much a day to each man; of which they keep three fourths to themselves, and it is the best part of their maintenance; such are those in Germany and other northern parts of Europe.

What you have told me (said my master), upon the subject of war, does indeed discover most admirably the effects of that reason you pretend to: however, it is happy that the shame is greater than the danger; and that nature hath left you utterly uncapable of doing much mischief.

For your mouths lying flat with your faces, you can hardly bite each other to any purpose, unless by consent. Then as to the claws upon your feet before and behind, they are so short and tender, that one of our

Yahoos would drive a dozen of yours before him. And therefore in recounting the numbers of those who have been killed in battle, I cannot but think that you have *said the thing which is not.*

I could not forbear shaking my head, and smiling a little at his ignorance. And being no stranger to the art of war, I gave him a description of cannons, culverins, muskets, carabines, pistols, bullets, powder, swords, bayonets, battles, sieges, retreats, attacks, under-mines, countermines, bombardments, sea fights; ships sunk with a thousand men, twenty thousand killed on each side; dying groans, limbs flying in the air, smoke, noise, confusion, trampling to death under horses' feet; flight, pursuit, victory; fields strewed with carcases left for food to dogs, and wolves, and birds of prey; plundering, stripping, ravishing, burning and destroying. And to set forth the valour of my own dear countrymen, I assured him, that I had seen them blow up a hundred enemies at once in a siege, and as many in a ship, and beheld the dead bodies come down in pieces from the clouds, to the great diversion of the spectators.

I was going on to more particulars, when my master commanded me silence. He said, whoever understood the nature of *Yahoos* might easily believe it possible for so vile an animal to be capable of every action I had named, if their strength and cunning equalled their malice. But as my discourse had increased his abhorrence of the whole species, so he found it gave him a disturbance in his mind, to which he was wholly a stranger before. He thought his ears being used to such abominable words, might by degrees admit them with less detestation. That although he hated the *Yahoos* of this country, yet he no more blamed them for their odious qualities, than he did a *gnnayh* (a bird of prey) for its cruelty, or a sharp stone for cutting his hoof. But when a creature pretending to reason could be capable of such enormities, he dreaded lest the corruption of that faculty might be worse than brutality itself. He seemed therefore confident, that instead of reason, we were only possessed of some quality fitted to increase our natural vices; as the reflection from a troubled stream returns the image of an ill-shapen body, not only larger, but more distorted.

He added, that he had heard too much upon the subject of war, both in this, and some former discourses. There was another point which a little perplexed him at present. I had informed him, that some of our crew left their country on account of being ruined by *Law;* that I had already explained the meaning of the word; but he was at a loss how it should come to pass, that the law which was intended for every man's preservation, should be any man's ruin. Therefore he desired to be farther satisfied what I meant by law, and the dispensers thereof, according to the present practice in my own country; because he thought nature and reason were sufficient guides for a reasonable animal, as we pretended to be, in showing us what we ought to do, and what to avoid.

I assured his Honour, that law was a science wherein I had not much conversed, further than by employing advocates, in vain, upon some injustices that had been done me: however, I would give him all the satisfaction I was able.

I said, there was a society of men among us, bred up from their youth in the art of proving by words multiplied for the purpose, that white is black, and black is white, according as they are paid. To this society all the rest of the people are slaves. For example, if my neighbour hath a mind to my cow, he hires a lawyer to prove that he ought to have my cow from me. I must then hire another to defend my right, it being against all rules of law that any man should be allowed to speak for himself. Now in this case, I, who am the right owner, lie under two great disadvantages. First, my lawyer, being practised almost from his cradle in defending falsehood, is quite out of his element when he would be an advocate for justice, which as an office unnatural, he always attempts with great awkwardness, if not with ill-will. The second disadvantage is, that my lawyer must proceed with great caution, or else he will be reprimanded by the judges, and abhorred by his brethren, as one that would lessen the practice of the law. And therefore I have but two methods to preserve my cow. The first is, to gain over my adversary's lawyer with a double fee; who will then betray his client, by insinuating that he hath justice on his side. The second way is for my lawyer to make my cause appear as unjust as he can, by allowing the cow to belong to my adversary: and this, if it be skilfully done, will certainly bespeak the favour of the bench.

Now, your Honour is to know, that these judges are persons appointed to decide all controversies of property, as well as for the trial of criminals, and picked out from the most dexterous lawyers, who are grown old or lazy, and having been biassed all their lives against truth and equity, are under such a fatal necessity of favouring fraud, perjury, and oppression, that I have known several of them refuse a large bribe from the side where justice lay, rather than injure the faculty, by doing any thing unbecoming their nature or their office.

It is a maxim among these lawyers, that whatever hath been done before, may legally be done again: and therefore they take special care to record all the decisions formerly made against common justice, and the general reason of mankind. These, under the name of *precedents*, they produce as authorities, to justify the most iniquitous opinions; and the judges never fail of directing accordingly.

In pleading, they studiously avoid entering into the merits of the cause; but are loud, violent, and tedious in dwelling upon all circumstances which are not to the purpose. For instance, in the case already mentioned: they never desire to know what claim or title my adversary hath to my cow; but whether the said cow were red or black; her horns long or short; whether the field I graze her in be round or square; whether she was milked at home or abroad; what diseases she is subject to, and the like; after which they consult precedents, adjourn the cause from time to time, and in ten, twenty, or thirty years, come to an issue.

It is likewise to be observed, that this society hath a peculiar cant and jargon of their own, that no other mortal can understand, and wherein all their laws are written, which they take special care to multiply; whereby they have wholly confounded the very essence of truth and falsehood, of right and wrong; so that it will take thirty years to decide whether the field left me by my ancestors for six generations belongs to me, or to a stranger three hundred miles off.

In the trial of persons accused for crimes against the state, the method is much more short and commendable: the judge first sends to sound the disposition of those in power, after which he can easily hang or save the criminal, strictly preserving all due forms of law.

Here my master interposing, said it was a pity, that creatures endowed with such prodigious abilities of mind as these lawyers, by the description I gave of them, must certainly be, were not rather encouraged to be instructors of others in wisdom and knowledge. In answer to which, I assured his Honour, that in all points out of their own trade, they were usually the most ignorant and stupid generation among us, the most despicable in common conversation, avowed enemies to all knowledge and learning, and equally disposed to pervert the general reason of mankind in every other subject of discourse, as in that of their own profession.

CHAPTER VI

A continuation of the state of England. *The character of a first or chief minister of state in* European *courts.*

My master was yet wholly at a loss to understand what motives could incite this race of lawyers to perplex, disquiet, and weary themselves, and engage in a confederacy of injustice, merely for the sake of injuring their fellow-animals; neither could he comprehend what I meant in saying they did it for hire. Whereupon I was at much pains to describe to him the use of money, the materials it was made of, and the value of the metals; that when a *Yahoo* had got a great store of this precious substance, he was able to purchase whatever he had a mind to; the finest clothing, the noblest houses, great tracts of land, the most costly meats and drinks, and have his choice of the most beautiful females. Therefore since money alone was able to perform all these feats, our *Yahoos* thought they could never have enough of it to spend or to save, as they found themselves inclined from their natural bent either to profusion or avarice. That the rich man enjoyed the fruit of the poor man's labour, and the latter were a thousand to one in proportion to the former. That the bulk of our people were forced to live miserably, by labouring every day for small wages to make a few live plentifully. I enlarged myself much on these and many other particulars to the same purpose; but his Honour was still to seek; for he went upon a supposition that all animals had a title to their share in the productions of the earth, and especially those who presided over the rest. Therefore he desired I would let him know, what these costly meats were, and how any of us happened to want them. Whereupon I enumerated as many sorts as came into my head, with the various methods of dressing them, which could not be done without sending vessels by sea to every part of the world, as well for liquors to drink, as for sauces, and innumerable other conveniences. I assured him, that this whole globe of earth must be at least three times gone round, before one of our better female *Yahoos* could get her breakfast, or a cup to put it in. He said, that must needs be a miserable country which cannot furnish food for its own inhabitants. But what he chiefly wondered at, was how such vast tracts of ground as I described should be wholly without fresh water, and the people put to the necessity of sending over the sea for drink. I replied, that England (the dear place of my nativity) was computed to produce three times the quantity of food, more than its inhabitants are able to consume, as well as liquors extracted from grain, or pressed out of the fruit of certain trees, which made excellent drink, and the same proportion in every other conveneince of life. But, in order to feed the luxury and intemperance of the males, and the vanity of the females, we sent away the greatest part of our necessary things to other countries, from whence in return we brought the materials of diseases, folly, and vice, to spend among ourselves. Hence it follows of necessity, that vast numbers of our people are compelled to seek their livelihood by begging, robbing, stealing, cheating, pimping, forswearing, flattering, suborning, forging, gaming, lying, fawning, hectoring, voting, scribbling, star-gazing, poisoning, whoring, canting, libelling, free-thinking, and the like occupations: every one of which terms, I was at much pains to make him understand.

That wine was not imported among us from foreign countries, to supply the want of water or other drinks, but because it was a sort of liquid which made us merry, by putting us out of our senses; diverted all melancholy thoughts, begat wild extravagant imaginations in the brain, raised our hopes, and banished our fears, suspended every office of reason for a time, and deprived us of the use of our limbs, till we fell into a profound sleep; although it must be confessed, that we always awaked sick and dispirited, and that the use of this liquor filled us with diseases, which made our lives uncomfortable and short.

But beside all this, the bulk of our people supported themselves by furnishing the necessities or conveniences of life to the rich, and to each other. For instance, when I am at home and dressed as I ought to be, I carry on my body the workmanship of an hundred tradesmen; the building and furniture of my house employ as many more, and five times the number to adorn my wife.

I was going on to tell him of another sort of people, who get their livelihood by attending the sick, having upon some occasions informed his Honour that many of my crew had died of diseases. But here it was with the utmost difficulty, that I brought him to apprehend what I meant. He could easily conceive, that a *Houyhnhnm* grew weak and heavy a few days before his death, or by some accident might hurt a limb. But that nature, who works all things to perfection, should suffer any pains to breed in our bodies, he thought impossible, and desired to know the reason of so unaccountable an evil. I told him, we fed on a thousand things which operated contrary to each other; that we eat when we were not hungry, and drank without the provocation of thirst; that we sat whole nights drinking strong liquors without eating a bit, which disposed us to sloth, inflamed our bodies, and precipitated or prevented digestion. That prostitute female *Yahoos* acquired a certain malady, which bred rottenness in the bones of those who fell into their embraces; that this and many other diseases were propagated from father to son, so that great numbers came into the world with complicated maladies upon them; that it would be endless to give him a catalogue of all diseases incident to human bodies; for they would not be fewer than five or six hundred, spread over every limb and joint; in short, every part, external and intestine, having diseases appropriated to each. To remedy which, there was a sort of people bred up among us, in the profession or pretence of curing the sick. And because I had some skill in the faculty, I would in gratitude to his Honour, let him know the whole mystery and method by which they proceed.

Their fundamental is, that all diseases arise from repletion, from whence they conclude, that a great evacuation of the body is necessary, either through the natural passage, or upwards at the mouth. Their next business is, from herbs, minerals, gums, oils, shells, salts, juices, seaweed, excrements, barks of trees, serpents, toads, frogs, spiders, dead men's flesh and bones, birds, beasts, and fishes, to form a composition for smell and taste the most abominable, nauseous, and detestable, they can possibly contrive, which the stomach immediately rejects with loathing; and this they call a vomit; or else from the same store-house, with some other poisonous additions, they command us to take in at the orifice above or below (just as the

physician then happens to be disposed) a medicine equally annoying and disgustful to the bowels; which relaxing the belly, drives down all before it, and this they call a purge, or a clyster. For nature (as the physicians allege) having intended the superior anterior orifice only for the intromission of solids and liquids, and the inferior posterior for ejection, these artists ingeniously considering that in all diseases nature is forced out of her seat, therefore to replace her in it, the
140 body must be treated in a manner directly contrary, by interchanging the use of each orifice; forcing solids and liquids in at the anus, and making evacuations at the mouth.

But, besides real diseases, we are subject to many that are only imaginary, for which the physicians have invented imaginary cures; these have their several names, and so have the drugs that are proper for them, and with these our female *Yahoos* are always infested.

One great excellency in this tribe is their skill at
150 prognostics,° wherein they seldom fail; their predictions in real diseases, when they rise to any degree of malignity, generally portending death, which is always in their power, when recovery is not: and therefore, upon any unexpected signs of amendment, after they have pronounced their sentence, rather than be accused as false prophets, they know how to approve their sagacity to the world by a seasonable dose.

They are likewise of special use to husbands and wives, who are grown weary of their mates; to eldest
160 sons, to great ministers of state, and often to princes.

I had formerly upon occasion discoursed with my master upon the nature of government in general, and particularly of our own excellent constitution, deservedly the wonder and envy of the whole world. But having here accidentally mentioned a minister of state, he commanded me some time after to inform him, what species of *Yahoo* I particularly meant by that appellation.

I told him, that a First or Chief Minister of State,
170 who was the person I intended to describe, was a creature wholly exempt from joy and grief, love and hatred, pity and anger; at least made use of no other passions but a violent desire of wealth, power, and titles; that he applies his words to all uses, except to the indication of his mind; that he never tells a truth, but with an intent that you should take it for a lie; nor a lie, but with a design that you should take it for a truth; that those he speaks worst of behind their backs, are in the surest way of preferment; and whenever he begins
180 to praise you to others or to yourself, you are from that day forlorn. The worst mark you can receive is a promise, especially when it is confirmed with an oath; after which every wise man retires, and gives over all hopes.

There are three methods by which a man may rise to be chief minister: the first is, by knowing how with prudence to dispose of a wife, a daughter, or a sister: the second, by betraying or undermining his predecessor: and the third is, by a furious zeal in public assemblies against the corruptions of the court. But a 190 wise prince would rather choose to employ those who practise the last of these methods; because such zealots prove always the most obsequious and subservient to the will and passions of their master. That these ministers having all employments at their disposal, preserve themselves in power, by bribing the majority of a senate or great council; and at last, by an expedient called an Act of Indemnity° (whereof I described the nature to him) they secure themselves from after-reckonings, and retire from the public, laden 200 with the spoils of the nation.

The palace of a chief minister is a seminary to breed up others in his own trade: the pages, lackeys, and porters, by imitating their master, become ministers of state in their several districts, and learn to excel in the three principal ingredients, of insolence, lying, and bribery. Accordingly, they have a subaltern° court paid to them by persons of the best rank, and sometimes by the force of dexterity and impudence, arrive through several gradations to be successors to their lord.   210

He is usually governed by a decayed wench, or favourite footman, who are the tunnels through which all graces are conveyed, and may properly be called, in the last resort, the governors of the kingdom.

One day in discourse my master, having heard me mention the nobility of my country, was pleased to make me a compliment which I could not pretend to deserve: that he was sure I must have been born of some noble family, because I far exceeded in shape, colour, and cleanliness, all the *Yahoos* of his nation, 220 although I seemed to fail in strength and agility, which must be imputed to my different way of living from those other brutes; and besides, I was not only endowed with the faculty of speech, but likewise with some rudiments of reason, to a degree, that with all his acquaintance I passed for a prodigy.

He made me observe, that among the *Houyhnhnms,* the white, the sorrel, and the iron-gray, were not so exactly shaped as the bay, the dapple-gray, and the black; nor born with equal talents of the mind, or a 230 capacity to improve them; and therefore continued always in the condition of servants, without ever aspiring to match out of their own race, which in that country would be reckoned monstrous and unnatural.

I made his Honour my most humble acknowledgments for the good opinion he was pleased to conceive of me; but assured him at the same time, that my birth was of the lower sort, having been born of plain honest parents, who were just able to give me a tolerable education; that nobility among us was altogether a differ- 240 ent thing from the idea he had of it; that our young noblemen are bred from their childhood in idleness and

198 **Act of Indemnity,** guaranteed freedom from prosecution for any actions of a specified official's tenure   207 **subaltern,** inferior

luxury; that as soon as years will permit, they consume their vigour, and contract odious diseases among lewd females; and when their fortunes are almost ruined, they marry some woman of mean birth, disagreeable person, and unsound constitution, merely for the sake of money, whom they hate and despise. That the productions of such marriages are generally scrofulous, rickety, or deformed children; by which means the family seldom continues above three generations, unless the wife takes care to provide a healthy father among her neighbours or domestics, in order to improve and continue the breed. That a weak diseased body, a meagre countenance, and sallow complexion, are the true marks of noble blood; and a healthy robust appearance is so disgraceful in a man of quality, that the world concludes his real father to have been a groom or a coachman. The imperfections of his mind run parallel with those of his body, being a composition of spleen, dullness, ignorance, caprice, sensuality, and pride.

Without the consent of this illustrious body, no law can be enacted, repealed, or altered; and these have the decision of all our possessions without appeal.

CHAPTER VII

The Author's great love of his native country. His master's observations upon the constitution and administration of England, *as described by the Author, with parallel cases and comparisons. His master's observations upon human nature.*

The reader may be disposed to wonder how I could prevail on myself to give so free a representation of my own species, among a race of mortals who are already too apt to conceive the vilest opinion of human kind, from that entire congruity betwixt me and their *Yahoos.* But I must freely confess, that the many virtues of those excellent quadrupeds placed in opposite view to human corruptions, had so far opened my eyes and enlarged my understanding, that I began to view the actions and passions of man in a very different light, and to think the honour of my own kind not worth managing; which, besides, it was impossible for me to do before a person of so acute a judgment as my master, who daily convinced me of a thousand faults in myself, whereof I had not the least perception before, and which with us would never be numbered even among human infirmities. I had likewise learned from his example an utter detestation of all falsehood or disguise; and truth appeared so amiable to me, that I determined upon sacrificing every thing to it.

Let me deal so candidly with the reader, as to confess, that there was yet a much stronger motive for the freedom I took in my representation of things. I had not been a year in this country, before I contracted such a love and veneration for the inhabitants, that I entered on a firm resolution never to return to human kind, but to pass the rest of my life among these admirable *Houyhnhnms* in the contemplation and practice of every virtue; where I could have no example or incitement to vice. But it was decreed by fortune, my perpetual enemy, that so great a felicity should not fall to my share. However, it is now some comfort to reflect, that in what I said of my countrymen, I extenuated their faults as much as I durst before so strict an examiner, and upon every article gave as favourable a turn as the matter would bear. For, indeed, who is there alive that will not be swayed by his bias and partiality to the place of his birth?

I have related the substance of several conversations I had with my master, during the greatest part of the time I had the honour to be in his service, but have indeed for brevity sake omitted much more than is here set down.

When I had answered all his questions, and his curiosity seemed to be fully satisfied; he sent for me one morning early, and commanding me to sit down at some distance (an honour which he had never before conferred upon me), he said, he had been very seriously considering my whole story, as far as it related both to myself and my country; that he looked upon us as a sort of animals to whose share, by what accident he could not conjecture, some small pittance of reason had fallen, whereof we made no other use than by its assistance to aggravate our natural corruptions, and to acquire new ones, which nature had not given us. That we disarmed ourselves of the few abilities she had bestowed, had been very successful in multiplying our original wants, and seemed to spend our whole lives in vain endeavours to supply them by our own inventions. That as to myself, was manifest I had neither the strength of agility of a common *Yahoo;* that I walked infirmly on my hinder feet; had found out a contrivance to make my claws of no use or defence, and to remove the hair from my chin, which was intended as a shelter from the sun and the weather. Lastly, that I could neither run with speed, nor climb trees like my brethren (as he called them) the *Yahoos* in this country.

That our institutions of government and law were plainly owing to our gross defects in reason, and by consequence, in virtue; because reason alone is sufficient to govern a rational creature; which was therefore a character we had no pretence to challenge, even from the account I had given of my own people; although he manifestly perceived, that in order to favour them, I had concealed many particulars, and often *said the thing which was not.*

He was the more confirmed in this opinion, because he observed, that as I agreed in every feature of my body with other *Yahoos,* except where it was to my real disadvantage in point of strength, speed and activity, the shortness of my claws, and some other particulars where nature had no part; so from the representation I had given him of our lives, our manners, and our actions, he found as near a resemblance in the disposition of our minds. He said the *Yahoos* were known to hate one another more than they did any different species of animals; and the reason usually assigned was the odiousness of their own shapes, which all 90 could see in the rest, but not in themselves. He had therefore begun to think it not unwise in us to cover our bodies, and by that invention conceal many of our own deformities from each other, which would else be hardly supportable. But he now found he had been mistaken, and that the dissensions of those brutes in his country were owing to the same cause with ours, as I had described them. For if (said he), you throw among five *Yahoos* as much food as would be sufficient for fifty, they will, instead of eating peaceably, fall to- 100 gether by the ears, each single one impatient to have all to itself; and therefore a servant was usually employed to stand by while they were feeding abroad, and those kept at home were tied at a distance from each other: that if a cow died of age or accident, before a *Houyhnhnm* could secure it for his own *Yahoos*, those in the neighbourhood would come in herds to seize it, and then would ensue such a battle as I had described, with terrible wounds made by their claws on both sides, although they seldom were able to kill 110 one another, for want of such convenient instruments of death as we had invented. At other times the like battles have been fought between the *Yahoos* of several neighbourhoods without any visible cause; those of one district watching all opportunities to surprise the next before they are prepared. But if they find their project hath miscarried, they return home, and, for want of enemies, engage in what I call a civil war among themselves.

That in some fields of his country, there are certain 120 shining stones of several colours, whereof the *Yahoos* are violently fond, and when part of these stones is fixed in the earth, as it sometimes happeneth, they will dig with their claws for whole days to get them out, then carry them away, and hide them by heaps in their kennels; but still looking round with great caution, for fear their comrades should find out their treasure. My master said, he could never discover the reason of this unnatural appetite, or how these stones could be of any use to a *Yahoo;* but now he believed it might pro- 130 ceed from the same principle of avarice which I had ascribed to mankind: that he had once, by way of experiment, privately removed a heap of these stones from the place where one of his *Yahoos* had buried it: whereupon, the sordid animal missing his treasure, by his loud lamenting brought the whole herd to the place, there miserably howled, then fell to biting and tearing the rest, began to pine away, would neither eat, nor sleep, nor work, till he ordered a servant privately to convey the stones into the same hole, and hide them as 140 before; which when his *Yahoo* had found, he presently

recovered his spirits and good humour, but took good care to remove them to a better hiding place, and hath ever since been a very serviceable brute.

My master farther assured me, which I also observed myself, that in the fields where the shining stones abound, the fiercest and most frequent battles are fought, occasioned by perpetual inroads of the neighbouring *Yahoos*.

He said, it was common when two *Yahoos* discov- 150 ered such a stone in a field, and were contending which of them should be the proprietor, a third would take the advantage, and carry it away from them both; which my master would needs contend to have some kind of resemblance with our suits at law; wherein I thought it for our credit not to undeceive him; since the decision he mentioned was much more equitable than many decrees among us; because the plaintiff and defendant there lost nothing beside the stone they contended for, whereas our courts of equity would never 160 have dismissed the cause while either of them had any thing left.

My master continuing his discourse, said, there was nothing that rendered the *Yahoos* more odious than their undistinguishing appetite to devour every thing that came in their way, whether herbs, roots, berries, the corrupted flesh of animals, or all mingled together: and it was peculiar in their temper, that they were fonder of what they could get by rapine or stealth at a greater distance, than much better food provided for them at home. If their prey held out, they would eat till 170 they were ready to burst, after which nature had pointed out to them a certain root that gave them a general evacuation.

There was also another kind of root very juicy, but somewhat rare and difficult to be found, which the *Yahoos* sought for with much eagerness, and would suck it with great delight; and it produced in them the same effects that wine hath upon us. It would make them sometimes hug, and sometimes tear one another; they would howl and grin, and chatter, and reel, and 180 tumble, and then fall asleep in the mud.

I did indeed observe, that the *Yahoos* were the only animals in this country subject to any diseases; which, however, were much fewer than horses have among us, and contracted not by any ill treatment they meet with, but by the nastiness and greediness of that sordid brute. Neither has their language any more than a general appellation for those maladies, which is borrowed from the name of the beast, and called *Hnea-Yahoo,* or *Yahoo's evil,* and the cure prescribed is a mixture of 190 their own dung and urine forcibly put down the *Yahoo's* throat. This I have since often known to have been taken with success, and do freely recommend it to my countrymen, for the public good, as an admirable specific against all diseases produced by repletion.

As to learning, government, arts, manufactures, and the like, my master confessed he could find little or no resemblance between the *Yahoos* of that country and those in ours. For he only meant to observe what parity there was in our natures. He had heard indeed some curious *Houyhnhnms* observe, that in most herds there was a sort of ruling *Yahoo* (as among us there is generally some leading or principal stag in a park), who was always more deformed in body, and mischievous in disposition, than any of the rest. That this leader had usually a favourite as like himself as he could get, whose employment was to lick his master's feet and posteriors, and drive the female *Yahoos* to his kennel; for which he was now and then rewarded with a piece of ass's flesh. This favourite is hated by the whole herd, and therefore to protect himself, keeps always near the person of his leader. He usually continues in office till a worse can be found; but the very moment he is discarded, his successor, at the head of all the *Yahoos* in that district, young and old, male and female come in a body, and discharge their excrements upon him from head to foot. But how far this might be applicable to our courts and favourites, and ministers of state, my master said I could best determine.

I durst make no return to this malicious insinuation, which debased human understanding below the sagacity of a common hound, who has judgment enough to distinguish and follow the cry of the ablest dog in the pack, without being ever mistaken.

My master told me, there were some qualities remarkable in the *Yahoos*, which he had not observed me to mention, or at least very slightly, in the accounts I had given him of human kind. He said, those animals, like other brutes, had their females in common; but in this they differed, that the she-*Yahoo* would admit the male while she was pregnant; and that the hees would quarrel and fight with the females as fiercely as with each other. Both which practices were such degrees of infamous brutality, that no other sensitive creature ever arrived at.

Another thing he wondered at in the *Yahoos,* was their strange disposition to nastiness and dirt, whereas there appears to be a natural love of cleanliness in all other animals. As to the two former accusations, I was glad to let them pass without any reply, because I had not a word to offer upon them in defence of my species, which otherwise I certainly had done from my own inclinations. But I could have easily vindicated human kind from the imputation of singularity upon the last article, if there had been any swine in that country (as unluckily for me there were not), which although it may be a sweeter quadruped than a *Yahoo,* cannot I humbly conceive in justice pretend to more cleanliness; and so his Honour himself must have owned, if he had seen their filthy way of feeding, and their custom of wallowing and sleeping in the mud.

My master likewise mentioned another quality which his servants had discovered in several *Yahoos,* and to him was wholly unaccountable. He said, a fancy would sometimes take a *Yahoo* to retire into a corner, to lie down and howl, and groan, and spurn away all that came near him, although he were young and fat, wanted neither food nor water; nor did the servants imagine what could possibly ail him. And the only remedy they found was to set him to hard work, after which he would infallibly come to himself. To this I was silent out of partiality to my own kind; yet here I could plainly discover the true seeds of spleen,° which only seizeth on the lazy, the luxurious, and the rich; who, if they were forced to undergo the same regimen, I would undertake for the cure.

His Honour had further observed, that a female *Yahoo* would often stand behind a bank or a bush, to gaze on the young males passing by, and then appear, and hide, using many antic gestures and grimaces, at which time it was observed that she had a most offensive smell; and when any of the males advanced, would slowly retire, looking often back, and with a counterfeit show of fear, run off into some convenient place where she knew the male would follow her.

At other times if a female stranger came among them, three or four of her own sex would get about her, and stare and chatter, and grin, and smell her all over; and then turn off with gestures that seemed to express contempt and disdain.

Perhaps my master might refine a little in these speculations, which he had drawn from what he observed himself, or had been told him by others; however, I could not reflect without some amazement, and much sorrow, that the rudiments of lewdness, coquetry, censure, and scandal, should have place by instinct in womankind.

I expected every moment, that my master would accuse the *Yahoos* of those unnatural appetites in both sexes, so common among us. But nature, it seems, hath not been so expert a school-mistress; and these politer pleasures are entirely the productions of art and reason, on our side of the globe.

CHAPTER VIII

The Author relates several particulars of the Yahoos. *The great virtues of the* Houyhnhnms. *The education and exercise of their youth. Their general assembly.*

As I ought to have understood human nature much better than I supposed it possible for my master to do, so it was easy to apply the character he gave of the *Yahoos* to myself and my countrymen; and I believed I could yet make farther discoveries from my own observation. I therefore often begged his favour to let me go among the herds of *Yahoos* in the neighbourhood, to which he always very graciously consented, being perfectly convinced that the hatred I bore those brutes would never suffer me to be corrupted by them; and

Chapter VII   263 **spleen,** melancholy, dejection, peevish temper

his Honour ordered one of his servants, a strong sorrel nag, very honest and good-natured, to be my guard, without whose protection I durst not undertake such adventures. For I have already told the reader how much I was pestered by those odious animals upon my first arrival. And I afterwards failed very narrowly three or four times of falling into their clutches, when I happened to stray at any distance without my hanger. And I have reason to believe they had some imagina-tion that I was of their own species, which I often assisted myself, by stripping up my sleeves, and showing my naked arms and breast in their sight, when my protector was with me. At which times they would approach as near as they durst, and imitate my actions after the manner of monkeys, but ever with great signs of hatred; as a tame jackdaw with cap and stockings is always persecuted by the wild ones, when he happens to be got among them.

They are prodigiously nimble from their infancy; however, I once caught a young male of three years old, and endeavoured by all marks of tenderness to make it quiet; but the little imp fell a squalling, and scratching, and biting with such violence, that I was forced to let it go; and it was high time, for a whole troop of old ones came about us at the noise, but find-ing the cub was safe (for away it ran), and my sorrel nag being by, they durst not venture near us. I ob-served the young animal's flesh to smell very rank, and the stink was somewhat between a weasel and a fox, but much more disagreeable. I forgot another cir-cumstance (and perhaps I might have the reader's par-don if it were wholly omitted), that while I held the odious vermin in my hands, it voided its filthy excre-ments of a yellow liquid substance, all over my clothes; but by good fortune there was a small brook hard by, where I washed myself as clean as I could; although I durst not come into my master's presence, until I were sufficiently aired.

But what I could discover, the *Yahoos* appear to be the most unteachable of all animals, their capacities never reaching higher than to draw or carry burdens. Yet I am of opinion, this defect ariseth chiefly from a perverse, restive disposition. For they are cunning, malicious, treacherous, and revengeful. They are strong and hardy, but of a cowardly spirit, and by con-sequence, insolent, abject, and cruel. It is observed, that the red-haired of both sexes are more libidinous and mischievous than the rest, whom yet they much exceed in strength and activity.

The *Houyhnhnms* keep the *Yahoos* for present use in huts not far from the house; but the rest are sent abroad to certain fields, where they dig up roots, eat several kinds of herbs, and search about for carrion, or sometimes catch weasels and *luhimuhs* (a sort of wild rat), which they greedily devour. Nature hath taught them to dig deep holes with their nails on the side of a rising ground, wherin they lie by themselves; only the kennels of the females are larger, sufficient to hold two or three cubs.

They swim from their infancy like frogs, and are able to continue long under water, where they often take fish, which the females carry home to their young. And upon this occasion, I hope the reader will pardon my relating an odd adventure.

Being one day abroad with my protector the sorrel nag, and the weather exceeding hot, I entreated him to let me bathe in a river that was near. He consented, and I immediately stripped myself stark naked, and went down softly into the stream. It happened that a young female *Yahoo*, standing behind a bank, saw the whole proceeding, and inflamed by desire, as the nag and I conjectured, came running with all speed, and leaped into the water, within five yards of the place where I bathed. I was never in my life so terribly frighted; the nag was grazing at some distance, not suspecting any harm. She embraced me after a most fulsome manner; I roared as loud as I could, and the nag came galloping towards me, whereupon she quit-ted her grasp, with the utmost reluctance, and leaped upon the opposite bank, where she stood gazing and howling all the time I was putting on my clothes.

This was matter of diversion to my master and his family, as well as of mortification to myself. For now I could no longer deny that I was a real *Yahoo* in every limb and feature, since the females had a natural pro-pensity to me, as one of their own species. Neither was the hair of this brute of a red colour (which might have been some excuse for an appetite a little irregular), but black as a sloe, and her countenance did not make an appearance altogether so hideous as the rest of the kind; for, I think, she could not be above eleven years old.

Having lived three years in this country, the reader I suppose will expect, that I should, like other travel-lers, give him some account of the manners and cus-toms of its inhabitants, which it was indeed my princi-pal study to learn.

As these noble *Houyhnhnms* are endowed by nature with a general disposition to all virtues, and have no conceptions or ideas of what is evil in a rational crea-ture, so their grand maxim is, to cultivate reason, and to be wholly governed by it. Neither is reason among them a point problematical as with us, where men can argue with plausibility on both sides of the question; but strikes you with immediate conviction; as it must needs do where it is not mingled, obscured, or discol-oured by passion and interest. I remember it was with extreme difficulty that I could bring my master to un-derstand the meaning of the word *opinion*, or how a point could be disputable; because reason taught us to affirm or deny only where we are certain; and beyond our knowledge we cannot do either. So that controversies, wranglings, disputes, and positiveness in false or dubious propositions, are evils unknown among the *Houyhnhnms*. In the like manner when I used to explain to him our several systems of natural philosophy, he would laugh that a creature pretending to reason, should value itself upon the knowledge of other people's conjectures, and in things, where that knowledge, if it were certain, could be of no use. Wherein he agreed entirely with the sentiments of Socrates, as Plato delivers them; which I mention as the highest honour I can do that prince of philosophers. I have often since reflected what destruction such a doctrine would make in the libraries of Europe; and how many paths to fame would be then shut up in the learned world.

Friendship and benevolence are the two principal virtues among the *Houyhnhnms;* and these not confined to particular objects, but universal to the whole race. For a stranger from the remotest part is equally treated with the nearest neighbour, and wherever he goes, looks upon himself as at home. They preserve decency and civility in the highest degrees, but are altogether ignorant of ceremony. They have no fondness for their colts or foals, but the care they take in educating them proceeds entirely from the dictates of reason. And I observed my master to show the same affection to his neighbour's issue that he had for his own. They will have it that nature teaches them to love the whole species, and it is reason only that maketh a distinction of persons, where there is a superior degree of virtue.

When the matron *Houyhnhnms* have produced one of each sex, they no longer accompany with their consorts, except they lose one of their issue by some casualty, which very seldom happens; but in such a case they meet again, or when the like accident befalls a person whose wife is past bearing, some other couple bestow him one of their own colts, and then go together again till the mother is pregnant. This caution is necessary to prevent the country from being overburthened with numbers. But the race of inferior *Houyhnhnms* bred up to be servants is not so strictly limited upon this article; these are allowed to produce three of each sex, to be domestics in the noble families.

In their marriages they are exactly careful to choose such colours as will not make any disagreeable mixture in the breed. Strength is chiefly valued in the male, and comeliness in the female; not upon the account of love, but to preserve the race from degenerating; for where a female happens to excel in strength, a consort is chosen with regard to comeliness. Courtship, love, presents, jointures,° settlements, have no place in their thoughts; or terms whereby to express them in their language. The young couple meet and are joined, merely because it is the determination of their parents and friends: it is what they see done every day, and they look upon it as one of the necessary actions of a reasonable being. But the violation of marriage, or any other unchastity, was never heard of: and the married pair pass their lives with the same friendship, and mutual benevolence that they bear to all others of the same species, who come in their way; without jealousy, fondness, quarrelling, or discontent.

In educating the youth of both sexes, their method is admirable, and highly deserves our imitation. These are not suffered to taste a grain of oats, except upon certain days, till eighteen years old; nor milk, but very rarely; and in summer they graze two hours in the morning, and as many in the evening, which their parents likewise observe: but the servants are not allowed above half that time, and a great part of their grass is brought home, which they eat at the most convenient hours, when they can be best spared from work.

Temperance, industry, exercise, and cleanliness, are the lessons equally enjoined to the young ones of both sexes: and my master thought it monstrous in us to give the females a different kind of education from the males, except in some articles of domestic management; whereby as he truly observed, one half of our natives were good for nothing but bringing children into the world: and to trust the care of our children to such useless animals, he said, was yet a greater instance of brutality.

But the *Houyhnhnms* train up their youth to strength, speed, and hardiness, by exercising them in running races up and down steep hills, and over hard stony grounds; and when they are all in a sweat, they are ordered to leap over head and ears into a pond or a river. Four times a year the youth of a certain district meet to show their proficiency in running and leaping, and other feats of strength and agility; where the victor is rewarded with a song made in his or her praise. On this festival the servants drive a herd of *Yahoos* into the field, laden with hay, and oats, and milk, for a repast to the *Houyhnhnms;* after which, these brutes are immediately driven back again, for fear of being noisome to the assembly.

Every fourth year, at the vernal equinox, there is a representative council of the whole nation, which meets in a plain about twenty miles from our house, and continues about five or six days. Here they enquire into the state and condition of the several districts; whether they abound or be deficient in hay or oats, or cows or *Yahoos*. And wherever there is any want (which is but seldom), it is immediately supplied by unanimous consent and contribution. Here likewise the regulation of children is settled: as for instance, if a *Houyhnhnm* hath two males, he changeth one of them with another that hath two females; and when a child hath been lost by any casualty, where the mother is past breeding, it is determined what family in the district shall breed another to supply the loss.

CHAPTER IX

A grand debate at the general assembly of the Houyhnhnms, *and how it was determined. The learning of the* Houyhnhnms. *Their buildings. Their manner of burials. The defectiveness of their language.*

One of these grand assemblies was held in my time, about three months before my departure, whither my master went as the representative of our district. In this council was resumed their old debate, and indeed, the only debate which ever happened in that country; whereof my master after his return gave me a very particular account.

The question to be debated was, whether the *Yahoos* should be exterminated from the face of the
10 earth. One of the members for the affirmative offered several arguments of great strength and weight, alleging, that as the *Yahoos* were the most filthy, noisome,° and deformed animal which nature ever produced, so they were the most restive and indocible, mischievous and malicious: they would privately suck the teats of the *Houyhnhnms*' cows, kill and devour their cats, trample down their oats and grass, if they were not continually watched, and commit a thousand other extravagancies. He took notice of a general tradition,
20 that *Yahoos* had not been always in that country; but, that many ages ago, two of these brutes appeared together upon a mountain; whether produced by the heat of the sun upon corrupted mud and slime, or from the ooze and froth of the sea, was never known. That these *Yahoos* engendered, and their brood in a short time grew so numerous as to over-run and infest the whole nation. That the *Houyhnhnms* to get rid of this evil, made a general hunting, and at last enclosed the whole herd; and destroying the elder, every *Houyhn-*
30 *hnm* kept two young ones in a kennel, and brought them to such a degree of tameness, as an animal so savage by nature can be capable of acquiring; using them for draught and carriage. That there seemed to be much truth in this tradition, and that those creatures could not be *Ylnhniamshy* (or *aborigines* of the land), because of the violent hatred the *Houyhnhnms*, as well as all other animals, bore them; which although their evil disposition sufficiently deserved, could never have arrived at so high a degree, if they had been
40 aborigines, or else they would have long since been rooted out. That the inhabitants taking a fancy to use the service of the *Yahoos*, had very imprudently neglected to cultivate the breed of asses, which were a comely animal, easily kept, more tame and orderly,

without any offensive smell, strong enough for labour, although they yield to the other in agility of body; and if their braying be no agreeable sound, it is far preferable to the horrible howlings of the *Yahoos*.

Several others declared their sentiments to the same purpose, when my master proposed an expedient to 50 the assembly, whereof he had indeed borrowed the hint from me. He approved of the tradition mentioned by the honourable member, who spoke before, and affirmed, that the two *Yahoos* said to be first seen among them, had been driven thither over the sea; that coming to land, and being forsaken by their companions, they retired to the mountains, and degenerating by degrees, became in process of time, much more savage than those of their own species in the country from whence these two originals came. The reason of 60 this assertion was, that he had now in his possession a certain wonderful *Yahoo* (meaning myself), which most of them had heard of, and many of them had seen. He then related to them, how he first found me; that my body was all covered with an artificial composure of the skins and hairs of other animals; that I spoke in a language of my own, and had thoroughly learned theirs: that I had related to him the accidents which brought me thither: that when he saw me without my covering, I was an exact *Yahoo* in ever part, 70 only of a whiter colour, less hairy, and with shorter claws. He added, how I had endeavoured to persuade him, that in my own and other countries the *Yahoos* acted as the governing, rational animal, and held the *Houyhnhnms* in servitude: that he observed in me all the qualities of a *Yahoo*, only a little more civilized by some tincture of reason, which however was in a degree as far inferior to the *Houyhnhnm* race, as the *Yahoos* of their country were to me: that, among other things, I mentioned a custom we had of castrating 80 *Houyhnhnms* when they were young, in order to render them tame; that the operation was easy and safe; that it was no shame to learn wisdom from brutes, as industry is taught by the ant, and building by the swallow. (For so I translate the word *lyhannh*, although it be a much larger fowl.) That this invention might be practised upon the younger *Yahoos* here, which, besides rendering them tractable and fitter for use, would in an age put an end to the whole species without destroying life. That in the mean time the 90 *Houyhnhnms* should be exhorted to cultivate the breed of asses, which, as they are in all respects more valuable brutes, so they have this advantage, to be fit for service at five years old, which the others are not till twelve.

This was all my master thought fit to tell me at that time, of what passed in the grand council. But he was pleased to conceal one particular, which related personally to myself, whereof I soon felt the unhappy effect, as the reader will know in its proper place, and 100 from whence I date all the succeeding misfortunes of my life.

Chapter IX   12 noisome, harmful

The *Houyhnhnms* have no letters, and consequently their knowledge is all traditional. But there happening few events of any moment among a people so well united, naturally disposed to every virtue, wholly governed by reason, and cut off from all commerce with other nations, the historical part is easily preserved without burthening their memories. I have already observed, that they are subject to no diseases, and therefore can have no need of physicians. However, they have excellent medicines composed of herbs, to cure accidental bruises and cuts in the pastern or frog of the foot by sharp stones, as well as other maims and hurts in the several parts of the body.

They calculate the year by the revolution of the sun and moon, but use no subdivision into weeks. They are well enough acquainted with the motions of those two luminaries, and understand the nature of eclipses; and this is the utmost progress of their astronomy.

In poetry they must be allowed to excel all other mortals; wherein the justness of their similes, and the minuteness, as well as exactness of their descriptions, are indeed inimitable. Their verses abound very much in both of these, and usually contain either some exalted notions of friendship and benevolence, or the praises of those who were victors in races, and other bodily exercises. Their buildings, although very rude and simple, are not inconvenient, but well contrived to defend them from all injuries of cold and heat. They have a kind of tree, which at forty years old loosens in the root, and falls with the first storm: it grows very straight, and being pointed like stakes with a sharp stone (for the *Houyhnhnms* know not the use of iron), they stick them erect in the ground about ten inches asunder, and then weave in oat-straw, or sometimes wattles betwixt them. The roof is made after the same manner, and so are the doors.

The *Houyhnhnms* use the hollow part between the pastern and the hoof of their fore-feet, as we do our hands, and this with greater dexterity than I could at first imagine. I have seen a white mare of our family thread a needle (which I lent her on purpose) with that joint. They milk their cows, reap their oats, and do all the work which requires hands, in the same manner. They have a kind of hard flints, which by grinding against other stones, they form into instruments, that serve instead of wedges, axes, and hammers. With tools made of these flints, they likewise cut their hay, and reap their oats, which there groweth naturally in several fields: the *Yahoos* draw home the sheaves in carriages, and the servants tread them in certain covered huts, to get out the grain, which is kept in stores. They make a rude kind of earthen and wooden vessels, and bake the former in the sun.

If they can avoid casualties, they die only of old age, and are buried in the obscurest places that can be found, their friends and relations expressing neither joy nor grief at their departure; nor does the dying person discover the least regret that he is leaving the world, any more than if he were upon returning home from a visit to one of his neighbours. I remember my master having once made an appointment with a friend and his family to come to his house upon some affair of importance; on the day fixed, the mistress and her two children came very late; she made two excuses, first for her husband, who, as she said, happened that very morning to *shnuwnh*. The word is strongly expressive in their language, but not easily rendered into English; it signifies, *to retire to his first mother*. Her excuse for not coming sooner was, that her husband dying late in the morning, she was a good while consulting her servants about a convenient place where his body should be laid; and I observed she behaved herself at our house as cheerfully as the rest. She died about three months after.

They live generally to seventy or seventy-five years, very seldom to fourscore: some weeks before their death they feel a gradual decay, but without pain. During this time they are much visited by their friends, because they cannot go abroad with their usual ease and satisfaction. However, about ten days before their death, which they seldom fail in computing, they return the visits that have been made them by those who are nearest in the neighbourhood, being carried in a convenient sledge drawn by *Yahoos;* which vehicle they use, not only upon this occasion, but when they grow old, upon long journeys, or when they are lamed by any accident. And therefore when the dying *Houyhnhnms* return those visits, they take a solemn leave of their friends, as if they were going to some remote part of the country, where they designed to pass the rest of their lives.

I know not whether it may be worth observing, that the *Houyhnhnms* have no word in their language to express any thing that is evil, except what they borrow from the deformities or ill qualities of the *Yahoos*. Thus they denote the folly of a servant, an omission of a child, a stone that cuts their feet, a continuance of foul or unseasonable weather, and the like, by adding to each the epithet of *Yahoo*. For instance, *Hhnm Yahoo, Whnaholm Yahoo, Ynlhmndwihlma Yahoo,* and an ill-contrived house *Ynholmhnmrohlnw Yahoo.*

I could with great pleasure enlarge further upon the manners and virtues of this excellent people; but intending in a short time to publish a volume by itself expressly upon that subject, I refer the reader thither. And in the mean time, proceed to relate my own sad catastrophe.

CHAPTER X

The Author's economy, and happy life among the Houyhnhnms. *His great improvement in virtue, by conversing with them. Their conversations. The Author has notice given him by his master that he must depart from the country. He falls into a swoon for grief, but submits. He contrives and finishes a canoe, by the help of a fellow-servant, and puts to sea at a venture.*

I had settled my little economy to my own heart's content. My master had ordered a room to be made for me after their manner, about six yards from the house; the sides and floors of which I plastered with clay, and covered with rush-mats of my own contriving; I had beaten hemp, which there grows wild, and made of it a sort of ticking: this I filled with the feathers of several birds I had taken with springs made of *Yahoos'* hairs, and were excellent food. I had worked two chairs with my knife, the sorrel nag helping me in the grosser and more laborious part. When my clothes were worn to rags, I made myself others with the skins of rabbits, and of a certain beautiful animal about the same size, called *nnuhnoh,* the skin of which is covered with a fine down. Of these I likewise made very tolerable stockings. I soled my shoes with wood which I cut from a tree, and fitted to the upper leather, and when this was worn out, I supplied it with the skins of *Yahoos* dried in the sun. I often got honey out of hollow trees, which I mingled with water, or eat with my bread. No man could more verify the truth of these two maxims, *That nature is very easily satisfied;* and *That necessity is the mother of invention.* I enjoyed perfect health of body, and tranquillity of mind; I did not feel the treachery of inconstancy of a friend, nor the injuries of a secret or open enemy. I had no occasion of bribing, flattering or pimping, to procure the favour of any great man or of his minion. I wanted no fence against fraud or oppression; here was neither physician to destroy my body, nor lawyer to ruin my fortune; no informer to watch my words and actions, or forge accusations against me for hire: here were no gibers, censurers, backbiters, pickpockets, highwaymen, housebreakers, attorneys, bawds, buffoons, gamesters, politicians, wits, splenetics, tedious talkers, controvertists, ravishers, murderers, robbers, virtuosos; no leaders or followers of party and faction; no encouragers to vice, by seducement or examples; no dungeon, axes, gibbets, whipping-posts, or pillories; no cheating shopkeepers or mechanics; no pride, vanity, or affectation; no fops, bullies, drunkards, strolling whores, or poxes; no ranting, lewd, expensive wives; no stupid, proud pedants; no importunate, overbearing, quarrelsome, noisy, roaring, empty, conceited, swearing companions; no scoundrels, raised from the dust for the sake of their vices, or nobility thrown into it on account of their virtues; no lords, fiddlers, judges, or dancing-masters.

I had the favour of being admitted to several *Houyhnhnms* who came to visit or dine with my master; where his Honour graciously suffered me to wait in the room, and listen to their discourse. Both he and his company would often descend to ask me questions, and receive my answers. I had also sometimes the honour of attending my master in his visits to others. I never presumed to speak, except in answer to a question; and then I did it with inward regret, because it was a loss of so much time for improving myself: but I was infinitely delighted with the station of an humble auditor in such conversations, where nothing passed but what was useful, expressed in the fewest and most significant words; where (as I have already said) the greatest decency was observed, without the least degree of ceremony; where no person spoke without being pleased himself, and pleasing his companions; where there was no interruption, tediousness, heat, or difference of sentiments. They have a notion, that when people are met together, a short silence doth much improve conversation: this I found to be true; for during those little intermissions of talk, new ideas would arise in their thoughts, which very much enlivened the discourse. Their subjects are generally on friendship and benevolence, or order and economy; sometimes upon the visible operations of nature, or ancient traditions; upon the bounds and limits of virtue; upon the unerring rules of reason, or upon some determinations to be taken at the next great assembly; and often upon the various excellencies of poetry. I may add, without vanity, that my presence often gave them sufficient matter for discourse, because it afforded my master an occasion of letting his friends into the history of me and my country, upon which they were all pleased to descant in a manner not very advantageous to human kind; and for that reason I shall not repeat what they said: only I may be allowed to observe, that his Honour, to my great admiration, appeared to understand the nature of *Yahoos* much better than myself. He went through all our vices and follies, and discovered many which I had never mentioned to him, by only supposing what qualities a *Yahoo* of their country, with a small proportion of reason, might be capable of exerting; and concluded, with too much probability, how vile as well as miserable such a creature must be.

I freely confess, that all the little knowledge I have of any value, was acquired by the lectures I received from my master, and from hearing the discourses of him and his friends; to which I should be prouder to listen, than to dictate to the greatest and wisest assembly in Europe. I admired the strength, comeliness, and speed of the inhabitants; and such a constellation of virtues in such amiable persons produced in me the highest veneration. At first, indeed, I did not feel that natural awe which the *Yahoos* and all other animals bear towards them; but it grew upon me by degrees, much sooner than I imagined, and was mingled with a respectful love and gratitude, that they would condescend to distinguish me from the rest of my species.

When I thought of my family, my friends, my countrymen, or human race in general, I considered them as they really were, *Yahoos* in shape and disposition, perhaps a little more civilized, and qualified with the gift of speech, but making no other use of reason, than to improve and multiply those vices, whereof their brethren in this country had only the share that nature allotted them. When I happened to behold the reflection of my own form in a lake or fountain, I turned away my face in horror and detestation of myself, and could better endure the sight of a common *Yahoo,* than of my own person. By conversing with the *Houyhnhnms,* and looking upon them with delight, I fell to imitate their gait and gesture, which is now grown into a habit, and my friends often tell me in a blunt way, that *I trot like a horse;* which, however, I take for a great compliment. Neither shall I disown, that in speaking I am apt to fall into the voice and manner of the *Houyhnhnms,* and hear myself ridiculed on that account without the least mortification.

In the midst of all this happiness, and when I looked upon myself to be fully settled for life, my master sent for me one morning a little earlier than his usual hour. I observed by his countenance that he was in some perplexity, and at a loss how to begin what he had to speak. After a short silence, he told me, he did not know how I would take what he was going to say; that in the last general assembly, when the affair of the *Yahoos* was entered upon, the representatives had taken offence at his keeping a *Yahoo* (meaning myself) in his family more like a *Houyhnhnm* than a brute animal. That he was known frequently to converse with me, as if he could receive some advantage or pleasure in my company; that such a practice was not agreeable to reason or nature, or a thing ever heard of before among them. The assembly did therefore exhort him, either to employ me like the rest of my species, or command me to swim back to the place from whence I came. That the first of these expedients was utterly rejected by all the *Houyhnhnms* who had ever seen me at his house or their own: for they alleged, that because I had some rudiments of reason, added to the natural pravity of those animals, it was to be feared, I might be able to seduce them into the woody and mountainous parts of the country, and bring them in troops by night to destroy the *Houyhnhnms'* cattle, as being naturally of the ravenous kind, and averse from labour.

My master added, that he was daily pressed by the *Houyhnhnms* of the neighbourhood to have the assembly's exhortation executed, which he could not put off much longer. He doubted it would be impossible for me to swim to another country, and therefore wished I would contrive some sort of vehicle resembling those I had described to him, that might carry me on the sea; in which work I should have the assistance of his own servants, as well as those of his neighbours. He concluded, that for his own part, he could have been content to keep me in his service as long as I lived; because he found I had cured myself of some bad habits and dispositions, by endeavouring, as far as my inferior nature was capable, to imitate the *Houyhnhnms.*

I should here observe to the reader, that a decree of the general assembly in this country is expressed by the word *hnheoayn,* which signifies an exhortation, as near as I can render it; for they have no conception how a rational creature can be compelled, but only advised, or exhorted; because no person can disobey reason, without giving up his claim to be a rational creature.

I was struck with the utmost grief and despair at my master's discourse; and being unable to support the agonies I was under, I fell into a swoon at his feet; when I came to myself, he told me, that he concluded that I had been dead (for these people are subject to no such imbecilities of nature). I answered, in a faint voice, that death would have been too great an happiness; that although I could not blame the assembly's exhortation, or the urgency of his friends; yet, in my weak and corrupt judgment, I thought it might consist with reason to have been less rigorous. That I could not swim a league, and probably the nearest land to theirs might be distant above an hundred: that many materials, necessary for making a small vessel to carry me off, were wholly wanting in this country, which, however, I would attempt in obedience and gratitude to his Honour, although I concluded the thing to be impossible, and therefore looked on myself as already devoted to destruction. That the certain prospect of an unnatural death was the least of my evils: for, supposing I should escape with life by some strange adventure, how could I think with temper of passing my days among *Yahoos,* and relapsing into my old corruptions, for want of examples to lead and keep me within the paths of virtue. That I knew too well upon what solid reasons all the determinations of the wise *Houyhnhnms* were founded, not to be shaken by arguments of mine, a miserable *Yahoo;* and therefore, after presenting him with my humble thanks for the offer of his servants' assistance in making a vessel, and desiring a reasonable time for so difficult a work, I told him I would endeavour to preserve a wretched being; and, if ever I returned to England, as not without hopes of being useful to my own species, by celebrating the praises of the renowned *Houyhnhnms,* and proposing their virtues to the imitation of mankind.

My master in a few words made me a very gracious reply, allowed me the space of two months to finish my boat; and ordered the sorrel nag, my fellow-servant (for so at this distance I may presume to call him) to follow my instructions, because I told my master, that his help would be sufficient, and I knew he had a tenderness for me.

In his company my first business was to go to that part of the coast where my rebellious crew had ordered

me to be set on shore. I got upon a height, and looking on every side into the sea, fancied I saw a small island, towards the north-east: I took out my pocket-glass, and could then clearly distinguish it about five leagues off, as I computed; but it appeared to the sorrel nag to
230 be only a blue cloud: for, as he had no conception of any country beside his own, so he could not be as expert in distinguishing remote objects at sea, as we who so much converse in that element.

After I had discovered this island, I considered no farther; but resolved it should, if possible, be the first place of my banishment, leaving the consequence to fortune.

I returned home, and consulting with the sorrel nag, we went into a copse at some distance, where I with
240 my knife, and he with a sharp flint fastened very artificially, after their manner, to a wooden handle, cut down several oak wattles about the thickness of a walking-staff, and some larger pieces. But I shall not trouble the reader with a particular description of my own mechanics; let it suffice to say, that in six weeks time, with the help of the sorrel nag, who performed the parts that required most labour, I finished a sort of Indian canoe, but much larger, covering it with the skins of *Yahoos* well stitched together, with hempen
250 threads of my own making. My sail was likewise composed of the skins of the same animal; but I made use of the youngest I could get, the older being too tough and thick; and I likewise provided myself with four paddles. I laid in a stock of boiled flesh, of rabbits and fowls, and took with me two vessels, one filled with milk, and the other with water.

I tried my canoe in a large pond near my master's house, and then corrected in it what was amiss; stopping all the chinks with *Yahoos'* tallow, till I found it
260 staunch, and able to bear me, and my freight. And when it was as complete as I could possibly make it, I had it drawn on a carriage very gently by *Yahoos* to the seaside, under the conduct of the sorrel nag, and another servant.

When all was ready, and the day came for my departure, I took leave of my master and lady, and the whole family, my eyes flowing with tears, and my heart quite sunk with grief. But his Honour, out of curiosity, and, perhaps (if I may speak it without van-
270 ity) partly out of kindness, was determined to see me in my canoe, and got several of his neighbouring friends to accompany him. I was forced to wait above an hour for the tide, and then observing the wind very fortunately bearing towards the island, to which I intended to steer my course, I took a second leave of my master: but as I was going to prostrate myself to kiss his hoof, he did me the honour to raise it gently to my mouth. I am not ignorant how much I have been censured for mentioning this last particular. For my de-
280 tractors are pleased to think it improbable, that so illustrious a person should descend to give so great a mark of distinction to a creature so inferior as I.

Neither have I forgot, how apt some travellers are to boast of extraordinary favours they have received. But if these censurers were better acquainted with the noble and courteous disposition of the *Houyhnhnms,* they would soon change their opinion.

I paid my respects to the rest of the *Houyhnhnms* in his Honour's company; then getting into my canoe, I pushed off from shore. 290

CHAPTER XI

The Author's dangerous voyage. He arrives at New Holland, *hoping to settle there. Is wounded with an arrow by one of the natives. Is seized and carried by force into a* Portuguese *ship. The great civilities of the Captain. The Author arrives at* England.

I began this desperate voyage on February 15, 1714–15, at 9 o'clock in the morning. The wind was very favourable; however, I made use at first only of my paddles; but considering I should soon be weary, and that the wind might chop about, I ventured to set up my little sail; and thus, with the help of the tide, I went at the rate of a league and a half an hour, as near as I could guess. My master and his friends continued on the shore, till I was almost out of sight; and I often heard the sorrel nag (who always loved me) crying out, 10 *Hnuy illa nyha majah Yahoo,* Take care of thyself, gentle *Yahoo.*

My design was, if possible, to discover some small island uninhabited, yet sufficient by my labour to furnish me with the necessaries of life, which I would have thought a greater happiness than to be first minister in the politest court of Europe; so horrible was the idea I conceived of returning to live in the society and under the government of *Yahoos.* For in such a solitude as I desired, I could at least enjoy my 20 own thoughts, and reflect with delight on the virtues of those inimitable *Houyhnhnms,* without any opportunity of degenerating into the vices and corruptions of my own species.

The reader may remember what I related when my crew conspired against me, and confined me to my cabin. How I continued there several weeks, without knowing what course we took; and when I was put ashore in the long boat, how the sailors told me with oaths, whether true or false, that they knew not in what 30 part of the world we were. However, I did then believe us to be about ten degrees southward of the Cape of Good Hope, or about forty-five degrees southern latitude, as I gathered from some general words I overheard among them, being I supposed to the south-east in their intended voyage to Madagascar. And although this were little better than conjecture, yet I resolved to steer my course eastward, hoping to reach the southwest coast of New Holland, and perhaps some such island as I desired, lying westward of it. The wind was full west, and by six in the evening I computed I had gone eastward at least eighteen leagues, when I spied a very small island about half a league off, which I soon reached. It was nothing but a rock with one creek, naturally arched by the force of tempests. Here I put in my canoe, and climbing up a part of the rock, I could plainly discover land to the east, extending from south to north. I lay all night in my canoe; and repeating my voyage early in the morning, I arrived in seven hours to the south-east point of New Holland. This confirmed me in the opinion I have long entertained, that the maps and charts place this country at least three degrees more to the east than it really is; which thought I communicated many years ago to my worthy friend Mr. Herman Moll, and gave him my reasons for it, although he hath rather chosen to follow other authors.

I saw no inhabitants in the place where I landed, and being unarmed, I was afraid of venturing far into the country. I found some shellfish on the shore, and eat them raw, not daring to kindle a fire, for fear of being discovered by the natives. I continued three days feeding on oysters and limpets, to save my own provisions; and I fortunately found a brook of excellent water, which gave me great relief.

On the fourth day, venturing out early a little too far, I saw twenty or thirty natives upon a height, not above five hundred yards from me. They were stark naked, men, women, and children round a fire, as I could discover by the smoke. One of them spied me, and gave notice to the rest; five of them advanced towards me, leaving the women and children at the fire. I made what haste I could to the shore, and getting into my canoe shoved off: the savages observing me retreat, ran after me; and before I could get far enough into the sea, discharged an arrow, which wounded me deeply on the inside of my left knee (I shall carry the mark to my grave). I apprehended the arrow might be poisoned, and paddling out of the reach of their darts (being a calm day), I made a shift to suck the wound, and dress it as well as I could.

I was at a loss what to do, for I durst not return to the same landing-place, but stood to the north, and was forced to paddle; for the wind, though very gentle, was against me, blowing north-west. As I was looking about for a secure landing-place, I saw a sail to the north-north-east, which appearing every minute more visible, I was in some doubt whether I should wait for them or no; but at last my detestation of the *Yahoo* race prevailed, and turning my canoe, I sailed and paddled together to the south, and got into the same creek from whence I set out in the morning, choosing rather to trust myself among these barbarians, than live with European *Yahoos*. I drew up my canoe as close as I could to the shore, and hid myself behind a stone by the little brook, which, as I have already said, was excellent water.

The ship came within half a league of this creek, and sent her long boat with vessels to take in fresh water (for the place it seems was very well known), but I did not observe it till the boat was almost on shore, and it was too late to seek another hiding-place. The seamen at their landing observed my canoe, and rummaging it all over, easily conjectured that the owner could not be far off. Four of them well armed searched every cranny and lurking-hole, till at last they found me flat on my face behind the stone. They gazed awhile in admiration at my strange uncouth dress; my coat made of skins, my wooden-soled shoes, and my furred stockings; from whence, however, they concluded I was not a native of the place, who all go naked. One of the seamen in Portuguese bid me rise, and asked who I was. I understood that language very well, and getting upon my feet, said, I was a poor *Yahoo*, banished from the *Houyhnhnms*, and desired they would please to let me depart. They admired to hear me answer them in their own tongue, and saw by my complexion I must be an European; but were at a loss to know what I mean by *Yahoos* and *Houyhnhnms*, and at the same time fell a laughing at my strange tone in speaking, which resembled the neighing of a horse. I trembled all the while betwixt fear and hatred. I again desired leave to depart, and was gently moving to my canoe; but they laid hold of me, desiring to know, what country I was of? whence I came? with many other questions. I told them, I was born in England, from whence I came about five years ago, and then their country and ours were at peace. I therefore hoped they would not treat me as an enemy, since I meant them no harm, but was a poor *Yahoo*, seeking some desolate place where to pass the remainder of his unfortunate life.

When they began to talk, I thought I never heard or saw any thing so unnatural; for it appeared to me as monstrous as if a dog or cow should speak in England, or a *Yahoo* in *Houyhnhnm-land*. The honest Portuguese were equally amazed at my strange dress, and the odd manner of delivering my words, which however they understood very well. They spoke to me with great humanity, and said they were sure their Captain would carry me *gratis* to Lisbon, from whence I might return to my own country; that two of the seamen would go back to the ship, inform the Captain of what they had seen, and receive his orders; in the mean time, unless I would give my solemn oath not to fly, they would secure me by force. I thought it best to comply with their proposal. They were very curious to know my story, but I gave them very little satisfaction; and they all conjectured that my misfortunes had impaired my reason. In two hours the boat, which went loaden with vessels of water, returned with the Captain's command to fetch me on board. I fell on my knees to preserve my liberty; but all was in vain, and the men having tied me with cords, heaved me into the boat, from whence I was taken into the ship, and from thence into the Captain's cabin.

His name was Pedro de Mendez; he was a very courteous and generous person; he entreated me to give some account of myself, and desired to know what I would eat or drink; said, I should be used as well as himself, and spoke so many obliging things, that I wondered to find such civilities from a *Yahoo.* However, I remained silent and sullen; I was ready to faint at the very smell of him and his men. At last I desired something to eat out of my own canoe; but he ordered me a chicken and some excellent wine, and then directed that I should be put to bed in a very clean cabin. I would not undress myself, but lay on the bedclothes, and in half an hour stole out, when I thought the crew was at dinner, and getting to the side of the ship was going to leap into the sea, and swim for my life, rather than continue among *Yahoos.* But one of the seamen prevented me, and having informed the Captain, I was chained to my cabin.

After dinner Don Pedro came to me, and desired to know my reason for so desperate an attempt; assured me he only meant to do me all the service he was able; and spoke so very movingly, that at last I descended to treat him like an animal which had some little portion of reason. I gave him a very short relation of my voyage; of the conspiracy against me by my own men; of the country where they set me on shore, and of my three years' residence there. All which he looked upon as if it were a dream or a vision; whereat I took great offence; for I had quite forgot the faculty of lying, so peculiar to *Yahoos* in all countries where they preside, and, consequently the disposition of suspecting truth in others of their own species. I asked him, whether it were the custom in his country to *say the thing that was not?* I assured him I had almost forgot what he meant by falsehood, and if I had lived a thousand years in *Houyhnhnm-land,* I should never have heard a lie from the meanest servant; that I was altogether indifferent whether he believed me or no; but however, in return for his favours, I would give so much allowance to the corruption of his nature, as to answer any objection he would please to make, and then he might easily discover the truth.

The Captain, a wise man, after many endeavours to catch me tripping in some part of my story, at last began to have a better opinion of my veracity. But he added, that since I professed so inviolable an attachment to truth, I must give him my word of honour to bear him company in this voyage, without attempting any thing against my life, or else he would continue me a prisoner till we arrived at Lisbon. I gave him the promise he required; but at the same time protested that I would suffer the greatest hardships rather than return to live among *Yahoos.*

Our voyage passed without any considerable accident. In gratitude to the Captain I sometimes sat with him at his earnest request, and strove to conceal my antipathy to human kind, although it often broke out, which he suffered to pass without observation. But the greatest part of the day, I confined myself to my cabin, to avoid seeing any of the crew. The Captain had often entreated me to strip myself of my savage dress, and offered to lend me the best suit of clothes he had. This I would not be prevailed on to accept, abhorring to cover myself with any thing that had been on the back of a *Yahoo.* I only desired he would lend me two clean shirts, which having been washed since he wore them, I believed would not so much defile me. These I changed every second day, and washed them myself.

We arrived at Lisbon, Nov. 5, 1715. At our landing the Captain forced me to cover myself with his cloak, to prevent the rabble from crowding about me. I was conveyed to his own house, and at my earnest request, he led me up to the highest room backwards. I conjured him to conceal from all persons what I had told him of the *Houyhnhnms,* because the least hint of such a story would not only draw numbers of people to see me, but probably put me in danger of being imprisoned, or burnt by the Inquisition. The Captain persuaded me to accept a suit of clothes newly made; but I would not suffer the tailor to take my measure; however, Don Pedro being almost my size, they fitted me well enough. He accoutred me with other necessaries all new, which I aired for twenty-four hours before I would use them.

The Captain had no wife, nor above three servants, none of which were suffered to attend at meals, and his whole deportment was so obliging, added to very good *human* understanding, that I really began to tolerate his company. He gained so far upon me, that I ventured to look out of the back window. By degrees I was brought into another room, from whence I peeped into the street, but drew my head back in a fright. In a week's time he seduced me down to the door. I found my terror gradually lessened, but my hatred and contempt seemed to increase. I was at last bold enough to walk the street in his company, but kept my nose well stopped with rue, or sometimes with tobacco.

In ten days, Don Pedro, to whom I had given some account of my domestic affairs, put it upon me as a matter of honour and conscience, that I ought to return to my native country, and live at home with my wife and children. He told me, there was an English ship in the port just ready to sail, and he would furnish me with all things necessary. It would be tedious to repeat his arguments, and my contradictions. He said it was altogether impossible to find such a solitary island as I desired to live in; but I might command in my own house, and pass my time in a manner as recluse as I pleased.

I complied at last, finding I could not do better. I left Lisbon the 24th day of November, in an English merchantman, but who was the master I never inquired. Don Pedro accompanied me to the ship, and lent me twenty pounds. He took kind leave of me, and embraced me at parting which I bore as well as I could. During this last voyage I had no commerce with the master or any of his men; but pretending I was sick, kept close in my cabin. On the fifth of December, 1715, we cast anchor in the Downs about nine in the morning, and at three in the afternoon I got safe to my house at Rotherhith.

My wife and family received me with great surprise and joy, because they concluded me certainly dead; but I must freely confess the sight of them filled me 280 only with hatred, disgust, and contempt, and the more by reflecting on the near alliance I had to them. For, although since my unfortunate exile from the *Houyhnhnm* country, I had compelled myself to tolerate the sight of *Yahoos*, and to converse with Don Pedro de Mendez; yet my memory and imagination were perpetually filled with the virtues and ideas of those exalted *Houyhnhnms*. And when I began to consider, that by copulating with one of the *Yahoo* species I had become a parent of more, it struck me with the utmost 290 shame, confusion, and horror.

As soon as I entered the house, my wife took me in her arms, and kissed me; at which, having not been used to the touch of that odious animal for so many years, I fell in a swoon for almost an hour. At the time I am writing it is five years since my last return to England: during the first year, I could not endure my wife or children in my presence, the very smell of them was intolerable; much less could I suffer them to eat in the same room. To this hour they dare not presume to 300 touch my bread, or drink out of the same cup, neither was I ever able to let one of them take me by the hand. The first money I laid out was to buy two young stonehorses,³ which I keep in a good stable, and next to them the groom is my greatest favourite; for I feel my spirits revived by the smell he contracts in the stable. My horses understand me tolerably well; I converse with them at least four hours every day. They are strangers to bridle or saddle; they live in great amity with me, and friendship to each other.

CHAPTER XII

The Author's veracity. His design in publishing this work. His censure of those travellers who swerve from the truth. The Author clears himself from any sinister ends in writing. An objection answered. The method of planting colonies. His native country commended. The right of the Crown to those countries described by the Author, is justified. The difficulty of conquering them. The Author takes his last leave of the reader; proposeth his manner of living for the future, gives good advice, and concludes.

Thus, gentle reader, I have given thee a faithful history of my travels for sixteen years and above seven months; wherein I have not been so studious of ornament as truth. I could perhaps like others have astonished thee with strange improbable tales; but I rather chose to relate plain matter of fact in the simplest manner and style; because my principal design was to inform, and not to amuse thee.

It is easy for us who travel into remote countries, which are seldom visited by Englishmen or other 10 Europeans, to form descriptions of wonderful animals both at sea and land. Whereas a traveller's chief aim should be to make men wiser and better, and to improve their minds by the bad as well as good example of what they deliver concerning foreign places.

I could heartily wish a law was enacted, that every traveller, before he were permitted to publish his voyages, should be obliged to make oath before the Lord High Chancellor that all he intended to print was absolutely true to the best of his knowledge; for then the 20 world would no longer be deceived as it usually is, while some writers, to make their works pass the better upon the public, impose the grossest falsities on the unwary reader. I have perused several books of travels with great delight in my younger days; but having since gone over most parts of the globe, and been able to contradict many fabulous accounts from my own observation, it hath given me a great disgust against this part of reading, and some indignation to see the credulity of mankind so impudently abused. 30 Therefore since my acquaintance were pleased to think my poor endeavours might not be unacceptable to my country, I imposed on myself as a maxim, never to be swerved from, that I would *strictly adhere to truth;* neither indeed can I be ever under the least temptation to vary from it, while I retain in my mind the lectures and example of my noble master, and the other illustrious *Houyhnhnms,* of whom I had so long the honour to be an humble hearer.

Nec si miserum Fortuna Sinonem 40
Finxit, vanum etiam, mendacemque improba finget.°

I know very well how little reputation is to be got by writings which require neither genius nor learning, nor indeed any other talent, except a good memory, or an exact journal. I know likewise, that writers of travels, like dictionary-makers, are sunk into oblivion by the weight and bulk of those who come after, and therefore lie uppermost. And it is highly probable, that such travellers who shall hereafter visit the countries described in this work of mine, may, by detecting my 50 errors (if there be any), and adding many new discoveries of their own, justle me out of vogue, and stand in my place, making the world forget that I was ever an author. This indeed would be too great a mortification if I wrote for fame: but, as my sole intention was the PUBLIC GOOD, I cannot be altogether disap-

Chapter XI 303 **stonehorses,** stallions, uncastrated male horses

Chapter XII 40–41 **Nec si . . . finget,** "Nor if base fortune has made Sinon wretched, will she also make him deceitful and false" (Vergil, *Aeneid,* II, 79–80)

pointed. For who can read of the virtues I have mentioned in the glorious *Houyhnhnms,* without being ashamed of his own vices, when he considers himself
60 as the reasoning, governing animal of his country? I shall say nothing of those remote nations where *Yahoos* preside; amongst which the least corrupted are the *Brobdingnagians,* whose wise maxims in morality and government it would be our happiness to observe. But I forbear descanting farther, and rather leave the judicious reader to his own remarks and applications.

I am not a little pleased that this work of mine can possibly meet with no censurers: for what objections can be made against a writer who relates only plain
70 facts that happened in such distant countries, where we have not the least interest with respect either to trade or negotiations? I have carefully avoided every fault with which common writers of travels are often too justly charged. Besides, I meddle not the least with any party, but write without passion, prejudice, or ill-will against any man or number of men whatsoever. I write for the noblest end, to inform and instruct mankind, over whom I may, without breach of modesty, pretend to some superiority, from the advantages I
80 received by conversing so long among the most accomplished *Houyhnhnms.* I write without any view towards profit or praise. I never suffer a word to pass that may look like reflection, or possibly give the least offence even to those who are most ready to take it. So that I hope I may with justice pronounce myself an author perfectly blameless, against whom the tribes of answerers, considerers, observers, reflecters, detecters, remarkers, will never be able to find matter for exercising their talents.
90 I confess, it was whispered to me, that I was bound in duty as a subject of England, to have given in a memorial to a Secretary of State, at my first coming over; because, whatever lands are discovered by a subject, belong to the Crown. But I doubt whether our conquests in the countries I treat of, would be as easy as those of Ferdinando Cortez over the naked Americans. The *Lilliputians* I think, are hardly worth the charge of a fleet and army to reduce them; and I question whether it might be prudent or safe to attempt the
100 *Brobdingnagians;* or whether an English army would be much at their ease with the Flying Island over their heads. The *Houyhnhnms,* indeed, appear not to be so well prepared for war, a science to which they are perfect strangers, and especially against missive weapons. However, supposing myself to be a minister of state, I could never give my advice for invading them. Their prudence, unanimity, unacquaintedness with fear, and their love of their country, would amply supply all defects in the military art. Imagine twenty
110 thousand of them breaking into the midst of an European army, confounding the ranks, overturning the carriages, battering the warriors' faces into mummy° by terrible yerks from their hinder hoofs; for they would well deserve the character given to Augustus: *Recalcitrat undique tutus.*° But instead of proposals for conquering that magnanimous nation, I rather wish they were in a capacity or disposition to send a sufficient number of their inhabitants for civilizing Europe, by teaching us the first principles of honour, justice, truth, temperance, public spirit, fortitude, chastity, 120 friendship, benevolence, and fidelity. The names of all which virtues are still retained among us in most languages and are to be met with in modern as well as ancient authors; which I am able to assert from my own small reading.

But I had another reason which made me less forward to enlarge his Majesty's dominions by my discoveries. To say the truth, I had conceived a few scruples with relation to the distributive justice of princes upon these occasions. For instance, a crew of pirates are driven 130 by a storm they know not whither; at length a boy discovers land from the topmast; they go on shore to rob and plunder; they see an harmless people, are entertained with kindness, they give the country a new name, they take formal possession of it for their king, they set up a rotten plank or a stone for a memorial, they murder two or three dozen of the natives, bring away a couple more by force for a sample, return home, and get their pardon. Here commences a new dominion acquired with a title by *divine right.* Ships 140 are sent with the first opportunity; the natives driven out or destroyed, their princes tortured to discover their gold; a free licence given to all acts of inhumanity and lust, the earth reeking with the blood of its inhabitants: and this execrable crew of butchers employed in so pious an expedition, is a *modern colony* sent to convert and civilize an idolatrous and barbarous people.

But this description, I confess, doth by no means affect the British nation, who may be an example to 150 the whole world for their wisdom, care, and justice in planting colonies; their liberal endowments for the advancement of religion and learning; their choice of devout and able pastors to propagate Christianity; their caution in stocking their provinces with people of sober lives and conversations from this the mother kingdom; their strict regard to the distribution of justice, in supplying the civil administration through all their colonies with officers of the greatest abilities, utter strangers to corruption; and to crown all, by send- 160 ing the most vigilant and virtuous governors, who have no other views than the happiness of the people over whom they preside, and the honour of the King their master.

112 **mummy,** a gummy mass   114–15 **Recalcitrat undique tutus,** "He kicks backward, on guard everywhere" (Horace, *Satires,* II, i, 20)

But, as those countries which I have described do not appear to have any desire of being conquered, and enslaved, murdered or driven out by colonies; nor abound either in gold, silver, sugar, or tobacco; I did humbly conceive, they were by no means proper objects of our zeal, our valour, or our interest. However, if those whom it more concerns think fit to be of another opinion, I am ready to depose, when I shall be lawfully called, that no European did ever visit these countries before me. I mean, if the inhabitants ought to be believed; unless a dispute may arise about the two *Yahoos*, said to have been seen many ages ago on a mountain in *Houyhnhnm-land*.

But, as to the formality of taking possession in my Sovereign's name, it never came once into my thoughts; and if it had, yet as my affairs then stood, I should perhaps in point of prudence and self-preservation, have put it off to a better opportunity.

Having thus answered the only objection that can ever be raised against me as a traveller, I here take a final leave of all my courteous readers, and return to enjoy my own speculations in my little garden at Redriff, to apply those excellent lessons of virtue which I learned among the *Houyhnhnms*; to instruct the *Yahoos* of my own family as far as I shall find them docible animals; to behold my figure often in a glass, and thus if possible habituate myself by time to tolerate the sight of a human creature: to lament the brutality of *Houyhnhnms* in my own country, but always treat their persons with respect, for the sake of my noble master, his family, his friends, and the whole *Houyhnhnm* race, whom these of ours have the honour to resemble in all their lineaments, however their intellectuals came to degenerate.

I began last week to permit my wife to sit at dinner with me, at the farthest end of a long table; and to answer (but with the utmost brevity) the few questions I asked her. Yet the smell of a *Yahoo* continuing very offensive, I always keep my nose well stopped with rue, lavender, or tobacco leaves. And although it be hard for a man late in life to remove old habits, I am not altogether out of hopes in some time to suffer a neighbour *Yahoo* in my company, without the apprehensions I am yet under of his teeth or his claws.

My reconcilement to the *Yahoo*-kind in general might not be so difficult, if they would be content with those vices and follies only which nature hath entitled them to. I am not in the least provoked at the sight of a lawyer, a pickpocket, a colonel, a fool, a lord, a gamester, a politician, a whore-master, a physician, an evidence, a suborner, an attorney, a traitor, or the like; this is all according to the due course of things: but when I behold a lump of deformity, and diseases both in body and mind, smitten with *pride*, it immediately breaks all the measures of my patience; neither shall I be ever able to comprehend how such an animal and such a vice could tally together. The wise and virtuous *Houyhnhnms*, who abound in all excellencies that can adorn a rational creature, have no name for this vice in their language, which hath no terms to express any thing that is evil, except those whereby they describe the detestable qualities of their *Yahoos*, among which they were not able to distinguish this of pride, for want of thoroughly understanding human nature, as it showeth itself in other countries, where that animal presides. But I, who had more experience, could plainly observe some rudiments of it among the wild *Yahoos*.

But the *Houyhnhnms*, who live under the government of reason, are no more proud of the good qualities they possess, than I should be for not wanting a leg or an arm, which no man in his wits would boast of, although he must be miserable without them. I dwell the longer upon this subject from the desire I have to make the society of an English *Yahoo* by any means not insupportable; and therefore I here entreat those who have any tincture of this absurd vice, that they will not presume to come in my sight.

(1726)

A MODEST PROPOSAL

For Preventing the Children of Poor People in Ireland from Being a Burden to Their Parents or Country, and for Making Them Beneficial to the Public

Swift was sick at heart over the deplorable condition of Ireland. In the preceding year (1728) he had published two of his numerous pieces on the subject of Irish grievances against England: *A Short View of the State of Ireland* and *On the Present Miserable State of Ireland*. In the former, he dwelt upon the ironic pathos of the fact that although Ireland had a fruitful soil and a mild climate, there was general desolation in the island. England, he said, was receiving all the revenues from Ireland without the slightest return to the Irish: "How long we shall be able to continue the payment I am not in the least certain: one thing I know, that when the hen is starved to death there will be no more golden eggs."

In *A Modest Proposal* Swift pretends to be one of the numerous tribe of economic "projectors" offering a "scheme" for solving the problem of poverty in Ireland.

It is a melancholy object to those who walk through this great town, or travel in the country, when they see the streets, the roads, and cabin doors crowded with beggars of the female sex, followed by three, four, or six children, all in rags and importuning every passenger for an alms. These mothers, instead of being able to work for their honest livelihood, are forced to employ all their time in strolling to beg sustenance for their helpless infants; who as they grow up either turn thieves, for want of work, or leave their dear native country to fight for the pretender° in Spain, or sell themselves to the Barbados.

I think it is agreed by all parties that this prodigious number of children in the arms, or on the backs, or at the heels of their mothers, and frequently of their fathers, is, in the present deplorable state of the kingdom, a very great additional grievance; and therefore whoever could find out a fair, cheap, and easy method of making these children sound, useful members of the commonwealth would deserve so well of the public as to have his statue set up for a preserver of the nation.

But my intention is very far from being confined to provide only for the children of professed beggars: it is of a much greater extent and shall take in the whole number of infants at a certain age who are born of parents in effect as little able to support them as those who demand our charity in the streets.

As to my own part, having turned my thoughts for many years upon this important subject and maturely weighed the several schemes of our projectors, I have always found them grossly mistaken in their computation. It is true, a child just dropped from its dam may be supported by her milk for a solar year, with little other nourishment: at most not above the value of two shillings which the mother may certainly get, or the value in scraps, by her lawful occupation of begging; and it is exactly at one year old that I propose to provide for them in such a manner, as, instead of being a charge upon their parents or the parish, or wanting food and raiment for the rest of their lives, they shall, on the contrary, contribute to the feeding and partly to the clothing of many thousands.

There is likewise another great advantage in my scheme, that it will prevent those voluntary abortions and that horrid practice of women murdering their bastard children, alas! too frequent among us, sacrificing the poor innocent babes, I doubt more to avoid the expense than the shame, which would move tears and pity in the most savage and inhuman breast.

The number of souls in this kingdom being usually reckoned one million and a half, of these I calculate there may be about two hundred thousand couple, whose wives are breeders; from which number I subtract thirty thousand couple, who are able to maintain their own children (although I apprehend there cannot be so many, under the present distresses of the kingdom), but this being granted, there will remain an hundred and seventy thousand breeders. I again subtract fifty thousand for those women who miscarry, or whose children die by accident or disease within the year. There only remains one hundred and twenty thousand children of poor parents annually born. The question therefore is, How this number shall be reared and provided for? which, as I have already said, under the present situation of affairs, is utterly impossible by all the methods hitherto proposed. For we can neither employ them in handicraft or agriculture; we neither build houses (I mean in the country) nor cultivate land: they can very seldom pick up a livelihood by stealing till they arrive at six years old, except where they are of towardly° parts; although I confess they learn the rudiments much earlier; during which time they can, however, be properly looked upon only as probationers; as I have been informed by a principal gentleman in the county of Cavan,° who protested to me that he never knew above one or two instances under the age of six, even in a part of the kingdom so renowned for the quickest proficiency in that art.

I am assured by our merchants that a boy or a girl before twelve years old is no salable commodity; and even when they come to this age they will not yield above three pounds, or three pounds and half a crown at most, on the exchange; which cannot turn to account either to the parents or kingdom, the charge of nutriment and rags having been at least four times that value.

I shall now therefore humbly propose my own thoughts, which I hope will not be liable to the least objection.

I have been assured by a very knowing American of my acquaintance in London that a young healthy child well nursed is at a year old a most delicious, nourishing, and wholesome food, whether stewed, roasted, baked, or boiled; and I make no doubt that it will equally serve in a fricassee or a ragout.

I do therefore humbly offer it to public consideration that of the hundred and twenty thousand children already computed, twenty thousand may be reserved for breed, whereof only one-fourth part to be males; which is more than we allow to sheep, black cattle, or swine; and my reason is that these children are seldom the fruits of marriage, a circumstance not much regarded by our savages; therefore one male will be sufficient to serve four females. That the remaining hundred thousand may, at a year old, be offered in sale to the persons of quality and fortune through the kingdom; always advising the mother to let them suck plentifully in the last month, so as to render them plump and fat for a good table. A child will make two dishes at an entertainment for friends; and when the family dines alone, the fore or hind quarter will make a

A Modest Proposal 11 pretender, James Stuart, son of King James II of England. He laid claim to the throne which his father had lost in the Revolution of 1688 and actually landed in Britain in 1715, but was defeated. He retired to the Continent where he and his son kept alive the "Jacobite" agitation, and where he intrigued not only with the King of France but with the French puppet sovereigns in Spain

71 towardly, ready to learn   75 Cavan, a county in Northern Ireland, bordering the present Republic of Eire

reasonable dish, and seasoned with a little pepper or salt will be very good boiled on the fourth day, especially in winter.

I have reckoned upon a medium that a child just born will weigh twelve pounds, and in a solar year, if tolerably nursed, will increase to twenty-eight pounds.

I grant this food will be somewhat dear, and therefore very proper for landlords, who, as they have already devoured most of the parents, seem to have the best title to the children.

Infant's flesh will be in season throughout the year, but more plentifully in March, and a little before and after: for we are told by a grave author, an eminent French physician, that fish being a prolific° diet, there are more children born in Roman Catholic countries about nine months after Lent than at any other season; therefore, reckoning a year after Lent, the markets will be more glutted than usual, because the number of popish infants is at least three to one in this kingdom: and therefore it will have one other collateral advantage, by lessening the number of papists among us.

I have already computed the charge of nursing a beggar's child (in which list I reckon all cottagers, laborers, and four-fifths of the farmers) to be about two shillings per annum, rags included; and I believe no gentleman would repine to give ten shillings for the carcass of a good fat child, which, as I have said, will make four dishes of excellent nutritive meat, when he has only some particular friend or his own family to dine with him. Thus the squire will learn to be a good landlord and grow popular among his tenants; the mother will have eight shillings net profit and be fit for work till she produces another child.

Those who are more thrifty (as I must confess the times require) may flay the carcass; the skin of which artificially dressed will make admirable gloves for ladies and summer boots for fine gentlemen.

As to our city of Dublin, shambles° may be appointed for this purpose in the most convenient parts of it, and butchers we may be assured will not be wanting; although I rather recommend buying the children alive and dressing them hot from the knife as we do roasting pigs.

A very worthy person, a true lover of his country, and whose virtues I highly esteem, was lately pleased, in discoursing on this matter, to offer a refinement upon my scheme. He said that many gentlemen of this kingdom, having of late destroyed their deer, he conceived that the want of venison might be well supplied by the bodies of young lads and maidens, not exceeding fourteen years of age nor under twelve; so great a number of both sexes in every country being now ready to starve for want of work and service; and these to be disposed of by their parents, if alive, or otherwise by their nearest relations. But with due deference to so excellent a friend and so deserving a patriot, I cannot be altogether in his sentiments; for as to the males, my American acquaintance assured me from frequent experience that their flesh was generally tough and lean, like that of our schoolboys, by continual exercise, and their taste disagreeable; and to fatten them would not answer the charge. Then as to the females, it would, I think, with humble submission be a loss to the public, because they soon would become breeders themselves: and besides, it is not improbable that some scrupulous people might be apt to censure such a practice (although indeed very unjustly), as a little bordering upon cruelty; which, I confess, has always been with me the strongest objection against any project, however so well intended.

But in order to justify my friend, he confessed that this expedient was put into his head by the famous Psalmanazar, a native of the island Formosa, who came from thence to London above twenty years ago: and in conversation told my friend that in his country when any young person happened to be put to death, the executioner sold the carcass to persons of quality as a prime dainty; and that in his time the body of a plump girl of fifteen, who was crucified for an attempt to poison the emperor, was sold to his imperial majesty's prime minister of state, and other great mandarins of the court, in joints from the gibbet, at four hundred crowns. Neither indeed can I deny that if the same use were made of several plump young girls in this town, who, without one single groat to their fortunes, cannot stir abroad without a chair, and appear at a playhouse and assemblies in foreign fineries which they never will pay for, the kingdom would not be the worse.

Some persons of a desponding spirit are in great concern about that vast number of poor people, who are aged, diseased, or maimed; and I have been desired to employ my thoughts, what course may be taken to ease the nation of so grievous an incumbrance. But I am not in the least pain upon that matter, because it is very well known that they are every day dying and rotting, by cold and famine, and filth and vermin, as fast as can be reasonably expected. And as to the young laborers, they are now in almost as hopeful a condition: they cannot get work, and consequently pine away for want of nourishment to a degree that if at any time they are accidentally hired to common labor, they have not strength to perform it; and thus the country and themselves are happily delivered from the evils to come.

I have too long digressed and therefore shall return to my subject. I think the advantages, by the proposal which I have made, are obvious and many, as well as of the highest importance.

For first, as I have already observed, it would

125 **prolific,** favorable to generating offspring   149 **shambles,** slaughterhouses

greatly lessen the number of papists, with whom we are yearly overrun, being the principal breeders of the nation, as well as our most dangerous enemies; and who stay at home on purpose to deliver the kingdom to the pretender, hoping to take their advantage by the absence of so many good protestants, who have chosen rather to leave their country than stay at home and pay tithes against their conscience to an episocopal curate.

Secondly, the poorer tenants will have something valuable of their own, which by law may be made liable to distress, and help to pay their landlord's rent; their corn and cattle being already seized, and money a thing unknown.

Thirdly, whereas the maintenance of a hundred thousand children, from two years old and upwards, cannot be computed at less than ten shilling a piece per annum, the nation's stock will be thereby increased fifty thousand pounds per annum, beside the profit of a new dish introduced to the tables of all gentlemen of fortune in the kingdom, who have any refinement in taste. And the money will circulate among ourselves, the goods being entirely of our own growth and manufacture.

Fourthly, the constant breeders, beside the gain of eight shillings sterling per annum by the sale of their children, will be rid of the charge of maintaining them after the first year.

Fifthly, this food would likewise bring great custom to taverns: where the vintners will certainly be so prudent as to procure the best receipts for dressing it to perfection, and consequently have their houses frequented by all the fine gentlemen, who justly value themselves upon their knowledge in good eating: and a skilful cook, who understands how to oblige his guests, will contrive to make it as expensive as they please.

Sixthly, this would be a great inducement to marriage, which all wise nations have either encouraged by rewards or enforced by laws and penalties. It would increase the care and tenderness of mothers toward their children, when they were sure of a settlement for life to the poor babes, provided in some sort by the public, to their annual profit instead of expense. We should see an honest emulation among the married women, which of them could bring the fattest child to the market. Men would become as fond of their wives during the time of their pregnancy as they are now of their mares in foal, their cows in calf, or sows when they are ready to farrow; nor offer to beat or kick them (as is too frequent a practice) for fear of a miscarriage.

Many other advantages might be enumerated. For instance, the addition of some thousand carcasses in our exportation of barreled beef, the propagation of swine's flesh, and improvement in the art of making good bacon, so much wanted among us by the great destruction of pigs, too frequent at our tables; which are no way comparable in taste or magnificence to a well-grown, fat, yearling child, which roasted whole will make a considerable figure at a lord mayor's feast, or any other public entertainment. But this and many others I omit, being studious of brevity.

Supposing that one thousand families in this city would be constant customers for infants' flesh, besides others who might have it at merry-meetings, particularly weddings and christenings, I compute that Dublin would take off annually about twenty thousand carcasses; and the rest of the kingdom (where probably they will be sold somewhat cheaper) the remaining eighty thousand.

I can think of no one objection that will possibly be raised against this proposal, unless it should be urged that the number of people will be thereby much lessened in the kingdom. This I freely own, and it was indeed one principal design in offering it to the world. I desire the reader will observe that I calculate my remedy for this one individual kingdom of Ireland, and for no other that ever was, is, or, I think, ever can be upon earth. Therefore let no man talk to me of other expedients: of taxing our absentees at five shillings a pound: of using neither clothes nor household furniture, except what is of our own growth and manufacture: of utterly rejecting the materials and instruments that promote foreign luxury: of curing the expensiveness of pride, vanity, idleness, and gaming in our women: of introducing a vein of parsimony, prudence, and temperance: of learning to love our country in the want of which we differ even from LAPLANDERS and the inhabitants of TOPINAMBOO: of quitting our animosities and factions, nor acting any longer like the Jews, who were murdering one another at the very moment their city was taken: of being a little cautious not to sell our country and conscience for nothing: of teaching landlords to have at least one degree of mercy toward their tenants: lastly, of putting a spirit of honesty, industry, and skill into our shop-keepers; who, if a resolution could now be taken to buy only our native goods, would immediately unite to cheat and exact upon us in the price, the measure, and the goodness, nor could ever yet be brought to make one fair proposal of just dealing, though often and earnestly invited to it.

Therefore, I repeat, let no man talk to me of these and the like expedients, till he has at least some glimpse of hope that there will be ever some hearty and sincere attempt to put them in practice.

But as to myself, having been wearied out for many years with offering vain, idle, visionary thoughts, and at length utterly despairing of success, I fortunately fell upon this proposal; which, as it is wholly new, so it has something solid and real, of no expense and little trouble, full in our own power, and whereby we can incur no danger in disobliging ENGLAND. For this kind of commodity will not bear exportation, the flesh being of too tender a consistence to admit a long continuance in salt, although perhaps I could name a country which would be glad to eat up our whole nation without it.

After all, I am not so violently bent upon my own 340 opinion as to reject any offer proposed by wise men, which shall be found equally innocent, cheap, easy, and effectual. But before something of that kind shall be advanced in contradiction to my scheme, and offering a better, I desire the author or authors will be pleased maturely to consider two points. First, as things now stand, how they will be able to find food and raiment for an hundred thousand useless mouths and backs. And secondly, there being a round million of creatures in human figure throughout this kingdom, 350 whose whole subsistence put into a common stock would leave them in debt two millions of pounds sterling, adding those who are beggars by profession to the bulk of farmers, cottagers, and laborers, with their wives and children, who are beggars in effect; I desire those politicians, who dislike my overture, and may perhaps be so bold as to attempt an answer, that they will first ask the parents of these mortals, whether they would not at this day think it a great happiness to have been sold for food at a year old in the manner I prescribe, and thereby have avoided such a perpetual 360 scene of misfortunes as they have since gone through by the oppression of landlords, the impossibility of paying rent without money or trade, the want of common sustenance, with neither house nor clothes to cover them from the inclemencies of the weather, and the most inevitable prospect of entailing the like or greater miseries upon their breed for ever.

I profess, in the sincerity of my heart, that I have not the least personal interest in endeavoring to promote this necessary work, having no other motive than the 370 public good of my country, by advancing our trade, providing for infants, relieving the poor, and giving some pleasure to the rich. I have no children by which I can propose to get a single penny; the youngest being nine years old, and my wife past child-bearing.
(1729)

JOSEPH ADDISON
1672–1719

RICHARD STEELE
1672–1729

Joseph Addison, the son of a churchman, attended Oxford and then began his literary career. He first won the attention of certain leaders in the Whig party. In 1699, Addison's patrons gave him the opportunity of traveling abroad, presumably to train himself for future diplomatic employment. With the death of King William III in 1702, however, the Whigs temporarily lost political power and Addison lost political support. Out of the party strife during the next few years, Addison emerged with *The Campaign* (1704), a poem in praise of the duke of Marlborough, a hero for his victory at Blenheim during the War of the Spanish Succession. The year 1706 saw the beginning of Addison's active political career. In spite of the fluctuating fortunes of the Whigs, who were not given much advantage until the death of Queen Anne in 1714, he eventually attained the post of Secretary of State in 1717. His late marriage just before to the countess of Warwick undoubtedly was a powerful aid to this important political appointment. Unfortunately, Addison was unable to enjoy his position long; he was forced to resign because of ill health and died in 1719.

Richard Steele, whose name is always associated with Addison's in literary pursuits, was born at Dublin in 1672, met Addison in school, and went with him to Oxford. Unlike his more conservative-minded friend, however, Steele did not wait to take a degree from the university but joined the army—an act for which he was promptly disinherited by his uncle. He remained in the army for some time, though not in active service, and rose to the rank of captain. His pamphlet *The Christian Hero* (1701) aroused the admiration of King William III. He turned next to the stage and wrote three plays of some popularity: *The Funeral* (1701), *The Lying Lover* (1703), and *The Tender Husband* (1705), all sentimental comedies.

By 1705, therefore, Steele had achieved greater success in literature than had Addison. Nevertheless, it was Addison's preoccupation with political preferment that got Steele his first taste of journalism, for Addison had Steele made official gazetteer for the Whigs; and the periodical *The Gazette,* appearing in May 1707, was the first definite recognition of the age that the periodical was more useful than the pamphlet for political controversy and exposition. In 1709, Steele began *The Tatler,* a newspaper for party politics and social comment that was published three times a week. The combination in Steele of political reporter and coffee house gossip was excellent for the journalistic success of *The Tatler;* but it was for Addison, with his greater stylistic dignity and more penetrating critical ability, to give the periodical something more than passing journalistic success. Nevertheless Steele, who was the first editor of *The Tatler,* under the pseudonym of Isaac Bickerstaff, furnished the initiative for most of the essays in *The Tatler* and should therefore be given preeminence in the founding of the periodical essay in England.

In January 1711, *The Tatler* was stopped for political reasons. Two months later, at the suggestion of Addison, a new periodical, *The Spectator,* made its debut. The chief distinction of *The Spectator* is the presence of the Sir Roger de Coverley papers, a series of sketches of the famous country squire and his circle, the Spectator Club, who are not only subjects for individual satire, but also mouthpieces for Addison's and Steele's observations. Sir Roger was pictured as a Tory, and thus the Whig editors could satirize their opponents, the losing party, through him. The conception of Sir Roger and his group was originally Steele's, but Addison gave variety, depth, and a satirical bent to the characterization. *The Spectator* ran until December 1712. Most of the essays in *The Tatler* were by Steele; most of those in *The Spectator* were by Addison, although the total of both *Tatler* and *Spectator* papers would show that Steele was more active than Addison. To both periodicals, moreover, many other writers of the time, such as Swift, contributed.

Neither Addison nor Steele ever subsequently matched the achievement of *The Tatler* or *The Spectator.* Addison's only other important work, the classical tragedy *Cato* (1713), was a popular and political success. Steele, on the other hand, went on in the field of journalism through a series of periodical ventures, most famous of which was *The Plebeian,* appearing first in 1718, in which he found himself in a position opposed politically to that of Addison. With the coming into power of the Whigs in 1714, Steele was rewarded with knighthood, but his telling literary work was finished. In 1724 Steele retired to his wife's estate in Wales and began to settle the debts that arose because of his improvident, generous nature. He died in 1729.

ON DUELLING (STEELE)

The Tatler, No. 25: Tuesday, June 7, 1709.

Quicquid agunt homines—
—nostri est farrago libelli.°——JUVENAL

A letter from a young lady, written in the most passionate terms, wherein she laments the misfortune of a gentleman, her lover, who was lately wounded in a duel, has turned my thoughts to that subject and inclined me to examine into the causes which precipitate men into so fatal a folly. And as it has been proposed to treat of subjects of gallantry in the article from hence and no one point in nature is more proper to be considered by the company who frequent this place than that of duels, it is worth our consideration to 10 examine into this chimerical, groundless humor and to lay every other thought aside, until we have stripped it of all its false pretenses to credit and reputation amongst men.

But I must confess, when I consider what I am going about, and run over in my imagination all the endless crowd of men of honor who will be offended at such a discourse, I am undertaking, methinks, a work worthy an invulnerable hero in romance, rather than a private gentleman with a single rapier: but as I am pretty well 20 acquainted by great opportunities with the nature of man and know of a truth that all men fight against their will, the danger vanishes and resolution rises upon this subject. For this reason, I shall talk very freely on a custom which all men wish exploded, though no man has courage enough to resist it.

But there is one unintelligible word, which I fear will extremely perplex my dissertation and I confess to you I find very hard to explain, which is the term "satisfaction." An honest country gentleman had the mis- 30 fortune to fall into company with two or three modern men of honor, where he happened to be very ill-treated; and one of the company, being conscious of his offense, sends a note to him in the morning and tells him he was ready to give him satisfaction. "This is fine doing," says the plain fellow; "last night he sent me away cursedly out of humor, and this morning he fancies it would be a satisfaction to be run through the body."

As the matter at present stands, it is not to do hand- 40 some actions denominates a man of honor; it is enough if he dares to defend ill ones. Thus you often see a common sharper° in competition with a gentleman of the first rank; though all mankind is convinced that a fighting gamester is only a pickpocket with the courage of a highwayman. One cannot with any patience reflect on the unaccountable jumble of persons and things in

On Duelling   Quicquid . . . libelli. "Whatever human beings do, that is the mixed material of our little book"   43 **sharper,** a cheat

this town and nation, which occasions very frequently that a brave man falls by a hand below that of a common hangman and yet his executioner escapes the clutches of the hangman for doing it. I shall, therefore, hereafter consider how the bravest men in other ages and nations have behaved themselves upon such incidents as we decide by combat; and show, from their practice, that this resentment neither has its foundation from true reason or solid fame; but is an imposture, made of cowardice, falsehood, and want of understanding. For this work, a good history of quarrels would be very edifying to the public and I apply myself to the town for particulars and circumstances within their knowledge which may serve to embellish the dissertation with proper cuts. Most of the quarrels I have ever known have proceeded from some valiant coxcomb's persisting in the wrong, to defend some prevailing folly and preserve himself from the ingenuousness of owning a mistake.

By this means it is called "giving a man satisfaction," to urge your offense against him with your sword; which puts me in mind of Peter's order to the keeper in *The Tale of a Tub:* "if you neglect to do all this, damn you and your generation for ever: and so we bid you heartily farewell." If the contradiction in the very terms of one of our challenges were as well explained and turned into downright English, would it not run after this manner?

"Sir:

"Your extraordinary behavior last night and the liberty you were pleased to take with me makes me this morning give you this, to tell you, because you are an ill-bred puppy, I will meet you in Hyde Park an hour hence; and because you want both breeding and humanity, I desire you would come with a pistol in your hand, on horseback, and endeavor to shoot me through the head, to teach you more manners. If you fail of doing me this pleasure, I shall say you are a rascal on every post in town: and so, sir, if you will not injure me more, I shall never forgive what you have done already. Pray, sir, do not fail of getting everything ready; and you will infinitely oblige, Sir, Your most obedient humble servant, etc."

THE SPECTATOR INTRODUCES HIMSELF TO THE READER (ADDISON)

The Spectator, No. 1: Thursday, March 1, 1711.

Non fumum ex fulgore, sed ex fumo dare lucem Cogitat, ut speciosa dehinc miracula promat.°
—HORACE

The Spectator Introduces   Non ... promat. "Not smoke from fire his object is to bring, But fire from smoke, a very different thing" (quoted from Horace's *Ars Poetica*)

I have observed that a reader seldom peruses a book with pleasure till he knows whether the writer of it be a black or a fair man, of a mild or choleric° disposition, married or a bachelor, with other particulars of the like nature that conduce very much to the right understanding of an author. To gratify this curiosity, which is so natural to a reader, I design this paper and my next as prefatory discourses to my following writings, and shall give some account in them of the several persons that are engaged in this work. As the chief trouble of compiling, digesting, and correcting will fall to my share, I must do myself the justice to open the work with my own history. I was born to a small hereditary estate, which, according to the tradition of the village where it lies, was bounded by the same hedges and ditches in William the Conqueror's time that it is at present, and has been delivered down from father to son whole and entire, without the loss or acquisition of a single field or meadow, during the space of six hundred years. There runs a story in the family that my mother dreamed that she was brought to bed of a judge: whether this might proceed from a lawsuit which was then depending° in the family, or my father's being a justice of the peace, I cannot determine; for I am not so vain as to think it presaged any dignity that I should arrive at in my future life, though that was the interpretation which the neighborhood put upon it. The gravity of my behavior at my very first appearance in the world seemed to favor my mother's dream: for, as she has often told me, I threw away my rattle before I was two months old, and would not make use of my coral till they had taken away the bells from it.

As for the rest of my infancy, there being nothing in it remarkable, I shall pass it over in silence. I find that, during my nonage, I had the reputation of a very sullen youth, but was always a favorite of my schoolmaster, who used to say *that my parts were solid and would wear well.* I had not been long at the University before I distinguished myself by a most profound silence; for during the space of eight years, excepting in the public exercises of the college, I scarce uttered the quantity of an hundred words; and indeed do not remember that I ever spoke three sentences together in my whole life. Whilst I was in this learned body, I applied myself with so much diligence to my studies that there are very few celebrated books, either in the learned or the modern tongues, which I am not acquainted with.

Upon the death of my father I was resolved to travel into foreign countries, and therefore left the University with the character of an odd, unaccountable fellow, that had a great deal of learning if I would but show it. An insatiable thirst after knowledge carried me into all

3 **choleric,** irritable. In ancient medical lore, a preponderance of bile (choler) produced an irascible disposition   23 **depending,** pending

the countries of Europe in which there was anything new or strange to be seen; nay, to such a degree was my curiosity raised that having read the controversies of some great men concerning the antiquities of Egypt, I made a voyage to Grand Cairo, on purpose to take the measure of a pyramid; and as soon as I had set 60 myself right in that particular, returned to my native country with great satisfaction.

I have passed my latter years in this city, where I am frequently seen in most public places, though there are not above half a dozen of my select friends that know me; of whom my next paper shall give a more particular account. There is no place of general sort wherein I do not often make my appearance; sometimes I am seen thrusting my head into a round of politicians at Will's,° and listening with great attention to the narra- 70 tives that are made in those little circular audiences. Sometimes I smoke a pipe at Child's, and whilst I seem attentive to nothing but *The Postman*,° overhear the conversation of every table in the room. I appear on Sunday nights at St. James's Coffee-House, and sometimes join the little committee of politics in the Inner room, as one who comes there to hear and improve. My face is likewise very well known at the Grecian, the Cocoa-Tree, and in the theaters both of Drury Lane and the Haymarket.° I have been taken for 80 a merchant upon the Exchange for above these ten years, and sometimes pass for a Jew in the assembly of stock-jobbers at Jonathan's. In short, wherever I see a cluster of people, I always mix with them, though I never open my lips but in my own club.

Thus I live in the world rather as a SPECTATOR of mankind than as one of the species; by which means I have made myself a speculative statesman, soldier, merchant, and artisan, without ever meddling with any practical part in life. I am very well versed in the 90 theory of an husband or a father, and can discern the errors in the economy, business, and diversion of others better than those who are engaged in them; as standers-by discover blots which are apt to escape those who are in the game. I never espoused any party with violence, and am resolved to observe an exact neutrality between the Whigs and Tories, unless I shall be forced to declare myself by the hostilities of either side. In short, I have acted in all the parts of my life as a looker-on, which is the character I intend to preserve 100 in this paper.

I have given the reader just so much of my history and character as to let him see I am not altogether unqualified for the business I have undertaken. As for other particulars in my life and adventures, I shall insert them in following papers as I shall see occasion. In the meantime, when I consider how much I have seen, read, and heard, I began to blame my own taciturnity: and since I have neither time nor inclination to communicate the fullness of my heart in speech, I am re- solved to do it in writing, and to print myself out, if 110 possible, before I die. I have been often told by my friends that it is a pity so many useful discoveries which I have made should be in the possession of a silent man. For this reason, therefore, I shall publish a sheetful of thoughts every morning for the benefit of my contemporaries; and if I can in any way contribute to the diversion or improvement of the country in which I live, I shall leave it, when I am summoned out of it, with the secret satisfaction of thinking that I have not lived in vain. 120

There are three very material points which I have not spoken to in this paper, and which, for several important reasons, I must keep to myself, at least for some time: I mean, an account of my name, my age, and my lodgings. I must confess I would gratify my reader in anything that is reasonable; but, as for these three particulars, though I am sensible they might tend very much to the embellishment of my paper, I cannot yet come to a resolution of communicating them to the public. They would indeed draw me out of that 130 obscurity which I have enjoyed for many years and expose me in public places to several salutes and civilities which have been always very disagreeable to me; for the greatest pain I can suffer is the being talked to and being stared at. It is for this reason, likewise, that I keep my complexion° and dress as very great secrets, though it is not impossible but I may make discoveries of both in the progress of the work I have undertaken.

After having been thus particular upon myself, I 140 shall in tomorrow's paper give an account of those gentlemen who are concerned with me in this work; for, as I have before intimated, a plan of it is laid and concerted (as all other matters of importance are) in a club. However, as my friends have engaged me to stand in the front, those who have a mind to correspond with me may direct their letters *To The Spectator, at Mr. Buckley's,° in Little Britain*. For I must further acquaint the reader that, though our club meets only on Tuesdays and Thursdays, we have appointed a 150 committee to sit every night for the inspection of all such papers as may contribute to the advancement of the public weal.

---

69 **Will's.** Most of the coffee houses, such as *Will's*, the *St. James*, the *Grecian*, and the *Cocoa-Tree*, have been described briefly. *Child's* was another coffee house frequented by the clergy; *Jonathan's* was used chiefly by brokers and bankers 72 **The Postman**, a mythical newsletter intended by Addison to typify all such current news-sheets, the forerunners of our modern newspaper 79 **Drury Lane . . . Haymarket**, at this time (1711), the two theaters of London. The *Drury Lane* was first opened in 1663, but was rebuilt after the Great Fire of London and was reopened in 1674. The *Haymarket* has been equally famous in London theatrical history

136 **complexion**, general appearance 148 **Mr. Buckley**, the senior partner of the firm which published *The Spectator*

THE SPECTATOR CLUB (STEELE)

The Spectator, No. 2: Friday, March 2, 1711.

> —Haec alii sex
> Vel plures uno conclamant ore.°

The first of our society is a gentleman of Worcester-shire, of ancient descent, a baronet; his name Sir Roger de Coverley. His great-grandfather was inventor of that famous country-dance which is called after him. All who know that shire are very well acquainted with the parts and merits of Sir Roger. He is a gentleman that is very singular in his behavior, but his singularities proceed from his good sense, and are contradictions to the manners of the world only as he
10 thinks the world is in the wrong. However, this humor creates him no enemies, for he does nothing with sourness of obstinacy; and his being unconfined to modes and forms makes him but the readier and more capable to please and oblige all who know him. When he is in town, he lives in Soho Square. It is said he keeps himself a bachelor by reason he was crossed in love by a perverse, beautiful widow of the next county to him. Before this disappointment, Sir Roger was what you call a fine gentleman, had often supped with my Lord
20 Rochester° and Sir George Etherege,° fought a duel upon his first coming to town, and kicked Bully Dawson° in a public coffee-house for calling him "youngster." But being ill-used by the above-mentioned widow, he was very serious for a year and a half; and though, his temper being naturally jovial, he at last got over it, he grew careless of himself, and never dressed afterward. He continues to wear a coat and doublet of the same cut that were in fashion at the time of his repulse, which, in his merry humors, he tells us, has
30 been in and out twelve times since he first wore it. 'Tis said Sir Roger grew humble in his desires after he had forgot this cruel beauty; but this is looked upon by his friends rather as matter of raillery than truth. He is now in his fifty-sixth year, cheerful, gay, and hearty; keeps a good house in both town and country; a great lover of mankind; but there is such a mirthful cast in his behavior that he is rather beloved than esteemed. His tenants grow rich, his servants look satisfied, all the young women profess love to him, and the young
40 men are glad of his company; when he comes into a house he calls the servants by their names, and talks

all the way upstairs to a visit. I must not omit that Sir Roger is a justice of the quorum;° that he fills the chair at a quarter-session° with great abilities; and, three months ago, gained universal applause by explaining a passage in the Game Act.

The gentleman next in esteem and authority among us is another bachelor, who is a member of the Inner Temple;° a man of great probity, wit, and understanding; but he has chosen his place of residence rather to 50 obey the direction of an old humorsome father, than in pursuit of his own inclinations. He was placed there to study the laws of the land, and is the most learned of any of the house in those of the stage. Aristotle and Longinus° are much better understood by him than Littleton or Coke.° The father sends up, every post, questions relating to marriage-articles, leases, and tenures, in the neighborhood; all which questions he agrees with an attorney to answer and take care of in the lump. He is studying the passions themselves, when he 60 should be inquiring into the debates among men which arise from them. He knows the argument of each of the orations of Demosthenes° and Tully,° but not one case in the reports of our own courts. No one ever took him for a fool, but none, except his intimate friends, know he has a great deal of wit. This turn makes him at once both disinterested and agreeable; as few of his thoughts are drawn from business, they are most of them fit for conversation. His taste of books is a little too just for the age he lives in; he has read all, but 70 approves of very few. His familiarity with the customs, manners, actions, and writings of the ancients makes him a very delicate observer of what occurs to him in the present world. He is an excellent critic, and the time of the play is his hour of business; exactly at five he passes through New Inn, crosses through Russell Court, and takes a turn at Will's till the play begins; he has his shoes rubbed and his periwig powdered at the barber's as you go into the Rose.° It is for the good of the audience when he is at a play, for the 80 actors have an ambition to please him.

The person of next consideration is Sir Andrew Freeport, a merchant of great eminence in the city of London,° a person of indefatigable industry, strong rea-

---

The Spectator Club   Haec . . . ore. "Six others or more cry out with one voice," a quotation from the seventh *Satire* of the Roman satirist Juvenal (60–140)
20 **Lord Rochester.** John Wilmot, Earl of Rochester (1647–1680), a courtier, man of fashion, and poet, perhaps the most notorious person in the court of Charles II **Sir George Etherege,** playwright of the Restoration (1635–1691), author of the three comedies, *The Comical Revenge, She Would If She Could,* and *The Man of Mode*   22 **Bully Dawson,** a notorious London sharper of the seventeenth century

43 **justice of the quorum,** justice of the peace in a county   44 **quartersession,** a meeting of a court every three months   49 **Inner Temple.** The Inns of Court were voluntary legal societies in London which had their origin toward the end of the thirteenth century. By the time of Elizabeth, they had become "a whole university, as it were, of students, practicers or pleaders, and judges of the laws of this realm," to quote a writer of the time. The Inns of Court were four in number: Lincoln's Inn, the Inner Temple, the Middle Temple, and Gray's Inn   54–55 **Aristotle and Longinus,** both famous Greek critics whose opinions were held in high esteem during the eighteenth century. Aristotle, "the father of all knowledge," lived from 384 to 322 B.C.; Longinus from A.D. 210 to 273   55–56 **Littleton or Coke.** Sir Thomas Littleton (1402–1481) was perhaps the greatest English jurist of the Middle Ages; Sir Edward Coke (1552–1634), who was in his day Lord Chief Justice, wrote a commentary on Littleton's treatise on Land Tenure   63 **Demosthenes** (384–322 B.C.), adjudged the greatest of ancient Greek orators   **Tully,** Marcus Tullius Cicero (106–43 B.C.), noted Roman orator, and for the eighteenth century probably the greatest of classical authorities on prose style   79 **the Rose,** a tavern adjoining Drury Lane Theater   84 **city of London,** in the central business district of London

son, and great experience. His notions of trade are noble and generous, and (as every rich man has usually some sly way of jesting which would make no great figure were he not a rich man) he calls the sea the British Common. He is acquainted with commerce in all its parts, and will tell you that it is a stupid and barbarous way to extend dominion by arms; for true power is to be got by arts and industry. He will often argue that if this part of our trade were well cultivated, we should gain from one nation; and if another, from another. I have heard him prove that diligence makes more lasting acquisitions than valor, and that sloth has ruined more nations than the sword. He abounds in several frugal maxims, among which the greatest favorite is, "A penny saved is a penny got." A general trader of good sense is pleasanter company than a general scholar; and Sir Andrew having a natural unaffected eloquence, the perspicuity of his discourse gives the same pleasure that wit would in another man. He has made his fortunes himself, and says that England may be richer than other kingdoms by as plain methods as he himself is richer than other men; though at the same time I can say this of him, that there is not a point in the compass but blows home a ship in which he is an owner.

Next to Sir Andrew in the club-room sits Captain Sentry, a gentleman of great courage, good understanding, but invincible modesty. He is one of those that deserve very well, but are very awkward at putting their talents within the observation of such as should take notice of them. He was some years a captain, and behaved himself with great gallantry in several engagements and at several sieges; but having a small estate of his own, and being next heir to Sir Roger, he has quitted a way of life in which no man can rise suitably to his merit who is not something of a courtier as well as a soldier. I have heard him often lament that in a profession where merit is placed in so conspicuous a view, impudence should get the better of modesty. When he has talked to this purpose I never heard him make a sour expression, but frankly confess that he left the world because he was not fit for it. A strict honesty and an even, regular behavior are in themselves obstacles to him that must press through crowds who endeavor at the same end with himself—the favor of a commander. He will, however, in this way of talk, excuse generals for not disposing according to men's desert, or inquiring into it, "For," says he, "that great man who has a mind to help me, has as many to break through to come at me as I have to come at him"; therefore he will conclude that the man who would make a figure, especially in a military way, must get over all false modesty, and assist his patron against the importunity of other pretenders by a proper assurance in his own vindication. He says it is a civil cowardice to be backward in asserting what you ought to expect, as it is a military fear to be slow in attacking when it is your duty. With this candor does

the gentleman speak of himself and others. The same frankness runs through all his conversation. The military part of his life has furnished him with many adventures, in the relation of which he is very agreeable to the company; for he is never overbearing, though accustomed to command men in the utmost degree below him; nor ever too obsequious from an habit of obeying men highly above him.

But that our society may not appear a set of humorists unacquainted with the gallantries and pleasures of the age, we have among us the gallant Will Honeycomb, a gentleman who, according to his years, should be in the decline of his life, but having ever been very careful of his person, and always had a very easy fortune, time has made but very little impression either by wrinkles on his forehead or traces in his brain. His person is well turned and of a good height. He is very ready at that sort of discourse with which men usually entertain women. He has all his life dressed very well, and remembers habits as others do men. He can smile when one speaks to him, and laughs easily. He knows the history of every mode, and can inform you from which of the French king's wenches our wives and daughters had this manner of curling their hair, that way of placing their hoods; whose frailty was covered by such a sort of petticoat, and whose vanity to show her foot made that part of the dress so short in such a year. In a word, all his conversation and knowledge has been in the female world. As other men of his age will take notice to you what such a minister said upon such and such an occasion, he will tell when the Duke of Monmouth° danced at court such a woman was then smitten, another was taken with him at the head of his troop in the Park. In all these important relations, he has ever about the same time received a kind glance or a blow of a fan from some celebrated beauty, mother of the present Lord Such-a-one. If you speak of a young commoner that said a lively thing in the House, he starts up: "He has good blood in his veins; Tom Mirabell, the rogue, cheated me in that affair; that young fellow's mother used me more like a dog than any woman I ever made advances to." This way of talking of his very much enlivens the conversation among us of a more sedate turn; and I find there is not one of the company but myself, who rarely speak at all, but speaks of him as of that sort of man who is usually called a well-bred, fine gentleman. To conclude his character, where women are not concerned, he is an honest, worthy man.

I cannot tell whether I am to account him whom I am next to speak of as one of our company, for he visits us but seldom; but when he does, it adds to every man else a new enjoyment of himself. He is a clergyman, a very philosophic man, of general learning, great sanctity of life, and the most exact good breeding. He has the misfortune to be of a very weak constitution, and

174 **Duke of Monmouth,** an illegitimate son of Charles II, greatly admired in English society for his manners and graceful dancing

consequently cannot accept of such cares and business as preferments in his function would oblige him to; he is therefore among divines what a chamber-counselor is among lawyers. The probity of his mind and the integrity of his life create him followers, as being eloquent or loud advances others. He seldom introduces the subject he speaks upon; but we are so far gone in years that he observes, when he is among us, an earnestness to have him fall on some divine topic, which he always treats with much authority, as one who has no interest in this world, as one who is hastening to the object of all his wishes and conceives hope from his decays and infirmities. These are my ordinary companions.

WESTMINSTER ABBEY (ADDISON)

The Spectator, No. 26: Friday, March 30, 1711.

Pallida mors aequo pulsat pede pauperum tabernas,
  Regnumque turres, O beate Sexti,
Vitae summa brevis spem nos vetat inchoare longam,
  Iam te premet nox, fabulaeque manes,
Et domus exilis Plutonia.°

When I am in a serious humor, I very often walk by myself in Westminster Abbey; where the gloominess of the place, and the use to which it is applied, with the solemnity of the building, and the condition of the people who lie in it, are apt to fill the mind with a kind of melancholy, or rather thoughtfulness, that is not disagreeable. I yesterday passed a whole afternoon in the churchyard, the cloisters, and the church, amusing myself with the tombstones and inscriptions that I met with in those several regions of the dead. Most of them recorded nothing else of the buried person, but that he was born upon one day and died upon another: the whole history of his life being comprehended in those two circumstances, that are common to all mankind. I could not but look upon these registers of existence, whether of brass or marble, as a kind of satire upon the departed persons; who had left no other memorial of them, but that they were born and that they died. They put me in mind of several persons mentioned in the battles of heroic poems, who have sounding names given them, for no other reason but that they may be killed, and are celebrated for nothing but being knocked on the head. Γλαῦκόν τε Μέδοντά τε Θερσίλοχόν τε.—Hom. *Glaucumque, Medontaque, Thersilochumque.*—Virg.° The life of these men is finely described in holy writ by "the path of an arrow," which is immediately closed up and lost.

Upon my going into the church, I entertained myself with the digging of a grave; and saw in every shovelful of it that was thrown up, the fragment of a bone or skull intermixt with a kind of fresh moldering earth, that some time or other had a place in the composition of a human body. Upon this I began to consider with myself what innumerable multitudes of people lay confused together under the pavement of that ancient cathedral; how men and women, friends and enemies, priests and soldiers, monks and prebendaries,° were crumbled amongst one another and blended together in the same common mass; how beauty, strength, and youth, with old age, weakness, and deformity, lay undistinguished in the same promiscuous heap of matter.

After having thus surveyed this great magazine of mortality, as it were, in the lump, I examined it more particularly by the accounts which I found on several of the monuments which are raised in every quarter of that ancient fabric. Some of them were covered with such extravagant epitaphs that, if it were possible for the dead person to be acquainted with them, he would blush at the praises which his friends have bestowed upon him. There are others so excessively modest that they deliver the character of the person departed in Greek or Hebrew, and by that means are not understood once in a twelvemonth. In the poetical quarter, I found there were poets who had no monuments, and monuments which had no poets. I observed, indeed, that the present war° had filled the church with many of these uninhabited monuments, which had been erected to the memory of persons whose bodies were perhaps buried in the plains of Blenheim, or in the bosom of the ocean.

I could not but be very much delighted with several modern epitaphs, which are written with great elegance of expression and justness of thought, and therefore do honor to the living as well as to the dead. As a foreigner is very apt to conceive an idea of the ignorance or politeness of a nation from the turn of their public monuments and inscriptions, they should be submitted to the perusal of men of learning and genius before they are put in execution. Sir Cloudesly Shovel's° monument has very often given me great offense: instead of the brave rough English Admiral, which was the distinguishing character of that plain gallant man, he is represented on his tomb by the figure of a beau, dressed in a long periwig, and reposing himself upon velvet cushions under a canopy of state. The inscription is answerable to the monument; for instead of celebrating the many remarkable actions he had performed in the service of his country, it acquaints us only with the manner of his death, in which it was impossible for him to reap any honor. The Dutch, whom we are apt to despise for want of genius, show an infinitely greater taste of antiquity and polite-

Westminster Abbey **Pallida . . . Plutonia,** quoted from Horace's *Odes,* I, iv. The translation by Thomas Creech (d. 1700) follows: With equal foot, rich friend, impartial fate/Knocks at the cottage and the palace-gate/Life's span forbids thee to extend thy cares,/And stretch thy hopes beyond thy years;/Night soon will seize, and you must quickly go/To story'd ghosts, and Pluto's house below   23–25 **Γλαῦκόν . . . Thersilochumque,** names of Greek heroes lost in the Trojan War, as cited by Homer and Vergil   37 **prebendaries,** persons who receive the revenues of a cathedral

56 **the present war,** the War of the Spanish Succession with France. One of the great victories won by the English in this war took place at Blenheim, Bavaria, in 1704   69–70 **Sir Cloudesly Shovel,** a noted British naval leader (1650–1707)

ness in their buildings and works of this nature than what we meet with in those of our own country. The monuments of their admirals, which have been erected at the public expense, represent them like themselves; and are adorned with rostral° crowns and naval ornaments, with beautiful festoons of sea-weed, shells, and coral.

But to return to our subject. I have left the repository of our English kings for the contemplation of another day, when I shall find my mind disposed for so serious an amusement. I know that entertainments of this nature are apt to raise dark and dismal thoughts in timorous minds and gloomy imaginations; but for my own part, though I am always serious, I do not know what it is to be melancholy; and can therefore take a view of nature in her deep and solemn scenes, with the same pleasure as in her most gay and delightful ones. By this means I can improve myself with those objects which others consider with terror. When I look upon the tombs of the great, every emotion of envy dies in me; when I read the epitaphs of the beautiful, every inordinate desire goes out; when I meet with the grief of parents upon a tomb-stone, my heart melts with compassion; when I see the tomb of the parents themselves, I consider the vanity of grieving for those whom we must quickly follow: when I see kings lying by those who deposed them, when I consider rival wits placed side by side, or the holy men that divided the world with their contests and disputes, I reflect with sorrow and astonishment on the little competitions, factions, and debates of mankind. When I read the several dates of the tombs, of some that died yesterday, and some six hundred years ago, I consider that great day when we shall all of us be contemporaries, and make our appearance together.

WIT: TRUE, FALSE, MIXED (ADDISON)

The Spectator, No. 62, Friday, May 11, 1711.

Scribendi recte sapere est et principium et fons.°
—HORACE, *Ars Poetica* 309

Mr. Locke° has an admirable reflection upon the difference of wit and judgment, whereby he endeavors to show the reason why they are not always the talents of the same person. His words are as follow: ''And hence, perhaps, may be given some reason of that common observation, that men who have a great deal of wit and prompt memories, have not always the clearest judgment, or deepest reason. For wit lying most in the assemblage of ideas, and putting those together with quickness and variety, wherein can be found any resemblance or congruity, thereby to make up pleasant pictures and agreeable visions in the fancy; judgment, on the contrary, lies quite on the other side, in separating carefully one from another, ideas wherein can be found the least difference, thereby to avoid being misled by similitude, and by affinity to take one thing for another. This is a way of proceeding quite contrary to metaphor and allusion; wherein, for the most part, lies that entertainment and pleasantry of wit which strikes so lively on the fancy, and is therefore so acceptable to all people.''

This is, I think, the best and most philosophical account that I have ever met with of wit, which generally, though not always, consists in such a resemblance and congruity of ideas as this author mentions. I shall only add to it, by way of explanation, that every resemblance of ideas is not that which we call wit, unless it be such an one that gives delight and surprise to the reader. These two properties seem essential to wit, more particularly the last of them. In order therefore that the resemblance in the ideas be wit, it is necessary that the ideas should not lie too near one another in the nature of things; for where the likeness is obvious, it gives no surprise. To compare one man's singing to that of another, or to represent the whiteness of any object by that of milk and snow, or the variety of its colors by those of the rainbow, cannot be called wit, unless, besides this obvious resemblance, there be some further congruity discovered in the two ideas that is capable of giving the reader some surprise. Thus when a poet tells us, the bosom of his mistress is as white as snow, there is no wit in the comparison; but when he adds, with a sigh, that it is as cold too, it then grows into wit. Every reader's memory may supply him with innumerable instances of the same nature. For this reason, the similitudes in heroic poets, who endeavor rather to fill the mind with great conceptions, than to divert it with such as are new and surprising, have seldom anything in them that can be called wit. Mr. Locke's account of wit, with this short explanation, comprehends most of the species of wit, as metaphors, similitudes, allegories, enigmas, mottoes, parables, fables, dreams, visions, dramatic writings, burlesque, and all the methods of allusion: as there are many other pieces of wit (how remote soever they may appear at first sight from the foregoing description) which upon examination will be found to agree with it.

As true wit generally consists in this resemblance and congruity of ideas, false wit chiefly consists in the resemblance and congruity sometimes of single letters, as in anagrams, chronograms,° lipograms,° and acrostics; sometimes of syllables, as in echoes and doggerel rhymes; sometimes of words, as in puns and quibbles; and sometimes of whole sentences or poems, cast into

---

87 **rostral,** of, or pertaining to, a rostrum   **Wit   Scribendi . . . fons.** ''The spring and fountain-head of writing well is wisdom''   1 **Mr. Locke,** in his *Essay Concerning Human Understanding,* II, 2

62 **chronograms,** a phrase or sentence in which certain letters, usually printed differently, express by their numerical values a date or epoch   **lipograms,** a composition from which the writer rejects all words with a certain letter or letters

the figures of eggs, axes, or altars: nay, some carry the notion of wit so far, as to ascribe it even to external mimicry; and to look upon a man as an ingenious person, that can resemble the tone, posture, or face of another.

As true wit consists in the resemblance of ideas, and false wit in the resemblance of words, according to the foregoing instances; there is another kind of wit which consists partly in the resemblance of ideas, and partly in the resemblance of words; which for distinction's sake I shall call mixed wit. This kind of wit is that which abounds in Cowley,° more than in any author that ever wrote. Mr. Waller has likewise a great deal of it. Mr. Dryden is very sparing in it. Milton had a genius much above it. Spenser is in the same class with Milton. The Italians, even in their epic poetry, are full of it. Monsieur Boileau,° who formed himself upon the ancient poets, has everywhere rejected it with scorn. If we look after mixed wit among the Greek writers, we shall find it nowhere but in the epigrammatists. There are indeed some strokes of it in the little poem ascribed to Musaeus,° which by that, as well as many other marks, betrays itself to be a modern composition. If we look into the Latin writers, we find none of this mixed wit in Virgil, Lucretius, or Catullus; very little in Horace, but a great deal of it in Ovid, and scarce anything else in Martial.

Out of the innumerable branches of mixed wit, I shall choose one instance which may be met with in all the writers of this class. The passion of love in its nature has been thought to resemble fire; for which reason the words fire and flame are made use of to signify love. The witty poets therefore have taken an advantage from the doubtful meaning of the word fire, to make an infinite number of witticisms. Cowley observing the cold regard of his mistress's eyes, and at the same time their power of producing love in him, considers them as burning-glasses made of ice; and finding himself able to live in the greatest extremities of love, concludes the torrid zone to be habitable. When his mistress has read his letter written in juice of lemon by holding it to the fire, he desires her to read it over a second time by love's flames. When she weeps, he wishes it were inward heat that distilled those drops from the limbec. When she is absent he is beyond eighty, that is, thirty degrees nearer the pole than when she is with him. His ambitious love is a fire that naturally mounts upwards; his happy love is the beams of heaven, and his unhappy love flames of hell. When it does not let him sleep, it is a flame that sends up no smoke; when it is opposed by counsel and advice, it is a fire that rages the more by the wind's blowing upon it. Upon the dying of a tree in which he had cut his loves, he observes that his written flames had burned up and withered the tree. When he resolves to give over his passion, he tells us that one burnt like him for ever dreads the fire. His heart is an Aetna, that instead of Vulcan's shop encloses Cupid's forge in it.° His endeavoring to drown his love in wine, is throwing oil upon the fire. He would insinuate to his mistress, that the fire of love, like that of the sun (which produces so many living creatures) should not only warm but beget. Love in another place cooks pleasure at his fire. Sometimes the poet's heart is frozen in every breast, and sometimes scorched in every eye. Sometimes he is drowned in tears, and burnt in love, like a ship set on fire in the middle of the sea.

The reader may observe in every one of these instances, that the poet mixes the qualities of fire with those of love; and in the same sentence speaking of it both as a passion, and as real fire, surprises the reader with those seeming resemblances or contradictions that make up all the wit in this kind of writing. Mixed wit therefore is a composition of pun and true wit, and is more or less perfect as the resemblance lies in the ideas or in the words: its foundations are laid partly in falsehood and partly in truth: reason puts in her claim for one half of it, and extravagance for the other. The only province therefore for this kind of wit, is epigram, or those little occasional poems that in their own nature are nothing else but a tissue of epigrams. I cannot conclude this head of mixed wit, without owning that the admirable poet out of whom I have taken the examples of it, had as much true wit as any author that ever writ; and indeed all other talents of an extraordinary genius.

It may be expected, since I am upon this subject, that I should take notice of Mr. Dryden's definition of wit; which, with all the deference that is due to the judgment of so great a man, is not so properly a definition of wit, as of good writing in general. Wit, as he defines it, is "a propriety of words and thoughts adapted to the subject." If this be a true definition of wit, I am apt to think that Euclid° was the greatest wit that ever set pen to paper: it is certain there never was a greater propriety of words and thoughts adapted to the subject, than what that author has made use of in his elements. I shall only appeal to my reader, if this definition agrees with any notion he has of wit: if it be a true one, I am sure Mr. Dryden was not only a better poet, but a greater wit than Mr. Cowley; and Virgil a much more facetious man than either Ovid or Martial.

Bouhours,° whom I look upon to be the most penetrating of all the French critics, has taken pains to show that it is impossible for any thought to be beautiful which is not just, and has not its foundation in the nature of things; that the basis of all wit is truth; and that no thought can be valuable, of which good sense is not the groundwork. Boileau has endeavored to inculcate the same notion in several parts of his writings,

---

77 **Cowley,** Abraham Cowley (1618–1667), English poet   82 **Boileau,** Nicolas Boileau-Despreaux (1636–1711), French poet and critic   87 **Musaeus,** Greek poet of fifth century A.D.

122–23 **Aetna . . . forge.** Mt. Aetna was the workshop of Vulcan   159 **Euclid,** Greek geometer of third century B.C.   168 **Bouhours,** French critic of the seventeenth century

both in prose and verse. This is that natural way of writing, that beautiful simplicity, which we so much admire in the compositions of the ancients; and which nobody deviates from, but those who want strength of genius to make a thought shine in its own natural beauties. Poets who want this strength of genius to give that majestic simplicity to nature, which we so much admire in the works of the ancients, are forced to hunt after foreign ornaments, and not to let any piece of wit of what kind soever escape them. I look upon these writers as Goths in poetry, who, like those in architecture, not being able to come up to the beautiful simplicity of the old Greeks and Romans, have endeavored to supply its place with all the extravagances of an irregular fancy. Mr. Dryden makes a very handsome observation on Ovid's writing a letter from Dido to Aeneas, in the following words: "Ovid" (says he, speaking of Virgil's fiction of Dido and Aeneas) "takes it up after him, even in the same age, and makes an ancient heroine of Virgil's new-created Dido; dictates a letter for her just before her death to the ungrateful fugitive; and, very unluckily for himself, is for measuring a sword with a man so much superior in force to him, on the same subject. I think I may be judge of this, because I have translated both. The famous author of the Art of Love° has nothing of his own; he borrows all from a greater master in his own profession, and, which is worse, improves nothing which he finds: nature fails him, and being forced to his old shift, he has recourse to witticism. This passes indeed with his soft admirers, and gives him the preference to Virgil in their esteem."

Were not I supported by so great an authority as that of Mr. Dryden, I should not venture to observe, that the taste of most of our English poets, as well as readers, is extremely Gothic. He quotes Monsieur Segrais° for a threefold distinction of the readers of poetry: in the first of which he comprehends the rabble of readers, whom he does not treat as such with regard to their quality, but to their numbers and the coarseness of their taste. His words are as follow: "Segrais has distinguished the readers of poetry, according to their capacity of judging, into three classes. [He might have said the same of writers too, if he had pleased.] In the lowest form he places those whom he calls *les petits esprits*, such things as are our upper-gallery audience in a play-house; who like nothing but the husk and rind of wit, prefer a quibble, a conceit, an epigram, before solid sense and elegant expression: these are mob-readers. If Virgil and Martial stood for parliament-men, we know already who would carry it. But though they make the greatest appearance in the field, and cry the loudest, the best on 't is they are but a sort of French Huguenots, or Dutch boors,° brought over in herds, but not naturalized; who have not lands of

two pounds per annum in Parnassus, and therefore are not privileged to poll. Their authors are of the same level, fit to represent them on a mountebank's stage, or to be masters of the ceremonies in a bear-garden: yet these are they who have the most admirers. But it often happens, to their mortification, that as their readers improve their stock of sense (as they may by reading better books, and by conversation with men of judgment), they soon forsake them."

I must not dismiss this subject without observing, that as Mr. Locke in the passage above-mentioned has discovered the most fruitful source of wit, so there is another of a quite contrary nature to it, which does likewise branch itself out into several kinds. For not only the resemblance but the opposition of ideas does very often produce wit; as I could show in several little points, turns, and antitheses, that I may possibly enlarge upon in some future speculation.

PARTY PATCHES° (ADDISON)

The Spectator, No. 81: Saturday, June 2, 1711.

Qualis ubi audito venantum murmure tigris
Horruit in maculas—°

About the middle of last winter I went to see an opera at the theater in the Haymarket, where I could not but take notice of two parties of very fine women, that had placed themselves in the opposite side-boxes, and seemed drawn up in a kind of battle array one against another. After a short survey of them, I found they were patched differently; the faces on one hand being spotted on the right side of the forehead, and those upon the other on the left. I quickly perceived that they cast hostile glances upon one another; and that their patches were placed in those different situations, as party-signals to distinguish friends from foes. In the middle boxes, between these two opposite bodies, were several ladies who patched indifferently on both sides of their faces, and seemed to sit there with no other intention but to see the opera. Upon inquiry I found that the body of Amazons° on my right hand were Whigs, and those on my left, Tories; and that those who had placed themselves in the middle boxes were a neutral party, whose faces had not yet declared themselves. These last, however, as I afterwards found, diminished daily, and took their party with one side or the other; insomuch that I observed in several of them, the patches, which were before dispersed equally, are now all gone over to the Whig or

201 **author of the Art of Love,** Ovid (c. 43 B.C.–A.D. 17), Roman poet
211 **Segrais,** Jean Regnault de Segrais (1624–1701), French poet and translator of Vergil   229 **French Huguenots, or Dutch boors,** recent, not acculturated, immigrant groups

Party Patches   Patches, small pieces of black silk or court-plaster, often fanciful in shape, worn on the face to hide a fault or, by contrast, to show off a complexion   **Qualis . . . maculas,** "like the tigress when, at the sound of the hunters, spots appear upon her skin"   17 **Amazons,** an ancient race of female warriors, famous in literature for their contests with the Greeks

Tory side of the face. The censorious say that the men, whose hearts are aimed at, are very often the occasions that one part of the face is thus dishonored, and lies under a kind of disgrace, while the other is so much set off and adorned by the owner; and that the patches turn to the right or to the left, according to the principles of the man who is most in favor. But whatever may be the motives of a few fantastical coquettes who do not patch for the public good so much as for their own private advantage, it is certain that there are several women of honor who patch out of principle, and with an eye to the interest of their country. Nay, I am informed that some of them adhere so steadfastly to their party, and are so far from sacrificing their zeal for the public to their passion for any particular person, that in a late draft of marriage articles a lady has stipulated with her husband that, whatever his opinions are, she shall be at liberty to patch on which side she pleases.

I must here take notice that Rosalinda, a famous Whig partisan, has most unfortunately a very beautiful mole on the Tory part of her forehead; which, being very conspicuous, has occasioned many mistakes, and given a handle to her enemies to misrepresent her face, as though it had revolted from the Whig interest. But, whatever this natural patch may seem to intimate, it is well known that her notions of government are still the same. This unlucky mole, however, has misled several coxcombs; and like the hanging out of false colors, made some of them converse with Rosalinda in what they thought the spirit of her party, when on a sudden she has given them an unexpected fire, that has sunk them all at once. If Rosalinda is unfortunate in her mole, Nigranilla is as unhappy in a pimple, which forces her, against her inclinations, to patch on the Whig side.

I am told that many virtuous matrons, who formerly have been taught to believe that this artificial spotting of the face was unlawful, are now reconciled by a zeal for their cause, to what they could not be prompted by a concern for their beauty. This way of declaring war upon one another puts me in mind of what is reported of the tigress, that several spots rise in her skin when she is angry, or as Mr. Cowley has imitated the verses that stand as the motto on this paper,

—She swells with angry pride,
And calls forth all her spots on ev'ry side.°

When I was in the theater the time above-mentioned, I had the curiosity to count the patches on both sides, and found the Tory patches to be about twenty stronger than the Whig; but to make amends for this small inequality, I the next morning found the whole puppet-show filled with faces spotted after the Whiggish manner. Whether or no the ladies had retreated hither in order to rally their forces I cannot tell; but the next night they came in so great a body to the opera that they outnumbered the enemy.

This account of party patches will, I am afraid, appear improbable to those who live at a distance from the fashionable world; but as it is a distinction of a very singular nature, and what perhaps may never meet with a parallel, I think I should not have discharged the office of a faithful Spectator had I not recorded it.

I have, in former papers, endeavored to expose this party-rage in women, as it only serves to aggravate the hatreds and animosities that reign among men, and in a great measure deprive the fair sex of those peculiar charms with which nature has endowed them.

When the Romans and Sabines° were at war, and just upon the point of giving battle, the women, who were allied to both of them, interposed with so many tears and entreaties, that they prevented the mutual slaughter which threatened both parties, and united them together in a firm and lasting peace.

I would recommend this noble example to our British ladies, at a time when their country is torn with so many unnatural divisions, that if they continue, it will be a misfortune to be born in it. The Greeks thought it so improper for women to interest themselves in competitions and contentions, that for this reason, among others, they forbade them, under pain of death, to be present at the Olympic games, notwithstanding these were the public diversions of all Greece.

As our English women excel those of all nations in beauty, they should endeavor to outshine them in all other accomplishments proper to the sex, and to distinguish themselves as tender mothers, and faithful wives, rather than as furious partisans. Female virtues are of a domestic turn. The family is the proper province for private women to shine in. If they must be showing their zeal for the public, let it not be against those who are perhaps of the same family, or at least of the same religion or nation, but against those who are the open, professed, undoubted enemies of their faith, liberty, and country. When the Romans were pressed with a foreign enemy, the ladies voluntarily contributed all their rings and jewels to assist the government under a public exigence, which appeared so laudable an action in the eyes of their countrymen, that from thenceforth it was permitted by a law to pronounce public orations at the funeral of a woman in praise of the deceased person, which till that time was peculiar to men. Would our English ladies, instead of sticking on a patch against those of their own country, show themselves so truly public-spirited as to sacrifice

71–72 **She swells . . . side,** from the *Davideis,* III, an epic poem by the seventeenth-century poet Abraham Cowley (1618–1667)

94 **Romans and Sabines.** The Sabines were an ancient people living in central Italy, the history of whom is bound up with the early history of the Romans. The story given here is legendary, but may easily have happened; if the Romans took many wives from the Sabines, it would account for the fact that there was a considerable relationship between the two people from the beginning of history. There were at least three wars, however, between the Romans and Sabines, at widely separated dates; this incident of the marrying of Sabine women by Romans supposedly occurred in the first war, shortly after the founding of Rome in the eighth century B.C.

every one her necklace against the common enemy, what decrees ought not to be made in favor of them?

Since I am recollecting upon this subject such passages as occur to my memory out of ancient authors, I cannot omit a sentence in the celebrated funeral oration of Pericles, which he made in honor of those brave Athenians that were slain in a fight with the Lacedaemonians.° After having addressed himself to
140 the several ranks and orders of his countrymen, and shown them how they should behave themselves in the public cause, he turns to the female part of his audience: "And as for you (says he) I shall advise you in very few words: Aspire only to those virtues that are peculiar to your sex; follow your natural modesty, and think it your greatest commendation not to be talked of one way or other."

A COUNTRY SUNDAY (ADDISON)

The Spectator, No. 112: Monday, July 9, 1711.

Ἀθανάτους μὲν πρῶτα θεοὺς, νόμῳ ὡς διάκειται,
Τίμα.°   —PYTHAGORAS

I am always very well pleased with a country Sunday, and think, if keeping holy the seventh day were only a human institution, it would be the best method that could have been thought of for the polishing and civilizing of mankind. It is certain the country people would soon degenerate into a kind of savages and barbarians were there not such frequent returns of a stated time in which the whole village meet together with their best faces, and in their cleanliest habits, to
10 converse with one another upon indifferent subjects, hear their duties explained to them, and join together in adoration of the Supreme Being. Sunday clears away the rust of the whole week, not only as it refreshes in their minds the notions of religion, but as it puts both the sexes upon appearing in their most agreeable forms, and exerting all such qualities as are apt to give them a figure in the eye of the village. A country fellow distinguishes himself as much in the churchyard as a citizen does upon the 'Change,° the
20 whole parish politics being generally discussed in that place either after sermon or before the bell rings.

My friend Sir Roger, being a good churchman, has beautified the inside of his church with several texts of his own choosing; he has likewise given a handsome pulpit-cloth, and railed in the communion-table at his own expense. He has often told me that, at his coming

to his estate, he found his parishioners very irregular; and that, in order to make them kneel and join in the responses, he gave every one of them a hassock and a common-prayer-book, and at the same time employed 30 an itinerant singing-master, who goes about the country for that purpose, to instruct them rightly in the tunes of the Psalms; upon which they now very much value themselves, and indeed outdo most of the country churches that I have ever heard.

As Sir Roger is landlord to the whole congregation, he keeps them in very good order, and will suffer nobody to sleep in it besides himself; for, if by chance he has been surprised into a short nap at sermon, upon recovering out of it he stands up and looks about him, 40 and if he sees anybody else nodding, either wakes them himself, or sends his servant to them. Several other of the old knight's particularities break out upon these occasions; sometimes he will be lengthening out a verse in the Singing-Psalms half a minute after the rest of the congregation have done with it; sometimes, when he is pleased with the matter of his devotion, he pronounces "Amen" three or four times to the same prayer; and sometimes stands up when everybody else is upon their knees, to count the congregation, or see if 50 any of his tenants are missing.

I was yesterday very much surprised to hear my old friend, in the midst of the service, calling out to one John Matthews to mind what he was about, and not disturb the congregation. This John Matthews, it seems, is remarkable for being an idle fellow, and at that time was kicking his heels for his diversion. This authority of the knight, though exerted in that odd manner which accompanies him in all circumstances of life, has a very good effect upon the parish, who are 60 not polite enough to see anything ridiculous in his behavior; besides that the general good sense and worthiness of his character makes his friends observe these little singularities as foils that rather set off than blemish his good qualities.

As soon as the sermon is finished, nobody presumes to stir till Sir Roger is gone out of the church. The knight walks down from his seat in the chancel between a double row of his tenants, that stand bowing to him on each side, and every now and then inquires how 70 such an one's wife, or mother, or son, or father do, whom he does not see at church—which is understood as a secret reprimand to the person that is absent.

The chaplain has often told me that, upon a catechizing day, when Sir Roger had been pleased with a boy that answers well, he has ordered a Bible to be given him next day for his encouragement, and sometimes accompanies it with a flitch of bacon to his mother. Sir Roger has likewise added five pounds a year to the clerk's place; and, that he may encourage the young fellows to make 80 themselves perfect in the church service, has promised, upon the death of the present incumbent, who is very old, to bestow it according to merit.

The fair understanding between Sir Roger and his

139 **Lacedaemonians,** Spartans. Sparta was the great rival of Athens among the ancient Greek cities. The Peloponnesian War was brought about largely by the rivalry of Athens and Sparta, and culminated in the defeat of the Athenians and the capture of their city in 404. *Pericles* (?–429 B.C.) was the greatest of Athenian rulers; the climax of ancient Greek literature is often alluded to as the Age of Pericles. **A Country Sunday** Ἀθανάτους, etc. "First, in obedience to thy country's rites, worship the immortal gods" 19 **'Change,** the London Stock Exchange, held during the time of Addison and Steele in Jonathan's Coffee House in Change Alley

chaplain, and their mutual concurrence in doing good, is the more remarkable because the very next village is famous for the differences and contentions that rise between the parson and the squire, who live in a perpetual state of war. The parson is always preaching at the squire, and the squire, to be revenged on the parson, never comes to church. The squire has made all his tenants atheists and tithe-stealers,° while the parson instructs them every Sunday in the dignity of his order, and insinuates to them in almost every sermon that he is a better man than his patron. In short, matters are come to such an extremity that the squire has not said his prayers either in public or in private this half year; and that the parson threatens him, if he does not mend his manners, to pray for him in the face of the whole congregation.

Feuds of this nature, though too frequent in the country, are very fatal to the ordinary people, who are so used to be dazzled with riches that they pay as much deference to the understanding of a man of an estate as of a man of learning; and are very hardly brought to regard any truth, how important soever it may be, that is preached to them, when they know there are several men of five hundred a year who do not believe it.

SIR ROGER AT THE ASSIZES (ADDISON)

The Spectator, No. 122: Friday, July 20, 1711.

Comes jucundus in via pro vehiculo est.°
—PUBL. SYR. FRAG.

A man's first care should be to avoid the reproaches of his own heart; his next, to escape the censures of the world. If the last interferes with the former, it ought to be entirely neglected; but otherwise there cannot be a greater satisfaction to an honest mind than to see those approbations which it gives itself seconded by the applauses of the public. A man is more sure of conduct when the verdict which he passes upon his own behavior is thus warranted and confirmed by the opinion of all that know him.

My worthy friend Sir Roger is one of those who is not only at peace within himself, but beloved and esteemed by all about him. He receives a suitable tribute for his universal benevolence to mankind, in the returns of affection and good-will, which are paid him by every one that lives within his neighborhood. I lately met with two or three odd instances of that general respect which is shown to the good old knight. He would needs carry Will Wimble and myself with him to the county assizes. As we were upon the road, Will Wimble joined a couple of plain men who rid before us and conversed with them for some time; during which my friend Sir Roger acquainted me with their characters.

"The first of them," says he, "that has a spaniel by his side is a yeoman of about an hundred pounds a year, an honest man. He is just within the game-act° and qualified to kill a hare or a pheasant. He knocks down a dinner with his gun twice or thrice a week; and by that means lives much cheaper than those who have not so good an estate as himself. He would be a good neighbor if he did not destroy so many partridges. In short he is a very sensible man; shoots flying,° and has been several times foreman of the petty jury.°

"That other that rides along with him is Tom Touchy, a fellow famous for 'taking the law' of everybody. There is not one in the town where he lives that he has not sued at a quarter-sessions. The rogue had once the impudence to go to law with the widow.° His head is full of costs, damages, and ejectments. He plagued a couple of honest gentlemen so long for a trespass in breaking one of his hedges, till he was forced to sell the ground it enclosed to defray the charges of the prosecution; his father left him fourscore pounds a year; but he has cast and been cast so often that he is not now worth thirty. I suppose he is going upon the old business of the willow tree."

As Sir Roger was giving me this account of Tom Touchy, Will Wimble and his two companions stopped short till we came up to them. After having paid their respects to Sir Roger, Will told him that Mr. Touchy and he must appeal to him upon a dispute that arose between them. Will, it seems, had been giving his fellow-traveler an account of his angling one day in such a hole; when Tom Touchy, instead of hearing out his story, told him that Mr. Such-a-one, if he pleased, might "take the law of him" for fishing in that part of the river. My friend Sir Roger heard them both, upon a round trot; and after having paused some time, told them, with the air of a man who would not give his judgment rashly, that "much might be said on both sides." They were neither of them dissatisfied with the knight's determination, because neither of them found himself in the wrong by it; upon which we made the best of our way to the assizes.

The court was sat before Sir Roger came; but notwithstanding all the justices had taken their places upon the bench, they made room for the old knight at the head of them; who, for his reputation in the country, took occasion to whisper in the judge's ear, that he was glad his lordship had met with so much good weather in his circuit. I was listening to the proceedings of the court with much attention, and infinitely pleased with that great appearance of solemnity which

92 **tithe-stealers,** those who do not pay their tithes. By not paying they may be said to "steal" from the church   **Sir Roger   Comes . . . est.** "An agreeable companion upon the road is as good as a coach" (quoted from some fragments by Publius Syrus, a Roman slave-poet)

27 **within the game-act.** The right to kill game depended upon one's income and social position; this law remained until 1831   33 **flying,** on the wing   34 **petty jury,** the jury that sits at a trial in an ordinary civil or criminal case   39 **the widow,** the object of Sir Roger's affections, frequently referred to in the papers

so properly accompanies such a public administration of our laws; when, after about an hour's sitting, I observed to my great surprise, in the midst of a trial, that my friend Sir Roger was getting up to speak. I was in some pain for him till I found he had acquitted himself
80 of two or three sentences, with a look of much business and great intrepidity.

Upon his first rising the court was hushed, and a general whisper ran among the country people that Sir Roger "was up." The speech he made was so little to the purpose that I shall not trouble my readers with an account of it; and I believe was not so much designed by the knight himself to inform the court as to give him a figure in my eye, and keep up his credit in the country.

90 I was highly delighted, when the court rose, to see the gentlemen of the country gathering about my old friend and striving who should compliment him most; at the same time that the ordinary people gazed upon him at a distance, not a little admiring his courage, that was not afraid to speak to the judge.

In our return home we met with a very odd accident which I cannot forbear relating, because it shows how desirous all who know Sir Roger are of giving him marks of their esteem. When we were arrived upon the
100 verge of his estate, we stopped at a little inn to rest ourselves and our horses. The man of the house had, it seems, been formerly a servant in the knight's family; and to do honor to his old master, had some time since, unknown to Sir Roger, put him up in a sign-post before the door; so that the knight's head had hung out upon the road about a week before he himself knew anything of the matter. As soon as Sir Roger was acquainted with it, finding that his servant's indiscretion proceeded wholly from affection and goodwill, he only
110 told him that he had made him too high a compliment; and when the fellow seemed to think that could hardly be, added with a more decisive look that it was too great an honor for any man under a duke; but told him at the same time that it might be altered with a very few touches and that he himself would be at the charge of it. Accordingly, they got a painter by the knight's directions to add a pair of whiskers to the face, and by a little aggravation of the features to change it into the *Saracen's Head.* I should not have known this story,
120 had not the inn-keeper, upon Sir Roger's alighting, told him in my hearing, that his honor's head was brought back last night with the alterations that he had ordered to be made in it. Upon this my friend with his usual cheerfulness related the particulars above-mentioned and ordered the head to be brought into the room. I could not forbear discovering greater expressions of mirth than ordinary upon the appearance of this monstrous face, under which, notwithstanding it was made to frown and stare in a most extraordinary manner, I
130 could still discover a distant resemblance of my old friend. Sir Roger, upon seeing me laugh, desired me to tell him truly if I thought it possible for people to know

him in that disguise. I at first kept my usual silence; but upon the knight's conjuring me to tell him whether it was not still more like himself than a Saracen, I composed my countenance in the best manner I could, and replied "that much might be said on both sides."

These several adventures, with the knight's behavior in them, gave me as pleasant a day as ever I met with in any of my travels.   140

A CONSIDERATION OF MILTON'S *PARADISE LOST* (ADDISON)

The Spectator, No. 267: Saturday, January 5, 1712.

Cedite, Romani scriptores, cedite Graii.°

There is nothing in nature so irksome as general discourses, especially when they turn chiefly upon words. For this reason I shall waive the discussion of that point which was started some years since, whether Milton's *Paradise Lost* may be called an heroic poem. Those who will not give it that title, may call it (if they please) a divine poem. It will be sufficient to its perfection, if it has in it all the beauties of the highest kind of poetry; and as for those who allege it is not an heroic poem, they advance no more to the 10 diminution of it, than if they should say Adam is not Aeneas, nor Eve Helen.

I shall therefore examine it by the rules of epic poetry, and see whether it falls short of the *Iliad* or *Aeneid* in the beauties which are essential to that kind of writing. The first thing to be considered in an epic poem is the fable, which is perfect or imperfect according as the action which it relates is more or less so. This action should have three qualifications in it. First, it should be but one action. Secondly, it should be an 20 entire action; and, thirdly, it should be a great action. To consider the action of the *Iliad, Aeneid,* and *Paradise Lost,* in these three several lights: Homer, to preserve the unity of his action, hastens into the midst of things, as Horace has observed.° Had he gone up to Leda's egg,° or begun much later, even at the rape of Helen, or the investing of Troy, it is manifest that the story of the poem would have been a series of several actions. He therefore opens his poem with the discord of his princes and artfully interweaves, in the several 30 succeeding parts of it, an account of everything material which relates to them and had passed before that

Milton's Paradise Lost   Cedite . . . Graii. "Give place, ye Roman and Greek writers" (quoted from the *Elegies* of the Roman poet Sextus Propertius, 50–16 B.C.)   25 **Horace has observed,** in his *Ars Poetica*   26 **Leda's egg.** It has been assumed here that the reader is familiar with the general outline of the narrative in the *Iliad* and the *Aeneid.* The Trojan War, which underlies both epics, had its primary cause in the abduction of Helen by Paris of Troy. But the enmity of Greeks and Trojans went beyond this particular episode; Addison implies here that it would be impractical for the epic poet, however, to go too far back in tracing the causes of the conflict. Helen was born miraculously from an egg delivered by her mother Leda (who had been wooed by Zeus in the disguise of a swan)

fatal dissension. After the same manner Aeneas makes his first appearance in the Tyrrhene seas,° and within sight of Italy, because the action proposed to be celebrated was that of his settling himself in Latium. But because it was necessary for the reader to know what had happened to him in the taking of Troy, and in the preceding parts of his voyage, Virgil makes his hero relate it by way of episode in the second and third books of the *Aeneid;* the contents of both which books come before those of the first book in the thread of the story, though for preserving this unity of action they follow them in the disposition of the poem. Milton, in imitation of these two great poets, opens his *Paradise Lost* with an infernal council plotting the fall of man, which is the action he proposed to celebrate; and as for those great actions, which preceded, in point of time, the battle of the angels, and the creation of the world, (which would have entirely destroyed the unity of the principal action, had he related them in the same order that they happened) he cast them into the fifth, sixth, and seventh books, by way of episode to this noble poem.

Aristotle himself allows that Homer has nothing to boast of as to the unity of his fable, though at the same time that great critic and philosopher endeavors to palliate this imperfection in the Greek poet by imputing it in some measure to the very nature of an epic poem. Some have been of opinion that the *Aeneid* also labors in this particular, and has episodes which may be looked upon as excrescences rather than as parts of the action. On the contrary, the poem which we have now under our consideration hath no other episodes than such as naturally arise from the subject, and yet is filled with such a multitude of astonishing incidents that it gives us at the same time a pleasure of the greatest variety and of the greatest simplicity; *uniform in its nature, though diversified in the execution.*

I must observe also, that as Virgil, in the poem which was designed to celebrate the original of the Roman empire, has described the birth of its great rival, the Carthaginian commonwealth; Milton, with the like art, in his poem on the fall of man, has related the fall of those angels who are his professed enemies. Besides the many other beauties in such an episode, its running parallel with the great action of the poem hinders it from breaking the unity so much as another episode would have done, that had not so great an affinity with the principal subject. In short, this is the same kind of beauty which the critics admire in the *Spanish Friar,* or the *Double Discovery,*° where the two different plots look like counter-parts and copies of one another.

The second qualification required in the action of an epic poem is that it should be an entire action. An action is entire when it is complete in all its parts; or as Aristotle describes it, when it consists of a beginning, a middle, and an end. Nothing should go before it, be intermixed with it, or follow after it, that is not related to it. As, on the contrary, no single step should be omitted in that just and regular process which it must be supposed to take from its original to its consummation. Thus we see the anger of Achilles in its birth, its continuance, and effects; and Aeneas's settlement in Italy carried on through all the oppositions in his way to it both by sea and land. The action in Milton excels (I think) both the former in this particular; we see it contrived in hell, executed upon earth, and punished by heaven. The parts of it are told in the most distinct manner and grow out of one another in the most natural method.

The third qualification of an epic poem is its greatness. The anger of Achilles was of such consequence that it embroiled the kings of Greece, destroyed the heroes of Troy, and engaged all the gods in factions. Aeneas's settlement in Italy produced the Caesars and gave birth to the Roman empire. Milton's subject was still greater than either of the former; it does not determine the fate of single persons or nations; but of a whole species. The united powers of hell are joined together for the destruction of mankind, which they effected in part, and would have completed, had not Omnipotence itself interposed. The principal actors are man in his greatest perfection, and woman in her highest beauty. Their enemies are the fallen angels; the Messiah their friend; and the Almighty their Protector. In short, everything that is great in the whole circle of being, whether within the verge of nature, or out of it, has a proper part assigned it in this admirable poem.

In poetry, as in architecture, not only the whole, but the principal members, and every part of them, should be great. I will not presume to say, that the book of games in the *Aeneid,* or that in the *Iliad,* are not of this nature; nor to reprehend Virgil's simile of the top, and many other of the same kind in the *Iliad,* as liable to any censure in this particular; but I think we may say, without derogating from those wonderful performances, that there is an unquestionable magnificence in every part of *Paradise Lost,* and indeed a much greater than could have been formed upon any pagan system.

But Aristotle, by the greatness of the action, does not only mean that it should be great in its nature, but also in its duration, or in other words, that it should have a due length in it, as well as what we properly call greatness. The just measure of this kind of magnitude he explains by the following similitude: An animal no bigger than a mite cannot appear perfect to the eye, because the sight takes it in at once and has only a confused idea of the whole, and not a distinct idea of all its parts; if on the contrary, you should suppose an animal of ten thousand furlongs in length, the eye would be so filled with a single part of it that it could not give the mind an idea of the whole. What these

34 **Tyrrhene seas,** in ancient geography, that part of the Mediterranean off the west coast of Italy   82 **Spanish . . . Discovery,** a tragedy by John Dryden, produced in 1681

animals are to the eye, a very short or a very long action would be to the memory. The first would be, as it were, lost and swallowed up by it, and the other difficult to be contained in it. Homer and Virgil have
150 shown their principal art in this particular; the action of the *Iliad,* and that of the *Aeneid,* were in themselves exceeding short but are so beautifully extended and diversified by the invention of episodes, and the machinery of gods, with the like poetical ornaments, that they make up an agreeable story, sufficient to employ the memory without overcharging it. Milton's action is enriched with such a variety of circumstances that I have taken as much pleasure in reading the contents of his books as in the best in-
160 vented story I ever met with. It is possible that the traditions on which the *Iliad* and the *Aeneid* were built had more circumstances in them than the history of the fall of man, as it is related in scripture. Besides, it was easier for Homer and Virgil to dash the truth with fiction, as they were in no danger of offending the religion of their country by it. But as for Milton, he had not only a very few circumstances upon which to raise his poem but was also obliged to proceed with the greatest caution in everything that he added out of his own
170 invention. And indeed, notwithstanding all the restraint he was under, he has filled his story with so many surprising incidents, which bear so close an analogy with what is delivered in holy writ, that it is capable of pleasing the most delicate reader without giving offense to the most scrupulous.

The modern critics have collected from several hints in the *Iliad* and *Aeneid* the space of time which is taken up by the action of each of those poems; but as a great part of Milton's story was translated in regions that lie
180 out of the reach of the sun and the sphere of day, it is impossible to gratify the reader with such a calculation, which indeed would be more curious than instructive, none of the critics, either ancient or modern, having laid down rules to circumscribe the action of an epic poem with any determined number of years, days, or hours.

This piece of criticism on Milton's *Paradise Lost* shall be carried on in the following Saturdays' papers.°

ON THE SCALE OF BEING (ADDISON)

The Spectator, No. 519, October 25, 1712.

*Inde hominum pecudumque genus, vitaeque volantum,
et quae marmoreo fert monstra sub aequore pontus.*°
—VIRGIL, *Aeneid* VI.728–29

187–88 **This . . . papers.** No fewer than twenty papers on Milton and *Paradise Lost* were published in *The Spectator*   **On the Scale of Being   Inde . . . pontus.** "From thence springs the race of men and of beasts, and the creatures of the air, and whatever monsters the sea supports beneath its smooth, marbled surface"

Though there is a great deal of pleasure in contemplating the material world, by which I mean that system of bodies into which nature has so curiously wrought the mass of dead matter, with the several relations which those bodies bear to one another, there is still, methinks, something more wonderful and surprising in contemplations on the world of life, by which I mean all those animals with which every part of the universe is furnished. The material world is only the shell of the universe: the world of life are its inhabi- 10 tants.

If we consider those parts of the material world which lie the nearest to us and are, therefore, subject to our observations and inquiries, it is amazing to consider the infinity of animals with which it is stocked. Every part of matter is peopled. Every green leaf swarms with inhabitants. There is scarce a single humor in the body of a man, or of any other animal, in which our glasses do not discover myriads of living creatures. The surface of animals is also covered with 20 other animals which are, in the same manner, the basis of other animals that live upon it; nay, we find in the most solid bodies, as in marble itself, innumerable cells and cavities that are crowded with such imperceptible inhabitants as are too little for the naked eye to discover. On the other hand if we look into the more bulky parts of nature, we see the seas, lakes, and rivers teeming with numberless kinds of living creatures. We find every mountain and marsh, wilderness and wood, plentifully stocked with birds and beasts, and 30 every part of matter affording proper necessaries and conveniences for the livelihood of multitudes which inhabit it.

The author of *The Plurality of Worlds*° draws a very good argument upon this consideration for the peopling of every planet, as indeed it seems very probable from the analogy of reason that, if no part of matter which we are acquainted with lies waste and useless, those great bodies, which are at such a distance from us, should not be desert and unpeopled, but rather that 40 they should be furnished with beings adapted to their respective situations.

Existence is a blessing to those beings only which are endowed with perception and is, in a manner, thrown away upon dead matter any further than as it is subservient to beings which are conscious of their existence. Accordingly we find from the bodies which lie under observation that matter is only made as the basis and support of animals and that there is no more of the one than what is necessary for the existence of 50 the other.

Infinite Goodness is of so communicative a nature that it seems to delight in the conferring of existence upon every degree of perceptive being. As this is a speculation which I have often pursued with great pleasure to myself, I shall enlarge farther upon it, by con-

34 **the author of The Plurality of Worlds,** Bernard le Fontenelle (1657–1757)

sidering that part of the scale of beings which comes within our knowledge.

There are some living creatures which are raised but just above dead matter. To mention only that species of shellfish, which are formed in the fashion of a cone, that grow to the surface of several rocks and immediately die upon their being severed from the place where they grow. There are many other creatures but one remove from these, which have no other sense besides that of feeling and taste. Others have still an additional one of hearing; others of smell, and others of sight. It is wonderful to observe by what a gradual progress the world of life advances through a prodigious variety of species before a creature is formed that is complete in all its senses; and, even among these, there is such a different degree of perfection in the sense which one animal enjoys, beyond what appears in another, that, though the sense in different animals be distinguished by the same common denomination, it seems almost of a different nature. If after this we look into the several inward perfections of cunning and sagacity, or what we generally call instinct, we find them rising after the same manner, imperceptibly, one above another, and receiving additional improvements, according to the species in which they are implanted. This progress in nature is so very gradual that the most perfect of an inferior species comes very near to the most imperfect of that which is immediately above it.

The exuberant and overflowing goodness of the Supreme Being, whose mercy extends to all his works, is plainly seen, as I have before hinted, from his having made so very little matter, at least what falls within our knowledge, that does not swarm with life. Nor is his goodness less seen in the diversity than in the multitude of living creatures. Had he only made one species of animals, none of the rest would have enjoyed the happiness of existence; he has, therefore, *specified* in his creation every degree of life, every capacity of being. The whole chasm in nature, from a plant to a man, is filled up with diverse kinds of creatures, rising one over another by such a gentle and easy ascent that the little transitions and deviations from one species to another are almost insensible. This intermediate space is so well husbanded and managed that there is scarce a degree of perception which does not appear in some one part of the world of life. Is the goodness or wisdom of the Divine Being more manifested in this his proceeding?

There is a consequence, besides those I have already mentioned, which seems very naturally deducible from the foregoing considerations. If the scale of being rises by such a regular progress so high as man, we may by a parity of reason suppose that it still proceeds gradually through those beings which are of a superior nature to him, since there is an infinitely greater space and room for different degrees of perfection between the Supreme Being and man than between

man and the most despicable insect. This consequence of so great a variety of beings which are superior to us, from that variety which is inferior to us, is made by Mr. Locke in a passage which I shall here set down after having premised that, notwithstanding there is such infinite room between man and his Maker for the creative power to exert itself in, it is impossible that it should ever be filled up, since there will be still an infinite gap or distance between the highest created being and the Power which produced him:

"That there should be more species of intelligent creatures above us than there are of sensible and material below, is probable to me from hence: That in all the visible corporeal world we see no chasms or no gaps. All quite down from us, the descent is by easy steps and a continued series of things that, in each remove, differ very little from the other. There are fishes that have wings and are not strangers to the airy region; and there are some birds that are inhabitants of the water, whose blood is cold as fishes and their flesh so like in taste that the scrupulous are allowed them on fish days. There are animals so near of kin both to birds and beasts that they are in the middle between both: amphibious animals link the terrestrial and aquatic together; seals live at land and at sea, and porpoises have the warm blood and entrails of a hog, not to mention what is confidently reported of mermaids or seamen. There are some brutes that seem to have as much knowledge and reason as some that are called men; and the animal and vegetable kingdoms are so nearly joined that, if you will take the lowest of one and the highest of the other, there will scarce be perceived any great difference between them; and so on, till we come to the lowest and the most inorganical parts of matter, we shall find everywhere that the several species are linked together and differ but in almost insensible degrees. And when we consider the infinite power and wisdom of the Maker, we have reason to think that it is suitable to the magnificent harmony of the universe and the great design and infinite goodness of the Architect, that the species of creatures should also, by gentle degrees, ascend upward from us toward his infinite perfection, as we see they gradually descend from us downward; which, if it be probable, we have reason to be persuaded that there are far more species of creatures above us than there are beneath, we being in degrees of perfection much more remote from the infinite being of God than we are from the lowest state of being and that which approaches nearest to nothing. And yet of all those distinct species we have no clear distinct ideas."

In this system of being, there is no creature so wonderful in its nature, and which so much deserves our particular attention, as man, who fills up the middle space between the animal and intellectual nature, the visible and invisible world, and is that link in the chain of beings which has been often termed the *nexus ut-*

riusque mundi.° So that he who, in one respect, is associated with angels and archangels, may look upon a Being of infinite perfection as his father, and the highest order of spirits as his brethren, and may, in another respect, say to corruption, "Thou art my father," and to the worm, "Thou art my mother and my sister."

ALEXANDER POPE
1688–1744

Alexander Pope was born in London in 1688, the son of a wealthy retired Roman Catholic merchant. Afflicted with tuberculosis of the spine while an infant, Pope was left hunchbacked and in fragile health for the rest of his life. Because of his religion, Pope did not have a formal education. He was trained at home by Catholic priests and attended Catholic schools, but he was mainly self-educated. He read Latin, Greek, French, and Italian. His precocious talents brought him attention at an early age; by 1705 his *Pastorals* (published in 1709) were circulating in manuscript among the best literary judges of the day. While the *Pastorals* were being circulated, he was already at work on a poem on the art of writing, *An Essay on Criticism*. Published in 1711, it received immediate acclaim because of its brilliantly polished epigrams. The success of the *Essay on Criticism* further increased Pope's wide circle of friends, among them Addison, Steele, Swift, Arbuthnot, and Gay. In 1712 he published *The Rape of the Lock*, a mock-heroic poem that sought to reconcile two Catholic families (a young man in one family had stolen a lock of hair from a young lady in another). In 1713 he announced his intent to do a verse translation of Homer. Published between 1715 and 1726, the translation was a critical and financial success. Dr. Johnson called it "the noblest version of poetry which the world has ever seen."

Pope soon found that the life of a wit was a life of fierce, sometimes vituperative, poetic combat. Either his person or his poems always seemed to be objects of attack by the critics of the day. This criticism reached something of a climax with his edition of Shakespeare published in 1725. In the spirit of the age, Pope edited the plays to accord with contemporary taste, but this practice was criticized by the scholar Lewis Theobald in the following year. Pope had had enough and defended his standards in the mock epic *The Dunciad* (first edition 1728; enlarged 1729; Book IV, 1743). Theobald was duly represented in it as the favorite son of the Goddess of Dullness.

171–72 **nexus utriusque mundi,** "the point of joining of both worlds"

By 1719 Pope had moved to Twickenham, in Middlesex, with his mother; there he spent the rest of his life. He frequently entertained such friends as Swift and often made visits to London. He was a passionate gardener who was frequently asked by his country friends to design and lay out their own grounds. During this time Pope began to contemplate a new, more philosophical work on the relations of man, nature, and society; published as *An Essay on Man* in the early 1730s, this ambitious work aroused much controversy. Pope was finally moved to make a reply to this controversy and to defend his own position as a satirist. He addressed his reply, an epistle in verse (1735), to Dr. John Arbuthnot; it is regarded today as one of the finest of his later poems. Pope's anxiety about prevailing literary standards first demonstrated in *The Dunciad* was shown once more in his last completed work, *The New Dunciad* (1742), the next year reprinted as the fourth book of a revised *Dunciad*. In this work Colley Cibber, a notorious English actor and dramatist also attacked by Johnson and Fielding, replaced Lewis Theobald. While at work on a revision of his poems for a new edition, he died at his home in Twickenham in 1744.

Pope is today considered the greatest English poet between Milton and Blake. He attempted with success each of the kinds of poetry acceptable in his day; he led his contemporaries in forming concepts of wit, taste, judgment, and genius; he brought the heroic couplet to a new level of concise statement and poetic validity. In his own time he was not only recognized as a great poet at home but was the first English poet to enjoy fame throughout the continent, witnessing translations of his poems into both modern and ancient languages.

from AN ESSAY ON CRITICISM

The accommodation of modern literary theory and practice to ancient rule and example is nowhere so urbanely and judiciously set forth in English as in Pope's *Essay on Criticism*. Though written when Pope was extremely young (he suggests the age of twelve), it is, in many ways, a very mature work. Its main outlines are traditional; they are based upon Horace's *Ars Poetica*, Boileau's *L'Art Poétique*, Quintillian's *Institutio Oratoria*, Ben Jonson's *Timber*, and John Dryden's Prefaces. But Pope does fulfill his own definition of "true wit":

> True wit is Nature to advantage dressed,
> What oft was thought, but ne'er so well
>   expressed. . . .

In Part I of the *Essay*, Pope explores the relationship of "wit" and art in the making of poetry; in Part II, he concerns himself mainly with the nature and effects of false "wit"; and in Part III (not printed here), he defines the good critic and provides a roll call of great critics of the past.

1

'Tis hard to say, if greater want of skill
Appear in writing or in judging ill;
But, of the two, less dangerous is the offense
To tire our patience, than mislead our sense.
Some few in that, but numbers err in this,
Ten censure wrong for one who writes amiss;
A fool might once himself alone expose,
Now one in verse makes many more in prose.

'Tis with our judgments as our watches; none
10 Go just alike, yet each believes his own.
In poets as true genius is but rare,
True taste as seldom is the critic's share;
Both must alike from Heaven derive their light,
These born to judge, as well as those to write.
Let such teach others who themselves excel,
And censure freely who have written well.
Authors are partial to their wit, 'tis true,
But are not critics to their judgment too?

Yet if we look more closely, we shall find
20 Most have the seeds of judgment in their mind:
Nature affords at least a glimmering light;
The lines, though touched but faintly, are drawn right.
But as the slightest sketch, if justly traced,
Is by ill-coloring but the more disgraced,
So by false learning is good sense defaced;
Some are bewildered in the maze of schools,
And some made coxcombs nature meant but fools.
In search of wit these lose their common sense,
And then turn critics in their own defense;
30 Each burns alike, who can, or cannot write,
Or with a rival's or an eunuch's spite.
All fools have still an itching to deride,
And fain would be upon the laughing side.
If Maevius° scribble in Apollo's spite,
There are who judge still worse than he can write.

Some have at first for wits, then poets passed,
Turned critics next, and proved plain fools at last.
Some neither can for wits nor critics pass,
As heavy mules are neither horse nor ass.
40 Those half-learned witlings, numerous in our isle,
As half-formed insects on the banks of Nile;°
Unfinished things, one knows not what to call,
Their generation's so equivocal;
To tell 'em, would a hundred tongues require,
Or one vain wit's, that might a hundred tire.

But you who seek to give and merit fame,
And justly bear a critic's noble name,

Be sure yourself and your own reach to know,
How far your genius, taste, and learning go;
Launch not beyond your depth, but be discreet, 50
And mark that point where sense and dullness meet.

Nature to all things fixed the limits fit,
And wisely curbed proud man's pretending wit.°
As on the land while here the ocean gains,
In other parts it leaves wide sandy plains;
Thus in the soul while memory prevails,
The solid power of understanding fails;
Where beams of warm imagination play,
The memory's soft figures melt away.
One science only will one genius fit; 60
So vast is art, so narrow human wit:
Not only bounded to peculiar arts,
But oft in those confined to single parts.
Like kings we lose the conquests gained before,
By vain ambition still to make them more;
Each might his several province well command,
Would all but stoop to what they understand.

First follow nature, and your judgment frame
By her just standard, which is still the same:
Unerring nature, still divinely bright, 70
One clear, unchanged, and universal light,
Life, force, and beauty, must to all impart,
At once the source, and end, and test of art.
Art from that fund each just supply provides,
Works without show, and without pomp presides:
In some fair body thus the informing soul
With spirits feeds, with vigor fills the whole,
Each motion guides, and every nerve sustains;
Itself unseen, but in the effects, remains.
Some, to whom Heaven in wit has been profuse, 80
Want as much more, to turn it to its use;
For wit and judgment often are at strife,
Though meant each other's aid, like man and wife.
'Tis more to guide than spur the Muse's steed;
Restrain his fury, than provoke his speed;
The winged courser, like a generous horse,
Shows most true mettle when you check his course.

Those rules of old discovered, not devised,
Are nature still, but nature methodized;
Nature, like liberty, is but restrained 90
By the same laws which first herself ordained.

Hear how learned Greece her useful rules indites,
When to repress, and when indulge our flights:
High on Parnassus'° top her sons she showed,
And pointed out those arduous paths they trod;
Held from afar, aloft, the immortal prize,
And urged the rest by equal steps to rise.

An Essay on Criticism   34 Maevius, an inferior Roman poet of the first century
41 half-formed . . . Nile. The Nile is noted for its periodic overflowings. Insects forming along its bank are prematurely destroyed

53 wit, a complex concept in the neoclassical age that is difficult to define. In a letter to Wycherley (26 December 1704), Pope says, "True wit, I believe, may be defined as greatness of thought, and a faculty of expression"   **94 Parnassus,** a mountain in Greece celebrated as the haunt of the Muses of poetry and music

Just precepts thus from great examples given,
She drew from them what they derived from Heaven.
100 The generous critic fanned the poet's fire,
And taught the world with reason to admire.
Then criticism the Muse's handmaid proved,
To dress her charms, and make her more beloved:
But following wits from that intention strayed,
Who could not win the mistress, wooed the maid;
Against the poets their own arms they turned,
Sure to hate most the men from whom they learned.
So modern 'pothecaries, taught the art
By doctor's bills to play the doctor's part,
110 Bold in the practice of mistaken rules,
Prescribe, apply, and call their masters fools.
Some on the leaves of ancient authors prey,
Nor time nor moths e'er spoiled so much as they.
Some dryly plain, without invention's aid,
Write dull receipts,° how poems may be made.
These leave the sense, their learning to display,
And those explain the meaning quite away.

You, then, whose judgment the right course would
      steer,
Know well each ancient's proper character;
120 His fable, subject, scope in every page;
Religion, country, genius of his age:
Without all these at once before your eyes,
Cavil you may, but never criticise.
Be Homer's works your study and delight,°
Read them by day, and meditate by night;
Thence form your judgment, thence your maxims
      bring,
And trace the Muses upward to their spring.
Still with itself compared, his text peruse;
And let your comment be the Mantuan Muse.°

130   When first young Maro in his boundless mind
A work to outlast immortal Rome designed,
Perhaps he seemed above the critic's law,
And but from nature's fountains scorned to draw:
But when to examine every part he came,
Nature and Homer were, he found, the same.
Convinced, amazed, he checks the bold design;
And rules as strict his labored work confine,
As if the Stagirite° o'erlooked each line;
Learn hence for ancient rules a just esteem;
140 To copy nature is to copy them.

Some beauties yet no precepts can declare,
For there's a happiness as well as care.
Music resembles poetry; in each
Are nameless graces which no methods teach,
And which a master-hand alone can reach.
If, where the rules not far enough extend,

(Since rules were made but to promote their end)
Some lucky license answer to the full
The intent proposed, that license is a rule.
Thus Pegasus,° a nearer way to take,   150
May boldly deviate from the common track;
From vulgar bounds with brave disorder part,
And snatch a grace beyond the reach of art,
Which without passing through the judgment, gains
The heart, and all its end at once attains.
In prospects thus, some objects please our eyes,
Which out of nature's common order rise,
The shapeless rock, or hanging precipice.
Great wits sometimes may gloriously offend,
And rise to faults true critics dare not mend.   160
But though the ancients thus their rules invade,
(As kings dispense with laws themselves have made)
Moderns, beware! or if you must offend
Against the precept, ne'er transgress its end;
Let it be seldom and compelled by need;
And have, at least, their precedent to plead.
The critic else proceeds without remorse,
Seizes your fame, and puts his laws in force.

I know there are,° to whose presumptuous thoughts
Those freer beauties, even in them, seem faults.   170
Some figures monstrous and mis-shaped appear,
Considered singly, or beheld too near,
Which, but proportioned to their light or place,
Due distance reconciles to form and grace.
A prudent chief not always must display
His powers in equal ranks, and fair array,
But with the occasion and the place comply,
Conceal his force, nay, seem sometimes to fly.
Those oft are stratagems which errors seem,
Nor is it Homer nods, but we that dream.   180

Still green with bays each ancient altar stands,
Above the reach of sacrilegious hands;
Secure from flames, from envy's fiercer rage,
Destructive war, and all-involving age.
See, from each clime the learned their incense bring!
Hear, in all tongues, consenting paeans ring!
In praise so just let every voice be joined,
And fill the general chorus of mankind.
Hail, bards triumphant! born in happier days;
Immortal heirs of universal praise!   190
Whose honors with increase of ages grow,
As streams roll down, enlarging as they flow;
Nations unborn your mighty names shall sound,
And worlds applaud that must not yet be found!
Oh, may some spark of your celestial fire,
The last, the meanest of your sons inspire,
(That on weak wings, from far, pursues your flights;
Glows while he reads, but trembles as he writes)

115 **receipts**, recipes   124 **Homer's works ... delight.** The "works" are, of course, the *Iliad* and the *Odyssey*   129 **Mantuan Muse,** the great Roman poet Vergil (70–19 B.C.), a native of Mantua, Italy, author of the *Aeneid* and didactic and lyric verse (the *Georgics* and *Eclogues*). His family name was *Maro* (cf. l. 130) 138 **Stagirite,** Aristotle (384–322 B.C.), so called from Stagira, his birthplace in Greece

150 **Pegasus,** the winged horse of classical mythology, finally conquered and ridden by Bellerophon. The winged horse is a symbol for poetic inspiration 169 **there are,** there are those to whom, etc.

To teach vain wits a science little known,
200 To admire superior sense, and doubt their own!

2

Of all the causes which conspire to blind
Man's erring judgment, and misguide the mind,
What the weak head with strongest bias rules,
Is pride, the never-failing vice of fools.
Whatever nature has in worth denied,
She gives in large recruits° of needful pride;
For as in bodies, thus in souls, we find
What wants in blood and spirits, swelled with wind:
Pride, where wit fails, steps in to our defense,
210 And fills up all the mighty void of sense.
If once right reason drives that cloud away,
Truth breaks upon us with resistless day.
Trust not yourself; but your defects to know,
Make use of every friend—and every foe.

A little learning is a dangerous thing;
Drink deep, or taste not the Pierian spring:°
There shallow draughts intoxicate the brain,
And drinking largely sobers us again.
Fired at first sight with what the Muse imparts,
220 In fearless youth we tempt the heights of arts,
While from the bounded level of our mind,
Short views we take, nor see the lengths behind;
But more advanced, behold with strange surprise
New distant scenes of endless science rise!
So pleased at first the towering Alps we try,
Mount o'er the vales, and seem to tread the sky,
The eternal snows appear already past,
And the first clouds and mountains seem the last;
But, those attained, we tremble to survey
230 The growing labors of the lengthened way,
The increasing prospect tires our wandering eyes,
Hills peep o'er hills, and Alps on Alps arise!

A perfect judge will read each work of wit
With the same spirit that its author writ:
Survey the whole, nor seek slight faults to find
Where nature moves, and rapture warms the mind;
Nor lose, for that malignant dull delight,
The generous pleasure to be charmed with wit.
But in such lays as neither ebb, nor flow,
240 Correctly cold, and regularly low,
That shunning faults, one quiet tenor keep;
We cannot blame indeed, but we may sleep.
In wit, as nature, what affects our hearts
Is not the exactness of peculiar parts;
'Tis not a lip, or eye, we beauty call,
But the joint force and full result of all.
Thus when we view some well-proportioned dome,

(The world's just wonder, and e'en thine, O Rome!)°
No single parts unequally surprise,
All comes united to the admiring eyes;   250
No monstrous height, or breadth, or length appear;
The whole at once is bold, and regular.

Whoever thinks a faultless piece to see,
Thinks what ne'er was, nor is, nor e'er shall be.
In every work regard the writer's end,
Since none can compass more than they intend;
And if the means be just, the conduct true,
Applause, in spite of trivial faults, is due;
As men of breeding, sometimes men of wit,
To avoid great errors, must the less commit: 260
Neglect the rules each verbal critic lays,
For not to know some trifles, is a praise.
Most critics, fond of some subservient art,
Still make the whole depend upon a part.
They talk of principles, but notions prize,
And all to one loved folly sacrifice.

Once on a time, La Mancha's knight,° they say,
A certain bard encountering on the way,
Discoursed in terms as just, with looks as sage,
As e'er could Dennis° of the Grecian stage;   270
Concluding all were desperate sots and fools,
Who durst depart from Aristotle's rules.
Our author, happy in a judge so nice,
Produced his play, and begged the knight's advice;
Made him observe the subject, and the plot,
The manners, passions, unities, what not?
All which, exact to rule, were brought about,
Were but a combat in the lists left out.
"What! leave the combat out?" exclaims the knight;
Yes, or we must renounce the Stagirite.   280
"Not so, by Heaven" (he answers in a rage),
"Knights, squires, and steeds, must enter on the
     stage."
So vast a throng the stage can ne'er contain.
"Then build a new, or act it in a plain."

Thus critics, of less judgment than caprice,
Curious not knowing, not exact but nice,
Form short ideas; and offend in arts
(As most in manners) by a love to parts.

Some to conceit alone their taste confine,
And glittering thoughts struck out at every line;   290
Pleased with a work where nothing's just or fit;
One glaring chaos and wild heap of wit.
Poets like painters, thus unskilled to trace
The naked nature and the living grace,
With gold and jewels cover every part,
And hide with ornaments their want of art.

206 **recruits**, additional supplies 216 **the Pierian spring.** Pieria, in Thessaly,
was considered the birthplace of the Muses. It was believed that the Muses were
originally nymphs, spirits who dwelt in forests, brooks, or fountains. To "drink" of
the Pierian spring would be to quaff inspiration

248 **wonder . . . Rome,** the Cathedral of St. Peter in Rome 267 **La Mancha's
knight,** Don Quixote, the hero of the celebrated Spanish mock romance of the
same name by Cervantes (1547–1616) 270 **Dennis,** John Dennis (1657–1734),
an English critic and dramatist who had written about Aristotle; he became a
lifelong foe of Pope

True wit is nature to advantage dressed,
What oft was thought, but ne'er so well expressed;
Something, whose truth convinced at sight we find,
300 That gives us back the image of our mind.
As shades more sweetly recommend the light,
So modest plainness sets off sprightly wit.
For works may have more wit than does 'em good,
As bodies perish through excess of blood.

Others for language all their care express,
And value books, as women, men, for dress:
Their praise is still—the style is excellent:
The sense, they humbly take upon content.
Words are like leaves; and where they most abound,
310 Much fruit of sense beneath is rarely found;
False eloquence, like the prismatic glass,
Its gaudy colors spreads on every place;
The face of nature we no more survey,
All glares alike, without distinction gay:
But true expression, like the unchanging sun,
Clears and improves whate'er it shines upon,
It gilds all objects, but it alters none.
Expression is the dress of thought, and still
Appears more decent, as more suitable;
320 A vile conceit in pompous words expressed,
Is like a clown in regal purple dressed:
For different styles with different subjects sort,
As several garbs with country, town, and court.
Some by old words to fame have made pretense,
Ancients in phrase, mere moderns in their sense;
Such labored nothings, in so strange a style,
Amaze the unlearned, and make the learnéd smile.
Unlucky, as Fungoso° in the play,
These sparks with awkward vanity display
330 What the fine gentlemen wore yesterday;
And but so mimic ancient wits at best,
As apes our grandsires, in their doublets dressed.
In words, as fashions, the same rule will hold;
Alike fantastic, if too new, or old:
Be not the first by whom the new are tried,
Nor yet the last to lay the old aside.

But most by numbers° judge a poet's song;
And smooth or rough, with them, is right or wrong:
In the bright Muse though thousand charms conspire,
340 Her voice is all these tuneful fools admire;
Who haunt Parnassus but to please their ear,
Not mend their minds; as some to church repair,
Not for the doctrine, but the music there.
These equal syllables alone require,
Though oft the ear the open vowels tire;
While expletives their feeble aid do join;
And ten low words oft creep in one dull line:
While they ring round the same unvaried chimes,
With sure returns of still expected rimes;

Where'er you find "the cooling western breeze,"   350
In the next line, it "whispers through the trees";
If crystal streams "with pleasing murmurs creep,"
The reader's threatened (not in vain) with "sleep":
Then, at the last and only couplet fraught
With some unmeaning thing they call a thought,
A needless Alexandrine° ends the song,
That, like a wounded snake, drags its slow length
    along.
Leave such to tune their own dull rimes, and know
What's roundly smooth or languishingly slow;
And praise the easy vigor of a line,   360
Where Denham's strength, and Waller's° sweetness
    join.
True ease in writing comes from art, not chance,
As those move easiest who have learned to dance.
'Tis not enough no harshness gives offense,
The sound must seem an echo to the sense:
Soft is the strain when Zephyr gently blows,
And the smooth stream in smoother numbers flows;
But when loud surges lash the sounding shore,
The hoarse, rough verse should like the torrent roar:°
When Ajax strives some rock's vast weight to throw, 370
The line too labors, and the words move slow;
Not so, when swift Camilla° scours the plain,
Flies o'er the unbending corn, and skims along the
    main.
Hear how Timotheus'° varied lays surprise,
And bid alternate passions fall and rise!
While, at each change, the son of Libyan Jove°
Now burns with glory, and then melts with love;
Now his fierce eyes with sparkling fury glow,
Now sighs steal out, and tears begin to flow:
Persians and Greeks like turns of nature found,   380
And the world's victor stood subdued by sound!
The power of music all our hearts allow,
And what Timotheus was, is Dryden now.

Avoid extremes; and shun the fault of such,
Who still are pleased too little or too much,
At every trifle scorn to take offense,
That always shows great pride, or little sense;
Those heads, as stomachs, are not sure the best,
Which nauseate all, and nothing can digest.
Yet let not each gay turn thy rapture move,   390
For fools admire, but men of sense approve:°
As things seem large which we through mists descry,
Dullness is ever apt to magnify.

356 **Alexandrine,** a line containing twelve syllables, iambic hexameter. The next line (l. 357) is an illustration. The name is derived from the fact that the important French medieval romance on Alexander the Great was written in this meter   361 **Denham ... Waller,** Sir John Denham (1615–1669) and Edmund Waller (1608–1687), both minor seventeenth-century poets, long praised as the originators of the closed couplet, developed by Dryden and perfected by Pope   369 **The hoarse . . . roar.** Pope is here trying to adapt the sound of the line to the sense (onomatopoeia)   370–72 **Ajax ... Camilla.** Ajax is a leading Greek hero in the Trojan War, noted for his great size and strength (cf. Homer's *Iliad*). *Camilla* is the swift-footed female warrior slain while fighting against the Trojan band in Italy (cf. Vergil's *Aeneid*)   374 **Timotheus,** the favorite musician of Alexander the Great (cf. Dryden's *Alexander's Feast*, ll. 158–160)   376 **son of Libyan Jove,** Alexander the Great (356–323 B.C.), King of Macedon, whom the priests of the Libyan Jupiter saluted as the son of their god. Historically, of course, Alexander was the son of King Philip of Macedon. There was a particularly powerful cult of Jupiter (Zeus) in Libya, Africa   391 **approve,** test

328 **Fungoso,** a foppish character in Ben Jonson's *Every Man Out of His Humor* (1599), who unsuccessfully tries to keep up with court fashions   337 **numbers,** verses

Some foreign writers, some our own despise;
The ancients only, or the moderns prize.
Thus wit, like faith, by each man is applied
To one small sect, and all are damned beside.
Meanly they seek the blessing to confine,
And force that sun but on a part to shine,
400 Which not alone the southern wit sublimes,
But ripens spirits in cold northern climes;
Which from the first has shone on ages past,
Enlights the present, and shall warm the last;
Though each may feel increases and decays,
And see now clearer and now darker days.
Regard not then if wit be old or new,
But blame the false, and value still the true.

Some ne'er advance a judgment of their own,
But catch the spreading notion of the town;
410 They reason and conclude by precedent,
And own stale nonsense which they ne'er invent.
Some judge of authors' names, not works, and then
Nor praise nor blame the writings, but the men.
Of all this servile herd the worst is he
That in proud dullness joins with quality,
A constant critic at the great man's board,
To fetch and carry nonsense for my lord.
What woeful stuff this madrigal would be,
In some starved hackney° sonneteer, or me?
420 But let a lord once own the happy lines,
How the wit brightens; how the style refines!
Before his sacred name flies every fault,
And each exalted stanza teems with thought!

The vulgar thus through imitation err;
As oft the learned by being singular;
So much they scorn the crowd, that if the throng
By chance go right, they purposely go wrong;
So schismatics° the plain believers quit,
And are but damned for having too much wit.
430 Some praise at morning what they blame at night;
But always think the last opinion right.
A Muse by these is like a mistress used,
This hour she's idolized, the next abused;
While their weak heads like towns unfortified,
'Twixt sense and nonsense daily change their side.
Ask them the cause; they're wiser still, they say;
And still tomorrow's wiser than today.
We think our fathers fools, so wise we grow;
Our wiser sons, no doubt, will think us so.
440 Once school-divines this zealous isle o'erspread;
Who knew most Sentences,° was deepest read;
Faith, Gospel, all seemed made to be disputed:
And none had sense enough to be confuted:

Scotists and Thomists,° now in peace remain,
Amidst their kindred cobwebs in Duck Lane;°
If faith itself has different dresses worn,
What wonder modes in wit should take their turn?
Oft, leaving what is natural and fit,
The current folly proves the ready wit;
And authors think their reputation safe,   450
Which lives as long as fools are pleased to laugh.

Some valuing those of their own side of mind,
Still make themselves the measure of mankind:
Fondly we think we honor merit then,
When we but praise ourselves in other men.
Parties in wit attend on those of state,
And public faction doubles private hate.
Pride, malice, folly, against Dryden rose,
In various shapes of parsons, critics, beaus;
But sense survived when merry jests were past;   460
For rising merit will buoy up at last.
Might he return, and bless once more our eyes,
New Blackmores° and new Milbourns° must arise:
Nay, should great Homer lift his awful head,
Zoilus° again would start up from the dead.
Envy will merit, as its shade, pursue;
But like a shadow, proves the substance true;
For envied wit, like Sol eclipsed, makes known
The opposing body's grossness, not its own.
When first that sun too powerful beams displays, 470
It draws up vapors which obscure its rays;
But even those clouds at last adorn its way,
Reflect new glories, and augment the day.

Be thou the first true merit to defend,
His praise is lost, who stays till all commend.
Short is the date, alas, of modern rimes,
And 'tis but just to let them live betimes.
No longer now that golden age appears,
When patriarch-wits survived a thousand years:
Now length of fame (our second life) is lost,   480
And bare threescore is all even that can boast;
Our sons their fathers' failing language see,
And such as Chaucer is, shall Dryden be.
So when the faithful pencil has designed
Some bright idea of the master's mind,
Where a new word leaps out at his command,
And ready nature waits upon his hand;
When the ripe colors soften and unite,
And sweetly melt into just shade and light;
When mellow years their full perfection give,   490
And each bold figure just begins to live,
The treacherous colors the fair art betray,
And all the bright creation fades away!

419 **hackney**, at first a horse for ordinary driving, then, figuratively, a drudge of any sort. As applied to a writer, the term means one who writes anything that comes his way in order to live. The combination "hackney writer" has been shortened to "hack writer" or "hack"   428 **schismatics**, people who promote schisms, disbeliefs or divisions in some body, particularly a religious one
441 **Sentences**, a reference to the *Book of Sentences*, a collection of religious precepts by Peter Lombard (fl. 1151)

444 **Scotists and Thomists**, disputing followers of Duns Scotus and St. Thomas Aquinas, scholastic philosophers of the thirteenth century   445 **Duck Lane**, a London street famous for its second-hand bookstores   463 **Blackmores**. Sir Richard Blackmore (1652–1729), physician and poet, had attacked Pope in *A Satire on Wit*   **Milbourns**. The Reverend Luke Milbourn (1649–1720), poet and translator, had criticized unfavorably Dryden's translation of Vergil   465 **Zoilus**, a Greek critic of the fourth century B.C., said to have been put to death for attacking Homer

Unhappy wit, like most mistaken things,
Atones not for that envy which it brings.
In youth alone its empty praise we boast,
But soon the short-lived vanity is lost:
Like some fair flower the early spring supplies,
That gaily blooms, but even in blooming dies.
500 What is this wit, which must our cares employ?
The owner's wife, that other men enjoy;
Then most our trouble still when most admired,
And still the more we give, the more required;
Whose fame with pains we guard, but lose with ease,
Sure some to vex, but never all to please;
'Tis what the vicious fear, the virtuous shun,
By fools 'tis hated, and by knaves undone!

If wit so much from ignorance undergo,
Ah, let not learning too commence its foe!
510 Of old, those met rewards who could excel,
And such were praised who but endeavored well:
Though triumphs were to generals only due,
Crowns were reserved to grace the soldiers too.
Now, they who reach Parnassus' lofty crown,
Employ their pains to spurn some others down;
And while self-love each jealous writer rules,
Contending wits become the sport of fools:
But still the worst with most regret commend,
For each ill author is as bad a friend.
520 To what base ends, and by what abject ways,
Are mortals urged through sacred lust of praise!
Ah, ne'er so dire a thirst of glory boast,
Nor in the critic let the man be lost.
Good-nature and good-sense must ever join;
To err is human, to forgive, divine.

But if in noble minds some dregs remain
Not yet purged off, of spleen and sour disdain:
Discharge that rage on more provoking crimes,
Nor fear a dearth in these flagitious° times.
530 No pardon vile obscenity should find,
Though wit and art conspire to move your mind;
But dullness with obscenity must prove
As shameful sure as impotence in love.
In the fat age of pleasure, wealth, and ease,
Sprung the rank weed, and thrived with large increase:
When love was all an easy Monarch's° care;
Seldom at council, never in a war:
Jilts ruled the state, and statesmen farces writ;
Nay, wits had pensions, and young lords had wit:
540 The fair sat panting at a courtier's play,
And not a mask went unimproved away:
The modest fan was lifted up no more,
And virgins smiled at what they blushed before.
The following license of a foreign reign
Did all the dregs of bold Socinus° drain;

Then unbelieving priests reformed the nation,
And taught more pleasant methods of salvation;
Where Heaven's free subjects might their rights dispute,
Lest God himself should seem too absolute;
Pulpits their sacred satire learned to spare,   550
And vice admired to find a flatterer there!
Encouraged thus, wit's Titans braved the skies,
And the press groaned with licensed blasphemies.
These monsters, critics! with your darts engage,
Here point your thunder, and exhaust your rage!
Yet shun their fault, who, scandalously nice,
Will needs mistake an author into vice;
All seems infected that the infected spy,
As all looks yellow to the jaundiced eye.
(1711)

THE RAPE OF THE LOCK

A quarrel between two prominent Catholic families had resulted from the cutting of a lock of hair from the head of Miss Arabella Fermor (pronounced *Farmer*) by Lord Petre. It was to heal the quarrel that Pope wrote the poem. Miss Fermor is Belinda; Lord Petre is the baron.

The enormous success of the first version (1712), which was written with great speed, convinced Pope to extend the poem from two cantos to five and to revise the original (1713).

The Rape of the Lock is a "mock epic," that is, a comic poem on an essentially trivial incident employing for the purpose of heightened comedy the elevated epic frame, corroborated by numerous allusions to serious episodes in Homer, Vergil, Shakespeare, and Milton. The traditional elements which provide the epic context are (1) the opening "proposition" or "invocation"; (2) parody of actual epic speeches; (3) epic similes; (4) a supernatural agent appearing in a dream; (5) the use of allegorical figures, given their appropriate setting; (6) the learned survey of a tract of knowledge; (7) the visit to the underworld; (8) the large-scale battle; (9) the epic denouement of strategy in war; and (10) the characteristic epic ending through *deus ex machina*.

Since this is a mock epic, Pope subjects the traditional epic elements to a process of diminution: for the epic protagonist, he presents a woman; in the place of the rape of Helen is a stolen lock of hair; epic meals become ceremonials around a silver tea set; trembling petticoats take the place of great shields. For the epic battle, he substitutes a game of cards upon a velvet plain and a fracas of fans, silks, and whalebone. In short, everything is made smaller in size and exquisitely feminine. The epical protagonist, Belinda, has hysterics, and the epical antagonist, the Hector-like baron, sneezes.

---

529 **flagitious,** corrupt, grossly wicked   536 **an easy Monarch,** the gay and dissolute Charles II, whose reign, referred to in the next few lines, covered the years 1660–1685   545 **Socinus,** the name of two Italian theologians, Laelius Socinus (1525–1562) and Faustus Socinus (1539–1604). They were the forerunners of modern Unitarianism

CANTO 1

What dire offense from amorous causes springs,
What mighty contests rise from trivial things,
I sing— This verse to Caryl, Muse! is due:
This, even Belinda may vouchsafe to view:
Slight is the subject, but not so the praise,
If she inspire, and he approve my lays.

Say what strange motive, goddess! could compel
A well-bred lord to assault a gentle belle?
Oh, say what stranger cause, yet unexplored,
10 Could make a gentle belle reject a lord?
In tasks so bold, can little men engage,
And in soft bosoms dwells such mighty rage?

Sol through white curtains shot a timorous ray,
And oped those eyes that must eclipse the day;
Now lap-dogs give themselves the rousing shake,
And sleepless lovers, just at twelve, awake;
Thrice rung the bell, the slipper knocked the ground,
And the pressed watch returned a silver sound.°
Belinda still her downy pillow pressed,
20 Her guardian sylph° prolonged the balmy rest:
'Twas he had summoned to her silent bed
The morning dream that hovered o'er her head;
A youth more glittering than a birth-night beau°
(That e'en in slumber caused her cheek to glow),
Seemed to her ear his winning lips to lay,
And thus in whispers said, or seemed to say:

"Fairest of mortals, thou distinguished care
Of thousand bright inhabitants of air!
If e'er one vision touched thy infant thought,
30 Of all the nurse and all the priest have taught
Of airy elves by moonlight shadows seen,°
The silver token, and the circled green,
Or virgins visited by angel powers,
With golden crowns and wreaths of heavenly flowers;
Hear and believe! thy own importance know,
Nor bound thy narrow views to things below.
Some secret truths, from learned pride concealed,
To maids alone and children are revealed;
What though no credit doubting wits may give?
40 The fair and innocent shall still believe.
Know, then, unnumbered spirits round thee fly,
The light militia of the lower sky:
These, though unseen, are ever on the wing,
Hang o'er the box, and hover round the Ring,°
Think what an equipage thou hast in air,
And view with scorn two pages and a chair.
As now your own, our beings were of old,

And once enclosed in woman's beauteous mold;
Thence, by a soft transition, we repair
From earthly vehicles to these of air.   50
Think not, when woman's transient breath is fled,
That all her vanities at once are dead;
Succeeding vanities she still regards,
And though she plays no more, o'erlooks the cards.
Her joy in gilded chariots, when alive,
And love of ombre,° after death survive.
For when the fair in all their pride expire,
To their first elements their souls retire:
The sprites of fiery termagants° in flame
Mount up, and take a salamander's° name.   60
Soft yielding minds to water glide away,
And sip, with nymphs, their elemental tea.
The graver prude sinks downward to a gnome,
In search of mischief still on earth to roam.
The light coquettes in sylphs aloft repair,
And sport and flutter in the fields of air.

"Know further yet; whoever fair and chaste
Rejects mankind, is by some sylph embraced;
For spirits, freed from mortal laws, with ease
Assume what sexes and what shapes they please.   70
What guards the purity of melting maids,
In courtly balls, and midnight masquerades,
Safe from the treacherous friend, the daring spark,°
The glance by day, the whisper in the dark,
When kind occasion prompts their warm desires,
When music softens, and when dancing fires?
'Tis but their sylph, the wise celestials know,
Though honor is the word with men below.
Some nymphs there are, too conscious of their face,
For life predestined to the gnomes' embrace.   80
These swell their prospects and exalt their pride,
When offers are disdained, and love denied:
Then gay ideas crowd the vacant brain,
While peers, and dukes, and all their sweeping train,
And garters, stars, and coronets appear,
And in soft sounds 'Your Grace' salutes their ear.
'Tis these that early taint the female soul,
Instruct the eyes of young coquettes to roll,
Teach infant cheeks a bidden blush to know,
And little hearts to flutter at a beau.   90

"Oft, when the world imagine women stray,
The sylphs through mystic mazes guide their way,
Through all the giddy circle they pursue,
And old impertinence expel by new.
What tender maid but must a victim fall
To one man's treat, but for another's ball?
When Florio speaks, what virgin could withstand,
If gentle Damon° did not squeeze her hand?

The Rape of the Lock   Canto 1   18 pressed . . . sound, a type of watch quite
common among the wealthier in the eighteenth century, in which a pressure upon
the stem would cause the watch to strike again the last hour   20 guardian sylph.
The sylphs and nymphs, lesser spirits of the air, take the place in this mock epic
of the gods and goddesses of classical mythology, who, in the pages of Homer
and Vergil, give aid and comfort to their protégés   23 birth-night beau, a courtier, who wore fine clothes on the sovereign's birthday   31 elves . . . seen, etc.
These few lines give a flash of "romantic" nature that is most unusual in Pope
44 box . . . Ring. The box is a box at the theater; the Ring is a circular driveway
or promenade in Hyde Park, London

56 ombre, a fashionable card game usually played by three people (see Canto 3,
25 ff.)   59 termagants. Termagant was originally a supposed deity of the Saracens. In the morality plays, in which Termagant appeared, he was always represented by a violent, brawling person. Hence the term eventually was applied to
any brawling person, and particularly to a scolding, shrewish, fiery woman
60 salamander. It was an old belief that salamanders could pass unharmed
through fire   73 spark, young man of elegant or foppish character   97–
98 Florio . . . Damon, traditional names for heroes in the pastoral literature of the
classics, and later for young swains

With varying vanities, from every part,
100 They shift the moving toyshop of their heart;
Where wigs with wigs, with sword-knots sword-knots
      strive,
Beaux banish beaux, and coaches coaches drive.
This erring mortals levity may call;
Oh, blind to truth! the sylphs contrive it all.

      "Of these am I, who thy protection claim,
A watchful sprite, and Ariel is my name.
Late, as I ranged the crystal wilds of air,
In the clear mirror of thy ruling star
I saw, alas! some dread event impend,
110 Ere to the main this morning sun descend,
But Heaven reveals not what, or how, or where:
Warned by the sylph, O pious maid, beware!
This to disclose is all thy guardian can:
Beware of all, but most beware of man!"

      He said; when Shock,° who thought she slept too
      long,
Leaped up, and waked his mistress with his tongue.
'Twas then, Belinda, if report say true,
Thy eyes first opened on a billet-doux;
Wounds, charms, and ardors were no sooner read,
120 But all the vision vanished from thy head.

      And now, unveiled, the toilet stands displayed,
Each silver vase in mystic order laid.
First, robed in white, the nymph intent adores,
With head uncovered, the cosmetic powers.
A heavenly image in the glass appears.
To that she bends, to that her eyes she rears;
The inferior priestess, at her altar's side,
Trembling begins the sacred rites of pride.
Unnumbered treasures ope at once, and here
130 The various offerings of the world appear;
From each she nicely culls with curious toil,
And decks the goddess with the glittering spoil.
This casket India's glowing gems unlocks,
And all Arabia breathes from yonder box.
The tortoise here and elephant unite,
Transformed to combs, the speckled, and the white.
Here files of pins extend their shining rows,
Puffs, powders, patches, bibles, billets-doux.
Now awful beauty puts on all its arms;
140 The fair each moment rises in her charms,
Repairs her smiles, awakens every grace,
And calls forth all the wonders of her face;
Sees by degrees a purer blush arise,
And keener lightnings quicken in her eyes.
The busy sylphs surround their darling care,
These set the head, and those divide the hair,
Some fold the sleeve, whilst others plait the gown;
And Betty's° praised for labors not her own.

115 **Shock,** Belinda's lap dog   148 **Betty,** a traditional name for a personal
maid; here, Belinda's

CANTO 2

      Not with more glories, in the ethereal plain,
The sun first rises o'er the purpled main,
Than, issuing forth, the rival of his beams
Launched on the bosom of the silver Thames.
Fair nymphs, and well-dressed youths around her
      shone,
But every eye was fixed on her alone.
On her white breast a sparkling cross she wore,
Which Jews might kiss, and infidels adore.
Her lively looks a sprightly mind disclose,
Quick as her eyes, and as unfixed as those;   10
Favors to none, to all she smiles extends;
Oft she rejects, but never once offends.
Bright as the sun, her eyes the gazers strike,
And, like the sun, they shine on all alike.
Yet graceful ease, and sweetness void of pride,
Might hide her faults, if belles had faults to hide;
If to her share some female errors fall,
Look on her face, and you'll forget 'em all.

      This nymph, to the destruction of mankind,
Nourished two locks, which graceful hung behind   20
In equal curls, and well conspired to deck
With shining ringlets the smooth ivory neck.
Love in these labyrinths his slaves detains,
And mighty hearts are held in slender chains.
With hairy springes, we the birds betray,
Slight lines of hair surprise the finny prey,
Fair tresses man's imperial race ensnare,
And beauty draws us with a single hair.

      The adventurous baron the bright locks admired;
He saw, he wished, and to the prize aspired.   30
Resolved to win, he meditates the way,
By force to ravish, or by fraud betray;
For when success a lover's toil attends,
Few ask, if fraud or force attained his ends.

      For this, ere Phoebus rose, he had implored
Propitious Heaven, and every power adored,
But chiefly Love—to Love an altar built,
Of twelve vast French romances, neatly gilt.
There lay three garters, half a pair of gloves;
And all the trophies of his former loves;   40
With tender billets-doux he lights the pyre,
And breathes three amorous sighs to raise the fire.
Then prostrate falls, and begs with ardent eyes
Soon to obtain, and long possess the prize;
The powers gave ear, and granted half his prayer,
The rest, the winds dispersed in empty air.

      But now secure the painted vessel glides,
The sunbeams trembling on the floating tides:
While melting music steals upon the sky,
And softened sounds along the waters die;   50
Smooth flow the waves, the zephyrs gently play,

Belinda smiled, and all the world was gay.
All but the sylph—with careful thoughts oppressed,
The impending woe sat heavy on his breast.
He summons straight his denizens of air;
The lucid squadrons round the sails repair:
Soft o'er the shrouds aërial whispers breathe,
That seemed but zephyrs to the train beneath.
Some to the sun their insect wings unfold,
60 Waft on the breeze, or sink in clouds of gold;
Transparent forms, too fine for mortal sight,
Their fluid bodies half dissolved in light.
Loose to the wind their airy garments flew,
Thin glittering textures of the filmy dew,
Dipped in the richest tincture of the skies,
Where light disports in ever-mingling dyes,
While every beam new transient colors flings,
Colors that change whene'er they wave their wings.
Amid the circle, on the gilded mast,
70 Superior° by the head, was Ariel placed;
His purple pinions opening to the sun,
He raised his azure wand, and thus begun.

"Ye sylphs and sylphids, to your chief give ear!
Fays, fairies, genii, elves, and demons, hear!
Ye know the spheres, and various tasks assigned
By laws eternal to the aërial kind.
Some in the fields of purest ether play,
And bask and whiten in the blaze of day.
Some guide the course of wandering orbs on high,
80 Or roll the planets through the boundless sky.
Some less refined, beneath the moon's pale light
Pursue the stars that shoot athwart the night,
Or suck the mists in grosser air below,
Or dip their pinions in the painted bow,
Or brew fierce tempests on the wintry main,
Or o'er the glebe distil the kindly rain.
Others on earth o'er human race preside,
Watch all their ways, and all their actions guide:
Of these the chief, the care of nations own,
90 And guard with arms divine the British throne.

"Our humbler province is to tend the fair.
Not a less pleasing, though less glorious care;
To save the powder from too rude a gale,
Nor let the imprisoned essences exhale;
To draw fresh colors from the vernal flowers;
To steal from rainbows ere they drop in showers,
A brighter wash; to curl their waving hairs,
Assist their blushes, and inspire their airs;
Nay, oft in dreams, invention we bestow,
100 To change a flounce, or add a furbelow.°

"This day, black omens threat the brightest fair
That e'er deserved a watchful spirit's care;
Some dire disaster, or by force, or slight;
But what, or where, the fates have wrapped in night.

Whether the nymph shall break Diana's law,°
Or some frail china jar receive a flaw;
Or stain her honor, or her new brocade;
Forget her prayers, or miss a masquerade;
Or lose her heart, or necklace, at a ball;
Or whether Heaven has doomed that Shock must fall. 110
Haste, then, ye spirits! to your charge repair;
The fluttering fan be Zephyretta's care;
The drops to thee, Brillante, we consign;
And, Momentilla, let the watch be thine;
Do thou, Crispissa, tend her favorite lock;
Ariel himself shall be the guard of Shock.

"To fifty chosen sylphs, of special note,
We trust the important charge, the petticoat:
Oft have we known that seven-fold fence to fail,
Though stiff with hoops, and armed with ribs of whale; 120
Form a strong line about the silver bound,
And guard the wide circumference around.

"Whatever spirit, careless of his charge,
His post neglects, or leaves the fair at large,
Shall feel sharp vengeance soon o'ertake his sins,
Be stopped in vials, or transfixed with pins;
Or plunged in lakes of bitter washes lie,
Or wedged whole ages in a bodkin's eye:
Gums and pomatums° shall his flight restrain,
While clogged he beats his silken wings in vain; 130
Or alum styptics with contracting power
Shrink his thin essence like a rivelled° flower:
Or, as Ixion fixed,° the wretch shall feel
The giddy motion of the whirling mill,
In fumes of burning chocolate shall glow,
And tremble at the sea that froths below!"

He spoke; the spirits from the sails descend;
Some, orb in orb, around the nymph extend;
Some thrid° the mazy ringlets of her hair;
Some hang upon the pendants of her ear; 140
With beating hearts the dire event they wait,
Anxious, and trembling for the birth of fate.

CANTO 3

Close by those meads, forever crowned with flow-
ers,
Where Thames with pride surveys his rising towers,
There stands a structure of majestic frame,°
Which from the neighboring Hampton takes its name.
Here Britain's statesmen oft the fall foredoom
Of foreign tyrants and of nymphs at home;

105 **Diana's law,** the law of chastity; Diana was the goddess of maidenhood
129 **Gums . . . pomatums,** perfumed ointments; pomatum was used particularly
for the hair   132 **rivelled,** withered   133 **Ixion fixed.** Ixion was a legendary
king who, for making love to Juno, wife of Jupiter and queen of the gods, was
fastened by Jupiter to an endlessly revolving wheel in Hades   139 **thrid,**
threaded, passed through   **Canto 3**   3 **structure . . . frame,** Hampton Court,
one of the royal palaces near London

Canto 2   70 **Superior,** above   100 **furbelow,** frill

Here thou, great Anna!° whom three realms obey,
Dost sometimes counsel take—and sometimes tea.°
Hither the heroes and the nymphs resort,
To taste awhile the pleasures of a court;
In various talk the instructive hours they passed,
Who gave the ball, or paid the visit last;
One speaks the glory of the British queen,
And one describes a charming Indian screen;
A third interprets motions, looks, and eyes;
At every word a reputation dies.
Snuff, or the fan, supply each pause of chat,
With singing, laughing, ogling, and all that.

Meanwhile, declining from the noon of day,
The sun obliquely shoots his burning ray;
The hungry judges soon the sentence sign,
And wretches hang that jurymen may dine;
The merchant from the Exchange returns in peace,
And the long labors of the toilet cease.
Belinda now, whom thirst of fame invites,
Burns to encounter two adventurous knights,
At ombre singly to decide their doom;
And swells her breast with conquests yet to come.
Straight the three bands prepare in arms to join,
Each band the number of the sacred nine.
Soon as she spreads her hand, the aërial guard
Descend, and sit on each important card:
First, Ariel perched upon a Matadore,°
Then each, according to the rank they bore;
For sylphs, yet mindful of their ancient race,
Are, as when women, wondrous fond of place.

Behold, four kings in majesty revered,
With hoary whiskers and a forky beard;
And four fair queens whose hands sustain a flower,
The expressive emblem of their softer power;
Four knaves in garbs succinct,° a trusty band,
Caps on their heads, and halberts° in their hand;
And parti-colored troops, a shining train,
Draw forth to combat on the velvet plain.

The skillful nymph reviews her force with care:
Let spades be trumps! she said, and trumps they were.

Now moved to war her sable Matadores,
In show like leaders of the swarthy Moors.
Spadillio first, unconquerable lord!
Led off two captive trumps, and swept the board.
As many more Manillio forced to yield,
And marched a victor from the verdant field.
Him Basto followed, but his fate more hard

Gained but one trump and one plebeian card.
With his broad saber next, a chief in years,
The hoary majesty of spades appears,
Puts forth one manly leg, to sight revealed,
The rest, his many-colored robe concealed.
The rebel knave, who dares his prince engage,
Proves the just victim of his royal rage.
Even mighty Pam, that kings and queens o'erthrew,
And mowed down armies in the fights of Loo,°
Sad chance of war! now destitute of aid,
Falls undistinguished by the victor spade!

Thus far both armies to Belinda yield;
Now to the baron fate inclines the field.
His warlike Amazon her host invades,
The imperial consort of the crown of spades,
The clubs black tyrant first her victim died,
Spite of his haughty mien, and barbarous pride:
What boots the regal circle on his head,
His giant limbs, in state unwieldy spread;
That long behind he trails his pompous robe,
And of all monarchs only grasps the globe?

The baron now his diamonds pours apace;
The embroidered king who shows but half his face
And his refulgent queen, with powers combined,
Of broken troops an easy conquest find.
Clubs, diamonds, hearts, in wild disorder seen,
With throngs promiscuous strew the level green.
Thus when dispersed a routed army runs,
Of Asia's troops, and Afric's sable sons,
With like confusion different nations fly,
Of various habit, and of various dye,
The pierced battalions disunited fall,
In heaps on heaps; one fate o'erwhelms them all.

The knave of diamonds tries his wily arts,
And wins (oh, shameful chance!) the queen of hearts.
At this the blood the virgin's cheek forsook,
A livid paleness spreads o'er all her look;
She sees, and trembles at the approaching ill,
Just in the jaws of ruin, and codille.°
And now (as oft in some distempered state)
On one nice° trick depends the general fate,
An ace of hearts steps forth; the king unseen
Lurked in her hand, and mourned his captive queen:
He springs to vengeance with an eager pace,
And falls like thunder on the prostrate ace.
The nymph exulting fills with shouts the sky;
The walls, the wood, and long canals reply.

Oh, thoughtless mortals! ever blind to fate,
Too soon dejected, and too soon elate.
Sudden, these honors shall be snatched away,
And cursed forever this victorious day.

---

7 **Anna,** Queen Anne, last of the Stuarts, whose reign from 1702 to 1714 is noteworthy because she was the first sovereign for whom the term ruler "of England, Scotland, and Wales" was an absolute reality. England and Scotland had been united politically in 1707   8 **tea,** pronounced to rhyme with obey   33 **Matadore,** one of the three highest cards in ombre; their names are given below. *Spadillio* (l. 49) was the ace of spades; *Manillio* (l. 51), the two of black trumps or the seven of red trumps; *Basto* (l. 53) was the ace of clubs   41 **succinct,** encircled by a girdle   42 **halberts,** halberds, long-handled, axlike weapons surmounted by a long point; they were used frequently in the armies of the fifteenth and sixteenth centuries

61-62 **Pam ... Loo.** Pam is the jack of clubs (*knave*), the highest card in the game of Loo   92 **codille,** failure to take the largest number of tricks   94 **nice,** possibly in the older sense of "foolish"; probably in the sense of "neat, precise, trim"

For lo! the board with cups and spoons is crowned,
The berries crackle, and the mill turns round;°
On shining altars of Japan° they raise
The silver lamp; the fiery spirits blaze:
From silver spouts the grateful liquors glide,
110 While China's earth receives the smoking tide:
At once they gratify their scent and taste,
And frequent cups prolong the rich repast.
Straight hover round the fair her airy band;
Some, as she sipped, the fuming liquor fanned,
Some o'er her lap their careful plumes displayed,
Trembling, and conscious of the rich brocade.
Coffee (which makes the politician wise,
And see through all things with his half-shut eyes)
Sent up in vapors to the baron's brain
120 New stratagems the radiant lock to gain.
Ah, cease rash youth! desist ere 'tis too late,
Fear the just gods, and think of Scylla's fate!
Changed to a bird, and sent to flit in air,
She dearly pays for Nisus' injured hair!°

But when to mischief mortals bend their will,
How soon they find fit instruments of ill!
Just then Clarissa drew with tempting grace
A two-edged weapon from her shining case;
So ladies in romance assist their knight,
130 Present the spear, and arm him for the fight.
He takes the gift with reverence, and extends
The little engine on his fingers' ends;
This just behind Belinda's neck he spread,
As o'er the fragrant steams she bends her head.
Swift to the lock a thousand sprites repair,
A thousand wings, by turns, blow back her hair;
And thrice they twitched the diamond in her ear;
Thrice she looked back, and thrice the foe drew near.
Just in that instant, anxious Ariel sought
140 The close recesses of the virgin's thought;
As on the nosegay in her breast reclined,
He watched the ideas rising in her mind,
Sudden he viewed, in spite of all her art,
An earthly lover lurking at her heart.
Amazed, confused, he found his power expired,
Resigned to fate, and with a sigh retired.

The peer now spreads the glittering forfex° wide,
To inclose the lock; now joins it, to divide.
Even then, before the fatal engine closed,
150 A wretched sylph too fondly interposed;
Fate urged the shears, and cut the sylph in twain,
(But airy substance soon unites again)
The meeting points the sacred hair dissever
From the fair head, forever, and forever!

Then flashed the living lightning from her eyes,
And screams of horror rend the affrighted skies.
Not louder shrieks to pitying Heaven are cast,
When husbands, or when lap-dogs breathe their last;
Or when rich China vessels, fallen from high,
In glittering dust and painted fragments lie!   160

"Let wreaths of triumph now my temples twine "
(The victor cried); "the glorious prize is mine!
While fish in streams, or birds delight in air,
Or in a coach and six the British fair,
As long as Atalantis shall be read,°
Or the small pillow grace a lady's bed,
While visits shall be paid on solemn days,
When numerous wax-lights in bright order blaze,
While nymphs take treats, or assignations give,
So long my honor, name, and praise shall live!   170
What Time would spare, from steel receives its date,
And monuments, like men, submit to fate!
Steel could the labor of the gods destroy,
And strike to dust the imperial towers of Troy;
Steel could the works of mortal pride confound,
And hew triumphal arches to the ground.
What wonder then, fair nymph! thy hairs should feel
The conquering force of unresisted steel?"

CANTO 4

But anxious cares° the pensive nymph oppressed,
And secret passions labored in her breast.
Not youthful kings in battle seized alive,
Not scornful virgins who their charms survive,
Not ardent lovers robbed of all their bliss,
Not ancient ladies when refused a kiss,
Not tyrants fierce that unrepenting die,
Not Cynthia° when her manteau's° pinned awry,
E'er felt such rage, resentment, and despair,
As thou, sad virgin, for thy ravished hair.   10
For, that sad moment, when the sylphs withdrew
And Ariel weeping from Belinda flew,
Umbriel, a dusky, melancholy sprite,
As ever sullied the fair face of light,
Down to the central earth, his proper scene,
Repaired to search the gloomy cave of Spleen.°

Swift on his sooty pinions flits the gnome,
And in a vapor reached the dismal dome.
No cheerful breeze this sullen region knows,
The dreaded east is all the wind that blows.   20
Here in a grotto, sheltered close from air,

106 **berries . . . round,** coffee berries ground in a handmill at the table
107 **altars of Japan,** small lacquered tables   122–24 **Scylla . . . Nisus . . . hair.**
In Greek legend, Scylla, the daughter of King Nisus of Megara, gave to an enemy
a lock of her father's hair, on which the safety of the state depended; for this offense she was changed into a bird. She must not be confused with Scylla, the
dreadful sea monster whose home was opposite the whirlpool Charybdis in the
Straits of Messina   147 **forfex,** shears, scissors

165 **Atalantis . . . read,** New Atalantis (1709), a popular book of contemporary
scandal and gossip, by Mrs. Mary Manley (1663–1724). The title of the book is
something of a play upon the title of Bacon's New Atlantis (1624). Bacon's work
was an account of a Utopia, or mythical kingdom, Atlantis; Mrs. Manley's was an
account of a woman's world of gossip   **Canto 4   1 anxious cares, etc.** This and
the following lines (1–10) afford some excellent examples of the neoclassical
"epithet." It is to be noted that virtually every noun has a single descriptive adjective in attendance   8 **Cynthia,** Diana, the goddess of chastity   **manteau,**
mantle   16 **Spleen,** melancholy, caprice, peevish temper

And screened in shades from day's detested glare,
She sighs forever on her pensive bed,
Pain at her side, and Megrim at° her head.
Two handmaids wait the throne, alike in place,
But differing far in figure and in face.
Here stood Ill-nature like an ancient maid,
Her wrinkled form in black and white arrayed;
With store of prayers, for mornings, nights, and noons,
30 Her hand is filled; her bosom with lampoons.

There Affectation, with a sickly mien,
Shows in her cheek the roses of eighteen,
Practiced to lisp, and hang the head aside,
Faints into airs, and languishes with pride,
On the rich quilt sinks with becoming woe,
Wrapped in a gown, for sickness, and for show.
The fair ones feel such maladies as these,
When each new night-dress gives a new disease.

A constant vapor o'er the palace flies;
40 Strange phantoms rising as the mists arise;
Dreadful, as hermit's dreams in haunted shades,
Or bright, as visions of expiring maids.
Now glaring fiends, and snakes on rolling spires,
Pale specters, gaping tombs, and purple fires:
Now lakes of liquid gold, Elysian scenes,
And crystal domes, and angels in machines.

Unnumbered throngs on every side are seen,
Of bodies changed to various forms by Spleen.
Here living tea-pots stand, one arm held out,
50 One bent; the handle this, and that the spout:
A pipkin° there, like Homer's tripod,° walks;
Here sighs a jar, and there a goose-pie talks;
Men prove with child, as powerful fancy works,
And maids, turned bottles, call aloud for corks.

Safe passed the gnome through this fantastic band,
A branch of healing spleenwort° in his hand.
Then thus addressed the power: "Hail, wayward
    queen!
Who rule the sex, to fifty from fifteen;
Parent of vapors° and of female wit,
60 Who give the hysteric, or poetic fit,
On various tempers act by various ways,
Make some take physic, others scribble plays;
Who cause the proud their visits to delay,
And send the godly in a pet to pray.
A nymph there is, that all thy power disdains,
And thousands more in equal mirth maintains.
But oh! if e'er thy gnome could spoil a grace,
Or raise a pimple on a beauteous face,
Like citron-waters° matrons' cheeks inflame,
70 Or change complexions at a losing game;

If e'er with airy horns I planted heads,°
Or rumpled petticoats, or tumbled beds,
Or caused suspicion when no soul was rude,
Or discomposed the head-dress of a prude,
Or e'er to costive lap-dog gave disease,
Which not the tears of brightest eyes could ease;
Hear me, and touch Belinda with chagrin,
That single act gives half the world the spleen.''

The goddess with a discontented air
Seems to reject him, though she grants his prayer.   80
A wondrous bag with both her hands she binds,
Like that where once Ulysses° held the winds;
There she collects the force of female lungs,
Sighs, sobs, and passions, and the war of tongues.
A vial next she fills with fainting fears,
Soft sorrows, melting griefs, and flowing tears.
The gnome rejoicing bears her gifts away,
Spreads his black wings, and slowly mounts to day.

Sunk in Thalestris'° arms the nymph he found,
Her eyes dejected and her hair unbound.   90
Full o'er their heads, the swelling bag he rent,
And all the furies issued at the vent.
Belinda burns with more than mortal ire,
And fierce Thalestris fans the rising fire.
''O wretched maid!'' she spread her hands, and cried,
(While Hampton's echoes, ''Wretched maid!'' replied)
''Was it for this you took such constant care
The bodkin, comb, and essence to prepare?
For this your locks in paper durance bound,
For this with torturing irons wreathed around?   100
For this with fillets strained your tender head,
And bravely bore the double loads of lead?
Gods! shall the ravisher display your hair,
While the fops envy, and the ladies stare!
Honor forbid! at whose unrivalled shrine
Ease, pleasure, virtue, all our sex resign.
Methinks already I your tears survey,
Already hear the horrid things they say,
Already see you a degraded toast,
And all your honor in a whisper lost!   110
How shall I, then, your helpless fame defend?
'Twill then be infamy to seem your friend!
And shall this prize, the inestimable prize,
Exposed through crystal to the gazing eyes,
And heightened by the diamond's circling rays,
On that rapacious hand forever blaze?
Sooner shall grass in Hyde Park Circus grow,
And wits take lodgings in the sound of Bow;°
Sooner let earth, air, sea, to chaos fall,
Men, monkeys, lap-dogs, parrots, perish all!''   120

24 **Megrim,** melancholy, depression   51 **pipkin,** a small jar   **Homer's tripod,** a self-moving tripod, described by Homer in the *Iliad*   56 **spleenwort,** maidenhair, an herb formerly used for the treatment of diseases of the spleen   59 **vapors,** spleen   69 **citron-waters,** citron brandy; older women could bring youthful color into their cheeks by drinking brandy

71 **horns . . . heads,** an allusion to the old belief that horns were supposed to grow on the heads of husbands with unfaithful wives   82 **Ulysses, etc.** Ulysses, during the course of his wanderings, visited the island of Eolus, god of the winds, and took away a bagful of the various winds to help him in his journey. The story is told in Homer's *Odyssey*   89 **Thalestris,** said to be Mrs. Gertrude Morley, friend to Arabella (Belinda) Fermor   118 **sound of Bow,** within sound of the bells of the church of St. Mary le Bow, traditionally the center of the city. The city was where the bourgeoisie lived as opposed to Westminster where the nobility and gentry lived

She said; then raging to Sir Plume repairs,
And bids her beau demand the precious hairs.
(Sir Plume, of amber snuff-box justly vain,
And the nice conduct of a clouded cane)°
With earnest eyes, and round unthinking face,
He first the snuff-box opened, then the case,
And thus broke out—"My lord, why, what the devil?
Z——ds!° damn the lock! 'fore Gad, you must be civil!
Plague on't! 'tis past a jest—nay prithee, pox!
130 Give her the hair," he spoke, and rapped his box.
"It grieves me much," replied the peer again,
"Who speaks so well should ever speak in vain.
But by this lock, this sacred lock, I swear,
(Which never more shall join its parted hair;
Which never more its honors shall renew,
Clipped from the lovely head where late it grew)
That while my nostrils draw the vital air,
This hand, which won it, shall forever wear."
He spoke, and speaking, in proud triumph spread
140 The long-contended honors of her head.

But Umbriel, hateful gnome! forbears not so;
He breaks the vial whence the sorrows flow.
Then see! the nymph in beauteous grief appears,
Her eyes half languishing, half drowned in tears;
On her heaved bosom hung her drooping head,
Which, with a sigh, she raised; and thus she said:

"Forever cursed be this detested day,
Which snatched my best, my favorite curl away!
Happy! ah, ten times happy had I been,
150 If Hampton Court these eyes had never seen!
Yet am not I the first mistaken maid,
By love of courts to numerous ills betrayed.
Oh, had I rather unadmired remained
In some lone isle or distant northern land;
Where the gilt chariot never marks the way,
Where none learn ombre, none e'er taste bohea!°
There kept my charms concealed from mortal eye,
Like roses, that in deserts bloom and die.
What moved my mind with youthful lords to roam?
160 Oh, had I stayed, and said my prayers at home!
'Twas this, the morning omens seemed to tell,
Thrice from my trembling hand the patch-box° fell;
The tottering china shook without a wind.
Nay, Poll sat mute, and Shock was most unkind!
A sylph, too, warned me of the threats of fate,
In mystic visions, now believed too late!
See the poor remnants of these slighted hairs!
My hands shall rend what e'en thy rapine spares;
These in two sable ringlets taught to break,
170 Once gave new beauties to the snowy neck;
The sister lock now sits uncouth, alone,
And in its fellow's fate foresees its own;
Unfurled it hangs, the fatal shears demands,

And tempts once more, thy sacrilegious hands.
Oh, hadst thou, cruel! been content to seize
Hairs less in sight, or any hairs but these!"

CANTO 5

She said; the pitying audience melt in tears.
But Fate and Jove had stopped the baron's ears.
In vain Thalestris with reproach assails,
For who can move when fair Belinda fails?
Not half so fixed the Trojan could remain,
While Anna begged and Dido raged in vain.°
Then grave Clarissa graceful waved her fan;
Silence ensued, and thus the nymph began:

"Say, why are beauties praised and honored most,
The wise man's passion, and the vain man's toast?   10
Why decked with all that land and sea afford,
Why angels called, and angel-like adored?
Why 'round our coaches crowd the white-gloved
        beaux,
Why bows the side-box from its inmost rows?
How vain are all these glories, all our pains,
Unless good sense preserve what beauty gains:
That men may say, when we the front-box grace:
'Behold the first in virtue as in face!'
Oh! if to dance all night, and dress all day,
Charmed the smallpox, or chased old age away;   20
Who would not scorn what housewife's cares produce,
Or who would learn one earthly thing of use?
To patch, nay ogle, might become a saint,
Nor could it sure be such a sin to paint.
But since, alas! frail beauty must decay,
Curled or uncurled, since locks will turn to gray;
Since painted, or not painted, all shall fade,
And she who scorns a man must die a maid;
What then remains but well our power to use,
And keep good humor still what'er we lose?   30
And trust me, dear! good humor can prevail,
When airs, and flights, and screams, and scolding fail.
Beauties in vain their pretty eyes may roll;
Charms strike the sight, but merit wins the soul."

So spoke the dame, but no applause ensued;
Belinda frowned, Thalestris called her prude.
"To arms, to arms!" the fierce virago cries,
And swift as lightning to the combat flies.
All side in parties, and begin th' attack;
Fans clap, silks rustle, and tough whale-bones crack;   40
Heroes' and heroines' shouts confusedly rise,
And bass and treble voices strike the skies.
No common weapons in their hands are found,
Like gods they fight, nor dread a mortal wound.

124 **clouded cane,** a walking stick with carvings in the shape of clouds
128 **Z---ds,** "zounds," a corruption of "God's wounds"   156 **bohea,** an expensive brand of tea   162 **patch-box,** a box containing patches of court plaster, which was used to decorate the face

Canto 5   5–6 Trojan . . . vain. The "Trojan" is Aeneas, hero of Vergil's *Aeneid,* who on command of Jupiter determined to leave Carthage in spite of the grief and pleas of Queen Dido of Carthage and of her sister Anna (*Aeneid,* IV, 4ff.)

So when bold Homer makes the gods engage,
And heavenly breasts with human passions rage;
'Gainst Pallas, Mars; Latona, Hermes arms;
And all Olympus rings with loud alarms:
Jove's thunder roars, Heaven trembles all around,
50 Blue Neptune° storms, the bellowing deeps resound:
Earth shakes her nodding towers, the ground gives
    way,
And the pale ghosts start at the flash of day!

    Triumphant Umbriel on a sconce's° height
Clapped his glad wings, and sat to view the fight:
Propped on their bodkin spears, the sprites survey
The growing combat, or assist the fray.

    While through the press enraged Thalestris flies,
And scatters death around from both her eyes,
A beau and witling perished in the throng,
60 One died in metaphor, and one in song.
"O cruel nymph! a living death I bear,"
Cried Dapperwit, and sunk beside his chair.
A mournful glance Sir Fopling° upwards cast,
"Those eyes are made so killing"—was his last.
Thus on Meander's flowery margin lies°
The expiring swan, and as he sings he dies.

    When bold Sir Plume had drawn Clarissa down,
Chloe stepped in and killed him with a frown;
She smiled to see the doughty hero slain,
70 But, at her smile, the beau revived again.
Now Jove suspends his golden scales in air,
Weighs the men's wits against the lady's hair;
The doubtful beam long nods from side to side;
At length the wits mount up, the hairs subside.

    See, fierce Belinda on the baron flies,
With more than usual lightning in her eyes;
Nor feared the chief the unequal fight to try,
Who sought no more than on his foe to die.
But this bold lord with manly strength endued,
80 She with one finger and a thumb subdued;
Just where the breath of life his nostrils drew,
A charge of snuff the wily virgin threw;
The gnomes direct, to every atom just,
The pungent grains of titillating dust.
Sudden, with starting tears each eye o'erflows,
And the high dome re-echoes to his nose.

    "Now meet thy fate, " incensed Belinda cried,
And drew a deadly bodkin from her side.
(The same, his ancient personage to deck,
90 Her great great grandsire wore about his neck,

In three seal-rings; which after, melted down,
Formed a vast buckle for his widow's gown;
Her infant grandame's whistle next it grew,
The bells she jingled, and the whistle blew;
Then in a bodkin graced her mother's hairs,
Which long she wore, and now Belinda wears.)

    "Boast not my fall," he cried, "insulting foe!
Thou by some other shalt be laid as low,
Nor think to die dejects my lofty mind;
All that I dread is leaving you behind!   100
Rather than so, ah, let me still survive,
And burn in Cupid's flames—but burn alive."

    "Restore the lock!" she cries; and all around
"Restore the lock!" the vaulted roofs rebound
Not fierce Othello in so loud a strain
Roared for the handkerchief that caused his pain.°
But see how oft ambitious aims are crossed,
And chiefs contend till all the prize is lost!
The lock, obtained with guilt, and kept with pain,
In every place is sought, but sought in vain: 110
With such a prize no mortal must be blessed,
So Heaven decrees! with Heaven who can contest?

    Some thought it mounted to the lunar sphere,
Since all things lost on earth are treasured there.
There heroes' wits are kept in ponderous vases,
And beaux' in snuff-boxes and tweezer cases.
There broken vows and death-bed alms are found,
And lovers' hearts with ends of riband bound,
The courtier's promises, and sick man's prayers,
The smiles of harlots, and the tears of heirs,   120
Cages for gnats, and chains to yoke a flea,
Dried butterflies, and tomes of casuistry.°

    But trust the Muse—she saw it upward rise,
Though marked by none but quick, poetic eyes:
(So Rome's great founder to the heavens withdrew,
To Proculus alone confessed in view)°
A sudden star, it shot through liquid air,
And drew behind a radiant trail of hair.
Not Berenice's locks first rose so bright,°
The heavens bespangling with disheveled light.   130
The sylphs behold it kindling as it flies,
And pleased pursue its progress through the skies.

    This the beau monde shall from the Mall survey,
And hail with music its propitious ray.
This the blest lover shall for Venus take,

47–50 **Pallas . . . Neptune,** *Pallas Athena* (Minerva), goddess of wisdom and war; *Mars,* god of war; *Latona,* mother of Apollo and goddess of the night; *Hermes* (Mercury), messenger of the gods; *Olympus,* a mountain in Thessaly, the home of the gods; *Neptune,* god of the sea   53 **sconce,** a bracket in a wall for holding candles   62 **Dapperwit . . . Sir Fopling.** *Dapperwit* was a ludicrous character in *Love in a Wood,* a comedy by William Wycherley (1640?–1715); *Sir Fopling* is a ludicrous character in *The Man of Mode,* a comedy by Sir George Etherege (1635?–1691?)   65 **Meander . . . lies.** The Meander is a river in Asia Minor, often mentioned in ancient poetry. It was noted for its extremely winding course

105–6 **Othello . . . pain.** Suspecting that Desdemona has given a highly prized handkerchief to Cassio, her supposed lover, Othello asks for it and becomes angry when Desdemona fails to produce it   122 **tomes of casuistry,** volumes of oversubtle reasoning about conscience and conduct   125–26 **Rome's . . . view.** The founder of Rome, Romulus, was carried in a storm to heaven by his father Mars, and was deified by the Romans. To the Roman senator Proculus, Romulus is said to have expressed a wish for deification as Quirinus. The story is told in *From the Founding of the City,* a history of Rome by the Roman Titus Livius (Livy) (59 B.C.–A.D. 17)   129 **Berenice's . . . bright.** Berenice was an Egyptian queen who dedicated her beautiful hair to Venus, goddess of love, for the safe return of her husband from war; the hair was changed into a comet. There is an astronomical constellation in the northern hemisphere known as *Coma Berenicis* (Berenice's hair)

And send up vows from Rosamonda's lake.°
This Partridge° soon shall view in cloudless skies.
When next he looks through Galileo's eyes;°
And hence the egregious wizard shall foredoom
140 The fate of Louis and the fall of Rome.°

  Then cease, bright nymph! to mourn thy ravished
      hair,
Which adds new glory to the shining sphere!
Not all the tresses that fair head can boast,
Shall draw such envy as the lock you lost.
For, after all the murders of your eye,
When, after millions slain, yourself shall die:
When those fair suns shall set, as set they must,
And all those tresses shall be laid in dust,
This lock, the Muse shall consecrate to fame,
150 And 'midst the stars inscribe Belinda's name.
(1712, 1714)

from AN ESSAY ON MAN

An Essay on Man is Pope's "theodicy"—a philosophical work which deals with the problem of the existence of evil in a world which was, presumably, the
creation of a benevolent God. It was written, then, according to Pope's own testimony, for the same reason
that Milton wrote *Paradise Lost,* "to vindicate the ways
of God to man." *An Essay on Man* is a segment of a
much more ambitious scheme of Pope's to devote his
writing to philosophical and ethical speculations.

  The *Essay* is dedicated to Henry St. John Viscount
Bolingbroke, who encouraged Pope to do the work
and who regularly discussed its underlying assumptions with him. The central thesis of the *Essay*—the
classical statement of eighteenth-century moral and
philosophical optimism—is stated in the closing lines
of Epistle I culminating in the italicized maxim,
"Whatever is, is right." Such a conclusion rests on the
premise that "it is inherently and absolutely good that
every kind of thing (however far down in the scale of
possibles) should actually be, as far as its existence is
logically conceivable, *i.e.,* involves no contradiction."
Pope finally does not deny the existence of evil but
rather asserts its necessity, and when he states or implies that this is "the best of all possible worlds," he
asserts not that it is absolutely good but that it is the
best conceivable.

EPISTLE I

Awake, my St. John! leave all meaner things
To low ambition, and the pride of kings.
Let us (since life can little more supply

Than just to look about us and to die)
Expatiate° free o'er all this scene of man;
A mighty maze! but not without a plan;
A wild, where weeds and flowers promiscuous shoot;
Or garden, tempting with forbidden fruit.
Together let us beat this ample field,
Try what the open, what the covert yield;   10
The latent tracts, the giddy heights, explore
Of all who blindly creep, or sightless soar;
Eye nature's walks, shoot folly as it flies,
And catch the manners living as they rise;
Laugh where we must, be candid where we can;
But vindicate the ways of God to man.°

I. Say first, of God above, or man below,
What can we reason, but from what we know?
Of man, what see we but his station here,
From which to reason, or to which refer?   20
Through worlds unnumbered though the God be
      known,
'Tis ours to trace him only in our own.
He, who through vast immensity can pierce,
See worlds on worlds compose one universe,
Observe how system into system runs,
What other planets circle other suns,
What varied being peoples every star,
May tell why Heaven has made us as we are.
But of this frame the bearings, and the ties,
The strong connections, nice dependencies,°   30
Gradations just, has thy pervading soul
Looked through? or can a part contain the whole?
Is the great chain, that draws all to agree,
And drawn supports, upheld by God, or thee?

II. Presumptuous man! the reason wouldst thou find,
Why formed so weak, so little, and so blind?
First, if thou canst, the harder reason guess,
Why formed no weaker, blinder, and no less?
Ask of thy mother earth, why oaks are made
Taller or stronger than the weeds they shade?   40
Or ask of yonder argent° fields above,
Why Jove's satellites are less than Jove?
  Of systems possible, if 'tis confessed
That wisdom infinite must form the best,
Where all must full or not coherent be,
And all that rises, rise in due degree;
Then, in the scale of reasoning life, 'tis plain,
There must be, somewhere, such a rank as man:
And all the question (wrangle e'er so long)
Is only this, if God has placed him wrong?   50
  Respecting man, whatever wrong we call,
May, must be right, as relative to all.
In human works, though labored on with pain,
A thousand movements scarce one purpose gain;

In God's, one single can its end produce;
Yet serves to second too some other use.
So man, who here seems principal alone,
Perhaps acts second to some sphere unknown,
Touches some wheel, or verges to some goal:
60 'Tis but a part we see, and not a whole.

When the proud steed shall know why man restrains
His fiery course, or drives him o'er the plains:
When the dull ox, why now he breaks the clod,
Is now a victim, and now Egypt's god:°
Then shall man's pride and dullness comprehend
His actions', passions', being's, use and end;
Why doing, suffering, checked, impelled; and why
This hour a slave, the next a deity.

Then say not man's imperfect, Heaven in fault;
70 Say rather, man's as perfect as he ought:
His knowledge measured to his state and place;
His time a moment, and a point his space.
If to be perfect in a certain sphere,
What matter, soon or late, or here or there?
The blest today is as completely so,
As who began a thousand years ago.

III. Heaven from all creatures hides the book of fate,
All but the page prescribed, their present state:
From brutes what men, from men what spirits know:
80 Or who could suffer being here below?
The lamb thy riot dooms to bleed today,
Had he thy reason, would he skip and play?
Pleased to the last, he crops the flowery food,
And licks the hand just raised to shed his blood.
O blindness to the future! kindly given,
That each may fill the circle marked by Heaven:
Who sees with equal eye, as God of all,
A hero perish, or a sparrow fall,
Atoms or systems into ruin hurled,
90 And now a bubble burst, and now a world.

Hope humbly then; with trembling pinions soar;
Wait the great teacher death: and God adore.
What future bliss, He gives not thee to know,
But gives that hope to be thy blessing now.
Hope springs eternal in the human breast:
Man never is, but always to be blest:
The soul, uneasy and confined from home,
Rests and expatiates in a life to come.
Lo, the poor Indian! whose untutored mind°
100 Sees God in clouds, or hears him in the wind:
His soul proud science never taught to stray
Far as the solar walk,° or Milky Way;
Yet simple nature to his hope has given,
Behind the cloud-topped hill, an humbler heaven;
Some safer world in depth of woods embraced,
Some happier island in the watery waste,
Where slaves once more their native land behold,
No fiends torment, no Christians thirst for gold.

To be, contents his natural desire,
He asks no angel's wing, no seraph's fire;   110
But thinks, admitted to that equal° sky,
His faithful dog shall bear him company.

IV. Go, wiser thou! and, in thy scale of sense,
Weigh thy opinion against Providence;
Call imperfection what thou fanciest such,
Say, here He gives too little, there too much:
Destroy all creatures for thy sport or gust,°
Yet cry, if man's unhappy, God's unjust;
If man alone engross not Heaven's high care,
Alone made perfect here, immortal there: 120
Snatch from his hand the balance and the rod,
Re-judge his justice, be the God of God.
In pride, in reasoning pride, our error lies;
All quit their sphere, and rush into the skies.
Pride still is aiming at the blest abodes,
Men would be angels, angels would be Gods.
Aspiring to be Gods, if angels fell,
Aspiring to be angels, men rebel:
And who but wishes to invert the laws
Of order, sins against th' eternal cause.   130

V. Ask for what end the heavenly bodies shine,
Earth for whose use? Pride answers, "'Tis for mine:
For me kind nature wakes her genial power,
Suckles each herb, and spreads out every flower;
Annual for me, the grape, the rose renew
The juice nectareous, and the balmy dew;
For me, the mine a thousand treasures brings;
For me, health gushes from a thousand springs;
Seas roll to waft me, suns to light me rise;
My foot-stool earth, my canopy the skies."   140
But errs not nature from his gracious end,
From burning suns when livid deaths descend,
When earthquakes swallow, or when tempests sweep
Towns to one grave, whole nations to the deep?
"No," 'tis replied, "the first Almighty Cause
Acts not by partial, but by general laws;
Th' exceptions few; some change since all began:
And what created perfect?"—Why then man?
If the great end be human happiness,
Then nature deviates; and can man do less?   150
As much that end a constant course requires
Of showers and sunshine, as of man's desires;
As much eternal springs and cloudless skies,
As men forever temperate, calm, and wise.
If plagues or earthquakes break not Heaven's design,
Why then a Borgia,° or a Catiline?°
Who knows but He, whose hand the lightning forms,
Who heaves old ocean, and who wings the storms;
Pours fierce ambition in a Caesar's mind,
Or turns young Ammon° loose to scourge mankind? 160

---

64 **Egypt's god.** The ox was a sacred animal in ancient Egypt   102 **solar walk,** the ecliptic, the path of the sun through the heavens

111 **equal,** impartial   117 **gust,** delight   156 **Borgia,** Cesare Borgia (1476–1507), Italian cardinal and military leader notorious for his cruelty, violence, and treachery   **Catiline,** the famous Roman conspirator and archenemy of Cicero during the first century B.C.   160 **young Ammon,** Alexander the Great, King of Macedon from 336–323 B.C., called the son of Jupiter Ammon; he was in reality the son of King Philip of Macedon (382–336 B.C.)

From pride, from pride, our very reasoning springs;
Account for moral as for natural things:
Why charge we Heaven in those, in these acquit?
In both, to reason right is to submit.
　　Better for us, perhaps, it might appear,
Were there all harmony, all virtue here;
That never air or ocean felt the wind;
That never passion discomposed the mind.
But all subsists by elemental strife;
170 And passions are the elements of life.
The general order, since the whole began
Is kept in nature, and is kept in man.

VI. What would this man? Now upward will he soar,
And, little less than angel,° would be more;
Now looking downwards, just as grieved appears
To want° the strength of bulls, the fur of bears.
Made for his use all creatures if he call,
Say what their use, had he the powers of all?
Nature to these, without profusion, kind,
180 The proper organs, proper powers assigned;
Each seeming want compensated of course,
Here with degrees of swiftness, there of force;
All in exact proportion to the state;
Nothing to add, and nothing to abate.
Each beast, each insect, happy in its own:
Is Heaven unkind to man, and man alone?
Shall he alone, whom rational we call,
Be pleased with nothing, if not blessed with all?
　　The bliss of man (could pride that blessing find)
190 Is not to act or think beyond mankind;
No powers of body or of soul to share,
But what his nature and his state can bear.
Why has not man a microscopic eye?°
For this plain reason, man is not a fly.
Say what the use, were finer optics given,
T' inspect a mite, not comprehend the heaven?
Or touch, if tremblingly alive all o'er,
To smart and agonize at every pore?
Or quick effluvia° darting through the brain,
200 Die of a rose in aromatic pain?
If nature thundered in his opening ears,
And stunned him with the music of the spheres,°
How would he wish that Heaven had left him still
The whispering zephyr, and the purling rill?
Who finds not Providence all good and wise,
Alike in what it gives, and what denies?

VII. Far as creation's ample range extends,
The scale of sensual, mental powers ascends:
Mark how it mounts, to man's imperial race,
210 From the green myriads in the peopled grass:
What modes of sight betwixt each wide extreme,

The mole's dim curtain, and the lynx's beam:
Of smell, the headlong lioness between,
And hound sagacious on the tainted green:
Of hearing, from the life that fills the flood,
To that which warbles through the vernal wood:
The spider's touch, how exquisitely fine!
Feels at each thread, and lives along the line:
In the nice° bee, what sense so subtly true
From poisonous herbs extracts the healing dew?　220
How instinct varies in the groveling swine,
Compared, half-reasoning elephant, with thine!
'Twixt that, and reason, what a nice barrier,
Forever separate, yet forever near!
Remembrance and reflection how allied;
What thin partitions sense from thought divide:
And middle natures, how they long to join,
Yet never pass th' insuperable line!
Without this just gradation, could they be
Subjected, these to those, or all to thee?　230
The powers of all subdued by thee alone,
Is not thy reason all these powers in one?

VIII. See, through this air, this ocean, and this earth,
All matter quick, and bursting into birth.
Above, how high progressive life may go!
Around, how wide! how deep extend below!
Vast chain of being! which from God began,
Natures ethereal, human, angel, man,
Beast, bird, fish, insect, what no eye can see,
No glass can reach; from Infinite to thee,　240
From thee to nothing.—On superior powers
Were we to press, inferior might on ours:
Or in the full creation leave a void,
Where, one step broken, the great scale's destroyed:
From nature's chain whatever link you strike,
Tenth or ten-thousandth, breaks the chain alike.
　　And, if each system in gradation roll
Alike essential to th' amazing whole,
The least confusion but in one, not all
That system only, but the whole must fall.　250
Let earth unbalanced from her orbit fly,
Planets and suns run lawless through the sky;
Let ruling angels from their spheres be hurled,
Being on being wrecked, and world on world;
Heaven's whole foundations to their center nod,
And nature tremble to the throne of God.
All this dread order break—for whom? for thee?
Vile worm!—O madness! Pride! Impiety!

IX. What if the foot, ordained the dust to tread,
Or hand, to toil, aspired to be the head?　260
What if the head, the eye, or ear repined
To serve mere engines to the ruling mind?
Just as absurd for any part to claim
To be another, in this general frame:
Just as absurd, to mourn the tasks or pains,

174 less than angel, suggested by the well-known verses: "What is man, that
thou art mindful of him? and the son of man, that thou visitest him? For thou hast
made him a little lower than the angels, and hast crowned him with glory and
honor" (Psalms, 8:4–5)　176 want, lack　193 a microscopic eye, possessing
the function of a microscope　199 effluvia, that which flows out, emanations
202 music of the spheres. The ancients believed that the stars made music as
they revolved in their spheres

219 nice, delicate, discriminating

The great directing mind of all ordains.
    All are but parts of one stupendous whole,
Whose body nature is, and God the soul;
That, changed through all, and yet in all the same;
270 Great in the earth, as in th' ethereal frame;
Warms in the sun, refreshes in the breeze,
Glows in the stars, and blossoms in the trees,
Lives through all life, extends through all extent,
Spreads undivided, operates unspent;
Breathes in our soul, informs our mortal part
As full, as perfect, in a hair as heart:
As full, as perfect, in vile man that mourns,
As the rapt Seraph that adores and burns:
To him no high, no low, no great, no small;
280 He fills, he bounds, connects, and equals all.

X. Cease then, nor order imperfection name:
Our proper bliss depends on what we blame.
Know thy own point: This kind, this due degree
Of blindness, weakness, Heaven bestows on thee.
Submit.—In this, or any other sphere,
Secure to be as blessed as thou canst bear:
Safe in the hand of one disposing power,
Or in the natal, or the mortal hour.
All nature is but art, unknown to thee;
290 All chance, direction, which thou canst not see;
All discord, harmony not understood;
All partial evil, universal good:
And, spite of pride, in erring reason's spite,
One truth is clear, *Whatever is, is right.*

EPISTLE II

I. Know then thyself, presume not God to scan,
The proper study of mankind is man.
Placed on this isthmus of a middle state,
A being darkly wise and rudely great:
With too much knowledge for the skeptic side,
With too much weakness for the stoic's pride,
He hangs between; in doubt to act, or rest;
In doubt to deem himself a god, or beast;
In doubt his mind or body to prefer;
10 Born but to die, and reasoning but to err;
Alike in ignorance, his reason such,
Whether he thinks too little, or too much:
Chaos of thought and passion, all confused;
Still by himself abused, or disabused;
Created half to rise, and half to fall;
Great lord of all things, yet a prey to all;
Sole judge of truth, in endless error hurled:
The glory, jest, and riddle of the world!
    Go, wondrous creature; mount where science
        guides,
20 Go, measure earth, weigh air, and state the tides;
Instruct the planets in what orbs to run,

Correct old Time, and regulate the sun;°
Go, soar with Plato to th' empyreal sphere,°
To the first good, first perfect, and first fair;
Or tread the mazy round his followers trod,
And quitting sense call imitating God;
As eastern priests in giddly circles run,°
And turn their heads to imitate the sun.
Go, teach Eternal Wisdom how to rule—
Then drop into thyself, and be a fool!   30
    Superior beings, when of late they saw
A mortal man unfold all nature's law,
Admired such wisdom in an earthly shape,
And showed a Newton, as we show an ape.
    Could he, whose rules the rapid comet bind,
Describe or fix one movement of his mind?
Who saw its fires here rise, and there descend,
Explain his own beginning or his end?
Alas! what wonder! Man's superior part
Unchecked may rise, and climb from art to art;   40
But when his own great work is but begun,
What reason weaves, by passion is undone.
    Trace science, then, with modesty thy guide;
First strip off all her equipage of pride;
Deduct what is but vanity or dress,
Or learning's luxury, or idleness,
Or tricks to show the stretch of human brain,
Mere curious pleasure, or ingenious pain;
Expunge the whole, or lop th' excrescent parts
Of all our vices have created arts;   50
Then see how little the remaining sum,
Which served the past, and must the times to come!

II. Two principles in human nature reign;
Self-love to urge, and reason to restrain;
Nor this a good, nor that a bad we call,
Each works its end to move or govern all:
And to their proper operation still
Ascribe all good; to their improper, ill.
    Self-love, the spring of motion, acts° the soul;
Reason's comparing balance rules the whole.   60
Man, but for that, no action could attend,
And, but for this, were active to no end:
Fixed like a plant on his peculiar spot,
To draw nutrition, propagate, and rot;
Or, meteor-like, flame lawless thro' the void,
Destroying others, by himself destroyed.
    Most strength the moving principle requires;
Active its task, it prompts, impels, inspires:
Sedate and quiet, the comparing° lies,
Formed but to check, deliberate, and advise.   70
Self-love still stronger, as its objects nigh;

Epistle II   22   regulate the sun. This refers to the reformation of the calendar, undertaken in Europe during the eighteenth century in order to make up the approximately twelve days that had been lost during the course of many centuries through the inaccurate Julian calendar formerly in use. The new Gregorian calendar, however, did not reach England until 1751   23   Plato . . . sphere. The *empyreal sphere* is the *primum mobile*, the outermost sphere, the abode of God; for Pope it is obviously the abode of Plato's archetypes of Ideas   27   eastern . . . run, an allusion to the whirling dervishes of the Orient   59   acts, actuates

Reason's at distance and in prospect lie:
That sees immediate good by present sense;
Reason, the future and the consequence.
Thicker than arguments, temptations throng,
At best more watchful this, but that more strong.
The action of the stronger to suspend,
Reason still use, to reason still attend.
Attention, habit, and experience gains;
80 Each strengthens reason, and self-love restrains.
    Let subtle schoolmen teach these friends to fight,
More studious to divide than to unite;
And grace and virtue, sense and reason split,
With all the rash dexterity of wit.
Wits, just like fools, at war about a name,
Have full as oft no meaning, or the same.
Self-love and reason to one end aspire,
Pain their aversion, pleasure their desire;
But greedy that, its object would devour,
90 This taste the honey, and not wound the flower:
Pleasure, or wrong or rightly understood,
Our greatest evil, or our greatest good.

III. Modes of self-love the passions we may call;
'Tis real good, or seeming, moves them all:
But since not every good we can divide,
And reason bids us for our own provide,
Passions, though selfish, if their means be fair,
List under reason, and deserve her care;
Those that imparted, court a nobler aim,
100 Exalt their kind, and take some virtue's name.
    In lazy apathy let stoics boast
Their virtue fixed: 'tis fixed as in a frost;
Contracted all, retiring to the breast;
But strength of mind is exercise, not rest:
The rising tempest puts in act the soul,
Parts it may ravage, but preserves the whole.
On life's vast ocean diversely we sail,
Reason the card,° but passion is the gale;
Nor God alone in the still calm we find,
110 He mounts the storm, and walks upon the wind.
    Passions, like elements, though born to fight,
Yet, mixed and softened, in his work unite:
These 'tis enough to temper and employ;
But what composes man, can man destroy?
Suffice that reason keep to nature's road,
Subject, compound them, follow her and God.
Love, hope, and joy, fair pleasure's smiling train,
Hate, fear, and grief, the family of pain,
These, mixed with art, and to due bounds confined,
120 Make and maintain the balance of the mind:
The lights and shades, whose well-accorded strife
Gives all the strength and color of our life.
    Pleasures are ever in our hands or eyes;
And when in act they cease, in prospect rise:

108 **card,** compass chart

Present to grasp, and future still to find,
The whole employ of body and of mind.
All spread their charms, but charm not all alike;
On different senses different objects strike;
Hence different passions more or less inflame,
As strong or weak the organs of the frame;   130
And hence one master-passion in the breast,
Like Aaron's serpent,° swallows up the rest.
    As man, perhaps, the moment of his breath,
Receives the lurking principle of death;
The young disease, that must subdue at length,
Grows with his growth, and strengthens with his
        strength:
So, cast and mingled with his very frame,
The mind's disease, its ruling passion, came;
Each vital humor which should feed the whole,
Soon flows to this, in body and in soul: 140
Whatever warms the heart, or fills the head,
As the mind opens, and its functions spread,
Imagination plies her dangerous art,
And pours it all upon the peccant° part.
Nature its mother, habit is its nurse;
Wit, spirit, faculties, but make it worse;
Reason itself but gives it edge and pow'r;
As Heaven's blest beam turns vinegar more sour.
    We, wretched subjects, though to lawful sway,
In this weak queen some favorite still obey;   150
Ah! if she lend not arms as well as rules,
What can she more than tell us we are fools?
Teach us to mourn our nature, not to mend,
A sharp accuser, but a helpless friend!
Or from a judge turn pleader, to persuade
The choice we make, or justify it made;
Proud of an easy conquest all along,
She but removes weak passions for the strong.
So, when small humors gather to a gout,
The doctor fancies he has driven them out.   160
    Yes, nature's road must ever be preferred;
Reason is here no guide, but still a guard;
'Tis hers to rectify, not overthrow,
And treat this passion more as friend than foe:
A mightier power the strong direction sends,
And several men impels to several ends:
Like varying winds by other passions tossed,
This drives them constant to a certain coast.
Let power or knowledge, gold or glory, please,
Or (oft more strong than all) the love of ease;   170
Through life 'tis followed, even at life's expense;
The merchant's toil, the sage's idolence,
The monk's humility, the hero's pride,
All, all alike find reason on their side.

132 **Aaron's serpent.** The reference is to *Exodus,* 7:10–12: "And Moses and
Aaron went in unto Pharaoh, and they did so as the Lord had commanded: and
Aaron cast down his rod before Pharaoh, and before his servants, and it became a
serpent. Then Pharaoh also called the wise men and the sorcerers: now the magicians of Egypt, they also did in like manner with their enchantments. For they cast
down every man his rod, and they became serpents: but Aaron's rod swallowed
up their rods"   144 **peccant,** diseased

Th' Eternal Art, educing good from ill,
Grafts on this passion our best principle:
'Tis thus the mercury of man is fixed,
Strong grows the virtue with his nature mixed;
The dross cements what else were too refined,
180 And in one interest body acts with mind.
    As fruits, ungrateful to the planter's care,
On savage stocks inserted, learn to bear,
The surest virtues thus from passions shoot,
Wild nature's vigor working at the root.
What crops of wit and honesty appear
From spleen, from obstinacy, hate, or fear!
See anger, zeal and fortitude supply;
Even avarice, prudence; sloth, philosophy;
Lust, through some certain strainers well refined,
190 Is gentle love, and charms all womankind;
Envy, to which th' ignoble mind's a slave,
Is emulation in the learned or brave;
Nor virtue, male or female, can we name,
But what will grow on pride, or grow on shame.
    Thus nature gives us (let it check our pride)
The virtue nearest to our vice allied;
Reason the bias turns to good from ill,
And Nero reigns a Titus,° if he will.
The fiery soul abhorred in Catiline,°
200 In Decius charms, in Curtius is divine:°
The same ambition can destroy or save,
And makes a patriot as it makes a knave.

IV. This light and darkness in our chaos joined,
What shall divide? The God within the mind.
    Extremes in nature equal ends produce,
In man they join to some mysterious use;
Though each by turns the other's bound invade,
As, in some well-wrought picture, light and shade,
And oft so mix, the difference is too nice
210 Where ends the virtue, or begins the vice.
    Fools! who from hence into the notion fall,
That vice or virtue there is none at all.
If white and black blend, soften, and unite
A thousand ways, is there no black or white?
Ask your own heart, and nothing is so plain;
'Tis to mistake them costs the time and pain.

V. Vice is a monster of so frightful mien,
As to be hated needs but to be seen;
Yet seen too oft, familiar with her face,
220 We first endure, then pity, then embrace.
But where th' extreme of vice, was ne'er agreed:
Ask where 's the north? at York, 'tis on the Tweed;

In Scotland, at the Orcades;° and there,
At Greenland, Zembla,° or the Lord knows where.
No creature owns it in the first degree,
But thinks his neighbor further gone than he;
Even those who dwell beneath its very zone,
Or never feel the rage, or never own;
What happier natures shrink at with affright
The hard inhabitant contends is right.   230

VI. Virtuous and vicious every man must be;
Few in th' extreme, but all in the degree.
The rogue and fool by fits is fair and wise;
And even the best, by fits, what they despise.
'Tis but by parts we follow good or ill;
For, vice or virtue, self directs it still;
Each individual seeks a several goal;
But Heaven's great view is one, and that the whole.
That counterworks each folly and caprice;
That disappoints th' effect of every vice;   240
That, happy frailties to all ranks applied,
Shame to the virgin, to the matron pride,
Fear to the statesman, rashness to the chief,
To kings presumption, and to crowds belief:
That, virtue's ends from vanity can raise,
Which seeks no interest, no reward but praise;
And build on wants, and on defects of mind,
The joy, the peace, the glory of mankind.
    Heaven, forming each on other to depend,
A master, or a servant, or a friend,   250
Bids each on other for assistance call,
Till one man's weakness grows the strength of all.
Wants, frailties, passions, closer still ally
The common interest, or endear the tie.
To these we owe true friendship, love sincere,
Each home-felt joy that life inherits here;
Yet from the same we learn, in its decline,
Those joys, those loves, those interests to resign:
Taught half by reason, half by mere decay,
To welcome death, and calmly pass away.   260
    Whate'er the passion—knowledge, fame, or pelf—
Not one will change his neighbor with himself.
The learned is happy nature to explore,
The fool is happy that he knows no more;
The rich is happy in the plenty given,
The poor contents him with the care of Heaven.
See the blind beggar dance, the cripple sing,
The sot a hero, lunatic a king;
The starving chemist° in his golden views
Supremely blest, the poet in his Muse.   270
    See some strange comfort every state attend.
And pride bestowed on all, a common friend:
See some fit passion every age supply,
Hope travels through, nor quits us when we die.
    Behold the child, by Nature's kindly law,
Pleased with a rattle, tickled with a straw;

---

198 **Nero . . . Titus.** The tyrant becomes a benefactor. Nero (37–68), was the corrupt, cruel, and perverted Roman emperor; Titus (40–81) had a brief but distinguished reign as emperor about a dozen years after Nero   199 **Catiline,** a famous Roman conspirator (108–62 B.C.), denounced and driven to destruction by Cicero   200 **Decius . . . divine.** Publius Decius Mus was consul of Rome in the year 340 B.C. during the war between the Romans and the Samnite-Latins. A vision had informed him that victory would lie on the side whose general should fall in battle. Decius therefore sacrificed himself by rushing recklessly into the thick of the combat. Curtius sacrificed himself similarly in 362 B.C. A great chasm had appeared in the Roman Forum and the soothsayers declared that it could be filled only if Rome's greatest treasure were thrown into it. Curtius leaped in, remarking that the greatest treasure of the city was a brave, self-sacrificing citizen

223 **Orcades,** the old name for the Orkney Islands, off the northeast coast of Scotland   224 **Zembla,** Nova Zembla, a large pair of islands off the northern coast of Russia within the Arctic Circle   269 **chemist,** alchemist

Some livelier plaything gives his youth delight,
A little louder, but as empty quite;
Scarfs, garters,° gold, amuse his riper stage,
280 And beads and prayer-books are the toys of age:
Pleased with this bauble still, as that before;
Till tired he sleeps, and life's poor play is o'er.
  Meanwhile Opinion gilds, with varying rays,
Those painted clouds that beautify our days;
Each want of happiness by hope supplied,
And each vacuity of sense by pride:
These build as fast as knowledge can destroy;
In Folly's cup still laughs the bubble joy;
One prospect lost, another still we gain;
290 And not a vanity is given in vain;
Even mean self-love becomes, by force divine,
The scale to measure others' wants by thine.
See, and confess, one comfort still must rise;
'Tis this, *Though man's a fool, yet God is wise!*
(1733)

EPISTLE TO DR. ARBUTHNOT

Dr. John Arbuthnot (1667–1735), prominent physician
and man of letters, was a lifelong friend of Pope. The
poem is a dialogue between the two. The immediate
occasion of the *Epistle* was the publication of the two
poems named in Pope's Advertisement below—the
first written probably by Lady Mary Wortley Montagu
and Lord John Hervey, the second by Hervey. Both
these writers had been previously attacked by Pope in
The Dunciad (1728). They are given another severe
lashing here.

ADVERTISEMENT

*This paper is a sort of bill of complaint, begun many
years since and drawn up by snatches, as the several
occasions offered. I had no thoughts of publishing it,
till it pleased some persons of rank and fortune (the
authors of* Verses to the Imitator of Horace, *and of an*
Epistle to a Doctor of Divinity from a Nobleman at
Hampton Court) *to attack, in a very extraordinary
manner, not only my writings (of which, being public,
the public is judge), but my person, morals, and fam-*
10 *ily, whereof, to those who know me not, a truer information may be requisite. Being divided between the
necessity to say something of myself and my own laziness to undertake so awkward a task, I thought it the
shortest way to put the last hand to this Epistle. If it
have anything pleasing, it will be that by which I am
most desirous to please, the truth and the sentiment;
and if anything offensive, it will be only to those I am
least sorry to offend, the vicious or the ungenerous.*
  Many will know their own pictures in it, there being
20 *not a circumstance but what is true; but I have for the*

most part spared their names, and they may escape
being laughed at if they please.
  *I would have some of them know it was owing to the
request of the learned and candid friend to whom it is
inscribed that I make not as free use of theirs as they
have done of mine. However, I shall have this advantage and honor on my side, that whereas, by their
proceeding, any abuse may be directed at any man, no
injury can possibly be done by mine, since a nameless
character can never be found out but by its truth and* 30
likeness.

P. Shut, shut the door, good John!° (fatigued, I said),
Tie up the knocker, say I'm sick, I'm dead.
The Dog-star° rages! nay 'tis past a doubt,
All Bedlam,° or Parnassus, is let out:
Fire in each eye, and papers in each hand,
They rave, recite, and madden round the land.
  What walls can guard me, or what shade can hide?
They pierce my thickets, through my Grot° they glide;
By land, by water, they renew the charge;
They stop the chariot, and they board the barge. 10
No place is sacred, not the Church is free;
E'en Sunday shines no Sabbath-day to me;
Then from the Mint° walks forth the man of rime,
Happy to catch me just at dinner-time.
  Is there a parson, much bemused in beer,
A maudlin poetess, a riming peer,
A clerk,° foredoomed his father's soul to cross,
Who pens a stanza, when he should *engross?*°
Is there, who, locked from ink and paper, scrawls
With desperate charcoal round his darkened walls? 20
All fly to Twit'nam,° and in humble strain
Apply to me, to keep them mad or vain.
Arthur,° whose giddy son neglects the laws,
Imputes to me and my damned works the cause:
Poor Cornus° sees his frantic wife elope,
And curses wit, and poetry, and Pope.
  Friend to my life (which did not you prolong,
The world had wanted many an idle song),
What drop or nostrum can this plague remove?
Or which must end me, a fool's wrath or love? 30
A dire dilemma! either way I'm sped,°
If foes, they write; if friends, they read me dead.
Seized and tied down to judge, how wretched I!
Who can't be silent, and who will not lie.
To laugh, were want of goodness and of grace,
And to be grave, exceeds all power of face.

Epistle to Dr. Arbuthnot 1 **John,** John Searl, Pope's household servant for many
years   3 **Dog-star,** Sirius, the most brilliant of the fixed stars. The sun, in its
travel through the sky during the course of the year, passes near Sirius in August.
The season of great heat was often marked by the incidence of rabies; hence the
association of Sirius with both dogs and madness   4 **Bedlam,** Bethlehem Hospital, asylum for the insane in London   8 **Grot,** an artificial grotto in Pope's
grounds at Twickenham, on the Thames just above London   13 **Mint,** a district
in London where debtors were safe from arrest; they were safe everywhere on
Sundays   17 **clerk,** here, a student of law   18 **engross,** write, in a large and
rather fancy hand, a formal document such as a legal writ   21 **Twit'nam,** the
popular pronunciation of Twickenham   23 **Arthur,** Arthur Moore (1666?–1730),
a prominent economist and politician, father of James Moore-Smythe, an extravagant fop and poetaster, who crossed Pope's path more than once   25 **Cornus,**
Sir Robert Walpole (1676–1745), the brilliant Whig prime minister. The name
Cornus is an insinuation by Pope that Walpole's wife was unfaithful to him, since
the word is derived from the Latin *cornus,* ''horn''   31 **sped,** done for

279 **garters,** referring to the badge of the Order of the Garter, the highest order in
English knighthood

I sit with sad civility, I read
With honest anguish, and an aching head;
And drop at last, but in unwilling ears,
40 This saving counsel "Keep your piece nine years."°
    "Nine years!" cries he, who high in Drury-Lane,
Lulled by soft zephyrs through the broken pane,
Rimes ere he wakes, and prints before term ends,°
Obliged by hunger, and request of friends:
"The piece, you think, is incorrect? why, take it,
I'm all submission, what you'd have it, make it."
    Three things another's modest wishes bound,
My friendship, and a prologue, and ten pound.
    Pitholeon° sends to me: "You know his Grace,
50 I want a patron; ask him for a place."
Pitholeon libeled me—"but here's a letter
Informs you, sir, 'twas when he knew no better.
Dare you refuse him? Curll° invites to dine,
He'll write a *Journal*, or he'll turn divine."
    Bless me! a packet.—"'Tis a stranger sues,
A virgin tragedy, an orphan Muse."
If I dislike it, "Furies, death and rage!"
If I approve, "Commend it to the stage."
There (thank my stars) my whole commission ends,
60 The players and I are, luckily, no friends,
Fired that the house reject him, "'Sdeath,° I'll print it,
And shame the fools——Your interest, sir, with
    Lintot!"°
Lintot, dull rogue! will think your price too much:
"Not, sir, if you revise it, and retouch."
All my demurs but double his attacks;
At last he whispers, "Do; and we go snacks."
Glad of a quarrel, straight I clap the door,
Sir, let me see your works and you no more.

'Tis sung, when Midas'° ears began to spring
70 (Midas, a sacred person and a king),
His very minister who spied them first,
(Some say his queen) was forced to speak, or burst.
And is not mine, my friend, a sorer case,
When every coxcomb perks them in my face?
A.° Good friend, forbear! you deal in dangerous things.
I'd never name queens, ministers, or kings;
Keep close to ears, and those let asses prick;
'Tis nothing—P. Nothing? if they bite and kick?
Out with it, *Dunciad!*° let the secret pass,
80 That secret to each fool, that he's an ass:
The truth once told (and wherefore should we lie?)

The queen of Midas slept, and so may I.
    You think this cruel? take it for a rule,
No creature smarts so little as a fool.
Let peals of laughter, Codrus!° round thee break,
Thou unconcerned canst hear the mighty crack:
Pit, box, and gallery in convulsions hurled,
Thou stand'st unshook amidst a bursting world.
Who shames a scribbler? break one cobweb through,
He spins the slight, self-pleasing thread anew: 90
Destroy his fib or sophistry, in vain;
The creature's at his dirty work again,
Throned in the center of his thin designs,
Proud of a vast extent of flimsy lines!
Whom have I hurt? has poet yet, or peer,
Lost the arched eye-brow, or Parnassian sneer?
And has not Colley° still his lord and whore?
His butchers Henley?° his freemasons Moore?°
Does not one table Bavius° still admit?
Still to one bishop, Philips° seem a wit?   100
Still Sappho°—A. Hold! for God's sake—you'll of-
    fend,
No names!—be calm!—learn prudence of a friend!
I too could write, and I am twice as tall;
But foes like these—P. One flatterer's worse than all.
Of all mad creatures, if the learned are right,
It is the slaver kills, and not the bite.
A fool quite angry is quite innocent:
Alas! 'tis ten times worse when they *repent*.
    One dedicates in high heroic prose,
And ridicules beyond a hundred foes: 110
One from all Grub Street° will my fame defend,
And, more abusive, calls himself my friend.
This prints my *letters*, that expects a bribe,
And others roar aloud, "Subscribe, subscribe."
    There are, who to my person pay their court:
I cough like Horace, and, though lean, am short,
Ammon's great son° one shoulder had too high,
Such Ovid's° nose, and "Sir! you have an eye"—
Go on, obliging creatures, make me see
All that disgraced my betters, met in me.   120
Say for my comfort, languishing in bed,
"Just so immortal Maro° held his head":
And when I die, be sure you let me know
Great Homer died three thousand years ago.
    Why did I write? what sin to me unknown
Dipped me in ink, my parents', or my own?
As yet a child, nor yet a fool to fame,

40 **Keep . . . years,** the advice of Horace in his *Ars Poetica,* l. 388 43 **term ends.** The *term* is the season of the sessions of law courts 49 **Pitholeon,** "the name of a foolish poet of Rhodes who pretended much to Greek" (Pope's note). He represents Leonard Welsted (1688–1747), a prolific writer and joint author of the libelous *One Epistle,* written in the early 1730's, which charged Pope with causing a lady's death. In *The Dunciad* (II, 207–210; III, 169–172), Pope accuses Welsted of squeezing money out of patrons by dedications 53 **Curll,** Edmund Curll (1675–1747), a piratical publisher, who did Pope several ill turns 61 **'Sdeath,** the oath formed from "God's death" 62 **Lintot,** Bernard Lintot (1675–1736), a publisher of many of Pope's works 69 **Midas,** a mythological king whose ears were changed to ass' ears because in a musical contest he gave the prize to Pan rather than to Apollo. In some accounts it was Midas' barber who told the secret of his ears; in Chaucer's *Wife of Bath's Tale,* it was the queen 75 **A.,** John Arbuthnot, the friend of Pope to whom this epistle was addressed. In addition to being a physician, he was an eminent mathematician and classical scholar, a prominent Tory politician, and a member of the famous Scriblerus Club, which numbered Pope, Addison, and Swift, among others 79 **Dunciad,** the masterpiece of personal satire written by Pope in two parts; the first appeared in 1728, the second in 1743

85 **Codrus,** a Roman poetaster ridiculed by Vergil; probably a fictitious name applied to poetasters in general 97 **Colley,** Colley Cibber (1671–1757), actor, dramatist, and poet laureate; for his various attacks upon Pope he was made the hero of the second version of Pope's *Dunciad* (1743) 98 **Henley,** John Henley (1692–1756), an eccentric and pompous London preacher who delivered a lecture before the Butchers Guild of London "in which he lauded the trade extravagantly" **Moore,** James Moore-Smythe, dandy and poetaster, the son of Arthur Moore mentioned in l. 23 99 **Bavius,** an inferior Roman poet of the first century A.D. 100 **bishop, Philips.** The bishop was Hugh Boulter (1672–1742), Archbishop of Armagh, Ireland, and friend and patron of Ambrose Philips (1675?–1749), Pope's rival in pastoral poetry 101 **Sappho,** the noted Greek lyric poetess of the seventh century B.C. The allusion here, however, is to Lady Mary Wortley Montagu (1689–1762), one of the most interesting and brilliant women of her time 111 **Grub Street,** famous as the abode of indigent writers 117 **Ammon's great son,** Alexander the Great, King of Macedon from 336 to 323 B.C., according to legend the son of Jupiter Ammon; his historical father was King Philip of Macedon (382–336 B.C.) 118 **Ovid,** the Roman didactic, lyric, and narrative poet (43 B.C.–A.D. 17) 122 **Maro,** the family name of Vergil (70–19 B.C.)

I lisped in numbers, for the numbers came.
I left no calling for this idle trade,
130 No duty broke, no father disobeyed.
The Muse but served to ease some friend, not wife,
To help me through this long disease, my life,
To second, Arbuthnot! thy art and care,
And teach the being you preserved, to bear.
  But why then publish? Granville° the polite,
And knowing Walsh,° would tell me I could write;
Well-natured Garth° inflamed with early praise;
And Congreve° loved, and Swift endured my lays;
The courtly Talbot,° Somers,° Sheffield,° read;
140 E'en mitered Rochester° would nod the head,
And St. John's° self (great Dryden's friends before)
With open arms received one poet more.
Happy my studies, when by these approved!
Happier their author, when by these beloved!
From these the world will judge of men and books,
Not from the Burnets,° Oldmixons,° and Cookes,°
  Soft were my numbers; who could take offense,
While pure description held the place of sense?
Like gentle Fanny's° was my flowery theme,
150 A painted mistress, or a purling stream.
Yet then did Gildon° draw his venal quill;—
I wished the man a dinner, and sat still.
Yet then did Dennis° rave in furious fret;
I never answered—I was not in debt.
If want provoked, or madness made them print,
I waged no war with Bedlam or the Mint.
  Did some more sober critic come abroad;
If wrong, I smiled; if right, I kissed the rod.
Pains, reading, study, are their just pretense,
160 And all they want is spirit, taste, and sense.
Commas and points they set exactly right,
And 'twere a sin to rob them of their mite.
Yet ne'er one sprig of laurel graced these ribalds,
From slashing Bentley° down to piddling Tibalds:°
Each wight who reads not, and but scans and spells,
Each word-catcher, that lives on syllables,
E'en such small critics some regard may claim,
Preserved in Milton's or in Shakespeare's name.
Pretty! in amber to observe the forms
170 Of hairs, or straws, or dirt, or grubs, or worms!

The things, we know, are neither rich nor rare,
But wonder how the devil they got there.
  Were others angry: I excused them too;
Well might they rage, I gave them but their due.
A man's true merit 'tis not hard to find;
But each man's secret standard in his mind,
That casting-weight° pride adds to emptiness,
This, who can gratify? for who can guess?
The bard° whom pilfered pastorals renown,
Who turns a Persian tale for half a crown,   180
Just writes to make his barrenness appear,
And strains, from hard-bound brains, eight lines a
    year;
He, who still wanting, though he lives on theft,
Steals much, spends little, yet has nothing left:
And he, who now to sense, now nonsense leaning,
Means not, but blunders round about a meaning:
And he, whose fustian's so sublimely bad,
It is not poetry, but prose run mad:
All these, my modest satire bade translate,
And owned that nine such poets made a Tate.°   190
How did they fume, and stamp, and roar, and chafe!
And swear, not Addison himself was safe.
  Peace to all such! but were there one° whose fires
True genius kindles, and fair fame inspires;
Blessed with each talent and each art to please,
And born to write, converse, and live with ease:
Should such a man, too fond to rule alone,
Bear, like the Turk, no brother near the throne,
View him with scornful, yet with jealous eyes,
And hate for arts that caused himself to rise;   200
Damn with faint praise, assent with civil leer,
And without sneering, teach the rest to sneer;
Willing to wound, and yet afraid to strike,
Just hint a fault, and hesitate dislike;
Alike reserved to blame, or to commend,
A timorous foe, and a suspicious friend;
Dreading e'en fools, by flatterers besieged,
And so obliging, that he ne'er obliged;
Like Cato,° give his little senate laws,
And sit attentive to his own applause;   210
While wits and Templars° every sentence raise,
And wonder with a foolish face of praise:——
Who but must laugh, if such a man there be?
Who would not weep, if Atticus° were he?
  What though my name stood rubric° on the walls
Or plastered posts, with claps,° in capitals?
Or smoking forth, a hundred hawkers' load,

135 **Granville,** George Granville (1667–1735), who had urged Pope to publish his *Windsor Forest* in 1713   136 **Walsh,** William Walsh (1663–1709), friend of both Dryden and Pope   137 **Garth,** Samuel Garth (1661–1719), physician and man of letters   138 **Congreve,** William Congreve (1670–1729), one of the most important of Restoration playwrights, author in particular of *The Way of the World* (1700) and *Love for Love* (1695), two brilliant social comedies   139 **Talbot,** Charles Talbot, Duke of Shrewsbury   **Somers,** John Somers, Lord Chancellor   **Sheffield,** John Sheffield, Duke of Buckingham. All those mentioned in this and the preceding line were prominent statesmen of the time who had encouraged Pope in his early work   140 **Rochester,** Francis Atterbury (1662–1732), Bishop of Rochester. The *miter* is the liturgical headdress of a bishop   141 **St. John,** Henry St. John (1678–1754), Viscount Bolingbroke, the statesman and political writer. It was he who gave Pope the encouragement for his *Essay on Man*   146 **Burnets.** We know nothing about this man except that he was a "writer of secret and scandalous history," to quote Pope's own phrase   **Oldmixons,** John Oldmixon (1673–1742), a contemporary historian and pamphleteer   **Cookes,** Thomas Cooke (1703–1756), who had attacked Pope in a pamphlet of 1725   149 **Fanny's.** *Fanny* is a contemptuous reference to Lord Hervey (1696–1743), the *Sporus* of 305 ff   151 **Gildon,** Charles Gildon (1665–1724), an abusive critic of Pope   153 **Dennis,** John Dennis (1657–1734), a reputable critic though a favorite object of Pope's satire   164 **Bentley,** Richard Bentley (1662–1742), noted critic and classical scholar at Cambridge, who published a poor edition of Milton's *Paradise Lost* in 1732   **Tibalds,** Lewis Theobald (1688–1744), minor poet and editor of Shakespeare; for his attack upon Pope's edition of Shakespeare he was made the hero of the first version of Pope's *Dunciad* (1728)

177 **casting-weight,** that which turns the scale   179 **The bard,** Ambrose Philips, who translated a book called *Persian Tales*   190 **Tate,** Nahum Tate (1652–1715), dramatist and poet laureate, known also for his hymn writing   193 **were there one, etc.** This characterization of Addison as *Atticus* (l. 214) is one of the most famous in all satiric literature. It shows Pope at his most skillful and perhaps at his fairest. Pope and Addison had many interests in common, but they differed in temperament and politics so that they finally drifted into mutual distrust. The culmination of their strained relations, this passage in the *Epistle to Arbuthnot*, was printed after Addison's death, although Pope indignantly denied that it had been written when the object of the attack could not answer   209 **Cato,** a Roman statesman, general, and writer (234–119 B.C.), and hero of Addison's classical tragedy *Cato* for which Pope had written the prologue   214 **Templars,** students of the temple, i.e., law students   214 **Atticus,** a Roman scholar and bookseller of the first century B.C.   215 **rubric,** in red. Names of new books were usually posted in red letters on the walls of the bookshops   216 **claps,** posters

Alexander Pope   547

On wings of winds came flying all abroad?
I sought no homage from the race that write;
220 I kept, like Asian monarchs, from their sight:
Poems I heeded (now be-rimed so long)
No more than thou, great George! a birthday song.
I ne'er with wits or witlings passed my days,
To spread about the itch of verse and praise;
Nor like a puppy, daggled° through the town,
To fetch and carry sing-song up and down;
Nor at rehearsals sweat, and mouthed, and cried,
With handkerchief and orange at my side;
But sick of fops, and poetry, and prate,
230 To Bufo,° left the whole Castalian state.°
    Proud as Apollo on his forkéd hill,°
Sat full-blown Bufo, puffed by every quill;
Fed with soft dedication all day long,
Horace and he went hand in hand in song.
His library (where busts of poets dead
And a true Pindar° stood without a head),
Received of wits an undistinguished race,
Who first his judgment asked, and then a place:
Much they extolled his pictures, much his seat,
240 And flattered every day, and some days eat:
Till grown more frugal in his riper days,
He paid some bards with port, and some with praise:
To some a dry rehearsal saw assigned,
And others (harder still) he paid in kind.
Dryden alone (what wonder?) came not nigh,
Dryden alone escaped this judging eye:
But still the great have kindness in reserve,
He helped to bury whom he helped to starve.
    May some choice patron bless each gray goose quill!
250 May every Bavius have his Bufo still!
So, when a statesman wants a day's defense,
Or envy holds a whole week's war with sense,
Or simple pride for flattery makes demands,
May dunce by dunce be whistled off my hands!
Blessed be the great! for those they take away,
And those they left me; for they left me Gay;°
Left me to see neglected genius bloom,
Neglected die, and tell it on his tomb:
Of all thy blameless life the sole return
260 My verse, and Queensbury° weeping o'er thy urn.
    Oh, let me live my own, and die so too!
(To live and die is all I have to do)
Maintain a poet's dignity and ease,
And see what friends, and read what books I please;

Above a patron, though I condescend
Sometimes to call a minister my friend.
I was not born for courts or great affairs;
I pay my debts, believe, and say my prayers;
Can sleep without a poem in my head;
Nor know, if Dennis be alive or dead.   270
    Why am I asked what next shall see the light?
Heavens! was I born for nothing but to write?
Has life no joys for me? or (to be grave)
Have I no friend to serve, no soul to save?
"I found him close with Swift"—"Indeed? no doubt"
(Cries prating Balbus),° "something will come out."
'Tis all in vain, deny it as I will.
"No, such a genius never can lie still";
And then for mine obligingly mistakes
The first lampoon Sir Will° or Bubo° makes.   280
Poor guiltless I! and can I choose but smile,
When every coxcomb knows me by my style?

    Cursed be the verse, how well soe'er it flow,
That tends to make one worthy man my foe,
Give virtue scandal, innocence a fear,
Or from the soft-eyed virgin steal a tear!
But he who hurts a harmless neighbor's peace,
Insults fallen worth, or beauty in distress,
Who loves a lie, lame slander helps about,
Who writes a libel, or who copies out: 290
That fop, whose pride affects a patron's name,
Yet absent, wounds an author's honest fame:
Who can your merit selfishly approve,
And show the sense of it without the love;
Who has the vanity to call you friend,
Yet wants the honor, injured, to defend;
Who tells whate'er you think, whate'er you say,
And, if he lie not, must at least betray:
Who to the Dean, and silver bell can swear,
And sees at Canons what was never there;   300
Who reads, but with a lust to misapply,
Make satire a lampoon, and fiction, lie.
A lash like mine no honest man shall dread,
But all such babbling blockheads in his stead.
    Let Sporus° tremble—A. What? that thing of silk,
Sporus, that mere white curd of ass's milk!
Satire or sense, alas! can Sporus feel?
Who breaks a butterfly upon a wheel?
P. Yet let me flap this bug with gilded wings,
This painted child of dirt, that stinks and stings;   310
Whose buzz the witty and the fair annoys,
Yet wit ne'er tastes, and beauty ne'er enjoys:
So well-bred spaniels civilly delight

225 **daggled,** wet, dirty, and limp   230 **Bufo,** probably Charles Montagu (1661–1715), Lord Halifax, poet, statesman, and patron of letters; an enemy of Pope   **Castalian state,** the realm of poetry, named from Castalia, a fountain on Mt. Parnassus, supposed to give inspiration to those who drank of it   231 **forkéd hill.** Apollo was god of both poetry and music   236 **Pindar,** a famous Greek lyric poet (522–443 B.C.) who gave his name to the elaborate form of exalted lyric known as the ode; the Pindaric ode, was imitated by Ben Jonson and by Thomas Gray. Pope is here ridiculing the affectation of antiquarians who often exhibited the headless trunks of statues of Plato, Homer, Pindar, etc.   256 **Gay,** for John Gay (1685–1732), poet and dramatist praised and befriended by Pope 260 **Queensbury,** Charles Douglas (1698–1778), Duke of Queensbury, a leader of fashion and patron of letters. Gay died in the house of the Duke and Duchess of Queensbury, who provided his monument in Westminster Abbey

276 **Balbus,** George Hay, seventh Earl of Kinnoul (d. 1758)   280 **Sir Will,** Sir William Yonge (d. 1755), fop and small poet. King George II called him "stinking Yonge." Pope was annoyed that verses by Yonge should be taken for his   **Bubo,** George Bubb Doddington (1691–1762), politician and promiscuous patron of letters   305 **Sporus,** Lord John Hervey, a court favorite. In history, Sporus was an effeminate favorite at the court of the Roman emperor Nero (37–68). The passage on Sporus is one of Pope's most vicious attacks

In mumbling of the game they dare not bite.
Eternal smiles his emptiness betray,
As shallow streams run dimpling all the way.
Whether in florid impotence he speaks,
And, as the prompter breathes, the puppet squeaks;
Or at the ear of Eve, familiar toad,
320 Half froth, half venom, spits himself abroad,
In puns, or politics, or tales, or lies,
Or spite, or smut, or rimes, or blasphemies.
His wit all see-saw, between that and this,
Now high, now low, now master up, now miss,
And he himself one vile antithesis.
Amphibious thing! that acting either part,
The trifling head or the corrupted heart,
Fop at the toilet, flatterer at the board,
Now trips a lady, and now struts a lord.
330 Eve's tempter thus the rabbins° have expressed,
A cherub's face, a reptile all the rest;
Beauty that shocks you, parts that none will trust;
Wit that can creep, and pride that licks the dust.
    Not fortune's worshiper, nor fashion's fool,
Not lucre's madman, nor ambition's tool,
Not proud, nor servile;—be one poet's praise,
That, if he pleased, he pleased by manly ways:
That flattery, e'en to kings, he held a shame,
And thought a lie in verse or prose the same.
340 That not in fancy's maze he wandered long,
But stooped to truth, and moralized his song:
That not for fame, but virtue's better end,
He stood the furious foe, the timid friend,
The damning critic, half-approving wit,
The coxcomb hit, or fearing to be hit;
Laughed at the loss of friends he never had,
The dull, the proud, the wicked, and the mad;
The distant threats of vengeance on his head,
The blow unfelt, the tear he never shed;
350 The tale revived, the lie so oft o'erthrown,
Th' imputed trash, and dullness not his own;
The morals blackened when the writings 'scape,
The libeled person, and the pictured shape;
Abuse, on all he loved, or loved him, spread,
A friend in exile, or a father dead;
The whisper, that to greatness still too near,
Perhaps, yet vibrates on his Sovereign's ear:—
Welcome for thee, fair virtue! all the past;
For thee, fair virtue! welcome e'en the last!
360   A. But why insult the poor, affront the great?
P. A knave's a knave, to me, in every state:
Alike my scorn, if he succeed or fail.
Sporus at court, or Japhet° in a jail,
A hireling scribbler, or a hireling peer,
Knight of the post corrupt,° or of the shire;

If on a pillory, or near a throne,
He gain his prince's ear, or lose his own.
    Yet soft by nature, more a dupe than wit,
Sappho can tell you how this man was bit;
This dreaded satirist Dennis will confess   370
Foe to his pride, but friend to his distress:
So humble, he has knocked at Tibbald's door,
Has drunk with Cibber, nay has rimed for Moore.
Full ten years slandered, did he once reply?
Three thousand suns went down on Welsted's lie.°
To please a mistress one aspersed his life;
He lashed him not, but let her be his wife.
Let Budgell° charge low Grub Street on his quill,
And write whate'er he pleased, except his will;
Let the two Curlls° of town and court, abuse   380
His father, mother, body, soul, and muse.
Yet why? that father held it for a rule,
It was a sin to call our neighbor fool;
That harmless mother thought no wife a whore:
Hear this, and spare his family, James Moore!°
Unspotted names, and memorable long!
If there be force in virtue, or in song.
    Of gentle blood (part shed in honor's cause,
While yet in Britain honor had applause)
Each parent sprung— A. What fortune, pray?—   390
    P. Their own,
And better got, than Bestia's° from the throne.
Born to no pride, inheriting no strife,
Nor marrying discord in a noble wife,
Stranger to civil and religious rage,
The good man walked innoxious through his age.
Nor courts he saw, no suits would ever try,
Nor dared an oath, nor hazarded a lie.
Unlearned, he knew no schoolman's subtle art,
No language, but the language of the heart.
By nature honest, by experience wise,   400
Healthy by temperance, and by exercise;
His life, though long to sickness past unknown,
His death was instant, and without a groan.
O grant me, thus to live, and thus to die!
Who sprung from kings shall know less joy than I.
    O friend! may each domestic bliss be thine!
Be no unpleasing melancholy mine:
Me, let the tender office long engage,
To rock the cradle of reposing age,
With lenient arts extend a mother's breath,   410
Make languor smile, and smooth the bed of death,
Explore the thought, explain the asking eye,

---

330 **rabbins,** Jewish rabbis   363 **Japhet,** Japhet Crooks, a notorious Londoner of Pope's day, imprisoned for forging deeds and wills   365 **Knight . . . corrupt.** The so-called knights of the post stood by the sheriff's pillars near the courts, ready to testify for pay to anything whatsoever

375 **Welsted's lie.** For Welsted, see l. 49 and note. The lie was told in 1730   378 **Budgell,** Eustace Budgell (1686–1737), a relative of Addison and author of thirty-seven of The Spectator papers. He was charged with forging a will to his own advantage   380 **two Curlls,** Edmund Curll and his son Henry. Both were unscrupulous publishers   385 **spare . . . Moore.** Pope had accused Moore's mother of unchastity   391 **Bestia,** probably the Duke of Marlborough, who was accused of making financial profit from the War of the Spanish Succession, which lasted intermittently from 1701 to 1713. L. Capurnius Besta was a Roman proconsul who in 111 B.C. accepted bribes from Jugurtha, King of Numidia (d. 104 B.C.), which sealed a dishonorable peace between the Roman republic and the wild kingdom of Numidia

And keep a while one parent from the sky!
On cares like these if length of days attend,
May Heaven, to bless those days, preserve my friend,
Preserve him social, cheerful, and serene,
And just as rich as when he served a queen.°
A. Whether that blessing be denied or given,
Thus far was right, the rest belongs to Heaven.
(1734; 1735)

from THE DUNCIAD°

First published in 1728, *The Dunciad* was modeled
upon Dryden's famous satirical poem *MacFlecknoe*, but
it is more elaborate in its mock-epic devices and in its
allusions to "dunces." In the first edition, Lewis
Theobald (1688–1744), who had criticized Pope's edition of Shakespeare (1725) and who was himself a
Shakespearean critic and editor, was elected by the
Goddess of Dullness to be king of her realm. In the
final, complete edition of 1743, Theobald was dethroned and Colley Cibber (1671–1757), actor, theater
manager, dramatist, poet laureate, was put in his
place. (As we have already noted, Book IV was not
added to *The Dunciad* until 1743.)

The modern reader of Pope's *Dunciad* is frequently put off by the many personal references and
allusions it contains. This need not be the case. Although scholars specializing in the eighteenth century
have by now identified most of the allusions, they are
not indispensable to a basic appreciation of the poem.
On many levels, the modern reader will find Pope's
satire quite relevant. Pope's portrait of Richard
Bentley, for example, will hold, in part at least, for any
contemporary academic pedant. Since Pope is ridiculing types as much as individuals, his satire remains
generally applicable today.

BOOK THE FOURTH

Argument

The Poet being, in this Book, to declare the Completion *of the* Prophecies *mention'd at the end of the
former, makes a new* Invocation; *as the greater Poets
are wont, when some high and worthy matter is to be
sung. He shews the Goddess coming in her Majesty, to
destroy* Order *and* Science, *and to substitute the
Kingdom of the Dull upon earth. How she leads captive the* Sciences, *and silenceth the* Muses; *and what
they be who succeed in their stead. All her Children,*

by a wonderful attraction, are drawn about her; and 10
bear along with them divers others, who promote her
Empire *by connivance, weak resistance, or discouragement of Arts; such as Half-wits, tasteless Admirers, vain Pretenders, the Flatterers of Dunces, or the
Patrons of them. All these crowd round her; one of
them offering to approach her, is driven back by a
Rival, but she commends and encourages both. The
first who speak in form are the* Genius's *of the*
Schools, *who assure her of their care to advance her
Cause, by confining Youth to* Words, *and keeping* 20
*them out of the way of real Knowledge. Their Address,
and her gracious Answer; with her Charge to them and
the Universities. The* Universities *appear by their proper Deputies, and assure her that the same method is
observ'd in the progress of* Education; *The speech of*
Aristarchus *on this subject. They are driven off by a
band of young Gentlemen return'd from* Travel *with
their* Tutors; *one of whom delivers to the Goddess, in a
polite oration, an account of the whole Conduct and
Fruits of their* Travels: *presenting to her at the same* 30
*time a young Nobleman perfectly accomplished. She
receives him graciously, and indues him with the
happy quality of* Want of Shame. *She sees loitering
about her a number of* Indolent Persons *abandoning
all business and duty, and dying with laziness: To these
approaches the* Antiquary Annius, *intreating her
to make them* Virtuosos, *and assign them over to him:
But* Mummius, *another Antiquary, complaining of his
fraudulent proceeding, she finds a method to reconcile
their difference. Then enter a Troop of people fantasti-* 40
*cally adorn'd, offering her strange and exotic pres-
ents: Amongst them, one stands forth and demands
justice on another, who had deprived him of one of the
greatest Curiosities in nature: but he justifies himself
so well, that the Goddess gives them both her approbation. She recommends to them to find proper
employment for the* Indolents *before-mentioned, in the
study of* Butterflies, Shells, Birds-nests, Moss, &c. *but
with particular caution, not to proceed beyond* Trifles,
to any useful or extensive views of Nature, or of the 50
Author of Nature. *Against the last of these apprehensions, she is secured by a hearty Address from the*
Minute Philosophers *and* Freethinkers, *one of whom
speaks in the name of the rest. The Youth thus instructed and principled, are delivered to her in a body,
by the hands of* Silenus; *and then admitted to taste the
Cup of the* Magus *her High Priest, which causes a
total oblivion of all Obligations, divine, civil, moral, or
rational. To these her Adepts she sends Priests, Attendants, and Comforters, of various kinds; confers on* 60
them Orders *and* Degrees; *and then dismissing them
with a speech, confirming to each his* Privileges *and
telling what she expects from each, concludes with a*
Yawn *of extraordinary virtue: The Progress and Ef-*

417 **served a queen.** Arbuthnot had been Queen Anne's favorite physician
The Dunciad. Pope himself wrote some notes for *The Dunciad;* they are used here
selectively, as they help to clarify the spirit of this intricately allusive poem. The
notes in quotation marks are Pope's

fects whereof on all Orders of men, and the Consummation of all, in the Restoration of Night *and* Chaos, *conclude the Poem.*

Yet, yet a moment, one dim Ray of Light
Indulge, dread Chaos, and eternal Night!
Of darkness visible° so much be lent,
As half to shew, half veil the deep Intent.
Ye Pow'rs!° whose Mysteries restor'd I sing,
To whom Time bears me on his rapid wing,
Suspend a while your Force inertly strong,°
Then take at once the Poet and the Song.
    Now flam'd the Dog-star's° unpropitious ray,
10 Smote ev'ry Brain, and wither'd ev'ry Bay;
Sick was the Sun, the Owl forsook his bow'r,
The moon-struck Prophet felt the madding hour:
Then rose the Seed of Chaos, and of Night,
To blot out Order, and extinguish Light,
Of dull and venal a new World to mold,
And bring Saturnian days of Lead and Gold.°
    She mounts the Throne: her head a Cloud conceal'd,
In broad Effulgence all below reveal'd,
('Tis thus aspiring Dulness ever shines)
20 Soft on her lap her Laureat son° reclines.
    Beneath her foot-stool, *Science* groans in Chains,
And *Wit* dreads Exile, Penalties and Pains.
There foam'd rebellious *Logic,* gagg'd and bound,
There, stript, fair *Rhet'ric* languish'd on the ground;
His blunted Arms by *Sophistry* are born,
And shameless *Billingsgate*° her Robes adorn.
Morality, by her false Guardians drawn,
Chicane° in Furs, and *Casuistry* in Lawn,
Gasps, as they straiten at each end the cord,
30 And dies, when Dulness gives her Page° the word.
Mad *Mathesis*° alone was unconfin'd,
Too mad for mere material chains to bind,
Now to pure Space lifts her extatic stare,
Now running round the Circle, finds it square.
But held in ten-fold bonds° the *Muses* lie,
Watch'd both by Envy's and by Flatt'ry's eye:
There to her heart sad Tragedy addrest
The dagger wont to pierce the Tyrant's breast;
But sober History restrain'd her rage,
40 And promis'd Vengeance on a barb'rous age.
There sunk Thalia,° nerveless, cold, and dead,
Had not her Sister Satyr held her head:

Nor cou'd'st thou, CHESTERFIELD!° a tear refuse,
Thou wept'st, and with thee wept each gentle Muse.
    When lo! a Harlot form° soft sliding by,
With mincing step, small voice, and languid eye;
Foreign her air, her robe's discordant pride
In patch-work flutt'ring, and her head aside.
By singing Peers up-held on either hand,
She tripp'd and laugh'd, too pretty much to stand;   50
Cast on the prostrate Nine° a scornful look,
Then thus in quaint Recitativo spoke.
    'O *Cara! Cara!* silence all that train:
Joy to great Chaos! let Division reign:
Chromatic tortures° soon shall drive them hence,
Break all their nerves, and fritter all their sense:
One Trill shall harmonize joy, grief, and rage,
Wake the dull Church, and lull the ranting Stage;
To the same notes thy sons shall hum, or snore,
And all thy yawning daughters cry, *encore.*   60
Another Phœbus, thy own Phœbus,° reigns,
Joys in my jiggs, and dances in my chains.
But soon, ah soon Rebellion will commence.
If Music meanly borrows aid from Sense:
Strong in new Arms, lo! Giant Handel° stands,
Like bold Briareus, with a hundred hands;
To stir, to rouze, to shake the Soul he comes,
And Jove's own Thunders follow Mars's Drums.
Arrest him, Empress; or you sleep no more'—
She heard, and drove him to th' Hibernian shore.   70
    And now had Fame's posterior Trumpet blown,
And all the Nations summon'd to the Throne.
The young, the old, who feel her inward sway,
One instinct seizes, and transports away.
None need a guide, by sure Attraction led,
And strong impulsive gravity of Head:
None want a place, for all their Centre found,
Hung to the Goddess, and coher'd around.
Not closer, orb in orb, conglob'd are seen
The buzzing Bees about their dusky Queen.   80
    The gath'ring number, as it moves along,
Involves a vast involuntary throng,
Who gently drawn, and struggling less and less,
Roll in her Vortex, and her pow'r confess.
Not those alone who passive own her laws,
But who, weak rebels, more advance her cause.
Whate'er of dunce in College or in Town
Sneers at another, in toupee or gown;
Whate'er of mungril° no one class admits,
A wit with dunces, and a dunce with wits.   90
    Nor absent they, no members of her state,
Who pay her homage in her sons, the Great;

3 **darkness visible,** *Paradise Lost* I, 63   5 **Ye Pow'rs,** Chaos and Night of l. 2
7 **Force inertly strong.** "Alluding to the *Vis inertiae of Matter,* which tho' it really be no Power, is yet the Foundation of all the Qualities and Attributes of that sluggish Substance"   9 **Dog-star's,** Sirius, the most brilliant of the fixed stars. The sun passes near Sirius in August. The season of great heat was often marked by the incidence of rabies; hence the association of Sirius with both dogs and madness   16 **Saturnian days of Lead and Gold.** Saturn presided over the ancient golden age. The new age will honor dullness with lead, and venality with gold 20 **her Laureat son,** Colley Cibber, the poet laureate   26 **Billingsgate,** the fishmarket. To such language has rhetoric sunk   28 **Chicane,** chicanery 30 **Page,** the last name of a famous hanging judge; also alludes to the custom of strangling criminals in Turkey by Pages   31 **Mad Mathesis.** "Alluding to the strange Conclusions some Mathematicians have deduced"   35 **ten-fold bonds,** the effect of a Licensing Act recently imposed   41 **Thalia,** muse of Comedy

43 **Chesterfield.** He opposed the Licensing Act in the House of Lords   45 **a Harlot form,** "the nature and genius of the Italian Opera." The section that follows is Pope's commentary on the musical tastes of his time   51 **the prostrate Nine,** the defeated Muses   55 **Chromatic tortures,** music which Pope considered only a trivial playing of tricks with notes   61 **thy own Phœbus,** a character in an opera has replaced Apollo   65 **Giant Handel,** Handel's music attacked Dulness; because he wrote music for a great variety of instruments, he is many-handed   89 **mungril,** mongrel, of no definable breed

Who false to Phœbus, bow the knee to Baal;°
Or impious, preach his Word without a call.
Patrons, who sneak from living worth to dead,
With-hold the pension, and set up the head;
Or vest dull Flatt'ry in the sacred Gown;
Or give from fool to fool the Laurel crown.
And (last and worst) with all the cant of wit,
100 Without the soul, the Muse's Hypocrit.
    There march'd the bard and blockhead, side by side,
Who rhym'd for hire, and patroniz'd for pride.
Narcissus,° prais'd with all a Parson's pow'r,
Look'd a white lilly sunk beneath a show'r.
There mov'd Montalto° with superior air;
His stretch'd-out arm display'd a Volume fair;
Courtiers and Patriots in two ranks divide,
Thro' both he pass'd, and bow'd from side to side:
But as in graceful act, with awful eye
110 Compos'd he stood, bold Benson° thrust him by:
On two unequal crutches propt he came,
Milton's on this, on that one Johnston's name.
The decent Knight retir'd with sober rage,
Withdrew his hand, and clos'd the pompous page.
[But (happy for him as the times went then)
Appear'd Apollo's May'r and Aldermen,
On whom three hundred gold-capt youths await,
To lug the pond'rous volume off in state.]
    When Dulness, smiling—'Thus revive the Wits!
120 But murder first, and mince them all to bits;°
As erst Medea (cruel, so to save!)
A new Edition of old Æson gave,
Let standard-Authors, thus, like trophies born,
Appear more glorious as more hack'd and torn,
And you, my Critics! in the chequer'd shade,
Admire new light thro' holes yourselves have made.
    'Leave not a foot of verse, a foot of stone,
A Page, a Grave, that they can call their own;
But spread, my sons, your glory thin or thick,
130 On passive paper, or on solid brick.
So by each Bard an Alderman shall sit,
A heavy Lord shall hang at ev'ry Wit,
And while on Fame's triumphal Car they ride,
Some Slave of mind be pinion'd to their side.'
    Now crowds on crowds around the Goddess press,
Each eager to present the first Address.°
Dunce scorning Dunce beholds the next advance,
But Fop shews Fop superior complaisance.
When lo! a Spectre rose,° whose index-hand
140 Held forth the Virtue of the dreadful wand;
His beaver'd brow a birchen garland wears,
Dropping with Infant's blood, and Mother's tears.
O'er ev'ry vein a shudd'ring horror runs;
Eton and Winton shake thro' all their Sons.

All Flesh is humbled, Westminster's bold race°
Shrink, and confess the Genius of the place:
The pale Boy-Senator yet tingling stands,
And holds his breeches close with both his hands.
    Then thus. 'Since Man from beast by Words is
        known,
Words are Man's province, Words we teach alone. 150
When Reason doubtful, like the Samian letter,°
Points him two ways, the narrower is the better.
Plac'd at the door of Learning, youth to guide,
We never suffer it to stand too wide.
To ask, to guess, to know, as they commence,
As Fancy opens the quick springs of Sense,
We ply the Memory, we load the brain,
Bind rebel Wit, and double chain on chain,
Confine the thought, to exercise the breath;
And keep them in the pale of Words till death. 160
Whate'er the talents, or howe'er design'd,
We hang one jingling padlock on the mind:
A Poet the first day, he dips his quill;
And what the last? a very Poet still.
Pity! the charm works only in our wall,
Lost, lost too soon in yonder House or Hall.°
There truant WYNDHAM ev'ry Muse gave o'er,°
There TALBOT sunk, and was a Wit no more!
How sweet an Ovid, MURRAY was our boast!
How many Martials were in PULT'NEY lost!° 170
Else sure some Bard, to our eternal praise,
In twice ten thousand rhyming nights and days,
Had reach'd the Work, the All that mortal can;
And South beheld that Master-piece of Man.'°
'Oh (cry'd the Goddess) for some pedant Reign!
Some gentle JAMES,° to bless the land again;
To stick the Doctor's Chair into the Throne,
Give law to Words, or war with Words alone,
Senates and Courts with Greek and Latin rule,
And turn the Council to a Grammar School! 180
For sure, if Dulness sees a grateful Day,
'Tis in the shade of Arbitrary Sway.
O! if my sons may learn one earthly thing,
Teach but that one, sufficient for a King;
That which my Priests, and mine alone, maintain,
Which as it dies, or lives, we fall, or reign:
May you, may Cam, and Isis° preach it long!
"The RIGHT DIVINE of Kings to govern wrong."'
    Prompt at the call, around the Goddess roll
Broad hats, and hoods, and caps,° a sable shoal: 190
Thick and more thick the black blockade extends,
A hundred head of Aristotle's friends.
Nor wert thou, Isis! wanting to the day,
    [Tho' Christ-church° long kept prudishly away.]

93 **Who false . . . Baal.** Those who are false to true poetry and worship dullness and venality   103 **Narcissus,** Lord Hervey   105 **Montalto,** "An eminent person of Quality, who was about to publish a very pompous Edition of a great Author"   110 **bold Benson.** "This man endeavoured to raise himself to Fame by erecting monuments, striking coins, and procuring translations, of Milton"   120 **mince them all to bits.** Pope castigates the practice of insignificant editors and publishers seeking fame by publishing bits and pieces of great authors   136 **first Address,** speech of welcome to the new ruler   139 **a Spectre rose,** a schoolmaster, with a schoolmaster's cane for directing and flogging

144–45 **Eton . . . bold race.** The alumni of famous English schools   151 **the Samian letter.** Pythagoras, from Samos, used Y as "an emblem of the different roads of Virtue and Vice"   166 **House or Hall,** the House of Commons and Westminster Hall   167–70 **Wyndham . . . Put'ney,** public figures who embody the lack of elegance in speaking   174 **South . . . Man.** "The famous Dr. South declared a perfect Epigram to be as difficult a performance as an Epic poem," which was said to be the greatest work of human nature   176 **gentle James,** James I   187 **Cam and Isis,** the rivers flowing through Cambridge and Oxford; hence, through synedoche, the universities   190 **Broad . . . caps,** academic dress   194 **Christ-church,** a Cambridge college

Each staunch Polemic, stubborn as a rock,
Each fierce Logician, still expelling Locke,
Came whip and spur, and dash'd thro' thin and thick
On German Nrouzaz, and Dutch Burgersdyck.°
As many quit the streams that murm'ring fall
200 To lull the sons of Marg'ret and Clare-hall,°
Where Bentley° late tempestuous wont to sport
In troubled waters, but now sleeps in Port.°
Before them march'd that awful Aristarch;°
Plow'd was his front with many a deep Remark:
His Hat, which never vail'd to human pride,
Walker with rev'rence took, and lay'd aside.
Low bow'd the rest: He, kingly, did but nod;
So upright Quakers please both Man and God.
'Mistress! dismiss that rabble from your throne:
210 Avaunt——is Aristarchus yet unknown?
Thy mighty Scholiast, whose unweary'd pains
Made Horace dull, and humbled Milton's strains.
Turn what they will to Verse, their toil is vain,
Critics like me shall make it Prose again.
Roman and Greek Grammarians! know your Better:
Author of something yet more great than Letter;
While tow'ring o'er your Alphabet, like Saul,
Stands our Digamma,° and o'er-tops them all.
'Tis true, on Words is still our whole debate,
220 Disputes of *Me* or *Te,* of *aut* or *at*,
To sound or sink in *cano,* O or A,
Or give up Cicero to C or K.
Let Freind affect to speak as Terence spoke,
And Alsop° never but like Horace joke.
For me, what Virgil, Pliny may deny,
Manilius or Solinus shall supply:
For Attic Phrase in Plato let them seek,
I poach in Suidas for unlicens'd Greek.
In ancient Sense if any needs will deal,
230 Be sure I give them Fragments, not a Meal;
What Gellius or Stobæus hash'd before,
Or chew'd by blind old Scholiasts o'er and o'er.
The critic Eye, that microscope of Wit,
Sees hairs and pores, examines bit by bit:
How parts relate to parts, or they to whole,
The body's harmony, the beaming soul,
Are things which Kuster, Burman, Wasse shall see,
When Man's whole frame is obvious to a *Flea*.
'Ah, think not, Mistress! more true Dulness lies
240 In Folly's Cap, than Wisdom's grave disguise.
Like buoys, that never sink into the flood,
On Learning's surface we but lie and nod.
Thine is the genuine head of many a house,
And much Divinity without a *Noũs*.

Nor could a BARROW work on ev'ry block,
Nor has one ATTERBURY° spoil'd the flock.
See! still thy own, the heavy Canon roll,
And Metaphysic smokes involve the Pole.°
For thee we dim the eyes, and stuff the head
With all such reading as was never read: 250
For thee explain a thing till all men doubt it,
And write about it, Goddess, and about it:
So spins the silk-worm small its slender store,
And labours till it clouds itself all o'er.
'What tho' we let some better sort of fool
Thrid ev'ry science, run thro' ev'ry school?
Never by tumbler thro' the hoops was shown
Such skill in passing all, and touching none.
He may indeed (if sober all this time)
Plague with Dispute, or persecute with Rhyme.   260
We only furnish what he cannot use,
Or wed to what he must divorce, a Muse:
Full in the midst of Euclid dip at once,
And petrify a Genius to a Dunce:
Or set on Metaphysic ground to prance,
Show all his paces, not a step advance.
With the same Cement, ever sure to bind,
We bring to one dead level ev'ry mind.
Then take him to devellop, if you can,
And hew the Block off, and get out the Man.°   270
But wherefore waste I words? I see advance
Whore, Pupil, and lac'd Governor from France.
Walker! our hat'—nor more he deign'd to say,
But, stern as Ajax' spectre, strode away.
In flow'd at once a gay embroider'd race,
And titt'ring push'd the Pedants off the place:
Some would have spoken, but the voice was drown'd
By the French horn, or by the op'ning hound.
The first came forwards, with as easy mien,
As if he saw St. James's° and the Queen.   280
When thus th' attendant Orator begun.
'Receive, great Empress! thy accomplish'd Son:
Thine from the birth, and sacred from the rod,
A dauntless infant! never scar'd with God.
The Sire saw, one by one, his Virtues wake:
The Mother begg'd the blessing of a Rake.
Thou gav'st that Ripeness, which so soon began,
And ceas'd so soon, he ne'er was Boy, nor Man.
Thro' School and College, thy kind cloud o'ercast,
Safe and unseen the young Æneas past: 290
Thence bursting glorious, all at once let down,
Stunn'd with his giddy Larum° half the town.
Intrepid then, o'er seas and lands he flew:
Europe he saw, and Europe saw him too.
There all thy gifts and graces we display,

198 **Crouzaz ... Burgersdyck,** Jean Pierre de Crousaz (1663–1748), Swiss philosopher and mathematician, attempted a confutation of the religious ideas in Pope's *Essay on Man.* Francis Burgersdyck (1590–1629), Dutch professor of logic and philosophy at Leyden. The two are being compared to draft horses
200 **Marg'ret and Clare-hall,** colleges at Cambridge   201 **Bentley,** see note on l. 164, *Epistle to Arbuthnot*   202 **in Port,** the wine as well as an end to a voyage
203 **Aristarch,** Aristarchus, "A famous Commentator and Corrector of Homer, whose name has been frequently used to signify a severe Critic"   218 **Digamma.** "Alludes to the boasted restoration of the Aeolic Digamma, in his long projected Edition of Homer"   223–24 **Freind ... Alsop,** contemporaries of Pope's who wrote in imitative Latin styles   225 The contrast that follows is between the minor critics and commentators, whom the speaker prefers, and the great authors
244 **Noũs,** Genius or natural acumen

245–46 **Barrow ... Atterbury,** "great Geniuses and eloquent Preachers"
248 **the Pole.** "Canon here, if spoken of *Artillery,* is in the plural number; if one of the *Canons of the House,* in the singular, and meant only of *one;* in which case I suspect the *Pole* to be a false reading, and that it should be the *Poll,* or *Head* of that Canon. It may be objected, that this is a mere Paronomasia, or Pun. But what of that? Is any figure of Speech more apposite to our gentle Goddess, or more frequently used by her and her Children, especially of the University?"
270 **hew ... Man.** "A notion of Aristotle, that there was originally in every block of marble a statue, which would appear on the removal of the superfluous parts"
280 **St. James's,** the court   292 **Larum,** a rushing forth with loud cries; cf. *alarm*

Thou, only thou, directing all our way!
To where the Seine, obsequious as she runs,
Pours at great Bourbon's feet her silken sons;
Or Tyber, now no longer Roman, rolls,
300 Vain of Italian Arts, Italian Souls:
To happy Convents, bosom'd deep in vines,
Where slumber Abbots, purple as their wines:
To Isles of fragrance, lilly-silver'd vales,
Diffusing languor in the panting gales:
To lands of singing, or of dancing slaves,
Love-whisp'ring woods, and lute-resounding waves.
But chief her shrine where naked Venus keeps,
And Cupids ride the Lyon of the Deeps;°
Where, eas'd of Fleets, the Adriatic main
310 Wafts the smooth Eunuch and enamour'd swain.
Led by my hand, he saunter'd Europe round,
And gather'd ev'ry Vice on Christian ground;
Saw ev'ry Court, heard ev'ry King declare
His royal Sense, of Op'ra's or the Fair;
The Stews and Palace equally explor'd,
Intrigu'd with glory, and with spirit whor'd;
Try'd all *hors-d'œuvres,* all *liqueurs* defin'd,
Judicious drank, and greatly-daring din'd;
Dropt the dull lumber of the Latin store,
320 Spoil'd his own language, and acquir'd no more;
All Classic learning lost on Classic ground;
And last turn'd *Air,* the Echo of a Sound!
See now, half-cur'd, and perfectly well-bred,
With nothing but a Solo in his head;
As much Estate, and Principle, and Wit,
As Jansen, Fleetwood, Cibber° shall think fit;
Stol'n from a Duel, follow'd by a Nun,
And, if a Borough chuse him, not undone;
See, to my country happy I restore
330 This glorious Youth, and add one Venus more.
Her too receive (for her my soul adores)
So may the sons of sons of sons of whores,
Prop thine, O Empress! like each neighbour Throne,
And make a long Posterity thy own.'
    Pleas'd, she accepts the Hero, and the Dame,
Wraps in her Veil, and frees from sense of Shame.
    Then look'd, and saw a lazy, lolling sort,
Unseen at Church, at Senate, or at Court,
Of ever-listless Loit'rers, that attend
340 No cause, no Trust, no Duty, and no Friend.
Thee too, my Paridel!° she mark'd thee there,
Stretch'd on the rack of a too easy chair,
And heard thy everlasting yawn confess
The Pains and Penalties of Idleness.
She pity'd! but her Pity only shed
Benigner influence on thy nodding head.
    But Annius,° crafty Seer, with ebon wand,
And well dissembled em'rald on his hand,
False as his Gems, and canker'd as his Coins,

Came, cramm'd with capon, from where Pollio dines. 350
Soft, as the wily Fox is seen to creep,
Where bask on sunny banks the simple sheep,
Walk round and round, now prying here, now there;
So he; but pious, whisper'd first his pray'r.
    'Grant, gracious Goddess! grant me still to cheat,
O may thy cloud still cover the deceit!
Thy choicer mists on this assembly shed,
But pour them thickest on the noble head.
So shall each youth, assisted by our eyes,
See other Cæsars, other Homers rise; 360
Thro' twilight ages hunt th' Athenian fowl,
Which Chalcis Gods, and mortals call an Owl,
Now see an Attys, now a Cecrops clear,
Nay, Mahomet! the Pigeon at thine ear;
Be rich in ancient brass, tho' not in gold,
And keep his Lares, tho' his house be sold;
To headless Phœbe his fair bride postpone,
Honour a Syrian Prince above his own;
Lord of an Otho, if I vouch it true;
Blest in one Niger, till he knows of two.' 370
    Mummius° o'erheard him; Mummius, Fool-renown'd,
Who like his Cheops stinks above the ground,
Fierce as a startled Adder, swell'd, and said,
Rattling an ancient Sistrum° at his head.
    'Speak'st thou of Syrian Princes? Traitor base!
Mine, Goddess! mine is all the horned race.
True, he had wit, to make their value rise;
From foolish Greeks to steal them, was as wise;
More glorious yet, from barb'rous hands to keep,
When Sallee Rovers chac'd him on the deep. 380
Then taught by Hermes, and divinely bold,
Down his own throat he risqu'd the Grecian gold;
Receiv'd each Demi-God, with pious care,
Deep in his Entrails—I rever'd them there,
I bought them, shrouded in that living shrine,
And, at their second birth, they issue mine.'
    'Witness great Ammon! by whose horns I swore,
(Reply'd soft Annius) this our paunch before
Still bears them, faithful; and that thus I eat,
Is to refund the Medals with the meat. 390
To prove me, Goddess! clear of all design,
Bid me with Pollio sup, as well as dine:
There all the Learn'd shall at the labour stand,
And Douglas° lend his soft, obstetric hand.'
    The Goddess smiling seem'd to give consent;
So back to Pollio, hand in hand, they went.
    Then thick as Locusts black'ning all the ground,
A tribe, with weeds and shells fantastic crown'd,
Each with some wond'rous gift approach'd the Pow'r,
A Nest, a Toad, a Fungus, or a Flow'r. 400
But far the foremost, two,° with earnest zeal,
And aspect ardent to the Throne appeal.

---

308 **the Lyon of the Deeps,** the winged Lion on the arms of Venice   326 **Jansen, Fleetwood, Cibber,** "Three very eminent persons, all managers of plays"   341 **my Paridel,** any idly wandering young man of means   347 **Annius,** stands for falsifiers and forgers, especially of coins and medals. The subjects chosen for the coins are obscure or unlikely

371 **Mummius,** another faker, one claiming, upon scanty or deceptive evidence, to own relics of dead monarchs   374 **Sistrum,** ancient musical instrument, a rattle of sorts   394 **Douglas,** "A physician of great Learning and no less Taste" 401 These two figures represent a petty approach to Nature, fixing on small, isolated pieces as they do

The first thus open'd: 'Hear thy suppliant's call,
Great Queen, and common Mother of us all!
Fair from its humble bed I rear'd this Flow'r,
Suckled, and chear'd, with air, and sun, and show'r,
Soft on the paper ruff its leaves I spread,
Bright with the gilded button tipt its head,
Then thron'd in glass, and nam'd it CAROLINE:
410 Each Maid cry'd, charming! and each Youth, divine!
Did Nature's pencil ever blend such rays,
Such vary'd light in one promiscuous blaze?
Now prostrate! dead! behold that Caroline:
No Maid cries, charming! and no Youth, divine!
And lo the wretch! whose vile, whose insect lust
Lay'd this gay daughter of the Spring in dust.
Oh punish him, or to th' Elysian shades
Dismiss my soul, where no Carnation fades.'
    He ceas'd and wept. With innocence of mien,
420 Th' Accus'd stood forth, and thus address'd the
        Queen.
    'Of all th' enamel'd race, whose silv'ry wing
Waves to the tepid Zephyrs of the spring,
Or swims along the fluid atmosphere,
Once brightest shin'd this child of Heat and Air.
I saw, and started from its vernal bow'r
The rising game, and chac'd from flow'r to flow'r.
It fled, I follow'd; now in hope, now pain;
It stopt, I stopt; it mov'd, I mov'd again.
At last it fix'd, 'twas on what plant it pleas'd,
430 And where it fix'd, the beauteous bird I seiz'd:
Rose or Carnation was below by care;
I meddle, Goddess! only in my sphere.
I tell the naked fact without disguise,
And, to excuse it, need but shew the prize;
Whose spoils this paper offers to your eye,
Fair ev'n in death! this peerless *Butterfly.*'
    'My sons! (she answer'd) both have done your parts:
Live happy both, and long promote our arts.
But hear a Mother, when she recommends
440 To your fraternal care, our sleeping friends.
The common Soul, of Heav'n's more frugal make,
Serves but to keep fools pert, and knaves awake:
A drowzy Watchman, that just gives a knock,
And breaks our rest, to tell us what's a clock.
Yet by some object ev'ry brain is stirr'd;
The dull may waken to a Humming-bird;
The most recluse, discreetly open'd find
Congenial matter in the Cockle-kind;
The mind, in Metaphysics at a loss,
450 May wander in a wilderness of Moss;
The head that turns at super-lunar things,
Poiz'd with a tail, may steer on Wilkins' wings.°
    'O! would the Sons of Men once think their Eyes
And Reason giv'n them but to study *Flies?*
See Nature in some partial narrow shape,
And let the Author of the Whole escape:

Learn but to trifle; or, who most observe,
To wonder at their Maker, not to serve.'
    'Be that my task (replies a gloomy Clerk,°   460
Sworn foe to Myst'ry, yet divinely dark;
Whose pious hope aspires to see the day
When Moral Evidence shall quite decay,
And damns implicit faith, and holy lies,
Prompt to impose, and fond to dogmatize:)
Let others creep by timid steps, and slow,
On plain Experience lay foundations low,
By common sense to common knowledge bred,
And last, to Nature's Cause thro' Nature led.
All-seeing in thy mists, we want no guide,
Mother of Arrogance, and Source of Pride!   470
We nobly take the high Priori Road,
And reason downward, till we doubt of God:
Make Nature still incroach upon his plan;
And shove him off as far as e'er we can:
Thrust some Mechanic Cause into his place;
Or bind in Matter, or diffuse in Space.
Or, at one bound o'er-leaping all his laws,
Make God Man's Image, Man the final Cause,
Find Virtue local, all Relation scorn,
See all in *Self,* and but for self be born: 480
Of nought so certain as our *Reason* still,
Of nought so doubtful as of *Soul* and *Will.*
Oh hide the God still more! and make us see
Such as Lucretius drew, a God like Thee:
Wrapt up in Self, a God without a Thought,
Regardless of our merit or default.
Or that bright Image to our fancy draw,
Which Theocles in raptur'd vision saw,
While thro' Poetic scenes the Genius roves,
Or wanders wild in Academic Groves;   490
That NATURE our Society adores,
Where Tindal dictates, and Silenus snores.'
    Rous'd at his name, up rose the bowzy Sire,
And shook from out his Pipe the seeds of fire;
Then snapt his box, and strok'd his belly down:
Rosy and rev'rend, tho' without a Gown.
Bland and familiar to the throne he came,
Led up the Youth, and call'd the Goddess *Dame.*
Then thus. 'From Priest-craft happily set free,
Lo! ev'ry finish'd Son returns to thee: 500
First slave to Words, then vassal to a Name,
Then dupe to Party; child and man the same;
Bounded by Nature, narrow'd still by Art,
A trifling head, and a contracted heart.
Thus bred, thus taught, how many have I seen,
Smiling on all, and smil'd on by a Queen.
Mark'd out for Honours, honour'd for their Birth,
To thee the most rebellious things on earth:
Now to thy gentle shadow all are shrunk,
All melted down, in Pension, or in Punk!°   510
So K★ so B★★ sneak'd into the grave,
A Monarch's half, and half a Harlot's slave.

---

452 **Wilkins wings.** "One of the first Projectors of the Royal Society, who,
among many enlarged and useful notions, entertained the extravagant hope of a
possibility to fly to the Moon"

459ff. Here Pope criticizes those who seek to find God through nature but more
often lose sight of God thereby   510 **Punk,** a prostitute

Poor W** nipt in Folly's broadest bloom,
Who praises now? his Chaplain on his Tomb.
Then take them all, oh take them to thy breast!
Thy *Magus,* Goddess! shall perform the rest.'
    With that, a WIZARD OLD his *Cup*° extends;
Which who so tastes, forgets his former friends,
Sire, Ancestors, Himself. One casts his eyes
520 Up to a *Star,* and like Endymion dies:
A *Feather* shooting from another's head,
Extracts his brain, and Principle is fled,
Lost is his God, his Country, ev'ry thing;
And nothing left but Homage to a King!
The vulgar herd turn off to roll with Hogs,
To run with Horses, or to hunt with Dogs;
But, sad example! never to escape
Their Infamy, still keep the human shape.
    But she, good Goddess, sent to ev'ry child
530 Firm Impudence, or Stupefaction mild;
And strait succeeded, leaving shame no room,
Cibberian forehead, or Cimmerian gloom.°
    Kind Self-conceit to some her glass applies,
Which no one looks in with another's eyes:
But as the Flatt'rer or Dependant paint,
Beholds himself a Patriot, Chief, or Saint.
    On others Int'rest her gay liv'ry flings,
Int'rest, that waves on Party-colour'd wings;
Turn'd to the Sun, she casts a thousand dyes,
540 And, as she turns, the colours fall or rise.
    Others the Syren Sisters warble round,
And empty heads console with empty sound.
No more, alas! the voice of Fame they hear,
The balm of Dulness trickling in their ear.
Great C **, H **, P **, R **, K *,
Why all your Toils? your Sons have learn'd to sing.
How quick Ambition hastes to ridicule!
The Sire is made a Peer, the Son a Fool.
    On some, a Priest succinct in amice white
550 Attends; all flesh is nothing in his sight!°
Beeves, at his touch, at once to jelly turn,
And the huge Boar is shrunk into an Urn:
The board with specious miracles he loads,
Turns Hares to Larks, and Pigeons into Toads.
Another (for in all what one can shine?)
Explains the *Seve* and *Verdeur* of the Vine.
What cannot copious Sacrifice attone?
Thy *Treufles,* Perigord! thy Hams, Bayonne!
With French Libation, and Italian Strain,
560 Wash Bladen white, and expiate Hays's stain.
Knight lifts the head, for what are crowds undone
To three essential Partriges in one?
Gone ev'ry blush, and silent all reproach,
Contending Princes mount them in their Coach.
    Next bidding all draw near on bended knees,
The Queen confers her *Titles* and *Degrees.*

Her children first of more distinguish'd sort,
Who study Shakespeare at the Inns of Court,
Impale a Glow-worm, or Vertù profess,
Shine in the dignity of F. R. S.°   570
Some, deep Free-Masons, join the silent race
Worthy to fill Pythagoras's place:
Some Botanists, or Florists at the least,
Or issue Members of an Annual feast.
Nor past the meanest unregarded, one
Rose a Gregorian, one a Gormogon.°
The last, not least in honour or applause,
Isis and Cam made Doctors of her Laws.
    Then blessing all, 'Go Children of my care!
To Practice now from Theory repair.   580
All my commands are easy, short and full:
My Sons! be proud, be selfish, and be dull.
Guard my Prerogative, assert my Throne:
This Nod confirms each Privilege your own.
The Cap and Switch be sacred to his Grace;
With Staff and Pumps the Marquis lead the Race;
From Stage to Stage the licens'd Earl may run,
Pair'd with his Fellow-Charioteer the Sun;
The learned Baron Butterflies design,
Or draw to silk Arachne's subtile line;   590
The Judge to dance his brother Sergeant call;
The Senator at Cricket urge the Ball;
The Bishop stow (Pontific Luxury!)
An hundred Souls of Turkeys in a pye;
The sturdy Squire to Gallic masters stoop,
And drown his Lands and Manors in a Soupe.
Others import yet nobler arts from France,
Teach Kings to fiddle, and make Senates dance.
Perhaps more high some daring son may soar,
Proud to my list to add one Monarch more;   600
And nobly conscious, Princes are but things
Born for First Ministers, as Slaves for Kings,
Tyrant supreme! shall three Estates command,
And MAKE ONE MIGHTY DUNCIAD OF THE LAND!'
    More she had spoke, but yawn'd—All Nature nods:
What Mortal can resist the Yawn of Gods?
Churches and Chapels instantly it reach'd;
(St. James's first, for leaden Gilbert° preach'd)
Then catch'd the Schools; the Hall scarce kept awake
The Convocation gap'd, but could not speak: 610
Lost was the Nation's Sense, nor could be found,
While the long solemn Unison went round:
Wide, and more wide, it spread o'er all the realm;
Ev'n Palinurus° nodded at the Helm:
The Vapour mild o'er each Committee crept;
Unfinish'd Treaties in each Office slept;
And Chiefless Armies doz'd out the Campaign;
And Navies yawn'd for Orders on the Main.
    O Muse! relate (for you can tell alone,
Wits have short Memories, and Dunces none)   620

---

517 **Wizard . . . Cup,** "The Cup of Self-love"   532 **Cibberian forehead, or Cimmerian gloom.** Pope has earlier used Cibber as the embodiment of Dullness. Cimmeria is the land of Stygian darkness   550 **all flesh . . . sight,** "The miracles of French cookery"

570 **F.R.S.,** initials standing for Fellow of the Royal Society   576 **Gormogon,** a member of a society imitating the Freemasons, founded early in the eighteenth century   608 **Gilbert,** a notable churchman   614 **Palinurus,** Aeneas' helmsman

Relate, who first, who last resign'd to rest;
Whose Heads she partly, whose completely blest;
What Charms could Faction, what Ambition lull,
The Venal quiet, and entrance the Dull;
'Till drown'd was Sense, and Shame, and Right, and
    Wrong—
O sing, and hush the Nations with thy Song!

* * * * *

In vain, in vain,—the all-composing Hour
Resistless falls: The Muse obeys the Pow'r.
She comes! she comes! the sable Throne behold
630 Of *Night* Primæval, and of *Chaos* old!
Before her, *Fancy*'s gilded clouds decay,
And all its varying Rain-bows die away.
Wit shoots in vain its momentary fires,
The meteor drops, and in a flash expires.
As one by one, at dread Medea's strain,
The sick'ning stars fade off th' ethereal plain;
As Argus' eyes by Hermes' wand opprest,

Clos'd one by one to everlasting rest;
Thus at her felt approach, and secret might,
Art after *Art* goes out, and all is Night.   640
See skulking *Truth* to her old Cavern fled,
Mountains of Casuistry heap'd o'er her head!
Philosophy, that lean'd on Heav'n before,
Shrinks to her second cause, and is no more.
Physic of *Metaphysic* begs defence,
And *Metaphysic* calls for aid on *Sense!*
See *Mystery* to *Mathematics* fly!
In vain! they gaze, turn giddy, rave, and die.
Religion blushing veils her sacred fires,
And unawares *Morality* expires.   650
Nor *public* Flame, nor *private*, dares to shine;
Nor *human* Spark is left, nor Glimpse *divine!*
Lo! thy dread Empire, CHAOS! is restor'd;
Light dies before thy uncreating word:
Thy hand, great Anarch! lets the curtain fall;
And Universal Darkness buries All.
(1743)

SAMUEL JOHNSON
1709–1784

Samuel Johnson was born in Lichfield in 1709, the son of an elderly and poor bookseller. He suffered from scrofula as a child, and ill health plagued him the rest of his life. He attended Lichfield and Stourbridge Grammar Schools and entered Pembroke College, Oxford. As a youth Johnson had frequently helped his father in the family bookstore, where he read voraciously; thus, by the time he entered Oxford in 1728, he was singularly well prepared for his studies. After only thirteen months, however, he was forced to leave the university because of his father's straitened circumstances; in 1731 his father died. Johnson published his first work in 1735, a translation into English from French of *A Voyage to Abyssinia* by Father Jerome Lobo (1593–1678), a Portuguese Jesuit missionary. In the same year Johnson married Elizabeth Porter, a widow twenty years his senior, and the couple then opened a school near Lichfield. When the school failed two years later, he set out for London with one of his pupils, the great future actor David Garrick (1717–1779).

From 1737 to 1746 Johnson worked doggedly at literary and journalistic projects, especially for *The Gentleman's Magazine.* He published *London,* his first substantial poem, an imitation of the third *Satire* of Juvenal, in 1738. Johnson's *Account of the Life of Mr. Richard Savage,* published anonymously in 1744, was the first of Johnson's prose works successful with the public; Richard Savage (1697?–1743), actor, playwright, and poet, had been one of Johnson's closest companions in his early years in London. In 1747 Johnson issued his ambitious *Plan of a Dictionary of the English Language;* eight and one-half years later, with the help of only six assistants, the work was completed. While at work on the *Dictionary,* Johnson also found time to write and publish another didactic poem, his best, *The Vanity of Human Wishes* (1749), and witnessed the production of his tragedy *Irene* by David Garrick (1749).

In 1750 Johnson, in imitation of *The Spectator,* brought out *The Rambler,* a twopenny sheet published twice a week which contained a single anonymous essay. Johnson was clear about the moral purpose of his periodical; he wanted to instruct—not to entertain. He published *The Rambler* for two years. In 1752 Mrs. Johnson died. Because of his debts, which he seemed to have throughout his life, he was forced to continue his activity as a journalist, writing many essays, reviews, and prefaces. This work culminated in a weekly essay, called "The Idler," which he contributed to the *Universal Chronicle* from 1758 to 1760. These essays on manners, morals, and literature enhanced his reputation as a moralist and social reformer.

In order to pay his mother's funeral expenses and debts, he composed *Rasselas, The Prince of Abyssinia* within the space of a single week in 1759. The setting was prompted by Lobo's *Voyage to Abyssinia. Rasselas* is a fine example of Johnson's fluent productivity and characteristic prose style. It was Johnson's only prose work that achieved immediate and widespread popularity.

In 1762 King George III bestowed a pension on Johnson, which much improved his financial position. The following year, on May 16, Johnson met James Boswell and inaugurated one of the most famous companionships in history. Though many others left valuable records of his life and character, Boswell's diary is unsurpassed in giving sustained, intimate glimpses of this witty conversationalist. In 1765 Johnson published his long-awaited edition of Shakespeare in eight volumes and also met the Thrales, a wealthy couple with whom he formed a most comforting friendship. Henry Thrale was a member of Parliament for Southwark; his wife was a famous London hostess. Johnson frequently spent weeks and even months at their country house where he enjoyed, among other solid comforts, intelligent conversation and good food. During the 1770s Johnson wrote a series of political pamphlets which express his essentially conservative and pragmatic philosophy. His life at this time was greatly given to his friends, particularly the group of literary and professional men who formed his famous Literary Club. Johnson's last published work, *The Lives of the English Poets,* appeared in two parts, in 1779 and 1781, respectively. He spent the remaining years of his life visiting and conversing with his increasingly small group of old friends. He died in London in 1784 and was buried in Westminster Abbey.

Johnson is today regarded not just as a great conversationalist or a great eccentric but as a great man of letters. As a literary critic, he was certainly the greatest of his century. His critical emphasis is practical rather than theoretical. His common sense and vast reading in English literature combine to make his judgments reasonable and literate. His prose style—known for its directness, balance, and periodic structures—has been judged his greatest achievement.

THE VANITY OF HUMAN WISHES

IN IMITATION OF THE TENTH SATIRE OF JUVENAL

Let Observation, with extensive view,
Survey mankind, from China to Peru;
Remark each anxious toil, each eager strife,
And watch the busy scenes of crowded life;
Then say how hope and fear, desire and hate
O'erspread with snares the clouded maze of fate,
Where wavering man, betrayed by venturous pride
To tread the dreary paths without a guide,
As treacherous phantoms in the mist delude,
Shuns fancied ills, or chases airy good;   10

How rarely Reason guides the stubborn choice,
Rules the bold hand, or prompts the suppliant voice;
How nations sink, by darling schemes oppressed,
When Vengeance listens to the fool's request.
Fate wings with every wish the afflictive dart,
Each gift of nature, and each grace of art;
With fatal heat impetuous courage glows,
With fatal sweetness elocution flows,
Impeachment stops the speaker's powerful breath,
And restless fire precipitates on death.   20

But scarce observed, the knowing and the bold
Fall in the general massacre of gold;
Wide-wasting pest! that rages unconfined,
And crowds with crimes the records of mankind;
For gold his sword the hireling ruffian draws,
For gold the hireling judge distorts the laws;
Wealth heaped on wealth, nor truth nor safety buys,
The dangers gather as the treasures rise.

Let History tell where rival kings command,
And dubious title shakes the madded° land,   30
When statutes glean the refuse of the sword,
How much more safe the vassal than the lord,
Low skulks the hind beneath the rage of power,
And leaves the wealthy traitor in the Tower,
Untouched his cottage, and his slumbers sound,
Though Confiscation's vultures hover round.

The needy traveler, serene and gay,
Walks the wild heath, and sings his toil away.
Does envy seize thee? crush the upbraiding joy,
Increase his riches and his peace destroy;   40
New fears in dire vicissitude invade,
The rustling brake° alarms, and quivering shade,
Nor light nor darkness bring his pain relief,
One shows the plunder, and one hides the thief.

Yet still one general cry the skies assails,
And gain and grandeur load the tainted gales;
Few know the toiling statesman's fear or care,
The insidious rival and the gaping heir.

Once more, Democritus,° arise on earth,
With cheerful wisdom and instructive mirth,   50
See motley life in modern trappings dressed,
And feed with varied fools the eternal jest:
Thou who couldst laugh where Want enchained
          Caprice,
Toil crushed Conceit, and man was of a piece;
Where Wealth unloved without a mourner died;
And scarce a sycophant was fed by Pride;
Where ne'er was known the form of mock debate,
Or seen a new-made mayor's unwieldy state;
Where change of favorites made no change of laws,
And senates heard before they judged a cause;   60
How wouldst thou shake at Britain's modish tribe,
Dart the quick taunt, and edge the piercing gibe?
Attentive truth and nature to descry,
And pierce each scene with philosophic eye,

The Vanity of Human Wishes   30 **madded,** maddened   42 **brake,** thicket of dense underbrush   49 **Democritus,** "the laughing philosopher" (fifth century B.C.)

To thee were solemn toys or empty show
The robes of pleasures and the veils of woe:
All aid the farce, and all thy mirth maintain,
Whose joys are causeless, or whose griefs are vain.
   Such was the scorn that filled the sage's mind,
70 Renewed at every glance on human kind;
How just that scorn ere yet thy voice declare,
Search every state, and canvass every prayer.
   Unnumbered suppliants crowd Preferment's gate,
Athirst for wealth, and burning to be great;
Delusive Fortune hears the incessant call,
They mount, they shine, evaporate, and fall.
On every stage the foes of peace attend,
Hate dogs their flight, and Insult mocks their end.
Love ends with hope, the sinking statesman's door
80 Pours in the morning worshiper no more;
For growing names the weekly scribbler lies,
To growing wealth the dedicator flies;
From every room descends the painted face,
That hung the bright palladium° of the place;
And smoked in kitchens, or in auctions sold,
To better features yields the frame of gold;
For now no more we trace in every line
Heroic worth, benevolence divine:
The form distorted justifies the fall,
90 And Detestation rids the indignant wall.
   But will not Britain hear the last appeal,
Sign her foes' doom, or guard her favorites' zeal?
Through Freedom's sons no more remonstrance rings,
Degrading nobles and controlling kings;
Our supple tribes repress their patriot throats,
And ask no questions but the price of votes,
With weekly libels° and septennial ale.°
Their wish is full to riot and to rail.
   In full-blown dignity, see Wolsey° stand,
100 Law in his voice, and fortune in his hand:
To him the church, the realm, their powers consign,
Through him the rays of regal bounty shine;
Turned by his nod the stream of honor flows,
His smile alone security bestows:
Still to new heights his restless wishes tower,
Claim leads to claim, and power advances power;
Till conquest unresisted ceased to please,
And rights submitted, left him none to seize.
At length his sovereign frowns—the train of state
110 Mark the keen glance, and watch the sign to hate.
Where'er he turns, he meets a stranger's eye,
His suppliants scorn him, and his followers fly;
At once is lost the pride of awful state,
The golden canopy, the glittering plate,
The regal palace, the luxurious board,
The liveried army, and the menial lord.
With age, with cares, with maladies oppressed,
He seeks the refuge of monastic rest.

Grief aids disease, remembered folly stings,
And his last sighs reproach the faith of kings.   120
   Speak thou, whose thoughts at humble peace repine,
Shall Wolsey's wealth, with Wolsey's end be thine?
Or liv'st thou now, with safer pride content,
The wisest justice on the banks of Trent?
For why did Wolsey, near the steeps of fate,
On weak foundations raise the enormous weight?
Why but to sink beneath misfortune's blow,
With louder ruin to the gulfs below?
   What gave great Villiers° to the assassin's knife,
And fixed disease on Harley's° closing life?   130
What murdered Wentworth,° and what exiled Hyde,°
By kings protected and to kings allied?
What but their wish indulged in courts to shine,
And power too great to keep or to resign?
   When first the college rolls receive his name,
The young enthusiast quits his ease for fame;
Resistless burns the fever of renown
Caught from the strong contagion of the gown:
O'er Bodley's° dome his future labors spread,
And Bacon's° mansion trembles o'er his head.   140
Are these thy views? proceed, illustrious youth,
And Virtue guard thee to the throne of Truth!
Yet should thy soul indulge the generous heat,
Till captive Science yields her last retreat;
Should Reason guide thee with her brightest ray,
And pour on misty Doubt resistless day;
Should no false kindness lure to loose delight,
Nor praise relax, nor difficulty fright;
Should tempting Novelty thy cell refrain,
And Sloth effuse her opiate fumes in vain;   150
Should Beauty blunt on fops her fatal dart,
Nor claim the triumph of a lettered heart;
Should no disease thy torpid veins invade,
Nor Melancholy's phantoms haunt thy shade;
Yet hope not life from grief or danger free,
Nor think the doom of man reversed for thee:
Deign on the passing world to turn thine eyes,
And pause a while from letters, to be wise;
There mark what ills the scholar's life assail,
Toil, envy, want, the patron, and the jail.   160
See nations slowly wise, and meanly just,
To buried merit raise the tardy bust.
If dreams yet flatter, once again attend,
Hear Lydiat's° life, and Galileo's° end.
   Nor deem, when Learning her last prize bestows,
The glittering eminence exempt from foes;
See when the vulgar 'scapes, despised or awed,

84 **palladium,** a statue of Pallas Athena, upon which the safety of Troy was supposed to depend   97 **weekly libels,** attacks in the weekly newspapers   **septennial ale,** ale given away by politicians at election time, at least every seven years   99 **Wolsey,** Thomas Cardinal Wolsey (1475?-1530), Lord Chancellor under Henry VIII

129 **Villiers,** George Villiers (1592-1628), 1st Duke of Buckingham and a royal favorite; he was assassinated   130 **Harley,** Robert Harley (1661-1724), 1st Earl of Oxford, one of Queen Anne's principal ministers. The year after her death he was imprisoned by the Whigs   131 **Wentworth,** Thomas Wentworth (1593-1641), 1st Earl of Strafford, and adviser to Charles I. Known as "Black Tom Tyrant," he was executed with Charles' assent in 1641   **Hyde,** Edward Hyde (1609-1674), Earl of Clarendon. He was the father-in-law of James II and Charles II's principal minister. Impeached in 1667, he fled to France   139 **Bodley's,** the Bodleian Library at Oxford   140 **Bacon,** Roger Bacon (1214?-1294), "the founder of English philosophy," was a learned professor at Oxford. Legend held that when a more learned man came to Oxford, Bacon's study would come crashing down   164 **Lydiat,** Thomas Lydiat (1572-1646), an Oxford scholar who died in want because of his sympathies for the Royalists   **Galileo,** Galileo Galilei (1564-1642), Italian astronomer and physicist imprisoned as a heretic by the Inquisition

Rebellion's vengeful talons seize on Laud.°
From meaner minds though smaller fines content,
170 The plundered palace, or sequestered rent;
Marked out by dangerous parts he meets the shock,
And fatal Learning leads him to the block:
Around his tomb let Art and Genius weep,
But hear his death, ye blockheads, hear and sleep.
    The festal blazes, the triumphal show,
The ravished standard, and the captive foe,
The senate's thanks, the gazette's pompous tale,
With force resistless o'er the brave prevail.
Such bribes the rapid Greek° o'er Asia whirled,
180 For such the steady Romans shook the world;
For such in distant lands the Britons shine,
And stain with blood the Danube or the Rhine;
This power has praise that virtue scarce can warm,
Till fame supplies the universal charm.
Yet Reason frowns on War's unequal game,
Where wasted nations raise a single name,
And mortgaged states their grandsires' wreaths regret
From age to age in everlasting debt;
Wreaths which at last the dear-bought right convey
190 To rust on medals, or on stones decay.
    On what foundation stands the warrior's pride,
How just his hopes, let Swedish Charles° decide;
A frame of adamant, a soul of fire,
No dangers fright him, and no labors tire;
O'er love, o'er fear, extends his wide domain,
Unconquered lord of pleasure and of pain;
No joys to him pacific scepters yield,
War sounds the trump, he rushes to the field;
Behold surrounding kings their powers combine,
200 And one capitulate, and one resign;
Peace courts his hand, but spreads her charms in vain;
"Think nothing gained," he cries, "till naught remain,
On Moscow's walls till Gothic standards fly,
And all be mine beneath the polar sky."
The march begins in military state,
And nations on his eye suspended wait;
Stern Famine guards the solitary coast,
And Winter barricades the realms of Frost;
He comes, nor want nor cold his course delay—
210 Hide, blushing Glory, hide Pultowa's day:
The vanquished hero leaves his broken bands,
And shows his miseries in distant lands;
Condemned a needy supplicant to wait,
While ladies interpose, and slaves debate.
But did not Chance at length her error mend?
Did no subverted empire mark his end?
Did rival monarchs give the fatal wound?
Or hostile millions press him to the ground?
His fall was destined to a barren strand,
220 A petty fortress, and a dubious hand:

He left the name at which the world grew pale,
To point a moral, or adorn a tale.
    All times their scenes of pompous woes afford,
From Persia's tyrant° to Bavaria's lord.
In gay hostility, and barbarous pride,
With half mankind embattled at his side,
Great Xerxes comes to seize the certain prey,
And starves exhausted regions in his way;
Attendant Flattery counts his myriads o'er,
Till counted myriads sooth his pride no more;   230
Fresh praise is tried till madness fires his mind,
The waves he lashes, and enchains the wind;
New powers are claimed, new powers are still
    bestowed,
Till rude resistance lops the spreading god;
The daring Greeks deride the martial show,
And heap their valleys with the gaudy foe;
The insulted sea with humbler thought he gains,
A single skiff to speed his flight remains;
The encumbered oar scarce leaves the dreaded coast
Through purple billows and a floating host.   240
    The bold Bavarian,° in a luckless hour,
Tries the dread summits of Caesarean power,
With unexpected legions bursts away,
And sees defenseless realms receive his sway;
Short sway! fair Austria spreads her mournful charms
The queen, the beauty, sets the world in arms;
From hill to hill the beacon's rousing blaze
Spreads wide the hope of plunder and of praise;
The fierce Croation, and the wild Hussar,
With all the sons of ravage crowd the war;   250
The baffled prince, in honor's flattering bloom
Of hasty greatness finds the fatal doom,
His foes' derision, and his subjects' blame,
And steals to death from anguish and from shame.
    Enlarge my life with multitude of days!
In health, in sickness, thus the suppliant prays;
Hides from himself his state, and shuns to know,
That life protracted is protracted woe.
Time hovers o'er, impatient to destroy,
And shuts up all the passages of joy;   260
In vain their gifts the bounteous seasons pour,
The fruit autumnal, and the vernal flower;
With listless eyes the dotard views the store,
He views, and wonders that they please no more;
Now pall the tasteless meats, and joyless wines,
And Luxury with sighs her slave resigns.
Approach, ye minstrels, try the soothing strain,
Diffuse the tuneful lenitives of pain:
No sounds, alas! would touch the impervious ear,
Though dancing mountains witnessed Orpheus near; 270
Nor lute nor lyre his feeble powers attend,
Nor sweeter music of a virtuous friend,

---

168 **Laud,** William Laud (1573–1645), Archbishop of Canterbury and a supporter of Charles I against Parliament; he was executed   179 **the rapid Greek,** Alexander the Great   192 **Swedish Charles, etc.** Charles XII of Sweden (1682–1718) was ambitious that "all be mine beneath the polar sky." Frederick IV of Denmark capitulated and Augustus II of Poland "resigned" (l. 200). Charles was defeated by the Russians (l. 216) at Pultowa and died in an attack on "a petty fortress" in Norway (ll. 219–220)

224 **Persia's tyrant, etc.** Xerxes, King of Persia from 485 to 465 B.C., bridged the Hellespont with boats and invaded Greece. At Thermopylae, a narrow pass between the mountains and the sea, a mere handful of Greeks and Spartans resisted for three days the vast army of the Persians (480 B.C.)   241 **bold Bavarian, etc.** Charles Albert, Elector of Bavaria, contested the crown of the Holy Roman Empire with the German archduchess Maria Theresa of Austria, thus causing the War of the Austrian Succession (1740–1748)

But everlasting dictates crowd his tongue,
Perversely grave, or positively wrong.
The still returning tale, and lingering jest,
Perplex the fawning niece and pampered guest,
While growing hopes scarce awe the gathering sneer,
And scarce a legacy can bribe to hear;
The watchful guests still hint the last offense;
280 The daughter's petulance, the son's expense,
Improve his heady rage with treacherous skill,
And mold his passions till they make his will.

Unnumbered maladies his joints invade,
Lay siege to life and press the dire blockade;
But unextinguished avarice still remains,
And dreaded losses aggravate his pains;
He turns, with anxious heart and crippled hands,
His bonds of debt, and mortgages of lands;
Or views his coffers with suspicious eyes,
290 Unlocks his gold, and counts it till he dies.

But grant, the virtues of a temperate prime
Bless with an age exempt from scorn or crime;
An age that melts with unperceived decay,
And glides in modest innocence away;
Whose peaceful day Benevolence endears,
Whose night congratulating Conscience cheers;
The general favorite as the general friend:
Such age there is, and who shall wish its end?

Yet even on this her load Misfortune flings,
300 To press the weary minutes' flagging wings;
New sorrow rises as the day returns,
A sister sickens, or a daughter mourns.
Now kindred Merit fills the sable bier,
Now lacerated Friendship claims a tear;
Year chases year, decay pursues decay,
Still drops some joy from withering life away;
New forms arise, and different views engage,
Superfluous lags the veteran on the stage,
Till pitying Nature signs the last release,
310 And bids afflicted Worth retire to peace.

But few there are whom hours like these await,
Who set unclouded in the gulfs of Fate.
From Lydia's monarch° should the search descend,
By Solon cautioned to regard his end,
In life's last scene what prodigies surprise,
Fears of the brave, and follies of the wise!
From Marlborough's° eyes the streams of dotage flow,
And Swift expires a driveler and a show.°
The teeming mother, anxious for her race,
320 Begs for each birth the fortune of a face:
Yet Vane° could tell what ills from beauty spring;
And Sedley° cursed the form that pleased a king.
Ye nymphs of rosy lips and radiant eyes,
Whom Pleasure keeps too busy to be wise,
Whom Joys with soft varieties invite,

313 **Lydia's monarch.** Croesus, last king of Lydia, was the wealthiest of men
("rich as Croesus"). He was warned by the philosopher Solon that a man cannot
claim happiness who has not ended his life happily. He lost his kingdom to Cyrus
of Persia   317 **Marlborough.** The 1st Duke of Marlborough, John Churchill
(1650–1722), passed from the life of a brilliant soldier to senility   318 **Swift . . .
show.** Jonathan Swift died *non compos mentis*   321 **Vane,** Anne Vane, mistress of
the Prince of Wales, son of George II   322 **Sedley,** Catherine Sedley, mistress of
James II

By day the frolic, and the dance by night;
Who frown with vanity, who smile with art,
And ask the latest fashion of the heart;
What care, what rules your heedless charms shall
        save,
Each nymph your rival, and each youth your slave?   330
Against your fame with Fondness Hate combines,
The rival batters, and the lover mines.
With distant voice neglected Virtue calls,
Less heard and less, the faint remonstrance falls;
Tired with contempt, she quits the slippery reign,
And Pride and Prudence take her seat in vain.
In crowd at once, where none the pass defend,
The harmless freedom, and the private friend.
The guardians yield, by force superior plied:
To Interest, Prudence; and to Flattery, Pride.   340
Now Beauty falls betrayed, despised, distressed,
And hissing Infamy proclaims the rest.

Where then shall Hope and Fear their objects find?
Must dull Suspense corrupt the stagnant mind?
Must helpless man, in ignorance sedate,
Roll darkling down the torrent of his fate?
Must no dislike alarm, no wishes rise,
No cries invoke the mercies of the skies?
Inquirer, cease; petitions yet remain,
Which Heaven may hear, nor deem religion vain.   350
Still raise for good the supplicating voice,
But leave to Heaven the measure and the choice.
Safe in His power, whose eyes discern afar
The secret ambush of a specious prayer.
Implore His aid, in His decisions rest,
Secure, what'er He gives, He gives the best.
Yet when the sense of sacred presence fires,
And strong devotion to the skies aspires,
Pour forth thy fervors for a healthful mind,
Obedient passions, and a will resigned,   360
For love, which scarce collective man can fill;
For patience sovereign o'er transmuted ill;
For faith, that panting for a happier seat,
Counts death kind Nature's signal of retreat;
These goods for man the laws of Heaven ordain,
These goods He grants, who grants the power to gain,
With these celestial Wisdom calms the mind,
And makes the happiness she does not find.

(1749)

ON THE DEATH OF DR. ROBERT LEVET

Condemn'd to hope's delusive mine,
    As on we toil from day to day,
By sudden blasts, or slow decline,
    Our social comforts drop away.

Well tried through many a varying year,
    See Levet to the grave descend;
Officious, innocent, sincere,
    Of ev'ry friendless name the friend.

Yet still he fills affection's eye,
10   Obscurely wise, and coarsely kind;
Nor, letter'd arrogance, deny
    Thy praise to merit unrefin'd.

When fainting nature call'd for aid,
    And hov'ring death prepar'd the blow,
His vig'rous remedy display'd
    The power of art without the show.

In misery's darkest caverns known,
    His useful care was ever nigh,
Where hopeless anguish pour'd his groan,
20   And lonely want retir'd to die.

No summons mock'd by chill delay,
    No petty gain disdain'd by pride,
The modest wants of ev'ry day
    The toil of ev'ry day supplied.

His virtues walk'd their narrow round,
    Nor made a pause, nor left a void;
And sure th' Eternal Master found
    The single talent well employ'd.

The busy day, the peaceful night,
30   Unfelt, uncounted, glided by;
His frame was firm, his powers were bright,
    Tho' now his eightieth year was nigh.

Then with no throbbing fiery pain,
    No cold gradations of decay,
Death broke at once the vital chain,
    And free'd his soul the nearest way.
    (1783)

from THE DICTIONARY

Johnson's *Dictionary* (1755) surpassed earlier dictionaries in precision of definition and in literary illustration. As stated in the original *Plan,* Johnson hoped to write "a dictionary by which the pronunciation of our language may be fixed, and its attainment facilitated; by which its purity may be preserved, its use ascertained, and its duration lengthened." What distinguishes Johnson's work is the range of reading by which he exemplifies the different shades of meaning of a particular word.

The following small sample of definitions from the *Dictionary* was chosen to highlight Johnson's lexicographical idiosyncrasies. Sometimes he gives a delicious flavor to his definitions by odd quirks of personal prejudice or humor, or by difficulties encountered in explaining the obvious.

It is not sufficient that a word is found [in the *Dictionary*], unless it be so combined as that its meaning is apparently determined by the tract and tenor of the sentence; such passages I have therefore chosen, and when it happened that any author gave a definition of a term, or such an explanation as is equivalent to a definition, I have placed his authority as a supplement to my own, without regard to the chronological order, that is otherwise observed. . . .

There is more danger of censure from the multiplic- 10 ity than paucity of examples; authorities will sometimes seem to have been accumulated without necessity or use, and perhaps some will be found, which might, without loss, have been omitted. But a work of this kind is not hastily to be charged with superfluities: those quotations which to careless or unskilful perusers appear only to repeat the same sense, will often exhibit, to a more accurate examiner, diversities of signification, or, at least, afford different shades of the same meaning: one will show the words applied to 20 persons, another to things; one will express an ill, another a good, and a third a neutral sense; one will prove the expression genuine from an ancient authour; another will show it elegant from a modern: a doubtful authority is corroborated by another of more credit; an ambiguous sentence is ascertained by a passage clear and determinate; the word, how often soever repeated, appears with new associates and different combinations, and every quotation contributes something to the stability or enlargement of the language. . . .   30

Thus I have laboured to settle the orthography, display the analogy, regulate the structures, and ascertain the signification of *English* words, to perform all the parts of a faithful lexicographer: but I have not always executed my own scheme, or satisfied my own expectations. The work, whatever proofs of diligence and attention it may exhibit, is yet capable of many improvements: the orthography which I recommend is still controvertible, the etymology which I adopt is uncertain, and perhaps frequently erroneous; the expla- 40 nations are sometimes too much contracted, and sometimes too much diffused, the significations are distinguished rather with subtilty than skill, and the attention is harassed with unnecessary minuteness.°

dry: desiccative.
dryness: siccity or aridity.
excise: a hateful tax levied upon commodities, and
    adjudged, not by the common judges of property,
    but wretches hired by those to whom excise is paid.
Grub Street: the name of a street in London, much
    inhabited by writers of small histories, *dictionaries,*
    and temporary poems; whence any mean production
    is called Grub Street.

The Dictionary   44 What follows is a selection of terms from *The Dictionary*

hatchet-faced: an ugly face; such, I suppose, as might be hewn out of a block by a hatchet.

lexicographer: a writer of dictionaries, a harmless drudge that busies himself in tracing the original and detailing the significance of words.

network: anything reticulated or decussated at equal distances with interstices between the intersections.

oats: a grain which in England is generally given to horses, but in Scotland supports the people.

patriotism: the last refuge of a scoundrel.

patron: one who countenances, supports, or protects. Commonly a wretch who supports with insolence, and is paid with flattery.

pension: an allowance made to anyone without an equivalent. In England it is generally understood to mean pay given to a state hireling for treason to his country.

pensioner: a slave of state, hired by a stipend to obey his master.

politician: a man of artifice; one deep of contrivance.

Redcoat: a name of contempt for a soldier.

thunder: a most bright flame rising on a sudden, moving with great violence, and with a very rapid velocity, through the air, according to any determination, and commonly ending with a loud noise or rattling.

Tory: one who adheres to the ancient constitution of the state, and the apostolical hierarchy of the Church of England, opposed to a Whig.

transpire: to escape from secrecy to notice, a sense lately innovated from France without necessity.

Whig: the name of a faction.

willow: a tree worn by forlorn lovers.

(1755)

from THE RAMBLER°

NO. 5. TUESDAY, 3 APRIL 1750.

Et nunc omnis ager, nunc omnis parturit arbos,
Nunc frondent silvae, nunc formosissimus annus.
Virgil, ECLOGUES, III. 56–57.

Now ev'ry field, now ev'ry tree is green;
Now genial nature's fairest face is seen.
Elphinston.

Every man is sufficiently discontented with some circumstances of his present state, to suffer his imagination to range more or less in quest of future happiness, and to fix upon some point of time, in which, by the removal of the inconvenience which now perplexes him, or acquisition of the advantage which he at present wants, he shall find the condition of his life very much improved.

When this time, which is too often expected with great impatience, at last arrives, it generally comes without the blessing for which it was desired; but we solace ourselves with some new prospect, and press forward again with equal eagerness.

It is lucky for a man, in whom this temper prevails, when he turns his hopes upon things wholly out of his own power; since he forbears then to precipitate his affairs, for the sake of the great event that is to complete his felicity, and waits for the blissful hour, with less neglect of the measures necessary to be taken in the mean time.

I have long known a person of this temper, who indulged his dream of happiness with less hurt to himself than such chimerical wishes commonly produce, and adjusted his scheme with such address, that his hopes were in full bloom three parts of the year, and in the other part never wholly blasted. Many, perhaps, would be desirous of learning by what means he procured to himself such a cheap and lasting satisfaction. It was gained by a constant practice of referring the removal of all his uneasiness to the coming of the next spring; if his health was impaired, the spring would restore it; if what he wanted was at a high price, it would fall its value in the spring.

The spring, indeed, did often come without any of these effects, but he was always certain that the next would be more propitious; nor was ever convinced that the present spring would fail him before the middle of summer; for he always talked of the spring as coming 'till it was past, and when it was once past, every one agreed with him that it was coming.

By long converse with this man, I am, perhaps, brought to feel immoderate pleasure in the contemplation of this delightful season; but I have the satisfaction of finding many, whom it can be no shame to resemble, infected with the same enthusiasm; for there is, I believe, scarce any poet of eminence, who has not left some testimony of his fondness for the flowers, the zephyrs, and the warblers of the spring. Nor has the most luxuriant imagination been able to describe the serenity and happiness of the golden age, otherwise than by giving a perpetual spring, as the highest reward of uncorrupted innocence.

There is, indeed, something inexpressibly pleasing, in the annual renovation of the world, and the new display of the treasures of nature. The cold and darkness of winter, with the naked deformity of every object on which we turn our eyes, make us rejoice at the succeeding season, as well for what we have escaped, as for what we may enjoy; and every budding flower,

The Rambler. This publication, which appeared every Tuesday and Saturday from March 1750 to March 1752, had mixed success. Public acceptance was rather slow at first. Some critics considered it superior to *The Spectator;* others thought that the style was often turgid and the vocabulary monotonous. Yet there was a general consensus among critics that the author of the papers was an acute observer and that his writing had a precise if weighty eloquence

which a warm situation brings early to our view, is considered by us as a messenger to notify the approach of more joyous days.

The spring affords to a mind, so free from the disturbance of cares or passions as to be vacant to calm amusements, almost every thing that our present state makes us capable of enjoying. The variegated verdure of the fields and woods, the succession of grateful odours, the voice of pleasure pouring out its notes on every side, with the gladness apparently conceived by every animal, from the growth of his food, and the clemency of the weather, throw over the whole earth an air of gaiety, significantly expressed by the smile of nature.

Yet there are men to whom these scenes are able to give no delight, and who hurry away from all the varieties of rural beauty, to lose their hours, and divert their thoughts by cards, or assemblies, a tavern dinner, or the prattle of the day.

It may be laid down as a position which will seldom deceive, that when a man cannot bear his own company there is something wrong. He must fly from himself, either because he feels a tediousness in life from the equipoise of an empty mind, which, having no tendency to one motion more than another but as it is impelled by some external power, must always have recourse to foreign objects; or he must be afraid of the intrusion of some unpleasing ideas, and, perhaps, is struggling to escape from the remembrance of a loss, the fear of a calamity, or some other thought of greater horror.

Those whom sorrow incapacitates to enjoy the pleasures of contemplation, may properly apply to such diversions, provided they are innocent, as lay strong hold on the attention; and those, whom fear of any future affliction chains down to misery, must endeavour to obviate the danger.

My considerations shall, on this occasion, be turned on such as are burthensome to themselves merely because they want subjects for reflexion, and to whom the volume of nature is thrown open, without affording them pleasure or instruction, because they never learned to read the characters.

A French author has advanced this seeming paradox, that "very few men know how to take a walk"; and, indeed, it is true, that few know how to take a walk with a prospect of any other pleasure, than the same company would have afforded them at home.

. There are animals that borrow their colour from the neighbouring body, and, consequently, vary their hue as they happen to change their place. In like manner it ought to be the endeavour of every man to derive his reflections from the objects about him; for it is to no purpose that he alters his position, if his attention continues fixed to the same point. The mind should be kept open to the access of every new idea, and so far disengaged from the predominance of particular thoughts, as easily to accommodate itself to occasional entertainment.

A man that has formed this habit of turning every new object to his entertainment, finds in the productions of nature an inexhaustible stock of materials upon which he can employ himself, without any temptations to envy or malevolence; faults, perhaps, seldom totally avoided by those, whose judgment is much exercised upon the works of art. He has always a certain prospect of discovering new reasons for adoring the sovereign author of the universe, and probable hopes of making some discovery of benefit to others, or of profit to himself. There is no doubt but many vegetables and animals have qualities that might be of great use, to the knowledge of which there is not required much force of penetration, or fatigue of study, but only frequent experiments, and close attention. What is said by the chymists of their darling mercury, is, perhaps, true of every body through the whole creation, that, if a thousand lives should be spent upon it, all its properties would not be found out.

Mankind must necessarily be diversified by various tastes, since life affords and requires such multiplicity of employments, and a nation of naturalists is neither to be hoped, or desired; but it is surely not improper to point out a fresh amusement to those who languish in health, and repine in plenty, for want of some source of diversion that may be less easily exhausted, and to inform the multitudes of both sexes, who are burthened with every new day, that there are many shows which they have not seen.

He that enlarges his curiosity after the works of nature, demonstrably multiplies the inlets to happiness; and, therefore, the younger part of my readers, to whom I dedicate this vernal speculation, must excuse me for calling upon them, to make use at once of the spring of the year, and the spring of life; to acquire, while their minds may be yet impressed with new images, a love of innocent pleasures, and an ardour for useful knowledge; and to remember, that a blighted spring makes a barren year, and that the vernal flowers, however beautiful and gay, are only intended by nature as preparatives to autumnal fruits.

NO. 154. SATURDAY, 7 SEPTEMBER 1751.

—*Tibi res antiquae laudis & artis*
Aggredior, sanctos ausus recludere fontes.
                    Virgil, GEORGICS, II. 174–75.

For thee my tuneful accents will I raise,
And treat of arts disclos'd in ancient days;

Once more unlock for thee the sacred spring.
                                    Dryden.

The direction of Aristotle to those that study politicks, is, first to examine and understand what has been written by the ancients upon government; then to cast their eyes round upon the world, and consider by what causes the prosperity of communities is visibly influenced, and why some are worse, and others better administered.

The same method must be pursued by him who hopes to become eminent in any other part of knowledge. The first task is to search books, the next to contemplate nature. He must first possess himself of the intellectual treasures which the diligence of former ages has accumulated, and then endeavour to encrease them by his own collections.

The mental disease of the present generation, is impatience of study, contempt of the great masters of ancient wisdom, and a disposition to rely wholly upon unassisted genius and natural sagacity. The wits of these happy days have discovered a way to fame, which the dull caution of our laborious ancestors durst never attempt; they cut the knots of sophistry which it was formerly the business of years to untie, solve difficulties by sudden irradiations of intelligence, and comprehend long processes of argument by immediate intuition.

Men who have flattered themselves into this opinion of their own abilities, look down on all who waste their lives over books, as a race of inferior beings condemned by nature to perpetual pupillage, and fruitlessly endeavouring to remedy their barrenness by incessant cultivation, or succour their feebleness by subsidiary strength. They presume that none would be more industrious than they, if they were not more sensible of deficiencies, and readily conclude, that he who places no confidence in his own powers, owes his modesty only to his weakness.

It is however certain that no estimate is more in danger of erroneous calculations than those by which a man computes the force of his own genius. It generally happens at our entrance into the world, that by the natural attraction of similitude, we associate with men like ourselves young, sprightly, and ignorant, and rate our accomplishments by comparison with theirs; when we have once obtained an acknowledged superiority over our acquaintances, imagination and desire easily extend it over the rest of mankind, and if no accident forces us into new emulations, we grow old, and die in admiration of ourselves.

Vanity, thus confirmed in her dominion, readily listens to the voice of idleness, and sooths the slumber of life with continual dreams of excellence and greatness.

A man elated by confidence in his natural vigour of fancy and sagacity of conjecture, soon concludes that he already possesses whatever toil and enquiry can confer. He then listens with eagerness to the wild objections which folly has raised against the common means of improvement; talks of the dark chaos of indigested knowledge; describes the mischievous effects of heterogeneous sciences fermenting in the mind; relates the blunders of lettered ignorance; expatiates on the heroick merit of those who deviate from prescription, or shake off authority; and gives vent to the inflations of his heart by declaring that he owes nothing to pedants and universities.

All these pretensions, however confident, are very often vain. The laurels which superficial acuteness gains in triumphs over ignorance unsupported by vivacity, are observed by Locke to be lost whenever real learning and rational diligence appear against her; the sallies of gaiety are soon repressed by calm confidence, and the artifices of subtilty are readily detected by those who having carefully studied the question, are not easily confounded or surprised.

But though the contemner of books had neither been deceived by others nor himself, and was really born with a genius surpassing the ordinary abilities of mankind; yet surely such gifts of providence may be more properly urged as incitements to labour, than encouragements to negligence. He that neglects the culture of ground, naturally fertile, is more shamefully culpable than he whose field would scarcely recompence his husbandry.

Cicero remarks, that not to know what has been transacted in former times is to continue always a child. If no use is made of the labours of past ages, the world must remain always in the infancy of knowledge. The discoveries of every man must terminate in his own advantage, and the studies of every age be employed on questions which the past generation had discussed and determined. We may with as little reproach borrow science as manufactures from our ancestors; and it is as rational to live in caves till our own hands have erected a palace, as to reject all knowledge of architecture, which our understandings will not supply.

To the strongest and quickest mind it is far easier to learn than to invent. The principles of arithmetick and geometry may be comprehended by a close attention in a few days; yet who can flatter himself that the study of a long life would have enabled him to discover them, when he sees them yet unknown to so many nations, whom he cannot suppose less liberally endowed with natural reason, than the Grecians or Egyptians?

Every science was thus far advanced towards perfection, by the emulous diligence of contemporary students, and the gradual discoveries of one age improving on another. Sometimes unexpected flashes of instruction were struck out by the fortuitous collision of happy incidents, or an involuntary concurrence of ideas, in which the philosopher to whom they happened had no other merit than that of knowing their value, and transmitting unclouded to posterity that light which had been kindled by causes out of his power. The happiness of these casual illuminations no man can promise to himself, because no endeavours can procure them; and therefore, whatever be our abilities or application, we must submit to learn from others what perhaps would have lain hid for ever from human penetration, had not some remote enquiry brought it to view; as treasures are thrown up by the ploughman and the digger in the rude exercise of their common occupations.

The man whose genius qualifies him for great undertakings, must at least be content to learn from books the present state of human knowledge; that he may not ascribe to himself the invention of arts generally known; weary his attention with experiments of which the event has been long registered; and waste, in attempts which have already succeeded or miscarried, that time which might have been spent with usefulness and honour upon new undertakings.

But though the study of books is necessary, it is not sufficient to constitute literary eminence. He that wishes to be counted among the benefactors of posterity, must add by his own toil to the acquisitions of his ancestors, and secure his memory from neglect by some valuable improvement. This can only be effected by looking out upon the wastes of the intellectual world, and extending the power of learning over regions yet undisciplined and barbarous; or by surveying more exactly her antient dominions, and driving ignorance from the fortresses and retreats where she skulks undetected and undisturbed. Every science has its difficulties which yet call for solution before we attempt new systems of knowledge; as every country has its forests and marshes, which it would be wise to cultivate and drain, before distant colonies are projected as a necessary discharge of the exuberance of inhabitants.

No man ever yet became great by imitation. Whatever hopes for the veneration of mankind must have invention in the design or the execution; either the effect must itself be new, or the means by which it is produced. Either truths hitherto unknown must be discovered, or those which are already known enforced by stronger evidence, facilitated by clearer method, or elucidated by brighter illustrations.

Fame cannot spread wide or endure long that is not rooted in nature, and manured by art. That which hopes to resist the blast of malignity, and stand firm against the attacks of time, must contain in itself some original principle of growth. The reputation which arises from the detail or transposition of borrowed

sentiments, may spread for a while, like ivy on the rind° of antiquity, but will be torn away by accident or contempt, and suffered to rot unheeded on the ground.

from THE PREFACE TO SHAKESPEARE°

The poet, of whose works I have undertaken the revision, may now begin to assume the dignity of an ancient, and claim the privilege of established fame and prescriptive veneration. He has long outlived his century, the term commonly fixed as the test of literary merit. Whatever advantages he might once derive from personal allusions, local customs, or temporary opinions, have for many years been lost; and every topick of merriment or motive of sorrow, which the modes of artificial life afforded him, now only obscure 10 the scenes which they once illuminated. The effects of favour and competition are at an end; the tradition of his friendships and his enmities has perished; his works support no opinion with arguments, nor supply any faction with invectives; they can neither indulge vanity nor gratify malignity, but are read without any other reason than the desire of pleasure, and are therefore praised only as pleasure is obtained; yet, thus unassisted by interest or passion, they have past through variations of taste and changes of manners, 20 and, as they devolved from one generation to another, have received new honours at every transmission.

But because human judgment, though it be gradually gaining upon certainty, never becomes infallible; and approbation, though long continued, may yet be only the approbation of prejudice or fashion; it is proper to inquire, by what peculiarities of excellence Shakespeare has gained and kept the favour of his countrymen.

Nothing can please many, and please long, but just 30 representations of general nature. Particular manners can be known to few, and therefore few only can judge how nearly they are copied. The irregular combinations of fanciful invention may delight a-while, by that novelty of which the common satiety of life sends us all in quest; but the pleasures of sudden wonder are soon exhausted, and the mind can only repose on the stability of truth.

Shakespeare is above all writers, at least above all modern writers, the poet of nature; the poet that holds 40 up to his readers a faithful mirrour of manners and of life. His characters are not modified by the customs of particular places, unpractised by the rest of the world; by the peculiarities of studies or professions, which can operate but upon small numbers; or by the accidents of transient fashions or temporary opinions: they are the genuine progeny of common humanity, such as

No. 154 164 **rind,** bark or surface **Preface to Shakespeare.** This preface, which appeared with Johnson's edition (1765) of Shakespeare's plays, is considered one of his best pieces of prose

the world will always supply, and observation will always find. His persons act and speak by the influence
50 of those general passions and principles by which all minds are agitated, and the whole system of life is continued in motion. In the writings of other poets a character is too often an individual; in those of Shakespeare it is commonly a species.

It is from this wide extension of design that so much instruction is derived. It is this which fills the plays of Shakespeare with practical axioms and domestick wisdom. It was said of Euripides, that every verse was a precept; and it may be said of Shakespeare, that
60 from his works may be collected a system of civil and oeconomical prudence. Yet his real power is not shewn in the splendour of particular passages, but by the progress of his fable, and the tenour of his dialogue; and he that tries to recommend him by select quotations will succeed like the pedant in Hierocles,° who, when he offered his house to sale, carried a brick in his pocket as a specimen.

It will not easily be imagined how much Shakespeare excells in accommodating his sentiments to real
70 life, but by comparing him with other authours. It was observed of the ancient schools of declamation, that the more diligently they were frequented, the more was the student disqualified for the world, because he found nothing there which he should ever meet in any other place. The same remark may be applied to every stage but that of Shakespeare. The theatre, when it is under any other direction, is peopled by such characters as were never seen, conversing in a language which was never heard, upon topicks which will
80 never arise in the commerce of mankind. But the dialogue of this authour is often so evidently determined by the incident which produces it, and is pursued with so much ease and simplicity, that it seems scarcely to claim the merit of fiction, but to have been gleaned by diligent selection out of common conversation, and common occurrences.

Upon every other stage the universal agent is love, by whose power all good and evil is distributed, and every action quickened or retarded. To bring a lover, a
90 lady and a rival into the fable; to entangle them in contradictory obligations, perplex them with oppositions of interest, and harrass them with violence of desires inconsistent with each other; to make them meet in rapture and part in agony; to fill their mouths with hyperbolical joy and outrageous sorrow; to distress them as nothing human ever was distressed; to deliver them as nothing human ever was delivered, is the business of a modern dramatist. For this, probability is violated, life is misrepresented, and language
100 is depraved. But love is only one of many passions, and as it has no great influence upon the sum of life, it has little operation in the dramas of a poet, who caught his ideas from the living world, and exhibited only what he saw before him. He knew, that any other passion, as it was regular or exorbitant, was a cause of happiness or calamity.

Characters thus ample and general were not easily discriminated and preserved, yet perhaps no poet ever kept his personages more distinct from each other. I will not say with Pope, that every speech may be as- 110 signed to the proper speaker, because many speeches there are which have nothing characteristical; but perhaps, though some may be equally adapted to every person, it will be difficult to find any that can be properly transferred from the present possessor to another claimant. The choice is right, when there is reason for choice.

Other dramatists can only gain attention by hyperbolical or aggravated characters, by fabulous and unexampled excellence or depravity, as the writers of 120 barbarous romances invigorated the reader by a giant and a dwarf; and he that should form his expectations of human affairs from the play, or from the tale, would be equally deceived. Shakespeare has no heroes; his scenes are occupied only by men, who act and speak as the reader thinks that he should himself have spoken or acted on the same occasion: Even where the agency is supernatural the dialogue is level with life. Other writers disguise the most natural passions and most frequent incidents; so that he who contemplates 130 them in the book will not know them in the world: Shakespeare approximates the remote, and familiarizes the wonderful; the event which he represents will not happen, but if it were possible, its effects would probably be such as he has assigned; and it may be said, that he has not only shewn human nature as it acts in real exigences, but as it would be found in trials, to which it cannot be exposed.

This therefore is the praise of Shakespeare, that his drama is the mirrour of life; that he who has mazed° his 140 imagination, in following the phantoms which other writers raise up before him, may here be cured of his delirious extasies, by reading human sentiments in human language; by scenes from which a hermit may estimate the transactions of the world, and a confessor predict the progress of the passions. . . .

Shakespeare's plays are not in the rigorous and critical sense either tragedies or comedies, but compositions of a distinct kind; exhibiting the real state of sublunary nature, which partakes of good and evil, joy 150 and sorrow, mingled with endless variety of proportion and innumerable modes of combination; and expressing the course of the world, in which the loss of one is the gain of another; in which, at the same time, the reveller is hasting to his wine, and the mourner burying his friend; in which the malignity of one is sometimes defeated by the frolick of another; and many mischiefs

65 **Hierocles**, a play

140 **mazed**, bewildered

and many benefits are done and hindered without design.

Out of this chaos of mingled purposes and casualties the ancient poets, according to the laws which custom had prescribed, selected some the crimes of men, and some their absurdities; some the momentous vicissitudes of life, and some the lighter occurrences; some the terrours of distress, and some the gayeties of prosperity. Thus rose the two modes of imitation, known by the names of tragedy and comedy, compositions intended to promote different ends by contrary means, and considered as so little allied, that I do not recollect among the Greeks or Romans a single writer who attempted both.

Shakespeare has united the powers of exciting laughter and sorrow not only in one mind but in one composition. Almost all his plays are divided between serious and ludicrous characters, and, in the successive evolutions of the design, sometimes produce seriousness and sorrow, and sometimes levity and laughter.

That this is a practice contrary to the rules of criticism will be readily allowed; but there is always an appeal open from criticism to nature. The end of writing is to instruct; the end of poetry is to instruct by pleasing. That the mingled drama may convey all the instruction of tragedy or comedy cannot be denied, because it includes both in its alternations of exhibition, and approaches nearer than either to the appearance of life, by shewing how great machinations and slender designs may promote or obviate one another, and the high and the low co-operate in the general system by unavoidable concatenation.

It is objected, that by this change of scenes the passions are interrupted in their progression, and that the principal event, being not advanced by a due graduation of preparatory incidents, wants at last the power to move, which constitutes the perfection of dramatick poetry. This reasoning is so specious, that it is received as true even by those who in daily experience feel it to be false. The interchanges of mingled scenes seldom fail to produce the intended vicissitudes of passion. Fiction cannot move so much, but that the attention may be easily transferred; and though it must be allowed that pleasing melancholy be sometimes interrupted by unwelcome levity, yet let it be considered likewise, that melancholy is often not pleasing, and that the disturbance of one man may be the relief of another; that different auditors have different habitudes; and that, upon the whole, all pleasure consists in variety. . . .

Shakespeare with his excellencies has likewise faults, and faults sufficient to obscure and overwhelm any other merit. I shall shew them in the proportion in which they appear to me, without envious malignity or superstitious veneration. No question can be more innocently discussed than a dead poet's pretensions to renown; and little regard is due to that bigotry which sets candour° higher than truth.

His first defect is that to which may be imputed most of the evil in books or in men. He sacrifices virtue to convenience, and is so much more careful to please than to instruct, that he seems to write without any moral purpose. From his writings indeed a system of social duty may be selected, for he that thinks reasonably must think morally; but his precepts and axioms drop casually from him; he makes no just distribution of good or evil, nor is always careful to shew in the virtuous a disapprobation of the wicked; he carries his persons indifferently through right and wrong, and at the close dismisses them without further care, and leaves their examples to operate by chance. This fault the barbarity of his age cannot extenuate; for it is always a writer's duty to make the world better, and justice is a virtue independant on time or place.

The plots are often so loosely formed, that a very slight consideration may improve them, and so carelessly pursued, that he seems not always fully to comprehend his own design. He omits opportunities of instructing or delighting which the train of his story seems to force upon him, and apparently rejects those exhibitions which would be more affecting, for the sake of those which are more easy.

It may be observed, that in many of his plays the latter part is evidently neglected. When he found himself near the end of his work, and in view of his reward, he shortened the labour, to snatch the profit. He therefore remits his efforts where he should most vigorously exert them, and his catastrophe is improbably produced or imperfectly represented.

He had no regard to distinction of time or place, but gives to one age or nation, without scruple, the customs, institutions, and opinions of another, at the expence not only of likelihood, but of possibility. These faults Pope has endeavoured, with more zeal than judgment, to transfer to his imagined interpolators. We need not wonder to find Hector quoting Aristotle, when we see the loves of Theseus and Hippolyta combined with the Gothick mythology of fairies. Shakespeare, indeed, was not the only violator of chronology, for in the same age Sidney, who wanted not the advantages of learning, has, in his *Arcadia,* confounded the pastoral with the feudal times, the days of innocence, quiet and security, with those of turbulence, violence and adventure.

In his comick scenes he is seldom very successful, when he engages his characters in reciprocations of smartness and contests of sarcasm; their jests are commonly gross, and their pleasantry licentious; neither his gentlemen nor his ladies have much delicacy, nor are sufficiently distinguished from his clowns by any appearance of refined manners.

216 **candour,** kindness

Whether he represented the real conversation of his time is not easy to determine; the reign of Elizabeth is commonly supposed to have been a time of stateliness, formality and reserve, yet perhaps the relaxations of that severity were not very elegant. There must, however, have been always some modes of gayety preferable to others, and a writer ought to chuse the best.

In tragedy his performance seems constantly to be worse, as his labour is more. The effusions of passion which exigence forces out are for the most part striking and energetick; but whenever he solicits his invention, or strains his faculties, the offspring of his throes is tumour,° meanness, tediousness, and obscurity.

In narration he affects a disproportionate pomp of diction and a wearisome train of circumlocution, and tells the incident imperfectly in many words, which might have been more plainly delivered in few. Narration in dramatick poetry is naturally tedious, as it is unanimated and inactive, and obstructs the progress of the action; it should therefore always be rapid, and enlivened by frequent interruption. Shakespeare found it an encumbrance, and instead of lightening it by brevity, endeavoured to recommend it by dignity and splendour.

His declamations or set speeches are commonly cold and weak, for his power was the power of nature; when he endeavoured, like other tragick writers, to catch opportunities of amplification, and instead of inquiring what the occasion demanded, to show how much his stores of knowledge could supply, he seldom escapes without the pity or resentment of his reader.

It is incident to him to be now and then entangled with an unwieldy sentiment, which he cannot well express, and will not reject; he struggles with it a while, and if it continues stubborn, comprises it in words such as occur, and leaves it to be disentangled and evolved by those who have more leisure to bestow upon it.

Not that always where the language is intricate the thought is subtle, or the image always great where the line is bulky; the equality of words to things is very often neglected, and trivial sentiments and vulgar ideas disappoint the attention, to which they are recommended by sonorous epithets and swelling figures.

But the admirers of this great poet have most reason to complain when he approaches nearest to his highest excellence, and seems fully resolved to sink them in dejection, and mollify them with tender emotions by the fall of greatness, the danger of innocence, or the crosses of love. What he does best, he soon ceases to do. He is not long soft and pathetick without some idle conceit, or contemptible equivocation. He no sooner begins to move, than he counteracts himself; and terrour and pity, as they are rising in the mind, are checked and blasted by sudden frigidity.

A quibble° is to Shakespeare, what luminous vapours° are to the traveller; he follows it at all adventures, it is sure to lead him out of his way, and sure to engulf him in the mire. It has some malignant power over his mind, and its fascinations are irresistible. Whatever be the dignity or profundity of his disquisition, whether he be enlarging knowledge or exalting affection, whether he be amusing attention with incidents, or enchaining it in suspense, let but a quibble spring up before him, and he leaves his work unfinished. A quibble is the golden apple for which he will always turn aside from his career, or stoop from his elevation. A quibble, poor and barren as it is, gave him such delight, that he was content to purchase it, by the sacrifice of reason, propriety and truth. A quibble was to him the fatal Cleopatra for which he lost the world, and was content to lose it.

It will be thought strange, that, in enumerating the defects of this writer, I have not yet mentioned his neglect of the unities; his violation of those laws which have been instituted and established by the joint authority of poets and of criticks.

For his other deviations from the art of writing, I resign him to critical justice, without making any other demand in his favour, than that which must be indulged to all human excellence; that his virtues be rated with his failings: But, from the censure which this irregularity may bring upon him, I shall, with due reverence to that learning which I must oppose, adventure to try how I can defend him.

His histories, being neither tragedies nor comedies, are not subject to any of their laws; nothing more is necessary to all the praise which they expect, than that the changes of action be so prepared as to be understood, that the incidents be various and affecting, and the characters consistent, natural and distinct. No other unity is intended, and therefore none is to be sought.

In his other works he has well enough preserved the unity of action. He has not, indeed, an intrigue regularly perplexed and regularly unravelled; he does not endeavour to hide his design only to discover it, for this is seldom the order of real events, and Shakespeare is the poet of nature: But his plan has commonly what Aristotle requires, a beginning, a middle, and an end; one event is concatenated with another, and the conclusion follows by easy consequence. There are perhaps some incidents that might be spared, as in other poets there is much talk that only fills up time upon the stage; but the general system makes gradual advances, and the end of the play is the end of expectation.

To the unities of time and place he has shewn no regard, and perhaps a nearer view of the principles on which they stand will diminish their value, and with-

---

282 **tumour** tumidity, pomposity

325 **quibble**, a pun   326 **luminous vapours**, will-o'-the-wisp

draw from them the veneration which, from the time of Corneille,° they have very generally received, by discovering that they have given more trouble to the poet, than pleasure to the auditor.

The necessity of observing the unities of time and place arises from the supposed necessity of making the drama credible. The criticks hold it impossible, that an action of months or years can be possibly believed to pass in three hours; or that the spectator can suppose himself to sit in the theatre, while ambassadors go and return between distant kings, while armies are levied and towns besieged, while an exile wanders and returns, or till he whom they saw courting his mistress, shall lament the untimely fall of his son. The mind revolts from evident falsehood, and fiction loses its force when it departs from the resemblance of reality.

From the narrow limitation of time necessarily arises the contraction of place. The spectator, who knows that he saw the first act at Alexandria, cannot suppose that he sees the next at Rome, at a distance to which not the dragons of Medea could, in so short a time, have transported him; he knows with certainty that he has not changed his place; and he knows that place cannot change itself; that what was a house cannot become a plain; that what was Thebes can never be Persepolis.

Such is the triumphant language with which a critick exults over the misery of an irregular poet, and exults commonly without resistance or reply. It is time therefore to tell him, by the authority of Shakespeare, that he assumes, as an unquestionable principle, a position, which, while his breath is forming it into words, his understanding pronounces to be false. It is false, that any representation is mistaken for reality; that any dramatick fable in its materiality was ever credible, or, for a single moment, was ever credited.

The objection arising from the impossibility of passing the first hour at Alexandria, and the next at Rome, supposes, that when the play opens the spectator really imagines himself at Alexandria, and believes that his walk to the theatre has been a voyage to Egypt, and that he lives in the days of Antony and Cleopatra. Surely he that imagines this may imagine more. He that can take the stage at one time for the palace of the Ptolemies, may take it in half an hour for the promontory of Actium. Delusion, if delusion be admitted, has no certain limitation; if the spectator can be once persuaded, that his old acquaintance are Alexander and Caesar, that a room illuminated with candles is the plain of Pharsalia, or the bank of Granicus, he is in a state of elevation above the reach of reason, or of truth, and from the heights of empyrean poetry, may despise the circumscriptions of terrestrial nature. There is no reason why a mind thus wandering in extasy should count the clock, or why an hour should not

be a century in that calenture of the brains that can make the stage a field.

The truth is, that the spectators are always in their senses, and know, from the first act to the last, that the stage is only a stage, and that the players are only players. They come to hear a certain number of lines recited with just gesture and elegant modulation. The lines relate to some action, and an action must be in some place; but the different actions that compleat a story may be in places very remote from each other; and where is the absurdity of allowing that space to represent first Athens, and then Sicily, which was always known to be neither Sicily nor Athens, but a modern theatre.

By supposition, as place is introduced, time may be extended; the time required by the fable elapses for the most part between the acts; for, of so much of the action as is represented, the real and poetical duration is the same. If, in the first act, preparations for war against Mithridates are represented to be made in Rome, the event of the war may, without absurdity, be represented, in the catastrophe, as happening in Pontus; we know that there is neither war, nor preparation for war; we know that we are neither in Rome nor Pontus; that neither Mithridates nor Lucullus are before us. The drama exhibits successive imitations of successive actions, and why may not the second imitation represent an action that happened years after the first; if it be so connected with it, that nothing but time can be supposed to intervene. Time is, of all modes of existence, most obsequious to the imagination; a lapse of years is as easily conceived as a passage of hours. In contemplation we easily contract the time of real actions, and therefore willingly permit it to be contracted when we only see their imitation.

It will be asked, how the drama moves, if it is not credited. It is credited with all the credit due to a drama. It is credited, whenever it moves, as a just picture of a real original; as representing to the auditor what he would himself feel, if he were to do or suffer what is there feigned to be suffered or to be done. The reflection that strikes the heart is not, that the evils before us are real evils, but that they are evils to which we ourselves may be exposed. If there be any fallacy, it is not that we fancy the players, but that we fancy ourselves unhappy for a moment; but we rather lament the possibility than suppose the presence of misery, as a mother weeps over her babe, when she remembers that death may take it from her. The delight of tragedy proceeds from our consciousness of fiction; if we thought murders and treasons real, they would please no more.

Imitations produce pain or pleasure, not because they are mistaken for realities, but because they bring realities to mind. When the imagination is recreated by a painted landscape, the trees are not supposed capable to give us shade, or the fountains coolness; but

° 381 **Corneille.** Corneille's *Discourse des trois unités* (1660) was the classic statement

we consider, how we should be pleased with such fountains playing beside us, and such woods waving over us. We are agitated in reading the history of Henry the Fifth, yet no man takes his book for the field of Agincourt. A dramatick exhibition is a book recited with concomitants that encrease or diminish its effect. Familiar comedy is often more powerful on the theatre, than in the page; imperial tragedy is always
500 less. The humour of Petruchio° may be heightened by grimace; but what voice or what gesture can hope to add dignity or force to the soliloquy of *Cato*.°

A play read, affects the mind like a play acted. It is therefore evident, that the action is not supposed to be real, and it follows that between the acts a longer or shorter time may be allowed to pass, and that no more account of space or duration is to be taken by the auditor of a drama, than by the reader of a narrative, before whom may pass in an hour the life of a hero, or
510 the revolutions of an empire.

Whether Shakespeare knew the unities, and rejected them by design, or deviated from them by happy ignorance, it is, I think, impossible to decide, and useless to enquire. We may reasonably suppose, that, when he rose to notice, he did not want the counsels and admonitions of scholars and criticks, and that he at last deliberately persisted in a practice, which he might have begun by chance. As nothing is essential to the fable, but unity of action, and as the unities of time and
520 place arise evidently from false assumptions, and, by circumscribing the extent of the drama, lessen its variety, I cannot think it much to be lamented, that they were not known by him, or not observed: Nor, if such another poet could arise, should I very vehemently reproach him, that his first act passed at Venice, and his next in Cyprus. Such violations of rules merely positive, become the comprehensive genius of Shakespeare, and such censures are suitable to the minute and slender criticism of Voltaire:

530 *Non usque adeo permiscuit imis*
Longus summa dies, ut non, si voce Metelli
Serventur leges, malint a Caesare tolli.°

Yet when I speak thus slightly of dramatick rules, I cannot but recollect how much wit and learning may be produced against me; before such authorities I am afraid to stand, not that I think the present question one of those that are to be decided by mere authority, but because it is to be suspected, that these precepts have not been so easily received but for better
540 reasons than I have yet been able to find. The result of my enquiries, in which it would be ludicrous to boast of impartiality, is, that the unities of time and place are not essential to a just drama, that though they may

sometimes conduce to pleasure, they are always to be sacrificed to the nobler beauties of variety and instruction; and that a play, written with nice observation of critical rules, is to be contemplated as an elaborate curiosity, as the product of superfluous and ostentatious art, by which is shewn, rather what is possible, than what is necessary. 550

He that, without diminution of any other excellence, shall preserve all the unities unbroken, deserves the like applause with the architect, who shall display all the orders of architecture in a citadel, without any deduction from its strength; but the principal beauty of a citadel is to exclude the enemy; and the greatest graces of a play, are to copy nature and instruct life.
(1765)

from THE LIVES OF THE ENGLISH POETS°

from DRYDEN

Dryden may be properly considered as the father of English criticism, as the writer who first taught us to determine upon principles the merit of composition. Of our former poets, the greatest dramatist° wrote without rules, conducted through life and nature by a genius that rarely misled, and rarely deserted him. Of the rest, those who knew the laws of propriety had neglected to teach them.

Two *Arts of English Poetry* were written in the days of Elizabeth by Webb° and Puttenham,° from which 10 something might be learned, and a few hints had been given by Jonson and Cowley;° but Dryden's *Essay on Dramatic Poetry*° was the first regular and valuable treatise on the art of writing.

He who, having formed his opinions in the present age of English literature, turns back to peruse this dialogue will not perhaps find much increase of knowledge, or much novelty of instruction; but he is to remember that critical principles were then in the hands of a few, who had gathered them partly from the an- 20 cients and partly from the Italians and French. The structure of dramatic poems was then not generally understood. Audiences applauded by instinct, and poets perhaps often pleased by chance.

A writer who obtains his full purpose loses himself

500 **Petruchio**, in Shakespeare's *The Taming of the Shrew*   502 **Cato**, the title character in a wooden tragedy by Joseph Addison   530–32 **Non . . . tolli.** In substance, the laws (rules) would rather be trampled on by a Caesar than sustained by a Metellus (Lucan)

The Lives of the English Poets. The idea for this work came from a group of London booksellers who decided to issue an edition of "all the English poets of reputation from Chaucer to the present day." They engaged Johnson, who was sixty-seven years old and pensioned, to write brief biographical and critical notes to precede the various selections of poetry. The booksellers chose the poets to be included; Johnson added only four names to their list. As Johnson progressed, the original scheme was modified, and the work was published for itself, without the selections from the poets. Johnson completed fifty-two sketches, which were published in ten volumes (1779, 1781) as *Prefaces Biographical and Critical to the Works of the English Poets*   **Dryden** 4 **greatest dramatist,** Shakespeare   10 **Webb,** William Webbe (b. 1550), author of *The Arte of English Poesie*, 1586   **Puttenham,** George Puttenham (d. 1590), supposed author of *The Arte of Poesie*, really written by his brother Richard   12 **Jonson and Cowley,** Ben Jonson (1573–1637) and Abraham Cowley (1618–1667)   12–13 **Essay . . . Poetry,** *Essay of Dramatic Poesy,* written in 1666

in his own luster. Of an opinion which is no longer doubted, the evidence ceases to be examined. Of an art universally practiced, the first teacher is forgotten. Learning once made popular is no longer learning; it
30 has the appearance of something which we have bestowed upon ourselves, as the dew appears to rise from the field which it refreshes.

To judge rightly of an author, we must transport ourselves to his time, and examine what were the wants of his contemporaries, and what were his means of supplying them. That which is easy at one time was difficult at another. Dryden at least imported his science and gave his country what it wanted before; or rather, he imported only the materials and manufac-
40 tured them by his own skill.

The dialogue on the drama was one of his first essays° of criticism, written when he was yet a timorous candidate for reputation, and therefore labored with that diligence which he might allow himself somewhat to remit when his name gave sanction to his positions, and his awe of the public was abated, partly by custom, and partly by success. It will not be easy to find, in all the opulence of our language, a treatise so artfully variegated with successive representations of op-
50 posite probabilities, so enlivened with imagery, so brightened with illustrations. His portraits of the English dramatists are wrought with great spirit and diligence. The account of Shakespeare may stand as a perpetual model of encomiastic° criticism; exact without minuteness, and lofty without exaggeration. The praise lavished by Longinus° on the attestation of the heroes of Marathon,° by Demosthenes,° fades away before it. In a few lines is exhibited a character so extensive in its comprehension, and so curious in its
60 limitations, that nothing can be added, diminished or reformed; nor can the editors and admirers of Shakespeare, in all their emulation of reverence, boast of much more than of having diffused and paraphrased this epitome of excellence, of having changed Dryden's gold for baser metal, of lower value though of greater bulk.

In this, and in all his other essays on the same subject, the criticism of Dryden is the criticism of a poet; not a dull collection of theorems, nor a rude detection
70 of faults, which perhaps the censor was not able to have committed; but a gay and vigorous dissertation, where delight is mingled with instruction, and where the author proves his right of judgment, by his power of performance.

The different manner and effect with which critical knowledge may be conveyed was perhaps never more clearly exemplified than in the performances of Rymer° and Dryden. It was said of a dispute between two mathematicians, "*malim cum Scaligero° errare, quam cum Clavio recte sapere,*" that *it was more eligible to* 80 *go wrong with one than right with the other.* A tendency of the same kind every mind must feel at the perusal of Dryden's prefaces and Rymer's discourses. With Dryden we are wandering in quest of Truth, whom we find, if we find her at all, dressed in the graces of elegance, and if we miss her, the labor of the pursuit rewards itself; we are led only through fragrance and flowers. Rymer, without taking a nearer, takes a rougher way; every step is to be made through thorns and brambles, and Truth, if we meet her, ap- 90 pears repulsive by her mien and ungraceful by her habit. Dryden's criticism has the majesty of a queen; Rymer's has the ferocity of a tyrant.

As he had studied with great diligence the art of poetry, and enlarged or rectified his notions, by experience perpetually increasing, he had his mind stored with principles and observations; he poured out his knowledge with little labor; for of labor, notwithstanding the multiplicity of his productions, there is sufficient reason to suspect that he was not a lover. 100 To write *con amore,* with fondness for the employment, with perpetual touches and retouches, with unwillingness to take leave of his own idea, and an unwearied pursuit of unattainable perfection, was, I think, no part of his character.

His criticism may be considered as general or occasional. In his general precepts, which depend upon the nature of things and the structure of the human mind, he may doubtless be safely recommended to the confidence of the reader; but his occasional and particular 110 positions were sometimes interested, sometimes negligent, and sometimes capricious. . . .

He is therefore by no means constant to himself. His defense and desertion of dramatic rime is generally known. Spence, in his remarks on Pope's *Odyssey,°* produces what he thinks an unconquerable quotation from Dryden's preface to the *Aeneid,* in favor of translating an epic poem into blank verse; but he forgets that when his author attempted the *Iliad,* some years afterwards,° he departed from his own decision, 120 and translated into rime.

When he has any objection to obviate, or any license to defend, he is not very scrupulous about what he asserts, nor very cautious, if the present purpose be served, not to entangle himself in his own sophistries. But when all arts are exhausted, like other hunted animals, he sometimes stands at bay; when he cannot disown the grossness of one of his plays, he declares that he knows not any law that prescribes morality to a comic poet. 130

His remarks on ancient or modern writers are not always to be trusted. His parallel of the versification of

42 **essays,** attempts   54 **encomiastic,** laudatory   56 **Longinus,** celebrated Greek critic and philosopher (c. A.D. 210–273)   57 **Marathon,** the famous battle between the Greeks and the Persians, 490 B.C.   **Demosthenes,** a noted Greek orator of the third century B.C.   77 **Rymer,** Thomas Rymer (1641–1713), critic and archeologist, chiefly remembered for his valuable collection of historical records. He published his *Tragedies of the Last Age Considered* in 1678; he was unfriendly to the plays of Shakespeare

79 **Scaligero,** Joseph Scaliger (1540–1609), referred to as the greatest scholar of modern times; an eminent Italian Renaissance linguist, philosopher, and mathematician   115 **Spence . . . Odyssey,** Joseph Spence (1699–1768), English critic; published his *Essay on Pope's Odyssey* in 1726   120 **some years afterwards.** Pope completed his *Odyssey* in 1726, his *Iliad* in 1718. Johnson is wrong

Ovid° with that of Claudian° has been very justly censured by Sewell.° His comparison of the first line of Virgil with the first of Statius° is not happier. Virgil, he says, is soft and gentle, and would have thought Statius mad if he had heard him thundering out

Quae superimposito moles geminata colosso.°

Statius perhaps heats himself, as he proceeds, to 140 exaggerations somewhat hyperbolical; but undoubtedly Virgil would have been too hasty if he had condemned him to straw for one sounding line. Dryden wanted an instance, and the first that occurred was impressed into the service.

What he wishes to say, he says at hazard; he cited *Gorbuduc,°* which he had never seen; gives a false account of Chapman's° versification; and discovers,° in the preface to his Fables, that he translated the first book of the *Iliad* without knowing what was in the 150 second.

It will be difficult to prove that Dryden ever made any great advances in literature. As having distinguished himself at Westminster under the tuition of Busby,° who advanced his scholars to a height of knowledge very rarely attained in grammar schools, he resided afterwards at Cambridge, it is not to be supposed that his skill in the ancient languages was deficient, compared with that of common students; but his scholastic acquisitions seem not proportionate to his 160 opportunities and abilities. He could not, like Milton or Cowley, have made his name illustrious merely by his learning. He mentions but few books, and those such as lie in the beaten track of regular study; from which if ever he departs, he is in danger of losing himself in unknown regions.

In his dialogue on the drama, he pronounces with great confidence that the Latin tragedy of *Medea°* is not Ovid's, because it is not sufficiently interesting and pathetic. He might have determined the question upon 170 surer evidence; for it is quoted by Quintilian° as the work of Seneca; and the only line which remains of Ovid's play, for one line is left us, is not there to be found. There was therefore no need of the gravity of conjecture, or the discussion of plot or sentiment, to find what was already known upon higher authority than such discussions can ever reach.

His literature, though not always free from ostentation, will be commonly found either obvious, and made his own by the art of dressing it; or superficial, 180 which, by what he gives, shows what he wanted; or erroneous, hastily collected, and negligently scattered.

Yet it cannot be said that his genius is ever unprovided of matter, or that his fancy languishes in penury of ideas. His works abound with knowledge, and sparkle with illustrations. There is scarcely any science or faculty that does not supply him with occasional images and lucky similitudes; every page discovers a mind very widely acquainted both with art and nature, and in full possession of great stores of intellectual wealth. Of him that knows much, it is 190 natural to suppose that he has read with diligence; yet I rather believe that the knowledge of Dryden was gleaned from accidental intelligence and various conversation, by a quick apprehension, a judicious selection, and a happy memory, a keen appetite of knowledge, and a powerful digestion; by vigilance that permitted nothing to pass without notice, and a habit of reflection that suffered nothing useful to be lost. A mind like Dryden's, always curious, always active, to which every understanding was proud to be associated, 200 and of which everyone solicited the regard, by an ambitious display of himself, had a more pleasant, perhaps a nearer way to knowledge than by the silent progress of solitary reading. I do not suppose that he despised books, or intentionally neglected them; but that he was carried out, by the impetuosity of his genius, to more vivid and speedy instructors; and that his studies were rather desultory and fortuitous than constant and systematical.

It must be confessed that he scarcely ever appears to want book-learning but when he mentions books; and 210 to him may be transferred the praise which he gives his master Charles.°

> His conversation, wit, and parts,
> His knowledge in the noblest useful arts,
> Were such, dead authors could not give,
> But habitudes of those that live;
> Who, lighting him, did greater lights receive,
> He drained from all, and all they knew,
> His apprehension quick, his judgment true;
> That the most learned with shame confess   220
> His knowledge more, his reading only less.

Of all this, however, if the proof be demanded, I will not undertake to give it; the atoms of probability, of which my opinion has been formed, lie scattered over all his works; and by him who thinks the question worth his notice, his works must be perused with very close attention.

Criticism, either didactic or defensive, occupies almost all his prose, except those pages which he has devoted to his patrons; but none of his prefaces were 230 ever thought tedious. They have not the formality of a settled style, in which the first half of a sentence betrays the other. The clauses are never balanced, nor the periods modeled; every word seems to drop by

133 **Ovid,** famous Roman poet (43 B.C.–A.D. 17)   **Claudian,** noted Latin poet (fourth century A.D.)   134 **Sewell,** George Sewell (d. 1726), a critic of the time of Pope   135 **Statius,** Roman poet (first century A.D.), author of the epic *Thebais*   138 **Quae,** etc. "With a colossus on top there is a double weight" (Statius' *Silvae,* I, l. 36)   146 **Gorbuduc,** *Gorboduc,* the first regular English tragedy, written by Thomas Norton (1532–1584) and Thomas Sackville (1536–1608)   147 **Chapman,** George Chapman (1559–1634), poet, dramatist, and translator of Homer   **discovers,** makes known   154 **Busby,** Richard Busby (1606–1695), headmaster of Westminster School, which Dryden attended   167 **Medea,** probably by the Roman tragedian Seneca (3 B.C.–A.D. 65)   170 **Quintilian,** celebrated Roman rhetorician and teacher of oratory (first century A.D.)

212 **Charles,** King Charles II, reigning from 1660 to 1685, whom Dryden praised extravagantly in *Astraea Redux* (1660), a poem inspired by the restoration of the monarchy

chance, though it falls into its proper place. Nothing is cold or languid; the whole is airy, animated, and vigorous: what is little, is gay; what is great, is splendid. He may be thought to mention himself too frequently; but while he forces himself upon our esteem, we cannot refuse him to stand high in his own. Everything is excused by the play of images and the sprightliness of expression. Though all is easy, nothing is feeble; though all seems careless, there is nothing harsh; and though since his earlier works more than a century has passed, they have nothing yet uncouth or obsolete.°

He who writes much will not easily escape a manner, such a recurrence of particular modes as may be easily noted. Dryden is always "another and the same"; he does not exhibit a second time the same elegances in the same form, nor appears to have any art other than that of expressing with clearness what he thinks with vigor. His style could not easily be imitated, either seriously or ludicrously; for, being always equable and always varied, it has no prominent or discriminative characters. The beauty who is totally free from disproportion of parts and features, cannot be ridiculed by an overcharged resemblance.

From his prose, however, Dryden derives only his accidental and secondary praise; the veneration with which his name is pronounced by every cultivator of English literature is paid to him as he refined the language, improved the sentiments, and tuned the numbers° of English Poetry.

After about half a century of forced thoughts and rugged meter, some advances towards nature and harmony had been already made by Waller and Denham; they had shown that long discourses in rime grew more pleasing when they were broken into couplets, and that verse consisted not only in the number but the arrangement of syllables.

But though they did much, who can deny that they left much to do? Their works were not many, nor were their minds of very ample comprehension. More examples of more modes of composition were necessary for the establishment of regularity, and the introduction of propriety in word and thought.

Every language of a learned nation necessarily divides itself into diction scholastic and popular, grave and familiar, elegant and gross; and from a nice distinction of these different parts arises a great part of the beauty of style. But if we except a few minds, the favorites of nature, to whom their own original rectitude was in the place of rules, this delicacy of selection was little known to our authors. Our speech lay before them in a heap of confusion, and every man took for every purpose what chance might offer him.

There was therefore before the time of Dryden no poetical diction, no system of words at once refined from the grossness of domestic use, and free from the harshness of terms appropriated to particular arts. Words too familiar, or too remote, defeat the purpose of a poet. From those sounds which we hear on small or on coarse occasions, we do not easily receive strong impressions, or delightful images; and words to which we are nearly strangers, whenever they occur, draw that attention on themselves which they should transmit to things.

Those happy combinations of words which distinguish poetry from prose had been rarely attempted; we had few elegances or flowers of speech; the roses had not yet been plucked from the bramble, or different colors had not yet been joined to enliven one another.

It may be doubted whether Waller and Denham could have overborne the prejudices which had long prevailed, and which even then were sheltered by the protection of Cowley. The new versification, as it was called, may be considered as owing its establishment to Dryden; from whose time it is apparent that English poetry has had no tendency to relapse to its former savageness. . . .

from POPE

. . . [Pope] professed to have learned his poetry from Dryden, whom, whenever an opportunity was presented, he praised through his whole life with unvaried liberality; and perhaps his character may receive some illustration if he be compared with his master.

Integrity of understanding and nicety of discernment were not allotted in a less proportion to Dryden than to Pope. The rectitude of Dryden's mind was sufficiently shown by the dismission° of his poetical prejudices, and the rejection of unnatural thoughts and rugged numbers. But Dryden never desired to apply all the judgment that he had. He wrote, and professed to write, merely for the people; and when he pleased others, he contented himself. He spent no time in struggles to rouse latent powers; he never attempted to make that better which was already good, nor often to mend what he must have known to be faulty. He wrote, as he tells us, with very little consideration; when occasion or necessity called upon him, he poured out what the present moment happened to supply, and, when once it had passed the press, ejected it from his mind; for when he had no pecuniary interest, he had no further solicitude.

Pope was not content to satisfy; he desired to excel, and therefore always endeavored to do his best: he did not court the candor, but dared the judgment of his reader, and, expecting no indulgence from others, he showed none to himself. He examined lines and words with minute and punctilious observation, and retouched every part with indefatigable diligence, till he had left nothing to be forgiven.

262 **tuned the numbers,** regularized the meter. Dryden established the closed couplet that had been introduced by Edmund Waller (1606–1687) and Sir John Denham (1615–1669)

Pope 9 **dismission,** laying aside

For this reason he kept his pieces very long in his hands, while he considered and reconsidered them. The only poems which can be supposed to have been written with such regard to the times as might hasten their publication were the two satires of *Thirty-eight;*° of which Docsley° told me that they were brought to him by the author, that they might be fairly copied. "Almost every line," he said, "was then written twice
40 over; I gave him a clean transcript, which he sent some time afterwards to me for the press, with almost every line written twice over a second time."

His declaration that his care for his works ceased at their publication was not strictly true. His parental attention never abandoned them; what he found amiss in the first edition, he silently corrected in those that followed. He appears to have revised the *Iliad,* and freed it from some of its imperfections; and the *Essay on Criticism* received many improvements after its first
50 appearance. It will seldom be found that he altered without adding clearness, elegance, or vigor. Pope had perhaps the judgment of Dryden; but Dryden certainly wanted the diligence of Pope.

In acquired knowledge, the superiority must be allowed to Dryden, whose education was more scholastic, and who before he became an author had been allowed more time for study, with better means of information. His mind has a larger range, and he collects his images and illustrations from a more extensive cir-
60 cumference of science. Dryden knew more of man in his general nature, and Pope in his local manners. The notions of Dryden were formed by comprehensive speculation, and those of Pope by minute attention. There is more dignity in the knowledge of Dryden, and more certainty in that of Pope.

Poetry was not the sole praise of either; for both excelled likewise in prose; but Pope did not borrow his prose from his predecessor. The style of Dryden is capricious and varied; that of Pope is cautious and
70 uniform. Dryden obeys the motions of his own mind; Pope constrains his mind to his own rules of composition. Dryden is sometimes vehement and rapid; Pope is always smooth, uniform, and gentle. Dryden's page is a natural field, rising into inequalities, and diversified by the varied exuberance of abundant vegetation; Pope's is a velvet lawn, shaven by the scythe, and leveled by the roller.

Of genius, that power which constitutes a poet; that quality without which judgment is cold, and knowl-
80 edge is inert; that energy which collects, combines, amplifies, and animates; the superiority must, with some hesitation, be allowed to Dryden. It is not to be inferred that of this poetical vigor Pope had only a little, because Dryden had more; for every other writer since Milton must give place to Pope; and even of Dryden it must be said, that, if he has brighter para-

graphs, he has not better poems. Dryden's performances were always hasty, either excited by some external occasion, or extorted by domestic necessity; he composed without consideration, and published 90 without correction. What his mind could supply at call, or gather in one excursion, was all that he sought, and all that he gave. The dilatory caution of Pope enabled him to condense his sentiments, to multiply his images, and to accumulate all that study might produce or chance might supply. If the flights of Dryden therefore are higher, Pope continues longer on the wing. If of Dryden's fire the blaze is brighter, of Pope's the heat is more regular and constant. Dryden often surpasses expectation, and Pope never falls below it. 100 Dryden is read with frequent astonishment, and Pope with perpetual delight.

This parallel will, I hope, when it is well considered, be found just; and if the reader should suspect me, as I suspect myself, of some partial fondness for the memory of Dryden, let him not too hastily condemn me; for meditation and inquiry may, perhaps, show him the reasonableness of my determination. . . .
(1779–1781)

JAMES BOSWELL
1740–1795

With the twentieth-century discovery and publication of his long lost journal, James Boswell, already well-known as Johnson's biographer, has come to be regarded as one of the world's great diarists as well. Boswell was born into an old and well-connected family in Edinburgh in 1740; his father was a lawyer who became a judge in 1754. The young Boswell was taught at home and then went through the arts course at the University of Edinburgh from 1753 to 1758; he switched to law in 1758. As early as 1762 he began keeping the journal that is the central expression of his personality. On a visit to London in 1763, Boswell was introduced to Samuel Johnson, whose works he had long admired and whom he had been trying to meet. Johnson was fifty-three years old when they met, Boswell twenty-two. After an adventurous and extensive tour of the Continent, Boswell was admitted to the bar in 1766; for seventeen years he practiced law in Edinburgh.

In 1768 Boswell gained fame through the publication of *An Account of Corsica, The Journal of a Tour to That Island; and Memoirs of Pascal Paoli.* In 1773 he was elected to The Club, the brilliant circle surrounding Dr. Johnson; later that year he made a tour with Johnson of the Hebrides. Although Johnson died in 1784, Boswell took his time in writing the biography. In 1786 Boswell moved to London, and thereafter had only a small legal practice. His principal business was writing Johnson's biography, although his work on it was irregular. Finally, in 1791, *The Life of Samuel Johnson, LL.D.* was published. He was at work on a new edition of the *Life* when he died in 1795.

His journals reveal Boswell to be a man with an insatiable thirst for experience, both savory and unsavory. He was a penetrating and reflective man, who observed life closely and ruminated on life objectively. He was a realistic autobiographer with, for some, a disquieting tendency to tell the truth about himself.

In writing the *Life*, Boswell made certain fundamental decisions without which Johnson could not have been "seen in this work more completely than any man who has ever lived": (1) he decided that "the extraordinary vigor and vivacity" of Johnson's mind "constituted one of the first features of his character"; (2) although for the most part he decided to tell the truth—to see his object as he in fact was—he did make Johnson conform to his own image, as the last sentence from the *Life* indicates, "the more his [Johnson's] character is considered, the more he will be regarded by the present age, and by posterity, with admiration and reverence"; (3) he decided to step back as much as possible and let the drama itself come forward—to "do the thing shall breed the thought,/ Nor wrong the thought, missing the mediate word"; and (4) he decided that he would not exclude details, an indirect form of editorializing, but would present them in all their minute abundance.

from LONDON JOURNAL°

Monday 16 May. Temple and his brother breakfasted with me. I went to Love's to try to recover some of the money which he owes me. But, alas, a single guinea was all I could get. He was just going to dinner, so I stayed and eat a bit, though I was angry at myself afterwards. I drank tea at Davies's in Russell Street, and about seven came in the great Mr. Samuel Johnson, whom I have so long wished to see. Mr. Davies introduced me to him. As I knew his mortal
10 antipathy at the Scotch, I cried to Davies, "Don't tell where I come from." However, he said, "From Scotland." "Mr. Johnson," said I, "indeed I come from Scotland, but I cannot help it." "Sir," replied he, "that, I find, is what a very great many of your countrymen cannot help." Mr. Johnson is a man of a most dreadful appearance. He is a very big man, is troubled with sore eyes, the palsy, and the king's evil.° He is very slovenly in his dress and speaks with a most uncouth voice. Yet his great knowledge and strength of
20 expression command vast respect and render him very

London Journal. For Boswell's rendering of this meeting in the *Life,* see "Boswell Introduced to Johnson." See notes there for specific information on individuals named   17 **the king's evil,** scrofula, so called because it was once thought to be cured by the king's touch

excellent company. He has great humour and is a worthy man. But his dogmatical roughness of manners is disagreeable. I shall mark what I remember of his conversation.

He said that people might be taken in once in imagining that an author is greater than other people in private life. "Uncommon parts require uncommon opportunities for their exertion.

"In barbarous society superiority of parts is of real consequence. Great strength or wisdom is of value to 30 an individual. But in more polished times you have people to do everything for money. And then there are a number of other superiorities, such as those of birth and fortune and rank, that dissipate men's attention and leave superiority of parts no extraordinary share of respect. And this is wisely ordered by Providence, to preserve a mediocrity.

"Lord Kames's *Elements* is a pretty essay and deserves to be held in some estimation, though it is chimerical. 40

"Wilkes is safe in the eye of the law. But he is an abusive scoundrel; and instead of sending my Lord Chief Justice to him, I would send a parcel of footmen and have him well ducked.

"The notion of liberty amuses the people of England and helps to keep off the *taedium vitae.* When a butcher says that he is in distress for his country, he has no uneasy feeling.

"Sheridan will not succeed at Bath, for ridicule has gone down before him, and I doubt Derrick is his 50 enemy."

I was sorry to leave him there at ten, when I had engaged to be at Dr. Pringle's, with whom I had a serious conversation much to my mind.

I stayed this night at Lord Eglinton's.

from THE LIFE OF SAMUEL JOHNSON, LL.D.

To write the Life of him who excelled all mankind in writing the lives of others, and who, whether we consider his extraordinary endowments, or his various works, has been equaled by few in any age, is an arduous, and may be reckoned in me a presumptuous, task.

Had Dr. Johnson written his own life, in conformity with the opinion which he has given, that every man's life may be best written by himself; had he employed in the preservation of his own history, that clearness of narration and elegance of language in which he has 10 embalmed so many eminent persons, the world would probably have had the most perfect example of biography that was ever exhibited. But although he at dif-

ferent times, in a desultory manner, committed to writing many particulars of the progress of his mind and fortunes, he never had persevering diligence enough to form them into a regular composition. Of these memorials a few have been preserved; but the greater part was consigned by him to the flames, a few
20 days before his death.

As I had the honor and happiness of enjoying his friendship for upwards of twenty years; as I had the scheme of writing his life constantly in view; as he was well apprised of this circumstance, and from time to time obligingly satisfied my inquiries, by communicating to me the incidents of his early years; as I acquired a facility in recollecting, and was very assiduous in recording, his conversation, of which the extraordinary vigor and vivacity constituted one of the
30 first features of his character; and as I have spared no pains in obtaining materials concerning him, from every quarter where I could discover that they were to be found, and have been favored with the most liberal communications by his friends; I flatter myself that few biographers have entered upon such a work as this, with more advantages; independent of literary abilities, in which I am not vain enough to compare myself with some great names who have gone before me in this kind of writing. . . .

40 Instead of melting down by materials into one mass, and constantly speaking in my own person, by which I might have appeared to have more merit in the execution of the work, I have resolved to adopt and enlarge upon the excellent plan of Mr. Mason, in his *Memoirs of Gray*. Wherever narrative is necessary to explain, connect, and supply, I furnish it to the best of my abilities; but in the chronological series of Johnson's life, which I trace as distinctly as I can, year by year, I produce, wherever it is in my power, his own minutes,
50 letters or conversation, being convinced that this mode is more lively, and will make my readers better acquainted with him, than even most of those were who actually knew him, but could know him only partially; whereas there is here an accumulation of intelligence from various points, by which his character is more fully understood and illustrated.

Indeed I cannot conceive a more perfect mode of writing any man's life, than not only relating all the most important events of it in their order, but inter-
60 weaving what he privately wrote, and said, and thought by which mankind are enabled as it were to see him live, and to "live o'er each scene" with him, as he actually advanced through the several stages of his life. Had his other friends been as diligent and ardent as I was, he might have been almost entirely preserved. As it is, I will venture to say that he will be seen in this work more completely than any man who has ever yet lived.

And he will be seen as he really was; for I profess to write, not his panegyric, which must be all praise, but 70 his Life; which, great and good as he was, must not be supposed to be entirely perfect. To be as he was, is indeed subject of panegyric enough to any man in this state of being; but in every picture there should be shade as well as light, and when I delineate him without reserve, I do what he himself recommended, both by his precept and his example.

"If the biographer writes from personal knowledge, and makes haste to gratify the public curiosity, there is danger lest his interest, his fear, his gratitude, or his 80 tenderness overpower his fidelity, and tempt him to conceal, if not to invent. There are many who think it an act of piety to hide the faults or failings of their friends, even when they can no longer suffer by their detection; we therefore see whole ranks of characters adorned with uniform panegyric, and not to be known from one another but by extrinsic and casual circumstances. 'Let me remember,' says Hale, 'when I find myself inclined to pity a criminal, that there is likewise a pity due to the country.' If we owe regard to 90 the memory of the dead, there is yet more respect to be paid to knowledge, to virtue and to truth."

What I consider as the peculiar value of the following work, is, the quantity it contains of Johnson's conversation; which is universally acknowledged to have been eminently instructive and entertaining; and of which the specimens that I have given upon a former occasion, have been received with so much approbation, that I have good grounds for supposing that the world will not be indifferent to more ample communi- 100 cations of a similar nature. . . .

Of one thing I am certain, that considering how highly the small portion which we have of the table-talk and other anecdotes of our celebrated writers is valued, and how earnestly it is regretted that we have not more, I am justified in preserving rather too many of Johnson's sayings, than too few; especially as from the diversity of dispositions it cannot be known with certainty beforehand, whether what may seem trifling to some, and perhaps to the collector himself, may not be 110 most agreeable to many; and the greater number that an author can please in any degree, the more pleasure does there arise to a benevolent mind.

To those who are weak enough to think this a degrading task, and the time and labor which have been devoted to it misemployed, I shall content myself with opposing the authority of the greatest man of any age, Julius Caesar, of whom Bacon observes, that "in his book of Apothegms which he collected, we see that he esteemed it more honor to make himself but a pair of 120 tables, to take the wise and pithy words of others, than to have every word of his own to be made an apothegm or an oracle."

Having said thus much by way of introduction, I commit the following pages to the candor of the Public. . . .

BOSWELL INTRODUCED TO JOHNSON (1763)

This is to me a memorable year; for in it I had the happiness to obtain the acquaintance of that extraordinary man whose memoirs I am now writing; an acquaintance which I shall ever esteem as one of the most fortunate circumstances in my life. Though then but two-and-twenty, I had for several years read his works with delight and instruction, and had the highest reverence for their author, which had grown up in my fancy into a kind of mysterious veneration, by figuring
10 to myself a state of solemn elevated abstraction, in which I supposed him to live in the immense metropolis of London. Mr. Gentleman, a native of Ireland, who passed some years in Scotland as a player, and as an instructor in the English language, a man whose talents and worth were depressed by misfortune, had given me a representation of the figure and manner of DICTIONARY JOHNSON! as he was then generally called; and during my first visit to London, which was for three months in 1760, Mr. Derrick the poet, who
20 was Gentleman's friend and countryman, flattered me with hopes that he would introduce me to Johnson, an honor of which I was very ambitious. But he never found an opportunity. . . .

Mr. Thomas Davies the actor, who then kept a bookseller's shop in Russell Street, Covent Garden,° told me that Johnson was very much his friend, and came frequently to his house, where he more than once invited me to meet him; but by some unlucky accident or other he was prevented from coming to us.
30 Mr. Thomas Davies was a man of good understanding and talents, with the advantage of a liberal education. Though somewhat pompous, he was an entertaining companion; and his literary performances have no inconsiderable share of merit. He was a friendly and very hospitable man. Both he and his wife (who has been celebrated for her beauty), though upon the stage for many years, maintained an uniform decency of character; and Johnson esteemed them, and lived in as easy an intimacy with them as with any family
40 which he used to visit. Mr. Davies recollected several of Johnson's remarkable sayings, and was one of the best of the many imitators of his voice and manner, while relating them. He increased my impatience more and more to see the extraordinary man whose works I highly valued, and whose conversation was reported to be so peculiarly excellent.

At last, on Monday the 16th of May, when I was sitting in Mr. Davies's back-parlor, after having drunk tea with him and Mrs. Davies, Johnson unexpectedly came into the shop;° and Mr. Davies having perceived 50 him through the glass door in the room in which we were sitting, advancing towards us, he announced his awful approach to me, somewhat in the manner of an actor in the part of Horatio, when he addresses Hamlet on the appearance of his father's ghost, "Look, my Lord, it comes."° I found that I had a very perfect idea of Johnson's figure, from the portrait of him painted by Sir Joshua Reynolds° soon after he had published his *Dictionary,*° in the attitude of sitting in his easy chair in deep meditation; which was the first picture his friend 60 did for him, which Sir Joshua very kindly presented to me, and from which an engraving has been made for this work. Mr. Davies mentioned my name, and respectfully introduced me to him. I was much agitated; and recollecting his prejudice against the Scotch, of which I had heard much, I said to Davies, "Don't tell where I come from."—"From Scotland," cried Davies, roguishly. "Mr. Johnson," said I, "I do indeed come from Scotland, but I cannot help it." I am willing to flatter myself that I meant this as light 70 pleasantry to soothe and conciliate him, and not as an humiliating abasement at the expense of my country. But however that might be, this speech was somewhat unlucky; for with that quickness of wit for which he was so remarkable, he seized the expression "come from Scotland," which I used in the sense of being of that country; and, as if I had said that I had come away from it, or left it, retorted, "That, Sir, I find is what a very great many of your countrymen cannot help." This stroke stunned me a good deal; and when we had 80 sat down, I felt myself not a little embarrassed, and apprehensive of what might come next. He then addressed himself to Davies: "What do you think of Garrick?° He has refused me an order for the play for Miss Williams,° because he knows the house will be full, and that an order would be worth three shillings." Eager to take any opening to get into conversation with him, I ventured to say, "O, Sir, I cannot think Mr. Garrick would grudge such a trifle to you." "Sir," said he, with a stern look, "I have known David Garrick longer 90 than you have done; and I know no right you have to talk to me on the subject." Perhaps I deserved this check; for it was rather presumptuous in me, an entire stranger, to express any doubt of the justice of his animadversion upon his old acquaintance and pupil.° I now felt myself much mortified, and began to think

50 **shop,** the bookseller's shop mentioned above   55–56 **Look . . . comes,** from Shakespeare's *Hamlet,* I. iv, 38   58 **Sir Joshua Reynolds,** the eminent portrait painter (1723–1792)   59 **Dictionary.** Johnson's *Dictionary* was completed in 1755   84 **Garrick,** David Garrick, the leading actor of his age (1717–1779) 85 **Miss Williams,** Anna Williams, a woman of rare talents, Johnson's friend and companion for many years. Up to this point in Boswell's *Life of Johnson,* she was mentioned as Mrs. Williams, "Mrs." being a common form of address for both married and unmarried women during the seventeenth and eighteenth centuries. Johnson uses both forms of address to her in his letters   92–95 **Perhaps . . . pupil.** Boswell's own note follows: "That this was a momentary sally against Garrick there can be no doubt; for at Johnson's desire he had, some years before, given a benefit-night at his theater to this very person, by which she had got two hundred pounds. Johnson, indeed, upon all other occasions, when I was in his company, praised the very liberal charity of Garrick. I once mentioned to him: 'It is observed, Sir, that you attack Garrick yourself but will suffer nobody else to do it.' JOHNSON (smiling): 'Why, Sir, that is true'"

The Life of Samuel Johnson, LL.D.   Boswell Introduced to Johnson   25 Covent Garden, a district in London once occupied by the Abbey of St. Peter, Westminster. The region until recently was occupied in part by a great market, and had further fame from the presence of the Covent Garden Theatre (built in 1731)—one of the best-known theaters in eighteenth-century London

that the hope which I had long indulged of obtaining his acquaintance was blasted. And, in truth, had not my ardor been uncommonly strong, and my resolution uncommonly persevering, so rough a reception might have deterred me forever from making any further attempts. Fortunately, however, I remained upon the field not wholly discomfited; and was soon rewarded by hearing some of his conversation of which I preserved the following short minute, without marking the questions and observations by which it was produced.

"People (he remarked) may be taken in once, who imagine that an author is greater in private life than other men. Uncommon parts require uncommon opportunities for their exertion."

"In barbarous society, superiority of parts is of real consequence. Great strength or great wisdom is of much value to an individual. But in more polished times there are people to do every thing for money; and then there are a number of other superiorities, such as those of birth and fortune, and rank, that dissipate men's attention, and leave no extraordinary share of respect for personal and intellectual superiority. This is wisely ordered by Providence, to preserve some equality among mankind."

"Sir, this book (*The Elements of Criticism,* which he had taken up,) is a pretty essay, and deserves to be held in some estimation, though much of it is chimerical."

Speaking of one° who with more than ordinary boldness attacked public measures and the royal family, he said,

"I think he is safe from the law, but he is an abusive scoundrel; and instead of applying to my Lord Chief Justice to punish him, I would send half a dozen footmen and have him well ducked."

"The notion of liberty amuses the people of England, and helps to keep off the *taedium vitae*. When a butcher tells you that *his heart bleeds for his country,* he has, in fact, no uneasy feeling."

"Sheridan will not succeed at Bath with his oratory. Ridicule has gone down before him, and, I doubt, Derrick is his enemy."

"Derrick may do very well, as long as he can outrun his character; but the moment his character gets up with him, it is all over."

It is, however, but just to record, that some years afterwards, when I reminded him of this sarcasm, he said, "Well, but Derrick has now got a character that he need not run away from."

I was highly pleased with the extraordinary vigor of his conversation, and regretted that I was drawn away from it by an engagement at another place. I had, for a part of the evening, been left alone with him, and had ventured to make an observation now and then, which he received very civilly; so that I was satisfied that though there was a roughness in his manner, there was

no ill-nature in his disposition. Davies followed me to the door, and when I complained to him a little of the hard blows which the great man had given me, he kindly took upon him to console me by saying, "Don't be uneasy. I can see he likes you very well."

BOSWELL'S FIRST CALL ON JOHNSON (1763)

A few days afterwards I called on Davies, and asked him if he thought I might take the liberty of waiting on Mr. Johnson at his chambers in the Temple. He said I certainly might, and that Mr. Johnson would take it as a compliment. So on Tuesday the 24th of May, after having been enlivened by the witty sallies of Messieurs Thornton, Wilkes, Churchill, and Lloyd,° with whom I had passed the morning, I boldly repaired to Johnson. His chambers were on the first floor of No. 1, Inner-Temple-lane, and I entered them with an impression given me by the Reverend Dr. Blair, of Edinburgh, who had been introduced to him not long before, and described his having "found the Giant in his den"; an expression which, when I came to be pretty well acquainted with Johnson, I repeated to him, and he was diverted at this picturesque account of himself. Dr. Blair had been presented to him by Dr. James Fordyce.° At this time the controversy concerning the pieces published by Mr. James Macpherson, as translations of Ossian,° was at its height. Johnson had all along denied their authenticity; and, what was still more provoking to their admirers, maintained that they had no merit. The subject having been introduced by Dr. Fordyce, Dr. Blair, relying on the internal evidence of their antiquity, asked Dr. Johnson whether he thought any man of a modern age could have written such poems? Johnson replied, "Yes, Sir, many men, many women, and many children." Johnson at this time, did not know that Dr. Blair had just published a Dissertation, not only defending their authenticity, but seriously ranking them with the poems of Homer and Virgil; and when he was afterwards informed of this circumstance, he expressed some displeasure at Dr. Fordyce's having suggested the topic, and said, "I am not sorry that they got thus much for their pains. Sir, it was like leading one to talk of a book, when the author is concealed behind the door."

He received me very courteously; but, it must be confessed that his apartment, and furniture, and morning dress, were sufficiently uncouth. His brown suit of clothes looked very rusty; he had on a little old shrivelled unpowdered wig, which was too small for his head; his shirt-neck and knees of his breeches were loose; his black worsted stockings ill drawn up; and he had a pair of unbuckled shoes by way of slippers. But

Boswell's First Call on Johnson 7 **Thornton . . . Lloyd.** All those mentioned here were literary wits and writers of the time: Bonnell Thornton (1724–1768); John Wilkes (1727–1797), champion of the rights of free representation in the government and friendly to the American cause in the revolution of 1776; Charles Churchill (1731–1764), author of the satiric poem *The Rosciad;* and Robert Lloyd (1733–1764) 11–18 **Blair . . . Fordyce.** Hugh Blair (1718–1800) was a noted preacher and critic, professor of rhetoric and *belles-lettres* at the University of Edinburgh; James Fordyce (1720–1796) was another popular preacher and a poet as well 19–20 **Macpherson . . . Ossian.** For Johnson's position on the question of the Ossianic poems, see his letter to Macpherson

125 **one,** Wilkes. See note on l. 7 of "Boswell's First Call on Johnson"

all these slovenly particularities were forgotten the moment that he began to talk. Some gentlemen, whom I do not recollect, were sitting with him; and when they went away, I also rose; but he said to me, "Nay, don't go."—"Sir," said I, "I am afraid that I intrude upon you. It is benevolent to allow me to sit and hear you." He seemed pleased with this compliment, which I sincerely paid him, and answered, "Sir, I am obliged to any man who visits me."—I have preserved the following short minute of what passed this day.

"Madness frequently discovers itself merely by unnecessary deviation from the usual modes of the world. My poor friend Smart° showed the disturbance of his mind, by falling upon his knees, and saying his prayers in the street, or in any other unusual place. Now although, rationally speaking, it is greater madness not to pray at all, than to pray as Smart did, I am afraid there are so many who do not pray, that their understanding is not called in question."

Concerning this unfortunate poet, Christopher Smart, who was confined in a mad-house, he had, at another time, the following conversation with Dr. Burney.—BURNEY.° "How does poor Smart do, Sir; is he likely to recover?" JOHNSON. "It seems as if his mind had ceased to struggle with the disease; for he grows fat upon it." BURNEY. "Perhaps, Sir, that may be from want of exercise." JOHNSON. "No, Sir; he has partly as much exercise as he used to have, for he digs in the garden. Indeed, before his confinement, he used for exercise to walk to the alehouse; but he was *carried* back again. I did not think he ought to be shut up. His infirmities were not noxious to society. He insisted on people praying with him; and I'd as lief pray with Kit Smart as anyone else. Another charge was, that he did not love clean linen; and I have no passion for it."

Johnson continued. "Mankind have a great aversion to intellectual labor; but even supposing knowledge to be easily attainable, more people would be content to be ignorant than would take even a little trouble to acquire it.

"The morality of an action depends on the motive from which we act. If I fling half a crown to a beggar with intention to break his head, and he picks it up and buys victuals with it, the physical effect is good; but, with respect to me, the action is very wrong. So, religious exercises, if not performed with an intention to please God, avail us nothing. As our Savior says of those who perform them from other motives, "Verily they have their reward.'"° . . .

Talking of Garrick, he said, "He is the first man in the world for sprightly conversation."

When I rose a second time, he again pressed me to stay, which I did.

He told me that he generally went abroad at four in the afternoon, and seldom came home till two in the morning. I took the liberty to ask if he did not think it wrong to live thus, and not make more use of his great talents. He owned it was a bad habit. On reviewing, at the distance of many years, my journal of this period, I wonder how, at my first visit, I ventured to talk to him so freely, and that he bore it with so much indulgence.

Before we parted, he was so good as to promise to favor me with his company one evening at my lodgings; and, as I took my leave, shook me cordially by the hand. It is almost needless to add, that I felt no little elation at having now so happily established an acquaintance of which I had been so long ambitious. . . .

OLIVER GOLDSMITH

As Dr. Oliver Goldsmith will frequently appear in this narrative, I shall endeavor to make my readers in some degree acquainted with his singular character. He was a native of Ireland, and a contemporary with Mr. Burke,° at Trinity College, Dublin, but did not then give much promise of future celebrity. He, however, observed to Mr. Malone,° that "though he made no great figure in mathematics, which was a study in much repute there, he could turn an Ode of Horace into English better than any of them." He afterwards studied physic at Edinburgh, and upon the Continent; and I have been informed, was enabled to pursue his travels on foot, partly by demanding at universities to enter the lists as a disputant, by which, according to the custom of many of them, he was entitled to the premium of a crown, when luckily for him his challenge was not accepted; so that, as I once observed to Dr. Johnson, he *disputed* his passage through Europe. He then came to England, and was employed successively in the capacities of an usher to an academy, a corrector of the press, a reviewer, and a writer for a newspaper. He had sagacity enough to cultivate assiduously the acquaintance of Johnson, and his faculties were gradually enlarged by the contemplation of such a model. To me and many others it appeared that he studiously copied the manner of Johnson, though, indeed, upon a smaller scale.

At this time I think he had published nothing with his name, though it was pretty generally known that one Dr. Goldsmith was the author of *An Enquiry into the Present State of Polite Learning in Europe,*° and of *The Citizen of the World,*° a series of letters supposed to be written from London by a Chinese. No man had the art of displaying with more advantage as a writer, whatever literary acquisitions he made. "*Nihil quod tetigit*

58 Smart. Christopher Smart (1722–1771), author of *A Song to David*, 1763, may have been the most distinguished religious poet of the age, a possibility which Johnson himself seems to have recognized   **68 Burney.** Charles Burney (1726–1814) was a musician as well as an author, but is known to posterity also as the father of Frances Burney (Madame d'Arblay), a novelist (1752–1840), whose *Evelina* (1778) and *Cecelia* (1782), to mention no other works, are excellent specimens of the novel of manners in the later eighteenth century   **94 Verily . . . reward,** from *Matthew*, 6:2

Oliver Goldsmith   5 **Mr. Burke,** Edmund Burke (1729–1797)   7 **Mr. Malone,** Edmund Malone (1741–1812), editor of Shakespeare and later a reviser of Boswell's *Life*   **30–31 An Enquiry . . . Europe,** a critical work by Oliver Goldsmith, 1759. Its general thesis was that literary criticism and literary decadence go hand in hand   **32 The Citizen of the World,** a series of letters contributed by Goldsmith to a newspaper called *The Public Ledger*, supposedly written by a Chinese traveler in London, impartially critical of English life and manners. The essays were later collected and published under the title *Letters from the Citizen of the World* (1762)

non ornavit.''° His mind resembled a fertile, but thin soil. There was a quick, but not a strong vegetation, of whatever chanced to be thrown upon it. No deep root could be struck. The oak of the forest did not grow there: but the elegant shrubbery and the fragrant parterre appeared in gay succession. It has been generally circulated and believed that he was a mere fool in conversation;° but, in truth, this has been greatly exaggerated. He had, no doubt, a more than common share of that hurry of ideas which we often find in his countrymen, and which sometimes produces a laughable confusion in expressing them. He was very much what the French call *un étourdi,*° and from vanity and an eager desire of being conspicuous wherever he was, he frequently talked carelessly without knowledge of the subject, or even without thought. His person was short, his countenance coarse and vulgar, his deportment that of a scholar awkwardly affecting the easy gentleman. Those who were in any way distinguished, excited envy in him to so ridiculous an excess, that the instances of it are hardly credible. When accompanying two beautiful young ladies° with their mother on a tour in France, he was seriously angry that more attention was paid to them than to him; and once at the exhibition of the *Fantoccini*° in London, when those who sat next him observed with what dexterity a puppet was made to toss a pike, he could not bear that it should have such praise, and exclaimed with some warmth, "Pshaw! I can do it better myself."

He, I am afraid, had no settled system of any sort, so that his conduct must not be strictly scrutinized; but his affections were social and generous, and when he had money he gave it away very liberally. His desire of imaginary consequence predominated over his attention to truth. When he began to rise into notice, he said he had a brother who was Dean of Durham,° a fiction so easily detected, that it is wonderful how he should have been so inconsiderate as to hazard it. He boasted to me at this time of the power of his pen in commanding money, which I believe was true in a certain degree, though in the instance he gave he was by no means correct. He told me that he had sold a novel for four hundred pounds. This was his *Vicar of Wakefield.* But Johnson informed me, that he had made the bargain for Goldsmith, and the price was sixty pounds. "And, Sir," said he, "a sufficient price too, when it was sold; for then the fame of Goldsmith had not been elevated, as it afterwards was, by his *Traveler;*° and the bookseller had such faint hopes of profit by his bargain, that he kept the manuscript by him a long time, and did not publish it till after the *Traveler* had appeared. Then, to be sure, it was accidentally worth more money."

Mrs. Piozzi° and Sir John Hawkins° have strangely misstated the history of Goldsmith's situation and Johnson's friendly interference, when this novel was sold. I shall give it authentically from Johnson's own exact narration:

"I received one morning a message from poor Goldsmith that he was in great distress, and as it was not in his power to come to me, begging that I would come to him as soon as possible. I sent him a guinea, and promised to come to him directly. I accordingly went as soon as I was dressed, and found that his landlady had arrested him for his rent, at which he was in a violent passion. I perceived that he had already changed my guinea, and had got a bottle of Madeira and a glass before him. I put the cork into the bottle, desired he would be calm, and began to talk to him of the means by which he might be extricated. He then told me that he had a novel ready for the press, which he produced to me. I looked into it, and saw its merit; told the landlady I should soon return, and having gone to a bookseller, sold it for sixty pounds. I brought Goldsmith the money, and he discharged his rent, not without rating his landlady in a high tone for having used him so ill."°

My next meeting with Johnson was on Friday the 1st of July, when he and I and Dr. Goldsmith supped together at the Mitre. I was before this time pretty well acquainted with Goldsmith, who was one of the brightest ornaments of the Johnsonian school. Goldsmith's respectful attachment to Johnson was then at its height; for his own literary reputation had not yet distinguished him so much as to excite a vain desire of competition with his great Master. He had increased my admiration of the goodness of Johnson's heart, by incidental remarks in the course of conversation, such as, when I mentioned Mr. Levet, who he entertained under his roof, "He is poor and honest, which is recommendation enough to Johnson"; and when I wondered that he was very kind to a man of whom I had heard a very bad character, "He is now become miserable, and that insures the protection of Johnson." . . .

He [Johnson] talked very contemptuously of Churchill's poetry, observing, that "it had a temporary currency, only from its audacity of abuse, and being filled with living names, and that it would sink into obliv-

---

35–36 **Nihil . . . ornavit.** "He touched nothing that he did not adorn" (from Johnson's epitaph on Goldsmith)   43 **fool in conversation,** an interesting echo of Goldsmith's own jocular reference to himself in the *Retaliation,* l. 16, with a pun on the word "fool"   48 **un étourdi,** a rattle-brained blunderer   57 **young ladies,** the Horneck sisters   60 **Fantoccini,** a famous puppet show   71 **Dean of Durham.** Goldsmith's near relative Dr. Isaac Goldsmith was Dean of Cloyne, Ireland, in 1747   83 **Traveler,** a didactic poem by Goldsmith (1764), attempting a survey of European culture; the poem brought Goldsmith both fame and money

89 **Mrs. Piozzi,** formerly Mrs. Henry Thrale, who after the death of her husband married Gabriel Piozzi, an Italian music master. The Thrales were intimate friends of Johnson, as the letter which Johnson wrote Mrs. Thrale at the time of her marriage to Piozzi well attests. Mrs. Piozzi's account of the Goldsmith matter is given in her *Anecdotes of Johnson*   **Sir John Hawkins,** a London attorney (1719–1789), who relates the incident in his *Life of Johnson*   112 **used him so ill.** Boswell's own note should be given here: "It may not be improper to annex here Mrs. Piozzi's account of this transaction, in her own words, as a specimen of the extreme inaccuracy with which all her anecdotes of Dr. Johnson are related, or rather discolored and distorted. 'I have forgotten the year, but it could scarcely, I think, be later than 1765 or 1766, that he [Johnson] was *called abruptly from our house after dinner,* and returning *in about three hours,* said he had been with an enraged author, whose landlady pressed him for payment within doors, while the bailiffs beset him without; that he was *drinking himself drunk* with Madeira, to drown care, and fretting over a novel, which, when *finished,* was to be his *whole fortune,* but *he could not get it done for distraction,* nor could he step out of doors to offer it for sale. Mr. Johnson, therefore, sent away the bottle, and went to the bookseller, recommending the performance, and desiring some *immediate relief,* which when he brought back to the writer, *he called the woman of the house directly to partake of punch and pass their time in merriment'* "

ion." I ventured to hint that he was not quite a fair judge, as Churchill had attacked him violently. JOHNSON. "Nay, Sir, I am a very fair judge. He did not attack me violently till he found I did not like his poetry; and his attack on me shall not prevent me from
140 continuing to say what I think of him, from an apprehension that it may be ascribed to resentment. No, Sir, I called the fellow a blockhead at first, and I will call him a blockhead still. However, I will acknowledge that I have a better opinion of him now, than I once had; for he has shown more fertility than I expected. To be sure, he is a tree that cannot produce good fruit: he only bears crabs. But, Sir, a tree that produces a great many crabs is better than a tree which produces only a few." . . .

BOSWELL'S APOLOGY

Let me here apologize for the imperfect manner in which I am obliged to exhibit Johnson's conversation at this period. In the early part of my acquaintance with him, I was so wrapt in admiration of his extraordinary colloquial talents, and so little accustomed to his peculiar mode of expression, that I found it extremely difficult to recollect and record his conversation with its genuine vigor and vivacity. In progress of time, when my mind was, as it were, *strongly impreg-*
10 *nated with the Johnsonian aether,* I could with much more facility and exactness, carry in my memory and commit to paper the exuberant variety of his wisdom and wit. . . .

BOSWELL'S PARTY AT THE MITRE

I had as my guests this evening at the Mitre tavern,° Dr. Johnson, Dr. Goldsmith, Mr. Thomas Davies, Mr. Eccles, an Irish gentleman, for whose agreeable company I was obliged to Mr. Davies, and the Reverend Mr. John Ogilvie, who was desirous of being in company with my illustrious friend, while I in my turn, was proud to have the honor of showing one of my countrymen upon what easy terms Johnson permitted me to live with him. . . .
10   "Bayle's *Dictionary*° is a very useful work for those to consult who love the biographical part of literature, which is what I love most."
    Talking of the eminent writers in Queen Anne's reign, he observed, "I think Dr. Arbuthnot° the first man among them. He was the most universal genius,

being an excellent physician, a man of deep learning, and a man of much humor. Mr. Addison° was, to be sure, a great man; his learning was not profound; but his morality, his humor, and his elegance of writing, set him very high."
20   Mr. Ogilvie was unlucky enough to choose for the topic of his conversation the praises of his native country. He began with saying, that there was very rich land around Edinburgh. Goldsmith, who had studied physic there, contradicted this, very untruly, with a sneering laugh. Disconcerted a little by this, Mr. Ogilvie then took a new ground, where, I suppose, he thought himself perfectly safe; for he observed that Scotland had a great many noble wild prospects. JOHNSON. "I believe, Sir, you have a great many.
30 Norway, too, has noble wild prospects; and Lapland is remarkable for prodigious noble wild prospects. But, Sir, let me tell you, the noblest prospect which a Scotchman ever sees, is the high road that leads him to England!" This unexpected and pointed sally produced a roar of applause. After all, however, those who admire the rude grandeur of nature, cannot deny it to Caledonia.

RELISH FOR GOOD EATING

At supper this night he talked of good eating with uncommon satisfaction. "Some people," said he, "have a foolish way of not minding, or pretending not to mind, what they eat. For my part, I mind my belly very studiously, and very carefully; for I look upon it, that he who does not mind his belly, will hardly mind anything else." He now appeared to me *Jean Bull philosophe,*° and he was for the moment, not only serious, but vehement. Yet I have heard him, upon other
10 occasions, talk with great contempt of people who were anxious to gratify their palates; and the 206th number of his *Rambler* is a masterly essay against gulosity.° His practice, indeed, I must acknowledge, may be considered as casting the balance of his different opinions upon this subject; for I never knew any man who relished good eating more than he did. When at table, he was totally absorbed in the business of the moment; his looks seemed riveted to his plate; nor would he, unless when in very high company, say one word, or even pay the least attention to what was said
20 by others, till he had satisfied his appetite; which was so fierce, and indulged with such intenseness, that while in the act of eating, the veins of his forehead swelled, and generally a strong perspiration was visible. To those whose sensations were delicate, this could not but be disgusting; and it was doubtless not very suitable to the character of a philosopher, who should be distinguished by self-command. But it must

Boswell's Party at the Mitre   1–5 **Mitre tavern . . . Ogilvie.** The people mentioned have been met with before, except for Mr. Eccles, "an Irish gentleman." For Johnson and Goldsmith no further note is necessary here; Mr. Thomas Davies was the actor at whose home Boswell first met Johnson; Mr. John Ogilvie was a Scottish minister with poetic pretensions. Boswell remarks in a note: "When I asked Dr. Johnson's permission to introduce him [Ogilvie], he obligingly agreed; adding, however, with a sly pleasantry, 'but he must give us none of his poetry'"   10 **Bayle's Dictionary,** the *Dictionnaire historique et critique* by Pierre Bayle (1647–1706), which is as much a résumé of the learning of the time as a dictionary   14 **Dr. Arbuthnot,** John Arbuthnot (1665?–1735), friend of Addison, Steele, Swift, and Pope. (See Pope's *Epistle to Dr. Arbuthnot*)

17 **Mr. Addison,** Joseph Addison (1672–1719), the essayist and journalist and man of affairs in the reign of Queen Anne   **Relish for Good Eating   7 Jean Bull philosophe,** John Bull, the typical Englishman, as philosopher   13 **gulosity,** excessive appetite, gluttony

be owned that Johnson, though he could be rigidly
30 *abstemious,* was not a *temperate* man either in eating
or drinking. He could refrain, but he could not use
moderately. He told me that he had fasted two days
without inconvenience, and that he had never been
hungry but once. They who beheld with wonder how
much he eat upon all occasions, when his dinner was
to his taste, could not easily conceive what he must
have meant by hunger; and not only was he remarkable for the extraordinary quantity which he eat, but he
was, or affected to be, a man of very nice discernment
40 in the science of cookery. He used to descant critically
on the dishes which had been at table where he had
dined or supped, and to recollect very minutely what
he had liked. I remember when he was in Scotland, his
praising *"Gordon's palates"*° (a dish of palates at the
Honorable Alexander Gordon's), with a warmth of expression which might have done honor to more important subjects. "As for Maclaurin's imitation° of a
made dish, it was a wretched attempt." He about the
same time was so much displeased with the perform-
50 ances of a nobleman's French cook, that he exclaimed
with vehemence, "I'd throw such a rascal into the
river"; and he then proceeded to alarm a lady at whose
house he was to sup, by the following manifesto of his
skill: "I, Madam, who live at a variety of good tables,
am a much better judge of cookery than any person
who has a very tolerable cook, but lives much at home;
for his palate is gradually adapted to the taste of his
cook; whereas, Madam, in trying by a wider range, I
can more exquisitely judge." When invited to dine,
60 even with an intimate friend, he was not pleased if
something better than a plain dinner was not prepared
for him. I have heard him say on such an occasion,
"This was a good dinner enough, to be sure; but it was
not a dinner to *ask* a man to." On the other hand, he
was wont to express, with great glee, his satisfaction
when he had been entertained quite to his mind. One
day when he had dined with his neighbor and landlord,
in Bolt Court, Mr. Allen, the printer, whose old
housekeeper had studied his taste in everything, he
70 pronounced this eulogy: "Sir, we could not have had a
better dinner, had there been a *Synod of Cooks.*"

While we were left by ourselves, after the Dutchman°
had gone to bed, Dr. Johnson talked of that studied
behavior which many have recommended and practiced. He disapproved of it; and said, "I never considered whether I should be a grave man, or a merry man,
but just let inclination, for the time, have its course."

He flattered me with some hopes that he would, in
the course of the following summer, come over to
80 Holland, and accompany me in a tour through the
Netherlands.

I teased him with fanciful apprehensions of unhappiness. A moth having fluttered round the candle, and
burnt itself, he laid hold of this little incident to admonish me; saying, with a sly look, and in a solemn but
a quiet tone, "That creature was its own tormentor,
and I believe its name was BOSWELL."

Next day we got to Harwich, to dinner; and my
passage in the packet-boat to Helvoetsluys° being secured, and my baggage put on board, we dined at our   90
inn by ourselves. I happened to say it would be terrible
if he should not find a speedy opportunity of returning
to London, and be confined in so dull a place.
JOHNSON. "Don't, Sir, accustom yourself to use big
words for little matters. It would *not* be *terrible,*
though I *were* to be detained some time here." The
practice of using words of disproportionate magnitude,
is, no doubt, too frequent everywhere; but, I think,
most remarkable among the French, of which, all who   100
have traveled in France must have been struck with
innumerable instances.

We went and looked at the church, and having gone
into it, and walked up to the altar, Johnson, whose
piety was constant and fervent, sent me to my knees,
saying, "Now that you are going to leave your native
country, recommend yourself to the protection of your
CREATOR and REDEEMER."

After we came out of the church, we stood talking
for some time together of Bishop Berkeley's ingenious   110
sophistry to prove the non-existence of matter,° and that
everything in the universe is merely ideal. I observed
that though we are satisfied his doctrine is not true, it
is impossible to refute it. I never shall forget the alacrity with which Johnson answered, striking his foot
with mighty force against a large stone, till he rebounded from it, "I refute it *thus.*" This was a stout
exemplification of the *first truths of Père Bouffier,*° or
the *original principles* of Reid and of Beattie;° without
admitting which, we can no more argue in meta-   120
physics, than we can argue in mathematics without axioms. To me it is not conceivable how Berkeley
can be answered by pure reasoning; but I know that
the nice and difficult task was to have been undertaken
by one of the most luminous minds of the present age,°
had not politics "turned him from calm philosophy
aside." What an admirable display of subtilty, united
with brilliance, might his contending with Berkeley
have afforded us! How must we, when we reflect on
the loss of such an intellectual feast, regret that he   130
should be characterized as the man,

89 **Helvoetsluys,** a seaport in The Netherlands 110–11 **Berkeley . . . matter,**
Bishop George Berkeley (1685–1753), churchman and metaphysician, author of
Principles of Human Knowledge (1710), which is based upon the "idealistic"
philosophy that nothing exists except in so far as it is perceived by the senses
118 **Père Bouffier.** Claude Bouffier (1661–1737), notable French writer on grammar and history, published in 1724 a *Traité des vérités premières,* which attempted
to discover the principles upon which all human knowledge is based. The core of
his philosophy is that of Descartes, a rational basis, but he partakes of some of the
views of Berkeley—the basis of all human knowledge and the foundation of every
other truth lie in the sense we have of our own existence and of what we feel
within ourselves   119 **Reid . . . Beattie,** Professor Thomas Reid (1710–1796), a
Scottish philosopher, the leading representative of the "school of common sense";
Dr. James Beattie (1735–1803), a poet and professor of moral philosophy at Aberdeen University   125 **luminous minds . . . age,** Edmund Burke (1729–1797),
famous statesman and orator

44 **palates,** things tasty or palatable. Johnson was in Scotland from August to
November 1773. Alexander Gordon was a wealthy Scot of the age, afterwards
Lord Rockville   47 **Maclaurin's imitation, etc.** This is an allusion to the effort of
John Maclaurin (1734–1796), a Scottish judge, afterwards Lord Dreghorn, to imitate the style of Johnson in Johnson's *Journey to the Western Islands* (1775). Of the
imitation Johnson said, "I could caricature my own style much better myself"
72 **the Dutchman,** a fellow passenger in the stagecoach to Harwich

Who, born for the universe, narrowed his mind,
And to party gave up what was meant for mankind?°

My revered friend walked down with me to the beach, where we embraced and parted with tenderness, and engaged to correspond by letters. I said, "I hope, Sir, you will not forget me in my absence." JOHNSON. "Nay, Sir, it is more likely you should forget me, than that I should forget you." As the vessel put out to sea, I kept my eyes upon him for a considerable time, while he remained rolling his majestic frame in his usual manner; and at last I perceived him walk back into the town, and he disappeared.

THE FEAR OF DEATH (1769)

When we were alone, I introduced the subject of death, and endeavored to maintain that the fear of it might be got over. I told him that David Hume° said to me he was no more uneasy to think he should *not be* after this life than that he *had not been* before he began to exist. JOHNSON. "Sir, if he really thinks so, his perceptions are disturbed; he is mad. If he does not think so, he lies. He may tell you he holds his finger in the flame of a candle without feeling pain; would you believe him? When he dies, he at least gives up all he has." BOSWELL. "Foote,° Sir, told me that when he was very ill he was not afraid to die." JOHNSON. "It is not true, Sir. Hold a pistol to Foote's breast, or to Hume's breast and threaten to kill them, and you'll see how they behave." BOSWELL. "But may we not fortify our minds for the approach of death?" Here I am sensible I was in the wrong, to bring before his view what he ever looked upon with horror; for although when in a celestial frame, in his *Vanity of Human Wishes,* he has supposed death to be "kind nature's signal for retreat," from this state of being to "a happier seat,"° his thoughts upon this awful change were in general full of dismal apprehensions. His mind resembled the vast amphitheater, the Coliseum at Rome. In the center stood his judgment, which, like a mighty gladiator, combated those apprehensions that, like the wild beasts of the arena, were all around in cells, ready to be let out upon him. After a conflict, he drives them back into their dens; but not killing them, they were still assailing him. To my question, whether we might not fortify our minds for the approach of death, he answered in a passion, "No, Sir, let it alone. It matters not how a man dies, but how he lives. The act of dying is not of importance; it lasts so short a time." He added, with an earnest look, "A man knows it must be so, and submits. It will do him no good to whine."

I attempted to continue the conversation. He was so provoked that he said, "Give us no more of this," and was thrown into such a state of agitation that he expressed himself in a way that alarmed and distressed me; showed an impatience that I should leave him, and when I was going away, called to me sternly, "Don't let us meet tomorrow."

I went home exceedingly uneasy. All the harsh observations which I had ever heard made upon his character crowded into my mind; and I seemed to myself like the man who had put his head into the lion's mouth a great many times with perfect safety, but at last had it bit off.

Next morning I sent him a note stating that I might have been in the wrong, but it was not intentionally; he was therefore, I could not help thinking, too severe upon me. That notwithstanding our agreement not to meet that day, I would call on him in my way to the city, and stay five minutes by my watch. "You are," said I, "in my mind, since last night, surrounded with cloud and storm. Let me have a glimpse of sunshine and go about my affairs in serenity and cheerfulness."

Upon entering his study, I was glad that he was not alone, which would have made our meeting more awkward. There were with him, Mr. Steevens° and Mr. Tyers,° both of whom I now saw for the first time. My note had, on his own reflection, softened him, for he received me very complacently; so that I unexpectedly found myself at ease, and joined in the conversation. . . .

Johnson spoke unfavorably of a certain pretty voluminous author, saying, "He used to write anonymous books, and then other books commending those books, in which there was something of rascality."

I whispered him, "Well, Sir, you are now in good humor." JOHNSON. "Yes, Sir." I was going to leave him, and had got as far as the staircase. He stopped me, and smiling, said, "Get you gone *in*"; a curious mode of inviting me to stay, which I accordingly did for some time longer.

This little incidental quarrel and reconciliation, which, perhaps, I may be thought to have detailed too minutely, must be esteemed as one of many proofs which his friends had, that though he might be charged with bad humor at times, he was always a good-natured man; and I have heard Sir Joshua Reynolds, a nice and delicate observer of manners, particularly remark that when upon any occasion Johnson had been rough to any person in company, he took the first opportunity of reconciliation, by drinking to him or addressing his discourse to him; but if he found his

---

133 **Who . . . mankind,** quoted from Goldsmith's *Retaliation,* ll. 31 and 32
The Fear of Death 3 **David Hume,** a Scottish historian and philosopher (1711–1776) 11 **Foote,** Samuel Foote (1720–1777), an English comedian and playwright 20 **kind . . . seat,** from Johnson's philosophic poem, *The Vanity of Human Wishes* (1749), ll. 363–364

61 **Mr. Steevens,** George Steevens (1736–1800), editor of Shakespeare 62 **Mr. Tyers,** Thomas Tyers (1726–1787), a dilettante author who published a biographical sketch of Johnson

dignified indirect overtures sullenly neglected, he was quite indifferent, and considered himself as having done all that he ought to do, and the other as now in the wrong.

HOW DR. JOHNSON AND MR. WILKES DINED TOGETHER (1776)

I am now to record a very curious incident in Dr. Johnson's life, which fell under my own observation; of which *pars magna fui*,° and which I am persuaded will, with the liberal-minded, be much to his credit.

My desire of being acquainted with celebrated men of every description, had made me, much about the same time, obtain an introduction to Dr. Samuel Johnson and to John Wilkes,° Esq. Two men more different could perhaps not be selected out of all mankind. They had even attacked one another with some asperity in their writings; yet I lived in habits of friendship with both. I could fully relish the excellence of each; for I have ever delighted in that intellectual chemistry, which can separate good qualities from evil in the same person.

Sir John Pringle,° "mine own friend and my Father's friend," between whom and Dr. Johnson I in vain wished to establish an acquaintance, as I respected and lived in intimacy with both of them, observed to me once, very ingeniously, "It is not in friendship as in mathematics, where two things, each equal to a third, are equal between themselves. You agree with Johnson as a middle quality, and you agree with me as a middle quality; but Johnson and I should not agree." Sir John was not sufficiently flexible; so I desisted; knowing, indeed, that the repulsion was equally strong on the part of Johnson; who, I know not from what cause, unless his being a Scotchman,° had formed a very erroneous opinion of Sir John. But I conceived an irresistible wish, if possible, to bring Dr. Johnson and Mr. Wilkes together. How to manage it, was a nice and difficult matter.

My worthy booksellers and friends, Messieurs Dilly in the Poultry,° at whose hospitable and well-covered table I have seen a greater number of literary men, than at any other, except that of Sir Joshua Reynolds,° had invited me to meet Mr. Wilkes and some more gentlemen, on Wednesday, May 15. "Pray (said I,) let us have Dr. Johnson."—"What with Mr. Wilkes? not for the world, (said Mr. Edward Dilly;) Dr. Johnson would never forgive me."—"Come, (said I,) if you'll let me negotiate for you, I will be answerable that all shall go well." DILLY. "Nay, if you will take it upon you, I am sure I shall be very happy to see them both here."

Notwithstanding the high veneration which I entertained for Dr. Johnson, I was sensible that he was sometimes a little actuated by the spirit of contradiction, and by means of that I hoped I should gain my point. I was persuaded that if I had come upon him with a direct proposal, "Sir, will you dine in company with Jack Wilkes?" he would have flown into a passion, and would probably have answered, "Dine with Jack Wilkes, Sir! I'd as soon dine with Jack Ketch."° I therefore, while we were sitting quietly by ourselves at his house in an evening, took occasion to open my plan thus:—"Mr. Dilly, Sir, sends his respectful compliments to you, and would be happy if you would do him the honor to dine with him on Wednesday next along with me, as I must soon go to Scotland." JOHNSON. "Sir, I am obliged to Mr. Dilly. I will wait upon him—" BOSWELL. "Provided, Sir, I suppose, that the company which he is to have, is agreeable to you." JOHNSON. "What do you mean, Sir? What do you take me for? Do you think I am so ignorant of the world, as to imagine that I am to prescribe to a gentleman what company he is to have at his table?" BOSWELL. "I beg your pardon, Sir, for wishing to prevent you from meeting people whom you might not like. Perhaps he may have some of what he calls his patriotic friends° with him." JOHNSON. "Well, Sir, and what then? What care *I* for his *patriotic friends?* Poh!" BOSWELL. "I should not be surprised to find Jack Wilkes there." JOHNSON. "And if Jack Wilkes *should* be there, what is that to *me*, Sir? My dear friend, let us have no more of this. I am sorry to be angry with you; but really it is treating me strangely to talk to me as if I could not meet any company whatever, occasionally." BOSWELL. "Pray, forgive me, Sir: I meant well. But you shall meet whoever comes, for me." Thus I secured him, and told Dilly that he would find him very well pleased to be one of his guests on the day appointed.

Upon the much expected Wednesday, I called on him about half an hour before dinner, as I often did when we were to dine out together, to see that he was ready in time, and to accompany him. I found him buffeting his books, as upon a former occasion, covered with dust, and making no preparation for going abroad. "How is this, Sir? (said I). Don't you recollect that you are to dine at Mr. Dilly's?" JOHNSON. "Sir, I did not think of going to Dilly's: it went out of my head. I have ordered dinner at home with Mrs. Wil-

How Dr. Johnson and Mr. Wilkes Dined Together   3 **pars magna fui,** in which I played a large part (quoted from the *Aeneid*, II, 5)   8 **John Wilkes,** a liberal, radical, and free-living Whig. Johnson was a conservative, respectable Tory   16 **Sir John Pringle,** a Scottish physician and Boswell's godfather (1707–1782)   28 **Scotchman.** Dr. Johnson made fun of Scots on all occasions, much to Boswell's discomfort   34 **Poultry,** a district east of Cheapside where poultry was sold in medieval and Elizabethan times   36 **Sir Joshua Reynolds,** famous portrait painter and member of the Johnson circle (1723–1792)

54 **Jack Ketch,** the public executioner who died in 1686. His successors inherited the name in popular slang. Of the imagined remark Boswell's note says: "This has been circulated as if actually said by Johnson, when the truth is, it was only *supposed* by me"   70 **patriotic friends.** Those Whigs who were most violently opposed to the autocracy of George III and his minister Lord North styled themselves patriots. Johnson, as a staunch Tory, disliked them heartily

liams."° BOSWELL. "But, my dear Sir, you know you were engaged to Mr. Dilly, and I told him so. He will expect you, and will be much disappointed if you don't come." JOHNSON. "You must talk to Mrs. Williams about this."

Here was a sad dilemma. I feared that what I was so confident I had secured, would yet be frustrated. He
100 had accustomed himself to show Mrs. Williams such a degree of humane attention, as frequently imposed some restraint upon him; and I knew that if she should be obstinate, he would not stir. I hastened downstairs to the blind lady's room, and told her I was in great uneasiness, for Dr. Johnson had engaged to me to dine this day at Mr. Dilly's, but that he had told me he had forgotten his engagement, and had ordered dinner at home. "Yes, Sir, (said she, pretty peevishly,) Dr. Johnson is to dine at home."—"Madam, (said I,) his
110 respect for you is such, that I know he will not leave you, unless you absolutely desire it. But as you have so much of his company, I hope you will be good enough to forego it for a day: as Mr. Dilly is a very worthy man, has frequently had agreeable parties at his house for Dr. Johnson, and will be vexed if the Doctor neglects him today. And then, Madam, be pleased to consider my situation; I carried the message, and I assured Mr. Dilly that Dr. Johnson was to come; and no doubt he has made a dinner, and invited
120 a company, and boasted of the honor he expected to have. I shall be quite disgraced if the Doctor is not there." She gradually softened to my solicitations, which were certainly as earnest as most entreaties to ladies upon any occasion, and was graciously pleased to empower me to tell Dr. Johnson, "That all things considered, she thought he should certainly go." I flew back to him, still in dust, and careless of what should be the event, "indifferent in his choice to go or stay;" but as soon as I had announced to him Mrs. Williams's
130 consent, he roared, "Frank,° a clean shirt," and was very soon drest. When I had him fairly seated in a hackney-coach with me, I exulted as much as a fortune-hunter who has got an heiress into a post-chaise with him to set out for Gretna-Green.°

When we entered Mr. Dilly's drawing-room, he found himself in the midst of a company he did not know. I kept myself snug and silent, watching how he would conduct himself. I observed him whispering to Mr. Dilly, "Who is that gentleman, sir?"—"Mr. Ar-
140 thur Lee."°—JOHNSON. "Too, too, too," (under his breath,) which was one of his habitual mutterings. Mr. Arthur Lee could not but be very obnoxious to Johnson, for he was not only a *patriot,* but an *Ameri-*

can. He was afterwards minister from the United States at the court of Madrid. "And who is the gentleman in lace?"—"Mr. Wilkes, Sir." This information confounded him still more; he had some difficulty to restrain himself, and taking up a book, sat down upon a window-seat and read, or at least kept his eye upon it intently for some time, till he composed himself. His 150 feelings, I dare say, were awkward enough. But he no doubt recollected his having rated me for supposing that he could be at all disconcerted by any company, and he, therefore, resolutely set himself to behave quite as an easy man of the world, who could adapt himself at once to the disposition and manners of those whom he might chance to meet.

The cheering sound of "Dinner is upon the table," dissolved his reverie, and we *all* sat down without any symptom of ill humor. There were present, beside Mr. 160 Wilkes, and Mr. Arthur Lee, who was an old companion of mine when he studied physic at Edinburgh, Mr. (now Sir John) Miller, Dr. Lettsom, and Mr. Slater, the druggist. Mr. Wilkes placed himself next to Dr. Johnson, and behaved to him with so much attention and politeness, that he gained upon him insensibly. No man eat more heartily than Johnson, or loved better what was nice and delicate. Mr. Wilkes was very assiduous in helping him to some fine veal. "Pray give me leave, Sir;—It is better here—A little of the 170 brown—Some fat, Sir—A little of the stuffing—Some gravy—Let me have the pleasure of giving you some butter—Allow me to recommend a squeeze of this orange;—or the lemon, perhaps, may have more zest."—"Sir, Sir, I am obliged to you, Sir," cried Johnson, bowing, and turning his head to him with a look for some time of "surly virtue,"° but, in a short while, of complacency.

Foote° being mentioned, Johnson said, "He is not a good mimic." One of the company added, "A merry 180 Andrew, a buffoon." JOHNSON. "But he has wit too, and is not deficient in ideas, or in fertility and variety of imagery, and not empty of reading; he has knowledge enough to fill up his part. One species of wit he has in an eminent degree, that of escape. You drive him into a corner with both hands; but he's gone, Sir, when you think you have got him—like an animal that jumps over your head. Then he has a great range for wit; he never lets truth stand between him and a jest, and he is sometimes mighty coarse. Garrick is under 190 many restraints from which Foote is free." WILKES. "Garrick's wit is more like Lord Chesterfield's."° JOHNSON. "The first time I was in company with Foote was at Fitzherbert's.° Having no good opinion of the fellow, I was resolved not to be pleased; and it is

93 **Mrs. Williams,** a blind friend of Mrs. Johnson's who lived in Johnson's house as a dependent. Every evening Johnson drank tea with her, and it was a signal favor to be invited by Johnson to attend   130 **Frank,** Johnson's servant
134 **Gretna-Green,** a village just over the border in Scotland to which couples went to get married because of the lax Scottish marriage laws   140 **Arthur Lee,** an American lawyer and English agent for the Massachusetts colony (1740-1792). He was an assistant to Benjamin Franklin and afterwards his successor. He helped to negotiate the treaty between France and America (1778)

177 **surly virtue,** "from Johnson's *London, a Poem,* V, 145"—Boswell's note
179 **Foote,** Samuel Foote (1720-1777), a popular comedian and dramatist
192 **Lord Chesterfield,** an English earl who was both statesman and author (1694-1773). His manners were elegant, his ethics cynical   194 **Fitzherbert,** William Fitzherbert, a friend of Johnson's

very difficult to please a man against his will. I went on eating my dinner pretty sullenly, affecting not to mind him. But the dog was so very comical, that I was obliged to lay down my knife and fork, throw myself back upon my chair, and fairly laugh it out. No, Sir, he was irresistible.° He upon one occasion experienced, in an extraordinary degree, the efficacy of his powers of entertaining. Amongst the many and various modes which he tried of getting money, he became a partner with a small-beer brewer, and he was to have a share of the profits for procuring customers amongst his numerous acquaintance. Fitzherbert was one who took his small-beer; but it was so bad that the servants resolved not to drink it. They were at some loss how to notify their resolution, being afraid of offending their master, who they knew liked Foote much as a companion. At last they fixed upon a little black boy, who was rather a favorite, to be their deputy, and deliver their remonstrance; and having invested him with the whole authority of the kitchen, he was to inform Mr. Fitzherbert, in all their names, upon a certain day, that they would drink Foote's small-beer no longer. On that day Foote happened to dine at Fitzherbert's, and this boy served at table; he was so delighted with Foote's stories, and merriment, and grimace, that when he went down stairs, he told them, 'This is the finest man I have ever seen. I will not deliver your message. I will drink his small-beer.' ''°

Somebody observed that Garrick could not have done this. WILKES. "Garrick would have made the small-beer still smaller. He is now leaving the stage; but he will play *Scrub*° all his life." I knew that Johnson would let nobody attack Garrick but himself, as Garrick said to me, and I had heard him praise his liberality; so to bring out his commendation of his celebrated pupil, I said, loudly, "I have heard Garrick is liberal." JOHNSON. ' Yes, Sir, I know that Garrick has given away more money than any man in England that I am acquainted with, and that not from ostentatious views. Garrick was very poor when he began life; so when he came to have money, he probably was very unskillful in giving away, and saved when he should not. But Garrick began to be liberal as soon as he could; and I am of opinion, the reputation of avarice which he has had, has been very lucky for him, and prevented his having many enemies. You despise a man for avarice, but do not hate him. Garrick might have been much better attacked for living with more splendor than is suitable to a player: if they had had the wit to have assaulted him in that quarter, they might have galled him more. But they have kept clamoring about his avarice, which has rescued him from much obloquy and envy."

Talking of the great difficulty of obtaining authentic information for biography, Johnson told us, "When I was a young fellow I wanted to write the 'Life of Dryden,' and in order to get materials, I applied to the only two persons then alive who had seen him; these were old Swinney,° and old Cibber.° Swinney's information was no more than this, 'That at Will's coffee-house Dryden had a particular chair for himself, which was set by the fire in winter, and was then called his winter-chair; and that it was carried out for him to the balcony in summer, and was then called his summer-chair.' Cibber could tell no more but 'That he remembered him a decent old man, arbiter of critical disputes at Will's.' You are to consider that Cibber was then at a great distance from Dryden, had perhaps one leg only in the room, and durst not draw in the other." BOSWELL. "Yet Cibber was a man of observation?" JOHNSON. "I think not." BOSWELL. "You will allow his 'Apology' to be well done." JOHNSON. "Very well done, to be sure, Sir. That book is a striking proof of the justice of Pope's remark:

'Each might his several province well command, Would all but stoop to what they understand.' ''

BOSWELL. "And his plays are good." JOHNSON. "Yes; but that was his trade; *l'esprit du corps;* he had been all his life among players and play-writers. I wondered that he had so little to say in conversation, for he had kept the best company, and learnt all that can be got by the ear. He abused Pindar° to me, and then showed me° an ode of his own, with an absurd couplet, making a linnet soar on an eagle's wing. I told him that when the ancients made a simile, they always made it like something real."

Mr. Wilkes remarked, that "among all the bold flights of Shakespeare's imagination, the boldest was making Birnamwood march to Dunsinane; creating a wood where there never was a shrub; a wood in Scotland! ha! ha! ha!" And he also observed, that "the clannish slavery of the Highlands of Scotland was the single exception to Milton's remark of 'The Mountain Nymph, sweet Liberty,' being worshipped in all hilly countries."—"When I was at Inverary (said he,) on a visit to my old friend Archibald, Duke of Argyle, his dependents congratulated me on being such a favorite of his Grace. I said, 'It is then, gentlemen, truly lucky for me; for if I had displeased the Duke, and he had wished it, there is not a Campbell° among you but would have been ready to bring John Wilkes's head to him in a charger. It would have been only

254 **Swinney,** Owen Swinney, former manager of Drury Lane, who died in 1754 **Cibber,** Colley Cibber (1671–1757), a popular actor-dramatist of the early eighteenth century   277 **Pindar,** a Greek lyric poet (522–443 B.C.), famous for his odes which he composed for the victors in athletic contests   278 **showed me.** Johnson had alluded to this episode in a conversation with Boswell at the Mitre Tavern, June 25, 1763. Pindar created superb word pictures, but Cibber's imitations were bombastic   295 **Campbell,** the Duke of Argyle, head of the Campbell clan

201 **irresistible.** 'Foote told me that Johnson said of him 'For loud obstreperous broad-faced mirth I know not his equal'"—Boswell's note   223 **small-beer,** weak beer   227 **Scrub,** a country servant in George Farquhar's *The Beaux' Stratagem* (1707)

'Off with his head! so much for *Aylesbury*.'°

I was then member for Aylesbury.'' . . .

300 Mr. Arthur Lee mentioned some Scotch who had taken possession of a barren part of America, and wondered why they should choose it. JOHNSON. "Why, Sir, all barrenness is comparative. The *Scotch* would not know it to be barren." BOSWELL. "Come, come, he is flattering the English. You have now been in Scotland, Sir, and say if you did not see meat and drink enough there." JOHNSON. "Why yes, Sir; meat and drink enough to give the inhabitants sufficient strength to run away from home." All these quick and 310 lively sallies were said sportively, quite in jest, and with a smile, which showed that he meant only wit. Upon this topic he and Mr. Wilkes could perfectly assimilate; here was a bond of union between them, and I was conscious that as both of them had visited Caledonia,° both were fully satisfied of the strange narrow ignorance of those who imagine that it is a land of famine. But they amused themselves with persevering in the old jokes. When I claimed a superiority for Scotland over England in one respect, that no man can 320 be arrested there for a debt merely because another swears it against him; but there must first be the judgment of a court of law ascertaining its justice; and that a seizure of the person, before judgment is obtained, can take place only, if his creditor should swear that he is about to fly from the country, or, as it is technically expressed, is *in meditatione fugæ*: WILKES. "That, I should think, may be safely sworn of all the Scotch nation." JOHNSON. (To Mr. Wilkes) "You must know, Sir, I lately took my friend Boswell, and showed him 330 genuine civilized life in an English provincial town. I turned him loose at Lichfield, my native city, that he might see for once real civility: for you know he lives among savages in Scotland, and among rakes in London." WILKES. "Except when he is with grave, sober, decent people, like you and me." JOHNSON. (smiling) "And we ashamed of him."

SECOND MEETING WITH WILKES (1781)

On Tuesday, May 8 [1781], I had the pleasure of again dining with him and Mr. Wilkes, at Mr. Dilly's. No *negotiation* was now required to bring them together; for Johnson was so well satisfied with the former interview, that he was very glad to meet Wilkes again, who was this day seated between Dr. Beattie° and Dr. Johnson; (between *Truth* and *Reason*, as General Paoli° said, when I told him of it.) WILKES. "I have been thinking, Dr. Johnson, that there should be a bill 10 brought into parliament that the controverted elections for Scotland should be tried in that country, at their own Abbey of Holy-Rood House, and not here; for the consequence of trying them here is, that we have an inundation of Scotchmen, who come up and never go back again. Now here is Boswell, who is come upon the election for his own county, which will not last a fortnight." JOHNSON. "Nay, Sir, I see no reason why they should be tried at all; for, you know, one Scotchman is as good as another." WILKES. "Pray, Boswell, how much may be got in a year by an Advocate at the 20 Scotch bar?" BOSWELL. "I believe, two thousand pounds." WILKES. "How can it be possible to spend that money in Scotland?" JOHNSON. "Why, Sir, the money may be spent in England; but there is a harder question. If one man in Scotland gets possession of two thousand pounds, what remains for all the rest of the nation?" WILKES. "You know, in the last war, the immense booty which Thurot carried off by the complete plunder of seven Scotch isles; he re-embarked with *three and six-pence*." Here again Johnson and 30 Wilkes joined in extravagant sportive raillery upon the supposed poverty of Scotland, which Dr. Beattie and I did not think it worth our while to dispute.

The subject of quotation being introduced, Mr. Wilkes censured it as pedantry. JOHNSON. "No, Sir, it is a good thing; there is a community of mind in it. Classical quotation is the *parole* of literary men all over the world." WILKES. "Upon the continent they all quote the vulgate Bible. Shakespeare is chiefly quoted here; and we quote also Pope, Prior, Butler, Waller, and 40 sometimes Cowley."

We talked of letter-writing. JOHNSON. "It is now become so much the fashion to publish letters, that, in order to avoid it, I put as little into mine as I can." BOSWELL. "Do what you will, Sir, you cannot avoid it. Should you even write as ill as you can, your letters would be published as curiosities:

'Behold a miracle! instead of wit,
See two dull lines with Stanhope's pencil writ.'''

He gave us an entertaining account of *Bet Flint*, a 50 woman of the town, who, with some eccentric talents and much effrontery, forced herself upon his acquaintance. "Bet (said he) wrote her own life in verse,° which she brought to me, wishing that I would furnish her with a preface to it. (Laughing.) I used to say of her, that she was generally slut and drunkard;—occasionally, whore and thief. She had, however, genteel lodgings, a spinnet on which she played, and a boy that walked before her chair. Poor Bet was taken up on a charge of stealing a counterpane, and tried at the Old 60 Bailey. Chief Justice——, who loved a wench, summed

298 **Aylesbury.** Wilkes was elected Member of Parliament from Aylesbury in 1757 and 1761. The quotation is a parody of a line in Cibber's adaptation of Shakespeare's *Richard III* 315 **Caledonia,** Scotland **Second Meeting with Wilkes** 6 **Dr. Beattie,** James Beattie (1735–1803), professor of moral philosophy at Aberdeen, and a poet 7 **General Paoli,** Pasquale Paoli (1725–1807), Corsican general, friend of Boswell

53 **verse.** "Johnson, whose memory was wonderfully retentive, remembered the first four lines of this curious production, which have been communicated to me by a young lady of his acquaintance: 'When first I drew my vital breath,/ A little minikin I came upon earth;/ And then I came from a dark abode,/ Into this gay and gaudy world.'"—Boswell's note

up favorably, and she was acquitted. After which, Bet said, with a gay and satisfied air, 'Now that the counterpane is *my own,* I shall make a petticoat of it.'"

THE ART OF CONVERSATION (1783)

Talking of conversation, he said, "There must, in the first place, be knowledge, there must be materials; in the second place, there must be a command of words; in the third place, there must be imagination, to place things in such views as they are not commonly seen in; and in the fourth place, there must be presence of mind, and a resolution that is not to be overcome by failures. This last is an essential requisite; for want of it many people do not excel in conversation. Now *I* want 10 it; I throw up the game upon losing a trick." I wondered to hear him talk thus of himself, and said, "I don't know, Sir, how this may be; but I am sure you beat other people's cards out of their hands." I doubt whether he heard this remark. While he went on talking triumphantly, I was fixed in admiration, and said to Mrs. Thrale, "Oh, for shorthand to take this down!" "You'll carry it all in your head," said she; "a long head is as good as shorthand."

It has been observed and wondered at, that Mr. 20 Charles Fox° never talked with any freedom in the presence of Dr. Johnson, though it is well known, and I myself can witness, that his conversation is various, fluent, and exceedingly agreeable. Johnson's own experience, however, of that gentleman's reserve was a sufficient reason for his going on thus: "Fox never talks in private company; not from any determination not to talk, but because he has not the first motion. A man who is used to the applause of the House of Commons has no wish for that of a private company. A 30 man accustomed to throw for a thousand pounds, if set down to throw for six-pence, would not be at the pains to count his dice. Burke's talk is the ebullition of his mind; he does not talk from a desire of distinction, but because his mind is full." . . .

KINDNESS (1783)

Johnson's love of little children, which he discovered° upon all occasions, calling them "pretty dears," and giving them sweetmeats, was an undoubted proof of the real humanity and gentleness of his disposition.

His uncommon kindness to his servants, and serious concern, not only for their comfort in this world, but their happiness in the next, was another unquestionable evidence of what all who were intimately acquainted with him knew to be true.

10 Nor would it be just, under this head, to omit the

The Art of Conversation   20 Mr. Charles Fox, an eminent English statesman and orator (1749–1806)   Kindness   1 discovered, uncovered, revealed

fondness which he showed for animals which he had taken under his protection. I never shall forget the indulgence with which he treated Hodge, his cat; for whom he himself used to go out and buy oysters, lest the servants having that trouble should take a dislike to the poor creature. I am, unluckily, one of those who have an antipathy to a cat, so that I am uneasy when in the room with one; and I own, I frequently suffered a good deal from the presence of this same Hodge. I recollect him one day scrambling up Dr. Johnson's breast, appa- 20 rently with much satisfaction, while my friend smiling and half-whistling, rubbed down his back, and pulled him by the tail; and when I observed he was a fine cat, saying, "Why yes, Sir, but I have had cats whom I liked better than this"; and then as if perceiving Hodge to be out of countenance, adding, "but he is a very fine cat, a very fine cat indeed."

This reminds me of the ludicrous account which he gave Mr. Langton, of the despicable state of a young gentleman of good family. "Sir, when I heard of him 30 last, he was running about town shooting cats." And then in a sort of kindly reverie, he bethought himself of his own favorite cat, and said, "But Hodge shan't be shot; no, no, Hodge shall not be shot." . . .

JOHNSON PREPARES FOR DEATH

My readers are now, at last, to behold Samuel Johnson preparing himself for that doom, from which the most exalted powers afford no exemption to man. Death had always been to him an object of terror; so that, though by no means happy, he still clung to life with an eagerness at which many have wondered. . . .

Dr. Heberden, Dr. Brocklesby, Dr. Warren, and Dr. Butter, physicians, generously attended him, without accepting of any fees, as did Mr. Cruikshank, surgeon; and all that could be done from professional skill and 10 ability, was tried, to prolong a life so truly valuable. He himself, indeed, having, on account of his very bad constitution, been perpetually applying himself to medical inquiries, united his own efforts with those of the gentlemen who attended him; and imagining that the dropsical collection of water which oppressed him might be drawn off by making incisions in his body, he, with his usual resolute defiance of pain, cut deep, when he thought that his surgeon had done it too tenderly.

About eight or ten days before his death, when Dr. 20 Brocklesby paid him his morning visit, he seemed very low and desponding, and said, "I have been as a dying man all night." He then emphatically broke out, in the words of Shakespeare:—

'Can'st thou not minister to a mind diseas'd;
Pluck from the memory a rooted sorrow;
Raze out the written troubles of the brain;
And, with some sweet oblivious antidote,

Cleanse the stuff'd bosom of that perilous stuff,
Which weighs upon the heart?'

To which Dr. Brocklesby readily answered, from the same great poet:—

'————————therein the patient
Must minister to himself.'

Johnson expressed himself much satisfied with the application. . . .

Amidst the melancholy clouds which hung over the dying Johnson, his characteristical manner showed itself on different occasions.

When Dr. Warren, in the usual style, hoped that he was better; his answer was, "No, Sir; you cannot conceive with what acceleration I advance towards death."

A man whom he had never seen before was employed one night to sit up with him. Being asked next morning how he liked his attendant, his answer was, "Not at all, Sir: the fellow's an idiot; he is as awkward as a turn-spit when first put into the wheel, and as sleepy as a dormouse."

Mr. Windham having placed a pillow conveniently to support him, he thanked him for his kindness, and said, "That will do,—all that a pillow can do." . . .

As he opened a note which his servant brought to him, he said, "An odd thought strikes me: we shall receive no letters in the grave."

He requested three things of Sir Joshua Reynolds:—To forgive him thirty pounds which he had borrowed of him; to read the Bible; and never to use his pencil on a Sunday. Sir Joshua readily acquiesced.

Indeed he showed the greatest anxiety for the religious improvement of his friends, to whom he discoursed of its infinite consequence. He begged of Mr. Hoole to think of what he had said, and to commit it to writing: and, upon being afterwards assured that this was done, pressed his hands, and in an earnest tone thanked him. Dr. Brocklesby having attended him with the utmost assiduity and kindness as his physician and friend, he was peculiarly desirous that this gentleman should not entertain any loose speculative notions, but be confirmed in the truths of Christianity, and insisted on his writing down in his presence, as nearly as he could collect it, the import of what passed on the subject: and Dr. Brocklesby having complied with the request, he made him sign the paper, and urged him to keep it in his own custody as long as he lived.

Johnson, with that native fortitude, which, amidst all his bodily distress and mental sufferings, never forsook him, asked Dr. Brocklesby, as a man in whom he had confidence, to tell him plainly whether he could recover. "Give me (said he,) a direct answer." The Doctor having first asked him if he could bear the whole truth, which way soever it might lead, and being answered that he could, declared that, in his opinion, he could not recover without a miracle. "Then, (said Johnson,) I will take no more physick, not even my opiates; for I have prayed that I may render up my soul to God unclouded." In this resolution he persevered, and, at the same time, used only the weakest kinds of sustenance. Being pressed by Mr. Windham to take somewhat more generous nourishment, lest too low a diet should have the very effect which he dreaded, by debilitating his mind, he said, "I will take any thing but inebriating sustenance."

The Reverend Mr. Strahan, who was the son of his friend, and had been always one of his great favorites, had, during his last illness, the satisfaction of contributing to soothe and comfort him. That gentleman's house, at Islington, of which he is Vicar, afforded Johnson, occasionally and easily, an agreeable change of place and fresh air; and he attended also upon him in town in the discharge of the sacred offices of his profession.

Mr. Strahan has given me the agreeable assurance, that, after being in much agitation, Johnson became quite composed, and continued so till his death.

Dr. Brocklesby, who will not be suspected of fanaticism, obliged me with the following accounts:—

"For some time before his death, all his fears were calmed and absorbed by the prevalence of his faith, and his trust in the merits and *propitiation* of JESUS CHRIST."

Johnson having thus in his mind the true Christian scheme, at once rational and consolatory, uniting justice and mercy in the DIVINITY, with the improvement of human nature, previous to his receiving the Holy Sacrament in his apartment, composed and fervently uttered this prayer:—

"Almighty and most merciful Father, I am now, as to human eyes, it seems, about to commemorate, for the last time, the death of thy Son JESUS CHRIST, our Saviour and Redeemer. Grant, O LORD, that my whole hope and confidence may be in his merits, and thy mercy; enforce and accept my imperfect repentance; make this commemoration available to the confirmation of my faith, the establishment of my hope, and the enlargement of my charity; and make the death of thy Son JESUS CHRIST effectual to my redemption. Have mercy upon me, and pardon the multitude of my offences. Bless my friends; have mercy upon all men. Support me, by thy Holy Spirit, in the days of weakness, and at the hour of death; and receive me, at my death, to everlasting happiness, for the sake of JESUS CHRIST. Amen."

Having . . . made his will on the 8th and 9th of December, and settled all his worldly affairs, he languished till Monday, the 13th of that month, when he expired, about seven o'clock in the evening, with so little apparent pain that his attendants hardly perceived when his dissolution took place.

A few days before his death, he had asked Sir John Hawkins, as one of his executors, where he should be buried; and on being answered, "Doubtless, in Westminster Abbey," seemed to feel a satisfaction, very natural to a poet; and indeed in my opinion very natural to every man of any imagination, who has no family sepulcher in which he can be laid with his fathers. Accordingly, upon Monday, December 20, his remains were deposited in that noble and renowned
10 edifice; and over his grave was placed a large blue flag-stone, with this inscription:

SAMUEL JOHNSON, LL.D.
Obiit XIII *die Decembris,*
Anno Domini
M.DCC.LXXXIV.
Aetatis suae LXXV.

His funeral was attended by a respectable number of his friends, particularly such of the members of the Literary Club° as were then in town; and was also hon-ored with the presence of several of the Reverend 20 Chapter of Westminster. Mr. Burke, Sir Joseph Banks, Mr. Windham, Mr. Langton, Sir Charles Bun-bury, and Mr. Colman, bore his pall. His school-fellow, Dr. Taylor, performed the mournful office of reading the burial service.

I trust, I shall not be accused of affectation, when I declare, that I find myself unable to express all that I felt upon the loss of such a "guide, philosopher, and friend."° I shall, therefore, not say one word of my own, but adopt those of an eminent friend, which he 30 uttered with an abrupt felicity, superior to all studied compositions: "He has made a chasm, which not only nothing can fill up, but which nothing has a tendency to fill up.—Johnson is dead.—Let us go to the next best:—there is nobody; no man can be said to put you in mind of Johnson." . . .

(1791)

Johnson's Funeral 19 **Literary Club,** Johnson's famous Circle, which included among others Reynolds, Burke, Garrick, Goldsmith, Boswell, and Gibbon the historian (1737–1794) 28–29 **guide . . . friend.** Cf. Pope's *Essay on Man,* IV, 390 ff.: "Shall then this verse to future age pretend / Thou wert my guide, philosopher, and friend? / That, urged by thee, I turned the tuneful art / From sounds to things, from fancy to the heart"

JAMES THOMSON
1700–1748

James Thomson was born in the parish of Ednam, Roxburghshire, Scotland. He went to Edinburgh University, and he wrote verse at an early age. Like most ambitious writers of the day, he went to London, where he shifted his interest in religious matters—in which his minister father had encouraged him—to literary pursuits.

Winter, his first important work, was brought to successful publication within a year after his introduction to London (1726). During the two years following he wrote *Summer, Spring,* and other poems, and produced the tragedy *Sophonisba. Autumn,* completing *The Seasons* in 1730, was followed in 1734 by his long poem *Liberty.*

Thomson was appointed Secretary of the Briefs, an obvious sinecure, in 1733. In 1737, the Prince of Wales, assessing his state of affairs to be "in a more poetic posture than formerly," granted Thomson a pension; thus, he was "obliged to write." During the years from 1738 to 1744 came the world-famous *Rule, Britannia!* and four plays. The dramas received only mixed approval. *The Castle of Indolence,* Thomson's last work, had its beginnings in a little piece by Thomson in which he joked at his own laziness; it became a very extensive piece of poetry and the finest of the many imitations of Spenser, which were in fashion at the time.

from THE SEASONS°

from WINTER

See, winter comes to rule the varied year,
Sullen and sad, with all his rising train—
Vapors, and clouds, and storms. Be these my theme;
These, that exalt the soul to solemn thought
And heavenly musing. Welcome, kindred glooms!
Cogenial horrors, hail! With frequent foot,
Pleased have I, in my cheerful morn of life,
When nursed by careless solitude I lived
And sung of nature with unceasing joy,

The Seasons. The four parts of *The Seasons* were first published separately in this order: Winter (1726), Summer (1727), Spring (1728), and Autumn (1730). They were later combined in logical order and republished several times with many additions and revisions. Thomson chose to write *The Seasons* in blank verse modeled after that of Milton rather than the closed couplets of Pope and thus helped to reintroduce blank verse as an important poetic medium

10 Pleased have I wandered through your rough domain;
   Trod the pure virgin-snows, myself as pure;
   Heard the winds roar, and the big torrent burst;
   Or seen the deep-fermenting tempest brewed
   In the grim evening-sky. Thus passed the time,
   Till through the lucid chambers of the south
   Looked out the joyous Spring—looked out and smiled.

     To thee, the patron of this first essay,
   The muse, O Wilmington!° renews her song.
   Since has she rounded the revolving year:
20 Skimmed the gay spring; on eagle-pinions borne,
   Attempted through the summer-blaze to rise;
   Then swept o'er autumn with the shadowy gale.
   And now among the wintry clouds again,
   Rolled in the doubling storm, she tries to soar,
   To swell her note with all the rushing winds,
   To suit her sounding cadence to the floods;
   As is her theme, her numbers wildly great.
   Thrice happy, could she fill thy judging ear
   With bold description and with manly thought!
30 Nor art thou skilled in awful schemes alone,
   And how to make a mighty people thrive;
   But equal goodness, sound integrity,
   A firm, unshaken, uncorrupted soul
   Amid a sliding age, and burning strong,
   Not vainly blazing, for thy country's weal,
   A steady spirit, regularly free—
   These, each exalting each, the statesman light
   Into the patriot; these, the public hope
   And eye to thee converting, bid the Muse
40 Record what envy dares not flattery call.

     Now, when the cheerless empire of the sky
   To Capricorn the Centaur-Archer° yields,
   And fierce Aquarius stains the inverted year—°
   Hung o'er that farthest verge of heaven, the sun
   Scarce spreads o'er ether° the dejected day.
   Faint are his gleams, and ineffectual shoot
   His struggling rays in horizontal lines
   Through the thick air; as clothed in cloudy storm,
   Weak, wan, and broad, he skirts the southern sky;
50 And, soon descending, to the long dark night,
   Wide-shading all, the prostrate world resigns.
   Nor is the night unwished; while vital heat,
   Light, life, and joy the dubious day forsake.
   Meantime, in sable cincture, shadows vast,
   Deep-tinged and damp, and congregated clouds,
   And all the vapory turbulence of heaven
   Involve the face of things. Thus winter falls,
   A heavy gloom oppressive o'er the world,
   Through nature shedding influence malign,

And rouses up the seeds of dark disease. 60
The soul of man dies in him, loathing life,
And black with more than melancholy views.
The cattle droop; and o'er the furrowed land,
Fresh from the plow, the dun discolored flocks,
Untended spreading, crop the wholesome root.
Along the woods, along the moorish fens,
Sighs the sad genius of the coming storm;
And up among the loose disjointed cliffs
And fractured mountains wild, the brawling brook
And cave, presageful, send a hollow moan, 70
Resounding long in listening fancy's ear.

   Then comes the father of the tempest forth,
Wrapped in black glooms. First, joyless rains obscure
Drive through the mingling skies with vapor foul,
Dash on the mountain's brow, and shake the woods
That grumbling wave below. The unsightly plain
Lies a brown deluge; as the low-bent clouds
Pour flood on flood, yet unexhausted still
Combine, and, deepening into night, shut up
The day's fair face. The wanderers of heaven, 80
Each to his home, retire; save those that love
To take their pastime in the troubled air,
Or skimming flutter round the dimply pool.
The cattle from the untasted fields return
And ask, with meaning low, their wonted stalls,
Or ruminate in the contiguous shade.
Thither the household feathery people crowd,
The crested cock, with all his female train,
Pensive and dripping; while the cottage-hind°
Hangs o'er the enlivening blaze, and taleful there 90
Recounts his simple frolic: much he talks,
And much he laughs, nor recks the storm that blows
Without, and rattles on his humble roof.

   Wide o'er the brim, with many a torrent swelled,
And the mixed ruin of its banks o'erspread,
At last the roused-up river pours along;
Resistless, roaring, dreadful, down it comes,
From the rude mountain and the mossy wild,
Tumbling through rocks abrupt, and sounding far;
Then o'er the sanded valley floating spreads, 100
Calm, sluggish, silent; till again, constrained
Between two meeting hills, it bursts a way
Where rocks and woods o'erhang the turbid stream;
There, gathering triple force, rapid and deep,
It boils, and wheels, and foams, and thunders through.

   Nature! great parent! whose unceasing hand
Rolls round the seasons of the changeful year,
How mighty, how majestic are thy works!
With what a pleasing dread they swell the soul,
That sees astonished, and astonished sings! 110
Ye too, ye winds! that now begin to blow
With boisterous sweep, I raise my voice to you.

Winter   **18 Wilmington.** *Winter* was dedicated to Sir Spencer Compton
(1673?–1743), later Earl of Wilmington   **42 Capricorn . . . Centaur-Archer,** two
constellations of the zodiac. When the sun passes from one constellation to the
next, the first is said to "yield" to the second. *Centaur-Archer* is Sagittarius. The
sun leaves Sagittarius about December 21, entering the sign of Capricorn (the
Goat); a month later it enters the sign of Aquarius (the Waterbearer)   **43 inverted year,** probably in the figurative sense of "upset" or "overthrown"; possibly
in the sense of "changed to the new (year)"   **45 ether,** in the general sense of
"the heavens"

89 cottage-hind, peasant in a cottage

Where are your stores, ye powerful beings! say,
Where your aërial magazines° reserved
To swell the brooding terrors of the storm?
In what far-distant region of the sky,
Hushed in deep silence, sleep you when 'tis calm?

When from the pallid sky the sun descends,
With many a spot, that o'er his glaring orb
120 Uncertain wanders, stained; red fiery streaks
Begin to flush around. The reeling clouds
Stagger with dizzy poise, as doubting yet
Which master to obey; while, rising slow,
Blank in the leaden-colored east, the moon
Wears a wan circle round her blunted horns.
Seen through the turbid, fluctuating air,
The stars obtuse° emit a shivering ray;
Or frequent seem to shoot athwart the gloom,
And long behind them trail the whitening blaze.
130 Snatched in short eddies, plays the withered leaf;
And on the flood the dancing feather floats.
With broadened nostrils to the sky upturned,
The conscious heifer snuffs the stormy gale.
E'en as the matron, at her nightly task,
With pensive labor draws the flaxen thread,
The wasted taper and the crackling flame
Foretell the blast. But chief the plumy race,
The tenants of the sky, its changes speak.
Retiring from the downs,° where all day long
140 They picked their scanty fare, a blackening train
Of clamorous rooks thick-urge their weary flight,
And seek the closing shelter of the grove.
Assiduous, in his bower, the wailing owl
Plies his sad song. The cormorant on high
Wheels from the deep, and screams along the land.
Loud shrieks the soaring hern;° and with wild wing
The circling sea-fowl cleave the flaky clouds.
Ocean, unequal pressed, with broken tide
And blind commotion heaves; while from the shore,
150 Eat into caverns by the restless wave,
And forest-rustling mountain comes a voice
That, solemn-sounding, bids the world prepare.
Then issues forth the storm with sudden burst,
And hurls the whole precipitated air
Down in a torrent. On the passive main
Descends the ethereal° force, and with strong gust
Turns from its bottom the discolored deep.
Through the black night that sits immense around,
Lashed into foam, the fierce-conflicting brine
160 Seems o'er a thousand raging waves to burn.
Meantime the mountain-billows, to the clouds
In dreadful tumult swelled, surge above surge,
Burst into chaos with tremendous roar,
And anchored navies from their stations drive
Wild as the winds, across the howling waste
Of mighty waters; now the inflated wave

Straining they scale, and now impetuous shoot
Into the secret chambers of the deep,
The wintry Baltic thundering o'er their head.
Emerging thence again, before the breath   170
Of full-exerted heaven they wing their course,
And dart on distant coasts—if some sharp rock
Or shoal insidious break not their career,°
And in loose fragments fling them floating round.

Nor less at land the loosened tempest reigns.
The mountain thunders, and its sturdy sons
Stoop to the bottom of the rocks they shade.
Lone on the midnight steep, and all aghast,
The dark wayfaring stranger breathless toils,
And, often falling, climbs against the blast.   180
Low waves the rooted forest, vexed, and sheds
What of its tarnished honors yet remain—
Dashed down and scattered, by the tearing wind's
Assiduous fury, its gigantic limbs.
Thus struggling through the dissipated grove,
The whirling tempest raves along the plain;
And, on the cottage thatched or lordly roof
Keen-fastening, shakes them to the solid base.
Sleep frighted flies; and round the rocking dome,
For entrance eager, howls the savage blast.   190
Then too, they say, through all the burdened air
Long groans are heard, shrill sounds, and distant
    sighs,
That, uttered by the demon of the night,
Warn the devoted wretch of woe and death.

Huge uproar lords it wide. The clouds, commixed
With stars swift-gliding, sweep along the sky.
All nature reels: till nature's king, who oft
Amid tempestuous darkness dwells alone,
And on the wings of the careering wind
Walks dreadfully serene, commands a calm;   200
Then straight air, sea, and earth are hushed at once.

As yet 'tis midnight deep. The weary clouds,
Slow-meeting, mingle into solid gloom.
Now, while the drowsy world lies lost in sleep,
Let me associate with the serious night,
And contemplation, her sedate compeer;
Let me shake off the intrusive cares of day,
And lay the meddling senses all aside.

Where now, ye lying vanities of life!
Ye ever-tempting, ever-cheating train!   210
Where are you now? and what is your amount?
Vexation, disappointment, and remorse.
Sad, sickening thought! and yet deluded man,
A scene of crude disjointed visions past,
And broken slumbers, rises still resolved,
With new-flushed hopes, to run the giddy round.

114 **magazines,** places for keeping something; specifically, storehouses for the
storms and thunders of heaven   127 **obtuse,** blunted, dulled in light
139 **downs,** treeless chalk uplands   146 **hern,** heron   156 **ethereal,** from the
heavens

173 **career,** wild flight

Father of light and life! thou Good Supreme!
O teach me what is good! teach me Thyself!
Save me from folly, vanity, and vice,
220 From every low pursuit; and feed my soul
With knowledge, conscious peace, and virtue pure—
Sacred, substantial, never-fading bliss!

The keener tempests come; and, fuming dun
From all the livid east or piercing north,
Thick clouds ascend, in whose capacious womb
A vapory deluge lies, to snow congealed.
Heavy they roll their fleecy world along,
And the sky saddens° with the gathered storm.
Through the hushed air the whitening shower
    descends,
230 At first thin-wavering; till at last the flakes
Fall broad and wide and fast, dimming the day
With a continual flow. The cherished fields
Put on their winter-robe of purest white.
'Tis brightness all; save where the new snow melts
Along the mazy current. Low the woods
Bow their hoar head; and, ere the languid sun
Faint from the west emits his evening ray,
Earth's universal face, deep-hid and chill,
Is one wild dazzling waste, that buries wide
240 The works of man. Drooping, the laborer-ox
Stands covered o'er with snow, and then demands
The fruit of all his toil. The fowls of heaven,
Tamed by the cruel season, crowd around
The winnowing store, and claim the little boon
Which Providence assigns them. One alone,
The redbreast, sacred to the household gods,
Wisely regardful of the embroiling sky,
In joyless fields and thorny thickets leaves
His shivering mates, and pays to trusted man
250 His annual visit. Half afraid, he first
Against the window beats; then brisk alights
On the warm hearth; then, hopping o'er the floor,
Eyes all the smiling family askance,
And pecks, and starts, and wonders where he is—
Till, more familiar grown, the table-crumbs
Attract his slender feet. The foodless wilds
Pour forth their brown inhabitants. The hare,
Though timorous of heart, and hard beset
By death in various forms, dark snares, and dogs,
260 And more unpitying men, the garden seeks,
Urged on by fearless want. The bleating kind°
Eye the bleak heaven, and next the glistening earth,
With looks of dumb despair; then, sad-dispersed,
Dig for the withered herb through heaps of snow.

Now, shepherds, to your helpless charge be kind;
Baffle the raging year, and fill their pens
With food at will; lodge them below the storm,
And watch them strict; for, from the bellowing east,
In this dire season, oft the whirlwind's wing

Sweeps up the burden of whole wintry plains   270
In one wide waft, and o'er the hapless flocks,
Hid in the hollow of two neighboring hills,
The billowy tempest whelms; till, upward urged,
The valley to a shining mountain swells,
Tipped with a wreath high-curling in the sky.

As thus the snows arise, and, foul and fierce,
All winter drives along the darkened air,
In his own loose-revolving fields the swain
Disastered stands; sees other hills ascend,
Of unknown joyless brow; and other scenes,   280
Of horrid prospect, shag the trackless plain;
Nor finds the river nor the forest hid
Beneath the formless wild; but wanders on
From hill to dale, still more and more astray—
Impatient flouncing through the drifted heaps,
Stung with the thoughts of home: the thoughts of home
Rust on his nerves and call their vigor forth
In many a vain attempt. How sinks his soul!
What black despair, what horror fills his heart,
When, for the dusky spot which fancy feigned   290
His tufted cottage rising through the snow,
He meets the roughness of the middle waste,
Far from the track and blest abode of man;
While round him night resistless closes fast,
And every tempest, howling o'er his head,
Renders the savage wilderness more wild.
Then throng the busy shapes into his mind
Of covered pits, unfathomably deep,
A dire descent! beyond the power of frost;
Of faithless bogs; of precipices huge,   300
Smoothed up with snow; and (what is land unknown,
What water) of the still unfrozen spring,
In the loose marsh or solitary lake,
Where the fresh fountain from the bottom boils.
These check his fearful steps; and down he sinks
Beneath the shelter of the shapeless drift,
Thinking o'er all the bitterness of death,
Mixed with the tender anguish nature shoots
Through the wrung bosom of the dying man—
His wife, his children, and his friends unseen.   310
In vain for him the officious° wife prepares
The fire fair-blazing and the vestment warm;
In vain his little children, peeping out
Into the mingling storm, demand their sire
With tears of artless innocence. Alas!
Nor wife nor children more shall he behold,
Nor friends, nor sacred home. On every nerve
The deadly winter seizes, shuts up sense,
And, o'er his inmost vitals creeping cold,
Lays him along the snows a stiffened corse,   320
Stretched out, and bleaching in the northern blast.

Ah! little think the gay licentious proud,
Whom pleasure, power, and affluence surround—

---

228 **saddens,** grows dark and heavy   261 **bleating kind,** sheep   311 **officious,** busy with duties

They, who their thoughtless hours in giddy mirth,
And wanton, often cruel, riot waste—
Ah! little think they, while they dance along,
How many feel, this very moment, death
And all the sad variety of pain;
How many sink in the devouring flood,
330 Or more devouring flame; how many bleed,
By shameful variance betwixt man and man;
How many pine in want, and dungeon-glooms,
Shut from the common air and common use
Of their own limbs; how many drink the cup
Of baleful grief, or eat the bitter bread
Of misery; sore pierced by wintry winds,
How many shrink into the sordid hut
Of cheerless poverty; how many shake
With all the fiercer tortures of the mind,
340 Unbounded passion, madness, guilt, remorse—
Whence, tumbled headlong from the height of life,
They furnish matter for the tragic muse;
Even in the vale, where wisdom loves to dwell,
With friendship, peace, and contemplation joined,
How many, racked with honest passions, droop
In deep retired distress; how many stand
Around the death-bed of their dearest friends,
And point the parting anguish! Thought fond man
Of these, and all the thousand nameless ills
350 That one incessant struggle render life,
One scene of toil, of suffering, and of fate,
Vice in his high career would stand appalled,
And heedless rambling impulse learn to think;
The conscious heart of charity would warm,
And her wide wish benevolence dilate;
The social tear would rise, the social sigh;
And, into clear perfection, gradual bliss,
Refining still, the social passions work.

And here can I forget the generous band°
360 Who, touched with human woe, redressive searched
Into the horrors of the gloomy jail?
Unpitied and unheard where misery moans,
Where sickness pines, where thirst and hunger burn,
And poor misfortune feels the lash of vice;
While in the land of liberty—the land
Whose every street and public meeting glow
With open freedom—little tyrants raged,
Snatched the lean morsel from the starving mouth,
Tore from cold wintry limbs the tattered weed,
370 E'en robbed them of the last of comforts, sleep,
The free-born Briton to the dungeon chained
Or, as the lust of cruelty prevailed,
At pleasure marked him with inglorious stripes,
And crushed out lives, by secret barbarous ways,
That for their country would have toiled or bled.
O great design! if executed well,
With patient care and wisdom-tempered zeal.
Ye sons of mercy! yet resume the search;

Drag forth the legal monsters into light,
Wrench from their hands oppression's iron rod,   380
And bid the cruel feel the pains they give.
Much still untouched remains; in this rank age,
Much is the patriot's weeding hand required.
The toils of law—what dark insidious men
Have cumbrous added to perplex the truth
And lengthen simple justice into trade—
How glorious were the day that saw these broke,
And every man within the reach of right! . . .
(1726; 1730)

RULE, BRITANNIA!

When Britain first, at Heaven's command,
    Arose from out the azure main,
This was the charter of the land,
    And guardian angels sung this strain—
        "Rule, Britannia, rule the waves;
        Britons never will be slaves."

The nations, not so blessed as thee,
    Must in their turns to tyrants fall;
While thou shalt flourish great and free,
    The dread and envy of them all.   10
        "Rule, Britannia, rule the waves;
        Britons never will be slaves."

Still more majestic shalt thou rise,
    More dreadful from each foreign stroke;
As the loud blast that tears the skies
    Serves but to root thy native oak.°
        "Rule," etc.

Thee haughty tyrants ne'er shall tame;
    All their attempts to bend thee down
Will but arouse thy generous flame,   20
    But work their woe and thy renown.
        "Rule," etc.

To thee belongs the rural reign;
    Thy cities shall with commerce shine;
All thine shall be the subject main,
    And every shore it circles thine.
        "Rule," etc.

The Muses, still with freedom found,
    Shall to thy happy coast repair;
Blessed isle! with matchless beauty crowned,   30
    And manly hearts to guard the fair.
        "Rule, Britannia, rule the waves;
        Britons never will be slaves."
(1740)

---

359 **generous band,** a committee appointed in 1729 to investigate the conditions of jails and prisons

Rule Britannia! 16 **oak,** from which were built the famous British men-of-war of the eighteenth century; also a symbol for the bravery of English seamen

THOMAS GRAY
1716–1771

The only one of a family of twelve children to survive infancy, Thomas Gray was born into a solid but unhappy home in London in 1716. His mother operated a shop in order to educate him. At the age of eight he was sent to Eton, where he formed two firm friendships—with Richard West, son of the Lord Chancellor of Ireland, and with Horace Walpole, son of the prime minister, Robert Walpole. From Eton, Gray proceeded to Cambridge, where he wrote good Latin verse. He left in 1738 without taking a degree and set out in 1739 with Robert Walpole on a long tour of the Continent. After a quarrel between the two, Gray returned to England in 1742, settled at Cambridge, and became a bachelor of civil law. Gray and Walpole, however, were later reconciled and remained friends for the rest of their lives.

In 1742 West died at the age of twenty-six; his death affected Gray deeply. It is thought by some scholars that Gray's melancholy over the death of his friend influenced his *Ode on a Distant Prospect of Eton College* and some of the stanzas of *Elegy Written in a*

Country Churchyard. The *Elegy*, published in 1751, was an instantaneous and overwhelming success. Dr. Johnson said that the *Elegy* "abounds with images which find a mirror in every mind, and with sentiments to which every bosom returns an echo." It has long been one of the most well-known and most popular poems in the English language. During the next twelve years, Gray quietly continued to write poetry: *The Progress of Poesy* and *The Bard* appeared in 1757; *The Fatal Sisters* and *The Descent of Odin*, in 1761. In the last of these poems, Gray was motivated by his strong interest and expertise in Norse and Celtic legends. Gray's health, always fragile, prompted him in 1765 to visit Scotland; he kept a lively account of his impressions during the trip. He came back to Cambridge to accept a professorship in modern history. Having suffered severely from gout, he died in 1771 and was buried in the country churchyard at Stoke Poges, Buckinghamshire, made famous in his *Elegy*.

ODE ON A DISTANT PROSPECT OF ETON COLLEGE°

Ye distant spires, ye antique towers,
  That crown the watery glade,
Where grateful Science still adores
  Her Henry's° holy shade;
And ye, that from the stately brow
Of Windsor's heights the expanse below
  Of grove, of lawn, of mead survey,
Whose turf, whose shade, whose flowers among
Wanders the hoary Thames along
10   His silver-winding way.

Ah, happy hills, ah, pleasing shade,
  Ah, fields beloved in vain,
Where once my careless childhood strayed.
  A stranger yet to pain!
I feel the gales, that from ye blow,
A momentary bliss bestow,
  As waving fresh their gladsome wing
My weary soul they seem to soothe,
And, redolent of joy and youth,
20   To breathe a second spring.

Say, Father Thames, for thou hast seen
  Full many a sprightly race
Disporting on thy margent° green
  The paths of pleasure trace,
Who foremost now delight to cleave
With pliant arm thy glassy wave?
  The captive linnet which enthral?
What idle progeny succeed
To chase the rolling circle's° speed,
  Or urge the flying ball?   30

While some on earnest business bent
  Their murmuring labors ply
Gainst graver hours, that bring constraint
  To sweeten liberty;
Some bold adventurers disdain
The limits of their little reign,
  And unknown regions dare descry;
Still as they run they look behind,
They hear a voice in every wind,
  And snatch a fearful joy.   40

Gay hope is theirs by fancy fed,

Eton College. Eton College, founded by King Henry VI in 1440, is situated in the valley of the Thames about twenty miles west of London. Windsor Castle stands on an eminence in the city of Windsor on the opposite side of the river. The college is also near the village of Stoke Poges, where Gray was living when he wrote this poem, shortly after the death of Richard West, his closest friend   **4 Her Henry,** Henry VI, who founded Eton College in 1440

23 **margent,** margin, bank   29 **rolling circle, etc.** The rolling circle is the hoop used in the game of rolling hoops. The flying ball (l. 30) is the cricket ball

Less pleasing when possessed;
The tear forgot as soon as shed,
  The sunshine of the breast;
Theirs buxom health of rosy hue,
Wild wit, invention ever-new,
  And lively cheer of vigor born;
The thoughtless day, the easy night,
The spirits pure, the slumbers light,
50 That fly the approach of morn.

Alas, regardless of their doom,
  The little victims play!
No sense have they of ills to come,
  Nor care beyond today;
Yet see how all around 'em wait
The ministers of human Fate,
  And black Misfortune's baleful train!
Ah, show them where in ambush stand,
To seize their prey, the murtherous band!
60 Ah, tell them they are men!

These shall the fury Passions tear,
  The vultures of the mind,
Disdainful Anger, pallid Fear,
  And Shame that skulks behind;
Or pining Love shall waste their youth,
Or Jealousy with rankling tooth,
  That inly gnaws the secret heart,
And Envy wan, and faded Care,
Grim-visaged comfortless Despair,
70 And Sorrow's piercing dart.

Ambition this shall tempt to rise,
  Then whirl the wretch from high,
To bitter Scorn a sacrifice,
  And grinning Infamy.
The stings of Falsehood those shall try,
And hard Unkindness' altered eye,
  That mocks the tear it forced to flow;
And keen Remorse with blood defiled,
And moody Madness laughing wild
80 Amid severest woe.

Lo! in the vale of years beneath
  A grisly troop are seen,
The painful family of Death,
  More hideous than their queen.
This racks the joints, this fires the veins,
That every laboring sinew strains,
  Those in the deeper vitals rage;
Lo, Poverty, to fill the band,
That numbs the soul with icy hand,
90 And slow-consuming Age.

To each his sufferings; all are men,
  Condemned alike to groan,
The tender for another's pain,
  The unfeeling for his own.

Yet ah! why should they know their fate?
Since sorrow never comes too late,
  And happiness too swiftly flies,
Thought would destroy their paradise.
No more; where ignorance is bliss,
  Tis folly to be wise.   100
(1742; 1747)

ELEGY WRITTEN
IN A COUNTRY CHURCHYARD

The curfew tolls the knell of parting day,
  The lowing herd wind slowly o'er the lea,
The plowman homeward plods his weary way,
  And leaves the world to darkness and to me.

Now fades the glimmering landscape on the sight,
  And all the air a solemn stillness holds,
Save where the beetle wheels his droning flight,
  And drowsy tinklings lull the distant folds;

Save that from yonder ivy-mantled tower
  The moping owl does to the moon complain   10
Of such as, wandering near her secret bower,
  Molest her ancient solitary reign.

Beneath those rugged elms, that yew-tree's shade,
  Where heaves the turf in many a moldering heap,
Each in his narrow cell forever laid,
  The rude forefathers of the hamlet sleep.

The breezy call of incense-breathing Morn,
  The swallow twittering from the straw-built shed,
The cock's shrill clarion, or the echoing horn,°
  No more shall rouse them from their lowly bed.   20

For them no more the blazing hearth shall burn,
  Or busy housewife ply her evening care;
No children run to lisp their sire's return,
  Or climb his knees the envied kiss to share.

Oft did the harvest to their sickle yield,
  Their furrow oft the stubborn glebe° has broke;
How jocund did they drive their team afield!
  How bowed the woods beneath their sturdy stroke!

Let not Ambition mock their useful toil,
  Their homely joys, and destiny obscure;   30
Nor Grandeur hear, with a disdainful smile,
  The short and simple annals of the poor.

The boast of heraldry, the pomp of power,
  And all that beauty, all that wealth e'er gave,
Awaits alike the inevitable hour:
  The paths of glory lead but to the grave.

Elegy   19 horn, the huntsman's horn   26 glebe, the sod in cultivated ground

Nor you, ye proud, impute to these the fault,
   If Memory o'er their tomb no trophies raise,
Where through the long-drawn aisle and fretted vault
40   The pealing anthem swells the note of praise.

Can storied urn° or animated° bust
   Back to its mansion call the fleeting breath?
Can Honor's voice provoke the silent dust,
   Or Flattery soothe the dull cold ear of Death?

Perhaps in this neglected spot is laid
   Some heart once pregnant with celestial fire;
Hands that the rod of empire might have swayed,
   Or waked to ecstasy the living lyre.

But Knowledge to their eyes her ample page
50   Rich with the spoils of time did ne'er unroll;
Chill Penury repressed their noble rage,
   And froze the genial current of the soul.

Full many a gem of purest ray serene
   The dark unfathomed caves of ocean bear;
Full many a flower is born to blush unseen,
   And waste its sweetness on the desert air.

Some village Hampden° that with dauntless breast
   The little tyrant of his fields withstood;
Some mute inglorious Milton° here may rest,
60   Some Cromwell° guiltless of his country's blood.

The applause of listening senates to command,
   The threats of pain and ruin to despise,
To scatter plenty o'er a smiling land,
   And read their history in a nation's eyes,

Their lot forbade; nor circumscribed alone
   Their growing virtues, but their crimes confined;
Forbade to wade through slaughter to a throne,
   And shut the gates of mercy on mankind,

The struggling pangs of conscious truth to hide,
70   To quench the blushes of ingenuous shame,
Or heap the shrine of Luxury and Pride
   With incense kindled at the Muse's flame.

Far from the madding crowd's ignoble strife,
   Their sober wishes never learned to stray;
Along the cool sequestered vale of life
   They kept the noiseless tenor of their way.

Yet ev'n these bones from insult to protect
   Some frail memorial still erected nigh,

With uncouth° rimes and shapeless sculpture decked,
   Implores the passing tribute of a sigh.   80

Their name, their years, spelt by the unlettered Muse,
   The place of fame and elegy supply;
And many a holy text around she strews,
   That teach the rustic moralist to die.

For who, to dumb Forgetfulness a prey,
   This pleasing anxious being e'er resigned,
Left the warm precincts of the cheerful day,
   Nor cast one longing, lingering look behind?

On some fond breast the parting soul relies,
   Some pious drops the closing eye requires;   90
Ev'n from the tomb the voice of Nature cries,
   Ev'n in our ashes live their wonted fires.

For thee,° who mindful of the unhonored dead
   Dost in these lines their artless tale relate;
If chance, by lonely Contemplation led,
   Some kindred spirit shall inquire thy fate,

Haply some hoary-headed swain may say,
   "Oft have we seen him at the peep of dawn
Brushing with hasty steps the dews away
   To meet the sun upon the upland lawn.   100

"There at the foot of yonder nodding beech,
   That wreathes its old fantastic roots so high,
His listless length at noontide would he stretch,
   And pore upon the brook that babbles by.

"Hard by yon wood, now smiling as in scorn,
   Muttering his wayward fancies he would rove,
Now drooping, woeful wan, like one forlorn,
   Or crazed with care, or crossed in hopeless love.

"One morn I missed him on the customed hill,
   Along the heath, and near his favorite tree;   110
Another came; nor yet beside the rill,
   Nor up the lawn, nor at the wood was he;

"The next with dirges due in sad array
   Slow through the church-way path we saw him
     borne.
Approach and read (for thou canst read) the lay,
   Graved on the stone beneath yon aged thorn."°

THE EPITAPH

Here rests his head upon the lap of Earth
   A youth to Fortune and to Fame unknown.
Fair Science frowned not on his humble birth,
   And Melancholy marked him for her own.   120

Large was his bounty, and his soul sincere,
    Heaven did a recompense as largely send;
He gave to Misery all he had, a tear,
    He gained from Heaven ('twas all he wished) a
        friend.

No farther seek his merits to disclose,
    Or draw his frailties from their dread abode,
(There they alike in trembling hope repose),
    The bosom of his Father and his God.
(1750; 1751)

WILLIAM COLLINS
1721–1759

Chichester, Sussex, was the birthplace of William
Collins. Showing an early aptitude for verse, he
began writing as a twelve-year-old student at Winchester. He matriculated at Magdalen College, Oxford,
but, possessing a genuine contempt for pedantry and
discipline, he left academic life upon receiving his degree.

Because young Collins was considered by his
guardian uncle to be too indolent for the army, the
Church was recommended for him and the title of a
curacy was secured. But Collins renounced taking holy
orders and instead went to London in 1744, a "literary
adventurer" with only a few pennies in his pocket. Of
his many literary projects, few materialized; he
planned tragedies and contemplated writing a history
of the revival of learning, but these remained in the
speculative stage. He did publish *Ode to Evening, How
Sleep the Brave,* and *Dirge in Cymbeline,* all appearing
in 1744 and 1746; these have since become his most
famous works. But in his own lifetime his *Ode to Fear,
Ode to Simplicity, On the Poetical Character,* and *On
the Popular Superstitions of the Highlands* were generally more favorably regarded. All these poems were
written between 1742 and 1752, although a few were
not published until after his death. A bookseller allowed Collins, on the credit of a projected translation
of Aristotle's *Poetics,* enough money to escape into the
country. Soon afterwards, however, at the death of
Collins' uncle, the poet was left an inheritance; the
advance was promptly repaid the bookseller and the
translation was abandoned. At this time, Collins began
to fail mentally and physically. Following a journey
into France, he is said to have been kept for some
time in an asylum in Chelsea; he returned to
Chichester only shortly before his death in 1759.

ODE TO SIMPLICITY

O thou, by Nature taught
    To breathe her genuine thought,
In numbers warmly pure, and sweetly strong;
    Who first, on mountains wild,
    In Fancy, loveliest child,
Thy babe, or Pleasure's, nursed the powers of song!

Thou, who, with hermit heart,
    Disdain'st the wealth of art,
And gauds,° and pageant weeds, and trailing pall;
    But com'st a decent maid,   10
    In Attic robe° arrayed,
O chaste, unboastful nymph, to thee I call;

By all the honeyed store
    On Hybla's thymy shore;°
By all her blooms, and mingled murmurs dear;
    By her whose lovelorn woe
    In evening musings slow
Soothed sweetly sad Electra's poet's° ear:

By old Cephisus° deep,
    Who spread his wavy sweep,   20
In warbled wanderings, round thy green retreat;
    On whose enameled side,
    When holy Freedom died,°
No equal haunt allured thy future feet.

O sister meek of Truth,
    To my admiring youth,
Thy sober aid and native charms infuse!
    The flowers that sweetest breathe,
    Though Beauty culled the wreath,
Still ask thy hand to range their ordered hues.   30

While Rome could none esteem
    But virtue's patriot theme,
You loved her hills, and led her laureat band:
    But stayed to sing alone
    To one distinguished throne;°
And turned thy face, and fled her altered land.

No more in hall or bower,
    The passions own thy power;
Love, only love, her forceless numbers mean;°
    For thou hast left her shrine;   40
    Nor olive more, nor vine,
Shall gain thy feet to bless the servile scene.

Ode to Simplicity   9 **gauds,** ornaments of dress   11 **Attic robe,** simple robe,
characteristic of Athenian life and art   14 **Hybla's . . . shore.** Mt. Hybla in Sicily
was celebrated in ancient poetry for the sweetness of its honey. *Thymy* is "grown
with thyme"   18 **Electra's poet,** Sophocles, great Greek tragedian of the fifth
century B.C. and author of *Electra.* In the play, Electra is comforted by the voice
of a nightingale   19 **Cephisus,** river in Greece near Athens   23 **When . . . died,**
when Greece was conquered by Alexander the Great (335 B.C.)   35 **one . . .
throne,** that of Augustus Caesar, patron of Vergil and Horace   39 **forceless . . .
mean,** an allusion to the artificial love poetry of the days of chivalry

Though taste, though genius, bless
To some divine excess,
Faints the cold work till thou inspire the whole;
What each, what all supply,
May court, may charm, our eye;
Thou, only thou, canst raise the meeting soul!

Of these let others ask,
50 To aid some mighty task,
I only seek to find thy temperate vale;
Where oft my reed° might sound
To maids and shepherds round,
And all thy sons, O Nature, learn my tale.
(1746)

ODE TO EVENING

If aught of oaten stop,° or pastoral song,
May hope, chaste Eve, to soothe thy modest ear,
Like thy own solemn springs,
Thy springs, and dying gales,

O nymph reserved, while now the bright-haired sun
Sits in yon western tent, whose cloudy skirts,
With brede° ethereal wove,
O'erhang his wavy bed:

Now air is hushed, save where the weak-eyed bat
10 With short, shrill shriek, flits by on leathern wing;
Or where the beetle winds
His small but sullen horn,

As oft he rises 'midst the twilight path,
Against the pilgrim borne in heedless hum:
Now teach me, maid composed,
To breathe some softened strain,

Whose numbers, stealing through thy darkening vale,
May, not unseemly, with its stillness suit,
As, musing slow, I hail
20 Thy genial loved return!

For when thy folding star° arising shows
His paly circlet, at his warning lamp
The fragrant Hours, and elves
Who slept in flowers the day,

And many a nymph who wreathes her brows with
sedge,
And sheds the freshening dew, and, lovelier still,
The pensive Pleasures sweet
Prepare thy shadowy car.

Then lead, calm votaress, where some sheety lake
Cheers the lone heath, or some time-hallowed pile,° 30
Or upland fallows gray
Reflect its last cool gleam.

But when chill blustering winds, or driving rain,
Forbid my willing feet, be mine the hut,
That from the mountain's side,
Views wilds, and swelling floods,

And hamlets brown, and dim-discovered spires;
And hears their simple bell, and marks o'er all
Thy dewy fingers draw
The gradual dusky veil. 40

While Spring shall pour his showers, as oft he wont,
And bathe thy breathing tresses, meekest Eve!
While Summer loves to sport
Beneath thy lingering light;

While sallow Autumn fills thy lap with leaves;
Or Winter, yelling through the troublous air,
Affrights thy shrinking train,°
And rudely rends thy robes;

So long, sure-found beneath the sylvan shed,
Shall Fancy, Friendship, Science, rose-lipped Health, 50
Thy gentlest influence own,
And hymn thy favorite name!
(1746)

OLIVER GOLDSMITH
1728–1774

Oliver Goldsmith was born in the Athlone country
in central Ireland. He went off to Dublin in 1744,
becoming a sizar (a student who acted as a servant to
other students in return for an allowance) at Trinity
College. Although he did not apply himself very seriously, he was granted a B.A. degree in 1749. He then
turned, in succession, to divinity, law, and medicine
but eventually gave up his studies and spent three
years rambling on the Continent. He returned to London claiming to have a medical degree, but his failure
to secure a medical position that would allow him to
support himself caused him to try literary hack work.

52 **reed,** symbol of pastoral poetry **Ode to Evening** 1 **If . . . stop,** if anything
played upon the shepherd's oat or pipe 7 **brede,** embroidery 21 **folding star,**
evening star

30 **pile,** large building; here, a church 47 **Affrights . . . train,** shortens the
evening

His *An Enquiry into the Present State of Polite Learning in Europe* appeared in 1759 and attracted some favorable attention. In this work he attempted to affirm that literary criticism was almost synonymous with literary decadence. Goldsmith contributed a series of letters, supposedly written to friends in the Orient by a Chinese traveler in London, to a newspaper; in 1762 this series was republished as *Letters from a Citizen of the World*. Although he earned some money from his writings, his generosity and improvidence kept him in debt. In 1766, as the story goes, Dr. Johnson himself took Goldsmith's manuscript of *The Vicar of Wakefield* to the publishers to pay Goldsmith's debt to his landlady. *The Vicar* was very favorably received. Goldsmith followed with three more successes—his collected essays (1767), *The Deserted Village* (1770), and *She Stoops to Conquer* (written 1771, produced 1773). Although public response to these works was flattering, their financial returns paid off a mere fraction of Goldsmith's large debts. After completing a masterly series of caricatures, *Retaliation*, he died in 1774.

THE DESERTED VILLAGE

The Deserted Village, like Gray's *Elegy*, is one of the most genuinely popular poems which the eighteenth century produced. The several themes of the poem give it broad appeal—a celebration of such homely virtues as self-reliance, a lamentation over the passing of an era, an indictment of the new age of the tyranny of trade, material luxury, and moral pride. Further, a comparison of Goldsmith's use of the heroic couplet with Pope's (say, in *An Essay on Man*), shows that a basic shift has taken place. Pope is sharp, crisp, rapid, and rational; Goldsmith is slow, suggestive, and sentimental. Although many of the characteristic devices of the heroic couplet can still be identified, genial sentiment has replaced epigrammatic sophistication.

Two fundamental revolutions which were taking place in England at the time Goldsmith was writing the poem were altering the conditions of ordinary life. The agricultural revolution, greatly accelerated by the Enclosure Acts, was driving people from the land; public lands were being "enclosed" and made part of large private estates. The small farmer, who had tilled public land and grazed his stock in public parks, was driven to the city or across the sea. The industrial revolution, which would make England into a nation of factory workers and shopkeepers, was beginning to gain momentum, with the result that England was about to undergo a very rapid and very painful urbanization. As Goldsmith saw, "Sweet Auburn" was soon to be replaced by the slums of London, Birmingham, and Manchester.

Sweet Auburn!° loveliest village of the plain,
Where health and plenty cheered the laboring swain,
Where smiling spring its earliest visit paid,
And parting summer's lingering blooms delayed;
Dear lovely bowers of innocence and ease,
Seats of my youth, when every sport could please;
How often have I loitered o'er thy green,
Where humble happiness endeared each scene!
How often have I paused on every charm,
The sheltered cot, the cultivated farm,   10
The never-failing brook, the busy mill,
The decent church that topped the neighboring hill;
The hawthorn bush, with seats beneath the shade,
For talking age and whispering lovers made!
How often have I blessed the coming day,
When toil, remitting, lent its turn to play,
And all the village train, from labor free,
Led up their sports beneath the spreading tree!
While many a pastime circled in the shade,
The young contending as the old surveyed;   20
And many a gambol frolicked o'er the ground,
And sleights of art and feats of strength went round;
And still, as each repeated pleasure tired,
Succeeding sports the mirthful band inspired—
The dancing pair that simply sought renown,
By holding out to tire each other down;
The swain mistrustless of his smutted face,
While secret laughter tittered round the place;
The bashful virgin's side-long looks of love;
The matron's glance, that would those looks reprove.   30
These were thy charms, sweet village! sports like
    these,
With sweet succession, taught e'en toil to please;
These round thy bowers their cheerful influence shed;
These were thy charms—but all these charms are fled.

Sweet smiling village, loveliest of the lawn,
Thy sports are fled, and all thy charms withdrawn;
Amidst thy bowers the tyrant's hand is seen,
And desolation saddens all thy green;
One only master grasps the whole domain,°
And half a tillage stints° thy smiling plain.   40
No more thy glassy brook reflects the day,
But, choked with sedges, works its weedy way;
Along thy glades, a solitary guest,
The hollow-sounding bittern guards its nest;
Amidst thy desert walks the lapwing flies,
And tires their echoes with unvaried cries;
Sunk are thy bowers in shapeless ruin all,
And the long grass o'ertops the moldering wall;
And, trembling, shrinking from the spoiler's hand,
Far, far away thy children leave the land.   50

The Deserted Village   1 **Sweet Auburn.** Auburn may have been suggested by the village of Lissoy, Ireland, Goldsmith's childhood home. But the name "Auburn" is a poetical name and little else; the village is a typical farm village in southern England   39 **grasps . . . domain.** The Enclosure Acts (1760–1774) excluded villagers from the use of grazing grounds formerly held to be common property   40 **stints,** restricts to scant allowance

Ill fares the land, to hastening ills a prey,
Where wealth accumulates, and men decay.
Princes and lords may flourish, or may fade;
A breath can make them, as a breath has made,
But a bold peasantry, their country's pride,
When once destroyed, can never be supplied.

A time there was, ere England's griefs began,
When every rood of ground maintained its man;
For him light labor spread her wholesome store,
60 Just gave what life required, but gave no more:
His best companions, innocence and health;
And his best riches, ignorance of wealth.

But times are altered; trade's unfeeling train
Usurp the land, and dispossess the swain;
Along the lawn, where scattered hamlets rose,
Unwieldy wealth and cumbrous pomp repose;
And every want to opulence allied,
And every pang that folly pays to pride.
Those gentle hours that plenty bade to bloom,
70 Those calm desires that asked but little room,
Those healthful sports that graced the peaceful scene,
Lived in each look, and brightened all the green—
These, far departing, seek a kinder shore,
And rural mirth and manners are no more.

Sweet Auburn! parent of the blissful hour,
Thy glades forlorn confess the tyrant's power.
Here, as I take my solitary rounds,
Amidst thy tangling walks and ruined grounds,
And, many a year elapsed, return to view
80 Where once the cottage stood, the hawthorn grew—
Remembrance wakes with all her busy train,
Swells at my breast, and turns the past to pain.

In all my wanderings round this world of care,
In all my griefs—and God has given my share—
I still had hopes, my latest hours to crown,
Amidst these humble bowers to lay me down;
To husband out life's taper at the close,
And keep the flame from wasting by repose;
I still had hopes, for pride attends us still,
90 Amidst the swains to show my book-learned skill,
Around my fire an evening group to draw,
And tell of all I felt, and all I saw;
And, as a hare, whom hounds and horns pursue,
Pants to the place from whence at first she flew,
I still had hopes, my long vexations past,
Here to return—and die at home at last.

O blest retirement, friend to life's decline,
Retreats from care, that never must be mine,
How happy he who crowns, in shades like these,
100 A youth of labor with an age of ease;
Who quits a world where strong temptations try,
And, since 'tis hard to combat, learns to fly!
For him no wretches, born to work and weep,

Explore the mine, or tempt the dangerous deep;
No surly porter stands, in guilty state,
To spurn imploring famine from the gate;
But on he moves to meet his latter end,
Angels around befriending virtue's friend;
Bends to the grave with unperceived decay,
While resignation gently slopes the way;   110
And, all his prospects brightening to the last,
His heaven commences ere the world be past!

Sweet was the sound, when oft, at evening's close,
Up yonder hill the village murmur rose.
There, as I passed with careless steps and slow,
The mingled notes came softened from below;
The swain responsive as the milkmaid sung,
The sober herd that lowed to meet their young;
The noisy geese that gabbled o'er the pool,
The playful children just let loose from school;   120
The watch-dog's voice that bayed the whispering
    wind,
And the loud laugh that spoke the vacant mind;—
These all in sweet confusion sought the shade,
And filled each pause the nightingale had made.
But now the sounds of population fail,
No cheerful murmurs fluctuate in the gale,
No busy steps the grass-grown footway tread,
For all the bloomy flush of life is fled—
All but yon widowed, solitary thing,
That feebly bends beside the plashy spring;   130
She, wretched matron—forced, in age for bread,
To strip the brook with mantling cresses spread,
To pick her wintry faggot from the thorn,
To seek her nightly shed, and weep till morn—
She only left of all the harmless train,
The sad historian of the pensive plain.

Near yonder copse, where once the garden smiled,
And still where many a garden-flower grows wild,
There, where a few torn shrubs the place disclose,
The village preacher's° modest mansion rose.   140
A man he was to all the country dear,
And passing rich with forty pounds a year.
Remote from towns he ran his godly race,
Nor e'er had changed, nor wished to change, his place;
Unpracticed he to fawn, or seek for power
By doctrines fashioned to the varying hour;
Far other aims his heart had learned to prize,
More skilled to raise the wretched than to rise.
His house was known to all the vagrant train;
He chid their wanderings, but relieved their pain;   150
The long-remembered beggar was his guest,
Whose beard descending swept his aged breast;
The ruined spendthrift, now no longer proud,
Claimed kindred there, and had his claims allowed;
The broken soldier, kindly bade to stay,
Sat by his fire, and talked the night away;—

140 **village preacher,** perhaps suggested by either Goldsmith's father or his
brother Henry

Wept o'er his wounds, or, tales of sorrow done,
Shouldered his crutch, and showed how fields were
    won.
Pleased with his guests, the good man learned to glow,
160 And quite forgot their vices in their woe;
Careless their merits or their faults to scan,
His pity gave ere charity began.

    Thus to relieve the wretched was his pride,
And e'en his failings leaned to virtue's side;
But in his duty prompt at every call,
He watched and wept, he prayed and felt for all;
And, as a bird each fond endearment tries
To tempt its new-fledged offspring to the skies,
He tried each art, reproved each dull delay,
170 Allured to brighter worlds, and led the way.

    Beside the bed where parting life was laid,
And sorrow, guilt, and pain, by turns dismayed,
The reverend champion stood. At his control,
Despair and anguish fled the struggling soul;
Comfort came down the trembling wretch to raise,
And his last faltering accents whispered praise.

    At church, with meek and unaffected grace,
His looks adorned the venerable place;
Truth from his lips prevailed with double sway,
180 And fools, who came to scoff, remained to pray.
The service past, around the pious man
With steady zeal, each honest rustic ran;
E'en children followed, with endearing wile,
And plucked his gown, to share the good man's smile;
His ready smile a parent's warmth expressed;
Their welfare pleased him, and their cares distressed:
To them his heart, his love, his griefs were given,
But all his serious thoughts had rest in heaven.
As some tall cliff that lifts its awful form,
190 Swells from the vale, and midway leaves the storm,
Though round its breast the rolling clouds are spread,
Eternal sunshine settles on its head.

    Beside yon straggling fence that skirts the way,
With blossomed furze unprofitably gay,
There, in his noisy mansion, skilled to rule,
The village master taught his little school.
A man severe he was, and stern to view;
I knew him well, and every truant knew;
Well had the boding tremblers learned to trace
200 The day's disasters in his morning face;
Full well they laughed with counterfeited glee
At all his jokes, for many a joke had he;
Full well the busy whisper, circling round,
Conveyed the dismal tidings when he frowned.
Yet he was kind, or if severe in aught,
The love he bore to learning was in fault.
The village all declared how much he knew;
'Twas certain he could write, and cipher too;
Lands he could measure, terms and tides presage,

And e'en the story ran that he could gauge.°   210
In arguing, too, the parson owned his skill,
For e'en though vanquished, he could argue still;
While words of learnéd length and thundering sound
Amazed the gazing rustics ranged around;
And still they gazed, and still the wonder grew,
That one small head could carry all he knew.
But past is all his fame;—the very spot,
Where many a time he triumphed, is forgot.

    Near yonder thorn, that lifts its head on high,
Where once the sign-post caught the passing eye,   220
Low lies that house where nut-brown drafts° inspired,
Where gray-beard mirth and smiling toil retired,
Where village statesmen talked with looks profound,
And news much older than their ale went round.
Imagination fondly stoops to trace
The parlor splendors of that festive place;
The whitewashed wall, the nicely-sanded floor,
The varnished clock that clicked behind the door
The chest, contrived a double debt to pay,
A bed by night, a chest of drawers by day,   230
The pictures placed for ornament and use,
The twelve good rules,° the royal game of goose,°
The hearth, except when winter chilled the day,
With aspen boughs, and flowers, and fennel, gay;—
While broken teacups, wisely kept for show,
Ranged o'er the chimney, glistened in a row.

    Vain transitory splendors! could not all
Reprieve the tottering mansion from its fall?
Obscure it sinks, nor shall it more impart
An hour's importance to the poor man's heart.   240
Thither no more the peasant shall repair,
To sweet oblivion of his daily care;
No more the farmer's news, the barber's tale,
No more the woodman's ballad shall prevail;
No more the smith his dusky brow shall clear,
Relax his ponderous strength, and lean to hear;
The host himself no longer shall be found
Careful to see the mantling bliss go round;
Nor the coy maid, half willing to be pressed,
Shall kiss the cup to pass it to the rest.   250

    Yes! let the rich deride, the proud disdain,
These simple blessings of the lowly train;
To me more dear, congenial to my heart,
One native charm, than all the gloss of art.
Spontaneous joys, where nature has its play,
The soul adopts, and owns their first-born sway;
Lightly they frolic o'er the vacant mind,
Unenvied, unmolested, unconfined:
But the long pomp, the midnight masquerade,
With all the freaks of wanton wealth arrayed,   260

210 **gauge,** measure; here, to survey   221 **nut-brown drafts,** draughts of ale
232 **twelve good rules,** rules of conduct printed on cards and meant to be hung
on walls. The legend goes that these rules were originally discovered in the rooms
of Charles I after his execution   **game of goose,** a dice game of the parcheesi
type, generally known by the French name *jeu de l'oie*

In these, ere triflers half their wish obtain,
The toiling pleasure sickens into pain;
And, e'en while fashion's brightest arts decoy,
The heart distrusting asks, if this be joy.

    Ye friends to truth, ye statesmen, who survey
The rich man's joys increase, the poor's decay,
'Tis yours to judge how wide the limits stand
Between a splendid and a happy land.
Proud swells the tide with loads of freighted ore,
270 And shouting folly hails them from her shore;
Hoards, e'en beyond the miser's wish, abound,
And rich men flock from all the world around.
Yet count our gains. This wealth is but a name
That leaves our useful products still the same.
Not so the loss. The man of wealth and pride
Takes up a space that many poor supplied;
Space for his lake, his park's extended bounds,
Space for his horses, equipage, and hounds;
The robe that wraps his limbs in silken sloth,
280 Has robbed the neighboring fields of half their growth;
His seat, where solitary sports are seen,
Indignant spurns° the cottage from the green;
Around the world each needful product flies,
For all the luxuries the world supplies;
While thus the land, adorned for pleasure all,
In barren splendor feebly waits the fall.

    As some fair female, unadorned and plain,
Secure to please while youth confirms her reign,
Slights every borrowed charm that dress supplies,
290 Nor shares with art the triumph of her eyes;
But when those charms are past, for charms are frail,
When time advances, and when lovers fail,
She then shines forth, solicitous to bless,
In all the glaring impotence of dress;
Thus fares the land by luxury betrayed;
In nature's simplest charms at first arrayed;—
But verging to decline, its splendors rise,
Its vistas strike, its palaces surprise;
While, scourged by famine, from the smiling land
300 The mournful peasant leads his humble band;
And while he sinks, without one arm to save,
The country blooms—a garden and a grave!

    Where, then, ah! where shall poverty reside,
To 'scape the pressure of contiguous pride?°
If to some common's fenceless limits strayed,
He drives his flock to pick the scanty blade,
Those fenceless fields the sons of wealth divide,
And e'en the bare-worn common° is denied.

    If to the city sped—what waits him there?
310 To see profusion that he must not share;

To see ten thousand baneful arts combined
To pamper luxury and thin mankind;
To see those joys the sons of pleasure know
Extorted from his fellow-creature's woe;
Here while the courtier glitters in brocade,
There the pale artist plies the sickly trade;
Here while the proud their long-drawn pomps display,
There the black gibbet glooms beside the way;
The dome where pleasure holds her midnight reign,
Here, richly decked, admits the gorgeous train;   320
Tumultuous grandeur crowds the blazing square,
The rattling chariots clash, the torches glare.
Sure scenes like these no troubles e'er annoy!
Sure these denote one universal joy!—
Are these thy serious thoughts?—ah, turn thine eyes
Where the poor houseless shivering female lies;
She once, perhaps, in village plenty blessed,
Has wept at tales of innocence distressed;
Her modest looks the cottage might adorn,
Sweet as the primrose peeps beneath the thorn;   330
Now lost to all, her friends, her virtue, fled,
Near her betrayer's door she lays her head,
And, pinched with cold, and shrinking from the
    shower,
With heavy heart deplores that luckless hour,
When idly first, ambitious of the town,
She left her wheel,° and robes of country brown.

    Do thine, sweet Auburn, thine, the loveliest train,
Do thy fair tribes participate° her pain?
E'en now, perhaps, by cold and hunger led,
At proud men's doors they ask a little bread!   340

    Ah, no. To distant climes, a dreary scene,
Where half the convex world intrudes between,
Through torrid tracts with fainting steps they go,
Where wild Altama° murmurs to their woe.
Far different there from all that charmed before,
The various terrors of that horrid shore;
Those blazing suns that dart a downward ray,
And fiercely shed intolerable day;
Those matted woods where birds forget to sing,
But silent bats in drowsy clusters cling;   350
Those poisonous fields, with rank luxuriance crowned,
Where the dark scorpion gathers death around;
Where at each step the stranger fears to wake
The rattling terrors of the vengeful snake;
Where crouching tigers wait their hapless prey,
And savage men more murderous still than they;
While oft in whirls the mad tornado flies,
Mingling the ravaged landscape with the skies.
Far different these from every former scene,
The cooling brook, the grassy-vested green,   360
The breezy covert of the warbling grove,
That only sheltered thefts of harmless love.

Good Heaven! what sorrows gloomed that parting
    day,
That called them from their native walks away;
When the poor exiles, every pleasure past,
Hung round their bowers, and fondly looked their last,
And took a long farewell, and wished in vain,
For seats like these beyond the western main;
And shuddering still to face the distant deep,
370 Returned and wept, and still returned to weep!
The good old sire the first prepared to go
To new-found worlds, and wept for others' woe;
But for himself, in conscious virtue brave,
He only wished for worlds beyond the grave.
His lovely daughter, lovelier in her tears,
The fond companion of his helpless years,
Silent went next, neglectful of her charms,
And left a lover's for a father's arms.
With louder plaints the mother spoke her woes,
380 And blessed the cot where every pleasure rose,
And kissed her thoughtless babes with many a tear,
And clasped them close, in sorrow doubly dear;
Whilst her fond husband strove to lend relief
In all the silent manliness of grief.

O luxury, thou cursed by Heaven's decree,
How ill exchanged are things like these for thee!
How do thy potions, with insidious joy,
Diffuse their pleasures only to destroy!
Kingdoms by thee to sickly greatness grown,
390 Boast of a florid vigor not their own;
At every draft more large and large they grow,
A bloated mass of rank unwieldy woe;
Till sapped their strength, and every part unsound,
Down, down they sink, and spread a ruin round.

E'en now the devastation is begun,
And half the business of destruction done;
E'en now, methinks, as pondering here I stand,
I see the rural virtues leave the land.
Down where yon anchoring vessel spreads the sail,
400 That idly waiting flaps with every gale,
Downward they move, a melancholy band,
Pass from the shore, and darken all the strand;
Contented toil, and hospitable care,
And kind connubial tenderness are there;
And piety with wishes placed above,
And steady loyalty, and faithful love.

And thou, sweet Poetry, thou loveliest maid,
Still first to fly where sensual joys invade!
Unfit, in these degenerate times of shame,
410 To catch the heart, or strike for honest fame;
Dear charming nymph, neglected and decried,
My shame in crowds, my solitary pride;
Thou source of all my bliss and all my woe,
That found'st me poor at first, and keep'st me so;
Thou guide by which the nobler arts excel,

Thou nurse of every virtue, fare thee well!
Farewell! and oh! where'er thy voice be tried,
On Torno's° cliffs, or Pambamarca's° side,
Whether where equinoctial fervors° glow,
Or winter wraps the polar world in snow,   420
Still let thy voice, prevailing over time,
Redress the rigors of th' inclement clime;
Aid slighted truth with thy persuasive strain;
Teach erring man to spurn the rage of gain;
Teach him that states, of native strength possessed,
Though very poor, may still be very blest;
That trade's proud empire hastes to swift decay,
As ocean sweeps the labored mole away;
While self-dependent power can time defy,
As rocks resist the billows and the sky.   430
(1770)

WILLIAM COWPER
1731–1800

William Cowper was born in the village of Great Berkhampstead in Hertfordshire, where his father was rector. His mother, Anne Donne Cowper, was descended from John Donne, the seventeenth-century poet. Cowper went to the Westminster School and then entered the legal profession, receiving a small government appointment. He was admitted to the bar in 1755, but had no real desire to practice law. From his childhood onward, Cowper's mental sensitivity was great. He suffered fits of intense depression and insanity throughout his life. He described one of his first fits this way: "I was struck with such a dejection of spirit as none but they who have felt the same can have the least conception of. Day and night I was upon the rack, lying down in horror and rising up in despair." Some time after the death of his father in 1756, Cowper attempted to kill himself and was committed to a private asylum. Two years later he was discharged and took up residence at Huntingdon in order to be near his younger brother, who was a fellow at Cambridge.

At Huntingdon, Cowper was fortunate to make the acquaintance of the Unwin family. He boarded with the family, and after the death of Morley Unwin in 1767, he remained as a boarder with the widow. Cowper and Mrs. Unwin soon moved to a smaller home in the nearby parish of Olney, where Cowper briefly became an assistant to the village curate. Another attack of insanity ended all his activity in the

418 **Torno,** the River Tornea (Tana) which flows into the Gulf of Bothnia, at the northern extremity of Sweden   **Pambamarca,** a mountain near Quito, Ecuador
419 **equinoctial fervors,** the intense heat of the equator

parish. But his first considerable publication, *Olney Hymns,* in 1779 stemmed from this period. His attack of madness was followed by a very peaceful period. The friendship of Mrs. Unwin and of a Lady Austen, a rich widow of the vicinity, brightened his life. At the age of fifty, he began a sudden streak of literary activity. In 1782 he published a volume of didactic poems. In 1785 he published *The Task,* which began as a mock-heroic description of a sofa in a country home but ended as a piece of spiritual autobiography. After the death of Mrs. Unwin in 1796, his mania returned, never to leave him until his death in 1800.

from THE TASK

The Task derives its title from the request of Cowper's friend, Lady Austen, that he write a poem in blank verse on the subject of the parlor sofa. In the "advertisement" to the poem, Cowper says that he obeyed: "and, having much leisure, connected another subject with it; and, pursuing the train of thought to which my situation and turn of mind led me, brought forth at length, instead of the trifle which I at first intended, a serious affair—a volume!"

The purpose of the poem, as stated by Cowper in a letter to William Unwin (October 10, 1784), was "to discountenance the modern enthusiasm after a London life, and to recommend rural ease and leisure as friendly to the cause of piety and virtue."

from BOOK I. THE SOFA°

. . . For I have loved the rural walk through lanes
110 Of grassy swarth, close cropped by nibbling sheep,
And skirted thick with intertexture firm
Of thorny boughs; have loved the rural walk
O'er hills, through valleys, and by rivers' brink,
E'er since a truant boy I passed my bounds
To enjoy a ramble on the banks of Thames;
And still remember, nor without regret
Of hours that sorrow since has much endeared,
How oft, my slice of pocket store consumed,
Still hungering, penniless and far from home,
120 I fed on scarlet hips and stony haws,
Or blushing crabs, or berries, that emboss
The bramble, black as jet, or sloes austere.°
Hard fare! but such as boyish appetite
Disdains not; nor the palate, undepraved
By culinary arts, unsavory deems.
No Sofa then awaited my return;
Nor Sofa then I needed. Youth repairs
His wasted spirits quickly, by long toil

Incurring short fatigue; and, though our years
As life declines speed rapidly away,   130
And not a year but pilfers as he goes
Some youthful grace that age would gladly keep:
A tooth or auburn lock, and by degrees
Their length and color from the locks they spare;
The elastic spring of an unwearied foot
That mounts the stile with ease, or leaps the fence,
That play of lungs, inhaling and again
Respiring freely the fresh air, that makes
Swift pace or steep ascent no toil to me,
Mine have not pilfered yet; nor yet impaired   140
My relish of fair prospect; scenes that soothed
Or charmed me young, no longer young, I find
Still soothing and of power to charm me still.
And witness, dear companion of my walks,°
Whose arm this twentieth winter I perceive
Fast locked in mine, with pleasure such as love,
Confirmed by long experience of thy worth
And well-tried virtues, could alone inspire—
Witness a joy that thou hast doubled long.
Thou knowest my praise of nature most sincere,   150
And that my raptures are not conjured up
To serve occasions of poetic pomp,
But genuine, and art partner of them all.
How oft upon yon eminence our pace
Has slackened to a pause, and we have borne
The ruffling wind, scarce conscious that it blew,
While admiration, feeding at the eye,
And still unsated, dwelt upon the scene.
Thence with what pleasure have we just discerned
The distant plow slow moving, and beside   160
His laboring team, that swerved not from the track,
The sturdy swain diminished to a boy!
Here Ouse,° slow winding through a level plain
Of spacious meads with cattle sprinkled o'er,
Conducts the eye along its sinuous course
Delighted. There, fast rooted in his bank,
Stand, never overlooked, our favorite elms,
That screen the herdsman's solitary hut;
While far beyond, and overthwart the stream
That, as with molten glass, inlays the vale,   170
The sloping land recedes into the clouds;
Displaying on its varied side the grace
Of hedge-row beauties numberless, square tower,
Tall spire, from which the sound of cheerful bells
Just undulates upon the listening ear,
Groves, heaths, and smoking villages remote.
Scenes must be beautiful, which daily viewed,
Please daily, and whose novelty survives
Long knowledge and the scrutiny of years—
Praise justly due to those that I describe.°   180

Nor rural sights alone, but rural sounds
Exhilarate the spirit and restore
The tone of languid nature. Mighty winds,

The Task   The Sofa. "A lady, fond of blank verse, demanded a poem of that kind from the author, and gave him the Sofa for a subject. He obeyed; and, having much leisure, connected another subject with it; and, pursuing the train of thought to which his situation and turn of mind led him, brought forth at length, instead of the trifle which he at first intended, a serious affair—a Volume!" (Cowper's note on the origin of the title)   122 austere, used here in the sense of "sour"

144 companion . . . walks, Mary Unwin   163 Ouse, small river in Sussex
180 those . . . describe, familiar scenes around Olney, Cowper's home

That sweep the skirt of some far-spreading wood
Of ancient growth, make music not unlike
The wash of ocean on his winding shore,
And lull the spirit while they fill the mind;
Unnumbered branches waving in the blast,
And all their leaves fast fluttering, all at once.
190 Nor less composure waits upon the roar
Of distant floods, or on the softer voice
Of neighboring fountain, or of rills that slip
Through the cleft rock, and, chiming as they fall
Upon loose pebbles, lose themselves at length
In matted grass, that with a livelier green
Betrays the secret of their silent course.
Nature inanimate employs sweet sounds,
But animated nature sweeter still,
To soothe and satisfy the human ear.
200 Ten thousand warblers cheer the day, and one
The livelong night: nor these alone, whose notes
Nice-fingered art must emulate in vain,
But cawing rooks, and kites that swim sublime
In still repeated circles, screaming loud,
The jay, the pie, and e'en the boding owl
That hails the rising moon, have charms for me.
Sounds inharmonious in themselves and harsh,
Yet heard in scenes where peace forever reigns,
And only there, please highly for their sake. . . .

Where finds philosophy her eagle eye,
With which she gazes at yon burning disk
Undazzled, and detects and counts his spots?
In London. Where her implements exact,
With which she calculates, computes, and scans,
All distance, motion, magnitude, and now
Measures an atom, and now girds a world?
720 In London. Where has commerce such a mart,
So rich, so thronged, so drained, and so supplied,
As London—opulent, enlarged, and still
Increasing London? Babylon of old
Not more the glory of the earth than she,
A more accomplished world's chief glory now.

She has her praise. Now mark a spot or two,
That so much beauty would do well to purge;
And show this queen of cities that so fair
May yet be foul; so witty, yet not wise.
730 It is not seemly, nor of good report,
That she is slack in discipline; more prompt
To avenge than to prevent the breach of law:
That she is rigid in denouncing° death
On petty robbers, and indulges life
And liberty, and oft-times honor too,
To peculators° of the public gold:
That thieves at home must hang, but he that puts
Into his overgorged and bloated purse
The wealth of Indian provinces escapes.°

Nor is it well, nor can it come to good,
That, through profane and infidel contempt   740
Of holy writ, she has presumed to annul
And abrogate, as roundly as she may,
The total ordinance and will of God;
Advancing fashion to the post of truth,
And centering all authority in modes
And customs of her own, till sabbath rites
Have dwindled into unrespected forms,
And knees and hassocks are well-nigh divorced.

God made the country, and man made the town.
What wonder then that health and virtue, gifts   750
That can alone make sweet the bitter draught
That life holds out to all, should most abound
And least be threatened in the fields and groves?
Possess ye, therefore, ye who, borne about
In chariots and sedans,° know no fatigue
But that of idleness, and taste no scenes
But such as art contrives, possess ye still
Your element; there only can ye shine,
There only minds like yours can do no harm.
Our groves were planted to console at noon   760
The pensive wanderer in their shades. At eve
The moonbeam, sliding softly in between
The sleeping leaves, is all the light they wish,
Birds warbling all the music. We can spare
The splendor of your lamps; they but eclipse
Our softer satellite. Your songs confound
Our more harmonious notes; the thrush departs
Scared, and the offended nightingale is mute.
There is a public mischief in your mirth;
It plagues your country. Folly such as yours,   770
Graced with a sword, and worthier of a fan,
Has made, what enemies could ne'er have done,
Our arch of empire, steadfast but for you,
A mutilated structure, soon to fall.

from BOOK II. THE TIME-PIECE

Oh, for a lodge in some vast wilderness,°
Some boundless contiguity of shade,
Where rumor of oppression and deceit,
Of unsuccessful or successful war,
Might never reach me more! My ear is pained,
My soul is sick, with every day's report
Of wrong and outrage with which earth is filled.
There is no flesh in man's obdurate heart,
It does not feel for man; the natural bond
Of brotherhood is severed as the flax   10
That falls asunder at the touch of fire.
He finds his fellow guilty of a skin
Not colored like his own; and, having power
To enforce the wrong, for such a worthy cause

732 **denouncing,** pronouncing. Petty crimes were at that time punishable by death in England   735 **peculators,** embezzlers   736 **he . . . escapes,** an allusion to the fortune made by the British East India Company in India after 1751

755 **sedans,** sedan chairs   **The Time-Piece**   1 **lodge . . . wilderness.** Cf. *Jeremiah,* 9:2 "Oh that I had in the wilderness a lodging place of wayfaring men; that I might leave my people, and go from them"

Dooms and devotes him as his lawful prey.
Lands intersected by a narrow frith°
Abhor each other. Mountains interposed
Make enemies of nations, who had else,
Like kindred drops, been mingled into one.
20 Thus man devotes° his brother, and destroys;
And, worse than all, and most to be deplored,
As human nature's broadest, foulest blot,
Chains him, and tasks him, and exacts his sweat
With stripes, that Mercy, with a bleeding heart,
Weeps when she sees inflicted on a beast.
Then what is man? And what man, seeing this,
And having human feelings, does not blush,
And hang his head, to think himself a man?
I would not have a slave to till my ground,
30 To carry me, to fan me while I sleep,
And tremble when I wake, for all the wealth
That sinews bought and sold have ever earned.
No: dear as freedom is, and in my heart's
Just estimation prized above all price,
I had much rather be myself the slave,
And wear the bonds, than fasten them on him.
We have no slaves at home.—Then why abroad?
And they themselves, once ferried o'er the wave
That parts us, are emancipate and loosed.
40 Slaves cannot breathe in England;° if their lungs
Receive our air, that moment they are free;
They touch our country, and their shackles fall.
That's noble, and bespeaks a nation proud
And jealous of the blessing. Spread it then,
And let it circulate through every vein
Of all your empire; that where Britain's power
Is felt, mankind may feel her mercy too. . . .

from BOOK III. THE GARDEN

I was a stricken deer that left the herd
Long since;° with many an arrow deep infixed
110 My panting side was charged, when I withdrew
To seek a tranquil death in distant shades.
There was I found by One Who had Himself
Been hurt by the archers. In His side He bore,
And in His hands and feet, the cruel scars.
With gentle force soliciting the darts,
He drew them forth, and healed, and bade me live.
Since then, with few associates, in remote
And silent woods I wander, far from those
My former partners of the peopled scene,
120 With few associates, and not wishing more.
Here much I ruminate, as much I may,
With other views of men and manners now
Than once, and others of a life to come.
I see that all are wanderers, gone astray

Each in his own delusions; they are lost
In chase of fancied happiness, still wooed
And never won; dream after dream ensues,
And still they dream that they shall still succeed,
And still are disappointed: rings the world
With the vain stir. I sum up half mankind,   130
And add two-thirds of the remainder half,
And find the total of their hopes and fears
Dreams, empty dreams. . . .

(1785)

16 **frith,** narrow arm of the sea   20 **devotes,** gives over to destruction
40 **Slaves . . . England.** The court decision that "slaves cannot breathe in England" was given by Lord Mansfield in 1772. The slave trade was not abolished until 1807, and slavery in the colonies was not ended until 1833
The Garden   109 **Long since.** Cowper's first breakdown came in 1763

The Romantic Period

From the Death of Samuel Johnson to the Accession of Victoria, 1784–1837

PART 4

Royal Pavilion, Brighton, designed by John Nash, completed in 1821

Romantic literature was the product of a turbulent and complex age that saw three great revolutions—the American (1776), the French (1789), and the Industrial (1770s to the present)—change the shape of Western culture. The notion of the "Romantic" is generally used in two different ways: in popular usage it refers to a permanent and recurrent characteristic of the human spirit, a tendency to idealism, imaginative speculation, and emotional indulgence; in its historical sense Romanticism denotes a period in European culture from the late eighteenth to the early nineteenth century in which radical changes occurred in intellectual, artistic, and social patterns. From the standpoint of English literary history, the most important of these changes occurred in poetry. In the space of merely forty years (1789–1830), six major poets emerged who permanently affected the nature of English language and literature. Wordsworth, Coleridge, and Blake may be regarded as the first generation of Romantic poets, doing their major work from 1790 to 1805. Shelley, Keats, and Byron are the second generation, working from 1810 to 1824. If we think of Elizabethan England as the great age of drama, the Victorian era as the great age of the novel, Romantic England was the great age of poetry.

Major literary and cultural changes do not, of course, occur in a vacuum. They arise in response to (and often generate) massive historical transformations in the material basis of life and in patterns of social and intellectual behavior. In order to understand the literary revolution called Romanticism, therefore, we must see it against the background of the other revolutions which ushered in what we now call "the modern world."

The Age of Revolution

Do ideas make history, or do historical events produce new ideas? Let us approach this chicken-and-egg question from the standpoint of the idealist, and trace some of the major changes in patterns of thinking in the late eighteenth century. The reliance on reason, the central tendency of seventeenth- and eighteenth-century philosophical writing, gradually diminished during the late eighteenth century as philosophers began to recognize the importance of man's other faculties. Two significant figures who questioned the extent to which rational contemplation could uncover truth were the French philosopher Jean Jacques Rousseau (1712–1778) and the German philosopher Immanuel Kant (1724–1804). In his essays and novels Rousseau challenged the idea that man should strive to be rational; truth is God, not a supernatural being, but a creative force or spirit that resides in man and nature. Any contemplation of this spirit must necessarily be inspiring, emotionally stimulating, and exalting. Since this creative spirit is present in nature and in man, it follows that man in a natural setting, as free as possible from artificial restraints imposed by the demands of society, is in his happiest possible state. According to Rousseau, the contemplation of nature—of natural landscape and natural phenomena—is the surest way to approach God; the more primitive man's environment, the closer he is to perfection. In his *Critique of Pure Reason* (1781) Kant unambiguously stated that reason has its limitations; when it fails, he said, one must rely on intuition and instinct.

Although new ideas about the nature of man de-emphasized reason, it was the application of reason to social problems that generated the stunning political revolutions. Reason called into question such notions as the divine right of kings and the superiority of the nobility over common men. Repressive political measures and shortsighted domination by the aristocracy provoked a violent political uprising in France in the

Tintern Abbey (1794?), a watercolor by Joseph M. W. Turner (1775–1851), whose subject matter here—the famous twelfth-century Gothic ruin in Wales—suggests the revival of interest in the Middle Ages that occurred during the Romantic period. In one sense, Romanticism was a reaction against the immediate past (the eighteenth century) and a revival of the more distant past, especially the Middle Ages. The pastoral landscape surrounding Tintern Abbey inspired Wordsworth's famous poem.

Dedham Vale with Ploughmen (1814–1817) by John Constable (1776–1837), English landscape painter known for his scenes of rural life. Constable was chiefly interested in capturing the changing qualities of the sky—light, wind, and clouds; in this oil painting the clouds, rather than the ploughmen, receive primary emphasis.

1790s. With its radical reduction of religious, political, and social forms of patriarchy, and its emphasis on liberty, fraternity, and equality, the early days of the French Revolution seemed to promise a new world. When the symbol of the French monarchy's oppression, the Bastille, fell on July 14, 1789, it fell to the people. Generals, armies, ministers, and other European nations were of course involved during various phases of the revolution, but to the imagination of the age it was a revolution of the common people. The first phase of the French Revolution—sometimes called the First Revolution—appeared to promise stable and progressive government. A year after the fall of the Bastille, things seemed to be progressing: moderates were in power and reform was proceeding. But a frightening phase soon supplanted moderacy. The government collapsed, and in 1793 the execution of Louis XVI shocked Europe. Then in 1794 came the Reign of Terror. The death of thousands of suspected royalists at the guillotine and the fact that many of these died because of factionalism within the revolution doubly disillusioned English observers and writers who had believed in the possibility of serious reform. English sympathy for the French experiment was at its lowest ebb in the period from 1799 to 1815, when Napoleon Bonaparte (1769–1821) committed French energies to the conquest of Europe.

The political situation in England during the early nineteenth century also differed radically from that of earlier periods, but not because of a popular uprising against harsh aristocratic rule. In fact, the ruling Hanovers of this period were largely ineffectual. George III, intermittently mad for years, was judged permanently incompetent in 1810; his son, George, became Prince Regent and later ruled from 1820 to 1830. George IV is remembered primarily for his unsuccessful attempt to divorce his wife, Caroline of Brunswick, and for his pursuits of pleasure. Though William IV did not provide much political leadership during his reign (1830–1837), liberal policies were established, largely due to the efforts of a growing national reform movement. Neither royal succession nor religious belief, however, aroused much political controversy. Rather, the nation was shaken by economic struggles, by class conflict. The Napoleonic wars did not reach English soil, but they left their mark, for anxiety about the possibility of English revolution initially occasioned repressive policies with severe restrictions on freedom of the press, speech, and assem-

Cottage Industry (1791), an engraving by William Hincks, shows the spinning, reeling, and boiling of yarn. In the seventeenth and eighteenth centuries, merchants often furnished materials and paid wages to rural laborers who worked in homes (cottages) to produce goods. Factories gradually replaced cottage industries in the nineteenth century.

The Romantic Period   **613**

bly. Moreover, the economic boom that war inflation and the Industrial Revolution brought to the middle class brought only higher prices to the poor. In the Luddite riots (1811, 1812, 1816), workers in northern England wrecked the machinery that they felt had destroyed their cottage industries. From 1815 to 1827 Liverpool was the site both of great turmoil and repressive policies that denied civil liberties to the working classes. In 1819 soldiers fired upon a mass meeting at St. Peter's Field near Manchester, killing eleven and wounding many more. This incident became known as the Peterloo Massacre, a sardonic reference to the famed British victory over Napoleon at Waterloo.

Revolution had seemed imminent for so long that political leaders finally initiated reforms from within the political system. The Reform Bill of 1832 began the needed readjustment of political seats to economic realities. It denied Parliamentary representation to fifty-six "rotten boroughs," districts where there was no longer a population sufficient to elect a representative to Parliament and where representatives had been appointed by the aristocracy. Further, it provided representation for the first time to one hundred and fifty-six communities, some of which—like Manchester and Birmingham—were quite populous. Though the Bill did not give the vote to the working class, it did extend the franchise to include large numbers of the middle class. Though it did not introduce democracy into England, it did make democracy ultimately possible. By the time eighteen-year-old Victoria ascended the throne in 1837, England had overcome its severe political crises. The need for social reform continued, but England had escaped a Reign of Terror like France's. Indeed, the reforms eventually passed by Parliament during the late 1820s and early 1830s were evolutionary (as opposed to revolutionary) in nature.

This view of a nineteenth-century textile factory (1820) shows children winding cotton. The use of child labor increased throughout the nineteenth century as the Industrial Revolution progressed. Children worked long hours performing menial jobs for shockingly low wages.

RADIO TIMES/HULTON PICTURE LIBRARY

Perhaps the most dramatic changes for England during the early nineteenth century were precipitated by what we commonly call the Industrial Revolution. The last decades of the eighteenth century witnessed the invention of machines that revolutionized the means of production. The spinning jenny and the power loom transformed cloth making from a cottage to a factory industry. Blast furnaces made the mass production of iron possible; steam engines offered a new source of power and transportation. Opportunities for work in growing factory towns—Manchester, Birmingham, Liverpool, Bristol, and the smaller industrial centers in Yorkshire, Lancashire, and Nottinghamshire—drew people from the land. As a result, England changed from a primarily agricultural nation into one that was primarily industrial and mercantile.

The Romantic Movement

Perhaps the most important generalization to remember about the Romantic Movement is that it was not a single, unified body of thought. There were as many Romanticisms as there were Romanticists, and any attempt to reduce this period to a few slogans about emotion, imagination, or "the love of nature" is bound to be false. Nevertheless, we can observe a common cluster of themes or problems which engaged the attention of artists and intellectuals in this era. European civilization was undergoing a drastic transformation in its basic assumptions about the nature of man, the structure of society, and the shape of reality. Many writers welcomed these changes and saw their work as contributing to and creating the new order. Others saw the change as deplorable and sought ways to revive the old forms in ways that could survive in the new world. Rarely did a single artist express a simple or straightforward version of one of these positions. Byron, for instance, was a political radical who supported revolution in Greece and admired Napoleon; yet he was poetically a conservative who thought of Wordsworth and Coleridge as deviations from the great tradition of English poetry represented by the classicism of Pope and Dryden. Wordsworth, who sympathized with the French Revolution in his youth, became a political conservative in his later years but sustained throughout his career a commitment to a new, experimental kind of poetry that he defined as a rebellion against the artificialities of eighteenth-century verse. The Romantic Movement is best understood, therefore, not as a single movement, but as a lively controversy which converged on a common set of challenges and problems.

One of the most pressing common problems was what might be called "the burden of the past." Though we have noted that the neoclassical age was in fact much more diverse than the label "Age of Rea-

Durham Cathedral, a watercolor by Thomas Girtin (1775–1802), one of a group of English painters who elevated the watercolor technique to a popular art form during the first half of the nineteenth century. Like other English landscape artists, Girtin made sketching tours of the British Isles, which furnished subjects for watercolors such as this. Girtin had already attained popularity as a painter when he died at twenty-seven; Turner reportedly remarked, "Had Girtin lived I should have starved."

son" suggests, many Romantic writers viewed the literature of the early eighteenth century as a dead weight of tradition to be discarded. The authoritative weight of classical precedents in literature, like the authority of church and state in society, was rejected in favor of poetic forms that seemed to reflect more fundamental aspects of the human spirit. The word *Romantic* itself indicates one of the main sources of this new search for fundamentals—the realm of Gothic or medieval culture. To eighteenth-century neoclassicists and rationalists, the notion of the Gothic suggested barbarism, superstition, and ignorance. To many Romantic writers, however, it suggested an age of faith, idealism, and adventure; more important, it provided a literary form, the quest-romance, which could be adapted to the needs of the new age.

The typical Romantic poem takes the basic element of the quest-romance, the journey through strange lands in search of an ideal object (often a woman), and internalizes it as a psychological quest for self-knowledge. The hero of the poem is no longer a knight in armor, but the poet himself, and the fields on which he does battle are the infinite realms of the human mind. The major poems of the Romantic Move-

Portrait of William Wordsworth (1842) by B. R. Haydon.

The Romantic Period　615

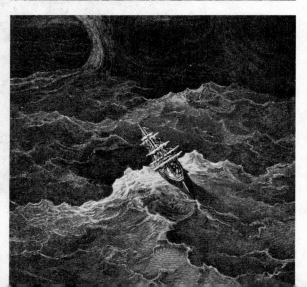

Three scenes from Coleridge's The Rime of the Ancient Mariner, *from engravings made in the 1870s by Gustave Doré (1832–1883), well-known French book illustrator. The Rime of the Ancient Mariner, Coleridge's most famous poem, appeared in the revolutionary* Lyrical Ballads *of 1798.*

ment—Wordsworth's *Prelude,* Coleridge's *Rime of the Ancient Mariner,* Shelley's *Prometheus Unbound,* Blake's *Jerusalem*—may all be regarded as psychological epics, attempts to explore the human mind as fully as Milton or Dante had explored the Christian universe, or as Homer had explored the world of Greek myth and military heroism.

Literary Theory

How did this Romantic spirit translate itself into new conceptions of literature? The first Romantic manifesto is Wordsworth's Preface to the second edition of the *Lyrical Ballads* (1800). This volume of poems by Wordsworth and Samuel Taylor Coleridge had aroused controversy with its initial 1798 appearance. In addition to the Preface Wordsworth's poetic contribution was twofold: a group of poems reminiscent of medieval ballads, simple in diction, plain in style, with rustic scenes and characters and frequent references to the tutelage of nature; and the contemplative poem *Tintern Abbey,* a blank-verse exploration of Wordsworth's own feelings on revisiting a favorite spot in the Wye river valley. Coleridge contributed the supernatural, imaginative ballad, *The Rime of the Ancient Mariner,* notable for its haunting atmosphere and its blend of modern and archaic language. The *Lyrical Ballads* provoked laughter and scorn among most traditional literary critics, but a second edition was issued in 1800.

In its day, Wordsworth's *Preface* was a revolutionary document in several respects: it espoused a novel, "experimental" kind of poetry which would dare to treat of "low" or "common" (and therefore "unpoetical") subjects; it denied any essential distinction between the language of poetry and prose and questioned the popular equation of poetry with metrical verse (after Wordsworth the prose-poem was at least a theoretical possibility); it denied the poet any special mystique other than heightened sensitivity to the world and defined poetry in plain terms as "a man speaking to men"; it emphasized the importance of disciplined meditation in the creative process and de-emphasized the imitation of classical precedents, particularly the ornate, artificial language of "poetic diction."

A common misconception about Wordsworth is that he advocated a sort of mindless and artless approach to poetry in his poetic theory. Nothing could be further from the truth. The "spontaneous overflow of powerful feeling" that he associated with poetic creation could be achieved only after sober thought and

View of the Lake District in northern England, which provided the inspiration for many of Wordsworth's poems. Wordsworth was born in the Lake District and spent most of his life in the region.

meditation. The result was a poetry that was highly crafted, not simply in terms of literary models and precedents but in relation to the evolving consciousness of its creator. Wordsworth's major poem, *The Prelude*, took its shape not from classical rules about the construction of an epic but from the inner necessity of his subject, "the growth of a poet's mind."

Another common misconception about Wordsworth (really a kind of half-truth) is that he was essentially a "Nature Poet." Most of his poems had rural settings, and he described himself as a "priest of nature." Nevertheless, he did not emphasize nature simply for its own sake but as a way of exploring fundamental aspects of human nature that had been obscured by the artificial roles of civilized society:

> Humble and rustic life was generally chosen, because, in that condition, the essential passions of the heart find a better soil in which they can attain their maturity, are less under restraint, and speak a plainer and more emphatic language; because in that condition of life our elementary feelings co-exist in a state of greater simplicity, and consequently may be more accurately contemplated.

Wordsworth was thus a poet of nature only as a way of being a more accurate poet of the human mind and heart.

It is a good measure of the diversity of the Romantic Movement that Coleridge, who collaborated with Wordsworth on the *Lyrical Ballads* and was his closest friend, vigorously disagreed with many of the ideas in the *Preface to the Lyrical Ballads*. On one issue, however, they and most of the other major English Romantic poets were in agreement: that poetry was a genuine contribution to knowledge, not merely a pretty ornament of polite society. Wordsworth called poetry "the first and last of all knowledge" in *The Preface* and suggested that it was as important as science. Coleridge, Shelley, Keats, and Blake would all have agreed with this notion. Romantic writers used the term *imagination* to designate this power of poetry to expand knowledge. For them it constituted a mental faculty which replaces and absorbs the classical ideas of reason and understanding. For classical thinkers, imagination was simply the power to make mental images, and it was subordinate to rational, analytical processes. For the Romantics, man was imaginative, more than rational—that is, capable of creation, invention, and inspiration.

Coleridge, with his religious sensibility, regarded imagination as the divine spark in mankind, the quality that makes us miniature analogues of the creator of the universe:

> The Imagination then, I consider either as primary, or secondary. The primary Imagination I hold to be the living power and prime Agent of all human perception, and as a repetition in the finite mind of the eternal act of creation in the infinite I Am.

Although Shelley was an atheist who would have argued with Coleridge on theological questions, he would have agreed on the centrality of imagination.

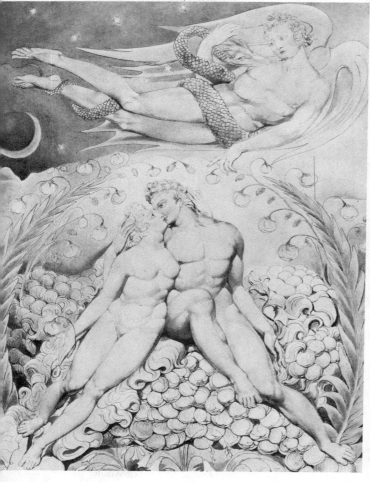

William Blake expressed his mystical vision in paintings and engravings as well as in his poetry. Right: "The Tyger," from his book of poems entitled Songs of Experience *(1794). Blake engraved the text and illustrated the pages of this and other volumes of his poems. Left: Satan with Adam and Eve (1808), one of Blake's watercolors for Milton's* Paradise Lost. *Among his many other book illustrations, his watercolor series for the Bible (1800–1805) and for Dante's Divine Comedy (1825–1827) are especially noteworthy.*

He expressed it as "the principle of synthesis" which "has for its object those forms which are common to universal nature and to existence itself"; it was defined in opposition to reason, the subordinate faculty of analytical thought:

Reason is the enumeration of quantities already known; imagination is the perception of the value of those quantities, both separately and as a whole. Reason respects the differences, and imagination the similitudes of things. Reason is to imagination as the instrument to the agent, as the body to the spirit, as the shadow to the substance.

Keats the agnostic declared that he was "certain of

nothing but of the holiness of the Heart's affections and the truth of Imagination." And Blake affirmed that "imagination . . . is the Human Existence itself."

Thus, though the Romantic theorists are not uniform in their use of terms or in their conception of the poet's role, they agree in the primacy given to the imagination as the power of poetry. The practice of these theorists, as we shall see, provides a corresponding continuity amid diversity.

Romantic Literature

The English, for all their native political conservatism, could not avoid the revolutionary ideas circulating at the end of the eighteenth and at the beginning of the nineteenth centuries. As discussed immediately above, these revolutionary ideas had a great impact on English theories of literature. The literature that was produced—both directly and indirectly—as a result of these theories is extremely complicated, with many paradoxes and crosscurrents of thought and emotion. We will turn first to poetry because it was the genre that was most affected by the new theories of literature popular during the age of revolution.

Poetry. Although the poetry of Robert Burns and William Blake appeared in the last quarter of the eighteenth century, it differs radically from the neoclassical style of many of their contemporaries. Burns' realistic satires relate well to traditional eighteenth-century poetry, but his emotional, lyric qualities, his use of the common Scottish dialect, and his rural life settings suggest a strong affinity with the Romantic movement. Blake, on the other hand, has only come to be understood in the twentieth century. An apocalyptic radical in both the verbal and visual arts (which he practiced with equal mastery), Blake was part of a movement toward linear abstraction in painting in the late eighteenth century and found his literary ties in the great allegorical myth-making poets Dante, Milton, and Spenser. Blake's early poetry, like that of Wordsworth and Coleridge, tended to imitate naive and primitive sources in medieval ballad and romance; his *Songs of Innocence and Experience* were literally songs to be performed with musical accompaniment. In his later poetry Blake developed a kind of synthetic mythology (mistakenly called "private" because it requires sustained study) which unites elements of a wide variety of mythologies (Greco-Roman, Judao-Christian, Hindu, Scandinavian, English folklore and legend, and occult, cabalistic lore) into a single cosmic myth about a "universal man." The work of Freud and Jung with dream symbolism and modern studies of comparative mythology, have made Blake's work much more accessible to modern readers than it was to his contemporaries, who regarded him as an eccentric genius.

Wordsworth and Coleridge, the so-called elder statesmen of the Romantic movement, continued to follow the directions established in the *Lyrical Ballads*. Wordsworth depicted the rustic life and the powers of nature; the masterpiece of his long career, *The Prelude*, was not published in its final form until 1850. Although weakened by drug addiction and an erratic private life, Coleridge published the marvelous "Kubla Kahn" and "Christabel" and devoted a great portion of his time to philosophy and literary criticism.

Wordsworth and Coleridge were separated from the younger group of Romantic poets by age and occasional disagreement. Byron, in his first important work, the satirical *English Bards and Scotch Reviewers*, pays his disrespects to what he considers their exaggerated renown. Wordsworth is to him a "mild apostate from

Portrait of Byron.

poetic rule," simple and inclined to the idiotic; Coleridge is obscure and "to turgid ode and tumid stanza dear." These unflattering sentiments Byron repeated with equal vehemence in his last work, *Don Juan*. Indeed, Byron said privately that this new scheme of poetry which excited the Romantics "was not worth a damn in itself." Clearly, Byron was no admirer of plain diction or rustic scenes; his talent, in a certain sense, could almost be called neoclassic, as his whip-lash satire and avowed admiration of Pope and Dryden make clear. In an age of emotional poetry, Byron's *Don Juan* seems anomalous, but it is one of the great satires of English literature.

One of Byron's contributions to Romanticism was his magnetic and glamorous personality. In *Childe Harold* and in his oriental tales he created the "Byronic hero," a young man who is moody, melodramatic, violent, tender, sinister, passionate, restless, and unsatisfied—a portrait of Byron himself. The reputation of his exploits attained almost mythic proportions even in his lifetime. As Byron's poetic talent developed, the satirical outlook in his poems became more prominent; yet one Romantic trait in his character did not change—his love of human liberty, for which he never ceased to fight in his dashing, spectacular manner.

Shelley shared his friend Byron's sense of political and social outrage—Shelley once spent time distributing revolutionary pamphlets in Ireland—but Shelley's poetry is quite unlike Byron's. Shelley's poetic theory moved him to sublime visions; Shelley spent his life as a poet recapturing those visions. Shelley regarded spiritual beauty, which is permanent and true, as the only real beauty. Only the shadow of beauty falls upon the earth, but it is beauty that makes existence worthwhile. His longer poems, such as *Prometheus Unbound* or *Hellas*, bring a violent revolutionary spirit that demands political and social upheaval into contact with this Platonic system of beauty. The harmonizing element is the love of

Portrait of Shelley (1819) by Amelia Curran.

Malthus (1766–1834) argued that population was growing faster than food supplies and therefore that starvation was inevitable unless forces tending to check the population, such as wars and disease, were allowed to operate. Jeremy Bentham's (1748–1832) doctrine of "the greatest good for the greatest number" and his constant testing of an idea or invention by the simple question, "What is the use of it?" (the utilitarian viewpoint) made him perhaps the most practically democratic theorist of his time. William Godwin (1756–1836) and Mary Wollstonecraft (1759–1797) were pioneer radicals imbued with the spirit of Rousseau. Intellectual and philosophical anarchists, they attacked all government and restraints upon human beings and advocated complete revolution, not by violence but by the application of reason to all social problems. Feminism was a growing concern of the period and was most clearly expressed in Wollstonecraft's *A Vindication of the Rights of Women* (1792). Godwin's influence upon Wordsworth and Coleridge was profound, particularly by way of Godwin's *Enquiry Concerning Political Justice* (1793). Shelley, later Godwin's son-in-law, derived many of his early rev-

humanity. In Shelley's shorter poems, the characteristic stamp of Platonic philosophy is evident, but here the poet's supreme lyrical gifts are most important. Few English poets can approach Shelley in melody, in finished harmony and sound effect, in fluency, and in fire and intensity.

The element of revolt evident in Byron and Shelley is absent in Keats, the youngest of the Romantic poets and first to die. Ill much of his adult life, Keats had a premonition of an early death that seemed to give him a superhuman delight in the senses, a well-known characteristic of his poetry. Like Shelley, Keats had a profound love of abstract beauty, but he also worshiped the warm, pulsing earthly beauty; the physical charm of both landscape and humanity could inspire him. In his brief but formidable career, he mastered many Romantic modes. His lyrical odes and sonnets reveal a concern with formal mastery, a common trait in this supposedly effusive period. His effective use of medieval material and ballad techniques suggests an affinity with Coleridge and indicates his admiration of Spenser. Keats' reputation grew after his death, and he had a formative influence on Tennyson, the first great poet of the Victorian period.

Prose. An age of profound social, political, and literary change invites commentary and criticism, and such was the case in the Romantic period. A number of journals were established in the early 1800s, and these provided forums for several interesting and important writers.

The social commentators of the period are numerous. Early in the era came Adam Smith's *Wealth of Nations* (1776), a landmark in the history of economic thought and a masterful analysis of capitalism. Thomas

John Martin's (1789–1851) Romantic painting The Bard *(1817), based upon a poem of the same name (1757) by Thomas Gray. Martin focuses our attention on the ethereal, dreamlike landscape.*

olutionary and socialistic views from the Godwin circle.

The rise of the personal essay parallels the development of Romantic poetry. The foremost essayists of the day, William Hazlitt, Thomas De Quincey, and Charles Lamb, refused to follow the traditional rules of the formal essay and the classical elements of rhetoric. Rather than convincing the reader of a point by logical argument, these writers were more interested in tracing the way their impressions and thoughts were transformed into beliefs. The structures of their essays, ostensibly haphazard when compared to the traditional formal essay, often represent "the growth of the writer's mind" in the way Wordsworth's *Prelude* traces the poet's development.

Hazlitt's most well-known volume of personal essays was *Table-Talk*, published in 1821. More aggressively learned than the other writers in this genre, Hazlitt's style is provocative, for his personal opinions were strongly felt and forcefully argued. In a piece such as "On Going on a Journey" readers can capture an attractive quality of the personal essay—the sense of listening to intelligent, sometimes intimate, conversation on a subject of general interest. Thomas De Quincey's *Confessions of an English Opium Eater*, published in 1821, brought him to popular attention. The majority of his best pieces were written for magazines and reflect the poetic quality that distinguished his prose, more sensuous in its movement, from the prose of the other two writers. Lamb, however, is responsible for most of the achievements of the genre and remains the most popular of the three today. His emotional warmth and lucidity of style are coupled with a wry sense of humor that together make such pieces as "The Two Races of Men" and "Poor Relations" a joy to read.

Fiction. The excellence of the Romantic period's poetry and prose nonfiction is in direct contrast to its prose fiction and drama. English drama was virtually nonexistent during this period and, with the exception of Jane Austen, the age's novelists are generally considered minor. For convenience we may divide the novels written after *Tristram Shandy* (1760–1767) into four general categories: the Gothic romance, the novel of purpose, the novel of manners, and the historical novel.

The fiction that most clearly portrays romantic tendencies and was the earliest to appear is the Gothic romance. To neoclassical writers and readers the term suggested the wild, the barbaric, and the primitive; specifically, it referred to the medievalism of a Gothic cathedral, and hence to the superstition of the Middle Ages, the mysterious and the unknown. The Gothic novel represents the Romantic return to the horror of

The Needles (1817–1818), a watercolor by John Sell Cotman (1782–1842), a prominent member of the Norwich School group of English landscape watercolorists. The geometrical figures and flattened space in Cotman's compositions prefigure techniques of modern artists such as Paul Cézanne.

the supernatural, the vaguely but monstrously sensational. Like the "graveyard" poetry of the late eighteenth century, it is a reaction against neoclassical rationalism. The first Gothic romance is *The Castle of Otranto* (1764) by Horace Walpole (1717–1797). The novel is both a whimsical fantasy and a serious exploration of themes basic to later Gothic fiction—the workings of fate, the power of guilt, the influence of the past, and, above all, the dark drives of the unconscious.

It was not until after the French Revolution that Gothic fiction became a major vogue in England, with the novels of Mrs. Anne Radcliffe. *The Mysteries of Udolpho* (1794) and *The Italian* (1797) enabled readers to feel the tingles of terror amid the security of a basically benign universe and with the guarantee of rational explanation. Three more subversive works followed: *The Monk* (1795) by Mathew Gregory Lewis; *Melmoth the Wanderer* (1820) by Charles Maturin, and *Frankenstein* (1816) by Mary Godwin Shelley. The poetic justice meted out to the "villains" cannot hide the extent to which characters are prey to emotions that they cannot control and that they share with us all. Gothic fiction was the first surfacing of those dark doubts about human potential and social efficacy that would enter much of English fiction before 1900.

In addition to the Gothic romance, the eighteenth-century novel of manners—a satirical picture, often

Valley of Aosta—Snowstorm, Avalanche, and Thunderstorm (1836–1837), an oil painting by Joseph M. W. Turner (1775–1851), prominent English landscape painter and watercolorist. Like Constable, Turner attempted in his canvases to portray changing atmospheric qualities and to express the emotional and spiritual qualities that they suggested. His technique was thus impressionistic rather than realistic.

Coming from Evening Church (1830), an oil painting by Samuel Palmer (1805–1881), known for his mystical landscapes, which were strongly influenced by Blake's illustrations. Palmer was a member of the Ancients, a group of English artists who admired the mysticism of Blake as well as the work of poets such as Vergil and Milton. The eminent Victorian art critic John Ruskin thought that Palmer was "deserving of the very highest place among followers of nature."

picaresque in structure, of English life and social customs—continued throughout the period. The most interesting writers of the genre were women. Frances Burney (1752–1840), the friend of Dr. Johnson, shows charm, narrative power, and shrewd portraiture in *Evelina* (1778), "the history of a young lad's entrance into the world." Maria Edgeworth (1760–1849) is a capable novelist whose specialities are the delineation of life among the Irish tenants of absentee landlords and the exposition of Irish folk manners, as in *Castle Rackrent* (1800) and *The Absentee* (1809). The greatest writer of the age transcends the rather loose description of a novelist of manners. Jane Austen (1775–1817) has all the satirical instincts of a neoclassicist: the remarkable clarity, the good sense, the humor, and the unusual detachment of her works belong to the preceding age. She insists that the moral life is inseparable from the social. Elizabeth Bennet in *Pride and Prejudice* and Emma Woodhouse in *Emma* learn that the discipline and humanity which make them good wives also allow them to assume their proper roles in their communities. Although Austen's tough-minded irony precludes sentimentality, all of life's day-to-day dangers and sorrows enter her apparently placid world. Jane Austen's early death cut short a talent which had already achieved major stature and remained unapproached in English fiction until the Victorian period.

The novel of purpose divides roughly into two kinds: those which had a pedagogic aim, and those which advocated social, political, or economic reform. Of the first kind, none is of first rank. The social revolutionary novel fared better and William Godwin's *Caleb Williams* (1794) is often considered one of the most underrated English novels. It pioneers the detective story format and combines radical ideas with deft insight into human psychology.

The historical novel found its ablest writer in Sir Walter Scott, who turned from poetry to fiction in 1814. *Waverly* is the first of nearly thirty novels written between then and Scott's death in 1832. Those on Scottish subjects are regarded as his best, though *Ivanhoe*, set in England in the days of Richard the Lionhearted, remains Scott's most popular work. Scott adjusts historical facts as he sees necessary, but the energy of his plots and his memorable characters compensate for a lack of intellectual vision and formal mastery. Scott's achievements gave to the novel a popular stature it had never before attained.

The merits of England's Romantic poets and writers are strongly debated even today, but the influence of their techniques and their changes in poetic language

An illustration of the Holme, a house in Regent's Park, London. It is a good example of the Regency style of architecture popular between 1810 and 1820, during the regency of George IV.

cannot be disputed. Many readers feel an affinity for the ways in which the period's artistic sensibilities reacted to the dramatic events and various revolutions surrounding them. Wordsworth prided himself on his desire to speak the language of common people and to share his innermost soul. Byron rebelled against the literary trend of his time and dreamed of helping an enslaved people by joining Greek insurgents in their struggle for independence. Shelley, who regarded himself as a visionary, became a kind of oracle for emerging British socialism. Blake, an obscure cult figure through the nineteenth century, has become a major influence on twentieth-century poetry and criticism. We—by way of the Victorians—are descendants of this first generation of the modern world; their problems remain our concerns.

ROBERT BURNS
1759–1796

Robert Burns was born in Ayrshire, a county in southwestern Scotland. He was the son of a hard-working farmer whose ambitious hopes for his children were blighted by poverty and discouragement. The childhood and boyhood of the poet consisted largely of a series of transient settlings and sudden uprootings on various unsuccessful farms. On all of them Burns labored as a plowboy. ''This kind of life,'' he himself said, ''the cheerless gloom of a hermit and the unceasing toil of a galley slave, brought me to my sixteenth year.'' It is probable that much of Burns' later fragile health and his untimely death at thirty-seven can be traced to his arduous life.

Although he was able to attend school from time to time, Burns chiefly educated himself. He was rather well read in great works of literature and enthusiastic about the songs, folklore, and native literary traditions of Scotland. For a time he eked out a living from the soil. In 1781 he became a flax dresser at Irvine, Ayrshire; there he received his introduction to town life.

In 1784 his father died, and Burns, with his brother Gilbert, resumed farm life on land previously leased at Mossgiel. He began a liaison there with Jean Armour, the daughter of a mason in the vicinity. This affair lasted intermittently for years, but the girl's father raised objections to their marriage. The publication of his first volume of poems at Kilmarnock in 1786, a collection including some of his most famous poems, made the obscure young peasant the literary rage; he visited Edinburgh, where he was wined and dined but regarded as a rustic prodigy.

The second edition of the *Poems* (1787) brought him enough money for two brief tours—one through the northern counties of England and the other into the Highlands. In the next year Burns took another farm in Dumfriesshire, lost money, wrote more poems, and finally married Jean Armour. In 1789 he became the exciseman of the district and later took a similar position in the town of Dumfries.

Burns' last year of literary activity (1792) was spent largely in collecting and editing traditional songs and ballads of ancient Scotland; he was responsible for the publication not only of the traditional texts of these ballads but of their melodies as well. Much of his editing resulted in virtually original compositions and added to his reputation as a great national poet. His growing sympathy with the ideas underlying the French Revolution, however, caused him to lose many friends. His health declined, and with that decline in health came irritability of temperament and an increased defiance of convention. He died in July 1796.

HOLY WILLIE'S PRAYER

O Thou, wha in the Heavens dost dwell,
Wha, as it pleases best Thysel',
Sends ane to heaven an' ten to hell
    A' for Thy glory,
And no for onie guid or ill
    They've done bafore Thee!

I bless and praise Thy matchless might,
Whan thousands Thou hast left in night,
That I am here before Thy sight,
    For gifts an' grace,   10
A burning an' a shining light,
    To a' this place.

What was I, or my generation,
That I should get sic exaltation?
I' wha deserv'd sic just damnation
    For broken laws,
Five thousand years 'fore my creation,
    Thro' Adam's cause!

When frae my mither's womb I fell,
Thou might hae plung'd me deep in hell,   20
To gnash my gums, to weep and wail,
    In burnin' lake,
Where damnéd devils roar and yell,
    Chain'd to a stake.

Yet I am here, a chosen sample,
To show Thy grace is great and ample;
I'm here a pillar in Thy temple,
    Strong as a rock,
A guide, a buckler, an example
    To a' Thy flock.   30

O Lord, Thou kens what zeal I bear,
When drinkers drink, and swearers swear,
And singin there and dancin here,
    Wi' great an' sma':
For I am keepit by Thy fear,
    Free frae them a'.

But yet, O Lord! confess I must:
At times I'm fash'd° wi' fleshly lust;
An' sometimes, too, wi' warldly trust,
    Vile self gets in;   40
But Thou remembers we are dust,
    Defil'd in sin.

O Lord! yestreen, Thou kens, wi' Meg—
Thy pardon I sincerely beg,
O! may it ne'er be a livin plague
    To my dishonor!

Holy Willie's Prayer 38 **fash'd,** beset

An' I'll ne'er lift a lawless leg
    Again upon her.

Besides I farther maun° allow,
50 Wi' Lizzie's lass, three times, I trow;
But, Lord, that Friday I was fou,°
    When I came near her,
Or else, Thou kens, Thy servant true
    Wad ne'er hae steered° her.

May be Thou lets this fleshly thorn
Beset Thy servant e'en and morn,
Lest he owre high and proud should turn,
    'Cause he's sae gifted;
If sae, Thy hand maun e'en be borne,
60   Until Thou lift it.

Lord, bless Thy chosen in this place,
For here Thou hast a chosen race;
But God confound their stubborn face,
    And blast their name,
Wha bring Thy elders to disgrace,
    An' public shame!

Lord, mind Gau'n Hamilton's deserts:
He drinks, an' swears, an' plays at cartes,
Yet has sae monie takin arts
70   Wi' grit and sma',
Frae God's ain Priest the people's hearts
    He steals awa'.

An' whan we chasten'd him therefore,
Thou kens how he bred sic a splore,°
As set the warld in a roar
    O' laughin at us;
Curse Thou his basket and his store,
    Kail° and potatoes!

Lord, hear my earnest cry an' pray'r
80 Against that Presbyt'ry o' Ayr!
Thy strong right hand, Lord, make it bare
    Upo' their heads;
Lord, weigh it down, an' dinna spare,
    For their misdeeds!

O Lord my God! that glib-tongu'd Aiken,
My very heart and flesh are quakin,
To think how we stood sweatin, shakin,
    An' pish'd wi' dread,
While he, wi' hingin lip an' snakin,°
90   Held up his head.

Lord, in the day of vengeance try him;
Lord, visit him wha did employ him,

And pass not in Thy mercy by 'em,
    Nor hear their pray'r:
But, for Thy people's sake, destroy 'em,
    An' dinna spare.

But, Lord, remember me and mine
Wi' mercies temp'ral and divine,
That I for gear° and grace may shine,
    Excelled by nane;°   100
And a' the glory shall be Thine,
    Amen, Amen.

(1785; 1808)

TO A MOUSE

ON TURNING UP HER NEST WITH THE PLOW,
NOVEMBER, 1785

Wee, sleekit, cowrin, tim'rous beastie,
O, what a panic's in thy breastie!
Thou need na start awa sae hasty
    Wi' bickering brattle!°
I wad be laith° to rin an' chase thee,
    Wi' murdering pattle!°

I'm truly sorry man's dominion
Has broken Nature's social union,
An' justifies that ill opinion
    Which makes thee startle   10
At me, thy poor, earth-born companion
    An' fellow-mortal!

I doubt na, whyles,° but thou may thieve;
What then? poor beastie, thou maun live:
A daimen icker in a thrave°
    'S a sma' request;
I'll get a blessin wi' the lave,°
    An' never miss 't!

Thy wee-bit housie, too, in ruin!
Its silly wa's the win's are strewin!   20
An' naething, now, to big° a new ane,
    O' foggage° green!
An' bleak December's win's ensuin,
    Baith snell° an' keen!

Thou saw the fields laid bare an' waste,
An' weary winter comin' fast,
An' cozie here, beneath the blast,
    Thou thought to dwell,

---

49 **maun,** must   51 **fou,** full, drunk   54 **steered,** meddled with   74 **sic a splore,** such a fuss   78 **Kail,** cabbage   89 **snakin,** sneering

99 **gear,** wealth   100 **nane,** none   **To a Mouse**   4 **Wi' . . . brattle,** with a sudden scamper   5 **wad be laith,** would be loath   6 **pattle,** paddle, used for cleaning the plow   13 **whyles,** sometimes   15 **daimen . . . thrave,** occasional ear or head of grain in a shock   17 **lave,** rest   21 **big,** build   22 **foggage,** coarse grass   24 **snell,** sharp, bitter

Till, crash! the cruel coulter° passed
      Out through thy cell.

That wee bit heap o' leaves an' stibble,
Hast cost thee monie a weary nibble!
Now thou's turned out, for a' thy trouble,
      But° house or hald,°
To thole° the winter's sleety dribble,
      An' cranreuch° cauld!

But Mousie, thou art no thy lane,°
In proving foresight may be vain:
The best-laid schemes o' mice an' men
      Gang aft agley,°
An' lea'e us naught but grief an' pain,
      For promised joy!

Still thou art blest, compared wi' me!
The present only toucheth thee:
But och! I backward cast my e'e,
      On prospects drear!
An' forward, though I canna see,
      I guess an' fear!

(1785; 1786)

TO A LOUSE

ON SEEING ONE ON A LADY'S BONNET AT CHURCH

Ha! wh'are ye gaun, ye crowlin ferlie?°
Your impudence protects you sairly;°
I canna say but ye strunt rarely,
      Owre gauze and lace,
Tho' faith! I fear ye dine but sparely
      On sic a place.

Ye ugly, creepin, blastit wonner,°
Detested, shunned by saunt an' sinner,
How dare ye set your fit upon her,
      Sae fine a lady?
Gae somewhere else, and seek your dinner
      On some poor body.

Swith,° in some beggar's hauffet° squattle;°
There ye may creep, and sprawl, and sprattle°
Wi' ither kindred jumping cattle,
      In shoals and nations;
Whare horn nor bane° ne'er dare unsettle
      Your thick plantations.

Now haud you there! ye're out o' sight,
Below the fatt'rils,° snug an' tight;
Na, faith ye yet! ye'll no be right
      Till ye've got on it,
The very tapmost tow'ring height
      O' Miss's bonnet.

My sooth! right bauld ye set your nose out,
As plump an' gray as onie grozet;°
O for some rank mercurial rozet,°
      Or fell red smeddum!°
I'd gie you sic a hearty dose o't,
      Wad dress your droddum!°

I wad na been surprised to spy
You on an auld wife's flainen toy;°
Or aiblins° some bit duddie° boy,
      On's wyliecoat;°
But Miss's fine Lunardi!° fie,
      How daur ye do't?

O Jenny, dinna toss your head,
An' set your beauties a' abread!°
Ye little ken what curséd speed
      The blastie's° makin!
Thae winks and finger-ends, I dread,
      Are notice takin!

O wad some Power the giftie gie us
To see oursels as ithers see us!
It wad frae monie a blunder free us,
      An' foolish notion:
What airs in dress an' gait wad lea'e us,
      An' ev'n devotion!

(1786)

AULD LANG SYNE°

Should auld acquaintance be forgot,
   And never brought to min'?
Should auld acquaintance be forgot,
   And auld lang syne?

CHORUS

For auld lang syne, my dear,
   For auld lang syne,
We'll tak a cup o' kindness yet
   For auld lang syne.

29 **coulter,** cutter attached to the beam of a plow   34 **But,** without   **hald,** abode   35 **thole,** endure   36 **cranreuch,** hoarfrost   37 **no thy lane,** not alone   40 **Gang aft agley,** often go awry   **To a Louse**   1 **crowlin ferlie,** crawling wonder   2 **sairly,** greatly   **blastit wonner,** blasted wonder   13 **Swith,** quick   **hauffet,** temple   **squattle,** settle   14 **sprattle,** scramble   17 **horn nor bane,** horn comb, bone comb

20 **fatt'rils,** ribbon ends   26 **grozet,** gooseberry   27 **rozet,** rosin   28 **smeddum,** powder   30 **droddum,** breech   32 **flainen toy,** flannel cap   33 **aiblins,** perhaps   **bit duddie,** small, ragged   34 **wyliecoat,** undervest   35 **Lunardi,** balloon bonnet, named after a noted balloonist   38 **abread,** abroad   40 **blastie,** blasted creature   **Auld Lang Syne,** Old Long Since, i.e., Old Times

And surely ye'll be your pint-stowp,°
10 And surely I'll be mine!
And we'll tak a cup o' kindness yet
    For auld lang syne.

We twa hae run about the braes,°
    And pu'd the gowans° fine;
But we've wandered monie a weary fit°
    Sin' auld lang syne.

We twa hae paidled° i' the burn,°
    From mornin' sun till dine;°
But seas between us braid hae roared
20   Sin' auld lang syne.

And there's a hand, my trusty fiere,°
    And gie's a hand o' thine;
And we'll tak a right guid-willie waught°
    For auld lang syne.
(1788; 1796)

TAM O'SHANTER

A TALE

Of Brownyis and of Bogillis° full is this Buke.
                    —Gawin Douglas

    When chapman billies° leave the street,
And drouthy° neebors neebors meet,
As market-days are wearing late,
An' folk begin to take the gate;°
While we sit bousing at the nappy,°
An' gettin fou° and unco happy,
We think na on the lang Scots miles,°
The mosses,° waters, slaps,° and stiles,
That lie between us and our hame,
10 Whare sits our sulky, sullen dame,
Gathering her brows like gathering storm,
Nursing her wrath to keep it warm.

    This truth fand° honest Tam o' Shanter,
As he frae Ayr ae night did canter:
(Auld Ayr, wham ne'er a town surpasses,
For honest men and bonie° lasses.)

    O Tam! had'st thou but been sae wise
As taen thy ain wife Kate's advice!
She tauld thee weel thou was a skellum,°

A bletherin,° blusterin, drunken blellum;°   20
That frae November till October,
Ae market-day thou was na sober;
That ilka melder° wi' the miller,
Thou sat as lang as thou had siller;°
That ev'ry naig was ca'd° a shoe on,
The smith and thee gat roaring fou on;
That at the Lord's house, even on Sunday,
Thou drank wi' Kirkton° Jean till Monday.
She prophesied, that, late or soon,
Thou would be found deep drowned in Doon;°   30
Or catched wi' warlocks in the mirk,°
By Alloway's auld haunted kirk.

    Ah, gentle dames! it gars me greet,°
To think how monie counsels sweet,
How monie lengthened sage advices,
The husband frae the wife despises!

    But to our tale:—Ae market night,
Tam had got planted unco° right,
Fast by an ingle,° bleezing finely,
Wi' reaming swats° that drank divinely;   40
And at his elbow, Souter° Johnie,
His ancient, trusty, drouthy° cronie:
Tam loe'd him like a very brither;
They had been fou for weeks thegither.
The night drave on wi' sangs and clatter;
And ay the ale was growing better:
The landlady and Tam grew gracious
Wi' secret favors, sweet and precious:
The souter tauld his queerest stories;
The landlord's laugh was ready chorus: 50
The storm without might rair and rustle,
Tam did na mind the storm a whistle.

    Care, mad to see a man sae happy,
E'en drowned himsel amang the nappy:
As bees flee hame wi' lades o' treasure,
The minutes winged their way wi' pleasure;
Kings may be blest, but Tam was glorious,
O'er a' the ills o' life victorious!

    But pleasures are like poppies spread,
You seize the flow'r, its bloom is shed;   60
Or like the snow falls in the river,
A moment white—then melts forever;
Or like the borealis race,
That flit ere you can point their place;
Or like the rainbow's lovely form
Evanishing amid the storm.
Nae man can tether time nor tide:
The hour approaches Tam maun ride—

---

9 **ye'll . . . pint-stowp.** You will pay for your pint of drink   13 **braes,** hill-sides   14 **gowans,** daisies   15 **fit,** foot, step   17 **paidled,** paddled, dabbled   **burn,** brook   18 **dine,** dinner time   21 **fiere,** friend   23 **right . . . waught,** hearty good-will draught   **Tam O'Shanter   Of Brownyis . . . Bogillis,** brownies and hob-goblins. The line is quoted from the Scottish Chaucerian poet's prologue to a transla-tion of Vergil's *Aeneid*   1 **chapman billies,** peddler comrades   2 **drouthy,** thirsty   4 **take the gate,** take the way, go home   5 **bousing at the nappy,** drinking ale   6 **fou,** full, drunk   7 **lang . . . miles.** The old Scottish mile was 216 yards longer than the English mile   8 **mosses,** bogs   **slaps,** gates   13 **fand,** found   16 **bonie,** winsome

19 **skellum,** good-for-nothing   20 **bletherin,** idly talking   **blellum,** babbler   23 **ilka melder,** every grinding   24 **siller,** silver, money   25 **ca'd,** nailed   28 **Kirkton,** any village near a church   30 **Doon,** a small stream near Burns' birthplace   31 **mirk,** dark   33 **gars me greet,** makes me weep   38 **unco,** very, exactly   39 **ingle,** fireplace   40 **reaming swats,** foaming new ale   41 **Souter,** cobbler   42 **drouthy,** thirsty

That hour, o' night's black arch the keystane,°
70 That dreary hour Tam mounts his beast in;
And sic a night he taks the road in,
As ne'er poor sinner was abroad in.

The wind blew as 'twad blawn its last;
The rattling showers rose on the blast;
The speedy gleams the darkness swallowed;
Loud, deep, and lang the thunder bellowed:
That night, a child might understand,
The Deil had business on his hand.

Weel mounted on his gray mare, Meg—
80 A better never lifted leg—
Tam skelpit° on thro' dub° and mire,
Despising wind and rain and fire;
Whiles holding fast his guid blue bonnet,
Whiles crooning o'er some auld Scots sonnet,
Whiles glow'ring round wi' prudent cares,
Lest bogles° catch him unawares.
Kirk-Alloway was drawing nigh,
Whare ghaists and houlets° nightly cry.

By this time he was cross the ford,
90 Whare in the snaw the chapman smoored;°
And past the birks° and meikle stane,°
Whare drunken Charlie brak's neck-bane;
And thro' the whins,° and by the cairn,°
Whare hunters fand the murdered bairn;°
And near the thorn, aboon the well,
Whare Mungo's mither hanged hersel.
Before him Doon pours all his floods;
The doubling storm roars thro' the woods;
The lightnings flash from pole to pole,
100 Near and more near the thunders roll;
When, glimmering thro' the groaning trees
Kirk-Alloway seemed in a bleeze:
Thro' ilka bore° the beams were glancing,
And loud resounded mirth and dancing.

Inspiring bold John Barleycorn!
What dangers thou canst make us scorn!
Wi' tippenny° we fear nae evil;
Wi' usquebae° we'll face the devil!
The swats sae reamed° in Tammie's noddle,
110 Fair play, he cared na deils a boddle.°
But Maggie stood right sair astonished,
Till, by the heel and hand admonished,
She ventured forward on the light;
And, wow! Tam saw an unco° sight!

Warlocks and witches in a dance;
Nae cotillion brent-new frae France,

But hornpipes,° jigs, strathspeys, and reels
Put life and mettle in their heels:
A winnock bunker° in the east,
There sat Auld Nick in shape o' beast;   120
A towsie tyke,° black, grim, and large,
To gie them music was his charge;
He screwed the pipes and gart them skirl,°
Till roof and rafters a' did dirl.°
Coffins stood round like open presses,
That shawed the dead in their last dresses;
And by some devilish cantraip sleight°
Each in its cauld hand held a light,
By which heroic Tam was able
To note upon the haly° table   130
A murderer's banes in gibbet airns;°
Twa span-lang, wee, unchristened bairns;
A thief, new-cutted frae a rape°—
Wi' his last gasp his gab° did gape;
Five tomahawks, wi' bluid red-rusted;
Five scymitars, wi' murder crusted;
A garter, which a babe had strangled;
A knife, a father's throat had mangled,
Whom his ain son o' life bereft—
The gray hairs yet stack to the heft;   140
Wi' mair o' horrible and awfu',
Which even to name wad be unlawfu'.

As Tammie glowered, amazed and curious,
The mirth and fun grew fast and furious:
The piper loud and louder blew,
The dancers quick and quicker flew;
They reeled, they set, they crossed, they cleekit,°
Till ilka carlin swat and reekit,°
And coost her duddies to the wark°
And linket at it in her sark!°   150

Now Tam, O Tam! had thae been queans,°
A' plump and strapping in their teens!
Their sarks, instead o' creeshie flannen,°
Been snaw-white seventeen hunder linen!°—
Thir breeks° o' mine, my only pair,
That ance were plush, o' guid blue hair,
I wad hae gien them aff my hurdies,°
For ae blink o' the bonie burdies!°

But wither'd beldams, auld and droll,
Rigwoodie° hags wad spean° a foal,   160
Louping and flinging on a crummock,°
I wonder didna turn thy stomach.

69 hour . . . keystane, midnight   81 skelpit, clattered   dub, puddle   86 bogles, hobgoblins   88 houlets, owls   90 smoored, smothered   91 birks, birches   meikle stane, great stone   93 whins, furze   cairn, pile of stones   94 bairn, child   103 ilka bore, every crevice   107 tippenny, two-penny ale   108 usquebae, whisky   109 swats sae reamed, ale so foamed   110 deils a boddle, devil a farthing   114 unco, strange

117 hornpipes, etc., lively Scottish dances   119 winnock bunker, window seat   121 towsie tyke, shaggy cur   123 gart them skirl, make them scream   124 dirl, ring, tingle   127 cantraip sleight, magic trick   130 haly, holy   131 banes in gibbet airns, bones in gibbet irons   133 rape, rope   134 gab, mouth   147 cleekit, caught hold of each other   148 ilka . . . reekit, each hag sweat and steamed   149 coost . . . wark, threw off her clothes for the work   150 linket . . . sark, went at it in her shirt   151 queans, young wenches   153 creeshie flannen, greasy flannel   154 seventeen . . . linen, fine linen, with 1700 threads to the width   155 Thir breeks, these breeches   157 hurdies, hips   158 burdies, lasses   160 Rigwoodie, lean, withered   spean, wean (out of disgust)   161 Louping . . . crummock, leaping and capering on a crooked staff

But Tam kend° what was what fu' brawlie;°
There was ae winsome wench and wawlie,°
That night enlisted in the core°
Lang after kend on Carrick° shore
(For monie a beast to dead she shot,
An' perished monie a bonie boat,
And shook baith meikle corn and bear,°
170 And kept the countryside in fear).
Her cutty sark,° o' Paisley harn,°
That while a lassie she had worn,
In longitude tho' sorely scanty,
It was her best, and she was vauntie.°
Ah! little kend thy reverend grannie,
That sark she coft° for her wee Nannie,
Wi' twa pund Scots ('twas a' her riches),
Wad ever graced a dance o' witches!

But here my Muse her wing maun cour,°
180 Sic flights are far beyond her power;
To sing how Nannie lap and flang,°
(A souple jade she was and strang,)
And how Tam stood like ane bewitched,
And thought his very een enriched;
Even Satan glowered and fidged fu' fain,°
And hotched° and blew wi' might and main:
Till first ae caper, syne anither,
Tam tint° his reason a' thegither,
And roars out, "Weel done, Cutty-sark!"
190 And in an instant all was dark:
And scarcely had he Maggie rallied,
When out the hellish legion sallied.

As bees bizz out wi' angry fyke,°
When plundering herds° assail their byke;°
As open° pussie's° mortal foes,
When, pop! she starts before their nose;
As eager runs the market-crowd,
When "Catch the thief!" resounds aloud;
So Maggie runs, the witches follow,
200 Wi' monie an eldritch° skriech and hollo.

Ah, Tam! ah, Tam! thou'll get thy fairin!°
In hell they'll roast thee like a herrin!
In vain thy Kate awaits thy comin!
Kate soon will be a woefu' woman!
Now, do thy speedy utmost, Meg,
And win the keystane of the brig:°
There at them thou thy tail may toss,
A running stream they dare na cross.
But ere the keystane she could make,
210 The fient° a tail she had to shake!
For Nannie, far before the rest,

Hard upon noble Maggie prest,
And flew at Tam wi' furious ettle;°
But little wist° she Maggie's mettle—
Ae spring brought aff her master hale,
But left behind her ain gray tail:
The carlin claught° her by the rump,
And left poor Maggie scarce a stump.

Now, wha this tale o' truth shall read,
Ilk man and mother's son, take heed,   220
Whene'er to drink you are inclined,
Or cutty-sarks run in your mind,
Think, ye may buy the joys o'er dear,
Remember Tam o' Shanter's Mare.
(1789;1791)

SCOTS, WHA HAE

Scots, wha hae wi' Wallace° bled,
Scots, wham Bruce° has aften led,
Welcome to your gory bed
        Or to victorie!

Now's the day, and now's the hour:
See the front o' battle lour,
See approach proud Edward's power—
        Chains and slaverie!

Wha will be a traitor knave?
Wha can fill a coward's grave?   10
Wha sae base as be a slave?—
        Let him turn, and flee!

Wha for Scotland's King and Law
Freedom's sword will strongly draw,
Freeman stand or freeman fa',
        Let him follow me!

By Oppression's woes and pains,
By your sons in servile chains,
We will drain our dearest veins.
        But they shall be free!   20

Lay the proud usurpers low!
Tyrants fall in every foe!
Liberty's in every blow!
        Let us do, or die!
(1793; 1794)

163 **kend**, knew   **fu' brawlie**, full well   164 **wawlie**, buxom   165 **core**, company   166 **Carrick**, southern district of Ayrshire   169 **corn and bear**, wheat and barley   171 **cutty sark**, short shirt   **Paisley harn**, coarse linen made in the town of Paisley   174 **vauntie**, proud   176 **coft**, bought   179 **maun cour**, must lower   181 **lap and flang**, jumped and kicked   185 **fidged fu' fain**, fidgeted with pleasure   186 **hotched**, jerked   188 **tint**, lost   193 **fyke**, fuss   194 **herds**, herdsmen   **byke**, hive   195 **open**, begin to bark   **pussie's**, the hare's   200 **eldritch**, unearthly   201 **fairin**, reward   206 **brig**, bridge   210 **fient**, devil

213 **ettle**, aim, intent   214 **wist**, knew   217 **claught**, seized   **Scots, Wha Hae**   1 **Wallace**, Scottish patriot and lifelong resister of the English at the time of Edward I   2 **Bruce**, King Robert the Bruce of Scotland, led the Scots to defeat the English at the Battle of Bannockburn in 1314

A RED, RED ROSE

O, my luve is like a red, red rose,
  That's newly sprung in June.
O, my luve is like the melodie,
  That's sweetly played in tune.

5 As fair art thou, my bonie lass,
  So deep in luve am I,
And I will luve thee still, my dear,
  Till a' the seas gang dry.

Till a' the seas gang dry, my dear,
10 And the rocks melt wi' the sun!
And I will luve thee still, my dear,
  While the sands o' life shall run.

And fare thee weel, my only luve,
  And fare thee weel a while!
15 And I will come again, my luve,
  Tho' it were ten thousand mile!
(1794; 1796)

A MAN'S A MAN FOR A' THAT

Is there, for honest poverty,
  That hings his head, an' a' that?
The coward slave, we pass him by,
  We dare be poor for a' that!
    For a' that, an' a' that,
      Our toils obscure, an' a' that;
    The rank is but the guinea's stamp;°
    The man's the gowd° for a' that.

What tho' on hamely fare we dine,
10 Wear hodden-gray,° an' a' that;
Gie fools their silks, and knaves their wine,
  A man's a man for a' that.
    For a' that, an' a' that,
      Their tinsel show, an' a' that;
    The honest man, tho' e'er sae poor,
    Is king o' men for a' that.

Ye see yon birkie,° ca'd a lord,
  Wha struts, an' stares, an' a' that;
Tho' hundreds worship at his word,
20 He's but a coof° for a' that.
    For a' that, an' a' that,
      His riband, star, an' a' that
    The man o' independent mind,
      He looks and laughs at a' that.

A prince can mak a belted knight,
  A marquis, duke, an' a' that;
But an honest man's aboon° his might,
  Guid faith he mauna fa'° that!
    For a' that, an' a' that,
      Their dignities, an' a' that,   30
    The pith o' sense, an' pride o' worth,
    Are higher rank than a' that.

Then let us pray that come it may,
  As come it will for a' that,
That sense and worth, o'er a' the earth,
  May bear the gree,° an' a' that.
    For a' that, an' a' that,
      It's coming yet, for a' that,
    That man to man, the warld o'er,
    Shall brothers be for a' that.   40
(1794; 1795)

WILLIAM BLAKE
1757–1827

William Blake, the son of a hosier, was born in London in 1757. He was brought up in a modest shopkeeper's household; his parents were Nonconformists, or dissenters, from the Anglican Church. Blake did not go to school but was taught by his mother and read extensively from a very early age. All his life he had a strongly visual mind and had the ability to see mental images as if they were solid figures. At the age of ten, he was sent to a good art school and a few years later was apprenticed to an engraver for the usual seven years. Upon completing his apprenticeship, he enrolled briefly as a student in the Royal Academy but left because he felt his artistic talents were being wasted. He then began to make his living by engraving for publishers and painting watercolors; this work remained his chief source of livelihood until his death.

During the 1770s Blake became friendly with a number of people who were unorthodox in their religious and social views. For the most part their politics were liberal; they were sympathetic to the American Revolution. Among the people he met with regularly were William Godwin (1756–1836), radical philosopher and writer; Mary Wollstonecraft (1759–1797), social reformer and champion of the oppressed; Thomas Paine (1737–1809), philosopher and active supporter of the American Revolution; and Joseph

---

A Man's a Man for A' That   7 **guinea's stamp,** imprint of the King's head on a coin as a statement of its value   8 **gowd,** gold   10 **hodden-gray,** coarse gray woolen cloth   17 **birkie,** young fellow   20 **coof,** fool

27 **aboon,** above   28 **mauna fa',** must not claim or get   36 **bear the gree,** have the prize

Priestly (1733–1804), Unitarian and rationalist thinker.

Blake had begun to write poetry while still a boy, and with the help of sympathetic friends, he published a small book called *Poetical Sketches by W.B.* in 1783. His publisher described the poems as "the production of untutored youth, commenced in his twelfth, and occasionally resumed by the author till his twentieth year." Using his own unique method, Blake engraved the text of his *Songs of Innocence* on small copper plates in 1789. He printed and colored the pages of the book by hand. In 1794 Blake brought out a sequel to this book, called *Songs of Experience.* Although neither of these books had much impact in his own lifetime, they were revolutionary works. It is unclear why they did not touch off the romantic storm that came so soon after when Wordsworth and Coleridge published the *Lyrical Ballads* (1798). One probable reason is that Blake's works were not sold or reviewed in the conventional way. Between 1790 and 1793 Blake was also working on a work of prose titled *The Marriage of Heaven and Hell.* This work included a series of "Proverbs of Hell," which developed in simple images the themes of the *Songs of Experience.* In the late 1790s Blake's fortunes fell, partly as a result of the economic depression resulting from England's war with France. Blake was sympathetic to the French cause and was known to be an opponent of his own government.

While staying in Felpham in 1803, Blake had an altercation with a private in a troop of dragoons stationed in the village. Blake apparently ordered the soldier out of his yard. Thereupon the soldier filed a complaint against Blake, accusing him of uttering seditious statements about king and country. Blake was eventually acquitted, but the event and the soldier haunted Blake's imagination. Later Blake would transform this incident in ominous fashion in *Jerusalem.* After 1804 Blake spent his time working on his two longest works—*Milton* (finished about 1808) and *Jerusalem* (finished in 1820). These works are very different from his earlier, lyric poems; they are long, unrhymed narratives that share a prophetic character. Blake's basic theme in these two later works, as in his earlier lyrics, is that man must free himself from conventional authority.

The later part of his life was primarily devoted to pictorial art. He held an exhibition of his paintings and watercolors in 1809, but it did not meet with success. His final years, however, were enriched by the admiration of a group of young painters, including John Linnell (1792–1882), Samuel Palmer (1805–1881), and Edward Calvert (1799–1883), who called themselves the Ancients and regarded Blake as a prophet. Blake was commissioned by friends to illustrate the works of other poets (Chaucer, Dante, and Gray) and the Bible (the Book of Job). He died relatively unknown in 1827 and was buried in an unmarked grave.

Blake's talent and achievement were not generally recognized for more than one hundred years after his death. In the interim he was highly regarded by fellow artists and poets such as Dante Gabriel Rossetti, Algernon Charles Swinburne, and William Butler Yeats. Today his reputation is firmly established. Though his work transcends simple labels, he can be classified as a romantic in his mystically imaginative creations in both verse and art and in the arresting emotional power of his lyric poetry. He was an extraordinarily gifted combination of poet, painter, and visionary who seized the pictorial element of an idea and translated it into the sensuous language of his deeply religious, though unorthodox, mysticism.

from POETICAL SKETCHES

TO THE EVENING STAR

Thou fair-haired angel of the evening,
Now, whilst the sun rests on the mountains, light
Thy bright torch of love; thy radiant crown
Put on, and smile upon our evening bed!
Smile on our loves, and while thou drawest the   5
Blue curtains of the sky, scatter thy silver dew
On every flower that shuts its sweet eyes
In timely sleep. Let thy west wind sleep on
The lake; speak silence with thy glimmering eyes,
And wash the dusk with silver. Soon, full soon,   10
Dost thou withdraw; then the wolf rages wide,
And the lion glares through the dun forest:
The fleeces of our flocks are covered with
Thy sacred dew; protect them with thine influence.

MY SILKS AND FINE ARRAY

My silks and fine array,
My smiles and languished air,
By love are driven away;
And mournful lean Despair
Brings me yew to deck my grave;   5
Such end true lovers have.

His face is fair as heaven
When springing buds unfold;
O why to him was't given,
Whose heart is wintry cold?   10
His breast is love's all-worshiped tomb,
Where all love's pilgrims come.

Bring me an ax and spade,
Bring me a winding-sheet;
15 When I my grave have made,
Let winds and tempests beat;
Then down I'll lie as cold as clay.
True love doth pass away!

SONG

How sweet I roam'd from field to field,
   And tasted all the summer's pride,
'Till I the prince of love beheld,
   Who in the sunny beams did glide!

5 He shew'd me lilies for my hair,
   And blushing roses for my brow;
He led me through his gardens fair,
   Where all his golden pleasures grow.

With sweet May dews my wings were wet,
10   And Phoebus fir'd my vocal rage;
He caught me in his silken net,
   And shut me in his golden cage.

He loves to sit and hear me sing,
   Then, laughing, sports and plays with me;
15 Then stretches out my golden wing,
   And mocks my loss of liberty.
(1783)

from SONGS OF INNOCENCE

INTRODUCTION

Piping down the valleys wild,
Piping songs of pleasant glee,
On a cloud I saw a child,
And he laughing said to me:

5 "Pipe a song about a Lamb!"
So I piped with merry cheer.
"Piper, pipe that song again";
So I piped: he wept to hear.

"Drop thy pipe, thy happy pipe;
10 Sing thy songs of happy cheer";
So I sang the same again,
While he wept with joy to hear.

"Piper, sit thee down and write
In a book, that all may read."
So he vanished from my sight,   15
And I plucked a hollow reed,

And I made a rural pen,
And I stained the water clear,
And I wrote my happy songs
Every child may joy to hear.   20

THE LAMB

   Little Lamb, who made thee?
   Dost thou know who made thee?
Gave thee life, and bid thee feed,
By the stream and o'er the mead;
Gave thee clothing of delight,   5
Softest clothing, woolly, bright;
Gave thee such a tender voice,
Making all the vales rejoice?
   Little Lamb, who made thee?
   Dost thou know who made thee?   10

   Little Lamb, I'll tell thee,
   Little Lamb, I'll tell thee:
He is calléd by thy name,
For He calls Himself a Lamb,
He is meek, and He is mild;   15
He became a little child.
I a child, and thou a lamb,
We are calléd by His name.
   Little Lamb, God bless thee!
   Little Lamb, God bless thee!   20

THE LITTLE BLACK BOY

My mother bore me in the southern wild,
And I am black, but O! my soul is white;
White as an angel is the English child,
But I am black, as if bereaved of light.

My mother taught me underneath a tree, 5
And, sitting down before the heat of day,
She took me on her lap and kisséd me,
And, pointing to the east, began to say:

"Look on the rising sun—there God does live,
And gives His light, and gives His heat away;   10
And flowers and trees and beasts and men receive
Comfort in morning, joy in the noonday.

"And we are put on earth a little space,
That we may learn to bear the beams of love;
15 And these black bodies and this sunburnt face
Is but a cloud, and like a shady grove.

"For when our souls have learned the heat to bear,
The cloud will vanish; we shall hear His voice,
Saying: 'Come out from the grove, My love and care,
20 And round My golden tent like lambs rejoice.'"

Thus did my mother say, and kisséd me;
And thus I say to little English boy.
When I from black and he from white cloud free,
And round the tent of God like lambs we joy,

25 I'll shade him from the heat, till he can bear
To lean in joy upon our Father's knee;
And then I'll stand and stroke his silver hair,
And be like him, and he will then love me.

THE CHIMNEY SWEEPER

When my mother died I was very young,
And my father sold me while yet my tongue,
Could scarcely cry weep weep weep weep.
So your chimneys I sweep & in soot I sleep.

5 There's little Tom Dacre, who cried when his head
That curl'd like a lambs back, was shav'd, so I said.
Hush Tom never mind it, for when your head's bare,
You know that the soot cannot spoil your white hair.

And so he was quiet, & that very night,
10 As Tom was a sleeping he had such a sight,
That thousands of sweepers Dick, Joe Ned & Jack
Were all of them lock'd up in coffins of black

And by came an Angel who had a bright key,
And he open'd the coffins & set them all free.
15 Then down a green plain leaping laughing they run
And wash in a river and shine in the Sun.

Then naked & white, all their bags left behind,
They rise upon clouds, and sport in the wind.
And the Angel told Tom if he'd be a good boy,
20 He'd have God for his father & never want joy.

And so Tom awoke and we rose in the dark
And got with our bags & our brushes to work.
Tho' the morning was cold, Tom was happy & warm,
So if all do their duty, they need not fear harm.

THE DIVINE IMAGE

To Mercy, Pity, Peace, and Love
All pray in their distress;
And to these virtues of delight
Return their thankfulness.

For Mercy, Pity, Peace, and Love   5
Is God, our Father dear,
And Mercy, Pity, Peace, and Love
Is man, His child and care.

For Mercy has a human heart,
Pity a human face,   10
And Love, the human form divine,
And Peace, the human dress.

Then every man, of every clime,
That prays in his distress,
Prays to the human form divine,   15
Love, Mercy, Pity, Peace.

And all must love the human form,
In heathen, Turk, or Jew;
Where Mercy, Love, and Pity dwell
There God is dwelling too.   20

HOLY THURSDAY

'Twas on a Holy Thursday,° their innocent faces clean,
The children walking two and two, in red and blue
    and green;
Gray-headed beadles° walked before, with wands as
    white as snow;
Till into the high dome of Paul's° they like Thames'
    waters flow.

Oh, what a multitude they seemed, these flowers of   5
    London town!
Seated in companies, they sit with radiance all their
    own.
The hum of multitudes was there, but multitudes
    of lambs,
Thousands of little boys and girls raising their inno-
    cent hands.

Now like a mighty wind they raise to Heaven the
    voice of song,
Or like harmonious thunderings the seats of Heaven   10
    among.

Holy Thursday   1 **Holy Thursday,** Thursday of Holy Week, the week before Easter.
Cf. this poem to "Holy Thursday" in *Songs of Experience.* The scene describes the
annual services in London for charity schoolchildren.   3 **beadles,** parish officers   4 **Paul's,** St. Paul's Cathedral, London

Beneath them sit the agéd men, wise guardians of
   the poor;
Then cherish pity, lest you drive an angel from your
   door.
(1789–90)

from SONGS OF EXPERIENCE

INTRODUCTION

Hear the voice of the Bard!
Who Present, Past, & Future sees
Whose ears have heard,
The Holy Word,
5 That walk'd among the ancient trees.

Calling the lapsed Soul
And weeping in the evening dew;
That might controll,
The starry pole;
10 And fallen fallen light renew!

O Earth O Earth return!
Arise from out the dewy grass;
Night is worn,
And the morn
15 Rises from the slumberous mass.

Turn away no more:
Why wilt thou turn away
The starry floor
The watry shore
20 Is giv'n thee till the break of day.

EARTH'S ANSWER

Earth rais'd up her head,
From the darkness dread & drear.
Her light fled:
Stony dread!
5 And her locks cover'd with grey despair.

Prison'd on watry shore
Starry Jealousy does keep my den
Cold and hoar
Weeping o'er
10 I hear the Father of the ancient men

Selfish father of men
Cruel jealous selfish fear
Can delight
Chain'd in night
The virgins of youth and morning bear.   15

Does spring hide its joy
When buds and blossoms grow?
Does the sower?
Sow by night?
Or the plowman in darkness plow?   20

Break this heavy chain,
That does freeze my bones around
Selfish! vain,
Eternal bane!
That free Love with bondage bound.   25

THE CLOD & THE PEBBLE

Love seeketh not Itself to please,
Nor for itself hath any care;
But for another gives its ease,
And builds a Heaven in Hells despair.

    So sang a little Clod of Clay,   5
    Trodden with the cattles feet:
    But a Pebble of the brook,
    Warbled out these metres meet.

Love seeketh only Self to please,
To bind another to its delight;   10
Joys in anothers loss of ease,
And builds a Hell in Heavens despite.

HOLY THURSDAY

Is this a holy thing to see,
In a rich and fruitful land,
Babes reducd to misery,
Fed with cold and usurous hand?

Is that trembling cry a song?   5
Can it be a song of joy?
And so many children poor?
It is a land of poverty!

And their sun does never shine.
And their fields are bleak & bare.   10
And their ways are fill'd with thorns.
It is eternal winter there.

For where-e'er the sun does shine,
And where-e'er the rain does fall:
15 Babe can never hunger there,
Nor poverty the mind appall.

THE CHIMNEY SWEEPER

A little black thing among the snow:
Crying weep, weep, in notes of woe!
Where are thy father & mother? say?
They are both gone up to the church to pray.

5 Because I was happy upon the heath,
And smil'd among the winters snow:
They clothed me in the clothes of death,
And taught me to sing the notes of woe.

And because I am happy, & dance & sing,
10 They think they have done me no injury:
And are gone to praise God & his Priest & King
Who make up a heaven of our misery.

THE SICK ROSE

O Rose thou art sick.
The invisible worm,
That flies in the night
In the howling storm:

5 Has found out thy bed
Of crimson joy:
And his dark secret love
Does thy life destroy.

THE FLY

Little Fly
Thy summers play,
My thoughtless hand
Has brush'd away.

5 Am not I
A fly like thee?
Or art not thou
A man like me?

For I dance
And drink & sing;   10
Till some blind hand
Shall brush my wing.

If thought is life
And strength & breath;
And the want   15
Of thought is death;

Then am I
A happy fly,
If I live,
Or if I die.   20

THE TYGER

Tyger Tyger, burning bright,
In the forests of the night;
What immortal hand or eye,
Could frame thy fearful symmetry?

In what distant deeps or skies   5
Burnt the fire of thine eyes!
On what wings dare he aspire?
What the hand, dare sieze the fire?

And what shoulder, & what art,
Could twist the sinews of thy heart? 10
And when thy heart began to beat,
What dread hand? & what dread feet?

What the hammer? what the chain,
In what furnace was thy brain?
What the anvil? what dread grasp,   15
Dare its deadly terrors clasp?

When the stars threw down their spears
And water'd heaven with their tears:
Did he smile his work to see?
Did he who made the Lamb make thee?   20

Tyger, Tyger burning bright,
In the forests of the night:
What immortal hand or eye,
Dare frame thy fearful symmetry?

AH! SUN-FLOWER

Ah Sun-flower! weary of time,
Who countest the steps of the Sun:

Seeking after that sweet golden clime
Where the travellers journey is done.

5 Where the Youth pined away with desire,
And the pale Virgin shrouded in snow:
Arise from their graves and aspire,
Where my Sun-flower wishes to go.

THE GARDEN OF LOVE

I went to the Garden of Love,
And saw what I never had seen:
A Chapel was built in the midst,
Where I used to play on the green.

5 And the gates of this Chapel were shut,
And Thou shalt not. writ over the door;
So I turn'd to the Garden of Love,
That so many sweet flowers bore,

And I saw it was filled with graves,
10 And tomb-stones where flowers should be:
And Priests in black gowns, were walking their
    rounds,
And binding with briars, my joys & desires.

LONDON

I wander thro' each charter'd° street,
Near where the charter'd Thames does flow.
And mark in every face I meet
Marks of weakness, marks of woe.

5 In every cry of every Man,
In every Infants cry of fear,
In every voice: in every ban,
The mind-forg'd manacles I hear

How the Chimney-sweepers cry
10 Every blackning Church appalls,
And the hapless Soldiers sigh,
Runs in blood down Palace walls

But most thro' midnight streets I hear
How the youthful Harlots curse
15 Blasts the new-born Infants tear
And blights with plagues the Marriage hearse

London   1 charter'd, privileged, protected by charter (cf. "Great Charter" or
Magna Carta)

THE HUMAN ABSTRACT

Pity would be no more,
If we did not make somebody Poor:
And Mercy no more could be,
If all were as happy as we;

And mutual fear brings peace;   5
Till the selfish loves increase.
Then Cruelty knits a snare,
And spreads his baits with care.

He sits down with holy fears,
And waters the ground with tears: 10
Then Humility takes its root
Underneath his foot.

Soon spreads the dismal shade
Of Mystery over his head;
And the Catterpiller and Fly,   15
Feed on the Mystery.

And it bears the fruit of Deceit,
Ruddy and sweet to eat;
And the Raven his nest has made
In its thickest shade.   20

The Gods of the earth and sea,
Sought thro' Nature to find this Tree
But their search was all in vain:
There grows one in the Human Brain

A POISON TREE

I was angry with my friend;
I told my wrath, my wrath did end.
I was angry with my foe:
I told it not, my wrath did grow.

And I waterd it in fears,   5
Night & morning with my tears:
And I sunned it with smiles,
And with soft deceitful wiles.

And it grew both day and night.
Till it bore an apple bright.   10
And my foe beheld it shine.
And he knew that it was mine.

And into my garden stole,
When the night had veild the pole;
In the morning glad I see;   15
My foe outstretchd beneath the tree.
(1794)

NEVER PAIN TO TELL THY LOVE

Never pain to tell thy love
Love that never told can be
For the gentle wind does move
Silently invisibly

5   I told my love I told my love
I told her all my heart
Trembling cold in ghastly fears
Ah she doth depart

Soon as she was gone from me
10 A traveller came by
Silently invisibly
O was no deny

I ASKED A THIEF

I askéd a thief to steal me a peach
He turned up his eyes
I ask'd a lithe° lady to lie her down
Holy & meek she cries—

5   As soon as I went
An angel came.
He wink'd at the thief
And smild at the dame—

And without one word said
10 Had a peach from the tree
And still as a maid
Enjoy'd the lady.
(1796)

AND DID THOSE FEET

And did those feet in ancient time.
Walk upon Englands mountains green:
And was the holy Lamb of God,
On Englands pleasant pastures seen!

5   And did the Countenance Divine,
Shine forth upon our clouded hills?
And was Jerusalem builded here,
Among these dark Satanic Mills?

Bring me my Bow of burning gold:
Bring me my Arrows of desire: 10
Bring me my Spear: O clouds unfold!
Bring me my Chariot of fire!

I will not cease from Mental Fight,
Nor shall my Sword sleep in my hand:
Till we have built Jerusalem,°   15
In Englands green & pleasant Land.
(1804–1810)

THE MARRIAGE OF HEAVEN AND HELL

PLATE 2
THE ARGUMENT.

Rintrah° roars & shakes his fires in the burdend air;
Hungry clouds swag on the deep

Once meek, and in a perilous path,
The just man kept his course along
The vale of death.   5
Roses are planted where thorns grow.
And on the barren heath
Sing the honey bees.

Then the perilous path was planted:
And a river, and a spring   10
On every cliff and tomb;
And on the bleached bones
Red clay brought forth.

Till the villain left the paths of ease,
To walk in perilous paths, and drive   15
The just man into barren climes.

Now the sneaking serpent walks
In mild humility.
And the just man rages in the wilds
Where lions roam.   20

Rintrah roars & shakes his fires in the burdend air;
Hungry clouds swag on the deep.

PLATE 3

    As a new heaven is begun, and it is now thirty-three
years since its advent: the Eternal Hell revives. And

And Did Those Feet   15 **Jerusalem**, the New Jerusalem, which will appear as the Bride of Christ the Lamb to mark the end of this fallen world and the beginning of a new heaven and earth. See *Revelation*, 21–22   **The Argument**   1 **Rintrah**, personification of the just wrath of the prophet Elijah

I Asked a Thief   3 **lithe**, gentle, agreeable

lo! Swedenborg° is the Angel sitting at the tomb; his writings are the linen clothes folded up. Now is the dominion of Edom,° & the return of Adam into Paradise; see Isaiah xxxiv & XXXV Chap:

Without Contraries is no progression. Attraction and Repulsion, Reason and Energy, Love and Hate, are necessary to Human existence.

From these contraries spring what the religious call Good & Evil. Good is the passive that obeys Reason [.] Evil is the active springing from Energy.

Good is Heaven. Evil is Hell.

PLATE 4

THE VOICE OF THE DEVIL

All Bibles or sacred codes. have been the causes of the following Errors.

1. That Man has two real existing principles Viz: a Body & a Soul.

2. That Energy. calld Evil. is alone from the Body. & that Reason. calld Good. is alone from the Soul.

3. That God will torment Man in Eternity for following his Energies. But the following Contraries to these are True

1 Man has no Body distinct from his Soul for that calld Body is a portion of Soul discernd by the five Senses, the chief inlets of Soul in this age

2 Energy is the only life and is from the Body and Reason is the bound or outward circumference of Energy.

3 Energy is Eternal Delight

PLATE 5

Those who restrain desire, do so because theirs is weak enough to be restrained; and the restrainer or reason usurps its place & governs the unwilling.

And being restraind it by degrees becomes passive till it is only the shadow of desire.

The history of this is written in Paradise Lost. & the Governor or Reason is call'd Messiah.

And the original Archangel or possessor of the command of the heavenly host, is calld the Devil or Satan and his children are call'd Sin & Death

But in the Book of Job Miltons Messiah° is call'd Satan.

For this history has been adopted by both parties

It indeed appear'd to Reason as if Desire was cast out, but the Devils account is, that the Messi[PL 6]ah fell. & formed a heaven of what he stole from the Abyss

This is shewn in the Gospel, where he prays to the Father to send the comforter or Desire that Reason may have Ideas to build on, the Jehovah of the Bible

being no other than he, who dwells in flaming fire. Know that after Christs death, he became Jehovah.

But in Milton; the Father is Destiny, the Son, a Ratio of the five senses. & the Holy-ghost, Vacuum!

Note. The reason Milton wrote in fetters when he wrote of Angels & God, and at liberty when of Devils & Hell, is because he was a true Poet and of the Devils party without knowing it

A MEMORABLE FANCY.

As I was walking among the fires of hell, delighted with the enjoyments of Genius; which to Angels look like torment and insanity. I collected some of their Proverbs: thinking that as the sayings used in a nation, mark its character, so the Proverbs of Hell, shew the nature of Infernal wisdom better than any description of buildings or garments.

When I came home; on the abyss of the five senses, where a flat sided steep frowns over the present world. I saw a mighty Devil folded in black clouds, hovering on the sides of the rock, with cor[PL 7]roding fires he wrote the following sentence now percieved by the minds of men, & read by them on earth.

> How do you know but ev'ry Bird that cuts the airy way,
> Is an immense world of delight, clos'd by your senses five?

PROVERBS OF HELL.

In seed time learn, in harvest teach, in winter enjoy.
Drive your cart and your plow over the bones of the dead.
The road of excess leads to the palace of wisdom.
Prudence is a rich ugly old maid courted by Incapacity.
He who desires but acts not, breeds pestilence.
The cut worm forgives the plow.
Dip him in the river who loves water.
A fool sees not the same tree that a wise man sees.
He whose face gives no light, shall never become a star.
Eternity is in love with the productions of time.
The busy bee has no time for sorrow.
The hours of folly are measur'd by the clock, but of wisdom: no clock can measure.
All wholsom food is caught without a net or a trap.
Bring out number weight & measure in a year of dearth.
No bird soars too high. if he soars with his own wings.
A dead body. revenges not injuries.
The most sublime act is to set another before you.
If the fool would persist in his folly he would become wise
Folly is the cloke of knavery.
Shame is Prides cloke.

Plate 3   3 Swedenborg, Emanuel Swedenborg (1688–1772), Swedish scientist, philosopher and mystic. He believed in the spiritual symbolism of the material world and his scriptural interpretation influenced Blake early in his career   5 Edom, another name for Esau, the disinherited son of Isaac   Plate 5   11 Milton's Messiah, John Milton, Paradise Lost; see Chapter III

PLATE 8

Prisons are built with stones of Law, Brothels with
  bricks of Religion.
The pride of the peacock is the glory of God.
The lust of the goat is the bounty of God.
The wrath of the lion is the wisdom of God.
5 The nakedness of woman is the work of God.
Excess of sorrow laughs. Excess of joy weeps.
The roaring of lions, the howling of wolves, the raging
  of the stormy sea, and the destructive sword. are
  portions of eternity too great for the eye of man.
The fox condemns the trap, not himself.
Joys impregnate. Sorrows bring forth.
10 Let man wear the fell of the lion. woman the fleece of
  the sheep.
The bird a nest, the spider a web, man friendship.
The selfish smiling fool. & the sullen frowning fool.
  shall be both thought wise. that they may be a rod.
What is now proved was once, only imagin'd.
The rat, the mouse, the fox, the rabbet; watch the
  roots, the lion, the tyger, the horse, the elephant,
  watch the fruits.
15 The cistern contains: the fountain overflows
One thought fills immensity.
Always be ready to speak your mind, and a base man
  will avoid you.
Every thing possible to be believ'd is an image of truth.
The eagle never lost so much time. as when he submitted to learn of the crow.

PLATE 9

The fox provides for himself. but God provides for the
  lion.
Think in the morning, Act in the noon, Eat in the
  evening, Sleep in the night.
He who has sufferd you to impose on him knows you.
As the plow follows words, so God rewards prayers.
5 The tygers of wrath are wiser than the horses of in-
  struction
Expect poison from the standing water.
You never know what is enough unless you know what
  is more than enough.
Listen to the fools reproach! it is a kingly title!
The eyes of fire, the nostrils of air, the mouth of water,
  the beard of earth.
10 The weak in courage is strong in cunning.
The apple tree never asks the beech how he shall grow,
  nor the lion. the horse, how he shall take his prey.
The thankful reciever bears a plentiful harvest.
If others had not been foolish, we should be so.
The soul of sweet delight, can never be defil'd,
15 When thou seest an Eagle, thou seest a portion of
  Genius. lift up thy head!
As the caterpiller chooses the fairest leaves to lay her

eggs on, so the priest lays his curse on the fairest
  joys.
To create a little flower is the labour of ages.
Damn. braces: Bless relaxes.
The best wine is the oldest. the best water the newest.
Prayers plow not! Praises reap not!   20
Joys laugh not! Sorrows weep not!

PLATE 10

The head Sublime, the heart Pathos, the genitals
  Beauty, the hands & feet Proportion.
As the air to a bird or the sea to a fish, so is contempt
  to the contemptible.
The crow wish'd every thing was black, the owl, that
  every thing was white.
Exuberance is Beauty.
If the lion was advise'd by the fox. he would be cun-
  ning.   5
Improve[me]nt makes strait roads, but the crooked
  roads without Improvement, are roads of Genius.
Sooner murder an infant in its cradle than nurse un-
  acted desires
Where man is not nature is barren.
Truth can never be told so as to be understood, and not
  be believ'd.
        Enough! or Too much

PLATE 11

  The ancient Poets animated all sensible objects with
Gods or Geniuses, calling them by the names and
adorning them with the properties of woods, rivers,
mountains, lakes, cities, nations, and whatever their
enlarged & numerous senses could percieve.   5
  And particularly they studied the genius of each city
& country. placing it under its mental deity.
  Till a system was formed, which some took advantage of & enslav'd the vulgar by attempting to realize
or abstract the mental deities from their objects; thus 10
began Priesthood.
  Choosing forms of worship from poetic tales.
  And at length they pronouncd that the Gods had
orderd such things.
  Thus men forgot that All deities reside in the human 15
breast.

PLATE 12
A MEMORABLE FANCY.

The Prophets Isaiah and Ezekiel° dined with me, and I
asked them how they dared so roundly to assert. that
God spake to them; and whether they did not think at
the time, that they would be misunderstood, & so be
the cause of imposition.
  Isaiah answer'd. I saw no God, nor heard any, in a

Plate 12   1 Isaiah and Ezekiel, Old Testament prophets

finite organical perception; but my senses discover'd the infinite in every thing, and as I was then perswaded, & remain confirm'd; that the voice of honest indignation is the voice of God, I cared not for consequences but wrote.

Then I asked: does a firm perswasion that a thing is so, make it so?

He replied. All poets believe that it does, & in ages of imagination this firm perswasion removed mountains; but many are not capable of a firm perswasion of any thing.

Then Ezekiel said. The philosophy of the east taught the first principles of human perception some nations held one principle for the origin & some another, we of Israel taught that the Poetic Genius (as you now call it) was the first principle and all the others merely derivative, which was the cause of our despising the Priests & Philosophers of other countries, and prophecying that all Gods [PL 13] would at last be proved to originate in ours & to be the tributaries of the Poetic Genius, it was this. that our great poet King David desired so fervently & invokes so patheticly, saying by this he conquers enemies & governs kingdoms; and we so loved our God. that we cursed in his name all the deities of surrounding nations, and asserted that they had rebelled; from these opinions the vulgar came to think that all nations would at last be subject to the jews.

This said he, like all firm perswasions, is come to pass, for all nations believe the jews code and worship the jews god, and what greater subjection can be

I heard this with some wonder, & must confess my own conviction. After dinner I ask'd Isaiah to favour the world with his lost works, he said none of equal value was lost. Ezekiel said the same of his.

I also asked Isaiah what made him go naked and barefoot three years? he answerd, the same that made our friend Diogenes the Grecian.°

I then asked Ezekiel. why he eat dung, & lay so long on his right & left side? he answerd. the desire of raising other men into a perception of the infinite this the North American tribes practise. & is he honest who resists his genius or conscience. only for the sake of present ease or gratification?

PLATE 14

The ancient tradition that the world will be consumed in fire at the end of six thousand years is true. as I have heard from Hell.

For the cherub with his flaming sword is hereby commanded to leave his guard at tree of life, and when he does, the whole creation will be consumed, and appear infinite. and holy whereas it now appears finite & corrupt.

---

44 **Diogenes the Grecian,** a philosopher of the fifth century B.C., about whom many legends are told; one is that he gave up clothing in pursuit of austerity and simplicity

This will come to pass by an improvement of sensual enjoyment.

But first the notion that man has a body distinct from his soul, is to be expunged; this I shall do, by printing in the infernal method, by corrosives, which in Hell are salutary and medicinal, melting apparent surfaces away, and displaying the infinite which was hid.

If the doors of perception were cleansed every thing would appear to man as it is, infinite.

For man has closed himself up, till he sees all things thro' narrow chinks of his cavern.

PLATE 15
A MEMORABLE FANCY

I was in a Printing house in Hell & saw the method in which knowledge is transmitted from generation to generation.

In the first chamber was a Dragon-Man, clearing away the rubbish from a caves mouth; within, a number of Dragons were hollowing the cave,

In the second chamber was a Viper folding round the rock & the cave, and others adorning it with gold silver and precious stones.

In the third chamber was an Eagle with wings and feathers of air, he caused the inside of the cave to be infinite, around were numbers of Eagle like men, who built palaces in the immense cliffs.

In the fourth chamber were Lions of flaming fire raging around & melting the metals into living fluids.

In the fifth chamber were Unnam'd forms, which cast the metals into the expanse.

There they were reciev'd by Men who occupied the sixth chamber, and took the forms of books & were arranged in libraries.

PLATE 16

The Giants who formed this world into its sensual existence and now seem to live in it in chains, are in truth. the causes of its life & the sources of all activity, but the chains are, the cunning of weak and tame minds. which have power to resist energy, according to the proverb, the weak in courage is strong in cunning.

Thus one portion of being, is the Prolific. the other, the Devouring: to the devourer it seems as if the producer was in his chains, but it is not so, he only takes portions of existence and fancies that the whole.

But the Prolific would cease to be Prolific unless the Devourer as a sea recieved the excess of his delights.

Some will say, Is not God alone the Prolific? I answer, God only Acts & Is, in existing beings or Men.

These two classes of men are always upon earth, & they should be enemies; whoever tries [PL 17] to reconcile them seeks to destroy existence.

Religion is an endeavour to reconcile the two.

Note. Jesus Christ did not wish to unite but to seperate them, as in the Parable of sheep and goats! & he says I came not to send Peace but a Sword.

Messiah or Satan or Tempter was formerly thought to be one of the Antediluvians° who are our Energies.

A MEMORABLE FANCY

An Angel came to me and said O pitiable foolish young man! O horrible! O dreadful state! consider the hot burning dungeon thou art preparing for thyself to all eternity, to which thou art going in such career.

I said, perhaps you will be willing to shew me my eternal lot & we will contemplate together upon it and see whether your lot or mine is most desirable

So he took me thro' a stable & thro' a church & down into the church vault at the end of which was a mill: thro' the mill we went, and came to a cave. down the winding cavern we groped our tedious way till a void boundless as a nether sky appeard beneath us. & we held by the roots of trees and hung over this immensity, but I said, if you please we will commit ourselves to this void, and see whether providence is here also, if you will not I will? but he answerd, do not presume O youngman but as we here remain behold thy lot which will soon appear when the darkness passes away

So I remaind with him sitting in the twisted [PL 18] root of an oak. he was suspended in a fungus which hung with the head downward into the deep;

By degrees we beheld the infinite Abyss, fiery as the smoke of a burning city; beneath us at an immense distance was the sun, black but shining[;] round it were fiery tracks on which revolv'd vast spiders, crawling after their prey; which flew or rather swum in the infinite deep, in the most terrific shapes of animals sprung from corruption. & the air was full of them, & seemd composed of them; these are Devils. and are called Powers of the air, I now asked my companion which was my eternal lot? he said, between the black & white spiders

But now, from between the black & white spiders a cloud and fire burst and rolled thro the deep blackning all beneath, so that the nether deep grew black as a sea & rolled with a terrible noise: beneath us was nothing now to be seen but a black tempest, till looking east between the clouds & the waves, we saw a cataract of blood mixed with fire and not many stones throw from us appeard and sunk again the scaly fold of a monstrous serpent[.] at last to the east, distant about three degrees appeard a fiery crest above the waves[.] slowly it reared like a ridge of golden rocks till we discoverd two globes of crimson fire, from which the sea fled away in clouds of smoke, and now we saw, it was the head of Leviathan,° his forehead was divided

into streaks of green & purple like those on a tygers forehead: soon we saw his mouth & red gills hang just above the raging foam tinging the black deep with beams of blood, advancing toward [PL 19] us with all the fury of a spiritual existence.

My friend the Angel climb'd up from his station into the mill; I remain'd alone, & then this appearance was no more, but I found myself sitting on a pleasant bank beside a river by moon light hearing a harper who sung to the harp, & his theme was, The man who never alters his opinion is like standing water, & breeds reptiles of the mind.

But I arose, and sought for the mill, & there I found my Angel, who surprised asked me, how I escaped?

I answerd. All that we saw was owing to your metaphysics:° for when you ran away, I found myself on a bank by moonlight hearing a harper, But now we have seen my eternal lot, shall I shew you yours? he laughd at my proposal; but I by force suddenly caught him in my arms, & flew westerly thro' the night, till we were elevated above the earths shadow: then I flung myself with him directly into the body of the sun, here I clothed myself in white, & taking in my hand Swedenborgs volumes sunk from the glorious clime, and passed all the planets till we came to saturn, here I staid to rest & then leap'd into the void, between saturn & the fixed stars.

Here said I! is your lot, in this space, if space it may be calld, Soon we saw the stable and the church, & I took him to the altar and open'd the Bible, and lo! it was a deep pit, into which I descended driving the Angel before me, soon we saw seven houses of brick, one we enterd; in it were a [PL 20] number of monkeys, baboons, & all of that species chaind by the middle, grinning and snatching at one another, but witheld by the shortness of their chains: however I saw that they sometimes grew numerous, and then the weak were caught by the strong and with a grinning aspect, first coupled with & then devourd, by plucking off first one limb and then another till the body was left a helpless trunk. this after grinning & kissing it with seeming fondness they devourd too; and here & there I saw one savourily picking the flesh off of his own tail; as the stench terribly annoyd us both we went into the mill, & I in my hand brought the skeleton of a body, which in the mill was Aristotles Analytics.°

So the Angel said: thy phantasy has imposed upon me & thou oughtest to be ashamed.

I answered: we impose on one another, & it is but lost time to converse with you whose works are only Analytics

Opposition is true Friendship.

Plate 16   24 **Antediluvians,** those who lived before the Flood; in a general sense, ancestors   71 **Leviathan,** an aquatic monster appearing in Hebrew poetry; also used as name for Satan

87 **metaphysics,** a system of thinking based on abstract general reasoning or on theoretic or a priori principles   117 **Aristotles Analytics.** The name itself gives an emphasis to analytic thought which Blake distrusts

PLATE 21

I have always found that Angels have the vanity to speak of themselves as the only wise; this they do with a confident insolence sprouting from systematic reasoning;

Thus Swedenborg boasts that what he writes is new; tho' it is only the Contents or Index of already publish'd books

A man carried a monkey about for a shew, & because he was a little wiser than the monkey, grew vain, and conciev'd himself as much wiser than seven men. It is so with Swedenborg; he shews the folly of churches & exposes hypocrites, till he imagines that all are religious. & himself the single [PL 22] one on earth that ever broke a net.

Now hear a plain fact: Swedenborg has not written one new truth: Now hear another: he has written all the old falshoods.

And now hear the reason. He conversed with Angels who are all religious, & conversed not with Devils who all hate religion, for he was incapable thro' his conceited notions.

Thus Swedenborgs writings are a recapitulation of all superficial opinions, and an analysis of the more sublime, but no further.

Have now another plain fact: Any man of mechanical talents may from the writings of Paracelsus° or Jacob Behmen,° produce ten thousand volumes of equal value with Swedenborg's. and from those of Dante or Shakespear, an infinite number.

But when he has done this, let him not say that he knows better than his master, for he only holds a candle in sunshine.

A MEMORABLE FANCY

Once I saw a Devil in a flame of fire. who arose before an Angel that sat on a cloud. and the Devil utterd these words.

The worship of God is. Honouring his gifts in other men each according to his genius. and loving the [PL 23] greatest men best, those who envy or calumniate great men hate God, for there is no other God.

The Angel hearing this became almost blue but mastering himself he grew yellow, & at last white pink & smiling, and then replied,

Thou Idolater, is not God One? & is not he visible in Jesus Christ? and has not Jesus Christ given his sanction to the law of ten commandments and are not all other men fools, sinners, & nothings?

The Devil answer'd; bray a fool in a morter with wheat. yet shall not his folly be beaten out of him: if Jesus Christ is the greatest man, you ought to love him in the greatest degree; now hear how he has given his

sanction to the law of ten commandments: did he not mock at the sabbath, and so mock the sabbaths God? murder those who were murderd because of him? turn away the law from the woman taken in adultery? steal the labor of others to support him? bear false witness when he omitted making a defence before Pilate? covet when he pray'd for his disciples, and when he bid them shake off the dust of their feet against such as refused to lodge them? I tell you, no virtue can exist without breaking these ten commandments.°. Jesus was all virtue, and acted from im[PL 24]pulse. not from rules.

When he had so spoken: I beheld the Angel who stretched out his arms embracing the flame of fire & he was consumed and arose as Elijah.

Note. This Angel, who is now become a Devil, is my particular friend: we often read the Bible together in its infernal or diabolical sense which the world shall have if they behave well

I have also: The Bible of Hell: which the world shall have whether they will or no.

One Law for the Lion & Ox is Oppression

PLATE 25
A SONG OF LIBERTY

1. The Eternal Female groand! it was heard over all the Earth:
2. Albions° coast is sick silent; the American meadows faint!
3. Shadows of Prophecy shiver along by the lakes and the rivers and mutter across the ocean? France rend down thy dungeon;
4. Golden Spain burst the barriers of old Rome;
5. Cast thy keys O Rome into the deep down falling, even to eternity down falling,
6. And weep
7. In her trembling hands she took the new born terror howling:
8. On those infinite mountains of light now barr'd out by the atlantic sea, the new born fire stood before the starry king!
9. Flag'd with grey brow'd snows and thunderous visages the jealous wings wav'd over the deep.
10. The speary hand burned aloft, unbuckled was the shield, forth went the hand of jealousy among the flaming hair, and [PL 26] hurl'd the new born wonder thro' the starry night.
11. The fire, the fire, is falling!
12. Look up! look up! O citizen of London. enlarge thy countenance; O Jew, leave counting gold! return to thy oil and wine; O African! black African! (go. winged thought widen his forehead.)
13. The fiery limbs, the flaming hair, shot like the sinking sun into the western sea.

Plate 21 26 **Paracelsus,** (1493–1541) noted physician and mystic philosopher 27 **Jacob Behmen,** Jacob Boehme (1575–1624), untutored shoemaker and great mystic

Plate 25 3 **Albions,** England's

14. Wak'd from his eternal sleep, the hoary element roaring fled away:

15. Down rushd beating his wings in vain the jealous king; his grey brow'd councellors, thunderous warriors, curl'd veterans, among helms, and shields, and chariots[,] horses, elephants: banners, castles, slings and rocks,

16. Falling, rushing, ruining! buried in the ruins, on Urthona's° dens.

17. All night beneath the ruins, then their sullen
40 flames faded emerge round the gloomy king,

18. With thunder and fire: leading his starry hosts thro' the waste wilderness [PL 27] he promulgates his ten commands, glancing his beamy eyelids over the deep in dark dismay,

19. Where the son of fire in his eastern cloud, while the morning plumes her golden breast,

20. Spurning the clouds written with curses, stamps the stony law to dust, loosing the eternal horses from the dens of night, crying

50 Empire is no more! and now the lion & wolf shall cease.

Chorus

Let the Prests of the Raven of dawn, no longer in deadly black. with hoarse note curse the sons of joy. Nor his accepted brethren whom, tyrant, he calls free: lay the bound or build the roof. Nor pale religious letchery call that virginity, that wishes but acts not!
    For every thing that lives is Holy
(1792)

from LETTERS

[TO] REVᵈ DR TRUSLER,
ENGLEFIELD GREEN, EGHAM, SURREY

    13 Hercules Buildings, Lambeth, August 23, 1799

Revᵈ Sir
    I really am sorry that you are falln out with the Spiritual World Especially if I should have to answer for it I feel very sorry that your Ideas & Mine on Moral Painting differ so much as to have made you angry with my method of Study. If I am wrong I am wrong in good company. I had hoped your plan comprehended All Species of this Art & Especially that you would not regret that Species which gives Existence to Every other. namely Visions of Eternity You say that I want somebody to Elucidate my Ideas. But you ought to 10 know that What is Grand is necessarily obscure to Weak men. That which can be made Explicit to the Idiot is not worth my care. The wisest of the Ancients considerd what is not too Explicit as the fittest for Instruction because it rouzes the faculties to act. I name Moses Solomon Esop Homer Plato

    But as you have favord me with your remarks on my Design permit me in return to defend it against a mistaken one, which is. That I have supposed Malevolence without a Cause.—Is not Merit in one a Cause of 20 Envy in another & Serenity & Happiness & Beauty a Cause of Malevolence. But Want of Money & the Distress of A Thief can never be alledged as the Cause of his Thievery. for many honest people endure greater hard ships with Fortitude We must therefore seek the Cause elsewhere than in want of Money for that is the Misers passion, not the Thiefs

    I have therefore proved your Reasonings Ill proportiond which you can never prove my figures to be. They are those of Michael Angelo Rafael & the Anti- 30 que & of the best living Models. I percieve that your Eye[s] is perverted by Caricature Prints, which ought not to abound so much as they do. Fun I love but too much Fun is of all things the most loathsom. Mirth is better than Fun & Happiness is better than Mirth—I feel that a Man may be happy in This World. And I know that This World Is a World of Imagination & Vision I see Every thing I paint In This World, but Every body does not see alike. To the Eyes of a Miser a Guinea° is more beautiful than the Sun & a bag worn 40 with the use of Money has more beautiful proportions than a Vine filled with Grapes. The tree which moves some to tears of joy is in the Eyes of others only a Green thing that stands in the way. Some See Nature all Ridicule & Deformity & by these I shall not regulate my proportions, & Some Scarce see Nature at all But to the Eyes of the Man of Imagination Nature is Imagination itself. As a man is So he Sees. As the Eye is formed such are its Powers You certainly Mistake when you say that the Visions of Fancy are not to be 50 found in This World. To Me This World is all One continued Vision of Fancy or Imagination & I feel Flatterd when I am told So. What is it sets Homer Virgil & Milton in so high a rank of Art. Why is the Bible more Entertaining & Instructive than any other book. Is it not because they are addressed to the Imagination which is Spiritual Sensation & but mediately to the Understanding or Reason Such is True Painting and such <was> alone valued by the Greeks & the best modern Artists. Consider what Lord Bacon says 60 "Sense sends over to Imagination before Reason have judged & Reason sends over to Imagination before the Decree can be acted." See Advancemᵗ of Learning° Part 2 P 47 of first Edition

    But I am happy to find a Great Majority of Fellow

38 **Urthona's** an old earth-spirit

Letter 40 **a Guinea,** a gold coin, worth 21s 63 **Advancemᵗ of Learning,** *Advancement of Learning* published by Francis Bacon in 1605

Mortals who can Elucidate My Visions & Particularly they have been Elucidated by Children who have taken a greater delight in contemplating my Pictures than I even hoped. Neither Youth nor Childhood is
70 Folly or Incapacity Some Children are Fools & so are some Old Men. But There is a vast Majority on the side of Imagination or Spiritual Sensation

To Engrave after another Painter is infinitely more laborious than to Engrave ones own Inventions. And of the Size you require my price has been Thirty Guineas & I cannot afford to do it for less. I had Twelve for the Head I sent you as a Specimen, but after my own designs I could do at least Six times the quantity of labour in the same time which will account
80 for the difference of price as also that Chalk Engraving is at least six times as laborious as Aqua tinta.° I have no objection to Engraving after another Artist. Engraving is the profession I was apprenticed to, & should never have attempted to live by any thing else If orders had not come in for my Designs & Paintings, which I have the pleasure to tell you are Increasing Every Day. Thus If I am a Painter it is not to be attributed to Seeking after. But I am contented whether I live by Painting or Engraving
90 I am Revd Sir Your very obedient servant

William Blake

WILLIAM WORDSWORTH
1770–1850

William Wordsworth was born in April 1770, in the village of Cockermouth in the Lake District of northern England. His father was an attorney and steward for a large estate. As a young boy he was sent as a boarder to the Hawkshead grammar school in the heart of the Lake District. There he was encouraged in his extensive reading and poetic inclination by the school's young headmaster, William Taylor. It was also there, in the school's unspoiled rural community, that Wordsworth formed his great, overriding attachment to nature; the pastoral scenes and mountain panoramas, together with the robust pursuits of boyhood, shaped Wordsworth's poetic imagination. He was to return to this rustic period of his life over and over again in his later poetry.

Since Wordsworth's parents had died by the time he was thirteen and had not left a large estate, he at-tended Cambridge on a scholarship. The academic life, however, was not really to Wordsworth's liking, and he completed his degree without distinction in 1791. His university years were interrupted briefly by a walking tour through France, Italy, Switzerland, and Germany in 1790. This trip provided him with important images and memories for his poetry.

After his graduation in 1791, the enthusiastic Wordsworth again visited France. His stay there throughout 1792 coincided with some of the most turbulent and exciting days of the French Revolution. During this time he had an affair with Annette Vallon, who gave birth to his child, Caroline, in December 1792.

In 1793 Wordsworth reluctantly returned to England because of a lack of money. His loyalties for some time were to be divided equally between France and England. He was influenced by the teachings of the French philosopher Jean Jacques Rousseau (1712–1778) and William Godwin (1756–1836), whose *Enquiry Concerning Political Justice* (1793) was the authoritative work for the little group of English revolutionists with whom Wordsworth was associated. Wordsworth and his beloved sister Dorothy settled at Racedown, Dorsetshire, in 1795. There he met Samuel Taylor Coleridge, and the two of them soon formed a close friendship. When Coleridge moved to Somersetshire (1797), Wordsworth and his sister followed.

In the next year the two men published jointly a collection of poems known simply as *Lyrical Ballads* (1798). Wordsworth's advertisement for the book claimed that its poems were "experiments" to determine "how far the language of conversation in the middle and lower classes of society is adapted to the purposes of poetic pleasure." The poems illustrated the revolutionary theories of Wordsworth and Coleridge as applied to poetry. The *Lyrical Ballads* was condemned by many as inadequate poetry, by others as "revolutionary," a term which by 1798 had become anathema to many English readers. In spite of adverse judgments, the *Lyrical Ballads* survived; a second edition appeared in 1800, to which Wordsworth added a preface which stated formally the new ideals of sincerity, democracy, "natural piety," and simple diction to which he and Coleridge dedicated themselves.

Between the first and second editions of the *Lyrical Ballads*, Wordsworth, his sister, and Coleridge visited a remote little town in Germany. Wordsworth used his physical isolation to good purpose—he wrote several of his finest lyrics, the "Lucy" series, and began work on his great long poem, *The Prelude*. Upon their return to England, Wordsworth and his sister returned to the Lake Country, settling in a small cottage in the village of Grasmere.

Wordsworth's ideas about the French Revolution, like those of many other young English revolutionists, underwent a considerable change with the advent of

---

81 **Aqua tinta,** a method of engraving on copper by use of a resinous solution and nitric acid, which produces effects resembling watercolor drawing

Napoleon. His relationship with Annette Vallon, from whom he had been cut off by the war between England and France, also changed; the couple decided not to marry. In 1802, the break with France and Vallon now more decided, Wordsworth married Mary Hutchinson, a close friend of his sister. By 1806 Wordsworth had completed all his major work on *The Prelude* (not published until 1850) and had finished his *Immortality Ode*.

His increasingly conservative turn of mind is evidenced by the fact that he became a distributor of stamps and thus an employee of the government in 1813. He remained by choice in the Lake Country, moving to Rydal Mount near Lake Windermere, where he spent the remainder of his long and peacefully idyllic life. He continued to work on poetry, though on nothing as important as his earlier work. In his seventies he became poet laureate (1843). His death in 1850 came long after the ideas for which he labored had been not only accepted but in many ways superseded.

With Coleridge, Wordsworth was an important poetic revolutionary both in practice and in his statements about poetry. He established himself in poems like *The Solitary Reaper* and his *Intimations Ode* as one of the most versatile and distinctive practitioners of the short, lyrical poem; in his "philosophic" works, notably *The Prelude*, he proved himself to be a master of the longer, extended poem as well. The nineteenth century prized his shorter poems, celebrating "simple primary affections and duties," to use his own phrase. Our own century has viewed the later philosophic works with more interest.

from LYRICAL BALLADS

LINES WRITTEN IN EARLY SPRING

I heard a thousand blended notes,
While in a grove I sate reclined,
In that sweet mood when pleasant thoughts
Bring sad thoughts to the mind.

5 To her fair works did Nature link
The human soul that through me ran;
And much it grieved my heart to think
What man has made of man.

Through primrose tufts, in that green bower,
10 The periwinkle trailed its wreaths;
And 'tis my faith that every flower
Enjoys the air it breathes.

The birds around me hopped and played,
Their thoughts I cannot measure—
But the least motion which they made,   15
It seemed a thrill of pleasure.

The budding twigs spread out their fan,
To catch the breezy air;
And I must think, do all I can,
That there was pleasure there.   20

If this belief from heaven be sent,
If such be Nature's holy plan,
Have I not reason to lament
What man has made of man?
(1798)

WE ARE SEVEN

—A simple Child,
That lightly draws its breath,
And feels its life in every limb,
What should it know of death?

I met a little cottage Girl:
She was eight years old, she said;
Her hair was thick with many a curl
That clustered round her head.

She had a rustic, woodland air,
And she was wildly clad: 10
Her eyes were fair, and very fair;
—Her beauty made me glad.

"Sisters and brothers, little Maid,
How many may you be?"
"How many? Seven in all," she said,
And wondering looked at me.

"And where are they? I pray you tell."
She answered, "Seven are we;
And two of us at Conway dwell,
And two are gone to sea.   20

"Two of us in the churchyard lie,
My sister and my brother;
And, in the churchyard cottage, I
Dwell near them with my mother."

"You say that two at Conway dwell,
And two are gone to sea,
Yet ye are seven! I pray you tell,
Sweet Maid, how this may be."

Then did the little Maid reply,
"Seven boys and girls are we;   30

Two of us in the churchyard lie,
Beneath the churchyard tree."

"You run about, my little Maid,
Your limbs they are alive;
If two are in the churchyard laid,
Then ye are only five."

"Their graves are green, they may be seen,"
The little Maid replied,
"Twelve steps or more from my mother's door,
40 And they are side by side.

"My stockings there I often knit,
My kerchief there I hem;
And there upon the ground I sit,
And sing a song to them.

"And often after sunset, sir,
When it is light and fair,
I take my little porringer,
And eat my supper there.

"The first that died was sister Jane;
50 In bed she moaning lay,
Till God released her of her pain;
And then she went away.

"So in the churchyard she was laid;
And, when the grass was dry,
Together round her grave we played,
My brother John and I.

"And when the ground was white with snow,
And I could run and slide,
My brother John was forced to go,
60 And he lies by her side."

"How many are you, then," said I,
"If they two are in heaven?"
Quick was the little Maid's reply,
"O master! we are seven."

"But they are dead; those two are dead!
Their spirits are in heaven!"
'Twas throwing words away; for still
The little Maid would have her will,
And said, "Nay, we are seven!"
(1798)

EXPOSTULATION AND REPLY

'Why, William, on that old grey stone,
Thus for the length of half a day,
Why, William, sit you thus alone,
And dream your time away?

'Where are your books?—that light bequeathed
To Beings else forlorn and blind!
Up! up! and drink the spirit breathed
From dead men to their kind.

'You look round on your Mother Earth,
As if she for no purpose bore you;   10
As if you were her first-born birth,
And none had lived before you!'

One morning thus, by Esthwaite lake,
When life was sweet, I knew not why,
To me my good friend° Matthew spake,
And thus I made reply:

'The eye—it cannot choose but see;
We cannot bid the ear be still;
Our bodies feel, wher'er they be,
Against or with our will.   20

'Nor less I deem that there are Powers
Which of themselves our minds impress;
That we can feed this mind of ours
In a wise passiveness.

'Think you, 'mid all this mighty sum
Of things for ever speaking,
That nothing of itself will come,
But we must still be seeking?

'—Then ask not wherefore, here, alone,
Conversing as I may,   30
I sit upon this old grey stone,
And dream my time away.'
(1798)

THE TABLES TURNED

Up! up! my Friend, and quit your books;
Or surely you'll grow double:
Up! up! my Friend, and clear your looks;
Why all this toil and trouble?

The sun, above the mountain's head,
A freshening lustre mellow
Through all the long green fields has spread,
His first sweet evening yellow.

Books! 'tis a dull and endless strife:
Come, hear the woodland linnet,   10
How sweet his music! on my life,
There's more of wisdom in it.

Expostulation and Reply   15 friend, William Hazlitt

And hark! how blithe the throstle sings!
He, too, is no mean preacher:
Come forth into the light of things,
Let Nature be your Teacher.

She has a world of ready wealth,
Our minds and hearts to bless—
Spontaneous wisdom breathed by health,
20 Truth breathed by cheerfulness.

One impulse from a vernal wood
May teach you more of man,
Of moral evil and of good,
Than all the sages can.

Sweet is the lore which Nature brings;
Our meddling intellect
Mis-shapes the beauteous forms of things:—
We murder to dissect.

Enough of Science and of Art;
30 Close up these barren leaves;
Come forth, and bring with you a heart
That watches and receives.
(1798)

LINES

COMPOSED A FEW MILES ABOVE TINTERN ABBEY°

Five years have past; five summers, with the length
Of five long winters! and again I hear
These waters, rolling from their mountain-springs
With a soft inland murmur.—Once again
Do I behold these steep and lofty cliffs,
That on a wild secluded scene impress
Thoughts of more deep seclusion; and connect
The landscape with the quiet of the sky.
The day is come when I again repose
10 Here, under this dark sycamore, and view
These plots of cottage-ground, these orchard-tufts,
Which at this season, with their unripe fruits,
Are clad in one green hue, and lose themselves
Mid groves and copses. Once again I see
These hedgerows, hardly hedgerows, little lines
Of sportive wood run wild: these pastoral farms,
Green to the very door; and wreaths of smoke
Sent up, in silence, from among the trees!
With some uncertain notice, as might seem
20 Of vagrant dwellers in the houseless woods,
Or of some Hermit's cave, where by his fire
The Hermit sits alone.
                    These beauteous forms,

Through a long absence, have not been to me
As is a landscape to a blind man's eye:
But oft, in lonely rooms, and 'mid the din
Of towns and cities, I have owed to them,
In hours of weariness, sensations sweet,
Felt in the blood, and felt along the heart;
And passing even into my purer mind,
With tranquil restoration—feelings too   30
Of unremembered pleasure: such, perhaps,
As have no slight or trivial influence
On that best portion of a good man's life,
His little, nameless, unremembered acts
Of kindness and of love. Nor less, I trust,
To them I may have owed another gift,
Of aspect more sublime; that blesséd mood,
In which the burthen of the mystery,
In which the heavy and the weary weight
Of all this unintelligible world,   40
Is lightened—that serene and blesséd mood,
In which the affections gently lead us on—
Until, the breath of this corporeal frame
And even the motion of our human blood
Almost suspended, we are laid asleep
In body, and become a living soul:
While with an eye made quiet by the power
Of harmony, and the deep power of joy,
We see into the life of things.
                    If this
Be but a vain belief, yet, oh! how oft—   50
In darkness and amid the many shapes
Of joyless daylight; when the fretful stir
Unprofitable, and the fever of the world,
Have hung upon the beatings of my heart—
How oft, in spirit, have I turned to thee,
O sylvan Wye!° thou wanderer through the woods,
How often has my spirit turned to thee!
  And now, with gleams of half-extinguished
      thought,
With many recognitions dim and faint,
And somewhat of a sad perplexity,   60
The picture of the mind revives again:
While here I stand, not only with the sense
Of present pleasure, but with pleasing thoughts
That in this moment there is life and food
For future years. And so I dare to hope,
Though changed, no doubt, from what I was when first
I came among these hills; when like a roe
I bounded o'er the mountains, by the sides
Of the deep rivers, and the lonely streams,
Wherever nature led: more like a man   70
Flying from something that he dreads than one
Who sought the thing he loved. For nature° then
(The coarser pleasures of my boyish days,
And their glad animal movements all gone by)
To me was all in all.—I cannot paint
What then I was. The sounding cataract

Lines   Tintern Abbey, famous ruin in Monmouthshire, which Wordsworth visited in
1793

56 Wye, river which runs past Tintern Abbey   72–111 For nature, etc. Cf. this
passage with ll. 175–203 of Wordsworth's Ode on Intimations of Immortality

Haunted me like a passion: the tall rock,
The mountain, and the deep and gloomy wood,
Their colors and their forms, were then to me
80 An appetite; a feeling and a love,
That had no need of a remoter charm,
By thought supplied, nor any interest
Unborrowed from the eye.—That time is past,
And all its aching joys are now no more,
And all its dizzy raptures. Nor for this
Faint I, nor mourn nor murmur; other gifts
Have followed; for such loss, I would believe,
Abundant recompense. For I have learned
To look on nature, not as in the hour
90 Of thoughtless youth; but hearing oftentimes
The still, sad music of humanity,
Nor harsh nor grating, though of ample power
To chasten and subdue. And I have felt
A presence that disturbs me with the joy
Of elevated thoughts; a sense sublime
Of something far more deeply interfused,
Whose dwelling is the light of setting suns,°
And the round ocean and the living air,
And the blue sky, and in the mind of man:
100 A motion and a spirit, that impels
All thinking things, all objects of all thought,
And rolls through all things. Therefore am I still
A lover of the meadows and the woods,
And mountains; and of all that we behold
From this green earth; of all the mighty world
Of eye, and ear—both what they half create,
And what perceive; well pleased to recognize
In nature and the language of the sense
The anchor of my purest thoughts, the nurse,
110 The guide, the guardian of my heart, and soul
Of all my moral being.
                        Nor perchance,
If I were not thus taught, should I the more
Suffer my genial spirits to decay:
For thou art with me here upon the banks
Of this fair river; thou my dearest Friend,°
My dear, dear Friend; and in thy voice I catch
The language of my former heart, and read
My former pleasures in the shooting lights
Of thy wild eyes. Oh! yet a little while
120 May I behold in thee what I was once,
My dear, dear Sister! and this prayer I make,
Knowing that Nature never did betray
The heart that loved her; 'tis her privilege,
Through all the years of this our life, to lead
From joy to joy: for she can so inform°
The mind that is within us, so impress
With quietness and beauty, and so feed
With lofty thoughts, that neither evil tongues,
Rash judgments, nor the sneers of selfish men,
130 Nor greetings where no kindness is, nor all

The dreary intercourse of daily life,
Shall e'er prevail against us, or disturb
Our cheerful faith, that all which we behold
Is full of blessings. Therefore let the moon
Shine on thee in thy solitary walk;
And let the misty mountain-winds be free
To blow against thee: and, in after years,
When these wild ecstasies shall be matured
Into a sober pleasure; when thy mind
Shall be a mansion for all lovely forms, 140
Thy memory be as a dwelling-place
For all sweet sounds and harmonies; oh! then,
If solitude, or fear, or pain, or grief,
Should be thy portion, with what healing thoughts
Of tender joy wilt thou remember me,
And these my exhortations! Nor, perchance—
If I should be where I no more can hear
Thy voice, nor catch from thy wild eyes these gleams
Of past existence—wilt thou then forget
That on the banks of this delightful stream 150
We stood together; and that I, so long
A worshiper of Nature, hither came
Unwearied in that service: rather say
With warmer love—oh! with far deeper zeal
Of holier love. Nor wilt thou then forget
That after many wanderings, many years
Of absence, these steep woods and lofty cliffs,
And this green pastoral landscape, were to me
More dear, both for themselves and for thy sake!
(1798)

STRANGE FITS OF PASSION HAVE I KNOWN°

Strange fits of passion have I known:
And I will dare to tell,
But in the Lover's ear alone,
What once to me befell.

When she I loved looked every day
Fresh as a rose in June,
I to her cottage bent my way,
Beneath an evening-moon.

Upon the moon I fixed my eye,
All over the wide lea; 10
With quickening pace my horse drew nigh
Those paths so dear to me.

And now we reached the orchard-plot;
And, as we climbed the hill,
The sinking moon to Lucy's cot
Came near, and nearer still.

---

97 **Whose . . . suns, etc.** Tennyson spoke of this line as giving the sense of "the permanent in the transitory" 115 **Friend,** Wordsworth's sister Dorothy 125 **inform,** inspire

Strange Fits. This and the four following poems are often grouped as the "Lucy Poems." The identity of Lucy remains a matter of speculation

In one of these sweet dreams I slept,
Kind Nature's gentlest boon!
And all the while my eyes I kept
20 On the descending moon.

My horse moved on; hoof after hoof
He raised, and never stopped:
When down behind the cottage roof,
At once, the bright moon dropped.

What fond and wayward thoughts will slide
Into a Lover's head!
"O mercy!" to myself I cried,
"If Lucy should be dead!"
(1799; 1800)

SHE DWELT
AMONG THE UNTRODDEN WAYS

She dwelt among the untrodden ways
  Beside the springs of Dove,°
A Maid whom there were none to praise
  And very few to love:

5 A violet by a mossy stone
  Half hidden from the eye!
—Fair as a star, when only one
  Is shining in the sky.

She lived unknown, and few could know
10   When Lucy ceased to be;
But she is in her grave, and, oh,
  The difference to me!
(1799; 1800)

I TRAVELED AMONG UNKNOWN MEN

I traveled among unknown men,
  In lands beyond the sea;
Nor, England! did I know till then
  What love I bore to thee.

5 'Tis past, that melancholy dream!
  Nor will I quit thy shore
A second time; for still I seem
  To love thee more and more.

Among thy mountains did I feel
10   The joy of my desire;

She Dwelt Among   2 Dove, river forming part of the boundary between the counties of Derby and Stafford

And she I cherished turned her wheel
  Beside an English fire.

Thy mornings showed, thy nights concealed
  The bowers where Lucy played;
And thine too is the last green field   15
  That Lucy's eyes surveyed.
(1801; 1807)

THREE YEARS SHE GREW
IN SUN AND SHOWER

Three years she grew in sun and shower,
Then Nature said, "A lovelier flower
On earth was never sown;
This Child I to myself will take;
She shall be mine, and I will make
A Lady of my own.

"Myself will to my darling be
Both law and impulse: and with me
The Girl, in rock and plain,
In earth and heaven, in glade and bower,   10
Shall feel an overseeing power
To kindle or restrain.

"She shall be sportive as the fawn
That wild with glee across the lawn,
Or up the mountains springs;
And hers shall be the breathing balm,
And hers the silence and the calm
Of mute insensate things.

"The floating clouds their state shall lend
To her; for her the willow bend;   20
Nor shall she fail to see
Even in the motions of the Storm
Grace that shall mold the Maiden's form
By silent sympathy.

"The stars of midnight shall be dear
To her; and she shall lean her ear
In many a secret place
Where rivulets dance their wayward round,
And beauty born of murmuring sound
Shall pass into her face.   30

"And vital feelings of delight
Shall rear her form to stately height,
Her virgin bosom swell;
Such thoughts to Lucy I will give
While she and I together live
Here in this happy dell."

Thus Nature spake.—The work was done.—
How soon my Lucy's race was run!
She died, and left to me
40 This heath, this calm, and quiet scene;
The memory of what has been,
And never more will be.
(1799; 1800)

A SLUMBER DID MY SPIRIT SEAL

A slumber did my spirit seal;
    I had no human fears:
She seemed a thing that could not feel
    The touch of earthly years.

5 No motion has she now, no force;
    She neither hears nor sees;
Rolled round in earth's diurnal° course,
    With rocks, and stones, and trees.
(1799; 1800)

NUTTING°

————————It seems a day
(I speak of one from many singled out)
One of those heavenly days that cannot die;
When, in the eagerness of boyish hope,
I left our cottage-threshold, sallying forth
With a huge wallet o'er my shoulders slung,
A nutting-crook in hand; and turned my steps
Toward some far-distant wood, a Figure quaint,
Tricked out in proud disguise of cast-off weeds°
10 Which for that service had been husbanded,
By exhortation of my frugal Dame—
Motley accoutrement, of power to smile
At thorns, and brakes, and brambles,—and, in truth,
More ragged than need was! O'er path-less rocks,
Through beds of matted fern, and tangled thickets,
Forcing my way, I came to one dear nook
Unvisited, where not a broken bough
Drooped with its withered leaves, ungracious sign
Of devastation; but the hazels rose
20 Tall and erect, with tempting clusters hung,
A virgin scene!—A little while I stood,
Breathing with such suppression of the heart
As joy delights in; and, with wise restraint
Voluptuous, fearless of a rival, eyed
The banquet;—or beneath the trees I sate

Among the flowers, and with the flowers I played:
A temper known to those who, after long
And weary expectation, have been blest
With sudden happiness beyond all hope.
Perhaps it was a bower beneath whose leaves   30
The violets of five seasons re-appear
And fade, unseen by any human eye;
Where fairy water-breaks do murmur on
Forever; and I saw the sparkling foam,
And—with my cheek on one of those green stones
That, fleeced with moss, under the shady trees,
Lay round me, scattered like a flock of sheep—
I heard the murmur and the murmuring sound,
In that sweet mood when pleasure loves to pay
Tribute to ease; and, of its joy secure,   40
The heart luxuriates with indifferent things,
Wasting its kindliness on stocks and stones,
And on the vacant air. Then up I rose,
And dragged to earth both branch and bough, with
    crash
And merciless ravage: and the shady nook
Of hazels, and the green and mossy bower,
Deformed and sullied, patiently gave up
Their quiet being: and, unless I now
Confound my present feelings with the past,
Ere from the mutilated bower I turned   50
Exulting, rich beyond the wealth of kings,
I felt a sense of pain when I beheld
The silent trees, and saw the intruding sky.—
Then, dearest Maiden, move along these shades
In gentleness of heart; with gentle hand
Touch—for there is a spirit in the woods.
(1798; 1800)

ELEGIAC STANZAS

*Suggested by a Picture of Peele Castle,° in a Storm, Painted
By Sir George Beaumont*

I was thy neighbor once, thou rugged Pile!
Four summer weeks I dwelt in sight of thee:
I saw thee every day; and all the while
Thy Form was sleeping on a glassy sea.

So pure the sky, so quiet was the air!
So like, so very like, was day to day!
Whene'er I looked, thy Image still was there;
It trembled, but it never passed away.

How perfect was the calm! it seemed no sleep;
No mood, which season takes away, or brings: 10

A Slumber Did   7 **diurnal,** daily
Nutting, refers to the activity of gathering nuts   9 **weeds,** clothes

Elegiac Stanzas   **Peele Castle,** castle on the coast of Lancashire. Wordsworth visited
a cousin near there. Beaumont, a friend of the poet, painted two pictures of it

I could have fancied that the mighty Deep
Was even the gentlest of all gentle Things.

Ah! then, if mine had been the painter's hand,
To express what then I saw; and add the gleam,
The light that never was, on sea or land,
The consecration, and the poet's dream;

I would have planted thee, thou hoary Pile
Amid a world how different from this!°
Beside a sea that could not cease to smile;
20 On tranquil land, beneath a sky of bliss.

Thou shouldst have seemed a treasure-house divine
Of peaceful years; a chronicle of heaven;—
Of all the sunbeams that did ever shine
The very sweetest had to thee been given.

A picture had it been of lasting ease,
Elysian quiet, without toil or strife;
No motion but the moving tide, a breeze,
Or merely silent Nature's breathing life.

Such, in the fond illusion of my heart,
30 Such picture would I at that time have made:
And seen the soul of truth in every part,
A steadfast peace that might not be betrayed.

So once it would have been—'tis so no more;°
I have submitted to a new control:
A power is gone, which nothing can restore;
A deep distress hath humanized my Soul.

Not for a moment could I now behold
A smiling sea, and be what I have been:
The feeling of my loss will ne'er be old;
40 This, which I know, I speak with mind serene.

Then, Beaumont, friend! who would have been the
    friend,
If he had lived, of him whom I deplore,
This work of thine I blame not, but commend;
This sea in anger, and that dismal shore.

O 'tis a passionate Work!—yet wise and well,
Well chosen is the spirit that is here;
That Hulk which labors in the deadly swell,
This rueful sky, this pageantry of fear!

And this huge Castle, standing here sublime,
50 I love to see the look with which it braves,
Cased in the unfeeling armor of old time,
The lightning, the fierce wind, and trampling waves.

Farewell, farewell the heart that lives alone,
Housed in a dream, at distance from the Kind!

---

18 **different from this,** different from the world of storm as shown in the picture 33 **no more.** Wordsworth's brother, John, went down with his ship on 5 February 1805

Such happiness, wherever it be known,
Is to be pitied; for 'tis surely blind.

But welcome fortitude, and patient cheer,
And frequent sights of what is to be borne!
Such sights, or worse, as are before me here.—
Not without hope we suffer and we mourn.   60
(1805; 1807)

from THE PRELUDE

In his preface to *The Excursion,* Wordsworth describes the occasion and the plan of *The Prelude:*

"Several years ago, when the author retired to his native mountains with the hope of being enabled to construct a literary work that might live, it was a reasonable thing that he should take a review of his own mind, and examine how far nature and education had qualified him for such an employment. As subsidiary to this preparation, he undertook to record, in verse, the origin and progress of his own powers, as far as he was acquainted with them. That work, addressed to a dear friend, most distinguished for his knowledge and genius, and to whom the author's intellect is deeply indebted, has been long finished; and the result of the investigation which gave rise to it, was a determination to compose a philosophical poem, containing views of man, nature, and society, and to be entitled *The Recluse,* as having for its principal subject the sensations and opinions of a poet living in retirement.

"The preparatory poem [*The Prelude*] is biographical, and conducts the history of the author's mind to the point when he was emboldened to hope that his faculties were sufficiently matured for entering upon the arduous labor which he had proposed to himself; and the two works [*The Prelude* and *The Recluse*] have the same kind of relation to each other, if he may so express himself, as the ante-chapel has to the body of a Gothic church. Continuing this allusion, he may be permitted to add, that his minor pieces, which have been long before the public, when they shall be properly arranged, will be found by the attentive reader to have such connection with the main work as may give them claim to be likened to the little cells, oratories, and sepulchral recesses, ordinarily included in those edifices."

Thus, *The Prelude* was to be the introduction to a larger work called *The Recluse;* in this larger work *The Excursion* was to be the second part. The project was not completed, but *The Prelude* and *The Excursion* remain as highly significant autobiographical poems.

The "dear friend" to whom *The Prelude* was addressed was Coleridge. The poem was not published until 1850, three months after Wordsworth's death.

BOOK I. INTRODUCTION—CHILDHOOD AND SCHOOL-TIME

Oh, there is° blessing in this gentle breeze,
A visitant that while it fans my cheek
Doth seem half-conscious of the joy it brings
From the green fields, and from yon azure sky.
Whate'er its mission, the soft breeze can come
To none more grateful than to me; escaped
From the vast city,° where I long had pined
A discontented sojourner: now free,
Free as a bird to settle where I will.
10 What dwelling shall receive me? in what vale
Shall be my harbor? underneath what grove
Shall I take up my home? and what clear stream
Shall with its murmur lull me into rest?
The earth is all before me.° With a heart
Joyous, nor scared at its own liberty,
I look about; and should the chosen guide
Be nothing better than a wandering cloud,
I cannot miss my way. I breathe again!
Trances of thought and mountings of the mind
20 Come fast upon me: it is shaken off,
That burthen of my own unnatural self,
The heavy weight of many a weary day
Not mine, and such as were not made for me.
Long months of peace (if such bold word accord
With any promises of human life),
Long months of ease and undisturbed delight
Are mine in prospect; whither shall I turn,
By road or pathway, or through trackless field,
Up-hill or down, or shall some floating thing
30 Upon the river point me out my course?

Dear Liberty! Yet what would it avail
But for a gift that consecrates the joy?
For I, methought, while the sweet breath of heaven
Was blowing on my body, felt within
A correspondent breeze, that gently moved
With quickening virtue, but is now become
A tempest, a redundant energy,
Vexing its own creation. Thanks to both,
And their congenial powers, that, while they join
40 In breaking up a long-continued frost,
Bring with them vernal promises, the hope
Of active days urged on by flying hours—
Days of sweet leisure, taxed with patient thought
Abstruse, nor wanting punctual service high,
Matins and vespers of harmonious verse!

Thus far, O Friend!° did I, not used to make
A present joy the matter of a song,
Pour forth that day my soul in measured strains
That would not be forgotten, and are here
Recorded: to the open fields I told   50
A prophecy: poetic numbers came
Spontaneously to clothe in priestly robe
A renovated spirit singled out,
Such hope was mine, for holy services.
My own voice cheered me, and, far more, the mind's
Internal echo of the imperfect sound;
To both I listened, drawing from them both
A cheerful confidence in things to come.

Content and not unwilling now to give
A respite to this passion, I paced on   60
With brisk and eager steps; and came, at length,
To a green shady place, where down I sate
Beneath a tree, slackening my thoughts by choice
And settling into gentler happiness.
'Twas autumn, and a clear and placid day,
With warmth, as much as needed, from a sun
Two hours declined toward the west; a day
With silver clouds, and sunshine on the grass,
And in the sheltered and the sheltering grove
A perfect stillness. Many were the thoughts   70
Encouraged and dismissed, till choice was made
Of a known Vale,° whither my feet should turn,
Nor rest till they had reached the very door
Of the one cottage which methought I saw.
No picture of mere memory ever looked
So fair; and while upon the fancied scene
I gazed with growing love, a higher power
Than Fancy gave assurance of some work
Of glory there forthwith to be begun,
Perhaps too there performed. Thus long I mused,   80
Nor e'er lost sight of what I mused upon,
Save when, amid the stately grove of oaks,
Now here, now there, an acorn, from its cup
Dislodged, through sere leaves rustled, or at once
To the bare earth dropped with a startling sound.
From that soft couch I rose not, till the sun
Had almost touched the horizon; casting then
A backward glance upon the curling cloud
Of city smoke, by distance ruralized;
Keen as a Truant or a Fugitive,   90
But as a Pilgrim resolute, I took,
Even with the chance equipment of that hour,
The road that pointed toward the chosen Vale.
It was a splendid evening, and my soul
Once more made trial of her strength, nor lacked
Aeolian visitations;° but the harp
Was soon defrauded, and the banded host
Of harmony dispersed in straggling sounds,
And lastly utter silence! "Be it so;

Book I 1–45 **Oh, there is, etc.** These lines were written in September 1795 on the way from Bristol to Racedown, over two years before the idea of *The Prelude* was conceived; the poem was written from 1798 through the summer of 1805   7 **vast city,** London, where Wordsworth lived from January to September in 1795   14 **earth . . . me.** One of the many echoes of Milton in the poem; cf. *Paradise Lost*, XII, 646: "The World was all before them, where to choose"

46 **Friend,** Samuel Taylor Coleridge   72 **Vale,** Racedown   96 **Aeolian visitations,** thoughts that come and go with the breeze, as sounds are produced when the wind strikes the Aeolian harp, named after Aeolus, god of winds

100 Why think of anything but present good?''
    So, like a home-bound laborer, I pursued
    My way beneath the mellowing sun, that shed
    Mild influence; nor left in me one wish
    Again to bend the Sabbath° of that time
    To a servile yoke. What need of many words?
    A pleasant loitering journey, through three days
    Continued, brought me to my hermitage.
    I spare to tell of what ensued, the life
    In common things—the endless store of things,
110 Rare, or at least so seeming, every day
    Found all about me in one neighborhood—
    The self-congratulation, and, from morn
    To night, unbroken cheerfulness serene.
    But speedily an earnest longing rose
    To brace myself to some determined aim,
    Reading or thinking; either to lay up
    New stores, or rescue from decay the old
    By timely interference: and therewith
    Came hopes still higher, that with outward life
120 I might endue some airy phantasies
    That had been floating loose about for years,
    And to such beings temperately deal forth
    The many feelings that oppressed my heart.
    That hope hath been discouraged; welcome light
    Dawns from the east, but dawns to disappear
    And mock me with a sky that ripens not
    Into a steady morning: if my mind,
    Remembering the bold promise of the past,
    Would gladly grapple with some noble theme,
130 Vain is her wish; where'er she turns she finds
    Impediments from day to day renewed.

    And now it would content me to yield up
    Those lofty hopes awhile, for present gifts
    Of humbler industry. But, oh, dear Friend!
    The Poet, gentle creature as he is,
    Hath, like the Lover, his unruly times;
    His fits when he is neither sick nor well,
    Though no distress be near him but his own
    Unmanageable thoughts: his mind, best pleased
140 While she as duteous as the mother dove
    Sits brooding, lives not always to that end,
    But like the innocent bird hath goadings on
    That drive her as in trouble through the groves;
    With me is now such passion to be blamed
    No otherwise than as it lasts too long.

    When, as becomes a man who would prepare
    For such an arduous work, I through myself
    Make rigorous inquisition, the report
    Is often cheering; for I neither seem
150 To lack that first great gift, the vital soul,
    Nor general Truths, which are themselves a sort
    Of Elements and Agents, Under-powers,
    Subordinate helpers of the living mind:

Nor am I naked of external things,
Forms, images, nor numerous other aids
Of less regard, though won perhaps with toil
And needful to build up a Poet's praise.
Time, place, and manners do I seek, and these
Are found in plenteous store, but nowhere such
As may be singled out with steady choice;   160
No little band of yet remembered names
Whom I, in perfect confidence, might hope
To summon back from lonesome banishment,
And make them dwellers in the hearts of men
Now living, or to live in future years.
Sometimes the ambitious Power of choice, mistaking
Proud spring-tide swellings for a regular sea,
Will settle on some British theme, some old
Romantic tale by Milton left unsung;°
More often turning to some gentle place   170
Within the groves of Chivalry,° I pipe
To shepherd swains, or seated harp in hand,
Amid reposing knights by a river side
Or fountain, listen to the grave reports
Of dire enchantments faced and overcome
By the strong mind, and tales of warlike feats,
Where spear encountered spear, and sword with
    sword
Fought, as if conscious of the blazonry
That the shield bore, so glorious was the strife;
Whence inspiration for a song that winds   180
Through ever-changing scenes of votive quest
Wrongs to redress, harmonious tribute paid
To patient courage and unblemished truth,
To firm devotion, zeal unquenchable,
And Christian meekness hallowing faithful loves.
Sometimes, more sternly moved, I would relate
How vanquished Mithridates° northward passed,
And, hidden in the cloud of years, became
Odin, the Father of a race by whom
Perished the Roman Empire: how the friends   190
And followers of Sertorius,° out of Spain
Flying, found shelter in the Fortunate Isles,
And left their usages, their arts and laws,
To disappear by a slow gradual death,
To dwindle and to perish one by one,
Starved in those narrow bounds: but not the soul
Of Liberty, which fifteen hundred years
Survived, and, when the European came
With skill and power that might not be withstood,
Did, like a pestilence, maintain its hold   200
And wasted down by glorious death that race
Of natural heroes: or I would record
How, in tyrannic times, some high-souled man,

168–169 **British theme . . . unsung.** Milton seriously considered writing an epic on the history of Britain before the Conquest and also a poem on King Arthur 171 **groves of Chivalry,** see Spenser's *Faerie Queene,* Bk. VI 187 **Mithridates,** king of Pontus, Asia Minor (120–63 B.C.); he was defeated by Pompey in 66 B.C. His identification with Odin, the supreme deity of Scandinavian mythology, was suggested to Wordsworth by a passage in Gibbon's *Decline and Fall of the Roman Empire* (Chap. 10) 191 **Sertorius,** a famous Roman general who resisted tyrannical rule for eight years, until he was assassinated in 72 B.C. On one of his journeys he landed in Spain, where he learned from sailors about the Fortunate Islands in the Atlantic, supposed to be the Canaries. Wordsworth read about him in Plutarch's *Lives*

104 **Sabbath,** calm, restfulness

Unnamed among the chronicles of kings,
Suffered in silence for Truth's sake; or tell,
How that one Frenchman,° through continued force
Of meditation on the inhuman deeds
Of those who conquered first the Indian Isles,
Went single in his ministry across
210 The Ocean; not to comfort the oppressed,
But, like a thirsty wind, to roam about
Withering the Oppressor: how Gustavus° sought
Help at his need in Dalecarlia's mines:
How Wallace° fought for Scotland; left the name
Of Wallace to be found, like a wild flower,
All over his dear Country; left the deeds
Of Wallace, like a family of Ghosts,
To people the steep rocks and river banks,
Her natural sanctuaries, with a local soul
220 Of independence and stern liberty.
Sometimes it suits me better to invent
A tale from my own heart, more near akin
To my own passions and habitual thoughts;
Some variegated story, in the main
Lofty, but the unsubstantial structure melts
Before the very sun that brightens it,
Mist into air dissolving! Then a wish,
My last and favorite aspiration, mounts
With yearning toward some philosophic song
230 Of Truth that cherishes our daily life;
With meditations passionate from deep
Recesses in man's heart, immortal verse
Thoughtfully fitted to the Orphean lyre;°
But from this awful burthen I full soon
Take refuge and beguile myself with trust
That mellower years will bring a riper mind
And clearer insight. Thus my days are passed
In contradiction; with no skill to part
Vague longing, haply bred by want of power,
240 From paramount impulse not to be withstood,
A timorous capacity from prudence,
From circumspection, infinite delay.
Humility and modest awe themselves
Betray me, serving often for a cloak
To a more subtle selfishness; that now
Locks every function up in blank reserve,
Now dupes me, trusting to an anxious eye
That with instrusive restlessness beats off
Simplicity and self-presented truth.
250 Ah! better far than this, to stray about
Voluptuously through fields and rural walks,
And ask no record of the hours, resigned
To vacant musing, unreproved neglect
Of all things, and deliberate holiday.
Far better never to have heard the name
Of zeal and just ambition, than to live

Baffled and plagued by a mind that every hour
Turns recreant to her task; takes heart again,
Then feels immediately some hollow thought
Hang like an interdict upon her hopes. 260
This is my lot; for either still I find
Some imperfection in the chosen theme,
Or see of absolute accomplishment
Much wanting, so much wanting, in myself,
That I recoil and droop, and seek repose
In listlessness from vain perplexity,
Unprofitably traveling toward the grave,
Like a false steward° who hath much received
And renders nothing back.
                              Was it for this
That one, the fairest of all rivers,° loved 270
To blend his murmurs with my nurse's song,
And, from his alder shades and rocky falls,
And from his fords and shallows, sent a voice
That flowed along my dreams? For this, didst thou,
O Derwent! winding among grassy holms°
Where I was looking on, a babe in arms,
Make ceaseless music that composed my thoughts
To more than infant softness, giving me
Amid the fretful dwellings of mankind
A foretaste, a dim earnest, of the calm 280
That Nature breathes among the hills and groves.

When he had left the mountains and received
On his smooth breast the shadow of those towers°
That yet survive, a shattered monument
Of feudal sway, the bright blue river passed
Along the margin of our terrace walk;
A tempting playmate whom we dearly loved.
Oh, many a time have I, a five years' child,
In a small mill-race severed from his stream,
Made one long bathing of a summer's day; 290
Basked in the sun, and plunged and basked again
Alternate, all a summer's day, or scoured
The sandy fields, leaping through flowery groves
Of yellow ragwort; or when rock and hill,
The woods, and distant Skiddaw's° lofty height,
Were bronzed with deepest radiance, stood alone
Beneath the sky, as if I had been born
On Indian plains, and from my mother's hut
Had run abroad in wantonness, to sport,
A naked savage, in the thunder-shower. 300

Fair seed-time had my soul, and I grew up
Fostered alike by beauty and by fear:
Much favored in my birthplace, and no less
In that belovéd Vale° to which erelong
We were transplanted—there were we let loose
For sports of wider range. Ere I had told

206 **Frenchman,** Dominique de Gourges, who sailed to Florida in 1568 to avenge the massacre of French colonists by the Spaniards   212 **Gustavus,** Gustavus I of Sweden (1496–1560), who freed his country from the tyranny of Denmark. He worked out his plans in Dalecarlia, a mining district in the west midlands of Sweden, where he often disguised himself as a peasant or a miner to escape capture by the Danes   214 **Wallace,** William Wallace (d. 1305), celebrated Scottish hero and patriot   233 **Orphean lyre,** an allusion to the famous lyre of Orpheus, mythological poet and musician, whose music could charm beasts and move trees and stones

268 **false steward,** an allusion to the parable of the talents. Two of the three stewards were faithful to their trust, but the third was false. See *Matthew* 25:14–30   270 **fairest of all rivers,** Derwent. Wordsworth was born at Cockermouth situated at the junction of two rivers—Cocker and Derwent   275 **holms,** low flat lands   283 **those towers,** of Cockermouth Castle   295 **Skiddaw,** a mountain in Cumberlandshire   304 **Vale,** Esthwaite, Lancashire, where Wordsworth attended Hawkshead school

Ten birthdays; when among the mountain-slopes
Frost, and the breath of frosty wind, had snapped
The last autumnal crocus, 'twas my joy
310 With store of springes° o'er my shoulder hung
To range the open heights where woodcocks run
Among the smooth green turf. Through half the night,
Scudding away from snare to snare, I plied
That anxious visitation;—moon and stars
Were shining o'er my head. I was alone,
And seemed to be a trouble to the peace
That dwelt among them. Sometimes it befell
In these night wanderings, that a strong desire
O'erpowered my better reason, and the bird
320 Which was the captive of another's toil
Became my prey; and when the deed was done,
I heard among the solitary hills
Low breathings coming after me, and sounds
Of undistinguishable motion, steps
Almost as silent as the turf they trod.

Nor less when spring had warmed the cultured Vale,°
Roved we as plunderers where the mother-bird
Had in high places built her lodge; though mean
Our object and inglorious, yet the end
330 Was not ignoble. Oh! when I have hung
Above the raven's nest, by knots of grass
And half-inch fissures in the slippery rock
But ill sustained, and almost (so it seemed)
Suspended by the blast that blew amain,
Shouldering the naked crag, oh, at that time
While on the perilous ridge I hung alone,
With what strange utterance did the loud dry wind
Blow through my ear! the sky seemed not a sky
Of earth—and with what motion moved the clouds!

340   Dust as we are, the immortal spirit grows
Like harmony in music; there is a dark
Inscrutable workmanship that reconciles
Discordant elements, makes them cling together
In one society. How strange that all
The terrors, pains, and early miseries,
Regrets, vexations, lassitudes interfused
Within my mind, should e'er have borne a part,
And that a needful part, in making up
The calm existence that is mine when I
350 Am worthy of myself! Praise to the end!
Thanks to the means which Nature deigned to employ;
Whether her fearless visitings, or those
That came with soft alarm, like hurtless light
Opening the peaceful clouds; or she may use
Severer interventions, ministry
More palpable, as best might suit her aim.

One summer evening (led by her°) I found
A little boat tied to a willow tree
Within a rocky cave, its usual home.

Straight I unloosed her chain, and stepping in   360
Pushed from the shore. It was an act of stealth
And troubled pleasure, nor without the voice
Of mountain-echoes did my boat move on;
Leaving behind her still, on either side,
Small circles glittering idly in the moon,
Until they melted all into one track
Of sparkling light. But now, like one who rows,
Proud of his skill, to reach a chosen point
With an unswerving line, I fixed my view
Upon the summit of a craggy ridge,   370
The horizon's utmost boundary; for above
Was nothing but the stars and the gray sky.
She was an elfin pinnace;° lustily
I dipped my oars into the silent lake,
And, as I rose upon the stroke, my boat
Went heaving through the water like a swan;
When, from behind that craggy steep till then
The horizon's bound, a huge peak, black and huge,
As if with voluntary power instinct
Upreared its head. I struck and struck again,   380
And growing still in stature the grim shape
Towered up between me and the stars, and still,
For so it seemed, with purpose of its own
And measured motion like a living thing,
Strode after me. With trembling oars I turned,
And through the silent water stole my way
Back to the covert of the willow tree;
There in her mooring-place I left my bark—
And through the meadows homeward went, in grave
And serious mood; but after I had seen   390
That spectacle, for many days, my brain
Worked with a dim and undetermined sense
Of unknown modes of being; o'er my thoughts
There hung a darkness, call it solitude
Or blank desertion. No familiar shapes
Remained, no pleasant images of trees,
Of sea or sky, no colors of green fields;
But huge and mighty forms, that do not live
Like living men, moved slowly through the mind
By day, and were a trouble to my dreams.   400

Wisdom and Spirit of the universe!
Thou Soul that art the eternity of thought,
That givest to forms and images a breath
And everlasting motion, not in vain
By day or star-light thus from my first dawn
Of childhood didst thou intertwine for me
The passions that build up our human soul;
Not with the mean and vulgar works of man,
But with high objects, with enduring things—
With life and nature—purifying thus   410
The elements of feeling and of thought,
And sanctifying, by such discipline,
Both pain and fear, until we recognize
A grandeur in the beatings of the heart.

310 springes, snares, traps   326 Vale, Yewdale, a valley near
Hawkshead   357 her, Nature

373 pinnace, light sailing vessel

Nor was this fellowship vouchsafed to me
With stinted kindness. In November days,
When vapors rolling down the valley made
A lonely scene more lonesome, among woods,
At noon and 'mid the calm of summer nights,
420 When, by the margin of the trembling lake,
Beneath the gloomy hills homeward I went
In solitude, such intercourse was mine;
Mine was it in the fields both day and night,
And by the waters, all the summer long.

And in the frosty season, when the sun
Was set, and visible for many a mile
The cottage windows blazed through twilight gloom,
I heeded not their summons: happy time
It was indeed for all of us—for me
430 It was a time of rapture! Clear and loud
The village clock tolled six—I wheeled about,
Proud and exulting like an untired horse
That cares not for his home. All shod with steel,
We hissed along the polished ice in games
Confederate, imitative of the chase
And woodland pleasures—the resounding horn,
The pack loud chiming, and the hunted hare.
So through the darkness and the cold we flew,
And not a voice was idle; with the din
440 Smitten, the precipices rang aloud;
The leafless trees and every icy crag
Tinkled like iron; while far distant hills
Into the tumult sent an alien sound
Of melancholy not unnoticed, while the stars
Eastward were sparkling clear, and in the west
The orange sky of evening died away.
Not seldom from the uproar I retired
Into a silent bay, or sportively
Glanced sideway, leaving the tumultuous throng,
450 To cut across the reflex of a star
That fled, and, flying still before me, gleamed
Upon the glassy plain; and oftentimes,
When we had given our bodies to the wind,
And all the shadowy banks on either side
Came sweeping through the darkness, spinning still
The rapid line of motion, then at once
Have I, reclining back upon my heels,
Stopped short; yet still the solitary cliffs
Wheeled by me—even as if the earth had rolled
460 With visible motion her diurnal round!
Behind me did they stretch in solemn train,
Feebler and feebler, and I stood and watched
Till all was tranquil as a dreamless sleep.

Ye Presences of Nature in the sky
And on the earth! Ye Visions of the hills!
And Souls of lonely places! can I think
A vulgar hope was yours when ye employed
Such ministry, when ye through many a year
Haunting me thus among my boyish sports,
470 On caves and trees, upon the woods and hills,

Impressed upon all forms the characters
Of danger or desire; and thus did make
The surface of the universal earth
With triumph and delight, with hope and fear,
Work like a sea?

                    Not uselessly employed,
Might I pursue this theme through every change
Of exercise and play, to which the year
Did summon us in his delightful round.

We were a noisy crew; the sun in heaven
Beheld not vales more beautiful than ours;   480
Nor saw a band in happiness and joy
Richer, or worthier of the ground they trod.
I could record with no reluctant voice
The woods of autumn, and their hazel bowers
With milk-white clusters hung; the rod and line,
True symbol of hope's foolishness, whose strong
And unreproved enchantment led us on
By rocks and pools shut out from every star,
All the green summer, to forlorn cascades
Among the windings hid of mountain brooks.   490
—Unfading recollections! at this hour
The heart is almost mine with which I felt,
From some hill-top on sunny afternoons,
The paper kite high among fleecy clouds
Pull at her rein like an impetuous courser;
Or, from the meadows sent on gusty days,
Beheld her breast the wind, then suddenly
Dashed headlong, and rejected by the storm.

Ye lowly cottages wherein we dwelt,
A ministration of your own was yours;   500
Can I forget you, being as you were
So beautiful among the pleasant fields
In which ye stood? or can I here forget
The plain and seemly countenance with which
Ye dealt out your plain comforts? Yet had ye
Delights and exultations of your own.
Eager and never weary we pursued
Our home-amusements by the warm peat-fire
At evening, when with pencil, and smooth slate
In square divisions parceled out and all   510
With crosses and with ciphers scribbled o'er,
We schemed and puzzled, head opposed to head
In strife too humble to be named in verse;
Or round the naked table, snow-white deal,°
Cherry or maple, sate in close array,
And to the combat, Loo° or Whist,° led on
A thick-ribbed army; not, as in the world,
Neglected and ungratefully thrown by
Even for the very service they had wrought,
But husbanded through many a long campaign.   520
Uncouth assemblage was it, where no few
Had changed their functions; some, plebeian cards
Which Fate, beyond the promise of their birth,

514 **deal,** pine or fir wood   516 **Loo,** a card game   **Whist,** a card game

Had dignified, and called to represent
The persons of departed potentates.
Oh, with what echoes on the board they fell!
Ironic diamonds—clubs, hearts, diamonds, spades,
A congregation piteously akin!
Cheap matter offered they to boyish wit,
530 Those sooty knaves, precipitated down
With scoffs and taunts, like Vulcan out of heaven:
The paramount ace, a moon in her eclipse,
Queens gleaming through their splendor's last decay,
And monarchs surly at the wrongs sustained
By royal visages. Meanwhile abroad
Incessant rain was falling, or the frost
Raged bitterly, with keen and silent tooth;
And, interrupting oft that eager game,
From under Esthwaite's splitting fields of ice
540 The pent-up air, struggling to free itself,
Gave out to meadow-grounds and hills a loud
Protracted yelling, like the noise of wolves
Howling in troops along the Bothnic Main.°

 Nor, sedulous as I have been to trace
How Nature by extrinsic passion first
Peopled the mind with forms sublime or fair,
And made me love them, may I here omit
How other pleasures have been mine, and joys
Of subtler origin; how I have felt,
550 Not seldom even in that tempestuous time,
Those hallowed and pure emotions of the sense
Which seem, in their simplicity, to own
An intellectual charm; that calm delight
Which, if I err not, surely must belong
To those first-born affinities that fit
Our new existence to existing things,
And, in our dawn of being, constitute
The bond of union between life and joy.

 Yes, I remember when the changeful earth,
560 And twice five summers on my mind had stamped
The faces of the moving year, even then
I held unconscious intercourse with beauty
Old as creation, drinking in a pure
Organic pleasure from the silver wreaths
Of curling mist, or from the level plain
Of waters colored by impending clouds.

 The sands of Westmoreland, the creeks and bays
Of Cumbria's° rocky limits, they can tell
How, when the Sea threw off his evening shade
570 And to the shepherd's hut on distant hills
Sent welcome notice of the rising moon,
How I have stood, to fancies such as these
A stranger, linking with the spectacle
No conscious memory of a kindred sight,
And bringing with me no peculiar sense
Of quietness or peace; yet have I stood,

543 **Bothnic Main,** Baltic Sea   568 **Cumbria,** Cumberlandshire, most of which
made up the ancient British kingdom of Cumbria

Even while mine eye hath moved o'er many a league
Of shining water, gathering as it seemed,
Through every hair-breadth in that field of light,
New pleasure like a bee among the flowers.   580

 Thus oft amid those fits of vulgar joy
Which, through all seasons, on a child's pursuits
Are prompt attendants, 'mid that giddy bliss
Which, like a tempest, works along the blood
And is forgotten; even then I felt
Gleams like the flashing of a shield; the earth
And common face of Nature spake to me
Rememberable things; sometimes, 'tis true,
By chance collisions and quaint accidents
(Like those ill-sorted unions, work supposed   590
Of evil-minded fairies), yet not vain
Nor profitless, if haply they impressed
Collateral objects and appearances,
Albeit lifeless then, and doomed to sleep
Until maturer seasons called them forth
To impregnate and to elevate the mind.
—And if the vulgar joy by its own weight
Wearied itself out of the memory,
The scenes which were a witness of that joy
Remained in their substantial lineaments   600
Depicted on the brain, and to the eye
Were visible, a daily sight; and thus
By the impressive discipline of fear,
By pleasure and repeated happiness,
So frequently repeated, and by force
Of obscure feelings representative
Of things forgotten, these same scenes so bright,
So beautiful, so majestic in themselves,
Though yet the day was distant, did become
Habitually dear, and all their forms   610
And changeful colors by invisible links
Were fastened to the affections.
                           I began
My story early—not misled, I trust,
By an infirmity of love for days
Disowned by memory—ere the birth of spring
Planting my snowdrops among winter snows:
Nor will it seem to thee, O Friend! so prompt
In sympathy, that I have lengthened out
With fond and feeble tongue a tedious tale.
Meanwhile, my hope has been that I might fetch   620
Invigorating thoughts from former years;
Might fix the wavering balance of my mind,
And haply meet reproaches too, whose power
May spur me on, in manhood now mature,
To honorable toil. Yet should these hopes
Prove vain, and thus should neither I be taught
To understand myself, nor thou to know
With better knowledge how the heart was framed
Of him thou lovest; need I dread from thee
Harsh judgments, if the song be loath to quit   630
Those recollected hours that have the charm
Of visionary things, those lovely forms

And sweet sensations that throw back our life,
And almost make remotest infancy
A visible scene, on which the sun is shining?

One end at least hath been attained; my mind
Hath been revived, and if this genial mood
Desert me not, forthwith shall be brought down
Through later years the story of my life.
640 The road lies plain before me;—'tis a theme
Single and of determined bounds; and hence
I choose it rather at this time, than work
Of ampler or more varied argument,
Where I might be discomfited and lost:
And certain hopes are with me, that to thee
This labor will be welcome, honored Friend!
(1798-99–1805; 1850)

from BOOK XII.°
IMAGINATION AND TASTE,
HOW IMPAIRED AND RESTORED

There are in our existence spots of time,
That with distinct pre-eminence retain
210 A renovating virtue, whence—depressed
By false opinion and contentious thought,
Or aught of heavier or more deadly weight,
In trivial occupations, and the round
Of ordinary intercourse—our minds
Are nourished and invisibly repaired;
A virtue, by which pleasure is enhanced,
That penetrates, enables us to mount,
When high, more high, and lifts us up when fallen.
This efficacious spirit chiefly lurks
220 Among those passages of life that give
Profoundest knowledge to what point, and how,
The mind is lord and master—outward sense
The obedient servant of her will. Such moments
Are scattered everywhere, taking their date
From our first childhood. I remember well,
That once, while yet my inexperienced hand
Could scarcely hold a bridle, with proud hopes
I mounted, and we journeyed towards the hills:
An ancient servant of my father's house
230 Was with me, my encourager and guide;
We had not traveled long, ere some mischance
Disjoined me from my comrade; and, through fear
Dismounting, down the rough and stony moor
I led my horse, and, stumbling on, at length
Came to a bottom, where in former times
A murderer had been hung in iron chains.
The gibbet-mast had moldered down, the bones
And iron case were gone; but on the turf,
Hard by, soon after that fell deed was wrought,

Some unknown hand had carved the murderer's name. 240
The monumental letters were inscribed
In times long past; but still, from year to year
By superstition of the neighborhood,
The grass is cleared away, and to this hour
The characters are fresh and visible:
A casual glance had shown them, and I fled,
Faltering and faint, and ignorant of the road:
Then, reascending the bare common, saw
A naked pool that lay beneath the hills,
The beacon on the summit, and, more near,   250
A girl, who bore a pitcher on her head,
And seemed with difficult steps to force her way
Against the blowing wind. It was, in truth,
An ordinary sight; but I should need
Colours and words that are unknown to man,
To paint the visionary dreariness
Which, while I looked all round for my lost guide
Invested moorland waste and naked pool,
The beacon crowning the lone eminence,
The female and her garments vexed and tossed   260
By the strong wind. When, in the blessèd hours
Of early love, the loved one at my side,
I roamed, in daily presence of this scene,
Upon the naked pool and dreary crags,
And on the melancholy beacon, fell
A spirit of pleasure and youth's golden gleam;
And think ye not with radiance more sublime
For these remembrances, and for the power
They had left behind? So feeling comes in aid
Of feeling, and diversity of strength   270
Attends us, if but once we have been strong.
Oh! mystery of man, from what a depth
Proceed thy honours. I am lost, but see
In simple childhood something of the base
On which thy greatness stands; but this I feel,
That from thyself it comes, that thou must give,
Else never canst receive. The days gone by
Return upon me almost from the dawn
Of life: the hiding-places of man's power
Open; I would approach them, but they close.   280
I see by glimpses now; when age comes on,
May scarcely see at all; and I would give,
While yet we may, as far as words can give,
Substance and life to what I feel, enshrining,
Such is my hope, the spirit of the Past
For future restoration.—Yet another
Of these memorials:—

           One Christmas-time,
On the glad eve of its dear holidays,
Feverish, and tired, and restless, I went forth
Into the fields, impatient for the sight   290
Of those led palfreys that should bear us home;
My brothers and myself. There rose a crag,
That, from the meeting-point of two highways
Ascending, overlooked them both, far stretched;
Thither, uncertain on which road to fix
My expectation, thither I repaired,

Book XII. In this book Wordsworth reviews the "impairment" and gradual restoration of his creative sensibility in response to the natural world; its climax is the celebrated description of the "spots of time," ordinary moments of experience which become illuminated with a profound significance through the imaginative power of the beholder

Scout-like, and gained the summit; 'twas a day
Tempestuous, dark, and wild, and on the grass
I sate half-sheltered by a naked wall;
300 Upon my right hand couched a single sheep,
Upon my left a blasted hawthorn stood;
With those companions at my side, I watched,
Straining my eyes intensely, as the mist
Gave intermitting prospect of the copse
And plain beneath. Ere we to school returned,—
That dreary time,—ere we had been ten days
Sojourners in my father's house, he died;
And I and my three brothers, orphans then,
Followed his body to the grave. The event,
310 With all the sorrow that it brought, appeared
A chastisement; and when I called to mind
That day so lately past, when from the crag
I looked in such anxiety of hope;
With trite reflections of morality,
Yet in the deepest passion, I bowed low
To God, Who thus corrected my desires;
And, afterwards, the wind and sleety rain,
And all the business of the elements,
The single sheep, and the one blasted tree,
320 And the bleak music from that old stone wall,
The noise of wood and water, and the mist
That on the line of each of those two roads
Advanced in such indisputable shapes;
All these were kindred spectacles and sounds
To which I oft repaired, and thence would drink,
As at a fountain; and on winter nights,
Down to this very time, when storm and rain
Beat on my roof, or, haply, at noon-day,
While in a grove I walk, whose lofty trees,
330 Laden with summer's thickest foliage, rock
In a strong wind, some working of the spirit,
Some inward agitations thence are brought,
Whate'er their office, whether to beguile
Thoughts over busy in the course they took,
Or animate an hour of vacant ease.

from BOOK XIII.
IMAGINATION AND TASTE,
HOW IMPAIRED AND RESTORED
(CONCLUDED)

From Nature doth emotion come, and moods
Of calmness equally are Nature's gift;
This is her glory; these two attributes
Are sister horns that constitute her strength.
Hence Genius, born to thrive by interchange
Of peace and excitation, finds in her
His best and purest friend; from her receives
That energy by which he seeks the truth,
From her that happy stillness of the mind
10 Which fits him to receive it when unsought.

Such benefit the humblest intellects
Partake of, each in their degree; 'tis mine
To speak, what I myself have known and felt;
Smooth task! for words find easy way, inspired
By gratitude, and confidence in truth.
Long time in search of knowledge did I range
The field of human life, in heart and mind
Benighted; but, the dawn beginning now
To reappear, 'twas proved that not in vain
I had been taught to reverence a power   20
That is the visible quality and shape
And image of right reason; that matures
Her processes by steadfast laws; gives birth
To no impatient or fallacious hopes,
No heat of passion or excessive zeal,
No vain conceits; provokes to no quick turns
Of self-applauding intellect; but trains
To meekness, and exalts by humble faith,
Holds up before the mind intoxicate
With present objects, and the busy dance   30
Of things that pass away, a temperate show
Of objects that endure; and by this course
Disposes her, when overfondly set
On throwing off incumbrances, to seek
In man, and in the frame of social life,
Whate'er there is desirable and good
Of kindred permanence, unchanged in form
And function, or, through strict vicissitude
Of life and death, revolving. Above all
Were re-established now those watchful thoughts   40
Which, seeing little worthy or sublime
In what the historian's pen so much delights
To blazon—power and energy detached
From moral purpose—early tutored me
To look with feelings of fraternal love
Upon the unassuming things that hold
A silent station in this beauteous world.

* * * * *

Here, calling up to mind what then I saw,
A youthful traveler, and see daily now
In the familiar circuit of my home,
Here might I pause, and bend in reverence
To Nature, and the power of human minds,
To men as they are men within themselves.
How oft high service is performed within,
When all the external man is rude in show—
Not like a temple rich with pomp and gold,
But a mere mountain chapel, that protects   230
Its simple worshipers from sun and shower.
Of these, said I, shall be my song; of these,
If future years mature me for the task,
Will I record the praises, making verse
Deal boldly with substantial things; in truth
And sanctity of passion, speak of these,
That justice may be done, obeisance paid
Where it is due: thus haply shall I teach,
Inspire; through unadulterated ears

240 Pour rapture, tenderness, and hope—my theme
No other than the very heart of man,
As found among the best of those who live,
Not unexalted by religious faith,
Nor uninformed by books, good books, though few,
In Nature's presence; thence may I select
Sorrow, that is not sorrow, but delight;
And miserable love, that is not pain
To hear of, for the glory that redounds
Therefrom to human kind, and what we are.
250 Be mine to follow with no timid step
Where knowledge leads me: it shall be my pride
That I have dared to tread this holy ground,
Speaking no dream, but things oracular;
Matter not lightly to be heard by those
Who to the letter of the outward promise
Do read the invisible soul; by men adroit
In speech, and for communion with the world
Accomplished; minds whose faculties are then
Most active when they are most eloquent,
260 And elevated most when most admired.
Men may be found of other mold than these,
Who are their own upholders, to themselves
Encouragement, and energy, and will,
Expressing liveliest thoughts in lively words
As native passion dictates.
(1799–1805; 1850)

MY HEART LEAPS UP WHEN I BEHOLD

My heart leaps up when I behold
   A rainbow in the sky:
So was it when my life began;
So is it now I am a man:
5 So be it when I shall grow old,
   Or let me die!
The Child is father of the Man;
And I could wish my days to be
Bound each to each by natural piety.°
(1802; 1807)

RESOLUTION AND INDEPENDENCE

According to Dorothy Wordsworth, the subject of this poem was a poor and crippled old man that she and her brother met in the course of one of their walks. "He had been hurt in driving a cart, his leg broken, his body driven over, his skull fractured." Wordsworth evidently saw in him some of the effects of the inexplicable harmful forces of nature. He himself said, speaking of *Resolution and Independence:* "I describe myself as having been exalted to the highest pitch of delight by the joyousness and beauty of nature; and then as depressed, even in the midst of those beautiful objects, to the lowest dejection and despair. A young poet in the midst of the happiness of nature is described as overwhelmed by the thoughts of the miserable reverses which have befallen the happiest of all men." Significant also is the last sentence in the passage: "I cannot conceive a figure more impressive than that of an old man like this . . . traveling alone among the mountains and all lonely places, carrying with him his own fortitude, and the necessities which an unjust state of society has laid upon him."

There was a roaring in the wind all night;
The rain came heavily and fell in floods;
But now the sun is rising calm and bright;
The birds are singing in the distant woods:
Over his own sweet voice the stock-dove broods;
The jay makes answer as the magpie chatters;
And all the air is filled with pleasant noise of waters.

All things that love the sun are out of doors;
The sky rejoices in the morning's birth;
The grass is bright with raindrops;—on the moors   10
The hare is running races in her mirth;
And with her feet she from the plashy° earth
Raises a mist, that, glittering in the sun,
Runs with her all the way wherever she doth run.

I was a traveler then upon the moor;
I saw the hare that raced about with joy;
I heard the woods and distant waters roar,
Or heard them not, as happy as a boy:
The pleasant season did my heart employ:
My old remembrances went from me wholly;   20
And all the ways of men so vain and melancholy.

But, as it sometimes chanceth, from the might
Of joy in minds that can no further go,
As high as we have mounted in delight
In our dejection do we sink as low,
To me that morning did it happen so;
And fears, and fancies, thick upon me came;
Dim sadness—and blind thoughts, I knew not, nor
   could name.

I heard the skylark warbling in the sky;
And I bethought me of the playful hare: 30
Even such a happy child of earth am I;
Even as these blissful creatures do I fare;
Far from the world I walk, and from all care;

My Heart Leaps Up   9 **piety,** reverence, affection

Resolution and Independence   12 **plashy,** swampy, marshy

But there may come another day to me—
Solitude, pain of heart, distress, and poverty.

My whole life I have lived in pleasant thought,
As if life's business were a summer mood;
As if all needful things would come unsought
To genial faith, still rich in genial good;
40 But how can he expect that others should
Build for him, sow for him, and at his call
Love him, who for himself will take no heed at all?

I thought of Chatterton,° the marvelous boy,
The sleepless soul that perished in his pride;
Of him who walked in glory and in joy°
Following his plow, along the mountain side:
By our own spirits are we deified:
We poets in our youth begin in gladness;
But thereof come in the end despondency and mad-
    ness.

50 Now, whether it were by peculiar grace,
A leading from above, a something given,
Yet it befell, that, in this lonely place,
When I with these untoward thoughts had striven,
Beside a pool bare to the eye of heaven
I saw a man before me unawares:
The oldest man he seemed that ever wore gray hairs.

As a huge stone is sometimes seen to lie
Couched on the bald top of an eminence;
Wonder to all who do the same espy,
60 By what means it could thither come, and whence;
So that it seems a thing endued with sense:
Like a sea-beast crawled forth, that on a shelf
Of rock or sand reposeth, there to sun itself;

Such seemed this man, not all alive nor dead,
Nor all asleep—in his extreme old age:
His body was bent double, feet and head
Coming together in life's pilgrimage;
As if some dire constraint of pain, or rage
Of sickness felt by him in times long past,
70 A more than human weight upon his frame had cast.

Himself he propped, limbs, body, and pale face,
Upon a long gray staff of shaven wood:
And, still as I drew near with gentle pace,
Upon the margin of that moorish° flood
Motionless as a cloud the old man stood;
That heareth not the loud winds when they call,
And moveth altogether, if it move at all.

At length, himself unsettling, he the pond
Stirred with his staff and fixedly did look
80 Upon the muddy water, which he conned,
As if he had been reading in a book:

43 **Chatterton,** Thomas Chatterton (1752–1770), a youthful poet who in despair and
poverty took his own life   45 **him . . . joy,** Robert Burns   74 **moorish,** marshy

And now a stranger's privilege I took;
And, drawing to his side, to him did say,
"This morning gives us promise of a glorious day."

A gentle answer did the old man make,
In courteous speech which forth he slowly drew;
And him with further words I thus bespake:
"What occupation do you there pursue?
This is a lonesome place for one like you."
Ere he replied, a flash of mild surprise   90
Broke from the sable orbs of his yet vivid eyes.

His words came feebly, from a feeble chest,
But each in solemn order followed each,
With something of a lofty utterance dressed;
Choice word, and measured phrase, above the reach
Of ordinary men; a stately speech;
Such as grave Livers do in Scotland use,
Religious men, who give to God and man their dues.

He told, that to these waters he had come
To gather leeches, being old and poor: 100
Employment hazardous and wearisome!
And he had many hardships to endure:
From pond to pond he roamed, from moor to moor;
Housing, with God's good help, by choice or chance;
And in this way he gained an honest maintenance.

The old man still stood talking by my side;
But now his voice to me was like a stream
Scarce heard; nor word from word could I divide;
And the whole body of the man did seem
Like one whom I had met with in a dream;   110
Or like a man from some far region sent,
To give me human strength, by apt admonishment.

My former thoughts returned: the fear that kills;
And hope that is unwilling to be fed;
Cold, pain and labor, and all fleshly ills;
And mighty poets in their misery dead.
Perplexed, and longing to be comforted,
My question eagerly did I renew,
"How is it that you live, and what is it you do?"

He with a smile did then his words repeat;   120
And said that, gathering leeches, far and wide
He traveled; stirring thus about his feet
The waters of the pools where they abide.
"Once I could meet with them on every side;
But they have dwindled long by slow decay;
Yet still I persevere, and find them where I may."

While he was talking thus, the lonely place,
The old man's shape, and speech, all troubled me:
In my mind's eye I seemed to see him pace
About the weary moors continually,   130
Wandering about alone and silently.
While I these thoughts within myself pursued,

He, having made a pause, the same discourse re-
    newed.

And soon with this he other matter blended,
Cheerfully uttered, with demeanor kind,
But stately in the main; and when he ended,
I could have laughed myself to scorn to find
In that decrepit man so firm a mind.
"God," said I, "be my help and stay secure;
140 I'll think of the leech-gatherer on the lonely moor!"
    (1802; 1807)

COMPOSED UPON WESTMINSTER BRIDGE

Earth has not anything to show more fair:
Dull would he be of soul who could pass by
A sight so touching in its majesty:
This City now doth like a garment wear
5 The beauty of the morning; silent, bare,
Ships, towers, domes, theaters, and temples lie
Open unto the fields, and to the sky;
All bright and glittering in the smokeless air.
Never did sun more beautifully steep
10 In his first splendor valley, rock, or hill;
Ne'er saw I, never felt, a calm so deep!
The river glideth at his own sweet will:
Dear God! the very houses seem asleep;
And all that mighty heart is lying still!
    (1802; 1807)

COMPOSED BY THE SEASIDE, NEAR CALAIS

Fair Star of evening, Splendor of the west,
Star of my Country!—on the horizon's brink
Thou hangest, stooping, as might seem, to sink
On England's bosom, yet well pleased to rest,
5 Meanwhile, and be to her a glorious crest
Conspicuous to the Nations. Thou, I think,
Shouldst be my Country's emblem; and shouldst wink,
Bright Star! with laughter on her banners, dressed
In thy fresh beauty. There! that dusky spot
10 Beneath thee, that is England; there she lies.
Blessings be on you both! one hope, one lot,
One life, one glory!—I, with many a fear
For my dear Country, many heartfelt sighs,
Among men who do not love her, linger here.
    (1802; 1807)

IT IS A BEAUTEOUS EVENING, CALM AND FREE

It is a beauteous evening, calm and free.
The holy time is quiet as a Nun,
Breathless with adoration: the broad sun
Is sinking down in its tranquillity;
The gentleness of heaven broods o'er the sea;   5
Listen! the mighty Being is awake,
And doth with his eternal motion make
A sound like thunder—everlastingly.
Dear Child!° dear Girl! that walkest with me here,°
If thou appear untouched by solemn thought,   10
Thy nature is not therefore less divine:
Thou liest in Abraham's bosom° all the year,
And worship'st at the Temple's inner shrine,
God being with thee when we know it not.
    (1802; 1807)

LONDON, 1802

Milton!° thou shouldst be living at this hour:
England hath need of thee: she is a fen
Of stagnant waters: altar, sword, and pen,
Fireside, the heroic wealth of hall and bower,°
Have forfeited their ancient English dower   5
Of inward happiness. We are selfish men:
Oh! raise us up, return to us again;
And give us manners, virtue, freedom, power.
Thy soul was like a Star, and dwelt apart:
Thou hadst a voice whose sound was like the sea,   10
Pure as the naked heavens, majestic, free;
So didst thou travel on life's common way
In cheerful godliness; and yet thy heart
The lowliest duties on herself did lay.
    (1802; 1807)

THE SOLITARY REAPER

Behold her, single in the field,
Yon solitary Highland lass!
Reaping and singing by herself;

It Is a Beauteous Evening   9 **Dear Child,** Caroline, the daughter of Wordsworth and Annette Vallon   **here,** on Calais beach, where the sonnet was composed   12 **in Abraham's bosom,** in the presence or favor of God   **London, 1802**   1 **Milton.** Milton was actively and conscientiously engaged in politics as well as poetry. Moreover, he too lived during a very troubled period in English history   4 **hall and bower.** The hall was the public dwelling of a Teutonic chieftain, and the bower the private apartments

Stop here, or gently pass!
Alone she cuts and binds the grain,
And sings a melancholy strain;
O listen! for the vale profound
Is overflowing with the sound.

No nightingale did ever chaunt
10 More welcome notes to weary bands
Of travelers in some shady haunt,
Among Arabian sands:
A voice so thrilling ne'er was heard
In springtime from the cuckoo-bird,
Breaking the silence of the seas
Among the farthest Hebrides.°

Will no one tell me what she sings?°—
Perhaps the plaintive numbers flow
For old, unhappy, far-off things,
20 And battles long ago:
Or is it some more humble lay,
Familiar matter of today?
Some natural sorrow, loss, or pain,
That has been, and may be again?

Whate'er the theme, the maiden sang
As if her song could have no ending;
I saw her singing at her work,
And o'er the sickle bending;—
I listened, motionless and still;
30 And, as I mounted up the hill,
The music in my heart I bore,
Long after it was heard no more.
(1803; 1807)

TO THE CUCKOO

O blithe Newcomer! I have heard,
I hear thee and rejoice.
O Cuckoo! shall I call thee Bird,
Or but a wandering Voice?

While I am lying on the grass,
Thy twofold shout I hear;
From hill to hill it seems to pass,
At once far off, and near.

Though babbling only to the Vale,
10 Of sunshine and of flowers,
Thou bringest unto me a tale
Of visionary hours.

Thrice welcome, darling of the Spring!
Even yet thou art to me
No bird, but an invisible thing,
A voice, a mystery;

The same when in my schoolboy days
I listened to; that Cry
Which made me look a thousand ways
In bush, and tree, and sky.   20

To seek thee did I often rove
Through woods and on the green;
And thou wert still a hope, a love;
Still longed for, never seen.

And I can listen to thee yet;
Can lie upon the plain
And listen, till I do beget
That golden time again.

O blessèd Bird! the earth we pace
Again appears to be   30
An unsubstantial, faery place;
That is fit home for thee!
(1802; 1807)

SHE WAS A PHANTOM
OF DELIGHT

She° was a phantom of delight
When first she gleamed upon my sight;
A lovely apparition, sent
To be a moment's ornament;
Her eyes as stars of twilight fair;
Like twilight's too, her dusky hair;
But all things else about her drawn
From May-time and the cheerful dawn;
A dancing shape, an Image gay,
To haunt, to startle, and waylay.   10

I saw her upon nearer view,
A spirit, yet a woman too!
Her household motions light and free,
And steps of virgin liberty;
A countenance in which did meet
Sweet records, promises as sweet;
A creature not too bright or good
For human nature's daily food:
For transient sorrows, simple wiles,
Praise, blame, love, kisses, tears, and smiles. 20

And now I see with eye serene
The very pulse of the machine;°
A being breathing thoughtful breath,
A Traveler between life and death;
The reason firm, the temperate will,
Endurance, foresight, strength, and skill,
A perfect woman, nobly planned,
To warn, to comfort, and command;
And yet a spirit still, and bright
30 With something of angelic light.
(1804; 1807)

I WANDERED LONELY AS A CLOUD

I wandered lonely as a cloud
That floats on high o'er vales and hills,
When all at once I saw a crowd,
A host, of golden daffodils;
Beside the lake, beneath the trees,
Fluttering and dancing in the breeze.

Continuous as the stars that shine
And twinkle on the Milky Way,
They stretched in never-ending line
10 Along the margin of a bay:
Ten thousand saw I at a glance,
Tossing their heads in sprightly dance.

The waves beside them danced; but they
Outdid the sparkling waves in glee:
A poet could not but be gay,
In such a jocund company:
I gazed—and gazed—but little thought
What wealth the show to me had brought:

For oft, when on my couch I lie
20 In vacant or in pensive mood,
They flash upon that inward eye
Which is the bliss of solitude;
And then my heart with pleasure fills,
And dances with the daffodils.
(1804; 1807)

TO A SKYLARK

Up with me! up with me into the clouds!
    For thy song, Lark, is strong;
Up with me, up with me into the clouds!
    Singing, singing,

With clouds and sky about thee ringing,
    Lift me, guide me till I find
That spot which seems so to thy mind.

I have walked through wildernesses dreary,
And today my heart is weary;
Had I now the wings of a Faery   10
Up to thee would I fly.
There is madness about thee, and joy divine
In that song of thine;
Lift me, guide me, high and high
To thy banqueting-place in the sky!

    Joyous as morning,
Thou art laughing and scorning;
Thou hast a nest for thy love and thy rest,
And, though little troubled with sloth,
Drunken Lark! thou wouldst be loath   20
To be such a traveler as I.
Happy, happy Liver,
With a soul as strong as a mountain river
Pouring out praise to the almighty Giver,
    Joy and jollity be with us both!

Alas! my journey, rugged and uneven,
Through prickly moors or dusty ways must wind;
But hearing thee, or others of thy kind,
As full of gladness and as free of heaven,
I, with my fate contented, will plod on,   30
And hope for higher raptures, when life's day is done.
(1805; 1807)

NUNS FRET NOT
AT THEIR CONVENT'S NARROW ROOM

Nuns fret not at their convent's narrow room;
And hermits are contented with their cells;
And students with their pensive citadels;°
Maids at the wheel, the weaver at his loom,
Sit blithe and happy; bees that soar for bloom,   5
High as the highest Peak of Furness-fells,°
Will murmur by the hour in foxglove bells:
In truth the prison, into which we doom
Ourselves, no prison is: and hence for me,
In sundry moods, 'twas pastime to be bound   10
Within the Sonnet's scanty plot of ground;
Pleased if some Souls (for such there needs must be)
Who have felt the weight of too much liberty,°
Should find brief solace there, as I have found.
(1807)

22 **machine,** body. The word *machine* had greater poetic value in Wordsworth's day than now

Nuns Fret Not   3 **pensive citadels,** retreats suitable for quiet thought   6 **Furness-fells,** upland tracts of Furness, on the coast of Lancashire   13 **weight . . . liberty.** Writing sonnets was especially helpful to Wordsworth in overcoming his early discursive style

THE WORLD IS TOO MUCH WITH US

The world is too much with us; late and soon,
Getting and spending, we lay waste our powers:
Little we see in Nature that is ours;
We have given our hearts away, a sordid boon!
5 The sea that bares her bosom to the moon;
The winds that will be howling at all hours,
And are up-gathered now like sleeping flowers;
For this, for everything, we are out of tune;
It moves us not.—Great God! I'd rather be
10 A Pagan suckled in a creed outworn;
So might I, standing on this pleasant lea,
Have glimpses that would make me less forlorn;
Have sight of Proteus° rising from the sea;
Or hear old Triton blow his wreathéd horn.
(1807)

ODE

ON INTIMATIONS OF IMMORTALITY FROM
RECOLLECTIONS OF EARLY CHILDHOOD

This ode is built upon a characteristically Wordsworthian version of the Platonic doctrine that all
knowledge is simply recollection. The following ex-
cerpts from Plato's *Phaedo* (in Jowett's translation) may
be helpful:

"Your favorite doctrine, Socrates, that knowledge is
simply recollection, if true, also necessarily implies a
previous time in which we learned that which we now
recollect. But this would be impossible unless our soul
was in some place before existing in the human form;
here then is another argument of the soul's immortality. . . . And if we acquired this knowledge before we
were born and were born having it, then we also
knew before we were born and at the instant of
birth. . . . If, after having acquired, we have not forgotten that which we acquired, then we must always
have been born with knowledge and shall always
continue to know as long as life lasts—for knowledge
is the acquiring and retaining knowledge and not
forgetting . . . But if the knowledge which we acquired
before birth was lost by us at birth, and if afterwards
by the use of the senses we recovered that which we
previously knew, will not that which we call learning
be a process of recovering our knowledge, and may
not this be rightly termed recollection by us?"

The Child is father of the Man;
And I could wish my days to be
Bound each to each by natural piety.°

The World Is Too Much with Us 13 **Proteus,** sea god in the service of Neptune, god of the sea. Triton (l. 14) is another sea god   **Ode on Intimations The Child . . . piety,** quoted from *My Heart Leaps Up*

1

There was a time when meadow, grove, and stream,
The earth, and every common sight,
To me did seem
Appareled in celestial light,
The glory and the freshness of a dream.
It is not now as it hath been of yore;—
Turn wheresoe'er I may,
By night or day,
The things which I have seen I now can see no more.

2

The Rainbow comes and goes,   10
And lovely is the Rose;
The Moon doth with delight
Look round her when the heavens are bare;
Waters on a starry night
Are beautiful and fair;
The sunshine is a glorious birth;
But yet I know, where'er I go,
That there hath passed away a glory from the earth.

3

Now, while the birds thus sing a joyous song,
And while the young lambs bound   20
As to the tabor's° sound,
To me alone there came a thought of grief:
A timely utterance gave that thought relief,
And I again am strong:
The cataracts blow their trumpets from the steep;
No more shall grief of mine the season wrong;°
I hear the Echoes through the mountains throng,
The Winds come to me from the fields of sleep,
And all the earth is gay;
Land and sea   30
Give themselves up to jollity,
And with the heart of May
Doth every Beast keep holiday;—
Thou Child of Joy,
Shout round me, let me hear thy shouts, thou happy
Shepherd-boy!

4

Ye blesséd Creatures, I have heard the call
Ye to each other make; I see
The heavens laugh with you in your jubilee;
My heart is at your festival,
My head hath its coronal,°   40
The fulness of your bliss, I feel—I feel it all.
Oh, evil day! if I were sullen
While Earth herself is adorning,
This sweet May-morning,
And the Children are culling
On every side,
In a thousand valleys far and wide,
Fresh flowers; while the sun shines warm,

21 **tabor,** small drum   26 **No . . . wrong,** because of lack of sympathy
40 **coronal,** garland

And the Babe leaps up on his Mother's arm—
50   I hear, I hear, with joy I hear!
    —But there's a Tree, of many, one,
A single Field which I have looked upon,
Both of them speak of something that is gone:
    The Pansy at my feet
    Doth the same tale repeat:
Whither is fled the visionary gleam?
Where is it now, the glory and the dream?

5

Our birth is but a sleep and a forgetting:
The Soul that rises with us, our life's Star,
60   Hath had elsewhere its setting,
    And cometh from afar:
    Not in entire forgetfulness,
    And not in utter nakedness,
But trailing clouds of glory do we come
    From God, who is our home:
Heaven lies about us in our infancy!
Shades of the prison-house begin to close
    Upon the growing Boy,
But he beholds the light, and whence it flows
70   He sees it in his joy;
The Youth, who daily farther from the east
    Must travel, still is Nature's priest,
    And by the vision splendid
    Is on his way attended;
At length the Man perceives it die away,
And fade into the light of common day.

6

Earth fills her lap with pleasures of her own;
Yearnings she hath in her own natural kind,
And even with something of a Mother's mind,
80   And no unworthy aim,
    The homely Nurse doth all she can
To make her Foster-child, her Inmate Man,
    Forget the glories he hath known,
And that imperial palace whence he came.

7

Behold the Child among his new-born blisses,
A six years' Darling of a pigmy size!
See, where 'mid work of his own hand he lies,
Fretted by sallies of his mother's kisses,
With light upon him from his father's eyes!
90 See, at his feet, some little plan or chart,
Some fragment from his dream of human life,
Shaped by himself with newly-learnèd art;
    A wedding or a festival,
    A mourning or a funeral,
    And this hath now his heart,
    And unto this he frames his song:
    Then will he fit his tongue
To dialogues of business, love, or strife;
    But it will not be long

Ere this be thrown aside,
    And with new joy and pride
The little Actor cons another part;°
Filling from time to time his "humorous° stage"
With all the Persons, down to palsied Age,
That Life brings with her in her equipage;
    As if his whole vocation
    Were endless imitation.

8

Thou, whose exterior semblance doth belie
    Thy Soul's immensity;
Thou best Philosopher, who yet dost keep
Thy heritage, thou Eye among the blind,
That, deaf and silent, read'st the eternal deep,°
Haunted forever by the eternal mind—
    Mighty Prophet! Seer blest!
    On whom those truths do rest,
Which we are toiling all our lives to find,
In darkness lost, the darkness of the grave;
Thou, over whom thy Immortality
Broods like the Day, a Master o'er a Slave,
A Presence which is not to be put by;
Thou little Child, yet glorious in the might
Of heaven-born freedom on thy being's height,
Why with such earnest pains dost thou provoke
The years to bring the inevitable yoke,
Thus blindly with thy blessedness at strife?
Full soon thy Soul shall have her earthly freight,
And custom lie upon thee with a weight,
Heavy as frost, and deep almost as life!

9

    Oh, joy! that in our embers
    Is something that doth live,
    That nature yet remembers
    What was so fugitive!
The thought of our past years in me doth breed
Perpetual benediction: not indeed
For that which is most worthy to be blest;
Delight and liberty, the simple creed
Of Childhood, whether busy or at rest,
With new-fledged hope still fluttering in his breast—
    Not for these I raise
    The song of thanks and praise;
    But for those obstinate questionings
    Of sense and outward things,
    Fallings from us, vanishings;
    Blank misgivings of a Creature
Moving about in worlds not realized,
High instincts before which our mortal nature
Did tremble like a guilty thing surprised:
    But for those first affections,
    Those shadowy recollections,

100

110

120

130

140

102 **Actor . . . part,** an allusion to Jaques' speech in *As You Like It,* II, vii, 139 ff.:
"All the world's a stage"   103 **humorous,** changeable, moody   112 **eternal deep,**
deep mysteries of eternity

Which, be they what they may,
  Are yet the fountain light of all our day,
  Are yet a master light of all our seeing;
    Uphold us, cherish, and have power to make
Our noisy years seem moments in the being
Of the eternal Silence: truths that wake,
    To perish never;
Which neither listlessness, nor mad endeavor,
    Nor Man nor Boy,
Nor all that is at enmity with joy,
Can utterly abolish or destroy!
    Hence in a season of calm weather
    Though inland far we be,
Our Souls have sight of that immortal sea
    Which brought us hither,
    Can in a moment travel thither,
And see the Children sport upon the shore,
And hear the mighty waters rolling evermore.

10

Then sing, ye Birds, sing, sing a joyous song!
    And let the young Lambs bound
    As to the tabor's sound!
We in thought will join your throng,
    Ye that pipe and ye that play,
    Ye that through your hearts today
    Feel the gladness of the May!
What though° the radiance which was once so bright
Be now forever taken from my sight,
  Though nothing can bring back the hour
Of splendor in the grass, of glory in the flower;
    We will grieve not, rather find
    Strength in what remains behind;
    In the primal sympathy
    Which having been must ever be;
    In the soothing thoughts that spring
    Out of human suffering;
    In the faith that looks through death,
In years that bring the philosophic mind.

11

And O, ye Fountains, Meadows, Hills, and Groves,
Forebode not any severing of our loves!
Yet in my heart of hearts I feel your might;
I only have relinquished one delight
To live beneath your more habitual sway.
I love the Brooks which down their channels fret,
Even more than when I tripped lightly as they;
The innocent brightness of a new-born Day
    Is lovely yet;
The Clouds that gather round the setting sun
Do take a sober coloring from an eye
That hath kept watch o'er man's mortality.
Another race hath been, and other palms are won.
Thanks to the human heart by which we live,

175–203 **What though,** etc. Cf. this passage with ll. 72–111 of *Lines Composed a Few Miles Above Tintern Abbey*

Thanks to its tenderness, its joys, and fears,
To me the meanest flower that blows can give
Thoughts that do often lie too deep for tears.
(1802–04; 1807)

SCORN NOT THE SONNET

Scorn not the Sonnet; Critic, you have frowned,
Mindless of its just honors; with this key
Shakespeare unlocked his heart; the melody
Of this small lute gave ease to Petrarch's wound;°
A thousand times this pipe did Tasso° sound;
With it Camoëns° soothed an exile's grief;
The Sonnet glittered a gay myrtle leaf
Amid the cypress with which Dante crowned
His visionary brow; a glowworm lamp,
It cheered mild Spenser, called from Faeryland
To struggle through dark ways; and when a damp
Fell round the path of Milton, in his hand
The Thing became a trumpet; whence he blew
Soul-animating strains—alas, too few!
(1827)

YEW TREES

There is a Yew Tree, pride of Lorton Vale,°
Which to this day stands single, in the midst
Of its own darkness, as it stood of yore:
Not loath to furnish weapons for the bands
Of Umfraville or Percy° ere they marched
To Scotland's heaths; or those that crossed the sea
And drew their sounding bows at Azincour,
Perhaps at earlier Crecy, or Poictiers.°
Of vast circumference and gloom profound
This solitary Tree! a living thing
Produced too slowly ever to decay;
Of form and aspect too magnificent
To be destroyed. But worthier still of note
Are those fraternal Four of Borrowdale,°
Joined in one solemn and capacious grove;
Huge trunks! and each particular trunk a growth
Of intertwisted fibers serpentine
Up-coiling, and inveterately convolved;°
Nor uninformed with Phantasy, and looks
That threaten the profane—a pillared shade,
Upon whose grassless floor of red-brown hue,
By sheddings from the pining umbrage tinged
Perennially—beneath whose sable roof
Of boughs, as if for festal purpose decked
With unrejoicing berries—ghostly Shapes

Scorn Not the Sonnet 4 **Petrarch's wound,** the wound of love, for Laura 5 **Tasso,** 16th century Italian poet 6 **Camoëns,** "banished from Lisbon because of his love for Donna Caterina" (Noyes) **Yew Trees** 1 **Lorton Vale,** in the Lake District; the other place names are in the vicinity 5 **Umfraville or Percy,** noble families in the north of England 8 **Azincour, Crecy, Poictiers,** English victories over the French in the Hundred Years' War 14 **fraternal Four of Borrowdale,** four large yew trees 18 **convolved,** enclosed in folds

May meet at noontide; Fear and trembling Hope,
Silence and Foresight; Death the Skeleton
And Time the Shadow—there to celebrate,
As in a natural temple scattered o'er
30 With altars undisturbed of mossy stone,
United worship; or in mute repose
To lie, and listen to the mountain flood
Murmuring from Glaramara's inmost caves.
(ca. 1803; 1815)

from PREFACE TO LYRICAL BALLADS

. . . The principal object, then, proposed in these poems° was to choose incidents and situations from common life, and to relate or describe them, throughout, as far as was possible in a selection of language really used by men, and at the same time to throw over them a certain coloring of imagination, whereby ordinary things should be presented to the mind in an unusual aspect; and, further, and above all, to make these incidents and situations interesting by tracing in 10 them, truly though not ostentatiously, the primary laws of our nature: chiefly, as far as regards the manner in which we associate ideas in a state of excitement. Humble and rustic life was generally chosen, because, in that condition, the essential passions of the heart find a better soil in which they can attain their maturity, are less under restraint, and speak a plainer and more emphatic language; because in that condition of life our elementary feelings co-exist in a state of greater simplicity, and, consequently, may be more 20 accurately contemplated, and more forcibly communicated; because the manners of rural life germinate from those elementary feelings, and, from the necessary character of rural occupations, are more easily comprehended, and are more durable; and, lastly, because in that condition the passions of men are incorporated with the beautiful and permanent forms of nature. The language, too, of these men has been adopted (purified indeed from what appear to be its real defects, from all lasting and rational causes of dis-30 like or disgust) because such men hourly communicate with the best objects from which the best part of language is originally derived; and because, from their rank in society and the sameness and narrow circle of their intercourse, being less under the influence of social vanity, they convey their feelings and notions in simple and unelaborated expressions. Accordingly, such a language, arising out of repeated experience and regular feelings, is a more permanent and a far more philosophical language than that which is fre-40 quently substituted for it by poets, who think that they are conferring honor upon themselves and their art, in proportion as they separate themselves from the sympathies of men, and indulge in arbitrary and capricious habits of expression, in order to furnish food for fickle tastes and fickle appetites of their own creation.

I cannot, however, be insensible to the present outcry against the triviality and meanness, both of thought and language, which some of my contemporaries° have occasionally introduced into their metrical compositions; and I acknowledge that this defect, where it 50 exists, is more dishonorable to the writer's own character than false refinement or arbitrary innovation, though I should contend at the same time that it is far less pernicious in the sum of its consequences. From such verses the poems in these volumes will be found distinguished at least by one mark of difference, that each of them has a worthy *purpose*. Not that I always began to write with a distinct purpose formally conceived; but habits of meditation have, I trust, so prompted and regulated my feelings that my descrip- 60 tions of such objects as strongly excite those feelings will be found to carry along with them a *purpose*. If this opinion be erroneous, I can have little right to the name of a poet. For all good poetry is the spontaneous overflow of powerful feelings: and though this be true, poems to which any value can be attached were never produced on any variety of subjects but by a man who, being possessed of more than usual organic sensibility, had also thought long and deeply. For our continued influxes of feeling are modified and directed by our 70 thoughts, which are indeed the representatives of all our past feelings; and, as by contemplating the relation of these general representatives to each other, we discover what is really important to men, so, by the repetition and continuance of this act, our feelings will be connected with important subjects, till at length, if we be originally possessed of much sensibility, such habits of mind will be produced, that, by obeying blindly and mechanically the impulses of those habits, we shall describe objects and utter sentiments, of such 80 a nature, and in such connection with each other, that the understanding of the reader must necessarily be in some degree enlightened, and his affections strengthened and purified.

It has been said that each of these poems has a purpose. Another circumstance must be mentioned which distinguishes these poems from the popular poetry of the day; it is this, that the feeling therein developed gives importance to the action and situation, and not the action and situation to the feeling. 90

A sense of false modesty shall not prevent me from asserting that the reader's attention is pointed to this mark of distinction, far less for the sake of these particular poems than from the general importance of the subject. The subject is indeed important! For the human mind is capable of being excited without the application of gross and violent stimulants; and he must have a very faint perception of its beauty and dignity who does not know this, and who does not further

Preface to Lyrical Ballads   1 **these poems,** those published in *Lyrical Ballads*   48 **contemporaries,** possibly a reference to Southey and Crabbe

know that one being is elevated above another, in proportion as he possesses this capability. It has therefore appeared to me that to endeavor to produce or enlarge this capability is one of the best services in which, at any period, a writer can be engaged; but this service, excellent at all times, is especially so at the present day. For a multitude of causes, unknown to former times are now acting with a combined force to blunt the discriminating powers of the mind, and, unfitting it for all voluntary exertion, to reduce it to a state of almost savage torpor. The most effective of these causes are the great national events° which are daily taking place, and the increasing accumulation of men in cities, where the uniformity of their occupations produces a craving for extraordinary incident, which the rapid communication of intelligence hourly gratifies. To this tendency of life and manners the literature and theatrical exhibitions of the country have conformed themselves. The invaluable works of our elder writers—I had almost said the works of Shakespeare and Milton—are driven into neglect by frantic novels,° sickly and stupid German tragedies,° and deluges of idle and extravagant stories in verse.°—When I think upon this degrading thirst after outrageous stimulation, I am almost ashamed to have spoken of the feeble endeavor made in these volumes to counteract it; and, reflecting upon the magnitude of the general evil, I should be oppressed with no dishonorable melancholy, had I not a deep impression of certain inherent and indestructible qualities of the human mind, and likewise of certain powers in the great and permanent objects that act upon it, which are equally inherent and indestructible; and were there not added to this impression a belief that the time is approaching when the evil will be systematically opposed, by men of greater powers, and with far more distinguished success.

Having dwelt thus long on the subjects and aim of these poems, I shall request the reader's permission to apprise him of a few circumstances relating to their *style*, in order, among other reasons, that he may not censure me for not having performed what I never attempted. The reader will find that personifications of abstract ideas rarely occur in these volumes; and are utterly rejected, as an ordinary device, to elevate the style and raise it above prose. My purpose was to imitate, and, as far as possible, to adopt the very language of men; and assuredly such personifications do not make any natural or regular part of that language. They are indeed, a figure of speech occasionally prompted by passion, and I have made use of them as such; but have endeavored utterly to reject them as a mechanical device of style, or as a family language

which writers in meter seem to lay claim to by prescription. I have wished to keep the reader in the company of flesh and blood, persuaded that by so doing I shall interest him. Others who pursue a different track will interest him likewise; I do not interfere with their claim, but wish to prefer a claim of my own. There will also be found in these volumes little of what is usually called poetic diction; as much pains has been taken to avoid it as is ordinarily taken to produce it; this has been done for the reason already alleged, to bring my language near to the language of men, and further, because the pleasure which I have proposed to myself to impart, is of a kind very different from that which is supposed by many persons to be the proper object of poetry. Without being culpably particular, I do not know how to give my reader a more exact notion of the style in which it was my wish and intention to write than by informing him that I have at all times endeavored to look steadily at my subject; consequently, there is, I hope, in these poems little falsehood of description, and my ideas are expressed in language fitted to their respective importance. Something must have been gained by this practice, as it is friendly to one property of all good poetry, namely, good sense: but it has necessarily cut me off from a large portion of phrases and figures of speech which from father to son have long been regarded as the common inheritance of poets. I have also thought it expedient to restrict myself still further, having abstained from the use of many expressions, in themselves proper and beautiful, but which have been foolishly repeated by bad poets, till such feelings of disgust are connected with them as it is scarcely possible by any art of association to overpower.

If in a poem there should be found a series of lines, or even a single line, in which the language, though naturally arranged and according to the strict laws of meter, does not differ from that of prose there is a numerous class of critics, who, when they stumble upon these prosaisms, as they call them, imagine that they have made a notable discovery, and exult over the poet as over a man ignorant of his own profession. Now these men would establish a canon of criticism which the reader will conclude he must utterly reject if he wishes to be pleased with these volumes. And it would be a most easy task to prove to him that not only the language of a large portion of every good poem, even of the most elevated character, must necessarily, except with reference to the meter, in no respect differ from that of good prose, but likewise that some of the most interesting parts of the best poems will be found to be strictly the language of prose when prose is well written. The truth of this assertion might be demonstrated by innumerable passages from almost all the poetical writings, even of Milton himself. To illustrate the subject in a general manner, I will here adduce a short composition of Gray, who was at the head of those who, by their reasonings, have attempted to

111 **national events,** such as the war with France, the Irish Rebellion, and the passage of important labor laws   121 **frantic novels,** such as Mrs. Radcliffe's *Mysteries of Udolpho* (1794) and other Gothic romances   **stupid . . . tragedies,** such as August Kotzebue's *Misanthropy and Repentance* (1790), known in England as *The Stranger*   122 **idle . . . verse,** a probable reference to such poems as *Maviad* (1795) and *Baviad* (1794), two satires by William Gifford, editor of the *Quarterly Review;* Landor's *Gebir* (1798); and Scott's translations of Bürger's *Lenore*

widen the space of separation betwixt Prose and Metrical composition, and was more than any other man curiously elaborate in the structure of his own poetic diction.

In vain to me the smiling mornings shine,
And reddening Phoebus lifts his golden fire;
The birds in vain their amorous descant join,
Or cheerful fields resume their green attire.
These ears, alas! for other notes repine;
220 *A different object do these eyes require;*
My lonely anguish melts no heart but mine;
And in my breast the imperfect joys expire;
Yet morning smiles the busy race to cheer,
And new-born pleasure brings to happier men;
The fields to all their wonted tribute bear;
To warm their little loves the birds complain.
I fruitless mourn to him that cannot hear,
And weep the more because I weep in vain.°

It will easily be perceived, that the only part of this
230 Sonnet which is of any value is the lines printed in Italics; it is equally obvious that, except in the rime and in the use of the single word "fruitless" for "fruitlessly," which is so far a defect, the language of these lines does in no respect differ from that of prose.

By the foregoing quotation it has been shown that the language of Prose may yet be well adapted to Poetry;° and it was previously asserted that a large portion of the language of every good poem can in no respect differ from that of good Prose. We will go
240 further. It may be safely affirmed that there neither is, nor can be, any *essential* difference between the language of prose and metrical composition. We are fond of tracing the resemblance between Poetry and Painting, and, accordingly, we call them Sisters; but where shall we find bonds of connection sufficiently strict to typify the affinity betwixt metrical and prose composition? They both speak by and to the same organs; the bodies in which both of them are clothed may be said to be of the same substance, their affections are
250 kindred, and almost identical, not necessarily differing even in degree; Poetry sheds no tears "such as Angels weep," but natural and human tears; she can boast of no celestial ichor° that distinguishes her vital juices from those of Prose; the same human blood circulates through the veins of them both.

If it be affirmed that rime and metrical arrangement of themselves constitute a distinction which overturns what has just been said on the strict affinity of metrical language with that of prose, and paves the way for
260 other artificial distinctions which the mind voluntarily

admits, I answer that the language of such poetry as is here recommended is, as far as is possible, a selection of the language really spoken by men; that this selection, wherever it is made with true taste and feeling, will of itself form a distinction far greater than would at first be imagined, and will entirely separate the composition from the vulgarity and meanness of ordinary life; and, if meter be superadded thereto, I believe that a dissimilitude will be produced altogether sufficient for the gratification of a rational mind. What other dis- 270 tinction would we have? Whence is it to come? And where is it to exist? Not, surely, where the poet speaks through the mouths of his characters—it cannot be necessary here, either for elevation of style, or any of its supposed ornaments; for, if the poet's subject be judiciously chosen, it will naturally, and upon fit occasion, lead him to passions the language of which, if selected truly and judiciously, must necessarily be dignified and variegated, and alive with metaphors and figures. I forbear to speak of an incongruity which 280 would shock the intelligent reader, should the poet interweave any foreign splendor of his own with that which the passion naturally suggests; it is sufficient to say that such addition is unnecessary. And, surely, it is more probable that those passages, which with propriety abound with metaphors and figures, will have their due effect, if, upon other occasions where the passions are of a milder character, the style also be subdued and temperate.

But, as the pleasure which I hope to give by the 290 poems now presented to the reader must depend entirely on just notions upon this subject, and, as it is in itself of high importance to our taste and moral feelings, I cannot content myself with these detached remarks. And if, in what I am about to say, it shall appear to some that my labor is unnecessary, and that I am like a man fighting a battle without enemies, such persons may be reminded, that, whatever be the language outwardly holden by men, a practical faith in the opinions which I am wishing to establish is almost un- 300 known. If my conclusions are admitted and carried as far as they must be carried if admitted at all, our judgments concerning the works of the greatest poets both ancient and modern will be far different from what they are at present, both when we praise, and when we censure; and our moral feelings influencing and influenced by these judgments will, I believe, be corrected and purified.

Taking up the subject, then, upon general grounds, let me ask, what is meant by the word poet? What is a 310 poet? To whom does he address himself? And what language is to be expected from him?—He is a man speaking to men: a man, it is true, endowed with more lively sensibility, more enthusiasm and tenderness, who has a greater knowledge of human nature, and a more comprehensive soul than are supposed to be common among mankind; a man pleased with his own passions and volitions, and who rejoices more than

228 **vain,** Gray's Sonnet on the Death of Richard West   237 **Poetry.** "I here use the word 'Poetry' (though against my own judgment) as opposed to the word 'Prose,' and synonymous with metrical composition. But much confusion has been introduced into criticism by this contradistinction of Poetry and Prose, instead of the more philosophical one of Poetry and Matter of Fact, or Science. The only strict antithesis to Prose is Meter; nor is this, in truth, a *strict* antithesis, because lines and passages of meter so naturally occur in writing prose, that it would be scarcely possible to avoid them, even were it desirable."—Wordsworth's note   253 **ichor,** ethereal fluid that flowed in the veins of the gods

other men in the spirit of life that is in him; delighting
320 to contemplate similar volitions and passions as manifested in the goings-on of the Universe, and habitually
impelled to create them where he does not find them.
To these qualities he has added a disposition to be
affected more than other men by absent things as if
they were present; an ability of conjuring up in himself
passions which are indeed far from being the same as
those produced by real events, yet (especially in those
parts of the general sympathy which are pleasing and
delightful) do more nearly resemble the passions pro-
330 duced by real events, than anything which, from the
motions of their own minds merely, other men are accustomed to feel in themselves—whence, and from
practice, he has acquired a greater readiness and
power in expressing what he thinks and feels, and
especially those thoughts and feelings which, by his
own choice or from the structure of his own mind,
arise in him without immediate external excitement.

But whatever portion of this faculty we may suppose
even the greatest poet to possess, there cannot be a
340 doubt that the language which it will suggest to him
must often, in liveliness and truth, fall short of that
which is uttered by men in real life, under the actual
pressure of those passions, certain shadows of which
the poet thus produces, or feels to be produced, in
himself.

However exalted a notion we would wish to cherish
of the character of a poet, it is obvious that while he
describes and imitates passions, his employment is in
some degree mechanical, compared with the freedom
350 and power of real and substantial action and suffering.
So that it will be the wish of the poet to bring his
feelings near to those of the persons whose feelings he
describes, nay, for short spaces of time, perhaps, to let
himself slip into an entire delusion, and even confound
and identify his own feelings with theirs; modifying
only the language which is thus suggested to him by a
consideration that he describes for a particular purpose, that of giving pleasure. Here, then, he will apply
the principle of selection which has been already in-
360 sisted upon. He will depend upon this for removing
what would otherwise be painful or disgusting in the
passion; he will feel that there is no necessity to trick
out or to elevate nature; and, the more industriously he
applies this principle, the deeper will be his faith that
no words, which *his* fancy or imagination can suggest,
will be to be compared with those which are the emanations of reality and truth.

But it may be said by those who do not object to the
general spirit of these remarks that, as it is impossible
370 for the poet to produce upon all occasions language as
exquisitely fitted for the passion as that which the real
passion itself suggests, it is proper that he should consider himself as in the situation of a translator, who
does not scruple to substitute excellencies of another
kind for those which are unattainable by him; and endeavors occasionally to surpass his original, in order to
make some amends for the general inferiority to which
he feels that he must submit. But this would be to
encourage idleness and unmanly despair. Further, it is
the language of men who speak of what they do not 380
understand; who talk of poetry as of a matter of
amusement and idle pleasure; who will converse with
us as gravely about a *taste* for poetry, as they express
it, as if it were a thing as indifferent as a taste for
rope-dancing, or Frontiniac or Sherry.° Aristotle, I have
been told, has said that poetry is the most philosophic
of all writing;° it is so; its object is truth, not individual
and local, but general and operative; not standing upon
external testimony, but carried alive into the heart by
passion; truth which is its own testimony, which gives 390
competence and confidence to the tribunal to which it
appeals, and receives them from the same tribunal.
Poetry is the image of man and nature. The obstacles
which stand in the way of the fidelity of the biographer
and historian, and of their consequent utility, are in-
calculably greater than those which are to be encountered by the poet who comprehends the dignity of his
art. The poet writes under one restriction only,
namely, the necessity of giving immediate pleasure to
a human being possessed of that information which 400
may be expected from him, not as a lawyer, a physician, a mariner, an astronomer, or a natural philosopher, but as a man. Except this one restriction, there is
no object standing between the poet and the image of
things; between this, and the biographer and historian,
there are a thousand.

Nor let this necessity of producing immediate pleasure be considered as a degradation of the poet's art. It
is far otherwise. It is an acknowledgment of the beauty
of the universe, an acknowledgment the more sincere, 410
because not formal, but indirect; it is a task light and
easy to him who looks at the world in the spirit of love;
further, it is a homage paid to the native and naked
dignity of man, to the grand elementary principle of
pleasure, by which he knows, and feels, and lives, and
moves. We have no sympathy but what is propagated
by pleasure—I would not be misunderstood; but
wherever we sympathize with pain, it will be found
that the sympathy is produced and carried on by subtle
combinations with pleasure. We have no knowledge, 420
that is, no general principles drawn from the contemplation of particular facts, but what has been built up
by pleasure, and exists in us by pleasure alone. The
man of science, the chemist and mathematician, whatever difficulties and disgusts they may have had to
struggle with, know and feel this. However painful
may be the objects with which the anatomist's knowledge is connected, he feels that his knowledge is pleasure; and where he has no pleasure, he has no knowledge. What then does the poet? He considers man and 430
the objects that surround him as acting and reacting

385 **Frontiniac or Sherry,** a French and a Spanish wine, respectively   **Aristotle . . . writing.** "Poetry is more philosophical and more serious than history."
—*Poetics,* 9,3

upon each other, so as to produce an infinite complexity of pain and pleasure; he considers man in his own nature and in his ordinary life as contemplating this with a certain quantity of immediate knowledge, with certain convictions, intuitions, and deductions, which from habit acquire the quality of intuitions; he considers him as looking upon this complex scene of ideas and sensations, and finding everywhere objects that immediately excite in him sympathies which, from the necessities of his nature, are accompanied by an overbalance of enjoyment.

To this knowledge which all men carry about with them, and to these sympathies in which, without any other discipline than that of our daily life, we are fitted to take delight, the poet principally directs his attention. He considers man and nature as essentially adapted to each other, and the mind of man as naturally the mirror of the fairest and most interesting properties of nature. And thus the poet, prompted by this feeling of pleasure, which accompanies him through the whole course of his studies, converses with general nature, with affections akin to those, which, through labor and length of time, the man of science has raised up in himself by conversing with those particular parts of nature which are the objects of his studies. The knowledge both of the poet and the man of science is pleasure; but the knowledge of the one cleaves to us as a necessary part of our existence, our natural and unalienable inheritance; the other is a personal and individual acquisition, slow to come to us, and by no habitual and direct sympathy connecting us with our fellow-beings. The man of science seeks truth as a remote and unknown benefactor; he cherishes and loves it in his solitude; the poet, singing a song in which all human beings join with him, rejoices in the presence of truth as our visible friend and hourly companion. Poetry is the breath and finer spirit of all knowledge; it is the impassioned expression which is in the countenance of all science. Emphatically may it be said of the poet, as Shakespeare hath said of man, "that he looks before and after."° He is the rock of defense for human nature; and upholder and preserver, carrying everywhere with him relationship and love. In spite of difference of soil and climate, of language and manners, of laws and customs, in spite of things silently gone out of mind and things violently destroyed; the poet binds together by passion and knowledge the vast empire of human society, as it is spread over the whole earth and over all time. The objects of the poet's thoughts are everywhere; though the eyes and senses of man are, it is true, his favorite guides, yet he will follow wheresoever he can find an atmosphere of sensation in which to move his wings. Poetry is the first and last of all knowledge—it is as immortal as the heart of man. If the labors of men of science should ever create any material revolution, direct or indirect, in our condition and in the impressions which we habitually receive, the poet will sleep then no more than at present; he will be ready to follow the steps of the man of science, not only in those general indirect effects, but he will be at his side, carrying sensation into the midst of the objects of science itself. The remotest discoveries of the chemist, the botanist, or mineralogist, will be as proper objects of the poet's art as any upon which it can be employed, if the time should ever come when these things shall be familiar to us, and the relations under which they are contemplated by the followers of these respective sciences shall be manifestly and palpably material to us as enjoying and suffering beings. If the time should ever come when what is now called science, thus familiarized to men, shall be ready to put on, as it were, a form of flesh and blood, the poet will lend his divine spirit to aid the transfiguration, and will welcome the being thus produced, as a dear and genuine inmate of the household of man.—It is not, then, to be supposed that anyone, who holds that sublime notion of poetry which I have attempted to convey, will break in upon the sanctity and truth of his pictures by transitory and accidental ornaments, and endeavor to excite admiration of himself by arts, the necessity of which must manifestly depend upon the assumed meanness of his subject.

What has been thus far said applies to poetry in general; but especially to those parts of composition where the poet speaks through the mouths of his characters; and upon this point it appears to authorize the conclusion that there are few persons of good sense, who would not allow that the dramatic parts of composition are defective, in proportion as they deviate from the real language of nature, and are colored by a diction of the poet's own, either peculiar to him as an individual poet or belonging simply to poets in general; to a body of men who, from the circumstance of their compositions being in meter, it is expected will employ a particular language.

It is not, then, in the dramatic parts of composition that we look for this distinction of language; but still it may be proper and necessary where the poet speaks to us in his own person and character. To this I answer by referring the reader to the description before given of a poet. Among the qualities there enumerated as principally conducing to form a poet is implied nothing differing in kind from other men, but only in degree. The sum of what was said is, that the poet is chiefly distinguished from other men by a greater promptness to think and feel without immediate external excitement and a greater power in expressing such thoughts and feelings as are produced in him in that manner. But these passions and thoughts and feelings are the general passions and thoughts and feelings of men. And with what are they connected? Undoubtedly with our moral sentiments and animal sensations, and with the causes which excite these; with the operations of the

471–72 **that . . . after,** from *Hamlet,* IV, iv, 37

elements and the appearances of the visible universe; with storm and sunshine, with the revolutions of the seasons, with cold and heat, with loss of friends and kindred, with injuries and resentments, gratitude and
550 hope, with fear and sorrow. These, and the like, are the sensations and objects which the poet describes, as they are the sensations of other men, and the objects which interest them. The poet thinks and feels in the spirit of human passions. How, then, can his language differ in any material degree from that of all other men who feel vividly and see clearly? It might be *proved* that it is impossible. But supposing this were not the case, the poet might then be allowed to use a peculiar language when expressing his feelings for his own
560 gratification, or that of men like himself. But poets do not write for poets alone, but for men. Unless therefore we are advocates for that admiration which subsists upon ignorance, and that pleasure which arises from hearing what we do not understand, the poet must descend from this supposed height; and, in order to excite rational sympathy, he must express himself as other men express themselves. To this it may be added, that while he is only selecting from the real language of men, or, which amounts to the same thing,
570 composing accurately in the spirit of such selection, he is treading upon safe ground, and we know what we are to expect from him. Our feelings are the same with respect to meter; for, as it may be proper to remind the reader, the distinction of meter is regular and uniform, and not, like that which is produced by what is usually called POETIC DICTION, arbitrary and subject to infinite caprices upon which no calculation whatever can be made. In the one case, the reader is utterly at the mercy of the poet, respecting what imagery or diction
580 he may choose to connect with the passion; whereas, in the other, the meter obeys certain laws to which the poet and reader both willingly submit because they are certain, and because no interference is made by them with the passion, but such as the concurring testimony of ages has shown to heighten and improve the pleasure which co-exists with it.

It will now be proper to answer an obvious question, namely: Why, professing these opinions, have I written in verse? To this, in addition to such answer as is
590 included in what has been already said, I reply, in the first place: Because, however I may have restricted myself, there is still left open to me what confessedly constitutes the most valuable object of all writing, whether in prose or verse—the great and universal passions of men, the most general and interesting of their occupations, and the entire world of nature before me to supply endless combinations of forms and imagery. Now, supposing for a moment that whatever is interesting in these objects may be as vividly de-
600 scribed in prose, why should I be condemned for attempting to superadd to such description the charm which, by the consent of all nations, is acknowledged to exist in metrical language? To this, by such as are

yet unconvinced, it may be answered that a very small part of the pleasure given by poetry depends upon the meter, and that it is injudicious to write in meter unless it be accompanied with the other artificial distinctions of style with which meter is usually accompanied, and that, by such deviation, more will be lost from the shock which will thereby be given to the reader's as-
610 sociations than will be counterbalanced by any pleasure which he can derive from the general power of numbers.° In answer to those who still contend for the necessity of accompanying meter with certain appropriate colors of style in order to the accomplishment of its appropriate end, and who also, in my opinion, greatly underrate the power of meter in itself, it might, perhaps, as far as relates to these volumes, have been almost sufficient to observe, that poems are extant, written upon more humble subjects, and in a still more
620 naked and simple style, which have continued to give pleasure from generation to generation. Now, if nakedness and simplicity be a defect, the fact here mentioned affords a strong presumption that poems somewhat less naked and simple are capable of affording pleasure at the present day; and, what I wished *chiefly* to attempt, at present, was to justify myself for having written under the impression of this belief. . . .

I have said that poetry is the spontaneous overflow of powerful feelings: it takes its origin from emotion
630 recollected in tranquillity; the emotion is contemplated till, by a species of reaction, the tranquillity gradually disappears, and an emotion, kindred to that which was before the subject of contemplation, is gradually produced, and does itself actually exist in the mind. In this mood successful composition generally begins, and in a mood similar to this it is carried on; but the emotion, of whatever kind and in whatever degree, from various causes, is qualified by various pleasures, so that in describing any passions whatsoever which are volun-
640 tarily described, the mind will, upon the whole, be in a state of enjoyment. If nature be thus cautious to preserve in a state of enjoyment a being so employed, the poet ought to profit by the lesson held forth to him and ought especially to take care that, whatever passions he communicates to his reader, those passions, if his reader's mind be sound and vigorous, should always be accompanied with an overbalance of pleasure. Now the music of harmonious metrical language, the sense of difficulty overcome, and the blind association of
650 pleasure which has been previously received from works of rime or meter of the same or similar construction, an indistinct perception perpetually renewed of language closely resembling that of real life, and yet, in the circumstance of meter, differing from it so widely—all these imperceptibly make up a complex feeling of delight which is of the most important use in tempering the painful feeling always found intermingled with powerful descriptions of the deeper passions.

613 **numbers,** the mechanics of verse, or verse itself

This effect is always produced in pathetic and impassioned poetry; while, in lighter compositions, the ease and gracefulness with which the poet manages his numbers are themselves confessedly a principal source of the gratification of the reader. All that it is *necessary* to say, however, upon this subject may be effected by affirming—what few persons will deny—that, of two descriptions, either of passions, manners, or characters, each of them equally well executed, the one in prose and the other in verse, the verse will be read a hundred times where the prose is read once.

Having thus explained a few of my reasons for writing in verse, and why I have chosen subjects from common life, and endeavored to bring my language near to the real language of men, if I have been too minute in pleading my own cause, I have at the same time been treating a subject of general interest; and for this reason a few words shall be added with reference solely to these particular poems and to some defects which will probably be found in them. I am sensible that my associations must have sometimes been particular instead of general, and that, consequently, giving to things a false importance, I may have sometimes written upon unworthy subjects; but I am less apprehensive on this account than that my language may frequently have suffered from those arbitrary connections of feelings and ideas with particular words and phrases from which no man can altogether protect himself. Hence I have no doubt, that, in some instances, feelings, even of the ludicrous, may be given to my readers by expressions which appeared to me tender and pathetic. Such faulty expressions, were I convinced they were faulty at present and that they must necessarily continue to be so, I would willingly take all reasonable pains to correct. But it is dangerous to make these alterations on the simple authority of a few individuals, or even of certain classes of men; for where the understanding of an author is not convinced, or his feelings altered, this cannot be done without great injury to himself: for his own feelings are his stay and support; and if he set them aside in one instance, he may be induced to repeat this act till his mind shall lose all confidence in itself, and become utterly debilitated. To this it may be added that the critic ought never to forget that he is himself exposed to the same errors as the poet, and, perhaps, in a much greater degree: for there can be no presumption in saying of most readers that it is not probable they will be so well acquainted with the various stages of meaning through which words have passed, or with the fickleness or stability of the relations of particular ideas to each other; and, above all, since they are so much less interested in the subject, they may decide lightly and carelessly.

Long as the reader has been detained, I hope he will permit me to caution him against a mode of false criticism which has been applied to poetry, in which the language closely resembles that of life and nature. Such verses have been triumphed over in parodies, of which Dr. Johnson's° stanza is a fair specimen:

I put my hat upon my head
And walked into the Strand,°
And there I met another man
Whose hat was in his hand.

Immediately under these lines let us place one of the most justly-admired stanzas of the *Babes in the Wood:*

These pretty Babes with hand in hand
Went wandering up and down;
But never more they saw the Man
Approaching from the Town.

In both these stanzas the words and the order of the words in no respect differ from the most unimpassioned conversation. There are words in both, for example, "the Strand," and "the Town," connected with none but the most familiar ideas; yet the one stanza we admit as admirable and the other as a fair example of the superlatively contemptible. Whence arises this difference? Not from the meter, not from the language, not from the order of the words; but the *matter* expressed in Dr. Johnson's stanza is contemptible. The proper method of treating trivial and simple verses, to which Dr. Johnson's stanza would be a fair parallelism, is not to say, this is a bad kind of poetry, or, this is not poetry; but, this wants sense; it is neither interesting in itself nor can *lead* to anything interesting; the images neither originate in that sane state of feeling which arises out of thought nor can excite thought or feeling in the reader. This is the only sensible manner of dealing with such verses. Why trouble yourself about the species till you have previously decided upon the genus? Why take pains to prove that an ape is not a Newton° when it is self-evident that he is not a man?

One request I must make of my reader, which is, that in judging these poems he would decide by his own feelings genuinely and not by reflection upon what will probably be the judgment of others. How common is it to hear a person say, I myself do not object to this style of composition, or this or that expression, but, to such and such classes of people it will appear mean or ludicrous! This mode of criticism, so destructive of all sound unadulterated judgment, is almost universal; let the reader then abide, independently, by his own feelings, and, if he finds himself affected, let him not suffer such conjectures to interfere with his pleasure. . . .

(1800)

719 **Dr. Johnson,** Samuel Johnson, who had little interest in ballads, the style of which he parodied in the lines quoted here 721 **Strand,** prominent street in London 751 **Newton,** Sir Isaac Newton (1642–1727), famous English mathematician, scientist, and natural philosopher

SAMUEL TAYLOR COLERIDGE 1772–1834

Coleridge was born in 1772 in Devonshire, the son of a clergyman. He was educated at Christ's Hospital, London, where he met Charles Lamb, and at Jesus College, Cambridge. At both school and university he read prodigiously, immersing himself particularly in works of imagination and visionary philosophy. Depressed over debts, Coleridge ran away from Cambridge and enlisted in the Dragoons under the name Silas Tomkyn Comberbacke. His brothers returned him to Cambridge, but he left without a degree in 1794, hoping to found, with his friend Robert Southey, the Pantisocracy, an ideal society to be established on the banks of the Susquehanna River in Pennsylvania. The plan fell through, largely for lack of money. Southey married Edith Fricker during this time; Coleridge, partly influenced by Southey, married Mrs. Southey's sister, Sarah. The latter marriage did not prove to be a happy one.

In 1796 Coleridge began writing for The Watchman, a short-lived radical paper. He also had his Juvenile Poems published in 1796. In 1797 he was granted an annuity by Thomas and Josiah Wedgwood, sons of the founder of the pottery firm. In 1795 he settled at Nether Stowey, Somersetshire, where he met Wordsworth and his sister, Dorothy. The years 1797 and 1798 were remarkably productive for Coleridge; during this time he composed The Rime of the Ancient Mariner, Christabel, "Kubla Khan," and "France: An Ode." In 1798 came the Lyrical Ballads (see headnote on Wordsworth for significance). Coleridge's chief contribution to the Ballads was The Rime of the Ancient Mariner, which was placed at the beginning of the collection.

Coleridge and the Wordsworths traveled to Germany in the winter of 1798; Coleridge studied German philosophy and read German literature at the University of Gottingen. The Wordsworths returned and settled at Grasmere. Coleridge returned and became estranged from his wife, who had never cared much for the Wordsworths. He fell hopelessly in love with Sara Hutchinson, the sister of Wordsworth's future wife, in late 1799. In 1800 Coleridge followed the Wordsworths to Grasmere and settled at Greta Hall, Keswick, twelve miles away. The arrival of Coleridge at Keswick coincided with an ebbing of his creative power and a growing dependence on opium. Although he was eventually able to free himself from his addiction, his abilities were nevertheless somewhat stunted. As Lamb observed, Coleridge was an "archangel a little damaged."

Partly as a result of his attempt to combine a platonic love for Sara with fidelity to his wife and family, Coleridge's mental and physical health deteriorated. In 1804 he left Keswick to become secretary to the governor of Malta, a move intended to improve his health. In 1806, when his health had in fact worsened, he returned to England. He lectured and began writing for newspapers; in addition, he single-handedly wrote and distributed The Friend, a periodical devoted largely to German criticism, metaphysics, and philology.

In 1810 he quarreled with Wordsworth because Wordsworth had apparently encouraged Sara, who had been acting as Coleridge's secretary, to retire to her brother's farm in order to avoid further psychological strain; Coleridge never saw Sara Hutchinson again. During the next few years he conducted a successful lecture series on Shakespeare and Milton. In 1816 Coleridge moved to Highgate, a suburb of London, where he lived in the house of James Gillman, a surgeon.

The Highgate years saw a brief period of sustained literary activity, generally considered his "philosophical" period. He published Biographia Literaria (1817); Zapolya, a dramatic piece (1817); a volume of essays enlarged from The Friend; various treatises on religious and philosophical subjects. He continued to lecture and enjoyed a sense of popular recognition. From 1819 until his death in 1834, he lived quietly with Dr. and Mrs. Gillman, receiving many distinguished visitors from England and America and acquiring his legendary reputation as a brilliant conversationalist. Coleridge was, and remains, an original in English literature. "The most wonderful man that I have ever known," Wordsworth declared at his old friend's death; and Lamb, voicing his own sense of the incomparable phenomenon of Coleridge, remarked, "Never saw I his likeness, nor probably the world can again."

PANTISOCRACY°

No more my visionary soul shall dwell
On joys that were; no more endure to weigh
The shame and anguish of the evil day,
Wisely forgetful! O'er the ocean swell
Sublime of Hope, I seek the cottag'd dell   5
Where Virtue calm with careless step may stray,
And dancing to the moonlight roundelay,
The wizard Passions weave an holy spell.
Eyes that have ach'd with Sorrow! Ye shall weep
Tears of doubt-mingled joy, like theirs who start   10
From Precipices of distemper'd sleep,

Pantisocracy. "The ideal social state that Coleridge and Southey planned to establish in America." (Noyes)

On which the fierce-eyed Fiends their revels keep,
And see the rising Sun, and feel it dart
New rays of pleasance trembling to the heart.
(1794; 1849)

THE EOLIAN HARP°

COMPOSED AT CLEVEDON, SOMERSETSHIRE°

My pensive Sara!° thy soft cheek reclined
Thus on mine arm, most soothing sweet it is
To sit beside our cot,° our cot o'ergrown
With white-flowered jasmin, and the broad-leaved
  myrtle,
(Meet emblems they of Innocence and Love!)
And watch the clouds, that late were rich with light,
Slow saddening round, and mark the star of eve
Serenely brilliant (such should Wisdom be)
Shine opposite! How exquisite the scents
Snatched from yon beanfield! and the world *so*
10   hushed!
The stilly murmur of the distant sea
Tells us of silence.
             And that simplest lute,°
Placed lengthways in the clasping casement, hark!
How by the desultory breeze caressed,
Like some coy maid half yielding to her lover,
It pours such sweet upbraiding, as must needs
Tempt to repeat the wrong! And now, its strings
Boldlier swept, the long sequacious° notes
Over delicious surges sink and rise,
20 Such a soft floating witchery of sound
As twilight elfins make, when they at eve
Voyage on gentle gales from fairyland,
Where melodies round honey-dropping flowers,
Footless and wild, like birds of paradise,°
Nor pause, nor perch, hovering on untamed wing!
O! the one life° within us and abroad,
Which meets all motion and becomes its soul,
A light in sound, a sound-like power in light,
Rhythm in all thought, and joyance every where—
30 Methinks, it should have been impossible
Not to love all things in a world so filled;
Where the breeze warbles, and the mute still air
Is Music slumbering on her instrument.

And thus, my love! as on the midway slope
Of yonder hill I stretch my limbs at noon,
Whilst through my half-closed eyelids I behold
The sunbeams dance, like diamonds, on the main,
And tranquil muse upon tranquility;
Full many a thought uncalled and undetained,
And many idle flitting fantasies,   40
Traverse my indolent and passive brain,
As wild and various as the random gales
That swell and flutter on this subject lute!
    And what if all of animated nature
Be but organic harps diversely framed,
That tremble into thought, as o'er them sweeps
Plastic and vast, one intellectual breeze,
At once the soul of each, and God of all?
    But thy more serious eye a mild reproof
Darts, O beloved woman! nor such thoughts 50
Dim and unhallowed dost thou not reject,
And biddest me walk humbly with my God.
Meek daughter in the family of Christ!
Well hast thou said and holily dispraised
These shapings of the unregenerate mind;
Bubbles that glitter as they rise and break
On vain philosophy's aye-babbling spring.
For never guiltless may I speak of him,
The Incomprehensible! save when with awe
I praise him, and with faith that inly *feels*; 60
Who with his saving mercies healed me,
A sinful and most miserable man,
Wildered and dark, and gave me to possess
Peace, and this cot, and thee, heart-honored maid!
(1795; 1796)

THIS LIME-TREE BOWER MY PRISON

Addressed to Charles Lamb, of the India House, London

"In the June of 1797 some long-expected friends° paid
a visit to the author's cottage, and on the morning of
their arrival, he met with an accident,° which disabled
him from walking during the whole time of their stay.
One evening, when they had left him for a few hours, he
composed the following lines in the garden-bower."
                     —Coleridge's note

Well, they are gone, and here must I remain,
This lime-tree bower my prison! I have lost
Beauties and feelings, such as would have been
Most sweet to my remembrance even when age
Had dimmed mine eyes to blindness! They, mean-
  while,
Friends, whom I never more may meet again,
On springy heath, along the hilltop edge,
Wander in gladness, and wind down, perchance,
To that still roaring dell of which I told;
The roaring dell, o'erwooded, narrow, deep, 10

The Eolian Harp, crude ancient harp consisting of strings stretched over a box
which is sounded by the wind. It was often used by the romantics as a symbol for
the creative process **Clevedon, Somersetshire,** village on the Bristol Channel
where Coleridge spent his honeymoon in 1795 1 **Sara,** Sara Fricker, Coleridge's
wife 3 **cot,** cottage 12 **lute,** Eolian harp 18 **sequacious,** successive
24 **birds of paradise,** legendary birds which, lacking feet, live on the wing and
feed on air 26–33 **O! the one life, etc.** These lines first appeared in the 1817
edition

This Lime-Tree Bower My Prison   **friends,** William and Dorothy Wordsworth
and Charles Lamb   **accident.** Coleridge's wife Sara "emptied a skillet of boiling
milk" on his foot

And only speckled by the midday sun;
Where its slim trunk the ash from rock to rock
Flings arching like a bridge;—that branchless ash,
Unsunned and damp, whose few poor yellow leaves
Ne'er tremble in the gale, yet tremble still,
Fanned by the waterfall! and there my friends
Behold the dark green file of long lank weeds,
That all at once (a most fantastic sight!)
Still nod and drip beneath the dripping edge
Of the blue clay stone.

20   Now my friends emerge
Beneath the wide wide heaven—and view again
The many-steepled tract magnificent
Of hilly fields and meadows, and the sea,
With some fair bark, perhaps, whose sails light up
The slip of smooth clear blue betwixt two isles
Of purple shadow! Yes! they wander on
In gladness all; but thou, methinks, most glad,
My gentle-hearted Charles!° for thou hast pined
And hungered after nature, many a year,
30 In the great city pent, winning thy way
With sad yet patient soul, through evil and pain
And strange calamity!° Ah! slowly sink
Behind the western ridge, thou glorious sun!
Shine in the slant beams of the sinking orb,
Ye purple heath flowers! richlier burn, ye clouds!
Live in the yellow light, ye distant groves!
And kindle, thou blue ocean! So my friend
Struck with deep joy may stand, as I have stood,
Silent with swimming sense; yea, gazing round
40 On the wide landscape, gaze till all doth seem
Less gross than bodily; and of such hues
As veil the Almighty Spirit, when yet he makes
Spirits perceive his presence.

                A delight
Comes sudden on my heart, and I am glad
As I myself were there! Nor in this bower,
This little lime-tree bower, have I not marked
Much that has soothed me. Pale beneath the blaze
Hung the transparent foliage; and I watched
Some broad and sunny leaf, and loved to see
50 The shadow of the leaf and stem above
Dappling its sunshine! And that walnut tree
Was richly tinged, and a deep radiance lay
Full on the ancient ivy which usurps
Those fronting elms, and now, with blackest mass
Makes their dark branches gleam a lighter hue
Through the late twilight: and though now the bat
Wheels silent by, and not a swallow twitters,
Yet still the solitary humblebee
Sings in the bean flower! Henceforth I shall know
60 That nature ne'er deserts the wise and pure;
No plot so narrow, be but nature there,

No waste so vacant, but may well employ
Each faculty of sense, and keep the heart
Awake to love and beauty! and sometimes
'Tis well to be bereft of promised good,
That we may lift the soul, and contemplate
With lively joy the joys we cannot share.
My gentle-hearted Charles! when the last rook
Beat its straight path along the dusky air
Homewards, I blest it! deeming its black wing   70
(Now a dim speck, now vanishing in light)
Had crossed the mighty orb's dilated glory,
While thou stood'st gazing; or, when all was still,
Flew creeking o'er thy head, and had a charm
For thee, my gentle-hearted Charles, to whom
No sound is dissonant which tells of life.
(1797; 1800)

THE RIME OF THE ANCIENT MARINER

IN SEVEN PARTS

The first edition of *Lyrical Ballads* (1798) contained this
poem anonymously; the second edition made some
changes to eliminate a few archaisms which Coleridge
had written in the original. It was not published separately under Coleridge's name until 1817; the marginal
gloss, which may have been written earlier, and the
Latin epigraph first appeared at this time. The genesis
of the poem has been described thoroughly by Coleridge in *Biographia Literaria* (Chapter XIV). Wordsworth
states that it was he who suggested the shooting of the
albatross, but the rudimentary inspiration for the narrative as a whole probably came from a pair of
seventeenth-century voyage narratives, the *Letters of
Saint Paulinus to Macarius* (1618) and Capt. T. James'
Strange and Dangerous Voyage (1633). The idea of the
albatross as a bird of good luck belongs to the folklore
of the sea.

*Facile credo,° plures esse Naturas invisibiles quam
visibiles in rerum universitate. Sed horum* [sic] *omnium familiam quis nobis enarrabit? et gradus et cog-
nationes et discrimina et singulorum munera? Quid
agunt? quae loca habitant? Harum rerum notitiam
semper ambivit ingenium humanum, nunquam attigit.
Juvat, interea, non diffiteor, quandoque in animo,
tanquam in tabula, majoris et melioris mundi im-
aginem contemplari: ne mens assuefacta hodiernae
vitae minutiis se contrabat nimis, et tota subsidat in
pusillas cogitationes. Sed veritati interea invigilandum*

---

28 **gentle-hearted Charles.** The epithet displeased Lamb, who humorously replied, "For God's sake, don't make me ridiculous any more by terming me gentle-hearted in print"   32 **strange calamity,** the periodic attacks of insanity suffered by Lamb's sister Mary, who had killed their mother in 1796

The Rime of the Ancient Mariner **Facile credo, etc.** This excerpt, adapted from
a curious work by Thomas Burnet (1635?–1715), concerns the reality of the unseen, of the "nether" dimension of human experience with which the poem is
concerned: "I readily believe that there are more invisible than visible things in
the universe. But who will tell us of their families, ranks, similarities and differences? What do they do? Where do they live? Human knowledge has always circled around the understanding of these things but has never achieved it. It is
pleasant, however, to contemplate at times, as in a picture, the image of a greater
and better world lest the mind, too accustomed to the details of everyday life,
become contracted and dwell completely on trivial things. But meanwhile we
must be watchful of truth and keep within certain limits so that we may distinguish truth from opinion, day from night."

est, modusque servandus, ut certa ab incertis, diem a nocte, distinguamus.

T. Burnet, Archaeol. Phil.

ARGUMENT

How a Ship having passed the Line was driven by storms to the cold Country towards the South Pole, and how from thence she made her course to the tropical Latitude of the Great Pacific Ocean, and of the strange things that befell: and in what manner the Ancyent Marinere came back to his own Country.

PART 1

It is an ancient Mariner,
And he stoppeth one of three. *An ancient Mariner*
"By the long gray beard and glittering *meeteth three Gallants*
eye, *bidden to a wedding-*
feast, and detaineth
Now wherefore stopp'st thou me? *one.*

"The Bridegroom's doors are opened wide,
And I am next of kin,
The guests are met, the feast is set:
May'st hear the merry din."

He holds him with his skinny hand;
10 "There was a ship," quoth he.
"Hold off! unhand me, gray-beard loon!"
Eftsoons° his hand dropt he.

He holds° him with his glittering eye— *The Wedding-Guest is*
The Wedding-Guest stood still, *spellbound by the eye*
And listens like a three years' child. *of the old seafaring*
man and constrained
The Mariner hath his will. *to hear his tale.*

The Wedding-Guest sat on a stone:
He cannot choose but hear;
And thus spake on that ancient man,
20 The bright-eyed Mariner.

"The ship was cheered, the harbor cleared,
Merrily did we drop
Below the kirk, below the hill,
Below the light-house top.

"The sun came up upon the left, *The Mariner tells how*
Out of the sea came he! *the ship sailed south-*
ward with a good wind
And he shone bright, and on the right *and fair weather, till it*
Went down into the sea. *reached the Line.*

"Higher and higher every day,
30 Till over the mast at noon°—"

The Wedding-Guest here beat his breast,
For he heard the loud bassoon.

The bride hath paced into the hall, *The Wedding-Guest*
Red as a rose is she; *heareth the bridal*
music; but the Mariner
Nodding their heads before her goes *continueth his tale.*
The merry minstrelsy.

The Wedding-Guest he beat his breast,
Yet he cannot choose but hear;
And thus spake on that ancient man,
The bright-eyed Mariner. 40

"And now the Storm-blast came, and *The ship driven by a*
he *storm toward the*
south pole.
Was tyrannous and strong:
He struck with his o'ertaking wings,
And chased us south along.

"With sloping masts and dipping prow,
As who pursued with yell and blow
Still treads the shadow of his foe,
And forward bends his head,
The ship drove fast, loud roared the blast,
And southward aye we fled. 50

"And now there came both mist and snow,
And it grew wondrous cold:
And ice, mast-high, came floating by,
As green as emerald.

"And through the drifts the snowy *The land of ice, and of*
clifts *fearful sounds where*
no living thing was to
Did send a dismal sheen: *be seen.*
Nor shapes of men nor beasts we
ken—
The ice was all between.°

"The ice was here, the ice was there,
The ice was all around: 60
It cracked and growled, and roared and howled,
Like noises in a swound!

"At length did cross an Albatross, *Till a great sea-bird,*
Thorough° the fog it came; *called the Albatross,*
came through the
As if it had been a Christian soul, *snow-fog, and was re-*
We hailed it in God's name. *ceived with great joy*
and hospitality.

"It ate the food it ne'er had eat,
And round and round it flew.
The ice did split with a thunder-fit;
The helmsman steered us through! 70

"And a good south wind sprung up *And lo! the Albatross*
behind; *proveth a bird of good*
omen, and followeth
The Albatross did follow, *the ship as it returned*
And every day, for food or play, *northward through fog*
Came to the mariners' hollo! *and floating ice.*

---

12 **eftsoons,** at once. Coleridge's use of such archaic words recalls the atmosphere of the old ballads   13–16 **He holds, etc.** Wordsworth stated that he wrote this stanza   30 **over . . . noon.** The ship is near the equator

58 **between,** between the ship and the land   64 **Thorough,** an old form of *through*

"In mist or cloud, on mast or shroud,°
It perched for vespers° nine;
Whiles all the night, through fog-smoke white,
Glimmered the white moon-shine."

"God save thee, ancient Mariner! *The ancient Mariner*
From the fiends, that plague thee *inhospitably killeth the*
80   thus!— *pious bird of good*
Why look'st thou so?"—"With my *omen.*
   cross-bow
I shot the Albatross!"

PART 2

"The Sun now rose° upon the right:
Out of the sea came he,
Still hid in mist, and on the left
Went down into the sea.

"And the good south wind still blew behind,
But no sweet bird did follow,
Nor any day for food or play
90 Came to the mariners' hollo!

"And I had done a hellish thing, *His shipmates cry out*
And it would work 'em woe: *against the ancient*
For all averred, I had killed the bird *Mariner, for killing the*
That made the breeze to blow. *bird of good luck.*
Ah, wretch! said they, the bird to slay,
That made the breeze to blow!

"Nor dim nor red, like God's own *But when the fog*
   head, *cleared off they justify*
The glorious Sun uprist: *the same, and thus*
Then all averred, I had killed the bird *make themselves ac-*
100 That brought the fog and mist. *complices in the*
'Twas right, said they, such birds to slay, *crime.*
That bring the fog and mist.

"The fair breeze blew, the white foam *The fair breeze con-*
   flew, *tinues; the ship enters*
The furrow followed free; *the Pacific Ocean, and*
We were the first that ever burst *sails northward, even*
Into that silent sea. *till it reaches the Line.*

"Down dropt the breeze, the sails *The ship hath been*
   dropt down, *suddenly becalmed.*
'Twas sad as sad could be;
And we did speak only to break
110 The silence of the sea!

"All in a hot and copper sky,
The bloody Sun, at noon,
Right up above the mast did stand,
No bigger than the Moon.

"Day after day, day after day,
We stuck, nor breath nor motion;
As idle as a painted ship
Upon a painted ocean.

"Water, water, everywhere, *And the Albatross be-*
And all the boards did shrink; *gins to be avenged.* 120
Water, water, everywhere,
Nor any drop to drink.

"The very deep did rot: O Christ!
That ever this should be!
Yea, slimy things did crawl with legs
Upon the slimy sea.

"About, about, in reel and rout
The death-fires° danced at night;
The water, like a witch's oils,
Burnt green, and blue and white. 130

"And some in dreams assured were *A Spirit had followed*
Of the Spirit that plagued us so; *them; one of the in-*
Nine fathom deep he had followed us *visible inhabitants of*
From the land of mist and snow. *this planet, neither*
departed souls nor
angels; concerning
whom the learned
Jew, Josephus, and
the Platonic Constan-
"And every tongue, through utter *tinopolitan, Michael*
   drought, *Psellus, may be con-*
Was withered at the root; *sulted. They are very*
We could not speak, no more than if *numerous, and there is*
We had been choked with soot. *no climate or element*
without one or more.

"Ah! well-a-day! what evil looks *The shipmates, in their*
Had I from old and young! *sore distress, would*
Instead of the cross, the Albatross *fain throw the whole* 140
About my neck was hung. *guilt on the ancient*
Mariner: in sign
whereof they hang the
dead seabird round his
neck.

PART 3

"There passed a weary time. Each throat
Was parched, and glazed each eye.
A weary time! a weary time!
How glazed each weary eye,
When looking westward, I beheld *The ancient Mariner*
A something in the sky. *beholdeth a sign in the*
element afar off.

"At first it seemed a little speck,
And then it seemed a mist; 150
It moved and moved, and took at last
A certain shape, I wist.°

"A speck, a mist, a shape, I wist!
And still it neared and neared:
As if it dodged a water-sprite,
It plunged and tacked and veered.

75 **shroud,** a rope running from the masthead to the side of the ship   76 **vespers,** evening   83 **Sun now rose.** The ship has rounded Cape Horn and is
headed north into the Pacific

128 **death-fires,** phosphorescent lights, considered omens of disaster. Perhaps
Coleridge had in mind the phenomenon known as St. Elmo's fire   152 **wist,**
thought, knew

"With throats unslaked, with black
    lips baked,
We could nor laugh nor wail;
Through utter drought all dumb we
    stood!

*At its nearer ap-
proach, it seemeth him
to be a ship; and at a
dear ransom he freeth
his speech from the
bonds of thirst.*

160 I bit my arm, I sucked the blood,
And cried, A sail! a sail!

"With throats unslaked, with black lips baked,
Agape they heard me call:
Gramercy!° they for joy did grin,   *A flash of joy;*
And all at once their breath drew in,
As they were drinking all.

"See! see! (I cried) she tacks no
    more!
Hither to work us weal—
Without a breeze, without a tide,
170 She steadies with upright keel!

*And horror follows.
For can it be a ship
that comes onward
without wind or tide?*

"The western wave was all aflame,
The day was well nigh done!
Almost upon the western wave
Rested the broad bright Sun;
When that strange shape drove suddenly
Betwixt us and the Sun.

"And straight the Sun was flecked
    with bars,   *It seemeth him but the
skeleton of a ship.*
(Heaven's Mother send us grace!)
As if through a dungeon-grate he peered
180 With broad and burning face.

"Alas! (thought I, and my heart beat loud)
How fast she nears and nears!
Are those her sails that glance in the Sun,
Like restless gossameres?°

"Are those her ribs through which the
    Sun   *And its ribs are seen
as bars on the face of
the setting Sun.*
Did peer, as through a grate?
And is that Woman all her crew?   *The Specter-Woman
and her Death-mate,
and no other on board
the skeleton ship.*
Is that a Death? and are there two?
Is Death that woman's mate?

190 "Her lips were red, her looks were free,
Her locks were yellow as gold: *Like vessel, like crew!*
Her skin was as white as leprosy,
The Night-mare Life-in-Death was she,
Who thicks man's blood with cold.

"The naked hulk alongside came,   *Death and Life-in-
Death have diced for
the ship's crew, and
she (the latter)
winneth the ancient
Mariner.*
And the twain were casting dice;
'The game is done! I've won! I've
    won!'
Quoth she, and whistles thrice.

"The Sun's rim dips; the stars rush
    out: *No twilight, within the
courts of the Sun.*
At one stride comes the dark;   200
With far-heard whisper, o'er the sea,
Off shot the specter-bark.

"We listened and looked sideways
    up!   *At the rising of the
Moon,*
Fear at my heart, as at a cup,
My life-blood seemed to sip!
The stars were dim, and thick the night,
The steersman's face by his lamp gleamed white;
From the sails the dew did drip—
Till clomb above the eastern bar
The hornéd Moon,° with one bright star   210
Within the nether tip.

"One after one, by the star-dogged   *One after another,*
    Moon,
Too quick for groan or sigh,
Each turned his face with a ghastly pang,
And cursed me with his eye.

"Four times fifty living men,   *His shipmates drop
down dead.*
(And I heard nor sigh nor groan)
With heavy thump, a lifeless lump,
They dropt down one by one.

"The souls did from their bodies fly—   *But Life-in-Death*   220
They fled to bliss or woe!   *begins her work on the
ancient Mariner.*
And every soul, it passed me by
Like the whizz of my cross-bow!"

PART 4

"I fear thee, ancient Mariner!   *The Wedding-Guest
feareth that a Spirit is
talking to him;*
I fear thy skinny hand!
And thou° art long, and lank, and
    brown,
As is the ribbed sea-sand.

"I fear thee and thy glittering eye,°   *But the ancient
Mariner assureth him
of his bodily life, and
proceedeth to relate
his horrible penance.*
And thy skinny hand, so brown."—
"Fear not, fear not, thou Wedding-
    Guest!   230
This body dropt not down.

"Alone, alone, all, all alone,
Alone on a wide, wide sea!
And never a saint took pity on
My soul in agony.

210–211 **Moon . . . tip.** "It is a common superstition among sailors that something evil is about to happen whenever a star dogs the moon."—Coleridge's
manuscript note   226–227 **And thou, etc.** Coleridge acknowledged indebtedness
to Wordsworth for these two lines   228 **glittering eye.** It is a commonplace of
European folklore that an evil person can do harm to another by fixing him with
his eye—the evil eye

164 **Gramercy,** great thanks   184 **gossameres,** fine spiderwebs

"The many men, so beautiful!   *He despiseth the*
And they all dead did lie: *creatures of the calm.*
And a thousand thousand slimy things
Lived on; and so did I.

240 "I looked upon the rotting sea,   *And envieth that they*
And drew my eyes away;   *should live, and so*
I looked upon the rotting deck,   *many lie dead.*
And there the dead men lay.

"I looked to Heaven, and tried to pray;
But or ever a prayer had gusht,
A wicked whisper came, and made
My heart as dry as dust.

"I closed my lids, and kept them close,
And the balls like pulses beat;
250 For the sky and the sea, and the sea and the sky
Lay like a load on my weary eye,
And the dead were at my feet.

"The cold sweat melted from their   *But the curse liveth for*
    limbs,   *him in the eye of the*
Nor rot nor reek did they: *dead men.*
The look with which they looked on me
Had never passed away.

"An orphan's curse would drag to hell
A spirit from on high;
But oh! more horrible than that
260 Is a curse in a dead man's eye!
Seven days, seven nights, I saw that
    curse,
And yet I could not die.

"The moving Moon went up the sky,   *In his loneliness and*
And nowhere did abide: *fixedness he yearneth*
Softly she was going up,   *towards the journey-*
And a star or two beside—   *ing Moon, and the*
                                      stars that still sojourn,
                                      yet still move onward;
"Her beams bemocked the sultry   *and everywhere the*
    main,   *blue sky belongs to*
Like April hoar-frost spread;   *them, and is their ap-*
But where the ship's huge shadow   *pointed rest, and their*
    lay,   *native country and*
270 The charméd water burnt alway   *their own natural*
A still and awful red.   *homes, which they*
                                      enter unannounced, as
                                      lords that are certainly
"Beyond the shadow of the ship,   *expected, and yet*
I watched the water-snakes: *there is a silent joy at*
They moved in tracks of shining   *their arrival.*
    white,
And when they reared, the elfish light   *By the light of the*
Fell off in hoary flakes.   *Moon he beholdeth*
                                          God's creatures of the
                                          great calm.
"Within the shadow of the ship
I watched their rich attire:
Blue, glossy green, and velvet black,

They coiled and swam; and every track   280
Was a flash of golden fire.

"O happy living things! no tongue   *Their beauty and their*
Their beauty might declare: *happiness.*
A spring of love gushed from my
    heart,
And I blessed them unaware;   *He blesseth them in*
Sure my kind saint took pity on me,   *his heart.*
And I blessed them unaware.

"The selfsame moment I could pray;   *The spell begins to*
And from my neck so free   *break.*
The Albatross fell off, and sank   290
Like lead into the sea."

PART 5

"Oh sleep! it is a gentle thing,
Beloved from pole to pole!
To Mary Queen the praise be given!
She sent the gentle sleep from Heaven,
That slid into my soul.

"The silly° buckets on the deck,   *By grace of the holy*
That had so long remained,   *Mother, the ancient*
I dreamt that they were filled with *Mariner is refreshed*
    dew;   *with rain.*
And when I awoke, it rained.   300

"My lips were wet, my throat was cold,
My garments all were dank;
Sure I had drunken in my dreams,
And still my body drank.

"I moved, and could not feel my limbs:
I was so light—almost
I thought that I had died in sleep,
And was a blessed ghost.

"And soon I heard a roaring wind: *He heareth sounds*
It did not come anear;   *and seeth strange*
But with its sound it shook the sails, *sights and commo-* 310
That were so thin and sere.   *tions in the sky and the*
                                      elements.

"The upper air burst into life!
And a hundred fire-flags° sheen,°
To and fro they were hurried about!
And to and fro, and in and out,
The wan stars danced between.

"And the coming wind did roar more loud,
And the sails did sigh like sedge;°
And the rain poured down from one black cloud; 320
The Moon was at its edge.

297 **silly**, innocent; by poetic extension, "unused," "empty"   314 **fire-flags**,
perhaps the Northern Lights   **sheen**, bright   319 **sedge**, coarse marsh grass

"The thick black cloud was cleft, and still
The Moon was at its side:
Like waters shot from some high crag,
The lightning fell with never a jag,
A river steep and wide.

"The loud wind never reached the
   ship,
Yet now the ship moved on!
Beneath the lightning and the Moon
330 The dead men gave a groan.

"They groaned, they stirred, they all uprose,
Nor spake, nor moved their eyes;
It had been strange, even in a dream,
To have seen those dead men rise.

"The helmsman steered, the ship moved on;
Yet never a breeze up blew;
The mariners all 'gan work the ropes,
Where they were wont to do;
They raised their limbs like lifeless tools—
340 We were a ghastly crew.

"The body of my brother's son
Stood by me, knee to knee:
The body and I pulled at one rope,
But he said nought to me."

"I fear thee, ancient Mariner!"
"Be calm, thou Wedding-Guest!
'Twas not those souls that fled in
   pain,
Which to their corses came again,
But a troop of spirits blest:

350 "For when it dawned—they dropped their arms,
And clustered round the mast;
Sweet sounds rose slowly through their mouths,
And from their bodies passed.

"Around, around, flew each sweet sound,
Then darted to the Sun;
Slowly the sounds came back again,
Now mixed, now one by one.

"Sometimes a-dropping from the sky
I heard the skylark sing;
360 Sometimes all little birds that are,
How they seemed to fill the sea and air
With their sweet jargoning!

"And now 'twas like all instruments,
Now like a lonely flute;
And now it is an angel's song,
That makes the heavens be mute.

The bodies of the ship's crew are inspired, and the ship moves on;

But not by the souls of the men, nor by demons of earth or middle air, but by a blessed troop of angelic spirits, sent down by the invocation of the guardian saint.

"It ceased; yet still the sails made on
A pleasant noise till noon,
A noise like of a hidden brook
In the leafy month of June,   370
That to the sleeping woods all night
Singeth a quiet tune.

"Till noon we quietly sailed on,
Yet never a breeze did breathe:
Slowly and smoothly went the ship,
Moved onward from beneath.

"Under the keel nine fathom deep,
From the land of mist and snow,
The Spirit slid: and it was he
That made the ship to go.
The sails at noon left off their tune,
And the ship stood still also.

"The Sun, right up above the mast,
Had fixed her to the ocean:
But in a minute she 'gan stir,
With a short uneasy motion—
Backwards and forwards half her length
With a short uneasy motion.

"Then like a pawing horse let go,
She made a sudden bound: 390
It flung the blood into my head,
And I fell down in a swound.

"How long in that same fit I lay,
I have not° to declare;
But ere my living life returned,
I heard, and in my soul discerned,
Two voices in the air.

"'Is it he?' quoth one, 'Is this the
   man?
By Him who died on cross,
With his cruel bow he laid full low   400
The harmless Albatross.

"'The Spirit who bideth by himself
In the land of mist and snow,
He loved the bird that loved the man
Who shot him with his bow.'

"The other was a softer voice,
As soft as honey-dew:
Quoth he, 'The man hath penance done,
And penance more will do.'"

The lonesome Spirit from the South Pole carries on the ship as far as the Line, in obedience to the angelic troop, but still requireth vengeance.   380

The Polar Spirit's fellow demons, the invisible inhabitants of the element, take part in his wrong; and two of them relate, one to the other that penance long and heavy for the ancient Mariner hath been accorded to the Polar Spirit, who returneth southward.

394 **have not,** have not the power or knowledge

PART 6

FIRST VOICE

410 "'But tell me, tell me! speak again,
Thy soft response renewing—
What makes that ship drive on so fast?
What is the ocean doing?'

SECOND VOICE

"'Still as a slave before his lord,
The ocean hath no blast;
His great bright eye most silently
Up to the Moon is cast—

"'If he may know which way to go;
For she guides him smooth or grim.
420 See, brother, see! how graciously
She looketh down on him.'

FIRST VOICE

"'But why drives on that ship so fast,
Without or wave or wind?'

The Mariner hath been cast into a trance; for the angelic power causeth the vessel to drive northward faster than human life could endure.

SECOND VOICE

"'The air is cut away before,
And closes from behind.'

"'Fly, brother, fly! more high, more high!
Or we shall be belated:
For slow and slow that ship will go,
When the Mariner's trance is abated.'

430 "I woke, and we were sailing on
As in a gentle weather:
'Twas night, calm night, the moon
   was high;
The dead men stood together.

The supernatural motion is retarded; the Mariner awakes, and his penance begins anew.

"All stood together on the deck,
For a charnel-dungeon° fitter:
All fixed on me their stony eyes,
That in the Moon did glitter.

"The pang, the curse, with which they died,
Had never passed away:
440 I could not draw my eyes from theirs,
Nor turn them up to pray.

435 **charnel-dungeon,** vault for bones of the dead

"And now this spell was snapt: once
   more
I viewed the ocean green,
And looked far forth, yet little saw
Of what had else been seen—

The curse is finally expiated.

"Like one, that on a lonesome road
Doth walk in fear and dread,
And having once turned round, walks on,
And turns no more his head;
Because he knows, a frightful fiend   450
Doth close behind him tread.

"But soon there breathed a wind on me,
Nor sound nor motion made:
Its path was not upon the sea,
In ripple or in shade.

"It raised my hair, it fanned my cheek
Like a meadow-gale of spring—
It mingled strangely with my fears,
Yet it felt like a welcoming.

"Swiftly, swiftly flew the ship,   460
Yet she sailed softly too:
Sweetly, sweetly blew the breeze—
On me alone it blew.

"Oh! dream of joy! is this indeed
The light-house top I see?
Is this the hill? is this the kirk?
Is this mine own countree?

And the ancient Mariner beholdeth his native country.

"We drifted o'er the harbor-bar,
And I with sobs did pray—
O let me be awake, my God!   470
Or let me sleep alway.

"The harbor-bay was clear as glass,
So smoothly it was strewn!
And on the bay the moonlight lay,
And the shadow of the Moon.

"The rock shone bright, the kirk no less,
That stands above the rock:
The moonlight steeped in silentness
The steady weathercock.

"And the bay was white with silent light 480
Till, rising from the same,
Full many shapes, that shadows were,
In crimson colors came.

The angelic spirits leave the dead bodies.

"A little distance from the prow
Those crimson shadows were:
I turned my eyes upon the deck—
Oh, Christ! what saw I there!

"Each corse lay flat, lifeless and flat,
And, by the holy rood!°
490 A man all light, a seraph-man,   *And appear in their*
On every corse there stood.   *own forms of light.*

"This seraph-band, each waved his hand:
It was a heavenly sight!
They stood as signals to the land,
Each one a lovely light;

"This seraph-band, each waved his hand,
No voice did they impart—
No voice; but oh! the silence sank
Like music on my heart.

500 "But soon I heard the dash of oars,
I heard the Pilot's cheer;
My head was turned perforce away,
And I saw a boat appear.

"The Pilot and the Pilot's boy,
I heard them coming fast:
Dear Lord in Heaven! it was a joy
The dead men could not blast.

"I saw a third—I heard his voice:
It is the Hermit good!
510 He singeth loud his godly hymns
That he makes in the wood.
He'll shrieve my soul, he'll wash away
The Albatross's blood."

PART 7

This Hermit good lives in that wood   *The Hermit of the*
Which slopes down to the sea.   *wood,*
How loudly his sweet voice he rears!
He loves to talk with marineres
That come from a far countree.

"He kneels at morn, and noon, and eve—
520 He hath a cushion plump:
It is the moss that wholly hides
The rotted old oak-stump.

"The skiff-boat neared: I heard them talk,
'Why, this is strange, I trow!
Where are those lights so many and fair,
That signal made but now?'

"'Strange, by my faith!' the Hermit   *Approacheth the ship*
said—   *with wonder.*
'And they answered not our cheer!
The planks looked warped! and see
those sails,

How thin they are and sere!   530
I never saw aught like to them,
Unless perchance it were

"'Brown skeletons of leaves that lag
My forest-brook along;
When the ivy-tod° is heavy with snow,
And the owlet whoops to the wolf below,
That eats the she-wolf's young.'

"'Dear Lord! it hath a fiendish look—
(The Pilot made reply)
I am a-feared'—'Push on, push on!'   540
Said the Hermit cheerily.

"The boat came closer to the ship,
But I nor spake nor stirred;
The boat came close beneath the ship,
And straight a sound was heard.

"Under the water it rumbled on,   *The ship suddenly*
Still louder and more dread: *sinketh.*
It reached the ship, it split the bay;
The ship went down like lead.

"Stunned by that loud and dreadful   *The ancient Mariner is*
sound,   *saved in the Pilot's*
Which sky and ocean smote,   *boat.*   550
Like one that hath been seven days drowned
My body lay afloat;
But swift as dreams, myself I found
Within the Pilot's boat.

"Upon the whirl, where sank the ship,
The boat spun round and round;
And all was still, save that the hill°
Was telling of the sound.

"I moved my lips—the Pilot shrieked   560
And fell down in a fit;
The holy Hermit raised his eyes,
And prayed where he did sit.

"I took the oars: the Pilot's boy,
Who now doth crazy go,
Laughed loud and long, and all the while
His eyes went to and fro.
'Ha! ha!' quoth he, 'full plain I see,
The Devil knows how to row.'

"And now, all in my own countree,   570
I stood on the firm land!
The Hermit stepped forth from the boat,
And scarcely he could stand.

489 **rood,** cross

535 **ivy-tod,** ivy bush   558–559 **hill . . . sound,** referring to the echo of the
cataclysm

"'O shrieve me, shrieve° me, holy man!'
The Hermit crossed his brow.° The ancient Mariner
earnestly entreateth
the Hermit to shrieve
him; and the penance
of life falls on him.
'Say quick,' quoth he, 'I bid thee
   say—
What manner of man art thou?'

"Forthwith this frame of mine was wrenched
With a woful agony,
580 Which forced me to begin my tale;
And then it left me free.

"Since then, at an uncertain hour, And ever and anon
throughout his future
life an agony con-
straineth him to travel
from land to land,
That agony returns;
And till my ghastly tale is told,
This heart within me burns.

"I pass, like night, from land to land;
I have strange power of speech;
That moment that his face I see,
I know the man that must hear me:
590 To him my tale I teach.

"What loud uproar bursts from that door!
The wedding-guests are there:
But in the garden-bower the bride
And bride-maids singing are:
And hark the little vesper bell,
Which biddeth me to prayer!

"O Wedding-Guest! this soul hath been
Alone on a wide, wide sea:
So lonely 'twas, that God himself
600 Scarce seeméd there to be.

"Oh sweeter than the marriage-feast,
'Tis sweeter far to me,
To walk together to the kirk
With a goodly company!—

"To walk together to the kirk,
And all together pray,
While each to his great Father bends,
Old men, and babes, and loving friends,
And youths and maidens gay!

610 "Farewell, farewell! but this I tell And to teach by his
own example love and
reverence to all things
that God made and
loveth.
To thee, thou Wedding-Guest!
He prayeth well, who loveth well
Both man and bird and beast.

"He prayeth best, who loveth best
All things both great and small;
For the dear God who loveth us,
He made and loveth all."

The Mariner, whose eye is bright,
Whose beard with age is hoar,

Is gone: and now the Wedding-Guest 620
Turned from the bridegroom's door.

He went like one that hath been stunned,
And is of sense forlorn:°
A sadder and a wiser man,
He rose the morrow morn.
(1797–1798; 1798)

CHRISTABEL

Coleridge never finished this poem, never even carried
it much beyond the beginning of the story. The first
part was composed as early as 1797; the second part,
which has very little relation to the first, not until
1800. The completed portions of the poem were finally published in 1816. Coleridge said of it in 1833:
"The reason of my not finishing Christabel is not that I
don't know how to do it—for I have, as I always had,
the whole plan entire from beginning to end in my
mind; but I fear I could not carry on with equal success the execution of the idea, an extremely subtle and
difficult one."

For the meter of Christabel, Coleridge used the
free four-stress line, divisible into two half lines of two
stresses each, that was an important characteristic of
Old English alliterative verse.

PART 1

'Tis the middle of night by the castle clock,
And the owls have awakened the crowing cock,
Tu—whit!——Tu—whoo!
And hark, again! the crowing cock,
How drowsily it crew.

Sir Leoline, the Baron rich,
Hath a toothless mastiff bitch;
From her kennel beneath the rock
She maketh answer to the clock,
Four for the quarters, and twelve for the hour; 10
Ever and aye, by shine and shower,
Sixteen short howls, not over loud;
Some say, she sees my lady's shroud.

Is the night chilly and dark?
The night is chilly, but not dark.
The thin gray cloud is spread on high,
It covers but not hides the sky.
The moon is behind, and at the full;
And yet she looks both small and dull.
The night is chill, the cloud is gray: 20

---

574 **shrieve,** hear confession, absolve, impose penance   575 **crossed his brow,** made the sign of the cross upon his forehead to avert evil

623 **of sense forlorn,** both saddened and stunned

'Tis a month before the month of May,
And the Spring comes slowly up this way.

The lovely lady, Christabel,
Whom her father loves so well,
What makes her in the wood so late,
A furlong from the castle gate?
She had dreams all yesternight
Of her own betrothéd knight;
And she in the midnight wood will pray
30 For the weal of her lover that's far away.

She stole along, she nothing spoke,
The sighs she heaved were soft and low,
And naught was green upon the oak
But moss and rarest mistletoe:
She kneels beneath the huge oak tree
And in silence prayeth she.

The lady sprang up suddenly,
The lovely lady, Christabel!
It moaned as near, as near can be,
40 But what it is she cannot tell.—
On the other side it seems to be,
Of the huge, broad-breasted, old oak tree.

The night is chill; the forest bare;
Is it the wind that moaneth bleak?
There is not wind enough in the air
To move away the ringlet curl
From the lovely lady's cheek—
There is not wind enough to twirl
The one red leaf, the last of its clan,
50 That dances as often as dance it can,
Hanging so light, and hanging so high,
On the topmost twig that looks up at the sky.

Hush, beating heart of Christabel!
Jesu Maria, shield her well!
She folded her arms beneath her cloak,
And stole to the other side of the oak.
  What sees she there?

There she sees a damsel bright,
Drest in a silken robe of white,
60 That shadowy in the moonlight shone:
The neck that made that white robe wan,
Her stately neck, and arms were bare;
Her blue-veined feet unsandalled were,
And wildly glittered here and there
The gems entangled in her hair.
I guess, 'twas frightful there to see
A lady so richly clad as she—
Beautiful exceedingly!

"Mary mother, save me now!"
70 (Said Christabel) "And who art thou?"
The lady strange made answer meet,

And her voice was faint and sweet:
"Have pity on my sore distress,
I scarce can speak for weariness":
"Stretch forth thy hand, and have no fear!"
Said Christabel, "How camest thou here?"
And the lady, whose voice was faint and sweet,
Did thus pursue her answer meet:

"My sire is of a noble line,
And my name is Geraldine: 80
Five warriors seized me yestermorn.
Me, even me, a maid forlorn:
They choked my cries with force and fright,
And tied me on a palfrey white.
The palfrey was as fleet as wind,
And they rode furiously behind.
They spurred amain, their steeds were white:
And once we crossed the shade of night.

As sure as Heaven shall rescue me,
I have no thought what men they be;   90
Nor do I know how long it is
(For I have lain entranced, I wis)
Since one, the tallest of the five,
Took me from the palfrey's back,
A weary woman, scarce alive.
Some muttered words his comrades spoke:
He placed me underneath this oak;
He swore they would return with haste;
Whither they went I cannot tell—
I thought I heard, some minutes past,   100
Sounds as of a castle bell.
Stretch forth thy hand (thus ended she),
And help a wretched maid to flee."

Then Christabel stretched forth her hand,
And comforted fair Geraldine:
"Oh well, bright dame! may you command
The service of Sir Leoline:
And gladly our stout chivalry
Will he send forth, and friends withal,
To guide and guard you safe and free   110
Home to your noble father's hall."

She rose: and forth with steps they passed
That strove to be, and were not, fast.
Her gracious stars the lady blest,
And thus spake on sweet Christabel:
"All our household are at rest,
The hall as silent as the cell;
Sir Leoline is weak in health,
And may not well awakened be,
But we will move as if in stealth,   120
And I beseech your courtesy,
This night, to share your couch with me."

They crossed the moat, and Christabel
Took the key that fitted well;

A little door she opened straight,
All in the middle of the gate;
The gate that was ironed within and without,
Where an army in battle array had marched out.
The lady sank,° belike through pain,
130 And Christabel with might and main
Lifted her up, a weary weight,
Over the threshold of the gate:
Then the lady rose again,
And moved as she were not in pain.

So free from danger, free from fear,
They crossed the court: right glad they were.
And Christabel devoutly cried
To the lady by her side,
"Praise we the Virgin all divine
140 Who hath rescued thee from thy distress!"
"Alas, alas!" said Geraldine,
"I cannot speak for weariness."
So free from danger, free from fear,
They crossed the court: right glad they were.

Outside her kennel the mastiff old
Lay fast asleep, in moonshine cold.
The mastiff old did not awake,
Yet she an angry moan did make!
And what can ail the mastiff bitch?
150 Never till now she uttered yell
Beneath the eye of Christabel.
Perhaps it is the owlet's scritch:
For what can ail the mastiff bitch?

They passed the hall, that echoes still,
Pass as lightly as you will!
The brands were flat, the brands were dying,
Amid their own white ashes lying;
But when the lady passed, there came
A tongue of light, a fit of flame;
160 And Christabel saw the lady's eye,
And nothing else saw she thereby,
Save the boss of the shield of Sir Leoline tall,
Which hung in a murky old niche in the wall.
"O softly tread," said Christabel,
"My father seldom sleepeth well."

Sweet Christabel her feet doth bare,
And jealous of the listening air,
They steal their way from stair to stair,
Now in glimmer, and now in gloom,
170 And now they pass the Baron's room,
As still as death, with stifled breath!
And now have reached her chamber door;
And now doth Geraldine press down
The rushes of the chamber floor.

The moon shines dim in the open air,
And not a moonbeam enters here.
But they without its light can see
The chamber carved so curiously,
Carved with figures strange and sweet,
All made out of the carver's brain, 180
For a lady's chamber meet:
The lamp with twofold silver chain
Is fastened to an angel's feet.

The silver lamp burns dead and dim;
But Christabel the lamp will trim.
She trimmed the lamp, and made it bright,
And left it swinging to and fro,
While Geraldine, in wretched plight,
Sank down upon the floor below.

"O weary lady, Geraldine, 190
I pray you, drink this cordial wine!
It is a wine of virtuous powers;
My mother made it of wild flowers."

"And will your mother pity me,
Who am a maiden most forlorn?"
Christabel answered—"Woe is me!
She died the hour that I was born.
I have heard the gray-haired friar tell,
How on her death-bed she did say,
That she should hear the castle-bell 200
Strike twelve upon my wedding-day.
O mother dear! that thou wert here!"
"I would," said Geraldine, "she were!"

But soon with altered voice, said she—
"Off, wandering mother!° Peak and pine!
I have power to bid thee flee."
Alas! what ails poor Geraldine?
Why stares she with unsettled eye?
Can she the bodiless dead espy?
And why with hollow voice cries she, 210
"Off, woman, off! this hour is mine—
Though thou her guardian spirit be,
Off, woman, off! 'tis given to me."

Then Christabel knelt by the lady's side,
And raised to heaven her eyes so blue—
"Alas!" said she, "this ghastly ride—
Dear lady! it hath wildered° you!"
The lady wiped her moist cold brow,
And faintly said, "'Tis over now!"

Again the wild-flower wine she drank: 220
Her fair large eyes 'gan glitter bright,
And from the floor whereon she sank,
The lofty lady stood upright;

Christabel 129-159 **The lady sank, etc.** These lines show Geraldine to be an evil spirit. She was unable, without aid, to cross the threshold, which had been blessed to keep evil spirits away; she refused to praise the Virgin (l. 142); the action of the fire (ll. 156-159) was caused by the presence of a supernatural being

205 **Off . . . mother.** Geraldine has the power to drive away the beneficent spirit of Christabel's mother   217 **wildered,** perplexed

She was most beautiful to see,
Like a lady of a far countree.

And thus the lofty lady spake—
"All they, who live in the upper sky,
Do love you, holy Christabel!
And you love them, and for their sake
230 And for the good which me befell,
Even I in my degree will try,
Fair maiden, to requite you well.
But now unrobe yourself; for I
Must pray, ere yet in bed I lie."

Quoth Christabel, "So let it be!"
And as the lady bade, did she.
Her gentle limbs did she undress,
And lay down in her loveliness.

But through her brain of weal and woe
240 So many thoughts moved to and fro,
That vain it were her lids to close:
So half-way from the bed she rose,
And on her elbow did recline
To look at the lady Geraldine.

Beneath the lamp the lady bowed,
And slowly rolled her eyes around;
Then drawing in her breath aloud,
Like one that shuddered, she unbound
The cincture° from beneath her breast:
250 Her silken robe, and inner vest,
Dropt to her feet, and full in view,
Behold! her bosom and half her side—
A sight to dream of, not to tell!
Oh, shield her! shield sweet Christabel!

Yet Geraldine nor speaks nor stirs;
Ah! what a stricken look was hers!
Deep from within she seems half-way
To lift some weight with sick assay,
And eyes the maid and seeks delay;
260 Then suddenly, as one defied,
Collects herself in scorn and pride,
And lay down by the maiden's side!—
And in her arms the maid she took,
      Ah, well-a-day!
And with low voice and doleful look
      These words did say:

"In the touch of this bosom there worketh a spell,
Which is lord of thy utterance, Christabel!
Thou knowest tonight, and wilt know tomorrow,
270 This mark of my shame, this seal of my sorrow:
      But vainly thou warrest,
      For this is alone in
      Thy power to declare,

That in the dim forest
   Thou heard'st a low moaning,
And found'st a bright lady, surpassingly fair:
And didst bring her home with thee in love and in
   charity,
To shield her and shelter her from the damp air."

THE CONCLUSION TO PART 1

It was a lovely sight to see
The lady Christabel, when she   280
Was praying at the old oak tree.
   Amid the jagged shadows
   Of mossy leafless bought,
   Kneeling in the moonlight,
   To make her gentle vows;
Her slender palms together prest,
Heaving sometimes on her breast;
Her face resigned to bliss or bale—
Her face, oh call it fair not pale,
And both blue eyes more bright than clear,   290
Each about to have a tear.

With open eyes (ah, woe is me!)
Asleep, and dreaming fearfully,
Fearfully dreaming, yet, I wis,°
Dreaming that alone, which is—
O sorrow and shame! Can this be she,
The lady, who knelt at the old oak tree?
And lo! the worker of these harms,
That holds the maiden in her arms,
Seems to slumber still and mild,   300
As a mother with her child.

A star hath set, a star hath risen,
O Geraldine! since arms of thine
Have been the lovely lady's prison.
O Geraldine! one hour was thine—
Thou'st had thy will! By tairn° and rill,
The night-birds all that hour were still.
But now they are jubilant anew,
From cliff and tower, tu—whoo! tu—whoo!
Tu—whoo! tu!—whoo! from wood and fell!   310

And see! the lady Christabel
Gathers herself from out her trance;
Her limbs relax, her countenance
Grows sad and soft; and smooth thin lids
Close o'er her eyes; and tears she sheds—
Large tears that leave the lashes bright!
And oft the while she seems to smile
As infants at a sudden light!

Yea, she doth smile, and she doth weep,
Like a youthful hermitess,   320

---

249 **cincture,** girdle

294 **wis,** think   306 **tairn,** tarn, mountain pool

Beauteous in a wilderness,
Who, praying always, prays in sleep.
And, if she move unquietly,
Perchance, 'tis but the blood so free
Comes back and tingles in her feet.
No doubt she hath a vision sweet.
What if her guardian spirit 'twere?
What if she knew her mother near?
But this she knows, in joys and woes,
330 That saints will aid if men will call:
For the blue sky bends over all!

PART 2

Each matin bell, the Baron saith,
Knells us back to a world of death.
These words Sir Leoline first said,
When he rose and found his lady dead:
These words Sir Leoline will say,
Many a morn to his dying day!

And hence the custom and law began,
That still at dawn the sacristan,
340 Who duly pulls the heavy bell,
Five and forty beads must tell
Between each stroke—a warning knell,
Which not a soul can choose but hear
From Bratha Head° to Wyndermere.

Saith Bracy the bard, "So let it knell!
And let the drowsy sacristan
Still count as slowly as he can!
There is no lack of such, I ween,
As well fill up the space between."
350 In Langdale Pike° and Witch's lair,

And Dungeon-ghyll° so foully rent,
With ropes of rock and bells of air
Three sinful sextons' ghosts are pent,
Who all give back, one after t' other,
The death-note to their living brother;
And oft too, by the knell offended,
Just as their one! two! three! is ended,
The devil mocks the doleful tale
With a merry peal from Borodale.

360 The air is still! through mist and cloud
That merry peal comes ringing loud;
And Geraldine shakes off her dread,
And rises lightly from the bed;
Puts on her silken vestments white,
And tricks her hair in lovely plight,
And nothing doubting of her spell
Awakens the lady Christabel.

"Sleep you, sweet lady Christabel?
I trust that you have rested well."

And Christabel awoke and spied   370
The same who lay down by her side—
Oh, rather say, the same whom she
Raised up beneath the old oak tree!
Nay, fairer yet; and yet more fair!
For she belike hath drunken deep
Of all the blessedness of sleep!
And while she spake, her looks, her air,
Such gentle thankfulness declare,
That (so it seemed) her girded vests
Grew tight beneath her heaving breasts.   380
"Sure I have sinned!" said Christabel,
"Now heaven be praised if all be well!"
And in low faltering tones, yet sweet,
Did she the lofty lady greet,
With such perplexity of mind
As dreams too lively leave behind.

So quickly she rose, and quickly arrayed
Her maiden limbs, and having prayed
That He, who on the cross did groan,
Might wash away her sins unknown,   390
She forthwith led fair Geraldine
To meet her sire, Sir Leoline.

The lovely maid and lady tall
Are pacing both into the hall,
And pacing on through page and groom,
Enter the Baron's presence-room.

The Baron rose, and while he prest
His gentle daughter to his breast,
With cheerful wonder in his eyes
The lady Geraldine espies,   400
And gave such welcome to the same,
As might beseem so bright a dame!

But when he heard the lady's tale,
And when she told her father's name,
Why waxed Sir Leoline so pale,
Murmuring o'er the name again,
Lord Roland de Vaux of Tryermaine?

Alas!° they had been friends in youth;
But whispering tongues can poison truth;
And constancy lives in realms-above;   410
And life is thorny; and youth is vain;
And to be wroth with one we love
Doth work like madness in the brain.
And thus it chanced, as I divine,
With Roland and Sir Leoline.
Each spake words of high disdain

344 **Bratha Head,** source of the river Bratha, which flows through the county of Westmorland into Lake Windermere. The other places named are in the Lake District, but the poem is not meant to be thus localized   350 **Pike,** peak, hill   351 **ghyll,** valley or ravine with a stream running through it

408–426 **Alas! they,** etc. Coleridge regarded this passage as "the best and sweetest" he ever wrote. It may have been suggested by his temporary estrangement from Southey

And insult to his heart's best brother:
They parted—ne'er to meet again!
But never either found another
420 To free the hollow heart from paining—
They stood aloof, the scars remaining,
Like cliffs which had been rent asunder;
A dreary sea now flows between—
But neither heat, nor frost, nor thunder,
Shall wholly do away, I ween,
The marks of that which once hath been.

Sir Leoline, a moment's space,
Stood gazing on the damsel's face:
And the youthful Lord of Tryermaine
430 Came back upon his heart again.

Oh then the Baron forgot his age,
His noble heart swelled high with rage;
He swore by the wounds in Jesu's side,
He would proclaim it far and wide,
With trump and solemn heraldy,
That they who thus had wronged the dame,
Were base as spotted infamy!
"And if they dare deny the same,
My herald shall appoint a week,
440 And let the recreant traitors seek
My tourney court—that there and then
I may dislodge their reptile souls

From the bodies and forms of men!"
He spake: his eye in lightning rolls!
For the lady was ruthlessly seized; and he kenned
In the beautiful lady the child of his friend!

And now the tears were on his face,
And fondly in his arms he took
Fair Geraldine, who met the embrace,
450 Prolonging it with joyous look.
Which when she viewed, a vision fell
Upon the soul of Christabel,
The vision of fear, the touch and pain!
She shrunk and shuddered, and saw again—
(Ah, woe is me! Was it for thee,
Thou gentle maid! such sights to see?)

Again she saw that bosom old,
Again she felt that bosom cold,
And drew in her breath with a hissing sound:
460 Whereat the Knight turned wildly round,
And nothing saw but his own sweet maid
With eyes upraised, as one that prayed.

The touch, the sight, had passed away,
And in its stead that vision blest,
Which comforted her after-rest
While in the lady's arms she lay,
Had put a rapture in her breast,
And on her lips and o'er her eyes

Spread smiles like light!
                    With new surprise,
"What ails then my belovéd child?"   470
The Baron said—His daughter mild
Made answer, "All will yet be well!"
I ween, she had no power to tell
Aught else: so mighty was the spell.

Yet he, who saw this Geraldine,
Had deemed her sure a thing divine.
Such sorrow with such grace she blended,
As if she feared she had offended
Sweet Christabel, that gentle maid!
And with such lowly tones she prayed,   480
She might be sent without delay
Home to her father's mansion.

                              "Nay!
Nay, by my soul!" said Leoline.
"Ho! Bracy, the bard, the charge be thine!
Go thou, with music sweet and loud,
And take two steeds with trappings proud,
And take the youth whom thou lov'st best
To bear thy harp, and learn thy song,
And clothe you both in solemn vest,
And over the mountains haste along,   490
Lest wandering folk, that are abroad,
Detain you on the valley road.
And when he has crossed the Irthing flood,
My merry bard! he hastes, he hastes
Up Knorren Moor, through Halegarth Wood,
And reaches soon that castle good
Which stands and threatens Scotland's wastes.

"Bard Bracy! bard Bracy! your horses are fleet
Ye must ride up the hall, your music so sweet
More loud than your horses' echoing feet!   500
And loud and loud to Lord Roland call,
Thy daughter is safe in Langdale hall!
Thy beautiful daughter is safe and free—
Sir Leoline greets thee thus through me.
He bids thee come without delay
With all thy numerous array;
And take thy lovely daughter home:
And he will meet thee on the way
With all his numerous array
White with their panting palfreys' foam: 510
And by mine honor! I will say,
That I repent me of the day
When I spake words of fierce disdain
To Roland de Vaux of Tryermaine!—
For since that evil hour hath flown,
Many a summer's sun hath shone;
Yet ne'er found I a friend again
Like Roland de Vaux of Tryermaine."

The lady fell, and clasped his knees,
Her face upraised, her eyes o'erflowing;   520

And Bracy replied, with faltering voice,
His gracious hail on all bestowing!—
"Thy words, thou sire of Christabel,
Are sweeter than my harp can tell;
Yet might I gain a boon of thee,
This day my journey should not be,
So strange a dream hath come to me;
That I had vowed with music loud
To clear yon wood from thing unblest,
530 Warned by a vision in my rest!
For in my sleep I saw that dove,
That gentle bird, whom thou dost love,

And call'st by thy own daughter's name—
Sir Leoline! I saw the same
Fluttering, and uttering fearful moan,
Among the green herbs in the forest alone.
Which when I saw and when I heard,
I wondered what might ail the bird
For nothing near it could I see,
Save the grass and green herbs underneath the old
540   tree.

"And in my dream methought I went
To search out what might there be found;
And what the sweet bird's trouble meant,
That thus lay fluttering on the ground.
I went and peered, and could descry
No cause for her distressful cry;
But yet for her dear lady's sake
I stooped, methought, the dove to take,
When lo! I saw a bright green snake
550 Coiled around its wings and neck.
Green as the herbs on which it couched,
Close by the dove's its head it crouched;
And with the dove it heaves and stirs,
Swelling its neck as she swelled hers!
I woke; it was the midnight hour,
The clock was echoing in the tower;
But though my slumber was gone by,
This dream it would not pass away—
It seems to live upon my eye!
560 And thence I vowed this self-same day,
With music strong and saintly song
To wander through the forest bare,
Lest aught unholy loiter there."

Thus Bracy said: the Baron, the while
Half-listening heard him with a smile;
Then turned to Lady Geraldine,
His eyes made up of wonder and love;
And said in courtly accents fine,
"Sweet maid, Lord Roland's beauteous dove,
570 With arms more strong than harp or song,
Thy sire and I will crush the snake!"
He kissed her forehead as he spake,
And Geraldine, in maiden wise,
Casting down her large bright eyes,

With blushing cheek and courtesy fine
She turned her from Sir Leoline;
Softly gathering up her train,
That o'er her right arm fell again;
And folded her arms across her chest,
And couched her head upon her breast,   580
And looked askance at Christabel—
Jesu Maria, shield her well!

A snake's small eye blinks dull and shy,
And the lady's eyes they shrunk in her head,
Each shrunk up to a serpent's eye,
And with somewhat of malice, and more of dread,
At Christabel she looked askance!—
One moment—and the sight was fled!
But Christabel in dizzy trance
Stumbling on the unsteady ground   590
Shuddered aloud, with a hissing sound;
And Geraldine again turned round,
And like a thing that sought relief,
Full of wonder and full of grief,
She rolled her large bright eyes divine
Wildly on Sir Leoline.

The maid, alas! her thoughts are gone,
She nothing sees—no sight but one!
The maid, devoid of guile and sin,
I know not how, in fearful wise   600
So deeply had she drunken in
That look, those shrunken serpent eyes,
That all her features were resigned
To this sole image in her mind;
And passively did imitate
That look of dull and treacherous hate!
And thus she stood, in dizzy trance,
Still picturing that look askance
With forced unconscious sympathy
Full before her father's view—   610
As far as such a look could be
In eyes so innocent and blue!

And when the trance was o'er, the maid
Paused awhile, and inly prayed:
Then falling at the Baron's feet,
"By my mother's soul do I entreat
That thou this woman send away!"
She said: and more she could not say:
For what she knew she could not tell,
O'ermastered by the mighty spell.   620

Why is thy cheek so wan and wild,
Sir Leoline? Thy only child
Lies at thy feet, thy joy, thy pride,
So fair, so innocent, so mild;
The same, for whom thy lady died!

O, by the pangs of her dear mother
Think thou no evil of thy child!

For her, and thee, and for no other,
She prayed the moment ere she died:
630 Prayed that the babe for whom she died,
Might prove her dear lord's joy and pride!
That prayer her deadly pangs beguiled,
　　Sir Leoline!
And wouldst thou wrong thy only child,
　　Her child and thine?

Within the Baron's heart and brain
If thoughts, like these, had any share,
They only swelled his rage and pain,
And did but work confusion there.
640 His heart was cleft with pain and rage,
His cheeks they quivered, his eyes were wild,
Dishonored thus in his old age;
Dishonored by his only child,
And all his hospitality
To the insulted daughter of his friend
By more than woman's jealousy
Brought thus to a disgraceful end—
He rolled his eye with stern regard
Upon the gentle minstrel bard,
650 And said in tones abrupt, austere—
"Why, Bracy! dost thou loiter here?
I bade thee hence!" The bard obeyed;
And turning from his own sweet maid,
The aged knight, Sir Leoline,
Led forth the lady Geraldine!

THE CONCLUSION TO PART 2

A little child,° a limber elf,
Singing, dancing to itself,
A fairy thing with red round cheeks,
That always finds, and never seeks,
660 Makes such a vision to the sight
As fills a father's eyes with light;
And pleasures flow in so thick and fast
Upon his heart, that he at last
Must needs express his love's excess
With words of unmeant bitterness.
Perhaps 'tis pretty to force together
Thoughts so all unlike each other;
To mutter and mock a broken charm,
To dally with wrong that does no harm.
670 Perhaps 'tis tender too and pretty
At each wild word to feel within
A sweet recoil of love and pity.
And what, if in a world of sin
(O sorrow and shame should this be true!)
Such giddiness of heart and brain
Comes seldom save from rage and pain,
So talks as it's mbst used to do.
(1797–1800; 1816)

656 **A little child, etc.** These lines have little connection with the rest of the
poem, and it is unlikely they were meant originally to be part of it. They were
sent to Southey in a letter dated May 6, 1801. They do not appear in any of the
three extant manuscripts of the poem

FROST AT MIDNIGHT

The frost performs its secret ministry,
Unhelped by any wind. The owlet's cry
Came loud—and hark, again! loud as before.
The inmates of my cottage, all at rest,
Have left me to that solitude, which suits
Abstruser musings: save that at my side
My cradled infant° slumbers peacefully.
'Tis calm indeed! so calm, that it disturbs
And vexes meditation with its strange
And extreme silentness. Sea, hill, and wood,　　10
This populous village! Sea, and hill, and wood,
With all the numberless goings-on of life,
Inaudible as dreams! the thin blue flame
Lies on my low-burnt fire, and quivers not;
Only that film,° which fluttered on the grate,
Still flutters there, the sole unquiet thing.
Methinks, its motion in this hush of nature
Gives it dim sympathies with me who live,
Making it a companionable form,
Whose puny flaps and freaks the idling spirit　　20
By its own moods interprets, everywhere
Echo or mirror seeking of itself,
And makes a toy of thought.

　　　　　　　　　But O! how oft,
How oft, at school,° with most believing mind,
Presageful, have I gazed upon the bars,
To watch that fluttering *stranger!* and as oft
With unclosed lids, already had I dreamt
Of my sweet birthplace, and the old church tower,
Whose bells, the poor man's only music, rang
From morn to evening, all the hot fair-day,　　30
So sweetly, that they stirred and haunted me

With a wild pleasure, falling on mine ear
Most like articulate sounds of things to come!
So gazed I, till the soothing things, I dreamt,
Lulled me to sleep, and sleep prolonged my dreams!
And so I brooded all the following morn,
Awed by the stern preceptor's° face, mine eye
Fixed with mock study on my swimming book:
Save if the door half opened, and I snatched
A hasty glance, and still my heart leaped up,　　40
For still I hoped to see the *stranger's* face,
Townsman, or aunt, or sister more beloved,
My playmate° when we both were clothed alike!

Dear babe, that sleepest cradled by my side,
Whose gentle breathings, heard in this deep calm,
Fill up the interspersèd vacancies
And momentary pauses of the thought!
My babe so beautiful! it thrills my heart

Frost at Midnight 7 **infant,** Hartley Coleridge, born in 1796　15 **film.** "In all
parts of the kingdom these films are called *strangers* and are supposed to portend
the arrival of some absent friend."—Coleridge's note　24 **school,** Christ's Hospital, London　37 **stern preceptor,** Boyer, Master of Christ's Hospital
43 **playmate,** Coleridge's sister Ann

With tender gladness, thus to look at thee,
50 And think that thou shalt learn far other lore,
And in far other scenes! For I was reared°
In the great city, pent 'mid cloisters dim,
And saw nought lovely but the sky and stars.
But *thou*, my babe! shalt wander like a breeze
By lakes and sandy shores, beneath the crags
Of ancient mountain, and beneath the clouds,
Which image in their bulk both lakes and shores
And mountain crags: so shalt thou see and hear
The lovely shapes and sounds intelligible
60 Of that eternal language, which thy God
Utters, who from eternity doth teach
Himself in all, and all things in himself.
Great universal Teacher! he shall mold
Thy spirit, and by giving make it ask.

Therefore all seasons shall be sweet to thee,
Whether the summer clothe the general earth
With greenness, or the redbreast sit and sing
Betwixt the tufts of snow on the bare branch
Of mossy apple tree, while the nigh thatch
70 Smokes in the sun-thaw; whether the eave-drops fall
Heard only in the trances of the blast,
Or if the secret ministry of frost
Shall hang them up in silent icicles,
Quietly shining to the quiet Moon.
(1798)

FEARS IN SOLITUDE

WRITTEN IN APRIL 1798,
DURING THE ALARM OF AN INVASION°

A green and silent spot, amid the hills,
A small and silent dell! O'er stiller place
No singing sky-lark ever poised himself.
The hills are heathy, save that swelling slope,
Which hath a gay and gorgeous covering on,
All golden with the never-bloomless furze,°
Which now blooms most profusely: but the dell,
Bathed by the mist, is fresh and delicate
As vernal corn-field, or the unripe flax,
10 When, through its half-transparent stalks, at eve,
The level sunshine glimmers with green light.
Oh! 'tis a quiet spirit-healing nook!
Which all, methinks, would love; but chiefly he,
The humble man, who, in his youthful years,
Knew just so much of folly, as had made
His early manhood more securely wise!
Here he might lie on fern or withered heath,
While from the singing lark (that sings unseen

The minstrelsy that solitude loves best),
And from the sun, and from the breezy air,   20
Sweet influences trembled o'er his frame;
And he, with many feelings, many thoughts,
Made up a meditative joy, and found
Religious meanings in the forms of Nature!
And so, his senses gradually wrapt
In a half sleep, he dreams of better worlds,
And dreaming hears thee still, O singing lark,
That singest like an angel in the clouds!

My God! it is a melancholy thing
For such a man, who would full fain preserve   30
His soul in calmness, yet perforce must feel
For all his human brethren—O my God!
It weighs upon the heart, that he must think
What uproar and what strife may now be stirring
This way or that way o'er these silent hills—
Invasion, and the thunder and the shout,
And all the crash of onset; fear and rage,
And undetermined conflict—even now,
Even now, perchance, and in his native isle:
Carnage and groans beneath this blessed sun!   40
We have offended, Oh! my countrymen!
We have offended very grievously,
And been most tyrannous. From east to west
A groan of accusation pierces Heaven!

The wretched plead against us; multitudes
Countless and vehement, the sons of God,
Our brethren! Like a cloud that travels on,
Steamed up from Cairo's swamps of pestilence,
Even so, my countrymen! have we gone forth
And borne to distant tribes slavery and pangs,   50
And, deadlier far, our vices, whose deep taint
With slow perdition murders the whole man,
His body and his soul! Meanwhile, at home,
All individual dignity and power
Engulfed in Courts, Committees, Institutions,
Associations and Societies,
A vain, speech-mouthing, speech-reporting Guild,
One Benefit-Club° for mutual flattery,
We have drunk up, demure as at a grace,
Pollutions from the brimming cup of wealth;   60
Contemptuous of all honourable rule,
Yet bartering freedom and the poor man's life
For gold, as at a market! The sweet words
Of Christian promise, words that even yet
Might stem destruction, were they wisely preached
Are muttered o'er by men, whose tones proclaim
How flat and wearisome they feel their trade:
Rank scoffers some, but most too indolent
To deem them falsehoods or to know their truth.
Oh! blasphemous! the Book of Life is made   70
A superstitious instrument, on which
We gabble o'er the oaths we mean to break,

51–53 **For I was reared, etc.** Cf. these lines with *The Prelude*, VII, 433–434: "I did not pine like one in cities bred,/As was thy melancholy lot, dear friend"
Fears in Solitude   invasion, in 1798 there were rumors of a planned invasion of England by the French   6 **furze**, an evergreen shrub with yellow flowers

58 **Benefit-Club**, an association whose members pay small sums regularly, so that they may receive financial aid in time of age or sickness

For all must swear—all and in every place,
College and wharf, council and justice-court;
All, all must swear, the briber and the bribed,
Merchant and lawyer, senator and priest,
The rich, the poor, the old man and the young;
All, all make up one scheme of perjury,
That faith doth reel; the very name of God
80 Sounds like a juggler's charm; and, bold with joy,
Forth from his dark and lonely hiding-place,
(Portentous sight!) the owlet Atheism,
Sailing on obscene wings athwart the noon,
Drops his blue-fringèd lids, and holds them close,
And hooting at the glorious sun in Heaven,
Cries out, 'Where is it?'

                    Thankless too for peace,
(Peace long preserved by fleets and perilous seas)
Secure from actual warfare, we have loved
To swell the war-whoop, passionate for war!
90 Alas! for ages ignorant of all
Its ghastlier workings, (famine or blue plague,
Battle, or siege, or flight through wintry snows,)
We, this whole people, have been clamorous
For war and bloodshed; animating sports,
The which we pay for as a thing to talk of,
Spectators and not combatants! No guess
Anticipative of a wrong unfelt,
No speculation on contingency,
However dim and vague, too vague and dim
100 To yield a justifying cause; and forth,
(Stuffed out with big preamble, holy names,
And adjurations of the God in Heaven,)
We send our mandates for the certain death
Of thousands and ten thousands! Boys and girls,
And women, that would groan to see a child
Pull off an insect's leg, all read of war,
The best amusement for our morning meal!
The poor wretch, who has learnt his only prayers
From curses, who knows scarcely words enough
110 To ask a blessing from his Heavenly Father,
Becomes a fluent phraseman, absolute
And technical in victories and defeats,
And all our dainty terms for fratricide;
Terms which we trundle smoothly o'er our tongues
Like mere abstractions, empty sounds to which
We join no feeling and attach no form!
As if the soldier died without a wound;
As if the fibres of this godlike frame
Were gored without a pang; as if the wretch,
120 Who fell in battle, doing bloody deeds,
Passed off to Heaven, translated and not killed;
As though he had no wife to pine for him,
No God to judge him! Therefore, evil days
Are coming on us, O my countrymen!
And what if all-avenging Providence,
Strong and retributive, should make us know
The meaning of our words, force us to feel

The desolation and the agony
Of our fierce doings?

                    Spare us yet awhile,
Father and God! O! spare us yet awhile!   130
Oh! let not English women drag their flight
Fainting beneath the burthen of their babes,
Of the sweet infants, that but yesterday
Laughed at the breast! Sons, brothers, husbands, all
Who ever gazed with fondness on the forms
Which grew up with you round the same fire-side,
And all who ever heard the sabbath-bells
Without the infidel's scorn, make yourselves pure!
Stand forth! be men! repel an impious foe,
Impious and false, a light yet cruel race,   140

Who laugh away all virtue. mingling mirth
With deeds of murder; and still promising
Freedom, themselves too sensual to be free,
Poison life's amities, and cheat the heart
Of faith and quiet hope, and all that soothes,
And all that lifts the spirit! Stand we forth;
Render them back upon the insulted ocean,
And let them toss as idly on its waves
As the vile sea-weed, which some mountain-blast
Swept from our shores! And oh! may we return   150
Not with a drunken triumph, but with fear,
Repenting of the wrongs with which we stung
So fierce a foe to frenzy!

                    I have told,
O Britons! O my brethren! I have told
Most bitter truth, but without bitterness.
Nor deem my zeal or factious or mistimed;
For never can true courage dwell with them,
Who, playing tricks with conscience, dare not look
At their own vices. We have been too long
Dupes of a deep delusion! Some, belike,   160
Groaning with restless enmity, expect
All change from change of constituted power;
As if a Government had been a robe,
On which our vice and wretchedness were tagged
Like fancy-points and fringes, with the robe
Pulled off at pleasure. Fondly these attach
A radical causation to a few
Poor drudges of chastising Providence,
Who borrow all their hues and qualities
From our own folly and rank wickedness,   170
Which gave them birth and nursed them. Others,
     meanwhile,
Dote with a mad idolatry; and all
Who will not fall before their images,
And yield them worship, they are enemies
Even of their country!

                  Such have I been deemed.—
But, O dear Britain! O my Mother Isle!

Needs must thou prove a name most dear and holy
To me, a son, a brother, and a friend,
A husband, and a father! who revere
180 All bonds of natural love, and find them all
Within the limits of thy rocky shores.
O native Britain! O my Mother Isle!
How shouldst thou prove aught else but dear and holy
To me, who from thy lakes and mountain-hills,
Thy clouds, thy quiet dales, thy rocks and seas,
Have drunk in all my intellectual life,
All sweet sensations, all ennobling thoughts,
All adoration of the God in nature,
All lovely and all honourable things,
190 Whatever makes this mortal spirit feel
The joy and greatness of its future being?
There lives nor form nor feeling in my soul
Unborrowed from my country! O divine
And beauteous island! thou hast been my sole
And most magnificent temple, in the which
I walk with awe, and sing my stately songs,
Loving the God that made me!—

                              May my fears,
My filial fears, be vain! and may the vaunts
And menace of the vengeful enemy
200 Pass like the gust, that roared and died away
In the distant tree: which heard, and only heard
In this low dell, bowed not the delicate grass.

    But now the gentle dew-fall sends abroad
The fruit-like perfume of the golden furze:
The light has left the summit of the hill,
Though still a sunny gleam lies beautiful,
Aslant the ivied beacon. Now farewell,
Farewell, awhile, O soft and silent spot!
On the green sheep-track, up the heathy hill,
210 Homeward I wind my way; and lo! recalled
From bodings that have well-nigh wearied me,
I find myself upon the brow, and pause
Startled! And after lonely sojourning
In such a quiet and surrounded nook,
This burst of prospect, here the shadowy main,
Dim-tinted, there the mighty majesty
Of that huge amphitheatre of rich
And elmy fields, seems like society—
Conversing with the mind, and giving it
220 A livelier impulse and a dance of thought!
And now, belovéd Stowey!° I behold
Thy church-tower, and, methinks, the four huge elms
Clustering, which mark the mansion of my friend;°
And close behind them, hidden from my view,
Is my own lowly cottage, where my babe
And my babe's mother dwell in peace! With light
And quickened footsteps thitherward I tend,
Remembering thee, O green and silent dell!

221 **Stowey,** Nether Stowey, the village where Coleridge lived   223 **my friend,** Thomas Poole

And grateful, that by nature's quietness
And solitary musings, all my heart
Is softened, and made worthy to indulge   230
Love, and the thoughts that yearn for human kind.
(1798; 1798)

KUBLA KHAN

OR A VISION° IN A DREAM.
A FRAGMENT

Kubla Khan contained in its first printing (1816) a rather lengthy and colorful preface, of which the following is the most significant part:

    "In the summer of the year 1797, the author, then in ill health, had retired to a lonely farmhouse between Porlock and Lynton, on the Exmoor confines of Somerset and Devonshire. In consequence of a slight indisposition, an anodyne had been prescribed, from the effects of which he fell asleep in his chair at the moment he was reading the following sentence, or words of the same substance, in *Purchas's Pilgrimage:* 'Here the Khan Kubla commanded a palace to be built, and a stately garden thereunto. And thus ten miles of fertile ground were inclosed with a wall.' The author continued for about three hours in a profound sleep, at least of the external senses, during which time he has the most vivid confidence that he could not have composed less than from two to three hundred lines; if that indeed can be called composition in which all the images rose up before him as *things,* with a parallel production of the correspondent expressions, without any sensation or consciousness of effort. On awaking he appeared to himself to have a distinct recollection of the whole, and taking his pen, ink, and paper, instantly and eagerly wrote down the lines that are here preserved. At this moment he was unfortunately called out by a person on business from Porlock, and detained by him above an hour, and on his return to his room, found, to his no small surprise and mortification, that though he still retained some vague and dim recollection of the general purport of the vision, yet, with the exception of some eight or ten scattered lines and images, all the rest had passed away like the images on the surface of a stream into which a stone had been cast, but, alas! without the after restoration of the latter!"

In Xanadu° did Kubla Khan°
A stately pleasure-dome decree:
Where Alph, the sacred river, ran
Through caverns measureless to man
    Down to a sunless sea.

Kubla Khan   1 **Xanadu,** region in Tartary   **Kubla Khan,** Cham or Emperor Kubla. He founded the Mogul dynasty in China in the thirteenth century

So twice five miles of fertile ground
With walls and towers were girdled round:
And here were gardens bright with sinuous rills,
Where blossomed many an incense-bearing tree;
10 And here were forests ancient as the hills,
Enfolding sunny spots of greenery.

But oh! that deep romantic chasm which slanted
Down the green hill athwart a cedarn cover!
A savage place! as holy and enchanted
As e'er beneath a waning moon was haunted
By woman wailing for her demon-lover!
And from this chasm, with ceaseless turmoil seething,
As if this earth in fast thick pants were breathing,
A mighty fountain momently° was forced;
20 Amid whose swift half-intermitted burst
Huge fragments vaulted like rebounding hail,
Or chaffy grain beneath the thresher's flail:
And 'mid these dancing rocks at once and ever
It flung up momently the sacred river.
Five miles meandering with a mazy motion
Through wood and dale the sacred river ran,
Then reached the caverns measureless to man,
And sank in tumult to a lifeless ocean:
And 'mid this tumult Kubla heard from far
30 Ancestral voices prophesying war!
    The shadow of the dome of pleasure
    Floated midway on the waves;
    Where was heard the mingled measure
    From the fountain and the caves.
It was a miracle of rare device,
A sunny pleasure-dome with caves of ice!

    A damsel with a dulcimer
    In a vision once I saw:
    It was an Abyssinian maid,
40 And on her dulcimer she played,
    Singing of Mount Abora.°
    Could I revive within me,
    Her symphony and song,
    To such a deep delight 'twould win me,
That with music loud and long,
I would build that dome in air,
That sunny dome! those caves of ice!
And all who heard should see them there,
And all should cry, Beware! Beware!
50 His flashing eyes, his floating hair!
Weave a circle round him thrice,
And close your eyes with holy dread,
For he on honey-dew hath fed,
And drunk the milk of Paradise.
(1797; 1816)

DEJECTION: AN ODE

This poem originated in a verse letter to Sara Hutchinson, sister of Wordsworth's fiancée, after Coleridge had heard the first stanzas of his friend's great *Intimations* ode in April 1802. Later the poem was addressed to Wordsworth and printed in *The Morning Post* on his wedding day, October 4, 1802, which was also the seventh anniversary of Coleridge's unhappy marriage to Sara Fricker. In this version Wordsworth was referred to as "Edmund," and that name occurred where "Lady" is found in the present text and where "Otway" appears in line 120. A still earlier version contained the name "William" throughout. An estrangement between the two poets was the cause of the later substitutions.

Late, late yestreen I saw the new Moon
    With the old Moon in her arms;
And I fear, I fear, my Master dear!
    We shall have a deadly storm.
                    Ballad of Sir Patrick Spence

I

Well! If the Bard was weather-wise, who made
    The grand old ballad of Sir Patrick Spence,
    This night, so tranquil now, will not go hence
Unroused by winds, that ply a busier trade
Than those which mold yon cloud in lazy flakes,
Or the dull sobbing draft, that moans and rakes
    Upon the strings of this Aeolian lute,°
    Which better far were mute;
    For lo! the new-moon winter bright!
    And overspread with phantom light,   10
    (With swimming phantom light o'erspread
    But rimmed and circled by a silver thread)
I see the old moon in her lap, foretelling
    The coming-on of rain and squally blast.
And oh! that even now the gust were swelling,
    And the slant night-shower driving loud and fast!
Those sounds which oft have raised me, whilst they
        awed,
    And sent my soul abroad,
Might now perhaps their wonted impulse give,
Might startle this dull pain, and make it move and live!   20

II

A grief without a pang, void, dark, and drear,
    A stifled, drowsy, unimpassioned grief,
    Which finds no natural outlet, no relief,
        In word, or sigh, or tear—
O Lady!° in this wan and heartless mood,
To other thoughts by yonder throstle wooed,

All this long eve, so balmy and serene,
Have I been gazing on the western sky,
And its peculiar tint of yellow green:
30 And still I gaze—and with how blank an eye!
And those thin clouds above, in flakes and bars,
That give away their motion to the stars;
Those stars, that glide behind them or between,
Now sparkling, now bedimmed, but always seen:
Yon crescent moon, as fixed as if it grew
In its own cloudless, starless lake of blue;
I see them all so excellently fair,
I see, not feel, how beautiful they are!

III

My genial spirits fail;
40   And what can these avail
To lift the smothering weight from off my breast?
It were a vain endeavor,
Though I should gaze forever
On that green light that lingers in the west:
I may not hope from outward forms to win
The passion and the life, whose fountains are within.

IV

O Lady! we receive but what we give,
And in our life alone does Nature live:
Ours is her wedding garment, ours her shroud!
50   And would we aught behold, of higher worth,
Than that inanimate cold world allowed
To the poor loveless ever-anxious crowd,
Ah! from the soul itself must issue forth
A light, a glory, a fair luminous cloud
Enveloping the earth—
And from the soul itself must there be sent
A sweet and potent voice, of its own birth,
Of all sweet sounds the life and element!

V

O pure of heart! thou need'st not ask of me
60 What this strong music in the soul may be!
What, and wherein it doth exist,
This light this glory, this fair luminous mist,
This beautiful and beauty-making power.
Joy, virtuous Lady! Joy that ne'er was given,
Save to the pure, and in their purest hour,
Life, and Life's effluence, cloud at once and shower,
Joy, Lady! is the spirit and the power,
Which wedding Nature to us gives in dower,
A new earth and new heaven,
70 Undreamt of by the sensual and the proud—
Joy is the sweet voice, Joy the luminous cloud—
We in ourselves rejoice!
And thence flows all that charms or ear or sight,
All melodies the echoes of that voice,
All colors a suffusion from that light.

VI

There was a time when, though my path was rough,
This joy within me dallied with distress,
And all misfortunes were but as the stuff
Whence Fancy made me dreams of happiness:
For Hope grew round me, like the twining vine,   80
And fruits, and foliage, not my own, seemed mine.
But now afflictions bow me down to earth:
Nor care I that they rob me of my mirth;
But oh! each visitation
Suspends what nature gave me at my birth,
My shaping spirit of Imagination.
For not to think of what I needs must feel,
But to be still and patient, all I can;
And haply by abstruse research to steal
From my own nature all the natural man—   90
This was my sole resource, my only plan:
Till that which suits a part infects the whole,
And now is almost grown the habit of my soul.

VII

Hence, viper thoughts, that coil around my mind,
Reality's dark dream!
I turn from you, and listen to the wind,
Which long has raved unnoticed. What a scream
Of agony by torture lengthened out
That lute sent forth! Thou Wind, that rav'st without,
Bare crag, or mountain-tairn, or blasted tree,   100
Or pine-grove whither woodman never clomb,
Or lonely house, long held the witches' home,
Methinks were fitter instruments for thee,
Mad Lutanist! who in this month of showers,
Of dark-brown gardens, and of peeping flowers,
Mak'st Devils' yule, with worse than wintry song,
The blossoms, buds, and timorous leaves among.
Thou actor, perfect in all tragic sounds!
Thou mighty poet, e'en to frenzy bold!
What tell'st thou now about?   110
'Tis of the rushing of an host in rout,
With groans of trampled men, with smarting
wounds—
At once they groan with pain, and shudder with the
cold!
But hush! there is a pause of deepest silence!
And all that noise, as of a rushing crowd,
With groans, and tremulous shudderings—all is
over—
It tells another tale, with sounds less deep and loud!
A tale of less affright,
And tempered with delight,
As Otway's° self had framed the tender lay—   120
'Tis of a little child°
Upon a lonesome wild,

120 **Otway,** Thomas Otway (1652–1685), Restoration tragic playwright, author of *The Orphan* 121 **a little child,** an allusion to Wordsworth's *Lucy Gray*

Not far from home, but she hath lost her way:
And now moans low in bitter grief and fear,
And now screams loud, and hopes to make her mother
    hear.

VIII

'Tis midnight, but small thoughts have I of sleep:
Full seldom may my friend such vigils keep!
Visit her, gentle Sleep! with wings of healing,
  And may this storm be but a mountain-birth,
130 May all the stars hang bright above her dwelling,
    Silent as though they watched the sleeping earth!
      With light heart may she rise,
      Gay fancy, cheerful eyes,
    Joy lift her spirit, joy attune her voice;
To her may all things live, from pole to pole,
Their life the eddying of her living soul!
  O simple spirit, guided from above,
Dear Lady! friend devoutest of my choice,
Thus mayest thou ever, evermore rejoice.
(1802)

THE PAINS OF SLEEP

Ere on my bed my limbs I lay,
It hath not been my use to pray
With moving lips or bended knees;
But silently, by slow degrees,
My spirit I to Love compose,
In humble trust mine eye-lids close,
With reverential resignation,
No wish conceived, no thought exprest,
Only a sense of supplication;
10 A sense o'er all my soul imprest
That I am weak, yet not unblest,
Since in me, round me, every where
Eternal Strength and Wisdom are.

But yester-night I prayed aloud
In anguish and in agony,
Up-starting from the fiendish crowd
Of shapes and thoughts that tortured me:
A lurid light, a trampling throng,
Sense of intolerable wrong,
20 And whom I scorned, those only strong!

Thirst of revenge, the powerless will
Still baffled, and yet burning still!
Desire with loathing strangely mixed
On wild or hateful objects fixed.
Fantastic passions! maddening brawl!
And shame and terror over all!
Deeds to be hid which were not hid,
Which all confused I could not know
Whether I suffered, or I did:
30 For all seemed guilt, remorse or woe,

My own or others still the same
Life-stifling fear, soul-stifling shame.

So two nights passed: the night's dismay
Saddened and stunned the coming day.
Sleep, the wide blessing, seemed to me
Distemper's worst calamity.
The third night, when my own loud scream
Had waked me from the fiendish dream,
O'ercome with sufferings strange and wild,
I wept as I had been a child;   40
And having thus by tears subdued
My anguish to a milder mood,
Such punishments, I said, were due
To natures deepliest stained with sin,—
For aye entempesting° anew
The unfathomable hell within,
The horror of their deeds to view,
To know and loathe, yet wish and do!
Such griefs with such men well agree,
But wherefore, wherefore fall on me?   50
To be beloved is all I need,
And whom I love, I love indeed.
(1803; 1816)

ON DONNE'S POETRY

With Donne, whose muse on dromedary trots,
Wreathe iron pokers into true-love knots;
Rhyme's sturdy cripple, fancy's maze and clue,
Wit's forge and fire-blast, meaning's press and screw.
(?1818)

from BIOGRAPHIA LITERARIA

CHARACTERISTICS OF SHAKESPEARE'S DRAMAS

In lectures of which amusement forms a large part of
the object, there are some peculiar difficulties. The
architect places his foundation out of sight, and the
musician tunes his instrument before he makes his
appearance; but the lecturer has to try his chords in the
presence of the assembly, an operation not likely, indeed, to produce much pleasure, but yet indispensably
necessary to a right understanding of the subject to be
developed.

    Poetry in essence is as familiar to barbarous as to 10
civilized nations. The Laplander and the savage Indian
are cheered by it as well as the inhabitants of London
and Paris; its spirit takes up and incorporates surrounding materials, as a plant clothes itself with soil

***

Pains of Sleep 45 **entempesting,** bringing into the condition of a tempest

and climate, whilst it exhibits the working of a vital principle within, independent of all accidental circumstances. And to judge with fairness of an author's works, we ought to distinguish what is inward and essential from what is outward and circumstantial. It is
20 essential to poetry that it be simple,° and appeal to the elements and primary laws of our nature; that it be sensuous, and by its imagery elicit truth at a flash; that it be impassioned, and be able to move our feelings and awaken our affections. In comparing different poets with each other, we should inquire which have brought into the fullest play our imagination and our reason, or have created the greatest excitement and produced the completest harmony. If we consider great exquisiteness of language and sweetness of meter alone, it is
30 impossible to deny to Pope the character of a delightful writer; but whether he be a poet must depend upon our definition of the word; and, doubtless, if everything that pleases be poetry, Pope's satires and epistles must be poetry. This I must say, that poetry, as distinguished from other modes of composition, does not rest in meter, and that it is not poetry if it make no appeal to our passions or our imagination. One character belongs to all true poets, that they write from a principle within, not originating in anything without;
40 and that the true poet's work in its form, its shapings, and its modifications, is distinguished from all other works that assume to belong to the class of poetry, as a natural from an artificial flower, or as the mimic garden of a child from an enameled meadow. In the former the flowers are broken from their stems and stuck into the ground; they are beautiful to the eye and fragrant to the sense, but their colors soon fade, and their odor is transient as the smile of the planter; while the meadow may be visited again and again with re-
50 newed delight; its beauty is innate in the soil, and its bloom is of the freshness of nature.

The next ground of critical judgment, and point of comparison, will be as to how far a given poet has been influenced by accidental circumstances. As a living poet must surely write, not for the ages past, but for that in which he lives, and those which are to follow, it is, on the one hand, natural that he should not violate, and on the other, necessary that he should not depend on, the mere manners and modes of his day. See how
60 little does Shakespeare leave us to regret that he was born in his particular age! The great era in modern times was what is called the Restoration of Letters; the ages preceding it are called the dark ages; but it would be more wise, perhaps, to call them the ages in which we were in the dark. It is usually overlooked that the supposed dark period was not universal, but partial and successive, or alternate; that the dark age of England was not the dark age of Italy, but that one country

was in its light and vigor, whilst another was in its gloom and bondage. But no sooner had the Reforma- 70 tion sounded through Europe like the blast of an archangel's trumpet, than from king to peasant there arose an enthusiasm for knowledge; the discovery of a manuscript became the subject of an embassy; Erasmus° read by moonlight, because he could not afford a torch, and begged a penny, not for the love of charity, but for the love of learning. The three great points of attention were religion, morals, and taste; men of genius as well as men of learning, who in this age need to be so widely distinguished, then alike became 80 copyists of the ancients; and this, indeed, was the only way by which the taste of mankind could be improved, or their understandings informed. Whilst Dante° imagined himself a humble follower of Virgil,° and Ariosto° of Homer,° they were both unconscious of that greater power working within them, which in many points carried them beyond their supposed originals. All great discoveries bear the stamp of the age in which they are made; hence we perceive the effects of the purer religion of the moderns, visible for the most part in their 90 lives; and in reading their works we should not content ourselves with the mere narratives of events long since passed, but should learn to apply their maxims and conduct to ourselves.

Having intimated that times and manners lend their form and pressure to genius, let me once more draw a slight parallel between the ancient and modern stage, the stages of Greece and of England. The Greeks were polytheists; their religion was local; almost the only object of their knowledge, art, and taste was their 100 gods; and, accordingly, their productions were, if the expression may be allowed, statuesque, whilst those of the moderns are picturesque. The Greeks reared a structure which in its parts, and as a whole, filled the mind with the calm and elevated impression of perfect beauty, and symmetrical proportions. The moderns also produced a whole, a more striking whole; but it was by blending materials and fusing the parts together. And as the Pantheon° is to York Minster or Westminster Abbey, so is Sophocles° compared with 110 Shakespeare; in the one a completeness, a satisfaction, an excellence, on which the mind rests with complacency; in the other a multitude of interlaced materials, great and little, magnificent and mean, accompanied, indeed, with the sense of a falling short of perfection, and yet, at the same time, so promising of our social and individual progression that we would not, if we could, exchange it for that repose of the mind which swells on the forms of symmetry in the acquiescent admiration of grace. This general characteristic of the 120 ancient and modern drama might be illustrated by a

Characteristics of Shakespeare's Dramas   20–23 simple . . . impassioned. Milton defined poetry as "simple, sensuous, passionate." Cf. the definitions in Shelley's Defense of Poetry and Wordsworth's Preface to Lyrical Ballads

74 Erasmus, Dutch classical scholar (1466–1536)   83 Dante, Italian poet (1265–1321)   84 Virgil, Roman poet (70–19 B.C.)   Ariosto, Italian poet (1474–1533)   85 Homer, ancient Greek poet, reputed author of the Iliad and the Odyssey   109 Pantheon, circular temple in Rome, built in 27 B.C. 110 Sophocles, Greek tragic dramatist of the fifth century B.C.

parallel of the ancient and modern music, the one consisting of melody arising from a succession only of pleasing sounds, the modern embracing harmony also, the result of combination and the effect of a whole.

I have said, and I say it again, that great as was the genius of Shakespeare, his judgment was at least equal to it. Of this anyone will be convinced, who attentively considers those points in which the dramas of Greece and England differ, from the dissimilitude of circumstances by which each was modified and influenced. The Greek stage had its origin in the ceremonies of a sacrifice, such as of the goat° to Bacchus, whom we most erroneously regard as merely the jolly god of wine; for among the ancients he was venerable, as the symbol of that power which acts without our consciousness in the vital energies of nature—the *vinum mundi*°—as Apollo° was that of the conscious agency of our intellectual being. The heroes of old under the influences of this Bacchic enthusiasm performed more than human actions; hence tales of the favorite champions soon passed into dialogue. On the Greek stage the chorus was always before the audience; the curtain was never dropped, as we should say; and change of place being therefore, in general, impossible, the absurd notion of condemning it merely as improbable in itself was never entertained by anyone. If we can believe ourselves at Thebes in one act, we may believe ourselves at Athens in the next. If a story lasts twenty-four hours or twenty-four years, it is equally improbable. There seems to be no just boundary but what the feelings prescribe. But on the Greek stage where the same persons were perpetually before the audience, great judgment was necessary in venturing on any such change. The poets never, therefore, attempted to impose on the senses by bringing places to men, but they did bring men to places, as in the well known instance in the *Eumenides*,° where, during an evident retirement of the chorus from the orchestra, the scene is changed to Athens, and Orestes° is first introduced in the temple of Minerva,° and the chorus of Furies° come in afterwards in pursuit of him.

In the Greek drama there were no formal divisions into scenes and acts; there were no means, therefore, of allowing for the necessary lapse of time between one part of the dialogue and another, and unity of time in a strict sense was, of course, impossible. To overcome that difficulty of accounting for time, which is effected on the modern stage by dropping a curtain, the judgment and great genius of the ancients supplied music and measured motion, and with the lyric ode filled up the vacuity. In the story of the *Agamemnon* of Aeschylus, the capture of Troy is supposed to be announced by a fire lighted on the Asiatic shore and the

transmission of the signal by successive beacons to Mycenae. The signal is first seen at the 21st line, and the herald from Troy itself enters at the 486th, and Agamemnon himself at the 783rd line. But the practical absurdity of this was not felt by the audience, who, in imagination stretched the minutes into hours, while they listened to the lofty narrative odes of the chorus which almost entirely filled up the interspace. Another fact deserves attention here, namely, that regularly on the Greek stage a drama, or acted story, consisted in reality of three dramas,° called together a trilogy, and performed consecutively in the course of one day. Now you may conceive a tragedy of Shakespeare's as a trilogy connected in one single representation. Divide *Lear* into three parts, and each would be a play with the ancients; or take the three Aeschylean dramas of *Agamemnon,* and divide them into, or call them, as many acts, and they together would be one play. The first act would comprise the usurpation of Aegisthus and the murder of Agamemnon; the second, the revenge of Orestes and the murder of his mother; and the third, the penance and absolution of Orestes;—occupying a period of twenty-two years.

The stage in Shakespeare's time was a naked room with a blanket for a curtain; but he made it a field for monarchs. That law of unity, which has its foundations, not in the factitious necessity of custom, but in nature itself, the unity of feeling, is everywhere and at all times observed by Shakespeare in his plays. Read *Romeo and Juliet:* all is youth and spring; youth with its follies, its virtues, its precipitancies; spring with its odors, its flowers, and its transiency. It is one and the same feeling that commences, goes through, and ends the play. The old men, the Capulets and the Montagues, are not common old men; they have an eagerness, a heartiness, a vehemence, the effect of spring; with Romeo, his change of passion, his sudden marriage, and his rash death, are all the effects of youth; whilst in Juliet, love has all that is tender and melancholy in the nightingale, all that is voluptuous in the rose, with whatever is sweet in the freshness of spring; but it ends with a long deep sigh like the last breeze of the Italian evening. This unity of feeling and character pervades every drama of Shakespeare.

It seems to me that his plays are distinguished from those of all other dramatic poets by the following characteristics:

1. Expectation in preference to surprise. It is like the true reading of the passage: "God said, Let there be light, and there was *light*";° not there *was* light. As the feeling with which we startle at a shooting star compared with that of watching the sunrise at the preestablished moment, such and so low is surprise compared with expectation.

2. Signal adherence to the great law of nature, that

133 **goat,** common sacrificial victim in the orgies of the devotees of Bacchus, god of wine and fertility   138 **vinum mundi,** wine of the world   **Apollo,** god of poetry and music   158 **Eumenides,** tragedy by Aeschylus, Greek dramatist of the fifth century B.C.; the incident occurs in Act V, 230–239   160 **Orestes,** son of the Greek king Agamemnon and Clytemnestra; he killed his mother and her lover Aegisthus in revenge for their murder of Agamemnon   161 **Minerva,** goddess of wisdom   162 **Furies,** deities of vengeance in Greek mythology

185 **three dramas,** Agamemnon, Choephorai, and Eumenides   223–224 **God . . . light,** from Genesis, 1:3   237 **precepts to Bertram,** in All's Well That Ends Well, I, i, 14

all opposites tend to attract and temper each other. Passion in Shakespeare generally displays libertinism, but involves morality; and if there are exceptions to this, they are, independently of their intrinsic value, all of them indicative of individual character, and, like the farewell admonitions of a parent, have an end beyond the parental relation. Thus the Countess's beautiful precepts to Bertram,° by elevating her character, raise that of Helena her favorite, and soften down the point in her which Shakespeare does not mean us not to see, but to see and to forgive, and at length to justify. And so it is in Polonius,° who is the personified memory of wisdom no longer actually possessed. This admirable character is always misrepresented on the stage. Shakespeare never intended to exhibit him as a buffoon; for although it was natural that Hamlet (a young man of fire and genius, detesting formality, and disliking Polonius on political grounds, as imagining that he had assisted his uncle in his usurpation) should express himself satirically; yet this must not be taken as exactly the poet's conception of him. In Polonius a certain induration of character had arisen from long habits of business; but take his advice to Laertes,° and Ophelia's reverence for his memory, and we shall see that he was meant to be represented as a statesman somewhat past his faculties—his recollections of life all full of wisdom, and showing a knowledge of human nature, whilst what immediately takes place before him and escapes from him is indicative of weakness.

But as in Homer all the deities are in armor, even Venus,° so in Shakespeare all the characters are strong. Hence real folly and dullness are made by him the vehicles of wisdom. There is no difficulty for one being a fool to imitate a fool; but to be, remain, and speak like a wise man and a great wit, and yet so as to give a vivid representation of a veritable fool—*hic labor, hoc opus est.*° A drunken constable is not uncommon, nor hard to draw; but see and examine what goes to make up a Dogberry.°

3. Keeping at all times in the high road of life. Shakespeare has no innocent adulteries, no interesting incests, no virtuous vice; he never renders that amiable which religion and reason alike teach us to detest, or clothe impurity in the garb of virtue, like Beaumont and Fletcher,° the Kotzebues° of the day. Shakespeare's fathers are roused by ingratitude, his husbands stung by unfaithfulness; in him, in short, the affections are wounded in those points in which all may, nay, must, feel. Let the morality of Shakespeare be contrasted with that of the writers of his own, or the succeeding, age, or of those of the present day, who boast their superiority in this respect. No one can dispute that the result of such a comparison is altogether in favor of Shakespeare; even the letters of women of high rank in his age were often coarser than his writings. If he occasionally disgusts a keen sense of delicacy, he never injures the mind; he neither excites nor flatters passion in order to degrade the subject of it; he does not use the faulty thing for a faulty purpose, nor carries on warfare against virtue by causing wickedness to appear as no wickedness through the medium of a morbid sympathy with the unfortunate. In Shakespeare vice never walks as in twilight; nothing is purposely out of its place; he inverts not the order of nature and propriety, does not make every magistrate a drunkard or glutton, nor every poor man meek, humane, and temperate; he has no benevolent butchers, nor any sentimental rat-catchers.

4. Independence of the dramatic interest on the plot. The interest in the plot is always in fact on account of the characters, not *vice versa,* as in almost all other writers; the plot is a mere canvass and no more. Hence arises the true justification of the same stratagem being used in regard to Benedict and Beatrice, the vanity in each being alike. Take away from the *Much Ado About Nothing* all that which is not indispensable to the plot, either as having little to do with it, or, at best, like Dogberry and his comrades, forced into the service when any other less ingeniously absurd watchmen and night-constables would have answered the mere necessities of the action; take away Benedict, Beatrice, Dogberry, and the reaction of the former on the character of Hero, and what will remain? In other writers the main agent of the plot is always the prominent character; in Shakespeare it is so, or is not so, as the character is in itself calculated, or not calculated, to form the plot. Don John is the main-spring of the plot of this play; but he is merely shown and then withdrawn.

5. Independence of the interest on the story as the groundwork of the plot. Hence Shakespeare never took the trouble of inventing stories. It was enough for him to select from those that had been already invented or recorded such as had one or other, or both, of two recommendations, namely, suitableness to his particular purpose, and their being parts of popular tradition—names of which we had often heard, and of their fortunes, and as to which all we wanted was, to see the man himself. So it is just the man himself, the Lear, the Shylock, the Richard, that Shakespeare makes us for the first time acquainted with. Omit the first scene in *Lear*, and yet everything will remain; so the first and second scenes in *The Merchant of Venice.* Indeed it is universally true.

6. Interfusion of the lyrical (that which in its very essence is poetical) not only with the dramatic, as in the plays of Metastasio,° where at the end of the scenes comes the *aria*° as the *exit* speech of the character, but also in and through the dramatic. Songs in Shake-

241 **Polonius,** the King's chamberlain and father of Ophelia and Laertes in *Hamlet*
252 **advice to Laertes,** in Act I, iii, 58–81   260 **Venus,** goddess of love
265–266 **hic . . . est,** this is the labor, this is the work (*Aeneid,* VI, 129)
268 **Dogberry,** stupid constable in *Much Ado About Nothing*   274 **Beaumont and Fletcher,** Francis Beaumont (1584–1616) and John Fletcher (1579–1625), mainly writers of tragicomedies and romances   **Kotzebues,** August Kotzebue (1761–1819), German writer of sentimental plays popular in England

336 **Metastasio,** Italian lyric dramatist (1698–1782)   337 **aria,** elaborate melody sung by a single voice

speare are introduced as songs only, just as songs are in real life, beautifully as some of them are characteristic of the person who has sung or called for them, as Desdemona's "Willow,"° and Ophelia's wild snatches, and the sweet carollings in *As You Like It*. But the whole of the *Midsummer-Night's Dream* is one continued specimen of the dramatized lyrical. And observe how exquisitely the dramatic of Hotspur:

Marry and I'm glad on't with all my heart;
I'd rather be a kitten and cry mew, &c.

melts away into the lyric of Mortimer:

I understand thy looks: that pretty Welsh
Which thou pour'st down from these swelling heavens
I am too perfect in, &c.

1 Henry IV, III, i

7. The characters of the *dramatis personae*, like those in real life, are to be inferred by the reader; they are not told to him. And it is well worth remarking that Shakespeare's characters, like those in real life, are very commonly misunderstood, and almost always

342 Willow, song of forsaken love in Othello, IV, iii, 41–57

understood by different persons in different ways. The causes are the same in either case. If you take only what the friends of the character say, you may be deceived, and still more so, if that which his enemies say; nay, even the character himself sees through the medium of his character, and not exactly as he is. Take all together, not omitting a shrewd hint from the clown, or the fool, and perhaps your impression will be right; and you may know whether you have in fact discovered the poet's own idea, by all the speeches receiving light from it, and attesting its reality by reflecting it.

Lastly, in Shakespeare the heterogeneous is united, as it is in nature. You must not suppose a pressure or passion always acting on or in the character. Passion in Shakespeare is that by which the individual is distinguished from others, not that which makes a different kind of him. Shakespeare followed the main march of the human affections. He entered into no analysis of the passions or faiths of men, but assured himself that such and such passions and faiths were grounded in our common nature, and not in the mere accidents of ignorance or disease. This is an important consideration and constitutes our Shakespeare the morning star, the guide and the pioneer, of true philosophy.
(1815; 1817)

CHARLES LAMB
1775–1834

Charles Lamb was born in London on February 10, 1775, the son of a clerk in the office of one of the leading lawyers of the city. His schooling was at Christ's Hospital, where Coleridge and Lamb were schoolmates. A speech impediment prevented Lamb from taking examinations for honors, and he was therefore excluded from taking a degree. He quit school at the age of fourteen and began to earn a living first at the South Sea House and then three years later at the East India House, where he became a valuable accountant for that great commercial organization upon which rested the foundations of the British Empire in the Orient. His professional life was spent in this position.

His personal life was marred by what Wordsworth called "strange calamities." He spent six weeks in an asylum (1795–1796), and the next year his only sister Mary killed their mother in a fit of madness. After being institutionalized, she was released to the care of her brother but was subject to recurrent attacks during which she had to be temporarily confined. Lamb took

care of her, and during her sane intervals, she became his constant companion and collaborated with him on some books for children, notably the *Tales from Shakespeare* (1807). Lamb was finally pensioned in 1825; after nine peaceful years of leisure, he died in 1834.

Lamb's avocation was always literature. He tried drama, with complete lack of success; he published a rather feeble prose tale called *Rosamund Gray* and some poetry. His finest work is the series of personal essays entitled the *Essays of Elia*, which appeared in *London Magazine* (1820–1823) and later in book form (1823). A second series, running from 1824 to 1825, was collected and printed in 1833, a year before his death. Elia is an artistic projection of elements in Lamb's own personality. The pseudonym he chose was the name of an Italian who was at that time a clerk in the South Sea House. Lamb was also responsible for an excellent series of essays on Shakespeare, the other important dramatic poets of the Elizabethan age, and the prose authors of the seventeenth century.

THE TWO RACES OF MEN

The human species, according to the best theory I can form of it is composed of two distinct races, *the men who borrow*, and *the men who lend*. To these two original diversities may be reduced all those impertinent classifications of Gothic and Celtic tribes, white men, black men, red men. All the dwellers upon earth, "Parthians, and Medes, and Elamites,"° flock hither, and do naturally fall in with one or other of these primary distinctions. The infinite superiority of the
10 former, which I choose to designate as the *great race*, is discernible in their figure, port, and a certain instinctive sovereignty. The latter are born degraded. "He shall serve his brethren."° There is something in the air of one of this cast, lean and suspicious; contrasting with the open, trusting, generous manners of the other.

Observe who have been the greatest borrowers of all ages—Alcibiades°—Falstaff°—Sir Richard Steele° —our late incomparable Brinsley°—what a family
20 likeness in all four!

What a careless, even deportment hath your borrower! what rosy gills! what a beautiful reliance on Providence doth he manifest—taking no more thought than lilies!° What contempt for money—accounting it (yours and mine especially) no better than dross. What a liberal confounding of those pedantic distinctions of *meum* and *tuum*!° or rather, what a noble simplification of language (beyond Tooke),° resolving these supposed opposites into one clear, intelligible pronoun adjec-
30 tive!—What near approaches doth he make to the primitive *community*—to the extent of one half of the principle at least!

He is the true taxer who "calleth all the world up to be taxed";° and the distance is as vast between him and *one of us* as subsisted betwixt the Augustan Majesty and the poorest obolary° Jew that paid it tribute-pittance at Jerusalem!—His exactions, too, have such a cheerful, voluntary air! So far removed from your sour parochial or state-gatherers—those ink-horn varlets,
40 who carry their want of welcome in their faces! He cometh to you with a smile, and troubleth you with no receipt; confining himself to no set season. Every day is his Candlemas, or his Feast of Holy Michael.° He applieth the *Lene tormentum*° of a pleasant look to your

purse—which to that gentle warmth expands her silken leaves, as naturally as the cloak of the traveler, for which sun and wind contended! He is the true Propontic which never ebbeth!° The sea which taketh handsomely at each man's hand. In vain the victim, whom he delighteth to honor, struggles with destiny; he is in 50 the net. Lend therefore cheerfully, O man ordained to lend—that thou lose not in the end, with thy worldly penny, the reversion promised. Combine not preposterously in thine own person the penalties of Lazarus and of Dives!°—but, when thou seest the proper authority coming, meet it smilingly, as it were half-way. Come, a handsome sacrifice! See how light *he* makes of it! Strain not courtesies with a noble enemy.

Reflections like the foregoing were forced upon my mind by the death of my old friend, Ralph Bigod,° Esq., 60 who departed this life on Wednesday evening, dying, as he had lived, without much trouble. He boasted himself a descendant from mighty ancestors of that name, who heretofore held ducal dignities in this realm. In his actions and sentiments he belied not the stock to which he pretended. Early in life he found himself invested with ample revenues, which, with that noble disinterestedness which I have noticed as inherent in men of the *great race*, he took almost immediate measures entirely to dissipate and bring to 70 nothing: for there is something revolting in the idea of a king holding a private purse; and the thoughts of Bigod were all regal. Thus furnished, by the very act of disfurnishment; getting rid of the cumbersome luggage of riches, more apt (as one sings)

To slacken virtue, and abate her edge
Than prompt her to do aught may merit praise;°

he set forth, like some Alexander, upon his great enterprise, "borrowing and to borrow"!°

In his periegesis, or triumphant progress throughout 80 this island, it has been calculated that he laid a tythe° part of the inhabitants under contribution. I reject this estimate as greatly exaggerated:—but having had the honor of accompanying my friend, divers times, in his perambulations about this vast city, I own I was greatly struck at first with the prodigious number of faces we met who claimed a sort of respectful acquaintance with us. He was one day so obliging as to explain the phenomenon. It seems these were his tributaries; feeders of his exchequer; gentlemen, his 90 good friends (as he was pleased to express himself), to whom he had occasionally been beholden for a loan.

The Two Races of Men 7 **Parthians . . . Elamites,** from *Acts*, 2:9 13 **He . . . brethren.** See *Genesis*, 9:25 18 **Alcibiades,** Athenian general and politician (450–404 B.C.) **Falstaff,** earthy character in Shakespeare's *Henry IV* and *The Merry Wives of Windsor* **Steele,** the eighteenth-century essayist and playwright 19 **Brinsley,** Richard Brinsley Sheridan (1751–1816), author of *The School for Scandal* 24 **taking . . . lilies,** See *Matthew*, 6:28–29 27 **meum and tuum,** mine and yours 28 **Tooke,** John Horne Tooke (1736–1812), English politician and philologist 34 **calleth . . . taxed.** Cf. *Luke*, 2:1: "And it came to pass in those days that there went out a decree from Caesar Augustus, that all the world should be taxed." The quotation should make clear the allusion in the following lines 36 **obolary,** having only an obolus, a small silver coin of ancient Greece and Asia Minor of extremely low monetary value 43 **Candlemas . . . Michael.** Candlemas, or the feast of the candles, celebrates the presentation of Christ in the Temple of Jerusalem and is observed on Midwinter Day (February 2); the Feast of Holy Michael, or Michaelmas, is celebrated on September 29 44 **Lene tormentum,** mild torture or gentle stimulus, quoted from Horace, *Odes*, III, 21, 13

48 **Propontic . . . ebbeth.** See Shakespeare's *Othello*, III, iii, 453. The Propontic, or Pontic Sea, is another name for the Black Sea 55 **Lazarus . . . Dives.** The parable of Lazarus, the pauper, and Dives, the rich man, is told in *Luke*, 16:19–31. Dives went to hell and Lazarus to heaven 60 **Ralph Bigod.** It has not been established that Bigod represents any real person 77 **To . . . praise,** quoted from Milton's *Paradise Regained*, II, 455–456 79 **borrowing . . . borrow,** adapted from *Revelation*, 6:2: "And I saw, and behold a white horse: and he that sat on him had a bow; and a crown was given unto him: and he went forth conquering, and to conquer" 81 **tythe,** tenth

Their multitudes did no way disconcert him. He rather took a pride in numbering them; and, with Comus, seemed pleased to be "stocked with so fair a herd."°

With such sources, it was a wonder how he contrived to keep his treasury always empty. He did it by force of an aphorism, which he had often in his mouth, that "money kept longer than three days stinks." So he made use of it while it was fresh. A good part he drank away (for he was an excellent toss-pot), some he gave away, the rest he threw away, literally tossing and hurling it violently from him—as boys do burrs, or as if it had been infectious—into ponds, or ditches, or deep holes—inscrutable cavities of the earth;—or he would bury it (where he would never seek it again) by a river's side under some bank, which (he would facetiously observe) paid no interest—but out away from him it must go peremptorily, as Hagar's offspring into the wilderness,° while it was sweet. He never missed it. The streams were perennial which fed his fisc.° When new supplies became necessary, the first person that had the felicity to fall in with him, friend or stranger, was sure to contribute to the deficiency. For Bigod had an *undeniable* way with him. He had a cheerful, open exterior, a quick jovial eye, a bald forehead, just touched with gray (*cana fides*).° He anticipated no excuse, and found none. And, waiving for awhile my theory as to the *great race,* I would put it to the most untheorizing reader, who may at times have disposable coin in his pocket, whether it is not more repugnant to the kindliness of his nature to refuse such a one as I am describing, than to say *no* to a poor petitionary rogue (your bastard borrower) who, by his mumping visnomy,° tells you that he expects nothing better, and, therefore, whose preconceived notions and expectations you do in reality so much less shock in the refusal.

When I think of this man; his fiery glow of heart; his swell of feeling; how magnificent, how *ideal* he was; how great at the midnight hour; and when I compare with him the companions with whom I have associated since, I grudge the saving of a few idle ducats, and think that I am fallen into the society of *lenders,* and *little men.*

To one like Elia, whose treasures are rather cased in leather covers than closed in iron coffers, there is a class of alienators more formidable than that which I have touched upon; I mean your *borrowers of books*—those mutilators of collections, spoilers of the symmetry of shelves, and creators of odd volumes. There is Comberbatch,° matchless in his depredations!

That foul gap in the bottom shelf facing you, like a great eye-tooth knocked out (you are now with me in my little back study in Bloomsbury, reader!), with the huge Switzer-like° tomes on each side (like the Guildhall giants,° in their reformed posture, guardant of nothing), once held the tallest of my folios, *Opera Bonaventurae,*° choice and massy divinity, to which its two supporters (school divinity also, but of a lesser calibre—Bellarmine,° and Holy Thomas°), showed but as dwarfs—itself an Ascapart°—that Comberbatch abstracted upon the faith of a theory he holds, which is more easy, I confess, for me to suffer by than to refute, namely, that "the title to property in a book (my Bonaventure, for instance) is in exact ratio to the claimant's powers of understanding and appreciating the same." Should he go on acting upon this theory, which of our shelves is safe?

The slight vacuum in the left-hand case—two shelves from the ceiling—scarcely distinguishable but by the quick eye of a loser—was whilom the commodious resting-place of Browne on *Urn Burial.*° C.° will hardly allege that he knows more about that treatise than I do, who introduced it to him, and was indeed the first (of the moderns) to discover its beauties—but so have I known a foolish lover to praise his mistress in the presence of a rival more qualified to carry her off than himself.—Just below, Dodsley's° dramas want their fourth volume, where *Vittoria Corrombona*° is! The remainder nine are as distasteful as Priam's refuse sons, when the Fates *borrowed Hector.*° Here stood *The Anatomy of Melancholy,*° in sober state.—There loitered *The Complete Angler,*° quiet as in life, by some stream side.—In yonder nook, *John Buncle,*° a widower-volume, with "eyes closed," mourns his ravished mate.

One justice I must do my friend, that if he sometimes, like the sea, sweeps away a treasure, at another time, sea-like, he throws up as rich an equivalent to match it. I have a small under-collection of this nature (my friend's gatherings in his various calls), picked up, he has forgotten at what odd places, and deposited with as little memory at mine. I take in these orphans, the twice-deserted. These proselytes of the gate are

146 **Switzerlike,** huge like the giant Swiss guards who protect the pope
147 **Guildhall giants,** referring to the colossal figures in the council hall at London known as Gog and Magog   149 **Opera Bonaventurae,** the works of St. Bonaventure, medieval scholastic philosopher (1221–1274) who was later canonized   151 **Bellarmine,** Robert Bellarmino, Jesuit theologian and cardinal (1542–1621)   **Holy Thomas,** St. Thomas Aquinas (c. 1225–1274), generally considered the greatest of medieval Catholic theologians and philosophers   152 **Ascapart,** giant conquered by Bevis of Hampton in a middle English romance
163 **Browne on Urn Burial,** Sir Thomas Browne (1605–1682), author of *Religio Medici* and other works   **C.,** Comberbatch, or Coleridge   169 **Dodsley,** Robert Dodsley (1703–1764), bookseller and editor; his collection of English drama, the most famous of the time, was first printed in 1744.   171 **Vittoria Corrombona,** or *The White Devil,* now better known by the English title, a grim and bloody tragedy (1612) by the Elizabethan playwright, John Webster   172 **Priam . . . Hector.** In the Trojan War, Hector, the favorite son of King Priam of Troy and the most illustrious of Trojan champions, was slain by the Greek hero Achilles. With nine of his fifty sons still living, Priam begged Achilles for the body of Hector. The incident is told in the *Iliad,* XXIV, 486 ff.   173 **The . . . Melancholy,** an exhaustive treatise (1621) on the causes, nature, and cure of melancholy by Robert Burton (1577–1640)   174 **The Complete Angler,** by Izaak Walton (1593–1683)
176 **John Buncle,** novel (1756–1766) of the picaresque type by Thomas Amory (1691?–1788). The reference in this line is to the fact that John Buncle, the hero of the book, made the statement that when one of his wives died he remained four days with his eyes shut. In the course of the novel, he embarked upon no less than seven matrimonial adventures

95 **stocked . . . herd,** quoted from Milton's *Comus,* 152   110 **Hagar's . . . wilderness.** Hagar was the handmaid of Sarah, the wife of Abraham (cf. *Genesis,* 16). Abraham's relations with Hagar, suggested by Sarah (who was then sterile), resulted in the son Ishmael. Sarah, reproved by her conscience, turned upon Hagar, who was banished (with the Lord's approval) into the wilderness, where Ishmael grew to be "a wild man; his hand against every man, and every man's hand against him"   111 **fisc,** treasury   117 **cana fides,** gray-haired fidelity; quoted from Vergil's *Aeneid,* I, 292   124–125 **mumping visnomy,** mumbling physiognomy, or face   142 **Comberbatch.** Coleridge at one time ran away from Cambridge and enlisted in the dragoons under the name of Silas Tomkyn Comberbacke. The reference here is undoubtedly to Coleridge, in spite of the slightly modified form of the pseudonym

welcome as the true Hebrews. There they stand in conjunction; natives, and naturalized. The latter seem as little disposed to inquire out their true lineage as I am.—I charge no warehouse-room for these deodands,° nor shall ever put myself to the ungentlemanly trouble of advertising a sale of them to pay expenses.

To lose a volume to C. carries some sense and meaning in it. You are sure that he will make one hearty meal on your viands, if he can give no account of the platter after it. But what moved thee, wayward, spiteful K.,° to be so importunate to carry off with thee, in spite of tears and adjurations to thee to forbear, the *Letters* of that princely woman, the thrice noble Margaret Newcastle?°—knowing at the time, and knowing that I knew also, thou most assuredly wouldst never turn over one leaf of the illustrious folio:—what but the mere spirit of contradiction, and childish love of getting the better of thy friend?—Then, worst cut of all! to transport it with thee to the Gallican land—

Unworthy land to harbor such a sweetness,
A virtue in which all ennobling thoughts dwelt,
Pure thoughts, kind thoughts, high thoughts, her sex's
    wonder!

—hadst thou not thy play-books, and books of jests and fancies, about thee, to keep thee merry, even as thou keepest all companies with thy quips and mirthful tales?—Child of the Green-room,° it was unkindly done of thee. Thy wife, too, that part-French, better-part Englishwoman!—that *she* could fix upon no other treatise to bear away, in kindly token of remembering us, than the works of Fulke Greville,° Lord Brooke—of which no Frenchman, nor woman of France, Italy, or England, was ever by nature constituted to comprehend a tittle! *Was there not Zimmerman° on Solitude?*

Reader, if haply thou art blessed with a moderate collection, be shy of showing it; or if thy heart overfloweth to lend them, lend thy books; but let it be to such as one as S.T.C.°—he will return them (generally anticipating the time appointed) with usury; enriched with annotations, tripling their value. I have had experience. Many are these precious MSS. of his—(in *matter* oftentimes, and almost in *quantity* not unfrequently vying with the originals)—in no very clerkly hand—legible in my Daniel;° in old Burton; in Sir Thomas Browne; and those abstruser cogitations of the Greville, now, alas! wandering in Pagan lands—I

counsel thee, shut not thy heart, nor thy library, against S.T.C.
(1820)

DREAM-CHILDREN: A REVERIE°

Children love to listen to stories about their elders, when *they* were children; to stretch their imagination to the conception of a traditionary great-uncle, or grandame, whom they never saw. It was in this spirit that my little ones crept about me the other evening to hear about their great-grandmother Field, who lived in a great house in Norfolk° (a hundred times bigger than that in which they and papa lived) which had been the scene—so at least it was generally believed in that part of the country—of the tragic incidents which they had lately become familiar with from the ballad of the Children in the Wood. Certain it is that the whole story of the children and their cruel uncle was to be seen fairly carved out in wood upon the chimney-piece of the great hall, the whole story down to the Robin Redbreasts,° till a foolish rich person pulled it down to set up a marble one of modern invention in its stead, with no story upon it. Here Alice put out one of her dear mother's looks, too tender to be called upbraiding. Then I went on to say how religious and how good their great-grandmother Field was, how beloved and respected by everybody, though she was not indeed the mistress of this great house, but had only the charge of it (and yet in some respects she might be said to be the mistress of it too) committed to her by the owner, who preferred living in a newer and more fashionable mansion which he had purchased somewhere in the adjoining county; but still she lived in it in a manner as if it had been her own, and kept up the dignity of the great house in a sort while she lived, which afterwards came to decay, and was nearly pulled down, and all its old ornaments stripped and carried away to the owner's other house, where they were set up, and looked as awkward as if someone were to carry away the old tombs they had seen lately at the Abbey, and stick them up in Lady C.'s tawdry gilt drawing-room. Here John smiled, as much as to say, "that would be foolish, indeed." And then I told how, when she came to die, her funeral was attended by a concourse of all the poor, and some of the gentry too, of the neighborhood for many miles round, to show their respect for her memory, because she had been such a good and religious woman; so good indeed that she knew all the Psaltery by heart, ay, and a great part of the Testament besides. Here little Alice spread her

190 **deodands,** in English law, things forfeited to the crown   197 **wayward, spiteful K.,** James Kenney (1780–1849), minor dramatist of the time   200 **Letters . . . Newcastle** the *Sociable Letters* of Margaret Cavendish, Lady Newcastle (c. 1625–1673)   212 **Green-room,** originally the dressing room of a theater, then applied to the stage as a whole   216 **Fulke Greville,** first Lord Brooke (1554–1628), Elizabethan poet, courtier, and statesman; friend of Queen Elizabeth and of Sir Philip Sidney in particular; one of the most famous Elizabethan gentlemen of the court   219 **Zimmerman,** Johann Georg van Zimmerman (1728–1795), Swiss physician and philosophical writer, best known for his monograph on solitude (1784–85)   224 **S.T.C.,** Samuel Taylor Coleridge   230 **Daniel,** Samuel Daniel, Elizabethan poet (1562–1619)

Dream Children. This essay was prompted by the death of Lamb's brother John on October 26, 1821. It is understandable that Lamb should turn in his hours of solitude to the thoughts of what his life might have been had he been able to marry Ann Simmons, his old sweetheart   7 **Norfolk.** Lamb's grandmother had been a housekeeper at Blakesware, Hertfordshire, not Norfolk. Lamb may have changed the county because the man who dismantled Blakesware, William Plumer, also lived in Hertfordshire and was alive when the essay was published   16 **Robin Redbreasts.** At the end of the ballad they cover the murdered children with leaves

hands.° Then I told what a tall, upright, graceful person their great-grandmother Field once was; and how in her youth she was esteemed the best dancer—here Alice's little right foot played an involuntary move-
50 ment, till upon my looking grave, it desisted—the best dancer, I was saying, in the county, till a cruel disease, called a cancer, came, and bowed her down with pain; but it could never bend her good spirits, or make them stoop, but they were still upright, because she was so good and religious. Then I told how she was used to sleep by herself in a lone chamber of the great lone house; and how she believed that an apparition of two infants° was to be seen at midnight gliding up and down the great staircase near where she slept, but she said
60 "those innocents would do her no harm"; and how frightened I used to be, though in those days I had my maid to sleep with me, because I was never half so good or religious as she—and yet I never saw the infants. Here John expanded all his eyebrows and tried to look courageous. Then I told how good she was to all her grandchildren, having us to the great house in the holidays, where I in particular used to spend many hours by myself, in gazing upon the old busts of the twelve Caesars, that had been emperors of Rome, till
70 the old marble heads would seem to live again, or I to be turned into marble with them; how I never could be tired with roaming about that huge mansion, with its vast empty rooms, with their worn-out hangings, fluttering tapestry, and carved oaken panels, with the gilding almost rubbed out—sometimes in the spacious old-fashioned gardens, which I had almost to myself, unless when now and then a solitary gardening man would cross me—and how the nectarines and peaches hung upon the walls without my ever offering to pluck
80 them, because they were forbidden fruit, unless now and then—and because I had more pleasure in strolling about among the old melancholy-looking yew-trees, or the firs, and picking up the red berries, and the fir apples,° which were good for nothing but to look at—or in lying about upon the fresh grass, with all the fine garden smells around me—or basking in the orangery, till I could almost fancy myself ripening too along with the oranges and the limes in that grateful warmth—or in watching the dace that darted to and fro in the
90 fish-pond, at the bottom of the garden, with here and there a great sulky pike hanging midway down the water in silent state, as if it mocked at their impertinent friskings°—I had more pleasure in these busy-idle diversions than in all the sweet flavors of peaches, nectarines, oranges, and such-like common baits of children. Here John slyly deposited back upon the plate a bunch of grapes which, not unobserved by Alice, he had meditated dividing with her, and both seemed willing to relinquish them for the present as irrelevant.
100 Then in somewhat a more heightened tone, I told how,

though their great-grandmother Field loved all her grandchildren, yet in an especial manner she might be said to love their uncle, John L——° because he was so handsome and spirited a youth, and a king to the rest of us; and, instead of moping about in solitary corners, like some of us, he would mount the most mettlesome horse he could get, when but an imp no bigger than themselves, and make it carry him half over the county in a morning, and join the hunters when there were any out—and yet he loved the old great house and gardens 110 too, but had too much spirit to be always pent up within their boundaries—and how their uncle grew up to man's estate as brave as he was handsome, to the admiration of everybody, but of their great-grandmother Field most especially; and how he used to carry me upon his back when I was a lame-footed boy—for he was a good bit older than me—many a mile when I could not walk for pain;—and how in after-life he became lame-footed too, and I did not always (I fear) make allowances enough for him when he was impa- 120 tient, and in pain, nor remember sufficiently how considerate he had been to me when I was lame-footed; and how when he died, though he had not been dead an hour, it seemed as if he had died a great while ago, such a distance there is betwixt life and death; and how I bore his death as I thought pretty well at first, but afterwards it haunted and haunted me; and though I did not cry or take it to heart as some do, and as I think he would have done if I had died, yet I missed him all day long, and knew not till then how much I had loved him. I missed 130 his kindness, and I missed his crossness, and wished him to be alive again, to be quarreling with him (for we quarreled sometimes), rather than not have him again, and was as uneasy without him, as he, their poor uncle, must have been when the doctor took off his limb.° Here the children fell a-crying, and asked if their little mourning which they had on was not for Uncle John, and they looked up, and prayed me not to go on about their uncle, but to tell them some stories about their pretty dead mother. Then I told how for seven long 140 years, in hope sometimes, sometimes in despair, yet persisting ever, I courted the fair Alice W——n;° and, as much as children could understand, I explained to them what coyness, and difficulty,° and denial meant in maidens—when suddenly, turning to Alice, the soul of the first Alice looked out at her eyes with such a reality of representment,° that I became in doubt which of them stood there before me, or whose that bright hair was; and while I stood gazing, both the children gradually grew fainter to my view, receding, and still reced- 150 ing till nothing at last but two mournful features were seen in the uttermost distance, which without speech, strangely impressed upon me the effects of speech: "We are not of Alice, nor of thee, nor are we children at all. The children of Alice call Bartrum° father. We

46 **spread her hands,** a sign of astonishment   58 **apparition of two infants,** an old legend of the Plumer family   84 **fir apples,** fir cones   93 **impertinent friskings.** The pike feeds upon dace

103 **John L——,** Lamb's brother John   135 **doctor . . . limb,** a detail of Lamb's imagination   142 **Alice W——n,** Winterton, probably Ann Simmons, Lamb's boyhood love   144 **difficulty,** shyness   147 **representment,** reincarnation 155 **Bartrum.** Ann Simmons married a man named Bartrum

are nothing; less than nothing, and dreams. We are only what might have been, and must wait upon the tedious shores of Lethe° millions of ages before we have existence and a name"—and immediately

160 awaking, I found myself quietly seated in my bachelor armchair, where I had fallen asleep, with the faithful Bridget unchanged by my side—but John L. (or James Elia)° was gone forever.

(1822)

POOR RELATIONS

A poor relation—is the most irrelevant thing in nature,—a piece of impertinent correspondency,—an odious approximation,—a haunting conscience,—a preposterous shadow, lengthening in the noontide of your prosperity,—an unwelcome remembrancer,—a perpetually recurring mortification,—a drain on your purse,—a more intolerable dun upon your pride,—a drawback upon success,—a rebuke to your rising,—a stain in your blood,—a blot on your scutcheon,—a

10 rent in your garment,—a death's head° at your banquet,—Agathocles' pot,°—a Mordecai in your gate,°—a Lazarus at your door,°—a lion in your path,°—a frog in your chamber,°—a fly in your ointment,°—a mote in your eye,°—a triumph to your enemy, an apology to your friends,—the one thing not needful,°—the hail in harvest,°—the ounce of sour in a pound of sweet.°

He is known by his knock. Your heart telleth you, "That is Mr ——." A rap, between familiarity and respect, that demands, and at the same time seems to

20 despair of, entertainment. He entereth smiling and—embarrassed. He holdeth out his hand to you to shake, and—draweth it back again. He casually looketh in about dinner-time—when the table is full. He offereth to go away, seeing you have company—but is induced to stay. He filleth a chair, and your visitor's two children are accommodated at a side table. He never cometh upon open days, when your wife says with some complacency, "My dear, perhaps Mr. —— will drop in today." He remembereth birthdays—and profes-

30 seth he is fortunate to have stumbled upon one. He declareth against fish, the turbot being small—yet suffereth himself to be importuned into a slice, against his first resolution. He sticketh by the port—yet will be prevailed upon to empty the remainder glass of claret, if a stranger press it upon him. He is a puzzle to the servants, who are fearful of being too obsequious, or not civil enough, to him. The guests think "they have seen him before." Everyone speculateth upon his condition; and the most part take him to be—a tide-

40 waiter.° He calleth you by your Christian name, to imply that his other is the same with your own. He is too familiar by half, yet you wish he had less diffidence. With half the familiarity, he might pass for a casual dependent; with more boldness, he would be in no danger of being taken for what he is. He is too humble for a friend; yet taketh on him more state than befits a client.° He is a worse guest than a country tenant, inasmuch as he bringeth up no rent—yet 'tis odds, from his garb and demeanor, that your guests take him for

50 one. He is asked to make one at the whist-table; refuseth on the score of poverty, and—resents being left out. When the company break up, he proffereth to go for a coach—and lets the servant go. He recollects your grandfather; and will thrust in some mean and quite unimportant anecdote of—the family. He knew it when it was not quite so flourishing as "he is blest in seeing it now." He reviveth past situations, to institute what he calleth—favorable comparisons. With a reflecting sort of congratulation, he will inquire the price

60 of your furniture; and insults you with a special commendation of your window-curtains. He is of opinion that the urn is the more elegant shape, but, after all, there was something more comfortable about the old tea-kettle—which you must remember. He dare say you must find a great convenience in having a carriage of your own, and appealeth to your lady if it is not so. Inquireth if you have had your arms done on vellum yet; and did not know, till lately, that such-and-such had been the crest of the family. His memory is unsea-

70 sonable; his compliments perverse; his talk a trouble; his stay pertinacious; and when he goeth away, you dismiss his chair into a corner, as precipitately as possible, and feel fairly rid of two nuisances.

There is a worse evil under the sun, and that is—a female Poor Relation. You may do something with the other; you may pass him off tolerably well; but your indigent she-relative is hopeless. "He is an old humorist,°" you may say, "and affects° to go threadbare. His circumstances are better than folks would

80 take them to be. You are fond of having a Character at your table, and truly he is one." But in the indications of female poverty there can be no disguise. No woman dresses below herself from caprice. The truth must out without shuffling. "She is plainly related to the L——s; or what does she at their house?" She is, in all probability, your wife's cousin. Nine times out of ten, at least, this is the case. Her garb is something between a gentlewoman and a beggar, yet the former evidently predominates. She is most provokingly humble,

90 and ostentatiously sensible to her inferiority. He may

---

158 **Lethe,** river of forgetfulness in Hades. In the *Aeneid* (VI, 703–751) Vergil tells how the soul, after drinking of Lethe, will return after many years to earth in a new body   163 **Bridget . . . James Elia,** names given by Lamb to his sister Mary and his brother John in *My Relations*
Poor Relations   10 **death's head,** an allusion to the Egyptian custom of having a coffin and representation of a corpse carried through a banquet hall to remind the guests of their necessary end   11 **Agathocles' pot.** Agathocles, tyrant of Sicily (361–289 B.C.), hated the sight of a pot because it reminded him that he was the son of a potter   **Mordecai . . . gate,** a reference to the vigils of Mordecai at the gates of King Ahasuerus to learn what happened to Esther; see *Esther,* 3:1–2; 5:11–13   12 **Lazarus . . . door.** Lazarus placed himself at the gate of a rich man to get the crumbs from his table; see *Luke,* 16:20   **lion . . . path.** See *1 Kings,* 13:24   **frog . . . chamber.** See *Exodus,* 8:3–4   13 **fly . . . ointment.** See *Ecclesiastes,* 10:1   14 **eye.** See *Matthew,* 7:3–5   **one . . . needful.** See *Luke,* 10:42   16 **hail in harvest.** See *Proverbs,* 26:1   **ounce . . . sweet,** from Spenser's *Faerie Queene,* I, iii, 30

39–40 **tide-waiter,** literally, a minor customs official who waits for the arrival of ships and enforces the revenue laws; here, one like Micawber in *David Copperfield* who waits for something lucky to turn up   47 **client,** dependent   78 **humorist,** eccentric person   **affects,** chooses

require to be repressed sometimes—*aliquando suf-flaminandus erat;*°—but there is no raising her. You send her soup at dinner, and she begs to be helped—after the gentlemen. Mr.—— requests the honor of taking wine with her; she hesitates between port and Madeira, and chooses the former—because he does. She calls the servant "Sir"; and insists on not troubling him to hold her plate. The housekeeper patronizes her. The children's governess takes upon her to correct her when she has mistaken the piano for a harpsichord.

Richard Amlet, Esq., in the play,° is a notable instance of the disadvantages to which this chimerical notion of *affinity constituting a claim to acquaintance* may subject the spirit of a gentleman. A little foolish blood is all that is betwixt him and a lady of great estate. His stars are perpetually crossed by the malignant maternity of an old woman, who persists in calling him "her son Dick." But she has wherewithal in the end to recompense his indignities, and float him again upon the brilliant surface, under which it had been her seeming business and pleasure all along to sink him. All men, besides, are not of Dick's temperament. I knew an Amlet in real life, who, wanting Dick's buoyancy, sank indeed. Poor W——° was of my own standing at Christ's,° a fine classic, and a youth of promise. If he had a blemish, it was too much pride; but its quality was inoffensive; it was not of that sort which hardens the heart, and serves to keep inferiors at a distance; it only sought to ward off derogation from itself. It was the principle of self-respect carried as far as it could go without infringing upon that respect which he would have everyone else equally maintain for himself. He would have you to think alike with him on this topic. Many a quarrel have I had with him, when we were rather older boys and our tallness° made us more obnoxious to observation in the blue clothes,° because I would not thread the alleys and blind ways of the town with him to elude notice, when we have been out together on a holiday in the streets of this sneering and prying metropolis. W—— went, sore with these notions, to Oxford, where the dignity and sweetness of a scholar's life, meeting with the alloy of a humble introduction, wrought in him a passionate devotion to the place, with a profound aversion from the society. The servitor's gown° (worse than his school array) clung to him with Nessian venom.° He thought himself ridiculous in a garb under which Latimer° must have walked erect, and in which Hooker,° in his young days, possibly flaunted in a vein

of no discommendable vanity. In the depth of college shades or in his lonely chamber, the poor student shrunk from observation. He found shelter among books, which insult not; and studies, that ask no questions of a youth's finances. He was lord of his library, and seldom cared for looking out beyond his domains. The healing influence of studious pursuits was upon him, to soothe and to abstract. He was almost a healthy man; when the waywardness of his fate broke out against him with a second and worse malignity. The father of W—— had hitherto exercised the humble profession of house-painter at N——,° near Oxford. A supposed interest with some of the heads of the colleges had now induced him to take up his abode in that city, with the hope of being employed upon some public works which were talked of. From that moment I read in the countenance of the young man the determination which at length tore him from academical pursuits forever. To a person unacquainted with our universities, the distance between the gownsmen and the townsmen, as they are called—the trading part of the latter especially—is carried to an excess that would appear harsh and incredible. The temperament of W——'s father was diametrically the reverse of his own. Old W—— was a little, busy, cringing tradesman, who, with his son upon his arm, would stand bowing and scraping, cap in hand, to anything that wore the semblance of a gown—insensible to the winks and opener remonstrances of the young man, to whose chamber-fellow or equal in standing, perhaps, he was thus obsequiously and gratuitously ducking. Such a state of things could not last. W—— must change the air of Oxford or be suffocated. He chose the former; and let the sturdy moralist, who strains the point of the filial duties as high as they can bear, censure the dereliction; he cannot estimate the struggle. I stood with W——, the last afternoon I ever saw him, under the eaves of his paternal dwelling. It was in the fine lane leading from the High-street to the back of —— College, where W—— kept his rooms. He seemed thoughtful and more reconciled. I ventured to rally him—finding him in a better mood—upon a representation of the artist Evangelist,° which the old man, whose affairs were beginning to flourish, had caused to be set up in a splendid sort of frame over his really handsome shop, either as a token of prosperity or badge of gratitude to his saint. W—— looked up at the Luke, and, like Satan, "knew his mounted sign—and fled."° A letter on his father's table the next morning announced that he had accepted a commission in a regiment about to embark for Portugal. He was among the first who perished before the walls of St. Sebastian.°

I do not know how, upon a subject which I began with treating half seriously, I should have fallen upon a

92 **aliquando . . . erat.** Sometimes he had to be checked   102 **the play,** *The Confederacy,* by Sir John Vanbrugh (1666–1726)   115 **Poor W——.** Lamb says elsewhere that W—— was his friend Favell, who "left Cambridge because he was ashamed of his father, who was a house-painter there"   116 **Christ's,** Christ's Hospital, where Lamb went to school   126 **our tallness.** Lamb was actually rather short   128 **blue clothes.** Boys at Christ's Hospital wore long blue coats and yellow stockings   136 **servitor's gown,** worn by undergraduates who waited tables at the Commons in return for partial support from College funds   137 **Nessian venom.** Hercules killed the centaur Nessus with a poisoned arrow and then died himself from wearing a shirt dipped in its envenomed blood   139 **Latimer,** Hugh Latimer (1488–1555), preacher and reformer, who had been a servitor at Cambridge   140 **Hooker,** Richard Hooker (1553–1600), English divine, who had been a servitor at Oxford

152 **N——,** a substitute for Cambridge   183 **artist Evangelist,** St. Luke, by tradition a painter as well as a physician   189 **knew . . . fled,** from Milton's *Paradise Lost,* IV, 1013   193 **St. Sebastian,** seaport on the north coast of Spain, taken by Wellington in 1813

recital so eminently painful; but this theme of poor relationship is replete with so much matter for tragic as well as comic associations that it is difficult to keep the account distinct without blending. The earliest impres-
200 sions which I received on this matter are certainly not attended with anything painful or very humiliating in the recalling. At my father's table (no very splendid one) was to be found, every Saturday, the mysterious figure of an aged gentleman, clothed in neat black, of a sad yet comely appearance. His deportment was of the essence of gravity; his words few or none; and I was not to make a noise in his presence. I had little inclination to have done so—for my cue was to admire in silence. A particular elbow-chair was appropriated to
210 him, which was in no case to be violated. A peculiar sort of sweet pudding, which appeared on no other occasion, distinguished the days of his coming. I used to think him a prodigiously rich man. All I could make out of him was that he and my father had been school-fellows a world ago at Lincoln, and that he came from the Mint.° The Mint I knew to be a place where all the money was coined—and I thought he was the owner of all that money. Awful ideas of the Tower twined themselves about his presence. He seemed above human
220 infirmities and passions. A sort of melancholy grandeur invested him. From some inexplicable doom I fancied him obliged to go about in an eternal suit of mourning; a captive, a stately being, let out of the Tower on Saturdays. Often have I wondered at the temerity of my father, who, in spite of an habitual general respect which we all in common manifested towards him, would venture now and then to stand up against him in some argument touching their youthful days. The houses of the ancient city of Lincoln are
230 divided (as most of my readers know) between the dwellers on the hill and in the valley. This marked distinction formed an obvious division between the boys who lived above (however brought together in a common school) and the boys whose paternal residence was on the plain; a sufficient cause of hostility in the code of these young Grotiuses.° My father had been a leading Mountaineer; and would still maintain the general superiority, in skill and hardihood, of the *Above Boys* (his own faction) over the *Below Boys* (so
240 were they called), of which party his contemporary had been a chieftain. Many and hot were the skirmishes on this topic—the only one upon which the old gentleman was ever brought out—and bad blood bred; even sometimes almost to the recommencement (so I expected) of actual hostilities. But my father, who scorned to insist upon advantages, generally contrived to turn the conversation upon some adroit by-commendation of the old Minster; in the general preference of which before all other cathedrals in the island, the
250 dweller on the hill and the plain-born could meet on a conciliating level, and lay down their less important differences. Once only I saw the old gentleman really ruffled, and I remembered with anguish the thought that came over me: "Perhaps he will never come here again." He had been pressed to take another plate of the viand which I have already mentioned as the indispensable concomitant of his visits. He had refused with a resistance amounting to rigor, when my aunt—an old Lincolnian, but who had something of this in common with my cousin Bridget, that she would 260 sometimes press civility out of season—uttered the following memorable application: "Do take another slice, Mr. Billet, for you do not get pudding every day." The old gentleman said nothing at the time; but he took occasion in the course of the evening, when some argument had intervened between them, to utter with an emphasis which chilled the company, and which chills me now as I write it—"Woman, you are superannuated!" John Billet did not survive long after the digesting of this affront, but he survived long 270 enough to assure me that peace was actually restored; and if I remember aright, another pudding was discreetly substituted in the place of that which had occasioned the offense. He died at the Mint (*anno* 1781), where he had long held what he accounted a comfortable independence; and with five pounds, fourteen shillings, and a penny, which were found in his *escritoire* after his decease, left the world, blessing God that he had enough to bury him and that he had never been obliged to any man for a sixpence. This was—a 280 Poor Relation.

(1823)

OLD CHINA

I have an almost feminine partiality for old china. When I go to see any great house, I enquire for the china-closet, and next for the picture gallery. I cannot defend the order of preference, but by saying, that we have all some taste or other, of too ancient a date to admit of our remembering distinctly that it was an acquired one. I can call to mind the first play, and the first exhibition, that I was taken to; but I am not conscious of a time when china jars and saucers were introduced into my imagination.   10

I had no repugnance then—why should I now have?—to those little, lawless, azure-tinctured grotesques, that under the notion of men and women, float about, uncircumscribed by any element, in that world before perspective—a china tea-cup.

I like to see my old friends—whom distance cannot diminish—figuring up in the air (so they appear to our optics), yet on *terra firma* still—for so we must in courtesy interpret that speck of deeper blue,—which the decorous artist, to prevent absurdity, had made to 20 spring up beneath their sandals.

216 **the Mint,** located near the Tower of London, the state prison   236 **young Grotiuses,** law students, after Hugo Grotius (1583–1645), Dutch authority on international law

I love the men with women's faces, and the women, if possible, with still more womanish expressions.

Here is a young and courtly Mandarin, handing tea to a lady from a salver—two miles off. See how distance seems to set off respect! And here the same lady, or another—for likeness is identity on tea-cups—is stepping into a little fairy boat, moored on the hither side of this calm garden river, with a dainty mincing foot, which in a right angle of incidence (as angles go in our world) must infallibly land her in the midst of a flowery mead—a furlong off on the other side of the same strange stream!

Farther on—if far or near can be predicated of their world—see horses, trees, pagodas, dancing the hays.°

Here—a cow and rabbit couchant,° and co-extensive—so objects show, seen through the lucid atmosphere of fine Cathay.°

I was pointing out to my cousin last evening, over our Hyson,° (which we are old fashioned enough to drink unmixed still of an afternoon) some of these *speciosa miracula*° upon a set of extraordinary old blue china (a recent purchase) which we were now for the first time using; and could not help remarking, how favourable circumstances had been to us of late years, that we could afford to please the eye sometimes with trifles of this sort—when a passing sentiment seemed to overshade the brows of my companion. I am quick at detecting these summer clouds in Bridget.°

"I wish the good old times would come again," she said, "when we were not quite so rich. I do not mean, that I want to be poor; but there was a middle state"—so she was pleased to ramble on,—"in which I am sure we were a great deal happier. A purchase is but a purchase, now that you have money enough and to spare. Formerly it used to be a triumph. When we coveted a cheap luxury (and, O! how much ado I had to get you to consent in those times!)—we were used to have a debate two or three days before, and to weigh the *for* and *against,* and think what we might spare it out of, and what saving we could hit upon, that should be an equivalent. A thing was worth buying then, when we felt the money that we paid for it."

"Do you remember the brown suit, which you made to hang upon you, till all your friends cried shame upon you, it grew so thread-bare—and all because of that folio Beaumont and Fletcher,° which you dragged home late at night from Barker's in Covent Garden? Do you remember how we eyed it for weeks before we could make up our minds to the purchase, and had not come to a determination till it was near ten o'clock of the Saturday night, when you set off from Islington, fearing you should be too late—and when the old bookseller with some grumbling opened his shop, and by the twinkling taper (for he was setting bedwards)

lighted out the relic from his dusty treasures—and when you lugged it home, wishing it were twice as cumbersome—and when you presented it to me—and when we were exploring the perfectness of it (*collating* you called it)—and while I was repairing some of the loose leaves with paste, which your impatience would not suffer to be left till daybreak—was there no pleasure in being a poor man? or can those neat black clothes which you wear now, and are so careful to keep brushed, since we have become rich and finical, give you half the honest vanity, with which you flaunted it about in that overworn suit—your old corbeau°—for four or five weeks longer than you should have done, to pacify your conscience for the mighty sum of fifteen—or sixteen shillings was it?—a great affair we thought it then—which you had lavished on the old folio. Now you can afford to buy any book that pleases you, but I do not see that you ever bring me home any nice old purchases now."

"When you came home with twenty apologies for laying out a less number of shillings upon that print after Leonardo,° which we christened the 'Lady Blanch'; when you looked at the purchase, and thought of the money—and thought of the money, and looked again at the picture—was there no pleasure in being a poor man? Now, you have nothing to do but to walk into Colnaghi's, and buy a wilderness of Leonardos. Yet do you?"

"Then, do you remember our pleasant walks to Enfield, and Potter's Bar, and Waltham, when we had a holyday—holydays, and all other fun, are gone, now we are rich—and the little hand-basket in which I used to deposit our day's fare of savoury cold lamb and salad—and how you would pry about at noontide for some decent house, where we might go in, and produce our store—only paying for the ale that you must call for—and speculate upon the looks of the landlady, and whether she was likely to allow us a table-cloth—and wish for such another honest hostess, as Izaak Walton has described many a one on the pleasant banks of the Lea, when he went a fishing—and sometimes they would prove obliging enough, and sometimes they would look grudgingly upon us—but we had cheerful looks still for one another, and would eat our plain food savorily, scarcely grudging Piscator° his Trout Hall? Now,—when we go out a day's pleasuring, which is seldom moreover, we *ride* part of the way—and go into a fine inn, and order the best of dinners, never debating the expense—which, after all, never has half the relish of those chance country snaps, when we were at the mercy of uncertain usage, and a precarious welcome."

"You are too proud to see a play anywhere now but in the pit. Do you remember where it was we used to sit, when we saw the *Battle of Hexham,* and the *Sur-*

Old China   35 **hays,** country dance with much interweaving of couples
36 **couchant,** lying down with head raised (from heraldry)   38 **Cathay,** China
40 **Hyson,** a Chinese green tea   42 **speciosa miracula,** shining marvels, from
Horace's *Ars Poetica,* 144   49 **Bridget,** Lamb's sister Mary   67 **Beaumont and
Fletcher,** Francis Beaumont (1584–1616) and John Fletcher (1579–1625), dramatic
collaborators

88 **corbeau,** a dark-green cloth   97 **Leonardo,** Leonardo da Vinci (1452–1519),
Italian painter, sculptor, architect, musician, engineer, mathematician, and scientist. The painting referred to is *Modesty and Vanity*   120 **Piscator,** the fisherman
in Izaak Walton's *The Complete Angler* (1653)

render of Calais,° and Bannister and Mrs. Bland in the *Children in the Wood*°—when we squeezed out our shillings a-piece to sit three or four times in a season in the one-shilling gallery—where you felt all the time that you ought not to have brought me—and more strongly I felt obligation to you for having brought me—and the pleasure was the better for a little shame—and when the curtain drew up, what cared we for our place in the house, or what mattered it where we were sitting, when our thoughts were with Rosalind° in Arden, or with Viola° at the Court of Illyria? You used to say, that the Gallery was the best place of all for enjoying a play socially—that the relish of such exhibitions must be in proportion to the infrequency of going—that the company we met there, not being in general readers of plays, were obliged to attend the more, and did attend, to what was going on, on the stage—because a word lost would have been a chasm, which it was impossible for them to fill up. With such reflections we consoled our pride then—and I appeal to you, whether, as a woman, I met generally with less attention and accommodation, than I have done since in more expensive situations in the house? The getting in indeed, and the crowding up those inconvenient staircases, was bad enough,—but there was still a law of civility to woman recognised to quite as great an extent as we ever found in the other passages—and how a little difficulty overcome heightened the snug seat, and the play, afterwards. Now we can only pay our money and walk in. You cannot see, you say, in the galleries now. I am sure we saw, and heard too, well enough then—but sight, and all, I think, is gone with our poverty."

"There was pleasure in eating strawberries, before they became quite common—in the first dish of peas, while they were yet dear—to have them for a nice supper, a treat. What treat can we have now? If we were to treat ourselves now—that is, to have dainties a little above our means, it would be selfish and wicked. It is very little more that we allow ourselves beyond what the actual poor can get at, that makes what I call a treat—when two people living together, as we have done, now and then indulge themselves in a cheap luxury, which both like; while each apologises, and is willing to take both halves of the blame to his single share. I see no harm in people making much of themselves in that sense of the word. It may give them a hint how to make much of others. But now—what I mean by the word—we never do make much of ourselves. None but the poor can do it. I do not mean the veriest poor of all, but persons as we were, just above poverty."

"I know what you were going to say, that it is mighty pleasant at the end of the year to make all meet,—and much ado we used to have every Thirty-first Night of December to account for our exceedings—many a long face did you make over your puzzled accounts, and in contriving to make it out how we had spent so much—or that we had not spent so much—or that it was impossible we should spend so much next year—and still we found our slender capital decreasing—but then, betwixt ways, and projects, and compromises of one sort or another, and talk of curtailing this charge, and doing without that for the future—and the hope that youth brings, and laughing spirits (in which you were never poor till now) we pocketed up our loss, and in conclusion, with 'lusty brimmers' (as you used to quote it out of *hearty cheerful Mr. Cotton,*° as you called him), we used to welcome in the 'coming guest.' Now we have no reckoning at all at the end of the old year—no flattering promises about the new year doing better for us."

Bridget is so sparing of her speech on most occasions, that when she gets into a rhetorical vein, I am careful how I interrupt it. I could not help, however, smiling at the phantom of wealth which her dear imagination had conjured up out of a clear income of a poor—hundred pounds a year. "It is true we were happier when we were poorer, but we were also younger, my cousin. I am afraid we must put up with the excess, for if we were to shake the superflux into the sea, we should not much mend ourselves. That we had much to struggle with, as we grew up together, we have reason to be most thankful. It strengthened, and knit our compact closer. We could never have been what we have been to each other, if we had always had the sufficiency which you now complain of. The resisting power—those natural dilations of the youthful spirit, which circumstances cannot straighten—with us are long since passed away. Competence to age is supplementary youth, a sorry supplement indeed, but I fear the best that is to be had. We must ride, where we formerly walked: live better, and lie softer—and shall be wise to do so—than we had means to do in those good old days you speak of. Yet could those days return—could you and I once more walk our thirty miles a-day—could Bannister and Mrs. Bland again be young, and you and I be young to see them—could the good old one-shilling gallery days return—they are dreams, my cousin, now—but could you and I at this moment, instead of this quiet argument, by our well-carpeted fire-side, sitting on this luxurious sofa—be once more struggling up those inconvenient stair cases, pushed about, and squeezed, and elbowed by the poorest rabble or poor gallery scramblers—could I once more hear those anxious shrieks of yours—and the delicious *Thank God, we are safe,* which always followed when the topmost stair, conquered, let in the first light of the whole cheerful theatre down beneath us—I know not the fathom line that ever touched a descent so deep as I would be willing to bury more

---

131 **The Battle of . . . Calais,** *The Battle of Hexham* and *The Surrender of Calais,* two comedies by George Colman (1762–1836)   132 **Children in the Wood,** a play by Thomas Morton (1764–1838)   140 **Rosalind,** character in Shakespeare's *As You Like It*   141 **Viola,** character in Shakespeare's *Twelfth Night*

199 **Mr. Cotton,** Charles Cotton (1630–1687); the quotations are from his poem *The New Year,* 49–50

wealth in than Crœsus° had, or the great Jew R——° is supposed to have, to purchase it. And now do just look at that merry little Chinese waiter holding an umbrella, big enough for a bed-tester, over the head of that pretty insipid half-Madonna-ish chit of a lady in that very blue summer house."

(1823)

WILLIAM HAZLITT
1778–1830

William Hazlitt, the son of a Unitarian minister, was born in Maidstone, April 10, 1778. Hazlitt was largely privately educated. Although his father would have liked to see his son in the ministry, Hazlitt was interested in philosophy and in painting. Indeed, he finally decided (1802) not only to undertake painting as a career but also to continue his study of metaphysics as a kind of second vocation. Although he never achieved a reputation as either a good painter or philosopher, the combination of these two interests apparently formed a third and very important one. Hazlitt developed an unusual ability as a critic from the logical processes of metaphysical thought and from the eye for color and form necessary to the art of painting.

Hazlitt's first important piece of writing, though a failure in metaphysics, was the *Essay on Principles of Human Action* (1807). Resigned to his failure as a philosopher, Hazlitt turned to general critical writing, contributing to various journals and grouping together a collection of essays known as *The Round Table*. His first achievement in literary criticism was *The Characters of Shakespeare's Plays* (1818); his most valuable miscellaneous collection of prose writings is *Table Talk* (1821). The years from 1807 to 1821, easily the most active period of Hazlitt's life, saw the writing of the three prose collections just mentioned and a considerable amount of lecturing, much of it on the Elizabethan playwrights, for whom Hazlitt shared the enthusiasm shown by Coleridge, Lamb, and De Quincey.

Hazlitt was extremely liberal, not to say radical, in his political tendencies. His liberalism usually meant unfavorable criticism of his work from the reviewers, particularly from those on the *Quarterly Review*. Nor did Hazlitt's private life help his isolated position. His first marriage was a dismal failure. In 1823, after he became involved with a servant girl, he and his wife separated, and he wrote *Liber Amoris*, an indiscreet account of the affair, which won him little sympathy.

He then left for the Continent, having somewhat casually contracted a second marriage in the meantime. Soon after (1825), he returned and published *The Spirit of the Age*. In the *Life of Napoleon* (1828–1830), Hazlitt clearly showed that he had passed his peak. He died on September 18, 1830. Hazlitt and Coleridge are regarded as the two most important literary critics of their day.

from MY FIRST ACQUAINTANCE WITH POETS

MEETING WITH COLERIDGE

My father was a Dissenting Minister at W——m° in Shropshire; and in the year 1798 (the figures that compose that date are to me like the "dreaded name of Demogorgon"°) Mr. Coleridge came to Shrewsbury, to succeed Mr. Rowe in the spiritual charge of a Unitarian congregation there. He did not come till late on the Saturday afternoon before he was to preach; and Mr. Rowe, who himself went down to the coach in a state of anxiety and expectation to look for the arrival of his successor, could find no one at all answering the 10 description but a round-faced man in a short black coat (like a shooting jacket) which hardly seemed to have been made for him, but who seemed to be talking at a great rate to his fellow-passengers. Mr. Rowe had scarce returned to give an account of his disappointment, when the round-faced man in black entered, and dissipated all doubts on the subject, by beginning to talk. He did not cease while he stayed; nor has he since, that I know of. He held the good town of Shrewsbury in delightful suspense for three weeks that 20 he remained there, "fluttering the *proud Salopians* like an eagle in dove-cote";° and the Welsh mountains that skirt the horizon with their tempestuous confusion agree to have heard no such mystic sounds since the days of

High-born Hoel's harp or soft Llewellyn's lay!°

As we passed along between W——m and Shrewsbury, and I eyed their blue tops seen through the wintry branches, or the red rustling leaves of the sturdy 30 oaktrees by the roadside, a sound was in my ears as of a siren's° song; I was stunned, startled with it, as from deep sleep; but I had no notion then that I should ever be able to express my admiration to others in motley

---

242 **Crœsus,** a king of Lydia (560–546 B.C.) noted for his great wealth **Jew R——,** Nathan Meyer Rothschild (1777–1836), who founded the English branch of the Rothschild banking house

Meeting With Coleridge 1 **W——m,** Wem, village near Shrewsbury 4 **dreaded . . . Demogorgon,** *Paradise Lost,* II, 964. Demogorgon was a mysterious infernal deity who controlled the fates of both gods and men 22 **fluttering . . . dove-cote,** Shakespeare, *Coriolanus,* V, vi, 115. Salopians are the inhabitants of Shropshire, from its old Latin name *Salopia* 26 **High-born . . . lay!** Gray, *The Bard,* 28, p. 57 31 **siren,** one of the sea nymphs said to inhabit an island near Italy and by their singing to lure mariners to destruction. The story of their attempts to lure Ulysses and his crew is told in Homer's *Odyssey,* XII

imagery or quaint allusion, till the light of his genius shone into my soul, like the sun's rays glittering in the puddles of the road. I was at that time dumb, inarticulate, helpless, like a worm by the wayside, crushed, bleeding, lifeless; but now, bursting from the deadly bands that bound them,

40 With Styx nine times round them,°

my ideas float on winged words, and as they expand their plumes, catch the golden light of other years. My soul has indeed remained in its original bondage, dark, obscure, with longings infinite and unsatisfied; my heart, shut up in the prison-house of this rude clay, has never found, nor will it ever find, a heart to speak to; but that my understanding also did not remain dumb and brutish, or at length found a language to express itself, I owe to Coleridge. But this is not to my pur-
50 pose.

My father lived ten miles from Shrewsbury, and was in the habit of exchanging visits with Mr. Rowe and with Mr. Jenkins of Whitchurch (nine miles farther on) according to the custom of Dissenting Ministers in each other's neighborhood. A line of communication is thus established, by which the flame of civil and religious liberty is kept alive, and nourishes its smoldering fire unquenchable, like the fires in the *Agamemnon*° of Aeschylus, placed at different stations, that waited for
60 ten long years to announce with their blazing pyramids the destruction of Troy. Coleridge had agreed to come over to see my father, according to the courtesy of the country, as Mr. Rowe's probable successor; but in the meantime I had gone to hear him preach the Sunday after his arrival. A poet and a philosopher getting up into a Unitarian pulpit to preach the Gospel was a romance in these degenerate days, a sort of revival of the primitive spirit of Christianity, which was not to be resisted.
70 It was in January, 1798, that I rose one morning before daylight, to walk ten miles in the mud, and went to hear this celebrated person preach. Never, the longest day I have to live, shall I have such another walk as this cold, raw, comfortless one, in the winter of the year 1798. *Il y a des impressions que ni le temps ni les circonstances peuvent effacer. Dusse-je vivre des siècles entiers, le doux temps de ma jeunesse ne peut renaître pour moi, ni s'effacer jamais dans ma mémoire.*° When I got there, the organ was playing the
80 100th psalm, and, when it was done, Mr. Coleridge rose and gave out his text, "And he went up into the mountain to pray, HIMSELF, ALONE."° As he gave out this text, his voice "rose like a steam of rich distilled perfumes,"° and when he came to the two last words,

which he pronounced loud, deep, and distinct, it seemed to me, who was then young, as if the sounds had echoed from the bottom of the human heart, and as if that prayer might have floated in solemn silence through the universe. The idea of St. John came into mind, "of one crying in the wilderness, who had his 90 loins girt about, and whose food was locusts and wild honey."° The preacher then launched into his subject, like an eagle dallying with the wind. The sermon was upon peace and war; upon church and state—not their alliance, but their separation—on the spirit of the world and the spirit of Christianity, not as the same, but as opposed to one another. He talked of those who had "inscribed the cross of Christ on banners dripping with human gore." He made a poetical and pastoral excursion—and to show the fatal effects of war, drew 100 a striking contrast between the simple shepherd boy, driving his team afield, or sitting under the hawthorn, piping to his flock, "as though he should never be old,"° and the same poor country-lad, crimped, kidnaped, brought into town, made drunk at an ale-house, turned into a wretched drummer-boy, with his hair sticking on end with powder and pomatum,° a long cue at his back, and tricked out in the loathsome finery of the profession of blood.

Such were the notes our once-loved poet sung.°   110

And for myself, I could not have been more delighted if I had heard the music of the spheres.° Poetry and Philosophy had met together. Truth and Genius had embraced,° under the eye and with the sanction of Religion. This was even beyond my hopes. I returned home well satisfied. The sun that was still laboring pale and wan through the sky, obscured by thick mists, seemed an emblem of the *good cause,*° and the cold dank drops of dew that hung half melted on the beard of the thistle had something genial and refreshing in 120 them; for there was a spirit of hope and youth in all nature that turned everything into good. The face of nature had not then the brand of JUS DIVINUM° on it:

Like to that sanguine flower inscribed with woe.°

On the Tuesday following, the half-inspired speaker came. I was called down into the room where he was, and went half-hoping, half-afraid. He received me very graciously, and I listened for a long time without uttering a word. I did not suffer in his opinion by my silence. "For those two hours," he afterwards was 130 pleased to say, "he was conversing with W. H.'s

40 **With . . . them,** Pope, *Ode on St. Cecilia's Day,* 90   58 **Agamemnon,** tragedy by Aeschylus, Greek dramatist (fifth century B.C.), in which fires are used to announce the fall of Troy   75–79 **Il y a des, etc.** There are impressions which neither times nor circumstances can efface. Were I enabled to live entire ages, the sweet days of my youth could not return for me, nor ever be obliterated from my memory (Rousseau, *Confessions,* II, 7)   82 **And . . . alone,** *John,* 6:15   84 **rose . . . perfumes,** Milton, *Comus,* 556

90–92 **of one . . . honey,** *Matthew,* 3:3–4   104 **as . . . old,** Sidney, *Arcadia,* 2   107 **pomatum,** perfumed ointment for the hair   110 **Such . . . sung,** Pope, *Epistle to Robert, Earl of Oxford,* 1   112 **music . . . spheres.** The ancients believed that the movement of the celestial planets produced music   114 **Truth . . . embraced.** Cf. *Psalms,* 85:10: "Mercy and truth are met together; righteousness and peace have kissed each other"   118 **good cause,** Liberty; the phrase had been popular during the time of the French Revolution   123 **Jus Divinum,** divine right, especially the divine right of kings   124 **Like . . . woe,** *Lycidas,* 106. The petals of the hyacinth (sanguine flower) were supposed to be marked with the exclamation Ai (alas), in lamentation for the Greek youth Hyacinthus, from whose blood the flower was said to have sprung

forehead!'' His appearance was different from what I had anticipated from seeing him before. At a distance, and in the dim light of the chapel, there was to me a strange wildness in his aspect, a dusky obscurity, and I thought him pitted with the small-pox. His complexion was at that time clear, and even bright—

As are the children of yon azure sheen.°

His forehead was broad and high, light as if built of
140 ivory, with large projecting eyebrows, and his eyes rolling beneath them like the sea with darkened luster. ''A certain tender bloom his face o'erspread,''° a purple tinge as we see it in the pale thoughtful complexions of the Spanish portrait-painters, Murillo and Velasquez.° His mouth was gross, voluptuous, open, eloquent; his chin good-humored and round; but his nose, the rudder of the face, the index of the will, was small, feeble, nothing—like what he has done. It might seem that the genius of his face as from a height surveyed and pro-
150 jected him (with sufficient capacity and huge aspiration) into the world unknown of thought and imagination, with nothing to support or guide his veering purpose, as if Columbus had launched his adventurous course for the New World in a scallop,° without oars or compass. So at least I comment on it after the event. Coleridge in his person was rather above the common size, inclining to the corpulent, or like Lord Hamlet, ''somewhat fat and pursy.°'' His hair (now, alas! gray) was then black and glossy as the raven's, and fell in
160 smooth masses over his forehead. This long pendulous hair is peculiar to enthusiasts, to those whose minds tend heavenward; and is traditionally inseparable (though of a different color) from the pictures of Christ. It ought to belong, as a character, to all who preach *Christ crucified*, and Coleridge was at that time one of those!

It was curious to observe the contrast between him and my father, who was a veteran in the cause and then declining into the vale of years. He had been a
170 poor Irish lad, carefully brought up by his parents, and sent to the University of Glasgow (where he studied under Adam Smith°) to prepare him for his future destination. It was his mother's proudest wish to see her son a Dissenting Minister. So if we look back to past generations (as far as eye can reach) we see the same hopes, fears, wishes, followed by the same disappointments, throbbing in the human hearts; and so we may see them (if we look forward) rising up forever, and disappearing, like vaporish bubbles, in the human
180 breast! After being tossed about from congregation to congregation in the heats of the Unitarian controversy and squabbles about the American war, he had been relegated to an obscure village, where he was to spend

the last thirty years of his life, far from the only converse that he loved, the talk about disputed texts of Scripture and the cause of civil and religious liberty. Here he passed his days, repining but resigned in the study of the Bible, and the perusal of the Commentators—huge folios, not easily got through, one of which would outlast a winter! Why did he pore on 190 these from morn to night (with the exception of a walk in the fields or a turn in the garden to gather broccoli plants or kidney-beans of his own rearing, with no small degree of pride and pleasure)? Here were ''no figures nor no fantasies''°—neither poetry nor philosophy—nothing to dazzle, nothing to excite modern curiosity; but to his lack-luster eyes there appeared, within the pages of the ponderous, unwieldy, neglected tomes, the sacred name of JEHOVAH in Hebrew capitals: pressed down by the weight of the 200 style, worn to the last fading thinness of the understanding, there were glimpses, glimmering notions of the patriarchal wanderings, with palm-trees hovering in the horizon, and processions of camels at the distance of three thousand years; there was Moses with the Burning Bush,° the number of the Twelve Tribes,° types, shadows, glosses on the law and the prophets; there were discussions (dull enough) on the age of Methuselah,° a mighty speculation! there were outlines, rude guesses at the shape of Noah's Ark° and of the 210 riches of Solomon's Temple;° questions as to the date of the creation, predictions of the end of all things; the great lapses of time, the strange mutations of the globe were unfolded with the voluminous leaf, as it turned over; and though the soul might slumber with an hieroglyphic veil of inscrutable mysteries drawn over it, yet it was in a slumber ill-exchanged for all the sharpened realities of sense, wit, fancy, or reason. My father's life was comparatively a dream; but it was a dream of infinity and eternity, of death, the resurrec- 220 tion, and a judgment to come!

No two individuals were ever more unlike than were the host and his guest. A poet was to my father a sort of nondescript: yet whatever added grace to the Unitarian cause was to him welcome. He could hardly have been more surprised or pleased if our visitor had worn wings. Indeed, his thoughts had wings; and as the silken sounds rustled round our little wainscoted parlor, my father threw back his spectacles over his forehead, his white hairs mixing with its sanguine hue; and a 230 smile of delight beamed across his rugged cordial face, to think that Truth had found a new ally in Fancy!° Besides, Coleridge seemed to take considerable notice of me, and that of itself was enough. He talked very

138 **As . . . sheen,** Thomson, *The Castle of Indolence,* II, 295   142 **A certain . . . o'erspread,** *ibid.,* 507. Thomson has *gloom* instead of *bloom*   144 **Murillo and Velasquez,** Spanish painters of the seventeenth century   154 **scallop,** a kind of sea shell   158 **pursy,** scant of breath, from *Hamlet,* V, ii, 298   172 **Adam Smith,** celebrated Scottish political economist (1723–1790)

195 **no . . . fantasies,** *Julius Caesar,* II, i, 231   206 **Moses . . . Bush,** a reference to the angel of the Lord that appeared in a burning bush to Moses. Cf. *Exodus,* 3:1–6   **Twelve Tribes,** of Israel; see *Genesis,* 49   209 **Methuselah,** Hebrew patriarch said to have lived 969 years. See *Genesis,* 5:27   210 **Noah's Ark,** described in *Genesis,* 6:14–16   211 **riches . . . Temple,** described in *1 Kings,* 6:20–35   232 **ally in Fancy.** "My father was one of those who mistook his talent after all. He used to be very much dissatisfied that I preferred his Letters to his Sermons. The last were forced and dry; the first came naturally from him. For ease, half-plays on words, and a supine, monkish, indolent pleasantry, I have never seen them equaled.''—Hazlitt's note

familiarly, but agreeably, and glanced over a variety of subjects. At dinner-time he grew more animated, and dilated in a very edifying manner on Mary Wollstonecraft° and Mackintosh.° The last, he said, he considered (on my father's speaking of his *Vindiciae Gallicae* as a capital performance) as a clever scholastic man—a master of the topics—or as the ready warehouseman of letters, who knew exactly where to lay his hand on what he wanted, though the goods were not his own. He thought him no match for Burke, either in style or matter. Burke was a metaphysician, Mackintosh a mere logician. Burke was an orator (almost a poet) who reasoned in figures, because he had an eye for nature: Mackintosh, on the other hand, was a rhetorician, who had only an eye to commonplaces. On this I ventured to say that I had always entertained a great opinion of Burke, and that (as far as I could find) the speaking of him with contempt might be made the test of a vulgar democratical mind. This was the first observation I ever made to Coleridge, and he said it was a very just and striking one. I remember the leg of Welsh mutton and the turnips on the table that day had the finest flavor imaginable. Coleridge added that Mackintosh and Tom Wedgwood (of whom, however, he spoke highly) had expressed a very indifferent opinion of his friend Mr. Wordsworth, on which he remarked to them—"He strides on so far before you that he dwindles in the distance!" Godwin had once boasted to him of having carried on an argument with Mackintosh for three hours with dubious success; Coleridge told him—"If there had been a man of genius in the room, he would have settled the question in five minutes." He asked me if I had ever seen Mary Wollstonecraft, and I said I had once for a few moments, and that she seemed to me to turn off Godwin's objections to something she advanced with quite a playful, easy air. He replied, that "this was only one instance of the ascendancy which people of imagination exercised over those of mere intellect." He did not rate Godwin very high (this was caprice or prejudice, real or affected) but he had a great idea of Mrs. Wollstonecraft's powers of conversation, none at all of her talent for book-making. We talked a little about Holcroft.° He had been asked if he was not much struck *with* him, and he said he thought himself in more danger of being struck *by* him. I complained that he would not let me get on at all, for he required a definition of every commonest word, exclaiming, "What do you mean by a *sensation*, Sir? What do you mean by an *idea*?" This, Coleridge said, was barricadoing° the road to truth—it was setting up a turnpike-gate at every step we took. I forgot a great number of things, many more than I remember; but the day passed off pleasantly, and the next morning Mr. Coleridge was to return to Shrewsbury. When I came down to breakfast, I found that he had just received a letter from his friend T. Wedgwood, making him an offer of £150 a year if he chose to waive his present pursuit, and devote himself entirely to the study of poetry and philosophy. Coleridge seemed to make up his mind to close with this proposal in the act of tying on one of his shoes. It threw an additional damp on his departure. It took the wayward enthusiast quite from us to cast him into Deva's° winding vales, or by the shores of old romance.° Instead of living at ten miles distance, of being the pastor of a Dissenting congregation at Shrewsbury, he was henceforth to inhabit the Hill of Parnassus,° to be a Shepherd on the Delectable Mountains.° Alas! I knew not the way thither, and felt very little gratitude for Mr. Wedgwood's bounty. I was presently relieved from the dilemma; for Mr. Coleridge, asking for a pen and ink, and going to a table to write something on a bit of card, advanced towards me with undulating step, and giving me the precious document, said that that was his address, *Mr. Coleridge, Nether Stowey, Somersetshire;* and that he should be glad to see me there in a few weeks' time, and, if I chose, would come half-way to meet me. I was not less surprised than the shepherd-boy (this simile is to be found in *Cassandra*°) when he sees a thunder-bolt fall close at his feet. I stammered out my acknowledgments and acceptance of this offer (I thought Mr. Wedgwood's annuity a trifle to it) as well as I could; and this mighty business being settled, the poet-preacher took leave, and I accompanied him six miles on the road. It was a fine morning in the middle of winter, and he talked the whole way. The scholar in Chaucer is described as going

—sounding on his way.°

So Coleridge went on his. In digressing, in dilating, in passing from subject to subject, he appeared to me to float in air, to slide on ice. He told me in confidence (going along) that he should have preached two sermons before he accepted the situation at Shrewsbury, one on Infant Baptism, the other on the Lord's supper, showing that he could not administer either, which would have effectually disqualified him for the object in view. I observed that he continually crossed me on the way by shifting from one side of the footpath to the other. This struck me as an odd movement; but I did not at that time connect it with any instability of purpose or involuntary change of principle, as I have done since. He seemed unable to keep on in a straight line.

---

238 **Mary Wollstonecraft,** English feminist writer (1759–1797) **Mackintosh,** Sir James Mackintosh (1765–1832), Scottish philosopher and historian in sympathy with the French Revolution; he published *Vindiciae Gallicae* (1791) in answer to Edmund Burke's *Reflections on the Revolution in France* (1790) 278 **Holcroft,** Thomas Holcroft (1745–1309), English dramatist, actor, and miscellaneous writer; also a prominent radical 284 **barricadoing,** barricading

298 **Deva,** old Latin name for the River Dee, in North Wales **by . . . romance.** Cf. Wordsworth's *A Narrow Girdle of Rough Stones and Crags,* 38: "Sole-sitting by the shores of old romance" 301 **inhabit . . . Parnassus,** become a poet. Parnassus is a mountain in Greece, celebrated as the haunt of the Muses of poetry and music 302 **Shepherd . . . Mountains.** In Bunyan's *Pilgrim's Progress,* Christian and Hopeful escape from Giant Despair and come to the Shepherds of the Delectable Mountains 313 **Cassandra,** French historical romance by La Calprenède (1610–1663) 323 **sounding . . . way,** from Chaucer's *Prologue* to *The Canterbury Tales,* 307

He spoke slightingly of Hume° (whose *Essay on Miracles* he said was stolen from an objection started in one of South's° sermons—*Credat Judaeus Apella!*°) I was not very much pleased at this account of Hume, for I had just been reading, with infinite relish, that completest of all metaphysical *choke-pears,* his *Treatise on Human Nature,* to which the *Essays,* in point of scholastic subtlety and close reasoning, are mere elegant trifling, light summer-reading. Coleridge even denied the excellence of Hume's general style, which I think betrayed a want of taste or candor. He however made me amends by the manner in which he spoke of Berkeley.° He dwelt particularly on his *Essay on Vision* as a masterpiece of analytical reasoning. So it undoubtedly is. He was exceedingly angry with Dr. Johnson for striking the stone with his foot, in allusion to this author's *Theory of Matter and Spirit,* and saying, "Thus I confute him, Sir."° Coleridge drew a parallel (I don't know how he brought about the connection) between Bishop Berkeley and Tom Paine.° He said the one was an instance of a subtle, the other of an acute mind, than which no two things could be more distinct. The one was a shop-boy's quality, the other the characteristic of a philosopher. He considered Bishop Butler° as a true philosopher, a profound and conscientious thinker, a genuine reader of nature and of his own mind. He did not speak of his *Analogy,* but of his *Sermons at the Rolls' Chapel,* of which I had never heard. Coleridge somehow always contrived to prefer the *unknown* to the *known.* In this instance he was right. The *Analogy* is a tissue of sophistry, of wire-drawn, theological special-pleading; the *Sermons* (with the Preface to them) are in a fine vein of deep, matured reflection, a candid appeal to our observation of human nature, without pedantry and without bias. I told Coleridge I had written a few remarks, and was sometimes foolish enough to believe that I had made a discovery on the same subject (the *Natural Disinterestedness of the Human Mind)°*—and I tried to explain my view of it to Coleridge, who listened with great willingness, but I did not succeed in making myself understood. I sat down to the task shortly afterwards for the twentieth time, got new pens and paper, determined to make clear work of it, wrote a few meager sentences in the skeleton-style of a mathematical demonstration, stopped half way down the second page; and, after trying in vain to pump up any words, images, notions, apprehensions, facts, or observations, from that gulf of abstraction in which I had plunged myself for four or five years preceding, gave up the attempt as labor in vain, and shed tears of helpless despondency on the blank unfinished paper. I can write fast enough now. Am I better than I was then? Oh, no! One truth discovered, one pang of regret at not being able to express it, is better than all the fluency and flippancy in the world. Would that I could go back to what I then was! Why can we not revive past times as we can revisit old places? If I had the quaint Muse of Sir Philip Sidney to assist me, I would write a *Sonnet to the Road between W——m and Shrewsbury,* and immortalize every step of it by some fond enigmatical conceit. I would swear that the very milestones had ears, and that Harmer-hill° stooped with all its pines to listen to a poet as he passed! I remember but one other topic of discourse in this walk. He mentioned Paley,° praised the naturalness and clearness of his style, but condemned his sentiments, thought him a mere time-serving casuist, and said that "the fact of his work on *Moral and Political Philosophy* being made a textbook in our Universities was a disgrace to the national character." We parted at the six-mile stone; and I returned homeward, pensive but much pleased. I had met with unexpected notice from a person whom I believed to have been prejudiced against me. "Kind and affable to me had been his condescension, and should be honored ever with suitable regard."° He was the first poet I had known, and he certainly answered to that inspired name. I had heard a great deal of his powers of conversation, and was not disappointed. In fact, I never met with anything at all like them, either before or since. I could easily credit the accounts which were circulated of his holding forth to a large party of ladies and gentlemen, an evening or two before, on the Berkeleian Theory, when he made the whole material universe look like a transparency of fine words; and another story (which I believe he has somewhere told himself°) of his being asked to a party at Birmingham,° of his smoking tobacco and going to sleep after dinner on a sofa, where the company found him to their no small surprise, which was increased to wonder when he started up of a sudden, and rubbing his eyes, looked about him, and launched into a three-hours' description of the third heaven, of which he had had a dream, very different from Mr. Southey's *Vision of Judgment,°* and also from that other *Vision of Judgment,* which Mr. Murray,° the Secretary of the Bridge-street Junto, has taken into his especial keeping!

On my way back I had a sound in my ears; it was the voice of Fancy—I had a light before me; it was the face of Poetry. The one still lingers there; the other has not quitted my side! Coleridge in truth met me halfway on the ground of philosophy, or I should not have been won over to his imaginative creed. I had an uneasy,

338 **Hume,** David Hume (1711–1776), famous Scottish philosopher. His *Essay on Miracles* shocked orthodox theologians of the period   340 **South,** Robert South (1634–1716), celebrated English divine   **Credat . . . Apella.** Let the Jew Apella—i.e., a credulous person—believe it: I shall not (Horace, *Satires,* I, v, 101)   350 **Berkeley,** George Berkeley (1685–1753), Irish bishop and idealistic philosopher   355 **Thus . . . Sir,** related in Boswell's *Life of Johnson*   357 **Tom Paine,** Anglo-American liberal political writer (1737–1809)   362 **Bishop Butler,** Joseph Butler (1692–1752), English theologian   376 **Natural . . . Mind,** not published until 1805

400 **Harmer-hill,** prominent hill on the road between Wem and Shrewsbury   403 **Paley,** William Paley (1743–1805), orthodox theologian and philosopher   412–414 **Kind . . . regard,** *Paradise Lost,* VIII, 648–650   424 **he . . . himself,** in *Biographia Literaria,* 10   425 **Birmingham,** large manufacturing city in Warwickshire   432 **Southey's Vision of Judgment,** describes the entrance of George III into heaven. The "other *Vision*" is Byron's ferocious satire of Southey's poem   433 **Mr. Murray,** John Murray (1778–1843), Byron's publisher. He was publisher also of the Tory *Quarterly Review.* The Bridge-Street Association was organized in 1821 to prevent seditious publications and acts

pleasurable sensation all the time, till I was to visit him. During those months the chill breath of winter gave me a welcoming; the vernal air was balm and inspiration to me. The golden sunsets, the silver star of evening, lighted me on my way to new hopes and prospects. *I was to visit Coleridge in the spring*. This circumstance was never absent from my thoughts, and mingled with all my feelings. I wrote to him at the time
450 proposed, and received an answer postponing my intended visit for a week or two, but very cordially urging me to complete my promise then. This delay did not damp, but rather increased my ardor. In the meantime I went to Llangollen Vale,° by way of initiating myself in the mysteries of natural scenery; and I must say I was enchanted with it. I had been reading Coleridge's description of England, in his fine *Ode on the Departing Year*, and I applied it, *con amore*,° to the objects before me. That valley was to me (in a manner)
460 the cradle of a new existence: in the river that winds through it, my spirit was baptized in the waters of Helicon!° . . .

(1823)

GEORGE NOEL GORDON, LORD BYRON
1788–1824

Byron was a legend all over Europe in his own lifetime. His international reputation was greater than that of any English literary contemporary, but it was based as much on his personality as on his poetry. The legendary public image of the man, the facts of his biography, and the self-dramatizations in his poetry are extraordinarily complex; they still fascinate readers and critics today.

Byron was born in London in 1788, the son of a famous rake, "mad Jack" Byron, and a rich Scottish heiress of uneven temperament, Catherine Gordon. Byron was born with a clubfoot, an affliction to which he remained very sensitive all his life but which did not seem to diminish his social attractiveness. He was sexually precocious, conceiving passions for two distant female cousins when he was only nine. At the age of ten he succeeded to the title of his great-uncle, the "wicked" Lord Byron, and inherited the ancestral estate of Newstead Abbey, Nottinghamshire, which had been presented to the Byrons by Henry VIII. He was sent to Harrow, one of England's most prestigious schools, and to Trinity College, Cambridge. Although he read widely at the university in English literature,

history, and books of travel, his main interest seemed to be the fashionable dissipation of a Regency lord. At the university he formed a close friendship with John Cam Hobhouse, who stirred his interest in liberal politics.

On reaching his majority in 1809, Byron took his seat in the House of Lords. He also published his first important poem, the satire *English Bards and Scotch Reviewers*, in which he ridiculed Wordsworth and Coleridge among other literary contemporaries. After the commotion caused by his satire, Byron and Hobhouse took an extensive tour of the eastern Mediterranean region, visiting Albania, Greece, and Asia Minor. The tour lasted two years, during which time Byron accumulated materials which he used in his later poetic works. His first use of these materials was in the first two cantos of *Childe Harold* (1812). The reception in London of *Childe Harold* was sensational; Byron suddenly found himself lionized in the best drawing rooms. The reasons for the poem's success are not hard to determine—it had great vigor and descriptive power, and it was extremely opportune, for it provided a kind of poetical guidebook to the Europe of Byron's own day. Moreover, there was an interestingly mysterious unhappiness which already was apparent in Byron's lines; the hero of *Childe Harold* was a melancholy young aristocrat with a proud, somewhat self-dramatizing attitude. The appeal of all this to his contemporaries was irresistible. In spite of Byron's denials, his reading audience insisted that the poem was largely autobiographical. As a result of the glamor attached to his name, the poet soon gained the reputation of being, as one mistress put it, "mad, bad, and dangerous to know."

Having found a real outlet for his natural poetic powers, Byron proceeded to follow it with great diligence. He launched upon a series of narrative poems, tales of adventure located for the most part in the Near East or the Mediterranean area. *The Giaour* (1813), *The Bride of Abydos* (1813), *The Corsair* (1814), *Lara* (1814), *The Siege of Corinth* (1816), *Parisina* (1816) are all "Oriental tales." Added to *Childe Harold* they made Byron distinctly the rage. The handsome Byron was soon besieged by women. He had numerous affairs, some no doubt as a result of female initiative. His most notorious liaison was with the eccentric Lady Caroline Lamb, but Byron was eventually repelled by her reckless indiscretions.

Nothing remained in Byron's quest for worldly happiness, it seemed, but a steadying love and an advantageous marriage. In January 1815 Byron married Isabella Millbanke: she was rich, beautiful, intelligent, morally earnest, and naive. The controversy over the causes of their bitter separation after only a year of marriage is still unsettled. The explanation by Byron was simply that they were incompatible, but the persistent rumor of Byron's intimate relations with his half-sister, Augusta Leigh, was doubtless an important

---

454 **Llangollen Vale,** in Wales, about thirty-five miles from Wem   458 **con amore,** with love   462 **Helicon,** mountain in Greece; it had two springs sacred to the Muses

factor in the dissolution of his marriage. Whatever the cause, the British public chose to believe the worst; Byron, virtually ostracized, went to the Continent, never returning to England.

After visiting with the poet Shelley and his circle in Switzerland for a time, Byron made his way to Italy, where he spent his time traveling from city to city and falling in and out of love. In Venice he is reported to have kept a virtual harem. Finally, in 1819, he settled into a liaison with the nineteen-year-old Countess Teresa Guiccioli, who gave him a steadiness he had never known before. His output of poetry in Italy, mostly under the influence of the Countess Guiccioli, was astonishing. *Childe Harold* was completed, and the satirical *Beppo* appeared the same year (1817); *Mazeppa* and *The Prisoner of Chillon* soon followed. *The Prophecy of Dante* and several poetic dramas like *Cain* appeared in 1821. Byron's satire *The Vision of Judgment* (1822) blasted not only the Poet Laureate Robert Southey but the older school of romantic poets like Wordsworth and Coleridge. But Byron's crowning achievement of his Italian days was *Don Juan,* on which he was engaged from 1818 until his death. Don Juan is perhaps a comic-epic panorama of Byron as a whole, his complex character blended into one romantic, cynical, satirical, amorous, adventurous, melodramatic, liberty-loving person who travels throughout Europe never satisfied.

In 1822 Byron, the Countess Guiccioli, and her family (the politically active Gambas) set up a household in Florence. There they were frequently visited by Shelley and Leigh Hunt (1784–1859), who was a coeditor with Byron of the literary periodical *The Liberal.* By 1823 Byron's interest in the periodical had waned and he had grown restive in his life with Teresa Guiccioli. Thus, he eagerly accepted an offer to act as the agent for the London Greek Committee in aiding the Greeks in their war for independence from the Turks. Byron tried to promote the finances for the cause in London, but he eventually aided the Greeks with his own money. While awaiting action in the rebellion at Missolonghi, he contracted a fever. He died on April 19, 1824. He was deeply mourned by the Greek people, who now consider him a national hero. His body was returned to England but was refused burial in Westminster Abbey because of his immorality. A memorial to Byron was finally placed in the Abbey in 1969.

WHEN WE TWO PARTED

When we two parted
  In silence and tears,
Half broken-hearted
  To sever for years,
Pale grew thy cheek and cold,
  Colder thy kiss;
Truly that hour foretold
  Sorrow to this.

The dew of the morning
10 Sunk chill on my brow—
It felt like the warning
  Of what I feel now.
Thy vows are all broken,
  And light is thy fame;
I hear thy name spoken,
  And share in its shame.

They name thee before me,
  A knell to mine ear;
A shudder comes o'er me—
20 Why wert thou so dear?
They know not I knew thee,
  Who knew thee too well—
Long, long shall I rue thee,
  Too deeply to tell.

In secret we met—
  In silence I grieve
That thy heart could forget,
  Thy spirit deceive,
If I should meet thee
  After long years,   30
How should I greet thee?—
  With silence and tears.
(1808; 1816)

SHE WALKS IN BEAUTY

She° walks in beauty, like the night
  Of cloudless climes and starry skies;
And all that's best of dark and bright
  Meet in her aspect and her eyes:
Thus mellowed to that tender light   5
  Which heaven to gaudy day denies.

One shade the more, one ray the less,
  Had half impaired the nameless grace
Which waves in every raven tress,
  Or softly lightens o'er her face;   10
Where thoughts serenely sweet express
  How pure, how dear their dwelling-place.

And on that cheek, and o'er that brow,
  So soft, so calm, yet eloquent,
The smiles that win, the tints that glow,   15
  But tell of days in goodness spent,
A mind at peace with all below,
  A heart whose love is innocent!
(1814; 1815)

She Walks in Beauty 1 **She,** Lady Wilmot Horton, who had appeared in an evening dress of black mourning with spangles

STANZAS FOR MUSIC

There's not a joy the world can give like that it takes
    away,
When the glow of early thought declines in feeling's
    dull decay;
'Tis not on youth's smooth cheek the blush alone,
    which fades so fast,
But the tender bloom of heart is gone, ere youth itself
    be past.

Then the few whose spirits float above the wreck of
    happiness
Are driven o'er the shoals of guilt or ocean of excess:
The magnet of their course is gone, or only points in
    vain
The shore to which their shivered sail shall never
    stretch again.

Then the mortal coldness of the soul like death itself
    comes down;
It cannot feel for others' woes, it dare not dream its
    own
That heavy chill has frozen o'er the fountain of our
    tears,
And though the eye may sparkle still, 'tis where the ice
    appears

Though wit may flash from fluent lips, and mirth dis-
    tract the breast,
Through midnight hours that yield no more their
    former hope of rest;
'Tis but as ivy-leaves around the ruined turret wreath,
All green and wildly fresh without, but worn and gray
    beneath.

Oh, could I feel as I have felt—or be what I have been,
Or weep as I could once have wept, o'er many a van-
    ished scene;
As springs, in deserts found, seem sweet, all brackish
    though they be,
So, midst the withered waste of life, those tears would
    flow to me.
(1815; 1816)

10

20

STANZAS FOR MUSIC

There be none of Beauty's daughters
    With a magic like thee;
And like music on the waters
    Is thy sweet voice to me:
When, as if its sound were causing
The charmèd ocean's pausing,
The waves lie still and gleaming,
And the lulled winds seem dreaming.

5

And the midnight moon is weaving
    Her bright chain o'er the deep;
Whose breast is gently heaving,
    As an infant's asleep:
So the spirit bows before thee,
To listen and adore thee;
With a full but soft emotion,
Like the swell of Summer's ocean.
(1816)

10

15

SONNET ON CHILLON°

The Castle of Chillon is situated at the eastern end of Lake Geneva, Switzerland. The poem, a dramatic monologue, was written in two days at a small inn where Byron and Shelley were detained by bad weather during a tour of the lake. François de Bonnivard (1493–1570) was a Swiss patriot and religious reformer. For his participation in an effort to make Geneva a republic, free from the control of Charles III, duke of Savoy, he was imprisoned in the Castle of Chillon from 1530 until he was released by his own party in 1536. Byron presents a romantic idealization of the few facts at his disposal. The brothers are imaginary.

Eternal Spirit of the chainless Mind!
    Brightest in dungeons, Liberty! thou art:
    For there thy habitation is the heart—
The heart which love of thee alone can bind;
And when thy sons to fetters are consigned—
    To fetters, and the damp vault's dayless gloom,
    Their country conquers with their martyrdom,
And Freedom's fame finds wings on every wind.
Chillon! thy prison is a holy place,
    And thy sad floor an altar—for 'twas trod,
Until his very steps have left a trace
    Worn, as if thy cold pavement were a sod,
By Bonnivard!°—May none those marks efface!
    For they appeal from tyranny to God.
(1816)

5

10

SO WE'LL GO NO MORE A-ROVING

So we'll go no more a-roving
    So late into the night,
Though the heart be still as loving,
    And the moon be still as bright.

For the sword outwears its sheath,
    And the soul wears out the breast,
And the heart must pause to breathe,
    And love itself have rest.

5

Sonnet on Chillon. 13 **Bonnivard,** Francois de Bonnivard (1493–1570), a Swiss patriot and religious reformer, who was imprisoned in Chillon for six years

Though the night was made for loving,
10   And the day returns too soon,
Yet we'll go no more a-roving
   By the light of the moon.
(1817; 1830)

from DON JUAN

The poem *Don Juan* owes its title and certain features
of its story to an old Spanish legend based on the
folklore theme of the universal lover. The legend had
been popular in Europe for centuries and had undergone a revival during the neoclassical age; there had
been a play by Molière (1622–1673) and an opera,
Don Giovanni, by Mozart (1756–1791). Byron's version, however, is highly original, presenting Juan as a
young innocent more sinned against than sinning. He
said in a letter to his friend Thomas Moore, dated
September 19, 1818: "I have finished the first Canto (a
long one of about 180 octaves) of a poem in the style
and manner of *Beppo*, encouraged by the good success
of the same. It is called *Don Juan*, and is meant to be
a little quietly facetious about everything. But I doubt
whether it is not—at least, as far as it has yet gone
—too free for these very modest days. However, I
shall try the experiment, anonymously; if it don't take,
it will be discontinued. It is dedicated to Southey in
good, simple, savage verse, upon the Laureate's politics, and the way he got them." The experiment was
successful, and the sixteen cantos appeared in steady
succession between 1818 and March 1824, less than a
month before Byron's death.

FRAGMENT°

I would to heaven that I were so much clay,
   As I am blood, bone, marrow, passion, feeling—
Because at least the past were passed away—
   And for the future—(but I write this reeling,
5 Having got drunk exceedingly today,
   So that I seem to stand upon the ceiling)
I say—the future is a serious matter—
And so—for God's sake—hock° and soda water!

DEDICATION

I

Bob Southey!° You're a poet—Poet-laureate,
   And representative of all the race;
Although 'tis true that you turn'd out a Tory at

Last,—yours has lately been a common case;
And now, my Epic Renegade! what are ye at?   5
   With all the Lakers,° in and out of place?
A nest of tuneful persons, to my eye
Like "four and twenty Blackbirds in a pye;

II

"Which pye being open'd they began to sing"
   (This old song and new simile holds good),   10
"A dainty dish to set before the King,"
   Or Regent,° who admires such kind of food;—
And Coleridge, too, has lately taken wing,°
   But like a hawk encumber'd with his hood,—
Explaining metaphysics to the nation—   15
I wish he would explain his Explanation.

III

You, Bob! are rather insolent, you know,
   At being disappointed in your wish
To supersede all warblers here below,
   And be the only Blackbird in the dish;   20
And then you overstrain yourself, or so,
   And tumble downward like the flying fish
Gasping on deck, because you soar too high, Bob,
And fall, for lack of moisture quite a-dry, Bob!

IV

And Wordsworth, in a rather long "Excursion"°   25
   (I think the quarto holds five hundred pages),
Has given a sample from the vasty version
   Of his new system to perplex the sages;
'Tis poetry—at least by his assertion,
   And may appear so when the dog-star rages—   30
And he who understands it would be able
To add a story to the Tower of Babel.

V

You—Gentlemen! by dint of long seclusion
   From better company, have kept your own
At Keswick,° and, through still continued fusion   35
   Of one another's minds, at last have grown
To deem as a most logical conclusion,
   That Poesy has wreaths for you alone:
There is a narrowness in such a notion,
Which makes me wish you'd change your lakes for
      ocean.   40

VI

I would not imitate the petty thought,
   Nor coin my self-love to so base a vice,
For all the glory your conversion brought,
   Since gold alone should not have been its price.
You have your salary: was't for that you wrought?   45

Fragment. This stanza was written on the back of part of the manuscript of Canto
I; it serves aptly as an epigraph   8 **hock,** white Rhine wine   **Dedication**
1 **Southey.** Southey, like Wordsworth and Coleridge, was at one time an ardent
Republican, but the excesses and failures of the French Revolution led him finally
to become a Tory

6 **Lakers,** Wordsworth, Coleridge, and others, so called from their residence in
the Lake District   12 **Regent,** the Prince of Wales, later George IV, who was
appointed when his father George III went insane in 1811. Southey was made
poet laureate in 1813   13 **Coleridge . . . wing,** a reference to his *Biographia
Literaria,* published in 1817   25 **Excursion,** title of a long poem by Wordsworth
35 **Keswick,** town in the Lake District where Southey joined Coleridge in 1803

And Wordsworth has his place in the Excise.°
You're shabby fellows—true—but poets still,
And duly seated on the immortal hill.

VII

Your bays° may hide the baldness of your brows—
50 Perhaps some virtuous blushes;—let them go—
To you I envy neither fruit nor boughs—
    And for the fame you would engross below,
The field is universal, and allows
    Scope to all such as feel the inherent glow:
55 Scott, Rogers, Campbell, Moore, and Crabbe,° will try
'Gainst you the question with posterity.

VIII

For me, who, wandering with pedestrian Muses,
    Contend not with you on the winged steed,°
I wish your fate may yield ye, when she chooses,
60 The fame you envy, and the skill you need;
And recollect a poet nothing loses
    In giving to his brethren their full meed
Of merit, and complaint of present days
Is not the certain path to future praise.

IX

65 He that reserves his laurels for posterity
    (Who does not often claim the bright reversion)
Has generally no great crop to spare it, he
    Being only injured by his own assertion;
And although here and there some glorious rarity
70 Arise like Titan° from the sea's immersion,
The major part of such appellants go
To—God knows where—for no one else can know.

X

If, fallen in evil days on evil tongues,°
    Milton appealed to the Avenger, Time,
75 If Time, the Avenger, execrates his wrongs,
    And makes the word "Miltonic" mean "*sublime*,"
He deign'd not to belie his soul in songs,
    Nor turn his very talent to a crime;
He did not loathe the Sire to laud the Son,°
80 But closed the tyrant-hater he begun.

XI

Think'st thou, could he—the blind Old Man—arise,
    Like Samuel° from the grave, to freeze once more
The blood of monarchs with his prophecies,
    Or be alive again—again all hoar
85 With time and trials, and those helpless eyes,
    And heartless daughters°—worn—and pale—and
        poor,

Would *he* adore a sultan? *he* obey
The intellectual eunuch Castlereagh?°

XII

Cold-blooded, smooth-faced, placid miscreant!
    Dabbling its sleek young hands in Erin's gore,   90
And thus for wider carnage taught to pant,
    Transferr'd to gorge upon a sister shore,
The vulgarest tool that Tyranny could want,
    With just enough of talent, and no more,
To lengthen fetters by another fix'd,   95
And offer poison long already mix'd.

XIII

An orator of such set trash of phrase
    Ineffably—legitimately vile,
That even its grossest flatterers dare not praise,
    Nor foes—all nations—condescend to smile;   100
Not even a sprightly blunder's spark can blaze
    From that Ixion° grindstone's ceaseless toil,
That turns and turns to give the world a notion
Of endless torments and perpetual motion.

XIV

A bungler even in its disgusting trade,   105
    And botching, patching, leaving still behind
Something of which its masters are afraid,
    States to be curb'd, and thoughts to be confined,
Conspiracy or Congress to be made—
    Cobbling at manacles for all mankind—   110
A tinkering slave-maker, who mends old chains,
With God and man's abhorrence for its gains.

XV

If we may judge of matter by the mind,
    Emasculated to the marrow *It*
Hath but two objects, how to serve, and bind,   115
    Deeming the chain it wears even men may fit,
Eutropius° of its many masters,—blind
    To worth as freedom, wisdom as to wit.
Fearless—because *no* feeling dwells in ice,
Its very courage stagnates to a vice.   120

XVI

Where shall I turn me not to *view* its bonds,
    For I will never *feel* them;—Italy!
Thy late reviving Roman soul desponds
    Beneath the lie this State-thing breathed o'er thee—
Thy clanking chain, and Erin's yet green wounds,   125
    Have voices—tongues to cry aloud for me.
Europe has slaves, allies, kings, armies still,
And Southey lives to sing them very ill.

---

46 **the Excise.** Wordsworth was made Distributor of Stamps for Westmorland in 1813, but he never had any connection with the excise   49 **bays,** wreaths of honor made from the leaves of the bay tree, a kind of laurel   55 **Scott . . . Crabbe,** all contemporary poets   58 **winged steed,** Pegasus, associated with poetic inspiration   70 **Titan,** one of a mythological race of giants said to have piled mountain on mountain to scale heaven   73 **fallen . . . tongues,** from *Paradise Lost,* VII, 26   79 **loathe . . . Son,** as Southey did with reference to George III and his son   82 **Samuel.** See *1 Samuel,* 28   86 **heartless daughters.** Milton is said to have received shameful treatment from his daughters

88 **Castlereagh,** Robert Stewart (1769–1822), Viscount Castlereagh, who as Foreign Secretary was noted for his cruelty and his contempt for anyone not of the aristocracy. At the time of the Irish Rebellion in 1798 he was charged with encouraging inhuman punishments of the rebels   102 **Ixion,** legendary Greek king who for boasting of the favors of Hera, wife of Zeus, was bound to an endlessly revolving wheel in Hades   117 **Eutropius,** Byzantine statesman surnamed "The Eunuch" who served as chamberlain to Arcadius on his succession to power as Emperor of the East in 395

XVII

Meantime, Sir Laureate, I proceed to dedicate,
130   In honest simple verse, this song to you.
And, if in flattering strains I do not predicate,
    'Tis that I still retain my "buff and blue;"°
My politics as yet are all to educate:
    Apostasy's so fashionable, too,
135 To keep *one* creed's a task grown quite Herculean:
    Is it not so, my Tory, Ultra-Julian?°

from CANTO 1

I

I WANT a hero: an uncommon want,
    When every year and month sends forth a new one,
Till, after cloying the gazettes with cant,
    The age discovers he is not the true one:
5 Of such as these I should not care to vaunt,
    I'll therefore take our ancient friend Don Juan—
We all have seen him, in the pantomime,
Sent to the devil somewhat ere his time. . . .

V

Brave men were living before Agamemnon°
    And since, exceeding valorous and sage,
35 A good deal like him too, though quite the same none;
    But then they shone not on the poet's page,
And so have been forgotten:—I condemn none,
    But can't find any in the present age
Fit for my poem (that is, for my new one);
40 So, as I said, I'll take my friend Don Juan.

VI

Most epic poets plunge "in medias res"°
    (Horace makes this the heroic turnpike road),
And then your hero tells, whene'er you please,
    What went before—by way of episode,
45 While seated after dinner at his ease,
    Beside his mistress in some soft abode,
Palace, or garden, paradise, or cavern,
Which serves the happy couple for a tavern.

VII

That is the usual method, but not mine—
50   My way is to begin with the beginning;
The regularity of my design
    Forbids all wandering as the worst of sinning,
And therefore I shall open with a line
    (Although it cost me half an hour in spinning)
55 Narrating somewhat of Don Juan's father,
    And also of his mother, if you'd rather. . . .

XXXVII

Dying intestate, Juan was sole heir
    To a chancery° suit, and messuages° and lands,   290
Which, with a long minority and care,
    Promised to turn out well in proper hands:
Inez became sole guardian, which was fair,
    And answer'd but to nature's just demands;
An only son left with an only mother   295
Is brought up much more wisely than another.

XXXVIII

Sagest of women, even of widows, she
    Resolved that Juan should be quite a paragon,
And worthy of the noblest pedigree:
    (His sire was of Castile, his dam from Aragon).   300
Then for accomplishments of chivalry,
    In case our lord the king should go to war again,
He learn'd the arts of riding, fencing, gunnery,
And how to scale a fortress—or a nunnery.

XXXIX

But that which Donna Inez most desired,   305
    And saw into herself each day before all
The learned tutors whom for him she hired,
    Was, that his breeding should be strictly moral:
Much into all his studies she inquired,
    And so they were submitted first to her, all,   310
Arts, sciences, no branch was made a mystery
To Juan's eyes, excepting natural history.

XL

The languages, especially the dead,
    The sciences, and most of all the abstruse,
The arts, at least all such as could be said   315
    To be the most remote from common use,
In all these he was much and deeply read:
    But not a page of anything that's loose,
Or hints continuation of the species,
Was ever suffer'd, lest he should grow vicious.   320

XLI

His classic studies made a little puzzle,
    Because of filthy loves of gods and goddesses,
Who in the earlier ages raised a bustle,
    But never put on pantaloons or bodices;
His reverend tutors had at times a tussle,   325
    And for their Æneids, Iliads, and Odysseys,
Were forced to make an odd sort of apology,
For Donna Inez dreaded the Mythology.

XLII

Ovid's° a rake, as half his verses show him,
    Anacreon's° morals are a still worse sample,   330

---

132 **buff and blue,** colors of the uniform of members of the Whig Club; hence the binding of the *Edinburgh Review,* the Whig organ   136 **Ultra-Julian.** "I allude not to our friend Landor's hero, the traitor Count Julian, but to Gibbon's hero vulgarly yclept 'The Apostate.'"—Byron's note. Julian was Roman emperor between 361 and 363; he was known as "Julian the Apostate" because he was a persistent enemy of Christianity. He publicly announced his conversion to paganism in 361   **Canto 1**   33 **Agamemnon,** king and leader of the Greek force at Troy in Homer's *Iliad*   41 **in medias res,** in the middle of things; from Horace's *Ars Poetica*

290 **chancery,** high court of equity in England with common-law functions **messuages,** dwellings and outbuildings   329 **Ovid,** Roman poet, satirist, and mythographer (43 B.C.–A.D. 18). Among his works is the *Ars Amatoria* (Art of Love) which, in three books, gives instructions on how to acquire and keep a lover   330 **Anacreon,** Greek lyric poet (572?–488 B.C.); wrote many short lyrics celebrating love and wine

Catullus° scarcely has a decent poem,
　I don't think Sappho's° Ode a good example,
Although Longinus° tells us there is no hymn
　Where the sublime soars forth on wings more ample;
335 But Virgil's° songs are pure, except that horrid one
　Beginning with "Formosum Pastor Corydon."

XLIII

Lucretius'° irreligion is too strong
　For early stomachs, to prove wholesome food;
I can't help thinking Juvenal° was wrong,
340 　Although no doubt his real intent was good,
For speaking out so plainly in his song,
　So much indeed as to be downright rude;
And then what proper person can be partial
To all those nauseous epigrams of Martial?°

XLIV

345 Juan was taught from out the best edition,
　Expurgated by learned men, who place,
Judiciously, from out the schoolboy's vision,
　The grosser parts; but, fearful to deface
Too much their modest bard by this omission,
350 　And pitying sore this mutilated case,
They only add them all in an appendix,
Which saves, in fact, the trouble of an index;

XLV

For there we have them all "at one fell swoop,"
　Instead of being scatter'd through the pages;
355 They stand forth marshall'd in a handsome troop,
　To meet the ingenuous youth of future ages,
Till some less rigid editor shall stoop
　To call them back into their separate cages,
Instead of standing staring all together,
360 Like garden gods—and not so decent either.

XLVI

The Missal too (it was the family Missal)
　Was ornamented in a sort of way
Which ancient mass-books often are, and this all
　Kinds of grotesques illumined; and how they,
365 Who saw those figures on the margin kiss all,
　Could turn their optics to the text and pray,
Is more than I know—But Don Juan's mother
Kept this herself, and gave her son another.

XLVII

Sermons he read, and lectures he endured,
370 　And homilies, and lives of all the saints;

To Jerome° and to Chrysostom° inured,
　He did not take such studies for restraints;
But how faith is acquired, and then insured,
　So well not one of the aforesaid paints
As Saint Augustine° in his fine Confessions,　　375
Which makes the reader envy his transgressions.

XLVIII

This, too, was a seal'd book to little Juan—
　I can't but say that his mamma was right,
If such an education was the true one.
　She scarcely trusted him from out her sight;　　380
Her maids were old, and if she took a new one,
　You might be sure she was a perfect fright,
She did this during even her husband's life—
I recommend as much to every wife.

XLIX

Young Juan wax'd in godliness and grace;　　385
　At six a charming child, and at eleven
With all the promise of as fine a face
　As e'er to man's maturer growth was given.
He studied steadily and grew apace,
　And seem'd, at least, in the right road to heaven,　　390
For half his days were pass'd at church, the other
Between his tutors, confessor, and mother.

L

At six, I said, he was a charming child,
　At twelve he was a fine, but quiet boy;
Although in infancy a little wild,　　395
　They tamed him down amongst them: to destroy
His natural spirit not in vain they toil'd,
　At least it seem'd so; and his mother's joy
Was to declare how sage, and still, and steady,
Her young philosopher was grown already.　　400

LI

I had my doubts, perhaps I have them still,
　But what I say is neither here nor there:
I knew his father well, and have some skill
　In character—but it would not be fair
From sire to son to augur good or ill:　　405
　He and his wife were an ill sorted pair—
But scandal's my aversion—I protest
Against all evil speaking, even in jest.

LII

For my part I say nothing—nothing—but
　This I will say—my reasons are my own—　　410
That if I had an only son to put
　To school (as God be praised that I have none),
'Tis not with Donna Inez I would shut
　Him up to larn his catechism alone,

331 **Catullus,** Roman lyric poet (84?–54 B.C.); addressed many of his poems to Lesbia, the one great passion of his life   332 **Sappho,** Greek lyric poet (fl. sixth century B.C.); of her nine books of lyric poems, all are lost except one ode to Aphrodite (Greek goddess of love and beauty) and a few fragments   333 **Longinus,** Greek Platonic philosopher and rhetorician (fl. third century A.D.); among his works is the famous essay *On the Sublime*   335 **Virgil,** Roman lyric and epic poet (70–19 B.C.); his second *Eclogue* begins with the words quoted in l. 336, "Handsome shepherd Corydon"   337 **Lucretius,** Roman philosophical poet (fl. first century B.C.); his great work is *De Rerum Natura* (Concerning the Nature of Things), a long didactic poem   339 **Juvenal,** Roman satirist (60?–?140); satirized the vices of Rome under the empire with brutal frankness   344 **Martial,** Roman epigrammatist (fl. first century A.D.)

371 **Jerome,** early Christian writer and Doctor of the Church (340?–420); published Latin version of the Bible (Vulgate) and wrote a large number of works interpreting the Bible   **Chrysostom,** Father of the Greek Church (345?–407); wrote many homilies, commentaries, and letters   375 **Augustine,** early Christian church father and philosopher (354–430); his autobiographical *Confessions* (Confessiones) treats his early profligate life in some detail

George Noel Gordon, Lord Byron

415 No—no—I'd send him out betimes to college,
    For there it was I pick'd up my own knowledge.

LIII

For there one learns—'tis not for me to boast,
    Though I acquired—but I pass over *that,*
As well as all the Greek I since have lost:
420   I say that there's the place—but "*Verbum sat,*"°
I think I pick'd up too, as well as most,
    Knowledge of matters—but no matter *what*—
I never married—but, I think, I know
That sons should not be educated so.

LIV

425 Young Juan now was sixteen years of age,
    Tall, handsome, slender, but well knit: he seem'd
Active, though not so sprightly, as a page;
    And everybody but his mother deem'd
Him almost man; but she flew in a rage
430   And bit her lips (for else she might have scream'd)
If any said so, for to be precocious
Was in her eyes a thing the most atrocious.

LV

Amongst her numerous acquaintance, all
    Selected for discretion and devotion,
435 There was the Donna Julia, whom to call
    Pretty were but to give a feeble notion
Of many charms in her as natural
    As sweetness to the flower, or salt to ocean,
Her zone to Venus, or his bow to Cupid,
440 (But this last simile is trite and stupid).

LVI

The darkness of her Oriental eye
    Accorded with her Moorish origin;
(Her blood was not all Spanish, by the by;
    In Spain, you know, this is a sort of sin).
445 When proud Granada fell, and, forced to fly,
    Boabdil° wept, of Donna Julia's kin
Some went to Africa, some stay'd in Spain,
Her great great grandmamma chose to remain.

LVII

She married (I forget the pedigree)
450   With an Hidalgo,° who transmitted down
His blood less noble than such blood should be;
    At such alliances his sires would frown,
In that point so precise in each degree
    That they bred *in and in,* as might be shown,
455 Marrying their cousins—nay, their aunts, and nieces,
Which always spoils the breed, if it increases.

LVIII

This heathenish cross restored the breed again,
    Ruin'd its blood, but much improved its flesh;
For from a root the ugliest in old Spain
    Sprung up a branch as beautiful as fresh;   460
The sons no more were short, the daughters plain:
    But there's a rumour which I fain would hush,
'Tis said that Donna Julia's grandmamma
Produced her Don more heirs at love than law.

LIX

However this might be, the race went on   465
    Improving still through every generation,
Until it centred in an only son,
    Who left an only daughter: my narration
May have suggested that this single one
    Could be but Julia (whom on this occasion   470
I shall have much to speak about), and she
Was married, charming, chaste, and twenty-three.

LX

Her eye (I'm very fond of handsome eyes)
    Was large and dark, suppressing half its fire
Until she spoke, then through its soft disguise   475
    Flash'd an expression more of pride than ire,
And love than either; and there would arise
    A something in them which was not desire,
But would have been, perhaps, but for the soul
Which struggled through and chasten'd down the
    whole.   480

LXI

Her glossy hair was cluster'd o'er a brow
    Bright with intelligence, and fair, and smooth;
Her eyebrow's shape was like the aërial bow,
    Her cheek all purple with the beam of youth,
Mounting, at times, to a transparent glow,   485
    As if her veins ran lightning; she, in sooth,
Possess'd an air and grace by no means common:
Her stature tall—I hate a dumpy woman.

LXII

Wedded she was some years, and to a man
    Of fifty, and such husbands are in plenty;   490
And yet, I think, instead of such a ONE
    'Twere better to have TWO of five-and-twenty,
Especially in countries near the sun:
    And now I think on't, "mi vien in mente,"°
Ladies even of the most uneasy virtue   495
Prefer a spouse whose age is short of thirty.

LXIII

'Tis a sad thing, I cannot choose but say,
    And all the fault of that indecent sun,
Who cannot leave alone our helpless clay,
    But will keep baking, broiling, burning on,   500
That howsoever people fast and pray,
    The flesh is frail, and so the soul undone:

---

420 **Verbum sat,** a word to the wise is sufficient   446 **Boabdil,** last Moorish
king of Granada; defeated and driven from Granada in 1492 by Ferdinand and
Isabella   450 **Hidalgo,** a member of the lower Spanish nobility

494 **mi vien in mente,** it comes to my mind

What men call gallantry, and gods adultery,
Is much more common where the climate's sultry.

LXIV

505 Happy the nations of the moral North!
  Where all is virtue, and the winter season
Sends sin, without a rag on, shivering forth
  ('Twas snow that brought St. Anthony° to reason);
Where juries cast up what a wife is worth,
510 By laying whate'er sum, in mulct, they please on
The lover, who must pay a handsome price,
Because it is a marketable vice.

LXV

Alfonso was the name of Julia's lord,
  A man well looking for his years, and who
515 Was neither much beloved nor yet abhorr'd:
  They lived together as most people do,
Suffering each other's foibles by accord,
  And not exactly either *one* or *two*;
Yet he was jealous, though he did not show it,
520 For jealousy dislikes the world to know it.

LXVI

Julia was—yet I never could see why—
  With Donna Inez quite a favourite friend;
Between their tastes there was small sympathy,
  For not a line had Julia ever penn'd:
525 Some people whisper (but, no doubt, they lie,
  For malice still imputes some private end)
That Inez had, ere Don Alfonso's marriage,
Forgot with him her very prudent carriage;

LXVII

And that still keeping up the old connexion,
530 Which time had lately render'd much more chaste,
She took his lady also in affection,
  And certainly this course was much the best:
She flatter'd Julia with her sage protection,
  And complimented Don Alfonso's taste;
535 And if she could not (who can?) silence scandal,
At least she left it a more slender handle.

LXVIII

I can't tell whether Julia saw the affair
  With other people's eyes, or if her own
Discoveries made, but none could be aware
540 Of this, at least no symptom e'er was shown;
Perhaps she did not know, or did not care,
  Indifferent from the first, or callous grown:
I'm really puzzled what to think or say,
She kept her counsel in so close a way.

LXIX

545 Juan she saw, and, as a pretty child,
  Caress'd him often—such a thing might be

Quite innocently done, and harmless styled,
  When she had twenty years, and thirteen he;
But I am not so sure I should have smiled
550 When he was sixteen, Julia twenty-three;
These few short years make wondrous alterations,
Particularly amongst sun-burnt nations.

LXX

Whate'er the cause might be, they had become
  Changed; for the dame grew distant, the youth shy,
555 Their looks cast down, their greetings almost dumb,
  And much embarrassment in either eye;
There surely will be little doubt with some
  That Donna Julia knew the reason why,
But as for Juan, he had no more notion
560 Than he who never saw the sea or ocean.

LXXI

Yet Julia's very coldness still was kind,
  And tremulously gentle her small hand
Withdrew itself from his, but left behind
  A little pressure, thrilling, and so bland
565 And slight, so very slight, that to the mind
  'Twas but a doubt; but ne'er magician's wand
Wrought change with all Armida's° fairy art
Like what this light touch left on Juan's heart.

LXXII

And if she met him, though she smiled no more,
570 She look'd a sadness sweeter than her smile,
As if her heart had deeper thoughts in store
  She must not own, but cherish'd more the while
For that compression in its burning core;
  Even innocence itself has many a wile,
575 And will not dare to trust itself with truth,
And love is taught hypocrisy from youth.

LXXIII

But passion most dissembles, yet betrays
  Even by its darkness; as the blackest sky
Foretells the heaviest tempest, it displays
580 Its workings through the vainly guarded eye,
And in whatever aspect it arrays
  Itself, 'tis still the same hypocrisy:
Coldness or anger, even disdain or hate,
Are masks it often wears, and still too late.

LXXIV

Then there were sighs, the deeper for suppression,
585 And stolen glances, sweeter for the theft,
And burning blushes, though for no transgression,
  Tremblings when met, and restlessness when left;
All these are little preludes to possession,
  Of which young passion cannot be bereft,
590 And merely tend to show how greatly love is
Embarrass'd at first starting with a novice.

---

508 **St. Anthony.** It was actually St. Francis of Assisi who controlled his lust with snow

567 **Armida,** sorceress in Tasso's *Jerusalem Delivered* (1575)

LXXV

Poor Julia's heart was in an awkward state;
  She felt it going, and resolved to make
595 The noblest efforts for herself and mate,
  For honour's, pride's, religion's, virtue's sake.
Her resolutions were most truly great,
  And almost might have made a Tarquin quake:
She pray'd the Virgin Mary for her grace,
600 As being the best judge of a lady's case.

LXXVI

She vow'd she never would see Juan more,
  And next day paid a visit to his mother,
And look'd extremely at the opening door,
  Which, by the Virgin's grace, let in another;
605 Grateful she was, and yet a little sore—
  Again it opens, it can be no other,
'Tis surely Juan now—No! I'm afraid
That night the Virgin was no further pray'd.

LXXVII

She now determined that a virtuous woman
610   Should rather face and overcome temptation,
That flight was base and dastardly, and no man
  Should ever give her heart the least sensation;
That is to say, a thought beyond the common
  Preference, that we must feel upon occasion,
615 For people who are pleasanter than others,
But then they only seem so many brothers.

LXXVIII

And even if by chance—and who can tell?
  The devil's so very sly—she should discover
That all within was not so very well,
620   And, if still free, that such or such a lover
Might please perhaps, a virtuous wife can quell
  Such thoughts, and be the better when they're over;
And if the man should ask, 'tis but denial:
I recommend young ladies to make trial.

LXXIX

625 And then there are such things as love divine,
  Bright and immaculate, unmix'd and pure,
Such as the angels think so very fine,
  And matrons, who would be no less secure,
Platonic, perfect, "just such love as mine:"
630   Thus Julia said—and thought so, to be sure;
And so I'd have her think, were I the man
On whom her reveries celestial ran.

LXXX

Such love is innocent, and may exist
  Between young persons without any danger:
635 A hand may first, and then a lip be kist;
  For my part, to such doings I'm a stranger,
But *hear* these freedoms form the utmost list
  Of all o'er which such love may be a ranger:

If people go beyond, 'tis quite a crime,
But not my fault—I tell them all in time.   640

LXXXI

Love, then, but love within its proper limits
  Was Julia's innocent determination
In young Don Juan's favour, and to him its
  Exertion might be useful on occasion;
And, lighted at too pure a shrine to dim its   645
  Ethereal lustre, with what sweet persuasion
He might be taught, by love and her together—
I really don't know what, nor Julia either.

LXXXII

Fraught with this fine intention, and well fenced
  In mail of proof—her purity of soul,   650
She, for the future of her strength convinced,
  And that her honour was a rock, or mole,
Exceeding sagely from that hour dispensed
  With any kind of troublesome control;
But whether Julia to the task was equal   655
Is that which must be mention'd in the sequel.

LXXXIII

Her plan she deem'd both innocent and feasible,
  And, surely, with a stripling of sixteen
Not scandal's fangs could fix on much that's seizable,
  Or if they did so, satisfied to mean   660
Nothing but what was good, her breast was peaceable:
  A quiet conscience makes one so serene!
Christians have burnt each other, quite persuaded
That all the Apostles would have done as they did.

LXXXIV

And if in the mean time her husband died,   665
  But Heaven forbid that such a thought should cross
Her brain, though in a dream! (and then she sigh'd)
  Never could she survive that common loss;
But just suppose that moment should betide,
  I only say suppose it—*inter nos.*°   670
(This should be *entre nous,* for Julia thought
In French, but then the rhyme would go for nought.)

LXXXV

I only say, suppose this supposition:
  Juan being then grown up to man's estate
Would fully suit a widow of condition,   675
  Even seven years hence it would not be too late
And in the interim (to pursue this vision)
  The mischief, after all, could not be great,
For he would learn the rudiments of love,
I mean the seraph way of those above.   680

LXXXVI

So much for Julia. Now we'll turn to Juan.
  Poor little fellow! he had no idea

670 **inter nos,** just between us

Of his own case, and never hit the true one;
  In feelings quick as Ovid's Miss Medea,°
685 He puzzled over what he found a new one,
    But not as yet imagined it could be a
Thing quite in course, and not at all alarming,
Which, with a little patience, might grow charming.

LXXXVII

Silent and pensive, idle, restless, slow,
690   His home deserted for the lonely wood,
Tormented with a wound he could not know,
  His, like all deep grief, plunged in solitude:
I'm fond myself of solitude or so,
  But then, I beg it may be understood,
695 By solitude I mean a Sultan's, not
  A hermit's, with a haram for a grot.°

LXXXVIII

"Oh Love! in such a wilderness as this,
  Where transport and security entwine,
Here is the empire of thy perfect bliss,
700   And here thou art a god indeed divine."
The bard I quote from does not sing amiss,
  With the exception of the second line,
For that same twining "transport and security"
Are twisted to a phrase of some obscurity.

LXXXIX

705 The poet meant, no doubt, and thus appeals
  To the good sense and senses of mankind,
The very thing which everybody feels,
  As all have found on trial, or may find,
That no one likes to be disturb'd at meals
710 Or love.—I won't say more about "entwined"
Or "transport," as we knew all that before,
But beg "Security" will bolt the door.

XC

Young Juan wander'd by the glassy brooks,
  Thinking unutterable things; he threw
715 Himself at length within the leafy nooks
  Where the wild branch of the cork forest grew;
There poets find materials for their books,
  And every now and then we read them through,
So that their plan and prosody are eligible,
720 Unless, like Wordsworth, they prove unintelligible.

XCI

He, Juan (and not Wordsworth), so pursued
  His self-communion with his own high soul,
Until his mighty heart, in its great mood,
  Had mitigated part, though not the whole
725 Of its disease; he did the best he could
  With things not very subject to control,

And turn'd, without perceiving his condition,
Like Coleridge, into a metaphysician.

XCII

He thought about himself, and the whole earth,
  Of man the wonderful, and of the stars,   730
And how the deuce they ever could have birth;
  And then he thought of earthquakes, and of wars,
How many miles the moon might have in girth,
  Of air-balloons, and of the many bars
To perfect knowledge of the boundless skies;— 735
And then he thought of Donna Julia's eyes.

XCIII

In thoughts like these true wisdom may discern
  Longings sublime, and aspirations high,
Which some are born with, but the most part learn
  To plague themselves withal, they know not why: 740
'Twas strange that one so young should thus concern
  His brain about the action of the sky;
If *you* think 'twas philosophy that this did,
I can't help thinking puberty assisted.

XCIV

He pored upon the leaves, and on the flowers, 745
  And heard a voice in all the winds; and then
He thought of wood-nymphs and immortal bowers,
  And how the goddesses came down to men:
He miss'd the pathway, he forgot the hours,
  And when he look'd upon his watch again, 750
He found how much old Time had been a winner—
He also found that he had lost his dinner.

XCV

Sometimes he turn'd to gaze upon his book,
  Boscan,° or Garcilasso;°—by the wind
Even as the page is rustled while we look, 755
  So by the poesy of his own mind
Over the mystic leaf his soul was shook,
  As if 'twere one whereon magicians bind
Their spells, and give them to the passing gale
According to some good old woman's tale. 760

XCVI

Thus would he while his lonely hours away
  Dissatisfied, nor knowing what he wanted;
Nor glowing reverie, nor poet's lay,
  Could yield his spirit that for which it panted,
A bosom whereon he his head might lay, 765
  And hear the heart beat with the love it granted,
With——several other things, which I forget,
Or which, at least, I need not mention yet.

XCVII

Those lonely walks, and lengthening reveries,
  Could not escape the gentle Julia's eyes; 770

---

684 **Ovid's Miss Medea.** See Ovid's *Metamorphoses* VII, 1. 9ff. 696 **grot,** grotto or cave   754 **Boscan,** Spanish poet (1493?–1542) **Garcilasso,** Spanish poet and soldier (1503–1536)

She saw that Juan was not at his ease;
  But that which chiefly may, and must surprise,
Is, that the Donna Inez did not tease
  Her only son with question or surmise;
775 Whether it was she did not see, or would not,
  Or, like all very clever people, could not.

XCVIII

This may seem strange, but yet 'tis very common;
  For instance—gentlemen, whose ladies take
Leave to o'erstep the written rights of woman,
  And break the——Which commandment is't they
780   break?
  (I have forgot the number, and think no man
  Should rashly quote, for fear of a mistake.)
I say, when these same gentlemen are jealous,
They make some blunder, which their ladies tell us.

XCIX

785 A real husband always is suspicious,
  But still no less suspects in the wrong place,
Jealous of some one who had no such wishes,
  Or pandering blindly to his own disgrace,
By harbouring some dear friend extremely vicious;
790   The last indeed's infallibly the case:
And when the spouse and friend are gone off wholly,
He wonders at their vice, and not his folly.

C

Thus parents also are at times short-sighted;
  Though watchful as the lynx, they ne'er discover,
795 The while the wicked world beholds delighted,
  Young Hopeful's mistress, or Miss Fanny's lover,
Till some confounded escapade has blighted
  The plan of twenty years, and all is over;
And then the mother cries, the father swears,
800 And wonders why the devil he got heirs.

CI

But Inez was so anxious, and so clear
  Of sight, that I must think, on this occasion,
She had some other motive much more near
  For leaving Juan to this new temptation,
805 But what that motive was, I shan't say here;
  Perhaps to finish Juan's education,
Perhaps to open Don Alfonso's eyes,
In case he thought his wife too great a prize.

CII

It was upon a day, a summer's day;—
810   Summer's indeed a very dangerous season,
And so is spring about the end of May;
  The sun, no doubt, is the prevailing reason;
But whatsoe'er the cause is, one may say,
  And stand convicted of more truth than treason,
That there are months which nature grows more merry
815   in,—
March has its hares, and May must have its heroine.

CIII

'Twas on a summer's day—the sixth of June:—
  I like to be particular in dates,
Not only of the age, and year, but moon;
  They are a sort of post-house, where the Fates 820
Change horses, making history change its tune,
  Then spur away o'er empires and o'er states,
Leaving at last not much besides chronology,
Excepting the post-obits of theology.

CIV

'Twas on the sixth of June, about the hour 825
  Of half-past six—perhaps still nearer seven—
When Julia sate within as pretty a bower
  As e'er held houri in that heathenish heaven
Described by Mahomet, and Anacreon Moore,°
  To whom the lyre and laurels have been given, 830
With all the trophies of triumphant song—
He won them well, and may he wear them long!

CV

She sate, but not alone; I know not well
  How this same interview had taken place,
And even if I knew, I should not tell— 835
  People should hold their tongues in any case;
No matter how or why the thing befell,
  But there were she and Juan, face to face—
When two such faces are so, 'twould be wise,
But very difficult, to shut their eyes. 840

CVI

How beautiful she look'd! her conscious heart
  Glow'd in her cheek, and yet she felt no wrong.
Oh Love! how perfect is thy mystic art,
  Strengthening the weak, and trampling on the
    strong!
How self-deceitful is the sagest part 845
  Of mortals whom thy lure hath led along!—
The precipice she stood on was immense,
So was her creed in her own innocence.

CVII

She thought of her own strength, and Juan's youth,
  And of the folly of all prudish fears, 850
Victorious virtue, and domestic truth,
  And then of Don Alfonso's fifty years:
I wish these last had not occurr'd, in sooth,
  Because that number rarely much endears,
And through all climes, the snowy and the sunny, 855
Sounds ill in love, whate'er it may in money.

CVIII

When people say, "I've told you *fifty* times,"
  They mean to scold, and very often do;
When poets say, "I've written *fifty* rhymes,"
  They make you dread that they'll recite them too; 860

829 **Anacreon Moore.** The Irish poet Thomas Moore (1779–1852) published a
translation of Anacreon's odes in 1800

In gangs of *fifty*, thieves commit their crimes;
   At *fifty* love for love is rare, 'tis true,
But then, no doubt, it equally as true is,
A good deal may be bought for *fifty* Louis.

CIX

865 Julia had honour, virtue, truth, and love
   For Don Alfonso; and she inly swore,
By all the vows below to powers above,
   She never would disgrace the ring she wore,
Nor leave a wish which wisdom might reprove;
870   And while she ponder'd this, besides much more,
One hand on Juan's carelessly was thrown,
Quite by mistake—she thought it was her own;

CX

Unconsciously she lean'd upon the other,
   Which play'd within the tangles of her hair;
875 And to contend with thoughts she could not smother
   She seem'd, by the distraction of her air.
'Twas surely very wrong in Juan's mother
   To leave together this imprudent pair,
She who for many years had watch'd her son so—
880 I'm very certain *mine* would not have done so.

CXI

The hand which still held Juan's, by degrees
   Gently, but palpably confirm'd its grasp,
As if it said, "Detain me, if you please;"
   Yet there's no doubt she only meant to clasp
885 His fingers with a pure Platonic squeeze;
   She would have shrunk as from a toad, or asp,
Had she imagined such a thing could rouse
A feeling dangerous to a prudent spouse.

CXII

I cannot know what Juan thought of this,
890   But what he did, is much what you would do;
His young lip thank'd it with a grateful kiss,
   And then, abash'd at its own joy, withdrew
In deep despair, lest he had done amiss,—
   Love is so very timid when 'tis new:
895 She blush'd, and frown'd not, but she strove to speak,
And held her tongue, her voice was grown so weak.

CXIII

The sun set, and up rose the yellow moon:
   The devil's in the moon for mischief; they
Who call'd her CHASTE, methinks, began too soon
900   Their nomenclature; there is not a day,
The longest, not the twenty-first of June,
   Sees half the business in a wicked way,
On which three single hours of moonshine smile—
And then she looks so modest all the while.

CXIV

905 There is a dangerous silence in that hour,
   A stillness, which leaves room for the full soul
To open all itself, without the power
   Of calling wholly back its self-control;
The silver light which, hallowing tree and tower,
   Sheds beauty and deep softness o'er the whole,   910
Breathes also to the heart, and o'er it throws
A loving languor, which is not repose.

CXV

And Julia sate with Juan, half embraced
   And half retiring from the glowing arm,
Which trembled like the bosom where 'twas placed;   915
   Yet still she must have thought there was no harm,
Or else 'twere easy to withdraw her waist;
   But then the situation had its charm,
And then——God knows what next—I can't go on;
I'm almost sorry that I e'er begun.   920

CXVI

Oh Plato!° Plato! you have paved the way,
   With your confounded fantasies, to more
Immoral conduct by the fancied sway
   Your system feigns o'er the controlless core
Of human hearts, than all the long array   925
   Of poets and romancers:—You're a bore,
A charlatan, a coxcomb—and have been,
At best, no better than a go-between.

CXVII

And Julia's voice was lost, except in sighs,
   Until too late for useful conversation;   930
The tears were gushing from her gentle eyes,
   I wish, indeed, they had not had occasion;
But who, alas! can love, and then be wise?
   Not that remorse did not oppose temptation;
A little still she strove, and much repented,   935
And whispering "I will ne'er consent"—con-
sented.

CXVIII

'Tis said that Xerxes° offer'd a reward
   To those who could invent him a new pleasure;
Methinks the requisition's rather hard,
   And must have cost his majesty a treasure: 940
For my part, I'm a moderate-minded bard
   Fond of a little love (which I call leisure);
I care not for new pleasures, as the old
Are quite enough for me, so they but hold.

CXIX

Oh Pleasure! you're indeed a pleasant thing,   945
   Although one must be damn'd for you, no doubt;
I make a resolution every spring

---

921 **Plato.** Byron is alluding to the conception of Platonic love, the love of souls and not of bodies   937 **Xerxes,** Persian king (fifth century B.C.)

Of reformation, ere the year run out,
But somehow, this my vestal vow takes wing,
950   Yet still, I trust, it may be kept throughout:
I'm very sorry, very much ashamed,
And mean, next winter, to be quite reclaim'd.

CXX

Here my chaste Muse a liberty must take—
    Start not! still chaster reader—she'll be nice hence-
955 Forward, and there is no great cause to quake;
    This liberty is a poetic licence,
Which some irregularity may make
    In the design, and as I have a high sense
Of Aristotle and the Rules, 'tis fit
960 To beg his pardon when I err a bit.

CXXI

This licence is to hope the reader will
    Suppose from June the sixth (the fatal day
Without whose epoch my poetic skill
    For want of facts would all be thrown away),
965 But keeping Julia and Don Juan still
    In sight, that several months have pass'd; we'll say
'Twas in November, but I'm not so sure
About the day—the era's more obscure.

CXXII

We'll talk of that anon.—'Tis sweet to hear
970   At midnight on the blue and moonlit deep
The song and oar of Adria's° gondolier,
    By distance mellow'd, o'er the waters sweep;
'Tis sweet to see the evening star appear;
    'Tis sweet to listen as the night-winds creep
975 From leaf to leaf; 'tis sweet to view on high
The rainbow, based on ocean, span the sky.

CXXIII

'Tis sweet to hear the watch-dog's honest bark
    Bay deep-mouth'd welcome as we draw near home;
'Tis sweet to know there is an eye will mark
980   Our coming, and look brighter when we come;
'Tis sweet to be awaken'd by the lark,
    Or lull'd by falling waters; sweet the hum
Of bees, the voice of girls, the song of birds,
The lisp of children, and their earliest words.

CXXIV

985 Sweet is the vintage, when the showering grapes
    In Bacchanal profusion reel to earth,
Purple and gushing; sweet are our escapes
    From civic revelry to rural mirth;
Sweet to the miser are his glittering heaps,
990   Sweet to the father is his first-born's birth,
Sweet is revenge—especially to women,
Pillage to soldiers, prize-money to seamen.

CXXV

Sweet is a legacy, and passing sweet
    The unexpected death of some old lady
Or gentleman of seventy years complete,   995
    Who've made "us youth" wait too—too long already
For an estate, or cash, or country seat,
    Still breaking, but with stamina so steady
That all the Israelites are fit to mob its
Next owner for their double-damn'd postobits.   1000

CXXVI

'Tis sweet to win, no matter how, one's laurels,
    By blood or ink; 'tis sweet to put an end
To strife; 'tis sometimes sweet to have our quarrels,
    Particularly with a tiresome friend:
Sweet is old wine in bottles, ale in barrels;   1005
    Dear is the helpless creature we defend
Against the world; and dear the schoolboy spot
We ne'er forget, though there we are forgot.

CXXVII

But sweeter still than this, than these, than all,
    Is first and passionate love—it stands alone,   1010
Like Adam's recollection of his fall;
    The tree of knowledge has been pluck'd—all's known—
And life yields nothing further to recall
    Worthy of this ambrosial sin, so shown,
No doubt in fable, as the unforgiven   1015
Fire which Prometheus filch'd for us from heaven.°

CXXVIII

Man's a strange animal, and makes strange use
    Of his own nature, and the various arts,
And likes particularly to produce
    Some new experiment to show his parts;   1020
This is the age of oddities let loose,
    Where different talents find their different marts;
You'd best begin with truth, and when you've lost your
Labour, there's a sure market for imposture.

CXXIX

What opposite discoveries we have seen!   1025
    (Signs of true genius, and of empty pockets.)
One makes new noses, one a guillotine,
    One breaks your bones, one sets them in their sockets;
But vaccination certainly has been
    A kind antithesis to Congreve's rockets,°   1030
With which the Doctor paid off an old pox,
By borrowing a new one from an ox.

---

971 **Adria,** the Adriatic

1016 **Fire . . . heaven.** According to Greek myth, Prometheus stole fire from heaven, gave it to man, and was consequently punished by Zeus   1030 **Congreve's rockets.** Sir William Congreve (1772–1828) invented a new explosive shell

CXXX

Bread has been made (indifferent) from potatoes;
　　And galvanism has set some corpses grinning,
1035 But has not answer'd like the apparatus
　　Of the Humane Society's beginning,
By which men are unsuffocated gratis:
　　What wondrous new machines have late been
　　　spinning!
I said the small pox has gone out of late;
1040 Perhaps it may be follow'd by the great.

CXXXI

'Tis said the great came from America;
　　Perhaps it may set out on its return,—
The population there so spreads, they say
　　'Tis grown high time to thin it in its turn,
1045 With war, or plague, or famine, any way,
　　So that civilisation they may learn;
And which in ravage the more loathsome evil is—
Their real lues,° or our pseudo-syphilis?

CXXXII

This is the patent age of new inventions
1050 　　For killing bodies, and for saving souls,
All propagated with the best intentions;
　　Sir Humphrey Davy's lantern, by which coals
Are safely mined for in the mode he mentions,°
　　Tombuctoo travels, voyages to the Poles,
1055 Are ways to benefit mankind, as true,
Perhaps, as shooting them at Waterloo.°

CXXXIII

Man's a phenomenon, one knows not what,
　　And wonderful beyond all wondrous measure;
'Tis pity though, in this sublime world, that
1060 　　Pleasure's a sin, and sometimes sin's a pleasure;
Few mortals know what end they will be at,
　　But whether glory, power, or love, or treasure,
The path is through perplexing ways, and when
The goal is gain'd, we die, you know—and then——

CXXXIV

1065 What then?—I do not know, no more do you—
　　And so good night.—Return we to our story:
'Twas in November, when fine days are few,
　　And the far mountains wax a little hoary,
And clap a white cape on their mantles blue;
1070 　　And the sea dashes round the promontory,
And the loud breaker boils against the rock,
And sober suns must set at five o'clock.

CXXXV

'Twas, as the watchmen say, a cloudy night;
　　No moon, no stars, the wind was low or loud

By gusts, and many a sparkling hearth was bright　1075
　　With the piled wood, round which the family crowd;
There's something cheerful in that sort of light,
　　Even as a summer sky's without a cloud:
I'm fond of fire, and crickets, and all that,
A lobster salad, and champagne, and chat.　1080

CXXXVI

'Twas midnight—Donna Julia was in bed,
　　Sleeping, most probably,—when at her door
Arose a clatter might awake the dead,
　　If they had never been awoke before,
And that they have been so we all have read,　1085
　　And are to be so, at the least, once more;—
The door was fasten'd, but with voice and fist
First knocks were heard, then "Madam—Madam—
　　hist!

CXXXVII

"For God's sake, Madam—Madam—here's my
　　master,
With more than half the city at his back—　1090
Was ever heard of such a curst disaster!
　　'Tis not my fault—I kept good watch—Alack!
Do pray undo the bolt a little faster—
　　They're on the stair just now, and in a crack
Will all be here; perhaps he yet may fly—　1095
Surely the window's not so *very* high!"

CXXXVIII

By this time Don Alfonso was arrived,
　　With torches, friends, and servants in great number;
The major part of them had long been wived,
　　And therefore paused not to disturb the slumber　1100
Of any wicked woman, who contrived
　　By stealth her husband's temples to encumber:°
Examples of this kind are so contagious,
Were *one* not punish'd, *all* would be outrageous.

CXXXIX

I can't tell how, or why, or what suspicion　1105
　　Could enter into Don Alfonso's head;
But for a cavalier of his condition
　　It surely was exceedingly ill-bred,
Without a word of previous admonition,
　　To hold a levee° round his lady's bed,　1110
And summon lackeys, arm'd with fire and sword,
To prove himself the thing he most abhorr'd.

CXL

Poor Donna Julia! starting as from sleep
　　(Mind—that I do not say—she had not slept),
Began at once to scream, and yawn, and weep;　1115
　　Her maid, Antonia, who was an adept,

1048 **lues,** syphilis　1052–1053 **Sir . . . mentions.** Sir Humphrey Davy, English chemist (1778–1829), invented the miner's safety lamp in 1815　1056 **Waterloo,** commune in central Belgium near Brussels; site of Napoleon's defeat by the British under Wellington and the Prussians under Blücher on 18 June 1815

1102 **temples to encumber.** Refers to the traditional horns of the cuckolded husband　1110 **levee,** reception held by a person of distinction upon arising from bed

Contrived to fling the bed-clothes in a heap,
  As if she had just now from out them crept:
I can't tell why she should take all this trouble
1120 To prove her mistress had been sleeping double.

CXLI

But Julia mistress, and Antonia maid,
  Appear'd like two poor harmless women, who
Of goblins, but still more of men afraid,
  Had thought one man might be deterr'd by two,
1125 And therefore side by side were gently laid,
  Until the hours of absence should run through,
And truant husband should return, and say,
"My dear, I was the first who came away."

CXLII

Now Julia found at length a voice, and cried,
1130   "In heaven's name, Don Alfonso, what d'ye mean?
Has madness seized you? would that I had died
  Ere such a monster's victim I had been!
What may this midnight violence betide,
  A sudden fit of drunkenness or spleen?
1135 Dare you suspect me, whom the thought would kill?
Search, then, the room!"—Alfonso said, "I will."

CXLIII

He search'd, *they* search'd, and rummaged
    everywhere,
  Closet and clothes-press, chest and windowseat,
And found much linen, lace, and several pair
1140   Of stockings, slippers, brushes, combs, complete,
With other articles of ladies fair,
  To keep them beautiful, or leave them neat:
Arras they prick'd and curtains with their swords,
And wounded several shutters, and some boards.

CXLIV

1145 Under the bed they search'd, and there they found—
  No matter what—it was not that they sought;
They open'd windows, gazing if the ground
  Had signs or footmarks, but the earth said nought;
And then they stared each other's faces round:
1150   'Tis odd, not one of all these seekers thought,
And seems to me almost a sort of blunder,
Of looking *in* the bed as well as under.

CXLV

During this inquisition Julia's tongue
  Was not asleep—"Yes, search and search," she
    cried,
1155 "Insult on insult heap, and wrong on wrong!
  It was for this that I became a bride!
For this in silence I have suffer'd long
  A husband like Alfonso at my side;

But now I'll bear no more, nor here remain,
If there be law or lawyers in all Spain.   1160

CXLVI

"Yes, Don Alfonso! husband now no more,
  If ever you indeed deserved the name,
Is't worthy of your years?—you have threescore—
  Fifty, or sixty, it is all the same—
Is't wise or fitting, causeless to explore   1165
  For facts against a virtuous woman's fame?
Ungrateful, perjured, barbarous Don Alfonso,
How dare you think your lady would go on so?

CXLVII

"Is it for this I have disdain'd to hold
  The common privileges of my sex?   1170
That I have chosen a confessor so old
  And deaf, that any other it would vex,
And never once he has had cause to scold,
  But found my very innocence perplex
So much, he always doubted I was married—   1175
How sorry you will be when I've miscarried!

CXLVIII

"Was it for this that no Cortejo e'er
  I yet have chosen from out the youth of Seville?
Is it for this I scarce went anywhere,
  Except to bull-fights, mass, play, rout, and revel?   1180
Is it for this, whate'er my suitors were,
  I favour'd none—nay, was almost uncivil?
Is it for this that General Count O'Reilly,
Who took Algiers, declares I used him vilely?

CXLIX

"Did not the Italian Musico Cazzani   1185
  Sing at my heart six months at least in vain?
Did not his countryman, Count Corniani,
  Call me the only virtuous wife in Spain?
Were there not also Russians, English, many?
  The Count Strongstroganoff I put in pain,   1190
And Lord Mount Coffeehouse, the Irish peer,
Who kill'd himself for love (with wine) last year.

CL

"Have I not had two bishops at my feet?
  The Duke of Ichar, and Don Fernan Nunez?
And is it thus a faithful wife you treat?   1195
  I wonder in what quarter now the moon is:
I praise your vast forbearance not to beat
  Me also, since the time so opportune is—
Oh, valiant man! with sword drawn and cock'd trigger,
Now, tell me, don't you cut a pretty figure?   1200

CLI

"Was it for this you took your sudden journey,

Under pretense of business indispensable,
With that sublime of rascals your attorney,
Whom I see standing there, and looking sensible
1205 Of having play'd the fool? though both I spurn, he
Deserves the worst, his conduct's less defensible,
Because, no doubt, 'twas for his dirty fee,
And not from any love to you nor me.

CLII

"If he comes here to take a deposition,
1210 By all means let the gentleman proceed;
You've made the apartment in a fit condition:—
There's pen and ink for you, sir, when you need—
Let everything be noted with precision,
I would not you for nothing should be fee'd—
1215 But as my maid's undrest, pray turn your spies out."
"Oh!" sobb'd Antonia, "I could tear their eyes out."

CLIII

"There is the closet, there the toilet, there
The antechamber—search them under, over;
There is the sofa, there the great arm-chair,
1220 The chimney—which would really hold a lover.
I wish to sleep, and beg you will take care
And make no further noise, till you discover
The secret cavern of this lurking treasure—
And when 'tis found, let me, too, have that pleasure.

CLIV

1225 "And now, Hidalgo! now that you have thrown
Doubt upon me, confusion over all,
Pray have the courtesy to make it known
Who is the man you search for? how d'ye call
Him? what's his lineage? let him but be shown—
1230 I hope he's young and handsome—is he tall?
Tell me—and be assured, that since you stain
Mine honour thus, it shall not be in vain.

CLV

"At least, perhaps, he has not sixty years,
At that age he would be too old for slaughter,
1235 Or for so young a husband's jealous fears—
(Antonia! let me have a glass of water.)
I am ashamed of having shed these tears,
They are unworthy of my father's daughter;
My mother dream'd not in my natal hour,
1240 That I should fall into a monster's power.

CLVI

"Perhaps 'tis of Antonia you are jealous,
You saw that she was sleeping by my side,
When you broke in upon us with your fellows;
Look where you please—we've nothing, sir, to
hide:
1245 Only another time, I trust, you'll tell us,

Or for the sake of decency abide
A moment at the door, that we may be
Drest to receive so much good company.

CLVII

"And now, sir, I have done, and say no more;
The little I have said may serve to show   1250
The guileless heart in silence may grieve o'er
The wrongs to whose exposure it is slow:—
I leave you to your conscience as before,
'Twill one day ask you, why you used me so?
God grant you feel not then the bitterest grief!   1255
Antonia! where's my pocket-handkerchief?"

CLVIII

She ceased, and turn'd upon her pillow; pale
She lay, her dark eyes flashing through their tears,
Like skies that rain and lighten; as a veil,
Waved and o'ershading her wan cheek, appears   1260
Her streaming hair; the black curls strive, but fail,
To hide the glossy shoulder, which uprears
Its snow through all;—her soft lips lie apart,
And louder than her breathing beats her heart.

CLIX

The Senhor Don Alfonso stood confused;   1265
Antonia bustled round the ransack'd room,
And, turning up her nose, with looks abused
Her master, and his myrmidons, of whom
Not one, except the attorney, was amused;
He, like Achates,° faithful to the tomb,   1270
So there were quarrels, cared not for the cause,
Knowing they must be settled by the laws.

CLX

With prying snub-nose, and small eyes, he stood,
Following Antonia's motions here and there,
With much suspicion in his attitude;   1275
For reputations he had little care;
So that a suit or action were made good,
Small pity had he for the young and fair,
And ne'er believed in negatives, till these
Were proved by competent false witnesses.   1280

CLXI

But Don Alfonso stood with downcast looks,
And, truth to say, he made a foolish figure;
When, after searching in five hundred nooks,
And treating a young wife with so much rigour,
He gain'd no point, except some self-rebukes,   1285
Added to those his lady with such vigour
Had pour'd upon him for the last half hour,
Quick, thick, and heavy—as a thunder-shower.

1270 **Achates,** the loyal and faithful companion of Aeneas in Vergil's *Aeneid*

CLXII

At first he tried to hammer an excuse,
1290   To which the sole reply was tears and sobs,
And indications of hysterics, whose
   Prologue is always certain throes, and throbs,
Gasps, and whatever else the owners choose:
   Alfonso saw his wife, and thought of Job's;
1295 He saw too, in perspective, her relations,
And then he tried to muster all his patience.

CLXIII

He stood in act to speak, or rather stammer,
   But sage Antonia cut him short before
The anvil of his speech received the hammer,
1300   With "Pray, sir, leave the room, and say no more,
Or madam dies."—Alfonso mutter'd, "D—n her."
   But nothing else, the time of words was o'er;
He cast a rueful look or two, and did,
He knew not wherefore, that which he was bid.

CLXIV

1305 With him retired his *"posse comitatus,"*°
   The attorney last, who linger'd near the door
Reluctantly, still tarrying there as late as
   Antonia let him—not a little sore
At this most strange and unexplain'd *"hiatus"*
1310   In Don Alfonso's facts, which just now wore
An awkward look; as he revolved the case,
The door was fasten'd in his legal face.

CLXV

No sooner was it bolted, than—Oh shame!
   Oh sin! Oh sorrow! and Oh womankind!
1315 How can you do such things and keep your fame,
   Unless this world, and t'other too, be blind?
Nothing so dear as an unfilch'd good name!
   But to proceed—for there is more behind:
With much heartfelt reluctance be it said,
1320 Young Juan slipp'd, half-smother'd, from the bed.

CLXVI

He had been hid—I don't pretend to say
   How, nor can I indeed describe the where—
Young, slender, and pack'd easily, he lay,
   No doubt, in little compass, round or square;
1325 But pity him I neither must nor may
   His suffocation by that pretty pair;
'Twere better, sure, to die so, than be shut
With maudlin Clarence in his Malmsey butt.°

CLXVII

And, secondly, I pity not, because
1330   He had no business to commit a sin,

Forbid by heavenly, fined by human laws,
   At least 'twas rather early to begin;
But at sixteen the conscience rarely gnaws
   So much as when we call our old debts in
At sixty years, and draw the accompts of evil,   1335
And find a deuced balance with the devil.

CLXVIII

Of his position I can give no notion:
   'Tis written in the Hebrew Chronicle,
How the physicians, leaving pill and potion,
   Prescribed, by way of blister, a young belle,   1340
When old King David's blood grew dull in motion,
   And that the medicine answer'd very well;
Perhaps 'twas in a different way applied,
For David lived, but Juan nearly died.

CLXIX

What's to be done? Alfonso will be back   1345
   The moment he has sent his fools away.
Antonia's skill was put upon the rack,
   But no device could be brought into play—
And how to parry the renew'd attack?
   Besides, it wanted but few hours of day: 1350
Antonia puzzled; Julia did not speak,
But press'd her bloodless lip to Juan's cheek.

CLXX

He turn'd his lip to hers, and with his hand
   Call'd back the tangles of her wandering hair;
Even then their love they could not all command,   1355
   And half forgot their danger and despair:
Antonia's patience now was at a stand—
   "Come, come, 'tis no time now for fooling there,"
She whisper'd, in great wrath—"I must deposit
This pretty gentleman within the closet: 1360

CLXXI

"Pray, keep your nonsense for some luckier night—
   Who can have put my master in this mood?
What will become on't—I'm in such a fright,
   The devil's in the urchin, and no good—
Is this a time for giggling? this a plight?   1365
   Why, don't you know that it may end in blood?
You'll lose your life, and I shall lose my place,
My mistress all, for that half-girlish face.

CLXXII

"Had it but been for a stout cavalier
   Of twenty-five or thirty—(come, make haste)   1370
But for a child, what piece of work is here!
   I really, madam, wonder at your taste—
(Come, sir, get in)—my master must be near:
   There, for the present, at the least, he's fast,
And if we can but till the morning keep   1375
Our counsel—(Juan, mind, you must not sleep)."

1305 **posse comitatus,** band of comrades   1328 **With . . . butt.** See Shake-speare's *Richard III*, I, iv. The Duke of Clarence is thrown into a butt or cask of Malmsey, a sweet wine, to drown

CLXXIII

Now, Don Alfonso entering, but alone,
　　Closed the oration of the trusty maid:
She loiter'd, and he told her to be gone,
1380　An order somewhat sullenly obey'd;
However, present remedy was none,
　　And no great good seem'd answer'd if she staid;
Regarding both with slow and sidelong view,
She snuff'd the candle, curtsied, and withdrew.

CLXXIV

1385 Alfonso paused a minute—then begun
　　Some strange excuses for his late proceeding:
He would not justify what he had done,
　　To say the best, it was extreme ill-breeding;
But there were ample reasons for it, none
1390　Of which he specified in this his pleading:
His speech was a fine sample, on the whole,
Of rhetoric, which the learn'd call "rigmarole."

CLXXV

Julia said nought; though all the while there rose
　　A ready answer, which at once enables
1395 A matron, who her husband's foible knows,
　　But a few timely words to turn the tables,
Which, if it does not silence, still must pose,—
　　Even if it should comprise a pack of fables;
'Tis to retort with firmness, and when he
1400 Suspects with one, do you reproach with three.

CLXXVI

Julia, in fact, had tolerable grounds,—
　　Alfonso's loves with Inez were well known;
But whether 'twas that one's own guilt confounds—
　　But that can't be, as has been often shown,
1405 A lady with apologies abounds;—
　　It might be that her silence sprang alone
From delicacy to Don Juan's ear,
To whom she knew his mother's fame was dear.

CLXXVII

There might be one more motive, which makes two,
1410　Alfonso ne'er to Juan had alluded,—
Mentioned his jealousy, but never who
　　Had been the happy lover, he concluded,
Conceal'd amongst his premises; 'tis true,
　　His mind the more o'er this its mystery brooded
1415 To speak of Inez now were, one may say,
Like throwing Juan in Alfonso's way.

CLXXVIII

A hint, in tender cases, is enough;
　　Silence is best: besides there is a tact—
(That modern phrase appears to me sad stuff,
1420　But it will serve to keep my verse compact)—
Which keeps, when push'd by questions rather rough,

A lady always distant from the fact:
The charming creatures lie with such a grace,
There's nothing so becoming to the face.

CLXXIX

They blush, and we believe them, at least I　　1425
　　Have always done so; 'tis of no great use,
In any case, attempting a reply,
　　For then their eloquence grows quite profuse;
And when at length they're out of breath, they sigh,
　　And cast their languid eyes down, and let loose　1430
A tear or two, and then we make it up;
And then—and then—and then—sit down and sup.

CLXXX

Alfonso closed his speech, and begg'd her pardon,
　　Which Julia half withheld, and then half granted,
And laid conditions, he thought very hard, on,　　1435
　　Denying several little things he wanted:
He stood like Adam lingering near his garden,
　　With useless penitence perplex'd and haunted,
Beseeching she no further would refuse,
When, lo! he stumbled o'er a pair of shoes.　　1440

CLXXXI

A pair of shoes!—what then? not much, if they
　　Are such as fit with ladies' feet, but these
(No one can tell how much I grieve to say)
　　Were masculine; to see them, and to seize,
Was but a moment's act.—Ah! well-a-day!　　1445
　　My teeth begin to chatter, my veins freeze—
Alfonso first examined well their fashion,
And then flew out into another passion.

CLXXXII

He left the room for his relinquish'd sword,
　　And Julia instant to the closet flew.　　1450
"Fly, Juan, fly! for heaven's sake—not a word—
　　The door is open—you may yet slip through
The passage you so often have explored—
　　Here is the garden-key—Fly—fly—Adieu!
Haste—haste! I hear Alfonso's hurrying feet—　　1455
Day has not broke—there's no one in the street."

CLXXXIII

None can say that this was not good advice,
　　The only mischief was, it came too late;
Of all experience 'tis the usual price,
　　A sort of income-tax laid on by fate:　　1460
Juan had reach'd the room-door in a trice,
　　And might have done so by the garden-gate,
But met Alfonso in his dressing-gown,
Who threaten'd death—so Juan knock'd him down.

CLXXXIV

Dire was the scuffle, and out went the light;　　1465
　　Antonia cried out "Rape!" and Julia "Fire!"

But now a servant stirr'd to aid the fight.
　　Alfonso, pommell'd to his heart's desire,
　　Swore lustily he'd be revenged this night;
1470　And Juan, too, blasphemed an octave higher;
　　His blood was up: though young, he was a Tartar,
　　And not at all disposed to prove a martyr.

CLXXXV

Alfonso's sword had dropp'd ere he could draw it,
　　And they continued battling hand to hand,
1475　For Juan very luckily ne'er saw it;
　　His temper not being under great command,
If at that moment he had chanced to claw it,
　　Alfonso's days had not been in the land
Much longer.—Think of husbands', lovers' lives!
1480　And how ye may be doubly widows—wives!

CLXXXVI

Alfonso grappled to detain the foe,
　　And Juan throttled him to get away,
And blood ('twas from the nose) began to flow;
　　At last, as they more faintly wrestling lay,
1485　Juan contrived to give an awkward blow,
　　And then his only garment quite gave way;
He fled, like Joseph,° leaving it; but there,
I doubt, all likeness ends between the pair.

CLXXXVII

Lights came at length, and men, and maids, who found
1490　An awkward spectacle their eyes before;
Antonia in hysterics, Julia swoon'd,
　　Alfonso leaning, breathless, by the door;
Some half-torn drapery scatter'd on the ground,
　　Some blood, and several footsteps, but no more:
1495　Juan the gate gain'd, turn'd the key about,
And liking not the inside, lock'd the out.

CLXXXVIII

Here ends this canto.—Need I sing, or say,
　　How Juan, naked, favour'd by the night,
Who favours what she should not, found his way,
1500　And reach'd his home in an unseemly plight?
The pleasant scandal which arose next day,
　　The nine days' wonder which was brought to light,
And how Alfonso sued for a divorce,
Were in the English newspapers, of course.

CLXXXIX

1505　If you would like to see the whole proceedings,
　　The depositions and the cause at full,
The names of all the witnesses, the pleadings
　　Of counsel to nonsuit, or to annul,
There's more than one edition, and the readings
1510　Are various, but they none of them are dull;

The best is that in short-hand ta'en by Gurney,°
Who to Madrid on purpose made a journey.

CXC

But Donna Inez, to divert the train
　　Of one of the most circulating scandals
That had for centuries been known in Spain,　　　1515
　　At least since the retirement of the Vandals,
First vow'd (and never had she vow'd in vain)
　　To Virgin Mary several pounds of candles;
And then, by the advice of some old ladies,
She sent her son to be shipp'd off from Cadiz.　　1520

CXCI

She had resolved that he should travel through
　　All European climes, by land or sea,
To mend his former morals, and get new,
　　Especially in France and Italy
(At least this is the thing most people do).　　　1525
　　Julia was sent into a convent: she
Grieved, but, perhaps, her feelings may be better
Shown in the following copy of her Letter:—

CXCII

"They tell me 'tis decided you depart:
　　'Tis wise—'tis well, but not the less a pain;　　1530
I have no further claim on your young heart,
　　Mine is the victim, and would be again:
To love too much has been the only art
　　I used;—I write in haste, and if a stain
Be on this sheet, 'tis not what it appears;　　　1535
My eyeballs burn and throb, but have no tears.

CXCIII

"I loved, I love you, for this love have lost
　　State, station, heaven, mankind's, my own esteem,
And yet cannot regret what it hath cost,
　　So dear is still the memory of that dream;　　　1540
Yet, if I name my guilt, 'tis not to boast,
　　None can deem harshlier of me than I deem:
I trace this scrawl because I cannot rest—
I've nothing to reproach or to request.

CXCIV

"Man's love is of man's life a thing apart,　　　1545
　　'Tis woman's whole existence; man may range
The court, camp, church, the vessel, and the mart;
Sword, gown, gain, glory, offer in exchange
Pride, fame, ambition, to fill up his heart,
　　And few there are whom these cannot estrange;　1550
Men have all these resources, we but one,
To love again, and be again undone.

CXCV

"You will proceed in pleasure, and in pride,
　　Beloved and loving many; all is o'er

1555 For me on earth, except some years to hide
     My shame and sorrow deep in my heart's core:
     These I could bear, but cannot cast aside
     The passion which still rages as before,—
     And so farewell—forgive me, love me—No,
1560 That word is idle now—but let it go.

CXCVI

"My breast has been all weakness, is so yet:
     But still I think I can collect my mind;
     My blood still rushes where my spirit's set,
     As roll the waves before the settled wind;
1565 My heart is feminine, nor can forget—
     To all, except one image, madly blind;
     So shakes the needle, and so stands the pole,
     As vibrates my fond heart to my fix'd soul.

CXCVII

"I have no more to say, but linger still,
1570 And dare not set my seal upon this sheet,
     And yet I may as well the task fulfil,
     My misery can scarce be more complete:
     I had not lived till now, could sorrow kill;
     Death shuns the wretch who fain the blow would
         meet,
1575 And I must even survive this last adieu,
     And bear with life to love and pray for you!"

CXCVIII

This note was written upon gilt-edge paper
     With a neat little crow-quill, slight and new;
     Her small white hand could hardly reach the taper,
1580 It trembled as magnetic needles do,
     And yet she did not let one tear escape her;
     The seal a sun-flower; *"Elle vous suit partout,"*°
     The motto cut upon a white cornelian;
     The wax was superfine, its hue vermilion.

CXCIX

1585 This was Don Juan's earliest scrape; but whether
     I shall proceed with his adventures is
     Dependent on the public altogether;
     We'll see however, what they say to this,
     Their favour in an author's cap's a feather,
1590 And no great mischief's done by their caprice;
     And if their approbation we experience,
     Perhaps they'll have some more about a year hence.

CC

My poem's epic, and is meant to be
     Divided in twelve books; each book containing,
1595 With love, and war, a heavy gale at sea,
     A list of ships, and captains, and kings reigning,
     New characters; the episodes are three:
     A panoramic view of hell's in training,

After the style of Virgil and of Homer,
So that my name of Epic's no misnomer.   1600

CCI

All these things will be specified in time,
     With strict regard to Aristotle's rules,°
The *Vade Mecum*° of the true sublime,
     Which makes so many poets, and some fools:
Prose poets like blank-verse, I'm fond of rhyme,   1605
     Good workmen never quarrel with their tools;
I've got new mythological machinery,
And very handsome supernatural scenery.

CCII

There's only one slight difference between
     Me and my epic brethren gone before,   1610
And here the advantage is my own, I ween°
     (Not that I have not several merits more,
But this will more peculiarly be seen);
     They so embellish, that 'tis quite a bore
Their labyrinth of fables to thread through,   1615
Whereas this story's actually true.

CCIII

If any person doubt it, I appeal
     To history, tradition, and to facts,
To newspapers, whose truth all know and feel,
     To plays in five, and operas in three acts;   1620
All these confirm my statement a good deal,
     But that which more completely faith exacts
Is, that myself, and several now in Seville,°
Saw Juan's last elopement with the devil.

CCIV

If ever I should condescend to prose,   1625
     I'll write poetical commandments, which
Shall supersede beyond all doubt all those
     That went before; in these I shall enrich
My text with many things that no one knows,
     And carry precept to the highest pitch: 1630
I'll call the work "Longinus° o'er a Bottle,
Or, Every Poet his *own* Aristotle."

CCV

Thou shalt believe in Milton, Dryden, Pope;
     Thou shalt not set up Wordsworth, Coleridge,
         Southey;
Because the first is crazed beyond all hope,   1635
     The second drunk, the third so quaint and mouthy:
With Crabbe it may be difficult to cope,
     And Campbell's Hippocrene° is somewhat drouthy:
Thou shalt not steal from Samuel Rogers,° nor
Commit—flirtation with the muse of Moore.   1640

1602 **Aristotle's rules,** rules regarding epic and narrative poetry put forth in the *Poetics*   1603 **Vade Mecum,** handbook; literally, "go with me"   1611 **ween,** think   1623 **Seville,** city in southwestern Spain   1631 **Longinus,** Greek Platonic philosopher and critic of the third century   1638 **Hippocrene,** fountain in Greece sacred to the Muses   1639 **Samuel Rogers,** contemporary minor poet

1582 **Elle ... partout.** She follows you everywhere

CCVI

Thou shalt not covet Mr. Sotheby's° Muse,
  His Pegasus,° nor anything that's his;
Thou shalt not bear false witness like "the Blues°"—
  (There's one, at least, is very fond of this);
1645 Thou shalt not write, in short, but what I choose;
  This is true criticism, and you may kiss—
Exactly as you please, or not,—the rod;
But if you don't, I'll lay it on, by G—d!

CCVII

If any person should presume to assert
1650   This story is not moral, first, I pray,
That they will not cry out before they're hurt,
  Then that they'll read it o'er again, and say
(But, doubtless, nobody will be so pert),
  That this is not a moral tale, though gay;
1655 Besides, in Canto Twelfth, I mean to show
The very place where wicked people go.

CCVIII

If, after all, there should be some so blind
  To their own good this warning to despise,
Led by some tortuosity of mind,
1660   Not to believe my verse and their own eyes,
And cry that they "the moral cannot find,"
  I tell him, if a clergyman, he lies;
Should captains the remark, or critics, make,
They also lie too—under a mistake.

CCIX

1665 The public approbation I expect,
  And beg they'll take my word about the moral,
Which I with their amusement will connect
  (So children cutting teeth receive a coral);
Meantime they'll doubtless please to recollect
1670   My epical pretensions to the laurel:
For fear some prudish readers should grow skittish,
I've bribed my grandmother's review—the British.

CCX

I sent it in a letter to the Editor,
  Who thank'd me duly by return of post—
1675 I'm for a handsome article his creditor;
  Yet, if my gentle Muse he please to roast,
And break a promise after having made it her,
  Denying the receipt of what it cost,
And smear his page with gall instead of honey,
1680 All I can say is—that he had the money.

CCXI

I think that with this holy new alliance
  I may ensure the public, and defy
All other magazines of art or science,
  Daily, or monthly, or three monthly; I

Have not essay'd to multiply their clients,   1685
  Because they tell me 'twere in vain to try,
And that the Edinburgh Review and Quarterly°
Treat a dissenting author very martyrly. . . .

from CANTO 2

I

Oh ye! who teach the ingenuous youth of nations,
  Holland, France, England, Germany, or Spain,
I pray ye flog them upon all occasions,
  It mends their morals, never mind the pain:
The best of mothers and of educations   5
  In Juan's case were but employ'd in vain,
Since, in a way that's rather of the oddest, he
Became divested of his native modesty.

II

Had he but been placed at a public school,°
  In the third form, or even in the fourth,   10
His daily task had kept his fancy cool,
  At least, had he been nurtured in the north.
Spain may prove an exception to the rule,
  But then exceptions always prove its worth—
A lad of sixteen causing a divorce   15
Puzzled his tutors very much, of course.

III

I can't say that it puzzles me at all,
  If all things be consider'd; first, there was
His lady-mother, mathematical,
  A——never mind;—his tutor, an old ass;   20
A pretty woman—(that's quite natural,
  Or else the thing had hardly come to pass)
A husband rather old, not much in unity
With his young wife—a time, and opportunity.

IV

Well—well; the world must turn upon its axis,   25
  And all mankind turn with it, heads or tails,
And live and die, make love and pay our taxes,
  And as the veering wind shifts, shift our sails;
The king commands us, and the doctor quacks us,
  The priest instructs, and so our life exhales,   30
A little breath, love, wine, ambition, fame,
Fighting, devotion, dust,—perhaps a name.

V

I said, that Juan had been sent to Cadiz°—
  A pretty town, I recollect it well—
'Tis there the mart of the colonial trade is,   35
  (Or was, before Peru learn'd to rebel,)
And such sweet girls—I mean, such graceful ladies,
  Their very walk would make your bosom swell;
I can't describe it, though so much it strike,
Nor liken it—I never saw the like: 40

1641 **Sotheby,** William Sotheby (1757–1833), English scholar and poet
1642 **Pegasus,** winged horse associated with poetic inspiration   1643 **the Blues,**
the Bluestockings, a name applied to a society of women affecting an interest in
literature and politics

1687 **Edinburgh Review and Quarterly.** Both magazines were hostile to Byron;
he attacked them in *English Bards and Scotch Reviewers* **Canto 2** 9 **public
school,** in England a private school like Eton 33 **Cadiz,** city on the southwest
coast of Spain

VI

An Arab horse, a stately stag, a barb°
  New broke, a cameleopard, a gazelle,
No—none of these will do;—and then their garb,
  Their veil and petticoat—Alas! to dwell
45 Upon such things would very near absorb
  A canto—then their feet and ankles,—well,
Thank Heaven I've got no metaphor quite ready,
(And so, my sober Muse—come, let's be steady—

VII

Chaste Muse!—well, if you must, you must)—the veil
50   Thrown back a moment with the glancing hand,
While the o'erpowering eye, that turns you pale,
  Flashes into the heart:—All sunny land
Of love! when I forget you, may I fail
  To——say my prayers—but never was there
      plann'd
55 A dress through which the eyes give such a volley,
Excepting the Venetian Fazzioli.°

VIII

But to our tale: the Donna Inez sent
  Her son to Cadiz only to embark;
To stay there had not answer'd her intent,
60   But, why?—we leave the reader in the dark—
'Twas for a voyage the young man was meant,
  As if a Spanish ship were Noah's ark,
To wean him from the wickedness of earth,
And send him like a dove of promise forth.°

IX

65 Don Juan bade his valet pack his things
  According to direction, then received
A lecture and some money: for four springs
  He was to travel; and though Inez grieved
(As every kind of parting has its stings),
70   She hoped he would improve—perhaps believed:
A letter, too, she gave (he never read it)
Of good advice—and two or three of credit.

X

In the mean time, to pass her hours away,
  Brave Inez now set up a Sunday school
75 For naughty children, who would rather play
  (Like truant rogues) the devil, or the fool;
Infants of three years old were taught that day,
  Dunces were whipt, or set upon a stool:
The great success of Juan's education
80 Spurr'd her to teach another generation.

XI

Juan embark'd—the ship got under way,
  The wind was fair, the water passing rough;
A devil of a sea rolls in that bay,

41 **barb,** Barbary horse, noted for speed and endurance 56 **Fazzioli.** "Literally, little handkerchiefs—the veils most availing of St. Mark." —Byron's note
64 **Dove . . forth,** a reference to the dove sent by Noah from the ark when he wanted to learn whether the waters were receding

As I, who've cross'd it oft, know well enough;
And, standing upon deck, the dashing spray   85
  Flies in one's face, and makes it weathertough:
And there he stood to take, and take again,
His first—perhaps his last—farewell of Spain.

XII

I can't but say it is an awkward sight
  To see one's native land receding through   90
The growing waters; it unmans one quite,
  Especially when life is rather new:
I recollect Great Britain's coast looks white,
  But almost every other country's blue,
When gazing on them, mystified by distance,   95
We enter on our nautical existence.

XIII

So Juan stood, bewilder'd on the deck:
  The wind sung, cordage strain'd, and sailors swore,
And the ship creak'd, the town became a speck,
  From which away so fair and fast they bore.   100
The best of remedies is a beef-steak
  Against sea-sickness: try it, sir, before
You sneer, and I assure you this is true,
For I have found it answer—so may you.

XIV

Don Juan stood, and, gazing from the stern,   105
  Beheld his native Spain receding far:
First partings form a lesson hard to learn,
  Even nations feel this when they go to war;
There is a sort of unexprest concern,
  A kind of shock that sets one's heart ajar: 110
At leaving even the most unpleasant people
And places, one keeps looking at the steeple.

XV

But Juan had got many things to leave,
  His mother, and a mistress, and no wife,
So that he had much better cause to grieve   115
  Than many persons more advanced in life;
And if we now and then a sigh must heave
  At quitting even those we quit in strife,
No doubt we weep for those the heart endears—
That is, till deeper griefs congeal our tears.   120

XVI

So Juan wept, as wept the captive Jews
  By Babel's waters, still remembering Sion:
I'd weep,—but mine is not a weeping Muse,
  And such light griefs are not a thing to die on;
Young men should travel, if but to amuse   125
  Themselves; and the next time their servants tie on
Behind their carriages their new portmanteau,
Perhaps it may be lined with this my canto.

XVII

And Juan wept, and much he sigh'd and thought,
  While his salt tears dropp'd into the salt sea,   130

"Sweets to the sweet;" (I like so much to quote;
    You must excuse this extract,—'tis where she,
The Queen of Denmark, for Ophelia brought
    Flowers to the grave;) and, sobbing often, he
135 Reflected on his present situation,
And seriously resolved on reformation.

XVIII

"Farewell, my Spain! a long farewell!" he cried,
    "Perhaps I may revisit thee no more,
But die, as many an exiled heart hath died,
140   Of its own thirst to see again thy shore:
Farewell, where Guadalquivir's waters glide!
    Farewell, my mother! and, since all is o'er,
Farewell, too, dearest Julia!—(here he drew
Her letter out again, and read it through.)

XIX

145 "And oh! if e'er I should forget, I swear—
    But that's impossible, and cannot be—
Sooner shall this blue ocean melt to air,
    Sooner shall earth resolve itself to sea,
Than I resign thine image, oh, my fair!
150   Or think of anything, excepting thee;
A mind diseased no remedy can physic—
(Here the ship gave a lurch, and he grew seasick.)

XX

"Sooner shall heaven kiss earth—(here he fell sicker)
    Oh, Julia! what is every other woe?—
155 (For God's sake let me have a glass of liquor;
    Pedro, Battista, help me down below.)
Julia, my love—(you rascal, Pedro, quicker)—
    Oh, Julia!—(this curst vessel pitches so)—
Beloved Julia, hear me still beseeching!"
160 (Here he grew inarticulate with retching.)

XXI

He felt that chilling heaviness of heart,
    Or rather stomach, which, alas! attends,
Beyond the best apothecary's art,
    The loss of love, the treachery of friends,
165 Or death of those we dote on, when a part
    Of us dies with them as each fond hope ends:
No doubt he would have been much more pathetic,
But the sea acted as a strong emetic.

XXII

Love's a capricious power: I've known it hold
170   Out through a fever caused by its own heat,
But be much puzzled by a cough and cold,
    And find a quinsy very hard to treat;
Against all noble maladies he's bold,
    But vulgar illnesses don't like to meet,
175 Nor that a sneeze should interrupt his sigh,
Nor inflammations redden his blind eye.

XXIII

But worst of all is nausea, or a pain
    About the lower region of the bowels;
Love, who heroically breathes a vein,
    Shrinks from the application of hot towels,   180
And purgatives are dangerous to his reign,
    Sea-sickness death: his love was perfect, how else
Could Juan's passion, while the billows roar,
Resist his stomach, ne'er at sea before?

XXIV

The ship, call'd the most holy "Trinidada,"   185
    Was steering duly for the port Leghorn;°
For there the Spanish family Moncada
    Were settled long ere Juan's sire was born:
They were relations, and for them he had a
    Letter of introduction, which the morn   190
Of his departure had been sent him by
His Spanish friends for those in Italy.

XXV

His suite consisted of three servants and
    A tutor, the licentiate Pedrillo,
Who several languages did understand,   195
    But now lay sick and speechless on his pillow,
And, rocking in his hammock, long'd for land,
    His headache being increased by every billow;
And the waves oozing through the port-hole made
His berth a little damp, and him afraid.   200

XXVI

'Twas not without some reason, for the wind
    Increased at night, until it blew a gale;
And though 'twas not much to a naval mind,
    Some landsmen would have look'd a little pale,
For sailors are, in fact, a different kind: 205
    At sunset they began to take in sail,
For the sky show'd it would come on to blow,
And carry away, perhaps, a mast or so.

XXVII

At one o'clock the wind with sudden shift
    Threw the ship right into the trough of the sea,   210
Which struck her aft, and made an awkward rift,
    Started the stern-post, also shatter'd the
Whole of her stern-frame, and, ere she could lift
    Herself from out her present jeopardy,
The rudder tore away: 'twas time to sound   215
The pumps, and there were four feet water found.

XXVIII

One gang of people instantly was put
    Upon the pumps, and the remainder set
To get up part of the cargo, and what not;
    But they could not come at the leak as yet;   220

186 **Leghorn,** a city in Tuscany, on the west coast of Italy

At last they did get at it really, but
　　Still their salvation was an even bet:
The water rush'd through in a way quite puzzling,
　　While they thrust sheets, shirts, jackets, bales of
　　　muslin,

XXIX

225 Into the opening; but all such ingredients
　　Would have been vain, and they must have gone
　　　down,
Despite of all their efforts and expedients,
　　But for the pumps: I'm glad to make them known
To all the brother tars who may have need hence,
230　　For fifty tons of water were upthrown
By them per hour, and they all had been undone,
But for the maker, Mr. Mann, of London.

XXX

As day advanced the weather seem'd to abate,
　　And then the leak they reckon'd to reduce,
235 And keep the ship afloat, though three feet yet
　　Kept two hand and one chain-pump still in use.
The wind blew fresh again: as it grew late
　　A squall came on, and while some guns broke loose,
A gust—which all descriptive power transcends—
240 Laid with one blast the ship on her beam ends.

XXXI

There she lay, motionless, and seem'd upset;
　　The water left the hold, and wash'd the decks,
And made a scene men do not soon forget;
　　For they remember battles, fires, and wrecks,
245　　Or any other thing that brings regret,
　　Or breaks their hopes, or hearts, or heads, or necks;
Thus drownings are much talk'd of by the divers,
And swimmers, who may chance to be survivors.

XXXII

Immediately the masts were cut away,
250　　Both main and mizen:° first the mizen went,
The main-mast follow'd; but the ship still lay
　　Like a mere log, and baffled our intent.
Foremast and bowsprit° were cut down, and they
　　Eased her at last (although we never meant
255 To part with all till every hope was blighted),
And then with violence the old ship righted.

XXXIII

It may be easily supposed, while this
　　Was going on, some people were unquiet,
That passengers would find it much amiss
260　　To lose their lives, as well as spoil their diet;
That even the able seaman, deeming his
　　Days nearly o'er, might be disposed to riot,
As upon such occasions tars will ask
For grog, and sometimes drink rum from the cask.

XXXIV

There's nought, no doubt, so much the spirit calms　265
　　As rum and true religion: thus it was,
Some plunder'd, some drank spirits, some sung
　　psalms,
　　The high wind made the treble, and as bass
The hoarse harsh waves kept time; fright cured the
　　qualms
Of all the luckless landsmen's sea-sick maws:　270
Strange sounds of wailing, blasphemy, devotion,
Clamour'd in chorus to the roaring ocean.

XXXV

Perhaps more mischief had been done, but for
　　Our Juan, who, with sense beyond his years,
Got to the spirit-room, and stood before　　275
　　It with a pair of pistols; and their fears,
As if Death were more dreadful by his door
　　Of fire than water, spite of oaths and tears,
Kept still aloof the crew, who, ere they sunk,
Thought it would be becoming to die drunk.　280

XXXVI

"Give us more grog," they cried, "for it will be
　　All one an hour hence." Juan answer'd, "No!
'Tis true that death awaits both you and me,
　　But let us die like men, not sink below
Like brutes:"—and thus his dangerous post kept he,　285
　　And none liked to anticipate the blow;
And even Pedrillo, his most reverend tutor,
Was for some rum a disappointed suitor.

XXXVII

The good old gentleman was quite aghast,
　　And made a loud and pious lamentation;　290
Repented all his sins, and made a last
　　Irrevocable vow of reformation;
Nothing should tempt him more (this peril past)
　　To quit his academic occupation,
In cloisters of the classic Salamanca,°　295
To follow Juan's wake, like Sancho Panca.°

XXXVIII

But now there came a flash of hope once more;
　　Day broke, and the wind lull'd: the masts were gone;
The leak increased; shoals round her, but no shore,　300
　　The vessel swam, yet still she held her own.
They tried the pumps again, and though before
　　Their desperate efforts seem'd all useless grown,
A glimpse of sunshine set some hands to bale—
The stronger pump'd, the weaker thrumm'd° a sail.

XXXIX

Under the vessel's keel the sail was pass'd,　305
　　And for the moment it had some effect;

250 **mizen,** aftermost mast of a three-masted ship　253 **bowsprit,** large spar
projecting forward from the stem of a ship

295 **Salamanca,** city in western Spain, the seat of a celebrated university
296 **Sancho Panca,** Sancho Panza, shrewd squire of the hero in *Don Quixote,* the
satirical romance by Cervantes (1547-1616)　304 **thrumm'd,** inserted short
pieces of rope yarn in canvas to give it a rough surface

But with a leak, and not a stick of mast,
    Nor rag of canvas, what could they expect?
But still 'tis best to struggle to the last,
    'Tis never too late to be wholly wreck'd:
And though 'tis true that man can only die once,
310 'Tis not so pleasant in the Gulf of Lyons.°

XL

There winds and waves had hurl'd them, and from
    thence,
    Without their will, they carried them away;
315 For they were forced with steering to dispense,
    And never had as yet a quiet day
On which they might repose, or even commence
    A jurymast° or rudder, or could say
The ship would swim an hour, which, by good luck,
320 Still swam—though not exactly like a duck.

XLI

The wind, in fact, perhaps, was rather less,
    But the ship labour'd so, they scarce could hope
To weather out much longer; the distress
    Was also great with which they had to cope
325 For want of water, and their solid mess
    Was scant enough: in vain the telescope
Was used—nor sail nor shore appear'd in sight,
Nought but the heavy sea, and coming night.

XLII

Again the weather threaten'd,—again blew
330 A gale, and in the fore and after hold
Water appear'd; yet, though the people knew
    All this, the most were patient, and some bold,
Until the chains and leathers were worn through
    Of all our pumps:—a wreck complete she roll'd,
335 At mercy of the waves, whose mercies are
Like human beings during civil war.

XLIII

Then came the carpenter, at last, with tears
    In his rough eyes, and told the captain, he
Could do no more: he was a man in years,
340 And long had voyaged through many a stormy sea,
And if he wept at length, they were not fears
    That made his eyelids as a woman's be,
But he, poor fellow, had a wife and children,
Two things for dying people quite bewildering.

XLIV

345 The ship was evidently settling now
    Fast by the head; and, all distinction gone,
Some went to prayers again, and made a vow
    Of candles to their saints—but there were none
To pay them with; and some look'd o'er the bow;
350 Some hoisted out the boats; and there was one

That begg'd Pedrillo for an absolution,
Who told him to be damn'd—in his confusion.

XLV

Some lash'd them in their hammocks; some put on
    Their best clothes, as if going to a fair;
Some cursed the day on which they saw the sun,   355
    And gnash'd their teeth, and howling, tore their hair;
And others went on as they had begun,
    Getting the boats out, being well aware
That a tight boat will live in a rough sea,
Unless with breakers close beneath her lee.   360

XLVI

The worst of all was, that in their condition,
    Having been several days in great distress,
'Twas difficult to get out such provision
    As now might render their long suffering less:
Men, even when dying, dislike inanition;   365
    Their stock was damaged by the weather's stress:
Two casks of biscuit, and a keg of butter,
Were all that could be thrown into the cutter.

XLVII

But in the long-boat they contrived to stow
    Some pounds of bread, though injured by the wet; 370
Water, a twenty-gallon cask or so:
    Six flasks of wine: and they contrived to get
A portion of their beef up from below,
    And with a piece of pork, moreover, met,
But scarce enough to serve them for a luncheon— 375
Then there was rum, eight gallons in a puncheon.°

XLVIII

The other boats, the yawl° and pinnace,° had
    Been stove in the beginning of the gale;
And the long-boat's condition was but bad,
    As there were but two blankets for a sail,   380
And one oar for a mast, which a young lad
    Threw in by good luck over the ship's rail;
And two boats could not hold, far less be stored,
To save one half the people then on board.

XLIX

'Twas twilight, and the sunless day went down   385
    Over the waste of waters; like a veil,
Which, if withdrawn, would but disclose the frown
    Of one whose hate is mask'd but to assail.
Thus to their hopeless eyes the night was shown,
    And grimly darkled o'er the faces pale,   390
And the dim desolate deep: twelve days had Fear
Been their familiar,° and now Death was here.

L

Some trial had been making at a raft,
    With little hope in such a rolling sea,

---

312 **Gulf of Lyons,** on the southern coast of France   318 **jurymast,** temporary mast   376 **puncheon,** a kind of large cask   377 **yawl,** ship's small boat   **pinnace,** light sailing vessel   392 **familiar,** attendant spirit

395 A sort of thing at which one would have laugh'd,
      If any laughter at such times could be,
    Unless with people who too much have quaff'd,
      And have a kind of wild and horrid glee,
    Half epileptical, and half hysterical:—
400 Their preservation would have been a miracle.

LI

    At half-past eight o'clock, booms,° hencoops, spars,
      And all things, for a chance, had been cast loose
    That still could keep afloat the struggling tars,
      For yet they strove, although of no great use:
405 There was no light in heaven but a few stars,
      The boats put off o'ercrowded with their crews;
    She gave a heel, and then a lurch to port,
    And, going down head foremost—sunk, in short.

LII

    Then rose from sea to sky the wild farewell—
410   Then shriek'd the timid, and stood still the brave—
    Then some leap'd overboard with dreadful yell,
      As eager to anticipate their grave;
    And the sea yawn'd around her like a hell,
      And down she suck'd with her the whirling wave,
415 Like one who grapples with his enemy,
    And strives to strangle him before he die.

LIII

    And first one universal shriek there rush'd,
      Louder than the loud ocean, like a crash
    Of echoing thunder; and then all was hush'd,
420   Save the wild wind and the remorseless dash
    Of billows; but at intervals there gush'd,
      Accompanied with a convulsive splash,
    A solitary shriek, the bubbling cry
    Of some strong swimmer in his agony. . . .

CXI

    How long in his damp trance young Juan lay
      He knew not, for the earth was gone for him,
    And time had nothing more of night nor day
      For his congealing blood, and senses dim;
885 And how this heavy faintness pass'd away
      He knew not, till each painful pulse and limb,
    And tingling vein, seem'd throbbing back to life,
    For Death, though vanquish'd, still retired with strife.

CXII

    His eyes he open'd, shut, again unclosed,
890   For all was doubt and dizziness; he thought
    He still was in the boat, and had but dozed,
      And felt again with his despair o'erwrought,
    And wish'd it death in which he had reposed,
      And then once more his feelings back were brought,
895 And slowly by his swimming eyes was seen
    A lovely female face of seventeen.

401 **booms.** long poles used to extend the bottoms of sails

CXIII

    'Twas bending close o'er his, and the small mouth
      Seem'd almost prying into his for breath;
    And chafing him, the soft warm hand of youth
      Recall'd his answering spirits back from death;   900
    And, bathing his chill temples, tried to soothe
      Each pulse to animation, till beneath
    Its gentle touch and trembling care, a sigh
    To these kind efforts made a low reply.

CXIV

    Then was the cordial pour'd, and mantle flung   905
      Around his scarce-clad limbs; and the fair arm
    Raised higher the faint head which o'er it hung;
      And her transparent cheek, all pure and warm,
    Pillow'd his death-like forehead; then she wrung
      His dewy curls, long drench'd by every storm;   910
    And watch'd with eagerness each throb that drew
    A sigh from his heaved bosom—and hers, too.

CXV

    And lifting him with care into the cave,
      The gentle girl, and her attendant,—one
    Young, yet her elder, and of brow less grave,   915
      And more robust of figure—then begun
    To kindle fire, and as the new flames gave
      Light to the rocks that roof'd them, which the sun
    Had never seen, the maid, or whatsoe'er
    She was, appear'd distinct, and tall, and fair.   920

CXVI

    Her brow was overhung with coins of gold,
      That sparkled o'er the auburn of her hair,
    Her clustering hair, whose longer locks were roll'd
      In braids behind; and though her stature were
    Even of the highest for a female mould,   925
      They nearly reach'd her heel; and in her air
    There was a something which bespoke command,
    As one who was a lady in the land.

CXVII

    Her hair, I said, was auburn; but her eyes
      Were black as death, their lashes the same hue,   930
    Of downcast length, in whose silk shadow lies
      Deepest attraction; for when to the view
    Forth from its raven fringe the full glance flies,
      Ne'er with such force the swiftest arrow flew;
    'Tis as the snake late coil'd, who pours his length, 935
    And hurls at once his venom and his strength.

CXVIII

    Her brow was white and low, her cheek's pure dye
      Like twilight rosy still with the set sun;
    Short upper lip—sweet lips! that make us sigh
      Ever to have seen such; for she was one   940
    Fit for the model of a statuary
      (A race of mere impostors, when all's done—

I've seen much finer women, ripe and real,
   Than all the nonsense of their stone ideal).

CXIX

945 I'll tell you why I say so, for 'tis just
   One should not rail without a decent cause:
There was an Irish lady, to whose bust
   I ne'er saw justice done, and yet she was
A frequent model; and if e'er she must
950   Yield to stern Time and Nature's wrinkling laws,
They will destroy a face which mortal thought
Ne'er compass'd, nor less mortal chisel wrought.

CXX

And such was she, the lady of the cave:
   Her dress was very different from the Spanish,
955 Simpler, and yet of colours not so grave;
   For, as you know, the Spanish women banish
Bright hues when out of doors, and yet, while wave
   Around them (what I hope will never vanish)
The basquina and the mantilla, they
960 Seem at the same time mystical and gay.

CXXI

But with our damsel this was not the case:
   Her dress was many-colour'd, finely spun;
Her locks curl'd negligently round her face,
   But through them gold and gems profusely shone:
965 Her girdle sparkled, and the richest lace
   Flow'd in her veil, and many a precious stone
Flash'd on her little hand; but, what was shocking,
Her small snow feet had slippers, but no stocking.

CXXII

The other female's dress was not unlike,
970   But of inferior materials: she
Had not so many ornaments to strike,
   Her hair had silver only, bound to be
Her dowry; and her veil, in form alike,
   Was coarser; and her air, though firm, less free;
975 Her hair was thicker, but less long; her eyes
As black, but quicker, and of smaller size.

CXXIII

And these two tended him, and cheer'd him both
   With food and raiment, and those soft attentions,
Which are—(as I must own)—of female growth,
980   And have ten thousand delicate inventions:
They made a most superior mess of broth,
   A thing which poesy but seldom mentions,
But the best dish that e'er was cook'd since Homer's
Achilles order'd dinner for new comers.°

CXXIV

985 I'll tell you who they were, this female pair,
   Lest they should seem princesses in disguise;

Besides, I hate all mystery, and that air
   Of clap-trap, which your recent poets prize;
And so, in short, the girls they really were
   They shall appear before your curious eyes,   990
Mistress and maid; the first was only daughter
Of an old man, who lived upon the water.

CXXV

A fisherman he had been in his youth,
   And still a sort of fisherman was he;
But other speculations were, in sooth,   995
   Added to his connexion with the sea,
Perhaps not so respectable, in truth:
   A little smuggling, and some piracy,
Left him, at last, the sole of many masters
Of an ill-gotten million of piastres.°   1000

CXXVI

A fisher, therefore, was he,—though of men,
   Like Peter the Apostle,—and he fish'd
For wandering merchant vessels, now and then,
   And sometimes caught as many as he wish'd;
The cargoes he confiscated, and gain   1005
   He sought in the slave-market too, and dish'd
Full many a morsel for that Turkish trade,
By which, no doubt, a good deal may be made.

CXXVII

He was a Greek, and on his isle had built
   (One of the wild and smaller Cyclades)°   1010
A very handsome house from out his guilt,
   And there he lived exceedingly at ease.
Heaven knows what cash he got, or blood he spilt,
   A sad old fellow was he, if you please;
But this I know, it was a spacious building,   1015
Full of barbaric carving, paint, and gilding.

CXXVIII

He had an only daughter, call'd Haidée,
   The greatest heiress of the Eastern Isles;
Besides, so very beautiful was she,
   Her dowry was as nothing to her smiles: 1020
Still in her teens, and like a lovely tree
   She grew to womanhood, and between whiles
Rejected several suitors, just to learn
How to accept a better in his turn.

CXXIX

And walking out upon the beach, below   1025
   The cliff,—towards sunset, on that day she found,
Insensible,—not dead, but nearly so,—
   Don Juan, almost famish'd, and half drown'd;
But being naked, she was shock'd, you know,
   Yet deem'd herself in common pity bound,   1030
As far as in her lay, "to take him in,
A stranger" dying, with so white a skin.

983–984 **since . . . comers.** Reference to the feast prepared by Achilles for
Ulysses, Ajax, and Phoenix in the ninth book of the *Iliad*

1000 **piastres,** pieces of eight (money)   1010 **Cyclades,** group of Aegean islands

CXXX

But taking him into her father's house
  Was not exactly the best way to save,
1035 But like conveying to the cat the mouse,
  Or people in a trance into their grave;
Because the good old man had so much "νους,°"
  Unlike the honest Arab thieves so brave,
He would have hospitably cured the stranger
1040 And sold him instantly when out of danger.

CXXXI

And therefore, with her maid, she thought it best
  (A virgin always on her maid relies)
To place him in the cave for present rest:
  And when, at last, he open'd his black eyes,
1045 Their charity increased about their guest;
  And their compassion grew to such a size,
It open'd half the turnpike gates to heaven—
(St. Paul says, 'tis the toll which must be given).

CXXXII

They made a fire,—but such a fire as they
1050 Upon the moment could contrive with such
Materials as were cast up round the bay,—
  Some broken planks, and oars, that to the touch
Were nearly tinder, since so long they lay
  A mast was almost crumbled to a crutch;
1055 But, by God's grace, here wrecks were in such plenty,
That there was fuel to have furnish'd twenty.

CXXXIII

He had a bed of furs, and a pelisse,
  For Haidée stripp'd her sables off to make
His couch; and, that he might be more at ease,
1060 And warm, in case by chance he should awake,
They also gave a petticoat apiece,
  She and her maid,—and promised by daybreak
To pay him a fresh visit, with a dish
For breakfast, of eggs, coffee, bread, and fish.

CXXXIV

1065 And thus they left him to his lone repose:
  Juan slept like a top, or like the dead,
Who sleep at last, perhaps (God only knows),
  Just for the present; and in his lull'd head
Not even a vision of his former woes
  Throbb'd in accursed dreams, which sometimes
1070 spread
Unwelcome visions of our former years,
Till the eye, cheated, opens thick with tears.

CXXXV

Young Juan slept all dreamless:—but the maid,
  Who smooth'd his pillow, as she left the den
1075 Look'd back upon him, and a moment staid,
  And turn'd, believing that he call'd again.

He slumber'd; yet she thought, at least she said
  (The heart will slip, even as the tongue and pen),
He had pronounced her name—but she forgot
That at this moment Juan knew it not.   1080

CXXXVI

And pensive to her father's house she went,
  Enjoining silence strict to Zoe, who
Better than her knew what, in fact, she meant,
  She being wiser by a year or two:
A year or two's an age when rightly spent,   1085
  And Zoe spent hers, as most women do,
In gaining all that useful sort of knowledge
Which is acquired in Nature's good old college.

CXXXVII

The morn broke, and found Juan slumbering still
  Fast in his cave, and nothing clash'd upon   1090
His rest: the rushing of the neighbouring rill,
  And the young beams of the excluded sun,
Troubled him not, and he might sleep his fill;
  And need he had of slumber yet, for none
Had suffer'd more—his hardships were comparative   1095
To those related in my grand-dad's "Narrative.°"

CXXXVIII

Not so Haidée: she sadly toss'd and tumbled,
  And started from her sleep, and, turning o'er
Dream'd of a thousand wrecks, o'er which she
  stumbled,
  And handsome corpses strew'd upon the shore;   1100
And woke her maid so early that she grumbled,
  And call'd her father's old slaves up, who swore
In several oaths—Armenian, Turk, and Greek—
They knew not what to think of such a freak.

CXXXIX

But up she got, and up she made them get,   1105
  With some pretence about the sun, that makes
Sweet skies just when he rises, or is set;
  And 'tis, no doubt, a sight to see when breaks
Bright Phœbus, while the mountains still are wet
  With mist, and every bird with him awakes,   1110
And night is flung off like a mourning suit
Worn for a husband,—or some other brute.

CXL

I say, the sun is a most glorious sight:
  I've seen him rise full oft, indeed of late
I have sat up on purpose all the night,   1115
  Which hastens, as physicians say, one's fate;
And so all ye, who would be in the right
  In health and purse, begin your day to date
From daybreak, and when coffin'd at fourscore
Engrave upon the plate, you rose at four.   1120

1096 **Narrative.** Reference to the shipwreck narrative written by Byron's grand-father

1037 **νους,** intelligence

CXLI

And Haidée met the morning face to face;
　Her own was freshest, though a feverish flush
Had dyed it with the headlong blood, whose race
　From heart to cheek is curb'd into a blush,
1125　Like to a torrent which a mountain's base,
　That overpowers some Alpine river's rush,
Checks to a lake, whose waves in circles spread;
Or the Red Sea—but the sea is not red.

CXLII

And down the cliff the island virgin came,
1130　And near the cave her quick light footsteps drew,
While the sun smiled on her with his first flame,
　And young Aurora° kiss'd her lips with dew,
Taking her for a sister; just the same
　Mistake you would have made on seeing the two,
1135　Although the mortal, quite as fresh and fair,
Had all the advantage, too, of not being air.

CXLIII

And when into the cavern Haidée stepp'd
　All timidly, yet rapidly, she saw
That like an infant Juan sweetly slept;
1140　And then she stopp'd, and stood as if in awe
(For sleep is awful), and on tiptoe crept
　And wrapt him closer, lest the air, too raw,
Should reach his blood, then o'er him still as death
Bent, with hush'd lips, that drank his scarcedrawn
　breath.

CXLIV

1145　And thus like to an angel o'er the dying
　Who die in righteousness, she lean'd; and there
All tranquilly the shipwreck'd boy was lying,
　As o'er him lay the calm and stirless air:
But Zoe the meantime some eggs was frying,
1150　Since, after all, no doubt the youthful pair
Must breakfast, and betimes—lest they should ask it,
She drew out her provision from the basket.

CXLV

She knew that the best feelings must have victual,
　And that a shipwreck'd youth would hungry be;
1155　Besides, being less in love, she yawn'd a little
　And felt her veins chill'd by the neighbouring sea;
And so, she cook'd their breakfast to a tittle;
　I can't say that she gave them any tea,
But there were eggs, fruit, coffee, bread, fish, honey,
1160　With Scio wine,—and all for love, not money.

CXLVI

And Zoe, when the eggs were ready, and
　The coffee made, would fain have waken'd Juan;
But Haidée stopp'd her with her quick small hand,

1132 **Aurora,** the Roman goddess of dawn

And without word, a sign her finger drew on
Her lip, which Zoe needs must understand;　　　　1165
　And, the first breakfast spoilt, prepared a new one,
Because her mistress would not let her break
That sleep which seem'd as it would ne'er awake.

CXLVII

For still he lay, and on his thin worn cheek
　A purple hectic play'd like dying day　　　　　　1170
On the snow-tops of distant hills; the streak
　Of sufferance yet upon his forehead lay,
Where the blue veins look'd shadowy, shrunk, and
　　weak;
　And his black curls were dewy with the spray,
Which weigh'd upon them yet, all damp and salt,　1175
Mix'd with the stony vapours of the vault.

CXLVIII

And she bent o'er him, and he lay beneath,
　Hush'd as the babe upon its mother's breast,
Droop'd as the willow when no winds can breath
　Lull'd like the depth of ocean when at rest,　　1180
Fair as the crowning rose of the whole wreath,
　Soft as the callow cygnet in its nest;
In short, he was a very pretty fellow,
Although his woes had turn'd him rather yellow.

CXLIX

He woke and gazed, and would have slept again,　1185
　But the fair face which met his eyes forbade
Those eyes to close, though weariness and pain
　Had further sleep a further pleasure made;
For woman's face was never form'd in vain
　For Juan, so that even when he pray'd　　　　　1190
He turn'd from grisly saints, and martyrs hairy,
To the sweet portraits of the Virgin Mary.

CL

And thus upon his elbow he arose,
　And look'd upon the lady, in whose cheek
The pale contended with the purple rose,　　　　1195
　As with an effort she began to speak;
Her eyes were eloquent, her words would pose,
　Although she told him, in good modern Greek,
With an Ionian accent, low and sweet,
That he was faint, and must not talk, but eat.　　1200

CLI

Now Juan could not understand a word,
　Being no Grecian; but he had an ear,
And her voice was the warble of a bird,
　So soft, so sweet, so delicately clear,
That finer, simpler music ne'er was heard;　　　　1205
　The sort of sound we echo with a tear,
Without knowing why—an overpowering tone,
Whence melody descends as from a throne.

CLII

And Juan gazed as one who is awoke
1210   By a distant organ, doubting if he be
Not yet a dreamer, till the spell is broke
   By the watchman, or some such reality,
Or by one's early valet's cursed knock;
   At least it is a heavy sound to me,
1215 Who like a morning slumber—for the night
Shows stars and women in a better light.

CLIII

And Juan, too, was help'd out from his dream,
   Or sleep, or whatsoe'er it was, by feeling
A most prodigious appetite; the steam
1220   Of Zoe's cookery no doubt was stealing
Upon his senses, and the kindling beam
   Of the new fire, which Zoe kept up, kneeling,
To stir her viands, made him quite awake
And long for food, but chiefly a beef-steak.

CLIV

1225 But beef is rare within these oxless isles;
   Goat's flesh there is, no doubt, and kid, and mutton,
And, when a holiday upon them smiles,
   A joint upon their barbarous spits they put on:
But this occurs but seldom, between whiles,
1230   For some of these are rocks with scarce a hut on;
Others are fair and fertile, among which
This, though not large, was one of the most rich.

CLV

I say that beef is rare, and can't help thinking
   That the old fable of the Minotaur°—
1235 From which our modern morals, rightly shrinking,
   Condemn the royal lady's taste who wore
A cow's shape for a mask—was only (sinking
   The allegory) a mere type, no more,
That Pasiphae promoted breeding cattle,
1240 To make the Cretans bloodier in battle.

CLVI

For we all know that English people are
   Fed upon beef—I won't say much of beer,
Because 'tis liquor only, and being far
   From this my subject, has no business here;
1245 We know, too, they are very fond of war,
   A pleasure—like all pleasures—rather dear;
So were the Cretans—from which I infer
That beef and battles both were owing to her.

CLVII

But to resume. The languid Juan raised
1250   His head upon his elbow, and he saw
A sight on which he had not lately gazed,

1234 **fable of the Minotaur.** In Greek mythology the Minotaur, a monster with
the head of a bull and the body of a man, was the offspring of Pasiphae, the wife
of King Minos of Crete, and a bull

As all his latter meals had been quite raw,
Three or four things, for which the Lord he praised,
   And, feeling still the famish'd vulture gnaw,
He fell upon whate'er was offer'd, like   1255
A priest, a shark, an alderman, or pike.

CLVIII

He ate, and he was well supplied; and she,
   Who watch'd him like a mother, would have fed
Him past all bounds, because she smiled to see
   Such appetite in one she had deem'd dead: 1260
But Zoe, being older than Haidée,
   Knew (by tradition, for she ne'er had read)
That famish'd people must be slowly nurst.
And fed by spoonfuls, else they always burst.

CLIX

And so she took the liberty to state,   1265
   Rather by deeds than words, because the case
Was urgent, that the gentleman, whose fate
   Had made her mistress quit her bed to trace
The sea-shore at this hour, must leave his plate,
   Unless he wish'd to die upon the place—   1270
She snatch'd it, and refused another morsel,
Saying, he had gorged enough to make a horse ill.

CLX

Next they—he being naked, save a tatter'd
   Pair of scarce decent trowsers—went to work,
And in the fire his recent rags they scatter'd,   1275
   And dress'd him, for the present, like a Turk,
Or Greek—that is, although it not much matter'd,
   Omitting turban, slippers, pistols, dirk,—
They furnish'd him, entire, except some stitches,
With a clean shirt, and very spacious breeches.   1280

CLXI

And then fair Haidée tried her tongue at speaking,
   But not a word could Juan comprehend,
Although he listen'd so that the young Greek in
   Her earnestness would ne'er have made an end;
And, as he interrupted not, went eking   1285
   Her speech out to her protégé and friend,
Till pausing at the last her breath to take,
She saw he did not understand Romaic.

CLXII

And then she had recourse to nods, and signs,
   And smiles, and sparkles of the speaking eye,   1290
And read (the only book she could) the lines
   Of his fair face, and found, by sympathy,
The answer eloquent, where the soul shines
   And darts in one quick glance a long reply;
And thus in every look she saw exprest   1295
A world of words, and things at which she guess'd.

CLXIII

And now, by dint of fingers and of eyes,
   And words repeated after her, he took

A lesson in her tongue; but by surmise,
1300   No doubt, less of her language than her look:
As he who studies fervently the skies
    Turns oftener to the stars than to his book,
Thus Juan learn'd his alpha beta better
From Haidée's glance than any graven letter.

CLXIV

1305 'Tis pleasing to be school'd in a strange tongue
    By female lips and eyes—that is, I mean,
When both the teacher and the taught are young,
    As was the case, at least, where I have been;
They smile so when one's right, and when one's wrong
1310   They smile still more, and then there intervene
Pressure of hands, perhaps even a chaste kiss;—
I learn'd the little that I know by this:

CLXV

That is, some words of Spanish, Turk, and Greek,
    Italian not at all, having no teachers;
1315 Much English I cannot pretend to speak,
    Learning that language chiefly from its preachers,
Barrow, South, Tillotson, whom every week
    I study, also Blair,° the highest reachers
Of eloquence in piety and prose—
1320 I hate your poets, so read none of those.

CLXVI

As for the ladies, I have nought to say,
    A wanderer from the British world of fashion,
Where I, like other "dogs, have had my day,"
    Like other men, too, may have had my passion—
1325 But that, like other things, has pass'd away,
    And all her fools whom I *could* lay the lash on:
Foes, friends, men, women, now are nought to me
But dreams of what has been, no more to be.

CLXVII

Return we to Don Juan. He begun
1330   To hear new words, and to repeat them; but
Some feelings, universal as the sun,
    Were such as could not in his breast be shut
More than within the bosom of a nun:
    He was in love,—as you would be, no doubt,
1335 With a young benefactress,—so was she,
Just in the way we very often see.

CLXVIII

And every day by daybreak—rather early
    For Juan, who was somewhat fond of rest—
She came into the cave, but it was merely
1340   To see her bird reposing in his nest;
And she would softly stir his locks so curly,
    Without disturbing her yet slumbering guest,

Breathing all gently o'er his cheek and mouth,
As o'er a bed of roses the sweet south.

CLXIX

And every morn his colour freshlier came,   1345
    And every day help'd on his convalescence;
'Twas well, because health in the human frame
    Is pleasant, besides being true love's essence,
For health and idleness to passion's flame
    Are oil and gunpowder; and some good lessons   1350
Are also learnt from Ceres° and from Bacchus,°
Without whom Venus will not long attack us.

CLXX

While Venus fills the heart (without heart really
    Love, though good always, is not quite so good),
Ceres presents a plate of vermicelli,—   1355
    For love must be sustain'd like flesh and blood,
While Bacchus pours out wine, or hands a jelly:
    Eggs, oysters, too, are amatory food;
But who is their purveyor from above
Heaven knows,—it may be Neptune, Pan, or Jove.   1360

CLXXI

When Juan woke he found some good things ready,
    A bath, a breakfast, and the finest eyes
That ever made a youthful heart less steady,
    Besides her maid's, as pretty for their size;
But I have spoken of all this already—   1365
    And repetition's tiresome and unwise,—
Well—Juan, after bathing in the sea,
Came always back to coffee and Haidée.

CLXXII

Both were so young, and one so innocent,
    That bathing pass'd for nothing; Juan seem'd   1370
To her, as 'twere, the kind of being sent,
    Of whom these two years she had nightly dream'd,
A something to be loved, a creature meant
    To be her happiness, and whom she deem'd
To render happy: all who joy would win   1375
Must share it,—Happiness was born a twin.

CLXXIII

It was such pleasure to behold him, such
    Enlargement of existence to partake
Nature with him, to thrill beneath his touch,
    To watch him slumbering, and to see him wake;   1380
To live with him for ever were too much;
    But then the thought of parting made her quake:
He was her own, her ocean-treasure, cast
Like a rich wreck—her first love, and her last.

CLXXIV

And thus a moon roll'd on, and fair Haidée   1385
    Paid daily visits to her boy, and took

1317–1318 **Barrow . . . Blair,** famous preachers: Isaac Barrow (1630–1677), English mathematician and theologian; Robert South (1634–1716), English court preacher; John Tillotson (1630–1694), English prelate and preacher; and Hugh Blair (1718–1800), Scottish Presbyterian clergyman

1351 **Ceres,** Roman goddess of agriculture   **Bacchus,** Greek god of wine

Such plentiful precautions, that still he
   Remain'd unknown within his craggy nook;
At last her father's prows put out to sea,
1390   For certain merchantmen upon the look,
Not as of yore to carry off an Io,°
But three Ragusan vessels bound for Scio.

CLXXV

Then came her freedom, for she had no mother,
   So that, her father being at sea, she was
1395 Free as a married woman, or such other
   Female, as where she likes may freely pass,
Without even the encumbrance of a brother,
   The freest she that ever gazed on glass:
I speak of Christian lands in this comparison,
1400 Where wives, at least, are seldom kept in garrison.

CLXXVI

Now she prolong'd her visits and her talk
   (For they must talk), and he had learnt to say
So much as to propose to take a walk,—
   For little had he wander'd since the day
1405 On which, like a young flower snapp'd from the stalk,
   Drooping and dewy on the beach he lay,—
And thus they walk'd out in the afternoon,
And saw the sun set opposite the moon.

CLXXVII

It was a wild and breaker-beaten coast,
1410   With cliffs above, and a broad sandy shore,
Guarded by shoals and rocks as by an host,
   With here and there a creek, whose aspect wore
A better welcome to the tempest-tost;
   And rarely ceased the haughty billow's roar,
1415 Save on the dead long summer days, which make
The outstretch'd ocean glitter like a lake.

CLXXVIII

And the small ripple spilt upon the beach
   Scarcely o'erpass'd the cream of your champagne,
When o'er the brim the sparkling bumpers reach,
1420   That spring-dew of the spirit! the heart's rain!
Few things surpass old wine; and they may preach
   Who please,—the more because they preach in
      vain,—
Let us have wine and women, mirth and laughter,
Sermons and soda-water the day after.

CLXXIX

1425 Man, being reasonable, must get drunk;
   The best of life is but intoxication:
Glory, the grape, love, gold, in these are sunk
   The hopes of all men, and of every nation;
Without their sap, how branchless were the trunk
1430   Of life's strange tree, so fruitful on occasion!

1391 **Io**, carried off by traders. Io was beloved by Zeus and persecuted by his jealous wife Hera

But to return,—Get very drunk; and when
You wake with headache, you shall see what then

CLXXX

Ring for your valet—bid him quickly bring
   Some hock and soda-water, then you'll know
A pleasure worthy Xerxes the great king;   1435
   For not the blest sherbet, sublimed with snow,
Nor the first sparkle of the desert spring,
   Nor Burgundy in all its sunset glow,
After long travel, ennui, love, or slaughter,
Vie with that draught of hock and soda-water.   1440

CLXXXI

The coast—I think it was the coast that I
   Was just describing—Yes, it *was* the coast—
Lay at this period quiet as the sky,
   The sands untumbled, the blue waves untost,
And all was stillness, save the sea-bird's cry,   1445
   And dolphin's leap, and little billow crost
By some low rock or shelve, that made it fret
Against the boundary it scarcely wet.

CLXXXII

And forth they wander'd, her sire being gone,
   As I have said, upon an expedition;   1450
And mother, brother, guardian, she had none,
   Save Zoe, who, although with due precision
She waited on her lady with the sun,
   Thought daily service was her only mission,
Bringing warm water, wreathing her long tresses,   1455
And asking now and then for cast-off dresses.

CLXXXIII

It was the cooling hour, just when the rounded
   Red sun sinks down behind the azure hill,
Which then seems as if the whole earth it bounded,
   Circling all nature, hush'd, and dim, and still,   1460
With the far mountain-crescent half surrounded
   On one side, and the deep sea calm and chill,
Upon the other, and the rosy sky,
With one star sparkling through it like an eye.

CLXXXIV

And thus they wander'd forth, and hand in hand,   1465
   Over the shining pebbles and the shells,
Glided along the smooth and harden'd sand,
   And in the worn and wild receptacles
Work'd by the storms, yet work'd as it were plann'd,
   In hollow halls, with sparry roofs and cells,   1470
They turn'd to rest; and, each clasp'd by an arm,
Yielded to the deep twilight's purple charm.

CLXXXV

They look'd up to the sky, whose floating glow
   Spread like a rosy ocean, vast and bright;
They gazed upon the glittering sea below,   1475
   Whence the broad moon rose circling into sight;

They heard the waves splash, and the wind so low,
   And saw each other's dark eyes darting light
Into each other—and, beholding this,
1480 Their lips drew near, and clung into a kiss;

CLXXXVI

A long, long kiss, a kiss of youth, and love,
   And beauty, all concentrating like rays
Into one focus, kindled from above;
   Such kisses as belong to early days,
1485 Where heart, and soul, and sense, in concert move,
   And the blood's lava, and the pulse a blaze,
Each kiss a heart-quake,—for a kiss's strength,
I think it must be reckon'd by its length.

CLXXXVII

By length I mean duration; theirs endured
   Heaven knows how long—no doubt they never
1490   reckon'd;
   And if they had, they could not have secured
   The sum of their sensations to a second:
They had not spoken; but they felt allured,
   As if their souls and lips each other beckon'd,
1495 Which, being join'd, like swarming bees they clung—
   Their hearts the flowers from whence the honey
     sprung.

CLXXXVIII

They were alone, but not alone as they
   Who shut in chambers think it loneliness;
The silent ocean, and the starlight bay,
1500   The twilight glow, which momently grew less,
The voiceless sands, and dropping caves, that lay
   Around them, made them to each other press,
As if there were no life beneath the sky
Save theirs, and that their life could never die.

CLXXXIX

1505 They fear'd no eyes nor ears on that lone beach,
   They felt no terrors from the night; they were
All in all to each other; though their speech
   Was broken words, they *thought* a language
     there,—
And all the burning tongues the passions teach
1510   Found in one sigh the best interpreter
Of nature's oracle—first love,—that all
Which Eve has left her daughters since her fall.

CXC

Haidée spoke not of scruples, ask'd no vows,
   Nor offer'd any; she had never heard
1515 Of plight and promises to be a spouse,
   Or perils by a loving maid incurr'd;
She was all which pure ignorance allows,
   And flew to her young mate like a young bird,
And never having dreamt of falsehood, she
1520 Had not one word to say of constancy.

CXCI

She loved, and was beloved—she adored,
   And she was worshipp'd; after nature's fashion,
Their intense souls, into each other pour'd,
   If souls could die, had perish'd in that passion,—
But by degrees their senses were restored,   1525
   Again to be o'ercome, again to dash on;
And, beating 'gainst *his* bosom, Haidée's heart
Felt as if never more to beat apart.

CXCII

Alas! they were so young, so beautiful,
   So lonely, loving, helpless, and the hour   1530
Was that in which the heart is always full,
   And, having o'er itself no further power,
Prompts deeds eternity cannot annul,
   But pays off moments in an endless shower
Of hell-fire—all prepared for people giving   1535
Pleasure or pain to one another living.

CXCIII

Alas! for Juan and Haidée! they were
   So loving and so lovely—till then never,
Excepting our first parents, such a pair
   Had run the risk of being damn'd for ever;   1540
And Haidée, being devout as well as fair,
   Had, doubtless, heard about the Stygian river,°
And hell and purgatory—but forgot
Just in the very crisis she should not.

CXCIV

They look upon each other, and their eyes   1545
   Gleam in the moonlight; and her white arm clasps
Round Juan's head, and his around her lies
   Half buried in the tresses which it grasps;
She sits upon his knee, and drinks his sighs,
   He hers, until they end in broken gasps;   1550
And thus they form a group that's quite antique,
Half naked, loving, natural, and Greek.

CXCV

And when those deep and burning moments pass'd,
   And Juan sunk to sleep within her arms,
She slept not, but all tenderly, though fast,   1555
   Sustain'd his head upon her bosom's charms;
And now and then her eye to heaven is cast,
   And then on the pale cheek her breast now warms,
Pillow'd on her o'erflowing heart, which pants
With all it granted, and with all it grants.   1560

CXCVI

An infant when it gazes on a light,
   A child the moment when it drains the breast,
A devotee when soars the Host° in sight,
   An Arab with a stranger for a guest,

1542 **Stygian river,** the river Styx in Hades   1563 **Host,** the communion wafer
in Roman Catholicism

1565 A sailor wher the prize has struck in fight,
　　A miser filling his most hoarded chest,
　　Feel rapture; but not such true joy are reaping
　　As they who watch o'er what they love while sleeping.

CXCVII

　　For there it lies so tranquil, so beloved,
1570　　All that it hath of life with us is living;
　　So gentle, stirless, helpless, and unmoved,
　　　And all unconscious of the joy 'tis giving;
　　All it hath felt, inflicted, pass'd, and proved,
　　　Hush'd into depths beyond the watcher's diving;
1575 There lies the thing we love with all its errors
　　And all its charms, like death without its terrors.

CXCVIII

　　The lady watch'd her lover—and that hour
　　　Of Love's, and Night's, and Ocean's solitude,
　　O'erflowed her soul with their united power;
1580　　Amidst the barren sand and rocks so rude
　　She and her wave-worn love had made their bower,
　　　Where nought upon their passion could intrude,
　　And all the stars that crowded the blue space
　　Saw nothing happier than her glowing face.

CXCIX

1585 Alas! the love of women! it is known
　　　To be a lovely and a fearful thing;
　　For all of theirs upon that die is thrown,
　　　And if 'tis lost, life hath no more to bring
　　To them but mockeries of the past alone,
1590　　And their revenge is as the tiger's spring,
　　Deadly, and quick, and crushing; yet, as real
　　Torture is theirs, what they inflict they feel.

CC

　　They are right; for man, to man so oft unjust,
　　　Is always so to women; one sole bond
1595 Awaits them, treachery is all their trust;
　　　Taught to conceal, their bursting hearts despond
　　Over their idol, till some wealthier lust
　　　Buys them in marriage—and what rests beyond?
　　A thankless husband, next a faithless lover,
1600 Then dressing, nursing, praying, and all's over.

CCI

　　Some take a lover, some take drams or prayers,
　　　Some mind their household, others dissipation,
　　Some run away, and but exchange their cares,
　　　Losing the advantage of a virtuous station;
1605 Few changes e'er can better their affairs,
　　　Theirs being an unnatural situation,
　　From the dull palace to the dirty hovel:
　　Some play the devil, and then write a novel.°

CCII

Haidée was Nature's bride, and knew not this:
　　Haidée was Passion's child, born where the sun　　1610
Showers triple light, and scorches even the kiss
　　Of his gazelle-eyed daughters; she was one
Made but to love, to feel that she was his
　　Who was her chosen: what was said or done
Elsewhere was nothing. She had nought to fear,　　1615
Hope, care, nor love beyond,—her heart beat
　　here. . . .

from CANTO 3

The Isles of Greece°

1

The isles of Greece, the isles of Greece!
　　Where burning Sappho° loved and sung,
Where grew the arts of war and peace,
　　Where Delos° rose, and Phoebus° sprung!
Eternal summer gilds them yet,　　5
But all, except their sun, is set.

2

The Scian and the Teian muse,°
　　The hero's harp, the lover's lute,
Have found the fame your shores refuse:
　　Their place of birth alone is mute　　10
To sounds which echo further west
Than your sires' "Islands of the Blest."°

3

The mountains look on Marathon°—
　　And Marathon looks on the sea;
And musing there an hour alone,　　15
　　I dreamed that Greece might still be free;
For standing on the Persians' grave,
I could not deem myself a slave.

4

A king° sat on the rocky brow
　　Which looks o'er sea-born Salamis;°　　20
And ships, by thousands, lay below,
　　And men in nations;—all were his!
He counted them at break of day—
And when the sun set, where were they?

5

And where are they? and where art thou,　　25
　　My country? On thy voiceless shore

1608 **Some . . . novel.** Reference to Lady Caroline Lamb (1785–1828) who became infatuated with Byron; their relationship lasted only nine months. She later wrote a novel, *Glenarvon* (1816), which contained a caricature portrait of him

Canto 3 The Isles of Greece. During the absence of Haidée's father, Juan and Haidée hold a feast at which the song given here is sung　2 **Sappho,** Greek lyric poet (fl. sixth century B.C.); she is known as the Tenth Muse　4 **Delos,** island off the coast of Greece　**Phoebus,** god of music and poetry　7 **Scian . . . muse,** Homer of the island of Scio, east of Greece, and Anacreon, Greek lyric poet (sixth century B.C.) of Teos, Asia Minor　12 **Islands of the Blest,** mythical islands said to lie in the Western Ocean where the favorites of the gods dwelt after death 13 **Marathon,** plain in Attica, Greece, the scene of the famous Greek victory over the Persian army in 490 B.C.　19 **king,** Xerxes, of Persia (486–465 B.C.) 20 **Salamis,** Greek island west of Athens where the Greeks destroyed the Persian fleet of Xerxes in 480 B.C.

The heroic lay is tuneless now—
    The heroic bosom beats no more!
    And must thy lyre, so long divine,
30 Degenerate into hands like mine?

6

'Tis something, in the dearth of fame,
    Though linked among a fettered race,
To feel at least a patriot's shame,
    Even as I sing, suffuse my face;
35 For what is left the poet here?
For Greeks a blush—for Greece a tear.

7

Must *we* but weep o'er days more blest?
    Must *we* but blush?—Our fathers bled.
Earth! render back from out thy breast
40   A remnant of our Spartan dead!
Of the three hundred grant but three,
To make a new Thermopylae!°

8

What, silent still? and silent all?
    Ah! no;—the voices of the dead
45 Sound like a distant torrent's fall,
    And answer, "Let one living head,
But one arise—we come, we come!"
'Tis but the living who are dumb.

9

In vain—in vain: strike other chords;
50   Fill high the cup with Samian° wine!
Leave battles to the Turkish hordes,
    And shed the blood of Scio's vine!
Hark! rising to the ignoble call—
How answers each bold Bacchanal!°

10

55 You have the Pyrrhic dance° as yet;
    Where is the Pyrrhic phalanx° gone?
Of two such lessons, why forget
    The nobler and the manlier one?
You have the letters Cadmus° gave—
60 Think ye he meant them for a slave?

11

Fill high the bowl with Samian wine!
    We will not think of themes like these!
It made Anacreon's° song divine:
    He served—but served Polycrates°—

A tyrant; but our masters then   65
Were still, at least, our countrymen.

12

The tyrant of the Chersonese°
    Was freedom's best and bravest friend;
That tyrant was Miltiades!°
    Oh! that the present hour would lend   70
Another despot of the kind!
Such chains as his were sure to bind.

13

Fill high the bowl with Samian wine!
    On Suli's° rock, and Parga's° shore,
Exists the remnant of a line   75
    Such as the Doric° mothers bore;
And there, perhaps, some seed is sown,
The Heracleidan° blood might own.

14

Trust not for freedom to the Franks—
    They have a king who buys and sells;   80
In native swords, and native ranks,
    The only hope of courage dwells:
But Turkish force, and Latin fraud,
Would break your shield, however broad.

15

Fill high the bowl with Samian wine!   85
    Our virgins dance beneath the shade—
I see their glorious black eyes shine;
    But gazing on each glowing maid,
My own the burning tear-drop laves,
To think such breasts must suckle slaves.   90

16

Place me on Sunium's° marbled steep,
    Where nothing, save the waves and I,
May hear our mutual murmurs sweep;
    There, swan-like,° let me sing and die:
A land of slaves shall ne'er be mine—   95
Dash down yon cup of Samian wine!

LXXXVII

Thus sung, or would, or could, or should have sung,
    The modern Greek, in tolerable verse;   690
If not like Orpheus° quite, when Greece was young,
    Yet in these times he might have done much worse:
His strain displayed some feeling—right or wrong;
    And feeling, in a poet, is the source
Of others' feeling; but they are such liars,   695
And take all colors—like the hands of dyers.

---

42 **Thermopylae,** pass in northern Greece where Leonidas and his band of Spartans made a valiant stand against the Persian army of Xerxes in 480 B.C.
50 **Samian,** from Samos, an island in the Aegean Sea 52 **Scio,** island in the Aegean Sea once famous for its wines 54 **Bacchanal,** devotee of Bacchus, god of wine 55 **Pyrrhic dance,** ancient war dance 56 **Pyrrhic phalanx,** that used by Pyrrhus, great Greek general (third century B.C.) 59 **Cadmus,** reputed founder of Thebes. He brought the old Phoenician alphabet of sixteen letters to Greece 63 **Anacreon,** famous Greek lyric poet (sixth century B.C.) 64 **Polycrates,** tyrant of Samos (sixth century B.C.) and patron of literature and art

67 **Chersonese,** peninsula of ancient Greece 69 **Miltiades,** famous Athenian general (fifth century B.C.) 74 **Suli,** mountainous district in European Turkey **Parga,** a seaport in Turkey 76 **Doric,** from Doris, an ancient province in northern Greece 78 **Heracleidan,** tracing back to Hercules, i.e., ancient Greek 91 **Sunium,** in ancient geography the promontory at the southeastern extremity of Attica, Greece 94 **swan-like.** The swan was said to sing melodiously when about to die 691 **Orpheus,** mythological poet and musician whose lyre could charm beasts and move trees and stones

LXXXVIII

But words are things, and a small drop of ink,
  Falling like dew, upon a thought, produces
That which makes thousands, perhaps millions, think;
700 'Tis strange, the shortest letter which man uses
Instead of speech, may form a lasting link
  Of ages; to what straits old Time reduces
Frail man, when paper—even a rag like this,
Survives himself, his tomb, and all that's his!

LXXXIX

705 And when his bones are dust, his grave a blank,
  His station, generation, even his nation,
Become a thing, or nothing, save to rank
  In chronological commemoration,
Some dull MS. oblivion long has sank,
710 Or graven stone found in a barrack's station
In digging the foundation of a closet,
May turn his name up, as a rare deposit.

XC

And glory long has made the sages smile;
  'Tis something, nothing, words, illusion, wind—
715 Depending more upon the historian's style
  Than on the name a person leaves behind:
Troy owes to Homer° what whist owes to Hoyle:°
  The present century was growing blind
To the great Marlborough's° skill in giving knocks,
720 Until his late Life by Archdeacon Coxe.°

XCI

Milton's the prince of poets—so we say;
  A little heavy, but no less divine:
An independent being in his day—
  Learned, pious, temperate in love and wine;
725 But his life falling into Johnson's way,°
  We're told this great high priest of all the Nine°
Was whipped at college—a harsh sire—odd spouse,
For the first Mrs. Milton left his house.

XCII

All these are, *certes*, entertaining facts,
  Like Shakespeare's stealing deer,° Lord Bacon's
730   bribes;°
Like Titus' youth,° and Caesar's earliest acts;
  Like Burns (whom Doctor Currie° well describes);
Like Cromwell's pranks;°—but although truth exacts
  These amiable descriptions from the scribes,

As most essential to their hero's story,   735
They do not much contribute to his glory.

XCIII

All are not moralists, like Southey, when
  He prated to the world of "Pantisocrasy";°
Or Wordsworth unexcised, unhired, who then
  Seasoned his peddler poems° with democracy;   740
Or Coleridge, long before his flighty pen
  Let to the Morning Post° its aristocracy;
When he and Southey, following the same path,
Espoused two partners° (milliners of Bath).

XCIV

Such names at present cut a convict figure,   745
  The very Botany Bay° in moral geography;
Their loyal treason, renegado rigor,
  Are good manure for their more bare biography;
Wordsworth's last quarto, by the way, is bigger
  Than any since the birthday of typography;   750
A drowsy, frowzy poem, called the "Excursion,"
Writ in a manner which is my aversion.

XCV

He there builds up a formidable dyke
  Between his own and others' intellect;
But Wordsworth's poem, and his followers, like   755
  Joanna Southcote's° Shiloh and her sect,
Are things which in this century don't strike
  The public mind—so few are the elect;
And the new births of both their stale virginities
Have proved but dropsies, taken for divinities.   760

XCVI

But let me to my story: I must own,
  If I have any fault, it is digression,
Leaving my people to proceed alone,
  While I soliloquize beyond expression:
But these are my addresses from the throne,   765
  Which put off business to the ensuing session:
Forgetting each omission is a loss to
The world, not quite so great as Ariosto.°

XCVII

I know that what our neighbors call "*longueurs*,"°
  (We've not so good a *word*, but have the *thing*,   770
In that complete perfection which insures
  An epic from Bob Southey every spring—)
Form not the true temptation which allures
  The reader; but 'twould not be hard to bring

---

717 **Troy . . . Homer.** Troy, an ancient city in Asia Minor, is the scene of Homer's *Iliad* **Hoyle,** Edmund Hoyle (1672–1769), famous writer on card games 719 **Marlborough,** John Churchill (1650–1722), Duke of Marlborough, famous English general who defeated the French in the Battle of Blenheim (Bavaria) in 1704 720 **Coxe,** William Coxe (1747–1832), English historian. His *Memoirs of the Duke of Marlborough* appeared in 1817–1819 725 **life . . . way.** Samuel Johnson included a life of Milton in his *Lives of the English Poets* (1779, 1781) 726 **the Nine,** the nine Muses 730 **stealing deer,** fictitious anecdote associated with Shakespeare's youth **Bacon's bribes.** Bacon was charged with accepting bribes and was excluded from Parliament 731 **Titus' youth.** The youth of Titus Vespasianus, Roman emperor (79–81), like that of Julius Caesar and that of Burns, was noted for its voluptuousness 732 **Currie,** James Currie (1756–1805), Scottish physician who wrote a life of Burns for the benefit of the Burns family 733 **Cromwell's pranks.** The youthful Cromwell was noted for robbing orchards

738 **Pantisocrasy,** name given to a scheme for an ideal community that Southey, Coleridge, and others planned in 1794 to establish in America 740 **peddler poems,** a reference to Wordsworth's *Peter Bell*, whose hero is a peddler 742 **Morning Post.** Coleridge began contributing to the *Morning Post* in 1798 744 **two partners.** Coleridge married Sara Fricker of Bath, and Southey married her sister Edith. They were not milliners at the time of their marriages in 1795 746 **Botany Bay,** inlet on the east coast of Australia, formerly used by the British as a convict station 756 **Joanna Southcote,** visionary who prophesied that she would give birth to a second Shiloh, or Messiah, on October 19, 1814. On that day she fell into a trance and died ten days later 768 **Ariosto,** famous Italian poet (1474–1533) 769 **longueurs,** tedious passages

775 Some fine examples of the *épopée*,°
To prove its grand ingredient is *ennui*.°

XCVIII

We learn from Horace,° "Homer sometimes sleeps";
    We feel without him, Wordsworth sometimes
        wakes—
To show with what complacency he creeps,
780   With his dear *"Wagoners,"*° around his lakes.
He wishes for "a boat" to sail the deeps—
    Of ocean?—No, of air; and then he makes
Another outcry for "a little boat,"°
And drivels seas to set it well afloat.

XCIX

785 If he must fain sweep o'er the ethereal plain,
    And Pegasus runs restive in his "Wagon,"
Could he not beg the loan of Charles's Wain?°
    Or pray Medea° for a single dragon?
Or if, too classic for his vulgar brain,
790   He feared his neck to venture such a nag on,
And he must needs mount nearer to the moon,
Could not the blockhead ask for a balloon?

C

"Peddlers," and "Boats," and "Wagons!" Oh! ye
        shades
    Of Pope and Dryden, are we come to this?
795 That trash of such sort not alone evades
    Contempt, but from the bathos' vast abyss
Floats scumlike uppermost, and these Jack Cades°
    Of sense and song above your graves may hiss—
The "little boatman" and his "Peter Bell"
800 Can sneer at him° who drew "Achitophel"!

CI

T' our tale.—The feast was over, the slaves gone,
    The dwarfs and dancing girls had all retired;
The Arab lore and poet's song were done,
    And every sound of revelry expired,
805 The lady and her lover, left alone,
    The rosy flood of twilight's sky admired;—
Ave Maria o'er the earth and sea,
That heavenliest hour of Heaven is worthiest thee!

CII

Ave Maria! blessèd be the hour
810   The time, the clime, the spot, where I so oft
Have felt that moment in its fullest power
    Sink o'er the earth so beautiful and soft,
While swung the deep bell in the distant tower,
    Or the faint dying day-hymn stole aloft,

And not a breath crept through the rosy air,   815
And yet the forest leaves seemed stirred with prayer.

CIII

Ave Maria! 'tis the hour of prayer!
    Ave Maria! 'tis the hour of love!
Ave Maria! may our spirits dare
    Look up to thine and to thy Son's above!   820
Ave Maria! oh that face so fair!
    Those downcast eyes beneath the Almighty Dove—
What though 'tis but a pictured image?—strike—
That painting is no idol—'tis too like.

CIV

Some kinder casuists are pleased to say,   825
    In nameless print—that I have no devotion;
But set those persons down with me to pray,
    And you shall see who has the properest notion
Of getting into heaven the shortest way;
    My altars are the mountains and the ocean,   830
Earth, air, stars—all that springs from the great
        Whole,
Who hath produced, and will receive the soul.

CV

Sweet hour of twilight!—in the solitude
    Of the pine forest, and the silent shore
Which bounds Ravenna's° immemorial wood,   835
    Rooted where once the Adrian wave flowed o'er,
To where the last Caesarean fortress stood,
    Evergreen forest! which Boccaccio's lore
And Dryden's lay° made haunted ground to me,
How have I loved the twilight hour and thee!   840

CVI

The shrill cicalas,° people of the pine,
    Making their summer lives one ceaseless song,
Were the sole echoes, save my steed's and mine,
    And vesper bell's that rose the boughs along;
The specter huntsman of Onesti's° line,   845
    His hell-dogs, and their chase, and the fair throng
Which learned from this example not to fly
From a true lover—shadowed my mind's eye.

CVII

Oh, Hesperus!° thou bringest all good things—
    Home to the weary, to the hungry cheer,   850
To the young bird the parent's brooding wings,
    The welcome stall to the o'erlabored steer;
Whate'er of peace about our hearthstone clings,
    Whate'er our household goods protect of dear,
Are gathered round us by thy look of rest;   855
Thou bring'st the child, too, to the mother's breast.

---

775 **épopée**, epic   776 **ennui**, languid weariness   777 **Horace**, famous Latin
poet (first century B.C.)   780 **Wagoners.** One of Wordsworth's poems is entitled
The Wagoner   783 **a little boat**, from the first stanza of *Peter Bell*   787 **Charles's
Wain**, a constellation known as the Big Dipper.   788 **Medea**, enchantress who
helped her lover Jason get the Golden Fleece   797 **Jack Cades.** Jack Cade was
the leader of "Cade's Rebellion," a political uprising in Kent in 1450   800 **him,**
Dryden, of whom Wordsworth was not fond

835 **Ravenna**, city and province in Italy   839 **Dryden's lay**, *Theodore and Hon-
oria*, tale of a specter huntsman who haunted the region of Ravenna; it is adapted
from Boccaccio's *Decameron*   841 **cicalas**, locusts   845 **Onesti**, hero of Boccaccio's story; he became Dryden's *Theodore*. The specter merely appeared to
Onesti; it was not of his line   849 **Hesperus**, the evening star in Greek mythology

Soft hour! which wakes the wish and melts the heart
  Of those who sail the seas, on the first day
When they from their sweet friends are torn apart;
860   Or fills with love the pilgrim on his way
As the far bell of vesper makes him start,
  Seeming to weep the dying day's decay;
Is this a fancy which our reason scorns?
Ah! surely nothing dies but something mourns! . . .
(1819–1820; 1820)

STANZAS WRITTEN ON THE ROAD BETWEEN FLORENCE AND PISA

Oh, talk not to me of a name great in story;
The days of our youth are the days of our glory;
And the myrtle and ivy° of sweet two-and-twenty
Are worth all your laurels, though ever so plenty.

5 What are garlands and crowns to th brow that is
  wrinkled?
'Tis but as a dead-flower with May-dew besprinkled.
Then away with all such from the head that is hoary!
What care I for the wreaths that can only give glory!

Oh Fame!—if I e'er took delight in thy praises,
10 'Twas less for the sake of thy high-sounding phrases,
Than to see the bright eyes of the dear one discover,
She thought that I was not unworthy to love her.

There chiefly I sought thee, there only I found thee;
Her glance was the best of the rays that surround thee;
When it sparkled o'er aught that was bright in my
15 story,
I knew it was love, and I felt it was glory.
(1821; 1830)

WHEN A MAN HATH NO FREEDOM

When a man hath no freedom to fight for at home,
  Let him combat for that of his neighbors;
Let him think of the glories of Greece and of Rome,
  And get knocked on the head for his labors.

5 To do good to mankind is the chivalrous plan,
  And is always as nobly requited;
Then battle for freedom wherever you can,
  And, if not shot or hanged, you'll get knighted.
(1820; 1824)

Stanzas Written on the Road 3 myrtle and ivy. The myrtle was a symbol of love;
ivy, of constancy in friendship

ON THIS DAY I COMPLETE MY THIRTY-SIXTH YEAR

'Tis time this heart should be unmoved,
  Since others it hath ceased to move;
Yet, though I cannot be beloved,
  Still let me love!

My days are in the yellow leaf;°
  The flowers and fruits of love are gone;
The worm, the canker, and the grief
  Are mine alone!

The fire that on my bosom preys
  Is lone as some volcanic isle;   10
No torch is kindled at its blaze—
  A funeral pile.

The hope, the fear, the jealous care,
  The exalted portion of the pain
And power of love, I cannot share,
  But wear the chain.

But 't is not thus—and 't is not here—
  Such thoughts should shake my soul, nor now,
Where glory decks the hero's bier,
  Or binds his brow.   20

The sword, the banner, and the field,
  Glory and Greece, around me see!
The Spartan, borne upon his shield,°
  Was not more free.

Awake! (not Greece—she is awake!)
  Awake, my spirit; Think through whom
Thy life-blood tracks its parent lake,°
  And then strike home!

Tread those reviving passions down,
  Unworthy manhood!—unto thee   30
Indifferent should the smile or frown
  Of beauty be.

If thou regrett'st thy youth, why live?
  The land of honorable death
Is here—up to the field, and give
  Away thy breath!

Seek out—less often sought than found—
  A soldier's grave,° for thee the best;
Then look around, and choose thy ground,
  And take thy rest.   40
(1824)

On This Day 5 My . . . leaf, from Macbeth, V, iii, 22: "my way of life/Is fall'n into
the sear, the yellow leaf" 23 Spartan . . . shield. In ancient Sparta it was the custom to carry home a fallen warrior on his shield 27 life-blood . . . lake. Byron's
mother was a descendant of James I; his father traced his ancestry to the heroes of the
days of William the Conqueror 38 A soldier's grave. Byron died on a military
expedition undertaken for the independence of Greece

PERCY BYSSHE SHELLEY
1792–1822

Shelley's personal life was tumultuous; his poetry sometimes is luminously clear, sometimes esoterically obscure. Revolutionary fervor and radical idealism characterize both his life and his poetry.

Shelley was born in 1792 in Sussex, the son of a wealthy, conservative country squire. He was sent to Eton, where he was something of a rebel; his classmates dubbed him "Mad Shelley." By the age of twelve he had collaborated with his sister on a collection of verse and had alone composed a Gothic novel, *Zastrozzi*. Soon after entering University College, Oxford, he met Thomas Jefferson Hogg (1792–1862), who remained a very close friend all his life. Shelley and Hogg were expelled from Oxford for circulating a radical pamphlet, *The Necessity of Atheism*. As a result of this evidence of nonconformity, Shelley's father wished to have little to do with his son. Shelley went to London, aided by his sister's pocket money.

In London Shelley met Harriet Westbrook, who soon became his wife. She accompanied him on a series of visits to Scotland, Ireland, and Wales, where Shelley was interested in supporting (with his pen and money) revolutionary causes. Shelley began corresponding with William Godwin (1756–1836), the author of *Political Justice* (1793), which Shelley regarded as the revolutionaries' bible. In 1812 he finally met Godwin in London, fell in love with his daughter Mary, the child of Godwin's brief and tragic marriage to Mary Wollstonecraft. Shelley proposed a living situation in which he, Mary, and Harriet would all live together, with Harriet playing a sisterly role. Harriet refused, returned to her own family, and eventually committed suicide by drowning in 1816. Shelley and Mary eloped to France, accompanied by Claire Clairmont, Mary's stepsister.

In 1813 Shelley published *Queen Mab*, a visionary and revolutionary poem which became a kind of manifesto for the English working classes in the nineteenth century. This poem articulated the main principles of the revolutionary, libertarian philosophy that Shelley was to remain faithful to for the rest of his life: an absolute hatred of all forms of tyranny and patriarchy, from the religious domination of priesthood, to the political oppression of monarchy, to the domestic slavery of unhappy marriage and male supremacy. Shelley pronounced himself a believer in free love, free politics, atheism, and vegetarianism, and promptly found himself the most scandalous figure in England—much more scandalous, in fact, than Byron, whose excesses were those of a rogue or libertine and did not emerge from a principled critique of the "respectable" way of doing things.

The inheritance that came from the death of his grandfather in 1815 left Shelley financially secure. Mary and Shelley took a house in Windsor Forest during 1816; it was there, during the early summer, that Shelley completed his first major poem, *Alastor, or the Spirit of Solitude*. The end of the summer found Mary and Shelley in a cottage on the shores of Lake Geneva, Switzerland, where they made friends with Byron. After returning to England in 1817, Shelley composed *Prince Athanase*, *Rosalind and Helen*, and *The Revolt of Islam*. This was a period of comparative peace for the Shelleys; they bought a house in Buckinghamshire and received many friends and relatives, including Leigh Hunt (1784–1859), William Godwin, Thomas Love Peacock (1785–1866), and Thomas Hogg. But life in England soon became uncomfortable for Shelley. His first wife having committed suicide, he was hounded as a villain. Everywhere he went he was met with loathing, and his health began to decline. In March 1818 he left England forever with Mary (now legally his wife).

The Shelleys settled in Italy. There he had leisure to study, write, and enjoy. The Italian years were very fertile—Shelley completed *Julian and Maddalo*, containing portraits of Byron and himself; *The Cenci*, a poetic tragedy; *Ode to the West Wind*; *Peter Bell the Third*, a satire on renegades from liberalism, such as he conceived Wordsworth and Coleridge to be; *The Mask of Anarchy*; and the great *Prometheus Unbound*, his poem of the triumph of the universal principle of good over the universal principle of evil. All this work was completed between 1818 and 1820.

In the last two years of his life Shelley wrote some of his finest lyrics, including *To a Skylark*, *To Night*, and the final *Chorus* to his drama *Hellas*. He also composed several longer works, *Epipsychidion*, *Defense of Poetry*, *Adonais*, and the unfinished *Triumph of Life*. Of these longer works, *Adonais*, his elegy on the death of Keats, is perhaps the greatest.

On July 8, 1822, Shelley and his friend Edward Williams, a retired lieutenant in the dragoons, set out on a boat trip on the Gulf of Spezia. A sudden squall blew up and sank the boat; ten days later their bodies were washed ashore. Byron and Hunt were present at the cremation of Shelley's body on the beach. His ashes were buried in the Protestant Cemetery at Rome, near Keats' grave.

MUTABILITY

We are as clouds that veil the midnight moon;
  How restlessly they speed, and gleam, and quiver,
Streaking the darkness radiantly!—yet soon
  Night closes round, and they are lost forever:

Or like forgotten lyres, whose dissonant strings   5
  Give various response to each varying blast,

To whose frail frame no second motion brings
    One mood or modulation like the last.

We rest—a dream has power to poison sleep;
10 We rise—one wandering thought pollutes the day;
We feel, conceive or reason, laugh or weep;
    Embrace fond woe, or cast our cares away:

It is the same!—For, be it joy or sorrow,
    The path of its departure still is free:
15 Man's yesterday may ne'er be like his morrow;
    Naught may endure but Mutability.
    (1815; 1816)

MONT BLANC°

I

The everlasting universe of things
Flows through the mind, and rolls its rapid waves—
Now dark, now glittering, now reflecting gloom,
Now lending splendour where, from secret springs,
The source of human thought its tribute brings
Of waters,—with a sound but half its own,
Such as a feeble brook will oft assume
In the wild woods, among the mountains lone,
Where waterfalls around it leap for ever,
10 Where woods and winds contend, and a vast river
Over its rocks ceaselessly bursts and raves.

II

Thus thou, Ravine of Arve—dark, deep Ravine;—
Thou many-coloured, many-voicèd vale,
Over whose pines and crags and caverns sail
Fast cloud-shadows and sunbeams;—awful scene
Where Power, in likeness of the Arve, comes down
From the ice-gulfs that gird his secret throne,
Bursting through these dark mountains like the flame
Of lightning through the tempest;—thou dost lie,
20 Thy giant brood of pines around thee clinging
(Children of elder time, in whose devotion
The chainless winds still come, and ever came
To drink their odours, and their mighty swinging
To hear—an old and solemn harmony),
Thine earthly rainbows stretched across the sweep
Of the aethereal waterfall, whose veil
Robes some unsculptured image (even the sleep,
The sudden pause which does inhabit thee
Which, when the voices of the desert fail
30 And its hues wane, doth blend them all and steep
Their period in its own eternity),
Thy caverns echoing to the Arve's commotion,
A loud, lone sound no other sound can tame;—
Thou art pervaded with that ceaseless motion,
Thou art the path of that unresting sound,

Dizzy Ravine! . . . . . . And, when I gaze on thee,
I seem as in a trance sublime and strange
To muse on my own separate fantasy,
My own, my human mind, which passively
Now renders and receives fast influencings,°   40
Holding an unremitting interchange
With the clear universe of things around—
One legion of wild thoughts, whose wandering wings
Now float above thy darkness, and now rest
Where that or thou art no unbidden guest,
In the still cave of the witch Poesy—
Seeking among the shadows that pass by
(Ghosts of all things that are) some shade of thee,
Some phantom, some faint image; till the breast
From which they fled recalls them, thou art there!   50

III

Some say that gleams of a remoter world
Visit the soul in sleep,—that death is slumber,
And that its shapes the busy thoughts outnumber
Of those who wake and live. I look on high:—
Has some unknown omnipotence unfurled
The veil of life and death? Or do I lie
In dream, and does the mightier world of sleep
Spread far around and inaccessibly
Its circles? For the very spirit fails,
Driven like a homeless cloud from steep to steep   60
That vanishes among the viewless gales!
Far, far above, piercing the infinite sky,
Mont Blanc appears,—still, snowy, and serene;
Its subject mountains their unearthly forms
Pile round it, ice and rock, broad vales between
Of frozen floods, unfathomable deeps,
Blue as the overhanging heaven, that spread
And wind among the accumulated steeps—
A desert peopled by the storms alone,
Save when the eagle brings some hunter's bone,   70
And the wolf tracks her there. How hideously
Its shapes are heaped around—rude, bare, and high,
Ghastly, and scarred, and riven!—Is this the scene
Where the old Earthquake-daemon taught her young
Ruin? Were these their toys? or did a sea
Of fire envelop once this silent snow?
None can reply—all seems eternal now.
The wilderness has a mysterious tongue
Which teaches awful doubt, or faith so mild,
So solemn, so serene, that man may be,   80
In such a faith, with nature reconciled,—
Thou hast a voice, great Mountain, to repeal
Large codes of fraud and woe not understood
By all, but which the wise, and great, and good
Interpret, or make felt, or deeply feel!

IV

The fields, the lakes, the forests, and the streams,
Ocean, and all the living things that dwell

Mont Blanc. Shelley viewed Mont Blanc from the bridge over the Arve. He says of the poem's composition: "It was composed under the immediate impression of the deep and powerful feelings excited by the objects which it attempts to describe . . ."

40 **influencings,** the exertions of influence

Within the daedal° earth; lightning, and rain,
Earthquake, and fiery flood, and hurricane;
90 The torpor of the year when feeble dreams
Visit the hidden buds, or dreamless sleep
Holds every future leaf and flower; the bound
With which from that detested trance they leap;
The works and ways of man, their death and birth,
And that of him and all that his may be;—
All things that move and breathe with toil and sound
Are born and die, revolve, subside, and swell.
Power dwells apart in its tranquillity,
Remote, serene, and inaccessible:
100 And *this*, the naked countenance of earth,
On which I gaze, even these primaeval mountains
Teach the adverting° mind. The glaciers creep
Like snakes that watch their prey, from their far foun-
tains,
Slow rolling on; there, many a precipice,
Frost and the Sun in scorn of mortal power
Have piled: dome, pyramid, and pinnacle,
A city of death, distinct with many a tower
And wall impregnable of beaming ice.
Yet not a city, but a flood of ruin
110 Is there, that from the boundaries of the sky
Rolls its perpetual stream; vast pines are strewing
Its destined path, or in the mangled soil
Branchless and shattered stand; the rocks, drawn
down
From yon remotest waste, have overthrown
The limits of the dead and living world,
Never to be reclaimed. The dwelling-place
Of insects, beasts, and birds becomes its spoil;
Their food and their retreat for ever gone,
So much of life and joy is lost. The race
120 Of man flies far in dread; his work and dwelling
Vanish, like smoke before the tempest's stream,
And their place is not known. Below, vast caves
Shine in the rushing torrents' restless gleam,
Which from those secret chasms in tumult welling
Meet in the vale, and one majestic River,
The breath and blood of distant lands, for ever
Rolls its loud waters to the ocean-waves,
Breathes its swift vapours to the circling air.

V

Mont Blanc yet gleams on high:—the power is there,
130 The still and solemn power of many sights,
And many sounds, and much of life and death.
In the calm darkness of the moonless nights,
In the lone glare of day, the snows descend
Upon that Mountain; none beholds them there,
Nor when the flakes burn in the sinking sun,
Or the star-beams dart through them. Winds contend
Silently there, and heap the snow with breath
Rapid and strong, but silently. Its home
The voiceless lightning in these solitudes

88 **daedal,** varied, variously adorned   102 **adverting,** paying attention to, taking
heed

Keeps innocently, and like vapour broods   140
Over the snow. The secret Strength of things
Which governs thought, and to the infinite dome
Of Heaven is as a law, inhabits thee.
And what were thou, and earth, and stars, and sea,
If to the human mind's imaginings
Silence and solitude were vacancy?
(1816; 1817)

HYMN TO INTELLECTUAL BEAUTY

Shelley based this poem upon the Platonic idea of
Eternal Beauty—in brief, a conception of absolute and
perfect beauty, "simple, pure, uncontaminated with
the intermixture of human flesh and colors, and all
other idle and unreal shapes attendant upon mortality." This absolute beauty, although invisible, is immortal and pervades everything; it can be perceived
by contemplating the beautiful, the good, and the true,
for "to him alone is accorded the prerogative of
bringing forth, not images and shadows of virtue, for
he is in contact not with a shadow, but reality, with
virtue itself, in the production and nourishment of
which he becomes dear to the gods, and, if such a
privilege is conceded to any human being, himself
immortal." The quotations are from Shelley's translation of Plato's *Symposium*. It may be added that Shelley takes the word "intellectual" in the general sense
of "spiritual"; "intellectual beauty," which is immortal, must be distinguished from mere "physical
beauty."

The awful shadow of some unseen Power
    Floats though unseen among us—visiting
    This various world with as inconstant wing
As summer winds that creep from flower to flower—
Like moonbeams that behind some piny mountain
        shower,
    It visits with inconstant glance
    Each human heart and countenance;
Like hues and harmonies of evening—
        Like clouds in starlight widely spread—
        Like memory of music fled—   10
        Like aught that for its grace may be
Dear, and yet dearer for its mystery.

Spirit of Beauty, that dost consecrate
    With thine own hues all thou dost shine upon
    Of human thought or form—where art thou gone?
Why dost thou pass away and leave our state,
This dim vast vale of tears, vacant and desolate?
        Ask why the sunlight not forever
        Weaves rainbows o'er yon mountain-river,
Why aught should fail and fade that once is shown,   20
        Why fear and dream and death and birth
        Cast on the daylight of this earth

Such gloom—why man has such a scope
For love and hate, despondency and hope?

No voice from some sublimer world hath ever
   To sage or poet these responses° given—
   Therefore the names of Demon,° Ghost, and Heaven,
Remain the records of their vain endeavor,
Frail spells—whose uttered charm might not avail to
     sever,
30   From all we hear and all we see,
    Doubt, chance, and mutability.
Thy light alone—like mist o'er mountains driven,
   Or music by the night-wind sent
   Through strings of some still instrument,
   Or moonlight on a midnight stream,
Gives grace and truth to life's unquiet dream.

Love, Hope, and Self-Esteem, like clouds depart
   And come, for some uncertain moments lent.
   Man were immortal, and omnipotent,
40 Didst thou, unknown and awful as thou art,
Keep with thy glorious train firm state within his heart.
    Thou messenger of sympathies,
    That wax and wane in lovers' eyes—
Thou—that to human thought art nourishment,
    Like darkness to a dying flame!
    Depart not as thy shadow came,
    Depart not—lest the grave should be,
Like life and fear, a dark reality.

While yet a boy I sought for ghosts, and sped
50   Through many a listening chamber, cave and ruin,
   And starlight wood, with fearful steps pursuing
Hopes of high talk with the departed dead.
I called on poisonous names with which our youth is
    fed;
    I was not heard—I saw them not—
    When musing deeply on the lot
Of life, at that sweet time when winds are wooing
    All vital things that wake to bring
    News of birds and blossoming—
    Sudden, thy shadow fell on me;
60 I shrieked, and clasped my hands in ecstasy!

I vowed that I would dedicate my powers
   To thee and thine—have I not kept the vow?
   With beating heart and streaming eyes, even now
I called the phantoms of a thousand hours
Each from his voiceless grave: they have in visioned
    bowers
    Of studious zeal or love's delight
    Outwatched with me the envious night—
They know that never joy illumed my brow
    Unlinked with hope that thou wouldst free
70   This world from its dark slavery,

That thou—O awful Loveliness,
Wouldst give whate'er these words cannot express.

The day becomes more solemn and serene
   When noon is past—there is a harmony
   In autumn, and a luster in its sky,
Which through the summer is not heard or seen,
As if it could not be, as if it had not been!
    Thus let thy power, which like the truth
    Of nature on my passive youth
Descended, to my onward life supply   80
    Its calm—to one who worships thee,
    And every form containing thee,
    Whom, Spirit fair, thy spells did bind
To fear himself, and love all human kind.
(1816; 1817)

OZYMANDIAS°

I met a traveler from an antique land
Who said: "Two vast and trunkless legs of stone
Stand in the desert. Near them, on the sand,
Half sunk, a shattered visage lies, whose frown,
And wrinkled lip, and sneer of cold command,   5
Tell that its sculptor well those passions read
Which yet survive, stamped on these lifeless things,
The hand that mocked them,° and the heart° that fed:
And on the pedestal these words appear:
'My name is Ozymandias, king of kings: 10
Look on my works, ye Mighty, and despair!'
Nothing beside remains. Round the decay
Of that colossal wreck, boundless and bare
The lone and level sands stretch far away."
(1817; 1818)

ENGLAND IN 1819

An old, mad, blind, despised, and dying king°—
Princes, the dregs of their dull race, who flow
Through public scorn—mud from a muddy spring—
Rulers who neither see, nor feel, nor know,
But leech-like to their fainting country cling,   5
Till they drop, blind in blood, without a blow—
A people starved and stabbed in the untilled field—
An army, which liberticide and prey
Makes as a two-edged sword to all who wield—
Golden and sanguine laws which tempt and slay;   10
Religion, Christless, Godless—a book sealed;
A Senate—Time's worst statute unrepealed°—
Are graves, from which a glorious Phantom° may
Burst, to illumine our tempestuous day.
(1819; 1839)

Hymn to Intellectual Beauty   26 **these responses,** responses to these questions   27 **Demon,** supernatural being of Greek mythology, conceived as holding a position between gods and men

Ozymandias. According to the statement of the Greek historian Diodorus Siculus (first century B.C.), the statue of Ozymandias was reputed to be the largest in Egypt and to bear the following inscription: "I am Ozymandias, the King of Kings; if any man wishes to know what I am and where I am buried, let him surpass me in some of my achievements"   8 **hand . . . them,** hand of the sculptor who imitated or reproduced them   **heart,** of Ozymandias, who nursed those passions   **England in 1819**   1 **king,** George III of England (1760–1820). He became hopelessly insane in 1810   12 **Time's . . . unrepealed,** law restricting the civil liberties of Roman Catholics; it was repealed in 1829   13 **Phantom,** liberty

ODE TO THE WEST WIND

1

O wild West Wind, thou breath of Autumn's being,
Thou, from whose unseen presence the leaves dead
Are driven, like ghosts from an enchanter fleeing.

Yellow, and black, and pale, and hectic red,
Pestilence-stricken multitudes: O thou,
Who chariotest to their dark wintry bed

The wingéd seeds, where they lie cold and low,
Each like a corpse within its grave, until
Thine azure sister of the Spring° shall blow

10 Her clarion o'er the dreaming earth, and fill
(Driving sweet buds like flocks to feed in air)
With living hues and odors plain and hill:

Wild Spirit, which art moving everywhere;
Destroyer and preserver; hear, oh, hear!

2

Thou on whose stream, mid the steep sky's commo-
tion,
Loose clouds like earth's decaying leaves are shed,
Shook from the tangled boughs of Heaven and Ocean,

Angels of rain and lightning: there are spread
On the blue surface of thine aëry surge,
20 Like the bright hair uplifted from the head

Of some fierce Maenad,° even from the dim verge
Of the horizon to the zenith's height,
The locks of the approaching storm. Thou dirge

Of the dying year, to which this closing night
Will be the dome of a vast sepulcher,
Vaulted with all thy congregated might

Of vapors, from whose solid atmosphere
Black rain, and fire, and hail will burst: oh, hear!

3

Thou who didst waken from his summer dreams
30 The blue Mediterranean, where he lay,
Lulled by the coil of his crystalline streams,

Beside a pumice° isle in Baiae's° bay,
And saw in sleep old palaces and towers
Quivering within the wave's intenser day,

All overgrown with azure moss and flowers
So sweet, the sense faints picturing them! Thou
For whose path the Atlantic's level powers

Cleave themselves into chasms, while far below
The sea-blooms and the oozy woods which wear
The sapless foliage of the ocean, know   40

Thy voice, and suddenly grow gray with fear,
And tremble and despoil themselves: oh, hear!°

4

If I were a dead leaf thou mightest bear,
If I were a swift cloud to fly with thee;
A wave to pant beneath thy power, and share

The impulse of thy strength, only less free
Than thou, O uncontrollable! If even
I were as in my boyhood, and could be

The comrade of thy wanderings over Heaven,
As then, when to outstrip thy skyey speed   50
Scarce seemed a vision; I would ne'er have striven

As thus with thee in prayer in my sore need.
Oh, lift me as a wave, a leaf, a cloud!
I fall upon the thorns of life! I bleed!

A heavy weight of hours has chained and bowed
One too like thee: tameless, and swift, and proud.

5

Make me thy lyre, even as the forest is:
What if my leaves are falling like its own!
The tumult of thy mighty harmonies

Will take from both a deep, autumnal tone,   60
Sweet though in sadness. Be thou, Spirit fierce,
My spirit! Be thou me, impetuous one!

Drive my dead thoughts over the universe
Like withered leaves to quicken a new birth!
And, by the incantation of this verse,

Scatter, as from an unextinguished hearth
Ashes and sparks, my words among mankind!
Be through my lips to unawakened earth

The trumpet of a prophecy! O Wind,
If Winter comes, can Spring be far behind?   70
(1819; 1820)

Ode to the West Wind   9 sister of the Spring, the south wind   **21 Maenad,** priestess of Bacchus, god of wine   **32. pumice,** light, porous volcanic substance
Baiae, small seaport in Italy near Naples

39–42 sea-blooms . . . hear. "The vegetation at the bottom of the sea, of rivers,
and of lakes, sympathizes with that of the land in the change of seasons, and is
consequently influenced by the winds which announce it."—Shelley's note

STANZAS°

WRITTEN IN DEJECTION, NEAR NAPLES

The sun is warm, the sky is clear,
  The waves are dancing fast and bright,
Blue isles and snowy mountains wear
  The purple noon's transparent might,
  The breath of the moist earth is light,
  Around its unexpanded buds;
  Like many a voice of one delight,
  The winds, the birds, the ocean floods,
The City's voice itself, is soft like Solitude's.

10 I see the Deep's untrampled floor
  With green and purple seaweeds strown;
I see the waves upon the shore,
  Like light dissolved in star-showers, thrown:
  I sit upon the sands alone—
  The lightning of the noontide ocean
  Is flashing round me, and a tone
  Arises from its measured motion,
How sweet! did any heart now share in my emotion.

Alas! I have nor hope nor health,
20 Nor peace within nor calm around,
Nor that content surpassing wealth
  The sage in meditation found,
  And walked with inward glory crowned—
  Nor fame, nor power, nor love, nor leisure.
  Others I see whom these surround—
  Smiling they live, and call life pleasure;—
To me that cup has been dealt in another measure.

Yet now despair itself is mild,
  Even as the winds and waters are;
30 I could lie down like a tired child,
  And weep away the life of care
  Which I have borne and yet must bear,
  Till death like sleep might steal on me,
  And I might feel in the warm air
  My cheek grow cold, and hear the sea
Breathe o'er my dying brain its last monotony.

Some might lament that I were cold,
  As I, when this sweet day is gone,
Which my lost heart, too soon grown old,
40 Insults with this untimely moan;
  They might lament—for I am one
  Whom men love not—and yet regret,
  Unlike this day, which, when the sun

Shall on its stainless glory set,
Will linger, though enjoyed, like joy in memory yet.
(1818; 1824)

THE INDIAN SERENADE

I arise from dreams of Thee
  In the first sweet sleep of night,
When the winds are breathing low
  And the stars are shining bright:
I arise from dreams of thee,
  And a spirit in my feet
Hath led me—who knows how?
  To thy chamber-window, Sweet!

The wandering airs, they faint
  On the dark, the silent stream—   10
The champak° odors fail
  Like sweet thoughts in a dream;
The nightingale's complaint,
  It dies upon her heart,
As I must die on thine,
  O beloved as thou art!

Oh, lift me from the grass!
  I die, I faint, I fail!
Let thy love in kisses rain
  On my lips and eyelids pale.   20
My cheek is cold and white, alas!
  My heart beats loud and fast;
Oh! press it close to thine again,
  Where it will break at last.
(1819; 1822)

from PROMETHEUS UNBOUND

ASIA

My soul is an enchanted boat,
  Which, like a sleeping swan, doth float
Upon the silver waves of thy sweet singing;
  And thine doth like an angel sit
  Beside a helm conducting it,
Whilst all the winds with melody are ringing.
  It seems to float ever, forever,
  Upon that many-winding river,
  Between mountains, woods, abysses,
  A paradise of wildernesses!   10
Till, like one in slumber bound,
Borne to the ocean, I float down, around,
Into a sea profound, of ever-spreading sound:

Stanzas Written in Dejection. In the first year of his stay in Italy (1818), Shelley suffered ill health; he was convinced that he was a victim of tuberculosis

Indian Serenade 11 **champak,** a species of magnolia, with very fragrant flowers

Meanwhile thy spirit lifts its pinions
   In music's most serene dominions;
Catching the winds that fan that happy heaven.
   And we sail on, away, afar,
   Without a course, without a star,
But, by the instinct of sweet music driven;
20   Till through Elysian° garden islets
   By thee, most beautiful of pilots,
   Where never mortal pinnace glided,
   The boat of my desire is guided:
Realms where the air we breathe is love,
Which in the winds and on the waves doth move,
Harmonizing this earth with what we feel above.

   We have passed Age's icy caves,
   And Manhood's dark and tossing waves,
And Youth's smooth ocean, smiling to betray:
30   Beyond the glassy gulfs we flee
   Of shadow-peopled Infancy,
Through Death and Birth, to a diviner day;
   A paradise of vaulted bowers,
   Lit by downward-gazing flowers,
   And watery paths that wind between
   Wildernesses calm and green,
Peopled by shapes too bright to see,
And rest, having beheld; somewhat like thee;
Which walk upon the sea, and chant melodiously!

DEMOGORGON°

This is the day, which down the void abysm
At the Earth-born's spell° yawns for Heaven's des-
   potism,
   And Conquest is dragged captive through the deep:
Love, from its awful throne of patient power
In the wise heart, from the last giddy hour
   Of dead endurance, from the slippery, steep,
And narrow verge of crag-like agony, springs
And folds over the world its healing wings.

Gentleness, Virtue, Wisdom, and Endurance,
10 These are the seals of that most firm assurance
   Which bars the pit over Destruction's strength;
And if, with infirm hand, Eternity,
Mother of many acts and hours, should free
   The serpent that would clasp her with his length;
These are the spells by which to reassume
An empire o'er the disentangled doom.

To suffer woes which Hope thinks infinite;
To forgive wrongs darker than death or night;
   To defy Power, which seems omnipotent;
20 To love, and bear; to hope till Hope creates
From its own wreck the thing it contemplates;

Neither to change, nor falter, nor repent;
This, like thy glory, Titan, is to be
Good, great and joyous, beautiful and free;
This is alone Life, Joy, Empire, and Victory.
(1818–19; 1820)

THE CLOUD

I bring fresh showers for the thirsting flowers,
   From the seas and the streams;
I bear light shade for the leaves when laid
   In their noonday dreams.
From my wings are shaken the dews that waken
   The sweet buds every one,
When rocked to rest on their mother's breast,
   As she dances about the sun.
I wield the flail of the lashing hail,
   And whiten the green plains under,   10
And then again I dissolve it in rain,
   And laugh as I pass in thunder.

I sift the snow on the mountains below,
   And their great pines groan aghast;
And all the night 'tis my pillow white,
   While I sleep in the arms of the blast.
Sublime on the towers of my skyey bowers,
   Lightning my pilot sits;
In a cavern under is fettered the thunder,
   It struggles and howls at fits;   20
Over earth and ocean, with gentle motion,
   This pilot is guiding me,
Lured by the love of the genii that move
   In the depths of the purple sea;
Over the rills, and the crags, and the hills,
   Over the lakes and the plains,
Wherever he dream, under mountain or stream,
   The Spirit he loves remains;
And I all the while bask in Heaven's blue smile,
   Whilst he is dissolving in rains.   30

The sanguine Sunrise, with his meteor eyes,
   And his burning plumes outspread,
Leaps on the back of my sailing rack,°
   When the morning star shines dead;
As on the jag of a mountain crag,
   Which an earthquake rocks and swings,
An eagle alit one moment may sit
   In the light of its golden wings.
And when Sunset may breathe, from the lit sea be-
   neath,
   Its ardors of rest and of love,   40
And the crimson pall of eve may fall
   From the depth of Heaven above,
With wings folded I rest, on mine airy nest,
   As still as a brooding dove.

Asia   20 **Elysian,** pertaining to Elysium, the abode of the blessed after death
Demogorgon, in *Prometheus Unbound,* the spirit of necessity   2 **Earth-born's
spell,** the spell of Prometheus, one of the Titans

The Cloud   33 **rack,** broken portion of cloud

That orbéd maiden with white fire laden,
  Whom mortals call the Moon,
Glides glimmering o'er my fleece-like floor,
  By the midnight breezes strewn;
And wherever the beat of her unseen feet,
50 Which only the angels hear,
May have broken the woof of my tent's thin roof,
  The stars peep behind her and peer;
And I laugh to see them whirl and flee,
  Like a swarm of golden bees,
When I widen the rent in my wind-built tent,
  Till the calm rivers, lakes, and seas,
Like strips of the sky fallen through me on high,
  Are each paved with the moon and these.°

I bind the Sun's throne with a burning zone,°
60 And the Moon's with a girdle of pearl;
The volcanoes are dim, and the stars reel and swim,
  When the whirlwinds my banner unfurl.
From cape to cape, with a bridge-like shape,
  Over a torrent sea,
Sunbeam-proof, I hang like a roof—
  The mountains its columns be.
The triumphal arch, through which I march,
  With hurricane, fire, and snow,
When the Powers of the air are chained to my chair,
70 Is the million-colored bow;
The sphere-fire above its soft colors wove,
  While the moist Earth was laughing below.

I am the daughter of Earth and Water,
  And the nursling of the Sky;
I pass through the pores of the ocean and shores,
  I change, but I cannot die.
For after the rain when with never a stain
  The pavilion of Heaven is bare,
And the winds and sunbeams with their convex gleams
80 Build up the blue dome of air,
I silently laugh at my own cenotaph,°
  And out of the caverns of rain,
Like a child from the womb, like a ghost from the
    tomb,
  I arise and unbuild it again.

(1820)

TO A SKYLARK

  Hail to thee, blithe Spirit!
    Bird thou never wert,
  That from Heaven, or near it,
    Pourest thy full heart
In profuse strains of unpremeditated art.

  Higher still and higher
    From the earth thou springest

Like a cloud of fire;
  The blue deep thou wingest,
And singing still dost soar, and soaring ever singest. 10

  In the golden lightning
    Of the sunken sun,
  O'er which clouds are bright'ning,
    Thou dost float and run;
Like an unbodied joy whose race is just begun.

  The pale purple even
    Melts around thy flight;
  Like a star of Heaven,
    In the broad daylight
Thou art unseen, but yet I hear thy shrill delight, 20

  Keen as are the arrows
    Of that silver sphere,
  Whose intense lamp narrows
    In the white dawn clear
Until we hardly see—we feel that it is there.

  All the earth and air
    With thy voice is loud,
  As, when night is bare,
    From one lonely cloud
The moon rains out her beams, and Heaven is over-
    flowed. 30

  What thou art we know not;
    What is most like thee?
  From rainbow clouds there flow not
    Drops so bright to see
As from thy presence showers a rain of melody.

  Like a Poet hidden
    In the light of thought,
  Singing hymns unbidden,
    Till the world is wrought
To sympathy with hopes and fears it heeded not: 40

  Like a high-born maiden
    In a palace tower,
  Soothing her love-laden
    Soul in secret hour
With music sweet as love, which overflows her bower:

  Like a glowworm golden
    In a dell of dew,
  Scattering unbeholden
    Its aëreal hue
Among the flowers and grass, which screen it from the
    view! 50

  Like a rose embowered
    In its own green leaves,
  By warm winds deflowered,
    Till the scent it gives

58 **these,** the stars 59 **zone,** girdle 81 **cenotaph,** an empty tomb that honors
someone lost or buried elsewhere; here, the blue dome of air

Makes faint with too much sweet those heavy-wingéd
    thieves:

    Sound of vernal showers
      On the twinkling grass,
    Rain-awakened flowers,
      All that ever was
60 Joyous, and clear, and fresh, thy music doth surpass:

    Teach us, Sprite or Bird,
      What sweet thoughts are thine:
    I have never heard
      Praise of love or wine
That panted forth a flood of rapture so divine.

    Chorus Hymeneal,
      Or triumphal chant,
    Matched with thine would be all
      But an empty vaunt,
70 A thing wherein we feel there is some hidden want.

    What objects are the fountains
      Of thy happy strain?
    What fields, or waves, or mountains?
      What shapes of sky or plain?
What love of thine own kind? what ignorance of pain?

    With thy clear keen joyance
      Languor cannot be:
    Shadow of annoyance
      Never came near thee:
80 Thou lovest—but ne'er knew love's sad satiety.

    Waking or asleep,
      Thou of death must deem
    Things more true and deep
      Than we mortals dream,
Or how could thy notes flow in such a crystal stream?

    We look before and after,
      And pine for what is not:
    Our sincerest laughter
      With some pain is fraught;
Our sweetest songs are those that tell of saddest
90   thought.

    Yet if we could scorn
      Hate, and pride, and fear;
    If we were things born
      Not to shed a tear,
I know not how thy joy we ever should come near.

    Better than all measures
      Of delightful sound,
    Better than all treasures
      That in books are found,
100 Thy skill to poet were, thou scorner of the ground!

    Teach me half the gladness
      That thy brain must know,
    Such harmonious madness
      From my lips would flow
The world should listen then—as I am listening now.
(1820)

MUTABILITY

The flower that smiles today
    Tomorrow dies;
All that we wish to stay
    Tempts and then flies.
What is this world's delight?
Lightning that mocks the night,
    Brief even as bright.

Virtue, how frail it is!
    Friendship how rare!
Love, how it sells poor bliss   10
    For proud despair!
But we, though soon they fall,
Survive their joy, and all
    Which ours we call
Whilst skies are blue and bright,
    Whilst flowers are gay,
Whilst eyes that change ere night
    Make glad the day;
Whilst yet the calm hours creep,
Dream thou—and from thy sleep   20
    Then wake to weep.
(1821; 1824)

A LAMENT

O world! O life! O time!
On whose last steps I climb,
    Trembling at that where I had stood before;
When will return the glory of your prime?
    No more—Oh, never more!   5

Out of the day and night
A joy has taken flight;
    Fresh spring, and summer, and winter hoar,
Move my faint heart with grief, but with delight
    No more—Oh, never more!   10
(1821; 1824)

ADONAIS

AN ELEGY ON THE DEATH OF JOHN KEATS

Keats' premature death from tuberculosis stirred many
of his contemporaries, particularly Byron and Shelley.
Some of them believed his death had been hastened, if

not directly caused, by a harsh review of Keats' early poem *Endymion* in the *Quarterly Review* for April 1818, three years before Keats' death. Such an idea hardly seems likely, as Byron himself admits:

> 'Tis very strange the mind, that fiery particle
> Should let itself be snuffed out by an article.
> —*Don Juan*, XI, 60

But to the emotional Shelley, who had also received considerable critical abuse and neglect, Keats had been murdered by his critics, and *Adonais*, the beautiful elegy on the death of Keats, is partly an oblique attack upon his "murderers," who, as Shelley saw it, had forced him "to drink poison."

The title of the poem is an adaptation of the name of Adonis, the beautiful youth loved by Venus and killed by a boar. The immediate sources of the poem, particularly at the beginning, are the *Lament for Adonis* by the Greek poet Bion of uncertain date and the *Lament for Bion* by the poet Moschus, who lived some time during the Alexandrian period of Greek literature (333–146 B.C.). Both Greek poets and Shelley follow the form of the memorial idyll by the Greek poet Theocritus (fl. 270 B.C.), which is distinctly pastoral poetry. Milton had done the same with his *Lycidas.*

I weep for Adonais—he is dead!
O, weep for Adonais! though our tears
Thaw not the frost which binds so dear a head!
And thou, sad Hour, selected from all years
To mourn our loss, rouse thy obscure compeers,°
And teach them thine own sorrow, say: "With me
Died Adonais; till the Future dares
Forget the Past, his fate and fame shall be
An echo and a light unto eternity!"

10 Where wert thou, mighty Mother,° when he lay,
When thy Son lay, pierced by the shaft which flies
In darkness? where was lorn Urania
When Adonais died? With veiléd eyes,
'Mid listening Echoes, in her Paradise
She sate, while one,° with soft enamored breath,
Rekindled all the fading melodies,
With which, like flowers that mock the corse beneath,
He had adorned and hid the coming bulk of Death.

Oh, weep for Adonais—he is dead!
20 Wake, melancholy Mother, wake and weep!
Yet wherefore? Quench within their burning bed
Thy fiery tears, and let thy loud heart keep
Like his, a mute and uncomplaining sleep;
For he is gone, where all things wise and fair
Descend;—oh, dream not that the amorous Deep
Will yet restore him to the vital air;

Death feeds on his mute voice, and laughs at our despair.

Most musical of mourners, weep again!
Lament anew, Urania!—He died,
Who was the Sire° of an immortal strain, 30
Blind, old, and lonely, when his country's pride,
The priest, the slave, and the liberticide,
Trampled and mocked with many a loathéd rite
Of lust and blood;° he went, unterrified,
Into the gulf of death; but his clear Sprite
Yet reigns o'er the earth; the third among the sons of light.°

Most musical of mourners, weep anew!
Not all to that bright station dared to climb;
And happier they their happiness who knew,
Whose tapers yet burn through that night of time 40
In which suns perished; others more sublime,
Struck by the envious wrath of man or god,
Have sunk, extinct in their refulgent prime;
And some yet live,° treading the thorny road,
Which leads, through toil and hate, to Fame's serene abode.

But now, thy youngest, dearest one, has perished—
The nursling of thy widowhood, who grew,
Like a pale flower by some sad maiden cherished,
And fed with true-love tears, instead of dew;
Most musical of mourners, weep anew! 50
Thy extreme° hope, the loveliest and the last,
The bloom, whose petals nipped before they blew
Died on the promise of the fruit, is waste;
The broken lily lies—the storm is overpast.

To that high Capital,° where kingly Death
Keeps his pale court in beauty and decay,
He came; and bought, with price of purest breath,
A grave among the eternal.—Come away!
Haste, while the vault of blue Italian day
Is yet his fitting charnel-roof! while still 60
He lies, as if in dewy sleep he lay;
Awake him not! surely he takes his fill
Of deep and liquid rest, forgetful of all ill.

He will awake no more, oh, never more!—
Within the twilight chamber spreads apace
The shadow of white Death, and at the door
Invisible Corruption waits to trace
His extreme way to her dim dwelling-place;
The eternal Hunger° sits, but pity and awe
Soothe her pale rage, nor dares she to deface 70
So fair a prey, till darkness, and the law
Of change, shall o'er his sleep the mortal curtain draw.

Adonais 5 **thy . . . compeers,** hours less memorable than the one that marked the death of Keats 10 **Mother,** Urania, muse of astronomy. Shelley here identifies her with Uranian Aphrodite, the spirit of lyric poetry and heavenly love 15 **one,** one echo

30 **the Sire,** Milton, of whose *Lycidas* Shelley's poem is reminiscent 31–34 **when . . . blood,** the Restoration period 36 **third . . . light.** According to Shelley's *Defense of Poetry,* Homer and Dante were the first and second epic poets 44 **some yet live,** such as Wordsworth and Byron 51 **extreme,** last 55 **Capital,** Rome, where Keats had gone for his health 69 **Hunger,** the corruption of the grave

Oh, weep for Adonais!—The quick Dreams,
The passion-wingéd Ministers of thought,
Who were his flocks, whom near the living streams
Of his young spirit he fed, and whom he taught
The love which was its music, wander not—
Wander no more, from kindling brain to brain,
But droop there, whence they sprung; and mourn their
lot
80 Round the cold heart, where, after their sweet pain,°
They ne'er will gather strength, or find a home again.

And one with trembling hands clasps his cold head,
And fans him with her moonlight wings, and cries;
"Our love, our hope, our sorrow, is not dead;
See, on the silken fringe of his faint eyes,
Like dew upon a sleeping flower, there lies
A tear some Dream has loosened from his brain."
Lost Angel of a ruined Paradise!
She knew not 'twas her own; as with no stain
90 She faded, like a cloud which had outwept its rain.

One from a lucid urn of starry dew
Washed his light limbs as if embalming them;
Another clipped her profuse locks, and threw
The wreath upon him, like an anadem,°
Which frozen tears instead of pearls begem;
Another in her wilful grief would break
Her bow and wingéd reeds, as if to stem
A greater loss with one which was more weak;
And dull the barbéd fire against his frozen cheek.

100 Another Splendor on his mouth alit,
That mouth, whence it was wont to draw the breath
Which gave it strength to pierce the guarded wit,
And pass into the panting heart beneath
With lightning and with music: the damp death
Quenched its caress upon his icy lips;
And, as a dying meteor stains a wreath
Of moonlight vapor, which the cold night clips,°
It flushed through his pale limbs, and passed to its
eclipse.

And others came . . . Desires and Adorations,
110 Wingéd Persuasions and veiled Destinies,
Splendors, and Glooms, and glimmering Incarnations
Of hopes and fears, and twilight Phantasies;
And Sorrow, with her family of Sighs,
And Pleasure, blind with tears, led by the gleam
Of her own dying smile instead of eyes,
Came in slow pomp;—the moving pomp might seem
Like pageantry of mist on an autumnal stream.

All he had loved, and molded into thought,
From shape, and hue, and odor, and sweet sound,
120 Lamented Adonais. Morning sought
Her eastern watch-tower, and her hair unbound,

Wet with the tears which should adorn the ground,
Dimmed the aëreal eyes that kindle day;
Afar the melancholy thunder moaned,
Pale Ocean in unquiet slumber lay,
And the wild Winds flew round, sobbing in their dis-
may.

Lost Echo° sits amid the voiceless mountains,
And feeds her grief with his remembered lay,
And will no more reply to winds or fountains,
Or amorous birds perched on the young green spray, 130
Or herdsman's horn, or bell at closing day;
Since she can mimic not his lips, more dear
Than those° for whose disdain she pined away
Into a shadow of all sounds—a drear
Murmur, between their songs, is all the woodmen
hear.

Grief made the young Spring wild, and she threw down
Her kindling buds, as if she Autumn were,
Or they dead leaves; since her delight is flown,
For whom should she have waked the sullen year?
To Phoebus° was not Hyacinth so dear   140
Nor to himself Narcissus,° as to both
Thou, Adonais: wan they stand and sere
Amid the faint companions of their youth,
With dew all turned to tears; odor, to sighing ruth.

Thy spirit's sister, the lorn nightingale°
Mourns not her mate with such melodious pain;
Not so the eagle, who like thee could scale
Heaven, and could nourish in the sun's domain
Her mighty youth with morning, doth complain,
Soaring and screaming round her empty nest,   150
As Albion° wails for thee: the curse of Cain°
Light on his head° who pierced thy innocent breast,
And scared the angel soul that was its earthly guest!

Ah, woe is me! Winter is come and gone,
But grief returns with the revolving year;
The airs and streams renew their joyous tone;
The ants, the bees, the swallows reappear;
Fresh leaves and flowers deck the dead Seasons' bier;
The amorous birds now pair in every brake,°
And build their mossy homes in field and brere;°   160
And the green lizard, and the golden snake,
Like unimprisoned flames, out of their trance awake.

Through wood and stream and field and hill and Ocean
A quickening life from the Earth's heart has burst

127 **Echo,** beautiful nymph of classical legend who for love of Narcissus pined
away into a mere voice 133 **those,** of Narcissus 140 **Phoebus,** Apollo, god of
music and poetry. He loved a beautiful youth named Hyacinthus, whom he accidentally killed with a quoit. Upon his death Hyacinthus was changed into a
flower 141 **Narcissus,** who fell in love with his own image as reflected in a
fountain. He was changed into a flower at his death because he refused the love
of Echo 145 **nightingale,** an allusion to Keats' *Ode to a Nightingale* and to the
melody of Keats' verse 151 **Albion,** poetic name for England **curse of Cain.**
For killing his brother Abel, Cain was condemned to be a homeless wanderer. To
the romantic poets, particularly Byron, he was the prototype of the artistic social
outcast 152 **his head,** the head of the critic. Shelley believed the death of Keats
was caused by attacks on his poetry 159 **brake,** thicket 160 **brere,** briar

80 **sweet pain,** birth pangs 94 **anadem,** crown 107 **clips,** embraces

As it has ever done, with change and motion,
From the great morning of the world when first
God dawned on Chaos; in its stream immersed,
The lamps of Heaven flash with a softer light;
All baser things pant with life's sacred thirst;
170 Diffuse themselves; and spend in love's delight,
The beauty and the joy of their renewéd might.

The leprous corpse, touched by this spirit tender,
Exhales itself in flowers of gentle breath;
Like incarnations of the stars, when splendor
Is changed to fragrance, they illumine death
And mock the merry worm that wakes beneath;
Nought we know, dies. Shall that alone which knows
Be as a sword consumed before the sheath
By sightless° lightning?—the intense atom glows
180 A moment, then is quenched in a most cold repose.

Alas! that all we loved of him should be,
But for our grief, as if it had not been,
And grief itself be mortal! Woe is me!
Whence are we, and why are we? of what scene
The actors or spectators? Great and mean
Meet massed in death, who lends what life must bor-
    row.
As long as skies are blue, and fields are green,
Evening must usher night, night urge the morrow,
Month follow month with woe, and year wake year to
    sorrow.

190 He will awake no more, oh, never more!
"Wake thou," cried Misery, "childless Mother, rise
Out of thy sleep, and slake, in thy heart's core,
A wound more fierce than his, with tears and sighs."
And all the Dreams that watched Urania's eyes,
And all the Echoes whom their sister's song
Had held in holy silence, cried: "Arise!"
Swift as a Thought by the snake Memory stung,
From her ambrosial rest the fading Splendor sprung.

She rose like an autumnal Night, that springs
200 Out of the East, and follows wild and drear
The golden Day, which, on eternal wings,
Even as a ghost abandoning a bier,
Had left the Earth a corpse. Sorrow and fear
So struck, so roused, so rapped Urania;
So saddened round her like an atmosphere
Of stormy mist; so swept her on her way
Even to the mournful place where Adonais lay.

Out of her secret Paradise she sped,
Through camps and cities rough with stone, and steel,
210 And human hearts, which to her aëry tread
Yielding not, wounded the invisible
Palms of her tender feet where'er they fell:

And barbéd tongues, and thoughts more sharp than
    they,
Rent the soft Form they never could repel,
Whose sacred blood, like the young tears of May,
Paved with eternal flowers that undeserving way.

In the death-chamber for a moment Death,
Shamed by the presence of that living Might,
Blushed to annihilation, and the breath
Revisited those lips, and Life's pale light   220
Flashed through those limbs, so late her dear delight.
"Leave me not wild and drear and comfortless,
As silent lightning leaves the starless night!
Leave me not!" cried Urania: her distress
Roused Death: Death rose and smiled, and met her
    vain caress.

"Stay yet awhile! speak to me once again;
Kiss me, so long but as a kiss may live;
And in my heartless breast° and burning brain
That word, that kiss, shall all thoughts else survive,
With food of saddest memory kept alive,   230
Now thou art dead, as if it were a part
Of thee, my Adonais! I would give
All that I am to be as thou now art!
But I am chained to Time, and cannot thence depart!

"O gentle child, beautiful as thou wert,
Why didst thou leave the trodden paths of men
Too soon, and with weak hands though mighty heart
Dare the unpastured dragon° in his den?
Defenseless as thou wert, oh, where was then
Wisdom and mirrored shield,° or scorn the spear?   240
Or hadst thou waited the full cycle, when
Thy spirit should have filled its crescent sphere,
The monsters of life's waste had fled from thee like
    deer.

"The herded wolves,° bold only to pursue;
The obscene ravens, clamorous o'er the dead;
The vultures to the conqueror's banner true
Who feed where Desolation first has fed,
And whose wings rain contagion;—how they fled,
When, like Apollo, from this golden bow
The Pythian of the age° one arrow sped   250
And smiled!—The spoilers tempt no second blow,
They fawn on the proud feet that spurn them lying low.

"The sun comes forth, and many reptiles spawn;
He sets, and each ephemeral insect then
Is gathered into death without a dawn,
And the immortal stars awake again;
So is it in the world of living men:

228 **heartless breast,** heartless because she had given her heart to Adonais
238 **unpastured dragon,** the harsh and insatiable world   240 **mirrored shield,** a
reference to the shield that protected the mythological hero Perseus from the fatal
gaze of the demon Gorgons and that enabled him to cut off Medusa's head as he
saw it by reflection   244 **herded wolves,** contemporary critics, who catered to
the political party in power   250 **Pythian of the age,** Byron, who had "slain"
the critics in his *English Bards and Scotch Reviewers* as Apollo did the Python

A godlike mind soars forth, in its delight
Making earth bare and veiling heaven, and when
It sinks, the swarms that dimmed or shared its light
Leave to its kindred lamps the spirit's awful night.''

Thus ceased she: and the mountain shepherds came,
Their garlands sere, their magic mantles rent;
The Pilgrim of Eternity,° whose fame
Over his living head like Heaven is bent,
An early but enduring monument,
Came, veiling all the lightnings of his song
In sorrow; from her wilds Ierne° sent
The sweetest lyrist of her saddest wrong,
And Love taught Grief to fall like music from his
    tongue.

Midst others of less note, came one frail Form,°
A phantom among men; companionless
As the last cloud of an expiring storm
Whose thunder is its knell; he, as I guess,
Had gazed on Nature's naked loveliness,
Actaeon-like,° and now he fled astray
With feeble steps o'er the world's wilderness,
And his own thoughts, along that rugged way,
Pursued, like raging hounds, their father and their
    prey.

A pardlike° Spirit beautiful and swift—
A Love in desolation masked;—a Power
Girt around with weakness; it can scarce uplift
The weight of the superincumbent hour;
It is a dying lamp, a falling shower,
A breaking billow;—even whilst we speak
Is it not broken? On the withering flower
The killing sun smiles brightly: on a cheek
The life can burn in blood, even while the heart may
    break.

His head was bound with pansies° overblown,
And faded violets, white, and pied, and blue;
And a light spear topped with a cypress cone,
Round whose rude shaft dark ivy-tresses grew
Yet dripping with the forest's noonday dew,
Vibrated, as the ever-beating heart
Shook the weak hand that grasped it; of that crew
He came the last, neglected and apart;
A herd-abandoned deer struck by the hunter's dart.

All stood aloof, and at his partial° moan
Smiled through their tears; well knew that gentle band
Who in another's fate now wept his own,
As in the accents of an unknown land°
He sung new sorrow; sad Urania scanned

The Stranger's mien, and murmured: ''Who art thou?''
He answered not, but with a sudden hand
Made bare his branded and ensanguined brow,
Which was like Cain's or Christ's—oh! that it should
    be so!°

What softer voice° is hushed over the dead?
Athwart what brow is that dark mantle thrown?
What form leans sadly o'er the white deathbed,
In mockery of monumental stone,   310
The heavy heart heaving without a moan?
If it be He, who, gentlest of the wise,
Taught, soothed, loved, honored the departed one,
Let me not vex, with inharmonious sighs,
The silence of that heart's accepted sacrifice.

Our Adonais has drunk poison—oh!
What deaf and viperous murderer could crown
Life's early cup with such a draught of woe?
The nameless worm° would now itself disown:
It felt, yet could escape, the magic tone   320
Whose prelude held all envy, hate, and wrong,
But what was howling in one breast alone,°
Silent with expectation of the song,
Whose master's hand is cold, whose silver lyre un-
    strung.

Live thou,° whose infamy is not thy fame!
Live! fear no heavier chastisement from me,
Thou noteless blot on a remembered name!
But be thyself, and know thyself to be!
And ever at thy season be thou free
To spill the venom when thy fangs o'erflow: 330
Remorse and Self-contempt shall cling to thee;
Hot Shame shall burn upon thy secret brow,
And like a beaten hound tremble thou shalt—as now.

Nor let us weep that our delight is fled
Far from these carrion kites that scream below;
He wakes or sleeps with the enduring dead;
Thou canst not soar where he is sitting now°—
Dust to the dust! but the pure spirit shall flow
Back to the burning fountain whence it came,
A portion of the Eternal, which must glow   340
Through time and change, unquenchably the same,
Whilst thy cold embers choke the sordid hearth of
    shame.

Peace, peace! he is not dead, he doth not sleep—
He hath awakened from the dream of life—
'Tis we, who lost in stormy visions, keep
With phantoms an unprofitable strife,

---

264 **Pilgrim of Eternity,** Byron, so called from his *Childe Harold's Pilgrim-age*   268 **Ierne,** Ireland. The reference is to Thomas Moore (1779–1852) and his *Irish Melodies*   271 **one frail Form,** Shelley himself   276 **Actaeon-like.** For gazing on Diana and her nymphs bathing, Actaeon the hunter was turned into a stag and killed by his own hounds   280 **pardlike,** leopardlike   289 **pansies, etc.** The pansy symbolizes thought; the violet, modesty; the cypress, mourning; the ivy, constancy in friendship   298 **partial,** fond, sympathetic   301 **accents . . . land,** the language of England, a land unknown to the Greek muse Urania

306 **oh . . . so.** Shelley means that he bore marks of cruel treatment such as the world gave to Cain, an enemy of the race, or to Christ, a benefactor   307 **softer voice,** that of Leigh Hunt, Keats's close friend and mentor   319 **nameless worm,** unnamed serpent. The harsh criticism of *Endymion* in the *Quarterly Review* was unsigned; it was written by J. W. Croker   322 **one breast alone,** that of the re-viewer just referred to. Harsher criticism, however, had appeared in *Blackwood's Magazine*, August 1818   325 **thou,** the critic of the *Quarterly Review*   337 **Thou . . . now,** an echo from *Paradise Lost*, IV, 828–829: ''Ye knew me once no mate/For you, there sitting where ye durst not soar''

And in mad trance, strike with our spirit's knife
Invulnerable nothings.—*We* decay
Like corpses in a charnel; fear and grief
350 Convulse us and consume us day by day,
And cold hopes swarm like worms within our living
    clay.

He has outsoared the shadow of our night;
Envy and calumny and hate and pain,
And that unrest which men miscall delight,
Can touch him not and torture not again;
From the contagion of the world's slow stain
He is secure, and now can never mourn
A heart grown cold, a head grown gray in vain;
Nor, when the spirit's self has ceased to burn,
360 With sparkless ashes load an unlamented urn.

He lives, he wakes—'tis Death is dead, not he;
Mourn not for Adonais.—Thou young Dawn,
Turn all thy dew to splendor, for from thee
The spirit thou lamentest is not gone;
Ye caverns and ye forests, cease to moan!
Cease, ye faint flowers and fountains, and thou Air,
Which like a mourning veil thy scarf hadst thrown
O'er the abandoned Earth, now leave it bare
Even to the joyous stars which smile on its despair!

370 He is made one with Nature: there is heard
His voice in all her music, from the moan
Of thunder, to the song of night's sweet bird;
He is a presence to be felt and known
In darkness and in light, from herb and stone,
Spreading itself where'er that Power may move
Which has withdrawn his being to its own;
Which wields the world with never-wearied love,
Sustains it from beneath, and kindles it above.

He is a portion of the loveliness
380 Which once he made more lovely: he doth bear
His part, while the one Spirit's plastic° stress
Sweeps through the dull dense world, compelling
    there,
All new successions to the forms they wear;°
Torturing th' unwilling dross that checks its flight
To its own likeness, as each mass may bear;
And bursting in its beauty and its might
From trees and beasts and men into the Heaven's
    light.

The splendors of the firmament of time
May be eclipsed, but are extinguished not;
390 Like stars to their appointed height they climb,
And death is a low mist which cannot blot
The brightness it may veil. When lofty thought
Lifts a young heart above its mortal lair,
And love and life contend in it, for what

Shall be its earthly doom, the dead live there
And move like winds of light on dark and stormy air.

The inheritors of unfulfilled renown
Rose from their thrones, built beyond mortal thought,
Far in the Unapparent. Chatterton°
Rose pale—his solemn agony had not   400
Yet faded from him; Sidney,° as he fought
And as he fell and as he lived and loved
Sublimely mild, a Spirit without spot,
Arose; and Lucan,° by his death approved:
Oblivion as they rose shrank like a thing reproved.

And many more, whose names on Earth are dark,
But whose transmitted effluence cannot die
So long as fire outlives the parent spark,
Rose, robed in dazzling immortality.
"Thou art become as one of us," they cry,   410
"It was for thee yon kingless sphere has long
Swung blind in unascended majesty,
Silent alone amid an Heaven of Song.
Assume thy wingéd throne, thou Vesper of our
    throng!"

Who mourns for Adonais? Oh, come forth,
Fond wretch! and know thyself and him aright.
Clasp with thy panting soul the pendulous Earth;
As from a center, dart thy spirit's light
Beyond all worlds, until its spacious might
Satiate the void circumference: then shrink   420
Even to a point within our day and night;
And keep thy heart light lest it make thee sink
When hope has kindled hope, and lured thee to the
    brink.

Or go to Rome, which is the sepulcher,
Oh, not of him, but of our joy: 'tis nought
That ages, empires, and religions there
Lie buried in the ravage they have wrought;
For such as he can lend—they borrow not
Glory from those who made the world their prey;
And he is gathered to the kings of thought   430
Who waged contention with their time's decay,
And of the past are all that cannot pass away.

Go thou to Rome—at once the Paradise,
The grave, the city, and the wilderness;
And where its wrecks like shattered mountains rise,
And flowering weeds, and fragrant copses dress
The bones of Desolation's nakedness
Pass, till the spirit of the spot shall lead
Thy footsteps to a slope of green access°

381 **plastic,** shaping 383 **forms they wear.** The spirit of love and beauty was
thought to permeate all matter and mold everything into its appropriate form

399 **Chatterton,** Thomas Chatterton (1752–1770), the young poet who in despair
and poverty killed himself. The romantics looked upon him as a genius blighted
by society's indifference 401 **Sidney,** Sir Philip Sidney (1554–1586), who died
from a battle wound at 32 404 **Lucan,** a Latin poet who killed himself at the
age of 26 to escape execution for taking part in a political conspiracy
439 **slope . . . access,** the Protestant cemetery where Keats was buried.
Shelley's ashes were buried near Keats shortly after the writing of *Adonais*

440 Where, like an infant's smile, over the dead
A light of laughing flowers along the grass is spread;

And gray walls molder round, on which dull Time
Feeds, like slow fire upon a hoary brand;
And one keen pyramid° with wedge sublime,
Pavilioning the dust of him who planned
This refuge for his memory, doth stand
Like flame transformed to marble; and beneath,
A field is spread, on which a newer band
Have pitched in Heaven's smile their camp of death,
Welcoming him we lose with scarce extinguished
450   breath.

Here pause: these graves are all too young° as yet
To have outgrown the sorrow which consigned
Its charge to each; and if the seal is set,
Here, on one fountain of a mourning mind,
Break it not thou! too surely shalt thou find
Thine own well full, if thou returnest home,
Of tears and gall. From the world's bitter wind
Seek shelter in the shadow of the tomb.
What Adonais is, why fear we to become?

460 The One remains, the many change and pass;
Heaven's light forever shines, Earth's shadows fly;
Life, like a dome of many-colored glass,
Stains the white radiance of Eternity,
Until Death tramples it to fragments.—Die,
If thou wouldst be with that which thou dost seek!°
Follow where all is fled!—Rome's azure sky,
Flowers, ruins, statues, music, words are weak
The glory they transfuse with fitting truth to speak.

Why linger, why turn back, why shrink, my Heart?
470 Thy hopes are gone before: from all things here
They have departed; thou shouldst now depart!
A light is passed from the revolving year,
And man, and woman; and what still is dear
Attracts to crush, repels to make thee wither.
The soft sky smiles—the low wind whispers near:
'Tis Adonais calls! oh, hasten thither,
No more let Life divide what Death can join together.

That Light whose smile kindles the Universe,
That Beauty in which all things work and move,
480 That Benediction which the eclipsing Curse
Of birth can quench not, that sustaining Love
Which through the web of being blindly wove
By man and beast and earth and air and sea,
Burns bright or dim, as each are mirrors of
The fire for which all thirst; now beams on me,
Consuming the last clouds of cold mortality.

The breath whose might I have invoked in song
Descends on me; my spirit's bark is driven,

Far from the shore, far from the trembling throng
Whose sails were never to the tempest given;   490
The massy earth and sphered skies are riven!
I am borne darkly, fearfully, afar;
Whilst, burning through the inmost veil of Heaven,
The soul of Adonais, like a star,
Beacons from the abode where the Eternal are.
(1821)

from **HELLAS**

FINAL CHORUS

The world's great age° begins anew,
  The golden years return,
The earth doth like a snake renew
  Her winter weeds° outworn;
Heaven smiles, and faiths and empires gleam,
Like wrecks of a dissolving dream.

A brighter Hellas° rears its mountains
  From waves serener far;
A new Peneus° rolls his fountains
  Against the morning star.   130
Where fairer Tempes° bloom, there sleep
Young Cyclads° on a sunnier deep.

A loftier Argo° cleaves the main,
  Fraught with a later prize;
Another Orpheus° sings again,
  And loves, and weeps, and dies.
A new Ulysses° leaves once more
Calypso for his native shore.

Oh, write no more the tale of Troy,
  If earth Death's scroll must be!   140
Nor mix with Laian rage° the joy
  Which dawns upon the free;
Although a subtler Sphinx renew
Riddles of death Thebes never knew.°

Another Athens shall arise,
  And to remoter time

444 **one . . . pyramid,** the tomb of Caius Cestius, built in the time of Augustus (27 B.C.–A.D. 14)   451 **too young.** Shelley's son William, who died in June 1819, was buried there. The cemetery was new   465 **that . . . seek,** absolute beauty

Final Chorus   121 **The world's great age.** At the end of the "great age" of the ancients the planets were to resume their original positions, and the history of the world was to repeat itself. The Golden Age was to return, to be followed by ages of degradation and evil   124 **weeds,** garments, particularly a widow's   127 **Hellas,** Greece   129 **Peneus,** river in Thessaly, Greece   131 **Tempes,** valley through which the Peneus flows   132 **Cyclads,** islands in the Aegean Sea   133 **Argo,** ship of the Argonauts, who accompanied Jason on his quest for the Golden Fleece   135 **Orpheus,** mythological poet and musician who went to the lower world to lead his wife Eurydice back to the upper world. He was given permission on the condition that he not look back until they reached the upper air. Orpheus did look back, and Eurydice disappeared   137 **Ulysses,** the hero of Homer's *Odyssey.* When shipwrecked, he was detained on an island by the nymph Calypso who promised him immortal youth if he would remain with her, but he refused   141 **Laian rage.** Upon hearing from the oracle that he would be killed by his son, King Laius of Thebes left the infant Oedipus in the woods. The boy was rescued and later slew his father unwittingly   144 **Sphinx . . . knew.** The Sphinx was a winged monster who killed all who could not solve her riddle. Oedipus solved it, and she threw herself down from a rock and died

Bequeath, like sunset to the skies,
　The splendor of its prime;
And leave, if nought so bright may live,
150 All earth can take or Heaven can give.

Saturn and Love° their long repose
　Shall burst, more bright and good
Than all who fell,° than One who rose,°
　Than many unsubdued;°
Not gold, not blood, their altar dowers,
But votive tears and symbol flowers.

Oh, cease! must hate and death return?
　Cease! must men kill and die?
Cease! drain not to its dregs the urn
160 　Of bitter prophecy.
The world is weary of the past,
Oh, might it die or rest at last!
(1821; 1822)

LINES

When the lamp is shattered,
The light in the dust lies dead—
　When the cloud is scattered,
The rainbow's glory is shed.
　When the lute is broken,
Sweet tones are remembered not;
　When the lips have spoken,
Loved accents are soon forgot.

　As music and splendor
10 Survive not the lamp and the lute,
　The heart's echoes render
No song when the spirit is mute—
　No song but sad dirges,
Like the wind through a ruined cell,
　Or the mournful surges
That ring the dead seaman's knell.

When hearts have once mingled
Love first leaves the well-built nest;
　The weak one is singled
20 To endure what it once possessed.
　O Love! who bewailest
The frailty of all things here,
　Why choose you the frailest
For your cradle, your home, and your bier?

　Its passions will rock thee
As the storms rock the ravens on high;
　Bright reason will mock thee,
Like the sun from a wintry sky.

From thy nest every rafter
Will rot, and thine eagle home　　　　30
　Leave thee naked to laughter,
When leaves fall and cold winds come.
(1822; 1824)

ESSAY ON LIFE

Life and the world, or whatever we call that which we are and feel, is an astonishing thing. The mist of familiarity obscures from us the wonder of our being. We are struck with admiration at some of its transient modifications, but it is itself the great miracle. What are changes of empires, the wreck of dynasties, with the opinions which supported them; what is the birth and the extinction of religious and of political systems, to life? What are the revolutions of the globe which we inhabit, and the operations of the elements of which it 10 is composed, compared with life? What is the universe of stars, and suns, of which this inhabited earth is one, and their motions, and their destiny, compared with life? Life, the great miracle, we admire not, because it is so miraculous. It is well that we are thus shielded by the familiarity of what is at once so certain and so unfathomable from an astonishment which would otherwise absorb and overawe the functions of that which is its object.

If any artist, I do not say had executed, but had 20 merely conceived in his mind the system of the sun, and the stars, and planets, they not existing, and had painted to us in words, or upon canvas, the spectacle now afforded by the nightly cope of heaven, and illustrated it by the wisdom of astronomy, great would be our admiration. Or had he imagined the scenery of this earth, the mountains, the seas, and the rivers; the grass, and the flowers, and the variety of the forms and masses of the leaves of the woods, and the colors which attend the setting and the rising sun, and the 30 hues of the atmosphere, turbid or serene, these things not before existing, truly we should have been astonished, and it would not have been a vain boast to have said of such a man, "Non merita nome di creatore, se non Iddio ed il Poeta."° But now these things are looked on with little wonder, and to be conscious of them with intense delight is esteemed to be the distinguishing mark of a refined and extraordinary person. The multitude of men care not for them. It is thus with Life—that which includes all.　　　　40

What is life? Thoughts and feelings arise, with or without our will, and we employ words to express them. We are born, and our birth is unremembered, and our infancy remembered but in fragments; we live on, and in living we lose the apprehension of life. How vain is it to think that words can penetrate the mystery of our being! Rightly used they may make evident our

---

151 **Saturn and Love,** supposed to have ruled in the Golden Age　153 **all who fell,** the gods of Greece, Asia, and Egypt　**One who rose,** Christ　154 **many unsubdued,** objects of the idolatry of China, India, etc.

On Life　35 **"Non merita . . . Poeta."** "No one deserves the name of a creator, save God and the Poet"—Tasso, sixteenth century Italian epic poet

ignorance to ourselves, and this is much. For what are we? Whence do we come? And whither do we go? Is birth the commencement, is death the conclusion of our being? What is birth and death?

The most refined abstractions of logic conduct to a view of life which, though startling to the apprehension, is in fact that which the habitual sense of its repeated combinations has extinguished in us. It strips, as it were, the painted curtain from this scene of things. I confess that I am one of those who am unable to refuse my assent to the conclusions of those philosophers who assert that nothing exists but as it is perceived.

It is a decision against which all our persuasions struggle, and we must be long convicted before we can be convinced that the solid universe of external things is "such stuff as dreams are made of."° The shocking absurdities of the popular philosophy of mind and matter, its fatal consequences in morals, and their violent dogmatism concerning the source of all things, had early conducted me to materialism. This materialism is a seducing system to young and superficial minds. It allows its disciples to talk and dispenses them from thinking. But I was discontented with such a view of things as it afforded; man is a being of high aspirations, "looking both before and after,"° whose "thoughts wander through eternity," disclaiming alliance with transience and decay; incapable of imagining to himself annihilation; existing but in the future and the past; being, not what he is, but what he has been and shall be. Whatever may be his true and final destination, there is a spirit within him at enmity with nothingness and dissolution. This is the character of all life and being. Each is at once the centre and the circumference, the point to which all things are referred, and the line in which all things are contained. Such contemplations as these, materialism and the popular philosophy of mind and matter alike forbid; they are only consistent with the intellectual system.

It is absurd to enter into a long recapitulation of arguments sufficiently familiar to those inquiring minds whom alone a writer on abstruse subjects can be conceived to address. Perhaps the most clear and vigorous statement of the intellectual system is to be found in Sir William Drummond's *Academical Questions*.° After such an exposition, it would be idle to translate into other words what could only lose its energy and fitness by the change. Examined point by point, and word by word, the most discriminating intellects have been able to discern no train of thoughts in the process of reasoning which does not conduct inevitably to the conclusion which has been stated.

What follows from the admission? It establishes no new truth, it gives us no additional insight into our hidden nature, neither its action nor itself. Philosophy,

impatient as it may be to build, has much work yet remaining as pioneer for the overgrowth of ages. It makes one step towards this object: it destroys error and the roots of error. It leaves, what it is too often the duty of the reformer in political and ethical questions to leave, a vacancy. It reduces the mind to that freedom in which it would have acted but for the misuse of words and signs, the instruments of its own creation. By signs, I would be understood in a wide sense, including what is properly meant by that term, and what I peculiarly mean. In this latter sense, almost all familiar objects are signs, standing not for themselves but for others in their capacity of suggesting one thought which shall lead to a train of thoughts. Our whole life is thus an education of error.

Let us recollect our sensations as children. What a distinct and intense apprehension had we of the world and of ourselves! Many of the circumstances of social life were then important to us which are now no longer so. But that is not the point of comparison on which I mean to insist. We less habitually distinguished all that we saw and felt, from ourselves. They seemed, as it were, to constitute one mass. There are some persons who in this respect are always children. Those who are subject to the state called reverie feel as if their nature were dissolved into the surrounding universe, or as if the surrounding universe were absorbed into their being. They are conscious of no distinction. And these are states which precede, or accompany, or follow an unusually intense and vivid apprehension of life. As men grow up this power commonly decays, and they become mechanical and habitual agents. Thus feelings and then reasonings are the combined result of a multitude of entangled thoughts and of a series of what are called impressions, planted by reiteration.

The view of life presented by the most refined deductions of the intellectual philosophy is that of unity. Nothing exists but as it is perceived. The difference is merely nominal between those two classes of thought which are vulgarly distinguished by the names of ideas and of external objects. Pursuing the same thread of reasoning, the existence of distinct individual minds, similar to that which is employed in now questioning its own nature, is likewise found to be a delusion. The words *I, you, they* are not signs of any actual difference subsisting between the assemblage of thoughts thus indicated, but are merely marks employed to denote the different modifications of the one mind.

Let it not be supposed that this doctrine conducts to the monstrous presumption that I, the person who now write and think, am that one mind. I am but a portion of it. The words *I* and *you* and *they* are grammatical devices invented simply for arrangement, and totally devoid of the intense and exclusive sense usually attached to them. It is difficult to find terms adequate to express so subtle a conception as that to which the Intellectual Philosophy has conducted us. We are on

64 **"such stuff . . . made of,"** *The Tempest*, IV, i, 156. The lines actually read: "such stuff/As dreams are made on" 73 **"looking . . . after,"** *Hamlet*, IV, iv, 37 92 **Academical Questions**, a discussion of Berkeley's idealist philosophy published in 1805

that verge where words abandon us, and what wonder if we grow dizzy to look down the dark abyss of how little we know.

The relations of *things* remain unchanged, by whatever system. By the word *things* is to be understood any object of thought—that is, any thought upon which any other thought is employed with an apprehension of distinction. The relations of these remain unchanged; and such is the material of our
170 knowledge.

What is the cause of life? That is, how was it produced, or what agencies distinct from life have acted or act upon life? All recorded generations of mankind have wearily busied themselves in inventing answers to this question; and the result has been—Religion. Yet, that the basis of all things cannot be, as the popular philosophy alleges, mind, is sufficiently evident. Mind, as far as we have any experience of its properties, and beyond that experience how vain is argu-
180 ment! cannot create, it can only perceive. It is said also to be the cause. But cause is only a word expressing a certain state of the human mind with regard to the manner in which two thoughts are apprehended to be related to each other. If any one desires to know how unsatisfactorily the popular philosophy employs itself upon this great question, they need only impartially reflect upon the manner in which thoughts develop themselves in their minds. It is infinitely improbable that the cause of mind, that is, of existence, is similar
190 to mind.

(1819)

from A DEFENSE OF POETRY

A poem is the very image of life expressed in its eternal truth. There is this difference between a story and a poem, that a story is a catalogue of detached facts, which have no other bond of connexion than time, place, circumstance, cause, and effect; the other is the creation of actions according to the unchangeable forms of human nature, as existing in the mind of the creator, which is itself the image of all other minds. The one is partial, and applies only to a definite period
10 of time, and a certain combination of events which can never again recur; the other is universal, and contains within itself the germ of a relation to whatever motives or actions have place in the possible varieties of human nature. Time, which destroys the beauty and the use of the story of particular facts, stript of the poetry which should invest them, augments that of Poetry, and for ever develops new and wonderful applications of the eternal truth which it contains. Hence epitomes° have been called the moths of just history; they eat out the
20 poetry of it. The story of particular facts is as a mirror which obscures and distorts that which should be

Defense   18 **epitomes,** abstracts, abridgments

beautiful; poetry is a mirror which makes beautiful that which is distorted.

The parts of a composition may be poetical, without the composition as a whole being a poem. A single sentence may be considered as a whole, though it may be found in the midst of a series of unassimilated portions; a single word may even be a spark of inextinguishable thought. And thus all the great historians, Herodotus, Plutarch, Livy, were poets; and although 30 the plan of these writers, especially that of Livy, restrained them from developing this faculty in its highest degree, they make copious and ample amends for their subjection, by filling all the interstices of their subjects with living images.

Having determined what is poetry, and who are poets, let us proceed to estimate its effects upon society.

Poetry is ever accompanied with pleasure: all spirits upon which it falls open themselves to receive the wis- 40 dom which is mingled with its delight. In the infancy of the world, neither poets themselves nor their auditors are fully aware of the excellence of poetry: for it acts in a divine and unapprehended manner, beyond and above consciousness; and it is reserved for future generations to contemplate and measure the mighty cause and effect in all the strength and splendour of their union. Even in modern times, no living poet ever arrived at the fulness of his fame; the jury which sits in judgment upon a poet, belonging as he does to all time, 50 must be composed of his peers; it must be impanneled by Time from the selectest of the wise of many generations. A Poet is a nightingale, who sits in darkness and sings to cheer its own solitude with sweet sounds; his auditors are as men entranced by the melody of an unseen musician, who feel that they are moved and softened, yet know not whence or why. The poems of Homer and his contemporaries were the delight of infant Greece; they were the elements of that social system which is the column upon which all succeeding 60 civilization has reposed. Homer embodied the ideal perfection of his age in human character; nor can we doubt that those who read his verses were awakened to an ambition of becoming like to Achilles, Hector, and Ulysses: the truth and beauty of friendship, patriotism, and persevering devotion to an object, were unveiled to their depths in these immortal creations: the sentiments of the auditors must have been refined and enlarged by a sympathy with such great and lovely impersonations, until from admiring they imitated, and 70 from imitation they identified themselves with the objects of their admiration.

* * * * *

The first part of these remarks has related to Poetry in its elements and principles; and it has been shewn, as well as the narrow limits assigned them would permit, that what is called poetry, in a restricted sense, has a common source with all other forms of order and

of beauty, according to which the materials of human life are susceptible of being arranged, and which is
80 Poetry in an universal sense.

The second part will have for its object an application of these principles to the present state of the cultivation of Poetry, and a defense of the attempt to idealize the modern forms of manners and opinions, and compel them into a subordination to the imaginative and creative faculty. For the literature of England, an energetic development of which has ever preceded or accompanied a great and free development of the national will, has arisen as it were from a new birth. In
90 spite of the low-thoughted envy which would undervalue contemporary merit, our own will be a memorable age in intellectual achievements, and we live among such philosophers and poets as surpass beyond comparison any who have appeared since the last national struggle for civil and religious liberty. The most unfailing herald, companion, and follower of the awakening of a great people to work a beneficial change in opinion or institution, is Poetry. At such periods there is an accumulation of the power of com-
100 municating and receiving intense and impassioned conceptions respecting man and nature. The persons in whom this power resides, may often as far as regards many portions of their nature, have little apparent correspondence with that spirit of good of which they are the ministers. But even whilst they deny and abjure, they are yet compelled to serve, the Power which is seated on the throne of their own soul. It is impossible to read the compositions of the most celebrated writers of the present day without being startled with the electric life which burns within their words. 110 They measure the circumference and sound the depths of human nature with a comprehensive and all-penetrating spirit, and they are themselves perhaps the most sincerely astonished at its manifestations; for it is less their spirit than the spirit of the age. Poets are the hierophants of an unapprehended inspiration; the mirrors of the gigantic shadows which futurity casts upon the present; the words which express what they understand not; the trumpets which sing to battle, and feel not what they inspire; the influence which is moved 120 not, but moves. Poets are the unacknowledged legislators of the world.

(1821)

JOHN KEATS
1795–1821

Keats' life and career were short but brilliant. He was born on October 31, 1795, in London, the first child of a head hostler at a livery stable who died when the boy was nine. In 1803 Keats entered the Clarke School at Enfield, where he befriended Charles Cowden Clarke, the headmaster's son, who encouraged Keats' reading of poetry, particularly Spenser, and introduced him to the theater. After spending his holidays nursing her, Keats saw his mother die of tuberculosis in 1810; this disease would eventually kill his brother and his grandmother, as well as Keats himself. Richard Abbey, a practically minded businessman, was appointed guardian of the Keats children upon the death of their mother. Abbey took Keats out of school and apprenticed him to an apothecary-surgeon. Keats eventually studied medicine and received a certificate to practice in 1816. But he increasingly felt doubts about his fitness for a medical career. Upon reaching the age of twenty-one in 1816, Keats informed the skeptical Abbey that he intended to abandon medicine for poetry.

Though he had begun to write poetry three years earlier, Keats was introduced by Clarke to Leigh Hunt's (1784–1859) literary circle in 1816. This same year he produced two poems of major promise, "On First Looking Into Chapman's Homer" and "Sleep and Poetry." These two poems, together with several others, were published as a book in 1817; Keats dedicated the book to Hunt, who praised Keats and Shelley in an article in *The Examiner*. Three lines from "Sleep and Poetry" are very significant in relation to Keats' short career:

O for ten years, that I may overwhelm
Myself in poesy; so I may do the deed
That my own soul has to itself decreed.

Keats had only half the time he requested; yet he nevertheless succeeded.

In 1818 Keats published his first long poem, *Endymion*, which was based on the Greek legend of the love of the moon goddess for a mortal. At this same time, personal and family difficulties began to cloud his life. Although his father had left the family a reasonably large estate, it was tied up in a Chancery suit for all of Keats' lifetime. In addition to financial worries, his brother Tom was dying from tuberculosis. Late in 1818 reviews of *Endymion* started to appear, all of them negative. The review in *Blackwood's Magazine* was the harshest and most irresponsible. Keats met these reviews with equanimity and proceeded to write the first two books of his poem

Hyperion during his brother's last months. During this period he fell in love with Frances (Fanny) Brawne, who lived with her widowed mother in Hampstead.

The year 1819 was both a prolific and great one for Keats. Beset by illness as a result of a strenuous walking tour through the Lake District, concerned with the financial problems of his whole family, and upset emotionally by his unresolved relationship with Fanny, Keats nevertheless managed to write his greatest poems in the first nine months of 1819. The poems written this year included "The Eve of St. Agnes," "La Belle Dame sans Merci," "To Psyche," "On Melancholy," "To a Nightingale," "On a Grecian Urn," "Lamia," and the unfinished The Fall of Hyperion. Late in the year he became officially engaged to Fanny. He also began to suffer from tuberculosis, caught while nursing his brother.

His volume Lamia, Isabella, The Eve of St. Agnes, and Other Poems was published in 1820 and received favorable reviews. Because he began to undergo increasingly severe lung hemorrhages, his doctor advised Keats to visit Italy, a milder climate in which the poet might attempt to recuperate. Accompanied by the young painter Joseph Severn (1793–1879), Keats went to Rome. Massive hemorrhages soon indicated that there was no hope. Keats wanted to commit suicide but was prevented by Severn. He died on February 21, 1821, and was buried in the Protestant Cemetery there. The words on his tombstone read: "Here lies one whose name was writ in water."

Keats' poetry and letters, which reveal him to be a talented letter writer and a provocative romantic literary theorist and critic, are an astonishing legacy for a man of twenty-five. He was afraid that he would leave no mark upon literature; yet he influenced the future course of English poetry more than any other romantic poet. His was, perhaps, the most premature death in the history of English literature.

ON FIRST LOOKING
INTO CHAPMAN'S HOMER°

Much have I traveled in the realms of gold,
And many goodly states and kingdoms seen;
Round many western islands have I been
Which bards in fealty to Apollo° hold.
5 Oft of one wide expanse had I been told
That deep-browed Homer ruled as his demesne;
Yet did I never breathe its pure serene
Till I heard Chapman speak out loud and bold:
Then felt I like some watcher of the skies
10 When a new planet swims into his ken;
Or like stout Cortez° when with eagle eyes

He stared at the Pacific—and all his men
Looked at each other with a wild surmise—
Silent, upon a peak in Darien.°
(1815; 1816)

TO ONE WHO HAS BEEN
LONG IN CITY PENT

To one who has been long in city pent
'Tis very sweet to look into the fair
And open face of heaven—to breathe a prayer
Full in the smile of the blue firmament.
Who is more happy, when, with heart's content,   5
Fatigued he sinks into some pleasant lair
Of wavy grass, and reads a debonair
And gentle tale of love and languishment?
Returning home at evening, with an ear
Catching the notes of Philomel°—an eye   10
Watching the sailing cloudlet's bright career,
He mourns that day so soon has glided by:
E'en like the passage of an angel's tear
That falls through the clear ether silently.
(1816; 1817)

ON SEEING THE ELGIN MARBLES°

My spirit is too weak—mortality
Weighs heavily on me like unwilling sleep,
And each imagined pinnacle and steep
Of godlike hardship tells me I must die
Like a sick eagle looking at the sky.   5
Yet 'tis a gentle luxury to weep
That I have not the cloudy winds to keep,
Fresh for the opening of the morning's eye.
Such dim-conceivéd glories of the brain
Bring round the heart an undescribable feud;   10
So do these wonders a most dizzy pain,
That mingles Grecian grandeur with the rude
Wasting of old Time—with a billowy main—
A sun—a shadow of a magnitude.
(1817)

WHEN I HAVE FEARS
THAT I MAY CEASE TO BE

When I have fears that I may cease to be
Before my pen has gleaned my teeming brain,
Before high piléd books, in charactry,°
Hold like rich garners the full-ripened grain;
When I behold, upon the night's starred face,   5

14 **Darien,** district forming the eastern part of the Isthmus of Panama
To One Who Has Been Long   10 **Philomel,** nightingale   **On Seeing the Elgin Marbles.** Thomas Bruce (1766–1841), Earl of Elgin, was a British diplomat who brought ancient Greek sculptures from the Parthenon during the years 1803 to 1812 and placed them in the British Museum. Keats derived much of his sympathy with Greek ideas of beauty and artistic permanence from these antiquities
When I Have Fears   3 **charactry,** characters, letters

On First Looking. A translation of Homer by George Chapman (1559?–1634), famous Elizabethan dramatist and translator of classics, which Keats and his friend Charles Cowden Clarke spent a night reading, inspired this sonnet   4 **Apollo,** god of poetry and music   11 **Cortez.** Balboa, not Cortez, discovered the Pacific Ocean

Huge cloudy symbols of a high romance,
And think that I may never live to trace
Their shadows, with the magic hand of chance;
And when I feel, fair creature of an hour!
10 That I shall never look upon thee more,
Never have relish in the faery power
Of unreflecting love!—then on the shore
Of the wide world I stand alone, and think
Till Love and Fame to nothingness do sink.
(1818; 1848)

IN A DREAR-NIGHTED DECEMBER

In a drear-nighted December,
Too happy, happy tree,
Thy branches ne'er remember
Their green felicity:
The north cannot undo them,
With a sleety whistle through them;
Nor frozen thawings glue them
From budding at the prime.

In a drear-nighted December,
10 Too happy, happy brook,
Thy bubblings ne'er remember
Apollo's° summer look;
But with a sweet forgetting,
They stay their crystal fretting,
Never, never petting°
About the frozen time.

Ah! would 'twere so with many
A gentle girl and boy!
But were there ever any
20 Writhed not at passéd joy?
To know the change and feel it,
When there is none to heal it,
Nor numbéd sense to steal it,
Was never said in rime.
(1817; 1829)

from ENDYMION

In this poem, completed in 1817, Keats follows the
general outline of the old classical myth of Endymion,
the tale of the moon goddess Diana's love for the
beautiful youth. But, as he was to do again in *Hyperion,* he enlarges the story by giving it a luxuriant descriptive background, heightens the emotional effects
wherever possible, and colors it with his own imagination; in other words, he romanticizes the story.
Along with the sonnet *On First Looking into Chapman's
Homer, Endymion* is the first important manifestation

by Keats of the interest in classical writers that was
common among romantic writers.

PROEM

A thing of beauty is a joy forever:
Its loveliness increases; it will never
Pass into nothingness; but still will keep
A bower quiet for us, and a sleep
Full of sweet dreams, and health, and quiet breathing.
Therefore, on every morrow, are we wreathing
A flowery band to bind us to the earth,
Spite of despondence, of the inhuman dearth
Of noble natures, of the gloomy days,
Of all the unhealthy and o'er-darkened ways   10
Made for our searching: yes, in spite of all,
Some shape of beauty moves away the pall
From our dark spirits. Such the sun, the moon,
Trees old, and young, sprouting a shady boon
For simple sheep; and such are daffodils
With the green world they live in; and clear rills
That for themselves a cooling covert make
'Gainst the hot season; the mid-forest brake,°
Rich with a sprinkling of fair musk-rose blooms:
And such too is the grandeur of the dooms°   20
We have imagined for the mighty dead;
All lovely tales that we have heard or read:
An endless fountain of immortal drink,
Pouring unto us from the heaven's brink.

Nor do we merely feel these essences
For one short hour; no, even as the trees
That whisper round a temple become soon
Dear as the temple's self, so does the moon,
The passion poesy, glories infinite,
Haunt us till they become a cheering light   30
Unto our souls, and bound to us so fast,
That, whether there be shine, or gloom o'ercast,
They always must be with us, or we die.

Therefore, 'tis with full happiness that I
Will trace the story of Endymion.
The very music of the name has gone
Into my being, and each pleasant scene
Is growing fresh before me as the green
Of our own valleys: so I will begin
Now while I cannot hear the city's din;   40
Now while the early budders are just new,
And run in mazes of the youngest hue
About old forests; while the willow trails
Its delicate amber; and the dairy pails
Bring home increase of milk. And, as the year
Grows lush in juicy stalks, I'll smoothly steer
My little boat, for many quiet hours,
With streams that deepen freshly into bowers.
Many and many a verse I hope to write,

In a Drear-Nighted December   12 **Apollo,** god of music and poetry   15 **petting,**
complaining

Proem   18 **brake,** thicket   20 **dooms,** destinies

Before the daisies, vermeil-rimmed and white,   50
Hide in deep herbage; and ere yet the bees
Hum about globes of clover and sweet peas,
I must be near the middle of my story.
O may no wintry season, bare and hoary,
See it half finished: but let Autumn bold,
With universal tinge of sober gold,
Be all about me when I make an end.
And now at once, adventuresome, I send
My herald thought into a wilderness:
There let its trumpet blow, and quickly dress   60
My uncertain path with green, that I may speed
Easily onward, thorough° flowers and weed.
(1817–1818; 1818)

ODE

Bards of Passion and of Mirth,
Ye have left your souls on earth!
Have ye souls in heaven too,
Double-lived in regions new?
Yes, and those of heaven commune
With the spheres of sun and moon;
With the noise of fountains wond'rous,
And the parle° of voices thund'rous;
With the whisper of heaven's trees
And one another, in soft ease   10
Seated on Elysian° lawns
Browsed by none but Dian's fawns;°
Underneath large blue-bells tented,
Where the daisies are rose-scented,
And the rose herself has got
Perfume which on earth is not;
Where the nightingale doth sing
Not a senseless, trancéd thing,
But divine melodious truth;
Philosophic numbers smooth;   20
Tales and golden histories
Of heaven and its mysteries.

Thus ye live on high, and then
On the earth ye live again;
And the souls ye left behind you
Teach us here, the way to find you,
Where your other souls are joying,
Never slumbered, never cloying.
Here, your earth-born souls still speak
To mortals, of their little week;   30
Of their sorrows and delights;
Of their passions and their spites;
Of their glory and their shame;
What doth strengthen and what maim.
Thus ye teach us, every day,
Wisdom, though fled far away.

Bards of Passion and of Mirth,
Ye have left your souls on earth!
Ye have souls in heaven too,
Double-lived in regions new!   40
(1819; 1820)

THE EVE OF ST. AGNES

St. Agnes was a saint martyred in Rome about the year
300. In the early days of the Catholic Church, on St.
Agnes' Day (January 21), the *Agnus Dei* ("Lamb of
God") from the Mass was chanted, and two lambs
were sacrificed, their wool to be woven later by nuns.
In the Middle Ages a legend developed that a girl
could find out about her future husband on St. Agnes'
Eve (January 20); as she lay on her back, with her
hands beneath her head, he would appear before her
in a dream, kiss her, and feast with her.

St. Agnes' Eve—Ah, bitter chill° it was!
The owl, for all his feathers, was a-cold;
The hare limped trembling through the frozen grass,
And silent was the flock in woolly fold:
Numb were the Beadsman's° fingers, while he told
His rosary,° and while his frosted breath,
Like pious incense from a censer old,
Seemed taking flight for heaven, without a death,
Past the sweet Virgin's picture, while his prayer he
    saith.

His prayer he saith, this patient, holy man;   10
Then takes his lamp, and riseth from his knees,
And back returneth, meager, barefoot, wan,
Along the chapel aisle by slow degrees:
The sculptured dead, on each side, seem to freeze,
Emprisoned in black, purgatorial rails:
Knights, ladies, praying in dumb orat'ries,°
He passeth by; and his weak spirit fails
To think how they may ache in icy hoods and mails.

Northward he turneth through a little door,
And scarce three steps, ere Music's golden tongue   20
Flattered to tears this aged man and poor;
But no—already had his death-bell rung:
The joys of all his life were said and sung:
His was harsh penance on St. Agnes' Eve:
Another way he went, and soon among
Rough ashes sat he for his soul's reprieve,
And all night kept awake, for sinners' sake to grieve.

That ancient Beadsman heard the prelude soft;
And so it chanced, for many a door was wide,
From hurry to and fro. Soon, up aloft,   30

The Eve of St. Agnes   1 bitter chill. St. Agnes' Eve, January 20, is supposed to be
the coldest night of the year   5 **Beadsman,** a poor man supported in an almshouse
and required to pray for its founder   **told His rosary,** numbered the beads on his
rosary as he recited salutations to the Virgin Mary   16 **dumb orat'ries,** small
chapels for prayer, called dumb because they contain statues

62 **thorough,** through   **Ode   8 parle,** talk, discourse   11 **Elysian,** of Elysium,
home of the blessed after death   12 **Dian's fawns.** The fawn was the favorite
animal of Diana, goddess of the moon and the chase

The silver, snarling trumpets 'gan to chide:
The level chambers, ready with their pride,
Were glowing to receive a thousand guests:
The carvéd angels, ever eager-eyed,
Stared, where upon their heads the cornice rests,
With hair blown back, and wings put cross-wise on
   their breasts.

At length burst in the argent° revelry,
With plume, tiara, and all rich array,
Numerous as shadows haunting faerily
40 The brain, new-stuffed, in youth, with triumphs gay
Of old romance. These let us wish away,
And turn, sole-thoughted, to one Lady there,
Whose heart had brooded, all that wintry day,
On love, and winged St. Agnes' saintly care,
As she had heard old dames full many times declare.

They told her how, upon St. Agnes' Eve,
Young virgins might have visions of delight,
And soft adorings from their loves receive
Upon the honeyed middle of the night,
50 If ceremonies due they did aright;
As, supperless to bed they must retire,
And couch supine their beauties, lily white;
Nor look behind, nor sideways, but require
Of Heaven with upward eyes for all that they desire.

Full of this whim was thoughtful Madeline:
The music, yearning like a god in pain,
She scarcely heard: her maiden eyes divine,
Fixed on the floor, saw many a sweeping train°
Pass by—she heeded not at all: in vain
60 Came many a tiptoe, amorous cavalier,
And back retired; not cooled by high disdain,
But she saw not: her heart was otherwhere;
She sighed for Agnes' dreams, the sweetest of the
   year.

She danced along with vague, regardless eyes,
Anxious her lips, her breathing quick and short:
The hallowed hour was near at hand: she sighs
Amid the timbrels,° and the thronged resort
Of whisperers in anger, or in sport;
'Mid looks of love, defiance, hate, and scorn,
70 Hoodwinked with faery fancy; all amort,°
Save to St. Agnes and her lambs unshorn,
And all the bliss to be before tomorrow morn.

So, purposing each moment to retire,
She lingered still. Meantime, across the moors,
Had come young Porphyro, with heart on fire
For Madeline. Beside the portal doors,
Buttressed from moonlight, stands he, and implores
All saints to give him sight of Madeline,
But for one moment in the tedious hours,

That he might gaze and worship all unseen;   80
Perchance speak, kneel, touch, kiss—in sooth such
   things have been.

He ventures in: let no buzzed whisper tell:
All eyes be muffled, or a hundred swords
Will storm his heart, Love's fev'rous citadel:
For him, those chambers held barbarian hordes,
Hyena foemen, and hot-blooded lords,
Whose very dogs would execrations howl
Against his lineage: not one breast affords
Him any mercy, in that mansion foul,
Save one old beldame, weak in body and in soul.   90

Ah, happy chance! the aged creature came,
Shuffling along with ivory-headed wand,
To where he stood, hid from the torch's flame,
Behind a broad hall-pillar, far beyond
The sound of merriment and chorus bland:
He startled her; but soon she knew his face,
And grasped his fingers in her palsied hand,
Saying, "Mercy, Porphyro! hie thee from this place;
They are all here tonight, the whole blood-thirsty race!

"Get hence! get hence! there's dwarfish Hildebrand; 100
He had a fever late, and in the fit
He curséd thee and thine, both house and land:
Then there's that old Lord Maurice, not a whit
More tame for his gray hairs—Alas me! flit!
Flit like a ghost away."—"Ah, Gossip° dear,
We're safe enough; here in this armchair sit,
And tell me how"—"Good Saints not here, not here;
Follow me, child, or else these stones will be thy
   bier."

He followed through a lowly archéd way,
Brushing the cobwebs with his lofty plume;   110
And as she muttered, "Well-a—well-a-day!"
He found him in a little moonlight room,
Pale, latticed, chill, and silent as a tomb.
"Now tell me where is Madeline," said he,
"O tell me, Angela, by the holy loom
Which none but secret sisterhood may see,
When they St. Agnes' wool are weaving, piously."

"St. Agnes! Ah! it is St. Agnes' Eve—
Yet men will murder upon holy days:
Thou must hold water in a witch's sieve,°   120
And be liege-lord of all the Elves and Fays,
To venture so: it fills me with amaze
To see thee, Porphyro!—St. Agnes' Eve!
God's help! my lady fair the conjuror plays
This very night: good angels her deceive!
But let me laugh awhile, I've mickle° time to grieve."

Feebly she laugheth in the languid moon,

---

37 **argent,** shining 58 **sweeping train,** long trailing dress 67 **timbrels,** small hand drums 70 **amort,** dead

105 **Gossip,** godmother, here, merely devoted friend 120 **hold . . . sieve,** a feat regarded as a sign of supernatural power 126 **mickle,** much, ample

While Porphyro upon her face doth look,
Like puzzled urchin on an aged crone
130 Who keepeth closed a wond'rous riddle-book,
As spectacled she sits in chimney nook.
But soon his eyes grew brilliant, when she told
His lady's purpose; and he scarce could brook
Tears, at the thought of those enchantments cold,
And Madeline asleep in lap of legends old.

Sudden a thought came like a full-blown rose,
Flushing his brow, and in his painéd heart
Made purple riot: then doth he propose
A stratagem that makes the beldame start:
140 "A cruel man and impious thou art:
Sweet lady, let her pray, and sleep, and dream
Alone with her good angels, far apart
From wicked men like thee. Go, go! I deem
Thou canst not surely be the same that thou didst
    seem."

"I will not harm her, by all saints I swear,"
Quoth Porphyro: "O may I ne'er find grace
When my weak voice shall whisper its last prayer,
If one of her soft ringlets I displace,
Or look with ruffian passion in her face:
150 Good Angela, believe me by these tears;
Or I will, even in a moment's space,
Awake, with horrid shout, my foemen's ears,
And beard them, though they be more fanged than
    wolves and bears."

"Ah! why wilt thou affright a feeble soul?
A poor, weak, palsy-stricken, churchyard thing,
Whose passing-bell may ere the midnight toll;
Whose prayers for thee, each morn and evening,
Were never missed." Thus plaining, doth she bring
A gentler speech from burning Porphyro;
160 So woeful, and of such deep sorrowing,
That Angela gives promise she will do
Whatever he shall wish, betide her weal or woe.

Which was, to lead him, in close secrecy,
Even to Madeline's chamber, and there hide
Him in a closet, of such privacy
That he might see her beauty unespied,
And win perhaps that night a peerless bride,
While legioned faeries paced the coverlet,
And pale enchantment held her sleepy-eyed.
170 Never on such a night have lovers met,
Since Merlin paid his Demon all the monstrous debt.°

"It shall be as thou wishest," said the Dame:
"All cates° and dainties shall be storéd there
Quickly on this feast-night: by the tambour frame°

Her own lute thou wilt see: no time to spare,
For I am slow and feeble, and scarce dare
On such a catering trust my dizzy head.
Wait here, my child, with patience; kneel in prayer
The while: Ah! thou must needs the lady wed,
Or may I never leave my grave among the dead."   180

So saying, she hobbled off with busy fear.
The lover's endless minutes slowly passed;
The Dame returned, and whispered in his ear
To follow her—with agéd eyes aghast
From fright of dim espial. Safe at last,
Through many a dusky gallery, they gain
The maiden's chamber, silken, hushed, and chaste;
Where Porphyro took covert, pleased amain.°
His poor guide hurried back with agues in her brain.

Her faltering hand upon the balustrade,   190
Old Angela was feeling for the stair,
When Madeline, St. Agnes' charméd maid,
Rose, like a missioned spirit, unaware:
With silver taper's light, and pious care,
She turned, and down the aged gossip led
To a safe level matting. Now prepare,
Young Porphyro, for gazing on that bed;
She comes, she comes again, like ring-dove frayed°
    and fled.

Out went the taper as she hurried in;
Its little smoke, in pallid moonshine, died: 200
She closed the door, she panted, all akin
To spirits of the air, and visions wide:
No uttered syllable, or, woe betide!
But to her heart, her heart was voluble,
Paining with eloquence her balmy side;
As though a tongueless nightingale should swell
Her throat in vain, and die, heart-stifled in her dell.

A casement high and triple-arched there was,
All garlanded with carven imag'ries
Of fruits, and flowers, and bunches of knot-grass,   210
And diamonded with panes of quaint device,
Innumerable of stains and splendid dyes,
As are the tiger-moth's deep-damasked wings;
And in the midst, 'mong thousand heraldries,
And twilight saints, and dim emblazonings,
A shielded scutcheon blushed with blood of queens
    and kings.

Full on this casement shone the wintry moon,
And threw warm gules° on Madeline's fair breast,
As down she knelt for heaven's grace and boon;
Rose-bloom fell on her hands, together pressed,   220
And on her silver cross soft amethyst,
And on her hair a glory, like a saint:
She seemed a splendid angel, newly dressed,

171 **Merlin . . . debt.** According to one legend Merlin, the magician of the Arthurian romances was the son of a demon. He paid the "debt" for his existence when he was killed by the enchantress Vivien, who used a magic spell he had taught her 173 **cates,** delicacies 174 **tambour frame,** embroidery frame in the shape of a drum

188 **amain,** exceedingly 198 **frayed,** frightened 218 **gules,** red tinctures; the term is from heraldry

Save wings, for heaven—Porphyro grew faint:
She knelt, so pure a thing, so free from mortal taint.

Anon his heart revives: her vespers done,
Of all its wreathéd pearls her hair she frees;
Unclasps her warméd jewels one by one;
Loosens her fragrant bodice; by degrees
230 Her rich attire creeps rustling to her knees:
Half-hidden, like a mermaid in sea-weed,
Pensive awhile she dreams awake, and sees,
In fancy, fair St. Agnes in her bed,
But dares not look behind, or all the charm is fled.

Soon, trembling, in her soft and chilly nest,
In sort of wakeful swoon, perplexed she lay,
Until the poppied warmth of sleep oppressed
Her soothéd limbs, and soul fatigued away;
Flown, like a thought, until the morrow-day;
240 Blissfully havened both from joy and pain;
Clasped like a missal where swart Paynims pray;°
Blinded alike from sunshine and from rain,
As though a rose should shut, and be a bud again.

Stol'n to this paradise, and so entranced,
Porphyro gazed upon her empty dress,
And listened to her breathing, if it chanced
To wake into a slumberous tenderness;
Which when he heard, that minute did he bless,
And breathed himself: then from the closet crept,
250 Noiseless as fear° in a wide wilderness,
And over the hushed carpet, silent, stepped,
And 'tween the curtains peeped, where, lo!—how fast
    she slept.

Then by the bedside, where the faded moon
Made a dim, silver twilight, soft he set
A table, and, half anguished, threw thereon
A cloth of woven crimson, gold, and jet—
O for some drowsy Morphean° amulet!
The boisterous, midnight, festive clarion,
The kettle-drum, and far-heard clarionet,
260 Affray his ears, though but in dying tone—
The hall door shuts again, and all the noise is gone.

And still she slept an azure-lidded sleep,
In blanchéd linen, smooth, and lavendered,°
While he from forth the closet brought a heap
Of candied apple, quince, and plum, and gourd;
With jellies soother° than the creamy curd,
And lucent syrups, tinct° with cinnamon;
Manna and dates, in argosy° transferred
From Fez;° and spicéd dainties, every one,
270 From silken Samarcand° to cedared Lebanon.°

241 **Clasped . . . pray,** closed like a Christian prayer book, which pagans would
have no occasion to use   250 **as fear,** as a person in fear   257 **Morphean,** sleep-
producing, from Morpheus, the son of Sleep and god of dreams   263 **lavendered,**
perfumed with lavender, a European mint   266 **soother,** softer, smoother
267 **tinct,** flavored   268 **argosy,** a large merchant ship   269 **Fez,** important
commercial city in northern Morocco   270 **Samarcand,** city in Turkestan, Asiatic
Russia, noted for its silks   **Lebanon,** mountain range in southern Syria, once famous for its forests of cedar

These delicates he heaped with glowing hand
On golden dishes and in baskets bright
Of wreathéd silver: sumptuous they stand
In the retiréd quiet of the night,
Filling the chilly room with perfume light.—
"And now, my love, my seraph fair, awake!
Thou art my heaven, and I thine eremite:°
Open thine eyes, for meek St. Agnes' sake,
Or I shall drowse beside thee, so my soul doth ache."

Thus whispering, his warm, unnervéd arm   280
Sank in her pillow. Shaded was her dream
By the dusk curtains—'twas a midnight charm
Impossible to melt as icéd stream:
The lustrous salvers in the moonlight gleam;
Broad golden fringe upon the carpet lies:
It seemed he never, never could redeem
From such a steadfast spell his lady's eyes;
So mused awhile, entoiled in wooféd phantasies.°

Awakening up, he took her hollow lute—
Tumultuous—and, in chords that tenderest be,   290
He played an ancient ditty, long since mute,
In Provence called "La belle dame sans merci";°
Close to her ear touching the melody;—
Wherewith disturbed, she uttered a soft moan:
He ceased—she panted quick—and suddenly
Her blue affrayéd eyes wide open shone:
Upon his knees he sank, pale as smooth-sculptured
    stone.

Her eyes were open, but she still beheld,
Now wide awake, the vision of her sleep:
There was a painful change, that nigh expelled   300
The blisses of her dream so pure and deep
At which fair Madeline began to weep,
And moan forth witless words with many a sigh;
While still her gaze on Porphyro would keep;
Who knelt, with joinéd hands and piteous eye,
Fearing to move or speak, she looked so dreamingly.

"Ah, Porphyro!" said she, "but even now
Thy voice was at sweet tremble in mine ear,
Made tuneable with ever sweetest vow;
And those sad eyes were spiritual and clear: 310
How changed thou art! how pallid, chill, and drear!
Give me that voice again, my Porphyro,
Those looks immortal, those complainings dear!
Oh, leave me not in this eternal woe,
For if thou diest, my Love, I know not where to go."

Beyond a mortal man impassioned far
At these voluptuous accents, he arose,
Ethereal, flushed, and like a throbbing star
Seen mid the sapphire heaven's deep repose;

277 **eremite,** hermit; here, devoted lover   288 **wooféd phantasies,** fancies woven
together like threads   292 **La belle . . . merci,** the beautiful lady without pity

320 Into her dream he melted, as the rose
   Blendeth its odor with the violet—
   Solution sweet: meantime the frost-wind blows
   Like Love's alarum pattering the sharp sleet
   Against the window-panes; St. Agnes' moon hath set.

   'Tis dark; quick pattereth the flaw-blown sleet;
   "This is no dream, my bride, my Madeline!"
   'Tis dark; the icéd gusts still rave and beat;
   "No dream, alas! alas! and woe is mine!
   Porphyro will leave me here to fade and pine.—
330 Cruel! what traitor could thee hither bring?
   I curse not, for my heart is lost in thine.
   Though thou forsakest a deceivéd thing;—
   A dove forlorn and lost with sick unprunéd wing."

   "My Madeline! sweet dreamer! lovely bride!
   Say, may I be for aye thy vassal blest?
   Thy beauty's shield, heart-shaped and vermeil-dyed?
   Ah, silver shrine, here will I take my rest
   After so many hours of toil and quest,
   A famished pilgrim—saved by miracle.
340 Though I have found, I will not rob thy nest
   Saving of thy sweet self; if thou think'st well
   To trust, fair Madeline, to no rude infidel.

   "Hark! 'tis an elfin storm from faery land,
   Of haggard seeming,° but a boon indeed:
   Arise—arise! the morning is at hand—
   The bloated wassailers will never heed—
   Let us away, my love, with happy speed;
   There are no ears to hear, or eyes to see—
   Drowned all in Rhenish° and the sleepy mead;°
350 Awake! arise! my love, and fearless be,
   For o'er the southern moors I have a home for thee."

   She hurried at his words, beset with fears,
   For there were sleeping dragons all around,
   At glaring watch, perhaps, with ready spears—
   Down the wide stairs a darkling way they found.—
   In all the house was heard no human sound.
   A chain-drooped lamp was flickering by each door;
   The arras,° rich with horseman, hawk, and hound,
   Fluttered in the besieging wind's uproar;
360 And the long carpets rose along the gusty floor.

   They glide, like phantoms, into the wide hall;
   Like phantoms to the iron porch they glide,
   Where lay the Porter, in uneasy sprawl,
   With a huge empty flagon by his side;
   The wakeful bloodhound rose, and shook his hide,
   But his sagacious eye an inmate owns:
   By one, and one, the bolts full easy slide—
   The chains lie silent on the footworn stones;—
   The key turns, and the door upon its hinges groans.

344 **haggard seeming,** wild appearance   349 **Rhenish,** wine from the vineyards of the Rhine   **mead,** fermented drink made from honey   358 **arras,** tapestry

And they are gone: aye, ages long ago   370
These lovers fled away into the storm.
That night the Baron dreamt of many a woe,
And all his warrior-guests, with shade and form
Of witch, and demon, and large coffin-worm,
Were long be-nightmared. Angela the old
Died palsy-twitched, with meager face deform;
The Beadsman, after thousand aves° told,
For aye unsought-for slept among his ashes cold.
(1819; 1820)

LA BELLE DAME SANS MERCI°

O what can ail thee, knight-at-arms!
   Alone and palely loitering!
The sedge° has withered from the lake,
   And no birds sing.

O what can ail thee, knight-at-arms!
   So haggard and so woe-begone?
The squirrel's granary is full,
   And the harvest's done.

I see a lily on thy brow
   With anguish moist and fever dew,   10
And on thy cheeks a fading rose
   Fast withereth too.

"I met° a lady in the meads,
   Full beautiful—a faery's child,
Her hair was long, her foot was light,
   And her eyes were wild.

"I made a garland for her head,
   And bracelets too, and fragrant zone;°
She looked at me as she did love,
   And made sweet moan.   20

"I set her on my pacing steed,
   And nothing else saw all day long.
For sidelong would she bend, and sing
   A faery's song.

"She found me roots of relish sweet,
   And honey wild and manna-dew;
And sure in language strange she said,
   'I love thee true.'

"She took me to her elfin grot,
   And there she wept and sighed full sore;   30
And there I shut her wild, wild eyes
   With kisses four.

377 **aves,** salutations to the Virgin Mary, counted on the beads of the rosary
La Belle Dame sans Merci, the beautiful lady without pity. The ancient folklore theme of the Fairy Lover was illustrated in the popular old ballad *Thomas Rhymer.* La Belle Dame is Keats's highly romantic treatment of the same theme   3 **sedge,** coarse marsh grass   13 **I met,** etc. The knight begins to speak here   18 **zone,** girdle

"And there she lulléd me asleep,
   And there I dreamed—ah! woe betide!—
The latest dream I ever dreamed
   On the cold hillside.

"I saw pale kings, and princes too,
   Pale warriors, death-pale were they all:
They cried—'La Belle Dame sans Merci
40   Hath thee in thrall!'

"I saw their starved lips in the gloam
   With horrid warning gapéd wide,
And I woke, and found me here
   On the cold hillside.

"And this is why I sojourn here
   Alone and palely loitering,
Though the sedge is withered from the lake,
   And no birds sing."
                              (1819; 1820)

TO SLEEP

O soft embalmer of the still midnight,
   Shutting, with careful fingers and benign,
Our gloom-pleased eyes, embower'd from the light,
   Enshaded in forgetfulness divine;
5 O soothest Sleep! if so it please thee, close,
   In midst of this thine hymn, my willing eyes,
Or wait the amen, ere thy poppy throws
   Around my bed its lulling charities;
Then save me, or the passed day will shine
10 Upon my pillow, breeding many woes;
   Save me from curious conscience, that still lords
Its strength for darkness, burrowing like a mole;
   Turn the key deftly in the oiled wards,
And seal the hushed casket of my soul.

ODE TO PSYCHE

The story of Cupid and Psyche is a late Greek romance of the Christian era. It is the story of the love of
a god for a mortal woman, but unlike the older tales
based on this theme, the story ends happily, for
Psyche, after untold hardships, wins a place beside
Cupid on Mount Olympus, the home of the Greek
gods.
      The letter which Keats wrote to his brother and
sister on the subject of this ode throws light on his
methods of writing: "The following poem . . . is the
first and the only one with which I have taken even
moderate pains. I have for the most part dash'd off my
lines in a hurry. This I have done leisurely—I think it
reads the more richly for it, and will I hope encourage
me to write other things in even a more peaceable and
healthy spirit."

O Goddess! hear these tuneless numbers, wrung
   By sweet enforcement and remembrance dear,
And pardon that thy secrets should be sung
   Even into thine own soft-conchéd° ear:
Surely I dreamt today, or did I see
   The wingéd Psyche with awakened eyes?
I wandered in a forest thoughtlessly,
   And, on the sudden, fainting with surprise,
Saw two fair creatures, couchéd side by side
   In deepest grass, beneath the whisp'ring roof   10
   Of leaves and trembled blossoms, where there ran
      A brooklet, scarce espied:

'Mid hushed, cool-rooted flowers, fragrant-eyed,
   Blue, silver-white, and budded Tyrian,°
They lay calm-breathing on the bedded grass;
   Their arms embracéd, and their pinions too;
Their lips touched not, but had not bade adieu,
   As if disjoinéd by soft-handed slumber,
And ready still past kisses to outnumber
   At tender eye-dawn of aurorean love: 20
      The wingéd boy° I knew;
   But who wast thou, O happy, happy dove?
      His Psyche true!

O latest born and loveliest vision far
   Of all Olympus'° faded hierarchy!
Fairer than Phoebe's sapphire-regioned star,°
   Or Vesper,° amorous glowworm of the sky;
Fairer than these, though temple thou hast none,
   Nor altar heaped with flowers;
Nor virgin-choir to make delicious moan   30
   Upon the midnight hours;
No voice, no lute, no pipe, no incense sweet
   From chain-swung censer teeming;
No shrine, no grove, no oracle, no heat
   Of pale-mouthed prophet dreaming.

O brightest! though too late for antique vows,
   Too, too late for the fond believing lyre,
When holy were the haunted forest boughs,
   Holy the air, the water, and the fire;
Yet even in these days so far retired   40
   From happy pieties, thy lucent fans,°
   Fluttering among the faint Olympians,
I see, and sing, by my own eyes inspired.
So let me be thy choir, and make a moan
      Upon the midnight hours;
Thy voice, thy lute, thy pipe, thy incense sweet
   From swinged censer teeming;
Thy shrine, thy grove, thy oracle, thy heat
   Of pale-mouthed prophet dreaming.

Yes, I will be thy priest, and build a fane   50

Ode to Psyche 4 **conchéd,** shell-shaped   14 **budded Tyrian,** with buds of
Tyrian purple   21 **wingéd boy,** Cupid, god of love   25 **Olympus,** home of the
gods   26 **Phoebe's . . . star,** the moon. Phoebe is Diana, goddess of the
moon   27 **Vesper,** Venus, when an evening star   41 **lucent fans,** transparent
wings

In some untrodden region of my mind,
Where branchéd thoughts, new grown with pleasant
    pain,
Instead of pines shall murmur in the wind:
Far, far around shall those dark-clustered trees
    Fledge the wild-ridgéd mountains steep by steep;°
And there by zephyrs, streams, and birds, and bees,
    The moss-lain Dryads° shall be lulled to sleep;
And in the midst of this wide quietness
A rosy sanctuary will I dress
60 With the wreathéd trellis of a working brain,
    With buds, and bells, and stars without a name,
With all the gardener Fancy e'er could feign,
    Who, breeding flowers, will never breed the same;
And there shall be for thee all soft delight
    That shadowy thought can win,
A bright torch, and a casement ope at night,
    To let the warm Love° in!
(1819; 1820)

ODE TO A NIGHTINGALE

My heart aches, and a drowsy numbness pains
    My sense, as though of hemlock I had drunk,
Or emptied some dull opiate to the drains
    One minute past, and Lethe-wards° had sunk:
'Tis not through envy of thy happy lot,
    But being too happy in thine happiness—
        That thou, light-wingéd Dryad° of the trees,
            In some melodious plot
Of beechen green, and shadows numberless,
10   Singest of summer in full-throated ease.

O, for a draught of vintage! that hath been
    Cooled a long age in the deep-delvéd earth,
Tasting of Flora° and the country green,
    Dance, and Provençal song,° and sunburnt mirth!
O for a beaker full of the warm South,
    Full of the true, the blushful Hippocrene,°
        With beaded bubbles winking at the brim,
            And purple-stainéd mouth;
That I might drink, and leave the world unseen,
20   And with thee fade away into the forest dim:

Fade far away, dissolve, and quite forget
    What thou among the leaves hast never known,
The weariness, the fever, and the fret
    Here, where men sit and hear each other groan;
Where palsy shakes a few, sad, last gray hairs,
    Where youth grows pale, and specter-thin, and dies;
    Where but to think is to be full of sorrow

And leaden-eyed despairs,
    Where Beauty cannot keep her lustrous eyes,
        Or new Love pine at them beyond tomorrow.   30

Away! away! for I will fly to thee,
    Not charioted by Bacchus° and his pards,
But on the viewless° wings of Poesy,
    Though the dull brain perplexes and retards:
Already with thee! tender is the night,
    And haply the Queen-Moon is on her throne,
        Clustered around by all her starry Fays;°
            But here there is no light,
Save what from heaven is with the breezes blown
    Through verdurous glooms and winding mossy
        ways.   40

I cannot see what flowers are at my feet,
    Now what soft incense hangs upon the boughs,
But, in embalméd° darkness, guess each sweet
    Wherewith the seasonable month endows
The grass, the thicket, and the fruit-tree wild;
    White hawthorn, and the pastoral eglantine;
        Fast fading violets covered up in leaves;
            And mid-May's eldest child,
The coming musk-rose, full of dewy wine,
    The murmurous haunt of flies on summer eves.   50

Darkling° I listen; and, for many a time,
    I have been half in love with easeful Death,
Called him soft names in many a muséd rime,
    To take into the air my quiet breath;
Now more than ever seems it rich to die,
    To cease upon the midnight with no pain,
        While thou art pouring forth thy soul abroad
            In such an ecstasy!
Still wouldst thou sing, and I have ears in vain—
    To thy high requiem become a sod.   60

Thou wast not born for death, immortal Bird!
    No hungry generations tread thee down;
The voice I hear this passing night was heard
    In ancient days by emperor and clown:
Perhaps the self-same song that found a path
    Through the sad heart of Ruth, when, sick for home,
        She stood in tears amid the alien corn;
            The same that oft-times hath
Charmed magic casements, opening on the foam
    Of perilous seas, in faery lands forlorn.   70

Forlorn! the very word is like a bell
    To toll me back from thee to my sole self,
Adieu! the fancy cannot cheat so well
    As she is famed to do, deceiving elf.
Adieu! adieu! thy plaintive anthem fades
    Past the near meadows, over the still stream,

---

55 **Fledge . . . steep.** "Keats puts nearly all that may be said of the pine into one verse, though they are only figurative pines of which he is speaking."—Ruskin, *Modern Painters*   57 **Dryads,** nymphs of the trees in Greek mythology   67 **the warm Love,** Cupid   **Ode to a Nightingale**   4 **Lethe-wards,** toward Lethe, the river of forgetfulness in Hades   7 **Dryad,** tree nymph   13 **Flora,** goddess of the flowers and the spring   14 **Provençal song.** The medieval lyric flourished in Provence, the home of the troubadours   16 **Hippocrene,** fountain on Mt. Helicon sacred to the Muses

32 **Bacchus,** god of wine, who was often represented as riding in a car drawn by leopards or other wild beasts   33 **viewless,** invisible   37 **Fays,** fairies   43 **embalméd,** balmy, fragrant   51 **Darkling,** in the dark, becoming dark

Up the hillside; and now 'tis buried deep
    In the next valley glades:
  Was it a vision, or a waking dream?
80   Fled is that music—Do I wake or sleep?
  (1819; 1820)

ODE ON A GRECIAN URN

According to tradition, the urn that inspired this famous ode was one still preserved in the garden of Holland House, a noted mansion in Kensington, London.
But there were many such treasures in the British
Museum, decorated with marble urns carved with figures in low relief (see ll. 41–42).

Thou still unravished bride of quietness,
    Thou foster-child of Silence and slow Time,
Sylvan historian, who canst thus express
    A flowery tale more sweetly than our rime:
What leaf-fringed legend haunts about thy shape
    Of deities or mortals, or of both,
        In Tempe° or the dales of Arcady?°
    What men or gods are these? What maidens loth?
What mad pursuit? What struggle to escape?
10   What pipes and timbrels? What wild ecstasy?

Heard melodies are sweet, but those unheard
    Are sweeter; therefore, ye soft pipes, play on;
Not to the sensual ear, but, more endeared,
    Pipe to the spirit ditties of no tone:
Fair youth, beneath the trees, thou canst not leave
    Thy song, nor ever can those trees be bare;
        Bold Lover, never, never canst thou kiss,
    Though winning near the goal—yet, do not grieve;
        She cannot fade, though thou hast not thy bliss,
20   Forever wilt thou love, and she be fair!

Ah, happy, happy boughs! that cannot shed
    Your leaves, nor ever bid the Spring adieu;
And, happy melodist, unwearièd,
    Forever piping songs forever new.
More happy love! more happy, happy love!
    Forever warm and still to be enjoyed,
        Forever panting, and forever young;
All breathing human passion far above,
    That leaves a heart high-sorrowful and cloyed,
30   A burning forehead, and a parching tongue.

Who are these coming to the sacrifice?
    To what green altar, O mysterious priest,
Lead'st thou that heifer lowing at the skies,
    And all her silken flanks with garlands dressed?
What little town by river or seashore,
    Or mountain-built with peaceful citadel,

Is emptied of this folk, this pious morn?
And, little town, thy streets forevermore
    Will silent be; and not a soul to tell
        Why thou art desolate, can e'er return.   40

O Attic shape! Fair attitude! with brede°
    Of marble men and maidens overwrought,
With forest branches and the trodden weed;
    Thou, silent form! dost tease us out of thought
As doth eternity: Cold Pastoral!°
    When old age shall this generation waste,
        Thou shalt remain, in midst of other woe
    Than ours, a friend to man, to whom thou say'st,
"Beauty is truth, truth beauty,—that is all
    Ye know on earth, and all ye need to know."   50
(1819; 1820)

ODE ON MELANCHOLY

The poem, although not published until 1820, was
written in 1819, after the disasters which befell Keats
in 1818. Keats wrote in a letter to a friend at the beginning of the year 1819: "I have been writing a little
now and then lately: but nothing to speak of—being
discontented and as it were moulting. Yet I do not
think I shall ever come to the rope or the pistol, for
after a day or two's melancholy, although I smoke
more and more my own insufficiency—I see by little
and little more of what is to be done, and how it is to
be done, should I ever be able to do it. On my soul,
there should be some reward for that continual *agonie
ennuyeuse.*"

No, no! go not to Lethe,° neither twist
    Wolf's-bane,° tight-rooted, for its poisonous wine;
Nor suffer thy pale forehead to be kissed
    By nightshade,° ruby grape of Proserpine;°
Make not your rosary of yew-berries,°
    Nor let the beetle,° nor the death-moth° be
        Your mournful Psyche,° nor the downy owl
A partner in your sorrow's mysteries;
    For shade to shade will come too drowsily,
        And drown the wakeful anguish of the soul.   10

But when the melancholy fit shall fall
    Sudden from heaven like a weeping cloud,
That fosters the droop-headed flowers all,
    And hides the green hill in an April shroud;
Then glut thy sorrow on a morning rose,
    Or on the rainbow of the salt sand-wave,
        Or on the wealth of globèd peonies;

41 **brede,** embroidery   45 **Cold Pastoral,** pastoral story in marble
Ode on Melancholy   1 **Lethe,** river of forgetfulness in Hades   2 **Wolf's-bane,**
poisonous plant   4 **nightshade,** poisonous herb   **Proserpine,** queen of the underworld   5 **yew-berries.** The yew is an emblem of mourning   6 **beetle.** The
sacred beetle of Egypt was regarded as a symbol of the resurrection of the soul
and hence was placed with the dead in coffins   **death-moth,** a moth with markings resembling a human skull   7 **Psyche,** the soul in classical mythology, symbolized by the butterfly

Ode on a Grecian Urn   7 **Tempe,** a beautiful valley in Thessaly, Greece   **Arcady,** Arcadia, a mountainous region in Greece celebrated in pastoral poetry as a
place of carefree shepherd life

Or if thy mistress some rich anger shows,
   Emprison her soft hand, and let her rave,
20   And feed deep, deep upon her peerless eyes.

She dwells with Beauty—Beauty that must die;
   And Joy, whose hand is ever at his lips
Bidding adieu; and aching Pleasure nigh,
   Turning to poison while the bee-mouth sips:
Ay, in the very temple of Delight
   Veiled Melancholy has her sovran shrine,
      Though seen of none save him whose strenuous
         tongue
   Can burst Joy's grape against his palate fine;
His soul shall taste the sadness of her might,
30   And be among her cloudy trophies hung.
(1819; 1820)

ODE ON INDOLENCE°

"THEY TOIL NOT, NEITHER DO THEY SPIN."°

I

One morn before me were three figures seen,
   With bowed necks, and joined hands, side-faced;
And one behind the other stepp'd serene,
   In placid sandals, and in white robes graced;
They pass'd, like figures on a marble urn,
   When shifted round to see the other side;
      They came again; as when the urn once more
Is shifted round, the first seen shades return;
   And they were strange to me, as may betide
10   With vases, to one deep in Phidian° lore.

II

How is it, Shadows! that I knew ye not?
   How came ye muffled in so hush a mask?
Was it a silent deep-disguised plot
   To steal away, and leave without a task
My idle days? Ripe was the drowsy hour;
   The blissful cloud of summer-indolence
      Benumb'd my eyes; my pulse grew less and less;
Pain had no sting, and pleasure's wreath no flower:
   O, why did ye not melt, and leave my sense
20   Unhaunted quite of all but—nothingness?

III

A third time came they by;—alas! wherefore?
   My sleep had been embroider'd with dim dreams;
My soul had been a lawn besprinkled o'er
   With flowers, and stirring shades, and baffled
      beams:

Ode on Indolence. Describing his mood at the time of composition of this poem, Keats wrote to his sister, "—The fibres of the brain are relaxed in common with the rest of the body. Neither poetry, nor ambition, nor love have any alertness of countenance as they pass by me; they seem rather like figures on a Greek vase . . ." **They toil not,** Matthew, 6:28   10 **Phidian,** of Phidias, famous Greek sculptor of fifth century B.C.

The morn was clouded, but no shower fell,
   Tho' in her lids hung the sweet tears of May;
   The open casement press'd a new-leav'd vine,
Let in the budding warmth and throstle's lay;
   O Shadows! 'twas a time to bid farewell!
      Upon your skirts had fallen no tears of mine.   30

IV

A third time pass'd they by, and, passing, turn'd
   Each one the face a moment whiles to me;
Then faded, and to follow them I burn'd
   And ached for wings because I knew the three;
The first was a fair Maid, and Love her name;
   The second was Ambition, pale of cheek,
      And ever watchful with fatigued eye;
The last, whom I love more, the more of blame
   Is heap'd upon her, maiden most unmeek,—
      I knew to be my demon Poesy.   40

V

They faded, and forsooth! I wanted wings:
   O folly! What is Love! and where is it?
And for that poor Ambition! it springs
   From a man's little heart's short fever-fit;
For Poesy!—no,—she has not a joy,—
   At least for me,—so sweet as drowsy noons,
      And evenings steep'd in honied indolence;
O, for an age so shelter'd from annoy,
   That I may never know how change the moons,
      Or hear the voice of busy common-sense!   50

VI

So, ye three Ghosts, adieu! Ye cannot raise
   My head cool-bedded in the flowery grass;
For I would not be dieted with praise,
   A pet-lamb in a sentimental farce!
Fade softly from my eyes, and be once more
   In masque-like figures on the dreamy urn;
      Farewell! I yet have visions for the night,
And for the day faint visions there is store;
   Vanish, ye Phantoms! from my idle spright,
      Into the clouds, and never more return!   60
(1819; 1820)

TO AUTUMN

Season of mists and mellow fruitfulness,
   Close bosom-friend of the maturing sun;
Conspiring with him how to load and bless
   With fruit the vines that round the thatch-eaves run;
To bend with apples the mossed cottage-trees,
   And fill all fruit with ripeness to the core;
      To swell the gourd, and plump the hazel shells
With a sweet kernel; to set budding more,
   And still more, later flowers for the bees,
   Until they think warm days will never cease,   10

For Summer has o'er-brimmed their clammy°
    cells.

Who hath not seen thee oft amid thy store?
    Sometimes whoever seeks abroad may find
Thee sitting careless on a granary floor,
    Thy hair soft-lifted by the winnowing wind;
Or on a half-reaped furrow sound asleep,
    Drowsed with the fume of poppies, while thy hook
        Spares the next swath and all its twinéd flowers:
And sometime like a gleaner thou dost keep
20   Steady thy laden head across a brook;
    Or by a cider-press, with patient look,
        Thou watchest the last oozings, hours by hours.

Where are the songs of Spring? Ay, where are they?
    Think not of them, thou hast thy music too—
While barréd clouds bloom the soft-dying day,
    And touch the stubble-plains with rosy hue;
Then in a wailful choir the small gnats mourn
    Among the river sallows,° borne aloft
        Or sinking as the light wind lives or dies;
30 And full-grown lambs loud bleat from hilly bourn;
    Hedge-crickets° sing; and now with treble soft
    The redbreast whistles from a garden-croft,°
        And gathering swallows twitter in the skies.
(1819; 1820)

BRIGHT STAR!
WOULD I WERE
STEADFAST AS THOU ART

Bright star! would I were steadfast as thou art—
Not in lone splendor hung aloft the night,
And watching, with eternal lids apart,
Like Nature's patient sleepless Eremite,
5 The moving waters at their priestlike task
Of pure ablution round earth's human shores,
Or gazing on the new soft fallen mask
Of snow upon the mountains and the moors—
No—yet still steadfast, still unchangeable,
10 Pillowed upon my fair love's ripening breast,
To feel forever its soft fall and swell,
Awake forever in a sweet unrest,
Still, still to hear her tender-taken breath,
And so live ever—or else swoon to death.
(1819; 1848)

To Autumn   11 **clammy**, soft, moist   28 **sallows**, willows   31 **Hedge-crickets**, grasshoppers   32 **garden-croft**, garden enclosure

---

from LETTERS

T. S. Eliot has called the letters of Keats "the most important ever written by an English poet." They are engrossing to read because of the insight they afford into Keats' development as a personality and as a poet, of course, but more often than not the letters are also significant documents of literary criticism.

TO BENJAMIN BAILEY°

(22 November 1817)

MY DEAR BAILEY,

. . . O I wish I was as certain of the end of all your troubles as that of your momentary start about the authenticity of the Imagination. I am certain of nothing but of the holiness of the Heart's affections and the truth of Imagination—What the imagination seizes as Beauty must be truth—whether it existed before or not—for I have the same Idea of all our Passions as of Love they are all in their sublime, creative of essential Beauty—In a Word, you may know my favorite Speculation by my first Book and the little song° I sent 10 in my last—which is a representation from the fancy of the probable mode of operating in these Matters—The Imagination may be compared to Adam's dream°—he awoke and found it truth. I am the more zealous in this affair, because I have never yet been able to perceive how any thing can be known for truth by consequitive reasoning—and yet it must be—Can it be that even the greatest Philosopher ever arrived at his goal without putting aside numerous objections—However it may be, O for a Life of Sensations rather than of Thoughts! 20 It is 'a Vision in the form of Youth' a Shadow of reality to come—and this consideration has further conv[i]nced me for it has come as auxiliary to another favorite Speculation of mine, that we shall enjoy ourselves here after by having what we called happiness on Earth repeated in a finer tone and so repeated—And yet such a fate can only befall those who delight in sensation rather than hunger as you do after Truth—Adam's dream will do here and seems to be a conviction that Imagination and its empyreal reflection is the same as 30 human Life and its spiritual repetition. But as I was saying—the simple imaginative Mind may have its rewards in the repeti[ti]on of its own silent Working coming continually on the spirit with a fine suddenness—to compare great things with small—have you never by being surprised with an old Melody—in a

---

To Benjamin Bailey. Benjamin Bailey (1794–1848) was one of Keats's closest friends. Keats had stayed with him in October at Oxford   10 **little song,** *O Sorrow,* from *Endymion*   13 **Adam's dream.** In *Paradise Lost,* VIII, 460–490, Adam dreams that Eve has been created, then awakes to find her real

delicious place—by a delicious voice, fe[l]t over again your very speculations and surmises at the time it first operated on your soul—do you not remember forming
40 to yourself the singer's face more beautiful that [*for* than] it was possible and yet with the elevation of the Moment you did not think so—even then you were mounted on the Wings of Imagination so high—that the Prototype must be here after—that delicious face you will see—What a time! I am continually running away from the subject—sure this cannot be exactly the case with a complex Mind—one that is imaginative and at the same time careful of its fruits—who would exist partly on sensation partly on thought—to whom
50 it is necessary that years should bring the philosophic Mind—such an one I consider your's and therefore it is necessary to your eternal Happiness that you not only drink this old Wine of Heaven which I shall call the redigestion of our most ethereal Musings on Earth; but also increase in knowledge and know all things. I am glad to hear you are in a fair Way for Easter—you will soon get through your unpleasant reading and then!—but the world is full of troubles and I have not much reason to think myself pesterd with many—I
60 think Jane or Marianne° has a better opinion of me than I deserve—for really and truly I do not think my Brothers illness connected with mine—you know more of the real Cause than they do—nor have I any chance of being rack'd as you have been°—you perhaps at one time thought there was such a thing as Worldly Happiness to be arrived at, at certain periods of time marked out—you have of necessity from your disposition been thus led away—I scarcely remember counting upon any Happiness—I look not for it if it be
70 not in the present hour—nothing startles me beyond the Moment. The setting sun will always set me to rights—or if a Sparrow come before my Window I take part in its existence and pick about the Gravel. The first thing that strikes me on hea[r]ing a Misfortune having befalled another is this. 'Well it cannot be helped.—he will have the pleasure of trying the resourses of his spirit, and I beg now my dear Bailey that hereafter should you observe any thing cold in me not to but [*for* put] it to the account of heartlessness but abstrac-
80 tion—for I assure you I sometimes feel not the influence of a Passion or Affection during a whole week—and so long this sometimes continues I begin to suspect myself and the genui[ne]ness of my feelings at other times—thinking them a few barren Tragedy-tears . . .

Your affectionate friend
John Keats—

---

60 **Jane or Marianne,** Jane and Marianne Reynolds, friends of Keats, who feared that he was coming down with tuberculosis, from which his brother Tom was suffering   64 **rack'd . . . been.** Bailey had recently had an unsuccessful love affair

TO GEORGE AND THOMAS KEATS

(21, 27 (?) December 1817)
Hampstead Sunday

MY DEAR BROTHERS,

. . . I spent Friday evening with Wells° & went the next morning to see *Death on the Pale horse*. It is a wonderful picture, when West's° age is considered; But there is nothing to be intense upon; no women one feels mad to kiss; no face swelling into reality. the excellence of every Art is its intensity, capable of making all disagreeables evaporate, from their being in close relationship with Beauty & Truth—Examine King Lear & you will find this examplified throughout; but in this picture we have unpleasantness without any 10 momentous depth of speculation excited, in which to bury its repulsiveness—The picture is larger than Christ rejected. . . .Brown° & Dilke° walked with me & back from the Christmas pantomime. I had not a dispute but a disquisition with Dilke, on various subjects; several things dovetailed in my mind, & at once it struck me, what quality went to form a Man of Achievement especially in Literature & which Shakespeare posessed so enormously—I mean *Negative Capability,* that is when man is capable of being in 20 uncertainties, Mysteries, doubts, without any irritable reaching after fact & reason—Coleridge, for instance, would let go by a fine isolated verisimilitude caught from the Penetralium° of mystery, from being incapable of remaining content with half knowledge. This pursued through Volumes would perhaps take us no further than this, that with a great poet the sense of Beauty overcomes every other consideration, or rather obliterates all consideration.

Shelley's poem is out, & there are words about its 30 being objected too, as much as Queen Mab was. Poor Shelley I think he has his Quota of good qualities, in sooth la!! Write soon to your most sincere friend & affectionate Brother.

John

TO JOHN HAMILTON REYNOLDS°

(3 February 1818)
Hampstead Tuesday

MY DEAR REYNOLDS,

. . . It may be said that we ought to read our Contemporaries. that Wordsworth &c should have their due from us. but for the sake of a few fine imaginative

To George and Thomas Keats   1 **Wells,** Charles Wells, former schoolmate of Keats's brother Tom   3 **West's,** Benjamin West (1738–1820), historical painter   13 **Brown,** Charles Brown, writer and friend of Keats   **Dilke,** Charles Dilke, writer and friend of Keats   24 **Penetralium,** signifying the most secret part of a temple   **To John Hamilton Reynolds.** Reynolds (1796–1852) was a poet, critic, and lawyer and a close friend of Keats

or domestic passages, are we to be bullied into a certain Philosophy engendered in the whims of an Egotist—Every man has his speculations, but every man does not brood and peacock over them till he makes a false coinage and deceives himself—Many a man can travel to the very bourne of Heaven, and yet want confidence to put down his halfseeing. Sancho will invent a Journey heavenward as well as any body. We hate poetry that has a palpable design upon us—and if we do not agree, seems to put its hand in its breeches pocket. Poetry should be great & unobtrusive, a thing which enters into one's soul, and does not startle it or amaze it with itself but with its subject.—How beautiful are the retired flowers! how would they lose their beauty were they to throng into the highway crying out, "admire me I am a violet! dote upon me I am a primrose!" Modern poets differ from the Elizabethans in this. Each of the moderns like an Elector of Hanover governs his petty state, & knows how many straws are swept daily from the Causeways in all his dominions & has a continual itching that all the Housewives should have their coppers well scoured: the antients were Emperors of vast Provinces, they had only heard of the remote ones and scarcely cared to visit them.—I will cut all this—I will have no more of Wordsworth or Hunt° in particular—Why should we be of the tribe of Manasseh, when we can wander with Esau?° why should we kick against the Pricks, when we can walk on Roses? Why should we be owls, when we can be Eagles? Why be teased with "nice Eyed wagtails",° when we have in sight "the Cherub Contemplation"?°—Why with Wordsworths "Matthew with a bough of wilding in his hand"° when we can have Jacques "under an oak° &c."?—The secret of the Bough of Wilding will run through your head faster than I can write it—Old Matthew spoke to him some years ago on some nothing, & because he happens in an Evening Walk to imagine the figure of the old man—he must stamp it down in black & white, and it is henceforth sacred—I don't mean to deny Wordsworth's grandeur & Hunt's merit but I mean to say we need not be teazed with grandeur & merit—when we can have them uncontaminated & unobtrusive. Let us have the old Poets, & robin Hood Your letter and its sonnets gave me more pleasure than will the 4th Book of Childe Harold & the whole of any body's life & opinions. In return for your dish of filberts, I have gathered a few Catkins, I hope they'll look pretty.

[Here follow *Robin Hood* and *Lines on the Mermaid Tavern*]

* * * * *

Yr sincere friend and Coscribbler
John Keats.

TO RICHARD WOODHOUSE°

(27 October 1818)

MY DEAR WOODHOUSE,

Your Letter gave me a great satisfaction; more on account of its friendliness, than any relish of that matter in it which is accounted so acceptable in the 'genus irritabile'.° The best answer I can give you is in a clerklike manner to make some observations on two principle points, which seem to point like indices into the midst of the whole pro and con, about genius, and views and atchievements and ambition and cœtera. 1st As to the poetical Character itself, (I mean that sort of which, if I am any thing, I am a Member; that sort distinguished from the wordsworthian or egotistical sublime; which is a thing per se and stands alone) it is not itself—it has no self—it is every thing and nothing—It has no character—it enjoys light and shade; it lives in gusto, be it foul or fair, high or low, rich or poor, mean or elevated—It has as much delight in conceiving an Iago° as an Imogen.° What shocks the virtuous philosop[h]er, delights the camelion Poet. It does no harm from its relish of the dark side of things any more than from its taste for the bright one; because they both end in speculation. A Poet is the most unpoetical of any thing in existence; because he has no Identity—he is continually in for—and filling some other Body—The Sun, the Moon, the Sea and Men and Women who are creatures of impulse are poetical and have about them an unchangeable attribute—the poet has none; no identity—he is certainly the most unpoetical of all God's Creatures. If then he has no self, and if I am a Poet, where is the Wonder that I should say I would write no more? Might I not at that very instant [have] been cogitating on the Characters of saturn and Ops? It is a wretched thing to confess; but is a very fact that not one word I ever utter can be taken for granted as an opinion growing out of my identical nature—how can it, when I have no nature? When I am in a room with People if I ever am free from speculating on creations of my own brain, then not myself goes home to myself: but the identity of every

29 **Hunt,** Leigh Hunt (1784–1859), poet and essayist   31 **Manasseh . . . Esau.** That is, why should we dwell in the cities when we can roam the fields? See *Genesis,* 25:27; *Numbers,* 32:33 ff.   34 **nice Eyed wagtails,** evidently a phrase from one of Reynolds's sonnets   35 **the Cherub Contemplation,** quoted from Milton's *Il Penseroso,* 54   36 **Matthew . . . hand,** quoted from Wordsworth's *The Two April Mornings,* 59–60; *wilding* is an uncultivated plant or weed   37 **under an oak,** referring to the melancholy Jaques in Shakespeare's *As You Like It,* II, i, 31

To Richard Woodhouse. Woodhouse was a lawyer with literary inclinations who made copies of many of Keats's poems and letters   4 **genus irritabile,** "the irritable tribe [of poets]," from Horace's *Epistles,* II, ii, 102   17 **Iago,** evil character in Shakespeare's *Othello*   **Imogen,** virtuous character in Shakespeare's *Cymbeline*

one in the room begins to [for so?] to press upon me
that, I am in a very little time an[ni]hilated—not only
among Men; it would be the same in a Nursery of
children: I know not whether I make myself wholly
understood: I hope enough so to let you see that no
dependence is to be placed on what I said that day.

In the second place I will speak of my views, and of
the life I purpose to myself—I am ambitious of doing
the world some good: if I should be spared that may be
the work of maturer years—in the interval I will assay
to reach to as high a summit in Poetry as the nerve
bestowed upon me will suffer. The faint conceptions I
have of Poems to come brings the blood frequently
into my forehead—All I hope is that I may not lose all
interest in human affairs—that the solitary indifference I feel for applause even from the finest Spirits,
will not blunt any acuteness of vision I may have. I do
not think it will—I feel assured I should write from the
mere yearning and fondness I have for the Beautiful
even if my night's labours should be burnt every
morning and no eye ever shine upon them. But even
now I am perhaps not speaking from myself; but from
some character in whose soul I now live. I am sure
however that this next sentence is from myself. I feel
your anxiety, good opinion and friendliness in the
highest degree, and am

Your's most sincerely
John Keats

TO GEORGE
AND GEORGIANA KEATS

(21 April 1819)

MY DEAR BROTHER & SISTER—

. . . The whole appears to resolve into this—that
Man is originally 'a poor forked creature'° subject to
the same mischances as the beasts of the forest, destined to hardships and disquietude of some kind or
other. If he improves by degrees his bodily ac-
com[m]odations and comforts—at each stage, at each
accent [for ascent] there are waiting for him a fresh set
of annoyances—he is mortal and there is still a heaven
with its Stars abov[e] his head. The most interesting
question that can come before us is, How far by the
persevering endeavours of a seldom appearing Socrates Mankind may be made happy—I can imagine
such happiness carried to an extreme—but what must
it end in?—Death—and who could in such a case bear
with death—the whole troubles of life which are now
frittered away in a series of years, would the[n] be

To George and Georgiana Keats 2 a poor . . . creature. Cf. Shakespeare's *King
Lear*, III, iv, 112–113: "Man is no more but such a poor, bare, forked animal as
thou art"

accumulated for the last days of a being who instead of
hailing its approach, would leave this world as Eve left
Paradise—But in truth I do not at all believe in this
sort of perfectibility—the nature of the world will not
admit of it—the inhabitants of the world will correspond to itself—Let the fish philosophise the ice away
from the Rivers in winter time and they shall be at
continual play in the tepid delight of summer. Look at
the Poles and at the sands of Africa, Whirlpools and
volcanoes—Let men exterminate them and I will say
that they may arrive at earthly Happiness—The point
at which Man may arrive is as far as the paral[l]el state
in inanimate nature and no further—For instance suppose a rose to have sensation, it blooms on a beautiful
morning it enjoys itself—but there comes a cold wind,
a hot sun—it can not escape it, it cannot destroy its
annoyances—they are as native to the world as itself:
no more can man be happy in spite, the world[l]y elements will prey upon his nature—The common cog-
nomen of this world among the misguided and
superstitious is 'a vale of tears' from which we are to
be redeemed by a certain arbit[r]ary interposition of
God and taken to Heaven—What a little circumscribe[d] straightened notion! Call the world if you
Please "The vale of Soul-making" Then you will find
out the use of the world (I am speaking now in the
highest terms for human nature admitting it to be immortal which I will here take for granted for the purpose of showing a thought which has struck me concerning it) I say 'Soul making' Soul as distinguished
from an Intelligence—There may be intelligences or
sparks of the divinity in millions—but they are not
Souls till they acquire identities, till each one is personally itself. I[n]telligences are atoms of perception—they know and they see and they are pure, in
short they are God—How then are Souls to be made?
How then are these sparks which are God to have
identity given them—so as ever to possess a bliss
peculiar to each ones individual existence? How, but
by the medium of a world like this? This point I sincerely wish to consider because I think it a grander system of salvation than the chrystain religion—or rather
it is a system of Spirit-creation—This is effected by
three grand materials acting the one upon the other for
a series of years. These three Materials are the *Intelligence*—the *human heart* (as distinguished from intelligence or Mind) and the *World* or *Elemental space*
suited for the proper action of *Mind and Heart* on each
other for the purpose of forming the *Soul* or *Intelligence destined to possess the sense of Identity*. I can
scarcely express what I but dimly perceive—and yet I
think I perceive it—that you may judge the more
clearly I will put it in the most homely form possible—I will call the *world* a School instituted for the
purpose of teaching little children to read—I will call

the *human heart* the *horn Book* used in that School—and I will call the *Child able to read, the Soul* made from that *school* and its *hornbook.* Do you not see how necessary a World of Pains and troubles is to school an Intelligence and make it a soul? A Place where the heart must feel and suffer in a thousand diverse ways! Not merely is the Heart a Hornbook, It is the Minds Bible, it is the Minds experience, it is the teat from which the Mind or intelligence sucks its identity—As various as the Lives of Men are—so various become their souls, and thus does God make individual beings, Souls, Identical Souls of the sparks of his own essence—This appears to me a faint sketch of a system of Salvation which does not affront our reason and humanity . . .

Your ever Affectionate Brother,
John Keats—

THOMAS DE QUINCEY
1785–1859

Thomas De Quincey was born near Manchester, the son of a rich merchant who died when the boy was young but who left a sizable estate, which seems to have lasted through De Quincey's lifetime. The boy was unusually precocious; he could write Greek fluently at the age of thirteen and could speak it with ease at fifteen. In spite of his proficiency, De Quincey abhorred his early schooling and briefly ran away to London. He went to Oxford, where his career was most irregular; he ran away again and in the second year of his course became addicted to opium, a habit brought on through the use of the drug to alleviate the pain of an annoying minor illness. Having studied brilliantly but erratically, he left Oxford in 1808 without a degree because he could not stand the emotional ordeal of the oral examination.

His interest in literature had been marked from the first. It was not surprising, therefore, that De Quincey was attracted to the company of Wordsworth and Coleridge. He went to the Lake District, took a home near Wordsworth at Grasmere, and remained there for about ten years, studying the classics and cultivating Coleridge and Wordsworth. During this time, however, he did no significant work. From Coleridge he acquired an interest in the Elizabethans and in German literature, at the time an almost unknown field. In 1817 he married a local girl and soon became the father of a large family. In 1820 he moved to London, where he renewed his acquaintance with Lamb which he had made in earlier days; he learned much from him about the English prose writers of the seventeenth century—Browne, Fuller, and Taylor.

De Quincey's *Confessions of an English Opium Eater* appeared in 1821. He had taken enormous quantities of opium at one time (1813) but had greatly reduced the daily allowance before his marriage, although there had been some relapses. The book sold very well. It was authentically intimate in a sensational way; it was exciting and romantic in its account of De Quincey's early days when he had fled to London from school and college; and it was written in a rich, sensuous and imaginative prose style. The remainder of De Quincey's output was originally written for periodicals, particularly *Blackwood's Magazine;* it consists of essays on personal, political, social, critical, historical, and even philosophical subjects.

De Quincey moved to Edinburgh in middle age and remained there until his death on December 8, 1859. His life was in keeping with his gentle, scholarly, eccentric character. His desire for solitude amounted at times almost to a craze, for he would abandon his living quarters and go away to some other place, locking the door behind him. Six such apartments, locked and stuffed with papers, were discovered after his death.

De Quincey's style is his chief contribution. It is always polished and, as De Quincey himself called it, "impassioned." Though such "impassioned" prose was not original with him, he was a radical innovator in the genre of poetic prose or prose poetry that rose to prominence in the modern period. "There is, first," said De Quincey, "the literature of knowledge, and, secondly, the literature of power. The function of the first is to teach; the function of the second is to move; the first is a rudder; the second, an oar or sail." De Quincey's best work belongs to the literature of power.

ON THE KNOCKING
AT THE GATE IN *MACBETH*

From my boyish days I had always felt a great perplexity on one point in *Macbeth.* It was this: the knocking at the gate which succeeds to the murder of Duncan produced to my feelings an effect for which I never could account. The effect was that it reflected back upon the murderer a peculiar awfulness and a depth of solemnity; yet, however obstinately I endeavored with my understanding to comprehend this, for many years I never could see *why* it should produce such an effect.

Here I pause for one moment to exhort the reader never to pay any attention to his understanding when it stands in opposition to any other faculty of his mind. The mere understanding, however useful and indispensable, is the meanest° faculty in the human mind and the most to be distrusted; and yet the great major-

On the Knocking at the Gate in *Macbeth*   15 **meanest,** lowest

ity of people trust to nothing else—which may do for ordinary life, but not for philosophical purposes. Of this, out of ten thousand instances that I might pro-
20 duce, I will cite one. Ask of any person whatsoever who is not previously prepared for the demand by a knowledge of perspective, to draw in the rudest way the commonest appearance which depends upon the laws of that science—as, for instance, to represent the effect of two walls standing at right angles to each other, or the appearance of the houses on each side of a street, as seen by a person looking down the street from one extremity. Now, in all cases, unless the person has happened to observe in pictures how it is that
30 artists produce these effects, he will be utterly unable to make the smallest approximation to it. Yet why? For he has actually seen the effect every day of his life. The reason is that he allows his understanding to overrule his eyes. His understanding, which includes no intuitive knowledge of the laws of vision, can furnish him with no reason why a line which is known and can be proved to be a horizontal line should not *appear* a horizontal line: a line that made any angle with the perpendicular less than a right angle would seem to
40 him to indicate that his houses were all tumbling down together. Accordingly he makes the line of his houses a horizontal line, and fails of course to produce the effect demanded. Here then is one instance out of many, in which not only the understanding is allowed to overrule the eyes, but where the understanding is positively allowed to obliterate the eyes, as it were; for not only does the man believe the evidence of his understanding in opposition to that of his eyes, but (what is monstrous) the idiot is not aware that his eyes ever
50 gave such evidence. He does not know that he has seen (and therefore *quoad* his consciousness° has *not* seen) that which he *has* seen every day of his life.

But to return from this digression. My understanding could furnish no reason why the knocking at the gate in *Macbeth* should produce any effect, direct or reflected. In fact, my understanding said positively that it could *not* produce any effect. But I knew better; I felt that it did; and I waited and clung to the problem until further knowledge should enable me to solve it.
60 At length, in 1812,° Mr. Williams° made his *début* on the stage of Ratcliffe Highway,° and executed those unparalleled murders which have procured for him such a brilliant and undying reputation. On which murders, by the way, I must observe, that in one respect they have had an ill effect, by making the connoisseur in murder very fastidious in his taste, and dissatisfied with anything that has been since done in that line. All other murders look pale by the deep crimson of his; and, as an amateur° once said to me in a querulous
70 tone, "There has been absolutely nothing *doing* since

his time, or nothing that's worth speaking of." But this is wrong, for it is unreasonable to expect all men to be great artists, and born with the genius of Mr. Williams. Now it will be remembered that in the first of these murders (that of the Marrs) the same incident (of a knocking at the door° soon after the work of extermination was complete) did actually occur which the genius of Shakespeare has invented; and all good judges, and the most eminent dilettanti,° acknowledged the felicity of Shakespeare's suggestion as soon 80 as it was actually realized. Here, then, was a fresh proof that I had been right in relying on my own feeling in opposition to my understanding; and again I set myself to study the problem. At length I solved it to my own satisfaction; and my solution is this—Murder, in ordinary cases, where the sympathy is wholly directed to the case of the murdered person, is an incident of coarse and vulgar horror; and for this reason—that it flings the interest exclusively upon the natural but ignoble instinct by which we cleave to life: an instinct 90 which, as being indispensable to the primal law of self-preservation, is the same in kind (though different in degree) amongst all living creatures. This instinct, therefore, because it annihilates all distinctions, and degrades the greatest of men to the level of "the poor beetle that we tread on,"° exhibits human nature in its most abject and humiliating attitude. Such an attitude would little suit the purposes of the poet. What then must he do? He must throw the interest on the murderer. Our sympathy° must be with *him* (of course I 100 mean a sympathy of comprehension, a sympathy by which we enter into his feelings, and are made to understand them—not a sympathy of pity or approbation). In the murdered person all strife of thought, all flux and reflux of passion and of purpose, are crushed by one overwhelming panic; the fear of instant death smites him "with its petrific° mace." But in the murderer, such a murderer as a poet will condescend to, there must be raging some great storm of passion—jealousy, ambition, vengeance, hatred—which will 110 create a hell within him; and into this hell we are to look.

In *Macbeth,* for the sake of gratifying his now enormous and teeming faculty of creation, Shakespeare has introduced two murderers: and, as usual in his hands, they are remarkably discriminated: but—though in Macbeth the strife of mind is greater than in his wife, the tiger spirit not so awake, and his feelings caught chiefly by contagion from her—yet, as both were finally involved in the guilt of murder, the mur- 120

51 **quoad his consciousness,** as far as his consciousness is concerned 60 **in 1812.** It was in December 1811; two families were murdered—the Marrs and the Williamsons **Mr. Williams,** John Williams, English seaman and notorious murderer of the early nineteenth century 61 **Ratcliffe Highway,** public thoroughfare in a disreputable quarter of the eastern wharf-district of London 69 **amateur,** here one who makes a study of murders

76 **knocking at the door,** by the servant of the Marrs, who had been sent out to buy oysters 79 **dilettanti,** lovers of the art of murder; literally, lovers of art 96 **the . . . on,** Shakespeare, *Measure for Measure*, III, i, 78 100 **sympathy.** "It seems almost ludicrous to guard and explain my use of a word in a situation where it would naturally explain itself. But it has become necessary to do so, in consequence of the unscholar-like use of the word *sympathy*, at present so general, by which, instead of taking it in its proper sense, as the act of reproducing in our minds the feelings of another, whether for hatred, indignation, love, pity, or approbation, it is made a mere synonym of the word *pity*; and hence, instead of saying 'sympathy *with* another,' many writers adopt the monstrous barbarism of 'sympathy *for* another.'"—De Quincey's note 107 **petrific,** petrifying. The phrase is from *Paradise Lost*, X, 293

derous mind of necessity is finally to be presumed in both. This was to be expressed; and on its own account, as well as to make it a more proportionable antagonist to the unoffending nature of their victim, "the gracious Duncan,"° and adequately to expound "the deep damnation of his taking off,"° this was to be expressed with peculiar energy. We were to be made to feel that the human nature—i.e., the divine nature of love and mercy, spread through the hearts of all creatures, and seldom utterly withdrawn from man—was gone, vanished, extinct, and that the fiendish nature had taken its place. And, as this effect is marvelously accomplished in the *dialogues* and *soliloquies* themselves, so it is finally consummated by the expedient under consideration; and it is to this that I now solicit the reader's attention. If the reader has ever witnessed a wife, daughter, or sister, in a fainting fit, he may chance to have observed that the most affecting moment in such a spectacle is *that* in which a sign and a stirring announce the recommencement of suspended life. Or, if the reader has ever been present in a vast metropolis on the day when some great national idol was carried in funeral pomp to his grave, and, chancing to walk near the course through which it passed, has felt powerfully, in the silence and desertion of the streets and in the stagnation of ordinary business, the deep interest which at that moment was possessing the heart of man—if all at once he should hear the death-like stillness broken up by the sound of wheels rattling away from the scene, and making known that the transitory vision was dissolved, he will be aware that at no moment was his sense of the complete suspension and pause in ordinary human concerns so full and affecting as at that moment when the suspension ceases, and the goings-on of human life are suddenly resumed. All action in any direction is best expounded, measured, and made apprehensible, by reaction. Now apply this to the case in *Macbeth*. Here, as I have said, the retiring of the human heart and the entrance of the fiendish heart was to be expressed and made sensible. Another world has stepped in; and the murderers are taken out of the region of human things, human purposes, human desires. They are transfigured: Lady Macbeth is "unsexed";° Macbeth has forgot that he was born of woman; both are conformed to the image of devils; and the world of devils is suddenly revealed. But how shall this be conveyed and made palpable? In order that a new world may step in, this world must for a time disappear. The murderers, and the murder, must be insulated—cut off by an immeasurable gulf from the ordinary tide and succession of human affairs—locked up and sequestered in some deep recess; we must be made sensible that the world of ordinary life is suddenly arrested—laid asleep—tranced—racked into a dread armistice; time must be annihilated; relation to things without abolished; and

all must pass self-withdrawn into a deep syncope° and suspension of earthly passion. Hence it is that, when the deed is done, when the work of darkness is perfect, then the world of darkness passes away like a pageantry in the clouds: the knocking at the gate is heard, and it makes known audibly that the reaction has commenced; the human has made its reflux upon the fiendish: the pulses of life are beginning to beat again; and the re-establishment of the goings-on of the world in which we live first makes us profoundly sensible of the awful parenthesis that had suspended them.

O mighty poet! Thy works are not as those of other men, simply and merely great works of art, but are also like the phenomena of nature, like the sun and the sea, the stars and the flowers, like frost and snow, rain and dew, hail-storm and thunder, which are to be studied with entire submission of our own faculties, and in the perfect faith that in them there can be no too much or too little, nothing useless or inert, but that, the farther we press in our discoveries, the more we shall see proofs of design and self-supporting arrangement where the careless eye had seen nothing but accident! (1823)

from THE POETRY OF POPE

LITERATURE OF KNOWLEDGE AND LITERATURE OF POWER

What is it that we mean by *literature?* Popularly, and amongst the thoughtless, it is held to include everything that is printed in a book. Little logic is required to disturb *that* definition. The most thoughtless person is easily made aware that in the idea of *literature* one essential element is—some relation to a general and common interest of man, so that what applies only to a local or professional or merely personal interest, even though presenting itself in the shape of a book, will not belong to literature. So far the definition is easily narrowed; and it is as easily expanded. For not only is much that takes a station in books not literature, but, inversely, much that really *is* literature never reaches a station in books. The weekly sermons of Christendom, that vast pulpit literature which acts so extensively upon the popular mind—to warn, to uphold, to renew, to comfort, to alarm—does not attain the sanctuary of libraries in the ten-thousandth part of its extent. The drama, again, as for instance the finest of Shakespeare's plays in England and all leading Athenian plays in the noontide of the Attic stage,° operated as a literature on the public mind, and were (according to the strictest letter of that term) *published* through the audiences° that witnessed their representation, some

125 **the gracious Duncan**, *Macbeth*, III, i, 66   126 **the deep . . . off**, *Macbeth*, I, vii, 20   164 **unsexed**, *Macbeth*, I, v, 42

177 **syncope**, cessation, swoon   **Literature of Knowledge and Literature of Power**   21 **noontide . . . stage,** the time of Aeschylus, Sophocles, and Euripides, famous Greek dramatists of the fifth century B.C.   24 **published . . . audiences.** "Charles I, for example, when *Prince of Wales,* and many others in his father's court, gained their known familiarity with Shakespeare—not through the original quartos, so slenderly diffused, nor through the first folio of 1623, but through the court representations of his chief dramas at Whitehall."—De Quincey's note

time before they were published as things to be read; and they were published in this scenical mode of publication with much more effect than they could have had as books during ages of costly copying or of costly printing.

30 Books, therefore, do not suggest an idea co-extensive and interchangeable with the idea of literature; since much literature, scenic, forensic, or didactic (as from lecturers and public orators), may never come into books, and much that does come into books may connect itself with no literary interest. But a far more important correction, applicable to the common vague idea of literature, is to be sought not so much in a better definition of literature as in a sharper distinction of the two functions which it fulfils. In that great social 40 organ which, collectively, we call literature, there may be distinguished two separate offices that may blend and often do so, but capable, severally, of a severe insulation, and naturally fitted for reciprocal repulsion. There is, first, the literature of *knowledge*, and secondly, the literature of *power*. The function of the first is to *teach*, the function of the second is to *move*; the first is a rudder, the second an oar or a sail. The first speaks to the mere discursive understanding; the second speaks ultimately, it may happen, to the higher 50 understanding or reason, but always through affections of pleasure and sympathy. Remotely, it may travel towards an object seated in what Lord Bacon calls *dry light*;° but, proximately, it does and must operate—else it ceases to be a literature of *power*—on and through that *humid* light which clothes itself in the mists and glittering *iris*° of human passions, desires, and genial emotions. Men have so little reflected on the higher functions of literature as to find it a paradox if one should describe it as a mean or subordinate pur-60 pose of books to give information. But this is a paradox only in the sense which makes it honorable to be paradoxical. Whenever we talk in ordinary language of seeking information or gaining knowledge, we understand the words as connected with something of absolute novelty. But it is the grandeur of all truth which can occupy a very high place in human interests that it is never absolutely novel to the meanest of minds: it exists eternally by way of germ or latent principle in the lowest as in the highest, needing to be 70 developed, but never to be planted. To be capable of transplantation is the immediate criterion of a truth that ranges on a lower scale. Besides which, there is a rarer thing than truth—namely, *power*, or deep sympathy with truth. What is the effect, for instance, upon society, of children? By the pity, by the tenderness, and by the peculiar modes of admiration, which connect themselves with the helplessness, with the innocence, and with the simplicity of children, not only are the primal affections strengthened and continually re-

newed, but the qualities which are dearest in the sight 80 of heaven—the frailty, for instance, which appeals to forbearance, the innocence which symbolizes the heavenly, and the simplicity which is most alien from the worldly—are kept up in perpetual remembrance, and their ideals are continually refreshed. A purpose of the same nature is answered by the higher literature, viz., the literature of power. What do you learn from *Paradise Lost?* Nothing at all. What do you learn from a cookery-book? Something new, something that you did not know before, in every paragraph. But would 90 you therefore put the wretched cookery-book on a higher level of estimation than the divine poem? What you owe to Milton is not any knowledge, of which a million separate items are still but a million of advancing steps on the same earthly level; what you owe is *power*—that is, exercise and expansion to your own latent capacity of sympathy with the infinite, where every pulse and each separate influx is a step upwards, a step ascending as upon a Jacob's ladder° from earth to mysterious altitudes above the earth. *All* the steps of 100 knowledge, from first to last, carry you further on the same plane, but could never raise you one foot above your ancient level of earth: whereas the very *first* step in power is a flight—is an ascending movement into another element where earth is forgotten.

Were it not that human sensibilities are ventilated and continually called out into exercise by the great phenomena of infancy, or of real life as it moves through chance and change, or of literature as it recombines these elements in the mimicries of poetry, 110 romance, etc., it is certain that, like any animal power or muscular energy falling into disuse, all such sensibilities would gradually droop and dwindle. It is in relation to these great *moral* capacities of man that the literature of power, as contradistinguished from that of knowledge, lives and has its field of action. It is concerned with what is highest in man; for the Scriptures themselves never condescended to deal by suggestion or co-operation with the mere discursive understanding: when speaking of man in his intellectual capacity, 120 the Scriptures speak not of the understanding, but of *"the understanding heart"*°—making the heart, i.e., the great *intuitive* (or nondiscursive) organ, to be the interchangeable formula for man in his highest state of capacity for the infinite. Tragedy, romance, fairy tale, or epopee,° all alike restore to man's mind the ideals of justice, of hope, of truth, of mercy, of retribution, which else (left to the support of daily life in its realities) would languish for want of sufficient illustration. 130

What is meant, for instance, by *poetic justice?* It does not mean a justice that differs by its object from the ordinary justice of human jurisprudence, for then it must be confessedly a very bad kind of justice; but it

---

53 **Bacon . . . light.** "Heraclitus the Obscure said: *The dry light was the best soul*—meaning, when the faculties intellectual are in vigor, not wet, nor, as it were, blooded by the affections."—Bacon, *Apothegms New and Old*, 268 56 **iris,** rainbow; from Iris, goddess of the rainbow

99 **Jacob's ladder.** In a dream Jacob beheld a ladder that reached from earth to heaven. See *Genesis*, 28:12 122 **the . . . heart,** *1 Kings*, 3:9, 12: "Give therefore thy servant an understanding heart to judge thy people" 126 **epopee,** epic poem

means a justice that differs from common forensic justice by the degree in which it attains its object—a justice that is more omnipotent over its own ends, as dealing, not with the refractory elements of earthly life, but with the elements of its own creation, and with materials flexible to its own purest preconceptions. It is certain that, were it not for the literature of power, these ideals would often remain amongst us as mere arid notional forms; whereas, by the creative forces of man put forth in literature, they gain a vernal life of restoration, and germinate into vital activities. The commonest novel, by moving in alliance with human fears and hopes, with human instincts of wrong and right, sustains and quickens those affections. Calling them into action, it rescues them from torpor. And hence the pre-eminence over all authors that merely *teach,* of the meanest that *moves,* or that teaches, if at all, indirectly by moving. The very highest work that has ever existed in the literature of knowledge is but a provisional work—a book upon trial and sufferance, and *quamdiu bene se gesserit.*° Let its teaching be even partially revised, let it be but expanded—nay, even let its teaching be but placed in a better order—and instantly it is superseded. Whereas the feeblest works in the literature of power, surviving at all, survive as finished and unalterable amongst men. For instance, the *Principia*° of Sir Isaac Newton was a book militant on earth from the first. In all stages of its progress it would have to fight for its existence: first, as regards absolute truth; secondly, when that combat was over, as regards its form or mode of presenting the truth. And as soon as a Laplace,° or anybody else, builds higher upon the foundations laid by this book, effectually he throws it out of the sunshine into decay and darkness; by weapons won from this book he superannuates and destroys this book, so that soon the name of Newton remains as a mere *nominis umbra,*° but his book, as a living power, has transmigrated into other forms. Now, on the contrary, the *Iliad,*° the *Prometheus* of Aeschylus, the *Othello* or *King Lear,* the *Hamlet* or *Macbeth,* and the *Paradise Lost,* are not militant, but triumphant forever, as long as the languages exist in which they speak or can be taught to speak. They never *can* transmigrate into new incarnations. To reproduce these in new forms, or variations, even if in some things they should be improved, would be to plagiarize. A good steam engine is properly superseded by a better. But one lovely pastoral valley is not superseded by another, nor a statue of Praxiteles by a statue of Michael Angelo.° These things are separated not by imparity but by disparity. They are not

thought of as unequal under the same standard, but as different in *kind,* and, if otherwise equal, as equal under a different standard. Human works of immortal beauty and works of nature in one respect stand on the same footing: they never absolutely repeat each other, never approach so near as not to differ, and they differ not as better and worse, or simply by more and less—they differ by undecipherable and incommunicable differences, that cannot be caught by mimicries, that cannot be reflected in the mirror of copies, that cannot become ponderable in the scales of vulgar comparison.

Applying these principles to Pope as a representative of fine literature in general, we would wish to remark the claim which he has, or which any equal writer has, to the attention and jealous winnowing of those critics in particular who watch over public morals. Clergymen, and all organs of public criticism put in motion by clergymen, are more especially concerned in the just appreciation of such writers, if the two canons are remembered which we have endeavored to illustrate, viz., that all works in this class, as opposed to those in the literature of knowledge, 1st, work by far deeper agencies, and 2dly, are more permanent; in the strictest sense they are κτήματα ἐς ἀεί:° and what evil they do, or what good they do, is commensurate with the national language, sometimes long after the nation has departed. At this hour, five hundred years since their creation, the tales of Chaucer, never equaled on this earth for their tenderness, and for life of picturesqueness, are read familiarly by many in the charming language of their natal day, and by others in the modernisations of Dryden, of Pope, and Wordsworth. At this hour, one thousand eight hundred years since their creation, the Pagan tales of Ovid,° never equaled on this earth for the gayety of their movement and the capricious graces of their narrative, are read by all Christendom. This man's people and their monuments are dust; but *he* is alive: he has survived them, as he told us that he had it in his commission to do, by a thousand years "and *shall* a thousand more."

All the literature of knowledge builds only groundnests, that are swept away by floods, or confounded by the plow; but the literature of power builds nests in aërial altitudes of temples sacred from violation, or of forests inaccessible to fraud. *This* is a great prerogative of the *power* literature; and it is a greater which lies in the mode of its influence. The *knowledge* literature, like the fashion of this world, passeth away. An Encyclopedia is its abstract; and, in this respect, it may be taken for its speaking symbol—that before one generation has passed, an Encyclopedia is superannuated; for it speaks through the dead memory and unimpassioned understanding, which have not the re-

155 **quamdiu . . . gesserit,** as long as it bore itself well   161 **Principia,** *The Mathematical Principles of Natural Philosophy,* published in 1687   166 **Laplace,** French astronomer and mathematician (1749–1827)   171 **nominis umbra,** shadow of a name   173 **Iliad,** the story of the Trojan War, by Homer   184 **Praxiteles . . . Michael Angelo.** The work of the Greek sculptor Praxiteles (fourth century B.C.) is noted for its grace and naturalness; that of the Italian Michelangelo (1475–1564) for its power

210 κτήματα ἐς αεί, permanent possessions   220 **Ovid,** famous Roman storyteller and poet (43 B.C.–A.D. 17)

pose of higher faculties, but are continually enlarging and varying their phylacteries.° But all literature properly so called—literature κατέξοχην°—for the very same reason that it is so much more durable than the literature of knowledge, is (and by the very same proportion it is) more intense and electrically searching in its impressions. The directions in which the tragedy of this planet has trained our human feelings to play, and the combinations into which the poetry of this planet has thrown our human passions of love and hatred, of admiration and contempt, exercise a power for bad or good over human life that cannot be contemplated, when stretching through many generations, without a sentiment allied to awe. And of this let everyone be assured—that he owes to the impassioned books which he has read many a thousand more of emotions than he can consciously trace back to them. Dim by their origination, these emotions yet arise in him and mold him through life, like forgotten incidents of his childhood.

(1848)

241 **phylacteries,** records; literally, boxes containing slips of parchment on which certain passages of scripture are written. They are bound on the forehead and left forearm by Jews at prayer   242 *κατέξοχην, par excellence,* preëminently

The Victorian Age

From the Accession of Victoria to the First World War, 1837–1914

PART 5

Crystal Palace, London, built by Sir Joseph Paxton for the Great Exhibition of 1851

The Victorian age is generally considered to have begun in 1837, the year that Queen Victoria (1819–1901) acceded to the throne. Although Victoria outlived almost everyone of her generation, it might be said that the Victorian age outlived even the queen and did not come to a close until the outbreak of the First World War in 1914. The era was one of rapid growth and social change. All over England, industry grew quickly and large urban centers soon expanded around the new factories. The lower class became more class-conscious, the middle class more powerful, and the upper class more vulnerable. For Victorian society, these changes were accomplished through wide-ranging political and social reform. For Victorian literature, these changes produced an enormous new readership drawn from all classes. The novels of Dickens, the poems of Tennyson and Swinburne, and the plays of Oscar Wilde could all find their own large, appreciative audience. The writers adapted the forms and sensibility of the Romantic period to the facts of modern industrialized life, and in the process achieved an unprecedented popularity and influence.

The Early Victorians

Both the Victorian task and the Victorian achievement have often been caricatured in the twentieth century. Indeed, the word *Victorian* still suggests intolerance, a simplistic belief in progress, sexual repression, and a humorless earnestness. Yet anyone approaching the literature of the period should be wary of such stereotypes. To suggest that the Victorians were intolerant of differences is to ignore the abundance of public debate on such issues as individual liberty, religion, science, evolution, education, and women's rights. These issues were debated not only in professional and intellectual circles, but in the public press. The solutions proposed in these controversies may at times reveal a too earnest and simplistic belief in progress, but they can also reveal the opposite. In Dickens' *David Copperfield*, for example, Mr. Micawber is ever armed with a new plan and an expectation of plenty, yet he is ever disappointed. And Dickens is only one of the many Victorian masters of humor.

While it is generally true that the early and mid-Victorians were prudish about sex, figures like Dr. George R. Drysdale spoke out for sexual realities and needs throughout the period, and many individuals undoubtedly refused to conform to conventional stereotypes. The treatment of sex became increasingly explicit as the century wore on—as in Swinburne's poems of the 1860s and Hardy's notorious novels, *Tess of the D'Urbervilles* (1891) and *Jude the Obscure* (1896). The stereotype of humorlessness is entirely unfounded—as witness the famous humor magazine *Punch;* the prevalence of cartoons, lampoons, comic songs, jokes, and music hall farce; the comic novels of

Queen Victoria, Prince Consort, and Eldest Children (1846), a portrait by Franz X. Winterhalter.

Dickens, Thackeray, and Trollope; and the childish humor of Gilbert and Sullivan's operettas, or Lewis Carroll's *Alice in Wonderland,* and of Edward Lear's nonsense verses.

Queen Victoria herself embodied many of the complexities of the age and has been much misunderstood. Her concern for the propriety of the court has received more emphasis than her realistic awareness of marital problems—the occasional exploitation of wives by their husbands, the difficulties of pregnancies and caring for infants, the advantages of the single life—that her letters to her daughter Vicky reveal. Although Victoria's displeasure with the growing feminist movement was real, her concern for the state of women was equally genuine. When she consented to receive chloroform during childbirth, her decision went against the belief that woman's suffering was imposed by God. Although her decision upset the clergy, the religious Victoria went ahead with an act that set a precedent for English women, many of whom found childbirth more difficult than she. When a well-intentioned clergyman suggested to Victoria after the death of her husband, Prince Albert (1819–1861), that she might console herself by being a Bride of Christ, Victoria replied, "Now that is what I call twaddle." Abandoning a simple view of Queen Victoria can help us escape the oversimplified connotation of the term *Victorian,* for just as there were many sides to the queen, so too there were many sides to her subjects and her age

The Social Challenge

The first decades of Victoria's reign were a time of great social unrest. Poor harvests and economic depressions throughout the 1830s and 1840s created a crisis that came to be known as the "Condition of England" question. Proposed solutions to the question were numerous, but two of the most important came from the Chartists and the anti–Corn Law proponents. Chartism was a radical political movement with a lower-class base. While the middle class received some relief from the Reform Bill of 1832, passed during the reign of William IV, the lower classes soon demanded further action. A People's Charter, or Carta, from which the Chartist movement derived its name, was drawn up. The People's Charter demanded six specific reforms: universal manhood suffrage, vote by ballot, annual Parliaments, payment of members of Parliament, abolition of property qualifications for membership in the House of Commons, and equal electoral districts. Though many of these reforms were eventually enacted by the end of the century, the Chartists themselves never seized political power. The dramatic climax of the movement came in 1848 when the

This cartoon, entitled Capital and Labour, *appeared in the humor magazine* Punch *in the 1840s. The top section of the cartoon satirizes the wealth and leisure of the upper class in nineteenth-century England; the bottom section portrays the poverty and misery of the working class.*

Chartist leader, Feargus O'Connor, gathered 500,000 men on the Kennington Common and threatened to march on Westminster. The government, in turn, rallied 70,000 special constables, augmented by troops, and effectively deflected the Chartists. The movement was once more unsuccessful in 1848 and subsequently declined, partly because of financial scandals in its management.

The anti–Corn Law proponents directed their energies to economic reform. Corn Laws were protective tariffs that prohibited the importation of grain at prices cheaper than the local product. The Corn Laws favored the landowners and hurt factory workers and also factory owners who had to pay higher wages because of the increased price of bread. Finally, in 1846, the Corn Laws were repealed as part of the victory of the industrial over the landowning interests. The industrialists favored free trade, since they knew they could export their products in a world that had not yet caught up with Britain industrially.

Through the next thirty years, the pattern of reform continued under the direction of two men, William Ewart Gladstone (1809–1898), the Liberal, and Benjamin Disraeli (1804–1881), the Conservative, who alternated as prime minister. Gladstone's reforms were aimed primarily toward political institutions, while Disraeli's addressed specific social problems. Gladstone advocated free trade and Home Rule for Ireland—two extremely controversial issues. Educational, judicial, and ballot reforms under Gladstone were followed by further reforms in laborers' rights and sanitation in Disraeli's term. Along with reform came prosperity. London became the financial center of the world. And when Victoria became "Empress of India" in 1876, England's international economic and political supremacy seemed assured.

The Religious Challenge

Political, social, and economic institutions were not the only targets of Victorian reform. The Established (Anglican) Church was under fire from various sides. The Oxford Movement called into question the whole theological and liturgical legitimacy of the Church of England. The Oxford Movement, named for its origin

The Albert Memorial in Kensington Gardens, London, designed by the English architect Sir George Gilbert Scott (1811–1878) as a memorial to Queen Victoria's husband, Prince Albert, who died in 1861. Completed in 1872, the memorial suggests the popularity of the Gothic revival in English architecture.

CAMERA PRESS

at Oxford University, was also called Tractarianism because the Oxford reformers published their doctrines in a series of *Tracts for the Times*, which began in September 1833 and ended with the famous *Tract XC* in 1841. The Tractarians insisted that the Anglican Church was Catholic not Protestant, and wanted to establish its spiritual independence from the increasingly middle-class, liberal state. The movement began under the leadership of John Keble, but found its most powerful supporter in John Henry Newman (1801–1890), fellow of Oriel College at Oxford and vicar of St. Mary's. Like Keble, Newman attacked the national apostasy from the pulpit and wrote many of the *Tracts for the Times*. Newman's *Tract XC* was regarded as a direct challenge to the Church of England, and it ultimately resulted in his resignation (1843) from St. Mary's. Two years later, Newman was received into the Church of Rome. With his conversion the Oxford Movement came to an end, although its influence continued to be felt in the Church of England.

From another quarter came the attack of the Higher Criticism. This movement was influenced by the Continental (particularly German) insistence that Old and New Testament materials came not from God but from cultural sources. Biblical stories were explained as mythic products of certain historical circumstances. Bishop John William Colenso's *Critical Examination of the Pentateuch*, published between 1862 and 1879, carried to the extreme the tendencies of the Higher Criticism, for he concluded that the books of the Pentateuch—and thus *Genesis* and *Exodus*—were forgeries of Hebrew writers, written after the exile of the Jews. While not all the proponents of Higher Criticism were so extreme, the movement challenged the authority of the Bible.

Beginning in the eighteenth century, Methodism had drawn many converts from the Established Church, and its growth in the nineteenth century was remarkable. Others who shared with the Methodists a strong belief in the emotional and biblical basis of religion chose to stay within the Church of England but formed their own separate group characterized as Low Church. Still another challenge to the Established Church was brought by the Broad Church group, which attempted to remedy what they felt was a damaging narrowness in Church doctrine. Men like Thomas Arnold (1795–1842) and Charles Kingsley (1819–1875) sought latitude on theological questions (hence their name "latitudinarian divines") while emphasizing ethical rigor and social consciousness.

To these various movements within Christianity must be added the more general experience of religious anxiety. The widespread phenomenon of a "crisis of faith" brought some Victorians to atheism, others to agnosticism, and still others to an ambivalent stance within their chosen sects. The Victorians differed from their eighteenth-century predecessors in that they *desired* the faith they could no longer maintain. Chris-

Throne (1846) in the House of Lords designed by A. W. N. Pugin (1812–1852), who was instrumental in reviving Gothic architecture in England. Architectural style had religious and moral as well as aesthetic implications in nineteenth-century England. For those Victorians disillusioned by the apparent materialism of their age, Gothic architecture came to symbolize Christianity and the presumed spiritual purity of the Middle Ages.

tianity—intensely felt, anxiously maintained, or finally lost—remained a paramount concern of the nineteenth century.

The Scientific Challenge

Victorian religion found yet another antagonist in science. Many orthodox Victorians still believed that God had created each distinct species and that the creation of the world had taken literally seven days. As the nineteenth century proceeded, such traditional notions of species and time were increasingly questioned. Erasmus Darwin (1731–1802), Charles Darwin's grandfather, had studied the species of botany and had produced in *Zoonomia* (1794–1796) an early exposition of some evolutionary principles. The fossil studies of Charles Lyell (1797–1875) in the 1830s suggested both that species may have evolved and that the world was much older than the Christian tradition held. Though Charles Darwin (1809–1882) first observed the problem of the variation of species in his studies of the Galapagos Islands in the '30s, it was his *Origin of the Species* in 1859 that precipitated full-scale controversy. Darwin maintained that separate species evolve as a result of the principles of natural selection, or survival of the fittest. Many more members of a species are born than can survive; some are endowed by chance with a characteristic essential to survival; they endure and reproduce that characteristic in their children. Contemporaries of Darwin proposed other explanations of the process, but Darwin's theory quickly proved to be the most influential among both scientists and the general public. Darwin allowed Thomas

An English Autumn Afternoon, an oil painting by the English artist Ford Madox Brown (1821–1893), who was associated with the Pre-Raphaelite Brotherhood in the 1850s. Dante Gabriel Rossetti was one of his pupils.

Henry Huxley (1825–1895) to take the lead in the public controversy. In addition to his Oxford debate with Bishop Samuel Wilberforce in 1866, Huxley wrote *Man's Place in Nature* (1863) and *Lay Sermons* (1870) to provide popular, nontechnical expositions of both the biological theory and it geological counterparts. On the side of the conservatives were many clergymen and writers, including Charles Kingsley, who attacked the biologists scathingly in *The Water Babies* (1863). The public debate over evolution marked for many Victorians a radical change in intellectual and religious life.

Dante Gabriel Rossetti's portrait (1855) of Robert Browning.

Early Victorian Literature

The literature of the first four decades of the Victorian period could not help but reflect the social and intellectual controversies of the time. Writers like Matthew Arnold and John Ruskin attacked the problems directly, while others, like Charles Dickens, George Eliot, and Alfred Tennyson, dramatized the challenges and conflicts in their works. The most popular form for this kind of dramatization was undoubtedly the novel; even a powerful politician like Disraeli felt called upon to express himself in this lengthy, fictional form. And though the poetry and prose of the time were certainly distinguished, it was the novel that ultimately proved to be the Victorians' special literary achievement.

Portrait of Tennyson by A. Arnault.

Poetry. The three most important poets of the early Victorian period followed closely the premises of their Romantic predecessors. Robert Browning shared with Shelley the desire to join philosophy and lyricism; Arnold carried forward Wordsworth's concerns with nature and society; Tennyson, in his careful meter and diction, was closest to Keats. Thematically the Victorians put less emphasis than the Romantics on primitivism and revolution, although they continued to be concerned with the past, particularly the medieval past. But the major Victorian themes were loneliness,

religious anxiety, and social change. Matthew Arnold expressed these themes most powerfully. In "Dover Beach," the speaker sees his unbelieving society as on a "darkling plain . . . Where ignorant armies clash by night." In "Stanzas from the Grand Chartreuse," Arnold describes his society as "between two worlds, one dead/and the other powerless to be born." "The Scholar Gypsy" offers one solution to the problem of loneliness, but the price is impossibly high for most people—retreat altogether from the world.

The loss of faith in established religion also contributed to this Victorian sense of loneliness. Tennyson's poem *In Memoriam* represents an attempt to resolve a crisis of belief felt with intensity by so many Victorians. Religious faith no longer consoled, and the vision of nature as "red in tooth and claw" denied also the healing and comforting effects of nature intimated by Wordsworth. The knowledge of extinct species left the individual all the more alone and threatened. The search for consolation in a lonely world made the medieval past seem especially attractive, but even when writers employed medieval settings, as in Tennyson's *Idylls of the King* (1859) and some of William Morris' medieval poems, the landscape was dominated by base human emotions. Art itself could be regarded as a form of escape, but many Victorian poets found themselves torn between their sense of an obligation to guide the public as poetic sages and their desire to lose themselves in their art.

To the Victorian poets, art offered the consolation that comes from recognition of rather than escape from the problems of the time. In the dramatic monologue, they developed a form that could express and contain the thematic elements that concerned them. First, the monologue allowed that exploration of the psyche that a reflective mind found relevant and exciting. Second, the dramatic quality of the form freed poets from what was becoming an increasing burden—the obligation to analyze and speak from the authoritative, virtually omniscient position of sage. It allowed the Victorian poet to suggest a variety of possible truths, forcing the reader to interpret the speaker's personality and moral state, to piece together a reality from a variety of clues.

The monologue creates an intense sense of community with the speaker, since readers must be closely involved with him or her to recognize and understand the conscious and unconscious nuances of the poem. But this form can likewise have a distancing effect, since our insight into the depths of the speaker may reveal unexpected horrors. Tennyson's and Arnold's monologues have the former effect, while Browning's often have the latter. It is Browning's distinctive achievement, however, that he finally has things both ways: our shocking insights in "My Last Duchess" or "Porphyria's Lover" cause us, almost in spite of ourselves, to recognize the universality of evil human traits. In an age when fiction was so popular, the dramatic monologue gave poetry the means to explore—in depth—the realm of character.

The Blessed Damozel, *a painting by Dante Gabriel Rossetti, who attempted to express the Pre-Raphaelite ideal of 'truth to nature' in his paintings as well as in his poetry.*

Oil painting of Matthew Arnold by the English artist George Frederic Watts (1817–1904).

Several individuals and groups rebelled against the conventional qualities of the Victorian poetic establishment. The largest group of rebels was the Pre-Raphaelite Brotherhood. The leaders of this group were Dante Gabriel Rossetti and John Everett Millais (1829–1896); Christina Rossetti and William Morris were also associated with the Brotherhood, and John Ruskin defended it valiantly against hostile reviewers. The P.R.B., as the Brotherhood signed itself, took its name from its objective: fidelity to nature as presented by the later medieval Italian painters before Raphael (1483–1520). The Pre-Raphaelite revolt against eighteenth-century academic painting was essentially

Romantic. But the Pre-Raphaelites' literal presentation of nature differed from that of the earlier Romantics. Indeed, both the painting and poetry of the P.R.B. were particularly Victorian blendings of the Romantic, the realistic, and the supernatural. But because their works contained little of the conventional spiritual and moral qualities of Victorian orthodoxy, the Pre-Raphaelites were vigorously attacked for their sensuousness. To many Victorian readers, Dante Gabriel Rossetti's sensuous Blessed Damozel hardly seemed a disembodied and spiritual figure. Long after its best work was over and the sensational attacks upon it had ceased, the principles and specimens of Pre-Raphaelitism continued to have a strong influence—an influence that can be felt in the early works of poets like William Butler Yeats and T. S. Eliot.

Prose. For the earliest Victorian prose writers, the "Condition of England" question posed by the economic and social turmoil of the '30s and '40s was a central concern. In succeeding decades the criticism of society and the development of the self continued to occupy prose writers. Thomas Carlyle attempted to convince his readers of the decline of the age. His picture of life in the medieval past, particularly in *Past and Present,* shows a life and society far more attractive and unified than contemporary life and society. The florid exaggerations of Carlyle's style may seem awkward and unconvincing today, but his popularity in the Victorian period and his influence on almost all

The embroidered chair (right) *and the stoneware vase* (left), *both decorated with portraits of Queen Victoria, were made in 1851 for the Great Exhibition, an international art exposition held in London. The bamboo-shaped handle and the engraved floral designs on the silver pitcher* (center) *reflect the nineteenth-century interest in Japanese art.*

the important Victorian writers in verse and prose cannot be overestimated. Even John Stuart Mill, whose style is quite the opposite of Carlyle's, was influenced by him. Mill aims for the lucidity and restraint appropriate to highly rational examination. He began from an early Utilitarian position and moved steadily forward to an increased awareness of the limitations of identifying happiness with pleasure, as championed by Jeremy Bentham (1748–1832). Emotional needs, he said, cannot be met by the moral arithmetic of pleasures. In his autobiography Mill argues for "Romantic" values. Autobiography was also the form in which John Henry Newman expressed his sense of the emotional crisis of the age. Newman combined Carlyle's passionate argumentativeness with Mill's love of lucidity in argument to become one of the great prose writers in English literature.

The works of two other Victorian prose writers, John Ruskin and Matthew Arnold, show the Victorian fondness for debating issues and the Victorian fear that prosperity and freedom might destroy, rather than liberate, the arts. Ruskin saw art as a reflection of the moral character of society. He began as a critic of art but eventually turned to broader, direct criticism of the values of society itself. His utter distaste for modern materialism made him so deadly a critic of the middle class that public pressure twice forced *Cornhill Magazine* to discontinue his essays. Matthew Arnold's turn from poetry to prose in his later years sprang from his desire to order the chaos, the potential anarchy, of the new, developing world. Arnold believed that if the energetic activism of "Hebraism" could be joined to the reflective knowledge of "Hellenism," then culture, not anarchy, would result. His writings on education, society, and art reflect his search for principles that he hoped would move society and criticism away from the turmoil of subjectivity.

Fiction.   The High Victorian novel is so ambitious a phenomenon that we can only sketch its development here. Perhaps the most noticeable feature of the Victorian novel is its diversity. It not only includes masterpieces like Thackeray's *Vanity Fair* and Eliot's *Middlemarch* but also an unceasing flow of lesser works. The twentieth-century distinction between "popular fiction" and "literature" was not made in the Victorian period. Victorian readers recognized the intelligence and erudition of a writer like George Eliot—qualities that clearly separated her from the mass of other novelists—but her novels nevertheless sold very well and attracted a wide readership. Moreover, the Victorian period produced a number of novelists whose work today seems to fit somewhere between "popular fiction" and "literature"—novelists like Wilkie Collins (1824–1889), with his exciting and well-constructed *The Woman in White* (1860); Elizabeth Gaskell (1810–1865), with her unfinished *Wives and Daughters* (1865); M. E. Braddon (1837–1915), with her much underrated *Lady Audley's Secret* (1862). All three of these authors wrote for an audience enlarged not only by a sharp rise in literacy but also by an intricate system of publication and sales. Most fiction appeared first in parts or numbers serialized in weekly or monthly periodicals or published separately in installments. After the parts were complete, the public could then either purchase the complete novels in expensive hardback editions or borrow them from enormous and influential libraries.

Victorian novels come in a variety of genres, many of which were derived from Romantic precedents. The immensely popular historical novels of writers like Charles Kingsley and Bulwer-Lytton (1803–1873), for example, owe a clear debt to Sir Walter Scott. Less melodramatic than either writer is Charles Reade, whose *The Cloister and the Hearth* (1861) achieves true power in its presentation of fifteenth-century Europe. The premier Victorian novelists contributed to the historical genre, but neither Dickens' *A Tale of Two Cities* (1859) nor Eliot's *Romola* (1865) represents either author's best work. Dickens rarely transcends the sensational and sentimental, and Eliot's historical accuracy becomes heavy and self-conscious. Thackeray's *The History of Henry Esmond* (1852), on the other hand, is perhaps the greatest historical novel in English. His sympathy for the eighteenth century allowed him to imitate neoclassical prose so accurately that the period seems to come to life not merely in descriptions of costume or events but in the very tones of speech and rhythm of prose. And in young Esmond's startling marriage to a woman old enough to be his mother, Thackeray manages to introduce a psychological complexity so often absent from this genre.

The motifs of Gothic fiction also found their way into the Victorian novel, and two authors raised the genre above even the highest Romantic standards. Emily Brontë's (1818–1848) *Wuthering Heights* (1847) is one of the finest novels of the century. It is a masterful combination of Gothic motifs, the Byronic hero, a wild romantic feeling of elemental nature, and a quietly subversive view of institutional Christianity. Less well known today is the work of Joseph Sheridan Le Fanu (1814–1873). Le Fanu's novels, such as *The*

Portrait of Emily Brontë done by her brother, Patrick (1817–1848).

House by the Churchyard (1863) and *Uncle Silas* (1864), were immensely popular, but his short stories truly establish him as a master of the Gothic genre. "Carmilla" (1872) in particular blends conventional vampire lore and psychological insight with a compression of detail and mastery of image.

Victorian interest in the quality of social life led to a flowering of the novel of romance. Aside from George Eliot, who will be discussed later, four writers were preeminent. Elizabeth Gaskell produces a charming picture of village life in *Cranford* (1853) and a complex study of family life in *Wives and Daughters* (1865). The novels of Anthony Trollope (1815–1882) take place in the fictional world of Barsetshire where the intricacies of clerical and domestic life are chronicled with accuracy, sympathy, and wit. In novels like *Jane Eyre* (1847) and *Villette* (1853), Charlotte Brontë (1816–1855) chronicles the daily lives of "ordinary" young women, but goes beyond earlier novelists of manners in insisting upon the passions (largely sexual) that exist beneath the polite surfaces of these seemingly simple heroines. The novels of George Meredith (1828–1909) also follow this subversive tradition. In *The Ordeal of Richard Feverel* (1859) he takes a conventional situation—a young person growing to maturity—and introduces major, finally unreconcilable conflicts between the natural impulses of youth and the repressive educational system of an overbearing father. Like Charlotte Brontë, Meredith presents with painful directness the anguish of contemporary sexuality. In his masterpiece, *The Egoist* (1879), Meredith employs a complex style and intricate image patterns that bring to the Victorian novel an almost poetic density.

Unquestionably, the three great masters of the Victorian novel were Charles Dickens (1817–1870), William Thackeray (1811–1863), and George Eliot (1819–1880). Of the three, Dickens was the most popular with the Victorian public and is probably the most difficult to evaluate today. For Dickens cannot really be judged by later critical standards, particularly those that emphasize economy of design and compression of detail. His is a different, more all-inclusive, more loosely woven type of art. Also, Dickens' novels are often read superficially; readers who are fascinated by his picturesque types and social "realities" often fail to see that beneath the well-known colorful surface are all the repressed drives of the Victorian period: incest, crime, desires to inflict and receive pain, adulation of and antagonism toward women. This father of ten children, who left his wife and took up with a young actress, wrote novels in which Victorian realities were in constant conflict with Victorian orthodoxies. *Bleak House* (1853), for example, ends with a happy couple, but as in most good comedies, their marriage does not resolve the social and psychological issues raised by the work. Even after his vision darkened and his personal life became more

work suffers from an increasing need to preach, he continued to experiment with form throughout his career.

George Eliot (born Mary Ann Evans) was perhaps the most learned of the great Victorian novelists. She translated the writings of the avant-garde German religious philosopher Ludwig Feuerbach (1804–1872), knew the positivist writings of the French philosopher Auguste Comte (1798–1857) thoroughly, and worked on the radical *Westminster Review*. What makes her best work so attractive is her ability to blend erudition with a profound love of nature and mankind. In *Adam Bede* (1859) Eliot combines contemporary Victorian themes of the fallen woman and Methodism with a reverence for rural life. In *The Mill on the Floss* (1860) nature is again powerfully present; it provides the setting for the conflicting emotions of a girl growing to maturity. In *Middlemarch* (1871–1872), Eliot portrays her belief that human aspiration is limited but not extinguished by contemporary life. The heroine of the novel, Dorothea Brooke, survives initial failures and achieves a life of unobtrusive service. In the process, Eliot celebrates the power of this unobtrusive service which allows everyone a chance for real, if limited heroism. Eliot's interweaving of multiple plots, her complex patterning of imagery, and her development of social and philosophical issues in *Middlemarch* make it the most intelligent and carefully wrought British novel of the period.

The Late Victorians

By the end of 1880, Eliot, Dickens, and Thackeray were dead, and the early Victorian era portrayed in their novels was likewise drawing to a close. The decades leading to the First World War saw new, steadily more violent upheaval on the domestic and foreign fronts. A fall in profit margins and increased competition from foreign markets (U.S. wheat in particular) made the economic outlook less positive than in earlier decades. Like Germany, France, and Belgium, England moved aggressively to expand its colonial empire. Earlier in the period, its foreign possessions had often seemed a liability, and the notion of eventual self-rule for the colonies had often been discussed. Enormous profits, however, now made foreign holdings seem more attractive, but these holdings also meant more foreign entanglements. The South African Boer War (1899–1902), a war notable for both its unpopularity at home and the inability of the British to immediately defeat the smaller forces of the Boers, was a direct result of England's push for territorial holdings.

Though the Third Reform Bill in 1884 extended the franchise again, adding more voters than the First and Second Reform Bills combined, political unrest grew. From the 1870s onward the long-exploited working

THE TATE GALLERY, LONDON

The Awakening Conscience *(1853), by the English artist William Holman Hunt (1827–1910), one of the founders of the Pre-Raphaelite Brotherhood in 1848. The painting is filled with symbolic details such as the cat and bird* (lower left) *and the musical score* (on the floor) *of Tennyson's poem "Tears, Idle Tears."*

complicated, Dickens tried desperately to make inherently tragic materials fit the English comic novel tradition, as in his last complete novel, *Our Mutual Friend* (1865).

Thackeray too struggled to adapt the form of the novel to his unique and evolving personality. Victorians considered him a merciless satirist who exposed the foibles of contemporary society. If today Thackeray sometimes seems too sentimental, the Victorian judgment remains accurate to this extent: Thackeray at his best recognizes and castigates many of the shams upon which society rests. In his greatest novel, the satirical *Vanity Fair* (1847–1848), Thackeray refuses both to elevate the heroine onto the traditional pedestal and to inflict upon her antagonist complete defeat. *Vanity Fair* is, as Thackeray says in the subtitle, a "novel without a hero." Although Thackeray's late

Too Early, an oil painting by James Jacques Tissot (1836–1902), a French artist who lived in London in the 1870s and who is famous for his many scenes of fashionable Victorian society.

classes achieved greater organization and power, particularly in the Trades Union Congress. Yet widespread poverty continued. In 1901, the social philanthropist Seebohm Rowntree (1871–1954), concluded in *Poverty: A Study of Town Life* that over 30 percent of the population of England lived below the poverty line. For the working-class poor, the increasing attraction of socialism eventually led to the formation of the Labour party in 1906. While the Labour party never gained

control of Parliament during the Victorian period, it did manage to aid the passage of valuable legislation such as the National Insurance Act of 1911, which provided workers with basic health and unemployment insurance.

At the same time, the Women's Rights Movement continued to gather strength. The Women's Social and Political Union, founded in 1903 and led by Emmeline (1858–1928) and Christobel (1880–1958) Pankhurst,

Lord Curzon (1859–1925), viceroy of India from 1898 to 1905, is pictured (seated, center) *with his first wife* (seated, fifth from left) *and with Indian notables in this photograph taken around the turn of the century, when British colonialism was at its height.*

WILLIAM MORRIS GALLERY

WILLIAM MORRIS GALLERY

William Morris was a craftsman and designer as well as a poet. He attempted in his designs to combine functional and aesthetic values to produce a useful art for all people, not just for wealthy patrons. William Morris and Company, a crafts firm formed in 1861 by Morris and some of his friends (including D. G. Rossetti), designed and produced furniture like the Sussex rush-seated chair (right) and objects of high craftsmanship like the candleholders, tiles, and embroidery (left). In addition, Morris established the Kelmscott Press in 1891 and developed an exquisite medieval bookmaking technique, as shown in these pages (top) from the Kelmscott edition of Chaucer's Canterbury Tales.

conducted an increasingly violent campaign for women's suffrage—a campaign that was not successful until the close of the First World War. Meanwhile, the Irish Question, unresolved throughout the century, also moved toward open warfare. The Act of Union in 1801 had insisted on England's supremacy and Ireland's subjection. Daniel O'Connell (1775–1847) and Charles Stewart Parnell (1846–1891) became powerful forces for independence, but neither succeeded. O'Connell failed because he was too early; Parnell, because involvement in a divorce case ruined him politically in Catholic Ireland. The House of Lords supported Protestant Northern Ireland and blocked repeated efforts to pass a Home Rule Bill. The agitation resulting from this impasse focused attention on the House of Lords, the traditional, ultra-conservative house of Parliament. In 1911 the Lords' veto power was removed, and a Home Rule Bill was passed (1914) amid much turbulence. The outbreak of the First World War, however, postponed freedom for Southern Ireland.

Victoria died in 1901, and her son Edward VII (1841–1910) proved to be an unexpectedly able leader. Edward devoted himself to strengthening Britain against the tremendous expansive force of the new German Empire. He worked to establish defensive alliances with other European nations to achieve a balance of power. This balance, however, proved too precarious to last. Four years after the death of Edward VII and the accession of his son George V (1865–1936), the First World War shook the world.

Late Victorian Literature

The literature of this transitional period was, not surprisingly, a literature of revolt—a revolt against what now seemed the earlier generation's smugness about their own achievements. The nature of the revolt can best be explained in terms of its extremes: realism and aestheticism. Realism had long been an essential part of English literature. Wordsworth and his eighteenth-century predecessors had attempted to portray nature and the common man as they existed in real life, and early Victorian novelists had detailed social abuses as precisely as possible. This tradition created a receptive climate for the theory of naturalism expressed by French writers, especially in Emile Zola's (1840–1902) prefaces and novels. Naturalism asserts that all consequences are the inevitable result of natural causes, and it instructs the writer to devote himself, like the scientist, to the credible portrayal of natural causes. Some naturalistic writers overcorrected the romantic tendencies of their fellow writers and often dealt exclusively with the seamy side of life. This is perhaps truer of the French than of the British, for few British writers accepted the full philosophical implications of Naturalism. What the British did maintain was a realistic point of view and a fierce determination to present the world in all its cruelty and sorrow.

At the other extreme was the Aesthetic Movement, which came to a climax in the last decade of the nineteenth century. "Art for art's sake," the credo of the Aesthetic Movement, developed from various sources. It was a popular notion earlier in France, for example, flowering in the theories of Theophile Gautier (1811–1872) and the practice of Gustave Flaubert (1821–1880). In England the Pre-Raphaelite Brotherhood had earlier exalted art and the artist; and though John Ruskin was both a realist and a moralist, he placed art at the center of life and made art the criterion for judging the quality of a society. Walter Pater, in his "Conclusion" to *Studies in the History of the Renaissance* (1873), emphasizes the subjectivity of experience and the need for fidelity to that experience through "art for art's sake." In the 1890s, aestheticism, dandyism, and art for art's sake were all parts of the revolt against the Victorian notion that art should serve only moral, social, and religious ends. The Aesthetic Movement was never large, but its writers were widely

The Private View at the Royal Academy (1881), a painting by William Powell Frith (1819–1909), an artist known for his realistic scenes of nineteenth-century social gatherings. Among the eminent Victorians pictured here are William Gladstone, Robert Browning, Anthony Trollope, and Oscar Wilde.

The Rape of the Lock *(1896), an illustration for Pope's mock-heroic poem of the same name, by the late Victorian English artist Aubrey Beardsley (1872–1898), noted for his black-and-white drawings of elongated, caricatured figures. Beardsley sympathized with the ideals of the Aesthetic Movement; many of his illustrations were published in the Movement's major periodical,* The Yellow Book.

read. Indeed, the Movement's first major periodical, *The Yellow Book* (1894–1897) quickly achieved an international reputation. The aesthetes were led by Oscar Wilde (1854–1900), whose epigrammatic brilliance made him a celebrity and whose sensational trial and imprisonment for homosexual offenses effectively ruined him. It also crippled a movement that has since been parodied repeatedly, but its achievements should not be underrated. Its fiction, poetry, and art have stood the test of time; and its precepts have led to the symbolism that characterizes some of the best twentieth-century literature.

Poetry. In their preference for aestheticism over realism, many English poets of the late Victorian period sought to convey their impressions by suggestion, as the French symbolist poets did, rather than by direct expression. Though more of these writers were impressionists than symbolists in the French sense, they shared the French desire to escape the commonplace and to convey delicately the mysterious spirit of a scene or feeling. Several poets, including Lionel Johnson (1867–1902), Ernest Dowson (1867–1900), Arthur Symons (1865–1945), and William

Butler Yeats, formed The Rhymers' Club in London in 1890. According to Yeats, the Rhymers endeavored "to express life at its intense moments alone." Gerard Manley Hopkins, an impressionist and Catholic mystic, combined a profound feeling for God ("God's Grandeur") and human suffering ("The Wreck of the Deutschland") with a brilliant capacity for formal innovation and turning natural objects into symbols ("The Windhover") to produce some of the finest poems in the language.

Fiction. With the exception of Oscar Wilde, whose short stories and novel, *The Picture of Dorian Grey* (1891), are really grounded in the Aesthetic Movement, most major late Victorian novelists practiced a kind of realism that approached naturalism. One of the most remarkable of these was Samuel Butler (1835–1902). After graduating from Cambridge and spending some years in New Zealand as a sheep rancher, Butler returned to England to settle down as a journalist and miscellaneous writer. His Utopian satire, *Erehwon* ("nowhere" spelled backwards), written in 1872, is a Swift-like attack on what he conceives to be the universal stagnation of thought that had settled on mid-Victorian England. His other novel, *The Way of All Flesh*, published posthumously in 1903, is a bitter attack on Victorian worship of the family as an institution.

George Gissing (1857–1903) infused into his novels much of the pessimism that he acquired from experience, from Zola, and from the German philosopher Schopenhauer (1788–1860). His early novels, such as *Workers of the Dawn* (1880) and *The Nether World* (1889), are studies of the industrial poor. Though he is better known for his semiautobiographical works, *The New Grub Street* (1891) and *The Private Papers of Henry Ryecroft* (1903), his novel on the plight of women, *The Odd Women* (1893), is in some respects his most complex creation and is only now receiving the attention it deserves.

Thomas Hardy (1840–1928) carried on Eliot's concern for rural life and Trollope's desire to fashion a fictional world (Hardy created Wessex as Trollope did Barsetshire) but with a particularly late Victorian naturalistic tone. In Hardy's universe, the natural and social environment combine to create for the individual a fate that he or she cannot escape. Human efforts often seem puny and ridiculous. At his best, Hardy unites a poetic instinct for image and a thorough knowledge of rural life. His strongest novels are unequalled in this period; his *Tess of the D'Urbervilles* (1891) stands as one of the most powerful novels of the century.

The second generation of late Victorian novelists carried naturalistic themes into the twentieth century. Arnold Bennett (1867–1931) and John Galsworthy (1867–1933), for example, were immensely popular in

This Victorian drawing room (c. 1890–1900) shows the Victorian taste for lavish brocade upholstery, gilt picture frames, ferns, and dark-paneled woodwork.

their time. In *The Old Wives Tale* (1908) Bennett shows a remarkable fidelity to detail and demonstrates journalistic genius. Galsworthy's two novel series, *The Forsyte Saga* (1906–1921) and *A Modern Comedy* (1929), provide a thorough analysis of the propertied man of the late Victorian period. Ironically, another naturalistic novelist, H. G. Wells (1866–1946), is popular today mainly because of his science-fiction works, *The Time Machine* (1895) and *The War of the Worlds* (1898); in his own time Wells' social novels, such as *Kipps* (1905) and *Tono-Bungay* (1909), were both popular and influential.

Drama. Like late Victorian novelists, late Victorian dramatists attempted to present life realistically. Just as English impressionists were influenced by the French symbolists and the English naturalists were influenced by Zola, English playwrights were influenced by the new naturalism of the great Norwegian dramatist Henrik Ibsen (1828–1906). In *A Doll's House* (1879), Ibsen dramatizes the problem of a woman who is forced to leave her egoistic husband in order to preserve her integrity and self-respect. In *Ghosts* (1881), he rejects the assertion that man and wife must remain inseparable; the tragedy results from a wife's conventional and lying loyalty to a worthless husband. Ibsen was initially quite unpopular in England, but since the

Walter Sickert's (1860–1942) Post-Impressionistic painting *Ennui* (1913), one of his many famous scenes depicting life in Camden Town, London.

THE FRICK COLLECTION

Portrait entitled Mrs. Frederick R. Leyland *done by the American-born artist James McNeill Whistler (1834–1903). His technique in painting the prominent British art patron shows both Impressionistic and Japanese influences.*

direct and frank treatment of human relationships had become common in the late Victorian novel, themes similar to his found their way into the theater of the 1890s.

Sir Henry Arthur Jones (1851–1929) and Sir Arthur Wing Pinero (1855–1929) were the leading society dramatists between 1890 and 1910. Most of their plays are concerned with social relationships and social problems. Pinero's most celebrated play, *The Second Mrs. Tanqueray* (1893), deals with the problem of whether a woman with a past can be admitted to polite society.

Another popular late Victorian dramatist, Oscar Wilde, rarely wrote plays that dealt with social problems directly. Though his *Lady Windermere's Fan* (1892) and *A Woman of No Importance* (1893) skirt social situations, they alternate between brilliant epigrams and melodramatic plots. Wilde's masterpiece, *The Importance of Being Earnest* (1895), is pure comedy—though one can detect a satire of Victorian earnestness. *The Importance of Being Earnest* ranks among the most brilliant and perfect comedies in English.

Although many writers at the turn of the century were moving gradually toward a complete rejection of earlier Victorian ideals, the final blow to the Victorian age did not come until the outbreak of the First World War in August 1914. For the next four years, novelists, poets, and dramatists directed their energies primarily to the war efforts. After the Armistice in November 1918, they returned to a changed world. The British empire was badly shaken, the Labour party was rising to prominence, and the landed aristocracy was losing its political power. The ideals and forms popular with the Romantics and Victorians no longer seemed adequate in this radically different society. Formal refinement was abandoned for formal experiment as writers attempted to develop new kinds of works and a new kind of language to express their disillusionment with the war and the civilization that had produced the war.

THOMAS CARLYLE
1795–1881

Though born in the same year as Keats, Carlyle is nevertheless grouped with younger writers because he added to the Romantic world view new, distinctively Victorian preoccupations. Carlyle, it should also be remembered, outlived Charles Dickens, William Makepeace Thackeray, and John Stuart Mill.

Carlyle was born in Ecclefechan, a village in southern Scotland. The son of a mason with strong Calvinist convictions, he was raised in a strict household. He attended his village school, was sent to Annan Academy, and eventually entered the University of Edinburgh (1809). His father intended him to enter the ministry of the Scottish Church, but Carlyle decided against it. Similarly, he gave up schoolteaching after a year's trial. He tried law at Edinburgh in 1819, but gave it up after three years. He seems at this time to have gone through a period of despondency and religious doubt.

About 1821 Carlyle underwent conversion to the Romantic world view, which he described later in fictionalized form in *Sartor Resartus*. He also began studying German thought and philosophy, especially the poets Schiller (1759–1805) and Goethe (1749–1832); he wrote a biography of Schiller in 1823–1824 and translated Goethe's novel *Wilhelm Meister* (1824). These works were followed by a series of articles on German literature which appeared in various periodicals in 1827. In 1826 Carlyle married Jane Welsh, and the two retired to her farm at Craigenputtock for a period of six years. During this time Carlyle worked on his fictionalized autobiography, *Sartor Resartus*, and wrote articles for the *Edinburgh Review*.

In 1834 the Carlyles moved to the Chelsea area of London. There he began work on an ambitious historical project, *The French Revolution*. The partially completed manuscript, lent to John Stuart Mill, was accidentally destroyed in a fire (1835). After working furiously for two more years, Carlyle finally published it to great popular and critical acclaim. Because of the success of *The French Revolution* (1837), Carlyle gave a series of public lectures. Of these the most famous were those on *Heroes, Hero-Worship, and the Heroic in History*, delivered in 1840 and published in 1841; they saliently expressed Carlyle's belief in individualism and the importance of great men to society and culture. *Chartism* (1839) and the *Latter-Day Pamphlets* (1850) presented his economic and social-political theories. *Past and Present* (1843) elaborated upon his earlier notions about the importance of the hero and of an organically unified society. Carlyle, naturally turning to Cromwell as the greatest English example of his ideal man, produced *The Letters and Speeches of Oliver Cromwell* in 1845. Likewise he focused upon another of his heroes in his biographical *History of Frederick II of Prussia, Called Frederick the Great* (1858–1865). Carlyle believed history to be "the essence of innumerable biographies."

In 1865 Carlyle was elected Lord Rector of Edinburgh University. Soon thereafter, Jane Carlyle died; he never completely recovered from her death. He lived the life of a partial recluse in the last fifteen years of his life. Although he published *The Early Kings of Norway* and *Portraits of John Knox* in 1875, he wrote comparatively little in his last years. He died in London in 1881 and was buried beside his parents at Ecclefechan.

Reared in an era of revolutionary change, when the old order was yielding to the new in an atmosphere of physical violence and philosophical chaos, Carlyle searched for a few basic premises which would give order to the social change he saw as necessary. He was a romantic by temperament and an iconoclast by necessity; every drift of nineteenth-century development ran contrary to his perception of what was right. Already forty-two when Victoria ascended the throne, he was virtually alone, deprived of the psychological reinforcement of sympathetic contemporaries. But he was popular with the younger generation of writers taking shape in the 1830s and 1840s—Dickens, Tennyson, Arnold, and Ruskin. Carlyle, especially the Carlyle of *Sartor Resartus* and *Past and Present* was, as Thomas Henry Huxley said, "a source of intellectual invigoration and moral stimulus and refreshment." It is not an exaggeration to say that Carlyle sensitized the social conscience of a whole generation of English writers.

The strong quality of Carlyle's personality finds natural reflection in the style of his writing. He was a nineteenth-century prophet whose style was—as Mill said—"an insane rhapsody." It has an echo of the utterances of the Old Testament prophets and abounds in vigorous figures of speech; it reflects Carlyle's fierce indignation and passionate love of truth.

from SARTOR RESARTUS

Sartor Resartus, Carlyle's "spiritual autobiography," is the best example of his social philosophy and prose style. The title means "The Tailor Retailored," and the "clothes philosophy" of the first part Carlyle took from Swift's similar ideas in *A Tale of a Tub*. *Sartor Resartus* is not a narrative in the ordinary sense of the word; it is a philosophical romance. The first part sets forth the idea that the universe is to be considered as "a large suit of clothes which invests everything"; the second is an autobiographical romance in which Carlyle, under the figure of a philosophical German named Diogenes Teufelsdröckh (God-begotten devil's dung), Professor of Things in General at the University of Weissnichtwo

(I know not where), sets forth his own spiritual doubts. In this second part Carlyle tells the story of his conversion in three chapters—"The Everlasting No," in which he rediscovers his will in his ability to defy the universe; "The Center of Indifference," in which he pursues experience for its own sake; and "The Everlasting Yea," in which he arrives at his new Romantic affirmations. The material and the style of this astonishing production kept some publishers from considering it; ultimately it appeared in *Fraser's Magazine* in 1833–1834. It nearly wrecked the magazine: subscriptions fell off, and critics damned it, one writer summarizing it as "a heap of clotted nonsense." It survived this storm of adverse criticism, however, and appeared in book form in New York in 1836 and in London in 1838. The "cracked and crazed" style, an "insane rhapsody" of figures, Germanisms, unusual words and phrases, increased its unpopularity. The style, however, had its desired effect, for it shocked a generation into a revision of its thoughts and actions.

THE EVERLASTING NO

Under the strange nebulous envelopment, wherein our Professor has now shrouded himself,° no doubt but his spiritual nature is nevertheless progressive, and growing for how can the "Son of Time," in any case, stand still? We behold him, through those dim years, in a state of crisis, of transition: his mad Pilgrimings, and general solution into aimless Discontinuity, what is all this but a mad Fermentation; wherefrom, the fiercer it is, the clearer product will one day evolve itself?

10 Such transitions are ever full of pain: thus the Eagle when he molts is sickly; and, to attain his new beak, must harshly dash-off the old one upon rocks. What Stoicism soever our Wanderer, in his individual acts and motions, may affect, it is clear that there is a hot fever of anarchy and misery raging within; coruscations of which flash out: as, indeed, how could there be other? Have we not seen him disappointed, bemocked of Destiny, through long years? All that the young heart might desire and pray for has been denied; nay,

20 as in the last worst instance, offered and then snatched away. Ever an "excellent Passivity"; but of useful, reasonable Activity, essential to the former as Food to Hunger, nothing granted: till at length, in this wild Pilgrimage, he must forcibly seize for himself an Activity, though useless, unreasonable. Alas, his cup of bitterness, which had been filling drop by drop, ever since that first "ruddy morning" in the Hinterschlag Gymnasium, was at the very lip; and then with that poison-drop, of the Towgood-and-Blumine business,° it

30 runs over, and even hisses over in a deluge of foam.

He himself says once, with more justice than origi-

nality: "Man is, properly speaking, based upon Hope; he has no other possession but Hope; this world of his is emphatically the 'Place of Hope.' " What, then, was our Professor's possession? We see him, for the present, quite shut-out from Hope; looking not into the golden orient, but vaguely all round into a dim copper firmament, pregnant with earthquake and tornado.

Alas, shut-out from Hope, in a deeper sense than we yet dream of! For, as he wanders wearisomely through 40 this world, he has now lost all tidings of another and higher. Full of religion, or at least of religiosity, as our Friend has since exhibited himself, he hides not that, in those days, he was wholly irreligious: "Doubt had darkened into Unbelief," says he; "shade after shade goes grimly over your soul, till you have the fixed, starless, Tartarean black.°" To such readers as have reflected, what can be called reflecting, on man's life, and happily discovered, in contradiction to much Profit-and-Loss Philosophy,° speculative and practical, 50 that Soul is *not* synonymous with Stomach; who understands, therefore, in our Friend's words, "that, for man's well-being, Faith is properly the one thing needful; how, with it, Martyrs, otherwise weak, can cheerfully endure the shame and the cross; and without it, Worldlings puke-up their sick existence, by suicide, in the midst of luxury": to such it will be clear that, for a pure moral nature, the loss of his religious Belief was the loss of everything. Unhappy young man! All wounds, the crush of long-continued Destitu- 60 tion, the stab of false Friendship and of false Love, all wounds in thy so genial heart, would have healed again, had not its life-warmth been withdrawn. Well might he exclaim, in his wild way: "Is there no God, then; but at best an absentee God, sitting idle, ever since the first Sabbath, at the outside of his Universe, and *see*ing it go?° Has the word Duty no meaning; is what we call Duty no divine Messenger and Guide, but a false earthly Fantasm, made-up of Desire and Fear, of emanations from the Gallows and from Doctor 70 Graham's° Celestial-Bed? Happiness of an approving Conscience! Did not Paul of Tarsus,° whom admiring men have since named Saint, feel that *he* was 'the chief of sinners'; and Nero of Rome,° jocund in spirit (*wohlgemuth*)°, spend much of his time in fiddling? Foolish Wordmonger and Motive-grinder, who in thy Logic-mill hast an earthly mechanism for the Godlike itself, and wouldst fain grind me out Virtue from the husks of Pleasure—I tell thee, Nay! To the unregenerate Prometheus Vinctus° of a man, it is ever the bit- 80 terest aggravation of his wretchedness that he is conscious of Virtue, that he feels himself the victim not of suffering only, but of injustice. What then? Is the heroic inspiration we name Virtue but some Passion;

47 **Tartarean black**, black as hell   50 **Profit-and-loss Philosophy,** Utilitarianism   64–67 **Is there . . . seeing it go,** allusion to eighteenth-century Deism   71 **Dr. Graham,** James Graham (1745–1794), a quack, professed to having invented a bed to cure sterility in married people   72 **Paul of Tarsus,** St. Paul, in *1 Timothy*, 1:15   74 **Nero of Rome,** the Emperor Nero, who fiddled while Rome burned (Tacitus' *Annals*, xiv, 14)   75 **wohlgemuth,** cheerful   80 **Prometheus Vinctus,** *Prometheus Bound*, a play by Aeschylus

The Everlasting No   1–2 **strange . . . himself,** that is, like the Wandering Jew, he is living out his sorrows, preparing for his "Altercation with the Devil"   29 **Towngood . . . business.** Teufelsdröckh had been thrown into a state of spiritual negation by the loss of his sweetheart, Blumine, to his friend Towngood

some bubble of the blood, bubbling in the direction others *profit* by? I know not: only this I know, If what thou namest Happiness be our true aim, then are we all astray. With Stupidity and sound Digestion man may front much. But what, in these dull unimaginative days, are the terrors of Conscience to the diseases of the Liver! Not on Morality, but on Cookery, let us build our stronghold: there brandishing our frying-pan, as censer, let us offer sweet incense to the Devil, and live at ease on the fat things *he* has provided for his Elect!''

Thus has the bewildered Wanderer to stand, as so many have done, shouting question after question into the Sibyl-cave of Destiny, and receive no Answer but an echo. It is all a grim Desert, this once-fair world of his; wherein is heard only the howling of wild-beasts, or the shrieks of despairing, hate-filled men; and no Pillar of Cloud by day, and no Pillar of Fire by night,° any longer guides the Pilgrim. To such length has the spirit of Inquiry carried him. ''But what boots it (*was thut's*)?'' cries he: ''it is but the common lot in this era. Not having come to spiritual majority prior to the *Siècle de Louis Quinze,*° and not being born purely a Loghead (*Dummkopf*), thou hadst no other outlook. The whole world is, like thee, sold to Unbelief; their old Temples of the Godhead, which for long have not been rainproof, crumble down; and men ask now: where is the Godhead; our eyes never saw him?''

Pitiful enough were it, for all these wild utterances, to call our Diogenes° wicked. Unprofitable servants as we all are, perhaps at no era of his life was he more decisively the Servant of Goodness, the Servant of God, than even now when doubting God's existence. ''One circumstance I note,'' says he: ''after all the nameless woe that Inquiry, which for me, what it is not always, was genuine Love of Truth, had wrought me, I nevertheless still loved Truth, and would bate no jot of my allegiance to her. 'Truth!' I cried, 'though the Heavens crush me for following her: no Falsehood! though a whole celestial Lubberland° were the price of Apostasy.' In conduct it was the same. Had a divine Messenger from the clouds, or miraculous Handwriting on the wall,° convincingly proclaimed to me *This thou shalt do,* with what passionate readiness, as I often thought, would I have done it, had it been leaping into the infernal Fire. Thus, in spite of all Motive-grinders, and Mechanical Profit-and-Loss Philosophies, with the sick ophthalmia and hallucination they had brought on, was the Infinite nature of Duty still dimly present to me: living without God in the world, of God's light I was not utterly bereft; if my as yet sealed eyes with their unspeakable longing, could nowhere see Him, nevertheless in my heart He was present, and His heaven-written Law still stood legible and sacred there.''

Meanwhile, under all these tribulations, and temporal and spiritual destitutions, what must the Wanderer, in his silent soul, have endured! ''The painfullest feeling,'' writes he, ''is that of your own Feebleness (*Unkraft*); ever, as the English Milton says, to be weak is the true misery.° And yet of your Strength there is and can be no clear feeling, save by what you have prospered in, by what you have done. Between vague wavering Capability and fixed indubitable Performance, what a difference! A certain inarticulate Self-consciousness dwells dimly in us; which only our Works can render articulate and decisively discernible. Our Works are the mirror wherein the spirit first sees its natural lineaments. Hence, too, the folly of that impossible Precept, *Know thyself,*° till it be translated into this partially possible one, *Know what thou canst work at.*

''But for me, so strangely unprosperous had I been, the net-result of my Workings amounted as yet simply to—Nothing. How then could I believe in my Strength, when there was as yet no mirror to see it in? Ever did this agitating, yet, as I now perceive, quite frivolous question, remain to me insoluble: Hast thou a certain Faculty, a certain Worth, such even as the most have not; or art thou the completest Dullard of these modern times? Alas, the fearful Unbelief is unbelief in yourself; and how could I believe? Had not my first, last Faith in myself, when even to me the Heavens seemed laid open, and I dared to love, been all-too cruelly belied? The speculative Mystery of Life grew ever more mysterious to me: neither in the practical Mystery had I made the slightest progress, but been everywhere buffeted, foiled, and contemptuously cast out. A feeble unit in the middle of a threatening Infinitude, I seemed to have nothing given me but eyes, whereby to discern my own wretchedness. Invisible yet impenetrable walls, as of Enchantment, divided me from all living: was there, in the wide world, any true bosom I could press trustfully to mine? O Heaven, No, there was none! I kept a lock upon my lips: why should I speak much with that shifting variety of so-called Friends, in whose withered, vain and too-hungry souls Friendship was but an incredible tradition? In such cases, your resource is to talk little, and that little mostly from the Newspapers. Now when I look back, it was a strange isolation I then lived in. The men and women around me, even speaking with me, were but Figures; I had, practically, forgotten that they were alive, that they were not merely automatic. In the midst of their crowded streets and assemblages, I walked solitary; and (except as it was my own heart, not another's, that I kept devouring) savage also, as the tiger in his jungle. Some comfort it would have been, could I, like a Faust,° have fancied myself tempted and tormented of the Devil; for a Hell, as I imag-

102 **Pillar . . . by night.** See *Exodus,* 13:21   107 **Siècle . . . Quinze,** the name of the Age of Reason and of a book by Voltaire   114 **Diogenes,** Greek Cynic philosopher c 412-c. 323 B.C.), legendary seeker after an honest man   124 **Lubberland,** land of plenty   127 **Handwriting . . . wall.** See *Daniel,* 5:5–28

145 **to be weak . . . misery,** *Paradise Lost,* I, 157   154 **Know thyself,** precept inscribed on the temple at Delphi   193 **Faust,** of Goethe's play. He was tempted by the Devil

ine, without Life, though only diabolic Life, were more frightful: but in our age of Down-pulling and Dis-belief, the very Devil has been pulled down, you cannot so much as believe in a Devil. To me the Universe was all void of Life, of Purpose, of Volition, even of 200 Hostility: it was one huge dead, immeasurable Steam-engine, rolling on, in its dead indifference, to grind me limb from limb. O, the vast, gloomy, solitary Golgotha,° and Mill of Death! Why was the Living banished thither companionless, conscious? Why, if there is no Devil; nay, unless the Devil is your God?''

A prey incessantly to such corrosions, might not, moreover, as the worst aggravation to them, the iron constitution even of a Teufelsdröckh threaten to fail? We conjecture that he has known sickness; and, in 210 spite of his locomotive habits, perhaps sickness of the chronic sort. Hear this, for example: ''How beautiful to die of broken-heart, on Paper! Quite another thing in practice; every window of your Feeling, even of your intellect, as it were, begrimed and mud-bespattered, so that no pure ray can enter; a whole Drug-shop in your inwards; the fordone soul drowning slowly in quagmires of Disgust!''

Putting all which external and internal miseries together, may we not find in the following sentences, 220 quite in our Professor's still vein, significance enough? ''From Suicide a certain aftershine (Nachschein) of Christianity withheld me: perhaps also a certain indolence of character; for, was not that a remedy I had at any time within reach? Often, however, was there a question present to me: Should some one now, at the turning of that corner, blow thee suddenly out of Space, into the other World, or other No-world, by pistol-shot—how were it? On which ground, too, I often, in sea-storms and sieged cities and other death-230 scenes, exhibited an imperturbability, which passed, falsely enough, for courage.''

''So had it lasted,'' concludes the Wanderer, ''so had it lasted as in bitter protracted Death-agony, through long years. The heart within me, unvisited by any heavenly dewdrop, was smoldering in sulphurous, slow-consuming fire. Almost since earliest memory I had shed no tear; or once only when I, murmuring half-audibly, recited Faust's Death-song, that wild Selig der den er im Siegesglanze findet° (Happy whom 240 he finds in Battle's splendor), and thought that of this last Friend° even I was not forsaken, that Destiny itself could not doom me not to die. Having no hope, neither had I any definite fear, were it of Man or of Devil: nay, I often felt as if it might be solacing, could the Arch-Devil himself, though in Tartarean terrors, but rise to me, that I might tell him a little of my mind. And yet, strangely enough, I lived in a continual, indefinite, pining fear; tremulous, pusillanimous, apprehensive of I knew not what; it seemed as if all things in the 250 Heavens above and the Earth beneath would hurt me;

as if the Heavens and the Earth were but boundless jaws of a devouring monster, wherein I, palpitating, waited, to be devoured.

''Full of such humor, and perhaps the miserablest man in the whole French Capital or Suburbs, was I, one sultry Dogday, after much perambulation, toiling along the dirty little Rue Saint-Thomas de l'Enfer, among civic rubbish enough, in a close atmosphere, and over pavements hot as Nebuchadnezzar's Furnace;° whereby doubtless my spirits were little 260 cheered; when, all at once, there rose a Thought in me, and I asked myself: 'What art thou afraid of? Wherefore, like a coward, dost thou forever pip and whimper, and go cowering and trembling? Despicable biped! what is the sum-total of the worst that lies before thee? Death? Well, Death; and say the pangs of Tophet too, and all that the Devil and Man may, will, or can do against thee! Hast thou not a heart; canst thou not suffer whatsoever it be; and, as a Child of Freedom, though outcast, trample Tophet itself under 270 thy feet, while it consumes thee? Let it come, then; I will meet it and defy it!' And as I so thought, there rushed like a stream of fire over my whole soul; and I shook base Fear away from me forever. I was strong, of unknown strength; a spirit, almost a god. Ever from that time, the temper of my misery was changed: not Fear or whining Sorrow was it, but Indignation and grim fire-eyed Defiance.

''Thus had the EVERLASTING NO (das ewige Nein) pealed authoritatively through all the recesses of my 280 Being, of my ME; and then was it that my whole ME stood up, in native God-created majesty, and with emphasis recorded its Protest. Such a Protest, the most important transaction in Life, may that same Indignation and Defiance, in a psychological point of view, be fitly called. The Everlasting No had said: 'Behold, thou art fatherless, outcast, and the Universe is mine (the Devil's)'; to which my whole ME now made answer: 'I am not thine, but Free, and forever hate thee!'

''It is from this hour that I incline to date my 290 Spiritual New-birth, or Baphometic Fire-baptism;° perhaps I directly thereupon began to be a Man.'' (II, 7)

CENTER OF INDIFFERENCE°

Though, after this ''Baphometic Fire-baptism'' of his, our Wanderer signifies that his Unrest was but increased; as, indeed, ''Indignation and Defiance,'' especially against things in general, are not the most peaceable inmates; yet can the Psychologist surmise that it was no longer a quite hopeless Unrest; that henceforth it had at least a fixed center to revolve

203 **Golgotha,** Calvary, where Jesus was crucified   239 **Selig . . . findet,** from Goethe's *Faust*, I, iv, 1573–1576   241 **last Friend,** death

260 **Nebuchadnezzar's Furnace.** See *Daniel*, 3:19   291 **Baphometic Fire-baptism,** a transformation by a flash of spiritual illumination. The idol Baphomet was the symbol of the Templars, a religious-military order established in Jerusalem in the twelfth century to protect Christian pilgrims   **Center of Indifference,** a term used in physics denoting the equatorial point between two extremes of a magnet

round. For the fire-baptized soul, long so scathed and thunder-riven, here feels its own Freedom, which feeling is its Baphometic Baptism: the citadel of its whole kingdom it has thus gained by assault, and will keep inexpugnable; outwards from which the remaining dominions, not indeed without hard battling, will doubtless by degrees be conquered and pacificated. Under another figure, we might say, if in that great moment, in the *Rue Saint-Thomas de l'Enfer,* the old inward Satanic School was not yet thrown out of doors, it received peremptory judicial notice to quit;—whereby, for the rest, its howl-chantings, Ernulphus-cursings,° and rebellious gnashings of teeth, might, in the meanwhile, become only the more tumultuous, and difficult to keep secret.

Accordingly, if we scrutinize these Pilgrimings well, there is perhaps discernible henceforth a certain incipient method in their madness.° Not wholly as a Specter does Teufelsdröckh now storm through the world; at worst as a specter-fighting Man, nay who will one day be a Specter-queller. If pilgriming restlessly to so many "Saints' Wells," and ever without quenching of his thirst, he nevertheless finds little secular wells, whereby from time to time some alleviation is ministered. In a word, he is now, if not ceasing, yet intermitting to "eat his own heart"; and clutches round him outwardly on the NOT-ME° for wholesomer food. Does not the following glimpse exhibit him in a much more natural state?

"Towns also and Cities, especially the ancient, I failed not to look upon with interest. How beautiful to see thereby, as through a long vista, into the remote Time! to have, as it were, an actual section of almost the earliest Past brought safe into the Present, and set before your eyes! There, in that old City, was a live ember of Culinary Fire put down, say only two thousand years ago; and there, burning more or less triumphantly, with such fuel as the region yielded, it has burnt, and still burns, and thou thyself seest the very smoke thereof. Ah! and the far more mysterious live ember of Vital Fire was then also put down there; and still miraculously burns and spreads; and the smoke and ashes thereof (in these Judgment-Halls and Churchyards), and its bellows-engines (in these Churches) thou still seest; and its flame, looking out from every kind countenance, and every hateful one, still warms thee or scorches thee.

"Of Man's Activity and Attainment the chief results are aeriform, mystic, and preserved in Tradition only: such are his Forms of Government, with the Authority they rest on; his Customs, or Fashions both of Cloth-habits and of Soul-habits; much more his collective stock of Handicrafts, the whole Faculty he has acquired of manipulating Nature: all these things, as indispensable and priceless as they are, cannot in any way be fixed under lock and key, but must flit, spirit-like, on impalpable vehicles, from Father to Son; if you demand sight of them, they are nowhere to be met with. Visible Ploughmen and Hammermen there have been, ever from Cain and Tubalcain° downwards: but where does your accumulated Agricultural, Metallurgic, and other Manufacturing SKILL lie warehoused? It transmits itself on the atmospheric air, on the sun's rays (by Hearing and by Vision); it is a thing aeriform, impalpable, of quite spiritual sort. In like manner, ask me not, Where are the LAWS; where is the GOVERNMENT? In vain wilt thou go to Schönbrunn, to Downing Street, to the Palais Bourbon:° thou findest nothing there but brick or stone houses, and some bundles of Papers tied with tape. Where, then, is that same cunningly-devised almighty GOVERNMENT of theirs to be laid hands on? Everywhere, yet nowhere: seen only in its works, this too is a thing aeriform, invisible; or if you will, mystic and miraculous. So spiritual (*geistig*) is our whole daily Life: all that we do springs out of Mystery, Spirit, invisible Force; only like a little Cloud-image, or Armida's Palace,° airbuilt, does the Actual body itself forth from the great mystic Deep.

"Visible and tangible products of the Past, again, I reckon-up to the extent of three: Cities, with their Cabinets and Arsenals; then tilled Fields, to either or to both of which divisions Roads with their Bridges may belong; and thirdly——Books. In which third truly, the last invented, lies a worth far surpassing that of the two others. Wondrous indeed is the virtue of a true Book. Not like a dead city of stones, yearly crumbling, yearly needing repair; more like a tilled field, but then a spiritual field: like a spiritual tree, let me rather say, it stands from year to year, and from age to age (we have Books that already number some hundred-and-fifty human ages); and yearly comes its new produce of leaves (Commentaries, Deductions, Philosophical, Political Systems; or were it only Sermons, Pamphlets, Journalistic Essays), every one of which is talismanic and thaumaturgic, for it can persuade men. O thou who art able to write a Book, which once in the two centuries or oftener there is a man gifted to do, envy not him whom they name City-builder, and inexpressibly pity him whom they name Conqueror or City-burner! Thou too art a Conqueror and Victor: but of the true sort, namely over the Devil: thou too hast built what will outlast all marble and metal, and be a wonder-bringing City of the Mind, a Temple and Seminary and Prophetic Mount, whereto all kindreds of the Earth will pilgrim.—Fool! why journeyest thou wearisomely, in thy antiquarian fervor, to gaze on the stone pyramids of Geeza, or the clay ones of Sacchara?° These stand there, as I can tell thee, idle and inert, looking over the Desert, foolishly

20 **Ernulphus-cursings,** an allusion to the curse of Ernulf (1040–1124), Bishop of Rochester, delineated in Sterne's *Tristram Shandy,* III, xi   24–25 **certain . . . madness,** *Hamlet,* II, ii, 211–212   34 **Not-me,** that is, the external, objective, physical world

67 **Cain and Tubalcain.** See *Genesis,* 4:1–22   74–75 **Schönbrunn . . . Palais Bourbon,** seats of government in Vienna, London, and Paris   84 **Armida's Palace,** palace of the enchantress in Tasso's *Jerusalem Delivered*   115–16 **pyramids . . . Sacchara,** pyramids near Cairo

enough, for the last three-thousand years: but canst thou not open thy Hebrew BIBLE, then, or even Luther's Version° thereof?''

No less satisfactory is his sudden appearance not in Battle, yet on some Battle-field; which, we soon gather, must be that of Wagram;° so that here, for once, is a certain approximation to distinctness of date. Omitting much, let us impart what follows:

"Horrible enough! A whole Marchfeld° strewed with shell-splinters, cannon-shot, ruined tumbrils, and dead men and horses; stragglers still remaining not so much as buried. And those red mould heaps: ay, there lie the Shells of Men, out of which all the Life and Virtue has been blown; and now are they swept together, and crammed-down out of sight, like blown Egg-shells! —Did Nature, when she bade the Donau bring down his mould-cargoes from the Carinthian and Carpathian Heights, and spread them out here into the softest, richest level—intend thee, O Marchfeld, for a corn-bearing Nursery, whereon her children might be nursed; or for a Cockpit, wherein they might the more commodiously be throttled and tattered? Were thy three broad Highways, meeting here from the ends of Europe, made for Ammunition-wagons, then? Were thy Wagrams and Stillfrieds but so many ready-built Casemates, wherein the house of Hapsburg might batter with artillery, and with artillery be battered? König Ottokar, amid yonder hillocks, dies under Rodolf's truncheon; here Kaiser Franz falls a-swoon under Napoleon's: within which five centuries, to omit the others, how has thy breast, fair Plain, been defaced and defiled! The greensward is torn-up and trampled-down; man's fond care of it, his fruit-trees, hedge-rows, and pleasant dwellings, blown away with gun powder; and the kind seedfield lies a desolate, hideous Place of Skulls.°—Nevertheless, Nature is at work; neither shall these Powder-Devilkins with their utmost devilry gainsay here: but all that gore and carnage will be shrouded-in, absorbed into manure; and next year the Marchfeld will be green, nay greener. Thrifty un-wearied Nature, ever out of our great waste educing some little profit of thy own—how dost thou, from the very carcass of the Killer, bring Life for the Living!°

"What, speaking in quite unofficial language, is the net-purport and upshot of war? To my own knowl-edge, for example, there dwell and toil, in the British village of Dumdrudge, usually some five-hundred souls. From these, by certain "Natural Enemies" of the French, there are successively selected, during the French war, say thirty able-bodied men. Dumdrudge, at her own expense, has suckled and nursed them: she has, not without difficulty and sorrow, fed them up to manhood, and even trained them to crafts, so that one can weave, another build, another hammer, and the weakest can stand under thirty stone avoirdupois. Nevertheless, amid much weeping and swearing, they are selected; all dressed in red; and shipped away, at the public charges, some two thousand miles, or say only to the south of Spain;° and fed there till wanted. And now to that same spot, in the south of Spain, are thirty similar French artisans, from a French Dum-drudge, in like manner wending, till at length, after infinite effort, the two parties come into actual jux-taposition; and Thirty stands fronting Thirty, each with a gun in his hand. Straightway the word "Fire!" is given, and they blow the souls out of one another; and in place of sixty brisk useful craftsmen, the world has sixty dead carcasses, which it must bury, and anew shed tears for. Had these men any quarrel? Busy as the Devil is, not the smallest! They lived far enough apart; were the entirest strangers; nay, in so wide a Universe, there was even, unconsciously, by Com-merce, some mutual helpfulness between them. How then? Simpleton! their Governors had fallen out; and, instead of shooting one another, had the cunning to make these poor blockheads shoot.—Alas, so is it in Deutschland, and hitherto in all other lands; still as of old, 'what devilry soever Kings do, the Greeks must pay the piper!'°—In that fiction of the English Smol-lett,° it is true, the final Cessation of War is perhaps prophetically shadowed forth; where the two Natural Enemies, in person, take each a Tobacco-pipe, filled with Brimstone; light the same, and smoke in one another's faces, till the weaker gives in: but from such predicted Peace-Era, what blood-filled trenches, and contentious centuries, may still divide us!''

Thus can the Professor, at least in lucid intervals, look away from his own sorrows, over the many-colored world, and pertinently enough note what is passing there. We may remark, indeed, that for the matter of spiritual culture, if for nothing else, perhaps few periods of his life were richer than this. Internally, there is the most momentous instructive Course of Practical Philosophy, with Experiments, going on; to-wards the right comprehension of which his Peripatetic habits, favorable to Meditation, might help him rather than hinder. Externally, again, as he wanders to and fro, there are, if for the longing heart little substance, yet for the seeing eye sights enough: in these so boundless Travels of his, granting that the Satanic School was even partially kept down, what an incredi-ble knowledge of our Planet, and its Inhabitants and their Works, that is to say, of all knowable things, might not Teufelsdröckh acquire!

"I have read in most Public Libraries," says he, "including those of Constantinople and Samarcand: in most Colleges, except the Chinese Mandarin ones, I

120 **Luther's Version,** published by Martin Luther, the religious reformer, in 1534–1535   123 **Wagram,** a village near Vienna where Napoleon defeated the Austrians   126 **Marchfeld,** a field near Vienna where the Austrians defeated the Bohemians in the thirteenth century and where Napoleon defeated the Austrians in the nineteenth   153 **Place of Skulls,** Calvary or Golgotha   160 **carcass . . . Living.** See *Judges,* 14:9

176 **south of Spain,** site of the British engagement against Napoleon in 1808–1809   195–196 **what devilry . . . piper,** from Horace's *Epistles,* I, ii, 14   197 **English Smollett,** Tobias G. Smollett (1721–1771), in *The Adventures of Fer-dinand Count Fathom,* Ch. 41

have studied, or seen that there was no studying. Unknown Languages have I oftenest gathered from their natural repertory, the Air, by my organ of Hearing; Statistics, Geographics, Topographics came, through the Eye, almost of their own accord. The ways of Man, how he seeks food, and warmth, and protection for himself, in most regions, are ocularly known to me. Like the great Hadrian,° I meted out much of the terraqueous Globe with a pair of Compasses that belonged to myself only.

"Of great Scenes why speak? Three summer days, I lingered reflecting, and even composing (*dichtete*), by the Pine-chasms of Vaucluse;° and in that clear Lakelet moistened my bread. I have sat under the Palm-trees of Tadmor;° smoked a pipe among the ruins of Babylon. The great Wall of China I have seen; and can testify that it is of gray brick, coped and covered with granite, and shows only second-rate masonry.—Great Events, also, have not I witnessed? Kings sweated-down (*ausgemergelt*) into Berlin-and-Milan Customhouse-Officers; the World well won, and the World well lost; oftener than once a hundred thousand individuals shot (by each other) in one day. All kindreds and peoples and nations dashed together and shifted and shoveled into heaps that they might ferment there, and in time unite. The birth-pangs of Democracy,° wherewith convulsed Europe was groaning in cries that reached Heaven, could not escape me.

"For great Men I have ever had the warmest predilection; and can perhaps boast that few such in this era have wholly escaped me. Great Men are the inspired (speaking and acting) Texts of that divine BOOK OF REVELATIONS, whereof a Chapter is completed from epoch to epoch, and by some named HISTORY; to which inspired Texts your numerous talented men, and your innumerable untalented men, are the better or worse exegetic Commentaries, and wagonload of too-stupid, heretical or orthodox, weekly Sermons. For my study the inspired Texts themselves! Thus did not I, in very early days, having disguised me as tavern-waiter, stand behind the field-chairs, under that shady Tree at Treisnitz° by the Jena Highway; waiting upon the great Schiller and greater Goethe; and hearing what I have not forgotten. For——"

——But at this point the Editor recalls his principle of caution, some time ago laid down, and must suppress much. Let not the sacredness of Laureled, still more, of Crowned Heads, be tampered with. Should we, at a future day, find circumstances altered, and the time come for Publication, then may these glimpses into the privacy of the Illustrious be conceded; which for the present were little better than treacherous, perhaps traitorous Eavesdroppings. Of Lord Byron, therefore, of Pope Pius,° Emperor Tarakwang,° and the "White Water-roses" (Chinese Carbonari°) with their mysteries, no notice here! Of Napoleon himself we shall only, glancing from afar, remark that Teufelsdröckh's relation to him seems to have been of very varied character. At first we find our poor Professor on the point of being shot as a spy; then taken into private conversation, even pinched on the ear, yet presented with no money; at last indignantly dismissed, almost thrown out of doors, as an "Ideologist." "He himself," says the Professor, "was among the completest Ideologists, at least Ideopraxists: in the Idea (*in der Idee*) he lived, moved, and fought. The man was a Divine Missionary, though unconscious of it; and preached, through the cannon's throat, that great doctrine, *La carrière ouverte aux talens* (The Tools to him that can handle them), which is our ultimate Political Evangel, wherein alone can liberty lie. Madly enough he preached, it is true, as Enthusiasts and first Missionaries are wont, with imperfect utterance, amid much frothy rant; yet as articulately perhaps as the case admitted. Or call him, if you will, an American Backwoodsman, who had to fell unpenetrated forests, and battle with innumerable wolves, and did not entirely forbear strong liquor, rioting, and even theft; whom, notwithstanding, the peaceful Sower will follow, and, as he cuts the boundless harvest, bless."

More legitimate and decisively authentic is Teufelsdröckh's appearance and emergence (we know not well whence) in the solitude of the North Cape, on that June Midnight. He has "a light-blue Spanish cloak" hanging round him, as his "most commodious, principal, indeed sole upper garment"; and stands there, on the World-promontory, looking over the infinite Brine, like a little blue Belfry (as we figure), now motionless indeed, yet ready, if stirred, to ring quaintest changes.

"Silence as of death," writes he; "for Midnight, even in the Arctic latitudes, has its character: nothing but the granite cliffs ruddy-tinged, the peaceable gurgle of that slow-heaving Polar Ocean, over which in the utmost North the great Sun hangs low and lazy, as if he too were slumbering. Yet is his cloud-couch wrought of crimson and cloth-of-gold; yet does his light stream over the mirror of waters, like a tremulous fire-pillar, shooting downwards to the abyss, and hide itself under my feet. In such moments, Solitude also is invaluable; for who would speak, or be looked on, when behind him lies all Europe and Africa, fast asleep, except the watchmen; and before him the silent Immensity, and Palace of the Eternal, whereof our Sun is but a porch-lamp?

"Nevertheless, in this solemn moment comes a man, or monster, scrambling from among the rock-

233 **Hadrian,** the Roman Emperor (76–138) who traveled extensively throughout the Empire   238 **Vaucluse,** the home of Petrarch in southeast France   240 **Tadmor,** Palmyra, an ancient city in Syria   251 **birth-pangs of Democracy,** allusion to the July Revolution in Paris in 1830   267 **Tree at Treisnitz,** rendezvous of the poet-philosophers Goethe and Schiller near Jena, Germany

279 **Pope Pius,** perhaps Pius VII, pope between 1800 and 1823   **Emperor Tarakwang,** Tao Kuang, who became Emperor of China in 1821   280 **White Water-roses . . . Carbonari,** Chinese and Italian revolutionary societies, respectively

hollows; and, shaggy, huge as the Hyperborean Bear, hails me in Russian speech: most probably, therefore, a Russian Smuggler. With courteous brevity, I signify my indifference to contraband trade, my humane intentions, yet strong wish to be private. In vain: the monster, counting doubtless on his superior stature, and minded to make sport for himself, or perhaps prof-
340 it, were it with murder, continues to advance, ever assailing me with his importunate train-oil breath, and now has advanced, till we stand both on the verge of the rock, the deep Sea rippling greedily down below. What argument will avail? On the thick Hyperborean, cherubic reasoning, seraphic eloquence were lost. Prepared for such extremity, I, deftly enough, whisk aside one step; draw out, from my interior reservoirs, a sufficient Birmingham Horse-pistol, and say, "Be so obliging as retire, Friend (*Er ziehe sich zurück,*
350 *Freund*), and with promptitude!" This logic even the Hyperborean understands; fast enough, with apologetic, petitionary growl, he sidles off; and, except for suicidal as well as homicidal purposes, need not return.

"Such I hold to be the genuine use of Gunpowder: that it makes all men alike tall. Nay, if thou be cooler, cleverer than I, if thou have more *Mind,* though all but no Body whatever, then canst thou kill me first, and art the taller. Hereby, at last, is the Goliath powerless,
360 and the David resistless;° savage Animalism is nothing, inventive Spiritualism is all.°

"With respect to Duels, indeed, I have my own ideas. Few things, in this so surprising world, strike me with more surprise. Two little visual Spectra of men, hovering with insecure enough cohesion in the midst of the UNFATHOMABLE, and to dissolve therein, at any rate, very soon—make pause at the distance of twelve paces asunder; whirl round; and, simultaneously by the cunningest mechanism, explode one
370 another into Dissolution; and off-hand become Air, and Non-extant! Deuce on it (*verdammt*), the little spitfires!—Nay, I think with old Hugo von Trimberg:° 'God must needs laugh outright, could such a thing be, to see his wondrous Manikins here below.' "

But amid these specialties, let us not forget the great generality, which is our chief quest here: How prospered the inner man of Teufelsdröckh under so much outward shifting? Does Legion° still lurk in him, though repressed; or has he exorcised that Devil's Brood? We
380 can answer that the symptoms continue promising. Experience is the grand spiritual Doctor; and with him Teufelsdröckh has now been long a patient, swallowing many a bitter bolus.° Unless our poor Friend belong to the numerous class of Incurables, which seems not likely, some cure will doubtless be effected. We should rather say that Legion, or the Satanic School, was now pretty well extirpated and cast out, but next to nothing

introduced in its room; whereby the heart remains, for the while, in a quiet but no comfortable state.

"At length, after so much roasting," thus writes our 390 Autobiographer, "I was what you might name calcined. Pray only that it be not rather, as is the more frequent issue, reduced to a *caput mortuum!*° But in any case, by mere dint of practice, I had grown familiar with many things. Wretchedness was still wretched; but I could now partly see through it, and despise it. Which highest mortal, in this inane Existence, had I not found a Shadow-hunter, or Shadow-hunted; and, when I looked through his brave garnitures, miserable enough? Thy wishes have all been 400 sniffed aside, thought I: but what, had they even been all granted! Did not the Boy Alexander° weep because he had not two Planets to conquer; or a whole Solar System; or after that, a whole Universe? *Ach Gott,* when I gazed into these Stars, have they not looked down on me as if with pity, from their serene spaces, like Eyes glistening with heavenly tears over the little lot of man! Thousands of human generations, all as noisy as our own, have been swallowed-up of Time, and there remains no wreck° of them any more; and 410 Arcturus and Orion and Sirius and the Pleiades° are still shining in their courses, clear and young, as when the Shepherd first noted them in the plain of Shinar.° Pshaw! what is this paltry little Dog-cage° of an Earth; what art thou that sittest whining there? Thou art still Nothing, Nobody; true; but who, then, is Something, Somebody? For thee the Family of Man has no use; it rejects thee; thou art wholly as a dissevered limb; so be it; perhaps it is better so!"

Too-heavy-laden Teufelsdröckh! Yet surely his 420 bands are loosening; one day he will hurl the burden far from him, and bound forth free and with a second youth.

"This," says our Professor, "was the CENTER OF INDIFFERENCE I had now reached; through which whoso travels from the Negative Pole to the Positive must necessarily pass."

(II, 8)

THE EVERLASTING YEA

"Temptations in the Wilderness!°" exclaims Teufelsdröckh. "Have we not all to be tried with such? Not so easily can the old Adam,° lodged in us by birth, be dispossessed. Our Life is compassed round with Necessity; yet is the meaning of Life itself no other than Freedom, than Voluntary Force: thus have we a warfare; in the beginning, especially, a hard-fought battle. For the God-given mandate, *Work thou in Well-doing,*° lies mysteriously written, in Promethean°

359–360 **Goliath . . . resistless.** See *1 Samuel,* 17   360–361 **savage Animalism . . . is all,** one of the foundation-principles in Carlyle's thought   372 **Hugo von Trimberg,** German schoolmaster and moral writer (1260–1309)   378 **Legion.** See *Mark,* 5:9   383 **bolus,** a large pill for sick animals

393 **caput mortuum,** death's head, or worthless leftovers   402 **Alexander,** Alexander the Great (356–323 B.C.)   410 **wreck,** remains   411 **Arcturus . . . Pleiades,** stars, star-clusters, and constellations   413 **Shepherd . . . Shinar.** See *Genesis,* 11:1-9. Shinar was the site of the Tower of Babel   414 **Dog-cage,** a wheel-shaped cage in which a dog turned the jack of a spit   **The Everlasting Yea** 1 **Temptations . . . Wilderness.** See *Matthew,* 4:1   3 **Adam, etc.** See *Colossians,* 3:9   8–9 **Work . . . Welldoing.** See *2 Thessalonians,* 3:13   9 **Promethean,** fire-bearing

Prophetic Characters, in our hearts; and leaves us no rest, night or day, till it be deciphered and obeyed; till it burn forth, in our conduct, a visible, acted Gospel of Freedom. And as the clay-given mandate, *Eat thou and be filled,* at the same time persuasively proclaims itself through every nerve—must not there be a confusion, a contest, before the better Influence can become the upper?

"To me nothing seems more natural than that the Son of Man, when such God-given mandate first prophetically stirs within him, and the Clay must now be vanquished, or vanquish—should be carried of the spirit into grim Solitudes, and there fronting the Tempter do grimmest battle with him; defiantly setting him at naught, till he yield and fly. Name it as we choose: with or without visible Devil, whether in the natural Desert of rocks and sands, or in the populous moral Desert of selfishness and baseness—to such Temptation are we all called. Unhappy if we are not! Unhappy if we are but Half-men, in whom that divine handwriting has never blazed forth, all-subduing, in true sun-splendor; but quivers dubiously amid meaner lights or smolders, in dull pain, in darkness, under earthly vapors!—Our Wilderness is the wide World in an Atheistic Century; our Forty Days are long years of suffering and fasting: nevertheless, to these also comes an end. Yes, to me also was given, if not Victory, yet the consciousness of Battle, and the resolve to persevere therein while life or faculty is left. To me also, entangled in the enchanted forests, demon-peopled, doleful of sight and of sound, it was given, after weariest wanderings, to work out my way into the higher sunlit slopes—of that Mountain which has no summit, or whose summit is in Heaven only!''

He says elsewhere, under a less ambitious figure, as figures are, once for all, natural to him: "Has not thy Life been that of most sufficient men (*tüchtigen Männer*) thou hast known in this generation? An outflush of foolish young Enthusiasm, like the first fallow crop, wherein are as many weeds as valuable herbs: this all parched away, under the Droughts of practical and spiritual Unbelief, as Disappointment, in thought and act, often-repeated gave rise to Doubt, and Doubt gradually settled into Denial! If I have had a second-crop, and now see the perennial greensward, and sit under umbrageous cedars, which defy all Drought (and Doubt); herein, too, be the Heavens praised, I am not without examples, and even exemplars.''

So that, for Teufelsdröckh also, there has been a "glorious revolution"°: these mad shadow-hunting and shadow-hunted Pilgrimings of his were but some purifying "Temptation in the Wilderness," before his Apostolic work (such as it was) could begin; which Temptation is now happily over, and the Devil once more worsted! Was "that high moment in the *Rue de l'Enfer,*'' then, properly the turning-point of the battle; when the Fiend said, *Worship me or be torn in shreds;* and was answered valiantly with an *Apage Satana?*° —Singular Teufelsdröckh, would thou hadst told thy singular story in plain words! But it is fruitless to look there, in those Paper-bags, for such. Nothing but innuendoes, figurative crochets: a typical Shadow, fitfully wavering, prophetico-satiric; no clear logical Picture. "How paint to the sensual eye," asks he once, "what passes in the Holy-of-Holies of Man's Soul; in what words, known to these profane times, speak even afar-off of the unspeakable?'' We ask in turn: Why perplex these times, profane as they are, with needless obscurity, by omission and by commission? Not mystical only is our Professor, but whimsical; and involves himself, now more than ever, in eye-bewildering *chiaroscuro.*° Successive glimpses, here faithfully imparted, our more gifted readers must endeavor to combine for their own behoof.

He says: "The hot Harmattan wind° had raged itself out; its howl went silent within me; and the long-deafened soul could now hear. I paused in my wild wanderings; and sat me down to wait, and consider; for it was as if the hour of change drew nigh. I seemed to surrender, to renounce utterly, and say: Fly, then, false shadows of Hope; I will chase you no more, I will believe you no more. And ye too, haggard specters of Fear, I care not for you; ye too are all shadows and a lie. Let me rest here: for I am way-weary and life-weary; I will rest here, were it but to die: to die or to live is alike to me; alike insignificant.''—And again: "Here, then, as I lay in that CENTER OF INDIFFERENCE; cast, doubtless by benignant upper Influence, into a healing sleep, the heavy dreams rolled gradually away, and I awoke to a new Heaven and a new Earth. The first preliminary moral Act, Annihilation of Self (*Selbsttödtung*), had been happily accomplished; and my mind's eyes were now unsealed, and its hands ungyved.°''

Might we not also conjecture that the following passage refers to his Locality, during this same "healing sleep"; that his Pilgrimstaff lies cast aside here, on "the high table-land"; and indeed that the repose is already taking wholesome effect on him? If it were not that the tone, in some parts, has more of riancy,° even of levity, than we could have expected! However, in Teufelsdröckh, there is always the strangest Dualism: light dancing, with guitar-music, will be going on in the fore-court, while by fits from within comes the faint whimpering of woe and wail. We transcribe the piece entire:

"Beautiful it was to sit there, as in my skyey Tent, musing and meditating; on the high table-land, in front of the Mountains; over me, as roof, the azure Dome, and around me, for walls, four azure-flowing curtains—namely, of the Four azure winds, on whose

---

59 **glorious revolution,** allusion to the English Revolution in 1688 whereby William and Mary came to the throne

67–68 **Apage Satana.** Get thee hence, Satan   81 **chiaroscuro,** light-and-shadow
84 **Harmattan wind,** a dry, dusty wind on the Atlantic coast of Africa
103 **ungyved,** unfettered   109 **riancy,** mirthfulness

bottom-fringes also I have seen gilding. And then to fancy the fair Castles that stood sheltered in these Mountain hollows; with their green flower-lawns, and white dames and damosels, lovely enough: or better still, the straw-roofed Cottages, wherein stood many a Mother baking bread, with her children round her:— all hidden and protectingly folded-up in the valley-folds; yet there and alive, as sure as if I beheld them. Or to see, as well as fancy, the nine Towns and Vil-
130 lages, that lay round my mountain-seat, which, in still weather, were wont to speak to me (by their steeple-bells) with metal tongue; and, in almost all weather, proclaimed their vitality by repeated Smoke-clouds; whereon, as on a culinary horologe, I might read the hour of the day. For it was the smoke of cookery, as kind housewives at morning, midday, eventide were boiling their husbands' kettles; and ever a blue pillar rose up into the air, successively or simultaneously, from each of the nine, saying, as plainly as smoke
140 could say: Such and such a meal is getting ready here. Not uninteresting! For you have the whole Borough, with all its love-makings and scandal-mongeries, con-tentions and contentments, as in miniature, and could cover it all with your hat.—If, in my wide Wayfarings, I had learned to look into the business of the World in its details, here perhaps was the place for combining it into general propositions, and deducing inferences therefrom.

"Often also could I see the black Tempest marching
150 in anger through the Distance: round some Schreck-horn,° as yet grim-blue, would the eddying vapor gather, and there tumultuously eddy, and flow down like a mad witch's hair; till, after a space, it vanished, and, in the clear sunbeam, your Schreckhorn stood smiling grim-white, for the vapor had held snow. How thou fermentest and elaboratest, in thy great ferment-ing-vat and laboratory of an Atmosphere, of a World, O Nature!—Or what is Nature? Ha! why do I not name thee GOD? Art not thou the "Living Garment of
160 God"? O Heavens, is it, in very deed, HE, then, that ever speaks through thee; that lives and loves in thee, that lives and loves in me?

"Fore-shadows, call them rather fore-splendors, of that Truth, and Beginning of Truths, fell mysteriously over my soul. Sweeter than Dayspring to the Ship-wrecked in Nova Zembla;° ah, like the mother's voice to her little child that strays bewildered, weeping, in unknown tumults; like soft streamings of celestial music to my too-exasperated heart, came that
170 Evangel. The Universe is not dead and demoniacal, a charnel-house with specters; but godlike, and my Father's!

"With other eyes, too, could I now look upon my fellow man; with an infinite Love, an infinite Pity. Poor, wandering, wayward man! Art thou not tired, and beaten with stripes, even as I am? Ever, whether thou bear the royal mantle or the beggar's gabardine, art thou not so weary, so heavy-laden; and thy Bed of Rest is but a Grave. O my Brother, my Brother, why cannot I shelter thee in my bosom, and wipe away all 180 tears from thy eyes! Truly, the din of many-voiced Life, which, in this solitude, with the mind's organ, I could hear, was no longer a maddening discord, but a melting one; like inarticulate cries, and sobbings of a dumb creature, which in the ear of Heaven are prayers. The poor Earth, with her poor joys, was now my needy Mother, not my cruel Stepdame. Man, with his so mad Wants and so mean Endeavors, had be-come the dearer to me; and even for his sufferings and his sins, I now first named him Brother. Thus was I 190 standing in the porch of that 'Sanctuary of Sorrow';° by strange, steep ways had I too been guided thither; and ere long its sacred gates would open, and the 'Divine Depth of Sorrow' lie disclosed to me.''

The Professor says he here first got eye on the Knot that had been strangling him, and straightway could unfasten it, and was free. "A vain interminable con-troversy," writes he, "touching what is at present called Origin of Evil, or some such thing, arises in every soul, since the beginning of the world; and in 200 every soul, that would pass from idle Suffering into actual Endeavoring, must first be put an end to. The most, in our time, have to go content with a simple, incomplete enough Suppression of this controversy; to a few some Solution of it is indispensable. In every new era, too, such Solution comes-out in different terms; and ever the Solution of the last era has become obsolete, and is found unserviceable. For it is man's nature to change his Dialect from century to century; he cannot help it though he would. The authentic 210 Church-Catechism of our present century has not yet fallen into my hands: meanwhile, for my own private behoof, I attempt to elucidate the matter so. Man's Unhappiness, as I construe, comes of his Greatness; it is because there is an Infinite in him, which with all his cunning he cannot quite bury under the Finite. Will the whole Finance Ministers and Upholsterers and Con-fectioners of modern Europe undertake, in jointstock company, to make one Shoeblack HAPPY? They can-not accomplish it, above an hour or two; for the 220 Shoeblack also has a Soul quite other than his Stomach; and would require, if you consider it, for his permanent satisfaction and saturation, simply this al-lotment, no more, and no less: God's infinite Universe altogether to himself, therein to enjoy infinitely, and fill every wish as fast as it rose. Oceans of Hoch-heimer,° a Throat like that of Ophiuchus:° speak not of them; to the infinite Shoeblack they are as nothing. No sooner is your ocean filled than he grumbles that it might have been of better vintage. Try him with half of 230

---

150 **Schreckhorn,** a chief Alpine summit in Switzerland   166 **Shipwrecked in Nova Zembla,** allusion to an ill-fated Dutch expedition (1596) to Nova Zembla, an arctic archipelago

191 **Sanctuary of Sorrow,** from Goethe's *Wilhelm Meister*   227 **Hochheimer,** Rhine wine from Hochheim   **Ophiuchus,** the constellation Serpentarius, a man holding a serpent in his hand

a Universe, of an Omnipotence, he sets to quarreling with the proprietor of the other half and declares himself the most maltreated of men.—Always there is a black spot in our sunshine: it is even as I said, the *Shadow of Ourselves*.

"But the whim we have of Happiness is somewhat thus. By certain valuations, and averages, of our own striking, we come upon some sort of average terrestrial lot; this we fancy belongs to us by nature, and of inde-
240 feasible right. It is simple payment of our wages, of our deserts; requires neither thanks nor complaint; only such *overplus* as there may be do we account Happiness; any *deficit* again is Misery. Now consider that we have the valuation of our own deserts ourselves, and what a fund of Self-conceit there is in each of us—do you wonder that the balance should so often dip the wrong way, and many a Blockhead cry: See there, what a payment; was ever worthy gentleman so used!—I tell thee, Blockhead, it all comes of thy Van-
250 ity; of what thou *fanciest* those same deserts of thine to be. Fancy that thou deservest to be hanged (as is most likely), thou wilt feel it happiness to be only shot: fancy that thou deservest to be hanged in a hair-halter, it will be a luxury to die in hemp.

"So true is it, what I then say, that *the Fraction of Life can be increased in value not so much by increasing your Numerator as by lessening your Denominator*. Nay, unless my Algebra deceive me, *Unity* itself divided by *Zero* will give *Infinity*. Make thy claim
260 of wages a zero, then; thou hast the world under thy feet. Well did the Wisest of our time° write: 'It is only with Renunciation (*Entsagen*) that Life, properly speaking, can be said to begin.'

"I asked myself: What is this that, ever since earliest years, thou hast been fretting and fuming, and lamenting and self-tormenting, on account of? Say it in a word: is it not because thou art not HAPPY? Because the THOU (sweet gentleman) is not sufficiently honored, nourished, soft-bedded, and lovingly cared for?
270 Foolish soul! What Act of Legislature was there that *thou* shouldst be Happy? A little while ago thou hadst no right to *be* at all. What if thou wert born and predestined not to be Happy, but to be Unhappy! Art thou nothing other than a Vulture, then, that fliest through the Universe seeking after somewhat to *eat;* and shrieking dolefully because carrion enough is not given thee? Close thy *Byron;* open thy *Goethe.*°"

"*Es leuchtet mir ein,*° I see a glimpse of it!" cries he elsewhere "there is in man a HIGHER than Love of
280 Happiness: he can do without Happiness, and instead thereof find Blessedness! Was it not to preach forth this same HIGHER that sages and martyrs, the Poet and the Priest, in all times, have spoken and suffered; bearing testimony, through life and through death, of the Godlike that is in Man, and how in the Godlike

only has he Strength and Freedom? Which God-inspired Doctrine art thou also honored to be taught; O Heavens! and broken with manifold merciful Afflictions, even till thou become contrite, and learn it! O, thank thy Destiny for these; thankfully bear what yet 290 remain: thou hadst need of them; the Self in thee needed to be annihilated. By benignant fever-paroxysms is Life rooting out the deep-seated chronic Disease, and triumphs over Death. On the roaring billows of Time, thou art not engulfed, but borne aloft into the azure of Eternity. Love not Pleasure; love God.° This is the EVERLASTING YEA, wherein all contradiction is solved: wherein whoso walks and works, it is well with him."

And again: "Small is it that thou canst trample the 300 Earth with its injuries under thy feet, as old Greek Zeno° trained thee: thou canst love the Earth while it injures thee, and even because it injures thee; for this a Greater than Zeno was needed, and he too was sent. Knowest thou that '*Worship of Sorrow*'?° The Temple° thereof, founded some eighteen centuries ago, now lies in ruins, overgrown with jungle, the habitation of doleful creatures: nevertheless, venture forward; in a low crypt, arched out of falling fragments, thou findest the Altar still there, and its sacred Lamp perennially 310 burning."

Without pretending to comment on which strange utterances, the Editor will only remark that there lies beside them much of a still more questionable character; unsuited to the general apprehension; nay wherein he himself does not see his way. Nebulous disquisitions on Religion, yet not without bursts of splendor; on the "perennial continuance of Inspiration"; on Prophecy; that there are "true Priests, as well as Baal-Priests,° in our own day": with more of the like 320 sort. We select some fractions, by way of finish to this farrago.

"Cease, my much-respected Herr von Voltaire,°" thus apostrophizes the Professor: "shut thy sweet voice; for the task appointed thee seems finished. Sufficiently hast thou demonstrated this proposition, considerable or otherwise: That the Mythus of the Christian Religion looks not in the eighteenth century as it did in the eighth. Alas, were thy six-and-thirty quartos and the six-and-thirty thousand other quartos and 330 folios, and flying sheets or reams, printed before and since on the same subject, all needed to convince us of so little! But what next? Wilt thou help us to embody the divine Spirit of that Religion in a new Mythus, in a new vehicle and vesture, that our Souls, otherwise too like perishing, may live? What! thou hast no faculty in that kind? Only a torch for burning, no hammer for building? Take our thanks, then, and—thyself away.

"Meanwhile what are antiquated Mythuses to me?

---

261 **Wisest of our time,** Goethe   277 **Close . . . Goethe,** a well-known Carlylean phrase, meaning to put aside Satanic self-consciousness and substitute spiritual illumination and commitment   278 **Es leuchtet mir ein,** from *Wilhelm Meister*

296–297 **Love . . . God.** See 2 *Timothy,* 3:4   302 **Zeno,** Greek Stoic philosopher of the third century B.C.   305 **Worship of Sorrow,** a phrase derived from Goethe, expressing the idea that suffering is one form of spiritual development **Temple, etc.** See *Isaiah,* 13:21   320 **Baal-Priests,** false priests (see *I Kings,* 18:17–40)   323 **Voltaire,** French skeptic (1694–1778)

340 Or is the God present, felt in my own heart, a thing which Herr von Voltaire will dispute out of me; or dispute into me? To the 'Worship of Sorrow' ascribe what origin and genesis thou pleasest, *has* not that Worship originated, and been generated; is it not *here?* Feel it in thy heart, and then say whether it is of God! This is Belief; all else is Opinion—for which latter whoso will let him worry and be worried."

"Neither," observes he elsewhere, "shall ye tear-out one another's eyes, struggling over 'Plenary Inspi-
350 ration,° and suchlike: try rather to get a little even Partial Inspiration, each of you for himself. One BIBLE I know, of whose Plenary Inspiration doubt is not so much as possible; nay with my own eyes I saw the God's-Hand writing it: thereof all other Bibles are but leaves—say, in Picture-Writing to assist the weaker faculty."

Or, to give the wearied reader relief, and bring it to an end, let him take the following perhaps more intelligible passage:
360 "To me, in this our life," says the Professor, "which is an internecine warfare with the Time-spirit, other warfare seems questionable. Hast thou in any way a Contention with thy brother, I advise thee, think well what the meaning thereof is. If thou gauge it to the bottom, it is simply this: 'Fellow, see! thou art taking more than thy share of Happiness in the world, something from *my* share: which, by the Heavens, thou shalt not; nay I will fight thee rather.'—Alas, and the whole lot to be divided is such a beggarly matter, truly
370 a 'feast of shells,'° for the substance has been spilled out: not enough to quench one Appetite; and the collective human species clutching at them!—Can we not, in all such cases, rather say: 'Take it, thou too-ravenous individual; take that pitiful additional fraction of a share, which I reckoned mine, but which thou so wantest; take it with a blessing: would to Heaven I had enough for thee!'—If Fichte's° *Wissenschaftslehre* be, 'to a certain extent, Applied Christianity,' surely to a still greater extent, so is this. We have here not a
380 Whole Duty of Man,° yet a Half Duty, namely the Passive half: could we but do it, as we can demonstrate it!

"But indeed Conviction, were it never so excellent, is worthless till it convert itself into Conduct. Nay properly Conviction is not possible till then; inasmuch as all Speculation is by nature endless, formless, a vortex amid vortices: only by a felt indubitable certainty of Experience does it find any center to revolve round, and so fashion itself into a system. Most true is it, as a wise man teaches us, that 'Doubt of any sort
390 cannot be removed except by Action.'° On which

ground, too, let him who gropes painfully in darkness or uncertain light, and prays vehemently that the dawn may ripen into day, lay this other precept well to heart, which to me was of invaluable service: 'Do the Duty *which lies nearest thee,'*° which thou knowest to be a Duty! Thy second Duty will already have become clearer.

"May we not say, however, that the hour of Spiritual Enfranchisement is even this: When your Ideal World, wherein the whole man has been dimly 400 struggling and inexpressibly languishing to work, becomes revealed, and thrown open; and you discover, with amazement enough, like the Lothario in *Wilhelm Meister,* that your 'America is here or nowhere'? The Situation that has not its Duty, its Ideal, was never yet occupied by man. Yes, here, in this poor, miserable, hampered, despicable Actual, wherein thou even now standest, here or nowhere is thy Ideal: work it out therefrom; and working, believe, live, be free. Fool! the Ideal is in thyself, the impediment too is in thyself: 410 thy Condition is but the stuff thou art to shape that same Ideal out of: what matters whether such stuff be of this sort or that, so the Form thou give it be heroic, be poetic? O thou that pinest in the imprisonment of the Actual, and criest bitterly to the gods for a kingdom wherein to rule and create, know this of a truth: the thing thou seekest is already with thee, 'here or nowhere,' couldst thou only see!

"But it is with man's Soul as it was with Nature: the beginning of Creation is—Light.° Till the eye have vi- 420 sion, the whole members are in bonds.° Divine moment, when over the tempest-tossed Soul, as once over the wild-weltering Chaos, it is spoken: Let there be Light! Ever to the greatest that has felt such moment, is it not miraculous and God-announcing; even as, under simpler figures, to the simplest and least. The mad primeval Discord is hushed; the rudely jumbled conflicting elements bind themselves into separate Firmaments: deep silent rock-foundations are built beneath; and the skyey vault with its everlasting 430 Luminaries above: instead of a dark wasteful Chaos, we have a blooming, fertile, heaven-encompassed World.

"I too could now say to myself: Be no longer a Chaos, but a World, or even Worldkin. Produce! Produce! Were it but the pitifullest infinitesimal fraction of a Product, produce it, in God's name! 'Tis the utmost thou hast in thee: out with it, then. Up, up! Whatsoever thy hand findeth to do, do it with thy whole might. Work while it is called Today; for the Night 440 cometh, wherein no man can work."° (II, 9)
(1833–1834)

349–350 **Plenary Inspiration,** the doctrine that the Bible is fully inspired in every respect   370 **feast of shells,** that is, shells from which the egg has been blown out   377 **Fichte,** Johann Gottlieb Fichte (1762–1814), post-Kantian philosopher, whose *Doctrine of Knowledge* appeared in 1794   380 **Whole Duty of Man,** an anonymous devotional work of the seventeenth century   389–390 **Doubt . . . Action,** from *Wilhelm Meister*

394–395 **Do the Duty . . . thee,** from *Wilhelm Meister*   420 **beginning . . . Light.** See *Genesis* 1:3   421 **whole members . . . bonds.** See *Matthew,* 6:22–23   438–441 **Whatsoever thy hand . . . work.** See *Ecclesiastes,* 9:10 and *John,* 9:4

from PAST AND PRESENT

The series of essays called *Past and Present* was first published in 1843. It belongs to the economic-social group of Carlyle's writings and is remarkable because it was written in only seven weeks. As the title implies, Carlyle attempted to gather from the past some good lessons for the present. To personalize the material in his usual manner, he compared Victorian conditions to those recorded in the ancient chronicle written by Jocelyn of Brakelond, English monk of Bury St. Edmunds, at the beginning of the thirteenth century. Jocelyn's Latin narrative of the fortunes of his own monastery contains a glowing account of the work of Abbot Samson, whom Carlyle admired greatly. Carlyle's comparison of past and present is almost entirely in favor of the past, the advantages of which are highly, but very artistically, exaggerated. Carlyle's direct comment on contemporary conditions includes attacks on his radical, legislating friends, and an exposition of his own theories of duty, responsibility, work, reward, capital, and labor—all vigorously presented in terms of abstract principle rather than concrete proposals.

DEMOCRACY

If the Serene Highnesses and Majesties do not take note of that, then, as I perceive, *that* will take note of itself! The time for levity, insincerity, and idle babble and play-acting, in all kinds, is gone by; it is a serious, grave time. Old long-vexed questions, not yet solved in logical words or parliamentary laws, are fast solving themselves in facts, somewhat unblessed to behold! This largest of questions, this question of Work and Wages, which ought, had we heeded Heaven's voice, 10 to have begun two generations ago or more, cannot be delayed longer without hearing Earth's voice. "Labour" will verily need to be somewhat "organized," as they say,—God knows with what difficulty. Man will actually need to have his debts and earnings a little better paid by man; which, let Parliaments speak of them, or be silent of them, are eternally his due from man, and cannot, without penalty and at length not without death-penalty, be withheld. How much ought to cease among us straightway; how much 20 ought to begin straightway, while the hours yet are!

Truly they are strange results to which this of leaving all to "Cash"; of quietly shutting up the God's Temple, and gradually opening wide-open the Mammon's Temple, with "Laissez-faire, and Every man for himself,"—have led us in these days! We have Upper, speaking Classes, who indeed do "speak" as never man spake before; the withered flimsiness, godless baseness and barrenness of whose Speech might of itself indicate what kind of Doing and practical Governing went on under it! For Speech is the gaseous 30 element out of which most kinds of Practice and Performance, especially all kinds of moral Performance, condense themselves, and take shape; as the one is, so will the other be. Descending, accordingly, into the Dumb Class in its Stockport Cellars and Poor-Law Bastilles, have we not to announce that they are hitherto unexampled in the History of Adam's Posterity?

Life was never a May-game for men: in all times the lot of the dumb millions born to toil was defaced with 40 manifold sufferings, injustices, heavy burdens, avoidable and unavoidable; not play at all, but hard work that made the sinews sore and the heart sore. As bond-slaves, *villani, bordarii, sochemanni,* nay indeed as dukes, earls and kings, men were oftentimes made weary of their life; and had to say, in the sweat of their brow and of their soul, Behold, it is not sport, it is grim earnest, and our back can bear no more! Who knows not what massacrings and harryings there have been; grinding, long-continuing, unbearable injustices,—till 50 the heart had to rise in madness, and some "*Eu Sachsen, nimith euer sachses,* You Saxons, out with your gully-knives, then!" You Saxons, some "arrestment," partial "arrestment of the Knaves and Dastards" has become indispensable!—The page of Dryasdust is heavy with such details.

And yet I will venture to believe that in no time, since the beginnings of Society, was the lot of those same dumb millions of toilers so entirely unbearable as it is even in the days now passing over us. It is not to 60 die, or even to die of hunger, that makes a man wretched; many men have died; all men must die,—the last exit of us all is in a Fire-Chariot of Pain. But it is to live miserable we know not why; to work sore and yet gain nothing; to be heart-worn, weary, yet isolated, unrelated, girt-in with a cold universal Laissez-faire: it is to die slowly all our life long, imprisoned in a deaf, dead, Infinite Injustice, as in the accursed iron belly of a Phalaris' Bull!° This is and remains for ever intolerable to all men whom God has made. Do we wonder at 70 French Revolutions, Chartisms, Revolts of Three Days? The times, if we will consider them, are really unexampled.

Never before did I hear of an Irish Widow reduced to "prove her sisterhood by dying of typhus-fever and infecting seventeen persons,"—saying in such undeniable way, "You *see,* I was your sister!" Sisterhood, brotherhood, was often forgotten; but not till the rise of these ultimate Mammon and Shotbelt° Gospels did I

Democracy   69 Phalaris' Bull, a brazen bull in which Phalaris, tyrant of Agrigentum (sixth century B.C.), punished criminals by burning a fire beneath it
79 Shotbelt, ammunition belt

ever see it so expressly denied. If no pious Lord or *Law-ward* would remember it, always some pious Lady (*"Hlaf dig,"* Benefactress, *"Loaf-giveress,"* they say she is,—blessings on her beautiful heart!) was there, with mild mother-voice and hand, to remember it; some pious thoughtful *Elder,* what we now call "Prester," *Presbyter* or "Priest," was there to put all men in mind of it, in the name of the God who had made all.

Not even in Black Dahomey° was it ever, I think, forgotten to the typhus-fever length. Mungo Park,° resourceless, had sunk down to die under the Negro Village-Tree, a horrible White object in the eyes of all. But in the poor Black Woman, and her daughter who stood aghast at him, whose earthly wealth and funded capital consisted of one small calabash of rice, there lived a heart richer than *"Laissez-faire"* they, with a royal munificence, boiled their rice for him; they sang all night to him, spinning assiduous on their cotton distaffs, as he lay to sleep: "Let us pity the poor white man; no mother has he to fetch him milk, no sister to grind him corn!" Thou poor black Noble One,—thou *Lady* too: did not a God make thee too; was there not in thee too something of a God!—

Gurth,° born thrall of Cedric the Saxon, has been greatly pitied by Dryasdust and others.° Gurth, with the brass collar round his neck, tending Cedric's pigs in the glades of the wood, is not what I call an exemplar of human felicity: but Gurth, with the sky above him, with the free air and tinted boscage and umbrage round him, and in him at least the certainty of supper and social lodging when he came home; Gurth to me seems happy, in comparison with many a Lancashire and Buckinghamshire man, of these days, not born thrall of anybody! Gurth's brass collar did not gall him: Cedric *deserved* to be his Master. The pigs were Cedric's, but Gurth too would get his parings of them. Gurth had the inexpressible satisfaction of feeling himself related indissolubly, though in a rude brass-collar way, to his fellow-mortals in this Earth. He had superiors, inferiors, equals.—Gurth is now "emancipated" long since; has what we call "Liberty." Liberty, I am told, is a Divine thing. Liberty when it becomes the "Liberty to die by starvation" is not so divine!

Liberty? The true liberty of a man, you would say, consisted in his finding out, or being forced to find out, the right path, and to walk thereon. To learn, or to be taught, what work he actually was able for; and then by permission, persuasion, and even compulsion, to set about doing of the same! That is his true blessedness, honour, "liberty" and maximum of wellbeing: if liberty be not that, I for one have small care about liberty. You do not allow a palpable madman to leap over precipices; you violate his liberty, you that are wise; and keep him, were it in strait-waistcoats, away

from the precipices! Every stupid, every cowardly and foolish man is but a less palpable madman: his true liberty were that a wiser man, that any and every wiser man, could, by brass collars, or in whatever milder or sharper way, lay hold of him when he was going wrong, and order and compel him to go a little righter. O, if thou really art my *Senior,* Seigneur, my *Elder,* Presbyter or Priest,—if thou art in very deed my *Wiser,* may a beneficent instinct lead and impel thee to "conquer" me, to command me! If thou do know better than I what is good and right, I conjure thee in the name of God, force me to do it; were it by never such brass collars, whips and handcuffs, leave me not to walk over precipices! That I have been called, by all the Newspapers, a "free man" will avail me little, if my pilgrimage have ended in death and wreck. O that the Newspapers had called me slave, coward, fool, or what it pleased their sweet voices to name me, and I had attained not death, but life!— Liberty requires new definitions.

A conscious abhorrence and intolerance of Folly, of Baseness, Stupidity, Poltroonery and all that brood of things, dwells deep in some men: still deeper in others an *un*conscious abhorrence and intolerance, clothed moreover by the beneficent Supreme Powers in what stout appetites, energies, egoisms so-called, are suitable to it;—these latter are your Conquerors, Romans, Normans, Russians, Indo-English; Founders of what we call Aristocracies. Which indeed have they not the most "divine right" to found;—being themselves very truly "Αριστοι, BRAVEST, BEST; and conquering generally a confused rabble of WORST, or at lowest, clearly enough, of WORSE? I think their divine right, tried, with affirmatory verdict, in the greatest Law-Court known to me, was good! A class of men who are dreadfully exclaimed against by Dryasdust; of whom nevertheless beneficent Nature has oftentimes had need; and may, alas, again have need.

When, across the hundredfold poor scepticisms, trivialisms, and constitutional cob-webberies of Dryasdust, you catch any glimpse of a William the Conqueror,° a Tancred of Hauteville° or such like,—do you not discern veritably some rude outline of a true God-made King; whom not the Champion of England cased in tin, but all Nature and the Universe were calling to the throne? It is absolutely necessary that he get thither. Nature does not mean her poor Saxon children to perish, of obesity, stupor or other malady, as yet: a stern Ruler and Line of Rulers therefore is called in,—a stern but most beneficent *perpetual House-Surgeon* is by Nature herself called in, and even the appropriate *fees* are provided for him! Dryasdust talks lamentably about Hereward° and the Fen Counties; fate of Earl Waltheof;° Yorkshire and the North re-

---

89 **Black Dahomey,** a cannibalistic West African state   90 **Mungo Park,** Scottish surgeon and African explorer (1771–1806)   104 **Gurth,** serf in Scott's novel *Ivanhoe* (1819)   105 **Dryasdust and others,** lifeless historians

175–176 **William the Conqueror,** William of Normandy, conqueror of the Anglo-Saxons in 1066   176 **Tancred of Hauteville,** Norman hero of the Crusade (1078?–1112) featured in Tasso's *Jerusalem Delivered* (1593)   187 **Hereward,** called the Wake, a romantic outlaw-hero of the eleventh century   188 **Earl Waltheof,** Earl of Northumberland, an eleventh-century political martyr, executed by William the Conqueror

duced to ashes; all of which is undoubtedly lamenta-
190 ble. But even Dryasdust apprises me of one fact: "A
child, in this William's reign, might have carried a
purse of gold from end to end of England." My erudite
friend, it is a fact which outweighs a thousand! Sweep
away thy constitutional, sentimental, and other cob-
webberies; look eye to eye, if thou still have any eye,
in the face of this big burly William Bastard: thou wilt
see a fellow of most flashing discernment, of most
strong lion-heart;—in whom, as it were, within a frame
of oak and iron, the gods have planted the soul of "a
200 man of genius"! Dost thou call that nothing? I call it an
immense thing!—Rage enough was in this Willelmus
Conquaestor, rage enough for his occasions;—and yet
the essential element of him, as of all such men, is not
scorching *fire,* but shining illuminative *light.* Fire and
light are strangely interchangeable; nay, at bottom, I
have found them different forms of the same most
godlike "elementary substance" in our world: a thing
worth stating in these days. The essential element of
this Conquaestor is, first of all, the most sun-eyed per-
210 ception of *what is* really what on this God's-Earth;—
which, thou wilt find, does mean at bottom "Justice,"
and "Virtues" not a few: *Conformity* to what the
Maker has seen good to make; that, I suppose, will
mean Justice and a Virtue or two?—

Dost thou think Willelmus Conquaestor would have
tolerated ten years' jargon, one hour's jargon, on the
propriety of killing Cotton-manufactures by partridge
Corn-Laws? I fancy, this was not the man to knock out
of his night's-rest with nothing but a noisy bedlamism
220 in your mouth! "Assist us still better to bush the partridges; strangle Plugson who spins the shirts?"—
"Par la Splendeur de Dieu!"—Dost thou think Willelmus Conquaestor, in this new time, with Steam-
engine Captains of Industry on one hand of him, and
Joe-Manton Captains of Idleness° on the other, would
have doubted which *was* really the BEST; which did
deserve strangling, and which not?

I have a certain indestructible regard for Willelmus
Conquaestor. A resident House-Surgeon, provided by
230 Nature for her beloved English People, and even furnished with the requisite fees, as I said; for he by no
means felt himself doing Nature's work, this Willelmus, but his own work exclusively! And his own work
withal it was; informed *"par la Splendeur de
Dieu."*—I say, it is necessary to get the work out of
such a man, however harsh that be! When a world, not
yet doomed for death, is rushing down to ever-deeper
Baseness and Confusion, it is a dire necessity of Nature's to bring in her ARISTOCRACIES, her BEST, even
240 by forcible methods. When their descendants or representatives cease entirely to *be* the Best, Nature's
poor world will very soon rush down again to Baseness; and it becomes a dire necessity of Nature's to
cast them out. Hence French Revolutions, Five-point

Charters,° Democracies, and a mournful list of *Et-
ceteras,* in these our afflicted times.

To what extent Democracy has now reached, how it
advances irresistible with ominous, ever-increasing
speed, he that will open his eyes on any province of
human affairs may discern. Democracy is everywhere 250
the inexorable demand of these ages, swiftly fulfilling
itself. From the thunder of Napoleon battles, to the
jabbering of Open-vestry° in St. Mary Axe, all things
announce Democracy. A distinguished man, whom
some of my readers will hear again with pleasure, thus
writes to me what in these days he notes from the
Wahngasse of Weissnichtwo, where our London
fashions seem to be in full vogue. Let us hear the Herr
Teufelsdröckh° again, were it but the smallest word!

"Democracy, which means despair of finding any 260
Heroes to govern you, and contented putting up with
the want of them,—alas, thou too, *mein Lieber,°* seest
well how close it is of kin to *Atheism,* and other sad
Isms: he who discovers no God whatever, how shall he
discover Heroes, the visible Temples of God?—
Strange enough meanwhile it is, to observe with what
thoughtlessness, here in our rigidly Conservative
Country, men rush into Democracy with full cry. Beyond doubt, his Excellenz the Titular-Herr Ritter
Kauderwälsch von Pferdefuss-Quacksalber,° he our 270
distinguished Conservative Premier himself, and all
but the thicker-headed of his Party, discern Democracy to be inevitable as death, and are even desperate
of delaying it much!

"You cannot walk the streets without beholding
Democracy announce itself: the very Tailor has become, if not properly Sansculottic, which to him would
be ruinous, yet a Tailor unconsciously symbolizing,
and prophesying with his scissors, the reign of Equality. What now is our fashionable coat? A thing of 280
superfinest texture, of deeply meditated cut; with
Malines-lace° cuffs; quilted with gold; so that a man can
carry, without difficulty, an estate of land on his back?
Keineswegs, By no manner of means! The Sumptuary
Laws° have fallen into such a state of desuetude as was
never before seen. Our fashionable coat is an am-
phibium between barn-sack and drayman's doublet.
The cloth of it is studiously coarse; the colour a
speckled soot-black or rust-brown grey;—the nearest
approach to a Peasant's. And for shape,—thou 290
shouldst see it! The last consummation of the year now
passing over us is definable as Three Bags; a big bag
for the body, two small bags for the arms, and by way
of collar a hem! The first Antique Cheruscan° who, of
felt-cloth or bear's-hide, with bone or metal needle, set
about making himself a coat, before Tailors had yet

225 **Joe-Manton . . . Idleness.** Joseph Manton was a London gunsmith from
whom the aristocrats bought their hunting pieces—hence, idle aristocracy

244–245 **Five-point Charters.** Actually, the People's Charter contained six points,
all calculated to bring about a democratic electorate   253 **Open-vestry,** vehicle
for expression of the will of the rate-paying parishioners—looked upon as a
democratic function   259 **Herr Teufelsdröckh,** author's pseudonym in *Sartor Resartus*   262 **mein Lieber,** my dear friend   270 **Kauderwälsch von Pferdefuss-
Quacksalber,** Gibberish von Horsefoot-Quack-doctor   282 **Malines-lace,** lace
made in Malines, near Brussels   284–285 **Sumptuary Laws,** laws intended to
curb extravagance in private life by limiting expenditures   294 **Cheruscan,**
member of an ancient German tribe

awakened out of Nothing,—did not he make it even so? A loose wide poke for body, with two holes to let out the arms; this was his original coat: to which holes it was soon visible that two small loose pokes, or sleeves, easily appended, would be an improvement.

"Thus has the Tailor-art, so to speak, overset itself, like most other things; changed its centre-of-gravity; whirled suddenly over from zenith to nadir. Your Stulz, with huge somerset, vaults from his high shop-board down to the depths of primal savagery,—carrying much along with him! For I will invite thee to reflect that the Tailor, as topmost ultimate froth of Human Society, is indeed swift-passing, evanescent, slippery to decipher; yet significant of much, nay of all. Topmost evanescent froth, he is churned up from the very lees, and from all intermediate regions of the liquor. The general outcome he, visible to the eye, of what men aimed to do, and were obliged and enabled to do, in this one public department of symbolizing themselves to each other by covering of their skins. A smack of all Human Life lies in the Tailor: its wild struggles towards beauty, dignity, freedom, victory; and how, hemmed in by Sedan and Huddersfield,° by Nescience, Dullness, Prurience, and other sad necessities and laws of Nature, it has attained just to this: Grey savagery of Three Sacks with a hem!

"When the very Tailor verges towards Sansculottism, is it not ominous? The last Divinity of poor mankind dethroning himself; sinking *his* taper too, flame downmost, like the Genius of Sleep or of Death; admonitory that Tailor-time shall be no more!—For, little as one could advise Sumptuary Laws at the present epoch, yet nothing is clearer than that where ranks do actually exist, strict division of costumes will also be enforced; that if we ever have a new Hierarchy and Aristocracy, acknowledged veritably as such, for which I daily pray Heaven, the Tailor will re-awaken; and be, by volunteering and appointment, consciously and unconsciously, a safeguard of that same."—Certain farther observations, from the same invaluable pen, on our never-ending changes of mode, our "perpetual nomadic and even ape-like appetite for change and mere change" in all the equipments of our existence, and the "fatal revolutionary character" thereby manifested, we suppress for the present. It may be admitted that Democracy, in all meanings of the word, is in full career; irresistible by any Ritter Kauderwälsch or other Son of Adam, as times go. "Liberty" is a thing men are determined to have.

But truly, as I had to remark in the mean while, "the liberty of not being oppressed by your fellow man" is an indispensable, yet one of the most insignificant fractional parts of Human Liberty. No man oppresses thee, can bid thee fetch or carry, come or go, without reason shown. True; from all men thou art emancipated: but from Thyself and from the Devil—? No man, wiser, unwiser, can make thee come or go: but thy own futilities, bewilderments, thy false appetites for Money, Windsor Georges° and such like? No man oppresses thee, O free and independent Franchiser: but does not this stupid Porter-pot oppress thee? No Son of Adam can bid thee come or go; but this absurd Pot of Heavy-wet,° this can and does! Thou art the thrall not of Cedric the Saxon, but of thy own brutal appetites, and this scoured dish of liquor. And thou pratest of thy "liberty"? Thou entire blockhead!

Heavy-wet and gin: alas, these are not the only kinds of thraldom. Thou who walkest in a vain show, looking out with ornamental dilettante sniff, and serene supremacy, at all Life and all Death; and amblest jauntily; perking up thy poor talk into crotchets, thy poor conduct into fatuous somnambulisms;—and *art* as an "enchanted Ape" under God's sky, where thou mightest have been a man, had proper Schoolmasters and Conquerors, and Constables with cat-o'-nine tails, been vouch-safed thee: dost thou call that "liberty"? Or your unreposing Mammonworshipper, again, driven, as if by Galvanisms,° by Devils and Fixed-Ideas, who rises early and sits late, chasing the impossible; straining every faculty to "fill himself with the east wind,"—how merciful were it, could you, by mild persuasion or by the severest tyranny so-called, check him in his mad path, and turn him into a wiser one! All painful tyranny, in that case again, were but mild "surgery"; the pain of it cheap, as health and life, instead of galvanism and fixed-idea, are cheap at any price.

Sure enough, of all paths a man could strike into, there *is,* at any given moment, a *best path* for every man; a thing which, here and now, it were of all things *wisest* for him to do;—which could he be but led or driven to do, he were then doing "like a man," as we phrase it; all men and gods agreeing with him, the whole Universe virtually exclaiming Well-done to him! His success, in such case, were complete; his felicity a maximum. This path, to find this path and walk in it, is the one thing needful for him. Whatsoever forwards him in that, let it come to him even in the shape of blows and spurnings, is liberty: whatsoever hinders him, were it wardmotes, open-vestries, poll-booths, tremendous cheers, rivers of heavy-wet, is slavery.

The notion that a man's liberty consists in giving his vote at election-hustings, and saying, "Behold now I too have my twenty-thousandth part of a Talker in our National Palaver;° will not all the gods be good to me?"—is one of the pleasantest! Nature nevertheless is kind at present; and puts it into the heads of many, almost of all. The liberty especially which has to purchase itself by social isolation, and each man standing separate from the other, having "no business

---

319 **Sedan and Huddersfield,** centers of cloth manufacture

355 **Windsor Georges,** that is, pomp, as in royal displays   359 **Heavy-wet,** slang for malt liquor   374 **Galvanisms,** electric shocks   401 **National Palaver,** Parliament

with him'' but a cash-account: this is such a liberty as the Earth seldom saw;—as the Earth will not long put up with, recommend it how you may. This liberty turns out, before it have long continued in action, with all men flinging up their caps round it, to be, for the Working Millions, a liberty to die by want of food; for the Idle Thousands and Units, alas, a still more fatal liberty to live in want of work; to have no earnest duty to do in this God's-World any more. What becomes of a man in such predicament? Earth's Laws are silent; and Heaven's speak in a voice which is not heard. No work, and the ineradicable need of work, give rise to new very wondrous life-philosophies, new very wondrous life-practices! Dilettantism, Pococurantism,° Beau-Brummelism,° with perhaps an occasional, half-mad, protesting burst of Byronism, establish themselves: at the end of a certain period,—if you go back to "the Dead Sea," there is, say our Moslem friends, a very strange "Sabbath-day" transacting itself there! —Brethren, we know but imperfectly yet, after ages of Constitutional Government, what Liberty and Slavery are.

Democracy, the chase of Liberty in that direction, shall go its full course; unrestrained by him of Pferdefuss-Quacksalber, or any of *his* household. The Toiling Millions of Mankind, in most vital need and passionate instinctive desire of Guidance, shall cast away False-Guidance; and hope, for an hour, that No-Guidance will suffice them: but it can be for an hour only. The smallest item of human Slavery is the oppression of man by his Mock-Superiors; the palpablest, but I say at bottom the smallest. Let him shake off such oppression, trample it indignantly under his feet; I blame him not, I pity and commend him. But oppression by your Mock-Superiors well shaken off, the grand problem yet remains to solve: That of finding government by your Real-Superiors! Alas, how shall we ever learn the solution of that, benighted, bewildered, sniffing, sneering, godforgetting unfortunates as we are? It is a work for centuries; to be taught us by tribulations, confusions, insurrections, obstructions; who knows if not by conflagration and despair! It is a lesson inclusive of all other lessons; the hardest of all lessons to learn.

One thing I do know: Those Apes, chattering on the branches by the Dead Sea, never got it learned; but chatter there to this day. To them no Moses need come a second time; a thousand Moseses would be but so many painted Phantasms, interesting Fellow-Apes of new strange aspect,—whom they would "invite to dinner," be glad to meet with in lion-soirées. To them the voice of Prophecy, of heavenly monition, is quite ended. They chatter there, all Heaven shut to them, to the end of the world. The unfortunates! Oh, what is dying of hunger, with honest tools in your hand, with a manful purpose in your heart, and much real labour lying round you done, in comparison? You honestly quit your tools; quit a most muddy confused coil of sore work, short rations, of sorrows, dispiritments and contradictions, having now honestly done with it all;—and await, not entirely in a distracted manner, what the Supreme Powers, and the Silences and the Eternities may have to say to you.

A second thing I know: This lesson will have to be learned,—under penalties! England will either learn it, or England also will cease to exist among Nations. England will either learn to reverence its Heroes, and discriminate them from its Sham-Heroes and Valets and gaslighted Histrios; and to prize them as the audible God's-voice, amid all inane jargons and temporary market-cries, and say to them with heart-loyalty, "Be ye King and Priest, and Gospel and Guidance for us": or else England will continue to worship new and ever-new forms of Quackhood,—and so, with what resiliences and reboundings matters little, go down to the Father of Quacks! Can I dread such things of England? Wretched, thick-eyed, gross-hearted mortals, why will ye worship lies, and "Stuffed Clothes-suits, created by the ninth-parts of men!" It is not your purses that suffer; your farm-rents, your commerces, your mill-revenues, loud as ye lament over these; no, it is not these alone, but a far deeper than these: it is your souls that lie dead, crushed down under despicable Nightmares, Atheisms, Brain-fumes; and are not souls at all, but mere succedanea° for *salt* to keep your bodies and their appetites from putrefying! Your cotton-spinning and thrice-miraculous mechanism, what is this too, by itself, but a larger kind of Animalism? Spiders can spin, Beavers can build and show contrivance: the Ant lays up accumulation of capital, and has, for aught I know, a Bank of Antland. If there is no soul in man higher than all that, did it reach to sailing on the cloud-rack and spinning sea-sand; then I say, man is but an animal, a more cunning kind of brute: he has no soul, but only a succedaneum for salt. Whereupon, seeing himself to be truly of the beasts that perish, he ought to admit it, I think;—and also straightway universally to kill himself; and so, in a manlike manner, at least, *end,* and wave these brute-worlds *his* dignified farewell!—

ARISTOCRACIES

To predict the Future, to manage the Present, would not be so impossible, had not the Past been so sacrilegiously mishandled; effaced, and what is worse, defaced! The Past cannot be seen; the Past, looked at through the medium of "Philosophical History" in these times, cannot even be *not* seen: it is misseen; affirmed to have existed—and to have been a godless impossibility. Your Norman Conquerors, true royal

420 **Pococurantism,** little-care-ism   421 **Beau-Brummelism,** dandyism, after Beau Brumme of the Regency (1811–1820)

491 **succedanea,** substitutes

souls, crowned kings as such, were vulturous irrational tyrants: your Becket° was a noisy egoist and
hypocrite; getting his brains spilt on the floor of Canterbury Cathedral, to secure the main chance—somewhat uncertain how! "Policy, Fanaticism"; or say
"Enthusiasm," even "honest-Enthusiasm"—ah yes,
of course:

The Dog, to gain his private ends,
Went mad, and bit the Man!°—

For in truth, the eye sees in all things "what it
brought with it the means of seeing." A godless century, looking back on centuries that were godly, produces portraitures more miraculous than any other. All
was inane discord in the Past; brute Force bore rule
everywhere; Stupidity, savage Unreason, fitter for
Bedlam than for a human World! Whereby indeed it
becomes sufficiently natural that the like qualities, in
new sleeker habiliments, should continue in our time
to rule. Millions enchanted in Bastille Workhouses;
Irish Widows proving their relationship by typhus-
fever: what would you have? It was ever so, or worse.
Man's History, was it not always even this: the cookery and eating-up of imbecile Dupedom by successful
Quackhood; the battle, with various weapons, of vulturous Quack and Tyrant against vulturous Tyrant and
Quack? No God was in the Past Time; nothing but
Mechanisms and Chaotic Brute-Gods: how shall the
poor "Philosophic Historian," to whom his own century is all godless, see any God in other centuries?

Men believe in Bibles, and disbelieve in them: but of
all Bibles the frightfulest to disbelieve in is this "Bible
of Universal History." This is the Eternal Bible and
God's Book, "which every born man," till once the
soul and eyesight are extinguished in him, "can and
must, with his own eyes, see the God's-Finger writing!" To discredit this, is an *infidelity* like no other.
Such infidelity you would punish, if not by fire and
faggot, which are difficult to manage in our times, yet
by the most peremptory order, To hold its peace till it
got something wiser to say. Why should the blessed
Silence be broken into noises, to communicate only
the like of this? If the Past have no God's-Reason in it,
nothing but Devil's-Unreason, let the Past be eternally
forgotten: mention *it* no more;—we whose ancestors
were all hanged, why should we talk of ropes!

It is, in brief, not true that men ever lived by Delirium, Hypocrisy, Injustice, or any form of Unreason,
since they came to inhabit this Planet. It is not true that
they ever did, or ever will, live except by the reverse
of these. Men will again be taught this. Their acted
History will then again be a Heroism; their written
History, what it once was, an Epic. Nay, forever it is
either such, or else it virtually is—Nothing. Were it

written in a thousand volumes, the Unheroic of such
volumes hastens incessantly to be forgotten: the net
content of an Alexandrian Library° of Unheroics is, and
will ultimately show itself to be, *zero*. What man is
interested to remember *it;* have not all men, at all
times, the liveliest interest to forget it?—"Revelations," if not celestial, then infernal, will teach us that
God is; we shall then, if needful, discern without difficulty that He has always been! The Dryasdust
Philosophisms and enlightened Skepticisms of the
Eighteenth Century, historical and other, will have to
survive for a while with the Physiologists, as a memorable *Nightmare-Dream*. All this haggard epoch, with
its ghastly Doctrines, and death's-head Philosophies
"teaching by example" or otherwise, will one day
have become, what to our Moslem friends their godless ages are, "the Period of Ignorance."

If the convulsive struggles of the last Half-Century
have taught poor struggling convulsed Europe any
truth, it may perhaps be this as the essence of innumerable others: That Europe requires a real Aristocracy, a real Priesthood, or it cannot continue to exist.
Huge French Revolutions, Napoleonisms, then Bour-
bonisms with their corollary of Three Days, finishing
in very unfinal Louis-Philippisms:° all this ought to be
didactic! All this may have taught us: That False
Aristocracies are insupportable; that No-Aristoc-
racies, Liberty-and-Equalities are impossible; that
True Aristocracies are at once, indispensable and not
easily attained.

Aristocracy and Priesthood, a Governing Class and
a Teaching Class: these two, sometimes separate, and
endeavoring to harmonize themselves, sometimes
conjoined as one, and the King a Pontiff-King: there
did no Society exist without these two vital elements,
there will none exist. It lies in the very nature of man:
you will visit no remotest village in the most republican country of the world, where virtually or actually
you do not find these two powers at work. Man, little
as he may suppose it, is necessitated to obey
superiors. He is a social being in virtue of this necessity; nay he could not be gregarious otherwise. He
obeys those whom he esteems better than himself,
wiser, braver; and will forever obey such; and even be
ready and delighted to do it.

The Wiser, Braver: these, a Virtual Aristocracy
everywhere and everywhen, do in all Societies that
reach any articulate shape, develop themselves in a
ruling class, an Actual Aristocracy, with settled modes
of operating, what are called laws and even *private-
laws* or privileges, and so forth; very notable to look
upon in this world.—Aristocracy and Priesthood, we
say, are sometimes united. For indeed the Wiser and
the Braver are properly but one class; no wise man but
needed first of all to be a brave man, or he never had

Aristocracies 10 **Becket,** Thomas a Becket (1118?–1170), first Chancellor under
Henry II and later Archbishop of Canterbury. He was killed in the cathedral by
supporters of Henry's cause against the Church 16–17 **The Dog . . . the Man**
from Oliver Goldsmith, "Elegy on the Death of a Mad Dog"

64 **Alexandrian Library.** The library of Alexandria, destroyed in the seventh century, was reknowned in the classical world for the size of its collection
86 **Louis-Philippisms.** Charles X, a Bourbon, was deposed in 1830, after a three-
day revolution, and replaced by Louis Philippe

been wise. The noble Priest was always a noble *Aristos* to begin with, and something more to end with. Your Luther, your Knox, your Anselm, Becket, Abbot Samson,° Samuel Johnson, if they had not been brave enough, by what possibility could they ever have been wise?—If, from accident and forethought, this your Actual Aristocracy have got discriminated into Two Classes, there can be no doubt but the Priest Class is the more dignified; supreme over the other, as governing head is over active hand. And yet in practice again, it is likeliest the reverse will be found arranged;—a sign that the arrangement is already vitiated; that a split is introduced into it, which will widen and widen till the whole be rent asunder.

In England, in Europe generally, we may say that these two Virtualities have unfolded themselves into Actualities, in by far the noblest and richest manner any region of the world ever saw. A spiritual Guideship, a practical Governorship, fruit of the grand conscious endeavors, say rather of the immeasurable unconscious instincts and necessities of men, have established themselves; very strange to behold. Everywhere, while so much has been forgotten, you find the King's Palace, and the Viceking's Castle, Mansion, Manorhouse; till there is not an inch of ground from sea to sea but has both its King and Viceking, long due series of Vicekings, its Squire, Earl, Duke or whatever the title of him—to whom you have given the land, that he may govern you in it.

More touching still, there is not a hamlet where poor peasants congregate, but, by one means and another, a Church-Apparatus has been got together—roofed edifice, with revenues and belfries; pulpit, reading-desk, with Books and Methods: possibility, in short, and strict prescription: That a man stand there and speak of spiritual things to men. It is beautiful;—even in its great obscuration and decadence, it is among the beautifulest, most touching objects one sees on the Earth. This Speaking Man has indeed, in these times, wandered terribly from the point; has, alas, as it were, totally lost sight of the point: yet, at bottom, whom have we to compare with him? Of all public functionaries boarded and lodged on the Industry of Modern Europe, is there one worthier of the board he has? A man even professing, and never so languidly making still some endeavor, to save the souls of men: contrast him with a man professing to do little but shoot the partridges of men! I wish he could find the point again, this Speaking One; and stick to it with tenacity, with deadly energy; for there is need of him yet! The Speaking Function, this of Truth coming to us with a living voice, nay in a living shape, and as a concrete practical exemplar: this, with all our Writing and Printing Functions, has a perennial place. Could he but find the point again—take the old spectacles off his nose, and looking up discover, almost in contact with him, what the *real* Satanas, and soul-devouring, world-devouring *Devil,* now is! Original Sin and such-like are bad enough, I doubt not: but distilled Gin, dark Ignorance, Stupidity, dark Corn-Law,° Bastille and Company, what are they! *Will* he discover our new real Satan, whom he has to fight; or go on droning through his old nose-spectacles about old extinct Satans; and never see the real one, till he *feel* him at his own throat and ours? That is a question, for the world! Let us not intermeddle with it here.

Sorrowful, phantasmal as this same Double Aristocracy of Teachers and Governors now looks, it is worth all men's while to know that the purport of it is and remains noble and most real. Dryasdust, looking merely at the surface, is greatly in error as to those ancient Kings. William Conqueror, William Rufus or Redbeard, Stephen Curthose himself much more Henry Beauclerc and our brave Plantagenet Henry:° the life of these men was not a vulturous Fighting; it was a valorous Governing—to which occasionally Fighting did, and alas must yet, though far seldomer now, superadd itself as an accident, a distressing impedimental adjunct. The fighting too was indispensable, for ascertaining who had the might over whom, the right over whom. By much hard fighting, as we once said, "the unrealities, beaten into dust, flew gradually off"; and left the plain reality and fact, "Thou stronger than I; thou wiser than I; thou king, and subject I," in a somewhat clearer condition.

Truly we cannot enough admire, in those Abbot-Samson and William Conqueror times, the arrangement they had made of their Governing Classes. Highly interesting to observe how the sincere insight, on their part, into what did, of primary necessity, behove to be accomplished, had led them to the way of accomplishing it, and in the course of time to get it accomplished! No imaginary Aristocracy would serve their turn; and accordingly they attained a real one. The Bravest men, who, it is ever to be repeated and remembered, are also on the whole the Wisest, Strongest, everyway Best, had here, with a respectable degree of accuracy, been got selected; seated each on his piece of territory, which was lent him, then gradually given him, that he might govern it. These Vicekings, each on his portion of the common soil of England, with a Head King over all, were a "Virtuality perfected into an Actuality" really to an astonishing extent.

For those were rugged stalwart ages; full of earnestness, of a rude God's-truth—nay, at any rate, their *quilting* was so unspeakably *thinner* than ours; Fact came swiftly on them, if at any time they had yielded to Phantasm! "The Knaves and Dastards" had to be "arrested" in some measure; or the world, almost within year and day, found that it could not live. The

---

120 **Abbot Samson,** monastic leader discussed by Carlyle in an earlier section of *Past and Present*

176 **Corn-Law,** restrictions on importation of foreign corn (grain). Such laws caused political controversy and economic distress   188–190 **William . . . Henry,** kings of England, 1066–1189

Knaves and Dastards accordingly were got arrested. Dastards upon the very throne had to be got arrested, and taken off the throne—by such methods as there were; by the roughest method, if there chanced to be no smoother one! Doubtless there was much harshness of operation, much severity; as indeed government and surgery are often somewhat severe. Gurth, born thrall of Cedric, it is like, got cuffs as often as pork-parings, if he misdemeaned himself; but Gurth did belong to Cedric: no human creature then went about connected with nobody; left to go his way into Bastilles or worse, under *Laissez-faire;* reduced to prove his relationship by dying of typhus-fever!—Days come when there is no King in Israel, but every man is his own king, doing that which is right in his own eyes;—and tarbarrels are burnt to "Liberty," "Ten-pound Franchise," and the like, with considerable effect in various ways!—

That Feudal Aristocracy, I say, was no imaginary one. To a respectable degree, its *Jarls,* what we now call Earls, were *Strong-Ones* in fact as well as etymology; its Dukes *Leaders;* its Lords *Law-wards.* They did all the Soldiering and Police of the country, all the Judging, Law-making, even the Church-Extension; whatsoever in the way of Governing, of Guiding and Protecting could be done. It was a Land Aristocracy; it managed the Governing of this English People, and had the reaping of the Soil of England in return. It is, in many senses, the Law of Nature, this same Law of Feudalism;—no right Aristocracy but a Land one! The curious are invited to meditate upon it in these days. Soldiering, Police, and Judging, Church-Extension, nay real Government and Guidance, all this was actually *done* by the Holders of the Land in return for their Land. How much of it is now done by them; done by anybody? Good Heavens, *"Laissez-faire,* Do ye nothing, eat your wages and sleep" is everywhere the passionate half-wise cry of this time; and they will not so much as do nothing, but must do mere Corn-Laws! We raise Fifty-two millions, from the general mass of us, to get our Governing done—or, alas, to get ourselves persuaded that it is done: and the "peculiar burden of the Land" is to pay, not all this, but to pay, as I learn, one twenty-fourth part of all this. Our first Chartist Parliament, or Oliver *Redivivus,*° you would say, will know where to lay the new taxes of England!—Or, alas, taxes? If we made the Holders of the Land pay every shilling still of the expense of Governing the Land, what were all that? The Land, by mere hired Governors, cannot be got governed. You cannot hire men to govern the Land; it is by mission not contracted for in the Stock-Exchange, but felt in their own hearts as coming out of Heaven, that men can govern a Land. The mission of a Land Aristocracy is a *sacred* one, in both the senses of that old word.

The footing it stands on, at present, might give rise to thoughts other than of Corn-Laws!—

But truly a "Splendor of God," as in William Conqueror's rough oath, did dwell in those old rude veracious ages; did inform, more and more, with a heavenly nobleness, all departments of their work and life. Phantasms could not yet walk abroad in mere Cloth Tailorage; they were at least Phantasms "on the rim of the horizon," penciled there by an eternal Lightbeam from within. A most "practical" Hero-worship went on, unconsciously or half-consciously, everywhere. A Monk Samson, with a maximum of two shillings in his pocket, could, without a ballot-box, be made a Viceking of, being seen to be worthy. The difference between a good man and a bad man was as yet felt to be, what it forever is, an immeasurable one. Who *durst* have elected a Pandarus Dogdraught, in those days, to any office, Carlton Club, Senatorship, or place whatsoever? It was felt that the arch Satanas and no other had a clear right of property in Pandarus; that it were better for you to have no hand in Pandarus, to keep out of Pandarus his neighborhood! Which is, to this hour, the mere fact; though for the present, alas, the forgotten fact. I think they were comparatively blessed times those, in their way! "Violence," "war," "disorder": well, what is war, and death itself, to such a perpetual life-in-death, and "peace, peace, where there is no peace"! Unless some Hero-worship, in its new appropriate form, can return, this world does not promise to be very habitable long.

Old Anselm,° exiled Archbishop of Canterbury, one of the purest-minded "men of genius," was traveling to make his appeal to Rome against King Rufus—a man of rough ways, in whom the "inner Lightbeam" shone very fitfully. It is beautiful to read, in Monk Eadmer,° how the continental populations welcomed and venerated this Anselm, as no French population now venerates Jean-Jacques° or giant-killing Voltaire; as not even an American population now venerates a Schnüspel the distinguished Novelist! They had, by phantasy and true insight, the intensest conviction that a God's-Blessing dwelt in this Anselm—as is my conviction too. They crowded round, with bent knees and enkindled hearts, to receive his blessing, to hear his voice, to see the light of his face. My blessings on them and on him!—but the notablest was a certain necessitous or covetous Duke of Burgundy, in straitened circumstances we shall hope—who reflected that in all likelihood this English Archbishop, going towards Rome to appeal, must have taken store of cash with him to bribe the Cardinals. Wherefore he of Burgundy, for his part, decided to lie in wait and rob him. "In an open space of a wood," some "wood" then

313 **Anselm,** Scholastic philosopher (1033–1109). Appointed Archbishop of Canterbury by William Rufus (1093). Subsequently exiled by Rufus and Henry I. Canonized in 1494   318 **Eadmer,** monk of Canterbury (d. 1124?), chronicler and biographer of Anselm   320 **Jean-Jacques,** Jean Jacques Rousseau (1712–1778), French philosopher and author

272 **Redivivus,** returned to life

green and growing, eight centuries ago, in Burgundian Land—this fierce Duke, with fierce steel followers, shaggy, savage, as the Russian bear, dashes out on the weak old Anselm; who is riding along there, on his small quiet-going pony; escorted only by Eadmer and another poor Monk on ponies; and, except small modicum of roadmoney, not a gold coin in his possession. The steel-clad Russian bear emerges, glaring: the old white-bearded man starts not—paces on unmoved, looking into him with those clear old earnest eyes, with that venerable sorrowful time-worn face; of whom no man or thing need be afraid, and who also is afraid of no created man or thing. The fire-eyes of his Burgundian Grace meet these clear eye-glances, convey them swift to his heart: he bethinks him that probably this feeble, fearless, hoary Figure has in it something of the Most High God; that probably he shall be damned if he meddle with it—that, on the whole, he had better not. He plunges, the rough savage, from his war-horse, down to his knees; embraces the feet of old Anselm: he too begs his blessing; orders men to escort him, guard him from being robbed, and under dread penalties see him safe on his way. *Per os Dei,*° as his Majesty was wont to ejaculate!

Neither is this quarrel of Rufus and Anselm, of Henry and Becket uninstructive to us. It was, at bottom, a great quarrel. For, admitting that Anselm was full of divine blessing, he by no means included in him all forms of divine blessing—there were far other forms withal, which he little dreamed of; and William Redbeard was unconsciously the representative and spokesman of these. In truth, could your divine Anselm, your divine Pope Gregory have had their way, the results had been very notable. Our Western World had all become a European Thibet, with one Grand Lama sitting at Rome; our one honorable business that of singing mass, all day and all night. Which would not in the least have suited us. The Supreme Powers willed it not so.

It was as if King Redbeard unconsciously, addressing Anselm, Becket, and the others, had said: "Right Reverend, your Theory of the Universe is indisputable by man or devil. To the core of our heart we feel that this divine thing, which you call Mother Church, does fill the whole world hitherto known, and is and shall be all our salvation and all our desire. And yet—and yet—Behold, though it is an unspoken secret, the world is *wider* than any of us think, Right Reverend! Behold, there are yet other immeasurable Sacrednesses in this that you call Heathenism, Secularity! On the whole I, in an obscure but most rooted manner, feel that I cannot comply with you. Western Thibet and perpetual mass-chanting—No. I am, so to speak, in the family-way; with child, of I know not what—certainly of something far different from this! I

have—*Per os Dei,* I have Manchester Cotton-trades, Bromwicham Iron-trades, American Commonwealths, Indian Empires, Steam Mechanisms, and Shakespeare Dramas, in my belly; and cannot do it, Right Reverend!"—So accordingly it was decided: and Saxon Becket spilt his life in Canterbury Cathedral, as Scottish Wallace° did on Tower-hill, and as generally a noble man and martyr has to do—not for nothing; no, but for a divine something other than *he* had altogether calculated. We will now quit this of the hard, organic, but limited Feudal Ages; and glance timidly into the immense Industrial Ages, as yet all inorganic, and in a quite pulpy condition, requiring desperately to harden themselves into some organism!

Our Epic having now become *Tools and the Man,*° it is more than usually impossible to prophesy the Future. The boundless Future does lie there, predestined, nay already extant though unseen; hiding, in its Continents of Darkness, "gladness and sorrow"; but the supremest intelligence of man cannot prefigure much of it—the united intelligence and effort of All Men in all coming generations, this alone will gradually prefigure it, and figure and form it into a seen fact! Straining our eyes hitherto, the utmost effort of intelligence sheds but some most glimmering dawn, a little way into its dark enormous Deeps: only huge outlines loom uncertain on the sight; and the ray of prophecy, at a short distance, expires. But may we not say, here as always, Sufficient for the day is the evil thereof! To shape the whole Future is not our problem; but only to shape faithfully a small part of it, according to rules already known. It is perhaps possible for each of us, who will with due earnestness inquire, to ascertain clearly what he, for his own part, ought to do: this let him, with true heart, do, and continue doing. The general issue will, as it has always done, rest well with a Higher Intelligence than ours.

One grand "outline," or even two, many earnest readers may perhaps, at this stage of the business, be able to prefigure for themselves—and draw some guidance from. One prediction, or even two, are already possible. For the Life-Tree Igdrasil,° in all its new developments, is the selfsame world-old Life-Tree: having found an element or elements there, running from the very roots of it in Hela's Realms, in the Well of Mimer and of the Three Nornas or TIMES, up to this present hour of it in our own hearts, we conclude that such will have to continue. A man has, in his own soul, an Eternal; can read something of the Eternal there, if he will look! He already knows what will continue; what cannot, by any means or appliance whatsoever, be made to continue!

One wide and widest "outline" ought really, in all

---

358 **Per os Dei,** from the mouth of God

397 **Wallace,** Scottish patriot (d. 1305)   405 **Tools and the Man,** Vergil's *Aeneid* begins "I sing of arms and the man." Carlyle wishes to contrast the classical and modern ages   432 **Igdrasil,** in Norse mythology a tree supposed to support the entire universe. Its roots are in hell, its trunk is in earth, and its branches are in heaven

ways, to be becoming clear to us; this namely: That a "Splendor of God," in one form or other, will have to unfold itself from the heart of these our Industrial Ages too; or they will never get themselves "organized"; but continue chaotic, distressed, distracted evermore, and have to perish in frantic suicidal dissolution. A
450 second "outline" or prophecy, narrower, but also wide enough, seems not less certain: That there will again *be* a King in Israel; a system of Order and Government; and every man shall, in some measure, see himself constrained to do that which is right in the King's eyes. This too we may call a sure element of the Future; for this too is of the Eternal;—this too is of the Present, though hidden from most; and without it no fiber of the Past ever was. An actual new Sovereignty, Industrial Aristocracy, real not imagi-
460 nary Aristocracy, is indispensable and indubitable for us.

But what an Aristocracy; on what new, far more complex and cunningly devised conditions than that old Feudal fighting one! For we are to bethink us that the Epic verily is not *Arms and the Man*, but *Tools and the Man*—an infinitely wider kind of Epic. And again we are to bethink us that men cannot now be bound to men by *brass-collars*—not at all: that this brass-collar method, in all figures of it, has vanished out of Europe
470 forevermore! Huge Democracy, walking the streets everywhere in its Sack Coat, has asserted so much; irrevocably, brooking no reply! True enough, man *is* forever the "born thrall" of certain men, born master of certain other men, born equal of certain others, let him acknowledge the fact or not. It is unblessed for him when he cannot acknowledge this fact; he is in the chaotic state, ready to perish, till he do get the fact acknowledged. But no man is, or can henceforth be, the brass-collar thrall of any man; you will have to bind
480 him by other, far nobler and cunninger methods. Once for all, he is to be loose of the brass-collar, to have a scope *as* wide as his faculties now are—will he not be all the usefuler to you in that new state? Let him go abroad as a trusted one, as a free one; and return home to you with rich earnings at night! Gurth could only tend pigs; this one will build cities, conquer waste worlds.—How, in conjunction with inevitable Democracy, indispensable Sovereignty is to exist: certainly it is the hugest question ever heretofore propounded to
490 Mankind! The solution of which is work for long years and centuries. Years and centuries, of one knows not what complexion;—blessed or unblessed, according as they shall, with earnest valiant effort, make progress therein, or, in slothful unveracity and dilettantism, only talk of making progress. For either progress therein, or swift and ever swifter progress towards dissolution, is henceforth a necessity.

It is of importance that this grand reformation were begun; that Corn-Law Debatings and other jargon, lit-
500 tle less than delirious in such a time, had fled far away, and left us room to begin! For the evil has grown prac-
tical, extremely conspicuous; if it be not seen and provided for, the blindest fool will have to feel it ere long. There is much that can wait; but there is something also that cannot wait. With millions of eager Working Men imprisoned in "Impossibility" and Poor-Law Bastilles, it is time that some means of dealing with them were trying to become "possible"! Of the Government of England, of all articulate-speaking functionaries, real and imaginary Aristocracies, of me 510 and of thee, it is imperatively demanded, "How do you mean to manage these men? Where are they to find a supportable existence? What is to become of them—and of you!" (IV, 1)
(1843)

JOHN HENRY CARDINAL NEWMAN 1801–1890

The son of a London banker, Newman was sent to an evangelical school with strong Calvinist tendencies. He later attended Trinity College, Oxford, and was made vicar of St. Mary's, Oxford, in 1828. For a time he was attracted to Liberalism, but in 1833 he became deeply involved with John Keble, Richard Froude, and others in the Oxford Movement. A high church movement within the Church of England, the Oxford Movement was started at Oxford in 1833 with the object of stressing the Catholic elements in the Anglican Church. Newman was one of its founders and intellectual leaders, contributing numerous books, including *Lectures on the Prophetical Office of the Church* (1837) and *University Sermons* (1843), and twenty-four of the famous *Tracts for the Times* (1833–1841), which were manifestos of the Movement. Bishop Richard Bagot of Oxford requested that the tracts be suspended; consequently, Newman resigned from St. Mary's in 1843. Gradually, he came to believe that "there are but two alternatives, the way to Rome and the way to atheism," and he chose the former.

In 1845 he was received into the Roman Catholic Church and a year later was ordained in Rome. He was regarded with suspicion by the more rigorous Roman Catholic clergy because of his seemingly liberal sympathies. Many Anglicans regarded him as a traitor not only to the Church of England but to England itself. His existence was not a happy one. In 1852 he was summoned to Ireland to be the first rector of the Catholic University in Dublin. There he gave his famous series of lectures, called *The Idea of a University*, in defense of liberal education. By virtue of its subject matter and sophisticated reasoning, *The Idea of* a *University* (published 1873) is the most compelling of Newman's books for the general reader. He resigned his post at the Catholic University in 1856; his role as editor of the Roman Catholic monthly, *The Rambler*, in which he encouraged critical scholarship among Catholics, angered Henry Edward Manning, later made a cardinal (1875) in the Roman Catholic Church. Thus, Newman became the most controversial religious figure of the Victorian period and one of its greatest prose stylists.

In 1864 he was verbally attacked by Charles Kingsley, an Anglican cleric and novelist of extreme anti-Catholic views. He responded to this attack by writing his autobiographical *Apologia pro Vita Sua* (1864), which justified the honesty of his life as an Anglican and which was a defense of his current religious opinions. Newman's autobiography is not only a revelation of his own personality but also a revelation of the personality of the age in which he lived. The *Apologia* was very widely read and favorably discussed by both Catholics and non-Catholics. It was greatly admired for its candor, fairness, interest, and beautiful style. It ended many of Newman's frustrations and assured his stature in the Roman Catholic Church. In 1870 he wrote *A Grammar of Assent*, which, though highly philosophical, was also well received. In 1878 Protestant Oxford elected him to an honorary fellowship in Trinity, his old college. He was made a cardinal in the Roman Church in 1879. He died in 1890. His influence in both the Catholic Church and the Church of England was, and is, great. His early treatise, *The Development of Christian Doctrine* (1845), was frequently and favorably quoted in the proceedings of the Second Vatican Council (1962–1965).

The moculated tone and clarity that distinguish Newman's prose style were achieved by great conscious effort. He described his habits of composition in a way that should reassure any writer struggling for clarity: "I write," he said, "I write again: I write a third time in the course of six months. Then I take the third: I literally fill the paper with corrections, so that another person could not read it. I then write it out fair for the printer. I put it by; I take it up; I begin to correct again it will not do. Alterations multiply, pages are re-written, little lines sneak in and crawl about. The whole page is disfigured; I write again; I cannot count how many times this process is repeated."

from THE IDEA OF A UNIVERSITY

From May 10 to June 7, 1852, Newman delivered nine lectures to the Catholics of Dublin. In the same year these lectures were published as *Discourses on the Scope and Nature of a University Education*. Afterwards they were revised and republished with a series of "Occasional Lectures and Essays on University Subjects" as *The Idea of a University* (1873).

The subject was not new to Newman. In 1841 Sir Robert Peel had delivered an address at the opening of a new library and reading room at Tamworth, in Staffordshire. Peel had seemed to Newman to say something like this: "Education is the cultivation of the intellect and heart, and Useful Knowledge is the great instrument of education. It is the parent of virtue, the nurse of religion; it exalts man to his highest perfection, and is the sufficient scope of his most earnest exertions." Under the pseudonym of "Catholicus," Newman set out to analyze and refute these arguments for "useful knowledge." He argued that secular knowledge was *not* the nurse of religion, was *not* a direct means of moral improvement, was *not* a principle of action. Newman worried that the liberals would substitute the subtle fault for the gross fault. To make knowledge the test of admirable men was to eliminate good and evil as criteria of judgment. According to Newman, rationalism, the philosophical basis of liberalism, was more concerned with concluding rightly than with right conclusions. Thus, his purpose was not to attack secular knowledge but to resist the pretense that secular knowledge could do more than it in fact could.

DISCOURSE V

KNOWLEDGE ITS OWN END

A university may be considered with reference either to its Students or to its Studies; and the principle, that all Knowledge is a whole and the separate Sciences parts of one, which I have hitherto been using in behalf of its studies, is equally important when we direct our attention to its students. Now then I turn to the students, and shall consider the education which, by virtue of this principle, a University will give them; and thus I shall be introduced, Gentlemen, to the second question, which I proposed to discuss, viz., whether 10 and in what sense its teaching, viewed relatively to the taught, carries the attribute of Utility along with it.

1.

I have said that all branches of knowledge are connected together, because the subject-matter of knowledge is intimately united in itself, as being the acts and the work of the Creator. Hence it is that the Sciences, into which our knowledge may be said to be cast, have multiplied bearings one on another, and an internal sympathy, and admit, or rather demand, comparison and adjustment. They complete, correct, balance each 20 other. This consideration, if well-founded, must be taken into account, not only as regards the attainment of truth, which is their common end, but as regards the influence which they exercise upon those whose education consists in the study of them. I have said already, that to give undue prominence to one is to be unjust to another; to neglect or supersede these is to divert those from their proper object. It is to unsettle the boundary lines between science and science, to 30 disturb their action, to destroy the harmony which binds them together. Such a proceeding will have a corresponding effect when introduced into a place of education. There is no science but tells a different tale, when viewed as a portion of a whole, from what it is likely to suggest when taken by itself, without the safeguard, as I may call it, of others.

Let me make use of an illustration. In the combination of colors, very different effects are produced by a difference in their selection and juxtaposition; red, 40 green, and white change their shades, according to the contrast to which they are submitted. And, in like manner, the drift and meaning of a branch of knowledge varies with the company in which it is introduced to the student. If his reading is confined simply to one subject, however such division of labor may favor the advancement of a particular pursuit, a point into which I do not here enter, certainly it has a tendency to contract his mind. If it is incorporated with others, it depends on those others as to the kind of influence which 50 it exerts upon him. Thus the Classics, which in England are the means of refining the taste, have in France subserved the spread of revolutionary and deistical doctrines. In Metaphysics, again, Butler's° *Analogy of Religion* which has had so much to do with the conversion of members of the University of Oxford, appeared to Pitt and others, who had received a different training, to operate only in the direction of infidelity. And so again, Watson,° Bishop of Llandaff, as I think he tells us in the narrative of his life, felt the science of 60 Mathematics to indispose the mind to religious belief, while others see in its investigations the best defense of the Christian Mysteries. In like manner, I suppose, Arcesilaus° would not have handled logic as Aristotle, nor Aristotle have criticized poets as Plato; yet reasoning and poetry are subject to scientific rules.

It is a great point then to enlarge the range of studies which a University professes, even for the sake of the students; and, though they cannot pursue every subject which is open to them, they will be the gainers by 70 living among those and under those who represent the whole circle. This I conceive to be the advantage of a seat of universal learning, considered as a place of education. An assemblage of learned men, zealous for their own sciences, and rivals of each other, are brought, by familiar intercourse and for the sake of intellectual peace, to adjust together the claims and relations of their respective subjects of investigation. They learn to respect, to consult, to aid each other. Thus is created a pure and clear atmosphere of thought, which the student also breathes, though in his 80 own case he only pursues a few sciences out of the multitude. He profits by an intellectual tradition, which is independent of particular teachers, which guides him in his choice of subjects, and duly interprets for him those which he chooses. He apprehends the great outlines of knowledge, the principles on which it rests, the scale of its parts, its lights and its shades, its great points and its little, as he otherwise cannot apprehend them. Hence it is that his education is called "Liberal." A habit of mind is formed which 90 lasts through life, of which the attributes are, freedom, equitableness, calmness, moderation, and wisdom; or what in a former Discourse I have ventured to call a philosophical habit. This then I would assign as the special fruit of the education furnished at a University, as contrasted with other places of teaching or modes of teaching. This is the main purpose of a University in its treatment of its students.

And now the question is asked me, What is the *use* of it? And my answer will constitute the main subject 100 of the Discourses which are to follow.

2.

Cautious and practical thinkers, I say, will ask of me, what, after all, is the gain of this Philosophy, of which I make such account, and from which I promise so much. Even supposing it to enable us to give the degree of confidence exactly due to every science respectively, and to estimate precisely the value of every truth which is anywhere to be found, how are we better for this master view of things, which I have been extolling? Does it not reverse the principle of the divi- 110 sion of labor? will practical objects be obtained better or worse by its cultivation? to what then does it lead? where does it end? what does it do? how does it profit? what does it promise? Particular sciences are respectively the basis of definite arts, which carry on to results tangible and beneficial the truths which are the subjects of the knowledge attained; what is the Art of this science of sciences? what is the fruit of such a Philosophy? what are we proposing to effect, what inducements do we hold out to the Catholic community, 120 when we set about the enterprise of founding a University?

I am asked what is the end of University Education, and of the Liberal or Philosophical Knowledge which I conceive it to impart: I answer, that what I have already said has been sufficient to show that it has a very tangible, real, and sufficient end, though the end cannot be divided from that knowledge itself. Knowledge is capable of being its own end. Such is the constitu-

53 **Butler,** Joseph Butler (1692–1752), Anglican divine   58 **Watson,** Richard Watson (1737–1816), defender of Christianity against Edward Gibbon and Tom Paine   63 **Arcesilaus,** Greek philosopher of the third century B.C.

tion of the human mind, that any kind of knowledge, if it be really such, is its own reward. And if this is true of all knowledge, it is true also of that special Philosophy, which I have made to consist in a comprehensive view of truth in all its branches, of the relations of science to science, of their mutual bearings, and their respective values. What the worth of such an acquirement is, compared with other objects which we seek—wealth or power or honor or the conveniences and comforts of life—I do not profess here to discuss; but I would maintain, and mean to show, that it is an object, in its own nature so really and undeniably good, as to be the compensation of a great deal of thought in the compassing, and a great deal of trouble in the attaining.

Now, when I say that Knowledge is, not merely a means to something beyond it, or the preliminary of certain arts into which it naturally resolves, but an end sufficient to rest in and to pursue for its own sake, surely I am uttering no paradox, for I am stating what is both intelligible in itself, and has ever been the common judgment of philosophers and the ordinary feeling of mankind. I am saying what at least the public opinion of this day ought to be slow to deny, considering how much we have heard of late years, in opposition to Religion, of entertaining, curious, and various knowledge. I am but saying what whole volumes have been written to illustrate, by a "selection from the records of Philosophy, Literature, and Art, in all ages and countries, of a body of examples, to show how the most unpropitious circumstances have been unable to conquer an ardent desire for the acquisition of knowledge."° That further advantages accrue to us and redound to others by its possession, over and above what it is in itself, I am very far indeed from denying; but, independent of these, we are satisfying a direct need of our nature in its very acquisition; and, whereas our nature, unlike that of the inferior creation, does not at once reach its perfection, but depends, in order to it, on a number of external aids and appliances, Knowledge, as one of the principal gifts or accessories by which it is completed, is valuable for what its very presence in us does for us after the manner of a habit, even though it be turned to no further account, nor subserve any direct end.

3.

Hence it is that Cicero, in enumerating the various heads of mental excellence, lays down the pursuit of Knowledge for its own sake, as the first of them. "This pertains most of all to human nature," he says, "for we are all of us drawn to the pursuit of Knowledge; in which to excel we consider excellent, whereas to mistake, to err, to be ignorant, to be deceived, is both an evil and a disgrace." And he considers Knowledge the very first object to which we are attracted, after the supply of our physical wants. After the calls and duties of our animal existence, as they may be termed, as regards ourselves, our family, and our neighbors, follows, he tells us, "the search after truth. Accordingly, as soon as we escape from the pressure of necessary cares, forthwith we desire to see, to hear, to learn; and consider the knowledge of what is hidden or is wonderful a condition of our happiness."°

This passage, though it is but one of many similar passages in a multitude of authors, I take for the very reason that it is so familiarly known to us; and I wish you to observe, Gentlemen, how distinctly it separates the pursuit of Knowledge from those ulterior objects to which certainly it can be made to conduce, and which are, I suppose, solely contemplated by the persons who would ask of me the use of a University or Liberal Education. So far from dreaming of the cultivation of Knowledge directly and mainly in order to our physical comfort and enjoyment, for the sake of life and person, of health, of the conjugal and family union, of the social tie and civil security, the great Orator implies, that it is only after our physical and political needs are supplied, and when we are "free from necessary duties and cares," that we are in a condition for "desiring to see, to hear, and to learn." Nor does he contemplate in the least degree the reflex or subsequent action of Knowledge, when acquired, upon those material goods which we set out by securing before we seek it; on the contrary, he expressly denies its bearing upon social life altogether, strange as such a procedure is to those who live after the rise of the Baconian philosophy, and he cautions us against such a cultivation of it as will interfere with our duties to our fellow-creatures. "All these methods," he says, "are engaged in the investigation of truth; by the pursuit of which to be carried off from public occupations is a transgression of duty. For the praise of virtue lies altogether in action; yet intermissions often occur, and then we recur to such pursuits; not to say that the incessant activity of the mind is vigorous enough to carry us on in the pursuit of knowledge, even without any exertion of our own." The idea of benefiting society by means of "the pursuit of science and knowledge," did not enter at all into the motives which he would assign for their cultivation.

This was the ground of the opposition which the elder Cato° made to the introduction of Greek Philosophy among his countrymen, when Carneades° and his companions, on occasion of their embassy, were charming the Roman youth with their eloquent

156–161 selection . . . knowledge, from *Pursuit of Knowledge under Difficulties,* by George Lillie Craik (1798–1866)

176–190 This pertains . . . happiness, "Cicero, *Offic. init.*"—Newman's note
229 Cato, Roman statesman (234–149 B.C.)   230 Carneades, Skeptic philosopher of the third century B.C. who held that man has no criterion for truth

expositions of it. The fit representative of a practical people, Cato estimated everything by what it produced; whereas the Pursuit of Knowledge promised nothing beyond Knowledge itself. He despised that refinement or enlargement of mind of which he had no experience.

4.

Things, which can bear to be cut off from everything else and yet persist in living, must have life in themselves; pursuits, which issue in nothing, and still maintain their ground for ages, which are regarded as admirable, though they have not as yet proved themselves to be useful, must have their sufficient end in themselves, whatever it turn out to be. And we are brought to the same conclusion by considering the force of the epithet, by which the knowledge under consideration is popularly designated. It is common to speak of "*liberal* knowledge," of the "*liberal* arts and studies," and of a "*liberal* education," as the especial characteristic or property of a University and of a gentleman; what is really meant by the word? Now, first, in its grammatical sense it is opposed to *servile*; and by "servile work" is understood, as our catechisms inform us, bodily labor, mechanical employment, and the like, in which the mind has little or no part. Parallel to such works are those arts, if they deserve the name of which the poet speaks,° which owe their origin and their method to hazard, not to skill; as, for instance, the practice and operations of an empiric. As far as this contrast may be considered as a guide into the meaning of the word, liberal knowledge and liberal pursuits are exercises of mind, of reason, of reflection.

But we want something more for its explanation, for there are bodily exercises which are liberal, and mental exercises which are not so. For instance, in ancient times the practitioners in medicine were commonly slaves; yet it was an art as intellectual in its nature, in spite of the pretense, fraud, and quackery with which it might then, as now, be debased, as it was heavenly in its aim. And so in like manner, we contrast a liberal education with a commercial education or a professional; yet no one can deny that commerce and the professions afford scope for the highest and most diversified powers of mind. There is then a great variety of intellectual exercises, which are not technically called "liberal"; on the other hand, I say, there are exercises of the body which do receive that appellation. Such, for instance, was the palaestra,° in ancient times; such the Olympic games, in which strength and dexterity of body as well as of mind gained the prize. In Xenophon° we read of the young Persian nobility being taught to ride on horseback and to speak the

truth—both being among the accomplishments of a gentleman. War, too, however rough a profession, has ever been accounted liberal, unless in cases when it becomes heroic, which would introduce us to another subject.

Now comparing these instances together, we shall have no difficulty in determining the principle of this apparent variation in the application of the term which I am examining. Manly games, or games of skill, or military prowess, though bodily, are, it seems, accounted liberal; on the other hand, what is merely professional, though highly intellectual, nay, though liberal in comparison of trade and manual labor, is not simply called liberal, and mercantile occupations are not liberal at all. Why this distinction? because that alone is liberal knowledge, which stands on its own pretentions, which is independent of sequel, expects no complement, refuses to be *informed* (as it is called) by any end, or absorbed into any art, in order duly to present itself to our contemplation. The most ordinary pursuits have this specific character, if they are self-sufficient and complete; the highest lose it, when they minister to something beyond them. It is absurd to balance, in point of worth and importance, a treatise on reducing fractures with a game of cricket or a fox-chase; yet of the two the bodily exercise has that quality which we call "liberal," and the intellectual has it not. And so of the learned professions altogether, considered merely as professions; although one of them be the most popularly beneficial, and another the most politically important, and the third the most intimately divine of all human pursuits, yet the very greatness of their end, the health of the body, or of the commonwealth, or of the soul, diminishes, not increases, their claim to the appellation "liberal," and that still more, if they are cut down to the strict exigencies of that end. If, for instance, Theology, instead of being cultivated as a contemplation, be limited to the purposes of the pulpit or be represented by the catechism, it loses—not its usefulness, not its divine character, not its meritoriousness (rather it increases these qualities by such charitable condescension)—but it does lose the particular attribute which I am illustrating; just as a face worn by tears and fasting loses its beauty, or a laborer's hand loses its delicateness;—for Theology thus exercised is not simple knowledge, but rather is an art or a business making use of Theology. And thus it appears that even what is supernatural need not be liberal, nor need a hero be a gentleman, for the plain reason that one idea is not another idea. And in like manner the Baconian Philosophy, by using its physical sciences in the service of man, does thereby transfer them from the order of Liberal Pursuits to, I do not say the inferior, but the distinct class of the Useful. And, to take a different instance, hence again, as is evident, whenever personal gain is the motive, still more distinctive an effect has it upon the character of a given

258 **of which . . . speaks,** Aristotle: "Art loves fate, and fate loves art"
280 **palaestra,** wrestling school   283 **Xenophon,** Greek historian in the Age of Pericles (fifth century B.C.), author of the *Anabasis*

pursuit; thus racing, which was a liberal exercise in Greece, forfeits its rank in times like these, so far as it is made the occasion of gambling.

All that I have been now saying is summed up in a few characteristic words of the great Philosopher.° "Of possessions," he says, "those rather are useful, which bear fruit; those *liberal, which tend to enjoyment.* By fruitful, I mean, which yield revenue; by enjoyable, 350 where *nothing accrues of consequence beyond the use.*"

5.

Do not suppose, Gentlemen, that in thus appealing to the ancients, I am throwing back the world two thousand years, and fettering Philosophy with the reasonings of paganism. While the world lasts, will Aristotle's doctrine on these matters last, for he is the oracle of nature and of truth. While we are men, we cannot help, to a great extent, being Aristotelians, for the great Master does but analyze the thoughts, feel-360 ings, views, and opinions of human kind. He has told us the meaning of our own words and ideas, before we were born. In many subject-matters, to think correctly, is to think like Aristotle; and we are his disciples whether we will or no, though we may not know it. Now, as to the particular instance before us, the word "liberal" as applied to Knowledge and Education, expresses a specific idea, which ever has been, and ever will be, while the nature of man is the same, just as the idea of the Beautiful is specific, or of the 370 Sublime, or of the Ridiculous, or of the Sordid. It is in the world now, it was in the world then; and, as in the case of the dogmas of faith, it is illustrated by a continuous historical tradition, and never was out of the world, from the time it came into it. There have indeed been differences of opinion from time to time, as to what pursuits and what arts came under that idea, but such differences are but an additional evidence of its reality. That idea must have a substance in it, which has maintained its ground amid these conflicts and 380 changes, which has ever served as a standard to measure things withal, which has passed from mind to mind unchanged, when there was so much to color, so much to influence any notion or thought whatever, which was not founded in our very nature. Were it a mere generalization, it would have varied with the subjects from which it was generalized; but though its subjects vary with the age, it varies not itself. The palaestra may seem a liberal exercise to Lycurgus,° and illiberal to Seneca;° coach-driving and prize-fighting 390 may be recognized in Elis,° and be condemned in England; music may be despicable in the eyes of certain moderns and be in the highest place with Aristotle and Plato—(and the case is the same in the particular ap-plication of the idea of Beauty, or of Goodness, or of Moral Virtue, there is a difference of tastes, a difference of judgments)—still these variations imply, instead of discrediting, the archetypal idea, which is but a previous hypothesis or condition, by means of which issue is joined between contending opinions, and without which there would be nothing to dispute about. 400

I consider, then, that I am chargeable with no paradox, when I speak of a Knowledge which is its own end, when I call it liberal knowledge, or a gentleman's knowledge, when I educate for it, and make it the scope of a University. And still less am I incurring such a charge, when I make this acquisition consist, not in Knowledge in a vague and ordinary sense, but in that Knowledge which I have especially called Philosophy or, in an extended sense of the word, Science; for whatever claims Knowledge has to be con- 410 sidered as a good, these it has in a higher degree when it is viewed not vaguely, not popularly, but precisely and transcendently as Philosophy. Knowledge, I say, is then especially liberal or sufficient for itself, apart from every external and ulterior object, when and so far as it is philosophical, and this I proceed to show.

6.

Now bear with me, Gentlemen, if what I am about to say, has at first sight a fanciful appearance. Philosophy, then, or Science, is related to Knowledge in this way: Knowledge is called by the name of Sci- 420 ence or Philosophy, when it is acted upon, informed, or if I may use a strong figure, impregnated by Reason. Reason is the principle of that intrinsic fecundity of Knowledge, which, to those who possess it, is its especial value, and which dispenses with the necessity of their looking abroad for any end to rest upon external to itself. Knowledge, indeed, when thus exalted into a scientific form, is also power; not only is it excellent in itself, but whatever such excellence may be, it is something more, it has a result beyond itself. 430 Doubtless; but that is a further consideration, with which I am not concerned. I only say that, prior to its being a power, it is a good; that it is, not only an instrument, but an end. I know well it may resolve itself into an art, and terminate in a mechanical process, and in tangible fruit; but it also may fall back upon that Reason, which informs it, and resolve itself into Philosophy. In one case it is called Useful Knowledge, in the other Liberal. The same person may cultivate it in both ways at once; but this again is a matter 440 foreign to my subject; here I do but say that there are two ways of using Knowledge, and in matter of fact those who use it in one way are not likely to use it in the other, or at least in a very limited measure. You see, then, here are two methods of Education; the end of the one is to be philosophical, of the other to be mechanical; the one rises towards general ideas, the other is exhausted upon what is particular and exter-

346 **the great philosopher, etc.,** Aristotle, in the *Rhetoric* 388 **Lycurgus,** Spartan lawgiver of the ninth century B.C. 389 **Seneca,** Roman lawgiver of the first century 390 **Elis,** first home of the Olympic games

nal. Let me not be thought to deny the necessity, or to decry the benefit, of such attention to what is particular and practical, as belongs to the useful or mechanical arts; life could not go on without them; we owe our daily welfare to them; their exercise is the duty of the many, and we owe to the many a debt of gratitude for fulfilling that duty. I only say that Knowledge, in proportion as it tends more and more to be particular, ceases to be Knowledge. It is a question whether Knowledge can in any proper sense be predicated of the brute creation; without pretending to metaphysical exactness of phraseology, which would be unsuitable to an occasion like this, I say, it seems to me improper to call that passive sensation, or perception of things, which brutes seem to possess, by the name of Knowledge. When I speak of Knowledge, I mean something intellectual, something which grasps what it perceives through the senses; something which takes a view of things; which sees more than the senses convey; which reasons upon what it sees, and while it sees; which invests it with an idea. It expresses itself, not in a mere enunciation, but by an enthymeme:° it is of the nature of science from the first, and in this consists its dignity. The principle of real dignity in Knowledge, its worth, its desirableness, considered irrespectively of its results, is this germ within it of a scientific or a philosophical process. This is how it comes to be an end in itself; this is why it admits of being called Liberal. Not to know the relative disposition of things is the state of slaves or children; to have mapped out the Universe is the boast, or at least the ambition, of Philosophy.

Moreover, such knowledge is not a mere extrinsic or accidental advantage, which is ours today and another's tomorrow, which may be got up from a book, and easily forgotten again, which we can command or communicate at our pleasure, which we can borrow for the occasion, carry about in our hand, and take into the market; it is an acquired illumination, it is a habit, a personal possession, and an inward endowment. And this is the reason, why it is more correct, as well as more usual, to speak of a University as a place of education, than of instruction, though, when knowledge is concerned, instruction would at first sight have seemed the more appropriate word. We are instructed, for instance, in manual exercises, in the fine and useful arts, in trades, and in ways of business; for these are methods, which have little or no effect upon the mind itself, are contained in rules committed to memory, to tradition, or to use, and bear upon an end external to themselves. But education is a higher word; it implies an action upon our mental nature, and the formation of a character; it is something individual and permanent, and is commonly spoken of in connection with religion and virtue. When, then, we speak of the communication of Knowledge as being Educa-

470 **enthymeme,** a syllogism in which one of the propositions or premises is understood but not stated

tion, we thereby really imply that that Knowledge is a state or condition of mind; and since cultivation of mind is surely worth seeking for its own sake, we are thus brought once more to the conclusion, which the word "Liberal" and the word "Philosophy" have already suggested, that there is a Knowledge, which is desirable, though nothing come of it, as being of itself a treasure, and a sufficient remuneration of years of labor.

7.

This, then, is the answer which I am prepared to give to the question with which I opened this Discourse. Before going on to speak of the object of the Church in taking up Philosophy, and the uses to which she puts it, I am prepared to maintain that Philosophy is its own end, and, as I conceive, I have now begun proving it. I am prepared to maintain that there is a knowledge worth possessing for what it is, and not merely for what it does; and what minutes remain to me today I shall devote to the removal of some portion of the indistinctness and confusion with which the subject may in some minds be surrounded.

It may be objected then, that, when we profess to seek Knowledge for some end or other beyond itself, whatever it be, we speak intelligibly; but that, whatever men may have said, however obstinately the idea may have kept its ground from age to age, still it is simply unmeaning to say that we seek Knowledge for its own sake, and for nothing else; for that it ever leads to something beyond itself, which therefore is its end, and the cause why it is desirable;—moreover, that this end is twofold, either of this world or of the next; that all knowledge is cultivated either for secular objects or for eternal; that if it is directed to secular objects, it is called Useful Knowledge, if to eternal, Religious or Christian Knowledge;—in consequence, that if, as I have allowed, this Liberal Knowledge does not benefit the body or estate, it ought to benefit the soul; but if the fact be really so, that it is neither a physical or a secular good on the one hand, nor a moral good on the other, it cannot be a good at all, and is not worth the trouble which is necessary for its acquisition.

And then I may be reminded that the professors of this Liberal or Philosophical Knowledge have themselves, in every age, recognized this exposition of the matter, and have submitted to the issue in which it terminates; for they have ever been attempting to make men virtuous; or, if not, at least have assumed that refinement of mind was virtue, and that they themselves were the virtuous portion of mankind. This they have professed on the one hand; and on the other, they have utterly failed in their professions, so as ever to make themselves a proverb among men, and a laughing stock both to the grave and the dissipated portion of mankind, in consequence of them. Thus they have furnished against themselves both the ground and the means of their own exposure, without

any trouble at all to anyone else. In a word, from the time that Athens was the University of the world, what has Philosophy taught men, but to promise without practicing, and to aspire without attaining? What has the deep and lofty thought of its disciples ended in but eloquent words? Nay, what has its teaching ever meditated, when it was boldest in its remedies for human ill, beyond charming us to sleep by its lessons, that we might feel nothing at all? like some melodious
570 air, or rather like those strong and transporting perfumes, which at first spread their sweetness over everything they touch, but in a little while do but offend in proportion as they once pleased us. Did Philosophy support Cicero under the disfavor of the fickle populace, or nerve Seneca to oppose an imperial tyrant? It abandoned Brutus,° as he sorrowfully confessed, in his greatest need, and it forced Cato,° as his panegyrist strangely boasts, into the false position of defying heaven. How few can be counted among its
580 professors, who, like Polemon,° were thereby converted from a profligate course, or like Anaxagoras,° thought the world well lost in exchange for its possession? The philosopher in *Rasselas*° taught a superhuman doctrine, and then succumbed without an effort to a trial of human affection.

"He discoursed," we are told, "with great energy on the government of the passions. His look was venerable, his action graceful, his pronunciation clear, and his diction elegant. He showed, with great strength of
590 sentiment and variety of illustration, that human nature is degraded and debased, when the lower faculties predominate over the higher. He communicated the various precepts given, from time to time, for the conquest of passion, and displayed the happiness of those who had obtained the important victory, after which man is no longer the slave of fear, nor the fool of hope. . . . He enumerated many examples of heroes immovable by pain or pleasure, who looked with indifference on those modes or accidents to which the
600 vulgar give the names of good and evil."

Rasselas in a few days found the philosopher in a room half darkened, with his eyes misty, and his face pale. "Sir," said he, "you have come at a time when all human friendship is useless; what I suffer cannot be remedied, what I have lost cannot be supplied. My daughter, my only daughter, from whose tenderness I expected all the comforts of my age, died last night of a fever." "Sir," said the prince, "mortality is an event by which a wise man can never be surprised; we know
610 that death is always near, and it should therefore always be expected." "Young man," answered the philosopher, "you speak like one who has never felt the pangs of separation." "Have you, then, forgot the precept," said Rasselas, "which you so powerfully

enforced? . . . consider that external things are naturally variable, but truth and reason are always the same." "What comfort," said the mourner, "can truth and reason afford me? Of what effect are they now, but to tell me that my daughter will not be restored?"

8.

Better, far better, to make no professions, you will 620 say, than to cheat others with what we are not, and to scandalize them with what we are. The sensualist, or the man of the world, at any rate is not the victim of fine words, but pursues a reality and gains it. The Philosophy of Utility, you will say, Gentlemen, has at least done its work; and I grant it—it aimed low, but it has fulfilled its aim. If that man of great intellect who has been its Prophet° in the conduct of life played false to his own professions, he was not bound by his philosophy to be true to his friend or faithful in his 630 trust. Moral virtue was not the line in which he undertook to instruct men; and though, as the poet° calls him, he were the "meanest" of mankind, he was so in what may be called his private capacity, and without any prejudice to the theory of induction. He had a right to be so, if he chose, for anything that the Idols of the den or the theater had to say to the contrary. His mission was the increase of physical enjoyment and social comfort;° and most wonderfully, most awfully has he fulfilled his conception and his design. Almost day by 640 day have we fresh and fresh shoots, and buds, and blossoms, which are to ripen into fruit, on that magical tree of Knowledge which he planted, and to which none of us perhaps, except the very poor, but owes, if not his present life, at least his daily food, his health, and general well-being. He was the divinely provided minister of temporal benefits to all of us so great, that, whatever I am forced to think of him as a man, I have not the heart, from mere gratitude, to speak of him severely. And in spite of the tendencies of his 650 philosophy, which are, as we see at this day, to depreciate, or to trample on Theology, he has himself, in his writings, gone out of his way, as if with a prophetic misgiving of those tendencies, to insist on it as the instrument of that beneficent Father, who, when He came on earth in visible form, took on Him first and most prominently the office of assuaging the bodily wounds of human nature. And truly, like the old mediciner in the tale, "he sat diligently at his work, and hummed, with cheerful countenance, a pious 660 song"; and then in turn "went out singing into the meadows so gayly, that those who had seen him from afar might well have thought it was a youth gathering flowers for his beloved, instead of an old physician gathering healing herbs in the morning dew."°

576 **Brutus,** famous friend of Julius Caesar to whom "Et tu, Brute" was addressed
577 **Cato,** Marcus Portius Cato (95–46 B.C.), object of Cicero's panegyric
580 **Polemon** Platonic philosopher of the third and fourth centuries B.C.
581 **Anaxagoras,** Greek philosopher of the Age of Pericles   583 **Rasselas,** didactic romance (1759) by Samuel Johnson

628 **Prophet,** Francis Bacon, who confessed to corruption as Lord Chancellor
632 **poet,** Alexander Pope, who called Bacon "the wisest, brightest, meanest of mankind"   639 **comfort.** "It will be seen that on the whole I agree with Lord Macaulay in his essay on Bacon's philosophy. I do not know whether he would agree with me."—Newman's note   658–665 **And truly . . . morning dew,** "Fouqué's *Unknown Patient*."—Newman's note. Baron de la Motte Fouqué (1777–1843) was a German poet and novelist

Alas, that men, in the action of life or in their heart of hearts, are not what they seem to be in their moments of excitement, or in their trances or intoxications of genius—so good, so noble, so serene! Alas, that Bacon too in his own way should after all be but the fellow of those heathen philosophers who in their disadvantages had some excuse for their inconsistency, and who surprise us rather in what they did say than in what they did not do! Alas, that he too, like Socrates or Seneca, must be stripped of his holy-day coat, which looks so fair, and should be but a mockery amid his most majestic gravity of phrase; and, for all his vast abilities, should, in the littleness of his own moral being, but typify the intellectual narrowness of his school! However, granting all this, heroism after all was not his philosophy: I cannot deny he has abundantly achieved what he proposed. His is simply a Method whereby bodily discomforts and temporal wants are to be most effectually removed from the greatest number; and already, before it has shown any signs of exhaustion, the gifts of nature, in their most artificial shapes and luxurious profusion and diversity, from all quarters of the earth, are, it is undeniable, by its means brought even to our doors, and we rejoice in them.

9.

Useful Knowledge then, I grant, has done its work; and Liberal Knowledge as certainly has not done its work—supposing, that is, as the objectors assume, its direct end, like Religious Knowledge, is to make men better; but this I will not for an instant allow, and unless I allow it, those objectors have said nothing to the purpose. I admit, rather I maintain, what they have been urging, for I consider Knowledge to have its end in itself. For all its friends, or its enemies, may say, I insist upon it, that it is as real a mistake to burden it with virtue or religion as with the mechanical arts. Its direct business is not to steel the soul against temptation, or to console it in affliction, any more than to set the loom in motion, or to direct the steam carriage; be it ever so much the means or the condition of both material and moral advancement, still, taken by and in itself, it as little mends our hearts as it improves our temporal circumstances. And if its eulogists claim for it such a power, they commit the very same kind of encroachment on a province not their own as the political economist who should maintain that his science educated him for casuistry or diplomacy. Knowledge is one thing, virtue is another; good sense is not conscience, refinement is not humility, nor is largeness and justness of view faith. Philosophy, however enlightened, however profound, gives no command over the passions, no influential motives, no vivifying principles. Liberal Education makes not the Christian, not the Catholic, but the gentleman. It is well to be a gentleman, it is well to have a cultivated intellect, a delicate taste, a candid, equitable, dispassionate mind, a noble and courteous bearing in the conduct of life;—these are the connatural qualities of a large knowledge; they are the objects of a University; I am advocating, I shall illustrate and insist upon them; but still, I repeat, they are no guarantee for sanctity or even for conscientiousness they may attach to the man of the world, to the profligate, to the heartless—pleasant, alas, and attractive as he shows when decked out in them. Taken by themselves, they do but seem to be what they are not; they look like virtue at a distance, but they are detected by close observers, and on the long run; and hence it is that they are popularly accused of pretense and hypocrisy, not, I repeat, from their own fault, but because their professors and their admirers persist in taking them for what they are not, and are officious in arrogating for them a praise to which they have no claim. Quarry the granite rock with razors, or moor the vessel with a thread of silk; then may you hope with such keen and delicate instruments as human knowledge and human reason to contend against these giants, the passion and the pride of man.

Surely we are not driven to theories of this kind in order to vindicate the value and dignity of Liberal Knowledge. Surely the real grounds on which its pretensions rest are not so very subtle or abstruse, so very strange or improbable. Surely it is very intelligible to say, and that is what I say here, that Liberal Education, viewed in itself, is simply the cultivation of the intellect as such, and its object is nothing more or less than intellectual excellence. Every thing has its own perfection, be it higher or lower in the scale of things; and the perfection of one is not the perfection of another. Things animate, inanimate, visible, invisible, all are good in their kind, and have a *best* of themselves, which is an object of pursuit. Why do you take such pains with your garden or your park? You see to your walks and turf and shrubberies; to your trees and drives; not as if you meant to make an orchard of the one, or corn or pasture land of the other, but because there is a special beauty in all that is goodly in wood, water, plain, and slope, brought all together by art into one shape, and grouped into one whole. Your cities are beautiful, your palaces, your public buildings, your territorial mansions, your churches; and their beauty leads to nothing beyond itself. There is a physical beauty and a moral: there is a beauty of person, there is a beauty of our moral being, which is natural virtue; and in like manner there is a beauty, there is a perfection, of the intellect. There is an ideal perfection in these various subject-matters, towards which individual instances are seen to rise, and which are the standards for all instances whatever. The Greek divinities and demigods, as the statuary has molded them, with their symmetry of figure, and their high forehead and their regular features, are the perfection of physical beauty. The heroes, of whom history tells, Alexander, or Caesar, or Scipio, or Saladin,° are the 780 representatives of that magnanimity or self-mastery which is the greatness of human nature. Christianity too has its heroes, and in the supernatural order, and we call them saints. The artist puts before him beauty of feature and form; the poet, beauty of mind; the preacher, the beauty of grace: then intellect too, I repeat, has its beauty, and it has those who aim at it. To open the mind, to correct it, to refine it, to enable it to know, and to digest, master, rule, and use its knowledge, to give it power over its own faculties, applica- 790 tion, flexibility, method, critical exactness, sagacity, resource, address, eloquent expression, is an object as intelligible (for here we are inquiring, not what the object of a Liberal Education is worth, nor what use the Church makes of it, but what it is in itself), I say, an object as intelligible as the cultivation of virtue, while, at the same time, it is absolutely distinct from it.

10.

This indeed is but a temporal object, and a transitory possession but so are other things in themselves which we make much of and pursue. The moralist will 800 tell us that man, in all his functions, is but a flower which blossoms and fades, except so far as a higher principle breathes upon him, and makes him and what he is immortal. Body and mind are carried on into an eternal state of being by the gifts of Divine Munificence; but at first they do but fail in a failing world; and if the powers of intellect decay, the powers of the body have decayed before them, and, as an Hospital or an Almshouse though its end be ephemeral, may be sanctified to the service of religion, so surely may a 810 University, even were it nothing more than I have as yet described it. We attain to heaven by using this world well though it is to pass away; we perfect our nature, not by undoing it, but by adding to it what is more than nature, and directing it towards aims higher than its own.

(1852)

from APOLOGIA PRO VITA SUA

Newman's "apology for," or defense of, his life was written as a reply to the Reverend Charles Kingsley, who had called Newman's intellectual honesty into question and had, through Newman, attacked the integrity of the Catholic clergy. The work was written under great physical and emotional strain and, in contrast to his usual method of composition, at great speed. It was issued between April 21 and June 2, 1864, as a series of pamphlets. When the work was revised for book publication (1864), much of the

polemic against Kingsley was deleted. The selection below was the first chapter of the book publication. Newman's statement in the preface about his perception of what he must ultimately do is instructive: "Yes, I said to myself, his very question is about my meaning: 'What does Dr. Newman mean?' It pointed in the very same direction as that into which my musings had turned me already. He asks what I *mean*; not about my words, not about my arguments, not about my actions, as his ultimate point, but about that living intelligence, by which I write, and argue, and act. He asks about my Mind and its Beliefs and its sentiments; and he shall be answered."

HISTORY OF MY RELIGIOUS OPINIONS TO THE YEAR 1833

It may easily be conceived how great a trial it is to me to write the following history of myself; but I must not shrink from the task. The words "Secretum meum mihi,"° keep ringing in my ears; but as men draw towards their end, they care less for disclosures. Nor is it the least part of my trial, to anticipate that my friends may, upon first reading what I have written, consider much in it irrelevant to my purpose; yet I cannot help thinking that, viewed as a whole, it will effect what I wish it to do. 10

I was brought up from a child to take great delight in reading the Bible; but I had no formal religious convictions till I was fifteen. Of course I had perfect knowledge of my Catechism.°

After I was grown up, I put on paper such recollections as I had of my thoughts and feelings on religious subjects, at the time that I was a child and a boy. Out of these I select two, which are at once the most definite among them, and also have a bearing on my later convictions. 20

In the paper to which I have referred, written either in the long vacation of 1820, or in October 1823, the following notices of my school days were sufficiently prominent in my memory for me to consider them worth recording:—"I used to wish the Arabian Tales were true: my imagination ran on unknown influences, on magical powers, and talismans. . . . I thought life might be a dream, or I an Angel, and all this world a deception, my fellow-angels by a playful device concealing themselves from me, and deceiving me with 30 the semblance of a material world."

Again, "Reading in the Spring of 1816 a sentence from [Dr. Watt's]° *Remnants of Time*, entitled 'the Saints unknown to the world,' to the effect, that 'there is nothing in their figure or countenance to distinguish

779 **Scipio or Saladin,** references to members of an illustrious Roman family of patricians and to Saladin, Sultan of Egypt (1137–1193)

History of My Religious Opinions to the Year 1833   3–4 **Secretum meum mihi,** my private life is my own affair   14 **Catechism,** the Anglican Catechism, contained in the *Book of Common Prayer*   33 **Dr. Watt,** Isaac Watt (1674–1748), popular theologian and hymn writer

them,' etc., etc., I supposed he spoke of Angels who lived in the world, as it were disguised."

The other remark is this: "I was very superstitious, and for some time previous to my conversion" [when I was fifteen] "used constantly to cross myself on going into the dark."

Of course I must have got this practice from some external source or other; but I can make no sort of conjecture whence; and certainly no one had ever spoken to me on the subject of the Catholic religion, which I only knew by name. The French master was an *emigré*° priest, but he was simply made a butt, as French masters too commonly were in that day, and spoke English very imperfectly. There was a Catholic family in the village, old maiden ladies we used to think; but I knew nothing but their name. I have of late years heard that there were one or two Catholic boys in the school; but either we were carefully kept from knowing this, or the knowledge of it made simply no impression on our minds. My brother will bear witness how free the school was from Catholic ideas.

I had once been into Warwick Street Chapel, with my father, who, I believe, wanted to hear some piece of music; all that I bore away from it was the recollection of a pulpit and a preacher and a boy swinging a censer.

When I was at Littlemore, I was looking over old copybooks of my school days, and I found among them my first Latin verse-book; and in the first page of it there was a device which almost took my breath away with surprise. I have the book before me now, and have just been showing it to others. I have written in the first page, in my schoolboy hand, "John H. Newman, February 11th, 1811, Verse Book"; then follow my first verses. Between "Verse" and "Book" I have drawn the figure of a solid cross upright, and next to it is, what may indeed be meant for a necklace, but what I cannot make out to be anything else than a set of beads suspended, with a little cross attached. At this time I was not quite ten years old. I suppose I got the idea from some romance, Mrs. Radcliffe's or Miss Porter's;° or from some religious picture; but the strange thing is, how, among the thousand objects which meet a boy's eyes, these in particular should so have fixed themselves in my mind, that I made them thus practically my own. I am certain there was nothing in the churches I attended, or the prayer books I read, to suggest them. It must be recollected that churches and prayer books were not decorated in those days as I believe they are now.

When I was fourteen, I read Paine's tracts against the Old Testament,° and found pleasure in thinking of the objections which were contained in them. Also, I read some of Hume's essays;° and perhaps that on Miracles. So at least I gave my father to understand; but perhaps it was a brag. Also, I recollect copying out some French verses, perhaps Voltaire's,° against the immortality of the soul, and saying to myself something like "How dreadful, but how plausible!"

When I was fifteen (in the autumn of 1816) a great change of thought took place in me. I fell under the influences of a definite creed, and received into my intellect impressions of dogma, which, through God's mercy, have never been effaced or obscured. Above and beyond the conversations and sermons of the excellent man, long dead, who was the human means of this beginning of divine faith in me, was the effect of the books which he put into my hands, all of the school of Calvin. One of the first books I read was a work of Romaine's;° I neither recollect the title nor the contents, except one doctrine, which of course I do not include among those which I believe to have come from a divine source, viz. the doctrine of final perseverance. I received it at once, and believed that the inward conversion of which I was conscious (and of which I still am more certain than that I have hands and feet) would last into the next life, and that I was elected to eternal glory. I have no consciousness that this belief had any tendency whatever to lead me to be careless about pleasing God. I retained it till the age of twenty-one, when it gradually faded away; but I believe that it had some influence on my opinions, in the direction of those childish imaginations which I have already mentioned, viz. in isolating me from the objects which surrounded me, in confirming me in my mistrust of the reality of material phenomena, and making me rest in the thought of two and two only supreme and luminously self-evident beings, myself and my Creator;—for while I considered myself predestined to salvation, I thought others simply passed over, not predestined to eternal death. I only thought of the mercy to myself.

The detestable doctrine last mentioned is simply denied and abjured, unless my memory strangely deceives me, by the writer who made a deeper impression on my mind than any other, and to whom (humanly speaking) I almost owe my soul—Thomas Scott° of Aston Sandford. I so admired and delighted in his writings, that, when I was an undergraduate, I thought of making a visit to his parsonage, in order to see a man whom I so deeply revered. I hardly think I could have given up the idea of this expedition, even after I had taken my degree; for the news of his death

---

47 **emigré,** a Royalist fugitive from the French Revolution   76–77 **Mrs. Radcliffe, Miss Porter,** Ann Radcliffe (1764–1823) and Jane Porter (1776–1850), authors of Gothic and other romances   86–87 **Paine's tracts ... Old Testament,** Thomas Paine (1737–1809), in *The Age of Reason*

89 **Hume's essays, etc.,** David Hume (1711–1776), historian and philosopher. "Of Miracles" appeared in *Enquiry Concerning Human Understanding* (1748)   92 **Voltaire,** French critic and skeptic (1694–1778)   105 **Romaine,** William Romaine (1714–1795), religious writer   132 **Thomas Scott.** Scott (1747–1821) was the author of a serial commentary on the Bible

in 1821 came upon me as a disappointment as well as a sorrow. I hung upon the lips of Daniel Wilson,° afterwards Bishop of Calcutta, as in two sermons at St. John's Chapel he gave the history of Scott's life and death. I had been possessed of his essays from a boy; his commentary I bought when I was an undergraduate.

What, I suppose, will strike any reader of Scott's history and writings, is his bold unworldliness and vigorous independence of mind. He followed truth wherever it led him, beginning with Unitarianism, and ending in a zealous faith in the Holy Trinity. It was he who first planted deep in my mind that fundamental truth of religion. With the assistance of Scott's essays, and the admirable work of Jones of Nayland,° I made a collection of Scripture texts in proof of the doctrine, with remarks (I think) of my own upon them, before I was sixteen; and a few months later I drew up a series of texts in support of each verse of the Athanasian Creed. These papers I have still.

Besides his unworldliness, what I also admired in Scott was his resolute opposition to Antinomianism,° and the minutely practical character of his writings. They show him to be a true Englishman, and I deeply felt his influence; and for years I used almost as proverbs what I considered to be the scope and issue of his doctrine, "Holiness before peace," and "Growth is the only evidence of life."

Calvinists make a sharp separation between the elect and the world; there is much in this that is parallel or cognate to the Catholic doctrine; but they go on to say, as I understand them, very differently from Catholicism,—that the converted and the unconverted can be discriminated by man, that the justified are conscious of their state of justification, and that the regenerate cannot fall away. Catholics on the other hand shade and soften the awful antagonism between good and evil, which is one of their dogmas, by holding that there are different degrees of justification, that there is a great difference in point of gravity between sin and sin, that there is the possibility and the danger of falling away, and that there is no certain knowledge given to any one that he is simply in a state of grace, and much less that he is to persevere to the end:—of the Calvinistic tenets the only one which took root in my mind was the fact of heaven and hell, divine favour and divine wrath, of the justified and the unjustified. The notion that the regenerate and the justified were one and the same, and that the regenerate, as such, had the gift of perseverance, remained with me not many years, as I have said already.

This main Catholic doctrine of the warfare between the city of God and the powers of darkness was also deeply impressed upon my mind by a work of a very opposite character, Law's° Serious Call.

From this time I have given a full inward assent and belief to the doctrine of eternal punishment, as delivered by our Lord Himself, in as true a sense as I hold that of eternal happiness; though I have tried in various ways to make that truth less terrible to the reason.

Now I come to two other works, which produced a deep impression on me in the same autumn of 1816, when I was fifteen years old, each contrary to each, and planting in me the seeds of an intellectual inconsistency which disabled me for a long course of years. I read Joseph Milner's° Church History, and was nothing short of enamoured of the long extracts from St. Augustine and the other Fathers which I found there. I read them as being the religion of the primitive Christians: but simultaneously with Milner I read Newton° on the Prophecies, and in consequence became most firmly convinced that the Pope was the Antichrist predicted by Daniel, St. Paul, and St. John. My imagination was stained by the effects of this doctrine up to the year 1843; it had been obliterated from my reason and judgment at an earlier date; but the thought remained upon me as a sort of false conscience. Hence came that conflict of mind, which so many have felt besides myself;—leading some men to make a compromise between two ideas, so inconsistent with each other— driving others to beat out the one idea or the other from their minds—and ending in my own case, after many years of intellectual unrest, in the gradual decay and extinction of one of them—I do not say in its violent death, for why should I not have murdered it sooner, if I murdered it at all?

I am obliged to mention, though I do it with great reluctance, another deep imagination, which at this time, the autumn of 1816, took possession of me— there can be no mistake about the fact;—viz. that it was the will of God that I should lead a single life. This anticipation, which has held its ground almost continuously ever since—with the break of a month now and a month then, up to 1829, and, after that date, without any break at all—was more or less connected, in my mind, with the notion that my calling in life would require such a sacrifice as celibacy involved; as, for instance, missionary work among the heathen, to which I had a great drawing for some years. It also strengthened my feeling of separation from the visible world, of which I have spoken above.

In 1822 I came under very different influences from those to which I had hitherto been subjected. At that

140 **Daniel Wilson**, Evangelical preacher (1778–1858) 152 **Jones of Nayland,** William Jones of Nayland, Suffolk (1726–1800), author of *The Catholic Doctrine of the Trinity* 159 **Antinomianism,** the belief that faith alone is necessary for salvation with its corollary that good works are not effective or obligatory

192 **Law,** William Law (1686–1761), author of *Serious Call to a Devout and Holy Life* (1728) 203 **Joseph Milner,** Evangelical divine (1744–1797), author of *History of the Church of Christ* (1794–1797) 207 **Newton,** Thomas Newton (1704–1782), Bishop of Bristol, author of a *Dissertation on the Prophecies* (1754)

time, Mr. Whately,° as he was then, afterwards Archbishop of Dublin, for the few months he remained in Oxford, which he was leaving for good, showed great kindness to me. He renewed it in 1825, when he became Principal of Alban Hall, making me his vice-principal and tutor. Of Dr. Whately I will speak presently, for from 1822 to 1825 I saw most of the present Provost of Oriel, Dr. Hawkins,° at that time Vicar of St. Mary's; and, when I took orders in 1824 and had a
250 curacy at Oxford, then, during the long vacations, I was especially thrown into his company. I can say with a full heart that I love him, and have never ceased to love him; and I thus preface what otherwise might sound rude, that in the course of the many years in which we were together afterwards, he provoked me very much from time to time, though I am perfectly certain that I have provoked him a great deal more. Moreover, in me such provocation was unbecoming, both because he was the head of my college, and be-
260 cause in the first years that I knew him, he had been in many ways of great service to my mind.

He was the first who taught me to weigh my words, and to be cautious in my statements. He led me to that mode of limiting and clearing my sense in discussion and in controversy, and of distinguishing between cognate ideas, and of obviating mistakes by anticipation, which to my surprise has been since considered, even in quarters friendly to me, to savour of the polemics of Rome. He is a man of most exact mind
270 himself, and he used to snub me severely, on reading, as he was kind enough to do, the first sermons that I wrote, and other compositions which I was engaged upon.

Then as to doctrine, he was the means of great additions to my belief. As I have noticed elsewhere, he gave me the *Treatise on Apostolical Preaching,* by Sumner,° afterwards Archbishop of Canterbury, from which I learned to give up my remaining Calvinism, and to receive the doctrine of Baptismal Regeneration.
280 In many other ways too he was of use to me, on subjects semi-religious and semi-scholastic.

It was Dr. Hawkins too who taught me to anticipate that, before many years were over, there would be an attack made upon the books and the canon of Scripture. I was brought to the same belief by the conversation of Mr. Blanco White,° who also led me to have freer views on the subject of inspiration than were usual in the Church of England at the time.

There is one other principle, which I gained from Dr.
290 Hawkins, more directly bearing upon Catholicism, than any that I have mentioned; and that is the doctrine of Tradition. When I was an undergraduate, I heard him preach in the University pulpit his celebrated sermon on the subject, and recollect how long it appeared to me, though he was at that time a very

striking preacher; but, when I read it and studied it as his gift, it made a most serious impression upon me. He does not go one step, I think, beyond the high Anglican doctrine, nay he does not reach it; but he does his work thoroughly, and his view was original 300 with him, and his subject was a novel one at the time. He lays down a proposition, self-evident as soon as stated, to those who have at all examined the structure of Scripture, viz. that the sacred text was never intended to teach doctrine, but only to prove it, and that, if we would learn doctrine, we must have recourse to the formularies of the Church; for instance to the Catechism, and to the Creeds. He considers, that, after learning from them the doctrines of Christianity, the inquirer must verify them by Scripture. This view, 310 most true in its outline, most fruitful in its consequences, opened upon me a large field of thought. Dr. Whately held it too. One of its effects was to strike at the root of the principle on which the Bible Society was set up. I belonged to its Oxford Association; it became a matter of time when I should withdraw my name from its subscription-list, though I did not do so at once.

It is with pleasure that I pay here a tribute to the memory of the Rev. William James, then Fellow of 320 Oriel; who, about the year 1823, taught me the doctrine of Apostolical Succession, in the course of a walk, I think, round Christ Church meadow: I recollect being somewhat impatient on the subject at the time.

It was at about this date, I suppose, that I read Bishop Butler's° *Analogy;* the study of which has been to so many, as it was to me, an era in their religious opinions. Its inculcation of a visible church, the oracle of truth and a pattern of sanctity, of the duties of ex- 330 ternal religion, and of the historical character of revelation, are characteristics of this great work which strike the reader at once; for myself, if I may attempt to determine what I most gained from it, it lay in two points, which I shall have an opportunity of dwelling on in the sequel; they are the underlying principles of a great portion of my teaching. First, the very idea of an analogy between the separate works of God leads to the conclusion that the system which is of less importance is economically or sacramentally connected with 340 the more momentous system, and of this conclusion the theory, to which I was inclined as a boy, viz. the unreality of material phenomena, is an ultimate resolution. At this time I did not make the distinction between matter itself and its phenomena, which is so necessary and so obvious in discussing the subject. Secondly, Butler's doctrine that probability is the guide of life, led me, at least under the teaching to which a few years later I was introduced, to the question of the logical cogency of faith, on which I have 350 written so much. Thus to Butler I trace those two prin-

241 **Mr. Whately,** Richard Whately (1787–1863), critic of religious dogma and supporter of Broad Church views   248 **Dr. Hawkins,** Edward Hawkins (1789–1882)   277 **Sumner,** John Bird Sumner (1780–1862)   286 **Mr. Blanco White,** Joseph Blanco White (1775–1841), theological writer

327 **Bishop Butler,** Joseph Butler (1692–1752), author of *Analogy of Religion* (1736)

ciples of my teaching, which have led to a charge against me both of fancifulness and of scepticism.

And now as to Dr. Whately. I owe him a great deal. He was a man of generous and warm heart. He was particularly loyal to his friends, and to use the common phrase, "all his geese were swans." While I was still awkward and timid in 1822, he took me by the hand, and acted the part to me of a gentle and encouraging instructor. He, emphatically, opened my mind, and taught me to think and to use my reason. After being first noticed by him in 1822, I became very intimate with him in 1825, when I was his vice-principal at Alban Hall. I gave up that office in 1826, when I became tutor of my college, and his hold upon me gradually relaxed. He had done his work towards me or nearly so, when he had taught me to see with my own eyes and to walk with my own feet. Not that I had not a good deal to learn from others still, but I influenced them as well as they me, and co-operated rather than merely concurred with them. As to Dr. Whately, his mind was too different from mine for us to remain long on one line. I recollect how dissatisfied he was with an article of mine in the *London Review,*° which Blanco White, good-humouredly, only called platonic. When I was diverging from him (which he did not like), I thought of dedicating my first book to him, in words to the effect that he had not only taught me to think, but to think for myself. He left Oxford in 1831; after that, as far as I can recollect, I never saw him but twice—when he visited the University; once in the street, once in a room. From the time that he left, I have always felt a real affection for what I must call his memory; for thenceforward he made himself dead to me. My reason told me that it was impossible that we could have got on together longer; yet I loved him too much to bid him farewell without pain. After a few years had passed, I began to believe that his influence on me in a higher respect than intellectual advance (I will not say through his fault) had not been satisfactory. I believe that he has inserted sharp things in his later works about me. They have never come in my way, and I have not thought it necessary to seek out what would pain me so much in the reading.

What he did for me in point of religious opinion, was first to teach me the existence of the Church, as a substantive body or corporation; next to fix in me those anti-Erastian° views of Church polity, which were one of the most prominent features of the Tractarian Movement. On this point, and, as far as I know, on this point alone, he and Hurrell Froude° intimately sympathised, though Froude's development of opinion here was of a later date. In the year 1826, in the course of a walk he said much to me about a work then just published, called *Letters on the Church by an Epis-copalian.* He said that it would make my blood boil. It was certainly a most powerful composition. One of our common friends told me, that, after reading it, he could not keep still, but went on walking up and down his room. It was ascribed at once to Whately; I gave eager expression to the contrary opinion; but I found the belief of Oxford in the affirmative to be too strong for me; rightly or wrongly I yielded to the general voice; and I have never heard, then or since, of any disclaimer of authorship on the part of Dr. Whately.

The main positions of this able essay are these; first that Church and State should be independent of each other:—he speaks of the duty of protesting "against the profanation of Christ's kingdom, by that *double usurpation,* the interference of the Church in temporals, of the State in spirituals" (p. 191); and, secondly, that the Church may justly and by right retain its property, though separated from the State. "The clergy," he says, p. 133, "though they ought not to be the hired servants of the Civil Magistrate, may justly retain their revenues; and the State, though it has no right of interference in spiritual concerns, not only is justly entitled to support from the ministers of religion, and from all other Christians, but would, under the system I am recommending, obtain it much more effectually." The author of this work, whoever he may be, argues out both these points with great force and ingenuity, and with a thorough-going vehemence, which perhaps we may refer to the circumstance, that he wrote, not *in propriâ personâ,*° but in the professed character of a Scotch Episcopalian. His work had a gradual, but a deep effect on my mind.

I am not aware of any other religious opinion which I owe to Dr. Whately. For his special theological tenets I had no sympathy. In the next year, 1827, he told me he considered that I was Arianising.° The case was this: though at that time I had not read Bishop Bull's° *Defensio* nor the Fathers, I was just then very strong for that ante-Nicene view° of the Trinitarian doctrine, which some writers, both Catholic and non-Catholic, have accused of wearing a sort of Arian exterior. This is the meaning of a passage in Froude's *Remains,*° in which he seems to accuse me of speaking against the Athanasian Creed. I had contrasted the two aspects of the Trinitarian doctrine, which are respectively presented by the Athanasian Creed and the Nicene. My criticisms were to the effect that some of the verses of the former Creed were unnecessarily scientific. This is a specimen of a certain disdain for antiquity which had been growing on me now for several years. It showed itself in some flippant language against the Fathers in the *Encyclopædia Metropolitana,*° about whom I knew

374 **article . . . London Review,** "Poetry, with Reference to Aristotle's *Poetics,*" in the *London Review* (1829)   398 **anti-Erastian,** from Thomas Erastus, sixteenth-century theologian who held that the state was supreme in ecclesiastical affairs   401 **Hurrell Froude,** Richard Hurrell Froude (1803–1836), brother of James Anthony Froude (editor of *Fraser's Magazine,* 1860–1874)

435 **in propriâ personâ,** in his own person   441 **Arianising,** that is, tending to deny the divinity of Christ   442 **Bishop Bull,** George Bull (1634–1710), author of *Defensio Fidei Nicaenae* (1685)   444 **ante-Nicene view,** etc. The Nicene Creed, adopted by the Council of Nicaea in 325 and confirmed by the second ecumenical council at Constantinople in 381, is a summary of the Christian faith, including the doctrine of three equal persons in one God   447 **Froude's Remains,** published in 1837–1839, included strictures on the Reformation and aroused hostility toward the Tractarian Movement   457 **Encyclopædia Metropolitana.** Newman wrote a few articles for this encyclopedia in 1824

little at the time, except what I had learnt as a boy from Joseph Milner. In writing on the Scripture Miracles in 1825-6, I had read Middleton° on the *Miracles* of the early Church, and had imbibed a portion of his spirit.

The truth is, I was beginning to prefer intellectual excellence to moral; I was drifting in the direction of liberalism. I was rudely awakened from my dream at the end of 1827 by two great blows—illness and bereavement.

In the beginning of 1829, came the formal break between Dr. Whately and me; Mr. Peel's attempted re-election was the occasion of it. I think in 1828 or 1827 I had voted in the minority, when the petition to Parliament against the Catholic claims° was brought into Convocation. I did so mainly on the views suggested to me by the theory of the *Letters of an Episcopalian*. Also I disliked the bigoted "two bottle orthodox,"° as they were invidiously called. I took part against Mr. Peel, on a simple academical, not at all an ecclesiastical or a political ground; and this I professed at the time. I considered that Mr. Peel had taken the University by surprise, that he had no right to call upon us to turn round on a sudden, and to expose ourselves to the imputation of time-serving, and that a great university ought not to be bullied even by a great Duke of Wellington. Also by this time I was under the influence of Keble° and Froude; who, in addition to the reasons I have given, disliked the duke's change of policy as dictated by liberalism.

Whately was considerably annoyed at me, and he took a humorous revenge, of which he had given me due notice beforehand. As head of a house, he had duties of hospitality to men of all parties; he asked a set of the least intellectual men in Oxford to dinner, and men most fond of port; he made me one of the party; placed me between Provost this, and Principal that, and then asked me if I was proud of my friends. However, he had a serious meaning in his act; he saw, more clearly than I could do, that I was separating from his own friends for good and all.

Dr. Whately attributed my leaving his *clientela* to a wish on my part to be the head of a party myself. I do not think that it was deserved. My habitual feeling then and since has been, that it was not I who sought friends, but friends who sought me. Never man had kinder or more indulgent friends than I have had, but I expressed my own feeling as to the mode in which I gained them, in this very year 1829, in the course of a copy of verses. Speaking of my blessings, I said, "Blessings of friends, which to my door, *unasked, unhoped,* have come." They have come, they have gone; they came to my great joy, they went to my great grief. He who gave, took away. Dr. Whately's impression about me, however, admits of this explanation:—

During the first years of my residence at Oriel, though proud of my college, I was not at home there. I was very much alone, and I used often to take my daily walk by myself. I recollect once meeting Dr. Copleston,° then provost, with one of the fellows. He turned round, and with the kind courteousness which sat so well on him, made me a bow and said "Nunquam minus solus, quàm cùm solus."° At that time indeed (from 1823) I had the intimacy of my dear and true friend Dr. Pusey, and could not fail to admire and revere a soul so devoted to the cause of religion, so full of good works, so faithful in his affections; but he left residence when I was getting to know him well. As to Dr. Whately himself, he was too much my superior to allow of my being at my ease with him; and to no one in Oxford at this time did I open my heart fully and familiarly. But things changed in 1826. At that time I became one of the tutors of my college, and this gave me position; besides, I had written one or two essays which had been well received. I began to be known. I preached my first University sermon. Next year I was one of the public examiners for the B.A. degree. It was to me like the feeling of spring weather after winter; and, if I may so speak, I came out of my shell; I remained out of it till 1841.

The two persons who knew me best at that time are still alive, beneficed clergymen; no longer my friends. They could tell better than any one else what I was in those years. From this time my tongue was, as it were, loosened, and I spoke spontaneously and without effort. A shrewd man, who knew me at this time, said, "Here is a man who, when he is silent, will never begin to speak; and when he once begins to speak, will never stop." It was at this time that I began to have influence, which steadily increased for a course of years. I gained upon my pupils, and was in particular intimate and affectionate with two of our probationer fellows, Robert I. Wilberforce° (afterwards archdeacon) and Richard Hurrell Froude. Whately then, an acute man, perhaps saw around me the signs of an incipient party of which I was not conscious myself. And thus we discern the first elements of that movement afterwards called Tractarian.

The true and primary author of it, however, as is usual with great motive-powers, was out of sight. Having carried off as a mere boy the highest honours of the university, he had turned from the admiration which haunted his steps, and sought for a better and holier satisfaction in pastoral work in the country. Need I say that I am speaking of John Keble? The first time that I was in a room with him was on occasion of my election to a fellowship at Oriel, when I was sent for into the tower, to shake hands with the provost and fellows. How is that hour fixed in my memory after the changes of forty-two years, forty-two this very day on

460 **Middleton,** Conyers Middleton (1683–1750), author of a liberal treatise, *Miracles* (1748), which maintained that post-apostolic miracles were unreal   471 **Catholic claims,** that is, for political emancipation, which was passed in 1829   474–475 **two bottle orthodox,** that is, as orthodox in politics and religion as in their taste for wine at table   484 **Keble,** John Keble (1792–1866), founder of the Oxford (or Tractarian) Movement

515 **Dr. Copleston,** Edward Copleston (1776–1849), prelate and pamphleteer   518–519 **Nunquam . . . solus,** never less alone than when alone   549 **Robert I. Wilberforce.** Wilberforce (1802–1857), the son of a leading Evangelical, joined the Roman Catholic Church

which I write! I have lately had a letter in my hands, which I sent at the time to my great friend, John Bowden,° with whom I passed almost exclusively my undergraduate years. "I had to hasten to the tower," I say to him, "to receive the congratulations of all the fellows. I bore it till Keble took my hand, and then felt so abashed and unworthy of the honour done me, that I seemed desirous of quite sinking into the ground." His had been the first name which I had heard spoken of, with reverence rather than admiration, when I came up to Oxford. When one day I was walking in High Street with my dear earliest friend just mentioned, with what eagerness did he cry out, "There's Keble!" and with what awe did I look at him! Then at another time I heard a master of arts of my college give an account how he had just then had occasion to introduce himself on some business to Keble, and how gentle, courteous, and unaffected Keble had been, so as almost to put him out of countenance. Then too it was reported, truly or falsely, how a rising man of brilliant reputation, the present Dean of St. Paul's, Dr. Milman, admired and loved him, adding, that somehow he was unlike any one else. However, at the time when I was elected Fellow of Oriel he was not in residence, and he was shy of me for years in consequence of the marks which I bore upon me of the evangelical and liberal schools. At least so I have ever thought. Hurrell Froude brought us together about 1828: it is one of the sayings preserved in his *Remains*,—"Do you know the story of the murderer who had done one good thing in his life? Well; if I was ever asked what good deed I had ever done, I should say that I had brought Keble and Newman to understand each other."

The *Christian Year* made its appearance in 1827. It is not necessary, and scarcely becoming, to praise a book which has already become one of the classics of the language. When the general tone of religious literature was so nerveless and impotent, as it was at that time, Keble struck an original note and woke up in the hearts of thousands a new music, the music of a school, long unknown in England. Nor can I pretend to analyse, in my own instance, the effect of religious teaching so deep, so pure, so beautiful. I have never till now tried to do so; yet I think I am not wrong in saying, that the two main intellectual truths which it brought home to me, were the same two, which I had learned from Butler, though recast in the creative mind of my new master. The first of these was what may be called, in a large sense of the word, the sacramental system; that is, the doctrine that material phenomena are both the types and the instruments of real things unseen,—a doctrine, which embraces, not only what Anglicans, as well as Catholics, believe about sacraments properly so called; but also the article of "the Communion of Saints" in its fullness; and likewise the mysteries of the faith. The

connection of this philosophy of religion with what is sometimes called "Berkeleyism"° has been mentioned above; I knew little of Berkeley at this time except by name; nor have I ever studied him.

On the second intellectual principle which I gained from Mr. Keble, I could say a great deal; if this were the place for it. It runs through very much that I have written, and has gained for me many hard names. Butler teaches us that probability is the guide of life. The danger of this doctrine, in the case of many minds, is, its tendency to destroy in them absolute certainty, leading them to consider every conclusion as doubtful, and resolving truth into an opinion, which it is safe to obey or to profess, but not possible to embrace with full internal assent. If this were to be allowed, then the celebrated saying, "O God, if there be a God, save my soul, if I have a soul!" would be the highest measure of devotion:—but who can really pray to a being, about whose existence he is seriously in doubt?

I considered that Mr. Keble met this difficulty by ascribing the firmness of assent which we give to religious doctrine, not to the probabilities which introduced it, but to the living power of faith and love which accepted it. In matters of religion, he seemed to say, it is not merely probability which makes us intellectually certain, but probability as it is put to account by faith and love. It is faith and love which give to probability a force which it has not in itself. Faith and love are directed towards an object; in the vision of that object they live; it is that object, received in faith and love, which renders it reasonable to take probability as sufficient for internal conviction. Thus the argument about probability, in the matter of religion, became an argument from personality, which in fact is one form of the argument from authority.

In illustration, Mr. Keble used to quote the words of the psalm: "I will guide thee with mine *eye*. Be ye not like to horse and mule, which have no understanding; whose mouths must be held with bit and bridle, lest they fall upon thee." This is the very difference, he used to say, between slaves, and friends or children. Friends do not ask for literal commands; but, from their knowledge of the speaker, they understand his half-words, and from love of him they anticipate his wishes. Hence it is, that in his poem for St. Bartholomew's Day, he speaks of the "Eye of God's word"; and in the note quotes Mr. Miller, of Worcester College, who remarks, in his Bampton lectures, on the special power of Scripture, as having "this eye, like that of a portrait, uniformly fixed upon us, turn where we will." The view thus suggested by Mr. Keble, is brought forward in one of the earliest of the *Tracts for the Times*. In No. 8 I say, "The Gospel is a Law of Liberty. We are treated as sons, not as servants; not subjected to a code of formal command-

---

568 **John Bowden.** Bowden (1798–1844) was the author of *Life of Gregory VII*

624 **Berkeleyism,** after George Berkeley (1685–1753), author of *Treatise Concerning Human Knowledge* in which he maintained that it was impossible to have knowledge of an object beyond what is learned through the senses

ments, but addressed as those who love God, and wish to please Him.''

680   I did not at all dispute this view of the matter, for I made use of it myself; but I was dissatisfied, because it did not go to the root of the difficulty. It was beautiful and religious, but it did not even profess to be logical; and accordingly I tried to complete it by considerations of my own, which are implied in my University sermons, *Essay on Ecclesiastical Miracles,* and *Essay on Development of Doctrine.* My argument is in outline as follows: that that absolute certitude which we were able to possess, whether as to the truths of natural 690 theology, or as to the fact of a revelation, was the result of an *assemblage* of concurring and converging probabilities, and that, both according to the constitution of the human mind and the will of its Maker; that certitude was a habit of mind, that certainty was a quality of propositions; that probabilities which did not reach to logical certainty, might create a mental certitude; that the certitude thus created might equal in measure and strength the certitude which was created by the strictest scientific demonstration; and that to 700 have such certitude might in given cases and to given individuals be a plain duty, though not to others in other circumstances:—

Moreover, that as there were probabilities which sufficed to create certitude, so there were other probabilities which were legitimately adapted to create opinion; that it might be quite as much a matter of duty in given cases and to given persons to have about a fact an opinion of a definite strength and consistency, as in the case of greater or of more numerous 710 probabilities it was a duty to have a certitude; that accordingly we were bound to be more or less sure, on a sort of (as it were) graduated scale of assent, viz. according as the probabilities attaching to a professed fact were brought home to us, and, as the case might be, to entertain about it a pious belief, or a pious opinion, or a religious conjecture, or at least a tolerance of such belief, or opinion, or conjecture in others; that on the other hand, as it was a duty to have a belief, of more or less strong texture, in given cases, so in other 720 cases it was a duty not to believe, not to opine, not to conjecture, not even to tolerate the notion that a professed fact was true, inasmuch as it would be credulity or superstition, or some other moral fault, to do so. This was the region of private judgment in religion; that is, of a private judgment, not formed arbitrarily and according to one's fancy or liking, but conscientiously, and under a sense of duty.

Considerations such as these throw a new light on the subject of Miracles, and they seem to have led me 730 to reconsider the view which I took of them in my essay in 1825-6. I do not know what was the date of this change in me, nor of the train of ideas on which it was founded. That there had been already great miracles, as those of Scripture, as the Resurrection, was a fact establishing the principle that the laws of nature

had sometimes been suspended by their Divine Author; and since what had happened once might happen again, a certain probability, at least no kind of improbability, was attached to the idea, taken in itself, of miraculous intervention in later times, and miraculous 740 accounts were to be regarded in connection with the verisimilitude, scope, instrument, character, testimony, and circumstances, with which they presented themselves to us; and, according to the final result of those various considerations, it was our duty to be sure, or to believe, or to opine, or to surmise, or to tolerate, or to reject, or to denounce. The main difference between my essay on Miracles in 1826 and my essay in 1842 is this: that in 1826 I considered that miracles were sharply divided into two classes, those 750 which were to be received, and those which were to be rejected; whereas in 1842 I saw that they were to be regarded according to their greater or less probability, which was in some cases sufficient to create certitude about them, in other cases only belief or opinion.

Moreover, the argument from analogy, on which this view of the question was founded, suggested to me something besides, in recommendation of the ecclesiastical miracles. It fastened itself upon the theory of church history which I had learned as a boy 760 from Joseph Milner. It is Milner's doctrine, that upon the visible Church come down from above, from time to time, large and temporary *Effusions* of divine grace. This is the leading idea of his work. He begins by speaking of the Day of Pentecost, as marking "the first of those *Effusions* of the Spirit of God, which from age to age have visited the earth since the coming of Christ" (vol. i. p. 3). In a note he adds that "in the term 'Effusion' there is not here included the idea of the miraculous or extraordinary operations of the 770 Spirit of God"; but still it was natural for me, admitting Milner's general theory, and applying to it the principle of analogy, not to stop short at his abrupt *ipse dixit,*° but boldly to pass forward to the conclusion, on other grounds plausible, that, as miracles accompanied the first effusion of grace, so they might accompany the later. It is surely a natural and on the whole, a true anticipation (though of course there are exceptions in particular cases), that gifts and graces go together; now, according to the ancient Catholic doctrine, the 780 gift of miracles was viewed as the attendant and shadow of transcendent sanctity: and more over, as such sanctity was not of every day's occurrence, nay further, as one period of church history differed widely from another, and, as Joseph Milner would say, there had been generations or centuries of degeneracy or disorder, and times of revival, and as one region might be in the mid-day of religious fervour, and another in twilight or gloom, there was no force in the popular argument, that, because we did not see miracles with 790 our own eyes, miracles had not happened in former

773 **ipse dixit.** He himself has said it

times, or were not now at this very time taking place in distant places:—but I must not dwell longer on a subject, to which in a few words it is impossible to do justice.

Hurrell Froude was a pupil of Keble's, formed by him, and in turn reacting upon him. I knew him first in 1826, and was in the closest and most affectionate friendship with him from about 1829 till his death in 1836. He was a man of the highest gifts—so truly many-sided, that it would be presumptuous in me to attempt to describe him, except under those aspects, in which he came before me. Nor have I here to speak of the gentleness and tenderness of nature, the playfulness, the free elastic force and graceful versatility of mind, and the patient winning considerateness in discussion, which endeared him to those to whom he opened his heart; for I am all along engaged upon matters of belief and opinion, and am introducing others into my narrative, not for their own sake, or because I love and have loved them, so much as because, and so far as, they have influenced my theological views. In this respect then, I speak of Hurrell Froude—in his intellectual aspect—as a man of high genius, brimful and overflowing with ideas and views, in him original, which were too many and strong even for his bodily strength, and which crowded and jostled against each other in their effort after distinct shape and expression. And he had an intellect as critical and logical as it was speculative and bold. Dying prematurely, as he did, and in the conflict and transition-state of opinion, his religious views never reached their ultimate conclusion, by the very reason of their multitude and their depth. His opinions arrested and influenced me, even when they did not gain my assent. He professed openly his admiration of the Church of Rome, and his hatred of the reformers. He delighted in the notion of an hierarchical system, of sacerdotal power and of full ecclesiastical liberty. He felt scorn of the maxim, "The Bible and the Bible only is the religion of Protestants"; and he gloried in accepting tradition as a main instrument of religious teaching. He had a high severe idea of the intrinsic excellence of virginity; and he considered the Blessed Virgin its great pattern. He delighted in thinking of the saints; he had a keen appreciation of the idea of sanctity, its possibility and its heights; and he was more than inclined to believe a large amount of miraculous interference as occurring in the early and middle ages. He embraced the principle of penance and mortification. He had a deep devotion to the Real Presence, in which he had a firm faith. He was powerfully drawn to the medieval church, but not to the primitive.

He had a keen insight into abstract truth; but he was an Englishman to the backbone in his severe adherence to the real and the concrete. He had a most classical taste, and a genius for philosophy and art; and he was fond of historical inquiry, and the politics of religion. He had no turn for theology as such. He had no

appreciation of the writings of the Fathers, of the detail or development of doctrine, of the definite traditions of the Church viewed in their matter, of the teaching of the ecumenical councils, or of the controversies out of which they arose. He took an eager, courageous view of things on the whole. I should say that his power of entering into the minds of others did not equal his other gifts; he could not believe, for instance, that I really held the Roman Church to be Antichristian. On many points he would not believe but that I agreed with him, when I did not. He seemed not to understand my difficulties. His were of a different kind, the contrariety between theory and fact. He was a high Tory of the cavalier stamp, and was disgusted with the Toryism of the opponents of the Reform Bill.° He was smitten with the love of the theocratic church; he went abroad and was shocked by the degeneracy which he thought he saw in the Catholics of Italy.

It is difficult to enumerate the precise additions to my theological creed which I derived from a friend to whom I owe so much. He made me look with admiration towards the Church of Rome, and in the same degree to dislike the Reformation. He fixed deep in me the idea of devotion to the Blessed Virgin, and he led me gradually to believe in the Real Presence.°

There is one remaining source of my opinions to be mentioned, and that far from the least important. In proportion as I moved out of the shadow of liberalism which had hung over my course, my early devotion towards the Fathers returned; and in the long vacation of 1828 I set about to read them chronologically, beginning with St. Ignatius and St. Justin.° About 1830 a proposal was made to me by Mr. Hugh Rose, who with Mr. Lyall° (afterwards Dean of Canterbury) was providing writers for a theological library, to furnish them with a history of the principal councils. I accepted it, and at once set to work on the Council of Nicæa. It was launching myself on an ocean with currents innumerable; and I was drifted back first to the ante-Nicene history, and then to the Church of Alexandria. The work at last appeared under the title of *The Arians of the Fourth Century;* and of its 422 pages, the first 117 consisted of introductory matter, and the Council of Nicæa did not appear till the 254th, and then occupied at most twenty pages.

I do not know when I first learnt to consider that antiquity was the true exponent of the doctrines of Christianity and the basis of the Church of England; but I take it for granted that Bishop Bull, whose works at this time I read, was my chief introduction to this

864 **Reform Bill.** The Reform Bill of 1832 extended the right to vote to many members of the middle class. Though it did not introduce democracy into England, it did make democracy ultimately possible   874 **the Real Presence,** that is, the actual presence of Christ in the bread and wine of the Eucharistic sacrament   881 **St. Ignatius and St. Justin.** Ignatius (d.c. 107) was Bishop of Antioch and Father of the Church; Justin was a Christian apologist (c. 100–c. 165)   882-883 **Mr. Hugh Rose . . . Mr. Lyall.** Hugh James Rose (1795–1838) was a theologian connected with the beginnings of Tractarianism. William Rowe Lyall (1788–1857) was the editor of the *Theological Library*

principle. The course of reading which I pursued in the composition of my work was directly adapted to develop it in my mind. What principally attracted me in the ante-Nicene period was the great Church of Alexandria, the historical centre of teaching in those times. Of Rome for some centuries comparatively little is known. The battle of Arianism was first fought in Alexandria; Athanasius,° the champion of the truth, was Bishop of Alexandria; and in his writings he refers to the great religious names of an earlier date, to Origen,° Dionysius,° and others who were the glory of its see, or of its school. The broad philosophy of Clement° and Origen carried me away; the philosophy, not the theological doctrine; and I have drawn out some features of it in my volume, with the zeal and freshness, but with the partiality of a neophyte. Some portions of their teaching, magnificent in themselves, came like music to my inward ear, as if the response to ideas, which, with little external to encourage them, I had cherished so long. These were based on the mystical or sacramental principle, and spoke of the various economies or dispensations of the eternal. I understood them to mean that the exterior world, physical and historical, was but the outward manifestation of realities greater than itself. Nature was a parable: Scripture was an allegory: pagan literature, philosophy, and mythology, properly understood, were but a preparation for the Gospel. The Greek poets and sages were in a certain sense prophets; for "thoughts beyond their thought to those high bards were given." There had been a divine dispensation granted to the Jews; there had been in some sense a dispensation carried on in favour of the Gentiles. He who had taken the seed of Jacob for His elect people, had not therefore cast the rest of mankind out of His sight. In the fullness of time both Judaism and Paganism had come to nought; the outward framework, which concealed yet suggested the living truth, had never been intended to last, and it was dissolving under the beams of the sun of justice behind it and through it. The process of change had been slow; it had been done not rashly, but by rule, and measure, "at sundry times and in divers manners," first one disclosure and then another, till the whole was brought into full manifestation. And thus room was made for the anticipation of further and deeper disclosures, of truths still under the veil of the letter, and in their season to be revealed. The visible world still remains without its divine interpretation; Holy Church in her sacraments and her hierarchical appointments, will remain even to the end of the world, only a symbol of those heavenly facts which fill eternity. Her mysteries are but the expressions in human language of truths to which the human mind is unequal. It is evident how much there was in all this in correspondence with the thoughts which had attracted me when I was young, and with the doctrine which I have already connected with the *Analogy* and the *Christian Year*.

I suppose it was to the Alexandrian school and to the early church that I owe in particular what I definitely held about the angels. I viewed them, not only as the ministers employed by the Creator in the Jewish and Christian dispensations, as we find on the face of Scripture, but as carrying on, as Scripture also implies, the economy of the visible world. I considered them as the real causes of motion, light, and life, and of those elementary principles of the physical universe, which, when offered in their developments to our senses, suggest to us the notion of cause and effect, and of what are called the laws of nature. I have drawn out this doctrine in my sermon for Michaelmas day, written not later than 1834. I say of the angels, "Every breath of air and ray of light and heat, every beautiful prospect is, as it were, the skirts of their garments, the waving of the robes of those whose faces see God." Again, I ask what would be the thoughts of a man who, "when examining a flower, or a herb, or a pebble, or a ray of light, which he treats as something so beneath him in the scale of existence, suddenly discovered that he was in the presence of some powerful being who was hidden behind the visible things he was inspecting, who, though concealing his wise hand, was giving them their beauty, grace, and perfection, as being God's instrument for the purpose, nay, whose robe and ornaments those objects were, which he was so eager to analyse?" and I therefore remark that "we may say with grateful and simple hearts with the Three Holy Children, 'O all ye works of the Lord, etc., etc., bless ye the Lord, praise Him, and magnify Him for ever.'"

Also, besides the hosts of evil spirits, I considered there was a middle race, δαιμόνια, neither in heaven, nor hell: partially fallen, capricious, wayward; noble or crafty, benevolent or malicious, as the case might be. They gave a sort of inspiration or intelligence to races, nations, and classes of men. Hence the action of bodies politic and associations, which is so different often from that of the individuals who compose them. Hence the character and the instinct of states and governments, of religious communities and communions. I thought they were inhabited by unseen intelligences. My preference of the personal to the abstract would naturally lead me to this view. I thought it countenanced by the mention of "the Prince of Persia"° in the Prophet Daniel, and I think I considered that it was of such intermediate beings that the Apocalypse° spoke, when it introduced "the Angels of the Seven Churches."

In 1837 I made a further development of this doctrine. I said to my great friend, Samuel Francis Wood, in a letter which came into my hands on his death, "I

907 **Athanasius**, St. Athanasius (296?–373), opponent of Arianism   909 **Origen**, Christian theologian in Alexandria (c. 185–c. 254)   910 **Dionysius**, the Great (c. 190–265), Bishop of Alexandria, student of Origen   911 **Clement**, of Alexandria (c. 150–c. 215), Greek Christian theologian

1003 **Prince of Persia.** See *Daniel*, 10:13   1005 **Apocalypse, etc.** See *Revelation*, 1

have an idea. The mass of the Fathers (Justin, Athenagoras, Irenæus, Clement, Tertullian, Origen, Lactantius, Sulpicius, Ambrose, Nazianzen), hold that, though Satan fell from the beginning, the Angels fell before the deluge, falling in love with the daughters of men. This has lately come across me as a remarkable solution of a notion which I cannot help holding. Dariel speaks as if each nation had its guardian Angel. I cannot but think that there are beings with a great deal of good in them, yet with great defects, who are the animating principles of certain institutions, etc., etc. . . . Take England, with many high virtues, and yet a low Catholicism. It seems to me that John Bull is a spirit neither of heaven nor hell. . . . Has not the Christian Church, in its parts, surrendered itself to one or other of these simulations of the truth? . . . How are we to avoid Scylla and Charybdis and go straight on to the very image of Christ?'' etc., etc.

I am aware that what I have been saying will, with many men, be doing credit to my imagination at the expense of my judgment—''Hippoclides doesn't care'';° I am not setting myself up as a pattern of good sense or of anything else: I am but vindicating myself from the charge of dishonesty.—There is indeed another view of the economy brought out, in the course of the same dissertation on the subject, in my History of the Arians, which has afforded matter for the latter imputation; but I reserve it for the concluding portion of my reply.

While I was engaged in writing my work upon the Arians, great events were happening at home and abroad, which brought out into form and passionate expression the various beliefs which had so gradually been winning their way into my mind. Shortly before, there had been a revolution in France; the Bourbons had been dismissed:° and I believed that it was unchristian for nations to cast off their governors, and, much more, sovereigns who had the divine right of inheritance. Again, the great Reform agitation was going around me as I wrote. The Whigs had come into power; Lord Grey° had told the bishops to set their house in order, and some of the prelates had been insulted and threatened in the streets of London. The vital question was how were we to keep the Church from being liberalised? there was such apathy on the subject in some quarters, such imbecile alarm in others; the true principles of churchmanship seemed so radically decayed, and there was such distraction in the councils of the clergy. The Bishop of London of the day, an active and openhearted man, had been for years engaged in diluting the high orthodoxy of the Church by the introduction of the Evangelical body into places of influence and trust. He had deeply of-

fended men who agreed with myself, by an off-hand saying (as it was reported) to the effect that belief in the Apostolical succession° had gone out with the non-jurors.° ''We can count you,'' he said to some of the gravest and most venerated persons of the old school. And the Evangelical party itself seemed, with their late success, to have lost that simplicity and unworldliness which I admired so much in Milner and Scott. It was not that I did not venerate such men as the then Bishop of Lichfield, and others of similar sentiments, who were not yet promoted out of the ranks of the clergy, but I thought little of them as a class. I thought they played into the hands of the Liberals. With the establishment thus divided and threatened, thus ignorant of its true strength, I compared that fresh vigorous power of which I was reading in the first centuries. In her triumphant zeal on behalf of that primeval mystery, to which I had had so great a devotion from my youth, I recognised the movement of my Spiritual Mother. ''Incessu patuit Dea.''° The self-conquest of her ascetics, the patience of her martyrs, the irresistible determination of her bishops, the joyous swing of her advance, both exalted and abashed me. I said to myself, ''Look on this picture and on that''; I felt affection for my own Church, but not tenderness; I felt dismay at her prospects, anger and scorn at her do-nothing perplexity. I thought that if Liberalism once got a footing within her, it was sure of the victory in the event. I saw that Reformation principles were powerless to rescue her. As to leaving her, the thought never crossed my imagination; still I ever kept before me that there was something greater than the Established Church, and that that was the Church Catholic and Apostolic, set up from the beginning, of which she was but the local presence and organ. She was nothing, unless she was this. She must be dealt with strongly, or she would be lost. There was need of a second Reformation.

At this time I was disengaged from college duties, and my health had suffered from the labour involved in the composition of my volume. It was ready for the press in July 1832, though not published till the end of 1833. I was easily persuaded to join Hurrell Froude and his father, who were going to the south of Europe for the health of the former.

We set out in December 1832. It was during this expedition that my verses which are in the Lyra Apostolica were written;—a few indeed before it, but not more than one or two of them after it. Exchanging, as I was, definite tutorial labours, and the literary quiet and pleasant friendships of the last six years, for foreign countries and an unknown future, I naturally was led to think that some inward changes, as well as some larger course of action, was coming upon me. At

1032–1033 **Hippoclides doesn't care.** According to Herodotus, this is what Hippoclides said when his would-be father-in-law told him that his foolishness had lost him his bride   1047 **Bourbons . . . dismissed.** Charles X was dethroned in the Revolution in France of July 27–29, 1830   1052 **Lord Grey,** Earl Grey (1764–1845), British Prime Minister, 1830–1834

1067 **Apostolical succession,** the doctrine of uninterrupted succession of bishops from the Apostles to the present time   1068 **non-jurors,** English and Scottish clergymen with benefices who refused to take the oath of allegiance to William and Mary and their successors   1084 **Incessu . . . Dea.** The goddess stood revealed by her walk

Whitchurch, while waiting for the down mail to Fal-
mouth, I wrote the verses about my Guardian Angel,
which begin with these words: "Are these the tracks of
some unearthly Friend?" and go on to speak of "the
vision" which haunted me:—that vision is more or
less brought out in the whole series of these compositions.

I went to various coasts of the Mediterranean,
parted with my friends at Rome; went down for the
second time to Sicily, at the end of April, and got back
to England by Palermo in the early part of July. The
strangeness of foreign life threw me back into myself; I
found pleasure in historical sites and beautiful scenes,
not in men and manners. We kept clear of Catholics
throughout our tour. I had a conversation with the
Dean of Malta, a most pleasant man, lately dead; but it
was about the Fathers, and the library of the great
church. I knew the Abbate Santini, at Rome, who did
no more than copy for me the Gregorian tones. Froude
and I made two calls upon Monsignore (now Cardinal)
Wiseman° at the Collegio Inglese, shortly before we left
Rome. I do not recollect being in a room with any
other ecclesiastics, except a priest at Castro-Giovanni
in Sicily, who called on me when I was ill, and with
whom I wished to hold a controversy. As to church
services, we attended the Tenebræ,° at the Sestine,° for
the sake of the Miserere;° and that was all. My general
feeling was, "All, save the spirit of man, is divine." I
saw nothing but what was external; of the hidden life
of Catholics I knew nothing. I was still more driven
back into myself, and felt my isolation. England was in
my thoughts solely, and the news from England came
rarely and imperfectly. The Bill for the Suppression of
the Irish Sees was in progress, and filled my mind. I
had fierce thoughts against the Liberals.

It was the success of the Liberal cause which fretted
me inwardly. I became fierce against its instruments
and its manifestations. A French vessel was at Algiers;
I would not even look at the tricolour. On my return,
though forced to stop a day in Paris, I kept indoors the
whole time, and all that I saw of that beautiful city
was what I saw from the diligence. The Bishop of
London had already sounded me as to my filling one of
the Whitehall preacherships, which he had just then
put on a new footing; but I was indignant at the line
which he was taking, and from my steamer I sent home
a letter declining the appointment by anticipation,
should it be offered to me. At this time I was specially
annoyed with Dr. Arnold,° though it did not last into
later years. Some one, I think, asked in conversation
at Rome, whether a certain interpretation of Scripture
was Christian? it was answered that Dr. Arnold took
it; I interposed, "But is *he* a Christian?" The subject
went out of my head at once; when afterwards I was

taxed with it I could say no more in explanation, than
that I thought I must have been alluding to some free
views of Dr. Arnold about the Old Testament:—I
thought I must have meant, "But who is to answer for
Arnold?" It was at Rome too that we began the *Lyra
Apostolica* which appeared monthly in the *British
Magazine*. The motto shows the feeling of both Froude
and myself at the time: we borrowed from M. Bunsen° a
Homer, and Froude chose the words in which Achilles, on returning to the battle, says, "You shall know
the difference, now that I am back again."

Especially when I was left by myself, the thought
came upon me that deliverance is wrought, not by the
many but by the few, not by bodies but by persons.
Now it was, I think, that I repeated to myself the
words, which had ever been dear to me from my
school days, "Exoriare aliquis!"°—now too, that
Southey's beautiful poem of *Thalaba,* for which I had
an immense liking, came forcibly to my mind. I began
to think that I had a mission. There are sentences of
my letters to my friends to this effect, if they are not
destroyed. When we took leave of Monsignore Wiseman, he had courteously expressed a wish that we
might make a second visit to Rome; I said with great
gravity, "We have a work to do in England." I went
down at once to Sicily, and the presentiment grew
stronger. I struck into the middle of the island, and fell
ill of a fever at Leonforte. My servant thought that I
was dying and begged for my last directions. I gave
them, as he wished; but I said, "I shall not die." I
repeated, "I shall not die, for I have not sinned against
light, I have not sinned against light."° I never have
been able to make out at all what I meant.

I got to Castro-Giovanni, and was laid up there for
nearly three weeks. Towards the end of May I set off
for Palermo, taking three days for the journey. Before
starting from my inn in the morning of May 26th or
27th, I sat down on my bed, and began to sob bitterly.
My servant, who had acted as my nurse, asked what
ailed me. I could only answer, "I have a work to do in
England."

I was aching to get home; yet for want of a vessel I
was kept at Palermo for three weeks. I began to visit
the churches, and they calmed my impatience, though
I did not attend any services. I knew nothing of the
presence of the Blessed Sacrament there. At last I got
off in an orange boat, bound for Marseilles. We were
becalmed a whole week in the Straits of Bonifacio.
Then it was that I wrote the lines, "Lead, kindly
light," which have since become well known. I was
writing verses the whole time of my passage. At length
I got to Marseilles, and set off for England. The fatigue
of traveling was too much for me, and I was laid up for
several days at Lyons. At last I got off again, and did
not stop night or day till I reached England, and my
mother's house. My brother had arrived from Persia

1139 **Wiseman,** Nicholas Patrick Stephen Wiseman (1802–1865), Catholic Cardinal Primate of England in 1850   1144 **Tenebrae,** special Holy Week services
commemorating the suffering of Christ   **Sestine,** the Sistine Chapel in the Vatican
1145 **Miserere,** musical setting of the Fifteenth Psalm (Vulgate)   1167 **Dr. Arnold,** Thomas Arnold (1795–1842), Master of Rugby School, father of Matthew
Arnold, and liberal student of Scripture

1180 **M. Bunsen,** Christian Charles Josias, Baron von Bunsen (1791–1860), envoy
to the Papal court   1189 **Exoriare aliquis.** May someone arise

only a few hours before. This was on the Tuesday. The following Sunday, July 14th, Mr. Keble preached the assize sermon in the University pulpit. It was published under the title of *National Apostasy*. I have ever considered and kept the day as the start of the religious movement of 1833.

(1864)

JOHN STUART MILL
1806–1873

John Stuart Mill was the son of James Mill, a leading historian, economist, and utilitarian philosopher, and he was educated exclusively at home in London under his father's direction. As a boy, he read Latin and Greek with ease and could discourse intelligently on mathematics, philosophy, and economics. So intensive was his education that he felt that when he started his career, he had "an advantage of a quarter of a century" over his contemporaries. He worked for twenty-two years for the East India House, rising to the position of chief examiner, and served in Parliament from 1865 to 1868. His primary interest, however, was writing.

Mill's books were important in his day, and most of them still are significant primary documents in political and economic discussions. But his reputation as a thinker in the nineteenth century was made by three books: his *System of Logic* (1843) became "the textbook of the Empirical School and the guide of all 'Radical' thinkers of the day"; his *Principles of Political Economy* (1848) became "the handbook of Victorian progressives who . . . thought that the 'state of polemical discussion' had now passed and that a great constructive era had dawned"; his *On Liberty* (1859) became, and remains, the great popular statement of utilitarianism which, according to Thomas Hardy, the students of the 1860s knew almost by heart. For later students of Mill, the *Autobiography* (1873) has taken on increasing importance as one of the principal documents, along with Carlyle's *Sartor Resartus* and Newman's *Apologia*, for reviewing the forces which shaped the Victorian mind.

Because of the temper of his mind and the austerity of his training, Mill's major sympathies lay with the philosophy known as utilitarianism, whose followers held that the useful was the good and that the determining consideration of right conduct should be the usefulness of its consequences. Although most utilitarians tended to be inflexible, Mill was noted for the liberal and inquiring spirit with which he handled the great questions of his time. Influenced by Carlyle and Coleridge, Mill tried to reconcile romanticism with utilitarianism. He was certainly the least rigid and most effective of all the social commentators in the utilitarian-liberal tradition.

Because Mill was a rationalist as well as a utilitarian, his prose style is characterized by precise statement and simple clarity. He can be the most lucid and intelligible of writers. By his own statement, he wrote all of his books twice. His is the style of mind speaking to mind, and, in contrast to Carlyle, he does not depend upon color or energy to accomplish his purposes.

from ON LIBERTY

In the first chapter of *On Liberty*, Mill stated that his object was "to assert one very simple principle, as entitled to govern absolutely the dealings of society with the individual in the way of compulsion and control, whether the means used be physical force in the form of legal penalties, or the moral coercion of public opinion. That principle is, that the sole end for which mankind are warranted, individually or collectively, in interfering with the liberty of action of any of their number, is self-protection. That the only purpose for which power can be rightfully exercised over any member of a civilized community, against his will, is to prevent harm to others." Thus, Mill carries the classical arguments for freedom of speech and publication one step further—to freedom of action.

The immediate predecessors of *On Liberty* in the late eighteenth and early nineteenth centuries were Jeremy Bentham's *Introduction to the Principles of Morals and Legislation* (1789) and the writings of Claude Henri Saint-Simon (1760–1825) and Auguste Comte (1798–1857). In the longer Western tradition, the book can be compared with Plato's *Republic*, Aristotle's *Politics*, Machiavelli's *Prince*, Hobbes' *Leviathan*, and Rousseau's *Social Contract*.

OF INDIVIDUALITY,
AS ONE OF THE ELEMENTS OF WELL-BEING

Such being the reasons which make it imperative that human beings should be free to form opinions, and to express their opinions without reserve; and such the baneful consequences to the intellectual, and through that to the moral nature of man, unless this liberty is either conceded, or asserted in spite of prohibition; let us next examine whether the same reasons do not require that men should be free to act upon their opinions—to carry these out in their lives, without hindrance, either physical or moral, from their fellow men, so long as it is at their own risk and peril. This last proviso is of course indispensable. No one pretends that actions should be as free as opinions. On the contrary, even opinions lose their immunity, when the circumstances in which they are expressed are such as to constitute their expression a positive instigation to some mischievous act. An opinion that corn-dealers are starvers of the poor, or that private property is robbery, ought to be unmolested when simply circulated through the press, but may justly incur punishment when delivered orally to an excited mob assembled before the house of a corn-dealer, or when handed about among the same mob in the form of a placard. Acts, of whatever kind, which, without justifiable cause, do harm to others, may be, and in the more important cases absolutely require to be, controlled by the unfavourable sentiments, and, when needful, by the active interference of mankind. The liberty of the individual must be thus far limited; he must not make himself a nuisance to other people. But if he refrains from molesting others in what concerns them, and merely acts according to his own inclination and judgement in things which concern himself, the same reasons which show that opinion should be free, prove also that he should be allowed, without molestation, to carry his opinions into practice at his own cost. That mankind are not infallible; that their truths, for the most part, are only half-truths; that unity of opinion, unless resulting from the fullest and freest comparison of opposite opinions, is not desirable, and diversity not an evil, but a good, until mankind are much more capable than at present of recognizing all sides of the truth, are principles applicable to men's modes of action, not less than to their opinions. As it is useful that while mankind are imperfect there should be different opinions, so is it that there should be different experiments of living; that free scope should be given to varieties of character, short of injury to others; and that the worth of different modes of life should be proved practically, when any one thinks fit to try them. It is desirable, in short, that in things which do not primarily concern others, individuality should assert itself. Where, not the person's own character, but the traditions or customs of other people are the rule of conduct, there is wanting one of the principal ingredients of human happiness, and quite the chief ingredient of individual and social progress.

In maintaining this principle, the greatest difficulty to be encountered does not lie in the appreciation of means towards an acknowledged end, but in the indifference of persons in general to the end itself. If it were felt that the free development of individuality is one of the leading essentials of well-being; that it is not only a co-ordinate element with all that is designated by the terms civilization, instruction, education, culture, but is itself a necessary part and condition of all those things; there would be no danger that liberty should be undervalued, and the adjustment of the boundaries between it and social control would pres-

ent no extraordinary difficulty. But the evil is, that individual spontaneity is hardly recognized by the common modes of thinking, as having any intrinsic worth, or deserving any regard on its own account. The majority, being satisfied with the ways of mankind as they now are (for it is they who make them what they are), cannot comprehend why those ways should not be good enough for everybody; and what is more, spontaneity forms no part of the ideal of the majority of moral and social reformers, but is rather looked on with jealousy, as a troublesome and perhaps rebellious obstruction to the general acceptance of what these reformers, in their own judgement, think would be best for mankind. Few persons, out of Germany, even comprehend the meaning of the doctrine which Wilhelm von Humboldt, so eminent both as a savant and as a politician, made the text of a treatise—that "the end of man, or that which is prescribed by the eternal or immutable dictates of reason, and not suggested by vague and transient desires, is the highest and most harmonious development of his powers to a complete and consistent whole"; that, therefore, the object "towards which every human being must ceaselessly direct his efforts, and on which especially those who design to influence their fellow men must ever keep their eyes, is the individuality of power and development"; that for this there are two requisites, "freedom, and variety of situations"; and that from the union of these arise "individual vigour and manifold diversity," which combine themselves in "originality."°

Little, however, as people are accustomed to a doctrine like that of Von Humboldt, and surprising as it may be to them to find so high a value attached to individuality, the question, one must nevertheless think, can only be one of degree. No one's idea of excellence in conduct is that people should do absolutely nothing but copy one another. No one would assert that people ought not to put into their mode of life, and into the conduct of their concerns, any impress whatever of their own judgement, or of their own individual character. On the other hand, it would be absurd to pretend that people ought to live as if nothing whatever had been known in the world before they came into it; as if experience had as yet done nothing towards showing that one mode of existence, or of conduct, is preferable to another. Nobody denies that people should be so taught and trained in youth, as to know and benefit by the ascertained results of human experience. But it is the privilege and proper condition of a human being, arrived at the maturity of his faculties, to use and interpret experience in his own way. It is for him to find out what part of recorded experience is properly applicable to his own circumstances and character. The traditions and customs of other people are, to a certain extent, evidence of

Of Individuality   85–100 **Wilhelm von Humboldt . . . originality**, identified by Mill himself as being from *The Sphere and Duties of Government*, by Baron Wilhelm von Humboldt (1767–1835), Prussian statesman and political theorist

what their experience has taught *them;* presumptive evidence, and as such, have a claim to his deference: but, in the first place, their experience may be too narrow; or they may not have interpreted it rightly. Secondly, their interpretation of experience may be correct, but unsuitable to him. Customs are made for customary circumstances, and customary characters; and his circumstances or his character may be uncustomary. Thirdly, though the customs be both good as customs, and suitable to him, yet to conform to custom, merely as custom, does not educate or develop in him any of the qualities which are the distinctive endowment of a human being. The human faculties of perception, judgement, discriminative feeling, mental activity, and even moral preference, are exercised only in making a choice. He who does anything because it is the custom makes no choice. He gains no practice either in discerning or in desiring what is best. The mental and moral, like the muscular powers, are improved only by being used. The faculties are called into no exercise by doing a thing merely because others do it, no more than by believing a thing only because others believe it. If the grounds of an opinion are not conclusive to the person's own reason, his reason cannot be strengthened, but is likely to be weakened, by his adopting it: and if the inducements to an act are not such as are consentaneous to his own feelings and character (where affection, or the rights of others, are not concerned) it is so much done towards rendering his feelings and character inert and torpid, instead of active and energetic.

He who lets the world, or his own portion of it, choose his plan of life for him, has no need of any other faculty than the ape-like one of imitation. He who chooses his plan for himself, employs all his faculties. He must use observation to see, reasoning and judgement to foresee, activity to gather materials for decision, discrimination to decide, and when he has decided, firmness and self-control to hold to his deliberate decision. And these qualities he requires and exercises exactly in proportion as the part of his conduct which he determines according to his own judgement and feelings is a large one. It is possible that he might be guided in some good path, and kept out of harm's way, without any of these things. But what will be his comparative worth as a human being? It really is of importance, not only what men do, but also what manner of men they are that do it. Among the works of man, which human life is rightly employed in perfecting and beautifying, the first in importance surely is man himself. Supposing it were possible to get houses built, corn grown, battles fought, causes tried, and even churches erected and prayers said, by machinery—by automatons in human form—it would be a considerable loss to exchange for these automatons even the men and women who at present inhabit the more civilized parts of the world, and who assuredly are but starved specimens of what nature can and will produce. Human nature is not a machine to be built after a model, and set to do exactly the work prescribed for it, but a tree, which requires to grow and develop itself on all sides, according to the tendency of the inward forces which make it a living thing.

It will probably be conceded that it is desirable people should exercise their understandings, and that an intelligent following of custom, or even occasionally an intelligent deviation from custom, is better than a blind and simply mechanical adhesion to it. To a certain extent it is admitted, that our understanding should be our own: but there is not the same willingness to admit that our desires and impulses should be our own likewise; or that to possess impulses of our own, and of any strength, is anything but a peril and a snare. Yet desires and impulses are as much a part of a perfect human being, as beliefs and restraints: and strong impulses are only perilous when not properly balanced; when one set of aims and inclinations is developed into strength, while others, which ought to co-exist with them, remain weak and inactive. It is not because men's desires are strong that they act ill; it is because their consciences are weak. There is no natural connexion between strong impulses and a weak conscience. The natural connexion is the other way. To say that one person's desires and feelings are stronger and more various than those of another, is merely to say that he has more of the raw material of human nature, and is therefore capable, perhaps of more evil, but certainly of more good. Strong impulses are but another name for energy. Energy may be turned to bad uses; but more good may always be made of an energetic nature, than of an indolent and impassive one. Those who have most natural feeling, are always those whose cultivated feelings may be made the strongest. The same strong susceptibilities which make the personal impulses vivid and powerful, are also the source from whence are generated the most passionate love of virtue, and the sternest self-control. It is through the cultivation of these, that society both does its duty and protects its interests: not by rejecting the stuff of which heroes are made, because it knows not how to make them. A person whose desires and impulses are his own—are the expression of his own nature, as it has been developed and modified by his own culture—is said to have a character. One whose desires and impulses are not his own, has no character, no more than a steam-engine has a character. If, in addition to being his own, his impulses are strong, and are under the government of a strong will, he has an energetic character. Whoever thinks that individuality of desires and impulses should not be encouraged to unfold itself, must maintain that society has no need of strong natures—is not the better for containing many persons who have much character—and that a high general average of energy is not desirable.

In some early states of society, these forces might

be, and were, too much ahead of the power which society then possessed of disciplining and controlling them. There has been a time when the element of spontaneity and individuality was in excess, and the social principle had a hard struggle with it. The difficulty then was, to induce men of strong bodies or minds to pay obedience to any rules which required them to control their impulses. To overcome this difficulty, law and discipline, like the Popes struggling against the Emperors, asserted a power over the whole man, claiming to control all his life in order to control his character—which society had not found any other sufficient means of binding. But society has now fairly got the better of individuality; and the danger which threatens human nature is not the excess, but the deficiency, of personal impulses and preferences. Things are vastly changed, since the passions of those who were strong by station or by personal endowment were in a state of habitual rebellion against laws and ordinances, and required to be rigorously chained up to enable the persons within their reach to enjoy any particle of security. In our times, from the highest class of society down to the lowest, every one lives under the eye of a hostile and dreaded censorship. Not only in what concerns others, but in what concerns only themselves, the individual or the family do not ask themselves—what do I prefer? or, what would suit my character and disposition? or, what would allow the best and highest in me to have fair play, and enable it to grow and thrive? They ask themselves, what is suitable to my position? what is usually done by persons of my station and pecuniary circumstances? or (worse still) what is usually done by persons of a station and circumstances superior to mine? I do not mean that they choose what is customary, in preference to what suits their own inclination. It does not occur to them to have any inclination, except for what is customary. Thus the mind itself is bowed to the yoke: even in what people do for pleasure, conformity is the first thing thought of; they like in crowds; they exercise choice only among things commonly done: peculiarity of taste, eccentricity of conduct, are shunned equally with crimes: until by dint of not following their own nature, they have no nature to follow: their human capacities are withered and starved: they become incapable of any strong wishes or native pleasures, and are generally without either opinions or feelings of home growth, or properly their own. Now is this, or is it not, the desirable condition of human nature?

It is so, on the Calvinistic theory. According to that, the one great offence of man is self-will. All the good of which humanity is capable is comprised in obedience. You have no choice; thus you must do, and no otherwise: "whatever is not a duty, is a sin." Human nature being radically corrupt, there is no redemption for any one until human nature is killed within him. To one holding this theory of life, crushing out any of the human faculties, capacities, and susceptibilities, is no evil: man needs no capacity, but that of surrendering himself to the will of God: and if he uses any of his faculties for any other purpose but to do that supposed will more effectually, he is better without them. This is the theory of Calvinism; and it is held, in a mitigated form, by many who do not consider themselves Calvinists; the mitigation consisting in giving a less ascetic interpretation to the alleged will of God; asserting it to be his will that mankind should gratify some of their inclinations; of course not in the manner they themselves prefer, but in the way of obedience, that is, in a way prescribed to them by authority; and, therefore, by the necessary conditions of the case, the same for all.

In some such insidious form there is at present a strong tendency to this narrow theory of life, and to the pinched and hidebound type of human character which it patronises. Many persons, no doubt, sincerely think that human beings thus cramped and dwarfed, are as their Maker designed them to be; just as many have thought that trees are a much finer thing when clipped into pollards,° or cut out into figures of animals, than as nature made them. But if it be any part of religion to believe that man was made by a good Being, it is more consistent with that faith to believe, that this Being gave all human faculties that they might be cultivated and unfolded, not rooted out and consumed, and that he takes delight in every nearer approach made by his creatures to the ideal conception embodied in them, every increase in any of their capabilities of comprehension, of action, or of enjoyment. There is a different type of human excellence from the Calvinistic; a conception of humanity as having its nature bestowed on it for other purposes than merely to be abnegated. "Pagan self-assertion" is one of the elements of human worth, as well as "Christian self-denial."° There is a Greek ideal of self-development, which the Platonic and Christian ideal of self-government blends with, but does not supersede. It may be better to be a John Knox than an Alcibiades, but it is better to be a Pericles° than either; nor would a Pericles, if we had one in these days, be without anything good which belonged to John Knox.

It is not by wearing down into uniformity all that is individual in themselves, but by cultivating it and calling it forth, within the limits imposed by the rights and interests of others, that human beings become a noble and beautiful object of contemplation; and as the works partake the character of those who do them, by the same process human life also becomes rich, diversified, and animating, furnishing more abundant aliment to high thoughts and elevating feelings, and strengthening the tie which binds every individual to

321 **pollards,** trees cut back nearly to the trunk to produce a dense mass of branches   334–336 **Pagan self-assertion . . . self-denial,** identified by Mill as from the *Essays* (1848) of John Sterling, minor social commentator and friend of Thomas Carlyle's, who wrote his biography   339–340 **John Knox . . . Pericles.** John Knox (1505–1572) was a Scottish Calvinistic reformer; Alcibiades (450?–404 B.C.) an Athenian politician and general; Pericles (c. 490–429 B.C.) an Athenian statesman who gave the age his name

the race, by making the race infinitely better worth belonging to. In proportion to the development of his individuality, each person becomes more valuable to himself, and is therefore capable of being more valuable to others. There is a greater fullness of life about his own existence, and when there is more life in the units there is more in the mass which is composed of them. As much compression as is necessary to prevent the stronger specimens of human nature from encroaching on the rights of others, cannot be dispensed with; but for this there is ample compensation even in the point of view of human development. The means of development which the individual loses by being prevented from gratifying his inclinations to the injury of others, are chiefly obtained at the expense of the development of other people. And even to himself there is a full equivalent in the better development of the social part of his nature, rendered possible by the restraint put upon the selfish part. To be held to rigid rules of justice for the sake of others, develops the feelings and capacities which have the good of others for their object. But to be restrained in things not affecting their good, by their mere displeasure, develops nothing valuable, except such force of character as may unfold itself in resisting the restraint. If acquiesced in, it dulls and blunts the whole nature. To give any fair play to the nature of each, it is essential that different persons should be allowed to lead different lives. In proportion as this latitude has been exercised in any age, has that age been noteworthy to posterity. Even despotism does not produce its worst effects, so long as individuality exists under it; and whatever crushes individuality is despotism, by whatever name it may be called, and whether it professes to be enforcing the will of God or the injunctions of men.

Having said that Individuality is the same thing with development, and that it is only the cultivation of individuality which produces, or can produce, well-developed human beings, I might here close the argument: for what more or better can be said of any condition of human affairs, than that it brings human beings themselves nearer to the best thing they can be? or what worse can be said of any obstruction to good, than that it prevents this? Doubtless, however, these considerations will not suffice to convince those who most need convincing; and it is necessary further to show, that these developed human beings are of some use to the undeveloped—to point out to those who do not desire liberty, and would not avail themselves of it, that they may be in some intelligible manner rewarded for allowing other people to make use of it without hindrance.

In the first place, then, I would suggest that they might possibly learn something from them. It will not be denied by anybody, that originality is a valuable element in human affairs. There is always need of persons not only to discover new truths, and point out when what were once truths are true no longer, but also to commence new practices, and set the example of more enlightened conduct, and better taste and sense in human life. This cannot well be gainsaid by anybody who does not believe that the world has already attained perfection in all its ways and practices. It is true that this benefit is not capable of being rendered by everybody alike: there are but few persons, in comparison with the whole of mankind, whose experiments, if adopted by others, would be likely to be any improvement on established practice. But these few are the salt of the earth; without them, human life would become a stagnant pool. Not only is it they who introduce good things which did not before exist; it is they who keep the life in those which already existed. If there were nothing new to be done, would human intellect cease to be necessary? Would it be a reason why those who do the old things should forget why they are done, and do them like cattle, not like human beings? There is only too great a tendency in the best beliefs and practices to degenerate into the mechanical; and unless there were a succession of persons whose ever-recurring originality prevents the grounds of those beliefs and practices from becoming merely traditional, such dead matter would not resist the smallest shock from anything really alive, and there would be no reason why civilisation should not die out, as in the Byzantine Empire.° Persons of genius, it is true, are, and are always likely to be, a small minority; but in order to have them, it is necessary to preserve the soil in which they grow. Genius can only breathe freely in an *atmosphere* of freedom. Persons of genius are, *ex vi termini,*° more individual than any other people—less capable, consequently, of fitting themselves, without hurtful compression, into any of the small number of moulds which society provides in order to save its members the trouble of forming their own character. If from timidity they consent to be forced into one of these moulds, and to let all that part of themselves which cannot expand under the pressure remain unexpanded, society will be little the better for their genius. If they are of a strong character, and break their fetters, they become a mark for the society which has not succeeded in reducing them to commonplace, to point at with solemn warning as "wild," "erratic," and the like; much as if one should complain of the Niagara river for not flowing smoothly between its banks like a Dutch canal.

I insist thus emphatically on the importance of genius, and the necessity of allowing it to unfold itself freely both in thought and in practice, being well aware that no one will deny the position in theory, but knowing also that almost every one, in reality, is totally indifferent to it. People think genius a fine thing if it enables a man to write an exciting poem, or paint a picture. But in its true sense, that of originality in

436 **Byzantine Empire,** the Eastern Empire after the fall of the Western Roman Empire in 476, with Constantinople as its capital   441 **ex vi termini,** by force of the term or by definition

thought and action, though no one says that it is not a thing to be admired, nearly all, at heart, think that they can do very well without it. Unhappily this is too natural to be wondered at. Originality is the one thing which unoriginal minds cannot feel the use of. They cannot see what it is to do for them: how should they? If they could see what it would do for them, it would not be originality. The first service which originality has to render them, is that of opening their eyes: which being once fully done, they would have a chance of being themselves original. Meanwhile, recollecting that nothing was ever yet done which some one was not the first to do, and that all good things which exist are the fruits of originality, let them be modest enough to believe that there is something still left for it to accomplish, and assure themselves that they are more in need of originality, the less they are conscious of the want.

In sober truth, whatever homage may be professed, or even paid, to real or supposed mental superiority, the general tendency of things throughout the world is to render mediocrity the ascendant power among mankind. In ancient history, in the middle ages, and in a diminishing degree through the long transition from feudality to the present time, the individual was a power in himself; and if he had either great talents or a high social position, he was a considerable power. At present individuals are lost in the crowd. In politics it is almost a triviality to say that public opinion now rules the world. The only power deserving the name is that of masses, and of governments while they make themselves the organ of the tendencies and instincts of masses. This is as true in the moral and social relations of private life as in public transactions. Those whose opinions go by the name of public opinion are not always the same sort of public: in America they are the whole white population; in England, chiefly the middle class. But they are always a mass, that is to say, collective mediocrity. And what is a still greater novelty, the mass do not now take their opinions from dignitaries in Church or State, from ostensible leaders, or from books. Their thinking is done for them by men much like themselves, addressing them or speaking in their name, on the spur of the moment, through the newspapers. I am not complaining of all this. I do not assert that anything better is compatible, as a general rule, with the present low state of the human mind. But that does not hinder the government of mediocrity from being mediocre government. No government by a democracy or a numerous aristocracy, either in its political acts or in the opinions, qualities, and tone of mind which it fosters, ever did or could rise above mediocrity, except in so far as the sovereign Many have let themselves be guided (which in their best times they always have done) by the counsels and influence of a more highly gifted and instructed One or Few. The initiation of all wise or noble things comes and must come from individuals; generally at first from some one individual. The honour and glory of the average man is that he is capable of following that initiative; that he can respond internally to wise and noble things, and be led to them with his eyes open. I am not countenancing the sort of "hero-worship" which applauds the strong man of genius for forcibly seizing on the government of the world and making it do his bidding in spite of itself. All he can claim is, freedom to point out the way. The power of compelling others into it, is not only inconsistent with the freedom and development of all the rest, but corrupting to the strong man himself. It does seem, however, that when the opinions of masses of merely average men are everywhere become or becoming the dominant power, the counterpoise and corrective to that tendency would be, the more and more pronounced individuality of those who stand on the higher eminences of thought. It is in these circumstances most especially, that exceptional individuals, instead of being deterred, should be encouraged in acting differently from the mass. In other times there was no advantage in their doing so, unless they acted not only differently, but better. In this age, the mere example of nonconformity, the mere refusal to bend the knee to custom, is itself a service. Precisely because the tyranny of opinion is such as to make eccentricity a reproach, it is desirable, in order to break through that tyranny, that people should be eccentric. Eccentricity has always abounded when and where strength of character has abounded; and the amount of eccentricity in a society has generally been proportional to the amount of genius, mental vigour, and moral courage it contained. That so few now dare to be eccentric marks the chief danger of the time.

I have said that it is important to give the freest scope possible to uncustomary things, in order that it may in time appear which of these are fit to be converted into customs. But independence of action, and disregard of custom, are not solely deserving of encouragement for the chance they afford that better modes of action, and customs more worthy of general adoption, may be struck out; nor is it only persons of decided mental superiority who have a just claim to carry on their lives in their own way. There is no reason that all human existence should be constructed on some one or some small number of patterns. If a person possesses any tolerable amount of common sense and experience, his own mode of laying out his existence is the best, not because it is the best in itself, but because it is his own mode. Human beings are not like sheep; and even sheep are not undistinguishably alike. A man cannot get a coat or a pair of boots to fit him, unless they are either made to his measure, or he has a whole warehouseful to choose from: and is it easier to fit him with a life than with a coat, or are human beings more like one another in their whole physical and spiritual conformation than in the shape of their feet? If it were only that people have diversities of taste, that is reason enough for not attempting to shape them all after one model. But different persons also require different conditions for their spiritual development; and can no more exist healthily in the same moral, than all the variety of plants can in the same physical, atmosphere and climate. The same things which are helps to one person towards the cultivation of his higher nature, are hindrances to another. The same mode of life is a healthy excitement to one, keeping all his faculties of action and enjoyment in their best order, while to another it is a distracting burthen, which suspends or crushes all internal life. Such are the differences among human beings in their sources of pleasure, their susceptibilities of pain, and the operation on them of different physical and moral agencies, that unless there is a corresponding diversity in their modes of life, they neither obtain their fair share of happiness, nor grow up to the mental, moral, and aesthetic stature of which their nature is capable. Why then should tolerance, as far as the public sentiment is concerned, extend only to tastes and modes of life which extort acquiescence by the multitude of their adherents? Nowhere (except in some monastic institutions) is diversity of taste entirely unrecognized; a person may without blame, either like or dislike rowing, or smoking, or music, or athletic exercises, or chess, or cards, or study, because both those who like each of these things, and those who dislike them, are too numerous to be put down. But the man, and still more the woman, who can be accused either of doing "what nobody does," or of not doing "what everybody does," is the subject of as much depreciatory remark as if he or she had committed some grave moral delinquency. Persons require to possess a title, or some other badge of rank, or of the consideration of people of rank, to be able to indulge somewhat in the luxury of doing as they like without detriment to their estimation. To indulge somewhat, I repeat: for whoever allow themselves much of that indulgence, incur the risk of something worse than disparaging speeches—they are in peril of a commission *de lunatico*, and of having their property taken from them and given to their relations.°

There is one characteristic of the present direction of public opinion, peculiarly calculated to make it in-

620-622 **de lunatico . . . relations.** "There is something both contemptible and frightful in the sort of evidence on which, of late years, any person can be judicially declared unfit for the management of his affairs; and after his death, his disposal of his property can be set aside, if there is enough of it to pay the expenses of litigation—which are charged on the property itself. All the minute details of his daily life are pried into, and whatever is found which, seen through the medium of the perceiving and describing faculties of the lowest of the low, bears an appearance unlike absolute commonplace, is laid before the jury as evidence of insanity, and often with success; the jurors being little, if at all, less vulgar and ignorant than the witnesses; while the judges, with that extraordinary want of knowledge of human nature and life which continually astonishes us in English lawyers, often help to mislead them. These trials speak volumes as to the state of feeling and opinion among the vulgar with regard to human liberty. So far from setting any value on individuality—so far from respecting the right of each individual to act in things indifferent, as seems good to his own judgment and inclinations, judges and juries cannot even conceive that a person in a state of sanity can desire such freedom. In former days, when it was proposed to burn atheists, charitable people used to suggest putting them in a mad-house instead: it would be nothing surprising now-a-days were we to see this done, and the doers applauding themselves, because, instead of persecuting for religion, they had adopted so humane and Christian a mode of treating these unfortunates, not without a silent satisfaction at their having thereby obtained their deserts."—Mill's note

tolerant of any marked demonstration of individuality. The general average of mankind are not only moderate in intellect, but also moderate in inclinations: they have no tastes or wishes strong enough to incline them to do anything unusual, and they consequently do not understand those who have, and class all such with the wild and intemperate whom they are accustomed to look down upon. Now, in addition to this fact which is general, we have only to suppose that a strong movement has set in towards the improvement of morals, and it is evident what we have to expect. In these days such a movement has set in; much has actually been effected in the way of increased regularity of conduct, and discouragement of excesses; and there is a philanthropic spirit abroad, for the exercise of which there is no more inviting field than the moral and prudential improvement of our fellow creatures. These tendencies of the times cause the public to be more disposed than at most former periods to prescribe general rules of conduct, and endeavour to make every one conform to the approved standard. And that standard, express or tacit, is to desire nothing strongly. Its ideal of character is to be without any marked character; to maim by compression, like a Chinese lady's foot, every part of human nature which stands out prominently, and tends to make the person markedly dissimilar in outline to commonplace humanity.

As is usually the case with ideals which exclude one-half of what is desirable, the present standard of approbation produces only an inferior imitation of the other half. Instead of great energies guided by vigorous reason, and strong feelings strongly controlled by a conscientious will, its result is weak feelings and weak energies, which therefore can be kept in outward conformity to rule without any strength either of will or of reason. Already energetic characters on any large scale are becoming merely traditional. There is now scarcely any outlet for energy in this country except business. The energy expended in this may still be regarded as considerable. What little is left from that employment, is expended on some hobby; which may be a useful, even a philanthropic hobby, but is always some one thing, and generally a thing of small dimensions. The greatness of England is now all collective: individually small, we only appear capable of anything great by our habit of combining; and with this our moral and religious philanthropists are perfectly contented. But it was men of another stamp than this that made England what it has been; and men of another stamp will be needed to prevent its decline.

The despotism of custom is everywhere the standing hindrance to human advancement, being in unceasing antagonism to that disposition to aim at something better than customary, which is called, according to circumstances, the spirit of liberty, or that of progress or improvement. The spirit of improvement is not always a spirit of liberty, for it may aim at forcing improvements on an unwilling people; and the spirit of liberty, in so far as it resists such attempts, may ally itself locally and temporarily with the opponents of improvement; but the only unfailing and permanent source of improvement is liberty, since by it there are as many possible independent centres of improvement as there are individuals. The progressive principle, however, in either shape, whether as the love of 690 liberty or of improvement, is antagonistic to the sway of Custom, involving at least emancipation from that yoke; and the contest between the two constitutes the chief interest of the history of mankind. The greater part of the world has, properly speaking, no history, because the despotism of Custom is complete. This is the case over the whole East. Custom is there, in all things, the final appeal; justice and right mean conformity to custom; the argument of custom no one, unless some tyrant intoxicated with power, thinks of resist- 700 ing. And we see the result. Those nations must once have had originality; they did not start out of the ground populous, lettered, and versed in many of the arts of life; they made themselves all this, and were then the greatest and most powerful nations of the world. What are they now? The subjects or dependents of tribes whose forefathers wandered in the forests when theirs had magnificent palaces and gorgeous temples, but over whom custom exercised only a divided rule with liberty and progress. A people, 710 it appears, may be progressive for a certain length of time, and then stop: when does it stop? When it ceases to possess individuality. If a similar change should befall the nations of Europe, it will not be in exactly the same shape: the despotism of custom with which these nations are threatened is not precisely stationariness. It proscribes singularity, but it does not preclude change, provided all change together. We have discarded the fixed costumes of our forefathers; every one must still dress like other people, but the fashion 720 may change once or twice a year. We thus take care that when there is change it shall be for change's sake, and not from any idea of beauty or convenience; for the same idea of beauty or convenience would not strike all the world at the same moment, and be simultaneously thrown aside by all at another moment. But we are progressive as well as changeable: we continually make new inventions in mechanical things, and keep them until they are again superseded by better; we are eager for improvement in politics, in education, 730 even in morals, though in this last our idea of improvement chiefly consists in persuading or forcing other people to be as good as ourselves. It is not progress that we object to; on the contrary, we flatter ourselves that we are the most progressive people who ever lived. It is individuality that we war against: we should think we had done wonders if we had made ourselves all alike; forgetting that the unlikeness of one person to another is generally the first thing which draws the attention of either to the imperfection of his 740 own type, and the superiority of another, or the possi-

bility, by combining the advantages of both, of producing something better than either. We have a warning example in China—a nation of much talent, and, in some respects, even wisdom, owing to the rare good fortune of having been provided at an early period with a particularly good set of customs, the work, in some measure, of men to whom even the most enlightened European must accord, under certain limitations, the title of sages and philosophers. They are remarkable, too, in the excellence of their apparatus for impress- 750 ing, as far as possible, the best wisdom they possess upon every mind in the community, and securing that those who have appropriated most of it shall occupy the posts of honour and power. Surely the people who did this have discovered the secret of human progressiveness, and must have kept themselves steadily at the head of the movement of the world. On the contrary, they have become stationary—have remained so for thousands of years; and if they are ever to be farther improved, it must be by foreigners. They have 760 succeeded beyond all hope in what English philanthropists are so industriously working at—in making a people all alike, all governing their thoughts and conduct by the same maxims and rules; and these are the fruits. The modern *régime* of public opinion is, in an unorganized form, what the Chinese educational and political systems are in an organized; and unless individuality shall be able successfully to assert itself against this yoke, Europe, notwithstanding its noble antecedents and its professed Christianity, will tend to 770 become another China.

What is it that has hitherto preserved Europe from this lot? What has made the European family of nations an improving, instead of a stationary portion of mankind? Not any superior excellence in them, which, when it exists, exists as the effect, not as the cause; but their remarkable diversity of character and culture. Individuals, classes, nations, have been extremely unlike one another: they have struck out a great variety of paths, each leading to something valu- 780 able; and although at every period those who travelled in different paths have been intolerant of one another, and each would have thought it an excellent thing if all the rest could have been compelled to travel his road, their attempts to thwart each other's development have rarely had any permanent success, and each has in time endured to receive the good which the others have offered. Europe is, in my judgement, wholly indebted to this plurality of paths for its progressive and many-sided development. But it already 790 begins to possess this benefit in a considerably less degree. It is decidedly advancing towards the Chinese ideal of making all people alike. M. de Tocqueville,° in his last important work, remarks how much more the Frenchmen of the present day resemble one another,

793 **M. de Tocqueville, etc.,** Alexis de Tocqueville (1805–1859), French political theorist and historian, author of *Democracy in America* (1835–1839) and *L'Ancien Régime et la Révolution* (1850), to which Mill refers

than did those even of the last generation. The same remark might be made of Englishmen in a far greater degree. In a passage already quoted from Wilhelm von Humboldt, he points out two things as necessary conditions of human development, because necessary to render people unlike one another; namely, freedom, and variety of situations. The second of these two conditions is in this country every day diminishing. The circumstances which surround different classes and individuals, and shape their characters, are daily becoming more assimilated. Formerly, different ranks, different neighbourhoods, different trades and professions, lived in what might be called different worlds; at present, to a great degree in the same. Comparatively speaking, they now read the same things, listen to the same things, see the same things, go to the same places, have their hopes and fears directed to the same objects, have the same rights and liberties, and the same means of asserting them. Great as are the differences of position which remain, they are nothing to those which have ceased. And the assimilation is still proceeding. All the political changes of the age promote it, since they all tend to raise the low and to lower the high. Every extension of education promotes it, because education brings people under common influences, and gives them access to the general stock of facts and sentiments. Improvements in the means of communication promote it, by bringing the inhabitants of distant places into personal contact, and keeping up a rapid flow of changes of residence between one place and another. The increase of commerce and manufactures promotes it, by diffusing more widely the advantages of easy circumstances, and opening all objects of ambition, even the highest, to general competition, whereby the desire of rising becomes no longer the character of a particular class, but of all classes. A more powerful agency than even all these, in bringing about a general similarity among mankind, is the complete establishment, in this and other free countries, of the ascendancy of public opinion in the State. As the various social eminences which enabled persons entrenched on them to disregard the opinion of the multitude gradually become levelled; as the very idea of resisting the will of the public, when it is positively known that they have a will, disappears more and more from the minds of practical politicians; there ceases to be any social support for nonconformity—any substantive power in society, which, itself opposed to the ascendancy of numbers, is interested in taking under its protection opinions and tendencies at variance with those of the public.

The combination of all these causes forms so great a mass of influences hostile to Individuality, that it is not easy to see how it can stand its ground. It will do so with increasing difficulty, unless the intelligent part of the public can be made to feel its value—to see that it is good there should be differences, even though not for the better, even though, as it may appear to them,

some should be for the worse. If the claims of Individuality are ever to be asserted, the time is now, while much is still wanting to complete the enforced assimilation. It is only in the earlier stages that any stand can be successfully made against the encroachment. The demand that all other people shall resemble ourselves grows by what it feeds on. If resistance waits till life is reduced *nearly* to one uniform type, all deviations from that type will come to be considered impious, immoral, even monstrous and contrary to nature. Mankind speedily become unable to conceive diversity, when they have been for some time unaccustomed to see it.

(1859)

from AUTOBIOGRAPHY

Mill's *Autobiography* is the history of its author's "honest exercise of [his] thinking faculties to whatever conclusions might result from it." He wrote it as a record of his education, of the transition of his opinions, and of his intellectual indebtedness to various people. So rigidly did Mill control that record that Carlyle spoke of it as "the life of a logic-chopping engine, little more of human in it than if it had been done by a thing of mechanised iron." The account of the experiences in Chapter V, printed here, is generally recognized as of key importance to an understanding of Mill.

A CRISIS IN MY MENTAL HISTORY. ONE STAGE ONWARD

For some years after this time° I wrote very little, and nothing regularly, for publication: and great were the advantages which I derived from the intermission. It was of no common importance to me, at this period, to be able to digest and mature my thoughts for my own mind only, without any immediate call for giving them out in print. Had I gone on writing, it would have much disturbed the important transformation in my opinions and character, which took place during those years. The origin of this transformation, or at least the process by which I was prepared for it, can only be explained by turning some distance back.

From the winter of 1821, when I first read Bentham,° and especially from the commencement of the *Westminster Review*, I had what might truly be called an object in life; to be a reformer of the world. My conception of my own happiness was entirely identified with this object. The personal sympathies I wished for were those of fellow labourers in this enterprise. I endeavoured to pick up as many flowers as I could by the way; but as a serious and permanent personal satisfaction to rest upon, my whole reliance was

A Crisis in My Mental History 1 **this time,** that is, 1828   13 **Bentham,** Jeremy Bentham (1748–1832), chief formulator of English Utilitarianism (sometimes called Benthamism)

placed on this; and I was accustomed to felicitate myself on the certainty of a happy life which I enjoyed, through placing my happiness in something durable and distant, in which some progress might be always making, while it could never be exhausted by complete attainment. This did very well for several years, during which the general improvement going on in the world and the idea of myself as engaged with others in struggling to promote it, seemed enough to fill up an interesting and animated existence. But the time came when I awakened from this as from a dream. It was in the autumn of 1826. I was in a dull state of nerves, such as everybody is occasionally liable to; unsusceptible to enjoyment or pleasurable excitement; one of those moods when what is pleasure at other times, becomes insipid or indifferent; the state, I should think, in which converts to Methodism usually are, when smitten by their first "conviction of sin." In this frame of mind it occurred to me to put the question directly to myself: "Suppose that all your objects in life were realized; that all the changes in institutions and opinions which you are looking forward to, could be completely effected at this very instant: would this be a great joy and happiness to you?" And an irrepressible self-consciousness distinctly answered, "No!" At this my heart sank within me: the whole foundation on which my life was constructed fell down. All my happiness was to have been found in the continual pursuit of this end. The end had ceased to charm, and how could there ever again be any interest in the means? I seemed to have nothing left to live for.

At first I hoped that the cloud would pass away of itself; but it did not. A night's sleep, the sovereign remedy for the smaller vexations of life, had no effect on it. I awoke to a renewed consciousness of the woful fact. I carried it with me into all companies, into all occupations. Hardly anything had power to cause me even a few minutes' oblivion of it. For some months the cloud seemed to grow thicker and thicker. The lines in Coleridge's "Dejection"—I was not then acquainted with them—exactly describe my case:

A grief without a pang, void, dark and drear,
A drowsy, stifled, unimpassioned grief,
Which finds no natural outlet or relief
In word, or sigh, or tear.°

In vain I sought relief from my favourite books; those memorials of past nobleness and greatness from which I had always hitherto drawn strength and animation. I read them now without feeling, or with the accustomed feeling *minus* all its charm; and I became persuaded, that my love of mankind, and of excellence for its own sake, had worn itself out. I sought no comfort by speaking to others of what I felt. If I had loved any one sufficiently to make confiding my griefs a necessity, I should not have been in the condition I was. I felt, too, that mine was not an interesting, or in any way respectable distress. There was nothing in it to attract sympathy. Advice, if I had known where to seek it, would have been most precious. The words of Macbeth to the physician° often occurred to my thoughts. But there was no one on whom I could build the faintest hope of such assistance. My father, to whom it would have been natural to me to have recourse in any practical difficulties, was the last person to whom, in such a case as this, I looked for help. Everything convinced me that he had no knowledge of any such mental state as I was suffering from, and that even if he could be made to understand it, he was not the physician who could heal it. My education, which was wholly his work, had been conducted without any regard to the possibility of its ending in this result; and I saw no use in giving him the pain of thinking that his plans had failed, when the failure was probably irremediable, and, at all events, beyond the power of *his* remedies. Of other friends, I had at that time none to whom I had any hope of making my condition intelligible. It was however abundantly intelligible to myself; and the more I dwelt upon it, the more hopeless it appeared.

My course of study had led me to believe, that all mental and moral feelings and qualities, whether of a good or of a bad kind, were the results of association; that we love one thing, and hate another, take pleasure in one sort of action or contemplation, and pain in another sort, through the clinging of pleasurable or painful ideas to those things, from the effect of education or of experience. As a corollary from this, I had always heard it maintained by my father, and was myself convinced, that the object of education should be to form the strongest possible associations of the salutary class; associations of pleasure with all things beneficial to the great whole, and of pain with all things hurtful to it. This doctrine appeared inexpugnable; but it now seemed to me, on retrospect, that my teachers had occupied themselves but superficially with the means of forming and keeping up these salutary associations. They seemed to have trusted altogether to the old familiar instruments, praise and blame, reward and punishment. Now, I did not doubt that by these means, begun early, and applied unremittingly, intense associations of pain and pleasure, especially of pain, might be created, and might produce desires and aversions capable of lasting undiminished to the end of life. But there must always be something artificial and casual in associations thus produced. The pains and pleasures thus forcibly associated with things, are not connected with them by any natural tie; and it is therefore, I thought, essential to the durability of these associations, that they should have become so intense and inveterate as to be practically indissoluble, before the habitual exercise of the

64–67 **A grief . . . tear,** from Coleridge, "Dejection: An Ode," 21–24

81 **words of Macbeth . . . physician,** "Canst thou not minister to a mind diseased . . . ?" (V, iii, 40–44)

power of analysis had commenced. For I now saw, or thought I saw, what I had always before received with incredulity—that the habit of analysis has a tendency to wear away the feelings: as indeed it has, when no other mental habit is cultivated, and the analysing spirit remains without its natural complements and correctives. The very excellence of analysis (I argued) is that it tends to weaken and undermine whatever is the result of prejudice; that it enables us mentally to separate ideas which have only casually clung together: and no associations whatever could ultimately resist this dissolving force, were it not that we owe to analysis our clearest knowledge of the permanent sequences in nature; the real connexions between Things, not dependent on our will and feelings; natural laws, by virtue of which, in many cases, one thing is inseparable from another in fact; which laws, in proportion as they are clearly perceived and imaginatively realized, cause our ideas of things which are always joined together in Nature, to cohere more and more closely in our thoughts. Analytic habits may thus even strengthen the associations between causes and effects, means and ends, but tend altogether to weaken those which are, to speak familiarly, a *mere* matter of feeling. They are therefore (I thought) favourable to prudence and clear-sightedness, but a perpetual worm at the root both of the passions and of the virtues; and, above all, fearfully undermine all desires, and all pleasures, which are the effects of association, that is, according to the theory I held, all except the purely physical and organic; of the entire insufficiency of which to make life desirable, no one had a stronger conviction than I had. These were the laws of human nature, by which, as it seemed to me, I had been brought to my present state. All those to whom I looked up, were of opinion that the pleasure of sympathy with human beings, and the feelings which made the good of others, and especially of mankind on a large scale, the object of existence, were the greatest and surest sources of happiness. Of the truth of this I was convinced, but to know that a feeling would make me happy if I had it, did not give me the feeling. My education, I thought, had failed to create these feelings in sufficient strength to resist the dissolving influence of analysis, while the whole course of my intellectual cultivation had made precocious and premature analysis the inveterate habit of my mind. I was thus, as I said to myself, left stranded at the commencement of my voyage, with a well-equipped ship and a rudder, but no sail; without any real desire for the ends which I had been so carefully fitted out to work for: no delight in virtue, or the general good, but also just as little in anything else. The fountains of vanity and ambition seemed to have dried up within me, as completely as those of benevolence. I had had (as I reflected) some gratification of vanity at too early an age: I had obtained some distinction, and felt myself of some importance, before the desire of distinction

and of importance had grown into a passion: and little as it was which I had attained, yet having been attained too early, like all pleasures enjoyed too soon, it had made me *blasé* and indifferent to the pursuit. Thus neither selfish nor unselfish pleasures were pleasures to me. And there seemed no power in nature sufficient to begin the formation of my character anew, and create in a mind now irretrievably analytic, fresh associations of pleasure with any of the objects of human desire.

These were the thoughts which mingled with the dry heavy dejection of the melancholy winter of 1826–7. During this time I was not incapable of my usual occupations. I went on with them mechanically, by the mere force of habit. I had been so drilled in a certain sort of mental exercise, that I could still carry it on when all the spirit had gone out of it. I even composed and spoke several speeches at the debating society, how, or with what degree of success, I know not. Of four years continual speaking at that society, this is the only year of which I remember next to nothing. Two lines of Coleridge, in whom alone of all writers I have found a true description of what I felt, were often in my thoughts, not at this time (for I had never read them), but in a later period of the same mental malady:

Work without hope draws nectar in a sieve,
And hope without an object cannot live.°

In all probability my case was by no means so peculiar as I fancied it, and I doubt not that many others have passed through a similar state; but the idiosyncrasies of my education had given to the general phenomenon a special character, which made it seem the natural effect of causes that it was hardly possible for time to remove. I frequently asked myself, if I could, or if I was bound to go on living, when life must be passed in this manner. I generally answered to myself, that I did not think I could possibly bear it beyond a year. When, however, not more than half that duration of time had elapsed, a small ray of light broke in upon my gloom. I was reading, accidentally, Marmontel's ''Memoires,''° and came to the passage which relates his father's death, the distressed position of the family, and the sudden inspiration by which he, then a mere boy, felt and made them feel that he would be everything to them—would supply the place of all that they had lost. A vivid conception of that scene and its feelings came over me, and I was moved to tears. From this moment my burden grew lighter. The oppression of the thought that all feeling was dead within me, was gone. I was no longer hopeless: I was not a stock or a stone. I had still, it seemed, some of the material out of which all worth of character, and all capacity for happiness, are made. Relieved from my ever present sense of ir-

215–217 **Work . . . cannot live,** from Coleridge, "Work Without Hope," 13–14
230 **Marmontel's "Memoires."** Jean François Marmontel (1723–1799) was a French writer and moralist whose *Mémoires d'un père* appeared in 1804

remediable wretchedness, I gradually found that the ordinary incidents of life could again give me some pleasure; that I could again find enjoyment, not intense, but sufficient for cheerfulness, in sunshine and sky, in books, in conversation, in public affairs; and that there was, once more, excitement, though of a 250 moderate kind, in exerting myself for my opinions, and for the public good. Thus the cloud gradually drew off, and I again enjoyed life: and though I had several relapses, some of which lasted many months, I never again was as miserable as I had been.

The experiences of this period had two very marked effects on my opinions and character. In the first place, they led me to adopt a theory of life, very unlike that on which I had before acted, and having much in common with what at that time I certainly had never 260 heard of, the anti-self-consciousness theory of Carlyle.° I never, indeed, wavered in the conviction that happiness is the test of all rules of conduct, and the end of life. But I now thought that this end was only to be attained by not making it the direct end. Those only are happy (I thought) who have their minds fixed on some object other than their own happiness; on the happiness of others, on the improvement of mankind, even on some art or pursuit, followed not as a means, but as itself an ideal end. Aiming thus at something 270 else, they find happiness by the way. The enjoyments of life (such was now my theory) are sufficient to make it a pleasant thing, when they are taken *en passant,* without being made a principal object. Once make them so, and they are immediately felt to be insufficient. They will not bear a scrutinizing examination. Ask yourself whether you are happy, and you cease to be so. The only chance is to treat, not happiness, but some end external to it, as the purpose of life. Let your self-consciousness, your scrutiny, your self-interroga- 280 tion, exhaust themselves on that; and if otherwise fortunately circumstanced you will inhale happiness with the air you breathe, without dwelling on it or thinking about it, without either forestalling it in imagination, or putting it to flight by fatal questioning. This theory now became the basis of my philosophy of life. And I still hold to it as the best theory for all those who have but a moderate degree of sensibility and of capacity for enjoyment, that is, for the great majority of mankind.°

290 The other important change which my opinions at this time underwent, was that I, for the first time, gave its proper place, among the prime necessities of human well-being, to the internal culture of the individual. I ceased to attach almost exclusive importance to the ordering of outward circumstances, and the training of the human being for speculation and for action.°

I had now learnt by experience that the passive susceptibilities needed to be cultivated as well as the ac-

tive capacities, and required to be nourished and enriched as well as guided. I did not, for an instant, lose 300 sight of, or undervalue, that part of the truth which I had seen before; I never turned recreant to intellectual culture, or ceased to consider the power and practice of analysis as an essential condition both of individual and of social improvement. But I thought that it had consequences which required to be corrected, by joining other kinds of cultivation with it. The maintenance of a due balance among the faculties, now seemed to me of primary importance. The cultivation of the feelings became one of the cardinal points in my 310 ethical and philosophical creed. And my thoughts and inclinations turned in an increasing degree towards whatever seemed capable of being instrumental to that object.

I now began to find meaning in the things which I had read or heard about the importance of poetry and art as instruments of human culture. But it was some time longer before I began to know this by personal experience. The only one of the imaginative arts in which I had from childhood taken great pleasure, was 320 music; the best effect of which (and in this it surpasses perhaps every other art) consists in exciting enthusiasm; in winding up to a high pitch those feelings of an elevated kind which are already in the character, but to which this excitement gives a glow and a fervour, which, though transitory at its utmost height, is precious for sustaining them at other times. This effect of music I had often experienced; but like all my pleasurable susceptibilities it was suspended during the gloomy period. I had sought relief again and again 330 from this quarter, but found none. After the tide had turned, and I was in process of recovery, I had been helped forward by music, but in a much less elevated manner. I at this time first became acquainted with Weber's *Oberon,*° and the extreme pleasure which I drew from its delicious melodies did me good, by showing me a source of pleasure to which I was as susceptible as ever. The good, however, was much impaired by the thought, that the pleasure of music (as is quite true of such pleasure as this was, that of mere 340 tune) fades with familiarity, and requires either to be revived by intermittence, or fed by continual novelty. And it is very characteristic both of my then state, and of the general tone of my mind at this period of my life, that I was seriously tormented by the thought of the exhaustibility of musical combinations. The octave consists only of five tones and two semitones, which can be put together in only a limited number of ways, of which but a small proportion are beautiful: most of these, it seemed to me, must have been already discov- 350 ered, and there could not be room for a long succession of Mozarts and Webers, to strike out, as these had done, entirely new and surpassingly rich veins of musical beauty. This source of anxiety may, perhaps,

260 **Carlyle.** See especially Carlyle's essay *Characteristics*   286–289 **And I still hold . . . mankind.** Mill's position here should be compared with Carlyle's in The *Everlasting Yea* in *Sartor Resartus*

335 **Weber's Oberon,** a popular English opera, first produced on April 12, 1826, composed by Carl Maria von Weber (1786–1826)

be thought to resemble that of the philosophers of Laputa,° who feared lest the sun should be burnt out. It was, however, connected with the best feature in my character, and the only good point to be found in my very unromantic and in no way honourable distress. For though my dejection, honestly looked at, could not be called other than egotistical, produced by the ruin, as I thought, of my fabric of happiness, yet the destiny of mankind in general was ever in my thoughts, and could not be separated from my own. I felt that the flaw in my life, must be a flaw in life itself; that the question was, whether, if the reformers of society and government could succeed in their objects, and every person in the community were free and in a state of physical comfort, the pleasures of life, being no longer kept up by struggle and privation, would cease to be pleasures. And I felt that unless I could see my way to some better hope than this for human happiness in general, my dejection must continue; but that if I could see such an outlet, I should then look on the world with pleasure; content as far as I was myself concerned, with any fair share of the general lot.

This state of my thoughts and feelings made the fact of my reading Wordsworth for the first time (in the autumn of 1828), an important event in my life. I took up the collection of his poems from curiosity, with no expectation of mental relief from it, though I had before resorted to poetry with that hope. In the worst period of my depression, I had read through the whole of Byron (then new to me), to try whether a poet, whose peculiar department was supposed to be that of the intenser feelings, could rouse any feeling in me. As might be expected, I got no good from this reading, but the reverse. The poet's state of mind was too like my own. His was the lament of a man who had worn out all pleasures, and who seemed to think that life, to all who possess the good things of it, must necessarily be the vapid, uninteresting thing which I found it. His Harold and Manfred had the same burden on them which I had; and I was not in a frame of mind to desire any comfort from the vehement sensual passion of his Giaours, or the sullenness of his Laras.° But while Byron was exactly what did not suit my condition, Wordsworth was exactly what did. I had looked into the *Excursion* two or three years before, and found little in it; and I should probably have found as little, had I read it at this time. But the miscellaneous poems, in the two-volume edition of 1815 (to which little of value was added in the latter part of the author's life), proved to be the precise thing for my mental wants at that particular juncture.

In the first place, these poems addressed themselves powerfully to one of the strongest of my pleasurable susceptibilities, the love of rural objects and natural scenery; to which I had been indebted not only for much of the pleasure of my life, but quite recently for relief from one of my longest relapses into depression. In this power of rural beauty over me, there was a foundation laid for taking pleasure in Wordsworth's poetry; the more so, as his scenery lies mostly among mountains, which, owing to my early Pyrenean excursion,° were my ideal of natural beauty. But Wordsworth would never have had any great effect on me, if he had merely placed before me beautiful pictures of natural scenery. Scott does this still better than Wordsworth, and a very second-rate landscape does it more effectually than any poet. What made Wordsworth's poems a medicine for my state of mind, was that they expressed, not mere outward beauty, but states of feeling, and of thought coloured by feeling, under the excitement of beauty. They seemed to be the very culture of the feelings, which I was in quest of. In them I seemed to draw from a source of inward joy, of sympathetic and imaginative pleasure, which could be shared in by all human beings; which had no connexion with struggle or imperfection, but would be made richer by every improvement in the physical or social condition of mankind. From them I seemed to learn what would be the perennial sources of happiness, when all the greater evils of life shall have been removed. And I felt myself at once better and happier as I came under their influence. There have certainly been, even in our own age, greater poets than Wordsworth; but poetry of deeper and loftier feeling could not have done for me at that time what his did. I needed to be made to feel that there was real, permanent happiness in tranquil contemplation. Wordsworth taught me this, not only without turning away from, but with a greatly increased interest in the common feelings and common destiny of human beings. And the delight which these poems gave me, proved that with culture of this sort, there was nothing to dread from the most confirmed habit of analysis. At the conclusion of the Poems came the famous Ode, falsely called Platonic, "Intimations of Immortality": in which, along with more than his usual sweetness of melody and rhythm, and along with the two passages of grand imagery but bad philosophy so often quoted, I found that he too had had similar experience to mine; that he also had felt that the first freshness of youthful enjoyment of life was not lasting; but that he had sought for compensation, and found it, in the way in which he was now teaching me to find it. The result was that I gradually, but completely, emerged from my habitual depression, and was never again subject to it. I long continued to value Wordsworth less according to his intrinsic merits, than by the measure of what he had done for me. Compared with the greatest poets, he may be said to be the poet of unpoetical natures, possessed of quiet and contemplative tastes. But unpoetical natures are precisely those which require poetic

---

355–356 **philosophers of Laputa,** that is, in *Gulliver's Travels,* Book III, where the satire is directed against philosophers and scientists gone to absurd speculative lengths   393–396 **Harold . . . Laras,** references to the gloomy heroes of Byron's poems

415–416 **my early . . . excursion.** In 1820–1821, Mill spent a year in France and found in the Pyrenees "the highest order of mountain scenery"

cultivation. This cultivation Wordsworth is much more fitted to give, than poets who are intrinsically far more poets than he.

It so fell out that the merits of Wordsworth were the occasion of my first public declaration of my new way of thinking, and separation from those of my habitual companions who had not undergone a similar change. The person with whom at that time I was most in the habit of comparing notes on such subjects was Roebuck,° and I induced him to read Wordsworth, in whom he also at first seemed to find much to admire: but I, like most Wordsworthians, threw myself into strong antagonism to Byron, both as a poet and as to his influence on the character. Roebuck, all whose instincts were those of action and struggle, had, on the contrary, a strong relish and great admiration of Byron, whose writings he regarded as the poetry of human life, while Wordsworth's, according to him, was that of flowers and butterflies. We agreed to have the fight out at our Debating Society, where we accordingly discussed for two evenings the comparative merits of Byron and Wordsworth, propounding and illustrating by long recitations our respective theories of poetry: Sterling also, in a brilliant speech, putting forward his particular theory. This was the first debate on any weighty subject in which Roebuck and I had been on opposite sides. The schism between us widened from this time more and more, though we continued for some years longer to be companions. In the beginning, our chief divergence related to the cultivation of the feelings. Roebuck was in many respects very different from the vulgar notion of a Benthamite or Utilitarian. He was a lover of poetry and of most of the fine arts. He took great pleasure in music, in dramatic performances, especially in painting, and himself drew and designed landscapes with great facility and beauty. But he never could be made to see that these things have any value as aids in the formation of character. Personally, instead of being, as Benthamites are supposed to be, void of feeling, he had very quick and strong sensibilities. But, like most Englishmen who have feelings, he found his feelings stand very much in his way. He was much more susceptible to the painful sympathies than to the pleasurable, and looking for his happiness elsewhere, he wished that his feelings should be deadened rather than quickened. And, in truth, the English character, and English social circumstances, make it so seldom possible to derive happiness from the exercise of the sympathies, that it is not wonderful if they count for little in an Englishman's scheme of life. In most other countries the paramount importance of the sympathies as a constituent of individual happiness is an axiom, taken for granted rather than needing any formal statement; but most English thinkers almost seem to regard them as necessary evils, required for keeping men's actions be-

nevolent and compassionate. Roebuck was, or appeared to be, this kind of Englishman. He saw little good in any cultivation of the feelings, and none at all in cultivating them through the imagination, which he thought was only cultivating illusions. It was in vain I urged on him that the imaginative emotion which an idea, when vividly conceived, excites in us, is not an illusion but a fact, as real as any of the other qualities of objects; and far from implying anything erroneous and delusive in our mental apprehension of the object, is quite consistent with the most accurate knowledge and most perfect practical recognition of all its physical and intellectual laws and relations. The intensest feeling of the beauty of a cloud lighted by the setting sun, is no hindrance to my knowing that the cloud is vapour of water, subject to all the laws of vapours in a state of suspension; and I am just as likely to allow for, and act on, these physical laws whenever there is occasion to do so, as if I had been incapable of perceiving any distinction between beauty and ugliness.

While my intimacy with Roebuck diminished, I fell more and more into friendly intercourse with our Coleridgian adversaries in the Society, Frederick Maurice° and John Sterling,° both subsequently so well known, the former by his writings, the latter through the biographies by Hare° and Carlyle. Of these two friends, Maurice was the thinker, Sterling the orator, and impassioned expositor of thoughts which, at this period, were almost entirely formed for him by Maurice.

With Maurice I had for some time been acquainted through Eyton Tooke,° who had known him at Cambridge, and although my discussions with him were almost always disputes, I had carried away from them much that helped to build up my new fabric of thought, in the same way as I was deriving much from Coleridge, and from the writings of Goethe and other German authors which I read during these years. I have so deep a respect for Maurice's character and purposes, as well as for his great mental gifts, that it is with some unwillingness I say anything which may seem to place him on a less high eminence than I would gladly be able to accord him. But I have always thought that there was more intellectual power wasted in Maurice than in any other of my contemporaries. Few of them certainly have had so much to waste. Great powers of generalization, rare ingenuity and subtlety, and a wide perception of important and unobvious truths, served him not for putting something better into the place of the worthless heap of received opinions on the great subjects of thought, but for proving to his own mind that the Church of England had known everything from the first, and that all the truths on the ground of which the Church and orthodoxy have been attacked (many of which he saw as clearly

475 **Roebuck,** John Arthur Roebuck (1801–1879), politician and social reformer

544 **Frederick Maurice,** Frederick Denison Maurice (1805–1872), popular theological writer and Christian socialist   545 **John Sterling,** essayist and poet (1806–1844), founder of a literary club bearing his name   547 **Hare,** Julius Charles Hare (1795–1855), religious philosopher and translator   552 **Eyton Tooke,** son of Thomas Tooke (1774–1858), an economist

as any one) are not only consistent with the Thirty-nine Articles, but are better understood and expressed in those Articles than by any one who rejects them. I have never been able to find any other explanation of this, than by attributing it to that timidity of conscience, combined with original sensitiveness of temperament, which has so often driven highly gifted men into Romanism from the need of a firmer support than they can find in the independent conclusions of their own judgment. Any more vulgar kind of timidity no one who knew Maurice would ever think of imputing to him, even if he had not given public proof of his freedom from it, by his ultimate collision with some of the opinions commonly regarded as orthodox, and by his noble origination of the Christian Socialist movement. The nearest parallel to him, in a moral point of view, is Coleridge, to whom, in merely intellectual power, apart from poetical genius, I think him decidedly superior. At this time, however, he might be described as a disciple of Coleridge, and Sterling as a disciple of Coleridge and of him. The modifications which were taking place in my old opinions gave me some points of contact with them; and both Maurice and Sterling were of considerable use to my development. With Sterling I soon became very intimate, and was more attached to him than I have ever been to any other man. He was indeed one of the most loveable of men. His frank, cordial, affectionate, and expansive character; a love of truth alike conspicuous in the highest things and the humblest; a generous and ardent nature which threw itself with impetuosity into the opinions it adopted, but was as eager to do justice to the doctrines and the men it was opposed to, as to make war on what it thought their errors; and an equal devotion to the two cardinal points of Liberty and Duty, formed a combination of qualities as attractive to me, as to all others who knew him as well as I did. With his open mind and heart, he found no difficulty in joining hands with me across the gulf which as yet divided our opinions. He told me how he and others had looked upon me (from hearsay information), as a "made" or manufactured man, having had a certain impress of opinion stamped on me which I could only reproduce; and what a change took place in his feelings when he found, in the discussion on Wordsworth and Byron, that Wordsworth, and all which that name implies, "belonged" to me as much as to him and his friends. The failure of his health soon scattered all his plans of life, and compelled him to live at a distance from London, so that after the first year or two of our acquaintance, we only saw each other at distant intervals. But (as he said himself in one of his letters to Carlyle) when we did meet it was like brothers. Though he was never, in the full sense of the word, a profound thinker, his openness of mind, and the moral courage in which he greatly surpassed Maurice, made him outgrow the dominion which Maurice and Coleridge had once exercised over his intellect; though he

retained to the last a great but discriminating admiration of both, and towards Maurice a warm affection. Except in that short and transitory phasis of his life, during which he made the mistake of becoming a clergyman, his mind was ever progressive: and the advance he always seemed to have made when I saw him after an interval, made me apply to him what Goethe said of Schiller, "er hatte eine furchtliche Fortschreitung."° He and I started from intellectual points almost as wide apart as the poles, but the distance between us was always diminishing: if I made steps towards some of his opinions, he, during his short life, was constantly approximating more and more to several of mine: and if he had lived, and had health and vigour to prosecute his ever assiduous self-culture, there is no knowing how much further this spontaneous assimilation might have proceeded.

After 1829 I withdrew from attendance on the Debating Society. I had had enough of speech-making, and was glad to carry on my private studies and meditations without any immediate call for outward assertion of their results. I found the fabric of my old and taught opinions giving way in many fresh places, and I never allowed it to fall to pieces, but was incessantly occupied in weaving it anew. I never, in the course of my transition, was content to remain, for ever so short a time, confused and unsettled. When I had taken in any new idea, I could not rest till I had adjusted its relation to my old opinions, and ascertained exactly how far its effect ought to extend in modifying or superseding them.

The conflicts which I had so often had to sustain in defending the theory of government laid down in Bentham's and my father's writings, and the acquaintance I had obtained with other schools of political thinking, made me aware of many things which that doctrine, professing to be a theory of government in general, ought to have made room for and did not. But these things, as yet, remained with me rather as corrections to be made in applying the theory to practice, than as defects in the theory. I felt that politics could not be a science of specific experience; and that the accusations against the Benthamic theory of *being* a theory, of proceeding *à priori*° by way of general reasoning, instead of Baconian experiment, showed complete ignorance of Bacon's principles, and of the necessary conditions of experimental investigation. At this juncture appeared in the *Edinburgh Review*, Macaulay's famous attack on my father's *Essay on Government*. This gave me much to think about. I saw that Macaulay's conception of the logic of politics was erroneous; that he stood up for the empirical mode of treating political phenomena, against the philosophical; that even in physical science his notions of philosophizing might have recognised Kepler, but

641–642 **er hatte ... Fortschreitung.** He had a terrible development   677 **à priori,** reasoning that proceeds from definitions and principles rather than from scientific observation and induction (*a posteriori*)

would have excluded Newton and Laplace. But I could not help feeling, that though the tone was unbecoming (an error for which the writer, at a later period, made the most ample and honourable amends), there was truth in several of his strictures on my father's treatment of the subject; that my father's premises were really too narrow, and included but a small number of the general truths, on which, in politics, the important consequences depend. Identity of interest between the governing body and the community at large, is not, in any practical sense which can be attached to it, the only thing on which good government depends; neither can this identity of interest be secured by the mere conditions of election. I was not at all satisfied with the mode in which my father met the criticisms of Macaulay. He did not, as I thought he ought to have done, justify himself by saying, "I was not writing a scientific treatise on politics, I was writing an argument for parliamentary reform." He treated Macaulay's argument as simply irrational; an attack upon the reasoning faculty; an example of the saying of Hobbes,° that when reason is against a man, a man will be against reason. This made me think that there was really something more fundamentally erroneous in my father's conception of philosophical method, as applicable to politics, than I had hitherto supposed there was. But I did not at first see clearly what the error might be. At last it flashed upon me all at once in the course of other studies. In the early part of 1830 I had begun to put on paper the ideas on Logic (chiefly on the distinctions among Terms, and the import of Propositions) which had been suggested and in part worked out in the morning conversations already spoken of.° Having secured these thoughts from being lost, I pushed on into the other parts of the subject, to try whether I could do anything further towards clearing up the theory of logic generally. I grappled at once with the problem of Induction, postponing that of Reasoning, on the ground that it is necessary to obtain premises before we can reason from them. Now, Induction is mainly a process for finding the causes of effects: and in attempting to fathom the mode of tracing causes and effects in physical science, I soon saw that in the more perfect of the sciences, we ascend, by generalization from particulars, to the tendencies of causes considered singly, and then reason downward from those separate tendencies, to the effect of the same causes when combined. I then asked myself, what is the ultimate analysis of this deductive process; the common theory of the syllogism evidently throwing no light upon it. My practice (learnt from Hobbes and my father) being to study abstract principles by means of the best concrete instances I could find, the Composition of Forces, in dynamics, occurred to me as the most complete example of the logical process I was investigating. On examining, accordingly, what the mind does when it applies the principle of the Composition of Forces, I found that it performs a simple act of addition. It adds the separate effect of the one force to the separate effect of the other, and puts down the sum of these separate effects as the joint effect. But is this a legitimate process? In dynamics, and in all the mathematical branches of physics, it is; but in some other cases, as in chemistry, it is not; and I then recollected that something not unlike this was pointed out as one of the distinctions between chemical and mechanical phenomena, in the introduction to that favourite of my boyhood, Thomson's° *System of Chemistry*. This distinction at once made my mind clear as to what was perplexing me in respect to the philosophy of politics. I now saw, that a science is either deductive or experimental, according as, in the province it deals with, the effects of causes when conjoined, are or are not the sums of the effects which the same causes produce when separate. It followed that politics must be a deductive science. It thus appeared, that both Macaulay and my father were wrong; the one in assimilating the method of philosophizing in politics to the purely experimental method of chemistry; while the other, though right in adopting a deductive method, had made a wrong selection of one, having taken as the type of deduction, not the appropriate process, that of the deductive branches of natural philosophy, but the inappropriate one of pure geometry, which, not being a science of causation at all, does not require or admit of any summing-up of effects. A foundation was thus laid in my thoughts for the principal chapters of what I afterwards published on the *Logic of the Moral Sciences;*° and my new position in respect to my old political creed, now became perfectly definite.

If I am asked, what system of political philosophy I substituted for that which, as a philosophy, I had abandoned, I answer, No system: only a conviction that the true system was something much more complex and many-sided than I had previously had any idea of, and that its office was to supply, not a set of model institutions, but principles from which the institutions suitable to any given circumstances might be deduced. The influences of European, that is to say, Continental, thought, and especially those of the reaction of the nineteenth century against the eighteenth, were now streaming in upon me. They came from various quarters: from the writings of Coleridge, which I had begun to read with interest even before the change in my opinions; from the Coleridgians with whom I was in personal intercourse; from what I had read of Goethe; from Carlyle's early articles in the *Edinburgh* and *Foreign Reviews,* though for a long time I saw nothing in these (as my father saw nothing in them to the last) but insane rhapsody. From these sources, and from the acquaintance I kept up with the

710 **Hobbes,** Thomas Hobbes (1588–1679), important British philosopher
722 **morning conversations . . . spoken of,** with his father, who served as his tutor

756 **Thomson,** Thomas Thomson (1773–1852), Scottish chemist 777 **Logic . . . Sciences,** *System of Logic* (1843)

French literature of the time, I derived, among other ideas which the general turning upside down of the opinions of European thinkers had brought uppermost, these in particular: That the human mind has a certain order of possible progress, in which some things must precede others, an order which governments and public instructors can modify to some, but not to an unlimited extent: that all questions of political institutions are relative, not absolute, and that different stages of human progress not only *will* have, but *ought* to have, different institutions: that government is always either in the hands, or passing into the hands, of whatever is the strongest power in society, and that what this power is, does not depend on institutions, but institutions on it: that any general theory or philosophy of politics supposes a previous theory of human progress, and that this is the same thing with a philosophy of history. These opinions, true in the main, were held in an exaggerated and violent manner by the thinkers with whom I was now most accustomed to compare notes, and who, as usual with a reaction, ignored that half of the truth which the thinkers of the eighteenth century saw. But though, at one period of my progress, I for some time undervalued that great century, I never joined in the reaction against it, but kept as firm hold of one side of the truth as I took of the other. The fight between the nineteenth century and the eighteenth always reminded me of the battle about the shield, one side of which was white and the other black. I marvelled at the blind rage with which the combatants rushed against one another. I applied to them, and to Coleridge himself, many of Coleridge's sayings about half truths; and Goethe's device, "many-sidedness,"° was one which I would most willingly, at this period, have taken for mine.

The writers by whom, more than by any others, a new mode of political thinking was brought home to me, were those of the St. Simonian school° in France. In 1829 and 1830 I became acquainted with some of their writings. They were then only in the earlier stages of their speculations. They had not yet dressed out their philosophy as a religion, nor had they organized their scheme of Socialism. They were just beginning to question the principle of hereditary property. I was by no means prepared to go with them even this length; but I was greatly struck with the connected view which they for the first time presented to me, of the natural order of human progress; and especially with their division of all history into organic periods and critical periods. During the organic periods (they said) mankind accept with firm conviction some positive creed, claiming jurisdiction over all their actions, and containing more or less of truth and adaptation to the needs of humanity. Under its influence they make all the progress compatible with the creed, and finally outgrow it; when a period follows of criticism and negation, in which mankind lose their old convictions without acquiring any new ones, of a general or authoritative character, except the conviction that the old are false. The period of Greek and Roman polytheism, so long as really believed in by instructed Greeks and Romans, was an organic period, succeeded by the critical or sceptical period of the Greek philosophers. Another organic period came in with Christianity. The corresponding critical period began with the Reformation, has lasted ever since, still lasts, and cannot altogether cease until a new organic period has been inaugurated by the triumph of a yet more advanced creed. These ideas, I knew, were not peculiar to the St. Simonians; on the contrary, they were the general property of Europe, or at least of Germany and France, but they had never, to my knowledge, been so completely systematized as by these writers, nor the distinguishing characteristics of a critical period so powerfully set forth; for I was not then acquainted with Fichte's° Lectures on "The Characteristics of the Present Age." In Carlyle, indeed, I found bitter denunciations of an "age of unbelief," and of the present age as such, which I, like most people at that time, supposed to be passionate protests in favour of the old modes of belief. But all that was true in these denunciations, I thought that I found more calmly and philosophically stated by the St. Simonians. Among their publications, too, there was one which seemed to me far superior to the rest; in which the general idea was matured into something much more definite and instructive. This was an early work of Auguste Comte, who then called himself, and even announced himself in the title-page as, a pupil of Saint Simon. In this tract M. Comte first put forth the doctrine, which he afterwards so copiously illustrated, of the natural succession of three stages in every department of human knowledge: first, the theological, next the metaphysical, and lastly, the positive stage; and contended, that social sciencz must be subject to the same law; that the feudal and Catholic system was the concluding phasis of the theological state of the social science, Protestantism the commencement, and the doctrines of the French Revolution the consummation, of the metaphysical; and that its positive state was yet to come. This doctrine harmonized well with my existing notions, to which it seemed to give a scientific shape. I already regarded the methods of physical science as the proper models for political. But the chief benefit which I derived at this time from the trains of thought suggested by the St. Simonians and by Comte, was, that I obtained a clearer conception than ever before of the peculiarities of an era of transition in opinion, and ceased to mistake the moral and intellectual characteristics of such an era, for the normal attributes of humanity. I looked forward, through

834 **many-sidedness,** *building,* or self-development, a doctrine expounded in *Wilhelm Meister*   838 **St. Simonian school,** followers of Claude Henri Saint-Simon (1760–1825), French founder of positivism

876 **Fichte,** Johann Gottlieb Fichte (1762–1814), one of the principal influencers of Carlyle's thought

the present age of loud disputes but generally weak convictions, to a future which shall unite the best qualities of the critical with the best qualities of the organic periods; unchecked liberty of thought, unbounded freedom of individual action in all modes not hurtful to others; but also, convictions as to what is right and wrong, useful and pernicious, deeply engraven on the feelings by early education and general unanimity of sentiment, and so firmly grounded in reason and in the true exigencies of life, that they shall not, like all former and present creeds, religious, ethical, and political, require to be periodically thrown off and replaced by others.

M. Comte soon left the St. Simonians, and I lost sight of him and his writings for a number of years. But the St. Simonians I continued to cultivate. I was kept *au courant*° of their progress by one of their most enthusiastic disciples, M. Gustave d'Eichthal, who about that time passed a considerable interval in England. I was introduced to their chiefs, Bazard and Enfantin, in 1830; and as long as their public teachings and proselytism continued, I read nearly everything they wrote. Their criticisms on the common doctrines of Liberalism seemed to me full of important truth; and it was partly by their writings that my eyes were opened to the very limited and temporary value of the old political economy, which assumes private property and inheritance as indefeasible facts, and freedom of production and exchange as the *dernier mot*° of social improvement. The scheme gradually unfolded by the St. Simonians, under which the labour and capital of society would be managed for the general account of the community, every individual being required to take a share of labour, either as thinker, teacher, artist, or producer, all being classed according to their capacity, and remunerated according to their work, appeared to me a far superior description of Socialism to Owen's.° Their aim seemed to me desirable and rational, however their means might be inefficacious; and though I neither believed in the practicability, nor in the beneficial operation of their social machinery, I felt that the proclamation of such an ideal of human society could not but tend to give a beneficial direction to the efforts of others to bring society, as at present constituted, nearer to some ideal standard. I honoured them most of all for what they have been most cried down for— the boldness and freedom from prejudice with which they treated the subject of family, the most important of any, and needing more fundamental alterations than remain to be made in any other great social institution, but on which scarcely any reformer has the courage to touch. In proclaiming the perfect equality of men and women, and an entirely new order of things in regard to their relations with one another, the St. Simonians, in common with Owen and Fourier,° have entitled themselves to the grateful remembrance of future generations.

In giving an account of this period of my life, I have only specified such of my new impressions as appeared to me, both at the time and since, to be a kind of turning points, marking a definite progress in my mode of thought. But these few selected points give a very insufficient idea of the quantity of thinking which I carried on respecting a host of subjects during these years of transition. Much of this, it is true, consisted in rediscovering things known to all the world, which I had previously disbelieved, or disregarded. But the rediscovery was to me a discovery, giving me plenary possession of the truths, not as traditional platitudes, but fresh from their source: and it seldom failed to place them in some new light, by which they were reconciled with, and seemed to confirm while they modified, the truths less generally known which lay in my early opinions, and in no essential part of which I at any time wavered. All my new thinking only laid the foundation of these more deeply and strongly, while it often removed misapprehension and confusion of ideas which had perverted their effect. For example, during the later returns of my dejection, the doctrine of what is called Philosophical Necessity weighed on my existence like an incubus. I felt as if I was scientifically proved to be the helpless slave of antecedent circumstances; as if my character and that of all others had been formed for us by agencies beyond our control, and was wholly out of our own power. I often said to myself, what a relief it would be if I could disbelieve the doctrine of the formation of character by circumstances; and remembering the wish of Fox° respecting the doctrine of resistance to governments, that it might never be forgotten by kings, nor remembered by subjects, I said that it would be a blessing if the doctrine of necessity could be believed by all *quoad* the characters of others, and disbelieved in regard to their own. I pondered painfully on the subject, till gradually I saw light through it. I perceived, that the word Necessity, as a name for the doctrine of Cause and Effect applied to human action, carried with it a misleading association; and that this association was the operative force in the depressing and paralysing influence which I had experienced: I saw that though our character is formed by circumstances, our own desires can do much to shape those circumstances; and that what is really inspiriting and ennobling in the doctrine of freewill, is the conviction that we have real power over the formation of our own character; that our will, by influencing some of our circumstances, can modify our future habits or capabilities of willing. All this was entirely consistent with the doctrine of circumstances, or rather, was that doctrine itself, properly understood. From that time I drew in my own mind, a clear distinction between the

928 **au courant,** informed, up-to-date   940 **dernier mot,** the last word
948 **Owen,** Robert Owen (1771–1858), socialistic theorist   966 **Fourier,** Charles
Fourier (1772–1837), French socialist

999 **Fox,** Charles James Fox (1749–1806), Whig statesman and humanitarian

doctrine of circumstances, and Fatalism; discarding altogether the misleading word Necessity. The theory, which I now for the first time rightly apprehended, ceased altogether to be discouraging, and besides the relief to my spirits, I no longer suffered under the burden, so heavy to one who aims at being a reformer in opinions, of thinking one doctrine true, and the contrary doctrine morally beneficial. The train of thought which had extricated me from this dilemma, seemed to me, in after years, fitted to render a similar service to others; and it now forms the chapter on Liberty and Necessity in the concluding Book of my system of Logic.

Again, in politics, though I no longer accepted the doctrine of the *Essay on Government* as a scientific theory; though I ceased to consider representative democracy as an absolute principle, and regarded it as a question of time, place, and circumstance; though I now looked upon the choice of political institutions as a moral and educational question more than one of material interests, thinking that it ought to be decided mainly by the consideration, what great improvement in life and culture stands next in order for the people concerned, as the condition of their further progress, and what institutions are most likely to promote that; nevertheless, this change in the premises of my political philosophy did not alter my practical political creed as to the requirements of my own time and country. I was as much as ever a Radical and Democrat for Europe, and especially for England. I thought the predominance of the aristocratic classes, the noble and the rich, in the English constitution, an evil worth any struggle to get rid of; not on account of taxes, or any such comparatively small inconvenience, but as the great demoralizing agency in the country. Demoralizing, first, because it made the conduct of the Government an example of gross public immorality, through the predominance of private over public interests in the State, and the abuse of the powers of legislation for the advantage of classes. Secondly, and in a still greater degree, because the respect of the multitude always attaching itself principally to that which, in the existing state of society, is the chief passport to power; and under English institutions, riches, hereditary or acquired, being the almost exclusive source of political importance; riches, and the signs of riches, were almost the only things really respected, and the life of the people was mainly devoted to the pursuit of them. I thought, that while the higher and richer classes held the power of government, the instruction and improvement of the mass of the people were contrary to the self-interest of those classes, because tending to render the people more powerful for throwing off the yoke: but if the democracy obtained a large, and perhaps the principal share, in the governing power, it would become the interest of the opulent classes to promote their education, in order to ward off really mischievous errors, and especially those which would

lead to unjust violations of property. On these grounds I was not only as ardent as ever for democratic institutions, but earnestly hoped that Owenite, St. Simonian, and all other anti-property doctrines might spread widely among the poorer classes; not that I thought those doctrines true, or desired that they should be acted on, but in order that the higher classes might be made to see that they had more to fear from the poor when uneducated, than when educated.

In this frame of mind the French Revolution of July° found me. It roused my utmost enthusiasm, and gave me, as it were, a new existence. I went at once to Paris, was introduced to Lafayette, and laid the groundwork of the intercourse I afterwards kept up with several of the active chiefs of the extreme popular party. After my return I entered warmly, as a writer, into the political discussions of the time; which soon became still more exciting, by the coming in of Lord Grey's Ministry,° and the proposing of the Reform Bill. For the next few years I wrote copiously in newspapers. It was about this time that Fonblanque,° who had for some time written the political articles in the Examiner, became the proprietor and editor of the paper. It is not forgotten with what verve and talent, as well as fine wit, he carried it on, during the whole period of Lord Grey's Ministry, and what importance it assumed as the principal representative, in the newspaper press, of Radical opinions. The distinguishing character of the paper was given to it entirely by his own articles, which formed at least three-fourths of all the original writing contained in it: but of the remaining fourth I contributed during those years a much larger share than any one else. I wrote nearly all the articles on French subjects, including a weekly summary of French politics, often extending to considerable length; together with many leading articles on general politics, commercial and financial legislation, and any miscellaneous subjects in which I felt interested, and which were suitable to the paper, including occasional reviews of books. Mere newspaper articles on the occurrences or questions of the moment, gave no opportunity for the development of any general mode of thought; but I attempted, in the beginning of 1831, to embody in a series of articles, headed "The Spirit of the Age," some of my new opinions, and especially to point out in the character of the present age, the anomalies and evils characteristic of the transition from a system of opinions which had worn out, to another only in process of being formed. These articles were, I fancy, lumbering in style, and not lively or striking enough to be, at any time, acceptable to newspaper readers; but had they been far more attractive, still, at that particular moment, when great political changes were impending, and engrossing all minds, these discussions were ill-timed, and missed

1090 **French Revolution of July,** in 1830   1099 **Lord Grey's Ministry,** the Whig Ministry under Earl Grey (1830–1834)   1101 **Fonblanque,** Albany Fonblanque (1793–1872), radical journalist

fire altogether. The only effect which I know to have been produced by them, was that Carlyle, then living in a secluded part of Scotland, read them in his solitude, and saying to himself (as he afterwards told me) 1140 "Here is a new Mystic," inquired on coming to London that autumn respecting their authorship; an inquiry which was the immediate cause of our becoming personally acquainted.

I have already mentioned Carlyle's earlier writings as one of the channels through which I received the influences which enlarged my early narrow creed; but I do not think that those writings, by themselves, would ever have had any effect on my opinions. What truths they contained, though of the very kind which I 1150 was already receiving from other quarters, were presented in a form and vesture less suited than any other to give them access to a mind trained as mine had been. They seemed a haze of poetry and German metaphysics, in which almost the only clear thing was a strong animosity to most of the opinions which were the basis of my mode of thought; religious scepticism, utilitarianism, the doctrine of circumstances, and the attaching any importance to democracy, logic, or political economy. Instead of my having been taught 1160 anything, in the first instance, by Carlyle, it was only in proportion as I came to see the same truths through media more suited to my mental constitution, that I recognised them in his writings. Then, indeed, the wonderful power with which he put them forth made a deep impression upon me, and I was during a long period one of his most fervent admirers; but the good his writings did me, was not as philosophy to instruct, but as poetry to animate. Even at the time when our acquaintance commenced, I was not sufficiently ad- 1170 vanced in my new modes of thought, to appreciate him fully; a proof of which is, that on his showing me the manuscript of *Sartor Resartus*, his best and greatest work, which he had just then finished, I made little of it; though when it came out about two years afterwards in *Fraser's Magazine* I read it with enthusiastic admiration and the keenest delight. I did not seek and cultivate Carlyle less on account of the fundamental differences in our philosophy. He soon found out that I was not "another mystic," and when for the sake of my 1180 own integrity I wrote to him a distinct profession of all those of my opinions which I knew he most disliked, he replied that the chief difference between us was that I "was as yet consciously nothing of a mystic." I do not know at what period he gave up the expectation that I was destined to become one; but though both his and my opinions underwent in subsequent years considerable changes, we never approached much nearer to each other's modes of thought than we were in the first years of our acquaintance. I did not, however, 1190 deem myself a competent judge of Carlyle. I felt that he was a poet, and that I was not; that he was a man of intuition, which I was not; and that as such, he not only saw many things long before me, which I could,

only when they were pointed out to me, hobble after and prove, but that it was highly probable he could see many things which were not visible to me even after they were pointed out. I knew that I could not see round him, and could never be certain that I saw over him; and I never presumed to judge him with any definiteness, until he was interpreted to me by one greatly 1200 the superior of us both—who was more a poet than he, and more a thinker than I—whose own mind and nature included his, and infinitely more.

Among the persons of intellect whom I had known of old, the one with whom I had now most points of agreement was the elder Austin.° I have mentioned that he always set himself in opposition to our early sectarianism; and latterly he had, like myself, come under new influences. Having been appointed Professor of Jurisprudence in the London University (now Univer- 1210 sity College), he had lived for some time at Bonn to study for his Lectures; and the influences of German literature and of the German character and state of society had made a very perceptible change in his views of life. His personal disposition was much softened; he was less militant and polemic; his tastes had begun to turn themselves towards the poetic and contemplative. He attached much less importance than formerly to outward changes; unless accompanied by a better cultivation of the inward nature. He had a strong 1220 distaste for the general meanness of English life, the absence of enlarged thoughts and unselfish desires, the low objects on which the faculties of all classes of the English are intent. Even the kind of public interests which Englishmen care for, he held in very little esteem. He thought that there was more practical good government, and (which is true enough) infinitely more care for the education and mental improvement of all ranks of the people, under the Prussian monarchy, than under the English representative government: 1230 and he held, with the French *Economistes,* that the real security for good government is "un peuple éclairé,"° which is not always the fruit of popular institutions, and which if it could be had without them, would do their work better than they. Though he approved of the Reform Bill, he predicted, what in fact occurred, that it would not produce the great immediate improvements in government, which many expected from it. The men, he said, who could do these great things, did not exist in the country. There were many 1240 points of sympathy between him and me, both in the new opinions he had adopted and in the old ones which he retained. Like me, he never ceased to be an utilitarian, and with all his love of the Germans, and enjoyment of their literature, never became in the smallest degree reconciled to the innate-principle metaphysics. He cultivated more and more a kind of German religion, a religion of poetry and feeling with little, if anything, of positive dogma; while, in politics (and here it

1206 **the elder Austin,** John Austin (1790–1859), writer about and professor of law   1232–1233 **un peuple éclairé,** an enlightened people

was that I most differed with him) he acquired an indifference, bordering on contempt, for the progress of popular institutions: though he rejoiced in that of Socialism, as the most effectual means of compelling the powerful classes to educate the people, and to impress on them the only real means of permanently improving their material condition, a limitation of their numbers. Neither was he, at this time, fundamentally opposed to Socialism in itself as an ultimate result of improvement. He professed great disrespect for what he called "the universal principles of human nature of the political economists," and insisted on the evidence which history and daily experience afford of the "extraordinary pliability of human nature" (a phrase which I have somewhere borrowed from him), nor did he think it possible to set any positive bounds to the moral capabilities which might unfold themselves in mankind, under an enlightened direction of social and educational influences. Whether he retained all these opinions to the end of life I know not. Certainly the modes of thinking of his later years, and especially of his last publication, were much more Tory in their general character than those which he held at this time.

My father's tone of thought and feeling, I now felt myself at a great distance from: greater, indeed, than a full and calm explanation and reconsideration on both sides, might have shown to exist in reality. But my father was not one with whom calm and full explanations on fundamental points of doctrine could be expected, at least with one whom he might consider as, in some sort, a deserter from his standard. Fortunately we were almost always in strong agreement on the political questions of the day, which engrossed a large part of his interest and of his conversation. On those matters of opinion on which we differed, we talked little. He knew that the habit of thinking for myself, which his mode of education had fostered, sometimes led me to opinions different from his, and he perceived from time to time that I did not always tell him *how* different. I expected no good, but only pain to both of us, from discussing our differences: and I never expressed them but when he gave utterance to some opinion or feeling repugnant to mine, in a manner which would have made it disingenuousness on my part to remain silent.

It remains to speak of what I wrote during these years, which, independently of my contributions to newspapers, was considerable. In 1830 and 1831 I wrote the five Essays since published under the title of "Essays on some Unsettled Questions of Political Economy," almost as they now stand, except that in 1833 I partially rewrote the fifth Essay. They were written with no immediate purpose of publication; and when, some years later, I offered them to a publisher, he declined them. They were only printed in 1844, after the success of the "System of Logic." I also resumed my speculations on this last subject, and puzzled myself, like others before me, with the great paradox of the discovery of new truths by general reasoning. As to the fact, there could be no doubt. As little could it be doubted, that all reasoning is resolvable into syllogisms, and that in every syllogism the conclusion is actually contained and implied in the premises. How, being so contained and implied, it could be new truth, and how the theorems of geometry, so different in appearance from the definitions and axioms, could be all contained in these, was a difficulty which no one, I thought, had sufficiently felt, and which, at all events, no one had succeeded in clearing up. The explanations offered by Whately° and others, though they might give a temporary satisfaction, always, in my mind, left a mist still hanging over the subject. At last, when reading a second or third time the chapters on Reasoning in the second volume of Dugald Stewart,° interrogating myself on every point, and following out, as far as I knew how, every topic of thought which the book suggested, I came upon an idea of his respecting the use of axioms in ratiocination, which I did not remember to have before noticed, but which now, in meditating on it, seemed to me not only true of axioms, but of all general propositions whatever, and to be the key of the whole perplexity. From this germ grew the theory of the Syllogism propounded in the Second Book of the *Logic;* which I immediately fixed by writing it out. And now, with greatly increased hope of being able to produce a work on Logic, of some originality and value, I proceeded to write the First Book, from the rough and imperfect draft I had already made. What I now wrote became the basis of that part of the subsequent Treatise; except that it did not contain the Theory of Kinds, which was a later addition, suggested by otherwise inextricable difficulties which met me in my first attempt to work out the subject of some of the concluding chapters of the Third Book. At the point which I had now reached I made a halt, which lasted five years. I had come to the end of my tether; I could make nothing satisfactory of Induction, at this time. I continued to read any book which seemed to promise light on the subject, and appropriated, as well as I could, the results; but for a long time I found nothing which seemed to open to me any very important vein of meditation.

In 1832 I wrote several papers for the first series of *Tait's Magazine,* and one for a quarterly periodical called the *Jurist,* which had been founded, and for a short time carried on, by a set of friends, all lawyers and law reformers, with several of whom I was acquainted. The paper in question is the one on the rights and duties of the States respecting Corporation and Church Property, now standing first among the collected *Dissertations and Discussions;* where one of my articles in *Tait,* "The Currency Juggle," also appears. In the whole mass of what I wrote previous to these,

1319 **Whately,** Richard Whately (1787–1863), author of *Logic* (1826)
1324 **Dugald Stewart,** Scottish moral philosopher (1753–1828)

there is nothing of sufficient permanent value to justify reprinting. The paper in the *Jurist*, which I still think a very complete discussion of the rights of the State over Foundations, showed both sides of my opinions, asserting as firmly as I should have done at any time, the doctrine that all endowments are natiomal property, 1370 which the government may and ought to control; but not, as I should once have done, condemning endowments in themselves, and proposing that they should be taken to pay off the national debt. On the contrary, I urged strenuously the importance of having a provision for education, not dependent on the mere demand of the market, that is, on the knowledge and discernment of average parents, but calculated to establish and keep up a higher standard of instruction than is likely to be spontaneously demanded by the buyers of 1380 the article. All these opinions have been confirmed and strengthened by the whole course of my subsequent reflections.

(1873)

ALFRED, LORD TENNYSON
1809-1892

Alfred Tennyson was born in Lincolnshire in 1809, the fourth of twelve children of an old Lincolnshire family. He was educated both at home by his father, an Anglican clergyman, and at the local grammar school; in 1827 he went to Trinity College, Cambridge. There he became a close intellectual, spiritual, and aesthetic friend of Arthur Henry Hallam who had an important intellectual influence on him. When Tennyson published *Poems, Chiefly Lyrical* in 1830, Hallam gave the book one of its few favorable reviews. Tennyson left Cambridge after the death of his father (1831) without taking a degree because of the family's financial straits. During this period, Tennyson's life seems to have been characterized by personal insecurity and poetic uncertainty. In 1832 he published *Poems*, which included "The Lotos-Eaters," "The Palace of Art," and "The Lady of Shallott."

In 1833, Tennyson received news that his young friend Hallam had died suddenly in Vienna. This was a severe shock to Tennyson. It came at a bad time— several members of his family were being treated for mental illness and his poems were generally receiving bad reviews. Tennyson withdrew into a period of silence in which he worked through his intellectual and emotional dilemmas and perfected his poetry. While attending the wedding of his brother Charles in 1836, he fell in love with his brother's wife's sister, Emily Sellwood. They immediately struck up a correspondence, but it was forbidden by Emily's father in 1840

because he did not approve of Tennyson's bohemianism and liberal intellectual and religious views. In 1842 Tennyson broke his long public silence of ten years and published *Poems*, in two volumes, one containing revised selections from his 1830 and 1832 collections, the other made up of new poems. The book was not well received, but it did win Tennyson a yearly pension from a patron, which helped to alleviate his financial worries. In 1847 he published his experimental narrative poem, *The Princess*.

The year 1850 neatly divides Tennyson's life into two halves. Not only is it the midpoint chronologically, but in that year he married Emily Sellwood, published his elegy *In Memoriam*, won the friendship of Queen Victoria, and succeeded Wordsworth as Poet Laureate. *In Memoriam*, a collection of poems on Hallam's death that had been published anonymously at first, was a great critical and public success.

After his marriage, his life became more secure and was outwardly rather uneventful. The Tennysons took a house in the Isle of Wight in 1853 and built a summer home at Aldworth in Surrey in 1868; Tennyson spent most of the rest of his life in semiseclusion in these two houses. His poetic output, however, continued for quite a while. In 1852 he published, in his role as Poet Laureate, an ode on the death of the duke of Wellington. In 1855 he published his experimental monologue *Maud*, considered by many critics to be his most innovative long poem. The first four books of *The Idylls of the King*, a large-scale Arthurian epic, appeared in 1859 and were immediately successful; completed in twelve books in 1888, this single poem occupied most of the second half of his career. Between 1874 and 1884 Tennyson turned his energies, rather unsuccessfully, to the stage by writing a number of poetic dramas. Tennyson reluctantly accepted a peerage in 1884. Three more volumes—*Tiresias and Other Poems*, 1885; *Locksley Hall Sixty Years After and Other Poems*, 1886; *Demeter and Other Poems*, 1889 —appeared before his death at Aldworth in 1892. He was buried in Westminster Abbey. *The Death of Oenone and Other Poems* appeared posthumously.

Tennyson's unquiet mind and heart together with his fine ear, superb poetic technique, and breadth of intellectual interest make him a great poet. Since he wrote "to the multitude and the happy few alike," he enjoyed extraordinary success in his own time. In the early part of the twentieth century, his reputation suffered from a revolutionary shift in poetic idiom. But Tennyson has come to be highly regarded again in the last few decades; he is now considered one of the greatest Victorian poets and one of the most influential for later poets such as T. S. Eliot.

Certain broad characteristics of Tennyson's poetry can be outlined: (1) there is a recurrent motif of individual isolation, coupled with a habitual use of voyage or odyssey; (2) there is a frequent use of an essentially dramatic technique within a lyrical frame—in other words, dramatic monologues, for which he is almost as well known as Browning; (3) there is an attempt to achieve a carefully controlled equilibrium between the public and the private obligations of the poet—most significantly in his two chief works, *In Memoriam* and the *Idylls of the King*; (4) there is an unusual quality of boldness and a continual experimentation with form in all its multiple phases, of which *Maud* and *The Princess* are extraordinary examples; (5) there is an attempt to resolve the persistent war between the ancients and the moderns by extensively employing antique fables as vehicles of modern historical and psychological exploration; and (6) there is a persistent dedication to the poetic principle that sound is the major vehicle of sense, although Tennyson knew that few people would truly hear the sound or surmise its significance.

The central questions in Tennyson's poetry are these: What is reality? What seems to be real, but is not? What is truth? How is one to take truth's measure? What is fact, what fable? How much of Christian teaching can we believe in a scientific age? What is a poet? What are the uses of poetry? Am I a poet? In an age which is antipoetic in its rejection of both fable and religion, what are the poet's responsibilities? Reduced to the two essential issues, Tennyson's questions are the questions of his age: Who am I? What can I believe?

THE KRAKEN°

Below the thunders of the upper deep;
Far, far beneath in the abysmal sea,
His ancient, dreamless, uninvaded sleep
The Kraken sleepeth: faintest sunlights flee
5 About his shadowy sides: above him swell
Huge sponges of millennial growth and height;
And far away into the sickly light,
From many a wondrous grot and secret cell
Unnumbered and enormous polypi°
10 Winnow with giant arms the slumbering green.
There hath he lain for ages and will lie
Battening upon huge seaworms in his sleep,
Until the latter fire shall heat the deep;
Then once by man and angels to be seen,
15 In roaring he shall rise and on the surface die.
(1830)

MARIANA

Mariana in the moated grange
　　　　　　　　　　(Measure for Measure)

With blackest moss the flower-plots
　Were thickly crusted, one and all:

The rusted nails fell from the knots
　That held the pear to the gable-wall.
The broken sheds looked sad and strange:
　Unlifted was the clinking latch;
　Weeded and worn the ancient thatch
Upon the lonely moated grange.°
　　She only said, 'My life is dreary,
　　　He cometh not,' she said;   10
　　She said, 'I am aweary, aweary,
　　　I would that I were dead!'

Her tears fell with the dews at even;
　Her tears fell ere the dews were dried;
She could not look on the sweet heaven,
　Either at morn or eventide.
After the flitting of the bats,
　When thickest dark did trance the sky,
　She drew her casement-curtain by,
And glanced athwart the glooming flats.°   20
　　She only said, 'The night is dreary,
　　　He cometh not,' she said;
　　She said, 'I am aweary, aweary,
　　　I would that I were dead!'

Upon the middle of the night,
　Waking she heard the night-fowl crow:
The cock sung out an hour ere light:
　From the dark fen the oxen's low
Came to her: without hope of change,
　In sleep she seemed to walk forlorn,   30
　Till cold winds woke the gray-eyed morn
About the lonely moated grange.
　　She only said, 'The day is dreary,
　　　He cometh not,' she said;
　　She said, 'I am aweary, aweary,
　　　I would that I were dead!'

About a stone-cast from the wall
　A sluice with blackened waters slept,
And o'er it many, round and small,
　The clustered marish-mosses° crept.   40
Hard by a poplar shook alway,
　All silver-green with gnarlèd bark:
　For leagues no other tree did mark
The level waste, the rounding gray.
　　She only said, 'My life is dreary,
　　　He cometh not,' she said;
　　She said, 'I am aweary, aweary,
　　　I would that I were dead!'

And ever when the moon was low,
　And the shrill winds were up and away,   50
In the white curtain, to and fro,
　She saw the gusty shadow sway.
But when the moon was very low,
　And wild winds bound within their cell,

Kraken, a fabulous Scandinavian sea monster　**9 polypi,** sea animals with sacklike bodies surrounded by tentacles; an octopus for example

Mariana　8 grange, farm　**20 flats,** flatlands　**40 marish-mosses,** marsh mosses

The shadow of the poplar fell
Upon her bed, across her brow.
   She only said, 'The night is dreary,
     He cometh not,' she said;
   She said, 'I am aweary, aweary,
60   I would that I were dead!'

All day within the dreamy house,
   The doors upon their hinges creaked;
The blue fly sung in the pane; the mouse
   Behind the mouldering wainscot shrieked,
Or from the crevice peered about.
Old faces glimmered through the doors,
Old footsteps trod the upper floors,
Old voices called her from without.
   She only said, 'My life is dreary,
70   He cometh not,' she said;
   She said, 'I am aweary, aweary,
     I would that I were dead!'

The sparrow's chirrup on the roof,
   The slow clock ticking, and the sound
Which to the wooing wind aloof
   The poplar made, did all confound
Her sense; but most she loathed the hour
When the thick-moted sunbeam lay
Athwart the chambers, and the day
80 Was sloping toward his western bower.
   Then, said she, 'I am very dreary,
     He will not come,' she said;
   She wept, 'I am aweary, aweary,
     Oh God, that I were dead!'

(1830)

THE LADY OF SHALOTT°

PART 1

On either side the river lie
Long fields of barley and of rye,
That clothe the wold° and meet the sky;
And through the field the road runs by
   To many-towered Camelot;°
And up and down the people go,
Gazing where the lilies blow°
Round an island there below,
   The island of Shalott.

10 Willows whiten,° aspens quiver,
Little breezes dusk and shiver
Through the wave that runs forever
By the island in the river
   Flowing down to Camelot.
Four gray walls, and four gray towers,
Overlook a space of flowers,
And the silent isle embowers
   The Lady of Shalott.

By the margin, willow-veiled,
Slide the heavy barges trailed   20
By slow horses; and unhailed
The shallop° flitteth silken-sailed
   Skimming down to Camelot:
But who hath seen her wave her hand?
Or at the casement seen her stand?
Or is she known in all the land,
   The Lady of Shalott?

Only reapers, reaping early
In among the bearded barley,
Hear a song that echoes cheerly   30
From the river winding clearly,
   Down to towered Camelot;
And by the moon the reaper weary,
Piling sheaves in uplands airy,
Listening, whispers, "'Tis the fairy
   Lady of Shalott."

PART 2

There she weaves by night and day
A magic web with colors gay.
She has heard a whisper say,
A curse is on her if she stay   40
   To look down to Camelot.
She knows not what the curse may be,
And so she weaveth steadily,
And little other care hath she,
   The Lady of Shalott.

And moving through a mirror° clear
That hangs before her all the year,
Shadows of the world appear.
There she sees the highway near
   Winding down to Camelot;   50
There the river eddy whirls,
And there the surly village-churls,
And the red cloaks of market girls,
   Pass onward from Shalott.

Sometimes a troop of damsels glad,
An abbot on an ambling pad,°
Sometimes a curly shepherd-lad,
Or long-haired page in crimson clad,
   Goes by to towered Camelot;

The Lady of Shalott. The exact meaning of the allegory in this poem is uncertain, but it is generally held that the lady is a poet or artist, the castle an ivory tower, the tapestry and the mirror metaphors for the creative imagination   3 wold, a plain 5 Camelot, the city of King Arthur's court, in Cornwall 7 blow, bloom 10 Willows whiten. The wind turns up the white underside of the leaves

22 shallop, light open boat 46 mirror, used in weaving to reflect the pattern hanging behind her and the finished tapestry on the loom 56 pad, an easy-gaited horse

60 And sometimes through the mirror blue
The knights come riding two and two;
She hath no loyal knight and true,
	The Lady of Shalott.

But in her web she still delights
To weave the mirror's magic sights,
For often through the silent nights
A funeral, with plumes and lights
	And music, went to Camelot;
Or when the moon was overhead,
70 Came two young lovers lately wed;
"I am half sick of shadows," said
	The Lady of Shalott.

PART 3

A bow-shot from her bower eaves,
He rode between the barley sheaves;
The sun came dazzling through the leaves,
And flamed upon the brazen greaves°
	Of bold Sir Lancelot.
A red-cross knight° forever kneeled
To a lady in his shield,
80 That sparkled on the yellow field,
	Beside remote Shalott.

The gemmy bridle glittered free,
Like to some branch of stars we see
Hung in the golden Galaxy.°
The bridle bells rang merrily
	As he rode down to Camelot;
And from his blazoned baldric° slung
A mighty silver bugle hung,
And as he rode his armor rung,
90	Beside remote Shalott.

All in the blue unclouded weather
Thick-jeweled shone the saddle-leather,
The helmet and the helmet-feather
Burned like one burning flame together
	As he rode down to Camelot;
As often through the purple night,
Below the starry clusters bright,
Some bearded meteor, trailing light,
	Moves over still Shalott.

100 His broad clear brow in sunlight glowed;
On burnished hooves his war horse trode;
From underneath his helmet flowed
His coal-black curls as on he rode,
	As he rode down to Camelot.
From the bank and from the river
He flashed into the crystal mirror,

"Tirra lirra," by the river
	Sang Sir Lancelot.

She left the web, she left the loom,
She made three paces through the room,	110
She saw the water lily bloom,
She saw the helmet and the plume,
	She looked down to Camelot.
Out flew the web and floated wide;
The mirror cracked from side to side;
"The curse is come upon me," cried
	The Lady of Shalott.

PART 4

In the stormy east wind straining,
The pale yellow woods were waning,
The broad stream in his banks complaining,	120
Heavily the low sky raining
	Over towered Camelot;
Down she came and found a boat
Beneath a willow left afloat,
And round about the prow she wrote
	The Lady of Shalott.

And down the river's dim expanse
Like some bold seër in a trance,
Seeing all his own mischance—
With a glassy countenance	130
	Did she look to Camelot.
And at the closing of the day
She loosed the chain, and down she lay;
The broad stream bore her far away,
	The Lady of Shalott.

Lying, robed in snowy white
That loosely flew to left and right—
The leaves upon her falling light—
Through the noises of the night
	She floated down to Camelot;	140
And as the boat-head wound along
The willowy hills and fields among,
They heard her singing her last song,
	The Lady of Shalott.

Heard a carol, mournful, holy,
Chanted loudly, chanted lowly,
Till her blood was frozen slowly,
And her eyes were darkened wholly,
	Turned to towered Camelot.
For ere she reached upon the tide	150
The first house by the waterside,
Singing in her song she died,
	The Lady of Shalott.

Under tower and balcony,
By garden wall and gallery,

---

76 **greaves,** armor for the legs   78 **A red-cross knight.** Cf. Spenser's *Faerie
Queene*   84 **Galaxy,** the Milky Way   87 **baldric,** a belt worn over the shoulder
to support a sword or bugle

A gleaming shape she floated by,
Dead-pale between the houses high,
   Silent into Camelot.
Out upon the wharfs they came,
160 Knight and burgher, lord and dame,
And round the prow they read her name,
   The Lady of Shalott.

Who is this? And what is here?
And in the lighted palace near
Died the sound of royal cheer;
And they crossed themselves for fear,
   All the knights at Camelot.
But Lancelot mused a little space;
He said, "She has a lovely face;
170 God in his mercy lend her grace,
   The Lady of Shalott."
   (1832; 1842)

THE LOTOS-EATERS°

"Courage!" he said, and pointed toward the land,
"This mounting wave will roll us shoreward soon."
In the afternoon they came unto a land
In which it seeméd always afternoon.
All round the coast the languid air did swoon,
Breathing like one that hath a weary dream.
Full-faced above the valley stood the moon;
And, like a downward smoke, the slender stream
Along the cliff to fall and pause and fall did seem.

10 A land of streams! some, like a downward smoke,
Slow-dropping veils of thinnest lawn, did go;
And some through wavering lights and shadows broke,
Rolling a slumbrous sheet of foam below.
They saw the gleaming river seaward flow
From the inner land; far off, three mountain-tops,
Three silent pinnacles of aged snow,
Stood sunset-flushed; and, dewed with showery drops,
Up-clomb the shadowy pine above the woven copse.

The charméd sunset lingered low adown
20 In the red West; through mountain clefts the dale
Was seen far inland, and the yellow down°
Bordered with palm, and many a winding vale
And meadow, set with slender galingale;°
A land where all things always seemed the same!
And round about the keel with faces pale,
Dark faces pale against that rosy flame,
The mild-eyed melancholy Lotos-eaters came.

Branches they bore of that enchanted stem,
Laden with flower and fruit, whereof they gave

To each, but whoso did receive of them   30
And taste, to him the gushing of the wave
Far far away did seem to mourn and rave
On alien shores; and if his fellow spake,
His voice was thin, as voices from the grave;
And deep-asleep he seemed, yet all awake,
And music in his ears his beating heart did make.

They sat them down upon the yellow sand
Between the sun and moon upon the shore;
And sweet it was to dream of Fatherland,
Of child, and wife, and slave; but evermore   40
Most weary seemed the sea, weary the oar,
Weary the wandering fields of barren foam.
Then someone said, "we will return no more";
And all at once they sang, "Our island home°
Is far beyond the wave; we will no longer roam."

CHORIC SONG

There is sweet music here that softer falls
Than petals from blown roses on the grass,
Or night-dews on still waters between walls
Of shadowy granite, in a gleaming pass;
Music that gentlier on the spirit lies,   50
Than tired eyelids upon tired eyes;
Music that brings sweet sleep down from the blissful
   skies.
Here are cool mosses deep,
And through the moss the ivies creep,
And in the stream the long-leaved flowers weep,
And from the craggy ledge the poppy hangs in sleep.

Why are we weighed upon with heaviness,
And utterly consumed with sharp distress,
While all things else have rest from weariness?
All things have rest; why should we toil alone,   60
We only toil, who are the first of things,
And make perpetual moan,
Still from one sorrow to another thrown;
Nor ever fold our wings,
And cease from wanderings,
Nor steep our brows in slumber's holy balm;
Nor harken what the inner spirit sings,
"There is no joy but calm!"—
Why should we only toil, the roof and crown of things?

Lo! in the middle of the wood,   70
The folded leaf is wooed from out the bud
With winds upon the branch, and there
Grows green and broad, and takes no care,
Sun-steeped at noon, and in the moon
Nightly dew-fed; and turning yellow
Falls, and floats adown the air.
Lo! sweetened with the summer light,

The Lotos-Eaters. The story of the Lotos-Eaters Tennyson took from a brief episode in Book IX of the *Odyssey*, which narrates how the sailors who ate of "the lotos' honeyed fruit" wished "never to leave the place but with the Lotos-Eaters there to stay, feed on Lotos and forget going home"   21 **down**, a tract of open upland. See l. 149   23 **galingale**, a kind of grasslike herb

44 **island home**, Ithaca, off the west coast of Greece

The full-juiced apple, waxing over-mellow,
Drops in a silent autumn night.
80 All its allotted length of days
The flower ripens in its place,
Ripens and fades, and falls, and hath no toil,
Fast-rooted in the fruitful soil.

Hateful is the dark-blue sky,
Vaulted o'er the dark-blue sea.
Death is the end of life; ah, why
Should life all labor be?
Let us alone. Time driveth onward fast,
And in a little while our lips are dumb.
90 Let us alone. What is it that will last?
All things are taken from us, and become
Portions and parcels of the dreadful past.
Let us alone. What pleasure can we have
To war with evil? Is there any peace
In ever climbing up the climbing wave?
All things have rest, and ripen toward the grave
In silence—ripen, fall, and cease;
Give us long rest or death, dark death, or dreamful
ease.

How sweet it were, hearing the downward stream
100 With half-shut eyes ever to seem
Falling asleep in a half-dream!
To dream and dream, like yonder amber light,
Which will not leave the myrrh-bush on the height;
To hear each other's whispered speech;
Eating the Lotos day by day,
To watch the crisping ripples on the beach,
And tender curving lines of creamy spray;
To lend our hearts and spirits wholly
To the influence of mild-minded melancholy;
110 To muse and brood and live again in memory,
With those old faces of our infancy
Heaped over with a mound of grass,
Two handfuls of white dust, shut in an urn of brass!

Dear is the memory of our wedded lives,
And dear the last embraces of our wives
And their warm tears; but all hath suffered change;
For surely now our household hearths are cold,
Our sons inherit us, our looks are strange,
And we should come like ghosts to trouble joy.
120 Or else the island princes° over-bold
Have eat our substance, and the minstrel sings
Before them of the ten years' war in Troy,
And our great deeds, as half-forgotten things.
Is there confusion in the little isle?
Let what is broken so remain.
The gods are hard to reconcile;
'Tis hard to settle order once again.
There is confusion worse than death,
Trouble on trouble, pain on pain,

Long labor unto aged breath,   130
Sore task to hearts worn out by many wars
And eyes grown dim with gazing on the pilot-stars.°

But, propped on beds of amaranth° and moly,°
How sweet—while warm airs lull us, blowing lowly—
With half-dropped eyelid still,
Beneath a heaven dark and holy,
To watch the long bright river drawing slowly
His waters from the purple hill—
To hear the dewy echoes calling
From cave to cave through the thick-twined vine— 140
To watch the emerald-colored water falling
Through many a woven acanthus-wreath° divine!
Only to hear and see the far-off sparkling brine,
Only to hear were sweet, stretched out beneath the
pine.

The Lotos blooms below the barren peak,
The Lotos blows by every winding creek;
All day the wind breathes low with mellower tone;
Through every hollow cave and alley lone
Round and round the spicy downs the yellow Lotos-
dust is blown.
We have had enough of action, and of motion we, 150
Rolled to starboard, rolled to larboard, when the surge
was seething free,
Where the wallowing monster spouted his foam-
fountains in the sea.
Let us swear an oath, and keep it with an equal mind,
In the hollow Lotos-land to live and lie reclined
On the hills like gods together, careless of mankind.
For they lie beside their nectar, and the bolts° are
hurled
Far below them in the valleys, and the clouds are
lightly curled
Round their golden houses, girdled with the gleaming
world;
Where they smile in secret, looking over wasted lands,
Blight and famine, plague and earthquake, roaring   160
deeps and fiery sands,
Clanging fights, and flaming towns, and sinking ships,
and praying hands.
But they smile, they find a music centered in a doleful
song
Steaming up, a lamentation and an ancient tale of
wrong,
Like a tale of little meaning though the words are
strong;
Chanted from an ill-used race of men that cleave the
soil,
Sow the seed, and reap the harvest with enduring toil,
Storing yearly little dues of wheat, and wine and oil;
Till they perish and they suffer—some, 'tis whis-
pered—down in hell

---

120 **island princes**, princes from other islands near Greece; these men were
courting Odysseus' wife, Penelope, in his absence, and living in his palace

132 **pilot-stars**, stars used as guides by sailors   133 **amaranth**, imaginary flower
supposed never to fade   **moly**, fabulous herb of magic power. It was given by
Hermes, messenger of the gods, to Odysseus as a protection against the enchantress Circe   142 **acanthus**, plant sacred to the gods   156 **bolts**, thunderbolts

Alfred, Lord Tennyson   **881**

Suffer endless anguish, others in Elysian valleys dwell,
170 Resting weary limbs at last on beds of asphodel.°
Surely, surely, slumber is more sweet than toil, the
     shore
Than labor in the deep mid-ocean, wind and wave and
     oar;
O rest ye, brother mariners, we will not wander more.
(1832; 1842)

YOU ASK ME, WHY,
THOUGH ILL AT EASE

You ask me, why, though ill at ease,
    Within this region I subsist,
    Whose spirits falter in the mist,
And languish for the purple seas.

It is the land that freemen till,
    That sober-suited Freedom chose,
    The land where, girt with friends or foes,
A man may speak the thing he will;

A land of settled government,
10   A land of just and old renown,
    Where Freedom slowly broadens down
From precedent to precedent;

Where faction seldom gathers head,
    But, by degrees to fullness wrought,
    The strength of some diffusive thought
Hath time and space to work and spread.

Should banded unions persecute
    Opinion, and induce a time
    When single thought is civil crime,
20 And individual freedom mute,

Though power should make from land to land
    The name of Britain trebly great—
    Though every channel of the State
Should fill and choke with golden sand—

Yet waft me from the harbor-mouth,
    Wild wind! I seek a warmer sky,
    And I will see before I die
The palms and temples of the South.
(c. 1833; 1842)

MORTE D'ARTHUR

So all day long the noise of battle rolled
Among the mountains by the winter sea;
Until King Arthur's table, man by man,

Had fallen in Lyonnesse° about their Lord,
King Arthur: then, because his wound was deep,
The bold Sir Bedivere uplifted him,
Sir Bedivere, the last of all his knights,
And bore him to a chapel nigh the field,
A broken chancel with a broken cross,   60
That stood on a dark strait of barren land.
On one side lay the Ocean, and on one
Lay a great water, and the moon was full.

Then spake King Arthur to Sir Bedivere:
'The sequel of today unsolders all
The goodliest fellowship of famous knights
Whereof this world holds record. Such a sleep
They sleep—the men I loved. I think that we
Shall never more, at any future time,
Delight our souls with talk of knightly deeds,   70
Walking about the gardens and the halls
Of Camelot,° as in the days that were.
I perish by this people which I made,—
Though Merlin° sware that I should come again
To rule once more—but let what will be, be,
I am so deeply smitten through the helm
That without help I cannot last till morn.
Thou therefore take my brand Excalibur,
Which was my pride: for thou rememberest how
In those old days, one summer noon, an arm   80
Rose up from out the bosom of the lake,
Clothed in white samite,° mystic, wonderful,
Holding the sword—and how I rowed across
And took it, and have worn it, like a king:
And, wheresoever I am sung or told
In aftertime, this also shall be known:
But now delay not: take Excalibur,
And fling him far into the middle mere:
Watch what thou seëst, and lightly bring me word.'

To him replied the bold Sir Bedivere: 90
'It is not meet, Sir King, to leave thee thus,
Aidless, alone, and smitten through the helm.
A little thing may harm a wounded man.
Yet I thy hest will all perform at full,
Watch what I see, and lightly bring thee word.'

So saying, from the ruined shrine he stept
And in the moon athwart the place of tombs,
Where lay the mighty bones of ancient men,
Old knights, and over them the sea-wind sang
Shrill, chill, with flakes of foam. He, stepping down   100
By zig-zag paths, and juts of pointed rock,
Came on the shining levels of the lake.

There drew he forth the brand Excalibur,
And o'er him, drawing it, the winter moon,
Brightening the skirts of a long cloud, ran forth

170 Elysian . . . asphodel. The Elysian Fields, the paradise of the Greeks, were
said by Homer to be covered with asphodels, or daffodils

Morte d'Arthur   55 Lyonnesse, an area between Cornwall and the Scilly Islands,
including Land's End   72 Camelot, in Cornwall, seat of Arthur's court
74 Merlin, the seer of Arthur's court   82 samite, heavy silk fabric

And sparkled keen with frost against the hilt:
For all the haft twinkled with diamond sparks,
Myriads of topaz-lights, and jacinth-work
Of subtlest jewellery. He gazed so long
110 That both his eyes were dazzled, as he stood,
This way and that dividing the swift mind,
In act to throw: but at the last it seemed
Better to leave Excalibur concealed
There in the many-knotted waterflags,
That whistled stiff and dry about the marge.
So strode he back slow to the wounded King.

Then spake King Arthur to Sir Bedivere:
'Hast thou performed my mission which I gave?
What is it thou hast seen? or what hast heard?'

120 And answer made the bold Sir Bedivere:
'I heard the ripple washing in the reeds,
And the wild water lapping on the crag.'

To whom replied King Arthur, faint and pale:
'Thou hast betrayed thy nature and thy name,
Not rendering true answer, as beseemed
Thy fëalty, nor like a noble knight:
For surer sign had followed, either hand,
Or voice, or else a motion of the mere.
This is a shameful thing for men to lie.
130 Yet now, I charge thee, quickly go again
As thou art lief° and dear, and do the thing
I bad thee watch, and lightly bring me word.'

Then went Sir Bedivere the second time
Across the ridge, and paced beside the mere,
Counting the dewy pebbles, fixed in thought;
But when he saw the wonder of the hilt,
How curiously and strangely chased, he smote
His palms together, and he cried aloud,

'And if indeed I cast the brand away,
140 Surely a precious thing, one worthy note,
Should thus be lost for ever from the earth,
Which might have pleased the eyes of many men.
What good should follow this, if this were done?
What harm, undone? deep harm to disobey,
Seeing obedience is the bond of rule.
Were it well to obey then, if a king demand
An act unprofitable, against himself?
The King is sick, and knows not what he does.
What record, or what relic of my lord
150 Should be to aftertime, but empty breath
And rumours of a doubt? but were this kept,
Stored in some treasure-house of mighty kings,
Some one might show it at a joust of arms,
Saying, "King Arthur's sword, Excalibur,
Wrought by the lonely maiden of the Lake.
Nine years she wrought it, sitting in the deeps

Upon the hidden bases of the hills."
So might some old man speak in the aftertime
To all the people, winning reverence.
But now much honour and much fame were lost.'   160

So spake he, clouded with his own conceit,
And hid Excalibur the second time,
And so strode back slow to the wounded King.

Then spoke King Arthur, breathing heavily:
'What is it thou hast seen? or what hast heard?'

And answer made the bold Sir Bedivere:
'I heard the water lapping on the crag,
And the long ripple washing in the reeds.'

To whom replied King Arthur, much in wrath:
'Ah, miserable and unkind, untrue,   170
Unknightly, traitor-hearted! Woe is me!
Authority forgets a dying king,
Laid widowed of the power in his eye
That bowed the will. I see thee what thou art,
For thou, the latest-left of all my knights,
In whom should meet the offices of all,
Thou wouldst betray me for the precious hilt;
Either from lust of gold, or like a girl
Valuing the giddy pleasure of the eyes.
Yet, for a man may fail in duty twice,   180
And the third time may prosper, get thee hence:
But, if thou spare to fling Excalibur,
I will arise and slay thee with my hands.'

Then quickly rose Sir Bedivere, and ran,
And, leaping down the ridges lightly, plunged
Among the bulrush-beds, and clutched the sword,
And strongly wheeled and threw it. The great brand
Made lightnings in the splendour of the moon,
And flashing round and round, and whirled in an arch,
Shot like a streamer of the northern morn,°   190
Seen where the moving isles of winter° shock
By night, with noises of the northern sea.
So flashed and fell the brand Excalibur:
But ere he dipt the surface, rose an arm
Clothed in white samite, mystic, wonderful,
And caught him by the hilt, and brandished him
Three times, and drew him under in the mere.
And lightly went the other to the King.

Then spoke King Arthur, drawing thicker breath:
'Now see I by thine eyes that this is done.   200
Speak out: what is it thou hast heard, or seen?'

And answer made the bold Sir Bedivere:
'Sir King, I closed mine eyelids, lest the gems
Should blind my purpose, for I never saw,
Nor shall see, here or elsewhere, till I die,

131 **lief,** precious, loved

190 **streamer of the northern morn,** the aurora borealis   191 **moving isles of winter,** icebergs

Not though I live three lives of mortal men,
So great a miracle as yonder hilt.
Then with both hands I flung him, wheeling him;
But when I looked again, behold an arm,
210 Clothed in white samite, mystic, wonderful,
That caught him by the hilt, and brandished him
Three times, and drew him under in the mere.'

And answer made King Arthur, breathing hard:
'My end draws nigh; 'tis time that I were gone.
Make broad thy shoulders to receive my weight,
And bear me to the margin; yet I fear
My wound hath taken cold, and I shall die.'

So saying, from the pavement he half rose,
Slowly, with pain, reclining on his arm,
220 And looking wistfully with wide blue eyes
As in a picture. Him Sir Bedivere
Remorsefully regarded through his tears,
And would have spoken, but he found not words,
Then took with care, and kneeling on one knee,
O'er both his shoulders drew the languid hands,
And rising bore him through the place of tombs.

But, as he walked, King Arthur panted hard,
Like one that feels a nightmare on his bed
When all the house is mute. So sighed the King,
230 Muttering and murmuring at his ear, 'Quick, quick!
I fear it is too late, and I shall die.'
But the other swiftly strode from ridge to ridge,
Clothed with his breath, and looking, as he walked,
Larger than human on the frozen hills.
He heard the deep behind him, and a cry
Before. His own thought drove him, like a goad.
Dry clashed his harness in the icy caves
And barren chasms, and all to left and right
The bare black cliff clanged round him, as he based
240 His feet on juts of slippery crag that rang
Sharp-smitten with the dint of armèd heels—
And on a sudden, lo! the level lake,
And the long glories of the winter moon.

Then saw they how there hove a dusky barge,
Dark as a funeral scarf from stem to stern,
Beneath them; and descending they were ware
That all the decks were dense with stately forms
Black-stoled, black-hooded, like a dream—by these
Three Queens with crowns of gold—and from them
        rose
250 A cry that shivered to the tingling stars,
And, as it were one voice, an agony
Of lamentation, like a wind, that shrills
All night in a waste land, where no one comes,
Or hath come, since the making of the world.

Then murmured Arthur, 'Place me in the barge,'
And to the barge they came. There those three Queens
Put forth their hands, and took the King, and wept.

But she, that rose the tallest of them all
And fairest, laid his head upon her lap,
And loosed the shattered casque, and chafed his
        hands,   260
And called him by his name, complaining loud,
And dropping bitter tears against his brow
Striped with dark blood: for all his face was white
And colourless, and like the withered moon
Smote by the fresh beam of the springing east;
And all his greaves and cuisses dashed with drops
Of onset; and the light and lustrous curls—
That made his forehead like a rising sun
High from the daïs-throne—were parched with dust;
Or, clotted into points and hanging loose,   270
Mixed with the knightly growth that fringed his lips.
So like a shattered column lay the King;
Not like that Arthur who, with lance in rest,
From spur to plume a star of tournament,
Shot through the lists at Camelot, and charged
Before the eyes of ladies and of kings.

Then loudly cried the bold Sir Bedivere,
'Ah! my Lord Arthur, whither shall I go?
Where shall I hide my forehead and my eyes?
For now I see the true old times are dead,   280
When every morning brought a noble chance,
And every chance brought out a noble knight.
Such times have been not since the light° that led
The holy Elders with the gift of myrrh.
But now the whole ROUND TABLE is dissolved
Which was an image of the mighty world;
And I, the last, go forth companionless,
And the days darken round me, and the years,
Among new men, strange faces, other minds.'

And slowly answered Arthur from the barge: 290
'The old order changeth, yielding place to new,
And God fulfils Himself in many ways,
Lest one good custom should corrupt the world.
Comfort thyself: what comfort is in me?
I have lived my life, and that which I have done
May He within Himself make pure! but thou,
If thou shouldst never see my face again,
Pray for my soul. More things are wrought by prayer
Than this world dreams of. Wherefore, let thy voice
Rise like a fountain for me night and day.   300
For what are men better than sheep or goats
That nourish a blind life within the brain,
If, knowing God, they lift not hands of prayer
Both for themselves and those who call them friend?
For so the whole round earth is every way
Bound by gold chains about the feet of God.
But now farewell. I am going a long way
With these thou seëst—if indeed I go—
(For all my mind is clouded with a doubt)
To the island-valley of Avilion;°   310

283 **light,** the Star of Bethlehem   310 **Avilion,** Avalon, an earthly paradise

Where falls not hail, or rain, or any snow,
Nor ever wind blows loudly; but it lies
Deep-meadowed, happy, fair with orchard-lawns
And bowery hollows crowned with summer sea,
Where I will heal me of my grievous wound.'

    So said he, and the barge with oar and sail
Moved from the brink, like some full-breasted swan
That, fluting a wild carol ere her death,
Ruffles her pure cold plume, and takes the flood
320 With swarthy webs. Long stood Sir Bedivere
Revolving many memories, till the hull
Looked one black dot against the verge of dawn,
And on the mere the wailing died away.

[THE EPIC]

Here ended Hall, and our last light, that long
Had winked and threatened darkness, flared and fell:
At which the Parson, sent to sleep with sound,
And waked with silence, grunted 'Good!' but we
Sat rapt: it was the tone with which he read—
Perhaps some modern touches here and there
330 Redeemed it from the charge of nothingness—
Or else we loved the man, and prized his work;
I know not: but we sitting, as I said,
The cock crew loud; as at that time of year
The lusty bird takes every hour for dawn:
Then Francis, muttering, like a man ill-used,
'There now—that's nothing!' drew a little back,
And drove his heel into the smouldered log,
That sent a blast of sparkles up the flue:
And so to bed; where yet in sleep I seemed
340 To sail with Arthur under looming shores,
Point after point; till on to dawn, when dreams
Begin to feel the truth and stir of day,
To me, methought, who waited with a crowd,
There came a bark that, blowing forward, bore
King Arthur, like a modern gentleman
Of stateliest port; and all the people cried,
'Arthur is come again: he cannot die.'
Then those that stood upon the hills behind
Repeated—'Come again, and thrice as fair;'
350 And, further inland, voices echoed—'Come
With all good things, and war shall be no more.'
At this a hundred bells began to peal,
That with the sound I woke, and heard indeed
The clear church-bells ring in the Christmas-morn.
(1833–34)

ULYSSES

It little profits that an idle king,
By this still hearth, among these barren crags,°
Matched with an aged wife,° I mete and dole

Unequal laws unto a savage race,
That hoard, and sleep, and feed, and know not me.
I cannot rest from travel; I will drink
Life to the lees. All times I have enjoyed
Greatly, have suffered greatly, both with those
That loved me, and alone; on shore, and when
Through scudding drifts the rainy Hyades°   10
Vexed the dim sea. I am become a name:
For always roaming with a hungry heart
Much have I seen and known—cities of men
And manners, climates, councils, governments,
Myself not least, but honored of them all—
And drunk delight of battle with my peers,
Far on the ringing plains of windy Troy.
I am a part of all that I have met;
Yet all experience is an arch wherethrough
Gleams that untraveled world whose margin fades 20
Forever and forever when I move.
How dull it is to pause, to make an end,
To rust unburnished, not to shine in use!
As though to breathe were life! Life piled on life
Were all too little, and of one to me
Little remains; but every hour is saved
From that eternal silence,° something more,
A bringer of new things; and vile it were
For some three suns to store and hoard myself,
And this gray spirit yearning in desire   30
To follow knowledge like a sinking star,
Beyond the utmost bound of human thought.
    This is my son, mine own Telemachus,
To whom I leave the scepter and the isle—
Well-loved of me, discerning to fulfill
This labor, by slow prudence to make mild
A rugged people, and through soft degrees
Subdue them to the useful and the good.
Most blameless is he, centered in the sphere
Of common duties, decent not to fail   40
In offices of tenderness, and pay
Meet adoration to my household gods,
When I am gone. He works his work, I mine.
    There lies the port; the vessel puffs her sail;
There gloom the dark, broad seas. My mariners,
Souls that have toiled, and wrought, and thought with
      me—
That ever with a frolic welcome took
The thunder and the sunshine, and opposed
Free hearts, free foreheads—you° and I are old;
Old age hath yet his honor and his toil.   50
Death closes all; but something ere the end,
Some work of noble note, may yet be done,
Not unbecoming men that strove with gods.
The lights begin to twinkle from the rocks;
The long day wanes; the slow moon climbs; the deep
Moans round with many voices. Come, my friends.
'Tis not too late to seek a newer world.

Ulysses 2 **crags,** on the bleak island of Ithaca, the home of Ulysses 3 **aged wife,** Penelope

10 **Hyades,** a group of seven stars in the constellation Taurus. They were associated with the rainy season 27 **eternal silence,** a pagan view of death
49 **you,** Ulysses' companions. The attitude expressed here is modern

Push off, and sitting well in order smite
The sounding furrows; for my purpose holds
60 To sail beyond the sunset, and the baths
Of all the western stars, until I die.
It may be that the gulfs will wash us down;
It may be we shall touch the Happy Isles,°
And see the great Achilles,° whom we knew.
Though much is taken, much abides; and though
We are not now that strength which in old days
Moved earth and heaven, that which we are, we are—
One equal temper of heroic hearts,
Made weak by time and fate, but strong in will
70 To strive, to seek, to find, and not to yield.
(1842)

TITHONUS°

The woods decay, the woods decay and fall,
The vapors weep their burthen to the ground,
Man comes and tills the field and lies beneath,
And after many a summer dies the swan.
Me only cruel immortality
Consumes; I wither slowly in thine arms,
Here at the quiet limit of the world,
A white-hair'd shadow roaming like a dream
The ever-silent spaces of the East,
10 Far-folded mists, and gleaming halls of morn.
  Alas! for this gray shadow, once a man—
So glorious in his beauty and thy choice,
Who madest him thy chosen, that he seem'd
To his great heart none other than a God!
I ask'd thee, "Give me immortality."
Then didst thou grant mine asking with a smile,
Like wealthy men who care not how they give.
But thy strong Hours° indignant work'd their wills,
And beat me down and marr'd and wasted me,
20 And tho' they could not end me, left me maim'd
To dwell in presence of immortal youth,
Immortal age beside immortal youth,
And all I was in ashes. Can thy love,
Thy beauty, make amends, tho' even now,
Close over us, the silver star,° thy guide,
Shines in those tremulous eyes that fill with tears
To hear me? Let me go; take back thy gift.
Why should a man desire in any way
To vary from the kindly° race of men,
30 Or pass beyond the goal of ordinance
Where all should pause, as is most meet for all?
  A soft air fans the cloud apart; there comes
A glimpse of that dark world where I was born.

Once more the old mysterious glimmer steals
From thy pure brows, and from thy shoulders pure,
And bosom beating with a heart renew'd.
Thy cheek begins to redden thro' the gloom,
Thy sweet eyes brighten slowly close to mine,
Ere yet they blind the stars, and the wild team°
Which love thee, yearning for thy yoke, arise,   40
And shake the darkness from their loosen'd manes,
And beat the twilight into flakes of fire.
  Lo! ever thus thou growest beautiful
In silence, then before thine answer given
Departest, and thy tears are on my cheek.
  Why wilt thou ever scare me with thy tears,
And make me tremble lest a saying learnt,
In days far-off, on that dark earth, be true?
"The Gods themselves cannot recall their gifts."
  Ay me! ay me! with what another heart   50
In days far-off, and with what other eyes
I used to watch—if I be he that watch'd—
The lucid outline forming round thee; saw
The dim curls kindle into sunny rings;
Changed with thy mystic change, and felt my blood
Glow with the glow that slowly crimson'd all
Thy presence and thy portals, while I lay,
Mouth, forehead, eyelids, growing dewy-warm
With kisses balmier than half-opening buds
Of April, and could hear the lips that kiss'd   60
Whispering I knew not what of wild and sweet,
Like that strange song I heard Apollo sing,
While Ilion° like a mist rose into towers.
  Yet hold me not for ever in thine East;
How can my nature longer mix with thine?
Coldly thy rosy shadows bathe me, cold
Are all thy lights, and cold my wrinkled feet
Upon thy glimmering thresholds, when the steam
Floats up from those dim fields about the homes
Of happy men that have the power to die,   70
And grassy barrows of the happier dead.
Release me, and restore me to the ground.
Thou seest all things, thou wilt see my grave;
Thou wilt renew thy beauty morn by morn,
I earth in earth forget these empty courts,
And thee returning on thy silver wheels.
(1842)

LOCKSLEY HALL°

Comrades, leave me here a little, while as yet 'tis early
  morn;
Leave me here, and when you want me, sound upon
  the bugle horn.

---

63 **Happy Isles,** the Islands of the Blessed, identified with the Elysian Fields as the abode of just men after death   64 **Achilles,** most famous of the Greek heroes in the Trojan War. After slaying Hector and dragging his body three times around the walls, Achilles was finally killed by Paris, wounded with a poisoned arrow in the heel, his only vulnerable spot. The arms of Achilles were awarded to Ulysses **Tithonus.** Tithonus was a Trojan prince loved by Eos, or Aurora, goddess of the dawn, to whom the monologue is addressed. She gave Tithonus eternal life without eternal rejuvenation. He prays for release from "cruel immortality," but "the Gods themselves cannot recall their gifts"   18 **Hours,** goddesses who control the seasons of all things   25 **silver star,** morning star   29 **kindly,** natural

39 **wild team,** the white horses which drew Aurora's golden chariot at the break of day   63 **Ilion,** Troy, built to the music of Apollo's lyre. This is probably the source of the idea that Camelot was built to music
Locksley Hall. "Locksley Hall," Tennyson said, "represents young life, its good side, its deficiencies, and its yearnings"

'Tis the place, and all around it, as of old, the curlews
  call,
Dreary gleams° about the moorland flying over
  Locksley Hall;

Locksley Hall, that in the distance overlooks the
  sandy tracts,
And the hollow ocean-ridges roaring into cataracts.

Many a night from yonder ivied casement, ere I went
  to rest,
Did I look on great Orion° sloping slowly to the west.

Many a night I saw the Pleiads,° rising through the
  mellow shade,
10 Glitter like a swarm of fireflies tangled in a silver braid.

Here about the beach I wandered, nourishing a youth
  sublime
With the fairy tales of science, and the long result of
  time;

When the centuries behind me like a fruitful land reposed;
When I clung to all the present for the promise that it
  closed;

When I dipped into the future far as human eye could
  see,
Saw the vision of the world and all the wonder that
  would be.—

In the spring a fuller crimson comes upon the robin's
  breast;
In the spring the wanton lapwing gets himself another
  crest;

In the spring a livelier iris changes on the burnished
  dove;°
20 In the spring a young man's fancy lightly turns to
  thoughts of love.

Then her cheek was pale and thinner than should be
  for one so young,
And her eyes on all my motions with a mute
  observance hung.

And I said, "My cousin Amy, speak and speak the
  truth to me;
Trust me, cousin, all the current of my being sets to
  thee."

On her pallid cheek and forehead came a color and a
  light,

As I have seen the rosy red flushing in the northern
  night.

And she turned—her bosom shaken with a sudden
  storm of sighs—
All the spirit deeply dawning in the dark of hazel
  eyes—

Saying, "I have hid my feelings, fearing they should do
  me wrong";
Saying, "Dost thou love me, cousin?" weeping, "I   30
  have loved thee long."

Love took up the glass of Time, and turned it in his
  glowing hands;
Every moment, lightly shaken, ran itself in golden
  sands.

Love took up the harp of Life, and smote on all the
  chords with might;
Smote the chord of Self, that, trembling, passed in
  music out of sight.

Many a morning on the moorland did we hear the
  copses ring,
And her whisper thronged my pulses with the fullness
  of the spring.

Many an evening by the waters did we watch the
  stately ships,
And our spirits rushed together at the touching of the
  lips.

O my cousin, shallow-hearted! O my Amy, mine no
  more!
O the dreary, dreary moorland! O the barren, barren 40
  shore!

Falser than all fancy fathoms,° falser than all songs
  have sung,
Puppet to a father's threat, and servile to a shrewish
  tongue!°

Is it well to wish thee happy?—having known me—to
  decline
On a range of lower feelings and a narrower heart than
  mine!

Yet it shall be, thou shalt lower to his level day by day,
What is fine within thee growing coarse to sympathize
  with clay.

As the husband is, the wife is; thou art mated with a
  clown,

---

4 **gleams,** probably in apposition to *curlews;* or the entire phrase may be taken as an absolute construction   8 **Orion,** a conspicuous constellation   9 **Pleiads,** group of seven stars in the constellation Taurus   19 **iris . . . dove.** The rainbow colors on the dove's neck become brighter during the mating season

41 **all fancy fathoms,** everything the imagination comprehends   42 **Puppet . . . tongue.** Her father and her mother forced her to marry another—a man of coarser nature

Alfred, Lord Tennyson   887

And the grossness of his nature will have weight to drag thee down.

He will hold thee, when his passion shall have spent its novel force,
50 Something better than his dog, a little dearer than his horse.

What is this? his eyes are heavy; think not they are glazed with wine.
Go to him, it is thy duty; kiss him, take his hand in thine.

It may be my lord is weary, that his brain is over-wrought;
Soothe him with thy finer fancies, touch him with thy lighter thought.

He will answer to the purpose, easy things to understand—
Better thou wert dead before me, though I slew thee with my hand!

Better thou and I were lying, hidden from the heart's disgrace,
Rolled in one another's arms, and silent in a last embrace.

Curséd be the social wants that sin against the strength of youth!
60 Curséd be the social lies that warp us from the living truth!

Curséd be the sickly forms that err from honest Nature's rule!
Curséd be the gold that gilds the straitened forehead of the fool!

Well—'tis well that I should bluster!—Hadst thou less unworthy proved—
Would to God—for I had loved thee more than ever wife was loved.

Am I mad, that I should cherish that which bears but bitter fruit?
I will pluck it from my bosom, though my heart be at the root.

Never—though my mortal summers to such length of years should come
As the many-wintered crow° that leads the clanging rookery home.

Where is comfort? in division of the records of the mind?

Can I part her from herself, and love her, as I knew 70 her, kind?

I remember one that perished; sweetly did she speak and move;
Such a one do I remember, whom to look at was to love.

Can I think of her as dead, and love her for the love she bore?
No—she never loved me truly; love is love for ever-more.

Comfort? comfort scorned of devils!° this is truth the poet sings,
That a sorrow's crown of sorrow is remembering happier things.°

Drug thy memories, lest thou learn it, lest thy heart be put to proof,
In the dead unhappy night, and when the rain is on the roof.

Like a dog, he° hunts in dreams, and thou art staring at the wall,
Where the dying night-lamp flickers, and the shadows 80 rise and fall.

Then a hand shall pass before thee, pointing to his drunken sleep,
To thy widowed marriage-pillows, to the tears that thou wilt weep.

Thou shalt hear the "Never, never," whispered by the phantom years,
And a song from out the distance in the ringing of thine ears;

And an eye shall vex thee looking ancient kindness on thy pain.
Turn thee, turn thee on thy pillow; get thee to thy rest again.

Nay, but Nature brings thee solace; for a tender voice will cry.
'Tis a purer life than thine, a lip to drain thy trouble dry.

Baby lips will laugh me down; my latest rival brings thee rest.
Baby fingers, waxen touches, press me from the 90 mother's breast.

Oh, the child too clothes the father with a dearness not his due.

68 **crow,** rook

75 **comfort . . . devils,** as in *Paradise Lost,* I and II   76 **That . . . things,** a favorite idea of the poets. Dante, *Inferno,* V, 121: "There is no greater sorrow than to remember happy times when one is in misery"   79 **he,** Amy's husband, a fox-hunting squire

Half is thine and half is his; it will be worthy of the
two.

Oh, I see thee old and formal, fitted to thy petty part,
With a little hoard of maxims preaching down a
daughter's heart.

"They were dangerous guides, the feelings—she
herself was not exempt—
Truly, she herself had suffered"—Perish in thy self-
contempt!

Overlive it—lower yet—be happy! wherefore should I
care?
I myself must mix with action, lest I wither by despair.

What is that which I should turn to, lighting upon days
like these?
100 Every door is barred with gold, and opens but to
golden keys.

Every gate is thronged with suitors, all the markets
overflow.
I have but an angry fancy; what is that which I should
do?

I had been content to perish, falling on the foeman's
ground,
When the ranks are rolled in vapor, and the winds are
laid° with sound.

But the jingling of the guinea helps the hurt that Honor
feels,
And the nations do but murmur, snarling at each
other's heels.

Can I but relive in sadness? I will turn that earlier
page.
Hide me from my deep emotion, O thou wondrous
Mother-age!

Make me feel the wild pulsation that I felt before the
strife,
110 When I heard my days before me, and the tumult of my
life;

Yearning for the large excitement that the coming
years would yield,
Eager-hearted as a boy when first he leaves his father's
field,

And at night along the dusky highway near and nearer
drawn,
Sees in heaven the light of London flaring like a dreary
dawn;

And his spirit leaps within him to be gone before him
then,
Underneath the light he looks at, in among the throngs
of men;

Men, my brothers, men the workers, ever reaping
something new;
That which they have done but earnest of the things
that they shall do.

For I dipped into the future, far as human eye could
see,
Saw the Vision of the world, and all the wonder that   120
would be;

Saw the heavens fill with commerce, argosies of magic
sails,
Pilots of the purple twilight, dropping down with costly
bales;

Heard the heavens fill with shouting, and there rained
a ghastly dew
From the nations' airy navies grappling in the central
blue;

Far along the world-wide whisper of the south wind
rushing warm,
With the standards of the peoples plunging through the
thunder-storm;

Till the war drum throbbed no longer, and the battle-
flags were furled
In the Parliament of man, the Federation of the world.°

There the common sense of most shall hold a fretful
realm in awe,
And the kindly earth shall slumber, lapped in universal   130
law.

So I triumphed ere my passion sweeping through me
left me dry,
Left me with the palsied heart, and left me with the
jaundiced° eye;

Eye, to which all order festers, all things here are out
of joint.
Science moves, but slowly, slowly, creeping on from
point to point;

Slowly comes a hungry people,° as a lion, creeping
nigher,
Glares at one that nods and winks behind a slowly
dying fire.

---

104 **winds are laid.** It was an old belief that the discharge of cannon during a
battle stilled the winds

128 **Parliament . . . world.** Cf. the idea of the present United Nations
132 **jaundiced,** prejudiced   135 **a hungry people,** an allusion to the "dangerous" advance of democracy felt in the discontent preceding the revolutions in
Europe in 1848—in France, in Germany, in Italy, in Austro-Hungary, and in Ireland

Yet I doubt not through the ages one increasing purpose runs,
And the thoughts of men are widened with the process of the suns.°

What is that to him that reaps not harvest of his youthful joys,
140 Though the deep heart of existence beat forever like a boy's?

Knowledge comes, but wisdom lingers, and I linger on the shore,
And the individual withers, and the world is more and more.°

Knowledge comes, but wisdom lingers, and he bears a laden breast,
Full of sad experience, moving toward the stillness of his rest.

Hark, my merry comrades call me, sounding on the bugle horn,
They to whom my foolish passion were a target for their scorn.

Shall it not be scorn to me to harp on such a moldered string?
I am shamed through all my nature to have loved so slight a thing.

Weakness to be wroth with weakness! woman's pleasure, woman's pain—
150 Nature made them blinder motions° bounded in a shallower brain.

Woman is the lesser man, and all thy passions, matched with mine,
Are as moonlight unto sunlight, and as water unto wine—

Here at least, where nature sickens, nothing. Ah, for some retreat
Deep in yonder shining Orient, where my life began to beat,

Where in wild Mahratta-battle fell my father° evil-starred—
I was left a trampled orphan, and a selfish uncle's ward.

Or to burst all links of habit—there to wander far away,
On from island unto island at the gateways of the day—

Larger constellations burning, mellow moons and happy skies,
Breadths of tropic shade and palms in cluster, knots of 160 Paradise;

Never comes the trader, never floats an European flag,
Slides the bird o'er lustrous woodland, swings the trailer from the crag;

Droops the heavy-blossomed bower, hangs the heavy-fruited tree—
Summer isles of Eden lying in dark-purple spheres of sea.

There methinks would be enjoyment more than in this march of mind,
In the steamship, in the railway, in the thoughts that shake mankind.

There the passions cramped no longer shall have scope and breathing space;
I will take some savage woman, she shall rear my dusky race.

Iron-jointed, supple-sinewed, they shall dive, and they shall run,
Catch the wild goat by the hair, and hurl their lances in 170 the sun;

Whistle back the parrot's call, and leap the rainbows of the brooks,
Not with blinded eyesight poring over miserable books—

Fool, again the dream, the fancy! I *know* my words are wild,
But I count the gray barbarian lower than the Christian child.

I, to herd with narrow foreheads, vacant of our glorious gains,
Like a beast with lower pleasures, like a beast with lower pains!

Mated with a squalid savage—what to me were sun or clime?
I the heir of all the ages, in the foremost files of time—

I that rather held it better men should perish one by one,
Than that earth should stand at gaze like Joshua's 180 moon in Ajalon!°

Not in vain the distance beacons.° Forward, forward let us range,

---

138 **process of the suns,** the passing of the years   141 **Knowledge . . . more,** new facts of life may crowd in but fundamental truths are constant; science and evolution show that the mass of humanity is more important than the individual   150 **motions,** impulses   155 **fell my father.** The hero is represented as having been born in India, the son of a British soldier who fell in battle against the Mahrattas, a people living in central and western India

180 **Joshua's . . . Ajalon.** From *Joshua,* 10:12-13: "Then spake Joshua . . . in the sight of Israel, Sun, stand thou still upon Gibeon; and thou, Moon, in the valley of Ajalon. And the sun stood still, and the moon stayed, until the people had avenged themselves upon their enemies"   181 **beacons,** lights a signal for advance

Let the great world spin forever down the ringing
    grooves° of change.

Through the shadow of the globe we sweep into the
    younger day;
Better fifty years of Europe than a cycle of Cathay.°

Mother-Age—for mine I knew not—help me as when
    life begun;
Rift the hills,° and roll the waters, flash the lightnings,
    weigh the sun.

Oh, I see the crescent promise of my spirit hath not
    set.
Ancient founts of inspiration well through all my fancy
    yet.

Howsoever these things be, a long farewell to
    Locksley Hall!
190 Now for me° the woods may wither, now for me the
    roof-tree fall.

Comes a vapor from the margin, blackening over heath
    and holt,
Cramming all the blast before it, in its breast a thun-
    derbolt.

Let it fall on Locksley Hall, with rain or hail, or fire or
    snow;
For the mighty wind arises, roaring seaward, and I go.
(1842)

THE EAGLE

FRAGMENT

He clasps the crag with crooked hands;
Close to the sun in lonely lands,
Ringed with the azure world, he stands.

The wrinkled sea beneath him crawls;
5 He watches from his mountain walls,
And like a thunderbolt he falls.
(1851)

BREAK, BREAK, BREAK

Break, break, break,
    On thy cold gray stones, O Sea!
And I would that my tongue could utter
    The thoughts that arise in me.

O well for the fisherman's boy,
    That he shouts with his sister at play!
O well for the sailor lad,
    That he sings in his boat on the bay!

And the stately ships go on
    To their haven under the hill;   10
But O for the touch of a vanished hand,°
    And the sound of a voice that is still!

Break, break, break,
    At the foot of thy crags, O Sea!
But the tender grace of a day that is dead
    Will never come back to me.
(1842)

from THE PRINCESS

Tennyson believed that normal human affections
should not be repressed by social patterns. *The Princess*, a semiburlesque narrative poem, recounts the
failure of a princess to carry out her plan of establishing a college for women only. A young prince, disguised as a girl, gains admission to the college but is
discovered and finds himself ultimately fighting in battle against warriors who have come to the aid of the
princess. He is defeated, but his very defeat brings him
victory, for the sympathy of the princess for the
wounded hero leads her to fall in love with him and
marry him. A child in the poem symbolizes the
triumph of natural affections over artificial ideas; the
princess loves the child even when she seems most
adamant in carrying on her plans for the college. The
songs in the poem suggest the moods of the action.
Some of these were inserted in the second edition of
1850.

SWEET AND LOW

Sweet and low, sweet and low,
    Wind of the western sea,
Low, low, breathe and blow,
    Wind of the western sea!
Over the rolling waters go,
Come from the dying moon, and blow,
    Blow him again to me;
While my little one, while my pretty one, sleeps.

Sleep and rest, sleep and rest,
    Father will come to thee soon;   10
Rest, rest, on mother's breast,
    Father will come to thee soon;

182 **grooves.** When Tennyson first rode on a railroad train in 1830, he thought
that the wheels ran in a groove. He stated that he composed this line at that time
184 **a cycle of Cathay,** a very long period spent in China   186 **Rift the hills,**
etc. This line probably refers to Francis Baily's experiments (1838–1842) for determining the mean density of the earth and the weight of the sun   190 **for me,**
as far as I am concerned

Break, Break, Break   11 **vanished hand.** Hallam's

Father will come to his babe in the nest,
Silver sails all out of the west
   Under the silver moon;
Sleep, my little one, sleep, my pretty one, sleep.

THE SPLENDOR FALLS ON CASTLE WALLS

The splendor falls on castle walls
   And snowy summits old in story;
The long light shakes across the lakes,
   And the wild cataract leaps in glory.
Blow, bugle, blow, set the wild echoes flying,
Blow, bugle; answer, echoes, dying, dying, dying.

O hark, O hear! how thin and clear,
   And thinner, clearer, farther going!
O sweet and far from cliff and scar
10   The horns of Elfland faintly blowing!
Blow, let us hear the purple glens replying,
Blow, bugle; answer, echoes, dying, dying, dying.

O love, they die in yon rich sky,
   They faint on hill or field or river;
Our echoes roll from soul to soul,
   And grow forever and forever.
Blow, bugle, blow, set the wild echoes flying,
And answer, echoes, answer, dying, dying, dying.

TEARS, IDLE TEARS

Tears, idle tears, I know not what they mean;
Tears from the depth of some divine despair
Rise in the heart, and gather to the eyes,
In looking on the happy autumn fields,
And thinking of the days that are no more.

Fresh as the first beam glittering on a sail,
That brings our friends up from the underworld,
Sad as the last which reddens over one
That sinks with all we love below the verge;
10 So sad, so fresh, the days that are no more.

Ah, sad and strange as in dark summer dawns
The earliest pipe of half-awakened birds
To dying ears, when unto dying eyes
The casement slowly grows a glimmering square;
So sad, so strange, the days that are no more.

Dear as remembered kisses after death,
And sweet as those by hopeless fancy feigned
On lips that are for others; deep as love,
Deep as first love, and wild with all regret;
20 O Death in Life, the days that are no more!

HOME THEY BROUGHT HER WARRIOR DEAD

Home they brought her warrior dead,
   She nor swooned nor uttered cry.
All her maidens, watching, said,
   "She must weep or she will die."

Then they praised him, soft and low,
   Called him worthy to be loved,
Truest friend and noblest foe;
   Yet she neither spoke nor moved.

Stole a maiden from her place,
   Lightly to the warrior stepped,   10
Took the face-cloth from the face;
   Yet she neither moved nor wept.

Rose a nurse of ninety years,
   Set his child upon her knee—
Like summer tempest came her tears—
   "Sweet my child, I live for thee."

ASK ME NO MORE

Ask me no more—the moon may draw the sea;
   The cloud may stoop from heaven and take the
      shape,
   With fold to fold, of mountain or of cape;
But O too fond, when have I answered thee?
     Ask me no more.

Ask me no more—what answer should I give?
   I love not hollow cheek or faded eye;
   Yet, O my friend, I will not have thee die!
Ask me no more, lest I should bid thee live;
     Ask me no more.   10

Ask me no more—thy fate and mine are sealed;
   I strove against the stream and all in vain;
   Let the great river take me to the main.
No more, dear love, for at a touch I yield;
     Ask me no more.

NOW SLEEPS THE CRIMSON PETAL

Now sleeps the crimson petal, now the white;
Nor waves the cypress in the palace walk;
Nor winks the gold fin in the porphyry font.
The firefly wakens; waken thou with me.

Now droops the milk-white peacock like a ghost,
And like a ghost she glimmers on to me.

Now lies the Earth all Danaë to the stars,°
And all thy heart lies open unto me.

Now Sleeps the Crimson Petal   7 **Now . . . stars.** The earth is compared to
Danaë, the princess whom Zeus in the form of a shower of gold visited in a tower
of brass in which her father had imprisoned her

Now slides the silent meteor on, and leaves
10 A shining furrow, as thy thoughts in me.

Now folds the lily all her sweetness up,
And slips into the bosom of the lake.
So fold thyself, my dearest, thou, and slip
Into my bosom and be lost in me.

COME DOWN, O MAID

Come down, O maid, from yonder mountain height.
What pleasure lives in height (the shepherd sang),
In height and cold, the splendor of the hills?
But cease to move so near the heavens, and cease
To glide a sunbeam by the blasted pine,
To sit a star upon the sparkling spire;
And come, for Love is of the valley, come,
For Love is of the valley, come thou down
And find him; by the happy threshold, he,
10 Or hand in hand with Plenty in the maize,
Or red with spirited purple of the vats,
Or foxlike in the vine,° nor cares to walk
With Death and Morning on the Silver Horns,°
Nor wilt thou snare him in the white ravine,
Nor find him dropped upon the firths of ice;°
That huddling slant in furrow-cloven° falls
To roll the torrent out of dusky doors.°
But follow; let the torrent dance thee down
To find him in the valley; let the wild
20 Lean-headed eagles yelp alone, and leave
The monstrous ledges there to slope, and spill
Their thousand wreaths of dangling water-smoke,
That like a broken purpose waste in air.
So waste not thou, but come; for all the vales
Await thee; azure pillars of the hearth°
Arise to thee; the children call, and I,
Thy shepherd, pipe, and sweet is every sound,
Sweeter thy voice, but every sound is sweet;
Myriads of rivulets hurrying through the lawn,
30 The moan of doves in immemorial elms,
And murmuring of innumerable bees.
(1850)

from IN MEMORIAM

In Memoriam makes the climactic statement on a
major question posed by Tennyson's early poetry:
what are the foundations for hope in a world in which
"all things will die"? In the first part Tennyson portrays
the obstacles to hope in his own despair over Hallam's
death and in his interpretation of pre-Darwinian

theory. Later, the tone of the work changes and moves
toward affirmation. Tennyson's development from despair to hope is marked by the different qualities of the
three Christmases celebrated after Hallam's death.
Tennyson states that we must follow the dictates of the
heart, not the mind; and the heart affirms the immortality of the soul and the power of love.

The traditional view of *In Memoriam* as essentially
autobiographical can be seriously challenged.
Throughout Tennyson's early poems, the poet sheds
"no tears of love, but tears that Love can die." In
1830 Tennyson published his *Supposed Confessions of a
Second-Rate Sensitive Mind*, in which he had asked the
question upon which, rationally, *In Memoriam* rests:

Shall we not look into the laws
Of life and death, and things that seem,
And things that be, and analyze
Our double nature, and compare
All creeds till we have found the one,
If one there be?

And quite explicitly these confessions are only "supposed." In 1833 Tennyson wrote *The Two Voices*, a
poem which bears such striking resemblances to *In
Memoriam* that it is often referred to as a "little *In
Memoriam*." In the same year he also wrote *Ulysses*.
When comparing *Ulysses* to *In Memoriam*, Tennyson
reportedly said: "There is more about myself in 'Ulysses,' which was written under the sense of loss and
that all had gone by, but that still life must be fought
out to the end." On the basis of this and other evidence, then, one can conclude that *In Memoriam* is
not an autobiographical poem and that the "I" of *In
Memoriam* is an imaginary poet-narrator, not Alfred
Tennyson.

Tennyson left a number of directives which provide some assistance in understanding the character of
In Memoriam: (a) it is "a kind of *Divina Commedia*,
ending in happiness"; (b) it attempts to portray "different moods of sorrow as in a drama"; (c) it expresses
the poet's conviction that "anxieties of heart" rising
out of fear, doubt, and suffering will find relief "only
through Faith in a God of Love"; (d) the poem is divided according to the Christmas sections: XXVIII,
LXXVIII, CIV; and (e) the poem falls into "nine natural
groups" marking the stages of his grief and his
thought: (1) I–VIII, (2) IX–XIX, (3) XX–XXVII, (4)
XXVIII–XLIX, (5) L–LVIII, (6) LIX–LXXI, (7) LXXII–
XCVIII, (8) XCIX–CIII, (9) CIV–CXXXI.

OBIIT MDCCCXXXIII

Strong Son of God, immortal Love,
    Whom we, that have not seen thy face,
    By faith, and faith alone, embrace,
Believing where we cannot prove;

Come Down, O Maid 12 **foxlike in the vine.** Cf. *The Song of Solomon,* 2:15:
"Take us the foxes, the little foxes, that spoil the vines: for our vines have tender
grapes" 13 **Silver Horns,** peaks of the mountains. The Silverhorn is a spur of
the Jungfrau, in the Alps 15 **firths of ice,** glaciers 16 **furrow-cloven,** split by
crevasses 17 **dusky doors,** the piled-up mass of refuse through which the stream
emerges at the foot of the glacier 25 **azure . . . hearth,** columns of blue smoke

Thine are these orbs° of light and shade;
　　Thou madest Life in man and brute;
　　Thou madest Death; and lo, thy foot
Is on the skull which thou hast made.

Thou wilt not leave us in the dust:
10　Thou madest man, he knows not why,
　　He thinks he was not made to die;
And thou hast made him: thou art just.

Thou seemest human and divine,
　　The highest, holiest manhood, thou.
　　Our wills are ours, we know not how;
Our wills are ours, to make them thine.

Our little systems° have their day;
　　They have their day and cease to be;
　　They are but broken lights of thee,
20 And thou, O Lord, art more than they.

We have but faith: we cannot know,
　　For knowledge is of things we see;
　　And yet we trust it comes from thee,
A beam in darkness: let it grow.

Let knowledge grow from more to more,
　　But more of reverence in us dwell;
　　That mind and soul, according well,
May make one music as before,°

But vaster. We are fools and slight;
30　We mock thee when we do not fear:
　　But help thy foolish ones to bear;
Help thy vain worlds to bear thy light.

Forgive what seem'd my sin in me,
　　What seem'd my worth since I began;
　　For merit lives from man to man,
And not from man, O Lord, to thee.

Forgive my grief for one removed,
　　Thy creature, whom I found so fair.
　　I trust he lives in thee, and there
40 I find him worthier to be loved.

Forgive these wild and wandering cries,
　　Confusions of a wasted° youth;
　　Forgive them where they fail in truth,
And in thy wisdom make me wise.
　　(1849; 1850)

I

I held it truth, with him who sings°
　　To one clear harp in divers tones,
　　That men may rise on stepping-stones
Of their dead selves to higher things.

But who shall so forecast the years
　　And find in loss a gain to match?
　　Or reach a hand thro' time to catch
The far-off interest of tears?

Let Love clasp Grief lest both be drown'd,
　　Let darkness keep her raven gloss.　　　10
　　Ah, sweeter to be drunk with loss,
To dance with Death, to beat the ground,

Than that the victor Hours should scorn
　　The long result of love, and boast,
　　"Behold the man that loved and lost,
But all he was is overworn."

II

Old yew, which graspest at the stones
　　That name the underlying dead,
　　Thy fibres net the dreamless head,
Thy roots are wrapt about the bones.　　　20

The seasons bring the flower again,
　　And bring the firstling to the flock;
　　And in the dusk of thee the clock
Beats out the little lives of men.

O, not for thee the glow, the bloom,
　　Who changest not in any gale,
　　Nor branding summer suns avail
To touch thy thousand years of gloom;

And gazing on thee, sullen tree,
　　Sick for° thy stubborn hardihood,　　　30
　　I seem to fail from out my blood
And grow incorporate into thee.

III

O Sorrow, cruel fellowship,
　　O Priestess in the vaults of Death,
　　O sweet and bitter in a breath,
What whispers from thy lying lip?

"The stars," she whispers, "blindly run;
　　A web is woven across the sky;
　　From out waste places comes a cry,
And murmurs from the dying sun;　　　40

"And all the phantom, Nature, stands—
　　With all the music in her tone,
　　A hollow echo of my own,—
A hollow form with empty hands."

And shall I take a thing so blind,
　　Embrace her as my natural good;
　　Or crush her, like a vice of blood,
Upon the threshold of the mind?

In Memoriam　5 **orbs,** planets　17 **systems,** of theology and philosophy
28 **as before,** before mind and soul were separated by modern skepticism
42 **wasted,** desolated　1 **him who sings,** Goethe, greatly admired by Tennyson
for his ability to work in many different styles

30 **Sick for,** yearning for

IV

To Sleep I give my powers away;
50 My will is bondsman to the dark;
    I sit within a helmless bark,
And with my heart I muse and say:

O heart, how fares it with thee now,
    That thou shouldst fail from thy desire,
    Who scarcely darest to inquire,
"What is it makes me beat so low?"

Something it is which thou hast lost,
    Some pleasure from thine early years.
    Break, thou deep vase of chilling tears,
60 That grief hath shaken into frost!

Such clouds of nameless trouble cross
    All night below the darken'd eyes;
    With morning wakes the will, and cries,
"Thou shalt not be the fool of loss."

V

I sometimes hold it half a sin
    To put in words the grief I feel;
    For words, like Nature, half reveal
And half conceal the Soul within.

But, for the unquiet heart and brain,
70 A use in measured language lies;
    The sad mechanic exercise,
Like dull narcotics, numbing pain.

In words, like weeds,° I'll wrap me o'er,
    Like coarsest clothes against the cold;
    But that large grief which these enfold
Is given in outline and no more.

VI

One writes, that "other friends remain,"
    That "loss is common to the race"—
    And common is the commonplace,
80 And vacant chaff well meant for grain.

That loss is common would not make
    My own less bitter, rather more.
    Too common! Never morning wore
To evening, but some heart did break.

O father, wheresoe'er thou be,
    Who pledgest now thy gallant son,
    A shot ere half thy draught be done,
Hath still'd the life that beat from thee.

O mother, praying God will save
90 Thy sailor,—while thy head is bow'd,
    His heavy-shotted hammock-shroud
Drops in his vast and wandering grave.

Ye know no more than I who wrought
    At that last hour to please him well;
    Who mused on all I had to tell,
And something written, something thought;

Expecting still his advent home;
    And ever met him on his way
    With wishes, thinking, "here to-day,"
Or "here to-morrow will he come."   100

O, somewhere, meek, unconscious dove,
    That sittest ranging golden hair;
    And glad to find thyself so fair,
Poor child, that waitest for thy love!

For now her father's chimney glows
    In expectation of a guest;
    And thinking "this will please him best,"
She takes a riband or a rose;

For he will see them on to-night;
    And with the thought her color burns;   110
    And having left the glass, she turns
Once more to set a ringlet right;

And, even when she turn'd, the curse
    Had fallen, and her future lord
    Was drown'd in passing thro' the ford,
Or kill'd in falling from his horse.

O, what to her shall be the end?
    And what to me remains of good?
    To her perpetual maidenhood,
And unto me no second friend.   120

VII

Dark house,° by which once more I stand
    Here in the long unlovely street,
    Doors, where my heart was used to beat
So quickly, waiting for a hand,

A hand that can be clasp'd no more—
    Behold me, for I cannot sleep,
    And like a guilty thing I creep
At earliest morning to the door.

He is not here; but far away
    The noise of life begins again,   130
    And ghastly thro' the drizzling rain
On the bald street breaks the blank day.

XIX

The Danube to the Severn° gave
    The darken'd heart that beat no more;
    They laid him by the pleasant shore,
And in the hearing of the wave.   360

---

73 **weeds,** mourning garments

121 **Dark house,** 67 Wimpole Street, London, where Hallam had lived
357 **The Danube . . . Severn.** Hallam died in Vienna, on the Danube; he was
buried on the banks of the Severn in southwest England

Alfred, Lord Tennyson   **895**

There twice a day the Severn fills;
 The salt sea-water passes by,
 And hushes half the babbling Wye,°
And makes a silence in the hills.

The Wye is hush'd nor moved along,
 And hush'd my deepest grief of all,
 When fill'd with tears that cannot fall,
I brim with sorrow drowning song.

370 The tide flows down, the wave again
 Is vocal in its wooded walls;
 My deeper anguish also falls,
And I can speak a little then.

XX

The lesser griefs that may be said,
 That breathe a thousand tender vows,
 Are but as servants in a house
Where lies the master newly dead;

Who speak their feeling as it is,
 And weep the fulness from the mind.
 "It will be hard," they say, "to find
380 Another service such as this."

My lighter moods are like to these,
 That out of words a comfort win;
 But there are other griefs within,
And tears that at their fountain freeze;

For by the hearth the children sit
 Cold in that atmosphere of death,
 And scarce endure to draw the breath,
Or like to noiseless phantoms flit;

But open converse is there none,
390 So much the vital spirits sink
 To see the vacant chair, and think,
"How good! how kind! and he is gone."

XXI

I sing to him that rests below,
 And, since the grasses round me wave,
 I take the grasses of the grave,
And make them pipes whereon to blow.

The traveller hears me now and then,
 And sometimes harshly will he speak:
 "This fellow would make weakness weak,
400 And melt the waxen hearts of men."

Another answers: "Let him be,
 He loves to make parade of pain,
 That with his piping he may gain
The praise that comes to constancy."

363 **Wye,** a tributary of the Severn and partly tidal. It becomes silent when the
tide flows in and "vocal" as it flows out

A third is wroth: "Is this an hour
 For private sorrow's barren song,
 When more and more the people throng
The chairs and thrones of civil power?

"A time to sicken and to swoon,
 When Science reaches forth her arms   410
 To feel from world to world, and charms
Her secret from the latest moon?"

Behold, ye speak an idle thing;
 Ye never knew the sacred dust.
 I do but sing because I must,
And pipe but as the linnets sing;

And one is glad; her note is gay,
 For now her little ones have ranged;
 And one is sad; her note is changed,
Because her brood is stolen away.   420

XXII

The path by which we twain did go,
 Which led by tracts that pleased us well,
 Thro' four sweet years arose and fell,
From flower to flower, from snow to snow;

And we with singing cheer'd the way,
 And, crown'd with all the season lent,
 From April on to April went,
And glad at heart from May to May.

But where the path we walk'd began
 To slant the fifth autumnal slope,   430
 As we descended following Hope,
There sat the Shadow fear'd of man;

Who broke our fair companionship,
 And spread his mantle dark and cold,
 And wrapt thee formless in the fold,
And dull'd the murmur on thy lip,

And bore thee where I could not see
 Nor follow, tho' I walk in haste,
 And think that somewhere in the waste
The Shadow sits and waits for me.   440

XXIII

Now, sometimes in my sorrow shut,
 Or breaking into song by fits,
 Alone, alone, to where he sits,
The Shadow cloak'd from head to foot,

Who keeps the keys of all the creeds,
 I wander, often falling lame,
 And looking back to whence I came,
Or on to where the pathway leads;

And crying, How changed from where it ran

450 Thro' lands where not a leaf was dumb,
    But all the lavish hills would hum
The murmur of a happy Pan;°

When each by turns was guide to each,
    And Fancy light from Fancy caught,
    And Thought leapt out to wed with Thought
Ere Thought could wed itself with Speech;

And all we met was fair and good,
    And all was good that Time could bring,
    And all the secret of the Spring
460 Moved in the chambers of the blood;

And many an old philosophy
    On Argive° heights divinely sang,
    And round us all the thicket rang
To many a flute of Arcady.°

XXIV

And was the day of my delight
    As pure and perfect as I say?
    The very source and fount of day
Is dash'd with wandering isles of night.

If all was good and fair we met,
470   This earth had been the Paradise
    It never look'd to human eyes
Since our first sun arose and set.

And is it that the haze of grief
    Makes former gladness loom so great?
    The lowness of the present state,
That sets the past in this relief?

Or that the past will always win
    A glory from its being far,
    And orb into the perfect star
480 We saw not when we moved therein?

XXV

I know that this was Life,—the track
    Whereon with equal feet we fared;
    And then, as now, the day prepared
The daily burden for the back.

But this it was that made me move
    As light as carrier-birds in air;
    I loved the weight I had to bear,
Because it needed help of Love;

Nor could I weary, heart or limb,
490   When mighty Love would cleave in twain
    The lading of a single pain,
And part it, giving half to him.

452 **Pan,** god of nature   462 **Argive,** Greek   464 **Arcady,** Arcadia, home of
the shepherd poets. Such references as this and the above carry on the pastoral
conventions of the elegy

XXVI

Still onward winds the dreary way;
    I with it, for I long to prove
    No lapse of moons can canker Love,
Whatever fickle tongues may say.

And if that eye which watches guilt
    And goodness, and hath power to see
    Within the green the moulder'd tree,
And towers fallen as soon as built—   500

O, if indeed that eye foresee
    Or see—in Him is no before—
    In more of life true life no more
And Love the indifference to be,

Then might I find, ere yet the morn
    Breaks hither over Indian seas,
    That Shadow waiting with the keys,
To shroud me from my proper scorn.

XXVII

I envy not in any moods
    The captive void of noble rage,   510
    The linnet born within the cage,
That never knew the summer woods;

I envy not the beast that takes
    His license in the field of time,
    Unfetter'd by the sense of crime,
To whom a conscience never wakes;

Nor, what may count itself as blest,
    The heart that never plighted troth
    But stagnates in the weeds of sloth;
Nor any want-begotten rest.   520

I hold it true, whate'er befall;
    I feel it, when I sorrow most;
    'T is better to have loved and lost
Than never to have loved at all.

XXVIII

The times draws near the birth of Christ.
    The moon is hid, the night is still;
    The Christmas bells from hill to hill
Answer each other in the mist.

Four voices of four hamlets round,
    From far and near, on mead and moor,   530
    Swell out and fail, as if a door
Were shut between me and the sound;

Each voice four changes on the wind,
    That now dilate, and now decrease,
    Peace and goodwill, goodwill and peace,
Peace and goodwill, to all mankind.

Alfred, Lord Tennyson   **897**

This year I slept and woke with pain,
  I almost wish'd no more to wake,
  And that my hold on life would break
540 Before I heard those bells again;

But they my troubled spirit rule,
  For they controll'd me when a boy;
  They bring me sorrow touch'd with joy,
The merry, merry bells of Yule.

XXIX

With such compelling cause to grieve
  As daily vexes household peace,
  And chains regret to his decease,
How dare we keep our Christmas-eve,

Which brings no more a welcome guest
550 To enrich the threshold of the night
  With shower'd largess of delight
In dance and song and game and jest?

Yet go, and while the holly boughs
  Entwine the cold baptismal font,
  Make one wreath more for Use and Wont,
That guard the portals of the house;

Old sisters of a day gone by,
  Gray nurses, loving nothing new—
  Why should they miss their yearly due
560 Before their time? They too will die.

XXX

With trembling fingers did we weave
  The holly round the Christmas hearth;
  A rainy cloud possess'd the earth,
And sadly fell our Christmas-eve.

At our old pastimes in the hall
  We gamboll'd, making vain pretence
  Of gladness, with an awful sense
Of one mute Shadow watching all.

We paused: the winds were in the beech;
570 We heard them sweep the winter land;
  And in a circle hand-in-hand
Sat silent, looking each at each.

Then echo-like our voices rang;
  We sung, tho' every eye was dim,
  A merry song we sang with him
Last year; impetuously we sang.

We ceased; a gentler feeling crept
  Upon us: surely rest is meet.
  "They rest," we said, "their sleep is sweet,"
580 And silence follow'd, and we wept.

Our voices took a higher range;
  Once more we sang: "They do not die
  Nor lose their mortal sympathy,
Nor change to us, although they change;

"Rapt from the fickle and the frail
  With gather'd power, yet the same,
  Pierces the keen seraphic flame
From orb to orb, from veil to veil."

Rise, happy morn, rise, holy morn,
  Draw forth the cheerful day from night: 590
  O Father, touch the east, and light
The light that shone when Hope was born.

XXXI

When Lazarus left his charnel-cave,
  And home to Mary's house return'd,
  Was this demanded—if he yearn'd
To hear her weeping by his grave?

"Where wert thou, brother, those four days?"
  There lives no record of reply,
  Which telling what it is to die
Had surely added praise to praise.   600

From every house the neighbors met,
  The streets were fill'd with joyful sound,
  A solemn gladness even crown'd
The purple brows of Olivet.

Behold a man raised up by Christ!
  The rest remaineth unreveal'd;
  He told it not, or something seal'd
The lips of that Evangelist.

XXXII

Her eyes are homes of silent prayer,
  Nor other thought her mind admits   610
  But, he was dead, and there he sits,
And he that brought him back is there.

Then one deep love doth supersede
  All other, when her ardent gaze
  Roves from the living brother's face,
And rests upon the Life indeed.

All subtle thought, all curious fears,
  Borne down by gladness so complete,
  She bows, she bathes the Saviour's feet
With costly spikenard and with tears.   620

Thrice blest whose lives are faithful prayers,
  Whose loves in higher love endure;
  What souls possess themselves so pure,
Or is there blessedness like theirs?

XXXIII

O thou° that after toil and storm
    Mayst seem to have reach'd a purer air,
    Whose faith has centre everywhere,
Nor cares to fix itself to form,

Leave thou thy sister when she prays
630 Her early heaven, her happy views;
    Nor thou with shadow'd hint confuse
A life that leads melodious days.

Her faith thro' form is pure as thine,
    Her hands are quicker unto good.
    O, sacred be the flesh and blood
To which she links a truth divine!

See thou, that countest reason ripe
    In holding by the law within,
    Thou fail not in a world of sin,
640 And even for want of such a type.

XXXIV

My own dim life should teach me this,
    That life shall live for evermore,
    Else earth is darkness at the core,
And dust and ashes all that is;

This round of green, this orb of flame,
    Fantastic beauty; such as lurks
    In some wild poet, when he works
Without a conscience or an aim.

What then were God to such as I?
650 'T were hardly worth my while to choose
    Of things all mortal, or to use
A little patience ere I die;

'T were best at once to sink to peace,
    Like birds the charming serpent draws,
    To drop head-foremost in the jaws
Of vacant darkness and to cease.

XXXV

Yet if° some voice that man could trust
    Should murmur from the narrow house,
    "The cheeks drop in, the body bows;
660 Man dies, nor is there hope in dust;"

Might I not say? "Yet even here,
    But for one hour, O Love, I strive
    To keep so sweet a thing alive."
But I should turn mine ears and hear

625–640 **O thou, etc.** These words are addressed to rationalistic liberals who
have put aside a dogmatic and ritualistic form of religion   657–680 **Yet if, etc.**
The dialogue in this section poses the central question: Is not Love a mockery if
physical death closes all? The poet is identifying Love with Christ; hence, the pagan imagery of lines 677–680

The moanings of the homeless sea,
    The sound of streams that swift or slow
    Draw down Æonian° hills, and sow
The dust of continents to be;

And Love would answer with a sigh,
    "The sound of that forgetful shore   670
    Will change my sweetness more and more,
Half-dead to know that I shall die."

O me, what profits it to put
    An idle case? If Death were seen
    At first as Death, Love had not been,
Or been in narrowest working shut,

Mere fellowship of sluggish moods,
    Or in his coarsest Satyr-shape
    Had bruised the herb and crush'd the grape,
And bask'd and batten'd in the woods.   680

L

Be near me when my light is low,
    When the blood creeps, and the nerves prick
    And tingle; and the heart is sick,
And all the wheels of being slow.

Be near me when the sensuous frame
    Is rack'd with pangs that conquer trust;   930
    And Time, a maniac scattering dust,
And Life, a Fury slinging flame.

Be near me when my faith is dry,
    And men the flies of latter spring,
    That lay their eggs, and sting and sing
And weave their petty cells and die.

Be near me when I fade away,
    To point the term of human strife,
    And on the low dark verge of life
The twilight of eternal day.   940

LI

Do we indeed desire the dead
    Should still be near us at our side?
    Is there no baseness we would hide?
No inner vileness that we dread?

Shall he for whose applause I strove,
    I had such reverence for his blame,
    See with clear eye some hidden shame
And I be lessen'd in his love?

I wrong the grave with fears untrue.
    Shall love be blamed for want of faith?   950
    There must be wisdom with great Death;
The dead shall look me thro' and thro'.

667 **Æonian,** eons old

Be near us when we climb or fall;
   Ye watch, like God, the rolling hours
   With larger other eyes than ours,
To make allowance for us all.

LXXIII

So many worlds, so much to do,
   So little done, such things to be,
   How know I what had need of thee,
For thou wert strong as thou wert true?

The fame is quench'd that I foresaw,
   The head hath miss'd an earthly wreath:
   I curse not Nature, no, nor Death;
For nothing is that errs from law.

We pass; the path that each man trod
1330   Is dim, or will be dim, with weeds.
   What fame is left for human deeds
In endless age? It rests with God.

O hollow wraith of dying fame,
   Fade wholly, while the soul exults,
   And self-infolds the large results
Of force that would have forged a name.

LXXIV

As sometimes in a dead man's face,
   To those that watch it more and more,
   A likeness, hardly seen before,
1340 Comes out—to some one of his race;

So, dearest, now thy brows are cold,
   I see thee what thou art, and know
   Thy likeness to the wise below,
Thy kindred with the great of old.

But there is more than I can see,
   And what I see I leave unsaid,
   Nor speak it, knowing Death has made
His darkness beautiful with thee.

LXXV

I leave thy praises unexpress'd
1350   In verse that brings myself relief,
   And by the measure of my grief
I leave thy greatness to be guess'd.

What practice howsoe'er expert
   In fitting aptest words to things,
   Or voice the richest-toned that sings,
Hath power to give thee as thou wert?

I care not in these fading days
   To raise a cry that lasts not long,
   And round thee with the breeze of song
1360 To stir a little dust of praise.

Thy leaf has perish'd in the green,
   And, while we breathe beneath the sun,
   The world which credits what is done
Is cold to all that might have been.

So here shall silence guard thy fame;
   But somewhere, out of human view,
   Whate'er thy hands are set to do
Is wrought with tumult of acclaim.

LXXVI

Take wings of fancy, and ascend,
   And in a moment set thy face   1370
   Where all the starry heavens of space
Are sharpen'd to a needle's end;

Take wings of foresight; lighten thro'
   The secular abyss to come,
   And lo, thy deepest lays are dumb
Before the mouldering of a yew;

And if the matin songs, that woke
   The darkness of our planet, last,
   Thine own shall wither in the vast,
Ere half the lifetime of an oak.   1380

Ere these have clothed their branchy bowers
   With fifty Mays, thy songs are vain;
   And what are they when these remain
The ruin'd shells of hollow towers?

LXXVII

What hope is here for modern rhyme
   To him who turns a musing eye
   On songs, and deeds, and lives, that lie
Foreshorten'd in the tract of time?

These mortal lullabies of pain
   May bind a book, may line a box,   1390
   May serve to curl a maiden's locks;
Or when a thousand moons shall wane

A man upon a stall may find,
   And, passing, turn the page that tells
   A grief, then changed to something else,
Sung by a long-forgotten mind.

But what of that? My darken'd ways
   Shall ring with music all the same;
   To breathe my loss is more than fame,
To utter love more sweet than praise.   1400

LXXVIII

Again at Christmas did we weave
   The holly round the Christmas hearth;
   The silent snow possess'd the earth,
And calmly fell our Christmas-eve.

The yule-clog sparkled keen with frost,
  No wing of wind the region swept,
  But over all things brooding slept
The quiet sense of something lost.

As in the winters left behind,
1410 Again our ancient games had place,
  The mimic picture's° breathing grace,
And dance and song and hoodman-blind.

Who show'd a token of distress?
  No single tear, no mark of pain—
  O sorrow, then can sorrow wane?
O grief, can grief be changed to less?

O last regret, regret can die!
  No—mixt with all this mystic frame,
  Her deep relations are the same,
1420 But with long use her tears are dry.

LXXXVII

I past beside the reverend walls°
  In which of old I wore the gown;
  I roved at random thro' the town,
And saw the tumult of the halls;

And heard once more in college fanes
1690 The storm their high-built organs make,
  And thunder-music, rolling, shake
The prophet blazon'd on the panes;

And caught once more the distant shout,
  The measured pulse of racing oars
  Among the willows; paced the shores
And many a bridge, and all about

The same gray flats again, and felt
  The same, but not the same; and last
  Up that long walk of limes I past
1700 To see the rooms in which he dwelt.

Another name was on the door.
  I linger'd; all within was noise
  Of songs, and clapping hands, and boys
That crash'd the glass and beat the floor;

Where once we held debate,° a band
  Of youthful friends, on mind and art,
  And labor, and the changing mart,
And all the framework of the land;

When one would aim an arrow fair,
1710 But send it slackly from the string;
  And one would pierce an outer ring,
And one an inner, here and there;

And last the master-bowman, he,
  Would cleave the mark. A willing ear
  We lent him. Who but hung to hear
The rapt oration flowing free

From point to point, with power and grace
  And music in the bounds of law,
  To those conclusions when we saw
The God within him light his face,   1720

And seem to lift the form, and glow
  In azure orbits heavenly-wise;
  And over those ethereal eyes
The bar° of Michael Angelo?

XCV

By night° we linger'd on the lawn,
  For underfoot the herb was dry;
  And genial warmth; and o'er the sky
The silvery haze of summer drawn;   1880

And calm that let the tapers burn
  Unwavering: not a cricket chirr'd;
  The brook alone far-off was heard,
And on the board the fluttering urn.

And bats went round in fragrant skies,
  And wheel'd or lit the filmy shapes
  That haunt the dusk, with ermine capes
And woolly breasts and beaded eyes;

While now we sang old songs that peal'd
  From knoll to knoll, where, couch'd at ease,   1890
  The white kine glimmer'd, and the trees
Laid their dark arms about the field.

But when those others, one by one,
  Withdrew themselves from me and night,
  And in the house light after light
Went out, and I was all alone,

A hunger seized my heart; I read
  Of that glad year which once had been,
  In those fallen leaves which kept their green,
The noble letters of the dead.   1900

And strangely on the silence broke
  The silent-speaking words, and strange
  Was love's dumb cry defying change
To test his worth; and strangely spoke

The faith, the vigor, bold to dwell
  On doubts that drive the coward back,
  And keen thro' wordy snares to track
Suggestion to her inmost cell.

1411 **mimic picture's,** a form of charade   1685 **reverend walls,** Trinity College, Cambridge   1705 **debate.** Tennyson and Hallam had belonged to a group called the "Apostles"

1724 **bar,** a prominent ridge of bone above the eyes   1877–1940 **By night, etc.** This section contains the first climax of reunion in the poem. The experience is mystical, but Tennyson very carefully prepares the setting to achieve psychological truth

So word by word, and line by line,
  1910   The dead man touch'd me from the past,
      And all at once it seem'd at last
The living soul was flash'd on mine,

And mine in this was wound, and whirl'd
      About empyreal heights of thought,
      And came on that which is, and caught
The deep pulsations of the world,

Æonian music measuring out
      The steps of Time—the shocks of Chance—
      The blows of Death. At length my trance
  1920 Was cancell'd, stricken thro' with doubt.

Vague words! but ah, how hard to frame
      In matter-moulded forms of speech,
      Or even for intellect to reach
Thro' memory that which I became;

Till now the doubtful dusk reveal'd
      The knolls once more where, couch'd at ease,
      The white kine glimmer'd, and the trees
Laid their dark arms about the field;

And suck'd from out the distant gloom
  1930   A breeze began to tremble o'er
      The large leaves of the sycamore,
And fluctuate all the still perfume,

And gathering freshlier overhead,
      Rock'd the full-foliaged elms, and swung
      The heavy-folded rose, and flung
The lilies to and fro, and said,

"The dawn, the dawn," and died away;
      And East and West, without a breath,
      Mixt their dim lights, like life and death,
  1940 To broaden into boundless day.

XCVI

You say, but with no touch of scorn,
      Sweet-hearted, you, whose light-blue eyes
      Are tender over drowning flies,
You tell me, doubt is Devil-born.

I know not: one indeed I knew
      In many a subtle question versed,
      Who touch'd a jarring lyre at first,
But ever strove to make it true;

Perplext in faith, but pure in deeds,
  1950   At last he beat his music out.
      There lives more faith in honest doubt,
Believe me, than in half the creeds.

He fought his doubts and gather'd strength,
      He would not make his judgment blind,

He faced the spectres of the mind
And laid them; thus he came at length

To find a stronger faith his own,
      And Power was with him in the night,
      Which makes the darkness and the light,
And dwells not in the light alone,   1960

But in the darkness and the cloud,
      As over Sinai's peaks of old,
      While Israel° made their gods of gold,
Altho' the trumpet blew so loud.

CV

To-night ungather'd let us leave
      This laurel, let this holly stand: 2190
      We live within the stranger's land,
And strangely falls our Christmas-eve.

Our father's dust is left alone
      And silent under other snows:
      There in due time the woodbine blows,
The violet comes, but we are gone.

No more shall wayward grief abuse
      The genial hour with mask and mime;
      For change of place, like growth of time,
Has broke the bond of dying use.   2200

Let cares that petty shadows cast,
      By which our lives are chiefly proved,
      A little spare the night I loved,
And hold it solemn to the past.

But let no footstep beat the floor,
      Nor bowl of wassail mantle warm;
      For who would keep an ancient form
Thro' which the spirit breathes no more?

Be neither song, nor game, nor feast;
      Nor harp be touch'd, nor flute be blown;   2210
      No dance, no motion, save alone
What lightens in the lucid East

Of rising worlds by yonder wood.
      Long sleeps the summer in the seed;
      Run out your measured arcs, and lead
The closing cycle rich in good.

CVI

Ring out, wild bells, to the wild sky,
      The flying cloud, the frosty light:
      The year is dying in the night;
Ring out, wild bells, and let him die.   2220

Ring out the old, ring in the new,

1963 **While Israel, etc.** The Israelites made a golden calf to worship while God was revealing the Commandments to Moses

Ring, happy bells, across the snow:
  The year is going, let him go;
Ring out the false, ring in the true.

Ring out the grief that saps the mind,
  For those that here we see no more;
  Ring out the feud of rich and poor,
Ring in redress to all mankind.

Ring out a slowly dying cause,
2230 And ancient forms of party strife;
  Ring in the nobler modes of life,
With sweeter manners, purer laws.

Ring out the want, the care, the sin,
  The faithless coldness of the times;
  Ring out, ring out my mournful rhymes,
But ring the fuller minstrel in.

Ring out false pride in place and blood,
  The civic slander and the spite;
  Ring in the love of truth and right,
2240 Ring in the common love of good.

Ring out old shapes of foul disease;
  Ring out the narrowing lust of gold;
  Ring out the thousand wars of old,
Ring in the thousand years of peace.

Ring in the valiant man and free,
  The larger heart, the kindlier hand;
  Ring out the darkness of the land,
Ring in the Christ that is to be.

CIX
Heart-affluence in discursive talk
2290 From household fountains never dry;
  The critic clearness of an eye
That saw thro' all the Muses' walk:

Seraphic intellect and force
  To seize and throw the doubts of man;
  Impassion'd logic, which outran
The hearer in its fiery course;

High nature amorous of the good,
  But touch'd with no ascetic gloom;
  And passion pure in snowy blood
2300 Thro' all the years of April blood;

A love of freedom rarely felt,
  Of freedom in her regal seat
  Of England; not the schoolboy heat,
The blind hysterics of the Celt;

And manhood fused with female grace
  In such a sort, the child would twine

A trustful hand, unask'd, in thine,
  And find his comfort in thy face;

All these have been, and thee mine eyes
  Have look'd on: if they look'd in vain,   2310
  My shame is greater who remain,
Nor let thy wisdom make me wise.

CXVIII
Contemplate all this work of Time,
  The giant laboring in his youth;   2470
  Nor dream of human love and truth,
As dying Nature's earth and lime;

But trust that those we call the dead
  Are breathers of an ampler day
  For ever nobler ends. They° say,
The solid earth whereon we tread

In tracts of fluent heat began,
  And grew to seeming-random forms,
  The seeming prey of cyclic storms,
Till at the last arose the man;   2480

Who throve and branch'd from clime to clime,
  The herald of a higher race,
  And of himself in higher place,
If so he type this work of time

Within himself, from more to more;
  Or, crown'd with attributes of woe
  Like glories, move his course, and show
That life is not as idle ore,

But iron dug from central gloom,
  And heated hot with burning fears,   2490
  And dipt in baths of hissing tears,
And batter'd with the shocks of doom

To shape and use. Arise and fly
  The reeling Faun, the sensual feast;
  Move upward, working out the beast,
And let the ape and tiger die.

CXXIV
That which we dare invoke to bless;
  Our dearest faith; our ghastliest doubt;
  He, They, One, All; within, without;
The Power in darkness whom we guess,—

I found Him not in world or sun,
  Or eagle's wing, or insect's eye,
  Nor thro' the questions men may try
The petty cobwebs we have spun.   2580

If e'er when faith had fallen asleep,

2475 **They,** geologists and astronomers

I heard a voice, "believe no more,"
And heard an ever-breaking shore
That tumbled in the Godless deep,

A warmth within the breast would melt
The freezing reason's colder part,
And like a man in wrath the heart
Stood up and answer'd, "I have felt."

No, like a child in doubt and fear:
2590   But that blind clamor made me wise;
Then was I as a child that cries,
But, crying, knows his father near;

And what I am beheld again
What is, and no man understands;
And out of darkness came the hands
That reach thro' nature, moulding men.

CXXVII

And all is well, tho' faith and form
Be sunder'd in the night of fear;
Well roars the storm to those that hear
A deeper voice across the storm,

Proclaiming social truth shall spread,
2630   And justice, even tho' thrice again
The red fool-fury of the Seine°
Should pile her barricades with dead.

But ill for him that wears a crown,
And him, the lazar, in his rags!
They tremble, the sustaining crags;
The spires of ice are toppled down,

And molten up, and roar in flood;
The fortress crashes from on high,
The brute earth lightens to the sky,
2640 And the great Æon sinks in blood,

And compass'd by the fires of hell;
While thou, dear spirit, happy star,
O'erlook'st the tumult from afar,
And smilest, knowing all is well.

CXXX

Thy voice is on the rolling air;
I hear thee where the waters run;
Thou standest in the rising sun,
And in the setting thou art fair.

What are thou then? I cannot guess;
But tho' I seem in star and flower
To feel thee some diffusive power,
I do not therefore love thee less.

My love involves the love before;
My love is vaster passion now;   2690
Tho' mix'd with God and Nature thou,
I seem to love thee more and more.

Far off thou art, but ever nigh;
I have thee still, and I rejoice;
I prosper, circled with thy voice;
I shall not lose thee tho' I die.

CXXXI

O living will that shalt endure
When all that seems shall suffer shock,
Rise in the spiritual rock,
Flow thro' our deeds and make them pure,   2700

That we may lift from out of dust
A voice as unto him that hears,
A cry above the conquer'd years
To one that with us works, and trust,

With faith that comes of self-control,
The truths that never can be proved
Until we close with all we loved,
And all we flow from, soul in soul.

EPILOGUE

O true and tried,° so well and long,
Demand not thou a marriage lay;   2710
In that it is thy marriage day
Is music more than any song.

Nor have I felt so much of bliss
Since first he told me that he loved
A daughter of our house, nor proved
Since that dark day a day like this;

Tho' I since then have number'd o'er
Some thrice three years; they went and came,
Remade the blood and changed the frame,
And yet is love not less, but more;   2720

No longer caring to embalm
In dying songs a dead regret,
But like a statue solid-set,
And moulded in colossal calm.

Regret is dead, but love is more
Than in the summers that are flown,
For I myself with these have grown
To something greater than before;

Which makes appear the songs I made

2631 **Seine,** reference to periodic revolutionary disorders in France, more specifically to the revolution of 1830

2709–2852 **O true and tried, etc.** The epilogue is addressed to Edward Lushington and is an epithalamium or marriage hymn. Tennyson is following elegiac tradition here, but he is also confirming his faith in human love

As echoes out of weaker times,
　　As half but idle brawling rhymes,
　　The sport of random sun and shade.

But where is she, the bridal flower,
　　That must be made a wife ere noon?
　　She enters, glowing like the moon
Of Eden on its bridal bower.

On me she bends her blissful eyes
　　And then on thee; they meet thy look
　　And brighten like the star that shook
2740 Betwixt the palms of Paradise.

O, when her life was yet in bud,
　　He too foretold the perfect rose.
　　For thee she grew, for thee she grows
For ever, and as fair as good.

And thou art worthy, full of power;
　　As gentle; liberal-minded, great,
　　Consistent; wearing all that weight
Of learning lightly like a flower.

But now set out: the noon is near,
2750　　And I must give away the bride;
　　She fears not, or with thee beside
And me behind her, will not fear.

For I that danced her on my knee,
　　That watch'd her on her nurse's arm,
　　That shielded all her life from harm,
At last must part with her to thee;

Now waiting to be made a wife,
　　Her feet, my darling, on the dead;
　　Their pensive tablets round her head,
2760 And the most living words of life

Breathed in her ear. The ring is on,
　　The "Wilt thou?" answer'd, and again
　　The "Wilt thou?" ask'd, till out of twain
Her sweet "I will" has made you one.

Now sign your names, which shall be read,
　　Mute symbols of a joyful morn,
　　By village eyes as yet unborn.
The names are sign'd, and overhead

Begins the clash and clang that tells
2770　　The joy to every wandering breeze;
　　The blind wall rocks, and on the trees
The dead leaf trembles to the bells.

O happy hour, and happier hours
　　Await them. Many a merry face
　　Salutes them—maidens of the place,
That pelt us in the porch with flowers.

O happy hour, behold the bride
　　With him to whom her hand I gave.
　　They leave the porch, they pass the grave
That has to-day its sunny side.　　　　　　2780

To-day the grave is bright for me,
　　For them the light of life increased,
　　Who stay to share the morning feast,
Who rest to-night beside the sea.

Let all my genial spirits advance
　　To meet and greet a whiter sun;
　　My drooping memory will not shun
The foaming grape of eastern France.

It circles round, and fancy plays,
　　And hearts are warm'd and faces bloom,　　2790
　　As drinking health to bride and groom
We wish them store of happy days.

Nor count me all to blame if I
　　Conjecture of a stiller guest,
　　Perchance, perchance, among the rest,
And, tho' in silence, wishing joy.

But they must go, the time draws on,
　　And those white-favor'd horses wait;
　　They rise, but linger; it is late;
Farewell, we kiss, and they are gone.　　　2800

A shade falls on us like the dark
　　From little cloudlets on the grass,
　　But sweeps away as out we pass
To range the woods, to roam the park,

Discussing how their courtship grew,
　　And talk of others that are wed,
　　And how she look'd, and what he said,
And back we come at fall of dew.

Again the feast, the speech, the glee,
　　The shade of passing thought, the wealth　　2810
　　Of words and wit, the double health,
The crowning cup, the three-times-three,

And last the dance;—till I retire.
　　Dumb is that tower which spake so loud,
　　And high in heaven the streaming cloud,
And on the downs a rising fire:

And rise, O moon, from yonder down,
　　Till over down and over dale
　　All night the shining vapor sail
And pass the silent-lighted town,　　　　　2820

The white-faced halls, the glancing rills,
　　And catch at every mountain head,

And o'er the friths that branch and spread
  Their sleeping silver thro' the hills;

And touch with shade the bridal doors,
  With tender gloom the roof, the wall;
  And breaking let the splendor fall
To spangle all the happy shores

By which they rest, and ocean sounds,
2830 And, star and system rolling past,
  A soul shall draw from out the vast
And strike his being into bounds,

And, moved thro' life of lower phase,
  Result in man, be born and think,
  And act and love, a closer link
Betwixt us and the crowning race

Of those that, eye to eye, shall look
  On knowledge; under whose command
  Is Earth and Earth's, and in their hand
2840 Is Nature like an open book;

No longer half-akin to brute,
  For all we thought and loved and did,
  And hoped, and suffer'd, is but seed
Of what in them is flower and fruit;

Whereof the man that with me trod
  This planet was a noble type
  Appearing ere the times were ripe,
That friend of mind who lives in God,

That God, which ever lives and loves,
2850 One God, one law, one element,
  And one far-off divine event,
To which the whole creation moves.
(1850)

from MAUD

COME INTO THE GARDEN, MAUD

Come into the garden, Maud,
  For the black bat, night, has flown,
Come into the garden, Maud,
  I am here at the gate alone;
And the woodbine spices are wafted abroad,
  And the musk of the rose is blown.

For a breeze of morning moves,
  And the planet of Love is on high,
Beginning to faint in the light that she loves
10 On a bed of daffodil sky,

To faint in the light of the sun she loves,
  To faint in his light, and to die.

All night have the roses heard
  The flute, violin, bassoon;
All night has the casement jessamine stirred
  To the dancers dancing in tune;
Till a silence fell with the waking bird,
  And a hush with the setting moon.

I said to the lily, "There is but one,
  With whom she has heart to be gay.   20
When will the dancers leave her alone?
  She is weary of dance and play."
Now half to the setting moon are gone,
  And half to the rising day;
Low on the sand and loud on the stone
  The last wheel echoes away.

I said to the rose, "The brief night goes
  In babble and revel and wine.
O young lord-lover, what sighs are those,
  For one that will never be thine?   30
But mine, but mine," so I sware to the rose,
  "Forever and ever, mine."

And the soul of the rose went into my blood,
  As the music clashed in the hall;
And long by the garden lake I stood,
  For I heard your rivulet fall
From the lake to the meadow and on to the wood,
  Our wood, that is dearer than all;

From the meadow your walks have left so sweet
  That whenever a March wind sighs   40
He sets the jewel-print of your feet
  In violets blue as your eyes,
To the woody hollows in which we meet
  And the valleys of Paradise.

The slender acacia would not shake
  One long milk-bloom on the tree;
The white lake-blossom fell into the lake
  As the pimpernel dozed on the lea;
But the rose was awake all night for your sake,
  Knowing your promise to me;   50
The lilies and roses were all awake,
  They sighed for the dawn and thee.

Queen rose of the rosebud garden of girls,
  Come hither, the dances are done,
In gloss of satin and glimmer of pearls,
  Queen lily and rose in one;
Shine out, little head, sunning over with curls,
  To the flowers, and be their sun.

There has fallen a splendid tear

60 From the passion-flower at the gate.
   She is coming, my dove, my dear;
      She is coming, my life, my fate.
   The red rose cries, "She is near, she is near";
      And the white rose weeps, "She is late";
   The larkspur listens, "I hear, I hear";
      And the lily whispers, "I wait."

   She is coming, my own, my sweet;
      Were it ever so airy a tread,
   My heart would hear her and beat,
70   Were it earth in an earthy bed;
   My dust would hear her and beat,
      Had I lain for a century dead,
   Would start and tremble under her feet,
      And blossom in purple and red.

O THAT 'TWERE POSSIBLE

   O that 'twere possible
   After long grief and pain
   To find the arms of my true love
   Round me once again!

   When I was wont to meet her
   In the silent woody places
   By the home that gave me birth,
   We stood tranced in long embraces
   Mixed with kisses sweeter, sweeter
10 Than anything on earth.

   A shadow flits before me,
   Not thou, but like to thee.
   Ah, Christ, that it were possible
   For one short hour to see
   The souls we loved, that they might tell us
   What and where they be!

   It leads me forth at evening,
   It lightly winds and steals
   In a cold white robe before me,
20 When all my spirit reels
   At the shouts, the leagues of lights,
   And the roaring of the wheels.

   Half the night I waste in sighs,
   Half in dreams I sorrow after
   The delight of early skies;
   In a wakeful doze I sorrow
   For the hand, the lips, the eyes,
   For the meeting of the morrow,
   The delight of happy laughter,
30 The delight of low replies.

   'Tis a morning pure and sweet,
   And a dewy splendor falls

On the little flower that clings
To the turrets and the walls;
'Tis a morning pure and sweet,
And the light and shadow fleet.
She is walking in the meadow,
And the woodland echo rings;
In a moment we shall meet.
She is singing in the meadow,   40
And the rivulet at her feet
Ripples on in light and shadow
To the ballad that she sings.

Do I hear her sing as of old,
My bird with the shining head,
My own dove with the tender eye?
But there rings on a sudden a passionate cry,
There is someone dying or dead,
And a sullen thunder is rolled;
For a tumult shakes the city,   50
And I wake, my dream is fled.
In the shuddering dawn, behold,
Without knowledge, without pity,
By the curtains of my bed
That abiding phantom cold!

Get thee hence, nor come again,
Mix not memory with doubt,
Pass, thou deathlike type of pain,
Pass and cease to move about!
'Tis the blot upon the brain   60
That *will* show itself without.

Then I rise, the eave-drops fall,
And the yellow vapors choke
The great city sounding wide;
The day comes, a dull red ball
Wrapped in drifts of lurid smoke
On the misty river-tide.

Through the hubbub of the market
I steal, a wasted frame;
It crosses here, it crosses there,   70
Through all that crowd confused and loud,
The shadow still the same;
And on my heavy eyelids
My anguish hangs like shame.

Alas for her that met me,
That heard me softly call,
Came glimmering through the laurels
At the quiet evenfall,
In the garden by the turrets
Of the old manorial hall!   80

Would the happy spirit descend
From the realms of light and song,
In the chamber or the street,

Alfred, Lord Tennyson   907

As she looks among the blest,
Should I fear to greet my friend
Or to say, "Forgive the wrong,"
Or to ask her, "Take me, sweet,
To the regions of thy rest"?

But the broad light glares and beats,
90 And the shadow flits and fleets
And will not let me be;
And I loathe the squares and streets,
And the faces that one meets,
Hearts with no love for me.
Always I long to creep
Into some still cavern deep,
There to weep, and weep, and weep
My whole soul out to thee.

OH, LET THE SOLID GROUND

Oh, let the solid ground
    Not fail beneath my feet
Before my life has found
    What some have found so sweet!
5 Then let come what come may,
What matter if I go mad,
    I shall have had my day.

Let the sweet heavens endure,
    Not close and darken above me
10 Before I am quite, quite sure
    That there is one to love me!
Then let come what come may
To a life that has been so sad—
    I shall have had my day.
(1854; 1857)

FLOWER IN THE CRANNIED WALL

Flower in the crannied wall,
I pluck you out of the crannies,
I hold you here, root and all, in my hand,
Little flower—but *if* I could understand
5 What you are, root and all, and all in all,
I should know what God and man is.
(1869)

from IDYLLS OF THE KING

PELLEAS AND ETTARRE

King Arthur made new knights to fill the gap
Left by the Holy Quest; and as he sat
In hall at old Caerleon,° the high doors

Pelleas and Ettarre 3 Caerleon, town in Monmouthshire, sometimes identified
with Camelot

Were softly sundered, and through these a youth,
Pelleas, and the sweet smell of the fields
Past, and the sunshine came along with him.

'Make me thy knight, because I know, Sir King,
All that belongs to knighthood, and I love.'
Such was his cry: for having heard the King
Had let proclaim a tournament—the prize   10
A golden circlet and a knightly sword,
Full fain had Pelleas for his lady won
The golden circlet, for himself the sword:
And there were those who knew him near the King,
And promised for him: and Arthur made him knight.

And this new knight, Sir Pelleas of the isles—
But lately come to his inheritance,
And lord of many a barren isle was he—
Riding at noon, a day or twain before,
Across the forest called of Dean, to find   20
Caerleon and the King, had felt the sun
Beat like a strong knight on his helm, and reeled
Almost to falling from his horse; but saw
Near him a mound of even-sloping side,
Whereon a hundred stately beeches grew,
And here and there great hollies under them;
But for a mile all round was open space,
And fern and heath: and slowly Pelleas drew
To that dim day, then binding his good horse
To a tree, cast himself down; and as he lay   30
At random looking over the brown earth
Through that green-glooming twilight of the grove,
It seemed to Pelleas that the fern without
Burnt as a living fire of emeralds,
So that his eyes were dazzled looking at it.

Then o'er it crost the dimness of a cloud
Floating, and once the shadow of a bird
Flying, and then a fawn; and his eyes closed.
And since he loved all maidens, but no maid
In special, half-awake he whispered, 'Where?   40
O where? I love thee, though I know thee not.
For fair thou art and pure as Guinevere,
And I will make thee with my spear and sword
As famous—O my Queen, my Guinevere,
For I will be thine Arthur when we meet.'

Suddenly wakened with a sound of talk
And laughter at the limit of the wood,
And glancing through the hoary boles, he saw,
Strange as to some old prophet might have seemed
A vision hovering on a sea of fire,   50
Damsels in divers colours like the cloud
Of sunset and sunrise, and all of them
On horses, and the horses richly trapt
Breast-high in that bright line of bracken stood:
And all the damsels talked confusedly,
And one was pointing this way, and one that,
Because the way was lost.

And Pelleas rose,
And loosed his horse, and led him to the light.
There she that seemed the chief among them said,
60 'In happy time behold our pilot-star!
Youth, we are damsels-errant, and we ride,
Armed as ye see, to tilt against the knights
There at Caerleon, but have lost our way:
To right? to left? straight forward? back again?
Which? tell us quickly.'

               Pelleas gazing thought,
'Is Guinevere herself so beautiful?'
For large her violet eyes looked, and her bloom
A rosy dawn kindled in stainless heavens,
And round her limbs, mature in womanhood;
70 And slender was her hand and small her shape;
And but for those large eyes, the haunts of scorn,
She might have seemed a toy to trifle with,
And pass and care no more. But while he gazed
The beauty of her flesh abashed the boy,
As though it were the beauty of her soul:
For as the base man, judging of the good,
Puts his own baseness in him by default
Of will and nature, so did Pelleas lend
All the young beauty of his own soul to hers,
80 Believing her; and when she spake to him,
Stammered, and could not make her a reply.
For out of the waste islands had he come,
Where saving his own sisters he had known
Scarce any but the women of his isles,
Rough wives, that laughed and screamed against the
    gulls,
Makers of nets, and living from the sea.

Then with a slow smile turned the lady round
And looked upon her people; and as when
A stone is flung into some sleeping tarn,
90 The circle widens till it lip the marge,°
Spread the slow smile through all her company.
Three knights were thereamong; and they too smiled,
Scorning him; for the lady was Ettarre,
And she was a great lady in her land.

Again she said, 'O wild and of the woods,
Knowest thou not the fashion of our speech?
Or have the Heavens but given thee a fair face,
Lacking a tongue?'

             'O damsel,' answered he,
'I woke from dreams; and coming out of gloom
100 Was dazzled by the sudden light, and crave
Pardon: but will ye to Caerleon? I
Go likewise: shall I lead you to the King?'

'Lead then,' she said; and through the woods they
    went.

And while they rode, the meaning in his eyes,
His tenderness of manner, and chaste awe,
His broken utterances and bashfulness,
Were all a burthen to her, and in her heart
She muttered, 'I have lighted on a fool,
Raw, yet so stale!' But since her mind was bent
On hearing, after trumpet blown, her name   110
And title, 'Queen of Beauty,' in the lists
Cried—and beholding him so strong, she thought
That peradventure he will fight for me,
And win the circlet: therefore flattered him,
Being so gracious, that he wellnigh deemed
His wish by hers was echoed; and her knights
And all her damsels too were gracious to him,
For she was a great lady.

             And when they reached
Caerleon, ere they past to lodging, she,
Taking his hand, 'O the strong hand,' she said,   120
'See! look at mine! but wilt thou fight for me,
And win me this fine circlet, Pelleas,
That I may love thee?'

             Then his helpless heart
Leapt, and he cried, 'Ay! wilt thou if I win?'
'Ay, that will I,' she answered, and she laughed,
And straitly nipt the hand,° and flung it from her;
Then glanced askew at those three knights of hers,
Till all her ladies laughed along with her.

'O happy world,' thought Pelleas, 'all, meseems,
Are happy; I the happiest of them all.'   130
Nor slept that night for pleasure in his blood,
And green wood-ways, and eyes among the leaves;
Then being on the morrow knighted, sware
To love one only. And as he came away,
The men who met him rounded on their heels
And wondered after him, because his face
Shone like the countenance of a priest of old
Against the flame about a sacrifice
Kindled by fire from heaven: so glad was he.

Then Arthur made vast banquets, and strange   140
    knights
From the four winds came in: and each one sat,
Though served with choice from air, land, stream, and
    sea,
Oft in mid-banquet measuring with his eyes
His neighbour's make and might: and Pelleas looked
Noble among the noble, for he dreamed
His lady loved him, and he knew himself
Loved of the King: and him his new-made knight
Worshipt, whose lightest whisper moved him more
Than all the rangèd reasons of the world.

Then blushed and brake the morning of the jousts, 150

90 lip the marge, touch the edge

126 nipt the hand, checked it sharply or pinched it

And this was called 'The Tournament of Youth:'
For Arthur, loving his young knight, withheld
His older and his mightier from the lists,
That Pelleas might obtain his lady's love,
According to her promise, and remain
Lord of the tourney. And Arthur had the jousts
Down in the flat field by the shore of Usk
Holden: the gilded parapets were crowned
With faces, and the great tower filled with eyes
160 Up to the summit, and the trumpets blew.
There all day long Sir Pelleas kept the field
With honour: so by that strong hand of his
The sword and golden circlet were achieved.

Then rang the shout his lady loved: the heat
Of pride and glory fired her face; her eye
Sparkled; she caught the circlet from his lance,
And there before the people crowned herself:
So for the last time she was gracious to him.

Then at Caerleon for a space—her look
170 Bright for all others, cloudier on her knight—
Lingered Ettarre: and seeing Pelleas droop,
Said Guinevere, 'We marvel at thee much,
O damsel, wearing this unsunny face
To him who won thee glory!' And she said,
'Had ye not held your Lancelot in your bower,
My Queen, he had not won.' Whereat the Queen,
As one whose foot is bitten by an ant,
Glanced down upon her, turned and went her way.

But after, when her damsels, and herself,
180 And those three knights all set their faces home,
Sir Pelleas followed. She that saw him cried,
'Damsels—and yet I should be shamed to say it—
I cannot bide Sir Baby. Keep him back
Among yourselves. Would rather that we had
Some rough old knight who knew the worldly way,
Albeit grizzlier than a bear, to ride
And jest with: take him to you, keep him off,
And pamper him with papmeat, if ye will,
Old milky fables of the wolf and sheep,
190 Such as the wholesome mothers tell their boys.
Nay, should ye try him with a merry one
To find his mettle, good: and if he fly us,
Small matter! let him.' This her damsels heard,
And mindful of her small and cruel hand,
They, closing round him through the journey home,
Acted her hest, and always from her side
Restrained him with all manner of device,
So that he could not come to speech with her.
And when she gained her castle, upsprang the bridge,
200 Down rang the grate of iron through the groove,
And he was left alone in open field.

'These be the ways of ladies,' Pelleas thought,
'To those who love them, trials of our faith.
Yea, let her prove me to the uttermost,

For loyal to the uttermost am I.'
So made his moan; and, darkness falling, sought
A priory not far off, there lodged, but rose
With morning every day, and, moist or dry,
Full-armed upon his charger all day long
Sat by the walls, and no one opened to him.   210

And this persistence turned her scorn to wrath.
Then calling her three knights, she charged them,
     'Out!
And drive him from the walls.' And out they came,
But Pelleas overthrew them as they dashed
Against him one by one; and these returned,
But still he kept his watch beneath the wall.

Thereon her wrath became a hate; and once,
A week beyond, while walking on the walls
With her three knights, she pointed downward, 'Look,
He haunts me—I cannot breathe—besieges me;   220
Down! strike him! put my hate into your strokes,
And drive him from my walls.' And down they went,
And Pelleas overthrew them one by one;
And from the tower above him cried Ettarre,
'Bind him, and bring him in.'

                              He heard her voice;
Then let the strong hand, which had overthrown
Her minion-knights, by those he overthrew
Be bounden straight, and so they brought him in.

Then when he came before Ettarre, the sight
Of her rich beauty made him at one glance   230
More bondsman in his heart than in his bonds.
Yet with good cheer he spake, 'Behold me, Lady,
A prisoner, and the vassal of thy will;
And if thou keep me in thy donjon here,
Content am I so that I see thy face
But once a day: for I have sworn my vows,
And thou hast given thy promise, and I know
That all these pains are trials of my faith,
And that thyself, when thou hast seen me strained
And sifted to the utmost, wilt at length   240
Yield me thy love and know me for thy knight.'

Then she began to rail so bitterly,
With all her damsels, he was stricken mute;
But when she mocked his vows and the great King,
Lighted on words: 'For pity of thine own self,
Peace, Lady, peace: is he not thine and mine?'
'Thou fool,' she said, 'I never heard his voice
But longed to break away. Unbind him now,
And thrust him out of doors; for save he be
Fool to the midmost marrow of his bones,   250
He will return no more.' And those, her three,
Laughed, and unbound, and thrust him from the gate.

And after this, a week beyond, again
She called them, saying, 'There he watches yet,

There like a dog before his master's door!
Kicked, he returns: do ye not hate him, ye?
Ye know yourselves: how can ye bide at peace,
Affronted with his fulsome innocence?
Are ye but creatures of the board and bed,
260 No men to strike? Fall on him all at once,
And if ye slay him I reck not: if ye fail,
Give ye the slave mine order to be bound,
Bind him as heretofore, and bring him in:
It may be ye shall slay him in his bonds.'

She spake; and at her will they couched their spears,
Three against one: and Gawain passing by,
Bound upon solitary adventure, saw
Low down beneath the shadow of those towers
A villainy, three to one: and through his heart
270 The fire of honour and all noble deeds
Flashed, and he called, 'I strike upon thy side—
The caitiffs!' 'Nay,' said Pelleas, 'but forbear;
He needs no aid who doth his lady's will.'

So Gawain, looking at the villainy done,
Forbore, but in his heat and eagerness
Trembled and quivered, as the dog, withheld
A moment from the vermin that he sees
Before him, shivers, ere he springs and kills.

And Pelleas overthrew them, one to three;
280 And they rose up, and bound, and brought him in.
Then first her anger, leaving Pelleas, burned
Full on her knights in many an evil name
Of craven, weakling, and thrice-beaten hound:
'Yet, take him, ye that scarce are fit to touch,
Far less to bind, your victor, and thrust him out,
And let who will release him from his bonds.
And if he comes again'—there she brake short;
And Pelleas answered, 'Lady, for indeed
I loved you and I deemed you beautiful,
290 I cannot brook to see your beauty marred
Through evil spite: and if ye love me not,
I cannot bear to dream you so forsworn:
I had liefer ye were worthy of my love,
Than to be loved again of you—farewell;
And though ye kill my hope, not yet my love,
Vex not yourself: ye will not see me more.'

While thus he spake, she gazed upon the man
Of princely bearing, though in bonds, and thought,
'Why have I pushed him from me? this man loves,
300 If love there be: yet him I loved not. Why?
I deemed him fool? yea, so? or that in him
A something—was it nobler than myself?—
Seemed my reproach? He is not of my kind.
He could not love me, did he know me well.
Nay, let him go—and quickly.' And her knights
Laughed not, but thrust him bounden out of door.

Forth sprang Gawain, and loosed him from his
    bonds,

And flung them o'er the walls; and afterward,
Shaking his hands, as from a lazar's° rag,
'Faith of my body,' he said, 'and art thou not—   310
Yea thou art he, whom late our Arthur made
Knight of his table; yea and he that won
The circlet? wherefore hast thou so defamed
Thy brotherhood in me and all the rest,
As let these caitiffs on thee work their will?'

And Pelleas answered, 'O, their wills are hers
For whom I won the circlet; and mine, hers,
Thus to be bounden, so to see her face,
Marred though it be with spite and mockery now,
Other than when I found her in the woods;   320
And though she hath me bounden but in spite,
And all to flout me, when they bring me in,
Let me be bounden, I shall see her face;
Else must I die through mine unhappiness.'

And Gawain answered kindly though in scorn,
'Why, let my lady bind me if she will,
And let my lady beat me if she will:
But an she send her delegate to thrall
These fighting hands of mine—Christ kill me then
But I will slice him handless by the wrist,   330
And let my lady sear the stump for him,
Howl as he may. But hold me for your friend:
Come, ye know nothing: here I pledge my troth,
Yea, by the honour of the Table Round,
I will be leal to thee and work thy work,
And tame thy jailing princess to thine hand.
Lend me thine horse and arms, and I will say
That I have slain thee. She will let me in
To hear the manner of thy fight and fall;
Then, when I come within her counsels, then   340
From prime to vespers will I chant thy praise
As prowest knight and truest lover, more
Than any have sung thee living, till she long
To have thee back in lusty life again,
Not to be bound, save by white bonds and warm,
Dearer than freedom. Wherefore now thy horse
And armour: let me go: be comforted:
Give me three days to melt her fancy, and hope
The third night hence will bring thee news of gold.'

Then Pelleas lent his horse and all his arms,   350
Saving the goodly sword, his prize, and took
Gawain's, and said, 'Betray me not, but help—
Art thou not he whom men call light-of-love?'

'Ay,' said Gawain, 'for women be so light.'
Then bounded forward to the castle walls,
And raised a bugle hanging from his neck,
And winded it, and that so musically
That all the old echoes hidden in the wall
Rang out like hollow woods at hunting-tide.

309 **lazar**, leper

Up ran a score of damsels to the tower;
'Avaunt,' they cried, 'our lady loves thee not.'
But Gawain lifting up his vizor said,
'Gawain am I, Gawain of Arthur's court,
And I have slain this Pelleas whom ye hate:
Behold his horse and armour. Open gates,
And I will make you merry.'

               And down they ran,
Her damsels, crying to their lady, 'Lo!
Pelleas is dead—he told us—he that hath
His horse and armour: will ye let him in?
He slew him! Gawain, Gawain of the court,
Sir Gawain—there he waits below the wall,
Blowing his bugle as who should say him nay.'

    And so, leave given, straight on through open door
Rode Gawain, whom she greeted courteously.
'Dead, is it so?' she asked. 'Ay, ay,' said he,
'And oft in dying cried upon your name.'
'Pity on him,' she answered, 'a good knight,
But never let me bide one hour at peace.'
'Ay,' thought Gawain, 'and you be fair enow:
But I to your dead man have given my troth,
That whom ye loathe, him will I make you love.'

    So those three days, aimless about the land,
Lost in a doubt, Pelleas wandering
Waited, until the third night brought a moon
With promise of large light on woods and ways.

    Hot was the night and silent; but a sound
Of Gawain ever coming, and this lay—
Which Pelleas had heard sung before the Queen,
And seen her sadden listening—vext his heart,
And marred his rest—'A worm within the rose.'

    'A rose, but one, none other rose had I,
A rose, one rose, and this was wondrous fair,
One rose, a rose that gladdened earth and sky,
One rose, my rose, that sweetened all mine air—
I cared not for the thorns; the thorns were there.

    'One rose, a rose to gather by and by,
One rose, a rose, to gather and to wear,
No rose but one—what other rose had I?
One rose, my rose; a rose that will not die,—
He dies who loves it,—if the worm be there.'

    This tender rhyme, and evermore the doubt,
'Why lingers Gawain with his golden news?'
So shook him that he could not rest, but rode
Ere midnight to her walls, and bound his horse
Hard by the gates. Wide open were the gates,
And no watch kept; and in through these he past,
And heard but his own steps, and his own heart
Beating, for nothing moved but his own self,
And his own shadow. Then he crost the court,

And spied not any light in hall or bower,
But saw the postern portal also wide
Yawning; and up a slope of garden, all
Of roses white and red, and brambles mixt
And overgrowing them, went on, and found,
Here too, all hushed below the mellow moon,
Save that one rivulet from a tiny cave
Came lightening downward, and so spilt itself
Among the roses, and was lost again.

    Then was he ware of three pavilions reared
Above the bushes, gilden-peakt: in one,
Red after revel, droned her lurdane knights
Slumbering, and their three squires across their feet:
In one, their malice on the placid lip
Frozen by sweet sleep, four of her damsels lay:
And in the third, the circlet of the jousts
Bound on her brow, were Gawain and Ettarre.

    Back, as a hand that pushes through the leaf
To find a nest and feels a snake, he drew:
Back, as a coward slinks from what he fears
To cope with, or a traitor proven, or hound
Beaten, did Pelleas in an utter shame
Creep with his shadow through the court again,
Fingering at his sword-handle until he stood
There on the castle-bridge once more, and thought,
'I will go back, and slay them where they lie.'

    And so went back, and seeing them yet in sleep
Said, 'Ye, that so dishallow the holy sleep,
Your sleep is death,' and drew the sword, and thought,
'What! slay a sleeping knight? the King hath bound
And sworn me to this brotherhood;' again,
'Alas that ever a knight should be so false.'
Then turned, and so returned, and groaning laid
The naked sword athwart their naked throats,
There left it, and them sleeping; and she lay,
The circlet of the tourney round her brows,
And the sword of the tourney across her throat.

    And forth he past, and mounting on his horse
Stared at her towers that, larger than themselves
In their own darkness, thronged into the moon.
Then crushed the saddle with his thighs, and clenched
His hands, and maddened with himself and moaned:

    'Would they have risen against me in their blood
At the last day? I might have answered them
Even before high God. O towers so strong,
Huge, solid, would that even while I gaze
The crack of earthquake shivering to your base
Split you, and Hell burst up your harlot roofs
Bellowing, and charred you through and through
    within,
Black as the harlot's heart—hollow as a skull!
Let the fierce east scream through your eyelet-holes,
And whirl the dust of harlots round and round

In dung and nettles! hiss, snake—I saw him there—
Let the fox bark, let the wolf yell. Who yells
Here in the still sweet summer night, but I—
I, the poor Pelleas whom she called her fool?
Fool, beast—he, she, or I? myself most fool;
Beast too, as lacking human wit—disgraced,
Dishonoured all for trial of true love—
Love?—we be all alike: only the King
470 Hath made us fools and liars. O noble vows!
O great and sane and simple race of brutes
That own no lust because they have no law!
For why should I have loved her to my shame?
I loathe her, as I loved her to my shame.
I never loved her, I but lusted for her—
Away—'
      He dashed the rowel into his horse,
And bounded forth and vanished through the night.

Then she, that felt the cold touch on her throat,
Awaking knew the sword, and turned herself
480 To Gawain: 'Liar, for thou hast not slain
This Pelleas! here he stood, and might have slain
Me and thyself.' And he that tells the tale
Says that her ever-veering fancy turned
To Pelleas, as the one true knight on earth,
And only lover; and through her love her life
Wasted and pined, desiring him in vain.

But he by wild and way, for half the night,
And over hard and soft, striking the sod
From out the soft, the spark from off the hard,
490 Rode till the star above the wakening sun,
Beside that tower where Percivale was cowled,
Glanced from the rosy forehead of the dawn.
For so the words were flashed into his heart
He knew not whence or wherefore: 'O sweet star,
Pure on the virgin forehead of the dawn!'
And there he would have wept, but felt his eyes
Harder and drier than a fountain bed
In summer: thither came the village girls
And lingered talking, and they come no more
500 Till the sweet heavens have filled it from the heights
Again with living waters in the change
Of seasons: hard his eyes; harder his heart
Seemed; but so weary were his limbs, that he,
Gasping, 'Of Arthur's hall am I, but here,
Here let me rest and die,' cast himself down,
And gulfed his griefs in inmost sleep; so lay,
Till shaken by a dream, that Gawain fired
The hall of Merlin, and the morning star
Reeled in the smoke, brake into flame, and fell.

510 He woke, and being ware of some one nigh,
Sent hands upon him, as to tear him, crying,
'False! and I held thee pure as Guinevere.'

But Percivale stood near him and replied,
'Am I but false as Guinevere is pure?

Or art thou mazed with dreams? or being one
Of our free-spoken Table hast not heard
That Lancelot'—there he checked himself and paused.

Then fared it with Sir Pelleas as with one
Who gets a wound in battle, and the sword
That made it plunges through the wound again,   520
And pricks it deeper: and he shrank and wailed,
'Is the Queen false?' and Percivale was mute.
'Have any of our Round Table held their vows?'
And Percivale made answer not a word.
'Is the King true?' 'The King!' said Percivale.
'Why then let men couple at once with wolves.
What! art thou mad?'

      But Pelleas, leaping up,
Ran through the doors and vaulted on his horse
And fled: small pity upon his horse had he,
Or on himself, or any, and when he met   530
A cripple, one that held a hand for alms—
Hunched as he was, and like an old dwarf-elm
That turns its back on the salt blast, the boy
Paused not, but overrode him, shouting, 'False,
And false with Gawain!' and so left him bruised
And battered, and fled on, and hill and wood
Went ever streaming by him till the gloom,
That follows on the turning of the world,
Darkened the common path: he twitched the reins,
And made his beast that better knew it, swerve   540
Now off it and now on; but when he saw
High up in heaven the hall that Merlin built,
Blackening against the dead-green stripes of even,
'Black nest of rats,' he groaned, 'ye build too high.'

Not long thereafter from the city gates
Issued Sir Lancelot riding airily,
Warm with a gracious parting from the Queen,
Peace at his heart, and gazing at a star
And marvelling what it was: on whom the boy,
Across the silent seeded meadow-grass   550
Borne, clashed: and Lancelot, saying, 'What name
    hast thou
That ridest here so blindly and so hard?'
'No name, no name,' he shouted, 'a scourge am I
To lash the treasons of the Table Round.'
'Yea, but thy name?' 'I have many names,' he cried:
'I am wrath and shame and hate and evil fame,
And like a poisonous wind I pass to blast
And blaze the crime of Lancelot and the Queen.'
'First over me,' said Lancelot, 'shalt thou pass.'
'Fight therefore,' yelled the youth, and either knight 560
Drew back a space, and when they closed, at once
The weary steed of Pelleas floundering flung
His rider, who called out from the dark field,
'Thou art false as Hell: slay me: I have no sword.'
Then Lancelot, 'Yea, between thy lips—and sharp;
But here will I disedge it by thy death.'
'Slay then,' he shrieked, 'my will is to be slain,'

And Lancelot, with his heel upon the fallen,
Rolling his eyes, a moment stood, then spake:
570 'Rise, weakling; I am Lancelot; say thy say.'

And Lancelot slowly rode his warhorse back
To Camelot, and Sir Pelleas in brief while
Caught his unbroken limbs from the dark field,
And followed to the city. It chanced that both
Brake into hall together, worn and pale.
There with her knights and dames was Guinevere.
Full wonderingly she gazed on Lancelot
So soon returned, and then on Pelleas, him
Who had not greeted her, but cast himself
580 Down on a bench, hard-breathing. 'Have ye fought?'
She asked of Lancelot. 'Ay, my Queen,' he said.
'And thou hast overthrown him?' 'Ay, my Queen.'
Then she, turning to Pelleas, 'O young knight,
Hath the great heart of knighthood in thee failed
So far thou canst not bide, unfrowardly,
A fall from *him*?' Then, for he answered not,
'Or hast thou other griefs? If I, the Queen,
May help them, loose thy tongue, and let me know.'
But Pelleas lifted up an eye so fierce
590 She quailed; and he, hissing 'I have no sword,'
Sprang from the door into the dark. The Queen
Looked hard upon her lover, he on her;
And each foresaw the dolorous day to be:
And all talk died, as in a grove all song
Beneath the shadow of some bird of prey;
Then a long silence came upon the hall,
And Modred thought, 'The time is hard at hand.'

CROSSING THE BAR

Sunset and evening star,
　And one clear call for me!
And may there be no moaning of the bar,
　When I put out to sea,

5 But such a tide as moving seems asleep,
　Too full for sound and foam,
When that which drew from out the boundless deep
　Turns again home.

Twilight and evening bell,
10 　And after that the dark!
And may there be no sadness of farewell,
　When I embark;

For though from out our bourne of Time and Place
　The flood may bear me far,
15 I hope to see my Pilot face to face
　When I have crossed the bar.
(1889)

ROBERT BROWNING
1812–1889

Browning was born in 1812 in Camberwell, near London, the son of a wealthy clerk in the Bank of England. Although he was sent to a boarding school for a while and was briefly enrolled at the University of London, his formal schooling was slight. Instead, he received a very broad but unsystematic education at home. His father taught him Latin and Greek and put his large and varied library at his son's disposal. His mother, a devout Congregationalist, attended to his religious education. As a youth, Browning especially enjoyed reading drama and history. After reading a volume of Shelley's lyrics in 1826, Browning decided that he wanted to become a poet. Aside from brief visits to Russia and Italy, Browning lived with his parents in London until 1846.

Browning's first published poem, *Pauline: A Fragment of a Confession* (1833), received some favorable reviews. But Browning was especially sensitive to John Stuart Mill's criticism of the work as "intense and morbid self-consciousness." Because of this criticism, Browning resolved to be less personal and intimate in his later work; he actively strove to be impersonal and objective. Browning next wrote *Paracelsus* (1835), which was the first of his poems to exhibit his passionate love of the Renaissance and its ideals of art and life. His next venture, a theatrical production called *Strafford* (1836), ran for only five nights. Between 1841 and 1846 Browning published seven more plays (in a series of pamphlets with the general title *Bells and Pomegranates*), but they met with little success. In 1840 he published *Sordello*, a long poem on the life of an Italian poet, which received very negative reviews; most critics found it "incomprehensible." Also published among the plays in *Bells and Pomegranates* were many fine poems, including "My Last Duchess," one of Browning's first and most successful ventures in the form for which he was to become famous—the dramatic monologue.

In 1845 Browning met Elizabeth Barrett, who had earlier praised him in one of her own poems. The most famous exchange of love letters of the nineteenth century ensued, and within a year they were secretly married. Though considered an invalid and a recluse, Elizabeth Barrett had managed to become a very popular Victorian poet; she was considerably more famous than Browning at the time of their marriage. For most of their married life, the Brownings made their home in Italy, at Casa Guidi in Florence; because she was not well, Mrs. Browning's doctors felt that the milder Italian climate would be good for her. Though their steady income (in the form of family allowances) was initially rather small, the two lived a comfortable life. During his married life, Browning wrote *Christmas*

Eve and Easter Day (1850), a long poem in which he works out his religious position against the alternatives of his time, and his greatest volume, *Men and Women* (1855), a collection of fifty-one of what are today considered his best and most typical poems. But at the time of publication, *Men and Women* received generally unfavorable notices. Mrs. Browning's health, never good, finally failed; she died in 1861. Browning immediately left Italy for London with his young son.

Upon returning to England, Browning prepared his wife's *Last Poems* for publication. In 1864 he published *Dramatis Personae*, which included "Rabbi Ben Ezra" and "Caliban upon Setebos." This volume was well received; Browning at last began to win a measure of public recognition. During the years 1868 and 1869, *The Ring and the Book* appeared in four installments. Browning based this work on a seventeenth-century murder case in Rome involving an aristocratic husband who brutally murdered his young wife. This long poem is organized as a series of dramatic monologues on different points of view toward the murder case. The enthusiastic public reception of *The Ring and the Book* established his reputation as one of the most important literary figures of his day. Thereafter he became quite a social figure, frequently sought after by the rich and famous. He spent his summers on the Continent, especially in Italy.

After 1869 he published six long poems and several volumes of shorter pieces, none of which are as attractive to modern readers as the works of his middle years. While visiting Venice in 1889, Browning became seriously ill and died soon after hearing of the favorable prepublication reception of his last collection of poems, *Asolando*. He was buried in Westminster Abbey.

Robert Browning did more to transmute the dominant tradition of English poetry than did any other major poet of his century. In his diction, formal structures, and assumptions about poetry, he has more in common with John Donne, T. S. Eliot, and Ezra Pound than with Spenser, Milton, Keats, and Tennyson: he abandoned the "sweet and lovely language" of the past. Browning also adopted the "technique of indirection," which has been so popular with twentieth-century poets. He explained and defended this technique at the end of *The Ring and the Book*:

. . . it is the glory and good of Art,
That Art remains the one way possible
Of speaking truth, to mouths like mine at least.

. . . Art may tell a truth
Obliquely, do the thing shall breed the thought,
Nor wrong the thought, missing the mediate
    word.
So may you paint your picture, twice show truth,
Beyond mere imagery on the wall,—. . .
So write a book shall mean beyond the facts.

His principal formal device for achieving indirection was the dramatic monologue, in which he tried to show "Action in Character, rather than Character in Action" and through which he could stress "incidents in the development of a human soul." Further, Browning was one of the most erudite of English poets, though his erudition was idiosyncratic because he was self-educated. His vast knowledge contributed to his poetry a quality of surprise and intellectual challenge.

Browning frequently used the grotesque in his poetry. The literary meaning of the term has been succinctly described as follows: "Its proper province would seem to be the exhibition of fanciful power by the artist; not beauty or truth in the literal sense at all, but inventive affluence of unreal yet absurdly comic forms, with just a flavour of the terrible added, to give a grim dignity, and save from the triviality of caricature." It is clear from Browning's use of the word in his own poetry that he was aware of the specific meaning of the term and deliberately worked for grotesque effect. "Caliban upon Setebos" is one of the best examples of Browning's use of the grotesque.

PORPHYRIA'S LOVER

The rain set early in tonight,
    The sullen wind was soon awake,
It tore the elm-tops down for spite,
    And did its worst to vex the lake:
    I listened with heart fit to break.
When glided in Porphyria; straight
    She shut the cold out and the storm,
And kneeled and made the cheerless grate
    Blaze up, and all the cottage warm;
    Which done, she rose, and from her form   10
Withdrew the dripping cloak and shawl,
    And laid her soiled gloves by, untied
Her hat and let the damp hair fall,
    And, last, she sat down by my side
    And called me. When no voice replied,
She put my arm about her waist,
    And made her smooth white shoulder bare,
And all her yellow hair displaced,
    And, stooping, made my cheek lie there,
    And spread, o'er all, her yellow hair,   20
Murmuring how she loved me—she
    Too weak, for all her heart's endeavor,
To set its struggling passion free
    From pride, and vainer ties dissever,
    And give herself to me forever.
But passion sometimes would prevail,
    Nor could tonight's gay feast restrain
A sudden thought of one so pale
    For love of her, and all in vain:

So, she was come through wind and rain.
   Be sure I looked up at her eyes
     Happy and proud; at last I knew
   Porphyria worshiped me: surprise
     Made my heart swell, and still it grew
     While I debated what to do.
   That moment she was mine, mine, fair,
     Perfectly pure and good: I found
   A thing to do, and all her hair
     In one long yellow string I wound
40   Three times her little throat around,
   And strangled her. No pain felt she;
     I am quite sure she felt no pain.
   As a shut bud that holds a bee,
     I warily oped her lids: again
     Laughed the blue eyes without a stain.
   And I untightened next the tress
     About her neck; her cheek once more
   Blushed bright beneath my burning kiss:
     I propped her head up as before,
50   Only, this time my shoulder bore
   Her head, which droops upon it still:
     The smiling rosy little head,
   So glad it has its utmost will,
     That all it scorned at once is fled,
     And I, its love, am gained instead!
   Porphyria's love: she guessed not how
     Her darling one wish would be heard.
   And thus we sit together now,
     And all night long we have not stirred,
60   And yet God has not said a word!
   (1834; 1836)

SOLILOQUY OF THE SPANISH CLOISTER

1

Gr-r-r—there go, my heart's abhorrence!
   Water your damned flowerpots, do!
If hate killed men, Brother Lawrence,
   God's blood,° would not mine kill you!
What? your myrtle bush wants trimming?
   Oh, that rose has prior claims—
Needs its leaden vase filled brimming?
   Hell dry you up with its flames!

2

At the meal we sit together:
10   *Salve tibi!*° I must hear
Wise talk of the kind of weather,
   Sort of season, time of year:
Not a plenteous cork crop: scarcely
   Dare we hope oak-galls,° *I doubt:*
What's the Latin name for "parsley"?
   What's the Greek name for Swine's Snout?

3

Whew! We'll have our platter burnished,
   Laid with care on our own shelf!
With a fire-new spoon we're furnished,
   And a goblet for ourself,   20
Rinsed like something sacrificial
   Ere 'tis fit to touch our chaps—
Marked with L. for our initial!
   (He-he! There his lily snaps!)

4

Saint, forsooth! While brown Dolores
   Squats outside the Convent bank
With Sanchicha, telling stories,
   Steeping tresses in the tank,
Blue-black, lustrous, thick like horsehairs,
   —Can't I see his dead eye glow,   30
Bright as 'twere a Barbary corsair's?°
   (That is, if he'd let it show!)

5

When he finishes refection,°
   Knife and fork he never lays
Cross-wise, to my recollection,
   As do I, in Jesu's praise.
I the Trinity illustrate,
   Drinking watered orange pulp—
In three sips the Arian° frustrate;
   While he drains his at one gulp.   40

6

Oh, those melons? If he's able
   We're to have a feast! so nice!
One goes to the Abbot's table,
   All of us get each a slice.
How go on your flowers? None double?
   Not one fruit-sort can you spy?
Strange!—And I, too, at such trouble,
   Keep them close-nipped on the sly!

7

There's a great text in Galatians,°
   Once you trip on it, entails   50
Twenty-nine distinct damnations,
   One sure, if another fails:
If I trip him just a-dying,
   Sure of heaven as sure can be,
Spin him round and send him flying
   Off to hell, a Manichee?°

8

Or, my scrofulous French novel
   On gray paper with blunt type!

31 **corsair,** fierce, lecherous pirate. The speaker is, of course, accusing Lawrence of his own perverseness, as l. 29 proves   33 **refection,** meal   39 **Arian,** heretic who denied the doctrine of the Trinity, three persons in one God   49 **Galatians.** *Galatians,* 5:19–21, enumerates "works of the flesh," which may or may not number twenty-nine. Browning may have taken a slight liberty for purposes of rhythm and rhyme   56 **Manichee,** heretic who posed an eternal warfare between the powers of light (the soul) and darkness (the body)

Soliloquy of the Spanish Cloister   4 **God's blood,** by the blood of Christ, an especially blasphemous oath   10 **Salve tibi,** hail to you   14 **oak-galls,** form of tree fungus

Simply glance at it, you grovel
60   Hand and foot in Belial's° gripe:
If I double down its pages
  At the woeful sixteenth print,
When he gathers his greengages,
  Ope a sieve and slip it in't?

9

Or, there's Satan!—one might venture
  Pledge one's soul° to him, yet leave
Such a flaw in the indenture
  As he'd miss till, past retrieve,
Blasted lay that rose-acacia
70   We're so proud of! *Hy, Zy, Hine*° . . .
'St, there's Vespers! *Plena gratiá*
  Ave, Virgo!° Gr-r-r—you swine!
(1842)

MY LAST DUCHESS

That's my last Duchess painted on the wall,
Looking as if she were alive. I call
That piece a wonder, now; Frà Pandolf's° hands
Worked busily a day, and there she stands.
Will 't please you sit and look at her? I said
"Frà Pandolf" by design, for never read
Strangers like you that pictured countenance,
The depth and passion of its earnest glance,
But to myself they turned (since none puts by
10 The curtain I have drawn for you, but I)
And seemed as they would ask me, if they durst,
How such a glance came there; so, not the first
Are you to turn and ask thus. Sir, 'twas not
Her husband's presence only, called that spot
Of joy into the Duchess' cheek; perhaps
Fra Pandolf chanced to say, "Her mantle laps
Over my lady's wrist too much," or "Paint
Must never hope to reproduce the faint
Half-flush that dies along her throat." Such stuff
20 Was courtesy, she thought, and cause enough
For calling up that spot of joy. She had
A heart—how shall I say?—too soon made glad,
Too easily impressed; she liked whate'er
She looked on, and her looks went everywhere.
Sir, 'twas all one!° My favor at her breast,
The dropping of the daylight in the West,
The bough of cherries some officious fool
Broke in the orchard for her, the white mule
She rode with round the terrace—all and each
30 Would draw from her alike the approving speech,
Or blush, at least. She thanked men—good! but
    thanked

Somehow—I know not how—as if she ranked
My gift of a nine-hundred-years-old name
With anybody's gift. Who'd stoop to blame
This sort of trifling? Even had you skill
In speech—which I have not—to make your will
Quite clear to such an one, and say, "Just this
Or that in you disgusts me; here you miss,
Or there exceed the mark"—and if she let
Herself be lessoned so, nor plainly set   40
Her wits to yours, forsooth, and made excuse—
E'en then would be some stooping; and I choose
Never to stoop. Oh, sir, she smiled, no doubt,
Whene'er I passed her; but who passed without
Much the same smile? This grew; I gave commands;
Then all smiles stopped together.° There she stands
As if alive. Will 't please you rise? We'll meet
The company below, then. I repeat,
The Count your master's known munificence
Is ample warrant that no just pretense   50
Of mine for dowry will be disallowed;
Though his fair daughter's self, as I avowed
At starting, is my object. Nay, we'll go
Together down, sir. Notice Neptune, though,
Taming a sea-horse, thought a rarity,
Which Claus of Innsbruck° cast in bronze for me!
(1842)

THE LOST LEADER

Just for a handful of silver he left us,
  Just for a riband to stick in his coat—
Found the one gift of which fortune bereft us,
  Lost all the others she lets us devote;
They, with the gold to give, doled him out silver,
  So much was theirs who so little allowed;
How all our copper had gone for his service!
  Rags—were they purple, his heart had been proud!

We that had loved him so, followed him, honored him,
  Lived in his mild and magnificent eye,   10
Learned his great language, caught his clear accents,
  Made him our pattern to live and to die!
Shakespeare was of us, Milton was for us,
  Burns, Shelley, were with us—they watch from
    their graves!
He alone breaks from the van and the freemen—
  He alone sinks to the rear and the slaves!

We shall march prospering—not through his presence;
  Songs may inspirit us—not from his lyre;
Deeds will be done—while he boasts his quiescence,
  Still bidding crouch whom the rest bade aspire;   20
Blot out his name, then, record one lost soul more,
  One task more declined, one more footpath untrod,

60 **Belial,** Satan   66 **Pledge one's soul,** etc. The speaker would dupe the devil to discomfort or destroy Lawrence   70 **Hy, Zy, Hine,** frequently interpreted as the sound of vesper bells   71 **Plena gratia, . . . Virgo!** Hail, Virgin, full of grace   **My Last Duchess**   3 **Frà Pandolf,** or Brother Pandolf, an imaginary painter   25–31 **Sir, 'twas,** etc. Browning's explanation of these lines was the following: "An excuse—mainly to himself—for taking revenge on one who had unwittingly wounded his absurdly pretentious vanity, by failing to recognize his superiority in even the most trifling matters"

45–46 **I gave . . . together.** Browning explained this cryptic passage as meaning that he had her put to death or shut up in a convent   56 **Claus of Innsbruck,** an unidentified craftsman from the Count of Tyrol's capital

One more devils'-triumph and sorrow for angels,
  One wrong more to man, one more insult to God!
Life's night begins; let him never come back to us!
  There would be doubt, hesitation, and pain,
Forced praise on our part—the glimmer of twilight,
  Never glad confident morning again!
Best fight on well, for we taught him—strike gallantly,
30 Menace our heart ere we master his own;
Then let him receive the new knowledge and wait us,
  Pardoned in heaven, the first by the throne!
(1845)

MEETING AT NIGHT

The gray sea and the long black land;
And the yellow half-moon large and low;
And the startled little waves that leap
In fiery ringlets from their sleep,
5 As I gain the cove with pushing prow,
And quench its speed i' the slushy sand.

Then a mile of warm sea-scented beach;
Three fields to cross till a farm appears;
A tap at the pane, the quick sharp scratch
10 And blue spurt of a lighted match,
And a voice less loud, through its joys and fears,
Than the two hearts beating each to each!
(1845)

PARTING AT MORNING

Round the cape of a sudden came the sea,
And the sun looked over the mountain's rim:
And straight was a path of gold for him,
And the need of a world of men for me.
(1845)

HOME-THOUGHTS, FROM ABROAD

Oh, to be in England
Now that April's there,
And whoever wakes in England
Sees, some morning, unaware,
That the lowest boughs and the brushwood sheaf
Round the elm-tree bole are in tiny leaf,
While the chaffinch sings on the orchard bough
In England—now!

And after April, when May follows,
10 And the whitethroat builds, and all the swallows!
Hark, where my blossomed pear-tree in the hedge
Leans to the field and scatters on the clover
Blossoms and dewdrops—at the bent spray's edge—
That's the wise thrush; he sings each song twice over,
Lest you should think he never could recapture

The first fine careless rapture!
And though the fields look rough with hoary dew,
All will be gay when noontide wakes anew
The buttercups, the little children's dower—
Far brighter than this gaudy melon-flower! 20
(1845)

HOME-THOUGHTS, FROM THE SEA

Nobly, nobly Cape Saint Vincent° to the Northwest
  died away;
Sunset ran, one glorious blood-red, reeking into Cadiz
  Bay;°
Bluish 'mid the burning water, full in face Trafalgar°
  lay;
In the dimmest northeast distance dawned Gibraltar°
  grand and gray;
"Here and here did England help me; how can I help 5
  England?"—say,
Whoso turns as I, this evening, turn to God to praise
  and pray,
While Jove's planet° rises yonder, silent over Africa.
(1845)

THE BISHOP ORDERS HIS TOMB AT SAINT PRAXED'S CHURCH°

ROME, 15—

Vanity,° saith the preacher, vanity!
Draw round my bed; is Anselm keeping back?
Nephews—sons mine . . . ah, God, I know not!
  Well—
She, men would have to be your mother once,
Old Gandolf° envied me, so fair she was!
What's done is done, and she is dead beside,
Dead long ago, and I am Bishop since,
And as she died so must we die ourselves,
And thence ye may perceive the world's a dream.
Life, how and what is it? As here I lie 10
In this state-chamber, dying by degrees,
Hours and long hours in the dead night, I ask,
"Do I live, am I dead?" Peace, peace seems all.
Saint Praxed's ever was the church for peace;
And so, about this tomb of mine. I fought
With tooth and nail to save my niche, ye know—
Old Gandolf cozened me, despite my care;

Home-Thoughts, from the Sea 1 **Cape Saint Vincent,** the southwestern point of Portugal, near which England won a naval victory over Spain in 1797 2 **Cadiz Bay,** on the southern coast of Spain, east of Cape St. Vincent, where an English fleet destroyed the second Spanish Armada in 1596 3 **Trafalgar,** a cape east of Cadiz Bay, off which Lord Nelson won his greatest victory over the French and Spanish fleets in 1805 4 **Gibraltar,** the famous British stronghold at the entrance to the Mediterranean. It was acquired from Spain by the Peace of Utrecht in 1713 7 **Jove's planet,** Jupiter
The Bishop Orders His Tomb. The church is named after the virgin St. Praxed, or Praxedes, a Christian saint of the first century. Both the bishop and the tomb are imaginary 1 **Vanity, etc.,** from *Ecclesiastes,* 1:2: "Vanity of vanities, saith the Preacher, vanity of vanities; all is vanity" 5 **Gandolf,** the Bishop's predecessor and rival

Shrewd was that snatch from out the corner South
He graced his carrion with, God curse the same!
20 Yet still my niche is not so cramped but thence
One sees the pulpit o' the epistle-side,°
And somewhat of the choir, those silent seats,
And up into the aëry dome where live
The angels, and a sunbeam's sure to lurk;
And I shall fill my slab of basalt° there,
And 'neath my tabernacle° take my rest,
With those nine columns round me, two and two,
The odd one at my feet where Anselm stands:
Peach-blossom marble° all, the rare, the ripe
30 As fresh-poured red wine of a mighty pulse.°
—Old Gandolf with his paltry onion-stone,°
Put me where I may look at him! True peach,
Rosy and flawless; how I earned the prize!
Draw close; that conflagration of my church—
What then? So much was saved if aught were missed!
My sons, ye would not be my death? Go dig
The white-grape vineyard where the oil-press stood,
Drop water gently till the surface sink,
And if ye find . . . Ah, God, I know not, I! . . .
40 Bedded in store of rotten fig-leaves soft,
And corded up in a tight olive-frail,°
Some lump, ah, God, of *lapis lazuli*,°
Big as a Jew's head cut off at the nape,
Blue as a vein o'er the Madonna's breast . . .
Sons, all have I bequeathed you, villas, all,
That brave Frascati° villa with its bath,
So, let the blue lump poise between my knees,
Like God the Father's globe on both his hands
Ye worship in the Jesu Church° so gay,
50 For Gandolf shall not choose but see and burst!
Swift as a weaver's shuttle fleet our years;°
Man goeth to the grave, and where is he?
Did I say basalt for my slab, sons? Black—
'Twas ever antique-black° I meant! How else
Shall ye contrast my frieze to come beneath?
The bas-relief in bronze ye promised me,
Those Pans° and Nymphs ye wot of, and perchance
Some tripod,° thyrsus,° with a vase or so,
The Savior at his sermon on the mount,°
60 Saint Praxed in a glory, and one Pan
Ready to twitch the Nymph's last garment off,
And Moses with the tables° . . . but I know
Ye mark me not! What do they whisper thee,
Child of my bowels, Anselm? Ah, ye hope
To revel down my villas while I gasp

Bricked o'er with beggar's moldy travertine°
Which Gandolf from his tomb-top chuckles at!
Nay, boys, ye love me—all of jasper,° then!
'Tis jasper ye stand pledged to, lest I grieve.
My bath must needs be left behind, alas! 70
One block, pure green as a pistachio-nut,
There's plenty jasper somewhere in the world—
And have I not Saint Praxed's ear to pray
Horses for ye, and brown° Greek manuscripts,
And mistresses with great smooth marbly limbs?
—That's if ye carve my epitaph aright
Choice Latin, picked phrase, Tully's every word,°
No gaudy ware like Gandolf's second line—
Tully, my masters? Ulpian° serves his need!
And then how I shall lie through centuries, 80
And hear the blessed mutter of the Mass,
And see God made and eaten all day long,°
And feel the steady candle-flame, and taste
Good strong thick stupefying incense-smoke!
For as I lie here, hours of the dead night,
Dying in state and by such slow degrees,
I fold my arms as if they clasped a crook,°
And stretch my feet forth straight as stone can point,
And let the bedclothes, for a mortcloth,° drop
Into great laps and folds of sculptor's work; 90
And as yon tapers dwindle, and strange thoughts
Grow, with a certain humming in my ears
About the life before I lived this life,
And this life too, popes, cardinals, and priests,
Saint Praxed at his° sermon on the mount,
Your tall pale mother with her talking eyes,
And new-found agate urns as fresh as day,
And marble's language, Latin pure, discreet—
Aha, ELUCESCEBAT° quoth our friend?
No Tully, said I, Ulpian at the best! 100
Evil and brief hath been my pilgrimage.
All *lapis*, all, sons! Else I give the Pope
My villas! Will ye ever eat my heart?
Ever your eyes were as a lizard's quick,
They glitter like your mother's for my soul,
Or ye would heighten my impoverished frieze,
Piece out its starved design, and fill my vase
With grapes, and add a visor° and a term,°
And to the tripod ye would tie a lynx
That in his struggle throws the thyrsus down. 110
To comfort me on my entablature
Whereon I am to lie till I must ask,
"Do I live, am I dead?" There, leave me, there!
For ye have stabbed me with ingratitude
To death—ye wish it—God, ye wish it! Stone—
Gritstone, a-crumble! Clammy squares which sweat
As if the corpse they keep were oozing through—

21 **the epistle-side,** the side of an altar from which the Epistle is read; the right-hand side as one faces the altar. The left is the gospel-side   25 **basalt,** hard rock of dark color   26 **tabernacle,** protecting canopy   29 **Peach-blossom marble,** exceptionally fire marble of a pinkish hue   30 **of . . . pulse,** of great strength   31 **onion-stone,** inferior greenish marble that easily splits into thin layers like those of the onion   41 **olive-frail,** basket for holding olives   42 **lapis lazuli,** valuable blue stone, stolen by the Bishop from his own church   46 **Frascati,** wealthy resort near Rome   49 **Jesu Church,** Il Gesu, the church of the Jesuits in Rome; it contains an image of God holding a globe made of lapis lazuli   51 **Swift . . . years,** from *Job*, 7:6: "My days are swifter than a weaver's shuttle, and are spent without hope"   54 **antique-black,** Nero-antico, a beautiful black marble   57 **Pans.** Pan was the god of flocks and pastures. The bas-relief was to contain a curious mixture of pagan and Christian symbols   58 **tripod,** the three-legged stool on which the priestess of Apollo sat when giving responses to persons consulting the oracle at Delphi   **thyrsus,** the staff used by followers of Bacchus, god of wine   59 **sermon on the mount,** found in *Matthew*, 5–7   62 **Moses . . . tables.** The account is found in *Exodus*, 24–34

66 **travertine,** white limestone   68 **jasper,** smooth dark-green stone   74 **brown,** brown with age   77 **Tully's . . . word,** in the style of Cicero (106–43 B.C.), i.e., the purest classic Latin   79 **Ulpian,** noted Roman jurist (170–229), whose Latin style was inferior to that of Cicero   82 **God . . . long,** in the sacrament of the Eucharist   87 **crook,** crozier, the pastoral staff of a bishop; it is the symbol of his office as shepherd of the flock   89 **mortcloth,** funeral pall   95 **his.** The Bishop's mind is confused; St. Praxed was a woman   99 **elucescebat,** he was famous. The Bishop hates the form of the word, the classic form being *elucebat*   108 **visor,** mask   **term,** combined bust and pedestal

And no more *lapis* to delight the world!
Well, go! I bless ye. Fewer tapers there,
120 But in a row; and, going, turn your backs—
Aye, like departing altar-ministrants,
And leave me in my church, the church for peace,
That I may watch at leisure if he leers—
Old Gandolf—at me, from his onion-stone,
As still he envied me, so fair she was!
(1845)

RABBI BEN EZRA°

Grow old along with me!
The best is yet to be,
The last of life, for which the first was made.
Our times are in his hand
Who saith, "A whole I planned;
Youth shows but half. Trust God; see all, nor be
    afraid!"

Not that,° amassing flowers,
Youth sighed, "Which rose make ours,
Which lily leave and then as best recall?"
10 Not that, admiring stars,
It yearned, "Nor Jove, nor Mars;
Mine be some figured flame which blends, transcends
    them all!"

Not for such hopes and fears
Annulling youth's brief years,
Do I remonstrate—folly wide the mark!
Rather I prize the doubt
Low kinds exist without,
Finished the finite clods, untroubled by a spark.

Poor vaunt of life indeed,
20 Were man but formed to feed
On joy, to solely seek and find and feast.
Such feasting ended, then
As sure an end to men;
Irks care the crop-full bird?° Frets doubt the maw-
    crammed beast?

Rejoice we are allied
To that which doth provide
And not partake, effect and not receive!
A spark disturbs our clod;
Nearer we hold of God
30 Who gives, than of his tribes that take, I must believe.

Then, welcome each rebuff
That turns earth's smoothness rough,
Each sting that bids nor sit nor stand but go!

Rabbi Ben Ezra. Rabbi Abraham Ibn Ezra was a distinguished Jewish philosopher, physician, astronomer, and poet of the twelfth century. Browning is said to have been faithful to the Rabbi's own writing, but it is also true that the poem provides a clear exposition of Browning's own philosophy of life   **7 Not that.** *Not that* of ll. 7 and 10 and *Not for* of l. 13 go with *Do I remonstrate* of l. 15   **24 Irks . . . bird.** Does care irk the crop-full bird?

Be our joys three parts pain!
Strive, and hold cheap the strain;
Learn, nor account the pang; dare, never grudge the
    throe!

For thence—a paradox
Which comforts while it mocks—
Shall life succeed in that it seems to fail:
What I aspired to be,   40
And was not, comforts me;°
A brute I might have been, but would not sink i' the
    scale.

What is he but a brute
Whose flesh has soul to suit,
Whose spirit works lest arms and legs want play?
To man, propose this test—
Thy body at its best,
How far can that project thy soul on its lone way?

Yet gifts should prove their use:
I own the Past profuse   50
Of power each side, perfection every turn;
Eyes, ears took in their dole,
Brain treasured up the whole;
Should not the heart beat once, "How good to live and
    learn"?

Not once beat, "Praise be thine!
I see the whole design,
I, who saw power, see now Love perfect too;
Perfect I call thy plan.
Thanks that I was a man!
Maker, remake, complete—I trust what thou shalt   60
    do!"

For pleasant° is this flesh;
Our soul, in its rose-mesh
Pulled ever to the earth, still yearns for rest.
Would we some prize might hold
To match those manifold
Possessions of the brute—gain most, as we did best!

Let us not always say,
"Spite of this flesh today
I strove, made head, gained ground upon the whole!"
As the bird wings and sings,   70
Let us cry, "All good things
Are ours, nor soul helps flesh more, now, than flesh
    helps soul!"

Therefore I summon age
To grant youth's heritage,
Life's struggle having so far reached its term.
Thence shall I pass, approved

40–41 What . . . me. Cf. *Andrea del Sarto*, ll. 97–98   **61–72 For pleasant, etc.** Cf. *Fra Lippo Lippi*, ll. 205–214

A man, for aye removed
From the developed brute—a god, though in the germ.

And I shall thereupon
80 Take rest, ere I be gone
Once more on my adventure brave and new;°
Fearless and unperplexed,
When I wage battle next,
What weapons to select, what armor to indue.°

Youth ended, I shall try
My gain or loss thereby;
Leave the fire ashes,° what survives is gold.
And I shall weigh the same,
Give life its praise or blame.
90 Young, all lay in dispute; I shall know, being old.

For note, when evening shuts,
A certain moment cuts
The deed off, calls the glory from the gray;
A whisper from the west
Shoots—"Add this to the rest,
Take it and try its worth. Here dies another day."

So, still within this life,
Though lifted o'er its strife,
Let me discern, compare, pronounce at last,
100 "This rage was right i' the main,
That acquiescence vain;
The Future I may face, now I have proved the Past."

For more is not reserved
To man, with soul just nerved
To act tomorrow what he learns today;
Here, work enough to watch
The Master work, and catch
Hints of the proper craft, tricks of the tool's true play.

As it was better, youth
110 Should strive, through acts uncouth,
Toward making, than repose on aught found made;
So, better, age, exempt
From strife, should know, than tempt
Further. Thou waitedst age; wait death nor be afraid!

Enough now, if the Right
And Good and Infinite
Be named here, as thou callest thy hand thine own,
With knowledge absolute,
Subject to no dispute
120 From fools that crowded youth, nor let thee feel alone.

Be there, for once and all,
Severed great minds from small,
Announced to each his station in the Past!

Was I,° the world arraigned,
Were they, my soul disdained,
Right? Let age speak the truth and give us peace at
    last!

Now, who shall arbitrate?
Ten men love what I hate,
Shun what I follow, slight what I receive;
Ten, who in ears and eyes   130
Match me. We all surmise,
They this thing, and I that; whom shall my soul
    believe?

Not on the vulgar mass
Called "work," must sentence pass—
Things done, that took the eye and had the price;
O'er which, from level stand,
The low world laid its hand,
Found straightway to its mind, could value in a trice:

But all, the world's coarse thumb
And finger failed to plumb,   140
So passed in making up the main account;
All instincts immature,
All purposes unsure,
That weighed not as his work, yet swelled the man's
    amount:

Thoughts hardly to be packed
Into a narrow act,
Fancies that broke through language and escaped;
All I could never be,
All, men ignored in me,
This, I was worth to God, whose wheel the pitcher   150
    shaped.

Aye, note that Potter's wheel,°
That metaphor! and feel
Why time spins fast, why passive lies our clay—
Thou, to whom fools propound,
When the wine makes its round,
"Since life fleets, all is change; the Past gone, seize
    today!"

Fool! All that is, at all,
Lasts ever, past recall;
Earth changes, but thy soul and God stand sure.
What entered into thee,   160
That was, is, and shall be.
Time's wheel runs back or stops; Potter and clay
    endure.

He fixed thee 'mid this dance
Of plastic circumstance,
This Present, thou, forsooth, would fain arrest—

---

81 **adventure . . new,** the life of an old person after the passions and problems
of youth are left behind   84 **to indue,** to put on   87 **Leave . . . ashes,** if the fire
leaves ashes

124 **Was I.** Supply *whom* after *I* and also after *they,* l. 125   151 **Potter's wheel.**
Cf. *Isaiah,* 64:8: "But now, O Lord, thou art our father; we are the clay, and thou
our potter; and we all are the work of thy hand"

Machinery just meant
To give thy soul its bent,
Try thee and turn thee forth, sufficiently impressed.

What though the earlier grooves,
170 Which ran the laughing loves
Around thy base, no longer pause and press?
What though, about thy rim,
Skull-things in order grim
Grow out, in graver mood, obey the sterner stress?

Look not thou down but up!
To uses of a cup,
The festal board, lamp's flash, and trumpet's peal,
The new wine's foaming flow,
The Master's lips aglow!
180 Thou, heaven's consummate cup, what needst thou
    with earth's wheel?

But I need, now as then,
Thee, God, who moldest men;
And since, not even while the whirl was worst,
Did I—to the wheel of life
With shapes and colors rife,
Bound dizzily—mistake my end, to slake Thy thirst.

So, take and use Thy work;
Amend what flaws may lurk,
What strain o' the stuff, what warpings past the aim!
190 My times be in Thy hand!
Perfect the cup as planned!
Let age approve of youth, and death complete the
    same!
(1864)

LOVE AMONG THE RUINS°

1

Where the quiet-coloured end of evening smiles
        Miles and miles
On the solitary pastures where our sheep
        Half-asleep
Tinkle homeward thro' the twilight, stray or stop
        As they crop—

2

Was the site once of a city great and gay,
        (So they say)
Of our country's very capital, its prince
10   Ages since
Held his court in, gathered councils, wielding far
        Peace or war.

3

Now—the country does not even boast a tree,

As you see,
To distinguish slopes of verdure, certain rills
        From the hills
Intersect and give a name to, (else they run
        Into one)

4

Where the domed and daring palace shot its spires
        Up like fires   20
O'er the hundred-gated circuit of a wall
        Bounding all,
Made of marble, men might march on nor be prest,
        Twelve abreast.

5

And such plenty and perfection, see, of grass
        Never was!
Such a carpet as, this summer-time, o'erspreads
        And embeds
Every vestige of the city, guessed alone,
        Stock or stone—   30

6

Where a multitude of men breathed joy and woe
        Long ago;
Lust of glory pricked their hearts up, dread of shame
        Struck them tame;
And that glory and that shame alike, the gold
        Bought and sold.

7

Now,—the single little turret that remains
        On the plains,
By the caper° overrooted, by the gourd
        Overscored,   40
While the patching houseleek's head of blossom winks
        Through the chinks—

8

Marks the basement whence a tower in ancient time
        Sprang sublime,
And a burning ring all round, the chariots traced
        As they raced,
And the monarch and his minions and his dames
        Viewed the games.

9

And I know, while thus the quiet-coloured eve
        Smiles to leave   50
To their folding, all our many-tinkling fleece
        In such peace,
And the slopes and rills in undistinguished grey
        Melt away—

10

That a girl with eager eyes and yellow hair

Waits me there
In the turret, whence the charioteers caught soul
　　　For the goal,
When the king looked, where she looks now, breath-
　　　less, dumb
60　　　Till I come.

11

But he looked upon the city, every side,
　　　Far and wide,
All the mountains topped with temples, all the glades'
　　　Colonnades,
All the causeys,° bridges, aqueducts,—and then,
　　　All the men!

12

When I do come, she will speak not, she will stand,
　　　Either hand
On my shoulder, give her eyes the first embrace
70　　　Of my face,
Ere we rush, ere we extinguish sight and speech
　　　Each on each.

13

In one year they sent a million fighters forth
　　　South and north,
And they built their gods a brazen pillar high
　　　As the sky,
Yet reserved a thousand chariots in full force—
　　　Gold, of course.

14

Oh, heart! oh, blood that freezes, blood that burns!
80　　　Earth's returns
For whole centuries of folly, noise and sin!
　　　Shut them in,
With their triumphs and their glories and the rest.
　　　Love is best!

(1855)

A TOCCATA OF GALUPPI'S°

O Galuppi, Baldassare, this is very sad to find!
I can hardly misconceive you; it would prove me deaf
　　and blind;
But although I take your meaning, 'tis with such a
　　heavy mind!

Here you come with your old music, and here's all the
　　good it brings.
What, they lived once thus at Venice where the mer-
　　chants were the kings,

Where St. Mark's is, where the Doges° used to wed the
　　sea with rings?

Aye, because the sea's the street there; and 'tis arched
　　by—what you call—
Shylock's bridge° with houses on it, where they kept
　　the carnival.
I was never out of England—it's as if I saw it all.

Did young people take their pleasure when the sea was　10
　　warm in May?
Balls and masks begun at midnight, burning ever to
　　mid-day,
When they made up fresh adventures for the morrow,
　　do you say?

Was a lady such a lady, cheeks so round and lips so
　　red—
On her neck the small face buoyant, like a bell-flower
　　on its bed,
O'er the breast's superb abundance where a man might
　　base his head?

Well, and it was graceful of them—they'd break talk
　　off and afford—
She, to bite her mask's black velvet—he, to finger on
　　his sword,
While you sat and played toccatas, stately at the
　　clavichord?°

What? Those lesser thirds° so plaintive, sixths di-
　　minished, sigh on sigh,
Told them something? Those suspensions, those solu-　20
　　tions—"Must we die?"
Those commiserating sevenths—"Life might last! we
　　can but try!"

"Were you happy?"—"Yes."—"And are you still as
　　happy?"—"Yes. And you?"
—"Then, more kisses!"—"Did I stop them, when a
　　million seemed so few?"
Hark, the dominant's persistence till it must be
　　answered to!

So, an octave struck the answer. Oh, they praised you,
　　I dare say!
"Brave Galuppi! that was music! good alike at grave
　　and gay!
I can always leave off talking when I hear a master
　　play!"

Then they left you for their pleasure; till in due time,
　　one by one,

---

65 **causeys,** walkways　**A Toccata of Galuppi's.** Baldassare Galuppi (1706–1785) was a noted popular Italian musician and composer. During his last years he was organist at St. Mark's Cathedral in Venice. Browning was very fond of playing his music. A toccata (Italian *toccare*, to touch) is a musical composition in a light and free style

6 **Doges.** The Doge was the chief magistrate of the city　8 **Shylock's bridge,** the Rialto, a bridge over the Grand Canal. Cf. Shakespeare's *Merchant of Venice* 18 **clavichord,** an old-fashioned instrument with keys and strings, the predecessor of the modern piano　19–24 **thirds, etc.** The technical musical terms in these lines are made clear by accompanying phrases

Some with lives that came to nothing, some with deeds
   as well undone,
30 Death stepped tacitly and took them where they never
   see the sun.

But when I sit down to reason, think to take my stand
   nor swerve,
While I triumph o'er a secret wrung from nature's
   close reserve,
In you come with your cold music till I creep through
   every nerve.

Yes, you, like a ghostly cricket, creaking where a
   house was burned:
"Dust° and ashes, dead and done with, Venice spent
   what Venice earned.
The soul, doubtless, is immortal—where a soul can be
   discerned.

"Yours, for instance: you know physics, something of
   geology,
Mathematics are your pastime; souls shall rise in their
   degree;
Butterflies may dread extinction—you'll not die, it
   cannot be!

40 "As for Venice and her people, merely born to bloom
   and drop,
Here on earth they bore their fruitage, mirth and folly
   were the crop;
What of soul was left, I wonder, when the kissing had
   to stop?

"Dust and ashes!" So you creak it, and I want the
   heart to scold.
Dear dead women, with such hair, too—what's become of all the gold
Used to hang and brush their bosoms? I feel chilly and
   grown old.
(1855)

TWO IN THE CAMPAGNA°

1

I wonder do you feel to-day
   As I have felt, since, hand in hand,
We sat down on the grass, to stray
   In spirit better through the land,
This morn of Rome and May?

2

For me, I touched a thought, I know,

Has tantalised me many times,
(Like turns of thread the spiders throw
   Mocking across our path) for rhymes
To catch at and let go.   10

3

Help me to hold it: first it left
   The yellowing fennel, run to seed
There, branching from the brickwork's cleft,
   Some old tomb's ruin: yonder weed
Took up the floating weft,

4

Where one small orange cup amassed
   Five beetles,—blind and green they grope
Among the honey-meal,—and last
   Everywhere on the grassy slope
I traced it. Hold it fast!   20

5

The champaign° with its endless fleece
   Of feathery grasses everywhere!
Silence and passion, joy and peace,
   An everlasting wash of air—
Rome's ghost since her decease.

6

Such life there, through such lengths of hours,
   Such miracles performed in play,
Such primal naked forms of flowers,
   Such letting Nature have her way
While Heaven looks from its towers.   30

7

How say you? Let us, O my dove,
   Let us be unashamed of soul,
As earth lies bare to heaven above.
   How is it under our control
To love or not to love?

8

I would that you were all to me,
   You that are just so much, no more—
Nor yours, nor mine,—nor slave nor free!
   Where does the fault lie? what the core
Of the wound, since wound must be?   40

9

I would I could adopt your will,
   See with your eyes, and set my heart
Beating by yours, and drink my fill
   At your soul's springs,—your part, my part
In life, for good and ill.

10

No. I yearn upward—touch you close,

35–43 **Dust, etc.** The quotation is what the music says to the speaker in the
monologue concerning the men and the women for whom life meant merely a
butterfly pleasure
Two in the Campagna. Campagna refers to the countryside around Rome, comprising about 800 square miles

21 **champaign,** field or campagna

Then stand away. I kiss your cheek,
  Catch your soul's warmth,—I pluck the rose
  And love it more than tongue can speak—
50 Then the good minute goes.

11

Already how am I so far
  Out of that minute? Must I go
Still like the thistle-ball, no bar,
  Onward, whenever light winds blow,
Fixed by no friendly star?

12

Just when I seemed about to learn!
  Where is the thread now? Off again!
The old trick! Only I discern—
  Infinite passion and the pain
60 Of finite hearts that yearn.
(1855)

MEMORABILIA°

Ah, did you once see Shelley plain,
  And did he stop and speak to you,
And did you speak to him again?
  How strange it seems and new!

But you were living before that,
  And also you are living after;
And the memory I started at—
  My starting moves your laughter!

I crossed a moor, with a name of its own
10   And a certain use in the world, no doubt,
Yet a hand's-breadth of it shines alone
  'Mid the blank miles round about;

For there I picked up on the heather,
  And there I put inside my breast
A molted feather, an eagle-feather!
  Well, I forget the rest.
(1855)

"CHILDE ROLAND
TO THE DARK TOWER CAME"°

My first thought was, he lied in every word,
  That hoary cripple, with malicious eye
  Askance to watch the working of his lie
On mine, and mouth scarce able to afford
Suppression of the glee, that pursed and scored
  Its edge, at one more victim gained thereby.

What else should he be set for, with his staff?
  What, save to waylay with his lies, ensnare
  All travelers who might find him posted there,
And ask the road? I guessed what skull-like laugh   10
Would break, what crutch 'gin write my epitaph
  For pastime in the dusty thoroughfare,

If at his counsel I should turn aside
  Into that ominous tract which, all agree,
  Hides the Dark Tower. Yet acquiescingly
I did turn as he pointed—neither pride
Nor hope rekindling at the end descried,
  So much as gladness that some end might be.

For, what with my whole world-wide wandering,
  What with my search drawn out through years, my   20
    hope
  Dwindled into a ghost not fit to cope
With that obstreperous joy success would bring—
I hardly tried now to rebuke the spring
  My heart made, finding failure in its scope.

As when a sick man very near to death
  Seems dead indeed, and feels begin and end
  The tears, and takes the farewell of each friend,
And hears one bid the other go, draw breath
Freelier outside ("since all is o'er," he saith,
  "And the blow fallen no grieving can amend"),   30

While some discuss if near the other graves
  Be room enough for this, and when a day
  Suits best for carrying the corpse away,
With care about the banners, scarves, and staves;
And still the man hears all, and only craves
  He may not shame such tender love and stay.

Thus, I had so long suffered in this quest,
  Heard failure prophesied so oft, been writ
  So many times among "The Band"—to wit,
The knights who to the Dark Tower's search ad-   40
    dressed
Their steps—that just to fail as they, seemed best,
  And all the doubt was now—should I be fit?

So, quiet as despair, I turned from him,
  That hateful cripple, out of his highway
  Into the path he pointed. All the day
Had been a dreary one at best, and dim
Was settling to its close, yet shot one grim
  Red leer to see the plain catch its estray.°

For mark! no sooner was I fairly found
  Pledged to the plain, after a pace or two,   50
  Than, pausing to throw backward a last view
O'er the safe road, 'twas gone; gray plain all round—

Memorabilia. Donald Smalley presents the following account from Browning: "I was one day in the shop of Hodgson, the well-known London bookseller, when a stranger came in who, in the course of conversation with the bookseller, spoke of something that Shelley had once said to him. Suddenly the stranger paused, and burst into laughter as he observed me staring at him with blanched face. . . ."

Childe Roland. A "childe" is a youth of noble birth. The poem is based on the lines in *King Lear* (III, iv, 154–156) spoken by Edgar, feigning madness, when Lear is about to enter the hovel on the hearth during the storm. "Childe Roland to the dark tower came, /His word was still—Fie, foh, and fum,/ I smell the blood of British man" 48 **estray,** the one who has strayed—namely, Childe Roland

Nothing but plain to the horizon's bound.
   I might go on; naught else remained to do.

So, on I went. I think I never saw
   Such starved ignoble nature; nothing throve;
   For flowers—as well expect a cedar grove!
But cockle,° spurge, according to their law
Might propagate their kind, with none to awe,
60   You'd think; a burr had been a treasure trove.

No! penury, inertness, and grimace,
   In some strange sort, were the land's portion. "See
   Or shut your eyes," said Nature peevishly,
"It nothing skills°—I cannot help my case;
'Tis the Last Judgment's fire must cure this place,
   Calcine° its clods, and set my prisoners free."

If there pushed any ragged thistle-stalk
   Above its mates, the head was chopped; the bents°
   Were jealous else. What made those holes and rents
70 In the dock's° harsh swarth leaves, bruised as to balk
All hope of greenness? 'Tis a brute must walk
   Pashing° their life out, with a brute's intents.

As for the grass, it grew as scant as hair
   In leprosy; thin dry blades pricked the mud,
   Which underneath looked kneaded up with blood.
One stiff blind horse,° his every bone a-stare,
Stood stupefied, however he came there—
   Thrust out past service from the devil's stud!

Alive? He might be dead for aught I know,
80   With that red gaunt and colloped° neck a-strain,
   And shut eyes underneath the rusty mane;
Seldom went such grotesqueness with such woe;
I never saw a brute I hated so;
   He must be wicked to deserve such pain.

I shut my eyes and turned them on my heart.
   As a man calls for wine before he fights,
   I asked one draft of earlier, happier sights,
Ere fitly I could hope to play my part.
Think first, fight afterwards—the soldier's art;
90   One taste of the old time sets all to rights.

Not it! I fancied Cuthbert's reddening face
   Beneath its garniture of curly gold,
   Dear fellow, till I almost felt him fold
An arm in mine to fix me to the place,
That way he used. Alas, one night's disgrace!
   Out went my heart's new fire and left it cold.

Giles then, the soul of honor—there he stands
   Frank as ten years ago when knighted first.

What honest man should dare (he said) he durst.
Good—but the scene shifts—faugh! what hangman   100
   hands
Pin to his breast a parchment? His own bands
   Read it. Poor traitor, spit upon and cursed!

Better this present than a past like that;
   Back therefore to my darkening path again!
   No sound, no sight as far as eye could strain.
Will the night send a howlet or a bat?
I asked—when something on the dismal flat
   Came to arrest my thoughts and change their train.

A sudden little river crossed my path
   As unexpected as a serpent comes.   110
   No sluggish tide congenial to the glooms;
This, as it frothed by, might have been a bath
For the fiend's glowing hoof—to see the wrath
   Of its black eddy bespate° with flakes and spumes.

So petty yet so spiteful! All along,
   Low scrubby alders kneeled down over it;
   Drenched willows flung them headlong in a fit
Of mute despair, a suicidal throng;
The river which had done them all the wrong,
   Whate'er that was, rolled by, deterred no whit.   120

Which, while I forded—good saints, how I feared
   To set my foot upon a dead man's cheek,
   Each step, or feel the spear I thrust to seek
For hollows, tangled in his hair or beard!
—It may have been a water rat I speared,
   But, ugh! it sounded like a baby's shriek.

Glad was I when I reached the other bank.
   Now for a better country. Vain presage!
   Who were the strugglers, what war did they wage,
Whose savage trample thus could pad° the dank   130
Soil to a plash?° Toads in a poisoned tank,
   Or wild cats in a red-hot iron cage—

The fight must so have seemed in that fell cirque.°
   What penned them there, with all the plain to
     choose?
   No footprint leading to that horrid mews,°
None out of it. Mad brewage set to work
Their brains, no doubt, like galley-slaves the Turk
   Pits for his pastime, Christians against Jews.

And more than that—a furlong on—why, there!
   What bad use was that engine for, that wheel,   140
   Or brake, not wheel—that harrow fit to reel
Men's bodies out like silk? with all the air
Of Tophet's° tool, on earth left unaware,
   Or brought to sharpen its rusty teeth of steel.

---

58 **cockle, spurge,** common wild shrubs   64 **skills,** matters   66 **Calcine,** reduce to powder by heat   68 **bents,** coarse grasses   70 **dock,** a kind of weed   72 **Pashing,** crushing   76 **One . . . horse.** The figure of a lean horse in a piece of tapestry in Browning's drawing room furnished this picture   80 **colloped,** marked with ridges

114 **bespate,** spattered   130 **pad,** tread down   131 **plash,** puddle   133 **cirque,** circle   135 **mews,** enclosure, pen   143 **Tophet,** an Old Testament name for hell

Then came a bit of stubbed ground, once a wood,
  Next a marsh, it would seem, and now mere earth
  Desperate and done with—so a fool finds mirth,
Makes a thing and then mars it, till his mood
Changes and off he goes!—within a rood,
150 Bog, clay, and rubble,° sand, and stark black dearth.

Now blotches rankling, colored gay and grim,
  Now patches where some leanness of the soil's
  Broke into moss or substances like boils;
Then came some palsied oak, a cleft in him
Like a distorted mouth that splits its rim
  Gaping at death, and dies while it recoils.

And just as far as ever from the end!
  Naught in the distance but the evening, naught
  To point my footstep further! At the thought
160 A great black bird, Apollyon's° bosom friend,
Sailed past, nor beat his wide wing dragon-penned°
  That brushed my cap—perchance the guide I
    sought.

For, looking up, aware I somehow grew,
  'Spite of the dusk, the plain had given place
  All round to mountains—with such name to grace
Mere ugly heights and heaps now stolen in view.
How thus they had surprised me—solve it, you!
  How to get from them was no clearer case.

Yet half I seemed to recognize some trick
170 Of mischief happened to me, God knows when—
  In a bad dream, perhaps. Here ended, then,
Progress this way. When, in the very nick
Of giving up, one time more, came a click
  As when a trap shuts—you're inside the den!

Burningly it came on me all at once,
  This was the place! those two hills on the right,
  Crouched like two bulls locked horn in horn in fight;
While to the left, a tall scalped mountain . . . Dunce,
Dotard, a-dozing at the very nonce,
180 After a life spent training for the sight!

What in the midst lay but the Tower itself?
  The round squat turret, blind as the fool's heart,
  Built of brown stone, without a counterpart
In the whole world. The tempest's mocking elf
Points to the shipman thus the unseen shelf
  He strikes on, only when the timbers start.

Not see? because of night, perhaps?—why, day
  Came back again for that! before it left,
  The dying sunset kindled through a cleft;
190 The hills, like giants at a hunting, lay

Chin upon hand, to see the game at bay—
  "Now stab and end the creature—to the heft!"

Not hear? when noise was everywhere! it tolled
  Increasing like a bell. Names in my ears,
  Of all the lost adventurers my peers—
How such a one was strong, and such was bold,
And such was fortunate, yet each of old
  Lost, lost! one moment knelled the woe of years.

There they stood, ranged along the hillsides, met
  To view the last of me, a living frame   200
  For one more picture! in a sheet of flame
I saw them and I knew them all. And yet
Dauntless the slug-horn to my lips I set,
  And blew. *"Childe Roland to the Dark Tower
   came."*

(1852; 1855)

FRA LIPPO LIPPI°

I am poor brother Lippo, by your leave!
You need not clap your torches to my face.
Zooks,° what's to blame? you think you see a monk!
What, 'tis past midnight, and you go the rounds,
And here you catch me at an alley's end
Where sportive ladies leave their doors ajar?
The Carmine's° my cloister; hunt it up,
Do—harry out, if you must show your zeal,
Whatever rat, there, haps on his wrong hole,
And nip each softling of a wee white mouse,   10
Weke, weke, that's crept to keep him company!
Aha, you know your betters! Then, you'll take
Your hand away that's fiddling on my throat,
And please to know me likewise. Who am I?
Why, one, sir, who is lodging with a friend
Three streets off—he's a certain . . . how d' ye call?
Master—a . . . Cosimo of the Medici,°
I' the house that caps the corner. Boh! you were best!
Remember and tell me, the day you're hanged,
How you affected such a gullet's gripe!   20
But you, sir, it concerns you that your knaves
Pick up a manner nor discredit you;
Zooks, are we pilchards,° that they sweep the streets
And count fair prize what comes into their net?
He's Judas to a tittle, that man is!
Just such a face! Why, sir, you make amends.
Lord, I'm not angry! Bid your hangdogs go
Drink out this quarter-florin° to the health

Fra Lippo Lippi. Browning was prompted to write this poem by a paragraph in Giorgio Vasari's *Lives of the Painters* (1550). It has to do principally with the efforts of his patron, Cosimo de' Medici to keep Filippo Lippi (1412–1469) off the streets. First he tried locking the door, but Lippo went out the window in the way described in the poem. His patron heard of the escapade and, rather than have a great painter break his neck in search of pleasure, he left the door unlocked 3 **Zooks,** an oath shortened from *Gadzooks, Godzooks;* the meaning of the second syllable is not clear 7 **The Carmine's.** Lippo entered the monastery of the Carmelite friars of the Carmine in Florence in 1420 17 **Cosimo of the Medici,** Cosimo de' Medici (1389–1464), rich Florentine banker, statesman, and patron of art and literature; the Medici palace, now known as the Palazzo Riccardi, is on the corner of Via Cavour and Via Gori 23 **pilchards,** cheap common fish 28 **quarter-florin,** small gold coin

150 **rubble,** broken stone 160 **Apollyon,** the devil; he is "the angel of the bottomless pit" in *Revelation,* 9 161 **dragon-penned,** furnished with feathers like those in a dragon's wing

Of the munificent House that harbors me
30 (And many more beside, lads! more beside!)
And all's come square again! I'd like his face—
His, elbowing on his comrade in the door
With the pike and lantern—for the slave that holds
John Baptist's head a-dangle by the hair°
With one hand ("Look you, now," as who should say)
And his weapon in the other, yet unwiped!
It's not your chance to have a bit of chalk,
A wood-coal or the like? or you should see!
Yes, I'm the painter, since you style me so.
40 What, brother Lippo's doings, up and down,
You know them and they take you? like enough!
I saw the proper twinkle in your eye—
'Tell you, I liked your looks at very first.
Let's sit and set things straight now, hip to haunch.
Here's spring come, and the nights one makes up
   bands
To roam the town and sing out carnival,°
And I've been three weeks shut within my mew,°
A-painting for the great man, saints and saints
And saints again. I could not paint all night—
50 Ouf! I leaned out of window for fresh air.
There came a hurry of feet and little feet,
A sweep of lute strings, laughs, and whifts of song°—
Flower o' the broom,
Take away love, and our earth is a tomb!
Flower o' the quince,
I let Lisa go, and what good in life since?
Flower o' the thyme—and so on. Round they went.
Scarce had they turned the corner when a titter
Like the skipping of rabbits by moonlight—three slim
   shapes,
60 And a face that looked up . . . zooks, sir, flesh and
   blood,
That's all I'm made of! Into shreds it went,
Curtain and counterpane and coverlet,
All the bed furniture—a dozen knots,
There was a ladder! Down I let myself,
Hands and feet, scrambling somehow, and so dropped,
And after them. I came up with the fun
Hard by Saint Laurence,° hail fellow, well met—
Flower o' the rose,
If I've been merry, what matter who knows?
70 And so as I was stealing back again
To get to bed and have a bit of sleep
Ere I rise up tomorrow and go work
On Jerome knocking at his poor old breast°
With his great round stone to subdue the flesh,
You snap me of a sudden. Ah, I see!

Though your eye twinkles still, you shake your head—
Mine's shaved—a monk, you say—the sting's in that!
If Master Cosimo announced himself,
Mum's the word naturally; but a monk!
Come, what am I a beast for? tell us, now! 80
I was a baby when my mother died
And father died and left me in the street.
I starved there, God knows how, a year or two
On fig skins, melon parings, rinds, and shucks,
Refuse and rubbish. One fine frosty day,
My stomach being empty as your hat,
The wind doubled me up, and down I went.
Old Aunt Lapaccia° trussed me° with one hand
(Its fellow was a stinger as I knew),
And so along the wall, over the bridge, 90
By the straight cut to the convent. Six words there,
While I stood munching my first bread that month:
"So, boy, you're minded," quoth the good fat father,
Wiping his own mouth—'twas refection time°—
"To quit this very miserable world?
Will you renounce" . . . "the mouthful of bread?"
   thought I;
By no means! Brief, they made a monk of me;
I did renounce the world, its pride and greed,
Palace, farm, villa, shop, and banking house,
Trash, such as these poor devils of Medici 100
Have given their hearts to—all at eight years old.
Well, sir, I found in time, you may be sure,
'Twas not for nothing—the good bellyful,
The warm serge, and the rope that goes all round,
And day-long blessed idleness beside!
"Let's see what the urchin's fit for"—that came next.
Not overmuch their way, I must confess.
Such a to-do! They tried me with their books;
Lord, they'd have taught me Latin in pure waste!
Flower o' the clove, 110
All the Latin I construe is "amo," I love!
But, mind you, when a boy starves in the streets
Eight years together, as my fortune was,
Watching folk's faces to know who will fling
The bit of half-stripped grape-bunch he desires,
And who will curse or kick him for his pains—
Which gentleman processional° and fine,
Holding a candle to the Sacrament,
Will wink and let him lift a plate and catch
The droppings of the wax to sell again, 120
Or holla for the Eight° and have him whipped—
How say I?—nay, which dog bites, which lets drop
His bone from the heap of offal in the street—
Why, soul and sense of him grow sharp alike;
He learns the look of things, and none the less
For admonition from the hunger pinch.
I had a store of such remarks, be sure,
Which, after I found leisure, turned to use.

33-34 **the slave . . . hair,** an imaginary picture; in Lippo's real picture of the be-heading of John the Baptist, the head is carried on a great platter by Salome, the daughter of Herodias. See *Matthew,* 14:1-12   46 **carnival,** period of gaiety pre-ceding Lent   47 **mew,** pen. (Lippo had been engaged to paint pictures in the palace and had been locked in a room until the work should be done)   52 **song.** The song that follows is a *stornello,* a kind of short folk song of the Italians, usu-ally improvised on the name of a flower or some other familiar object   67 **Saint Laurence,** the Church of San Lorenzo   73 **Jerome . . . breast.** Saint Jerome (340?-420) was the most learned of the early Fathers of the Latin Church. He lived in the desert for several years as a penance for his youthful sins. Early Chris-tian art depicted him on his knees before a crucifix, beating his breast with a stone

88 **Aunt Lapaccia,** Mona Lapaccia, his father's sister   **trussed me,** lifted me up   94 **refection time,** lunch time   117 **gentleman processional, etc.,** gentleman wearing fine robes and walking in the religious procession   121 **the Eight,** the magistrates who governed Florence

I drew men's faces on my copy books,
130 Scrawled them within the antiphonary's marge,°
Joined legs and arms to the long music-notes,°
Found eyes and nose and chin for A's and B's,
And made a string of pictures of the world
Betwixt the ins and outs of verb and noun,
On the wall, the bench, the door. The monks looked
      black.
"Nay," quoth the Prior, "turn him out, d'ye say?
In no wise. Lose a crow and catch a lark.
What if at last we get our man of parts,
We Carmelites,° like those Camaldolese
140 And Preaching Friars, to do our church up fine
And put the front° on it that ought to be!"
And hereupon he bade me daub away.
Thank you! my head being crammed, the walls a
      blank,
Never was such prompt disemburdening.
First, every sort of monk, the black and white,
I drew them, fat and lean; then, folk at church,
From good old gossips waiting to confess
Their cribs° of barrel droppings, candle ends—
To the breathless fellow at the altar foot,
150 Fresh from his murder, safe° and sitting there
With the little children round him in a row
Of admiration, half for his beard and half
For that white anger of his victim's son
Shaking a fist at him with one fierce arm,
Signing himself with the other because of Christ°
(Whose sad face on the cross sees only this
After the passion° of a thousand years),
Till some poor girl, her apron o'er her head
(Which the intense eyes looked through), came at eve
160 On tiptoe, said a word, dropped in a loaf,
Her pair of earrings, and a bunch of flowers
(The brute took growling), prayed, and so was gone.
I painted all, then cried, "'Tis ask and have;
Choose, for more's ready!"—laid the ladder flat,
And showed my covered bit of cloister wall.
The monks closed in a circle and praised loud
Till checked, taught what to see and not to see,
Being simple bodies—"That's the very man!
Look at the boy who stoops to pat the dog!
170 That woman's like the Prior's niece who comes
To care about his asthma; it's the life!"
But there my triumph's straw-fire flared and funked;°
Their betters took their turn to see and say;
The Prior and the learned pulled a face

And stopped all that in no time. "How? what's here?
Quite from the mark of painting, bless us all!
Faces, arms, legs, and bodies like the true
As much as pea and pea! It's devil's game!
Your business is not to catch men with show,
With homage to the perishable clay,   180
But lift them over it, ignore it all,
Make them forget there's such a thing as flesh.
Your business is to paint the souls of men—
Man's soul, and it's a fire, smoke . . . no, it's not . .
It's vapor done up like a new-born babe
(In that shape when you die it leaves your mouth)-
It's . . . well, what matters talking, it's the soul!
Give us no more of body than shows soul!
Here's Giotto,° with his Saint a-praising God,
That sets us praising—why not stop with him?   190
Why put all thoughts of praise out of our head
With wonder at lines, colors, and what not?
Paint the soul, never mind the legs and arms!
Rub all out, try at it a second time.
Oh, that white smallish female with the breasts,
She's just my niece . . . Herodias,° I would say—
Who went and danced and got men's heads cut off!
Have it all out!" Now, is this sense, I ask?
A fine way to paint soul, by painting body
So ill the eye can't stop there, must go further   200
And can't fare worse! Thus, yellow does for white
When what you put for yellow's simply black,
And any sort of meaning looks intense
When all beside itself means and looks naught.
Why can't a painter lift each foot in turn,
Left foot and right foot, go a double step,
Make his flesh liker and his soul more like,
Both in their order? Take the prettiest face,
The Prior's niece . . . patron saint—is it so pretty
You can't discover if it means hope, fear,   210
Sorrow, or joy? won't beauty go with these?
Suppose I've made her eyes all right and blue,
Can't I take breath and try to add life's flash,
And then add soul and heighten them threefold?
Or say there's beauty with no soul at all
(I never saw it—put the case the same);
If you get simple beauty and naught else,
You get about the best thing God invents—
That's somewhat; and you'll find the soul you have
      missed,
Within yourself, when you return him thanks.   220
"Rub all out!" Well, well, there's my life, in short,
And so the thing has gone on ever since.
I'm grown a man no doubt, I've broken bounds;
You should not take a fellow eight years old
And make him swear to never kiss the girls.
I'm my own master, paint now as I please—
Having a friend, you see, in the Corner-house!

130 **antiphonary's marge,** the margins of the books used by the choir 131 **long
music-notes.** The medieval music notes were square or oblong with long stems
139 **Carmelites, etc.** The Carmelites were monks of the Order of Mount Carmel,
in Syria; the Camaldolese belonged to the convent of Camaldoli, near Florence;
the Preaching Friars are the Dominicans, named after St. Dominic; they were
called Brothers Preachers by Pope Innocent III in 1215. These orders owned various monasteries and churches and were eager to possess the greatest religious
paintings 141 **the front, etc.** The façade of the Church of the Medici in Florence (San Lorenzo), designed by Michelangelo, has never been finished but presents ragged brickwork, waiting for its marble veneer 148 **Their cribs, etc.,**
small thefts of wine, wax, etc. 150 **safe,** because he is in a sacred place, which
by the law of the medieval church protected him from arrest 154-155 **Shaking
. . . Christ.** Revenge and religion are at war in him 157 **passion,** suffering
172 **funked,** smoked

189 **Giotto,** Giotto di Bondone (1267?–1337), famous Florentine painter, architect, and sculptor. He expressed the soul in his paintings and cared nothing for
realistic art. Lippo and Guidi (l. 276) introduced realism, which Lippo here defends 196 **Herodias,** Salome's mother

Lord, it's fast holding by the rings in front°—
Those great rings serve more purposes than just
230 To plant a flag in, or tie up a horse!
And yet the old schooling sticks, the old grave eyes
Are peeping o'er my shoulder as I work,
The heads shake still—"It's art's decline, my son!
You're not of the true painters, great and old;
Brother Angelico's° the man, you'll find;
Brother Lorenzo° stands his single peer—
Fag on at flesh, you'll never make the third!"
Flower o' the pine,
You keep your mistr . . . manners, and I'll stick to
mine!
240 I'm not the third, then; bless us, they must know!
Don't you think they're the likeliest to know,
They with their Latin? So, I swallow my rage,
Clench my teeth, suck my lips in tight, and paint
To please them—sometimes do and sometimes don't;
For, doing most, there's pretty sure to come
A turn, some warm eve finds me at my saints—
A laugh, a cry, the business of the world
(*Flower o' the peach,*
Death for us all, and his own life for each!)—
250 And my whole soul revolves, the cup runs over,
The world and life's too big to pass for a dream,
And I do these wild things in sheer despite,
And play the fooleries you catch me at,
In pure rage! The old mill-horse, out at grass
After hard years, throws up his stiff heels so,
Although the miller does not preach to him
The only good of grass is to make chaff.
What would men have? Do they like grass or no—
May they or mayn't they? All I want's the thing
260 Settled forever one way. As it is,
You tell too many lies and hurt yourself;
You don't like what you only like too much,
You do like what, if given you at your word,
You find abundantly detestable.
For me, I think I speak as I was taught;
I always see the garden and God there
A-making man's wife; and, my lesson learned—
The value and significance of flesh—
I can't unlearn ten minutes afterwards.

270 You understand me; I'm a beast, I know.
But see, now—why, I see as certainly
As that the morning star's about to shine,
What will hap some day. We've a youngster here
Comes to our convent, studies what I do,
Slouches and stares and lets no atom drop.
His name is Guidi°—he'll not mind the monks—
They call him Hulking Tom; he lets them talk;
He picks my practice up—he'll paint apace,

I hope so—though I never live so long,
I know what's sure to follow. You be judge!   280
You speak no Latin more than I, belike;
However, you're my man, you've seen the world—
The beauty and the wonder and the power,
The shapes of things, their colors, lights, and shades,
Changes, surprises—and God made it all!
—For what? Do you feel thankful, aye or no,
For this fair town's face, yonder river's line,
The mountain round it and the sky above,
Much more the figures of man, woman, child,
These are the frame to? What's it all about?   290
To be passed over, despised? or dwelt upon,
Wondered at? Oh, this last of course!—you say.
But why not do as well as say—paint these
Just as they are, careless what comes of it?
God's works—paint any one, and count it crime
To let a truth slip. Don't object, "His works
Are here already; nature is complete:
Suppose you reproduce her—which you can't—
There's no advantage! you must beat her, then."
For, don't you mark? we're made so that we love   300
First when we see them painted, things we have
     passed
Perhaps a hundred times nor cared to see;
And so they are better, painted—better to us,
Which is the same thing. Art was given for that;
God uses us to help each other so,
Lending our minds out. Have you noticed, now,
Your cullion's° hanging face? A bit of chalk,
And trust me but you should, though! How much
     more,
If I drew higher things with the same truth!
That were to take the Prior's pulpit-place,   310
Interpret God to all of you! Oh, oh,
It makes me mad to see what men shall do
And we in our graves! This world's no blot for us,
Nor blank; it means intensely, and means good—
To find its meaning is my meat and drink.
"Aye, but you don't so instigate to prayer!"
Strikes in the Prior; "when your meaning's plain,
It does not say to folk—remember matins,
Or, mind you fast next Friday!" Why, for this
What need of art at all? A skull and bones,   320
Two bits of stick nailed crosswise, or, what's best,
A bell to chime the hour with does as well.
I painted a Saint Laurence° six months since
At Prato,° splashed the fresco in fine style;
"How looks my painting, now the scaffold's down?"
I ask a brother. "Hugely," he returns—
"Already not one phiz of your three slaves
Who turn the Deacon off his toasted side,
But's scratched and prodded to our heart's content,
The pious people have so eased their own   330
With coming to say prayers there in a rage;

228 **the rings in front,** large iron rings on the front of the palace. Lippo used
them in climbing in and out of his window   235 **Brother Angelico,** Fra
Angelico, Giovanni da Fiesole (1387–1455), greatest of the medieval school of religious artists who "painted souls"   236 **Brother Lorenzo,** Lorenzo Monaco, a
painter of the Order of the Camaldolese, who also "painted souls"   276 **Guidi,**
Tommaso Guidi, or Masaccio (1401–1428), nicknamed Hulking Tom. He is said
to have been the first Italian artist to paint a nude figure. He was Lippo's master

307 **cullion,** a low fellow   323 **a Saint Laurence,** a picture of St. Laurence, who
was martyred in 258 by being burned to death on a gridiron   324 **At Prato.**
Some of Lippo's most important work is in the Cathedral at Prato, a town near
Florence

We get on fast to see the bricks beneath.
Expect another job this time next year,
For pity and religion grow i' the crowd—
Your painting serves its purpose!'' Hang the fools!

   —That is—you'll not mistake an idle word
Spoke in a huff by a poor monk, God wot,
Tasting the air this spicy night, which turns
The unaccustomed head like Chianti wine!
340 Oh, the church knows! don't misreport me, now!
It's natural a poor monk out of bounds
Should have his apt word to excuse himself;
And hearken how I plot to make amends.
I have bethought me: I shall paint a piece
. . . There's for you! Give me six months, then go, see
Something in Sant' Ambrogio's!° Bless the nuns!
They want a cast o' my office. I shall paint°
God in the midst, Madonna and her babe,
Ringed by a bowery, flowery angel brood,
350 Lilies and vestments and white faces, sweet
As puff on puff of grated orris root
When ladies crowd to Church at midsummer.
And then i' the front, of course a saint or two—
Saint John,° because he saves the Florentines,
Saint Ambrose, who puts down in black and white
The convent's friends and gives them a long day,
And Job,° I must have him there past mistake,
The man of Uz (and Us without the z,
Painters who need his patience). Well, all these
360 Secured at their devotion, up shall come
Out of a corner° when you least expect,
As one by a dark stair into a great light,
Music and talking, who but Lippo! I!—
Mazed, motionless, and moonstruck—I'm the man!
Back I shrink—what is this I see and hear?
I, caught up with my monk's-things by mistake,
My old serge gown and rope that goes all round,
I, in this presence, this pure company!
Where's a hole, where's a corner for escape?
370 Then steps a sweet angelic slip of a thing
Forward, puts out a soft palm: "Not so fast!"
—Addresses the celestial presence, "Nay,
He made you and devised you, after all,
Though he's none of you! Could Saint John there
    draw—
His camel-hair° make up a painting-brush?
We come to brother Lippo for all that,
Iste perfecit opus!°'' So, all smile—
I shuffle sideways with my blushing face
Under the cover of a hundred wings
380 Thrown like a spread of kirtles° when you're gay

And play hot cockles,° all the doors being shut,
Till, wholly unexpected, in there pops
The hothead husband! Thus I scuttle off
To some safe bench behind, not letting go
The palm of her, the little lily thing
That spoke the good word for me in the nick,
Like the Prior's niece . . . Saint Lucy, I would say.
And so all's saved for me, and for the church
A pretty picture gained. Go, six months hence!
Your hand, sir, and good-by; no lights, no lights!   390
The street's hushed, and I know my own way back,
Don't fear me! There's the gray beginning. Zooks!
(1855)

ANDREA DEL SARTO°

CALLED "THE FAULTLESS PAINTER"

But do not let us quarrel any more,
No, my Lucrezia; bear with me for once.
Sit down and all shall happen as you wish.
You turn your face, but does it bring your heart?
I'll work then for your friend's friend, never fear,
Treat his own subject after his own way,
Fix his own time, accept too his own price,
And shut the money into this small hand
When next it takes mine. Will it? tenderly?
Oh, I'll content him—but tomorrow, Love!   10
I often am much wearier than you think,
This evening more than usual, and it seems
As if—forgive now—should you let me sit
Here by the window with your hand in mine
And look a half-hour forth on Fiesole,°
Both of one mind, as married people use,
Quietly, quietly the evening through,
I might get up tomorrow to my work
Cheerful and fresh as ever. Let us try.
Tomorrow, how you shall be glad for this!   20
Your soft hand is a woman of itself,
And mine the man's bared breast she curls inside.
Don't count the time lost, neither; you must serve
For each of the five pictures we require—
It saves a model.° So! keep looking so—
My serpentining beauty, rounds on rounds!
—How could you ever prick those perfect ears,
Even to put the pearl there! oh, so sweet—
My face, my moon, my everybody's moon,
Which everybody looks on and calls his,   30
And, I suppose, is looked on by in turn,

346 **Sant' Ambrogio's,** Saint Ambrose's Church in Florence. St. Ambrose was a famous church leader during the fourth century. He became Bishop of Milan in 374   347–352 **I shall paint, etc.** The picture described is *The Coronation of the Virgin,* now in the Academy of Fine Arts, Florence. The model for the Virgin was Lucrezia Buti, Lippo's mistress   354 **Saint John,** St. John the Baptist, the patron saint of Florence   357 **Job.** Cf. *Job,* 1:1: "There was a man in the land of 'Uz, whose name was Job"   361–363 **Out of a corner . . . I.** Lippo's head appears in the lower right-hand corner of the picture   374–375 **Saint John . . . camel-hair.** Cf. *Mark,* 1:6: "And John was clothed with camel's hair"   377 **Iste . . . opus,** this one did the work. The inscription is on a scroll in the picture   380 **kirtles,** tunics, coats

381 **hot cockles,** an old English game in which a blindfolded player tries to guess who strikes him   **Andrea del Sarto.** Andrea d'Agnolo di Francesco (1486–1531) was called "del Sarto" because he was the son of a tailor *(sarto).* The perfection of his frescoes in the Church of the Annunziata in Florence won him the title of "The Faultless Painter." In 1512 he married Lucrezia del Fede, whose influence led Andrea to neglect his artwork. The poem is based upon the account of Andrea found in Vasari's *Lives of the Painters*   15 **Fiesole,** suburb of Florence   23–25 **you . . . model.** Lucrezia is discernible in nearly all the women of Andrea's pictures

Robert Browning   931

While she looks—no one's: very dear, no less.
You smile? why, there's my picture ready made,
There's what we painters call our harmony!
A common grayness silvers everything—
All in a twilight, you and I alike—
You, at the point of your first pride in me
(That's gone, you know), but I, at every point;
My youth, my hope, my art, being all toned down
40 To yonder sober pleasant Fiesole.
There's the bell clinking from the chapel-top;
That length of convent-wall across the way
Holds the trees safer, huddled more inside;
The last monk leaves the garden; days decrease,
And autumn grows, autumn in everything.
Eh? the whole seems to fall into a shape
As if I saw alike my work and self
And all that I was born to be and do,
A twilight-piece. Love, we are in God's hand.
50 How strange now looks the life he makes us lead;
So free we seem, so fettered fast we are!
I feel he laid the fetter; let it lie!
This chamber, for example—turn your head—
All that's behind us! You don't understand,
Nor care to understand, about my art,
But you can hear at least when people speak;
And that cartoon, the second from the door—
It is the thing, Love! so such thing should be—
Behold Madonna!—I am bold to say.
60 I can do with my pencil what I know,
What I see, what at bottom of my heart
I wish for, if I ever wish so deep—
Do easily, too—when I say perfectly,
I do not boast, perhaps; yourself are judge,
Who listened to the Legate's talk° last week,
And just as much they used to say in France.
At any rate, 'tis easy, all of it!
No sketches first, no studies—that's long past;
I do what many dream of all their lives—
70 Dream? strive to do, and agonize to do,
And fail in doing. I could count twenty such
On twice your fingers, and not leave this town,
Who strive—you don't know how the others strive
To paint a little thing like that you smeared
Carelessly passing with your robes afloat—
Yet do much less, so much less, Someone says
(I know his name, no matter)—so much less!
Well, less is more, Lucrezia; I am judged.
There burns a truer light of God in them,
80 In their vexed, beating, stuffed, and stopped-up brain,
Heart, or whate'er else, than goes on to prompt
This low-pulsed forthright° craftsman's hand of mine.
Their works drop groundward, but themselves, I
    know,
Reach many a time a heaven that's shut to me,
Enter and take their place there sure enough,
Though they come back and cannot tell the world.

My works are nearer heaven, but I sit here.
The sudden blood of these men! at a word—
Praise them, it boils; or blame them, it boils too.
I, painting from myself and to myself,   90
Know what I do, am unmoved by men's blame
Or their praise either. Somebody remarks
Morello's° outline there is wrongly traced,
His hue mistaken; what of that? or else,
Rightly traced and well ordered; what of that?
Speak as they please, what does the mountain care?
Ah, but a man's reach should exceed his grasp,
Or what's a heaven for?° All is silver-gray,
Placid and perfect with my art: the worse!
I know both what I want and what might gain,   100
And yet how profitless to know, to sigh,
"Had I been two, another and myself,
Our head would have o'erlooked the world!" No
    doubt.
Yonder's a work now, of that famous youth,
The Urbinate,° who died five years ago.
('Tis copied; George Vasari° sent it me.)
Well, I can fancy how he did it all,
Pouring his soul, with kings and popes to see,
Reaching, that heaven might so replenish him,
Above and through his art—for it gives way: 110
That arm is wrongly put—and there again—
A fault to pardon in the drawing's lines,
Its body, so to speak: its soul is right,
He means right—that, a child may understand.
Still, what an arm! and I could alter it;
But all the play, the insight, and the stretch—
Out of me, out of me! And wherefore out?
Had you enjoined them on me, given me soul,
We might have risen to Rafael, I and you!
Nay, Love, you did give all I asked, I think—   120
More than I merit, yes, by many times.
But had you—oh, with the same perfect brow,
And perfect eyes, and more than perfect mouth,
And the low voice my soul hears, as a bird
The fowler's pipe, and follows to the snare—
Had you, with these the same, but brought a mind!
Some women do so. Had the mouth there urged,
"God and the glory! never care for gain.
The present by the future, what is that?
Live for fame, side by side with Agnolo!°   130
Rafael is waiting; up to God, all three!"
I might have done it for you. So it seems;
Perhaps not. All is as God overrules.
Beside, incentives come from the soul's self;
The rest avail not. Why do I need you?
What wife had Rafael, or has Agnolo?
In this world, who can do a thing, will not;
And who would do it, cannot, I perceive;

---

93 **Morello,** high peak of the Apennines, north of Florence   97–98 **Ah . . . for?**
Cf. *Rabbi Ben Ezra,* ll. 40–41   105 **The Urbinate,** Raphael Sanzio (1483–1520),
one of the greatest of Italian painters; he was born in the city of Urbino
106 **George Vasari,** pupil of Andrea and author of *The Lives of the Most Eminent
Painters, Sculptors, and Architects* (1512–1574)   130 **Agnolo,** Michelangelo
(1475–1564), celebrated as painter, sculptor, architect, and poet

65 **the Legate's talk.** The legate was the representative of the pope   82 **forth-
right,** unswerving

Yet the will's somewhat—somewhat, too, the
    power—
140 And thus we half-men struggle. At the end,
God, I conclude, compensates, punishes.
'Tis safer for me, if the award be strict,
That I am something underrated here,
Poor this long while, despised, to speak the truth.
I dared not, do you know, leave home all day,
For fear of chancing on the Paris lords.
The best is when they pass and look aside;
But they speak sometimes; I must bear it all.
Well may they speak! That Francis,° that first time,
150 And that long festal year at Fontainebleau!
I surely then could sometimes leave the ground,
Put on the glory, Rafael's daily wear,
In that humane great monarch's golden look—
One finger in his beard or twisted curl
Over his mouth's good mark that made the smile;
One arm about my shoulder, round my neck;
The jingle of his gold chain in my ear—
I painting proudly with his breath on me,
All his Court round him, seeing with his eyes,
160 Such frank French eyes, and such a fire of souls
Profuse, my hand kept plying by those hearts;
And, best of all, this, this, this face beyond,
This in the background, waiting on my work,
To crown the issue with a last reward!
A good time, was it not, my kingly days?
And had you not grown restless . . . but I know—
'Tis done and past; 'twas right, my instinct said;
Too live the life grew, golden and not gray,
And I'm the weak-eyed bat no sun should tempt
170 Out of the grange whose four walls make his world.
How could it end in any other way?
You called me, and I came home to your heart.
The triumph was—to reach and stay there; since
I reached it ere the triumph, what is lost?
Let my hands frame your face in your hair's gold,
You beautiful Lucrezia that are mine!
"Rafael did this, Andrea painted that;
The Roman's° is the better when you pray,
But still the other's Virgin was his wife"—
180 Men will excuse me. I am glad to judge
Both pictures in your presence; clearer grows
My better fortune, I resolve to think.
For, do you know, Lucrezia, as God lives,
Said one day Agnolo, his very self,
To Rafael . . . I have known it all these years . . .
(When the young man was flaming out his thoughts
Upon a palace-wall for Rome to see,
Too lifted up in heart because of it),°
"Friend, there's a certain sorry little scrub
190 Goes up and down our Florence, none cares how,

149 **That Francis,** Francis I of France (1515–1547). He had invited Andrea to
come to Fontainebleau, the seat of the richest of the royal palaces. While engaged
upon important work there, Andrea was suddenly called home by Lucrezia. He
was given money with which to secure works of art for the French king, but he
purchased a house with it for Lucrezia   178 **The Roman's,** Raphael's
186–188 **When . . . it,** probably a reference to Raphael's decorations made in
certain rooms of the Vatican under Julius II (1443–1513)

Who, were he set to plan and execute
As you are, pricked on by your popes and kings,
Would bring the sweat into that brow of yours!"
To Rafael's!—And indeed the arm is wrong.
I hardly dare . . . yet, only you to see,
Give the chalk here—quick, thus the line should go!
Ay, but the soul! he's Rafael! rub it out!
Still, all I care for, if he spoke the truth
(What he? why, who but Michel Agnolo?
Do you forget already words like those?),   200
If really there was such a chance, so lost—
Is, whether you're—not grateful—but more pleased.
Well, let me think so. And you smile indeed!
This hour has been an hour! Another smile?
If you would sit thus by me every night,
I should work better, do you comprehend?
I mean that I should earn more, give you more.
See, it is settled dusk now; there's a star;
Morello's gone, the watch-lights show the wall,
The cue-owls° speak the name we call them by.   210
Come from the window, love—come in, at last,
Inside the melancholy little house
We built to be so gay with. God is just.
King Francis may forgive me; oft at nights
When I look up from painting, eyes tired out,
The walls become illumined, brick from brick
Distinct, instead of mortar, fierce bright gold,
That gold of his I did cement them with!
Let us but love each other. Must you go?
That Cousin° here again? he waits outside?   220
Must see you—you, and not with me? Those loans?
More gaming debts to pay? you smiled for that?
Well, let smiles buy me! have you more to spend?
While hand and eye and something of a heart
Are left me, work's my ware, and what's it worth?
I'll pay my fancy. Only let me sit
The gray remainder of the evening out,
Idle, you call it, and muse perfectly
How I could paint, were I but back in France,
One picture, just one more—the Virgin's face,   230
Not yours this time! I want you at my side
To hear them—that is, Michel Agnolo—
Judge all I do and tell you of its worth.
Will you? Tomorrow, satisfy your friend.
I take the subjects for his corridor,
Finish the portrait out of hand—there, there,
And throw him in another thing or two
If he demurs; the whole should prove enough
To pay for this same Cousin's freak. Beside—
What's better and what's all I care about—   240
Get you the thirteen scudi° for the ruff!
Love, does that please you? Ah, but what does he,
The Cousin! what does he to please you more?
    I am grown peaceful as old age tonight.
I regret little, I would change still less.
Since there my past life lies, why alter it?

210 **cue-owls,** small European owls   220 **Cousin,** a euphemism for *lover.* Cf.
ll. 29–32   241 **scudi,** small coins

The very wrong to Francis!—it is true
I took his coin, was tempted, and complied,
And built this house and sinned, and all is said.
250 My father and my mother died of want.
Well, had I riches of my own? you see
How one gets rich! Let each one bear his lot.
They were born poor, lived poor, and poor they died;
And I have labored somewhat in my time
And not been paid profusely. Some good son
Paint my two hundred pictures—let him try!
No doubt, there's something strikes a balance. Yes,
You loved me quite enough, it seems tonight.
This must suffice me here. What would one have?
260 In heaven, perhaps, new chances, one more chance—
Four great walls in the New Jerusalem,°
Meted on each side by the angel's reed,
For Leonard,° Rafael, Agnolo, and me
To cover—the three first without a wife,
While I have mine! So—still they overcome
Because there's still Lucrezia—as I choose.

    Again the Cousin's whistle! Go, my Love.
(1855)

CALIBAN UPON SETEBOS°

OR, NATURAL THEOLOGY IN THE ISLAND

*"Thou thoughtest that I was altogether such an one as
  thyself."*

['Will° sprawl, now that the heat of day is best,
Flat on his belly in the pit's much mire,
With elbows wide, fists clenched to prop his chin.
And, while he kicks both feet in the cool slush,
And feels about his spine small eft-things° course,
Run in and out each arm, and make him laugh;
And while above his head a pompion-plant,°
Coating the cave-top as a brow its eye,
Creeps down to touch and tickle hair and beard,
10 And now a flower drops with a bee inside,
And now a fruit to snap at, catch and crunch—
He looks out o'er yon sea, which sunbeams cross
And recross till they weave a spider-web
(Meshes of fire, some great fish breaks at times),

And talks to his own self, howe'er he please,
Touching that other, whom his dam called God.
Because to talk about Him,° vexes—ha,
Could He but know! and time to vex is now,°
When talk is safer than in winter-time.
Moreover Prosper and Miranda sleep   20
In confidence he drudges at their task;
And it is good to cheat the pair, and gibe,
Letting the rank tongue blossom into speech.]

Setebos, Setebos, and Setebos!
'Thinketh He dwelleth i' the cold o' the moon.

'Thinketh He made it, with the sun to match,
But not the stars; the stars came otherwise;
Only made clouds, winds, meteors, such as that;
Also this isle, what lives and grows thereon,
And snaky sea which rounds and ends the same.   30

'Thinketh, it came of being ill at ease;
He hated that He cannot change His cold,
Nor cure its ache. 'Hath° spied an icy fish
That longed to 'scape the rock-stream where she lived,
And thaw herself within the lukewarm brine
O' the lazy sea her stream thrusts far amid,
A crystal spike 'twixt two warm walls of wave;
Only, she ever sickened, found repulse
At the other kind of water, not her life
(Green-dense and dim-delicious, bred o' the sun),   40
Flounced back from bliss she was not born to breathe,
And in her old bounds buried her despair,
Hating and loving warmth alike: so He.

'Thinketh, He made thereat the sun, this isle,
Trees and the fowls here, beast and creeping thing;
Yon otter, sleek-wet, black, lithe as a leech;
Yon auk, one fire-eye in a ball of foam,
That floats and feeds; a certain badger brown
He hath watched hunt with that slant white-wedge eye
By moonlight; and the pie° with the long tongue   50
That pricks deep into oakwarts for a worm,
And says a plain word when she finds her prize,
But will not eat the ants; the ants themselves
That build a wall of seeds and settled stalks
About their hole—He made all these and more,
Made all we see, and us, in spite; how else?
He could not, Himself, make a second self
To be His mate—as well have made Himself;
He would not make what He mislikes or slights,
An eyesore to Him, or not worth His pains;   60
But did, in envy, listlessness, or sport,
Make what Himself would fain, in a manner, be—
Weaker in most points, stronger in a few,
Worthy, and yet mere playthings all the while,
Things He admires and mocks too—that is it.
Because, so brave, so better though they be,

---

261 **the New Jerusalem.** For a description of the New Jerusalem and its walls, see *Revelation,* 21:10–21 263 **Leonard,** Leonardo da Vinci (1452–1519), one of the greatest of Italian painters **Caliban upon Setebos.** Caliban is a kind of semi-intelligent monster, one of the servants of Prospero and his daughter Miranda on the island in Shakespeare's *The Tempest.* Caliban was the son of the witch Sycorax, who worshiped Setebos, the god of the Patagonians. The epigraph is from *Psalms,* 50: 21; it is spoken by God to the wicked. Caliban talks in the third person to avoid responsibility for his meditations. Thus "he," with a lower-case *h,* refers to Caliban; "Him," with an upper-case *H,* refers to Setebos. Caliban even omits his own pronominal reference entirely to avoid culpability in the eyes of Setebos. Toward the end (ll. 202 ff.), he forgets his caution and uses the personal pronoun 1–23 **'Will . . . speech.** In these lines Caliban describes his physical background and the reason for his theological speculations. In most of the poem he speaks of himself in the third person 5 **eft-things,** lizard-like animals 7 **pompion-plant,** a vine of the pumpkin family

17 **Him.** Pronouns referring to Setebos are capitalized 18 **time . . . now,** in summer, when Setebos is likely to be away from the island; in winter he would usually be at home, on or near the island 33 **'Hath.** He (Caliban) hath 50 **pie,** magpie

It nothing skills if He begin to plague.
Look now, I melt a gourd-fruit into mash,
And honeycomb and pods, I have perceived,
70 Which bite like finches when they bill and kiss—
Then, when froth rises bladdery,° drink up all,
Quick, quick, till maggots scamper through my brain;
Last, throw me on my back i' the seeded thyme,
And wanton, wishing I were born a bird.
Put case,° unable to be what I wish,
I yet could make a live bird out of clay;
Would not I take clay, pinch my Caliban
Able to fly?—for, there, see, he hath wings,
And great comb like the hoopoe's° to admire,
80 And there, a sting to do his foes offense;
There, and I will that he begin to live,
Fly to yon rock-top, nip me off the horns
Of grigs° high up that make the merry din,
Saucy through their veined wings, and mind me not.
In which feat, if his leg snapped, brittle clay,
And he lay stupid-like—why, I should laugh;
And if he, spying me, should fall to weep,
Beseech me to be good, repair his wrong,
Bid his poor leg smart less or grow again—
90 Well, as the chance were, this might take or else
Not take my fancy; I might hear his cry,
And give the manikin three sound legs for one,
Or pluck the other off, leave him like an egg,
And lessoned he was mine and merely clay.
Were this no pleasure, lying in the thyme,
Drinking the mash, with brain become alive,
Making and marring clay at will? So He.

'Thinketh, such shows nor right nor wrong in Him,
Nor kind, nor cruel; He is strong and Lord.
100 'Am strong myself compared to yonder crabs
That march now from the mountain to the sea;
'Let twenty pass, and stone the twenty-first,
Loving not, hating not, just choosing so.°
'Say, the first straggler that boasts purple spots
Shall join the file, one pincer twisted off;
'Say, this bruised fellow shall receive a worm,
And two worms he whose nippers end in red;
As it likes me each time, I do. So He.

Well then, 'supposeth He is good i' the main,
110 Placable if His mind and ways were guessed,
But rougher than His handiwork, be sure!
Oh, He hath made things worthier than Himself,
And envieth that, so helped, such things do more
Than He who made them! What consoles but this?
That they, unless through Him, do naught at all,

And must submit; what other use in things?
'Hath cut a pipe of pithless elder-joint

That, blown through, gives exact the scream o' the jay
When from her wing you twitch the feathers blue;
Sound this, and little birds that hate the jay   120
Flock within stone's throw, glad their foe is hurt.
Put case such pipe could prattle and boast forsooth,
"I catch the birds, I am the crafty thing,
I make the cry my maker cannot make
With his great round mouth; he must blow through
    mine!"
Would not I smash it with my foot? So He.
But wherefore rough, why cold and ill at ease?
Aha, that is a question! Ask, for that,
What knows—the something over Setebos
That made Him, or He, may be, found and fought,   130
Worsted, drove off, and did to nothing, perchance.
There may be something quiet o'er His head,
Out of His reach, that feels nor joy nor grief,
Since both derive from weakness in some way.
I joy because the quails come; would not joy
Could I bring quails here when I have a mind;
This Quiet, all it hath a mind to, doth.
'Esteemeth stars the outposts of its couch,
But never spends much thought nor care that way.
It may look up, work up—the worse for those   140
It works on! 'Careth but for Setebos
The many-handed as a cuttle-fish,
Who, making Himself feared through what He does,
Looks up, first, and perceives he cannot soar
To what is quiet and hath happy life;
Next looks down here, and out of very spite
Makes this a bauble-world to ape yon real,
These good things to match those as hips do grapes.
'Tis solace making baubles, aye, and sport.
Himself peeped late, eyed Prosper at his books   150
Careless and lofty, lord now of the isle;
Vexed, 'stitched a book of broad leaves, arrow-
    shaped,
Wrote thereon, he knows what, prodigious words;
Has peeled a wand and called it by a name;
Weareth at whiles for an enchanter's robe
The eyed skin of a supple oncelot;°
And hath an ounce sleeker than youngling mole,
A four-legged serpent he makes cower and couch,
Now snarl, now hold its breath and mind his eye,
And saith she is Miranda and my wife.   160
'Keeps for his Ariel° a tall pouch-bill crane
He bids go wade for fish and straight disgorge;
Also a sea-beast, lumpish, which he snared,
Blinded the eyes of, and brought somewhat tame,
And split its toe-webs, and now pens the drudge
In a hole o' the rock and calls him Caliban—
A bitter heart that bides its time and bites.
'Plays thus at being Prosper in a way,
Taketh his mirth with make-believes. So He.

His dam held that the Quiet made all things   170

---

71 **bladdery,** in bladder-like bubbles   75 **Put case, etc.** If Caliban were the Creator, he would do things out of spite or envy, or as an exercise of absolute will; so does Setebos   79 **hoopoe,** a kind of bird with a beautiful crest   83 **grigs,** crickets   103 **Loving . . . so.** This line and ll. 98–108 correspond with the Calvinistic doctrine of election and reprobation, whereby some persons are predestined to eternal life and others to eternal death

156 **oncelot,** the ounce, or snow leopard   161 **Ariel,** an airy spirit in the service of Prospero

Robert Browning   935

Which Setebos vexed only; 'holds not so.
Who made them weak, meant weakness He might vex.
Had He meant other, while His hand was in,
Why not make horny eyes no thorn could prick,
Or plate my scalp with bone against the snow,
Or overscale my flesh 'neath joint and joint,
Like an orc's° armor? Aye—so spoil His sport!
He is the One now; only He doth all.

'Saith, He may like, perchance, what profits Him.
180 Aye, himself loves what does him good; but why?
'Gets good no otherwise. This blinded beast
Loves whoso places flesh-meat on his nose,
But, had he eyes, would want no help, but hate
Or love, just as it liked him; He hath eyes.
Also it pleaseth Setebos to work,
Use all His hands, and exercise much craft,
By no means for the love of what is worked.
'Tasteth, himself, no finer good i' the world
When all goes right, in this safe summer-time,
190 And he wants little, hungers, aches not much,
Than trying what to do with wit and strength.
'Falls to make something; 'piled yon pile of turfs,
And squared and stuck there squares of soft white
chalk,
And, with a fish-tooth, scratched a moon on each,
And set up endwise certain spikes of tree,
And crowned the whole with a sloth's skull a-top,
Found dead i' the woods, too hard for one to kill.
No use at all i' the work, for work's sole sake;
'Shall some day knock it down again. So He.

200 'Saith He is terrible; watch His feats in proof!
One hurricane will spoil six good months' hope.
He hath a spite against me, that I know,
Just as He favors Prosper, who knows why?
So it is, all the same, as well I find.
'Wove wattles° half the winter, fenced them firm
With stone and stake to stop she-tortoises
Crawling to lay their eggs here; well, one wave,
Feeling the foot of Him upon its neck,
Gaped as a snake does, lolled out its large tongue,
210 And licked the whole labor flat—so much for spite.
'Saw a ball flame down late (yonder it lies)
Where, half an hour before, I slept i' the shade.
Often they scatter sparkles; there is force!
'Dug up a newt He may have envied once
And turned to stone, shut up inside a stone.
Please Him and hinder this?—What Prosper does?
Aha, if He would tell me how! Not He!
There is the sport; discover how or die!
All need not die, for of the things o' the isle
220 Some flee afar, some dive, some run up trees.
Those at His mercy—why, they please Him most
When . . . when . . . well, never try the same way
twice!

Repeat what act has pleased, He may grow wroth.
You must not know His ways, and play Him off,
Sure of the issue. 'Doth the like himself:
'Spareth a squirrel that it nothing fears
But steals the nut from underneath my thumb,
And when I threat, bites stoutly in defense;
'Spareth an urchin that contrariwise,
Curls up into a ball, pretending death   230
For fright at my approach—the two ways please.
But what would move my choler more than this,
That either creature counted on its life
Tomorrow and next day and all days to come,
Saying, forsooth, in the inmost of its heart,
"Because he did so yesterday with me,
And otherwise with such another brute,
So must he do henceforth and always."—Aye?
Would teach the reasoning couple what "must"
means!
'Doth as he likes, or wherefore Lord? So He.   240

'Conceiveth all things will continue thus,
And we shall have to live in fear of Him
So long as He lives, keeps His strength; no change,
If He have done His best, make no new world
To please Him more, so leave off watching this—
If He surprise not even the Quiet's self
Some strange day—or, suppose, grow into it
As grubs grow butterflies; else, here we are,
And there is He, and nowhere help at all.

'Believeth with the life, the pain shall stop.   250
His dam held different, that after death
He both plagued enemies and feasted friends:
Idly! He doth His worst in this our life,
Giving just respite lest we die through pain,
Saving last pain for worst—with which, an end.
Meanwhile, the best way to escape His ire
Is, not to seem too happy. 'Sees, himself,
Yonder two flies, with purple films and pink,
Bask on the pompion-bell above; kills both.
'Sees two balck painful beetles roll their ball   260
On head and tail as if to save their lives;
Moves them the stick away they strive to clear.

Even so, 'would have Him misconceive, suppose
This Caliban strives hard and ails no less,
And always, above all else, envies Him;
Wherefore he mainly dances on dark nights,
Moans in the sun, gets under holes to laugh,
And never speaks his mind save housed as now:
Outside, 'groans, curses. If He caught me here,
O'erheard this speech, and asked, "What chucklest   270
at?"
'Would, to appease Him, cut a finger off,
Or of my three kid yearlings burn the best,
Or let the toothsome apples rot on tree,
Or push my tame beast for the orc to taste—
While myself lit a fire, and made a song

177 **orc**, a sea monster   205 **wattles**, twigs

And sung it, "*What I hate, be consecrate*
To celebrate Thee and Thy state, no mate
For Thee; what see for envy in poor me?"
Hoping the while, since evils sometimes mend,
280 Warts rub away, and sores are cured with slime,
That some strange day, will either the Quiet catch
And conquer Setebos, or likelier He
Decrepit may doze, doze, as good as die.

[What, what? A curtain o'er the world at once!
Crickets stop hissing; not a bird—or yes,
There scuds His raven that has told Him all!
It was fool's play, this prattling! Ha! The wind
Shoulders the pillared dust, death's house o' the move,
And fast invading fires begin! White blaze—
290 A tree's head snaps—and there, there, there, there,
there,
His thunder follows! Fool to gibe at Him!
Lo! 'Lieth flat and loveth Setebos!
'Maketh his teeth meet through his upper lip,
Will let those quails fly, will not eat this month
One little mess of whelks, so he may 'scape!]
(1864)

PROSPICE°

Fear death?—to feel the fog in my throat,
    The mist in my face,
When the snows begin, and the blasts denote
    I am nearing the place,
The power of the night, the press of the storm,
    The post of the foe;
Where he stands, the Arch Fear in a visible form,
    Yet the strong man must go.
For the journey is done and the summit attained,
10   And the barriers fall,
Though a battle's to fight ere the guerdon be gained,
    The reward of it all.
I was ever a fighter, so—one fight more,
    The best and the last!
I would hate that death bandaged my eyes, and fore-
    bore,
    And bade me creep past.
No! let me taste the whole of it, fare like my peers,
    The heroes of old,
Bear the brunt, in a minute pay glad life's arrears
20   Of pain, darkness, and cold.
For sudden the worst turns the best to the brave,
    The black minute's at end,
And the elements' rage, the fiend-voices that rave,
    Shall dwindle, shall blend,
Shall change, shall become first a peace out of pain,

Prospice. The title of this poem, written shortly after the death of Mrs. Browning, means *Look Forward*

Then a light, then thy breast,
O thou soul of my soul! I shall clasp thee again,
    And with God be the rest!
(1861; 1864)

from THE RING AND THE BOOK

PROEM

O lyric Love, half angel and half bird,
And all a wonder and a wild desire—
Boldest of hearts that ever braved the sun,
Took sanctuary within the holier blue,
And sang a kindred soul out to his face—
Yet human at the red-ripe of the heart—
When the first summons from the darkling earth
Reached thee amid thy chambers, blanched their blue,
And bared them of the glory—to drop down,
To toil for man, to suffer or to die—   10
This is the same voice: can thy soul know change?
Hail then, and hearken from the realms of help!
Never may I commence my song, my due
To God who best taught song by gift of thee,
Except with bent head and beseeching hand—
That still, despite the distance and the dark,
What was, again may be; some interchange
Of grace, some splendor once thy very thought,
Some benediction anciently thy smile:
—Never conclude, but raising hand and head   20
Thither where eyes, that cannot reach, yet yearn
For all hope, all sustainment, all reward,
Their utmost up and on—so blessing back
In those thy realms of help, that heaven thy home,
Some whiteness which, I judge, thy face makes proud,
Some wanness where, I think, thy foot may fall!
(1869)

EPILOGUE TO ASOLANDO

At the midnight in the silence of the sleep-time,
    When you set your fancies free,
Will they pass to where—by death, fools think, im-
        prisoned—
Low he lies who once so loved you, whom you loved
        so,
    —Pity me?

Oh, to love so, be so loved, yet so mistaken!
    What had I on earth to do
With the slothful, with the mawkish, the unmanly?
Like the aimless, helpless, hopeless, did I drivel—   10
    Being—who?

One who never turned his back but marched breast
    forward,
  Never doubted clouds would break,
Never dreamed, though right were worsted, wrong
    would triumph,
Held we fall to rise, are baffled to fight better,
    Sleep to wake.

No! At noonday, in the bustle of man's work-time,
  Greet the unseen with a cheer!
Bid him forward, breast and back as either should be,
"Strive and thrive!" cry, "Speed—fight on, fare ever
    There as here!"
(1889)

ELIZABETH BARRETT BROWNING 1806–1861

Elizabeth Barrett's life up to her forty-first year has frequently been the subject of story and drama. An injury to her spine when she was fifteen, the shock of her brother Edward's death by drowning in 1840, and her father's insistence that none of his daughters should marry caused her to become a recluse. While confined at home, she read Hebrew and Greek and wrote poetry. On September 12, 1846, she became Mrs. Robert Browning by a secret marriage. One week later she left her home at 50 Wimpole Street, London, where she had been dominated by her overly protective father, for Casa Guidi in Florence.

Browning was attracted to Elizabeth Barrett not only by her poetry but by the quality of her mind. The Brownings were not only ideal lovers; they were also intellectual companions, for they understood and admired each other's poetry. She was already considered a rival of Tennyson before Browning, then an obscure poet, came to know her. Her scholarship had been displayed in her *Essay on Mind; with Other Poems*, published when she was twenty, and in a translation of Aeschylus' *Prometheus Bound* in 1833. *The Seraphim and Other Poems*, obviously written under Byron's influence, was published in 1838. It was the volume called *Poems* (1844) that attracted Browning to her work and to her. "The Cry of the Children" and "Cry of the Human," both from this volume, express her deep and almost painful social sympathy. In "Lady Geraldine's Courtship" her allusion to Browning's work, which was seldom read, flattered and touched him.

While she was engaged, Barrett had written some sonnets to Robert; as Mrs. Browning she added to these, and in 1850 she gave him the *Sonnets from the Portuguese* as a gift. The intimate nature of these love poems is revealed in the title, for Browning had playfully called her his "little Portuguese" in reference to her dark complexion. Her reputation today rests mainly on this sonnet sequence.

Mrs. Browning's concern for liberal causes resulted in an interest in Italian political affairs that was shared by her husband. Her political interest and the delicacy of her health kept her from writing as much in the last years of her life as she had done earlier. Her *Last Poems* was published in 1862, a year after her death. She was buried in Florence.

from SONNETS FROM THE PORTUGUESE

1

I thought once how Theocritus° had sung
Of the sweet years, the dear and wished-for years,
Who each one in a gracious hand appears
To bear a gift for mortals, old or young;
And, as I mused it in his antique tongue,   5
I saw, in gradual vision through my tears,
The sweet, sad years, the melancholy years,
Those of my own life, who by turns had flung
A shadow across me. Straightway I was 'ware,
So weeping, how a mystic Shape did move   10
Behind me, and drew me backward by the hair;
And a voice said in mastery, while I strove—
"Guess now who holds thee?"—"Death,"° I said.
  But, there,
The silver answer rang—"Not Death, but Love."

14

If thou must love me, let it be for naught
Except for love's sake only. Do not say
"I love her for her smile—her look—her way
Of speaking gently—for a trick of thought
That falls in well with mine, and certes brought   5
A sense of pleasant ease on such a day"—
For these things in themselves, Beloved, may
Be changed, or change for thee—and love, so
  wrought,
May be unwrought so. Neither love me for
Thine own dear pity's wiping my cheeks dry—   10
A creature might forget to weep, who bore
Thy comfort long, and lose thy love thereby!
But love me for love's sake, that evermore
Thou mayst love on, through love's eternity.

20

Belovéd, my Belovéd, when I think
That thou wast in the world a year ago,

Sonnet 1   1 **Theocritus,** famous Greek pastoral poet of the third century B.C.
13 **Death.** Miss Barrett had been an invalid for years

What time I sat alone here in the snow
5 And saw no footprint, heard the silence sink
No moment at thy voice, but, link by link,
Went counting all my chains as if that so
They never could fall off at any blow
Struck by thy possible hand,—why, thus I drink
10 Of life's great cup of wonder! Wonderful,
Never to feel thee thrill the day or night
With personal act or speech,—nor ever cull
Some prescience of thee with the blossoms white
Thou sawest growing! Atheists are as dull,
Who cannot guess God's presence out of sight.

43

How do I love thee? Let me count the ways.
I love thee to the depth and breadth and height
My soul can reach, when feeling out of sight
5 For the ends of Being and ideal Grace.
I love thee to the level of everyday's
Most quiet need, by sun and candle-light.
I love thee freely, as men strive for Right;
I love thee purely, as they turn from Praise.
10 I love thee with the passion put to use
In my old griefs, and with my childhood's faith.
I love thee with a love I seemed to lose
With my lost saints—I love thee with the breath,
Smiles, tears, of all my life!—and, if God choose,
I shall but love thee better after death.
(1845–1846; 1850)

EMILY BRONTË
1818–1848

Victorian literature provided several examples of
literary families in which more than one member
was talented—the Tennysons, the Newmans, the Rossettis, and the Brontës. The three Brontë sisters—
Charlotte (1816–1855), Emily (1818–1848), and Anne
(1819–1849)—were the children of an impoverished
but well-educated and intelligent clergyman of
Haworth in Yorkshire. All three became novelists, but
Charlotte was the most famous of the three in her
time.

The lives of all three sisters were outwardly uneventful. After their mother died in 1821, they were
left very much to themselves at home. The girls were
avid readers and loved to ramble on the desolate
Yorkshire moors. They were sent to very strict boarding schools, which left them with many harsh
memories. When they were at home, however, the
three happily indulged in imaginative games involving
the make-believe kingdoms of Angria and Gondal;
they kept extended chronicles of the romantic goings-on that took place in them. It is clear that Emily's
contributions to the Poems—published in 1846 by the
three sisters under the pseudonyms Currer, Ellis, and
Acton Bell (Emily was "Ellis")—had their origin in the
imaginary kingdom of Gondal, which strongly resembled Yorkshire. Anne and Charlotte generously admitted that the genuine poetry in Poems was Emily's. The
publication of this volume preceded by only two
months the publication of Emily's novel Wuthering
Heights, in which the strange love experiences of
Heathcliff and Catherine Earnshaw closely resemble
the love experiences depicted in Poems.

The personal lives of the Brontë sisters were in
many ways tragic. All three attempted to become
schoolteachers, but none seemed to possess the required temperament; the school opened in the parsonage at Haworth in 1844 attracted no pupils. Their
book of Poems was published at their own expense
and received few reviews and even fewer sales. With
the exception of the sisters' novels (including Wuthering Heights by Emily, Jane Eyre by Charlotte, and
Agnes Grey by Anne), their efforts met with little success. While attending her brother's funeral (he died at
the age of thirty) in 1848, Emily caught a cold that
eventually led to tuberculosis; she died the same year
at thirty. Anne, Emily's closest friend, died of the same
disease a year later at twenty-nine. Charlotte, after
marrying the curate assigned to her father's church in
Haworth, died during pregnancy in 1855 at
thirty-nine.

REMEMBRANCE

Cold in the earth—and the deep snow piled above
    thee,
Far, far removed, cold in the dreary grave!
Have I forgot, my only Love, to love thee,
Severed at last by Time's all-severing wave?

Now when alone, do my thoughts no longer hover
Over the mountains, on that northern shore,
Resting their wings where heath and fern-leaves cover
Thy noble heart forever, ever more?

Cold in the earth—and fifteen wild Decembers,
From those brown hills, have melted into spring; 10
Faithful, indeed, is the spirit that remembers
After such years of change and suffering!

Sweet Love of youth, forgive, if I forget thee,
While the world's tide is bearing me along;

Other desires and other hopes beset me,
Hopes which obscure, but cannot do thee wrong!

No later light has lightened up my heaven,
No second morn has ever shone for me;
All my life's bliss from thy dear life was given,
20 All my life's bliss is in the grave with thee.

But, when the days of golden dreams had perished,
And ev'n Despair was powerless to destroy;
Then did I learn how existence could be cherished,
Strengthened, and fed without the aid of joy.

Then did I check the tears of useless passion—
Weaned my young soul from yearning after thine;
Sternly denied its burning wish to hasten
Down to that tomb already more than mine.

And, even yet, I dare not let it languish,
30 Dare not indulge in memory's rapturous pain;
Once drinking deep of that divinest anguish,
How could I seek the empty world again?
(1845; 1846)

THE NIGHT IS DARKENING

The night is darkening round me,
  The wild winds coldly blow;
But a tyrant spell has bound me,
  And I cannot, cannot go.

5 The giant trees are bending
  Their bare boughs weighed with snow;
The storm is fast descending,
  And yet I cannot go.

Clouds beyond clouds above me,
10 Wastes beyond wastes below;
But nothing drear can move me:
  I will not, cannot go.
(1846)

OFTEN REBUKED,
YET ALWAYS BACK RETURNING

Often rebuked, yet always back returning
  To those first feelings that were born with me,
And leaving busy chase of wealth and learning
  For idle dreams of things which cannot be:

Today, I will seek not the shadowy region;
  Its unsustaining vastness waxes drear;
And visions rising, legion after legion,
  Bring the unreal world too strangely near.

I'll walk, but not in old heroic traces,
  And not in paths of high morality,
And not among the half-distinguished faces, 10
  The clouded forms of long-past history.

I'll walk where my own nature would be leading—
  It vexes me to choose another guide—
Where the gray flocks in ferny glens are feeding,
  Where the wild wind blows on the mountain-side.

What have those lonely mountains° worth revealing?
  More glory and more grief than I can tell:
The earth that wakes one human heart to feeling
  Can center both the worlds of Heaven and Hell. 20
(1850)

NO COWARD SOUL IS MINE

No coward soul is mine,
No trembler in the world's storm-troubled sphere;
  I see Heaven's glories shine,
And faith shines equal, arming me from fear.

  O God within my breast,
Almighty, ever-present Deity!
  Life—that in me has rest,
As I—undying Life—have power in Thee!

  Vain are the thousand creeds
That move men's hearts—unutterably vain; 10
  Worthless as withered weeds,
Or idlest froth amid the boundless main,

  To waken doubt in one
Holding so fast by Thine infinity;
  So surely anchored on
The steadfast rock of immortality.

  With wide-embracing love
Thy spirit animates eternal years,
  Pervades and broods above,
Changes, sustains, dissolves, creates, and rears. 20

  Though earth and man were gone,
And suns and universes ceased to be,
  And Thou were left alone,
Every existence would exist in Thee.

  There is not room for Death,
Nor atom that his might could render void;
  Thou—Thou art Being and Breath,
And what Thou art may never be destroyed.
(1850)

Often Rebuked, Yet Always Back Returning 17 **those lonely mountains,** the moors in Yorkshire, where Emily Brontë lived

JOHN RUSKIN
1819–1900

John Ruskin was born in London in 1819. His father was a prosperous wine merchant who gave his son an unusually sheltered childhood. The father personally tutored his son in the eighteenth-century classics and encouraged his appreciation for art and his talent for drawing. As a youth, Ruskin spent many hours looking at pictures in the galleries in and around London, especially the Dulwich College Picture Gallery. Mrs. Ruskin, intensely religious like her husband, read the Bible to her son daily. Several family tours of the Continent exposed the young Ruskin to significant art and architecture. In 1836 Ruskin matriculated at Christ Church College, Oxford, where he won the Newdigate Poetry Prize. Because of a generous allowance from his father, he began to collect pictures by the noted English landscape artist J. M. W. Turner (1775–1851). In the spring of 1840 Ruskin was advised to spend the winter abroad for health reasons; he and his parents soon departed for Italy, where he befriended several painters and made many sketches. His health improved; he returned to Oxford and graduated in 1842. The family spent the following summer in the French Alps, where Ruskin began a book in defense of Turner, whose recent exhibition at the Royal Academy had met with severe criticism. The book, the first volume of *Modern Painters*, was published in 1843 when Ruskin was twenty-four; it met with considerable success. Ruskin again visited Italy in 1845 but this time without his parents. On this visit he became quite taken by medieval architecture in the northern region and made many excellent sketches.

When he returned to England, he worked on the second volume of *Modern Painters*, which appeared in 1846. After yet another trip to Italy, he became engaged to Euphemia Chalmers Grey. They were married in 1848, but the marriage was annulled in 1854 on the grounds of Ruskin's impotence. *The Seven Lamps of Architecture*, a book on the essential qualities of Gothic architecture, was published in 1849. The first volume of *The Stones of Venice*, published in 1851, discussed the moral and spiritual forces at work in Venetian architecture. In this same year Ruskin defended the Pre-Raphaelite Brotherhood, a group of young English artists formed in opposition to the accepted academic school of painting, in a series of letters to the London *Times*. Ruskin soon came to know Dante Gabriel Rossetti, Edward Burne-Jones, and John Everett Millais, all members of the Brotherhood. Ruskin published the third and fourth volumes of *Modern Painters* in 1856. He then offered his services to help organize the paintings Turner had left to the National Gallery when he died in 1851. Volume five of *Modern Painters* was issued in 1860, when Ruskin was beginning his decline into intermittent spells of madness.

In 1862 he issued in book form *Unto This Last*, a series of essays on the nature of wealth which opposed the fashionable laissez-faire economic doctrines of the time and received harsh criticism. *Unto This Last* marks a definite break in his career—everything he wrote prior to it was concerned primarily with aesthetics; everything he wrote after it (*Sesame and Lilies*, 1865; *The Crown of Wild Olive*, 1866; *Time and Tide*, 1867; *Fors Clavigera*, 1871–1874; *Munera Pulveris*, 1872) was concerned primarily with ethics. But the trend toward the social and the economic criticism that forms the great body of Ruskin's later writing is apparent in his earlier writing on art, especially in the famous chapter, "The Nature of Gothic," in *The Stones of Venice*. His theory of aesthetics was ethical, for he believed that great art had to be moral and could only emerge from a just society in which manual labor is respected as creative. Ruskin's philosophy, in fact, was essentially consistent throughout his life.

Despite his gradually declining state of mind and strength of purpose, he remained active and was named Slade Professor of Fine Arts at Oxford in 1869. Fits of illness interrupted his work and his busy lecture schedule. He suffered an attack of acute mania in 1878 and resigned his professorship the following year. He managed to complete his autobiography, *Praeterita* (1885–1889), before a final attack of disabling madness. He died in 1900.

Ruskin's essays on art are smooth, ornate, almost too elaborate; in those on economic theory, however, he seems to have imitated his mentor, Thomas Carlyle, and the richness of his earlier manner disappeared. His reading of the English poets, especially Wordsworth, his thorough familiarity with the Bible, and his training as a painter influenced his style. The accuracy, the detail, the color, and the ornateness of his language are those of an artist, even if the cadences of his sentences suggest the Old Testament. Ruskin exerted an enormous influence in the spheres of art, economics, politics, and morals. His admirers included such prominent writers of the Victorian period as William Morris, Walter Pater, and Oscar Wilde, as well as such diverse figures as Marcel Proust and Mahatma Gandhi.

from THE STONES OF VENICE

According to Ruskin, *The Stones of Venice* was written "to show that certain right states of temper and moral feeling were the magic powers by which all good architecture, without exception, had been produced. *The Stones of Venice* had, from beginning to end, no other aim than to show that the Gothic architecture of Venice had risen out of, and indicated in all its features, a state of pure national faith, and of domestic virtue; and that its Renaissance architecture had arisen out of, and in all its features indicated, a state of concealed national infidelity, and of domestic corruption." The chapter included here, which Ruskin called "precisely and accurately the most important in the whole book," reveals Ruskin turning from criticism of art to criticism of society.

from THE NATURE OF GOTHIC

1. If the reader will look back to the division of our subject which was made in the first chapter of the first volume, he will find that we are now about to enter upon the examination of that school of Venetian architecture which forms an intermediate step between the Byzantine and Gothic forms; but which I find may be conveniently considered in its connection with the latter style. In order that we may discern the tendency of each step of this change, it will be wise in the outset to endeavour to form some general idea of its final result. We know already what the Byzantine architecture is from which the transition was made, but we ought to know something of the Gothic architecture into which it led. I shall endeavour therefore to give the reader in this chapter an idea, at once broad and definite, of the true nature of *Gothic* architecture, properly so called; not of that of Venice only, but of universal Gothic: for it will be one of the most interesting parts of our subsequent inquiry, to find out how far Venetian architecture reached the universal or perfect type of Gothic, and how far it either fell short of it, or assumed foreign and independent forms.

2. The principal difficulty in doing this arises from the fact that every building of the Gothic period differs in some important respect from every other; and many include features which, if they occurred in other buildings, would not be considered Gothic at all; so that all we have to reason upon is merely, if I may be allowed so to express it, a greater or less degree of Gothicness in each building we examine. And it is this Gothicness,—the character which, according as it is found more or less in a building, makes it more or less Gothic,—of which I want to define the nature; and I feel the same kind of difficulty in doing so which would be encountered by any one who undertook to explain, for instance, the nature of Redness, without any actually red thing to point to, but only orange and purple things. Suppose he had only a piece of heather and a dead oak-leaf to do it with. He might say, the colour which is mixed with the yellow in this oak-leaf, and with the blue in this heather, would be red, if you had it separate; but it would be difficult, nevertheless, to make the abstraction perfectly intelligible: and it is so in a far greater degree to make the abstraction of the Gothic character intelligible, because that character itself is made up of many mingled ideas, and can consist only in their union. That is to say, pointed arches do not constitute Gothic, nor vaulted roofs, nor flying buttresses, nor grotesque sculptures; but all or some of these things, and many other things with them, when they come together so as to have life.

3. Observe also, that, in the definition proposed, I shall only endeavour to analyse the idea which I suppose already to exist in the reader's mind. We all have some notion, most of us a very determined one, of the meaning of the term Gothic; but I know that many persons have this idea in their minds without being able to define it: that is to say, understanding generally that Westminster Abbey is Gothic, and St. Paul's is not, that Strasburg Cathedral is Gothic, and St. Peter's is not, they have, nevertheless, no clear notion of what it is that they recognise in the one or miss in the other, such as would enable them to say how far the work at Westminster or Strasburg is good and pure of its kind; still less to say of any nondescript building, like St. James's Palace or Windsor Castle, how much right Gothic element there is in it, and how much wanting. And I believe this inquiry to be a pleasant and profitable one; and that there will be found something more than usually interesting in tracing out this grey, shadowy, many-pinnacled image of the Gothic spirit within us; and discerning what fellowship there is between it and our Northern hearts. And if, at any point of the inquiry, I should interfere with any of the reader's previously formed conceptions, and use the term Gothic in any sense which he would not willingly attach to it, I do not ask him to accept, but only to examine and understand, my interpretation, as necessary to the intelligibility of what follows in the rest of the work.

4. We have, then, the Gothic character submitted to our analysis, just as the rough mineral is submitted to that of the chemist, entangled with many other foreign substances, itself perhaps in no place pure, or ever to be obtained or seen in purity for more than an instant; but nevertheless a thing of definite and separate nature, however inextricable or confused in appearance. Now observe: the chemist defines his mineral by two separate kinds of character; one external, its crystalline form, hardness, lustre, etc.; the other internal, the proportions and nature of its constituent atoms. Exactly in the same manner, we shall find that Gothic architecture has external forms, and internal elements. Its elements are certain mental tendencies of the builders, legibly expressed in it; as fancifulness, love of variety, love of richness, and such others. Its external forms are pointed arches, vaulted roofs, etc. And unless both the elements and the forms are there, we have no right to call the style Gothic. It is not enough that it has the Form, if it have not also the power and life. It is not enough that it has the Power, if it have not the form. We must therefore inquire into each of these

characters successively; and determine first, what is the Mental Expression, and secondly, what the Material Form, of Gothic architecture, properly so called.

First. Mental Power of Expression. What characters, we have to discover, did the Gothic builders love, or instinctively express in their work, as distinguished from all other builders?

5. Let us go back for a moment to our chemistry, and note that, in defining a mineral by its constituent parts, it is not one nor another of them, that can make up the mineral, but the union of all: for instance, it is neither in charcoal, nor in oxygen, nor in lime, that there is the making of chalk, but in the combination of all three in certain measures; they are all found in very different things from chalk, and there is nothing like chalk either in charcoal or in oxygen, but they are nevertheless necessary to its existence.

So in the various mental characters which make up the soul of Gothic. It is not one nor another that produces it; but their union of certain measures. Each one of them is found in many other architectures besides Gothic; but Gothic cannot exist where they are not found, or, at least, where their place is not in some way supplied. Only there is this great difference between the composition of the mineral, and of the architectural style, that if we withdraw one of its elements from the stone, its form is utterly changed, and its existence as such and such a mineral is destroyed; but if we withdraw one of its mental elements from the Gothic style, it is only a little less Gothic than it was before, and the union of two or three of its elements is enough already to bestow a certain Gothicness of character, which gains in intensity as we add the others, and loses as we again withdraw them.

6. I believe, then, that the characteristic or moral elements of Gothic are the following, placed in the order of their importance:

1. Savageness.   4. Grotesqueness.
2. Changefulness.   5. Rigidity.
3. Naturalism.   6. Redundance.

These characters are here expressed as belonging to the building; as belonging to the builder, they would be expressed thus:—1. Savageness, or Rudeness. 2. Love of Change. 3. Love of Nature. 4. Disturbed Imagination. 5. Obstinacy. 6. Generosity. And I repeat, that the withdrawal of any one, or any two, will not at once destroy the Gothic character of a building, but the removal of a majority of them will. I shall proceed to examine them in their order.

7. SAVAGENESS. I am not sure when the word ''Gothic'' was first generically applied to the architecture of the North; but I presume that, whatever the date of its original usage, it was intended to imply reproach, and express the barbaric character of the nations among whom that architecture arose. It never implied that they were literally of Gothic lineage, far less that their architecture had been originally invented by the Goths themselves; but it did imply that they and their buildings together exhibited a degree of sternness and rudeness, which, in contradistinction to the character of Southern and Eastern nations, appeared like a perpetual reflection of the contrast between the Goth and the Roman in their first encounter. And when that fallen Roman, in the utmost impotence of his luxury, and insolence of his guilt, became the model for the imitation of civilised Europe, at the close of the so-called Dark ages, the word Gothic became a term of unmitigated contempt, not unmixed with aversion. From that contempt, by the exertion of the antiquaries and architects of this century, Gothic architecture has been sufficiently vindicated; and perhaps some among us, in our admiration of the magnificent science of its structure, and sacredness of its expression, might desire that the term of ancient reproach should be withdrawn, and some other, of more apparent honourableness, adopted in its place. There is no chance, as there is no need, of such a substitution. As far as the epithet was used scornfully, it was used falsely; but there is no reproach in the word, rightly understood; on the contrary, there is a profound truth, which the instinct of mankind almost unconsciously recognises. It is true, greatly and deeply true, that the architecture of the North is rude and wild; but it is not true, that, for this reason, we are to condemn it, or despise. Far otherwise: I believe it is in this very character that it deserves our profoundest reverence.

8. The charts of the world which have been drawn up by modern science have thrown into a narrow space the expression of a vast amount of knowledge, but I have never yet seen any one pictorial enough to enable the spectator to imagine the kind of contrast in physical character which exists between Northern and Southern countries. We know the differences in detail, but we have not that broad glance and grasp which would enable us to feel them in their fulness. We know that gentians grow on the Alps, and olives on the Apennines; but we do not enough conceive for ourselves that variegated mosaic of the world's surface which a bird sees in its migration, that difference between the district of the gentian and of the olive which the stork and the swallow see far off, as they lean upon the sirocco wind. Let us, for a moment, try to raise ourselves even above the level of their flight, and imagine the Mediterranean lying beneath us like an irregular lake, and all its ancient promontories sleeping in the sun: here and there an angry spot of thunder, a grey stain of storm, moving upon the burning field; and here and there a fixed wreath of white volcano smoke, surrounded by its circle of ashes; but for the most part a great peacefulness of light, Syria and Greece, Italy and Spain, laid like pieces of a golden pavement into the sea-blue, chased, as we stoop nearer to them, with bossy beaten work of mountain chains, and glowing

softly with terraced gardens, and flowers heavy with frankincense, mixed among masses of laurel, and orange, and plumy palm, that abate with their grey-green shadows the burning of the marble rocks, and of the ledges of porphyry sloping under lucent sand. Then let us pass farther towards the north, until we see the orient colours change gradually into a vast belt of rainy green, where the pastures of Switzerland, and poplar valleys of France, and dark forests of the Danube and Carpathians stretch from the mouths of the Loire to those of the Volga, seen through clefts in grey swirls of rain-cloud and flaky veils of the mist of the brooks, spreading low along the pasture lands: and then, farther north still, to see the earth heave into mighty masses of leaden rock and heathy moor, bordering with a broad waste of gloomy purple that belt of field and wood, and splintering into irregular and grisly islands amidst the northern seas, beaten by storm, and chilled by ice-drift, and tormented by furious pulses of contending tide, until the roots of the last forests fail from among the hill ravines, and the hunger of the north wind bites their peaks into barrenness; and, at last, the wall of ice, durable like iron, sets, deathlike, its white teeth against us out of the polar twilight. And, having once traversed in thought this gradation of the zoned iris of the earth in all its material vastness, let us go down nearer to it, and watch the parallel change in the belt of animal life: the multitudes of swift and brilliant creatures that glance in the air and sea, or tread the sands of the southern zone; striped zebras and spotted leopards, glistening serpents, and birds arrayed in purple and scarlet. Let us contrast their delicacy and brilliancy of colour, and swiftness of motion, with the frost-cramped strength, and shaggy covering, and dusky plumage of the northern tribes; contrast the Arabian horse with the Shetland, the tiger and leopard with the wolf and bear, the antelope with the elk, the bird of paradise with the osprey: and then, submissively acknowledging the great laws by which the earth and all that it bears are ruled throughout their being, let us not condemn, but rejoice in the expression by man of his own rest in the statutes of the lands that gave him birth. Let us watch him with reverence as he sets side by side the burning gems, and smooths with soft sculpture the jasper pillars, that are to reflect a ceaseless sunshine, and rise into a cloudless sky: but not with less reverence let us stand by him, when, with rough strength and hurried stroke, he smites an uncouth animation out of the rocks which he has torn from among the moss of the moorland, and heaves into the darkened air the pile of iron buttress and rugged wall, instinct with work of an imagination as wild and wayward as the northern sea; creations of ungainly shape and rigid limb, but full of wolfish life; fierce as the winds that beat, and changeful as the clouds that shade them.

There is, I repeat, no degradation, no reproach in this, but all dignity and honourableness: and we should err grievously in refusing either to recognise as an essential character of the existing architecture of the North, or to admit as a desirable character in that which it yet may be, this wildness of thought, and roughness of work; this look of mountain brotherhood between the cathedral and the Alp; this magnificence of sturdy power, put forth only the more energetically because the fine finger-touch was chilled away by the frosty wind, and the eye dimmed by the moor-mist, or blinded by the hail; this outspeaking of the strong spirit of men who may not gather redundant fruitage from the earth, nor bask in dreamy benignity of sunshine, but must break the rock for bread, and cleave the forest for fire, and show, even in what they did for their delight, some of the hard habits of the arm and heart that grew on them as they swung the axe or pressed the plough.

9. If, however, the savageness of Gothic architecture, merely as an expression of its origin among Northern nations, may be considered, in some sort, a noble character, it possesses a higher nobility still, when considered as an index, not of climate, but of religious principle.

In the thirteenth and fourteenth paragraphs of Chapter XXI. of the first volume of this work, it was noticed that the systems of architectural ornament, properly so called, might be divided into three:—1. Servile ornament, in which the execution or power of the inferior workman is entirely subjected to the intellect of the higher;—2. Constitutional ornament, in which the executive inferior power is, to a certain point, emancipated and independent, having a will of its own, yet confessing its inferiority and rendering obedience to higher powers;—and 3. Revolutionary ornament, in which no executive inferiority is admitted at all. I must here explain the nature of these divisions at somewhat greater length.

Of Servile ornament, the principal schools are the Greek, Ninevite, and Egyptian; but their servility is of different kinds. The Greek master-workman was far advanced in knowledge and power above the Assyrian or Egyptian. Neither he nor those for whom he worked could endure the appearance of imperfection in anything; and, therefore, what ornament he appointed to be done by those beneath him was composed of mere geometrical forms,—balls, ridges, and perfectly symmetrical foliage,—which would be executed with absolute precision by line and rule, and were as perfect in their way, when completed, as his own figure sculpture. The Assyrian and Egyptian, on the contrary, less cognisant of accurate form in anything, were content to allow their figure sculpture to be executed by inferior workmen, but lowered the method of its treatment to a standard which every workman could reach, and then trained him by discipline so rigid, that there was no chance of his falling beneath the standard appointed. The Greek gave to the lower workman no subject which he could not perfectly execute. The Assyrian gave him subjects which he could only execute imperfectly, but fixed a legal standard for his imperfection. The workman was, in both systems, a slave.°

10. But in the medieval, or especially Christian, system of ornament, this slavery is done away with altogether; Christianity having recognised, in small things as well as great, the individual value of every soul. But it not only recognises its value; it confesses its imperfection, in only bestowing dignity upon the acknowledgment of unworthiness. That admission of lost power and fallen nature, which the Greek or Ninevite felt to be intensely painful, and, as far as might be, altogether refused, the Christian makes daily and hourly, contemplating the fact of it without fear, as tending, in the end, to God's greater glory. Therefore, to every spirit which Christianity summons to her service, her exhortation is: Do what you can, and confess frankly what you are unable to do; neither let your effort be shortened for fear of failure, nor your confession silenced for fear of shame. And it is, perhaps, the principal admirableness of the Gothic schools of architecture, that they thus receive the results of the labour of inferior minds; and out of fragments full of imperfection, and betraying that imperfection in every touch, indulgently raise up a stately and unaccusable whole.

11. But the modern English mind has this much in common with that of the Greek, that it intensely desires, in all things, the utmost completion or perfection compatible with their nature. This is a noble character in the abstract, but becomes ignoble when it causes us to forget the relative dignities of that nature itself, and to prefer the perfectness of the lower nature to the imperfection of the higher; not considering that as, judged by such a rule, all the brute animals would be preferable to man, because more perfect in their functions and kind, and yet are always held inferior to him, so also in the works of man, those which are more perfect in their kind are always inferior to those which are, in their nature, liable to more faults and shortcomings. For the finer the nature, the more flaws it will show through the clearness of it; and it is a law of this universe, that the best things shall be seldomest seen in their best form. The wild grass grows well and strongly, one year with another; but the wheat is, according to the greater nobleness of its nature, liable to the bitterer blight. And therefore, while in all things that we see, or do, we are to desire perfection, and strive for it, we are nevertheless not to set the meaner thing, in its narrow accomplishment, above the nobler thing, in its mighty progress; not to esteem smooth minuteness above shattered majesty; not to prefer mean victory to honourable defeat; not to lower the level of our aim, that we may the more surely enjoy the complacency of success. But above all, in our dealings with the souls of other men, we are to take care how we check, by severe requirement of narrow caution, efforts which might otherwise lead to a noble issue; and, still more, how we withhold our admiration from great excellencies, because they are mingled with rough faults. Now, in the make and nature of every man, however rude or simple, whom we employ in manual labour, there are some powers for better things: some tardy imagination, torpid capacity of emotion, tottering steps of thought, there are, even at the worst; and in most cases it is all our own fault that they *are* tardy or torpid. But they cannot be strengthened, unless we are content to take them in their feebleness, and unless we prize and honour them in their imperfection above the best and most perfect manual skill. And this is what we have to do with all our labourers; to look for the *thoughtful* part of them, and get that out of them, whatever we lose for it, whatever faults and errors we are obliged to take with it. For the best that is in them cannot manifest itself, but in company with much error. Understand this clearly: You can teach a man to draw a straight line, and to cut one; to strike a curved line, and to carve it; and to copy and carve any number of given lines or forms, with admirable speed and perfect precision; and you find his work perfect of its kind: but if you ask him to think about any of those forms, to consider if he cannot find any better in his own head, he stops; his execution becomes hesitating; he thinks, and ten to one he thinks wrong; ten to one he makes a mistake in the first touch he gives to his work as a thinking being. But you have made a man of him for all that. He was only a machine before, an animated tool.

12. And observe, you are put to stern choice in this matter. You must either make a tool of the creature, or a man of him. You cannot make both. Men were not intended to work with the accuracy of tools, to be precise and perfect in all their actions. If you will have that precision out of them, and make their fingers measure degrees like cog-wheels, and their arms strike curves like compasses, you must unhumanise them. All the energy of their spirits must be given to make cogs and compasses of themselves. All their attention and strength must go to the accomplishment of the mean act. The eye of the soul must be bent upon the finger-point, and the soul's force must fill all the invisible nerves that guide it, ten hours a day, that it may not err from its steely precision, and so soul and sight be worn away, and the whole human being be lost at last—a heap of sawdust, so far as its intellectual work in this world is concerned; saved only by its Heart, which cannot go into the form of cogs and compasses, but expands, after the ten hours are over, into fireside humanity. On the other hand, if you will make a man of

The Nature of Gothic   336 a slave. "The third kind of ornament, the Renaissance, is that in which the inferior detail becomes principal, the executor of every minor portion being required to exhibit skill and possess knowledge as great as that which is possessed by the master of the design; and in the endeavour to endow him with this skill and knowledge, his own original power is overwhelmed, and the whole building becomes a wearisome exhibition of well-educated imbecility. We must fully inquire into the nature of this form of error, when we arrive at the examination of the Renaissance schools."—Ruskin's note

the working creature, you cannot make a tool. Let him but begin to imagine, to think, to try to do anything worth doing; and the engine-turned precision is lost at once. Out come all his roughness, all his dulness, all his incapability; shame upon shame, failure upon failure, pause after pause: but out comes the whole majesty of him also; and we know the height of it only, when we see the clouds settling upon him. And, whether the clouds be bright or dark, there will be transfiguration behind and within them.

13. And now, reader, look round this English room of yours, about which you have been proud so often, because the work of it was so good and strong, and the ornaments of it so finished. Examine again all those accurate mouldings, and perfect polishings, and unerring adjustments of the seasoned wood and tempered steel. Many a time you have exulted over them, and thought how great England was, because her slightest work was done so thoroughly. Alas! if read rightly, these perfectnesses are signs of a slavery in our England a thousand times more bitter and more degrading than that of the scourged African, or helot Greek.° Men may be beaten, chained, tormented, yoked like cattle, slaughtered like summer flies, and yet remain in one sense, and the best sense, free. But to smother their souls within them, to blight and hew into rotting pollards° the suckling branches of their human intelligence, to make the flesh and skin which, after the worm's work on it, is to see God, into leathern thongs to yoke machinery with,—this is to be slave-masters indeed; and there might be more freedom in England, though her feudal lords' lightest words were worth men's lives, and though the blood of the vexed husbandman dropped in the furrows of her fields, than there is while the animation of her multitudes is sent like fuel to feed the factory smoke, and the strength of them is given daily to be wasted into the fineness of a web, or racked into the exactness of a line.

14. And, on the other hand, go forth again to gaze upon the old cathedral front, where you have smiled so often at the fantastic ignorance of the old sculptors: examine once more those ugly goblins, and formless monsters, and stern statues, anatomiless and rigid; but do not mock at them, for they are signs of the life and liberty of every workman who struck the stone; a freedom of thought, and rank in scale of being, such as no laws, no charters, no charities can secure; but which it must be the first aim of all Europe at this day to regain for her children.

15. Let me not be thought to speak wildly or extravagantly. It is verily this degradation of the operative into a machine, which, more than any other evil of the times, is leading the mass of the nations everywhere into vain, incoherent, destructive struggling for a freedom of which they cannot explain the nature to themselves. Their universal outcry against wealth, and against nobility, is not forced from them either by the pressure of famine, or the sting of mortified pride. These do much, and have done much in all ages; but the foundations of society were never yet shaken as they are at this day. It is not that men are ill fed, but that they have no pleasure in the work by which they make their bread, and therefore look to wealth as the only means of pleasure. It is not that men are pained by the scorn of the upper classes, but they cannot endure their own; for they feel that the kind of labour to which they are condemned is verily a degrading one, and makes them less than men. Never had the upper classes so much sympathy with the lower, or charity for them, as they have at this day, and yet never were they so much hated by them: for, of old, the separation between the noble and the poor was merely a wall built by law; now it is a veritable difference in level of standing, a precipice between upper and lower grounds in the field of humanity, and there is pestilential air at the bottom of it. I know not if a day is ever to come when the nature of right freedom will be understood, and when men will see that to obey another man, to labour for him, yield reverence to him or to his place, is not slavery. It is often the best kind of liberty,—liberty from care. The man who says to one, Go, and he goeth, and to another, Come, and he cometh, has, in most cases, more sense of restraint and difficulty than the man who obeys him. The movements of the one are hindered by the burden on his shoulder; of the other, by the bridle on his lips: there is no way by which the burden may be lightened; but we need not suffer from the bridle if we do not champ at it. To yield reverence to another, to hold ourselves and our lives at his disposal, is not slavery; often, it is the noblest state in which a man can live in this world. There is, indeed, a reverence which is servile, that is to say irrational or selfish: but there is also noble reverence, that is to say, reasonable and loving; and a man is never so noble as when he is reverent in this kind; nay, even if the feeling pass the bounds of mere reason, so that it be loving, a man is raised by it. Which had, in reality, most of the serf nature in him,—the Irish peasant who was lying in wait yesterday for his landlord, with his musket muzzle thrust through the ragged hedge; or that old mountain servant, who, 200 years ago, at Inverkeithing, gave up his own life and the lives of his seven sons for his chief?°—as each fell, calling forth his brother to the death, "Another for Hector!" And therefore, in all ages and all countries, reverence has been paid and sacrifice made by men to each other, not only without complaint, but rejoicingly; and famine, and peril, and

464 **helot Greek,** a slave   469 **pollards,** trees cut back to the trunk so as to produce a dense mass of branches

541–546 **the Irish . . . chief.** "Vide Preface to 'Fair Maid of Perth.'"—Ruskin's note, referring to Scott's novel

sword, and all evil, and all shame, have been borne willingly in the causes of masters and kings; for all these gifts of the heart ennobled the men who gave, not less than the men who received them, and nature prompted, and God rewarded the sacrifice. But to feel their souls withering within them, unthanked, to find their whole being sunk into an unrecognised abyss, to be counted off into a heap of mechanism, numbered with its wheels, and weighed with its hammer 560 strokes;—this nature bade not,—this God blesses not,—this humanity for no long time is able to endure.

16. We have much studied and much perfected, of late, the great civilised invention of the division of labour; only we give it a false name. It is not, truly speaking, the labour that is divided; but the men:—Divided into mere segments of men—broken into small fragments and crumbs of life; so that all the little piece of intelligence that is left in a man is not enough to make a pin, or a nail, but exhausts itself in making the 570 point of a pin, or the head of a nail. Now it is a good and desirable thing, truly, to make many pins in a day; but if we could only see with what crystal sand their points were polished,—sand of human soul, much to be magnified before it can be discerned for what it is,—we should think there might be some loss in it also. And the great cry that rises from all our manufacturing cities, louder than their furnace blast, is all in very deed for this,—that we manufacture everything there except men; we blanch cotton, and 580 strengthen steel, and refine sugar, and shape pottery; but to brighten, to strengthen, to refine, or to form a single living spirit, never enters into our estimate of advantages. And all the evil to which that cry is urging our myriads can be met only in one way: not by teaching nor preaching, for to teach them is but to show them their misery, and to preach to them, if we do nothing more than preach, is to mock at it. It can be met only by a right understanding, on the part of all classes, of what kinds of labour are good for men, 590 raising them, and making them happy; by a determined sacrifice of such convenience, or beauty, or cheapness as is to be got only by the degradation of the workman; and by equally determined demand for the products and results of healthy and ennobling labour.

17. And how, it will be asked, are these products to be recognised, and this demand to be regulated? Easily: by the observance of three broad and simple rules:

1. Never encourage the manufacture of any article not absolutely necessary, in the production of which 600 *Invention* has no share.

2. Never demand an exact finish for its own sake, but only for some practical or noble end.

3. Never encourage imitation or copying of any kind, except for the sake of preserving record of great works.

The second of these principles is the only one which directly rises out of the consideration of our immediate subject; but I shall briefly explain the meaning and extent of the first also, reserving the enforcement of the third for another place. 610

1. Never encourage the manufacture of anything not necessary, in the production of which invention has no share.

For instance. Glass beads are utterly unnecessary, and there is no design or thought employed in their manufacture. They are formed by first drawing out the glass into rods; these rods are chopped up into fragments of the size of beads by the human hand, and the fragments are then rounded in the furnace. Then men who chop up the rods sit at their work all day, their 620 hands vibrating with a perpetual and exquisitely timed palsy, and the beads dropping beneath their vibration like hail. Neither they, nor the men who draw out the rods or fuse the fragments, have the smallest occasion for the use of any single human faculty; and every young lady, therefore, who buys glass beads is engaged in the slave-trade, and in a much more cruel one than that which we have so long been endeavouring to put down.

But glass cups and vessels may become the subjects 630 of exquisite invention; and if in buying these we pay for the invention, that is to say for the beautiful form, or colour, or engraving, and not for mere finish of execution, we are doing good to humanity.

18. So, again, the cutting of precious stones, in all ordinary cases, requires little exertion of any mental faculty; some tact and judgment in avoiding flaws, and so on, but nothing to bring out the whole mind. Every person who wears cut jewels merely for the sake of their value is, therefore, a slave-driver. 640

But the working of the goldsmith, and the various designing of grouped jewellery and enamel-work, may become the subject of the most noble human intelligence. Therefore, money spent in the purchase of well-designed plate, of precious engraved vases, cameos, or enamels, does good to humanity; and, in work of this kind, jewels may be employed to heighten its splendour; and their cutting is then a price paid for the attainment of a noble end, and thus perfectly allowable. 650

19. I shall perhaps press this law farther elsewhere, but our immediate concern is chiefly with the second, namely, never to demand an exact finish, when it does not lead to a noble end. For observe, I have only dwelt upon the rudeness of Gothic, or any other kind of imperfectness, as admirable, where it was impossible to get design or thought without it. If you are to have the thought of a rough and untaught man, you must have it in a rough and untaught way; but from an educated man, who can without effort express his thoughts in an 660 educated way, take the graceful expression, and be thankful. Only *get* the thought, and do not silence the

peasant because he cannot speak good grammar, or until you have taught him his grammar. Grammar and refinement are good things, both, only be sure of the better thing first. And thus in art, delicate finish is desirable from the greatest masters, and is always given by them. In some places Michael Angelo, Leonardo, Phidias, Perugino, Turner, all finished with the most exquisite care; and the finish they give always leads to the fuller accomplishment of their noble purposes. But lower men than these cannot finish, for it requires consummate knowledge to finish consummately, and then we must take their thoughts as they are able to give them. So the rule is simple: Always look for invention first, and after that, for such execution as will help the invention, and as the inventor is capable of without painful effort, and *no more*. Above all, demand no refinement of execution where there is no thought, for that is slaves' work, unredeemed. Rather choose rough work than smooth work, so only that the practical purpose be answered, and never imagine there is reason to be proud of anything that may be accomplished by patience and sand-paper.

20. I shall only give one example, which however will show the reader what I mean, from the manufacture already alluded to, that of glass. Our modern glass is exquisitely clear in its substance, true in its form, accurate in its cutting. We are proud of this. We ought to be ashamed of it. The old Venice glass was muddy, inaccurate in all its forms, and clumsily cut, if at all. And the old Venetian was justly proud of it. For there is this difference between the English and Venetian workman, that the former thinks only of accurately matching his patterns, and getting his curves perfectly true and his edges perfectly sharp, and becomes a mere machine for rounding curves and sharpening edges, while the old Venetian cared not a whit whether his edges were sharp or not, but he invented a new design for every glass that he made, and never moulded a handle or a lip without a new fancy in it. And therefore, though some Venetian glass is ugly and clumsy enough, when made by clumsy and uninventive workmen, other Venetian glass is so lovely in its forms that no price is too great for it; and we never see the same form in it twice. Now you cannot have the finish and the varied form too. If the workman is thinking about his edges, he cannot be thinking of his design; if of his design, he cannot think of his edges. Choose whether you will pay for the lovely form or the perfect finish, and choose at the same moment whether you will make the worker a man or a grindstone.

21. Nay, but the reader interrupts me,—"If the workman can design beautifully, I would not have him kept at the furnace. Let him be taken away and made a gentleman, and have a studio, and design his glass there, and I will have it blown and cut for him by common workmen, and so I will have my design and my finish too."

All ideas of this kind are founded upon two mistaken suppositions: the first, that one man's thoughts can be, or ought to be, executed by another man's hands; the second, that manual labour is a degradation, when it is governed by intellect.

On a large scale, and in work determinable by line and rule, it is indeed both possible and necessary that the thoughts of one man should be carried out by the labour of others; in this sense I have already defined the best architecture to be the expression of the mind of manhood by the hands of childhood. But on a smaller scale, and in a design which cannot be mathematically defined, one man's thoughts can never be expressed by another: and the difference between the spirit of touch of the man who is inventing, and of the man who is obeying directions, is often all the difference between a great and a common work of art. How wide the separation is between original and second-hand execution, I shall endeavour to show elsewhere; it is not so much to our purpose here as to mark the other and more fatal error of despising manual labour when governed by intellect; for it is no less fatal an error to despise it when thus regulated by intellect, than to value it for its own sake. We are always in these days endeavouring to separate the two; we want one man to be always thinking, and another to be always working, and we call one a gentleman, and the other an operative; whereas the workman ought often to be thinking, and the thinker often to be working, and both should be gentlemen, in the best sense. As it is, we make both ungentle, the one envying, the other despising, his brother; and the mass of society is made up of morbid thinkers, and miserable workers. Now it is only by labour that thought can be made healthy, and only by thought that labour can be made happy, and the two cannot be separated with impunity. It would be well if all of us were good handicraftsmen in some kind, and the dishonour of manual labour done away with altogether; so that though there should still be a trenchant distinction of race between nobles and commoners, there should not, among the latter, be a trenchant distinction of employment, as between idle and working men, or between men of liberal and illiberal professions. All professions should be liberal, and there should be less pride felt in peculiarity of employment, and more in excellence of achievement. And yet more, in each several profession, no master should be too proud to do its hardest work. The painter should grind his own colours; the architect work in the mason's yard with his men; the master-manufacturer be himself a more skilful operative than any man in his mills; and the distinction between one man and another be only in experience and skill, and the authority and wealth which these must naturally and justly obtain.

22. I should be led far from the matter in hand, if I were to pursue this interesting subject. Enough, I trust, has been said to show the reader that the rude-

ness or imperfection which at first rendered the term "Gothic" one of reproach is indeed, when rightly understood, one of the most noble characters of Christian architecture, and not only a noble but an *essential* one. It seems a fantastic paradox, but it is nevertheless a most important truth, that no architecture can be truly noble which is *not* imperfect. And this is easily demonstrable. For since the architect, whom we will suppose capable of doing all in perfection, cannot execute the whole with his own hands, he must either make slaves of his workmen in the old Greek, and present English fashion, and level his work to a slave's capacities, which is to degrade it; or else he must take his workmen as he finds them, and let them show their weaknesses together with their strength, which will involve the Gothic imperfection, but render the whole work as noble as the intellect of the age can make it.

23. But the principle may be stated more broadly still. I have confined the illustration of it to architecture, but I must not leave it as if true of architecture only. Hitherto I have used the words imperfect and perfect merely to distinguish between work grossly unskilful, and work executed with average precision and science; and I have been pleading that any degree of unskilfulness should be admitted, so only that the labourer's mind had room for expression. But, accurately speaking, no good work whatever can be perfect, and *the demand for perfection is always a sign of a misunderstanding of the ends of art.*

24. This for two reasons, both based on everlasting laws. The first, that no great man ever stops working till he has reached his point of failure; that is to say, his mind is always far in advance of his powers of execution, and the latter will now and then give way in trying to follow it; besides that he will always give to the inferior portions of his work only such inferior attention as they require; and according to his greatness he becomes so accustomed to the feeling of dissatisfaction with the best he can do, that in moments of lassitude or anger with himself he will not care though the beholder be dissatisfied also. I believe there has only been one man who would not acknowledge this necessity, and strove always to reach perfection, Leonardo; the end of his vain effort being merely that he would take ten years to a picture, and leave it unfinished. And therefore, if we are to have great men working at all, or less men doing their best, the work will be imperfect, however beautiful. Of human work none but what is bad can be perfect, in its own bad way.°

25. The second reason is, that imperfection is in some sort essential to all that we know of life. It is the sign of life in a mortal body, that is to say, of a state of progress and change. Nothing that lives is, or can be, rigidly perfect; part of it is decaying, part nascent. The foxglove blossom,—a third part bud, a third part past,

a third part in full bloom,—is a type of the life of this world. And in all things that live there are certain irregularities and deficiencies which are not only signs of life, but sources of beauty. No human face is exactly the same in its lines on each side, no leaf perfect in its lobes, no branch in its symmetry. All admit irregularity as they imply change; and to banish imperfection is to destroy expression, to check exertion, to paralyse vitality. All things are literally better, lovelier, and more beloved for the imperfections which have been divinely appointed, that the law of human life may be Effort, and the law of human judgment, Mercy.

Accept this then for a universal law, that neither architecture nor any other noble work of man can be good unless it be imperfect; and let us be prepared for the otherwise strange fact, which we shall discern clearly as we approach the period of the Renaissance, that the first cause of the fall of the arts of Europe was a relentless requirement of perfection, incapable alike either of being silenced by veneration for greatness, or softened into forgiveness of simplicity.

Thus far then of the Rudeness or Savageness, which is the first mental element of Gothic architecture. It is an element in many other healthy architectures also, as in Byzantine and Romanesque; but true Gothic cannot exist without it.

26. The second mental element above named was CHANGEFULNESS, or Variety.

I have already enforced the allowing independent operation to the inferior workman, simply as a duty to *him*, and as ennobling the architecture by rendering it more Christian. We have now to consider what reward we obtain for the performance of this duty, namely, the perpetual variety of every feature of the building.

Wherever the workman is utterly enslaved, the parts of the building must of course be absolutely like each other; for the perfection of his execution can only be reached by exercising him in doing one thing, and giving him nothing else to do. The degree in which the workman is degraded may be thus known at a glance, by observing whether the several parts of the building are similar or not; and if, as in Greek work, all the capitals are alike, and all the mouldings unvaried, then the degradation is complete; if, as in Egyptian or Ninevite work, though the manner of executing certain figures is always the same, the order of design is perpetually varied, the degradation is less total; if, as in Gothic work, there is perpetual change both in design and execution, the workman must have been altogether set free.

27. How much the beholder gains from the liberty of the labourer may perhaps be questioned in England, where one of the strongest instincts in nearly every mind is that Love of Order which makes us desire that our house windows should pair like our carriage horses, and allows us to yield our faith unhesitatingly to architectural theories which fix a form for everything, and forbid variation from it. I would not im-

827 **bad way.** "The Elgin marbles are supposed by many persons to be 'perfect.' In the most important portions they indeed approach perfection, but only there. The draperies are unfinished, the hair and wool of the animals are unfinished, and the entire bas-reliefs of the frieze are roughly cut."—Ruskin's note

peach love of order: it is one of the most useful elements of the English mind; it helps us in our commerce and in all purely practical matters; and it is in many cases one of the foundation stones of morality. Only do not let us suppose that love of order is love of art. It is true that order, in its highest sense, is one of the necessities of art, just as time is a necessity of music; but love of order has no more to do with our right enjoyment of architecture or painting, than love of punctuality with the appreciation of an opera. Experience, I fear, teaches us that accurate and methodical habits in daily life are seldom characteristic of those who either quickly perceive, or richly possess, the creative powers of art; there is, however, nothing inconsistent between the two instincts, and nothing to hinder us from retaining our business habits, and yet fully allowing and enjoying the noblest gifts of Invention. We already do so, in every other branch of art except architecture, and we only do *not* so there because we have been taught that it would be wrong. Our architects gravely inform us that, as there are four rules of arithmetic, there are five orders of architecture; we, in our simplicity, think that this sounds consistent, and believe them. They inform us also that there is one proper form for Corinthian capitals, another for Doric, and another for Ionic. We, considering that there is also a proper form for the letters A, B, and C, think that this also sounds consistent, and accept the proposition. Understanding, therefore, that one form of the said capitals is proper, and no other, and having a conscientious horror of all impropriety, we allow the architect to provide us with the said capitals, of the proper form, in such and such a quantity, and in all other points to take care that the legal forms are observed; which having done, we rest in forced confidence that we are well housed.

28. But our higher instincts are not deceived. We take no pleasure in the building provided for us, resembling that which we take in a new book or a new picture. We may be proud of its size, complacent in its correctness, and happy in its convenience. We may take the same pleasure in its symmetry and workmanship as in a well-ordered room, or a skilful piece of manufacture. And this we suppose to be all the pleasure that architecture was ever intended to give us. The idea of reading a building as we would read Milton or Dante, and getting the same kind of delight out of the stones as out of the stanzas, never enters our minds for a moment. And for good reason:—There is indeed rhythm in the verses, quite as strict as the symmetries or rhythm of the architecture, and a thousand times more beautiful, but there is something else than rhythm. The verses were neither made to order, nor to match, as the capitals were; and we have therefore a kind of pleasure in them other than a sense of propriety. But it requires a strong effort of common sense to shake ourselves quit of all that we have been taught for the last two centuries, and wake to the perception of a truth just as simple and certain as it is new: that great art, whether expressing itself in words, colours, or stones, does *not* say the same thing over and over again; that the merit of architectural, as of every other art, consists in its saying new and different things; that to repeat itself is no more a characteristic of genius in marble than it is of genius in print; and that we may, without offending any laws of good taste, require of an architect, as we do of a novelist, that he should be not only correct, but entertaining.

Yet all this is true, and self-evident; only hidden from us, as many other self-evident things are, by false teaching. Nothing is a great work of art, for the production of which either rules or models can be given. Exactly so far as architecture works on known rules, and from given models, it is not an art, but a manufacture; and it is, of the two procedures, rather less rational (because more easy) to copy capitals or mouldings from Phidias, and call ourselves architects, than to copy heads and hands from Titian, and call ourselves painters.

29. Let us then understand at once, that change or variety is as much a necessity to the human heart and brain in buildings as in books; that there is no merit, though there is some occasional use, in monotony; and that we must no more expect to derive either pleasure or profit from an architecture whose ornaments are one pattern, and whose pillars are of one proportion, than we should out of a universe in which the clouds were all of one shape, and the trees all of one size.

30. And this we confess in deeds, though not in words. All the pleasure which the people of the nineteenth century take in art, is in pictures, sculpture, minor objects of virtù, or medieval architecture, which we enjoy under the term picturesque: no pleasure is taken anywhere in modern buildings, and we find all men of true feeling delighting to escape out of modern cities into natural scenery: hence, as I shall hereafter show, that peculiar love of landscape which is characteristic of the age. It would be well, if, in all other matters, we were as ready to put up with what we dislike, for the sake of compliance with established law, as we are in architecture.

31. How so debased a law ever came to be established, we shall see when we come to describe the Renaissance schools: here we have only to note, as the second most essential element of the Gothic spirit, that it broke through that law wherever it found it in existence; it not only dared, but delighted in, the infringement of every servile principle; and invented a series of forms of which the merit was, not merely that they were new, but that they were *capable of perpetual novelty*. The pointed arch was not merely a bold variation from the round, but it admitted of millions of variations in itself; for the proportions of a pointed arch are changeable to infinity, while a circular arch is always the same. The grouped shaft was not merely a bold variation from the single one, but it admitted of

millions of variations in its grouping, and in the proportions resultant from its grouping. The introduction of tracery was not only a startling change in the treatment of window lights, but admitted endless changes in the interlacement of the tracery bars themselves. So that, while in all living Christian architecture the love of variety exists, the Gothic schools exhibited that love in culminating energy; and their influence, wherever it extended itself, may be sooner and farther traced by this character than by any other; the tendency to the adoption of Gothic types being always first shown by greater irregularity and richer variation in the forms of the architecture it is about to supersede, long before the appearance of the pointed arch or of any other recognisable *outward* sign of the Gothic mind.

32. We must, however, herein note carefully what distinction there is between a healthy and a diseased love of change; for as it was in healthy love of change that the Gothic architecture rose, it was partly in consequence of diseased love of change that it was destroyed. In order to understand this clearly, it will be necessary to consider the different ways in which change and monotony are presented to us in nature; both having their use, like darkness and light, and the one incapable of being enjoyed without the other: change being most delightful after some prolongation of monotony, as light appears most brilliant after the eyes have been for some time closed.

33. I believe that the true relations of monotony and change may be most simply understood by observing them in music. We may therein notice, first, that there is a sublimity and majesty in monotony which there is not in rapid or frequent variation. This is true throughout all nature. The greater part of the sublimity of the sea depends on its monotony; so also that of desolate moor and mountain scenery; and especially the sublimity of motion, as in the quiet, unchanged fall and rise of an engine beam. So also there is sublimity in darkness which there is not in light.

34. Again, monotony after a certain time, or beyond a certain degree, becomes either uninteresting or intolerable, and the musician is obliged to break it in one of two ways: either while the air or passage is perpetually repeated, its notes are variously enriched and harmonised; or else, after a certain number of repeated passages, an entirely new passage is introduced, which is more or less delightful according to the length of the previous monotony. Nature, of course, uses both these kinds of variation perpetually. The sea-waves, resembling each other in general mass, but none like its brother in minor divisions and curves, are a monotony of the first kind; the great plain, broken by an emergent rock or clump of trees, is a monotony of the second.

35. Farther: in order to the enjoyment of the change in either case, a certain degree of patience is required from the hearer or observer. In the first case, he must be satisfied to endure with patience the recurrence of the great masses of sound or form, and to seek for entertainment in a careful watchfulness of the minor details. In the second case, he must bear patiently the infliction of the monotony for some moments, in order to feel the full refreshment of the change. This is true even of the shortest musical passage in which the element of monotony is employed. In cases of more majestic monotony, the patience required is so considerable that it becomes a kind of pain,—a price paid for the future pleasure.

36. Again: the talent of the composer is not in the monotony, but in the changes: he may show feeling and taste by his use of monotony in certain places or degrees; that is to say, by his *various* employment of it; but it is always in the new arrangement or invention that his intellect is shown, and not in the monotony which relieves it.

Lastly: if the pleasure of change be too often repeated, it ceases to be delightful, for then change itself becomes monotonous, and we are driven to seek delight in extreme and fantastic degrees of it. This is the diseased love of change of which we have above spoken.

37. From these facts we may gather generally that monotony is, and ought to be, in itself painful to us, just as darkness is; that an architecture which is altogether monotonous is a dark or dead architecture; and, of those who love it, it may be truly said, "they love darkness rather than light." But monotony in certain measure, used in order to give value to change, and, above all, that *transparent* monotony which, like the shadows of a great painter, suffers all manner of dimly suggested form to be seen through the body of it, is as essential in architectural as in all other composition; and the endurance of monotony has about the same place in a healthy mind that the endurance of darkness has: that is to say, as a strong intellect will have pleasure in the solemnities of storm and twilight, and in the broken and mysterious lights that gleam among them, rather than in mere brilliancy and glare, while a frivolous mind will dread the shadow and the storm; and as a great man will be ready to endure much darkness of fortune in order to reach greater eminence of power or felicity, while an inferior man will not pay the price; exactly in like manner a great mind will accept, or even delight in, monotony which would be wearisome to an inferior intellect, because it has more patience and power of expectation, and is ready to pay the full price for the great future pleasure of change. But in all cases it is not that the noble nature loves monotony, any more than it loves darkness or pain. But it can bear with it, and receives a high pleasure in the endurance or patience, a pleasure necessary to the well-being of this world; while those who will not submit to the temporary sameness, but rush from one change to another, gradually dull the edge of change itself, and bring a shadow and weariness over the whole world from which there is no more escape.

38. From these general uses of variety in the economy of the world, we may at once understand its use and abuse in architecture. The variety of the Gothic schools is the more healthy and beautiful, because in many cases it is entirely unstudied, and results, not from the mere love of change, but from practical necessities. For in one point of view Gothic is not only the best, but the *only rational* architecture, as being that which can fit itself most easily to all services, vulgar or noble. Undefined in its slope of roof, height of shaft, breadth of arch, or disposition of ground plan, it can shrink into a turret, expand into a hall, coil into a staircase, or spring into a spire, with undegraded grace and unexhausted energy; and whenever it finds occasion for change in its form or purpose, it submits to it without the slightest sense of loss either to its unity or majesty,—subtle and flexible like a fiery serpent, but ever attentive to the voice of the charmer. And it is one of the chief virtues of the Gothic builders, that they never suffered ideas of outside symmetries and consistencies to interfere with the real use and value of what they did. If they wanted a window, they opened one; a room, they added one; a buttress, they built one; utterly regardless of any established conventionalities of external appearance, knowing (as indeed it always happened) that such daring interruptions of the formal plan would rather give additional interest to its symmetry than injure it. So that, in the best times of Gothic, a useless window would rather have been opened in an unexpected place for the sake of the surprise, than a useful one forbidden for the sake of symmetry. Every successive architect, employed upon a great work, built the pieces he added in his own way, utterly regardless of the style adopted by his predecessors; and if two towers were raised in nominal correspondence at the sides of a cathedral front, one was nearly sure to be different from the other, and in each the style at the top to be different from the style at the bottom.

39. These marked variations were, however, only permitted as part of the great system of perpetual change which ran through every member of Gothic design, and rendered it as endless a field for the beholder's inquiry, as for the builder's imagination: change, which in the best schools is subtle and delicate, and rendered more delightful by intermingling of a noble monotony; in the more barbaric schools is somewhat fantastic and redundant; but, in all, a necessary and constant condition of the life of the school. Sometimes the variety is in one feature, sometimes in another; it may be in the capitals or crockets, in the niches or the traceries, or in all together, but in some one or other of the features it will be found always. If the mouldings are constant, the surface sculpture will change; if the capitals are of a fixed design, the traceries will change; if the traceries are monotonous, the capitals will change; and if even, as in some fine schools, the early English for example, there is the slightest approxima-tion to an unvarying type of mouldings, capitals, and floral decoration, the variety is found in the disposition of the masses, and in the figure sculpture.

40. I must now refer for a moment, before we quit the consideration of this, the second mental element of Gothic, to the opening of the third chapter of the "Seven Lamps of Architecture," in which the distinction was drawn (—2) between man gathering and man governing; between his acceptance of the sources of delight from nature, and his development of authoritative or imaginative power in their arrangement: for the two mental elements, not only of Gothic, but of all good architecture, which we have just been examining, belong to it, and are admirable in it, chiefly as it is, more than any other subject of art, the work of man, and the expression of the average power of man. A picture or poem is often little more than a feeble utterance of man's admiration of something out of himself; but architecture approaches more to a creation of his own, born of his necessities, and expressive of his nature. It is also, in some sort, the work of the whole race, while the picture or statue is the work of one only, in most cases more highly gifted than his fellows. And therefore we may expect that the first two elements of good architecture should be expressive of some great truths commonly belonging to the whole race, and necessary to be understood or felt by them in all their work that they do under the sun. And observe what they are: the confession of Imperfection, and the confession of Desire of Change. The building of the bird and the bee needs not express anything like this. It is perfect and unchanging. But just because we are something better than birds or bees, our building must confess that we have not reached the perfection we can imagine, and cannot rest in the condition we have attained. If we pretend to have reached either perfection or satisfaction, we have degraded ourselves and our work. God's work only may express that; but ours may never have that sentence written upon it,—"And behold, it was very good." And, observe again, it is not merely as it renders the edifice a book of various knowledge, or a mine of precious thought, that variety is essential to its nobleness. The vital principle is not the love of *Knowledge,* but the love of *Change.* It is that strange *disquietude* of the Gothic spirit that is its greatness; that restlessness of the dreaming mind, that wanders hither and thither among the niches, and flickers feverishly around the pinnacles, and frets and fades in labyrinthine knots and shadows along wall and roof, and yet is not satisfied, nor shall be satisfied. The Greek could stay in his triglyph furrow, and be at peace; but the work of the Gothic heart is fretwork still, and it can neither rest in, nor from, its labour, but must pass on, sleeplessly, until its love of change shall be pacified for ever in the change that must come alike on them that wake and them that sleep.

41. The third constituent element of the Gothic mind was stated to be NATURALISM; that is to say, the

love of natural objects for their own sake, and the effort to represent them frankly, unconstrained by artistical laws.

This characteristic of the style partly follows in necessary connection with those named above. For, so soon as the workman is left free to represent what subjects he chooses, he must look to the nature that is round him for material, and will endeavour to represent it as he sees it, with more or less accuracy according to the skill he possesses, and with much play of fancy, but with small respect for law. There is, however, a marked distinction between the imaginations of the Western and Eastern races, even when both are left free; the Western, or Gothic, delighting most in the representation of facts, and the Eastern (Arabian, Persian, and Chinese) in the harmony of colours and forms. Each of these intellectual dispositions has its particular forms of error and abuse, which, though I have often before stated, I must here again briefly explain; and this the rather, because the word Naturalism is, in one of its senses, justly used as a term of reproach, and the questions respecting the real relations of art and nature are so many and so confused throughout all the schools of Europe at this day, that I cannot clearly enunciate any single truth without appearing to admit, in fellowship with it, some kind of error, unless the reader will bear with me in entering into such an analysis of the subject as will serve us for general guidance.

42. We are to remember, in the first place, that the arrangement of colours and lines is an art analogous to the composition° of music, and entirely independent of the representation of facts. Good colouring does not necessarily convey the image of anything but itself. It consists in certain proportions and arrangements of rays of light, but not in likenesses to anything. A few touches of certain greys and purples laid by a master's hand on white paper, will be good colouring; as more touches are added beside them, we may find out that they were intended to represent a dove's neck, and we may praise, as the drawing advances, the perfect imitation of the dove's neck. But the good colouring does not consist in that imitation, but in the abstract qualities and relations of the grey and purple.

In like manner, as soon as a great sculptor begins to shape his work out of the block, we shall see that its lines are nobly arranged, and of noble character. We may not have the slightest idea for what the forms are intended, whether they are of man or beast, of vegetation or drapery. Their likeness to anything does not affect their nobleness. They are magnificent forms,

and that is all we need care to know of them, in order to say whether the workman is a good or bad sculptor.

43. Now the noblest art is an exact unison of the abstract value, with the imitative power, of forms and colours. It is the noblest composition, used to express the noblest facts. But the human mind cannot in general unite the two perfections: it either pursues the fact to the neglect of the composition, or pursues the composition to the neglect of the fact.

44. And it is intended by the Deity that it *should* do this; the best art is not always wanted. Facts are often wanted without art, as in a geological diagram; and art often without facts, as in a Turkey carpet. And most men have been made capable of giving either one or the other, but not both; only one or two, the very highest, can give both.

Observe then. Men are universally divided, as respects their artistical qualifications, into three great classes; a right, a left, and a centre. On the right side are the men of facts, on the left the men of design,° in the centre the men of both.

The three classes of course pass into each other by imperceptible gradations. The men of facts are hardly ever altogether without powers of design; the men of design are always in some measure cognisant of facts; and as each class possesses more or less of the powers of the opposite one, it approaches to the character of the central class. Few men, even in that central rank, are so exactly thronged on the summit of the crest that they cannot be perceived to incline in the least one way or the other, embracing both horizons with their glance. Now each of these classes has, as I above said, a healthy function in the world, and correlative diseases or unhealthy functions; and, when the work of either of them is seen in its morbid condition, we are apt to find fault with the class of workmen, instead of finding fault only with the particular abuse which has perverted their action.

* * * * *

What, then, are the diseased operations to which the three classes of workmen are liable?

46. Primarily, two; affecting the two inferior classes:

First, When either of those two classes Despises the other;

Second, When either of the two classes Envies the other; producing, therefore, four forms of dangerous error.

First, when the men of facts despise design. This is the error of the common Dutch painters, of merely imitative painters of still life, flowers, etc., and other men who, having either the gift of accurate imitation or strong sympathies with nature, suppose that all is done when the imitation is perfected or sympathy ex-

1271 **composition.** "I am always afraid to use this word 'Composition'; it is so utterly misused in the general parlance respecting art. Nothing is more common than to hear divisions of art into 'form, composition, and colour,' or 'light and shade and composition,' or 'sentiment and composition,' or it matters not what else and composition; the speakers in each case attaching a perfectly different meaning to the word, generally an indistinct one, and always a wrong one. Composition is, in plain English, 'putting together,' and it means the putting together of lines, of forms, of colours, of shades, or of ideas. Painters compose in colour, compose in thought, compose in form, and compose in effect; the word being of use merely in order to express a scientific, disciplined, and inventive arrangement of any of these, instead of a merely natural or accidental one."—Ruskin's note

1310 **design.** "Design is used in this place as expressive of the power to arrange lines and colours nobly. By facts, I mean facts perceived by the eye and mind, not facts accumulated by knowledge."—Ruskin's note

pressed. A large body of English landscapists come into this class, including most clever sketches from nature, who fancy that to get a sky of true tone, and a gleam of sunshine or sweep of shower faithfully expressed, is all that can be required of art. These men are generally themselves answerable for much of their deadness of feeling to the higher qualities of composition. They probably have not originally the high gifts of design, but they lose such powers as they originally possessed by despising, and refusing to study, the results of great power of design in others. Their knowledge, as far as it goes, being accurate, they are usually presumptuous and self-conceited, and gradually become incapable of admiring anything but what is like their own works. They see nothing in the works of great designers but the faults, and do harm almost incalculable in the European society of the present day by sneering at the compositions of the greatest men of the earlier ages, because they do not absolutely tally with their own ideas of "Nature."

47. The second form of error is when the men of design despise facts. All noble design must deal with facts to a certain extent, for there is no food for it but in nature. The best colourist invents best by taking hints from natural colours; from birds, skies, or groups of figures. And if, in the delight of inventing fantastic colour and form, the truths of nature are wilfully neglected, the intellect becomes comparatively decrepit, and that state of art results which we find among the Chinese. The Greek designers delighted in the facts of the human form, and became great in consequence; but the facts of lower nature were disregarded by them, and their inferior ornament became, therefore, dead and valueless.

48. The third form of error is when the men of facts envy design: that is to say, when, having only imitative powers, they refuse to employ those powers upon the visible world around them; but, having been taught that composition is the end of art, strive to obtain the inventive powers which nature has denied them, study nothing but the works of reputed designers, and perish in a fungous growth of plagiarism and laws of art.

Here was the great error of the beginning of this century; it is the error of the meanest kind of men that employ themselves in painting, and it is the most fatal of all, rendering those who fall into it utterly useless, incapable of helping the world with either truth or fancy, while, in all probability, they deceive it by base resemblances of both, until it hardly recognises truth or fancy when they really exist.

49. The fourth form of error is when the men of design envy facts; that is to say, when the temptation of closely imitating nature leads them to forget their own proper ornamental function, and when they lose the power of the composition for the sake of graphic truth; as, for instance, in the hawthorn moulding so

often spoken of round the porch of Bourges° Cathedral, which, though very lovely, might perhaps, as we saw above, have been better, if the old builder, in his excessive desire to make it look like hawthorn, had not painted it green.

50. It is, however, carefully to be noted, that the two morbid conditions to which the men of facts are liable are much more dangerous and harmful than those to which the men of design are liable. The morbid state of men of design injures themselves only; that of the men of facts injures the whole world. The Chinese porcelain-painter is, indeed, not so great a man as he might be, but he does not want to break everything that is not porcelain: but the modern English fact-hunter, despising design, wants to destroy everything that does not agree with his own notions of truth, and becomes the most dangerous and despicable of iconoclasts, excited by egotism instead of religion. Again: the Bourges sculptor, painting his hawthorns green, did indeed somewhat hurt the effect of his own beautiful design, but did not prevent any one from loving hawthorn: but Sir George Beaumont,° trying to make Constable° paint grass brown *instead* of green, was setting himself between Constable and nature, blinding the painter, and blaspheming the work of God.

* * * * *

68. There is, however, one direction in which the Naturalism of the Gothic workmen is peculiarly manifested; and this direction is even more characteristic of the school than the Naturalism itself; I mean their peculiar fondness for the forms of Vegetation. In rendering the various circumstances of daily life, Egyptian and Ninevite sculpture is as frank and as diffuse as the Gothic. From the highest pomps of state or triumphs of battle, to the most trivial domestic arts and amusements, all is taken advantage of to fill the field of granite with the perpetual interest of a crowded drama; and the early Lombardic and Romanesque sculpture is equally copious in its description of the familiar circumstances of war and the chase. But in all the scenes portrayed by the workmen of these nations, vegetation occurs only as an explanatory accessary; the reed is introduced to mark the course of the river, or the tree to mark the covert of the wild beast, or the ambush of the enemy, but there is no especial interest in the forms of the vegetation strong enough to induce them to make it a subject of separate and accurate study. Again, among the nations who followed the arts of design exclusively, the forms of foliage introduced were meagre and general, and their real intricacy and life were neither admired nor expressed. But to the

1400 **Bourges,** in central France   1421 **George Beaumont,** landscape painter and patron of art (1753–1827)   1422 **Constable,** John Constable (1776–1837), English landscape painter

Gothic workman the living foliage became a subject of intense affection, and he struggled to render all its characters with as much accuracy as was compatible with the laws of his design and the nature of his material, not unfrequently tempted in his enthusiasm to transgress the one and disguise the other.

69. There is a peculiar significance in this, indicative both of higher civilisation and gentler temperament, than had before been manifested in architecture.
1460 Rudeness, and the love of change, which we have insisted upon as the first elements of Gothic, are also elements common to all healthy schools. But here is a softer element mingled with them, peculiar to the Gothic itself The rudeness or ignorance which would have been painfully exposed in the treatment of the human form, are still not so great as to prevent the successful rendering of the wayside herbage; and the love of change, which becomes morbid and feverish in following the haste of the hunter, and the rage of the
1470 combatant, is at once soothed and satisfied as it watches the wandering of the tendril, and the budding of the flower. Nor is this all: the new direction of mental interest marks an infinite change in the means and the habits of life. The nations whose chief support was in the chase, whose chief interest was in the battle, whose chief pleasure was in the banquet, would take small care respecting the shapes of leaves and flowers; and notice little in the forms of the forest trees which sheltered them, except the signs indicative of
1480 the wood which would make the toughest lance, the closest roof, or the clearest fire. The affectionate observation of the grace and outward character of vegetation is the sure sign of a more tranquil and gentle existence, sustained by the gifts, and gladdened by the splendour, of the earth. In that careful distinction of species, and richness of delicate and undisturbed organisation, which characterise the Gothic design, there is the history of rural and thoughtful life, influenced by habitual tenderness, and devoted to subtle inquiry; and
1490 every discriminating and delicate touch of the chisel, as it rounds the petal or guides the branch, is a prophecy of the development of the entire body of the natural sciences, beginning with that of medicine, of the recovery of literature, and the establishment of the most necessary principles of domestic wisdom and national peace.

70. I have before alluded to the strange and vain supposition, that the original conception of Gothic architecture had been derived from vegetation,—from
1500 the symmetry of avenues, and the interlacing of branches. It is a supposition which never could have existed for a moment in the mind of any person acquainted with early Gothic; but, however idle as a theory, it is most valuable as a testimony to the character of the perfected style. It is precisely because the reverse of this theory is the fact, because the

Gothic did not arise out of, but developed itself into, a resemblance to vegetation, that this resemblance is so instructive as an indication of the temper of the builders. It was no chance suggestion of the form of an 1510 arch from the bending of a bough, but a gradual and continual discovery of a beauty in natural forms which could be more and more perfectly transferred into those of stone, that influenced at once the heart of the people, and the form of the edifice. The Gothic architecture arose in massy and mountainous strength, axe-hewn, and iron-bound, block heaved upon block by the monk's enthusiasm and the soldier's force; and cramped and stanchioned into such weight of grisly wall, as might bury the anchoret in darkness, and beat 1520 back the utmost storm of battle, suffering but by the same narrow crosslet the passing of the sunbeam, or of the arrow. Gradually, as that monkish enthusiasm became more thoughtful, and as the sound of war became more and more intermittent beyond the gates of the convent or the keep, the stony pillar grew slender and the vaulted roof grew light, till they had wreathed themselves into the semblance of the summer woods at their fairest, and of the dead field-flowers, long trodden down in blood, sweet monumental statues were 1530 set to bloom for ever, beneath the porch of the temple, or the canopy of the tomb.

71. Nor is it only as a sign of greater gentleness or refinement of mind, but as a proof of the best possible direction of this refinement, that the tendency of the Gothic to the expression of vegetative life is to be admired. That sentence of Genesis, "I have given thee every green herb for meat,"° like all the rest of the book, has a profound symbolical as well as a literal meaning. It is not merely the nourishment of the body, 1540 but the food of the soul, that is intended. The green herb is, of all nature, that which is most essential to the healthy spiritual life of man. Most of us do not need fine scenery; the precipice and the mountain peak are not intended to be seen by all men,—perhaps their power is greatest over those who are unaccustomed to them. But trees, and fields, and flowers were made for all, and are necessary for all. God has connected the labour which is essential to the bodily sustenance, with the pleasures which are healthiest for the heart; and 1550 while He made the ground stubborn, He made its herbage fragrant, and its blossoms fair. The proudest architecture that man can build has no higher honour than to bear the image and recall the memory of that grass of the field which is, at once, the type and the support of his existence; the goodly building is then most glorious when it is sculptured into the likeness of the leaves of Paradise; and the great Gothic spirit, as we showed it to be noble in its disquietude, is also noble in its hold of nature; it is, indeed, like the dove of 1560

1537–1538 **I have . . . meat.** See *Genesis*, 1:30

Noah, in that she found no rest upon the face of the waters,—but like her in this also, "Lo, IN HER MOUTH WAS AN OLIVE BRANCH, PLUCKED OFF."°

72. The fourth essential element of the Gothic mind was above stated to be the sense of the GROTESQUE; but I shall defer the endeavour to define this most curious and subtle character until we have occasion to examine one of the divisions of the Renaissance schools, which was morbidly influenced by it (Vol. III Chap. III). It is the less necessary to insist upon it here, because every reader familiar with Gothic architecture must understand what I mean, and will, I believe, have no hesitation in admitting that the tendency to delight in fantastic and ludicrous, as well as in sublime, images, is a universal instinct of the Gothic imagination.

73. The fifth element above named was RIGIDITY; and this character I must endeavour carefully to define, for neither the word I have used, nor any other that I can think of, will express it accurately. For I mean, not merely stable, but *active* rigidity; the peculiar energy which gives tension to movement, and stiffness to resistance, which makes the fiercest lightning forked rather than curved, and the stoutest oak-branch angular rather than bending, and is as much seen in the quivering of the lance as in the glittering of the icicle.

74. I have before had occasion (Vol. I Chap. XIII — viii) to note some manifestations of this energy or fixedness; but it must be still more attentively considered here, as it shows itself throughout the whole structure and decoration of Gothic work. Egyptian and Greek buildings stand, for the most part, by their own weight and mass, one stone passively incumbent on another: but in the Gothic vaults and traceries there is a stiffness analogous to that of the bones of a limb, or fibres of a tree; an elastic tension and communication of force from part to part, and also a studious expression of this throughout every visible line of the building. And, in like manner, the Greek and Egyptian ornament is either mere surface engraving, as if the face of the wall had been stamped with a seal, or its lines are flowing, lithe, and luxuriant; in either case, there is no expression of energy in the framework of the ornament itself. But the Gothic ornament stands out in prickly independence, and frosty fortitude, jutting into crockets, and freezing into pinnacles; here starting up into a monster, there germinating into a blossom; anon knitting itself into a branch, alternately thorny, bossy, and bristly, or writhed into every form of nervous entanglement; but, even when most graceful, never for an instant languid, always quickset; erring, if at all, ever on the side of brusquerie.

*　*　*　*　*

78. Last, because the least essential, of the constituent elements of this noble school, was placed that of REDUNDANCE,—the uncalculating bestowal of the wealth of its labour. There is, indeed, much Gothic, and that of the best period, in which this element is hardly traceable, and which depends for its effect almost exclusively on loveliness of simple design and grace of uninvolved proportion: still, in the most characteristic buildings, a certain portion of their effect depends upon accumulation of ornament; and many of those which have most influence on the minds of men, have attained it by means of this attribute alone. And although, by careful study of the school, it is possible to arrive at a condition of taste which shall be better contented by a few perfect lines than by a whole façade covered with fretwork, the building which only satisfies such a taste is not to be considered the best. For the very first requirement of Gothic architecture being, as we saw above, that it shall both admit the aid, and appeal to the admiration, of the rudest as well as the most refined minds, the richness of the work is, paradoxical as the statement may appear, a part of its humility. No architecture is so haughty as that which is simple; which refuses to address the eye, except in a few clear and forceful lines; which implies, in offering so little to our regards, that all it has offered is perfect; and disdains, either by the complexity or the attractiveness of its features, to embarrass our investigation, or betray us into delight. That humility, which is the very life of the Gothic school, is shown not only in the imperfection, but in the accumulation, of ornament. The inferior rank of the workman is often shown as much in the richness, as the roughness, of his work; and if the co-operation of every hand, and the sympathy of every heart, are to be received, we must be content to allow the redundance which disguises the failure of the feeble, and wins the regard of the inattentive. There are, however, far nobler interests mingling, in the Gothic heart, with the rude love of decorative accumulation: a magnificent enthusiasm, which feels as if it never could do enough to reach the fulness of its ideal; and unselfishness of sacrifice, which would rather cast fruitless labour before the altar than stand idle in the market; and, finally, a profound sympathy with the fulness and wealth of the material universe, rising out of that Naturalism whose operation we have already endeavoured to define. The sculptor who sought for his models among the forest leaves, could not but quickly and deeply feel that complexity need not involve the loss of grace, nor richness that of repose; and every hour which he spent in the study of the minute and various work of Nature, made him feel more forcibly the barrenness of what was best in that of man: nor is it to be wondered at, that, seeing her perfect and exquisite creations poured forth in a profusion which conception could not grasp nor calculation sum, he should think that it ill became him to be niggardly of his own rude craftsmanship; and where he saw throughout the

1562–1563 **Lo, in her mouth . . . off.** See *Genesis*, 8:11

universe a faultless beauty lavished on measureless spaces of broidered field and blooming mountain, to grudge his poor and imperfect labour to the few stones that he had raised one upon another, for habitation or memorial. The years of his life passed away before his task was accomplished; but generation succeeded generation with unwearied enthusiasm, and the cathedral front was at last lost in the tapestry of its traceries, like a rock among the thickets and herbage of spring.

*　*　*　*　*

106. We have now, I believe, obtained a sufficiently accurate knowledge both of the spirit and form of Gothic architecture; but it may, perhaps, be useful to the general reader, if, in conclusion, I set down a few plain and practical rules for determining, in every instance, whether a given building be good Gothic or not, and, if not Gothic, whether its architecture is of a kind which will probably reward the pains of careful examination.

107. First. Look if the roof rises in a steep gable, high above the walls. If it does not do this, there is something wrong; the building is not quite pure Gothic, or has been altered.

108. Secondly. Look if the principal windows and doors have pointed arches with gables over them. If not pointed arches, the building is not Gothic; if they have not any gables over them, it is either not pure, or not first-rate.

If, however, it has the steep roof, the pointed arch, and gable all united, it is nearly certain to be a Gothic building of a very fine time.

109. Thirdly. Look if the arches are cusped, or apertures foliated. If the building has met the first two conditions, it is sure to be foliated somewhere; but, if not everywhere, the parts which are unfoliated are imperfect, unless they are large bearing arches, or small and sharp arches in groups, forming a kind of foliation by their own multiplicity, and relieved by sculpture and rich mouldings. The upper windows, for instance, in the east end of Westminster Abbey are imperfect for want of foliation. If there be no foliation anywhere, the building is assuredly imperfect Gothic.

110. Fourthly. If the building meets all the first three conditions, look if its arches in general, whether of windows and doors, or of minor ornamentation, are carried on *true shafts with bases and capitals*. If they are, then the building is assuredly of the finest Gothic style. It may still, perhaps, be an imitation, a feeble copy, or a bad example, of a noble style; but the manner of it, having met all these four conditions, is assuredly first-rate.

If its apertures have not shafts and capitals, look if they are plain openings in the walls, studiously simple, and unmoulded at the sides. . . . If so, the building may still be of the finest Gothic, adapted to some domestic or military service. But if the sides of the window be moulded, and yet there are no capitals at the spring of the arch, it is assuredly of an inferior school.

This is all that is necessary to determine whether the building be of a fine Gothic style. The next tests to be applied are in order to discover whether it be good architecture or not: for it may be very impure Gothic, and yet very noble architecture; or it may be very pure Gothic, and yet, if a copy, or originally raised by an ungifted builder, very bad architecture.

If it belong to any of the great schools of colour, its criticism becomes as complicated, and needs as much care, as that of a piece of music, and no general rules for it can be given; but if not—

111. First. See if it looks as if it had been built by strong men; if it has the sort of roughness, and largeness, and nonchalance, mixed in places with the exquisite tenderness which seems always to be the sign-manual of the broad vision, and massy power of men who can see *past* the work they are doing, and betray here and there something like disdain for it. If the building has this character, it has much already in its favour; it will go hard but it proves a noble one. If it has not this, but is altogether accurate, minute, and scrupulous in its workmanship, it must belong to either the very best or the very worst of schools: the very best, in which exquisite design is wrought out with untiring and conscientious care, as in the Giottesque Gothic; or the very worst, in which mechanism has taken the place of design. It is more likely, in general, that it should belong to the worst than the best: so that, on the whole, very accurate workmanship is to be esteemed a bad sign; and if there is nothing remarkable about the building but its precision, it may be passed at once with contempt.

112. Secondly. Observe if it be irregular, its different parts fitting themselves to different purposes, no one caring what becomes of them, so that they do their work. If one part always answers accurately to another part, it is sure to be a bad building; and the greater and more conspicuous the irregularities, the greater the chances are that it is a good one.

*　*　*　*　*

113. Thirdly. Observe if all the traceries, capitals, and other ornaments are of perpetually varied design. If not, the work is assuredly bad.

114. Lastly. *Read* the sculpture. Preparatory to reading it, you will have to discover whether it is legible (and, if legible, it is nearly certain to be worth reading). On a good building, the sculpture is *always* so set, and on such a scale, that at the ordinary distance from which the edifice is seen, the sculpture shall be thoroughly intelligible and interesting. In order to accomplish this, the uppermost statues will be ten or twelve feet high, and the upper ornamentation will be colossal, increasing in fineness as it descends, till on the foundation it will often be wrought as if for a precious cabinet in a king's chamber; but the spectator

will not notice that the upper sculptures are colossal. He will merely feel that he can see them plainly, and make them all out at his ease.

And having ascertained this, let him set himself to read them. Thenceforward the criticism of the building is to be conducted precisely on the same principles as that of a book; and it must depend on the knowledge, feeling, and not a little on the industry and perseverance of the reader, whether, even in the case of the best works, he either perceive them to be great, or feel them to be entertaining.

(1853)

from THE CROWN OF WILD OLIVE

LECTURE II.

TRAFFIC.

(Delivered in the Town Hall, Bradford.)

My good Yorkshire friends, you asked me down here among your hills that I might talk to you about this Exchange you are going to build: but earnestly and seriously asking you to pardon me, I am going to do nothing of the kind. I cannot talk, or at least can say very little, about this same Exchange. I must talk of quite other things, though not willingly;—I could not deserve your pardon, if when you invited me to speak on one subject, I wilfully spoke on another. But I cannot speak, to purpose, of anything about which I do not care; and most simply and sorrowfully I have to tell you, in the outset, that I do *not* care about this Exchange of yours.

If, however, when you sent me your invitation, I had answered, 'I won't come, I don't care about the Exchange of Bradford,' you would have been justly offended with me, not knowing the reasons of so blunt a carelessness. So I have come down, hoping that you will patiently let me tell you why, on this, and many other such occasions, I now remain silent, when formerly I should have caught at the opportunity of speaking to a gracious audience.

In a word, then, I do not care about this Exchange,—because *you* don't; and because you know perfectly well I cannot make you. Look at the essential circumstances of the case, which you, as business men, know perfectly well, though perhaps you think I forget them. You are going to spend 30,000*l*., which to you, collectively, is nothing: the buying a new coat is, as to the cost of it, a much more important matter of consideration to me than building a new Exchange is to you. But you think you may as well have the right thing for your money. You know there are a great many odd styles of architecture about; you don't want

to do anything ridiculous; you hear of me, among others, as a respectable architectural man-milliner: and you send for me, that I may tell you the leading fashion; and what is, in our shops, for the moment, the newest and sweetest thing in pinnacles.

Now, pardon me for telling you frankly, you cannot have good architecture merely by asking people's advice on occasion. All good architecture is the expression of national life and character; and it is produced by a prevalent and eager national taste, or desire for beauty. And I want you to think a little of the deep significance of this word 'taste;' for no statement of mine has been more earnestly or oftener controverted than that good taste is essentially a moral quality. 'No,' say many of my antagonists, 'taste is one thing, morality is another. Tell us what is pretty; we shall be glad to know that; but preach no sermons to us.'

Permit me, therefore, to fortify this old dogma of mine somewhat. Taste is not only a part and an index of morality—it is the *only* morality. The first, and last, and closest trial question to any living creature is, 'What do you like?' Tell me what you like, and I'll tell you what you are. Go out into the street, and ask the first man or woman you meet, what their 'taste' is, and if they answer candidly, you know them, body and soul. 'You, my friend in the rags, with the unsteady gait, what do *you* like?' 'A pipe and a quartern of gin.' I know you. 'You, good woman, with the quick step and tidy bonnet, what do you like?' 'A swept hearth and a clean tea-table, and my husband opposite me, and a baby at my breast.' Good, I know you also. 'You, little girl with the golden hair and the soft eyes, what do you like?' 'My canary, and a run among the wood hyacinths.' 'You, little boy with the dirty hands and the low forehead, what do you like?' 'A shy at the sparrows, and a game at pitch farthing.' Good; we know them all now. What more need we ask?

'Nay,' perhaps you answer: 'we need rather to ask what these people and children do, than what they like. If they *do* right, it is no matter that they like what is wrong; and if they *do* wrong, it is no matter that they like what is right. Doing is the great thing; and it does not matter that the man likes drinking, so that he does not drink; nor that the little girl likes to be kind to her canary, if she will not learn her lessons; nor that the little boy likes throwing stones at the sparrows, if he goes to the Sunday school.' Indeed, for a short time, and in a provisional sense, this is true. For if, resolutely, people do what is right, in time they come to like doing it. But they only are in a right moral state when they *have* come to like doing it; and as long as they don't like it, they are still in a vicious state. The man is not in health of body who is always thirsting for the bottle in the cupboard, though he bravely bears his thirst; but the man who heartily enjoys water in the morning and wine in the evening, each in its proper quantity and time. And the entire object of true education is to make people not merely *do* the right things, but *enjoy* the right things—not merely industrious, but to love industry—not merely learned, but to love knowledge—not merely pure, but to love purity—not merely just, but to hunger and thirst after justice.

But you may answer or think, 'Is the liking for outside ornaments,—for pictures, or statues, or furniture, or architecture,—a moral quality?' Yes, most surely, if a rightly set liking. Taste for *any* pictures or statues is not a moral quality, but taste for good ones is. Only here again we have to define the word 'good.' I don't mean by 'good,' clever—or learned—or difficult in the doing. Take a picture by Teniers,° of sots quarrelling over their dice: it is an entirely clever picture; so clever that nothing in its kind has ever been done equal to it; but it is also an entirely base and evil picture. It is an expression of delight in the prolonged contemplation of a vile thing, and delight in that is an 'unmannered,' or 'immoral' quality. It is 'bad taste' in the profoundest sense—it is the taste of the devils. On the other hand, a picture of Titian's, or a Greek statue, or a Greek coin, or a Turner landscape, expresses delight in the perpetual contemplation of a good and perfect thing. That is an entirely moral quality—it is the taste of the angels. And all delight in art, and all love of it, resolve themselves into simple love of that which deserves love. That deserving is the quality which we call 'loveliness'—(we ought to have an opposite word, hateliness, to be said of the things which deserve to be hated); and it is not an indifferent nor optional thing whether we love this or that; but it is just the vital function of all our being. What we *like* determines what we *are*, and is the sign of what we are; and to teach taste is inevitably to form character. As I was thinking over this, in walking up Fleet Street the other day, my eye caught the title of a book standing open in a bookseller's window. It was—'On the necessity of the diffusion of taste among all classes.' 'Ah,' I thought to myself 'my classifying friend, when you have diffused your taste, where will your classes be? The man who likes what you like, belongs to the same class with you, I think. Inevitably so. You may put him to other work if you choose, but, by the condition you have brought him into, he will dislike the other work as much as you would yourself. You get hold of a scavenger, or a costermonger, who enjoyed the Newgate Calendar° for literature, and "Pop goes the Weasel" for music. You think you can make him like Dante and Beethoven? I wish you joy of your lessons; but if you do, you have made a gentleman of him:—he won't like to go back to his costermongering.'

And so completely and unexceptionally is this so, that, if I had time to-night, I could show you that a nation cannot be affected by any vice, or weakness, without expressing it, legibly, and for ever, either in bad art, or by want of art; and that there is no na-

tional virtue, small or great, which is not manifestly expressed in all the art which circumstances enable the people possessing that virtue to produce. Take, for instance, your great English virtue of enduring and patient courage. You have at present in England only one art of any consequence—that is, iron-working. You know thoroughly well how to cast and hammer iron. Now, do you think in those masses of lava which you build volcanic cones to melt, and which you forge at the mouths of the Infernos you have created; do you think, on those iron plates, your courage and endurance are not written for ever—not merely with an iron pen, but on iron parchment? And take also your great English vice—European vice—vice of all the world —vice of all other worlds that roll or shine in heaven, bearing with them yet the atmosphere of hell—the vice of jealousy, which brings competition into your commerce, treachery into your councils, and dishonour into your wars—that vice which has rendered for you, and for your next neighbouring nation, the daily occupations of existence no longer possible, but with the mail upon your breasts and the sword loose in its sheath; so that, at last, you have realised for all the multitudes of the two great peoples who lead the so-called civilisation of the earth,—you have realised for them all, I say, in person and in policy, what was once true only of the rough Border riders of your Cheviot hills—

'They carved at the meal
With gloves of steel,
And they drank the red wine
   through the helmet barr'd;—

do you think that this national shame and dastardliness of heart are not written as legibly on every rivet of your iron armour as the strength of the right hands that forged it? Friends, I know not whether this thing be the more ludicrous or the more melancholy. It is quite unspeakably both. Suppose, instead of being now sent for by you, I had been sent for by some private gentleman, living in a suburban house, with his garden separated only by a fruit-wall from his next door neighbour's; and he had called me to consult with him on the furnishing of his drawing-room. I begin looking about me, and find the walls rather bare; I think such and such a paper might be desirable—perhaps a little fresco here and there on the ceiling—a damask curtain or so at the windows. 'Ah,' says my employer, 'damask curtains, indeed! That's all very fine, but you know I can't afford that kind of thing just now!' 'Yet the world credits you with a splendid income!' 'Ah, yes,' says my friend, 'but do you know, at present, I am obliged to spend it nearly all in steel-traps?' 'Steel-traps! for whom?' 'Why, for that fellow on the other side the wall, you know: we're very good friends, capital friends; but we are obliged to keep our traps set on both sides of the wall; we could not possi-

Traffic 104 **Teniers,** famous seventeenth century Flemish painter 138 **Newgate Calendar,** a famous collection of memoirs of notorious prisoners. Newgate was a London prison

John Ruskin 959

bly keep on friendly terms without them, and our spring guns. The worst of it is, we are both clever fellows enough; and there's never a day passes that we don't find out a new trap, or a new gun-barrel, or something; we spend about fifteen millions a year each in our traps, take it all together; and I don't see how we're to do with less.' A highly comic state of life for two private gentlemen! but for two nations, it seems to me, not wholly comic? Bedlam would be comic, perhaps, if there were only one madman in it; and your Christmas pantomime is comic, when there is only one clown in it; but when the whole world turns clown, and paints itself red with its own heart's blood instead of vermilion, it is something else than comic, I think.

Mind, I know a great deal of this is play, and willingly allow for that. You don't know what to do with yourselves for a sensation: fox-hunting and cricketing will not carry you through the whole of this unendurably long mortal life: you liked pop-guns when you were schoolboys, and rifles and Armstrongs are only the same things better made: but then the worst of it is, that what was play to you when boys, was not play to the sparrows; and what is play to you now, is not play to the small birds of State neither; and for the black eagles, you are somewhat shy of taking shots at them, if I mistake not.

I must get back to the matter in hand, however. Believe me, without farther instance, I could show you, in all time, that every nation's vice, or virtue, was written in its art: the soldiership of early Greece; the sensuality of late Italy; the visionary religion of Tuscany; the splendid human energy and beauty of Venice. I have no time to do this to-night (I have done it elsewhere before now); but I proceed to apply the principle to ourselves in a more searching manner.

I notice that among all the new buildings that cover your once wild hills, churches and schools are mixed in due, that is to say, in large proportion, with your mills and mansions and I notice also that the churches and schools are almost always Gothic, and the mansions and mills are never Gothic. Will you allow me to ask precisely the meaning of this? For, remember, it is peculiarly a modern phenomenon. When Gothic was invented, houses were Gothic as well as churches; and when the Italian style superseded the Gothic, churches were Italian as well as houses. If there is a Gothic spire to the cathedral of Antwerp, there is a Gothic belfry to the Hôtel de Ville at Brussels; if Inigo Jones builds an Italian Whitehall, Sir Christopher Wren builds an Italian St. Paul's. But now you live under one school of architecture, and worship under another. What do you mean by doing this? Am I to understand that you are thinking of changing your architecture back to Gothic; and that you treat your churches experimentally, because it does not matter what mistakes you make in a church? Or am I to understand that you consider Gothic a pre-eminently sacred and beautiful model of building, which you think, like the fine frankincense, should be mixed for the tabernacle only, and reserved for your religious services? For if this be the feeling, though it may seem at first as if it were graceful and reverent, you will find that, at the root of the matter, it signifies neither more nor less than that you have separated your religion from your life.

For consider what a wide significance this fact has; and remember that it is not you only, but all the people of England, who are behaving thus just now.

You have all got into the habit of calling the church 'the house of God.' I have seen, over the doors of many churches, the legend actually carved, 'This is the house of God, and this is the gate of heaven.' Now, note where that legend comes from, and of what place it was first spoken. A boy leaves his father's house to go on a long journey on foot, to visit his uncle; he has to cross a wild hill-desert; just as if one of your own boys had to cross the wolds of Westmoreland, to visit an uncle at Carlisle. The second or third day your boy finds himself somewhere between Hawes and Brough, in the midst of the moors, at sunset. It is stony ground, and boggy; he cannot go one foot farther that night. Down he lies, to sleep, on Wharnside, where best he may, gathering a few of the stones together to put under his head;—so wild the place is, he cannot get anything but stones. And there, lying under the broad night, he has a dream; and he sees a ladder set up on the earth, and the top of it reaches to heaven, and the angels of God are ascending and descending upon it. And when he wakes out of his sleep, he says, 'How dreadful is this place; surely, this is none other than the house of God, and this is the gate of heaven.' This PLACE observe; not this church; not this city; not this stone, even, which he puts up for a memorial—the piece of flint on which his head has lain. But this place; this windy slope of Wharnside; this moorland hollow, torrent-bitten, snow-blighted; this any place where God lets down the ladder. And how are you to know where that will be? or how are you to determine where it may be, but by being ready for it always? Do you know where the lightning is to fall next? You do know that, partly; you can guide the lightning; but you cannot guide the going forth of the Spirit, which is that lightning when it shines from the east to the west.

But the perpetual and insolent warping of that strong verse to serve a merely ecclesiastical purpose, is only one of the thousand instances in which we sink back into gross Judaism. We call our churches 'temples.' Now, you know, or ought to know, they are not temples. They have never had, never can have, anything whatever to do with temples. They are 'synagogues'—'gathering places'—where you gather yourselves together as an assembly; and by not calling them so, you again miss the force of another mighty text—'Thou, when thou prayest, shalt not be as the hypocrites are; for they love to pray standing in the churches' [we should translate it], 'that they may be seen of men. But thou, when thou prayest, enter into thy closet, and when thou hast shut thy door, pray to thy Father,'—which is, not in chancel nor in aisle, but 'in secret.'

Now, you feel, as I say this to you—I know you feel—as if I were trying to take away the honour of your churches. Not so; I am trying to prove to you the honour of your houses and your hills; I am trying to show you—not that the Church is not sacred—but that the whole Earth is. I would have you feel, what careless, what constant, what infectious sin there is in all modes of thought, whereby, in calling your churches only 'holy,' you call your hearths and homes profane; and have separated yourselves from the heathen by casting all your household gods to the ground, instead of recognising, in the place of their many and feeble Lares, the presence of your One and Mighty Lord and Lar.

'But what has all this to do with our Exchange?' you ask me, impatiently. My dear friends, it has just everything to do with it; on these inner and great questions depend all the outer and little ones; and if you have asked me down here to speak to you, because you had before been interested in anything I have written, you must know that all I have yet said about architecture was to show this. The book I called 'The Seven Lamps' was to show that certain right states of temper and moral feeling were the magic powers by which all good architecture, without exception, had been produced. 'The Stones of Venice' had, from beginning to end, no other aim than to show that the Gothic architecture of Venice had arisen out of, and indicated in all its features, a state of pure national faith, and of domestic virtue; and that its Renaissance architecture had arisen out of, and in all its features indicated, a state of concealed national infidelity, and of domestic corruption. And now, you ask me what style is best to build in; and how can I answer, knowing the meaning of the two styles, but by another question—do you mean to build as Christians or as Infidels? And still more—do you mean to build as honest Christians or as honest Infidels? as thoroughly and confessedly either one or the other? You don't like to be asked such rude questions. I cannot help it; they are of much more importance than this Exchange business; and if they can be at once answered, the Exchange business settles itself in a moment. But, before I press them farther, I must ask leave to explain one point clearly. In all my past work, my endeavour has been to show that good architecture is essentially religious—the production of a faithful and virtuous, not of an infidel and corrupted people. But in the course of doing this, I have had also to show that good architecture is not *ecclesiastical*. People are so apt to look upon religion as the business of the clergy, not their own, that the moment they hear of anything depending on 'religion,' they think it must also have depended on the priesthood; and I have had to take what place was to be occupied between these two errors,

and fight both, often with seeming contradiction. Good architecture is the work of good and believing men; therefore, you say, at least some people say, 'Good architecture must essentially have been the work of the clergy, not of the laity.' No—a thousand times no; good architecture has always been the work of the commonalty, *not* of the clergy. What, you say, those glorious cathedrals—the pride of Europe—did their builders not form Gothic architecture? No; they corrupted Gothic architecture. Gothic was formed in the baron's castle, and the burgher's street. It was formed by the thoughts, and hands, and powers of free citizens and soldier kings. By the monk it was used as an instrument for the aid of his superstition; when that superstition became a beautiful madness, and the best hearts of Europe vainly dreamed and pined in the cloister, and vainly raged and perished in the crusade—through that fury of perverted faith and wasted war, the Gothic rose also to its loveliest, most fantastic, and, finally, most foolish dreams; and, in those dreams, was lost.

I hope, now, that there is no risk of your misunderstanding me when I come to the gist of what I want to say to-night—when I repeat, that every great national architecture has been the result and exponent of a great national religion. You can't have bits of it here, bits there—you must have it everywhere, or nowhere. It is not the monopoly of a clerical company—it is not the exponent of a theological dogma—it is not the hieroglyphic writing of an initiated priesthood; it is the manly language of a people inspired by resolute and common purpose, and rendering resolute and common fidelity to the legible laws of an undoubted God.

Now, there have as yet been three distinct schools of European architecture. I say, European, because Asiatic and African architectures belong so entirely to other races and climates, that there is no question of them here; only, in passing, I will simply assure you that whatever is good or great in Egypt, and Syria, and India, is just good or great for the same reasons as the buildings on our side of the Bosphorus. We Europeans, then, have had three great religions: the Greek, which was the worship of the God of Wisdom and Power; the Mediæval, which was the Worship of the God of Judgment and Consolation; the Renaissance, which was the worship of the God of Pride and Beauty; these three we have had—they are past,—and now, at last, we English have got a fourth religion, and a God of our own, about which I want to ask you. But I must explain these three old ones first.

I repeat, first, the Greeks essentially worshipped the God of Wisdom; so that whatever contended against their religion,—to the Jews a stumbling block,—was to the Greeks—*Foolishness*.

The first Greek idea of Deity was that expressed in the word, of which we keep the remnant in our words 'Di-urnal' and 'Di-vine'—the god of *Day*, Jupiter the revealer. Athena is his daughter, but especially daughter of the Intellect, springing armed from the head. We are only with the help of recent investigation beginning to penetrate the depth of meaning couched under the Athenaic symbols: but I may note rapidly, that her ægis, the mantle with the serpent fringes, in which she often, in the best statues, is represented as folding up her left hand for better guard, and the Gorgon on her shield, are both representative mainly of the chilling horror and sadness (turning men to stone, as it were,) of the outmost and superficial spheres of knowledge—that knowledge which separates, in bitterness, hardness, and sorrow, the heart of the full-grown man from the heart of the child. For out of imperfect knowledge spring terror, dissension, danger, and disdain; but from perfect knowledge, given by the full-revealed Athena, strength and peace, in sign of which she is crowned with the olive spray, and bears the resistless spear.

This, then, was the Greek conception of purest Deity, and every habit of life, and every form of his art developed themselves from the seeking this bright, serene, resistless wisdom; and setting himself, as a man, to do things evermore rightly and strongly; not with any ardent affection or ultimate hope; but with a resolute and continent energy of will, as knowing that for failure there was no consolation, and for sin there was no remission. And the Greek architecture rose unerring, bright, clearly defined, and self-contained.

Next followed in Europe the great Christian faith, which was essentially the religion of Comfort. Its great doctrine is the remission of sins; for which cause it happens, too often, in certain phases of Christianity, that sin and sickness themselves are partly glorified, as if, the more you had to be healed of, the more divine was the healing. The practical result of this doctrine, in art, is a continual contemplation of sin and disease, and of imaginary states of purification from them; thus we have an architecture conceived in a mingled sentiment of melancholy and aspiration, partly severe, partly luxuriant, which will bend itself to every one of our needs, and every one of our fancies, and be strong or weak with us, as we are strong or weak ourselves. It is, of all architecture, the basest, when base people build it—of all, the noblest, when built by the noble.

And now note that both these religions—Greek and Mediæval—perished by falsehood in their own main purpose. The Greek religion of Wisdom perished in a false philosophy—'Oppositions of science, falsely so called.' The Mediæval religion of Consolation perished in false comfort; in remission of sins given lyingly. It was the selling of absolution that ended the Mediæval faith; and I can tell you more, it is the selling of absolution which, to the end of time, will mark false Christianity. Pure Christianity gives her remission of sins only by *ending* them; but false Christianity gets her remission of sins by *compounding for* them. And there are many ways of compounding for them. We English have beautiful little quiet ways of buying absolution, whether in low Church or high, far more cunning than any of Tetzel's trading.°

Then, thirdly, there followed the religion of Pleasure, in which all Europe gave itself to luxury, ending in death. First, *bals masqu´es* in every saloon, and then guillotines in every square. And all these three worships issue in vast temple building. Your Greek worshipped Wisdom, and built you the Parthenon—the Virgin's temple. The Mediæval worshipped Consolation, and built you Virgin temples also—but to our Lady of Salvation. Then the Revivalist worshipped beauty, of a sort, and built you Versailles, and the Vatican. Now, lastly, will you ask me what *we* worship, and what *we* build?

You know we are speaking always of the real, active, continual, national worship; that by which men act while they live; not that which they talk of when they die. Now, we have, indeed, a nominal religion, to which we pay tithes of property and sevenths of time; but we have also a practical and earnest religion, to which we devote nine-tenths of our property and sixth-sevenths of our time. And we dispute a great deal about the nominal religion; but we are all unanimous about this practical one, of which I think you will admit that the ruling goddess may be best generally described as the 'Goddess of Getting-on,' or 'Britannia of the Market.' The Athenians had an 'Athena Agoraia,' or Minerva of the Market; but she was a subordinate type of their goddess, while our Britannia Agoraia is the principal type of ours. And all your great architectural works, are, of course, built to her. It is long since you built a great cathedral; and how you would laugh at me, if I proposed building a cathedral on the top of one of these hills of yours, taking it for an Acropolis! But your railroad mounds prolonged masses of Acropolis; your railroad stations, vaster than the Parthenon, and innumerable; your chimneys, how much more mighty and costly than cathedral spires! your harbour-piers; your warehouses; your exchanges!—all these are built to your great Goddess of 'Getting-on;' and she has formed, and will continue to form, your architecture, as long as you worship her; and it is quite vain to ask me to tell you how to build to *her*; you know far better than I.

There might indeed, on some theories, be a conceivably good architecture for Exchanges—that is to say if there were any heroism in the fact or deed of exchange, which might be typically carved on the outside of your building. For, you know, all beautiful architecture must be adorned with sculpture or painting; and for sculpture or painting, you must have a subject. And hitherto it has been a received opinion among the nations of the world that the only right subjects for either, were *heroisms* of some sort. Even on his pots and his flagons, the Greek put a Hercules slaying lions,

495 **Tetzel's trading.** Johann Tetzel (1460–1519), a German Dominican monk, was appointed by Archbishop Albert of Mainz to sell (trade in) indulgences (remissions of part or all of the temporal punishment that according to Roman Catholicism is due for sins)

or an Apollo slaying serpents, or Bacchus slaying melancholy giants, and earth-born despondencies. On his temples, the Greek put contests of great warriors in founding states, or of gods with evil spirits. On his houses and temples alike, the Christian put carvings of angels conquering devils; or of hero-martyrs exchanging this world for another; subject inappropriate, I think, to our manner of exchange here. And the Master of Christians not only left his followers without any orders as to the sculpture of affairs of exchange on the outside of buildings, but gave some strong evidence of his dislike of affairs of exchange within them. And yet there might surely be a heroism in such affairs; and all commerce become a kind of selling of doves, not impious. The wonder has always been great to me, that heroism has never been supposed to be in anywise consistent with the practice of supplying people with food, or clothes, rather with that of quartering oneself upon them for food, and stripping them of their clothes. Spoiling of armour is an heroic deed in all ages; but the selling of clothes, old, or new, has never taken any colour of magnanimity. Yet one does not see why feeding the hungry and clothing the naked should ever become base businesses, even when engaged in on a large scale. If one could contrive to attach the notion of conquest to them anyhow? so that, supposing there were anywhere an obstinate race, who refused to be comforted, one might take some pride in giving them compulsory comfort; and as it were, 'occupying a country' with one's gifts, instead of one's armies? If one could only consider it as much a victory to get a barren field sown, as to get an eared field stripped; and contend who should build villages, instead of who should 'carry' them. Are not all forms of heroism, conceivable in doing these serviceable deeds? You doubt who is strongest? It might be ascertained by push of spade, as well as push of sword. Who is wisest? There are witty things to be thought of in planning other business than campaigns. Who is bravest? There are always the elements to fight with stronger than men; and nearly as merciless. The only absolutely and unapproachably heroic element in the soldier's work seems to be—that he is paid little for it—and regularly: while you traffickers, and exchangers, and others occupied in presumably benevolent business, like to be paid much for it—and by chance. I never can make out how it is that a knight-errant does not expect to be paid for his trouble, but a pedlar-errant always does;—that people are willing to take hard knocks for nothing, but never to sell ribands cheap;—that they are ready to go on fervent crusades to recover the tomb of a buried God, never on any travels to fulfil the orders of a living God;—that they will go anywhere barefoot to preach their faith, but must be well bribed to practise it, and are perfectly ready to give the Gospel gratis, but never the loaves and fishes. If you chose to take the matter up on any such soldierly principle, to do your commerce, and

your feeding of nations, for fixed salaries; and to be as particular about giving people the best food, and the best cloth, as soldiers are about giving them the best gunpowder, I could carve something for you on your exchange worth looking at. But I can only at present suggest decorating its frieze with pendant purses; and making its pillars broad at the base for the sticking of bills. And in the innermost chambers of it there might be a statue of Britannia of the Market, who may have, perhaps advisably, a partridge for her crest, typical at once of her courage in fighting for noble ideas; and of her interest in game; and round its neck the inscription in golden letters, 'Perdix fovit quæ non peperit.'° Then, for her spear, she might have a weaver's beam; and on her shield, instead of her Cross, the Milanese boar, semi-fleeced, with the town of Gennesaret proper, in the field and the legend 'In the best market,' and her corslet, of leather, folded over her heart in the shape of a purse, with thirty slits in it for a piece of money to go in at, on each day of the month. And I doubt not but that people would come to see your exchange, and its goddess, with applause.

Nevertheless, I want to point out to you certain strange characters in this goddess of yours. She differs from the great Greek and Mediæval deities essentially in two things—first, as to the continuance of her presumed power; secondly, as to the extent of it.

1st, as to the Continuance.

The Greek Goddess of Wisdom gave continual increase of wisdom, as the Christian Spirit of Comfort (or Comforter) continual increase of comfort. There was no question, with these, of any limit or cessation of function. But with your Agora Goddess, that is just the most important question. Getting on—but where to? Gathering together—but how much? Do you mean to gather always—never to spend? If so, I wish you joy of your goddess, for I am just as well off as you, without the trouble of worshipping her at all. But if you do not spend, somebody else will—somebody else must. And it is because of this (among many other such errors) that I have fearlessly declared your so-called science of Political Economy to be no science; because, namely, it has omitted the study of exactly the most important branch of the business—the study of spending. For spend you must, and as much as you make, ultimately. You gather corn:—will you bury England under a heap of grain; or will you, when you have gathered, finally eat? You gather gold:—will you make your house-roofs of it, or pave your streets with it? That is still one way of spending it. But if you keep it, that you may get more, I'll give you more; I'll give you all the gold you want—all you can imagine—if you can tell me what you'll do with it. You shall have thousands of gold pieces;—thousands of thousands —millions—mountains, of gold: where will you keep them? Will you put an Olympus of silver upon a golden

619 **Perdix ... peperit,** a plover cherished that which she did not bring forth

Pelion—make Ossa° like a wart? Do you think the rain and dew would then come down to you, in the streams from such mountains, more blessedly than they will down the mountains which God has made for you, of moss and whinstone? But it is not gold that you want to gather! What is it? greenbacks? No; not those neither. What is it then—is it ciphers after a capital I? Cannot you practise writing ciphers, and write as many as you want? Write ciphers for an hour every morning, in a big book, and say every evening, I am worth all those noughts more than I was yesterday. Won't that do? Well, what in the name of Plutus is it you want? Not gold, not greenbacks, not ciphers after a capital I? You will have to answer, after all, 'No; we want, somehow or other, money's *worth*.' Well, what is that? Let your Goddess of Getting-on discover it, and let her learn to stay therein.

II. But there is yet another question to be asked respecting this Goddess of Getting-on. The first was of the continuance of her power; the second is of its extent.

Pallas° and the Madonna were supposed to be all the world's Pallas, and all the world's Madonna. They could teach all men, and they could comfort all men. But, look strictly into the nature of the power of your Goddess of Getting-on; and you will find she is the Goddess—not of everybody's getting on—but only of somebody's getting on. This is a vital, or rather deathful, distinction. Examine it in your own ideal of the state of national life which this Goddess is to evoke and maintain. I asked you what it was, when I was last here;—you have never told me. Now, shall I try to tell you?

Your ideal of human life then is, I think, that it should be passed in a pleasant undulating world, with iron and coal everywhere underneath it. On each pleasant bank of this world is to be a beautiful mansion, with two wings; and stables, and coach-houses; a moderately sized park; a large garden and hot-houses; and pleasant carriage drives through the shrubberies. In this mansion are to live the favoured votaries of the Goddess; the English gentleman, with his gracious wife, and his beautiful family; always able to have the boudoir and the jewels for the wife, and the beautiful ball dresses for the daughters, and hunters for the sons, and a shooting in the Highlands for himself. At the bottom of the bank, is to be the mill; not less than a quarter of a mile long, with a steam engine at each end, and two in the middle, and a chimney three hundred feet high. In this mill are to be in constant employment from eight hundred to a thousand workers, who never drink, never strike, always go to church on Sunday, and always express themselves in respectful language.

Is not that, broadly, and in the main features, the kind of thing you propose to yourselves? It is very pretty indeed seen from above; not at all so pretty, seen from below. For, observe, while to one family this deity is indeed the Goddess of Getting on, to a thousand families she is the Goddess of *not* Getting on. 'Nay,' you say, 'they have all their chance.' Yes, so has every one in a lottery, but there must always be the same number of blanks. 'Ah! but in a lottery it is not skill and intelligence which take the lead, but blind chance.' What then! do you think the old practice, that 'they should take who have the power, and they should keep who can,' is less iniquitous, when the power has become power of brains instead of fist? and that, though we may not take advantage of a child's or a woman's weakness, we may of a man's foolishness? 'Nay, but finally, work must be done, and some one must be at the top, some one at the bottom.' Granted, my friends. Work must always be, and captains of work must always be; and if you in the least remember the tone of any of my writings, you must know that they are thought unfit for this age, because they are always insisting on need of government, and speaking with scorn of liberty. But I beg you to observe that there is a wide difference between being captains or governors of work, and taking the profits of it. It does not follow, because you are general of an army, that you are to take all the treasure, or land, it wins (if it fight for treasure or land); neither, because you are king of a nation, that you are to consume all the profits of the nation's work. Real kings, on the contrary, are known invariably by their doing quite the reverse of this,—by their taking the least possible quantity of the nation's work for themselves. There is no test of real kinghood so infallible as that. Does the crowned creature live simply, bravely, unostentatiously? probably he *is* a King. Does he cover his body with jewels, and his table with delicates? in all probability he is *not* a King. It is possible he may be, as Solomon was; but that is when the nation shares his splendour with him. Solomon made gold, not only to be in his own palace as stones, but to be in Jerusalem as stones. But even so, for the most part, these splendid kinghoods expire in ruin, and only the true kinghoods live, which are of royal labourers governing loyal labourers; who, both leading rough lives, establish the true dynasties. Conclusively you will find that because you are king of a nation, it does not follow that you are to gather for yourself all the wealth of that nation; neither, because you are king of a small part of the nation, and lord over the means of its maintenance—over field, or mill, or mine, are you to take all the produce of that piece of the foundation of national existence for yourself.

You will tell me I need not preach against these things for I cannot mend them. No, good friends, I cannot; but you can, and you will; or something else can and will. Do you think these phenomena are to stay always in their present power or aspect? All his-

663 **Pelion . . . Ossa.** The giants, in their war with the gods on Olympus, are said to have piled one of these mountains on top of the other   684 **Pallas,** name given to Athena, goddess of wisdom, in classical mythology

tory shows, on the contrary, that to be the exact thing they never can do. Change *must* come; but it is ours to determine whether change of growth, or change of death. Shall the Parthenon be in ruins on its rock, and Bolton priory in its meadow, but these mills of yours be the consummation of the buildings of the earth, and their wheels be as the wheels of eternity? Think you that 'men may come, and men may go,' but—mills—go on for ever? Not so; out of these, better or worse shall come; and it is for you to choose which.

I know that none of this wrong is done with deliberate purpose. I know, on the contrary, that you wish your workmen well; that you do much for them, and that you desire to do more for them, if you saw your way to it safely. I know that many of you have done, and are every day doing, whatever you feel to be in your power; and that even all this wrong and misery are brought about by a warped sense of duty, each of you striving to do his best, without noticing that this best is essentially and centrally the best for himself, not for others. And all this has come of the spreading of that thrice accursed, thrice impious doctrine of the modern economist, that 'To do the best for yourself, is finally to do the best for others.' Friends, our great Master said not so; and most absolutely we shall find this world is not made so. Indeed, to do the best for others, is finally to do the best for ourselves; but it will not do to have our eyes fixed on that issue. The Pagans had got beyond that. Hear what a Pagan says of this matter; hear what were, perhaps, the last written words of Plato,—if not the last actually written (for this we cannot know), yet assuredly in fact and power his parting words—in which, endeavouring to give full crowning and harmonious close to all his thoughts, and to speak the sum of them by the imagined sentence of the Great Spirit, his strength and his heart fail him, and the words cease, broken off for ever. It is the close of the dialogue called 'Critias,' in which he describes, partly from real tradition, partly in ideal dream, the early state of Athens; and the genesis, and order, and religion, of the fabled isle of Atlantis; in which genesis he conceives the same first perfection and final degeneracy of man, which in our own Scriptural tradition is expressed by saying that the Sons of God intermarried with the daughters of men, for he supposes the earliest race to have been indeed the children of God; and to have corrupted themselves, until 'their spot was not the spot of his children.' And this, he says, was the end; that indeed through many generations, so long as the God's nature in them yet was full, they were submissive to the sacred laws, and carried themselves lovingly to all that had kindred with them in divineness; for their uttermost spirit was faithful and true, and in every wise great; so that, in all meekness of wisdom, they dealt with each other, and took all the chances of life; and despising all things except virtue, they cared little what happened day by day, and *bore lightly the*

burden of gold and of possessions; for they saw that, if only their common love and virtue increased, all these things would be increased together with them; but to set their esteem and ardent pursuit upon material possession would be to lose that first, and their virtue and affection together with it. And by such reasoning, and what of the divine nature remained in them, they gained all this greatness of which we have already told; but when the God's part of them faded and became extinct, being mixed again and again, and effaced by the prevalent mortality; and the human nature at last exceeded, they then became unable to endure the courses of fortune; and fell into shapelessness of life, and baseness in the sight of him who could see, having lost everything that was fairest of their honour; while to the blind hearts which could not discern the true life, tending to happiness, it seemed that they were then chiefly noble and happy, being filled with all iniquity of inordinate possession and power. Whereupon, the God of Gods, whose Kinghood is in laws, beholding a once just nation thus cast into misery, and desiring to lay such punishment upon them as might make them repent into restraining, gathered together all the gods into his dwelling-place, which from heaven's centre overlooks whatever has part in creation; and having assembled them, he said'—

The rest is silence. So ended are the last words of the chief wisdom of the heathen, spoken of this idol of riches; this idol of yours; this golden image high by measureless cubits, set up where your green fields of England are furnace-burnt into the likeness of the plain of Dura:° this idol, forbidden to us, first of all idols, by our own Master and faith; forbidden to us also by every human lip that has ever, in any age or people, been accounted of as able to speak according to the purposes of God. Continue to make that forbidden deity your principal one, and soon no more art, no more science, no more pleasure will be possible. Catastrophe will come; or worse than catastrophe, slow mouldering and withering into Hades. But if you can fix some conception of a true human state of life to be striven for—life for all men as for yourselves—if you can determine some honest and simple order of existence; following those trodden ways of wisdom, which are pleasantness, and seeking her quiet and withdrawn paths, which are peace;—then, and so sanctifying wealth into 'commonwealth,' all your art, your literature, your daily labours, your domestic affection, and citizen's duty, will join and increase into one magnificent harmony. You will know then how to build, well enough; you will build with stone well, but with flesh better; temples not made with hands, but riveted of hearts; and that kind of marble, crimson-veined, is indeed eternal.

(1866)

862 **Dura**, plain, near Babylon, where Nebuchadnezzar (c. 605–562 B.C.) set up a golden image. See *Daniel* 3:1

MATTHEW ARNOLD
1822–1888

Matthew Arnold was born in Laleham, Middlesex, England, the eldest son of Thomas Arnold (1795–1842), the distinguished headmaster of Rugby School and the leading educator of his generation in England. The young Arnold attended his father's school, where he won the Rugby Poetry Prize. He was a scholarship student at Balliol College, Oxford, where he won the Newdigate Poetry Prize. After graduating from Oxford, Arnold became private secretary to Lord Lansdowne, an important cabinet official in the government. In 1849 he published his first volume of poems, *The Strayed Reveller and Other Poems by A.*, but soon withdrew the volume. Shortly thereafter (1851) he accepted a government position as Inspector of Schools, which he held for almost all of the rest of his life. Although Arnold found much of his work as a school inspector to be drudgery, his natural instincts for teaching and preaching, together with his puritan sense of duty, allowed him to generally enjoy his role as a missionary for culture in the state schools. Arnold was successful in his government career and was asked to extend his study of schools to those on the Continent; he published his findings concerning foreign educational procedures and methods in a series of monographs between 1861 and 1867. In 1852 another volume of verse, *Empedocles on Etna and Other Poems*, was published, like the first, simply under the initial "A." It is interesting to note that Arnold's poetry and criticism, which have earned him such high regard in literary studies, were written in his spare time from official government duties.

In 1853 he published *Poems*, a collection which failed to include *Empedocles on Etna*. In the preface, which has been called one of the most important critical documents of the nineteenth century, Arnold set out to explain why he had omitted *Empedocles*. This preface is a forerunner of his later criticism in its insistence upon the classic virtues of universality, impersonality, and unity rather than the Romantic values of self-absorption, self-division, and despair in *Empedocles*. Arnold's criticism disapproved of his own best poetry, which remained Romantic. In 1855 Arnold published *Poems, Second Series*. He had the distinction of being the first layman elected to the Professorship of Poetry at Oxford (1857), a position he held for the next ten years. *Merope*, a verse drama in imitation of the ancient Greeks, appeared in 1858. A series of Oxford lectures entitled *On Translating Homer* came out in 1861, followed by another series, *On the Study of Celtic Literature*, in 1867. Arnold also published *New Poems* in 1867 but composed little poetry after the publication of this volume.

Arnold recognized his limitations as a poet. As he wrote to his sister in 1853: "Fret not yourself to make my poems square in all their parts, but like what you can my darling. The true reason why parts suit you while others do not is that my poems are fragments —*i.e.* that I am fragments, while you are whole; the whole effect of my poems is quite vague and indeterminate—this is their weakness . . . a person who has any inward completeness can at best only like parts of them; in fact such a person stands firmly and knows what he is about while the poems stagger weakly and are at their wits end. I shall do better some day I hope—meanwhile . . . do not plague yourself to find a consistent meaning for these last; which in fact they do not possess through my weakness." Critics have generally agreed with Arnold's judgment of his poetry. Paradoxically, the fact that Arnold's poems generally lack the complete harmony and formal integrity of great poetry increases their value to the student of the Victorian temperament. Arnold's poetry reflects his acute awareness of "the bewildering confusion" of his times—the disappearance of traditional values, the flow of false tendencies, the increasing estrangement of the individual from society.

Arnold established his reputation as the leading literary critic of his day with *Essays in Criticism* (1865). He reinforced that reputation with *Culture and Anarchy: An Essay in Political and Social Criticism* (1869), *St. Paul and Protestantism* (1870), *Literature and Dogma* (1873), *God and the Bible* (1875), and *Last Essays on Church and Religion* (1877). He was both a prolific and a popular critic in his own time.

Modern literary critics have frequently commented upon the fact that when Arnold the critic was born, Arnold the poet died. The shift was at first gradual. He continued to refine and apply the critical principles that he had first formulated in the preface to his *Poems* of 1853, finally giving a social orientation to his literary criticism in *The Function of Criticism at the Present Time*, written explicitly as an introduction to *Essays in Criticism*. His careful and exact reports to the Education Department contained his observations of the middle classes in their schools. By the mid-1860s, he had become an expert on education. He turned to the broader issues and began to say to the middle classes: "Your whole future depends on your giving a public establishment to your education and thus getting your minds more opened and your characters more dignified." The ferment which Arnold witnessed among the dissenting middle classes seemed to give him a chance to do something important. The step from here to general criticism of politics and society was not difficult; it was certainly a natural one for Arnold's flexible mind.

The critic in prose spoke with a firmer voice than the critic in poetry. The resolute tone of the 1853 preface persisted throughout Arnold's life as a literary critic. Two basic principles guided Arnold's literary criticism: his immense faith in poetry and his determination to introduce "a little order into this [modern] chaos by establishing in any quarter a single sound rule of criticism, a single rule which clearly marks what is right as right and what is wrong as wrong." To achieve this, Arnold relied on three essential qualities: on *intellectual curiosity*—the "disinterested love of a free play of the mind on all subjects for its own sake"; on *literary conscience*—that quality which asks, not whether one is amused or pleased or moved "by a work of art or mind," but whether one is "*right* in being amused with it, and in applauding it, and in being moved by it"; and on *faith in the qualitative distinction*—"Of this quality the world is impatient; it chafes against it, rails at it, hates it;—it ends by receiving its influence, and by undergoing its law. This quality at last inexorably corrects the world's blunders, and fixes the world's ideals."

Arnold carried his faith in the qualitative distinction over into his social criticism. He felt that it was necessary to call the world's social and political reformers back to first principles so that outmoded institutions—laws, dogmas, customs—could be transformed on a rational basis. For an expansive, reforming generation to proceed on bases other than first principles was, he felt, anarchy—intellectually and socially. But the only way to get back to first principles was to explore the world's best knowledge and the world's best wisdom. Hence, Arnold's definition of culture (a return to first principles) is a knowledge of the best that has been thought (literature and philosophy) and known (science). But it was culture with a "social idea"—not only a *knowledge* of the best but also a *will* to make that best prevail.

In 1883-1884 Arnold accepted a government pension and undertook a lecture tour of the United States; his *Discourses in America* was published in 1885. He retired the following year and died in Liverpool in 1888. He was buried in his native Laleham.

TO A FRIEND

Who prop, thou ask'st, in these bad days, my mind?
He much, the old man,° who, clearest-souled of men,
Saw The Wide Prospect,° and the Asian Fen,°
And Tmolus' hill,° and Smyrna bay,° though blind.
5 Much he, whose friendship I not long since won,
That halting slave,° who in Nicopolis
Taught Arrian, when Vespasian's brutal son
Cleared Rome of what most shamed him. But be his°
My special thanks, whose even-balanced soul,

From first youth tested up to extreme old age,   10
Business could not make dull, nor Passion wild:
Who saw life steadily, and saw it whole;
The mellow glory of the Attic stage;
Singer of sweet Colonus, and its child.
(1849)

IN HARMONY WITH NATURE

TO A PREACHER

"In harmony with Nature?" Restless fool,
Who with such heat dost preach what were to thee,
When true, the last impossibility—
To be like Nature strong, like Nature cool!
Know, man hath all which Nature hath, but more,   5
And in that *more* lie all his hopes of good.
Nature is cruel, man is sick of blood;
Nature is stubborn, man would fain adore;
Nature is fickle, man hath need of rest;
Nature forgives no debt, and fears no grave;   10
Man would be mild, and with safe conscience blest.
Man must begin, know this, where Nature ends;
Nature and man can never be fast friends.
Fool, if thou canst not pass her, rest her slave!
(1849)

THE FORSAKEN MERMAN

Come, dear children, let us away;
Down and away below!
Now my brothers call from the bay,
Now the great winds shoreward blow,
Now the salt tides seaward flow;
Now the wild white horses play,
Champ and chafe and toss in the spray.
Children dear, let us away!
This way, this way!

Call her once before you go—   10
Call once yet!
In a voice that she will know:
"Margaret! Margaret!"°
Children's voices should be dear
(Call once more) to a mother's ear;
Children's voices, wild with pain—
Surely she will come again!
Call her once and come away;
This way, this way!
"Mother dear, we cannot stay!   20
The wild white horses foam and fret."
Margaret! Margaret!

To a Friend   2 **the old man,** Homer, who was said to be blind   3 **The Wide Prospect,** Europe   **Asian Fen,** the marshy, low-lying districts along the rivers in Asia Minor   4 **Tmolus' hill,** mountain in Lydia, Asia Minor   **Smyrna bay.** Smyrna, one of the many towns that claimed to be the birthplace of Homer, is the chief seaport of Asia Minor   6 **slave,** Epictetus (c. 60–120), the Stoic philosopher, who was lame and at one time a slave. He lived at Nicopolos, Greece, after he was banished from Rome by the Emperor Domitian, the brutal son of Vespasian. One of the pupils of Epictetus was Arrian, a famous philosopher and historian   8 **his,** reference to Sophocles (497–406 B.C.), the Athenian dramatist whose plays are noted for their serenity. He was born at Colonus (l. 14), a village near Athens

The Forsaken Merman   13 **Margaret,** a favorite name with Arnold; it means sea pearl

Come, dear children, come away down;
Call no more!
One last look at the white-walled town,
And the little gray church on the windy shore,
Then come down!
She will not come though you call all day;
Come away, come away!

30 Children dear, was it yesterday
We heard the sweet bells over the bay?
In the caverns where we lay,
Through the surf and through the swell,
The far-off sound of a silver bell?
Sand-strewn caverns, cool and deep,
Where the winds are all asleep;
Where the spent lights quiver and gleam,
Where the salt weed sways in the stream,
Where the sea-beasts, ranged all round,
40 Feed in the ooze of their pasture-ground;
Where the sea-snakes coil and twine,
Dry their mail and bask in the brine;
Where great whales come sailing by,
Sail and sail, with unshut eye,
Round the world for ever and aye?
When did music come this way?
Children dear, was it yesterday?

Children dear, was it yesterday
(Call yet once) that she went away?
50 Once she sate with you and me,
On a red gold throne in the heart of the sea,
And the youngest sate on her knee.
She combed its bright hair, and she tended it well,
When down swung the sound of a far-off bell.
She sighed, she looked up through the clear green sea;
She said: "I must go, for my kinsfolk pray
In the little gray church on the shore today.
'Twill be Easter-time in the world—ah me!
And I lose my poor soul, Merman! here with thee."
60 I said: "Go up, dear heart, through the waves;
Say thy prayer, and come back to the kind sea-caves!"
She smiled, she went up through the surf in the bay.
Children dear, was it yesterday?

Children dear, were we long alone?
"The sea grows stormy, the little ones moan;
Long prayers," I said, "in the world they say;
Come!" I said; and we rose through the surf in the bay.
We went up the beach, by the sandy down
Where the sea-stocks° bloom, to the white-walled
town;
70 Through the narrow paved streets, where all was still,
To the little gray church on the windy hill.
From the church came a murmur of folk at their
prayers,
But we stood without in the cold blowing airs.

We climbed on the graves, on the stones worn with
rains,
And we gazed up the aisle through the small leaded
panes.
She sate by the pillar; we saw her clear:
"Margaret, hist! come quick, we are here!
Dear heart," I said, "we are long alone;
The sea grows stormy, the little ones moan."
But, ah, she gave me never a look,   80
For her eyes were sealed to the holy book!
Loud prays the priest; shut stands the door.°
Come away, children, call no more!
Come away, come down, call no more!

Down, down, down!
Down to the depths of the sea!
She sits at her wheel in the humming town,
Singing most joyfully.
Hark what she sings: "O joy, O joy,
For the humming street, and the child with its toy!   90
For the priest, and the bell, and the holy well;°
For the wheel where I spun,
And the blessed light of the sun!"
And so she sings her fill,
Singing most joyfully,
Till the spindle drops from her hand,
And the whizzing wheel stands still.
She steals to the window, and looks at the sand,
And over the sand at the sea;
And her eyes are set in a stare;   100
And anon there breaks a sigh,
And anon there drops a tear,
From a sorrow-clouded eye,
And a heart sorrow-laden,
A long, long sigh;
For the cold strange eyes of a little Mermaiden
And the gleam of her golden hair.

Come away, away, children;
Come, children, come down!
The hoarse wind blows coldly;   110
Lights shine in the town.
She will start from her slumber
When gusts shake the door;
She will hear the winds howling,
Will hear the waves roar.
We shall see, while above us
The waves roar and whirl,
A ceiling of amber,
A pavement of pearl.
Singing: "Here came a mortal,   120
But faithless was she!
And alone dwell forever
The kings of the sea."

But, children, at midnight,
When soft the winds blow,
When clear falls the moonlight,
When spring-tides are low;
When sweet airs come seaward
From heaths starred with broom,
130 And high rocks throw mildly
On the blanched sands a gloom;
Up the still, glistening beaches,
Up the creeks we will hie,
Over banks of bright seaweed
The ebb-tide leaves dry.
We will gaze, from the sand-hills,
At the white, sleeping town;
At the church on the hillside—
And then come back down,
140 Singing: "There dwells a loved one,
But cruel is she!
She left lonely forever
The kings of the sea."
(1849)

MEMORIAL VERSES

APRIL 1850

Goethe in Weimar sleeps, and Greece,
Long since, saw Byron's struggle cease.
But one such death remained to come;
The last poetic voice is dumb—
We stand today by Wordsworth's tomb.

When Byron's eyes were shut in death,
We bowed our head and held our breath.
He taught us little; but our soul
Had *felt* him like the thunder's roll.
10 With shivering heart the strife we saw
Of passion with eternal law;
And yet with reverential awe
We watched the fount of fiery life
Which served for that Titanic strife.°

When Goethe's death was told, we said:
Sunk, then, is Europe's sagest head.
Physician of the iron age,°
Goethe has done his pilgrimage.
He took the suffering human race,
20 He read each wound, each weakness clear;
And struck his finger on the place,
And said *Thou ailest here, and here!*
He looked on Europe's dying hour

Of fitful dream and feverish power;
His eye plunged down the weltering strife,
The turmoil of expiring life—
He said: *The end is everywhere,
Art still has truth, take refuge there!*
And he was happy, if to know
Causes of things, and far below   30
His feet to see the lurid flow
Of terror, and insane distress,
And headlong fate, be happiness.°

And Wordsworth!—Ah, pale ghosts, rejoice!
For never has such soothing voice
Been to your shadowy world conveyed,
Since erst, at morn, some wandering shade
Heard the clear song of Orpheus come
Through Hades, and the mournful gloom.
Wordsworth has gone from us—and ye,   40
Ah, may ye feel his voice as we!
He too upon a wintry clime
Had fallen—on this iron time
Of doubts, disputes, distractions, fears.
He found us when the age had bound
Our souls in its benumbing round;
He spoke, and loosed our heart in tears.
He laid us, as we lay at birth,
On the cool flowery lap of earth;
Smiles broke from us, and we had ease;   50
The hills were round us, and the breeze
Went o'er the sun-lit fields again;
Our foreheads felt the wind and rain.
Our youth returned; for there was shed
On spirits that had long been dead,
Spirits dried up and closely furled,
The freshness of the early world.

Ah! since dark days still bring to light
Man's prudence and man's fiery might,
Time may restore us in his course   60
Goethe's sage mind and Byron's force;
But where will Europe's latter hour
Again find Wordsworth's healing power?
Others will teach us how to dare,
And against fear our breast to steel;
Others will strengthen us to bear—
But who, ah! who, will make us feel?
The cloud of mortal destiny,
Others will front it fearlessly—
But who, like him, will put it by?   70

Keep fresh the grass upon his grave,
O Rotha,° with thy living wave!
Sing him thy best! for few or none
Hears thy voice right, now he is gone.
(1850)

Memorial Verses   14 Titanic strife. Byron was noted for his fiery, passionate nature, and the word *Titanic* is fittingly applied to him. The Titans were superhuman beings of great size who rebelled against the gods   17 iron age, so called because of the terrible years of the French Revolution and the period following. To Goethe they seemed to portend the destruction of Europe

29-33 And he . . . happiness. These lines were translated from Vergil's *Georgics*, II, 490-492   72 Rotha, small stream near Grasmere, Westmoreland, where Wordsworth is buried

ISOLATION. TO MARGUERITE

We were apart; yet, day by day,
I bade my heart more constant be.
I bade it keep the world away,
And grow a home for only thee;
Nor feared but thy love likewise grew,
Like mine, each day, more tried, more true.

The fault was grave! I might have known,
What far too soon, alas! I learned—
The heart can bind itself alone,
10 And faith may oft be unreturned.
Self-swayed our feelings ebb and swell—
Thou lov'st no more;—Farewell! Farewell!

Farewell!—and thou, thou lonely heart,
Which never yet without remorse
Even for a moment didst depart
From thy remote and spheréd course
To haunt the place where passions reign—
Back to thy solitude again!

Back! with the conscious thrill of shame
20 Which Luna° felt, that summer-night,
Flash through her pure immortal frame,
When she forsook the starry height
To hang over Endymion's sleep
Upon the pine-grown Latmian steep.

Yet she, chaste queen, had never proved
How vain a thing is mortal love,
Wandering in heaven, far removed.
But thou hast long had place to prove
This truth—to prove, and make thine own:
30 "Thou hast been, shalt be, art alone."

Or, if not quite alone, yet they
Which touch thee are unmating things—
Ocean and clouds and night and day;
Lorn autumns and triumphant springs;
And life, and others' joy and pain,
And love, if love, of happier men.

Of happier men—for they, at least,
Have *dreamed* two human hearts might blend
In one, and were through faith released
40 From isolation without end
Prolonged; nor knew, although not less
Alone than thou, their loneliness.
(1855)

TO MARGUERITE—CONTINUED

Yes! in the sea of life enisled,
With echoing straits between us thrown,
Dotting the shoreless watery wild,
We mortal millions live *alone*.
The islands feel the enclasping flow,
And then their endless bounds they know.

But when the moon their hollows lights,
And they are swept by balms of spring,
And in their glens, on starry nights,
The nightingales divinely sing;   10
And lovely notes, from shore to shore,
Across the sounds and channels pour—

Oh! then a longing like despair
Is to their farthest caverns sent;
For surely once, they feel, we were
Parts of a single continent!
Now round us spreads the watery plain—
Oh, might our marges meet again!

Who ordered that their longing's fire
Should be, as soon as kindled, cooled?   20
Who renders vain their deep desire?—
A god, a god their severance ruled!
And bade betwixt their shores to be
The unplumbed, salt, estranging sea.
(1852)

THE BURIED LIFE

Light flows our war of mocking words, and yet,
Behold, with tears mine eyes are wet!
I feel a nameless sadness o'er me roll.
Yes, yes, we know that we can jest,
We know, we know that we can smile!
But there's a something in this breast,
To which thy light words bring no rest,
And thy gay smiles no anodyne.
Give me thy hand, and hush awhile,
And turn those limpid eyes on mine,   10
And let me read there, love! thy inmost soul.

Alas! is even love too weak
To unlock the heart, and let it speak?
Are even lovers powerless to reveal
To one another what indeed they feel?
I knew the mass of men concealed
Their thoughts, for fear that if revealed
They would by other men be met
With blank indifference, or with blame reproved;
I knew they lived and moved   20

Tricked in disguises, alien to the rest
Of men, and alien to themselves—and yet
The same heart beats in every human breast!
But we, my love!—doth a like spell benumb
Our hearts, our voices?—must we too be dumb?

Ah! well for us, if even we,
Even for a moment, can get free
Our heart, and have our lips unchained;
For that which seals them hath been deep-ordained!
30 Fate, which foresaw
How frivolous a baby man would be—
By what distractions he would be possessed,
How he would pour himself in every strife,
And well-nigh change his own identity—
That it might keep from his capricious play
His genuine self, and force him to obey
Even in his own despite his being's law,
Bade through the deep recesses of our breast
The unregarded river of our life
40 Pursue with indiscernible flow its way;
And that we should not see
The buried stream, and seem to be
Eddying at large in blind uncertainty,
Though driving on with it eternally.

But often, in the world's most crowded streets,
But often, in the din of strife,
There rises an unspeakable desire
After the knowledge of our buried life;
A thirst to spend our fire and restless force
50 In tracking out our true, original course;
A longing to inquire
Into the mystery of this heart which beats
So wild, so deep in us—to know
Whence our lives come and where they go.
And many a man in his own breast then delves,
But deep enough, alas! none ever mines.
And we have been on many thousand lines,
And we have shown, on each, spirit and power;
But hardly have we, for one little hour,
60 Been on our own line, have we been ourselves—
Hardly had skill to utter one of all
The nameless feelings that course through our breast,
But they course on forever unexpressed.
And long we try in vain to speak and act
Our hidden self, and what we say and do
Is eloquent, is well—but 'tis not true!
And then we will no more be racked
With inward striving, and demand
Of all the thousand nothings of the hour
70 Their stupefying power;
Ah yes, and they benumb us at our call!
Yet still, from time to time, vague and forlorn,
From the soul's subterranean depth upborne

As from an infinitely distant land,
Come airs, and floating echoes, and convey
A melancholy into all our day.

Only—but this is rare—
When a belovéd hand is laid in ours,
When, jaded with the rush and glare
Of the interminable hours,   80
Our eyes can in another's eyes read clear,
When our world-deafened ear
Is by the tones of a loved voice caressed—
A bolt is shot back somewhere in our breast,
And a lost pulse of feeling stirs again;
The eye sinks inward, and the heart lies plain,
And what we mean, we say, and what we would, we
    know.
A man becomes aware of his life's flow,
And hears its winding murmur; and he sees
The meadows where it glides, the sun, the breeze.   90

And there arrives a lull in the hot race
Wherein he doth forever chase
That flying and elusive shadow, rest.
An air of coolness plays upon his face,
And an unwonted calm pervades his breast.
And then he thinks he knows
The hills where his life rose,
And the sea where it goes.
(1852)

A SUMMER NIGHT

In the deserted, moon-blanch'd street,
How lonely rings the echo of my feet!
Those windows, which I gaze at, frown,
Silent and white, unopening down,
Repellent as the world;—but see,
A break between the housetops shows
The moon! and, lost behind her, fading dim
Into the dewy dark obscurity
Down at the far horizon's rim,
Doth a whole tract of heaven disclose!   10

And to my mind the thought
Is on a sudden brought
Of a past night, and a far different scene.
Headlands stood out into the moonlit deep
As clearly as at noon;
The spring-tide's brimming flow
Heaved dazzlingly between;
Houses, with long white sweep,
Girdled the glistening bay;
Behind, through the soft air,   20
The blue haze-cradled mountains spread away,

That night was far more fair—
But the same restless pacings to and fro,
And the same vainly throbbing heart was there,
And the same bright, calm moon.

And the calm moonlight seems to say:
Hast thou then still the old unquiet breast,
Which neither deadens into rest,
Nor ever feels the fiery glow
30 *That whirls the spirit from itself away,*
But fluctuates to and fro,
Never by passion quite possess'd
And never quite benumb'd by the world's sway?—
And I, I know not if to pray
Still to be what I am, or yield and be
Like all the other men I see.

For most men in a brazen prison live,
Where, in the sun's hot eye,
With heads bent o'er their toil, they languidly
40 Their lives to some unmeaning taskwork give,
Dreaming of nought beyond their prison-wall.
And as, year after year,
Fresh products of their barren labour fall
From their tired hands, and rest
Never yet comes more near,
Gloom settles slowly down over their breast;
And while they try to stem
The waves of mournful thought by which they are
    prest,
Death in their prison reaches them,
50 Unfreed, having seen nothing, still unblest.

And the rest, a few,
Escape their prison and depart
On the wide ocean of life anew.
There the freed prisoner, where'er his heart
Listeth, will sail;
Nor doth he know how there prevail,
Despotic on that sea,
Trade-winds which cross it from eternity.
Awhile he holds some false way, undebarr'd
60 By thwarting signs, and braves
The freshening wind and blackening waves.
And then the tempest strikes him; and between
The lightning-bursts is seen
Only a driving wreck,
And the pale master on his spar-strewn deck
With anguish'd face and flying hair
Grasping the rudder hard,
Still bent to make some port he knows not where,
Still standing for some false, impossible shore.
70 And sterner comes the roar
Of sea and wind, and through the deepening gloom
Fainter and fainter wreck and helmsman loom,
And he too disappears, and comes no more.

Is there no life, but these alone?
Madman or slave, must man be one?

Plainness and clearness without shadow of stain!
Clearness divine!
Ye heavens, whose pure dark regions have no sign
Of languor, though so calm, and, though so great,
Are yet untroubled and unpassionate;   80
Who, though so noble, share in the world's toil,
And, though so task'd, keep free from dust and soil!
I will not say that your mild deeps retain
A tinge, it may be, of their silent pain
Who have long'd deeply once, and long'd in vain—
But I will rather say that you remain
A world above man's head, to let him see
How boundless might his soul's horizons be,
How vast, yet of what clear transparency!
How it were good to abide there, and breathe free; 90
How fair a lot to fill
Is left to each man still!
(1852)

PHILOMELA

Hark! ah, the nightingale—
The tawny-throated!
Hark, from that moonlit cedar what a burst!
What triumph! hark!—what pain!

O wanderer from a Grecian shore,
Still, after many years, in distant lands,
Still nourishing in thy bewildered brain
That wild, unquenched, deep-sunken, old-world
    pain—
Say, will it never heal?
And can this fragrant lawn   10
With its cool trees, and night,
And the sweet, tranquil Thames,
And moonshine, and the dew,
To thy racked heart and brain
Afford no balm?

Dost thou tonight behold,
Here, through the moonlight on this English grass,
The unfriendly palace in the Thracian wild?
Dost thou again peruse
With hot cheeks and seared eyes   20
The too clear web, and thy dumb sister's shame?
Dost thou once more assay
Thy flight, and feel come over thee,
Poor fugitive, the feathery change
Once more, and once more seem to make resound
With love and hate, triumph and agony,

Lone Daulis,° and the high Cephissian vale?
  Listen, Eugenia°—
    How thick the bursts come crowding through the
      leaves?
30 Again—thou hearest?
  Eternal passion!
  Eternal pain!

(1853)

THE SCHOLAR-GYPSY

Go, for they call you, shepherd, from the hill;
  Go, shepherd, and untie the wattled cotes!°
    No longer leave thy wistful flock unfed,
    Nor let thy bawling fellows rack their throats,
      Nor the cropped herbage shoot another head.
        But when the fields are still,
    And the tired men and dogs all gone to rest,
      And only the white sheep are sometimes seen
    Cross and recross the strips of moon-blanched
      green,
10   Come, shepherd, and again begin the quest!°

Here, where the reaper was at work of late—
  In this high field's dark corner, where he leaves
    His coat, his basket, and his earthen cruse,
    And in the sun all morning binds the sheaves,
      Then here, at noon, comes back his stores to
        use—
        Here will I sit and wait,
    While to my ear from uplands far away
      The bleating of the folded flocks is borne,
    With distant cries of reapers in the corn°—
20   All the live murmur of a summer's day.

Screened is this nook o'er the high, half-reaped field,
  And here till sun-down, shepherd! will I be.
    Through the thick corn the scarlet poppies peep
    And round green roots and yellowing stalks I see
      Pale pink convolvulus° in tendrils creep;
        And air-swept lindens yield
    Their scent, and rustle down their perfumed show-
      ers
    Of bloom on the bent grass where I am laid,
    And bower me from the August sun with shade;
30   And the eye travels down to Oxford's towers.

And near me on the grass lies Glanvil's book°—
  Come let me read the oft-read tale again!
    The story of the Oxford scholar poor,

Of pregnant parts° and quick inventive brain,
  Who, tired of knocking at preferment's door,
    One summer-morn forsook
His friends, and went to learn the gypsy-lore,
    And roamed the world with that wild brother-
      hood,
    And came, as most men deemed, to little good,
But came to Oxford and his friends no more.   40

But once, years after, in the country-lanes,
  Two scholars, whom at college erst he knew,
    Met him, and of his way of life inquired;
    Whereat he answered that the gypsy-crew,
      His mates, had arts to rule as they desired
        The workings of men's brains,
    And they can bind them to what thoughts they
      will.
        "And I," he said, "the secret of their art,
    When fully learned, will to the world impart;
    But it needs heaven-sent moments for this skill."   50

This said, he left them, and returned no more.—
  But rumors hung about the country-side,
    That the lost scholar long was seen to stray,
    Seen by rare glimpses, pensive and tongue-tied
      In hat of antique shape, and cloak of gray,
        The same the gypsies wore.
    Shepherds had met him on the Hurst° in spring;
      At some lone alehouse in the Berkshire° moors,
    On the warm ingle-bench,° the smock-frocked
      boors
    Had found him seated at their entering.   60

But 'mid their drink and clatter, he would fly.
  And I myself seem half to know thy looks,
    And put the shepherds, wanderer! on thy trace;
    And boys who in lone wheatfields scare the rooks
      I ask if thou hast passed their quiet place;
        Or in my boat I lie
    Moored to the cool bank in the summer-heats,
      'Mid wide grass meadows which the sunshine
      fills,
    And watch the warm, green-muffled Cumner hills,
    And wonder if thou haunt'st their shy retreats.   70

For most, I know, thou lov'st retired ground!
  Thee at the ferry Oxford riders blithe,
    Returning home on summer nights, have met
    Crossing the stripling Thames at Bab-lock-hithe,°
      Trailing in the cool stream thy fingers wet,
      As the punt's rope chops round;°

Philomela 27 **Daulis,** the scene of the tragedy, in Phocis, Greece. The Cephissus was the chief river of Phocis 28 **Eugenia,** an imaginary person
The Scholar-Gypsy. Arnold drew the story for this poem from *The Vanity of Dogmatizing* (1661), an attack on scholastic philosophy written by Joseph Glanvil (1636–1680) 2 **wattled cotes,** sheepfolds built of wattles, interwoven twigs 10 **the quest,** the search for the Scholar-Gypsy, who is supposed still to haunt the vicinity 19 **corn,** wheat, grain 25 **convolvulus,** a kind of morning-glory 31 **Glanvil's book,** *The Vanity of Dogmatizing*

34 **pregnant parts,** inventive faculties 57 **Hurst,** Cumner Hurst, a prominent hill in the parish of Cumner, southwest of Oxford 58 **Berkshire,** a county south of Oxford 59 **ingle-bench,** bench in the chimney corner 74 **Bab-lock-hithe,** a ferry over the Thames about two miles west of the village of Cumner 76 **punt's . . . round.** The Scholar-Gypsy is seen reposing in a boat moored to the bank. The punt, or ferryboat, is pulled across the stream by a rope, and the boat moves in a kind of curve. The rope "chops" or suddenly shifts with the wind or the current

And leaning backward in a pensive dream,
  And fostering in thy lap a heap of flowers
  Plucked in shy fields and distant Wychwood° bowers,
80 And thine eyes resting on the moonlit stream.

And then they land, and thou art seen no more!—
  Maidens, who from the distant hamlets come
  To dance around the Fyfield elm in May,°
  Oft through the darkening fields have seen thee roam,
  Or cross a stile into the public way.
    Oft thou hast given them store
  Of flowers—the frail-leafed, white anemone,
  Dark bluebells drenched with dews of summer eves,
  And purple orchises with spotted leaves—
90 But none hath words she can report of thee.

And, above Godstow Bridge,° when hay-time's here
  In June, and many a scythe in sunshine flames,
  Men who through those wide fields of breezy grass
  Where black-winged swallows haunt the glittering Thames,
  To bathe in the abandoned lasher pass,°
    Have often passed thee near
  Sitting upon the river bank o'ergrown;
  Marked thine outlandish garb, thy figure spare,
  Thy dark vague eyes, and soft abstracted air—
100 But, when they came from bathing, thou wast gone!

At some lone homestead in the Cumner hills,
  Where at her open door the housewife darns,
  Thou hast been seen, or hanging on a gate
  To watch the threshers in the mossy barns.
    Children, who early range these slopes and late
    For cresses from the rills,
  Have known thee eying, all an April-day,
  The springing pastures and the feeding kine;
  And marked thee, when the stars come out and shine,
110 Through the long dewy grass move slow away.

In autumn, on the skirts of Bagley Wood°—
  Where most the gypsies by the turf-edged way
  Pitch their smoked tents, and every bush you see
  With scarlet patches tagged and shreds of gray,°
  Above the forest-ground called Thessaly°—
    The blackbird, picking food,
  Sees thee, nor stops his meal, nor fears at all;
  So often has he known thee past him stray,
  Rapt, twirling in thy hand a withered spray,

And waiting for the spark from heaven to fall.   120

And once, in winter, on the causeway chill
  Where home through flooded fields foot-travelers go,
  Have I not passed thee on the wooden bridge,
  Wrapped in thy cloak and battling with the snow,
  Thy face tow'rd Hinksey° and its wintry ridge?
    And thou hast climbed the hill,
  And gained the white brow of the Cumner range;
  Turned once to watch, while thick the snowflakes fall,
  The line of festal light in Christ-Church hall°—
  Then sought thy straw in some sequestered grange.   130

But what—I dream! Two hundred years are flown
  Since first thy story ran through Oxford halls,
  And the grave Glanvil did the tale inscribe
  That thou wert wandered from the studious walls
  To learn strange arts, and join a gypsy tribe;
    And thou from earth art gone
  Long since, and in some quiet churchyard laid—
  Some country-nook, where o'er thy unknown grave
  Tall grasses and white flowering nettles wave,
  Under a dark, red-fruited yew-tree's shade.   140

—No, no, thou hast not felt the lapse of hours!
  For what wears out the life of mortal men?
  'Tis that from change to change their being rolls;
  'Tis that repeated shocks, again, again,
  Exhaust the energy of strongest souls
    And numb the elastic powers,
  Till having used our nerves with bliss and teen,°
  And tired upon a thousand schemes our wit,
  To the just-pausing Genius° we remit
  Our worn-out life, and are—what we have been.   150

Thou hast not lived, why should'st thou perish, so?
  Thou hadst one aim, one business, one desire;
    Else wert thou long since numbered with the dead!
  Else hadst thou spent, like other men, thy fire!
  The generations of thy peers are fled,
    And we ourselves shall go;
  But thou possessest an immortal lot,
  And we imagine thee exempt from age
  And living as thou liv'st on Glanvil's page,
  Because thou hadst—what we, alas! have not.   160

For early didst thou leave the world, with powers
  Fresh undiverted to the world without,
    Firm to their mark, not spent on other things;
  Free from the sick fatigue, the languid doubt,

79 **Wychwood,** a forest ten miles northwest of Oxford 83 **Fyfield . . . May,** a reference to the maypole dance at Fyfield, a village six miles southwest of Oxford. The large elm was a landmark for all the countryside 91 **Godstow Bridge,** about two miles up the Thames River from Oxford 95 **lasher pass,** pool below a dam 111 **Bagley Wood,** southwest of Oxford; it was a favorite of Arnold's father 114 **scarlet patches . . . gray.** The bright-colored tattered garments of the gypsies were hung on the bushes 115 **Thessaly,** a piece of forest ground near Bagley Wood

125 **Hinksey,** a village south of Oxford 129 **Christ-Church hall,** the dining-hall in Christ Church College, Oxford 147 **teen,** sorrow 149 **just-pausing Genius.** According to the ancients the Genius of a man was his spirit or guardian angel. The phrase may mean that the Genius pauses just for a moment before departing, or that the even-handed Spirit of the world impartially ends individual lives

Which much to have tried, in much been baffled,
   brings.
   O life unlike to ours!
Who fluctuate idly without term or scope,
   Of whom each strives nor knows for what he
      strives,
   And each half lives a hundred different lives;
170 Who wait like thee, but not, like thee, in hope.

   Thou waitest for the spark from heaven! and we,
   Light half-believers of our casual creeds,
      Who never deeply felt, nor clearly willed,
   Whose insight never has borne fruit in deeds,
      Whose vague resolves never have been fulfilled;
         For whom each year we see
   Breeds new beginnings, disappointments new;
      Who hesitate and falter life away,
      And lose tomorrow the ground won today—
180 Ah! do not we, wanderer! await it too?

   Yes, we await it!—but it still delays,
   And then we suffer! and amongst us one,
      Who most hast suffered,° takes dejectedly
   His seat upon the intellectual throne;
      And all his store of sad experience he
         Lays bare of wretched days;
   Tells us his misery's birth and growth and signs,
      And how the dying spark of hope was fed,
      And how the breast was soothed, and how the
         head,
190 And all his hourly varied anodynes.°

   This for our wisest! and we others pine,
   And wish the long unhappy dream would end,
      And waive all claim to bliss, and try to bear;
   With close-lipped patience for our only friend,
      Sad patience, too near neighbor to despair—
         But none has hope like thine!
   Thou through the fields and through the woods dost
      stray,
      Roaming the country-side, a truant boy,
      Nursing thy project in unclouded joy,
200 And every doubt long blown by time away.

   O born in days when wits were fresh and clear,
   And life ran gayly as the sparkling Thames;
      Before this strange disease of modern life,
   With its sick hurry, its divided aims,
      Its heads o'ertaxed, its palsied hearts, was rife—
         Fly hence, our contact fear!
   Still fly, plunge deeper in the bowering wood!
      Averse, as Dido did with gesture stern
      From her false friend's approach in Hades turn,°
210 Wave us away, and keep thy solitude!

Still nursing the unconquerable hope,
   Still clutching the inviolable shade,
      With a free, onward impulse brushing through,
   By night, the silvered branches of the glade—
      Far on the forest-skirts, where none pursue,
         On some mild pastoral slope
   Emerge, and resting on the moonlit pales
      Freshen thy flowers as in former years
      With dew, or listen with enchanted ears,
   From the dark dingles,° to the nightingales!   220

   But fly our paths, our feverish contact fly!
   For strong the infection of our mental strife,
      Which, though it gives no bliss, yet spoils for rest;
   And we should win thee from thy own fair life,
      Like us distracted, and like us unblest.
         Soon, soon thy cheer would die,
   Thy hopes grow timorous, and unfixed thy powers,
      And thy clear aims be cross and shifting made;
      And then thy glad perennial youth would fade,
   Fade, and grow old at last, and die like ours.   230

   Then fly our greetings, fly our speech and smiles!
   —As some grave Tyrian trader,° from the sea,
      Descried at sunrise an emerging prow
   Lifting the cool-haired creepers° stealthily,
      The fringes of a southward-facing brow
         Among the Aegean isles;°
   And saw the merry Grecian coaster come,
      Freighted with amber grapes, and Chian wine,°
      Green, bursting figs, and tunnies° steeped in
         brine—
   And knew the intruders on his ancient home,   240

   The young light-hearted masters of the waves—
      And snatched his rudder, and shook out more sail;
      And day and night held on indignantly
   O'er the blue Midland waters° with the gale,
      Betwixt the Syrtes° and soft Sicily,
         To where the Atlantic raves
   Outside the western straits;° and unbent sails
      There, where down cloudy cliffs, through sheets
         of foam,
      Shy traffickers, the dark Iberians° come;
   And on the beach undid his corded bales.   250

(1853)

STANZAS
FROM THE GRANDE CHARTREUSE°

Through Alpine meadows soft-suffused
With rain, where thick the crocus blows,

182–190 one ... suffered, etc. These lines have been applied to Carlyle or Tennyson   190 anodynes, pain-soothing drugs   208–209 Dido ... turn. Dido, Queen of Carthage, killed herself because she was deserted by Aeneas. On his journey through Hades, Aeneas met the shade of Dido, but she turned scornfully away from him (Aeneid, VI, 450–471)

220 dingles, wooded dells   232 Tyrian trader. The Phoenicians of the city of Tyre were the chief traders in the Mediterranean from 900 to 700 B.C. They were gradually displaced by the Greeks   234 cool-haired creepers, foliage overhanging the entrance to some cavern or inlet   236 Aegean isles, islands in the Aegean Sea, between Greece and Asia Minor   238 Chian wine, wine from Chios, an island in the Aegean Sea   239 tunnies, a kind of large fish   244 Midland waters, Mediterranean Sea   245 Syrtes, the Gulf of Sidra, on the northeast coast of Africa   247 western straits, Strait of Gibraltar   249 Iberians, early inhabitants of Spain and Portugal   Stanzas from the Grand Chartreuse, the Grand Chartreuse Carthusian monastery in the French Alps

Past the dark forges long disused,
The mule-track from Saint Laurent goes.
The bridge is cross'd, and slow we ride,
Through forest, up the mountain-side.

The autumnal evening darkens round,
The wind is up, and drives the rain;
While, hark! far down, with strangled sound
10 Doth the Dead Guier's stream° complain,
Where that wet smoke, among the woods,
Over his boiling cauldron broods.

Swift rush the spectral vapours white
Past limestone scars with ragged pines,
Showing—then blotting from our sight!—
Halt—through the cloud-drift something shines!
High in the valley, wet and drear,
The huts of Courrerie appear.

Strike leftward! cries our guide; and higher
20 Mounts up the stony forest-way.
At last the encircling trees retire;
Look! through the showery twilight grey
What pointed roofs are these advance?—
A palace of the Kings of France?

Approach, for what we seek is here!
Alight, and sparely sup, and wait
For rest in this outbuilding near;
Then cross the sward and reach that gate.
Knock; pass the wicket! Thou art come
30 To the Carthusians' world-famed home.

The silent courts, where night and day
Into their stone-carved basins cold
The splashing icy fountains play—
The humid corridors behold!
Where, ghostlike in the deepening night,
Cowl'd forms brush by in gleaming white.

The chapel, where no organ's peal
Invests the stern and naked prayer—
With penitential cries they kneel
40 And wrestle; rising then, with bare
And white uplifted faces stand,
Passing the Host from hand to hand;

Each takes, and then his visage wan
Is buried in his cowl once more.
The cells!—the suffering Son of Man°
Upon the wall—the knee-worn floor—
And where they sleep, that wooden bed,
Which shall their coffin be, when dead!

The library, where tract and tome
50 Not to feed priestly pride are there,

To hymn the conquering march of Rome,
Nor yet to amuse, as ours are!
They paint of souls the inner strife,
Their drops of blood, their death in life.

The garden, overgrown—yet mild,
See, fragrant herbs are flowering there!
Strong children of the Alpine wild
Whose culture is the brethren's care;
Of human tasks their only one,
And cheerful works beneath the sun.   60

Those halls, too, destined to contain
Each its own pilgrim-host of old,
From England, Germany, or Spain—
All are before me! I behold
The House, the Brotherhood austere!
—And what am I, that I am here?

For rigorous teachers seized my youth,
And purged its faith, and trimm'd its fire,
Show'd me the high, white star of Truth,
There bade me gaze, and there aspire.   70
Even now their whispers pierce the gloom:
What dost thou in this living tomb?

Forgive me, masters of the mind!
At whose behest I long ago
So much unlearnt, so much resign'd—
I come not here to be your foe!
I seek these anchorites,° not in ruth,°
To curse and to deny your truth;

Not as their friend, or child, I speak!
But as, on some far northern strand,   80
Thinking of his own Gods, a Greek
In pity and mournful awe might stand
Before some fallen Runic stone°—
For both were faiths, and both are gone.

Wandering between two worlds, one dead,
The other powerless to be born,
With nowhere yet to rest my head,
Like these, on earth I wait forlorn.
Their faith, my tears, the world deride—
I come to shed them at their side.   90

Oh, hide me in your gloom profound,
Ye solemn seats of holy pain!
Take me, cowl'd forms, and fence me round,
Till I possess my soul again;
Till free my thoughts before me roll,
Not chafed by hourly false control!

For the world cries your faith is now
But a dead time's exploded dream;

10 **Dead Guier's stream,** a literal translation of the French name of the river, *Guiers Mort*   45 **the suffering Son of Man,** Christ

77 **anchorites,** individuals who live in seclusion for religious reasons   **ruth,** pity
83 **Runic stone.** A stone engraved with the straight-line alphabet of early Germanic tribes. Hence, something that once carried meaning and now seems inscrutable

My melancholy, sciolists° say,
100 Is a pass'd mode, an outworn theme—
As if the world had ever had
A faith, or sciolists been sad!

Ah, if it *be* pass'd, take away,
At least, the restlessness, the pain;
Be a man henceforth no more a prey
To these out-dated stings again!
The nobleness of grief is gone—
Ah, leave us not the fret alone!

But—if you cannot give us ease—
110 Last of the race of them who grieve
Here leave us to die out with these
Last of the people who believe!
Silent, while years engrave the brow;
Silent—the best are silent now.

Achilles ponders in his tent,
The kings of modern thought are dumb;
Silent they are, though not content,
And wait to see the future come.
They have the grief men had of yore,
120 But they contend and cry no more.

Our fathers water'd with their tears
This sea of time whereon we sail,
Their voices were in all men's ears
Who pass'd within their puissant hail.
Still the same ocean round us raves,
But we stand mute, and watch the waves.

For what avail'd it, all the noise
And outcry of the former men?—
Say, have their sons achieved more joys,
130 Say, is life lighter now than then?
The sufferers died, they left their pain—
The pangs which tortured them remain.

What helps it now, that Byron bore,
With haughty scorn which mock'd the smart,
Through Europe to the Ætolian shore°
The pageant of his bleeding heart?
That thousands counted every groan,
And Europe made his woe her own?

What boots it, Shelley! that the breeze
140 Carried thy lovely wail away,
Musical through Italian trees
Which fringe thy soft blue Spezzian bay?°
Inheritors of thy distress
Have restless hearts one throb the less?

Or are we easier, to have read,
O Obermann!° the sad, stern page,

Which tells us how thou hidd'st thy head
From the fierce tempest of thine age
In the lone brakes of Fontainebleau,
Or chalets near the Alpine snow?   150

Ye slumber in your silent grave!—
The world, which for an idle day
Grace to your mood of sadness gave,
Long since hath flung her weeds away.
The eternal trifler breaks your spell;
But we—we learnt your lore too well!

Years hence, perhaps, may dawn an age,
More fortunate, alas! than we,
Which without hardness will be sage,
And gay without frivolity.   160
Sons of the world, oh, speed those years;
But, while we wait, allow our tears!

Allow them! We admire with awe
The exulting thunder of your race;
You give the universe your law,
You triumph over time and space!
Your pride of life, your tireless powers,
We laud them, but they are not ours.

We are like children rear'd in shade
Beneath some old-world abbey wall,   170
Forgotten in a forest-glade,
And secret from the eyes of all.
Deep, deep the greenwood round them waves,
Their abbey, and its close of graves!

But, where the road runs near the stream,
Oft through the trees they catch a glance,
Of passing troops in the sun's beam—
Pennon, and plume, and flashing lance!
Forth to the world those soldiers fare,
To life, to cities, and to war!   180

And through the wood, another way,
Faint bugle-notes from far are borne,
Where hunters gather, staghounds bay,
Round some fair forest-lodge at morn.
Gay dames are there, in sylvan green;
Laughter and cries—those notes between!

The banners flashing through the trees
Make their blood dance and chain their eyes;
That bugle-music on the breeze
Arrests them with a charm'd surprise.   190
Banner by turns and bugle woo:
Ye shy recluses, follow too!

O children, what do ye reply?—
'Action and pleasure, will ye roam
Through these secluded dells to cry

99 **sciolists,** superficial learners   135 **Ætolian shore,** where Byron died
142 **Spezzian bay,** where Shelley died   146 **Obermann,** hero of Senancour's
novel of that name (1804)

Matthew Arnold 977

And call us?—but too late ye come!
Too late for us your call ye blow,
Whose bent was taken long ago.

'Long since we pace this shadow'd nave;
200 We watch those yellow tapers shine,
Emblems of hope over the grave,
In the high altar's depth divine;
The organ carries to our ear
Its accents of another sphere.

'Fenced early in this cloistral round
Of reverie, of shade, of prayer,
How should we grow in other ground?
How can we flower in foreign air?
—Pass, banners, pass, and bugles, cease;
210 And leave our desert to its peace!'
(1855)

THYRSIS

A monody, to commemorate the author's friend, Arthur Hugh Clough, who died at Florence, 1861

How changed is here each spot man makes or fills!
In the two Hinkseys° nothing keeps the same;
The village street its haunted mansion lacks,
And from the sign is gone Sibylla's° name
And from the roofs the twisted° chimney-stacks—
Are ye too changed, ye hills?
See, 'tis no foot of unfamiliar men
Tonight from Oxford up your pathway strays!
Here came I often, often, in old days—
10 Thyrsis and I; we still had Thyrsis then.

Runs it not here, the track by Childsworth Farm,°
Past the high wood, to where the elm-tree crowns
The hill behind whose ridge the sunset flames?
The signal-elm,° that looks on Ilsley Downs,°
The Vale, the three lone weirs,° the youthful
Thames?°—
This winter's eve is warm,
Humid the air! leafless, yet soft as spring,
The tender purple spray on copse and briers!
And that sweet city° with her dreaming spires,
20 She needs not June for beauty's heightening,

Lovely all times she lies, lovely tonight!—
Only, methinks, some loss of habit's power

Befalls me wandering through this upland dim;
Once passed I blindfold here, at any hour;
Now seldom come I, since I came with him.
That single elm tree bright
Against the west—I miss it! it is gone?
We prized it dearly; while it stood, we said,
Our friend, the gypsy-scholar,° was not dead;
While the tree lived, he in these fields lived on.   30

Too rare, too rare, grow now my visits here,
But once I knew each field, each flower, each stick;
And with the country folk acquaintance made
By barn in threshing-time, by new-built rick.
Here, too, our shepherd-pipes° we first assayed.
Ah me! this many a year
My pipe is lost,° my shepherd's holiday!
Needs must I lose them, needs with heavy heart
Into the world and wave of men depart;
But Thyrsis of his own will went away.°   40

It irked him to be here; he could not rest.
He loved each simple joy the country yields,
He loved his mates; but yet he could not keep,
For that a shadow lowered on the fields,
Here with the shepherds and the silly° sheep.
Some life of men unblest
He knew, which made him droop, and filled his
head.
He went; his piping took a troubled sound
Of storms that rage° outside our happy ground;
He could not wait their passing, he is dead.   50

So, some tempestuous morn in early June,
When the year's primal burst of bloom is o'er,
Before the roses and the longest day—
When garden-walks and all the grassy floor
With blossoms red and white of fallen May
And chestnut flowers are strewn—
So have I heard the cuckoo's parting cry,
From the wet field, through the vexed garden-
trees,
Come with the volleying rain and tossing breeze:
The bloom is gone, and with the bloom go I!   60

Too quick despairer, wherefore wilt thou go?
Soon will the high midsummer pomps° come on.
Soon will the musk carnations break and swell,
Soon shall we have gold-dusted snapdragon,
Sweet-William with his homely cottage-smell,
And stocks° in fragrant blow;
Roses that down the alleys shine afar,
And open, jasmine-muffled lattices,

Thyrsis   2 **two Hinkseys,** villages southwest of Oxford across the river
4 **Sibylla,** the first name of a woman who kept this lodging house near Oxford
5 **twisted,** set at an angle   11 **Childsworth Farm,** modern Chilswell Farm, three
miles from Oxford   14 **signal-elm.** This famous tree has frequently been identified with an oak tree standing at the top of the knoll on the Oxford side of the
ridge; but a large elm a short distance below the summit of the ridge better fits
the description   **Ilsley Downs.** Ilsley is a parish in West Berkshire   15 **weirs,**
dams   **youthful Thames.** The Thames River is about fifty yards wide at Oxford
19 **sweet city,** Oxford

29 **gypsy-scholar.** See *The Scholar-Gypsy* and title note   35 **shepherd-pipes,** the
usual pastoral symbol for poetry   36–37 **many a year . . . lost.** Arnold had not
published any poetry for nine years   40 **Thyrsis . . . away.** Clough resigned his
fellowship in Oriel College, Oxford, in 1848, partly on religious grounds
45 **silly,** simple   49 **storms that rage.** Much of the poetry of Clough reflects his
spiritual struggles   62 **pomps,** shows, displays   66 **stocks,** gillyflowers

And groups under the dreaming garden-trees,
70 And the full moon, and the white evening-star.

He hearkens not! light comer, he is flown!
    What matters it? next year he will return,
    And we shall have him in the sweet spring days,
    With whitening hedges, and uncrumpling fern,
    And bluebells trembling by the forest-ways,
        And scent of hay new-mown.
    But Thyrsis never more we swains shall see;
    See him come back, and cut a smoother reed,
    And blow a strain the world at last shall heed—
80 For Time, not Corydon, hath conquered thee!

Alack, for Corydon no rival now!—
    But when Sicilian shepherds° lost a mate,
    Some good survivor with his flute would go,
    Piping a ditty sad for Bion's fate;
    And cross the unpermitted ferry's flow,°
        And relax Pluto's° brow,
    And make leap up with joy the beauteous head
    Of Proserpine, among whose crownéd hair
    Are flowers first opened on Sicilian air,
90 And flute his friend, like Orpheus,° from the dead.

O easy access to the hearer's grace
    When Dorian° shepherds sang to Proserpine!
    For she herself had trod Sicilian fields,
    She knew the Dorian water's gush divine,
    She knew each lily white which Enna yields,
        Each rose with blushing face;
    She loved the Dorian pipe, the Dorian strain.
    But, ah, of our poor Thames she never heard!
    Her foot the Cumner° cowslips never stirred;
100 And we should tease her with our plaint in vain!

Well! wind-dispersed and vain the words will be,
    Yet, Thyrsis, let me give my grief its hour
    In the old haunt, and find our tree-topped hill!
    Who, if not I, for questing here hath power?
    I know the wood which hides the daffodil,
        I know the Fyfield tree,°
    I know what white, what purple fritillaries°
    The grassy harvest of the river-fields,
    Above by Ensham,° down by Sandford, yields,
110 And what sedged brooks are Thames's tributaries;

I know these slopes; who knows them if not I?—
    But many a dingle° on the loved hillside,
        With thorns once studded, old, white-blossomed
            trees,

Where thick the cowslips grew, and far descried
    High towered the spikes of purple orchises,
        Hath since our day put by
    The coronals of that forgotten time;
    Down each green bank hath gone the plowboy's
        team,
    And only in the hidden brookside gleam
Primroses, orphans of the flowery prime.   120

Where is the girl, who by the boatman's door,
    Above the locks, above the boating throng,
    Unmoored our skiff when through the Wytham
        flats,°
    Red loosestrife and blond meadow-sweet among
    And darting swallows and light water-gnats,
        We tracked the shy Thames shore?
    Where are the mowers, who, as the tiny swell
    Of our boat passing heaved the river-grass,
    Stood with suspended scythe to see us pass?—
They are all gone, and thou art gone as well!   130

Yes, thou art gone! and round me too the night
    In ever-nearing circle weaves her shade.
    I see her veil draw soft across the day,
    I feel her slowly chilling breath invade
        The cheek grown thin, the brown hair sprent° with
            gray;
        I feel her finger light
    Laid pausefully° upon life's headlong train—
    The foot less prompt to meet the morning dew,
    The heart less bounding at emotion new,
    And hope, once crushed, less quick to spring again. 140

And long the way appears, which seemed so short
    To the less practiced eye of sanguine youth;
    And high the mountain-tops, in cloudy air,
    The mountain-tops, where is the throne of Truth,
    Tops in life's morning-sun so bright and bare!
        Unbreachable the fort
    Of the long-battered world uplifts its wall;
    And strange and vain the earthly turmoil grows,
    And near and real the charm of thy repose,
    And night as welcome as a friend would fall.   150

But hush! the upland hath a sudden loss
    Of quiet!—Look, adown the dusk hillside,
    A troop of Oxford hunters going home,
    As in old days, jovial and talking, ride!
        From hunting with the Berkshire° hounds they
            come.
        Quick! let me fly, and cross
    Into yon farther field;—'Tis done; and see,
    Backed by the sunset, which doth glorify
    The orange and pale violet evening sky,
    Bare on its lonely ridge, the Tree!° the Tree!   160

---

82 **Sicilian shepherds**, pastoral poets of Sicily; a reference to the lament for Bion, a Sicilian pastoral poet, written by his friend Moschus, second century B.C. 85 **unpermitted . . . flow**, the River Styx, over which only the dead were permitted to pass 86 **Pluto**, the god of the underworld. He is said to have carried off Proserpine to be his wife. He found her in the vale of Enna (l. 95), in Sicily, where she was gathering lilies and violets 90 **Orpheus.** Orpheus' skill won him back his love, Eurydice, though he subsequently lost her again 92 **Dorian**, Sicilian 99 **Cumner**, hills near Oxford 106 **Fyfield tree**, a giant elm near the village of Fyfield, six miles southwest of Oxford 107 **fritillaries**, lily-like flowers 109 **Ensham**, Eynsham, a village northwest of Oxford. Sanford is south of Oxford 112 **dingle**, wooded dell

123 **Wytham flats**, about two miles northwest of Oxford, between the village of Wytham and the Thames 135 **sprent**, sprinkled 137 **pausefully**, so as to make it pause 155 **Berkshire**, a county south of Oxford 160 **the Tree**. See ll. 12–14

I take the omen! Eve lets down her veil,
  The white fog creeps from bush to bush about,
    The west unflushes, the high stars grow bright,
    And in the scattered farms the lights come out.
  I cannot reach the signal-tree tonight,
      Yet, happy omen, hail!
  Hear it from thy broad lucent Arno-vale°
    (For there thine earth-forgetting eyelids keep
    The morningless and unawakening sleep
170   Under the flowery oleanders, pale),

  Hear it, O Thyrsis, still our tree is there!—
    Ah, vain! These English fields, this upland dim,
    These brambles pale with mist engarlanded,
  That lone, sky-pointing tree, are not for him;
    To a boon° southern country he is fled,
      And now in happier air,
  Wandering with the great Mother's° train divine
    (And purer or more subtle soul than thee,
    I trow, the mighty Mother doth not see)
180   Within a folding of the Apennine,

  Thou hearest the immortal chants of old!—
    Putting his sickle to the perilous grain
    In the hot cornfield of the Phrygian king,°
  For thee the Lityerses-song again
    Young Daphnis with his silver voice doth sing;
      Sings his Sicilian fold,
  His sheep, his hapless love, his blinded eyes—
    And how a call celestial round him rang,
    And heavenward from the fountain-brink he
      sprang,
190   And all the marvel of the golden skies.

There thou art gone, and me thou leavest here
  Sole in these fields! yet will I not despair.
    Despair I will not, while I yet descry
  'Neath the mild canopy of English air
    That lonely tree against the western sky.
      Still, still these slopes, 'tis clear,
  Our gypsy-scholar haunts, outliving thee!
    Fields where soft sheep from cages pull the hay,
    Woods with anemones in flower till May,
200   Know him a wanderer still; then why not me?

A fugitive and gracious light he seeks,
  Shy to illumine;° and I seek it too.
    This does not come with houses or with gold,
  With place, with honor, and a flattering crew;
    'Tis not in the world's market bought and sold—
      But the smooth-slipping weeks

Drop by, and leave its seeker still untired;
  Out of the heed of mortals he is gone,
  He wends unfollowed, he must house alone;
Yet on he fares, by his own heart imspired.   210

Thou too, O Thyrsis, on like quest wast bound;
  Thou wanderedst with me for a little hour!
    Men gave thee nothing; but this happy quest,
  If men esteemed thee feeble, gave thee power,
    If men procured thee trouble, gave thee rest.
      And this rude Cumner ground,
  Its fir-topped Hurst,° its farms, its quiet fields,
    Here cam'st thou in thy jocund youthful time,
    Here was thine height of strength, thy golden
      prime!
  And still the haunt beloved a virtue yields.   220

What though the music of thy rustic flute
  Kept not for long its happy, country tone;
    Lost it too soon, and learned a stormy note
  Of men contention-tossed, of men who groan,
    Which tasked thy pipe too sore, and tired thy
      throat—
      It failed, and thou wast mute!
  Yet hadst thou alway visions of our light,
    And long with men of care thou couldst not stay,
    And soon thy foot resumed its wandering way,
  Left human haunt, and on alone till night.   230

Too rare, too rare, grow now my visits here!
  'Mid city-noise, not, as with thee of yore,
    Thyrsis! in reach of sheep-bells is my home.
  —Then through the great town's harsh, heart-
      wearying roar,
    Let in thy voice a whisper often come,
      To chase fatigue and fear:
  Why faintest thou? I wandered till I died.
    Roam on! The light we sought is shining still.
    Dost thou ask proof? Our tree yet crowns the hill,
  Our scholar travels yet the loved hillside.   240
(1866)

DOVER BEACH

The sea is calm tonight,
The tide is full, the moon lies fair
Upon the straits;—on the French coast the light
Gleams and is gone; the cliffs of England stand,
Glimmering and vast, out in the tranquil bay.
Come to the window, sweet is the night-air!

Only, from the long line of spray
Where the sea meets the moon-blanched land,
Listen! you hear the grating roar
Of pebbles which the waves draw back, and fling,   10

---

167 **Arno.** Clough died in Italy and was buried in Florence by the Arno River
175 **boon,** rich, benign   177 **great Mother,** Cybele, the goddess of nature and
the mother of the gods   183 **Phrygian king,** Lityerses, who made strangers contest with him in reaping grain; if he defeated them he put them to death. The
Sicilian shepherd Daphnis (l. 185), son of Hermes, messenger of the gods, engaged in such a contest in order to release his mistress, who was in the power of
the king. Hercules reaped the grain for Daphnis and killed Lityerses. The
Lityerses-song connected with the tradition used to be sung by Greek grain reapers. Another tradition represented Daphnis as having been blinded by a nymph
whose love he slighted. Hermes raised Daphnis to Olympus and marked by a
fountain the place of his ascent   202 **Shy to illumine,** reluctant to shine forth

217 **Hurst,** a prominent hill in the parish of Cumner

At their return, up the high strand,
Begin, and cease, and then again begin,
With tremulous cadence slow, and bring
The eternal note of sadness in.

Sophocles° long ago
Heard it on the Aegean, and it brought
Into his mind the turbid ebb and flow
Of human misery; we
Find also in the sound a thought,
20 Hearing it by this distant northern sea.

The Sea of Faith
Was once, too, at the full, and round earth's shore
Lay like the folds of a bright girdle furled.
But now I only hear
Its melancholy, long, withdrawing roar,
Retreating, to the breath
Of the night-wind, down the vast edges drear
And naked shingles° of the world.

Ah, love, let us be true
30 To one another! for the world, which seems
To lie before us like a land of dreams,
So various, so beautiful, so new,
Hath really neither joy, nor love, nor light,
Nor certitude, nor peace, nor help for pain:
And we are here as on a darkling plain
Swept with confused alarms of struggle and flight,
Where ignorant armies clash by night.
(1867)

PREFACE TO POEMS, 1853

This preface marks the beginning of Matthew Arnold's
career as a prose writer and literary critic. Among
other reasons, it is important to the history of criticism
as the most explicit rejection of romanticism that the
age had thus far produced.

In two small volumes of Poems, published anonymously, one in 1849, the other in 1852,° many of the
Poems which compose the present volume have already appeared. The rest are now published for the
first time.

I have, in the present collection, omitted the poem
from which the volume published in 1852 took its title.
I have done so, not because the subject of it was a
Sicilian Greek° born between two and three thousand
10 years ago, although many persons would think this a
sufficient reason. Neither have I done so because I
had, in my own opinion, failed in the delineation which
I intended to effect. I intended to delineate the feelings

of one of the last of the Greek religious philosophers,
one of the family of Orpheus° and Musæus,° having survived his fellows, living on into a time when the habits
of Greek thought and feeling had begun fast to change,
character to dwindle, the influence of the Sophists° to
prevail. Into the feelings of a man so situated there
entered much that we are accustomed to consider as 20
exclusively modern; how much the fragments of Empedocles himself which remain to us are sufficient at
least to indicate. What those who are familiar only
with the great monuments of early Greek genius suppose to be its exclusive characteristics, have disappeared; the calm, the cheerfulness, the disinterested
objectivity have disappeared; the dialogue of the mind
with itself has commenced; modern problems have
presented themselves; we hear already the doubts, we
witness the discouragement, of Hamlet and of Faust.° 30

The representation of such a man's feelings must be
interesting if consistently drawn. We all naturally take
pleasure, says Aristotle,° in any imitation or representation whatever; this is the basis of our love of poetry;
and we take pleasure in them, he adds, because all
knowledge is naturally agreeable to us; not to the
philosopher only, but to mankind at large. Every representation, therefore, which is consistently drawn
may be supposed to be interesting, inasmuch as it
gratifies this natural interest in knowledge of all kinds. 40
What is *not* interesting is that which does not add to
our knowledge of any kind; that which is vaguely conceived and loosely drawn; a representation which is
general, indeterminate, and faint, instead of being particular, precise, and firm.

Any accurate representation may therefore be expected to be interesting; but, if the representation be a
poetical one, more than this is demanded. It is demanded not only that it shall interest, but also that it
shall inspirit and rejoice the reader; that it shall convey 50
a charm, and infuse delight. For the Muses, as Hesiod°
says, were born that they might be "a forgetfulness of
evils, and a truce from cares": and it is not enough that
the poet should add to the knowledge of men, it is
required of him also that he should add to their happiness. "All art," says Schiller,° "is dedicated to joy, and
there is no higher and no more serious problem than
how to make men happy. The right art is that alone
which creates the highest enjoyment."

A poetical work, therefore, is not yet justified when 60
it has been shown to be an accurate and therefore interesting representation; it has to be shown also that it
is a representation from which men can derive enjoyment. In presence of the most tragic circumstances,
represented in a work of art, the feeling of enjoyment,
as is well known, may still subsist: the representation

Dover Beach   15 Sophocles, famous Greek tragic dramatist of the fifth century
B.C. The reference is to a passage in *Antigone*, 583 ff.   28 shingles, beaches
covered with shingles, large stones   Preface to Poems, 1853   2 one in . . .
1852, *The Strayed Reveller, and Other Poems* (1849) and *Empedocles on Etna, and
Other Poems* (1852)   9 Sicilian Greek, Empedocles (c. 500–c. 430 B.C.)

15 Orpheus, son of Apollo, poet and musician   Musæus, son of Apollo
18 Sophists, Greek philosophers whose extremists ran to adroit and sometimes
specious reasoning   30 Hamlet . . . Faust, in Shakespeare's *Hamlet* and Goethe's
Faust   33 says Aristotle, in his *Poetics*   51 Hesiod, Greek poet (eighth century
B.C.?). His *Theogony* is a history of the gods.   56 Schiller, German romantic poet
(1759–1805). The quotation is from his preface to *Die Braut von Messina*

of the most utter calamity, of the liveliest anguish, is not sufficient to destroy it; the more tragic the situation, the deeper becomes the enjoyment; and the situation is more tragic in proportion as it becomes more terrible.

What then are the situations, from the representation of which, though accurate, no poetical enjoyment can be derived? They are those in which the suffering finds no vent in action; in which a continuous state of mental distress is prolonged, unrelieved by incident, hope, or resistance; in which there is everything to be endured, nothing to be done. In such situations there is inevitably something morbid, in the description of them something monotonous. When they occur in actual life, they are painful, not tragic; the representation of them in poetry is painful also.

To this class of situations, poetically faulty as it appears to me, that of Empedocles, as I have endeavoured to represent him, belongs; and I have therefore excluded the poem from the present collection.

And why, it may be asked, have I entered into this explanation respecting a matter so unimportant as the admission or exclusion of the poem in question? I have done so, because I was anxious to avow that the sole reason for its exclusion was that which has been stated above; and that it has not been excluded in deference to the opinion which many critics of the present day appear to entertain against subjects chosen from distant times and countries: against the choice, in short, of any subjects but modern ones.

"The poet," it is said,° and by an intelligent critic, "the poet who would really fix the public attention must leave the exhausted past and draw his subjects from matters of present import, and *therefore* both of interest and novelty."

Now this view I believe to be completely false. It is worth examining, inasmuch as it is a fair sample of a class of critical dicta everywhere current at the present day, having a philosophical form and air, but no real basis in fact; and which are calculated to vitiate the judgment of readers of poetry, while they exert, so far as they are adopted, a misleading influence on the practice of those who make it.

What are the eternal objects of poetry, among all nations and at all times? They are actions; human actions; possessing an inherent interest in themselves, and which are to be communicated in an interesting manner by the art of the poet. Vainly will the latter imagine that he has everything in his own power; that he can make an intrinsically inferior action equally delightful with a more excellent one by his treatment of it. He may indeed compel us to admire his skill, but his work will possess, within itself, an incurable defect.

The poet, then, has in the first place to select an excellent action; and what actions are the most excel-

lent? Those, certainly, which most powerfully appeal to the great primary human affections: to those elementary feelings which subsist permanently in the race, and which are independent of time. These feelings are permanent and the same; that which interests them is permanent and the same also. The modernness or antiquity of an action, therefore, has nothing to do with its fitness for poetical representation; this depends upon its inherent qualities. To the elementary part of our nature, to our passions, that which is great and passionate is eternally interesting; and interesting solely in proportion to its greatness and to its passion. A great human action of a thousand years ago is more interesting to it than a smaller human action of to-day, even though upon the representation of this last the most consummate skill may have been expended, and though it has the advantage of appealing by its modern language, familiar manners, and contemporary allusions, to all our transient feelings and interests. These, however, have no right to demand of a poetical work that it shall satisfy them; their claims are to be directed elsewhere. Poetical works belong to the domain of our permanent passions; let them interest these, and the voice of all subordinate claims upon them is at once silenced.

Achilles, Prometheus, Clytemnestra, Dido,°—what modern poem presents personages as interesting, even to us moderns, as these personages of an "exhausted past"? We have the domestic epic dealing with the details of modern life which pass daily under our eyes; we have poems representing modern personages in contact with the problems of modern life, moral, intellectual, and social; these works have been produced by poets the most distinguished of their nation and time; yet I fearlessly assert that *Hermann and Dorothea, Childe Harold, Jocelyn,* the *Excursion,*° leave the reader cold in comparison with the effect produced upon him by the latter books of the *Iliad,* by the *Oresteia,* or by the episode of Dido. And why is this? Simply because in the three last-named cases the action is greater, the personages nobler, the situations more intense: and this is the true basis of the interest in a poetical work, and this alone.

It may be urged, however, that past actions may be interesting in themselves, but that they are not to be adopted by the modern poet, because it is impossible for him to have them clearly present to his own mind, and he cannot therefore feel them deeply, nor represent them forcibly. But this is not necessarily the case. The externals of a past action, indeed, he cannot know with the precision of a contemporary; but his business is with its essentials. The outward man of Œdipus or of Macbeth, the houses in which they lived, the ceremonies of their courts, he cannot accurately figure to

98 **it is said,** "in the *Spectator* of April 2, 1853: The words quoted were not used with reference to poems of mine." —Arnold's note

148 **Achilles . . . Dido,** figures from classical mythology. *Achilles* is the hero of Homer's *Iliad; Prometheus,* Titanic friend of man; *Clytemnestra,* wife of Agamemnon (Aeschylus' *Oresteia*); *Dido,* queen of Carthage (Vergil's *Aeneid*) 157–
158 **Herman . . . Excursion,** respectively, long narrative poems by Goethe, Byron, Lamartine, and Wordsworth

himself; but neither do they essentially concern him. His business is with their inward man; with their feelings and behaviour in certain tragic situations, which engage their passions as men; these have in them nothing local and casual; they are as accessible to the modern poet as to a contemporary.

The date of an action, then, signifies nothing; the action itself its selection and construction, that is what is all-important. This the Greeks understood far more clearly than we do. The racial difference between their poetical theory and ours consists, as it appears to me, in this: that, with them, the poetical character of the action in itself, and the conduct of it, was the first consideration; with us, attention is fixed mainly on the value of the separate thoughts and images which occur in the treatment of an action. They regarded the whole; we regard the parts. With them the action predominated over the expression of it; with us the expression predominates over the action. Not that they failed in expression, or were inattentive to it; on the contrary, they are the highest models of expression, the unapproached masters of the *grand style*.° But their expression is so excellent because it is so admirably kept in its right degree of prominence; because it is so simple and so well subordinated; because it draws its force directly from the pregnancy of the matter which it conveys. For what reason was the Greek tragic poet confined to so limited a range of subjects? Because there are so few actions which unite in themselves, in the highest degree, the conditions of excellence: and it was not thought that on any but an excellent subject could an excellent poem be constructed. A few actions, therefore, eminently adapted for tragedy, maintained almost exclusive possession of the Greek tragic stage. Their significance appeared inexhaustible; they were as permanent problems, perpetually offered to the genius of every fresh poet. This, too, is the reason of what appears to us moderns a certain baldness of expression in Greek tragedy; of the triviality with which we often reproach the remarks of the chorus, where it takes part in the dialogue: that the action itself, the situation of Orestes, or Merope, or Alcmæon,° was to stand the central point of interest, unforgotten, absorbing, principal; that no accessories were for a moment to distract the spectator's attention from this; that the tone of the parts was to be perpetually kept down, in order not to impair the grandiose effect of the whole. The terrible old mythic story on which the drama was founded stood, before he entered the theatre, traced in its bare outlines upon the spectator's mind; it stood in his memory as a group of statuary, faintly seen, at the end of a long and dark vista: then came the poet, embodying outlines, developing situations, not a word wasted, not a sentiment capriciously thrown in; stroke upon stroke, the drama proceeded; the light deepened upon the group; more and more it revealed itself to the riveted gaze of the spectator, until at last, when the final words were spoken, it stood before him in broad sunlight, a model of immortal beauty.

This was what a Greek critic demanded; this was what a Greek poet endeavoured to effect. It signified nothing to what time an action belonged. We do not find that the *Persæ*° occupied a particularly high rank among the dramas of Æschylus because it represented a matter of contemporary interest; this was not what a cultivated Athenian required. He required that the permanent elements of his nature should be moved; and dramas of which the action, though taken from a long-distant mythic time, yet was calculated to accomplish this in a higher degree than that of the *Persæ*, stood higher in his estimation accordingly. The Greeks felt, no doubt, with their exquisite sagacity of taste, that an action of present times was too near them, too much mixed up with what was accidental and passing, to form a sufficiently grand, detached, and self-subsistent object for a tragic poem. Such objects belonged to the domain of the comic poet, and of the lighter kinds of poetry. For the more serious kinds, for *pragmatic* poetry, to use an excellent expression of Polybius,° they were more difficult and severe in the range of subjects which they permitted. Their theory and practice alike, the admirable treatise of Aristotle, and the unrivalled works of their poets, exclaim with a thousand tongues—"All depends upon the subject; choose a fitting action, penetrate yourself with the feeling of its situations; this done, everything else will follow."

But for all kinds of poetry alike there was one point on which they were rigidly exacting: the adaptability of the subject to the kind of poetry selected, and the careful construction of the poem.

How different a way of thinking from this is ours! We can hardly at the present day understand what Menander° meant, when he told a man who inquired as to the progress of his comedy that he had finished it, not having yet written a single line, because he had constructed the action of it in his mind. A modern critic would have assured him that the merit of his piece depended on the brilliant things which arose under his pen as he went along. We have poems which seem to exist merely for the sake of single lines and passages; not for the sake of producing any total impression. We have critics who seem to direct their attention merely to detached expressions, to the language about the action, not to the action itself. I verily think that the majority of them do not in their hearts believe that there is such a thing as a total-impression to be derived from a poem at all, or to be demanded from a poet; they think the term a commonplace of

198 **grand style**, a phrase made famous by Arnold in *Last Words on Translating Homer*   213 **situation of . . . Alcmæon**, Orestes and Alcmæon avenged the murder of their fathers, Merope of her husband

240 **Persæ**, Aeschylus' drama on the Greeks' war against the Persians   257 **Polybius**, Greek historian (205–123 B.C.)   271 **Menander**, Greek poet and dramatist (342–292 B.C.)

metaphysical criticism. They will permit the poet to select any action he pleases, and to suffer that action to go as it will, provided he gratifies them with occasional bursts of fine writing, and with a shower of isolated thoughts and images. That is, they permit him to leave their poetical sense ungratified, provided that he gratifies their rhetorical sense and their curiosity. Of his neglecting to gratify these, there is little danger. He needs rather to be warned against the danger of attempting to gratify these alone; he needs rather to be perpetually reminded to prefer his action to everything else; so to treat this, as to permit its inherent excellences to develop themselves, without interruption from the intrusion of his personal peculiarites; most fortunate when he most entirely succeeds in effacing himself, and in enabling a noble action to subsist as it did in nature.

But the modern critic not only permits a false practice; he absolutely prescribes false aims. ''A true allegory of the state of one's own mind in a representative history,'' the poet is told, ''is perhaps the highest thing that one can attempt in the way of poetry.'' And accordingly he attempts it. An allegory of the state of one's own mind, the highest problem of an art which imitates actions! No, assuredly, it is not, it never can be so: no great poetical work has ever been produced with such an aim. *Faust* itself, in which something of the kind is attempted, wonderful passages as it contains, and in spite of the unsurpassed beauty of the scenes which relate to Margaret, *Faust* itself, judged as a whole, and judged strictly as a poetical work, is defective: its illustrious author, the greatest poet of modern times, the greatest critic of all times, would have been the first to acknowledge it; he only defended his work, indeed, by asserting it to be ''something incommensurable.''°

The confusion of the present times is great, the multitude of voices counselling different things bewildering, the number of existing works capable of attracting a young writer's attention and of becoming his models, immense. What he wants is a hand to guide him through the confusion, a voice to prescribe to him the aim which he should keep in view, and to explain to him that the value of the literary works which offer themselves to his attention is relative to their power of helping him forward on his road towards this aim. Such a guide the English writer at the present day will nowhere find. Failing this, all that can be looked for, all indeed that can be desired, is, that his attention should be fixed on excellent models; that he may reproduce, at any rate, something of their excellence, by penetrating himself with their works and by catching their spirit, if he cannot be taught to produce what is excellent independently.

Foremost among these models for the English writer

stands Shakespeare: a name the greatest perhaps of all poetical names; a name never to be mentioned without reverence. I will venture, however, to express a doubt whether the influence of his works, excellent and fruitful for the readers of poetry, for the great majority, has been an unmixed advantage to the writers of it. Shakespeare indeed chose excellent subjects—the world could afford no better than *Macbeth,* or *Romeo and Juliet,* or *Othello;* he had no theory respecting the necessity of choosing subjects of present import, or the paramount interest attaching to allegories of the state of one's own mind; like all great poets, he knew well what constituted a poetical action; like them, wherever he found such an action, he took it; like them, too, he found his best in past times. But to these general characteristics of all great poets he added a special one of his own; a gift, namely, of happy, abundant, and ingenious expression, eminent and unrivalled: so eminent as irresistibly to strike the attention first in him, and even to throw into comparative shade his other excellences as a poet. Here has been the mischief. These other excellences were his fundamental excellences *as a poet;* what distinguishes the artist from a mere amateur, says Goethe, is *Architectonicé* in the highest sense; that power of execution which creates, forms, and constitutes: not the profoundness of single thoughts, nor the richness of imagery, not the abundance of illustration. But these attractive accessories of a poetical work being more easily seized than the spirit of the whole, and these accessories being possessed by Shakespeare in an unequalled degree, a young writer having recourse to Shakespeare as his model runs great risk of being vanquished and absorbed by them, and, in consequence, of reproducing, according to the measure of his power, these, and these alone. Of this preponding quality of Shakespeare's genius, accordingly, almost the whole of modern English poetry has, it appears to me, felt the influence. To the exclusive attention on the part of his imitators to this it is in a great degree owing, that of the majority of modern poetical works the details alone are valuable, the composition worthless. In reading them one is perpetually reminded of that terrible sentence on a modern French poet,—*il dit tout ce qu'il veut, mais malheureusement il n' a rien à dire.*°

Let me give an instance of what I mean. I will take it from the works of the very chief among those who seem to have been formed in the school of Shakespeare; of one whose exquisite genius and pathetic death render him forever interesting. I will take the poem of *Isabella, or the Pot of Basil,* by Keats. I choose this rather than the *Endymion,* because the latter work (which a modern critic has classed with the *Faery Queen!*), although undoubtedly there blows through it the breath of genius, is yet as a whole so utterly in-

322 **something incommensurable,** from Johann Eckermann's *Conversations with Goethe* (1836–1848)

385–386 **il . . . dire.** He says all that he wishes, but unfortunately he has nothing to say

coherent, as not strictly to merit the name of a poem at all. The poem of *Isabella,* then, is a perfect treasure-house of graceful and felicitous words and images: almost in every stanza there occurs one of those vivid and picturesque turns of expression, by which the object is made to flash upon the eye of the mind, and which thrill the reader with a sudden delight. This one short poem contains, perhaps, a greater number of happy single expressions which one could quote than all the extant tragedies of Sophocles. But the action, the story? The action in itself is an excellent one; but so feebly is it conceived by the poet, so loosely constructed, that the effect produced by it, in and for itself, is absolutely null. Let the reader, after he has finished the poem of Keats, turn to the same story in the *Decameron:*° he will then feel how pregnant and interesting the same action has become in the hands of a great artist, who above all things delineates his object; who subordinates expression to that which it is designed to express.

I have said that the imitators of Shakespeare, fixing their attention on his wonderful gift of expression, have directed their imitation to this, neglecting his other excellences. These excellences, the fundamental excellences of poetical art, Shakespeare no doubt possessed them,—possessed many of them in a splendid degree; but it may perhaps be doubted whether even he himself did not sometimes give scope to his faculty of expression to the prejudice of a higher poetical duty. For we must never forget that Shakespeare is the great poet he is from his skill in discerning and firmly conceiving an excellent action, from his power of intensely feeling a situation, of intimately associating himself with a character; not from his gift of expression, which rather even leads him astray, degenerating sometimes into a fondness for curiosity of expression, into an irritability of fancy, which seems to make it impossible for him to say a thing plainly, even when the press of the action demands the very directest language, or its level character the very simplest. Mr. Hallam,° than whom it is impossible to find a saner and more judicious critic, has had the courage (for at the present day it needs courage) to remark, how extremely and faultily difficult Shakespeare's language often is. It is so: you may find main scenes in some of his greatest tragedies, *King Lear,* for instance, where the language is so artificial, so curiously tortured, and so difficult, that every speech has to be read two or three times before its meaning can be comprehended. This over-curiousness of expression is indeed but the excessive employment of a wonderful gift,—of the power of saying a thing in a happier way than any other man; nevertheless, it is carried so far that one understands what M. Guizot° meant when he said that

411–412 turn . . . Decameron, the fourth day, fifth novel of Boccaccio's famous collection of stories   437 Mr. Hallam, Henry Hallam (1777–1859), distinguished historian   450 Guizot, François Pierre Guillaume Guizot (1787–1874), French historian and literary scholar

Shakespeare appears in his language to have tried all styles except that of simplicity. He has not the severe and scrupulous self-restraint of the ancients, partly, no doubt, because he has a far less cultivated and exacting audience. He has indeed a far wider range than they had, a far richer fertility of thought; in this respect he rises above them. In his strong conception of his subject, in the genuine way in which he is penetrated with it, he resembles them, and is unlike the moderns. But in the accurate limitation of it, the conscientious rejection of superfluities, the simple and rigorous development of it from the first line of his work to the last, he falls below them, and comes nearer to the moderns. In his chief works, besides what he has of his own, he has the elementary soundness of the ancients; he has their important action and their large and broad manner; but he has not their purity of method. He is therefore a less safe model; for what he has of his own is personal, and inseparable from his own rich nature; it may be imitated and exaggerated, it cannot be learned or applied as an art. He is above all suggestive; more valuable, therefore, to young writers as men than as artists. But clearness of arrangement, rigour of development, simplicity of style,—these may to a certain extent be learned; and these may, I am convinced, be learned best from the ancients, who, although infinitely less suggestive than Shakespeare, are thus, to the artist, more instructive.

What then, it will be asked, are the ancients to be our sole models? the ancients with their comparatively narrow range of experience, and their widely different circumstances? Not, certainly, that which is narrow in the ancients, nor that in which we can no longer sympathize. An action like the action of the *Antigone* of Sophocles, which turns upon the conflict between the heroine's duty to her brother's corpse and that to the laws of her country, is no longer one in which it is possible that we should feel a deep interest. I am speaking too, it will be remembered, not of the best sources of intellectual stimulus for the general reader, but of the best models of instruction for the individual writer. This last may certainly learn of the ancients, better than anywhere else, three things which it is vitally important for him to know—the all-importance of the choice of a subject; the necessity of accurate construction; and the subordinate character of expression. He will learn from them how unspeakably superior is the effect of the one moral impression left by a great action treated as a whole, to the effect produced by the most striking single thought or by the happiest image. As he penetrates into the spirit of the great classical works, as he becomes gradually aware of their intense significance, their noble simplicity, and their calm pathos, he will be convinced that it is this effect, unity and profoundness of moral impression, at which the ancient poets aimed; that it is this which constitutes the grandeur of their works, and which makes them immortal. He will desire to direct his own efforts towards producing the same effect. Above all, he will deliver himself from the jargon of modern criticism, and escape the danger of producing poetical works conceived in the spirit of the passing time, and which partake of its transitoriness.

The present age makes great claims upon us; we owe it service, it will not be satisfied without our admiration. I know not how it is, but their commerce with the ancients appears to me to produce, in those who constantly practise it, a steadying and composing effect upon their judgment, not of literary works only, but of men and events in general. They are like persons who have had a very weighty and impressive experience; they are more truly than others under the empire of facts, and more independent of the language current among those with whom they live. They wish neither to applaud nor to revile their age; they wish to know what it is, what it can give them, and whether this is what they want. What they want, they know very well; they want to educe and cultivate what is best and noblest in themselves; they know, too, that this is no easy task—χαλεπὸν, as Pitticus said, χαλεπὸν ἐσθλὸν 'ἔμμεναι°—and they ask themselves sincerely whether their age and its literature can assist them in the attempt. If they are endeavouring to practise any art, they remember the plain and simple proceedings of the old artists, who attained their grand results by penetrating themselves with some noble and significant action, not by inflating themselves with a belief in the preeminent importance and greatness of their own times. They do not talk of their mission, nor of interpreting their age, nor of the coming poet; all this, they know, is the mere delirium of vanity; their business is not to praise their age, but to afford to the men who live in it the highest pleasure which they are capable of feeling. If asked to afford this by means of subjects drawn from the age itself, they ask what special fitness the present age has for supplying them. They are told that it is an era of progress, an age commissioned to carry out the great ideas of industrial development and social amelioration. They reply that with all this they can do nothing; that the elements they need for the exercise of their art are great actions, calculated powerfully and delightfully to affect what is permanent in the human soul; that so far as the present age can supply such actions, they will gladly make use of them; but that an age wanting in moral grandeur can with difficulty supply such, and an age of spiritual discomfort with difficulty be powerfully and delightfully affected by them.

A host of voices will indignantly rejoin that the present age is inferior to the past neither in moral grandeur nor in spiritual health. He who possesses the discipline I speak of will content himself with remembering the judgments passed upon the present age, in this respect, by the men of strongest head and widest culture whom it has produced; by Goethe and by Niebuhr.° It will be sufficient for him that he knows the opinions held by these two great men respecting the present age and its literature; and that he feels assured in his own mind that their aims and demands upon life were such as he would wish, at any rate, his own to be; and their judgment as to what is impeding and disabling such as he may safely follow. He will not, however, maintain a hostile attitude towards the false pretensions of his age: he will content himself with not being overwhelmed by them. He will esteem himself fortunate if he can succeed in banishing from his mind all feelings of contradiction, and irritation, and impatience; in order to delight himself with the contemplation of some noble action of a heroic time, and to enable others, through his representation of it, to delight in it also.

I am far indeed from making any claim, for myself, that I possess this discipline; or for the following poems, that they breathe its spirit. But I say, that in the sincere endeavour to learn and practise, amid the bewildering confusion of our times, what is sound and true in poetical art, I seemed to myself to find the only sure guidance, the only solid footing, among the ancients. They, at any rate, knew what they wanted in art, and we do not. It is this uncertainty which is disheartening, and not hostile criticism. How often have I felt this when reading words of disparagement or of cavil: that it is the uncertainty as to what is really to be aimed at which makes our difficulty, not the dissatisfaction of the critic, who himself suffers from the same uncertainty. *Non me tua fervida terrent Dicta; . . . Dii me terrent, et Jupiter hostis.°*

Two kinds of *dilettanti*, says Goethe, there are in poetry: he who neglects the indispensable mechanical part, and thinks he has done enough if he shows spirituality and feeling; and he who seeks to arrive at poetry merely by mechanism, in which he can acquire an artisan's readiness, and is without soul and matter. And he adds, that the first does most harm to art, and the last to himself. If we must be *dilettanti:* if it is impossible for us, under the circumstances amidst which we live, to think clearly, to feel nobly, and to delineate firmly: if we cannot attain to the mastery of the great artists;—let us, at least, have so much respect for our art as to prefer it to ourselves. Let us not bewilder our successors; let us transmit to them the practice of poetry, with its boundaries and wholesome regulative laws, under which excellent works may again, perhaps, at some future time, be produced, not yet fallen into oblivion through our neglect, not yet condemned and cancelled by the influence of their eternal enemy, caprice.

(1853)

530–531 χαλεπὸν . . . 'ἔμμεναι. It is hard to be excellent. *Pittacus* (c. 650–569 B.C.) was one of the Seven Sages of Greece

565 **Niebuhr,** Barthold Georg Niebuhr (1776–1831), German historian, statesman, and critic   595–596 **Non . . . hostis.** Your hot words do not frighten me; . . . The gods frighten me, and Jupiter as an enemy (Vergil's *Aeneid, XII*)

THE FUNCTION OF CRITICISM
AT THE PRESENT TIME

The essay printed first in *Essays in Criticism* and reprinted here was actually written last; it shows the principles toward which Arnold had been working. It contains, moreover, a sign of the many directions, other than the purely literary, in which Arnold's critical thinking was to lead him: social conditions, science, philosophy, religion. Arnold used the term *essays* in the sense of "attempts" or "specimens."

Many objections have been made to a proposition which, in some remarks of mine on translating Homer, I ventured to put forth; a proposition about criticism, and its importance at the present day. I said: "Of the literature of France and Germany, as of the intellect of Europe in general, the main effort, for now many years, has been a critical effort; the endeavour, in all branches of knowledge, theology, philosophy, history, art, science, to see the object as in itself it really is." I
10 added, that owing to the operation in English literature of certain causes, "almost the last thing for which one would come to English literature is just that very thing which now Europe most desires,—criticism"; and that the power and value of English literature was thereby impaired. More than one rejoinder declared that the importance I here assigned to criticism was excessive, and asserted the inherent superiority of the creative effort of the human spirit over its critical effort. And the other day, having been led by a Mr. Shairp's° ex-
20 cellent notice of Wordsworth to turn again to his biography, I found, in the words of this great man, whom I, for one, must always listen to with the profoundest respect, a sentence passed on the critic's business, which seems to justify every possible disparagement of it. Wordsworth says in one of his letters:—

"The writers in these publications" (the Reviews), "while they prosecute their inglorious employment, cannot be supposed to be in a state of mind very favourable for being affected by the finer influences of
30 a thing so pure as genuine poetry."

And a trustworthy reporter of his conversation quotes a more elaborate judgment to the same effect:—

"Wordsworth holds the critical power very low, infinitely lower than the inventive; and he said to-day that if the quantity of time consumed in writing critiques on the works of others were given to original composition, of whatever kind it might be, it would be much better employed; it would make a man find out
40 sooner his own level, and it would do infinitely less

The Function of Criticism at the Present Time   19 **Shairp,** John Campbell Shairp (1819–1885), critic and professor of poetry at Oxford (1877–1884), whose notice —"Wordsworth: The Man and the Poet"—had appeared in the *North British Review* for August 1864

mischief. A false or malicious criticism may do much injury to the minds of others; a stupid invention, either in prose or verse, is quite harmless."

It is almost too much to expect of poor human nature, that a man capable of producing some effect in one line of literature, should, for the greater good of society, voluntarily doom himself to impotence and obscurity in another. Still less is this to be expected from men addicted to the composition of the "false or malicious criticism" of which Wordsworth speaks. 50 However, everybody would admit that a false or malicious criticism had better never have been written. Everybody, too, would be willing to admit, as a general proposition, that the critical faculty is lower than the inventive. But is it true that criticism is really, in itself, a baneful and injurious employment; is it true that all time given to writing critiques on the works of others would be much better employed if it were given to original composition, of whatever kind this may be? Is it true that Johnson had better have gone on pro- 60 ducing more *Irenes* instead of writing his *Lives of the Poets;* nay, is it certain that Wordsworth himself was better employed in making his Ecclesiastical Sonnets than when he made his celebrated Preface,° so full of criticism, and criticism of the works of others? Wordsworth was himself a great critic, and it is to be sincerely regretted that he has not left us more criticism; Goethe was one of the greatest of critics, and we may sincerely congratulate ourselves that he has left us so much criticism. Without wasting time over the 70 exaggeration which Wordsworth's judgment on criticism clearly contains, or over an attempt to trace the causes,—not difficult, I think, to be traced,—which may have led Wordsworth to this exaggeration, a critic may with advantage seize an occasion for trying his own conscience, and for asking himself of what real service, at any given moment, the practice of criticism either is or may be made to his own mind and spirit, and to the minds and spirits of others.

The critical power is of lower rank than the creative. 80 True; but in assenting to this proposition, one or two things are to be kept in mind. It is undeniable that the exercise of a creative power, that a free creative activity, is the highest function of man; it is proved to be so by man's finding in it his true happiness. But it is undeniable, also, that men may have the sense of exercising this free creative activity in other ways than in producing great works of literature or art; if it were not so, all but a very few men would be shut out from the true happiness of all men. They may have it in well- 90 doing, they may have it in learning, they may have it even in criticising. This is one thing to be kept in mind. Another is, that the exercise of the creative power in the production of great works of literature or art, however high this exercise of it may rank, is not at all

64 **celebrated Preface,** *Preface* to the second edition (1800) of *Lyrical Ballads*

epochs and under all conditions possible; and that therefore labour may be vainly spent in attempting it, which might with more fruit be used in preparing for it, in rendering it possible. This creative power works with elements, with materials; what if it has not those materials, those elements, ready for its use? In that case it must surely wait till they are ready. Now, in literature,—I will limit myself to literature, for it is about literature that the question arises,—the elements with which the creative power works are ideas; the best ideas on every matter which literature touches, current at the time. At any rate we may lay it down as certain that in modern literature no manifestation of the creative power not working with these can be very important or fruitful. And I say *current* at the time, not merely accessible at the time; for creative literary genius does not principally show itself in discovering new ideas, that is rather the business of the philosopher. The grand work of literary genius is a work of synthesis and exposition, not of analysis and discovery; its gift lies in the faculty of being happily inspired by a certain intellectual and spiritual atmosphere, by a certain order of ideas, when it finds itself in them; of dealing divinely with these ideas, presenting them in the most effective and attractive combinations,—making beautiful works with them, in short. But it must have the atmosphere, it must find itself amidst the order of ideas, in order to work freely; and these it is not so easy to command. This is why great creative epochs in literature are so rare, this is why there is so much that is unsatisfactory in the productions of many men of real genius; because, for the creation of a masterwork of literature two powers must concur, the power of the man and the power of the moment, and the man is not enough without the moment; the creative power has, for its happy exercise, appointed elements, and those elements are not in its own control.

Nay, they are more within the control of the critical power. It is the business of the critical power, as I said in the words already quoted, "in all branches of knowledge, theology, philosophy, history, art, science, to see the object as in itself it really is." Thus it tends, at last, to make an intellectual situation of which the creative power can profitably avail itself. It tends to establish an order of ideas, if not absolutely true, yet true by comparison with that which it displaces; to make the best ideas prevail. Presently these new ideas reach society, the touch of truth is the touch of life, and there is a stir and growth everywhere; out of this stir and growth come the creative epochs of literature.

Or, to narrow our range, and quit these considerations of the general march of genius and of society,— considerations which are apt to become too abstract and impalpable,—every one can see that a poet, for instance, ought to know life and the world before dealing with them in poetry; and life and the world being in modern times very complex things, the crea-

tion of a modern poet, to be worth much, implies a great critical effort behind it; else it must be a comparatively poor, barren, and short-lived affair. This is why Byron's poetry had so little endurance in it, and Goethe's so much; both Byron and Goethe had a great productive power, but Goethe's was nourished by a great critical effort providing the true materials for it, and Byron's was not; Goethe knew life and the world, the poet's necessary subjects, much more comprehensively and thoroughly than Byron. He knew a great deal more of them, and he knew them much more as they really are.

It has long seemed to me that the burst of creative activity in our literature, through the first quarter of this century, had about it in fact something premature; and that from this cause its productions are doomed, most of them, in spite of the sanguine hopes which accompanied and do still accompany them, to prove hardly more lasting than the productions of far less splendid epochs. And this prematureness comes from its having proceeded without having its proper data, without sufficient materials to work with. In other words, the English poetry of the first quarter of this century, with plenty of energy, plenty of creative force, did not know enough. This makes Byron so empty of matter, Shelley so incoherent, Wordsworth even, profound as he is, yet so wanting in completeness and variety. Wordsworth cared little for books, and disparaged Goethe. I admire Wordsworth, as he is, so much that I cannot wish him different; and it is vain, no doubt, to imagine such a man different from what he is, to suppose that he *could* have been different. But surely the one thing wanting to make Wordsworth an even greater poet than he is,—his thought richer, and his influence of wider application,—was that he should have read more books, among them, no doubt, those of that Goethe whom he disparaged without reading him.

But to speak of books and reading may easily lead to a misunderstanding here. It was not really books and reading that lacked to our poetry at this epoch: Shelley had plenty of reading, Coleridge had immense reading. Pindar and Sophocles,°—as we all say so glibly, and often with so little discernment of the real import of what we are saying,—had not many books; Shakespeare was no deep reader. True; but in the Greece of Pindar and Sophocles, in the England of Shakespeare, the poet lived in a current of ideas in the highest degree animating and nourishing to the creative power; society was, in the fullest measure, permeated by fresh thought, intelligent and alive. And this state of things is the true basis for the creative power's exercise, in this it finds its data, its materials, truly ready for its hand; all the books and reading in the world are only valuable as they are helps to this. Even when this does not actually exist, books and reading may enable a man to

196 **Pindar and Sophocles,** Greek writers. Pindar (522–448? B.C.) is noted for his odes, Sophocles (496?–406 B.C.) for his dramas

construct a kind of semblance of it in his own mind, a world of knowledge and intelligence in which he may live and work. This is by no means an equivalent to the artist for the nationally diffused life and thought of the epochs of Sophocles or Shakespeare; but, besides that it may be a means of preparation for such epochs, it does really constitute, if many share in it, a quickening and sustaining atmosphere of great value. Such an atmosphere the many-sided learning and the long and widely combined critical effort of Germany formed for Goethe, when he lived and worked. There was no national glow of life and thought there as in the Athens of Pericles° or the England of Elizabeth. That was the poet's weakness. But there was a sort of equivalent for it in the complete culture and unfettered thinking of a large body of Germans. That was his strength. In the England of the first quarter of this century there was neither a national glow of life and thought, such as we had in the age of Elizabeth, nor yet a culture and a force of learning and criticism such as were to be found in Germany. Therefore the creative power of poetry wanted, for success in the highest sense, materials and a basis; a thorough interpretation of the world was necessarily denied to it.

At first sight it seems strange that out of the immense stir of the French Revolution and its age should not have come a crop of works of genius equal to that which came out of the stir of the great productive time of Greece, or out of that of the Renascence, with its powerful episode the Reformation. But the truth is that the stir of the French Revolution took a character which essentially distinguished it from such movements as these. These were, in the main, disinterestedly intellectual and spiritual movements; movements in which the human spirit looked for its satisfaction in itself and in the increased play of its own activity. The French Revolution took a political, practical character. The movement, which went on in France under the old *régime,* from 1700 to 1789, was far more really akin than that of the Revolution itself to the movement of the Renascence; the France of Voltaire and Rousseau° told far more powerfully upon the mind of Europe than the France of the Revolution. Goethe reproached this last expressly with having ''thrown quiet culture back.'' Nay, and the true key to how much in our Byron, even in our Wordsworth, is this!—that they had their source in a great movement of feeling, not in a great movement of mind. The French Revolution, however,—that object of so much blind love and so much blind hatred,—found undoubtedly its motive-power in the intelligence of men, and not in their practical sense: this is what distinguishes it from the English Revolution of Charles the First's time.° This is what makes it a more spiritual event than our Revolution, an event of much more powerful and world-wide

interest, though practically less successful; it appeals to an order of ideas which are universal, certain, permanent. 1789 asked of a thing, Is it rational? 1642 asked of a thing, Is it legal? or, when it went furthest, Is it according to conscience? This is the English fashion, a fashion to be treated, within its own sphere, with the highest respect; for its success, within its own sphere, has been prodigious. But what is law in one place is not law in another; what is law here today is not law even here tomorrow; and as for conscience, what is binding on one man's conscience is not binding on another's. The old woman who threw her stool at the head of the surpliced minister in St. Giles' Church at Edinburgh obeyed an impulse to which millions of the human race may be permitted to remain strangers.° But the prescriptions of reason are absolute, unchanging, of universal validity; *to count by tens is the easiest way of counting*—that is a proposition of which every one, from here to the Antipodes, feels the force; at least I should say so if we did not live in a country where it is not impossible that any morning we may find a letter in the *Times* declaring that a decimal coinage is an absurdity. That a whole nation should have been penetrated with an enthusiasm for pure reason, and with an ardent zeal for making its prescriptions triumph, is a very remarkable thing, when we consider how little of mind, or anything so worthy and quickening as mind, comes into the motives which alone, in general, impel great masses of men. In spite of the extravagant direction given to this enthusiasm, in spite of the crimes and follies in which it lost itself, the French Revolution derives from the force, truth, and universality of the ideas which it took for its law, and from the passion with which it could inspire a multitude for these ideas, a unique and still living power; it is,—it will probably long remain,—the greatest, the most animating event in history. And as no sincere passion for the things of the mind, even though it turn out in many respects an unfortunate passion, is ever quite thrown away and quite barren of good, France has reaped from hers one fruit—the natural and legitimate fruit though not precisely the grand fruit she expected: she is the country in Europe where *the people* is most alive.

But the mania for giving an immediate political and practical application to all these fine ideas of the reason was fatal. Here an Englishman is in his element: on this theme we can all go on for hours. And all we are in the habit of saying on it has undoubtedly a great deal of truth. Ideas cannot be too much prized in and for themselves, cannot be too much lived with; but to transport them abruptly into the world of politics and practice, violently to revolutionise this world to their bidding,—that is quite another thing. There is the world of ideas and there is the world of practice; the French are often for suppressing the one and the En-

---

222 **Pericles,** political leader of the era (495?–429 B.C.)   250–252 **France . . . Rousseau,** that is pre-Revolutionary France   262 **English . . . time,** that is, the second quarter of the seventeenth century

276–279 **old woman . . . strangers,** Jenny, or Janet, Geddes, protesting the new church service prescribed by Charles I for Scotland

glish the other; but neither is to be suppressed. A member of the House of Commons said to me the other day: "That a thing is an anomaly, I consider to be no objection to it whatever." I venture to think he was wrong; that a thing is an anomaly *is* an objection to it, but absolutely and in the sphere of ideas: it is not necessarily, under such and such circumstances, or at such and such a moment, an objection to it in the sphere of politics and practice. Joubert° has said beautifully: "C'est la force et le droit qui règlent toutes choses dans le monde; la force en attendant le droit." (Force and right are the governors of this world; force till right is ready.) *Force till right is ready;* and till right is ready, force, the existing order of things, is justified, is the legitimate ruler. But right is something moral, and implies inward recognition, free assent of the will; we are not ready for right,—*right,* so far as we are concerned, *is not ready,*—until we have attained this sense of seeing it and willing it. The way in which for us it may change and transform force, the existing order of things, and become, in its turn, the legitimate ruler of the world, should depend on the way in which, when our time comes, we see it and will it. Therefore for other people enamoured of their own newly discerned right, to attempt to impose it upon us as ours, and violently to substitute their right for our force, is an act of tyranny, and to be resisted. It sets at nought the second great half of our maxim, *force till right is ready.* This was the grand error of the French Revolution; and its movement of ideas, by quitting the intellectual sphere and rushing furiously into the political sphere, ran, indeed, a prodigious and memorable course, but produced no such intellectual fruit as the movement of ideas of the Renascence, and created, in opposition to itself, what I may call an *epoch of concentration.* The great force of that epoch of concentration was England; and the great voice of that epoch of concentration was Burke.° It is the fashion to treat Burke's writings on the French Revolution as superannuated and conquered by the event; as the eloquent but unphilosophical tirades of bigotry and prejudice. I will not deny that they are often disfigured by the violence and passion of the moment, and that in some directions Burke's view was bounded, and his observation therefore at fault. But on the whole, and for those who can make the needful corrections, what distinguishes these writings is their profound, permanent, fruitful, philosophical truth. They contain the true philosophy of an epoch of concentration, dissipate the heavy atmosphere which its own nature is apt to engender round it, and make its resistance rational instead of mechanical.

But Burke is so great because, almost alone in England, he brings thought to bear upon politics, he saturates politics with thought. It is his accident that his ideas were at the service of an epoch of concentration,

not of an epoch of expansion; it is his characteristic that he so lived by ideas, and had such a source of them welling up within him, that he could float even an epoch of concentration and English Tory politics with them. It does not hurt him that Dr. Price° and the Liberals were enraged with him; it does not even hurt him that George the Third and the Tories were enchanted with him. His greatness is that he lived in a world which neither English Liberalism nor English Toryism is apt to enter;—the world of ideas, not the world of catchwords and party habits. So far is it from being really true of him that he "to party gave up what was meant for mankind," that at the very end of his fierce struggle with the French Revolution, after all his invectives against its false pretensions, hollowness, and madness, with his sincere convictions of its mischievousness, he can close a memorandum on the best means of combating it, some of the last pages he ever wrote,—the *Thoughts on French Affairs,* in December 1791,—with these striking words:—

"The evil is stated, in my opinion, as it exists. The remedy must be where power, wisdom, and information, I hope, are more united with good intentions than they can be with me. I have done with this subject, I believe, for ever. It has given me many anxious moments for the last two years. *If a great change is to be made in human affairs, the minds of men will be fitted to it; the general opinions and feelings will draw that way. Every fear, every hope will forward it; and then they who persist in opposing this mighty current in human affairs, will appear rather to resist the decrees of Providence itself, than the mere designs of men. They will not be resolute and firm, but perverse and obstinate."*

That return of Burke upon himself has always seemed to me one of the finest things in English literature, or indeed in any literature. That is what I call living by ideas: when one side of a question has long had your earnest support, when all your feelings are engaged, when you hear all round you no language but one, when your party talks this language like a steam-engine and can imagine no other,—still to be able to think, still to be irresistibly carried, if so it be, by the current of thought to the opposite side of the question, and, like Balaam,° to be unable to speak anything *but what the Lord has put in your mouth.* I know nothing more striking, and I must add that I know nothing more un-English.

For the Englishman in general is like my friend the Member of Parliament, and believes, point-blank, that for a thing to be an anomaly is absolutely no objection to it whatever. He is like the Lord Auckland° of

329 **Joubert,** Joseph Joubert (1754–1824), French aphorist and author of *Pensées de J. Joubert*   358 **Burke,** Edmund Burke (1729–1797), English statesman

381 **Dr. Price,** Richard Price (1723–1791), noncomformist minister and liberal commentator on morals, politics, and economics   421 **Balaam,** diviner who was rebuked by the ass he rode and blessed the Israelites when he had been commanded to curse them   428 **Lord Auckland,** William Eden, first Baron Auckland (1744–1814), author and diplomat

Burke's day, who, in a memorandum on the French
Revolution, talks of certain "miscreants, assuming the
name of philosophers, who have presumed themselves
capable of establishing a new system of society." The
Englishman has been called a political animal, and he
values what is political and practical so much that
ideas easily become objects of dislike in his eyes, and
thinkers, "miscreants," because ideas and thinkers
have rashly meddled with politics and practice. This
would be all very well if the dislike and neglect confined themselves to ideas transported out of their own
sphere, and meddling rashly with practice; but they are
inevitably extended to ideas as such, and to the whole
life of intelligence; practice is everything, a free play of
the mind is nothing. The notion of the free play of the
mind upon all subjects being a pleasure in itself, being
an object of desire, being an essential provider of elements without which a nation's spirit, whatever compensations it may have for them, must, in the long run,
die of inanition, hardly enters into an Englishman's
thoughts. It is noticeable that the word *curiosity,*
which in other languages is used in a good sense, to
mean, as a high and fine quality of man's nature, just
this disinterested love of a free play of the mind on all
subjects, for its own sake,—it is noticeable, I say, that
this word has in our language no sense of the kind, no
sense but a rather bad and disparaging one. But criticism, real criticism, is essentially the exercise of this
very quality. It obeys an instinct prompting it to try to
know the best that is known and thought in the world,
irrespectively of practice, politics, and everything of
the kind; and to value knowledge and thought as they
approach this best, without the intrusion of any other
considerations whatever. This is an instinct for which
there is, I think, little original sympathy in the practical
English nature, and what there was of it has undergone
a long benumbing period of blight and suppression in
the epoch of concentration which followed the French
Revolution.

But epochs of concentration cannot well endure for
ever; epochs of expansion, in the due course of things,
follow them. Such an epoch of expansion seems to be
opening in this country. In the first place all danger of a
hostile forcible pressure of foreign ideas upon our
practice has long disappeared; like the traveller in the
fable,° therefore, we begin to wear our cloak a little
more loosely. Then, with a long peace, the ideas of
Europe steal gradually and amicably in, and mingle,
though in infinitesimally small quantities at a time,
with our own notions. Then, too, in spite of all that is
said about the absorbing and brutalising influence of
our passionate material progress, it seems to me indisputable that this progress is likely, though not certain,
to lead in the end to an apparition of intellectual life;
and that man, after he has made himself perfectly
comfortable and has now to determine what to do with

himself next, may begin to remember that he has a
mind, and that the mind may be made the source of
great pleasure. I grant it is mainly the privilege of faith,
at present, to discern this end to our railways, our
business, and our fortune-making; but we shall see if,
here as elsewhere, faith is not in the end the true
prophet. Our ease, our travelling, and our unbounded
liberty to hold just as hard and securely as we please to
the practice to which our notions have given birth, all
tend to beget an inclination to deal a little more freely
with these notions themselves, to canvass them a little,
to penetrate a little into their real nature. Flutterings of
curiosity, in the foreign sense of the word, appear
amongst us, and it is in these that criticism must look
to find its account. Criticism first; a time of true creative activity, perhaps,—which, as I have said, must
inevitably be preceded amongst us by a time of
criticism,—hereafter, when criticism has done its
work.

It is of the last importance that English criticism
should clearly discern what rule for its course, in order
to avail itself of the field now opening to it, and to
produce fruit for the future, it ought to take. The rule
may be summed up in one word,—*disinterestedness.*
And how is criticism to show disinterestedness? By
keeping aloof from what is called "the practical view
of things"; by resolutely following the law of its own
nature, which is to be a free play of the mind on all
subjects which it touches. By steadily refusing to lend
itself to any of those ulterior, political, practical considerations about ideas, which plenty of people will be
sure to attach to them, which perhaps ought often to be
attached to them, which in this country at any rate are
certain to be attached to them quite sufficiently, but
which criticism has really nothing to do with. Its business is, as I have said, simply to know the best that is
known and thought in the world, and by in its turn
making this known, to create a current of true and
fresh ideas. Its business is to do this with inflexible
honesty, with due ability; but its business is to do no
more, and to leave alone all questions of practical consequences and applications, questions which will
never fail to have due prominence given to them. Else
criticism, besides being really false to its own nature,
merely continues in the old rut which it has hitherto
followed in this country, and will certainly miss the
chance now given to it. For what is at present the bane
of criticism in this country? It is that practical considerations cling to it and stifle it. It subserves interests
not its own. Our organs of criticism are organs of men
and parties having practical ends to serve, and with
them those practical ends are the first thing and the
play of mind the second; so much play of mind as is
compatible with the prosecution of those practical
ends is all that is wanted. An organ like the *Revue des
Deux Mondes,* having for its main function to understand and utter the best that is known and thought in
the world, existing, it may be said, as just an organ for

473–474 **traveller . . . fable,** that is, in Aesop's fable of the wind and the sun

a free play of the mind, we have not. But we have the *Edinburgh Review*, existing as an organ of the old Whigs, and for as much play of mind as may suit its being that; we have the *Quarterly Review*, existing as an organ of the Tories, and for as much play of mind as may suit its being that; we have the *British Quarterly Review*, existing as an organ of the political Dissenters, and for as much play of mind as may suit its being that; we have the *Times*, existing as an organ of the common, satisfied, well-to-do Englishman, and for as much play of mind as may suit its being that. And so on through all the various fractions, political and religious, of our society; every fraction has, as such, its organ of criticism, but the notion of combining all fractions in the common pleasure of a free disinterested play of mind meets with no favour. Directly this play of mind wants to have more scope, and to forget the pressure of practical considerations a little, it is checked, it is made to feel the chain. We saw this the other day in the extinction, so much to be regretted, of the *Home and Foreign Review*. Perhaps in no organ of criticism in this country was there so much knowledge, so much play of mind; but these could not save it. The *Dublin Review* subordinates play of mind to the practical business of English and Irish Catholicism, and lives. It must needs be that men should act in sects and parties, that each of these sects and parties should have its organ, and should make this organ subserve the interests of its action; but it would be well, too, that there should be a criticism, not the minister of these interests, not their enemy, but absolutely and entirely independent of them. No other criticism will ever attain any real authority or make any real way towards its end,—the creating a current of true and fresh ideas.

It is because criticism has so little kept in the pure intellectual sphere, has so little detached itself from practice, has been so directly polemical and controversial, that it has so ill accomplished, in this country, its best spiritual work; which is to keep man from a self-satisfaction which is retarding and vulgarising, to lead him towards perfection, by making his mind dwell upon what is excellent in itself, and the absolute beauty and fitness of things. A polemical practical criticism makes men blind even to the ideal imperfection of their practice, makes them willingly assert its ideal perfection, in order the better to secure it against attack; and clearly this is narrowing and baneful for them. If they were reassured on the practical side, speculative considerations of ideal perfection they might be brought to entertain, and their spiritual horizon would thus gradually widen. Sir Charles Adderley° says to the Warwickshire farmers:—

"Talk of the improvement of breed! Why, the race we ourselves represent, the men and women, the old Anglo-Saxon race, are the best breed in the whole world . . . The absence of a too enervating climate, too unclouded skies, and a too luxurious nature, has produced so vigorous a race of people, and has rendered us so superior to all the world."

Mr. Roebuck° says to the Sheffield cutlers:—

"I look around me and ask what is the state of England? Is not property safe? Is not every man able to say what he likes? Can you not walk from one end of England to the other in perfect security? I ask you whether, the world over or in past history, there is anything like it? Nothing. I pray that our unrivalled happiness may last."

Now obviously there is a peril for poor human nature in words and thoughts of such exuberant self-satisfaction, until we find ourselves safe in the streets of the Celestial City.

"Das wenige verschwindet leicht dem Blicke,
Der vorwärts sieht, wie viel noch übrig bleibt—"

says Goethe; "the little that is done seems nothing when we look forward and see how much we have yet to do." Clearly this is a better line of reflection for weak humanity, so long as it remains on this earthly field of labour and trial.

But neither Sir Charles Adderley nor Mr. Roebuck is by nature inaccessible to considerations of this sort. They only lose sight of them owing to the controversial life we all lead, and the practical form which all speculation takes with us. They have in view opponents whose aim is not ideal, but practical; and in their zeal to uphold their own practice against these innovators, they go so far as even to attribute to this practice an ideal perfection. Somebody has been wanting to introduce a six-pound franchise, or to abolish church-rates, or to collect agricultural statistics by force, or to diminish local self-government. How natural, in reply to such proposals, very likely improper or ill-timed, to go a little beyond the mark and to say stoutly, "Such a race of people as we stand, so superior to all the world! The old Anglo-Saxon race, the best breed in the whole world! I pray that our unrivalled happiness may last! I ask you whether, the world over or in past history, there is anything like it?" And so long as criticism answers this dithyramb by insisting that the old Anglo-Saxon race would be still more superior to all others if it had no church-rates, or that our unrivalled happiness would last yet longer with a six-pound franchise, so long will the strain, "The best breed in the whole world!" swell louder and louder, everything ideal and refining will be lost out of sight, and both the assailed and their critics will remain in a sphere, to say the truth, perfectly unvital, a sphere in which spiritual progression is impossible. But let criticism leave church-rates and the franchise alone, and in the most candid spirit, without

---

593 **Charles Adderley,** first Baron Norton (1814–1905), Conservative politician   602 **Roebuck,** John Arthur Roebuck (1801–1879), prominent radical reformer

a single lurking thought of practical innovation, confront with our dithyramb this paragraph on which I stumbled in a newspaper immediately after reading Mr. Roebuck:—

"A shocking child murder has just been committed at Nottingham. A girl named Wragg left the workhouse there on Saturday morning with her young illegitimate child. The child was soon afterwards found dead on Mapperly Hills, having been strangled. Wragg is in custody."

Nothing but that; but, in juxtaposition with the absolute eulogies of Sir Charles Adderley and Mr. Roebuck, how eloquent, how suggestive are those few lines! "Our old Anglo-Saxon breed, the best in the whole world!"—how much that is harsh and ill-favoured there is in this best! *Wragg!* If we are to talk of ideal perfection, of "the best in the whole world," has any one reflected what a touch of grossness in our race, what an original shortcoming in the more delicate spiritual perceptions, is shown by the natural growth amongst us of such hideous names,—Higginbottom, Stiggins, Bugg! In Ionia and Attica° they were luckier in this respect than "the best race in the world"; by the Ilissus° there was no Wragg, poor thing! And "our unrivalled happiness";—what an element of grimness, bareness, and hideousness mixes with it and blurs it; the workhouse, the dismal Mapperly Hills,—how dismal those who have seen them will remember;—the gloom, the smoke, the cold, the strangled illegitimate child! "I ask you whether, the world over or in past history, there is anything like it?" Perhaps not, one is inclined to answer; but at any rate, in that case, the world is very much to be pitied. And the final touch,—short, bleak and inhuman: *Wragg is in custody.* The sex lost in the confusion of our unrivalled happiness; or (shall I say?) the superfluous Christian name lopped off by the straightforward vigour of our Anglo-Saxon breed! There is profit for the spirit in such contrasts as this; criticism serves the cause of perfection by establishing them. By eluding sterile conflict, by refusing to remain in the sphere where alone narrow and relative conceptions have any worth and validity, criticism may diminish its momentary importance, but only in this way has it a chance of gaining admittance for those wider and more perfect conceptions to which all its duty is really owed. Mr. Roebuck will have a poor opinion of an adversary who replies to his defiant songs of triumph only by murmuring under his breath, *Wragg is in custody;* but in no other way will these songs of triumph be induced gradually to moderate themselves, to get rid of what in them is excessive and offensive, and to fall into a softer and truer key.

It will be said that it is a very subtle and indirect action which I am thus prescribing for criticism, and that, by embracing in this manner the Indian virtue of detachment and abandoning the sphere of practical life, it condemns itself to a slow and obscure work. Slow and obscure it may be, but it is the only proper work of criticism. The mass of mankind will never have any ardent zeal for seeing things as they are; very inadequate ideas will always satisfy them. On these inadequate ideas reposes, and must repose, the general practice of the world. That is as much as saying that whoever sets himself to see things as they are will find himself one of a very small circle; but it is only by this small circle resolutely doing its own work that adequate ideas will ever get current at all. The rush and roar of practical life will always have a dizzying and attracting effect upon the most collected spectator, and tend to draw him into its vortex; most of all will this be the case where that life is so powerful as it is in England. But it is only by remaining collected, and refusing to lend himself to the point of view of the practical man, that the critic can do the practical man any service; and it is only by the greatest sincerity in pursuing his own course, and by at last convincing even the practical man of his sincerity, that he can escape misunderstandings which perpetually threaten him.

For the practical man is not apt for fine distinctions, and yet in these distinctions truth and the highest culture greatly find their account. But it is not easy to lead a practical man,—unless you reassure him as to your practical intentions, you have no chance of leading him,—to see that a thing which he has always been used to look at from one side only, which he greatly values, and which, looked at from that side, quite deserves, perhaps, all the prizing and admiring which he bestows upon it,—that this thing, looked at from another side, may appear much less beneficent and beautiful, and yet retain all its claims to our practical allegiance. Where shall we find language innocent enough, how shall we make the spotless purity of our intentions evident enough, to enable us to say to the political Englishman that the British Constitution itself, which, seen from the practical side, looks such a magnificent organ of progress and virtue, seen from the speculative side,—with its compromises, its love of facts, its horror of theory, its studied avoidance of clear thoughts,—that, seen from this side, our august Constitution sometimes looks,—forgive me, shade of Lord Somers!°—a colossal machine for the manufacture of Philistines? How is Cobbett° to say this and not be misunderstood, blackened as he is with the smoke of a lifelong conflict in the field of political practice? how is Mr. Carlyle to say it and not be misunderstood, after his furious raid into this field with his *Latter-day Pamphlets?*° how is Mr. Ruskin, after his pugnacious political economy? I say, the critic must keep out of the region of immediate practice in the political, social,

673 **Ionia and Attica,** districts in classical Greece   675 **Ilissus,** a river near Athens

754 **Lord Somers,** John Somers, Baron Somers (1651–1716) great champion of the English Constitution   755 **Cobbett,** William Cobbett (1762–1835), violent democratic writer   760 **Latter-day Pamphlets,** pamphlets by Thomas Carlyle (see p. 599) of an extremely conservative bent published in 1850

humanitarian sphere if he wants to make a beginning for that more free speculative treatment of things, which may perhaps one day make its benefits felt even in this sphere, but in a natural and thence irresistible manner.

Do what he will, however, the critic will still remain exposed to frequent misunderstandings, and nowhere so much as in this country. For here people are particularly indisposed even to comprehend that without this free disinterested treatment of things, truth and the highest culture are out of the question. So immersed are they in practical life, so accustomed to take all their notions from this life and its processes, that they are apt to think that truth and culture themselves can be reached by the processes of this life, and that it is an impertinent singularity to think of reaching them in any other. "We are all *terræ filii*,"° cries their eloquent advocate; "all Philistines together. Away with the notion of proceeding by any other course than the course dear to the Philistines; let us have a social movement, let us organise and combine a party to pursue truth and new thought, let us call it *the liberal party,* and let us all stick to each other, and back each other up. Let us have no nonsense about independent criticism, and intellectual delicacy, and the few and the many. Don't let us trouble ourselves about foreign thought; we shall invent the whole thing for ourselves as we go along. If one of us speaks well, applaud him; if one of us speaks ill, applaud him too; we are all in the same movement, we are all liberals, we are all in pursuit of truth." In this way the pursuit of truth becomes really a social, practical, pleasurable affair, almost requiring a chairman, a secretary, and advertisements; with the excitement of an occasional scandal, with a little resistance to give the happy sense of difficulty overcome; but, in general, plenty of bustle and very little thought. To act is so easy, as Goethe says; to think is so hard! It is true that the critic has many temptations to go with the stream, to make one of the party movement, one of these *terræ filii;* it seems ungracious to refuse to be a *terræ filius* when so many excellent people are; but the critic's duty is to refuse, or, if resistance is vain, at least to cry with Obermann: *Périssons en résistant.*°

How serious a matter it is to try and resist, I had ample opportunity of experiencing when I ventured some time ago to criticise the celebrated first volume of Bishop Colenso.° The echoes of the storm which was then raised I still, from time to time, hear grumbling round me. That storm arose out of a misunderstanding almost inevitable. It is a result of no little culture to attain to a clear perception that science and religion are two wholly different things. The multitude will for ever confuse them; but happily that is of no great real importance, for while the multitude imagines itself to live by its false science, it does really live by its true religion. Dr. Colenso, however, in his first volume did all he could to strengthen the confusion, and to make it dangerous. He did this with the best intentions, I freely admit, and with the most candid ignorance that this was the natural effect of what he was doing; but, says Joubert, "Ignorance, which in matters of morals extenuates the crime, is itself, in intellectual matters, a crime of the first order." I criticised Bishop Colenso's speculative confusion. Immediately there was a cry raised: "What is this? here is a liberal attacking a liberal. Do not you belong to the movement? are you not a friend of truth? Is not Bishop Colenso in pursuit of truth? then speak with proper respect of his book. Dr. Stanley° is another friend of truth, and you speak with proper respect of his book; why make these invidious differences? both books are excellent, admirable, liberal; Bishop Colenso's perhaps the most so, because it is the boldest, and will have the best practical consequences for the liberal cause. Do you want to encourage to the attack of a brother liberal his, and your, and our implacable enemies, the *Church and State Review* or the *Record,* — the High Church rhinoceros and the Evangelical hyena? Be silent, therefore; or rather speak, speak as loud as ever you can! and go into ecstasies over the eighty and odd pigeons."

But criticism cannot follow this coarse and indiscriminate method. It is unfortunately possible for a man in pursuit of truth to write a book which reposes upon a false conception. Even the practical consequences of a book are to genuine criticism no recommendation of it, if the book is, in the highest sense, blundering. I see that a lady° who herself, too, is in pursuit of truth, and who writes with great ability, but a little too much, perhaps, under the influence of the practical spirit of the English liberal movement, classes Bishop Colenso's book and M. Renan's° together, in her survey of the religious state of Europe, as facts of the same order, works, both of them, of "great importance"; "great ability, power, and skill"; Bishop Colenso's, perhaps, the most powerful; at least, Miss Cobbe gives special expression to her gratitude that to Bishop Colenso "has been given the strength to grasp, and the courage to teach, truths of such deep import." In the same way, more than one popular writer has compared him to Luther. Now it is just this kind of false estimate which the critical spirit is, it seems to me, bound to resist. It is really the strongest possible proof of the low ebb at which, in England, the critical spirit is, that while the critical hit in the religious literature of Germany is Dr. Strauss's° book, in that of France M. Renan's book, the book of Bishop Colenso is the critical hit in the religious liter-

779 **terrae filii,** sons of the earth   806 **Périssons en résistant.** "Let us die resisting." E. P. de Senancour (1770–1846), author of *Obermann,* was a major influence on Arnold   810 **Colenso,** John William Colenso (1814–1883), Bishop of Natal, author of *The Pentateuch and Book of Joshua Critically Examined* (1862), a work in historical criticism of the Bible which caused much religious furor

832 **Stanley,** Arthur Penrhyn Stanley (1815–1881), Dean of Westminster and great friend of Arnold's father   850 **a lady,** Frances Power Cobbe (1822–1904), writer on religious and moral subjects   854 **Renan,** Ernest Renan (1823–1892), French philologist and historian, author of *Vie de Jésus* (1863)   868 **Strauss,** David Friedrich Strauss (1808–1874); the book alluded to is *Das Leben Jesu* (1835)

ature of England. Bishop Colenso's book reposes on a total misconception of the essential elements of the religious problem, as that problem is now presented for solution. To criticism, therefore, which seeks to have the best that is known and thought on this problem, it is, however well meant, of no importance whatever. M. Renan's book attempts a new synthesis of the elements furnished to us by the Four Gospels. It attempts, in my opinion, a synthesis, perhaps prema-
880 ture, perhaps impossible, certainly not successful. Up to the present time, at any rate, we must acquiesce in Fleury's sentence on such recastings of the Gospel story: *Quiconque s'imagine la pouvoir mieux écrire, ne l'entend pas.*° M. Renan had himself passed by anticipation a like sentence on his own work, when he said: "If a new presentation of the character of Jesus were offered to me, I would not have it; its very clearness would be, in my opinion, the best proof of its insufficiency." His friends may with perfect justice
890 rejoin that at the sight of the Holy Land, and of the actual scene of the Gospel-story, all the current of M. Renan's thoughts may have naturally changed, and a new casting of that story irresistibly suggested itself to him; and that this is just a case for applying Cicero's maxim: Change of mind is not inconsistency—*nemo doctus unquam mutationem consilii inconstantiam dixit esse.*° Nevertheless, for criticism, M. Renan's first thought must still be the truer one, as long as his new casting so fails more fully to commend itself, more
900 fully (to use Coleridge's happy phrase about the Bible) to *find* us. Still M. Renan's attempt is, for criticism, of the most real interest and importance, since, with all its difficulty, a fresh synthesis of the New Testament *data*—not making war on them, in Voltaire's fashion, not a leaving them out of mind, in the world's fashion, but the putting a new construction upon them, the taking them from under the old, traditional, conventional point of view and placing them under a new one,—is the very essence of the religious problem, as
910 now presented; and only by efforts in this direction can it receive a solution.

Again, in the same spirit in which she judges Bishop Colenso, Miss Cobbe, like so many earnest liberals of our practical race, both here and in America, herself sets vigorously about a positive reconstruction of religion, about making a religion of the future out of hand, or at least setting about making it. We must not rest, she and they are always thinking and saying, in negative criticism, we must be creative and construc-
920 tive; hence we have such works as her recent *Religious Duty,* and works still more considerable, perhaps, by others, which will be in every one's mind. These works often have much ability; they often spring out of sincere convictions, and a sincere wish to do good; and they sometimes, perhaps, do good. Their fault is (if I

may be permitted to say so) one which they have in common with the British College of Health, in the New Road. Every one knows the British College of Health; it is that building with the lion and the statue of the Goddess Hygeia before it; at least I am sure about the lion, though I am not absolutely certain about the 930 Goddess Hygeia. This building does credit, perhaps, to the resources of Dr. Morrison° and his disciples; but it falls a good deal short of one's idea of what a British College of Health ought to be. In England, where we hate public interference and love individual enterprise, we have a whole crop of places like the British College of Health; the grand name without the grand thing. Unluckily, creditable to individual enterprise as they are, they tend to impair our taste by making us forget what more grandiose, noble, or beautiful character 940 properly belongs to a public institution. The same may be said of the religions of the future of Miss Cobbe and others. Creditable, like the British College of Health, to the resources of their authors, they yet tend to make us forget what more grandiose, noble, or beautiful character properly belongs to religious constructions. The historic religions, with all their faults, have had this; it certainly belongs to the religious sentiment, when it truly flowers, to have this; and we impoverish our spirit if we allow a religion of the future without it. 950 What then is the duty of criticism here? To take the practical point of view, to applaud the liberal movement and all its works,—its New Road religions of the future into the bargain,—for their general utility's sake? By no means; but to be perpetually dissatisfied with these works, while they perpetually fall short of a high and perfect ideal.

For criticism, these are elementary laws; but they never can be popular, and in this country they have been very little followed, and one meets with immense 960 obstacles in following them. That is a reason for asserting them again and again. Criticism must maintain its independence of the practical spirit and its aims. Even with well-meant efforts of the practical spirit it must express dissatisfaction, if in the sphere of the ideal they seem impoverishing and limiting. It must not hurry on to the goal because of its practical importance. It must be patient, and know how to wait; and flexible, and know how to attach itself to things and how to withdraw from them. It must be apt to study 970 and praise elements that for the fulness of spiritual perfection are wanted, even though they belong to a power which in the practical sphere may be maleficent. It must be apt to discern the spiritual shortcomings or illusions of powers that in the practical sphere may be beneficent. And this without any notion of favouring or injuring, in the practical sphere, one power or the other; without any notion of playing off, in this sphere, one power against the other. When one looks, for instance, at the English Divorce Court,—an 980

882–883 **Quiconque . . . pas.** "Whoever thinks he can write it better does not understand it"; from Claude Fleury (1640–1723), *Discours sur l'histoire ecclésiastique* 895–896 **nemo . . . esse.** No learned person has ever said that change of mind is inconsistency (*Letters to Atticus*)

932 **Morrison,** James Morrison (1770–1840), seller of Morrison's Pills as universal cure-alls

institution which perhaps has its practical conveniences, but which in the ideal sphere is so hideous; an institution which neither makes divorce impossible nor makes it decent, which allows a man to get rid of his wife, or a wife of her husband, but makes them drag one another first, for the public edification, through a mire of unutterable infamy,—when one looks at this charming institution, I say, with its crowded trials, its newspaper reports, and its money compensations, this institution in which the gross unregenerate British Philistine has indeed stamped an image of himself,—one may be permitted to find the marriage theory of Catholicism refreshing and elevating. Or when Protestantism, in virtue of its supposed rational and intellectual origin, gives the law to criticism too magisterially, criticism may and must remind it that its pretensions, in this respect, are illusive and do it harm; that the Reformation was a moral rather than an intellectual event; that Luther's theory of grace no more exactly reflects the mind of the spirit than Bossuet's° philosophy of history reflects it; and that there is no more antecedent probability of the Bishop of Durham's° stock of ideas being agreeable to perfect reason than of Pope Pius the Ninth's. But criticism will not on that account forget the achievements of Protestantism in the practical and moral sphere; nor that, even in the intellectual sphere, Protestantism, though in a blind and stumbling manner, carried forward the Renaissance, while Catholicism threw itself violently across its path.

I lately heard a man of thought and energy contrasting the want of ardour and movement which he now found amongst young men in this country with what he remembered in his own youth, twenty years ago. "What reformers we were then!" he exclaimed; "What a zeal we had! how we canvassed every institution in Church and State, and were prepared to remodel them all on first principles!" He was inclined to regret, as a spiritual flagging, the lull which he saw. I am disposed rather to regard it as a pause in which the turn to a new mode of spiritual progress is being accomplished. Everything was long seen, by the young and ardent amongst us, in inseparable connection with politics and practical life. We have pretty well exhausted the benefits of seeing things in this connection, we have got all that can be got by so seeing them. Let us try a more disinterested mode of seeing them; let us betake ourselves more to the serener life of the mind and spirit. This life, too, may have its excesses and dangers; but they are not for us at present. Let us think of quietly enlarging our stock of true and fresh ideas, and not, as soon as we get an idea or half an idea, be running out with it into the street, and trying to make it rule there. Our ideas will, in the end, shape the world all the better for maturing a little. Perhaps in

fifty years' time it will in the English House of Commons be an objection to an institution that it is an anomaly, and my friend the Member of Parliament will shudder in his grave. But let us in the meanwhile rather endeavour that in twenty years' time it may, in English literature, be an objection to a proposition that it is absurd. That will be a change so vast, that the imagination almost fails to grasp it. *Ab integro sæclorum nascitur ordo.*°

If I have insisted so much on the course which criticism must take where politics and religion are concerned, it is because, where these burning matters are in question, it is more likely to go astray. I have wished, above all, to insist on the attitude which criticism should adopt towards things in general; on its right tone and temper of mind. But then comes another question as to the subject-matter which literary criticisms should most seek. Here, in general, its course is determined for it by the idea which is the law of its being; the idea of a disinterested endeavour to learn and propagate the best that is known and thought in the world, and thus to establish a current of fresh and true ideas. By the very nature of things, as England is not all the world, much of the best that is known and thought in the world cannot be of English growth, must be foreign; by the nature of things, again, it is just this that we are least likely to know, while English thought is streaming in upon us from all sides, and takes excellent care that we shall not be ignorant of its existence. The English critic of literature, therefore, must dwell much on foreign thought, and with particular heed on any part of it, which, while significant and fruitful in itself, is for any reason specially likely to escape him. Again, judging is often spoken of as the critic's one business, and so in some sense it is; but the judgment which almost insensibly forms itself in a fair and clear mind, along with fresh knowledge, is the valuable one; and thus knowledge, and ever fresh knowledge, must be the critic's great concern for himself. And it is by communicating fresh knowledge, and letting his own judgment pass along with it,—but insensibly, and in the second place, not the first, as a sort of companion and clue, not as an abstract lawgiver,—that the critic will generally do most good to his readers. Sometimes, no doubt, for the sake of establishing an author's place in literature, and his relation to a central standard (and if this is not done, how are we to get at our *best in the world?*), criticism may have to deal with a subject-matter so familiar that fresh knowledge is out of the question, and then it must be all judgment; an enunciation and detailed application of principles. Here the great safeguard is never to let oneself become abstract, always to retain an intimate and lively consciousness of the truth of what one is saying, and, the moment this fails us, to be sure that something is wrong. Still under all circumstances, this

1000 **Bossuet,** Jacques Bénigne Bossuet (1627–1704), French bishop and author who believed that all of history demonstrated that God had ordered events for the good of Christianity   1003 **Bishop of Durham,** Charles Thomas Baring (1807–1879)

1043–1044 **Ab . . . ordo.** Order is born from the renewal of the ages (Vergil, *Fourth Eclogue*)

mere judgment and application of principles is, in itself, not the most satisfactory work to the critic; like mathematics, it is tautological, and cannot well give us, like fresh learning, the sense of creative activity.

But stop, some one will say; all this talk is of no practical use to us whatever; this criticism of yours is not what we have in our minds when we speak of criticism; when we speak of critics and criticism, we mean critics and criticism of the current English literature of the day; when you offer to tell criticism its function, it is to this criticism that we expect you to address yourself. I am sorry for it, for I am afraid I must disappoint these expectations. I am bound by my own definition of criticism: *a disinterested endeavour to learn and propagate the best that is known and thought in the world.* How much of current English literature comes into this "best that is known and thought in the world"? Not very much, I fear; certainly less, at this moment, than of the current literature of France or Germany. Well, then, am I to alter my definition of criticism, in order to meet the requirements of a number of practising English critics, who, after all, are free in their choice of a business? That would be making criticism lend itself just to one of those alien practical considerations, which, I have said, are so fatal to it. One may say, indeed, to those who have to deal with the mass—so much better disregarded—of current English literature, that they may at all events endeavour, in dealing with this, to try it, so far as they can, by the standard of the best that is known and thought in the world; one may say, that to get anywhere near this standard, every critic should try and possess one great literature, at least, besides his own; and the more unlike his own, the better. But, after all, the criticism I am really concerned with,—the criticism which alone can much help us for the future, the criticism which, throughout Europe, is at the present day meant, when so much stress is laid on the importance of criticism and the critical spirit,—is a criticism which regards Europe as being, for intellectual and spiritual purposes, one great confederation, bound to a joint action and working to a common result; and whose members have, for their proper outfit, a knowledge of Greek, Roman, and Eastern antiquity, and of one another. Special, local, and temporary advantages being put out of account, that modern nation will in the intellectual and spiritual sphere make most progress, which most thoroughly carries out this program. And what is that but saying that we too, all of us, as individuals, the more thoroughly we carry it out, shall make the more progress?

There is so much inviting us!—what are we to take? what will nourish us in growth towards perfection? That is the question which, with the immense field of life and of literature lying before him, the critic has to answer; for himself first, and afterwards for others. In this idea of the critic's business the essays brought together in the following pages have had their origin; in this idea, widely different as are their subjects, they have, perhaps, their unity.

I conclude with what I said at the beginning: to have the sense of creative activity is the great happiness and the great proof of being alive, and it is not denied to criticism to have it; but then criticism must be sincere, simple, flexible, ardent, ever widening its knowledge. Then it may have, in no contemptible measure, a joyful sense of creative activity; a sense which a man of insight and conscience will prefer to what he might derive from a poor, starved, fragmentary, inadequate creation. And at some epochs no other creation is possible.

Still, in full measure, the sense of creative activity belongs only to genuine creation; in literature we must never forget that. But what true man of letters ever can forget it? It is no such common matter for a gifted nature to come into possession of a current of true and living ideas, and to produce amidst the inspiration of them, that we are likely to underrate it. The epochs of Æschylus and Shakespeare make us feel their preeminence. In an epoch like those is, no doubt, the true life of literature; there is the promised land, towards which criticism can only beckon. That promised land it will not be ours to enter, and we shall die in the wilderness: but to have desired to enter it, to have saluted it from afar, is already, perhaps, the best distinction among contemporaries; it will certainly be the best title to esteem with posterity.

(1865)

from CULTURE AND ANARCHY

Culture and Anarchy initially appeared in six installments in 1867 and 1868. The first, entitled *Culture and Its Enemies,* appeared in July 1867; the remainder, under the title *Anarchy and Authority,* appeared in January, February, June, July, and August 1868. After the first article had appeared—now *Sweetness and Light*—Arnold purposely waited for the critics' reactions so that he could synthesize and answer their criticisms. Thus, in his second chapter, Arnold could reply not only to the utilitarian liberalism of the day but also to its on-the-spot proponents. This fact accounts for Arnold's repeated apology that he is not a philosopher and is not to be expected to provide philosophical completeness: he employs "the simple unsystematic way which best suits my taste and my powers."

Arnold rebuts the "selfish matrix" of utilitarian liberalism. The utilitarians spoke of the "self"; Arnold spoke of the "best self." The utilitarians assumed a state of nature; Arnold assumed a state of cultivation. The utilitarians were quantitative; Arnold was qualitative. The utilitarians argued that things would turn out right without human intervention; Arnold understood that if there was to be any hope of things turning out right, the best and the best-informed people of each age must make a colossal effort to bring them round. At the heart of the difference between Arnold and the Liberals were two quite distinct concepts of the self.

HEBRAISM AND HELLENISM

This fundamental ground° is our preference of doing to thinking. Now this preference is a main element in our nature, and as we study it we find ourselves opening up a number of large questions on every side.

Let me go back for a moment to Bishop Wilson, who says: "First, never go against the best light you have; secondly, take care that your light be not darkness." We show, as a nation, laudable energy and persistence in walking according to the best light we have, but are
10 not quite careful enough, perhaps, to see that our light be not darkness. This is only another version of the old story that energy is our strong point and favourable characteristic, rather than intelligence. But we may give to this idea a more general form still, in which it will have a yet larger range of application. We may regard this energy driving at practice, this paramount sense of the obligation of duty, self-control, and work, this earnestness in going manfully with the best light we have, as one force. And we may regard the intelli-
20 gence driving at those ideas which are, after all, the basis of right practice, the ardent sense for all the new and changing combinations of them which man's development brings with it, the indomitable impulse to know and adjust them perfectly, as another force. And these two forces we may regard as in some sense rivals,—rivals not by the necessity of their own nature, but as exhibited in man and his history,—and rivals dividing the empire of the world between them. And to give these forces names from the two races of men
30 who have supplied the most signal and splendid manifestations of them, we may call them respectively the forces of Hebraism and Hellenism. Hebraism and Hellenism,—between these two points of influence moves our world. At one time it feels more powerfully the attraction of one of them, at another time of the other; and it ought to be, though it never is, evenly and happily balanced between them.

The final aim of both Hellenism and Hebraism, as of all great spiritual disciplines, is no doubt the same:
40 man's perfection or salvation. The very language which they both of them use in schooling us to reach this aim is often identical. Even when their language indicates by variation,—sometimes a broad variation, often a but slight and subtle variation,—the different courses of thought which are uppermost in each discipline, even then the unity of the final end and aim is still apparent. To employ the actual words of that discipline with which we ourselves are all of us most familiar, and the words of which, therefore, come most home to us, that final end and aim is "that we might be
50 partakers of the divine nature." These are the words of a Hebrew apostle, but of Hellenism and Hebraism alike this is, I say, the aim. When the two are confronted, as they very often are confronted, it is nearly always with what I may call a rhetorical purpose; the speaker's whole design is to exalt and enthrone one of the two, and he uses the other only as a foil and to enable him the better to give effect to his purpose. Obviously, with us, it is usually Hellenism which is thus reduced to minister to the triumph of Hebraism.
60 There is a sermon on Greece and the Greek spirit by a man never to be mentioned without interest and respect, Frederick Robertson,° in which this rhetorical use of Greece and the Greek spirit, and the inadequate exhibition of them necessarily consequent upon this, is almost ludicrous, and would be censurable if it were not to be explained by the exigencies of a sermon. On the other hand, Heinrich Heine,° and other writers of his sort, give us the spectacle of the tables completely turned, and of Hebraism brought in just as a foil and
70 contrast to Hellenism, and to make the superiority of Hellenism more manifest. In both these cases there is injustice and misrepresentation. The aim and end of both Hebraism and Hellenism is, as I have said, one and the same, and this aim and end is august and admirable.

Still, they pursue this aim by very different courses. The uppermost idea with Hellenism is to see things as they really are; the uppermost idea with Hebraism is conduct and obedience. Nothing can do away with this
80 ineffaceable difference. The Greek quarrel with the body and its desires is, that they hinder right thinking; the Hebrew quarrel with them is, that they hinder right acting. "He that keepeth the law, happy is he";° "Blessed is the man that feareth the Eternal, that delighteth greatly in his commandments";°—that is the Hebrew notion of felicity; and, pursued with passion and tenacity, this notion would not let the Hebrew rest till, as is well known, he had at last got out of the law a network of prescriptions to enwrap his whole life, to
90 govern every moment of it, every impulse, every action. The Greek notion of felicity, on the other hand, is perfectly conveyed in these words of a great French moralist: "C'est le bonheur des hommes,"°—when? when they abhor that which is evil?—no; when they exercise themselves in the law of the Lord day and night?—no; when they die daily?—no; when they walk about the New Jerusalem° with palms in their hands?—no; but when they think aright, when their thought hits: "quand ils pensent juste." At the bottom
100 of both the Greek and the Hebrew notion is the desire,

Hebraism and Hellenism   1 This fundamental ground. Arnold had ended the preceding chapter, *Barbarians, Philistines, Populace*, as follows: "We see how our habits and practice oppose themselves to such a recognition [of right reason], and the many inconveniences which we therefore suffer. But now let us try to go a little deeper, and find, beneath our actual habits and practice, the very ground and cause out of which they spring"

63 Frederick Robertson, author and distinguished clergyman (1816–1853) 68 Heinrich Heine, German poet and critic (1797–1856) from whom Arnold probably derived the terms "Hebraism and Hellenism"   84 He that . . . he. See *Proverbs*, 29:18   85–86 Blessed . . . commandments. See *Psalms*, 112:1 94 C'est . . . hommes. It is happiness for men when they think right   98 New Jerusalem, that is, the Celestial City of *Revelation*, 21:2

native in man, for reason and the will of God, the feeling after the universal order,—in a word, the love of God. But, while Hebraism seizes upon certain plain, capital intimations of the universal order, and rivets itself, one may say, with unequalled grandeur of earnestness and intensity on the study and observance of them, the bent of Hellenism is to follow, with flexible activity, the whole play of the universal order, to be
110 apprehensive of missing any part of it, of sacrificing one part to another, to slip away from resting in this or that intimation of it, however capital. An unclouded clearness of mind, an unimpeded play of thought, is what this bent drives at. The governing idea of Hellenism is *spontaneity of consciousness;* that of Hebraism, *strictness of conscience.*

Christianity changed nothing in this essential bent of Hebraism to set doing above knowing. Self-conquest, self-devotion, the following not our own individual
120 will, but the will of God, *obedience,* is the fundamental idea of this form, also, of the discipline to which we have attached the general name of Hebraism. Only, as the old law and the network of prescriptions with which it enveloped human life were evidently a motive-power not driving and searching enough to produce the result aimed at,—patient continuance in well-doing, self-conquest,—Christianity substituted for them boundless devotion to that inspiring and affecting pattern of self-conquest offered by Jesus
130 Christ; and by the new motive-power, of which the essence was this, though the love and admiration of Christian churches have for centuries been employed in varying, amplifying, and adoring the plain description of it, Christianity, as St. Paul truly says, "establishes the law,"° and in the strength of the ampler power which she has thus supplied to fulfil it, has accomplished the miracles, which we all see, of her history.

So long as we do not forget that both Hellenism and
140 Hebraism are profound and admirable manifestations of man's life, tendencies, and powers, and that both of them aim at a like final result, we can hardly insist too strongly on the divergence of line and of operation with which they proceed. It is a divergence so great that it most truly, as the prophet Zechariah says,° "has raised up thy sons, O Zion, against thy sons, O Greece!"° The difference whether it is by doing or by knowing that we set most store, and the practical consequences which follow from this difference, leave
150 their mark on all the history of our race and of its development. Language may be abundantly quoted from both Hellenism and Hebraism to make it seem that one follows the same current as the other towards the same goal. They are, truly, borne towards the same goal; but the currents which bear them are infinitely different. It is true, Solomon will praise knowing: "Understanding is a well-spring of life unto him that

hath it."° And in the New Testament, again, Jesus Christ is a "light,"° and "truth makes us free."° It is true, Aristotle will undervalue knowing: "In what 160 concerns virtue," says he, "three things are necessary—knowledge, deliberate will, and perseverance; but, whereas the two last are all-important, the first is a matter of little importance."° It is true that with the same impatience with which St. James enjoins a man to be not a forgetful hearer, but a *doer of the work,*° Epictetus° exhorts us to *do* what we have demonstrated to ourselves we ought to do; or he taunts us with futility, for being armed at all points to prove that lying is wrong, yet all the time continuing to lie. It is true 170 Plato, in words which are almost the words of the New Testament or the Imitation, calls life a learning to die.° But underneath the superficial agreement the fundamental divergence still subsists. The understanding of Solomon is "the walking in the way of the commandments"; this is "the way of peace," and it is of this that blessedness comes. In the New Testament, the truth which gives us the peace of God and makes us free, is the love of Christ constraining us to crucify, as he did, and with a like purpose of moral regeneration, 180 the flesh with its affections and lusts, and thus establishing, as we have seen, the law. The moral virtues, on the other hand, are with Aristotle but the porch and access to the intellectual, and with these last is blessedness. That partaking of the divine life, which both Hellenism and Hebraism, as we have said, fix as their crowning aim, Plato expressly denies to the man of practical virtue merely, of self-conquest with any other motive than that of perfect intellectual vision. He reserves it for the lover of pure knowledge, of seeing 190 things as they really are,—the φιλομαθής.

Both Hellenism and Hebraism arise out of the wants of human nature, and address themselves to satisfying those wants. But their methods are so different, they lay stress on such different points, and call into being by their respective disciplines such different activities, that the face which human nature presents when it passes from the hands of one of them to those of the other, is no longer the same. To get rid of one's ignorance, to see things as they are, and by seeing them as 200 they are to see them in their beauty, is the simple and attractive ideal which Hellenism holds out before human nature; and from the simplicity and charm of this ideal, Hellenism, and human life in the hands of Hellenism, is invested with a kind of aërial ease, clearness, and radiancy; they are full of what we call sweetness and light. Difficulties are kept out of view, and the beauty and rationalness of the ideal have all our thoughts. "The best man is he who most tries to perfect himself, and the happiest man is he who most 210 feels that he *is* perfecting himself,"°—this account of

134–135 **Christianity ... law.** See *Romans,* 3:31   145 **prophet ... says.** See *Zechariah,* 9:13

157–158 **Understanding ... it.** See *Proverbs,* 16:22   159 **light.** See *John,* 1:4-9   **truth ... free.** See *John,* 8:32   160–164 **In ... importance,** from Aristotle's *Nichomachean Ethics,* II, iv   166 **not ... work.** See *James,* 1:25   167 **Epictetus,** Greek Stoic philosopher (fl. c. 90 A.D.)   171–172 **Plato ... to die,** in the *Phaedo*   209–211 **The best man ... himself,** from Xenophon's *Memorabilia*

the matter by Socrates, the true Socrates of the *Memorabilia*, has something so simple, spontaneous, and unsophisticated about it, that it seems to fill us with clearness and hope when we hear it. But there is a saying which I have heard attributed to Mr. Carlyle° about Socrates,—a very happy saying, whether it is really Mr. Carlyle's or not,—which excellently marks the essential point in which Hebraism differs from
220 Hellenism. "Socrates," this saying goes, "is terribly *at ease in Zion.*°" Hebraism,—and here is the source of its wonderful strength,—has always been severely preoccupied with an awful sense of the impossibility of being at ease in Zion; of the difficulties which oppose themselves to man's pursuit or attainment of that perfection of which Socrates talks so hopefully, and, as from this point of view one might almost say, so glibly. It is all very well to talk of getting rid of one's ignorance, of seeing things in their reality, seeing them in
230 their beauty; but how is this to be done when there is something which thwarts and spoils all our efforts?

This something is *sin;* and the space which sin fills in Hebraism, as compared with Hellenism, is indeed prodigious. This obstacle to perfection fills the whole scene, and perfection appears remote and rising away from earth, in the background. Under the name of sin, the difficulties of knowing oneself and conquering oneself which impede man's passage to perfection, become, for Hebraism, a positive, active entity hostile to
240 man, a mysterious power which I heard Dr. Pusey° the other day, in one of his impressive sermons, compare to a hideous hunchback seated on our shoulders, and which it is the main business of our lives to hate and oppose. The discipline of the Old Testament may be summed up as a discipline teaching us to abhor and flee from sin; the discipline of the New Testament, as a discipline teaching us to die to it. As Hellenism speaks of thinking clearly, seeing things in their essence and beauty, as a grand and precious feat for man to
250 achieve, so Hebraism speaks of becoming conscious of sin, of wakening to a sense of sin, as a feat of this kind. It is obvious to what wide divergence these differing tendencies, actively followed, must lead. As one passes and repasses from Hellenism to Hebraism, from Plato to St. Paul, one feels inclined to rub one's eyes and ask oneself whether man is indeed a gentle and simple being, showing the traces of a noble and divine nature; or an unhappy chained captive, labouring with groanings that cannot be uttered to free himself from
260 the body of this death.

Apparently it was the Hellenic conception of human nature which was unsound, for the world could not live by it. Absolutely to call it unsound, however, is to fall into the common error of its Hebraising enemies; but it was unsound at that particular moment of man's development, it was premature. The indispensable basis of conduct and self-control, the platform upon which alone the perfection aimed at by Greece can come into bloom, was not to be reached by our race so easily; centuries of probation and discipline were needed to 270 bring us to it. Therefore the bright promise of Hellenism faded, and Hebraism ruled the world. Then was seen that astonishing spectacle, so well marked by the often-quoted words of the prophet Zechariah, when men of all languages and nations took hold of the skirt of him that was a Jew, saying:—"*We will go with you, for we have heard that God is with you.*"° And the Hebraism which thus received and ruled a world all gone out of the way and altogether become unprofitable, was, and could not but be, the later, the more 280 spiritual, the more attractive development of Hebraism. It was Christianity; that is to say, Hebraism aiming at self-conquest and rescue from the thrall of vile affections, not by obedience to the letter of a law, but by conformity to the image of a self-sacrificing example. To a world stricken with moral enervation Christianity offered its spectacle of an inspired self-sacrifice; to men who refused themselves nothing, it showed one who refused himself everything;—"*my Saviour banished joy!*" says George Herbert.° When the *alma* 290 *Venus,* the life-giving and joy-giving power of nature, so fondly cherished by the Pagan world, could not save her followers from self-dissatisfaction and ennui, the severe words of the apostle came bracingly and refreshingly: "Let no man deceive you with vain words, for because of these things cometh the wrath of God upon the children of disobedience."° Through age after age and generation after generation, our race, or all that part of our race which was most living and progressive, was *baptized into a death;*° and endeavoured, 300 by suffering in the flesh, to cease from sin. Of this endeavour, the animating labours and afflictions of early Christianity, the touching asceticism of mediæval Christianity, are the great historical manifestations. Literary monuments of it, each in its own way incomparable, remain in the Epistles of St. Paul, in St. Augustine's *Confessions,* and in the two original and simplest books of the *Imitation.*°

Of two disciplines laying their main stress, the one, on clear intelligence, the other, on firm obedience; the 310 one, on comprehensively knowing the grounds of one's duty, the other, on diligently practising it; the one, on taking all possible care (to use Bishop Wilson's words again) that the light we have be not darkness, the other, that according to the best light we have we diligently walk,—the priority naturally belongs to that discipline which braces all man's moral powers, and founds for him an indispensable basis of character. And, therefore, it is justly said of the Jewish people, who were charged with setting powerfully forth that 320 side of the divine order to which the words *conscience*

216 **Mr. Carlyle,** Thomas Carlyle   221 **Zion,** the hill in Jerusalem on which the temple of the Lord stood   240 **Dr. Pusey,** Edward Pusey (1800–1882), one of the leaders of the Oxford Movement

276–277 **We will . . . you.** See *Romans,* 8:26   290 **George Herbert.** religious poet (1593–1633), in his poem *The Size*   295–297 **Let . . . disobedience.** See *Ephesians,* 5:6   300 **baptized . . . death.** See *Romans,* 6:3   307–308 **two original . . . Imitation.** "The two first books."—Arnold's note

and *self-conquest* point, that they were "entrusted with the oracles of God";° as it is justly said of Christianity, which followed Judaism and which set forth this side with a much deeper effectiveness and a much wider influence, that the wisdom of the old Pagan world was foolishness° compared to it. No words of devotion and admiration can be too strong to render thanks to these beneficent forces which have so borne forward humanity in its appointed work of coming to the knowledge and possession of itself; above all, in those great moments when their action was the wholesomest and the most necessary.

But the evolution of these forces, separately and in themselves, is not the whole evolution of humanity,—their single history is not the whole history of man; whereas their admirers are always apt to make it stand for the whole history. Hebraism and Hellenism are, neither of them, the *law* of human development, as their admirers are prone to make them; they are, each of them, *contributions* to human development,—august contributions, invaluable contributions; and each showing itself to us more august, more invaluable, more preponderant over the other, according to the moment in which we take them, and the relation in which we stand to them. The nations of our modern world, children of that immense and salutary movement which broke up the Pagan world, inevitably stand to Hellenism in a relation which dwarfs it, and to Hebraism in a relation which magnifies it. They are inevitably prone to take Hebraism as the law of human development, and not as simply a contribution to it, however precious. And yet the lesson must perforce be learned, that the human spirit is wider than the most priceless of the forces which bear it onward, and that to the whole development of man Hebraism itself is, like Hellenism, but a contribution.

Perhaps we may help ourselves to see this clearer by an illustration drawn from the treatment of a single great idea which has profoundly engaged the human spirit, and has given it eminent opportunities for showing its nobleness and energy. It surely must be perceived that the idea of immortality, as this idea rises in its generality before the human spirit, is something grander, truer, and more satisfying, than it is in the particular forms by which St. Paul, in the famous fifteenth chapter of the Epistle to the Corinthians, and Plato, in the *Phædo,* endeavour to develop and establish it. Surely we cannot but feel, that the argumentation with which the Hebrew apostle goes about to expound this great idea is, after all, confused and inconclusive; and that the reasoning, drawn from analogies of likeness and equality, which is employed upon it by the Greek philosopher, is over-subtle and sterile. Above and beyond the inadequate solutions which Hebraism and Hellenism here attempt, extends the immense and august problem itself, and the human

spirit which gave birth to it. And this single illustration may suggest to us how the same thing happens in other cases also.

But meanwhile, by alternations of Hebraism and Hellenism, of a man's intellectual and moral impulses, of the effort to see things as they really are, and the effort to win peace by self-conquest, the human spirit proceeds; and each of these two forces has its appointed hours of culmination and seasons of rule. As the great movement of Christianity was a triumph of Hebraism and man's moral impulses, so the great movement which goes by the name of the Renascence° was an uprising and reinstatement of man's intellectual impulses and of Hellenism. We in England, the devoted children of Protestantism, chiefly know the Renascence by its subordinate and secondary side of the Reformation. The Reformation has been often called a Hebraising revival, a return to the ardour and sincereness of primitive Christianity. No one, however, can study the development of Protestantism and of Protestant churches without feeling that into the Reformation too,—Hebraising child of the Renascence and offspring of its fervour, rather than its intelligence, as it undoubtedly was,—the subtle Hellenic leaven of the Renascence found its way, and that the exact respective parts, in the Reformation, of Hebraism and of Hellenism, are not easy to separate. But what we may with truth say is, that all which Protestantism was to itself clearly conscious of, all which it succeeded in clearly setting forth in words, had the characters of Hebraism rather than of Hellenism. The Reformation was strong, in that it was an earnest return to the Bible and to doing from the heart the will of God as there written. It was weak, in that it never consciously grasped or applied the central idea of the Renascence,—the Hellenic idea of pursuing, in all lines of activity, the law and science, to use Plato's words, of things as they really are. Whatever direct superiority, therefore, Protestantism had over Catholicism was a moral superiority, a superiority arising out of its greater sincerity and earnestness,—at the moment of its apparition at any rate,—in dealing with the heart and conscience. Its pretensions to an intellectual superiority are in general quite illusory. For Hellenism, for the thinking side in man as distinguished from the acting side, the attitude of mind of Protestantism towards the Bible in no respect differs from the attitude of mind of Catholicism towards the Church. The mental habit of him who imagines that Balaam's ass spoke,° in no respect differs from the mental habit of him who imagines that a Madonna of wood or stone winked; and the one, who says that God's Church makes him believe what he believes, and the other, who says that God's Word makes him believe what he believes, are for the philosopher perfectly alike in not

322–323 **entrusted . . . God.** See *Romans,* 3:2   326–327 **that the wisdom . . . foolishness** See *1 Corinthians,* 3:19

389 **Renascence.** "I have ventured to give the foreign *Renaissance*—destined to become of more common use amongst us as the movement which it denotes comes, as it will come, increasingly to interest us—an English form."—Arnold's note   426–427 **him . . . spoke.** See *Numbers,* 22:22-35

really and truly knowing, when they say *God's Church* and *God's Word,* what it is they say, or whereof they affirm.

In the sixteenth century, therefore, Hellenism re-entered the world, and again stood in presence of Hebraism,—a Hebraism renewed and purged. Now, it has not been enough observed, how, in the seventeenth century, a fate befell Hellenism in some respects analogous to that which befell it at the commencement of our era. The Renascence, that great reawakening of Hellenism, that irresistible return of humanity to nature and to seeing things as they are, which in art, in literature, and in physics, produced such splendid fruits, had, like the anterior Hellenism of the Pagan world, a side of moral weakness and of relaxation or insensibility of the moral fibre, which in Italy showed itself with the most startling plainness, but which in France, England, and other countries was very apparent too. Again this loss of spiritual balance, this exclusive preponderance given to man's perceiving and knowing side, this unnatural defect of his feeling and acting side, provoked a reaction. Let us trace that reaction where it most nearly concerns us.

Science has now made visible to everybody the great and pregnant elements of difference which lie in race, and in how signal a manner they make the genius and history of an Indo-European people vary from those of a Semitic people. Hellenism is of Indo-European growth, Hebraism is of Semitic growth; and we English, a nation of Indo-European stock, seem to belong naturally to the movement of Hellenism. But nothing more strongly marks the essential unity of man, than the affinities we can perceive, in this point or that, between members of one family of peoples and members of another. And no affinity of this kind is more strongly marked than that likeness in the strength and prominence of the moral fibre, which, notwithstanding immense elements of difference, knits in some special sort the genius and history of us English, and our American descendants across the Atlantic, to the genius and history of the Hebrew people. Puritanism, which has been so great a power in the English nation, and in the strongest part of the English nation, was originally the reaction in the seventeenth century of the conscience and moral sense of our race, against the moral indifference and lax rule of conduct which in the sixteenth century came in with the Renascence. It was a reaction of Hebraism against Hellenism; and it powerfully manifested itself, as was natural, in a people with much of what we call a Hebraising turn, with a signal affinity for the bent which was the master-bent of Hebrew life. Eminently Indo-European by its *humour,* by the power it shows, through this gift, of imaginatively acknowledging the multiform aspects of the problem of life, and of thus getting itself unfixed from its own over-certainty, of smiling at its own over-tenacity, our race has yet (and a great part of its strength lies here), in matters of practical life and moral conduct, a strong share of the assuredness, the tenacity, the intensity of the Hebrews. This turn manifested itself in Puritanism, and has had a great part in shaping our history for the last two hundred years. Undoubtedly it checked and changed amongst us that movement of the Renascence which we see producing in the reign of Elizabeth such wonderful fruits. Undoubtedly it stopped the prominent rule and direct development of that order of ideas which we call by the name of Hellenism, and gave the first rank to a different order of ideas. Apparently, too, as we said of the former defeat of Hellenism, if Hellenism was defeated, this shows that Hellenism was imperfect, and that its ascendency at that moment would not have been for the world's good.

Yet there is a very important difference between the defeat inflicted on Hellenism by Christianity eighteen hundred years ago, and the check given to the Renascence by Puritanism. The greatness of the difference is well measured by the difference in force, beauty, significance, and usefulness, between primitive Christianity and Protestantism. Eighteen hundred years ago it was altogether the hour of Hebraism. Primitive Christianity was legitimately and truly the ascendent force in the world at that time, and the way of mankind's progress lay through its full development. Another hour in man's development began in the fifteenth century, and the main road of his progress then lay for a time through Hellenism. Puritanism was no longer the central current of the world's progress, it was a side stream crossing the central current and checking it. The cross and the check may have been necessary and salutary, but that does not do away with the essential difference between the main stream of man's advance and a cross or a side stream. For more than two hundred years the main stream of man's advance has moved towards knowing himself and the world, seeing things as they are, spontaneity of consciousness; the main impulse of a great part, and that the strongest part, of our nation has been towards strictness of conscience. They have made the secondary the principal at the wrong moment, and the principal they have at the wrong moment treated as secondary. This contravention of the natural order has produced, as such contravention always must produce, a certain confusion and false movement, of which we are now beginning to feel, in almost every direction, the inconvenience. In all directions our habitual courses of action seem to be losing efficaciousness, credit, and control, both with others and even with ourselves. Everywhere we see the beginnings of confusion, and we want a clue to some sound order and authority. This we can only get by going back upon the actual instincts and forces which rule our life, seeing them as they really are, connecting them with other instincts and forces, and enlarging our whole view and rule of life.

(1869)

from THE STUDY OF POETRY

From his periodical essays, Arnold had chosen the contents of *Essays in Criticism, Second Series,* before his death. Here Arnold comments on the generation which established the direction of nineteenth-century English literature.

The Study of Poetry was written as the general introduction to an extended anthology of English poetry called *The English Poets* (edited, in 4 volumes, by T. H. Ward), and the essay bears some mark of this purpose. It is not an exaggeration to say that, for two generations of nonspecialists, the canon of English poetry was set by Ward's anthology or that the vocabulary of academic criticism was shaped by Arnold's essay.

"The future of poetry is immense, because in poetry, where it is worthy of its high destinies, our race, as time goes on, will find an ever surer and surer stay. There is not a creed which is not shaken, not an accredited dogma which is not shown to be questionable, not a received tradition which does not threaten to dissolve. Our religion has materialized itself in the fact, in the supposed fact; it has attached its emotion to the fact, and now the fact is failing it. But for poetry
10 the idea is everything; the rest is a world of illusion, of divine illusion. Poetry attaches its emotion to the idea; the idea *is* the fact. The strongest part of our religion today is its unconscious poetry."°

Let me be permitted to quote these words of my own, as uttering the thought which should, in my opinion, go with us and govern us in all our study of poetry. In the present work it is the course of one great contributory stream to the world-river of poetry that we are invited to follow. We are here invited to trace
20 the stream of English poetry. But whether we set ourselves, as here, to follow only one of the several streams that make the mighty river of poetry, or whether we seek to know them all, our governing thought should be the same. We should conceive of poetry worthily, and more highly than it has been the custom to conceive of it. We should conceive of it as capable of higher uses, and called to higher destinies, than those which in general men have assigned to it hitherto. More and more mankind will discover that
30 we have to turn to poetry to interpret life for us, to console us, to sustain us. Without poetry, our science will appear incomplete; and most of what now passes with us for religion and philosophy will be replaced by poetry. Science, I say, will appear incomplete without it. For finely and truly does Wordsworth call poetry "the impassioned expression which is in the countenance of all science";° and what is a countenance without its expression? Again, Wordsworth finely and truly calls poetry "the breath and finer spirit of all knowl-
40 edge": our religion, parading evidences such as those on which the popular mind relies now; our philosophy, pluming itself on its reasonings about causation and finite and infinite being; what are they but the shadows and dreams and false shows of knowledge? The day will come when we shall wonder at ourselves for having trusted to them, for having taken them seriously; and the more we perceive their hollowness, the more we shall prize "the breath and finer spirit of knowledge" offered to us by poetry.

But if we conceive thus highly of the destinies of
50 poetry, we must also set our standard for poetry high, since poetry, to be capable of fulfilling such high destinies, must be poetry of a high order of excellence. We must accustom ourselves to a high standard and to a strict judgment. Sainte-Beuve° relates that Napoleon one day said, when somebody was spoken of in his presence as a charlatan: "Charlatan as much as you please; but where is there *not* charlatanism?"— "Yes," answers Sainte-Beuve, "in politics, in the art of governing mankind, that is perhaps true. But in the
60 order of thought, in art, the glory, the eternal honor is that charlatanism shall find no entrance; herein lies the inviolableness of that noble portion of man's being." It is admirably said, and let us hold fast to it. In poetry, which is thought and art in one, it is the glory, the eternal honor, that charlatanism shall find no entrance; that this noble sphere be kept inviolate and inviolable. Charlatanism is for confusing or obliterating the distinctions between excellent and inferior, sound and unsound or only half-sound, true and untrue or only
70 half-true. It is charlatanism, conscious or unconscious, whenever we confuse or obliterate these. And in poetry, more than anywhere else, it is unpermissible to confuse or obliterate them. For in poetry the distinction between excellent and inferior, sound and unsound or only half-sound, true and untrue or only half-true, is of paramount importance. It is of paramount importance because of the high destinies of poetry. In poetry, as a criticism of life under the conditions fixed for such a criticism by the laws of poetic
80 truth and poetic beauty, the spirit of our race will find, we have said, as time goes on and as other helps fail, its consolation and stay. But the consolation and stay

The Study of Poetry   1–13 The future . . . poetry, quoted in condensed form, from the introduction Arnold wrote to *The Hundred Greatest Men* (1879)

36–37 the impassioned . . . science, in the Preface to *Lyrical Ballads* (1800)
55 Sainte-Beuve, Charles Augustin Sainte-Beuve (1804–1869), French critic, in *Les Cahiers*

will be of power in proportion to the power of the criticism of life. And the criticism of life will be of power in proportion as the poetry conveying it is excellent rather than inferior, sound rather than unsound or half-sound, true rather than untrue or half-true.

The best poetry is what we want; the best poetry will be found to have a power of forming, sustaining, and delighting us, as nothing else can. A clearer, deeper sense of the best in poetry, and of the strength and joy to be drawn from it, is the most precious benefit which we can gather from a poetical collection such as the present. And yet in the very nature and conduct of such a collection there is inevitably something which tends to obscure in us the consciousness of what our benefit should be, and to distract us from the pursuit of it. We should therefore steadily set it before our minds at the outset, and should compel ourselves to revert constantly to the thought of it as we proceed.

Yes; constantly in reading poetry, a sense for the best, the really excellent, and of the strength and joy to be drawn from it, should be present in our minds and should govern our estimate of what we read. But this real estimate, the only true one, is liable to be superseded, if we are not watchful, by two other kinds of estimate, the historic estimate and the personal estimate, both of which are fallacious. A poet or a poem may count to us historically, they may count to us on grounds personal to ourselves, and they may count to us really. They may count to us historically. The course of development of a nation's language, thought, and poetry is profoundly interesting; and by regarding a poet's work as a stage in this course of development we may easily bring ourselves to make it of more importance as poetry than in itself it really is, we may come to use a language of quite exaggerated praise in criticizing it; in short, to overrate it. So arises in our poetic judgments the fallacy caused by the estimate which we may call historic. Then, again, a poet or a poem may count to us on grounds personal to ourselves. Our personal affinities, liking, and circumstances have great power to sway our estimate of this or that poet's work, and to make us attach more importance to it as poetry than in itself it really possesses, because to us it is, or has been, of high importance. Here also we overrate the object of our interest, and apply to it a language of praise which is quite exaggerated. And thus we get the source of a second fallacy in our poetic judgments—the fallacy caused by an estimate which we may call personal.

Both fallacies are natural. It is evident how naturally the study of the history and development of a poetry may incline a man to pause over reputations and works once conspicuous but now obscure, and to quarrel with a careless public for skipping, in obedience to mere tradition and habit, from one famous name or work in its national poetry to another, ignorant of what it misses, and of the reason for keeping what it keeps, and of the whole process of growth in its poetry. The French have become diligent students of their own early poetry, which they long neglected; the study makes many of them dissatisfied with their so-called classical poetry, the court-tragedy of the seventeenth century, a poetry which Pellisson° long ago reproached with its want of the true poetic stamp, with its *politesse stérile et rampante,*° but which nevertheless has reigned in France as absolutely as if it had been the perfection of classical poetry indeed. The dissatisfaction is natural; yet a lively and accomplished critic, M. Charles d'Héricault,° the editor of Clément Marot,° goes too far when he says that "the cloud of glory playing round a classic is a mist as dangerous to the future of a literature as it is intolerable for the purposes of history." "It hinders," he goes on, "it hinders us from seeing more than one single point, the culminating and exceptional point; the summary, fictitious and arbitrary, of a thought and of a work. It substitutes a halo for a physiognomy, it puts a statue where there was once a man, and hiding from us all trace of the labor, the attempts, the weaknesses, the failures, it claims not study but veneration; it does not show us how the thing is done, it imposes upon us a model. Above all, for the historian this creation of classic personages is inadmissible; for it withdraws the poet from his time, from his proper life, it breaks historical relationships, it blinds criticism by conventional admiration, and renders the investigation of literary origins unacceptable. It gives us a human personage no longer, but a God seated immovable amidst His perfect work, like Jupiter on Olympus; and hardly will it be possible for the young student, to whom such work is exhibited at such a distance from him, to believe that it did not issue ready made from that divine head."

All this is brilliantly and tellingly said, but we must plead for a distinction. Everything depends on the reality of a poet's classic character. If he is a dubious classic, let us sift him; if he is a false classic, let us explode him. But if he is a real classic, if his work belongs to the class of the very best (for this is the true and right meaning of the word *classic, classical*), then the great thing for us is to feel and enjoy his work as deeply as ever we can, and to appreciate the wide difference between it and all work which has not the same high character. This is what is salutary, this is what is formative; this is the great benefit to be got from the study of poetry. Everything which interferes with it, which hinders it, is injurious. True, we must read our classic with open eyes, and not with eyes blinded with superstition; we must perceive when his work comes short, when it drops out of the class of the very best, and we must rate it, in such cases, at its proper value. But the use of this negative criticism is not in itself, it is entirely in its enabling us to have a clearer sense and a deeper enjoyment of what is truly

146 **Pellisson,** Paul Pellisson (1624–1693), French author and critic 147–148 **politesse . . . rampante,** civility barren and bombastic 152 **d'Héricault,** French journalist and critic. His edition of Marot was published in 1868 **Clément Marot,** French poet at the court of Francis I (1496–1544)

excellent. To trace the labor, the attempts, the weaknesses, the failures of a genuine classic, to acquaint oneself with his time and his life and his historical relationship, is mere literary dilettantism unless it has that clear sense and deeper enjoyment for its end. It may be said that the more we know about a classic the better we shall enjoy him; and, if we lived as long as Methuselah and had all of us heads of perfect clearness and wills of perfect steadfastness, this might be true in fact as it is plausible in theory. But the case here is much the same as the case with the Greek and Latin studies of our schoolboys. The elaborate philological groundwork which we require them to lay is in theory an admirable preparation for appreciating the Greek and Latin authors worthily. The more thoroughly we lay the groundwork, the better we shall be able, it may be said, to enjoy the authors. True, if time were not so short, and schoolboys' wits not so soon tired and their power of attention exhausted; only, as it is, the elaborate philological preparation goes on, but the authors are little known and less enjoyed. So with the investigator of "historic origins" in poetry. He ought to enjoy the true classic all the better for his investigations; he often is distracted from the enjoyment of the best, and with the less good he overbusies himself, and is prone to overrate it in proportion to the trouble which it has cost him.

The idea of tracing historic origins and historical relationships cannot be absent from a compilation like the present. And naturally the poets to be exhibited in it will be assigned to those persons for exhibition who are known to prize them highly, rather than to those who have no special inclination towards them. Moreover the very occupation with an author, and the business of exhibiting him, disposes us to affirm and amplify his importance. In the present work, therefore, we are sure of frequent temptation to adopt the historic estimate, or the personal estimate, and to forget the real estimate; which latter, nevertheless, we must employ if we are to make poetry yield us its full benefit. So high is that benefit, the benefit of clearly feeling and of deeply enjoying the really excellent, the truly classic in poetry, that we do well, I say, to set it fixedly before our minds as our object in studying poets and poetry, and to make the desire of attaining it the one principle to which, as the *Imitation* says, whatever we may read or come to know, we always return. *Cum multa legeris et cognoveris, ad unum semper oportet redire principium.*°

The historic estimate is likely in especial to affect our judgment and our language when we are dealing with ancient poets; the personal estimate when we are dealing with poets our contemporaries, or at any rate modern. The exaggerations due to the historic estimate are not in themselves, perhaps, of very much gravity.

Their report hardly enters the general ear; probably they do not always impose even on the literary men who adopt them. But they lead to a dangerous abuse of language. So we hear Caedmon, amongst our own poets, compared to Milton.° I have already noticed the enthusiasm of one accomplished French critic for "historic origins." Another eminent French critic, M. Vitet,° comments upon that famous document of the early poetry of his nation, the *Chanson de Roland.*° It is indeed a most interesting document. The *joculator* or *jongleur*° Taillefer, who was with William the Conqueror's army at Hastings,° marched before the Norman troops, so said the tradition, singing "of Charlemagne and of Roland and of Oliver, and of the vassals who died at Roncevaux"; and it is suggested that in the *Chanson de Roland* by one Turoldus or Théroulde,° a poem preserved in a manuscript of the twelfth century in the Bodleian Library at Oxford, we have certainly the matter, perhaps even some of the words, of the chant which Taillefer sang. The poem has vigor and freshness; it is not without pathos. But M. Vitet is not satisfied with seeing in it a document of some poetic value, and of very high historic and linguistic value; he sees in it a grand and beautiful work, a monument of epic genius. In its general design he finds the grandiose conception, in its details he finds the constant union of simplicity with greatness, which are the marks, he truly says, of the genuine epic, and distinguish it from the artificial epic of literary ages. One thinks of Homer; this is the sort of praise which is given to Homer, and justly given. Higher praise there cannot well be, and it is the praise due to epic poetry of the highest order only, and to no other. Let us try, then, the *Chanson de Roland* at its best. Roland, mortally wounded, lays himself down under a pine-tree, with his face turned towards Spain and the enemy—

De plusurs choses à remembrer li prist,
De tantes teres cume li bers cunquist,
De dulce France, des humes de sun lign,
De Carlemagne sun seignor ki l'nurrit.°

That is primitive work, I repeat, with an undeniable poetic quality of its own. It deserves such praise, and such praise is sufficient for it. But now turn to Homer—

Ὥς φάτο, τοὺς δ' ἤδη κατέχεν φυσίζοος αἶα
ἐν Λακεδαίμονι αὖθι, φίλῃ ἐν πατρίδι γαίῃ°

255 **Caedmon . . . Milton.** Caedmon (died c. 680) also wrote a poem based on *Genesis*   259 **Vitet,** Ludoric Vitet (1802–1873), French man of letters and politician   260 **Chanson de Roland,** French folk epic of the eleventh century   262 **jongleur,** jester, a wandering minstrel   263 **Hastings,** the battle in which the Normans conquered the Anglo-Saxons   268 **Théroulde,** perhaps the scribe who copied the manuscript   288–291 **De plusurs . . . l'nurrit.** "Then began he to call many things to remembrance—all the lands which his valour conquered, and pleasant France, and the men of his lineage, and Charlemagne his liege lord who nourished him' (*Chanson de Roland,* iii, 939–942)."—Arnold's note   296–297 **"Ὥς . . . γαίῃ.** "'So said she, they long since in Earth's soft arms were reposing,/There, in their own dear land, their fatherland, Lacedaemon'—*Iliad,* iii, 243, 244 (translated by Dr. Hawtrey)"—Arnold's note

244–245 **Cum . . . principium.** When you have read and learned many things, you ought always to return to the one principle (Thomas à Kempis, d. 1471, *Imitation of Christ,* famous devotional book)

We are here in another world, another order of poetry altogether; here is rightly due such supreme praise as that which M. Vitet gives to the *Chanson de Roland.* If our words are to have any meaning, if our judgments are to have any solidity, we must not heap that supreme praise upon poetry of an order immeasurably inferior.

Indeed there can be no more useful help for discovering what poetry belongs to the class of the truly excellent, and can therefore do us most good, than to have always in one's mind lines and expressions of the great masters, and to apply them as a touchstone to other poetry. Of course we are not to require this other poetry to resemble them; it may be very dissimilar. But if we have any tact we shall find them, when we have lodged them well in our minds, an infallible touchstone for detecting the presence or absence of high poetic quality, and also the degree of this quality, in all other poetry which we may place beside them. Short passages, even single lines, will serve our turn quite sufficiently. Take the two lines which I have just quoted from Homer, the poet's comment on Helen's mention of her brothers;—or take his

Α δειλώ, τί σφῶι δόμεν Πηλῆι ἄνακτι
θνητῷ; ὑμεῖς δ ἐστὸν ἀγήρω τ᾿ἀθανάτω τε.
ἤ ἵνα δυστήνοισι μετ᾿ἀνδράσιν ἄλγε᾿ἔχητον;°

the address of Zeus to the horses of Peleus;—or take finally his

Καὶ σέ, γέρον, τὸ πρὶν μὲν ἀκούομεν ὄλβιον εἶναι°

the words of Achilles to Priam, a suppliant before him. Take that incomparable line and a half of Dante, Ugolino's tremendous words:

Io no piangeva; sì dentro impietrai.
Piangevan elli° . . .

take the lovely words of Beatrice to Virgil:

Io son fatta da Dio, sua mercè, tale,
Che la vostra miseria non mi tange,
Nè fiamma d'esto incendio non m'assale° . . .

take the simple, but perfect, single line:

In la sua volontade è nostra pace.°

Take of Shakespeare a line or two of Henry the

Fourth's expostulation with sleep:

Wilt thou upon the high and giddy mast
Seal up the ship-boy's eyes, and rock his brains
In cradle of the rude imperious surge° . . .

and take, as well, Hamlet's dying request to Horatio:

If thou didst ever hold me in thy heart,
Absent thee from felicity awhile,
And in this harsh world draw thy breath in pain,
To tell my story° . . .

Take of Milton that Miltonic passage:

Darkened so, yet shone
Above them all the archangel; but his face
Deep scars of thunder had intrenched, and care
Sat on his faded cheek° . . .

add two such lines as:

And courage never to submit or yield
And what is else not to be overcome° . . .

and finish with the exquisite close to the loss of Proserpine, the loss

. . . which cost Ceres all that pain
To seek her through the world.°

These few lines, if we have tact and can use them, are enough even of themselves to keep clear and sound our judgments about poetry, to save us from fallacious estimates of it, to conduct us to a real estimate.

The specimens I have quoted differ widely from one another, but they have in common this: the possession of the very highest poetical quality. If we are thoroughly penetrated by their power, we shall find that we have acquired a sense enabling us, whatever poetry may be laid before us, to feel the degree in which a high poetical quality is present or wanting there. Critics give themselves great labor to draw out what in the abstract constitutes the characters of a high quality of poetry. It is much better simply to have recourse to concrete examples;—to take specimens of poetry of the high, the very highest quality, and to say: The characters of a high quality poetry are what is expressed *there.* They are far better recognized by being felt in the verse of the master, than by being perused in the prose of the critic. Nevertheless if we are urgently pressed to give some critical account of them, we may safely, perhaps, venture on laying down, not indeed how and why the characters arise,

---

321–323 'Α . . ἔχητον. "'Ah, unhappy pair, w y gave we you to King Peleus, to a mortal? but ye are without old age, and immortal. Was it that with men born to misery ye might have sorrow?' (*Iliad*, xvii, 443–445)."—Arnold's note   326 **Καὶ . . . εἶναι.** "'Nay, and thou too, old man, in former days wast, as we hear, happy' (*Iliad*, xxiv, 543)."—Arnold's note   330–331 **Io . . . elli.** "I wailed not, so of stone I grew within;—they wailed' (*Inferno,* xxxiii, 39, 40)."—Arnold's note
333–335 **Io . . . m'assale.** "'Of such sort hath God, thanked be His mercy, made me, that your misery toucheth me no:, neither doth the flame of this fire strike me' (*Inferno,* ii, 91–93)."—Arnold's note   337 **In . . . pace.** "'In His will is our peace' (*Paradiso,* iii, 84)."—Arnold's note

340–342 **Wilt . . . surge,** *II Henry IV,* III, i, 18–20   344–347 **If . . . story,** *Hamlet,* V, ii, 357–360   349–352 **Darkened . . . cheek,** *Paradise Lost,* I, 599–602
354–355 **And courage . . . overcome,** *Paradise Lost,* I, 108–109   358–359 **which . . . world,** *Paradise Lost,* IV, 271–272

but where and in what they arise. They are in the matter and substance of the poetry, and they are in its manner and style. Both of these, the substance and matter on the one hand, the style and manner on the other, have a mark, an accent of high beauty, worth, and power. But if we are asked to define this mark and accent in the abstract, our answer must be: No, for we should thereby be darkening the question, not clearing it. The mark and accent are given by the substance and matter of that poetry, by the style and manner of that poetry, and of all other poetry which is akin to it in quality.

Only one thing we may add as to the substance and matter of poetry, guiding ourselves by Aristotle's profound observation that the superiority of poetry over history consists in its possessing a higher truth and a higher seriousness (φιλοσοφώτερον καὶ σπουδαιότερον).° Let us add, therefore, to what we have said, this: that the substance and matter of the best poetry acquire their special character from pos-

sessing, in an eminent degree, truth and seriousness. We may add yet further, what is in itself evident, that to the style and manner of the best poetry their special character, their accent, is given by their diction, and, even yet more, by their movement. And though we distinguish between the two characters, the two accents, of superiority, yet they are nevertheless vitally connected one with the other. The superior character 410 of truth and seriousness, in the matter and substance of the best poetry, is inseparable from the superiority of diction and movement marking its style and manner. The two superiorities are closely related, and are in steadfast proportion one to the other. So far as high poetic truth and seriousness are wanting to a poet's matter and substance, so far also, we may be sure, will a high poetic stamp of diction and movement be wanting to his style and manner. In proportion as this high stamp of diction and movement, again, is absent from 420 a poet's style and manner, we shall find, also, that high poetic truth and seriousness are absent from his substance and matter. . . .
(1880)

399–400 **φιλοσοφώτερον . . . σπουδαιότερον**, Aristotle, *Poetics*, IX, "more philosophical and more serious"

GEORGE MEREDITH
1828–1909

Meredith was born in Portsmouth in 1828. His father was a tailor who was apparently not in a position to do much for his son. After one year in a German school in 1843–1844, he was apprenticed to a London lawyer. But the profession of law did not attract him, and in 1848 he took up journalism and began sending his verses to the magazines. A year later he married the daughter of the poet Thomas Love Peacock. His wife proved to be a very difficult, temperamental woman, and after ten years of disagreeing together they finally separated. This losing marital struggle formed the basis of the fifty connected poems which he called *Modern Love* (1862). If the following sequence is a correct reflection of his experience, neither Meredith nor his wife was entirely responsible for their breakup:

In tragic life, God wot,
No villain need be! Passions spin the plot;
We are betrayed by what is false within.

Two years later Meredith married Marie Vulliamy. The Merediths settled in Surrey, where the poet-novelist lived and wrote for the rest of his life.

Although he is primarily known today as a novelist of penetrating psychological insight (*The Ordeal of Richard Feverel*, 1859; *Beauchamp's Career*, 1876; *The Egoist*, 1879), some of the main themes of his art appear in the titles of his long list of poems—from *Poems* (1851) to *A Reading of Life, with Other Poems* (1901). Between these dates *Modern Love* was issued with other poems in 1862; *Poems and Lyrics of the Joy of Earth* in 1883, *Ballads and Poems of Tragic Life* in 1887, *A Reading of Earth* the year following; *The Empty Purse, and Other Poems* in 1892, and *Odes in Contribution to the Song of French History* in 1898.

from MODERN LOVE°

1

By this he knew she wept with waking eyes:
That, at his hand's light quiver by her head,
The strange low sobs that shook their common bed
Were called into her with a sharp surprise,
And strangled mute, like little gaping snakes,   5
Dreadfully venomous to him. She lay
Stone-still, and the long darkness flowed away
With muffled pulses. Then, as midnight makes
Her giant heart of Memory and Tears
Drink the pale drug of silence, and so beat   10

Modern Love. This is a series of sixteen-line poems recording the thoughts and feelings of a husband and wife who loved each other once, but whose love has long been dying. The husband sometimes speaks in his own person as "I"

Sleep's heavy measure, they from head to feet
Were moveless, looking through their dead black
    years,
By vain regret scrawled over the blank wall.
Like sculptured effigies they might be seen
15 Upon their marriage-tomb, the sword between;
Each wishing for the sword that severs all.

13

"I play for Seasons, not Eternities!"
Says Nature, laughing on her way. "So must
All those whose stake is nothing more than dust!"
And lo, she wins, and of her harmonies
5 She is full sure! Upon her dying rose
She drops a look of fondness, and goes by,
Scarce any retrospection in her eye;
For she the laws of growth most deeply knows,
Whose hands bear, here, a seed-bag—there, an urn.
10 Pledged she herself to aught, 'twould mark her end!
This lesson of our only visible friend
Can we not teach our foolish hearts to learn?
Yes! yes!—but, oh, our human rose is fair
Surpassingly! Lose calmly Love's great bliss,
15 When the renewed forever of a kiss
Whirls life within the shower of loosened hair!

16

In our old shipwrecked days there was an hour,
When in the firelight steadily aglow,
Joined slackly, we beheld the red chasm grow
Among the clicking coals. Our library-bower
5 That eve was left to us; and hushed we sat
As lovers to whom Time is whispering.
From sudden-opened doors we heard them sing;
The nodding elders mixed good wine with chat.
Well knew we that Life's greatest treasure lay
10 With us, and of it was our talk. "Ah, yes!
Love dies!" I said (I never thought it less).
She yearned to me that sentence to unsay.
Then when the fire domed blackening, I found
Her cheek was salt against my kiss, and swift
15 Up the sharp scale of sobs her breast did lift.—
Now am I haunted by that taste! that sound!

29

Am I failing? For no longer can I cast
A glory round about this head of gold.
Glory she wears, but springing from the mold;
Not like the consecration of the Past!
5 Is my soul beggared? Something more than earth
I cry for still; I cannot be at peace
In having Love upon a mortal lease.
I cannot take the woman at her worth!
Where is the ancient wealth wherewith I clothed
10 Our human nakedness, and could endow

With a spiritual splendor a white brow
That else had grinned at me the fact I loathed?
A kiss is but a kiss now! and no wave
Of a great flood that whirls me to the sea.
But, as you will! we'll sit contentedly,   15
And eat our pot of honey on the grave.

43

Mark where the pressing wind shoots javelin-like
Its skeleton shadow on the broad-backed wave!
Here is a fitting spot to dig Love's grave;
Here where the ponderous breakers plunge and strike,
And dart their hissing tongues high up the sand: 5
In hearing of the ocean, and in sight
Of those ribbed wind-streaks running into white.
If I the death of Love had deeply planned,
I never could have made it half so sure,
As by the unblest kisses which upbraid   10
The full-waked sense; or failing that, degrade!
'Tis morning; but no morning can restore
What we have forfeited. I see no sin;
The wrong is mixed. In tragic life, God wot,
No villain need be! Passions spin the plot;   15
We are betrayed by what is false within.

44

They say that Pity in Love's service dwells,
A porter at the rosy temple's gate.
I missed him going: but it is my fate
To come upon him now beside his wells;
Whereby I know that I Love's temple leave,   5
And that the purple doors have closed behind.
Poor soul! if, in those early days unkind,
Thy power to sting had been but power to grieve,
We now might with an equal spirit meet,
And not be matched like innocence and vice.   10
She for the Temple's worship has paid price,
And takes the coin of Pity as a cheat.
She sees through simulation to the bone:
What's best in her impels her to the worst:
Never, she cries, shall Pity soothe Love's thirst,   15
Or foul hypocrisy for truth atone.

47

We saw the swallows gathering in the sky,
And in the osier-isle° we heard them noise.
We had not to look back on summer joys,
Or forward to a summer of bright dye;
But in the largeness of the evening earth   5
Our spirits grew as we went side by side.
The hour became her husband and my bride.
Love, that had robbed us so, thus blessed our dearth!
The pilgrims of the year waxed very loud

Poem 47 2 **osier-isle**, island overgrown with osiers, or willows

10 In multitudinous chatterings, as the flood
Full brown came from the West, and like pale blood
Expanded to the upper crimson cloud.
Love, that had robbed us of immortal things,
This little moment mercifully gave,
15 Where I have seen across the twilight wave
The swan sail with her young beneath her wings.

48

Their sense is with their senses all mixed in,
Destroyed by subtleties these women are!
More brain, O Lord, more brain! or we shall mar
Utterly this fair garden we might win.
5 Behold! I looked for peace, and thought it near.
Our inmost hearts had opened, each to each
We drank the pure daylight of honest speech.
Alas! that was the fatal draft, I fear.
For when of my lost Lady came the word,
10 This woman, O this agony of flesh!
Jealous devotion bade her break the mesh,
That I might seek that other like a bird.
I do adore the nobleness! despise
The act! She has gone forth, I know not where.
15 Will the hard world my sentience of her share?
I feel the truth; so let the world surmise.

50

Thus piteously Love closed what he begat:
The union of this ever-diverse pair!
These two were rapid falcons in a snare,
Condemned to do the flitting of the bat.
5 Lovers beneath the singing sky of May,
They wandered once, clear as the dew on flowers.
But they fed not on the advancing hours;
Their hearts held cravings for the buried day.
Then each applied to each that fatal knife,
10 Deep questioning, which probes to endless dole.
Ah, what a dusty answer gets the soul
When hot for certainties in this our life!—
In tragic hints here see what evermore
Moves dark as yonder midnight ocean's force,
15 Thundering like ramping hosts of warrior horse,
To throw that faint thin line upon the shore!

(1862)

LUCIFER IN STARLIGHT

On a starred night Prince Lucifer uprose.
Tired of his dark dominion, swung the fiend
Above the rolling ball, in cloud part screened,
Where sinners hugged their specter of repose.
5 Poor prey to his hot fit of pride were those.
And now upon his western wing he leaned,
Now his huge bulk o'er Afric's sands careened,

Now the black planet shadowed Arctic snows.
Soaring through wider zones that pricked his scars°
With memory of the old revolt from Awe,   10
He reached a middle height, and at the stars,
Which are the brain of heaven, he looked, and sank.
Around the ancient track marched, rank on rank,
The army of unalterable law.

(1883)

DANTE GABRIEL ROSSETTI
1828–1882

Rossetti was born in London, the son of an exiled
Italian patriot and man of letters. He attended
King's College School from 1837 to 1843. Finding
himself intensely interested in painting, he then
studied at Cary's Art Museum and became in 1846 a
student at the Royal Academy. Subsequently he
painted for a short time in the studio of his friend Ford
Madox Brown (1821–1893). Although his first dedication was to painting, he was also an omnivorous
reader. Before he was twenty, he had completed a
number of translations of Italian poets and had composed some original verse. Rossetti was largely responsible for establishing in 1848 the English Pre-Raphaelite Brotherhood, a group formed in order to carry on a
Romantic revolt against Victorian academic painting.
The seven other members of the Brotherhood, except
for Rossetti's brother, William Michael Rossetti, were
all students at the Royal Academy. They preferred
medieval and early Renaissance painting before
Raphael to baroque and neoclassical painting. The
term Pre-Raphaelite soon became synonymous with a
romanticized medieval past.

Pre-Raphaelitism also had its literary side. In 1850
Rossetti contributed to *The Germ*, the magazine of the
Brotherhood, eleven of his finest lyrics, including "The
Blessed Damozel." In this year he also became acquainted with Elizabeth Siddal, a strikingly beautiful
young woman who sat as a model for his painting and
served as an inspiration for his poetry. Three years later the two became engaged, but, because of Rossetti's
financial circumstances, they were not married until
1860. Siddal had the pale, lilylike beauty which was
the incarnation of the romantic mood as the Pre-
Raphaelites conceived it. The marriage ended tragi-
cally in 1862 with Siddal's death from an overdose of
laudanum. Rossetti's grief was so great that he buried

Lucifer in Starlight 9 **scars,** received in his battle with the angels and in his fall
from heaven

in her coffin a bundle of manuscript poems of which he kept no copy.

In 1861 he published a group of translations, *The Early Italian Poets*, to modest success. In 1869 Rossetti arranged to recover the poems he had buried with Siddal; they were published the following year under the title *Poems*. The volume included his sonnet sequence *The House of Life*, a record of his love for his wife, and other lyrics. He was a neurotic by temperament, and this tendency increased after his wife's death. Failing eyesight cut him off from painting, and he increasingly turned to poetry in his later years. To cure insomnia he began taking chloral; this treatment brought on hallucinations and fits of depression. He spent his last years almost in seclusion and died in 1882, just a year after the appearance of his last volume, *Ballads and Sonnets*.

Dante Gabriel Rossetti was primarily a painter, secondarily a poet, and the mark of the painter is evident in his poems. *The Blessed Damozel* provides a revealing example. In the first two stanzas, the blessed damozel can be *seen* leaning against the bar of heaven, clothed in white, her hair "lying down her back," "yellow like ripe corn." Rossetti draws the reader's attention to her dark, liquid eyes; in the third stanza, he gives the reader an indication of their shape and of their importance as an index to her soul. In precision of detail, in love of sensuous beauty, in vague symbolism—all used to present a frozen image of a lady in an attitude—the reader sees the Pre-Raphaelite painter turned poet.

Rossetti produced significant poetry in two other forms: the sonnet and the ballad. He was explicit about the type of situation or subject matter that drew him to these forms: "I must confess of a need, in narrative dramatic poetry (unless so simple in structure as *Auld Robin Gray*), of something rather 'exciting,' and indeed I believe something of the 'romantic' element, to rouse my mind to anything like the moods produced by personal emotion on my own life. . . . Not that I would place the expressions of pure love and life, or of any calm, gradual feeling or experience, one step below their place,—the very highest; but I think them better conveyed at less length, and chiefly as from oneself." Thus, he employed the ballad for his "narrative dramatic" poems and the sonnet for his "personal emotion."

THE BLESSED DAMOZEL°

The blessed damozel leaned out
  From the gold bar of heaven;
Her eyes were deeper than the depth

Of waters stilled at even;
She had three lilies in her hand,
  And the stars in her hair were seven.

Her robe, ungirth from clasp to hem,
  No wrought flowers did adorn,
But a white rose of Mary's gift,
  For service meetly worn;°   10
Her hair that lay along her back
  Was yellow like ripe corn.

Herseemed° she scarce had been a day
  One of God's choristers;
The wonder was not yet quite gone
  From that still look of hers;
Albeit, to them she left, her day
  Had counted as ten years.

(To *one* it is ten years of years.
  . . . Yet now, and in this place,   20
Surely she leaned o'er me—her hair
  Fell all about my face. . . .
Nothing: the autumn fall of leaves.
  The whole year sets apace.)

It was the rampart of God's house
  That she was standing on;
By God built over the sheer depth
  The which is Space begun;
So high, that looking downward thence
  She scarce could see the sun.   30

It lies in heaven, across the flood
  Of ether, as a bridge.
Beneath, the tides of day and night
  With flame and darkness ridge
The void, as low as where this earth
  Spins like a fretful midge.°

Around her, lovers, newly met
  'Mid deathless love's acclaims,
Spoke evermore among themselves
  Their heart-remembered names;
And the souls mounting up to God   40
  Went by her like thin flames.

And still she bowed herself and stooped
  Out of the circling charm;
Until her bosom must have made
  The bar she leaned on warm,
And the lilies lay as if asleep
  Along her bended arm.

From the fixed place of heaven she saw
  Time like a pulse shake fierce   50
Through all the worlds. Her gaze still strove

The Blessed Damozel. Rossetti designed this poem as a complement to Edgar Allan Poe's *The Raven* (1845), which represents a lover yearning hopelessly for "a sainted maiden whom the angels name Lenore." "I saw," he said, "that Poe had done the utmost it was possible to do with the grief of the lover on earth, and so I determined to reverse the conditions, and give utterance to the yearning of the loved one in heaven"

10 **For . . . worn,** fittingly worn in the service of the Virgin Mary   13 **Herseemed,** it seemed to her   36 **midge,** a kind of small gnat

Within the gulf to pierce
Its path; and now she spoke as when
   The stars sang in their spheres.

The sun was gone now; the curled moon
   Was like a little feather
Fluttering far down the gulf; and now
   She spoke through the still weather.
Her voice was like the voice the stars
60   Had when they sang together.

(Ah, sweet! Even now, in that bird's song,
   Strove not her accents there,
Fain to be harkened? When those bells
   Possessed the midday air,
Strove not her steps to reach my side
   Down all the echoing stair?)

"I wish that he were come to me,
   For he will come," she said.
"Have I not prayed in heaven?—on earth,
70   Lord, Lord, has he not prayed?
Are not two prayers a perfect strength?
   And shall I feel afraid?

"When round his head the aureole clings,
   And he is clothed in white,
I'll take his hand and go with him
   To the deep wells of light;
As unto a stream we will step down,
   And bathe there in God's sight.

"We two will stand beside that shrine,
80   Occult, withheld, untrod,
Whose lamps are stirred continually
   With prayers sent up to God;
And see our old prayers, granted, melt
   Each like a little cloud.

"We two will lie i' the shadow of
   That living mystic tree°
Within whose secret growth the Dove°
   Is sometimes felt to be,
While every leaf that His plumes touch
90   Saith His Name audibly.

"And I myself will teach to him,
   I myself, lying so,
The songs I sing here; which his voice
   Shall pause in, hushed and slow,
And find some knowledge at each pause,
   Or some new thing to know."

(Alas! We two, we two, thou say'st!
   Yea, one wast thou with me
That once of old. But shall God lift

To endless unity   100
The soul whose likeness with thy soul
   Was but its love for thee?)

"We two," she said, "will seek the groves
   Where the lady Mary is,
With her five handmaidens, whose names
   Are five sweet symphonies,
Cecily, Gertrude, Magdalen,
   Margaret, and Rosalys.°

"Circlewise sit they, with bound locks
   And foreheads garlanded;   110
Into the fine cloth white like flame
   Weaving the golden thread,
To fashion the birth-robes for them
   Who are just born, being dead.

"He shall fear, haply, and be dumb;
   Then will I lay my cheek
To his, and tell about our love,
   Not once abashed or weak;
And the dear Mother will approve
   My pride, and let me speak.   120

"Herself shall bring us, hand in hand,
   To Him round whom all souls
Kneel, the clear-ranged unnumbered heads
   Bowed with their aureoles;
And angels meeting us shall sing
   To their citherns and citoles.°

"There will I ask of Christ the Lord
   Thus much for him and me—
Only to live as once on earth
   With Love, only to be,   130
As then awhile, forever now,
   Together, I and he."

She gazed and listened and then said,
   Less sad of speech than mild—
"All this is when he comes." She ceased.
   The light thrilled toward her, filled
With angels in strong, level flight.
   Her eyes prayed, and she smiled.

(I saw her smile.) But soon their path
   Was vague in distant spheres;   140
And then she cast her arms along
   The golden barriers,
And laid her face between her hands,
   And wept. (I heard her tears.)
(1847; 1850, 1856, 1870)

---

86 **living . . . tree,** the tree of life (see *Revelation,* 22) 87 **Dove,** a symbol of the Holy Spirit, the third member of the Trinity; cf. *Luke,* 3:22

107–108 **Cecily . . . Rosalys.** These are names of famous Christian saints. *St. Cecilia* (third century) is the patron saint of the blind and of musicians; *St. Gertrude* (seventh century) is the patron saint of travelers; *St. Mary Magdalen* is the patron saint of penitents; *St. Margaret* (third century) is the chosen type of female innocence and meekness; *St. Rosalie* (twelfth century) is the patron saint of the city of Palermo, Sicily 126 **citherns and citoles,** medieval stringed musical instruments

JENNY°

Vengeance of Jenny's case! Fie on her! Never name
her child!—(Mrs. Quickly.)°

Lazy laughing languid Jenny,
Fond of a kiss and fond of a guinea,
Whose head upon my knee to-night
Rests for a while, as if grown light
With all our dances and the sound
To which the wild tunes spun you round:
Fair Jenny mine, the thoughtless queen
Of kisses which the blush between
Could hardly make much daintier;
10 Whose eyes are as blue skies, whose hair
Is countless gold incomparable:
Fresh flower, scarce touched with signs that tell
Of Love's exuberant hotbed:—Nay,
Poor flower left torn since yesterday
Until to-morrow leave you bare;
Poor handful of bright spring-water
Flung in the whirlpool's° shrieking face;
Poor shameful Jenny, full of grace
Thus with your head upon my knee;—
20 Whose person or whose purse may be
The lodestar of your reverie?

This room of yours, my Jenny, looks
A change from mine so full of books,
Whose serried ranks hold fast, forsooth,
So many captive hours of youth,—
The hours they thieve from day and night
To make one's cherished work come right,
And leave it wrong for all their theft,
Even as to-night my work was left:
30 Until I vowed that since my brain
And eyes of dancing° seemed so fain,
My feet should have some dancing too:—
And thus it was I met with you.
Well, I suppose 'twas hard to part,
For here I am. And now, sweetheart,
You seem too tired to get to bed.

It was a careless life I led
When rooms like this were scarce so strange
Not long ago. What breeds the change,—
40 The many aims or the few years?
Because to-night it all appears
Something I do not know again.

The cloud's not danced out of my brain,—
The cloud that made it turn and swim
While hour by hour the books grew dim.
Why, Jenny, as I watch you there,—
For all your wealth of loosened hair,
Your silk ungirdled and unlac'd
And warm sweets° open to the waist,
All golden in the lamplight's gleam,— 50
You know not what a book you seem,
Half-read by lightning in a dream!
How should you know, my Jenny? Nay,
And I should be ashamed to say:—
Poor beauty, so well worth a kiss!
But while my thought runs on like this
With wasteful whims more than enough,
I wonder what you're thinking of.

If of myself you think at all,
What is the thought?—conjectural 60
On sorry matters best unsolved?—
Or inly is each grace revolved
To fit me with a lure?—or (sad
To think!) perhaps you're merely glad
That I'm not drunk or ruffianly
And let you rest upon my knee.

For sometimes, were the truth confess'd,
You're thankful for a little rest,—
Glad from the crush to rest within,
From the heart-sickness and the din 70
Where envy's voice at virtue's pitch
Mocks you because your gown is rich;
And from the pale girl's dumb rebuke,
Whose ill-clad grace and toil-worn look
Proclaim the strength that keeps her weak,°
And other nights than yours bespeak;
And from the wise unchildish elf,
To schoolmate lesser than himself
Pointing you out, what thing you are:—
Yes, from the daily jeer and jar, 80
From shame and shame's outbraving too,
Is rest not sometimes sweet to you?—
But most from the hatefulness of man,
Who spares not to end what he began,
Whose acts are ill and his speech ill,
Who, having used you at his will,
Thrusts you aside, as when I dine
I serve the dishes and the wine.

Well, handsome Jenny mine, sit up:
I've filled our glasses, let us sup, 90
And do not let me think of you,
Lest shame of yours suffice for two.
What, still so tired? Well, well then, keep
Your head there, so you do not sleep;
But that the weariness may pass

Jenny. One of Rossetti's most famous and controversial ballads was the poem
Jenny. The reviewers of his day singled out this poem for abuse, an abuse which
Rossetti himself had predicted. He said of the poem: "there are a few things—and
notably a poem called *Jenny*—which will raise objection in some quarters. I only
know that they have been written neither recklessly nor aggressively (moods
which I think are sure to result in the ruin of Art), but from a true impulse to deal
with subjects which seem to me capable of being brought rightly within Art's
province. Of my own position I feel sure, and so wait the final result without apprehension." *Jenny* is the furthest Rossetti ever went in the poetry of social criticism   **Vengeance . . . child.** See *The Merry Wives of Windsor*, IV, i, 61
17 **whirlpool,** of vice   30–31 **brain . . . dancing,** i.e., from overwork

49 **sweets,** breasts   75 **strength . . . weak.** Her strength (virtue) restricts her to a
life of hard work and poor food, which keeps her weak

And leave you merry, take this glass,
Ah! lazy lily hand, more bless'd
If ne'er in rings it had been dress'd
Nor ever by a glove conceal'd!

100   Behold the lilies of the field,
They toil not neither do they spin;
(So doth the ancient text° begin,—
Not of such rest as one of these
Can share.) Another rest and ease
Along each summer-sated path
From its new lord the garden hath,
Than that whose spring in blessings ran
Which praised the bounteous husbandman,
Ere yet, in days of hankering breath,
110 The lilies sickened unto death.

    What, Jenny, are your lilies dead?
Aye, and the snow-white leaves are spread
Like winter on the garden-bed.
But you had roses left in May,—
They were not gone too. Jenny, nay,
But must your roses die, and those
Their purfled buds that should unclose?
Even so; the leaves are curled apart,
Still red as from the broken heart,
120 And here's the naked stem of thorns.

    Nay, nay, mere words. Here nothing warns
As yet of winter. Sickness here
Or want alone could waken fear,—
Nothing but passion wrings a tear.
Except when there may rise unsought
Haply at times a passing thought
Of the old days which seem to be
Much older than any history
That is written in any book;
130 When she would lie in fields and look
Along the ground through the blown grass,
And wonder where the city was,
Far out of sight, whose broil and bale
They told her then for a child's tale.

    Jenny, you know the city now.
A child can tell the tale there, how
Some things which are not yet enroll'd
In market-lists are bought and sold
Even till the early Sunday light,
140 When Saturday night is market-night
Everywhere, be it dry or wet,
And market-night in the Haymarket.°
Our learned London children know,
Poor Jenny, all your pride and woe;
Have seen your lifted silken skirt
Advertise dainties through the dirt;
Have seen your coach-wheels splash rebuke

On virtue; and have learned your look
When, wealth and health slipped past, you stare
Along the streets alone, and there,   150
Round the long park, across the bridge,
The cold lamps at the pavement's edge
Wind on together and apart,
A fiery serpent for your heart.

    Let the thoughts pass, an empty cloud!
Suppose I were to think aloud,—
What if to her all this were said?
Why, as a volume seldom read
Being opened halfway shuts again,
So might the pages of her brain   160
Be parted at such words, and thence
Close back upon the dusty sense.
For is there hue or shape defin'd
In Jenny's desecrated mind,
Where all contagious currents meet,
A Lethe of the middle street?°
Nay, it reflects not any face,
Nor sound is in its sluggish pace,
But as they coil those eddies clot,
And night and day remember not.   170

    Why, Jenny, you're asleep at last!
Asleep, poor Jenny, hard and fast,—
So young and soft and tired; so fair,
With chin thus nestled in your hair,
Mouth quiet, eyelids almost blue
As if some sky of dreams shone through!

    Just as another woman sleeps!
Enough to throw one's thoughts in heaps
Of doubt and horror,—what to say
Or think,—this awful secret sway,   180
The potter's power over the clay!
Of the same lump (it has been said)
For honour and dishonour made,
Two sister vessels. Here is one.

    My cousin Nell is fond of fun,
And fond of dress, and change, and praise,
So mere a woman in her ways:
And if her sweet eyes rich in youth
Are like her lips that tell the truth,
My cousin Nell is fond of love.   190
And she's the girl I'm proudest of.
Who does not prize her, guard her well?
The love of change, in cousin Nell,
Shall find the best and hold it dear:
The unconquered mirth turn quieter
Not through her own, through others' woe:
The conscious pride of beauty glow
Beside another's pride in her,
One little part of all they share.

200 For Love himself shall ripen these
In a kind soil to just increase
Through years of fertilising peace.

Of the same lump (as it is said)
For honour and dishonour made,
Two sister vessels. Here is one.

It makes a goblin of the sun.

So pure,—so fall'n! How dare to think
Of the first common kindred link?
Yet, Jenny, till the world shall burn
210 It seems that all things take their turn;
And who shall say but this fair tree
May need, in changes that may be,
Your children's children's charity?
Scorned then, no doubt, as you are scorn'd!
Shall no man hold his pride forewarn'd
Till in the end, the Day of Days,
At Judgment, one of his own race,
As frail and lost as you, shall rise,—
His daughter, with his mother's eyes?

220 How Jenny's clock ticks on the shelf!
Might not the dial scorn itself
That has such hours to register?
Yet as to me, even so to her
Are golden sun and silver moon,
In daily largesse of earth's boon,
Counted for life-coins to one tune.
And if, as blindfold fates are toss'd,
Through some one man this life be lost,
Shall soul not somehow pay for soul?

230 Fair shines the gilded aureole
In which our highest painters place
Some living woman's simple face.
And the stilled features thus descried
As Jenny's long throat droops aside,—
The shadows where the cheeks are thin,
And pure wide curve from ear to chin,—
With Raffael's, Leonardo's hand
To show them to men's souls, might stand,
Whole ages long, the whole world through,
240 For preachings of what God can do.
What has man done here? How atone,
Great God, for this which man has done?
And for the body and soul which by
Man's pitiless doom must now comply
With lifelong hell, what lullaby
Of sweet forgetful second birth
Remains? All dark. No sign on earth
What measure of God's rest endows
The many mansions of His house.

250 If but a woman's heart might see
Such erring heart unerringly

For once! But that can never be.

Like a rose shut in a book
In which pure women may not look,
For its base pages claim control
To crush the flower within the soul;
Where through each dead rose-leaf that clings,
Pale as transparent Psyche-wings,°
To the vile text, are traced such things
As might make lady's cheek indeed   260
More than a living rose to read;
So nought save foolish foulness may
Watch with hard eyes the sure decay;
And so the life-blood of this rose,
Puddled with shameful knowledge, flows
Through leaves no chaste hand may unclose:
Yet still it keeps such faded show
Of when 't was gathered long ago,
That the crushed petals' lovely grain,
The sweetness of the sanguine stain,   270
Seen of a woman's eyes, must make
Her pitiful heart, so prone to ache,
Love roses better for its sake:—
Only that this can never be:—
Even so unto her sex is she.

Yet, Jenny, looking long at you,
The woman almost fades from view.
A cipher of man's changeless sum
Of lust, past, present, and to come,
Is left. A riddle that one shrinks   280
To challenge from the scornful sphinx.

Like a toad within a stone°
Seated while Time crumbles on;
Which sits there since the earth was curs'd
For Man's transgression at the first;
Which, living through all centuries,
Not once has seen the sun arise;
Whose life, to its cold circle charmed,
The earth's whole summers have not warmed;
Which always—whitherso the stone   290
Be flung—sits there, dead, blind, alone;—
Aye, and shall not be driven out
Till that which shuts him round about
Break at the very Master's stroke,
And the dust thereof vanish as smoke,
And the seed of Man vanish as dust:—
Even so within this world is Lust.

Come, come, what use in thoughts like this?
Poor little Jenny, good to kiss,—
You'd not believe by what strange roads   300
Thought travels, when your beauty goads
A man to-night to think of toads!
Jenny, wake up . . . Why, there's the dawn!

258 **Psyche-wings,** moth wings, but also an allusion to the soul 282 **toad . . . stone,** fossil

And there's an early waggon drawn
To market, and some sheep that jog
Bleating before a barking dog;
And the old streets come peering through
Another night that London knew;
And all as ghostlike as the lamps.

310 So on the wings of day decamps
My last night's frolic. Glooms begin
To shiver off as lights creep in
Past the gauze curtains half drawn-to,
And the lamp's doubled shade grows blue,—
Your lamp, my Jenny, kept alight,
Like a wise virgin's, all one night!
And in the alcove coolly spread
Glimmers with dawn your empty bed;
And yonder your fair face I see
320 Reflected lying on my knee,
Where teems with first foreshadowings
Your pier-glass scrawled with diamond rings:°
And on your bosom all night worn
Yesterday's rose now droops forlorn,
But dies not yet this summer morn.

And now without, as if some word
Had called upon them that they heard,
The London sparrows far and nigh
Clamour together suddenly;
330 And Jenny's cage-bird grown awake
Here in their song his part must take,
Because here too the day doth break.

And somehow in myself the dawn
Among stirred clouds and veils withdrawn
Strikes greyly on her. Let her sleep.
But will it wake her if I heap
These cushions thus beneath her head
Where my knee was? No,—there's your bed,
My Jenny, while you dream. And there
340 I lay among your golden hair
Perhaps the subject of your dreams,
These golden coins.
                    For still one deems
That Jenny's flattering sleep confers
New magic on the magic purse,—
Grim web, how clogged with shrivelled flies!
Between the threads fine fumes arise
And shape their pictures in the brain.
There roll no streets in glare and rain,
Nor flagrant man-swine whets his tusk;
350 But delicately sighs in musk
The homage of the dim boudoir;
Or like a palpitating star
Thrilled into song, the opera-night
Breathes faint in the quick pulse of light;
Or at the carriage-window shine

Rich wares for choice; or, free to dine,
Whirls through its hour of health (divine
For her) the concourse of the Park.
And though in the discounted dark
Her functions there and here are one,   360
Beneath the lamps and in the sun
There reigns at least the acknowledged belle
Apparelled beyond parallel.
Ah Jenny, yes, we know your dreams.

For even the Paphian Venus° seems
A goddess o'er the realms of love,
When silver-shrined in shadowy grove:
Aye, or let offerings nicely plac'd
But hide Priapus° to the waist,
And whoso looks on him shall see   370
An eligible deity.

Why, Jenny, waking here alone
May help you to remember one,
Though all the memory's long outworn
Of many a double-pillowed morn.
I think I see you when you wake,
And rub your eyes for me, and shake
My gold, in rising, from your hair,
A Danaë° for a moment there.

Jenny, my love rang true! for still   380
Love at first sight is vague, until
That tinkling makes him audible.

And must I mock you to the last,
Ashamed of my own shame,—aghast
Because some thoughts not born amiss
Rose at a poor fair face like this?
Well, of such thoughts so much I know:
In my life, as in hers, they show,
By a far gleam which I may near,
A dark path I can strive to clear.   390

Only one kiss. Good-bye, my dear.
(1848; 1870)

SISTER HELEN

"Why did you melt your waxen man,
                    Sister Helen?
Today is the third since you began."
"The time was long, yet the time ran,
                    Little brother."
          (O Mother, Mary Mother,
Three days today, between Hell and Heaven!)

"But if you have done your work aright,

---

322 **scrawled . . . rings.** Her lovers scratched their names on her mirror

365 **Paphian Venus.** Venus was said to have appeared from the foam at Paphos on the island of Crete, where she reigned over erotic rites   369 **Priapus,** personification of lust   379 **Danaë,** the daughter of the king of the Argos who was seduced by Zeus; he appeared to her in a golden shower

Sister Helen,
10 You'll let me play, for you said I might."
"Be very still in your play tonight,
        Little brother."
    (O Mother, Mary Mother,
Third night, tonight, between Hell and Heaven!)

"You said it must melt ere vesper-bell,
        Sister Helen;
If now it be molten, all is well."
"Even so—nay, peace! you cannot tell,
        Little brother."
20 (O Mother, Mary Mother,
Oh, what is this, between Hell and Heaven?)

"Oh, the waxen knave was plump today,
        Sister Helen;
How like dead folk he has dropped away!"
"Nay now, of the dead what can you say,
        Little brother?"
    (O Mother, Mary Mother,
What of the dead, between Hell and Heaven?)

"See, see, the sunken pile of wood,
30   Sister Helen,
Shines through the thinned wax red as blood!"
"Nay now, when looked you yet on blood,
        Little brother?"
    (O Mother, Mary Mother,
How pale she is, between Hell and Heaven!)

"Now close your eyes, for they're sick and sore,
        Sister Helen,
And I'll play without the gallery door."
"Aye, let me rest—I'll lie on the floor,
40   Little brother."
    (O Mother, Mary Mother,
What rest tonight, between Hell and Heaven?)

"Here high up in the balcony,
        Sister Helen,
The moon flies face to face with me."
"Aye, look and say whatever you see,
        Little brother."
    (O Mother, Mary Mother,
What sight tonight, between Hell and Heaven?)

50 "Outside it's merry in the wind's wake,
        Sister Helen;
In the shaken trees the chill stars shake."
"Hush, heard you a horse-tread as you spake,
        Little brother?"
    (O Mother, Mary Mother,
What sound tonight, between Hell and Heaven?)

"I hear a horse-tread, and I see,
        Sister Helen,
Three horsemen that ride terribly."

"Little brother, whence come the three,   60
        Little brother?"
    (O Mother, Mary Mother,
Whence should they come, between Hell and
    Heaven?)

"They come by the hill-verge from Boyne Bar,°
        Sister Helen,
And one draws nigh, but two are afar."
"Look, look, do you know them who they are,
        Little brother?"
    (O Mother, Mary Mother,
Who should they be, between Hell and Heaven?)   70

"Oh, it's Keith of Eastholm rides so fast,
        Sister Helen,
For I know the white mane on the blast."
"The hour has come, has come at last,
        Little brother!"
    (O Mother, Mary Mother,
Her hour at last, between Hell and Heaven!)

"He has made a sign and called Halloo!
        Sister Helen,
And he says that he would speak with you."   80
"Oh, tell him I fear the frozen dew,
        Little brother."
    (O Mother, Mary Mother,
Why laughs she thus, between Hell and Heaven?)

"The wind is loud, but I hear him cry,
        Sister Helen,
That Keith of Ewern's like to die."
"And he and thou, and thou and I,
        Little brother."
    (O Mother, Mary Mother,   90
And they and we, between Hell and Heaven!)

"Three days ago, on his marriage-morn,
        Sister Helen,
He sickened, and lies since then forlorn."
"For bridegroom's side is the bride a thorn,
        Little brother?"
    (O Mother, Mary Mother,
Cold bridal cheer, between Hell and Heaven!)

"Three days and nights now he has lain abed,
        Sister Helen,   100
And he prays in torment to be dead."
"The thing may chance, if he have prayed,
        Little brother!"
    (O Mother, Mary Mother,
If he have prayed, between Hell and Heaven!)

"But he has not ceased to cry today,
        Sister Helen,

Sister Helen   64 **Boyne Bar,** a famous sand bar at the mouth of the Boyne River, Leinster, Ireland

That you should take your curse away."
"*My* prayer was heard—he need but pray,
    Little brother!"
110
   (O Mother, Mary Mother,
Shall God not hear, between Hell and Heaven?)

"But he says, till you take back your ban,
    Sister Helen,
His soul would pass, yet never can."
"Nay then, shall I slay a living man,
    Little brother?"
   (O Mother, Mary Mother,
A living soul between Hell and Heaven!)

120 "But he calls forever on your name,
    Sister Helen,
And says that he melts before a flame."
"My heart for his pleasure fared the same,
    Little brother."
   (O Mother, Mary Mother,
Fire at the heart, between Hell and Heaven!)

"Here's Keith of Westholm riding fast,
    Sister Helen,
For I know the white plume on the blast."
130 "The hour, the sweet hour I forecast,
    Little brother!"
   (O Mother, Mary Mother,
Is the hour sweet, between Hell and Heaven!)

"He stops to speak, and he stills his horse,
    Sister Helen;
But his words are drowned in the wind's course."
"Nay hear, nay hear, you must hear perforce,
    Little brother!"
   (O Mother, Mary Mother,
140 *What word now heard, between Hell and Heaven!)*

"Oh, he says that Keith of Ewern's cry,
    Sister Helen,
Is ever to see you ere he die."
"In all that his soul sees, there am I,
    Little brother!"
   (O Mother, Mary Mother,
The soul's one sight, between Hell and Heaven!)

"He sends a ring and a broken coin,°
    Sister Helen,
150 And bids you mind the banks of Boyne."
"What else he broke will he ever join,
    Little brother?"
   (O Mother, Mary Mother,
No, never joined, between Hell and Heaven!)

"He yields you these and craves full fain,
    Sister Helen,

148 **broken coin.** The two had broken a coin, and each had kept half as a pledge

You pardon him in his mortal pain."
"What else he took will he give again,
    Little brother?"
   (O Mother, Mary Mother,   160
Not twice to give, between Hell and Heaven!)

"He calls your name in an agony,
    Sister Helen,
That even dead Love must weep to see."
"Hate, born of Love, is blind as he,
    Little brother!"
   (O Mother, Mary Mother,
Love turned to hate, between Hell and Heaven!)

"Oh, it's Keith of Keith now that rides fast,
    Sister Helen,   170
For I know the white hair on the blast."
"The short, short hour will soon be past,
    Little brother!"
   (O Mother, Mary Mother,
Will soon be past, between Hell and Heaven!)

"He looks at me and he tries to speak,
    Sister Helen,
But oh! his voice is sad and weak!"
"What here should the mighty Baron seek,
    Little brother?"   180
   (O Mother, Mary Mother,
Is this the end, between Hell and Heaven?)

"Oh! his son still cries, if you forgive,
    Sister Helen,
The body dies, but the soul shall live."
"Fire shall forgive me as I forgive,
    Little brother!"
   (O Mother, Mary Mother,
As she forgives, between Hell and Heaven!)

"Oh, he prays you, as his heart would rive,   190
    Sister Helen,
To save his dear son's soul alive."
"Fire cannot slay it; it shall thrive,
    Little brother!"
   (O Mother, Mary Mother,
Alas, alas, between Hell and Heaven!)

"He cries to you, kneeling in the road,
    Sister Helen,
To go with him for the love of God!"
"The way is long to his son's abode,   200
    Little brother."
   (O Mother, Mary Mother,
The way is long, between Hell and Heaven!)

"A lady's here, by a dark steed brought,
    Sister Helen,
So darkly clad, I saw her not."
"See her now or never see aught,

Little brother!''
(O Mother, Mary Mother,
210 *What more to see, between Hell and Heaven!)*

"Her hood falls back, and the moon shines fair,
                    Sister Helen,
On the Lady of Ewern's golden hair."
"Blest hour of my power and her despair,
                    Little brother!"
(O Mother, Mary Mother,
Hour blest and banned, between Hell and Heaven!)

"Pale, pale her cheeks, that in pride did glow,
                    Sister Helen,
220 'Neath the bridal-wreath three days ago."
"One morn for pride and three days for woe,
                    Little brother!"
(O Mother, Mary Mother,
Three days, three nights, between Hell and Heaven!)

"Her clasped hands stretch from her bending head,
                    Sister Helen;
With the loud wind's wail her sobs are wed."
"What wedding-strains hath her bridal-bed,
                    Little brother?"
230   *(O Mother, Mary Mother,*
What strain but death's, between Hell and Heaven!)

"She may not speak, she sinks in a swoon,
                    Sister Helen—
She lifts her lips and gasps on the moon."
"Oh! might I but hear her soul's blithe tune,
                    Little brother!"
(O Mother, Mary Mother,
Her woe's dumb cry, between Hell and Heaven!)

"They've caught her to Westholm's saddle-bow,
240   Sister Helen,
And her moonlit hair gleams white in its flow."
"Let it turn whiter than winter snow,
                    Little brother!"
(O Mother, Mary Mother,
Woe-withered gold, between Hell and Heaven!)

"O Sister Helen, you heard the bell,
                    Sister Helen!
More loud than the vesper-chime it fell."
"No vesper-chime, but a dying knell,
250   Little brother!"
(O Mother, Mary Mother,
His dying knell, between Hell and Heaven!)

"Alas! but I fear the heavy sound,
                    Sister Helen;
Is it in the sky or in the ground?"

"Say, have they turned their horses round,
                    Little brother?"
(O Mother, Mary Mother,
What would she more, between Hell and Heaven?)

"They have raised the old man from his knee,   260
                    Sister Helen,
And they ride in silence hastily."
"More fast the naked soul doth flee,
                    Little brother!"
(O Mother, Mary Mother,
The naked soul, between Hell and Heaven!)

"Flank to flank are the three steeds gone,
                    Sister Helen,
But the lady's dark steed goes alone."
"And lonely her bridegroom's soul hath flown,   270
                    Little brother."
(O Mother, Mary Mother,
The lonely ghost, between Hell and Heaven!)

"Oh, the wind is sad in the iron chill,
                    Sister Helen,
And weary sad they look by the hill."
"But Keith of Ewern's sadder still,
                    Little brother!"
(O Mother, Mary Mother,
Most sad of all, between Hell and Heaven!)   280

"See, see, the wax has dropped from its place,
                    Sister Helen,
And the flames are winning up apace!"
"Yet here they burn but for a space,
                    Little brother!"
(O Mother, Mary Mother,
Here for a space, between Hell and Heaven!)

"Ah! what white thing at the door has crossed,
                    Sister Helen?
Ah! what is this that sighs in the frost?"   290
"A soul that's lost as mine is lost,
                    Little brother!"
(O Mother, Mary Mother,
Lost, lost, all lost, between Hell and Heaven!)
(1851–1852; 1853, 1870)

THE WOODSPURGE

The wind flapped loose, the wind was still,
Shaken out dead from tree and hill:
I had walked on at the wind's will,—
I sat now, for the wind was still.

5 Between my knees my forehead was,—
  My lips, drawn in, said not Alas!
  My hair was over in the grass,
  My naked ears heard the day pass.

  My eyes, wide open, had the run
10 Of some ten weeds to fix upon;
  Among those few, out of the sun,
  The woodspurge flowered, three cups in one.

  From perfect grief there need not be
  Wisdom or even memory:
15 One thing then learnt remains to me,—
  The woodspurge has a cup of three.
  (1856; 1870)

from **THE HOUSE OF LIFE°**

THE SONNET

A sonnet is a moment's monument—
Memorial from the Soul's eternity
To one dead deathless hour. Look that it be,
Whether for lustral rite° or dire portent,
5 *Of its own arduous fullness reverent.*
Carve it in ivory or in ebony,
As Day or Night may rule; and let Time see
Its flowering crest impearled and orient.
A sonnet is a coin; its face reveals
10 *The Soul—its converse, to what Power 'tis due:—*
Whether for tribute to the august appeals
Of Life, or dower in Love's high retinue,
It serve; or 'mid the dark wharf's cavernous breath,
In Charon's palm it pay the toll to Death.°

2. BRIDAL BIRTH

As when desire, long darkling, dawns, and first
  The mother looks upon the newborn child,
  Even so my Lady stood at gaze and smiled
When her soul knew at length the Love it nurs'd.
5 Born with her life, creature of poignant thirst
  And exquisite hunger, at her heart Love lay
  Quickening in darkness, till a voice that day
Cried on him, and the bonds of birth were burst.

Now, shadowed by his wings, our faces yearn
  Together, as his full-grown feet now range   10
    The grove, and his warm hands our couch pre-
     pare:
Till to his song our bodiless souls in turn
  Be born his children, when Death's nuptial change
  Leaves us for light the halo of his hair.

6. THE KISS

What smouldering senses in death's sick delay
  Or seizure of malign vicissitude
  Can rob this body of honor, or denude
This soul of wedding-raiment worn to-day?
For lo! even now my lady's lips did play   5
  With these my lips such consonant interlude
  As laurelled Orpheus longed for when he wooed
The half-drawn hungering face with that last lay.°

I was a child beneath her touch,—a man
  When breast to breast we clung, even I and she,—   10
  A spirit when her spirit looked through me,—
A god when all our life-breath met to fan
Our life-blood, till love's emulous ardors ran,
  Fire within fire, desire in deity.

6a. NUPTIAL SLEEP

At length their long kiss severed, with sweet smart:
  And as the last slow sudden drops are shed
  From sparkling eaves when all the storm has fled,
So singly flagged the pulses of each heart.
Their bosoms sundered, with the opening start   5
  Of married flowers to either side outspread
  From the knit stem; yet still their mouths, burnt red,
Fawned on each other where they lay apart.

Sleep sank them lower than the tide of dreams,
  And their dreams watched them sink, and slid away.   10
Slowly their souls swam up again, through gleams
  Of watered light and dull drowned waifs of day;
Till from some wonder of new woods and streams
  He woke, and wondered more: for there she lay.

18. GENIUS IN BEAUTY

Beauty like hers is genius. Not the call
Of Homer's or of Dante's heart sublime—
Not Michael's° hand furrowing the zones of time—

The House of Life. These sonnets were written during a period of thirty-three years—1848–1881. The title came from Rossetti's interest in astrology, according to which the heavens were regarded as divided into "houses," the most important of which was the "house of human life" **The Sonnet** 4 **lustral rite,** ceremony of purification 14 **Charon's . . . Death.** Charon was the boatman who ferried the souls of the dead over the Styx, one of the rivers of Hades. His pay was a coin found in the mouth of the passenger

Sonnet 6 7–8 **Orpheus . . . last lay.** Orpheus had won his love, Eurydice, back from Hades by his music. He was granted the chance to regain Eurydice if he could refrain from looking at her until he had led her back to sunlight. Orpheus could not resist, and Eurydice vanished forever **Sonnet 18** 3 **Michael,** Michelangelo (1475–1564) celebrated Italian painter, sculptor, and architect. The reference is to his figures of "Day," "Evening," "Night," etc.

Is more with compassed mysteries musical;
5   Nay, not in Spring's or Summer's sweet footfall
More gathered gifts exuberant Life bequeathes
Than doth this sovereign face, whose love-spell
      breathes
Even from its shadowed contour on the wall.
As many men are poets in their youth,
10 But for one sweet-strung soul the wires prolong
Even through all change the indomitable song;
So in like wise the envenomed years, whose tooth
Rends shallower grace with ruin void of ruth,
Upon this beauty's power shall wreak no wrong.

19. SILENT NOON

Your hands lie open in the long, fresh grass—
The finger-points look through like rosy blooms;
Your eyes smile peace. The pasture gleams and
      glooms
'Neath billowing skies that scatter and amass.
5   All round our nest, far as the eye can pass,
Are golden kingcup-fields with silver edge
Where the cow-parsley skirts the hawthorn hedge.
'Tis visible silence, still as the hour-glass.
Deep in the sun-searched growths the dragon-fly
10 Hangs like a blue thread loosened from the sky—
So this winged hour is dropped to us from above.
Oh! clasp we to our hearts, for deathless dower,
This close-companioned inarticulate hour
When twofold silence was the song of love.

24. PRIDE OF YOUTH

Even as a child, of sorrow that we give
The dead, but little in his heart can find,
Since without need of thought to his clear mind
Their turn it is to die and his to live—
5   Even so the winged New Love smiles to receive
Along his eddying plumes the auroral wind,
Nor, foward glorying, casts one look behind
Where night-rack shrouds the Old Love fugitive.
There is a change in every hour's recall,
10 And the last cowslip in the fields we see
On the same day with the first corn-poppy.
Alas for hourly change! Alas for all
The loves that from his hand proud Youth lets fall,
Even as the beads of a told° rosary!

36. LIFE-IN-LOVE

Not in thy body is thy life at all,
   But in this lady's lips and hands and eyes;
   Through these she yields thee life that vivifies

Sonnet 24   14 **told,** counted

What else were sorrow's servant and death's thrall.
Look on thyself without her, and recall   5
   The waste remembrance and forlorn surmise
   That lived but in a dead-drawn breath of sighs
O'er vanished hours and hours eventual.

Even so much life hath the poor tress of hair
   Which, stored apart, is all love hath to show   10
   For heart-beats and for fire-heats long ago;
Even so much life endures unknown, even where,
'Mid change the changeless night environeth,
Lies all that golden hair undimmed in death.

49. WILLOWWOOD°   I

I sat with Love upon a woodside well,
   Leaning across the water, I and he;
   Nor ever did he speak nor looked at me,
But touched his lute wherein was audible
The certain secret thing he had to tell: 5
   Only our mirrored eyes met silently
   In the low wave; and that sound came to be
The passionate voice I knew; and my tears fell.

And at their fall, his eyes beneath grew hers;
And with his foot and with his wing-feathers   10
   He swept the spring that watered my heart's drouth
Then the dark ripples spread to waving hair,
And as I stooped, her own lips rising there
   Bubbled with brimming kisses at my mouth.

50. WILLOWWOOD   II

And now Love sang: but his was such a song
   So meshed with half-remembrance hard to free,
   As souls disused in death's sterility
May sing when the new birthday tarries long,
And I was made aware of a dumb throng   5
   That stood aloof, one form by every tree,
   All mournful forms, for each was I or she,
The shades of those our days that had no tongue.

They looked on us, and knew us and were known;
   While fast together, alive from the abyss,   10
   Clung the soul-wrung implacable close kiss;
And pity of self through all made broken moan
Which said, "For once, for once, for once alone!"
   And still Love sang, and what he sang was this:—

51. WILLOWWOOD   III

"O ye, all ye that walk in Willowwood,
   That walk with hollow faces burning white;
What fathom-depth of soul-struck widowhood,
   What long, what longer hours, one lifelong night,
Ere ye again, who so in vain have wooed   5

Sonnet 49. The willow symbolizes mourning. The title of this series of sonnets is poetical for "the woodland of weeping"

Your last hope lost, who so in vain invite
Your lips to that their unforgotten food,
  Ere ye, ere ye again shall see the light!

Alas! the bitter banks in Willowwood,
10 With tear-spurge wan, with blood-wort burning red:
Alas! if ever such a pillow could
  Steep deep the soul in sleep till she were dead,—
Better all life forget her than this thing,
That Willowwood should hold her wandering!"

53. WITHOUT HER

What of her glass without her? The blank gray
There where the pool is blind of the moon's face.
Her dress without her? The tossed empty space
Of cloud-rack whence the moon has passed away.
5 Her paths without her? Day's appointed sway
Usurped by desolate night. Her pillowed place
Without her? Tears, ah me! for love's good grace,
And cold forgetfulness of night or day.
What of the heart without her? Nay, poor heart,
10 Of thee what word remains ere speech be still?

A wayfarer by barren ways and chill,
Steep ways and weary, without her thou art,
Where the long cloud, the long wood's counterpart,
Sheds doubled darkness up the laboring hill.

101. THE ONE HOPE

When vain desire at last and vain regret
  Go hand in hand to death, and all is vain,
  What shall assuage the unforgotten pain
And teach the unforgetful to forget?
Shall Peace be still a sunk stream long unmet,—   5
  Or may the soul at once in a green plain
  Stoop through the spray of some sweet life-fountain
And cull the dew-drenched flowering amulet?

Ah, when the wan soul in that golden air
  Between the scriptured petals softly blown   10
  Peers breathless for the gift of grace unknown,—
Ah! let none other alien spell soe'er
But only the one Hope's one name be there,—
  Not less nor more, but even that word alone.
(1881)

CHRISTINA ROSSETTI
1830–1894

Christina Rossetti was Italian by parentage and English by environment. Her father, Gabriel Rossetti, was an Italian expatriate and scholar who settled in London in 1825 and married Frances Polidori, the daughter of an Italian father and English mother. The Rossettis had four children; Dante Gabriel was the eldest and Christina the youngest. Christina was somewhat eclipsed in her own time by her brilliant brother and by the group of painters and poets with whom she associated, but she wrote poetry that has given her a secure place in Victorian literature.

As a child, Christina remained quietly at home and received no education beyond what she acquired from her mother and from her own habit of diligent reading. But her girlhood was far from drab. Italian painters, musicians, and writers came to the Rossetti home; the Rossetti children thus had unusually strong contacts with literature and art. In addition, her brother's friendship with Ford Madox Brown, Holman Hunt, and other painters enabled her to sit as a model for all these young artists. They considered her an excellent model because her pale, sensitive features and dark hair characterized their ideal of female beauty. Most of the group wrote poetry, and this provided for her another link with them. Seven of her early lyrics ap-

peared in the Pre-Raphaelite magazine, The Germ, in 1850. After these poems were published, she maintained a long silence, shyly permitting her brother and his friends to eclipse her. In 1862, however, she published in one volume the poems that she had been writing since 1848. The book was entitled Goblin Market, and Other Poems and contains in the goblin story her most famous single poem and some of the best of her lyrics. Her devout Anglicanism and religious intensity twice prevented her marriage—once (1850) to James Collinson, who was associated with the Pre-Raphaelites and who became a Roman Catholic, and on another occasion (1864) to Charles Cayley, one of her father's pupils, whom she found not religious enough. A journey to Normandy in 1861 and one to Switzerland and Italy in 1865 were her sole excursions to the Continent. The year after her return from Italy, where, she said, "all was music," she published The Prince's Progress. In 1871 an almost fatal illness made her an invalid, and from then until her death in 1894 she saw few people and rarely ventured out except to attend the Anglican services in a neighboring church. In these trying years her naturally religious spirit deepened in intensity, and much of her work was devotional in subject and mood. Sing-Song, a collection of verse for children, appeared in 1872. *Annus Domini* (1874) was distinctly religious, and *A Pageant* (1881) largely so. *Time Flies* (1885) was a mixture of prose and verse; her last publication, *The Face of the Deep* (1892), revealed in its curious interpretation of the Apocalypse the persistent mysticism of her nature.

SONG°

When I am dead, my dearest,
 Sing no sad songs for me;
Plant thou no roses at my head,
 Nor shady cypress tree.°
5 Be the green grass above me
 With showers and dewdrops wet;
And if thou wilt, remember,
 And if thou wilt, forget.

I shall not see the shadows,
10 I shall not feel the rain;
I shall not hear the nightingale
 Sing on as if in pain.
And dreaming through the twilight
 That doth not rise nor set,
15 Haply I may remember,
 And haply may forget.
  (1848; 1862)

GOBLIN MARKET

The following remarks of William Michael Rossetti may help to explain the central theme of the poem:

"I have more than once heard Christina say that she did not mean anything profound by this fairy-tale—it is not a moral apologue consistently carried out in detail. Still the incidents are such as to be at any rate suggestive, and different minds may be likely to read different messages into them. I find at times that people do not see the central point of the story, such as the authoress intended it; and she has expressed it too, but perhaps not with due emphasis. The foundation of the narrative is this: That the goblins tempt women to eat their luscious but uncanny fruits; that a first taste produces a rabid craving for a second taste; but that the second taste is never accorded, and, in default of it, the woman pines away and dies. Then comes the central point: Laura having tasted the fruits once, and being at death's door through inability to get a second taste, her sister Lizzie determines to save her at all hazards; so she goes to the goblins, refuses to eat their fruits, and beguiles them into forcing the fruits upon her with so much insistency that her face is all smeared and steeped with the juices; she gets

Laura to kiss and suck these juices off her face, and Laura, having thus obtained the otherwise impossible second taste, rapidly recovers."

Morning and evening
Maids heard the goblins cry,
"Come buy our orchard fruits,
Come buy, come buy:
Apples and quinces,
Lemons and oranges,
Plump unpecked cherries,
Melons and raspberries,
Bloom-down-cheeked peaches,
Swart-headed mulberries,   10
Wild free-born cranberries,
Crab-apples, dewberries,
Pineapples, blackberries,
Apricots, strawberries—
All ripe together
In summer weather—
Morns that pass by,
Fair eves that fly;
Come buy, come buy:
Our grapes fresh from the vine,   20
Pomegranates full and fine,
Dates and sharp bullaces,°
Rare pears and greengages,°
Damsons° and bilberries,°
Taste them and try;
Currants and gooseberries,
Bright-fire-like barberries,
Figs to fill your mouth,
Citrons from the South,
Sweet to tongue and sound to eye;   30
Come buy, come buy."

Evening by evening
Among the brook-side rushes,
Laura bowed her head to hear,
Lizzie veiled her blushes;
Crouching close together
In the cooling weather,
With clasping arms and cautioning lips,
With tingling cheeks and finger tips.
"Lie close," Laura said,   40
Pricking up her golden head.
"We must not look at goblin men,
We must not buy their fruits;
Who knows upon what soil they fed
Their hungry thirsty roots?"
"Come buy," call the goblins
Hobbling down the glen.
"Oh," cried Lizzie, "Laura, Laura,
You should not peep at goblin men.
Lizzie covered up her eyes,   50

Song. Cf. Shakespeare's Sonnet 71 **4 cypress tree.** The cypress is a symbol of mourning; it is a common tree in graveyards

Goblin Market 22 **bullaces,** small European plums 23 **greengages,** greenish-yellow plums 24 **Damsons,** small dark-purple plums **bilberries,** whortleberries (similar to blueberries)

Covered close lest they should look;
Laura reared her glossy head,
And whispered like the restless brook:
"Look, Lizzie, look, Lizzie,
Down the glen tramp little men.
One hauls a basket,
One bears a plate,
One lugs a golden dish
Of many pounds' weight.
60 How fair the vine must grow
Whose grapes are so luscious!
How warm the wind must blow
Through those fruit bushes!"
"No," said Lizzie, "No, no, no;
Their offers should not charm us,
Their evil gifts would harm us."

She thrust a dimpled finger
In each ear, shut eyes and ran.
Curious Laura chose to linger,
70 Wondering at each merchant man.
One had a cat's face,
One whisked a tail,
One tramped at a rat's pace,
One crawled like a snail,
One like a wombat° prowled obtuse and furry,
One like a ratel° tumbled hurry-skurry.
She heard a voice like voice of doves
Cooing all together;
They sounded kind and full of loves
80 In the pleasant weather.

Laura stretched her gleaming neck
Like a rush-imbedded swan,
Like a lily from the beck,°
Like a moonlit poplar branch,
Like a vessel at the launch
When its last restraint is gone.

Backward up the mossy glen
Turned and trooped the goblin men,
With their shrill repeated cry,
90 "Come buy, come buy."
When they reached where Laura was,
They stood stock still upon the moss,
Leering at each other,
Brother with queer brother;
Signaling each other,
Brother with sly brother.
One set his basket down,
One reared his plate;
One began to weave a crown
100 Of tendrils, leaves, and rough nuts brown.
(Men sell not such in any town);
One heaved the golden weight

Of dish and fruit to offer her;
"Come buy, come buy" was still their cry.
Laura stared but did not stir,
Longed but had no money.
The whisk-tailed merchant bade her taste
In tones as smooth as honey,
The cat-faced purred,
The rat-paced spoke a word   110
Of welcome, and the snail-paced even was heard;
One parrot-voiced and jolly
Cried, "Pretty Goblin" still for "Pretty Polly";
One whistled like a bird.

But sweet-tooth Laura spoke in haste:
"Good folk, I have no coin;
To take were to purloin.
I have no copper in my purse,
I have no silver either,
And all my gold is on the furze   120
That shakes in windy weather
Above the rusty heather."
"You have much gold upon your head,"
They answered all together;
"Buy from us with a golden curl."
She clipped a precious golden lock,
She dropped a tear more rare than pearl,
Then sucked their fruit globes fair or red.
Sweeter than honey from the rock,
Stronger than man-rejoicing wine,   130
Clearer than water flowed that juice;
She never tasted such before,
How should it cloy with length of use?
She sucked and sucked and sucked the more
Fruits which that unknown orchard bore;
She sucked until her lips were sore;
Then flung the emptied rinds away,
But gathered up one kernel stone,
And knew not was it night or day
As she turned home alone.   140

Lizzie met her at the gate,
Full of wise upbraidings:
"Dear, you should not stay so late,
Twilight is not good for maidens;
Should not loiter in the glen
In the haunts of goblin men.
Do you not remember Jeanie,
How she met them in the moonlight,
Took their gifts both choice and many,
Ate their fruits and wore their flowers   150
Plucked from bowers
Where summer ripens at all hours?
But ever in the moonlight
She pined and pined away;
Sought them by night and day,
Found them no more, but dwindled and grew gray;
Then fell with the first snow,
While to this day no grass will grow

75 **wombat,** an animal native to Australia that looks like a small bear. It carries
its young in a pouch, like the kangaroo   76 **ratel,** a South African animal, like
the badger in size, form, and habits   83 **beck,** a small brook

Where she lies low;
160 I planted daisies there a year ago
That never blow.

You should not loiter so."
"Nay, hush," said Laura;
"Nay, hush, my sister.
I ate and ate my fill,
Yet my mouth waters still.
Tomorrow night I will
Buy more"; and kissed her.
"Have done with sorrow;
170 I'll bring you plums tomorrow
Fresh on their mother twigs,
Cherries worth getting;
You cannot think what figs
My teeth have met in,
What melons icy-cold
Piled on a dish of gold
Too huge for me to hold,
What peaches with a velvet nap,
Pellucid grapes without one seed.
180 Odorous indeed must be the mead
Whereon they grow, and pure the wave they drink
With lilies at the brink,
And sugar-sweet their sap."

Golden head by golden head,
Like two pigeons in one nest
Folded in each other's wings,
They lay down in their curtained bed;
Like two blossoms on one stem,
Like two flakes of new-fallen snow,
190 Like two wands of ivory
Tipped with gold for awful kings.
Moon and stars gazed in at them,
Winds sang to them lullaby,
Lumbering owls forebore to fly,
Not a bat flapped to and fro
Round their nest;
Cheek to cheek and breast to breast
Locked together in one nest.

Early in the morning
200 When the first cock crowed his warning,
Neat like bees, as sweet and busy,
Laura rose with Lizzie;
Fetched in honey, milked the cows,
Aired and set to rights the house,
Kneaded cakes of whitest wheat,
Cakes for dainty mouths to eat,
Next churned butter, whipped up cream,
Fed their poultry, sat and sewed;
Talked as modest maidens should—
210 Lizzie with an open heart,
Laura in an absent dream,
One content, one sick in part;

One warbling for the mere bright day's delight,
One longing for the night.

At length slow evening came.
They went with pitchers to the reedy brook;
Lizzie most placid in her look,
Laura most like a leaping flame.
They drew the gurgling water from its deep.
Lizzie plucked purple and rich golden flags,   220
Then turning homeward said: "The sunset flushes
Those furthest loftiest crags;
Come, Laura, not another maiden lags.
No willful squirrel wags;
The beasts and birds are fast asleep."

But Laura loitered still among the rushes,
And said the bank was steep,
And said the hour was early still,
The dew not fallen, the wind not chill;
Listening ever, but not catching   230
The customary cry,
"Come buy, come buy,"
With its iterated jingle
Of sugar-baited words;
Not for all her watching
Once discerning even one goblin
Racing, whisking, tumbling, hobbling—
Let alone the herds
That used to tramp along the glen,
In groups or single,   240
O brisk fruit-merchant men.

Till Lizzie urged, "O Laura, come;
I hear the fruit-call, but I dare not look.
You should not loiter longer at this brook;
Come with me home.
The stars rise, the moon bends her arc,
Each glowworm winks her spark.
Let us get home before the night grows dark,
For clouds may gather
Though this is summer weather,   250
Put out the lights and drench us through;
Then if we lost our way what should we do?"

Laura turned cold as stone
To find her sister heard that cry alone,
That goblin cry,
"Come buy our fruits, come buy."
Must she then buy no more such dainty fruit?
Must she no more such succous° pasture find,
Gone deaf and blind?
Her tree of life drooped from the root;   260
She said not one word in her heart's sore ache;
But peering through the dimness, naught discerning,
Trudged home, her pitcher dripping all the way;

258 **succous**, juicy

So crept to bed, and lay
Silent till Lizzie slept;
Then sat up in a passionate yearning,
And gnashed her teeth for balked desire, and wept
As if her heart would break.

Day after day, night after night,
270 Laura kept watch in vain
In sullen silence of exceeding pain.
She never caught again the goblin cry,
"Come buy, come buy";
She never spied the goblin men
Hawking their fruits along the glen.
But when the noon waxed bright
Her hair grew thin and gray;
She dwindled, as the fair full moon doth turn
To swift decay and burn
280 Her fire away.

One day, remembering her kernel-stone,
She set it by a wall that faced the south;
Dewed it with tears, hoped for a root,
Watched for a waxing shoot,
But there came none.
It never saw the sun,
It never felt the trickling moisture run;
While with sunk eyes and faded mouth
She dreamed of melons, as a traveler sees
290 False waves in desert drouth
With shade of leaf-crowned trees,
And burns the thirstier in the sandful breeze.

She no more swept the house,
Tended the fowls, or cows,
Fetched honey, kneaded cakes of wheat,
Brought water from the brook;
But sat down listless in the chimney-nook
And would not eat.

Tender Lizzie could not bear
300 To watch her sister's cankerous care,
Yet not to share.
She night and morning
Caught the goblins' cry:
"Come buy our orchard fruits,
Come buy, come buy."
Beside the brook, along the glen,
She heard the tramp of goblin men,
The voice and stir
Poor Laura could not hear;
310 Longed to buy fruit to comfort her,
But feared to pay too dear.
She thought of Jeanie in her grave,
Who should have been a bride;
But who for joys brides hope to have
Fell sick and died
In her gay prime,

In earliest winter time,
With the first glazing rime,
With the first snow-fall of crisp winter time.

Till Laura dwindling   320
Seemed knocking at Death's door.
Then Lizzie weighed no more
Better and worse;
But put a silver penny in her purse,
Kissed Laura, crossed the heath with clumps of furze
At twilight, halted by the brook,
And for the first time in her life
Began to listen and look.

Laughed every goblin
When they spied her peeping;   330
Came toward her hobbling,
Flying, running, leaping,
Puffing and blowing,
Chuckling, clapping, crowing,
Clucking and gobbling,
Mopping and mowing,
Full of airs and graces,
Pulling wry faces,
Demure grimaces,
Cat-like and rat-like   340
Ratel- and wombat-like,
Snail-paced in a hurry,
Parrot-voiced and whistler,
Helter-skelter, hurry-skurry,
Chattering like magpies,

Fluttering like pigeons,
Gliding like fishes—
Hugged her and kissed her,
Squeezed and caressed her,
Stretched up their dishes,   350
Panniers, and plates:
"Look at our apples
Russet and dun,
Bob at our cherries,
Bite at our peaches,
Citrons and dates,
Grapes for the asking,
Pears red with basking
Out in the sun,
Plums on their twigs;   360
Pluck them and suck them—
Pomegranates, figs."

"Good folk," said Lizzie,
Mindful of Jeanie,
"Give me much and many";
Held out her apron,
Tossed them her penny.
"Nay, take a seat with us,
Honor and eat with us,"

They answered, grinning;
"Our feast is but beginning.
Night yet is early,
Warm and dew-pearly,
Wakeful and starry.
Such fruits as these
No man can carry;
Half their bloom would fly,
Half their dew would dry,
Half their flavor would pass by.
Sit down and feast with us,
Be welcome guest with us,
Cheer you and rest with us."—
"Thank you," said Lizzie, "but one waits
At home alone for me;
So without further parleying,
If you will not sell me any
Of your fruits though much and many,
Give me back my silver penny
I tossed you for a fee."—
They began to scratch their pates,
No longer wagging, purring,
But visibly demurring,
Grunting and snarling.
One called her proud,
Cross-grained, uncivil;
Their tones waxed loud,
Their looks were evil.
Lashing their tails,
They trod and hustled her,
Elbowed and jostled her,
Clawed with their nails,
Barking, mewing, hissing, mocking,
Tore her gown and soiled her stocking,
Twitched her hair out by the roots,
Stamped upon her tender feet,
Held her hands and squeezed their fruits
Against her mouth to make her eat.

White and golden Lizzie stood,
Like a lily in a flood—
Like a rock of blue-veined stone
Lashed by tides obstreperously—
Like a beacon left alone
In a hoary, roaring sea,
Sending up a golden fire—
Like a fruit-crowned orange-tree
White with blossoms honey-sweet
Sore beset by wasp and bee—
Like a royal virgin town
Topped with gilded dome and spire
Close beleaguered by a fleet
Mad to tug her standard down.

One may lead a horse to water;
Twenty cannot make him drink.

Though the goblins cuffed and caught her,
Coaxed and fought her,
Bullied and besought her,
Scratched her, pinched her black as ink,
Kicked and knocked her,
Mauled and mocked her,
Lizzie uttered not a word;
Would not open lip from lip
Lest they should cram a mouthful in;
But laughed in heart to feel the drip
Of juice that siruped all her face,
And lodged in dimples of her chin,
And streaked her neck which quaked like curd.
At last the evil people,
Worn out by her resistance,
Flung back her penny, kicked their fruit
Along whichever road they took,
Not leaving root or stone or shoot;
Some writhed into the ground,
Some dived into the brook
With ring and ripple,
Some scudded on the gale without a sound,
Some vanished in the distance.

In a smart, ache, tingle,
Lizzie went her way;
Knew not was it night or day;
Sprang up the bank, tore through the furze,
Threaded copse and dingle,
And heard her penny jingle
Bouncing in her purse—
Its bounce was music to her ear.
She ran and ran
As if she feared some goblin man
Dogged her with gibe or curse
Or something worse;
But not one goblin skurried after,
Nor was she pricked by fear;
The kind heart made her windy-paced
That urged her home quite out of breath with haste
And inward laughter.

She cried, "Laura," up the garden,
"Did you miss me?
Come and kiss me.
Never mind my bruises,
Hug me, kiss me, suck my juices
Squeezed from goblin fruits for you,
Goblin pulp and goblin dew.
Eat me, drink me, love me;
Laura, make much of me;
For your sake I have braved the glen
And had to do with goblin merchant men."

Laura started from her chair,
Flung her arms up in the air,

Clutched her hair:
"Lizzie, Lizzie, have you tasted
For my sake the fruit forbidden?
480 Must your light like mine be hidden,
Your young life like mine be wasted,
Undone in mine undoing,
And ruined in my ruin,
Thirsty, cankered, goblin-ridden?"—
She clung about her sister,
Kissed and kissed and kissed her;
Tears once again
Refreshed her shrunken eyes,
Dropping like rain
490 After long sultry drouth;
Shaking with anguish fear, and pain,
She kissed and kissed her with a hungry mouth.

Her lips began to scorch,
That juice was wormwood to her tongue,
She loathed the feast.
Writhing as one possessed, she leaped and sung,
Rent all her robe, and wrung
Her hands in lamentable haste,
And beat her breast.
500 Her locks streamed like the torch
Borne by a racer at full speed,
Or like the mane of horses in their flight,
Or like an eagle when she stems the light
Straight toward the sun,
Or like a caged thing freed,
Or like a flying flag when armies run.

Swift fire spread through her veins, knocked at her
    heart,
Met the fire smoldering there
And overbore its lesser flame;
510 She gorged on bitterness without a name—
Ah, fool, to choose such part
Of soul-consuming care!
Sense failed in the mortal strife;
Like the watch-tower of a town
Which an earthquake shatters down,
Like a lightning-stricken mast,
Like a wind-uprooted tree
Spun about,
Like a foam-topped waterspout
520 Cast down headlong in the sea,
She fell at last;
Pleasure past and anguish past,
Is it death or is it life?

Life out of death.
That night long Lizzie watched by her,
Counted her pulse's flagging stir,
Felt for her breath,
Held water to her lips, and cooled her face
With tears and fanning leaves.
But when the first birds chirped about their eaves, 530
And early reapers plodded to the place
Of golden sheaves,
And dew-wet grass
Bowed in the morning winds so brisk to pass,
And new buds with new day
Opened of cup-like lilies on the stream,
Laura awoke as from a dream,
Laughed in the innocent old way,
Hugged Lizzie but not twice or thrice;
Her gleaming locks showed not one thread of gray, 540
Her breath was sweet as May,
And light danced in her eyes.

Days, weeks, months, years
Afterwards, when both were wives
With children of their own;
Their mother-hearts beset with fears,
Their lives bound up in tender lives;
Laura would call the little ones
And tell them of her early prime,
Those pleasant days long gone 550
Of not-returning time;
Would talk about the haunted glen,
The wicked quaint fruit-merchant men,
Their fruits like honey to the throat
But poison in the blood
(Men sell not such in any town);
Would tell them how her sister stood
In deadly peril to do her good,
And win the fiery antidote;
Then joining hands to little hands 560
Would bid them cling together—
"For there is no friend like a sister
In calm or stormy weather;
To cheer one on the tedious way,
To fetch one if one goes astray,
To lift one if one totters down,
To strengthen whilst one stands."
(1859; 1862)

AFTER DEATH

The curtains were half drawn, the floor was swept
    And strewn with rushes, rosemary and may
    Lay thick upon the bed on which I lay,
    Where through the lattice ivy-shadows crept.
    He leaned above me, thinking that I slept   5
        And could not hear him; but I heard him say,
        'Poor child, poor child': and as he turned away
    Came a deep silence, and I knew he wept.
    He did not touch the shroud, or raise the fold
        That hid my face, or take my hand in his,   10

Or ruffle the smooth pillows for my head:
    He did not love me living; but once dead
    He pitied me; and very sweet it is
To know he still is warm though I am cold.
(1849)

AN APPLE GATHERING

I plucked pink blossoms from mine apple-tree
    And wore them all that evening in my hair;
Then in due season when I went to see,
    I found no apples there.

With dangling basket all along the grass
    As I had come I went the self-same track;
My neighbors mocked me while they saw me pass
    So empty-handed back.

Lilian and Lilias smiled in trudging by,
10   Their heaped-up basket teased me like a jeer;
Sweet-voiced they sang beneath the sunset sky—
    Their mother's home was near.

Plump Gertrude passed me with her basket full,
    A stronger hand than hers helped it along;
A voice talked with her through the shadows cool
    More sweet to me than song.

Ah Willie, Willie, was my love less worth
    Than apples with their green leaves piled above?
I counted rosiest apples on the earth
20   Of far less worth than love.

So once it was with me you stooped to talk,
    Laughing and listening in this very lane;
To think that by this way we used to walk
    We shall not walk again!

I let my neighbors pass me, ones and twos
    And groups; the latest said the night grew chill,
And hastened. But I loitered; while the dews
    Fell fast I loitered still.
(1857; 1862)

A BETTER RESURRECTION

I have no wit, no words, no tears;
    My heart within me like a stone
Is numbed too much for hopes or fears.

Look right, look left, I dwell alone;
I lift mine eyes, but dimmed with grief
    No everlasting hills° I see.
My life is in the falling leaf;°
    O Jesus, quicken me.

My life is like a faded leaf,
    My harvest dwindled to a husk;   10
Truly my life is void and brief
    And tedious in the barren dusk;
My life is like a frozen thing,
    No bud nor greenness can I see;
Yet rise it shall—the sap of Spring;
    O Jesus, rise in me.

My life is like a broken bowl,
    A broken bowl that cannot hold
One drop of water for my soul
    Or cordial in the searching cold;   20
Cast in the fire the perished thing;
    Melt and remold it, till it be
A royal cup for Him, my King;
    O Jesus, drink of me.
(1857; 1862)

UPHILL

Does the road wind uphill all the way?
    Yes, to the very end.
Will the day's journey take the whole long day?
    From morn to night, my friend.

But is there for the night a resting-place?
    A roof for when the slow dark hours begin.
May not the darkness hide it from my face?
    You cannot miss that inn.

Shall I meet other wayfarers at night?
    Those who have gone before.   10
Then must I knock, or call when just in sight?
    They will not keep you standing at that door.°

Shall I find comfort, travel-sore and weak?
    Of labor you shall find the sum.
Will there be beds for me and all who seek?
    Yea, for all who come.
(1858; 1861)

A Better Resurrection   5 **lift . . . hills.** Cf. *Psalms*, 121:1: "I will lift up mine eyes unto the hills, from whence cometh my help"   7 **life . . . leaf.** Cf. *Macbeth*, V, iii, 22–23: "My way of life/ Is fall'n into the sear, the yellow leaf"
Uphill   11–12 **knock . . . door,** from *Revelation*, 3:20: "Behold, I stand at the door and knock"

WILLIAM MORRIS
1834-1896

William Morris was born in 1834 of a large and wealthy family. After preparatory school he went to Exeter College, Oxford. There he became interested in John Ruskin's writings on architecture; he was particularly influenced by the chapter "The Nature of Gothic" from *The Stones of Venice.* After graduation, he worked in the offices of an Oxford architect and financed the first issues of *The Oxford and Cambridge Magazine,* which printed many of his early poems. In the course of his life his vast energies were channeled in several directions: Morris was a designer, businessman, craftsman, weaver, pioneer socialist, and poet. Early in his career he was associated with Dante Gabriel Rossetti and the Pre-Raphaelite Brotherhood in its second phase—the phase that began in 1857 when he, Rossetti, and Edward Burne-Jones were commissioned to paint the walls of the Oxford Union. In 1861 he and a small group of friends, including Rossetti, started the crafts firm of Morris, Marshall, Faulkner & Company, later (1874) reorganized simply as Morris & Company. Morris started giving public lectures on the arts in 1877. In the latter years of his life he was very actively engaged in socialist causes; he was a founder of the Socialist League and the Hammersmith Socialist Society. Although very busy with his socialist work, his interest in the arts never waned. In 1891 he started The Kelmscott Press, whose edition of *The Works of Geoffrey Chaucer* is considered one of the greatest examples of the art of bookmaking. Morris, most likely worn out by his many activities, died in Hammersmith in 1896.

The first of Morris' publications was *The Defense of Guenevere and Other Poems* (1858), which reprinted many of the earlier poems that appeared in *The Oxford and Cambridge Magazine.* This early book was characterized by a Pre-Raphaelite style. His *Life and Death of Jason* (1867), written in heroic couplets, was a romantic treatment of the Greek tale of Jason and Medea. In *The Earthly Paradise* (1868–1870) he combined in a prologue, epilogue, and twenty-four tales an equal number of Greek legends and Norse sagas. His framework in this poem suggests the influence of Chaucer's *Canterbury Tales.* Two journeys to Iceland inspired what may be regarded as his greatest long poem, *Sigurd the Volsung* (1876), a retelling of the great Norse saga in four books of anapestic couplets. After his excursion into socialistic writing, he undertook an amazing series of light prose romances, adorned with lyrics, that are totally different from any type of writing that appeared elsewhere in Victorian

England: *The House of the Wolfings* (1889), *The Story of the Glittering Plain* (1890), *The Roots of the Mountains* (1890), *The Wood Beyond the World* (1894), *Child Christopher* (1895), *The Well at the World's End* (1896), *The Water of the Wondrous Isles* (1897), and *The Story of the Sundering Flood* (1898). Morris retained his eagerness for expressing beauty throughout his career. These last writings have the same flavor of remote and pensive beauty as his long poems have.

THE DEFENSE OF GUENEVERE°

But, knowing now that they would have her speak,
She threw her wet hair backward from her brow,
Her hand close to her mouth touching her cheek,

As though she had had there a shameful blow,
And feeling it shameful to feel aught but shame
All through her heart, yet felt her cheek burned so,

She must a little touch it; like one lame
She walked away from Gauwaine, with her head
Still lifted up; and on her cheek of flame

The tears dried quick; she stopped at last and said: 10
"O knights and lords, it seems but little skill°
To talk of well-known things past now and dead.

"God wot° I ought to say, I have done ill,
And pray you all forgiveness heartily!
Because you must be right, such great lords; still

"Listen—suppose your time were come to die,
And you were quite alone and very weak;
Yea, laid a-dying, while very mightily

"The wind was ruffling up the narrow streak
Of river through your broad lands running well;   20
Suppose a hush should come, then someone speak:

"'One of these cloths is heaven, and one is hell;
Now choose one cloth forever—which they be,
I will not tell you; you must somehow tell

"'Of your own strength and mightiness; here, see!'
Yea, yea, my lord, and you to ope your eyes,
At foot of your familiar bed to see

"A great God's angel standing, with such dyes,

The Defense of Guenevere. In this poem Morris represents Arthur's queen as defending herself against the charge of adultery with Sir Launcelot which was brought against her by Sir Gauwaine. This was her second trial on the same charge; at the first she was saved by Launcelot, who slew her accuser, Sir Mellyagraunce, in a trial by combat (see ll. 166–219). Morris drew the general material for his poem from Malory's *Morte Darthur* but changed many details
11 skill, reason, wisdom   **13 wot,** knows

Not known on earth, on his great wings, and hands,
30 Held out two ways, light from the inner skies

"Showing him well, and making his commands
Seem to be God's commands, moreover, too,
Holding within his hands the cloths on wands;

"And one of these strange choosing cloths was blue,
Wavy and long, and one cut short and red;
No man could tell the better of the two.

"After a shivering half-hour you said:
'God help! heaven's color, the blue'; and he said,
  'hell.'
Perhaps you would then roll upon your bed,

40 "And cry to all good men that loved you well,
'Ah, Christ! if only I had known, known, known';
Launcelot went away, then I could tell,

"Like wisest man how all things would be, moan,
And roll and hurt myself, and long to die,
And yet fear much to die for what was sown.

"Nevertheless, you, O Sir Gauwaine, lie;°
Whatever may have happened through these years,
God knows I speak truth, saying that you lie."

Her voice was low at first, being full of tears,
50 But as it cleared, it grew full loud and shrill,
Growing a windy shriek in all men's ears,

A ringing in their startled brains, until
She said that Gauwaine lied, then her voice sunk,
And her great eyes began again to fill,

Though still she stood right up, and never shrunk,
But spoke on bravely, glorious lady fair!
Whatever tears her full lips may have drunk,

She stood, and seemed to think, and wrung her hair,
Spoke out at last with no more trace of shame,
60 With passionate twisting of her body there:

"It chanced upon a day that Launcelot came
To dwell at Arthur's court—at Christmas-time
This happened; when the heralds sung his name,

"Son of King Ban of Benwick, seemed to chime
Along with all the bells that rang that day,
O'er the white roofs, with little change of rime.

"Christmas and whitened winter passed away,
And over me the April sunshine came,
Made very awful with black hail-clouds; yea,

"And in the summer I grew white with flame,   70
And bowed my head down; autumn, and the sick
Sure knowledge things would never be the same,

"However often spring might be most thick
Of blossoms and buds, smote on me, and I grew
Careless of most things, let the clock tick, tick,

"To my unhappy pulse, that beat right through
My eager body; while I laughed out loud,
And let my lips curl up at false or true,

"Seemed cold and shallow without any cloud.
Behold, my judges, then the cloths° were brought;   80
While I was dizzied thus, old thoughts would crowd,

"Belonging to the time ere I was bought
By Arthur's great name and his little love;
Must I give up forever then, I thought,

"That which I deemed would ever round me move
Glorifying all things; for a little word,
Scarce ever meant at all, must I now prove

"Stone-cold forever? Pray you, does the Lord
Will that all folks should be quite happy and good?
I love God now a little, if this cord   90

"Were broken, once for all what striving could
Make me love anything in earth or heaven?
So day by day it grew, as if one should

"Slip slowly down some path worn smooth and even,
Down to a cool sea on a summer day;
Yet still in slipping there was some small leaven

"Of stretched hands catching small stones by the way,
Until one surely reached the sea at last,
And felt strange new joy as the worn head lay

"Back, with the hair like sea-weed; yea, all past   100
Sweat of the forehead, dryness of the lips,
Washed utterly out by the dear waves o'ercast,

"In the lone sea, far off from any ships!
Do I not know now of a day in spring?
No minute of that wild day ever slips

"From out my memory; I hear thrushes sing,
And wheresoever I may be, straightway
Thoughts of it all come up with most fresh sting.

"I was half mad with beauty on that day,
And went, without my ladies, all alone,   110
In a quiet garden walled round every way;

"I was right joyful of that wall of stone,
That shut the flowers and trees up with the sky,
And trebled all the beauty; to the bone—

"Yea, right through to my heart, grown very shy
With wary thoughts—it pierced, and made me glad,
Exceedingly glad, and I knew verily,

"A little thing just then had made me mad;
I dared not think, as I was wont to do,
120 Sometimes, upon my beauty; if I had

"Held out my long hand up against the blue,
And, looking on the tenderly darkened fingers,
Thought that by rights one ought to see quite through,

"There, see you, where the soft still light yet lingers,
Round by the edges; what should I have done,
If this had joined with yellow spotted singers,°

"And startling green drawn upward by the sun?
But shouting, loosed out, see now! all my hair,
And trancedly stood watching the west wind run

130 "With faintest half-heard breathing sound—why there
I lose my head e'en now in doing this.
But shortly listen: In that garden fair

"Came Launcelot walking; this is true, the kiss
Wherewith we kissed in meeting that spring day,
I scarce dare talk of the remembered bliss,

"When both our mouths went wandering in one way,
And aching sorely, met among the leaves;
Our hands, being left behind, strained far away.

"Never within a yard of my bright sleeves
140 Had Launcelot come before—and now so nigh!
After that day why is it Guenevere grieves?

"Nevertheless, you, O Sir Gauwaine, lie,
Whatever happened on through all those years—
God knows I speak truth, saying that you lie.

"Being such a lady, could I weep these tears
If this were true? A great queen such as I,
Having sinned this way, straight her conscience sears;

"And afterwards she liveth hatefully,
Slaying and poisoning—certes never weeps;
150 Gauwaine, be friends now, speak me lovingly.

"Do I not see how God's dear pity creeps
All through your frame, and trembles in your mouth?
Remember in what grave your mother° sleeps,

"Buried in some place far down in the south,
Men are forgetting as I speak to you;
By her head, severed in that awful drouth

"Of pity that drew Agravaine's fell blow,
I pray your pity! let me not scream out
Forever after, when the shrill winds blow

"Through half your castle-locks! let me not shout   160
Forever after in the winter night
When you ride out alone! in battle-rout

"Let not my rusting tears make your sword light!
Ah! God of mercy, how he turns away!
So, ever must I dress me to the fight,

"So—let God's justice work! Gauwaine, I say,
See me hew down your proofs; yea, all men know,
Even as you said, how Mellyagraunce one day,

"One bitter day in la Fausse Garde,° for so
All good knights held it after, saw—   170
Yea, sirs, by cursed unknightly outrage,° though

"You, Gauwaine, held his word without a flaw,
This Mellyagraunce saw blood upon my bed—
Whose blood then pray you? is there any law

"To make a queen say why some spots of red
Lie on her coverlet? or will you say,
'Your hands are white, lady, as when you wed,

"'Where did you bleed?' and must I stammer out—
'Nay,
I blush indeed, fair lord, only to rend
My sleeve up to my shoulder, where there lay   180

"'A knife-point last night': so must I defend
The honor of the Lady Guenevere?
Not so, fair lords, even if the world should end

"This very day, and you were judges here
Instead of God. Did you see Mellyagraunce
When Launcelot stood by him?—what white fear

"Curdled his blood, and how his teeth did dance,
His side sink in? as my knight cried and said:
'Slayer of unarmed men, here is a chance!

"'Setter of traps,° I pray you guard your head;   190
By God, I am so glad to fight with you,
Stripper of ladies, that my hand feels lead

"'For driving weight; hurrah now! draw and do,

126 yellow . . singers, thrushes (l. 106)   153 your mother. According to Mal-
ory she was Morgawse, Arthur's sister. She was slain by her son Sir Gaheris (not
Agravaine) when he found her faithless to her husband, King Lot, in Orkney
(Morte Darthur X, 24)

169 la Fausse Garde, the false prison in which Mellyagraunce had held her
171 unknightly outrage. Mellyagraunce had entered the chamber of Guenevere
before she was up   190 Setter of traps. Mellyagraunce had trapped Launcelot

For all my wounds are moving in my breast,
And I am getting mad with waiting so.'

"He struck his hands together o'er the beast,
Who fell down flat, and groveled at his feet,
And groaned at being slain so young. 'At least,'

"My knight said, 'Rise you, sir, who are so fleet
200 At catching ladies; half-armed will I fight,
My left side all uncovered!' Then, I weet,°

"Up sprang Sir Mellyagraunce with great delight
Upon his knave's face; not until just then
Did I quite hate him, as I saw my knight

"Along the lists look to my stake and pen
With such a joyous smile, it made me sigh
From agony beneath my waist-chain, when

"The fight began, and to me they drew nigh;
Even Sir Launcelot kept him on the right,
210 And traversed warily, and ever high

"And fast leapt caitiff's sword, until my knight
Sudden threw up his sword to his left hand,
Caught it, and swung it; that was all the fight,

"Except a spout of blood on the hot land;
For it was hottest summer; and I know
I wondered how the fire, while I should stand,

"And burn,° against the heat, would quiver so,
Yards above my head; thus these matters went;
Which things were only warnings of the woe

220 "That fell on me. Yet Mellyagraunce was shent,°
For Mellyagraunce had fought against the Lord;
Therefore, my lords, take heed lest you be blent°

"With all his wickedness—say no rash word
Against me, being so beautiful; my eyes,
Wept all away to gray, may bring some sword

"To drown you in your blood; see my breast rise,
Like waves of purple sea, as here I stand;
And how my arms are moved in wonderful wise;

"Yea, also at my full heart's strong command,
230 See through my long throat how the words go up
In ripples to my mouth; how in my hand

"The shadow lies like wine within a cup
Of marvelously colored gold; yea, now
This little wind is rising, look you up,

"And wonder how the light is falling so
Within my moving tresses. Will you dare
When you have looked a little on my brow,

"To say this thing is vile? or will you care
For any plausible lies of cunning woof,
When you can see my face with no lie there   240

"Forever? Am I not a gracious proof?—
'But in your chamber Launcelot was found'°—
Is there a good knight then would stand aloof,

"When a queen says with gentle queenly sound,
'O true as steel, come now and talk with me;
I love to see your step upon the ground

"'Unwavering; also well I love to see
That gracious smile light up your face, and hear
Your wonderful words, that all mean verily

"'The thing they seem to mean. Good friend, so dear   250
To me in everything, come here tonight,
Or else the hours will pass most dull and drear.

"'If you come not, I fear this time I might
Get thinking overmuch of times gone by,
When I was young, and green hope was in sight;

"'For no man cares now to know why I sigh;
And no man comes to sing me pleasant songs,
Nor any brings me the sweet flowers that lie

"'So thick in the gardens; therefore one so longs
To see you, Launcelot, that we may be   260
Like children once again, free from all wrongs

"'Just for one night.' Did he not come to me?
What thing could keep true Launcelot away
If I said, 'Come'? There was one less than three

"In my quiet room that night, and we were gay;
Till sudden I rose up, weak, pale, and sick,
Because a bawling broke our dream up; yea,

"I looked at Launcelot's face and could not speak
For he looked helpless, too, for a little while;
Then I remember how I tried to shriek,   270

"And could not, but fell down; from tile to tile
The stones they threw up rattled o'er my head
And made me dizzier; till within a while

"My maids were all about me, and my head
On Launcelot's breast was being soothed away
From its white chattering, until Launcelot said . . .

---

201 **weet,** observed, knew   216–217 **while . . . burn.** Upon the testimony of
Mellyagraunce she was sentenced to be burned. The appearance and the victory
of Launcelot saved her   220 **shent,** destroyed   222 **blent,** blinded

242 **But . . . found.** For the story of the fight in Guenevere's chamber, see Malory's *Morte Darthur,* XX, 4

"By God! I will not tell you more today—
Judge any way you will; what matters it?
You know quite well the story of that fray,

280 "How Launcelot stilled their bawling, the mad fit°
That caught up Gauwaine, all, all, verily,
But just that which would save me;° these things flit.

"Nevertheless, you, O Sir Gauwaine, lie;
Whatever may have happened these long years,
God knows I speak truth, saying that you lie!

"All I have said is truth, by Christ's dear tears."
She would not speak another word, but stood
Turned sideways, listening, like a man who hears

His brother's trumpet sounding through the wood
290 Of his foes' lances. She leaned eagerly,
And gave a slight spring sometimes, as° she could

At last hear something really; joyfully
Her cheek grew crimson, as the headlong speed
Of the roan charger drew all men to see
The knight who came was Launcelot at good need.°
(1858)

THE HAYSTACK IN THE FLOODS°

Had she come all the way for this,
To part at last without a kiss?
Yea, had she borne the dirt and rain
That her own eyes might see him slain
Beside the haystack in the floods?

Along the dripping leafless woods,
The stirrup touching either shoe,
She rode astride as troopers do;
With kirtle° kilted to her knee,
10 To which the mud splash'd wretchedly;

And the wet dripp'd from every tree
Upon her head and heavy hair,
And on her eyelids broad and fair;
The tears and rain ran down her face.
By fits and starts they rode apace,
And very often was his place
Far off from her; he had to ride
Ahead, to see what might betide
When the roads cross'd; and sometimes, when
20 There rose a murmuring from his men,

Had to turn back with promises;
Ah me! she had but little ease;
And often for pure doubt and dread
She sobb'd, made giddy in the head
By the swift riding; while, for cold,
Her slender fingers scarce could hold
The wet reins; yea, and scarcely, too,
She felt the foot within her shoe
Against the stirrup: all for this,   30
To part at last without a kiss
Beside the haystack in the floods.

For when they near'd that old soak'd hay,
They saw across the only way
That Judas, Godmar, and the three
Red running° lions dismally
Grinn'd from his pennon, under which,
In one straight line along the ditch,
They counted thirty heads.

                                    So then,
While Robert turn'd round to his men,
She saw at once the wretched end,   40
And, stooping down, tried hard to rend
Her coif° the wrong way from her head,
And hid her eyes; while Robert said:
"Nay, love, 'tis scarcely two to one,
At Poictiers° where we made them run
So fast—why, sweet my love, good cheer,
The Gascon frontier is so near,
Nought after this."

                        But, "O," she said,
"My God! my God! I have to tread
The long way back without you; then   50
The court at Paris; those six men;°
The gratings of the Chatelet;°
The swift Seine on some rainy day
Like this, and people standing by,
And laughing, while my weak hands try
To recollect how strong men swim.
All this, or else a life with him,
For which I should be damned at last,
Would God that this next hour were past!"

He answer'd not, but cried his cry,   60
"St. George for Marny!" cheerily;
And laid his hand upon her rein.
Alas! no man of all his train
Gave back that cheery cry again;
And, while for rage his thumb beat fast
Upon his sword-hilt, some one cast
About his neck a kerchief long,
And bound him.

280 **mad fit.** Gauwaine was not present   282 **that . . . me,** her innocence
291 **as,** as if   295 **knight . . . need.** Launcelot and his kinsmen rescued the
Queen from the fire   **The Haystack in the Floods.** Sir Robert de Marny, an English knight who had fought at Poictiers (1356), is riding through France with his
mistress Jehane and his men. They meet Godmar, a French knight, who has been
waiting for them   9 **kirtle,** shirt

35 **running,** rampant   42 **coif,** cap   45 **Poictiers.** The English had won even
though outnumbered   51 **those six men,** judges   52 **Chatelet,** a prison in Paris

Then they went along
To Godmar; who said: "Now, Jehane,
70 Your lover's life is on the wane
So fast, that, if this very hour
You yield not as my paramour,
He will not see the rain leave off—
Nay, keep your tongue from gibe and scoff,
Sir Robert, or I slay you now."

She laid her hand upon her brow,
Then gazed upon the palm, as though
She thought her forehead bled, and—"No!"
She said, and turn'd her head away,
80 As there were nothing else to say,
And everything were settled: red
Grew Godmar's face from chin to head:
"Jehane, on yonder hill there stands
My castle, guarding well my lands:
What hinders me from taking you,
And doing that I list to do
To your fair wilful body, while
Your knight lies dead?"

                    A wicked smile
Wrinkled her face, her lips grew thin,
90 A long way out she thrust her chin:
"You know that I should strangle you
While you were sleeping; or bite through
Your throat, by God's help—ah!" she said,
"Lord Jesus, pity your poor maid!
For in such wise they hem me in,
I cannot choose but sin and sin,
Whatever happens: yet I think
They could not make me eat or drink,
And so should I just reach my rest."
100 "Nay, if you do not my behest,
O Jehane! though I love you well,"
Said Godmar, "would I fail to tell
All that I know?" "Foul lies," she said.
"Eh? lies my Jehane? by God's head,
At Paris folks would deem them true!
Do you know, Jehane, they cry for you:
'Jehane the brown! Jehane the brown!
Give us Jehane to burn or drown!'—
Eh—gag me Robert!—sweet my friend,
110 This were indeed a piteous end
For those long fingers, and long feet,
And long neck, and smooth shoulders sweet:
An end that few men would forget
That saw it—So, an hour yet:
Consider, Jehane, which to take
Of life or death!"

                    So, scarce awake,
Dismounting, did she leave that place,
And totter some yards: with her face
Turn'd upward to the sky she lay,
120 Her head on a wet heap of hay,

And fell asleep: and while she slept
And did not dream, the minutes crept
Round to the twelve again; but she,
Being waked at last, sigh'd quietly,
And strangely childlike came, and said:
"I will not." Straightway Godmar's head,
As though it hung on strong wires, turn'd
Most sharply round, and his face burn'd.

For Robert—both his eyes were dry,   130
He could not weep, but gloomily
He seem'd to watch the rain; yea, too,
His lips were firm; he tried once more
To touch her lips; she reach'd out, sore
And vain desire so tortured them,
The poor grey lips, and now the hem
Of his sleeve brush'd them.

                    With a start
Up Godmar rose, thrust them apart;
From Robert's throat he loosed the bands
Of silk and mail; with empty hands
Held out, she stood and gazed, and saw,   140
The long bright blade without a flaw
Glide out from Godmar's sheath, his hand
In Robert's hair; she saw him bend
Back Robert's head; she saw him send
The thin steel down; the blow told well,
Right backward the knight Robert fell,
And moan'd as dogs do, being half dead,
Unwitting, as I deem: so then
Godmar turn'd grinning to his men,
Who ran, some five or six, and beat   150
His head to pieces at their feet.

Then Godmar turn'd again and said:
"So, Jehane, the first fitte° is read!
Take note, my lady, that your way
Lies backward to the Chatelet!"
She shook her head and gazed awhile
At her cold hands with a rueful smile,
As though this thing had made her mad.

This was the parting that they had
Beside the haystack in the floods.   160
(1858)

CONCERNING GEFFRAY TESTE NOIRE°

And if you meet the Canon of Chimay,
    As going to Ortaise you well may do,
Greet him from John of Castel Neuf, and say,
    All that I tell you, for all this is true.

153 **fitte,** part (of a tale)   **Concerning Geffray Teste Noire.** The places and
names of the framing story are drawn largely from the Froissart chronicles of
fourteenth-century France. In the 1370s outlaws not infrequently plundered villages and captured castles as Geffray does

This Geffray Teste Noire was a Gascon thief,
　　Who, under shadow of the English name,
Pilled all such towns and countries as were lief
　　To King Charles and St. Denis; thought it blame

If anything escaped him; so my lord
10　The Duke of Berry sent Sir John Bonne Lance,
And other knights, good players with the sword,
　　To check this thief and give the land a chance.

Therefore we set our bastides° round the tower
　　That Geffray held, the strong thief! like a king,
High perch'd upon the rock of Ventadour,
　　Hopelessly strong by Christ! It was mid spring,

When first I joined the little army there
　　With ten good spears; Auvergne is hot, each day
We sweated armed before the barrier;
20　Good feats of arms were done there often—eh?

Your brother was slain there? I mind me now,
　　A right good man-at-arms, God pardon him!
I think 'twas Geffray smote him on the brow
　　With some spiked axe, and while he totter'd, dim

About the eyes, the spear of Alleyne Roux°
　　Slipped through his camaille° and his throat; well,
　　　well!
Alleyne is paid now; your name Alleyne too?
　　Mary! how strange—but this tale I would tell—

For spite of all our bastides, damned Blackhead°
30　Would ride abroad whene'er he chose to ride,
We could not stop him; many a burgher bled
　　Dear gold all round his girdle; far and wide

The villayns dwelt in utter misery
　　'Twixt us and thief Sir Geffray; hauled this way
By Sir Bonne Lance at one time, he gone by,
　　Down comes this Teste Noire on another day,

And therefore they dig up the stone, grind corn,
　　Hew wood, draw water, yea, they lived, in short,
As I said just now, utterly forlorn,
40　Till this our knave and Blackhead was out-fought.

So Bonne Lance fretted, thinking of some trap
　　Day after day, till on a time he said:
"John of Newcastle, if we have good hap,
　　We catch our thief in two days." "How?" I said.

"Why, Sir, to-day he rideth out again,
　　Hoping to take well certain sumpter mules
From Carcassonne, going with little train,
　　Because, forsooth, he thinketh us mere fools;

"But if we set an ambush in some wood,
　　He is but dead: so, Sir, take thirty spears　　　　50
To Verville forest, if it seem you good."
　　Then felt I like the horse in Job,° who hears

The dancing trumpet sound, and we went forth;
　　And my red lion on the spear-head flapped,
As faster than the cool wind we rode north,
　　Towards the wood of Verville; thus it happed.

We rode a soft pace on that day, while spies
　　Got news about Sir Geffray; the red wine
Under the road-side bush was clear; the flies,
　　The dragon-flies I mind me most, did shine　　　60

In brighter arms than ever I put on;
　　So—"Geffray," said our spies, "would pass that
　　　way
Next day at sundown:" then he must be won;
　　And so we enter'd Verville wood next day,

In the afternoon; through it the highway runs,
　　'Twixt copses of green hazel, very thick,
And underneath, with glimmering of suns,
　　The primroses are happy; the dews lick

The soft green moss. "Put cloths about your arms,
　　Lest they should glitter; surely they will go　　70
In a long thin line, watchful for alarms,
　　With all their carriages of booty; so—

"Lay down my pennon in the grass—Lord God!
　　What have we lying here? will they be cold,
I wonder, being so bare, above the sod,
　　Instead of under? This was a knight too, fold

"Lying on fold of ancient rusted mail;
　　No plate at all, gold rowels to the spurs,
And see the quiet gleam of turquoise pale
　　Along the ceinture; but the long time blurs　　80

"Even the tinder of his coat to nought,
　　Except these scraps of leather; see how white
The skull is, loose within the coif! He fought
　　A good fight, maybe, ere he was slain quite.

"No armour on the legs too; strange in faith—
　　A little skeleton for a knight, though—ah!
This one is bigger, truly without scathe°
　　His enemies escaped not—ribs driven out far—

"That must have reach'd the heart, I doubt—how
　　　now,
　　What say you, Aldovrand—a woman? why?"　　90
"Under the coif a gold wreath on the brow,
　　Yea, see the hair not gone to powder, lie,

---

13 **bastides,** temporary huts built during a siege　25 **Alleyne Roux,** Geffray's
nephew and heir　26 **camaille,** chain mail covering the throat　29 **Blackhead,**
Morris' translation of Teste Noire

52 **Job,** Job, 39:24-25　87 **scathe,** pity

"Golden, no doubt, once—yea, and very small
    This for a knight; but for a dame, my lord,
These loose-hung bones seem shapely still, and tall,
    Didst ever see a woman's bones, my lord?"

Often, God help me! I remember when
    I was a simple boy, fifteen years old,
The Jacquerie° froze up the blood of men
100   With their fell deeds, not fit now to be told:

God help again! we enter'd Beauvais town,
    Slaying them fast, whereto I help'd, mere boy
As I was then; we gentles cut them down,
    These burners and defilers, with great joy.

Reason for that, too: in the great church there
    These fiends had lit a fire, that soon went out,
The church at Beauvais being so great and fair—
    My father, who was by me, gave a shout

Between a beast's howl and a woman's scream,
110   Then, panting, chuckled to me: "John, look! look!
Count the dames' skeletons!" from some bad dream
    Like a man just awaked, my father shook;

And I, being faint with smelling the burnt bones,
    And very hot with fighting down the street,
And sick of such a life, fell down, with groans
    My head went weakly nodding to my feet.

—An arrow had gone through her tender throat,
    And her right wrist was broken; then I saw
The reason why she had on that war-coat,
120   Their story came out clear without a flaw;

For when he knew that they were being waylaid,
    He threw it over her, yea, hood and all;
Whereby he was much hack'd, while they were stay'd
    By those their murderers; many an one did fall

Beneath his arm, no doubt, so that he clear'd
    Their circle, bore his death-wound out of it;
But as they rode, some archer least afear'd
    Drew a strong bow, and thereby she was hit.

Still as he rode he knew not she was dead,
130   Thought her but fainted from her broken wrist,
He bound with his great leathern belt—she bled?
    Who knows! he bled too, neither was there miss'd

The beating of her heart, his heart beat well
    For both of them, till here, within this wood,
He died scarce sorry; easy this to tell;
    After these years the flowers forget their blood.—

99 **Jacquerie**, peasant rebellion in France in the 1350s

How could it be? never before that day,
    However much a soldier I might be,
Could I look on a skeleton and say
    I care not for it, shudder not—now see,   140

Over those bones I sat and pored for hours,
    And thought, and dream'd, and still I scarce could
        see
The small white bones that lay upon the flowers,
    But evermore I saw the lady; she

With her dear gentle walking leading in,
    By a chain of silver twined about her wrists,
Her loving knight, mounted and arm'd to win
    Great honour for her, fighting in the lists.

O most pale face, that brings such joy and sorrow
    Into men's hearts—yea, too, so piercing sharp   150
That joy is, that it marcheth nigh to sorrow
    For ever—like an overwinded harp.—

Your face must hurt me always; pray you now,
    Doth it not hurt you too? seemeth some pain
To hold you always, pain to hold your brow
    So smooth, unwrinkled ever; yea again,

Your long eyes where the lids seem like to drop,
    Would you not, lady, were they shut fast, feel
Far merrier? there so high they will not stop,
    They are most sly to glide forth and to steal   160

Into my heart; *I kiss their soft lids there,*
    And in green gardens scarce can stop my lips
From wandering on your face, but that your hair
    Falls down and tangles me, back my face slips.

Or say your mouth—I saw you drink red wine
    Once at a feast; how slowly it sank in,
As though you fear'd that some wild fate might twine
    Within that cup, and slay you for a sin.

And when you talk your lips do arch and move
    In such wise that a language new I know   170
Besides their sound; they quiver, too, with love
    When you are standing silent; know this, too,

I saw you kissing once, like a curved sword
    That bites with all its edge, did your lips lie,
Curled gently, slowly, long time could afford
    For caught-up breathings; like a dying sigh

They gather'd up their lines and went away,
    And still kept twitching with a sort of smile,
As likely to be weeping presently,—
    Your hands too—how I watch'd them all the while!   180

"Cry out St. Peter now," quoth Aldovrand;
  I cried, "St. Peter!" broke out from the wood
With all my spears; we met them hand to hand,
  And shortly slew them; natheless, by the rood,

We caught no Blackhead then, or any day;
  Months after that he died at last in bed,
From a wound pick'd up at a barrier-fray;
  That same year's end a steel bolt in the head,

And much bad living kill'd Teste Noire at last;
190 John Froissart knoweth he is dead by now,
No doubt, but knoweth not this tale just past;
  Perchance then you can tell him what I show.

In my new castle, down beside the Eure,
  There is a little chapel of squared stone,
Painted inside and out; in green nook pure
  There did I lay them, every wearied bone;

And over it they lay, with stone-white hands
  Clasped fast together, hair made bright with gold;
This Jaques Picard, known through many lands,
200 Wrought cunningly; he's dead now—I am old.
(1858)

from THE EARTHLY PARADISE

AN APOLOGY°

Of Heaven or Hell° I have no power to sing;
I cannot ease the burden of your fears,
Or make quick-coming death a little thing,
Or bring again the pleasure of past years;
Nor for my words shall ye forget your tears,
Or hope again for aught that I can say—
The idle singer of an empty day.

But rather, when aweary of your mirth,
From full hearts still unsatisfied ye sigh,
10 And, feeling kindly unto all the earth,
Grudge every minute as it passes by,
Made the more mindful that the sweet days die—
Remember me a little then, I pray,
The idle singer of an empty day.

The heavy trouble, the bewildering care
That weighs us down who live and earn our bread,
These idle verses have no power to bear,
So let me sing of names remembered,
Because they, living not, can ne'er be dead,
Or long time take their memory quite away   20
From us poor singers of an empty day.

Dreamer of dreams, born out of my due time,
Why should I strive to set the crooked straight?
Let it suffice me that my murmuring rime,
Beats with light wing against the ivory gate,°
Telling a tale not too importunate
To those who in the sleepy region stay,
Lulled by the singer of an empty day.

Folk say, a wizard to a northern king
At Christmas-tide such wondrous things did show,   30
That through one window men beheld the spring,
And through another saw the summer glow,
And through a third the fruited vines a-row,
While still, unheard, but in its wonted way,
Piped the drear wind of that December day.

So with this Earthly Paradise it is,
If ye will read aright, and pardon me,
Who strive to build a shadowy isle of bliss
Midmost the beating of the steely sea,
Where tossed about all hearts of men must be;   40
Whose ravening monsters mighty men shall slay—
Not the poor singer of an empty day.
(1868-1870)

THE DAY IS COMING

Come hither, lads, and harken, for a tale there is to
  tell,
Of the wonderful days a-coming, when all shall be
  better than well.

And the tale shall be told of a country, a land in the
  midst of the sea,
And folk shall call it England in the days that are going
  to be.

There more than one in a thousand in the days that are
  yet to come,
Shall have some hope of the morrow, some joy of the
  ancient home.

For then—laugh not, but listen to this strange tale of
  mine—

The Earthly Paradise. In this poem Morris employed the familiar medieval device
of a framework to bind together a series of tales. The enveloping action has to do
with a band of medieval mariners who set out from Europe to find a country in
which they came happy. They chance upon an island, the "Earthly Paradise,"
where live the descendants of Greeks who had colonized the country centuries
before. At each of a series of banquets, which occur twice a month, the mariners
relate some medeval romance, or the hosts tell an ancient Greek legend
An Apology 1 Of Heaven or Hell. Morris disclaims equality with earlier poets
who used these themes—Vergil, Dante, Milton

25 **the ivory gate.** The house of Morpheus, god of sleep, had two gates through
which dreams issued. True dreams passed through a gate of horn; false dreams,
through a gate of ivory

All folk that are in England shall be better lodged than
   swine.

Then a man shall work and bethink him, and rejoice in
   the deeds of his hand,
Nor yet come home in the even too faint and weary to
10   stand.

Men in that time a-coming shall work and have no fear
For tomorrow's lack of earning and the hunger-wolf
   anear.

I tell you this for a wonder, that no man then shall be
   glad
Of his fellow's fall and mishap to snatch at the work he
   had,

For that which the worker winneth shall then be his
   indeed,
Nor shall half be reaped for nothing by him that sowed
   no seed.

O strange new wonderful justice! But for whom shall
   we gather the gain?
For ourselves and for each of our fellows, and no hand
   shall labor in vain.

Then all Mine and all Thine shall be Ours, and no more
   shall any man crave
For riches that serve for nothing but to fetter a friend
20   for a slave.

And what wealth then shall be left us when none shall
   gather gold
To buy his friend in the market, and pinch and pine the
   sold?

Nay, what save the lovely city, and the little house on
   the hill,
And the wastes and the woodland beauty, and the
   happy fields we till;

And the homes of ancient stories, the tombs of the
   mighty dead;
And the wise men seeking out marvels, and the poet's
   teeming head;

And the painter's hand of wonder; and the marvelous
   fiddle-bow,
And the banded choirs of music—all those that do and
   know.

For all these shall be ours and all men's; nor shall any
   lack a share
Of the toil and the gain of living in the days when the
30   world grows fair.

Ah! such are the days that shall be! But what are the
   deeds of today,
In the days of the years we dwell in, that wear our lives
   away?

Why, then, and for what are we waiting? There are
   three words to speak—
We will it—and what is the foeman but the dream-
   strong wakened and weak?

O why and for what are we waiting? while our brothers
   droop and die,
And on every wind of the heavens a wasted life goes
   by.

How long shall they reproach us where crowd on
   crowd they dwell,
Poor ghosts of the wicked city, the gold-crushed,
   hungry hell?

Through squalid life they labored, in sordid grief they
   died,
Those sons of a mighty mother, those props of
   England's pride.   40

They are gone; there is none can undo it, nor save our
   souls from the curse;
But many a million cometh, and shall they be better or
   worse?

It is we must answer and hasten, and open wide the
   door
For the rich man's hurrying terror, and the slow-foot
   hope of the poor.

Yea, the voiceless wrath of the wretched, and their
   unlearned discontent,
We must give it voice and wisdom till the waiting-tide
   be spent.

Come, then, since all things call us, the living and the
   dead,
And o'er the weltering tangle a glimmering light is
   shed.

Come, then, let us cast off fooling, and put by ease and
   rest,
For the Cause alone is worthy till the good days bring
   the best.   50

Come, join in the only battle wherein no man can fail,
Where whoso fadeth and dieth, yet his deed shall still
   prevail.

Ah! come cast off all fooling, for this, at least, we
   know:

That the Dawn and the Day is coming, and forth the
  Banners go.

(1884)

ALGERNON CHARLES SWINBURNE
1837–1909

Algernon Charles Swinburne, the son of an admiral
in the British Navy, was born in London in 1837.
He spent most of his youth on the Isle of Wight and at
his grandfather's estate in Northumberland. He was
educated at Eton and at Balliol College, Oxford,
though he left without taking a degree. An allowance
from his father allowed Swinburne to pursue a literary
life. After traveling for a year in Italy in 1864, he published his first book of poetry, *Atlanta in Calydon*
(1865), which commanded great critical and popular
attention. His next publication, *Poems and Ballads* (First
Series) (1866), however, caused a great uproar because of its frank sensuousness and paganism. The
London magazine *Punch* referred to the author of
Poems and Ballads as "Mr. Swineborn." A Second and
Third Series, which appeared in 1878 and 1889 respectively, were noticeably less sensual than the First
Series. During this period Swinburne also wrote
dramas (*Chastelard*, 1865; *Bothwell*, 1874; and *Mary
Stuart*, 1881), many poems on Italian freedom, a few
poems on nature, and an important series of critical
studies (*William Blake*, 1868; *Shakespeare*, 1880; *Victor
Hugo*, 1886; *Ben Jonson*, 1889). Swinburne's personal
life during the sixties and seventies was dominated by
his abnormal temperament and alcoholism. He suffered a complete nervous breakdown in 1879 and was
taken into the custody of Theodore Watts-Dunton
(1832–1914), a literary critic and poet, for the rest of
his life. After 1880 Swinburne continued to write, av-
eraging almost a volume a year for the remainder of
his life, but these writings did not meet with the same
success as those published before 1880. Swinburne's
poetry is today known for its richness of sound—a
sound so overpowering that it sometimes obscures the
sense.

Swinburne is a difficult figure to approach with
proper critical disinterestedness. To some of the young
rebels of his day he was a god to be idolized, and
they went about reverently "chanting these new astonishing melodies." To most of his older contemporaries he was an object of critical contempt: Tennyson called him "Master Swinburne"; Arnold called

him "a sort of pseudo-Shelley"; Carlyle thought his
poetry was "the miaulings of a delirious cat"; Browning considered his poetry "a fuzz of words." Perhaps
of that older generation, John Ruskin was the only one
who found Swinburne's poetry "glorious."

In the twentieth century, however, Swinburne has
found some strong champions. T. S. Eliot said: "The
bad poet dwells partly in a world of objects, and
partly in a world of words, and he never can get them
to fit. Only a man of genius could dwell so exclusively
and consistently among words as Swinburne." The
distinguished critic I. A. Richards (1893–   ) has
written that Swinburne "is indeed a very suitable poet
in whom to study the subordination, distortion and
occultation of sense through the domination of verbal
feeling. But the lapses of sense are very rarely so flagrant, so undisguised, that the reader, swept by on the
swift and splendid roundabout of the verse, is forced
to notice them. And more often than not, when the
reader thinks he has detected some nonsense, or some
inconsequent distortion of sense, he will, if he
examines it, be troubled to find it is he who is at
fault."

With Swinburne began, suddenly and sensationally,
the revolt against Victorian assumptions and Victorian
concerns. He criticized the main drift of his age and
rebelled against both the realities and the suggested
literary remedies. His outlook, from as early as 1865,
was deeply antagonistic to the notions of even such
comparatively enlightened "believers" as Tennyson
and Browning:

And most things are so wrong
That all things must be right.
This satisfies our Browning,
And that delights our Tennyson:
And soothed Britannia simpers in serene applause.

from ATALANTA IN CALYDON°

WHEN THE HOUNDS OF SPRING

When the hounds of spring are on winter's traces,
  The mother of months° in meadow or plain
Fills the shadows and windy places
  With lisp of leaves and ripple of rain;

Atalanta in Calydon, concerns the famous hunt for the wild boar which was sent,
according to legend, by Artemis, revengeful goddess of the moon, to ravage Calydon, a province in ancient Greece. Meleager killed the beast and presented the
spoils of victory to Atalanta, an Arcadian huntress with whom he had fallen in love.
When Toxeus and Plexippus, brothers of Queen Althaea, Meleager's mother, attempted to rob the huntress of her prize, their nephew slew them. On hearing of
the tragedy, Meleager's mother burned to ashes the fagot upon which her son's
life depended, and which she had carefully preserved up to that time. The opening chorus of the drama, "When the Hounds of Spring," is sung by a group of
maidens from Aetolia, an ancient Greek province   **When the Hounds of Spring**
2 **mother of months,** Artemis, goddess of the moon

And the brown bright nightingale amorous
Is half assuaged for Itylus,°
For the Thracian ships and the foreign faces,
    The tongueless vigil, and all the pain.

Come with bows bent and with emptying of quivers,
10   Maiden most perfect, lady of light,
With a noise of winds and many rivers,
    With a clamor of waters, and with might;
Bind on thy sandals, O thou most fleet,
Over the splendor and speed of thy feet;
For the faint east quickens, the wan west shivers,
    Round the feet of the day and the feet of the night.

Where shall we find her, how shall we sing to her,
    Fold our hands round her knees, and cling?
Oh, that man's heart were as fire and could spring to
        her,
20   Fire, or the strength of the streams that spring!
For the stars and the winds are unto her
As raiment, as songs of the harp-player;
For the risen stars and the fallen cling to her,
    And the southwest wind and the west wind sing.

For winter's rains and ruins are over,
    And all the season of snows and sins;
The days dividing lover and lover,
    The light that loses, the night that wins;°
And time remembered is grief forgotten,
30 And frosts are slain and flowers begotten,
And in green underwood and cover
    Blossom by blossom the spring begins.

The full streams feed on flower of rushes,
    Ripe grasses trammel a traveling foot,
The faint fresh flame of the young year flushes
    From leaf to flower and flower to fruit;
And fruit and leaf are as gold and fire,
And the oat° is heard above the lyre,
And the hoofèd heel of a satyr° crushes
40   The chestnut-husk at the chestnut-root.

And Pan° by noon and Bacchus° by night,
    Fleeter of foot than the fleet-foot kid,
Follows with dancing and fills with delight
    The Maenad° and the Bassarid;°
And soft as lips that laugh and hide
The laughing leaves of the trees divide,
And screen from seeing and leave in sight
    The god pursuing, the maiden hid.°

The ivy falls with the Bacchanal's hair
    Over her eyebrows hiding her eyes;   50
The wild vine slipping down leaves bare
    Her bright breast shortening into sighs;
The wild vine slips with the weight of its leaves,
But the berried ivy catches and cleaves
To the limbs that glitter, the feet that scare
    The wolf that follows, the fawn that flies.

(1865)

BEFORE THE BEGINNING OF YEARS

Before the beginning of years
    There came to the making of man
Time, with a gift of tears;
    Grief, with a glass that ran;
Pleasure, with pain for leaven;
    Summer, with flowers that fell;
Remembrance fallen from heaven,
    And madness risen from hell;
Strength without hands to smite;
    Love that endures for a breath;   10
Night, the shadow of light,
    And life, the shadow of death.

And the high gods took in hand
    Fire, and the falling of tears,
And a measure of sliding sand
    From under the feet of the years;
And froth and drift of the sea;
    And dust of the laboring earth;
And bodies of things to be
    In the houses of death and of birth;   20
And wrought with weeping and laughter,
    And fashioned with loathing and love,
With life before and after
    And death beneath and above,
For a day and a night and a morrow,
    That his strength might endure for a span
With travail and heavy sorrow,
    The holy spirit of man.

From the winds of the north and the south
    They gathered as unto strife;   30
They breathed upon his mouth,
    They filled his body with life;
Eyesight and speech they wrought
    For the veils of the soul therein,
A time° for labor and thought,
    A time to serve and to sin;
They gave him light in his ways,
    And love, and a space for delight,
And beauty and length of days,
    And night, and sleep in the night.   40
His speech is a burning fire;

With his lips he travaileth;
In his heart is a blind desire,
    In his eyes foreknowledge of death;
He weaves, and is clothed with derision;
    Sows, and he shall not reap;
His life is a watch or a vision
    Between a sleep and a sleep.

(1865)

ITYLUS°

Swallow, my sister, O sister swallow,
    How can thine heart be full of the spring?
    A thousand summers are over and dead.
What hast thou found in the spring to follow?
    What hast thou found in thine heart to sing?
    What wilt thou do when the summer is shed?

O swallow, sister, O fair swift swallow,
    Why wilt thou fly after spring to the south,
    The soft south whither thine heart is set?
10 Shall not the grief of the old time follow?
    Shall not the song thereof cleave to thy mouth?
    Hast thou forgotten ere I forget?

Sister, my sister, O fleet sweet swallow,
    Thy way is long to the sun and the south;
    But I, fulfilled of my heart's desire,
Shedding my song upon height, upon hollow,
    From tawny body and sweet small mouth
    Feed the heart of the night with fire.

I the nightingale all spring through,
20   O swallow, sister, O changing swallow,
    All spring through till the spring be done,
Clothed with the light of the night on the dew,
    Sing, while the hours and the wild birds follow,
    Take flight and follow and find the sun.

Sister, my sister, O soft light swallow,
    Though all things feast in the spring's guest-
            chamber,
    How hast thou heart to be glad thereof yet?
For where thou fliest I shall not follow,
    Till life forget and death remember,
30   Till thou remember and I forget.

Swallow, my sister, O singing swallow,
    I know not how thou hast heart to sing.
    Hast thou the heart? is it all past over?
Thy lord the summer is good to follow,
    And fair the feet of thy lover the spring:
    But what wilt thou say to the spring thy lover?

Itylus. See title note for Arnold's "Philomela" for a summary of the myth

O swallow, sister, O fleeting swallow,
    My heart in me is a molten ember
    And over my head the waves have met.
But thou wouldst tarry or I would follow,   40
    Could I forget or thou remember,
    Couldst thou remember and I forget.

O sweet stray sister, O shifting swallow,
    The heart's division divideth us.
    Thy heart is light as a leaf of a tree;
But mine goes forth among sea-gulfs hollow
    To the place of the slaying of Itylus,
    The feast of Daulis, the Thracian sea.

O swallow, sister, O rapid swallow,
    I pray thee sing not a little space.   50
    Are not the roofs and the lintels wet?
The woven web that was plain to follow,
    The small slain body, the flowerlike face,
    Can I remember if thou forget?

O sister, sister, thy first-begotten!
    The hands that cling and the feet that follow,
    The voice of the child's blood crying yet
Who hath remembered me? who hath forgotten?
    Thou hast forgotten, O summer swallow,
    But the world shall end when I forget.   60

(1866)

HYMN TO PROSERPINE°

(AFTER THE PROCLAMATION IN ROME
OF THE CHRISTIAN FAITH)

Vicisti, Galilæe.

I have lived long enough, having seen one thing, that
    love hath an end;
Goddess° and maiden and queen, be near me now and
    befriend.
Thou art more than the day or the morrow, the seasons
    that laugh or that weep;
For these give joy and sorrow; but thou, Proserpina,
    sleep.
Sweet is the treading of wine, and sweet the feet of the
    dove;°
But a goodlier gift is thine than foam of the grapes or
    love.
Yea, is not even Apollo, with hair and harpstring of
    gold,

Hymn to Proserpine. A biographer and critic of Swinburne, Samuel C. Chew, has put this poem into perspective: "The Heraclitean doctrine that all things are in flux and that nothing remains . . . is at the foundation of 'Hymn to Proserpine,' sung by an Epicurean after the proclamation of Christianity at Rome. Proserpine is the goddess of Change; she has overcome Olympus; in the end she will conquer Christianity." The Emperor Julian is said to have uttered the motto for the poem ("Thou hast conquered, Galilean") on his deathbed in 363. Swinburne called the poem "the deathsong of spiritual decadence" 2 **Goddess,** queen of the lower world, wife of Pluto, kidnapped child of Ceres 5 **dove,** bird sacred to Venus

A bitter God to follow, a beautiful God to behold?
I am sick of singing: the bays° burn deep and chafe: I am fain
To rest a little from praise and grievous pleasure and
pain.
For the Gods we know not of, who give us our daily breath,
We know they are cruel as love or life, and lovely as death.
O Gods dethroned and deceased, cast forth, wiped out in a day!
From your wrath is the world released, redeemed from your chains, men say.
New Gods are crowned in the city; their flowers have broken your rods;
They are merciful, clothed with pity, the young compassionate Gods.
But for me their new device is barren, the days are bare;
Things long past over suffice, and men forgotten that were.
Time and the Gods are at strife; ye dwell in the midst thereof.
20 Draining a little life from the barren breasts of love.
I say to you, cease, take rest; yea, I say to you all, be at peace,
Till the bitter milk of her breast and the barren bosom shall cease.
Wilt thou yet take all, Galilean? but these thou shalt not take,
The laurel, the palms and the pæan, the breasts of the nymphs in the brake;
Breasts more soft than a dove's, that tremble with tenderer breath;
And all the wings of the Loves, and all the joy before death;
All the feet of the hours that sound as a single lyre,
Dropped and deep in the flowers, with strings that flicker like fire.
More than these wilt thou give, things fairer than all these things?
30 Nay, for a little we live, and life hath mutable wings.
A little while and we die; shall life not thrive as it may?
For no man under the sky lives twice, outliving his day.
And grief is a grievous thing, and a man hath enough of his tears:
Why should he labour, and bring fresh grief to blacken his years?
Thou hast conquered, O pale Galilean; the world has grown grey from thy breath;
We have drunken of things Lethean,° and fed on the fullness of death.

Laurel is green for a season, and love is sweet for a day;
But love grows bitter with treason, and laurel outlives not May.
Sleep, shall we sleep after all? for the world is not sweet in the end;
For the old faiths loosen and fall, the new years ruin and rend. 40
Fate is a sea without shore, and the soul is a rock that abides;
But her ears are vexed with the roar and her face with the foam of the tides.
O lips that the live blood faints in, the leavings of racks and rods!
O ghastly glories of saints, dead limbs of gibbeted Gods!°
Though all men abase them before you in spirit, and all knees bend,
I kneel not neither adore you, but standing, look to the end.
All delicate days and pleasant, all spirits and sorrows are cast
Far out with the foam of the present that sweeps to the surf of the past:
Where beyond the extreme sea-wall, and between the remote sea-gates,
Waste water washes, and tall ships founder, and deep 50 death waits:
Where, mighty with deepening sides, clad about with the seas as with wings,
And impelled of invisible tides, and fulfilled of unspeakable things,
White-eyed and poisonous-finned, shark-toothed and serpentine-curled,
Rolls, under the whitening wind of the future, the wave of the world.
The depths stand naked in sunder behind it, the storms flee away;
In the hollow before it the thunder is taken and snared as a prey;
In its sides is the north-wind bound; and its salt is of all men's tears;
With light of ruin, and sound of changes, and pulse of years:
With travail of day after day, and with trouble of hour upon hour;
And bitter as blood is the spray; and the crests are as fangs that devour: 60
And its vapour and storm of its steam as the sighing of spirits to be;
And its noise as the noise in a dream; and its depth as the roots of the sea:
And the height of its heads as the height of the utmost stars of the air:

---

9 **bays,** laurel crown   36 **Lethean,** causing forgetfulness, from Lethe, the river of forgetfulness in Hades

44 **gibbeted Gods,** the crucified Christ

And the ends of the earth at the might thereof tremble,
  and time is made bare.
Will ye bridle the deep sea with reins, will ye chasten
  the high sea with rods?
Will ye take her to chain her with chains, who is older
  than all ye Gods?
All ye as a wind shall go by, as a fire shall ye pass and
  be past;
Ye are Gods, and behold, ye shall die, and the waves
  be upon you at last.
In the darkness of time, in the deeps of the years, in
  the change of things,
Ye shall sleep as a slain man sleeps, and the world
70 shall forget you for kings.
Though the feet of thine high priests tread where thy
  lords and our forefathers trod,
Though these that were Gods are dead, and thou being
  dead art a God,
Though before thee the throned Cytherean° be fallen,
  and hidden her head,
Yet thy kingdom shall pass, Galilean, thy dead shall go
  down to thee dead.
Of the maiden thy mother men sing as a goddess with
  grace clad around;
Thou art throned where another was king; where
  another was queen she is crowned.
Yea, once we had sight of another: but now she is
  queen, say these.
Not as thine, not as thine was our mother, a blossom of
  flowering seas,
Clothed round with the world's desire as with raiment,
  and fair as the foam,
And fleeter than kindled fire, and a goddess, and
80 mother of Rome.
For thine came pale and a maiden, and sister to sorrow; but ours,
Her deep hair heavily laden with odour and colour of
  flowers,
White rose of the rose-white water, a silver splendour,
  a flame,
Bent down unto us that besought her, and earth grew
  sweet with her name.
For thine came weeping, a slave among slaves, and
  rejected; but she
Came flushed from the full-flushed wave, and imperial,
  her foot on the sea.
And the wonderful waters knew her, the winds and the
  viewless ways,
And the roses grew rosier, and bluer the sea-blue
  stream of the bays.
Ye are fallen, our lords, by what token? we wist that
  ye should not fall.
Ye were all so fair that are broken; and one more fair
90 than ye all.

73 **Cytherean,** Venus or Aphrodite, mother of Rome

But I turn to her still, having seen she shall surely
  abide in the end;
Goddess and maiden and queen, be near me now and
  befriend.
O daughter of earth, of my mother, her crown and
  blossom of birth,
I am also, I also, thy brother; I go as I came unto earth.
In the night where thine eyes are as moons are in
  heaven, the night where thou art,
Where the silence is more than all tunes, where sleep
  overflows from the heart,
Where the poppies° are sweet as the rose in our world,
  and the red rose is white,
And the wind falls faint as it blows with the fume of the
  flowers of the night,
And the murmur of spirits that sleep in the shadow of
  Gods from afar
Grows dim in thine ears and deep as the deep dim soul
  of a star,   100
In the sweet low light of thy face, under heavens
  untrod by the sun,
Let my soul with their souls find place, and forget what
  is done and undone.
Thou art more than the Gods who number the days of
  our temporal breath;
For these give labour and slumber; but thou,
  Proserpina, death.
Therefore now at thy feet I abide for a season in
  silence. I know
I shall die as my fathers died, and sleep as they sleep;
  even so.
For the glass of the years is brittle wherein we gaze for
  a span;
A little soul for a little bears up this corpse which is
  man.
So long I endure, no longer; and laugh not again,
  neither weep.
For there is no God found stronger than death; and
  death is a sleep.   110
(1866)

FAUSTINE°

Ave Faustina Imperatrix, morituri te salutant.°

Lean back, and get some minutes' peace;
  Let your head lean
Back to the shoulder with its fleece
  Of locks, Faustine.

97 **poppies,** flowers of sleep or oblivion, sacred to Proserpine **Faustine.** Faustina
(c. 125–176) was the wife of Marcus Aurelius, notorious for her profligacy **Ave
... salutant,** Hail, Faustina, Empress, we who are about to die salute you. Traditionally, the salute of gladiators to the attendant rulers

The shapely silver shoulder stoops,
   Weighed over clean
With state of splendid hair that droops
   Each side, Faustine.

Let me go over your good gifts
10   That crown you queen;
A queen whose kingdom ebbs and shifts
   Each week, Faustine.

Bright heavy brows well gathered up:
   White gloss and sheen;
Carved lips that make my lips a cup
   To drink, Faustine,

Wine and rank poison, milk and blood,
   Being mixed therein
Since first the devil threw dice with God
20   For you, Faustine.

Your naked new-born soul, their stake,
   Stood blind between;
God said "let him that wins her take
   And keep Faustine."

But this time Satan throve, no doubt;
   Long since, I ween,
God's part in you was battered out;
   Long since, Faustine.

The die rang sideways as it fell,
30   Rang cracked and thin,
Like a man's laughter heard in hell
   Far down, Faustine,

A shadow of laughter like a sigh,
   Dead sorrow's kin;
So rang, thrown down, the devil's die
   That won Faustine.

A suckling of his breed you were,
   One hard to wean;
But God, who lost you, left you fair,
40   We see, Faustine.

You have the face that suits a woman
   For her soul's screen—
The sort of beauty that's called human
   In hell, Faustine.

You could do all things but be good
   Or chaste of mien;
And that you would not if you could,
   We know, Faustine.

Even he who cast seven devils out
   Of Magdalene°
Could hardly do as much, I doubt,   50
   For you, Faustine.

Did Satan make you to spite God?
   Or did God mean
To scourge with scorpions for a rod
   Our sins, Faustine?

I know what queen at first you were,
   As though I had seen
Red gold and black imperious hair
   Twice crown Faustine.   60

As if your fed sarcophagus
   Spared flesh and skin,
You come back face to face with us,
   The same Faustine.

She loved the games men played with death,
   Where death must win;
As though the slain man's blood and breath
   Revived Faustine.

Nets caught the pike, pikes tore the net;
   Lithe limbs and lean   70
From drained-out pores dripped thick red sweat
   To soothe Faustine.

She drank the steaming drift and dust
   Blown off the scene;
Blood could not ease the bitter lust
   That galled Faustine.

All round the foul fat furrows reeked,
   Where blood sank in;
The circus splashed and seethed and shrieked
   All round Faustine.   80

But these are gone now: years entomb
   The dust and din;
Yea, even the bath's fierce reek and fume
   That slew Faustine.

Was life worth living then? and now
   Is life worth sin?
Where are the imperial years? and how
   Are you Faustine?

Your soul forgot her joys, forgot
   Her times of teen;   90

49–50 **he who cast . . . Magdalene.** By the nineteenth century and even earlier, the woman taken in adultery, the woman who washes Christ's feet with her hair, and several other women in the Gospels had been combined into one, Mary Magdalene

Yea, this life likewise will you not
    Forget, Faustine?

For in the time we know not of
    Did fate begin
Weaving the web of days that wove
    Your doom, Faustine.

The threads were wet with wine, and all
    Were smooth to spin;
They wove you like a Bacchanal,°
100   The first Faustine.

And Bacchus cast your mates and you
    Wild grapes to glean;
Your flower-like lips were dashed with dew
    From his, Faustine.

Your drenched loose hands were stretched to hold
    The vine's wet green,
Long ere they coined in Roman gold
    Your face, Faustine.

Then after change of soaring feather
110   And winnowing fin,
You woke in weeks of feverish weather,
    A new Faustine.

A star upon your birthday burned,
    Whose fierce serene
Red pulseless planet never yearned
    In heaven, Faustine.

Stray breaths of Sapphic song° that blew
    Through Mitylene°
Shook the fierce quivering blood in you
120   By night, Faustine.

The shameless nameless love that makes
    Hell's iron gin
Shut on you like a trap that breaks
    The soul, Faustine.

And when your veins were void and dead,
    What ghosts unclean
Swarmed round the straitened barren bed
    That hid Faustine?

What sterile growths of sexless root
130   Or epicene?°
What flower of kisses without fruit
    Of love, Faustine?

What adders came to shed their coats?
    What coiled obscene
Small serpents with soft stretching throats
    Caressed Faustine?

But the time came of famished hours,
    Maimed loves and mean,
This ghastly thin-faced time of ours,
    To spoil Faustine.   140

You seem a thing that hinges hold,
    A love-machine
With clockwork joints of supple gold—
    No more, Faustine.

Not godless, for you serve one God,
    The Lampsacene,°
Who metes the gardens with his rod;
    Your lord, Faustine.

If one should love you with real love
    (Such things have been,   150
Things your fair face knows nothing of,
    It seems, Faustine);

That clear hair heavily bound back,
    The lights wherein
Shift from dead blue to burnt-up black;
    Your throat, Faustine,

Strong, heavy, throwing out the face
    And hard bright chin
And shameful scornful lips that grace
    Their shame, Faustine,   160

Curled lips, long since half kissed away,
    Still sweet and keen;
You'd give him—poison shall we say?
    Or what, Faustine?
(1866)

THE LEPER

Nothing is better, I well think,
    Than love; the hidden well-water
Is not so delicate to drink:
    This was well seen of me and her.

I served her in a royal house;
    I served her wine and curious meat.
For will to kiss between her brows
    I had no heart to sleep or eat.

99 **Bacchanal,** drunken revelry in honor of Bacchus, god of wine   117 **Sapphic song,** celebrations of the love of women   118 **Mitylene,** Sappho's birthplace on Lesbos   130 **epicene,** lacking characteristics of either sex

146 **Lampsacene.** Lampsacus, city in Asia Minor, chief seat of the cult of Priapus

Mere scorn God knows she had of me;
10   A poor scribe, nowise great or fair,
Who plucked his clerk's hood back to see
    Her curled-up lips and amorous hair.

I vex my head with thinking this.
    Yea, though God always hated me,
And hates me now that I can kiss
    Her eyes, plait up her hair to see

How she then wore it on the brows,
    Yet am I glad to have her dead
Here in this wretched wattled house°
20   Where I can kiss her eyes and head.

Nothing is better, I well know,
    Than love; no amber in cold sea
Or gathered berries under snow:
    That is well seen of her and me.

Three thoughts I make my pleasure of:
    First I take heart and think of this:
That knight's gold hair she chose to love,
    His mouth she had such will to kiss.

Then I remember that sundawn
30   I brought him by a privy way
Out at her lattice,° and thereon
    What gracious words she found to say.

(Cold rushes for such little feet—
    Both feet could lie into my hand.
A marvel was it of my sweet
    Her upright body could so stand.)

"Sweet friend, God give you thank and grace;
    Now am I clean and whole of shame,
Nor shall men burn me in the face
40   For my sweet fault that scandals them."

I tell you over word by word.
    She, sitting edgewise on her bed,
Holding her feet, said thus. The third,
    A sweeter thing than these, I said.

God, that makes time and ruins it,
    And alters not, abiding God,
Changed with disease her body sweet,
    The body of love wherein she abode.

Love is more sweet and comelier
50   Than a dove's throat strained out to sing.
All they spat out and cursed at her
    And cast her forth for a base thing.

They cursed her, seeing how God had wrought
    This curse to plague her, a curse of his.
Fools were they surely, seeing not
    How sweeter than all sweet she is.

He that had held her by the hair,
    With kissing lips blinding her eyes,
Felt her bright bosom, strained and bare,
    Sigh under him, with short mad cries   60

Out of her throat and sobbing mouth
    And body broken up with love,
With sweet hot tears his lips were loth
    Her own should taste the savour of,

Yea, he inside whose grasp all night
    Her fervent body leapt or lay,
Stained with sharp kisses red and white,
    Found her a plague to spurn away.

I hid her in this wattled house,
    I served her water and poor bread.   70
For joy to kiss between her brows
    Time upon time I was nigh dead.

Bread failed; we got but well-water
    And gathered grass with dropping seed.
I had such joy of kissing her,
    I had small care to sleep or feed.

Sometimes when service made me glad
    The sharp tears leapt between my lids,
Falling on her, such joy I had
    To do the service God forbids.   80

"I pray you let me be at peace,
    Get hence, make room for me to die."
She said that: her poor lip would cease,
    Put up to mine, and turn to cry.

I said, "Bethink yourself how love
    Fared in us twain, what either did;
Shall I unclothe my soul thereof?
    That I should do this, God forbid."

Yea, though God hateth us, he knows
    That hardly in a little thing   90
Love faileth of the work it does
    Till it grow ripe for gathering.

Six months, and now my sweet is dead
    A trouble takes me; I know not
If all were done well, all well said,
    No word or tender deed forgot.

Too sweet, for the least part in her,

To have shed life out by fragments; yet,
Could the close mouth catch breath and stir,
I might see something I forget.

Six months, and I sit still and hold
In two cold palms her cold two feet.
Her hair, half grey half ruined gold,
Thrills me and burns me in kissing it.

Love bites and stings me through, to see
Her keen face made of sunken bones.
Her worn-off eyelids madden me,
That were shot through with purple once.

She said, "Be good with me; I grow
So tired for shame's sake, I shall die
If you say nothing:" even so.
And she is dead now, and shame put by.

Yea, and the scorn she had of me
In the old time, doubtless vexed her then.
I never should have kissed her. See
What fools God's anger makes of men!

She might have loved me a little too,
Had I been humbler for her sake.
But that new shame could make love new
She saw not—yet her shame did make.

I took too much upon my love,
Having for such mean service done
Her beauty and all the ways thereof,
Her face and all the sweet thereon.

Yea, all this while I tended her,
I know the old love held fast his part:
I know the old scorn waxed heavier,
Mixed with sad wonder, in her heart.

It may be all my love went wrong—
A scribe's work writ awry and blurred,
Scrawled after the blind evensong—
Spoilt music with no perfect word.

But surely I would fain have done
All things the best I could. Perchance
Because I failed, came short of one,
She kept at heart that other man's.

I am grown blind with all these things:
It may be now she hath in sight
Some better knowledge; still there clings
The old question. Will not God do right?

(1866)

THE GARDEN OF PROSERPINE

Here, where the world is quiet;
    Here, where all trouble seems
Dead winds' and spent waves' riot
    In doubtful dreams of dreams;
I watch the green field growing
For reaping folk and sowing,
For harvest-time and mowing,
    A sleepy world of streams.

I am tired of tears and laughter,
    And men that laugh and weep;   10
Of what may come hereafter
    For men that sow to reap;
I am weary of days and hours,
Blown buds of barren flowers,°
Desires and dreams and powers
    And everything but sleep.

Here life has death for neighbor,
    And far from eye or ear
Wan waves and wet winds labor,
    Weak ships and spirits steer;   20
They drive adrift, and whither
They wot° not who make thither;
But no such winds blow hither,
    And no such things grow here.

No growth of moor or coppice,
    No heather-flower or vine,
But bloomless buds of poppies,°
    Green grapes of Proserpine,
Pale beds of blowing rushes
Where no leaf blooms or blushes   30
Save this whereout she crushes
    For dead men deadly wine.

Pale, without name or number,
    In fruitless fields of corn,°
They bow themselves and slumber
    All night till light is born;
And like a soul belated,
In hell and heaven unmated,
By cloud and mist abated
    Comes out of darkness morn.   40

Though one were strong as seven,
    He too with death shall dwell,

The Garden of Proserpine. In Greek mythology Proserpine was the goddess and
queen of the lower world. She was the daughter of Zeus and Demeter, or Ceres,
goddess of the harvest, and was carried off by Pluto while she was gathering
flowers in the Vale of Enna in Sicily. Her mother wandered over the whole earth
in search of her. On Demeter's prayer to Zeus that Proserpine be allowed to return to the upper world, Zeus permitted her to spend six months of the year on
earth; her alternate periods on earth and in Hades symbolize the changes of the
seasons 14 **Blown . . . flowers,** blossoming flowers that will produce no fruit.
They are used as a symbol of unfulfilled desires and dreams 22 **wot,** know
27 **poppies.** Proserpine was often represented with a crown of poppies on her
head (l. 50) 34 **corn,** grain, wheat

Nor wake with wings in heaven,
  Nor weep for pains in hell;
Though one were fair as roses,
His beauty clouds and closes;
And well though love reposes,
  In the end it is not well.

Pale, beyond porch and portal,
50 Crowned with calm leaves, she stands
Who gathers all things mortal
  With cold immortal hands;
Her languid lips are sweeter
Than love's who fears to greet her
To men that mix and meet her
  From many times and lands.

She waits for each and other,
  She waits for all men born;
Forgets the earth her mother,
60 The life of fruits and corn;
And spring and seed and swallow
Take wing for her and follow
Where summer song rings hollow
  And flowers are put to scorn.

There go the loves that wither,
  The old loves with wearier wings;
And all dead years draw thither,
  And all disastrous things;
Dead dreams of days forsaken,
70 Blind buds that snows have shaken,
Wild leaves that winds have taken,
  Red strays of ruined springs.

We are not sure of sorrow,
  And joy was never sure;
Today will die tomorrow;
  Time stoops to no man's lure;
And love, grown faint and fretful,
With lips but half regretful
Sighs, and with eyes forgetful
80 Weeps that no loves endure.

From too much love of living,
  From hope and fear set free,
We thank with brief thanksgiving
  Whatever gods may be
That no life lives forever;
That dead men rise up never;
That even the weariest river
  Winds somewhere safe to sea.

Then star nor sun shall waken,
90 Nor any change of light;
Nor sound of waters shaken,

Nor any sound or sight;
Nor wintry leaves nor vernal,
Nor days nor things diurnal;°
Only the sleep eternal
  In an eternal night.

(1866)

A FORSAKEN GARDEN

In a coign° of the cliff between lowland and highland,
  At the sea-down's edge between windward and lee,
Walled round with rocks as an inland island,
  The ghost of a garden fronts the sea.
A girdle of brushwood and thorn encloses
  The steep square slope of the blossomless bed
Where the weeds that grew green from the graves of its
    roses
    Now lie dead.

The fields fall southward, abrupt and broken,
  To the low last edge of the long lone land.   10
If a step should sound or a word be spoken,
  Would a ghost not rise at the strange guest's hand?
So long have the gray bare walks lain guestless,
  Through branches and briars if a man make way,
He shall find no life, but the sea-wind's, restless
    Night and day.

The dense hard passage is blind and stifled
  That crawls by a track none turn to climb
To the strait waste place that the years have rifled
  Of all but the thorns that are touched not of time.   20
The thorns he spares when the rose is taken;
  The rocks are left when he wastes the plain.
The wind that wanders, the weeds wind-shaken,
    These remain.

Not a flower to be pressed of the foot that falls not;
  As the heart of a dead man the seed-plots are dry;
From the thicket of thorns whence the nightingale calls
    not,
  Could she call, there were never a rose to reply
Over the meadows that blossom and wither
  Wings but the note of a sea-bird's song;   30
Only the sun and the rain come hither
  All year long.

The sun burns sear and the rain dishevels
  One gaunt bleak blossom of scentless breath.
Only the wind here hovers and revels
  In a round where life seems barren as death.
Here there was laughing of old, there was weeping,

94 **diurnal,** belonging to daylight
A Forsaken Garden   1 **coign,** corner, projection

Haply, of lovers none ever will know,
Whose eyes went seaward a hundred sleeping Years
ago.

40 Heart handfast in heart as they stood, "Look thither,"
Did he whisper? "look forth from the flowers to the
sea;
For the foam-flowers endure when the rose-blossoms
wither,
And men that love lightly may die—but we?"
And the same wind sang and the same waves
whitened,
And or ever the garden's last petals were shed,
In the lips that had whispered, the eyes that had
lightered,
Love was dead.

Or they loved their life through, and then went
whither?
And were one to the end—but what end who
knows?
50 Love deep as the sea as a rose must wither,
As the rose-red seaweed that mocks the rose.
Shall the dead take thought for the dead to love them?
What love was ever as deep as a grave?
They are loveless now as the grass above them
Or the wave.

All are at one now, roses and lovers,
Not known of the cliffs and the fields and the sea.
Not a breath of the time that has been hovers
In the air now soft with a summer to be.
60 Not a breath shall there sweeten the seasons hereafter
Of the flowers or the lovers that laugh now or weep,
When as they that are free now of weeping and
laughter
We shall sleep.

Here death may deal not again forever;
Here change may come not till all change end.
From the graves they have made they shall rise up
never,
Who have left naught living to ravage and rend.
Earth, stones, and thorns of the wild ground growing,
While the sun and the rain live, these shall be;
70 Till a last wind's breath upon all these blowing
Roll the sea.

Till the slow sea rise and the sheer cliff crumble,
Till terrace and meadow the deep gulfs drink,
Till the strength of the waves of the high tides humble
The fields that lessen, the rocks that shrink,
Here now in his triumph where all things falter,
Stretched out on the spoils that his own hand
spread,

As a god self-slain on his own strange altar,
Death lies dead.

(1876)

HERTHA°

I am that which began;
Out of me the years roll;
Out of me God and man;
I am equal and whole;
God changes, and man, and the form of them bodily;
I am the soul.

Before ever land was,
Before ever the sea,
Or soft hair of the grass,
Or fair limbs of the tree,
Or the flesh-colored fruit of my branches, I was, and
thy soul was in me.   10

First life on my sources
First drifted and swam;
Out of me are the forces
That save it or damn;
Out of me man and woman, and wild-beast and bird;
before God was, I am.°

Beside or above me
Naught is there to go;
Love or unlove me,
Unknow me or know,
I am that which unloves me and loves; I am stricken,
and I am the blow.   20

I the mark that is missed
And the arrows that miss,
I the mouth that is kissed
And the breath in the kiss,
The search, and the sought, and the seeker, the soul
and the body that is.

I am that thing which blesses
My spirit elate;
That which caresses
With hands uncreate
My limbs unbegotten that measure the length of the
measure of fate.   30

But what thing dost thou now,
Looking Godward, to cry,

Hertha. In Germanic mythology Hertha was goddess of the earth and of fertility
and growth; Swinburne conceived of her as the personification of the world soul
15 before . . . am. Cf. Exodus, 3:14: "And God said unto Moses, I am that I
am"; also John, 8:58: "Jesus said unto them, Verily, verily, I say unto you, Before
Abraham was, I am"

"I am I, thou art thou,
    I am low, thou art high"?
I am thou, whom thou seekest to find him; find thou
    but thyself, thou art I.

    I the grain and the furrow,
        The plow-cloven clod
    And the plowshare drawn thorough,
        The germ and the sod,
    The deed and the doer, the seed and the sower, the
40   dust which is God.

    Hast thou known° how I fashioned thee,
        Child, underground?
    Fire that impassioned thee,
        Iron that bound,
Dim changes of water, what thing of all these hast thou
    known of or found?

    Canst thou say in thine heart
        Thou hast seen with thine eyes
    With what cunning of art
        Thou wast wrought in what wise,
By what force of what stuff thou wast shapen, and
50   shown on my breast to the skies?

    Who hath given, who hath sold it thee,
        Knowledge of me?
    Hath the wilderness told it thee?
        Hast thou learnt of the sea?
Hast thou communed in spirit with night? Have the
    winds taken counsel with thee?

    Have I set such a star
        To show light on thy brow
    That thou sawest from afar
        What I show to thee now?
Have ye spoken as brethren together, the sun and the
60   mountains and thou?

    What is here, dost thou know it?
        What was, hast thou known?
    Prophet nor poet
        Nor tripod nor throne°
Nor spirit nor flesh can make answer, but only thy
    mother alone.

    Mother, not maker,
        Born, and not made;°
    Though her children forsake her,
        Allured or afraid,
Praying prayers to the God of their fashion, she stirs
70   not for all that have prayed.

    A creed is a rod,
        And a crown is of night;
    But this thing is God,
        To be man with thy might,
To grow straight in the strength of thy spirit, and live
    out thy life as the light.

    I am in thee to save thee,
        As my soul in thee saith;
    Give thou as I gave thee,
        Thy life-blood and breath,
Green leaves of thy labor, white flowers of thy
    thought, and red fruit of thy death.   80

    Be the ways of thy giving
        As mine were to thee;
    The free life of thy living,
        Be the gift of it free;
Not as servant to lord, nor as master to slave, shalt
    thou give thee to me.

    O children of banishment,
        Souls overcast,
    Were the lights° ye see vanish meant
        Alway to last,
Ye would know not the sun overshining the shadows
    and stars overpast.   90

    I that saw where ye trod
        The dim paths of the night
    Set the shadow called God
        In your skies to give light;
But the morning of manhood is risen, and the shadow-
    less soul is in sight.

    The tree many-rooted°
        That swells to the sky
    With frondage red-fruited,
        The life-tree am I;
In the buds of your lives is the sap of my leaves; ye
    shall live and not die.   100

    But the gods of your fashion
        That take and that give,
    In their pity and passion
        That scourge and forgive,
They are worms that are bred in the bark that falls
    off; they shall die and not live.

    My own blood is what stanches
        The wounds in my bark;
    Stars caught in my branches
        Make day of the dark,
And are worshiped as suns till the sunrise shall tread
    out their fires as a spark.   110

<hr/>

41–60 **Hast thou known, etc.** With these questions compare the words spoken to
Job by the Lord out of the whirlwind (*Job*, 38–39)   64 **Nor . . . throne,** neither
priest nor king. The tripod was the altar, supported on three legs, on which the
priestesses of Apollo at Delphi sat when they delivered their oracles   67 **Born
. . . made.** These lines are a protest against the idea of a single act of creation.
Swinburne conceives nature as a continuous process of evolution

88 **lights,** religious creeds and dogmas   96 **The tree many-rooted,** the mighty
ash tree Yggdrasil, supposed, in Norse mythology, to support the entire universe.
It represents the whole of the universe, for its roots are in hell, its trunk is in earth,
and its branches are in heaven

Where dead ages hide under
    The live roots of the tree,
In my darkness the thunder
    Makes utterance of me;
In the clash of my boughs with each other ye hear the
    waves sound of the sea.

That noise is of Time,
    As his feathers are spread
And his feet set to climb
    Through the boughs overhead,
And my foliage rings round him and rustles, and
120   branches are bent with his tread.

The storm-winds of ages
    Blow through me and cease,
The war-wind that rages,
    The spring-wind of peace,
Ere the breath of them roughen my tresses, ere one
    of my blossoms increase.

All sounds of all changes,
    All shadows and lights
On the world's mountain-ranges
    And stream-riven heights,
Whose tongue is the wind's tongue and language of
130   storm-clouds on earth-shaking nights;

All forms of all faces,
    All works of all hands
In unsearchable places
    Of time-stricken lands,
All death and all life, and all reigns and all ruins,
    drop through me as sands.

Though sore be my burden
    And more than ye know,
And my growth have no guerdon
    But only to grow,
Yet I fail not of growing for lightnings above me or
140   death-worms below.

These too have their part in me,
    As I too in these;
Such fire is at heart in me,
    Such sap is this tree's,
Which hath in it all sounds and all secrets of infinite
    lands and of seas.

In the spring-colored hours
    When my mind was as May's,
There brake forth of me flowers
    By centuries of days,
Strong blossoms with perfume of manhood shot out
150   from my spirit as rays.

And the sound of them springing
    And smell of their shoots

Were as warmth and sweet singing
    And strength to my roots;
And the lives of my children made perfect with free-
    dom of soul were my fruits.

I bid you but be;
    I have need not of prayer;
I have need of you free
    As your mouths of mine air;
That my heart may be greater within me, beholding
    the fruits of me fair.   160

More fair than strange fruit is
    Of faiths ye espouse;
In me only the root is
    That blooms in your boughs;
Behold now your God that ye made you, to feed him
    with faith of your vows.

In the darkening and whitening
    Abysses adored,
With dayspring and lightning
    For lamp and for sword,
God thunders in heaven, and his angels are red with
    the wrath of the Lord.   170

O my sons, O too dutiful
    Toward gods not of me,
Was not I enough beautiful?
    Was it hard to be free?
For behold, I am with you, am in you and of you;
    look forth now and see.

Lo, winged with world's wonders,
    With miracles shod,
With the fires of his thunders
    For raiment and rod,
God trembles in heaven, and his angels are white
    with the terror of God.   180

For his twilight° is come on him,
    His anguish is here;
And his spirits gaze dumb on him,
    Grown gray from his fear;
And his hour taketh hold on him stricken, the last
    of his infinite year.

Thought made him and breaks him,
    Truth slays and forgives;
But to you, as time takes him,
    This new thing it gives,
Even love, the beloved Republic, that feeds upon
    freedom and lives.   190

181 **his twilight.** The idea of the twilight of the gods is derived from Norse mythology. This is the period, known as Ragnarok, which involves the destruction of the universe. After this period a new heaven and a new earth will arise out of the sea

For truth only is living,
　　Truth only is whole,
And the love of his giving
　　Man's polestar and pole;
Man, pulse of my center, and fruit of my body, and
　　seed of my soul;

One birth of my bosom;
　　One beam of mine eye;
One topmost blossom
　　That scales the sky;
Man, equal and one with me, man that is made of me,
　　man that is I.

(1871)

WALTER HORATIO PATER
1839–1894

Walter Pater was the second son of Richard Glode Pater, a physician in the East End of London. He had his elementary schooling at King's School, Canterbury, and entered Queen's College, Oxford, in 1858. Four years later he became a private tutor at Oxford, and six years later a Fellow of Brasenose College. Pater remained at Oxford until 1885, when he moved with his sisters, who had been keeping house for him, to London. He returned to Oxford a year before his death in 1894 and completed his last work there.

Pater was a fastidious master of prose style. None of his work appeared in print until he was twenty-eight when, in 1867, the *Westminster Review* published his essay on Winckelmann (1717–1768), a famous German classical art critic. After this, he wrote essays fairly steadily, and in 1873 they were gathered into his first volume, *Studies in the History of the Renaissance*, a series of discussions of the spirit of the Renaissance through exemplary works of painting, sculpture, and literature. The volume contained an introduction and conclusion that became manifestos of late Victorian aestheticism. An interval of twelve years followed before the appearance of *Marius the Epicurean*, a philosophical romance of a young Roman of the early Roman empire who evolves through aestheticism and Epicureanism toward Christianity. The book was Pater's defense against the charges of hedonism brought upon him by the conclusion to *The Renaissance*, in which he had advised his readers to burn "with a hard gentle flame." In 1887 he published his *Imaginary Portraits*—four in number—and two years later the collection of critical essays called *Appreciations*, on Shakespeare, Wordsworth, and others. *Plato and Platonism*, in some respects a return to his first love, philosophy, was issued in 1893. *The Child in the*

House (1894) is an imaginative, autobiographical treatment of the sensitive boy. *Greek Studies* and *Gaston de Latour*—left unfinished—were published after his death.

Pater's criticism has its roots in his philosophy of life. He began his intellectual career with philosophy, and Plato and Goethe were probably the greatest literary influences in his life. But from philosophy his interest narrowed to aesthetics, the study of the principles of beauty in art and literature. His philosophy of life led him to believe that the highest wisdom lay in extracting from literature and art a heightened sense of life, an ecstasy of beauty. He became, in a sense, a connoisseur of beauty. His criticisms took the form of discovering the best in literature and art and of revealing these master strokes in *appreciations* of the craftsmen. This continued contemplation of the best gave him a soundness and quickness of judgment that made possible such discriminating definitions as the lucid distinction between the classical and the romantic, which penetrates to the core of both and makes clear the beauty of each.

from THE RENAISSANCE

PREFACE

Many attempts have been made by writers on art and poetry to define beauty in the abstract, to express it in the most general terms, to find some universal formula for it. The value of these attempts has most often been in the suggestive and penetrating things said by the way. Such discussions help us very little to enjoy what has been well done in art or poetry, to discriminate between what is more and what is less excellent in them, or to use words like beauty, excellence, art, poetry, with a more precise meaning than they would 10 otherwise have. Beauty, like all other qualities presented to human experience, is relative; and the definition of it becomes unmeaning and useless in proportion to its abstractness. To define beauty, not in the most abstract but in the most concrete terms possible, to find not its universal formula, but the formula which expresses most adequately this or that special manifestation of it, is the aim of the true student of aesthetics.

"To see the object as in itself it really is," has been 20 justly said to be the aim of all true criticism whatever; and in aesthetic criticism the first step towards seeing one's object as it really is, is to know one's own impression as it really is, to discriminate it, to realize it distinctly. The objects with which aesthetic criticism deals—music, poetry, artistic and accomplished forms of human life—are indeed receptacles of so many powers or forces: they possess, like the products of nature, so many virtues or qualities. What is this song or picture, this engaging personality presented in life or in a book, to me? What effect does it really produce on me? Does it give me pleasure? and if so, what sort or degree of pleasure? How is my nature modified by its presence, and under its influence? The answers to these questions are the original facts with which the aesthetic critic has to do; and, as in the study of light, of morals, of number, one must realize such primary data for one's self, or not at all. And he who experiences these impressions strongly, and drives directly at the discrimination and analysis of them, has no need to trouble himself with the abstract question what beauty is in itself, or what its exact relation to truth or experience—metaphysical questions, as unprofitable as metaphysical questions elsewhere. He may pass them all by as being, answerable or not, of no interest to him.

The aesthetic critic, then, regards all the objects with which he has to do, all works of art, and the fairer forms of nature and human life, as powers or forces producing pleasurable sensations, each of a more or less peculiar or unique kind. This influence he feels, and wishes to explain, by analyzing and reducing it to its elements. To him, the picture, the landscape, the engaging personality in life or in a book, "La Gioconda," the hills of Carrara, Pico of Mirandola,° are valuable for their virtues, as we say, in speaking of a herb, a wine, a gem; for the property each has of affecting one with a special, a unique, impression of pleasure. Our education becomes complete in proportion as our susceptibility to these impressions increases in depth and variety. And the function of the aesthetic critic is to distinguish, to analyze, and separate from its adjuncts, the virtue by which a picture, a landscape, a fair personality in life or in a book, produces this special impression of beauty or pleasure, to indicate what the source of that impression is, and under what conditions it is experienced. His end is reached when he has disengaged that virtue, and noted it, as a chemist notes some natural element, for himself and others; and the rule for those who would reach this end is stated with great exactness in the words of a recent critic of Sainte-Beuve: *De se borner à connaître de près les belles choses, et à s'en nourrir en exquis amateurs en humanistes accomplis.*°

What is important, then, is not that the critic should possess a correct abstract definition of beauty for the intellect, but a certain kind of temperament, the power of being deeply moved by the presence of beautiful objects. He will remember always that beauty exists in many forms. To him all periods, types, schools of taste, are in themselves equal. In all ages there have been some excellent workmen, and some excellent work done. The question he asks is always: In whom did the stir, the genius, the sentiment of the period find itself? where was the receptacle of its refinement, its elevation, its taste? "The ages are all equal," says William Blake, "but genius is always above its age."

Often it will require great nicety to disengage this virtue from the commoner elements with which it may be found in combination. Few artists, not Goethe or Byron even, work quite cleanly, casting off all debris, and leaving us only what the heat of their imagination has wholly fused and transformed. Take, for instance, the writings of Wordsworth. The heat of his genius, entering into the substance of his work, has crystallized a part, but only a part, of it; and in that great mass of verse there is much which might well be forgotten. But scattered up and down it, sometimes fusing and transforming entire compositions, like the stanzas on *Resolution and Independence,* or the *Ode on the Recollections of Childhood,* sometimes, as if at random, depositing a fine crystal here or there, in a matter it does not wholly search through and transmute, we trace the action of his unique, incommunicable faculty, that strange, mystical sense of a life in natural things, and of man's life as a part of nature, drawing strength and color and character from local influences, from the hills and streams, and from natural sights and sounds. Well! that is the *virtue,* the active principle in Wordsworth's poetry; and then the function of the critic of Wordsworth is to follow up that active principle, to disengage it, to mark the degree in which it penetrates his verse.

The subjects of the following studies are taken from the history of the *Renaissance,* and touch what I think the chief points in that complex, many-sided movement. I have explained in the first of them what I understand by the word, giving it a much wider scope than was intended by those who originally used it to denote that revival of classical antiquity in the fifteenth century which was only one of many results of a general excitement and enlightening of the human mind, but of which the great aim and achievements of what, as Christian art, is often falsely opposed to the Renaissance, were another result. This outbreak of the human spirit may be traced far into the Middle Age itself, with its motives already clearly pronounced, the care for physical beauty, the worship of the body, the breaking down of those limits which the religious system of the Middle Age imposed on the heart and the imagination. I have taken as an example of this movement, this earlier Renaissance within the Middle Age itself, and as an expression of its qualities, two little compositions in early French; not because they constitute the best possible expression of them, but because they help the unity of my series, inasmuch as the Renaissance ends also in France, in French poetry, in

The Renaissance   Preface   54–55 "La Gioconda," the hills of Carrara, Pico of Mirandola, the name given to Leonardo da Vinci's portrait of Mona Lisa; marble quarry region; fifteenth century Italian humanist and philosopher   72–74 **De se borner . . . accomplis.** To restrict themselves to knowing first hand beautiful things, and from these to develop themselves as exquisite amateurs, as accomplished humanists

a phase of which the writings of Joachim du Bellay° are
in many ways the most perfect illustration. The Renaissance, in truth, put forth in France an aftermath, a wonderful later growth, the products of which have to the full that subtle and delicate sweetness which belongs to a refined and comely decadence, just as its earliest phases have the freshness which belongs to all periods of growth in art, the charm of *ascêsis,* of the austere and serious girding of the loins in youth.

But it is in Italy, in the fifteenth century, that the interest of the Renaissance mainly lies—in that solemn fifteenth century which can hardly be studied too much, not merely for its positive results in the things of the intellect and the imagination, its concrete works of art, its special and prominent personalities, with their profound aesthetic charm, but for its general spirit and character, for the ethical qualities of which it is a consummate type.

The various forms of intellectual activity which together make up the culture of an age, move for the most part from different starting points, and by unconnected roads. As products of the same generation they partake indeed of a common character, and unconsciously illustrate each other; but of the producers themselves, each group is solitary, gaining what advantage or disadvantage there may be in intellectual isolation. Art and poetry, philosophy and the religious life, and that other life of refined pleasure and action in the conspicuous places of the world, are each of them confined to its own circle of ideas, and those who prosecute either of them are generally little curious of the thoughts of others. There come, however, from time to time, eras of more favorable conditions, in which the thoughts of men draw nearer together than is their wont, and the many interests of the intellectual world combine in one complete type of general culture. The fifteenth century in Italy is one of these happier eras, and what is sometimes said of the age of Pericles is true of that of Lorenzo:° it is an age productive in personalities, many-sided, centralized, complete. Here, artists and philosophers and those whom the action of the world has elevated and made keen, do not live in isolation, but breathe a common air, and catch light and heat from each other's thoughts. There is a spirit of general elevation and enlightenment in which all alike communicate. The unity of this spirit gives unity to all the various products of the Renaissance; and it is to this intimate alliance with mind, this participation in the best thoughts which that age produced, that the art of Italy in the fifteenth century owes much of its grave dignity and influence.

I have added an essay on Winckelmann,° as not incongruous with the studies which precede it, because Winckelmann, coming in the eighteenth century, really belongs in spirit to an earlier age. By his enthusiasm for the things of the intellect and the imagination for their own sake, by his Hellenism, his lifelong struggle to attain to the Greek spirit, he is in sympathy with the humanists of a previous century. He is the last fruit of the Renaissance, and explains in a striking way its motive and tendencies.

"LA GIOCONDA"°

"La Gioconda" is, in the truest sense, Leonardo's masterpiece, the revealing instance of his mode of thought and work. In suggestiveness, only the "Melancholia" of Dürer° is comparable to it; and no crude symbolism disturbs the effect of its subdued and graceful mystery. We all know the face and hands of the figure, set in its marble chair, in that circle° of fantastic rocks, as in some faint light under sea. Perhaps of all ancient pictures time has chilled it least. As often happens with works in which invention seems to reach its limit, there is an element in it given to, not invented by, the master. In that inestimable folio of drawings, once in the possession of Vasari,° were certain designs by Verrocchio,° faces of such impressive beauty that Leonardo in his boyhood copied them many times. It is hard not to connect with these designs of the elder, by-past master, as with its germinal principle, the unfathomable smile, always with a touch of something sinister in it, which plays over all Leonardo's work. Besides, the picture is a portrait. From childhood we see this image defining itself on the fabric of his dreams, and but for express historical testimony, we might fancy that this was but his ideal lady, embodied and beheld at last. What was the relationship of a living Florentine to this creature of his thought? By what strange affinities had the dream and the person grown up thus apart, and yet so closely together? Present from the first incorporeally in Leonardo's brain, dimly traced in the designs of Verrocchio, she is found present at last in Il Giocondo's house. That there is much of mere portraiture in the picture is attested by the legend that by artificial means, the presence of mimes° and flute-players, that subtle expression was protracted on the face. Again, was it in four years and by renewed labor never really completed, or in four months and as by stroke of magic, that the image was projected?

The presence that rose thus so strangely beside the waters, is expressive of what in the ways of a thousand years men had come to desire. Hers is the head upon

139 **Joachim du Bellay,** French poet and critic (1522–1560)   176–177 **age of Pericles . . . of Lorenzo.** Pericles ruled Athens in the fifth century B.C.; Lorenzo de Medici was a Renaissance Florentine ruler and patron of the arts
190 **Winckelmann,** eighteenth century German scholar who founded the modern study of Greek sculptures and antiquities

"**La Gioconda.**" Leonardo da Vinci, Italian painter, architect, musician, scientist, engineer, painted the portrait known as *La Gioconda* between 1503 and 1506 in Florence. His subject was the beautiful Mona (or Madonna, or Lady) Lisa, "the young, third wife of Francesco del Giocondo," a Florentine nobleman. La Gioconda's rapt expression, Leonardo explained, came from the effect of soft music which was played while he painted her. The painting is now in the collection of the Louvre in Paris   4 **Dürer,** Albrecht Dürer (1471–1582), the greatest artist of the Renaissance in Germany; he was a painter, an engraver, a sculptor, and an architect. His *Melancholia* is a copperplate engraving   7 **circle,** a kind of natural amphitheater   13 **Vasari,** Giorgio Vasari (1511–1574), Italian architect, painter, and writer on art   14 **Verrocchio,** Andrea Verrocchio (1435–1488), Italian sculptor and painter   32 **mimes,** jesters, clowns

which all "the ends of the world are come,"° and the eyelids are a little weary. It is a beauty wrought out from within upon the flesh, the deposit, little cell by cell, of strange thoughts and fantastic reveries and exquisite passions. Set it for a moment beside one of those white Greek goddesses or beautiful women of antiquity, and how would they be troubled by this beauty, into which the soul with all its maladies has passed! All the thoughts and experience of the world
50 have etched and molded there, in that which they have of power to refine and make expressive the outward form, the animalism° of Greece, the lust of Rome, the mysticism of the Middle Age with its spiritual ambition and imaginative loves, the return of the Pagan world,° the sins of the Borgias.° She is older than the rocks among which she sits; like the vampire,° she has been dead many times, and learned the secrets of the grave; and has been a diver in deep seas, and keeps their fallen day° about her; and trafficked for strange webs
60 with Eastern merchants, and, as Leda,° was the mother of Helen of Troy, and, as Saint Anne, the mother of Mary; and all this has been to her but as the sound of lyres and flutes, and lives only in the delicacy with which it has molded the changing lineaments, and tinged the eyelids and the hands. The fancy of a perpetual life, sweeping together ten thousand experiences, is an old one; and modern philosophy has conceived the idea of humanity as wrought upon by, and summing up in itself, all modes of thought and life.
70 Certainly Lady Lisa might stand as the embodiment of the old fancy, the symbol of the modern idea.

THE SCHOOL OF GIORGIONE

It is the mistake of much popular criticism to regard poetry, music, and painting—all the various products of art—as but translations into different languages of one and the same fixed quantity of imaginative thought, supplemented by certain technical qualities of colour, in painting; of sound, in music; of rhythmical words, in poetry. In this way, the sensuous element in art, and with it almost everything in art that is essentially artistic, is made a matter of indifference; and a
10 clear apprehension of the opposite principle—that the sensuous material of each art brings with it a special phase or quality of beauty, untranslatable into the forms of any other, an order of impressions distinct in kind—is the beginning of all true æsthetic criticism.

For, as art addresses not pure sense, still less the pure intellect, but the "imaginative reason" through the senses, there are differences of kind in æsthetic beauty, corresponding to the differences in kind of the gifts of sense themselves. Each art, therefore, having its own peculiar and untranslatable sensuous charm, 20 has it own special mode of reaching the imagination, its own special responsibilities to its material. One of the functions of æsthetic criticism is to define these limitations; to estimate the degree in which a given work of art fulfils its responsibilities to its special material; to note in a picture that true pictorial charm, which is neither a mere poetical thought or sentiment, on the one hand, nor a mere result of communicable technical skill in colour or design, on the other; to define in a poem that true poetical quality, which is 30 neither descriptive nor meditative merely, but comes of an inventive handling of rhythmical language, the element of song in the singing; to note in music the musical charm, that essential music, which presents no words, no matter of sentiment or thought, separable from the special form in which it is conveyed to us.

To such a philosophy of the variations of the beautiful, Lessing's° analysis of the spheres of sculpture and poetry, in the *Laocoön,* was an important contribution. But a true appreciation of these things is possible only in 40 the light of a whole system of such art-casuistries. Now painting is the art in the criticism of which this truth most needs enforcing, for it is in popular judgments on pictures that the false generalisation of all art into forms of poetry is most prevalent. To suppose that all is mere technical acquirement in delineation or touch, working through and addressing itself to the intelligence, on the one side, or a merely poetical, or what may be called literary interest, addressed also to the pure intelligence, on the other:—this is the way of most spectators, and of 50 many critics, who have never caught sight all the time of that true pictorial quality which lies between, unique pledge, as it is, of the possession of the pictorial gift, that inventive or creative handling of pure line and colour, which, as almost always in Dutch painting, as often also in the works of Titian or Veronese, is quite independent of anything definitely poetical in the subject it accompanies. It is the *drawing*—the design projected from that peculiar pictorial temperament or constitution, in which, while it may possibly be ignorant of 60 true anatomical proportions, all things whatever, all poetry, all ideas however abstract or obscure, float up as visible scene or image: it is the *colouring*—that weaving of light, as of just perceptible gold threads, through the dress, the flesh, the atmosphere, in Titian's *Lace-girl,* that staining of the whole fabric of the thing with a new, delightful physical quality. This *drawing,* then—the arabesque traced in the air by Tintoret's flying figures, by Titian's forest branches; this colouring—the magic conditions of light and hue in the atmo- 70

41 **the ends . . . come,** from *1 Corinthians,* 10:11   52 **animalism,** the doctrine that men are animals; the worship of physical form   54 **the return . . . world.** Near the end of the Middle Ages, Christianity lost much of its influence over the lives of the people   55 **Borgias,** a fifteenth-century family in Italy notorious for its violence, treachery, vices, and crimes. Leonardo served them in numerous ways   56 **vampire,** in medieval belief the reanimated body of a dead person, supposed to come from the grave and to wander about at night sucking the blood of persons asleep, thus causing their death and gaining a horrible immortality for itself   59 **their fallen day,** the gloom that prevails at great depths in the sea   60 **Leda,** in Greek mythology the wife of the Spartan king Tyndareus and mistress of Zeus. Helen of Troy, regarded as the most beautiful woman of her time, was faithless to her husband Menelaus. Thus, in its relation to Leda and Helen and to St. Anne and Mary, the face of La Gioconda reveals elements of the beautiful wanton wife and the saintly mother

The School of Giorgione   38 **Lessing,** eighteenth-century German critic and dramatist

sphere of Titian's *Lace-girl,* or Rubens's *Descent from the Cross:*—these essential pictorial qualities must first of all delight the sense, delight it as directly and sensuously as a fragment of Venetian glass; and through this delight alone become the vehicle of whatever poetry or science may lie beyond them in the intention of the composer. In its primary aspect, a great picture has no more definite message for us than an accidental play of sunlight and shadow for a few moments on the wall or
80 floor: is itself, in truth, a space of such fallen light, caught as the colours are in an Eastern carpet, but refined upon, and dealt with more subtly and exquisitely than by nature itself. And this primary and essential condition fulfilled, we may trace the coming of poetry into painting, by fine gradations upwards; from Japanese fan-painting, for instance, where we get, first, only abstract colour; then, just a little interfused sense of the poetry of flowers; then, sometimes, perfect flower-painting; and so, onwards, until in Titian we
90 have, as his poetry in the *Ariadne,* so actually a touch of true childlike humour in the diminutive, quaint figure with its silk gown, which ascends the temple stairs, in his picture of the *Presentation of the Virgin,* at Venice.

But although each art has thus its own specific order of impressions, and an untranslatable charm, while a just apprehension of the ultimate differences of the arts is the beginning of æsthetic criticism; yet it is noticeable that, in its special mode of handling its given material, each art may be observed to pass into the
100 condition of some other art, by what German critics term an *Anders-streben*°—a partial alienation from its own limitations, through which the arts are able, not indeed to supply the place of each other, but reciprocally to lend each other new forces.

Thus some of the most delightful music seems to be always approaching to figure, to pictorial definition. Architecture, again, though it has its own laws—laws esoteric enough, as the true architect knows only too well—yet sometimes aims at fulfilling the conditions of
110 a picture, as in the *Arena* chapel;° or of sculpture, as in the flawless unity of Giotto's tower at Florence; and often finds a true poetry, as in those strangely twisted staircases of the *châteaux* of the country of the Loire, as if it were intended that among their odd turnings the actors in a theatrical mode of life might pass each other unseen; there being a poetry also of memory and of the mere effect of time, by which architecture often profits greatly. Thus, again, sculpture aspires out of the hard limitation of pure form towards colour, or its equiva-
120 lent; poetry also, in many ways, finding guidance from the other arts, the analogy between a Greek tragedy and a work of Greek sculpture, between a sonnet and a relief, of French poetry generally with the art of engraving, being more than mere figures of speech; and all the arts in common aspiring towards the principle of music; music being the typical, or ideally consummate art, the object of the great *Anders-streben* of all art, of all that is artistic, or partakes of artistic qualities.

All art constantly aspires towards the condition of music. For a while in all other kinds of art it is possible 130 to distinguish the matter from the form, and the understanding can always make this distinction, yet it is the constant effort of art to obliterate it. That the mere matter of a poem, for instance, its subject, namely, its given incidents or situation—that the mere matter of a picture, the actual circumstances of an event, the actual topography of a landscape—should be nothing without the form, the spirit, of the handling, that this form, this mode of handling, should become an end in itself, should penetrate every part of the matter: this is 140 what all art constantly strives after, and achieves in different degrees.

This abstract language becomes clear enough, if we think of actual examples. In an actual landscape we see a long white road, lost suddenly on the hill-verge. That is the matter of one of the etchings of M. Alphonse Legros:° only, in this etching, it is informed by an indwelling solemnity of expression, seen upon it or half-seen, within the limits of an exceptional moment, or caught from his own mood perhaps, but which he 150 maintains as the very essence of the thing, throughout his work. Sometimes a momentary tint of stormy light may invest a homely or too familiar scene with a character which might well have been drawn from the deep places of the imagination. Then we might say that this particular effect of light, this sudden inweaving of gold thread through the texture of the haystack, and the poplars, and the grass, gives the scene artistic qualities, that it is like a picture. And such tricks of circumstance are commonest in landscape which has 160 little salient character of its own; because, in such scenery, all the material details are so easily absorbed by that informing expression of passing light, and elevated, throughout their whole extent, to a new and delightful effect by it. And hence, the superiority, for most conditions of the picturesque, of a river-side in France to a Swiss valley, because, on the French river-side, mere topography, the simple material, counts for so little, and, all being very pure, untouched, and tranquil in itself, mere light and shade 170 have such easy work in modulating it to one dominant tone. The Venetian landscape, on the other hand, has in its material conditions much which is hard, or harshly definite; but the masters of the Venetian school have shown themselves little burdened by them. Of its Alpine background they retain certain abstracted elements only, of cool colour and tranquillising line; and they use its actual details, the brown windy turrets, the straw-coloured fields, the forest arabesques, but as the notes of a music which duly 180 accompanies the presence of their men and women, presenting us with the spirit or essence only of a cer-

---

101 **Anders-streben,** to strive in some other way   110 **Arena chapel,** in Padua, the site of famous frescoes by Giotto

147 **Alphonse Legros,** French painter and etcher contemporary with Pater

tain sort of landscape—a country of the pure reason or half-imaginative memory.

Poetry, again, works with words addressed in the first instance to the pure intelligence; and it deals, most often, with a definite subject or situation. Sometimes it may find a noble and quite legitimate function in the conveyance of moral or political aspiration, as often in the poetry of Victor Hugo. In such instances it is easy enough for the understanding to distinguish between the matter and the form, however much the matter, the subject, the element which is addressed to the mere intelligence, has been penetrated by the informing, artistic spirit. But the ideal types of poetry are those in which this distinction is reduced to its *minimum;* so that lyrical poetry, precisely because in it we are least able to detach the matter from the form, without a deduction of something from that matter itself, is, at least artistically, the highest and most complete form of poetry. And the very perfection of such poetry often appears to depend, in part, on a certain suppression or vagueness of mere subject, so that the meaning reaches us through ways not distinctly traceable by the understanding, as in some of the most imaginative compositions of William Blake, and often in Shakespeare's songs, as pre-eminently in that song of Mariana's page in *Measure for Measure,* in which the kindling force and poetry of the whole play seems to pass for a moment into an actual strain of music.

And this principle holds good of all things that partake in any degree of artistic qualities, of the furniture of our houses, and of dress, for instance, of life itself, of gesture and speech, and the details of daily intercourse; these also, for the wise, being susceptible of a suavity and charm, caught from the way in which they are done, which gives them a worth in themselves. Herein, again, lies what is valuable and justly attractive, in what is called the fashion of a time, which elevates the trivialities of speech, and manner, and dress, into "ends in themselves," and gives them a mysterious grace and attractiveness in the doing of them.

Art, then, is thus always striving to be independent of the mere intelligence, to become a matter of pure perception, to get rid of its responsibilities to its subject or material; the ideal examples of poetry and painting being those in which the constituent elements of the composition are so welded together, that the material or subject no longer strikes the intellect only; nor the form, the eye or the ear only; but form and matter, in their union or identity, present one single effect to the "imaginative reason," that complex faculty for which every thought and feeling is twin-born with its sensible analogue or symbol.

It is the art of music which most completely realises this artistic ideal, this perfect identification of matter and form. In its consummate moments, the end is not distinct from the means, the form from the matter, the subject from the expression; they inhere in and completely saturate each other; and to it, therefore, to the condition of its perfect moments, all the arts may be supposed constantly to tend and aspire. In music, then, rather than in poetry, is to be found the true type or measure of perfected art. Therefore, although each art has its incommunicable element, its untranslatable order of impressions, its unique mode of reaching the "imaginative reason," yet the arts may be represented as continually struggling after the law or principle of music, to a condition which music alone completely realises; and one of the chief functions of æsthetic criticism, dealing with the products of art, new or old, is to estimate the degree in which each of those products approaches, in this sense, to musical law.

By no school of painters have the necessary limitations of the art of painting been so unerringly though instinctively apprehended, and the essence of what is pictorial in a picture so justly conceived, as by the school of Venice; and the train of thought suggested in what has been now said is, perhaps, a not unfitting introduction to a few pages about Giorgione, who, though much has been taken by recent criticism from what was reputed to be his work, yet, more entirely than any other painter, sums up, in what we know of himself and his art, the spirit of the Venetian school.

The beginnings of Venetian painting link themselves to the last, stiff, half-barbaric splendours of Byzantine decoration, and are but the introduction into the crust of marble and gold on the walls of the *Duomo°* of Murano, or of Saint Mark's, of a little more of human expression. And throughout the course of its later development, always subordinate to architectural effect, the work of the Venetian school never escaped from the influence of its beginnings. Unassisted, and therefore unperplexed, by naturalism, religious mysticism, philosophical theories, it had no Giotto, no Angelico, no Botticelli. Exempt from the stress of thought and sentiment, which taxed so severely the resources of the generations of Florentine artists, those earlier Venetian painters, down to Carpaccio and the Bellini, seem never for a moment to have been so much as tempted to lose sight of the scope of their art in its strictness, or to forget that painting must be before all things decorative, a thing for the eye, a space of colour on the wall, only more dexterously blent than the marking of its precious stone or the chance interchange of sun and shade upon it;—this, to begin and end with; whatever higher matter of thought, or poetry, or religious reverie might play its part therein, between. At last, with final mastery of all the technical secrets of his art, and with somewhat more than "a spark of the divine fire" to his share, comes Giorgione. He is the inventor of *genre,* of those easily movable pictures which serve neither for uses of devotion, nor of allegorical or historic teaching—little groups of real

269 **Duomo**, cathedral

men and women, amid congruous furniture or landscape—morsels of actual life, conversation or music or play, but refined upon or idealised, till they come to seem like glimpses of life from afar. Those spaces of more cunningly blent colour, obediently filling their places, hitherto, in a mere architectural scheme, Giorgione detaches from the wall. He frames them by the hands of some skilful carver, so that people may move them readily and take with them where they go, as one might a poem in manuscript, or a musical instrument, to be used, at will, as a means of self-education, stimulus or solace, coming like an animated presence, into one's cabinet, to enrich the air as with some choice aroma, and, like persons, live with us, for a day or a lifetime. Of all art such as this, art which has played so large a part in men's culture since that time, Giorgione is the initiator. Yet in him too that old Venetian clearness or justice, in the apprehension of the essential limitations of the pictorial art, is still undisturbed. While he interfuses his painted work with a high-strung sort of poetry, caught directly from a singularly rich and high-strung sort of life, yet in his selection of subject, or phase of subject, in the subordination of mere subject to pictorial design, to the main purpose of a picture, he is typical of that aspiration of all the arts towards music, which I have endeavoured to explain,—towards the perfect identification of matter and form.

Born so near to Titian, though a little before him, that these two companion pupils of the aged Giovanni Bellini may almost be called contemporaries, Giorgione stands to Titian in something like the relationship of Sordello to Dante, in Browning's poem. Titian, when he leaves Bellini, becomes, in turn, the pupil of Giorgione. He lives in constant labour more than sixty years after Giorgione is in his grave; and with such fruit, that hardly one of the greater towns of Europe is without some fragment of his work. But the slightly older man, with his so limited actual product (what remains to us of it seeming, when narrowly explained, to reduce itself to almost one picture, like Sordello's one fragment of lovely verse), yet expresses, in elementary motive and principle, that spirit—itself the final acquisition of all the long endeavours of Venetian art—which Titian spreads over his whole life's activity.

And, as we might expect, something fabulous and illusive has always mingled itself in the brilliancy of Giorgione's fame. The exact relationship to him of many works—drawings, portraits, painted idylls—often fascinating enough, which in various collections went by his name, was from the first uncertain. Still, six or eight famous pictures at Dresden, Florence and the Louvre, were with no doubt attributed to him, and in these, if anywhere, something of the splendour of the old Venetian humanity seemed to have been preserved. But of those six or eight famous pictures it is now known that only one is certainly from Giorgione's hand. The accomplished science of the subject has come at last, and, as in other instances, has not made the past more real for us, but assured us only that we possess less of it than we seemed to possess. Much of the work on which Giorgione's immediate fame depended, work done for instantaneous effect, in all probability passed away almost within his own age, like the frescoes on the facade of the *fondaco dei Tedeschi* at Venice, some crimson traces of which, however, still give a strange additional touch of splendour to the scene of the *Rialto*. And then there is a barrier or borderland, a period about the middle of the sixteenth century, in passing through which the tradition miscarries, and the true outlines of Giorgione's work and person are obscured. It became fashionable for wealthy lovers of art, with no critical standard of authenticity, to collect so-called works of Giorgione, and a multitude of imitations came into circulation. And now, in the "new Vasari," the great traditional reputation, woven with so profuse demand on men's admiration, has been scrutinised thread by thread; and what remains of the most vivid and stimulating of Venetian masters, a live flame, as it seemed, in those old shadowy times, has been reduced almost to a name by his most recent critics.

Yet enough remains to explain why the legend grew up above the name, why the name attached itself, in many instances, to the bravest work of other men. The *Concert* in the *Pitti* Palace, in which a monk, with cowl and tonsure, touches the keys of a harpsichord, while a clerk, placed behind him, grasps the handle of the viol, and a third, with cap and plume, seems to wait upon the true interval for beginning to sing, is undoubtedly Giorgione's. The outline of the lifted finger, the trace of the plume, the very threads of the fine linen, which fasten themselves on the memory, in the moment before they are lost altogether in that calm unearthly glow, the skill which has caught the waves of wandering sound, and fixed them for ever on the lips and hands—these are indeed the master's own; and the criticism which, while dismissing so much hitherto believed to be Giorgione's, has established the claims of this one picture, has left it among the most precious things in the world of art.

It is noticeable that the "distinction" of this *Concert,* its sustained evenness of perfection, alike in design, in execution, and in choice of personal type, becomes for the "new Vasari" the standard of Giorgione's genuine work. Finding here sufficient to explain his influence, and the true seal of mastery, its authors assign to Pellegrino da San Daniele the *Holy Family* in the Louvre, in consideration of certain points where it comes short of this standard. Such shortcoming, however, will hardly diminish the spectator's enjoyment of a singular charm of liquid air, with which the whole picture seems instinct, filling the eyes and lips, the very garments, of its sacred personages, with some wind-searched brightness and energy; of which fine air the blue peak, clearly defined in the distance, is, as it were, the visible pledge. Similarly, another favourite picture in the Louvre, the subject of a delightful sonnet by a poet whose own painted work often comes to mind as one ponders over these precious things—the *Fête Champêtre,* is assigned to an imitator of Sebastian del Piombo; and the *Tempest,* in the Academy at Venice, to Paris Bordone, or perhaps to "some advanced craftsman of the sixteenth century." From the gallery at Dresden, the *Knight embracing a Lady,* where the knight's broken gauntlets seem to mark some well-known pause in a story we would willingly hear the rest of, is conceded to "a Brescian hand," and *Jacob meeting Rachel* to a pupil of Palma. And then, whatever their charm, we are called on to give up the *Ordeal,* and the *Finding of Moses* with its jewel-like pools of water, perhaps to Bellini.

Nor has the criticism, which thus so freely diminishes the number of his authentic works, added anything important to the well-known outline of the life and personality of the man: only, it has fixed one or two dates, one or two circumstances, a little more exactly. Giorgione was born before the year 1477, and spent his childhood at Castelfranco, where the last crags of the Venetian Alps break down romantically, with something of park-like grace, to the plain. A natural child of the family of the Barbarelli by a peasant-girl of Vedelago, he finds his way early into the circle of notable persons—people of courtesy. He is initiated into those differences of personal type, manner, and even of dress, which are best understood there—that "distinction" of the *Concert* of the *Pitti* Palace. Not far from his home lives Catherine of Cornara, formerly Queen of Cyprus; and, up in the towers which still remain, Tuzio Costanzo, the famous *condottiere*—a picturesque remnant of medieval manners, amid a civilisation rapidly changing. Giorgione paints their portraits; and when Tuzio's son, Matteo, dies in early youth, adorns in his memory a chapel in the church of Castelfranco, painting on this occasion, perhaps, the altar-piece, foremost among his authentic works, still to be seen there, with the figure of the warrior-saint, Liberale, of which the original little study in oil, with the delicately gleaming, silver-grey armour, is one of the greater treasures of the National Gallery. In that figure, as in some other knightly personages attributed to him, people have supposed the likeness of the painter's own presumably gracious presence. Thither, at last, he is himself brought home from Venice, early dead, but celebrated. It happened, about his thirty-fourth year, that in one of those parties at which he entertained his friends with music, he met a certain lady of whom he became greatly enamoured, and "they rejoiced greatly," says Vasari, "the one and the other, in their loves." And two quite different legends concerning it agree in this, that it was through this lady he came by his death; Ridolfi relating that, being robbed of her by one of his pupils, he died of grief at the double treason; Vasari, that she being secretly stricken of the plague, and he making his visits to her as usual, Giorgione took the sickness from her mortally, along with her kisses, and so briefly departed.

But although the number of Giorgione's extant works has been thus limited by recent criticism, all is not done when the real and the traditional elements in what concerns him have been discriminated; for, in what is connected with a great name, much that is not real is often very stimulating. For the æsthetic philosopher, therefore, over and above the real Giorgione and his authentic extant works, there remains the *Giorgionesque* also—an influence, a spirit or type in art, active in men so different as those to whom many of his supposed works are really assignable. A veritable school, in fact, grew together out of all those fascinating works rightly or wrongly attributed to him; out of many copies from, or variations on him, by unknown or uncertain workmen, whose drawings and designs were, for various reasons, prized as his; out of the immediate impression he made upon his contemporaries, and with which he continued in men's minds; out of many traditions of subject and treatment, which really descend from him to our own time, and by retracing which we fill out the original image. Giorgione thus becomes a sort of impersonation of Venice itself, its projected reflex or ideal, all that was intense or desirable in it crystallising about the memory of this wonderful young man.

And now, finally, let me illustrate some of the characteristics of this *School of Giorgione,* as we may call it, which, for most of us, notwithstanding all that negative criticism of the "new Vasari," will still identify itself with those famous pictures at Florence, at Dresden and Paris. A certain artistic ideal is there defined for us—the conception of a peculiar aim and procedure in art, which we may understand as the *Giorgionesque,* wherever we find it, whether in Venetian work generally, or in work of our own time. Of this the *Concert,* that undoubted work of Giorgione in the *Pitti* Palace, is the typical instance, and a pledge authenticating the connexion of the school, and the spirit of the school, with the master.

I have spoken of a certain interpenetration of the matter or subject of a work of art with the form of it, a condition realised absolutely only in music, as the condition to which every form of art is perpetually aspiring. In the art of painting, the attainment of this ideal condition, this perfect interpenetration of the subject with the elements of colour and design, depends, of course, in great measure, on dexterous choice of that subject, or phase of subject; and such choice is one of the secrets of Giorgione's school. It is the school of *genre,* and employs itself mainly with "painted idylls," but, in the production of this pictorial poetry, exercises a wonderful tact in the selecting of such matter as lends itself most readily and entirely to pictorial form, to complete expression by drawing and colour. For although its productions are painted poems, they belong to a sort of poetry which tells itself without an articulated story. The master is pre-eminent for the resolution, the ease and quickness, with which he reproduces instantaneous motion—the lacing-on of armour, with the head bent back so stately—the fainting lady—the embrace, rapid as the kiss, caught with death itself from dying lips—some momentary conjunction of mirrors and polished armour and still water, by which all the sides of a solid image are exhibited at once, solving that casuistical question whether painting can present an object as completely as sculpture. The sudden act, the rapid transition of thought, the passing expression—this he arrests with that vivacity which Vasari has attributed to him, *il fuoco Giorgionesco,* as he terms it. Now it is part of the ideality of the highest sort of dramatic poetry, that it presents us with a kind of profoundly significant and animated instants, a mere gesture, a look, a smile, perhaps—some brief and wholly concrete moment—into which, however, all the motives, all the interests and effects of a long history, have condensed themselves, and which seem to absorb past and future in an intense consciousness of the present. Such ideal instants the school of Giorgione selects, with its admirable tact, from that feverish, tumultuously coloured world of the old citizens of Venice—exquisite pauses in time, in which, arrested thus, we seem to be spectators of all the fullness of existence, and which are like some consummate extract or quintessence of life.

It is to the law or condition of music, as I said, that all art like this is really aspiring; and, in the school of Giorgione, the perfect moments of music itself, the making or hearing of music, song or its accompaniment, are themselves prominent as subjects. On that background of the silence of Venice, so impressive to the modern visitor, the world of Italian music was then forming. In choice of subject, as in all besides, the *Concert* of the *Pitti* Palace is typical of everything that Giorgione, himself an admirable musician, touched with his influence. In sketch or finished picture, in various collections, we may follow it through many intricate variations—men fainting at music; music at the pool-side while people fish, or mingled with the sound of the pitcher in the well, or heard across running water, or among the flocks; the tuning of instruments; people with intense faces, as if listening, like those described by Plato in an ingenious passage of the *Republic,* to detect the smallest interval of musical sound, the smallest undulation in the air, or feeling for music in thought on a stringless instrument, ear and finger refining themselves infinitely, in the appetite for sweet sound; a momentary touch of an instrument in the twilight, as one passes through some unfamiliar room, in a chance company.

In these then, the favourite incidents of Giorgione's school, music or the musical intervals in our existence, life itself is conceived as a sort of listening—listening to music, to the reading of Bandello's novels, to the sound of water, to time as it flies. Often such moments are really our moments of play, and we are surprised at the unexpected blessedness of what may seem our least important part of time; not merely because play is in many instances that to which people really apply their own best powers, but also because at such times, the stress of our servile, everyday attentiveness being relaxed, the happier powers in things without are permitted free passage, and have their way with us. And so, from music, the school of Giorgione passes often to the play which is like music; to those masques in which men avowedly do but play at real life, like children "dressing up," disguised in the strange old Italian dresses, parti-coloured, or fantastic with embroidery and furs, of which the master was so curious a designer, and which, above all the spotless white linen at wrist and throat, he painted so dexterously.

But when people are happy in this thirsty land water will not be far off; and in the school of Giorgione, the presence of water—the well, or marble-rimmed pool, the drawing or pouring of water, as the woman pours it from a pitcher with her jewelled hand in the *Fête Champêtre,* listening, perhaps, to the cool sound as it falls, blent with the music of the pipes—is as characteristic, and almost as suggestive, as that of music itself. And the landscape feels, and is glad of it also—a landscape full of clearness, of the effects of water, of fresh rain newly passed through the air, and collected into the grassy channels. The air, moreover, in the school of Giorgione, seems as vivid as the people who breathe it, and literally empyrean, all impurities being burnt out of it, and no taint, no floating particle of anything but its own proper elements allowed to subsist within it.

Its scenery is such as in England we call "park scenery," with some elusive refinement felt about the rustic buildings, the choice grass, the grouped trees, the undulations deftly economised for graceful effect. Only, in Italy all natural things are as it were woven through and through with gold thread, even the cypress revealing it among the folds of its blackness. And it is with gold dust, or gold thread, that these Venetian painters seem to work, spinning its fine filaments, through the solemn human flesh, away into the white plastered walls of the thatched huts. The harsher details of the mountains recede to a harmonious distance, the one peak of rich blue above the horizon remaining but as the sensible warrant of that due coolness which is all we need ask here of the Alps, with their dark rains and streams. Yet what real, airy space, as the eye passes from level to level, through the long-drawn valley in which Jacob embraces Rachel among the flocks! Nowhere is there a truer instance of that balance, that modulated unison of landscape and persons—of the human image and its accessories—already noticed as characteristic of the Venetian school, so that, in it, neither personage nor scenery is ever a mere pretext for the other.

Something like this seems to me to be the *vraie vérité°* about Giorgione, if I may adopt a servicable expression, by which the French recognise those more liberal and durable impressions which, in respect of any really considerable person or subject, anything that has at all intricately occupied men's attention, lie beyond, and must supplement, the narrower range of the strictly ascertained facts about it. In this, Giorgione is but an illustration of a valuable general caution we may abide by in all criticism. As regards Giorgione himself, we have indeed to take note of all those negations and exceptions, by which, at first sight, a "new Vasari" seems merely to have confused our apprehension of a delightful object, to have explained away in our inheritance from past time what seemed of high value there. Yet it is not with a full understanding even of those exceptions that one can leave off just at this point. Properly qualified, such exceptions are but a salt of genuineness in our knowledge; and beyond all those strictly ascertained facts, we must take note of that indirect influence by which one like Giorgione, for instance, enlarges his permanent efficacy and really makes himself felt in our culture. In a just impression of that, is the essential truth, the *vraie vérité,* concerning him.

CONCLUSION

Λέγει που Ἡράκλειτος ὅτι πάντα χωρεῖ καὶ οὐδὲν μένει°

To regard all things and principles of things as inconstant modes or fashions has more and more become the tendency of modern thought. Let us begin with that which is without—our physical life. Fix upon it in one of its more exquisite intervals, the moment, for instance, of delicious recoil from the flood of water in summer heat. What is the whole physical life in that moment but a combination of natural elements to which science gives their names? But those elements, phosphorus and lime and delicate fibers, are present not in the human body alone: we detect them in places most remote from it. Our physical life is a perpetual motion of them—the passage of the blood, the waste and repairing of the lenses of the eye, the modification of the tissues of the brain under every ray of light and sound—processes which science reduces to simpler

and more elementary forces. Like the elements of which we are composed, the action of these forces extends beyond us: it rusts iron and ripens corn.° Far out on every side of us those elements are broadcast, driven in many currents; and birth and gesture° and death and the springing of violets from the grave are but a few out of ten thousand resultant combinations. That clear, perpetual outline of face and limb is but an image of ours, under which we group them—a design in a web, the actual threads of which pass out beyond it. This at least of flamelike our life has, that it is but the concurrence, renewed from moment to moment, of forces parting sooner or later on their ways.

Or, if we begin with the inward world of thought and feeling, the whirlpool is still more rapid, the flame more eager and devouring. There it is no longer the gradual darkening of the eye, the gradual fading of color from the wall—movements of the shore-side, where the water flows down indeed, though in apparent rest—but the race of the midstream, a drift of momentary acts of sight and passion and thought. At first sight experience seems to bury us under a flood of external objects, pressing upon us with a sharp and importunate reality, calling us out of ourselves in a thousand forms of action. But when reflection begins to play upon those objects they are dissipated under its influence; the cohesive force seems suspended like some trick of magic; each object is loosed into a group of impressions—color, odor, texture—in the mind of the observer. And it we continue to dwell in thought on this world, not of objects in the solidity with which language invests them, but of impressions, unstable, flickering, inconsistent, which burn and are extinguished with our consciousness of them, it contracts still further: the whole scope of observation is dwarfed into the narrow chamber of the individual mind. Experience, already reduced to a group of impressions, is ringed round for each one of us by that thick wall of personality through which no real voice has ever pierced on its way to us, or from us to that which we can only conjecture to be without. Every one of those impressions is the impression of the individual in his isolation, each mind keeping as a solitary prisoner its own dream of a world. Analysis goes a step farther still, and assures us that those impressions of the individual mind to which, for each one of us, experience dwindles down, are in perpetual flight; that each of them is limited by time, and that as time is infinitely divisible, each of them is infinitely divisible also; all that is actual in it being a single moment, gone while we try to apprehend it, of which it may ever be more truly said that it has ceased to be than that it is. To such a tremulous wisp constantly reforming itself on the stream, to a single sharp impression, with a sense in it, a relic more or less fleeting, of such moments

648 **vraie vérité,** true truth **Conclusion** Λέγει ποu, **etc.** Heraclitus says somewhere that everything flows and nothing remains (Plato, *Cratylus*)

19 **corn,** grain, wheat   21 **gesture,** bearing, behavior

gone by, what is real in our life fines itself down. It is with this movement, with the passage and dissolution of impressions, images, sensations, that analysis leaves off—that continual vanishing away, that strange, perpetual weaving and unweaving of ourselves.

Philosophiren, says Novalis, *ist dephlegmatisiren, vivificiren.*° The service of philosophy, of speculative culture, towards the human spirit is to rouse, to startle it to a life of constant and eager observation. Every moment some form grows perfect in hand or face; some tone on the hills or the sea is choicer than the rest; some mood of passion or insight or intellectual excitement is irresistibly real and attractive to us—for that moment only. Not the fruit of experience, but experience itself, is the end. A counted number of pulses only is given to us of a variegated, dramatic life. How may we see in them all that is to be seen in them by the finest senses? How shall we pass most swiftly from point to point, and be present always at the focus where the greatest number of vital forces unite in their purest energy?

To burn always with this hard, gemlike flame, to maintain this ecstasy, is success in life. In a sense it might even be said that our failure is to form habits: for, after all, habit is relative to a stereotyped world,° and meantime it is only the roughness of the eye that makes any two persons, things, situations, seem alike. While all melts under our feet, we may well grasp at any exquisite passion, or any contribution to knowledge that seems by a lifted horizon to set the spirit free for a moment, or any stirring of the senses, strange dyes, strange colors, and curious odors, or work of the artist's hands, or the face of one's friend. Not to discriminate every moment some passionate attitude in those about us, and in the very brilliancy of their gifts some tragic dividing of forces on their ways, is, on this short day of frost and sun, to sleep before evening. With this sense of the splendor of our experience and of its awful brevity, gathering all we are into one desperate effort to see and touch, we shall hardly have time to make theories about the things we see and touch. What we have to do is to be forever curiously testing new opinions and courting new impressions, never acquiescing in a facile orthodoxy of Comte,° or of Hegel,° or of our own. Philosophical theories or ideas, as points of view, instruments of criticism, may help us to gather up what might otherwise pass unregarded by us. "Philosophy is the microscope of thought." The theory or idea or system which requires of us the sacrifice of any part of this experience, in consideration of some interest into which we cannot enter, or some

abstract theory we have not identified with ourselves, or of what is only conventional, has no real claim upon us.

One of the most beautiful passages of Rousseau is that in the sixth book of the *Confessions*, where he describes the awakening in him of the literary sense. An undefinable taint of death had clung always about him, and now in early manhood he believed himself smitten by mortal disease. He asked himself how he might make as much as possible of the interval that remained; and he was not biased by anything in his previous life when he decided that it must be by intellectual excitement, which he found just then in the clear, fresh writings of Voltaire.° Well! we are all *condamnés*° as Victor Hugo° says: we are all under sentence of death but with a sort of indefinite reprieve—*les hommes sont tous condamnés à mort avec des sursis indéfinis:*° we have an interval, and then our place knows us no more. Some spend this interval in listlessness, some in high passions, the wisest, at least among "the children of this world," in art and song. For our one chance lies in expanding that interval, in getting as many pulsations as possible into the given time. Great passions may give us this quickened sense of life, ecstasy and sorrow of love, the various forms of enthusiastic activity, disinterested or otherwise, which come naturally to many of us. Only be sure it is passion—that it does yield you this fruit of a quickened, multiplied consciousness. Of such wisdom, the poetic passion, the desire of beauty, the love of art for its own sake, has most. For art comes to you proposing frankly to give nothing but the highest quality to your moments as they pass, and simply for those moments' sake.

(1868; 1873)

GERARD MANLEY HOPKINS 1844–1889

Born in 1844 into a High Church family, Hopkins attended Highgate School, where he showed promise both as a scholar and as a poet. He entered Balliol College, Oxford, in 1863 and graduated with high honors in 1867. There he was attracted by the aestheticism of Walter Pater but more particularly by the intensely religious atmosphere of the Oxford Movement. In his last year at Oxford, impressed by the example of John Henry Newman, he converted to Roman Catholicism. After a brief teaching experience at Newman's Oratory School, he entered the Jesuit

78–79 **Philosophiren, etc.,** to be a philosopher is to rid oneself of apathy, to become alive. Novalis was the pseudonym of Friedrich von Hardenberg (1772–1801), German romantic poet and novelist   97 **habit . . . world,** habit becomes fixed as man in his world becomes stereotyped   116 **Comte,** celebrated French philosopher (1798–1857) who held that science is the key to the temple of truth because it abides rigorously by fact   117 **Hegel,** famous German philosopher (1770–1831) in whom idealistic philosophy found its peak of intellectual acceptance

137 **Voltaire,** French philosopher and skeptic (1694–1778)   138 **condamnés,** condemned   **Victor Hugo,** celebrated French poet and novelist (1802–1885), the recognized leader of the romantic school of the nineteenth century in France   140–141 **les hommes, etc.** Pater has just given the translation of the quotation, which is from the scene at the barricade in *Les Misérables*

Order as a novitiate in 1868. To show the immediate impact of the new ascetic discipline imposed upon him, he burned all his early verse.

While Hopkins was still in this discipline, his rector, knowing his poetic capabilities, encouraged him to continue writing poetry. Throughout his life, he was uncertain about being a poet; he felt that poetry might be incompatible with his vocation. The drowning of five German nuns in the shipwreck of the steamer *Deutschland* (1875) inspired him to write a memorial poem, and from then until his death he wrote poems from time to time.

After his ordination in 1877, he held a variety of posts as preacher and minor administrator in London, Oxford, Liverpool, and Glasgow. In a letter to the poet Robert Bridges (1844–1930), he made the revealing comment: "I am going to preach tomorrow . . . what I am putting not at all so plainly to the rest of the world . . . in a sonnet." He gave himself unsparingly to the religious duties to which he had dedicated himself. He tried, though unsuccessfully, to become a composer of religious music; he taught the classics at a Jesuit preparatory school, Stonyhurst; and he spent the last few years of his life as Professor of Greek at University College in Dublin. He died of typhoid fever in Dublin in 1889.

Hopkins lived during the last part of the Victorian era, but his poetry owes little to that environment. It is intensely personal and highly original, and often difficult even for an age familiar with poetic compression. His bold poetic devices and verbal eccentricities, his often obscure imagery, and his subtle rhythms all tend to obtrude between the poet and the reader. Convinced that the rather startling innovations in Hopkins' poetry (which had been left in manuscript at the time of the poet's death) would meet with indifference or ridicule if given too soon to the literary world, Robert Bridges, his literary executor, delayed its publication until 1918, thirty or more years after most of it had been written. Not until the 1930s and 1940s, however, did his poetry come to be appreciated. Hopkins today has a secure position as both a Victorian and a twentieth-century poet.

An effort to understand how Hopkins combined thought and feeling in words and rhythmical patterns will yield rich rewards. He tried to make language revivify experience, and used word clusters instead of conventional grammatical constructions; his intense emotion expresses itself in a word instead of a phrase. He modified syntax to suit his purposes: a noun may become a verb, or a verb a noun; and the primary accent of a word may be shifted into a secondary one. Alliteration is often a conspicuous device, as are also internal rhymes and repetitions.

Some of his poems, as he himself pointed out, were written in what he called "sprung rhythm," which is measured by feet of one to four syllables, with the stress always on the first syllable of the foot. Although the number of stresses is fixed, the number of feet is variable. He explained further that this rhythm provides greater flexibility in the verse by allowing any one kind of foot to follow any other kind. "It is natural in sprung rhythm," he added, "for the lines to be *rove over*, that is, for the scanning of each line immediately to take up that of the one before, so that if the first has one or more syllables at its end, the other must have so many the less at its beginning; and in fact the scanning runs on without break from the beginning, say, of a stanza to the end, and all the stanza is one long strain, though written in lines asunder." Excellent examples of sprung rhythm can be found in *The Wreck of the Deutschland* or *The Windhover*.

Perhaps more important than any other consideration in reading the poetry of Hopkins, however, is an understanding of the concept which he called *inscape*. He believed that every object in nature is worthy of consideration as poetic material because it is highly individualized and different from all other objects. To render its uniqueness is to render its life, its spirit. This individualizing—called inscape—requires precision in language, imagery, and even prosodic effect, to say nothing of a strategic deployment of both words and phrases. All this must be achieved in terms of the dynamic rather than the passive. "One of two kinds of clearness one should have—either the meaning to be felt without effort as fast as one reads or else, if dark at first reading, when once made out, *to explode*."

THE WRECK OF THE DEUTSCHLAND

Disregarding at least for the moment Hopkins' division of the poem into two parts, one may have less difficulty in interpreting the outlines of the work if one divides it into four sections: the second and third sections deal with the actual shipwreck of the *Deutschland* in the Thames estuary in December 1875, while the first and last sections emphasize the glory of God and the necessity for accepting with faith God's will. The following sketch may be helpful.

The first section, lines 1–80, is a poetic essay on the infiniteness of God and on the intuitive knowledge that man, the dependent finite creature, acquires through the contemplation of this omnipotence and awesomeness. This knowledge leads him to grasp the beauty and love of God, who can be comprehended through terror and grief as well as through beauty and happiness. The Incarnation and the Passion, moreover, have taught the human heart and mind the true significance of suffering and loss—a paradox, no doubt, but an inescapable one.

In the second section, lines 81–136, the *Deutschland*, with her emigrants and exiles bound for America, is struck unexpectedly by a hurricane of wind and snow and is driven onto a sandbank. For a whole night, without any chance to seek help, the passengers and crew of the crippled, sinking ship are pummeled by the waves and the wind, and many perish.

In the third section, lines 137–248, a nun is heard calling upon Christ to "come quickly" (l. 191). (She was one of the five Franciscan exiles driven from Germany by the discriminatory anti-Catholic Falk Laws of 1875. The number five reminds the poet of the Five Wounds of Christ, a symbol of sacrifice and heavenly reward.) What does this nun mean? She represents all suffering mankind. It is not so much danger from which man seeks to escape—danger can be stimulating—but rather the monotonous daily round of work and frustration. Such deliverance can come only from Christ, whose failure and frustration meant victory; his Passion redeemed an otherwise "unshapeable" existence (l. 227). The nun was right: the tragedy and pain in life make clear and are in turn made clear by the Redemption. This nun represents a second Virgin Birth—a rebirth of the significance of Christ.

In the fourth section, lines 249–280, the poet returns to the thoughts of the first section. He repeats his adoration of the majesty and the unknowable wisdom of God.

To the happy memory of five
Franciscan Nuns exiles by the Falk Laws°
drowned between midnight
and morning of Dec. 7th, 1875

PART THE FIRST

1

Thou mastering me
God! giver of breath and bread;
World's strand, sway of the sea;
    Lord of living and dead;
Thou hast bound bones and veins in me, fastened me flesh,
And after it almost unmade, what with dread,
    Thy doing: and dost thou touch me afresh?
Over again I feel thy finger and find thee.

2

    I did say yes
10   O at lightning and lashed rod;
Thou heardst me truer than tongue confess
    Thy terror, O Christ, O God;
Thou knowest the walls, altar and hour and night:
The swoon of a heart that the sweep and the hurl of thee trod
    Hard down with a horror of height:

And the midriff astrain with leaning of, laced with fire of stress.

3

    The frown of his face
Before me, the hurtle of hell
Behind, where, where was a, where was a place?
    I whirled out wings that spell°   20
And fled with a fling of the heart to the heart of the Host.
My heart, but you were dovewinged, I can tell,
    Carrier-witted, I am bold to boast,
To flash from the flame to the flame then, tower from the grace' to the grace.

4

    I am soft sift
In an hourglass—at the wall
Fast, but mined with a motion, a drift,
    And it crowds and it combs to the fall;
I steady as a water in a well, to a poise, to a pane,
But roped° with, always, all the way down from the   30 tall
    Fells or flanks of the voel,° a vein
Of the gospel proffer, a pressure, a principle, Christ's gift.

5

    I kiss my hand
To the stars, lovely-asunder
Starlight, wafting him out of it; and
    Glow, glory in thunder;
Kiss my hand to the dappled-with-damson west:
Since, tho' he is under the world's splendour and wonder,
    His mystery must be instressed, stressed;
For I greet him the days I meet him, and bless when I   40 understand.

6

    Not out of his bliss
Springs the stress felt
Nor first from heaven (and few know this)
    Swings the stroke dealt—
Stroke and a stress that stars and storms deliver,
That guilt is hushed by, hearts are flushed by and melt—
    But it rides time like riding a river
(And here the faithful waver, the faithless fable and miss).

7

    It dates from day
Of his going in Galilee;   50
Warm-laid grave of a womb-life grey;
    Manger, maiden's knee;

The Wreck of the Deutschland   **Falk Laws.** Paul Falk (1827–1898), as Minister of Worship and Instruction in Germany, closed all monasteries in Prussia in May 1875 and expelled all members of religious orders from the country, except those who cared for the sick. The act was part of a bitter conflict between the government and the Catholic Church in Germany

20 **that spell,** in that brief interval   30 **roped,** forced into the shape of a rope, as in a thin waterfall   31 **voel,** a mountain in north Wales

The dense and the driven Passion, and frightful
    sweat;
Thence the discharge of it, there its swelling to be,
    Though felt before, though in high flood yet—
What none would have known of it, only the heart,
    being hard at bay,

8

    Is out with it! Oh,
      We lash with the best or worst
    Word last! How a lush-kept plush-capped sloe
60   Will, mouthed to flesh-burst,
Gush!—flush the man, the being with it, sour or
    sweet,
    Brim, in a flash, full!—Hither then, last or first,
      To hero of Calvary, Christ,'s feet—
Never ask if meaning it, wanting it, warned of it—men
    go.

9

    Be adored among men,
      God, three-numberèd form;
    Wring thy rebel, dogged in den,
      Man's malice, with wrecking and storm.
Beyond saying sweet, past telling of tongue,
70   Thou art lightning and love, I found it, a winter and
    warm;
    Father and fondler of heart thou hast wrung:
Hast thy dark descending and most art merciful then.

10

    With an anvil-ding
      And with fire in him forge thy will
    Or rather, rather then, stealing as Spring
      Through him, melt him but master him still:
    Whether at once, as once at a crash Paul,°
    Or as Austin,° a lingering-out swéet skîll,
      Make mercy in all of us, out of us all
80 Mastery, but be adored, but be adored King.

PART THE SECOND

11

    'Some find me a sword; some
      The flange and the rail; flame,
    Fang, or flood' goes Death on drum,
      And storms bugle his fame.
But wé dream we are rooted in earth—Dust!
Flesh falls within sight of us, we, though our flower
    the same,
    Wave with the meadow, forget that there must
The sour scythe cringe, and the blear° share° come.

12

    On Saturday sailed from Bremen,
      American-outward-bound,   90
    Take settler and seamen, tell° men with women,
      Two hundred souls in the round—
O Father, not under thy feathers nor ever as
    guessing
The goal was a shoal, of a fourth the doom to be
    drowned;
    Yet did the dark side of the bay of thy blessing
Not vault them, the millions of rounds of thy mercy
    not reeve° even them in?

13

    Into the snows she sweeps,
      Hurling the haven behind,
    The Deutschland, on Sunday; and so the sky
      keeps,
    For the infinite air is unkind,   100
And the sea flint-flake, black-backed in the regular
    blow,
Sitting Eastnortheast, in cursed quarter, the wind;
    Wiry and white-fiery and whirlwind-swivellèd
    snow
Spins to the widow-making unchilding unfathering
    deeps.

14

    She drove in the dark to leeward,
      She struck—not a reef or a rock
    But the combs° of a smother of sand: night drew
      her
      Dead to the Kentish Knock;°
And she beat the bank down with her bows and the
    ride of her keel:
The breakers rolled on her beam with ruinous shock; 110
    And canvas and compass, the whorl° and the wheel
Idle for ever to waft her or wind her with, these she
    endured.

15

    Hope had grown grey hairs,
      Hope had mourning on,
    Trenched with tears, carved with cares,
      Hope was twelve hours gone;
And frightful a nightfall folded rueful a day
Nor rescue, only rocket and lightship, shone,
    And lives at last were washing away:
To the shrouds they took,—they shook in the hurling 120
    and horrible airs.

16

    One stirred from the rigging to save
      The wild woman-kind below,

---

77 **crash Paul,** "Master him as you once mastered Paul by crashing him to the
ground." Saul of Tarsus was converted to Christianity by a sudden vision while he
was traveling to Damascus. He then assumed the name of Paul; see *Acts*, 9:1–9
78 **Austin,** St. Augustine (354–430), a celebrated Church father. His conversion
was rational and deliberate 88 **blear,** hazy, indistinct **share,** the plowshare
which cuts the ground at the bottom of the furrow

91 **tell,** count 96 **reeve,** fasten them in, as with a rope 107 **combs,** ridges
108 **Kentish Knock,** a sandbank near the mouth of the Thames River
111 **whorl,** propeller

With a rope's end round the man, handy and
  brave—
He was pitched to his death at a blow,
For all his dreadnought breast and braids of thew:°
They could tell him for hours, dandled the to and fro
Through the cobbled foam-fleece, what could he
  do
With the burl° of the fountains of air, buck° and the
  flood of the wave?

17

They fought with God's cold—
130 And they could not and fell to the deck
  (Crushed them) or water (and drowned them) or
    rolled
  With the sea-romp over the wreck.
Night roared, with the heart-break hearing a heart-
  broke rabble,
The woman's wailing, the crying of child without
  check—
  Till a lioness arose breasting the babble,
A prophetess towered in the tumult, a virginal tongue
  told.

18

Ah, touched in your bower of bone
  Are you! turned for an exquisite smart,
Have you! make words break from me here all
  alone,
140 Do you!—mother of being in me, heart.
O unteachably after° evil, but uttering truth;
  Why, tears! is it? tears, such a melting, a madrigal°
    start!
  Never-eldering revel and river of youth,
What can it be, this glee? the good you have there of
  your own?

19

Sister, a sister calling
  A master, her master and mine!—
And the inboard seas run swirling and hawling;°
  The rash smart sloggering brine
Blinds her; but she that weather sees one thing, one;
150 Has one fetch° in her: she rears herself to divine
  Ears, and the call of the tall nun
To the men in the tops and the tackle rode over the
  storm's brawling.

20

She was first of a five and came
  Of a coifèd sisterhood.
(O Deutschland, double a desperate name!
  O world wide of its good!°

But Gertrude,° lily, and Luther,° are two of a town,
  Christ's lily and beast of the waste wood:
From life's dawn it is drawn down,
Abel is Cain's brother and breasts they have sucked 160
  the same.°)

21

Loathed for a love men knew in them,°
  Banned by the land of their birth,
Rhine refused them. Thames would ruin them;
  Surf, snow, river, and earth
Gnashed: but thou art above, thou Orion° of light;
Thy unchancelling° poising palms were weighing the
  worth,
  Thou martyr-master: in thy sight
Storm flakes were scroll-leaved flowers, lily show-
  ers—sweet heaven was astrew in them.

22

Five! the finding° and sake
  And cipher of suffering Christ. 170
Mark, the mark is of man's make
  And the word of it Sacrificed.
But he scores it in scarlet himself on his own bespo-
  ken,
  Before-time-taken, dearest prizèd and priced—
  Stigma, signal, cinquefoil° token
For lettering of the lamb's fleece, ruddying of the
  rose-flake.

23

Joy fall to thee, father Francis,°
  Drawn to the Life that died;
With the gnarls of the nails in thee, niche of the
  lance, his
  Lovescape° crucified 180
And seal of his seraph-arrival! and these thy
  daughters
And five-livèd and leavèd° favour and pride,
  And sisterly sealed in wild waters,
To bathe in his fall-gold mercies, to breathe in his all-
  fire glances.

24

Away in the loveable west,
  On a pastoral forehead° of Wales,

157 **Gertrude,** a German mystic and saint (1256?–1302?) who lived in a convent near Eisleben, birthplace of Martin Luther (1483–1546). Her visions are recorded in her *Insinuationes,* published in 1662.   **Luther,** the great Protestant leader ("beast of the waste wood," l. 158) was excommunicated in 1520 for denying the supremacy of the Pope   160 **Abel . . . the same.** Abel and his brother and murderer Cain were both suckled by Eve; see *Genesis,* 4:1–12   161 **them,** the five nuns (ll. 153–154)   165 **Orion,** in classical mythology, a famous hunter of huge size; after his death he became perhaps the most famous of winter constellations in the northern hemisphere. The thought here seems to be that God, as a hunter, drove the nuns from their formerly safe place in Germany so that their bravery and devotion might be tested   166 **unchancelling,** not canceling, not revoking   169 **finding,** mark or device. The poet calls attention to the fact that the number of nuns, five, corresponds to the Five Wounds of Christ   175 **cinquefoil,** a decorative design having five points   177 **Francis,** St. Francis of Assisi (1181?–1226), founder of the Franciscan order, to which the nuns belonged   180 **Lovescape,** the pattern of the Five Wounds of Christ, which was the stigma on the body of St. Francis   182 **five . . . leaved,** a further reference to the cinquefoil (l. 175)   186 **pastoral forehead,** St. Bruno's College, located on a hill in the Vale of Clwyd, in northern Wales

125 **thew,** muscle   128 **burl,** fullness   **buck,** bucking, plunging   141 **after,** make after   142 **madrigal,** used here with reference to the joyous quality of most Elizabethan madrigals; hence, joyful   147 **hawling,** an onomatopoetic coinage   150 **fetch,** stratagem, device   156 **wide . . . good,** unfriendly to what is good for it

I was under a roof here, I was at rest,
    And they the prey of the gales;
She to the black-about air, to the breaker, the
    thickly
190 Falling flakes, to the throng that catches and quails
    Was calling 'O Christ, Christ, come quickly':
The cross to her° she calls Christ to her, christens her
    wild-worst Best.

25

    The majesty! what did she mean?
      Breathe, arch° and original Breath.
    Is it love in her of the being as her lover had been?
      Breathe, body of lovely Death.
    They were else-minded then, altogether, the men
Woke thee with a *we are perishing* in the weather of
    Gennesareth.°
    Or is it that she cried for the crown then,
The keener to come at° the comfort for feeling the
200   combating keen?

26

    For how to the heart's cheering
      The down-dugged ground-hugged grey
    Hovers off, the jay-blue heavens appearing
      Of pied and peeled May!
    Blue-beating and hoary-glow height; or night, still
    higher,
    With belled fire and the moth-soft Milky Way,
    What by your measure is the heaven of desire,
The treasure never eyesight got, nor was ever guessed
    what for the hearing?°

27

    No, but it was not these.
210   The jading and jar of the cart,
    Time's tasking, it is fathers that asking for ease
      Of the sodden-with-its-sorrowing heart,
    Not danger, electrical horror; then further it finds
    The appealing of the Passion is tenderer in prayer
    apart:
    Other, I gather, in measure her mind's
Burden, in wind's burly° and beat of endragonèd seas.

28

    But how shall I . . . make me room there:
      Reach me a . . .Fancy, come faster—
    Strike you the sight of it? look at it loom there,
220   Thing that she . . . there then! the Master,
    Ipse,° the only one, Christ, King, Head:
He was to cure the extremity where he had cast her;

Do, deal, lord it with living and dead;
Let him ride, her pride, in his triumph, despatch and
    have done with his doom there.

29

    Ah! there was a heart right
      There was single eye!°
    Read the unshapeable shock night
      And knew the who and the why;
    Wording it how but by him that present and past,
    Heaven and earth are word of, worded by?—   230
      The Simon Peter of a soul! to the blast
Tarpeian-fast, but a blown beacon of light.°

30

    Jesu, heart's light,
      Jesu, maid's son,
    What was the feast followed the night
      Thou hadst glory of this nun?—
    Feast of the one woman without stain.°
    For so conceivèd, so to conceive thee is done;°
    But here was heart-throe, birth of a brain,
Word, that heard and kept thee and uttered thee out- 240
right.

31

    Well, she has thee for the pain, for the
      Patience; but pity of the rest of them!
    Heart, go and bleed at a bitterer vein for the
      Comfortless unconfessed of them—
    No not uncomforted: lovely-felicitous Providence
    Finger of a tender of, O of a feathery delicacy, the
    breast of the
    Maiden could obey so, be a bell to, ring of it, and
Startle the poor sheep back! is the shipwrack then a
    harvest, does tempest carry the grain for thee?

32

    I admire thee, master of the tides,
      Of the Yore-flood,° of the year's fall,   250
    The recurb and the recovery of the gulf's sides,°
      The girth of it and the wharf of it and the wall;°
    Stanching, quenching ocean of a motionable mind;
    Ground of being, and granite° of it: past all
      Grasp God, throned behind
Death with a sovereignty that heeds but hides, bodes°
    but abides;

226 **single eye.** "The light of the body is the eye; if therefore thine eye be single, thy whole body shall be full of light"—*Matthew*, 6:22   231–232 **The Simon . . . light.** The references here are to the personal qualities of the nun—her steadfast devotion, her fear, and her surpassing example to her doomed fellow passengers. Peter, one of Christ's twelve apostles, was originally called Simon, but Jesus, having in mind his solid, steadfast character, changed his name to Peter ("rock"), saying: "Thou art Peter, and upon this rock I will build my church"—*Matthew*, 16:18. Tarpeia is a famous peaklike rock on the Capitoline Hill in ancient Rome, named after Tarpeaia, who was hurled from it because she was a traitor 237 **Feast . . . stain**, the Feast of the Immaculate Conception of the Blessed Virgin Mary, which comes on December 8 (the day following the disaster of the *Deutschland*) 238 **For so . . . done.** The nun is also a virgin, like Mary 250 **Yore-flood**, Noah's flood, the Deluge; see *Genesis*, 6–8 251 **recurb . . . sides**, the stemming and restemming of the waves and flood. "Or who shut up the sea with doors, when it brake forth, as if it had issued out of the womb?"—*Job*, 38:8 252 **wharf . . . wall**, the restraining factors 254 **granite.** The restless human mind finds peace only in the granite of God 256 **bodes**, portends

192 **the cross to her.** She identifies her own suffering with that of Christ on the Cross 194 **arch**, chief 198 **weather of Gennesareth.** When the disciples in a ship on the Lake of Gennesareth were frightened by a heavy storm, Jesus astonished them by walking to them on the water and calming the waves and winds. The lake is better known as the Sea of Galilee. See *Matthew*, 14:22–34 200 **come at**, attain, reach 208 **treasure . . . hearing.** "Eye hath not seen, nor ear heard, neither have entered into the heart of man, the things which God hath prepared for them that love him"—*1 Corinthians*, 2:9 216 **burly**, bluster 221 **Ipse**, Himself

33

With a mercy that outrides
The all of water, an ark
For the listener; for the lingerer with a love glides
Lower than death and the dark;
A vein for the visiting of the past-prayer, pent in
prison,
The-last-breath penitent spirits—the uttermost mark
Our passion-plungèd giant risen,
The Christ of the Father compassionate, fetched° in
the storm of his strides.

34

Now burn, new born to the world,
Double-naturèd name,
The heaven-flung, heart-fleshed, maiden-furled
Miracle-in-Mary-of-flame,
Mid-numbered He° in three of the thunder-throne!
Not a dooms-day dazzle in his coming nor dark as he
came;
Kind, but royally reclaiming his own;
A released shower, let flash to the shire,° not a
lightning of fire hard-hurled.

35

Dame, at our door
Drowned, and among our shoals,
Remember us in the roads, the heaven-haven of
the Reward:
Our King back, oh, upon English souls!
Let him easter in us, be a dayspring to the dimness
of us, be a crimson-cresseted east,
More brightening her, rare-dear Britain, as his reign
rolls,
Pride, rose, prince, hero of us, high-priest,
Our hearts' charity's hearth's fire, our thoughts'
chivalry's throng's Lord.
(1876–1889; 1918)

GOD'S GRANDEUR

The world is charged with the grandeur of God.
It will flame out, like shining from shook foil;
It gathers to a greatness, like the ooze of oil
Crushed.° Why do men then now not reck his rod?°
Generations have trod, have trod, have trod;
And all is seared with trade; bleared, smeared with
toil;
And wears man's smudge and shares man's smell:
the soil

Is bare now, nor can foot feel, being shod.

And for all this, nature is never spent;
There lives the dearest freshness deep down things; 10
And though the last lights off the black West went,
Oh, morning, at the brown brink eastward,
springs—
Because the Holy Ghost over the bent
World broods with warm breast and with ah! bright
wings.
(1877; 1918)

THE STARLIGHT NIGHT

Look at the stars! look, look up at the skies!
O look at all the fire-folk sitting in the air!
The bright boroughs, the circle-citadels there!
Down in dim woods the diamond delves!° the elves'-
eyes!
The gray lawns cold where gold, where quick-gold lies! 5
Wind-beat white-beam!° airy abeles° set on a flare!
Flake-doves sent floating forth at a farmyard
scare!—
Ah well! it is all a purchase, all is a prize.
Buy then! bid then!—What?°—Prayer, patience, alms,
vows.
Look, look: a May-mess,° like on orchard boughs! 10
Look! March-bloom, like on mealed-with-yellow
sallows!
These are indeed the barn;° withindoors house
The shocks.° This piece-bright paling° shuts the Spouse
Christ home, Christ and his mother and all his
hallows.°
(1877; 1918)

THE SEA AND THE SKYLARK

On ear and ear two noises too old to end
Trench°—right, the tide that ramps against the shore;
With a flood or a fall, low lull-off or all roar,
Frequenting there while moon shall wear and wend.

Left hand, off land, I hear the lark ascend, 5
His rash-fresh re-winded new-skeinèd score

264 **fetched.** The subject is *giant* (l. 263)   269 **Mid-numbered He,** Christ, the second in the formula, "the Father, the Son, and the Holy Ghost"   272 **shire,** region   **God's Grandeur**   3–4 **ooze . . . Crushed,** oil from crushed olives   4 **reck his rod,** heed his commandments

The Starlight Night   4 **delves.** *Delf* is an obsolete word meaning hollow, pit, mine   6 **white-beam,** a small tree with leaves white on the underside   **abeles,** white poplars   9 **What.** He is asking what price he should offer   10 **May-mess,** a medley, like blossoms in May   12 **barn.** Cf. *Matthew,* 13:30—". . . and in the time of harvest I will say to the reapers, Gather ye together first the tares, and bind them into bundles to burn them; but gather the wheat into my barn"   13 **shocks,** sheaves   **piece-bright paling,** a fence or enclosing element, each part of which is bright. In another poem, *The Elopement,* Hopkins refers to the stars as "packed so close that night/ They seemed to press and stare/ And gather in like hurdles bright/ The liberties of air"   14 **hallows,** saints   **The Sea and the Skylark**   2 **Trench,** cut and divide

In crisps° of curl off wild winch whirl, and pour
And pelt music, till none's to spill nor spend.°

How these two shame this shallow and frail town!
10   How ring right out our sordid turbid time,
Being pure! We, life's pride and cared-for crown,

Have lost that cheer and charm of earth's past
   prime:
Our make and making° break, are breaking, down
   To man's last dust, drain fast toward man's first
   slime.
(1877; 1918)

THE WINDHOVER°

TO CHRIST OUR LORD

I caught this morning morning's minion,° kingdom of
   daylight's dauphin,° dapple-dawn-drawn
      Falcon, in his riding
Of the rolling level underneath him steady air, and
   striding
High there, how he rung upon the rein of a wimpling
   wing°
5 In his ecstasy! then off, off forth on a swing,
   As a skate's heel sweeps smooth on a bow-bend: the
      hurl and gliding
   Rebuffed the big wind. My heart in hiding
Stirred for a bird—the achieve of, the mastery of the
   thing!
Brute beauty and valor and act, oh, air, pride, plume,
   here
   Buckle! AND the fire that breaks from thee then, a
10   billion
Times told lovelier, more dangerous, O my chevalier!

No wonder of it: shéer plód makes plow down sillion°
Shine, and blue-bleak embers, ah, my dear,
   Fall, gall themselves, and gash gold-vermilion.
(1877; 1918)

PIED BEAUTY

Glory be to God for dappled things—
   For skies of couple-color as a brinded° cow;
      For rose-moles all in stipple° upon trout that swim;
Fresh-firecoal chestnut-falls;° finches' wings;
   Landscape plotted and pieced°—fold, fallow, and
      plow;   5
   And all trades, their gear and tackle and trim.°

All things counter,° original, spare,° strange;
   Whatever is fickle, freckled (who knows how?)
      With swift, slow; sweet, sour; adazzle, dim;
He fathers-forth whose beauty is past change:°   10
      Praise him.
(1877; 1918)

HURRAHING IN HARVEST

Summer ends now; now, barbarous in beauty, the
   stooks° rise
Around; up above, what wind-walks! what lovely be-
   haviour
Of silk-sack clouds! has wilder, wilful-wavier
Meal-drift° moulded ever and melted across skies?

I walk, I lift up, I lift up heart, eyes,   5
Down all that glory in the heavens to glean our
   Saviour;
And, éyes, heárt, what looks, what lips yet gave you a
Rapturous love's greeting of realer, of rounder replies?

And the azurous hung hills are his world-wielding
   shoulder
Majestic—as a stallion stalwart, very-violet-sweet!— 10
These things, these things were here and but the be-
   holder
Wanting; which two when they once meet,
The heart rears wings bold and bolder
And hurls for him, O half hurls earth for him off under
   his feet.
(1877; 1918)

5–8 **Left . . . spend.** It is worth quoting Hopkins' explanation of this stanza made in a letter to Robert Bridges (1882): "*Rash-fresh* [l. 6] . . . means a headlong and exciting new snatch of singing, resumption by the lark of his song, which by turns he gives over and takes up again all day long, and this goes on, the sonnet says, through time, without ever losing its first freshness, being a thing both new and old. . . . The *skein* [is] the lark's song, which from his height gives the impression of something falling to the earth and not vertically quite, but tricklingly or wavingly, something as a skein of silk ribbed by having been wound on a narrow card or on a notched holder or as twine or fishing-tackle unwinding from a reel or *winch* [l. 7] or as pearls strung on a horsehair: the laps or folds are the notes or short measures and bars of them. The same is called a *score* in the musical sense." The passage affords an excellent example of what Hopkins would call *inscape* 7 **crisps,** curly wisps, referring to the trill of the bird's song 13 **make and making,** achievement and effort **The Windhover.** The windhover is a kestrel, or sparrow-hawk 1 **minion,** darling, favorite 2 **dauphin,** prince; originally, the heir to the throne of France 4 **rung . . . wing.** The bird's rapidly beating wings rang like a bell as it hovered **wimpling,** rippling 10 **Buckle.** The following note is by W. H. Gardner in the third edition of *Poems of Gerard Manley Hopkins* (Oxford, 1948), p. 228: "In one or all of its diverse but possible meanings (1. fasten together; 2. engage the enemy; 3. bend, crumple), this imperative (possibly indicative) verb seems to apply *directly* to the kestrel and *obliquely* to Christ, to whom the poem is dedicated (cf. 'O my chevalier' and 'ah my dear,' ll. 11 and 13). Through Christ, moreover, 'Buckle' comes home again to the poet-disciple himself, for the adverb 'here' (l. 9) can mean 'in this bird' and in my heart 'in hiding' (l. 7), i.e., dedicated to Christ but 'emotionally repressed,' perhaps 'shrinking from danger.' Thus, in the sestet, the concept of disciplined physical activity merges into that of disciplined spiritual activity—the beauty of sacrifice (l. 14)"

12 **sillion,** the ridge between two furrows of plowed land **Pied Beauty** 2 **brinded,** brindled, streaked 3 **stipple,** a method in painting of applying color in dots 4 **chestnut-falls,** chestnuts newly stripped of their husks 5 **plotted and pieced,** divided into fields 6 **trim,** equipment 7 **counter,** contrary to what is expected **spare,** rare 10 **whose . . . change.** Cf. *James,* 1:17: "Every good gift is from above, and cometh down from the Father of lights, with whom is no variableness, neither shadow of turning" **Hurrahing in Harvest** 1 **stooks,** shocks of grain 4 **Meal-drift,** sand drift

PEACE

When will you ever, Peace, wild wood-dove, shy
    wings shut,
Your round me roaming end, and under be my boughs?
When, when, Peace, will you, Peace? I'll not play
    hypocrite
To own my heart:° I yield you do come sometimes; but
5 That piecemeal peace is poor peace. What pure peace
    allows
Alarms of wars, the daunting wars, the death of it?

O surely, reaving Peace,° my Lord should leave in lieu
Some good! And so he does leave Patience exquisite,
That plumes to Peace thereafter. And when Peace here
    does house,
10 He comes with work to do, he does not come to coo,
    He comes to brood and sit.
    (1879; 1918)

SPRING AND FALL

TO A YOUNG CHILD

Márgarét, are you gríeving
Over Goldengrove unleaving?°
Leáves, líke the things of man, you
With your fresh thoughts care for, can you?
5 Ah! ás the heart grows older
It will come to such sights colder
By and by, nor spare a sigh
Though worlds of wanwood leafmeal lie;°
And yet you wíll weep and know why.
10 Now no matter, child, the name:
Sórrow's spríngs áre the same,
Nor mouth had, no nor mind, expressed
What heart heard of, ghost guessed:
It ís the blight man was born for,
15 It is Margaret you mourn for.
    (1880; 1918)

INVERSNAID°

This darksome burn,° horseback brown,
His rollrock highroad roaring down,
In coop° and in comb° the fleece of his foam
Flutes° and low to the lake falls home.

A windpuff-bonnet of fáwn-fróth   5
Turns and twindles° over the broth
Of a pool so pitchblack, féll-fRÓwning,
It rounds and rounds Despair to drowning.

Degged° with dew, dappled with dew
Are the groins of the braes that the brook treads   10
    through,
Wiry heathpacks,° flitches° of fern,
And the beadbonny ash that sits over the burn.

What would the world be, once bereft
Of wet and of wildness? Let them be left,
Oh, let them be left, wildness and wet;   15
Long live the weeds and the wilderness yet.
(1881; 1918)

CARRION COMFORT

Not, I'll not, carrion comfort, Despair, not feast on
    thee;
Not untwist—slack they may be—these last strands of
    man
In me ór, most weary, cry I can no more. I can;
Can something, hope, wish day come, not choose not
    to be.
But ah, but O thou terrible, why wouldst thou rude on
    me   5
Thy wring-world right foot rock? lay a lion-limb
    against me? scan
With darksome devouring eyes my bruiséd bones? and
    fan,
O in turns of tempest, me heaped there; me frantic to
    avoid thee and flee?

  Why? That my chaff might fly; my grain lie, sheer
    and clear.
Nay in all that toil, that coil,° since (seems) I kissed the
    rod,   10
Hand rather, my heart lo! lapped strength, stole joy,
    would laugh, chéer.
Cheer whom though? the hero whose heaven-handling
    flung me, fóot tród
Me? or me that fought him? O which one? is it each
    one? That night, that year
Of now done darkness I wretch lay wrestling with (my
    God!) my God.
(c. 1886; 1918)

Peace 4 **To own my heart,** to my own heart 7 **reaving Peace,** when God takes Peace away **Spring and Fall** 2 **unleaving,** losing (its) leaves 8 **worlds . . . lie,** though worlds of dark woods lie barren, leaf by leaf. *Leafmeal* seems to be formed on the analogy of *piecemeal* or *inchmeal,* "piece by piece," "inch by inch" **Inversnaid,** a hamlet on the east shore of Loch Lomond, Scotland 1 **burn,** brook 3 **coop,** a hollow or enclosed place **comb,** the crest of a wave, water pouring over the rocks at its highest point 4 **Flutes,** forms streaks or channels

6 **twindles,** a portmanteau word formed from "twists" and "dwindles" 9 **Degged,** sprinkled, dampened 11 **heathpacks,** clumps of heather **flitches,** ragged patches, tufts, or clumps **Carrion Comfort** 10 **coil,** confusion, conflict

NO WORST, THERE IS NONE

No worst, there is none. Pitched past pitch of grief,
More pangs will, schooled as forepangs, wilder wring.
Comforter, where, where is your comforting?
Mary, mother of us, where is your relief?
5 My cries heave, herds-long;° huddle in a main, a chief
Woe, world-sorrow;° on an age-old anvil wince and
    sing—
Then lull, then leave off. Fury had shrieked 'No ling-
ering! Let me be fell; force° I must be brief.'

    O the mind, mind has mountains; cliffs of fall
10 Frightful, sheer, no-man-fathomed. Hold them cheap
Man who ne'er hung there. Nor does long our small
Durance° deal with that steep or deep. Here! creep,
Wretch, under a comfort serves in a whirlwind: all
Life death does end and each day dies with sleep.
(1885; 1918)

I WAKE AND FEEL THE FELL OF DARK

I wake and feel the fell° of dark, not day.
What hours, O what black hoürs we have spent
This night! what sights you, heart, saw; ways you
    went!
And more must, in yet longer light's delay.
5   With witness I speak this. But where I say
Hours I mean years, mean life. And my lament
Is cries countless, cries like dead letters sent
To dearest him that lives alas! away.

    I am gall, I am heartburn. God's most deep decree
10 Bitter would have me taste: my taste was me;
Bones built in me, flesh filled, blood brimmed the
    curse.
    Selfyeast of spirit a dull dough sours.° I see
The lost are like this, and their scourge to be
As I am mine, their sweating selves; but worse.°
(c. 1885; 1918)

MY OWN HEART
LET ME MORE HAVE PITY ON

My own heart let me more have pity on; let
Me live to my sad self hereafter kind,
Charitable; not live this tormented mind
With this tormented mind tormenting yet.

I cast for comfort I can no more get   5
By groping round my comfortless, than blind
Eyes in their dark can day or thirst can find
Thirst's all-in-all in all a world of wet.

Soul, self; come, poor Jackself,° I do advise
You, jaded, let be; call off thoughts awhile   10
Elsewhere; leave comfort root-room; let joy size

At God knows when to God knows what; whose smile
's not wrung, see you; unforeseen times rather—as
    skies
Betweenpie° mountains—lights a lovely mile.
(c. 1885; 1918)

TO R. B.°

The fine delight that fathers thought; the strong
Spur, live and lancing like the blowpipe flame,
Breathes once and, quenchéd faster than it came,
Leaves yet the mind a mother of immortal song.
Nine months she then, nay years, nine years she long 5
Within her wears, bears, cares, and combs° the same:
The widow of an insight lost she lives, with aim
Now known and hand at work now never wrong.

    Sweet fire and sire of muse, my soul needs this;
I want the one rapture of an inspiration.   10
O then if in my lagging lines you miss
The roll, the rise, the carol, the creation,
My winter world, that scarcely breathes that bliss
Now, yields you, with some sighs, our explanation.
(1889; 1918)

No Worst, There Is None   5 herds-long. Troubles do not come singly, but in herds   6 world-sorrow. Cf. German *Weltschmerz*   8 force, perforce, of necessity   12 Durance, powers of endurance   I Wake and Feel the Fell of Dark 1 fell, huge and cruel falling; the various senses of this word are blended 12 Selfyeast . . . sours. The spirit should serve as a leaven to the material being, but now it is soured by a preoccupation with the self   14 but worse. Damned souls are in a worse situation

My Own Heart Let Me More Have Pity On   9 Jackself, his everyday self 14 Betweenpie. W. H. Gardner notes that this is "a strange word, in which *pie* apparently makes a compound verb with *between*, meaning, 'as the sky seen between dark mountains is brightly dappled,' the grammar such as *intervariegates* would make."   To R. B.   R. B., Robert Bridges, who reports that this was the last poem sent to him by Hopkins   6 combs. This was the word in the original poem, which Bridges changed to *molds*. Combs can be taken in the sense of either (1) to clean and unravel (as in combing hair) or (2) to store to mature (as in honeycomb). It is more than probable that Hopkins had both senses in mind

The Modern Period

From the First World War to the Present, 1914–

Queen Elizabeth Hall, London, completed in 1967, is part of the South Bank, a music and arts complex begun in 1951

World War I marks the end of an age. The period following it was an era of profound change for most of the countries of the world, but it was especially so for England. The First World War was a military and political event that changed the map of Europe. In the end there were victors and vanquished, of course, but principally victims. England was both victor and victim. There was a brief period of optimism after the war, but this was soon challenged by international and domestic crises. During the modern era Britain witnessed the gradual dissolution of its empire and the formation of a loosely joined commonwealth. Only twenty-one years after the so-called Great War, the world was once again plunged into global conflict, and again England was at the center. Once again England emerged both victor and victim. After the war England underwent a series of financial crises and at the same time suffered loss of world prestige. Many British colonies and territories gained their independence. The British economy is today plagued by high inflation and unemployment. England no longer stands among the major world powers.

These profound changes in the geography and politics of the empire have had important implications for English literature. Beginning with the war poetry of Wilfred Owen (1893–1918) and others, modern English literature took on pervasive tones of irony and anxiety, and expressed moods of sobriety and pathos that many writers believed were intrinsic to the human condition in the modern world. It would be incorrect to think of these qualities as uniquely modern, of course, but their new currency in modern literature suggests a movement away from the relatively self-confident view of the world that was characteristic of the nineteenth century.

Modern England

In the nineteenth century England's industrial might, its financial strength, and its smoothly functioning and stable government made it possible for the nation to play a unique role in human affairs. The very size of the British empire meant that Englishmen were involved in developments all over the globe. Enlarged and consolidated in the nineteenth century, the British empire consisted at its peak of thirteen million square miles of land—the largest empire known in history. The beginning of the dissolution of this empire can be traced back as far as the events surrounding the First World War.

The First World War

Today most historians agree that it is virtually impossible to explain the First World War in terms of the actions of any one of the great powers—Germany, Aus-

Police carry away Emmeline Pankhurst (1858–1928), the leader of the Women's Suffrage Movement in England, after her arrest during a suffragettes' demonstration at Buckingham Palace on May 21, 1914. British women did not achieve full voting rights until 1928.

A munitions worker loading a shell in July 1915 at Vickers, Ltd., a famous British armaments manufacturer.

tria-Hungary, Bulgaria, and Turkey on the one hand; England, France, and Russia on the other. Rather, all the major participating nations in some measure must accept responsibility for the outbreak of the war. The atmosphere of anguish and gloom prevalent in England in the last days of peace is reflected in a passage from the autobiography of Sir Edward Grey (1862–1933), the British foreign secretary:

A friend came to see me on one of the evenings of the last week [before the war]—he thinks it was on Monday, August 3. We were standing at the window of my room in the Foreign Office. It was getting dusk, and the lamps were being lit in the space below on which we were looking. My friend recalls that I remarked on this with the words: "The lamps are going out all over Europe; we shall not see them lit again in our lifetime."

For more than four years the science, industry, wealth, and power of Europe were concentrated upon destruction. The Great War of 1914–1918 was a total war—a war fought not only on land, sea, and in the air but also on home fronts far from military conflict. The campaigns fought at the beginning of the war—Marne and Tannenberg and, a little later, the Dardanelles and Jutland—ended any hope of a quick

British soldiers (1916) in the trenches, where much of the fighting in World War I occurred. Wilfred Owen (1893–1918) was among the many prominent English writers who lost their lives in the war.

victory on either side. The belligerents were condemned to the grinding horror of a war of attrition and stalemate. With the entrance of the United States into the war in the spring of 1917, however, this standoff finally ended. In the autumn of 1918 Germany collapsed and sued for peace.

At eleven o'clock on the morning of 11 November 1918, the guns became silent in the war "to make the world safe for democracy." It soon became evident, however, that the cessation of fighting on that first Armistice Day was no more than an indefinite truce—if indeed it could be called that—which was to last only slightly more than twenty years. For the victorious British troops, 11 November meant returning home to a joyful conqueror's welcome.

Between the Wars

Britain spent the first few years after Armistice Day in a hopeful effort to pick up the fragments of the old way of life which the war had shattered. "A land fit for heroes to live in" became its immediate slogan. The unemployment incidental to the return of hundreds of thousands of veterans to civilian life was anticipated and relieved for a time by a modest dole, but this measure soon proved inadequate.

The 1920s were not a tranquil period for Britain. During these dismal years unemployment and bitter labor disputes disrupted the nation. In 1924 Ramsay MacDonald (1866–1937) became Britain's first Labour prime minister. The goal of the Labour party was to introduce socialism slowly and within a democratic framework. During four years of power the Labour government registered some success in foreign affairs but at home generated little dynamism in solving Britain's critical economic problems. Following MacDonald's defeat at the polls in October 1924, Britain was for the next five years led by a Conservative government under Stanley Baldwin (1867–1947), who was even less successful than his predecessor in providing vigorous leadership. Thus, the decade following the victory in 1918 saw an absence of consensus about economic development and reform and a seeming inability to measure up to the demands of a difficult new age.

During this period serious tensions, mainly generated by demands for home rule, were emerging in various parts of the British empire, in Ireland, India, Ceylon, Burma, and Egypt. In 1918 militant Irish nationalists issued a declaration of independence for an Irish Republic. For three years Ireland was in turmoil with fighting between the nationalists and British troops and then among various Irish factions over the peace terms with Britain in 1921. These terms established the Irish Free State in the south with the status of a dominion. In the north, however, Ulster with its pro-British majority remained tied to Britain. During the next three decades southern Ireland gradually and peacefully severed all constitutional ties with Britain. The ultimate fate of Ulster remains unsettled as the bloodshed between the Protestant majority and Catholic minority continues to this day.

An ominous trend was the growing antagonism between the Arab inhabitants of mandated Palestine and

Princess Elizabeth (later Queen Elizabeth II) is seated between her grandparents, King George V and Queen Mary, in this 1933 photograph. Elizabeth's mother, the duchess of York, is facing Queen Mary.

Hunger marchers stopping for a meal on their way to London (1936). During the 1930s, groups of British workers conducted hunger marches to protest the high rate of unemployment.

the Jewish Zionist immigrants. A happier development was Britain's recognition in 1931, in the Statute of Westminster, of a new national status for the dominions (Canada, Australia, New Zealand, and South Africa). Henceforth, the dominions and Great Britain were held together only by loyalty to the crown and by a common language, legal principles, traditions, and economic interests. Collectively these states were now known as the British Commonwealth of Nations.

It was inevitable that the world depression that began in the late 1920s would have catastrophic effects in highly industrialized and heavily populated Britain. In two years exports and imports declined 35 percent, and three million unemployed roamed the streets of the factory towns.

A Labour administration, with Ramsay MacDonald as prime minister, took office in 1929. Little was accomplished, and unemployment became more widespread as the depression deepened. When the Labour government fell, MacDonald retained his office by becoming the leader of a national coalition government, which was primarily Conservative. The bulk of the Labour party constituted the opposition.

Nothing spectacular was undertaken, but the country did "muddle through." By 1937 a substantial measure of prosperity had been regained. To achieve this comeback, much of what remained of laissez-faire policy was discarded. The government now regulated

the currency, exacted high tariffs, gave farmers subsidies, and imposed heavy taxes. The rich had a large proportion of their income taxed away, and what might be left at death was decimated by inheritance taxes.

Despite improvements in the economic picture, an increasing demand for the extension of the welfare state existed. There were pleas for expanded educational and health facilities, better accident and unemployment insurance, and more adequate pensions. A survey of Britain's social services made in 1941 by the noted economist William Beveridge recommended a comprehensive system of social insurance. This plan served as the blueprint for Britain's post–Second World War legislation that provided free health care and free education for everyone.

Neville Chamberlain (1869–1940) became prime minister in 1937, and at this time Britain's foreign policy began to take precedence over its domestic policies. Having a sincere and passionate horror of war, Chamberlain determined to explore every possibility for reaching an equitable understanding with the rapidly growing totalitarian powers of Germany and Italy. Chamberlain persisted in trying to ease international tension despite snubs from those he wished to placate and also warnings from some of his colleagues in the British foreign office. Chamberlain's policies had some support in England because of a widespread and

UPI

These British soldiers crossing the English Channel were among the 198,000 British troops evacuated from the French city of Dunkirk between May 29 and June 3, 1940.

Ruins of the Coventry Cathedral, one of many important buildings in English cities destroyed by German air raids during the Battle of Britain (August 1940–April 1941).

RADIO TIMES HULTON PICTURE LIBRARY

extremely fierce desire for peace, arising from the general war weariness and disillusionment suffered after the First World War. But Chamberlain's policies of accommocation and appeasement were merely delaying tactics. When German forces invaded Poland on 1 September 1939, Britain could no longer afford to back down; it declared war against Germany. France took similar action. After an interval of only twenty-one years, Europe was again plunged into conflict.

The Second World War

The war can be divided into a series of stages. During 1939 and 1940 Germany virtually mastered Europe. Only Britain, now under the able wartime leadership of Winston Churchill (1874–1965), remained a defiant and lonely opponent. Churchill became the voice and symbol of a new and indomitable Britain. Following the fall of France, the United States made every effort to aid Britain and then Russia to forestall domination of the world by totalitarian powers.

These powers came perilously close to winning in the summer of 1942. After a sneak attack against the United States base at Pearl Harbor, the Japanese invaded island after island in the Pacific. Hitler marched through Russia to the outskirts of Stalingrad. In North Africa British troops were pushed back into Egypt by German forces. By the end of 1942, however, the tide began to turn with an Allied victory in North Africa and a Nazi debacle in the icy streets of Stalingrad. Italy surrendered, the Germans withdrew from Russia, and the Americans went on the offensive in the Pacific. Germany surrendered in May 1945; the Japanese in August.

The Postwar Years

Although England won the war, the postwar years were hard. The country in 1945 was in a state of near bankruptcy. During the war England had incurred huge losses of overseas investments and a marked decline in foreign trade. Moreover, its problems were increased by inefficient industrial management and featherbedding among trade unions, while its expensive but attractive welfare-state programs could only be paid for by a favorable balance of international payments. But imports kept exceeding exports, threatening the position of Britain's currency and creating balance-of-payment crises. These years of anxiety marked a whole generation of writers.

Perhaps Britain's most notable postwar achievement was the peaceful liquidation of its once vast empire. This imperial loss, coupled with domestic economic problems, caused British statesmen to develop a new posture in world affairs, such as seeking closer ties with countries across the English Channel. In 1971 Britain accepted an official invitation to join the

Sir Winston Churchill (1874–1965), British prime minister from 1940 to 1945 and from 1951 to 1953, flashes a "V" sign—a symbol for Allied victory—in this World War II photograph.

Common Market, a decision taken despite a split in British public opinion regarding its future impact on the country's domestic economy.

During the 1970s, Britain's most critical domestic problem was the failure of the electorate to give either of the major parties, Conservative or Labour, a majority in the House of Commons and a cabinet with enough strength and confidence to attack the country's worsening economic problems. These included an annual inflation rate of nearly 20 percent, high unemployment, and a $10 billion balance-of-payments deficit caused in large part by the inflated worldwide cost of crude oil. The battle with inflation has been and continues to be a hard one. As one contemporary observer has put it: "It has been said of the British that they are incapable of admitting defeat, which is why in the end they always win. But there can be no doubt that Britain faces the most serious challenge in her recent history as a liberal democracy."

Modern Literature

Modern British writers have understood and reflected the period's overall sense of dislocation. Sometimes they have responded to specific causes of upheaval and controversy such as war and political outrage. At other times they have sought ways to express the era's new discoveries and insights. Modern psychological theory, stemming in large part from the pioneering

Pelagos (1946) by Barbara Hepworth, one of the earliest and most prominent abstract sculptors in England. Her work in the '40s explored the counterplay between mass and space in sculpture, as this piece illustrates. Note that the sculptural space is accented and defined by the taut strings at the top of the loop.

work of Sigmund Freud (1856–1939), for example, has profoundly changed the presentation in fiction of the workings of the human mind. Most major modern writers have shown a dissatisfaction with Western civilization unmatched in even the most anxious works of the nineteenth century. Moreover, modern writers have felt, for the most part, increasingly alienated from the public. Ironic, esoteric, and outrightly antagonistic works recur throughout the period.

The most important watershed for modern literary history is the Second World War. By its end, Thomas Hardy, A. E. Housman, Joseph Conrad, D. H. Lawrence, James Joyce, and Virginia Woolf were dead; and T. S. Eliot and E. M. Forster had completed their major work. Of writers generally recognized as significant, only two who figured prominently on the prewar scene continued to produce long after it—W. H. Auden and Graham Greene.

The eclipse of England.

Because we are so close in time to twentieth-century literature, it is difficult to present that literature in clearcut categories, stages, and schools. An important first fact, though, is that many of the most significant writers are not English. Joseph Conrad (1857–1924) and T. S. Eliot were Polish and American, respectively; Bernard Shaw (1856–1950), William Butler Yeats (1865–1939), and James Joyce (1882–1941) were Irish. What is more, many British writers have chosen to live in exile. W. H. Auden (1907–1973), D. H. Lawrence (1885–1930), Malcolm Lowry (1909–1957), and Ford Madox Ford (1873–1939) all spent some of their last years in North

America. Others have taken the general insulation of English culture as a major theme for their art. For example, in *A Passage to India* (1924) E. M. Forster (1879–1970) chose a young Indian doctor as his protagonist and did so to help reveal the limitations of the colonial British mentality. Furthermore, especially in recent years, a number of fine works have been written in English by members of what were colonized peoples. In particular there are the novels of Chinua Achebe (born in Nigeria, 1930–   ) and of V. S. Naipaul (born in Trinidad, 1932–   ). Of crucial importance to modern British literature, however, were the Irish writers who were part of what is today known as the Irish Renaissance.

The Irish Renaissance.

The Irish Renaissance was a conscious literary movement which coincided with the struggle for Irish independence. The founder and leader of this movement was William Butler Yeats, and an earnest group of poets, dramatists, essayists, and novelists became associated with him from about 1890 on. The movement attempted to create a unity of spirit and national consciousness among the Irish people by reviving their romantic past and by interpreting their modern situation in works written in both Gaelic (the national language of Ireland) and English. Some notable Irish writers—Shaw and Joyce, for example—remained largely outside the movement, but they too contributed by frequently focusing their art upon Irish problems and concerns. Irish writers were prolific in drama, poetry, and prose.

Foremost among the dramatists of the Irish Renaissance is Bernard Shaw. Although born in Dublin, he lived most of his life in London. He once remarked, "England had conquered Ireland; so there was nothing for it but to come over and conquer England." In going to London, Shaw was following in the footsteps of

William Butler Yeats in 1932.

his great Irish theatrical predecessors, William Congreve (1670–1729) and Richard Sheridan (1751–1816). Shaw was among the first in London to recognize the greatness of the Norwegian playwright Henrik Ibsen (1828–1902). What Shaw admired in Ibsen—a savage attack upon the bourgeoisie and a use of theater for social debate—he adopted for his own dramatic credo. In his more than twenty plays and in his elaborate prefaces, Shaw attempted to intellectually provoke his audience. As a thinker, Shaw addressed himself to modern issues before they came into fashion and rejected old ideas which had become dogma. For example, he rejected theatrical realism and championed psychological realism, and he rejected society's accepted notions of femininity. And if he did not actually change the world in the way in which he hoped, he certainly did change the scope and nature of English drama. His best plays are generally considered to be *Arms and the Man* (1894), *Caesar and Cleopatra* (1899), *Major Barbara* (1907), *Pygmalion* (1913), and *Saint Joan* (1923).

Bernard Shaw.

While Shaw entertained London, others flourished at home. The Irish National Theatre Society, later the famous Abbey Theatre of Dublin, was founded in 1902 by W. B. Yeats, Lady Gregory (1852–1932), and several others. In addition to Lady Gregory's lucrative comedies, the Abbey Theatre staged the plays of John Millington Synge (1871–1909), Sean O'Casey (1880–1964), and Yeats himself. Synge sought to enrich his language with the diction and rhythms of folk speech. His greatest play, *The Playboy of the Western World* (1907), mirrors the credulity, superstition, and brutality, as well as the charm, of the Irish peasantry. O'Casey's early plays were also tied strongly to the life

and speech of the Irish poor. Set against the background of the Irish revolution, his best works, *Juno and the Paycock* (1924) and *The Plough and the Stars* (1926), combine in sharp, often startling juxtaposition the tragic and the comic. Yeats' plays, by contrast, make no claim to realism. Instead, they provide a vision by which Yeats' countrymen could transform Ireland and themselves. In *Kathleen ni Houlihan* (1902), for example, Yeats' lyrical patriotism is eloquently represented.

The two most important Irish dramas since the Second World War, *Waiting for Godot* (1952) by Samuel Beckett (1906–   ) and *The Hostage* (1958) by Brendan Behan (1923–1964), had their premieres outside Ireland. Beckett lives in Paris, writes in French, and then translates his own work into English. *Godot* reveals Beckett's basic sense of life as dirty, boring, and incomprehensible. But there is also a lyric beauty in his language and a nobility in his characters' fortitude. As one of his characters comments, "We have kept our appointment and that's an end to that. . . . How many people can say as much?" As a youth, Brendan Behan belonged to the Irish Republican Army (I.R.A.) and was imprisoned by the British. *The Hostage* depicts violence and imprisonment with trenchant Irish humor and a broad improvisational style. With Behan's death the center of modern English language theater swung back to London.

William Butler Yeats is the premier poet of the Irish Renaissance. As a young poet he shared in the enervated romanticism of the 1890s, but many of his primary concerns were Irish: he collected and wrote Irish tales and drew upon the heroic past of Irish legend in his verse. When he says in "Easter, 1916" that "a terrible beauty is born," he is not only referring to the literal Easter Rebellion against the British; he is also characterizing the poetry necessary to celebrate that rebellion. Many of his poems, especially "Easter, 1916" and "Meditations in Time of Civil War" (1922), derive part of their power from Yeats' conscious role as the articulator of the emotions and ideals of his

James Joyce.

people. By turning in the 1920s to the great figures of the Irish literary past—George Berkeley (1685–1753), Oliver Goldsmith (1730–1774), and Jonathan Swift (1667–1745)—Yeats attempted to assimilate the great Irish tradition into contemporary literature. By making a poetry "cold and passionate as the dawn," Yeats achieved that blend of distance and immediacy necessary for telling and embodying the multiple truths of major poetry and of a turbulent history.

What Yeats is to modern poetry, James Joyce is to the modern novel. Although Joyce lived his adult life as an exile, Ireland remained his obsession. He wrote short stories, novellas, and novels; and in all three his subject is Irish life. The short story collection *Dubliners* (1914) begins "There was no hope for him this time" and ends "the dead." The intervening pages present what Joyce the young exile saw as the death agonies of his homeland. In the last tale of *Dubliners*, "The Dead," Joyce has tempered some of his early rage. He manages to present not only the dying and ridiculous aspects of Irish life but also the source of his own strength: that interaction with love and death in a culture that brings new life to the consciousness. In its compression of detail and complexity of symbol, "The Dead" stands as one of the major achievements of its author and of the age.

Ulysses (1922) is an even greater achievement. This seven-hundred-page novel combines a microscopically accurate picture of Irish life and a mythical overview of human endeavors. Each section of the novel corresponds to a book of *The Odyssey* by Homer (probably eighth century B.C.); even the minor characters and the city streets are analogous to figures and locales in the Greek epic. The epic analogue is just one of several devices that Joyce employs to develop what he considers the primary theme of modern life: a tendency to fragmentation and isolation.

Joyce's fellow exile and friend, Samuel Beckett, has sustained his mentor's standard of formal innovation and fearless scrutiny of modern life. In Beckett's finest fiction—the trilogy *Molloy* (1951), *Malone Dies* (1951), and *The Unnameable* (1953)—he combines Joyce's concern for stream of consciousness with an older philosophical concern about the relationship between mind and body. The variously named protagonist of the trilogy begins his fictional life in good physical health and in a comfortable bourgeois setting but then loses both the bicycle on which he journeys and the use of his legs. He then spends much time trying by conscious rumination to discover if he has any body left, and ends as a disembodied consciousness trying to talk himself into existence. Together Joyce and

Sculptor Henry Moore's Recumbent Figure *opens up masses and studies space relationships. Moore has achieved an international reputation by being an innovator in material and form and a traditionalist in subject matter. His humanistic sculpture is noted for its psychological content as well as for the respect shown for the organic nature of material.*

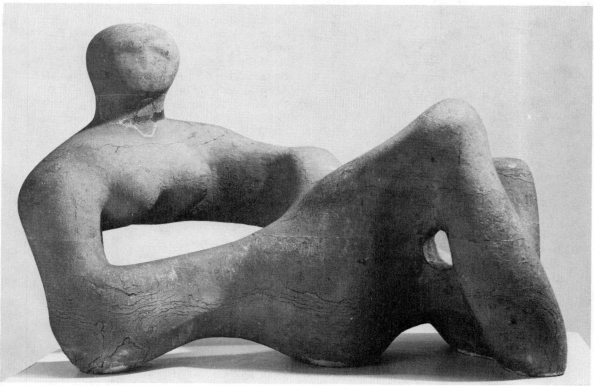

Beckett have exerted an immeasurable influence on modern fiction in all countries of the world.

Poetry. The pessimism of British poetry before 1930 is striking because it appears in the work of two distinct generations. Thomas Hardy and A. E. Housman, born in 1840 and 1859 respectively, speak from a thorough familiarity with the Victorian period. Wilfred Owen and T. S. Eliot reached manhood during World War I: Owen died in 1918 and Eliot developed his full potential in the years immediately after. Housman's poetry reveals an obsessive sense of human frailty; again and again youth is struck down by early death. Owen, who could have been one of Housman's subjects, expresses in his work the bitterness of men whose friends and companions have gone off to a supposedly glorious war and are blown to bits by the newly improved machinery of mass warfare. Hardy's poetry combines in many ways the concerns of Housman and Eliot. His early poems explore man's helplessness faced with uncaring, complacent Fate. His later works do not change in attitude, but they do incorporate materials which are products of man's "progress": the sinking of the Titanic and massive artillery practice, for example.

Those who survived the First World War were scarred by it. For this generation T. S. Eliot was the principal spokesman. With their abrupt transitions, recondite allusions, striking images, and sudden dictional shifts Eliot's poems aptly convey the period's sense of dislocation. He replaces the soft romanticism of contemporary gentility with a biting irony appropriate for a very grim reality; in fact, the title of his early masterpiece *The Waste Land* (1922) provides a sober epithet for postwar society. An earlier poem— "The Love Song of J. Alfred Prufrock" (1915)—reflects the hesitations of men caught in a time when any action was seemingly ineffectual. Ezra Pound, an American poet who spent almost all his adult life in Europe,

W. H. Auden.

was an important figure in this period, and a decisive influence on both Yeats and Eliot.

In spite of the extraordinary and lasting success of his early work, Eliot continued to develop his craft and to explore his experience. Moving steadily toward religion and hope, he mastered a less recondite, though still very learned poetry which was more accessible to the community. *Four Quartets* (1944) provides some transitions where his earlier poetry left only gulfs; with laborious honesty, Eliot finds some consolation in tradition and suffering.

The next two generations of British poets, those of the '30s and those of the '50s, have not been accorded the same literary recognition as their predecessors have. W. H. Auden burst forth in 1930 with a technical command and a personal touch that made him the heir of Yeats and Eliot. Auden expressed more clearly than other poets the sense of the thirties, a decade of radical politics and anxious psychology. His eye for detail, his ability to convey an ironic insight by a surprising joining of noun and adjective, and his wide-ranging knowledge of the English poetic tradition helped him to write poetry that was always intelligent and almost always very attractive. He engaged in a steady exploration of new poetic (and prose) forms, and his vision underwent a steady growth (toward religion, like Eliot). And yet reviewers, with rare unanimity, have consistently criticized Auden's poetry as "uneven." Although almost every collection has produced lines and passages of the highest order, very few poems sustain the effect throughout. At times there seems to be almost too much wit, too much skill; the cleverness makes the reader unsure how to take the line. On the other hand, Auden's strengths remain substantial. His best poems do hold together, and he combines great technical ability with an increasingly moderated sense of self-importance.

Among other poets of the '30s, Robert Graves (1895–   ) maintained a steady production of

T. S. Eliot.

An early-morning view of a Liverpool street (1954). This industrial, predominantly working-class city in northwest England even today looks much as it did in the nineteenth century.

touches nature and mystery in a way unmatched by the poets of the Movement. Hughes' later verse, however, has shown a limiting penchant for system and statement. The poets of the most recent generation have not had time for a full hearing, but Seamus Heaney (1939–   ) and Geoffrey Hill (1932–   ) seem substantial and promising.

Fiction. Like modern poetry, modern British fiction witnessed the emergence of a number of major figures in the first decades of the century—Joseph Conrad, D. H. Lawrence, E. M. Forster, and Virginia Woolf— apart from James Joyce, already mentioned.

Despite the fact that much of his best work predates 1914, Conrad belongs to the modern period; his thematic and formal concerns were similar to those of the writers who came to prominence after his death. Thematically, Conrad shared the dark vision of Hardy, Owen, and Eliot. He saw the corrupting power of politics: in *The Heart of Darkness* (1902) the dark heart is not only the interior of Africa but also the aspirations of colonializing "civilization," particularly the British empire; in *The Secret Agent* (1907) and *Under Western Eyes* (1911) the small minds of international politics shape large events. Conrad avoids the simplification of locating danger only in external forces and political life. He sees inscrutability and darkness as a very condition of our perceptions. He is scrupulous in his determination to deal honestly with life but is

A scene from Tony Richardson's British film A Taste of Honey *(1961), which focuses on the relationship between an unmarried pregnant schoolgirl and a homosexual boy.* A Taste of Honey *was one of many starkly realistic British films during the '50s and '60s that focused on working-class life.*

tough-minded, beautifully honed poetry. The other major poet of the '30s was Dylan Thomas (1914–1953). In one sense, his poetry is, like Eliot's, difficult. However, the difficulty is caused not by esoteric allusions, as in Eliot's poetry, but by syntactic compression and imagistic density. Despite their apparently rhapsodic effusiveness, both syntax and imagery are ordered with extreme care. The dense integration of formal components reflects Thomas' almost mystical sense of the oneness of nature and of man's place in that oneness.

Thomas' place as a major poet seems secure; the stature of those who have followed him is less clear. Poetry in the '50s reacted severely against what it considered the excesses of its predecessors. The "Movement" rejected myth and esoteric allusion and sought to promote common sense and a certain austerity. It replaced the seventeenth-century metaphysical poets beloved by Eliot with the precise and clean-edged eighteenth-century Augustans. Donald Davie (1922–   ) has been the chief spokesman for this group, and Philip Larkin (1922–   ) the chief poet. Larkin's extremely conservative choice of verse forms reflects his (and the Movement's) sense of the narrow bounds of human possibility. Larkin's contemporary, Ted Hughes (1930–   ), in some of his early poetry

skeptical about the mind's competence to do so. To embody the problematic and limited nature of man's perception, Conrad demonstrates considerable formal innovation. His characters have difficulty seeing both because desires and fears blind them and because their experience is variegated. In *Lord Jim* (1900), for example, the protagonist jumps overboard because he is sure his ship is sinking; only later does he learn that it does not. The rendering of this event and its aftermath is further complicated by Conrad's use of a narrator; this narrator gathers information firsthand, is told facts by others, recounts much of the story to listeners, and later sends to one of the listeners a written narrative which is augmented by documents from the protagonist's life. The very form of the novel indicates the difficulty of knowing a human being and places upon the reader much of the burden of creating meaning by putting together events intelligibly. This concern with point of view is one of Conrad's greatest legacies to fiction. Another is the symbolic quality of narrative. In Conrad's best works, objects and movements carry larger meanings than their immediate causes suggest. In *The Heart of Darkness*, for example, the protagonist begins a journey to find a colonial outpost; to be sure, he finds it, but, on another level, he also finds the horrible interior landscape of modern man's life.

Like Conrad, Lawrence is unquestionably a major talent. His response to modern industrialized society was to affirm the instincts and impulses of man. He was aware of a conflict in modern man, a conflict between what he termed "Law" and "Love." "Every work of art," he said, "adheres to some system of morality. But if it really be a work of art, it must contain the essential criticism of the morality to which it adheres. . . . The degree to which the system of morality, or the metaphysic, is submitted to criticism within the work of art makes the lasting value and satisfaction of that work." At times, it must be admitted, Lawrence's work fails by his own standards.

In Mexico, New Mexico, and Australia, among other places, Lawrence sought to escape modern industrial society and to explore the "primitive" in the individual and in culture. He pursued his vision of experience in his poems, short stories, novellas, and novels. The censors of his day believed that he was preoccupied with sex and obsessed with destructive relationships. But in novels such as *Sons and Lovers* (1913), *The Rainbow* (1915), and *Women in Love* (1920), Lawrence focuses on how well his characters understand their deepest human drives, especially as those drives are affected by personal demands and society's expectations. In this sense, Lawrence shared with Joyce and other modern writers a concern with the more elusive movements of the human mind, developing techniques to reveal the "inner life" of the individual.

Virginia Woolf was a perceptive literary theorist,

critic, and reviewer. Her disapproval of several popular novelists of her day was based upon her belief that they were too concerned with fiction as a social statement and not enough concerned with how fiction might reflect human character—especially the character of the mind. Woolf felt that writers could better speak to readers by recording the striking detail and conveying the telling moment in an individual's life rather than by informing readers of the individual's manners, wealth, or social position. Like Joyce, her concern with the flow of time and the multiplicity of human identity found expression in experimentation with stream of consciousness techniques. Like Joyce in *Ulysses*, Woolf in *Mrs. Dalloway* (1925) follows characters through a single day and records their manifold impressions. Her rendering of life in time goes even further in *To the Lighthouse* (1927), the central section of which lyrically portrays the passage of time in an empty house. One of Woolf's chief commitments was to the inner lives of women. Woolf knew that, "modern" as her age was, its economic,

The Irish-born Francis Bacon is often considered to be the most important figure painter in the British Isles since World War II. His subjects are frequently diseased, deformed, or monstrous. This painting, entitled Study for Portrait on Folding Bed, *has a disturbing, indeed horrifying, impact. The formal dignity and traditional arrangement of his compositions throws his obvious torment into sharp relief.*

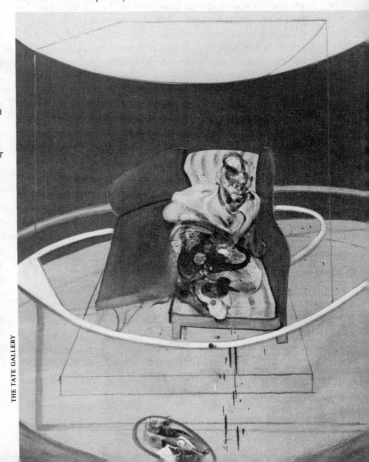

D. H. Lawrence.

THE BETTMANN ARCHIVE

and drawing critical attention in the 1930s, mixes an instinct for the contemporary scene with a witty style and a capacity to use the power and range of symbol. At his best he has a great gift for portraying human suffering with currency and immediacy. Sometimes, however, his characters seem determined by ideas. Still, in works like *Brighton Rock* (1938), *The Power and the Glory* (1940), and *The Heart of the Matter* (1948) he makes the high art of the great early modern novelists available to a larger public, and yet does not sacrifice that art's complexity or his own individuality.

A fresh group of writers emerged in the 1950s. Kingsley Amis (1922–), John Wain (1925–), John Braine (1922–), and Alan Sillitoe (1928–) expose with fury the false promises and hypocrisy of post-war English society. Because these writers sometimes seem to have only anger as their subject and because they react against formal innovation (and even, at times, against stylistic competence), they often seem quite limited. While Doris Lessing (1919–) shares their social concerns, she is not "angry" in the same sense. She explores from a Marxist point of view the problems of modern society and from a feminist point of view the problems of sexual relations. At the opposite extreme from these contemporary writers who lack style and wit are those who seem to have too much. Muriel Spark (1918–), Iris Murdoch (1919–), and William Golding (1911–) are writers of great skill and wit but, with the possible exception of Golding's *The Lord of the Flies* (1954), their work remains interesting rather than overwhelming. A possible bridge between these two limited traditions is the twelve-novel sequence *A Dance to the Music of Time* (1951–1975) by Anthony Powell (1905–), which scrutinizes and traces an entire generation without losing wit or formal control.

political, social, and intellectual habits created an environment in which the inner life was often the only true life that many women had. It was, then, by being a psychological novelist that Woolf was able to affirm the uniqueness and integrity of the individual and illuminate the lives of women.

Among those who have appeared since 1930, Malcolm Lowry comes close to the achievements of the best earlier fiction. In *Under the Volcano* (1947) Lowry joins many of the strongest elements of this century's finest literature and adds the personal component of his own dark vision. Like Eliot, he introduces details of arcane mythology; and like Conrad, Joyce, and Lawrence, he dares to write with a large, self-conscious style that utilizes the symbolic potential of language. Lowry's thematic use of alcoholism emphasizes further the collapse, repressiveness, and incomprehensibility which he, like so many modern writers, sees in both public and private life.

Graham Greene (1904–) was also influenced by earlier writers, but his works reflect his many personal and moral concerns. Greene, who began writing

Drama. Unlike fiction and poetry, modern British drama has gained in strength since the Second World War. Earlier efforts achieved at best qualified success. The dramas of John Galsworthy (1867–1933) debate social questions earnestly but lack the power essential for realistic theater. The plays of Noël Coward (1899–1973), whose wittiness once seemed so ironically tough, sometimes seem sentimental and inadequate to the social issues they raise. With *Murder in the Cathedral* (1935) T. S. Eliot managed an effective blend of poetry and ritual, but his later efforts, aimed at social comedy and box office appeal, met with much less success. Christopher Fry's (1907–) verse dramas appeared in the late 1940s, but their poetry has a tendency to decorate the action instead of helping to render new dramatic experience.

In 1956 John Osborne (1929–), the first of the "angry young men," came forward with his famous *Look Back in Anger.* Other playwrights soon followed

Graham Greene.

CAMERA PRESS, LTD.

in his footsteps—Shelagh Delaney (1939–   ) with *A Taste of Honey*, John Arden (1930–   ) with *Live Like Pigs*, and Arnold Wesker (1932–   ) with *Chicken Soup with Barley*, all in 1958. That year also saw the first appearance of the man who is the most important of the young playwrights, though his plays differ quite strongly from those of his peers. Harold Pinter (1930–   ) expresses a contemporary sense of dislocation by using the most complex techniques of Continental antirealist theater. Like Beckett, Pinter uses brilliantly compressed language to convey characters isolated not only from others but from themselves. In *The Birthday Party* (1958), *The Caretaker* (1960), and *The Homecoming* (1966), Pinter achieves an understated horror beyond any of the angry writers. Pinter may already be the greatest English-born dramatist of the century. He also works in film.

Pinter and his contemporaries write in an ambiance that could hardly be more congenial for playwrights. A large number of excellent actors, a variety of first-rate theaters, and serious directors and producers, such as Joan Littlewood (1914–   ), Peter Brook (1925–   ), and Peter Hall (1930–   ), make Britain fertile soil for dramatists. With the appearance of

British actor David Hemmings photographs high-fashion models in this scene from the popular and critically acclaimed movie Blow-Up *(1966), filmed in England and directed by the prominent Italian cinematographer Michelangelo Antonioni (1912–   ).*

David Hockney, one of the leading British pop artists of the '60s and '70s, uses a myriad of techniques in his paintings. Note the flat surfaces and stark mise-en-scène in this portrait entitled Mr. and Mrs. Clark and Percy.

The popular British musical group the Beatles, who helped to establish rock as a prominent new musical form in the 1960s.

John Arden's magnificent *Serjeant Musgrave's Dance* in 1959, the emergence of a steady stream of new talents—including Tom Stoppard (1937–   ) and Edward Bond (1934–   )—and the wider availability of Continental and American influences, drama has become contemporary Britain's strongest genre.

Modern British literature reflects a world far different from that which most Victorians knew, far different from that which earlier centuries produced. It is a world not of the British empire but of the commonwealth. A world of international community has altered the idea of what being "English" is. Writers as different in origin and art as Graham Greene and Doris Lessing, for example, are among those now working in the long tradition which holds that the quality of life is enhanced by an ability to express ideas about it.

THOMAS HARDY
1840–1928

Thomas Hardy was born in Dorsetshire in the southwest of England, a part of the country which he used as the background for so much of his fiction and poetry and for which he revived the name of the old Anglo-Saxon kingdom of Wessex. He attended local schools until he was sixteen, when he was apprenticed to a local architect and church restorer. Hardy put much of his spare time into the study of Latin and Greek and became acquainted with William Barnes (1800–1886), a local dialect poet. Hardy apparently gave some thought at this time to becoming a cleric, but in 1862 he actively followed the profession of architect by becoming a junior assistant to Sir Arthur Blomfield (1829–1899), an important Gothic revivalist architect, in London. He enjoyed the opportunities the city afforded for art and literature and at the same time won two prizes for architectural design.

In 1867 he left London and returned to Dorsetshire because of poor health. Though he still considered himself an architect, he began to write novels and poems. Hardy inaugurated his career with *Desperate Remedies* (1871), the first of fourteen novels which, over the next twenty-five years, established him as a first-rate novelist and allowed him to give up architecture and rely on writing as a career. He divided his novels into three groups based upon their type and technique: novels of ingenuity—*Desperate Remedies* (1871), *The Hand of Ethelberta* (1876), *A Laodicean* (1882); novels of character and environment—*Under the Greenwood Tree* (1872), *Far from the Madding Crowd* (1874), *The Return of the Native* (1878), *The Mayor of Casterbridge* (1886), *The Woodlanders* (1887), *Tess of the D'Urbervilles* (1891), *Jude the Obscure* (1896); romances and fantasies—*A Pair of Blue Eyes* (1873), *The Trumpet-Major* (1880), *Two on a Tower* (1882), *The Well Beloved* (1897). The reception of his outspoken novel *Jude the Obscure* by the English and American public was so hostile that Hardy completely abandoned the writing of novels, composing only poetry during the remaining thirty years of his life.

Hardy was a poet before he was a novelist and only the impossibility of getting his early poems published led him to prose fiction. In 1898, while living in a house that he designed in Dorsetshire, he published *Wessex Poems*. In 1902 appeared *Poems of the Past and the Present*. The next year the first part of a gigantic poetic enterprise, *The Dynasts*, was published, and this vast epic-drama of the Napoleonic Wars continued to occupy his attention for five years, the second section appearing in 1906 and the third and last in 1908. *Time's Laughingstocks and Other Verses* was issued in 1909, and *Satires of Circumstance*, containing some of his best poetry, in 1914. Hardy was awarded the Order of Merit in 1910. He continued to write poetry almost up to his death in 1928. His ashes were placed in Westminster Abbey, and his heart was buried in a church near his birthplace.

The poems of Thomas Hardy are plain in style, lacking the expansiveness of expression of many Victorian lyrics. They have as a result a certain bleak, almost angular, quality and an intense concentration and economy of expression. Many of them are barbed with satire. They reveal Hardy as a post-Victorian author who was a realist in technique and a pessimist in ideas, but who believed that the world could become better. His function in literature, he thought, was to bring about this change by assaulting human cruelty and by attacking the "robustious swaggering of optimism," which is "at bottom cowardly and insincere."

HAP

If but some vengeful god would call to me
From up the sky, and laugh: "Thou suffering thing,
Know that thy sorrow is my ecstasy,
That thy love's loss is my hate's profiting!"

Then would I bear it, clench myself, and die,   5
Steeled by the sense of ire unmerited;
Half-eased in that a Powerfuller than I
Had willed and meted me the tears I shed.

But not so. How arrives it joy lies slain,
And why unblooms the best hope ever sown?—   10
Crass Casualty obstructs the sun and rain,
And dicing Time° for gladness casts a moan. . . .
These purblind° Doomsters had as readily strown
Blisses about my pilgrimage as pain.
(1866; 1898)

NEUTRAL TONES

We stood by a pond that winter day,
And the sun was white, as though chidden° of God,
And a few leaves lay on the starving sod;
   —They had fallen from an ash, and were gray.

Your eyes on me were as eyes that rove   5
Over tedious riddles of years ago;
And some words played between us to and fro
   On which lost the more by our love.

The smile on your mouth was the deadest thing
Alive enough to have strength to die;   10

Hap   12 **dicing Time,** time that gambles with us   13 **purblind,** wholly blind
Neutral Tones   2 **chidden,** scolded

And a grin of bitterness swept thereby
    Like an ominous bird a-wing. . . .

Since then, keen lessons that love deceives
And wrings with wrong, have shaped to me
15 Your face, and the God-curst sun, and a tree,
    And a pond edged with grayish leaves.
(1867; 1898)

THE DARKLING THRUSH

I leant upon a coppice gate°
    When Frost was specter-gray,
And Winter's dregs made desolate
    The weakening eye of day.
The tangled bine-°stems scored the sky
    Like strings of broken lyres,
And all mankind that haunted nigh
    Had sought their household fires.

The land's sharp features seemed to be
10   The Century's corpse° outleant,
His crypt the cloudy canopy,
    The wind his death lament.
The ancient pulse of germ and birth
    Was shrunken hard and dry,
And every spirit upon earth
    Seemed fervorless as I.

At once a voice arose among
    The bleak twigs overhead
In a full-hearted evensong
20   Of joy illimited;
An aged thrush, frail, gaunt, and small,
    In blast-beruffled plume,
Had chosen thus to fling his soul
    Upon the growing gloom.

So little cause for carolings
    Of such ecstatic sound
Was written on terrestrial things
    Afar or nigh around,
That I could think there trembled through
30   His happy good-night air
Some blessed Hope, whereof he knew
    And I was unaware.
(1900; 1900)

THE MAN HE KILLED

"Had he and I but met
    By some old ancient inn,
We should have sat us down to wet
    Right many a nipperkin!°

"But ranged as infantry,
    And staring face to face,
I shot at him as he at me,
    And killed him in his place.

"I shot him dead because—
    Because he was my foe,   10
Just so—my foe of course he was;
    That's clear enough; although

"He thought he'd 'list,° perhaps,
    Off-hand like—just as I—
Was out of work—had sold his traps—
    No other reason why.

"Yes; quaint and curious war is!
    You shoot a fellow down
You'd treat if met where any bar is,
    Or help to half-a-crown.°"   20
(1909)

THOUGHTS OF PHENA

AT NEWS OF HER DEATH

Not a line of her writing have I,
    Not a thread of her hair,
No mark of her late time as dame in her dwelling,
    whereby
    I may picture her there;
And in vain do I urge my unsight
    To conceive my lost prize
At her close, whom I knew when her dreams were
    upbrimming with light,
    And with laughter her eyes.   10

What scenes spread around her last days,
    Sad, shining, or dim?
Did her gifts and compassions enray and enarch° her
    sweet ways
    With an aureate nimb?°
Or did life-light decline from her years,
    And mischances control
Her full day-star; unease, or regret, or forebodings, or
    fears
    Disennoble her soul?   20

Thus I do but the phantom retain
    Of the maiden of yore
As my relic; yet haply the best of her—fined in my
    brain
    It may be the more

The Darkling Thrush 1 coppice gate, gate leading to the thicket 5 bine, a kind of climbing plant 10 Century's corpse, the dead body of the nineteenth century; the poem was written in 1900 The Man He Killed 4 nipperkin, a half pint of ale

13 'list, enlist in the army 20 half-a-crown, currently worth a bit less than twenty-five cents Thoughts of Phena 13 enray and enarch, to cast their rays upon, to arch over 15 nimb, a nimbus or halo

That no line of her writing have I,
     Nor a thread of her hair,
No mark of her late time as dame in her dwelling,
     whereby
     I may picture her there.
     (1890)

THE RUINED MAID

"O 'melia, my dear, this does everything crown!
Who could have supposed I should meet you in Town?
And whence such fair garments, such prosperi-ty?"—
"O didn't you know I'd been ruined?" said she.

—"You left us in tatters, without shoes or socks,
Tired of digging potatoes, and spudding up docks;
And now you've gay bracelets and bright feathers
    three!"—
"Yes: that's how we dress when we're ruined," said
    she.

—"At home in the barton° you said 'thee' and 'thou,'
And 'thik oon,' and 'theäs oon,' and 't'other'; but now
Your talking quite fits 'ee for high compa-ny!"—
"Some polish is gained with one's ruin," said she.

—"Your hands were like paws then, your face blue
    and bleak
But now I'm bewitched by your delicate cheek,
And your little gloves fit as on any la-dy!"—
"We never do work when we're ruined," said she.

—"You used to call home-life a hag-ridden dream,
And you'd sigh, and you'd sock;° but at present you
    seem
To know not of megrims or melancho-ly!"—
"True. One's pretty lively when ruined," said she.

—"I wish I had feathers, a fine sweeping gown,
And a delicate face, and could strut about Town!"—
"My dear—a raw country girl, such as you be,
Cannot quite expect that. You ain't ruined," said she.
(1866)

THE VOICE OF THE THORN

I
When the thorn on the down
Quivers naked and cold,
And the mid-aged and old
Pace the path there to town,
In these words dry and drear
It seems to them sighing:

"O winter is trying
To sojourners here!"

II
When it stands fully tressed
On a hot summer day,
And the ewes there astray
Find its shade a sweet rest,
By the breath of the breeze
It inquires of each farer:
"Who would not be sharer
Of shadow with these?"

III
But by day or by night,
And in winter or summer,
Should I be the comer
Along that lone height,
In its voicing to me
Only one speech is spoken:
"Here once was nigh broken
A heart, and by thee."
(1909)

AFTER A JOURNEY

Hereto I come to view a voiceless ghost;
    Whither, O whither will its whim now draw me?
Up the cliff, down, till I'm lonely, lost,
    And the unseen waters' ejaculations awe me.
Where you will next be there's no knowing,
    Facing round about me everywhere,
        With your nut-coloured hair,
And gray eyes, and rose-flush coming and going.

Yes: I have re-entered your olden haunts at last;
    Through the years, through the dead scenes I have
        tracked you;
What have you now found to say of our past—
    Scanned across the dark space wherein I have
        lacked you?
Summer gave us sweets, but autumn wrought divi-
        sion?
    Things were not lastly as firstly well
        With us twain, you tell?
But all's closed now, despite Time's derision.

I see what you are doing: you are leading me on
    To the spots we knew when we haunted here to-
        gether,
The waterfall, above which the mist-bow shone
    At the then fair hour in the then fair weather,
And the cave just under, with a voice still so hollow
    That it seems to call out to me from forty years ago,
        When you were all aglow,
And not the thin ghost that I now frailly follow!

The Ruined Maid 9 **barton,** farmyard   18 **sock,** sigh

Ignorant of what there is flitting here to see,
　The waked birds preen and the seals flop lazily,
Soon you will have, Dear, to vanish from me,
　For the stars close their shutters and the dawn
　　　　whitens hazily.
Trust me, I mind not, though Life lours,°
30　The bringing me here; nay, bring me here again!
　　I am just the same as when
Our days were a joy, and our paths through flowers.
(1914)

DURING WIND AND RAIN

　　They sing their dearest songs—
　　He, she, all of them—yea,
　　Treble and tenor and bass,
　　　And one to play;
　　With the candles mooning each face. . . .
　　　Ah, no; the years O!
How the sick leaves reel down in throngs!

　　They clear the creeping moss—
　　Elders and juniors—aye,
10　Making the pathways neat
　　　And the garden gay;
　　And they build a shady seat. . . .
　　　Ah, no; the years, the years;
See, the white storm-birds wing across!

　　They are blithely breakfasting all—
　　Men and maidens—yea,
　　Under the summer tree,
　　　With a glimpse of the bay,
　　While pet fowl come to the knee. . . .
20　　Ah, no; the years O!
And the rotten rose is ript from the wall.

　　They change to a high new house,
　　He, she, all of them—aye,
　　Clocks and carpets and chairs
　　　On the lawn all day,
　　And brightest things that are theirs. . . .
　　　Ah, no; the years, the years;
Down their carved names the rain-drop ploughs.
(1917)

AN ANCIENT TO ANCIENTS

Where once we danced, where once we sang,
　　Gentlemen,
The floors are sunken, cobwebs hang,
And cracks creep; worms have fed upon
The doors.　Yea, sprightlier times were then

Than now, with harps and tabrets gone,
　　Gentlemen!

Where once we rowed, where once we sailed,
　　Gentlemen,
And damsels took the tiller, veiled　　　　　　　10
Against too strong a stare (God wot°
Their fancy, then or anywhen!)
Upon that shore we are clean forgot,
　　Gentlemen!

We have lost somewhat, afar and near,
　　Gentlemen,
The thinning of our ranks each year
Affords a hint we are nigh undone,
That we shall not be ever again
The marked of many, loved of one,　　　　　　20
　　Gentlemen.

In dance the polka hit our wish,
　　Gentlemen,
The paced quadrille,° the spry schottische,°
"Sir Roger."°—And in opera spheres
The "Girl" (the famed "Bohemian"),°
And "Trovatore,"° held the ears,
　　Gentlemen.

This season's paintings do not please,
　　Gentlemen,　　　　　　　　　　　　　　　30
Like Etty, Mulready, Maclise;°
Throbbing romance has waned and wanned;
No wizard wields the witching pen
Of Bulwer, Scott, Dumas, and Sand,°
　　Gentlemen.

The bower we shrined to Tennyson,
　　Gentlemen,
Is roof-wrecked;° damps there drip upon
Sagged seats, the creeper-nails° are rust,
The spider is sole denizen;　　　　　　　　　40
Even she who voiced those rhymes is dust,
　　Gentlemen!

We who met sunrise sanguine-souled,
　　Gentlemen,
Are wearing weary. We are old;
These younger press; we feel our rout
Is imminent to Aïdes'° den,—

An Ancient to Ancients　11 **wot,** knows　24 **quadrille,** a dance for four couples　**schottische,** outdated dance (like the quadrille)　25 **Sir Roger,** Sir Roger de Coverley, an old-fashioned country dance　26 **Bohemian,** *The Bohemian Girl* was an opera by Michael William Balfe (1808–1870), an Irish composer and singer, produced in London in 1843　27 **Trovatore,** an opera (1853) by Giuseppi Verdi (1813–1901), an important Italian composer　31 **Etty . . . Maclise,** English and Irish painters of the early nineteenth century—William Etty (1787–1849), William Mulready (1786–1863), Daniel Maclise (1806–1870)　34 **Bulwer . . . Sand,** nineteenth-century English and French novelists—Edward Bulwer-Lytton (1803–1873), Sir Walter Scott (1771–1832), Alexander Dumas (1802–1870), George Sand (1804–1876)　36–38 **bower . . . wrecked,** a reference to the decline in favor, in certain critical circles, of the poetry of Tennyson after his death　39 **creeper-nails,** the nails which fasten the vine to the wall　47 **Aïdes,** Hades, god of the Greek underworld

After a Journey　29 **lours,** scowls, looks threatening

That evening shades are stretching out,
    Gentlemen!

50 And yet, though ours be failing frames,
    Gentlemen,
So were some others' history names,
Who trode their track light-limbed and fast
As these youth, and not alien
From enterprise, to their long last,
    Gentlemen.

Sophocles, Plato, Socrates,
    Gentlemen,
Pythagoras, Thucydides,
60 Herodotus, and Homer,—yea,
Clement, Augustin, Origen,°
Burnt brightlier towards their setting-day,
    Gentlemen.

And ye, red-lipped and smooth-browed; list,
    Gentlemen;
Much is there waits you we have missed;
Much lore we leave you worth the knowing,
Much, much has lain outside our ken:
Nay, rush not: time serves: we are going,
70   Gentlemen.
    (1922)

"AH, ARE YOU DIGGING ON MY GRAVE?"

"Ah, are you digging on my grave
    My loved one?—planting rue?°"
—"No; yesterday he went to wed
One of the brightest wealth has bred.
'It cannot hurt her now,' he said,
    'That I should not be true.'"

"Then who is digging on my grave?
    My nearest dearest kin?"
—"Ah, no; they sit and think, 'What use!
10 What good will planting flowers produce?
No tendance of her mound can loose
    Her spirit from Death's gin.°'"

"But some one digs upon my grave?
    My enemy?—prodding sly?"
—"Nay; when she heard you had passed the Gate
That shuts on all flesh soon or late,
She thought you no more worth her hate,
    And cares not where you lie."

"Then, who is digging on my grave?
20   Say—since I have not guessed!"

—"O it is I, my mistress dear,
Your little dog, who still lives near,
And much I hope my movements here
    Have not disturbed your rest?"

"Ah, yes! *You* dig upon my grave . . .
    Why flashed it not on me
That one true heart was left behind!
What feeling do we ever find
To equal among human kind   30
    A dog's fidelity!"

"Mistress, I dug upon your grave
    To bury a bone, in case
I should be hungry near this spot
When passing on my daily trot.
I am sorry, but I quite forgot
    It was your resting-place."
    (1914)

THE OXEN

Christmas Eve, and twelve of the clock.
    "Now they are all on their knees,"
An elder said as we sat in a flock
    By the embers in hearthside ease.

We pictured the meek mild creatures where   5
    They dwelt in their strawy pen,
Nor did it occur to one of us there
    No doubt they were kneeling then.

So fair a fancy few would weave
    In these years! Yet, I feel,   10
If someone said on Christmas Eve,
    "Come; see the oxen kneel,

"In the lonely barton° by yonder coomb°
    Our childhood used to know,"
I should go with him in the gloom,   15
    Hoping it might be so.
    (1915; 1917)

FOR LIFE I HAD NEVER CARED GREATLY

For life I had never cared greatly,
    As worth a man's while;
    Peradventures unsought,
    Peradventures that finished in nought,
Had kept me from youth and through manhood till
    lately
    Unwon by its style.

57-61 **Sophocles . . . Origen,** Greek authors and philosophers and Christian
fathers of the church who had in common a profitable old age
"Ah, Are You Digging on My Grave?"   2 **rue,** an herb with bitter leaves; the
symbol of sorrow   12 **gin,** trap

The Oxen   13 **barton,** farmyard   **coomb,** a valley between steep hills

In earliest years—why I know not—
  I viewed it askance;
  Conditions of doubt,
10 Conditions that leaked slowly out,
May haply have bent me to stand and to show not
  Much zest for its dance.

  With symphonies soft and sweet color
  It courted me then,
  Till evasions seemed wrong,
  Till evasions gave in to its song,
And I warmed, until living aloofly loomed duller
  Than life among men.

  Anew I found nought to set eyes on,
20 When, lifting its hand,
  It uncloaked a star,
  Uncloaked it from fog-damps afar,
And showed its beams burning from pole to horizon
  As bright as a brand.

  And so, the rough highway forgetting,
  I pace hill and dale
  Regarding the sky,
  Regarding the vision on high,
And thus re-illumed have no humor for letting
30 My pilgrimage fail.
  (1917)

THE CONVERGENCE OF THE TWAIN°

(LINES ON THE LOSS OF THE "TITANIC")

1

In a solitude of the sea
Deep from human vanity,
And the Pride of Life that planned her, stilly couches
  she.

2

Steel chambers, late the pyres
Of her salamandrine fires,
Cold currents thrid,° and turn to rhythmic tidal lyres.

3

Over the mirrors meant
To glass the opulent

The sea-worm crawls—grotesque, slimed, dumb, indifferent.

4

Jewels in joy designed   10
To ravish the sensuous mind
Lie lightless, all their sparkles bleared and black and
  blind.

5

Dim moon-eyed fishes near
Gaze at the gilded gear
And query: "What does this vaingloriousness down
  here?" . . .

6

Well: while was fashioning
This creature of cleaving wing,
The Immanent Will° that stirs and urges everything

7

Prepared a sinister mate
For her—so gaily great—   20
A Shape of Ice, for the time far and dissociate.

8

And as the smart ship grew
In stature, grace, and hue,
In shadowy silent distance grew the Iceberg too.

9

Alien they seemed to be;
No mortal eye could see
The intimate welding of their later history,

10

Or sign that they were bent
By paths coincident
On being anon twin halves of one august event,   30

11

Till the Spinner of the Years
Said "Now!" And each one hears,
And consummation comes, and jars two hemispheres.
(1913; 1914)

SNOW IN THE SUBURBS

  Every branch big with it,
  Bent every twig with it;
  Every fork like a white web-foot;
  Every street and pavement mute;

The Convergence of the Twain. Shortly before midnight on the evening of April
14, 1912, the White Star liner *Titanic*, at the time the largest ship in the world
and supposedly unsinkable, on her maiden voyage to New York rammed into an
iceberg in mid-Atlantic. A little less than three hours later she sank, carrying to
their deaths more than 1500 persons. The circumstances of the event fit beautifully into Hardy's deterministic philosophy   6 **thrid,** pass through, thread their
way

18 **Immanent Will,** the force which drives the world, according to Hardy's
philosophy

Some flakes have lost their way, and grope back
    upward, when
Meeting those meandering down they turn and de-
    scend again.
  The palings are glued together like a wall,
  And there is no waft of wind with the fleecy fall.

    A sparrow enters the tree,
10   Whereon immediately
A snow-lump thrice his own slight size
Descends on him and showers his head and eyes,

    And overturns him,
    And near inurns° him,
  And lights on a nether twig, when its brush
Starts off a volley of other lodging lumps with a rush.

    The steps are a blanched slope,
    Up which, with feeble hope,
A black cat comes, wide-eyed and thin;
20   And we take him in.
  (1925)

BERNARD SHAW
1856–1950

"Things have not happened to me," Shaw once said; "on the contrary, it is I who have happened to things." Shaw's public image was that of a witty and somewhat arrogant iconoclast—socialist, vegetarian, antivivisectionist. Although there was a certain amount of eccentricity in some of these poses, Shaw was always seriously concerned with solving mankind's problems.

Shaw was born in Dublin in1856 into a genteel but rather unsuccessful family of English ancestry. He attended both Protestant and Catholic day schools, but was working in a land agent's office before he was sixteen. Shaw went to London in 1876, where he began spending his time in the reading room of the British Museum, attending lectures in the evening to further his self-education, and writing unsuccessful novels. No publisher in London would accept the manuscript for his first novel, *Immaturity*. During the '80s, however, Shaw began to find himself. He became a leading force behind the Fabian Society, a middle-class socialist group; he edited and contributed to one of the classic Socialist books, *Fabian Essays in Socialism*, in 1889. During this period he also became

a platform speaker of unusual ability; he spoke without pay to crowds of all sizes, usually on behalf of socialist causes. Shaw became drama critic for the *Saturday Review* in 1895, a position that enabled him to voice his opinions on what drama should be and to learn the techniques that would allow him to develop the possibilities of drama in his own work. He was a critic of passionate objectivity who contended that the critic should be "the man who becomes your personal enemy on the sole provocation of a bad performance, and will only be appeased by good performances." He publicized the works of the Norwegian dramatist Henrik Ibsen (1828–1906) as part of his continuing effort to broaden the intellectual quality of the London theater.

Shaw began to write his own plays in the '90s. Since his caustic wit was generally directed at things traditionally considered too sacred for ridicule (marriage, parenthood, heroism), most of his early plays were banned by the censor or refused production. Thus, he soon thought that his plays should be directed toward readers as well as toward a live audience. His play prefaces and extended stage directions are an important part of the argument of the plays. His plays are, for the most part, "problem plays"; that is, each play takes up a particular social question by presenting a dramatic enactment of both the problem and the solution. For example, *Mrs. Warren's Profession* (1898) is concerned with prostitution. *Arms and the Man* (1898) considers the disparity between the realities of war and the romantic images of it. Some of Shaw's plays, however, have a larger focus than a single social problem. *Pygmalion* (1913) is a humane comedy about love and class that was Shaw's greatest commercial success (later made into the musical *My Fair Lady*). *Saint Joan* (1923) is both a chronicle play and a tragedy that won Shaw the Nobel Prize for literature in 1925. His sense of the comic and his skill in argumentation eventually won him a public who demanded that his works be performed. By the time of World War I, his plays were highly successful on stage. Some of Shaw's best-known plays are *Caesar and Cleopatra* (1901), *The Devil's Disciple* (1901), *Man and Superman* (1903), *Major Barbara* (1907), *Androcles and the Lion* (1916), *Heartbreak House* (1919), and *Back to Methuselah* (1921). Although all Shaw's plays are entertaining, he always thought of them mainly as vehicles for presenting his ideas.

In addition to his many plays, Shaw was also the author of four early novels, several books on political subjects, and many essays on a wide variety of topics. He was an advocate of spelling reform and in his own writings used such devices as omitting apostrophes in some contractions; he insisted that his publishers retain these changes. He remained an active writer for most of his ninety-four years. He died in 1950 at his

---

Snow in the Suburbs   14 **inurns,** puts in an urn, buries

country home at Ayot St. Lawrence, a village in Hertfordshire in southeast England. He maintained his indomitable persona until the very end of his life; his will stipulated that the money in his estate be used to promote a more rational system of English spelling.

ARMS AND THE MAN°

Arms and the Man (1898) stands as Shaw's commentary on the power of the romantic image to blind us to reality. Can a "brave soldier" eat chocolate creams? Can a "brave soldier" hide in a woman's bedroom to save his life? Can a "brave soldier" trade horses faster than the next man? Shaw's commentary has broad implications; it extends beyond the distorted images of the reality of war to all pretensions that make the remote seem wondrous and the near-at-hand humdrum. His witty jokes about the Balkan adulation of Viennese manners and fashions are the most obvious evidence of his attack on pretense, but the attack cuts more deeply as it comes to examine the reasons why marriage, romance, and sexuality do not always happily coexist. Though the specific problems in *Arms and the Man* are comically resolved, the general issues that are raised remain serious.

ACT I

Night: A lady's bedchamber in Bulgaria, in a small town near the Dragoman Pass, late in November in the year 1885. Through an open window with a little balcony a peak of the Balkans, wonderfully white and beautiful in the starlit snow, seems quite close at hand, though it is really miles away. The interior of the room is not like anything to be seen in the west of Europe. It is half rich Bulgarian, half cheap Viennese. Above the head of the bed, which stands against a little wall cutting off the left hand corner of the room, is a painted wooden shrine, blue and gold, with an ivory image of Christ, and a light hanging before it in a pierced metal ball suspended by three chains. The principal seat, placed towards the other side of the room and opposite the window, is a Turkish ottoman. The counterpane and hangings of the bed, the window curtains, the little carpet, and all the ornamental textile fabrics in the room are oriental and gorgeous: the paper on the walls is occidental and paltry. The washstand, against the wall on the side nearest the ottoman and window, consists of an enamelled iron basin with a pail beneath it in a painted metal frame, and a single towel on the rail at the side. The dressing table, between the bed and the window, is a common pine table, covered with a cloth of many colors, with an expensive toilet mirror on it. The door is on the side nearest the bed; and there is a chest of drawers between. This chest of drawers is also covered by a variegated native cloth; and on it there is a pile of paper backed novels, a box of chocolate creams, and a miniature easel with a large photograph of an extremely handsome officer, whose lofty bearing and magnetic glance can be felt even from the portrait. The room is lighted by a candle on the chest of drawers, and another on the dressing table with a box of matches beside it.

The window is hinged doorwise and stands wide open. Outside, a pair of wooden shutters, opening outwards, also stand open. On the balcony a young lady, intensely conscious of the romantic beauty of the night, and of the fact that her own youth and beauty are part of it, is gazing at the snowy Balkans. She is in her nightgown, well covered by a long mantle of furs, worth, on a moderate estimate, about three times the furniture of her room.

Her reverie is interrupted by her mother, Catherine Petkoff, a woman over forty, imperiously energetic, with magnificent black hair and eyes, who might be a very splendid specimen of the wife of a mountain farmer, but is determined to be a Viennese lady, and to that end wears a fashionable tea gown on all occasions.

CATHERINE [*entering hastily, full of good news*] Raina! [*She pronounces it Rah-eena, with the stress on the ee*]. Raina! [*She goes to the bed, expecting to find Raina there*]. Why, where—? [*Raina looks into the room*]. Heavens, child! are you out in the night air instead of in your bed? You'll catch your death. Louka told me you were asleep.

RAINA [*dreamily*] I sent her away. I wanted to be alone. The stars are so beautiful! What is the matter?

CATHERINE. Such news! There has been a battle. 10

RAINA [*her eyes dilating*] Ah! [*She comes eagerly to Catherine*].

CATHERINE. A great battle at Slivnitza! A victory! And it was won by Sergius.

RAINA [*with a cry of delight*] Ah! [*They embrace rapturously*] Oh, mother! [*Then, with sudden anxiety*] Is father safe?

CATHERINE. Of course: he sends me the news. Sergius is the hero of the hour, the idol of the regiment.

RAINA. Tell me, tell me. How was it? [*Ecstatically*] 20 Oh, mother! mother! mother! [*She pulls her mother down on the ottoman; and they kiss one another frantically*].

CATHERINE [*with surging enthusiasm*] You cant guess how splendid it is. A cavalry charge! think of that! He defied our Russian commanders—acted without orders—led a charge on his own responsibility—headed it himself—was the first man to sweep through their guns. Cant you see it, Raina: our gallant splendid Bulgarians with their swords and eyes flash- 30 ing, thundering down like an avalanche and scattering the wretched Serbs and their dandified Austrian officers like chaff. And you! you kept Sergius waiting a

Arms and the Man. The title is a translation of the first two words of Vergil's (70–19 B.C.) *Aeneid,* "*Arma virumque*" year before you would be betrothed to him. Oh, if you have a drop of Bulgarian blood in your veins, you will worship him when he comes back.

RAINA. What will he care for my poor little worship after the acclamations of a whole army of heroes? But no matter: I am so happy! so proud! [She rises and walks about excitedly]. It proves that all our ideas were real after all.

CATHERINE [indignantly] Our ideas real! What do you mean?

RAINA. Our ideas of what Sergius would do. Our patriotism. Our heroic ideals. I sometimes used to doubt whether they were anything but dreams. Oh, what faithless little creatures girls are! When I buckled on Sergius's sword he looked so noble: it was treason to think of disillusion or humiliation or failure. And yet—and yet— [She sits down again suddenly] Promise me you'll never tell him.

CATHERINE. Dont ask me for promises until I know what I'm promising.

RAINA. Well, it came into my head just as he was holding me in his arms and looking into my eyes, that perhaps we only had our heroic ideas because we are so fond of reading Byron and Pushkin,° and because we were so delighted with the opera that season at Bucharest. Real life is so seldom like that! indeed never, as far as I knew it then. [Remorsefully] Only think, mother: I doubted him: I wondered whether all his heroic qualities and his soldiership might not prove mere imagination when he went into a real battle. I had an uneasy fear that he might cut a poor figure there beside all those clever officers from the Tsar's court.

CATHERINE. A poor figure! Shame on you! The Serbs have Austrian officers who are just as clever as the Russians; but we have beaten them in every battle for all that.

RAINA [laughing and snuggling against her mother] Yes: I was only a prosaic little coward. Oh, to think that it was all true! that Sergius is just as splendid and noble as he looks! that the world is really a glorious world for women who can see its glory and men who can act its romance! What happiness! what unspeakable fulfilment!

They are interrupted by the entry of Louka, a handsome proud girl in a pretty Bulgarian peasant's dress with double apron, so defiant that her servility to Raina is almost insolent. She is afraid of Catherine, but even with her goes as far as she dares.

LOUKA. If you please, madam, all the windows are to be closed and the shutters made fast. They say there may be shooting in the streets. [Raina and Catherine rise together, alarmed]. The Serbs are being chased right back through the pass; and they say they may run into the town. Our cavalry will be after them; and our people will be ready for them, you may be sure, now theyre running away. [She goes out on the balcony,

and pulls the outside shutters to; then steps back into the room].

CATHERINE [businesslike, her housekeeping instincts aroused] I must see that everything is made safe downstairs.

RAINA. I wish our people were not so cruel. What glory is there in killing wretched fugitives?

CATHERINE. Cruel! Do you suppose they would hesitate to kill you—or worse?

RAINA [to Louka] Leave the shutters so that I can just close them if I hear any noise.

CATHERINE [authoritatively, turning on her way to the door] Oh no, dear: you must keep them fastened. You would be sure to drop off to sleep and leave them open. Make them fast, Louka.

LOUKA. Yes, madam. [She fastens them].

RAINA. Dont be anxious about me. The moment I hear a shot, I shall blow out the candles and roll myself up in bed with my ears well covered.

CATHERINE. Quite the wisest thing you can do, my love. Goodnight.

RAINA. Goodnight. [Her emotion comes back for a moment]. Wish me joy [They kiss]. This is the happiest night of my life—if only there are no fugitives.

CATHERINE. Go to bed, dear; and dont think of them. [She goes out].

LOUKA [secretly, to Raina] If you would like the shutters open, just give them a push like this [she pushes them: they open: she pulls them to again]. One of them ought to be bolted at the bottom; but the bolt's gone.

RAINA [with dignity, reproving her] Thanks, Louka; but we must do what we are told. [Louka makes a grimace]. Goodnight.

LOUKA [carelessly] Goodnight. [She goes out, swaggering].

Raina, left alone, takes off her fur cloak and throws it on the ottoman. Then she goes to the chest of drawers, and adores the portrait there with feelings that are beyond all expression. She does not kiss it or press it to her breast, or shew it any mark of bodily affection; but she takes it in her hands and elevates it, like a priestess.

RAINA [looking up at the picture] Oh, I shall never be unworthy of you any more, my soul's hero: never, never, never. [She replaces it reverently. Then she selects a novel from the little pile of books. She turns over the leaves dreamily; finds her page; turns the book inside out at it; and, with a happy sigh, gets into bed and prepares to read herself to sleep. But before abandoning herself to fiction, she raises her eyes once more, thinking of the blessed reality, and murmurs] My hero! my hero!

A distant shot breaks the quiet of the night. She starts, listening; and two more shots, much nearer, follow, startling her so that she scrambles out of bed, and hastily blows out the candle on the chest of drawers. Then, putting her fingers in her ears, she runs to

57 **Byron and Pushkin,** George Gordon, Lord Byron (1788–1824), English romantic poet, and Alexander Pushkin (1799–1837), Russian poet often compared to Byron in style. In the works of both poets, dashing, romantic military figures appear

the dressing table, blows out the light there, and hur-
ries back to bed in the dark, nothing being visible but
150 *the glimmer of the light in the pierced ball before the*
image, and starlight seen through the slits at the top of
the shutters. The firing breaks out again: there is a
startling fusillade quite close at hand. Whilst it is still
echoing, the shutters disappear, pulled open from
without; and for an instant the rectangle of snowy
starlight flashes out with the figure of a man silhouet-
ted in black upon it. The shutters close immediately;
and the room is dark again. But the silence is now
broken by the sound of panting. Then there is a scratch
160 *and the flame of a match is seen in the middle of the*
room.

RAINA [*crouching on the bed*] Who's there? [*The match is out instantly*]. Who's there? Who is that?

A MAN'S VOICE [*in the darkness, subduedly, but threateningly*] Sh—sh! Dont call out; or youll be shot. Be good; and no harm will happen to you. [*She is heard leaving her bed, and making for the door*]. Take care: it's no use trying to run away.

RAINA. But who—

170 THE VOICE [*warning*] Remember: if you raise your voice my revolver will go off. [*Commandingly*]. Strike a light and let me see you. Do you hear. [*Another moment of silence and darkness as she retreats to the chest of drawers. Then she lights a candle; and the mystery is at an end. He is a man of about 35, in a deplorable plight, bespattered with mud and blood and snow, his belt and the strap of his revolver-case keep-ing together the torn ruins of the blue tunic of a Ser-bian artillery officer. All that the candlelight and his*
180 *unwashed unkempt condition make it possible to dis-cern is that he is of middling stature and undistin-guished appearance, with strong neck and shoulders, roundish obstinate looking head covered with short crisp bronze curls, clear quick eyes and good brows and mouth, hopelessly prosaic nose like that of a strong minded baby, trim soldierlike carriage and energetic manner, and with all his wits about him in spite of his desperate predicament: even with a sense of the humor of it, without, however, the least inten-*
190 *tion of trifling with it or throwing away a chance. Reckoning up what he can guess about Raina: her age, her social position, her character, and the extent to which she is frightened, he continues, more politely but still most determinedly*] Excuse my disturbing you; but you recognize my uniform? Serb! If I'm caught I shall be killed. [*Menacingly*] Do you understand that?

RAINA. Yes.

THE MAN. Well I dont intend to get killed if I can help it. [*Still more formidably*] Do you understand
200 that? [*He locks the door quickly but quietly*].

RAINA [*disdainfully*] I suppose not. [*She draws her-self up superbly, and looks him straight in the face, adding with cutting emphasis*] Some soldiers, I know, are afraid to die.

THE MAN [*with grim goodhumor*] All of them, dear

lady, all of them, believe me. It is our duty to live as long as we can. Now, if you raise an alarm—

RAINA [*cutting him short*] You will shoot me. How do you know that *I* am afraid to die?

THE MAN [*cunningly*] Ah; but suppose I dont shoot 210 you, what will happen then? A lot of your cavalry will burst into this pretty room of yours and slaughter me here like a pig; for I'll fight like a demon: they shant get me into the street to amuse themselves with: I know what they are. Are you prepared to receive that sort of company in your present undress? [*Raina, suddenly conscious of her nightgown, instinctively shrinks, and gathers it more closely about her neck. He watches her, and adds, pitilessly*] Hardly presentable, eh? [*She turns to the ottoman. He raises his pistol instantly,* 220 *and cries*] Stop! [*She stops*]. Where are you going?

RAINA [*with dignified patience*] Only to get my cloak.

THE MAN [*passing swiftly to the ottoman and snatching the cloak*] A good idea! I'll keep the cloak; and youll take care that nobody comes in and sees you without it. This is a better weapon than the revolver: eh? [*He throws the pistol down on the ottoman*].

RAINA [*revolted*] It is not the weapon of a gentleman!

THE MAN. It's good enough for a man with only you 230 to stand between him and death. [*As they look at one another for a moment, Raina hardly able to believe that even a Serbian officer can be so cynically and selfishly unchivalrous, they are startled by a sharp fusillade in the street. The chill of imminent death hushes the man's voice as he adds*] Do you hear? If you are going to bring those blackguards in on me you shall receive them as you are.

Clamor and disturbance. The pursuers in the street batter at the house door, shouting Open the door! 240 Open the door! Wake up, will you! *A man servant's voice calls to them angrily from within.* This is Major Petkoff's house: you cant come in here; *but a renewal of the clamor, and a torrent of blows on the door, end with his letting a chain down with a clank, followed by a rush of heavy footsteps and a din of triumphant yells, dominated at last by the voice of Catherine, indig-nantly addressing an officer with* What does this mean, sir? Do you know where you are? *The noise subsides suddenly.*
250

LOUKA [*outside, knocking at the bedroom door*] My lady! my lady! get up quick and open the door. If you dont they will break it down.

The fugitive throws up his head with the gesture of a man who sees that it is all over with him, and drops the manner he has been assuming to intimidate Raina.

THE MAN [*sincerely and kindly*] No use, dear: I'm done for. [*Flinging the cloak to her*] Quick! wrap your-self up: theyre coming.

RAINA. Oh, thank you. [*She wraps herself up with* 260 *intense relief*].

THE MAN [*between his teeth*] Dont mention it.

RAINA [*anxiously*] What will you do?

THE MAN [grimly] The first man in will find out. Keep out of the way; and dont look. It wont last long; but it will not be nice. [He draws his sabre and faces the door, waiting].

RAINA [impulsively] I'll help you. I'll save you.

THE MAN. You cant.

270 RAINA. I can. I'll hide you. [She drags him towards the window]. Here! behind the curtains.

THE MAN [yielding to her] Theres just half a chance, if you keep your head.

RAINA [drawing the curtain before him] S-sh! [She makes for the ottoman].

THE MAN [putting out his head] Remember—

RAINA [running back to him] Yes?

THE MAN.—nine soldiers out of ten are born fools.

RAINA. Oh! [She draws the curtain angrily before 280 him].

THE MAN [looking out at the other side] If they find me, I promise you a fight: a devil of a fight.

She stamps at him. He disappears hastily. She takes off her cloak, and throws it across the foot of the bed. Then, with a sleepy, disturbed air, she opens the door. Louka enters excitedly.

LOUKA. One of those beasts of Serbs has been seen climbing up the waterpipe to your balcony. Our men want to search for him; and they are so wild and drunk 290 and furious. [She makes for the other side of the room to get as far from the door as possible]. My lady says you are to dress at once, and to—[She sees the revolver lying on the ottoman, and stops, petrified].

RAINA [as if annoyed at being disturbed] They shall not search here. Why have they been let in?

CATHERINE [coming in hastily] Raina, darling: are you safe? Have you seen anyone or heard anything?

RAINA. I heard the shooting. Surely the soldiers will not dare come in here?

300 CATHERINE. I have found a Russian officer, thank Heaven: he knows Sergius. [Speaking through the door to someone outside] Sir: will you come in now. My daughter will receive you.

A young Russian officer, in Bulgarian uniform, enters, sword in hand.

OFFICER [with soft feline politeness and stiff military carriage] Good evening, gracious lady. I am sorry to intrude; but there is a Serb hiding on the balcony. Will you and the gracious lady your mother please to with- 310 draw whilst we search?

RAINA [petulantly] Nonsense, sir: you can see that there is no one on the balcony. [She throws the shutters wide open and stands with her back to the curtain where the man is hidden, pointing to the moonlit balcony. A couple of shots are fired right under the window; and a bullet shatters the glass opposite Raina, who winks and gasps, but stands her ground; whilst Catherine screams, and the officer, with a cry of Take care! rushes to the balcony].

320 THE OFFICER [on the balcony, shouting savagely down to the street] Cease firing there, you fools: do you hear? Cease firing, damn you! [He glares down for a moment; then turns to Raina, trying to resume his polite manner]. Could anyone have got in without your knowledge? Were you asleep?

RAINA. No: I have not been to bed.

THE OFFICER [impatiently, coming back into the room] Your neighbors have their heads so full of runaway Serbs that they see them everywhere. [Politely] Gracious lady: a thousand pardons. Good- 330 night. [Military bow, which Raina returns coldly. Another to Catherine, who follows him out].

Raina closes the shutters. She turns and sees Louka, who has been watching the scene curiously.

RAINA. Dont leave my mother, Louka, until the soldiers go away.

Louka glances at Raina, at the ottoman, at the curtain; then purses her lips secretively, laughs insolently, and goes out. Raina, highly offended by this demonstration, follows her to the door, and shuts it behind 340 her with a slam, locking it violently. The man immediately steps out from behind the curtain, sheathing his sabre. Then, dismissing the danger from his mind in a businesslike way, he comes affably to Raina.

THE MAN. A narrow shave; but a miss is as good as a mile. Dear young lady: your servant to the death. I wish for your sake I had joined the Bulgarian army instead of the other one. I am not a native Serb.

RAINA [haughtily] No: you are one of the Austrians who set the Serbs on to rob us of our national liberty, 350 and who officer their army for them. We hate them!

THE MAN. Austrian! not I. Dont hate me, dear young lady. I am a Swiss, fighting merely as a professional soldier. I joined the Serbs because they came first on the road from Switzerland. Be generous: youve beaten us hollow.

RAINA. Have I not been generous?

THE MAN. Noble! Heroic! But I'm not saved yet. This particular rush will soon pass through; but the pursuit will go on all night by fits and starts. I must 360 take my chance to get off in a quiet interval. [Pleasantly] You dont mind my waiting just a minute or two, do you?

RAINA [putting on her most genteel society manner] Oh, not at all. Wont you sit down?

THE MAN. Thanks. [He sits on the foot of the bed].

Raina walks with studied elegance to the ottoman and sits down. Unfortunately she sits on the pistol, and jumps up with a shriek. The man, all nerves, shies like a frightened horse to the other side of the room. 370

THE MAN [irritably] Dont frighten me like that. What is it?

RAINA. Your revolver! It was staring that officer in the face all the time. What an escape!

THE MAN [vexed at being unnecessarily terrified] Oh, is that all?

RAINA [staring at him rather superciliously as she conceives a poorer and poorer opinion of him, and feels proportionately more and more at her ease] I am

380 sorry I frightened you. [*She takes up the pistol and hands it to him*]. Pray take it to protect yourself against me.

THE MAN [*grinning wearily at the sarcasm as he takes the pistol*] No use, dear young lady: theres nothing in it. It's not loaded. [*He makes a grimace at it, and drops it disparagingly into his revolver case*].

RAINA. Load it by all means.

THE MAN. Ive no ammunition. What use are cartridges in battle? I always carry chocolate instead; and 390 I finished the last cake of that hours ago.

RAINA [*outraged in her most cherished ideals of manhood*] Chocolate! Do you stuff your pockets with sweets—like a schoolboy—even in the field?

THE MAN [*grinning*] Yes: isnt it contemptible? [*Hungrily*] I wish I had some now.

RAINA. Allow me. [*She sails away scornfully to the chest of drawers, and returns with the box of confectionery in her hand*]. I am sorry I have eaten all except these. [*She offers him the box*].

400 THE MAN [*ravenously*] Youre an angel! [*He gobbles the contents*]. Creams! Delicious! [*He looks anxiously to see whether there are any more. There are none: he can only scrape the box with his fingers and suck them. When that nourishment is exhausted he accepts the inevitable with pathetic goodhumor, and says, with grateful emotion*] Bless you, dear lady! You can always tell an old soldier by the inside of his holsters and cartridge boxes. The young ones carry pistols and cartridges: the old ones, grub. Thank you. [*He hands 410 back the box. She snatches it contemptuously from him and throws it away. He shies again, as if she had meant to strike him*]. Ugh! Dont do things so suddenly, gracious lady. It's mean to revenge yourself because I frightened you just now.

RAINA [*loftily*] Frighten me! Do you know, sir, that though I am only a woman, I think I am at heart as brave as you.

THE MAN. I should think so. You havnt been under fire for three days as I have. I can stand two days 420 without shewing it much; but no man can stand three days: I'm as nervous as a mouse. [*He sits down on the ottoman, and takes his head in his hands*]. Would you like to see me cry?

RAINA [*alarmed*] No.

THE MAN. If you would, all you have to do is to scold me just as if I were a little boy and you my nurse. If I were in camp now, theyd play all sorts of tricks on me.

RAINA [*a little moved*] I'm sorry. I wont scold you. [*Touched by the sympathy in her tone, he raises his 430 head and looks gratefully at her: immediately draws back and says stiffly*] You must excuse me: our soldiers are not like that. [*She moves away from the ottoman*].

THE MAN. Oh yes they are. There are only two sorts of soldiers: old ones and young ones. Ive served fourteen years: half of your fellows never smelt powder before. Why, how is it that youve just beaten us?

Sheer ignorance of the art of war, nothing else. [*Indignantly*] I never saw anything so unprofessional.

RAINA [*ironically*] Oh! was it unprofessional to beat 440 you?

THE MAN. Well, come! is it professional to throw a regiment of cavalry on a battery of machine guns, with the dead certainty that if the guns go off not a horse or man will ever get within fifty yards of the fire? I couldnt believe my eyes when I saw it.

RAINA [*eagerly turning to him, as all her enthusiasm and her dreams of glory rush back on her*] Did you see the great cavalry charge? Oh, tell me about it. Describe it to me. 450

THE MAN. You never saw a cavalry charge, did you?

RAINA. How could I?

THE MAN. Ah, perhaps not. No: of course not! Well, it's a funny sight. It's like slinging a handful of peas against a window pane: first one comes; then two or three close behind him; and then all the rest in a lump.

RAINA [*her eyes dilating as she raises her clasped hands ecstatically*] Yes, first One! the bravest of the brave!

THE MAN [*prosaically*] Hm! you should see the poor 460 devil pulling at his horse.

RAINA. Why should he pull at his horse?

THE MAN [*impatient of so stupid a question*] It's running away with him, of course: do you suppose the fellow wants to get there before the others and be killed? Then they all come. You can tell the young ones by their wildness and their slashing. The old ones come bunched up under the number one guard: they know that theyre mere projectiles, and that it's no use trying to fight. The wounds are mostly broken knees, 470 from the horses cannoning together.

RAINA Ugh! But I dont believe the first man is a coward. I know he is a hero!

THE MAN [*goodhumoredly*] Thats what youd have said if youd seen the first man in the charge today.

RAINA [*breathless, forgiving him everything*] Ah, I knew it! Tell me. Tell me about him.

THE MAN. He did it like an operatic tenor. A regular handsome fellow, with flashing eyes and lovely moustache, shouting his war-cry and charging like Don 480 Quixote at the windmills. We did laugh.

RAINA. You dared to laugh!

THE MAN. Yes; but when the sergeant ran up as white as a sheet, and told us theyd sent us the wrong ammunition, and that we couldnt fire a round for the next ten minutes, we laughed at the other side of our mouths. I never felt so sick in my life; though Ive been in one or two very tight places. And I hadnt even a revolver cartridge: only chocolate. We'd no bayonets: nothing. Of course, they just cut us to bits. And there 490 was Don Quixote° flourishing like a drum major,

491 **Don Quixote,** main character in a satirical romance of the same name by Miguel de Cervantes Saavedra (1547-1616). Don Quixote is a man whose wits become so disordered through the reading of romances that he sees himself called to seek adventure. He sees ordinary objects through romantic eyes—hence he charges at windmills, thinking them giants. The soldier uses the name scornfully, for one out of touch with the reality of war

thinking he'd done the cleverest thing ever known, whereas he ought to be courtmartialled for it. Of all the fools ever let loose on a field of battle, that man must be the very maddest. He and his regiment simply committed suicide; only the pistol missed fire: thats all.

RAINA [*deeply wounded, but steadfastly loyal to her ideals*] Indeed! Would you know him again if you ever
500 saw him?

THE MAN. Shall I ever forget him!

She again goes to the chest of drawers. He watches her with a vague hope that she may have something more for him to eat. She takes the portrait from its stand and brings it to him.

RAINA. That is a photograph of the gentleman—the patriot and hero—to whom I am betrothed.

THE MAN [*recognizing it with a shock*] I'm really very sorry. [*Looking at her*] Was it fair to lead me on?
510 [*He looks at the portrait again*] Yes: thats Don Quixote: not a doubt of it. [*He stifles a laugh.*]

RAINA [*quickly*] Why do you laugh?

THE MAN [*apologetic, but still greatly tickled*] I didnt laugh, I assure you. At least I didnt mean to. But when I think of him charging the windmills and imagining he was doing the finest thing—[*He chokes with suppressed laughter*].

RAINA [*sternly*] Give me back the portrait, sir.

THE MAN [*with sincere remorse*] Of course. Cer-
520 tainly. I'm really very sorry. [*He hands her the picture. She deliberately kisses it and looks him straight in the face before returning to the chest of drawers to replace it. He follows her, apologizing*]. Perhaps I'm quite wrong, you know: no doubt I am. Most likely he had got wind of the cartridge business somehow, and knew it was a safe job.

RAINA That is to say, he was a pretender and a coward! You did not dare say that before.

THE MAN [*with a comic gesture of despair*] It's no
530 use, dear lady: I cant make you see it from the professional point of view. [*As he turns away to get back to the ottoman, a couple of distant shots threaten renewed trouble*].

RAINA [*sternly, as she sees him listening to the shots*] So much the better for you!

THE MAN [*turning*] How?

RAINA. You are my enemy; and you are at my mercy. What would I do if I were a professional soldier?
540 THE MAN. Ah, true, dear young lady: youre always right. I know how good youve been to me: to my last hour I shall remember those three chocolate creams. It was unsoldierly; but it was angelic.

RAINA [*coldly*] Thank you. And now I will do a soldierly thing. You cannot stay here after what you have just said about my future husband; but I will go out on the balcony and see whether it is safe for you to climb down into the street. [*She turns to the window*].

THE MAN [*changing countenance*] Down that water-

pipe! Stop! Wait! I cant! I darent! The very thought of 550 it makes me giddy. I came up it fast enough with death behind me. But to face it now in cold blood—! [*He sinks on the ottoman*]. It's no use: I give up: I'm beaten. Give the alarm. [*He drops his head on his hands in the deepest dejection*].

RAINA [*disarmed by pity*] Come: dont be disheartened. [*She stoops over him almost maternally: he shakes his head*]. Oh, you are a very poor soldier: a chocolate cream soldier! Come, cheer up! it takes less courage to climb down than to face capture: remember 560 that.

THE MAN [*dreamily, lulled by her voice*] No: capture only means death; and death is sleep: oh, sleep, sleep, sleep, undisturbed sleep! Climbing down the pipe means doing something—exerting myself—thinking! Death ten times over first.

RAINA [*softly and wonderingly, catching the rhythm of his weariness*] Are you as sleepy as that?

THE MAN. Ive not had two hours undisturbed sleep since I joined. I havnt closed my eyes for forty-eight 570 hours.

RAINA [*at her wit's end*] But what am I to do with you?

THE MAN [*staggering up, roused by her desperation*] Of course. I must do something. [*He shakes himself; pulls himself together; and speaks with rallied vigor and courage*]. You see, sleep or no sleep, hunger or no hunger, tired or not tired, you can always do a thing when you know it must be done. Well, that pipe must be got down: [*he hits himself on the chest*] do you hear 580 that, you chocolate cream soldier? [*He turns to the window*].

RAINA [*anxiously*] But if you fall?

THE MAN. I shall sleep as if the stones were a feather bed. Goodbye. [*He makes boldly for the window; and his hand is on the shutter when there is a terrible burst of firing in the street beneath*].

RAINA [*rushing to him*] Stop! [*She seizes him recklessly, and pulls him quite round*]. Theyll kill you.

THE MAN [*coolly, but attentively*] Never mind: this 590 sort of thing is all in my day's work. I'm bound to ta⌐ my chance. [*Decisively*] Now do what I tell ⌐ out the candle; so that they shant see ⌐ open the shutters. And keep a⌐ whatever you do. If the⌐ shot at me.

RAINA [⌐
brigh⌐
indiff⌐

THE ⌐
shakes ⌐
dear you⌐
done?

RAINA. ⌐
him firmly b⌐
ment she rele⌐
the window ag⌐

1102

The Modern Period

651 **Ernani**, an opera by Gius⌐
(1802–1865) tragedy, Hernani,
honor of his word, elements made⌐

dont k⌐
RAINA⌐
great scen⌐
you are tom⌐
660 terest enemy,
to give him up.

exclaiming] Please! [*He becomes motionless, like a hypnotized rabbit, his fatigue gaining fast on him. She releases him, and addresses him patronizingly*]. Now listen. You must trust to our hospitality. You do not yet know in whose house you are. I am a Petkoff.

THE MAN. A pet what?

RAINA [*rather indignantly*] I mean that I belong to the family of the Petkoffs, the richest and best known in our country.

THE MAN. Oh yes, of course. I beg your pardon. The Petkoffs, to be sure. How stupid of me!

RAINA. You know you never heard of them until this moment. How can you stoop to pretend!

THE MAN. Forgive me: I'm too tired to think; and the change of subject was too much for me. Dont scold me.

RAINA. I forgot. It might make you cry. [*He nods, quite seriously. She pouts and then resumes her patronizing tone*]. I must tell you that my father holds the highest command of any Bulgarian in our army. He is [*proudly*] a Major.

THE MAN [*pretending to be deeply impressed*] A Major! Bless me! Think of that!

RAINA. You shewed great ignorance in thinking that it was necessary to climb up to the balcony because ours is the only private house that has two rows of windows. There is a flight of stairs inside to get up and down by.

THE MAN. Stairs! How grand! You live in great luxury indeed, dear young lady.

RAINA. Do you know what a library is?

THE MAN. A library? A roomful of books?

RAINA. Yes. We have one, the only one in Bulgaria.

THE MAN. Actually a real library! I should like to see that.

RAINA [*affectedly*] I tell you these things to shew you that you are not in the house of ignorant country folk who would kill you the moment they saw your Serbian uniform, but among civilized people. We go to Bucharest every year for the opera season; and I have spent a whole month in Vienna.

THE MAN. I saw that, dear young lady. I saw at once that you knew the world.

RAINA. Have you ever seen the opera of Ernani?°

THE MAN. Is that the one with the devil in it in red velvet, and a soldiers' chorus?

RAINA [*contemptuously*] No!

THE MAN [*stifling a heavy sigh of weariness*] Then I ___ now it.

___ I thought you might have remembered the ___ where Ernani, flying from his foes just as ___ ight, takes refuge in the castle of his bit- ___ an old Castilian noble. The noble refuses ___ His guest is sacred to him.

___eppi Verdi (1813–1901) based on Victor Hugo's ___he plot concerns a betrothed soldier and the ___ fun of by Shaw later in the play

THE MAN [*quickly, waking up a little*] Have your people got that notion?

RAINA [*with dignity*] My mother and I can understand that notion, as you call it. And if instead of threatening me with your pistol as you did you had simply thrown yourself as a fugitive on our hospitality, you would have been as safe as in your father's house.

THE MAN. Quite sure?

RAINA [*turning her back on him in disgust*] Oh, it is useless to try to make you understand.

THE MAN. Dont be angry: you see how awkward it would be for me if there was any mistake. My father is a very hospitable man: he keeps six hotels; but I couldnt trust him as far as that. What about your father?

RAINA. He is away at Slivnitza fighting for his country. I answer for your safety. There is my hand in pledge of it. Will that reassure you? [*She offers him her hand*].

THE MAN [*looking dubiously at his own hand*] Better not touch my hand, dear young lady. I must have a wash first.

RAINA [*touched*] That is very nice of you. I see that you are a gentleman.

THE MAN [*puzzled*] Eh?

RAINA. You must not think I am surprised. Bulgarians of really good standing—people in our position—wash their hands nearly every day. So you see I can appreciate your delicacy. You may take my hand. [*She offers it again*].

THE MAN [*kissing it with his hands behind his back*] Thanks, gracious young lady: I feel safe at last. And now would you mind breaking the news to your mother? I had better not stay here secretly longer than is necessary.

RAINA. If you will be so good as to keep perfectly still whilst I am away.

THE MAN. Certainly. [*He sits down on the ottoman*].

Raina goes to the bed and wraps herself in the fur cloak. His eyes close. She goes to the door. Turning for a last look at him, she sees that he is dropping off to sleep.

RAINA [*at the door*] You are not going asleep, are you? [*He murmurs inarticulately: she runs to him and shakes him*]. Do you hear? Wake up: you are falling asleep.

THE MAN. Eh? Falling aslee—? Oh no: not the least in the world: I was only thinking. It's all right: I'm wide awake.

RAINA [*severely*] Will you please stand up while I am away. [*He rises reluctantly*]. All the time, mind.

THE MAN [*standing unsteadily*] Certainly. Certainly: you may depend on me.

Raina looks doubtfully at him. He smiles weakly. She goes reluctantly, turning again at the door, and almost catching him in the act of yawning. She goes out.

THE MAN [drowsily] Sleep, sleep, sleep, sleep,
720 slee— [The words trail off into a murmur. He wakes
again with a shock on the point of falling]. Where am
I? Thats what I want to know: where am I? Must keep
awake. Nothing keeps me awake except danger: remember that: [intently] danger, danger, danger, dan—
[trailing off again: another shock] Wheres danger?
Mus' find it. [He starts off vaguely round the room in
search of it]. What am I looking for? Sleep—
danger—dont know. [He stumbles against the bed].
Ah yes: now I know. All right now. I'm to go to bed,
730 but not to sleep. Be sure not to sleep, because of
danger. Not to lie down either, only sit down. [He sits
on the bed. A blissful expression comes into his face].
Ah! [With a happy sigh he sinks back at full length;
lifts his boots into the bed with a final effort; and falls
fast asleep instantly].

Catherine comes in, followed by Raina.

RAINA [looking at the ottoman] He's gone! I left him
here.

CATHERINE. Here! Then he must have climbed down
740 from the—

RAINA [seeing him] Oh! [She points].

CATHERINE [scandalized] Well! [She strides to the
bed, Raina following until she is opposite her on the
other side]. He's fast asleep. The brute!

RAINA [anxiously] Sh!

CATHERINE [shaking him] Sir! [Shaking him again,
harder] Sir!! [Vehemently, shaking very hard] Sir!!!

RAINA [catching her arm] Dont, mamma: the poor
darling is worn out. Let him sleep.

750 CATHERINE [letting him go, and turning amazed to
Raina] The poor darling! Raina!!! [She looks sternly at
her daughter].

The man sleeps profoundly.

ACT II

The sixth of March, 1886. In the garden of Major Petkoff's house. It is a fine spring morning: the garden
looks fresh and pretty. Beyond the paling the tops of a
couple of minarets can be seen, shewing that there is a
valley there, with the little town in it. A few miles
further the Balkan mountains rise and shut in the landscape. Looking towards them from within the garden,
the side of the house is seen on the left, with a garden
door reached by a little flight of steps. On the right the
stable yard, with its gateway, encroaches on the garden. There are fruit bushes along the paling and
house, covered with washing spread out to dry. A path
runs by the house, and rises by two steps at the corner,
where it turns out of sight. In the middle, a small table,
with two bent wood chairs at it, is laid for breakfast
with Turkish coffee pot, cups, rolls, etc.; but the cups
have been used and the bread broken. There is a
wooden garden seat against the wall on the right.

Louka, smoking a cigaret, is standing between the
table and the house, turning her back with angry disdain on a man servant who is lecturing her. He is a
middle-aged man of cool temperament and low but
clear and keen intelligence, with the complacency of
the servant who values himself on his rank in servitude, and the imperturbability of the accurate cal-
culator who has no illusions. He wears a white Bulgarian costume: jacket with embroidered border, sash,
wide knickerbockers, and decorated gaiters. His head
is shaved up to the crown, giving him a high Japanese
forehead. His name is Nicola.

NICOLA. Be warned in time, Louka: mend your
manners. I know the mistress. She is so grand that she
never dreams that any servant could dare be disrespectful to her; but if she once suspects that you are
defying her, out you go.

LOUKA. I do defy her. I will defy her. What do I care
for her?

NICOLA. If you quarrel with the family, I never can
marry you. It's the same as if you quarrelled with me!

LOUKA. You take her part against me, do you?   10

NICOLA [sedately] I shall always be dependent on
the good will of the family. When I leave their service
and start a shop in Sofia, their custom will be half my
capital: their bad word would ruin me.

LOUKA. You have no spirit. I should like to catch
them saying a word against me!

NICOLA [pityingly] I should have expected more
sense from you, Louka. But youre young: youre
young!

LOUKA. Yes; and you like me the better for it, dont 20
you? But I know some family secrets they wouldnt
care to have told, young as I am. Let them quarrel with
me if they dare!)

NICOLA [with compassionate superiority] Do you
know what they would do if they heard you talk like
that?

LOUKA. What could they do?

NICOLA. Discharge you for untruthfulness. Who
would believe any stories you told after that? Who
would give you another situation? Who in this house 30
would dare be seen speaking to you ever again? How
long would your father be left on his little farm? [She
impatiently throws away the end of her cigaret, and
stamps on it]. Child: you dont know the power such
high people have over the like of you and me when we
try to rise out of our poverty against them. [He goes
close to her and lowers his voice]. Look at me, ten
years in their service. Do you think I know no secrets?
I know things about the mistress that she wouldnt have
the master know for a thousand levas. I know things 40
about him that she wouldnt let him hear the last of for
six months if I blabbed them to her. I know things
about Raina that would break off her match with Sergius if—

LOUKA [*turning on him quickly*] How do you know? I never told you!

NICOLA [*opening his eyes cunningly*] So thats your little secret, is it? I thought it might be something like that. Well, you take my advice and be respectful; and make the mistress feel that no matter what you know or dont know, she can depend on you to hold your tongue and serve the family faithfully. Thats what they like; and thats how youll make most out of them.

LOUKA [*with searching scorn*] You have the soul of a servant, Nicola.

NICOLA [*complacently*] Yes: thats the secret of success in service.

A loud knocking with a whip handle on a wooden door is heard from the stable yard.

MALE VOICE OUTSIDE. Hollo! Hollo there! Nicola!

LOUKA. Master! back from the war!

NICOLA [*quickly*] My word for it, Louka, the war's over. Off with you and get some fresh coffee. [*He runs out into the stable yard*].

LOUKA [*as she collects the coffee pot and cups on the tray, and carries it into the house*] Youll never put the soul of a servant into me.

Major Petkoff comes from the stable yard, followed by Nicola. He is a cheerful, excitable, insignificant, unpolished man of about 50, naturally unambitious except as to his income and his importance in local society, but just now greatly pleased with the military rank which the war has thrust on him as a man of consequence in his town. The fever of plucky patriotism which the Serbian attack roused in all the Bulgarians has pulled him through the war; but he is obviously glad to be home again.

PETKOFF [*pointing to the table with his whip*] Breakfast out here, eh?

NICOLA. Yes, sir. The mistress and Miss Raina have just gone in.

PETKOFF [*sitting down and taking a roll*] Go in and say Ive come; and get me some fresh coffee.

NICOLA. It's coming, sir. [*He goes to the house door. Louka, with fresh coffee, a clean cup, and a brandy bottle on her tray, meets him*]. Have you told the mistress?

LOUKA. Yes: she's coming.

Nicola goes into the house. Louka brings the coffee to the table.

PETKOFF. Well: the Serbs havnt run away with you, have they?

LOUKA. No, sir.

PETKOFF. Thats right. Have you brought me some cognac?

LOUKA [*putting the bottle on the table*] Here, sir.

PETKOFF. Thats right. [*He pours some into his coffee*].

Catherine, who, having at this early hour made only a very perfunctory toilet, wears a Bulgarian apron over a once brilliant but now half worn-out dressing gown, and a colored handkerchief tied over her thick black hair, comes from the house with Turkish slippers on her bare feet, looking astonishingly handsome and stately under all the circumstances. Louka goes into the house.

CATHERINE. My dear Paul: what a surprise for us! [*She stoops over the back of his chair to kiss him*]. Have they brought you fresh coffee?

PETKOFF. Yes: Louka's been looking after me. The war's over. The treaty was signed three days ago at Bucharest; and the decree for our army to demobilize was issued yesterday.

CATHERINE [*springing erect, with flashing eyes*] Paul: have you let the Austrians force you to make peace?

PETKOFF [*submissively*] My dear: they didnt consult me. What could *I* do? [*She sits down and turns away from him*]. But of course we saw to it that the treaty was an honorable one. It declares peace—

CATHERINE [*outraged*] Peace!

PETKOFF [*appeasing her*]—but not friendly relations: remember that. They wanted to put that in; but I insisted on its being struck out. What more could I do?

CATHERINE. You could have annexed Serbia and made Prince Alexander° Emperor of the Balkans. Thats what I would have done.

PETKOFF. I dont doubt it in the least, my dear. But I should have had to subdue the whole Austrian Empire first; and that would have kept me too long away from you. I missed you greatly.

CATHERINE [*relenting*] Ah! [*She stretches her hand affectionately across the table to squeeze his*].

PETKOFF. And how have you been, my dear?

CATHERINE. Oh, my usual sore throats: thats all.

PETKOFF [*with conviction*] That comes from washing your neck every day. Ive often told you so.

CATHERINE. Nonsense, Paul!

PETKOFF [*over his coffee and cigaret*] I dont believe in going too far with these modern customs. All this washing cant be good for the health: it's not natural. There was an Englishman at Philippopolis who used to wet himself all over with cold water every morning when he got up. Disgusting! It all comes from the English: their climate makes them so dirty that they have to be perpetually washing themselves. Look at my father! he never had a bath in his life; and he lived to be ninety-eight, the healthiest man in Bulgaria. I don't mind a good wash once a week to keep up my position; but once a day is carrying the thing to a ridiculous extreme.

CATHERINE. You are a barbarian at heart still, Paul. I hope you behaved yourself before all those Russian officers.

PETKOFF. I did my best. I took care to let them know that we have a library.

CATHERINE. Ah; but you didnt tell them that we have an electric bell in it? I have had one put up.

126 **Prince Alexander,** Prince Alexander Joseph of Battenberg (1857–1893), first prince of Bulgaria (1879–1886)

PETKOFF. Whats an electric bell?

160 CATHERINE. You touch a button; something tinkles in the kitchen; and then Nicola comes up.

PETKOFF. Why not shout for him?

CATHERINE. Civilized people never shout for their servants. Ive learnt that while you were away.

PETKOFF. Well, I'll tell you something Ive learnt too. Civilized people dont hang out their washing to dry where visitors can see it; so youd better have all that [indicating the clothes on the bushes] put somewhere else

170 CATHERINE. Oh, thats absurd, Paul: I dont believe really refined people notice such things.

SERGIUS [knocking at the stable gates] Gate, Nicola!

PETKOFF. Theres Sergius. [Shouting] Hollo, Nicola!

CATHERINE. Oh, dont shout, Paul: it really isnt nice.

PETKOFF. Bosh! [He shouts louder than before] Nicola!

NICOLA [appearing at the house door] Yes, sir.

PETKOFF. Are you deaf? Dont you hear Major Saranoff knocking? Bring him round this way. [He
180 pronounces the name with the stress on the second syllable: Sarahnoff].

NICOLA. Yes, major. [He goes into the stable yard].

PETKOFF. You must talk to him, my dear, until Raina takes him off our hands. He bores my life out about our not promoting him. Over my head, if you please.

CATHERINE. He certainly ought to be promoted when he marries Raina. Besides, the country should insist on having at least one native general.

190 PETKOFF. Yes; so that he could throw away whole brigades instead of regiments. It's no use, my dear: he hasnt the slightest chance of promotion until we're quite sure that the peace will be a lasting one.

NICOLA [at the gate, announcing] Major Sergius Saranoff! [He goes into the house and returns presently with a third chair, which he places at the table. He then withdraws].

Major Sergius Saranoff, the original of the portrait in Raina's room, is a tall romantically handsome man,
200 with the physical hardihood, the high spirit, and the susceptible imagination of an untamed mountaineer chieftain. But his remarkable personal distinction is of a characteristically civilized type. The ridges of his eyebrows, curving with an interrogative twist round the projections at the outer corners; his jealously observant eye; his nose, thin, keen, and apprehensive in spite of the pugnacious high bridge and large nostril; his assertive chin, would not be out of place in a Parisian saloon, shewing that the clever imaginative bar-
210 barian has an acute critical faculty which has been thrown into intense activity by the arrival of western civilization in the Balkans. The result is precisely what the advent of nineteenth century thought first produced in England: to wit, Byronism. By his brooding on the perpetual failure, not only of others, but of himself, to live up to his ideals; by his consequent cynical scorn for humanity; by his jejune credulity as to the absolute validity of his concepts and the unworthiness of the world in disregarding them; by his wincings and mockeries under the sting of the petty 220 disillusions which every hour spent among men brings to his sensitive observation, he has acquired the half tragic, half ironic air, the mysterious moodiness, the suggestion of a strange and terrible history that has left nothing but undying remorse, by which Childe Harold° fascinated the grandmothers of his English contemporaries. It is clear that here or nowhere is Raina's ideal hero. Catherine is hardly less enthusiastic about him than her daughter, and much less reserved in shewing her enthusiasm. As he enters from 230 the stable gate, she rises effusively to greet him. Petkoff is distinctly less disposed to make a fuss about him.

PETKOFF. Here already, Sergius! Glad to see you.

CATHERINE. My dear Sergius! [She holds out both her hands].

SERGIUS [kissing them with a scrupulous gallantry] My dear mother, if I may call you so.

PETKOFF [drily] Mother-in-law, Sergius: mother-in-law! Sit down; and have some coffee. 240

SERGIUS. Thank you: none for me. [He gets away from the table with a certain distaste for Petkoff's enjoyment of it, and posts himself with conscious dignity against the rail of the steps leading to the house].

CATHERINE. You look superb. The campaign has improved you, Sergius. Everybody here is mad about you. We were all wild with enthusiasm about that magnificent cavalry charge.

SERGIUS [with grave irony] Madam: it was the cradle and the grave of my military reputation. 250

CATHERINE. How so?

SERGIUS. I won the battle the wrong way when our worthy Russian generals were losing it the right way. In short, I upset their plans, and wounded their self-esteem. Two Cossack colonels had their regiments routed on the most correct principles of scientific warfare. Two major-generals got killed strictly according to military etiquette. The two colonels are now major-generals; and I am still a simple major.

CATHERINE. You shall not remain so, Sergius. The 260 women are on your side; and they will see that justice is done you.

SERGIUS. It is too late. I have only waited for the peace to send in my resignation.

PETKOFF [dropping his cup in amazement] Your resignation!

CATHERINE. Oh, you must withdraw it!

SERGIUS [with resolute measured emphasis, folding his arms] I never withdraw.

PETKOFF [vexed] Now who could have supposed 270 you were going to do such a thing?

SERGIUS [with fire] Everyone that knew me. But

226 **Childe Harold,** world weary hero of Byron's poem (1812) of the same name

enough of myself and my affairs. How is Raina; and where is Raina?

RAINA [*suddenly coming round the corner of the house and standing at the top of the steps in the path*] Raina is here.

She makes a charming picture as they turn to look at her. She wears an underdress of pale green silk,
280 *draped with an overdress of thin ecru canvas embroidered with gold. She is crowned with a dainty eastern cap of gold tinsel. Sergius goes impulsively to meet her. Posing regally, she presents her hand: he drops chivalrously on one knee and kisses it.*

PETKOFF [*aside to Catherine, beaming with parental pride*] Pretty, isnt it? She always appears at the right moment.

CATHERINE [*impatiently*] Yes: she listens for it. It is an abominable habit.

290 *Sergius leads Raina forward with splendid gallantry. When they arrive at the table, she turns to him with a bend of the head: he bows; and thus they separate, he coming to his place, and she going behind her father's chair.*

RAINA [*stooping and kissing her father*] Dear father! Welcome home!

PETKOFF [*patting her cheek*] My little pet girl. [*He kisses her. She goes to the chair left by Nicola for Sergius, and sits down*].

300 CATHERINE. And so youre no longer a soldier, Sergius.

SERGIUS. I am no longer a soldier. Soldiering, my dear madam, is the coward's art of attacking mercilessly when you are strong, and keeping out of harm's way when you are weak. That is the whole secret of successful fighting. Get your enemy at a disadvantage; and never, on any account, fight him on equal terms.

PETKOFF. They wouldnt let us make a fair stand-up
310 fight of it. However, I suppose soldiering has to be a trade like any other trade.

SERGIUS. Precisely. But I have no ambition to shine as a tradesman; so I have taken the advice of that bagman of a captain that settled the exchange of prisoners with us at Pirot, and given it up.

PETKOFF. What! that Swiss fellow? Sergius: Ive often thought of that exchange since. He over-reached us about those horses.

SERGIUS. Of course he over-reached us. His father
320 was a hotel and livery stable keeper; and he owed his first step to his knowledge of horse-dealing. [*With mock enthusiasm*] Ah, he was a soldier: every inch a soldier! If only I had bought the horses for my regiment instead of foolishly leading it into danger, I should have been a field-marshal now!

CATHERINE. A Swiss? What was he doing in the Serbian army?

PETKOFF. A volunteer, of course: keen on picking up his profession. [*Chuckling*] We shouldnt have been
330 able to begin fighting if these foreigners hadnt shewn

us how to do it: we knew nothing about it; and neither did the Serbs. Egad, there'd have been no war without them!

RAINA. Are there many Swiss officers in the Serbian Army?

PETKOFF. No. All Austrians, just as our officers were all Russians. This was the only Swiss I came across. I'll never trust a Swiss again. He humbugged us into giving him fifty ablebodied men for two hundred worn out chargers. They werent even eatable! 340

SERGIUS. We were two children in the hands of that consummate soldier, Major: simply two innocent little children.

RAINA. What was he like?

CATHERINE. Oh, Raina, what a silly question!

SERGIUS. He was like a commercial traveller° in uniform. Bourgeois to his boots!

PETKOFF [*grinning*] Sergius: tell Catherine that queer story his friend told us about how he escaped after Slivnitza. You remember. About his being hid by 350 two women.

SERGIUS [*with bitter irony*] Oh yes: quite a romance! He was serving in the very battery I so unprofessionally charged. Being a thorough soldier, he ran away like the rest of them, with our cavalry at his heels. To escape their sabres he climbed a waterpipe and made his way into the bedroom of a young Bulgarian lady. The young lady was enchanted by his persuasive commercial traveller's manners. She very modestly entertained him for an hour or so, and then called in 360 her mother lest her conduct should appear unmaidenly. The old lady was equally fascinated; and the fugitive was sent on his way in the morning, disguised in an old coat belonging to the master of the house, who was away at the war.

RAINA [*rising with marked stateliness*] Your life in the camp has made you coarse, Sergius. I did not think you would have repeated such a story before me. [*She turns away coldly*].

CATHERINE [*also rising*] She is right, Sergius. If such 370 women exist, we should be spared the knowledge of them.

PETKOFF. Pooh! nonsense! what does it matter?

SERGIUS [*ashamed*] No, Petkoff: I was wrong. [*To Raina, with earnest humility*] I beg your pardon. I have behaved abominably. Forgive me, Raina. [*She bows reservedly*]. And you too, madam. [*Catherine bows graciously and sits down. He proceeds solemnly, again addressing Raina*] The glimpses I have had of the seamy side of life during the last few months have 380 made me cynical; but I should not have brought my cynicism here: least of all into your presence, Raina. I—[*Here, turning to the others, he is evidently going to begin a long speech when the Major interrupts him*].

PETKOFF. Stuff and nonsense, Sergius! Thats quite enough fuss about nothing: a soldier's daughter should

346 **commercial traveller,** traveling salesman

be able to stand up without flinching to a little strong conversation. [*He rises*]. Come: it's time for us to get to business. We have to make up our minds how those three regiments are to get back to Philippopolis: theres no forage for them on the Sofia route. [*He goes towards the house*]. Come along. [*Sergius is about to follow him when Catherine rises and intervenes*].

CATHERINE. Oh, Paul, cant you spare Sergius for a few moments? Raina has hardly seen him yet. Perhaps I can help you to settle about the regiments.

SERGIUS [*protesting*] My dear madam, impossible: you—

CATHERINE [*stopping him playfully*] You stay here, my dear Sergius: theres no hurry. I have a word or two to say to Paul. [*Sergius instantly bows and steps back*]. Now, dear [*taking Petkoff's arm*]: come and see the electric bell.

PETKOFF. Oh, very well, very well.

They go into the house together affectionately. Sergius, left alone with Raina, looks anxiously at her, fearing that she is still offended. She smiles, and stretches out her arms to him.

SERGIUS [*hastening to her*] Am I forgiven?

RAINA [*placing her hands on his shoulders as she looks up at him with admiration and worship*] My hero! My king!

SERGIUS. My queen! [*He kisses her on the forehead*].

RAINA. How I have envied you, Sergius! You have been out in the world, on the field of battle, able to prove yourself there worthy of any woman in the world; whilst I have had to sit at home inactive—dreaming—useless—doing nothing that could give me the right to call myself worthy of any man.

SERGIUS. Dearest: all my deeds have been yours. You inspired me. I have gone through the war like a knight in a tournament with his lady looking down at him!

RAINA. And you have never been absent from my thoughts for a moment. [*Very solemnly*] Sergius: I think we two have found the higher love. When I think of you, I feel that I could never do a base deed, or think an ignoble thought.

SERGIUS. My lady and my saint! [*He clasps her reverently*].

RAINA [*returning his embrace*] My lord and my—

SERGIUS. Sh—sh! Let me be the worshipper, dear. You little know how unworthy even the best man is of a girl's pure passion!

RAINA. I trust you. I love you. You will never disappoint me, Sergius. [*Louka is heard singing within the house. They quickly release each other*]. I cant pretend to talk indifferently before her: my heart is too full. [*Louka comes from the house with her tray. She goes to the table, and begins to clear it, with her back turned to them*]. I will get my hat; and then we can go out until lunch time. Wouldnt you like that?

SERGIUS. Be quick. If you are away five minutes, it will seem five hours. [*Raina runs to the top of the steps, and turns there to exchange looks with him and wave him a kiss with both hands. He looks after her with emotion for a moment; then turns slowly away, his face radiant with the loftiest exaltation. The movement shifts his field of vision, into the corner of which there now comes the tail of Louka's double apron. His attention is arrested at once. He takes a stealthy look at her, and begins to twirl his moustache mischievously, with his left hand akimbo on his hip. Finally, striking the ground with his heels in something of a cavalry swagger, he strolls over to the other side of the table, opposite her, and says*] Louka: do you know what the higher love is?

LOUKA [*astonished*] No, sir.

SERGIUS. Very fatiguing thing to keep up for any length of time, Louka. One feels the need of some relief after it.

LOUKA [*innocently*] Perhaps you would like some coffee, sir? [*She stretches her hand across the table for the coffee pot*].

SERGIUS [*taking her hand*] Thank you, Louka.

LOUKA [*pretending to pull*] Oh, sir, you know I didnt mean that. I'm surprised at you!

SERGIUS [*coming clear of the table and drawing her with him*] I am surprised at myself, Louka. What would Sergius, the hero of Slivnitza, say if he saw me now? What would Sergius, the apostle of the higher love, say if he saw me now? What would the half dozen Sergiuses who keep popping in and out of this handsome figure of mine say if they caught us here? [*Letting go her hand and slipping his arm dexterously round her waist*] Do you consider my figure handsome, Louka?

LOUKA. Let me go, sir. I shall be disgraced. [*She struggles: he holds her inexorably*]. Oh, will you let go?

SERGIUS [*looking straight into her eyes*] No.

LOUKA. Then stand back where we cant be seen. Have you no common sense?

SERGIUS. Ah! thats reasonable. [*He takes her into the stableyard gateway, where they are hidden from the house*].

LOUKA [*plaintively*] I may have been seen from the windows: Miss Raina is sure to be spying about after you.

SERGIUS [*stung: letting her go*] Take care, Louka. I may be worthless enough to betray the higher love; but do not you insult it.

LOUKA [*demurely*] Not for the world, sir, I'm sure. May I go on with my work, please, now?

SERGIUS [*again putting his arm round her*] You are a provoking little witch, Louka. If you were in love with me, would you spy out of windows on me?

LOUKA. Well, you see, sir, since you say you are half a dozen different gentlemen all at once, I should have a great deal to look after.

SERGIUS [*charmed*] Witty as well as pretty. [*He tries to kiss her*].

LOUKA [avoiding him] No: I dont want your kisses. Gentlefolk are all alike: you making love to me behind Miss Raina's back; and she doing the same behind yours.

SERGIUS [recoiling a step] Louka!

LOUKA. It shews how little you really care.

SERGIUS [dropping his familiarity, and speaking with
510 freezing politeness] If our conversation is to continue, Louka, you will please remember that a gentleman does not discuss the conduct of the lady he is engaged to with her maid.

LOUKA. It's so hard to know what a gentleman considers right. I thought from your trying to kiss me that you had given up being so particular.

SERGIUS [turning from her and striking his forehead as he comes back into the garden from the gateway] Devil! devil!

520 LOUKA. Ha! ha! I expect one of the six of you is very like me, sir; though I am only Miss Raina's maid. [She goes back to her work at the table, taking no further notice of him].

SERGIUS [speaking to himself] Which of the six is the real man? thats the question that torments me. One of them is a hero, another a buffoon, another a humbug, another perhaps a bit of a blackguard. [He pauses, and looks furtively at Louka as he adds, with deep bitterness] And one, at least, is a coward: jealous, like all
530 cowards. [He goes to the table]. Louka.

LOUKA. Yes?

SERGIUS. Who is my rival?

LOUKA. You shall never get that out of me, for love or money.

SERGIUS. Why?

LOUKA. Never mind why. Besides, you would tell that I told you; and I should lose my place.

SERGIUS [holding out his right hand in affirmation] No! on the honor of a—[He checks himself; and his
540 hand drops, nerveless, as he concludes sardonically]—of a man capable of behaving as I have been behaving for the last five minutes. Who is he?

LOUKA. I dont know. I never saw him. I only heard his voice through the door of her room.

SERGIUS. Damnation! How dare you?

LOUKA [retreating] Oh, I mean no harm: youve no right to take up my words like that. The mistress knows all about it. And I tell you that if that gentleman ever comes here again, Miss Raina will marry him,
550 whether he likes it or not. I know the difference between the sort of manner you and she put on before one another and the real manner.

Sergius shivers as if she had stabbed him. Then, setting his face like iron, he strides grimly to her, and grips her above the elbows with both hands.

SERGIUS. Now listen you to me.

LOUKA [wincing] Not so tight: youre hurting me.

SERGIUS. That doesnt matter. You have stained my honor by making me a party to your eavesdropping.
560 And you have betrayed your mistress.

LOUKA [writhing] Please—

SERGIUS. That shews that you are an abominable little clod of common clay, with the soul of a servant. [He lets her go as if she were an unclean thing, and turns away, dusting his hands of her, to the bench by the wall, where he sits down with averted head, meditating gloomily].

LOUKA [whimpering angrily with her hands up her sleeves, feeling her bruised arms] You know how to hurt with your tongue as well as with your hands. But I 570 dont care, now Ive found out that whatever clay I'm made of, youre made of the same. As for her, she's a liar; and her fine airs are a cheat; and I'm worth six of her. [She shakes the pain off hardily; tosses her head; and sets to work to put the things on the tray].

He looks doubtfully at her. She finishes packing the tray, and laps the cloth over the edges, so as to carry all out together. As she stoops to lift it, he rises.

SERGIUS. Louka! [She stops and looks defiantly at him]. A gentleman has no right to hurt a woman under 580 any circumstances. [With profound humility, uncovering his head] I beg your pardon.

LOUKA. That sort of apology may satisfy a lady. Of what use is it to a servant?

SERGIUS [rudely crossed in his chivalry, throws it off with a bitter laugh, and says slightingly] Oh! you wish to be paid for the hurt? [He puts on his shako, and takes some money from his pocket].

LOUKA [her eyes filling with tears in spite of herself] No: I want my hurt made well. 590

SERGIUS [sobered by her tone] How?

She rolls up her left sleeve; clasps her arm with the thumb and fingers of her right hand; and looks down at the bruise. Then she raises her head and looks straight at him. Finally, with a superb gesture, she presents her arm to be kissed. Amazed, he looks at her; at the arm; at her again; hesitates; and then, with shuddering intensity, exclaims Never! and gets away as far as possible from her.

Her arm drops. Without a word, and with unaffected 600 dignity, she takes her tray, and is approaching the house when Raina returns, wearing a hat and jacket in the height of the Vienna fashion of the previous year, 1885. Louka makes way proudly for her, and then goes into the house.

RAINA. I'm ready. Whats the matter? [Gaily] Have you been flirting with Louka?

SERGIUS [hastily] No, no. How can you think such a thing?

RAINA [ashamed of herself] Forgive me, dear: it was 610 only a jest. I am so happy today.

He goes quickly to her, and kisses her hand remorsefully. Catherine comes out and calls to them from the top of the steps.

CATHERINE [coming down to them] I am sorry to disturb you, children; but Paul is distracted over those three regiments. He doesnt know how to send them to Philippopolis; and he objects to every suggestion of

mine. You must go and help him, Sergius. He is in the
library.

RAINA [*disappointed*] But we are just going out for a
walk.

SERGIUS. I shall not be long. Wait for me just five
minutes. [*He runs up the steps to the door*].

RAINA [*following him to the foot of the steps and
looking up at him with timid coquetry*] I shall go round
and wait in full view of the library windows. Be sure
you draw father's attention to me. If you are a moment
longer than five minutes, I shall go in and fetch you,
regiments or no regiments.

SERGIUS [*laughing*] Very well. [*He goes in*].

*Raina watches him until he is out of her sight. Then,
with a perceptible relaxation of manner, she begins to
pace up and down the garden in a brown study.*

CATHERINE. Imagine their meeting that Swiss and
hearing the whole story! The very first thing your
father asked for was the old coat we sent him off in. A
nice mess you have got us into!

RAINA [*gazing thoughtfully at the gravel as she
walks*] The little beast!

CATHERINE. Little beast! What little beast?

RAINA. To go and tell! Oh, if I had him here, I'd
cram him with chocolate creams til he couldnt ever
speak again!

CATHERINE. Dont talk such stuff. Tell me the truth,
Raina. How long was he in your room before you came
to me?

RAINA [*whisking round and recommencing her
march in the opposite direction*] Oh, I forget.

CATHERINE. You cannot forget! Did he really climb
up after the soldiers were gone; or was he there when
that officer searched the room?

RAINA. No. Yes: I think he must have been there
then.

CATHERINE. You think! Oh, Raina! Raina! Will
anything ever make you straightforward? If Sergius
finds out, it will be all over between you.

RAINA [*with cool impertinence*] Oh, I know Sergius
is your pet. I sometimes wish you could marry him
instead of me. You would just suit him. You would pet
him, and spoil him, and mother him to perfection.

CATHERINE [*opening her eyes very widely indeed*]
Well, upon my word!

RAINA [*capriciously: half to herself*] I always feel a
longing to do or say something dreadful to him—to
shock his propriety—to scandalize the five senses out
of him. [*To Catherine, perversely*] I dont care whether
he finds out about the chocolate cream soldier or not. I
half hope he may. [*She again turns and strolls flip-
pantly away up the path to the corner of the house*].

CATHERINE. And what should I be able to say to
your father, pray?

RAINA [*over her shoulder, from the top of the two
steps*] Oh, poor father! As if he could help himself!
[*She turns the corner and passes out of sight*].

CATHERINE [*looking after her, her fingers itching*]

Oh, if you were only ten years younger! [*Louka comes
from the house with a salver, which she carries hanging down by her side*]. Well?

LOUKA. Theres a gentleman just called, madam. A
Serbian officer.

CATHERINE [*flaming*] A Serb! And how dare he—
[*checking herself bitterly*] Oh, I forgot. We are at
peace now. I suppose we shall have them calling every
day to pay their compliments. Well: if he is an officer
why dont you tell your master? He is in the library
with Major Saranoff. Why do you come to me?

LOUKA. But he asks for you, madam. And I dont
think he knows who you are: he said the lady of the
house. He gave me this little ticket for you. [*She takes
a card out of her bosom; puts it on the salver; and
offers it to Catherine*].

CATHERINE [*reading*] "Captain Bluntschli"? Thats a
German name.

LOUKA. Swiss, madam, I think.

CATHERINE [*with a bound that makes Louka jump
back*] Swiss! What is he like?

LOUKA [*timidly*] He has a big carpet bag, madam.

CATHERINE. Oh Heavens! he's come to return the
coat. Send him away: say we're not at home: ask him
to leave his address and I'll write to him. Oh stop: that
will never do. Wait! [*She throws herself into a chair to
think it out. Louka waits*]. The master and Major
Saranoff are busy in the library, arnt they?

LOUKA. Yes, madam.

CATHERINE [*decisively*] Bring the gentleman out
here at once. [*Peremptorily*] And be very polite to him.
Dont delay. Here [*impatiently snatching the salver
from her*]: leave that here; and go straight back to him.

LOUKA. Yes, madam [*going*].

CATHERINE. Louka!

LOUKA [*stopping*] Yes, madam.

CATHERINE. Is the library door shut?

LOUKA. I think so, madam.

CATHERINE. If not, shut it as you pass through.

LOUKA. Yes, madam [*going*].

CATHERINE. Stop! [*Louka stops*]. He will have to go
that way [*indicating the gate of the stableyard*]. Tell
Nicola to bring his bag here after him. Dont forget.

LOUKA [*surprised*] His bag?

CATHERINE. Yes: here: as soon as possible.
[*Vehemently*] Be quick! [*Louka runs into the house.
Catherine snatches her apron off and throws it behind
a bush. She then takes up the salver and uses it as a
mirror, with the result that the handkerchief tied round
her head follows the apron. A touch to her hair and a
shake to her dressing gown make her presentable*].
Oh, how? how? how can a man be such a fool! Such a
moment to select! [*Louka appears at the door of the
house, announcing* Captain Bluntschli. *She stands
aside at the top of the steps to let him pass before she
goes in again. He is the man of the midnight adventure
in Raina's room, clean, well brushed, smartly uni-
formed, and out of trouble, but still unmistakably the*

same man. *The moment Louka's back is turned, Catherine swoops on him with impetuous, urgent, coaxing appeal*]. Captain Bluntschli: I am very glad to see you; but you must leave this house at once. [*He raises his eyebrows*]. My husband has just returned with my future son-in-law; and they know nothing. If they did, the consequences would be terrible. You are a foreigner: you do not feel our national animosities as we do. We still hate the Serbs: the effect of the peace on my husband has been to make him feel like a lion baulked of his prey. If he discovers our secret, he will never forgive me; and my daughter's life will hardly be safe. Will you, like the chivalrous gentleman and soldier you are, leave at once before he finds you here?

BLUNTSCHLI [*disappointed, but philosophical*] At once, gracious lady. I only came to thank you and return the coat you lent me. If you will allow me to take it out of my bag and leave it with your servant as I pass out, I need detain you no further. [*He turns to go into the house*].

CATHERINE [*catching him by the sleeve*] Oh, you must not think of going back that way. [*Coaxing him across to the stable gates*] This is the shortest way out. Many thanks. So glad to have been of service to you. Good-bye.

BLUNTSCHLI. But my bag?

CATHERINE. It shall be sent on. You will leave me your address.

BLUNTSCHLI. True. Allow me. [*He takes out his card-case, and stops to write his address, keeping Catherine in an agony of impatience. As he hands her the card, Petkoff, hatless, rushes from the house in a fluster of hospitality, followed by Sergius*].

PETKOFF [*as he hurries down the steps*] My dear Captain Bluntschli—

CATHERINE. Oh Heavens! [*She sinks on the seat against the wall*].

PETKOFF [*too preoccupied to notice her as he shakes Bluntschli's hand heartily*] Those stupid people of mine thought I was out here, instead of in the—haw!—library [*he cannot mention the library without betraying how proud he is of it*]. I saw you through the window. I was wondering why you didnt come in. Saranoff is with me: you remember him, dont you?

SERGIUS [*saluting humorously, and then offering his hand with great charm of manner*] Welcome, our friend the enemy!

PETKOFF. No longer the enemy, happily. [*Rather anxiously*] I hope youve called as a friend, and not about horses or prisoners.

CATHERINE. Oh, quite as a friend, Paul. I was just asking Captain Bluntschli to stay to lunch; but he declares he must go at once.

SERGIUS [*sardonically*] Impossible, Bluntschli. We want you here badly. We have to send on three cavalry regiments to Philippopolis; and we dont in the least know how to do it.

BLUNTSCHLI [*suddenly attentive and businesslike*] Philippopolis? The forage is the trouble, I suppose.

PETKOFF [*eagerly*] Yes: thats it. [*To Sergius*] He sees the whole thing at once.

BLUNTSCHLI. I think I can shew you how to manage that.

SERGIUS. Invaluable man! Come along! [*Towering over Bluntschli, he puts his hand on his shoulder and takes him to the steps, Petkoff following*].

Raina comes from the house as Bluntschli puts his foot on the first step.

RAINA. Oh! The chocolate cream soldier!

Bluntschli stands rigid. Sergius, amazed, looks at Raina, then at Petkoff, who looks back at him and then at his wife.

CATHERINE [*with commanding presence of mind*] My dear Raina, dont you see that we have a guest here? Captain Bluntschli: one of our new Serbian friends.

Raina bows: Bluntschli bows.

RAINA. How silly of me! [*She comes down into the centre of the group, between Bluntschli and Petkoff*]. I made a beautiful ornament this morning for the ice pudding; and that stupid Nicola has just put down a pile of plates on it and spoilt it. [*To Bluntschli, winningly*] I hope you didnt think that you were the chocolate cream soldier, Captain Bluntschli.

BLUNTSCHLI [*laughing*] I assure you I did. [*Stealing a whimsical glance at her*] Your explanation was a relief.

PETKOFF [*suspiciously, to Raina*] And since when, pray, have you taken to cooking?

CATHERINE. Oh, whilst you were away. It is her latest fancy.

PETKOFF [*testily*] And has Nicola taken to drinking? He used to be careful enough. First he shews Captain Bluntschli out here when he knew quite well I was in the library; and then he goes downstairs and breaks Raina's chocolate soldier. He must—[*Nicola appears at the top of the steps with the bag. He descends; places it respectfully before Bluntschli; and waits for further orders. General amazement. Nicola, unconscious of the effect he is producing, looks perfectly satisfied with himself. When Petkoff recovers his power of speech, he breaks out at him with*] Are you mad, Nicola?

NICOLA [*taken aback*] Sir?

PETKOFF. What have you brought that for?

NICOLA. My lady's orders, major. Louka told me that—

CATHERINE [*interrupting him*] My orders! Why should I order you to bring Captain Bluntschli's luggage out here? What are you thinking of, Nicola?

NICOLA [*after a moment's bewilderment, picking up the bag as he addresses Bluntschli with the very perfection of servile discretion*] I beg your pardon, captain, I am sure. [*To Catherine*] My fault, madam: I

hope youll overlook it. [*He bows, and is going to the*
steps with the bag, when Petkoff addresses him an-
850 grily*].

PETKOFF. Youd better go and slam that bag, too,
down on Miss Raina's ice pudding! [*This is too much
for Nicola. The bag drops from his hand almost on his
master's toes, eliciting a roar of*] Begone, you butter-
fingered donkey.

NICOLA [*snatching up the bag, and escaping into the
house*] Yes, major.

CATHERINE. Oh, never mind, Paul: dont be angry.

860 PETKOFF [*blustering*] Scoundrel! He's got out of
hand while I was away. I'll teach him. Infernal
blackguard! The sack next Saturday! I'll clear out the
whole establishment—[*He is stifled by the caresses of
his wife and daughter, who hang round his neck, petting him*].

CATHERINE ⎫ [*together*] ⎧ Now, now, now, it mustnt be
RAINA ⎭ ⎩ Wow, wow, wow: not on your
⎧ angry. He meant no harm. Be good to
⎪ first day at home. I'll make another ice
870 ⎨ please me, dear. Sh-sh-sh-sh!
⎪ pudding. Tch-ch-ch!

PETKOFF [*yielding*] Oh well, never mind. Come,
Bluntschli: lets have no more nonsense about going
away. You know very well youre not going back to
Switzerland yet. Until you do go back you'll stay with
us.

RAINA. Oh, do, Captain Bluntschli.

PETKOFF [*to Catherine*] Now, Catherine: it's of you
he's afraid. Press him; and he'll stay.

880 CATHERINE. Of course I shall be only too delighted if
[*appealingly*] Captain Bluntschli really wishes to stay.
He knows my wishes.

BLUNTSCHLI [*in his driest military manner*] I am at
madam's orders.

SERGIUS [*cordially*] That settles it!

PETKOFF [*heartily*] Of course!

RAINA. You see you must stay.

BLUNTSCHLI [*smiling*] Well, if I must, I must.
Gesture of despair from Catherine.

ACT III

*In the library after lunch. It is not much of a library. Its
literary equipment consists of a single fixed shelf
stocked with old paper covered novels, broken backed,
coffee stained, torn and thumbed; and a couple of little
hanging shelves with a few gift books on them: the rest
of the wall space being occupied by trophies of war and
the chase. But it is a most comfortable sitting room. A
row of three large windows shews a mountain
panorama, just now seen in one of its friendliest aspects in the mellowing afternoon light. In the corner
next the right hand window a square earthenware*

*stove, a perfect tower of glistening pottery, rises nearly
to the ceiling and guarantees plenty of warmth. The
ottoman is like that in Raina's room, and similarly
placed; and the window seats are luxurious with decorated cushions. There is one object, however, hopelessly out of keeping with its surroundings. This is a
small kitchen table, much the worse for wear, fitted as
a writing table with an old canister full of pens, an
eggcup filled with ink, and a deplorable scrap of heavily
used pink blotting paper.*

*At the side of this table, which stands to the left of
anyone facing the window, Bluntschli is hard at work
with a couple of maps before him, writing orders. At the
head of it sits Sergius, who is supposed to be also at
work, but is actually gnawing the feather of a pen, and
contemplating Bluntschli's quick, sure, businesslike
progress with a mixture of envious irritation at his own
incapacity and awestruck wonder at an ability which
seems to him almost miraculous, though its prosaic
character forbids him to esteem it. The Major is comfortably established on the ottoman, with a newspaper
in his hand and the tube of his hookah within easy
reach. Catherine sits at the stove, with her back to
them, embroidering. Raina, reclining on the divan, is
gazing in a daydream out at the Balkan landscape, with
a neglected novel in her lap.*

*The door is on the same side as the stove, farther
from the window. The button of the electric bell is at the
opposite side, behind Bluntschli.*

PETKOFF [*looking up from his paper to watch how they
are getting on at the table*] Are you sure I cant help you
in any way, Bluntschli?

BLUNTSCHLI [*without interrupting his writing or
looking up*] Quite sure, thank you. Saranoff and I will
manage it.

SERGIUS [*grimly*] Yes: we'll manage it. He finds out
what to do; draws up the orders; and I sign em. Division
of labor! [*Bluntschli passes him a paper*]. Another one?
Thank you. [*He plants the paper squarely before him; 10
sets his chair carefully parallel to it; and signs with his
cheek on his elbow and his protruded tongue following
the movements of his pen*]. This hand is more accustomed to the sword than to the pen.

PETKOFF. It's very good of you, Bluntschli: it is indeed, to let yourself be put upon in this way. Now are
you quite sure I can do nothing?

CATHERINE [*in a low warning tone*] You can stop
interrupting, Paul.

PETKOFF [*starting and looking round at her*] Eh? 20
Oh! Quite right, my love: quite right. [*He takes his
newspaper up again, but presently lets it drop*]. Ah,
you havnt been campaigning, Catherine: you dont
know how pleasant it is for us to sit here, after a good
lunch, with nothing to do but enjoy ourselves. Theres
only one thing I want to make me thoroughly comfortable.

CATHERINE. What is that?

PETKOFF. My old coat. I'm not at home in this one: I feel as if I were on parade.

CATHERINE. My dear Paul, how absurd you are about that old coat! It must be hanging in the blue closet where you left it.

PETKOFF. My dear Catherine, I tell you Ive looked there. Am I to believe my own eyes or not? [*Catherine rises and crosses the room to press the button of the electric bell*]. What are you shewing off that bell for? [*She looks at him majestically, and silently resumes her chair and her needlework*]. My dear: if you think the obstinacy of your sex can make a coat out of two old dressing gowns of Raina's, your waterproof, and my mackintosh, youre mistaken. Thats exactly what the blue closet contains at present.

Nicola presents himself.

CATHERINE. Nicola: go to the blue closet and bring your master's old coat here: the braided one he wears in the house.

NICOLA. Yes, madam. [*He goes out*].

PETKOFF. Catherine.

CATHERINE. Yes, Paul.

PETKOFF. I bet you any piece of jewellery you like to order from Sofia against a week's housekeeping money that the coat isnt there.

CATHERINE. Done, Paul!

PETKOFF [*excited by the prospect of a gamble*] Come: heres an opportunity for some sport. Wholl bet on it? Bluntschli: I'll give you six to one.

BLUNTSCHLI [*imperturbably*] It would be robbing you, major. Madam is sure to be right. [*Without looking up, he passes another batch of papers to Sergius*].

SERGIUS [*also excited*] Bravo, Switzerland! Major: I bet my best charger against an Arab mare for Raina that Nicola finds the coat in the blue closet.

PETKOFF [*eagerly*] Your best char—

CATHERINE [*hastily interrupting him*] Dont be foolish, Paul. An Arabian mare will cost you 50,000 levas.

RAINA [*suddenly coming out of her picturesque revery*] Really, mother, if you are going to take the jewellery, I dont see why you should grudge me my Arab.

Nicola comes back with the coat, and brings it to Petkoff, who can hardly believe his eyes.

CATHERINE. Where was it, Nicola?

NICOLA. Hanging in the blue closet, madam.

PETKOFF. Well, I am d—

CATHERINE [*stopping him*] Paul!

PETKOFF. I could have sworn it wasnt there. Age is beginning to tell on me. I'm getting hallucinations. [*To Nicola*] Here: help me to change. Excuse me, Bluntschli. [*He begins changing coats, Nicola acting as valet*]. Remember: I didnt take that bet of yours, Sergius. Youd better give Raina that Arab steed your-self, since youve roused her expectations. Eh, Raina? [*He looks round at her; but she is again rapt in the landscape. With a little gush of parental affection and pride, he points her out to them, and says*] She's dreaming, as usual.

SERGIUS. Assuredly she shall not be the loser.

PETKOFF. So much the better for her. *I* shant come off so cheaply, I expect. [*The change is now complete. Nicola goes out with the discarded coat*]. Ah, now I feel at home at last. [*He sits down and takes his newspaper with a grunt of relief*].

BLUNTSCHLI [*to Sergius, handing a paper*] Thats the last order.

PETKOFF [*jumping up*] What! Finished?

BLUNTSCHLI. Finished.

PETKOFF [*with childlike envy*] Havnt you anything for me to sign?

BLUNTSCHLI. Not necessary. His signature will do.

PETKOFF [*inflating his chest and thumping it*] Ah well, I think weve done a thundering good day's work. Can I do anything more?

BLUNTSCHLI. You had better both see the fellows that are to take these. [*Sergius rises*] Pack them off at once; and shew them that Ive marked on the orders the time they should hand them in by. Tell them that if they stop to drink or tell stories—if theyre five minutes late, theyll have the skin taken off their backs.

SERGIUS [*stiffening indignantly*] I'll say so. [*He strides to the door*]. And if one of them is man enough to spit in my face for insulting him, I'll buy his discharge and give him a pension. [*He goes out*].

BLUNTSCHLI [*confidentially*] Just see that he talks to them properly, major, will you?

PETKOFF [*officiously*] Quite right, Bluntschli, quite right. I'll see to it. [*He goes to the door importantly, but hesitates on the threshold*]. By the bye, Catherine, you may as well come too. Theyll be far more frightened of you than of me.

CATHERINE [*putting down her embroidery*] I daresay I had better. You would only splutter at them. [*She goes out, Petkoff holding the door for her and following her*].

BLUNTSCHLI. What an army! They make cannons out of cherry trees; and the officers send for their wives to keep discipline! [*He begins to fold and docket the papers*].

Raina, who has risen from the divan, marches slowly down the room with her hands clasped behind her, and looks mischievously at him.

RAINA. You look ever so much nicer than when we last met. [*He looks up, surprised*]. What have you done to yourself?

BLUNTSCHLI. Washed; brushed; good night's sleep and breakfast. Thats all.

RAINA. Did you get back safely that morning?

BLUNTSCHLI. Quite, thanks.

RAINA. Were they angry with you for running away from Sergius's charge?

BLUNTSCHLI [grinning] No: they were glad; because theyd all just run away themselves.

RAINA [going to the table, and leaning over it towards him] It must have made a lovely story for them: all that about me and my room.

BLUNTSCHLI. Capital story. But I only told it to one of them: a particular friend.

RAINA. On whose discretion you could absolutely rely?

BLUNTSCHLI. Absolutely.

RAINA. Hm! He told it all to my father and Sergius the day you exchanged the prisoners. [She turns away and strolls carelessly across to the other side of the room].

BLUNTSCHLI [deeply concerned, and half incredulous] No! You dont mean that, do you?

RAINA [turning, with sudden earnestness] I do indeed. But they dont know that it was in this house you took refuge. If Sergius knew, he would challenge you and kill you in a duel!

BLUNTSCHLI. Bless me! then dont tell him.

RAINA. Please be serious, Captain Bluntschli. Can you not realize what it is to me to deceive him? I want to be quite perfect with Sergius: no meanness, no smallness, no deceit. My relation to him is the one really beautiful and noble part of my life. I hope you can understand that.

BLUNTSCHLI [sceptically] You mean that you wouldnt like him to find out that the story about the ice pudding was a—a—a—You know.

RAINA [wincing] Ah, dont talk of it in that flippant way. I lied: I know it. But I did it to save your life. He would have killed you. That was the second time I ever uttered a falsehood. [Bluntschli rises quickly and looks doubtfully and somewhat severely at her]. Do you remember the first time?

BLUNTSCHLI. I! No. Was I present?

RAINA. Yes; and I told the officer who was searching for you that you were not present.

BLUNTSCHLI. True. I should have remembered it.

RAINA [greatly encouraged] Ah, it is natural that you should forget it first. It cost you nothing: it cost me a lie! A lie!

She sits down on the ottoman, looking straight before her with her hands clasped round her knee. Bluntschli, quite touched, goes to the ottoman with a particularly reassuring and considerate air, and sits down beside her.

BLUNTSCHLI. My dear young lady, dont let this worry you. Remember: I'm a soldier. Now what are the two things that happen to a soldier so often that he comes to think nothing of them? One is hearing people tell lies [Raina recoils]: the other is getting his life saved in all sorts of ways by all sorts of people.

RAINA [rising in indignant protest] And so he becomes a creature incapable of faith and of gratitude.

BLUNTSCHLI [making a wry face] Do you like gratitude? I dont. If pity is akin to love, gratitude is akin to the other thing.

RAINA. Gratitude! [Turning on him] If you are incapable of gratitude you are incapable of any noble sentiment. Even animals are grateful. Oh, I see now exactly what you think of me! You were not surprised to hear me lie. To you it was something I probably did every day! every hour!! That is how men think of women. [She paces the room tragically].

BLUNTSCHLI [dubiously] Theres reason in everything. You said youd told only two lies in your whole life. Dear young lady: isnt that rather a short allowance? I'm quite a straightforward man myself; but it wouldnt last me a whole morning.

RAINA [staring haughtily at him] Do you know, sir, that you are insulting me?

BLUNTSCHLI. I cant help it. When you strike that noble attitude and speak in that thrilling voice, I admire you; but I find it impossible to believe a single word you say.

RAINA [superbly] Captain Bluntschli!

BLUNTSCHLI [unmoved] Yes?

RAINA [standing over him, as if she could not believe her senses] Do you mean what you said just now? Do you know what you said just now?

BLUNTSCHLI. I do.

RAINA [gasping] I! I!!! [She points to herself incredulously, meaning "I, Raina Petkoff tell lies!" He meets her gaze unflinchingly. She suddenly sits down beside him, and adds, with a complete change of manner from the heroic to a babyish familiarity] How did you find me out?

BLUNTSCHLI [promptly] Instinct, dear young lady. Instinct, and experience of the world.

RAINA [wonderingly] Do you know, you are the first man I ever met who did not take me seriously?

BLUNTSCHLI. You mean, dont you, that I am the first man that has ever taken you quite seriously?

RAINA. Yes: I suppose I do mean that. [Cosily, quite at her ease with him] How strange it is to be talked to in such a way! You know, Ive always gone on like that.

BLUNTSCHLI. You mean the—?

RAINA. I mean the noble attitude and the thrilling voice. [They laugh together]. I did it when I was a tiny child to my nurse. She believed in it. I do it before my parents. They believe in it. I do it before Sergius. He believes in it.

BLUNTSCHLI. Yes: he's a little in that line himself, isnt he?

RAINA [startled] Oh! Do you think so?

BLUNTSCHLI. You know him better than I do.

RAINA. I wonder—I wonder is he? If I thought that—! [*Discouraged*] Ah, well: what does it matter? I suppose now youve found me out, you despise me.

BLUNTSCHLI [*warmly, rising*] No, my dear young lady, no, no, no a thousand times. It's part of your youth: part of your charm. I'm like all the rest of them: the nurse, your parents, Sergius: I'm your infatuated admirer.

RAINA [*pleased*] Really?

BLUNTSCHLI [*slapping his breast smartly with his hand, German fashion*] Hand aufs Herz!° Really and truly.

RAINA [*very happy*] But what did you think of me for giving you my portrait?

BLUNTSCHLI [*astonished*] Your portrait! You never gave me your portrait.

RAINA [*quickly*] Do you mean to say you never got it?

BLUNTSCHLI. No. [*He sits down beside her, with renewed interest, and says, with some complacency*] When did you send it to me?

RAINA [*indignantly*] I did not send it to you. [*She turns her head away, and adds, reluctantly*] It was in the pocket of that coat.

BLUNTSCHLI [*pursing his lips and rounding his eyes*] Oh-o-oh! I never found it. It must be there still.

RAINA [*springing up*] There still! for my father to find the first time he puts his hand in his pocket! Oh, how could you be so stupid?

BLUNTSCHLI [*rising also*] It doesnt matter: I suppose it's only a photograph: how can he tell who it was intended for? Tell him he put it there himself.

RAINA [*bitterly*] Yes: that is so clever! isnt it? [*Distractedly*] Oh! what shall I do?

BLUNTSCHLI. Ah, I see. You wrote something on it. That was rash.

RAINA [*vexed almost to tears*] Oh, to have done such a thing for you, who care no more—except to laugh at me—oh! Are you sure nobody has touched it?

BLUNTSCHLI. Well. I cant be quite sure. You see, I couldnt carry it about with me all the time: one cant take much luggage on active service.

RAINA. What did you do with it?

BLUNTSCHLI. When I got through to Pirot I had to put it in safe keeping somehow. I thought of the railway cloak room; but thats the surest place to get looted in modern warfare. So I pawned it.

RAINA. Pawned it!!!

BLUNTSCHLI. I know it doesnt sound nice; but it was much the safest plan. I redeemed it the day before yesterday. Heaven only knows whether the pawnbroker cleared out the pockets or not.

RAINA [*furious: throwing the words right into his face*] You have a low shopkeeping mind. You think of things that would never come into a gentleman's head.

259 **Hand aufs Herz,** German expression meaning "hand on heart" or "cross my heart"

BLUNTSCHLI [*phlegmatically*] Thats the Swiss national character, dear lady. [*He returns to the table*].

RAINA. Oh, I wish I had never met you. [*She flounces away, and sits at the window fuming*].

Louka comes in with a heap of letters and telegrams on her salver, and crosses, with her bold free gait, to the table. Her left sleeve is looped up to the shoulder with a brooch, shewing her naked arm, with a broad gilt bracelet covering the bruise.

LOUKA [*to Bluntschli*] For you. [*She empties the salver with a fling on to the table*]. The messenger is waiting. [*She is determined not to be civil to an enemy, even if she must bring him his letters*].

BLUNTSCHLI [*to Raina*] Will you excuse me: the last postal delivery that reached me was three weeks ago. These are the subsequent accumulations. Four telegrams: a week old. [*He opens one*]. Oho! Bad news!

RAINA [*rising and advancing a little remorsefully*] Bad news?

BLUNTSCHLI. My father's dead. [*He looks at the telegram with his lips pursed, musing on the unexpected changes in his arrangements. Louka crosses herself hastily*].

RAINA. Oh, how very sad!

BLUNTSCHLI. Yes: I shall have to start for home in an hour. He has left a lot of big hotels behind him to be looked after. [*He takes up a fat letter in a long blue envelope*]. Here's a whacking letter from the family solicitor. [*He pulls out the enclosures and glances over them*]. Great Heavens! Seventy! Two hundred! [*In a crescendo of dismay*] Four hundred! Four thousand!! Nine thousand six hundred!!! What on earth am I to do with them all?

RAINA [*timidly*] Nine thousand hotels?

BLUNTSCHLI. Hotels! nonsense. If you only knew! Oh, it's too ridiculous! Excuse me: I must give my fellow orders about starting. [*He leaves the room hastily, with the documents in his hand*].

LOUKA [*knowing instinctively that she cannot annoy Raina by disparaging Bluntschli*] He has not much heart that Swiss. He has not a word of grief for his poor father.

RAINA [*bitterly*] Grief! A man who has been doing nothing but killing people for years! What does he care? What does any soldier care? [*She goes to the door, restraining her tears with difficulty*].

LOUKA. Major Saranoff has been fighting too; and he has plenty of heart left. [*Raina, at the door, draws herself up haughtily and goes out*]. Aha! I thought you wouldnt get much feeling out of your soldier. [*She is following Raina when Nicola enters with an armful of logs for the stove*].

NICOLA [*grinning amorously at her*] Ive been trying all the afternoon to get a minute alone with you, my girl. [*His countenance changes as he notices her arm*]. Why, what fashion is that of wearing your sleeve, child?

LOUKA [*proudly*] My own fashion.

NICOLA. Indeed! If the mistress catches you, she'll talk to you. [*He puts the logs down, and seats himself comfortably on the ottoman*].

LOUKA. Is that any reason why you should take it on yourself to talk to me?

NICOLA. Come! dont be so contrary with me. Ive some good news for you. [*She sits down beside him. He takes out some paper money. Louka, with an eager gleam in her eyes, tries to snatch it; but he shifts it quickly to his left hand, out of her reach*]. See! a twenty leva bill! Sergius gave me that, out of pure swagger. A fool and his money are soon parted. Theres ten levas more. The Swiss gave me that for backing up the mistress's and Raina's lies about him. He's no fool, he isnt. You should have heard old Catherine downstairs as polite as you please to me, telling me not to mind the Major being a little impatient; for they knew what a good servant I was—after making a fool and liar of me before them all! The twenty will go to our savings and you shall have the ten to spend if youll only talk to me so as to remind me I'm a human being. I get tired of being a servant occasionally.

LOUKA. Yes: sell your manhood for 30 levas, and buy me for 10! [*Rising scornfully*] Keep your money. You were born to be a servant. I was not. When you set up your shop you will only be everybody's servant instead of somebody's servant. [*She goes moodily to the table and seats herself regally in Sergius's chair*].

NICOLA [*picking up his logs, and going to the stove*] Ah, wait til you see. We shall have our evenings to ourselves; and I shall be master in my own house, I promise you. [*He throws the logs down and kneels at the stove*].

LOUKA. You shall never be master in mine.

NICOLA [*turning, still on his knees, and squatting down rather forlornly on his calves, daunted by her implacable disdain*] You have a great ambition in you, Louka. Remember: if any luck comes to you, it was I that made a woman of you.

LOUKA. You!

NICOLA [*scrambling up and going at her*] Yes, me. Who was it made you give up wearing a couple of pounds of false black hair on your head and reddening your lips and cheeks like any other Bulgarian girl! I did. Who taught you to trim your nails, and keep your hands clean, and be dainty about yourself, like a fine Russian lady? Me: do you hear that? me! [*She tosses her head defiantly; and he turns away, adding, more coolly*] Ive often thought that if Raina were out of the way, and you just a little less of a fool and Sergius just a little more of one, you might come to be one of my grandest customers, instead of only being my wife and costing me money.

LOUKA. I believe you would rather be my servant than my husband. You would make more out of me. Oh, I know that soul of yours.

NICOLA [*going closer to her for greater emphasis*] Never you mind my soul; but just listen to my advice. If you want to be a lady, your present behavior to me wont do at all, unless when we're alone. It's too sharp and impudent; and impudence is a sort of familiarity: it shews affection for me. And dont you try being high and mighty with me, either. Youre like all country girls: you think it's genteel to treat a servant the way I treat a stableboy. Thats only your ignorance; and dont you forget it. And dont be so ready to defy everybody. Act as if you expected to have your own way, not as if you expected to be ordered about. The way to get on as a lady is the same as the way to get on as a servant: youve got to know your place: thats the secret of it. And you may depend on me to know my place if you get promoted. Think over it, my girl. I'll stand by you: one servant should always stand by another.

LOUKA [*rising impatiently*] Oh, I must behave in my own way. You take all the courage out of me with your cold-blooded wisdom. Go and put those logs on the fire: thats the sort of thing you understand.

Before Nicola can retort, Sergius comes in. He checks himself a moment on seeing Louka; then goes to the stove.

SERGIUS [*to Nicola*] I am not in the way of your work, I hope.

NICOLA [*in a smooth, elderly manner*] Oh no, sir: thank you kindly. I was only speaking to this foolish girl about her habit of running up here to the library whenever she gets a chance, to look at the books. Thats the worst of her education, sir: it gives her habits above her station. [*To Louka*] Make that table tidy, Louka, for the Major. [*He goes out sedately*].

Louka, without looking at Sergius, pretends to arrange the papers on the table. He crosses slowly to her, and studies the arrangement of her sleeve reflectively.

SERGIUS. Let me see: is there a mark there? [*He turns up the bracelet and sees the bruise made by his grasp. She stands motionless, not looking at him: fascinated, but on her guard*]. Ffff! Does it hurt?

LOUKA. Yes.

SERGIUS. Shall I cure it?

LOUKA [*instantly withdrawing herself proudly, but still not looking at him*] No. You cannot cure it now.

SERGIUS [*masterfully*] Quite sure? [*He makes a movement as if to take her in his arms*].

LOUKA. Dont trifle with me, please. An officer should not trifle with a servant.

SERGIUS [*indicating the bruise with a merciless stroke of his forefinger*] That was no trifle, Louka.

LOUKA [*flinching; then looking at him for the first time*] Are you sorry?

SERGIUS [*with measured emphasis, folding his arms*] I am never sorry.

LOUKA [*wistfully*] I wish I could believe a man could be as unlike a woman as that. I wonder are you really a brave man?

SERGIUS [*unaffectedly, relaxing his attitude*] Yes: I am a brave man. My heart jumped like a woman's at the first shot; but in the charge I found that I was brave. Yes: that at least is real about me.

LOUKA. Did you find in the charge that the men whose fathers are poor like mine were any less brave than the men who are rich like you.

SERGIUS [with bitter levity] Not a bit. They all slashed and cursed and yelled like heroes. Psha! the courage to rage and kill is cheap. I have an English bull terrier who has as much of that sort of courage as the whole Bulgarian nation, and the whole Russian nation at its back. But he lets my groom thrash him, all the same. Thats your soldier all over! No, Louka: your poor men can cut throats; but they are afraid of their officers; they put up with insults and blows; they stand by and see one another punished like children: aye, and help to do it when they are ordered. And the officers!!! Well [with a short harsh laugh] I am an officer. Oh, [fervently] give me the man who will defy to the death any power on earth or in heaven that sets itself up against his own will and conscience: he alone is the brave man.

LOUKA. How easy it is to talk! Men never seem to me to grow up: they all have schoolboy's ideas. You dont know what true courage is.

SERGIUS [ironically] Indeed! I am willing to be instructed. [He sits on the ottoman, sprawling magnificently].

LOUKA. Look at me! how much am I allowed to have my own will? I have to get your room ready for you: to sweep and dust, to fetch and carry. How could that degrade me if it did not degrade you to have it done for you? But [with subdued passion] if I were Empress of Russia, above everyone in the world, then!! Ah then, though according to you I could shew no courage at all, you should see, you should see.

SERGIUS. What would you do, most noble Empress?

LOUKA. I would marry the man I loved, which no other queen in Europe has the courage to do. If I loved you, though you would be as far beneath me as I am beneath you, I would dare to be the equal of my inferior. Would you dare as much if you loved me? No: if you felt the beginnings of love for me you would not let it grow. You would not dare: you would marry a rich man's daughter because you would be afraid of what other people would say of you.

SERGIUS [bounding up] You lie: it is not so, by all the stars! If I loved you, and I were the Czar himself, I would set you on the throne by my side. You know that I love another woman, a woman as high above you as heaven is above earth. And you are jealous of her.

LOUKA. I have no reason to be. She will never marry you now. The man I told you of has come back. She will marry the Swiss.

SERGIUS [recoiling] The Swiss!

LOUKA. A man worth ten of you. Then you can come to me; and I will refuse you. You are not good enough for me. [She turns to the door].

SERGIUS [springing after her and catching her fiercely in his arms] I will kill the Swiss; and afterwards I will do as I please with you.

LOUKA [in his arms, passive and steadfast] The Swiss will kill you, perhaps. He has beaten you in love. He may beat you in war.

SERGIUS [tormentedly] Do you think I believe that she—she! whose worst thoughts are higher than your best ones, is capable of trifling with another man behind my back?

LOUKA. Do you think she would believe the Swiss if he told her now that I am in your arms?

SERGIUS [releasing her in despair] Damnation! Oh, damnation! Mockery! mockery everywhere! everything I think is mocked by everything I do. [He strikes himself frantically on the breast]. Coward! liar! fool! Shall I kill myself like a man, or live and pretend to laugh at myself? [She again turns to go]. Louka! [She stops near the door]. Remember: you belong to me.

LOUKA [turning] What does that mean? An insult?

SERGIUS [commandingly] It means that you love me, and that I have had you here in my arms, and will perhaps have you there again. Whether that is an insult I neither know nor care: take it as you please. But [vehemently] I will not be a coward and a trifler. If I choose to love you, I dare marry you, in spite of all Bulgaria. If these hands ever touch you again, they shall touch my affianced bride.

LOUKA. We shall see whether you dare keep your word. And take care. I will not wait long.

SERGIUS [again folding his arms and standing motionless in the middle of the room] Yes: we shall see. And you shall wait my pleasure.

Bluntschli, much preoccupied, with his papers still in his hand, enters, leaving the door open for Louka to go out. He goes across to the table, glancing at her as he passes. Sergius, without altering his resolute attitude, watches him steadily. Louka goes out, leaving the door open.

BLUNTSCHLI [absently, sitting at the table as before, and putting down his papers] Thats a remarkable looking young woman.

SERGIUS [gravely, without moving] Captain Bluntschli.

BLUNTSCHLI. Eh?

SERGIUS. You have deceived me. You are my rival. I brook no rivals. At six oclock I shall be in the drilling-ground on the Klissoura road, alone, on horseback, with my sabre. Do you understand?

BLUNTSCHLI [staring, but sitting quite at his ease] Oh, thank you: thats a cavalry man's proposal. I'm in the artillery; and I have the choice of weapons. If I go,

I shall take a machine gun. And there shall be no mistake about the cartridges this time.

SERGIUS [flushing, but with deadly coldness] Take care, sir. It is not our custom in Bulgaria to allow invitations of that kind to be trifled with.

BLUNTSCHLI [warmly] Pooh! dont talk to me about Bulgaria. You dont know what fighting is. But have it your own way. Bring your sabre along. I'll meet you.

SERGIUS [fiercely delighted to find his opponent a man of spirit] Well said. Switzer. Shall I lend you my best horse?

BLUNTSCHLI. No: damn your horse! thank you all the same, my dear fellow. [Raina comes in, and hears the next sentence]. I shall fight you on foot. Horseback's too dangerous: I dont want to kill you if I can help it.

RAINA [hurrying forward anxiously] I have heard what Captain Bluntschli said, Sergius. You are going to fight. Why? [Sergius turns away in silence, and goes to the stove, where he stands watching her as she continues, to Bluntschli] What about?

BLUNTSCHLI. I dont know: he hasnt told me. Better not interfere, dear young lady. No harm will be done: Ive often acted as sword instructor. He wont be able to touch me; and I'll not hurt him. It will save explanations. In the morning I shall be off home; and youll never see me or hear of me again. You and he will then make it up and live happily ever after.

RAINA [turning away deeply hurt, almost with a sob in her voice] I never said I wanted to see you again.

SERGIUS [striding forward] Ha! That is a confession.

RAINA [haughtily] What do you mean?

SERGIUS. You love that man!

RAINA [scandalized] Sergius!

SERGIUS. You allow him to make love to you behind my back, just as you treat me as your affianced husband behind his. Bluntschli: you knew our relations; you deceived me. It is for that I call you to account, not for having received favors I never enjoyed.

BLUNTSCHLI [jumping up indignantly] Stuff! Rubbish! I have received no favors. Why, the young lady doesnt even know whether I'm married or not.

RAINA [forgetting herself] Oh! [Collapsing on the ottoman] Are you?

SERGIUS. You see the young lady's concern, Captain Bluntschli. Denial is useless. You have enjoyed the privilege of being received in her own room, late at night—

BLUNTSCHLI [interrupting him pepperily] Yes, you blockhead she received me with a pistol at her head. Your cavalry were at my heels. I'd have blown out her brains if she'd uttered a cry.

SERGIUS [taken aback] Bluntschli! Raina: is this true?

RAINA [rising in wrathful majesty] Oh, how dare you, how dare you?

BLUNTSCHLI. Apologize, man: apologize. [He resumes his seat at the table].

SERGIUS [with the old measured emphasis, folding his arms] I never apologize!

RAINA [passionately] This is the doing of that friend of yours, Captain Bluntschli. It is he who is spreading this horrible story about me. [She walks about excitedly].

BLUNTSCHLI. No: he's dead. Burnt alive.

RAINA [stopping, shocked] Burnt alive!

BLUNTSCHLI. Shot in the hip in a woodyard. Couldnt drag himself out. Your fellows' shells set the timber on fire and burnt him, with a half a dozen other poor devils in the same predicament.

RAINA. How horrible!

SERGIUS. And how ridiculous! Oh, war! war! the dream of patriots and heroes! A fraud, Bluntschli. A hollow sham, like love.

RAINA [outraged] Like love! You say that before me!

BLUNTSCHLI. Come, Saranoff: that matter is explained.

SERGIUS. A hollow sham, I say. Would you have come back here if nothing had passed between you except at the muzzle of your pistol? Raina is mistaken about your friend who was burnt. He was not my informant.

RAINA. Who then? [Suddenly guessing the truth] Ah, Louka! my maid! my servant! You were with her this morning all that time after—after—Oh, what sort of god is this I have been worshipping! [He meets her gaze with sardonic enjoyment of her disenchantment. Angered all the more, she goes closer to him, and says, in a lower, intenser tone] Do you know that I looked out of the window as I went upstairs, to have another sight of my hero; and I saw something I did not understand then. I know now that you were making love to her.

SERGIUS [with grim humor] You saw that?

RAINA. Only too well. [She turns away, and throws herself on the divan under the centre window, quite overcome].

SERGIUS [cynically] Raina: our romance is shattered. Life's a farce.

BLUNTSCHLI [to Raina, whimsically] You see: he's found himself out now.

SERGIUS [going to him] Bluntschli: I have allowed you to call me a blockhead. You may now call me a coward as well. I refuse to fight you. Do you know why?

BLUNTSCHLI. No; but it doesnt matter. I didnt ask the reason when you cried on; and I dont ask the reason now that you cry off. I'm a professional soldier: I fight when I have to, and am very glad to get out of it when I havnt to. Youre only an amateur: you think fighting's an amusement.

SERGIUS [*sitting down at the table, nose to nose with him*] You shall hear the reason all the same, my professional. The reason is that it takes two men—real men—men of heart, blood and honor—to make a genuine combat. I could no more fight with you than I could make love to an ugly woman. Youve no magnetism: youre not a man: youre a machine.

BLUNTSCHLI [*apologetically*] Quite true, quite true. I always was that sort of chap. I'm very sorry.

SERGIUS. Psha!

BLUNTSCHLI. But now that youve found that life isnt a farce, but something quite sensible and serious, what further obstacle is there to your happiness?

RAINA [*rising*] You are very solicitous about my happiness and his. Do you forget his new love—Louka? It is not you that he must fight now, but his rival, Nicola.

SERGIUS. Rival!! [*bounding half across the room*].

RAINA. Dont you know that theyre engaged?

SERGIUS. Nicola! Are fresh abysses opening? Nicola!!

RAINA [*sarcastically*] A shocking sacrifice, isnt it? Such beauty! such intellect! such modesty! wasted on a middle-aged servant man. Really, Sergius, you cannot stand by and allow such a thing. It would be unworthy of your chivalry.

SERGIUS [*losing all self-control*] Viper! Viper! [*He rushes to and fro, raging*].

BLUNTSCHLI. Look here, Saranoff: youre getting the worst of this.

RAINA [*getting angrier*] Do you realize what he has done, Captain Bluntschli? He has set this girl as a spy on us; and her reward is that he makes love to her.

SERGIUS. False! Monstrous!

RAINA. Monstrous! [*Confronting him*] Do you deny that she told you about Captain Bluntschli being in my room?

SERGIUS. No; but—

RAINA [*interrupting*] Do you deny that you were making love to her when she told you?

SERGIUS. No; but I tell you—

RAINA [*cutting him short contemptuously*] It is unnecessary to tell us anything more. That is quite enough for us. [*She turns away from him and sweeps majestically back to the window*].

BLUNTSCHLI [*quietly, as Sergius, in an agony of mortification, sinks on the ottoman, clutching his averted head between his fists*] I told you you were getting the worst of it, Saranoff.

SERGIUS. Tiger cat!

RAINA [*running excitedly to Bluntschli*] You hear this man calling me names, Captain Bluntschli?

BLUNTSCHLI. What else can he do, dear lady? He must defend himself somehow. Come [*very persuasively*]: dont quarrel. What good does it do?

Raina, with a gasp, sits down on the ottoman, and after a vain effort to look vexedly at Bluntschli, falls a victim to her sense of humor, and actually leans back babyishly against the writhing shoulder of Sergius.

SERGIUS. Engaged to Nicola! Ha! ha! Ah well, Bluntschli, you are right to take this huge imposture of a world coolly.

RAINA [*quaintly to Bluntschli, with an intuitive guess at his state of mind*] I daresay you think us a couple of grown-up babies, dont you?

SERGIUS [*grinning savagely*] He does: he does. Swiss civilization nursetending Bulgarian barbarism, eh?

BLUNTSCHLI [*blushing*] Not at all, I assure you. I'm only very glad to get you two quieted. There! there! let's be pleasant and talk it over in a friendly way. Where is this other young lady?

RAINA. Listening at the door, probably.

SERGIUS [*shivering as if a bullet had struck him, and speaking with quiet but deep indignation*] I will prove that that, at least, is a calumny. [*He goes with dignity to the door and opens it. A yell of fury bursts from him as he looks out. He darts into the passage, and returns dragging in Louka, whom he flings violently against the table, exclaiming*] Judge her, Bluntschli. You, the cool impartial man: judge the eavesdropper.

Louka stands her ground, proud and silent.

BLUNTSCHLI [*shaking his head*] I mustnt judge her. I once listened myself outside a tent when there was a mutiny brewing. It's all a question of the degree of provocation. My life was at stake.

LOUKA. My love was at stake. I am not ashamed.

RAINA [*contemptuously*] Your love! Your curiosity, you mean.

LOUKA [*facing her and retorting her contempt with interest*] My love, stronger than anything you can feel, even for your chocolate cream soldier.

SERGIUS [*with quick suspicion, to Louka*] What does that mean?

LOUKA [*fiercely*] It means—

SERGIUS [*interrupting her slightingly*] Oh, I remember: the ice pudding. A paltry taunt, girl!

Major Petkoff enters, in his shirtsleeves.

PETKOFF. Excuse my shirtsleeves, gentlemen. Raina: somebody has been wearing that coat of mine: I'll swear it. Somebody with a differently shaped back. It's all burst open at the sleeve. Your mother is mending it. I wish she'd make haste: I shall catch cold. [*He looks more attentively at them*]. Is anything the matter?

RAINA. No. [*She sits down at the stove, with a tranquil air*].

SERGIUS. Oh no. [*He sits down at the end of the table, as at first*].

BLUNTSCHLI [*who is already seated*] Nothing. Nothing.

PETKOFF [*sitting down on the ottoman in his old place*] Thats all right. [*He notices Louka*]. Anything the matter, Louka?

LOUKA. No, sir.

PETKOFF [*genially*] Thats all right. [*He sneezes*] Go and ask your mistress for my coat, like a good girl, will you?

Nicola enters with the coat. Louka makes a pretence of having business in the room by taking the little table with the hookah away to the wall near the windows.

RAINA [*rising quickly as she sees the coat on Nicola's arm*] Here it is, papa. Give it to me, Nicola; and do you put some more wood on the fire. [*She takes the coat, and brings it to the Major, who stands up to put it on. Nicola attends to the fire*].

PETKOFF [*to Raina, teasing her affectionately*] Aha! Going to be very good to poor old papa just for one day after his return from the wars, eh?

RAINA [*with solemn reproach*] Ah, how can you say that to me, father?

PETKOFF. Well, well, only a joke, little one. Come: give me a kiss. [*She kisses him*]. Now give me the coat.

RAINA. No: I am going to put it on for you. Turn your back. [*He turns his back and feels behind him with his arms for the sleeves. She dexterously takes the photograph from the pocket and throws it on the table before Bluntschli, who covers it with a sheet of paper under the very nose of Sergius, who looks on amazed, with his suspicions roused in the highest degree. She then helps Petkoff on with his coat*]. There, dear! Now are you comfortable?

PETKOFF. Quite, little love. Thanks. [*He sits down; and Raina returns to her seat near the stove*]. Oh, by the bye, I've found something funny. Whats the meaning of this? [*He puts his hand into the picked pocket*]. Eh? Hallo! [*He tries the other pocket*]. Well, I could have sworn—! [*Much puzzled, he tries the breast pocket*]. I wonder—[*trying the original pocket*]. Where can it—? [*He rises, exclaiming*] Your mother's taken it!.

RAINA [*very red*] Taken what?

PETKOFF. Your photograph, with the inscription: "Raina, to her Chocolate Cream Soldier: a Souvenir." Now you know theres something more in this than meets the eye; and I'm going to find it out. [*Shouting*] Nicola!

NICOLA [*coming to him*] Sir!

PETKOFF. Did you spoil any pastry of Miss Raina's this morning?

NICOLA. You heard Miss Raina say that I did, sir.

PETKOFF. I know that, you idiot. Was it true?

NICOLA. I am sure Miss Raina is incapable of saying anything that is not true, sir.

PETKOFF. Are you? Then I'm not. [*Turning to the others*] Come: do you think I dont see it all? [*He goes to Sergius, and slaps him on the shoulder*]. Sergius: youre the chocolate cream soldier, arnt you?

SERGIUS [*starting up*] I! A chocolate cream soldier! Certainly not.

PETKOFF. Not! [*He looks at them. They are all very serious and very conscious*]. Do you mean to tell me that Raina sends things like that to other men?

SERGIUS [*enigmatically*] The world is not such an innocent place as we used to think, Petkoff.

BLUNTSCHLI [*rising*] It's all right, Major. I'm the chocolate cream soldier. [*Petkoff and Sergius are equally astonished*]. The gracious young lady saved my life by giving me chocolate creams when I was starving: shall I ever forget their flavour! My late friend Stolz told you the story at Pirot. I was the fugitive.

PETKOFF. You! [*He gasps*]. Sergius: do you remember how those two women went on this morning when we mentioned it? [*Sergius smiles cynically. Petkoff confronts Raina severely*]. Youre a nice young woman, arnt you?

RAINA [*bitterly*] Major Saranoff has changed his mind. And when I wrote that on the photograph, I did not know that Captain Bluntschli was married.

BLUNTSCHLI [*startled into vehement protest*] I'm not married.

RAINA [*with deep reproach*] You said you were.

BLUNTSCHLI. I did not. I positively did not. I never was married in my life.

PETKOFF [*exasperated*] Raina: will you kindly inform me, if I am not asking too much, which of these gentlemen you are engaged to?

RAINA. To neither of them. This young lady [*introducing Louka, who faces them all proudly*] is the object of Major Saranoff's affections at present.

PETKOFF. Louka! Are you mad, Sergius? Why, this girl's engaged to Nicola.

NICOLA. I beg your pardon, sir. There is a mistake. Louka is not engaged to me.

PETKOFF. Not engaged to you, you scoundrel! Why, you had twenty-five levas from me on the day of your betrothal; and she had that gilt bracelet from Miss Raina.

NICOLA [*with cool unction*] We gave it out so, sir. But it was only to give Louka protection. She had a soul above her station; and I have been no more than her confidential servant. I intend, as you know, sir, to set up a shop later on in Sofia; and I look forward to her custom and recommendation should she marry into the nobility. [*He goes out with impressive discretion, leaving them all staring after him*].

PETKOFF [*breaking the silence*] Well, I am—hm!

SERGIUS. This is either the finest heroism or the most crawling baseness. Which is it, Bluntschli?

BLUNTSCHLI. Never mind whether it's heroism or baseness. Nicola's the ablest man Ive met in Bulgaria. I'll make him manager of a hotel if he can speak French and German.

LOUKA [*suddenly breaking out at Sergius*] I have been insulted by everyone here. You set them the example. You owe me an apology.

Sergius, like a repeating clock of which the spring
930 *has been touched, immediately begins to fold his arms.*

BLUNTSCHLI [*before he can speak*] It's no use. He never apologizes.

LOUKA. Not to you, his equal and his enemy. To me, his poor servant, he will not refuse to apologize.

SERGIUS [*approvingly*] You are right. [*He bends his knee in his grandest manner*] Forgive me.

LOUKA. I forgive you. [*She timidly gives him her hand, which he kisses*]. That touch makes me your
940 affianced wife.

SERGIUS [*springing up*] Ah! I forgot that.

LOUKA [*coldly*] You can withdraw if you like.

SERGIUS. Withdraw! Never! You belong to me. [*He puts his arm about her*].

Catherine comes in and finds Louka in Sergius's arms, with all the rest gazing at them in bewildered astonishment.

CATHERINE. What does this mean?

Sergius releases Louka.

950 PETKOFF. Well, my dear, it appears that Sergius is going to marry Louka instead of Raina. [*She is about to break out indignantly at him: he stops her by exclaiming testily*] Dont blame me: Ive nothing to do with it. [*He retreats to the stove*].

CATHERINE. Marry Louka! Sergius: you are bound by your word to us!

SERGIUS [*folding his arms*] Nothing binds me.

BLUNTSCHLI [*much pleased by this piece of common sense*] Saranoff: your hand. My congratulations.
960 These heroics of yours have their practical side after all. [*To Louka*] Gracious young lady: the best wishes of a good Republican! [*He kisses her hand, to Raina's great disgust, and returns to his seat*].

CATHERINE. Louka: you have been telling stories.

LOUKA. I have done Raina no harm.

CATHERINE [*haughtily*] Raina!

Raina, equally indignant, almost snorts at the liberty.

LOUKA. I have a right to call her Raina: she calls me
970 Louka. I told Major Saranoff she would never marry him if the Swiss gentleman came back.

BLUNTSCHLI [*rising, much surprised*] Hallo!

LOUKA [*turning to Raina*] I thought you were fonder of him than of Sergius. You know best whether I was right.

BLUNTSCHLI. What nonsense! I assure you, my dear Major, my dear Madam, the gracious young lady simply saved my life, nothing else. She never cared two straws for me. Why, bless my heart and soul, look at the young lady and look at me. She, rich, young, 980 beautiful, with her imagination full of fairy princes and noble natures and cavalry charges and goodness knows what! And I, a commonplace Swiss soldier who hardly knows what a decent life is after fifteen years of barracks and battles: a vagabond, a man who has spoiled all his chances in life through an incurably romantic disposition, a man—

SERGIUS [*starting as if a needle had pricked him and interrupting Bluntschli in incredulous amazement*] Excuse me, Bluntschli: what did you say had spoiled your 990 chances in life?

BLUNTSCHLI [*promptly*] An incurably romantic disposition. I ran away from home twice when I was a boy. I went into the army instead of into my father's business. I climbed the balcony of this house when a man of sense would have dived into the nearest cellar. I came sneaking back here to have another look at the young lady when any other man of my age would have sent the coat back—

PETKOFF. My coat! 1000

BLUNTSCHLI. —yes: thats the coat I mean—would have sent it back and gone quietly home. Do you suppose I am the sort of fellow a young girl falls in love with? Why, look at our ages! I'm thirty-four: I dont suppose the young lady is much over seventeen. [*This estimate produces a marked sensation, all the rest turning and staring at one another. He proceeds innocently*] All that adventure which was life or death to me, was only a schoolgirl's game to her—chocolate 1010 creams and hide and seek. Heres the proof! [*He takes the photograph from the table*]. Now, I ask you, would a woman who took the affair seriously have sent me this and written on it "Raina, to her Chocolate Cream Soldier: a Souvenir"? [*He exhibits the photograph triumphantly, as if it settled the matter beyond all possibility of refutation*].

PETKOFF. Thats what I was looking for. How the deuce did it get there? [*He comes from the stove to look at it, and sits down at the ottoman*].

BLUNTSCHLI [*to Raina, complacently*] I have put 1020 everything right, I hope, gracious young lady.

RAINA [*going to the table to face him*] I quite agree with your account of yourself. You are a romantic idiot. [*Bluntschli is unspeakably taken aback*]. Next time, I hope you will know the difference between a schoolgirl of seventeen and a woman of twenty-three.

BLUNTSCHLI [*stupefied*] Twenty-three!

Raina snaps the photograph contemptuously from his hand; tears it up; throws the pieces in his face; and sweeps back to her former place. 1030

SERGIUS [*with grim enjoyment of his rival's discomfiture*] Bluntschli: my one last belief is gone. Your sagacity is a fraud, like everything else. You have less sense than even I!

BLUNTSCHLI [*overwhelmed*] Twenty-three! Twenty-three!! [*He considers*]. Hm! [*Swiftly making up his mind and coming to his host*] In that case, Major Petkoff, I beg to propose formally to become a suitor for your daughter's hand, in place of Major Saranoff retired.

RAINA. You dare!

BLUNTSCHLI. If you were twenty-three when you said those things to me this afternoon, I shall take them seriously.

CATHERINE [loftily polite] I doubt, sir, whether you quite realize either my daughter's position or that of Major Sergius Saranoff, whose place you propose to take. The Petkoffs and the Saranoffs are known as the richest and most important families in the country. Our position is almost historical: we can go back for twenty years.

PETKOFF. Oh never mind that, Catherine. [To Bluntschli] We should be most happy, Bluntschli, if it were only a question of your position; but hang it, you know, Raina is accustomed to a very comfortable establishment. Sergius keeps twenty horses.

BLUNTSCHLI. But who wants twenty horses? We're not going to keep a circus.

CATHERINE [severely] My daughter, sir, is accustomed to a first-rate stable.

RAINA. Hush, mother: you're making me ridiculous.

BLUNTSCHLI. Oh well, if it comes to a question of an establishment, here goes! [He darts impetuously to the table; seizes the papers in the blue envelope; and turns to Sergius] How many horses did you say?

SERGIUS. Twenty, noble Switzer.

BLUNTSCHLI. I have two hundred horses. [They are amazed]. How many carriages?

SERGIUS. Three.

BLUNTSCHLI. I have seventy. Twenty-four of them will hold twelve inside, besides two on the box, without counting the driver and conductor. How many tablecloths have you?

SERGIUS. How the deuce do I know?

BLUNTSCHLI. Have you four thousand?

SERGIUS. No.

BLUNTSCHLI. I have. I have nine thousand six hundred pairs of sheets and blankets, with two thousand four hundred eider-down quilts. I have ten thousand knives and forks, and the same quantity of dessert spoons. I have three hundred servants. I have six palatial establishments, besides two livery stables, a tea garden, and a private house. I have four medals for distinguished services; I have the rank of an officer and the standing of a gentleman; and I have three native languages. Shew me any man in Bulgaria that can offer as much!

PETKOFF [with childish awe] Are you Emperor of Switzerland?

BLUNTSCHLI. My rank is the highest known in Switzerland: I am a free citizen.

CATHERINE. Then, Captain Bluntschli, since you are my daughter's choice—

RAINA [mutinously] He's not.

CATHERINE [ignoring her]—I shall not stand in the way of her happiness. [Petkoff is about to speak] That is Major Petkoff's feeling also.

PETKOFF. Oh, I shall be only too glad. Two hundred horses! Whew!

SERGIUS. What says the lady?

RAINA [pretending to sulk] The lady says that he can keep his tablecloths and his omnibuses. I am not here to be sold to the highest bidder. [She turns her back on him].

BLUNTSCHLI. I wont take that answer. I appealed to you as a fugitive, a beggar, and a starving man. You accepted me. You gave me your hand to kiss, your bed to sleep in, and your roof to shelter me.

RAINA. I did not give them to the Emperor of Switzerland.

BLUNTSCHLI. Thats just what I say. [He catches her by the shoulders and turns her face-to-face with him]. Now tell us whom you did give them to.

RAINA [succumbing with a shy smile] To my chocolate cream soldier.

BLUNTSCHLI [with a boyish laugh of delight] Thatll do. Thank you. [He looks at his watch and suddenly becomes businesslike]. Time's up, Major. Youve managed those regiments so well that youre sure to be asked to get rid of some of the infantry of the Timok division. Send them home by way of Lom Palanka. Saranoff: dont get married until I come back: I shall be here punctually at five in the evening on Tuesday fortnight. Gracious ladies [his heels click] good evening. [He makes them a military bow, and goes].

SERGIUS. What a man! Is he a man!

(1894)

A. E. HOUSMAN
1859–1936

Alfred Edward Housman was born in Worcestershire, but he said that he had "a sentimental feeling for Shropshire because its hills were our western horizon." At Oxford from 1877 to 1881, he attained success in classical studies, but failed to pass his Honors degree examination because he was in a state of emotional turmoil caused by his love for a fellow student. In 1882 he went to London where for ten years he held a post in the Patent Office; during that period many long evenings were spent in reading Latin and Greek in the British Museum. Published studies in the minor Latin poets resulted in his appointment in 1892 to a professorship in Latin in University College, London, and to a similar position at Cambridge in 1911. Between 1886 and 1905 Housman lived in Highgate, London, where he wrote A Shropshire Lad. Most of the poems were composed in 1895 during a great burst of creative activity just prior to publication. The title was suggested by a friend, A. W. Pollard, in place of the less attractive *Poems by Terence Hearsay*. In an autobiographical note, Housman says: "The Shropshire Lad is an imaginary figure, with something of my temper and view of life. Very little in the book is autobiographical." It was not until 1922 that Housman's next book, *Last Poems*, appeared. He died in 1936, and in the autumn of the same year his final work, *More Poems*, was issued by his brother.

Although Housman listed his chief sources as Shakespeare's songs, the Scottish border ballads, and the German poet Heinrich Heine (1797–1856), his verse distinctly shows a Latin influence. Housman spent almost thirty years working on his annotated edition of the early Roman poet Manilius; he had a worldwide reputation as an authority on Latin and Greek. His poetry has a flawless economy and simplicity. He often turns to the classical theme that youth and spring and all beautiful things must come to an end. There is frequently an undertone of fatalism in his compact verse.

from A SHROPSHIRE LAD

2. LOVELIEST OF TREES

Loveliest of trees, the cherry now
Is hung with bloom along the bough,
And stands about the woodland ride
Wearing white for Eastertide.

5 Now, of my threescore years and ten,
Twenty will not come again,
And take from seventy springs a score,
It only leaves me fifty more.

And since to look at things in bloom
10 Fifty springs are little room,
About the woodlands I will go
To see the cherry hung with snow.

13. WHEN I WAS ONE-AND-TWENTY

When I was one-and-twenty
 I heard a wise man say,
"Give crowns and pounds and guineas,°
 But not your heart, away;
5 Give pearls away and rubies,
 But keep your fancy free."
But I was one-and-twenty—
 No use to talk to me.

When I was one-and-twenty
 I heard him say again,   10
"The heart out of the bosom
 Was never given in vain;
'Tis paid with sighs a plenty
 And sold for endless rue."
And I am two-and-twenty,   15
 And oh, 'tis true, 'tis true.

19. TO AN ATHLETE DYING YOUNG

The time you won your town the race
We chaired you through the market-place;
Man and boy stood cheering by,
And home we brought you shoulder-high.

Today, the road all runners come,
Shoulder-high° we bring you home,
And set you at your threshold down,
Townsman of a stiller town.

Smart lad, to slip betimes away
From fields where glory does not stay   10
And early though the laurel° grows
It withers quicker than the rose.

Eyes the shady night has shut
Cannot see the record cut,
And silence sounds no worse than cheers
After earth has stopped the ears.

Now you will not swell the rout
Of lads that wore their honors out,
Runners whom renown outran
And the name died before the man.   20

So set, before its echoes fade,
The fleet foot on the sill of shade,
And hold to the low lintel up
The still-defended challenge-cup.

And round that early-laureled head
Will flock to gaze the strengthless dead,
And find unwithered on its curls
The garland briefer than a girl's.

21. BREDON HILL°

In summertime on Bredon
 The bells they sound so clear;
Round both the shires they ring them
 In steeples far and near,
 A happy noise to hear.

Here of a Sunday morning
  My love and I would lie,
And see the colored counties,°
And hear the larks so high
10 About us in the sky.

The bells would ring to call her
  In valleys miles away:
"Come all to church, good people;
  Good people, come and pray."
But here my love would stay.

And I would turn and answer
  Among the springing thyme,°
"Oh, peal upon our wedding,
  And we will hear the chime,
20 And come to church in time."

But when the snows at Christmas
  On Bredon top were strown,
My love rose up so early
  And stole out unbeknown
And went to church alone.

They tolled the one bell only,
  Groom there was none to see,
The mourners followed after,
  And so to church went she,
30 And would not wait for me.

The bells they sound on Bredon,
  And still the steeples hum,
"Come all to church, good people"—
  Oh, noisy bells, be dumb;
I hear you; I will come.

40. INTO MY HEART

Into my heart an air that kills
  From yon far country blows;
What are those blue remembered hills,
  What spires, what farms are those?

5 That is the land of lost content,
  I see it shining plain,
The happy highways where I went
  And cannot come again.

49. THINK NO MORE, LAD

Think no more, lad; laugh, be jolly.
  Why should men make haste to die?
Empty heads and tongues a-talking

Make the rough road easy walking,
And the feather pate of folly   5
  Bears the falling sky.

Oh, 'tis jesting, dancing, drinking
  Spins the heavy world around.
If young hearts were not so clever,
Oh, they would be young forever.   10
Think no more; 'tis only thinking
  Lays lads underground.

62. TERENCE, THIS IS STUPID STUFF

"Terence, this is stupid stuff:
You eat your victuals fast enough;
There can't be much amiss, 'tis clear,
To see the rate you drink your beer.
But oh, good Lord, the verse you make,
It gives a chap the bellyache.
The cow, the old cow, she is dead;
It sleeps well, the horned head:
We poor lads, 'tis our turn now
To hear such tunes as killed the cow.   10
Pretty friendship 'tis to rhyme
Your friends to death before their time
Moping melancholy mad.
Come, pipe a tune to dance to, lad."

  Why, if 'tis dancing you would be,
There's brisker pipes than poetry.
Say, for what were hop-yards meant,
Or why was Burton built on Trent?°
Oh, many a peer of England brews
Livelier liquor than the Muse,   20
And malt does more than Milton can
To justify God's ways to man.
Ale, man, ale's the stuff to drink
For fellows whom it hurts to think:
Look into the pewter pot
To see the world as the world's not.
And faith, 'tis pleasant till 'tis past:
The mischief is that 'twill not last.
Oh, I have been to Ludlow° Fair
And left my necktie God knows where,   30
And carried half way home, or near,
Pints and quarts of Ludlow beer.
Then the world seemed none so bad,
And I myself a sterling lad;
And down in lovely muck I've lain,
Happy till I woke again.
Then I saw the morning sky—
Heigho, the tale was all a lie;
The world, it was the old world yet,
I was I, my things were wet,   40
And nothing now remained to do
But begin the game anew.

---

8 **counties.** From Bredon Hill may be seen the variegated landscape of five counties—Worcestershire, Gloucestershire, Herefordshire, Warwickshire, and Oxfordshire   17 **thyme,** a mint plant

Terence, This Is Stupid Stuff   18 **Burton built on Trent,** famous brewery town
29 **Ludlow,** a town in Shropshire

Therefore, since the world has still
Much good, but much less good than ill,
And while the sun and moon endure
Luck's a chance, but trouble's sure,
I'd face it as a wise man would,
And train for ill and not for good.
'Tis true, the stuff I bring for sale
50 Is not so brisk a brew as ale;
'Out of a stem that scored the hand
I wrung it in a weary land.
But take it—if the smack is sour,
The better for the embittered hour;
It should do good to heart and head
When your soul is in my soul's stead;
And I will friend you, if I may,
In the dark and cloudy day.

There was a king reigned in the East;°
60 There, when kings will sit to feast,
They get their fill before they think
With poisoned meat and poisoned drink.
He gathered all that springs to birth
From the many-venomed earth;
First a little, thence to more,
He sampled all her killing store;
And easy, smiling, seasoned sound,
Sate the king when healths went round.
They put arsenic in his meat
70 And stared aghast to watch him eat;
They poured strychnine in his cup
And shook to see him drink it up.
They shook, they stared as white's their shirt;
Them it was their poison hurt.
—I tell the tale that I heard told.
Mithridates, he died old.
(1896)

from LAST POEMS

20. THE NIGHT IS FREEZING FAST

The night is freezing fast,
  To-morrow comes December;
    And winterfalls of old
Are with me from the past;
5   And chiefly I remember
    How Dick would hate the cold.

Fall, winter, fall; for he,
  Prompt hand and headpiece clever,
    Has woven a winter robe,
10 And made of earth and sea

59 **a king . . . East,** Mithridates of Pontus, reigned 120–63 B.C.

His overcoat for ever,
  And wears the turning globe.
(1922)

from MORE POEMS

THEY SAY MY VERSE IS SAD

They say my verse is sad: no wonder;
  Its narrow measure spans
Tears of eternity, and sorrow,
  Not mine, but man's.

This is for all ill-treated fellows   5
  Unborn and unbegot,
For them to read when they're in trouble
  And I am not.

9. WHEN GREEN BUDS HANG

When green buds hang in the elm like dust
  And sprinkle the lime like rain,
Forth I wander, forth I must,
  And drink of life again.
Forth I must by hedgerow bowers   5
  To look at the leaves uncurled
And stand in the fields where cuckoo-flowers
  Are lying about the world.
(1936)

JOSEPH CONRAD
1857–1924

Although born of Polish parents in what is now the Soviet Ukraine, Joseph Conrad (born Jozef Teodor Konrad Korzeniowski) became not only a British subject but also one of the greatest novelists in the English language.

Both his parents, who as Polish patriots and nationalists had suffered exile and privation at the hands of the Russians, had died by the time Conrad was twelve. He was subsequently raised by his maternal uncle, Tadeusz Bobrowski, who proved to be a kind, generous, and firm guardian. Stories of adventure, translations of books by James Fenimore Cooper, Sir Walter Scott, and Charles Dickens fed young Conrad's yearning for freedom and excitement. He was sent to school in Cracow but was bored and, by 1872, desired a life on the sea. A year later his uncle sent him to Switzerland with a tutor, whose job was to talk Conrad out of his romantic folly. But in 1874, with money and contacts supplied by his uncle, Conrad left Poland for Marseilles and service in the French Mercantile Marine. After three years at Marseilles and in the West Indies, he transferred to a British ship, and in June of his twenty-first year, knowing only such English as he may have picked up on the ship, he first set foot on English soil.

During the next few years, Conrad spent all his spare time on shipboard learning the English language, largely by studying newspapers. After passing the appropriate examinations, he was promoted to the rank of master seaman in 1886, the same year he became a British subject. For the next eight years, he served as one of the commanding officers on British merchant ships sailing to Australia, South Africa, South America, and the Orient. In 1890 he made a perilous journey to the Congo, where among other mishaps he contracted a devastating fever and also nearly drowned. He never completely recovered from the ill effects of this adventure. During all these years, however, while on sea voyages, in various ports and inside the Congo, Conrad was storing up incidents, experiences, and vivid impressions of character, which he used later in his novels and stories.

Returning to England early in 1891, Conrad spent several months in a hospital in London in pain and depression. He made two short voyages in 1892 and 1893, on one of which he came to know the English novelist John Galsworthy (1867–1933). Conrad read to Galsworthy a few chapters of a novel which he had started several years before, and Galsworthy encouraged him to continue writing. In January 1894 he left the marine service and settled in London. By May he had finished his first novel, *Almayer's Folly*, which was published in 1895. Heartened by the success of this book and by the further praise of Galsworthy, he began a second novel and dedicated himself to a life of writing. Although the critics were sympathetic, he achieved no popular success until *Chance* (1914). The success of this book caused his earlier novels to be more widely read and appreciated. He continued his writing as his popularity increased. In 1923 he made a visit to the United States and was appropriately received as one of the most famous living novelists. He died at his home in Bishopbourne, near Canterbury in southeast England, the following year.

"Art itself," Conrad wrote in the preface to *The Nigger of the Narcissus*, "may be defined as a single-minded attempt to render the highest kind of justice to the visible universe, by bringing to light the truth, manifold and one, underlying its every aspect. It is an attempt to find in its forms, in its colors, in its lights, in its shadows, in the aspect of the matter, and in the facts of life what of each is fundamental, what is enduring and essential—their one illuminating and con-

vincing quality—the very truth of their existence. . . . My task which I am trying to achieve is, by the power of the written word to make you hear, to make you feel—it is, before all, to make you see. That—and no more, and it is everything. If I succeed, you shall find there according to your deserts: encouragement, consolation, fear, charm—all you demanded—and, perhaps, also that glimpse of truth for which you have forgotten to ask. To snatch in a moment of courage, from the remorseless rush of time, a passing phase of life, is only the beginning of the task. The task approached in tenderness and faith is to hold up unquestioningly, without choice and without fear, the rescued fragment before all eyes in the light of a sincere mood. It is to show its vibration, its color, its form; and through its movement, its form, and its color, reveal the substance of its truth—disclose the inspiring secret: the stress and passion within the core of each convincing movement. In a single-minded attempt of that kind, if one be deserving and fortunate, one may perchance attain to such clearness of sincerity that at last the presented vision of regret or pity, of terror or mirth, shall awaken in the hearts of the beholders that feeling of unavoidable solidarity; of the solidarity in mysterious origin, in toil, in joy, in hope, in uncertain fate, which binds men to each other and all mankind to the visible world." Conrad held to these principles throughout his career.

Conrad's novels include *Almayer's Folly* (1895), *An Outcast of the Islands* (1896), *The Nigger of the Narcissus* (1897), *Lord Jim* (1900), *Nostromo* (1904), *The Secret Agent* (1908), *Under Western Eyes* (1911), *Chance* (1914), *Victory* (1915), *The Shadow Line* (1917), *The Arrow of Gold* (1918), *The Rescue* (1920), *The Rover* (1924), and *Suspense* (incomplete, 1925). He also achieved success as a writer of short stories, published in various collections; among the best-known individual stories are *The Lagoon, Heart of Darkness, Typhoon, The End of the Tether, The Secret Sharer, The Brute, A Warrior's Soul*, and *Prince Roman*. He also published two valuable autobiographical sketches: *The Mirror of the Sea* (1906) and *A Personal Record* (1912); and two volumes of essays: *Notes on Life and Letters* (1921) and *Last Essays* (1926).

THE SECRET SHARER

I

On my right hand there were lines of fishing stakes resembling a mysterious system of half-submerged bamboo fences, incomprehensible in its division of the domain of tropical fishes, and crazy of aspect as if abandoned forever by some nomad tribe of fishermen now gone to the other end of the ocean; for there was no sign of human habitation as far as the eye could reach. To the left a group of barren islets, suggesting ruins of stone walls, towers, and blockhouses, had its foundations set in a blue sea that itself looked solid, so still and stable did it lie below my feet; even the track of light from the westering sun shone smoothly, without that animated glitter which tells of an imperceptible ripple. And when I turned my head to take a parting glance at the tug which had just left us anchored outside the bar, I saw the straight line of the flat shore joined to the stable sea, edge to edge, with a perfect and unmarked closeness, in one leveled floor half brown, half blue under the enormous dome of the sky. Corresponding in their insignificance to the islets of the sea, two small clumps of trees, one on each side of the only fault in the impeccable joint, marked the mouth of the river Meinam we had just left on the first preparatory stage of our homeward journey; and, far back of the inland level, a larger and loftier mass, the grove surrounding the great Paknam pagoda, was the only thing on which the eye could rest from the vain task of exploring the monotonous sweep of the horizon. Here and there gleams as of a few scattered pieces of silver marked the windings of the great river; and on the nearest of them, just within the bar, the tug steaming right into the land became lost to my sight, hull and funnel and masts, as though the impassive earth had swallowed her up without an effort, without a tremor. My eye followed the light cloud of her smoke, now here, now there, above the plain, according to the devious curves of the stream, but always fainter and farther away, till I lost it at last behind the miter-shaped hill of the great pagoda. And then I was left alone with my ship, anchored at the head of the Gulf of Siam.

She floated at the starting point of a long journey, very still in an immense stillness, the shadows of her spars flung far to the eastward by the setting sun. At that moment I was alone on her decks. There was not a sound in her—and around us nothing moved, nothing lived, not a canoe on the water, not a bird in the air, not a cloud in the sky. In this breathless pause at the threshold of a long passage we seemed to be measuring our fitness for a long and arduous enterprise, the appointed task of both our existences to be carried out, far from all human eyes, with only sky and sea for spectators and for judges.

There must have been some glare in the air to interfere with one's sight, because it was only just before the sun left us that my roaming eyes made out beyond the highest ridges of the principal islet of the group something which did away with the solemnity of perfect solitude. The tide of darkness flowed on swiftly; and with tropical suddenness a swarm of stars came out above the shadowy earth, while I lingered yet, my hand resting lightly on my ship's rail as if on the shoulder of a trusted friend. But, with all that multitude of celestial bodies staring down at one, the comfort of quiet communion with her was gone for good. And there were also disturbing sounds by this time— voices, footsteps forward; the steward flitted along the main-deck, a busily ministering spirit; a hand bell tinkled urgently under the poop deck. . . .

I found my two officers waiting for me near the supper table, in the lighted cuddy.° We sat down at once, and as I helped the chief mate, I said:

"Are you aware that there is a ship anchored inside the islands? I saw her mastheads above the ridges as the sun went down."

He raised sharply his simple face, overcharged by a terrible growth of whisker, and emitted his usual ejaculations: "Bless my soul, sir! You don't say so!"

My second mate was a round-cheeked, silent young man, grave beyond his years, I thought; but as our eyes happened to meet I detected a slight quiver on his lips. I looked down at once. It was not my part to encourage sneering on board my ship. It must be said, too, that I knew very little of my officers. In consequence of certain events of no particular significance, except to myself, I had been appointed to the command only a fortnight before. Neither did I know much of the hands forward. All these people had been together for eighteen months or so, and my position was that of the only stranger on board. I mention this because it has some bearing on what is to follow. But what I felt most was my being a stranger to the ship; and if all the truth must be told, I was somewhat of a stranger to myself. The youngest man on board (barring the second mate), and untried as yet by a position of the fullest responsibility, I was willing to take the adequacy of the others for granted. They had simply to be equal to their tasks; but I wondered how far I should turn out faithful to that ideal conception of one's own personality every man sets up for himself secretly.

Meantime the chief mate, with an almost visible effect of collaboration on the part of his round eyes and frightful whiskers, was trying to evolve a theory of the anchored ship. His dominant trait was to take all things into earnest consideration. He was of a painstaking turn of mind. As he used to say, he "liked to account to himself" for practically everything that came in his way, down to a miserable scorpion he had found in his cabin a week before. The why and the wherefore of that scorpion—how it got on board and came to select his room rather than the pantry (which was a dark place and more what a scorpion would be partial to), and how on earth it managed to drown itself in the inkwell of his writing desk—had exercised him infinitely. The ship within the islands was much more easily accounted for; and just as we were about to rise from table he made his pronouncement. She was, he

The Secret Sharer 71 **cuddy,** a small cabin or "saloon" (term used below) under the poop deck (the deck in the stern of the vessel)

doubted not, a ship from home lately arrived. Probably she drew too much water to cross the bar except at the top of spring tides. Therefore she went into that natural harbor to wait for a few days in preference to remaining in an open roadstead.

"That's so," confirmed the second mate, suddenly, in his slightly hoarse voice. "She draws over twenty feet. She's the Liverpool ship *Sephora* with a cargo of coal. Hundred and twenty-three days from Cardiff."

We looked at him in surprise.

"The tugboat skipper told me when he came on board for your letters, sir," explained the young man. "He expects to take her up the river the day after tomorrow."

After thus overwhelming us with the extent of his information he slipped out of the cabin. The mate observed regretfully that he "could not account for that young fellow's whins." What prevented him telling us all about it at once, he wanted to know.

I detained him as he was making a move. For the last two days the crew had had plenty of hard work, and the night before they had very little sleep. I felt painfully that I—a stranger—was doing something unusual when I directed him to let all hands turn in without setting an anchor watch. I proposed to keep on deck myself till one o'clock or thereabouts. I would get the second mate to relieve me at that hour.

"He will turn out the cook and the steward at four," I concluded, "and then give you a call. Of course at the slightest sign of any sort of wind we'll have the hands up and make a start at once."

He concealed his astonishment. "Very well, sir." Outside the cuddy he put his head in the second mate's door to inform him of my unheard-of caprice to take a five hours' anchor watch on myself. I heard the other raise his voice incredulously—"What? The Captain himself?" Then a few more murmurs, a door closed, then another. A few moments later I went on deck.

My strangeness, which had made me sleepless, had prompted that unconventional arrangement, as if I had expected in those solitary hours of the night to get on terms with the ship of which I knew nothing, manned by men of whom I knew very little more. Fast alongside a wharf, littered like any ship in port with a tangle of unrelated things, invaded by unrelated shore people, I had hardly seen her yet properly. Now, as she lay cleared for sea, the stretch of her main-deck seemed to me very fine under the stars. Very fine, very roomy for her size, and very inviting. I descended the poop and paced the waist, my mind picturing to myself the coming passage through the Malay Archipelago, down the Indian Ocean, and up the Atlantic. All its phases were familiar enough to me, every characteristic, all the alternatives which were likely to face me on the high seas—everything! . . . except the novel responsibility of command. But I took heart from the reasonable thought that the ship was like other ships, the men like other men, and that the sea was not likely to keep any special surprises expressly for my discomfiture.

Arrived at that comforting conclusion, I bethought myself of a cigar and went below to get it. All was still down there. Everybody at the after end of the ship was sleeping profoundly. I came out again on the quarter-deck, agreeably at ease in my sleeping suit on that warm breathless night, barefooted, a glowing cigar in my teeth, and, going forward, I was met by the profound silence of the fore end of the ship. Only as I passed the door of the forecastle I heard a deep, quiet, trustful sigh of some sleeper inside. And suddenly I rejoiced in the great security of the sea as compared with the unrest of the land, in my choice of that untempted life presenting no disquieting problems, invested with an elementary moral beauty by the absolute straightforwardness of its appeal and by the singleness of its purpose.

The riding light in the forerigging burned with a clear, untroubled, as if symbolic, flame, confident and bright in the mysterious shades of the night. Passing on my way aft along the other side of the ship, I observed that the rope side ladder, put over, no doubt, for the master of the tug when he came to fetch away our letters, had not been hauled in as it should have been. I became annoyed at this, for exactitude in some small matters is the very soul of discipline. Then I reflected that I had myself peremptorily dismissed my officers from duty, and by my own act had prevented the anchor watch being formally set and things properly attended to. I asked myself whether it was wise ever to interfere with the established routine of duties even from the kindest of motives. My action might have made me appear eccentric. Goodness only knew how that absurdly whiskered mate would "account" for my conduct, and what the whole ship thought of that informality of their new captain. I was vexed with myself.

Not from compunction certainly, but, as it were mechanically, I proceeded to get the ladder in myself. Now a side ladder of that sort is a light affair and comes in easily, yet my vigorous tug, which should have brought it flying on board, merely recoiled upon my body in a totally unexpected jerk. What the devil! . . . I was so astounded by the immovableness of that ladder that I remained stockstill, trying to account for it to myself like that imbecile mate of mine. In the end, of course, I put my head over the rail.

The side of the ship made an opaque belt of shadow on the darkling glassy shimmer of the sea. But I saw at once something elongated and pale floating very close to the ladder. Before I could form a guess a faint flash of phosphorescent light, which seemed to issue suddenly from the naked body of a man, flickered in the sleeping water with the elusive, silent play of summer lightning in a night sky. With a gasp I saw revealed to my stare a pair of feet, the long legs, a broad livid back immersed right up to the neck in a greenish cadaverous glow. One hand, awash, clutched the bottom rung of the ladder. He was complete but for the head. A headless corpse! The cigar dropped out of my gaping mouth with a tiny plop and a short hiss quite audible in the absolute stillness of all things under heaven. At that I suppose he raised up his face, a dimly pale oval in the shadow of the ship's side. But even then I could only barely make out down there the shape of his black-haired head. However, it was enough for the horrid, frost-bound sensation which had gripped me about the chest to pass off. The moment of vain exclamations was past, too. I only climbed on the spare spar and leaned over the rail as far as I could, to bring my eyes nearer to that mystery floating alongside.

As he hung by the ladder, like a resting swimmer, the sea lightning played about his limbs at every stir; and he appeared in it ghastly, silvery, fishlike. He remained as mute as a fish, too. He made no motion to get out of the water, either. It was inconceivable that he should not attempt to come on board, and strangely troubling to suspect that perhaps he did not want to. And my first words were prompted by just that troubled incertitude.

"What's the matter?" I asked in my ordinary tone, speaking down to the face upturned exactly under mine.

"Cramp," it answered, no louder. Then slightly anxious, "I say, no need to call anyone."

"I was not going to," I said.

"Are you alone on deck?"

"Yes."

I had somehow the impression that he was on the point of letting go the ladder to swim away beyond my ken—mysterious as he came. But, for the moment, this being appearing as if he had risen from the bottom of the sea (it was certainly the nearest land to the ship) wanted only to know the time. I told him. And he, down there, tentatively:

"I suppose your captain's turned in?"

"I am sure he isn't," I said.

He seemed to struggle with himself, for I heard something like the low, bitter murmur of doubt. "What's the good?" His next words came out with a hesitating effort.

"Look here, my man. Could you call him out quietly?"

I thought the time had come to declare myself.

"*I* am the captain."

I heard a "By Jove!" whispered at the level of the water. The phosphorescence flashed in the swirl of the water all about his limbs, his other hand seized the ladder.

"My name's Leggatt."

The voice was calm and resolute. A good voice. The self-possession of that man had somehow induced a corresponding state in myself. It was very quietly that I remarked:

"You must be a good swimmer."

"Yes. I've been in the water practically since nine o'clock. The question for me now is whether I am to let go this ladder and go on swimming till I sink from exhaustion, or—to come on board here."

I felt this was no mere formula of desperate speech, but a real alternative in the view of a strong soul. I should have gathered from this that he was young; indeed, it is only the young who are ever confronted by such clear issues. But at the time it was pure intuition on my part. A mysterious communication was established already between us two—in the face of that silent, darkened tropical sea. I was young, too; young enough to make no comment. The man in the water began suddenly to climb up the ladder, and I hastened away from the rail to fetch some clothes.

Before entering the cabin I stood still, listening in the lobby at the foot of the stairs. A faint snore came through the closed door of the chief mate's room. The second mate's door was on the hook, but the darkness in there was absolutely soundless. He, too, was young and could sleep like a stone. Remained the steward, but he was not likely to wake up before he was called. I got a sleeping suit out of my room and, coming back on deck, saw the naked man from the sea sitting on the main hatch, glimmering white in the darkness, his elbows on his knees and his head in his hands. In a moment he had concealed his damp body in a sleeping suit of the same gray-stripe pattern as the one I was wearing and followed me like my double on the poop. Together we moved right aft, barefooted, silent.

"What is it?" I asked in a deadened voice, taking the lighted lamp out of the binnacle,° and raising it to his face.

"An ugly business."

He had rather regular features; a good mouth; light eyes under somewhat heavy, dark eyebrows; a smooth, square forehead; no growth on his cheeks; a small, brown mustache, and a well-shaped, round chin. His expression was concentrated, meditative, under the inspecting light of the lamp I held up to his face; such as a man thinking hard in solitude might wear. My sleeping suit was just right for his size. A well-knit young fellow of twenty-five at most. He caught his lower lip with the edge of white, even teeth.

"Yes," I said, replacing the lamp in the binnacle. The warm, heavy tropical night closed upon his head again.

"There's a ship over there," he murmured.

"Yes, I know. The *Sephora*. Did you know of us?"

"Hadn't the slightest idea. I am the mate of her—" He paused and corrected himself. "I should say I *was*."

"Aha! Something wrong?"

"Yes. Very wrong indeed. I've killed a man."

324 **binnacle**, a stand or case containing the ship's compass, usually placed just in front of the steering wheel

"What do you mean? Just now?"

"No, on the passage. Weeks ago. Thirty-nine south. When I say a man—"

350 "Fit of temper," I suggested, confidently.

The shadowy, dark head, like mine, seemed to nod imperceptibly above the ghostly gray of my sleeping suit. It was, in the night, as though I had been faced by my own reflection in the depths of a somber and immense mirror.

"A pretty thing to have to own up to for a Conway boy,°" murmured my double, distinctly.

"You're a Conway boy?"

"I am" he said, as if startled. Then, slowly
360 ... "Perhaps you too—"

It was so; but being a couple of years older I had left before he joined. After a quick interchange of dates a silence fell; and I thought suddenly of my absurd mate with his terrific whiskers and the "Bless my soul—you don't say so" type of intellect. My double gave me an inkling of his thoughts by saying: "My father's a parson in Norfolk. Do you see me before a judge and jury on that charge? For myself I can't see the necessity. There are fellows that an angel from heaven—And I
370 am not that. He was one of those creatures that are just simmering all the time with a silly sort of wickedness. Miserable devils that have no business to live at all. He wouldn't do his duty and wouldn't let anybody else do theirs. But what's the good of talking! You know well enough the sort of ill-conditioned snarling cur—"

He appeared to me as if our experiences had been as identical as our clothes. And I knew well enough the pestiferous danger of such a character where there are no means of legal repression. And I knew well enough
380 also that my double there was no homicidal ruffian. I did not think of asking him for details, and he told me the story roughly in brusque, disconnected sentences. I needed no more. I saw it all going on as though I were myself inside that other sleeping suit.

"It happened while we were setting a reefed foresail, at dusk. Reefed foresail! You understand the sort of weather. The only sail we had left to keep the ship running; so you may guess what it had been like for days. Anxious sort of job, that. He gave me some of
390 his cursed insolence at the sheet. I tell you I was overdone with this terrific weather that seemed to have no end to it. Terrific, I tell you—and a deep ship.° I believe the fellow himself was half crazed with funk. It was no time for gentlemanly reproof, so I turned round and felled him like an ox. He up and at me. We closed just as an awful sea made for the ship. All hands saw it coming and took to the rigging, but I had him by the throat, and went on shaking him like a rat, the men above us yelling, 'Look out! look out!' Then a crash as
400 if the sky had fallen on my head. They say that for over

ten minutes hardly anything was to be seen of the ship—just the three masts and a bit of the forecastle head and of the poop all awash driving along in a smother of foam. It was a miracle that they found us, jammed together behind the forebits.° It's clear that I meant business, because I was holding him by the throat still when they picked us up. He was black in the face. It was too much for them. It seems they rushed us aft together, gripped as we were, screaming 'Murder!' like a lot of lunatics, and broke into the 410 cuddy. And the ship running for her life, touch and go all the time, any minute her last in a sea fit to turn your hair gray only a-looking at it. I understand that the skipper, too, started raving like the rest of them. The man had been deprived of sleep for more than a week, and to have this sprung on him at the height of a furious gale nearly drove him out of his mind. I wonder they didn't fling me overboard after getting the carcass of their precious shipmate out of my fingers. They had rather a job to separate us, I've been told. A suffi- 420 ciently fierce story to make an old judge and a respectable jury sit up a bit. The first thing I heard when I came to myself was the maddening howling of that endless gale, and on that the voice of the old man. He was hanging on to my bunk, staring into my face out of his sou'wester.

"'Mr. Leggatt, you have killed a man. You can act no longer as chief mate of this ship.'"

His care to subdue his voice made it sound monotonous. He rested a hand on the end of the skylight to 430 steady himself with, and all that time did not stir a limb, so far as I could see. "Nice little tale for a quiet tea party," he concluded in the same tone.

One of my hands, too, rested on the end of the skylight; neither did I stir a limb, so far as I knew. We stood less than a foot from each other. It occurred to me that if old "Bless my soul—you don't say so" were to put his head up the companion and catch sight of us, he would think he was seeing double, or imagine himself come upon a scene of weird witchcraft; the strange 440 captain having a quiet confabulation by the wheel with his own gray ghost. I became very much concerned to prevent anything of the sort. I heard the other's soothing undertone.

"My father's a parson in Norfolk," it said. Evidently he had forgotten he had told me this important fact before. Truly a nice little tale.

"You had better slip down into my stateroom now," I said, moving off stealthily. My double followed my movements; our bare feet made no sound; I let him in, 450 closed the door with care, and, after giving a call to the second mate, returned on deck for my relief.

"Not much sign of any wind yet," I remarked when he approached.

---

356 **Conway boy** The Conway was the training school of merchant marine officers which Leggatt and the protagonist had attended   392 **deep ship,** a ship heavily laden and therefore deep in the water

405 **forebits.** Bits are heavy vertical beams running from keel to main deck and a little above; their tops are useful for securing ropes, hawsers, etc. The forebits would be those bits found at the foot of the foremast

"No, sir. Not much," he assented, sleepily, in his hoarse voice, with just enough deference, no more, and barely suppressing a yawn.

"Well, that's all you have to look out for. You have got your orders."

460 "Yes, sir."

I paced a turn or two on the poop and saw him take up his position face forward with his elbow in the ratlines of the mizzen rigging before I went below. The mate's faint snoring was still going on peacefully. The cuddy lamp was burning over the table on which stood a vase with flowers, a polite attention from the ship's provision merchant—the last flowers we should see for the next three months at the very least. Two bunches of bananas hung from the beam symmetri-
470 cally, one on each side of the rudder casing. Everything was as before in the ship—except that two of her captain's sleeping suits were simultaneously in use, one motionless in the cuddy, the other keeping very still in the captain's stateroom.

It must be explained here that my cabin had the form of the capital letter L, the door being within the angle and opening into the short part of the letter. A couch was to the left, the bed place to the right; my writing desk and the chronometers' table faced the door. But
480 anyone opening it, unless he stepped right inside, had no view of what I call the long (or vertical) part of the letter. It contained some lockers surmounted by a bookcase; and a few clothes, a thick jacket or two, caps, oilskin coat, and such like, hung on hooks. There was at the bottom of that part a door opening into my bathroom, which could be entered also directly from the saloon. But that way was never used.

The mysterious arrival had discovered the advantage of this particular shape. Entering my room,
490 lighted strongly by a big bulkhead lamp swung on gimbals° above my writing desk, I did not see him anywhere till he stepped out quietly from behind the coats hung in the recessed part.

"I heard somebody moving about, and went in there at once," he whispered.

I, too, spoke under my breath.

"Nobody is likely to come in here without knocking and getting permission."

He nodded. His face was thin and the sunburn
500 faded, as though he had been ill. And no wonder. He had been, I heard presently, kept under arrest in his cabin for nearly seven weeks. But there was nothing sickly in his eyes or in his expression. He was not a bit like me, really; yet, as we stood leaning over my bed place, whispering side by side, with our dark heads together and our backs to the door, anybody bold enough to open it stealthily would have been treated to the uncanny sight of a double captain busy talking in whispers with his other self.

510 "But all this doesn't tell me how you came to hang

491 **gimbals,** devices that permit objects to incline freely in any direction

on to our side ladder," I inquired, in the hardly audible murmurs we used, after he had told me something more of the proceedings on board the *Sephora* once the bad weather was over.

"When we sighted Java Head I had had time to think all those matters out several times over. I had six weeks of doing nothing else, and with only an hour or so every evening for a tramp on the quarter-deck."

He whispered, his arms folded on the side of my bed place, staring through the open port. And I could 520 imagine perfectly the manner of this thinking out—a stubborn if not a steadfast operation; something of which I should have been perfectly incapable.

"I reckoned it would be dark before we closed with the land," he continued, so low that I had to strain my hearing near as we were to each other, shoulder touching shoulder almost. "So I asked to speak to the old man. He always seemed very sick when he came to see me—as if he could not look me in the face. You know, that foresail saved the ship. She was too deep to 530 have run long under bare poles. And it was I that managed to set it for him. Anyway, he came. When I had him in my cabin—he stood by the door looking at me as if I had the halter round my neck already—I asked him right away to leave my cabin door unlocked at night while the ship was going through Sunda Straits. There would be the Java coast within two or three miles, off Angier Point. I wanted nothing more. I've had a prize for swimming my second year in the Conway."
540

"I can believe it," I breathed out.

"God only knows why they locked me in every night. To see some of their faces you'd have thought they were afraid I'd go about at night strangling people. Am I a murdering brute? Do I look it? By Jove! If I had been he wouldn't have trusted himself like that into my room. You'll say I might have chucked him aside and bolted out, there and then—it was dark already. Well, no. And for the same reason I wouldn't think of trying to smash the door. There would have 550 been a rush to stop me at the noise, and I did not mean to get into a confounded scrimmage. Somebody else might have got killed—for I would not have broken out only to get chucked back, and I did not want any more of that work. He refused, looking more sick than ever. He was afraid of the men, and also of that old second mate of his who had been sailing with him for years—a gray-headed old humbug; and his steward, too, had been with him devil knows how long—seventeen years or more—a dogmatic sort of loafer who hated me like 560 poison, just because I was the chief mate. No chief mate ever made more than one voyage in the *Sephora*, you know. Those two old chaps ran the ship. Devil only knows what the skipper wasn't afraid of (all his nerve went to pieces altogether in that hellish spell of bad weather we had)—of what the law would do to him—of his wife, perhaps. Oh, yes! she's on board. Though I don't think she would have meddled. She would have been only too glad to have me out of the ship in any way. The 'brand of Cain'° business, don't you see. That's all right. I was ready enough to go off wandering on the face of the earth—and that was price enough to pay for an Abel of that sort. Anyhow, he wouldn't listen to me. 'This thing must take its course. I represent the law here.' He was shaking like a leaf. 'So you won't?' 'No!' 'Then I hope you will be able to sleep on that,' I said, and turned my back on him. 'I wonder that *you* can,' cries he, and locks the door.

"Well after that, I couldn't. Not very well. That was three weeks ago. We have had a slow passage through the Java Sea; drifted about Carimata for ten days. When we anchored here they thought, I suppose, it was all right. The nearest land (and that's five miles) is the ship's destination; the consul would soon set about catching me; and there would have been no object in bolting to these islets there. I don't suppose there's a drop of water on them. I don't know how it was, but tonight that steward, after bringing me my supper, went out to let me eat it, and left the door unlocked. And I ate it—all there was, too. After I had finished I strolled out on the quarter-deck. I don't know that I meant to do anything. A breath of fresh air was all I wanted, I believe. Then a sudden temptation came over me. I kicked off my slippers and was in the water before I had made up my mind fairly. Somebody heard the splash and they raised an awful hullabaloo. 'He's gone! Lower the boats! He's committed suicide! No, he's swimming.' Certainly I was swimming. It's not so easy for a swimmer like me to commit suicide by drowning. I landed on the nearest islet before the boat left the ship's side. I heard them pulling about in the dark, hailing, and so on, but after a bit they gave up. Everything quieted down and the anchorage became as still as death. I sat down on a stone and began to think. I felt certain they would start searching for me at daylight. There was no place to hide on those stony things—and if there had been, what would have been the good? But now I was clear of that ship, I was not going back. So after a while I took off all my clothes, tied them up in a bundle with a stone inside, and dropped them in the deep water on the outer side of that islet. That was suicide enough for me. Let them think what they liked, but I didn't mean to drown myself. I meant to swim till I sank—but that's not the same thing. I struck out for another of these little islands, and it was from that one that I first saw your riding light. Something to swim for. I went on easily, and on the way I came upon a flat rock a foot or two above water. In the daytime, I dare say, you might make it out with a glass from your poop. I scrambled up on it and rested myself for a bit. Then I made another start. That last spell must have been over a mile."

His whisper was getting fainter and fainter, and all the time he stared straight out through the porthole, in which there was not even a star to be seen. I had not interrupted him. There was something that made comment impossible in his narrative, or perhaps in himself; a sort of feeling, a quality, which I can't find a name for. And when he ceased, all I found was a futile whisper: "So you swam for our light?"

"Yes—straight for it. It was something to swim for. I couldn't see any stars low down because the coast was in the way, and I couldn't see the land, either. The water was like glass. One might have been swimming in a confounded thousand-feet deep cistern with no place for scrambling out anywhere; but what I didn't like was the notion of swimming round and round like a crazed bullock before I gave out; and as I didn't mean to go back . . . No. Do you see me being hauled back, stark naked, off one of these little islands by the scruff of the neck and fighting like a wild beast? Somebody would have got killed for certain, and I did not want any of that. So I went on. Then your ladder—"

"Why didn't you hail the ship?" I asked, a little louder.

He touched my shoulder lightly. Lazy footsteps came right over our heads and stopped. The second mate had crossed from the other side of the poop and might have been hanging over the rail for all we knew.

"He couldn't hear us talking—could he?" My double breathed into my very ear, anxiously.

His anxiety was in answer, a sufficient answer, to the question I had put to him. An answer containing all the difficulty of that situation. I closed the porthole quietly, to make sure. A louder word might have been overheard.

"Who's that?" he whispered then.

"My second mate. But I don't know much more of the fellow than you do."

And I told him a little about myself. I had been appointed to take charge while I least expected anything of the sort, not quite a fortnight ago. I didn't know either the ship or the people. Hadn't had the time in port to look about me or size anybody up. And as to the crew, all they knew was that I was appointed to take the ship home. For the rest, I was almost as much of a stranger on board as himself, I said. And at the moment I felt it most acutely. I felt that it would take very little to make me a suspect person in the eyes of the ship's company.

He had turned about meantime; and we, the two strangers in the ship, faced each other in identical attitudes.

"Your ladder—" he murmured, after a silence. "Who'd have thought of finding a ladder hanging over at night in a ship anchored out here! I felt just then a very unpleasant faintness. After the life I've been leading for nine weeks, anybody would have got out of condition. I wasn't capable of swimming round as far as your rudder chains. And, lo and behold! there was a

570 **brand of Cain.** According to the story of the first murder, as told in the Old Testament, the murderer Cain was given a special mark or stigma to bear through life indicating his mortal crime. There is more than one reference to this story in Conrad's tale; see *Genesis*, 4

ladder to get hold of. After I gripped it I said to myself, 'What's the good?' When I saw a man's head looking over I thought I would swim away presently and leave him shouting—in whatever language it was. I didn't mind being looked at. I—I liked it. And then you speaking to me so quietly—as if you had expected me—made me hold on a little longer. It had been a confounded lonely time—I don't mean while swimming. I was glad to talk a little to somebody that didn't belong to the *Sephora*. As to asking for the captain, that was a mere impulse. It could have been no use, with all the ship knowing about me and the other people pretty certain to be round here in the morning. I don't know—I wanted to be seen, to talk with somebody, before I went on. I don't know what I would have said. . . . 'Fine night, isn't it?' or something of the sort.''

"Do you think they will be round here presently?" I asked with some incredulity.

"Quite likely," he said, faintly.

He looked extremely haggard all of a sudden. His head rolled on his shoulders.

"H'm. We shall see then. Meantime get into that bed," I whispered. "Want help? There."

It was a rather high bed place with a set of drawers underneath. This amazing swimmer really needed the lift I gave him by seizing his leg. He tumbled in, rolled over on his back, and flung one arm across his eyes. And then, with his face nearly hidden, he must have looked exactly as I used to look in that bed. I gazed upon my other self for a while before drawing across carefully the two green serge curtains which ran on a brass rod. I thought for a moment of pinning them together for greater safety, but I sat down on the couch, and once there I felt unwilling to rise and hunt for a pin. I would do it in a moment. I was extremely tired, in a peculiarly intimate way, by the strain of stealthiness, by the effort of whispering and the general secrecy of this excitement. It was three o'clock by now and I had been on my feet since nine, but I was not sleepy; I could not have gone to sleep. I sat there, fagged out, looking at the curtains, trying to clear my mind of the confused sensation of being in two places at once, and greatly bothered by an exasperating knocking in my head. It was a relief to discover suddenly that it was not in my head at all, but on the outside of the door. Before I could collect myself the words "Come in" were out of my mouth, and the steward entered with a tray, bringing in my morning coffee. I had slept, after all, and I was so frightened that I shouted, "This way! I am here, steward," as though he had been miles away. He put down the tray on the table next the couch and only then said, very quietly, "I can see you are here, sir." I felt him give me a keen look, but I dared not meet his eyes just then. He must have wondered why I had drawn the curtains of my bed before going to sleep on the couch. He went out, hooking the door open as usual.

I heard the crew washing decks above me. I knew I would have been told at once if there had been any wind. Calm, I thought, and I was doubly vexed. Indeed, I felt dual more than ever. The steward reappeared suddenly in the doorway. I jumped up from the couch so quickly that he gave a start.

"What do you want here?"

"Close your port, sir—they are washing decks."

"It is closed," I said, reddening.

"Very well, sir." But he did not move from the doorway and returned my stare in an extraordinary, equivocal manner for a time. Then his eyes wavered, all his expression changed, and in a voice unusually gentle, almost coaxingly:

"May I come in to take the empty cup away, sir?"

"Of course!" I turned my back on him while he popped in and out. Then I unhooked and closed the door and even pushed the bolt. This sort of thing could not go on very long. The cabin was as hot as an oven, too. I took a peep at my double, and discovered that he had not moved, his arm was still over his eyes; but his chest heaved; his hair was wet; his chin glistened with perspiration. I reached over him and opened the port.

"I must show myself on deck," I reflected.

Of course, theoretically, I could do what I liked, with no one to say nay to me within the whole circle of the horizon; but to lock my cabin door and take the key away I did not dare. Directly I put my head out of the companion I saw the group of my two officers, the second mate barefooted, the chief mate in long India-rubber boots, near the break of the poop, and the steward halfway down the poop ladder talking to them eagerly. He happened to catch sight of me and dived, the second ran down on the main-deck shouting some order or other, and the chief mate came to meet me, touching his cap.

There was a sort of curiosity in his eye that I did not like. I don't know whether the steward had told them that I was "queer" only, or downright drunk, but I know the man meant to have a good look at me. I watched him coming with a smile which, as he got into point-blank range, took effect and froze his very whiskers. I did not give him time to open his lips.

"Square the yards by lifts and braces before the hands go to breakfast."

It was the first particular order I had given on board that ship; and I stayed on deck to see it executed, too. I had felt the need of asserting myself without loss of time. That sneering young cub got taken down a peg or two on that occasion, and I also seized the opportunity of having a good look at the face of every foremast man as they filed past me to go to the after braces. At breakfast time, eating nothing myself, I presided with such frigid dignity that the two mates were only too glad to escape from the cabin as soon as decency permitted; and all the time the dual working of my mind distracted me almost to the point of insanity. I was constantly watching myself, my secret self, as dependent on my actions as my own personality, sleeping in that bed, behind that door which faced me as I sat at the head of the table. It was very much like being mad, only it was worse because one was aware of it.

I had to shake him for a solid minute, but when at last he opened his eyes it was in the full possession of his senses, with an inquiring look.

"All's well so far," I whispered. "Now you must vanish into the bathroom."

He did so, as noiseless as a ghost, and then I rang for the steward, and facing him boldly, directed him to tidy up my stateroom while I was having my bath—"and be quick about it." As my tone admitted of no excuses, he said, "Yes, sir," and ran off to fetch his dustpan and brushes. I took a bath and did most of my dressing, splashing, and whistling softly for the steward's edification, while the secret sharer of my life stood drawn up bolt upright in that little space, his face looking very sunken in daylight, his eyelids lowered under the stern, dark line of his eyebrows drawn together by a slight frown.

When I left him there to go back to my room the steward was finishing dusting. I sent for the mate and engaged him in some insignificant conversation. It was, as it were, trifling with the terrific character of his whiskers; but my object was to give him an opportunity for a good look at my cabin. And then I could at last shut, with a clear conscience, the door of my stateroom and get my double back into the recessed part. There was nothing else for it. He had to sit still on a small folding stool, half smothered by the heavy coats hanging there. We listened to the steward going into the bathroom out of the saloon, filling the water bottles there, scrubbing the bath, setting things to rights, whisk, bang, clatter—out again into the saloon—turn the key—click. Such was my scheme for keeping my second self invisible. Nothing better could be contrived under the circumstances. And there we sat; I at my writing desk ready to appear busy with some papers, he behind me out of sight of the door. It would not have been prudent to talk in daytime; and I could not have stood the excitement of that queer sense of whispering to myself. Now and then, glancing over my shoulder, I saw him far back there, sitting rigidly on the low stool, his bare feet close together, his arms folded, his head hanging on his breast—and perfectly still. Anybody would have taken him for me.

I was fascinated by it myself. Every moment I had to glance over my shoulder. I was looking at him when a voice outside the door said:

"Beg pardon, sir."

"Well!" . . . I kept my eyes on him, and so when the voice outside the door announced, "There's a ship's boat coming our way, sir," I saw him give a start—the first movement he had made for hours. But he did not raise his bowed head.

"All right. Get the ladder over."

I hesitated. Should I whisper something to him? But

what? His immobility seemed to have been never disturbed. What could I tell him he did not know already? . . . Finally I went on deck.

II

The skipper of the *Sephora* had a thin red whisker all round his face, and the sort of complexion that goes with hair of that color; also the particular, rather smeary shade of blue in his eyes. He was not exactly a showy figure; his shoulders were high, his stature but middling—one leg slightly more bandy than the other. He shook hands, looking vaguely around. A spiritless tenacity was his main characteristic, I judged. I behaved with a politeness which seemed to disconcert him. Perhaps he was shy. He mumbled to me as if he were ashamed of what he was saying; gave his name (it was something like Archbold—but at this distance of years I hardly am sure), his ship's name, and a few other particulars of that sort, in the manner of a criminal making a reluctant and doleful confession. He had had terrible weather on the passage out—terrible—terrible—wife aboard, too.

By this time we were seated in the cabin and the steward brought in a tray with a bottle and glasses. "Thanks! No." Never took liquor. Would have some water, though. He drank two tumblerfuls. Terrible thirsty work. Ever since daylight had been exploring the islands round his ship.

"What was that for—fun?" I asked, with an appearance of polite interest.

"No!" He sighed. "Painful duty."

As he persisted in his mumbling and I wanted my double to hear every word, I hit upon the notion of informing him that I regretted to say I was hard of hearing.

"Such a young man, too!" he nodded, keeping his smeary blue, unintelligent eyes fastened upon me. "What was the cause of it—some disease?" he inquired, without the least sympathy and as if he thought that, if so, I'd got no more than I deserved.

"Yes; disease," I admitted in a cheerful tone which seemed to shock him. But my point was gained, because he had to raise his voice to give me his tale. It is not worth while to record that version. It was just over two months since all this had happened, and he had thought so much about it that he seemed completely muddled as to its bearings, but still immensely impressed.

"What would you think of such a thing happening on board your own ship? I've had the *Sephora* for these fifteen years. I am a well-known shipmaster."

He was densely distressed—and perhaps I should have sympathized with him if I had been able to detach my mental vision from the unsuspected sharer of my cabin as though he were my second self. There he was on the other side of the bulkhead, four or five feet from us, no more, as we sat in the saloon. I looked politely at Captain Archbold (if that was his name), but it was the other I saw, in a gray sleeping suit, seated on a low stool, his bare feet close together, his arms folded, and every word said between us falling into the ears of his dark head bowed on his chest.

"I have been at sea now, man and boy, for seven-and-thirty years, and I've never heard of such a thing happening in an English ship. And that it should be my ship. Wife on board, too."

I was hardly listening to him.

"Don't you think," I said, "that the heavy sea which, you told me, came aboard just then might have killed the man? I have seen the sheer weight of a sea kill a man very neatly, by simply breaking his neck."

"Good God!" he uttered, impressively, fixing his smeary blue eyes on me. "The sea! No man killed by the sea ever looked like that." He seemed positively scandalized at my suggestion. And as I gazed at him certainly not prepared for anything original on his part, he advanced his head close to mine and thrust his tongue out at me so suddenly that I couldn't help starting back.

After scoring over my calmness in this graphic way he nodded wisely. If I had seen the sight, he assured me, I would never forget it as long as I lived. The weather was too bad to give the corpse a proper sea burial. So next day at dawn they took it up on the poop, covering its face with a bit of bunting; he read a short prayer, and then, just as it was, in its oilskins and long boots, they launched it amongst those mountainous seas that seemed ready every moment to swallow up the ship herself and the terrified lives on board of her.

"That reefed foresail saved you," I threw in.

"Under God—it did," he exclaimed fervently. "It was by a special mercy, I firmly believe, that it stood some of those hurricane squalls."

"It was the setting of that sail which—" I began.

"God's own hand in it," he interrupted me. "Nothing less could have done it. I don't mind telling you that I hardly dared give the order. It seemed impossible that we could touch anything without losing it, and then our last hope would have been gone."

The terror of that gale was on him yet. I let him go on for a bit, then said, casually—as if returning to a minor subject:

"You were very anxious to give up your mate to the shore people, I believe?"

He was. To the law. His obscure tenacity on that point had in it something incomprehensible and a little awful; something, as it were, mystical, quite apart from his anxiety that he should not be suspected of "countenancing any doings of that sort." Seven-and-thirty virtuous years at sea, of which over twenty of immaculate command, and the last fifteen in the *Sephora*, seemed to have laid him under some pitiless obligation.

"And you know," he went on, groping shame-facedly amongst his feelings, "I did not engage that young fellow. His people had some interest with my owners. I was in a way forced to take him on. He looked very smart, very gentlemanly, and all that. But do you know—I never liked him, somehow. I am a plain man. You see, he wasn't exactly the sort for the chief mate of a ship like the *Sephora*."

I had become so connected in thoughts and impressions with the secret sharer of my cabin that I felt as if I, personally, were being given to understand that I, too, was not the sort that would have done for the chief mate of a ship like the *Sephora*. I had no doubt of it in my mind.

"Not at all the style of man. You understand," he insisted, superfluously, looking hard at me.

I smiled urbanely. He seemed at a loss for a while.

"I suppose I must report a suicide."

"Beg pardon?"

"Sui-cide! That's what I'll have to write to my owners directly I get in."

"Unless you manage to recover him before tomorrow," I assented, dispassionately. . . . "I mean, alive."

He mumbled something which I really did not catch, and I turned my ear to him in a puzzled manner. He fairly bawled:

"The land—I say, the mainland is at least seven miles off my anchorage."

"About that."

My lack of excitement, of curiosity, of surprise, of any sort of pronounced interest, began to arouse his distrust. But except for the felicitous pretense of deafness I had not tried to pretend anything. I had felt utterly incapable of playing the part of ignorance properly, and therefore was afraid to try. It is also certain that he had brought some ready-made suspicions with him, and that he viewed my politeness as a strange and unnatural phenomenon. And yet how else could I have received him? Not heartily! That was impossible for psychological reasons, which I need not state here. My only object was to keep off his inquiries. Surlily? Yes, but surliness might have provoked a point-blank question. From its novelty to him and from its nature, punctilious courtesy was the manner best calculated to restrain the man. But there was the danger of his breaking through my defense bluntly. I could not, I think, have met him by a direct lie, also for psychological (not moral) reasons. If he had only known how afraid I was of his putting my feeling of identity with the other to the test! But, strangely enough—(I thought of it only afterwards)—I believe that he was not a little disconcerted by the reverse side of that weird situation, by something in me that reminded him of the man he was seeking—suggested a mysterious similitude to the young fellow he had distrusted and disliked from the first.

However that might have been, the silence was not very prolonged. He took another oblique step.

"I reckon I had no more than a two-mile pull to your ship. Not a bit more."

"And quite enough, too, in this awful heat," I said.

1030 Another pause full of mistrust followed. Necessity, they say, is mother of invention, but fear, too, is not barren of ingenious suggestions. And I was afraid he would ask me point-blank for news of my other self.

"Nice little saloon, isn't it?" I remarked, as if noticing for the first time the way his eyes roamed from one closed door to the other. "And very well fitted out, too. Here, for instance," I continued, reaching over the back of my seat negligently and flinging the door open, "is my bathroom."

1040 He made an eager movement, but hardly gave it a glance. I got up, shut the door of the bathroom, and invited him to have a look round, as if I were very proud of my accommodation. He had to rise and be shown round, but he went through the business without any raptures whatever.

"And now we'll have a look at my stateroom," I declared, in a voice as loud as I dared to make it, crossing the cabin to the starboard side with purposely heavy steps.

1050 He followed me in and gazed around. My intelligent double had vanished. I played my part.

"Very convenient—isn't it?"

"Very nice. Very comf . . ." He didn't finish and went out brusquely as if to escape from some unrighteous wiles of mine. But it was not to be. I had been too frightened not to feel vengeful; I felt I had him on the run, and I meant to keep him on the run. My polite insistence must have had something menacing in it, because he gave in suddenly. And I did not let him off

1060 a single item; mate's room, pantry, storerooms, the very sail locker which was also under the poop—he had to look into them all. When at last I showed him out on the quarter-deck he drew a long, spiritless sigh, and mumbled dismally that he must really be going back to his ship now. I desired my mate, who had joined us, to see to the captain's boat.

The man of whiskers gave a blast on the whistle which he used to wear hanging round his neck, and yelled, "*Sephora's* away!" My double down there in

1070 my cabin must have heard, and certainly could not feel more relieved than I. Four fellows came running out from somewhere forward and went over the side, while my own men, appearing on deck too, lined the rail. I escorted my visitor to the gangway ceremoniously, and nearly overdid it. He was a tenacious beast. On the very ladder he lingered, and in that unique, guiltily conscientious manner of sticking to the point:

"I say . . . you . . . you don't think that—"

I covered his voice loudly:

"Certainly not. . . . I am delighted. Good-by." 1080

I had an idea of what he meant to say, and just saved myself by the privilege of defective hearing. He was too shaken generally to insist, but my mate, close witness of that parting, looked mystified and his face took on a thoughtful cast. As I did not want to appear as if I wished to avoid all communication with my officers, he had the opportunity to address me.

"Seems a very nice man. His boat's crew told our chaps a very extraordinary story, if what I am told by the steward is true. I suppose you had it from the 1090 captain, sir?"

"Yes. I had a story from the captain."

"A very horrible affair—isn't it, sir?"

"It is."

"Beats all these tales we hear about murders in Yankee ships."

"I don't think it beats them. I don't think it resembles them in the least."

"Bless my soul—you don't say so! But of course I've no acquaintance whatever with American ships, 1100 not I, so I couldn't go against your knowledge. It's horrible enough for me. . . . But the queerest part is that those fellows seemed to have some idea the man was hidden aboard here. They had really. Did you ever hear of such a thing?"

"Preposterous—isn't it?"

We were walking to and fro athwart the quarter-deck. No one of the crew forward could be seen (the day was Sunday), and the mate pursued:

"There was some little dispute about it. Our chaps 1110 took offense. 'As if we would harbor a thing like that,' they said. 'Wouldn't you like to look for him in our coalhole?' Quite a tiff. But they made it up in the end. I suppose he did drown himself. Don't you, sir?"

"I don't suppose anything."

"You have no doubt in the matter, sir?"

"None whatever."

I left him suddenly. I felt I was producing a bad impression, but with my double down there it was most trying to be on deck. And it was almost as trying 1120 to be below. Altogether a nerve-trying situation. But on the whole I felt less torn in two when I was with him. There was no one in the whole ship whom I dared take into my confidence. Since the hands had got to know his story, it would have been impossible to pass him off for anyone else, and an accidental discovery was to be dreaded now more than ever. . . .

The steward being engaged in laying the table for dinner, we could talk only with our eyes when I first went down. Later in the afternoon we had a cautious 1130 try at whispering. The Sunday quietness of the ship was against us; the stillness of air and water around her was against us; the elements, the men were against us—everything was against us in our secret partnership; time itself—for this could not go on forever. The very trust in Providence was, I suppose, denied to his guilt. Shall I confess that this thought cast me down very much? And as to the chapter of accidents which counts for so much in the book of success, I could only hope that it was closed. For what favorable accident could be expected?

"Did you hear everything?" were my first words as soon as we took up our position side by side, leaning over my bed place.

He had. And the proof of it was his earnest whisper, "The man told you he hardly dared to give the order."

I understood the reference to be to that saving foresail.

"Yes. He was afraid of it being lost in the setting."

"I assure you he never gave the order. He may think he did, but he never gave it. He stood there with me on the break of the poop after the main topsail blew away, and whimpered about our last hope—positively whimpered about it and nothing else—and the night coming on! To hear one's skipper go on like that in such weather was enough to drive any fellow out of his mind. It worked me up into a sort of desperation. I just took it into my own hands and went away from him, boiling, and— But what's the use telling you? *You* know! . . . Do you think that if I had not been pretty fierce with them I should have got the men to do anything? Not It! The bo's'n perhaps? Perhaps! It wasn't a heavy sea—it was a sea gone mad! I suppose the end of the world will be something like that; and a man may have the heart to see it coming once and be done with it—but to have to face it day after day— I don't blame anybody. I was precious little better than the rest. Only—I was an officer of that old coal wagon, anyhow—"

"I quite understand," I conveyed that sincere assurance into his ear. He was out of breath with whispering; I could hear him pant slightly. It was all very simple. The same strung-up force which had given twenty-four men a chance, at least, for their lives, had, in a sort of recoil, crushed an unworthy mutinous existence.

But I had no leisure to weigh the merits of the matter—footsteps in the saloon, a heavy knock. "There's enough wind to get under way with, sir." Here was the call of a new claim upon my thoughts and even upon my feelings.

"Turn the hands up," I cried through the door. "I'll be on deck directly."

I was going out to make the acquaintance of my ship. Before I left the cabin our eyes met—the eyes of the only two strangers on board. I pointed to the recessed part where the campstool awaited him and laid my finger on my lips. He made a gesture—somewhat vague—a little mysterious, accompanied by a faint smile, as if of regret.

This is not the place to enlarge upon the sensations of a man who feels for the first time a ship move under his feet to his own independent word. In my case they were not unalloyed. I was not wholly alone with my command; for there was that stranger in my cabin. Or rather, I was not completely and wholly with her. Part of me was absent. That mental feeling of being in two places at once affected me physically as if the mood of secrecy had penetrated my very soul. Before an hour had elapsed since the ship had begun to move, having occasion to ask the mate (he stood by my side) to take a compass bearing of the pagoda, I caught myself reaching up to his ear in whispers. I say I caught myself, but enough had escaped to startle the man. I can't describe it otherwise than by saying that he shied. A grave, preoccupied manner, as though he were in possession of some perplexing intelligence, did not leave him henceforth. A little later I moved away from the rail to look at the compass with such a stealthy gait that the helmsman noticed it—and I could not help noticing the unusual roundness of his eyes. These are trifling instances, though it's to no commander's advantage to be suspected of ludicrous eccentricities. But I was also more seriously affected. There are to a seaman certain words, gestures, that should in given conditions come as naturally, as instinctively as the winking of a menaced eye. A certain order should spring on to his lips without thinking; a certain sign should get itself made, so to speak, without reflection. But all unconscious alertness had abandoned me. I had to make an effort of will to recall myself back (from the cabin) to the conditions of the moment. I felt that I was appearing an irresolute commander to those people who were watching me more or less critically.

And, besides, there were the scares. On the second day out, for instance, coming off the deck in the afternoon (I had straw slippers on my bare feet) I stopped at the open pantry door and spoke to the steward. He was doing something there with his back to me. At the sound of my voice he nearly jumped out of his skin, as the saying is, and incidentally broke a cup.

"What on earth's the matter with you?" I asked, astonished.

He was extremely confused. "Beg your pardon, sir. I made sure you were in your cabin."

"You see I wasn't."

"No, sir. I could have sworn I had heard you moving in there not a moment ago. It's most extraordinary . . . very sorry, sir."

I passed on with an inward shudder. I was so identified with my secret double that I did not even mention the fact in those scanty, fearful whispers we exchanged. I suppose he had made some slight noise of some kind or other. It would have been miraculous if he hadn't at one time or another. And yet, haggard as he appeared, he looked always perfectly self-controlled, more than calm—almost invulnerable. On my suggestion he remained almost entirely in the bathroom, which, upon the whole, was the safest place. There could be really no shadow of an excuse for anyone ever wanting to go in there, once the steward had done with it. It was a very tiny place. Sometimes he reclined on the floor, his legs bent, his head sustained on one elbow. At others I would find him on the campstool, sitting in his gray sleeping suit with his cropped dark hair like a patient, unmoved convict. At night I would smuggle him into my bed place, and we would whisper together, with the regular footfalls of the officer of the watch passing and repassing over our heads. It was an infinitely miserable time. It was lucky that some tins of fine preserves were stowed in a locker in my stateroom; hard bread I could always get hold of; and so he lived on stewed chicken, *pâté de foie gras,* asparagus, cooked oysters, sardines—on all sort of abominable sham delicacies out of tins. My early-morning coffee he always drank; and it was all I dared do for him in that respect.

Every day there was the horrible maneuvering to go through so that my room and then the bathroom should be done in the usual way. I came to hate the sight of the steward, to abhor the voice of that harmless man. I felt that it was he who would bring on the disaster of discovery. It hung like a sword over our heads.

The fourth day out, I think (we were then working down the east side of the Gulf of Siam, tack for tack, in light winds and smooth water)—the fourth day, I say, of this miserable juggling with the unavoidable, as we sat at our evening meal, that man, whose slightest movement I dreaded, after putting down the dishes ran up on deck busily. This could not be dangerous. Presently he came down again; and then it appeared that he had remembered a coat of mine which I had thrown over a rail to dry after having been wetted in a shower which had passed over the ship in the afternoon. Sitting stolidly at the head of the table I became terrified at the sight of the garment on his arm. Of course he made for my door. There was no time to lose.

"Steward," I thundered. My nerves were so shaken that I could not govern my voice and conceal my agitation. This was the sort of thing that made my terrifically whiskered mate tap his forehead with his forefinger. I had detected him using that gesture while talking on deck with a confidential air to the carpenter. It was too far to hear a word, but I had no doubt that this pantomime could only refer to the strange new captain.

"Yes, sir," the pale-faced steward turned resignedly to me. It was this maddening course of being shouted at, checked without rhyme or reason, arbitrarily chased out of my cabin, suddenly called into it, sent flying out of his pantry on incomprehensible errands, that accounted for the growing wretchedness of his expression.

"Where are you going with that coat?"

"To your room, sir."

"Is there another shower coming?"

"I'm sure I don't know, sir. Shall I go up again and see, sir?"

"No! never mind."

My object was attained, as of course my other self in there would have heard everything that passed. During this interlude my two officers never raised their eyes off their respective plates; but the lip of that confounded cub, the second mate, quivered visibly.

I expected the steward to hook my coat on and come out at once. He was very slow about it; but I dominated my nervousness sufficiently not to shout after him. Suddenly I became aware (it could be heard plainly enough) that the fellow for some reason or other was opening the door of the bathroom. It was the end. The place was literally not big enough to swing a cat in. My voice died in my throat and I went stony all over. I expected to hear a yell of surprise and terror, and made a movement, but had not the strength to get on my legs. Everything remained still. Had my second self taken the poor wretch by the throat? I don't know what I could have done next moment if I had not seen the steward come out of my room, close the door, and then stand quietly by the sideboard.

"Saved," I thought. "But, no! Lost! Gone! He was gone!"

I laid my knife and fork down and leaned back in my chair. My head swam. After a while, when sufficiently recovered to speak in a steady voice, I instructed my mate to put the ship round at eight o'clock himself.

"I won't come on deck," I went on. "I think I'll turn in, and unless the wind shifts I don't want to be disturbed before midnight. I feel a bit seedy."

"You did look middling bad a little while ago," the chief mate remarked without showing any great concern.

They both went out, and I stared at the steward clearing the table. There was nothing to be read on that wretched man's face. But why did he avoid my eyes, I asked myself. Then I thought I should like to hear the sound of his voice.

"Steward!"

"Sir!" Startled as usual.

"Where did you hang up that coat?"

"In the bathroom, sir." The usual anxious tone. "It's not quite dry yet, sir."

For some time longer I sat in the cuddy. Had my double vanished as he had come? But of his coming

there was an explanation, whereas his disappearance would be inexplicable. . . . I went slowly into my dark room, shut the door, lighted the lamp, and for a time dared not turn round. When at last I did I saw him standing bolt-upright in the narrow recessed part. It would not be true to say I had a shock, but an irresist-
1360 ible doubt of his bodily existence flitted through my mind. Can it be, I asked myself, that he is not visible to other eyes than mine? It was like being haunted. Motionless, with a grave face, he raised his hands slightly at me in a gesture which meant clearly, "Heavens! what a narrow escape!" Narrow indeed. I think I had come creeping quietly as near insanity as any man who has not actually gone over the border. That gesture restrained me, so to speak.

The mate with the terrific whiskers was now putting
1370 the ship on the other tack. In the moment of profound silence which follows upon the hands going to their stations I heard on the poop his raised voice: "Hard alee!" and the distant shout of the order repeated on the main-deck. The sails, in that light breeze, made but a faint fluttering noise. It ceased. The ship was coming round slowly: I held my breath in the renewed stillness of expectation; one wouldn't have thought that there was a single living soul on her decks. A sudden brisk shout, "Mainsail haul!" broke the spell, and in the
1380 noisy cries and rush overhead of the men running away with the main brace we two, down in my cabin, came together in our usual position by the bed place.

He did not wait for my question. "I heard him fumbling here and just managed to squat myself down in the bath," he whispered to me. "The fellow only opened the door and put his arm in to hang the coat up. All the same—"

"I never thought of that," I whispered back, even more appalled than before at the closeness of the
1390 shave, and marveling at that something unyielding in his character which was carrying him through so finely. There was no agitation in his whisper. Whoever was being driven distracted, it was not he. He was sane. And the proof of his sanity was continued when he took up the whispering again.

"It would never do for me to come to life again."

It was something that a ghost might have said. But what he was alluding to was his old captain's reluctant admission of the theory of suicide. It would obviously
1400 serve his turn—if I had understood at all the view which seemed to govern the unalterable purpose of his action.

"You must maroon me as soon as ever you can get amongst these islands off the Cambodge° shore," he went on.

"Maroon you! We are not living in a boy's adventure tale," I protested. His scornful whispering took me up.

"We aren't indeed! There's nothing of a boy's tale in

this. But there's nothing else for it. I want no more. 1410 You don't suppose I am afraid of what can be done to me? Prison or gallows or whatever they may please. But you don't see me coming back to explain such things to an old fellow in a wig and twelve respectable tradesmen, do you? What can they know whether I am guilty or not—or of *what* I am guilty, either? That's my affair. What does the Bible say? 'Driven off the face of the earth.'° Very well, I am off the face of the earth now. As I came at night so I shall go."

"Impossible!" I murmured. "You can't." 1420

"Can't? . . . Not naked like a soul on the Day of Judgment. I shall freeze on to this sleeping suit. The Last Day is not yet—and . . . you have understood thoroughly. Didn't you?"

I felt suddenly ashamed of myself. I may say truly that I understood—and my hesitation in letting that man swim away from my ship's side had been a mere sham sentiment, a sort of cowardice.

"It can't be done now till next night," I breathed out. "The ship is on the off-shore tack and the wind 1430 may fail us."

"As long as I know that you understand," he whispered. "But of course you do. It's a great satisfaction to have got somebody to understand. You seem to have been there on purpose." And in the same whisper, as if we two whenever we talked had to say things to each other which were not fit for the world to hear, he added, "It's very wonderful."

We remained side by side talking in our secret way—but sometimes silent or just exchanging a whis- 1440 pered word or two at long intervals. And as usual he stared through the port. A breath of wind came now and again into our faces. The ship might have been moored in dock, so gently and on an even keel she slipped through the water, that did not murmur even at our passage, shadowy and silent like a phantom sea.

At midnight I went on deck, and to my mate's great surprise put the ship round on the other tack. His terrible whiskers flitted round me in silent criticism. I certainly should not have done it if it had been only a 1450 question of getting out of that sleepy gulf as quickly as possible. I believe he told the second mate, who relieved him, that it was a great want of judgment. The other only yawned. That intolerable cub shuffled about so sleepily and lolled against the rails in such a slack, improper fashion that I came down on him sharply.

"Aren't you properly awake yet?"

"Yes, sir! I am awake."

"Well, then, be good enough to hold yourself as if you were. And keep a lookout. If there's any current 1460 we'll be closing with some islands before daylight."

The east side of the gulf is fringed with islands, some solitary, others in groups. On the blue background of the high coast they seem to float on silvery patches of calm water, arid and gray, or dark green and rounded

---

1404 **Cambodge,** Cambodian

1418 **Driven . . . earth.** Cf. *Genesis,* 4:14

like clumps of evergreen bushes, with the larger ones, a mile or two long, showing the outlines of ridges, ribs of gray rock under the dank mantle of matted leafage. Unknown to trade, to travel, almost to geography, the manner of life they harbor is an unsolved secret. There must be villages—settlements of fishermen at least —on the largest of them, and some communication with the world is probably kept up by native craft. But all that forenoon, as we headed for them, fanned along by the faintest of breezes, I saw no sign of man or canoe in the field of the telescope I kept on pointing at the scattered group.

At noon I gave no orders for a change of course, and the mate's whiskers became much concerned and seemed to be offering themselves unduly to my notice. At last I said:

"I am going to stand right in. Quite in—as far as I can take her."

The stare of extreme surprise imparted an air of ferocity also to his eyes, and he looked truly terrific for a moment.

"We're not doing well in the middle of the gulf," I continued, casually. "I am going to look for the land breezes tonight."

"Bless my soul! Do you mean, sir, in the dark amongst the lot of all them islands and reefs and shoals?"

"Well—if there are any regular land breezes at all on this coast one must get close inshore to find them, mustn't one?"

"Bless my soul!" he exclaimed again under his breath. All that afternoon he wore a dreamy, contemplative appearance which in him was a mark of perplexity. After dinner I went into my stateroom as if I meant to take some rest. There we two bent our dark heads over a half-unrolled chart lying on my bed.

"There," I said. "It's got to be Koh-ring. I've been looking at it ever since sunrise. It has got two hills and a low point. It must be inhabited. And on the coast opposite there is what looks like the mouth of a biggish river—with some towns, no doubt, not far up. It's the best chance for you that I can see."

"Anything. Koh-ring let it be."

He looked thoughtfully at the chart as if surveying chances and distances from a lofty height—and following with his eyes his own figure wandering on the blank land of Cochin-China,° and then passing off that piece of paper clean out of sight into uncharted regions. And it was as if the ship had two captains to plan her course for her. I had been so worried and restless running up and down that I had not had the patience to dress that day. I had remained in my sleeping suit, with straw slippers and a soft floppy hat. The closeness of the heat in the gulf had been most oppressive, and the crew were used to seeing me wandering in that airy attire.

"She will clear the south point as she heads now," I whispered into his ear. "Goodness only knows when, though, but certainly after dark. I'll edge her in to half a mile, as far as I may be able to judge in the dark—"

"Be careful," he murmured, warningly—and I realized suddenly that all my future, the only future for which I was fit, would perhaps go irretrievably to pieces in any mishap to my first command.

I could not stop a moment longer in the room. I motioned him to get out of sight and made my way on the poop. That unplayful cub had the watch. I walked up and down for a while thinking things out, then beckoned him over.

"Send a couple of hands to open the two quarter-deck ports," I said, mildly.

He actually had the impudence, or else so forgot himself in his wonder at such an incomprehensible order, as to repeat:

"Open the quarter-deck ports! What for, sir?"

"The only reason you need concern yourself about is because I tell you to do so. Have them open wide and fastened properly."

He reddened and went off, but I believe made some jeering remark to the carpenter as to the sensible practice of ventilating a ship's quarter-deck. I know he popped into the mate's cabin to impart the fact to him because the whiskers came on deck, as it were by chance, and stole glances at me from below—for signs of lunacy or drunkenness, I suppose.

A little before supper, feeling more restless than ever, I rejoined, for a moment, my second self. And to find him sitting so quietly was surprising, like something against nature, inhuman.

I developed my plan in a hurried whisper.

"I shall stand in as close as I dare and then put her round. I will presently find means to smuggle you out of here into the sail locker, which communicates with the lobby. But there is an opening, a sort of square for hauling the sails out, which gives straight on the quarter-deck and which is never closed in fine weather, so as to give air to the sails. When the ship's way is deadened in stays° and all the hands are aft at the main braces you will have a clear road to slip out and get overboard through the open quarter-deck port. I've had them both fastened up. Use a rope's end to lower yourself into the water so as to avoid a splash—you know. It could be heard and cause some beastly complication."

He kept silent for a while, then whispered, "I understand."

"I won't be there to see you go," I began with an effort. "The rest . . . I only hope I have understood, too."

"You have. From first to last"—and for the first time there seemed to be a faltering, something strained in his whisper. He caught hold of my arm, but the

---

1512 **Cochin-China.** In the days of the French colonization known as Indochina, this is the territory now known as South Vietnam

1563 **deadened in stays.** With the use of ropes, the sails are deadened so as to allow the ship to go from one tack into another

ringing of the supper bell made me start. He didn't though; he only released his grip.

1580 After supper I didn't come below again till well past eight o'clock. The faint, steady breeze was loaded with dew; and the wet, darkened sails held all there was of propelling power in it. The night, clear and starry, sparkled darkly, and the opaque, lightless patches shifting slowly against the low stars were the drifting islets. On the port bow there was a big one more distant and shadowily imposing by the great space of sky it eclipsed.

1590 On opening the door I had a back view of my very own self looking at a chart. He had come out of the recess and was standing near the table.

"Quite dark enough," I whispered.

He stepped back and leaned against my bed with a level, quiet glance. I sat on the couch. We had nothing to say to each other. Over our heads the officer of the watch moved here and there. Then I heard him move quickly. I knew what that meant. He was making for the companion; and presently his voice was outside my door.

1600 "We are drawing in pretty fast, sir. Land looks rather close."

"Very well," I answered. "I am coming on deck directly."

I waited till he was gone out of the cuddy, then rose. My double moved too. The time had come to exchange our last whispers, for neither of us was ever to hear each other's natural voice.

"Look here!" I opened a drawer and took out three sovereigns. "Take this anyhow. I've got six and I'd 1610 give you the lot, only I must keep a little money to buy some fruit and vegetables for the crew from native boats as we go through Sunda Straits."

He shook his head.

"Take it," I urged him, whispering desperately. "No one can tell what—"

He smiled and slapped meaningly the only pocket of the sleeping jacket. It was not safe, certainly. But I produced a large old silk handkerchief of mine, and tying the three pieces of gold in a corner, pressed it on 1620 him. He was touched, I supposed, because he took it at last and tied it quickly round his waist under the jacket, on his bare skin.

Our eyes met; several seconds elapsed, till, our glances still mingled, I extended my hand and turned the lamp out. Then I passed through the cuddy, leaving the door of my room wide open. . . . "Steward!"

He was still lingering in the pantry in the greatness of his zeal, giving a rub-up to a plated cruet stand the last thing before going to bed. Being careful not to 1630 wake up the mate, whose room was opposite, I spoke in an undertone.

He looked round anxiously. "Sir!"

"Can you get me a little hot water from the galley?"

"I am afraid, sir, the galley fire's been out for some time now."

"Go and see."

He flew up the stairs.

"Now," I whispered, loudly, into the saloon—too loudly, perhaps, but I was afraid I couldn't make a sound. He was by my side in an instant—the double 1640 captain slipped past the stairs—through a tiny dark passage . . . a sliding door. We were in the sail locker, scrambling on our knees over the sails. A sudden thought struck me. I saw myself wandering barefooted, bareheaded, the sun beating on my dark poll. I snatched off my floppy hat and tried hurriedly in the dark to ram it on my other self. He dodged and fended off silently. I wonder what he thought had come to me before he understood and suddenly desisted. Our hands met gropingly, lingered united in a steady, mo- 1650 tionless clasp for a second. . . . No word was breathed by either of us when they separated.

I was standing quietly by the pantry door when the steward returned.

"Sorry, sir. Kettle barely warm. Shall I light the spirit lamp?"

"Never mind."

I came out on deck slowly. It was now a matter of conscience to shave the land as close as possible—for now he must go overboard whenever the ship was put 1660 in stays. Must! There could be no going back for him. After a moment I walked over to leeward and my heart flew into my mouth at the nearness of the land on the bow. Under any other circumstances I would not have held on a minute longer. The second mate had followed me anxiously.

I looked on till I felt I could command my voice.

"She will weather," I said then in a quiet tone.

"Are you going to try that, sir?" he stammered out incredulously. 1670

I took no notice of him and raised my tone just enough to be heard by the helmsman.

"Keep her good full."

"Good full, sir."

The wind fanned my cheek, the sails slept, the world was silent. The strain of watching the dark loom of the land grow bigger and denser was too much for me. I had shut my eyes—because the ship must go closer. She must! The stillness was intolerable. Were we standing still? 1680

When I opened my eyes the second view started my heart with a thump. The black southern hill of Kohring seemed to hang right over the ship like a towering fragment of the everlasting night. On that enormous mass of blackness there was not a gleam to be seen, not a sound to be heard. It was gliding irresistibly towards us and yet seemed already within reach of the hand. I saw the vague figures of the watch grouped in the waist, gazing in awed silence.

1690 "Are you going on, sir?" inquired an unsteady voice at my elbow.

I ignored it. I had to go on.

"Keep her full. Don't check her way. That won't do now," I said, warningly.

"I can't see the sails very well," the helmsman answered me. in strange, quavering tones.

Was she close enough? Already she was, I won't say in the shadow of the land, but in the very blackness of it, already swallowed up as it were, gone too close to 1700 be recalled, gone from me altogether.

"Give the mate a call," I said to the young man who stood at my elbow as still as death. "And turn all hands up."

My tone had a borrowed loudness reverberated from the height of the land. Several voices cried out together: "We are all on deck, sir."

Then stillness again, with the great shadow gliding closer, towering higher, without a light, without a sound. Such a hush had fallen on the ship that she 1710 might have been a bark of the dead floating in slowly under the very gate of Erebus.°

"My God! Where are we?"

It was the mate moaning at my elbow. He was thunderstruck, and as it were deprived of the moral support of his whiskers. He clapped his hands and absolutely cried out, "Lost!"

"Be quiet," I said, sternly.

He lowered his tone, but I saw the shadowy gesture of his despair. "What are we doing here?"

1720 "Looking for the land wind."

He made as if to tear his hair, and addressed me recklessly.

"She will never get out. You have done it, sir. I knew it'd end in something like this. She will never weather, and you are too close now to stay. She'll drift ashore before she's round. O my God!"

I caught his arm as he was raising it to batter his poor devoted head, and shook it violently.

"She's ashore already," he wailed, trying to tear 1730 himself away.

"Is she? . . . Keep good full there!"

"Good full, sir," cried the helmsman in a frightened, thin, childlike voice.

I hadn't let go the mate's arm and went on shaking it. "Ready about, do you hear? You go forward"— shake—"and stop there"—shake—"and hold your noise"—shake—"and see these head-sheets properly overhauled"—shake, shake—shake.

And all the time I dared not look towards the land 1740 lest my heart should fail me. I released my grip at last and he ran forward as if fleeing for dear life.

I wondered what my double there in the sail locker thought of this commotion. He was able to hear everything—and perhaps he was able to understand why, on my conscience, it had to be thus close—no less. My first order "Hard alee!" re-echoed ominously under the towering shadow of Koh-ring as if I had shouted in a mountain gorge. And then I watched the land intently. In that smooth water and light wind it was impossible to feel the ship coming-to. No! I could 1750 not feel her. And my second self was making now ready to ship out and lower himself overboard. Perhaps he was gone already. . .?

The great black mass brooding over our very mastheads began to pivot away from the ship's side silently. And now I forgot the secret stranger ready to depart, and remembered only that I was a total stranger to the ship. I did not know her. Would she do it? How was she to be handled?

I swung the mainyard and waited helplessly. She 1760 was perhaps stopped, and her very fate hung in the balance, with the black mass of Koh-ring like the gate of the everlasting night towering over her taffrail.° What would she do now? Had she way on her yet? I stepped to the side swiftly, and on the shadowy water I could see nothing except a faint phosphorescent flash revealing the glassy smoothness of the sleeping surface. It was impossible to tell—and I had not learned yet the feel of my ship. Was she moving? What I needed was something easily seen, a piece of paper, 1770 which I could throw overboard and watch. I had nothing on me. To run down for it I didn't dare. There was no time. All at once my strained, yearning stare distinguished a white object floating within a yard of the ship's side. White on the black water. A phosphorescent flash passed under it. What was that thing? . . . I recognized my own floppy hat. It must have fallen off his head . . . and he didn't bother. Now I had what I wanted—the saving mark for my eyes. But I hardly thought of my other self, now gone from 1780 the ship, to be hidden forever from all friendly faces, to be a fugitive and a vagabond on the earth,° with no brand of the curse on his sane forehead to stay a slaying hand . . . too proud to explain.

And I watched the hat—the expression of my sudden pity for his mere flesh. It had been meant to save his homeless head from the dangers of the sun. And now—behold—it was saving the ship, by serving me for a mark to help out the ignorance of my strangeness. Ha! It was drifting forward, warning me just in time 1790 that the ship had gathered sternway.°

"Shift the helm," I said in a low voice to the seaman standing still like a statue.

The man's eyes glistened wildly in the binnacle light as he jumped round to the other side and spun round the wheel.

1711 **Erebus,** in Homeric mythology, the abode of the dead

1763 **taffrail,** the rail across the ship's stern 1782 **fugitive . . . earth,** another reference to the story of Cain; see *Genesis,* 4:14 1791 **gathered sternway,** moved backwards

I walked to the break of the poop. On the over-shadowed deck all hands stood by the forebraces
1800 waiting for my order. The stars ahead seemed to be gliding from right to left. And all was so still in the world that I heard the quiet remark, "She's round," passed in a tone of intense relief between two seamen.

"Let go and haul."

The foreyards ran round with a great noise, amidst cheery cries. And now the frightful whiskers made themselves heard giving various orders. Already the ship was drawing ahead. And I was alone with her. Nothing! no one in the world should stand now be-tween us, throwing a shadow on the way of silent
1810 knowledge and mute affection, the perfect communion of a seaman with his first command.

Walking to the taffrail, I was in time to make out, on the very edge of a darkness thrown by a towering black mass like the very gateway of Erebus—yes, I was in time to catch an evanescent glimpse of my white hat left behind to mark the spot where the secret sharer of my cabin and of my thoughts, as though he were my second self, had lowered himself into the water to take his punishment: a free man, a proud swimmer striking
1820 out for a new destiny.

(1909; 1912)

WILFRED OWEN
1893–1918

Wilfred Owen was killed at the age of twenty-five while leading his men across the Sambre Canal, in France, on November 4, 1918, one week before World War I ended. Owen was born in Oswestry, Shropshire, in 1893. His only formal education was secured at Birkenhead Institute, Liverpool.

Owen served in the war for two periods—first, in 1916–1917 until he was incapacitated and sent to a war hospital in Scotland; second, after his recovery, for most of 1918. He was awarded the Military Cross for gallantry under fire a month before he was killed.

Many of Owen's poems were written while he was recuperating in the hospital. While there, too, he be-came acquainted with Siegfried Sassoon, a young poet from whom he received much encouragement. Both wrote realistic and passionate poems condemning all the waste and horror of war, which they had seen at close range. It was Sassoon who collected and pub-lished Owen's poems two years after his death. In his foreword for the volume, Owen said, "Above all I am not concerned with Poetry. My subject is War, and the pity of War. The Poetry is in the pity. . . . All a Poet can do today is warn. That is why the true Poets must be truthful."

STRANGE MEETING

It seemed that out of battle I escaped
Down some profound dull tunnel, long since scooped
Through granites which titanic wars had groined.
Yet also there encumbered sleepers groaned,
Too fast in thought or death to be bestirred.
Then, as I probed them, one sprang up, and stared
With piteous recognition in fixed eyes,
Lifting distressful hands as if to bless.
And by his smile, I knew that sullen hall;
By his dead smile I knew we stood in Hell.   10
With a thousand pains that vision's face was grained;
Yet no blood reached there from the upper ground,
And no guns thumped, or down the flues made moan.
"Strange friend," I said, "here is no cause to mourn."
"None," said the other, "save the undone years,
The hopelessness. Whatever hope is yours,
Was my life also; I went hunting wild
After the wildest beauty in the world,
Which lies not calm in eyes, or braided hair,
But mocks the steady running of the hour,   20
And if it grieves, grieves richlier than here.
For by my glee might many men have laughed,
And of my weeping something had been left,
Which must die now. I mean the truth untold,
The pity of war, the pity war distilled.
Now men will go content with what we spoiled,
Or, discontent, boil bloody, and be spilled.
They will be swift with swiftness of the tigress,
None will break ranks, though nations trek from prog-
        ress.
Courage was mine, and I had mystery,   30
Wisdom was mine, and I had mastery;
To miss the march of this retreating world
Into vain citadels that are not walled.
Then when much blood had clogged their chariot
        wheels
I would go up and wash them from sweet wells,
Even with truths that lie too deep for taint.
I would have poured my spirit without stint
But not through wounds; not on the cess° of war.
Foreheads of men have bled where no wounds were.
I am the enemy you killed, my friend.   40
I knew you in this dark; for so you frowned
Yesterday through me as you jabbed and killed.
I parried; but my hands were loath and cold.
Let us sleep now. . . ."
(1918; 1920)

INSENSIBILITY

I

Happy are men who yet before they are killed
Can let their veins run cold.

Strange Meeting   38 cess, luck

Whom no compassion fleers
Or makes their feet
Sore on the alleys cobbled with their brothers.
The front line withers,
But they are troops who fade, not flowers
For poets' tearful fooling:
Men, gaps for filling:
10 Losses who might have fought
Longer; but no one bothers.

II

And some cease feeling
Even themselves or for themselves.
Dullness best solves
The tease and doubt of shelling,
And Chance's strange arithmetic
Comes simpler than the reckoning of their shilling.
They keep no check on armies' decimation.

III

Happy are these who lose imagination:
20 They have enough to carry with ammunition.
Their spirit drags no pack,
Their old wounds save with cold can not more ache.
Having seen all things red,
Their eyes are rid
Of the hurt of the colour of blood for ever.
And terror's first constriction over,
Their hearts remain small-drawn.
Their senses in some scorching cautery of battle
Now long since ironed,
30 Can laugh among the dying, unconcerned.

IV

Happy the soldier home, with not a notion
How somewhere, every dawn, some men attack,
And many sighs are drained.
Happy the lad whose mind was never trained:
His days are worth forgetting more than not.
He sings along the march
Which we march taciturn, because of dusk,
The long, forlorn, relentless trend
From larger day to huger night.

V

40 We wise, who with a thought besmirch
Blood over all our soul,
How should we see our task
But through his blunt and lashless eyes?
Alive, he is not vital overmuch;
Dying, not mortal overmuch;
Nor sad, nor proud,
Nor curious at all.
He cannot tell
Old men's placidity from his.

VI

50 But cursed are dullards whom no cannon stuns,
That they should be as stones;

Wretched are they, and mean
With paucity that never was simplicity.
By choice they made themselves immune
To pity and whatever moans in man
Before the last sea and the hapless stars;
Whatever mourns when many leave these shores;
Whatever shares
The eternal reciprocity of tears.
(1918; 1920)

MENTAL CASES

Who are these? Why sit they here in twilight?
Wherefore rock they, purgatorial shadows,
Drooping tongues from jaws that slob their relish,
Baring teeth that leer like skulls' teeth wicked?
Stroke on stroke of pain,—but what slow panic,
Gouged these chasms round their fretted sockets?
Ever from their hair and through their hands' palms
Misery swelters. Surely we have perished
Sleeping, and walk hell; but who these hellish?

—These are men whose minds the Dead have   10
   ravished.
Memory fingers in their hair of murders,
Multitudinous murders they once witnessed.
Wading sloughs of flesh these helpless wander,
Treading blood from lungs that had loved laughter.
Always they must see these things and hear them,
Batter of guns and shatter of flying muscles,
Carnage incomparable, and human squander,
Rucked° too thick for these men's extrication.

Therefore still their eyeballs shrink tormented
Back into their brains, because on their sense   20
Sunlight seems a blood-smear; night comes blood-
   black;
Dawn breaks open like a wound that bleeds afresh.
—Thus their heads wear this hilarious, hideous,
Awful falseness of set-smiling corpses.
—Thus their hands are plucking at each other;
Picking at the rope-knouts of their scourging;
Snatching after us who smote them, brother,
Pawing us who dealt them war and madness.
(1918; 1920)

DULCE ET DECORUM EST°

Bent double, like old beggars under sacks,
Knock-kneed, coughing like hags, we cursed through
   sludge,
Till on the haunting flares we turned our backs,

Mental Cases   18 Rucked, piled in a heap   Dulce et Decorum Est. The title in its full form (see ll. 27–28) means "It is sweet and honorable to die for one's country." It is quoted from Horace, *Odes*, III, 2, 13

And towards our distant rest began to trudge.
Men marched asleep. Many had lost their boots,
But limped on, blood-shod. All went lame, all blind;
Drunk with fatigue; deaf even to the hoots
Of gas-shells dropping softly behind.

Gas! GAS! Quick, boys—An ecstasy of fumbling,
10 Fitting the clumsy helmets just in time,
But someone still was yelling out and stumbling
And floundering like a man in fire or lime.—
Dim through the misty panes and thick green light,
As under a green sea, I saw him drowning.

In all my dreams before my helpless sight
He plunges at me, guttering, choking, drowning.

If in some smothering dreams, you too could pace
Behind the wagon that we flung him in,
And watch the white eyes writhing in his face,
20 His hanging face, like a devil's sick of sin;
If you could hear, at every jolt, the blood
Come gargling from the froth-corrupted lungs,
Bitten as the cud
Of vile, incurable sores on innocent tongues,—
My friend, you would not tell with such high zest
To children ardent for some desperate glory,
The old Lie: *Dulce et decorum est
Pro patria mori.*
(1920)

WILLIAM BUTLER YEATS
1865–1939

William Butler Yeats was born in Dublin of
Anglo-Irish parents. His father was a distinguished portrait painter and a member of the Royal
Hibernian Academy. After attending schools in Hammersmith, London, and in Dublin, Yeats studied
painting but soon turned to writing. He spent many
summers with maternal relatives in County Sligo, Ireland, which he later used as the setting for many of his
poems. His first poems and articles went to the *Dublin
University Review* and other Irish periodicals. In 1888
he moved to London. The next year he published his
first volume of verse, *The Wanderings of Oisin and
Other Poems.* His interest in both the ancient culture
and the contemporary political and social problems of
his native country was always intense and expressed
itself in many ways. He helped to organize Irish literary societies in London and Dublin and, with the
novelist George Moore (1852–1933) and others, established the Irish Literary Theater, which became in
1904 the famous Abbey Theater, home of the Irish
Players.

In 1897 he published *The Secret Rose,* a prose collection of Irish legends and tales. Remarkable lyrics
appeared in *Poems* (1895) and *The Wind Among the
Reeds* (1899). His greatest eminence is as a lyric poet,
but his most notable contributions to the Irish literary
movement are in the field of the drama. His plays
move in an atmosphere of Gaelic legend and are
usually in verse. His first play, *The Countess Cathleen,*
was a romantic drama written in 1892, but his best-
known dramatic work is a one-act play-poem entitled
The Land of Heart's Desire (1894). At this point, he
broke his early attachment to the symbolist movement
but experimented continuously, writing numerous volumes of poetry and plays. Among them are *The Green
Helmet and Other Poems* (1910), *Poems Written in Discouragement* (1913), *Responsibilities: Poems and a Play*
(1914), and *Reveries over Childhood and Youth* (1915).
However, Yeats' most mature development, both in
writing and in public affairs, came in the 1920s. In
1922 he was elected senator in the new Irish Free
State, and in 1923 he was awarded the Nobel Prize
for literature. The pinnacle of his poetic achievement
came in the collection *The Tower* (1928). In later years
he made a restless attempt to construct a philosophic
justification for his beliefs in the reality of dreams and
the life of the spirit. *A Vision,* published in 1925 in a
private edition and revised in 1937, records Yeats'
mystical and metaphysical view of history and reflects his interest in theosophy, magic, Swedenborg-
ianism, and astrology. He died January 28, 1939, and
was buried at Roquebrune, France, but in 1948 his
body was brought back to Drumcliff Churchyard in
Sligo.

Yeats was influenced by many poets, notably Blake,
Shelley, the Pre-Raphaelites, and the French symbolists. But just as many influenced him, he influenced
many. Soon after his death, the poet T. S. Eliot described Yeats as "the greatest poet of our time—certainly the greatest poet in this language, and so far as I
am able to judge, in any language." Even as a young
man, Yeats was a leading figure in literary circles in
England, Ireland, and France. In the '90s and the first
decade of this century, he was the most influential figure in the Irish Renaissance. His work brought him
into contact with James Joyce, Ezra Pound, and finally
with W. H. Auden, the spokesman of a new era in
poetry.

THE ROSE OF THE WORLD

Who dreamed that beauty passes like a dream?
For these red lips, with all their mournful pride,
Mournful that no new wonder may betide,

Troy passed away in one high funeral gleam,°
5 And Usna's children died.°

We and the laboring world are passing by;
Amid men's souls, that waver and give place,
Like the pale waters in their wintry race,
Under the passing stars, foam of the sky,
10 Lives on this lonely face.

Bow down, archangels, in your dim abode.
Before you were, or any hearts to beat,
Weary and kind, one lingered by His seat;
He° made the world to be a grassy road
15 Before her wandering feet.
(1893)

THE LAKE ISLE OF INNISFREE°

I will arise and go now, and go to Innisfree,
And a small cabin build there, of clay and wattles°
      made;
Nine bean rows° will I have there, a hive for the honey
      bee,
And live alone in the bee-loud glade.

5 And I shall have some peace there, for peace comes
      dropping slow,
Dropping from the veils of the morning to where the
      cricket sings;
There midnight's all a glimmer, and noon a purple
      glow,
And evening full of the linnet's wings.

I will arise and go now, for always night and day
10 I hear lake water lapping with low sounds by the shore;
While I stand on the roadway, or on the pavements
      gray,
I hear it in the deep heart's core.
(1893)

SEPTEMBER, 1913°

What need you, being come to sense,
But fumble in a greasy till
And add the halfpence to the pence
And prayer to shivering prayer, until

You have dried the marrow from the bone;
For men were born to pray and save:
Romantic Ireland's dead and gone,
It's with O'Leary° in the grave.

Yet they were of a different kind,
The names that stilled your childish play,   10
They have gone about the world like wind,
But little time had they to pray
For whom the hangman's rope was spun,
And what, God help us, could they save?
Romantic Ireland's dead and gone,
It's with O'Leary in the grave.

Was it for this the wild geese spread
The grey wing upon every tide;
For this that all that blood was shed,
For this Edward Fitzgerald died,   20
And Robert Emmet and Wolfe Tone,°
All that delirium of the brave?
Romantic Ireland's dead and gone,
It's with O'Leary in the grave.

Yet could we turn the years again,
And call those exiles as they were
In all their loneliness and pain,
You'd cry, 'Some woman's yellow hair
Has maddened every mother's son':
They weighed so lightly what they gave.   30
But let them be, they're dead and gone,
They're with O'Leary in the grave.
(1914)

THE MAGI

Now as at all times I can see in the mind's eye,
In their stiff, painted clothes, the pale unsatisfied ones
Appear and disappear in the blue depth of the sky
With all their ancient faces like rain-beaten stones,
And all their helms of silver hovering side by side,   5
And all their eyes still fixed, hoping to find once more,
Being by Calvary's turbulence unsatisfied,
The uncontrollable mystery on the bestial floor.°
(1913; 1914)

THE WILD SWANS AT COOLE

The trees are in their autumn beauty,
The woodland paths are dry,
Under the October twilight the water
Mirrors a still sky;
Upon the brimming water among the stones
Are nine-and-fifty swans.

The Rose of the World   4 Troy . . . gleam. It was the beauty of Helen that occasioned the Trojan War and the burning of Troy, as related in Homer's *Iliad*
5 Usna's . . . died. Naoise, a son of Usna, was in love with Deirdre, a heroine
of Irish legends. King Conchobar of Ulster desired her for his wife, and Naoise
and his two brothers carried her off to Scotland. Lured back by Conchobar, the
brothers were treacherously slain, and Deirdre killed herself in sorrow   **14 He,**
God   **The Lake Isle of Innisfree.** Innisfree is an island in Lough Gill, a lake in the
county of Sligo, Ireland   **2 wattles,** interwoven sticks and twigs   **September
1913.** The imminence of Home rule in Ireland early in 1913 led to the prospect
of civil war between Southern Ireland, which wanted independence, and Northern Ireland, which did not. In September 1913 came an Irish general strike. Temporizing measures failed to bring peace, but the advent of World War I a few
months later caused a temporary suspension of the crisis. Yeats here is deploring
the economic side of the conflict. The poem was originally subtitled 'On reading
much of the correspondence against the Art Gallery' and contrasts present political leadership with past glory

8 O'Leary. John O'Leary, Irish nationalist who had died in 1907   **20–21 Edward
Fitzgerald . . . Tone.** All three are eighteenth-century Irish nationalists, whose
deaths were related to their politics, either directly or indirectly—Edward Fitzgerald
(1763–1798), Robert Emmet (1778–1803), Theobald Wolfe Tone (1763–1798)
The Magi   8 mystery . . . floor, the Christ child in the stable at Bethlehem

The nineteenth autumn has come upon me
Since I first made my count;
I saw, before I had well finished,
All suddenly mount
And scatter wheeling in great broken rings
Upon their clamorous wings.

I have looked upon those brilliant creatures,
And now my heart is sore.
All's changed since I, hearing at twilight,
The first time on this shore,
The bell-beat of their wings above my head,
Trod with a lighter tread.

Unwearied still, lover by lover,
They paddle in the cold
Companionable streams or climb the air;
Their hearts have not grown old;
Passion or conquest, wander where they will,
Attend upon them still.

But now they drift on the still water
Mysterious, beautiful;
Among what rushes will they build,
By what lake's edge or pool
Delight men's eyes when I awake some day
To find they have flown away?
(1919)

EASTER, 1916°

I have met them at close of day
Coming with vivid faces
From counter or desk among grey
Eighteenth-century houses.
I have passed with a nod of the head
Or polite meaningless words,
Or have lingered awhile and said
Polite meaningless words,
And thought before I had done
Of a mocking tale or a gibe
To please a companion
Around the fire at the club,
Being certain that they and I
But lived where motley is worn:
All changed, changed utterly:
A terrible beauty is born.

That woman's° days were spent
In ignorant good will,
Her nights in argument
Until her voice grew shrill.
What voice more sweet than hers

When, young and beautiful,
She rode to harriers?
This man° had kept a school
And rode our wingèd horse;
This other his helper° and friend
Was coming into his force;
He might have won fame in the end,
So sensitive his nature seemed,
So daring and sweet his thought.
The other man° I had dreamed
A drunken, vainglorious lout.
He had done most bitter wrong
To some who are near my heart,
Yet I number him in the song;
He, too, had resigned his part
In the casual comedy;
He, too, has been changed in his turn,
Transformed utterly:
A terrible beauty is born.

Hearts with one purpose alone
Through summer and winter seem
Enchanted to a stone
To trouble the living stream.
The horse that comes from the road,
The rider, the birds that range
From cloud to tumbling cloud,
Minute by minute they change;
A shadow of cloud on the stream
Changes minute by minute;
A horse-hoof slides on the brim,
And a horse plashes within it;
The long-legged moor-hens dive,
And hens to moor-cocks call;
Minute by minute they live:
The stone's in the midst of all.

Too long a sacrifice
Can make a stone of the heart.
O when may it suffice?
That is Heaven's part, our part
To mutter name upon name,
As a mother names her child
When sleep at last has come
On limbs that had run wild.
Was it but nightfall?
No, no, not night but death;
Was it needless death after all?
For England may keep faith
For all that is done and said.
We know their dream; enough
To know they dreamed and are dead;
And what if excess of love
Bewildered them till they died?

Easter, 1916. The Easter Rebellion of 1916 was a brief (24 April to 29 April) but fierce revolt against British rule in Ireland organized by a nationalist group known as the Irish Republican Brotherhood. British reprisals against the nationalists were equally fierce   17 **That woman,** Constance Gore-Booth Markiewicz (1868–1927), commander in the Irish Republican Brotherhood and wife of a Polish count. Arrested and jailed by the British after the Rebellion

24 **This man,** Patrick Pearse (1879–1916), schoolmaster and poet involved in Irish nationalist politics. Executed by the British. The "winged horse" is Pegasus, symbol of poetic inspiration   26 **his helper,** Thomas MacDonagh (1878–1916), a young writer. Executed by the British   31 **the other man,** John McBride, whom Maud Gonne married and later separated from. Executed by the British for his participation in the Easter Rebellion

I write it out in a verse—
MacDonagh and MacBride
And Connolly° and Pearse
Now and in time to be,
Wherever green is worn,
Are changed, changed utterly:
80 A terrible beauty is born.
(1916; 1921)

THE SECOND COMING°

Turning and turning in the widening gyre
The falcon cannot hear the falconer;
Things fall apart: the center cannot hold;
Mere anarchy is loosed upon the world,
The blood-dimmed tide is loosed, and everywhere
The ceremony of innocence is drowned;
The best lack all conviction, while the worst
Are full of passionate intensity.

Surely some revelation is at hand;
10 Surely the Second Coming is at hand.
The Second Coming! Hardly are those words out
When a vast image out of *Spiritus Mundi*°
Troubles my sight: somewhere in sands of the desert
A shape with lion body and the head of a man,
A gaze blank and pitiless as the sun,
Is moving its slow thighs, while all about it
Reel shadows of the indignant desert birds.
The darkness drops again; but now I know
That twenty centuries of stony sleep
20 Were vexed to nightmare by a rocking cradle,
And what rough beast, its hour come round at last,
Slouches towards Bethlehem to be born?
(1921)

SAILING TO BYZANTIUM°

That is no country for old men. The young
In one another's arms, birds in the trees
(Those dying generations) at their song,
The salmon-falls, the mackerel-crowded seas,°
Fish, flesh, or fowl, commend all summer long
Whatever is begotten, born, and dies.

Caught in that sensual music, all neglect
Monuments of unaging intellect.

An aged man is but a paltry thing,
A tattered coat upon a stick, unless   10
Soul clap its hands and sing, and louder sing
For every tatter in its mortal dress;
Nor is there singing school but studying
Monuments of its own magnificence;
And therefore I have sailed the seas and come
To the holy city of Byzantium.

O sages, standing in God's holy fire
As in the gold mosaic of a wall,
Come from the holy fire, perne in a gyre,°
And be the singing-masters of my soul.   20
Consume my heart away—sick with desire
And fastened to a dying animal
It knows not what it is—and gather me
Into the artifice of eternity.

Once out of nature I shall never take
My bodily form from any natural thing,
But such a form as Grecian goldsmiths make
Of hammered gold and gold enamelling
To keep a drowsy emperor awake;
Or set upon a golden bough° to sing   30
To lords and ladies of Byzantium
Of what is past, or passing, or to come.
(1928)

from MEDITATIONS IN TIME OF CIVIL WAR

I

ANCESTRAL HOUSES

Surely among a rich man's flowering lawns,
Amid the rustle of his planted hills,
Life overflows without ambitious pains;
And rains down life until the basin spills,
And mounts more dizzy high the more it rains
As though to choose whatever shape it wills
And never stoop to a mechanical
Or servile shape, at others' beck and call.

Mere dreams, mere dreams! Yet Homer had not sung
Had he not found it certain beyond dreams   10
That out of life's own self-delight had sprung
The abounding glittering jet; though now it seems
As if some marvellous empty sea-shell flung
Out of the obscure dark of the rich streams,
And not a fountain, were the symbol which
Shadows the inherited glory of the rich.

76 **Connolly,** James Connolly (1870–1916), famous Irish labor leader. Executed by the British   **The Second Coming.** Various interpretations have been put upon the event designated as the second coming of Christ. Although the expression is not found in Scripture, synonyms of the event and allusions to it have been identified. One definition in the *Dictionary of the Bible* calls it "an Advent at the end of the age to judge the world, to destroy evil, to reward the saints, and to establish the Kingdom of Glory"   12 **Spiritus Mundi,** the soul of the world, the organizing principle of the physical universe. Yeats uses the phrase also to mean the Great Memory, a form of universal subconscious holding the memories of the human race   **Sailing to Byzantium.** In ancient geography Byzantium was a Greek city founded in the seventh century B.C. As Constantinople it became the capital of the Roman Empire and later of the Byzantine, or Eastern, Empire. The present name of the city is Istanbul. In the poem the city is presented symbolically as the ideal journey's end for the old, since it was the one place in all the world in which the forces of body, mind, and spirit existed in proper balance. In *A Vision* Yeats expressed the belief that "in early Byzantium, maybe never before nor since in recorded history, religious, aesthetic, and practical life were one"   4 **salmon-falls . . . seas,** a reference to the spawning period of salmon, which are noted for jumping up waterfalls at that time, and of mackerel, which crowd up streams

19 **perne in a gyre,** spool in a circular or spiral motion   30 **golden bough.** "I have read somewhere that in the Emperor's palace at Byzantium was a tree made of gold and silver, and artificial birds that sang."—Yeats' note

Some violent bitter man, some powerful man
Called architect and artist in, that they,
Bitter and violent men, might rear in stone
20 The sweetness that all longed for night and day,
The gentleness none there had ever known;
But when the master's buried mice can play,
And maybe the great-grandson of that house,
For all its bronze and marble, 's but a mouse.

O what if gardens where the peacock strays
With delicate feet upon old terraces,
Or else all Juno from an urn displays
Before the indifferent garden deities;
O what if levelled lawns and gravelled ways
30 Where slippered Contemplation finds his ease
And Childhood a delight for every sense,
But take our greatness with our violence?

What if the glory of escutcheoned doors,
And buildings that a haughtier age designed,
The pacing to and fro on polished floors
Amid great chambers and long galleries, lined
With famous portraits of our ancestors;
What if those things the greatest of mankind
Consider most to magnify, or to bless,
40 But take our greatness with our bitterness?
(1928)

NINETEEN HUNDRED AND NINETEEN

I

Many ingenious lovely things are gone
That seemed sheer miracle to the multitude,
Protected from the circle of the moon
That pitches common things about. There stood
Amid the ornamental bronze and stone
An ancient image made of olive wood—
And gone are Phidias'° famous ivories
And all the golden grasshoppers and bees.

We too had many pretty toys when young:
10 A law indifferent to blame or praise,
To bribe or threat; habits that made old wrong
Melt down, as it were wax in the sun's rays;
Public opinion ripening for so long
We thought it would outlive all future days.
O what fine thought we had because we thought
That the worst rogues and rascals had died out.

All teeth were drawn, all ancient tricks unlearned,
And a great army but a showy thing;
What matter that no cannon had been turned
20 Into a ploughshare? Parliament and king

Nineteen Hundred and Nineteen   7 Phidias, regarded as greatest of ancient
Greek sculptors (fifth century B.C.)

Thought that unless a little powder burned
The trumpeters might burst with trumpeting
And yet it lack all glory; and perchance
The guardsmen's drowsy chargers would not prance.

Now days are dragon-ridden, the nightmare
Rides upon sleep: a drunken soldiery
Can leave the mother, murdered at her door,
To crawl in her own blood, and go scot-free;
The night can sweat with terror as before
We pieced our thoughts into philosophy,   30
And planned to bring the world under a rule,
Who are but weasels fighting in a hole.

He who can read the signs nor sink unmanned
Into the half-deceit of some intoxicant
From shallow wits; who knows no work can stand,
Whether health, wealth or peace of mind were spent
On master-work of intellect or hand,
No honour leave its mighty monument,
Has but one comfort left: all triumph would
But break upon his ghostly solitude.   40

But is there any comfort to be found?
Man is in love and loves what vanishes,
What more is there to say? That country round
None dared admit, if such a thought were his,
Incendiary or bigot could be found
To burn that stump on the Acropolis,
Or break in bits the famous ivories
Or traffic in the grasshoppers or bees.

II

When Loie Fuller's Chinese dancers enwound
A shining web, a floating ribbon of cloth,   50
It seemed that a dragon of air
Had fallen among dancers, had whirled them round
Or hurried them off on its own furious path;
So the Platonic Year
Whirls out new right and wrong,
Whirls in the old instead;
All men are dancers and their tread
Goes to the barbarous clangour of a gong.

III

Some moralist or mythological poet
Compares the solitary soul to a swan;   60
I am satisfied with that,
Satisfied if a troubled mirror show it,
Before that brief gleam of its life be gone,
An image of its state;
The wings half spread for flight,
The breast thrust out in pride
Whether to play, or to ride
Those winds that clamour of approaching night.

A man in his own secret meditation
Is lost amid the labyrinth that he has made   70

In art or politics;
Some Platonist affirms that in the station
Where we should cast off body and trade
The ancient habit sticks,
And that if our works could
But vanish with our breath
That were a lucky death,
For triumph can but mar our solitude.

The swan has leaped into the desolate heaven:
80 That image can bring wildness, bring a rage
To end all things, to end
What my laborious life imagined, even
The half-imagined, the half-written page;
O but we dreamed to mend
Whatever mischief seemed
To afflict mankind, but now
That winds of winter blow
Learn that we were crack-pated when we dreamed.

            IV
We, who seven years ago
90 Talked of honour and of truth,
Shriek with pleasure if we show
The weasel's twist, the weasel's tooth.°

            V
Come let us mock at the great
That had such burdens on the mind
And toiled so hard and late
To leave some monument behind,
Nor thought of the levelling wind.

Come let us mock at the wise;
With all those calendars whereon
100 They fixed old aching eyes,
They never saw how seasons run,
And now but gape at the sun.

Come let us mock at the good
That fancied goodness might be gay,
And sick of solitude
Might proclaim a holiday:
Wind shrieked—and where are they?

Mock mockers after that
That would not lift a hand maybe
110 To help good, wise or great
To bar that foul storm out, for we
Traffic in mockery.

            VI
Violence upon the roads: violence of horses;
Some few have handsome riders, are garlanded
On delicate sensitive ear or tossing mane,
But wearied running round and round in their courses

92 **weasel's tooth**, men seem to be reduced to animals fighting in a hole

All break and vanish, and evil gathers head:
Herodias' daughters° have returned again,
A sudden blast of dusty wind and after
Thunder of feet, tumult of images,   120
Their purpose in the labyrinth of the wind;
And should some crazy hand dare touch a daughter
All turn with amorous cries, or angry cries,
According to the wind, for all are blind.
But now wind drops, dust settles; thereupon
There lurches past, his great eyes without thought
Under the shadow of stupid straw-pale locks,
That insolent fiend Robert Artisson
To whom the love-lorn Lady Kyteler° brought
Bronzed peacock feathers, red combs of her cocks. 130
(1919)

LEDA AND THE SWAN°

A sudden blow: the great wings beating still
Above the staggering girl, her thighs caressed
By the dark webs, her nape caught in his bill,
He holds her helpless breast upon his breast.

How can those terrified vague fingers push
The feathered glory from her loosening thighs?
And how can body, laid in that white rush,
But feel the strange heart beating where it lies?

A shudder in the loins engenders there
The broken wall, the burning roof and tower   10
And Agamemnon dead.°
                    Being so caught up,
So mastered by the brute blood of the air,
Did she put on his knowledge with his power
Before the indifferent beak could let her drop?
(1925)

AMONG SCHOOL CHILDREN

I walk through the long schoolroom questioning,
A kind old nun in a white hood replies;
The children learn to cipher and to sing,
To study reading-books and history,
To cut and sew, be neat in everything
In the best modern way—the children's eyes
In momentary wonder stare upon
A sixty year old smiling public man.

118 **Herodias' daughters,** examples of unnatural chaos and violence
128–129 **Robert Artisson . . . Lady Kyteler.** Artisson was a fourteenth-century incubus (a spirit that has sexual intercourse with women while they sleep) summoned up by Lady Kyteler to be her lover   **Leda and the Swan.** In classical
mythology Leda, wife of the Spartan king Tyndareus, was beloved by Zeus, who
visited her in the form of a swan. From their mating was born the beautiful Helen
of Troy. The abduction of Helen from her husband, Menelaus, by Paris, who fled
with her to Troy, was the cause of the legendary Trojan War   10–11 **broken
wall . . . dead,** well-known incidents in the Greek attack upon Troy in the Trojan
War. Agamemnon was the brother of Menelaus and the commander of the allied
Greek forces. While he was absent from home, his wife, Clytemnestra, another
daughter of Leda and Zeus, fell in love with Aegisthus. Upon his return from Troy,
Agamemnon was killed either by his wife or (according to Homer) by Aegisthus

I dream of a Ledaean° body, bent
10 Above a sinking fire, a tale that she
Told of a harsh reproof, or trivial event
That changed some childish day to tragedy—
Told, and it seemed that our two natures blent
Into a sphere from youthful sympathy,
Or else, to alter Plato's parable,°
Into the yolk and white of the one shell.

And thinking of that fit of grief or rage
I look upon one child or t'other there
And wonder if she stood so at that age—
20 For even daughters of the swan° can share
Something of every paddler's° heritage—
And had that color upon cheek or hair;
And thereupon my heart is driven wild:
She stands before me as a living child.

Her present image floats into the mind—
Did quattrocento° finger fashion it
Hollow of cheek as though it drank the wind
And took a mess of shadows for its meat?
And I though never of Ledaean kind
30 Had pretty plumage once—enough of that,
Better to smile on all that smile, and show
There is a comfortable kind of old scarecrow.

What youthful mother, a shape upon her lap
Honey of generation had betrayed,
And that must sleep, shriek, struggle to escape
As recollection or the drug decide,
Would think her son, did she but see that shape
With sixty or more winters on its head,
A compensation for the pang of his birth,
40 Or the uncertainty of his setting forth?

Plato thought nature but a spume° that plays
Upon a ghostly paradigm° of things;
Solider Aristotle° played the taws°
Upon the bottom of a king of kings;
World-famous golden-thighed Pythagoras°
Fingered upon a fiddle stick or strings
What a star sang and careless Muses heard:
Old clothes upon old sticks to scare a bird.

Both nuns and mothers worship images,
But those the candles light are not as those   50
That animate a mother's reveries,
But keep a marble or a bronze repose.
And yet they too break hearts—O Presences
That passion, piety or affection knows,
And that all heavenly glory symbolize—
O self-born mockers of man's enterprise;

Labor° is blossoming or dancing where
The body is not bruised to pleasure soul,
Nor beauty born out of its own despair,
Nor blear-eyed wisdom out of midnight oil.   60
O chestnut tree, great rooted blossomer,
Are you the leaf, the blossom or the bole?°
O body swayed to music, O brightening glance,
How can we know the dancer from the dance?
(1928)

COOLE PARK, 1929°

I meditate upon a swallow's flight,
Upon an aged woman and her house,
A sycamore and lime-tree lost in night
Although that western cloud is luminous,
Great works constructed there in nature's spite
For scholars and for poets after us,
Thoughts long knitted into a single thought,
A dance-like glory that those walls begot.

There Hyde° before he had beaten into prose
That noble blade the Muses buckled on,   10
There one° that ruffled in a manly pose
For all his timid heart, there that slow man,
That meditative man, John Synge,° and those
Impetuous men, Shawe-Taylor and Hugh Lane°
Found pride established in humility,
A scene well set and excellent company.

They came like swallows and like swallows went,
And yet a woman's powerful character
Could keep a swallow to its first intent;
And half a dozen in formation there,   20
That seemed to whirl upon a compass-point,
Found certainty upon the dreaming air,
The intellectual sweetness of those lines
That cut through time or cross it withershins.

Here, traveller, scholar, poet, take your stand
When all those rooms and passages are gone,
When nettles wave upon a shapeless mound
And saplings root among the broken stone,

Among School Children   9 **Ledaean**, like Leda, whose graceful figure was a subject of medieval art. See *Leda and the Swan.* The poet is thinking of his beloved, Maud Gonne   15 **Plato's parable.** Plato was a famous Greek philosopher of the fourth century B.C. This is probably a reference to the satirical discourse on the nature of man as related by Plato in the *Symposium,* 189 ff. As there presented, the sexes were three—male, female, and androgynous (union of the two). The last was a spherical creature, who, because of an attack upon the gods, was "cut in two as you might divide an egg with a hair." Plato frequently refers to the blending of mutually sympathetic natures. Such a union is symbolized by Yeats in the yolk and the white of an egg   20 **daughters of the swan**, symbolic for beautiful children   21 **paddler,** figurative for child of low birth   26 **quattrocento,** of the supreme fifteenth-century period of Italian art   41 **spume,** froth or foam   42 **ghostly paradigm,** spiritual model or pattern   43 **Aristotle,** the most celebrated and influential of the Greek philosophers (384–322 B.C.). He is regarded as more down-to-earth than the idealistic Plato   **played the taws,** plied the whip. Aristotle was practical enough as a teacher of Alexander the Great (the king of kings, 356–322 B.C.) to give the young prince the flogging that he needed   45 **Pythagoras,** famous Greek philosopher and mathematician of the sixth century B.C., said to have had a golden thigh. He is credited with the invention of the lyre. He is the example of the mystic, with his creation of the theory concerning the music of the spheres. All of these philosophies—of Plato, of Aristotle, and of Pythagoras—are in contrast to the solid reality of birth and death

57 **Labor,** child-birth   62 **bole,** tree trunk   **Coole Park, 1929.** Coole Park was the ancestral home of Yeats's friend, Lady Gregory (1859?–1932), the aged woman of l. 2   9 **Hyde,** Douglas Hyde (1860–1949), contemporary Irish writer, pioneer in the movement for revival of the Irish language and literature. Later President of Ireland (1938–1945)   11–12 **One . . . heart,** Yeats himself   13 **John Synge,** Irish playwright (1871–1909), best known for *The Playboy of the Western World*   14 **Shawe-Taylor and Hugh Lane,** nephews of Lady Gregory. They are the "travellers" of l. 25

And dedicate—eyes bent upon the ground,
30 Back turned upon the brightness of the sun
And all the sensuality of the shade—
A moment's memory to that laurelled head.°
(1933)

FOR ANNE GREGORY

"Never shall a young man,
Thrown into despair
By those great honey-colored
Ramparts at your ear,
5 Love you for yourself alone
And not your yellow hair."

"But I can get a hair-dye
And set such color there,
Brown, or black, or carrot,
10 That young men in despair
May love me for myself alone
And not my yellow hair."

"I heard an old religious man
But yesternight declare
15 That he had found a text to prove
That only God, my dear,
Could love you for yourself alone
And not your yellow hair."
(1931; 1932)

BYZANTIUM

The unpurged images of day recede;°
The Emperor's drunken soldiery are abed;
Night resonance recedes, night-walkers' song
After great cathedral gong;
A starlit or a moonlit dome disdains
All that man is,
All mere complexities,
The fury and the mire of human veins.

Before me floats an image, man or shade,
10 Shade more than man, more image than a shade;
For Hades' bobbin bound in mummy-cloth°
May unwind the winding path;
A mouth that has no moisture and no breath
Breathless mouths may summon;
I hail the superhuman;
I call it death-in-life and life-in-death.

Miracle, bird or golden handiwork,
More miracle than bird or handiwork,
Planted on the star-lit golden bough,°
Can like the cocks of Hades crow, 20
Or, by the moon embittered, scorn aloud
In glory of changeless metal
Common bird or petal
And all complexities of mire or blood.

At midnight on the Emperor's pavement flit
Flames that no faggot feeds, nor steel has lit,
Nor storm disturbs, flames begotten of flame,
Where blood-begotten spirits come
And all complexities of fury leave,
Dying into a dance, 30
An agony of trance,
An agony of flame that cannot singe a sleeve.

Astraddle on the dolphin's mire and blood,
Spirit after spirit! The smithies break the flood,
The golden smithies° of the Emperor!
Marbles of the dancing floor
Break bitter furies of complexity,
Those images that yet
Fresh images beget,
That dolphin-torn, that gong-tormented sea. 40
(1930)

CRAZY JANE TALKS WITH THE BISHOP°

I met the Bishop on the road
And much said he and I.
'Those breasts are flat and fallen now,
Those veins must soon be dry;
Live in a heavenly mansion, 5
Not in some foul sty.'

'Fair and foul are near of kin,
And fair needs foul,' I cried.
'My friends are gone, but that's a truth
Nor grave nor bed denied, 10
Learned in bodily lowliness
And in the heart's pride.

'A woman can be proud and stiff
When on love intent;
But Love has pitched his mansion in 15
The place of excrement;
For nothing can be sole or whole
That has not been rent.'
(1933)

32 **that laurelled head,** Lady Gregory was a playwright **Byzantium** 1 **recede.**
The scene is set in the evening 11 **Hades' ... cloth.** Yeats' early notes for the
poem mention "a walking mummy," which fits well into the poem's concern with
flesh-spirit and life-death relations

17–19 **bird ... bough.** Cf. the golden bird of Yeats' "Sailing to Byzantium,"
another image of the relation of artifice and life 35 **the golden smithies,** the
workshops where the mosaic pavement described in stanzas 4 and 5 is made
Crazy Jane Talks with the Bishop. Yeats wrote a series of poems on Crazy Jane,
many of which concern the relation between physicality and spirituality

LAPIS LAZULI°

(FOR HARRY CLIFTON)

I have heard that hysterical women say
They are sick of the palette and fiddle-bow.
Of poets that are always gay,
For everybody knows or else should know
That if nothing drastic is done
Aeroplane and Zeppelin will come out,
Pitch like King Billy° bomb-balls in
Until the town lie beaten flat.

All perform their tragic play,
10 There struts Hamlet, there is Lear,
That's Ophelia, that Cordelia;
Yet they, should the last scene be there,
The great stage curtain about to drop,
If worthy their prominent part in the play,
Do not break up their lines to weep.
They know that Hamlet and Lear are gay;
Gaiety transfiguring all that dread.
All men have aimed at, found and lost;
Black out; Heaven blazing into the head:
20 Tragedy wrought to its uttermost.
Though Hamlet rambles and Lear rages,
And all the drop-scenes drop at once
Upon a hundred thousand stages,
It cannot grow by an inch or an ounce.

On their own feet they came, or on shipboard,
Camel-back, horse-back, ass-back, mule-back,
Old civilisations put to the sword.
Then they and their wisdom went to rack:
No handiwork of Callimachus,°
30 Who handled marble as if it were bronze,
Made draperies that seemed to rise
When sea-wind swept the corner, stands;
His long lamp-chimney shaped like the stem
Of a slender palm, stood but a day;
All things fall and are built again,
And those that build them again are gay.

Two Chinamen, behind them a third,
Are carved in lapis lazuli,
Over them flies a long-legged bird,
40 A symbol of longevity;
The third, doubtless a serving-man,
Carries a musical instrument.

Every discoloration of the stone,
Every accidental crack or dent,
Seems a water-course or an avalanche,
Or lofty slope where it still snows
Though doubtless plum or cherry-branch
Sweetens the little half-way house
Those Chinamen climb towards, and I
Delight to imagine them seated there;   50
There, on the mountain and the sky,
On all the tragic scene they stare.
One asks for mournful melodies;
Accomplished fingers begin to play.
Their eyes mid many wrinkles, their eyes,
Their ancient, glittering eyes, are gay.
(1939)

THE CIRCUS ANIMALS' DESERTION

I

I sought a theme and sought for it in vain,
I sought it daily for six weeks or so.
Maybe at last, being but a broken man,
I must be satisfied with my heart, although
Winter and summer till old age began
My circus animals were all on show,
Those stilted boys, that burnished chariot,
Lion and woman and the Lord knows what.°

II

What can I but enumerate old themes?
First that sea-rider Oisin° led by the nose   10
Through three enchanted islands, allegorical dreams,
Vain gaiety, vain battle, vain repose,
Themes of the embittered heart, or so it seems,
That might adorn old songs or courtly shows;
But what cared I that set him on to ride,
I, starved for the bosom of his faery bride?°

And then a counter-truth filled out its play,
The Countess Cathleen was the name I gave it;
She, pity-crazed, had given her soul away,
But masterful Heaven had intervened to save it.   20
I thought my dear° must her own soul destroy,
So did fanaticism and hate enslave it,
And this brought forth a dream and soon enough
This dream itself had all my thought and love.

And when the Fool and Blind Man stole the bread
Cuchulain° fought the ungovernable sea;
Heart-mysteries there, and yet when all is said

Lapis Lazuli. Harry Clifton had given Yeats a lapis lazuli medallion on which was carved the figure of an old man and a servant   7 **King Billy.** In 1690, King Billy (William III of England) pitched in bomb-balls at the Battle of the Boyne. Yeats also wishes us to think of Kaiser Wilhelm II (1859–1941) from the Zeppelin reference. The references are clearly to point to destructive times for a civilization   29 **Callimachus,** Greek sculptor of late fifth century B.C.

The Circus Animals' Desertion   6–8 **circus animals . . . knows what,** the subjects of his early poetry, referred to as a menagerie   10 **Oisin,** legendary warrior bard of the Fenians, third century A.D., and the subject of much early work by Yeats   16 **faery bride.** Yeats identified Maud Gonne with Niamh, Oisin's bride   21 **my dear,** Maud Gonne   26 **Cuchulain** (pronounced Cuhoo-lin), Irish legendary hero of Ulster, of great strength and of remarkable beauty

It was the dream itself enchanted me:
Character isolated by a deed
To engross the present and dominate memory.
Players and painted stage took all my love,
And not those things that they were emblems of.

III

Those masterful images because complete
Grew in pure mind, but out of what began?
A mound of refuse or the sweepings of a street,
Old kettles, old bottles, and a broken can,
Old iron, old bones, old rags, that raving slut
Who keeps the till. Now that my ladder's gone,
I must lie down where all the ladders start,
In the foul rag-and-bone shop of the heart.
(1939)

CUCHULAIN COMFORTED°

A man that had six mortal wounds, a man
Violent and famous, strode among the dead;
Eyes stared out of the branches and were gone.

Then certain Shrouds that muttered head to head
Came and were gone. He leant upon a tree
As though to meditate on wounds and blood.

A Shroud that seemed to have authority
Among those bird-like things came, and let fall
A bundle of linen. Shrouds by two and three

Came creeping up because the man was still.
And thereupon that linen-carrier said:
'Your life can grow much sweeter if you will

'Obey our ancient rule and make a shroud;
Mainly because of what we only know
The rattle of those arms makes us afraid.

'We thread the needles' eyes, and all we do
All must together do.' That done, the man
Took up the nearest and began to sew.

'Now must we sing and sing the best we can,
But first you must be told our character:
Convicted cowards all, by kindred slain

'Or driven from home and left to die in fear.'
They sang, but had nor human tunes nor words,
Though all was done in common as before;

They had changed their throats and had the throats of
  birds.
(1939)

Cuchulain Comforted. See "The Circus Animals' Desertion," l. 26

UNDER BEN BULBEN°

I

Swear by what the sages spoke
Round the Mareotic Lake°
That the Witch of Atlas° knew,
Spoke and set the cocks a-crow.

Swear by those horsemen, by those women
Complexion and form prove superhuman,
That pale, long-visaged company
That air in immortality
Completeness of their passions won;
Now they ride the wintry dawn°
Where Ben Bulben sets the scene.

Here's the gist of what they mean.

II

Many times man lives and dies
Between his two eternities,
That of race and that of soul,
And ancient Ireland knew it all.
Whether man die in his bed
Or the rifle knock him dead,
A brief parting from those dear
Is the worst man has to fear.
Though grave-diggers' toil is long,
Sharp their spades, their muscles strong,
They but thrust their buried men
Back in the human mind again.

III

You that Mitchel's prayer° have heard,
'Send war in our time, O Lord!'
Know that when all words are said
And a man is fighting mad,
Something drops from eyes long blind,
He completes his partial mind,
For an instant stands at ease,
Laughs aloud, his heart at peace.
Even the wisest man grows tense
With some sort of violence
Before he can accomplish fate,
Know his work or choose his mate.

IV

Poet and sculptor, do the work,
Nor let the modish painter shirk
What his great forefathers did,

Under Ben Bulben. Ben Bulben is a mountain in County Sligo, Ireland
2 **Mareotic Lake,** Lake Mareotis, salt lake in northern Egypt near Alexandria.
Groups of philosophers lived around the lake in the first and third centuries A.D.;
hence the lake is a symbol of philosophy   3 **Witch of Atlas,** fanciful, fantastic
poem by Shelley (1820). In Yeats' poem the witch is a symbol of the occult
10 **Now . . . dawn,** folk, belief that supernatural horsemen ride from mountain to mountain   25 **Mitchel's prayer.** John Mitchel (d. 1875) was an Irish
revolutionary. The quotation is from his *Jail Journal*

40 Bring the soul of man to God,
Make him fill the cradles right.

Measurement began our might:
Forms a stark Egyptian thought,
Forms that gentler Phidias° wrought.
Michael Angelo° left a proof
On the Sistine Chapel roof,
Where but half-awakened Adam
Can disturb globe-trotting Madam
Till her bowels are in heat,
50 Proof that there's a purpose set
Before the secret working mind:
Profane perfection of mankind.

Quattrocento° put in paint
On backgrounds for a God or Saint
Gardens where a soul's at ease;
Where everything that meets the eye,
Flowers and grass and cloudless sky,
Resemble forms that are or seem
When sleepers wake and yet still dream,
60 And when it's vanished still declare,
With only bed and bedstead there,
That heavens had opened.
                              Gyres° run on;
When that greater dream had gone
Calvert and Wilson, Blake and Claude,°
Prepared a rest for the people of God,
Palmer's phrase,° but after that
Confusion fell upon our thought.

                    V

Irish poets, learn your trade,
Sing whatever is well made,
70 Scorn the sort now growing up
All out of shape from toe to top,
Their unremembering hearts and heads
Base-born products of base beds.
Sing the peasantry, and then
Hard-riding country gentlemen,
The holiness of monks, and after
Porter-drinkers' randy laughter;
Sing the lords and ladies gay
That were beaten into the clay
80 Through seven heroic centuries;
Cast your mind on other days
That we in coming days may be
Still the indomitable Irishry.

                    VI

Under bare Ben Bulben's head
In Drumcliff churchyard Yeats is laid.
An ancestor was rector there
Long years ago, a church stands near,
By the road an ancient cross.
No marble, no conventional phrase;
On limestone quarried near the spot   90
By his command these words are cut:
        Cast a cold eye
        On life, on death.
        Horseman, pass by!

(1938)

VIRGINIA WOOLF
1882–1941

When Virginia Stephen was born, her godfather
wrote some verses expressing the hope that she
would be "a sample of Heredity." This was no small
wish, for she was the daughter of a distinguished
writer and critic, Sir Leslie Stephen, the granddaughter
of the novelist Thackeray, and was related to the Darwins, Stracheys, and other eminent scholarly families.

A brilliant young woman, she grew up in a literary
atmosphere and was educated at home by her father.
The famous group of intellectuals that came to be
known as the "Bloomsbury Group" originated in
gatherings of Cambridge University graduates and their
friends at the house (in the Bloomsbury district of London) where Virginia was living with her sister and two
brothers. She married one of the young men, Leonard
Woolf, in 1912. Five years later, the Woolfs started the
Hogarth Press. It became a successful publishing
house, publishing not only Virginia Woolf's own first
short stories but also the early works of T. S. Eliot,
E. M. Forster, and other important authors. It also introduced the psychological works of Sigmund Freud
(1856–1939) to English readers. Virginia Woolf suffered a nervous breakdown in her thirties and from
then on worried that the illness would strike again.
She was depressed by the outbreak of World War II,
and despite the best efforts of her husband and friends,
she began to feel the symptoms of another collapse. In
1941 she committed suicide by drowning near her
home in Sussex.

Woolf was an author who made an original contribution to the form of the novel. Although her early
fiction (*The Voyage Out*, 1915; *Night and Day*, 1919)
is fairly conventional in its treatment of chronology, in
her later work (*Mrs. Dalloway*, 1925; *To the Lighthouse*, 1927) she manipulates point of view and narrative flow in an attempt to recreate the fluidity of hu-

44 **Phidias**, regarded as the greatest of ancient Greek sculptors (fifth century B.C.)
45 **Michael Angelo**, Michelangelo (1475–1564), famous Italian sculptor,
painter, architect, and poet of the High Renaissance   53 **Quattrocento**, stands
here for fifteenth-century Italian art   63 **Gyres**, spiral motions or forms. Yeats
preferred to see history as a series of revolving gyres; his was a cyclical theory of
history   64 **Calvert and Wilson, Blake and Claude.** Calvert may be Denis Calvert, sixteenth-century Flemish painter, or Edward Calvert, nineteenth-century
visionary artist and disciple of Blake. Richard Wilson was an eighteenth-century
British landscape painter. William Blake (1757–1827) was the famous English artist, poet, and visionary. Claude Lorrain was a seventeenth-century French landscape painter   66 **Palmer's phrase.** Samuel Palmer (1805–1881) was an English
landscape painter and a disciple of Blake. He used the phrase to describe Blake's
illustrations for Vergil's *Eclogues*

man experience. She believed that much imaginative literature is false to life because it relates episodes artificially—in a straight line—whereas human experiences are actually comprised of many vivid impressions that bombard us from all sides. *The Waves* (1931), *The Years* (1937), and *Between the Acts* (1941) carry her even further in the direction of a quasi-poetic symbolic fiction. She also wrote a great deal of distinguished literary criticism and many essays, some of which deal with women's emancipation.

THE MARK ON THE WALL

Perhaps it was the middle of January in the present year that I first looked up and saw the mark on the wall. In order to fix a date it is necessary to remember what one saw. So now I think of the fire; the steady film of yellow light upon the page of my book; the three chrysanthemums in the round glass bowl on the mantelpiece. Yes, it must have been the wintertime, and we had just finished our tea, for I remember that I was smoking a cigarette when I looked up and saw the
10 mark on the wall for the first time. I looked up through the smoke of my cigarette and my eye lodged for a moment upon the burning coals, and that old fancy of the crimson flag flapping from the castle tower came into my mind, and I thought of the cavalcade of red knights riding up the side of the black rock. Rather to my relief the sight of the mark interrupted the fancy, for it is an old fancy, an automatic fancy, made as a child perhaps. The mark was a small round mark, black upon the white wall, about six or seven inches
20 above the mantelpiece.

How readily our thoughts swarm upon a new object, lifting it a little way, as ants carry a blade of straw so feverishly, and then leave it. . . . If that mark was made by a nail, it can't have been for a picture, it must have been for a miniature—the miniature of a lady with white powdered curls, powder-dusted cheeks, and lips like red carnations. A fraud of course, for the people who had this house before us would have chosen pictures in that way—an old picture for an old
30 room. That is the sort of people they were—very interesting people, and I think of them so often, in such queer places, because one will never see them again, never know what happened next. They wanted to leave this house because they wanted to change their style of furniture, so he said, and he was in process of saying that in his opinion art should have ideas behind it when we were torn asunder, as one is torn from the old lady about to pour out tea and the young man about to hit the tennis ball in the back garden of the suburban
40 villa as one rushes past in the train.

But for that mark, I'm not sure about it; I don't believe it was made by a nail after all; it's too big, too round, for that. I might get up, but if I got up and looked at it, ten to one I shouldn't be able to say for certain: because once a thing's done, no one ever knows how it happened. Oh! dear me, the mystery of life; the inaccuracy of thought! The ignorance of humanity! To show how very little control of our possessions we have—what an accidental affair this living is
50 after all our civilization—let me just count over a few of the things lost in one lifetime, beginning, for that seems always the most mysterious of losses—what cat would gnaw, what rat would nibble—three pale blue canisters of bookbinding tools? Then there were the bird cages, the iron hoops, the steel skates, the Queen Anne coal scuttle, the bagatelle board, the hand organ—all gone, and jewels, too. Opals and emeralds, they lie about the roots of turnips. What a scraping paring affair it is to be sure! The wonder is that I've
60 any clothes on my back, that I sit surrounded by solid furniture at this moment. Why, if one wants to compare life to anything, one must liken it to being blown through the Tube° at fifty miles an hour—landing at the other end without a single hairpin in one's hair! Shot out at the feet of God entirely naked! Tumbling head over heels in the asphodel meadows like brown paper parcels pitched down a shoot in the post office! With one's hair flying back like the tail of a race horse. Yes, that seems to express the rapidity of life, the perpetual
70 waste and repair; all so casual, all so haphazard. . . .

But after life. The slow pulling down of thick green stalks so that the cup of the flower, as it turns over, deluges one with purple and red light. Why, after all, should one not be born there as one is born here, helpless, speechless, unable to focus one's eyesight, groping at the roots of the grass, at the toes of the Giants? As for saying which are trees, and which are men and women, or whether there are such things, that one won't be in a condition to do for fifty years or so.
80 There will be nothing but spaces of light and dark, intersected by thick stalks, and rather higher up perhaps, rose-shaped blots of an indistinct color—dim pinks and blues—which will, as time goes on, become more definite, become—I don't know what. . . .

And yet that mark on the wall is not a hole at all. It may even be caused by some round black substance, such as a small rose leaf, left over from the summer, and I, not being a very vigilant housekeeper—look at the dust on the mantelpiece, for example, the dust
90 which, so they say, buried Troy three times over, only fragments of pots utterly refusing annihilation, as one can believe.

The tree outside the window taps very gently on the pane. . . . I want to think quietly, calmly, spaciously, never to be interrupted, never to have to rise from my chair, to slip easily from one thing to another, without any sense of hostility, or obstacle. I want to sink deeper and deeper, away from the surface, with its hard separate facts. To steady myself, let me catch hold of the first idea that passes . . . Shakes-
100

The Mark on the Wall   63 **the Tube,** the subway

peare. . . . Well, he will do as well as another. A man who sat himself solidly in an armchair, and looked into the fire, so— A shower of ideas fell perpetually from some very high Heaven down through his mind. He leant his forehead on his hand, and people, looking in through the open door—for this scene is supposed to take place on a summer's evening— But how dull this is, this historical fiction! It doesn't interest me at all. I wish I could hit upon a pleasant track of thought, a 110 track indirectly reflecting credit upon myself, for those are the pleasantest thoughts, and very frequent even in the minds of modest mouse-colored people, who believe genuinely that they dislike to hear their own praises. They are not thoughts directly praising oneself; that is the beauty of them; they are thoughts like this:

"And then I came into the room. They were discussing botany. I said how I'd seen a flower growing on a dust heap on the site of an old house in Kingsway. The 120 seed, I said, must have been sown in the reign of Charles the First.° What flowers grew in the reign of Charles the First?" I asked— (But I don't remember the answer.) Tall flowers with purple tassels to them perhaps. And so it goes on. All the time I'm dressing up the figure of myself in my own mind, lovingly, stealthily, not openly adoring it, for if I did that, I should catch myself out, and stretch my hand at once for a book in self-protection. Indeed, it is curious how instinctively one protects the image of oneself from 130 idolatry or any other handling that could make it ridiculous, or too unlike the original to be believed in any longer. Or is it not so very curious after all? It is a matter of great importance. Suppose the looking glass smashes, the image disappears, and the romantic figure with the green of forest depths all about it is there no longer, but only that shell of a person which is seen by other people—what an airless, shallow, bald, prominent world it becomes! A world not to be lived in. As we face each other in omnibuses and under- 140 ground railways we are looking into the mirror; that accounts for the vagueness, the gleam of glassiness, in our eyes. And the novelists in future will realize more and more the importance of these reflections, for of course there is not one reflection but an almost infinite number; those are the depths they will explore, those the phantoms they will pursue, leaving the description of reality more and more out of their stories, taking a knowledge of it for granted, as the Greeks did and Shakespeare perhaps—but these generalizations are 150 very worthless. The military sound of the word is enough. It recalls leading articles, cabinet ministers—a whole class of things indeed which, as a child, one thought the thing itself, the standard thing, the real thing, from which one could not depart save at the risk of nameless damnation. Generalizations bring back

somehow Sunday in London, Sunday afternoon walks, Sunday luncheons, and also ways of speaking of the dead, clothes, and habits—like the habit of sitting all together in one room until a certain hour, although nobody liked it. There was a rule for everything. The 160 rule for tablecloths at that particular period was that they should be made of tapestry with little yellow compartments marked upon them, such as you may see in photographs of the carpets in the corridors of the royal palaces. Tablecloths of a different kind were not real tablecloths. How shocking, and yet how wonderful it was to discover that these real things, Sunday luncheons, Sunday walks, country houses, and table-cloths were not entirely real, were indeed half phantoms, and the damnation which visited the disbeliever 170 in them was only a sense of illegitimate freedom. What now takes the place of those things I wonder, those real standard things? Men perhaps, should you be a woman; the masculine point of view which governs our lives, which sets the standard, which establishes Whitaker's Table of Precedency,° which has become, I suppose, since the war, half a phantom to many men and women, which soon, one may hope, will be laughed into the dustbin where the phantoms go, the mahogany sideboards and the Landseer prints,° Gods 180 and Devils, Hell and so forth, leaving us all with an intoxicating sense of illegitimate freedom—if freedom exists. . . .

In certain lights that mark on the wall seems actually to project from the wall. Nor is it entirely circular. I cannot be sure, but it seems to cast a perceptible shadow, suggesting that if I ran my finger down that strip of the wall it would, at a certain point, mount and descend a small tumulus, a smooth tumulus like those barrows on the South Downs° which are, they say, 190 either tombs or camps. Of the two I should prefer them to be tombs, desiring melancholy like most English people, and finding it natural at the end of a walk to think of the bones stretched beneath the turf. . . . There must be some book about it. Some antiquary must have dug up those bones and given them a name. . . . What sort of a man is an antiquary, I wonder? Retired Colonels for the most part, I daresay, leading parties of aged laborers to the top here, examining clods of earth and stone, and getting into correspon- 200 dence with the neighboring clergy, which, being opened at breakfast time, gives them a feeling of importance, and the comparison of arrowheads necessitates cross-country journeys to the county towns, an agreeable necessity both to them and to their elderly wives, who wish to make plum jam or to clean out the study, and have every reason for keeping that great question of the camp or the tomb in perpetual suspen-

121 **the reign of Charles the First,** King of England, 1625–1649

176 **Whitaker's Table of Precedency.** *Whitaker's Almanack,* still being published, is a standard British reference work. The Table of Precedency lists the ceremonial priority or order of various ranks of society   180 **Landseer prints,** Edwin Henry Landseer (1802–1873), English animal painter   190 **South Downs,** treeless undulating chalklands of southern and southeastern England

sion, while the Colonel himself feels agreeably philosophic in accumulating evidence on both sides of the question. It is true that he does finally incline to believe in the camp; and, being opposed, indites a pamphlet which he is about to read at the quarterly meeting of the local society when a stroke lays him low, and his last conscious thoughts are not of wife or child, but of the camp and that arrowhead there, which is now in the case at the local museum, together with the foot of a Chinese murderess, a handful of Elizabethan nails, a great many Tudor clay pipes, a piece of Roman pottery, and the wineglass that Nelson° drank out of—proving I really don't know what.

No, no, nothing is proved, nothing is known. And if I were to get up at this very moment and ascertain that the mark on the wall is really—what shall we say?—the head of a gigantic old nail, driven in two hundred years ago, which has now, owing to the patient attrition of many generations of housemaids, revealed its head above the coat of paint, and is taking its first view of modern life in the sight of a white-walled firelit room, what should I gain?— Knowledge? Matter for further speculation? I can think sitting still as well as standing up. And what is knowledge? What are our learned men save the descendants of witches and hermits who crouched in caves and in woods brewing herbs, interrogating shrewmice and writing down the language of the stars? And the less we honor them as our superstitions dwindle and our respect for beauty and health of mind increases. . . . Yes, one could imagine a very pleasant world. A quiet, spacious world, with the flowers so red and blue in the open fields. A world without professors or specialists or housekeepers with the profiles of policemen, a world which one could slice with one's thought as a fish slices the water with his fin, grazing the stems of the water lilies, hanging suspended over nests of white sea eggs. . . . How peaceful it is down here, rooted in the center of the world and gazing up through the gray waters, with their sudden gleams of light, and their reflections—if it were not for Whitaker's Almanack—if it were not for the Table of Precedency!

I must jump up and see for myself what that mark on the wall really is—a nail, a rose leaf, a crack in the wood?

Here is nature once more at her old game of self-preservation. This train of thought, she perceives, is threatening mere waste of energy, even some collision with reality, for who will ever be able to lift a finger against Whitaker's Table of Precedency? The Archbishop of Canterbury is followed by the Lord High Chancellor; the Lord High Chancellor is followed by the Archbishop of York. Everybody follows somebody, such is the philosophy of Whitaker; and the great thing is to know who follows whom. Whitaker

220 **Nelson,** Admiral Horatio Nelson (1758–1805), British national naval hero

knows, and let that, so Nature counsels, comfort you, instead of enraging you; and if you can't be comforted, if you must shatter this hour of peace, think of the mark on the wall.

I understand Nature's game—her prompting to take action as a way of ending any thought that threatens to excite or to pain. Hence, I suppose, comes our slight contempt for men of action—men, we assume, who don't think. Still, there's no harm in putting a full stop to one's disagreeable thoughts by looking at a mark on the wall.

Indeed, now that I have fixed my eyes upon it, I feel that I have grasped a plank in the sea; I feel a satisfying sense of reality which at once turns the two Archbishops and the Lord High Chancellor to the shadows of shades. Here is something definite, something real. Thus, waking from a midnight dream of horror, one hastily turns on the light and lies quiescent, worshiping the chest of drawers, worshiping solidity, worshiping reality, worshiping the impersonal world which is a proof of some existence other than ours. That is what one wants to be sure of. . . . Wood is a pleasant thing to think about. It comes from a tree; and trees grow, and we don't know how they grow. For years and years they grow, without paying any attention to us, in meadows, in forests, and by the side of rivers—all things one likes to think about. The cows swish their tails beneath them on hot afternoons; they paint rivers so green that when a moorhen dives one expects to see its feathers all green when it comes up again. I like to think of the fish balanced against the stream like flags blown out; and of water beetles slowly raising domes of mud upon the bed of the river. I like to think of the tree itself: first of the close dry sensation of being wood; then the grinding of the storm; then the slow, delicious ooze of sap; I like to think of it, too, on winter's nights standing in the empty field with all leaves close-furled, nothing tender exposed to the iron bullets of the moon, a naked mast upon an earth that goes tumbling, tumbling, all night long. The song of birds must sound very loud and strange in June; and how cold the feet of insects must feel upon it, as they make laborious progresses up the creases of the bark, or sun themselves upon the thin green awning of the leaves, and look straight in front of them with diamond-cut red eyes. . . . One by one the fibers snap beneath the immense cold pressure of the earth, then the last storm comes and, falling, the highest branches drive deep into the ground again. Even so, life isn't done with; there are a million patient, watchful lives still for a tree, all over the world, in bedrooms, in ships, on the pavement, living rooms, where men and women sit after tea, smoking cigarettes. It is full of peaceful thoughts, happy thoughts, this tree. I should like to take each one separately—but something is getting in the way. . . . Where was I? What has it all been about? A tree? A river? The

Downs? Whitaker's Almanack? The fields of as- phodel? I can't remember a thing. Everything's mov- ing, falling, slipping, vanishing. . . . There is a vast upheaval of matter. Someone is standing over me and saying:

"I'm going out to buy a newpaper."

"Yes?"

"Though it's no good buying newpapers. . . . Nothing ever happens. Curse this war; God damn this war! . . . All the same, I don't see why we should have a snail on our wall."

Ah, the mark on the wall! It was a snail.

(1919; 1921)

D. H. LAWRENCE
1885–1930

David Herbert Lawrence was born in Eastwood, Nottinghamshire, in 1885. His father was a poor coal miner, and his mother was a schoolteacher who also wrote poetry. He attended Nottingham High School, was a clerk for a while, and taught in various places while writing poetry. When some of his first poems were submitted to the *English Review*, Ford Madox Ford, the editor, was so impressed that he ar- ranged with young Lawrence for a novel, which was published in 1911 as *The White Peacock*. It was a promising effort.

During this period, he had fallen in love with the aristocratic Frieda von Richtofen Weekley, sister of the chief German flying ace of the First World War and wife of Ernest Weekley, the lexicographer. The two went to the Continent, where Lawrence's second novel, *The Trespasser*, was completed and where they spent the winter in Italy. Eventually, after Frieda's divorce, they married and returned to England. In the mean- time, Lawrence had published a volume of ro- mantic poetry and was working feverishly on his new novel, *Sons and Lovers* (1913). Although the first pub- lisher that Lawrence approached rejected it as a "dirty book," *Sons and Lovers* was ultimately very successful.

Lawrence spent the war years at various places in England, having been rejected three times for military service because of tuberculosis. But these years were far from unproductive. *The Rainbow* (1915) caused a sensation; it was the first of Lawrence's novels to pre- sent sex situations in frank language. In the following year, Lawrence was in Cornwall, where a volume of poems on his life with Frieda, *Look! We Have Come Through* (1917), increased the controversy already be- gun by *The Rainbow*. Since he was regarded as a "queer" and possibly a German spy by the people of the neighborhood, he found it wiser to move away from Cornwall.

Never happy in England, Lawrence left the country after the Armistice and returned only for a few brief visits. He moved first to Italy, living at Capri and Sicily from 1920 to 1922. There he produced some short stories, an excellent novel—*Women in Love* (1920)— and a history—*Movements in European History* (1921) —under the pseudonym of Lawrence H. Davidson. He began traveling around the world in 1922, going to Ceylon, Australia, New Zealand, Tahiti, San Francisco, and then to Taos, New Mexico. His desire to build a new social existence at Taos was reminiscent of the idealistic dreams of Rousseau and Coleridge. "Let us all live together," he wrote, "and create a new world." But the paradise at Taos was broken up by a devoted admirer, Mabel Dodge Luhan. She and Frieda Lawrence became jealous of each other, and Law- rence was greatly harrassed by her presence. He spent part of the winter of 1923 in Chapala, near Guadala- jara, Mexico. After a trip to Europe, he returned, bringing another admirer, Dorothy Brett; again, condi- tions in the New Mexican retreat were far from har- monious. He spent another winter in Mexico, this time at Oaxaca.

Lawrence's final departure from the United States (1925) was an admission that his social dream had failed, for he never returned. He became seriously ill and went to Italy and the French Riviera. There he wrote, painted, and met the English novelist Aldous Huxley (1894–1963). During these last five years of his life, he managed to create an international scandal with *Lady Chatterley's Lover* (1928), a novel recounting an English lady's love for her husband's gamekeeper. Its blunt language made it unacceptable to English publishers. It was immediately banned, and only since 1960 has the ban been lifted. Lawrence was disgusted, as Hardy had been with the reception of *Jude the Obscure* in 1895, and did little more writing. He died of tuberculosis in a sanatorium near Antibes, France, in 1930.

Lawrence's experiences in Ceylon, Australia, the United States, and Mexico furnished settings that he could describe in brilliant contrast to those of his stories of English life. But his theme remained essen- tially unchanged. The struggle of the human being in love, caused by the tension between the sexual and spiritual expression of love, is what lies at the core of most of his fiction. In addition to novels, he wrote many distinguished short stories, poetry, literary criti- cism, and travel books.

PIANO

Softly, in the dusk, a woman is singing to me;
Taking me back down the vista of years, till I see
A child sitting under the piano, in the boom of the
   tingling strings
And pressing the small, poised feet of a mother who
   smiles as she sings.

5 In spite of myself, the insidious mastery of song
Betrays me back, till the heart of me weeps to belong
To the old Sunday evenings at home, with winter out-
   side
And hymns in the cozy parlor, the tinkling piano our
   guide.

So now it is vain for the singer to burst into clamor
10 With the great black piano appassionato.° The glamor
Of childish days is upon me, my manhood is cast
Down in the flood of remembrance, I weep like a child
   for the past.
(1918)

WINTRY PEACOCK

There was thin, crisp snow on the ground, the sky was
blue, the wind very cold, the air clear. Farmers were
just turning out the cows for an hour or so in the midday, and the smell of cowsheds was unendurable as I
entered Tible. I noticed the ash-twigs up in the sky
were pale and luminous, passing into the blue. And
then I saw the peacocks. There they were in the road
before me, three of them, and tailless, brown, speckled
birds, with dark-blue necks and ragged crests. They
10 stepped archly over the filigree snow, and their bodies
moved with slow motion, like small, light, flat-bot-
tomed boats. I admired them, they were curious. Then
a gust of wind caught them, heeled them over as if they
were three frail boats, opening their feathers like
ragged sails. They hopped and skipped with discomfort, to get out of the draught of the wind. And then, in
the lee of the walls, they resumed their arch, wintry
motion, light and unballasted now their tails were
gone, indifferent. They were indifferent to my pres-
20 ence. I might have touched them. They turned off to
the shelter of an open shed.

As I passed the end of the upper house, I saw a
young woman just coming out of the back door. I had
spoken to her in the summer. She recognised me at
once, and waved to me. She was carrying a pail,
wearing a white apron that was longer than her preposterously short skirt, and she had on the cotton bonnet. I took off my hat to her and was going on. But she
put down her pail and darted with a swift, furtive
movement after me. 30

"Do you mind waiting a minute?" she said. "I'll be
out in a minute."

She gave me a slight, odd smile, and ran back. Her
face was long and sallow and her nose rather red. But
her gloomy black eyes softened caressively to me for a
moment, with that momentary humility which makes a
man lord of the earth.

I stood in the road, looking at the fluffy, dark-red
young cattle that mooed and seemed to bark at me.
They seemed happy, frisky cattle, a little impudent, 40
and either determined to go back into the warm shed,
or determined not to go back. I could not decide
which.

Presently the woman came forward again, her head
rather ducked. But she looked up at me and smiled,
with that odd, immediate intimacy, something witch-
like and impossible.

"Sorry to keep you waiting," she said. "Shall we
stand in this cart-shed—it will be more out of the
wind." 50

So we stood among the shafts of the open cart-shed
that faced the road. Then she looked down at the
ground, a little sideways, and I noticed a small black
frown on her brows. She seemed to brood for a moment. Then she looked straight into my eyes, so that I
blinked and wanted to turn my face aside. She was
searching me for something and her look was too near.
The frown was still on her keen, sallow brow.

"Can you speak French?" she asked me abruptly.

"More or less," I replied. 60

"I was supposed to learn it at school," she said.
"But I don't know a word." She ducked her head and
laughed, with a slightly ugly grimace and a rolling of
her black eyes.

"No good keeping your mind full of scraps," I
answered.

But she had turned aside her sallow, long face, and
did not hear what I said. Suddenly again she looked at
me. She was searching. And at the same time she
smiled at me, and her eyes looked softly darkly, with 70
infinite trustful humility into mine. I was being cajoled.

"Would you mind reading a letter for me, in
French," she said, her face immediately black and
bitter-looking. She glanced at me, frowning.

"No at all," I said.

"It's a letter to my husband," she said, still
scrutinising.

I looked at her, and didn't quite realise. She looked
too far into me, my wits were gone. She glanced
round. Then she looked at me shrewdly. She drew a 80
letter from her pocket, and handed it to me. It was
addressed from France to Lance-Corporal Gotye, at

Piano 10 **appassionato,** in an impassioned manner

Tible. I took out the letter and began to read it, as mere words. "*Mon cher* Alfred"°—it might have been a bit of a torn newspaper. So I followed the script: the trite phrases of a letter from a French-speaking girl to an English soldier. "I think of you always, always. Do you think sometimes of me?" And then I vaguely realised that I was reading a man's private correspon-
90 dence. And yet, how could one consider these trivial, facile French phrases private! Nothing more trite and vulgar in the world, than such a love-letter—no newspaper more obvious.

Therefore I read with a callous heart the effusions of the Belgian damsel. But then I gathered my attention. For the letter went on: "*Notre chere petit bébé*—our dear little baby was born a week ago. Almost I died, knowing you were far away, and perhaps forgetting the fruit of our perfect love. But the child comforted me.
100 He has the smiling eyes and virile air of his English father. I pray to the Mother of Jesus to send me the dear father of my child, that I may see him with my child in his arms, and that we may be united in holy family love. Ah, my Alfred, can I tell you how I miss you, how I weep for you. My thoughts are with you always, I think of nothing but you, I live for nothing but you and our dear baby. If you do not come back to me soon, I shall die, and our child will die. But no, you cannot come back to me. But I can come to you, come
110 to England with our child. If you do not wish to present me to your good mother and father, you can meet me in some town, some city, for I shall be so frightened to be alone in England with my child, and no one to take care of us. Yet I must come to you, I must bring my child, my little Alfred to his father, the big, beautiful Alfred that I love so much. Oh, write and tell me where I shall come. I have some money, I am not a penniless creature. I have money for myself and my dear baby——"

120 I read to the end. It was signed: "Your very happy and still more unhappy Elise." I suppose I must have been smiling.

"I can see it makes you laugh," said Mrs. Goyte, sardonically. I looked up at her.

"It's a love-letter, I know that," she said. "There's too many 'Alfreds' in it."

"One too many," I said.

"Oh, yes—— And what does she say—Eliza? We know her name's Eliza, that's another thing." She
130 grimaced a little, looking up at me with a mocking laugh.

"Where did you get this letter?" I said.

"Postman gave it me last week."

"And is your husband at home?"

"I expect him home to-night. He's been wounded, you know, and we've been applying for him home. He was home about six weeks ago—he's been in Scotland since then. Oh, he was wounded in the leg. Yes, he's

all right, a great strapping fellow. But he's lame, he limps a bit. He expects he'll get his discharge—but I 140 don't think he will. We married? We've been married six years—and he joined up the first day of the war. Oh, he thought he'd like the life. He's been through the South African War. No, he was sick of it, fed up. I'm living with his father and mother—I've no home of my own now. My people had a big farm—over a thousand acres—in Oxfordshire. Not like here—no. Oh, they're very good to me, his father and mother. Oh, yes, they couldn't be better. They think more of me than of their own daughters. But it's not like being in a place of your 150 own, is it? You can't *really* do as you like. No, there's only me and his father and mother at home. Before the war? Oh, he was anything. He had a good education—but he liked the farming better. Then he was a chauffeur. That's how he knew French. He was driving in France for a long time——"

At this point the peacocks came round the corner on a puff of wind.

"Hello, Joey!" she called, and one of the birds came forward, on delicate legs. Its grey speckled back was 160 very elegant, it rolled its full, dark-blue neck as it moved to her. She crouched down. "Joey, dear," she said, in an odd, saturnine caressive voice, "you're bound to find me, aren't you?" She put her face forward, and the bird rolled his neck, almost touching her face with his beak, as if kissing her.

"He loves you," I said.

She twisted her face up at me with a laugh.

"Yes," she said, "he loves me, Joey does,"—then, to the bird—"and I love Joey, don't I. I *do* love Joey." 170 And she smoothed his feathers for a moment. Then she rose, saying: "He's an affectionate bird."

I smiled at the roll of her "bir-rrd".

"Oh, yes, he is," she protested. "He came with me from my home seven years ago. Those others are his descendants—but they're not like Joey—*are they, dee-urr?*" Her voice rose at the end with a witch-like cry.

Then she forgot the bird in the cart-shed and turned to business again. 180

"Won't you read that letter?" she said. "Read it, so that I know what it says."

"It's rather behind his back," I said.

"Oh, never mind him," she cried. "He's been behind my back long enough—all these four years. If he never did no worse things behind my back than I do behind his, he wouldn't have cause to grumble. You read me what it says."

Now I felt a distinct reluctance to do as she bid, and yet I began—"My dear Alfred." 190

"I guessed that much," she said. "Eliza's dear Alfred." She laughed. "How do you say it in French? *Eliza?*"

I told her, and she repeated the name with great contempt—*Elise*.

"Go on," she said. "You're not reading."

So I began—"I have been thinking of you some-times—have you been thinking of me——?"

"Of several others as well, beside her, I'll wager," said Mrs. Goyte.

"Probably not," said I, and continued. "A dear lit-tle baby was born here a week ago. Ah, can I tell you my feelings when I take my darling little brother into my arms——"

"I'll bet it's *his*," cried Mrs. Goyte.

"No," I said. "It's her mother's."

"Don't you believe it," she cried. "It's a blind. You mark, it's her own right enough—and his."

"No," I said, "it's her mother's." "He has sweet smiling eyes, but not like your beautiful English eyes——"

She suddenly struck her hand on her skirt with a wild motion, and bent down, doubled with laughter. Then she rose and covered her face with her hand.

"I'm forced to laugh at the beautiful English eyes," she said.

"Aren't his eyes beautiful?" I asked.

"Oh, yes—*very!* Go on!—*Joey, dear, dee-urr, Joey!*"—this to the peacock.

—"Er—We miss you very much. We all miss you. We wish you were here to see the darling baby. Ah, Alfred, how happy we were when you stayed with us. We all loved you so much. My mother will call the baby Alfred so that we shall never forget you——"

"Of course it's his right enough," cried Mrs. Goyte.

"No," I said. "It's the mother's. Er—My mother is very well. My father came home yester-day—on leave. He is delighted with his son, my little brother, and wishes to have him named after you, be-cause you were so good to us all in that terrible time, which I shall never forget. I must weep now when I think of it. Well, you are far away in England, and perhaps I shall never see you again. How did you find your dear mother and father? I am so happy that your wound is better, and that you can nearly walk——"

"How did he find his dear *wife?*" cried Mrs. Goyte. "He never told her he had one. Think of taking the poor girl in like that!"

"We are so pleased when you write to us. Yet now you are in England you will forget the family you served so well——"

"A bit too well—eh, *Joey?*" cried the wife.

"If it had not been for you we should not be alive now, to grieve and to rejoice in this life, that is so hard for us. But we have recovered some of our losses, and no longer feel the burden of poverty. The little Alfred is a great comfort to me. I hold him to my breast and think of the big, good Alfred, and I weep to think that those times of suffering were perhaps the times of a great happiness that is gone for ever."

"Oh, but isn't it a shame, to take a poor girl in like that!" cried Mrs. Goyte. "Never to let on that he was married, and raise her hopes—I call it beastly, I do."

"You don't know," I said. "You know how anxious women are to fall in love, wife or no wife. How could he help it, if she was determined to fall in love with him?"

"He could have helped it if he'd wanted."

"Well," I said, "we aren't all heroes."

"Oh, but that's different! The big, good Alfred!— did ever you hear such tommy-rot in your life! Go on—what does she say at the end?"

"Er—We shall be pleased to hear of your life in England. We all send many kind regards to your good parents. I wish you all happiness for your future days. Your very affectionate and ever-grateful, Elise."

There was silence for a moment, during which Mrs. Goyte remained with her head dropped, sinister and abstracted. Suddenly she lifted her face, and her eyes flashed.

"Oh, but I call it beastly, I call it mean, to take a girl in like that."

"Nay," I said. "Probably he hasn't taken her in at all. Do you think those French girls are such poor innocent things? I guess she's a great deal more downy° than he."

"Oh, he's one of the biggest fools that ever walked," she cried.

"There you are!" said I.

"But it's his child right enough," she said.

"I don't think so," said I.

"I'm sure of it."

"Oh, well," I said, "if you prefer to think that way."

"What other reason has she for writing like that——?"

I went out into the road and looked at the cattle.

"Who is this driving the cows?" I said. She too came out.

"It's the boy from the next farm," she said.

"Oh, well," said I, "those Belgian girls! You never know where their letters will end. And, after all, it's his affair—you needn't bother."

"Oh——!" she cried with scorn—"it's not *me* that bothers. But it's the nasty meanness of it—me writing him such loving letters"—she put her hand before her face, and laughed malevolently—"and sending him parcels all the time. You bet he fed that gurrl on my parcels—I know he did. It's just like him. I'll bet they laughed together over my letters. I'll bet anything they did——"

"Nay," said I. "He'd burn your letters for fear they'd give him away."

There was a black look on her yellow face. Suddenly a voice was heard calling. She poked her head out of the shed, and answered coolly:

"All right!" Then turning to me: "That's his mother looking after me."

She laughed into my face, witch-like, and we turned down the road.

275 **downy**, wide-awake, knowing

When I awoke, the morning after this episode, I found the house darkened with deep, soft snow, which had blown against the large west windows, covering them with a screen. I went outside, and saw the valley all white and ghastly below me, the trees beneath black and thin-looking like wire, the rockfaces dark between the glistening shroud, and the sky above sombre, heavy, yellowish-dark, much too heavy for this world below of hollow bluey whiteness figured 320 with black. I felt I was in a valley of the dead. And I sensed I was a prisoner, for the snow was everywhere deep, and drifted in places. So all the morning I remained indoors, looking up the drive at the shrubs so heavily plumed with snow, at the gate-posts raised high with a foot or more of extra whiteness. Or I looked down into the white-and-black valley that was utterly motionless and beyond life, a hollow sarcophagus.

Nothing stirred the whole day—no plume fell off the 330 shrubs, the valley was as abstracted as a grove of death. I looked over at the tiny, half-buried farms away on the bare uplands beyond the valley hollow, and I thought of Tible in the snow, of the black witch-like little Mrs. Goyte. And the snow seemed to lay me bare to influences I wanted to escape.

In the faint glow of the half-clear light that came about four o'clock in the afternoon, I was roused to see a motion in the snow away below, near where the thorn trees stood very black and dwarfed, like a little 340 savage group, in the dismal white. I watched closely. Yes, there was a flapping and a struggle—a big bird, it must be, labouring in the snow. I wondered. Our biggest birds, in the valley, were the large hawks that often hung flickering opposite my windows, level with me, but high above some prey on the steep valley-side. This was much too big for a hawk—too big for any known bird. I searched in my mind for the largest English wild bird, geese, buzzards.

Still it laboured and strove, then was still, a dark 350 spot, then struggled again. I went out of the house and down the steep slope, at risk of breaking my leg between the rocks. I knew the ground so well—and yet I got well shaken before I drew near the thorn trees.

Yes, it was a bird. It was Joey. It was the grey-brown peacock with a blue neck. He was snow-wet and spent.

"Joey—Joey, de-urr!" I said, staggering unevenly towards him. He looked so pathetic, rowing and struggling in the snow, too spent to rise, his blue neck 360 stretching out and lying sometimes on the snow, his eye closing and opening quickly, his crest all battered.

"Joey dee-urr!" I said caressingly to him. And at last he lay still, blinking, in the surged and furrowed snow, whilst I came near and touched him, stroked him, gathering him under my arm. He stretched his long, wetted neck away from me as I held him, none the less he was quiet in my arm, too tired, perhaps, to

struggle. Still he held his poor, crested head away from me, and seemed sometimes to droop, to wilt, as if he might suddenly die. 370

He was not so heavy as I expected, yet it was a struggle to get up to the house with him again. We set him down, not too near the fire, and gently wiped him with cloths. He submitted, only now and then stretched his soft neck away from us, avoiding us helplessly. Then we set warm food by him. I *put* it to his beak, tried to make him eat. But he ignored it. He seemed to be ignorant of what we were doing, recoiled inside himself inexplicably. So we put him in a basket with cloths, and left him crouching oblivious. His food 380 we put near him. The blinds were drawn, the house was warm, it was night. Sometimes he stirred, but mostly he huddled still, leaning his queer crested head on one side. He touched no food, and took no heed of sounds or movements. We talked of brandy or stimulants. But I realised we had best leave him alone.

In the night, however, we heard him thumping about. I got up anxiously with a candle. He had eaten some food, and scattered more, making a mess. And he was perched on the back of a heavy arm-chair. So I 390 concluded he was recovered, or recovering.

The next day was clear, and the snow had frozen, so I decided to carry him back to Tible. He consented, after various flappings, to sit in a big fish-bag with his battered head peeping out with wild uneasiness. And so I set off with him slithering down into the valley, making good progress down in the pale shadow beside the rushing waters, then climbing painfully up the arrested white valley-side, plumed with clusters of young pine trees, into the paler white radiance of the 400 snowy, upper regions, where the wind cut fine. Joey seemed to watch all the time with wide, anxious, unseeing eye, brilliant and inscrutable. As I drew near to Tible township he stirred violently in the bag, though I do not know if he recognised the place. Then, as I came to the sheds, he looked sharply from side to side, and stretched his neck out long. I was a little afraid of him. He gave a loud, vehement yell, opening his sinister beak, and I stood still, looking at him as he struggled in the bag, shaken myself by his struggles, yet not 410 thinking to release him.

Mrs. Goyte came darting past the end of the house, her head sticking forward in sharp scrutiny. She saw me, and came forward.

"Have you got Joey!" she cried sharply, as if I were a thief.

I opened the bag, and he flopped out, flapping as if he hated the touch of the snow now. She gathered him up, and put her lips to his beak. She was flushed and handsome, her eyes bright, her hair slack, thick, but 420 more witch-like than ever. She did not speak.

She had been followed by a grey-haired woman with a round, rather sallow face and a slightly hostile bearing.

"Did you bring him with you, then?" she asked sharply. I answered that I had rescued him the previous evening.

From the background slowly approached a slender man with a grey moustache and large patches on his trousers.

"You've got 'im back 'gain, ah see," he said to his daughter-in-law. His wife explained how I had found Joey.

"Ah," went on the grey man. "It wor our Alfred scarred him off, back your life. He must'a flyed ower t'valley. Tha ma' thank thy stars as 'e wor fun,° Maggie. 'E'd a bin froze. They a bit nesh,° you know," he concluded to me.

"They are," I answered. "This isn't their country."

"No, it isna," replied Mr. Goyte. He spoke very slowly and deliberately, quietly, as if the soft pedal were always down in his voice. He looked at his daughter-in-law as she crouched, flushed and dark, before the peacock, which would lay its long blue neck for a moment along her lap. In spite of his grey moustache and thin grey hair, the elderly man had a face young and almost delicate, like a young man's. His blue eyes twinkled with some inscrutable source of pleasure, his skin was fine and tender, his nose delicately arched. His grey hair being slightly ruffled, he had a debonair look, as of a youth who is in love.

"We mun tell 'im it's come," he said slowly, and turning he called: "Alfred—Alfred! Wheer's ter gotten to?"°

Then he turned again to the group.

"Get up then, Maggie, lass, get up wi' thee. Tha ma'es too much o' th' bod."°

A young man approached, wearing rough khaki and knee-breeches. He was Danish-looking, broad at the loins.

"I's come back then," said the father to the son; "leastwise, he's bin browt back, flyed ower the Griff Low."

The son looked at me. He had a devil-may-care bearing, his cap on one side, his hands stuck in the front pockets of his breeches. But he said nothing.

"Shall you come in a minute, Master," said the elderly woman, to me.

"Ay, come in an' ha'e a cup o' tea or summat. You'll do wi' summat, carrin' that bod. Come on, Maggie wench, let's go in."

So we went indoors, into the rather stuffy, overcrowded living-room, that was too cosy, and too warm. The son followed last, standing in the doorway. The father talked to me. Maggie put out the tea-cups. The mother went into the dairy again.

"Tha'lt rouse thysen° up a bit again, now, Maggie," the father-in-law said—and then to me: "'Ers not bin very bright sin' Alfred come whoam,° an' the bod flyed awee. 'E come whoam a Wednesday night, Alfred did. But ay, you knowed, didna yer. Ay, 'e comed 'a Wednesday—an' I reckon there wor a bit of a to-do between 'em worn't there, Maggie?"

He twinkled maliciously to his daughter-in-law, who flushed, brilliant and handsome.

"Oh, be quiet, father. You're wound up, by the sound of you," she said to him, as if crossly. But she could never be cross with him.

"'Ers got 'er colour back this mornin'," continued the father-in-law slowly. "It's bin heavy weather wi' 'er this last two days. 'Ay—'er's bin north-east° sin' 'er seed you a Wednesday."

"Father, do stop talking. You'd wear the leg off an iron pot. I can't think where you've found your tongue, all of a sudden," said Maggie, with caressive sharpness.

"Ah've found it wheer I lost it. Aren't goin' ter come in an' sit thee down, Alfred?"

But Alfred turned and disappeared.

"'E's got th' monkey on 'is back ower this letter job," said the father secretly to me. "Mother, 'er knows nowt about it. Lot o' tom-foolery, isn't it? Ay! What's good o'makkin' a peck o' trouble over what's far enough off, an' ned niver come no nigher. No—not a smite o' use. That's what I tell 'er. 'Er should ta'e no notice on't. Ty, what can y' expect."

The mother came in again, and the talk became general. Maggie flashed her eyes at me from time to time, complacent and satisfied, moving among the men. I paid her little compliments, which she did not seem to hear. She attended to me with a kind of sinister witch-like graciousness, her dark head ducked between her shoulders, at once humble and powerful. She was happy as a child attending to her father-in-law and to me. But there was something ominous between her eyebrows, as if a dark moth were settled there—and something ominous in her bent, hulking bearing.

She sat on a low stool by the fire, near her father-in-law. Her head was dropped, she seemed in a state of abstraction. From time to time she would suddenly recover, and look up at us, laughing and chatting. Then she would forget again. Yet in her hulked black forgetting she seemed very near to us.

The door having been opened, the peacock came slowly in, prancing calmly. He went near to her and crouched down, coiling his blue neck. She glanced at him, but almost as if she did not observe him. The bird sat silent, seeming to sleep, and the woman also sat hulked and silent, seemingly oblivious. Then once more there was a heavy step, and Alfred entered. He looked at his wife, and he looked at the peacock crouching by her. He stood large in the doorway, his

436 'e wor fun, he was found   437 nesh, soft, susceptible to cold
453 Wheer's ter gotten to?, where's he gone?   457 Tha ma'es too much 'o' th' bod, you make too much fuss over the bird   477 thysen, thyself

479 whoam, home   491 bin north-east, been stormy

hands stuck in front of him, in his breeches pockets. Nobody spoke. He turned on his heel and went out again.

I rose also to go. Maggie started as if coming to herself.

"Must you go?" she asked, rising and coming near to me, standing in front of me, twisting her head side-
540 ways and looking up at me. "Can't you stop a bit longer? We can all be cosy to-day, there's nothing to do outdoors." And she laughed, showing her teeth oddly. She had a long chin.

I said I must go. The peacock uncoiled and coiled again his long blue neck, as he lay on the hearth. Maggie still stood close in front of me, so that I was acutely aware of my waistcoat buttons.

"Oh, well," she said, "you'll come again, won't you? Do come again."
550 I promised.

"Come to tea one day—yes, do!"

I promised—one day.

The moment I went out of her presence I ceased utterly to exist for her—as utterly as I ceased to exist for Joey. With her curious abstractedness she forgot me again immediately. I knew it as I left her. Yet she seemed almost in physical contact with me while I was with her.

The sky was all pallid again, yellowish. When I went
560 out there was no sun; the snow was blue and cold. I hurried away down the hill, musing on Maggie. The road made a loop down the sharp face of the slope. As I went crunching over the laborious snow I became aware of a figure striding down the steep scarp° to intercept me. It was a man with his hands in front of him, half stuck in his breeches pockets, and his shoulders square—a real farmer of the hills; Alfred, of course. He waited for me by the stone fence.

"Excuse me," he said as I came up.
570 I came to a halt in front of him and looked into his sullen blue eyes. He had a certain odd haughtiness on his brows. But his blue eyes stared insolently at me.

"Do you know anything about a letter—in French —that my wife opened—a letter of mine——?"

"Yes," said I. "She asked me to read it to her."

He looked square at me. He did not know exactly how to feel.

"What was there in it?" he asked.

"Why?" I said. "Don't you know?"
580 "She makes out she's burnt it," he said.

"Without showing it you?" I asked.

He nodded slightly. He seemed to be meditating as to what line of action he should take. He wanted to know the contents of the letter: he must know: and therefore he must ask me, for evidently his wife had taunted him. At the same time, no doubt, he would like

to wreak untold vengeance on my unfortunate person. So he eyed me, and I eyed him, and neither of us spoke. He did not want to repeat his request to me. And yet I only looked at him, and considered. 590

Suddenly he threw back his head and glanced down the valley. Then he changed his position—he was a horse-soldier. Then he looked at me more confidentially.

"She burnt the blasted thing before I saw it," he said.

"Well," I answered slowly, "she doesn't know herself what was in it."

He continued to watch me narrowly. I grinned to myself. 600

"I didn't like to read her out what there was in it," I continued.

He suddenly flushed so that the veins in his neck stood out, and he stirred again uncomfortably.

"The Belgian girl said her baby had been born a week ago, and that they were going to call it Alfred," I told him.

He met my eyes. I was grinning. He began to grin, too.

"Good luck to her," he said. 610

"Best of luck," said I.

"And what did you tell *her?*" he asked.

"That the baby belonged to the old mother—that it was brother to your girl, who was writing to you as a friend of the family."

He stood smiling, with the long, subtle malice of a farmer.

"And did she take it in?" he asked.

"As much as she took anything else."

He stood grinning fixedly. Then he broke into a 620 short laugh.

"Good for *her!*" he exclaimed cryptically.

And then he laughed aloud once more, evidently feeling he had won a big move in his contest with his wife.

"What about the other woman?" I asked.

"Who?"

"Elise."

"Oh"—he shifted uneasily—"she was all right——" 630

"You'll be getting back to her," I said.

He looked at me. Then he made a grimace with his mouth.

"Not me," he said. "Back your life it's a plant."°

"You don't think the *cher petit bébé* is a little Alfred?"

"It might be," he said.

"Only might?"

"Yes—an' there's lots of mites in a pound of cheese." He laughed boisterously but uneasily. 640

---

564 **scarp,** the steep face of a hill

634 **Back your life . . . plant,** a trick, to convince him he is the father of the baby

"What did she say, exactly?" he asked.

I began to repeat, as well as I could, the phrases of the letter:

"*Mon cher Alfred—Figure-toi comme je suis desolée—*"°

He listened with some confusion. When I had finished all I could remember, he said:

"They know how to pitch you out a letter, those Belgian lasses."

"Practice," said I.

650 "They get plenty," he said.

There was a pause.

"Oh, well," he said. "I've never got that letter, anyhow."

The wind blew fine and keen, in the sunshine, across the snow. I blew my nose and prepared to depart.

"And *she* doesn't know anything?" he continued, jerking his head up the hill in the direction of Tible.

"She knows nothing but what I've said—that is, if she really burnt the letter."

660 "I believe she burnt it," he said, "for spite. She's a little devil, she is. But I shall have it out with her." His jaw was stubborn and sullen. Then suddenly he turned to me with a new note.

"Why?" he said. "Why didn't you wring that b—— peacock's neck—that b—— Joey?"

"Why?" I said. "What for?"

"I hate the brute," he said. "I had a shot at him——"

I laughed. He stood and mused.

670 "Poor little Elise," he murmured.

"Was she small—petite?" I asked. He jerked up his head.

"No," he said. "Rather tall."

"Taller than your wife, I suppose."

Again he looked into my eyes. And then once more he went into a loud burst of laughter that made the still, snow-deserted valley clap again.

"God, it's a knock-out!" he said, thoroughly amused. Then he stood at ease, one foot out, his hands

680 in his breeches pockets, in front of him, his head thrown back, a handsome figure of a man.

"But I'll do that blasted Joey in——" he mused.

I ran down the hill, shouting with laughter.

(1924)

THE ROCKING-HORSE WINNER

There was a woman who was beautiful, who started with all the advantages, yet she had no luck. She married for love, and the love turned to dust. She had bonny children, yet she felt they had been thrust upon her, and she could not love them. They looked at her

644 **Mon cher Alfred . . . desolée,** My dear Alfred, imagine to yourself how heartbroken I was.

coldly, as if they were finding fault with her. And hurriedly she felt she must cover up some fault in herself. Yet what it was that she must cover up she never knew. Nevertheless, when her children were present, she always felt the centre of her heart go hard. This 10 troubled her, and in her manner she was all the more gentle and anxious for her children, as if she loved them very much. Only she herself knew that at the centre of her heart was a hard little place that could not feel love, no, not for anybody. Everybody else said of her: "She is such a good mother. She adores her children." Only she herself, and her children themselves, knew it was not so. They read it in each other's eyes.

There were a boy and two little girls. They lived in a pleasant house, with a garden, and they had discreet 20 servants, and felt themselves superior to anyone in the neighbourhood.

Although they lived in style, they felt always an anxiety in the house. There was never enough money. The mother had a small income, and the father had a small income, but not nearly enough for the social position which they had to keep up. The father went into town to some office. But though he had good prospects, these prospects never materialised. There was always the grinding sense of the shortage of 30 money, though the style was always kept up.

At last the mother said: "I will see if *I* can't make something." But she did not know where to begin. She racked her brains, and tried this thing and the other, but could not find anything successful. The failure made deep lines come into her face. Her children were growing up, they would have to go to school. There must be more money, there must be more money. The father, who was always very handsome and expensive in his tastes, seemed as if he never 40 *would* be able to do anything worth doing. And the mother, who had a great belief in herself, did not succeed any better, and her tastes were just as expensive.

And so the house came to be haunted by the unspoken phrase: *There must be more money! There must be more money!* The children could hear it all the time, though nobody said it aloud. They heard it at Christmas, when the expensive and splendid toys filled the nursery. Behind the shining modern rocking-horse, behind the smart doll's house, a voice would start 50 whispering: "There *must* be more money! There *must* be more money!" And the children would stop playing, to listen for a moment. They would look into each other's eyes, to see if they had all heard. And each one saw in the eyes of the other two that they too had heard. "There *must* be more money! There *must* be more money!"

It came whispering from the springs of the still-swaying rocking-horse, and even the horse, bending his wooden, champing head, heard it. The big doll, 60 sitting so pink and smirking in her new pram, could hear it quite plainly, and seemed to be smirking all the more self-consciously because of it. The foolish puppy, too, that took the place of the teddy-bear, he was looking so extraordinarily foolish for no other reason but that he heard the secret whisper all over the house: "There *must* be more money!"

Yet nobody ever said it aloud. The whisper was everywhere, and therefore no one spoke it. Just as no one ever says: "We are breathing!" in spite of the fact that breath is coming and going all the time.

"Mother," said the boy Paul one day, "why don't we keep a car of our own? Why do we always use uncle's, or else a taxi?"

"Because we're the poor members of the family," said the mother.

"But why *are* we, mother?"

"Well—I suppose," she said slowly and bitterly, "it's because your father has no luck."

The boy was silent for some time.

"Is luck money, mother?" he asked, rather timidly.

"No, Paul. Not quite. It's what causes you to have money."

"Oh!" said Paul vaguely. "I thought when Uncle Oscar said *filthy lucker,* it meant money."

"*Filthy lucre* does mean money," said the mother. "But it's lucre, not luck."

"Oh!" said the boy. "Then what *is* luck, mother?"

"It's what causes you to have money. If you're lucky you have money. That's why it's better to be born lucky than rich. If you're rich, you may lose your money. But if you're lucky, you will always get more money."

"Oh! Will you? And is father not lucky?"

"Very unlucky, I should say," she said bitterly.

The boy watched her with unsure eyes.

"Why?" he asked.

"I don't know. Nobody ever knows why one person is lucky and another unlucky."

"Don't they? Nobody at all? Does *nobody* know?"

"Perhaps God. But He never tells."

"He ought to, then. And aren't you lucky either, mother?"

"I can't be, if I married an unlucky husband."

"But by yourself, aren't you?"

"I used to think I was, before I married. Now I think I am very unlucky indeed."

"Why?"

"Well—never mind! Perhaps I'm not really," she said.

The child looked at her to see if she meant it. But he saw, by the lines of her mouth, that she was only trying to hide something from him.

"Well, anyhow," he said stoutly, "I'm a lucky person."

"Why?" said his mother, with a sudden laugh.

He stared at her. He didn't even know why he had said it.

"God told me," he asserted, brazening it out.

"I hope He did, dear!" she said, again with a laugh, but rather bitter.

"He did, mother!"

"Excellent!" said the mother, using one of her husband's exclamations.

The boy saw she did not believe him; or rather, that she paid no attention to his assertion. This angered him somewhere, and made him want to compel her attention.

He went off by himself, vaguely, in a childish way, seeking for the clue to 'luck'. Absorbed, taking no heed of other people, he went about with a sort of stealth, seeking inwardly for luck. He wanted luck, he wanted it, he wanted it. When the two girls were playing dolls in the nursery, he would sit on his big rocking-horse, charging madly into space, with a frenzy that made the little girls peer at him uneasily. Wildly the horse careered, the waving dark hair of the boy tossed, his eyes had a strange glare in them. The little girls dared not speak to him.

When he had ridden to the end of his mad little journey, he climbed down and stood in front of his rocking-horse, staring fixedly into its lowered face. Its red mouth was slightly open, its big eye was wide and glassy-bright.

"Now!" he would silently command the snorting steed. "Now, take me to where there is luck! Now take me!"

And he would slash the horse on the neck with the little whip he had asked Uncle Oscar for. He *knew* the horse could take him to where there was luck, if only he forced it. So he would mount again and start on his furious ride, hoping at last to get there. He knew he could get there.

"You'll break your horse, Paul!" said the nurse.

"He's always riding like that! I wish he'd leave off!" said his elder sister Joan.

But he only glared down on them in silence. Nurse gave him up. She could make nothing of him. Anyhow, he was growing beyond her.

One day his mother and his Uncle Oscar came in when he was on one of his furious rides. He did not speak to them.

"Hallo, you young jockey! Riding a winner?" said his uncle.

"Aren't you growing too big for a rocking-horse? You're not a very little boy any longer, you know," said his mother.

But Paul only gave a blue glare from his big, rather close-set eyes. He would speak to nobody when he was in full tilt. His mother watched him with an anxious expression on her face.

At last he suddenly stopped forcing his horse into the mechanical gallop and slid down.

"Well, I got there!" he announced fiercely, his blue eyes still flaring, and his sturdy long legs straddling apart.

"Where did you get to?" asked his mother.

"Where I wanted to go," he flared back at her.

"That's right, son!" said Uncle Oscar. "Don't you stop till you get there. What's the horse's name?"

"He doesn't have a name," said the boy.

"Gets on without all right?" asked the uncle.

"Well, he has different names. He was called Sansovino last week."

"Sansovino, eh? Won the Ascot. How did you know this name?"

"He always talks about horse-races with Bassett," said Joan.

The uncle was delighted to find that his small nephew was posted with all the racing news. Bassett, the young gardener, who had been wounded in the left foot in the war and had got his present job through Oscar Cresswell, whose batman° he had been, was a perfect blade of the 'turf'. He lived in the racing events, and the small boy lived with him.

Oscar Cresswell got it all from Bassett.

"Master Paul comes and asks me, so I can't do more than tell him sir," said Bassett, his face terribly serious, as if he were speaking of religious matters.

"And does he ever put anything on a horse he fancies?"

"Well—I don't want to give him away—he's a young sport, a fine sport, sir. Would you mind asking him himself? He sort of takes a pleasure in it, and perhaps he'd feel I was giving him away, sir, if you don't mind."

Bassett was serious as a church.

The uncle went back to his nephew and took him off for a ride in the car.

"Say, Paul, old man, do you ever put anything on a horse?" the uncle asked.

The boy watched the handsome man closely.

"Why, do you think I oughtn't to?" he parried.

"Not a bit of it! I thought perhaps you might give me a tip for the Lincoln."

The car sped on into the country, going down to Uncle Oscar's place in Hampshire.

"Honour bright?" said the nephew.

"Honour bright, son!" said the uncle.

"Well, then, Daffodil."

"Daffodil! I doubt it, sonny. What about Mirza?"

"I only know the winner," said the boy. "That's Daffodil."

"Daffodil, eh?"

There was a pause. Daffodil was an obscure horse comparatively.

"Uncle!"

"Yes, son?"

"You won't let it go any further, will you? I promised Bassett."

"Bassett be damned, old man! What's he got to do with it?"

"We're partners. We've been partners from the first. Uncle, he lent me my first five shillings, which I lost. I promised him, honour bright, it was only between me and him; only you gave me that ten-shilling note I started winning with, so I thought you were lucky. You won't let it go any further, will you?"

The boy gazed at his uncle from those big, hot, blue eyes, set rather close together. The uncle stirred and laughed uneasily.

"Right you are, son! I'll keep your tip private. Daffodil, eh? How much are you putting on him?"

"All except twenty pounds," said the boy. "I keep that in reserve."

The uncle thought it a good joke.

"You keep twenty pounds in reserve, do you, you young romancer? What are you betting, then?"

"I'm betting three hundred," said the boy gravely. "But it's between you and me, Uncle Oscar! Honour bright?"

The uncle burst into a roar of laughter.

"It's between you and me all right, you young Nat Gould," he said, laughing. "But where's your three hundred?"

"Bassett keeps it for me. We're partners."

"You are, are you! And what is Bassett putting on Daffodil?"

"He won't go quite as high as I do, I expect. Perhaps he'll go a hundred and fifty."

"What, pennies?" laughed the uncle.

"Pounds," said the child, with a surprised look at his uncle. "Bassett keeps a bigger reserve than I do."

Between wonder and amusement Uncle Oscar was silent. He pursued the matter no further, but he determined to take his nephew with him to the Lincoln races.

"Now, son," he said, "I'm putting twenty on Mirza, and I'll put five on for you on any horse you fancy. What's your pick?"

"Daffodil, uncle."

"No, not the fiver on Daffodil!"

"I should if it was my own fiver," said the child.

"Good! Good! Right you are! A fiver for me and a fiver for you on Daffodil."

The child had never been to a race-meeting before, and his eyes were blue fire. He pursed his mouth tight and watched. A Frenchman just in front had put his money on Lancelot. Wild with excitement, he flayed his arms up and down, yelling *"Lancelot! Lancelot!"* in his French accent.

Daffodil came in first, Lancelot second, Mirza third. The child, flushed and with eyes blazing, was curiously serene. His uncle brought him four five-pound notes, four to one.

"What am I to do with these?" he cried, waving them before the boy's eyes.

"I suppose we'll talk to Bassett," said the boy. "I expect I have fifteen hundred now; and twenty in reserve; and this twenty."

His uncle studied him for some moments.

"Look here, son!" he said. "You're not serious about Bassett and that fifteen hundred, are you?"

"Yes, I am. But it's between you and me, uncle. Honour bright?"

"Honour bright all right, son! But I must talk to Bassett."

"If you'd like to be a partner, uncle, with Bassett and me, we could all be partners. Only, you'd have to promise, honour bright, uncle, not to let it go beyond us three. Bassett and I are lucky, and you must be lucky, because it was your ten shillings I started winning with. . . ."

Uncle Oscar took both Bassett and Paul into Richmond Park for an afternoon, and there they talked.

"It's like this, you see, sir," Bassett said. "Master Paul would get me talking about racing events, spinning yarns, you know, sir. And he was always keen on knowing if I'd made or if I'd lost. It's about a year since, now, that I put five shillings on Blush of Dawn for him: and we lost. Then the luck turned, with that ten shillings he had from you: that we put on Singhalese. And since that time, it's been pretty steady, all things considering. What do you say, Master Paul?"

"We're all right when we're sure," said Paul. "It's when we're not quite sure that we go down."

"Oh, but we're careful then," said Bassett.

"But when are you *sure*?" smiled Uncle Oscar.

"It's Master Paul, sir," said Bassett in a secret, religious voice. "It's as if he had it from heaven. Like Daffodil, now, for the Lincoln. That was as sure as eggs."

"Did you put anything on Daffodil?" asked Oscar Cresswell.

"Yes, sir. I made my bit."

"And my nephew?"

Bassett was obstinately silent, looking at Paul.

"I made twelve hundred, didn't I, Bassett? I told uncle I was putting three hundred on Daffodil."

"That's right," said Bassett, nodding.

"But where's the money?" asked the uncle.

"I keep it safe locked up, sir. Master Paul he can have it any minute he likes to ask for it."

"What, fifteen hundred pounds?"

"And twenty! And *forty,* that is, with the twenty he made on the course."

"It's amazing!" said the uncle.

"If Master Paul offers you to be partners, sir, I would, if I were you: if you'll excuse me," said Bassett.

Oscar Cresswell thought about it.

"I'll see the money," he said.

They drove home again, and, sure enough, Bassett came round to the garden-house with fifteen hundred pounds in notes. The twenty pounds reserve was left with Joe Glee, in the Turf Commission deposit.

"You see, it's all right, uncle, when I'm *sure*! Then we go strong, for all we're worth. Don't we, Bassett?"

"We do that, Master Paul."

"And when are you sure?" said the uncle, laughing.

"Oh, well, sometimes I'm *absolutely* sure, like about Daffodil," said the boy; "and sometimes I have an idea; and sometimes I haven't even an idea, have I, Bassett? Then we're careful, because we mostly go down."

"You do, do you! And when you're sure, like about Daffodil, what makes you sure, sonny?"

"Oh, well, I don't know," said the boy uneasily. "I'm sure, you know, uncle; that's all."

"It's as if he had it from heaven, sir," Bassett reiterated.

"I should say so!" said the uncle.

But he became a partner. And when the Leger was coming on Paul was 'sure' about Lively Spark, which was a quite inconsiderable horse. The boy insisted on putting a thousand on the horse, Bassett went for five hundred, and Oscar Cresswell two hundred. Lively Spark came in first, and the betting had been ten to one against him. Paul had made ten thousand.

"You see," he said, "I was absolutely sure of him."

Even Oscar Cresswell had cleared two thousand.

"Look here, son," he said, "this sort of thing makes me nervous."

"It needn't, uncle! Perhaps I shan't be sure again for a long time."

"But what are you going to do with your money?" asked the uncle.

"Of course," said the boy, "I started it for mother. She said she had no luck, because father is unlucky, so I thought if *I* was lucky, it might stop whispering."

"What might stop whispering?"

"Our house. I *hate* our house for whispering."

"What does it whisper?"

"Why—why"—the boy fidgeted—"why, I don't know. But it's always short of money, you know, uncle."

"I know it, son, I know it."

"You know people send mother writs,° don't you, uncle?"

"I'm afraid I do," said the uncle.

"And then the house whispers, like people laughing at you behind your back. It's awful, that is! I thought if I was lucky——"

"You might stop it," added the uncle.

The boy watched him with big blue eyes, that had an uncanny cold fire in them, and he said never a word.

"Well, then!" said the uncle. "What are we doing?"

"I shouldn't like mother to know I was lucky," said the boy.

"Why not, son?"

"She'd stop me."

390 **writs,** legal summonses to pay debts

"I don't think she would."

"Oh!"—and the boy writhed in an odd way—"I *don't* want her to know, uncle."

"All right, son! We'll manage it without her knowing."

They managed it very easily. Paul, at the other's suggestion, handed over five thousand pounds to his uncle, who deposited it with the family lawyer, who was then to inform Paul's mother that a relative had put five thousand pounds into his hands, which sum was to be paid out a thousand pounds at a time, on the mother's birthday, for the next five years.

"So she'll have a birthday present of a thousand pounds for five successive years," said Uncle Oscar. "I hope it won't make it all the harder for her later."

Paul's mother had her birthday in November. The house had been 'whispering' worse than ever lately, and, even in spite of his luck, Paul could not bear up against it. He was very anxious to see the effect of the birthday letter, telling his mother about the thousand pounds.

When there were no visitors, Paul now took his meals with his parents, as he was beyond the nursery control. His mother went into town nearly every day. She had discovered that she had an odd knack of sketching furs and dress materials, so she worked secretly in the studio of a friend who was the chief 'artist' for the leading drapers. She drew the figures of ladies in furs and ladies in silk and sequins for the newspaper advertisements. This young woman artist earned several thousand pounds a year, but Paul's mother only made several hundreds, and she was again dissatisfied. She so wanted to be first in something, and she did not succeed, even in making sketches for drapery advertisements.

She was down to breakfast on the morning of her birthday. Paul watched her face as she read her letters. He knew the lawyer's letter. As his mother read it, her face hardened and became more expressionless. Then a cold, determined look came on her mouth. She hid the letter under the pile of others, and said not a word about it.

"Didn't you have anything nice in the post for your birthday, mother?" said Paul.

"Quite moderately nice," she said, her voice cold and absent.

She went away to town without saying more.

But in the afternoon Uncle Oscar appeared. He said Paul's mother had had a long interview with the lawyer, asking if the whole five thousand could not be advanced at once, as she was in debt.

"What do you think, uncle?" said the boy.

"I leave it to you, son."

"Oh, let her have it, then! We can get some more with the other," said the boy.

"A bird in the hand is worth two in the bush, laddie!" said Uncle Oscar.

"But I'm sure to *know* for the Grand National; or the Lincolnshire; or else the Derby. I'm sure to know for *one* of them," said Paul.

So Uncle Oscar signed the agreement, and Paul's mother touched the whole five thousand. Then something very curious happened. The voices in the house suddenly went mad, like a chorus of frogs on a spring evening. There were certain new furnishings, and Paul had a tutor. He was *really* going to Eton, his father's school, in the following autumn. There were flowers in the winter, and a blossoming of the luxury Paul's mother had been used to. And yet the voices in the house, behind the sprays of mimosa and almond-blossom, and from under the piles of iridescent cushions, simply trilled and screamed in a sort of ecstasy: "There *must* be more money! Oh-h-h; there *must* be more money. Oh, now, now-w! Now-w-w—there *must* be more money!—more than ever! More than ever!"

It frightened Paul terribly. He studied away at his Latin and Greek with his tutor. But his intense hours were spent with Bassett. The Grand National had gone by: he had not 'known', and had lost a hundred pounds. Summer was at hand. He was in agony for the Lincoln. But even for the Lincoln he didn't 'know', and he lost fifty pounds. He became wild-eyed and strange, as if something were going to explode in him.

"Let it alone, son! Don't you bother about it!" urged Uncle Oscar. But it was as if the boy couldn't really hear what his uncle was saying.

"I've got to know for the Derby! I've got to know for the Derby!" the child reiterated, his big blue eyes blazing with a sort of madness.

His mother noticed how overwrought he was.

"You'd better go to the seaside. Wouldn't you like to go now to the seaside, instead of waiting? I think you'd better," she said, looking down at him anxiously, her heart curiously heavy because of him.

But the child lifted his uncanny blue eyes.

"I couldn't possibly go before the Derby, mother!" he said. "I couldn't possibly!"

"Why not?" she said, her voice becoming heavy when she was opposed. "Why not? You can still go from the seaside to see the Derby with your Uncle Oscar, if that's what you wish. No need for you to wait here. Besides, I think you care too much about these races. It's a bad sign. My family has been a gambling family, and you won't know till you grow up how much damage it has done. But it has done damage. I shall have to send Bassett away, and ask Uncle Oscar not to talk racing to you, unless you promise to be reasonable about it: go away to the seaside and forget it. You're all nerves!"

"I'll do what you like, mother, so long as you don't send me away till after the Derby," the boy said.

"Send you away from where? Just from this house?"

"Yes," he said, gazing at her.

"Why, you curious child, what makes you care about this house so much, suddenly? I never knew you loved it."

He gazed at her without speaking. He had a secret within a secret, something he had not divulged, even to Bassett or to his Uncle Oscar.

But his mother, after standing undecided and a little bit sullen for some moments, said:

"Very well, then! Don't go to the seaside till after the Derby, if you don't wish it. But promise me you won't let your nerves go to pieces. Promise you won't think so much about horse-racing and *events,* as you call them!"

"Oh no," said the boy casually. "I won't think much about them, mother. You needn't worry. I wouldn't worry, mother, if I were you."

"If you were me and I were you," said his mother, "I wonder what we *should* do!"

"But you know you needn't worry, mother, don't you?" the boy repeated.

"I should be awfully glad to know it," she said wearily.

"Oh, well, you *can,* you know. I mean, you *ought* to know you needn't worry," he insisted.

"Ought I? Then I'll see about it," she said.

Paul's secret of secrets was his wooden horse, that which had no name. Since he was emancipated from a nurse and a nursery-governess, he had had his rocking-horse removed to his own bedroom at the top of the house.

"Surely you're too big for a rocking-horse!" his mother had remonstrated.

"Well, you see, mother, till I can have a *real* horse, I like to have *some* sort of animal about," had been his quaint answer.

"Do you feel he keeps you company?" she laughed.

"Oh yes! He's very good, he always keeps me company, when I'm there," said Paul.

So the horse, rather shabby, stood in an arrested prance in the boy's bedroom.

The Derby was drawing near, and the boy grew more and more tense. He hardly heard what was spoken to him, he was very frail, and his eyes were really uncanny. His mother had sudden strange seizures of uneasiness about him. Sometimes, for half an hour, she would feel a sudden anxiety about him that was almost anguish. She wanted to rush to him at once, and know he was safe.

Two nights before the Derby, she was at a big party in town, when one of her rushes of anxiety about her boy, her first-born, gripped her heart till she could hardly speak. She fought with the feeling, might and main, for she believed in common sense. But it was too strong. She had to leave the dance and go downstairs to telephone to the country. The children's nursery-governess was terribly surprised and startled at being rung up in the night.

"Are the children all right, Miss Wilmot?"

"Oh yes, they are quite all right."

"Master Paul? Is he all right?"

"He went to bed as right as a trivet. Shall I run up and look at him?"

"No," said Paul's mother reluctantly. "No! Don't trouble. It's all right. Don't sit up. We shall be home fairly soon." She did not want her son's privacy intruded upon.

"Very good," said the governess.

It was about one o'clock when Paul's mother and father drove up to their house. All was still. Paul's mother went to her room and slipped off her white fur cloak. She had told her maid not to wait up for her. She heard her husband downstairs, mixing a whisky and soda.

And then, because of the strange anxiety at her heart, she stole upstairs to her son's room. Noiselessly she went along the upper corridor. Was there a faint noise? What was it?

She stood, with arrested muscles, outside his door, listening. There was a strange, heavy, and yet not loud noise. Her heart stood still. It was a soundless noise, yet rushing and powerful. Something huge, in violent, hushed motion. What was it? What in God's name was it? She ought to know. She felt that she knew the noise. She knew what it was.

Yet she could not place it. She couldn't say what it was. And on and on it went, like a madness.

Softly, frozen with anxiety and fear, she turned the doorhandle.

The room was dark. Yet in the space near the window, she heard and saw something plunging to and fro. She gazed in fear and amazement.

Then suddenly she switched on the light, and saw her son, in his green pyjamas, madly surging on the rocking-horse. The blaze of light suddenly lit him up, as he urged the wooden horse, and lit her up, as she stood, blonde, in her dress of pale green and crystal, in the doorway.

"Paul!" she cried. "Whatever are you doing?"

"It's Malabar!" he screamed in a powerful, strange voice. "It's Malabar!"

His eyes blazed at her for one strange and senseless second, as he ceased urging his wooden horse. Then he fell with a crash to the ground, and she, all her tormented motherhood flooding upon her, rushed to gather him up.

But he was unconscious, and unconscious he remained, with some brain-fever. He talked and tossed, and his mother sat stonily by his side.

"Malibar! It's Malabar! Bassett, Bassett, I *know*! It's Malabar!"

So the child cried, trying to get up and urge the rocking-horse that gave him his inspiration.

"What does he mean by Malabar?" asked the heart-frozen mother.

"I don't know," said the father stonily.

"What does he mean by Malabar?" she asked her brother Oscar.

"It's one of the horses running for the Derby," was the answer.

And, in spite of himself, Oscar Cresswell spoke to Bassett, and himself put a thousand on Malabar: at 640 fourteen to one.

The third day of the illness was critical: they were waiting for a change. The boy, with his rather long, curly hair, was tossing ceaselessly on the pillow. He neither slept nor regained consciousness, and his eyes were like blue stones. His mother sat, feeling her heart had gone, turned actually into a stone.

In the evening, Oscar Cresswell did not come, but Bassett sent a message, saying could he come up for one moment, just one moment? Paul's mother was 650 very angry at the intrusion, but on second thoughts she agreed. The boy was the same. Perhaps Bassett might bring him to consciousness.

The gardener, a shortish fellow with a little brown moustache and sharp little brown eyes, tiptoed into the room, touched his imaginary cap to Paul's mother, and stole to the bedside, staring with glittering, smallish eyes at the tossing, dying child.

"Master Paul!" he whispered. "Master Paul! Malabar came in first all right, a clean win. I did as you 660 told me. You've made over seventy thousand pounds, you have; you've got over eighty thousand. Malabar came in all right, Master Paul."

"Malabar! Malabar! Did I say Malabar, mother? Did I say Malabar? Do you think I'm lucky, mother? I knew Malabar, didn't I? Over eighty thousand pounds! I call that lucky, don't you, mother? Over eighty thousand pounds! I knew, didn't I know I knew? Malabar came in all right. If I ride my horse till I'm sure, then I tell you, Bassett, you can go as high as you 670 like. Did you go for all you were worth, Bassett?"

"I went a thousand on it, Master Paul."

"I never told you, mother, that if I can ride my horse, and *get there,* then I'm absolutely sure—oh, absolutely! Mother, did I ever tell you? I *am* lucky!"

"No, you never did," said his mother.

But the boy died in the night.

And even as he lay dead, his mother heard her brother's voice saying to her: "My God, Hester, you're eighty-odd thousand to the good, and a poor 680 devil of a son to the bad. But, poor devil, poor devil, he's best gone out of a life where he rides his rocking-horse to find a winner."

(1926)

BAVARIAN GENTIANS

Not every man has gentians° in his house
in Soft September, at slow, Sad Michaelmas.°

Bavarian Gentians 1 gentians, flowers, showy and usually blue 2 Michaelmas, September 29, the feast of St. Michael the Archangel

Bavarian gentians, big and dark, only dark
darkening the daytime torchlike with the smoking
    blueness of Pluto's° gloom,
ribbed and torchlike, with their blaze of darkness 5
    spread blue
down flattening into points, flattened under the sweep
    of white day
torch-flower of the blue-smoking darkness, Pluto's
    dark-blue daze,
black lamps from the halls of Dis,° burning dark blue,
giving off darkness, blue darkness, as Demeter's° pale
    lamps give off light,
lead me then, lead me the way. 10

Reach me a gentian, give me a torch
let me guide myself with the blue, forked torch of this
    flower
down the darker and darker stairs, where blue is
    darkened on blueness.
even where Persephone° goes, just now, from the
    frosted September
to the sightless realm where darkness was awake upon 15
    the dark
and Persephone herself is but a voice
or a darkness invisible enfolded in the deeper dark
of the arms Plutonic, and pierced with the passion of
    dense gloom,
among the splendor of torches of darkness, shedding
    darkness on the lost bride and her groom.

(1923)

SNAKE

A snake came to my water trough
On a hot, hot day, and I in pajamas for the heat,
To drink there.

In the deep, strange-scented shade of the great dark
    carob tree
I came down the steps with my pitcher
And must wait, must stand and wait, for there he was
    at the trough before me.

He reached down from a fissure in the earth-wall in the
    gloom
And trailed his yellow-brown slackness soft-bellied
    down, over the edge of the stone trough
And rested his throat upon the stone bottom,
And where the water had dripped from the tap, in a
    small clearness, 10
He sipped with his straight mouth,
Softly drank through his straight gums, into his slack
    long body,
Silently.

4 Pluto, the Greek god of the lower world 8 Dis, Roman counterpart to the Greek Pluto 9 Demeter, Persephone's (l. 14) mother, goddess of agriculture 14 Persephone, daughter of Zeus and Demeter, carried off to Hades by Pluto to be his queen

Someone was before me at my water trough,
And I, like a second-comer, waiting.

He lifted his head from his drinking, as cattle do,
And looked at me vaguely, as drinking cattle do,
And flickered his two-forked tongue from his lips, and
   mused a moment,
And stooped and drank a little more,
Being earth-brown, earth-golden from the burning
20   bowels of the earth
On the day of Sicilian July, with Etna smoking.

The voice of my education said to me
He must be killed,
For in Sicily the black black snakes are innocent, the
   gold are venomous.

And voices in me said, If you were a man
You would take a stick and break him now, and finish
   him off.

But must I confess how I liked him,
How glad I was he had come like a guest in quiet, to
   drink at my water trough
And depart peaceful, pacified, and thankless
30 Into the burning bowels of this earth?

Was it cowardice, that I dared not kill him?
Was it perversity, that I longed to talk to him?
Was it humility, to feel so honored?
I felt so honored.

And yet those voices:
If you were not afraid, you would kill him!
And truly I was afraid, I was most afraid,
But even so, honored still more
That he should seek my hospitality
40 From out the dark door of the secret earth.

He drank enough
And lifted his head, dreamily, as one who has drunken,
And flickered his tongue like a forked night on the air,
   so black,
Seeming to lick his lips,
And looked around like a god, unseeing, into the air,
And slowly turned his head,
And slowly, very slowly, as if thrice adream
Proceeded to draw his slow length curving round
And climb the broken bank of my wall-face.

50 And as he put his head into that dreadful hole,
And as he slowly drew up, snake-easing his shoulders,
   and entered further,
A sort of horror, a sort of protest against his with-
   drawing into that horrid black hole,
Deliberately going into the blackness, and slowly
   drawing himself after,
Overcame me now his back was tuned.

I looked round, I put down my pitcher,
I picked up a clumsy log
And threw it at the water trough with a clatter.

I think it did not hit him;
But suddenly that part of him that was left behind con-
   vulsed in undignified haste,
Writhed like lightning, and was gone   60
Into the black hole, the earth-lipped fissure in the
   wall-front
At which, in the intense still noon, I stared with fasci-
   nation.

And immediately I regretted it.
I thought how paltry, how vulgar, what a mean act!
I despised myself and the voices of my accursed hu-
   man education.

And I thought of the albatross,
And I wished he would come back, my snake.

For he seemed to me again like a king,
Like a king in exile, uncrowned in the underworld,
Now due to be crowned again.   70

And so, I missed my chance with one of the lords
Of life.
And I have something to expiate:
A pettiness.
(1923)

JAMES JOYCE
1882–1941

The eldest son of a large middle-class family, James
Joyce was born in a suburb of Dublin, Ireland, in
1882. His father was a civil servant, continually in financial difficulties; his mother was conventionally pious. But Joyce was given the best education available.
From the age of six to the age of nine he attended the
prestigious Clongowes Wood College, in Clane; from
the age of eleven to the age of sixteen he attended
Belvedere College, Dublin. Both of these preparatory
schools were run by the Jesuits and were considered
normal roads to the priesthood. He then went on to
the Jesuit-staffed University College, Dublin, where he
made a definite break with the Church, studying
neither philosophy nor theology but concentrating on
modern languages. He received his bachelor's degree
in 1902.

During his years of study, he showed marked originality and independence; he displayed a special talent
for creative writing and facility in a dozen or more

languages. Joyce's first serious writing was an essay on Henrik Ibsen, published in 1900 in *The Fortnightly Review*. His interest in Ibsen and other non-Irish writers led him to oppose the movement for the establishment of a national theater for Ireland. The success of his Ibsen article strengthened his resolution to become a writer.

In 1902 Joyce left Ireland on what proved to be a long, self-imposed exile. He returned twice: in 1903, because of his mother's fatal illness; and in 1912, in an attempt to publish one of his books. In Paris in 1902 Joyce gave up the idea of financing his writing career by becoming a doctor because he lacked the necessary funds. He also abandoned the notion of preparing for a career as a singer. In 1904 he taught at the Clifton School, Dalkey, Ireland. That same year he fell in love with Nora Barnacle, a Dublin chambermaid; the two moved to Trieste, where Joyce taught in the Berlitz School. Joyce and Nora remained on the Continent for the rest of their lives. Joyce bowed to convention and officially married Nora in 1931; they had two children.

Joyce was initially unable to find a publisher for some early poems, but a thin volume of lyrics, *Chamber Music*, was published in 1907. In addition, a Dublin publisher finally published Joyce's group of stories based on Dublin life under the title *Dubliners* in 1914. These masterly sketches of incidents, people, and dramatic episodes in many ways foreshadow his longer and more individualistic works.

Joyce's first novel, *A Portrait of the Artist as a Young Man*, a semiautobiographical account of the author's youthful years, first appeared serially in *The Egoist*, an English periodical, and then was published in book form in 1916 with the imprint "Dublin, 1904—Trieste, 1914." During the next few years, Joyce began to suffer from a series of eye ailments that plagued him for the rest of his life; he endured twenty-five eye operations that sometimes entailed periods of total blindness. Nevertheless, he worked on a long sequel to *A Portrait—Ulysses*, begun in Trieste in 1914 and finished in Paris in 1921. Expurgated portions were printed in *The Egoist*, and twenty-three installments appeared in the United States in *The Little Review* between 1918 and 1920. Three were confiscated by the United States Post Office, and the publishers were fined for allegedly sending immoral matter through the mails. In 1922 the novel was published in Paris. Five hundred copies were burned in New York by the United States Post Office; a similar number were confiscated by British Customs. These actions served only to stimulate public interest in what was described by some as "an infamously obscene book" and by others as the "greatest fiction of the twentieth century." After the ban was removed in 1933 by United States District Court Judge Woolsey in a historic decision, the novel circulated freely in America and soon afterwards in England.

Portions of Joyce's next novel, *Finnegans Wake* (1939), appeared first in Paris in periodicals under the title *Work in Progress*. This book, which occupied Joyce for fifteen years or more, follows the strenuous stylistic experimentation of *Ulysses*.

When he could, Joyce supported his family by working as a language teacher; at other times he had to depend on the charity of relatives and friends. He earned almost nothing from his writings until his later years. Joyce left Paris with his family in 1940, following the outbreak of World War II. After a brief stay in southern France, he managed to get to Zurich, Switzerland, where he died in January 1941.

Joyce wrote frankly, and his vocabulary is often startling. He made use of a great variety of narrative modes and prose styles, and he mercilessly parodied everything he saw as clichéd and worn-out. He was interested both in the individual mind, whose random thought-flow he sought to render by a technique which came to be called stream of consciousness, and in the collective memory of mankind, a treasure that he felt was stored up in myths, jokes, tall tales, and in ordinary language itself.

THE DEAD

Lily, the caretaker's daughter, was literally run off her feet. Hardly had she brought one gentleman into the little pantry behind the office on the ground floor and helped him off with his overcoat than the wheezy hall-door bell clanged again and she had to scamper along the bare hallway to let in another guest. It was well for her she had not to attend to the ladies also. But Miss Kate and Miss Julia had thought of that and had converted the bathroom upstairs into a ladies' dressing-room. Miss Kate and Miss Julia were there, 10 gossiping and laughing and fussing, walking after each other to the head of the stairs, peering down over the banisters and calling down to Lily to ask her who had come.

It was always a great affair, the Misses Morkan's annual dance. Everybody who knew them came to it, members of the family, old friends of the family, the members of Julia's choir, any of Kate's pupils that were grown up enough, and even some of Mary Jane's pupils too. Never once had it fallen flat. For years and 20 years it had gone off in splendid style, as long as anyone could remember, ever since Kate and Julia, after the death of their brother Pat, had left the house in Stoney Batter and taken Mary Jane, their only niece, to live with them in the dark, gaunt house on Usher's Island, the upper part of which they had rented from Mr. Fulham, the corn-factor on the ground floor. That was a good thirty years ago if it was a day. Mary Jane, who was then a little girl in short clothes, was now the main prop of the household, for she had the organ in 30 Haddington Road. She had been through the Academy and gave a pupils' concert every year in the upper room of the Ancient Concert Rooms. Many of her pupils belonged to the better-class families on the Kingstown and Dalkey line. Old as they were, her aunts also did their share. Julia, though she was quite grey, was still the leading soprano in Adam and Eve's, and Kate, being too feeble to go about much, gave music lessons to beginners on the old square piano in the back room. Lily, the caretaker's daughter, did housemaid's work for them. Though their life was modest, they believed in eating well; the best of everything: diamond-bone sirloins, three-shilling tea and the best bottled stout. But Lily seldom made a mistake in the orders, so that she got on well with her three mistresses. They were fussy, that was all. But the only thing they would not stand was back answers.

Of course, they had good reason to be fussy on such a night. And then it was long after ten o'clock and yet there was no sign of Gabriel and his wife. Besides they were dreadfully afraid that Freddy Malins might turn up screwed.° They would not wish for worlds that any of Mary Jane's pupils should see him under the influence; and when he was like that it was sometimes very hard to manage him. Freddy Malins always came late, but they wondered what could be keeping Gabriel: and that was what brought them every two minutes to the banisters to ask Lily had Gabriel or Freddy come.

"O, Mr. Conroy," said Lily to Gabriel when she opened the door for him, "Miss Kate and Miss Julia thought you were never coming. Good-night, Mrs. Conroy."

"I'll engage they did," said Gabriel, "but they forget that my wife here takes three mortal hours to dress herself."

He stood on the mat, scraping the snow from his goloshes, while Lily led his wife to the foot of the stairs and called out:

"Miss Kate, here's Mrs. Conroy."

Kate and Julia came toddling down the dark stairs at once. Both of them kissed Gabriel's wife, said she must be perished alive, and asked was Gabriel with her.

"Here I am as right as the mail, Aunt Kate! Go on up. I'll follow," called out Gabriel from the dark.

He continued scraping his feet vigorously while the three women went upstairs, laughing, to the ladies' dressing-room. A light fringe of snow lay like a cape on the shoulders of his overcoat and like toecaps on the toes of his goloshes; and, as the buttons of his overcoat slipped with a squeaking noise through the snow-stiffened frieze, a cold, fragrant air from out-of-doors escaped from crevices and folds.

"Is it snowing again, Mr. Conroy?" asked Lily.

She had preceded him into the pantry to help him off with his overcoat. Gabriel smiled at the three syllables

The Dead   52 screwed, drunk

she had given his surname and glanced at her. She was a slim, growing girl, pale in complexion and with hay-coloured hair. The gas in the pantry made her look still paler. Gabriel had known her when she was a child and used to sit on the lowest step nursing a rag doll.

"Yes, Lily," he answered, "and I think we're in for a night of it."

He looked up at the pantry ceiling, which was shaking with the stamping and shuffling of feet on the floor above, listened for a moment to the piano and then glanced at the girl, who was folding his overcoat carefully at the end of a shelf.

"Tell me, Lily," he said in a friendly tone, "do you still go to school?"

"O no, sir," she answered. "I'm done schooling this year and more."

"O, then," said Gabriel gaily, "I suppose we'll be going to your wedding one of these fine days with your young man, eh?"

The girl glanced back at him over her shoulder and said with great bitterness:

"The men that is now is only all palaver and what they can get out of you."

Gabriel coloured, as if he felt he had made a mistake and, without looking at her, kicked off his goloshes and flicked actively with his muffler at his patent-leather shoes.

He was a stout, tallish young man. The high colour of his cheeks pushed upwards even to his forehead, where it scattered itself in a few formless patches of pale red; and on his hairless face there scintillated restlessly the polished lenses and the bright gilt rims of the glasses which screened his delicate and restless eyes. His glossy black hair was parted in the middle and brushed in a long curve behind his ears where it curled slightly beneath the groove left by his hat.

When he had flicked lustre into his shoes he stood up and pulled his waistcoat down more tightly on his plump body. Then he took a coin rapidly from his pocket.

"O Lily," he said, thrusting it into her hands, "it's Christmas-time, isn't it? Just . . . here's a little . . ."

He walked rapidly towards the door.

"O no, sir!" cried the girl, following him. "Really, sir, I wouldn't take it."

"Christmas-time! Christmas-time!" said Gabriel, almost trotting to the stairs and waving his hand to her in deprecation.

The girl, seeing that he had gained the stairs, called out after him:

"Well, thank you, sir."

He waited outside the drawing-room door until the waltz should finish, listening to the skirts that swept against it and to the shuffling of feet. He was still discomposed by the girl's bitter and sudden retort. It had cast a gloom over him which he tried to dispel by arranging his cuffs and the bows of his tie. He then took

from his waistcoat pocket a little paper and glanced at the headings he had made for his speech. He was undecided about the lines from Robert Browning, for he feared they would be above the heads of his hearers. Some quotation that they would recognise from Shakespeare or from the Melodies° would be better.
150 The indelicate clacking of the men's heels and the shuffling of their soles reminded him that their grade of culture differed from his. He would only make himself ridiculous by quoting poetry to them which they could not understand. They would think that he was airing his superior education. He would fail with them just as he had failed with the girl in the pantry. He had taken up a wrong tone. His whole speech was a mistake from first to last, an utter failure.

Just then his aunts and his wife came out of the
160 ladies' dressing-room. His aunts were two small, plainly dressed old women. Aunt Julia was an inch or so the taller. Her hair, drawn low over the tops of her ears, was grey; and grey also, with darker shadows, was her large flaccid face. Though she was stout in build and stood erect, her slow eyes and parted lips gave her the appearance of a woman who did not know where she was or where she was going. Aunt Kate was more vivacious. Her face, healthier than her sister's, was all puckers and creases, like a shrivelled red ap-
170 ple, and her hair, braided in the same old-fashioned way, had not lost its ripe nut colour.

They both kissed Gabriel frankly. He was their favourite nephew, the son of their dead elder sister, Ellen, who had married T. J. Conroy of the Port and Docks.

"Gretta tells me you're not going to take a cab back to Monkstown tonight, Gabriel," said Aunt Kate.

"No," said Gabriel, turning to his wife, "we had quite enough of that last year, hadn't we? Don't you
180 remember, Aunt Kate, what a cold Gretta got out of it? Cab windows rattling all the way, and the east wind blowing in after we passed Merrion. Very jolly it was. Gretta caught a dreadful cold."

Aunt Kate frowned severely and nodded her head at every word.

"Quite right, Gabriel, quite right," she said. "You can't be too careful."

"But as for Gretta there," said Gabriel, "she'd walk home in the snow if she were let."
190 Mrs. Conroy laughed.

"Don't mind him, Aunt Kate," she said. "He's really an awful bother, what with green shades for Tom's eyes at night and making him do the dumbbells, and forcing Eva to eat the stirabout. The poor child! And she simply hates the sight of it! . . . O, but you'll never guess what he makes me wear now!"

She broke out into a peal of laughter and glanced at her husband, whose admiring and happy eyes had been wandering from her dress to her face and hair. The two aunts laughed heartily, too, for Gabriel's solicitude 200 was a standing joke with them.

"Goloshes!" said Mrs. Conroy. "That's the latest. Whenever it's wet underfoot I must put on my goloshes. Tonight even, he wanted me to put them on, but I wouldn't. The next thing he'll buy me will be a diving suit."

Gabriel laughed nervously and patted his tie reassuringly, while Aunt Kate nearly doubled herself, so heartily did she enjoy the joke. The smile soon faded from Aunt Julia's face and her mirthless eyes were 210 directed towards her nephew's face. After a pause she asked:

"And what are goloshes, Gabriel?"

"Goloshes, Julia!" exclaimed her sister. "Goodness me, don't you know what goloshes are? You wear them over your . . . over your boots, Gretta, isn't it?"

"Yes," said Mrs. Conroy. "Guttapercha things. We both have a pair now. Gabriel says everyone wears them on the Continent."

"O, on the Continent," murmured Aunt Julia, nod- 220 ding her head slowly.

Gabriel knitted his brows and said, as if he were slightly angered:

"It's nothing very wonderful, but Gretta thinks it very funny because she says the word reminds her of Christy Minstrels."

"But tell me, Gabriel," said Aunt Kate, with brisk tact. "Of course, you've seen about the room. Gretta was saying . . ."

"O, the room is all right," replied Gabriel. "I've 230 taken one in the Gresham."

"To be sure," said Aunt Kate, "by far the best thing to do. And the children, Gretta, you're not anxious about them?"

"O, for one night," said Mrs. Conroy. "Besides, Bessie will look after them."

"To be sure," said Aunt Kate again. "What a comfort it is to have a girl like that, one you can depend on! There's that Lily, I'm sure I don't know what has come over her lately. She's not the girl she was at all." 240

Gabriel was about to ask his aunt some questions on this point, but she broke off suddenly to gaze after her sister, who had wandered down the stairs and was craning her neck over the banisters.

"Now, I ask you," she said almost testily, "where is Julia going? Julia! Julia! Where are you going?"

Julia, who had gone half way down one flight, came back and announced blandly: "Here's Freddy."

At the same moment a clapping of hands and a final flourish of the pianist told that the waltz had ended. 250 The drawing-room door was opened from within and some couples came out. Aunt Kate drew Gabriel aside hurriedly and whispered into his ear.

"Slip down, Gabriel, like a good fellow and see if

149 **Melodies**, Irish Melodies, a collection of lyrics about Ireland and the Irish written by Thomas Moore (1779–1852) and adapted to well known Irish folksongs

he's all right, and don't let him up if he's screwed. I'm sure he's screwed. I'm sure he is."

Gabriel went to the stairs and listened over the banisters. He could hear two persons talking in the pantry. Then he recognised Freddy Malins' laugh. He went down the stairs noisily.

"It's such a relief," said Aunt Kate to Mrs. Conroy, "that Gabriel is here. I always feel easier in my mind when he's here. . . . Julia, there's Miss Daly and Miss Power will take some refreshment. Thanks for your beautiful waltz, Miss Daly. It made lovely time."

A tall wizen-faced man, with a stiff grizzled moustache and swarthy skin, who was passing out with his partner, said:

"And may we have some refreshment too, Miss Morkan?"

"Julia," said Aunt Kate summarily, "and here's Mr. Browne and Miss Furlong. Take them in, Julia, with Miss Daly and Miss Power."

"I'm the man for the ladies," said Mr. Browne, pursing his lips until his moustache bristled and smiling in all his wrinkles. "You know, Miss Morkan, the reason they are so fond of me is—"

He did not finish his sentence, but, seeing that Aunt Kate was out of earshot, at once led the three young ladies into the back room. The middle of the room was occupied by two square tables placed end to end, and on these Aunt Julia and the caretaker were straightening and smoothing a large cloth. On the sideboard were arrayed dishes and plates, and glasses and bundles of knives and forks and spoons. The top of the closed square piano served also as a sideboard for viands and sweets. At a smaller sideboard in one corner two young men were standing, drinking hop-bitters.

Mr. Browne led his charges thither and invited them all, in jest, to some ladies' punch, hot, strong and sweet. As they said they never took anything strong, he opened three bottles of lemonade for them. Then he asked one of the young men to move aside, and, taking hold of the decanter, filled out for himself a goodly measure of whisky. The young men eyed him respectfully while he took a trial sip.

"God help me," he said, smiling, "it's the doctor's orders."

His wizened face broke into a broader smile, and the three young ladies laughed in musical echo to his pleasantry, swaying their bodies to and fro, with nervous jerks of their shoulders. The boldest said:

"O, now, Mr. Browne, I'm sure the doctor never ordered anything of the kind."

Mr. Browne took another sip of his whisky and said, with sidling mimicry:

"Well, you see, I'm like the famous Mrs. Cassidy, who is reported to have said: 'Now, Mary Grimes, if I don't take it, make me take it, for I feel I want it.'"

His hot face had leaned forward a little too confidently and he had assumed a very low Dublin accent so that the young ladies, with one instinct, received his speech in silence. Miss Furlong, who was one of Mary Jane's pupils, asked Miss Daly what was the name of the pretty waltz she had played; and Mr. Browne, seeing that he was ignored, turned promptly to the two young men who were more appreciative.

A red-faced young woman, dressed in pansy, came into the room, excitedly clapping her hands and crying:

"Quadrilles! Quadrilles!"

Close on her heels came Aunt Kate, crying:

"Two gentlemen and three ladies, Mary Jane!"

"O, here's Mr. Bergin and Mr. Kerrigan," said Mary Jane. "Mr. Kerrigan, will you take Miss Power? Miss Furlong, may I get you a partner, Mr. Bergin. O, that'll just do now."

"Three ladies, Mary Jane," said Aunt Kate.

The two young gentlemen asked the ladies if they might have the pleasure, and Mary Jane turned to Miss Daly.

"O, Miss Daly, you're really awfully good, after playing for the last two dances, but really we're so short of ladies tonight."

"I don't mind in the least, Miss Morkan."

"But I've a nice partner for you, Mr. Bartell D'Arcy, the tenor. I'll get him to sing later on. All Dublin is raving about him."

"Lovely voice, lovely voice!" said Aunt Kate.

As the piano had twice begun the prelude to the first figure Mary Jane led her recruits quickly from the room. They had hardly gone when Aunt Julia wandered slowly into the room, looking behind her at something.

"What is the matter, Julia?" asked Aunt Kate anxiously. "Who is it?"

Julia, who was carrying in a column of table-napkins, turned to her sister and said, simply, as if the question had surprised her:

"It's only Freddy, Kate, and Gabriel with him."

In fact right behind her Gabriel could be seen piloting Freddy Malins across the landing. The latter, a young man of about forty, was of Gabriel's size and build, with very round shoulders. His face was fleshy and pallid, touched with colour only at the thick hanging lobes of his ears and at the wide wings of his nose. He had coarse features, a blunt nose, a convex and receding brow, tumid and protruded lips. His heavy-lidded eyes and the disorder of his scanty hair made him look sleepy. He was laughing heartily in a high key at a story which he had been telling Gabriel on the stairs and at the same time rubbing the knuckles of his left fist backwards and forwards into his left eye.

"Good evening, Freddy," said Aunt Julia.

Freddy Malins bade the Misses Morkan good-evening in what seemed an offhand fashion by reason of the habitual catch in his voice and then, seeing that Mr. Browne was grinning at him from the sideboard, crossed the room on rather shaky legs and began to repeat in an undertone the story he had just told to Gabriel.

"He's not so bad, is he?" said Aunt Kate to Gabriel.

Gabriel's brows were dark, but he raised them quickly and answered:

"O, no, hardly noticeable."

"Now, isn't he a terrible fellow!" she said. "And his poor mother made him take the pledge° on New Year's Eve. But come on, Gabriel, into the drawing-room."

Before leaving the room with Gabriel she signalled to Mr. Browne by frowning and shaking her forefinger in warning to and fro. Mr. Browne nodded in answer and, when she had gone, said to Freddy Malins:

"Now, then, Teddy, I'm going to fill you out a good glass of lemonade just to buck you up."

Freddy Malins, who was nearing the climax of his story, waved the offer aside impatiently but Mr. Browne, having first called Freddy Malins' attention to a disarray in his dress, filled out and handed him a full glass of lemonade. Freddy Malins' left hand accepted the glass mechanically, his right hand being engaged in the mechanical readjustment of his dress. Mr. Browne, whose face was once more wrinkling with mirth, poured out for himself a glass of whisky while Freddy Malins exploded, before he had well reached the climax of his story, in a kink of high-pitched bronchitic laughter and, setting down his untasted and overflowing glass, began to rub the knuckles of his left fist backwards and forwards into his left eye, repeating words of his last phrase as well as his fit of laughter would allow him.

Gabriel could not listen while Mary Jane was playing her Academy piece, full of runs and difficult passages, to the hushed drawing-room. He liked music but the piece she was playing had no melody for him and he doubted whether it had any melody for the other listeners, though they had begged Mary Jane to play something. Four young men, who had come from the refreshment-room to stand in the doorway at the sound of the piano, had gone away quietly in couples after a few minutes. The only persons who seemed to follow the music were Mary Jane herself, her hands racing along the keyboard or lifted from it at the pauses like those of a priestess in momentary imprecation, and Aunt Kate standing at her elbow to turn the page.

Gabriel's eyes, irritated by the floor, which glittered with beeswax under the heavy chandelier, wandered to the wall above the piano. A picture of the balcony scene in *Romeo and Juliet* hung there and beside it was a picture of the two murdered princes in the Tower which Aunt Julia had worked in red, blue and brown wools when she was a girl. Probably in the school they had gone to as girls that kind of work had been taught for one year. His mother had worked for him as a

birthday present a waistcoat of purple tabinet,° with little foxes' heads upon it, lined with brown satin and having round mulberry buttons. It was strange that his mother had had no musical talent though Aunt Kate used to call her the brains carrier of the Morkan family. Both she and Julia had always seemed a little proud of their serious and matronly sister. Her photograph stood before the pierglass. She held an open book on her knees and was pointing out something in it to Constantine who, dressed in a man-o'-war suit, lay at her feet. It was she who had chosen the names of her sons for she was very sensible of the dignity of family life. Thanks to her, Constantine was now senior curate in Balbriggan and, thanks to her, Gabriel himself had taken his degree in the Royal University. A shadow passed over his face as he remembered her sullen opposition to his marriage. Some slighting phrases she had used still rankled in his memory; she had once spoken of Gretta as being country cute and that was not true of Gretta at all. It was Gretta who had nursed her during all her last long illness in their house at Monkstown.

He knew that Mary Jane must be near the end of her piece for she was playing again the opening melody with runs of scales after every bar and while he waited for the end the resentment died down in his heart. The piece ended with a trill of octaves in the treble and a final deep octave in the bass. Great applause greeted Mary Jane as, blushing and rolling up her music nervously, she escaped from the room. The most vigorous clapping came from the four young men in the doorway who had gone away to the refreshment-room at the beginning of the piece but had come back when the piano had stopped.

Lancers were arranged. Gabriel found himself partnered with Miss Ivors. She was a frank-mannered talkative young lady, with a freckled face and prominent brown eyes. She did not wear a low-cut bodice and the large brooch which was fixed in the front of her collar bore on it an Irish device and motto.

When they had taken their places she said abruptly:

"I have a crow to pluck with you."

"With me?" said Gabriel.

She nodded her head gravely.

"What is it?" asked Gabriel, smiling at her solemn manner.

"Who is G. C.?" answered Miss Ivors, turning her eyes upon him.

Gabriel coloured and was about to knit his brows, as if he did not understand, when she said bluntly:

"O, innocent Amy! I have found out that you write for *The Daily Express*. Now, aren't you ashamed of yourself?"

"Why should I be ashamed of myself?" asked Gabriel, blinking his eyes and trying to smile.

---

377 **the pledge,** a solemn promise not to drink

424 **tabinet,** a kind of poplin cloth

"Well, I'm ashamed of you," said Miss Ivors
480 frankly. "To say you'd write for a paper like that. I
didn't think you were a West Briton.°"

A look of perplexity appeared on Gabriel's face. It
was true that he wrote a literary column every
Wednesday in *The Daily Express,* for which he was
paid fifteen shillings. But that did not make him a West
Briton surely. The books he received for review were
almost more welcome than the paltry cheque. He
loved to feel the covers and turn over the pages of
newly printed books. Nearly every day when his
490 teaching in the college was ended he used to wander
down the quays to the second-hand booksellers, to
Hickey's on Bachelor's Walk, to Webb's or Massey's
on Aston's Quay, or to O'Clohissey's in the by-street.
He did not know how to meet her charge. He wanted
to say that literature was above politics. But they were
friends of many years' standing and their careers had
been parallel, first at the University and then as
teachers: he could not risk a grandiose phrase with
her. He continued blinking his eyes and trying to smile
500 and murmured lamely that he saw nothing political in
writing reviews of books.

When their turn to cross had come he was still
perplexed and inattentive. Miss Ivors promptly took
his hand in a warm grasp and said in a soft friendly
tone:

"Of course, I was only joking. Come, we cross
now."

When they were together again she spoke of the
University question and Gabriel felt more at ease. A
510 friend of hers had shown her his review of Browning's
poems. That was how she had found out the secret: but
she liked the review immensely. Then she said suddenly:

"O, Mr. Conroy, will you come for an excursion to
the Aran Isles this summer? We're going to stay there
a whole month. It will be splendid out in the Atlantic.
You ought to come. Mr. Clancy is coming, and Mr.
Kilkelly and Kathleen Kearney. It would be splendid
for Gretta too if she'd come. She's from Connacht,
520 isn't she?"

"Her people are," said Gabriel shortly.

"But you will come, won't you?" said Miss Ivors,
laying her warm hand eagerly on his arm.

"The fact is," said Gabriel, "I have just arranged to
go—"

"Go where?" asked Miss Ivors.

"Well, you know, every year I go for a cycling tour
with some fellows and so—"

"But where?" asked Miss Ivors.

530 "Well, we usually go to France or Belgium or
perhaps Germany," said Gabriel awkwardly.

481 **West Briton,** one not in sympathy with the Irish nationalist movement, although living in Ireland

"And why do you go to France and Belgium," said
Miss Ivors, "instead of visiting your own land?"

"Well," said Gabriel, "it's partly to keep in touch
with the languages and partly for a change."

"And haven't you your own language to keep in
touch with—Irish?" asked Miss Ivors.

"Well," said Gabriel, "if it comes to that, you
know, Irish is not my language."

Their neighbours had turned to listen to the cross- 540
examination. Gabriel glanced right and left nervously
and tried to keep his good humour under the ordeal
which was making a blush invade his forehead.

"And haven't you your own land to visit," continued Miss Ivors, "that you know nothing of, your
own people, and your own country?"

"O, to tell you the truth," retorted Gabriel suddenly, "I'm sick of my own country, sick of it!"

"Why?" asked Miss Ivors.

Gabriel did not answer for his retort had heated him. 550

"Why?" repeated Miss Ivors.

They had to go visiting together and, as he had not
answered her, Miss Ivors said warmly:

"Of course, you've no answer."

Gabriel tried to cover his agitation by taking part in
the dance with great energy. He avoided her eyes for
he had seen a sour expression on her face. But when
they met in the long chain he was surprised to feel his
hand firmly pressed. She looked at him from under her
brows for a moment quizzically until he smiled. Then, 560
just as the chain was about to start again, she stood on
tiptoe and whispered into his ear:

"West Briton!"

When the lancers were over Gabriel went away to a
remote corner of the room where Freddy Malins'
mother was sitting. She was a stout feeble old woman
with white hair. Her voice had a catch in it like her
son's and she stuttered slightly. She had been told that
Freddy had come and that he was nearly all right. Gabriel asked her whether she had had a good crossing. 570
She lived with her married daughter in Glasgow and
came to Dublin on a visit once a year. She answered
placidly that she had had a beautiful crossing and that
the captain had been most attentive to her. She spoke
also of the beautiful house her daughter kept in Glasgow, and of all the friends they had there. While her
tongue rambled on Gabriel tried to banish from his
mind all memory of the unpleasant incident with Miss
Ivors. Of course the girl or woman, or whatever she
was, was an enthusiast but there was a time for all 580
things. Perhaps he ought not to have answered her like
that. But she had no right to call him a West Briton
before people, even in joke. She had tried to make him
ridiculous before people, heckling him and staring at
him with her rabbit's eyes.

He saw his wife making her way towards him

through the waltzing couples. When she reached him she said into his ear:

"Gabriel, Aunt Kate wants to know won't you carve the goose as usual. Miss Daly will carve the ham and I'll do the pudding."

"All right," said Gabriel.

"She's sending in the younger ones first as soon as this waltz is over so that we'll have the table to ourselves."

"Were you dancing?" asked Gabriel.

"Of course I was. Didn't you see me? What row had you with Molly Ivors?"

"No row. Why? Did she say so?"

"Something like that. I'm trying to get that Mr. D'Arcy to sing. He's full of conceit, I think."

"There was no row," said Gabriel moodily, "only she wanted me to go for a trip to the west of Ireland and I said I wouldn't."

His wife clasped her hands excitedly and gave a little jump.

"O, do go, Gabriel," she cried. "I'd love to see Galway again."

"You can go if you like," said Gabriel coldly.

She looked at him for a moment, then turned to Mrs. Malins and said:

"There's a nice husband for you, Mrs. Malins."

While she was threading her way back across the room Mrs. Malins, without adverting to the interruption, went on to tell Gabriel what beautiful places there were in Scotland and beautiful scenery. Her son-in-law brought them every year to the lakes and they used to go fishing. Her son-in-law was a splendid fisher. One day he caught a beautiful big fish and the man in the hotel cooked it for their dinner.

Gabriel hardly heard what she said. Now that supper was coming near he began to think again about his speech and about the quotation. When he saw Freddy Malins coming across the room to visit his mother Gabriel left the chair free for him and retired into the embrasure of the window. The room had already cleared and from the back room came the clatter of plates and knives. Those who still remained in the drawing-room seemed tired of dancing and were conversing quietly in little groups. Gabriel's warm trembling fingers tapped the cold pane of the window. How cool it must be outside! How pleasant it would be to walk out alone, first along by the river and then through the park! The snow would be lying on the branches of the trees and forming a bright cap on the top of the Wellington Monument. How much more pleasant it would be there than at the supper-table!

He ran over the headings of his speech: Irish hospitality, sad memories, the Three Graces, Paris, the quotation from Browning. He repeated to himself a phrase he had written in his review: "One feels that one is listening to a thought-tormented music." Miss Ivors had praised the review. Was she sincere? Had she really any life of her own behind all her propagandism? There had never been any ill-feeling between them until that night. It unnerved him to think that she would be at the supper-table, looking up at him while he spoke with her critical quizzing eyes. Perhaps she would not be sorry to see him fail in his speech. An idea came into his mind and gave him courage. He would say, alluding to Aunt Kate and Aunt Julia: "Ladies and Gentlemen, the generation which is now on the wane among us may have had its faults but for my part I think it had certain qualities of hospitality, of humour, of humanity, which the new and very serious and hypereducated generation that is growing up around us seems to me to lack." Very good: that was one for Miss Ivors. What did he care that his aunts were only two ignorant old women?

A murmur in the room attracted his attention. Mr. Browne was advancing from the door, gallantly escorting Aunt Julia, who leaned upon his arm, smiling and hanging her head. An irregular musketry of applause escorted her also as far as the piano and then, as Mary Jane seated herself on the stool, and Aunt Julia, no longer smiling, half turned so as to pitch her voice fairly into the room, gradually ceased. Gabriel recognised the prelude. It was that of an old song of Aunt Julia's—*Arrayed for the Bridal*. Her voice, strong and clear in tone, attacked with great spirit the runs which embellish the air and though she sang very rapidly she did not miss even the smallest of the grace notes. To follow the voice, without looking at the singer's face, was to feel and share the excitement of swift and secure flight. Gabriel applauded loudly with all the others at the close of the song and loud applause was borne in from the invisible supper-table. It sounded so genuine that a little colour struggled into Aunt Julia's face as she bent to replace in the music-stand the old leather-bound songbook that had her initials on the cover. Freddy Malins, who had listened with his head perched sideways to hear her better, was still applauding when everyone else had ceased and talking animatedly to his mother who nodded her head gravely and slowly in acquiescence. At last, when he could clap no more, he stood up suddenly and hurried across the room to Aunt Julia whose hand he seized and held in both his hands, shaking it when words failed him or the catch in his voice proved too much for him.

"I was just telling my mother," he said, "I never heard you sing so well, never. No. I never heard your voice so good as it is tonight. Now! Would you believe that now? That's the truth. Upon my word and honour that's the truth. I never heard your voice sound so fresh and so . . . so clear and fresh, never."

Aunt Julia smiled broadly and murmured something about compliments as she released her hand from his grasp. Mr. Browne extended his open hand towards 700 her and said to those who were near him in the manner of a showman introducing a prodigy to an audience:

"Miss Julia Morkan, my latest discovery!"

He was laughing very heartily at this himself when Freddy Malins turned to him and said:

"Well, Browne, if you're serious you might make a worse discovery. All I can say is I never heard her sing half so well as long as I am coming here. And that's the honest truth."

"Neither did I," said Mr. Browne. "I think her 710 voice has greatly improved."

Aunt Julia shrugged her shoulders and said with meek pride:

"Thirty years ago I hadn't a bad voice as voices go."

"I often told Julia," said Aunt Kate emphatically, "that she was simply thrown away in that choir. But she never would be said by me."

She turned as if to appeal to the good sense of the others against a refractory child while Aunt Julia gazed 720 in front of her, a vague smile of reminiscence playing on her face.

"No," continued Aunt Kate, "she wouldn't be said or led by anyone, slaving there in that choir night and day, night and day. Six o'clock on Christmas morning! And all for what?"

"Well, isn't it for the honour of God, Aunt Kate?" asked Mary Jane, twisting round on the piano stool and smiling.

Aunt Kate turned fiercely on her niece and said:
730 "I know all about the honour of God, Mary Jane, but I think it's not at all honourable for the pope to turn out the women out of the choirs that have slaved there all their lives and put little whipper-snappers of boys over their heads. I suppose it is for the good of the Church if the pope does it. But it's not just, Mary Jane, and it's not right."

She had worked herself into a passion and would have continued in defence of her sister for it was a sore subject with her but Mary Jane, seeing that all the 740 dancers had come back, intervened pacifically:

"Now, Aunt Kate, you're giving scandal to Mr. Browne who is of the other persuasion."

Aunt Kate turned to Mr. Browne, who was grinning at this allusion to his religion, and said hastily:

"O, I don't question the pope's being right. I'm only a stupid old woman and I wouldn't presume to do such a thing. But there's such a thing as common everyday politeness and gratitude. And if I were in Julia's place I'd tell that Father Healey straight up to his face . . ."
750 "And besides, Aunt Kate," said Mary Jane, "we really are all hungry and when we are hungry we are all very quarrelsome."

"And when we are thirsty we are also quarrelsome," added Mr. Browne.

"So that we had better go to supper," said Mary Jane, "and finish the discussion afterwards."

On the landing outside the drawing-room Gabriel found his wife and Mary Jane trying to persuade Miss Ivors to stay for supper. But Miss Ivors, who had put on her hat and was buttoning her cloak, would not 760 stay. She did not feel in the least hungry and she had already overstayed her time.

"But only for ten minutes, Molly," said Mrs. Conroy. "That won't delay you."

"To take a pick itself,"° said Mary Jane, "after all your dancing."

"I really couldn't," said Miss Ivors.

"I am afraid you didn't enjoy yourself at all," said Mary Jane hopelessly.

"Ever so much, I assure you," said Miss Ivors, 770 "but you really must let me run off now."

"But how can you get home?" asked Mrs. Conroy.

"O, it's only two steps up the quay."

Gabriel hesitated a moment and said:

"If you will allow me, Miss Ivors, I'll see you home if you are really obliged to go."

But Miss Ivors broke away from them.

"I won't hear of it," she cried. "For goodness' sake go in to your suppers and don't mind me. I'm quite well able to take care of myself." 780

"Well, you're the comical girl, Molly," said Mrs. Conroy frankly.

"*Beannacht libh,*"° cried Miss Ivors, with a laugh, as she ran down the staircase.

Mary Jane gazed after her, a moody puzzled expression on her face, while Mrs. Conroy leaned over the banisters to listen for the hall-door. Gabriel asked himself was he the cause of her abrupt departure. But she did not seem to be in ill humour: she had gone away laughing. He stared blankly down the staircase. 790

At the moment Aunt Kate came toddling out of the supper-room, almost wringing her hands in despair.

"Where is Gabriel?" she cried. "Where on earth is Gabriel? There's everyone waiting in there, stage to let, and nobody to carve the goose!"

"Here I am, Aunt Kate!" cried Gabriel, with sudden animation, "ready to carve a flock of geese, if necessary."

A fat brown goose lay at one end of the table and at the other end, on a bed of creased paper strewn with 800 sprigs of parsley, lay a great ham, stripped of its outer skin and peppered over with crust crumbs, a neat paper frill round its shin and beside this was a round of spiced beef. Between these rival ends ran parallel lines of side-dishes: two little minsters° of jelly, red and yel-

765 **take . . . itself,** to have a snack   783 **Beannacht libh,** good-bye to you
805 **minsters,** serving-dishes

low; a shallow dish full of blocks of blancmange and red jam, a large green leaf-shaped dish with a stalk-shaped handle, on which lay bunches of purple raisins and peeled almonds, a companion dish on which lay a solid rectangle of Smyrna figs, a dish of custard topped with grated nutmeg, a small bowl full of chocolates and sweets wrapped in gold and silver papers and a glass vase in which stood some tall celery stalks. In the centre of the table there stood, as sentries to a fruit-stand which upheld a pyramid of oranges and American apples, two squat old-fashioned decanters of cut glass, one containing port and the other dark sherry. On the closed square piano a pudding in a huge yellow dish lay in waiting and behind it were three squads of bottles of stout and ale and minerals, drawn up according to the colours of their uniforms, the first two black, with brown and red labels, the third and smallest squad white, with transverse green sashes.

Gabriel took his seat boldly at the head of the table and, having looked to the edge of the carver, plunged his fork firmly into the goose. He felt quite at ease now for he was an expert carver and liked nothing better than to find himself at the head of a well-laden table.

"Miss Furlong, what shall I send you?" he asked. "A wing or a slice of the breast?"

"Just a small slice of the breast."

"Miss Higgins, what for you?"

"O, anything at all, Mr. Conroy."

While Gabriel and Miss Daly exchanged plates of goose and plates of ham and spiced beef Lily went from guest to guest with a dish of hot floury potatoes wrapped in a white napkin. This was Mary Jane's idea and she had also suggested apple sauce for the goose but Aunt Kate had said that plain roast goose without any apple sauce had always been good enough for her and she hoped she might never eat worse. Mary Jane waited on her pupils and saw that they got the best slices and Aunt Kate and Aunt Julia opened and carried across from the piano bottles of stout and ale for the gentlemen and bottles of minerals for the ladies. There was a great deal of confusion and laughter and noise, the noise of orders and counter-orders, of knives and forks, of corks and glass-stoppers. Gabriel began to carve second helpings as soon as he had finished the first round without serving himself. Everyone protested loudly so that he compromised by taking a long draught of stout for he found the carving hot work. Mary Jane settled down quietly to her supper but Aunt Kate and Aunt Julia were still toddling round the table, walking on each other's heels, getting in each other's way and giving each other unheeded orders. Mr. Browne begged of them to sit down and eat their suppers and so did Gabriel but they said there was time enough, so that, at last, Freddy Malins stood up and, capturing Aunt Kate, plumped her down on her chair amid general laughter.

When everyone had been well served Gabriel said, smiling:

"Now, if anyone wants a little more of what vulgar people call stuffing let him or her speak."

A chorus of voices invited him to begin his own supper and Lily came forward with three potatoes which she had reserved for him.

"Very well," said Gabriel amiably, as he took another preparatory draught, "kindly forget my existence, ladies and gentlemen, for a few minutes."

He set to his supper and took no part in the conversation with which the table covered Lily's removal of the plates. The subject of talk was the opera company which was then at the Theatre Royal. Mr. Bartell D'Arcy, the tenor, a dark-complexioned young man with a smart moustache, praised very highly the leading contralto of the company but Miss Furlong thought she had a rather vulgar style of production. Freddy Malins said there was a Negro chieftain singing in the second part of the Gaiety pantomime who had one of the finest tenor voices he had ever heard.

"Have you heard him?" he asked Mr. Bartell D'Arcy across the table.

"No," answered Mr. Bartell D'Arcy carelessly.

"Because," Freddy Malins explained, "now I'd be curious to hear your opinion of him. I think he has a grand voice."

"It takes Teddy to find out the really good things," said Mr. Browne familiarly to the table.

"And why couldn't he have a voice too?" asked Freddy Malins sharply. "Is it because he's only a black?"

Nobody answered this question and Mary Jane led the table back to the legitimate opera. One of her pupils had given her a pass for *Mignon.*° Of course it was very fine, she said, but it made her think of poor Georgina Burns.° Mr. Browne could go back farther still, to the old Italian companies that used to come to Dublin—Tietjens, Ilma de Murzka, Campanini, the great Trebelli, Giuglini, Ravelli, Aramburo.° Those were the days, he said, when there was something like singing to be heard in Dublin. He told too of how the top gallery of the old Royal used to be packed night after night, of how one night an Italian tenor had sung five encores to *Let me like a Soldier fall,*° introducing a high C every time, and of how the gallery boys would sometimes in their enthusiasm unyoke the horses from the carriage of some great *prima donna* and pull her themselves through the streets to her hotel. Why did

896 **Mignon,** a popular opera by Ambroise Thomas (1811–1896), first produced in 1866   898 **Georgina Burns,** a fictitious Dublin singer   900–901 **Tietjens . . . Aramburo.** Some of the singers named here are historical, others can no longer be traced and may well be fictitious. Therese Tietjens (1831–1877) was a German soprano; Ilma de Murska (Murzka) (1836–1889) was a Croatian soprano; Zelie Gilbert (pseud. Trebelli) (1838–1892) was a French mezzo-soprano; and Italo Campanini (1845–1896) and Antonio Giuglini (1827–1865) Italian operatic tenors. Ravelli and Aramburo are no longer identifiable, and Parkinson (ll. 24–25) is fictitious   906 **Let . . . fall,** an extremely popular aria for tenor from the opera *Maritana* (1845) by William Vincent Wallace (1812–1865)

they never play the grand old operas now, he asked, *Dinorah,*° *Lucrezia Borgia?*° Because they could not get the voices to sing them: that was why.

"O, well," said Mr. Bartell D'Arcy, "I presume there are as good singers today as there were then."

"Where are they?" asked Mr. Browne defiantly.

"In London, Paris, Milan," said Mr. Bartell D'Arcy warmly. "I suppose Caruso,° for example, is quite as good, if not better than any of the men you have men-
920 tioned."

"Maybe so," said Mr. Browne. "But I may tell you I doubt it strongly."

"O, I'd give anything to hear Caruso sing," said Mary Jane.

"For me," said Aunt Kate, who had been picking a bone, "there was only one tenor. To please me, I mean. But I suppose none of you ever heard of him."

"Who was he, Miss Morkan?" asked Mr. Bartell D'Arcy politely.

930 "His name," said Aunt Kate, "was Parkinson. I heard him when he was in his prime and I think he had then the purest tenor voice that was ever put into a man's throat."

"Strange," said Mr. Bartell D'Arcy. "I never even heard of him."

"Yes, yes, Miss Morkan is right," said Mr. Browne. "I remember hearing of old Parkinson but he's too far back for me."

"A beautiful, pure, sweet, mellow English tenor,"
940 said Aunt Kate with enthusiasm.

Gabriel having finished, the huge pudding was transferred to the table. The clatter of forks and spoons began again. Gabriel's wife served out spoonfuls of the pudding and passed the plates down the table. Midway down they were held up by Mary Jane, who replenished them with raspberry or orange jelly or with blancmange and jam. The pudding was of Aunt Julia's making and she received praises for it from all quarters. She herself said that it was not quite brown
950 enough.

"Well, I hope, Miss Morkan," said Mr. Browne, "that I'm brown enough for you because, you know, I'm all brown."

All the gentlemen, except Gabriel, ate some of the pudding out of compliment to Aunt Julia. As Gabriel never ate sweets the celery had been left for him. Freddy Malins also took a stalk of celery and ate it with his pudding. He had been told that celery was a capital thing for the blood and he was just then under
960 doctor's care. Mrs. Malins, who had been silent all through the supper, said that her son was going down to Mount Melleray in a week or so. The table then spoke of Mount Melleray, how bracing the air was down there, how hospitable the monks were and how they never asked for a penny-piece from their guests.

"And do you mean to say," asked Mr. Browne incredulously, "that a chap can go down there and put up there as if it were a hotel and live on the fat of the land and then come away without paying anything?"

"O, most people give some donation to the monas- 970
tery when they leave," said Mary Jane.

"I wish we had an institution like that in our Church," said Mr. Browne candidly.

He was astonished to hear that the monks never spoke, got up at two in the morning and slept in their coffins. He asked what they did it for.

"That's the rule of the order," said Aunt Kate firmly.

"Yes, but why?" asked Mr. Browne.

Aunt Kate repeated that it was the rule, that was all. 980
Mr. Browne still seemed not to understand. Freddy Malins explained to him, as best he could, that the monks were trying to make up for the sins committed by all the sinners in the outside world. The explanation was not very clear for Mr. Browne grinned and said:

"I like that idea very much but wouldn't a comfortable spring bed do them as well as a coffin?"

"The coffin," said Mary Jane, "is to remind them of their last end."

As the subject had grown lugubrious it was buried in 990
a silence of the table during which Mrs. Malins could be heard saying to her neighbour in an indistinct undertone:

"They are very good men, the monks, very pious men."

The raisins and almonds and figs and apples and oranges and chocolates and sweets were now passed about the table and Aunt Julia invited all the guests to have either port or sherry. At first Mr. Bartell D'Arcy refused to take either but one of his neighbours nudged 1000
him and whispered something to him upon which he allowed his glass to be filled. Gradually as the last glasses were being filled the conversation ceased. A pause followed, broken only by the noise of the wine and by unsettlings of chairs. The Misses Morkan, all three, looked down at the tablecloth. Someone coughed once or twice and then a few gentlemen patted the table gently as a signal for silence. The silence came and Gabriel pushed back his chair and stood up.

The patting at once grew louder in encouragement 1010
and then ceased altogether. Gabriel leaned his ten trembling fingers on the tablecloth and smiled nervously at the company. Meeting a row of upturned faces he raised his eyes to the chandelier. The piano was playing a waltz tune and he could hear the skirts sweeping against the drawing-room door. People, perhaps, were standing in the snow on the quay outside, gazing up at the lighted windows and listening to the waltz music. The air was pure there. In the distance lay the park where the trees were weighted with 1020
snow. The Wellington Monument wore a gleaming cap of snow that flashed westward over the white field of Fifteen Acres.

912 **Dinorah,** an opera (1859) by the German composer Jakob Meyerbeer (1791–1864)   **Lucrezia Borgia,** an opera (1833) by the Italian composer Gaetano Donizetti (1798–1848)   918 **Caruso,** Enrico Caruso (1873–1921), the most famous operatic tenor of his generation

He began:

"Ladies and Gentlemen,

"It has fallen to my lot this evening, as in years past, to perform a very pleasing task but a task for which I am afraid my poor powers as a speaker are all too inadequate."

1030 "No, no!" said Mr. Browne.

"But, however that may be, I can only ask you tonight to take the will for the deed and to lend me your attention for a few moments while I endeavour to express to you in words what my feelings are on this occasion.

"Ladies and Gentlemen, it is not the first time that we have gathered together under this hospitable roof, around this hospitable board. It is not the first time that we have been the recipients—or perhaps, I had 1040 better say, the victims—of the hospitality of certain good ladies."

He made a circle in the air with his arm and paused. Everyone laughed or smiled at Aunt Kate and Aunt Julia and Mary Jane who all turned crimson with pleasure. Gabriel went on more boldly:

"I feel more strongly with every recurring year that our country has no tradition which does it so much honour and which it should guard so jealously as that of its hospitality. It is a tradition that is unique as far as 1050 my experience goes (and I have visited not a few places abroad) among the modern nations. Some would say, perhaps, that with us it is rather a failing than anything to be boasted of. But granted even that, it is, to my mind, a princely failing, and one that I trust will long be cultivated among us. Of one thing, at least, I am sure. As long as this one roof shelters the good ladies aforesaid—and I wish from my heart it may do so for many and many a long year to come—the tradition of genuine warm-hearted courteous Irish hospi-1060 tality, which our forefathers have handed down to us and which we in turn must hand down to our descendants, is still alive among us."

A hearty murmur of assent ran round the table. It shot through Gabriel's mind that Miss Ivors was not there and that she had gone away discourteously: and he said with confidence in himself:

"Ladies and Gentlemen,

"A new generation is growing up in our midst, a generation actuated by new ideas and new principles. 1070 It is serious and enthusiastic for these new ideas and its enthusiasm, even when it is misdirected, is, I believe, in the main sincere. But we are living in a sceptical and, if I may use the phrase, a thought-tormented age: and sometimes I fear that this new generation, educated or hypereducated as it is, will lack those qualities of humanity, of hospitality, of kindly humour which belonged to an older day. Listening tonight to the names of all those great singers of the past it seemed to me, I must confess, that we were living in a 1080 less spacious age. Those days might, without exaggeration, be called spacious days: and if they are gone

beyond recall let us hope, at least, that in gatherings such as this we shall still speak of them with pride and affection, still cherish in our hearts the memory of those dead and gone great ones whose fame the world will not willingly let die."

"Hear, hear!" said Mr. Browne loudly.

"But yet," continued Gabriel, his voice falling into a softer inflection, "there are always in gatherings such as this sadder thoughts that will recur to our minds: 1090 thoughts of the past, of youth, of changes, of absent faces that we miss here tonight. Our path through life is strewn with many such sad memories: and were we to brood upon them always we could not find the heart to go on bravely with our work among the living. We have all of us living duties and living affections which claim, and rightly claim, our strenuous endeavours.

"Therefore, I will not linger on the past. I will not let any gloomy moralising intrude upon us here tonight. Here we are gathered together for a brief moment from 1100 the bustle and rush of our everyday routine. We are met here as friends, in the spirit of good-fellowship, as colleagues, also to a certain extent, in the true spirit of *camaraderie,* and as the guest of—what shall I call them?—the Three Graces of the Dublin musical world."

The table burst into applause and laughter at this allusion. Aunt Julia vainly asked each of her neighbours in turn to tell her what Gabriel had said.

"He says we are the Three Graces, Aunt Julia," 1110 said Mary Jane.

Aunt Julia did not understand but she looked up, smiling, at Gabriel, who continued in the same vein:

"Ladies and Gentlemen,

"I will not attempt to play tonight the part that Paris° played on another occasion. I will not attempt to choose between them. The task would be an invidious one and one beyond my poor powers. For when I view them in turn, whether it be our chief hostess herself, whose good heart, whose too good heart, has become 1120 a byword with all who know her, or her sister, who seems to be gifted with perennial youth and whose singing must have been a surprise and a revelation to us all tonight, or, last but not least, when I consider our youngest hostess, talented, cheerful, hard-working and the best of nieces, I confess, Ladies and Gentlemen, that I do not know to which of them I should award the prize."

Gabriel glanced down at his aunts and, seeing the large smile on Aunt Julia's face and the tears which 1130 had risen to Aunt Kate's eyes, hastened to his close. He raised his glass of port gallantly, while every member of the company fingered a glass expectantly, and said loudly:

"Let us toast them all three together. Let us drink to their health, wealth, long life, happiness and prosperity and may they long continue to hold the proud and

1115 **Paris,** a reference to the award for beauty given to the goddess Venus by Paris, prince of Troy; he was obliged to judge among Venus, Juno, and Minerva

self-won position which they hold in their profession and the position of honour and affection which they hold in our hearts.''

All the guests stood up, glass in hand, and turning towards the three seated ladies, sang in unison, with Mr. Browne as leader:

> For they are jolly gay fellows,
> For they are jolly gay fellows,
> For they are jolly gay fellows,
> Which nobody can deny.

Aunt Kate was making frank use of her handkerchief and even Aunt Julia seemed moved. Freddy Malins beat time with his pudding-fork and the singers turned towards one another, as if in melodious conference, while they sang with emphasis:

> Unless he tells a lie,
> Unless he tells a lie,

Then, turning once more towards their hostesses, they sang:

> For they are jolly gay fellows,
> For they are jolly gay fellows,
> For they are jolly gay fellows,
> Which nobody can deny.

The acclamation which followed was taken up beyond the door of the supper-room by many of the other guests and renewed time after time, Freddy Malins acting as officer with his fork on high.

The piercing morning air came into the hall where they were standing so that Aunt Kate said:

"Close the door, somebody. Mrs. Malins will get her death of cold."

"Browne is out there, Aunt Kate," said Mary Jane.

"Browne is everywhere," said Aunt Kate, lowering her voice.

Mary Jane laughed at her tone.

"Really," she said archly, "he is very attentive."

"He has been laid on here like the gas," said Aunt Kate in the same tone, "all during the Christmas."

She laughed herself this time good-humouredly and then added quickly:

"But tell him to come in, Mary Jane, and close the door. I hope to goodness he didn't hear me."

At that moment the hall-door was opened and Mr. Browne came in from the doorstep, laughing as if his heart would break. He was dressed in a long green overcoat with mock astrakhan cuffs and collar and wore on his head an oval fur cap. He pointed down the snow-covered quay from where the sound of shrill prolonged whistling was borne in.

"Teddy will have all the cabs in Dublin out," he said.

Gabriel advanced from the little pantry behind the office, struggling into his overcoat and, looking round the hall, said:

"Gretta not down yet?"

"She's getting on her things, Gabriel," said Aunt Kate.

"Who's playing up there?" asked Gabriel.

"Nobody. They're all gone."

"O no, Aunt Kate," said Mary Jane. "Bartell D'Arcy and Miss O'Callaghan aren't gone yet."

"Someone is fooling at the piano anyhow," said Gabriel.

Mary Jane glanced at Gabriel and Mr. Browne and said with a shiver:

"It makes me feel cold to look at you two gentlemen muffled up like that. I wouldn't like to face your journey home at this hour."

"I'd like nothing better this minute," said Mr. Browne stoutly, "than a rattling fine walk in the country or a fast drive with a good spanking goer between the shafts."

"We used to have a very good horse and trap at home," said Aunt Julia sadly.

"The never-to-be-forgotten Johnny," said Mary Jane, laughing.

Aunt Kate and Gabriel laughed too.

"Why, what was wonderful about Johnny?" asked Mr. Browne.

"The late lamented Patrick Morkan, our grandfather, that is," explained Gabriel, "commonly known in his later years as the old gentleman, was a glueboiler."

"O, now, Gabriel," said Aunt Kate, laughing, "he had a starch mill."

"Well, glue or starch," said Gabriel, "the old gentleman had a horse by the name of Johnny. And Johnny used to work in the old gentleman's mill, walking round and round in order to drive the mill. That was all very well; but now comes the tragic part about Johnny. One fine day the old gentleman thought he'd like to drive out with the quality to a military review in the park."

"The Lord have mercy on his soul," said Aunt Kate compassionately.

"Amen," said Gabriel. "So the old gentleman, as I said, harnessed Johnny and put on his very best tall hat and his very best stock collar and drove out in grand style from his ancestral mansion somewhere near Back Lane, I think."

Everyone laughed, even Mrs. Malins, at Gabriel's manner and Aunt Kate said:

"O, now, Gabriel, he didn't live in Back Lane really. Only the mill was there."

"Out from the mansion of his forefathers," continued Gabriel, "he drove with Johnny. And everything went on beautifully until Johnny came in sight of King Billy's statue: and whether he fell in love with the horse King Billy sits on or whether he thought he was back again in the mill, anyhow he began to walk round the statue."

Gabriel paced in a circle round the hall in his goloshes amid the laughter of the others.

"Round and round he went," said Gabriel, "and the old gentleman, who was a very pompous old gentleman, was highly indignant. 'Go on, sir! What do you mean, sir? Johnny! Johnny! Most extraordinary conduct! Can't understand the horse!'"

The peal of laughter which followed Gabriel's imitation of the incident was interrupted by a resounding knock at the hall-door. Mary Jane ran to open it and let in Freddy Malins. Freddy Malins, with his hat well back on his head and his shoulders humped with cold, was puffing and steaming after his exertions.

"I could only get one cab," he said.

"O, we'll find another along the quay," said Gabriel.

"Yes," said Aunt Kate. "Better not keep Mrs. Malins standing in the draught."

Mrs. Malins was helped down the front steps by her son and Mr. Browne and, after many manoeuvres, hoisted into the cab. Freddy Malins clambered in after her and spent a long time settling her on the seat, Mr. Browne helping him with advice. At last she was settled comfortably and Freddy Malins invited Mr. Browne into the cab. There was a good deal of confused talk, and then Mr. Browne got into the cab. The cabman settled his rug over his knees, and bent down for the address. The confusion grew greater and the cabman was directed differently by Freddy Malins and Mr. Browne, each of whom had his head out through a window of the cab. The difficulty was to know where to drop Mr. Browne along the route, and Aunt Kate, Aunt Julia and Mary Jane helped the discussion from the doorstep with cross-directions and contradictions and abundance of laughter. As for Freddy Malins he was speechless with laughter. He popped his head in and out of the window every moment to the great danger of his hat, and told his mother how the discussion was progressing, till at last Mr. Browne shouted to the bewildered cabman above the din of everybody's laughter:

"Do you know Trinity College?"

"Yes, sir," said the cabman.

"Well, drive bang up against Trinity College gates," said Mr. Browne, "and then we'll tell you where to go. You understand now?"

"Yes, sir," said the cabman.

"Make like a bird for Trinity College."

1245 **King Billy**, William III of England, who reigned from 1688 to 1702 and suppressed the Jacobite rebellion in Ireland at the Battle of the Boyne in 1690

"Right, sir," said the cabman.

The horse was whipped up and the cab rattled off along the quay amid a chorus of laughter and adieus.

Gabriel had not gone to the door with the others. He was in a dark part of the hall gazing up the staircase. A woman was standing near the top of the first flight, in the shadow also. He could not see her face but he could see the terra-cotta and salmon-pink panels of her skirt which the shadow made appear black and white. It was his wife. She was leaning on the banisters, listening to something. Gabriel was surprised at her stillness and strained his ear to listen also. But he could hear little save the noise of laughter and dispute on the front steps, a few chords struck on the piano and a few notes of a man's voice singing.

He stood still in the gloom of the hall, trying to catch the air that the voice was singing and gazing up at his wife. There was grace and mystery in her attitude as if she were a symbol of something. He asked himself what is a woman standing on the stairs in the shadow, listening to distant music, a symbol of. If he were a painter he would paint her in that attitude. Her blue felt hat would show off the bronze of her hair against the darkness and the dark panels of her skirt would show off the light ones. *Distant Music* he would call the picture if he were a painter.

The hall-door was closed; and Aunt Kate, Aunt Julia and Mary Jane came down the hall, still laughing.

"Well, isn't Freddy terrible?" said Mary Jane. "He's really terrible."

Gabriel said nothing but pointed up the stairs towards where his wife was standing. Now that the hall-door was closed the voice and the piano could be heard more clearly. Gabriel held up his hand for them to be silent. The song seemed to be in the old Irish tonality and the singer seemed uncertain both of his words and of his voice. The voice, made plaintive by distance and by the singer's hoarseness, faintly illuminated the cadence of the air with words expressing grief.

> O, the rain falls on my heavy locks
> And the dew wets my skin,
> My babe lies cold . . .

"O," exclaimed Mary Jane. "It's Bartell D'Arcy singing and he wouldn't sing all the night. O, I'll get him to sing a song before he goes."

"O, do, Mary Jane," said Aunt Kate.

Mary Jane brushed past the others and ran to the staircase, but before she reached it the singing stopped and the piano was closed abruptly.

"O, what a pity!" she cried. "Is he coming down, Gretta?"

Gabriel heard his wife answer yes and saw her come

down towards them. A few steps behind her were Mr. Bartell D'Arcy and Miss O'Callaghan.

"O, Mr. D'Arcy," cried Mary Jane, "it's downright mean of you to break off like that when we were all in raptures listening to you."

"I have been at him all the evening," said Miss O'Callaghan, "and Mrs. Conroy, too, and he told us he had a dreadful cold and couldn't sing."

"O, Mr. D'Arcy," said Aunt Kate, "now that was a great fib to tell."

"Can't you see that I'm as hoarse as a crow?" said Mr. D'Arcy roughly.

He went into the pantry hastily and put on his overcoat. The others, taken aback by his rude speech, could find nothing to say. Aunt Kate wrinkled her brows and made signs to the others to drop the subject. Mr. D'Arcy stood swathing his neck carefully and frowning.

"It's the weather," said Aunt Julia, after a pause.

"Yes, everybody has colds," said Aunt Kate readily, "everybody."

"They say," said Mary Jane, "we haven't had snow like it for thirty years; and I read this morning in the newspapers that the snow is general all over Ireland."

"I love the look of snow," said Aunt Julia sadly.

"So do I," said Miss O'Callaghan. "I think Christmas is never really Christmas unless we have the snow on the ground."

"But poor Mr. D'Arcy doesn't like the snow," said Aunt Kate, smiling.

Mr. D'Arcy came from the pantry, fully swathed and buttoned, and in a repentant tone told them the history of his cold. Everyone gave him advice and said it was a great pity and urged him to be very careful of his throat in the night air. Gabriel watched his wife, who did not join in the conversation. She was standing right under the dusty fanlight and the flame of the gas lit up the rich bronze of her hair, which he had seen her drying at the fire a few days before. She was in the same attitude and seemed unaware of the talk about her. At last she turned towards them and Gabriel saw that there was colour on her cheeks and that her eyes were shining. A sudden tide of joy went leaping out of his heart.

"Mr. D'Arcy," she said, "what is the name of that song you were singing?"

"It's called *The Lass of Aughrim*," said Mr. D'Arcy, "but I couldn't remember it properly. Why? Do you know it?"

"*The Lass of Aughrim*," she repeated. "I couldn't think of the name."

"It's a very nice air," said Mary Jane. "I'm sorry you were not in voice tonight."

"Now, Mary Jane," said Aunt Kate, "don't annoy Mr. D'Arcy. I won't have him annoyed."

Seeing that all were ready to start she shepherded them to the door, where good-night was said:

"Well, good-night, Aunt Kate, and thanks for the pleasant evening."

"Good-night, Gabriel. Good-night Gretta!"

"Good-night, Aunt Kate, and thanks ever so much. Good-night, Aunt Julia."

"O, good-night, Gretta, I didn't see you."

"Good-night, Mr. D'Arcy. Good-night, Miss O'Callaghan."

"Good-night, Miss Morkan."

"Good-night, again."

"Good-night, all. Safe home."

"Good-night. Good-night."

The morning was still dark. A dull, yellow light brooded over the houses and the river; and the sky seemed to be descending. It was slushy underfoot; and only streaks and patches of snow lay on the roofs, on the parapets of the quay and on the area railings. The lamps were still burning redly in the murky air and, across the river, the palace of the Four Courts stood out menacingly against the heavy sky.

She was walking on before him with Mr. Bartell D'Arcy, her shoes in a brown parcel tucked under one arm and her hands holding her skirt up from the slush. She had no longer any grace of attitude, but Gabriel's eyes were still bright with happiness. The blood went bounding along his veins; and the thoughts went rioting through his brain, proud, joyful, tender, valorous.

She was walking on before him so lightly and so erect that he longed to run after her noiselessly, catch her by the shoulders and say something foolish and affectionate into her ear. She seemed to him so frail that he longed to defend her against something and then to be alone with her. Moments of their secret life together burst like stars upon his memory. A heliotrope envelope was lying beside his breakfast-cup and he was caressing it with his hand. Birds were twittering in the ivy and the sunny web of the curtain was shimmering along the floor: he could not eat for happiness. They were standing on the crowded platform and he was placing a ticket inside the warm palm of her glove. He was standing with her in the cold, looking in through a grated window at a man making bottles in a roaring furnace. It was very cold. Her face, fragrant in the cold air, was quite close to his; and suddenly he called out to the man at the furnace:

"Is the fire hot, sir?"

But the man could not hear with the noise of the furnace. It was just as well. He might have answered rudely.

A wave of yet more tender joy escaped from his heart and went coursing in warm flood along his arteries. Like the tender fire of stars moments of their life together, that no one knew of or would ever know of, broke upon and illumined memory. He longed to recall to her those moments, to make her forget the years of their dull existence together and remember only their moments of ecstasy. For the years, he felt, had not quenched his soul or hers. Their children, his writing, her household cares had not quenched all their souls' tender fire. In one letter that he had written to her then he had said: "Why is it that words like these seem to me so dull and cold? Is it because there is no word tender enough to be your name?"

Like distant music these words that he had written years before were borne towards him from the past. He longed to be alone with her. When the others had gone away, when he and she were in the room in the hotel, then they would be alone together. He would call her softly:

"Gretta!"

Perhaps she would not hear at once: she would be undressing. Then something in his voice would strike her. She would turn and look at him. . . .

At the corner of Winetavern Street they met a cab. He was glad of its rattling noise as it saved him from conversation. She was looking out of the window and seemed tired. The others spoke only a few words, pointing out some building or street. The horse galloped along wearily under the murky morning sky, dragging his old rattling box after his heels, and Gabriel was again in a cab with her, galloping to catch the boat, galloping to their honeymoon.

As the cab drove across O'Connell Bridge Miss O'Callaghan said:

"They say you never cross O'Connell Bridge without seeing a white horse."

"I see a white man this time," said Gabriel.

"Where?" asked Mr. Bartell D'Arcy.

Gabriel pointed to the statue, on which lay patches of snow. Then he nodded familiarly to it and waved his hand.

"Good-night, Dan," he said gaily.

When the cab drew up before the hotel, Gabriel jumped out and, in spite of Mr. Bartell D'Arcy's protest, paid the driver. He gave the man a shilling over his fare. The man saluted and said:

"A prosperous New Year to you, sir."

"The same to you," said Gabriel cordially.

She leaned for a moment on his arm in getting out of the cab and while standing at the curbstone, bidding the others good-night. She leaned lightly on his arm, as lightly as when she had danced with him a few hours before. He had felt proud and happy then, happy that she was his, proud of her grace and wifely carriage. But now, after the kindling again of so many memories, the first touch of her body, musical and strange and perfumed, sent through him a keen pang of lust. Under cover of her silence he pressed her arm closely to his side; and, as they stood at the hotel door, he felt that they had escaped from their lives and duties, escaped from home and friends and run away together with wild and radiant hearts to a new adventure.

An old man was dozing in a great hooded chair in the hall. He lit a candle in the office and went before them to the stairs. They followed him in silence, their feet falling in soft thuds on the thickly carpeted stairs. She mounted the stairs behind the porter, her head bowed in the ascent, her frail shoulders curved as with a burden, her skirt girt tightly about her. He could have flung his arms about her hips and held her still, for his arms were trembling with desire to seize her and only the stress of his nails against the palms of his hands held the wild impulse of his body in check. The porter halted on the stairs to settle his guttering candle. They halted, too, on the steps below him. In the silence Gabriel could hear the falling of the molten wax into the tray and the thumping of his own heart against his ribs.

The porter led them along a corridor and opened a door. Then he set his unstable candle down on a toilet-table and asked at what hour they were to be called in the morning.

"Eight," said Gabriel.

The porter pointed to the tap of the electric-light and began a muttered apology, but Gabriel cut him short.

"We don't want any light. We have light enough from the street. And I say," he added, pointing to the candle, "you might remove that handsome article, like a good man."

The porter took up his candle again, but slowly, for he was surprised by such a novel idea. Then he mumbled good-night and went out. Gabriel shot the lock to.

A ghastly light from the street lamp lay in a long shaft from one window to the door. Gabriel threw his overcoat and hat on a couch and crossed the room towards the window. He looked down into the street in order that his emotion might calm a little. Then he turned and leaned against a chest of drawers with his back to the light. She had taken off her hat and cloak and was standing before a large swinging mirror, unhooking her waist. Gabriel paused for a few moments, watching her, and then said:

"Gretta!"

She turned away from the mirror slowly and walked along the shaft of light towards him. Her face looked so serious and weary that the words would not pass Gabriel's lips. No, it was not the moment yet.

"You look tired," he said.

"I am a little," she answered.

"You don't feel ill or weak?"

"No, tired: that's all."

She went on to the window and stood there, looking out. Gabriel waited again and then, fearing that diffidence was about to conquer him, he said abruptly:

"By the way, Gretta!"

"What is it?"

"You know that poor fellow Malins?" he said quickly.

"Yes. What about him?"

"Well, poor fellow, he's a decent sort of chap, after all," continued Gabriel in a false voice. "He gave me back that sovereign I lent him, and I didn't expect it, really. It's a pity he wouldn't keep away from that Browne, because he's not a bad fellow, really."

He was trembling now with annoyance. Why did she seem so abstracted? He did not know how he could begin. Was she annoyed, too, about something? If she would only turn to him or come to him of her own accord! To take her as she was would be brutal. No, he must see some ardour in her eyes first. He longed to be master of her strange mood.

"When did you lend him the pound?" she asked, after a pause.

Gabriel strove to restrain himself from breaking out into brutal language about the sottish Malins and his pound. He longed to cry to her from his soul, to crush her body against his, to overmaster her. But he said:

"O, at Christmas, when he opened that little Christmas-card shop in Henry Street."

He was in such a fever of rage and desire that he did not hear her come from the window. She stood before him for an instant, looking at him strangely. Then, suddenly raising herself on tiptoe and resting her hands lightly on his shoulders, she kissed him.

"You are a very generous person, Gabriel," she said.

Gabriel, trembling with delight at her sudden kiss and at the quaintness of her phrase, put his hands on her hair and began smoothing it back, scarcely touching it with his fingers. The washing had made it fine and brilliant. His heart was brimming over with happiness. Just when he was wishing for it she had come to him of her own accord. Perhaps her thoughts had been running with his. Perhaps she had felt the impetuous desire that was in him, and then the yielding mood had come upon her. Now that she had fallen to him so easily, he wondered why he had been so diffident.

He stood, holding her head between his hands. Then, slipping one arm swiftly about her body and drawing her towards him, he said softly:

"Gretta, dear, what are you thinking about?"

She did not answer nor yield wholly to his arm. He said again, softly:

"Tell me what it is, Gretta. I think I know what is the matter. Do I know?"

She did not answer at once. Then she said in an outburst of tears:

"O, I am thinking about that song, *The Lass of Aughrim*."

She broke loose from him and ran to the bed and, throwing her arms across the bed-rail, hid her face. Gabriel stood stock-still for a moment in astonishment and then followed her. As he passed in the way of the cheval-glass he caught sight of himself in full length, his broad, well-filled shirt-front, the face whose expression always puzzled him when he saw it in a mirror, and his glimmering gilt-rimmed eyeglasses. He halted a few paces from her and said:

"What about the song? Why does that make you cry?"

She raised her head from her arms and dried her eyes with the back of her hand like a child. A kinder note than he had intended went into his voice.

"Why, Gretta?" he asked.

"I am thinking about a person long ago who used to sing that song."

"And who was the person long ago?" asked Gabriel, smiling.

"It was a person I used to know in Galway when I was living with my grandmother," she said.

The smile passed away from Gabriel's face. A dull anger began to gather again at the back of his mind and the dull fires of his lust began to glow angrily in his veins.

"Someone you were in love with?" he asked ironically.

"It was a young boy I used to know," she answered, "named Michael Furey. He used to sing that song, *The Lass of Aughrim*. He was very delicate."

Gabriel was silent. He did not wish her to think that he was interested in this delicate boy.

"I can see him so plainly," she said, after a moment. "Such eyes as he had: big, dark eyes! And such an expression in them—an expression!"

"O, then, you are in love with him?" said Gabriel.

"I used to go out walking with him," she said, "when I was in Galway."

A thought flew across Gabriel's mind.

"Perhaps that was why you wanted to go to Galway with that Ivors girl?" he said coldly.

She looked at him and asked in surprise:

"What for?"

Her eyes made Gabriel feel awkward. He shrugged his shoulders and said:

"How do I know? To see him, perhaps."

She looked away from him along the shaft of light towards the window in silence.

"He is dead," she said at length. "He died when he was only seventeen. Isn't it a terrible thing to die so young as that?"

"What was he?" asked Gabriel, still ironically.

"He was in the gasworks," she said.

Gabriel felt humiliated by the failure of his irony and by the evocation of this figure from the dead, a boy in the gasworks. While he had been full of memories of their secret life together, full of tenderness and joy and desire, she had been comparing him in her mind with another. A shameful consciousness of his own person assailed him. He saw himself as a ludicrous figure, acting as a pennyboy for his aunts, a nervous, well-meaning sentimentalist, orating to vulgarians and idealising his own clownish lusts, the pitiable fatuous fellow he had caught a glimpse of in the mirror. Instinctively he turned his back more to the light lest she might see the shame that burned upon his forehead.

He tried to keep up his tone of cold interrogation, but his voice when he spoke was humble and indifferent.

"I suppose you were in love with this Michael Furey, Gretta," he said.

"I was great with him at that time," she said.

Her voice was veiled and sad. Gabriel, feeling now how vain it would be to try to lead her whither he had purposed, caressed one of her hands and said, also sadly:

"And what did he die of so young, Gretta? Consumption, was it?"

"I think he died for me," she answered.

A vague terror seized Gabriel at this answer, as if, at that hour when he had hoped to triumph, some impalpable and vindictive being was coming against him, gathering forces against him in its vague world. But he shook himself free of it with an effort of reason and continued to caress her hand. He did not question her again, for he felt that she would tell him of herself. Her hand was warm and moist: it did not respond to his touch, but he continued to caress it just as he had caressed her first letter to him that spring morning.

"It was in the winter," she said, "about the beginning of the winter when I was going to leave my grandmother's and come up here to the convent. And he was ill at the time in his lodgings in Galway and wouldn't be let out, and his people in Oughterard were written to. He was in decline, they said, or something like that. I never knew rightly."

She paused for a moment and sighed.

"Poor fellow," she said. "He was very fond of me and he was such a gentle boy. We used to go out together, walking, you know, Gabriel, like the way they do in the country. He was going to study singing only for his health. He had a very good voice, poor Michael Furey."

"Well; and then?" asked Gabriel.

"And then when it came to the time for me to leave Galway and come up to the convent he was much worse and I wouldn't be let see him so I wrote him a letter saying I was going up to Dublin and would be back in the summer, and hoping he would be better then."

She paused for a moment to get her voice under control, and then went on:

"Then the night before I left, I was in my grandmother's house in Nuns' Island, packing up, and I heard gravel thrown up against the window. The window was so wet I couldn't see, so I ran downstairs as I was and slipped out the back into the garden and there was the poor fellow at the end of the garden, shivering."

"And did you not tell him to go back?" asked Gabriel.

"I implored of him to go home at once and told him he would get his death in the rain. But he said he did not want to live. I can see his eyes as well as well! He was standing at the end of the wall where there was a tree."

"And did he go home?" asked Gabriel.

"Yes, he went home. And when I was only a week in the convent he died and he was buried in Oughterard, where his people came from. O, the day I heard that, that he was dead!"

She stopped, choking with sobs, and overcome by emotion, flung herself face downward on the bed, sobbing in the quilt. Gabriel held her hand for a moment longer, irresolutely, and then, shy of intruding on her grief, let it fall gently and walked quietly to the window.

She was fast asleep.

Gabriel, leaning on his elbow, looked for a few moments unresentfully on her tangled hair and half-open mouth, listening to her deep-drawn breath. So she had had that romance in her life: a man had died for her sake. It hardly pained him now to think how poor a part he, her husband, had played in her life. He watched her while she slept, as though he and she had never lived together as man and wife. His curious eyes rested long upon her face and on her hair: and, as he thought of what she must have been then, in that time of her first girlish beauty, a strange, friendly pity for her entered his soul. He did not like to say even to himself that her face was no longer beautiful, but he knew that it was no longer the face for which Michael Furey had braved death.

Perhaps she had not told him all the story. His eyes moved to the chair over which she had thrown some of her clothes. A petticoat string dangled to the floor. One boot stood upright, its limp upper fallen down: the fellow of it lay upon its side. He wondered at his riot of emotions of an hour before. From what had it proceeded? From his aunt's supper, from his own foolish speech, from the wine and dancing, the merrymaking when saying good-night in the hall, the pleasure of the walk along the river in the snow. Poor Aunt Julia! She, too, would soon be a shade with the shade of Patrick Morkan and his horse. He had caught that haggard look upon her face for a moment when she was singing *Arrayed for the Bridal*. Soon, perhaps, he would be sitting in that same drawing-room, dressed in black, his silk hat on his knees. The blinds would be drawn down and Aunt Kate would be sitting beside him, crying and blowing her nose and telling him how Julia had died. He would cast about in his mind for some words that might console her, and would find only lame and useless ones. Yes, yes: that would happen very soon.

The air of the room chilled his shoulders. He stretched himself cautiously along under the sheets and lay down beside his wife. One by one, they were all becoming shades. Better pass boldly into that other world, in the full glory of some passion, than fade and wither dismally with age. He thought of how she who lay beside him had locked in her heart for so many years that image of her lover's eyes when he had told her that he did not wish to live.

Generous tears filled Gabriel's eyes. He had never 1810 felt like that himself towards any woman, but he knew that such a feeling must be love. The tears gathered more thickly in his eyes and in the partial darkness he imagined he saw the form of a young man standing under a dripping tree. Other forms were near. His soul had approached that region where dwell the vast hosts of the dead. He was conscious of, but could not apprehend, their wayward and flickering existence. His own identity was fading out into a grey impalpable world: the solid world itself, which these dead had one 1820 time reared and lived in, was dissolving and dwindling.

A few light taps upon the pane made him turn to the window. It had begun to snow again. He watched sleepily the flakes, silver and dark, falling obliquely against the lamplight. The time had come for him to set out on his journey westward. Yes, the newspapers were right: snow was general all over Ireland. It was falling on every part of the dark central plain, on the treeless hills, falling softly upon the Bog of Allen and, farther westward, softly falling into the dark mutinous 1830 Shannon waves. It was falling, too, upon every part of the lonely churchyard on the hill where Michael Furey lay buried. It lay thickly drifted on the crooked crosses and headstones, on the spears of the little gate, on the barren thorns. His soul swooned slowly as he heard the snow falling faintly through the universe and faintly falling, like the descent of their last end, upon all the living and the dead.

(1914)

CLAY

The matron had given her leave to go out as soon as the women's tea was over and Maria looked forward to her evening out. The kitchen was spick and span: the cook said you could see yourself in the big copper boilers. The fire was nice and bright and on one of the side-tables were four very big barmbracks.° These barmbracks seemed uncut; but if you went closer you would see that they had been cut into long thick even slices and were ready to be handed round at tea. Maria 10 had cut them herself.

Maria was a very, very small person indeed but she had a very long nose and a very long chin. She talked a little through her nose, always soothingly: *"Yes, my dear,"* and *"No, my dear."* She was always sent for when the women quarreled over their tubs and always succeeded in making peace. One day the matron had said to her:

"Maria, you are a veritable peacemaker!"

Clay 6 **barmbracks,** cakes especially baked for Halloween, with fortune-telling favors baked inside

And the sub-matron and two of the Board ladies had heard the compliment. And Ginger Mooney was al- 20 ways saying what she wouldn't do to the dummy who had charge of the irons if it wasn't for Maria. Everyone was so fond of Maria.

The women would have their tea at six o'clock and she would be able to get away before seven. From Ballsbridge to the Pillar, twenty minutes; from the Pillar to Drumcondra, twenty minutes; and twenty minutes to buy the things. She would be there before eight. She took out her purse with the silver clasps and read again the words *A Present from Belfast*. She was very 30 fond of that purse because Joe had brought it to her five years before when he and Alphy had gone to Belfast on a Whit-Monday trip. In the purse were two half-crowns and some coppers. She would have five shillings clear after paying tram fare. What a nice evening they would have, all the children singing! Only she hoped that Joe wouldn't come in drunk. He was so different when he took any drink.

Often he had wanted her to go and live with them; but she would have felt herself in the way (though 40 Joe's wife was ever so nice with her) and she had become accustomed to the life of the laundry. Joe was a good fellow. She had nursed him and Alphy too; and Joe used often say:

"Mamma is mamma but Maria is my proper mother."

After the break-up at home the boys had got her that position in the *Dublin by Lamplight* laundry, and she liked it. She used to have such a bad opinion of Protestants but now she thought they were very nice 50 people, a little quiet and serious, but still very nice people to live with. Then she had her plants in the conservatory and she liked looking after them. She had lovely ferns and wax-plants and, whenever anyone came to visit her, she always gave the visitor one or two slips from her conservatory. There was one thing she didn't like and that was the tracts on the walls; but the matron was such a nice person to deal with, so genteel.

When the cook told her everything was ready she 60 went into the women's room and began to pull the big bell. In a few minutes the women began to come in by twos and threes, wiping their steaming hands in their petticoats and pulling down the sleeves of their blouses over their red steaming arms. They settled down before their huge mugs which the cook and the dummy filled up with hot tea, already mixed with milk and sugar in huge tin cans. Maria superintended the distribution of the barmbrack and saw that every woman got her four slices. There was a great deal of laughing 70 and joking during the meal. Lizzie Fleming said Maria was sure to get the ring and, though Fleming had said that for so many Hallow Eves, Maria had to laugh and say she didn't want any ring or man either; and when she laughed her gray-green eyes sparkled with disappointed shyness and the tip of her nose nearly met the tip of her chin. Then Ginger Mooney lifted up her mug of tea and proposed Maria's health while all the other women clattered with their mugs on the table, and said she was sorry she hadn't a sup of porter to drink it in. And Maria laughed again till the tip of her nose nearly met the tip of her chin and till her minute body nearly shook itself asunder because she knew that Mooney meant well though, of course, she had the notions of a common woman.

But wasn't Maria glad when the women had finished their tea and the cook and the dummy had begun to clear away the tea-things! She went into her little bedroom and, remembering that the next morning was a mass morning, changed the hand of the alarm from seven to six. Then she took off her working skirt and her house-boots and laid her best skirt out on the bed and her tiny dress-boots beside the foot of the bed. She changed her blouse too and, as she stood before the mirror, she thought of how she used to dress for mass on Sunday morning when she was a young girl; and she looked with quaint affection at the diminutive body which she had so often adorned. In spite of its years she found it a nice tidy little body.

When she got outside the streets were shining with rain and she was glad of her old brown waterproof. The tram was full and she had to sit on the little stool at the end of the car, facing all the people, with her toes barely touching the floor. She arranged in her mind all she was going to do and thought how much better it was to be independent and to have your own money in your pocket. She hoped they would have a nice evening. She was sure they would but she could not help thinking what a pity it was Alphy and Joe were not speaking. They were always falling out now but when they were boys together they used to be the best of friends: but such was life.

She got out of her tram at the Pillar and ferreted her way quickly among the crowds. She went into Downes's cake-shop but the shop was so full of people that it was a long time before she could get herself attended to. She bought a dozen of mixed penny cakes, and at last came out of the shop laden with a big bag. Then she thought what else would she buy: she wanted to buy something really nice. They would be sure to have plenty of apples and nuts. It was hard to know what to buy and all she could think of was cake. She decided to buy some plumcake but Downes's plumcake had not enough almond icing on top of it so she went over to a shop in Henry Street. Here she was a long time in suiting herself and the stylish young lady behind the counter, who was evidently a little annoyed by her, asked her was it wedding cake she wanted to buy. That made Maria blush and smile at the young lady; but the young lady took it all very seriously and finally cut a thick slice of plumcake, parceled it up and said:

"Two-and-four, please."

She thought she would have to stand in the Drumcondra tram because none of the young men seemed to notice her but an elderly gentleman made room for her. He was a stout gentleman and he wore a brown hard hat; he had a square red face and a grayish moustache. Maria thought he was a colonel-looking gentleman and she reflected how much more polite he was than the young men who simply stared straight before them. The gentleman began to chat with her about Hallow Eve and the rainy weather. He supposed the bag was full of good things for the little ones and said it was only right that the youngsters should enjoy themselves while they were young. Maria agreed with him and favored him with demure nods and hems. He was very nice with her, and when she was getting out at the Canal Bridge she thanked him and bowed, and he bowed to her and raised his hat and smiled agreeably; and while she was going up along the terrace, bending her tiny head under the rain, she thought how easy it was to know a gentleman even when he has a drop taken.

Everybody said: "O, here's Maria!" when she came to Joe's house. Joe was there, having come home from business, and all the children had their Sunday dresses on. There were two big girls in from next door and games were going on. Maria gave the bag of cakes to the eldest boy, Alphy, to divide and Mrs. Donnelly said it was too good of her to bring such a big bag of cakes and made all the children say:

"Thanks, Maria."

But Maria said she had brought something special for papa and mamma, something they would be sure to like, and began to look for her plumcake. She tried in Downes's bag and then in the pockets of her waterproof and then on the hallstand but nowhere could she find it. Then she asked all the children had any of them eaten it—by mistake, of course—but the children all said no and looked as if they did not like to eat cakes if they were to be accused of stealing. Everybody had a solution for the mystery and Mrs. Donnelly said it was plain that Maria had left it behind her in the tram. Maria, remembering how confused the gentleman with the grayish moustache had made her, colored with shame and vexation and disappointment. At the thought of the failure of her little surprise and of the two and fourpence she had thrown away for nothing she nearly cried outright.

But Joe said it didn't matter and made her sit down by the fire. He was very nice with her. He told her all that went on in his office, repeating for her a smart answer which he had made to the manager. Maria did not understand why Joe laughed so much over the answer he had made but she said that the manager must have been a very overbearing person to deal with. Joe said he wasn't so bad when you knew how to take him, that he was a decent sort so long as you didn't rub him the wrong way. Mrs. Donnelly played the piano for the children and they danced and sang. Then the two next-door girls handed round the nuts.

Nobody could find the nutcrackers and Joe was nearly getting cross over it and asked how did they expect Maria to crack nuts without a nutcracker. But Maria said she didn't like nuts and that they weren't to bother about her. Then Joe asked would she take a bottle of stout and Mrs. Donnelly said there was port wine too in the house if she would prefer that. Maria
200 said she would rather they didn't ask her to take anything; but Joe insisted.

So Maria let him have his way and they sat by the fire talking over old times and Maria thought she would put in a good word for Alphy. But Joe cried that God might strike him stone dead if ever he spoke a word to his brother again and Maria said she was sorry she had mentioned the matter. Mrs. Donnelly told her husband it was a great shame for him to speak that way of his own flesh and blood but Joe said that Alphy was
210 no brother of his and there was nearly being a row on the head of it. But Joe said he would not lose his temper on account of the night it was and asked his wife to open some more stout. The two next-door girls had arranged some Hallow Eve games and soon everything was merry again. Maria was delighted to see the children so merry and Joe and his wife in such good spirits. The next-door girls put some saucers on the table and then led the children up to the table, blindfold. One got the prayer-book and the other three
220 got the water; and when one of the next-door girls got the ring Mrs. Donnelly shook her finger at the blushing girl as much as to say: O, I know all about it! They insisted then on blindfolding Maria and leading her up to the table to see what she would get; and, while they were putting on the bandage, Maria laughed and laughed again till the tip of her nose nearly met the tip of her chin.

They led her up to the table amid laughing and joking and she put her hand out in the air as she was told to
230 do. She moved her hand about here and there in the air and descended on one of the saucers. She felt a soft wet substance with her fingers and was surprised that nobody spoke or took off her bandage. There was a pause for a few seconds; and then a great deal of scuffling and whispering. Somebody said something about the garden, and at last Mrs. Donnelly said something very cross to one of the next-door girls and told her to throw it out at once: that was no play. Maria understood that it was wrong that time and so she had
240 to do it over again: and this time she got the prayer-book.

After that Mrs. Donnelly played Miss McCloud's Reel for the children and Joe made Maria take a glass of wine. Soon they were all quite merry again and Mrs. Donnelly said Maria would enter a convent before the year was out because she had got the prayer-book. Maria had never seen Joe so nice to her as he was that night, so full of pleasant talk and reminiscences. She said they were all very good to her.
250 At last the children grew tired and sleepy and Joe

asked Maria would she not sing some little song before she went, one of the old songs. Mrs. Donnelly said "Do, please, Maria!" and so Maria had to get up and stand beside the piano. Mrs. Donnelly bade the children be quiet and listen to Maria's song. Then she played the prelude and said "Now, Maria!" and Maria, blushing very much, began to sing in a tiny quavering voice. She sang I Dreamt that I Dwelt,° and when she came to the second verse she sang again:

> I dreamt that I dwelt in marble halls 260
>   With vassals and serfs at my side,
> And of all who assembled within those walls
>   That I was the hope and the pride.

> I had riches too great to count; could boast
>   Of a high ancestral name,
> But I also dreamt, which pleased me most,
>   That you loved me still the same.

But no one tried to show her her mistake; and when she had ended her song Joe was very much moved. He said that there was no time like the long ago and no 270 music for him like poor old Balfe, whatever other people might say; and his eyes filled up so much with tears that he could not find what he was looking for and in the end he had to ask his wife to tell him where the corkscrew was.

(1915)

T. S. ELIOT
1888–1965

Thomas Stearns Eliot was born in St. Louis, Missouri, into a branch of a distinguished Boston family. He lived in St. Louis until he was eighteen and attended Smith Academy; then, after a brief period at Milton Academy, near Boston, he entered Harvard in 1906. He received the bachelor's degree in 1909 and the master's degree a year later. At Harvard he was most influenced by the humanism of Irving Babbitt (1865–1933) and the philosophy of George Santayana (1863–1952). He continued his graduate work, first at the Sorbonne in Paris, then back at Harvard, and finally at Merton College, Oxford, eventually settling in England. He finished his dissertation, entitled *Knowledge and Experience in the Philosophy of F. H. Bradley*, but the First World War prevented his return to Harvard to take his final ral examination for the Ph.D. In London Eliot taught briefly at the Highgate School be-

---

258 **I Dreamt That I Dwelt,** a well-known song from the opera *The Bohemian Girl* (1843) by Michael William Balfe (l. 271) (1808–1870), Irish musician and composer poser

fore becoming a clerk in Lloyds Bank. In 1925 he joined the London publishing firm of Faber and Faber and was made a director of the firm in 1929. His interest in literature, particularly in poetry and criticism, had always been marked. By 1917 he had attracted enough attention among poets and readers of poetry to be named an assistant editor of *The Egoist*, a periodical founded by Ezra Pound (1885–1972), who was a pioneer in the imagist school of contemporary poetry. Pound's encouragement and poetic discernment did much for Eliot; in fact, Eliot's first volume of prose studies, *Ezra Pound, His Metric and Poetry* (1917) is a tribute to the poet Eliot called his master.

In 1917 Eliot also published his first volume of poetry, *Prufrock and Other Observations*. The most famous poem in the volume is the title poem, "The Love Song of J. Alfred Prufrock," which is today considered the first example of "modernism" in English. He issued another collection, *Poems*, in 1919. Two more volumes, one coming out in 1925 and the other in 1936, are cumulative collections including pieces from as far back as Eliot's Harvard days. *Three Critical Essays* (1919) and *The Sacred Wood* (1920) firmly established Eliot's position as a literary critic. In *The Sacred Wood* he gave clear evidence that he was by taste and nature an antisentimental, antiromantic classicist dedicated to finish in form and to balance and symmetry in expression. "Tradition and the Individual Talent," an essay that first appeared in *The Sacred Wood*, is regarded by some critics to be as historically important as Wordsworth's "Preface." Eliot's impact on criticism has few parallels anywhere in history.

In 1922 Eliot achieved an international reputation with the publication of *The Waste Land*. The poem is neither an outright allegory nor a plain narrative but rather a difficult mixture of associations, tags of quotations, bursts of conversation, descriptions, and fragmentary interior monologues. Its influence has been great. The poem caught so aptly the spirit of disillusionment prevailing after the First World War that it gave its name to a whole trend in the literature of the '20s and early '30s. Eliot also founded his own quarterly magazine, *The Criterion*, in 1922. Until its discontinuation in 1939, it was regarded as the most distinguished international journal of criticism in its time. Eliot published in the pages of *The Criterion* many of his essays, which were later gathered together in various volumes.

Eliot became a naturalized British subject in 1927, and in the foreword to *For Lancelot Andrewes* (1928) he declared himself to be "an Anglo-Catholic in religion, a classicist in literature, and a royalist in politics." This statement initially seemed in strong contrast to the pessimism evidenced in *The Waste Land*. But this new Eliot made his position clear in nearly all of his important works written during the '30s. In 1930 he published *Ash Wednesday*, a poem concerned with the tortuous conflict between Eliot's poetic intelligence and his desire to attain a state of grace. *The Rock* (1934) unmistakably sounds the call for a return to Christian spiritual values. His verse drama on the story of Thomas à Becket, the archbishop of Canterbury assassinated in 1170, entitled *Murder in the Cathedral* (1935), is further evidence that in Eliot the twentieth century had found a most articulate religious poet.

The four poems—*East Coker* (1940), *Burnt Norton* (1941), *The Dry Salvages* (1941), and *Little Gidding* (1942)—that were published together in 1943 as *Four Quartets* express both Eliot's desire for emotional security through religion and his still older pessimism. *Four Quartets* is generally considered to be his poetic masterpiece.

In addition to *Murder in the Cathedral*, Eliot published four other verse dramas that deal either explicitly or implicitly with religious themes: *The Family Reunion* (1939), *The Cocktail Party* (1950), *The Confidential Clerk* (1954), and *The Elder Statesman* (1959). Critical reaction to these plays has been varied, but most of them were popular successes. Although composed in verse, the plays, when well performed, capture the rhythms of conventional speech.

In 1948 Eliot received the Nobel Prize for literature and the Order of Merit from King George VI. After 1947 he occupied chairs of poetry at Harvard and Princeton and elsewhere. Because he wrote no major poetry in the last twenty-three years of his life, Eliot is thought of as a poet principally of the decades between the First and Second World Wars; he represented, better than any other important poet of his generation, the intellectual, social, and philosophical moods of his time. His consummate skill in treating traditional forms assures his longevity as a poet and spokesman for the whole first half of the twentieth century. He died in London in 1965.

THE LOVE SONG
OF J. ALFRED PRUFROCK

J. Alfred Prufrock is the embodiment of a type of man notorious in the early part of this century—blasé, intellectual, sensitive, but completely incapable of action or even of decision. The poem is Prufrock's fragmentary soliloquy, as he walks the streets in the evening, reluctant to come to a decision about love—or, for that matter, about anything. He imagines bits of conversation, typical drawing room scenes; he thinks of death. And with death in his mind, love and intellectual inquiry become empty.

S'io credesse che mia risposta fosse
A persona che mai tornasse al mondo,
Questa fiamma staria senza piu scosse.

Ma perciocche giammai di questo fondo
Non torno vivo alcun, s'i'odo il vero,
Senza tema d'infamia ti rispondo.°

Let us go then, you and I,
When the evening is spread out against the sky
Like a patient etherised upon a table;
Let us go, through certain half-deserted streets,
The muttering retreats
Of restless nights in one-night cheap hotels
And sawdust restaurants with oyster-shells:
Streets that follow like a tedious argument
Of insidious intent
10 To lead you to an overwhelming question . . .
Oh, do not ask, "What is it?"
Let us go and make our visit.

In the room the women come and go
Talking of Michelangelo.°

The yellow fog that rubs its back upon the window-
    panes,
The yellow smoke° that rubs its muzzle on the
    window-panes
Licked its tongue into the corners of the evening,
Lingered upon the pools that stand in drains,
Let fall upon its back the soot that falls from chimneys,
20 Slipped by the terrace, made a sudden leap,
And seeing that it was a soft October night,
Curled once about the house, and fell asleep.

And indeed there will be time
For the yellow smoke that slides along the street,
Rubbing its back upon the window-panes;
There will be time, there will be time
To prepare a face to meet the faces that you meet;
There will be time to murder and create,
And time for all the works and days° of hands
30 That lift and drop a question on your plate;
Time for you and time for me,
And time yet for a hundred indecisions,
And for a hundred visions and revisions,
Before the taking of a toast and tea.

In the room the women come and go
Talking of Michelangelo.

And indeed there will be time
To wonder, "Do I dare?" and, "Do I dare?"
Time to turn back and descend the stair,
40 With a bald spot in the middle of my hair—

[They will say: "How his hair is growing thin!"]
My morning coat, my collar mounting firmly to the
    chin,
My necktie rich and modest, but asserted by a simple
    pin—
[They will say: "But how his arms and legs are thin!"]
Do I dare
Disturb the universe?
In a minute there is time
For decisions and revisions which a minute will
    reverse.

For I have known them all already, known them all:—
Have known the evenings, mornings, afternoons,   50
I have measured out my life with coffee spoons;
I know the voices dying with a dying fall
Beneath the music from a farther room.
    So how should I presume?

And I have known the eyes already, known them all—
The eyes that fix you in a formulated phrase,
And when I am formulated, sprawling on a pin,
When I am pinned and wriggling on the wall,
Then how should I begin
To spit out all the butt-ends of my days and ways?   60
    And how should I presume?

And I have known the arms already, known them all—
Arms that are braceleted and white and bare
[But in the lamplight, downed with light brown hair!]
Is it perfume from a dress
That makes me so digress?
Arms that lie along a table, or wrap about a shawl.
    And should I then presume?
    And how should I begin?

                *   *   *   *   *

Shall I say, I have gone at dusk through narrow streets   70
And watched the smoke that rises from the pipes
Of lonely men in shirt-sleeves, leaning out of
    windows? . . .

I should have been a pair of ragged claws
Scuttling across the floors of silent seas.

                *   *   *   *   *

And the afternoon, the evening, sleeps so peacefully!
Smoothed by long fingers,
Asleep . . . tired . . . or it malingers,
Stretched on the floor, here beside you and me.
Should I, after tea and cakes and ices,
Have the strength to force the moment to its crisis?   80
But though I have wept and fasted, wept and prayed,
Though I have seen my head [grown slightly bald]
    brought in upon a platter,°

The Love Song of J. Alfred Prufrock   S'io . . . rispondo. "If I could believe that
my answer might be to a person who should ever return into the world, this flame
would stand without more quiverings; but inasmuch as, if I hear the truth, never
from this depth did any living man return, without fear of infamy I answer
thee."—Dante, *Inferno*, XXVII, ll. 61–66   14 **Michelangelo**, the great Renaissance artist (1475–1564), here used as a symbol for a topic of conversation about
art   16 **yellow smoke.** The extended image of yellow fog is a figure which the
French symbolists associated with the ugly and unpleasant aspects of the city
29 **works and days,** probably an allusion to *Works and Days* by Hesiod (eighth
century B.C.), a poem celebrating daily farm life and offering numerous moral
precepts

82 **my head . . . platter,** a reference to the execution of St. John the Baptist at the
importuning of Salome. Cf. *Mark*, 6, especially verses 27 and 28

I am no prophet—and here's no great matter;
I have seen the moment of my greatness flicker,
And I have seen the eternal Footman hold my coat,
   and snicker,
And in short, I was afraid.

And would it have been worth it, after all,
After the cups, the marmalade, the tea,
Among the porcelain, among some talk of you and me,
90 Would it have been worth while,
To have bitten off the matter with a smile,
To have squeezed the universe into a ball
To roll it toward some overwhelming question,
To say: "I am Lazarus,° come from the dead,
Come back to tell you all, I shall tell you all"—
If one, settling a pillow by her head,
   Should say: "That is not what I meant at all.
   That is not it, at all."

And would it have been worth it, after all,
100 Would it have been worth while,
After the sunsets and the dooryards and the sprinkled
   streets,
After the novels, after the teacups, after the skirts that
   trail along the floor—
And this, and so much more?—
It is impossible to say just what I mean!
But as if a magic lantern° threw the nerves in patterns
   on a screen:
Would it have been worth while
If one, setting a pillow or throwing off a shawl,
And turning toward the window, should say:
   "That is not it at all,
110   That is not what I meant, at all."

* * * * *

No! I am not Prince Hamlet, nor was meant to be;
Am an attendant lord, one that will do
To swell a progress, start a scene or two,
Advise the prince; no doubt, an easy tool,
Deferential, glad to be of use,
Politic, cautious, and meticulous;
Full of high sentence,° but a bit obtuse;
At times, indeed, almost ridiculous—
Almost, at times, the Fool.

120 I grow old . . . I grow old . . .
I shall wear the bottoms of my trousers rolled.

Shall I part my hair behind? Do I dare to eat a peach?
I shall wear white flannel trousers, and walk upon the
   beach.
I have heard the mermaids singing, each to each.

I do not think that they will sing to me.

I have seen them riding seaward on the waves
Combing the white hair of the waves blown back
When the wind blows the water white and black.

We have lingered in the chambers of the sea
By sea-girls wreathed with seaweed red and brown   130
Till human voices wake us, and we drown.°
(1910–1911; 1915)

SWEENEY AMONG THE NIGHTINGALES°

ὤμοι, πέπληγμαι καιρίαν πληγὴν ἔσω°

Apeneck Sweeney° spreads his knees
Letting his arms hang down to laugh,
The zebra stripes along his jaw
Swelling to maculate° giraffe.

   The circles of the stormy moon
Slide westward toward the River Plate,°
Death and the Raven° drift above
And Sweeney guards the hornéd gate.°

   Gloomy Orion and the Dog°
Are veiled; and hushed the shrunken seas;   10
The person in the Spanish cape
Tries to sit on Sweeney's knees

   Slips and pulls the table cloth
Overturns a coffee-cup,
Reorganized upon the floor
She yawns and draws a stocking up;

   The silent man in mocha brown
Sprawls at the window-sill and gapes;
The waiter brings in oranges
Bananas figs and hothouse grapes;   20

94 **Lazarus,** the young man who was resurrected by Christ. Cf. *John*, 11:1–46
105 **magic lantern,** early nonelectric device that projected images from a transparent slide   117 **Full of high sentence.** In the Prologue to the *Canterbury Tales*, Geoffrey Chaucer described the speech of the Clerk of Oxford as being "full of high sentence" (weighty thoughts)

131 **drown.** In Greek and Roman mythology, the Sirens lured men into caverns beneath the sea by their enchanting songs; when the songs ended, the men drowned   **Sweeney Among the Nightingales.** This poem contrasts the vulgarity of the present age with the heroic periods of history. Lust, cruelty, and violence, says Eliot, have always existed in the world, but in heroic ages they were the result of grand passions, while in the present they are characterized by unheroic action and lack of faith in anything   ὤμοι . . . ἔσω. "Ay me! I am smitten with a mortal blow." The passage is quoted from Aeschylus' *Agamemnon*   1 **Sweeney,** the primitive in man; note animal references to *apeneck* (l. 1), *zebra* (l. 3), *giraffe* (l. 4). He is in some kind of peril   4 **maculate,** spotted, striped   6 **River Plate,** Rio de la Plata, dividing Argentina from Uruguay   7 **Raven,** the small constellation Corvus, in the southern hemisphere. In this line the conjunction of Death and the Raven suggests the bird of death hovering above Sweeney   8 **hornéd gate,** in classical legend, the gate of horn in Hades, through which unpleasant but true dreams came to the upper world. Cf. Vergil, *Aeneid*, VI, 893–896. In this poem it is also perhaps the gate of death   9 **Orion and the Dog,** the two great winter constellations of Orion and Canis Major, in the latter of which is located the brilliant star Sirius (the Dog Star). In classical myth, Orion, the famous hunter, was in love with Merope and tried to carry her off, but was slain by her father. The sun god Apollo restored him to life, but he was killed again by Diana, the moon goddess and goddess of chastity. He then became a constellation, but the moon daily kills him with Diana's darts. King Agamemnon (l. 38) once killed one of Diana's harts; she took revenge on him

The silent vertebrate in brown
Contracts and concentrates, withdraws;
Rachel *née* Rabinovitch
Tears at the grapes with murderous paws;

She and the lady in the cape
Are suspect, thought to be in league;
Therefore the man with heavy eyes
Declines the gambit,° shows fatigue,

Leaves the room and reappears
30 Outside the window, leaning in,
Branches of wistaria
Circumscribe a golden grin;

The host with someone indistinct
Converses at the door apart,
The nightingales are singing near
The Convent of the Sacred Heart,°

And sang within the bloody wood°
When Agamemnon cried aloud,
And let their liquid siftings fall
40 To stain the stiff dishonoured shroud.
(1920)

JOURNEY OF THE MAGI°

'A cold coming we had of it,
Just the worst time of the year
For a journey, and such a long journey:
The ways deep and the weather sharp,
The very dead of winter.'
And the camels galled, sore-footed, refractory,
Lying down in the melting snow.
There were times we regretted
The summer palaces on slopes, the terraces,
10 And the silken girls bringing sherbet.
Then the camel men cursing and grumbling
And running away, and wanting their liquor and
    women,
And the night-fires going out, and the lack of shelters,
And the cities hostile and the towns unfriendly
And the villages dirty and charging high prices:
A hard time we had of it.
At the end we preferred to travel all night,
Sleeping in snatches,
With the voices singing in our ears, saying
20 That this was all folly.

Then at dawn we came down to a temperate valley,
Wet, below the snow line, smelling of vegetation;
With a running stream and a water-mill beating the
    darkness,
And three trees on the low sky,
And an old white horse galloped away in the meadow.
Then we came to a tavern with vine-leaves over the
    lintel,
Six hands at an open door dicing for pieces of silver,
And feet kicking the empty wine-skins.
But there was no information, and so we continued
And arrived at evening, not a moment too soon   30
Finding the place; it was (you may say) satisfactory.

All this was a long time ago, I remember,
And I would do it again, but set down
This set down
This: were we led all that way for
Birth or Death? There was a Birth, certainly,
We had evidence and no doubt. I had seen birth and
    death,
But had thought they were different; this Birth was
Hard and bitter agony for us, like Death, our death.
We returned to our places, these Kingdoms,   40
But no longer at ease here, in the old dispensation,
With an alien people clutching their gods.
I should be glad of another death.
(1927)

THE WASTE LAND°

"Nam Sibyllam quidem Cumis ego ipse oculis meis vidi
in ampulla pendere, et cum illi pueri dicerent: Σίβνλλα
τί θέλεις; respondebat illa: ἀποθανεῖν θέλω."°
                For Ezra Pound°
                il miglior fabbro.°

I. THE BURIAL OF THE DEAD

April is the cruellest month, breeding
Lilacs out of the dead land, mixing
Memory and desire, stirring
Dull roots with spring rain.
Winter kept us warm, covering
Earth in forgetful snow, feeding
A little life with dried tubers.

---

28 **gambit,** opening move in a chess game   35–36 **nightingales . . . Heart.** Note the juxtaposition of the Christian and the pagan. The nightingales recall the legend of Philomela, who was turned into a nightingale after she was raped by her brother-in-law, Tereus   37 **bloody wood.** Agamemnon was actually murdered in a bath. However, there is a telescoping of suggestion here of Agamemnon's murder with the wood where Philomela was ravished and also with the wood of Nemi, where, according to the first chapter of Sir James Frazer's *The Golden Bough,* the old priest of the grove was killed by his young successor, who was in turn killed when he grew old   **The Journey of the Magi.** The speaker in the poem is one of the three wise men who journeyed from the east to Bethlehem to worship the infant Jesus. Cf. *Matthew* 2:1–12

The Waste Land. "Not only the title, but the plan and a good deal of the incidental symbolism of the poem were suggested by Miss Jessie L. Weston's book on the Grail Legend: *From Ritual to Romance* (Cambridge). . . . To another work of anthropology I am indebted in general, one which has influenced our generation profoundly; I mean *The Golden Bough*"—Eliot's note   **Nam Sibyllam . . . θέλω.** For indeed I myself once, with my own eyes, saw the Sybill hanging in a cage, and when the boys said to her "Sibyll, what do you want?" she responded, "I want to die." The quotation is from the *Satyricon* by Petronius, Roman writer of first century A.D.   **Ezra Pound,** expatriate American poet (1885–1972) who helped Eliot revise "The Waste Land"   **il miglior fabbro,** the better maker or craftsman. The words are spoken of the poet Arnaut Daniel in Dante's *Purgatorio,* Canto 26, l. 117

Summer surprised us, coming over the Starnbergersee°
With a shower of rain; we stopped in the colonnade,
10 And went on in sunlight, into the Hofgarten,°
And drank coffee, and talked for an hour.
Bin gar keine Russin, stamm' aus Litauen, echt
    deutsch.°
And when we were children, staying at the archduke's,
My cousin's, he took me out on a sled,
And I was frightened. He said, Marie,
Marie, hold on tight. And down we went.
In the mountains, there you feel free.
I read, much of the night, and go south in the winter.

    What are the roots that clutch, what branches grow
20 Out of this stony rubbish? Son of man,°
You cannot say, or guess, for you know only
A heap of broken images, where the sun beats,
And the dead tree gives no shelter, the cricket no
    relief,°
And the dry stone no sound of water. Only
There is shadow under this red rock,
(Come in under the shadow of this red rock),
And I will show you something different from either
Your shadow at morning striding behind you
Or your shadow at evening rising to meet you;
30 I will show you fear in a handful of dust.
        Frisch weht der Wind
        Der Heimat zu
        Mein Irisch Kind,
        Wo weilest du?°
"You gave me hyacinths first a year ago;
"They called me the hyacinth girl."
—Yet when we came back, late, from the Hyacinth
    garden,
Your arms full, and your hair wet, I could not
Speak, and my eyes failed, I was neither
40 Living nor dead, and I knew nothing,
Looking into the heart of light, the silence.
Oed' und leer das Meer.°

    Madame Sosostris, famous clairvoyante,
Had a bad cold, nevertheless
Is known to be the wisest woman in Europe,
With a wicked pack of cards.° Here, said she,
Is your card, the drowned Phoenician Sailor,°
(Those are pearls that were his eyes.° Look!)

Here is Belladonna,° the Lady of the Rocks,
The lady of situations.   50
Here is the man with three staves, and here the Wheel,
And here is the one-eyed merchant, and this card,
Which is blank, is something he carries on his back,
Which I am forbidden to see. I do not find
The Hanged Man. Fear death by water.
I see crowds of people, walking round in a ring.
Thank you. If you see dear Mrs. Equitone,
Tell her I bring the horoscope myself:
One must be so careful these days.

    Unreal City,   60
Under the brown fog of a winter dawn,
A crowd flowed over London Bridge, so many,
I had not thought death had undone so many.°
Sighs, short and infrequent, were exhaled,
And each man fixed his eyes before his feet.
Flowed up the hill and down King William Street,
To where Saint Mary Woolnoth kept the hours
With a dead sound on the final stroke of nine.
There I saw one I knew, and stopped him, crying:
    "Stetson!
"You who were with me in the ships at Mylae!°   70
"That corpse you planted last year in your garden,
"Has it begun to sprout? Will it bloom this year?
"Or has the sudden frost disturbed its bed?
"Oh keep the Dog far hence,° that's friend to men,
"Or with his nails he'll dig it up again!
"You! hypocrite lecteur!—mon semblable,—mon
    frère!"°

II. A GAME OF CHESS

The Chair she sat in, like a burnished throne,°
Glowed on the marble, where the glass
Held up by standards wrought with fruited vines
From which a golden Cupidon peeped out   80
(Another hid his eyes behind his wing)
Doubled the flames of sevenbranched candelabra
Reflecting light upon the table as
The glitter of her jewels rose to meet it,
From satin cases poured in rich profusion;
In vials of ivory and coloured glass
Unstoppered, lurked her strange synthetic perfumes,
Unguent, powdered, or liquid—troubled, confused
And drowned the sense in odours; stirred by the air
That freshened from the window, these ascended   90
In fattening the prolonged candle-flames,
Flung their smoke into the laquearia,°
Stirring the pattern on the coffered ceiling.
Huge sea-wood fed with copper

---

8 **Starnbergersee,** a lake near Munich   10 **Hofgarten,** public park in Munich
12 **Bin . . . deutsch,** I am not Russian, I come from Lithuania, pure German
20 "Cf. *Ezekiel,* 2:1"—Eliot's note   23 "Cf. *Ecclesiastes* 12:5"—Eliot's note
31–34 **Frisch . . . du,** "Fresh blows the wind toward home. My Irish child, where
do you roam?" Lines from a song which opens *Tristan and Isolde,* an opera by
Richard Wagner (1813–1883)   42 **Oed' . . . Meer.** A line from the third act of
Tristan and Isolde in which Tristan lies sick and dying and
awaiting Isolde's ship; a shepherd lookout can only report, "Desolate and empty
is the sea"   46 **wicked pack of cards,** the Tarot deck, cards used for fortune-
telling. Eliot reported that he changed the significance of some cards for his own
purposes: "The Hanged Man, a member of the traditional pack, fits my purpose in
two ways: because he is associated in my mind with the Hanged God of Frazer
[author of *The Golden Bough*—ed. note], and because I associate him with the
hooded figure in the passage of the disciples to Emmaus in Part V. The Phoenician Sailor and the Merchant appear later; also the 'crowds of people,' and Death
by Water is executed in Part IV. The Man with Three Staves (an authentic member
of the Tarot pack) I associate, quite arbitrarily, with the Fisher King himself"
47 **Phoenician Sailor.** See Part IV   48 **Those . . . eyes.** Line from Shakespeare's
The Tempest (I, ii, 398) in which Ariel reminds Ferdinand of his drowned father,
Alonso

49 **Belladonna,** Italian for "Beautiful Lady"; also poisonous plant of the nightshade family   63 **I had . . . so many.** "Cf. *Inferno* III, 55–57"—Eliot's note
70 **Mylae,** battle in the First Punic War (260 B.C.)   74 "Cf. the Dirge in Webster's *White Devil*"—Eliot's note   76 **hypocrite . . . frère,** "Hypocritical
reader—my double or likeness—my brother." The quotation is from Baudelaire's
Preface to *Fleurs du Mal*   77 "Cf. *Antony and Cleopatra,* II, ii, l. 190"—Eliot's
note   92 **laquearia,** a paneled ceiling

Burned green and orange, framed by the coloured
   stone,
In which sad light a càrvèd dolphin swam.
Above the antique mantel was displayed
As though a window gave upon the sylvan scene
The change of Philomel,° by the barbarous king
100 So rudely forced; yet there the nightingale°
Filled all the desert with inviolable voice
And still she cried, and still the world pursues,
"Jug Jug"° to dirty ears.
And other withered stumps of time
Were told upon the walls; staring forms
Leaned out, leaning, hushing the room enclosed.
Footsteps shuffled on the stair.
Under the firelight, under the brush, her hair
Spread out in fiery points
110 Glowed into words, then would be savagely still.

    "My nerves are bad to-night. Yes, bad. Stay with
   me.
   "Speak to me. Why do you never speak. Speak.
    "What are you thinking of? What thinking? What?
"I never know what you are thinking. Think."

    I think we are in rats' alley°
Where the dead men lost their bones.

    "What is that noise?"
               The wind under the door.
   "What is that noise now? What is the wind doing?"
120   Nothing again nothing.
                              "Do
   "You know nothing? Do you see nothing? Do you
   remember
   "Nothing?"

    I remember
Those are pearls that were his eyes.
"Are you alive, or not? Is there nothing in your
   head?"
                                 But

O O O O that Shakespeherian Rag—
It's so elegant
130 So intelligent
"What shall I do now? What shall I do?"
"I shall rush out as I am, and walk the street
"With my hair down, so. What shall we do to-mor-
   row?
"What shall we ever do?"
                   The hot water at ten.
And if it rains, a closed car at four.
And we shall play a game of chess,

Pressing lidless eyes and waiting for a knock upon the
   door.

   When Lil's husband got demobbed,° I said—
I didn't mince my words, I said to her myself,   140
HURRY UP PLEASE ITS TIME°
Now Albert's coming back, make yourself a bit smart.
He'll want to know what you done with that money he
   gave you
To get yourself some teeth. He did, I was there.
You have them all out, Lil, and get a nice set,
He said, I swear, I can't bear to look at you.
And no more can't I, I said, and think of poor Albert,
He's been in the army four years, he wants a good
   time,
And if you don't give it him, there's others will, I said.
Oh is there, she said. Something o' that, I said.   150
Then I'll know who to thank, she said, and give me a
   straight look.
HURRY UP PLEASE ITS TIME
If you don't like it you can get on with it, I said.
Others can pick and choose if you can't.
But if Albert makes off, it won't be for lack of telling.
You ought to be ashamed, I said, to look so antique.
(And her only thirty-one.)
I can't help it, she said, pulling a long face,
It's them pills I took, to bring it off, she said.
(She's had five already, and nearly died of young
   George.)   160
The chemist said it would be all right, but I've never
   been the same.
You are a proper fool, I said.
Well, if Albert won't leave you alone, there it is, I said,
What you get married for if you don't want children?
HURRY UP PLEASE ITS TIME
Well, that Sunday Albert was home, they had a hot
   gammon,°
And they asked me in to dinner, to get the beauty of it
   hot—
HURRY UP PLEASE ITS TIME
HURRY UP PLEASE ITS TIME
Goonight Bill. Goonight Lou. Goonight May.
   Goonight.   170
Ta ta. Goonight. Goonight.
Good night, ladies, good night, sweet ladies, good
   night, good night.

III. THE FIRE SERMON

The river's tent is broken: the last fingers of leaf
Clutch and sink into the wet bank. The wind
Crosses the brown land, unheard. The nymphs are
   departed.
Sweet Thames, run softly, till I end my song.°

---

99 **Philomel,** see Ovid, *Metamorphoses* VI, 565. Ovid tells how Philomela was raped by the angry Tereus, her sister's husband. Tereus cut out Philomela's tongue. Philomela was later changed into a nightingale (l. 100) 100 "Cf. Part III, l. 204"—Eliot's note 103 **Jug Jug,** traditional representation of nightingale's song in Elizabethan poetry; also a sexual vulgarism 115 "Cf. Part III, l. 195"—Eliot's note

139 **demobbed,** slang for "demobilized," discharged from the army 141 **Hurry . . . time,** traditional call of English bartender at closing time 166 **gammon,** ham 176 "V. Spenser, *Prothalamion*"—Eliot's note

The river bears no empty bottles, sandwich papers,
Silk handkerchiefs, cardboard boxes, cigarette ends
Or other testimony of summer nights. The nymphs are
     departed
180 And their friends, the loitering heirs of city directors;
Departed, have left no addresses.
By the waters of Leman° I sat down and wept . . .
Sweet Thames, run softly till I end my song,
Sweet Thames, run softly, for I speak not loud or long.
But at my back in a cold blast I hear
The rattle of the bones, and chuckle spread from ear to
     ear.°
A rat crept softly through the vegetation
Dragging its slimy belly on the bank
While I was fishing in the dull canal
190 On a winter evening round behind the gashouse
Musing upon the king my brother's wreck
And on the king my father's death before him.°
White bodies naked on the low damp ground
And bones cast in a little low dry garret,
Rattled by the rat's foot only, year to year.
But at my back from time to time I hear
The sound of horns and motors, which shall bring
Sweeney to Mrs. Porter in the spring.
O the moon shone bright on Mrs. Porter
200 And on her daughter
They wash their feet in soda water°
Et O ces voix d'enfants, chantant dans la coupole!°

     Twit twit twit
Jug jug jug jug jug jug
So rudely forc'd.
Tereu°

     Unreal City
Under the brown fog of a winter noon
Mr. Eugenides, the Smyrna° merchant
210 Unshaven, with a pocket full of currants
C.i.f. London: documents at sight,°
Asked me in demotic French
To luncheon at the Cannon Street Hotel
Followed by a weekend at the Metropole.

     At the violet hour, when the eyes and back
Turn upward from the desk, when the human engine
     waits
Like a taxi throbbing waiting,

I Tiresias,° though blind, throbbing between two lives,
Old man with wrinkled female breasts, can see
At the violet hour, the evening hour that strives   220
Homeward, and brings the sailor home from sea,
The typist home at teatime, clears her breakfast, lights
Her stove, and lays out food in tins.
Out of the window perilously spread
Her drying combinations° touched by the sun's last
     rays,
On the divan are piled (at night her bed)
Stockings, slippers, camisoles, and stays.
I Tiresias, old man with wrinkled dugs
Perceived the scene, and foretold the rest—
I too awaited the expected guest.   230
He, the young man carbuncular, arrives,
A small house agent's clerk, with one bold stare,
One of the low on whom assurance sits
As a silk hat on a Bradford° millionaire.
The time is now propitious, as he guesses,
The meal is ended, she is bored and tired,
Endeavours to engage her in caresses
Which still are unreproved, if undesired.
Flushed and decided, he assaults at once;
Exploring hands encounter no defence;   240
His vanity requires no response,
And makes a welcome of indifference.
(And I Tiresias have foresuffered all
Enacted on this same divan or bed;
I who have sat by Thebes° below the wall
And walked among the lowest of the dead.)
Bestows one final patronising kiss,
And gropes his way, finding the stairs unlit . . .

     She turns and looks a moment in the glass,
Hardly aware of her departed lover;   250
Her brain allows one half-formed thought to pass:
"Well now that's done: and I'm glad it's over."
When lovely woman stoops to folly° and
Paces about her room again, alone,
She smoothes her hair with automatic hand,
And puts a record on the gramophone.

     "This music crept by me upon the waters"°
And along the Strand, up Queen Victoria Street.
O City city, I can sometimes hear
Beside a public bar in Lower Thames Street,   260
The pleasant whining of a mandoline
And a clatter and a chatter from within
Where fishmen lounge at noon: where the walls

182 **Leman.** See Psalms 137:1: "By the rivers of Babylon, there we sat down, yea, we wept, when we remembered Zion." Leman here stands for Lake Geneva, close to Lausanne, Switzerland, where Eliot wrote parts of the poem. "Leman" also means "lover"   185–186 **But . . . ear.** Parody of Marvell's "To His Coy Mistress": "But at my back I always hear / Time's winged chariot hurrying near" (ll. 21–22)   192 "Cf. *The Tempest*, I, ii"—Eliot's note   199–201 **O . . . water.** "I do not know the origin of the ballad from which these lines are taken: it was reported to me from Sydney, Australia"—Eliot's note. Lines from an obscene Australian ballad   202 **Et . . . coupole.** "And oh the voices of the children, singing in the cupola." A line from the sonnet "Parsifal" by Paul Verlaine (1844–1896), French symbolist poet   206 **Tereu.** A reference to Tereus who raped Philomela. Like "Jug Jug," "Tereu" is a traditional representation of nightingale's song in Elizabethan poetry   209 **Smyrna,** a seaport in Turkey   210–211 "The currants were quoted at a price 'carriage and insurance free to London'; and the Bill of Lading etc. were to be handed to the buyer upon payment of the sight draft"—Eliot's note

218 **Tiresias.** "Tiresias, although a mere spectator and not indeed a 'character,' is yet the most important personage in the poem, uniting all the rest"—Eliot's note. Tiresias is a mythological character who, as reported in Ovid's *Metamorphoses*, was changed from a man to a woman, and, subsequently, was changed from a woman back to a man   225 **combinations,** one piece undergarment   234 **Bradford,** an industrial town in Yorkshire where some fast fortunes were made   245 **Thebes.** Tiresias lived in Thebes; he was the blind man who knew that the curse placed on Thebes stemmed from the unknowing incest of Oedipus and Jocasta (Sophocles, *Oedipus the King*)   253 **When . . . folly.** "V. Goldsmith, the song in *The Vicar of Wakefield*"—Eliot's note. The song runs as follows: "When lovely woman stoops to folly, / And finds too late that men betray, / What charm can soothe her melancholy, / What act can wash her guilt away? / The only art her guilt to cover, / To hide her shame from every eye, / To give repentance to her lover / And wring his bosom—is to die"   257 "V. *The Tempest*, as above"—Eliot's note. See Act I, ii

Of Magnus Martyr hold
Inexplicable splendour of Ionian white and gold.°

  The river sweats°
 Oil and tar
 The barges drift
 With the turning tide
270 Red sails
 Wide
 To leeward, swing on the heavy spar.
 The barges wash
 Drifting logs
 Down Greenwich reach°
 Past the Isle of Dogs.°
   Weialala leia
   Wallala leialala

  Elizabeth and Leicester
280 Beating oars
 The stern was formed
 A gilded shell
 Red and gold
 The brisk swell
 Rippled both shores
 Southwest wind
 Carried down stream
 The peal of bells
 White towers
290   Weialala leia
   Wallala leialala

"Trams and dusty trees.
Highbury° bore me. Richmond and Kew
Undid me. By Richmond I raised my knees
Supine on the floor of a narrow canoe."

"My feet are at Moorgate, and my heart
Under my feet. After the event
He wept. He promised 'a new start.'
I made no comment. What should I resent?"

300 "On Margate Sands.
I can connect
Nothing with nothing.
The broken fingernails of dirty hands.
My people humble people who expect
Nothing."
   la la

To Carthage° then I came

Burning° burning burning burning
O Lord Thou pluckest me out°
O Lord Thou pluckest   310

burning

IV. DEATH BY WATER

Phlebas the Phoenician, a fortnight dead,
Forgot the cry of gulls, and the deep sea swell
And the profit and loss.
    A current under sea
Picked his bones in whispers. As he rose and fell
He passed the stages of his age and youth
Entering the whirlpool.
    Gentile or Jew
O you who turn the wheel and look to windward, 320
Consider Phlebas, who was once handsome and tall as
 you.

V. WHAT THE THUNDER SAID

After the torchlight red on sweaty faces
After the frosty silence in the gardens
After the agony in stony places°
The shouting and the crying
Prison and palace and reverberation
Of thunder of spring over distant mountains
He who was living is now dead°
We who were living are now dying
With a little patience   330

 Here is no water but only rock
Rock and no water and the sandy road
The road winding above among the mountains
Which are mountains of rock without water
If there were water we should stop and drink
Amongst the rock one cannot stop or think
Sweat is dry and feet are in the sand
If there were only water amongst the rock
Dead mountain mouth of carious teeth that cannot spit
Here one can neither stand nor lie nor sit 340
There is not even silence in the mountains
But dry sterile thunder without rain

263–265 **where . . . gold.** Description of the interior of the church of St. Magnus Martyr, designed by Sir Christopher Wren (1632–1723), renowned English architect 266 "The song of the (three) Thames-daughters begins here"—Eliot's note 275 **Greenwich reach.** Greenwich is a borough of London on the south bank of the Thames 276 **Isle of Dogs,** peninsula opposite Greenwich 293 **Highbury.** The references in this and the next six lines refer to locales in the vicinity of London or the Thames

307 "V. St. Augustine's *Confessions:* 'to Carthage then I came, where a cauldron of unholy loves sang all about mine ears'"—Eliot's note. St. Augustine (354–430) was an early church father and philosopher who had an unregenerate, indeed infamous, youth 308 "The complete text of the Buddha's Fire Sermon (which corresponds in importance to the Sermon on the Mount) from which these words are taken, will be found translated in the late Henry Clarke Warren's *Buddhism in Translation* (Harvard Oriental Series)"—Eliot's note 309 "From St. Augustine's *Confessions* again"—Eliot's note 322–328 **After . . . dead.** These lines refer to the betrayal, passion, and death of Christ as set forth in the New Testament. 324 **Stony places,** refers to the garden of Gethsemane

There is not even solitude in the mountains
But red sullen faces sneer and snarl
From doors of mudcracked houses
                                  If there were water

    And no rock
    If there were rock
    And also water
350 And water
    A spring
    A pool among the rock
    If there were the sound of water only
    Not the cicada°
    And dry grass singing
    But sound of water over a rock
    Where the hermit-thrush sings in the pine trees
    Drip drop drip drop drop drop drop
    But there is no water

360 Who is the third who walks always beside you?°
    When I count, there are only you and I together
    But when I look ahead up the white road
    There is always another one walking beside you
    Gliding wrapt in a brown mantle, hooded
    I do not know whether a man or a woman
    —But who is that on the other side of you?

    What is that sound high in the air
    Murmur of maternal lamentation
    Who are those hooded hordes swarming
370 Over endless plains, stumbling in cracked earth
    Ringed by the flat horizon only
    What is the city over the mountains
    Cracks and reforms and bursts in the violet air
    Falling towers
    Jerusalem Athens Alexandria
    Vienna London
    Unreal

    A woman drew her long black hair out tight
    And fiddled whisper music on those strings
380 And bats with baby faces in the violet light
    Whistled, and beat their wings
    And crawled head downward down a blackened wall
    And upside down in air were towers
    Tolling reminiscent bells, that kept the hours
    And voices singing out of empty cisterns and
        exhausted wells.

In this decayed hole among the mountains
In the faint moonlight, the grass is singing

Over the tumbled graves, about the chapel
There is the empty chapel, only the wind's home.
It has no windows, and the door swings,   390
Dry bones can harm no one.
Only a cock stood on the rooftree
Co co rico co co rico
In a flash of lightning. Then a damp gust
Bringing rain

    Ganga° was sunken, and the limp leaves
Waited for rain, while the black clouds
Gathered far distant, over Himavant.°
The jungle crouched, humped in silence.
Then spoke the thunder   400
DA
Datta:° what have we given?
My friend, blood shaking my heart
The awful daring of a moment's surrender
Which an age of prudence can never retract
By this, and this only, we have existed
Which is not to be found in our obituaries
Or in memories draped by the beneficent spider
Or under seals broken by the lean solicitor
In our empty rooms   410
DA
Dayadhvam: I have heard the key
Turn in the door once and turn once only
We think of the key, each in his prison
Thinking of the key, each confirms a prison
Only at nightfall, aethereal rumours
Revive for a moment a broken Coriolanus°
DA
Damyata: The boat responded
Gaily, to the hand expert with sail and oar   420
The sea was calm, your heart would have responded
Gaily, when invited, beating obedient
To controlling hands

                        I sat upon the shore
Fishing, with the arid plain behind me
Shall I at least set my lands in order?
London Bridge is falling down falling down falling
    down
Poi s'ascose nel foco che gli affina°
Quando fiam uti chelidon°—O swallow swallow
Le Prince d'Aquitaine à la tour abolie°   430

---

396 **Ganga,** the sacred river Ganges in India   398 **Himavant,** mountain peak in
the Himalayas   402 "'Datta, dayadhvam, damyata' (Give, sympathise, control).
The fable of the meaning of the Thunder is found in the *Brihadaranyaka —Upanishad,* 5, 1. The Upanishads are a group of poetic dialogues on metaphysics
written after the Vedas (oldest scriptures of Hinduism) and in part commenting on
them   417 **Coriolanus.** Shakespeare's example of a man exiled by pride;
banished from his own city, Coriolanus went over to the enemy and led them in
an attack against it   428–429 "V. *Purgatorio,* XXVI, 148. 'Ara vos prec per
aquella valor / que vos guida al som de l'escalina / sovegna vos a temps de ma
dolor. / Poi s'ascose nel foco che gli affina'"—Eliot's note. The last line reads,
"Then he hid him in the fire which refines them"   429 **Quando . . . chelidon,**
when shall I be as the swallow? From the medieval Latin poem *Pervigilium Ven-
eris*   430 **Le . . . abolie,** the Prince of Aquitaine in the broken tower

---

354 **cicada.** A reference to *Ecclesiastes* 12:5: "Also when they shall be afraid of
that which is high and fears shall be in the way, and the almond tree shall
flourish, and the grasshopper shall be a burden, and desire shall fail: because man
goeth to his long home, and the mourners go about the streets"   360 "The following lines were stimulated by the account of one of the Antarctic expeditions (I
forget which, but think one of Shackleton's): it was related that the party of
explorers, at the extremity of their strength, had the constant delusion that there
was *one more member* than could actually be counted"—Eliot's note

These fragments I have shored against my ruins
Why then Ile fit you. Hieronymo's mad againe.°
Datta. Dayadhvam. Damyata.
     Shantih° shantih shantih
(1922)

from FOUR QUARTETS°

LITTLE GIDDING°

I

Midwinter spring is its own season
Sempiternal° though sodden towards sundown,
Suspended in time, between pole and tropic.
When the short day is brightest, with frost and fire,
The brief sun flames the ice, on pond and ditches,
In windless cold that is the heart's heat,
Reflecting in a watery mirror
A glare that is blindness in the early afternoon.
And glow more intense than blaze of branch, or
    brazier,
10 Stirs the dumb spirit: no wind, but pentecostal fire°
In the dark time of the year. Between melting and
    freezing
The soul's sap quivers. There is no earth smell
Or smell of living thing. This is the spring time
But not in time's covenant. Now the hedgerow
Is blanched for an hour with transitory blossom
Of snow, a bloom more sudden
Than that of summer, neither budding nor fading,
Not in the scheme of generation.
Where is the summer, the unimaginable
20 Zero summer?

        If you came this way,
Taking the route you would be likely to take
From the place you would be likely to come from,
If you came this way in may time, you would find the
    hedges
White again, in May, with voluptuary sweetness.
It would be the same at the end of the journey,

If you came at night like a broken king,
If you came by day not knowing what you came for,
It would be the same, when you leave the rough road
And turn behind the pig-sty to the dull facade   30
And the tombstone. And what you thought you came
    for
Is only a shell, a husk of meaning
From which the purpose breaks only when it is fulfilled
If at all. Either you had no purpose
Or the purpose is beyond the end you figured
And is altered in fulfillment. There are other places
Which also are the world's end, some at the sea jaws,
Or over a dark lake, in a desert or a city—
But this is the nearest, in place and time,
Now and in England.   40

        If you came this way,
Taking any route, starting from anywhere,
At any time or at any season,
It would always be the same: you would have to put off
Sense and notion. You are not here to verify,
Instruct yourself, or inform curiosity
Or carry report. You are here to kneel
Where prayer has been valid. And prayer is more
Than an order of words, the conscious occupation
Of the praying mind, or the sound of the voice praying.   50
And what the dead had no speech for, when living,
They can tell you, being dead: the communication
Of the dead is tongued with fire beyond the language of
    the living.
Here, the intersection of the timeless moment
In England and nowhere. Never and always.

II

Ash on an old man's sleeve
Is all the ash the burnt roses leave.
Dust in the air suspended
Marks the place where a story ended.
Dust inbreathed was a house—
The wall, the wainscot and the mouse.   60
The death of hope and despair,
    This is the death of air.

  There are flood and drouth
Over the eyes and in the mouth,
Dead water and dead sand
Contending for the upper hand.
The parched eviscerate soil
Gapes at the vanity of toil,
Laughs without mirth.   70
    This is the death of earth.

  Water and fire succeed
The town, the pasture and the weed.
Water and fire deride
The sacrifice that we denied.
Water and fire shall rot
The marred foundations we forgot,

432 "V. Kyd's *Spanish Tragedy*"—Eliot's note. *The Spanish Tragedy* (subtitled "Hieronymo's Mad Againe") is the best known play by the English dramatist Thomas Kyd (1557?–?1595); his play is a fine example of revenge tragedy 434 "Shantih. Repeated as here, a formal ending to an Upanishad. 'The peace which passeth understanding' is our equivalent to this word"—Eliot's note **Four Quartets.** The *Four Quartets* are four related poems (*Burnt Norton, East Coker, The Dry Salvages,* and *Little Gidding*), each named after a place Eliot visited, and each in the form of a musical quartet. Each deals with some aspect of the relation between time and eternity, the meaning of history, and the moments of illumination in which the human spirit achieves the moment of timeless insight **Little Gidding.** The title is derived from the name of a small Anglican religious community founded in 1625 and destroyed in 1647, in the course of the English Civil War. Many of the lines are made more comprehensible if one remembers that *Little Gidding* was written during the Second World War, the great fires of which in London undoubtedly reminded Eliot of the supremacy of fire as a destructive element. The "broken king" of l. 27 is Charles I, who stopped at Little Gidding following his defeat at the Battle of Naseby (1645) 2 **Sempiternal,** everlasting, eternal 10 **pentecostal fire.** On the Pentecost day (seventh Sunday following Easter) after the death and resurrection of Christ, the apostles heard "a sound from heaven as of a rushing mighty wind. . . . And there appeared unto them cloven tongues like as of fire. . . . And they were all filled with the Holy Ghost." See *Acts*, 2:2–4

Of sanctuary and choir.
    This is the death of water and fire.

80   In the uncertain hour before the morning
    Near the ending of interminable night
    At the recurrent end of the unending
After the dark dove with the flickering tongue
    Had passed below the horizon of his homing
    While the dead leaves still rattled on like tin
Over the asphalt where no other sound was
    Between three districts whence the smoke arose
    I met one walking, loitering and hurried
As if blown towards me like the metal leaves
90   Before the urban dawn wind unresisting.
    And as I fixed upon the down-turned face
That pointed scrutiny with which we challenge
    The first-met stranger in the waning dusk
    I caught the sudden look of some dead master
Whom I had known, forgotten, half recalled
    Both one and many; in the brown baked features
    The eyes of a familiar compound ghost°
Both intimate and unidentifiable.
    So I assumed a double part, and cried
    And heard another's voice cry: 'What! are *you*
100   here?'
Although we were not. I was still the same,
    Knowing myself yet being someone other—
    And he a face still forming; yet the words sufficed
To compel the recognition they preceded.
    And so, compliant to the common wind,
    Too strange to each other for misunderstanding,
In concord at this intersection time
    Of meeting nowhere, no before and after,
    We trod the pavement in a dead patrol.
110 I said: 'The wonder that I feel is easy,
    Yet ease is cause of wonder. Therefore speak:
    I may not comprehend, may not remember.'
And he: 'I am not eager to rehearse
    My thought and theory which you have forgotten.
    These things have served their purpose: let them be.
So with your own, and pray they be forgiven
    By others, as I pray you to forgive
    Both bad and good. Last season's fruit is eaten
And the fullfed beast shall kick the empty pail.
120   For last year's words belong to last year's language
    And next year's words await another voice.
But, as the passage now presents no hindrance
    To the spirit unappeased and peregrine°
    Between two worlds become much like each other,
So I find words I never thought to speak
    In streets I never thought I should revisit
    When I left my body on a distant shore.
Since our concern was speech, and speech impelled us
    To purify the dialect of the tribe°
130   And urge the mind to aftersight and foresight,

Let me disclose the gifts reserved for age
    To set a crown upon your lifetime's effort.
    First, the cold friction of expiring sense
Without enchantment, offering no promise
    But bitter tastelessness of shadow fruit
    As body and soul begin to fall asunder.
Second, the conscious impotence of rage
    At human folly, and the laceration
    Of laughter at what ceases to amuse.
And last, the rending pain of re-enactment   140
    Of all that you have done, and been; the shame
    Of motives late revealed, and the awareness
Of things ill done and done to others' harm
    Which once you took for exercise of virtue.
    Then fools' approval stings, and honour stains.
From wrong to wrong the exasperated spirit
    Proceeds, unless restored by that refining fire
    Where you must move in measure, like a dancer.'
The day was breaking. In the disfigured street
    He left me, with a kind of valediction,   150
    And faded on the blowing of the horn.°

III

There are three conditions which often look alike
Yet differ completely, flourish in the same hedgerow:
Attachment to self and to things and to persons,
    detachment
From self and from things and from persons; and,
    growing between them, indifference
Which resembles the others as death resembles life,
Being between two lives—unflowering, between
The live and the dead nettle. This is the use of
    memory:
For liberation—not less of love but expanding
Of love beyond desire, and so liberation   160
From the future as well as the past. Thus, love of a
    country
Begins as attachment to our own field of action
And comes to find that action of little importance
Though never indifferent. History may be servitude,
History may be freedom. See, now they vanish,
The faces and places, with the self which, as it could,
    loved them,
To become renewed, transfigured, in another pattern.

    Sin is Behovely,° but
All shall be well, and
All manner of thing shall be well.   170
If I think, again, of this place,
And of people, not wholly commendable,
Of no immediate kin or kindness,
But some of peculiar genius,
All touched by a common genius,
United in the strife which divided them;

---

97 **ghost.** Cf. Shakespeare, *Sonnet 59*, l. 9: "that affable familiar ghost"
123 **peregrine,** foreign   129 **To purify . . . tribe,** from *The Tomb of Edgar Poe* by
the French poet Stéphane Mallarmé

151 **faded . . . horn.** Cf. *Hamlet*, I, i, 157: "It faded on the crowing of the cock."
The horn is the all clear signal after an air raid   168 **Behovely,** fitting. This passage is drawn from the writings of Juliana of Norwich, a fourteenth-century religious writer, considered one of the greatest English mystics

If I think of a king° at nightfall,
Of three men, and more, on the scaffold
And a few who died forgotten
180 In other places, here and abroad,
And of one who died blind and quiet,
Why should we celebrate
These dead men more than the dying?
It is not to ring the bell backward
Nor is it an incantation
To summon the spectre of a Rose.
We cannot revive old factions
We cannot restore old policies
Or follow an antique drum.
190 These men, and those who opposed them
And those whom they opposed
Accept the constitution of silence
And are folded in a single party.
Whatever we inherit from the fortunate
We have taken from the defeated
What they had to leave us—a symbol:
A symbol perfected in death.
And all shall be well and
All manner of thing shall be well
200 By the purification of the motive
In the ground of our beseeching.

IV

The dove descending breaks the air
With flame of incandescent terror
Of which the tongues declare
The one discharge from sin and error.
The only hope, or else despair
    Lies in the choice of pyre or pyre—
    To be redeemed from fire by fire.

Who then devised the torment? Love.
210 Love is the unfamiliar Name
Behind the hands that wove
The intolerable shirt of flame°
Which human power cannot remove.
    We only live, only suspire
    Consumed by either fire or fire.

V

What we call the beginning is often the end
And to make an end is to make a beginning.
The end is where we start from. And every phrase
And sentence that is right (where every word is at
    home,
220 Taking its place to support the others,
The word neither diffident nor ostentatious,
An easy commerce of the old and the new,
The common word exact without vulgarity,
The formal word precise but not pedantic,

The complete consort° dancing together)
Every phrase and every sentence is an end and a
    beginning,
Every poem an epitaph. And any action
Is a step to the block, to the fire, down the sea's throat
Or to an illegible stone: and that is where we start.
We die with the dying: 230
See, they depart, and we go with them.
We are born with the dead:
See, they return, and bring us with them.
The moment of the rose and the moment of the yew-
    tree
Are of equal duration. A people without history
Is not redeemed from time, for history is a pattern
Of timeless moments. So, while the light fails
On a winter's afternoon, in a secluded chapel
History is now and England.
With the drawing of this Love and the voice of this
    Calling   240

    We shall not cease from exploration
And the end of all our exploring
Will be to arrive where we started
And know the place for the first time.
Through the unknown, remembered gate
When the last of earth left to discover
Is that which was the beginning;
At the source of the longest river
The voice of the hidden waterfall
And the children in the apple-tree   250
Not known, because not looked for
But heard, half-heard, in the stillness
Between two waves of the sea.
Quick now, here, now, always—
A condition of complete simplicity
(Costing not less than everything)
And all shall be well and
All manner of thing shall be well
When the tongues of flame are in-folded
Into the crowned knot of fire   260
And the fire and the rose are one.
(1942)

from THE SACRED WOOD

TRADITION AND THE INDIVIDUAL TALENT

I

In English writing we seldom speak of tradition,
though we occasionally apply its name in deploring its
absence. We cannot refer to "the tradition" or to "a
tradition"; at most, we employ the adjective in saying
that the poetry of So-and-so is "traditional" or even

177 **king,** Charles I. He and his advisors, Archbishop Laud and the Earl of Strafford (l. 178), were executed in 1649   212 **shirt of flame.** Deianira gave her husband Hercules the poisoned shirt of Nessus with the mistaken belief that it would
increase his love for her. Instead, it corroded his flesh so agonizingly that he
burned himself to death

225 **consort.** This word means both *company* and *harmony of sounds*. Both
meanings are to be taken here

"too traditional." Seldom, perhaps, does the word appear except in a phrase of censure. If otherwise, it is vaguely approbative, with the implication, as to the work approved, of some pleasing archaeological reconstruction. You can hardly make the word agreeable to English ears without this comfortable reference to the reassuring science of archaeology.

Certainly the word is not likely to appear in our appreciations of living or dead writers. Every nation, every race, has not only its own creative, but its own critical turn of mind; and is even more oblivious of the shortcomings and limitations of its critical habits than of those of its creative genius. We know, or think we know, from the enormous mass of critical writing that has appeared in the French language the critical method or habit of the French; we only conclude (we are such unconscious people) that the French are "more critical" than we, and sometimes even plume ourselves a little with the fact, as if the French were the less spontaneous. Perhaps they are; but we might remind ourselves that criticism is as inevitable as breathing, and that we should be none the worse for articulating what passes in our minds when we read a book and feel an emotion about it, for criticizing our own minds in their work of criticism. One of the facts that might come to light in this process is our tendency to insist, when we praise a poet, upon those aspects of his work in which he least resembles anyone else. In these aspects or parts of his work we pretend to find what is individual, what is the peculiar essence of the man. We dwell with satisfaction upon the poet's difference from his predecessors, especially his immediate predecessors; we endeavour to find something that can be isolated in order to be enjoyed. Whereas if we approach a poet without this prejudice we shall often find that not only the best, but the most individual parts of his work may be those in which the dead poets his ancestors, assert their immortality most vigorously. And I do not mean the impressionable period of adolescence, but the period of full maturity.

Yet if the only form of tradition, of handing down, consisted in following the ways of the immediate generation before us in a blind or timid adherence to its successes, "tradition" should positively be discouraged. We have seen many such simple currents soon lost in the sand; and novelty is better than repetition. Tradition is a matter of much wider significance. It cannot be inherited, and if you want it you must obtain it by great labour. It involves, in the first place, the historical sense, which we may call nearly indispensable to anyone who would continue to be a poet beyond his twenty-fifth year; and the historical sense involves a perception, not only of the pastness of the past, but of its presence the historical sense compels a man to write not merely with his own generation in his bones, but with a feeling that the whole of the literature of Europe from Homer and within it the whole of the

literature of his own country has a simultaneous existence and composes a simultaneous order. This historical sense, which is a sense of the timeless as well as of the temporal and of the timeless and of the temporal together, is what makes a writer traditional. And it is at the same time what makes a writer most acutely conscious of his place in time, of his contemporaneity.

No poet, no artist of any art, has his complete meaning alone. His significance, his appreciation is the appreciation of his relation to the dead poets and artists. You cannot value him alone; you must set him, for contrast and comparison, among the dead. I mean this as a principle of aesthetic, not merely historical, criticism. The necessity that he shall conform, that he shall cohere, is not one-sided; what happens when a new work of art is created is something that happens simultaneously to all the works of art which preceded it. The existing monuments form an ideal order among themselves, which is modified by the introduction of the new (the really new) work of art among them. The existing order is complete before the new work arrives; for order to persist after the supervention of novelty, the *whole* existing order must be, if ever so slightly, altered; and so the relations, proportions, values of each work of art toward the whole are readjusted; and this is conformity between the old and the new. Whoever has approved this idea of order, of the form of European, of English literature, will not find it preposterous that the past should be altered by the present as much as the present is directed by the past. And the poet who is aware of this will be aware of great difficulties and responsibilities.

In a peculiar sense he will be aware also that he must inevitably be judged by the standards of the past. I say judged, not amputated, by them; not judged to be as good as, or worse or better than, the dead; and certainly not judged by the canons of dead critics. It is a judgment, a comparison, in which two things are measured by each other. To conform merely would be for the new work not really to conform at all; it would not be new, and would therefore not be a work of art. And we do not quite say that the new is more valuable because it fits in; but its fitting in is a test of its value—a test, it is true, which can only be slowly and cautiously applied, for we are none of us infallible judges of conformity. We say: it appears to conform, and is perhaps individual, or it appears individual, and may conform; but we are hardly likely to find that it is one and not the other.

To proceed to a more intelligible exposition of the relation of the poet to the past: he can neither take the past as a lump, an indiscriminate bolus,° nor can he form himself wholly on one or two private admirations, nor can he form himself wholly upon one preferred period. The first course is inadmissible, the second is an important experience of youth, and the third is a

Tradition and the Individual Talent 115 **bolus,** a rounded mass, a large pill

120 pleasant and highly desirable supplement. The poet must be very conscious of the main current, which does not at all flow invariably through the most distinguished reputations. He must be quite aware of the obvious fact that art never improves, but that the material of art is never quite the same. He must be aware that the mind of Europe—the mind of his own country—a mind which he learns in time to be much more important than his own private mind—is a mind which changes, and that this change is a development
130 which abandons nothing *en route,* which does not superannuate either Shakespeare, or Homer, or the rock drawing of the Magdalenian draughtsmen.° That this development, refinement perhaps, complication certainly, is not, from the point of view of the artist, any improvement. Perhaps not even an improvement from the point of view of the psychologist or not to the extent which we imagine; perhaps only in the end based upon a complication in economics and machinery. But the difference between the present and the
140 past is that the conscious present is an awareness of the past in a way and to an extent which the past's awareness of itself cannot show.

Some one said: "The dead writers are remote from us because we *know* so much more than they did." Precisely, and they are that which we know.

I am alive to a usual objection to what is clearly part of my programme for the *métier* of poetry. The objection is that the doctrine requires a ridiculous amount of erudition (pedantry), a claim which can be rejected by
150 appeal to the lives of poets in any pantheon. It will even be affirmed that much learning deadens or perverts poetic sensibility. While, however, we persist in believing that a poet ought to know as much as will not encroach upon his necessary receptivity and necessary laziness, it is not desirable to confine knowledge to whatever can be put into a useful shape for examinations, drawing-rooms, or the still more pretentious modes of publicity. Some can absorb knowledge, the more tardy must sweat for it. Shakespeare acquired
160 more essential history from Plutarch° than most men could from the whole British Museum. What is to be insisted upon is that the poet must develop or procure the consciousness of the past and that he should continue to develop this consciousness throughout his career.

What happens is a continual surrender of himself as he is at the moment to something which is more valuable. The progress of an artist is a continual self-sacrifice, a continual extinction of personality.
170 There remains to define this process of depersonali-

zation and its relation to the sense of tradition. It is in this depersonalization that art may be said to approach the condition of science. I shall, therefore, invite you to consider, as a suggestive analogy, the action which takes place when a bit of finely filiated° platinum is introduced into a chamber containing oxygen and sulphur dioxide.

II

Honest criticism and sensitive appreciation is directed not upon the poet but upon the poetry. If we attend to the confused cries of the newspaper critics 180 and the susurrus° of popular repetition that follows, we shall hear the names of poets in great numbers; if we seek not Blue-book° knowledge but the enjoyment of poetry, and ask for a poem, we shall seldom find it. In the last article I tried to point out the importance of the relation of the poem to other poems by other authors, and suggested the conception of poetry as a living whole of all the poetry that has ever been written. The other aspect of this Impersonal theory of poetry is the relation of the poem to its author. And I hinted, by an 190 analogy, that the mind of the mature poet differs from that of the immature one not precisely in any valuation of "personality," not being necessarily more interesting, or having "more to say," but rather by being a more finely perfected medium in which special, or very varied, feelings are at liberty to enter into new combinations.

The analogy was that of the catalyst.° When the two gases previously mentioned are mixed in the presence of a filament of platinum, they form sulphurous acid. 200 This combination takes place only if the platinum is present; nevertheless the newly formed acid contains no trace of platinum, and the platinum itself is apparently unaffected; has remained inert, neutral, and unchanged. The mind of the poet is the shred of platinum. It may partly or exclusively operate upon the experience of the man himself; but, the more perfect the artist, the more completely separate in him will be the man who suffers and the mind which creates; the more perfectly will the mind digest and transmute the pas- 210 sions which are its material.

The experience, you will notice, the elements which enter the presence of the transforming catalyst, are of two kinds: emotions and feelings. The effect of a work of art upon the person who enjoys it is an experience different in kind from any experience not of art. It may be formed out of one emotion, or may be a combination of several; and various feelings, inhering for the writer in particular words or phrases or images, may be added to compose the final result. Or great poetry 220 may be made without the direct use of any emotion whatever: composed out of feelings solely. Canto XV

132 **Magdalenian draughtsmen,** the men who drew in the Magdalenian Age. The name *Magdalenian* is applied to a stage of the Stone Age and is named from the archaeological remains found at La Madeleine in the Dordogne, France. The Magdalenian workmen used tools of horn and bone and attained a high quality of craftsmanship 160 **Plutarch,** the important Greek biographer (46?-?120). His major work is the *Parallel Lives* of twenty-three Greeks and twenty-three Romans. The work was translated into French during the Renaissance and from the French into English by Sir Thomas North (1579). North's translation was Shakespeare's main source of classical learning; it was from the *Lives* that he derived material for his *Julius Caesar, Coriolanus,* and *Antony and Cleopatra*

175 **filiated,** drawn out like a fine wire   181 **susurrus,** rustling whisper 183 **Blue-book,** official British government publication   198 **catalyst,** a substance that initiates a chemical reaction but is unaffected by it

of the *Inferno* (Brunetto Latini)° is a working up of the emotion evident in the situation; but the effect, though single as that of any work of art, is obtained by considerable complexity of detail. The last quatrain gives an image, a feeling attaching to an image, which "came," which did not develop simply out of what precedes, but which was probably in suspension in the poet's mind until the proper combination arrived for it to add itself to. The poet's mind is in fact a receptacle for seizing and storing up numberless feelings, phrases, images, which remain there until all the particles which can unite to form a new compound are present together.

If you compare several representative passages of the greatest poetry you see how great is the variety of types of combination, and also how completely any semi-ethical criterion of "sublimity" misses the mark. For it is not the "greatness," the intensity, of the emotions, the components, but the intensity of the artistic process, the pressure, so to speak, under which the fusion takes place, that counts. The episode of Paolo and Francesca° employs a definite emotion, but the intensity of the poetry is something quite different from whatever intensity in the supposed experience it may give the impression of. It is no more intense, furthermore, than Canto XXVI, the voyage of Ulysses, which has not the direct dependence upon an emotion. Great variety is possible in the process of transmutation of emotion: the murder of Agamemnon,° or the agony of Othello, gives an artistic effect apparently closer to a possible original than the scenes from Dante. In the *Agamemnon*, the artistic emotion approximates to the emotion of an actual spectator; in *Othello* to the emotion of the protagonist himself. But the difference between art and the event is always absolute; the combination which is the murder of Agamemnon is probably as complex as that which is the voyage of Ulysses. In either case there has been a fusion of elements. The ode of Keats contains a number of feelings which have nothing particular to do with the nightingale, but which the nightingale, partly, perhaps, because of its attractive name, and partly because of its reputation, served to bring together.

The point of view which I am struggling to attack is perhaps related to the metaphysical theory of the substantial unity of the soul: for my meaning is, that the poet has, not a "personality" to express, but a medium and not a personality, in which impressions and experiences combine in peculiar and unexpected ways. Impressions and experiences which are impor-

tant for the man may take no place in the poetry, and those which become important in the poetry may play quite a negligible part in the man, the personality.

I will quote a passage which is unfamiliar enough to be regarded with fresh attention in the light—or darkness—of these observations:

> And now methinks° I could e'en chide myself
> For doating on her beauty, though her death   280
> Shall be revenged after no common action.
> Does the silkworm expend her yellow labours
> For thee? For thee does she undo herself?
> Are lordships sold to maintain ladyships
> For the poor benefit of a bewildering minute?
> Why does yon fellow falsify highways,
> And put his life between the judge's lips,
> To refine such a thing—keeps horse and men
> To beat their valours for her? . . .

In this passage (as is evident if it is taken in its context) there is a combination of positive and negative emotions: an intensely strong attraction toward beauty and an equally intense fascination by the ugliness which is contrasted with it and which destroys it. This balance of contrasted emotion is in the dramatic situation to which the speech is pertinent, but that situation alone is inadequate to it. This is, so to speak, the structural emotion, provided by the drama. But the whole effect, the dominant tone, is due to the fact that a number of floating feelings, having an affinity to this emotion by no means superficially evident, have combined with it to give us a new art emotion.

It is not in his personal emotions, the emotions provoked by particular events in his life, that the poet is in any way remarkable or interesting. His particular emotions may be simple, or crude, or flat. The emotion in his poetry will be a very complex thing, but not with the complexity of the emotions of people who have very complex or unusual emotions in life. One error, in fact, of eccentricity in poetry is to seek for new human emotions to express; and in this search for novelty in the wrong place it discovers the perverse. The business of the poet is not to find new emotions, but to use the ordinary ones and, in working them up into poetry, to express feelings which are not in actual emotions at all. And emotions which he has never experienced will serve his turn as well as those familiar to him. Consequently, we must believe that "emotion recollected in tranquillity"° is an inexact formula. For it is neither emotion, nor recollection, nor, without distortion of meaning, tranquillity. It is a concentration, and a new thing resulting from the concentration, of a very great number of experiences which to the practical and ac-

223 **Brunetto Latini,** a great Florentine scholar (1210?–?1294), teacher of the Italian poet Dante Alighieri (1265–1321). Dante greatly admired Brunetto's learning but deplored his worldliness and vices and therefore depicts him in Canto XV of the *Inferno* among those who are being punished for sodomy   244 **Paolo and Francesca.** The tragic story of these two lovers, ill-starred in life and condemned after death to whirl about in Hell on the ceaseless blasts of unsatisfied desire, is told by Dante in his *Inferno*, V, 75 ff.   251 **Agamemnon,** a hero of the Greeks in the Trojan War. After the sack of Troy he returned to his home in Argos, where he was murdered by his faithless wife, Clytemnestra, and her lover, Aegisthus. Subsequently this murder was avenged by Agamemnon's son, Orestes. The tragic story was the subject of a play by Aeschylus (525–456 B.C.)

279–289 **And now methinks, etc.,** spoken by Vindici in *The Revenger's Tragedy* (1607) by Cyril Tourneur (1575?–1626), III, v, 71–82   318–319 **emotion . . . tranquillity,** In the Preface to the *Lyrical Ballads*, Wordsworth states that poetry "takes its origin from emotion recollected in tranquillity"

tive person would not seem to be experiences at all; it is a concentration which does not happen consciously or of deliberation. These experiences are not "recollected," and they finally unite in an atmosphere which is "tranquil" only in that it is a passive attending upon the event. Of course this is not quite the whole story. There is a great deal, in the writing of poetry, which must be conscious and deliberate. In fact, the bad poet is usually unconscious where he ought to be conscious, and conscious where he ought to be unconscious. Both errors tend to make him "personal." Poetry is not a turning loose of emotion, but an escape from emotion; it is not the expression of personality, but an escape from personality. But, of course, only those who have personality and emotions know what it means to want to escape from these things.

III

340 ὁ δὲ νοῦς, ἴσως, θειότερόν τι καὶ ἀπαθές ἐστιν°

This essay proposes to halt at the frontier of metaphysics or mysticism, and confine itself to such practical conclusions as can be applied by the responsible person interested in poetry. To divert interest from the poet to the poetry is a laudable aim: for it would conduce to a juster estimation of actual poetry, good and bad. There are many people who appreciate the expression of sincere emotion in verse, and there is a smaller number of people who can appreciate technical excellence. But very few know when there is expression of *significant* emotion, emotion which has its life in the poem and not in the history of the poet. The emotion of art is impersonal. And the poet cannot reach this impersonality without surrendering himself wholly to the work to be done. And he is not likely to know what is to be done unless he lives in what is not merely the present, but the present moment of the past, unless he is conscious, not of what is dead, but of what is already living.

(1920)

W. H. AUDEN
1907–1973

Wystan Hugh Auden was born in York in 1907. His father was a doctor, and his mother had been a nurse. The family was devoutly Anglican. After finishing the usual preparatory school course, Auden entered Christ Church, Oxford, in 1925. While there, he became interested in literature and in writing and

attracted great attention as a poet. He also became friends with such other literary intellectuals as C. Day-Lewis (1904–1972), Louis MacNeice (1907–1963), and Stephen Spender (1909–   ). At this time he also became interested in revolutionary politics and fell away from both Anglicanism and Christianity. After graduation he spent a year in Berlin, where he became enamored of German writers and their works, especially the plays of Bertolt Brecht (1898–1956). Upon returning to England, he taught school for five years. During 1935–1936 he was employed by the General Post Office in making documentary films.

In the thirties Auden published several books: his first volume, *Poems*, in 1930; an analysis of contemporary life, *The Orators*, in 1932; a satirical drama, *The Dance of Death*, in 1933; and with Christopher Isherwood (1904–   ), English critic and novelist and a personal friend, two satirical dramas—*The Dog Beneath the Skin*, in 1935, and *The Ascent of F 6*, in 1936; and a volume of miscellaneous verse, *Look, Stranger*, in 1936 (published in the United States as *On This Island*, 1937).

Always a wide reader and a keen social observer, Auden found rich material for his varied creative purposes. His journey to Iceland in 1936 with MacNeice resulted in a joint account of their experiences in *Letters from Iceland* (1937). A visit to China with Isherwood in 1938 furnished material for *Journey to a War* (1939). Another satirical drama, *On the Frontier*, in collaboration with Isherwood, and *Selected Poems* appeared in 1938. In 1939 Auden and Isherwood decided to settle in the United States, where for two years Auden was a member of the staff of the New School for Social Research in New York. Subsequently Auden became an American citizen. His change of citizenship was accompanied by changes in intellectual and religious perspectives as well. *The Double Man* (1940) depicted his thoughts on the verge of a new commitment to Christianity. In 1944 he wrote the religious Christmas oratory *For the Time Being*. He published his *Collected Poetry* in 1945. His new intellectual perspective is perhaps best illustrated in *The Age of Anxiety* (1947), which won him the Pulitzer Prize in 1948.

After 1948 Auden fell into a pattern of leaving New York during the summer months and residing at various spots on the Continent. His publishing remained prolific. *Nones* appeared in 1952, and *The Shield of Achilles* (1955), *The Old Man's Road* (1956), *The Dyer's Hand* (1957), *Five Poems* (1960), *Homage to Clio* (1960), and *Elegy for Young Lovers* (1961) followed in succession. Among the many honors that Auden received during this period was the professorship of poetry at Oxford (1956–1961). More poems, *City Without Walls*, followed in 1969. In 1970 Auden published a commonplace book, *A Certain World*. Auden spent his last months at Christ Church, Oxford, where he died in 1973.

340 ὃ . . . ἔστιν. Possibly the mind is too divine, and is therefore unaffected —Aristotle's *On the Soul*, I, iv (translation by W. S. Hert)

AS I WALKED OUT ONE EVENING

As I walked out one evening,
   Walking down Bristol Street,
The crowds upon the pavement
   Were fields of harvest wheat.

And down by the brimming river
   I heard a lover sing
Under an arch of the railway:
   'Love has no ending.

'I'll love you dear, I'll love you
10   Till China and Africa meet,
And the river jumps over the mountain
   And the salmon sing in the street,

'I'll love you till the ocean
   Is folded and hung up to dry
And the seven stars° go squawking
   Like geese about the sky.

'The years shall run like rabbits,
   For in my arms I hold
The Flower of the Ages,
20   And the first love of the world.'

But all the clocks in the city
   Began to whirr and chime:
'O let not Time deceive you,
   You cannot conquer Time.

'In the burrows of the Nightmare
   Where Justice naked is,
Time watches from the shadow
   And coughs when you would kiss.

'In headaches and in worry
30   Vaguely life leaks away,
And Time will have his fancy
   To-morrow or to-day.

'Into many a green valley
   Drifts the appalling snow;
Time breaks the threaded dances
   And the diver's brilliant bow.

'O plunge your hands in water,
   Plunge them in up to the wrist;
Stare, stare in the basin
40   And wonder what you've missed.

'The glacier knocks in the cupboard,
   The desert sighs in the bed,
And the crack in the tea-cup opens
   A lane to the land of the dead.

'Where the beggars raffle the banknotes
   And the Giant is enchanting to Jack,
And the Lily-white Boy is a Roarer,
   And Jill goes down on her back.°

'O look, look in the mirror,
   O look in your distress;   50
Life remains a blessing
   Although you cannot bless.

'O stand, stand at the window
   As the tears scald and start;
You shall love your crooked neighbour
   With your crooked heart.'

It was late, late in the evening,
   The lovers they were gone;
The clocks had ceased their chiming,
   And the deep river ran on.   60
(1938)

LULLABY

Lay your sleeping head, my love,
Human on my faithless arm;
Time and fevers burn away
Individual beauty from
Thoughtful children, and the grave
Proves the child ephemeral:
But in my arms till break of day
Let the living creature lie,
Mortal, guilty, but to me
The entirely beautiful.   10

Soul and body have no bounds:
To lovers as they lie upon
Her tolerant enchanted slope
In their ordinary swoon,
Grave the vision Venus sends
Of supernatural sympathy,
Universal love and hope;
While an abstract insight wakes
Among the glaciers and the rocks
The hermit's carnal ecstasy.   20

Certainty, fidelity
On the stroke of midnight pass
Like vibrations of a bell
And fashionable madmen raise
Their pedantic boring cry:
Every farthing of the cost,
All the dreaded cards foretell,
Shall be paid, but from this night
Not a whisper, not a thought,
Not a kiss nor look be lost.   30

As I Walked Out One Evening   15 **seven stars,** the Pleiades, the seven daughters of Atlas turned according to Greek mythology into a group of stars

45–48 **Where . . . back.** The world of nursery rhyme (Jack and Jill) and fairy tale (Jack the Giant-Killer) turned awry

Beauty, midnight, vision dies:
Let the winds of dawn that blow
Softly round your dreaming head
Such a day of welcome show
Eye and knocking heart may bless,
Find our mortal world enough;
Noons of dryness find you fed
By the involuntary powers,
Nights of insult let you pass
40 Watched by every human love.
(1937)

IF I COULD TELL YOU

Time will say nothing but I told you so,
Time only knows the price we have to pay;
If I could tell you I would let you know.

If we should weep when clowns put on their show,
If we should stumble when musicians play,
Time will say nothing but I told you so.

There are no fortunes to be told, although,
Because I love you more than I can say,
If I could tell you I would let you know.

The winds must come from somewhere when they
10   blow,
There must be reasons why the leaves decay;
Time will say nothing but I told you so.

Perhaps the roses really want to grow,
The vision seriously intends to stay;
If I could tell you I would let you know.

Suppose the lions all get up and go,
And all the brooks and soldiers run away;
Will Time say nothing but I told you so?
If I could tell you I would let you know.
(1941)

THE FALL OF ROME

(FOR CYRIL CONNOLLY)

The piers are pummelled by the waves;
In a lonely field the rain
Lashes an abandoned train;
Outlaws fill the mountain caves.

Fantastic grow the evening gowns;
Agents of the Fisc° pursue

The Fall of Rome   6 **Fisc,** state treasury

Absconding tax-defaulters through
The sewers of provincial towns.

Private rites of magic send
The temple prostitutes to sleep;   10
All the literati keep
An imaginary friend.

Cerebrotonic° Cato° may
Extol the Ancient Disciplines,
But the muscle-bound Marines
Mutiny for food and pay.

Caesar's double-bed is warm
As an unimportant clerk
Writes *I DO NOT LIKE MY WORK*
On a pink official form.   20

Unendowed with wealth or pity,
Little birds with scarlet legs,
Sitting on their speckled eggs,
Eye each flu-infected city.

Altogether elsewhere, vast
Herds of reindeer move across
Miles and miles of golden moss,
Silently and very fast.
(1947)

SEPTEMBER 1, 1939°

I sit in one of the dives
On Fifty-second Street
Uncertain and afraid
As the clever hopes expire
Of a low dishonest decade:
Waves of anger and fear
Circulate over the bright
And darkened lands of the earth,
Obsessing our private lives;
The unmentionable odour of death   10
Offends the September night.

Accurate scholarship can
Unearth the whole offence
From Luther until now
That has driven a culture mad,
Find what occurred at Linz,
What huge imago made
A psychopathic god:
I and the public know

13 **Cerebrotonic,** marked by predominance of intellectual over social or physical
factors and by sensitivity, introversion, and shyness   **Cato,** Roman statesman
known as Cato the Censor (234–149 B.C.)   **September 1, 1939.** The date of the
invasion of Poland by the forces of the Third Reich. As a result of this invasion,
both England and France declared war on Germany on September 3

20 What all schoolchildren learn,
Those to whom evil is done
Do evil in return.

Exiled Thucydides° knew
All that a speech can say
About Democracy,
And what dictators do,
The elderly rubbish they talk
To an apathetic grave;
Analysed all in his book,
30 The enlightenment driven away,
The habit-forming pain,
Mismanagement and grief:
We must suffer them all again.

Into this neutral air
Where blind skyscrapers use
Their full height to proclaim
The strength of Collective Man,
Each language pours its vain
Competitive excuse:
40 But who can live for long
In an euphoric dream;
Out of the mirror they stare,
Imperialism's face
And the international wrong.

Faces along the bar
Cling to their average day:
The lights must never go out,
The music must always play,
All the conventions conspire
50 To make this fort assume
The furniture of home;
Lest we should see where we are,
Lost in a haunted wood,
Children afraid of the night
Who have never been happy or good.

The windiest militant trash
Important Persons shout
Is not so crude as our wish:
What mad Nijinsky wrote
60 About Diaghilev°
Is true of the normal heart;
For the error bred in the bone
Of each woman and each man
Craves what it cannot have,
Not universal love
But to be loved alone.

From the conservative dark
Into the ethical life

The dense commuters come,
Repeating their morning vow; 70
"I *will* be true to the wife,
I'll concentrate more on my work,"
And helpless governors wake
To resume their compulsory game:
Who can release them now,
Who can reach the deaf,
Who can speak for the dumb?

Defenceless under the night
Our world in stupor lies;
Yet, dotted everywhere, 80
Ironic points of light
Flash out wherever the Just
Exchange their messages:
May I, composed like them
Or Eros and of dust,
Beleaguered by the same
Negation and despair,
Show an affirming flame.
(1939)

IN MEMORY OF W. B. YEATS

1

He disappeared in the dead of winter:°
The brooks were frozen, the air-ports almost deserted,
And snow disfigured the public statues;
The mercury sank in the mouth of the dying day.
O all the instruments agree
The day of his death was a dark cold day.

Far from his illness
The wolves ran on through the evergreen forests,
The peasant river was untempted by the fashionable
quays;
By mourning tongues 10
The death of the poet was kept from his poems.

But for him it was his last afternoon as himself,
An afternoon of nurses and rumors;
The provinces of his body revolted,
The squares of his mind were empty,
Silence invaded the suburbs,
The current of his feeling failed: he became his
admirers.°

Now he is scattered among a hundred cities
And wholly given over to unfamiliar affections;
To find his happiness in another kind of wood 20
And be punished under a foreign code of conscience.
The words of a dead man
Are modified in the guts of the living.

23 **Thucydides,** Greek historian and orator of the fifth century B.C. Considered the greatest historian of antiquity. The book referred to in l. 29 is his *History of the Peloponnesian War* 59–60 **What . . . Diaghilev.** Waslaw Nijinsky (1890–1950) was a famous Russian ballet dancer. He first appeared in Paris in 1909 with Sergei Diaghilev's (1872–1929) Ballet Russe. Diaghilev was a famous ballet producer and art critic. His relationship with Diaghilev was stormy, and Nijinsky's career came to an end in 1919 when he became insane

In Memory of W. B. Yeats 1 **He . . . winter.** Yeats died on the French Riviera on January 28, 1939

But in the importance and noise of tomorrow
When the brokers are roaring like beasts on the floor of
    the Bourse,°
And the poor have the sufferings to which they are
    fairly accustomed,
And each in the cell of himself is almost convinced of
    his freedom;
A few thousand will think of this day
As one thinks of a day when one did something slightly
    unusual.

30 O all the instruments agree
The day of his death was a dark cold day.

                            2
You were silly like us: your gift survived it all;
The parish of rich women,° physical decay,
Yourself; mad Ireland hurt you into poetry.
Now Ireland has her madness and her weather still,
For poetry makes nothing happen: it survives
In the valley of its saying where executives
Would never want to tamper; it flows south
From ranches of isolation and the busy griefs,
40 Raw towns that we believe and die in; it survives,
A way of happening, a mouth.

                            3
Earth, receive an honored guest;
William Yeats is laid to rest:
Let the Irish vessel lie
Emptied of its poetry.

Time° that is intolerant
Of the brave and innocent,
And indifferent in a week
To a beautiful physique,

50 Worships language and forgives
Everyone by whom it lives;
Pardons cowardice, conceit,
Lays its honors at their feet.

Time that with this strange excuse
Pardoned Kipling and his views,°
And will pardon Paul Claudel,
Pardons him for writing well.

In the nightmare of the dark
All the dogs of Europe bark,°
60 And the living nations wait,
Each sequestered in its hate;

Intellectual disgrace
Stares from every human face,
And the seas of pity lie
Locked and frozen in each eye.

Follow, poet, follow right
To the bottom of the night,
With your unconstraining voice
Still persuade us to rejoice;

With the farming of a verse   70
Make a vineyard of the curse,°
Sing of human unsuccess
In a rapture of distress;

In the deserts of the heart
Let the healing fountain start,
In the prison of his days
Teach the free man how to praise.
(1940)

MUSÉE DES BEAUX ARTS°

About suffering they were never wrong,
The Old Masters: how well they understood
Its human position; how it takes place
While someone else is eating or opening a window or
    just walking dully along;
How, when the aged are reverently, passionately
    waiting
For the miraculous birth, there always must be
Children who did not specially want it to happen,
    skating
On a pond at the edge of the wood:
They never forgot
That even the dreadful martyrdom must run its course 10
Anyhow in a corner, some untidy spot
Where the dogs go on with their doggy life and the
    torturer's horse
Scratches its innocent behind on a tree.

In Breughel's° Icarus, for instance: how everything
    turns away
Quite leisurely from the disaster; the ploughman may
Have heard the splash, the forsaken cry,
But for him it was not an important failure; the sun
    shone
As it had to on the white legs disappearing into the
    green

25 **Bourse**, the Paris stock exchange   33 **parish of rich women.** An allusion to
the fact that in his early years, and even in his later life, Yeats counted wealthy
women among his patrons   46–57 **Time . . . well.** These three stanzas were deleted from Auden's 1966 edition of his *Collected Poems*   55 **Pardoned . . . views.**
Both Rudyard Kipling (1865–1936) and the French poet Paul Claudel (1868–1955)
(l. 56) were known for their reactionary politics. Auden regards them as tokens of
poets who were politically and morally in the wrong, but still writers, members of
his "family" as it were   59 **All . . . bark.** World War II was to begin in September 1939

71 **vineyard . . . curse,** a reference to the expulsion of Adam and Eve from the
Garden of Eden. The metaphor represents the making of good out of bad
Musée des Beaux Arts. The title means "Museum of Fine Arts," which is the
name of the museum in Brussels owning Brueghel's *Icarus*   14 **Brueghel,** Pieter
Brueghel (1520?–1569), famous Flemish painter. Icarus was an Athenian youth
who tried to escape from Crete with his father by the use of artificial wings. He
flew too near the sun; the wax of the wings melted and he fell into the sea and
was drowned

Water; and the expensive delicate ship that must have
    seen
20 Something amazing, a boy falling out of the sky,
    Had somewhere to get to and sailed calmly on.
    (1940)

IN PRAISE OF LIMESTONE

If it form the one landscape that we the inconstant
    ones,
    Are consistently homesick for, this is chiefly
Because it dissolves in water. Mark these rounded
    slopes
    With their surface fragrance of thyme and beneath
A secret system of caves and conduits; hear these
    springs
    That spurt out everywhere with a chuckle
Each filling a private pool for its fish and carving
    Its own little ravine whose cliffs entertain
The butterfly and the lizard; examine this region
10   Of short distances and definite places:
What could be more like Mother or a fitter background
    For her son, for the nude young male who lounges
Against a rock displaying his dildo,° never doubting
    That for all his faults he is loved, whose works are
    but
Extensions of his power to charm? From weathered
    outcrop
    To hill-top temple, from appearing waters to
Conspicuous fountains, from a wild to a formal
    vineyard,
    Are ingenious but short steps that a child's wish
To receive more attention than his brothers, whether
20   By pleasing or teasing, can easily take.

Watch, then, the band of rivals as they climb up and
    down
    Their steep stone gennels° in twos and threes, some-
    times
Arm in arm, but never, thank God, in step; or engaged
    On the shady side of a square at midday in
Voluble discourse, knowing each other too well to
    think
    There are any important secrets, unable
To conceive a god whose temper-tantrums are moral
    And not to be pacified by a clever line
Or a good lay: for, accustomed to a stone that
    responds,
30   They have never had to veil their faces in awe
Of a crater whose blazing fury could not be fixed;
    Adjusted to the local needs of valleys
Where everything can be touched or reached by
    walking,
    Their eyes have never looked into infinite space

Through the lattice-work of a nomad's comb; born
    lucky,
    Their legs have never encountered the fungi
And insects of the jungle, the monstrous forms and
    lives
    With which we have nothing, we like to hope, in
    common.
So, when one of them goes to the bad, the way his
    mind works
    Remains comprehensible: to become a pimp   40
Or deal in fake jewellery or ruin a fine tenor voice
    For effects that bring down the house, could happen
    to all
But the best and the worst of us . . .
                              That is why, I suppose,
    The best and worst never stayed here long but
    sought
Immoderate soils where the beauty was not so
    external,
    The light less public and the meaning of life
Something more than a mad camp. 'Come!' cried the
    granite wastes,
    'How evasive is your humour, how accidental
Your kindest kiss, how permanent is death.'
    (Saints-to-be
    Slipped away sighing.) 'Come!' purred the clays and
    gravels.   50
'On our plains there is room for armies to drill; rivers
    Wait to be tamed and slaves to construct you a tomb
In the grand manner; soft as the earth is mankind and
    both
    Need to be altered.' (Intendant Caesars rose and
Left, slamming the door.) But the really reckless were
    fetched
    By an older colder voice, the oceanic whisper:
'I am the solitude that asks and promises nothing;
    That is how I shall set you free. There is no love;
There are only the various envies, all of them sad.'
    They were right, my dear, all those voices were right 60
And still are; this land is not the sweet home that it
    looks,
    Nor its peace the historical calm of a site
Where something was settled once and for all: A
    backward
    And dilapidated province, connected
To the big busy world by a tunnel, with a certain
    Seedy appeal, is that all it is now? Not quite:
It has a worldly duty which in spite of itself
    It does not neglect, but calls into question
All the Great Powers assumed; it disturbs our rights.
    The poet,
    Admired for his earnest habit of calling   70
The sun the sun, his mind Puzzle, is made uneasy
    By these solid statues which so obviously doubt
His antimythological myth; and these gamins,°
    Pursuing the scientist down the tiled colonnade

In Praise of Limestone   13 **dildo,** phallus   22 **gennels,** narrow passageways   73 **gamins,** street urchins

With such lively offers, rebuke his concern for
    Nature's
    Remotest aspects: I, too, am reproached, for what
And how much you know. Not to lose time, not to get
    caught,
    Not to be left behind, not, please! to resemble
The beasts who repeat themselves, or a thing like
    water
80   Or stone whose conduct can be predicted, these
Are our Common Prayer, whose greatest comfort is
    music
    Which can be made anywhere, is invisible,
And does not smell. In so far as we have to look
    forward
    To death as a fact, no doubt we are right: But if
Sins can be forgiven, if bodies rise from the dead,
    These modifications of matter into
Innocent athletes and gesticulating fountains,
    Made solely for pleasure, make a further point:
The blessed will not care what angle they are regarded
    from,
90   Having nothing to hide. Dear, I know nothing of
Either, but when I try to imagine a faultless love
    Or the life to come, what I hear is the murmur
Of underground streams, what I see is a limestone
    landscape.

(1948)

GRAHAM GREENE
1904–

Graham Greene was born in Hertfordshire in 1904, the son of the headmaster of Berkhamsted School. He attended his father's school but was unhappy there and ran away. He was subsequently sent for treatment to a London psychoanalyst in whose house he lived for six happy months. He went on to Balliol College, Oxford, where he published a book of verse, *Babbling April* in 1925, the year he took his degree. The following year he converted from Anglicanism to Roman Catholicism, which was to have an important influence on his later fiction, and began a career as a journalist. After spending some time on the staff of the London *Times,* he decided in 1929 to become a free-lance writer and critic. From 1937 to 1941 he served as movie and literary critic of the *Spectator.* During World War II he served in the Foreign Office.

His work may be divided, to use his own classification, into "entertainments" and "novels." The former are, for the most part, literary thrillers, such as *A Gun for Sale* (1936), *The Ministry of Fear* (1943), and *The*

Third Man (1949), a screenplay. His entertainments deal with situations of secrecy and betrayal, spies and espionage. In his more serious novels, among them *Brighton Rock* (1938), *The Power and the Glory* (1940), *The Heart of the Matter* (1948), *The End of the Affair* (1951), and *A Burnt-Out Case* (1961), Greene reflects on his religious convictions and probes the nature of good and evil on both the personal and doctrinal level. *Our Man in Havana* (1958) is a spoof of his spy novels. He is also the author of several plays, movie scripts, and many excellent short stories. He is equally at ease dealing with the decaying inner cities of modern England or the remote interiors of tropical countries or sophisticated Continental settings. His most recent novels are *Travels with My Aunt* (1970), *The Honorary Consul* (1973), and *The Human Factor* (1978). Greene now lives alternately in Paris and Antibes, France.

THE DESTRUCTORS

I

It was on the eve of August Bank Holiday° that the latest recruit became the leader of the Wormsley Common Gang. No one was surprised except Mike, but Mike at the age of nine was surprised by everything. "If you don't shut your mouth," somebody once said to him, "you'll get a frog down it." After that Mike had kept his teeth tightly clamped except when the surprise was too great.

The new recruit had been with the gang since the beginning of the summer holidays, and there were pos- 10 sibilities about his brooding silence that all recognized. He never wasted a word even to tell his name until that was required of him by the rules. When he said "Trevor" it was a statement of fact, not as it would have been with the others a statement of shame or defiance. Nor did anyone laugh except Mike, who finding himself without support and meeting the dark gaze of the newcomer opened his mouth and was quiet again. There was every reason why T., as he was afterwards referred to, should have been an object of mock- 20 ery—there was his name (and they substituted the initial because otherwise they had no excuse not to laugh at it), the fact that his father, a former architect and present clerk, had "come down in the world" and that his mother considered herself better than the neighbours. What but an odd quality of danger, of the unpredictable, established him in the gang without any ignoble ceremony of initiation?

The gang met every morning in an impromptu car-park, the site of the last bomb of the first blitz. The 30 leader, who was known as Blackie, claimed to have

---

The Destructors   1 **Bank Holiday,** an official holiday in England: the banks are closed

heard it fall, and no one was precise enough in his dates to point out that he would have been one year old and fast asleep on the down platform of Wormsley Common Underground Station. On one side of the car-park leant the first occupied house, number 3, of the shattered Northwood Terrace—literally leant, for it had suffered from the blast of the bomb and the side walls were supported on wooden struts. A smaller bomb and some incendiaries had fallen beyond, so that the house stuck up like a jagged tooth and carried on the further wall relics of its neighbour, a dado,° the remains of a fireplace. T., whose words were almost confined to voting "Yes" or "No" to the plan of operations proposed each day by Blackie, once startled the whole gang by saying broodingly, "Wren° built that house, father says."

"Who's Wren?"

"The man who built St. Paul's."

"Who cares?" Blackie said. "It's only old Misery's."

Old Misery—whose real name was Thomas—had once been a builder and decorator. He lived alone in the crippled house, doing for himself: once a week you could see him coming back across the common with bread and vegetables, and once as the boys played in the car-park he put his head over the smashed wall of his garden and looked at them.

"Been to the loo,°" one of the boys said, for it was common knowledge that since the bombs fell something had gone wrong with the pipes of the house and Old Misery was too mean to spend money on the property. He could do the redecorating himself at cost price, but he had never learnt plumbing. The loo was a wooden shed at the bottom of the narrow garden with a star-shaped hole in the door: it had escaped the blast which had smashed the house next door and sucked out the window-frames of No. 3.

The next time the gang became aware of Mr. Thomas was more surprising. Blackie, Mike, and a thin yellow boy, who for some reason was called by his surname Summers, met him on the common coming back from the market. Mr. Thomas stopped them. He said glumly, "You belong to the lot that play in the car-park?"

Mike was about to answer when Blackie stopped him. As the leader he had responsibilities. "Suppose we are?" he said ambiguously.

"I got some chocolates," Mr. Thomas said. "Don't like 'em myself. Here you are. Not enough to go round, I don't suppose. There never is," he added with sombre conviction. He handed over three packets of Smarties.

The gang were puzzled and perturbed by this action and tried to explain it away. "Bet someone dropped them and he picked 'em up," somebody suggested.

"Pinched 'em and then got in a bleeding funk,°" another thought aloud.

"It's a bribe," Summers said. "He wants us to stop bouncing balls on his wall."

"We'll show him we don't take bribes," Blackie said, and they sacrificed the whole morning to the game of bouncing that only Mike was young enough to enjoy. There was no sign from Mr. Thomas.

Next day T. astonished them all. He was late at the rendezvous, and the voting for that day's exploit took place without him. At Blackie's suggestion the gang was to disperse in pairs, take buses at random, and see how many free rides could be snatched from unwary conductors (the operation was to be carried out in pairs to avoid cheating). They were drawing lots for their companions when T. arrived.

"Where you been, T.?" Blackie asked. "You can't vote now. You know the rules."

"I've been *there*," T. said. He looked at the ground, as though he had thoughts to hide.

"Where?"

"At Old Misery's." Mike's mouth opened and then hurriedly closed again with a click. He had remembered the frog.

"At Old Misery's?" Blackie said. There was nothing in the rules against it, but he had a sensation that T. was treading on dangerous ground. He asked hopefully, "Did you break in?"

"No. I rang the bell."

"And what did you say?"

"I said I wanted to see his house."

"What did he do?"

"He showed it me."

"Pinch anything?"

"No."

"What did you do it for then?"

The gang had gathered round: it was as though an impromptu court were to form and to try some case of deviation. T. said, "It's a beautiful house," and still watching the ground, meeting no one's eyes, he licked his lips first one way, then the other.

"What do you mean, a beautiful house?" Blackie asked with scorn.

"It's got a staircase two hundred years old like a corkscrew. Nothing holds it up."

"What do you mean, nothing holds it up. Does it float?"

"It's to do with opposite forces, Old Misery said."

"What else?"

"There's panelling."

"Like in the Blue Boar?"

---

42 **dado,** the lower part of an interior wall when specially decorated or faced
46 **Wren,** Christopher Wren (1631–1723), famous English architect who proposed plans for rebuilding London after the Great Fire of 1666. He designed and rebuilt St. Paul's Cathedral as well as fifty-two other churches in London   59 **loo,** toilet

87 **funk,** state of panic or paralyzing fear

"Two hundred years old."

"Is Old Misery two hundred years old?"

140　Mike laughed suddenly and then was quiet again. The meeting was in a serious mood. For the first time since T. had strolled into the car-park on the first day of the holidays his position was in danger. It only needed a single use of his real name and the gang would be at his heels.

"What did you do it for?" Blackie asked. He was just, he had no jealousy, he was anxious to retain T. in the gang if he could. It was the word "beautiful" that worried him—that belonged to a class world that you 150　could still see parodied at the Wormsley Common Empire by a man wearing a top hat and a monocle, with a haw-haw accent. He was tempted to say, "My dear Trevor, old chap," and unleash his hell hounds. "If you'd broken in," he said sadly—that indeed would have been an exploit worthy of the gang.

"This was better," T. said. "I found out things." He continued to stare at his feet, not meeting anybody's eye, as though he were absorbed in some dream he was unwilling—or ashamed—to share.

160　"What things?"

"Old Misery's going to be away all tomorrow and Bank Holiday."

Blackie said with relief, "You mean we could break in?"

"And pinch things?" somebody asked.

Blackie said, "Nobody's going to pinch things. Breaking in—that's good enough, isn't it? We don't want any court stuff."

"I don't want to pinch anything," T. said. "I've got 170　a better idea."

"What is it?"

T. raised eyes, as grey and disturbed as the drab August day. "We'll pull it down," he said. "We'll destroy it."

Blackie gave a single hoot of laughter and then, like Mike, fell quiet, daunted by the serious implacable gaze. "What'd the police be doing all the time?" he said.

"They'd never know. We'd do it from inside. I've 180　found a way in." He said with a sort of intensity, "We'd be like worms, don't you see, in an apple. When we came out again there'd be nothing there, no staircase, no panels, nothing but just walls, and then we'd make the walls fall down—somehow."

"We'd go to jug,°" Blackie said.

"Who's to prove? And anyway we wouldn't have pinched anything." He added without the smallest flicker of glee, "There wouldn't be anything to pinch after we'd finished."

190　"I've never heard of going to prison for breaking things," Summers said.

"There wouldn't be time," Blackie said. "I've seen housebreakers at work."

"There are twelve of us," T. said. "We'd organize."

"None of us know how—"

"I know," T. said. He looked across at Blackie, "Have you got a better plan?"

"Today," Mike said tactlessly, "we're pinching free rides—"　200

"Free rides," T. said. "You can stand down, Blackie, if you'd rather. . . ."

"The gang's got to vote."

"Put it up then."

Blackie said uneasily, "It's proposed that tomorrow and Monday we destroy Old Misery's house."

"Here, here," said a fat boy called Joe.

"Who's in favour?"

T. said, "It's carried."

"How do we start?" Summers asked.　210

"He'll tell you," Blackie said. It was the end of his leadership. He went away to the back of the car-park and began to kick a stone, dribbling it this way and that. There was only one old Morris° in the park, for few cars were left there except lorries:° without an attendant there was no safety. He took a flying kick at the car and scraped a little paint off the rear mudguard. Beyond, paying no more attention to him than to a stranger, the gang had gathered round T.; Blackie was dimly aware of the fickleness of favour. He thought of 220　going home, of never returning, of letting them all discover the hollowness of T.'s leadership, but suppose after all what T. proposed was possible—nothing like it had ever been done before. The fame of the Wormsley Common car-park gang would surely reach around London. There would be headlines in the papers. Even the grown-up gangs who ran the betting at the all-in wrestling and the barrow-boys would hear with respect of how Old Misery's house had been destroyed. Driven by the pure, simple, and altruistic am-　230　bition of fame for the gang, Blackie came back to where T. stood in the shadow of Misery's wall.

T. was giving his orders with decision: it was as though this plan had been with him all his life, pondered through the seasons, now in his fifteenth year crystallized with the pain of puberty. "You," he said to Mike, "bring some big nails, the biggest you can find, and a hammer. Anyone else who can better bring a hammer and a screwdriver. We'll need plenty of them. Chisels too. We can't have too many chisels.　240　Can anybody bring a saw?"

"I can," Mike said.

"Not a child's saw," T. said. "A real saw."

Blackie realized he had raised his hand like any ordinary member of the gang.

"Right, you bring one, Blackie. But now there's a difficulty. We want a hacksaw."

"What's a hacksaw?" someone asked.

"You can get 'em at Woolworth's," Summers said.

185 **jug,** jail

214 **Morris,** trade name for a common English car　215 **lorries,** trucks

The fat boy called Joe said gloomily, "I knew it would end in a collection."

"I'll get one myself," T. said. "I don't want your money. But I can't buy a sledge-hammer."

Blackie said, "They are working on number fifteen. I know where they'll leave their stuff for Bank Holiday."

"Then that's all," T. said. "We meet here at nine sharp."

"I've got to go to church," Mike said.

"Come over the wall and whistle. We'll let you in."

II

On Sunday morning all were punctual except Blackie, even Mike. Mike had had a stroke of luck. His mother felt ill, his father was tired after Saturday night, and he was told to go to church alone with many warnings of what would happen if he strayed. Blackie had had difficulty in smuggling out the saw, and then in finding the sledge-hammer at the back of number 15. He approached the house from a lane at the rear of the garden, for fear of the policeman's beat along the main road. The tired evergreens kept off a stormy sun: another wet Bank Holiday was being prepared over the Atlantic, beginning in swirls of dust under the trees. Blackie climbed the wall into Misery's garden.

There was no sign of anybody anywhere. The loo stood like a tomb in a neglected graveyard. The curtains were drawn. The house slept. Blackie lumbered nearer with the saw and the sledge-hammer. Perhaps after all nobody had turned up: the plan had been a wild invention: they had woken wiser. But when he came close to the back door he could hear a confusion of sound, hardly louder than a hive in swarm: a clickety-clack, a bang bang bang, a scraping, a creaking, a sudden painful crack. He thought, It's true, and whistled.

They opened the back door to him and he came in. He had at once the impression of organization, very different from the old happy-go-lucky ways under his leadership. For a while he wandered up and down stairs looking for T. Nobody addressed him: he had a sense of great urgency, and already he could begin to see the plan. The interior of the house was being carefully demolished without touching the outer walls. Summers with hammer and chisel was ripping out the skirting-boards in the ground floor dining-room: he had already smashed the panels of the door. In the same room Joe was heaving up the parquet blocks, exposing the soft wood floor-boards over the cellar. Coils of wire came out of the damaged skirting and Mike sat happily on the floor, clipping the wires.

On the curved stairs two of the gang were working hard with an inadequate child's saw on the banisters—when they saw Blackie's big saw they signalled for it wordlessly. When he next saw them a quarter of the banisters had been dropped into the hall. He found T. at last in the bathroom—he sat moodily in the least cared-for room in the house, listening to the sounds coming up from below.

"You've really done it," Blackie said with awe. "What's going to happen?"

"We've only just begun," T. said. He looked at the sledge-hammer and gave his instructions. "You stay here and break the bath and the wash-basin. Don't bother about the pipes. They come later."

Mike appeared at the door. "I've finished the wire, T.," he said.

"Good. You've just got to go wandering round now. The kitchen's in the basement. Smash all the china and glass and bottles you can lay hold of. Don't turn on the taps—we don't want a flood—yet. Then go into all the rooms and turn out drawers. If they are locked get one of the others to break them open. Tear up any papers you find and smash all the ornaments. Better take a carving-knife with you from the kitchen. The bedroom's opposite here. Open the pillows and tear up the sheets. That's enough for the moment. And you, Blackie, when you've finished in here crack the plaster in the passage up with your sledge-hammer."

"What are you going to do?" Blackie asked.

"I'm looking for something special," T. said.

It was nearly lunch-time before Blackie had finished and went in search of T. Chaos had advanced. The kitchen was a shambles of broken glass and china. The dining-room was stripped of parquet, the skirting was up, the door had been taken off its hinges, and the destroyers had moved up a floor. Streaks of light came in through the closed shutters where they worked with the seriousness of creators—and destruction after all is a form of creation. A kind of imagination had seen this house as it had now become.

Mike said, "I've got to go home for dinner."

"Who else?" T. asked, but all the others on one excuse or another had brought provisions with them.

They squatted in the ruins of the room and swapped unwanted sandwiches. Half an hour for lunch and they were at work again. By the time Mike returned, they were on the top floor, and by six the superficial damage was completed. The doors were all off, all the skirtings raised, the furniture pillaged and ripped and smashed—no one could have slept in the house except on a bed of broken plaster. T. gave his orders—eight o'clock next morning—and to escape notice they climbed singly over the garden wall, into the car-park. Only Blackie and T. were left; the light had nearly gone, and when they touched a switch, nothing worked—Mike had done his job thoroughly.

"Did you find anything special?" Blackie asked.

T. nodded. "Come over here," he said, "and look." Out of both pockets he drew bundles of pound notes. "Old Misery's savings," he said. "Mike ripped out the mattress, but he missed them."

"What are you going to do? Share them?"

"We aren't thieves," T. said. "Nobody's going to steal anything from this house. I kept these for you and me—a celebration." He knelt down on the floor and counted them out—there were seventy in all.

"We'll burn them," he said, "one by one," and taking it in turns they held a note upwards and lit the top corner, so that the flame burnt slowly towards their fingers. The grey ash floated above them and fell on their heads like age. "I'd like to see Old Misery's face when we are through," T. said.

"You hate him a lot?" Blackie asked.

"Of course I don't hate him," T. said. "There'd be no fun if I hated him." The last burning note illuminated his brooding face. "All this hate and love," he said, "it's soft, it's hooey. There's only things, Blackie," and he looked round the room crowded with the unfamiliar shadows of half things, broken things, former things. "I'll race you home, Blackie," he said.

III

Next morning the serious destruction started. Two were missing—Mike and another boy whose parents were off to Southend and Brighton in spite of the slow warm drops that had begun to fall and the rumble of thunder in the estuary like the first guns of the old blitz. "We've got to hurry," T. said.

Summers was restive. "Haven't we done enough?" he said. "I've been given a bob for slot machines. This is like work."

"We've hardly started," T. said. "Why, there's all the floors left, and the stairs. We haven't taken out a single window. You voted like the others. We are going to *destroy* this house. There won't be anything left when we've finished."

They began again on the first floor picking up the top floor-boards next to the outer wall, leaving the joists exposed. Then they sawed through the joists and retreated into the hall, as what was left of the floor heeled and sank. They had learnt with practice, and the second floor collapsed more easily. By the evening an odd exhilaration seized them as they looked down the great hollow of the house. They ran risks and made mistakes: when they thought of the windows it was too late to reach them. "Cor," Joe said, and dropped a penny down into the dry rubble-filled well. It cracked and span among the broken glass.

"Why did we start this?" Summers asked with astonishment; T. was already on the ground, digging at the rubble, clearing a space along the outer wall. "Turn on the taps," he said. "It's too dark for anyone to see now, and in the morning it won't matter." The water overtook them on the stairs and fell through the floorless rooms.

It was then they heard Mike's whistle at the back. "Something's wrong," Blackie said. They could hear his urgent breathing as they unlocked the door.

"The bogies?"° Summers asked.

"Old Misery," Mike said. "He's on his way." He

put his head between his knees and retched. "Ran all the way," he said with pride.

"But why?" T. said. "He told me . . ." He protested with the fury of the child he had never been, "It isn't fair."

"He was down at Southend," Mike said, "and he was on the train coming back. Said it was too cold and wet." He paused and gazed at the water. "My, you've had a storm here. Is the roof leaking?"

"How long will he be?"

"Five minutes. I gave Ma the slip and ran."

"We better clear," Summers said. "We've done enough, anyway."

"Oh, no, we haven't. Anybody could do this—" "This" was the shattered hollowed house with nothing left but the walls. Yet walls could be preserved. Façades were valuable. They could build inside again more beautifully than before. This could again be a home. He said angrily, "We've got to finish. Don't move. Let me think."

"There's no time," a boy said.

"There's got to be a way," T. said. "We couldn't have got this far . . ."

"We've done a lot," Blackie said.

"No. No, we haven't. Somebody watch the front."

"We can't do any more."

"He may come in at the back."

"Watch the back too." T. began to plead. "Just give me a minute and I'll fix it. I swear I'll fix it." But his authority had gone with his ambiguity. He was only one of the gang. "Please," he said.

"Please," Summers mimicked him, and then suddenly struck home with the fatal name. "Run along home, Trevor."

T. stood with his back to the rubble like a boxer knocked groggy against the ropes. He had no words as his dreams shook and slid. Then Blackie acted before the gang had time to laugh, pushing Summers backward. "I'll watch the front, T.," he said, and cautiously he opened the shutters of the hall. The grey wet common stretched ahead, and the lamps gleamed in the puddles. "Someone's coming, T. No, it's not him. What's your plan, T.?"

"Tell Mike to go out to the loo and hide close beside it. When he hears me whistle he's got to count ten and start to shout."

"Shout what?"

"Oh, 'Help,' anything."

"You hear, Mike," Blackie said. He was the leader again. He took a quick look between the shutters. "He's coming, T."

"Quick, Mike. The loo. Stay here, Blackie, all of you till I yell."

"Where are you going, T.?"

"Don't worry. I'll see to this. I said I would, didn't I?"

Old Misery came limping off the common. He had mud on his shoes and he stopped to scrape them on the

---

416 **bogies**, police

pavement's edge. He didn't want to soil his house, which stood jagged and dark between the bomb-sites, saved so narrowly, as he believed, from destruction. Even the fan-light had been left unbroken by the bomb's blast. Somewhere somebody whistled. Old Misery looked sharply round. He didn't trust whistles. A child was shouting: it seemed to come from his own garden. Then a boy ran into the road from the car-park. "Mr. Thomas," he called, "Mr. Thomas."

"What is it?"

"I'm terribly sorry, Mr. Thomas. One of us got taken short, and we thought you wouldn't mind, and now he can't get out."

"What do you mean, boy?"

"He got stuck in your loo."

"He'd no business—Haven't I seen you before?"

"You showed me your house."

"So I did. So I did. That doesn't give you the right to—"

"Do hurry, Mr. Thomas. He'll suffocate."

"Nonsense. He can't suffocate. Wait till I put my bag in."

"I'll carry your bag."

"Oh, no, you don't. I carry my own."

"This way, Mr. Thomas."

"I can't get in the garden that way. I've got to go through the house."

"But you can get in the garden this way, Mr. Thomas. We often do."

"You often do?" He followed the boy with a scandalized fascination. "When? What right . . ."

"Do you see . . . ? The wall's low."

"I'm not going to climb walls into my own garden. It's absurd."

"This is how we do it. One foot here, one foot there, and over." The boy's face peered down, an arm shot out, and Mr. Thomas found his bag taken and deposited on the other side of the wall.

"Give me back my bag," Mr. Thomas said. From the loo a boy yelled and yelled. "I'll call the police."

"Your bag's all right, Mr. Thomas. Look. One foot there. On your right. Now just above. To your left." Mr. Thomas climbed over his own garden wall. "Here's your bag, Mr. Thomas."

"I'll have the wall built up," Mr. Thomas said, "I'll not have you boys coming over here, using my loo." He stumbled on the path, but the boy caught his elbow and supported him. "Thank you, thank you, my boy," he murmured automatically. Somebody shouted again through the dark. "I'm coming, I'm coming," Mr. Thomas called. He said to the boy beside him, "I'm not unreasonable. Been a boy myself. As long as things are done regular. I don't mind you playing round the place Saturday mornings. Sometimes I like company. Only it's got to be regular. One of you asks leave and I say Yes. Sometimes I'll say No. Won't feel like it. And you come in at the front door and out at the back. No garden walls."

"Do get him out, Mr. Thomas."

"He won't come to any harm in my loo," Mr. Thomas said, stumbling slowly down the garden. "Oh, my rheumatics," he said. "Always get 'em on Bank Holiday. I've got to go careful. There's loose stones here. Give me your hand. Do you know what my horoscope said yesterday? 'Abstain from any dealings in first half of week. Danger of serious crash.' That might be on this path," Mr. Thomas said. "They speak in parables and double meanings." He paused at the door of the loo. "What's the matter in there?" he called. There was no reply.

"Perhaps he's fainted," the boy said.

"Not in my loo. Here, you, come out," Mr. Thomas said, and giving a great jerk at the door he nearly fell on his back when it swung easily open. A hand first supported him and then pushed him hard. His head hit the opposite wall and he sat heavily down. His bag hit his feet. A hand whipped the key out of the lock and the door slammed. "Let me out," he called, and heard the key turn in the lock. "A serious crash," he thought, and felt dithery and confused and old.

A voice spoke to him softly through the star-shaped hole in the door. "Don't worry, Mr. Thomas," it said, "we won't hurt you, not if you stay quiet."

Mr. Thomas put his head between his hands and pondered. He had noticed that there was only one lorry in the car-park, and he felt certain that the driver would not come for it before the morning. Nobody could hear him from the road in front, and the lane at the back was seldom used. Anyone who passed there would be hurrying home and would not pause for what they would certainly take to be drunken cries. And if he did call "Help," who, on a lonely Bank Holiday evening, would have the courage to investigate? Mr. Thomas sat on the loo and pondered with the wisdom of age.

After a while it seemed to him that there were sounds in the silence—they were faint and came from the direction of his house. He stood up and peered through the ventilation-hole—between the cracks in one of the shutters he saw a light, not the light of a lamp, but the wavering light that a candle might give. Then he thought he heard the sound of hammering and scraping and chipping. He thought of burglars—perhaps they had employed the boy as a scout, but why should burglars engage in what sounded more and more like a stealthy form of carpentry? Mr. Thomas let out an experimental yell, but nobody answered. The noise could not even have reached his enemies.

IV

Mike had gone home to bed, but the rest stayed. The question of leadership no longer concerned the gang. With nails, chisels, screwdrivers, anything that was sharp and penetrating they moved around the inner walls worrying at the mortar between the bricks. They started too high, and it was Blackie who hit on the damp course and realized the work could be halved if they weakened the joints immediately above. It was a long, tiring, unamusing job, but at last it was finished. The gutted house stood there balanced on a few inches of mortar between the damp course and the bricks.

There remained the most dangerous task of all, out in the open at the edge of the bomb-site. Summers was sent to watch the road for passers-by, and Mr. Thomas, sitting on the loo, heard clearly now the sound of sawing. It no longer came from his house, and that a little reassured him. He felt less concerned. Perhaps the other noises too had no significance.

A voice spoke to him through the hole. "Mr. Thomas."

"Let me out," Mr. Thomas said sternly.

"Here's a blanket," the voice said, and a long grey sausage was worked through the hole and fell in swathes over Mr. Thomas's head.

"There's nothing personal," the voice said. "We want you to be comfortable tonight."

"Tonight," Mr. Thomas repeated incredulously.

"Catch," the voice said. "Penny buns—we've buttered them, and sausage-rolls. We don't want you to starve, Mr. Thomas."

Mr. Thomas pleaded desperately. "A joke's a joke, boy. Let me out and I won't say a thing. I've got rheumatics. I got to sleep comfortable."

"You wouldn't be comfortable, not in your house, you wouldn't. Not now."

"What do you mean, boy?" but the footsteps receded. There was only the silence of night: no sound of sawing. Mr. Thomas tried one more yell, but he was daunted and rebuked by the silence—a long way off an owl hooted and made away again on its muffled flight through the soundless world.

At seven next morning the driver came to fetch his lorry. He climbed into the seat and tried to start the engine. He was vaguely aware of a voice shouting, but it didn't concern him. At last the engine responded and he backed the lorry until it touched the great wooden shore that supported Mr. Thomas's house. That way he could drive right out and down the street without reversing. The lorry moved forward, was momentarily checked as though something were pulling it from behind, and then went on to the sound of a long rumbling crash. The driver was astonished to see bricks bouncing ahead of him, while stones hit the roof of his cab. He put on his brakes. When he climbed out the whole landscape had suddenly altered. There was no house beside the car-park, only a hill of rubble. He went round and examined the back of his car for damage, and found a rope tied there that was still twisted at the other end round part of a wooden strut.

The driver again became aware of somebody shouting. It came from the wooden erection which was the nearest thing to a house in that desolation of broken brick. The driver climbed the smashed wall and unlocked the door. Mr. Thomas came out of the loo. He was wearing a grey blanket to which flakes of pastry adhered. He gave a sobbing cry. "My house," he said. "Where's my house?"

"Search me," the driver said. His eye lit on the remains of a bath and what had once been a dresser and he began to laugh. There wasn't anything left anywhere.

"How dare you laugh," Mr. Thomas said. "It was my house. My house."

"I'm sorry," the driver said, making heroic efforts, but when he remembered the sudden check to his lorry, the crash of bricks falling, he became convulsed again. One moment the house had stood there with such dignity between the bomb-sites like a man in a top hat, and then, bang, crash, there wasn't anything left—not anything. He said, "I'm sorry. I can't help it, Mr. Thomas. There's nothing personal, but you got to admit it's funny."

(1954)

SAMUEL BECKETT 1906–

Samuel Beckett was born in a suburb of Dublin in 1906, the son of an Anglo-Irish, middle-class couple. He was educated at Trinity College, Dublin, where he studied Romance languages. After a brief period of schoolteaching in Belfast, he became a lecteur in English at the École Normale Supérieure in Paris in 1928. While in Paris, he became friends with the self-exiled novelist James Joyce. After returning to Ireland for a short while to take a teaching position at Trinity College, Beckett traveled for six years in England, France, Germany, and Italy. In 1930 Beckett published *Whoroscope*, a long poem on the French philosopher René Descartes (1596–1650). In 1934 he published a group of ten short stories under the title *More Pricks than Kicks*; a collection of poems, *Echo's Bones*, appeared in 1935. In 1937 Beckett decided to settle permanently in Paris, where a year later he published his first novel, *Murphy*. He remained in Paris during the early years of the Second World War and became a member of an underground resistance group. After the war he wrote prolifically, publishing several works: *Malloy* (French 1951, English 1955), *Malone Dies* (French 1951, English 1955), *The Unnamable* (French 1953, English 1958), *Waiting for Godot* (French 1952, English 1954). It was with the huge success of his play *Waiting for Godot*, rather than the publication of any of his novels, that Beckett took his place on the international literary scene. He had further success with the plays *Endgame* (French 1957, English 1958) and *Krapp's Last Tape* (1958). Though some of his works were originally written in English, the majority were written first in French and later translated (by Beckett) into English. Beckett is also the author of several radio plays, television plays, and film scripts. Many critics today consider his trilogy of novels (*Malloy, Malone Dies, The Unnamable*) to be his greatest achievement. He received the Nobel Prize for Literature in 1969. Beckett now lives and writes in Paris.

Beckett has described the area of human experience that is consistently presented in his fiction and in his plays in this manner: "My little exploration is that whole zone of being that has always been set aside by artists as something unusable—as something by definition incompatible with art." His characters are usually trapped, encumbered, and incapacitated; they seem to be surrounded by trash and chaos but are, somehow, incredibly resilient. His work, though almost deceptively simple on the surface, reveals an extremely rigorous philosophical bent. Beckett frequently calls attention to the illusion and futility that may undermine even the most seemingly satisfactory lives.

DANTE AND THE LOBSTER

It was morning and Belacqua was stuck in the first of the canti in the moon.° He was so bogged that he could move neither backward nor forward. Blissful Beatrice was there, Dante also, and she explained the spots on the moon to him. She shewed him in the first place where he was at fault, then she put up her own explanation. She had it from God, therefore he could rely on its being accurate in every particular. All he had to do was to follow her step by step. Part one, the refutation,
10 was plain sailing. She made her point clearly, she said what she had to say without fuss or loss of time. But part two, the demonstration, was so dense that Belacqua could not make head or tail of it. The disproof, the reproof, that was patent. But then came the proof, a rapid shorthand of the real facts, and Belacqua was bogged indeed. Bored also, impatient to get on to Piccarda. Still he pored over the enigma, he would not concede himself conquered, he would understand at least the meanings of the words, the order in which
20 they were spoken and the nature of the satisfaction that they conferred on the misinformed poet, so that when they were ended he was refreshed and could raise his heavy head, intending to return thanks and make formal retraction of his old opinion.

He was still running his brain against this impenetrable passage when he heard midday strike. At once he switched his mind off its task. He scooped his fin-

gers under the book and shovelled it back till it lay wholly on his palms. The *Divine Comedy* face upward on the lectern of his palms. Thus disposed he raised it 30 under his nose and there he slammed it shut. He held it aloft for a time, squinting at it angrily, pressing the boards inwards with the heels of his hands. Then he laid it aside.

He leaned back in his chair to feel his mind subside and the itch of this mean quodlibet° die down. Nothing could be done until his mind got better and was still, which gradually it did and was. Then he ventured to consider what he had to do next. There was always something that one had to do next. Three large obliga- 40 tions presented themselves. First lunch, then the lobster, then the Italian lesson. That would do to be going on with. After the Italian lesson he had no very clear idea. No doubt some niggling curriculum had been drawn up by someone for the late afternoon and evening, but he did not know what. In any case it did not matter. What did matter was: one, lunch; two, the lobster; three, the Italian lesson. That was more than enough to be going on with.

Lunch, to come off at all, was a very nice affair. If 50 his lunch was to be enjoyable, and it could be very enjoyable indeed, he must be left in absolute tranquillity to prepare it. But if he were disturbed now, if some brisk tattler were to come bouncing in now big with a big idea or a petition, he might just as well not eat at all, for the food would turn to bitterness on his palate, or, worse again, taste of nothing. He must be left strictly alone, he must have complete quiet and privacy, to prepare the food for his lunch.

The first thing to do was to lock the door. Now 60 nobody could come at him. He deployed an old *Herald* and smoothed it out on the table. The rather handsome face of McCabe the assassin stared up at him. Then he lit the gas-ring and unhooked the square flat toaster, asbestos grill, from its nail and set it precisely on the flame. He found he had to lower the flame. Toast must not on any account be done too rapidly. For bread to be toasted as it ought, through and through, it must be done on a mild steady flame. Otherwise you only charred the outside and left the pith as sodden as be- 70 fore. If there was one thing he abominated more than another it was to feel his teeth meet in a bathos of pith and dough. And it was so easy to do the thing properly. So, he thought, having regulated the flow and adjusted the grill, by the time I have the bread cut that will be just right. Now the long barrel-loaf came out of its biscuit-tin and had its end evened off on the face of McCabe. Two inexorable drives with the bread-saw and a pair of neat rounds of raw bread, the main elements of his meal, lay before him, awaiting his plea- 80 sure. The stump of the loaf went back into prison, the crumbs, as though there were no such thing as a sparrow in the wide world, were swept in a fever away, and the slices snatched up and carried to the grill. All these preliminaries were very hasty and impersonal.

It was now that real skill began to be required, it was at this point that the average person began to make a hash of the entire proceedings. He laid his cheek against the soft of the bread, it was spongy and warm, alive. But he would very soon take that plush feel off it, by God but he would very quickly take that fat white look off its face. He lowered the gas a suspicion and plaqued one flabby slab plump down on the glowing fabric, but very pat and precise, so that the whole resembled the Japanese flag. Then on top, there not being room for the two to do evenly side by side, and if you did not do them evenly you might just as well save yourself the trouble of doing them at all, the other round was set to warm. When the first candidate was done, which was only when it was black through and through, it changed places with its comrade, so that now it in its turn lay on top, done to a dead end, black and smoking, waiting till as much could be said of the other.

For the tiller of the field the thing was simple,° he had it from his mother. The spots were Cain with his truss of thorns, dispossessed, cursed from the earth, fugitive and vagabond. The moon was that countenance fallen and branded, seared with the first stigma of God's pity, that an outcast might not die quickly. It was a mix-up in the mind of the tiller, but that did not matter. It had been good enough for his mother, it was good enough for him.

Belacqua on his knees before the flame, poring over the grill, controlled every phase of the broiling. It took time, but if a thing was worth doing at all it was worth doing well, that was a true saying. Long before the end the room was full of smoke and the reek of burning. He switched off the gas, when all that human care and skill could do had been done, and restored the toaster to its nail. This was an act of dilapidation, for it seared a great weal° in the paper. This was hooliganism pure and simple. What the hell did he care? Was it his wall? The same hopeless paper had been there fifty years. It was livid with age. It could not be disimproved.

Next a thick paste of Savora,° salt and Cayenne on each round, well worked in while the pores were still open with the heat. No butter, God forbid, just a good foment of mustard and salt and pepper on each round. Butter was a blunder, it made the toast soggy. Buttered toast was all right for Senior Fellows and Salvationists, for such as had nothing but false teeth in their heads. It was no good at all to a fairly strong young rose like Belacqua. This meal that he was at such pains to make ready, he would devour it with a sense of rapture and victory, it would be like smiting

the sledded Polacks° on the ice. He would snap at it with closed eyes, he would gnash it into a pulp, he would vanquish it utterly with his fangs. Then the anguish of pungency, the pang of the spices, as each mouthful died, scorching his palate, bringing tears.

But he was not yet all set, there was yet much to be done. He had burnt his offering, he had not fully dressed it. Yes, he had put the horse behind the tumbrel.

He clapped the toasted rounds together, he brought them smartly together like cymbals, they clave the one to the other on the viscid salve of Savora. Then he wrapped them up for the time being in any old sheet of paper. Then he made himself ready for the road.

Now the great thing was to avoid being accosted. To be stopped at this stage and have conversational nuisance committed all over him would be a disaster. His whole being was straining forward towards the joy in store. If he were accosted now he might just as well fling his lunch into the gutter and walk straight back home. Sometimes his hunger, more of mind, I need scarcely say, than of body, for this meal amounted to such a frenzy that he would not have hesitated to strike any man rash enough to buttonhole and baulk him, he would have shouldered him out of his path without ceremony. Woe betide the meddler who crossed him when his mind was really set on this meal.

He threaded his way rapidly, his head bowed, through a familiar labyrinth of lanes and suddenly dived into a little family grocery. In the shop they were not surprised. Most days, about this hour, he shot in off the street in this way.

The slab of cheese was prepared. Separated since morning from the piece, it was only waiting for Belacqua to call and take it. Gorgonzola cheese. He knew a man who came from Gorgonzola, his name was Angelo. He had been born in Nice but all his youth had been spent in Gorgonzola. He knew where to look for it. Every day it was there, in the same corner, waiting to be called for. They were very decent obliging people.

He looked sceptically at the cut of cheese. He turned it over on its back to see was the other side any better. The other side was worse. They had laid it better side up, they had practised that little deception. Who shall blame them? He rubbed it. It was sweating. That was something. He stooped and smelt it. A faint fragrance of corruption. What good was that? He didn't want fragrance, he wasn't a bloody gourmet, he wanted a good stench. What he wanted was a good green stenching rotten lump of Gorgonzola cheese, alive, and by God he would have it.

He looked fiercely at the grocer.

---

105 **tiller . . . simple,** the unlearned have their own explanation for the spots on the moon   122 **weal,** welt   126 **Savora,** a kind of mustard

37 **sledded Polacks.** Cf. *Hamlet* I, i, 63. The elder Hamlet vigorously defeated the "sledded Polacks" on the ice

190 "What's that?" he demanded.

The grocer writhed.

"Well?" demanded Belacqua, he was without fear when roused. "is that the best you can do?"

"In the length and breadth of Dublin" said the grocer "you won't find a rottener bit this minute."

Belacqua was furious. The impudent dogsbody, for two pins he would assault him.

"It won't do" he cried "do you hear me, it won't do at all. I won't have it." He ground his teeth.

200 The grocer, instead of simply washing his hands like Pilate, flung out his arms in a wild crucified gesture of supplication. Sullenly Belacqua undid his packet and slipped the cadaverous tablet of cheese between the hard cold black boards of the toast. He stumped to the door where he whirled round however.

"You heard me?" he cried.

"Sir" said the grocer. This was not a question, nor yet an expression of acquiescence. The tone in which it was let fall made it quite impossible to know what 210 was in the man's mind. It was a most ingenious riposte.

"I tell you" said Belacqua with great heat "this won't do at all. If you can't do better than this" he raised the hand that held the packet "I shall be obliged to go for my cheese elsewhere. Do you mark me?"

"Sir" said the grocer.

He came to the threshold of his store and watched the indignant customer hobble away. Belacqua had a spavined gait, his feet were in ruins, he suffered with 220 them almost continuously. Even in the night they took no rest, or next to none. For then the cramps took over from the corns and hammer-toes, and carried on. So that he would press the fringes of his feet desperately against the end-rail of the bed or, better again, reach down with his hand and drag them up and back towards the instep. Skill and patience could disperse the pain, but there it was, complicating his night's rest.

The grocer without closing his eyes or taking them off the receding figure, blew his nose in the skirt of his 230 apron. Being a warm-hearted human man he felt sympathy and pity for this queer customer who always looked ill and dejected. But at the same time he was a small tradesman, don't forget that, with a small tradesman's sense of personal dignity and what was what. Thruppence, he cast it up, thruppence worth of cheese per day, one and a tanner per week. No, he would fawn on no man for that, no, not on the best in the land. He had his pride.

Stumbling along by devious ways towards the lowly 240 public° where he was expected, in the sense that the entry of his grotesque person would provoke no comment or laughter, Belacqua gradually got the upper hand of his choler. Now that lunch was as good as a *fait accompli,*° because the incontinent bosthoons of his own class, itching to pass on a big idea or inflict an appointment, were seldom at large in this shabby quarter of the city, he was free to consider items two and three, the lobster and the lesson, in closer detail.

At a quarter to three he was due at the school. Say five to three. The public closed, the fishmonger 250 reopened, at half-past two. Assuming then that his lousy old bitch of an aunt had given her order in good time that morning, with strict injunctions that it should be ready and waiting so that her blackguard boy should on no account be delayed when he called for it first thing in the afternoon, it would be time enough if he left the public as it closed, he could remain on till the last moment. Benissimo. He had half-a-crown. That was two pints of draught anyway and perhaps a bottle to wind up with. Their bottled stout was particularly 260 excellent and well up. And he would still be left with enough coppers to buy a *Herald* and take a tram if he felt tired or was pinched for time. Always assuming, of course, that the lobster was all ready to be handed over. God damn these tradesmen, he thought, you can never rely on them. He had not done an exercise but that did not matter. His Professoressa was so charming and remarkable. Signorina Adriana Ottolenghi! He did not believe it possible for a woman to be more intelligent or better informed than the little Ottolenghi. So he 270 had set her on a pedestal in his mind, apart from other women. She had said last day that they would read *Il Cinque Maggio*° together. But she would not mind if he told her, as he proposed to, in Italian, he would frame a shining phrase on his way from the public, that he would prefer to postpone the *Cinque Maggio* to another occasion. Manzoni was an old woman, Napoleon was another. *Napoleone di mezza calzetta, fa l'amore a Giacominetta.*° Why did he think of Manzoni as an old woman? Why did he do him that injustice? 280 Pellico° was another. They were all old maids, suffragettes. He must ask his Signorina where he could have received that impression, that the 19th century in Italy was full of old hens trying to cluck like Pindar.° Carducci° was another. Also about the spots on the moon. If she could not tell him there and then she would make it up, only too gladly, against the next time. Everything was all set now and in order. Bating,° of course, the lobster, which had to remain an incalculable factor. He must just hope for the best. And 290

244 **fait accompli,** something which has already been done, and can't be undone   273 **Il Cinque Maggio,** an ode (1821) on the death of Napoleon by the Italian writer Alessandro Manzoni (1785–1873)   278–279 **Napoleone . . . Giacominetta,** small town Napoleon makes love to Giacominetta. A sentence in contrast to the elevated tone of *Il Cinque Maggio*   281 **Pellico,** Silvio Pellico (1789–1854), Italian writer, editor, and patriot   284 **Pindar,** Greek lyric poet (522?–443 B.C.)   285 **Carducci,** Giosuè Carducci (1835–1907), Italian poet and professor of literary history. He was a staunch classicist who attempted to introduce classical metrical schemes into Italian poetry. Awarded Nobel Prize for literature in 1906   288 **Bating,** with the exception

240 **public,** pub

expect the worst, he thought gaily, diving into the public, as usual.

Belacqua drew near to the school, quite happy, for all had gone swimmingly. The lunch had been a notable success, it would abide as a standard in his mind. Indeed he could not imagine its ever being superseded. And such a pale soapy piece of cheese to prove so strong! He must only conclude that he had been abusing himself all these years in relating the strength of cheese directly to its greenness. We live and learn, that was a true saying. Also his teeth and jaws had been in heaven, splinters of vanquished toast spraying forth at each gnash. It was like eating glass. His mouth burned and ached with the exploit. Then the food had been further spiced by the intelligence, transmitted in a low tragic voice across the counter by Oliver the improver, that the Malahide° murderer's petition for mercy, signed by half the land, having been rejected, the man must swing at dawn in Mountjoy° and nothing could save him. Ellis the hangman was even now on his way. Belacqua, tearing at the sandwich and swilling the precious stout, pondered on McCabe in his cell.

The lobster was ready after all, the man handed it over instanter, and with such a pleasant smile. Really a little bit of courtesy and goodwill went a long way in this world. A smile and a cheerful word from a common working-man and the face of the world was brightened. And it was so easy, a mere question of muscular control.

"Lepping" he said cheerfully, handing it over.

"Lepping?" said Belacqua. What on earth was that?

"Lepping fresh, sir" said the man, "fresh in this morning."

Now Belacqua, on the analogy of mackerel and other fish that he had heard described as lepping fresh when they had been taken but an hour or two previously, supposed the man to mean that the lobster had very recently been killed.

Signorina Adriana Ottolenghi was waiting in the little front room off the hall, which Belacqua was naturally inclined to think of rather as the vestibule. That was her room, the Italian room. On the same side, but at the back, was the French room. God knows where the German room was. Who cared about the German room anyway?

He hung up his coat and hat, laid the long knobby brown-paper parcel on the hall-table, and went prestly in to the Ottolenghi.

After about half-an-hour of this and that obiter, she complimented him on his grasp of the language.

"You make rapid progress" she said in her ruined voice.

There subsisted as much of the Ottolenghi as might be expected to of the person of a lady of a certain age

who had found being young and beautiful and pure more of a bore than anything else.

Belacqua, dissembling his great pleasure, laid open the moon enigma.

"Yes" she said "I know the passage. It is a famous teaser. Off-hand I cannot tell you, but I will look it up when I get home."

The sweet creature! She would look it up in her big Dante when she got home. What a woman!

"It occurred to me" she said "apropos of I don't know what, that you might do worse than make up Dante's rare movements of compassion in Hell. That used to be" her past tenses were always sorrowful "a favourite question."

He assumed an expression of profundity.

"In that connexion" he said "I recall one superb pun anyway:

'qui vive la pietà quando è ben morta . . .'"

She said nothing.

"Is it not a great phrase?" he gushed.

She said nothing.

"Now" he said like a fool "I wonder how you could translate that?"

Still she said nothing. Then:

"Do you think" she murmured "it is absolutely necessary to translate it?"

Sounds as of conflict were borne in from the hall. Then silence. A knuckle tambourined on the door, it flew open and lo it was Mlle Glain, the French instructress, clutching her cat, her eyes out on stalks, in a state of the greatest agitation.

"Oh" she gasped "forgive me. I intrude, but what was in the bag?"

"The bag?" said the Ottolenghi.

Mlle Glain took a French step forward.

"The parcel" she buried her face in the cat "the parcel in the hall."

Belacqua spoke up composedly.

"Mine" he said, "a fish."

He did not know the French for lobster. Fish would do very well. Fish had been good enough for Jesus Christ, Son of God, Saviour. It was good enough for Mlle Glain.

"Oh" said Mlle Glain, inexpressibly relieved, "I caught him in the nick of time." She administered a tap to the cat. "He would have tore it to flitters."

Belacqua began to feel a little anxious.

"Did he actually get at it?" he said.

"No no" said Mlle Glain "I caught him just in time. But I did not know" with a blue-stocking snigger "what it might be, so I thought I had better come and ask."

Base prying bitch.

The Ottolenghi was faintly amused.

"Puisqu'il n'y a pas de mal . . ."° she said with great fatigue and elegance.

307 **Malahide,** town near Dublin   309 **Mountjoy,** a Dublin prison   399 **Puisqu'il . . . mal,** seeing that there is no harm in it

"Heureusement"° it was clear at once that Mlle Glain was devout "heureusement."

Chastening the cat with little skelps° she took herself off. The grey hairs of her maidenhead screamed at Belacqua. A devout, virginal blue-stocking, honing after a penny's worth of scandal.

"Where were we?" said Belacqua.

But Neapolitan patience has its limits.

"Where are we ever?" cried the Ottolenghi "where 410 we were, as we were."

Belacqua drew near to the house of his aunt. Let us call it Winter, that dusk may fall now and a moon rise. At the corner of the street a horse was down and a man sat on its head. I know, thought Belacqua, that that is considered the right thing to do. But why? A lamplighter flew by on his bike, tilting with his pole at the standards, jousting a little yellow light into the evening. A poorly dressed couple stood in the bay of a pretentious gateway, she sagging against the railings, 420 her head lowered, he standing facing her. He stood up close to her, his hands dangled by his sides. Where we were, though Belacqua, as we were. He walked on gripping his parcel. Why not piety and pity both, even down below? Why not mercy and Godliness together? A little mercy in the stress of sacrifice, a little mercy to rejoice against judgment. He thought of Jonah and the gourd and the pity of a jealous God on Nineveh. And poor McCabe, he would get it in the neck at dawn. What was he doing now, how was he feeling? He 430 would relish one more meal, one more night.

His aunt was in the garden, tending whatever flowers die at that time of year. She embraced him and together they went down into the bowels of the earth, into the kitchen in the basement. She took the parcel and undid it and abruptly the lobster was on the table, on the oilcloth, discovered.

"They assured me it was fresh" said Belacqua.

Suddenly he saw the creature move, this neuter creature. Definitely it changed its position. His hand 440 flew to his mouth.

"Christ!" he said "it's alive."

His aunt looked at the lobster. It moved again. It made a faint nervous act of life on the oilcloth. They stood above it, looking down on it, exposed cruciform on the oilcloth. It shuddered again. Belacqua felt he would be sick.

"My God" he whined "it's alive, what'll we do?"

The aunt simply had to laugh. She bustled off to the pantry to fetch her smart apron, leaving him goggling 450 down at the lobster, and came back with it on and her sleeves rolled up, all business.

"Well" she said "it is to be hoped so, indeed."

"All this time" muttered Belacqua. Then, suddenly aware of her hideous equipment: "What are you going to do?" he cried.

"Boil the beast" she said, "what else?"

"But it's not dead" protested Belacqua "you can't boil it like that."

She looked at him in astonishment. Had he taken leave of his senses? 460

"Have sense" she said sharply, "lobsters are always boiled alive. They must be." She caught up the lobster and laid it on its back. It trembled. "They feel nothing" she said.

In the depths of the sea it had crept into the cruel pot. For hours, in the midst of its enemies, it had breathed secretly. It had survived the Frenchwoman's cat and his witless clutch. Now it was going alive into scalding water. It had to. Take into the air my quiet breath. 470

Belacqua looked at the old parchment of her face, grey in the dim kitchen.

"You make a fuss" she said angrily "and upset me and then lash into it for your dinner."

She lifted the lobster clear of the table. It had about thirty seconds to live.

Well, thought Belacqua, it's a quick death, God help us all.

It is not.

(1934)

DYLAN THOMAS
1914–1953

Dylan Marlais Thomas was born in Wales in 1914 and educated at Swansea Grammar School, where his father taught English. He published *Eighteen Poems* in 1934 and *Twenty-Five Poems* in 1936. *The Map of Love* and *The World I Breathe* both appeared in 1939, *New Poems* in 1943, and *Death and Entrances* in 1946. During the Second World War Thomas was a documentary film editor for the British Broadcasting Company. He came to America in 1950 for a short visit and returned in January 1952 for an extended lecture tour. An extraordinary reader of poetry, he was enthusiastically received in dozens of American colleges and universities. Although the seemingly carefree bohemian life-style he adopted for public purposes made him a very popular and colorful figure, his private life was full of emotional trauma; he had frequent bouts with despair and often drank excessively. He died in 1953 in New York of an alcoholic overdose.

In his first poems, Thomas showed an unquestionable affinity for the surrealistic and for imagery drawn from primitive Celtic rituals of rebirth and sacrifice. In his later poems, he gained greater control of style and metaphor without losing any of the typical Celtic "magic of words."

Thomas died at the age of thirty-nine, and the body

of his work is small. There are only ninety-two poems in his *Collected Poems* (1953), all of them short lyrics. *The Doctor and the Devils* (1953), a filmscript, and *Under Milk Wood* (1954), a verse play for broadcasting; three chapters of an uncompleted novel, *Adventures in the Skin Trade* (1941); seven tales in prose, included in *The Map of Love* (1939); a thinly veiled autobiography, *Portrait of the Artist as a Young Dog* (1940) make up the rest of his creative output. Some of his short lyrics are among the finest that have been produced in this century. Few can remain unmoved by the richness of sound and metaphor, the startlingly fresh refurbishing of stale diction and syntax; many would agree with Sir Herbert Read's judgment of Thomas' poetry—"the most absolute poetry that has been written in our time."

THE FORCE THAT THROUGH THE GREEN FUSE DRIVES THE FLOWER

The force that through the green fuse drives the flower
Drives my green age; that blasts the roots of trees
Is my destroyer.
And I am dumb to tell the crooked rose
My youth is bent by the same wintry fever.

The force that drives the water through the rocks
Drives my red blood; that dries the mouthing streams
Turns mine to wax.
And I am dumb to mouth unto my veins
10 How at the mountain spring the same mouth sucks.

The hand that whirls the water in the pool
Stirs the quicksand; that ropes the blowing wind
Hauls my shroud sail.
And I am dumb to tell the hanging man
How of my clay is made the hangman's lime.

The lips of time leech to the fountain head;
Love drips and gathers, but the fallen blood
Shall calm her sores.
And I am dumb to tell a weather's wind
20 How time has ticked a heaven round the stars.

And I am dumb to tell the lover's tomb
How at my sheet goes the same crooked worm.
(1934; 1952)

TO-DAY, THIS INSECT, AND THE WORLD I BREATHE

To-day, this insect, and the world I breathe,
Now that my symbols have outelbowed space,
Time at the city spectacles, and half
The dear, daft time I take to nudge the sentence,

In trust and tale have I divided sense,
Slapped down the guillotine, the blood-red double
Of head and tail made witnesses to this
Murder of Eden and green genesis.

The insect certain is the plague of fables.

This story's monster has a serpent caul,   10
Blind in the coil scrams round the blazing outline,
Measures his own length on the garden wall
And breaks his own shell in the last shocked beginning;
A crocodile before the chrysalis,
Before the fall from love the flying heartbone,
Winged like a sabbath ass this children's piece
Uncredited blows Jericho on Eden.

The insect fable is the certain promise.

Death: death of Hamlet and the nightmare madmen,
An air-drawn windmill on a wooden horse,   20
John's beast,° Job's patience, and the fibs of vision,°
Greek in the Irish sea the ageless voice:

'Adam I love, my madmen's love is endless,
No tell-tale lover has an end more certain,
All legends' sweethearts on a tree of stories,
My cross of tales behind the fabulous curtain.'
(1936)

DO NOT GO GENTLE INTO THAT GOOD NIGHT

Do not go gentle into that good night,
Old age should burn and rave at close of day;
Rage, rage against the dying of the light.

Though wise men at their end know dark is right,
Because their words had forked no lightning they
Do not go gentle into that good night.

Good men, the last wave by, crying how bright
Their frail deeds might have danced in a green bay,
Rage, rage against the dying of the light.

Wild men who caught and sang the sun in flight,   10
And learn, too late, they grieved it on its way,
Do not go gentle into that good night.

Grave men, near death, who see with blinding sight
Blind eyes could blaze like meteors and be gay,
Rage, rage against the dying of the light.

To-day, This Insect   8–21 **Murder of Eden . . . vision.** These lines contain a series of metaphors and allusions to illustrate how violence and evil break in upon the ideal peaceful condition of life typified by the Garden of Eden. This violence and evil is "the insect" of the poem. Jericho, the Old Testament city destroyed by Joshua (see the Biblical *Book of Joshua*), illustrates human destruction (l. 17); the windmill and the horse (l. 20), as well as the "fibs of vision" (l. 21) illustrate the dangers of impractical or false visions or ideals, as typified in Don Quixote's adventures   21 **John's beast,** the Beast referred to in the *Book of Revelation,* the apocalyptic vision of St. John the Evangelist

And you, my father, there on the sad height,
Curse, bless, me now with your fierce tears, I pray.
Do not go gentle into that good night.
Rage, rage against the dying of the light.
(1952)

FERN HILL

Now as I was young and easy under the apple boughs
About the lilting house and happy as the grass was
    green,
  The night above the dingle° starry,
      Time let me hail and climb
  Golden in the heydays of his eyes,
And honoured among wagons I was prince of the apple
    towns
And once below a time I lordly had the trees and
    leaves
        Trail with daisies and barley
  Down the rivers of the windfall light.

10 And as I was green and carefree, famous among the
    barns
About the happy yard and singing as the farm was
    home,
  In the sun that is young once only,
      Time let me play and be
  Golden in the mercy of his means,
And green and golden I was huntsman and herdsman,
    the calves
Sang to my horn, the foxes on the hills barked clear
    and cold,
        And the sabbath rang slowly
  In the pebbles of the holy streams.

All the sun long it was running, it was lovely, the hay
Fields high as the house, the tunes from the chimneys,
20   it was air,
  And playing, lovely and watery
      And fire green as grass.
  And nightly under the simple stars
As I rode to sleep the owls were bearing the farm
    away,
All the moon long I heard, blessed among stables, the
    nightjars
  Flying with the ricks, and the horses
      Flashing into the dark.

And then to awake, and the farm, like a wanderer
    white
With the dew, come back, the cock on his shoulder: it
    was all
30   Shining, it was Adam and maiden,
      The sky gathered again
  And the sun grew round that very day.

Fern Hill   3 **dingle**, small wooded valley

So it must have been after the birth of the simple light
In the first, spinning place, the spellbound horses
    walking warm
  Out of the whinnying green stable
      On to the fields of praise.

And honoured among foxes and pheasants by the gay
    house
Under the new made clouds and happy as the heart
    was long,
  In the sun born over and over,
      I ran my heedless ways,   40
  My wishes raced through the house high hay
And nothing I cared, at my sky blue trades, that time
    allows
In all his tuneful turning so few and such morning
    songs
  Before the children green and golden
      Follow him out of grace,

Nothing I cared, in the lamb white days, that time
    would take me
Up to the swallow thronged loft by the shadow of my
    hand,
  In the moon that is always rising,
      Nor that riding to sleep
  I should hear him fly with the high fields   50
And wake to the farm forever fled from the childless
    land.
Oh as I was young and easy in the mercy of his means,
      Time held me green and dying
  Though I sang in my chains like the sea.
(1946)

IN MY CRAFT OR SULLEN ART

In my craft or sullen art
Exercised in the still night
When only the moon rages
And the lovers lie abed
With all their griefs in their arms,
I labor by singing light
Not for ambition or bread
Or the strut and trade of charms
On the ivory stages
But for the common wages   10
Of their most secret heart.

Not for the proud man apart
From the raging moon I write
On these spindrift pages
Nor for the towering dead
With their nightingales and psalms
But for the lovers, their arms
Round the griefs of the ages,
Who pay no praise or wages
Nor heed my craft or art.   20
(1946)

A REFUSAL TO MOURN THE DEATH, BY FIRE, OF A CHILD IN LONDON

Never until the mankind making
Bird beast and flower
Fathering and all humbling darkness
Tells with silence the last light breaking
And the still hour
Is come of the sea tumbling in harness

And I must enter again the round
Zion of the water bead
And the synagogue of the ear of corn°
10   Shall I let pray the shadow of a sound
Or sow my salt seed
In the least valley of sackcloth to mourn

The majesty and burning of the child's death.
I shall not murder
The mankind of her going with a grave truth
Nor blaspheme down the stations of the breath
With any further
Elegy of innocence and youth.

Deep with the first dead lies London's daughter,
20   Robed in the long friends,
The grains beyond age, the dark veins of her mother,
Secret by the unmourning water
Of the riding Thames.
After the first death, there is no other.
(1946; 1952)

DORIS LESSING
1919–

Doris Lessing was born of British parents in 1919 in Persia, where her father served as a captain in the British army. When she was five years old, her family moved to a farm in southern Rhodesia, which subsequently served as the setting for many of her short stories. She came to England in 1949 and has remained there ever since. As a young adult she was active in the Communist party and she remains today sympathetic to political activists of the left. Many of her fictions are concerned with characters who are involved with contemporary political and social upheaval.

She is the author of more than twenty books—novels, stories, reportage, poems, and plays. *The Grass*

Is Singing, her first published book, brought her short stories to public attention in 1950. The Martha Quest tetralogy, collected as *Children of Violence* (1964–1965), and *The Golden Notebook* (1962) are her most well-known works; the latter is often regarded as her best novel. Among her notable recent works are *Briefing for a Descent into Hell* (1971), *The Memoirs of a Survivor* (1975), and *Collected Stories* (1978). Lessing's fiction is generally known for its sensitive examination of women's identity and sexuality, as well as for its stark portrayal of economic and political realities.

A MAN AND TWO WOMEN

Stella's friends the Bradfords had taken a cheap cottage in Essex for the summer, and she was going down to visit them. She wanted to see them, but there was no doubt there was something of a letdown (and for them too) in the English cottage. Last summer Stella had been wandering with her husband around Italy; had seen the English couple at a café table, and found them sympathetic. They all liked each other, and the four went about for some weeks, sharing meals, hotels, trips. Back in London the friendship had not, 10 as might have been expected, fallen off. Then Stella's husband departed abroad, as he often did, and Stella saw Jack and Dorothy by herself. There were a great many people she might have seen, but it was the Bradfords she saw most often, two or three times a week, at their flat or hers. They were at ease with each other. Why were they? Well, for one thing they were all artists—in different ways. Stella designed wallpapers and materials; she had a name for it.

The Bradfords were real artists. He painted, she 20 drew. They had lived mostly out of England in cheap places around the Mediterranean. Both from the North of England, they had met at art school, married at twenty, had taken flight from England, then returned to it, needing it, then off again: and so on, for years, in the rhythm of so many of their kind, needing, hating, loving England. There had been seasons of real poverty, while they lived on *pasta* or bread or rice, and wine and fruit and sunshine, in Majorca, southern Spain, Italy, North Africa. 30

A French critic had seen Jack's work, and suddenly he was successful. His show in Paris, then one in London, made money; and now he charged in the hundreds where a year or so ago he charged ten or twenty guineas. This had deepened his contempt for the values of the markets. For a while Stella thought that this was the bond between the Bradfords and herself. They were so very much, as she was, of the new generation of artists (and poets and playwrights and novelists) who had one thing in common, a cool derision about 40 the racket. They were so very unlike (they felt) the older generation with their Societies and their Lunches

A Refusal to Mourn the Death   8–9 **Zion . . . corn.** These complex images deal with the natural and supernatural worlds. Zion is the heavenly Jerusalem. To return to the water bead, to find it Zion or the fruition of hopes, is to imagine returning to the primal liquid of creation. When rows of corn are all we know of gathering together, then the poet will mourn. Both images seem to be intended as impossibilities

and their salons and their cliques: their atmosphere of connivance with the snobberies of success. Stella, too, had been successful by a fluke. Not that she did not consider herself talented; it was that others as talented were unfêted, and unbought. When she was with the Bradfords and other fellow spirits, they would talk about the racket, using each other as yardsticks or fellow consciences about how much to give in, what to give, how to use without being used, how to enjoy without becoming dependent on enjoyment.

Of course Dorothy Bradford was not able to talk in quite the same way, since she had not yet been "discovered"; she had not "broken through." A few people with discrimination bought her unusual delicate drawings, which had a strength that was hard to understand unless one knew Dorothy herself. But she was not at all, as Jack was, a great success. There was a strain here, in the marriage, nothing much; it was kept in check by their scorn for their arbitrary rewards of "the racket." But it was there, nevertheless.

Stella's husband had said: "Well, I can understand that, it's like me and you—you're creative, whatever that may mean, I'm just a bloody TV journalist." There was no bitterness in this. He was a good journalist, and besides he sometimes got the chance to make a good small film. All the same, there was that between him and Stella, just as there was between Jack and his wife.

After a time Stella saw something else in her kinship with the couple. It was that the Bradfords had a close bond, bred of having spent so many years together in foreign places, dependent on each other because of their poverty. It had been a real love marriage, one could see it by looking at them. It was now. And Stella's marriage was a real marriage. She understood she enjoyed being with the Bradfords because the two couples were equal in this. Both marriages were those of strong, passionate, talented individuals; they shared a battling quality that strengthened them, not weakened them.

The reason why it had taken Stella so long to understand this was that the Bradfords had made her think about her own marriage, which she was beginning to take for granted, sometimes even found exhausting. She had understood, through them, how lucky she was in her husband; how lucky they all were. No marital miseries; nothing of (what they saw so often in friends) one partner in a marriage victim to the other, resenting the other; no claiming of outsiders as sympathisers or allies in an unequal battle.

There had been a plan for these four people to go off again to Italy or Spain, but then Stella's husband departed, and Dorothy got pregnant. So there was the cottage in Essex instead, a bad second choice, but better, they all felt, to deal with a new baby on home ground, at least for the first year. Stella, telephoned by Jack (on Dorothy's particular insistence, he said), offered and received commiserations on its being only Essex and not Majorca or Italy. She also received sympathy because her husband had been expected back this weekend, but had wired to say he wouldn't be back for another month, probably—there was trouble in Venezuela. Stella wasn't really forlorn; she didn't mind living alone, since she was always supported by knowing her man would be back. Besides, if she herself were offered the chance of a month's "trouble" in Venezuela, she wouldn't hesitate, so it wasn't fair . . . fairness characterised their relationship. All the same, it was nice that she could drop down (or up) to the Bradfords, people with whom she could always be herself, neither more nor less.

She left London at midday by train, armed with food unobtainable in Essex: salamis, cheeses, spices, wine. The sun shone, but it wasn't particularly warm. She hoped there would be heating in the cottage, July or not.

The train was empty. The little station seemed stranded in a green nowhere. She got out, cumbered by bags full of food. A porter and a stationmaster examined, then came to succour her. She was a tallish, fair woman, rather ample; her soft hair, drawn back, escaped in tendrils, and she had great helpless-looking blue eyes. She wore a dress made in one of the materials she had designed. Enormous green leaves laid hands all over her body, and fluttered about her knees. She stood smiling, accustomed to men running to wait on her, enjoying them enjoying her. She walked with them to the barrier where Jack waited, appreciating the scene. He was a smallish man, compact, dark. He wore a blue-green summer shirt, and smoked a pipe and smiled, watching. The two men delivered her into the hands of the third, and departed, whistling, to their duties.

Jack and Stella kissed, then pressed their cheeks together.

"Food," he said, "food," relieving her of the parcels.

"What's it like here, shopping?"

"Vegetables all right, I suppose."

Jack was still Northern in this: he seemed brusque, to strangers; he wasn't shy, he simply hadn't been brought up to enjoy words. Now he put his arm briefly around Stella's waist, and said: "Marvellous, Stell, marvellous." They walked on, pleased with each other. Stella had with Jack, her husband had with Dorothy, these moments, when they said to each other wordlessly: If I were not married to my husband, if you were not married to your wife, how delightful it would be to be married to you. These moments were not the least of the pleasures of this four-sided friendship.

"Are you liking it down here?"

"It's what we bargained for."

There was more than his usual shortness in this, and she glanced at him to find him frowning. They were walking to the car, parked under a tree.

"How's the baby?"

"Little bleeder never sleeps, he's wearing us out,
160 but he's fine."

The baby was six weeks old. Having the baby was a definite achievement: getting it safely conceived and born had taken a couple of years. Dorothy, like most independent women, had had divided thoughts about a baby. Besides, she was over thirty and complained she was set in her ways. All this—the difficulties, Dorothy's hesitations—had added up to an atmosphere which Dorothy herself described as "like wondering if some damned horse is going to take the
170 fence." Dorothy would talk, while she was pregnant, in a soft staccato voice: "Perhaps I don't really want a baby at all? Perhaps I'm not fitted to be a mother? Perhaps . . . and if so . . . and how . . . ?"

She said: "Until recently Jack and I were always with people who took it for granted that getting pregnant was a disaster, and now suddenly all the people we know have young children and baby-sitters and . . . perhaps . . . if . . ."

Jack said: "You'll feel better when it's born."
180 Once Stella had heard him say, after one of Dorothy's long troubled dialogues with herself: "Now that's enough, that's enough, Dorothy." He had silenced her, taking the responsibility.

They reached the car, got in. It was a second-hand job recently bought. "They" (being the press, the enemy generally) "wait for us" (being artists or writers who have made money) "to buy flashy cars." They had discussed it, decided that *not* to buy an expensive car if they felt like it would be allowing themselves to
190 be bullied; but bought a second-hand one after all. Jack wasn't going to give *them* so much satisfaction, apparently.

"Actually we could have walked," he said, as they shot down a narrow lane, "but with these groceries, it's just as well."

"If the baby's giving you a tough time, there can't be much time for cooking." Dorothy was a wonderful cook. But now again there was something in the air as he said: "Food's definitely not too good just now. You
200 can cook supper, Stell, we could do with a good feed."

Now Dorothy hated anyone in her kitchen, except, for certain specified jobs, her husband; and this was surprising.

"The truth is, Dorothy's worn out," he went on, and now Stella understood he was warning her.

"Well, it is tiring," said Stella soothingly.

"You were like that?"

Like that was saying a good deal more than just worn out, or tired, and Stella understood that Jack was
210 really uneasy. She said, plaintively humorous: "You two always expect me to remember things that happened a hundred years ago. Let me think. . . ."

She had been married when she was eighteen, got pregnant at once. Her husband had left her. Soon she had married Philip, who also had a small child from a former marriage. These two children, her daughter, seventeen, his son, twenty, had grown up together.

She remembered herself at nineteen, alone, with a small baby. "Well, I was alone," she said. "That makes a difference. I remember I was exhausted. Yes,
220 I was definitely irritable and unreasonable."

"Yes," said Jack, with a brief reluctant look at her.

"All right, don't worry," she said, replying aloud as she often did to things that Jack had not said aloud.

"Good," he said.

Stella thought of how she had seen Dorothy, in the hospital room, with the new baby. She had sat up in bed, in a pretty bed jacket, the baby beside her in a basket. He was restless. Jack stood between basket and bed, one large hand on his son's stomach. "Now,
230 you just shut up, little bleeder," he had said, as he grumbled. Then he had picked him up, as if he'd been doing it always, held him against his shoulder, and, as Dorothy held her arms out, had put the baby into them. "Want your mother, then? Don't blame you."

That scene, the ease of it, the way the two parents were together, had, for Stella, made nonsense of all the months of Dorothy's self-questioning. As for Dorothy, she had said, parodying the expected words but meaning them: "He's the most beautiful baby ever
240 born. I can't imagine why I didn't have him before."

"There's the cottage," said Jack. Ahead of them was a small labourer's cottage, among full green trees, surrounded by green grass. It was painted white, had four sparkling windows. Next to it a long shed or structure that turned out to be a greenhouse.

"The man grew tomatoes," said Jack. "Fine studio now."

The car came to rest under another tree.

"Can I just drop in to the studio?"
250 "Help yourself." Stella walked into the long, glass-roofed shed. In London Jack and Dorothy shared a studio. They had shared huts, sheds, any suitable building, all around the Mediterranean. They always worked side by side. Dorothy's end was tidy, exquisite, Jack's lumbered with great canvases, and he worked in a clutter. Now Stella looked to see if this friendly arrangement continued, but as Jack came in behind her he said: "Dorothy's not set herself up yet. I miss her, I can tell you."
260 The greenhouse was still partly one: trestles with plants stood along the ends. It was lush and warm.

"As hot as hell when the sun's really going, it makes up. And Dorothy brings Paul in sometimes, so he can get used to a decent climate young."

Dorothy came in, at the far end, without the baby. She had recovered her figure. She was a small dark woman, with neat, delicate limbs. Her face was white, with scarlet rather irregular lips, and black glossy brows, a little crooked. So while she was not pretty,
270 she was lively and dramatic-looking. She and Stella had their moments together, when they got pleasure

from contrasting their differences, one woman so big and soft and blond, the other so dark and vivacious.

Dorothy came forward through shafts of sunlight, stopped, and said: "Stella, I'm glad you've come." Then forward again, to a few steps off, where she stood looking at them. "You two look good together," she said, frowning. There was something heavy and overemphasised about both statements, and Stella said: "I was wondering what Jack had been up to."

"Very good, I think," said Dorothy, coming to look at the new canvas on the easel. It was of sunlit rocks, brown and smooth, with blue sky, blue water, and people swimming in spangles of light. When Jack was in the South he painted pictures that his wife described as "dirt and grime and misery"—which was how they both described their joint childhood background. When he was in England he painted scenes like these. "Like it? It's good, isn't it?" said Dorothy.

"Very much," said Stella. She always took pleasure from the contrast between Jack's outward self—the small, self-contained little man who could have vanished in a moment into a crowd of factory workers in, perhaps Manchester, and the sensuous bright pictures like these.

"And you?" asked Stella.

"Having a baby's killed everything creative in me—quite different from being pregnant," said Dorothy, but not complaining of it. She had worked like a demon while she was pregnant.

"Have a heart," said Jack, "he's only just got himself born."

"Well, I don't care," said Dorothy. "That's the funny thing, I *don't* care." She said this flat, indifferent. She seemed to be looking at them both again from a small troubled distance. "You two look good together," she said, and again there was the small jar.

"Well, how about some tea?" said Jack, and Dorothy said at once: "I made it when I heard the car. I thought better inside, it's not really hot in the sun." She led the way out of the greenhouse, her white linen dress dissolving in lozenges of yellow light from the glass panes above, so that Stella was reminded of the white limbs of Jack's swimmers disintegrating under sunlight in his new picture. The work of these two people was always reminding one of each other, or each other's work, and in all kinds of ways: they were so much married, so close.

The time it took to cross the space of rough grass to the door of the little house was enough to show Dorothy was right: it was really chilly in the sun. Inside two electric heaters made up for it. There had been two little rooms downstairs, but they had been knocked into one fine low-ceilinged room, stone-floored, whitewashed. A tea table, covered with a purple checked cloth, stood waiting near a window where flowering bushes and trees showed through clean panes. Charming. They adjusted the heaters and ar-

ranged themselves so they could admire the English countryside through glass. Stella looked for the baby; Dorothy said: "In the pram at the back." Then she asked: "Did yours cry a lot?"

Stella laughed and said again: "I'll try to remember."

"We expect you to guide and direct, with all your experience," said Jack.

"As far as I can remember, she was a little demon for about three months, for no reason I could see, then suddenly she became civilised."

"Roll on the three months," said Jack.

"Six weeks to go," said Dorothy, handling teacups in a languid indifferent manner Stella found new in her.

"Finding it tough going?"

"I've never felt better in my life," said Dorothy at once, as if being accused.

"You look fine."

She looked a bit tired, nothing much; Stella couldn't see what reason there was for Jack to warn her. Unless he meant the languor, a look of self-absorption? Her vivacity, a friendly aggressiveness that was the expression of her lively intelligence, was dimmed. She sat leaning back in a deep air-chair, letting Jack manage things, smiling vaguely.

"I'll bring him in in a minute," she remarked, listening to the silence from the sunlit garden at the back.

"Leave him," said Jack. "He's quiet seldom enough. Relax, woman, and have a cigarette."

He lit a cigarette for her, and she took it in the same vague way, and sat breathing out smoke, her eyes half closed.

"Have you heard from Philip?" she asked, not from politeness, but with sudden insistence.

"Of course she has, she got a wire," said Jack.

"I want to know how she feels," said Dorothy. "How do you feel, Stell?" She was listening for the baby all the time.

"Feel about what?"

"About his not coming back."

"But he is coming back, it's only a month," said Stella, and heard, with surprise, that her voice sounded edgy.

"You see?" said Dorothy to Jack, meaning the words, not the edge on them.

At this evidence that she and Philip had been discussed, Stella felt, first, pleasure: because it was pleasurable to be understood by two such good friends; then she felt discomfort, remembering Jack's warning.

"See what?" she asked Dorothy, smiling.

"That's enough now," said Jack to his wife in a flash of stubborn anger, which continued the conversation that had taken place.

Dorothy took direction from her husband, and kept quiet a moment, then seemed impelled to continue: "I've been thinking it must be nice, having your husband go off, then come back. Do you realise Jack and I haven't been separated since we married? That's over ten years. Don't you think there's something awful in two grown people stuck together all the time like Siamese twins?'' This ended in a wail of genuine appeal to Stella.

"No, I think it's marvellous.''

"But you don't mind being alone so much?''

"It's not *so* much, it's two or three months in a year. Well of course I mind. But I enjoy being alone, really. But I'd enjoy it too if we were together all the time. I envy you two.'' Stella was surprised to find her eyes wet with self-pity because she had to be without her husband another month.

"And what does he think?'' demanded Dorothy. "What does Philip think?''

Stella said: "Well, I think he likes getting away from time to time—yes. He likes intimacy, he enjoys it, but it doesn't come as easily to him as it does to me.'' She had never said this before because she had never thought about it. She was annoyed with herself that she had had to wait for Dorothy to prompt her. Yet she knew that getting annoyed was what she must not do, with the state Dorothy was in, whatever it was. She glanced at Jack for guidance, but he was determinedly busy on his pipe.

"Well, I'm like Philip,'' announced Dorothy. "Yes, I'd love it if Jack went off sometimes. I think I'm being stifled being shut up with Jack day and night, year in year out.''

"Thanks,'' said Jack, short but good-humoured.

"No, but I mean it. There's something humiliating about two adult people never for one second out of each other's sight.''

"Well,'' said Jack, "when Paul's a bit bigger, you buzz off for a month or so and you'll appreciate me when you get back.''

"It's not that I don't appreciate you, it's not that at all,'' said Dorothy, insistent, almost strident, apparently fevered with restlessness. Her languor had quite gone, and her limbs jerked and moved. And now the baby, as if he had been prompted by his father's mentioning him, let out a cry. Jack got up, forestalling his wife, saying: "I'll get him.''

Dorothy sat, listening for her husband's movements with the baby, until he came back, which he did, supporting the infant sprawled against his shoulder with a competent hand. He sat down, let his son slide onto his chest, and said: "There now, you shut up and leave us in peace a bit longer.'' The baby was looking up into his face with the astonished expression of the newly born, and Dorothy sat smiling at both of them. Stella understood that her restlessness, her repeated curtailed movements, meant that she longed—more, needed—to have the child in her arms, have its body against hers. And Jack seemed to feel this, because Stella could have sworn it was not a conscious deci-

sion that made him rise and slide the infant into his wife's arms. Her flesh, her needs, had spoken direct to him without words, and he had risen at once to give her what she wanted. This silent instinctive conversation between husband and wife made Stella miss her own husband violently, and with resentment against fate that kept them apart so often. She ached for Philip.

Meanwhile Dorothy, now the baby was sprawled softly against her chest, the small feet in her hand, seemed to have lapsed into good humour. And Stella, watching, remembered something she really had forgotten: the close, fierce physical tie between herself and her daughter when she had been a tiny baby. She saw this bond in the way Dorothy stroked the small head that trembled on its neck as the baby looked up into his mother's face. Why, she remembered it was like being in love, having a new baby. All kinds of forgotten or unused instincts woke in Stella. She lit a cigarette, took herself in hand; set herself to enjoy the other woman's love affair with her baby instead of envying her.

The sun, dropping into the trees, struck the windowpanes; and there was a dazzle and a flashing of yellow and white light into the room, particularly over Dorothy in her white dress and the baby. Again Stella was reminded of Jack's picture of the white-limbed swimmers in sun-dissolving water. Dorothy shielded the baby's eyes with her hand and remarked dreamily: "This is better than any man, isn't it, Stell? Isn't it better than any man?''

"Well—no,'' said Stella laughing. "No, not for long.''

"If you say so, you should know . . . but I can't imagine ever . . . tell me, Stell, does your Philip have affairs when he's away?''

"For God's sake!'' said Jack, angry. But he checked himself.

"Yes, I am sure he does.''

"Do you mind?'' asked Dorothy, loving the baby's feet with her enclosing palm.

And now Stella was forced to remember, to think about having minded, minding, coming to terms, and the ways in which she now did not mind.

"I don't think about it,'' she said.

"Well, I don't think I'd mind,'' said Dorothy.

"Thanks for letting me know,'' said Jack, short despite himself. Then he made himself laugh.

"And you, do you have affairs while Philip's away?''

"Sometimes. Not really.''

"Do you know, Jack was unfaithful to me this week,'' remarked Dorothy, smiling at the baby.

"That's *enough*,'' said Jack, really angry.

"No it isn't enough, it isn't. Because what's awful is, I don't care.''

"Well why should you care, in the circumstances?''

Jack turned to Stella. "There's a silly bitch Lady Edith lives across that field. She got all excited, real live artists living down her lane. Well Dorothy was lucky, she had an excuse in the baby, but I had to go to her silly party. Booze flowing in rivers, and the most incredible people—you know. If you read about them in a novel you'd never believe . . . but I can't remember much after about twelve."

"Do you know what happened?" said Dorothy. "I was feeding the baby, it was terribly early. Jack sat straight up in bed and said: 'Jesus, Dorothy, I've just remembered, I screwed that silly bitch Lady Edith on her brocade sofa.'"

Stella laughed. Jack let out a snort of laughter. Dorothy laughed, an unscrupulous chuckle of appreciation. Then she said seriously: "But that's the point, Stella—the thing is, I don't care a tuppenny damn."

"But why should you?" asked Stella.

"But it's the first time he ever has, and surely I should have minded?"

"Don't you be too sure of that," said Jack, energetically puffing his pipe. "Don't be too sure." But it was only for form's sake, and Dorothy knew it, and said: "Surely I should have cared, Stell?"

"No. You'd have cared if you and Jack weren't so marvellous together. Just as I'd care if Philip and I weren't. . . ." Tears came running down her face. She let them. These were her good friends; and besides, instinct told her tears weren't a bad thing, with Dorothy in this mood. She said, sniffing: "When Philip gets home, we always have a flaming bloody row in the first day or two, about something unimportant, but what it's really about, and we know it, is that I'm jealous of any affair he's had and vice versa. Then we go to bed and make up." She wept, bitterly, thinking of this happiness, postponed for a month, to be succeeded by the delightful battle of their day to day living.

"Oh Stella," said Jack. "Stell . . ." He got up, fished out a handkerchief, dabbed her eyes for her. "There, love, he'll be back soon."

"Yes, I know. It's just that you two are so good together and whenever I'm with you I miss Philip."

"Well, I suppose we're good together?" said Dorothy, sounding surprised. Jack, bending over Stella with his back to his wife, made a warning grimace, then stood up and turned, commanding the situation. "It's nearly six. You'd better feed Paul. Stella's going to cook supper."

"Is she? How nice," said Dorothy. "There's everything in the kitchen, Stella. How lovely to be looked after."

"I'll show you our mansion," said Jack.

Upstairs were two small white rooms. One was the bedroom, with their things and the baby's in it. The other was an overflow room, jammed with stuff. Jack picked up a large leather folder off the spare bed and said: "Look at these, Stell." He stood at the window, back to her, his thumb at work in his pipe bowl, looking into the garden. Stella sat on the bed, opened the folder and at once exclaimed: "When did she do these?"

"The last three months she was pregnant. Never seen anything like it, she just turned them out one after the other."

There were a couple of hundred pencil drawings, all of two bodies in every kind of balance, tension, relationship. The two bodies were Jack's and Dorothy's, mostly unclothed, but not all. The drawings startled, not only because they marked a real jump forward in Dorothy's achievement, but because of their bold sensuousness. They were a kind of chant, or exaltation about the marriage. The instinctive closeness, the harmony of Jack and Dorothy, visible in every movement they made towards or away from each other, visible even when they were not together, was celebrated here with a frank, calm triumph.

"Some of them are pretty strong," said Jack, the Northern working-class boy reviving in him for a moment's puritanism.

But Stella laughed, because the prudishness masked pride: some of the drawings were indecent.

In the last few of the series the woman's body was swollen in pregnancy. They showed her trust in her husband, whose body, commanding hers, stood or lay in positions of strength and confidence. In the very last Dorothy stood turned away from her husband, her two hands supporting her big belly, and Jack's hands were protective on her shoulders.

"They are marvellous," said Stella.

"They are, aren't they."

Stella looked, laughing, and with love, towards Jack; for she saw that his showing her the drawings was not only pride in his wife's talent; but that he was using this way of telling Stella not to take Dorothy's mood too seriously. And to cheer himself up. She said, impulsively: "Well that's all right then, isn't it?"

"What? Oh yes, I see what you mean, yes, I think it's all right."

"Do you know what?" said Stella, lowering her voice. "I think Dorothy's guilty because she feels unfaithful to you."

"What?"

"No, I mean, with the baby, and that's what it's all about."

He turned to face her, troubled, then slowly smiling. There was the same rich unscrupulous quality of appreciation in that smile as there had been in Dorothy's laugh over her husband and Lady Edith. "You think so?" They laughed together, irrepressibly and loudly.

"What's the joke?" shouted Dorothy.

"I'm laughing because your drawings are so good," shouted Stella.

"Yes, they are, aren't they?" But Dorothy's voice

changed to flat incredulity: "The trouble is, I can't imagine how I ever did them, I can't imagine ever being able to do it again."

"Downstairs," said Jack to Stella, and they went down to find Dorothy nursing the baby. He nursed with his whole being, all of him in movement. He was wrestling with the breast, thumping Dorothy's plump pretty breast with his fists. Jack stood looking down at the two of them, grinning. Dorothy reminded Stella of a cat, half closing her yellow eyes to stare over her kittens at work on her side, while she stretched out a paw where claws sheathed and unsheathed themselves, making a small rip-rip-rip on the carpet she lay on.

"You're a savage creature," said Stella, laughing.

Dorothy raised her small vivid face and smiled. "Yes, I am," she said, and looked at the two of them calm, and from a distance, over the head of her energetic baby.

Stella cooked supper in a stone kitchen, with a heater brought by Jack to make it tolerable. She used the good food she had brought with her, taking trouble. It took some time, then the three ate slowly over a big wooden table. The baby was not asleep. He grumbled for some minutes on a cushion on the floor, then his father held him briefly, before passing him over, as he had done earlier, in response to his mother's need to have him close.

"I'm supposed to let him cry," remarked Dorothy. "But why should he? If he were an Arab or an African baby he'd be plastered to my back."

"And very nice too," said Jack. "I think they come out too soon into the light of day, they should just stay inside for about eighteen months, much better all around."

"Have a heart," said Dorothy and Stella together, and they all laughed; but Dorothy added, quite serious: "Yes, I've been thinking so too."

This good nature lasted through the long meal. The light went cool and thin outside; and inside they let the summer dusk deepen, without lamps.

"I've got to go quite soon," said Stella, with regret.

"Oh, no, you've got to stay!" said Dorothy, strident. It was sudden, the return of the woman who made Jack and Dorothy tense themselves to take strain.

"We all thought Philip was coming. The children will be back tomorrow night, they've been on holiday."

"Then stay till tomorrow, I *want* you," said Dorothy, petulant.

"But I can't," said Stella.

"I never thought I'd want another woman around, cooking in my kitchen, looking after me, but I do," said Dorothy, apparently about to cry.

"Well, love, you'll have to put up with me," said Jack.

"Would you mind, Stell?"

"Mind *what*?" asked Stella, cautious.

"Do you find Jack attractive?"

"Very."

"Well I know you do. Jack, do you find Stella attractive?"

"Try me," said Jack, grinning; but at the same time signalling warnings to Stella.

"Well, then!" said Dorothy.

"A *ménage à trois*?" asked Stella laughing. "And how about my Philip? Where does he fit in?"

"Well, if it comes to that, I wouldn't mind Philip myself," said Dorothy, knitting her sharp black brows and frowning.

"I don't blame you," said Stella, thinking of her handsome husband.

"Just for a month, till he comes back," said Dorothy. "I tell you what, we'll abandon this silly cottage, we must have been mad to stick ourselves away in England in the first place. The three of us'll just pack up and go off to Spain or Italy with the baby."

"And what else?" enquired Jack, good-natured at all costs, using his pipe as a safety valve.

"Yes, I've decided I approve of polygamy," announced Dorothy. She had opened her dress and the baby was nursing again, quietly this time, relaxed against her. She stroked his head, softly, softly, while her voice rose and insisted at the other two people: "I never understood it before, but I do now. I'll be the senior wife, and you two can look after me."

"Any other plans?" enquired Jack, angry now. "You just drop in from time to time to watch Stella and me have a go, is that it? Or are you going to tell us when we can go off and do it, give us your gracious permission?"

"Oh I don't care what you do, that's the point," said Dorothy, sighing, sounding forlorn, however.

Jack and Stella, careful not to look at each other, sat waiting.

"I read something in the newspaper yesterday, it struck me," said Dorothy, conversational. "A man and two women living together—here, in England. They are both his wives, they consider themselves his wives. The senior wife has a baby, and the younger wife sleeps with him—well, that's what it looked like, reading between the lines."

"You'd better stop reading between lines," said Jack. "It's not doing you any good."

"No, I'd like it," insisted Dorothy. "I think our marriages are silly. Africans and people like that, they know better, they've got some sense."

"I can just see you if I did make love to Stella," said Jack.

"Yes!" said Stella, with a short laugh which, against her will, was resentful.

"But I wouldn't mind," said Dorothy, and burst into tears.

"Now, Dorothy, that's enough," said Jack. He got

up, took the baby, whose sucking was mechanical now, and said: "Now listen, you're going right upstairs and you're going to sleep. This little stinker's full as a tick, he'll be asleep for hours, that's my bet."

"I don't feel sleepy," said Dorothy, sobbing.

"I'll give you a sleeping pill, then."

Then started a search for sleeping pills. None to be found.

"That's just like us," wailed Dorothy, "we don't
740 even have a sleeping pill in the place. . . . Stella, I wish you'd stay, I really do. Why can't you?"

"Stella's going in just a minute, I'm taking her to the station," said Jack. He poured some Scotch into a glass, handed it to his wife and said: "Now drink that, love, and let's have an end of it. I'm getting fed-up." He sounded fed-up.

Dorothy obediently drank the Scotch, got unsteadily from her chair and went slowly upstairs. "Don't let him cry," she demanded, as she disappeared.

750 "Oh you silly bitch," he shouted after her. "When have I let him cry? Here, you hold on a minute," he said to Stella, handing her the baby. He ran upstairs.

Stella held the baby. This was almost for the first time, since she sensed how much another woman's holding her child made Dorothy's fierce new possessiveness uneasy. She looked down at the small, sleepy, red face and said softly: "Well, you're causing a lot of trouble, aren't you?"

Jack shouted from upstairs: "Come up a minute,
760 Stell." She went up, with the baby. Dorothy was tucked up in bed, drowsy from the Scotch, the bedside light turned away from her. She looked at the baby, but Jack took it from Stella.

"Jack says I'm a silly bitch," said Dorothy, apologetic, to Stella.

"Well, never mind, you'll feel different soon."

"I suppose so, if you say so. All right, I *am* going to sleep," said Dorothy, in a stubborn, sad little voice. She turned over, away from them. In the last flare of
770 her hysteria she said: "Why don't you two walk to the station together? It's a lovely night."

"We're going to," said Jack, "don't worry."

She let out a weak giggle, but did not turn. Jack carefully deposited the now sleeping baby in the bed, about a foot from Dorothy. Who suddenly wriggled over until her small, defiant white back was in contact with the blanketed bundle that was her son.

Jack raised his eyebrows at Stella: but Stella was looking at mother and baby, the nerves of her memory
780 filling her with sweet warmth. What right had this woman, who was in possession of such delight, to torment her husband, to torment her friend, as she had been doing—what right had she to rely on their decency as she did?

Surprised by these thoughts, she walked away downstairs, and stood at the door into the garden, her eyes shut, holding herself rigid against tears.

She felt a warmth on her bare arm—Jack's hand.

She opened her eyes to see him bending towards her, concerned.

"It'd serve Dorothy right if I did drag you off into the bushes. . . ."

"Wouldn't have to drag me," she said; and while the words had the measure of facetiousness the situation demanded, she felt his seriousness envelop them both in danger.

The warmth of his hand slid across her back, and she turned towards him under its pressure. They stood together, cheeks touching, scents of skin and hair mixing with the smells of warmed grass and leaves.

She thought: What is going to happen now will blow Dorothy and Jack and that baby sky-high; it's the end of my marriage; I'm going to blow everything to bits. There was almost uncontrollable pleasure in it.

She saw Dorothy, Jack, the baby, her husband, the two halfgrown children, all dispersed, all spinning downwards through the sky like bits of debris after an explosion.

Jack's mouth was moving along her cheek towards her mouth, dissolving her whole self in delight. She saw, against closed lids, the bundled baby upstairs, and pulled back from the situation, exclaiming energetically: "Damn Dorothy, damn her, damn her, I'd like to kill her. . . ."

And he, exploding into reaction, said in a low furious rage: "Damn you both! I'd like to wring both your bloody necks. . . ."

Their faces were at a foot's distance from each other, their eyes staring hostility. She thought that if she had not had the vision of the helpless baby they would now be in each other's arms—generating tenderness and desire like a couple of dynamos, she said to herself, trembling with dry anger.

"I'm going to miss my train if I don't go," she said.

"I'll get your coat," he said, and went in, leaving her defenceless against the emptiness of the garden.

When he came out, he slid the coat around her without touching her, and said: "Come on, I'll take you by car." He walked away in front of her to the car, and she followed meekly over rough lawn. It really was a lovely night.

(1958)

PHILIP LARKIN
1922–

Philip Larkin was born in Coventry in 1922 and was educated at Oxford on a scholarship. His first book of poems, *The North Ship* (1945), was surprisingly free of the studied bookishness and gloomy rhetoric that characterized so much English verse of the forties. Larkin has said that the verse of Thomas Hardy, with its commonplace subjects and its quiet pessimistic tone, was influential for him. He became well known with his publication of *The Less Deceived*, a collection of poems, in 1955. His other works include, in addition to two novels, *The Whitsun Weddings* (1964), *The Explosion* (1970), and *High Windows* (1974). Larkin is now librarian at the University of Hull, Yorkshire, and is the jazz critic of the *Daily Telegraph*.

POETRY OF DEPARTURES

Sometimes you hear, fifth-hand,
As epitaph:
*He chucked up everything
And just cleared off,*
And always the voice will sound
Certain you approve
This audacious, purifying,
Elemental move.

And they are right, I think.
10 We all hate home
And having to be there:
I detest my room,
Its specially-chosen junk,
The good books, the good bed,
And my life, in perfect order:
So to hear it said

He walked out on the whole crowd
Leaves me flushed and stirred,
Like *Then she undid her dress*
20 Or *Take that you bastard;*
Surely I can, if he did?
And that helps me stay
Sober and industrious.
But I'd go today,

Yes, swagger the nut-strewn roads,
Crouch in the fo'c'sle
Stubbly with goodness, if
It weren't so artificial,
Such a deliberate step backwards
30 To create an object:
Books; china; a life
Reprehensibly perfect.
(1955)

DECEPTIONS

'Of course I was drugged, and so heavily I did not regain my consciousness till the next morning. I was horrified to discover that I had been ruined, and for

some days I was inconsolable, and cried like a child to be killed or sent back to my aunt.' —Mayhew,° *London Labour and the London Poor.*

Even so distant, I can taste the grief,
Bitter and sharp with stalks, he made you gulp.
The sun's occasional print, the brisk brief
Worry of wheels along the street outside
Where bridal London bows the other way, 5
And light, unanswerable and tall and wide,
Forbids the scar to heal, and drives
Shame out of hiding. All the unhurried day
Your mind lay open like a drawer of knives.

Slums, years, have buried you. I would not dare 10
Console you if I could. What can be said,
Except that suffering is exact, but where
Desire takes charge, readings will grow erratic?
For you would hardly care
That you were less deceived, out on that bed, 15
Than he was, stumbling up the breathless stair
To burst into fulfilment's desolate attic.
(1955)

THE WHITSUN WEDDINGS

That Whitsun,° I was late getting away:
    Not till about
One-twenty on the sunlit Saturday
Did my three-quarters-empty train pull out,
All windows down, all cushions hot, all sense
Of being in a hurry gone. We ran
Behind the backs of houses, crossed a street
Of blinding windscreens, smelt the fish-dock; thence
The river's level drifting breadth began,
Where sky and Lincolnshire and water meet. 10

All afternoon, through the tall heat that slept
    For miles inland,
A slow and stopping curve southwards we kept.
Wide farms went by, short-shadowed cattle, and
Canals with floatings of industrial froth;
A hothouse flashed uniquely: hedges dipped
And rose: and now and then a smell of grass
Displaced the reek of buttoned carriage-cloth
Until the next town, new and nondescript,
Approached with acres of dismantled cars. 20

At first, I didn't notice what a noise
    The weddings made
Each station that we stopped at: sun destroys
The interest of what's happening in the shade,

Deceptions   **Mayhew**, Henry Mayhew (1812–1887), English journalist who chronicled Victorian lower-class life. His chief work, *London Labour and the London Poor*, was published between 1851 and 1864   **The Whitsun Weddings** 1 **Whitsun**, Pentecost, Christian feast celebrated on the seventh Sunday after Easter; commemorates the descent of the Holy Spirit on the apostles

And down the long cool platforms whoops and skirls
I took for porters larking with the mails,
And went on reading. Once we started, though,
We passed them, grinning and pomaded, girls
In parodies of fashion, heels and veils,
30 All posed irresolutely, watching us go,

As if out on the end of an event
  Waving goodbye
To something that survived it. Struck, I leant
More promptly out next time, more curiously,
And saw it all again in different terms:
The fathers with broad belts under their suits
And seamy foreheads; mothers loud and fat;
An uncle shouting smut; and then the perms,
The nylon gloves and jewellery-substitutes,
40 The lemons, mauves, and olive-ochres that

Marked off the girls unreally from the rest.
  Yes, from cafés
And banquet-halls up yards, and bunting-dressed
Coach-party annexes, the wedding-days
Were coming to an end. All down the line
Fresh couples climbed aboard: the rest stood round;
The last confetti and advice were thrown,
And, as we moved, each face seemed to define
Just what it saw departing: children frowned
50 At something dull; fathers had never known

Success so huge and wholly farcical;
  The women shared
The secret like a happy funeral;
While girls, gripping their handbags tighter, stared
At a religious wounding. Free at last,
And loaded with the sum of all they saw,
We hurried towards London, shuffling gouts of steam.
Now fields were building-plots, and poplars cast
Long shadows over major roads, and for
60 Some fifty minutes, that in time would seem

Just long enough to settle hats and say
  I nearly died,
A dozen marriages got under way.
They watched the landscape, sitting side by side
—An Odeon went past, a cooling tower,
And someone running up to bowl—and none
Thought of the others they would never meet
Or how their lives would all contain this hour.
I thought of London spread out in the sun,
70 Its postal districts packed like squares of wheat:

There we were aimed. And as we raced across
  Bright knots of rail
Past standing Pullmans, walls of blackened moss
Came close, and it was nearly done, this frail
Travelling coincidence; and what it held
Stood ready to be loosed with all the power

That being changed can give. We slowed again,
And as the tightened brakes took hold, there swelled
A sense of falling, like an arrow-shower
Sent out of sight, somewhere becoming rain.   80
(1964)

TED HUGHES
1930–

Ted Hughes, born in Yorkshire, was brought up in the West Country. He took a degree at Cambridge, where he was primarily interested in folklore and anthropology. He is an English poet with considerable American experience. He has taught in the United States, and in 1956 he married an American poet, the late Sylvia Plath. Presently he is editor of the magazine *Modern Poetry in Translation* and publishes poetry for both adults and children.

    He has published many volumes of poetry, including *The Hawk in the Rain* (1957), *Lupercal* (1960), *Wodwo* (1968), *Crow* (1970), and *Eat Crow* (1972). His poetry shows the influences of, among others, Thomas Hardy, D. H. Lawrence, and Robert Graves (1895–). He frequently writes of the savagery and cunning of animals and of similar qualities in human beings. His viewpoint is always unsentimental, sometimes to the point of harshness.

THE THOUGHT-FOX

I imagine this midnight moment's forest:
Something else is alive
Beside the clock's loneliness
And this blank page where my fingers move.

Through the window I see no star:
Something more near
Though deeper within darkness
Is entering the loneliness:

Cold, delicately as the dark snow
A fox's nose touches twig, leaf;   10
Two eyes serve a movement, that now
And again now, and now, and now

Sets neat prints into the snow
Between trees, and warily a lame
Shadow lags by stump and in hollow
Of a body that is bold to come

Across clearings, an eye,
A widening deepening greenness,
Brilliantly, concentratedly,
20 Coming about its own business

Till, with a sudden sharp hot stink of fox
It enters the dark hole of the head.
The window is starless still; the clock ticks,
The page is printed.
(1957)

THE JAGUAR

The apes yawn and adore their fleas in the sun.
The parrots shriek as if they were on fire, or strut
Like cheap tarts to attract the stroller with the nut.
Fatigued with indolence, tiger and lion

Lie still as the sun. The boa-constrictor's coil
Is a fossil. Cage after cage seems empty, or
Stinks of sleepers from the breathing straw.
It might be painted on a nursery wall.

But who runs like the rest past these arrives
10 At a cage where the crowd stands, stares, mesmerized,
As a child at a dream, at a jaguar hurrying enraged
Through prison darkness after the drills of his eyes

On a short fierce fuse. Not in boredom—
The eye satisfied to be blind in fire,
By the bang of blood in the brain deaf the ear—
He spins from the bars, but there's no cage to him

More than to the visionary his cell:
His stride is wildernesses of freedom:
The world rolls under the long thrust of his heel.
20 Over the cage floor the horizons come.
(1957)

HAWK ROOSTING

I sit in the top of the wood, my eyes closed.
Inaction, no falsifying dream
Between my hooked head and hooked feet:
Or in sleep rehearse perfect kills and eat.

The convenience of the high trees!
The air's buoyancy and the sun's ray
Are of advantage to me;
And the earth's face upward for my inspection.

My feet are locked upon the rough bark.
10 It took the whole of Creation
To produce my foot, my each feather:
Now I hold Creation in my foot

Or fly up, and revolve it all slowly—
I kill where I please because it is all mine.
There is no sophistry in my body:
My manners are tearing off heads—

The allotment of death.
For the one path of my flight is direct
Through the bones of the living.
No arguments assert my right: 20

The sun is behind me.
Nothing has changed since I began.
My eye has permitted no change.
I am going to keep things like this.
(1960)

KING OF CARRION

His palace is of skulls.

His crown is the last splinters
Of the vessel of life.

His throne is the scaffold of bones, the hanged thing's
Rack and final stretcher.   5

His robe is the black of the last blood.

His kingdom is empty—

The empty world, from which the last cry
Flapped hugely, hopelessly away
Into the blindness and dumbness and deafness of the   10
    gulf

Returning, shrunk, silent

To reign over silence.
(1970)

GEOFFREY HILL
1932–

Geoffrey Hill was born in Worcestershire in 1932
and educated at Keble College, Oxford. He has
published three major volumes of poetry: For the Unfallen: Poems 1952–1958 (1959), King Log (1968), and
Mercian Hymns (1971). Hill has been called "a poet of
pain and economy." He is one of the few English poets
to speak eloquently and with dignity about the horrors
of modern European history. He presently teaches English at Leeds University.

GENESIS

I

Against the burly air I strode,
Where the tight ocean heaves its load,
Crying the miracles of God.

And first I brought the sea to bear
Upon the dead weight of the land;
And the waves flourished at my prayer,
The rivers spawned their sand.

And where the streams were salt and full
The tough pig-headed salmon strove,
10 Curbing the ebb and the tide's pull,
To reach the steady hills above.

II

The second day I stood and saw
The osprey plunge with triggered claw,
Feathering blood along the shore,
To lay the living sinew bare.

And the third day I cried: 'Beware
The soft-voiced owl, the ferret's smile,
The hawk's deliberate stoop in air,
Cold eyes, and bodies hooped in steel,
20 Forever bent upon the kill.'

III

And I renounced, on the fourth day,
This fierce and unregenerate clay,

Building as a huge myth for man
The watery Leviathan,°

And made the glove-winged albatross
Scour the ashes of the sea
Where Capricorn and Zero cross,°
A brooding immortality—
Such as the charmed phoenix° has
30 In the unwithering tree.

IV

The phoenix burns as cold as frost;
And, like a legendary ghost,
The phantom-bird goes wild and lost,
Upon a pointless ocean tossed.

So, the fifth day, I turned again
To flesh and blood and the blood's pain.

V

On the sixth day, as I rode

In haste about the works of God,
With spurs I plucked the horse's blood.

By blood we live, the hot, the cold,   40
To ravage and redeem the world:
There is no bloodless myth will hold.

And by Christ's blood are men made free
Though in close shrouds their bodies lie
Under the rough pelt of the sea;°

Though Earth has rolled beneath her weight
The bones that cannot bear the light.
(1952; 1959)

IN MEMORY OF JANE FRASER

When snow like sheep lay in the fold
And winds went begging at each door,
And the far hills were blue with cold,
And a cold shroud lay on the moor,

She kept the siege. And every day   5
We watched her brooding over death
Like a strong bird above its prey.
The room filled with the kettle's breath.

Damp curtains glued against the pane
Sealed time away. Her body froze   10
As if to freeze us all, and chain
Creation to a stunned repose.

She died before the world could stir.
In March the ice unloosed the brook
And water ruffled the sun's hair,   15
And a few sprinkled leaves unshook.
(1953; 1959)

ANNUNCIATIONS

1

The Word has been abroad, is back, with a tanned look
From its subsistence in the stiffening-mire.
Cleansing has become killing, the reward
Touchable, overt, clean to the touch.
Now at a distance from the steam of beasts,
The loathly neckings and fat shook spawn
(Each specimen-jar fed with delicate spawn)
The searchers with the curers sit at meat
And are satisfied. Such precious things put down
And the flesh eased through turbulence the soul   10
Purples itself; each eye squats full and mild

Genesis 24 **Leviathan**, sea monster who symbolized evil in the Old Testament and Christian literature 27 **Capricorn . . . cross.** See Coleridge's *The Rime of the Ancient Mariner* 29 **phoenix**, mythical bird that died only to rise from its own ashes

44–45 **Though . . . sea.** Bodies buried at sea are sewn into a weighted shroud

While all who attend to fiddle or to harp
For betterment, flavour their decent mouths
With gobbets of the sweetest sacrifice.

2

O Love, subject of the mere diurnal grind,
Forever being pledged to be redeemed,
Expose yourself for charity; be assured
The body is but husk and excrement.
Enter these deaths according to the law,

O visited women, possessed sons! Foreign lusts   20
Infringe our restraints; the changeable
Soldiery have their goings-out and comings-in
Dying in abundance. Choicest beasts
Suffuse the gutters with their colourful blood.
Our God scatters corruption. Priests, martyrs,
Parade to this imperious theme: 'O Love,
You know what pains succeed; be vigilant; strive
To recognize the damned among your friends.'

(1961)

DEFINITIONS OF LITERARY TERMS

Words within entries in SMALL CAPITAL LETTERS refer you to other entries in the *Definitions of Literary Terms.*

alexandrine (See HEXAMETER.)

allegory, a NARRATIVE either in VERSE or prose, in which characters, action, and sometimes SETTING represent abstract concepts apart from the literal meaning of the story. The underlying meaning has moral, social, religious, or political significance, and the characters are often PERSONIFICATIONS of abstract ideas such as charity, hope, greed, or envy. Spenser's *The Faerie Queene* is a good example of allegory.

alliteration, the repetition of consonant sounds at the beginnings of words or within words, particularly in accented syllables. It can be used to reinforce meaning, unify thought, or simply for musical effect. "They called him *Gr*endel, a demon *gr*im" (*Beowulf,* line 99).

allusion, a brief reference to a person, event, or place, real or fictitious, or to a work of art. In Dryden's "To the Memory of Mr. Oldham," the reference to Marcellus, the promising young nephew of the emperor Augustus who died before he could succeed his uncle, is an allusion. In Auden's "Musée des Beaux Arts," there is an allusion to *Icarus,* a painting by Brueghel and to the Greek myth which inspired the painting.

analogy, a comparison made between two items, situations or ideas that are somewhat alike but unlike in most respects. Frequently an unfamiliar or complex object or idea will be explained through comparison to a familiar or simpler one. In "Of Studies," Bacon makes an analogy between the growth of natural human abilities and that of plants in nature.

anapest, a three-syllable metrical FOOT consisting of two unaccented syllables followed by an accented syllable. In the following line, the feet are divided by slashes, and since there are four feet, the line can be described as *anapestic* TETRAMETER.

Like a child / from the womb, / like a ghost / from the tomb . . .

Shelley, "The Cloud," line 83

anaphora, the repetition of a word or phrase at the beginning of successive clauses.

anastrophe, inversion of the usual order of the parts of a sentence, primarily for emphasis or to achieve a certain rhythm or rhyme. "About the woodlands I will go" (Housman, "Loveliest of Trees") is a reversal or inversion of the normal order of subject-verb-object (complement), "I will go about the woodlands."

antagonist, a character in a story or play who opposes the chief character or PROTAGONIST. In *Beowulf* Grendel is an antagonist, as is the Devil in *Paradise Lost.*

antithesis, a contrast or opposition in meaning, emphasized by a parallel in grammatical structure. In Pope's *The Rape of the Lock,* the grammatical parallelism is strengthened by alliteration:

Resolved to win, he meditates the way,
By force to ravish, or by fraud betray.

aphorism, a brief saying embodying a moral, such as Pope's "Some praise at morning what they blame at night, / But always think the last opinion right," from *An Essay on Criticism.*

apostrophe, a figure of speech in which an absent person, an abstract concept, or an inanimate object is directly addressed. "Milton! thou shouldst be living at this hour . . ." is an example of the first (Wordsworth's "London, 1802"); "Death, be not proud . . ." is an example of the second (Donne, "Holy Sonnet 10"); and "O sylvan Wye! thou wanderer through the woods . . ." is an example of the third (Wordsworth's "Tintern Abbey").

archetype, an image, story-pattern, or character type which recurs frequently in literature and evokes strong, often unconscious, associations in the reader. For example, the wicked witch, the enchanted prince, and the sleeping beauty are character types widely dispersed throughout folk tales and literature. Coleridge's "Kubla Khan" derives much of its power from its use of archetypal images such as the "deep romantic chasm," the "demon lover," the "sacred river," "ancestral voices prophesying war," and the "damsel with a dulcimer." The story of a hero who undertakes a dangerous quest (see *Beowulf* or *Sir Gawain and the Green Knight*) is a recurrent story pattern.

argument, a prose summary or synopsis of what is in a poem or play, both with regard to PLOT and meaning. See Milton's arguments in *Paradise Lost.*

assonance, the repetition of similar vowel sounds followed by different consonant sounds in stressed syllables or words. It is often used instead of RHYME. *Hate* and *great* are examples of rhyme; *hate* and *grade* are examples of assonance. In ". . . that hoard, and sleep, and feed, and know not me" (Tennyson, "Ulysses") the words *sleep, feed,* and *me* are assonant.

atmosphere, the MOOD of a literary work. An author establishes atmosphere partly through description of SETTING or landscape, and partly by the objects chosen to be described, as in the first eighteen lines of *The General Prologue* to *The Canterbury Tales,* where an atmosphere of rebirth and renewal is created by Chaucer.

autobiography (See BIOGRAPHY.)

ballad, a NARRATIVE passed on in the oral tradition. It often makes use of repetition and dialogue. A ballad whose author is unknown is called a *folk ballad.* If the author is known, the ballad is called a *literary ballad.* Coleridge's *The Rime of the Ancient Mariner* is perhaps the greatest of all English literary ballads.

ballad stanza, a STANZA usually consisting of four alternating lines of IAMBIC TETRAMETER and TRIMETER and rhyming the second and fourth lines.

It is an ancient Mariner,
And he stoppeth one of three.
"By thy long gray beard and glittering eye,
Now wherefore stopp'st thou me?

   Coleridge, *The Rime of the Ancient Mariner*

biography, any account of a person's life. See Boswell's life of *Johnson. Autobiography* is the story of all or part of a person's life written by the person who lived it. See Mill's *Autobiography.*

blank verse, unrhymed IAMBIC PENTAMETER, a line of five feet. Shakespeare's *The Tempest* and Milton's *Paradise Lost* are written in blank verse.

I máy / assért / Etér- / nal Próv- / ídence,

And jús- / tify / the wáys / of Gód / to mén.

   Milton, *Paradise Lost,* lines 25–26

burlesque (See SATIRE.)

cacophony, a succession of harsh, discordant sounds in either poetry or prose, used to achieve a specific effect. Note the harshness of sound and difficulty of articulation in these lines:

And all is seared with trade; bleared, smeared with toil;
And wears man's smudge and shares man's smell: the soil

Is bare now, nor can foot feel, being shod.

   Hopkins, "God's Grandeur"

caesura, a pause usually near the middle in a line of verse, usually indicated by the sense of the line, and often greater than a normal pause. For purposes of study, the mark indicating a caesura is two short vertical lines (||). A caesura can be indicated by punctuation, the grammatical construction of a sentence, or the placement of lines on a page. It is used to add variety to regular METER and therefore to add emphasis to certain words.

Born but to die, || and reas'ning but to err;
Alike in ignorance, || his reason such,
Whether he thinks too little, || or too much:
Chaos of thought and passion, || all confused;
Still by himself abused, || or disabused . . .

   Pope, *An Essay on Man*

The caesura was a particularly important device in Anglo-Saxon poetry, where each line had a caesura in the middle, but it is a technique used in most forms of poetry, such as the SONNET, the HEROIC COUPLET, and BLANK VERSE.

caricature, exaggeration of prominent features of appearance or character.

carpe diem (kär′pe dē′əm), Latin for "seize the day," the name applied to a THEME frequently found in LYRIC poetry: enjoy life's pleasures while you are able. See Herrick's "To the Virgins, To Make Much of Time."

characterization, the method an author uses to acquaint a reader with his or her characters. A character's physical traits and personality may be described, a character's speech and behavior may be described, or the thoughts and feelings of a character or the reactions of other characters to an individual may be shown. Any or all of these methods may be used in the same work.

cliché, an expression or phrase that is so overused as to become trite and meaningless: *white as snow, black as coal, cold as ice* are examples. A line from a famous writer may be quoted so often that it becomes a cliché. For example, Pope's "A little learning is a dangerous thing . . ." from *An Essay on Criticism.*

climax, as a term of dramatic structure, the decisive or turning point in a story or play when the action changes course and begins to resolve itself. In *Hamlet,* the hesitation and failure of the hero to kill Claudius at prayer in Act III is often regarded as the climax of the play. In *Macbeth,* the banquet scene in Act III where the ghost of Banquo appears to Macbeth is often regarded as the climax. Not every story or play has this kind of dramatic climax. Sometimes a character may simply resolve a problem in his or her mind. At times there is no resolution of the PLOT; the climax then comes when a character realizes that a resolution is impossible. (See also PLOT.) The term is also used to mean the point of greatest interest in a work, where the reader or audience has the most intense emotional response.

comedy, a play written primarily to amuse the audience. In addition to arousing laughter, comic writing often appeals to the intellect. Thus the comic mode has often been used to "instruct" the audience about the follies of certain social conventions and human foibles, as is done in Shaw's *Arms and the Man.* When so used, the comedy tends toward SATIRE.

comedy of ideas, a comedy in which the humor lies in ideas more than in situations. See *Arms and the Man.*

conceit, an elaborate and surprising *figure of speech* comparing two very dissimilar things. It usually involves intellectual cleverness and ingenuity. In the last three STANZAS of "A Valediction: Forbidding Mourning," Donne compares his soul and that of his love to the two legs or branches of a draftsman's compass used to make a circle. The previously unseen likeness as developed by the poet helps us to see and understand the subject described (the relationship of the lovers' souls) more clearly.

connotation, the emotional associations surrounding a word, as opposed to its literal meaning or DENOTATION. Some connotations are fairly general, others quite personal. Shakespeare's Sonnet 30 uses the connotative powers of language to create a mood of longing for lost beauties of the past that survive only in the poet's memory. Many of the words used by Shakespeare in this sonnet suggest associations that cluster around a sense of loss.

consonance, the repetition of consonant sounds that are preceded by different vowel sounds.

For*l*orn! the very word is like a be*ll*
To to*ll* me back from thee to my so*l*e se*l*f.

Keats, "Ode to a Nightingale"

Consonance is an effective device for linking sound, mood, and meaning. In the lines above, the *l* sounds reinforce the melancholy mood.

couplet, a pair of rhyming lines with identical meter.

Know then thyself, presume not God to scan:
The proper study of mankind is man.

Pope, *An Essay on Man*

When a couplet includes a complete unified thought, usually ending with a period, it is called a closed couplet.

dactyl, a three-syllable metrical FOOT consisting of an accented syllable followed by two unaccented syllables.

denotation, the strict, literal meaning of a word. (See CONNOTATION.)

denouement, the resolution of the PLOT. The word is derived from a French word meaning literally "to untie."

diary, a record of daily happenings written by a person for his or her own use. The diarist is moved by a need to record daily routine and confess innermost thoughts. The diary makes up in immediacy and frankness what it lacks in artistic shape and coherence. See the diary of Pepys.

diction, the author's choice of words or phrases in a literary work. This choice involves both the CONNOTATIVE and denotative meaning of a word as well as levels of usage.

dramatic convention, any of several devices which the audience accepts as a substitution for reality in a dramatic work. For instance, the audience accepts that an interval between acts may represent hours, days, weeks, months, or years; that a bare stage may be a meadow; that an invisible scaffold rather than a house supports a balcony; that an audible dialogue is supposed to represent whispered conversation; or that a rosy spotlight signals the dawn.

dramatic irony (See IRONY.)

dramatic monologue, a LYRIC poem in which the speaker addresses someone whose replies are not recorded. Sometimes the one addressed seems to be present, sometimes not. See Browning's "Porphyria's Lover" or "My Last Duchess."

elegy, a solemn, reflective poem, usually about death, written in a formal style. See Gray's "Elegy Written in a Country Churchyard."

end rhyme, the rhyming of words at the ends of lines of poetry. (See RHYME.)

end-stopped line, a line of poetry that contains a complete thought, thus necessitating the use of a semicolon, colon, or period at the end:

Good nature and good sense must ever join;
To err is human, to forgive divine.

Pope, *An Essay on Criticism*

(See also RUN-ON LINE.)

enjambment (See RUN-ON LINE.)

envoy, a short concluding stanza that serves to sum up a poem.

epic, a long NARRATIVE poem (originally handed down in oral tradition, later a literary form) dealing with great heroes and adventures, having a national, worldwide, or cosmic setting, involving supernatural forces, and written in a deliberately ceremonial STYLE. See *Beowulf* or *Paradise Lost.*

epigram, any short, witty verse or saying, often ending with a wry twist.

'Tis with our judgments as our watches; none
Go just alike, yet each believes his own.

Pope, An Essay on Criticism

epilogue, concluding section added to a work, serving to round out or interpret it. See the Epilogue to Tennyson's *In Memoriam.*

epithet, an adjective or adjectival phrase used to define a special quality of a person or thing. The term is also applied to a characterizing phrase that stands in place of a noun.

essay, a brief composition that presents a personal point of view. An essay may present a viewpoint through formal analysis and argument, as in Bacon's "Of Studies," or it may be more informal in style, as in Lamb's "Old China."

euphony, a combination of pleasing sounds in poetry or prose.

I cannot see what flowers are at my feet,
   Nor what soft incense hangs upon the boughs,
But, in embalmèd darkness, guess each sweet
   Wherewith the seasonable month endows
The grass, the thicket, and the fruit tree wild . . .

Keats, "Ode to a Nightingale"

(See also CACOPHONY.)

extended metaphor, a figure of speech that is developed at great length, often through a whole work or a great part of it. It is common in poetry but is used in prose as well. Wyatt's "Whoso List to Hunt," contains an extended metaphor, with the hunter representing the love-struck poet and the deer representing the poet's beloved. (See METAPHOR.)

eye-rhymes, words whose endings are spelled alike, and in most instances were once pronounced alike, but now have a different pronunciation: alone—done, daughter—laughter.

fable, a brief tale, in which the characters are often animals, told to point out a moral truth. Dryden's *The Hind and the Panther* is an example of a fable.

fantasy, a work that takes place in an unreal world, concerns incredible characters, or employs physical and scientific principles not yet discovered. There are elements of fantasy in Swift's *Gulliver's Travels.*

figurative language, language used in a nonliteral way to express a suitable relationship between essentially unlike things. When Burns says that his love is "like a red, red rose," he is using figurative language or a *figure of speech.* The more common figures of speech are SIMILE, METAPHOR, PERSONIFICATION, HYPERBOLE, and SYNECDOCHE.

flashback, interruption of the narrative to show an episode that happened before that particular point in the story. Most of the narrative in *Paradise Lost* is a flashback.

foil, a character whose traits are the opposite of those of another character and who thus points up the strengths or weaknesses of another character.

folk ballad (See BALLAD.)

folklore, the customs, legends, songs, and tales of a people or nation.

foot, a group of syllables in VERSE usually consisting of one accented syllable and the unaccented syllable(s) associated with it. (A foot may occasionally, for variety, have two accented syllables—see SPONDEE—or two unaccented syllables—the *pyrrhic.*) In the following lines the feet are divided by slashes:

Come live/ with me / and be / my Love,
And we / will all / the plea- / sures prove.

Marlowe, "The Passionate Shepherd to His Love"

The most common line lengths are five feet (PENTAMETER), four feet (TETRAMETER), and three feet (TRIMETER). The quoted lines above are IAMBIC TETRAMETER. (See also RHYTHM.)

foreshadowing, a hint given to the reader of what is to come.

frame, a NARRATIVE device presenting a story or group of stories within the frame of a larger narrative. The frame provides continuity for the group of stories. The pilgrimage in Chaucer's *The Canterbury Tales* is the frame unifying the stories told by the pilgrims.

free verse, a type of poetry that differs from conventional VERSE forms in being "free" from a fixed pattern of METER and RHYME, but using RHYTHM and other poetic devices. See Eliot's "The Love Song of J. Alfred Prufrock."

genre, a form or type of literary work. For example, the novel, the short story, and the poem are all genres. The term is a very loose one, however, so that subheadings under these would themselves also be called genres, for instance, EPIC.

heroic couplet, a pair of rhymed verse lines in IAMBIC PENTAMETER.

Trust not yourself: but your defects to know,
Make use of every friend—and every foe.

Pope, An Essay on Criticism

heroic simile, a SIMILE sustained for several lines and suggesting the heroic in nature or quality. See *Paradise Lost,* lines 196–210.

hexameter, a verse line of six feet. Spenser, in *The Faerie Queene,* uses a STANZA consisting of nine lines, the first eight of which are IAMBIC PENTAMETER and the last of which is a hexameter.

Most loath- / some, filth- / y, foul, /
   and full / of vile / disdain.

Spenser, The Faerie Queene

Six iambic feet make an Alexandrine.

homily, a sermon, or serious moral talk. See Donne's "Meditation 17."

hyperbole, a figure of speech involving great exaggeration. The effect may be serious or comic. See Marvell's description of his "vegetable love" in "To His Coy Mistress."

iamb, a two-syllable metrical FOOT consisting of one unaccented syllable followed by one accented syllable. The *iambic* foot is the most common meter in English poetry.

> For God's / sake, hold / your tongue, /
>   and let / me love . . .
>
> Donne, "The Canonization"

imagery, the sensory details that provide vividness in a literary work and tend to arouse emotions or feelings in a reader which abstract language does not. Shakespeare's Sonnet 130 is rich in specific, concrete details that appeal to the senses.

inference, a reasonable conclusion about the behavior of a character or the meaning of an event drawn from the limited information presented by the author.

in medias res (in mä′dē äs räs′), Latin for "in the middle of things." In a traditional EPIC the opening scene often begins in the middle of the action. Milton's *Paradise Lost* opens with Satan and his angels already defeated and in Hell; later in the poem the story of the battle between Satan and the forces of Heaven, which led to this defeat, is told. This device may be used in any NARRATIVE form, not just the epic.

internal rhyme, rhyming words or accented syllables within a line which may or may not have a rhyme at the end of the line as well: "We three shall flee across the sea to Italy."

inversion (See ANASTROPHE.)

invocation, the call on a deity or muse (classical goddess that inspired a poet) for help and inspiration found at the beginning of traditional EPIC poems. Milton, in *Paradise Lost,* instead of invoking one of the traditional muses of poetry calls upon the "Heavenly Muse" (line 6).

irony, the term used to describe a contrast between what appears to be and what really is. In *verbal irony,* the intended meaning of a statement or work is different from (often the opposite of) what the statement or work literally says, as in Swift's "A Modest Proposal." *Understatement,* in which an opinion is expressed less emphatically than it might be, is a form of verbal irony, often used for humorous or cutting effect; for example, "He's not the brightest man in the world," meaning "He is stupid." *Irony of situation* refers to an occurrence that is contrary to what is expected or intended, as in Hardy's "Ah, Are You Digging on My Grave." *Dramatic irony* refers to a situation in which events or facts not known to a character on stage or in a fictional work are known to another character and the audience or reader. The supreme example of dramatic irony is Sophocles' *Oedipus Tyrannus,* in which the hero unknowingly builds up the elaborate structure for his own undoing.

journal, a formal record of a person's daily experiences. It is less intimate or personal than a DIARY and more chronological than an autobiography. See Defoe's *A Journal of the Plague Year* for a fictional attempt to create the impression of an actual journal.

kenning, metaphorical compound word used as a poetic device. In *Beowulf* there are many examples of kennings. The king is the "ring-giver," the rough sea is the "whale-road," and the calm sea is the "swan-road."

literary ballad (See BALLAD.)

lyric, a poem, usually short, that expresses some basic emotion or state of mind. It usually creates a single impression and is highly personal. It may be rhymed or unrhymed. SONNETS are lyric poems. Other examples of lyrics are Burns' "A Red, Red Rose," and most of the shorter poems of the Romantics.

maxim (See APHORISM.)

memoir, a form of autobiography that is more concerned with personalities, events, and actions of public importance than with the private life of the writer.

metaphor, a figure of speech involving an implied comparison. In "Meditation 17" Donne compares the individual to a chapter in a book and, later, to a piece of a continent. (See also SIMILE and FIGURATIVE LANGUAGE.)

metaphysical poetry, poetry exhibiting a highly intellectual style that is witty, subtle, and sometimes fantastic, particularly in the use of CONCEITS. See especially the work of Donne.

meter, the pattern of stressed and unstressed syllables in poetry. (See RHYTHM.)

metonymy, a figure of speech in which a specific term naming an object is substituted for another word with which it is closely associated. For example, "the crown" stands for a king, and the term "Milton" stands for the works Milton wrote, in the sentence, "I have read all of Milton."

mock-heroic (also called *mock-epic*), a SATIRE using the form and style of an EPIC poem to treat a trivial incident. There are mock-heroic elements in Byron's *Don Juan.*

monologue (See SOLILOQUY and DRAMATIC MONOLOGUE.)

mood, the overall ATMOSPHERE or prevailing emotional aura of a work. Keats' "The Eve of St. Agnes" might be described as having a hypnotic, dreamlike atmosphere or mood. (See TONE for a comparison.)

motif, a character, incident, idea, or object that recurs in various works or in various parts of the same work. In Shakespeare's sonnets the nature and effect of time is a recurrent motif.

myth, a traditional story connected with the religion of a people, usually attempting to account for something in nature. Milton's *Paradise Lost* has mythic elements in its attempts to interpret aspects of the universe.

narrative, a story or account of an event or a series of events. It may be told either in poetry or prose; it may be either fictional or true. Defoe's *A Journal of the Plague Year* is a narrative, as is Milton's *Paradise Lost.*

narrator, the teller of a story. A narrator's attitude toward his or her subject is capable of much variation; it can range from one of apparent indifference to one of extreme conviction and feeling. When a narrator appears to have some bias regarding his or her subject, it becomes especially important not to automatically assume that the narrator and the author are to be regarded as the same person. (See also PERSONA and POINT OF VIEW.)

naturalism, writing that depicts events as rigidly determined by the forces of heredity and environment. The world described tends to be bleak. There are elements of naturalism in the work of Thomas Hardy and D. H. Lawrence.

neo-classicism, writing that shows the influence of the Greek and Roman classics. The term is often applied to English literature of the eighteenth century.

novel, a long work of NARRATIVE prose fiction dealing with characters, situations, and SETTINGS that imitate those of real life. Among the authors in this text who have written novels are Emily Brontë, Thomas Hardy, Joseph Conrad, D. H. Lawrence, James Joyce, Virginia Woolf, Graham Greene, and Doris Lessing. Conrad's *The Secret Sharer* is considered a short novel by some, although it is more properly classified as a long short story.

ode, a long LYRIC poem, formal in style and complex in form, often written in commemoration or celebration of a special quality, object, or occasion. See Shelley's "Ode to the West Wind" and Keats' "Ode on a Grecian Urn."

onomatopoeia, word(s) used in such a way that the sound of the word(s) imitates the sound of the thing spoken of. Some single words in which sound suggests meaning: "hiss," "smack," "buzz," and "hum." An example in which sound echoes sense throughout the whole phrase: "The murmurous haunt of flies on summer eves." (Keats' "Ode to a Nightingale.")

ottava rima, a STANZA pattern consisting of eight IAMBIC PENTAMETER lines rhyming *abababcc*. Byron's *Don Juan* is written in ottava rima.

oxymoron, a paradoxical statement that combines two terms that are ordinarily opposites:

O Death in Life, the days that are no more!

Tennyson, "Tears, Idle Tears"

parable, a brief fictional work which illustrates an abstract idea or teaches some lesson or truth. It differs from a FABLE in that the characters in it are generally people rather than animals; it differs from an ALLEGORY in that its characters do not necessarily represent abstract qualities. Chaucer's *The Wife of Bath's Tale* has elements of the parable.

paradox, a statement, often metaphorical, that seems to be self-contradictory but which has valid meaning:

When I lie tangled in her hair
    And fettered to her eye,
The birds that wanton in the air
    Know no such liberty.

Lovelace, "To Althea, from Prison"

parody (See SATIRE.)

pastoral poetry, a conventional form of LYRIC poetry presenting an idealized picture of rural life. See Marlowe's "The Passionate Shepherd to His Love."

pathetic fallacy, a term used by Ruskin to signify the attribution to nonhuman objects of human traits.

pentameter, a metrical line of five feet. (See also FOOT.)

When tó / the sés- / sions óf / sweet sí- /
    lent thought . . .

Shakespeare, Sonnet 30

persona, the mask or voice of the author or the author's creation in a particular work. (See also NARRATOR and POINT OF VIEW.)

personification, the representation of abstractions, ideas, animals, or inanimate objects as human beings by endowing them with human qualities. Death is personified in Donne's "Holy Sonnet 10." Personification is one kind of FIGURATIVE LANGUAGE.

Petrarchan sonnet (See SONNET.)

plot, in the simplest sense, a series of happenings in a literary work; but it is often used to refer to the action as it is organized around a conflict and builds through complication to a CLIMAX followed by a DENOUEMENT or resolution. See Marlowe's *Doctor Faustus.*

point of view, the relation between the teller of the story and the characters in it. The teller, or NARRATOR, may be a character in the story, in which case it is told from the *first-person* point of view. A writer who describes, in the *third person*, the thoughts and actions of any or all of the characters as the need arises is said to use the *omniscient* point of view. A writer who, in the *third person*, follows along with one character and tends to view events from that person's perspective is said to use a *limited omniscient* point of view. An author who describes only what can be seen, like a newspaper reporter, is said to use the *dramatic* point of view. (See also NARRATOR and PERSONA.)

prologue, section which precedes the main body of a work and serves as an introduction. See *The General Prologue* to *The Canterbury Tales.*

propaganda, writing that directly advocates a certain doctrine as the solution to some social or political problem.

protagonist, the leading character in a literary work.

pun, a play on words. Also known as *paronomasia.*

quatrain, verse STANZA of four lines. This stanza may take many forms, according to line lengths and RHYME patterns.

> The curfew tolls the knell of parting day,
> The lowing herd wind slowly o'er the lea,
> The plowman homeward plods his weary way,
> And leaves the world to darkness and to me.

> Gray, "Elegy Written in a Country Churchyard"

realism, a way of representing life that emphasizes ordinary people in everyday experiences.

refrain, the repetition of one or more lines in each STANZA of a poem.

rhyme, exact repetition of sounds in at least the final accented syllables of two or more words.

> Let such teach others who themselves ex*cel,*
> And censure freely who have written *well.*

> Pope, *An Essay on Criticism*

If the rhyme sound is the accented last syllable of the line, the rhyme is called masculine. If the very last syllable of the line is unaccented, the rhyme is called feminine. (See also RHYME SCHEME, INTERNAL RHYME, END RHYME, and SLANT RHYME.)

rhyme scheme, any pattern of rhyme in a STANZA. For purposes of study, the pattern is labeled as shown below, with the first rhyme labeled *a,* as are all the words rhyming with it; the second rhyme labeled *b,* the third rhyme *c,* and so on.

> Drink to me only with thine eyes,   *a*
>   And I will pledge with mine;   *b*
> Or leave a kiss but in the cup,   *c*
>   And I'll not look for wine.   *b*
> The thirst that from the soul doth rise   *a*
>   Doth ask a drink divine;   *b*
> But might I of Jove's nectar sup,   *c*
>   I would not change for thine.   *b*

> Jonson, "Song to Celia"

rhythm, the arrangement of stressed and unstressed sounds in speech or writing into patterns. Rhythm, or meter, may be regular or it may vary within a line or work. The four most common meters are IAMB or *iambus* ($\smallsmile\,/$), TROCHEE ($/\,\smallsmile$), ANAPEST ($\smallsmile\,\smallsmile\,/$), and DACTYL ($/\,\smallsmile\,\smallsmile$).

romance, a long narrative in VERSE or prose that originated in the Middle Ages. Its main elements are adventure, love, and magic. There are elements of romance in *Sir Gawain and the Green Knight* and *The Faerie Queene,* particularly in their ATMOSPHERE and SETTING.

romanticism, unlike REALISM, romanticism tends to portray the uncommon. The material selected tends to deal with extraordinary people in unusual experiences. In romantic literature there is often a stress on the past and an emphasis on nature.

run-on line, a line in which the thought continues beyond the end of the poetic line. There should be no pause after *thine* in the first line:

> For sure our souls were near allied, and thine
> Cast in the same poetic mould with mine.

> Dryden, "To the Memory of Mr. Oldham"

The process of creating run-on lines is sometimes referred to as *enjambment.*

sarcasm, the use of language to hurt or ridicule. It is less subtle in TONE than IRONY. Boswell, in the *Life of Johnson,* reports that when he first met Johnson he said (knowing Johnson's aversion to Scotland): "I do indeed come from Scotland, but I cannot help it." To which Johnson replied: "That, Sir, I find is what a very great many of your countrymen cannot help." Johnson's retort is an example of sarcasm.

satire, the technique that employs wit to ridicule a subject, usually some social institution or human foible, with the intention to inspire reform. SARCASM and IRONY are often used in writing satire. *Burlesque* and *parody* are closely related to satire. *Burlesque* is a literary or dramatic work that ridicules people, actions, or their literary works by mimickry and exaggeration. *Parody,* a kind of burlesque, is humorous imitation of serious writing, usually for the purpose of making the style of an author appear ridiculous. Swift's poetry and prose and Byron's *Don Juan* provide good examples of satire.

scansion, the marking off of lines of poetry into feet, indicating the stressed and unstressed syllables. (See RHYTHM and FOOT.)

setting, the time (both time of day and period in history) and place in which the action of a narrative occurs. The setting may be suggested through dialogue and action, or it may be described by the NARRATOR or one of the characters. Setting contributes strongly to the MOOD or ATMOSPHERE and plausibility of a work. Setting is important, for example, in Wordsworth's "Lines Composed a Few Miles Above Tintern Abbey."

Shakespearean sonnet (See SONNET.)

simile, a *figure of speech* involving a comparison using *like* or *as:*

> And now, like amorous birds of prey,
> Rather at once our time devour . . .

Marvell, "To His Coy Mistress"

In this example the similarity between the lovers and the birds of prey is their hungry appetite. (See METAPHOR for comparison.)

slant rhyme, rhyme in which the vowel sounds are not quite identical, as in the first and third lines below.

> And I untightened next the tress
>   About her neck; her cheek once more
> Blushed bright beneath my burning kiss:
>   I propped her head up as before,
>   Only, this time my shoulder bore . . .

Browning, "Porphyria's Lover"

soliloquy, a DRAMATIC CONVENTION that allows a character alone on stage to speak his or her thoughts aloud. If someone else is on stage, and the character's words are unheard, the soliloquy becomes an *aside.* See Shakespeare's *The Tempest* for examples. (Compare with DRAMATIC MONOLOGUE.)

sonnet, a LYRIC poem with a traditional form of fourteen IAMBIC PENTAMETER lines. Sonnets fall into two groups, according to their RHYME SCHEMES. The *Italian* or *Petrarchan* (after the Italian poet Petrarch) sonnet is usually rhymed *abbaabba/cdecde* (with variations permitted in the *cdecde* rhyme scheme), forming basically a two-part poem of eight lines *(octave)* and six lines *(sestet)* respectively. These two parts are played off against each other in a great variety of ways. See Wyatt's "Whoso List to Hunt." The *English* or *Shakespearean* sonnet is usually rhymed *abab/cdcd/efef/gg,* presenting a four-part structure in which an idea or theme is developed in three stages and then brought to a conclusion in the COUPLET. See Shakespeare's sonnets.

speaker (See NARRATOR.)

Spenserian stanza (See HEXAMETER.)

spondee, a metrical FOOT of two accented syllables (´ ´). It serves occasionally as a substitute foot to vary the meter, as in the third foot below.

> As yet / but knock, / breathe, shine, /
>   and seek / to mend . . .

Donne, "Holy Sonnet 14"

sprung rhythm, metrical form which consists of scanning the accented or stressed syllables without regard to the number of unstressed syllables in a FOOT. A foot may have from one to four syllables, with the accent always on the first syllable of the foot. The term was invented and the technique developed by Gerard Manley Hopkins. The following line is scanned according to Hopkins' theory:

> And for all / this, / nature is / never / spent . . .

Hopkins, "God's Grandeur"

The first foot has three syllables, the second foot one, the third foot three, the fourth foot two, and the fifth foot one, with the accent on the first syllable of each foot.

stanza, a group of lines which are set off and form a division in a poem, sometimes linked with other stanzas by RHYME. Hopkins' "Pied Beauty" has two stanzas.

stereotype, a conventional character, PLOT, or SETTING, which thus possesses little or no individuality, but which may be used for a purpose.

stream of consciousness, the recording or re-creation of a character's flow of thought. Raw images, perceptions, memories come and go in seemingly random, but actually controlled, fashion, much as they do in people's minds. See Joyce's *The Dead.*

style, the distinctive handling of language by an author. It involves the specific choices made with regard to DICTION, syntax, FIGURATIVE LANGUAGE, etc.

surrealism, a term used in both painting and literature to apply to incongruous and dreamlike IMAGERY and sequences which are associated with the unconscious. Eliot's "The Hollow Men" contains examples of surrealism.

symbol, something relatively concrete, such as an object, action, character, or scene, which signifies something relatively abstract, such as a concept or idea. In Yeats' "Sailing to Byzantium" the city is a symbol of the ideal unity of all aspects of life—religious, aesthetic, practical, intellectual.

synecdoche, a *figure of speech* in which a part stands for the whole, as in "hired *hands,*" in which *hands* (the part) stands for the whole (those who do manual labor—labor with their hands). The term also refers to a figurative expression in which the whole stands for a part, as in "call the *law,*" in which *law* (the whole) represents the police (a part of the whole system of law).

tercet, also called *triplet,* a STANZA of three rhyming lines.

> Whenas in silks my Julia goes,
> Then, then (methinks) how sweetly flows
> That liquefaction of her clothes.

Herrick, "Upon Julia's Clothes"

terza rima, a verse form with a three-line STANZA rhyming *aba, bcb, cdc,* etc.

Thou who didst waken from his summer dreams
The blue Mediterranean, where he lay,
Lulled by the coil of his crystalline streams,

Beside a pumice isle in Baiae's bay,
And saw in sleep old palaces and towers
Quivering within the wave's intenser day . . .

Shelley, "Ode to the West Wind"

tetrameter, a metrical line of four feet.

Had we / but world / enough, / and time . . .

Marvell, "To His Coy Mistress"

tone, the author's attitude toward his or her subject matter and toward the audience. In *The General Prologue* to *The Canterbury Tales*, Chaucer's tone is both sympathetic and ironic. He pretends to be an innocent observer, supplying details about each pilgrim in haphazard manner; yet these details, when carefully weighed, have a telling ironic force. The irony, however, is blended with humor and compassion.

tragedy, dramatic or narrative writing in which the main character suffers disaster after a serious and significant struggle but faces his or her downfall in such a way as to attain heroic stature. See Marlowe's *Doctor Faustus*.

trimeter, metrical line of three feet.

Down to / a sun- / less sea.

Coleridge, "Kubla Khan"

triplet (See TERCET.)

trochee (trō′kē), metrical foot made up of one accented syllable followed by an unaccented syllable.

verbal irony (See IRONY.)

verse, in its most general sense a synonym for *poetry*. Verse may also be used to refer to poetry carefully composed as to RHYTHM and RHYME SCHEME, but of inferior literary value. Sometimes the word *verse* is used to mean a *line* or STANZA of poetry.

vignette, a literary sketch or verbal description, a brief incident or scene.

voice (See PERSONA.)

ACKNOWLEDGMENTS

(continued from copyright page)

publishers, and The Society of Authors as the literary representative of the Estate of A. E. Housman. "Strange Meeting," "Insensibility," "Mental Cases," and "Dulce et Decorum Est" from *The Poems of Wilfred Owen*, edited by Edmund Blunden. Copyright Chatto & Windus Ltd., 1946, 1963. Reprinted by permission of New Directions Publishing Corporation, The Owen Estate and Chatto & Windus Ltd. *The Secret Sharer* from *'Twixt Land and Sea* by Joseph Conrad. Reprinted by permission of the Joseph Conrad Estate. "Sailing to Byzantium," "Ancestral Houses," "1919," "Leda and the Swan," and "Among School Children" reprinted with permission of Macmillan Publishing Co., Inc., M. B. Yeats, Miss Anne Yeats, and the Macmillan Co. of London and Basingstoke from *Collected Poems* by William Butler Yeats. Copyright 1928 by Macmillan Publishing Co., Inc., renewed 1956 by Georgie Yeats. "Coole Park, 1929," "For Anne Gregory," "Byzantium," "Crazy Jane Talks with the Bishop" reprinted with permission of Macmillan Publishing Co., Inc., M. B. Yeats, Miss Anne Yeats, and the Macmillan Co. of London & Basingstoke from *Collected Poems* by William Butler Yeats. Copyright 1933 by Macmillan Publishing Co., Inc., renewed 1961 by Bertha Georgie Yeats. "Easter 1916" and "The Second Coming" reprinted with permission of Macmillan Publishing Co., Inc., M. B. Yeats, Miss Anne Yeats, and the Macmillan Co. of London & Basingstoke from *Collected Poems* by William Butler Yeats. Copyright 1924 by Macmillan Publishing Co., Inc., renewed 1952 by Bertha Georgie Yeats. "The Wild Swans at Coole" reprinted with permission of Macmillan Publishing Co., Inc., M. B. Yeats, Miss Anne Yeats, and the Macmillan Co. of London & Basingstoke from *Collected Poems* by William Butler Yeats. Copyright 1919 by Macmillan Publishing Co., Inc., renewed 1947 by Bertha Georgie Yeats. "September, 1913" and "The Magi" reprinted with permission of Macmillan Publishing Co., Inc., M. B. Yeats, Miss Anne Yeats, and the Macmillan Co. of London & Basingstoke from *Collected Poems* by William Butler Yeats. Copyright 1916 by Macmillan Publishing Co., Inc. renewed 1944 by Bertha Georgie Yeats. "The Rose of the World" and "The Lake Isle of Innisfree" reprinted with permission of Macmillan Publishing Co., Inc., M. B. Yeats, Miss Anne Yeats, and the Macmillan Co. of London and Basingstoke from *Collected Poems* by William Butler Yeats. Copyright 1906 by Macmillan Publishing Co., Inc., renewed 1934 by William Butler Yeats. "Lapis Lazuli," "The Circus Animals' Desertion," "Cuchulain Comforted," "Under Ben Bulben" reprinted with permission of Macmillan Publishing Co., Inc., M. B. Yeats, Miss Anne Yeats, and the Macmillan Co. of London & Basingstoke from *Collected Poems* by William Butler Yeats. Copyright 1940 by Georgie Yeats, renewed 1968 by Bertha Georgie Yeats, Michael Butler Yeats, and Anne Yeats. "The Mark on the Wall" from *A Haunted House and Other Stories* by Virginia Woolf. Copyright, 1944, 1972, by Harcourt Brace Jovanovich, Inc. Reprinted by permission of Harcourt Brace Jovanovich, Inc., the Author's Literary Estate and The Hogarth Press Ltd. "The Rocking-Horse Winner" from *The Complete Short Stories of D. H. Lawrence*, Vol. III. (British titles *The Collected Short Stories of D. H. Lawrence*). Copyright 1933 by the Estate of D. H. Lawrence, 1961 by Angelo Ravagli and C. M. Weekley, Executors of the Estate of Frieda Lawrence Ravagli. Reprinted by permission of the Viking Press and Laurence Pollinger Ltd. "Wintry Peacock" from *The Complete Short Stories of D. H. Lawrence*, Vol II (British title: *The Collected Short Stories of D. H. Lawrence*). Copyright 1922 by Thomas B. Seltzer, Inc., 1950 by Frieda Lawrence. Reprinted by permission of The Viking Press, the Estate of the late Mrs. Frieda Lawrence, and Laurence Pollinger, Ltd. "Piano," "Bavarian Gentians," and "Snake" from *The Complete Poems of D. H. Lawrence* edited by Vivian de Sola Pinto and F. Warren Roberts. Copyright 1954, 1971 by Angelo Ravagli and C. M. Weekley, Executors of the Estate of Frieda Lawrence Ravagli. Reprinted by permission of The Viking Press and Laurence Pollinger Ltd. "The Dead" and "Clay" from *Dubliners* by James Joyce. Originally published by B. W. Huebsch, Inc. in 1916. Copyright 1967 by the Estate of James Joyce. All rights reserved. Reprinted by permission of The Viking

Press. "The Love Song of J. Alfred Prufrock," "Sweeney Among the Nightingales," "Journey of the Magi," and "The Waste Land" from *Collected Poems 1909–1962* by T. S. Eliot, copyright 1936, by Harcourt Brace Jovanovich, Inc.; copyright 1963, 1964 by T. S. Eliot. Reprinted by permission of Harcourt Brace Jovanovich and Faber and Faber Ltd. "Tradition and the Individual Talent" from *Selected Essays 1917–1932* by T. S. Eliot, copyright 1932, 1936, 1950 by Harcourt Brace Jovanovich, Inc.; renewed, 1960, 1964 by T. S. Eliot. Reprinted by permission of Harcourt Brace Jovanovich, Inc. and Faber and Faber Ltd. "Little Gidding" from *Four Quartets*, copyright 1943 by T. S. Eliot; renewed 1971 by Esme Valerie Eliot. Reprinted by permission of Harcourt Brace Jovanovich, Inc. and Faber and Faber Ltd. "In Praise of Limestone." Copyright 1951 by W. H. Auden. Reprinted from *Collected Poems*, by W. H. Auden, edited by Edward Mendelson, by permission of Random House, Inc. "The Fall of Rome." Copyright 1947 by W. H. Auden. Reprinted from *Collected Poems*, by W. H. Auden, edited by Edward Mendelson, by permission of Random House, Inc. "If I Could Tell You." Copyright 1945 by W. H. Auden. Reprinted from *Collected Poems*, by W. H. Auden, edited by Edward Mendelson, by permission of Random House, Inc. and Faber and Faber Ltd. "September 1, 1939." Copyright 1940 by W. H. Auden. Reprinted from *The English Auden*, by W. H. Auden, edited by Edward Mendelson, by permission of Random House, Inc. and Faber and Faber Ltd. "As I Walked Out One Evening," "In Memory of W. B. Yeats," and "Musée des Beaux Arts." Copyright 1940 and renewed 1968 by W. H. Auden. Reprinted from *Collected Poems*, by W. H. Auden, edited by Edward Mendelson, by permission of Random House, Inc. and Faber and Faber Ltd. "Lullaby." Copyright 1968 by W. H. Auden. Reprinted from *City Without Walls and Other Poems* (British title: *Collected Poems*) by W. H. Auden, by permission of Random House, Inc. and Faber and Faber Ltd. "The Destructors" from *Collected Stories* by Graham Greene. Copyright © 1955 by Graham Greene. Reprinted by permission of The Viking Press and Laurence Pollinger Ltd. for The Bodley Head and William Heinemann Ltd. "Dante and the Lobster" from *More Pricks Than Kicks* by Samuel Beckett. Reprinted by permission of Grove Press, Inc. and Calder and Boyars Ltd. All Rights Reserved. (First published by Chatto and Windus, London, 1934.) "The force that through the green fuse drives the flower," "Today, this insect," "Do Not Go Gentle," "Fern Hill," "In My Craft," and "A Refusal to Mourn" from *The Poems of Dylan Thomas*. Copyright 1939, 1946 by New Directions Publishing Corporation. Copyright 1952 by Dylan Thomas. Reprinted by permission of New Directions Publishing Corporation, J. M. Dent & Sons Ltd., and the Trustees for the Copyrights of the late Dylan Thomas. "A Man and Two Women." Copyright © 1958, 1962, 1963 by Doris Lessing. Reprinted by permission of Simon & Schuster, a Division of Gulf & Western Corporation and Curtis Brown Ltd. "The Whitsun Weddings" from *The Whitsun Weddings* by Philip Larkin. Copyright 1964 by Philip Larkin. Reprinted by permission of Faber and Faber Ltd. "Deceptions" and "Poetry of Departures" from *The Less Deceived* by Philip Larkin. Reprinted by permission of The Marvell Press, England. "Hawk Roosting" from *Selected Poems* by Ted Hughes (British title: *Lupercal*). Copyright © 1959 by Ted Hughes. Reprinted by permission of Harper & Row, Publishers, Inc. and Faber and Faber Ltd. "The Thought Fox" and "The Jaguar" from *Selected Poems* by Ted Hughes. Copyright © 1957 by Ted Hughes. Reprinted by permission of Harper & Row, Publishers, Inc. "King of Carrion" from *Crow* by Ted Hughes. Copyright © 1971 by Ted Hughes. Reprinted by permission of Harper & Row, Publishers, Inc. and Faber and Faber Ltd. "Genesis" and "In Memory of Jane Fraser" from *Somewhere Is Such a Kingdom: Poems 1952–1971* (British title: *For the Unfallen*) by Geoffrey Hill. Copyright © 1959, 1964, 1968, 1971, 1975 by Geoffrey Hill. Reprinted by permission of Houghton Mifflin Company and Andre Deutsch Limited. "Annunciations" from *Somewhere Is Such a Kingdom: Poems 1952–1971* (British title: *King Log*) by Geoffrey Hill. Copyright © 1959, 1964, 1968, 1971, 1975 by Geoffrey Hill. Reprinted by permission of Houghton Mifflin Company and Andre Deutsch Limited.

INDEX OF AUTHORS AND TITLES

INDEX OF FIRST LINES